MW01009338

[features]

GENESIS

The Beginning of the World

1 ·In the beginning [or In the beginning when] God created [Cthis Hebrew verb is used only when God is the one creating] the ·sky [heavens] and the earth. 2·The [or...the] earth ·had no form and was empty [or was a formless void]. Darkness covered the ·ocean [deep], and ·God's Spirit [or a mighty wind] was ·moving [hovering] over the water.

3Then God said, "Let there be light," and there was light. 4God saw that the light was good, so he ·divided [separated] the light from the darkness. 5God ·named [called] the light "day" and the darkness "night." ·Evening passed, and morning came [LThere was evening and there was morning; Cin the OT a day begins at nightfall]. This was the first day.

6Then God said, "Let there be ·something to divide the water in two [La firmament/dome/expanse in the midst of the waters to separate/divide the waters from the waters]." 7So God made the ·air [Lfirmament; dome; expanse; Crain clouds] and placed some of the water above the ·air [Lfirmament; dome; expanse] and some below it [Creferring to the rain and the oceans, lakes, and rivers]. 8God ·named [called] the ·air [Lfirmament/dome/expanse] "·sky [heaven]." Evening passed, and morning came [1:5]. This was the second day.

9Then God said, "Let the water under the ·sky [heavens] be gathered together so the dry land will appear." And it happened. 10God ·named [called] the dry land "earth" and [Lhe called] the water that was gathered together "seas." God saw that this was good.

11Then God said, "Let the earth produce ·plants [vegetation]—some to make grain for seeds and ·others to make fruits with seeds in them. Every seed will produce more of its own kind of plant [Lfruit trees on earth bearing fruit according to its own kind/species that has seed in them]." And it happened. 12The earth ·produced [brought forth] plants with grain for seeds and trees that made fruits with seeds in them. ·Each seed grew its own kind of plant [L...according to its kind/species]. God saw that all this was good. 13Evening passed, and morning came [1:5]. This was the third day.

14Then God said, "Let there be lights in the ·sky [Lfirmament/dome/expanse of the heavens] to ·separate [divide] day from night. ·These lights will be used for [LThey will be] signs, seasons, days, and years. 15They will be in the ·sky [Lfirmament/dome/expanse] to give light to the earth." And it happened.

16So God made the two ·large [great] lights. He made the ·brighter [Lgreater] light to rule the day and made the ·smaller [lesser] light to rule the night. ·He also made the stars [L...and the stars]. 17God put all these in the sky to shine on the earth, 18to rule over the day and over the night, and to ·separate [divide] the light from the darkness. God saw that all

these things were good. 19Evening passed, and morning came [1:5]. This was the fourth day.

20Then God said, "Let the water ·be filled with living things [Lswarm with living creatures], and let birds fly in the ·air [Lfirmament/dome/expanse] above the earth."

21So God created [1:1] the large sea ·animals [or monsters] and every living thing that ·moves [Lswarms] in the sea. The sea is filled with these living things, with each one ·producing more of its own kind [Laccording to its kind/species]. He also ·made [or created; 1:1] every bird that flies, and each bird ·produced more of its own kind [Laccording to its kind/species]. God saw that this was good. 22God blessed them and said, "·Have many young ones so that you may grow in number [TBe fruitful and multiply]. ·Fill [...and fill] the water of the seas, and let the birds ·grow in number [multiply] on the earth." 23Evening passed, and morning came [1:5]. This was the fifth day.

24Then God said, "Let the earth be filled with ·animals [living creatures], ·each producing more of its own kind [Laccording to their kind/species]. Let there be ·tame animals [beasts; livestock] and small crawling animals and wild animals, ·and let each produce more of its kind [Laccording to their kind/species]." And it happened.

25So God made the wild animals, the ·tame animals [beasts; livestock], and all the small crawling animals ·to produce more of their own kind [Laccording to their kind/species]. God saw that this was good.

26Then God said, "Let us make human beings in our image and likeness. And let them ·rule [Thave dominion] over the fish in the sea and the birds in the ·sky [heavens], over the ·tame animals [beasts; livestock], over all the earth, and over all the small crawling animals on the earth."

27So God created [1:1] ·human beings [Tman; Cthe Hebrew *adam* can mean human beings, humankind, person, man, or the proper name Adam] in his image [Creflecting God's nature/character and representing him in the world]. In the image of God he created them. He created them male and female. 28God blessed them and said [Lto them], "·Have many children and grow in number [TBe fruitful and multiply]. ·Fill [...and fill] the earth and ·be its master [subdue it]. ·Rule [THave dominion] over the fish in the sea and over the birds in the ·sky [heavens] and over every living thing that moves on the earth."

29God said, "Look, I have given you all the plants that have grain for seeds [Lon the face of the earth] and all the trees whose fruits have seeds in them. They will be food for you. 30I have given all the green plants as food for every wild animal, every bird of the ·air [sky; heavens], and every small ·crawling [creeping] animal." And it happened. 31God looked at everything he had made, and it was ·very [exceedingly] good. Evening passed, and morning came [1:5]. This was the sixth day.

The Seventh Day—Rest

2 So the ·sky [heavens], the earth, and all ·that filled them [Ltheir hosts] were ·finished [completed]. 2By the seventh day God ·finished [completed] the work he had been doing, so he ·rested [or ceased] from all his work [Lhe had done]. 3God blessed the seventh day and ·made it a holy day [consecrated it; set it apart], because on that day he ·rested [or ceased] from all the work he had done in creating [1:1] the world.

People

4·This is the story [LThese are the generations; Cintroduces a new section of the book; see also 5:1; 6:9; 10:1; 11:10, 27; 25:12, 19; 36:1, 9] of the

LITERAL MEANINGS
of words and phrases from the original languages offer additional understanding

REFERENCES
help you compare scriptures

EXPANDED TRANSLATIONS
bring out the meaning of words and offer alternative wordings

contents

the old testament

the new testament

Abbreviations used in

The

[expanded]

Bible™

Abbreviation	Book	Page
Acts	Acts	1643
Amos	Amos	1376
1 Chr.	1 Chronicles	554
2 Chr.	2 Chronicles	600
Col.	Colossians	1792
1 Cor.	1 Corinthians	1728
2 Cor.	2 Corinthians	1752
Dan.	Daniel	1323
Deut.	Deuteronomy	243
Eccl.	Ecclesiastes	969
Eph.	Ephesians	1777
Esth.	Esther	692
Ex.	Exodus	78
Ezek.	Ezekiel	1244
Ezra	Ezra	653
Gal.	Galatians	1768
Gen.	Genesis	1
Hab.	Habakkuk	1412
Hag.	Haggai	1424
Heb.	Hebrews	1823
Hos.	Hosea	1349
Is.	Isaiah	996
James	James	1844
Jer.	Jeremiah	1121
Job	Job	705
Joel	Joel	1368
John	John	1599
1 John	1 John	1864
2 John	2 John	1871
3 John	3 John	1872
Jon.	Jonah	1393
Josh.	Joshua	295
Jude	Jude	1873
Judg.	Judges	329
1 Kin.	1 Kings	463
2 Kin.	2 Kings	510
Lam.	Lamentations	1230
Lev.	Leviticus	140

Abbreviation	Book	Page
Luke	Luke	1541
Mal.	Malachi	1441
Mark	Mark	1507
Matt.	Matthew	1449
Mic.	Micah	1396
Nah.	Nahum	1407
Neh.	Nehemiah	669
Num.	Numbers	186
Obad.	Obadiah	1390
1 Pet.	1 Peter	1851
2 Pet.	2 Peter	1859
Phil.	Philippians	1786
Philem.	Philemon	1821
Prov.	Proverbs	911
Ps.	Psalms	761
Rev.	Revelation	1876
Rom.	Romans	1701
Ruth	Ruth	367
1 Sam.	1 Samuel	373
2 Sam.	2 Samuel	421
Song	Song of Songs	986
1 Thess.	1 Thessalonians	1798
2 Thess.	2 Thessalonians	1803
1 Tim.	1 Timothy	1806
2 Tim.	2 Timothy	1813
Titus	Titus	1818
Zech.	Zechariah	1427
Zeph.	Zephaniah	1418

Special Abbreviations

OT	Old Testament
NT	New Testament
AD	Anno Domini (in the year of our Lord)
BC	Before Christ
LXX	The Septuagint (a Greek translation of the OT)
cf.	confer (compare)

An Introduction to The [expanded] Bible™

More Than an Ordinary Translation

The Bible is the most influential literary work in human history, an unparalleled collection of poetry, prose, history, narrative, laws, psalms, proverbs, prophecy, and letters. Yet the Bible is much more than a great library. It is also the inspired and authoritative Word of God—his message to human beings. God speaks to us through his Word. It is critical, therefore, that it be understood.

Most people, however, do not read the Bible in its original languages. The Bible was originally written in Hebrew (the Old Testament) and Greek (the New Testament), with parts in Aramaic. As the most important book of all time, the Bible has been translated into hundreds of other languages, including, in the case of *The Expanded Bible*, English.

No translation is ever completely successful, however, whether of the Bible or any other text. All translations fall short for a variety of reasons. First, no two languages are equivalent in their vocabulary, sounds, rhythms, idioms, or underlying structure. Nor are any two cultures out of which languages arise equivalent in their way of understanding and expressing reality, their value systems, or their social and political organization, among other factors. Second, the meaning of a text includes much more than its abstract thought. The sounds and rhythms of words, word play and puns, emotional overtones, metaphor, figurative language, and tone are just some of the other devices that carry meaning. No translation can transfer all these things from one language to another. Third, all translation requires interpretation. One cannot convey meaning in a second language without first deciding what it means in the original. This step of interpretation in translation is unavoidable and imperfect; equally skilled and well-meaning scholars will interpret differently. Fourth, a traditional translation requires one to choose a single possibility—whether of a word or an interpretation—when in fact two or more may be plausible.

The Expanded Bible, while also imperfect, helps with all of these problems inherent in translation. It allows the reader to see multiple possibilities for words, phrases, and interpretations. Rather than opting for one choice, it shows many. It can, for instance, show both an original metaphor and a more prosaic understanding of that metaphor. It can show a second or third way of understanding the meaning of a word, phrase, verse, or passage. It can provide comments that give the historical, cultural, linguistic, or theological background that an English-language reader may lack. When helpful, it provides the most literal renderings to show what a translator has to work with.

With so many English translations available, some may ask why we need another. In many ways this is not another translation. Instead, it offers additional information that allows readers to see how translation communicates meaning. Readers see, in a clear and concise format, much of what a translator sees while working to be as faithful to the text as possible. The goal of this approach is not to suggest that a text can mean whatever anyone wants it to mean (it cannot), but to show that the Bible in its original languages is rich, multi-layered, and profound. *The Expanded Bible* does not overcome all the limitations of translation, but it allows more of the features of the original text to come across into English than any ordinary translation can.

Approaches to Translation

All translations of the Bible wish to be clear, accurate, and readable. Different translations emphasize different approaches to reaching that goal. Some emphasize reproducing as closely as possible in a modern language the structure of the original language (including word order, sentence length, and groupings of words in clauses and phrases). This approach, often called *formal equivalence*, favors being as literal as possible in finding single meanings for words, preserves idioms and metaphors (even if they convey little to a modern reader), and tends to expect the reader to work hard to understand the meaning of the text.

Another approach emphasizes that meaning in language is conveyed by groups of words working together. This approach, often called *functional equivalence* or *meaning-based translation*, tries less to find the single meaning of each word in the original, and more to understand and convey the meaning of entire phrases, clauses and sentences. To use an example from a modern language, the Spanish phrase *¿Como se llama?*, translated literally, would be something like "How yourself call?" This would be a poor translation. A more accurate, though less literal, rendering would be "What's your name?" *Meaning-based translation* theory claims this situation occurs frequently in all translation, including in translation of the biblical languages.

One place *meaning-based* translations differ from *formal equivalence* translations is in their treatment of gender. The New Testament Greek word *adelphoi*, for instance, sometimes means "brothers" (male siblings), but also commonly means simply "siblings" or "brothers and sisters"—referring to Christian believers. When the context in the original language calls for it, *The Expanded Bible* uses English terms that refer to both sexes. If multiple interpretations are possible, it shows alternatives.

Although both *formal* and *functional equivalence* translation theories have benefits, and impassioned advocates, every translation in fact uses both approaches. Even the most literal translation sacrifices literalness for meaning when it must, and even the most meaning-based or idiomatic translation is literal when the literal is clear and readable. One of the virtues of *The Expanded Bible* is that it represents the best of both approaches, offering idiomatic renderings to clearly convey the meaning of the text, and literal alternatives to show underlying structural features and allow the reader to assess the choices a more meaning-based translation has made. Ultimately, no translation serves the goals of clarity, accuracy, and readability better than *The Expanded Bible.*

How to Use *The Expanded Bible*

The Expanded Bible incorporates within each line the information one would find in a variety of Bible reference works, making it possible to read and study the Bible at the same time. The base text is a modified version of the *New Century Version*, a clear and accurate, meaning-based (functional-equivalent) Bible version. This base text appears in bold-faced type. Alternate interpretations of words, phrases, or idioms (and other information) are placed in brackets in lighter type. For Expansions, Alternates, certain Literals, and certain Traditionals (see below), a bullet (·) is used to show where to begin the replacement of a word or words before the set of brackets with the word or words within the set of brackets. The Literals and Traditionals that are not associated with a bullet do not require to be substituted for any word or words in the base text, but are just to be added.

The easiest way to learn to use *The Expanded Bible* is simply to read it. One may wish to read a verse or passage first using only **the bolded text**, then go back and read it again using the expanded material. The **markers** (sigla) used are simple and the method is quite intuitive:

[ ] EXPANSION: Other possible ways of translating a word, phrase, clause, or sentence. Expansions are enclosed within a set of brackets [ ], and provide synonyms, different nuances, or sometimes more sophisticated diction.

Hebrews 4:12 **God's word is alive and ·working** [active; powerful; effective] **and is sharper than a double-edged sword.**

[*or*] **ALTERNATE:** A different translation possibility that takes the meaning of the original language in a different direction than the base text does. Alternates provide information not possible in a standard translation, which must choose between possibilities for its main text. These are signaled by an *or* within a set of brackets: [*or*].

Hebrews 11:1–2 **Faith means ·being sure** [the assurance; *or* the tangible reality; *or* the sure foundation] **of the things we hope for and ·knowing that something is real even if we do not see it** [the conviction/assurance/evidence about things not seen]. [2]**Faith is the reason ·we remember** [*or* God commended/approved] **·great people who lived in the past** [the people of old; the ancients; our spiritual ancestors].

L **LITERAL:** A more literal rendering of the original language, allowing the reader to see why translations make varying choices. These are signaled by a superscript [L] within a bracket: [[L]].

Ephesians 5:6 **Do not let anyone ·fool** [deceive] **you ·by telling you things that are not true** [*or* with shallow philosophies; [L]with empty words], **because these things will bring God's ·anger** [wrath] **on ·those who do not obey him** [[L]the children/sons of disobedience].

T **TRADITIONAL:** Provides familiar terms and well-known renderings from past translations, especially those in the King James tradition. Signaled by a superscript [T] within a bracket: [[T]].

1 Corinthians 13:12 **Now we see a ·dim** [obscure; *or* indirect] **reflection, as ·if we were looking into a mirror** [[T]through a glass darkly], **but then we shall see ·clearly** [[L]face to face].

C **COMMENT:** Briefly provides historical, cultural, theological, or other explanatory information to help readers better understand a verse or passage. These are signaled by superscript [C] within a bracket: [[C]]. (There is no bullet in the base text for these because no replacement is required.)

Ephesians 5:25–26 **Husbands, love your wives as Christ loved the church and gave himself for her** [26]**to ·make her holy** [sanctify her], **cleansing her in the washing of water by the word** [[C]the "washing" may refer to (1) baptism; (2) spiritual cleansing (Titus 3:5); or (3) an analogy drawn from the Jewish prenuptial bath (Ezek. 16:8-14); the "word" may be (1) the Gospel; (2) a baptismal formula, or (3) the confession of the one baptized].

Gen. 1:1 **REFERENCE:** Provides cross-references to parallel passages, quotations from or allusions to another part of the Bible. These usually appear within a bracket. (There is no bullet in the base text for these because no replacement is required.)

Matthew 4:7 **Jesus answered him, "It also says in the Scriptures, 'Do not ·test** [tempt] **the Lord your God** [Deut. 6:16].'"

n **TEXTUAL VARIANT:** Footnoted material that shows significant differences in various manuscripts in the original languages. Signaled by a superscript [n] that leads to a footnote at the bottom of the page. (In some cases a passage in the base text is enclosed within vertical lines, indicating what is not contained in certain early manuscripts, as the footnote indicates.)

Matthew 6:13 |**The kingdom, the power, and the glory are yours forever. Amen.**|[n]

6:13 The kingdom . . . Amen. Some early Greek copies do not contain this passage.

The illuminating possibilities of *The Expanded Bible* method are most apparent when these different devices are used in close succession. Each device builds on the previous one to help us understand difficult passages and bring out the richness of the text more fully than any standard translation can: Romans 3:21–25

21 **But now ·God's way to make people right with him** [Lthe righteousness of God]
·without [apart from] **the law has been ·shown to us** [revealed; made known], **a way ·told**
to us [testified to; attested] **by the law and the prophets.** 22 **·God makes people right with**
himself [LThis righteousness comes] **through ·their faith in** [or the faithfulness of] **Jesus**
Christ. This is true for all who believe in Christ, because ·all people are the same [there
is no distinction/difference; Cbetween Jews and Gentiles]: 23 [LFor; Because] **Everyone has**
sinned and ·fallen short [*or* is not worthy of] **of God's ·glorious standard** [or glorious
presence; Lglory], 24 **and all need to be ·made right with God** [justified; declared righ-
teous] **as a free gift by his grace, ·by being set free from sin** [Lthrough the redemption
that is] **·through** [*or* in] **Jesus Christ.** 25 **God ·sent** [*or* appointed; *or* presented] **him ·to die**
in our place to take away our sins [as a sacrifice of atonement; *or* as the mercy seat; Tas a
propitiation; Cthe Greek term could mean the place where sacrificial blood was dripped
(the mercy seat) or the sacrifice itself; it implies an atoning sacrifice that turns away
divine wrath].

About the scholars

Tremper Longman III (Ph.D., Yale) is the Robert H. Gundry Professor of Biblical Studies at Westmont College. He has written numerous articles and authored or coauthored over twenty books, including commentaries on Song of Songs, Ecclesiastes, Daniel, Nahum, and Jeremiah and Lamentations; *How to Read Psalms; How to Read Proverbs; How to Read Genesis; and How to Read Exodus.* He coedited and wrote articles for *The Dictionary of the Old Testament: Wisdom, Poetry and Writings.* In addition, he is one of the main translators of the New Living Translation and has served as a consultant on other translations of the Bible including the Message, the New Century Version, and the Holman Christian Standard Bible.

Mark L. Strauss (Ph.D., Aberdeen) is professor of New Testament at Bethel Seminary San Diego, where he has served since 1994. He is the author or coauthor of various books and articles, including *Four Portraits, One Jesus: An Introduction to Jesus and the Gospels; How to Read the Bible in Changing Times; How to Choose a Translation for All It's Worth* (with Gordon D. Fee); *Mark* in the *Expositor's Bible Commentary, Revised Edition* (with Walter Wessel); *The Essential Bible Companion* (with John Walton); *Distorting Scripture? The Challenge of Bible Translation and Gender Accuracy; Luke* in the *Zondervan Illustrated Bible Background Commentary;* and *The Davidic Messiah in Luke-Acts.* Dr. Strauss has a heart for ministry and preaches and teaches regularly at churches, conferences, and colleges.

Daniel Taylor (Ph.D., Emory) is the author of ten books, including *The Myth of Certainty; Letters to My Children; Tell Me a Story: The Life-Shaping Power of Our Stories;* and, most recently, *Creating a Spiritual Legacy: Passing On Your Stories, Values, and Wisdom.* He speaks frequently at conferences, colleges, retreats, and churches on a variety of topics. Dr. Taylor is also cofounder of The Legacy Center, an organization devoted to helping individuals and organizations identify and preserve the values and stories that have shaped their lives. He is a contributing editor of *Books and Culture.*

Old Testament

GENESIS

The Beginning of the World

1 ·In the beginning [*or* In the beginning when] God created [Cthis
Hebrew verb is used only when God is the one creating] the ·sky
[heavens] and the earth. 2·The [*or*...the] earth ·had no form and was
empty [*or* was a formless void]. Darkness covered the ·ocean [deep], and
·God's Spirit [*or* a mighty wind] was ·moving [hovering] over the water.
3Then God said, "Let there be light," and there was light. 4God saw
that the light was good, so he ·divided [separated] the light from the
darkness. 5God ·named [called] the light "day" and the darkness "night."
·Evening passed, and morning came [LThere was evening and there was
morning; Cin the OT a day begins at nightfall]. This was the first day.
6Then God said, "Let there be ·something to divide the water in two [La
firmament/dome/expanse in the midst of the waters to separate/divide the
waters from the waters]." 7So God made the ·air [Lfirmament; dome;
expanse; Crain clouds] and placed some of the water above the ·air
[Lfirmament; dome; expanse] and some below it [Creferring to the rain
and the oceans, lakes, and rivers]. 8God ·named [called] the ·air
[Lfirmament/dome/expanse] "·sky [heaven]." Evening passed, and morning came [1:5]. This was the second day.
9Then God said, "Let the water under the ·sky [heavens] be gathered
together so the dry land will appear." And it happened. 10God ·named
[called] the dry land "earth" and [Lhe called] the water that was gathered
together "seas." God saw that this was good.
11Then God said, "Let the earth produce ·plants [vegetation]—some to
make grain for seeds and ·others to make fruits with seeds in them. Every
seed will produce more of its own kind of plant [Lfruit trees on earth bearing fruit according to its own kind/species that has seed in them]." And it
happened. 12The earth ·produced [brought forth] plants with grain for
seeds and trees that made fruits with seeds in them. ·Each seed grew its own
kind of plant [L...according to its kind/species]. God saw that all this was
good. 13Evening passed, and morning came [1:5]. This was the third day.
14Then God said, "Let there be lights in the ·sky [Lfirmament/dome/
expanse of the heavens] to ·separate [divide] day from night. ·These lights
will be used for [LThey will be] signs, seasons, days, and years. 15They will
be in the ·sky [Lfirmament/dome/expanse] to give light to the earth." And
it happened.
16So God made the two ·large [great] lights. He made the ·brighter
[Lgreater] light to rule the day and made the ·smaller [lesser] light to rule
the night. ·He also made the stars [L...and the stars]. 17God put all these
in the sky to shine on the earth, 18to rule over the day and over the night,
and to ·separate [divide] the light from the darkness. God saw that all

these things were good. 19Evening passed, and morning came [1:5]. This
was the fourth day.
20Then God said, "Let the water ·be filled with living things [Lswarm
with living creatures], and let birds fly in the ·air [Lfirmament/dome/
expanse] above the earth."
21So God created [1:1] the large sea ·animals [*or* monsters] and every
living thing that ·moves [Lswarms] in the sea. The sea is filled with these
living things, with each one ·producing more of its own kind [Laccording
to its kind/species]. He also ·made [*or* created; 1:1] every bird that flies, and
each bird ·produced more of its own kind [Laccording to its kind/species].
God saw that this was good. 22God blessed them and said, "·Have many
young ones so that you may grow in number [TBe fruitful and multiply].
·Fill [...and fill] the water of the seas, and let the birds ·grow in number
[multiply] on the earth." 23Evening passed, and morning came [1:5]. This
was the fifth day.
24Then God said, "Let the earth be filled with ·animals [living crea-
tures], ·each producing more of its own kind [Laccording to their kind/
species]. Let there be ·tame animals [beasts; livestock] and small crawling
animals and wild animals, ·and let each produce more of its kind
[Laccording to their kind/species]." And it happened.
25So God made the wild animals, the ·tame animals [beasts; livestock],
and all the small crawling animals ·to produce more of their own kind
[Laccording to their kind/species]. God saw that this was good.
26Then God said, "Let us make human beings in our image and likeness. And let them ·rule [Thave dominion] over the fish in the sea and the
birds in the ·sky [heavens], over the ·tame animals [beasts; livestock], over
all the earth, and over all the small crawling animals on the earth."
27So God created [1:1] ·human beings [Tman; Cthe Hebrew *adam* can
mean human beings, humankind, person, man, or the proper name
Adam] in his image [Creflecting God's nature/character and representing
him in the world]. In the image of God he created them. He created them
male and female. 28God blessed them and said [Lto them], "·Have many
children and grow in number [TBe fruitful and multiply]. ·Fill [...and fill]
the earth and ·be its master [subdue it]. ·Rule [THave dominion] over the
fish in the sea and over the birds in the ·sky [heavens] and over every living thing that moves on the earth."
29God said, "Look, I have given you all the plants that have grain for
seeds [Lon the face of the earth] and all the trees whose fruits have seeds
in them. They will be food for you. 30I have given all the green plants as
food for every wild animal, every bird of the ·air [sky; heavens], and every
small ·crawling [creeping] animal." And it happened. 31God looked at
everything he had made, and it was ·very [exceedingly] good. Evening
passed, and morning came [1:5]. This was the sixth day.

The Seventh Day—Rest

2 So the ·sky [heavens], the earth, and all ·that filled them [Ltheir
hosts] were ·finished [completed]. 2By the seventh day God ·fin-
ished [completed] the work he had been doing, so he ·rested [*or* ceased]
from all his work [Lhe had done]. 3God blessed the seventh day and ·made
it a holy day [consecrated it; set it apart], because on that day he ·rested
[*or* ceased] from all the work he had done in creating [1:1] the world.

The First People

4·This is the story [LThese are the generations; Cintroduces a new section of the book; see also 5:1; 6:9; 10:1; 11:10, 27; 25:12, 19; 36:1, 9] of the

creation of the ·sky [heavens] and the earth. When the ·LORD God [Yahweh Elohim; [C]Elohim is the common term for God; LORD (capital letters) represents the divine name YHWH, usually pronounced "Yahweh"; see Ex. 3:14–15] first made the earth and the ·sky [heavens], 5there were still no plants on the earth. Nothing was growing in the fields because the LORD God had not yet made it rain on the land. And there was no person to ·care for [*or* till; work] the ground, 6but a ·mist [*or* stream] would rise up from the earth and water all the ground.

7Then the LORD God took dust from the ground and formed a man from it [[C]there is wordplay between "ground" (*adama*) and "man" (*adam*)]. He breathed the breath of life into the man's nose, and the man became a living person. 8·Then the LORD God [*or* The LORD God had] planted a garden in the east [[C]probably east of Palestine], in a place called Eden [[C]related to a word meaning "luxurious"], and put the man he had formed into it. 9The LORD God caused every ·beautiful [[L]desirous to see] tree and every tree that was good for food to grow out of the ground. In the middle of the garden, God put the tree ·that gives life [[T]of life] and also the tree ·that gives the knowledge [[T]of the knowledge] of good and evil.

10A river flowed through Eden and watered the garden. From there the river ·branched out [divides] to become four ·rivers [[L]heads]. 11The first river, named Pishon [[C]otherwise unknown], flows around the whole land of Havilah [[C]otherwise unknown], where there is gold. 12The gold of that land is excellent. Bdellium [[C]a sweet-smelling resin like myrrh] and onyx [[C]a precious stone] are also found there. 13The second river, named Gihon [[C]a small stream in Jerusalem (1 Kin. 1:33), but here perhaps referring to another river], flows around the whole land of Cush [[C]often referring to Ethiopia, but here likely a place in Mesopotamia; see 10:7]. 14The third river, named Tigris [[C]a major river in Mesopotamia], flows out of Assyria [[C]in northern Mesopotamia (present-day Iraq)] toward the east. The fourth river is the Euphrates [[C]a major river in Mesopotamia; the location of Eden is uncertain, but this passage suggests Mesopotamia].

15The LORD God [[L]took and] put ·the man [*or* Adam; 1:27] in the garden of Eden to ·care for [*or* till] it and ·work [take care of; look after] it. 16The LORD God commanded him, "You may eat the fruit from ·any tree [*or* all the trees] in the garden, 17but you must not eat the fruit from the tree ·which gives the [[T]of the] knowledge of good and evil [[C]eating from this tree would make Adam, not God, the determiner of right and wrong]. If you ever eat fruit from that tree, you will [[L]certainly] die!"

The First Woman

18Then the LORD God said, "It is not good for the man to be alone. I will make a helper [[C]in the sense of a partner or ally; the word does not imply subordinate status; see Ps. 79:9] who ·is right for [is suitable for; corresponds with] him."

19From the ground God formed every ·wild animal [[L]animal of the field] and every bird in the ·sky [heavens], and he brought them to the man ·so the man could name them [[L]to see what he would call them]. Whatever the man called each living thing, that became its name. 20The man gave names to all the ·tame animals [beasts; livestock], to the birds in the ·sky [heavens], and to all the ·wild animals [[L]animals of the field]. But ·Adam [*or* the man; 1:27] did not find a helper that was right for him [2:18]. 21So the LORD God caused ·the man to sleep very deeply [[L]a deep sleep to fall on the man/Adam], and while he was asleep, God removed one of the man's ·ribs [or sides]. Then God closed up the man's skin at the place where he took the ·rib [or side]. 22The LORD God used the ·rib [or side] from the man to ·make [Lbuild; construct] a woman, and then he brought the woman to the man.

23And the man said,

"·Now, this is someone whose bones came from my bones,
whose body came from my body [LAt last, this is bone of my bones
and flesh of my flesh].
·I will call her [LShe will be called] 'woman [CHebrew '*ishshah*],'
because she was taken out of man [CHebrew '*ish*]."

24So a man will leave his father and mother [Cin the sense of a new primary loyalty] and be united with his wife, and the two will become one ·body [Tflesh].

25The man and his wife were naked, but they were not ashamed.

The Beginning of Sin

3 Now the ·snake [serpent] was the most ·clever [shrewd; cunning; crafty] of all the wild animals the LORD God had made. One day the snake said to the woman, "Did God really say that you must not eat fruit from any tree in the garden?"

2The woman answered the snake [3:1], "We may eat fruit from the trees in the garden. 3But God told us, 'You must not eat fruit from the tree that is in the middle of the garden [Cthe tree of the knowledge of good and evil]. You must not even touch it [CEve was adding to the divine command], or you will die.'"

4But the snake [3:1] said to the woman, "You will [Lmost certainly] not die. 5[LFor] God knows that if you eat ·the fruit from that tree [Lfrom it], [Lyour eyes will be opened and] you will ·learn about [experience; Lknow about] good and evil and you will be like God!"

6The woman saw that the tree was ·beautiful [Lpleasing to the eyes], that its fruit was good ·to eat [Lfor food], and that it would make her wise. So she took some of its fruit and ate it. She also gave some of the fruit to her husband who was with her [Capparently he was present but silent while the woman spoke to the snake], and he ate it.

7Then, ·it was as if their eyes [Lthe eyes of both of them] were opened. They ·realized [knew] they were naked, so they sewed fig leaves together and made ·something to cover [Lloincloths for] themselves [Rom. 5:12–21].

8Then they heard the [Lsound of the] LORD God walking in the garden during the cool part of the day, and the man and his wife hid from the LORD God among the trees in the garden. 9But the LORD God called to the man and said, "Where are you?"

10The man answered, "I heard ·you walking in the garden [Lyour voice/sound], and I was afraid because I was naked, so I hid."

11·God [LHe] asked, "Who told you that you were naked? Did you eat fruit from the tree from which I commanded you not to eat?"

12The man said, "You gave this woman to me and she gave me fruit from the tree, so I ate it."

13Then the LORD God said to the woman, "·How could you have done such a thing [What is this you have done]?"

She answered, "The snake ·tricked [deceived; 1 Tim. 2:14] me, so I ate the fruit."

14The LORD God said to the ·snake [serpent],

"Because you did this,
a curse will be put on you.
You will be cursed as no other animal, ·tame [beasts; livestock] or ·wild [Lof the field], will ever be.
You will ·crawl [go] on your ·stomach [belly],
and you will eat dust all the days of your life.
15I will ·make you and the woman
enemies to each other [Tplace hostility/enmity between you and the woman].
Your ·descendants [Lseed] and her ·descendants [Lseed]
will be enemies.
·One of her descendants [LHe] will crush your head,
and you will ·bite [strike; Tbruise; Lcrush] his heel [Rom. 16:20; Rev. 12:9]."
16Then God said to the woman,
"I will ·cause you to have much trouble [*or* increase your pain]
·when you are pregnant [in childbearing],
and when you give birth to children,
you will have great pain.
You will greatly desire [Cthe word implies a desire to control; 4:7] your husband,
but he will rule over you."
17Then God said to ·the man [*or* Adam; 1:27], "You listened to what
your wife said, and you ate fruit from the tree from which I commanded
you not to eat.
"·So I will put a curse on [Cursed is] the ground,
and you will have to ·work very hard [toil; labor] for your food.
In pain you will eat its food
all the days of your life.
18The ground will produce thorns and ·weeds [thistles] for you,
and you will eat the plants of the field.
19·You will sweat and work hard for [LBy the sweat of your brow you will eat] your food.
Later you will return to the ground,
because you were taken from it.
You are dust,
and ·when you die, you will return to the dust [Tto dust you will return; 1 Cor. 15:21–22, 40–45]."
20The man named his wife Eve [Cthe name derives from an early form of
the verb "to live"], because she was the mother of all the living.
21The LORD God made clothes from animal skins for ·the man [*or*
Adam; 1:27] and his wife and dressed them. 22Then the LORD God said,
"Humans have become like one of us [Creferring to the supernatural heavenly beings, God and the angels]; they know good and evil. We must keep them from [Lputting forth their hand and taking and] eating some of the fruit from the tree of life, or they will live forever." 23So the LORD
God ·forced [expelled] Adam out of the garden of Eden to ·work [till; *or* care for; 2:5] the ground from which he was taken. 24After God ·forced
[drove] humans out of the garden, he placed ·angels [Lcherubim; Cparticularly powerful spiritual beings] and a sword of fire that flashed

around in every direction on its eastern border. ·This kept people from getting [...to guard the way] **to the tree of life.**

The First Family

4 ·Adam [LThe man; 1:27] **·had sexual relations with** [Lknew] **his wife Eve, and she ·became pregnant** [conceived] **and gave birth to Cain. Eve said, "With the LORD's help, I have ·given birth to** [Lproduced; *or* acquired; Cthe verb resembles Cain's name] **a man." 2After that, Eve gave birth to Cain's brother Abel** [Cresembles the word for vapor or breath]. **Abel took care of flocks, and Cain ·became a farmer** [Lwas a tiller/worker of the ground].

3·Later [In due course; LAt the end of the days], **Cain brought some ·food** [produce; fruit] **from the ground as a ·gift** [tribute; Lev. 2] **to God. 4Abel brought the ·best parts** [fat portions; Lev. 3:16] **from some of the firstborn of his flock** [Heb. 11:4]. **The LORD ·accepted** [looked with favor on] **Abel and his ·gift** [tribute], **5but he did not ·accept** [look with favor on] **Cain and his ·gift** [tribute]. **So Cain became very angry and ·felt rejected** [*or* felt dejected; Lhis face/countenance fell].

6The LORD asked Cain, "Why are you angry? Why ·do you look so unhappy [Lhas your face/countenance fallen; 4:5]? **7If you do things ·well** [correctly; appropriately], **·I will** [Lwill I not...?] **accept you, but if you do not do them ·well** [correctly; appropriately], **sin is ·ready to attack you** [Lcrouching at the door]. **Sin ·wants** [desires to control; 3:16] **you, but you must rule over it."**

8Cain said to his brother Abel, "Let's go out into the field."[n] **While they were out in the field, Cain ·attacked** [Lrose up against] **his brother Abel and killed him** [Matt. 23:35; Luke 11:51; Heb. 12:24; 1 John 3:11–12; Jude 11].

9Later, the LORD said to Cain, "Where is your brother Abel?"

Cain answered, "I don't know. ·Is it my job to take care of my brother [TAm I my brother's keeper]**?"**

10Then the LORD said, "What have you done? Your brother's blood is crying out to me from the ground. 11And now you will be cursed ·in your work with [Land banished from] **the ground, ·the same ground where your brother's blood fell and where your hands killed him** [Lwhich has opened its mouth to take the blood of your brother from your hand]. **12You will ·work** [till] **the ground, but it will not ·grow good crops** [Lyield its strength] **for you anymore, and you will ·wander around** [be a fugitive and a wanderer/homeless wanderer] **on the earth."**

13Then Cain said to the LORD, "This punishment is more than I can ·stand [bear]! **14Today you have forced me ·to stop working** [Lfrom] **the ground, and now I ·must hide from you** [*or* will be hidden from your face]. **I ·must wander around** [Lwill be a fugitive and wanderer/homeless wanderer] **on the earth, and anyone who ·meets** [finds] **me can kill me."**

15The LORD said to Cain, "No! If anyone kills you, I will ·punish [avenge] **that person seven times more." Then the LORD put a mark** [Cthe nature of the mark is uncertain] **on Cain warning anyone who ·met** [finds] **him not to kill him.**

Cain's Family

16So Cain went away from the LORD and lived in the land of Nod [Cresembles a Hebrew word meaning "wanderer"], **east of Eden. 17He ·had sexual relations with** [Lknew; 4:1] **his wife, and she ·became pregnant** [conceived] **and gave birth to Enoch. At that time ·Cain** [Lhe] **was building a city, which he named after his son Enoch. 18·Enoch had a son named**

4:8 Cain...field This sentence appears in some Greek copies, but not in the Hebrew text.

[LTo Enoch was born; Cand so through the rest of the genealogy] **Irad, Irad had a son named Mehujael, Mehujael had a son named Methushael, and Methushael had a son named Lamech.**

19**Lamech ·married** [Ltook] **two ·women** [*or* wives], [Lthe name of the first was] **Adah and** [Lthe name of the second was] **Zillah.** 20**Adah gave birth to Jabal, who ·became the first person to** [Lwas the father of those who] **live in tents and raise ·cattle** [livestock]. 21**Jabal's brother was Jubal, the ·first person to** [Lfather of all who] **play the ·harp** [*or* lyre] **and ·flute** [pipe]. 22**Zillah gave birth to Tubal-Cain, who made tools out of bronze and iron. The sister of Tubal-Cain was Naamah.**

23**Lamech said to his wives:**

"Adah and Zillah, hear my voice!
You wives of Lamech, listen to what I say.
I killed a man for wounding me,
a young man for hitting me.
24**If ·Cain's killer is punished** [LCain is avenged] **seven times** [4:15],
then ·Lamech's killer will be punished [LLamech will be avenged]
seventy-seven times." [CLamech falsely thought he could get away with murder.]

Adam and Eve Have a New Son

25**Adam ·had sexual relations with** [Lknew; 4:1] **his wife Eve again, and she gave birth to a son. She named him Seth** [Crelated to the Hebrew word for "give" or "appoint"] **and said, "God has ·given** [appointed for] **me another child. He will take the place of Abel, who was killed by Cain."**
26**Seth also had a son, and they named him Enosh. At that time people began to ·pray to** [Lcall on the name of] **the LORD.**

Adam's Family History

5 **This is the ·family history** [Lbook of the generations; see 2:4] **of Adam. When God created ·human beings** [humankind; Tman; CHebrew *Adam;* 1:27–28], **he made them in his own likeness.** 2**He created them male and female, and on that day he blessed them and named them ·human beings** [humankind; *or* Adam; Tman].

3**When Adam was 130 years old, he became the father of another son in his likeness and image** [Cindicating he was like Adam and that he also bore God's image], **and Adam named him Seth** [4:25]. 4**After Seth was born, Adam lived 800 years and had other sons and daughters.** 5**So Adam lived a total of 930 years, and then he died** [Cthe long lives in this genealogy indicate God's blessing; these names are also in Jesus' genealogy in Luke 3:36–38].

6**When Seth was 105 years old, he had a son named Enosh.** 7**After Enosh was born, Seth lived 807 years and had other sons and daughters.** 8**So Seth lived a total of 912 years, and then he died.**

9**When Enosh was 90 years old, he had a son named Kenan.** 10**After Kenan was born, Enosh lived 815 years and had other sons and daughters.** 11**So Enosh lived a total of 905 years, and then he died.**

12**When Kenan was 70 years old, he had a son named Mahalalel.** 13**After Mahalalel was born, Kenan lived 840 years and had other sons and daughters.** 14**So Kenan lived a total of 910 years, and then he died.**

15**When Mahalalel was 65 years old, he had a son named Jared.** 16**After Jared was born, Mahalalel lived 830 years and had other sons and daughters.** 17**So Mahalalel lived a total of 895 years, and then he died.**

18**When Jared was 162 years old, he had a son named Enoch.** 19**After Enoch was born, Jared lived 800 years and had other sons and daughters.**

20 So Jared lived a total of 962 years, and then he died.

21 When Enoch was 65 years old, he had a son named Methuselah. 22 After Methuselah was born, Enoch walked with God 300 years more and had other sons and daughters. 23 So Enoch lived a total of 365 years. 24 Enoch walked with God [C he had a close relationship with God; Heb. 11:5–6]; one day Enoch could not be found, because God took him [C like Elijah (2 Kin. 2:11), he did not die].

25 When Methuselah was 187 years old, he had a son named Lamech. 26 After Lamech was born, Methuselah lived 782 years and had other sons and daughters. 27 So Methuselah lived a total of 969 years, and then he died.

28 When Lamech was 182, he had a son. 29 Lamech named his son Noah [C the name resembles the Hebrew word for "rest"] and said, "He will ·comfort us in [*or* give us rest from] our work, which comes from the ground the LORD has cursed [3:17–19]." 30 After Noah was born, Lamech lived 595 years and had other sons and daughters. 31 So Lamech lived a total of 777 years, and then he died.

32 After Noah was 500 years old, he became the father of Shem, Ham, and Japheth [9:18–29; 10].

The Human Race Grows More Evil

6 The number of people on earth began to ·grow [multiply], and daughters were born to them. 2 When the ·sons of God [C may refer to godly men among Seth's descendants (ch. 5), or noble men, or angels] saw that ·these girls [L the daughters of men/human beings; C either evil women among Cain's descendants (4:17–24), poor women, or simply mortal women] were beautiful, they married any of them they chose [C though their identity is unclear, their marriage clearly violated a boundary]. 3 The LORD said, "My Spirit will not ·remain in [*or* contend with] human beings forever, because they are ·flesh [mortal]. ·They will live [L Their days will be] only 120 years."

4 The ·Nephilim [L fallen ones; C the significance of the name is unclear] were on the earth in those days and also later. That was when the sons of God ·had sexual relations with [L came in to] the daughters of ·human beings [T man; C Hebrew: Adam; 1:27–28]. These women gave birth to children ·who became famous [L men of a name] and were the mighty warriors of long ago. [C The Nephilim of Num. 13:31–33, though not related genealogically, were giants, suggesting these pre-flood Nephilim were also.]

5 The LORD saw that the human beings on the earth were very ·wicked [evil] and that ·everything they thought about [L every inclination of their mind/heart] was ·evil [wicked]. 6 He ·was sorry [regretted] he had made human beings on the earth, and his heart was filled with pain. 7 So the LORD said, "I will ·destroy [wipe/blot out; exterminate] all human beings that I ·made [created; 1:1] on the earth. And I will destroy every animal and everything that ·crawls [creeps] on the earth and the birds of the ·air [sky; heavens], because I ·am sorry [regret] I have made them." 8 But Noah ·pleased [L found grace/favor in the eyes of] the LORD.

Noah and the Great Flood

9 This is the family history [2:4] of Noah. Noah was a ·good [righteous; just] man, the most ·innocent [blameless; Job 1:1] man of his ·time [generation], and he walked with God [5:24]. 10 He had three sons: Shem, Ham, and Japheth [9:18–10:32].

11 ·People on earth [L The earth] did what ·God said was evil [L was corrupt before God], and ·violence was everywhere [L the earth was filled

with violence]. 12When God saw that [Lthe earth was corrupt because]
·everyone [Lall flesh] on the earth ·did only evil [Lwas corrupt], 13God said
to Noah, "·I have decided to bring an end to all living creatures [LThe end
of all flesh is coming before me]. Because people have made the earth full
of violence, I will destroy all of them from the ·earth [land]. 14·Build
[Make] ·a boat [Lan ark] of ·cypress [*or* gopher; Cthe precise meaning is
uncertain] wood for yourself. Make rooms in it and cover it inside and
outside with ·tar [pitch]. 15This is how ·big I want you to build the boat
[Lyou should make it]: ·four hundred fifty feet [Lthree hundred cubits]
long, ·seventy-five feet [Lfifty cubits] wide, and ·forty-five feet [Lthirty
cubits] high. 16Make an opening around the top of the boat [Cprobably a
window] that is ·eighteen inches [La cubit] high from the edge of the roof
down. Put a door in the side of the boat. Make an ·upper, middle, and
lower [Llower, second, and third] deck in it. 17I will bring a flood of water
on the earth to destroy all ·living things [Lflesh] that live under ·the sky
[heaven], including everything that has the breath of life. Everything on
the earth will die. 18But I will ·make [establish] an ·agreement [covenant;
treaty] with you—you, your sons, your wife, and your sons' wives will all
go into the boat. 19Also, you must bring into the ·boat [Lark] two of ·every
living thing [Lall flesh], male and female. Keep them alive with you. 20Two
of every kind of bird, animal, and ·crawling [creeping] thing will come to
you to be kept alive. 21Also ·gather [take] some of every kind of food and
store it on the boat as food for you and the animals."

22Noah did everything that God commanded him.

The Flood Begins

7 Then the LORD said to Noah, "I have seen that you ·are the best
person [alone are righteous] among ·the people of this time [Lthis
generation], so you and your ·family [household] can go into the ·boat
[ark]. 2Take with you seven pairs, each male with its female, of every kind
of clean [Cin a ritual sense; Lev. 11] animal, and take one pair, each male
with its female, of every kind of unclean animal. 3Take seven pairs of all
the birds of the ·sky [heavens], each male with its female. This will allow
all these animals to continue living on the earth after the flood. 4Seven
days from now I will send rain on the earth. It will rain forty days and
forty nights, and I will ·wipe off [blot out] from the ·earth [Lface of the
ground] every living thing that I have made."

5Noah did everything the LORD commanded him.

6Noah was six hundred years old when the [Lwater of the] flood came
[Lon the earth]. 7He and his wife and his sons and their wives went into
the ·boat [ark] to escape the waters of the flood. 8The clean animals [7:2],
the unclean animals, the birds, and everything that ·crawls [creeps] on
the ground 9came to Noah. They went into the ·boat [ark] in groups of
two, male and female, just as God had commanded Noah. 10Seven days
later the ·flood started [Lwaters of the flood came on the earth].

11When Noah was six hundred years old, the flood started. On the seventeenth day of the second month of that year the ·underground springs
[Lfountains/springs of the deep] ·split [burst] open, and the ·clouds [flood-
gates; Lwindows] in the ·sky [heavens] ·poured out rain [Lwere opened].
12The rain fell on the earth for forty days and forty nights.

13On that same day Noah and his wife, his sons Shem, Ham, and
Japheth [9:18—10:32], and their wives went into the ·boat [ark]. 14They
had every kind of wild and tame animal, every kind of animal that ·crawls

[creeps] on the earth, and ·every kind of bird [Levery bird, every winged
creature]. 15·Every creature [LAll flesh] that had the breath of life came to
Noah in the ·boat [ark] in groups of two. 16One male and one female of
·every living thing [Lall flesh] came, just as God had commanded Noah.
Then the LORD ·closed the door behind them [Lshut them in].

17·Water flooded the earth [LThe flood continued] for forty days, and
as it rose it lifted the ·boat [ark] off the ground. 18The water continued to
rise [Land increase], and the ·boat [ark] floated on ·it above the earth [Lthe
face of the waters]. 19The water rose so much [Lover the earth] that even
the highest mountains under the ·sky [heavens] were covered by it. 20It
continued to rise until it was more than ·twenty feet [Lfifteen cubits]
above the mountains.

21All ·living things [Lflesh] that moved on the earth died. This included
all the birds, tame animals, wild animals, and [Lswarming] creatures that
swarm on the earth, as well as all human beings. 22So everything on dry
land that had the breath of life in ·it [Lits nostrils] died. 23God ·destroyed
[blotted/wiped out] from the earth every living thing that was on the
·land [Lface of the ground]—every man, animal, ·crawling [creeping]
thing, and bird of the ·sky [heavens]. All that ·was left [survived] was
Noah and what was with him in the ·boat [ark]. 24And the waters continued to cover the earth for one hundred fifty days.

The Flood Ends

8 But God remembered Noah and all the ·wild [beasts] and ·tame
animals [cattle] with him in the ·boat [ark]. He made a wind
·blow [pass] over the earth, and the water ·went down [subsided]. 2The
·underground springs [Lfountains/springs of the deep] stopped flowing,
and the ·clouds [floodgates; Lwindows] in the ·sky [heavens] ·stopped
pouring down rain [Lwere closed and the rain from the sky/heavens were
restrained]. 3-4The water that covered the earth began to ·go down
[recede]. After one hundred fifty days ·it [Lthe waters] had ·gone down
[abated] so much that the ·boat [ark] touched land again. It came to rest
on one of the mountains of Ararat [Cin ancient Urartu, present-day eastern Turkey] on the seventeenth day of the seventh month. 5The water
continued to ·go down [recede] so that by the first day of the tenth month
the tops of the mountains could be seen.

6Forty days later Noah opened the ·window [hatch] he had made in the
·boat [ark], and 7he sent out a raven. It ·flew [Lwent] here and there until
the water had dried up from the earth. 8Then Noah sent out a dove to find
out if the water had ·dried up [subsided] from the ground. 9The dove
could not find a place to ·land [Lset/rest its foot] because water still covered the earth, so it came back to the ·boat [ark]. Noah reached out his
hand and took the bird and brought it back into the boat.

10After [Lwaiting] seven days Noah again sent out the dove from the ·boat
[ark], 11and that evening it came back to him with a fresh olive leaf in its
·mouth [beak]. Then Noah knew that the ·ground was almost dry [Lwaters
had subsided from the ground]. 12·Seven days later [LAfter waiting another
seven days] he sent the dove out again, but this time it did not come back.

13When Noah was six hundred and one years old, in the first day of the
first month of that year, the water was dried up from the ·land [earth].
Noah removed the covering of the ·boat [ark] and saw that the ·land
[Lface of the ground] was dry. 14By the twenty-seventh day of the second
month the ·land [earth] was completely dry.

[15]Then God said to Noah, [16]"You and your wife, your sons, and their
wives should go out of the ·boat [ark]. [17]Bring every ·animal [[L]living thing
of all flesh] out of the ·boat [ark] with you—the birds, ·animals [beasts;
livestock], and everything that crawls on the earth. ·Let them have many
young ones so that they might […so they may swarm on earth and be
fruitful and] ·grow in number [multiply; 1:22]."
[18]So Noah went out with his sons, his wife, and his sons' wives. [19]Every
·animal [living thing], everything that ·crawls [creeps] on the earth, and
every bird [[L]and everything that crawls/creeps] went out of the ·boat [ark]
by families.
[20]Then Noah built an altar [[C]a place to offer sacrifices] to the LORD. He
took some of all the clean [[C]in a ritual sense] birds and ·animals [beasts;
livestock], and he ·burned them on the altar as offerings to God [[L]offered
a whole burnt offering on the altar; Lev. 1]. [21]The LORD ·was pleased with
these sacrifices [[L]smelled the sweet savor/smell] and said ·to himself [[L]in
his heart], "I will never again curse the ground because of human beings.
·Their thoughts [The inclination of their hearts] are evil even ·when [from
the time] they are young, but I will never again destroy every living thing
on the earth as I did this time.
[22]"As long as the earth continues,
planting and harvest,
cold and hot,
summer and winter,
day and night
will not stop."

The New Beginning

9 Then God blessed Noah and his sons and said to them, "·Have
many children; grow in number [[T]Be fruitful and multiply] and
fill the earth [1:22, 29]. [2]Every ·animal [living thing] on earth, every bird
in the ·sky [heavens], every animal that crawls on the ground, and every
fish in the sea will ·respect [fear] and ·fear [dread; be terrified of] you. I
have given them ·to you [[L]into your hand].
[3]"Everything that moves, everything that is alive, is yours for food.
Earlier I gave you the green plants [1:29–30], but now I give you everything for food. [4]But you must not eat ·meat [flesh] that still has blood in
it, because blood ·gives [[L]is] life [Lev. 3:17; 7:26–27; 17:10–14]. [5]I will
·demand [require; [L]seek] blood for life. I will ·demand [require; [L]seek] the
life of any animal that kills a person, and I will ·demand [require; [L]seek]
the life of anyone who takes another person's life.
[6]"Whoever ·kills [[L]sheds the blood of] a human being
will ·be killed [[L]have his blood shed] by a human being,
because God made humans
in ·his own image [[L]the image of God; 1:26–27].
[7]"As for you, Noah, ·I want you and your family to have many children,
to grow in number on the earth, and to become many [[L]be fruitful and
multiply, swarm/teem over the earth and multiply on it; 9:1]."
[8]Then God said to Noah and his sons, [9]"·Now [*or* Look] I am making my
·agreement [covenant; treaty; 6:18] with you and your ·people [seed] ·who
will live after you [[L]after you], [10]and with every living thing that is with
you—the birds, the ·tame [livestock; cattle] and the wild animals, and with
everything that came out of the ·boat [ark] with you—with every living
thing on earth. [11]I ·make [establish] this ·agreement [covenant; treaty; 6:18]

with you: ·I will never again destroy all living things by a flood [La flood will
never again cut off all flesh]. A flood will never again destroy the earth."
12And God said, "This is the sign [Ca symbol that represents this relationship between God and Noah; 17:11; Ex. 31:13, 17] of the ·agreement
[covenant; treaty; 6:18] between me and you and every living creature that
is with you for all future generations. 13I am putting my ·rainbow [bow;
Cmay represent God hanging up his weapon after warring against human-
ity] in the clouds as the sign of the ·agreement [covenant; treaty; 6:18]
between me and the earth. 14When I bring clouds over the earth and a
·rainbow [bow] appears in them, 15I will remember my ·agreement [cove-
nant; treaty; 6:18] between me and you and every living thing [Lof all
flesh]. [LThe waters of the] Floods will never again destroy all ·life on the
earth [Lflesh]. 16When the ·rainbow [bow] appears in the clouds, I will see
it and I will remember the ·agreement that continues forever [Leternal cov-
enant] between me and every living thing [Lof all flesh] on the earth."
17So God said to Noah, "·The rainbow [LThis] is a ·sign [9:12] of the
·agreement [covenant; treaty; 6:18] that I made with all living things
on earth."

Noah and His Sons

18The sons of Noah who came out of the ·boat [ark] with him were
Shem, Ham, and Japheth. (Ham was the father of Canaan.) 19These three
men were Noah's sons, and all the people on earth ·came [spread out; Csee
the genealogy in ch. 10] from these three sons.
20Noah ·became a farmer [Lwas the first man of the ground/soil] and
planted a vineyard. 21When he drank ·wine made from his grapes [Lthe
wine], he became drunk and lay ·naked [uncovered] in his tent. 22Ham,
the father of Canaan, looked at his naked father and told his [Ltwo] brothers outside [Can act of disrespect; he should have helped his father, as in
the next verse]. 23Then Shem and Japheth got a coat and, carrying it on
both their shoulders, they walked backwards into the tent and covered
[Lthe nakedness of] their father. They turned their faces away so that they
did not see their father's nakedness [Cthey acted appropriately according
to ancient custom].
24Noah ·was sleeping because of the wine. When he woke up [woke up
from his wine] and ·learned [Lhe knew] what his youngest son, Ham, had
done to him, 25he said,

"May there be a curse on Canaan [Cthe ancestor and representative of
the inhabitants of Palestine that Israel displaced at the time of the
conquest of the Promised Land; Josh. 1–12]!
May he be the lowest ·slave [servant] to his brothers."
26Noah also said,
"May the LORD, the God of Shem, be ·praised [blessed]!
May Canaan be Shem's ·slave [servant; LShem is the ancestor of Israel].
27May God ·give more land to [make space for; Cthe verb sounds like his
name] Japheth.
May Japheth live in Shem's tents,
and may Canaan be their slave [10:2–4; 1 Chr. 1:5–7]."

28After the flood Noah lived 350 years. 29·He lived a total of [LAll the
days of Noah were] 950 years, and then he died.

Nations Grow and Spread

10 ·This is the family history [LThese are the generations; 2:4] of
Shem, Ham, and Japheth, the sons of Noah. After the flood
·these three men had sons [Lsons were born to them].

Japheth's Sons

2The sons of Japheth were Gomer, Magog, Madai [Cancestor of the Medes]**, Javan, Tubal, Meshech, and Tiras.**

3The sons of Gomer [Cancestor of the Cimmerians] **were Ashkenaz** [Cancestor of the Scythians]**, Riphath, and Togarmah.**

4The sons of Javan were Elishah, Tarshish, Kittim [Cancestor of the people of Cyprus]**, and ·Rodanim** [LDodanim; see 1 Chr. 1:7]. **5·Those who lived in the lands around the Mediterranean Sea** [LThe people of the coastlands] **·came** [spread] **from these sons of Japheth. All the ·families** [clans] **grew and became different nations, each nation with its own land and its own language.**

Ham's Sons

6The sons of Ham [Cancestors of near neighbors and rivals of Israel] **were Cush** [Cancestor of the Ethiopians]**, Mizraim** [Cancestor of the Egyptians]**, Put** [Cperhaps ancestor of the Libyans]**, and Canaan.**

7The sons of Cush were Seba, Havilah, Sabtah, Raamah, and Sabteca.

The sons of Raamah were Sheba and Dedan [Csome of their descendants were the people around the Red Sea and southern Arabia].

8Cush also had a descendant named Nimrod, who became a very powerful man on earth. 9He was a ·great [mighty] **hunter before the LORD, which is why people say someone is "like Nimrod, a ·great** [mighty] **hunter before the LORD." 10·At first Nimrod's kingdom covered** [LThe beginning of his kingdom was] **Babylon, ·Erech** [*or* Uruk]**, Akkad, and Calneh** [Cwell-known cities in southern Mesopotamia] **in the land of ·Babylonia** [LShinar]. **11From there he went to Assyria** [Cin northern Mesopotamia]**, where he built the cities of Nineveh, ·Rehoboth Ir** [*or* that is a great city]**, and Calah. 12He also built Resen, the great city between Nineveh and Calah.**

13Mizraim [10:6] **was the father of the ·Ludites** [Cprobably the Lydians]**, Anamites, Lehabites, Naphtuhites, 14Pathrusites, Casluhites, and the ·people of Crete** [LCaphtorites]. **(The Philistines came from the ·Casluhites** [*or* Caphtorites].**)**

15Canaan [Cthe son of Ham whom Noah cursed; 9:25–27] **was the father of Sidon** [Cname of a famous coastal city in Syria]**, his first son, and of Heth** [Cancestor of the Hittites, important inhabitants of Asia Minor]. **16He was also the father of the Jebusites** [Cpre-Israelite inhabitants of Jerusalem]**, Amorites, Girgashites, 17Hivites, Arkites, Sinites, 18Arvadites, Zemarites, and Hamathites** [Cpeoples who lived in Syria-Palestine before the Israelites]. **The ·families** [clans] **of the Canaanites scattered. 19Their land reached from Sidon to Gerar as far as Gaza, and then to Sodom, Gomorrah, Admah, and Zeboiim, as far as Lasha.**

20All these people were the sons of Ham, and all these ·families [clans] **had their own languages, their own lands, and their own nations.**

Shem's Sons

21Shem, Japheth's older brother, also had sons. One of his descendants was the father of all the sons of Eber [Cthe Israelites were descended from Shem through Eber].

22The sons of Shem were Elam [Ca country east of Mesopotamia]**, Asshur** [Cin northern Mesopotamia]**, Arphaxad, Lud, and Aram** [Cnorth of Israel in Syria].

23The sons of Aram were Uz, Hul, Gether, and Meshech.

24Arphaxad was the father of Shelah, who was the father of Eber. 25Eber was the father of two sons—one named Peleg [Crelated to the Hebrew word for "divided"]**, because the earth was divided during his life, and the other was named Joktan.**

26 Joktan was the father of Almodad, Sheleph, Hazarmaveth, Jerah, 27 Hadoram, Uzal, Diklah, 28 Obal, Abimael, Sheba, 29 Ophir, Havilah, and Jobab. All these people were the sons of Joktan. 30 They lived in the area between Mesha and Sephar in the hill country in the East.

31 These are the people from the ·family [clans] of Shem, arranged by ·families [clans], languages, countries, and nations.

32 This is the list of the ·families [clans] from the sons of Noah, arranged according to their nations. From these ·families [clans] came all the nations who ·spread [branched out] across the earth after the flood.

The Languages Confused

11 At this time the whole world spoke one language, and everyone used the same words. 2 As people ·moved [migrated] ·from the east [*or* eastward; 2:8; 4:16], they found a plain in the land of ·Babylonia [LShinar] and settled there.

3 They said to each other, "Let's make bricks and ·bake [burn; fire] them ·to make them hard [thoroughly; Cin ancient times builders used mud-brick]." So they used bricks instead of stones, and ·tar [bitumen] instead of mortar. 4 Then they said to each other, "Let's build a city and a tower for ourselves, whose top will reach high into ·the sky [heaven; Ca ziggurat or stepped pyramid at whose top was a temple thought to be in heaven]. We will ·become famous [Lmake for ourselves a reputation/name]. Then we will not be scattered over all the earth."

5 The LORD came down to see the city and the tower that the ·people [Lsons of man] had built. 6 The LORD said, "Now, these people are ·united [Lone], all speaking ·the same [Lone] language. This is only the beginning of what they will do. ·They will be able to do anything they want [LNothing they want to do will be impossible for them]. 7 Come, let us go down and confuse their language [Lthere] so they will not be able to understand each other."

8 So the LORD scattered them from there over all the earth, and they ·stopped [ceased] building the city. 9 The place is called Babel [Csounds like the Hebrew word for "confused"] since that is where the LORD confused the language of the whole world. So the LORD caused them to spread out from there over the whole world.

The Story of Shem's Family

10 This is the ·family history [Lbook of the generations; 2:4] of Shem [9:18; 10:21–31]. Two years after the flood, when Shem was 100 years old, his son Arphaxad [10:22] was born. 11 After that, Shem lived 500 years and had other sons and daughters.

12 When Arphaxad was 35 years old, his son Shelah [10:24] was born. 13 After that, Arphaxad lived 403 years and had other sons and daughters.

14 When Shelah was 30 years old, his son Eber [10:21, 24] was born. 15 After that, Shelah lived 403 years and had other sons and daughters.

16 When Eber was 34 years old, his son Peleg [10:25] was born. 17 After that, Eber lived 430 years and had other sons and daughters.

18 When Peleg was 30 years old, his son Reu was born. 19 After that, Peleg lived 209 years and had other sons and daughters.

20 When Reu was 32 years old, his son Serug was born. 21 After that, Reu lived 207 years and had other sons and daughters.

22 When Serug was 30 years old, his son Nahor was born. 23 After that, Serug lived 200 years and had other sons and daughters.

24 When Nahor was 29 years old, his son Terah was born. 25 After that, Nahor lived 119 years and had other sons and daughters.

26After Terah was 70 years old, his sons Abram, Nahor, and Haran were
born.

The Story of Terah's Family

27·This is the family history [LThese are the generations; 2:4] of Terah.
Terah was the father of Abram, Nahor, and Haran. Haran was the father
of Lot. 28While his father, Terah, was still alive, Haran died in Ur [Ca major
city in southern Mesopotamia] ·in Babylonia [Lof the Chaldeans; CChaldea
was another name for Babylon], where he was born. 29Abram and Nahor
both ·married [Ltook wives]. Abram's wife was named Sarai, and Nahor's
wife was named Milcah. She was the daughter of Haran, who was the
father of both Milcah and Iscah. 30Sarai ·was not able to have children
[was barren; had no children].
31Terah took his son Abram, his grandson Lot (Haran's son), and his
daughter-in-law Sarai (Abram's wife) and moved out of Ur of ·Babylonia
[Lthe Chaldeans; 11:28]. They had planned to go to the land of Canaan,
but when they reached the city of Haran [Ca city in northern Syria], they
settled there.
32Terah lived to be 205 years old, and then he died in Haran.

God Calls Abram

12 The LORD said to Abram, "Leave your country, your relatives,
and your father's ·family [Lhouse], and go to the land I will
show you [CCanaan, the Promised Land].
2I will make you a great nation,
and I will bless you.
I will make ·you famous [Lyour name great],
·and [*or* so that] you will be a blessing to others.
3I will bless those who bless you,
and I will place a curse on those who ·harm [*or* curse] you.
And all the ·people [families; clans] on earth
will be blessed through you [Cthe promises of the Abrahamic covenant]."
4So Abram left Haran [11:31] as the LORD had told him, and Lot went
with him. At this time Abram was 75 years old. 5He took his wife Sarai, ·his
nephew [Lthe son of his brother] Lot, and everything they owned, as well as
all the ·servants [Lpeople] they had gotten in Haran. They set out from
Haran, planning to go to the land of Canaan, and in time they arrived there.
6Abram ·traveled [passed] through that land as far as the great oak [*or*
terebinth] tree of Moreh at Shechem [Ca town in northern Palestine]. The
Canaanites were living in the land at that time. 7The LORD appeared to
Abram and said, "I will give this land to your ·descendants [Lseed]." So
Abram built an altar [Ca place to offer sacrifices] there to the LORD, who
had appeared to him. 8Then he traveled from Shechem to the mountain
east of Bethel [Ca town in the central hill country south of Shechem] and
set up his tent there. Bethel was to the west, and Ai [Ca town near Bethel]
was to the east. There Abram built another altar to the LORD and ·
worshiped him [Lcalled on the name of the LORD]. 9After this, he traveled
on toward ·southern Canaan [Lthe Negev; 13:1].

Abram Goes to Egypt

10At this time there was ·not much food [La famine] in the land, so
Abram went down to Egypt to ·live [Lsojourn] because ·there was so little
food [Lthe famine was severe]. 11Just before they arrived in Egypt, he said
to his wife Sarai, "I know you are a very beautiful woman. 12When the

Egyptians see you, they will say, 'This woman is his wife.' Then they will kill me but let you live. [13]Tell them you are my sister so that things will go well with me and I may be allowed to live because of you [20:1–18; 26; CAbram did not trust God to protect him]."

[14]When Abram came to Egypt, the Egyptians saw that Sarai was very beautiful. [15]The Egyptian officers saw her and ·told the king of Egypt how beautiful she was [Lthey praised her]. They took her to the king's palace, and [16]the king was kind to Abram ·because he thought Abram was her brother [Lon account of her]. He gave Abram sheep, cattle, male and female donkeys, male and female servants, and camels.

[17]But the LORD sent terrible ·diseases [plagues] on the king and all the people in his house because of Abram's wife Sarai. [18]So the king sent for Abram and said, "What have you done to me? Why didn't you tell me Sarai was your wife? [19]Why did you say, 'She is my sister' so that I made her my wife? Now, here is your wife. Take ·her [Lyour wife] and ·leave [go]!" [20]Then the king commanded his men to make Abram leave Egypt; so Abram and his wife left with everything they owned.

Abram and Lot Separate

13 So Abram, his wife, and Lot ·left [Lcame up from] Egypt, taking everything they owned, and traveled ·to southern Canaan [Linto the Negev; Ca somewhat desolate area]. [2]Abram was very rich in cattle, silver, and gold.

[3]He ·left [Lwent by stages from] ·southern Canaan [Lthe Negev] and went back to Bethel where ·he had camped before [Lhis tent had been], between Bethel and Ai [12:8], [4]and where he had built an altar [Lat first]. So he ·worshiped [Lcalled on the name of] the LORD there.

[5]During this time Lot was traveling with Abram, and Lot also had flocks, herds, and tents. [6]Abram and Lot had so many ·animals [Lpossessions] that the land could not support both of them together, [7]so Abram's herdsmen and Lot's herdsmen began to argue. The Canaanites and the Perizzites were living in the land at this time.

[8]Abram said to Lot, "There should be no arguing between you and me, or between your herdsmen and mine, because we are ·brothers [relatives]. [9]We should separate. ·The whole land is [LIs not the whole land…?] there in front of you. If you go to the left, I will go to the right. If you go to the right, I will go to the left."

[10]Lot looked all around and saw the whole Jordan ·Valley [*or* plain; region] and that there was much water there. It was like the LORD's garden [Cthe garden of Eden], like the land of Egypt in the direction of Zoar [Cname meaning "small," in the vicinity of Sodom and Gomorrah; 14:2, 17; 19:23–24]. (This was before the LORD destroyed Sodom and Gomorrah [19:1–29].) [11]So Lot chose to move east and live in the Jordan Valley [13:10]. In this way Abram and Lot separated. [12]Abram lived in the land of Canaan, but Lot lived among the cities in the Jordan Valley [13:10], ·very near to [Lhe moved his tent near] Sodom. [13]Now the people of Sodom were very evil and were always sinning against the LORD.

[14]After Lot ·left [Lhad separated from him], the LORD said to Abram, "Look all around you—to the north and south and east and west. [15]All this land that you see I will give to you and your ·descendants [Lseed] forever. [16]I will make your ·descendants [Lseed] as many as the dust of the earth. If anyone could count the dust on the earth, he could count your ·people [Lseed]. [17]Get up! Walk through ·all [Lthe length and width of] this land because I am now giving it to you."

18 So Abram moved his tents and went to live near the great ·trees [L oaks; *or* terebinths] of Mamre [C an area near Hebron, named after an Amorite leader; 14:13, 24] at the city of Hebron [C nineteen miles south of Jerusalem]. There he built an altar to the LORD.

Lot Is Captured

14 Now Amraphel was king of ·Babylonia [L Shinar], Arioch was king of Ellasar [C possibly in Mesopotamia], Kedorlaomer was king of Elam [C located on the Iranian plateau], and Tidal was king of Goiim [C possibly a people otherwise known as the Umman-manda]. 2 All these kings went to war against several other kings: Bera king of Sodom, Birsha king of Gomorrah, Shinab king of Admah, Shemeber king of Zeboiim, and the king of Bela. (Bela is also called Zoar.) [C Sodom and Gomorrah were located in the vicinity of the Dead Sea, and the other named cities are thought to have been nearby.]

3 These kings who were attacked united their armies in the Valley of Siddim (·now [L that is] the ·Dead [L Salt] Sea). 4 They had served Kedorlaomer for twelve years, but in the thirteenth year, they all ·turned [rebelled] against him. 5 Then in the fourteenth year, Kedorlaomer and the kings with him came and ·defeated [subdued] the ·Rephaites [*or* Rephaim; C an especially warlike tribe in Canaan] in Ashteroth Karnaim, the Zuzites in Ham, and the Emites in Shaveh Kiriathaim [C the Zuzites and Emites were likely related to the Rephaites; Deut. 2:10–11]. 6 They also defeated the Horites in the mountains of ·Edom [L Seir; C a region outside of Palestine on the southeastern coast of the Dead Sea] to El Paran (near the ·desert [wilderness]). 7 Then they turned back and went to En Mishpat (that is, Kadesh). They ·defeated [subdued] all the Amalekites [C a fearsome tribe in pre-Israelite Canaan], as well as the Amorites who lived in Hazazon Tamar.

8 At that time the kings of Sodom, Gomorrah, Admah, Zeboiim, and Bela went out to fight in the Valley of Siddim. (Bela is called Zoar.) 9 They fought against Kedorlaomer king of Elam, Tidal king of Goiim, Amraphel king of ·Babylonia [L Shinar], and Arioch king of Ellasar—four kings fighting against five. 10 There were many ·tar [bitumen] pits in the Valley of Siddim. When the kings of Sodom and Gomorrah and their armies ·ran away [fled], some of the soldiers fell into the tar pits, but the others ·ran away [fled] to the mountains.

11 Now Kedorlaomer and his armies took everything the people of Sodom and Gomorrah owned, including their food, and left. 12 They took Lot, Abram's ·nephew [L son of his brother] who was living in Sodom, and ·everything he owned [L his possessions/goods]. Then they left. 13 One of the men who was not captured went to Abram, the Hebrew, and told him what had happened. At that time Abram was camped near the ·great trees [L oaks; *or* terebinths] of Mamre the Amorite. Mamre was a brother of Eshcol and Aner, and they had all made an ·agreement to help [covenant/treaty with] Abram.

Abram Rescues Lot

14 When Abram learned that ·Lot [L his relative/brother] had been captured, he called out his 318 trained men who had been born in his camp. He led the men and ·chased the enemy [went in pursuit] all the way to the town of Dan [C in the far north of Palestine]. 15 That night he divided his men into groups, and ·they made a surprise attack against the enemy [L he subdued/defeated/struck them]. They chased them all the way to Hobah, north of Damascus [C a major city in Syria]. 16 Then Abram brought back

·everything the enemy had stolen [Lall their possessions/goods], the women and the other people, and Lot, and ·everything Lot owned [Lhis goods/possessions].

17After defeating Kedorlaomer and the kings who were with him, Abram ·went home [Lreturned]. As he was returning, the king of Sodom came out to meet him in the Valley of Shaveh (now called King's Valley [Csomewhere in the vicinity of Jerusalem]).

18Melchizedek king of ·Salem [Cprobably an old name of Jerusalem] brought out bread and wine. He was a priest for God Most High [Ps. 110; Heb. 5:6–10; 6:20—7:28] 19and blessed Abram, saying,

"Abram, may you be blessed by God Most High,
 the ·God [Lone] who made heaven and earth.
20And ·we praise [Lblessed be] God Most High,
 who has ·helped you to defeat your enemies [Ldelivered your enemies
 into your hand]."

Then Abram gave Melchizedek a ·tenth [tithe] of everything he had brought back from the battle.

21The king of Sodom said to Abram, "You may keep ·all these things [the goods/possessions] for yourself. Just give me my people who were captured."

22But Abram said to the king of Sodom, "I ·make a promise [Llifted my hand; Ca gesture of swearing] to the LORD, the God Most High, who made heaven and earth. 23I promise that I will not keep anything that is yours. I will not keep even a thread or a sandal strap [Cthat is, not the smallest thing] so that you cannot say, 'I made Abram rich.' 24I will keep nothing but the food my young men have eaten. But give Aner, Eshcol, and Mamre their share of what we won, because they went with me into battle."

God's Covenant with Abram

15 After these things happened, the LORD spoke his word to Abram in a vision: "Abram, don't be afraid. I will ·defend [Lbe a shield to] you, and ·I will give you a great reward [Lyour reward will be great]."

2But Abram said, "Lord GOD [CHebrew *Adonai Yahweh;* combination of covenant name YHWH (2:4) with common Hebrew word for "sir," "lord," or "master"], what can you give me? I ·have no son [am childless], so my ·slave [servant] Eliezer from Damascus [Ca major city in Syria] will ·get everything I own after I die [be my heir; Ca household servant would take care of a childless couple in their old age and in turn inherit their possessions]." 3Abram said, "Look, you have given me no son, so a slave born in my house will ·inherit everything I have [be my heir]."

4Then the LORD spoke his word to Abram: "He will not be the one to inherit what you have. You will have a son of your own who will inherit what you have."

5Then God led Abram outside and said, "Look at the ·sky [heavens]. There are so many stars you cannot count them. Your ·descendants [Lseed] also will be too many to count."

6Abram ·believed [put his trust/faith in] the LORD. And the LORD ·accepted Abram's faith, and that faith made him right with God [Tcounted/credited it as righteousness; Rom. 4:3, 9, 22; Gal. 3:6; James 2:23].

7God said to Abram, "I am the LORD who led you out of Ur of ·Babylonia

[Lthe Chaldeans] so that I could give you this land ·to own [Las a possession; 12:1–3]."

8But Abram said, "Lord GOD, how can I ·be sure [Lknow] that I will ·own this land [possess/inherit it]?"

9·The LORD [LHe] said to Abram, "Bring me a three-year-old cow, a three-year-old goat, a three-year-old ·male sheep [ram], a ·dove [turtledove], and a young pigeon."

10Abram brought them all to God. Then Abram ·killed the animals and cut each of them into two pieces [Lsplit them down the middle], laying each half opposite the other half. But he did not cut the birds in half. 11Later, ·large birds [*or* birds of prey] flew down to eat the ·animals [Lcarcasses], but Abram chased them away [Cperhaps representing later enemies of Israel].

12As the sun was ·going down [setting], Abram fell into a deep sleep. While he was asleep, a very ·terrible [*or* frightening] darkness came. 13Then the LORD said to Abram, "You can be sure that your ·descendants [Lseed] will be ·strangers [sojourners; wanderers; resident aliens] in a land they don't own. The people there will make them slaves and ·be cruel to [oppress] them for four hundred years. 14But I will ·punish [judge] the nation ·where they are slaves [Lwhich they serve]. Then your ·descendants [Lseed] will leave that land, taking great ·wealth [possessions] with them. 15And you, Abram, will ·die [Lgo to your fathers/ancestors] in peace and will be buried at an old age. 16·After your great-great-grandchildren are born [LAfter the fourth generation], ·your people [Lthey] will come ·to this land [Lhere] again. It will take that long, because ·I am not yet going to punish the Amorites for their evil behavior [Tthe iniquity of the Amorites is not yet complete; CAmorites is one name for the pre-Israelite inhabitants of Canaan]."

17After the sun went down, it was very dark. Suddenly a smoking firepot and a blazing torch [Cfire and smoke often represent God] passed between the ·halves of the dead animals [Lpieces; Ca self-curse ritual; by passing between the pieces of the sacrifice, one vowed to keep an agreement or suffer the same fate as the animals]. 18So on that day the LORD ·made an agreement [Lcut a covenant/treaty; 6:18] with Abram and said, "I will give to your ·descendants [Lseed] the land between the river of Egypt and the great river Euphrates. 19This is the land of the Kenites, Kenizzites, Kadmonites, 20Hittites, Perizzites, Rephaites, 21Amorites, Canaanites, Girgashites, and Jebusites [Cthe name of peoples who lived in pre-Israelite Canaan]."

Ishmael Is Born

16 Sarai, Abram's wife, had no children, but she had a slave girl from Egypt named Hagar. 2Sarai said to Abram, "Look, the LORD has ·not allowed me to have [Lprevented/restrained me from having] children, so ·have sexual relations with [Lgo to] my slave girl. If she has a child, maybe I can ·have my own family [reproduce; have a child; Lbuild] through her [Ctaking a second wife or concubine was common for a childless couple at the time]."

Abram did what Sarai said. 3It was after he had lived ten years in Canaan that Sarai gave Hagar to her husband Abram as a ·wife [*or* concubine]. (Hagar was her slave girl from Egypt.)

4Abram ·had sexual relations with [Lwent in to] Hagar, and she ·became pregnant [conceived]. When Hagar learned she ·was pregnant [conceived], she began to ·treat [look on] her mistress Sarai ·badly [with contempt]. 5Then Sarai said to Abram, "·This is your fault [LMay the

wrong/violence done to me be on you]. I gave my slave girl ·to you [into
your embrace; Linto your lap], and when she ·became pregnant
[Lconceived], she began to ·treat [look on] me ·badly [with contempt]. Let
the LORD ·decide who is right—[judge between] you or me."
6But Abram said to Sarai, "·You are Hagar's mistress [LYour slave girl is
in your hand/power]. Do ·anything you want [Lwhat is good in your eyes]
to her." Then Sarai ·was hard on [afflicted; abused] Hagar, and Hagar ·ran
away [Lfled from her presence].
7The ·angel [messenger] of the LORD [Cthe angel of the Lord was either
a representative of the Lord or the Lord himself; v. 13; Judg. 6:11, 14]
found Hagar beside a spring of water in the ·desert [wilderness], by the
road to Shur [Clikely a location in southern Canaan; 20:1; 25:18; Ex. 15:22;
1 Sam. 15:7]. 8·The angel [LHe] said, "Hagar, Sarai's slave girl, where have
you come from? Where are you going?"
Hagar answered, "I am ·running away [fleeing] from my mistress Sarai."
9The ·angel [messenger] of the LORD [16:7] said to her, "Go home to
your mistress and ·obey [submit to] her." 10The angel of the LORD also
said, "I will ·give you so many descendants [Lgreatly multiply your seed so
that] they cannot be counted."
11The ·angel [messenger] added,

"You ·are now pregnant [have conceived],
and you will ·have [Lgive birth to] a son.
You will name him Ishmael [Csounds like the verb "to hear"],
because the LORD has heard ·your cries [Lof your affliction].
12Ishmael will be ·like a wild donkey [La wild donkey/ass of a man].
·He [LHis hand] will be against everyone,
and ·everyone [Leveryone's hand] will be against him.
He will ·attack [Ldwell against] all his brothers."

13The slave girl gave a name to the LORD who spoke to her: "You are
'·God who sees me [*or* God of seeing; Hebrew *El-Roi*]'" because she said
to herself, "Have I really seen God who sees me?" 14So the well there,
between Kadesh [Calso known as Kadesh Barnea in northeast Sinai] and
Bered [Clocation unknown], was called Beer Lahai Roi [Cthe well of the
Living One who sees me].
15Hagar gave birth to a son for Abram, and Abram named ·him [Lhis
son which Hagar bore him] Ishmael. 16Abram was eighty-six years old
when Hagar gave birth to Ishmael.

Proof of the Covenant

17 When Abram was ninety-nine years old, the LORD appeared
to him and said, "I am ·God Almighty [LEl Shaddai]. ·Obey
[LWalk before] me and ·do what is right [Lbe innocent/blameless; Job
1:1]. 2I will make an ·agreement [covenant; treaty; 6:18] between ·us
[Lme and you], and I will make you ·the ancestor of many people
[Lexceedingly numerous]."
3Then Abram ·bowed facedown on the ground [Lfell on his face]. God said
to him, 4"I am making my ·agreement [covenant; treaty; 6:18] with you: I
will make you the father of ·many [La host/multitude of] nations. 5I am
changing your name from Abram [Cmeaning "exalted father"] to Abraham
[Csounds like "father of a multitude" in Hebrew] because I am making you a
father of ·many [La host/multitude of] nations. 6I will ·give you many descendants [Lcause you to be exceedingly fruitful; 1:22]. ·New nations will be born
from you [LI will make nations of you], and kings will come from you. 7And

I will make an ·agreement [covenant; treaty; 6:18] **between me and you and**
all your ·descendants [Lseed] **·from now on** [*or* forever]**: I will be your God**
and the God of all your descendants. 8You live in the land of Canaan now as
a ·stranger [sojourner; wanderer; resident alien]**, but I will give you and your**
·descendants [Lseed] **all this land ·forever** [Las a permanent possesssion]**. And**
I will be the God of your ·descendants [Lseed]**.**"

9**Then God said to Abraham, "You and your ·descendants** [seed] **must**
·keep [obey; guard] **this ·agreement** [covenant; treaty; 6:18] **·from now on**
[Lthroughout their generations]. 10**This is my ·agreement** [covenant;
treaty; 6:18] **with you and all your ·descendants** [Lseed]**, which you must**
·obey [keep; guard]**: Every male among you must be circumcised** [Cthe
ritual of membership in the covenant/treaty]. 11**·Cut away** [Circumcise]
[Lthe flesh of] **your foreskin ·to show that you are prepared to follow the**
agreement [Las a sign of the covenant/treaty] **between me and you.** 12**·From**
now on [LThroughout your generations] **when a baby boy is eight days**
old, you will circumcise him. This includes any ·boy born among your
people [Lhouse-born slave] **or any who is ·your slave** [Lbought with money
from a foreigner]**, who is not one of your ·descendants** [Lseed].
13**Circumcise every baby boy whether he is born in your ·family** [Lhouse]
or bought ·as a slave [Lwith money from a foreigner]**. ·Your bodies will be**
marked to show that you are part of my agreement [L…so that my cove-
nant/treaty might be in your flesh as a covenant/treaty] **that lasts forever.**
14**Any** [Luncircumcised] **male ·who** [Lwhose foreskin] **is not circumcised**
will be cut off from his people, because he has broken my ·agreement
[covenant; treaty; 6:18]."

Isaac—the Promised Son

15**God said to Abraham, "I will change the name of Sarai** [Cmeaning
"princess" in her native dialect; 11:29]**, your wife, to Sarah** [Calso meaning
"princess," but in a dialect of Canaan, signifying her transition to the
Promised Land]. 16**I will bless her and give ·her a son, and you will be the**
father [Lfrom her to you a son]**. She will ·be the mother of** [give rise to]
many nations. Kings of nations will come from her."

17**Abraham ·bowed facedown on the ground** [Lfell on his face] **and**
laughed. He ·said to himself [thought; Lsaid in his heart]**, "Can a man have**
a child when he is a hundred years old? Can Sarah give birth to a child
when she is ninety?" 18**Then Abraham said to God, "Please let Ishmael ·be**
the son you promised [Llive before you]**.**"

19**God said, "·No,** [*or* Yes, but] **Sarah your wife will have a son, and you will**
name him Isaac [Crelated to the verb meaning "to laugh"]**. I will make my**
·agreement [covenant; treaty; 6:18] **with him to be an ·agreement that con-**
tinues forever [eternal covenant/treaty] **with all his ·descendants** [Lseed].

20**"As for Ishmael, I have heard you. I will bless him and ·give him many**
descendants [Lmake him fruitful]**. And I will cause their numbers to grow**
greatly. He will be the father of twelve great ·leaders [princes; chiefs;
25:16]**, and I will make him into a great nation.** 21**But I will make my**
·agreement [covenant; treaty; 6:18] **with Isaac, the son whom Sarah will**
have at this same time next year." 22**After ·God** [Lhe] **finished talking with**
Abraham, God ·rose and left him [Lwent up from Abraham].

23**Then Abraham ·gathered** [Ltook] **Ishmael, all the males ·born in his**
camp [Lof his house]**, and ·the slaves he had bought** [Lthose bought with
money]**. So that day Abraham circumcised** [Lthe flesh of his foreskin of]
every man and boy in his camp as God had told him to do. 24**Abraham**

was ninety-nine years old when he ·was circumcised [Lcircumcised the flesh of his foreskin]. 25And Ishmael, his son, was thirteen years old when he was circumcised [Lin the flesh of his foreskin]. 26Abraham and his son were circumcised on the same day. 27Also on that day all the men in Abraham's camp were circumcised, including all those born in his ·camp [Lhouse] and all ·the slaves he had bought from other nations [Lall those bought of a stranger].

The Three Visitors

18 Later, the LORD again appeared to Abraham near the ·great trees [Loaks; *or* terebinths] of Mamre [Can area near Hebron, named after Amorite leader; 14:13, 24]. Abraham was sitting at the entrance of his tent ·during the hottest part [Lin the heat] of the day. 2He ·looked up [Lraised his eyes] and saw three men standing near him. When Abraham saw them, he ran from [Lthe entrance of] his tent to meet them. He bowed facedown on the ground before them 3and said, "·Sir [My lord], if ·you think well of me [LI have found grace in your eyes], please ·stay awhile with me, [Ldo not pass by] your servant. 4I will bring some water so all of you can wash your feet. You may rest under the tree, 5and I will get some bread for you so you can regain your strength. Then you may ·continue your journey [Lpass by]."

The three men said, "That is fine. Do as you said." [CIn the ancient Near East, hospitality towards strangers was a very imporant value.]

6Abraham hurried to the tent where Sarah was and said to her, "Hurry, ·prepare [Ltake and knead] ·twenty quarts [Lthree seahs] of fine flour, and make ·it into loaves of bread [Lcakes]." 7Then Abraham ran to his herd and took one of his ·best [Ltender and good/choice] calves. He gave it to a servant, who hurried ·to kill it and to prepare it for food [Lto prepare it]. 8Abraham gave the three men the calf that had been ·cooked [Lprepared] and milk curds and milk. While they ate, he stood under the tree near them.

9The men asked Abraham, "Where is your wife Sarah?"

"There, in the tent," said Abraham.

10Then ·the LORD [Lhe] said, "I will certainly return to you ·about this time a year from now [*or* in due time; Labout the living time]. At that time your wife Sarah will have a son."

Sarah was listening at the entrance of the tent which was behind him. 11Abraham and Sarah were very old. Since ·Sarah was past the age when women normally have children [Lit had stopped being with Sarah after the manner of women; Cshe had reached menopause], 12she laughed ·to herself [inwardly], "·My husband and I are too old [LI am worn out and my husband is too old] to have ·a baby [Lpleasure]."

13Then the LORD said to Abraham, "Why did Sarah laugh? Why did she say, 'I am too old to have a baby'? 14Is anything too hard for the LORD? No! I will return to you ·at the right time a year from now [*or* in due time; Labout the living time], and Sarah will have a son."

15Sarah was afraid, so she ·lied [denied it] and said, "I didn't laugh."

But the LORD said, "No. You did laugh."

16Then the men got up to leave and ·started out [Llooked] toward Sodom. Abraham walked along with them a short time to send them on their way.

Abraham's Bargain with God

17The LORD said, "Should I ·tell [Lhide from] Abraham what I am going to do now? 18·Abraham's children [LAbraham] will certainly become a great and powerful nation, and all nations on earth will be blessed through

him [12:1–3]. 19I have ·chosen [Lknown] him so he would command his children and his ·descendants [Lhousehold] to ·live [Lkeep] the way the LORD
wants them to, ·to live right and be fair [L...by doing righteousness and jus-
tice]. Then I, the LORD, will give Abraham what I promised him."
20Then the LORD said, "·I have heard many complaints [LThe outcry is
great] against the people of Sodom and Gomorrah [14:2]. ·They are very
evil [LTheir sin is very great/heavy]. 21I will go down and see if they ·are as
bad as I have heard [Lhave done according to the outcry which has come
to me]. If not, I will know."
22So the men turned and went toward Sodom, but Abraham stood
there before the LORD. 23Then Abraham approached him and asked, "Do
you plan to ·destroy [sweep away] the ·good people [righteous] along
with the ·evil ones [wicked]? 24What if there are fifty ·good people [righ-
teous] in that city? Will you still ·destroy it [sweep it away]? Surely you
will ·save [spare] the ·city [Lplace] for the fifty ·good people [righteous]
living there. 25·Surely [LIt would be a desecration for you!] you will not
·destroy [Lkill; slay] the ·good people [righteous] along with the ·evil ones
[wicked]; then they would be treated the same. You are the judge of all the
earth. Won't you do what is ·right [just]?"
26The LORD said, "If I find fifty ·good people [righteous] in the city of
Sodom, I will ·save [spare] the whole ·city [Lplace] because of them."
27Then Abraham [Lanswered and] said, "Though I am only dust and
ashes, I have been brave to speak to the Lord. 28What if ·there are only forty-
five good people [Lfive of the fifty righteous are lacking] in the city? Will you
destroy the whole city for the lack of five ·good people [righteous]?"
The LORD said, "If I find forty-five there, I will not destroy the city."
29Again Abraham said to him, "If you find only forty ·good people
[righteous] there, will you destroy the city?"
The LORD said, "If I find forty, I will not destroy it."
30Then Abraham said, "Lord, please don't be angry with me, but let
me ask you this. If you find only thirty ·good people [righteous] in the
city, will you destroy it?"
He said, "If I find thirty ·good people [righteous] there, I will not
destroy the city."
31Then Abraham said, "I have been brave to speak to the Lord. But
what if there are twenty ·good people [righteous] in the city?"
He answered, "If I find twenty there, I will not destroy the city."
32Then Abraham said, "Lord, please don't be angry with me, but let me
bother you this one last time. What if you find ten there?"
He said, "If I find ten there, I will not destroy it."
33When the LORD finished speaking to Abraham, he left, and Abraham
returned ·home [Lto his place].

Lot Leaves Sodom

19 The two ·angels [messengers] came to Sodom in the evening
as Lot was sitting near the ·city gate [Lgate of Sodom; Cthe
administrative center of a city]. When he saw them, he got up ·and went
to [to meet] them and bowed facedown on the ground. 2Lot said, "·Sirs
[My lords], please come to ·my [Lyour servant's] house and spend the
night. There you can wash your feet, and then ·tomorrow you may [Lyou
can get up early and] continue your journey."
The ·angels [messengers] answered, "No, we will spend the night in the
city's public square."

3But Lot ·begged them [entreated/urged them strongly] to come, so
they ·agreed [Lturned aside to him] and went to his house. Then Lot prepared a ·meal [feast; banquet] for them. He baked ·bread without yeast
[unleavened bread], and they ate it.
4Before ·bedtime [Lthey lay down], men both young and old and from
every part of Sodom surrounded Lot's house. 5They called to Lot, "Where
are the two men who came to you tonight? Bring them out to us so we can
·have sexual relations with [Lknow] them."
6Lot went ·outside [Lout the door] to them, closing the door behind him.
7He said, "No, my brothers! Do not do this evil thing. 8Look! I have two
daughters who have never ·slept with [had sexual relations with; Lknown] a
man. I will give them to you, and you may do anything you want with them.
But please don't do anything to these men. They have come ·to my house,
and I must protect them [Lunder the shelter/shade of my roof]."
9The men around the house answered, "·Move out of the way [Stand
back]!" Then they said to each other, "This ·man Lot [fellow; Lone] came
to our city as a ·stranger [sojourner; wanderer; resident alien], and now he
wants to ·tell us what to do [Ljudge us]!" They said to Lot, "We will do
worse things to you than to them." They started pushing him back and
were ready to break down the door.
10But ·the two men staying with Lot [Lthe men] ·opened the door,
[Lreached out their hands and] pulled him back inside the house, and
then closed the door. 11They struck those outside the door with ·blind-
ness [a blinding flash], so the men, both ·young and old [Lsmall and great],
could not find the door.
12The two men said to Lot, "Do you have ·any other relatives in this city
[Lanyone else here]? Do you have any sons-in-law, sons, daughters, or any
other relatives? If you do, ·tell them to leave now [get them out of this
place], 13because we are about to destroy this ·city [Lplace]. ·The LORD has
heard of all the evil that is here [LGreat is the outcry against them before
the LORD], so he has sent us to destroy it."
14So Lot went out and said to his future sons-in-law who were pledged
to marry his daughters, "·Hurry and leave this city [LGet up and get out
of this place]! The LORD is about to destroy it!" But ·they [Lhis sons-in-
law] thought Lot was joking.
15·At dawn the next morning [LAs morning dawned], the ·angels [mes-
sengers] ·begged [urged] Lot to hurry. They said, "Go! Take your wife and
your two daughters with you so you will not be ·destroyed [swept away]
when the city is punished."
16But Lot ·delayed [lingered; dawdled]. So the two men ·took [grabbed;
seized] the hands of Lot, his wife, and his two daughters and led them
safely out of the city. So the LORD was merciful to Lot and his family.
17After they brought them out of the city, one of the men said, "·Run
[Flee] for your lives! Don't look back or stop anywhere in the ·valley [*or*
plain]. Run to the mountains, or you will be ·destroyed [swept away]."
18But Lot said to one of them, "·Sir, please don't force me to go so far
[LOh no, my lord]! 19·You have been merciful [LYour servant has found
grace in your eyes] and ·kind to me [Lyou have shown great kindness to
me] and have saved my life. But I can't ·run [flee] to the mountains. The
disaster will catch me, and I will die. 20Look, that little town over there is
·not too far away [Lnear enough to flee to]. Let me run there. It's really just
a little town, and ·I'll be safe there [Lmy life will be saved/spared]."

21The angel said to Lot, "Very well, I will ·allow you to do this also [show you this favor; Llift up your face]. I will not ·destroy that town [Loverthrow the town of which you speak]. 22But run there fast, because I cannot ·destroy Sodom [Ldo anything] until you are safely in that town." (That town is named Zoar, because it is little [CZoar sounds like the Hebrew word for "little"].)

Sodom and Gomorrah Are Destroyed

23The sun had already ·come up [Lrisen over the earth] when Lot entered Zoar. 24The LORD sent a rain of ·burning sulfur [sulfur and fire] down from ·the sky [heaven] on Sodom and Gomorrah 25and ·destroyed [overturned] those cities. He also ·destroyed [overturned] the whole ·Jordan Valley [valley; *or* plain], everyone living in the cities, and even all the plants.

26At that point Lot's wife looked back. When she did, she became a pillar of salt.

27Early the next morning, Abraham got up and went to the place where he had stood before the LORD. 28He looked down toward Sodom and Gomorrah and all the ·Jordan Valley [Lvalley; *or* plain] and saw smoke rising from the land, like smoke from a furnace.

29God destroyed the cities in the ·valley [*or* plain], but he remembered what Abraham had asked. So ·God saved Lot's life, but he [Lhe sent Lot out of the overthrow/upheaval when he] ·destroyed [overturned] the city where Lot had lived [Deut. 29:23; Is. 1:9; 13:19; Jer. 50:40; Amos 4:11; Matt. 10:15; 11:23–24; Jude 1:7; Rev. 11:8].

Lot and His Daughters

30Lot was afraid to continue living in Zoar, so he and his two daughters went to live in the mountains in a cave. 31One day the ·older daughter [Lfirstborn] said to the younger, "Our father is old. ·Everywhere on the earth women and men marry, but there are no men around here for us to marry [LThere is no man on earth to come into us according to the way of all the earth]. 32Let's get our father ·drunk [Lto drink wine] and ·have sexual relations [Lwe will lie] with him. ·We can use him to have children and continue our family [L…so we may preserve offspring/seed through our father]."

33That night the two girls ·got their father drunk [Lmade their father drink wine], and the ·older daughter [Lfirstborn] went and ·had sexual relations [Llay] with him. But Lot did not know when she lay down or when she got up.

34The next day the ·older daughter [Lfirstborn] said to the younger, "Last night I ·had sexual relations [lay] with my father. Let's get him ·drunk [Lto drink wine] again tonight so you can go and ·have sexual relations [Llay] with him, too. In this way we can ·use our father to have children to continue our family [preserve offspring/seed through our father]." 35So that night they got their father ·drunk [Lto drink wine] again, and the younger daughter went and ·had sexual relations [Llay] with him. Again, Lot did not know when she lay down or when she got up.

36So both of Lot's daughters ·became pregnant [conceived] by their father. 37The older daughter gave birth to a son and named him Moab. He is the ancestor of all the Moabite people who are still living today [Clocated to the east of the Dead Sea in what is today Jordan; the name sounds like "from the father" in Hebrew]. 38The younger daughter also gave birth to a son and named him Ben-Ammi [Csounds like "son of my relative" in Hebrew]. He is the father of all the Ammonite people [Clocated just north of Moab; Moab and Ammon were enemies of Israel] who are still living today [Cat the time this was written].

Abraham Tricks Abimelech

20 Abraham left Hebron [13:18] and traveled to ·southern Canaan [Lthe Negev; 13:1] where he stayed awhile between Kadesh [16:14] and Shur [16:7]. When he ·moved to [sojourned/lived as an alien in] Gerar [Cnorth of Kadesh and Shur; present-day Tell Abu Hureirah], 2he said to people about Sarah his wife, "She is my sister" [12:10–20; 26:1–11]. Abimelech king of Gerar heard this, so he sent some servants to take her. 3But one night God spoke to Abimelech in a dream and said, "You will die. The woman you took is married."

4But Abimelech had not gone near Sarah, so he said, "Lord, would you ·destroy [Lkill; slay] an innocent nation? 5·Abraham himself told [LDid he not tell…?] me, 'This woman is my sister,' and ·she also said [Ldid she not also say…?], 'He is my brother.' I ·am innocent and did not know I was doing anything wrong [Ldid this with a pure conscience/blameless heart and innocent hands]."

6Then God said to Abimelech in the dream, "Yes, I know you did ·not realize what you were doing [this with a pure conscience/Lblameless heart]. So I ·did not allow you to sin [restrained you from sinning] against me and touch her. 7Give ·Abraham [Lthe man] his wife back. He is a prophet [Cone who interceded for others]. He will pray for you, and you will not die. But if you do not give Sarah back, you and all ·your family [Lwho belong to you] will surely die."

8So early the next morning, Abimelech called all his ·officers [Lservants] and told them everything that had happened in the dream. They were very afraid. 9Then Abimelech called Abraham to him and said, "What have you done to us? What ·wrong [offense; sin] did I do against you? Why did you bring this ·trouble [great offense/guilt; Lgreat sin] to my kingdom? You should not have done these things to me. 10What ·were you thinking [possessed you] that caused you to do this?"

11Then Abraham answered, "I thought no one in this place ·respected [feared] God and that someone would kill me to get ·Sarah [Lmy wife]. 12And it is true that she is my sister. She is the daughter of my father, but she is not the daughter of my mother, and she became my wife. 13When God ·told me to leave my father's house and wander in many different places [Lcaused me to wander from my father's home; 12:1], I told Sarah, 'You must ·do a special favor for [*or* show loyalty to] me. Everywhere we go tell people, "He is my brother." ' "

14Then Abimelech gave Abraham some sheep, cattle, and male and female slaves. He also gave Sarah, Abraham's wife, back to him 15and said, "·Look around you at my land [LMy land is before you]. You may live anywhere you want."

16Abimelech said to Sarah, "I gave your brother Abraham ·twenty-five pounds [Lone thousand pieces] of silver ·to make up for any wrong that people may think about you [L—a covering of the eyes to all who are with you; Can indication that nothing improper happened]. I want everyone to know that you are innocent."

17Then Abraham prayed to God, and God healed Abimelech, his wife, and his servant girls so they could have children. 18The LORD had ·kept all the women in Abimelech's house from having children [Lclosed up every womb of the house of Abimelech] ·as a punishment on Abimelech for taking [Lon account of] Abraham's wife Sarah.

A Baby for Sarah

21 The LORD ·cared for [visited] Sarah as he had said and did for her what he had promised. 2Sarah ·became pregnant

[conceived] and gave birth to a son for Abraham in his old age. Everything happened at the time God had said it would. 3Abraham named his son Isaac, the son Sarah gave birth to. 4He circumcised [17:10] Isaac when he was eight days old as God had commanded.

5Abraham was one hundred years old when his son Isaac was born. 6And Sarah said, "God has made me laugh [Cthe name Isaac is related to a Hebrew word meaning "laugh"]. Everyone who hears about this will laugh ·with [*or* at] me. 7No one thought that I would ·be able to have Abraham's child [Lsuckle/nurse children], but even though Abraham is old I have given him a son."

Hagar and Ishmael Leave

8Isaac grew, and when he ·became old enough to eat food [was weaned], Abraham gave a great feast [Lon the day of his weaning]. 9But Sarah saw ·Ishmael [Lthe son of Hagar the Egyptian] ·making fun of Isaac [laughing; *or* playing]. 10So Sarah said to Abraham, "·Throw [Drive] out this slave woman and her son. Her son should not inherit anything; my son Isaac should receive it all [Gal. 4:21—5:1]."

11This ·troubled [distressed; upset] Abraham very much because Ishmael was also his son. 12But God said to Abraham, "Don't be ·troubled [distressed; upset] about the boy and the slave woman. Do ·whatever [all] Sarah tells you. ·The descendants I promised you will be from [LThe seed will be named for you through] Isaac. 13I will also make the ·descendants of Ishmael [Lthe son of your slave woman] into a great nation because he is your ·son [Lseed], too."

14Early the next morning Abraham [Lgot up and] took some food and a ·leather bag full [skin] of water. He gave them to Hagar and sent her away. Carrying these things and her son [Lon her shoulder], Hagar went and wandered [Cthe verb may imply moving aimlessly and without hope] in the ·desert [wilderness] of Beersheba [Can area in the northern part of the Negev, southern Canaan].

15Later, when all the water was ·gone [finished] from the ·bag [skin], Hagar put her son under a bush. 16Then she went a good way off, the distance of a bowshot, and sat down across from him. She thought, "My son will die, and I cannot watch this happen." She sat there across from him and began to cry.

17God heard the ·boy crying [Lsound/voice of the boy], and God's ·angel [messenger; 16:7] called to Hagar from heaven. He said, "What is wrong, Hagar? Don't be afraid! God has heard the ·boy crying [Lthe sound/voice of the boy] there. 18·Help [Get up and lift] him up and take him by the hand. I will make ·his descendants [Lhim] into a great nation." [CIshmael is considered the ancestor of the Arab people.]

19Then God [Lopened her eyes and] showed Hagar a well of water. So she went to the well and filled her ·bag [skin] with water and gave the boy a drink.

20God was with the boy as he grew up. Ishmael lived in the ·desert [wilderness] and became an archer. 21He lived in the Desert of Paran [Ca region in the eastern Sinai peninsula], and his mother found a wife for him in Egypt [CHagar's original homeland].

Abraham's Bargain with Abimelech

22·Then [At that time] Abimelech came with Phicol, the commander of his army, and said to Abraham, "God is with you in everything you do. 23So ·make a promise to me here before [swear to me by] God that you will ·be fair [Lnot deal falsely] with me and my children and my descendants. Be

·kind [loyal] to me and to this land where you have lived as a ·stranger [sojourner; wanderer; resident alien]—as ·kind [loyal] as I have been to you."

24And Abraham said, "I ·promise [swear]." 25Then Abraham ·complained to [reproved; reproached] Abimelech about Abimelech's servants who had seized a well of water.

26But Abimelech said, "I don't know who did this. You never told me [Land I have not heard] about this before today."

27Then Abraham gave Abimelech some sheep and cattle, and they made an ·agreement [covenant; treaty]. 28Abraham also put seven female lambs ·in front of Abimelech [Lapart by themselves].

29Abimelech asked Abraham, "Why did you put these seven female lambs by themselves?"

30Abraham answered, "Accept these lambs from ·me [Lmy hand] to ·prove that you believe [verify/witness that] I dug this well."

31So that place was called Beersheba [21:14; Cmeaning either "well of seven" or "well of promise"] because they ·made a promise to each other [swore an oath] there.

32After Abraham and Abimelech ·made the agreement [Lcut a covenant/treaty] at Beersheba, Abimelech and Phicol, the commander of his army, went back to the land of the Philistines [Ca region on the southern Mediterranean coast of Canaan].

33Abraham planted a tamarisk tree at Beersheba and prayed to the Lord, the ·God who lives forever [eternal God]. 34And Abraham lived as a ·stranger [wanderer; sojourner; resident alien] in the land of the Philistines for ·a long time [Lmany days].

God Tests Abraham

22 After these things God tested ·Abraham's faith [LAbraham]. God said to him, "Abraham!"

And he answered, "Here I am."

2Then God said, "Take your ·only [*or* precious] son, Isaac, the son you love, and go to the land of Moriah [2 Chr. 3:1; Cthe temple would later be built here]. Offer him as a whole burnt offering on one of the mountains I will tell you about."

3Abraham got up early in the morning and saddled his donkey. He took Isaac and two ·servants [*or* young men] with him. After he cut the wood for the sacrifice, they went to the place God had told them to go. 4On the third day Abraham ·looked up [Llifted his eyes] and saw the place in the distance. 5He said to his ·servants [*or* young men], "Stay here with the donkey. My son and I will go over there and worship, and then we will come back to you."

6Abraham took the wood for the ·sacrifice [Lwhole burnt offering] and ·gave it to his son to carry [Lplaced it on his son], but he himself took the knife and the ·fire [*or* tinder]. So he and his son went on together.

7Isaac said to his father Abraham, "Father!"

Abraham answered, "Yes, my son."

Isaac said, "We have the ·fire [*or* tinder] and the wood, but where is the ·lamb [sheep] ·we will burn as a sacrifice [Lfor the whole burnt offering]?"

8Abraham answered, "God will ·give us [provide; Lsee for] the ·lamb [sheep] for the ·sacrifice [whole burnt offering], my son."

So Abraham and his son went on together 9and came to the place

God had told him about. Abraham built an altar there. He ·laid [arranged] the wood on it and then ·tied up [bound] his son Isaac and laid him on the wood on the altar. 10Then Abraham [Lsent his hand and] took his knife and was about to ·kill [slaughter] his son.

11But the ·angel [messenger] of the LORD [16:7] called to him from heaven and said, "Abraham! Abraham!"

Abraham answered, "Yes."

12The angel said, "Don't ·kill [Lsend out your hand against] your son or ·hurt [Ldo anything to] him in any way. Now I can see that you ·trust [Lfear] God and that you have not ·kept [withheld] your son, your ·only [*or* precious] son, from me [Heb. 11:17–19; James 2:21–23]."

13Then Abraham ·looked up [Llifted his eyes] and saw ·a [*or* another] ·male sheep [ram] caught in a ·bush [thicket] by its horns. So Abraham went and took the sheep offering it as a whole burnt offering to God, ·and his son was saved [L. . . in the place of his son]. 14So Abraham named that place The LORD ·Provides [*or* Sees; CHebrew: Yahweh Yireh]. Even today people say, "On the mountain of the LORD it will be ·provided [*or* seen]."

15The ·angel [messenger] of the LORD [16:7] called to Abraham from heaven a second time 16and said, "The LORD says, 'Because you did not ·keep back [withhold] your son, your ·only [precious] son, from me, I ·make you this promise by my own name [Lswear by myself]: 17I will surely bless you and ·give you many descendants [Lmultiply your seed]. They will be as many as the stars in the ·sky [heavens] and the sand on the seashore, and they will ·capture [Lpossess] the ·cities [Lgates] of their enemies. 18Through your ·descendants [Lseed] all the nations on the earth will be blessed, because you ·obeyed [listened to] me [12:1–3].'"

19Then Abraham returned to his ·servants [young men]. They all traveled back to Beersheba, and Abraham ·stayed there [Lresided in Beersheba; 21:14].

20After these things happened, someone told Abraham: "·Your brother Nahor and his wife Milcah have children now [LMilcah has born sons to Nahor your brother; 11:29]. 21The ·first son [firstborn] is Uz, and ·the second [Lhis brother] is Buz. ·The third son is [...and] Kemuel (the father of Aram). 22Then there are Kesed, Hazo, Pildash, Jidlaph, and Bethuel." 23Bethuel became the father of Rebekah. Milcah was the mother of these eight sons, and Nahor, Abraham's brother, was the father. 24Also Nahor had four other sons by his ·slave woman [concubine; Ca secondary wife] Reumah. Their names were Tebah, Gaham, Tahash, and Maacah [CNahor's offspring may have been the ancestors of the Aramaean tribes in Syria].

Sarah Dies

23 Sarah lived to be one hundred twenty-seven years old [Lsuch were the years of Sarah's life]. 2She died in Kiriath Arba (that is, Hebron [Ccity nineteen miles south of Jerusalem]) in the land of Canaan. Abraham ·was very sad [mourned] and cried because of her. 3After a while he got up from the side of his ·wife's body [Ldead] and went to talk to the Hittites [Cone of the many groups that made up the population of Canaan at the time, notable in that they were not Semitic as the others were]. He said, 4"I am only a ·stranger [sojourner; wanderer; resident alien] and a ·foreigner [settler; Cthe combination of terms indicates a resident alien] here. Sell me some ·of your land [property for a burial place] so that I can bury my ·dead wife [Ldead]."

5The Hittites answered Abraham, 6"·Sir [My lord], you are a ·great
leader [mighty prince; *or* prince of God; Ca man of wealth and power
even though he owned no land] among us. You may have the ·best [choic-
est] place we have to bury your dead. You may have any of our burying
places that you want, and none of us will stop you from burying your
·dead wife [Ldead]."
7Abraham rose and bowed to the people of the land, the Hittites. 8He
said to them, "If you truly ·want to help me [are willing for me to] bury
my ·dead wife [Ldead] here, ·speak to [entreat] Ephron, the son of Zohar
for me. 9Ask him to sell me the cave of Machpelah at the edge of his field.
I will pay him the full price. You can be the witnesses that I am buying it
as a burial place."
10Ephron was sitting among the Hittites at the city gate [Cplace where
commercial transactions took place]. He answered Abraham [Lin the
hearing of the Hittites], 11"No, ·sir [my Lord]. [LHear me,] I will give you
the ·land [field] and the cave that is in it, with these people as witnesses.
Bury your ·dead wife [Ldead]."
12Then Abraham bowed down before the ·Hittites [Lpeople of the
land]. 13He said to Ephron ·before [Lin the hearing of] all the people,
"·Please let me [LListen to me. I will] pay you the full price for the field.
Accept my money, and I will bury my dead there."
14Ephron answered Abraham, 15"·Sir [My Lord], [LListen to me,] the
land is worth ·ten pounds [L400 shekels] of silver, ·but I won't argue with
you over the price [Lwhat is that between you and me?]. Take the land, and
bury your ·dead wife [Ldead]."
16Abraham ·agreed [listened] and paid Ephron in front of the Hittite
witnesses. He weighed out the full price, ·ten pounds [L400 shekels] of
silver, and they counted the weight as the traders normally did.
17-18So Ephron's field in Machpelah, east of Mamre, was sold. Abraham
became the owner of the field, the cave in it, and all the trees that were in
the field. The sale was made at the city gate, with the Hittites as witnesses
[Cthe first land actually owned by Abraham]. 19After this, Abraham buried
his wife Sarah in the cave in the field of Machpelah, near Mamre. (Mamre
was later called Hebron in the land of Canaan.) 20So Abraham bought the
field and the cave in it from the Hittites to use as a burying place.

A Wife for Isaac

24 Abraham was now very old, ·along in years [Lgoing in days],
and the LORD had blessed him in every way. 2Abraham said to
his oldest servant [Lin his house], who was in charge of everything he
owned, "Put your hand under my ·leg [Lthigh; Ca euphemism for male
genitalia, expressing commitment to keep a promise]. 3·Make a promise
to me before [Swear to me by] the LORD, the God of heaven and [Lthe God
of] earth. Don't get a wife for my son from the ·Canaanite girls [Ldaughters
of the Canaanites] who live around here. 4Instead, go back to my country,
to the land of my relatives, and get a wife for my son Isaac."
5The servant said to him, "·What if [Perhaps] this woman does not
want to return with me to this land? Then, should I take your son with me
back to your homeland?"
6Abraham said to him, "No! ·Don't take [LBe careful not to take] my
son back there. 7The LORD, the God of heaven, brought me from the home
of my father and the land of my relatives. And he ·promised [swore to]
me, 'I will give this land to your ·descendants [Lseed].' The LORD will send

his ·angel [messenger] before you to help you get a wife for my son there.
8If the ·girl [woman] won't come back with you, you will be ·free [declared
innocent] from this promise. But you must not take my son back there."
9So the servant put his hand under his master's ·leg [Lthigh; 24:2] and
·made a promise [swore] to Abraham about this.
10The servant took ten of Abraham's camels and left, carrying with
him many ·different kinds of beautiful gifts [Lgoods of his master]. He
went to ·northwestern Mesopotamia [LAram-Naharaim; Ca region near
the Habor and Euphrates rivers, about a month's journey away] to
·Nahor's city [*or* the city of Nahor]. 11In the evening, when the women
come out to get water [Cmost ancient towns had a single source of water
for the community], he made the camels kneel down at the well outside
the city.
12The servant said, "LORD, God of my master Abraham, ·allow me to
find a wife for his son [Lgrant me good fortune] today. Please show this
·kindness [loyalty] to my master Abraham. 13Here I am, standing by the
spring, and the ·girls [Ldaughters of the men] from the city are coming
out to get water. 14·I will say to one of them [LLet the girl to whom I will
say…], 'Please put your jar down so I can drink.' Then let her say, 'Drink,
and I will also give water to your camels.' If that happens, I will know she
is the ·right one [the one appointed/selected] for your servant Isaac and
that you have shown ·kindness [loyalty] to my master."
15Before the servant had finished ·praying [Lspeaking], Rebekah, the
daughter of Bethuel, came out of the city. (Bethuel was the son of
Milcah and Nahor, Abraham's brother [11:27–30].) Rebekah was carrying her water jar on her shoulder. 16She was ·very pretty [extremely
beautiful], a virgin; she had never ·had sexual relations with [Lknown] a
man. She went down to the spring and filled her jar, then came back up.
17The servant ran to her and said, "Please give me a little ·water [sip]
from your jar."
18Rebekah said, "Drink, ·sir [my master]." She quickly lowered the jar
·from her shoulder [Lon her hand] and gave him a drink. 19After ·he finished drinking [Lshe let him drink all he wanted], Rebekah said, "I will
also pour some water for your camels [Luntil they have finished drink-
ing]." 20So she quickly ·poured [emptied] all the water from her jar into
the drinking trough for the camels. Then she kept running to the well
until she had given all the camels enough to drink.
21The ·servant [Lman] quietly ·watched [stared at] her. He wanted to
·be sure [Llearn whether or not] the LORD had made his trip successful.
22After the camels had finished drinking, he gave Rebekah a gold ·ring
[Lnose-ring; *or* earring] weighing ·one-fifth of an ounce [Lone half shekel]
and two gold arm bracelets weighing about ·four ounces [Lten shekels]
each. 23He asked, "·Who is your father [LTell me whose daughter you are]?
Is there a place in his house for me and my men to spend the night?"
24Rebekah answered, "·My father is [LThe daughter of] Bethuel, the son
of Milcah and Nahor." 25Then she said, "And, yes, we have ·straw for your
camels [Lplenty of straw and feed] and a place for you to spend the night."
26The servant bowed and worshiped the LORD 27and said, "Blessed is
the LORD, the God of my master Abraham. The LORD ·has been kind and
truthful to him [Lhas not abandoned his kindness/loyalty and truthful-
ness/faithfulness to my master] and has led me to my master's relatives."

28Then Rebekah ran and told her mother's family about all these
things. 29She had a brother named Laban, who ran out to Abraham's servant, who was still at the spring. 30Laban had heard what she had said and
had seen the ·ring [Lnose-ring; *or* earring] and the bracelets on his sister's
arms. So he ran out to the well, and there was the man standing by the
camels at the spring. 31Laban said, "·Sir [LO blessed one], ·you are welcome to come in [Lcome]; ·you don't have to stand [Lwhy are standing…?]
outside. I have ·prepared [Lcleared out] the house for you and also a place
for your camels."

32So Abraham's servant went into the house. After Laban unloaded the
camels and gave them straw and ·food [fodder], he gave water to
Abraham's servant so he and the men with him could wash their feet.
33Then ·Laban gave the servant food [Lthe food was set before him], but
the servant said, "I will not eat until I have told you why I came."

So Laban said, "Then tell us."

34He said, "I am Abraham's servant. 35The Lord has greatly blessed my
master in everything [12:3], and he has become a rich man. The Lord
has given him many flocks of sheep, herds of cattle, silver and gold, male
and female servants, camels, and horses. 36Sarah, my master's wife, gave
birth to a son when she was old [21:1–7], and my master has given everything he owns to that son. 37My master had me ·make a promise to him
[swear] and said, 'Don't get a wife for my son from the Canaanite ·girls
[Ldaughters] ·who live around here [Lin whose land I live]. 38Instead, you
must go to my father's ·people [house] and to my family. There you must
·get [take] a wife for my son.' 39I said to my master, 'What if the woman
will not come back with me?' 40But he said, 'I ·serve [Lwalk before] the
Lord, who will send his ·angel [*or* messenger] with you and will ·help you
[Lmake your way successful]. You will ·get [take] a wife for my son from
my family and my father's ·people [Lhouse]. 41Then you will be ·free
[innocent] from ·the promise [Lmy oath]. But if they will not give you a
wife for my son, you will be ·free [innocent] from ·this promise [Lmy
oath].'

42"Today I came to this spring. I said, 'Lord, God of my master
Abraham, please make my ·trip [way] successful. 43I am standing by this
spring. I will wait for a young woman to come out to ·get [draw] water,
and I will say, "Please give me water from your jar to drink." 44Then let
her say, "Drink this water, and I will also draw water for your camels." By
this I will know the Lord has chosen her for my master's son.'

45"Before I finished ·my silent prayer [Lspeaking in my heart/mind],
Rebekah came out of the city with her water jar on her shoulder. She went
down to the spring and drew water. I said to her, 'Please give me a drink.'
46She quickly lowered the jar from her shoulder and said, 'Drink this. I
will also water your camels.' So I drank, and she watered my camels too.
47When I asked her, '·Who is your father [LWhose daughter are you]?' she
answered, '·My father is [LThe daughter of] Bethuel son of Milcah and
Nahor.' Then I put the ring in her nose and the bracelets on her arms,
48and I bowed my head and ·thanked [worshipped] the Lord. I ·praised
[blessed] the Lord, the God of my master Abraham, because he ·led
[guided] me on the right road to get the granddaughter of my master's
brother for his son. 49Now, tell me, will you be ·kind [loyal] and ·truthful
[faithful] to my master? And if not, tell me so. Then I will ·know what I
should do [Lturn to the right hand or to the left]."

50 Laban and Bethuel answered, "This ·is clearly [Lhas come out] from
the LORD, and we cannot ·change what must happen [Lspeak to you good
or evil]. 51 Rebekah is ·yours [Lbefore you]. Take her and go. Let her marry
your master's son as the LORD has ·commanded [spoken]."
52 When Abraham's servant heard these words, he bowed facedown on
the ground before the LORD. 53 Then he gave Rebekah gold and silver jewelry and clothes. He also gave expensive gifts to her brother and mother.
54 The servant and the men with him ate and drank and spent the night
there. When they got up the next morning, the servant said, "·Now let me
go [LSend me] back to my master."
55 Rebekah's mother and her brother said, "Let ·Rebekah [Lthe girl] stay
with us at least ten days. After that she may go."
56 But the servant said to them, "Do not ·make me wait [delay/hinder],
because the LORD has made my ·trip [way] successful. Now ·let me go
[Lsend me] back to my master."
57 Rebekah's brother and mother said, "We will call Rebekah and ask
her ·what she wants to do [Lat her mouth]." 58 They called her and asked
her, "Do you want to go with this man now?"
She said, "·Yes, I do [LI will go]."
59 So they ·allowed Rebekah and her nurse to go [Lsent Rebekah their
sister and her nurse] with Abraham's servant and his men. 60 They blessed
Rebekah and said,

"Our sister, may you ·be the mother of thousands of people [Lthousands
of myriads],
and may your ·descendants [Lseed] ·capture [inherit; possess] the
·cities of their enemies [Lgates of those who hate us]."

61 Then Rebekah and her servant girls ·got on [Lrose up and mounted]
the camels and followed the servant and his men. So the servant took
Rebekah and left.
62 At this time Isaac had left Beer Lahai Roi [16:14] and was living in
·southern Canaan [LNegev]. 63 One evening when he went out to the field
to ·think [meditate; reflect; *or* walk], he ·looked up [Lraised his eyes] and
saw camels coming. 64 Rebekah also ·looked [Lraised her eyes] and saw
Isaac. Then she ·jumped down [Lfell] from the camel 65 and asked the servant, "Who is that man walking in the field to meet us?"
The servant answered, "That is my master." So Rebekah covered her
face with her veil.
66 The servant told Isaac everything that had happened. 67 Then Isaac
brought Rebekah into the tent of Sarah, his mother, and she became
his wife. Isaac loved her very much, and so he was comforted after his
mother's death.

Abraham's Family

25 Abraham married again, and his new wife was Keturah [1
Chr. 1:32]. 2 She gave birth to Zimran, Jokshan, Medan,
Midian [Cancestor of the Midianites, the tribe into which Moses mar-
ried; Ex. 3:1], Ishbak, and Shuah [Cancestor of the tribe of Job's friend
Bildad; Job 2:11]. 3 Jokshan was the father of Sheba and Dedan [Is. 21:13;
Jer. 49:8; Ezek. 27:20]. Dedan's descendants were the people of Assyria,
Letush, and Leum. 4 The sons of Midian were Ephah, Epher, Hanoch,
Abida, and Eldaah. All these were descendants of Keturah. 5 Abraham
·left [gave] everything he owned to Isaac. 6 But ·before Abraham died
[Lwhile he was still alive], he did give gifts to the sons of his ·other wives

[concubines], **then sent them to the East to be away from Isaac** [Cto prevent rivalry over Abraham's inheritance].

7·**Abraham lived to be** [LThese are the days of the years of the life of Abraham] **one hundred seventy-five years old.** 8**He ·breathed his last breath** [expired] **and died at an old age, ·after a long and satisfying life** [Lan old man and full of years; he was gathered to his people/relatives; Cburied in the family plot, though may imply joining his ancestors in the afterlife]. 9**His sons Isaac and Ishmael buried him in the cave of Machpelah in the field of Ephron east of Mamre. (Ephron was the son of Zohar the Hittite.)** 10**So Abraham was buried with his wife Sarah in the same field that he had bought from the Hittites** [23:1–20]. 11**After Abraham died, God blessed his son Isaac. Isaac was now living at Beer Lahai Roi** [16:14].

12·**This is the family history** [LThese are the generations; 2:4] **of Ishmael, Abraham's son. (Hagar, Sarah's Egyptian servant, ·was Ishmael's mother** [Lbore him to Abraham].) 13**These are the names of Ishmael's sons in the order they were born: Nebaioth, the ·first son** [firstborn], **then Kedar, Adbeel, Mibsam,** 14**Mishma, Dumah, Massa,** 15**Hadad, Tema, Jetur, Naphish, and Kedemah.** 16**These were Ishmael's sons, and these are the names of the ·tribal leaders** [Ltwelve princes/chieftains according to their tribes; 17:20] **listed according to their ·settlements** [villages] **and camps.** 17·**Ishmael lived** [LThese are the years of the life of Ishmael] **one hundred thirty-seven years and then ·breathed his last breath** [expired] **and died** [Land was gathered to his people/relatives; 25:8]. 18**His descendants lived from Havilah to Shur, which is east of Egypt stretching toward Assyria** [Cthe area from the northern Sinai to the border of western Mesopotamia, the area of Arab tribes]. **They often ·attacked** [*or* settled among; Lfell on] **the descendants of his brothers.**

Isaac's Family

19·**This is the family history** [LThese are the generations; 2:4] **of Isaac. Abraham ·had a son named** [*or* was the father of] **Isaac.** 20**When Isaac was forty years old, he ·married** [Ltook as a wife] **Rebekah** [ch. 24], **·who came from northwestern Mesopotamia** [Lthe Aramean from Paddan-aram]. **She was Bethuel's daughter and the sister of Laban the Aramean.** 21**Isaac's wife ·could not have children** [was barren], **so Isaac ·prayed to** [entreated; interceded with] **the LORD for her. The LORD heard Isaac's prayer, and Rebekah ·became pregnant** [conceived].

22**While she was pregnant, the ·babies** [Lchildren] **struggled inside her. She asked, "·Why is this happening to me** [LIf thus, why this, I—; Cthe Hebrew is uncertain]?" **Then she went to ·get an answer from** [Lseek; inquire of] **the LORD.**

23**The LORD said to her,**

"Two nations are in your ·body [Lwomb],
and two groups of people ·will be taken from you [Lare being divided within your body].
One group will be stronger than the other,
and the older will serve the younger [Rom. 9:10–13]."

24**When the time came, ·Rebekah gave birth to twins** [Lthere were twins in her womb]. 25**The first baby ·was born** [Lcame out] **red. Since his skin was like a hairy robe, he was named Esau** [Csounds like "hairy" in Hebrew]. 26**When ·the second baby** [Lhis brother] **·was born** [Lcame out], **·he** [Lhis hand] **was ·holding on to** [gripping; grabbing] **Esau's heel, so that baby was named Jacob** [Csounds like Hebrew for "heel"; grabbing a heel is a

Hebrew idiom for tricking someone]. Isaac was sixty years old when they were born.

27**When the boys grew up, Esau became a ·skilled** [experienced] **hunter. He ·loved to be out in the fields** [Lwas a man of the fields]. **But Jacob was a ·quiet** [*or* mild; *or* blameless] **man ·and stayed among the** [Lliving in] **tents.** 28**Isaac loved Esau because ·he hunted the wild animals that Isaac enjoyed eating** [Lgame was in his (Isaac's) mouth]. **But Rebekah loved Jacob.**

29**One day Jacob was ·boiling a pot of vegetable soup** [*or* preparing stew]. **Esau came in from hunting in the fields, ·weak from hunger** [famished; starving]. 30**So Esau said to Jacob, "Let me ·eat** [gulp down] **some of that red ·soup** [*or* stuff], **because I am ·weak with hunger** [famished; starving]." **(That is why people call him Edom** [Csounds like Hebrew for "red"].**)**

31**But Jacob said, "·First** [LAs the day; Can idiom meaning, "First of all…"] **·sell** [*or* exchange with] **me your ·rights as the firstborn son** [birthright; Cthe firstborn had special inheritance rights and became the head of the family in the next generation]."

32**Esau said, "I am ·almost dead from hunger** [Lgoing to die]. **·If I die, all of my father's wealth will not help me** [LWhat will my birthright be to me?]."

33**But Jacob said, "First** [v. 31], **·promise** [swear to] **me that you will give it to me." So Esau ·made a promise to Jacob** [Lswore to him] **and ·sold** [exchanged] **his ·part of their father's wealth** [Lbirthright] **to Jacob.** 34**Then Jacob gave Esau bread and ·vegetable soup** [stew], **and he ate and drank, and then left. So Esau ·showed how little he cared about his rights as the firstborn son** [Ldespised/showed contempt toward his birthright; Heb. 12:16–17].

Isaac Lies to Abimelech

26 Now there was a ·time of hunger [Lfamine] **in the land, besides the ·time of hunger** [Lformer famine] **that happened during Abraham's life. So Isaac went to the town of Gerar** [20:1] **to see Abimelech king of the Philistines.** 2**The LORD appeared to Isaac and said, "Don't go down to Egypt, but ·live** [settle; dwell] **in the land where I tell you to live.** 3**·Stay** [Sojourn; Live as an alien] **in this land, and I will be with you and bless you** [12:3]. **I will give you and your ·descendants** [Lseed] **all these lands, and I will ·keep** [fulfill] **the oath I made to Abraham your father.** 4**I will ·give you many descendants** [Lmultiply your seed], **as hard to count as the stars in the sky, and I will give them all these lands. Through your ·descendants** [Lseed] **all the nations on the earth will be blessed** [12:1–3]. 5**I will do this because your father Abraham ·obeyed me** [Llistened to my voice]. **He did what I said and obeyed my ·instructions** [charge], **my commands, my teachings, and my ·rules** [instructions; laws]."

6**So Isaac ·stayed** [resided; settled] **in Gerar** [20:1]. 7**His wife Rebekah was very beautiful, and the men of that place asked Isaac about her. Isaac said, "She is my sister," because he was afraid to tell them she was his wife. He thought they might kill him so they could have her** [12:10–20; 20:1–18].

8**Isaac lived there a long time. One day as Abimelech king of the Philistines looked out his window, he saw Isaac ·holding** [fondling; playing with; Ca word related to the name Isaac] **his wife Rebekah tenderly.** 9**Abimelech called for Isaac and said, "This woman is your wife. Why did you say she was your sister?"**

Isaac said to him, "I ·was afraid you would kill me so you could have [Lthought I might die because of] **her."**

10 Abimelech said, "What have you done to us? One of our ·men [Lpeople] might have ·had sexual relations [lain] with your wife. Then ·we would have been guilty of a great sin [Lyou would have brought guilt/punishment on us]."

11 So Abimelech ·warned [commanded] ·everyone [all the people], "Anyone who touches this man or his wife will be put to death."

Isaac Becomes Rich

12 Isaac planted seed in that land, and that year he gathered ·a great harvest [La hundredfold]. The LORD blessed him very much, 13 and ·he [Lthe man] became rich. He ·gathered more wealth [grew richer and richer] until he became a very rich man. 14 He had so many slaves and flocks and herds that the Philistines envied him. 15 So they stopped up all the wells the servants of Isaac's father Abraham had dug. (They had dug them ·when Abraham was alive [Lin the days of Abraham his father].) The Philistines filled those wells with ·dirt [dust]. 16 And Abimelech said to Isaac, "Leave ·our country [Lmy people] because you have become much more powerful than we are."

17 So Isaac ·left that place [Lwent from there] and camped in the ·Valley [Wadi] of Gerar and ·lived [resided; settled] there. 18 ·Long before this time Abraham [LIn the days of Abraham his father they] had dug many wells, but after he died, the Philistines filled them with ·dirt [dust]. So Isaac dug those wells again and gave them the same names his father had given them. 19 Isaac's servants dug a well in the ·valley [wadi], ·from which a spring of water flowed [Land discovered springing/living water]. 20 But the ·herdsmen [shepherds] of Gerar ·argued [contended] with ·them [Lthe shepherds of Isaac] and said, "This water is ours." So Isaac named that well ·Argue [Contention; CHebrew: Esek] because they ·argued [contended] with him. 21 Then ·his servants [Lthey] dug another well. When the people also ·argued about it [contended], Isaac named that well ·Fight [Hebrew: Sitnah]. 22 He moved from there and dug another well. No one ·argued about [contended] this one, so he named it Room Enough [CHebrew: Rehoboth]. Isaac said, "Now the LORD has made room for us, and we will be ·successful [fruitful; 1:22] in this land."

23 From there Isaac went [Lup] to Beersheba [21:14]. 24 The LORD appeared to him that night and said, "I am the God of your father Abraham. Don't be afraid, because I am with you [Cindicating that the covenant with Abraham would be continued with Isaac]. I will bless you and ·give you many descendants [multiply your seed] because of my servant Abraham." 25 So Isaac built an altar [Ca place of sacrifice] and ·worshiped [Lcalled on the name of] the LORD there. He also ·made a camp [Lpitched his tent] there, and his servants dug a well.

26 Abimelech came from Gerar to see Isaac. He brought with him Ahuzzath, ·who advised him [his advisor/friend], and Phicol, the commander of his army. 27 Isaac asked them, "Why have you come to see me? You ·were my enemy [hate me] and ·forced me to leave your country [Lsent me away from you]."

28 They answered, "Now we ·know [Lclearly see] that the LORD is with you. Let us swear an oath to each other. Let us ·make [Lcut] an ·agreement [covenant; treaty] with you 29 that since we did not ·hurt [Ltouch] you, you will not ·hurt [harm] us. We were good to you and sent you away in peace. Now the LORD has blessed you."

30 So Isaac ·prepared food [made a banquet/feast] for them, and they all

ate and drank [Ccustomary to celebrate the signing of the treaty]. 31Early the next morning the men swore an oath to each other. Then Isaac sent them away, and they left in peace.

32That day Isaac's servants came and told him about the well they had dug, saying, "We found water in that well." 33So Isaac named it Shibah [Csounds like Hebrew for "seven" or "promise"] and that city is called Beersheba [21:14] even now.

34When Esau was forty years old, he married two Hittite women—Judith daughter of Beeri and Basemath daughter of Elon. 35These women brought much ·sorrow [bitterness] to Isaac and Rebekah [Cbecause Esau had married outside the people of God].

Jacob Tricks Isaac

27 When Isaac was old, his ·eyesight was poor [Leyes were dim], so he could not see clearly. One day he called his older son Esau to him and said, "[LMy] Son."

Esau answered, "Here I am."

2Isaac said, "I am old and don't know ·when I might die [Lthe day of my death]. 3So take your weapons, your ·bow and arrows [Lquiver and your bow], and go hunting in the field for ·an animal for me to eat [Lgame for me]. 4When you prepare the tasty food that I love, bring it to me, and I will eat. Then I will bless you before I die." 5So Esau went out in the field to hunt [Lfor game to bring it].

Rebekah was listening as Isaac said this to his son Esau. 6She said to her son Jacob, "Listen, I heard your father saying to your brother Esau, 7'·Kill an animal [LBring me game] and prepare some tasty food for me to eat. Then I will bless you in the presence of the LORD before I die.' 8So ·obey [listen to] me, my son, and do what I ·tell [command] you. 9Go out to our ·goats [Lflock] and bring me two ·of the best young ones [choice goats]. I will prepare them just the way your father ·likes [loves] them. 10Then you will ·take the food [Lbring them] to your father, and he will bless you before he dies."

11But Jacob said to his mother Rebekah, "My brother Esau is a hairy man, and I am smooth! 12If my father ·touches me, he will know I am not Esau [Lfeels me...]. Then he will not bless me but will place a curse on me because ·I tried to trick him [Lhe will think I am mocking him]."

13So ·Rebekah [Lhis mother] said to him, "·If your father puts a curse on you, I will accept the blame [LLet your curse be on me]. Just do what I said. Go get the goats for me."

14So Jacob went out and got ·two goats [Lthem] and brought them to his mother, and ·she cooked them in the special way [Lhis mother prepared a tasty meal just as] ·Isaac [Lhis father] ·enjoyed [loved]. 15She took the best clothes of her older son Esau that were in the house and put them on the younger son Jacob. 16She also took the skins of the goats and put them on Jacob's hands and [Lthe smoothness of his] neck. 17Then she gave Jacob the tasty food and the bread she had made.

18Jacob went in to his father and said, "[LMy] Father."

And his father said, "Yes, my son. Who are you?"

19Jacob said to him, "I am Esau, your ·first son [firstborn]. I have done what you told me. Now ·sit up [Lget up and sit down] and eat some ·meat of the animal [game] I hunted for you. Then bless me."

20But Isaac asked his son, "How did you find ·and kill the animal [Lit] so quickly?"

Jacob answered, "Because the LORD your God ·helped me to find it
[Lwent before me]."
21 Then Isaac said to Jacob, "Come near so I can ·touch [feel] you, my
son. Then I will know if you are really my son Esau [Lor not]."
22 So Jacob came near to Isaac his father. Isaac ·touched [felt] him and
said, "Your voice ·sounds like [Lis] Jacob's voice, but your hands ·are hairy
like [Lare] the hands of Esau." 23 Isaac did not ·know it was [recognize]
Jacob, because his hands were hairy like Esau's hands, so Isaac blessed
him. 24 Isaac asked, "Are you really my son Esau?"
Jacob answered, "Yes, I am."
25 Then Isaac said, "Bring ·me the food [Lit to me], and I will eat ·it [Lmy
son's game] and bless you." So Jacob gave him the food, and he ate. Jacob
gave him wine, and he drank. 26 Then Isaac [Lhis father] said to him, "My
son, come near and kiss me." 27 So Jacob went to his father and kissed him.
When Isaac smelled Esau's clothes, he blessed him and said,

"[LSee,] The smell of my son
is like the smell of the field
that the LORD has blessed.
28 May God give you ·plenty of rain [Lthe dew of heaven]
and ·good soil [Lthe fatness/richness/fertility of the earth]
so that you will have plenty of grain and new wine.
29 May nations serve you
and peoples bow down to you.
May you be master over your brothers,
and may your mother's sons bow down to you.
May everyone who curses you be cursed,
and may everyone who blesses you be blessed [12:3; Heb. 11:20]."

30 Isaac [Lhad just] finished blessing Jacob. Then, just as Jacob left his
father Isaac, Esau came in from hunting. 31 He also prepared some tasty
food and brought it to his father. He said [Lto his father], "Father, rise
and eat ·the food that your son killed for you [Lyour son's game] and
then bless me."
32 Isaac his father asked him, "Who are you?"
He answered, "I am your son—your firstborn son—Esau."
33 Then Isaac trembled ·greatly [violently] and said, "Then who was it
that hunted ·the animals [game] and brought me food before you came?
I ate it, and I blessed him, and ·it is too late now to take back my blessing
[Lhe will indeed be blessed]."
34 When Esau heard the words of his father, he let out a loud and bitter
cry. He said to his father, "Bless me—me, too, my father [Heb. 12:17]!"
35 But Isaac said, "Your brother came and ·tricked [deceived; defrauded]
me. He has taken your blessing."
36 Esau said, "Jacob [Csounds like Hebrew for "heel" or "deceive"; 25:26]
is the right name for him. He has ·tricked me [deceived me; Lbeen at my
heel] these two times. He took away my ·share of everything you own
[birthright], and now he has taken away my blessing." Then Esau asked,
"Haven't you ·saved [reserved] a blessing for me?"
37 Isaac answered [Land said to Esau], "I gave Jacob the power to be
master over you, and all his brothers will be his servants. And I kept ·him
strong [sustained him] with grain and new wine. ·There is nothing left to
give you [LWhat can I do for you…?], my son."
38 But Esau ·continued [Lsaid to his father], "Do you have only one

blessing, Father? Bless me, too, Father!" Then Esau ·began to cry out loud
[Llifted his voice and wept; Heb. 12:17].
39Isaac his father said to him,
"You will live far away from the ·best [fatness; richness; fertility of the]
land,
far from the ·rain [Lthe dew of heaven; 27:28].
40You will live by using your sword,
and you will ·be a slave to [serve] your brother.
But when you ·struggle [*or* become restless],
you will break ·free from him [Lhis yoke from your neck; Heb. 11:20]."
41After that Esau ·hated [held a grudge against] Jacob because of the
blessing ·from Isaac [Lwith which his father blessed him]. He thought ·to
himself [Lin his heart], "·My father will soon die, and I will be sad for him
[LThe days of mourning for my father are near]. Then I will kill Jacob
[Lmy brother]."
42Rebekah ·heard about Esau's plan to kill Jacob [Lwas told the words of
Esau her oldest son]. So she sent for Jacob [Lher younger son] and ·said to
[informed] him, "Listen, your brother Esau is ·comforting himself [con-
soling himself; *or* wants to execute his anger against you] by planning to
kill you. 43So, my son, ·do what I say [Llisten to my voice]. My brother
Laban is living in Haran. ·Go to him at once [LGet up and flee to him]!
44·Stay [Live; Reside] with him for a while, until your brother ·is not so
angry [calms down]. 45In time, your brother will not be angry, and he will
forget what you did to him. Then I will send a servant to bring you back. I
don't want to lose both of my sons on the same day."
46Then Rebekah said to Isaac, "I am ·tired of [weary of my life due to]
·Hittite women [Lthe daughters of the Hittites]. If Jacob marries one of
·these Hittite women [Lthe daughters of the Hittites] here in this land, ·I
want to die [why would I want to live?]."

Jacob Searches for a Wife

28 Isaac called Jacob and blessed him and commanded him
[Land said to him], "You must not marry a ·Canaanite woman
[Ldaughter of Canaan]. 2·Go [LGet up and go] to the house of Bethuel,
your mother's father, in ·northwestern Mesopotamia [LPaddan-aram;
25:20]. Laban, your mother's brother, lives there. Marry one of his
daughters. 3May God Almighty bless you and ·give you many
children [Lmake you fruitful and multiply you; 1:22], and may you
become a ·group [assembly; congregation; company] of many peoples.
4May he give you and your ·descendants [Lseed] the blessing of Abraham
so that you may ·own [possess] the land ·where you are now living as
a stranger [Lof your wandering/sojourn/alien status], the land God
gave to Abraham." 5So Isaac sent Jacob to ·northwestern Mesopotamia
[LPaddan-aram], to Laban the brother of Rebekah. Bethuel the Aramean
was the father of Laban and Rebekah, and Rebekah was the mother of
Jacob and Esau.
6Esau ·learned [Lsaw] that Isaac had blessed Jacob and sent him to
·northwestern Mesopotamia [LPaddan-aram] to find a wife there. He also
·learned [Lsaw] that Isaac had commanded Jacob not to marry a
·Canaanite woman [Ldaughter of Canaan] 7and that Jacob had ·obeyed
[listened to] his father and mother and had gone to ·northwestern
Mesopotamia [LPaddan-aram]. 8So Esau saw that ·his father Isaac did not
want his sons to marry Canaanite women [Cthe daughters of Canaan were

bad/evil in the eyes of his father Isaac]. 9Now Esau already had wives, but he went to Ishmael son of Abraham, and he married Mahalath, Ishmael's daughter. Mahalath was the sister of Nebaioth.

Jacob's Dream at Bethel

10Jacob left Beersheba [21:14] and set out for Haran [11:31]. 11When he came to a place, he spent the night there because the sun had set. He found a stone and laid his head on it ·to go to sleep [L and lay down in that place]. 12Jacob dreamed that there was a ·ladder [*or* stairway; *or* ramp] resting on the earth and reaching up into heaven, and he saw ·angels [messengers] of God ·going up and coming down [ascending and descending on] ·the ladder [L it; John 1:51]. 13Then Jacob saw the Lord standing above the ladder [28:12], and he said, "I am the Lord, the God of Abraham your grandfather, and the God of Isaac. I will give you and your ·descendants [L seed] the ·land [ground] on which you are now ·sleeping [lying; 12:1–3]. 14Your ·descendants [L seed] will be as many as the dust of the earth [13:16]. They will spread west and east, north and south, and all the ·families [clans] of the earth will ·be blessed [*or* bless themselves] through you and your ·descendants [seed]. 15I am with you and will ·protect [guard] you everywhere you go and will bring you back to this land. I will not ·leave [abandon; forsake] you until I have done what I have promised you."

16Then Jacob woke from his sleep and said, "Surely the Lord is in this place, but I did not know it." 17He was afraid and said, "This place frightens me! It is surely the house of God and the gate of heaven."

18Jacob rose early in the morning and took the stone ·he had slept on [L which was under his head] and set it up ·on its end [L as a pillar; 31:13, 45; 35:14, 20; Ex. 24:4; C a practice later prohibited because similar to Canaanite religion (Ex. 23:24; 34:13; Deut. 12:3)]. Then he poured olive oil on the top of it. 19·At first [Formerly], the name of that city was Luz, but Jacob named it Bethel [C "house of God"].

20Then Jacob ·made a promise [L vowed a vow]. He said, "I want God to be with me and to ·protect [guard] me on this journey. I want him to give me food to eat and clothes to wear 21so I will be able to return ·in peace [*or* safely] to my father's house. If the Lord does these things, he will be my God. 22This stone which I have set up ·on its end [L as a pillar] will be the house of God. And I will give God ·one-tenth [a tithe] of all he gives me."

Jacob Arrives in Northwestern Mesopotamia

29 Then Jacob ·continued his journey [L lifted his feet] and came to the land of the people of the East [C the area of the Arameans on the northern Euphrates]. 2He looked and saw a well in the field and three flocks of sheep lying nearby, because they drank water from this well. A large stone covered the mouth of the well. 3When all the flocks would gather there, ·the shepherds [L they] would roll the stone away from the well and water the sheep. Then they would put the stone back in its place.

4Jacob said to the shepherds there, "My brothers, where are you from?"

They answered, "We are from Haran [11:31]."

5Then Jacob asked, "Do you know Laban, ·grandson [descendant] of Nahor?"

They answered, "We know him."

6Then Jacob asked, "How is he?"

They answered, "He is well. Look, his daughter Rachel is coming now with his sheep."

7Jacob said, "But look, it is still ·the middle of the day [broad daylight].

It is not time for the sheep to be gathered for the night, so give them water
and let them go back into the pasture."
8But they said, "We cannot do that until all the flocks are gathered. Then
we will roll away the stone from the mouth of the well and water the sheep."
9While ·Jacob [Lhe] was talking with ·the shepherds [Lthem], Rachel
came with her father's sheep, because ·it was her job to care for the sheep
[Lshe was a shepherdess]. 10When Jacob saw Laban's daughter Rachel and
Laban's sheep, he went to the well and rolled the stone from its mouth
and watered Laban's sheep. Now Laban was the brother of Rebekah,
Jacob's mother. 11Then Jacob kissed Rachel and [Llifted his voice and]
cried. 12He told her that he was from her father's family and that he was
the son of Rebekah. So Rachel ran home and told her father.
13When Laban heard the news about his sister's son Jacob, he ran to
meet him. Laban hugged him and kissed him and brought him to his
house, where Jacob told Laban everything that had happened.
14Then Laban said, "You are my own ·flesh and blood [Lbone and flesh]."

Jacob Is Tricked

Jacob stayed there a month. 15Then Laban said to Jacob, "You are my
relative, but ·it is not right for you to work for me without pay [Lshould
you serve me for nothing?]. What ·would you like me to pay you [will
your wages be]?"
16Now Laban had two daughters. The older was Leah, and the younger
was Rachel. 17Leah had ·weak eyes [frail/tender eyes; Clikely means unat-
tractive], but Rachel was very beautiful. 18Jacob loved Rachel, so he said
to Laban, "·Let me marry your younger daughter Rachel. If you will, I
will work seven years for you [LI will work for seven years for your
younger daughter Rachel]."
19Laban said, "It would be better for ·her to marry you [Lme to give her
to you] than someone else, so stay here with me." 20So Jacob worked for
Laban seven years so he could marry Rachel. But they seemed like just a
few days to him because he loved Rachel very much.
21After seven years Jacob said to Laban, "Give me ·Rachel [Lmy woman/
wife] so that I may ·marry [Lgo to] her. ·The time I promised to work for
you is over [LMy days are fulfilled]."
22So Laban gave a ·feast [banquet] for all the people there. 23That evening he brought his daughter Leah to Jacob, and ·they had sexual relations
[Lhe (Jacob) went into her]. 24(Laban gave his slave girl Zilpah to his
daughter to be her ·servant [Lslave girl].) 25In the morning when Jacob
saw that ·he had had sexual relations with [Lit was] Leah, he said to Laban,
"What have you done to me? I worked hard for you so that I could marry
Rachel! Why did you ·trick [deceive; defraud] me?"
26Laban said, "In our ·country [Lplace] we do not allow the younger
daughter to marry before the ·older daughter [Lfirstborn]. 27But complete the full week of ·the marriage ceremony with Leah [Lthis one], and
I will give you ·Rachel [Lthe other one] to marry also. But you must serve
me another seven years."
28So Jacob did this, and when he had completed the week ·with Leah
[Lof this one], Laban gave him his daughter Rachel as a wife. 29(Laban
gave his slave girl Bilhah to his daughter Rachel to be her ·servant [Lslave
girl].) 30So Jacob ·had sexual relations with [Lwent to] Rachel also, and
Jacob loved Rachel more than Leah. Jacob worked for Laban for another
seven years.

Jacob's Family Grows

[31]When the LORD saw ·that Jacob loved Rachel more than Leah [LLeah was unloved/hated], he ·made it possible for Leah to have children [Lopened up her womb], but ·not Rachel [LRachel was barren]. [32]Leah ·became pregnant [conceived] and gave birth to a son. She named him Reuben [Csounds like "seen my troubles" in Hebrew], because she said, "The LORD has seen my ·troubles [distress]. Surely now my husband will love me."

[33]Leah ·became pregnant [conceived] again and gave birth to another son. She named him Simeon [Csounds like "has heard" in Hebrew] and said, "The LORD has heard that I am ·not loved [*or* hated], so he has given me this son."

[34]Leah ·became pregnant [conceived] again and gave birth to another son. She named him Levi [Csounds like "be close to" in Hebrew] and said, "Now, surely my husband will ·be close [bind/attach himself] to me, because I have given him three sons."

[35]Then Leah gave birth to another son. She named him Judah [Csounds like "praise" in Hebrew], because she said, "Now I will praise the LORD." Then Leah stopped having children.

30 When Rachel saw that she was not having children for Jacob, she ·envied [was jealous of] her sister Leah. She said to Jacob, "Give me children, or I'll die!" [2]Jacob became angry with her and said, "·Can I do what only God can do [LAm I in the place of God]? He ·is the one who has kept you from having children [Lhas withheld the fruit of your womb]."

[3]Then Rachel said, "Here is my slave girl Bilhah. ·Have sexual relations with [LGo to] her so she can ·give birth to a child for me [Lbear a child on my knees]. Then I can ·have my own family [Lbe built up] through her."

[4]So Rachel gave Bilhah, her slave girl, to Jacob as a ·wife [*or* concubine], and he ·had sexual relations with [Lwent to] her. [5]Bilhah ·became pregnant [conceived] and gave Jacob a son. [6]Rachel said, "God has ·judged me innocent [vindicated me]. He has listened to my prayer and has given me a son," so she named him Dan [Csounds like "he has judged" in Hebrew].

[7]Bilhah ·became pregnant [conceived] again and gave Jacob a second son. [8]Rachel said, "I have ·struggled [*or* wrestled] hard with my sister, and I have won." So she named that son Naphtali [Csounds like "my struggle/wrestling" in Hebrew].

[9]Leah saw that she had stopped having children, so she gave her slave girl Zilpah to Jacob as a ·wife [*or* concubine]. [10]When Zilpah, the slave girl of Leah, ·got pregnant [conceived] and had a son, [11]Leah said, "·I am lucky [Good fortune]," so she named him Gad [Csounds like "lucky" in Hebrew]. [12]Zilpah, the slave girl of Leah, gave birth to another son, [13]and Leah said, "I am very ·happy [*or* blessed]! Now women will call me ·happy [*or* blessed]," so she named him Asher [Csounds like "happy/blessed" in Hebrew].

[14]During the wheat harvest Reuben went into the field and found some mandrake plants [Can aphrodisiac, also thought to increase fertility] and brought them to his mother Leah. But Rachel said to Leah, "Please give me some of your son's mandrakes."

[15]Leah answered, "·You have already [LIs it a minor matter that you have] taken away my husband, and now you are trying to take away my son's mandrakes."

But Rachel answered, "If you will give me your son's mandrakes, you may ·sleep [Llie] with Jacob tonight."

[16]When Jacob came in from the field ·that night [in the evening], Leah

went out to meet him. She said, “You will ·have sexual relations with
[Lcome to] me tonight because I have ·paid for [bought; hired] you with
my son’s mandrakes.” So Jacob ·slept [Llay] with her that night.
17Then God ·answered Leah’s prayer [Lheard Leah], and she ·became
pregnant [Lconceived] again. She gave birth to a fifth son 18and said, “God
has given me what I ·paid for [bought; hired], because I gave my slave girl
to my husband.” So Leah named her son Issachar [Csounds like “paid for”
in Hebrew].
19Leah ·became pregnant [conceived] again and gave birth to a sixth
son. 20·She [LLeah] said, “God has given me a fine ·gift [dowry]. Now
surely Jacob will ·honor [exalt] me, because I have given him six sons,” so
she named him Zebulun [Csounds like “honor” in Hebrew]. 21Later Leah
gave birth to a daughter and named her Dinah [ch. 34].
22Then God remembered Rachel and ·answered her prayer [Lheard
her], ·making it possible for her to have children [Land opened her womb].
23When she ·became pregnant [conceived] and gave birth to a son, she
said, “God has taken away my ·shame [reproach],” 24and she named him
Joseph [Csounds like “he adds” in Hebrew]. Rachel said, “I wish the Lord
would ·give [Ladd to] me another son.”

Jacob Tricks Laban

25·After the birth of [At the time that Rachel gave birth to] Joseph,
Jacob said to Laban, “Now ·let me [Lsend me away that I might] go to my
own home and country. 26Give me my wives and my children and let me
go. I have earned them by working for you, and you know that I have
served you well.”
27Laban said to him, “If I have ·pleased you [Lfound grace in your eyes],
please stay. I ·know [*or* have learned by divination that] the Lord has
blessed me because of you. 28·Tell me what I should pay you [Name your
price], and I will give it to you.”
29Jacob answered, “You know that I have worked hard for you, and
[Lhow] your ·flocks [herds; *or* cattle] have ·grown while I cared for them
[Lhave done with me]. 30When I came, you had little, but now you have
·much [Lincreased many times]. ·Every time I did something for you
[Wherever I turned; LAt my feet], the Lord blessed you. But when will I be
able to do something for my own ·family [household; Lhouse]?”
31Laban asked, “Then what should I give you?”
Jacob answered, “I don’t want you to give me anything. Just do this one
thing, and I will come back and ·take care of [Lfeed and watch] your flocks.
32Today let me ·go [pass] through all your flocks. I will ·take [remove]
every speckled or spotted sheep, every black lamb, and every spotted or
speckled goat. That will be my ·pay [wage; hire]. 33In the future ·you can
easily see if I am honest [Lmy honesty/righteousness will answer for me].
When you come to look at my flocks, if I have any goat that isn’t speckled
or spotted or any lamb that isn’t black, you will know I stole it.”
34Laban answered, “Agreed! We will do what you ·ask [Lsay].” 35But that
day Laban ·took away [removed] all the male goats that had streaks or
spots, all the speckled and spotted female goats (all those that had white
on them), and all the black sheep. He told his sons to ·watch over [take
charge of] them. 36Then he took these animals to a place that was three
days’ journey away from Jacob. Jacob ·took care of [pastured] all the
flocks that were left.
37So Jacob cut ·green [fresh] ·branches [rods] from poplar, almond,

and plane trees and peeled off some of the bark so that the ·branches [rods] had white stripes on them. 38He put the ·branches [rods] in front of the flocks at the watering ·places [troughs]. When the animals came to drink, they ·also mated there [Lwere in heat], 39so the flocks mated in front of the branches [rods]. Then the young that were born were streaked, speckled, or spotted [Csince nothing in Jacob's strategy would have produced this result, God must have done it]. 40Jacob separated the young animals from the others, and he made them face the streaked and dark animals in Laban's flock. Jacob kept his animals separate from Laban's. 41When the stronger animals in the flock were ·mating [Lin heat], Jacob put the ·branches [rods] before their eyes so they would mate near the branches. 42But when the ·weaker [feebler] animals ·mated [Lwere in heat], Jacob did not put the ·branches [rods] there. So the animals born from the ·weaker [feebler] animals were Laban's, and those born from the stronger animals were Jacob's. 43In this way ·Jacob [Lthe man] became very rich. He had large flocks, many male and female servants, camels, and donkeys.

Jacob Runs Away

31 One day Jacob heard Laban's sons talking. They said, "Jacob has taken everything our father owned, and ·in this way he has become rich [Lhe has gotten all this wealth from our father]." 2Then Jacob ·noticed [saw] that Laban was not as friendly as he had been before. 3The LORD said to Jacob, "Go back to the land ·where your ancestors lived [Lof your fathers and your birthplace], and I will be with you [Cindicating Jacob's covenant with God]."

4So Jacob ·told [Lsent for] Rachel and Leah to meet him in the field where he kept his flocks. 5He said to them, "I have seen that your father is not as friendly with me as he used to be, but the God of my father has been with me. 6You both know that I have ·worked [served] ·as hard as I could [Lwith all my power/strength] for your father, 7but he ·cheated [mocked; deceived] me and changed my ·pay [wages] ten times. But God has not allowed your father to harm me. 8When Laban said, 'You can have all the speckled animals as your ·pay [wages],' all the animals gave birth to speckled young ones. But when he said, 'You can have all the streaked animals as your ·pay [wages],' all the flocks gave birth to streaked babies [30:37–43]. 9So God has taken the ·animals [livestock] away from your father and has given them to me.

10"I had a dream during the season when the flocks were ·mating [Lin heat]. I saw that the only male goats who were ·mating [mounting; Lgoing up] were streaked, speckled, or spotted. 11The ·angel [messenger] of God [16:7] spoke to me in that dream and said, 'Jacob!' I answered, 'Yes!' 12The ·angel [messenger] said, '·Look [LRaise up your eyes and see]! Only the streaked, speckled, or spotted male goats are ·mating [mounting; Lgoing up]. I have seen all ·the wrong things [Lthat which] Laban has been doing to you. 13I am the God ·who appeared to you at [Lof] Bethel, where you ·poured olive oil on [anointed] the ·stone you set up on end [pillar; 28:18–19] and where you made a ·promise [vow] to me. Now I want you to leave ·here [Lthis land] and go back to the land where you were born.' "

14Rachel and Leah answered Jacob, "·Our father has nothing to give us when he dies [LIs there any lot/portion or inheritance still in our father's house?]. 15He has ·treated [considered] us like ·strangers [*or* foreigners]. He sold us to you, and ·then he spent all of the money you paid for us [Ldevoured the money]. [16]God took all this wealth from our father, and now it belongs to us and our children. So do whatever God has told you to do."

[17]So Jacob [[L]rose up and] put his children and his wives on camels, [18]and they began their journey back to Isaac, his father, in the land of Canaan. All the flocks of animals that Jacob owned walked ahead of them. He carried ·everything [all the property] with him that he had gotten while he lived in ·northwestern Mesopotamia [[L]Paddan-aram].

[19]While Laban was gone to ·cut the wool from [shear] his sheep, Rachel stole the ·idols [[L]teraphim; [C]probably his household gods] that belonged to ·him [[L]her father]. [20]And Jacob ·tricked [deceived; [L]stole the heart of] Laban the Aramean by not telling him he was ·leaving [fleeing]. [21]·Jacob and his family [[L]He and all that was his] ·left quickly [fled], crossed the ·Euphrates River [[L]River; [C]the northern Euphrates separated Mesopotamia from Syria], and traveled toward the mountains of Gilead [[C]the northernmost part of Palestine].

[22]Three days later ·Laban learned [[L]it was told/reported to Laban] that Jacob had ·run away [fled], [23]so he ·gathered [[L]took] his ·relatives [[L]brothers] and began to ·chase [pursue] him. After seven days Laban ·found [caught up with] him in the mountains of Gilead. [24]That night God came to Laban the Aramean in a dream and said, "Be careful! Do not say anything to Jacob, good or bad."

The Search for the Stolen Idols

[25]So Laban caught up with Jacob. Now Jacob had ·made his camp [[L]pitched his tent] in the mountains, so Laban and his ·relatives [[L]brothers] ·set up their camp [pitched] in the mountains of Gilead. [26]Laban said to Jacob, "What have you done? You ·cheated me [deceived me; [L]stole my heart] and ·took [[L]carried away] my daughters as if you had captured them ·in a war [[L]with a sword]. [27]Why did you ·run away secretly [sneak off] and ·trick [deceive; [L]steal from] me? Why didn't you tell me? Then I could have sent you away with joy and singing and with the music of tambourines and ·harps [lyres]. [28]You did not even let me kiss my ·grandchildren [[L]sons] and my daughters good-bye. You were very foolish to do this! [29]I have the power to harm you, but last night the God of your father spoke to me and warned me not to say anything to you, good or bad. [30]I know you want to go back to ·your home [[L]the house of your father], but why did you steal my ·idols [[L]gods; 31:19]?"

[31]Jacob answered [[L]and said to] Laban, "I left without telling you, because I was afraid you would ·take [forcibly remove] your daughters away from me. [32]If you find anyone here who has taken your ·idols [gods], that person will ·be killed [[L]not live]! ·Your [[L]Our] ·relatives [[L]brothers] will be my witnesses. You may look for anything that belongs to you and take anything that is yours." (Now Jacob did not know that Rachel had stolen Laban's idols.)

[33]So Laban ·looked [[L]went] in Jacob's tent, in Leah's tent, and in the tent where the two slave women stayed, but he did not find his idols. When he left Leah's tent, he went into Rachel's tent. [34]Rachel had hidden the ·idols [teraphim; 31:19] inside her camel's saddle and was sitting on them. Although Laban looked through the whole tent, he did not find them.

[35]Rachel said to her father, "Father, don't be angry with me. I am not able to stand up before you because ·I am having my monthly period [[L]the way of women is on me]." So Laban ·looked through the camp [[L]searched], but he did not find ·his idols [[L]the teraphim].

[36]Then Jacob became very angry and accused Laban and said, "What ·wrong have I done [is my offense]? What ·law have I broken [Lis my sin] to cause you to ·chase [hotly pursue] me? [37]You have ·looked [felt] through everything I own, but you have found nothing that belongs to you. If you have found anything, show it to everyone. Put it in front of your ·relatives [Lbrothers] and my ·relatives [Lbrothers], and let them ·decide which one of us is right [judge between us]. [38]I have ·worked for [Lbeen with] you now for twenty years. During all that time none of the ·lambs [ewes] and kids ·died during birth [miscarried], and I have not eaten any of the ·male sheep [rams] from your flocks. [39]Any time an animal was killed by wild beasts, I did not bring it to you, but made up for the loss myself. You made me pay for any animal that was stolen during the day or night. [40]In the daytime the ·sun [heat] ·took away my strength [Lconsumed me], and at night I was cold and ·could not sleep [Lsleep fled from my eyes]. [41]I [Lwas in your house and] worked like a slave for you for twenty years— the first fourteen to get your two daughters and the last six to earn your flocks. During that time you changed my ·pay [wages] ten times. [42]But the God of my father, the God of Abraham and the ·God [LFear; Ca title for God; Prov. 1:7] of Isaac, was with me. Otherwise, you would have sent me away with nothing. But he saw the ·trouble [affliction] I had and the hard work I did, and last night he ·corrected [admonished; reproved] you."

Jacob and Laban's Treaty

[43]Laban said to Jacob, "·These girls [LThe daughters] are my daughters. ·Their children belong to me [LThe sons are my sons], and ·these flocks are mine [Lthe flocks are my flocks]. Everything you see here belongs to me, but ·I can do nothing to keep [Lwhat can I do about…?] my daughters and their children. [44]·Let us make [LCome, let us cut] ·an agreement [a covenant/treaty; 6:18], and let ·us set up a pile of stones to remind us of it [Lit be a witness between us]."

[45]So Jacob took a large rock and set it ·up on its end [Las a pillar]. [46]·He [LJacob] told his ·relatives [Lbrothers] to gather rocks, so they took the rocks and ·piled them up [made a pile/mound/heap]; then they ·ate [feasted] beside the pile [Ctreaties were often celebrated by a feast]. [47]Laban named that place in his language A Pile to Remind Us [Jegar-sahadutha; Che spoke Aramaic], and Jacob called the place Galeed [Cthe Hebrew version of the Aramaic name].

[48]Laban said to Jacob, "This ·pile of rocks [mound; heap] will ·remind us of the agreement [Lbe a witness] between us." That is why the place was called ·A Pile to Remind Us [Galeed]. [49]It was also called Mizpah [Csounds like "watch" in Hebrew], because Laban said, "Let the LORD watch over us while we are ·separated [absent] from each other. [50]Remember that God is our witness even if no one else is around us. He will know if you ·harm [abuse] my daughters or ·marry [take] other women. [51]Here is the ·pile of rocks [mound; heap] that I have ·put [thrown up] between us and here is the ·rock I set up on end [pillar]. [52]This ·pile of rocks [mound; heap] and this ·rock set on end [pillar] will ·remind us of our agreement [Lbe a witness]. I will never go past this ·pile [mound; heap] to hurt you, and you must never come to my side of them to hurt me. [53]Let the God of Abraham, who is the God of Nahor and the God of their ·ancestors [fathers], ·punish either of us if we break this agreement [Ljudge between us]."

So Jacob made a promise ·in the name of the God whom his father Isaac worshiped [Lby the fear of his father Isaac]. [54]Then Jacob ·killed an

animal and offered it as [L offered] a sacrifice on the mountain, and he
invited his ·relatives [L brothers] to share in the meal [31:46]. After they
finished eating, they spent the night on the mountain. 55 Early the next
morning Laban kissed his ·grandchildren [L sons] and his daughters and
blessed them, and then he left to return ·home [L to his place].

Jacob Meets Esau

32 When Jacob also went his way, the ·angels [messengers] of
God met him. 2 When he saw them, he said, "This is the camp
of God!" So he named that place Mahanaim [C sounds like "two camps"
in Hebrew; a city in the hill country of Gilead; Josh. 13:26, 30].
3 Jacob's brother Esau was living in the area called Seir in the country of
Edom [14:6]. Jacob sent messengers to Esau, 4 telling them, "Give this
message to my ·master [lord] Esau: 'This is what Jacob, your servant, says:
I have ·lived [sojourned; lived as an alien] with Laban and have ·remained
[*or* been detained] there until now. 5 I have cattle, donkeys, flocks, and
male and female servants. I send this message to ·you [my master/lord]
·and ask you to accept us [L to find grace in your eyes].'"
6 The messengers returned to Jacob and said, "We went to your brother
Esau. He is coming to meet you and has four hundred men with him."
7 Then Jacob was very afraid and ·worried [distressed]. He divided the
people who were with him and all the flocks, herds, and camels into two
camps. 8 Jacob thought, "Esau might come and ·destroy [strike; attack]
one camp, but the ·other camp can run away and [L the camp that is left]
·be saved [escape]."
9 Then Jacob said, "God of my father Abraham! God of my father Isaac!
LORD, ·you told [did you not tell…?] me to return to my country and my
family. You said that you would treat me well. 10 I am not worthy of the
·kindness [loyalty; covenant love] and ·continual goodness [faithfulness]
you have shown ·me [L your servant]. The first time I traveled across the
Jordan River, I had only my walking stick, but now I own enough to have
two camps. 11 Please ·save [rescue; deliver] me from [L the hand of] my
brother Esau. I am afraid he will come and ·kill [strike; attack] all of us,
even the mothers with the children. 12 You said to me, 'I will treat you well
and will make your ·children [L seed] as many as the sand of the seashore
[22:17]. There will be too many to count.'"
13 Jacob stayed there for the night and prepared ·a gift [*or* tribute] for
Esau from what he had with him: 14 two hundred female goats and twenty
male goats, two hundred ·female sheep [ewes] and twenty ·male sheep
[rams], 15 thirty female camels and their young, forty cows and ten bulls,
twenty female donkeys, and ten male donkeys. 16 Jacob gave each separate
flock of animals to one of his servants and said to them, "·Go [Pass] ahead
of me and keep some space between each herd." 17 Jacob gave them their
orders. To the servant with the first group of animals he said, "My brother
Esau will come to you and ask, '·Whose servant are you [L To whom do
you belong]? Where are you going and whose ·animals are these [L are
these ahead of you]?' 18 Then you will answer, 'They belong to your servant Jacob. He sent them as a ·gift [*or* tribute] to you, my ·master [lord]
Esau, and he also is coming behind us.'"
19 Jacob ordered the second servant, the third servant, and all the ·other
servants [L others who followed the droves of animals] to do the same
thing. He said, "Say the same thing to Esau when you meet him. 20 Say,
'Your servant Jacob is coming behind us.'" Jacob thought, "If I send ·these

gifts [*or* this tribute] ahead of me, maybe ·Esau will forgive me [LI will appease/propitiate him]. Then when I see ·him [Lhis face], perhaps he will accept me." 21So Jacob ·sent [passed ahead of him] the ·gifts [*or* tribute] to Esau, but he himself stayed that night in the camp.

Jacob Wrestles with God

22During the night Jacob rose and crossed the Jabbok River [Ca tributary of the Jordan about 15 miles north of the Dead Sea in the Transjordan] at the crossing, taking with him his two wives, his two slave girls, and his eleven sons. 23He sent his family and everything he had across the ·river [wadi; ravine]. 24So Jacob was alone, and a man came and wrestled with him until ·the sun came up [daybreak]. 25When the man saw he could not defeat Jacob, he struck Jacob's ·hip [hip socket] and put it out of joint [Las he wrestled with him]. 26Then he said to Jacob, "Let me go. ·The sun is coming up [Daybreak is coming]."

But Jacob said, "I will ·let you go if you will [Lnot let you go unless you] bless me."

27The man said to him, "What is your name?"

And he answered, "Jacob."

28Then the man said, "Your name will no longer be Jacob. Your name will now be Israel [Csounds like "he wrestled/fought/strove with God" in Hebrew], because you have ·wrestled [fought; strove] with God and with people, and you have ·won [prevailed]."

29Then Jacob asked him, "Please tell me your name."

But ·the man [Lhe] said, "Why do you ask my name?" Then he blessed Jacob there.

30So Jacob named that place Peniel [Csounds like "face of God" in Hebrew], saying, "I have seen God face to face, but my life was ·saved [spared]." 31Then the sun rose as he was leaving that place, and Jacob was limping because of his ·leg [hip]. 32So even today the people of Israel do not eat the muscle that is on the hip joint of animals [Cthe sciatic muscle], because Jacob was touched there.

Jacob Shows His Bravery

33 Jacob ·looked up [Lraised his eyes] and saw Esau coming, and with him were four hundred men. So Jacob divided his children among Leah, Rachel, and the two slave girls. 2Jacob put the slave girls with their children first, then Leah and her children behind them, and Rachel and Joseph last [Cleast favorite to most favorite]. 3Jacob himself ·went out [passed] in front of them and bowed down flat on the ground seven times ·as he was walking toward [*or* until he came near] his brother.

4But Esau ran to meet Jacob and ·put his arms around [hugged] him and ·hugged him [Lfell on his neck]. Then Esau kissed him, and they both cried. 5When ·Esau looked up [Lhe raised his eyes] and saw the women and children, he asked, "Who are these people with you?"

Jacob answered, "These are the children God has graciously given me, your servant."

6Then the two slave girls and their children came up to Esau and bowed down flat on the earth before him. 7Leah and her children also came up to Esau and also bowed down flat on the earth. Last of all, Joseph and Rachel came up to Esau, and they, too, bowed down flat before him.

8Esau said, "·I saw many herds as I was coming here. Why did you bring them [LWhat is all this camp that I encountered]?"

Jacob answered, "They were to ·please you, my master [Lfind grace/favor in the eyes of my master/lord]."

9But Esau said, "I already have enough, my brother. Keep what you have."
10Jacob said, "No! Please! If I have ·pleased you [Lfound grace/favor in your eyes], then ·accept the gift I give you [Ltake my gift/tribute from my hand]. ·I am very happy to see your face again. It [LSeeing your face] is like seeing the face of God, because you have accepted me. 11So I beg you to accept the ·gift [present; Lblessing] I give you. God has been very ·good [gracious; favorable] to me, and I have ·more than [all that] I need." And because ·Jacob begged [he urged him], Esau ·accepted [took] the gift.

12Then Esau said, "Let us be going. I will travel with you."

13But Jacob said to him, "My ·master [Llord], you know that the children are ·weak [soft; frail]. And I must be careful with my flocks ·and their young ones [Land herds that are nursing]. If I ·force them to go too far [push them too fast] in one day, ·all the animals [the entire flock] will die. 14So, my ·master [lord], you ·go [pass] on ahead of me, your servant. I will follow you slowly and let the animals and the children set the speed at which we travel. I will meet you, my ·master [lord], in ·Edom [LSeir; 14:6]."

15So Esau said, "Then let me leave some of my people with you."

"No, thank you," said Jacob. "·I only want to please you, my master [LWhy should I find such grace/favor in the eyes of my master/lord?]." 16So that day Esau started back to ·Edom [LSeir; 14:6]. 17But Jacob went to Succoth, where he built a house for himself and ·shelters [booths] for his animals. That is why the place was named Succoth [Csounds like "shelter" in Hebrew].

18Jacob left ·northwestern Mesopotamia [LPaddan-aram] and arrived safely at the city of Shechem [12:6] in the land of Canaan. There he camped ·east of [Lbefore] the city. 19He bought a ·part [parcel; portion] of the field where he had camped from the sons of Hamor father of Shechem for one hundred ·pieces of silver [Lqesitah; Can uncertain monetary unit; Josh. 24:32; John 4:5, 6, 12; Acts 7:16]. 20He ·built [erected] an altar there and named it ·after God, the God of Israel [LEl-Elohe-Israel].

Dinah Is Attacked

34 At this time Dinah, the daughter of Leah ·and [Lwhom she bore to] Jacob [30:21], went out to ·visit [see; *or* be seen with] the ·women [Ldaughters] of the land. 2When Shechem son of Hamor the Hivite [Cone of the tribes that inhabited Canaan], the ·ruler [prince] of the land, saw her, he took her and ·forced her to have sexual relations with him [lay with her and humiliated/violated her]. 3·Shechem fell in love with Dinah [LHis soul was bound to Dinah daugher of Jacob and he loved her], and he spoke kindly to her. 4He told his father, Hamor, "Please get this girl for me ·so I can marry her [Las a wife]."

5Jacob ·learned how [Lheard that] ·Shechem [Lhe] had ·disgraced [defiled; made unclean] his daughter, but since his sons were out in the field with the cattle, Jacob ·said nothing [was silent] until they came home. 6While he waited, Hamor father of Shechem went to talk with Jacob.

7When Jacob's sons heard what had happened, they came in from the field. They were [Lupset/shocked/pained and] very angry that Shechem had done ·such a wicked thing [sacrilege; Lfolly] to Israel. It was wrong for him to ·have sexual relations [Llie] with Jacob's daughter; a thing like this should not be done.

8But Hamor talked to Dinah's brothers and said, "My son Shechem is deeply ·in love with [attached/bound to] Dinah. Please ·let him marry her

[Lgive her to him as a wife]. 9·Marry [Make marriages/Intermarry with] our people. Give your women [Ldaughters] to ·our men as wives [Lus] and take our ·women [Ldaughters] for ·your men as wives [Lyourselves]. 10You can live in the same land with us. You will be free to own land and to trade here."

11Shechem also talked to ·Jacob [Lher father] and to Dinah's brothers and said, "·Please accept my offer [LLet me find grace/favor in your eyes]. I will give anything you ask. 12Ask as much as you want for the ·payment for the bride [bridal payment and gift; Ctraditional payments to the family], and I will give it to you. Just ·let me marry Dinah [Lgive me the girl as a wife]."

13Jacob's sons answered Shechem and his father ·with lies [deceitfully; with duplicity], because Shechem had ·disgraced [defiled; made unclean] their sister Dinah. 14The brothers said to them, "We cannot allow you [Lto do this thing] to ·marry our sister [Lgive our sister as a wife], because you are not circumcised. That would be a ·disgrace [reproach; shame] to us. 15But we will ·allow you to marry her [Lconsent] if you do this one thing: Every man in your town must be circumcised like us [17:10]. 16Then ·your men can marry our women [Lwe will give our daughers to you], and ·our men can marry your women [Lwe will take your daughters for ourselves], and we will live in your land and become one people. 17If you ·refuse [Ldo not listen/obey us] to be circumcised, we will take ·Dinah [Lour daughter] and ·leave [go]."

18What they asked seemed fair to Hamor and Shechem [Lthe son of Hamor]. 19So ·Shechem quickly went to be circumcised [Lthe man did not delay to do this thing] because he ·loved [delighted in] Jacob's daughter.

Now Shechem was the most ·respected [honored] man in ·his family [Lhis father's house]. 20So Hamor and Shechem [Lhis son] went to the gate of their city and spoke to the men of their city, saying, 21"These people want to be friends with us. So let them live in our land and trade here. ·There is enough land [LThe land is broad on both sides] for all of us. Let us ·marry their women [Ltake their daughters as wives for ourselves], and ·we can let them marry our women [Lgive them our daughters]. 22But we must agree to one thing: All our men must be circumcised as they are. Then they will agree to live in our land, and we will be one people. 23If we do this, their cattle and their animals will belong to us. Let us do what they say, and they will stay in our land." 24All the people who had come to the city gate heard this. They agreed with Hamor and Shechem [Lhis son], and every man was circumcised.

25Three days later the men who were circumcised were still in pain. Two of Jacob's sons, Simeon and Levi (Dinah's brothers), took their swords and made a ·surprise [*or* bold] attack on the city, killing all the men there. 26They killed Hamor and his son Shechem and then took Dinah out of Shechem's house and left. 27Jacob's sons came upon the dead bodies and ·stole everything that was in [plundered] the city, ·to pay them back for what Shechem had done to [Lbecause they had disgraced/defiled/made unclean] their sister. 28So the brothers took the flocks, herds, and donkeys, and everything in the city and in the fields. 29They ·took [Lcaptured and plundered] every valuable thing the people owned, even their wives and children and everything in the houses.

30Then Jacob said to Simeon and Levi, "You have caused me a lot of trouble. ·Now the Canaanites and the Perizzites who live in the land will hate me [LI will be a stench among the inhabitants of the land, among the

Canaanites and the Perizzites]. Since there are only a few of us, if they join together to attack us, my people and I will be destroyed."

31But the brothers said, "·We will not allow our sister to be treated [Should they treat our sister…?] like a ·prostitute [whore]."

Jacob in Bethel

35 God said to Jacob, "·Go [LRise up and go up] to the city of Bethel [12:8] and live there. Make an altar to the God who appeared to you there when you were ·running away [fleeing] from your brother Esau [28:1–22]."

2So Jacob said to his ·family [household] and to all who were with him, "Put away the foreign gods you have, and ·make yourselves clean [purify yourselves], and change your clothes. 3We will ·leave here and go [Lrise up and go up] to Bethel. There I will build an altar to God, who ·has helped [Lanswered] me ·during my time of trouble [Lin the day of my distress]. He has been with me [Can indication of a covenant relationship] everywhere I have gone." 4So they gave Jacob all the foreign gods ·they had [in their possession; Lin their hands], and the earrings ·they were wearing [Lon their ears], and he hid them under the ·great tree [Loak; *or* terebinth; 12:6] near the town of Shechem. 5Then Jacob and his sons left there. But ·God caused the people in the nearby cities to be afraid [Lthe terror of God was on the surrounding cities], so they did not ·follow [pursue] them. 6And Jacob and all the people who were with him went to Luz, which is now called Bethel, in the land of Canaan. 7There Jacob built an altar and named the place ·Bethel, after God [El-Bethel; *or* "God of Bethel"], because God had appeared to him there when he was ·running [fleeing] from his brother.

8Deborah, Rebekah's nurse, died and was buried under the oak tree at Bethel, so they named that place ·Oak of Crying [LAllon-bacuth].

Jacob's New Name

9When Jacob came back from ·northwestern Mesopotamia [LPaddan-aram], God appeared to him again and blessed him. 10God said to him, "Your name is Jacob, but you will not be called Jacob any longer. Your new name will be Israel." So he called him Israel [32:28]. 11God said to him, "I am ·God Almighty [LEl Shaddai]. ·Have many children [LBe fruitful] and ·grow in number [Lmultiply; 1:22] as a nation. ·You will be the ancestor of many nations [LA company/assembly of nations will come from you] and kings [Lwill spring from your loins]. 12The same land I gave to Abraham and Isaac I will give to you and your ·descendants [Lseed; 12:2]." 13Then God ·left him [Lwent up from him in the place where he spoke with him]. 14Jacob set up a ·stone on edge [Lpillar, a stone pillar] in that place where God had talked to him, and he poured a drink offering and olive oil on it to make it special for God. 15And Jacob named the place Bethel [C"house of God"].

Rachel Dies Giving Birth

16·Jacob and his group [LThey] ·left [departed from] Bethel. ·Before they came to [*or* While still some distance from] Ephrath [Cnear Bethlehem four miles south of Jerusalem; 35:19], Rachel began giving birth to her baby [Land had hard labor], 17but she was having ·much trouble [hard labor]. When ·Rachel's nurse [Lthe midwife] saw this, she said, "Don't be afraid, Rachel. You are giving birth to another son." 18Rachel gave birth to the son, but she herself died. As she lay dying, she named the boy ·Son of My Suffering [Ben-oni], but Jacob called him Benjamin [C"son of my right hand/the south"].

19 Rachel was buried on the road to Ephrath, ·a district of [*or* which is] Bethlehem, 20 and Jacob set up a pillar on her grave. It is the pillar of Rachel's grave to this day. 21 Then Israel [CJacob's new name] continued his journey and ·camped [Lpitched his tent] just south of ·Migdal Eder [*or* the tower of Eder; CEder means "the flock"; perhaps located near Jerusalem; Mic. 4:8].

22 While Israel was there, Reuben ·had sexual relations [Llay] with Israel's ·slave woman [concubine] Bilhah, and Israel heard about it [49:3–4].

The Family of Israel

Jacob had twelve sons. 23 He had six sons by his wife Leah: Reuben, his ·first son [firstborn], then Simeon, Levi, Judah, Issachar, and Zebulun.

24 He had two sons by his wife Rachel: Joseph and Benjamin.

25 He had two sons by Rachel's slave girl Bilhah: Dan and Naphtali.

26 And he had two sons by Leah's slave girl Zilpah: Gad and Asher.

These are Jacob's sons who were born in ·northwestern Mesopotamia [LPaddan-aram].

27 Jacob went to his father Isaac at Mamre near Hebron [13:18; 18:1; 23:17–18; 25:9], where Abraham and Isaac had ·lived [sojourned; lived as an alien]. 28 Isaac lived one hundred eighty years. 29 So Isaac breathed his last breath and died [Land was gathered to his people/relatives; 25:8] when he was very old [Land full of days], and his sons Esau and Jacob buried him.

Esau's Family

36 ·This is the family history [LThese are the generations; 2:4] of Esau (also called Edom [25:30]). 2 Esau ·married [Ltook] women from the ·land [Ldaughters] of Canaan: Adah daughter of Elon the Hittite; and Oholibamah daughter of Anah, the son of Zibeon the Hivite; 3 and Basemath [26:34], Ishmael's daughter, the sister of Nebaioth.

4 Adah gave birth to Eliphaz for Esau. Basemath gave him Reuel, 5 and Oholibamah gave him Jeush, Jalam, and Korah. These were Esau's sons who were born in the land of Canaan.

6 Esau took his wives, his sons, his daughters, and all the people who lived with him, his herds and other animals, and all the ·belongings [property] he had ·gotten [acquired] in Canaan, and he went to a land away from his brother Jacob. 7 ·Esau and Jacob's [LFor their] ·belongings [property] were becoming too many for them to live ·in the same land [together]. The land where they had ·lived [sojourned; lived as aliens] could not support both of them, because they had too many herds. 8 So Esau lived in the mountains of ·Edom [LSeir; 14:6]. (Esau is also named Edom [25:30].)

9 ·This is the family history [LThese are the generations; 2:4] of Esau. He is the ·ancestor [father] of the Edomites, who live in the mountains of ·Edom [LSeir].

10 ·Esau's sons were [LThese are the names of the sons of Esau:] Eliphaz, son of Adah and Esau, and Reuel, son of Basemath and Esau.

11 Eliphaz had five sons: Teman, Omar, Zepho, Gatam, and Kenaz. 12 Eliphaz also had a ·slave woman [concubine] named Timna, and Timna and Eliphaz gave birth to Amalek. These were Esau's ·grandsons [descendants; Lsons] by his wife Adah.

13 Reuel had four sons: Nahath, Zerah, Shammah, and Mizzah. These were Esau's grandsons by his wife Basemath.

14 Esau's third wife was Oholibamah the daughter of Anah. (Anah was the son of Zibeon.) Esau and Oholibamah gave birth to Jeush, Jalam, and Korah.

15 These were the ·leaders [chiefs; *or* clans] that came from Esau: Esau's

should take one-fifth of all the food that is grown during the seven ·good
years [years of plenty]. 35They should gather all the food that is produced
during the good years that are coming, and under the king's ·authority
[control; Lhand] they should store the grain in the cities and guard it.
36That food ·should be saved to use [shall serve as a reserve] during the
seven years of ·hunger [famine] that will come on the land of Egypt. Then
the people in Egypt will not ·die [Lbe cut off] during the seven years of
·hunger [famine]."

Joseph Is Made Ruler over Egypt

37·This seemed like a very good idea to the king [LThe thing/word was
good in the eyes of Pharaoh], and all his ·officers [servants] agreed. 38And
·the king asked them [LPharaoh said to his servants], "Can we find a ·bet-
ter man than Joseph to take this job [Lman like this man]? God's spirit is
truly in him!"
39So ·the king [LPharaoh] said to Joseph, "God has shown you all this.
There is no one as wise and ·understanding [discerning] as you are, so 40I
will put you in charge of my ·palace [house]. All the people will obey your
orders, and only [Lin terms of the throne] I will be greater than you."
41Then ·the king [LPharaoh] said to Joseph, "Look! I have put you in
charge of all the land of Egypt." 42Then ·the king [LPharaoh] took off
·from his own finger his ring with the royal seal on it [Lhis signet ring; Ca
form of identification], and he put it on Joseph's finger. He gave Joseph
fine linen clothes to wear, and he put a gold chain around Joseph's neck
[Call symbols of authority]. 43·The king had Joseph [LHe made him] ride
in the second royal chariot, and people walked ahead of his chariot calling, "Bow down [Can Egyptian word of uncertain meaning]!" By doing
these things, the king put Joseph in charge of all of Egypt.
44The king said to him, "I am ·the king [LPharaoh], and I say that no
one in all the land of Egypt may lift a hand or a foot without your permission." 45·The king [LPharaoh] gave Joseph the name Zaphenath-Paneah
[Cmay mean "the god said, 'let him live' "; showing the Egyptians' acceptance of him]. He also gave Joseph a wife named Asenath, who was the
daughter of Potiphera, priest of On [Can important city seven miles
northeast of Cairo also known as Heliopolis, a center of the worship of the
sun]. So Joseph ·traveled through [*or* rose over] all the land of Egypt.
46Joseph was thirty years old when he ·began serving [Lstood before the
Pharaoh] the king of Egypt. And he ·left the king's court [Lwent out from
before Pharaoh] and traveled through all the land of Egypt. 47During the
seven ·good years [years of plenty], the ·crops in the land grew well [land
produced much; Lland made by handfuls]. 48And Joseph gathered all the
food produced in Egypt during those seven years of good crops and stored
the food in the cities. In every city he stored grain that had been grown in
the fields around that city. 49Joseph stored much grain, as much as the sand
of the seashore—so much that he could not ·measure [count] it.
50Joseph's wife was Asenath daughter of Potiphera, the priest of On
[41:45]. Before the years of ·hunger [famine] came, Joseph and Asenath
had two sons. 51Joseph named the ·first son [firstborn] Manasseh [Csounds
like "made me forget" in Hebrew] and said, "God has made me forget all
the troubles I have had and all ·my father's family [Lthe house of my
father]." 52Joseph named the second son Ephraim [Crelated to the Hebrew
word for "fruitful"; 1:22] and said, "God has ·given me children [Lmade
me fruitful] in the land of my ·troubles [afflictions]."

53The seven years of ·good crops [plenty] came to an end in the land of Egypt. 54Then the seven years of ·hunger [famine] began, just as Joseph had said. In all the lands people had ·nothing to eat [famine], but in Egypt there was ·food [bread]. 55The ·time of hunger [famine] became terrible in all of Egypt, and the people cried to ·the king [LPharaoh] for food. He said to all the Egyptians, "Go to Joseph and do whatever he tells you."

56The ·hunger [famine] was ·everywhere in that part of the world [Lover all the face of the earth]. And Joseph opened ·the storehouses [Leverything that was in them] and sold grain to the people of Egypt, because the ·time of hunger [famine] became ·terrible [severe] in Egypt. 57And all the people in that part of the world came to Joseph in Egypt to buy grain because the ·hunger [famine] was ·terrible [severe] everywhere in ·that part of the [Lthe] world.

The Dreams Come True

42 Jacob ·learned [Lsaw] that there was grain in Egypt, so he said to his sons, "Why are you just sitting here looking at one another? 2I have heard that there is grain in Egypt. Go down there and buy grain for us to eat, so that we will live and not die."

3So ten of Joseph's brothers went down to buy grain from Egypt. 4But Jacob did not send Benjamin, Joseph's brother, with them, because he was afraid that ·something terrible [a fatal accident; harm; tragedy] might happen to him. 5Along with many other people, the sons of Israel [CJacob's other name] went to Egypt to buy grain, because ·the people in the land of Canaan were also hungry [Lthere was famine in the land of Canaan].

6Now Joseph was ·governor [administrator] over ·Egypt [Lthe land]. He was the one who sold the grain to people ·who came to buy it [Lof the land/earth]. So Joseph's brothers came to him and bowed facedown on the ground before him. 7When Joseph saw his brothers, he ·knew who they were [recognized them], but he ·acted as if he didn't know them [treated them as strangers/foreigners]. He asked ·unkindly [harshly], "Where do you come from?"

They answered, "We have come from the land of Canaan to buy food."

8Joseph ·knew they were [recognized] his brothers, but they did not ·know who he was [recognize him]. 9And Joseph remembered his dreams ·about his brothers bowing to him [Lwhich he dreamed about them; 37:5–11]. He said to them, "You are spies! You came to ·learn where the nation is weak [Lsee the nakedness of the land]!"

10But his brothers said to him, "No, my ·master [lord]. We come as your servants just to buy food. 11We are all sons of the same father. We are honest men, not spies."

12Then Joseph said to them, "No! You have come to ·learn where this nation is weak [Lsee the nakedness of the land]!"

13And they said, "·We [LYour servants] are ·ten of twelve [Ltwelve] brothers, sons of the same father, and we live in the land of Canaan. Our ·youngest [smallest] brother is there with our father right now, and ·our other brother is gone [Lone is no more]."

14But Joseph said to them, "·I can see I was right [LIt is as I spoke to you]! You are spies! 15But ·I will give you a way to prove you are telling the truth [Lin this way you will be tested]. As surely as ·the king [LPharaoh] lives, you will not ·leave [go out from] this place ·until [*or* unless] your ·youngest [smallest] brother comes here. 16One of you must go and get your brother. The rest of you will stay here in prison. We will ·see if you are telling the truth [Ltest your words/statements]. If not, as surely as ·the king [LPharaoh] lives, you are spies." 17Then Joseph put them all in ·prison [the guardhouse] for three days.

18On the third day Joseph said to them, "[LFor] I ·am a God-fearing man [fear God]. Do this and I will let you live: 19If you are honest men, let one of your brothers stay here in ·prison [the guardhouse] while the rest of you go and carry grain ·back to feed your hungry families [Lfor your families because of the famine]. 20Then bring your ·youngest [smallest] brother back here to me. If you do this, ·I will know you are telling the truth [Lyour words will be confirmed], and you will not die."

The brothers agreed to this. 21They said to each other, "[LAlas,] We are ·being punished [*or* guilty] for what we did to our brother. We saw ·his trouble [the distress of his soul], and he ·begged us to save him [pleaded with us], but we ·refused to [Ldid not] listen. That is why we are in this ·trouble [distress] now."

22Then Reuben said to them, "·I told [LDid I not tell...?] you not to ·harm [wrong; sin against] the ·boy [child], but you ·refused to [Ldid not] listen to me. So now ·we are being punished for what we did to him [Lthere is a reckoning for his blood]."

23When Joseph talked to his brothers, he used an ·interpreter [*or* intermediary], so they did not know that Joseph understood what they were saying. 24Then Joseph left them and cried. After a short time he went back and spoke to them. He took Simeon and ·tied [bound] him ·up while the other brothers watched [Lbefore their eyes]. 25Joseph ·told his servants [Lgave the command/order] to fill his brothers' bags with grain and to put ·the money the brothers had paid for the grain [Ltheir silver] back in their bags. ·The servants [LThey] were also to give them ·what they would need [provisions] for their trip back home. And ·the servants [Lthey] did this.

26So the brothers ·put [lifted] the grain on their donkeys and left. 27When ·they stopped for the night [at the lodging place], one of the brothers opened his sack to get ·food [fodder] for his donkey. Then he saw his ·money [silver] in the top of the sack. 28He said to the other brothers, "·The money I paid for the grain [LMy money/silver] has been put back. Here it is in [Lthe mouth of] my sack!"

The brothers ·were very frightened [Llost heart and trembled]. They said to each other, "What has God done to us?"

The Brothers Return to Jacob

29The brothers went to their father Jacob in the land of Canaan and told him everything that had happened. 30They said, "The master of that land spoke ·unkindly [harshly] to us. He accused us of spying on his country, 31but we told him that we were honest men, not spies. 32We told him that we ·were ten of twelve [Lare twelve] brothers—sons of one father. We said that one of our brothers was ·gone [Lno more] and that our ·youngest [smallest] brother was with our father in Canaan.

33"Then the master of the land said to us, 'Here is a way I can know you are honest men: Leave one of your brothers with me, and take grain to feed ·your hungry [Lbecause of the famine for your] families, and go. 34And bring your ·youngest [smallest] brother to me so I will know you are not spies but honest men. Then I will give you back your brother whom you leave with me, and you can ·move about freely [*or* trade] in our land.'"

35As the brothers emptied their sacks, each of them ·found his money

[saw his bundle of money/silver] in his sack. When they and their father
saw it, they were afraid.
36Their father Jacob said to them, "You are ·robbing [bereaving] me of
all my children. Joseph is ·gone [Lno more], Simeon is ·gone [Lno more],
and now you want to take Benjamin away, too. Everything is against me."
37Then Reuben said to his father, "You may put my two sons to death if
I don't bring Benjamin back to you. ·Trust him to my care [LPut him in
my hands], and I will bring him back to you."
38But Jacob said, "·I will not allow Benjamin to go [LMy son will not go
down] with you. His brother is dead, and he ·is the only son left from my
wife Rachel [Lalone is left]. I am afraid something ·terrible [disastrous;
tragic] might happen to him during the trip to Egypt. Then ·I would be
sad until the day I die [Lyou would bring my gray hair down to Sheol in
anguish]."

The Brothers Go Back to Egypt

43 ·Still no food grew in the land of Canaan [LThe famine was
heavy/severe in the land]. 2When ·Jacob's family [Lthey] had
eaten all the grain they had brought from Egypt, Jacob said to them,
"Go to Egypt again and buy a little more ·grain [Lfood] for us to eat."
3But Judah said to Jacob, "The ·governor of that country [man] strongly
warned us, '·If you don't bring your brother back with you, you will not be
allowed to see me [LYou may not see my face unless your brother is with
you].' 4If you will send ·Benjamin [Lour brother] with us, we will go down
and buy food for you. 5But if you ·refuse to send Benjamin [Lare not send-
ing], we will not go. The ·governor of that country [Lman] ·warned [Lsaid
to] us that ·we would not see him if we didn't bring Benjamin with us
[Lyou will not see my face unless your brother is with you]."
6Israel [Canother name for Jacob; 32:28] said, "Why did you tell the
man you had another brother? You have ·caused me a lot of trouble
[wronged/harmed me]."
7The brothers answered, "He questioned us ·carefully [*or* specifically]
about ourselves and our family. He asked us, 'Is your father still alive? Do
you have another brother?' We just answered his questions. How could
we know he would ask us to bring our other brother to him?"
8Then Judah said to his father ·Jacob [LIsrael; 32:28], "Send ·Benjamin
[Lthe lad/child] with me, and we will ·go at once [Lrise up and go] so that
we, you, and our ·children [little ones] may live and not die. 9I will ·guar-
antee you that he will be safe [Lbe a guarantee for him], and I will be
personally ·responsible [accountable] for him. If I don't bring him back
to you, ·you can blame me [LI will be condemned before you] all my life.
10If we had not ·wasted all this time [been delayed], we could have already
·made two trips [returned twice]."
11Then their father ·Jacob [LIsrael; 32:28] said to them, "If it has to be
that way, then do this: Take some of the best ·foods [products] in our land
in your packs. Give them to the man as a gift: some balm, some honey,
·spices [*or* gum], ·myrrh [*or* resin], pistachio nuts, and almonds. 12Take
twice as much ·money [silver] ·with you this time [Lin your hands], and
take back the ·money [silver] that was returned to you in [Lthe mouth of]
your sacks last time. Maybe it was a ·mistake [Lerror; oversight]. 13And
take ·Benjamin [Lyour brother] with you. Now ·leave and go [Lrise up and
return] to the man. 14I pray that God Almighty will cause the ·governor
[Lman] to be ·merciful to [compassionate toward] you and that he will

allow ·Simeon [Lyour other brother] and Benjamin to come back with
you. If I am ·robbed of my children [bereaved], then I am ·robbed of them
[bereaved]!"
15So the ·brothers [Lmen] took the ·gifts [*or* tribute]. They also took
twice ·as much money as they had taken the first time [Lthe money/silver
in their hand], and they took Benjamin. They ·hurried [Lrose up and
went] down to Egypt and stood before Joseph.
16When Joseph saw Benjamin with them, he said to the ·servant in
charge of [Lone over] his house, "Bring those men into my house. ·Kill
[Slaughter] an animal and prepare a meal. Those men will eat with me
today at noon." 17The ·servant [Lman] did as Joseph told him and brought
the men to Joseph's house.
18The ·brothers [Lmen] were afraid when they were brought to Joseph's
house and thought, "We were brought here because of the money that
was ·put [returned; replaced] in our sacks on the first trip. He wants to
·attack [Lfall on] us, make us slaves, and take our donkeys." 19So the brothers went to the ·servant in charge of [Lone over] Joseph's house and spoke
to him at the ·door [entrance] of the house. 20They said, "·Master [Lord],
we came here ·once before [the first time] to buy food. 21While we were
going home, ·we stopped for the night and [Lat the lodging place] when
we opened our sacks each of us found all his ·money [silver in its weight]
in his sack [42:26–28]. We brought that ·money [silver] ·with us to give it
[Lin our hands] back to you. 22And we have brought ·more [additional]
money to pay for the food we want to buy this time. We don't know who
put that money in our sacks."
23But the servant answered, "·It's all right [LPeace be with you]. Don't
be afraid. Your God, the God of your father, must have put the ·money
[silver; Ltreasure] in your sacks. I got the ·money [silver] you paid me for
the grain last time." Then the servant brought Simeon out to them.
24The ·servant [Lman] ·led [brought] the men into Joseph's house and
gave them water, and they washed their feet. Then he gave their donkeys
·food to eat [fodder]. 25The men prepared their ·gift [tribute] to give to
Joseph when he arrived at noon, because they had heard they were going
to eat with him there.
26When Joseph came home, the brothers gave him the ·gift [tribute]
·they had brought [Lin their hand] into the house and bowed down to the
ground in front of him. 27Joseph asked them how they were doing. He
said, "How is your aged father you told me about? Is he still alive?"
28The brothers answered, "Your servant, our father, is well. He is still
alive." And they bowed low ·before Joseph to show him respect [Land
did obeisance].
29When ·Joseph [Lhe lifted his eyes and] saw his brother Benjamin,
·who had the same mother as he [Lthe son of his mother], Joseph asked,
"Is this your ·youngest [smallest] brother you told me about?" Then he
said to Benjamin, "God be ·good [gracious] to you, my son!" 30Then
Joseph hurried off because he ·had to hold back the tears [Lwas overwhelmed with affection] when he saw his brother Benjamin. So Joseph
went into his room and cried there. 31Then he washed his face and came
out. He controlled himself and said, "Serve the meal."
32So they served Joseph ·at one table [Lby himself], his brothers ·at
another table [Lby themselves], and the Egyptians who ate with him ·at
another table [Lby themselves]. ·This was because Egyptians did not like

Hebrews and never ate with them [LFor the Egyptians could not eat with
Hebrews, for it was an abomination to the Egyptians]. 33Joseph's brothers
were seated in front of him ·in order of their ages [Lthe firstborn according to his birthright], ·from oldest to youngest [Lthe youngest according to
his youth]. They looked at each other because they were so amazed.
34·Food [Portions] from Joseph's table was taken to them, but Benjamin
was given five times more food than the others. Joseph's brothers ate and
·drank freely [celebrated with drinking] with him.

Joseph Sets a Trap

44 Then Joseph gave a command to the ·servant in charge of
[Lone over] his house. He said, "Fill the men's sacks with as
much ·grain [Lfood] as they can carry, and put each man's ·money [sil-
ver] into his sack with the grain. 2Put my silver ·cup [goblet] in the sack
of the ·youngest [smallest] brother, along with his ·money [silver] for the
grain." ·The servant [LHe] did what Joseph told him.

3At dawn the ·brothers [Lmen] were sent away with their donkeys. 4They
were not far from the city when Joseph said to the ·servant in charge of
[Lone over] his house, "·Go after [LGet up and pursue] the men. When you
catch up with them, say, 'Why have you paid back evil for good? 5·The cup
you have stolen is the one [LIs this not what…?] my ·master [lord] uses for
drinking and for ·explaining dreams [divination; Cperhaps by pouring oil
in water as a means of telling the future (called lecanomancy)]. ·You [LIs
not what you…?] have done a very wicked thing!' "

6So ·the servant [Lhe] caught up with ·the brothers [Lthem] and said to
them ·what Joseph had told him to say [Lthese words].

7But the brothers said to the servant, "Why do ·you [my master/lord]
say these things? ·We would not [LFar be it from your servants to] do anything like that! 8We brought back to you from the land of Canaan the
·money [silver] we found in our sacks. ·So surely we would not [LWhy
would we…?] steal silver or gold from your ·master's [lord's] house. 9If
·you find that silver cup in the sack of one of [Lit is found with one of] us,
then let him die, and we will be your ·slaves [servants]."

10·The servant [LHe] said, "·We will do [It will be] as you say, but only
the man who has taken the cup will become my ·slave [servant]. The rest
of you ·may go free [will be innocent]."

11Then every brother quickly lowered his sack to the ground and opened
·it [Ltheir sack]. 12·The servant [LHe] searched the sacks, ·going from [start-
ing with] the oldest brother to [Land ending with] the ·youngest [smallest],
and found the ·cup [goblet] in Benjamin's sack. 13The brothers tore their
clothes [Ca sign of mourning; they were afraid for Benjamin's life]. Then
they ·put their sacks back on [Lloaded] the donkeys and returned to
the city.

14When Judah and his brothers ·went back to [arrived at] Joseph's
house, Joseph was still there, so ·the brothers bowed facedown [Lthey fell]
on the ground before him. 15Joseph said to them, "What have you done?
Didn't you know that a man like me can ·learn things by signs and dreams
[Lpractice divination]?"

16Judah said, "·Master [My lord], what can we say? What can we tell
you? And how can we ·show we are not guilty [justify ourselves]? God has
·uncovered [Lfound out] our guilt, so all of us will be ·your slaves [Lslaves/
servants of my master/lord], not just ·Benjamin [Lthe one in whose hand
the cup/goblet was found]."

17But Joseph said, "·I will not make you all slaves [LFar be it from me
that I should do that]! Only the man ·who stole the cup [Lin whose hand
the cup/goblet was found] will be my ·slave [servant]. The rest of you may
go back ·safely [*or* in peace] to your father."

18Then Judah ·went to Joseph [Lapproached him] and said, "·Master
[My lord], please let ·me [Lyour servant] speak ·plainly to you [La word in
your ears], and please don't be angry with ·me [Lyour servant]. ·I know that
you are as powerful as the king of Egypt [LYou are like Pharaoh] himself.
19·When we were here before, you asked us [LMy master/lord asked his ser-
vants], 'Do you have a father or a brother?' 20And we answered ·you [Lmy
master/lord], 'We have an old father. And we have a younger brother, ·who
was born when our father was old [Lof his old age]. ·This youngest son's
[LHis] brother is dead, so he is the only one of his mother's children left
alive, and ·our [Lhis] father loves him very much.' 21Then you said to ·us
[Lyour servants], 'Bring ·that brother [Lhim] to me. I want to ·see [Lset my
eyes on] him.' 22And we said to ·you [Lmy master/lord], 'That young boy
cannot leave his father, because if he leaves him, his father would die.'
23But you said to ·us [your servants], 'If you don't bring your youngest
brother [Lwith you], you will not be allowed to see ·me [Lmy face] again.'
24So we went back to [Lyour servant] our father and told him ·what you
had said [Lthe words of my master/lord].

25"Later, our father said, '·Go again [Return] and buy us a little more
food.' 26We said to our father, 'We cannot go without our ·youngest
[smallest] brother. Without our ·youngest [smallest] brother, we will not
be allowed to see the ·governor [Lface of the man].' 27Then [Lyour ser-
vant] my father said to us, 'You know that my ·wife Rachel gave [Lwife
bore] me two sons. 28When one son left me, I thought, "Surely he has
been torn apart by a wild animal," and I haven't seen him since. 29Now
you want to take this son away from ·me [Lmy face/presence] also. But
something ·terrible [tragic; disastrous] might happen to him, and ·I
would be miserable until the day I die [Lyou would bring my gray head
down to Sheol in sorrow].' 30Now what will happen if we go home to
[Lyour servant] our father without our ·youngest [smallest] brother? ·He
is so important in our father's life [LAnd his life/soul is so bound up in
his life/soul] that 31when our father sees the young boy is not with us, he
will die. ·And it will be our fault. We will cause the great sorrow that kills
our father [LYour servants will have brought the gray head of your servant to Sheol in grief].

32"·I gave my father a guarantee that the young boy would be safe [LFor
your servant provided surety for the young boy for his father]. I said to my
father, 'If I don't bring him back to you, ·you can blame me [LI will be
condemned before my father] all my life.' 33So now, please allow ·me
[Lyour servant] to stay here and be your ·slave [Lservant in place of the
young boy], and let the young boy go back home with his brothers. 34I
cannot go back to my father if the boy is not with me. I couldn't stand to
see my father ·that sad [suffer]."

Joseph Reveals Who He Is

45 Joseph could not ·control [*or* express] himself in front of ·his
servants [Lall those standing around him] any longer, so he
cried out, "Have everyone leave me." ·When only the brothers were left
with Joseph [LSo no one was standing around him when], he ·told them
who he was [Lrevealed himself to his brothers]. 2Joseph cried so loudly

that the Egyptians heard him, and the ·people in the king's palace [Lhouse of Pharaoh] heard about it. 3·He [LJoseph] said to his brothers, "I am Joseph. Is my father still alive?" But the brothers could not answer him, because they were ·very afraid of [*or* startled by] him.

4So Joseph said to them, "Come close to me." When the brothers came close to him, he said to them, "I am your brother Joseph, whom you sold as a slave to go to Egypt [37:25–28]. 5Now don't be ·worried [in anguish; distressed] or angry with yourselves because you sold me here. God sent me here ahead of you to ·save [preserve] people's lives. 6·No food has grown on the land [LThe famine has been in the land] for two years now, and there will be five more years without ·planting [Lplowing] or harvest. 7So God sent me here ahead of you to ·make sure you have some descendants left [Lpreserve a remnant for you] on earth and to keep you alive in ·an amazing way [La great deliverance]. 8So it was not you who sent me here, but God [50:19–20]. God has made me ·the highest officer of the king of Egypt [Lfather to Pharaoh]. I am ·in charge [master; lord] of his palace, and I am the ·master [ruler] of all the land of Egypt.

9"So leave quickly and go to my father. Tell him, 'Your son Joseph says: God has made me ·master [lord] over all Egypt. Come down to me ·quickly [without delay]. 10Live in the land of Goshen [Cthe northeast area of the Nile Delta] where you will be near me. Your children, your grandchildren, your flocks and herds, and all that you have will also be near me. 11I will ·care for [sustain; maintain] you ·during the next five years of hunger [Lfor there are still five years of famine] so that you and your family and all that you have will not ·starve [Lbecome impoverished].'

12"Now you can see for yourselves, and so can my brother Benjamin, that ·the one speaking to you is really Joseph [Lmy mouth is speaking to you]. 13So tell my father about ·how powerful I have become [Lmy glory/prestige/status] in Egypt. Tell him about everything you have seen. Now hurry and bring him back to me." 14Then Joseph ·hugged [Lfell on the neck of] his brother Benjamin and cried, and Benjamin cried ·also [Lon his neck]. 15And Joseph kissed all his brothers and cried ·as he hugged them [Lover them]. After this, his brothers talked with him.

16When the king of Egypt and his ·officers [servants] ·learned [Lheard the report] that Joseph's brothers had come, ·they were very happy [Lit was good in their eyes]. 17So ·the king [LPharaoh] said to Joseph, "Tell your brothers to load their ·animals [donkeys] and go back to the land of Canaan 18and bring their father and their ·families [Lhouseholds] back here to me. I will give them the best land in Egypt, and they will eat the ·best food we have here [Lfat of the land; Ezek. 34:3; 39:19]. 19·Tell [Command] them to take some wagons from Egypt for their ·children [little ones] and their wives and to bring their father back also. 20Tell them not to ·worry [be troubled] about bringing any of their things with them, because we will give them the best of what we have in Egypt."

21So the sons of Israel did this. Joseph gave them wagons as the king had ordered and ·food [provisions] for ·their trip [the way]. 22He gave each ·brother [Lof them] a change of clothes, but he gave Benjamin five changes of clothes and about ·seven and one-half pounds [Lthree hundred pieces] of silver. 23Joseph also sent his father ten donkeys loaded with the best things from Egypt and ten female donkeys loaded with grain, bread, and other food for his father ·on his trip back [Lfor the way].

[24]Then Joseph told his brothers to go. As they were leaving, he said to them, "Don't quarrel on the way home."

[25]So the brothers left Egypt and went to their father Jacob in the land of Canaan. [26]They told him, "Joseph is still alive and is the ruler over all the land of Egypt." ·Their father [LHis heart] was ·shocked [stunned] and did not believe them. [27]But when the brothers told him everything Joseph had said, and when Jacob saw the wagons Joseph had sent to carry him back to Egypt, ·he felt better [Lthe spirit of Jacob their father came alive/revived]. [28]Israel [CJacob's other name; 32:28] said, "·Now I believe you [Enough!]. My son Joseph is still alive, and I will go and see him before I die."

Jacob Goes to Egypt

46 So ·Israel [CJacob's other name; 32:28] took all he had and ·started his trip [departed]. He went to Beersheba [21:14], where he offered sacrifices to the God of his father Isaac. [2]During the night God spoke to Israel in a vision and said, "Jacob, Jacob."

And Jacob answered, "Here I am."

[3]Then God said, "I am God, the God of your father. Don't be afraid to go to Egypt, because I will make ·your descendants [Lyou] a great nation there [12:1–3]. [4]I will go to Egypt with you, and I will bring you ·out of Egypt [Lup] again. Joseph's own hands will close your eyes when you die."

[5]Then Jacob left Beersheba. The sons of Israel loaded their father, their ·children [little ones], and their wives in the wagons ·the king of Egypt [LPharaoh] had sent. [6]They also took their farm animals and everything they had gotten in Canaan. So Jacob went to Egypt with all his ·descendants [Lseed]—[7]his sons and grandsons, his daughters and granddaughters. He took all his ·family [Lseed] to Egypt with him.

Jacob's Family

[8]Now these are the names of the ·children [sons] of Israel who went into Egypt (Jacob and his descendants).

Reuben was Jacob's ·first son [Lfirstborn]. [9]Reuben's sons were Hanoch, Pallu, Hezron, and Carmi.

[10]Simeon's sons were Jemuel, Jamin, Ohad, Jakin, Zohar, and Shaul (Simeon's son by a Canaanite woman).

[11]Levi's sons were Gershon, Kohath, and Merari.

[12]Judah's sons were Er, Onan, Shelah, Perez, and Zerah (but Er and Onan had died in the land of Canaan [38:1–11]). Perez's sons were Hezron and Hamul.

[13]Issachar's sons were Tola, Puah, Jashub, and Shimron.

[14]Zebulun's sons were Sered, Elon, and Jahleel.

[15]These are the sons of Leah and Jacob born in ·northwestern Mesopotamia [LPaddan-aram], in addition to his daughter Dinah [34:1]. There were thirty-three persons in this part of Jacob's family.

[16]Gad's sons were Zephon, Haggi, Shuni, Ezbon, Eri, Arodi, and Areli.

[17]Asher's sons were Imnah, Ishvah, Ishvi, and Beriah, and their sister was Serah. Beriah's sons were Heber and Malkiel.

[18]These are Jacob's sons by Zilpah, the slave girl whom Laban gave to his daughter Leah [29:24]. There were sixteen persons in this part of Jacob's family.

[19]The sons of Jacob's wife Rachel were Joseph and Benjamin. [20]In Egypt, Joseph became the father of Manasseh and Ephraim by his wife Asenath, the daughter of Potiphera, priest of On [41:45].

[21]Benjamin's sons were Bela, Beker, Ashbel, Gera, Naaman, Ehi, Rosh, Muppim, Huppim, and Ard.

22 These are the sons of Jacob by his wife Rachel. There were fourteen persons in this part of Jacob's family.

23 Dan's son was Hushim.

24 Naphtali's sons were Jahziel, Guni, Jezer, and Shillem.

25 These are Jacob's sons by Bilhah, the slave girl whom Laban gave to his daughter Rachel [29:29]. There were seven persons in this part of Jacob's family.

26 So the total number of ·Jacob's direct descendants [Lthose who came from the thigh/loins of Jacob] who went to Egypt was sixty-six, not counting the wives of Jacob's sons. 27 Joseph had two sons born in Egypt, so the total number in the family of Jacob in Egypt was seventy.

Jacob Arrives in Egypt

28 Jacob sent Judah ahead of him to ·see [*or* lead the way to] Joseph in Goshen [45:10]. When Jacob and his people came into the land of Goshen, 29 Joseph prepared his chariot and went to meet his father Israel in Goshen. As soon as Joseph saw his father, he ·hugged him [Lfell on his neck], and cried there for a long time.

30 Then Israel said to Joseph, "Now I am ready to die, because I have seen your face and I know you are still alive."

31 Joseph said to his brothers and his father's ·family [household], "I will go and tell ·the king [LPharaoh] you are here. I will say, 'My brothers and my father's ·family [household] have left the land of Canaan and have come here to me. 32 They are shepherds and take care of ·farm animals [livestock], and they have brought their flocks and their herds and everything they own with them.' 33 When ·the king [LPharaoh] calls you, he will ask, 'What work do you do?' 34 This is what you should tell him: 'We, your servants, have taken care of ·farm animals [livestock] all our lives. Our ·ancestors [fathers] did the same thing.' Then ·the king [Lhe] will allow you to settle in the land of Goshen, ·away from the Egyptians, because they don't like to be near shepherds [Lfor all shepherds of flocks are an abomination to the Egyptians]."

Jacob Settles in Goshen

47 Joseph went in and spoke to ·the king [LPharaoh] and said, "My father and my brothers have arrived from Canaan with their flocks and herds and everything they own. They are now in the land of Goshen [45:10]." 2 Joseph ·chose [took] five of his brothers to ·introduce [present] to ·the king [LPharaoh].

3 ·The king [LPharaoh] said to his brothers, "What work do you do?"

And they said to him, "We, your servants, are shepherds, just as our ·ancestors [fathers] were." 4 They said to ·the king [LPharaoh], "We have come to ·live [sojourn; reside as aliens] in this land, because there is no ·grass in the land of Canaan for our animals to eat [Lpasturage for the flocks of your servants], and the ·hunger [famine] is ·terrible [severe; heavy] there. So please allow ·us [Lyour servants] to live in the land of Goshen."

5 Then ·the king [LPharaoh] said to Joseph, "Your father and your brothers have come to you, 6 and ·you may choose any place in Egypt for them to live [Lthe land of Egypt is before you]. Give your father and your brothers the best land; let them live in the land of Goshen. And if any of them are skilled shepherds, put them in charge of my ·sheep and cattle [Llivestock]."

7 Then Joseph brought in his father Jacob and ·introduced him to the king [Lhe stood before Pharaoh], and Jacob blessed ·the king [LPharaoh].

8 Then ·the king [LPharaoh] said to Jacob, "How ·old are you [Lmany of the days are the years of your life]?"

9 **Jacob said to him, "My life has been spent ·wandering from place to place** [sojourning; residing as an alien]**. It has been short and filled with trouble—only one hundred thirty years. My ·ancestors** [fathers] **·lived** [Lwandered; sojourned; lived as an alien] **much longer than I."** 10 **Then Jacob blessed ·the king** [LPharaoh] **and ·left** [Lwent out from before the Pharaoh].

11 **Joseph obeyed the king and ·gave his father and brothers** [Lsettled his father and brothers and gave them a possession in] **the best land in Egypt, near the city of Rameses** [Ca city built later during the time of Moses in the Nile Delta region; Ex. 1:11]. 12 **And Joseph gave his father, his brothers, and ·everyone who lived with them** [Lall his father's household] **the food ·they needed** [Laccording to their little ones/dependents].

Joseph Buys Land for the King

13 **The ·hunger became worse** [Lfamine was severe/intense/heavy], **and since there was no food anywhere in the land, Egypt and Canaan ·became very poor** [Lwilted; languished]. 14 **Joseph ·collected** [gathered] **all the ·money** [silver] **that was to be found in Egypt and Canaan. People paid for the grain they were buying, and Joseph brought that ·money** [silver] **to ·the king's** [LPharaoh's] **palace.** 15 **After some time, when the people in Egypt and Canaan had no ·money** [silver] **left, ·they** [Lall Egypt] **went to Joseph and said, "Please give us food. Our money is gone, ·and if we don't eat, we will** [Lwhy should we...?] **die here in front of you."**

16 **Joseph answered, "Since you have no ·money** [silver], **give me your ·farm animals** [livestock], **and I will give you food in return** [Lfor your livestock]**."** 17 **So people brought their ·farm animals** [livestock] **to Joseph, and he gave them food in exchange for their horses, sheep, goats, cattle, and donkeys. And he ·kept them alive by trading** [supplied them with] **food for their ·farm animals** [livestock] **that year.**

18 **·The next year** [LWhen that year ended] **the people came to Joseph** [Lin the second year] **and said, "·You know** [LWe cannot hide from my master/lord that] **we have no money left, and all our ·animals** [Lherds of cattle] **belong to you. ·We have** [LBefore our master/lord there is] **nothing left except our bodies and our land.** 19 **·Surely both we and our land will** [LWhy should we and our land...?] **die here in front of you. Buy us and our land in exchange for food, and we will be ·slaves** [servants] **to ·the king** [LPharaoh], **together with our land. Give us seed to plant so that we will live and not die, and the land will not become ·a desert** [desolate]**."**

20 **So Joseph bought all the land in Egypt for ·the king** [LPharaoh; CJoseph's plan led to the tremendous power of the Pharaoh in Egypt and the world]. **Every Egyptian sold Joseph his field, because the ·hunger** [famine] **was very ·great** [strong; intense]. **So the land ·became the king's** [belonged to the Pharaoh], 21 **and Joseph made the people ·slaves**[n] **from one end of Egypt to the other.** 22 **The only land he did not buy was the land the priests owned. They did not need to sell their land because ·the king** [LPharaoh] **·paid them** [gave them an allowance] **for their work. So they had money to buy food.**

23 **Joseph said to the people, "Now I have bought you and your land for ·the king** [LPharaoh], **so I will give you seed and you can plant ·your fields** [Lthe land]. 24 **At harvest time you must give one-fifth to ·the king** [LPharaoh]. **You may keep four-fifths for yourselves to use as seed for the field and as food for yourselves, your families, and your ·children** [little ones]**."**

25 **The people said, "You have ·saved our lives** [allowed us to live]. **If ·you**

47:21 slaves Some Greek copies read "slaves." The Hebrew text reads "move to cities."

like [Lwe have found favor in the eyes of my master/lord], **we will become
slaves of ·the king** [LPharaoh]**."**
**26So Joseph made a law in Egypt, which continues today: One-fifth of
everything from the land belongs to ·the king** [LPharaoh]**. The only land
·the king** [LPharaoh] **did not get was the priests' land.**

"Don't Bury Me in Egypt"

27The Israelites continued to live in the land of Goshen [45:10] **in
Egypt. There they got possessions and ·had many children** [Lwere fruitful]
and ·grew in number [greatly multiplied; 1:22]**.**
**28Jacob lived in Egypt seventeen years, so he lived to be one hundred
forty-seven years old. 29When Israel** [Canother name for Jacob; 32:28]
**knew he soon would die, he called his son Joseph to him and said to him,
"If ·you love me** [LI have found grace in your eyes], **put your hand under
my ·leg** [Lthigh; Ca euphemism for male genitalia; this was a commitment
to keep a promise]. **·Promise me** [LDeal with me according to loyalty and
faithfulness that] **you will not bury me in Egypt. 30When I ·die** [Llie with
my fathers/ancestors], **carry me out of Egypt, and bury me ·where my
ancestors are buried** [Lin their burial place]**."**
Joseph answered, "I will do as you say."
31Then Jacob said, "·Promise [Swear to] **me." And ·Joseph promised** [he
swore to] **him that he would do this** [50:7–14]. **Then Israel worshiped as
he leaned on the top of his ·walking stick** [staff; *or* bed]**.**[n]

Blessings for Manasseh and Ephraim

48 ·Some time later [LAnd after these things] **Joseph ·learned**
[was told] **that his father was very sick, so he took his two
sons Manasseh and Ephraim ·and went to his father** [Lwith him]**. 2When
Joseph arrived, someone told Jacob, "Your son Joseph has come to see
you." ·Jacob** [LIsrael; another name for Jacob; 32:28] **·was weak, so he
·used all** [Lsummoned] **his strength and sat up on his bed.**
3Then Jacob said to Joseph, "God Almighty appeared to me at Luz
[Canother name for Bethel] **in the land of Canaan and blessed me there**
[28:19; 35:9–15]**. 4He said to me, 'I will ·give you many children** [Lmake you
fruitful and multiply you; 1:28]**. I will make you ·the father** [La company; an
assembly] **of many peoples, and I will give your ·descendants** [Lseed] **this
land ·forever** [as a permanent possession]**.' 5Your two sons, who were born
here in Egypt before I came, will be counted as my own sons. Ephraim and
Manasseh will be my sons just as Reuben and Simeon are my sons** [Chis two
oldest children]**. 6But if you have other children, they will be your own, and
·their land will be part of the land given to Ephraim and Manasseh** [Lthey
will be recorded according to the name of their brothers in regard to their
inheritance]**. 7When I came from northwestern Mesopotamia** [LPaddan],
Rachel died in the land of Canaan, as we were traveling toward Ephrath
[35:16, 19]**. This made me very sad, and I buried her there beside the road
to Ephrath." (Today Ephrath is Bethlehem.)**
8Then Israel saw Joseph's sons and said, "Who are these boys?"
**9Joseph said to his father, "They are my sons that God has given me
here in ·Egypt** [Lthis place]**."**
Israel said, "Bring your sons to me so I may bless them."
10At this time Israel's eyesight was ·bad [Lheavy] **because he was old.
So Joseph brought the boys close to him, and Israel kissed the boys and
·put his arms around** [embraced] **them. 11He said to Joseph, "I thought**

47:31 walking stick Some Greek copies read "walking stick." The Hebrew text reads "bed."

I would never see ·you alive [Lyour face] again, and now God has ·let me see you and [Lshown me] also your ·children [Lseed]." 12Then Joseph moved his sons off ·Israel's lap [Lhis knees] and bowed facedown to the ground. 13He put Ephraim on his right side and Manasseh on his left. (So Ephraim was near Israel's left hand, and Manasseh was near Israel's right hand.) Joseph brought the boys close to Israel. 14But Israel ·crossed his arms and put his [Lsent forth and placed his] right hand on the head of Ephraim, who was younger. He put his left hand on the head of Manasseh, the firstborn son. 15And Israel blessed Joseph and said,

"My ·ancestors [fathers] Abraham and Isaac ·served [Lwalked before] our God,
and like a shepherd God has led me all my life.
16He was the Angel who ·saved [redeemed] me from all ·my troubles [harm].
Now I pray that he will bless these boys.
May my name be known through these boys,
and may the names of my ancestors Abraham and Isaac be known through them.
May they ·have many descendants [grow into a large group] on the earth."

17When Joseph saw that his father put his right hand on Ephraim's head, he ·didn't like it [Lthought it was wrong]. So he took hold of his father's hand, wanting to move it from Ephraim's head to Manasseh's head. 18Joseph said to his father, "·You are doing it wrong, Father, since Manasseh [LNo, my Father, for this] is the firstborn son. Put your right hand on his head."

19But his father refused and said, "I know, my son, I know. Manasseh will be great and ·have many descendants [Lbecome great]. But his younger brother will be greater, and his ·descendants [Lseed] will ·be enough to make a nation [Lbecome the fullness of nations; CEphraim would become the dominant tribe in northern Israel]."

20So ·Israel [Lhe] blessed them that day and said,

"When a blessing is given in Israel, they will say:
'May God make you like Ephraim and Manasseh.'"

In this way he ·made Ephraim greater than [Lset Ephraim before] Manasseh.

21Then Israel said to Joseph, "Look at me; I am about to die. But God will be with you and will take you back to the land of your fathers. 22I have given you something that I did not give your brothers—the land of Shechem [*or* mountain slope; 12:6] that I took from the Amorite people with my sword and my bow [perhaps 34:1–31]."

Jacob Blesses His Sons

49 Then Jacob called his sons to him. He said, "·Come here to [LGather around] me, and I will tell you what will happen to you in the ·future [Ldays to come].

2"·Come [LAssemble] together and listen, sons of Jacob.
Listen to Israel [Canother name for Jacob; 32:28], your father."

3"Reuben, my ·first son [firstborn], you are my strength.
·Your birth showed I could be a father [L...and the first of my virility/vigor].
·You have the highest position among my sons [L...excelling in pride/rank/authority],
and you are the most powerful [L...excelling in power].

[4]**But you are ·uncontrolled** [unstable] **like water** [[C]often a symbol of chaos or evil],
so you will no longer ·lead your brothers [[L]excel].
This is because you got into your father's bed
and ·shamed me by having sexual relations with my slave girl [[L]you defiled it by going up on my couch; 35:22].

[5]**"Simeon and Levi are brothers**
who used their ·swords [*or* circumcision knives; *or* counsels; *or* treaties; ch. 34] **to do violence.**
[6]**I will not join their secret talks,**
and I will not ·meet with them to plan evil [[L]join them in their assembly].
They killed men because they were angry,
and they ·crippled [hamstrung] **oxen ·just for fun** [*or* at will; 34:25–31].
[7]**May their anger be cursed, because it is too ·violent** [severe; strong; intense].
May their violence be cursed, because it is too ·cruel [harsh].
I will divide them up among the tribes of Jacob
and scatter them through all the tribes of Israel [[C]neither Simeon nor Levi received a tribal allotment in the Promised Land; Josh. 13–22].

[8]**"Judah, your brothers will praise you** [[C]the Hebrew verb for "praise" sounds like the name Judah].
·You will grab your enemies by the neck [[L]Your hand will be on the neck of your enemies],
and ·your brothers [[L]the sons of your father] **will bow down to you.**
[9]**Judah is like a ·young lion** [lion cub].
You have ·returned from killing [[L]come up from the prey], **my son.**
Like a lion, he stretches out and ·lies down to rest [crouches],
and [[L]like a lioness] **·no one is brave enough to** [who will…?] **wake him.**
[10]**·Kings will come from Judah's family** [[L]No one will turn aside the scepter from Judah; [C]a scepter is a symbol of kingship];
·someone from Judah will always be on the throne [[L]the ruler's staff/mace from between his feet; [C]anticipates the rise of a perpetual kingship from the tribe of Judah; 2 Sam. 7].
Judah will rule until ·Shiloh comes [*or* he comes to Shiloh; *or* he comes to whom it belongs; *or* tribute comes to him],
and the ·nations [peoples] **will obey him.**
[11]**He ties his donkey to a grapevine,**
his young donkey to the best ·branch [vine].
He ·can afford to use wine to wash his clothes [[L]washes his clothes in wine]
and the ·best wine [[L]blood of grapes] **to wash his robes.**
[12]**His eyes are dark like the color of wine,**
and his teeth are as white as the color of milk.

[13]**"Zebulun will live ·near** [[L]at the shore/coast of] **the sea.**
His ·shore [coast] **will be a safe place for ships,**
and his land will reach as far as Sidon [10:15].

14"Issachar is like a strong donkey
who lies down ·while carrying his load [*or* between the pack saddles].
15When he sees his ·resting place [camp] is good
and how pleasant his land is,
he will put his ·back [Lshoulder] to the load
and become a slave [Lat forced labor].

16"Dan will ·rule [judge; *or* contend for; Cthe Hebrew verb for "judge" sounds like the name Dan] his own people
like ·the other [Lone of the] tribes in Israel.
17Dan will be like a snake by the side of the road,
a ·dangerous snake [viper] lying near the path.
That snake bites a horse's ·leg [heel; hoof],
and the rider is thrown off backward.

18"LORD, I wait for your ·salvation [*or* victory].

19"·Robbers [*or* Raiders] will ·attack [raid] Gad [Cthe Hebrew word for "raiders" sounds like the name Gad],
but he will ·defeat them and drive them away [Lraid them at their heels].

20"Asher's land will grow much ·good [*or* rich] food;
he will grow ·food fit for a king [kingly delicacies].

21"Naphtali is like a female deer that runs free,
that has ·beautiful fawns [*or* beautiful words].

22"Joseph is like a ·grapevine that produces much fruit [*or* fruitful bough/tree; *or* foal of a wild donkey]
a ·healthy vine [*or* fruitful bough/tree; *or* foal of a wild donkey]
·watered by [Lby] a spring,
·whose branches grow over the wall [*or* a wild donkey on a hillside].
23Archers attack him violently
and shoot at him angrily,
24but ·he aims his bow well [Lhis bow remains taut].
His arms ·are made strong [*or* were snapped].
·He gets his power from [L...by the hands of] the Mighty God of Jacob
·and his strength from [*or* by the name of] the Shepherd, the Rock of Israel.
25Your father's God helps you.
God Almighty blesses you.
He blesses you with ·rain [Lblessings] from above,
with ·water from springs below [Lthe blessings of the deep that crouches below],
with ·many babies born to your wives
and many young ones born to your animals [Lthe blessings of breasts and womb]
26The blessings of your father are greater
than the blessings of the ·oldest [*or* eternal] mountains,
greater than the ·good things [delight] of the long-lasting hills.
May these blessings rest on the head of Joseph,

on the forehead of the one who was ·separated from [*or* prince among]
his brothers [CEphraim would become the dominant tribe in
northern Israel].

27"Benjamin is like a hungry wolf.
In the morning he eats ·what he has caught [prey],
and in the evening he divides ·what he has taken [the plunder]."

28These are the twelve tribes of Israel, and this is what their father said to them. He gave each son the blessing that was ·right [suitable; appropriate] for him. 29Then Israel gave them a command and said, "I am about to ·die [Lbe gathered to my people/relatives; 25:8]. Bury me with my ·ancestors [fathers] in the cave in the field of Ephron the Hittite [23:7–20; 25:9]. 30That cave is in the field of Machpelah east of Mamre in the land of Canaan. Abraham bought the field and cave from Ephron the Hittite for a ·burying place [burial site]. 31Abraham and Sarah his wife are buried there. Isaac and Rebekah his wife are buried there, and I buried my wife Leah there. 32The field and the cave in it were bought from the Hittite people." 33After Jacob finished ·talking to [*or* instructing] his sons, he lay down. He put his feet back on the bed, took his last breath, and ·died [Lwas gathered to his people/relatives; 25:8].

Jacob's Burial

50 When Jacob died, Joseph ·hugged [Lfell on the face of] his father and cried over him and kissed him. 2He commanded the doctors who served him to ·prepare his father's body [embalm his father], so the doctors ·prepared Jacob's body to be buried [Lembalmed Israel; Canother name for Jacob; 32:28]. 3It took the doctors forty days to ·prepare his body [embalm him] (the usual time it took). And the Egyptians ·had a time of sorrow for Jacob that lasted [Lwept over him for] seventy days.

4When this time of ·sorrow had ended [Lweeping passed], Joseph spoke to ·the king's officers [Lhousehold of Pharaoh] and said, "If ·you think well of me [LI have found grace in your eyes], please ·tell this to the king [Lspeak now in the ear of Pharaoh]: 5'When my father was near death, ·I made a promise to him [Lmy father made me swear] that I would bury him in a cave in the land of Canaan, in a burial place that he cut out for himself. So please let me go and bury my father, and then I will return.'"

6·The king [LPharaoh] answered, "·Keep your promise. Go [LAs he made you swear, go] and bury your father."

7So Joseph went to bury his father. All ·the king's officers [Lservants of Pharaoh], the elders of his ·court [Lhouse], and all the elders of Egypt went with Joseph. 8·Everyone who lived with [LAll the house of] Joseph and his brothers went with him, as well as ·everyone who lived with [Lall the house of] his father. They left only their ·children [little ones], their flocks, and their herds in the land of Goshen [45:10]. 9They went with Joseph in chariots and on horses. It was a very large ·group [camp].

10When they came to ·the threshing floor of Atad [*or* Goren-ha-atad; *or* the threshing floor of the bramble], near the Jordan River, they ·cried loudly and bitterly for his father [Llamented there with a great and exceedingly strong lament]. Joseph's time of ·sorrow [mourning] continued for seven days. 11The people that lived in Canaan saw the ·sadness [mourning] at the threshing floor of Atad [*or* Goren-ha-atad; *or* threshing floor of the bramble] and said, "Those Egyptians are ·showing great sorrow [intense in their mourning]!" So now that place is named ·Sorrow of the Egyptians [*or* Abel-mizraim].

12So Jacob's sons did as their father commanded. 13His sons carried ·his body [Lhim] to the land of Canaan and buried ·it [*or* him] in the cave in the field of Machpelah near Mamre. Abraham had bought this cave and field from Ephron the Hittite to use as a burial ·place [site]. 14After Joseph buried his father, he returned to Egypt, along with his brothers and everyone who had gone with him to bury his father.

The Brothers Fear Joseph

15·After Jacob [LThe brothers of Joseph saw that their father had] died, ·Joseph's brothers [Land they] said, "What if Joseph ·is still angry with [holds a grudge against] us? We did many wrong things to him. What if he plans to pay us back?" 16So they ·sent a message to [instructed; commanded] Joseph that said, "Your father gave this command before he died. 17He said to us, 'You have done wrong and have sinned and done evil to Joseph. Tell Joseph to forgive you, his brothers.' So now, Joseph, we beg you to forgive our wrong. We are the servants of the God of your father." When Joseph received the message, he cried.

18And his brothers went to him and bowed low before him and said, "We are your slaves."

19Then Joseph said to them, "Don't be afraid. ·Can I do what only God can do [Am I in the place of God]? 20You meant ·to hurt [to harm; *or* evil against] me, but God ·turned your evil into [Lmeant it for] good to save the lives of many people, which is being done. 21So don't be afraid. I will take care of you and your ·children [little ones]." So Joseph ·comforted [consoled; reassured] his brothers and spoke kind words to them.

22Joseph continued to live in Egypt with all ·his father's family [Lthe house of his father]. ·He died when he was [LJoseph lived until he was] one hundred ten years old. 23·During Joseph's life Ephraim had children and grandchildren [LJoseph saw Ephraim's children to the third generation], and Joseph's son Manasseh had a son named Makir. ·Joseph accepted Makir's children as his own [LThe children of Makir were born on his knees].

The Death of Joseph

24Joseph said to his brothers, "I am about to die, but God will ·take care of [provide for] you. He will ·lead you out of [bring you up from] this land to the land he ·promised [swore] to Abraham, Isaac, and Jacob." 25Then Joseph had the sons of Israel ·make a promise [swear]. He said, "·Promise [Swear to] me that you will ·carry [bring up] my bones with you out of Egypt."

26Joseph died when he was one hundred ten years old. ·Doctors prepared his body for burial [LDoctors embalmed him], and then they put him in a coffin in Egypt.

EXODUS

Jacob's Family Grows Strong

1 When Jacob went to Egypt, he took his sons, and ·each son took his own family [L…their households] with him. These are the names of the sons of Israel: 2Reuben, Simeon, Levi, Judah, 3Issachar, Zebulun, Benjamin, 4Dan, Naphtali, Gad, and Asher. 5There was a total of seventy people who ·were descendants [Lcame out of the loins/thigh] of Jacob [Gen. 46:26–27]. Jacob's son Joseph was already in Egypt.

6Some time later, Joseph and his brothers died, along with all ·the people who had lived at that same time [Lthat generation]. 7But the ·people [Lsons; children] of Israel ·had many children [Lwere fruitful], and ·their number grew greatly [Lthey became a teeming swarm and multiplied]. They became very strong, and the ·country of Egypt [Lland] was filled with them [Gen. 1:28].

Trouble for the People of Israel

8Then a new king ·began to rule [Lrose over] Egypt, who did not know who Joseph was [Cidentification uncertain; may refer to Ahmose in 16th century BC]. 9·This king [LHe] said to his people, "Look! The people of Israel are too many and ·too strong for us to handle [Lstronger than us]! 10If we don't ·make plans against [deal wisely/shrewdly with] them, the number of their people will grow even more. Then if there is a war, they might join ·our enemies [Lthose who hate us] and fight us and ·escape [Lgo up] from the country!"

11So ·the Egyptians made life hard for the Israelites [Lthey afflicted/oppressed them with hard labor]. They put slave masters over them, who forced the Israelites to build the cities Pithom and Rameses as ·supply centers [storage cities] for ·the king [LPharaoh]. 12But the harder ·the Egyptians forced the Israelites to work [Lthey afflicted/oppressed them], the more ·the Israelites grew in number [they multiplied] and spread out. So ·the Egyptians became very afraid of them [Lthey dreaded the sons/Tchildren of Israel] 13and ·demanded even more of them [Lthe Egyptians ruthlessly forced the sons/Tchildren of Israel to labor]. 14They made their lives ·bitter [miserable]. They forced the Israelites to work hard to make bricks and mortar and to do all kinds of work in the fields. ·The Egyptians were not merciful to them in all their painful work [LThey ruthlessly forced them to work].

15Two Hebrew ·nurses [midwives] named Shiphrah and Puah were told by the king [Cnot the Pharaoh of 1:8; perhaps fifteenth or thirteenth century BC—if the latter, probably Rameses], 16"When you ·are helping the Hebrew women give birth to their babies [act as midwives for the Hebrew women], ·watch [observe them on the birthstool; *or* look at the stones; Ca euphemism for testicles]! If the baby is a girl, let her live, but if it is a boy, kill him!" 17But the ·nurses [midwives] feared God, so they did not do as the king [Lof Egypt] told them; they let all the boy babies live. 18Then the king of Egypt sent for the ·nurses [midwives] and said, "Why did you do this? Why did you let the boys live?"

19The ·nurses [midwives] said to ·him [LPharaoh], "The Hebrew women are ·much stronger than [Lnot like] the Egyptian women. They are ·strong [vigorous; hardy]. They give birth to their babies before we can get there." 20God ·was good [showed favor] to the ·nurses [midwives]. And the Hebrew people continued to grow in number, so they became even stronger. 21Because the ·nurses [midwives] feared God [Prov. 1:7], he gave them families of their own.

22So ·the king [LPharaoh] commanded all his people, "Every time a boy is born to the Hebrews, you must throw him into the Nile River, but let all the girl babies live."

Baby Moses

2 Now a man from the ·family [Lhouse] of Levi ·married a woman who was also from the family [Ltook a daughter] of Levi. 2She ·became pregnant [conceived] and gave birth to a son. When she saw how ·wonderful the baby [good/handsome/healthy he] was, she hid him for three months. 3But after three months she was not able to hide the baby any longer, so she got a ·basket [ark] made of ·reeds [papyrus] and covered it with ·tar so that it would float [bitumen and pitch]. She put the baby in the basket. Then she put the basket among the ·tall stalks of grass [Lreeds] at the edge of the ·Nile River [Lriver]. 4The baby's sister stood ·a short distance away [afar off] to see what would happen to him.

5Then the daughter of ·the king of Egypt [LPharaoh] came to the river to ·take a bath [wash], and her servant girls were walking beside the river. When she saw the ·basket [ark] in the ·tall grass [reeds] she sent her slave girl to get it. 6She opened the basket and saw the baby boy. He was crying, so she ·felt sorry [had pity] for him and said, "This is one of the Hebrew babies."

7Then the baby's sister asked ·the king's [LPharaoh's] daughter, "Would you like me to go and find a Hebrew woman to nurse the baby for you?"

8·The king's [LPharaoh's] daughter said, "Go!" So the girl went and got the baby's own mother [CMoses not only survived but was raised by his own mother].

9·The king's [LPharaoh's] daughter said to the woman, "Take this baby and nurse him for me, and I will pay you." So the woman took her baby and nursed him. 10When the child ·grew older [Lwas weaned], the woman took him to the ·king's [LPharaoh's] daughter, and she adopted the baby as her own son. The king's daughter named him Moses [Csounds like the Hebrew word for "draw/pull up"], because she had ·pulled [drawn] him out of the water.

Moses Tries to Help

11Moses ·grew and became a man [Lgrew up]. One day he ·visited his people [Lwent out among his brothers/relatives/kin] and saw ·that they were forced to work very hard [Ltheir hard/forced labor]. He saw an Egyptian beating a Hebrew man, one of Moses' ·own people [Lbrothers; relatives; kin]. 12Moses looked all around and saw that no one was watching, so he killed the Egyptian and hid his body in the sand.

13The ·next [Lsecond] day Moses returned and saw two Hebrew men fighting each other. He said to the one that was in the wrong, "Why are you hitting one of your ·own people [friends; neighbors]?"

14The man answered, "Who made you ·our ruler [Lprince over people] and judge? Are you going to kill me as you killed the Egyptian?"

Moses was afraid and thought, "·Now everyone knows what I did [LIndeed the deed is known]."

15When ·the king [LPharaoh] heard ·what Moses had done [Lof the thing], he ·tried [sought] to kill him. But Moses ·ran away [fled] from ·the king [LPharaoh] and went to live in the land of Midian [Cprobably in the eastern Sinai peninsula or in western Arabia]. There he sat down near a well.

Moses in Midian

16There was a priest in Midian [CJethro; also known as Reuel] who had seven daughters. His daughters went to that well to ·get [draw] water to fill the water troughs for their father's flock. 17Some shepherds came and ·chased [drove] the girls away, but Moses defended the girls and watered their flock.

18When they went back to their father Reuel [Canother name for Jethro], he asked them, "Why have you come home early today?"

19The girls answered, "·The shepherds chased us away, but an Egyptian defended us [LAn Egyptian man rescued us from the hand of shepherds]. He ·got [drew] water for us and watered our flock."

20He asked his daughters, "Where is this man? Why did you ·leave [abandon; forsake] him? Invite him to eat with us."

21Moses agreed to stay with Jethro, and he gave his daughter Zipporah to Moses to be his wife. 22She gave birth to a son. Moses named him Gershom [Csounds like "stranger/resident alien there" in Hebrew], because Moses was a stranger in a ·land that was not his own [foreign land].

23After a long time, the king of Egypt died. The people of Israel groaned, because ·they were forced to work very hard [of their work/slavery]. ·When they cried for help, God heard them [LTheir plea for help rose up to God because of their work/slavery]. 24God heard their ·cries [groaning], and he remembered ·the agreement he had made [his covenant] with Abraham, Isaac, and Jacob [Gen. 12:1–3]. 25God saw the ·troubles of the people [Lsons; children] of Israel, and he ·was concerned about [took note of] them.

The Burning Bush

3 One day Moses was ·taking care of [shepherding; grazing] Jethro's flock. (Jethro was the priest of Midian and also Moses' father-in-law.) When Moses led the flock to the west side of the ·desert [wilderness], he came to ·Sinai [LHoreb; Canother name for Mount Sinai], the mountain of God. 2There the ·angel [messenger] of the LORD appeared to him in flames of fire coming out of a bush. Moses saw that the bush was on fire, but it was not ·burning up [consumed]. 3So Moses said, "I will ·go closer to [Lturn aside to see] this ·strange [*or* marvelous; great] thing. ·How can a bush continue burning without burning up [Why does not the bush burn]?"

4When the LORD saw Moses was ·coming [Lturning aside] to look at it, God called to him from the bush, "Moses, Moses!"

And Moses said, "Here I am."

5Then God said, "Do not come any closer. Take off your sandals [Lfrom your feet], because the place where you are standing is holy ground. 6I am the God of your ·ancestors [fathers; Lfather]—the God of Abraham, the God of Isaac, and the God of Jacob." Moses ·covered [hid] his face because he was afraid to look at God.

7The LORD said, "I have seen the ·troubles [affliction; *or* humiliation]

my people have suffered in Egypt, and I have heard their cries ·when the
Egyptian slavemasters hurt them [Lbefore their foremen/taskmasters]. I
·am concerned about [Lknow] their pain, 8and I have come down to ·save
[rescue; deliver] them from the Egyptians. I will bring them out of that
land and lead them to a good land with lots of room—a ·fertile land
[Lland flowing with milk and honey; Can image of abundant fertility]. It is
the land of the Canaanites, Hittites, Amorites, Perizzites, Hivites, and
Jebusites. 9I have heard the cries of the people of Israel, and I have seen
the way the Egyptians have ·made life hard for [oppressed] them. 10So
now I am sending you to ·the king of Egypt [LPharaoh]. Go! Bring my
people, the Israelites, out of Egypt!"

11But Moses said to God, "·I am not a great man! How can I go to the
king [LWho am I that I should go to Pharaoh] and ·lead [bring] the
Israelites out of Egypt?"

12God said, "I will be with you. This will be the ·proof [sign] that I am
sending you: After you lead the people out of Egypt, all of you will ·wor-
ship me [Lserve God] on this mountain."

13Moses said to God, "When I go to the Israelites, I will say to them,
'The God of your ancestors sent me to you.' What if the people say, 'What
is his name [Cnames signified a person's essence, character, or reputa-
tion]?' What should I tell them?"

14Then God said to Moses, "I AM WHO I AM" [CThese Hebrew words are
related to the name Yahweh, usually translated "LORD," and suggest that
God eternally lives and is always with his people]. When you go to the
people of Israel, tell them, 'I AM sent me to you.' "

15God ·also [*or* again] said to Moses, "This is what you should tell the
people: 'The LORD is the God of your ·ancestors [fathers]—the God of
Abraham, the God of Isaac, and the God of Jacob. He sent me to you.'
This will always be my name, ·by which people from now on will know
me [Lthis is my title for all generations].

16"Go and gather the elders of Israel and tell them this: 'The LORD, the
God of your ·ancestors [fathers] Abraham, Isaac, and Jacob, has appeared to
me. He said, I ·care about you, and I have seen [have paid attention to you
and to] what has happened to you in Egypt. 17I ·promised [Lsaid] I would
take you out of your ·troubles [affliction; *or* humiliation] in Egypt. I will lead
you to the land of the Canaanites, Hittites, Amorites, Perizzites, Hivites, and
Jebusites—a ·fertile land [Lland flowing with milk and honey; 3:8].'

18"The elders will listen to you. And then you and the elders of Israel
will go to the king of Egypt and tell him, 'The LORD, the God of the
Hebrews, ·appeared to [Lmet with] us. Let us travel three days into the
·desert [wilderness] to offer sacrifices to the LORD our God.'

19"But I know that the king of Egypt will not let you go. Only ·a great
power will force him to let you go [Lby a strong hand], 20so I will ·use my
great power against Egypt [Lstretch forth my hand]. I will strike Egypt
with all the ·miracles [wonders] that will happen in that land. After I do
that, he will let you go. 21I will cause the Egyptians to ·think well of [be
favorable toward] the Israelites. So when you leave, ·they will give gifts to
your people [Lyou will not leave emptyhanded; 12:35–36]. 22Each woman
should ask her Egyptian neighbor and any Egyptian woman living in her
house for gifts—silver, gold, and clothing. You should put those gifts on
your ·children [Lsons and daughters] when you leave Egypt. In this way
you will ·take with you the riches of [plunder] the Egyptians."

Proof for Moses

4 **Then Moses answered, "What if ·the people of Israel** [Lthey] **do not ·believe** [trust] **me or listen to ·me** [Lmy voice]**? What if they say, 'The LORD did not appear to you'?"**

2**The LORD said to him, "What is that in your hand?"**

Moses answered, "It is my ·walking stick [staff; Crepresenting the presence of God]**."**

3**The LORD said, "Throw it on the ground."**

So Moses threw it on the ground, and it became a ·snake [serpent]**. Moses ·ran** [fled] **from the ·snake** [serpent], 4**but the LORD said to him, "·Reach out** [LSend out your hand] **and ·grab** [grasp; catch] **the ·snake** [serpent] **by its tail." When ·Moses** [Lhe] **·reached out** [Lsent out his hand] **and ·took hold of** [snatched] **·the snake** [Lit], **it again became a ·stick** [staff] **in his hand.** 5**The LORD said, "This is so that the ·Israelites** [Lthey] **will ·believe** [trust] **that the LORD appeared to you. I am the God of their ·ancestors** [fathers], **the God of Abraham, the God of Isaac, and the God of Jacob."**

6**Then the LORD said to Moses, "Put your hand inside your ·coat** [cloak; Lbosom]**." So Moses put his hand inside his ·coat** [cloak; Lbosom]**. When he took it out, it was ·white** [Llike snow] **with ·a skin disease** [Tleprosy; Cthe word is used for a variety of skin diseases]**.**

7**Then he said, "Now put your hand inside your ·coat** [cloak; Lbosom] **again." So Moses put his hand inside his ·coat** [cloak; Lbosom] **again. When he took it out** [Lof his coat/cloak/bosom], **·his hand was healthy again, like the rest of his skin** [Lit was restored like his flesh]**.**

8**Then the LORD said, "If the people do not ·believe** [trust] **you or ·pay attention to** [listen to the evidence of] **the first ·miracle** [sign], **they may ·believe** [trust] **you when you show them this second ·miracle** [sign]**.** 9**After these two ·miracles** [signs], **if they still do not ·believe** [trust] **or listen to ·you** [Lyour voice], **take some water from the Nile River and pour it on the dry ground. The water will become blood ·when it touches** [Lon] **the ground."**

10**But Moses said to the LORD, "Please, Lord, I have never been a ·skilled speaker** [Lman of words]**. Even now, after talking to you, I cannot speak well. I ·speak slowly and can't find the best words** [Lhave a heavy/slow mouth and a heavy/slow tongue]**."**

11**Then the LORD said to him, "Who made a person's mouth? And who makes someone deaf or ·not able to speak** [mute]**? Or who gives a person sight or blindness? It is I, the LORD.** 12**Now go! I will ·help you speak** [Lbe with your mouth], **and I will teach you what to say."**

13**But Moses said, "Please, Lord, send someone ·else** [Lyou want to send]**."**

14**The LORD became angry with Moses and said, "**[LDo I not know that…?] **Your brother Aaron, from the family of Levi, is a ·skilled** [fluent; smooth] **speaker. He is already coming to meet you, and ·he will be happy** [Lhis heart will rejoice] **when he sees you.** 15**You will speak to Aaron and ·tell him what to say** [Lplace your words in his mouth]**. I will ·help both of you to speak** [Lbe with your mouth and with his mouth] **and will teach you what to do.** 16**Aaron will speak to the people for you. ·You will tell him what God says, and he will speak for you** [LHe will be your mouth and you will be like God to him]**.** 17**Take your ·walking stick** [staff; 4:2] **·with you** [Lin your hand], **and use it to do the ·miracles** [signs]**."**

Moses Returns to Egypt

18 Moses went back to Jethro, his father-in-law, and said to him, "Let me
go back to my ·people [relatives; brothers; kindred] in Egypt. I want to see
if they are still alive."
Jethro said to Moses, "·Go! I wish you well [LGo in peace]."
19 While Moses was still in Midian, the LORD said to him, "Go back to
Egypt, because the men who ·wanted to kill you [Lwere seeking your life]
are dead now."
20 So Moses took his wife and his sons, put them on a donkey, and
started back to Egypt. He took ·with him [Lin his hand] the ·walking stick
[staff] of God.
21 The LORD said to Moses, "When you get back to Egypt, do all the
miracles I have ·given you the power to do [Lset in our hand]. Show them
to ·the king of Egypt [LPharaoh]. But I will ·make the king very stubborn
[Lharden his heart], and he will not let the people go. 22 Then say to ·the
king [LPharaoh], '·This is what [Thus] the LORD says: Israel is my firstborn
son [Cthe privileged child]. 23 I told you to let my son go so he may ·wor-
ship [serve] me. But you refused to let Israel go, so I will kill your firstborn
son [11:1–10].' "
24 ·As Moses was on his way to Egypt [LOn the way], he stopped at a
resting place for the night. The LORD met him there and tried to kill him.
25 But Zipporah took a flint knife and ·circumcised [Lcut the foreskin of]
her son. Taking the skin, she touched Moses' feet [Ca euphemism for his
genitalia] with it and said to him, "You are a bridegroom of blood to me."
26 She said, "You are a bridegroom of blood," ·because she had to circumcise her son [Lby circumcision]. So the LORD let Moses alone [Cthis event is
difficult to interpret, but shows that circumcision is important to God].
27 Meanwhile the LORD said to Aaron, "Go out into the ·desert [wilder-
ness] to meet Moses." When Aaron went, he met Moses at Sinai, the
mountain of God, and kissed him. 28 Moses ·told [reported to] Aaron
everything the LORD had said to him when he sent him to Egypt. He also
told him about the miracles [signs] which the LORD had commanded him
to do.
29 Moses and Aaron gathered all the elders of the ·Israelites [Lsons/
Tchildren of Israel], 30 and Aaron told them everything that the LORD had
told Moses. Then Moses did the ·miracles [signs] for all the people to see,
31 and the ·Israelites [Lpeople] ·believed [trusted]. When they heard that
the LORD was concerned about them and had seen their ·troubles [afflic-
tions; humiliation], they bowed down and worshiped him.

Moses and Aaron Before Pharaoh

5 After Moses and Aaron talked to the people, they went to ·the
king of Egypt [LPharaoh] and said, "This is what the LORD, the
God of Israel, says: 'Let my people go so they may ·hold a feast [celebrate
a festival; *or* make a pilgrimage] for me in the ·desert [wilderness].' "
2 But ·the king of Egypt [LPharaoh] said, "Who is the LORD? Why should
I ·obey him [Llisten to his voice] and let Israel go? I do not know the LORD,
and I will not let Israel go."
3 Then Aaron and Moses said, "The God of the Hebrews has met with
us. Now let us travel three days into the ·desert [wilderness] to offer sacrifices to the LORD our God. If we don't do this, he may kill us with a
·disease [pestilence; plague] or in war."
4 But the king [Lof Egypt] said to them, "Moses and Aaron, why are you
taking the people away from their work? Go back to your ·jobs [labor]!

[5]·There are very many Hebrews [LThey are more numerous than the people of the land], and now you want them to quit working!"

[6]That same day ·the king [LPharaoh] gave a command to the slave masters and ·foremen [supervisors]. [7]He said, "Don't give the people straw to make bricks as you used to do. Let them gather their own straw. [8]But they must still make the same number of bricks as they did before. Do not accept fewer. They have become lazy, and that is why they ·are asking me [cry; whine], 'Let us go to offer sacrifices to our God.' [9]Make these people work harder and ·keep them busy [Lthey will labor on it]; then they will ·not have time to listen to the lies of Moses [Lpay no attention to false words/reports]."

[10]So the slave masters [Lof the people] and ·foremen [supervisors] went ·to the Israelites [Lout] and said [Lto the people], "This is what ·the king [LPharaoh] says: I will no longer give you straw. [11]Go and get your own straw wherever you can find it. But ·you must make as many bricks as you made before [Lyour work will not dimish at all]." [12]So the people ·went everywhere in [Lscattered throughout] Egypt ·looking for dry stalks [Lgathering stubble] to use for straw. [13]The slave masters ·kept forcing the people to work harder [Lwere urgent]. They said, "You must ·make just as many bricks [Lfinish your work, the same daily assignment] as you did when you were given straw." [14]·The king's [LPharaoh's] slave masters had made the Israelite ·foremen [supervisors] responsible for the work the people did. The Egyptian slave masters beat these men and asked them, "Why ·aren't you making as many bricks as you made in the past [Ldid you not complete the number of bricks yesterday and today, as you did before]?"

[15]Then the Israelite ·foremen [supervisors] went to ·the king [LPharaoh] and ·complained [protested], "Why are you treating us, your servants, this way? [16]You give ·us [Lyour servants] no straw, but we are commanded to make bricks. Our slave masters beat us, but it is your own people's ·fault [offense; sin]."

[17]·The king [LHe] answered, "You are lazy! ·You don't want to work [LLazy]! ·That is why you ask to leave here [LTherefore you say, "Let us go…"] and make sacrifices to the Lord. [18]Now, go back to work! We will not give you any straw, but you must make just as many bricks as you did before."

[19]The Israelite ·foremen [supervisors] knew they were in trouble, because ·the king had told them [Lthey were told], "You must make just as many bricks each day as you did before." [20]As they were leaving the meeting with ·the king [LPharaoh], they met Moses and Aaron, who were waiting for them. [21]So they said to Moses and Aaron, "May the Lord ·punish you [Llook on you and judge]. You ·caused the king and his officers to hate us [Lhave made us a bad odor in the eyes of Pharaoh and his servants]. You have ·given them an excuse [Lplaced a sword in their hands] to kill us."

Moses Complains to God

[22]Then Moses returned to the Lord and said, "Lord, why have you brought this ·trouble [evil; harm] on your people? Is this why you sent me here? [23]I went to ·the king [LPharaoh] ·and said what you told me to say [Lto speak in your name], but ever since that time he has ·made the people suffer [harmed/mistreated this people]. And you have done nothing to ·save them [rescue/deliver your people]."

6 Then the LORD said to Moses, "Now you will see what I will do to
·the king of Egypt [LPharaoh]. ·I will use my great power against
him, and [LBy a mighty hand] he will let my people go. ·Because of my
power, [LBy a mighty hand] he will force them out of his country."
2Then God said to Moses, "I am the LORD. 3I appeared to Abraham,
Isaac, and Jacob by the name ·God Almighty [El Shaddai], but they did
not know me by my name, ·the LORD [Yahweh]. 4I also ·made [established]
my ·agreement [covenant; treaty; Cthe covenant with Abraham; Gen.
12:1–3] with them to give them the land of Canaan. They ·lived in that
land, but it was not their own [Lsojourned; wandered as aliens]. 5Now I
have heard the ·cries [groans; moans] of the ·Israelites [Lsons of Israel],
whom the Egyptians are treating as slaves, and I remember my ·agree-
ment [covenant]. 6So tell the ·people [Lsons; children] of Israel that I say
to them, 'I am the LORD. I will bring you out from the hard work the
Egyptians force you to do. I will rescue you, so you will not be slaves to
the Egyptians. I will ·free [redeem] you by my ·great power [Loutstretched
arm], and ·I will punish the Egyptians terribly [Lwith great/mighty judg-
ments]. 7I will make you my own people, and I will be your God [Cthe
heart or essence of the covenant]. You will know that I am the LORD your
God, the One who ·saves you [Lbrought you out] from the hard work the
Egyptians force you to do. 8I will ·lead [bring] you to the land that I
·promised [swore; Llifted my hand to give; Cto take an oath] to Abraham,
Isaac, and Jacob, and I will give you that land to own. I am the LORD.' "
9So Moses told this to the ·Israelites [Lsons/Tchildren of Israel], but they
would not listen to him. ·They were discouraged [Their spirits were bro-
ken], and their slavery was ·hard [cruel].
10Then the LORD said to Moses, 11"Go tell Pharaoh the king of Egypt
that he must let the ·Israelites [Lsons/Tchildren of Israel] leave his land."
12But Moses answered, "[LIf] The Israelites will not listen to me, so
surely ·the king [LPharaoh] will not listen to me either. I am ·not a good
speaker [Luncircumcised of lips]."
13But the LORD spoke to Moses and Aaron and gave them orders about
the ·Israelites [Lsons/Tchildren of Israel] and [LPharaoh] the king of Egypt.
He commanded them to ·lead [bring] the ·Israelites [Lsons/Tchildren of
Israel] out of Egypt.

Families of Israel

14These are the ·leaders [heads] of the ·families of Israel [Ltheir father's/
ancestors' household]:
Israel's first son, Reuben, had four sons: Hanoch, Pallu, Hezron, and
Carmi. These are the ·family groups [clans] of Reuben.
15Simeon's sons were Jemuel, Jamin, Ohad, Jakin, Zohar, and Shaul, the
son of a Canaanite woman. These are the ·family groups [clans] of Simeon.
16Levi lived one hundred thirty-seven years. These are the names of his
sons according to their family history: Gershon, Kohath, and Merari.
17Gershon had two sons, Libni and Shimei, with their ·families [clans].
18Kohath lived one hundred thirty-three years. The sons of Kohath
were Amram, Izhar, Hebron, and Uzziel.
19The sons of Merari were Mahli and Mushi.
These are the ·family groups [clans] of Levi, according to their family
history.
20Amram married his father's sister Jochebed, who gave birth to Aaron
and Moses. Amram lived one hundred thirty-seven years.

21Izhar's sons were Korah, Nepheg, and Zicri.
22Uzziel's sons were Mishael, Elzaphan, and Sithri.
23Aaron married Elisheba, the daughter of Amminadab and the sister
of Nahshon. Elisheba gave birth to Nadab, Abihu, Eleazar, and Ithamar.
24The sons of Korah were Assir, Elkanah, and Abiasaph. These are the
·family groups [clans] of the Korahites.
25Eleazar son of Aaron married a daughter of Putiel, and she gave birth
to Phinehas.

These are the ·leaders [heads] of the ·family groups [clans] of the Levites.
26This was the Aaron and Moses to whom the LORD said, "·Lead [Bring]
the people of Israel out of Egypt by their ·divisions [hosts; companies; Ca
military term]." 27Aaron and Moses are the ones who talked to Pharaoh
the king of Egypt and told him to let the Israelites leave Egypt.

God Repeats His Call to Moses

28The LORD spoke to Moses in the land of Egypt 29and said, "I am the
LORD. Tell Pharaoh the king of Egypt everything I tell you."
30But Moses answered, "I am ·not a good speaker [Luncircumcised of
lips]. ·The king [LPharaoh] will not listen to me."

7 The LORD said to Moses, "I have made you ·like God [LGod] to
·the king of Egypt [LPharaoh], and your brother Aaron will be like
a prophet for you [Cjust as God would speak to people through prophets
so Moses would speak to Pharaoh through Aaron]. 2Tell Aaron your
brother everything that I command you, and let him tell ·the king of
Egypt [LPharaoh] to let the ·Israelites [Lsons/Tchildren of Israel] leave his
·country [land]. 3But I will ·make the king stubborn [Lharden the heart of
Pharaoh]. I will ·do many miracles [Lmultiply my signs and wonders] in
Egypt, 4but ·he will still refuse to listen [LPharaoh will not listen to you].
So then I will ·punish Egypt terribly [Lplace my hand on Egypt with great
judgments], and I will lead my ·divisions [hosts; companies; 6:26], my
people the Israelites, out of ·that land [Lthe land of Egypt]. 5I will ·punish
Egypt with my power [Lextend my hand against Egypt], and I will bring
the ·Israelites [Lsons/Tchildren of Israel] ·out of that land [Lfrom their
midst]. Then the Egyptians will know I am the LORD."
6Moses and Aaron did just as the LORD had commanded them. 7Moses
was eighty years old and Aaron was eighty-three when they spoke to ·the
king [LPharaoh].

Aaron's Walking Stick Becomes a Snake

8The LORD said to Moses and Aaron, 9"Moses, when ·the king [LPharaoh]
asks you to do a ·miracle [wonder], tell Aaron to [Ltake and] throw his
·walking stick [staff] down in front of ·the king [LPharaoh], and it will
become a ·snake [serpent; 4:3–5; Csymbols of dangerous power in Egypt;
Pharaoh's headdress had a serpent at its crest]."
10So Moses and Aaron went to ·the king [LPharaoh] as the LORD had
commanded. Aaron threw his ·walking stick [staff] down in front of ·the
king [LPharaoh] and his officers, and it became a ·snake [serpent].
11So ·the king [LPharaoh] called in his wise men and his ·magicians
[sorcerers], and with their ·tricks [magic arts] the Egyptian magicians
were able to do the same thing [Cshowing that they had spiritual powers
supporting them]. 12They threw their ·walking sticks [staffs] on the
ground, and their ·sticks [staffs] became snakes. But Aaron's ·stick [staff]
swallowed theirs [Cshowing God's power was superior]. 13Still the king
·was stubborn [Lhardened his heart] and refused to listen to Moses and
Aaron, just as the LORD had said.

The Water Becomes Blood

14Then the LORD said to Moses, "·The king is being stubborn [LPharaoh's heart is hard/heavy] and refuses to let the people go. 15In the morning ·the king [LPharaoh] will go out to the ·Nile River [Lwater]. Go meet him by the edge of the ·river [LNile], and take with you the ·walking stick [staff] that became a ·snake [serpent]. 16Tell him: The LORD, the God of the Hebrews, sent me to you. He said, 'Let my people go ·worship [serve] me in the ·desert [wilderness].' Until now you have not listened. 17This is what the LORD says: 'This is how you will know that I am the LORD. I will strike the water of the Nile River with this ·stick [staff] in my hand, and the water will change into blood. 18Then the fish in the Nile will die, and the river will begin to stink. The Egyptians will not be able to drink the water from the Nile.' "

19The LORD said to Moses, "Tell Aaron: 'Take the ·walking stick [staff] in your hand and stretch your hand over the rivers, canals, ponds, and pools in Egypt.' The water will become blood everywhere in Egypt, both in wooden buckets and in stone jars."

20So Moses and Aaron did just as the LORD had commanded. In front of ·the king [LPharaoh] and his officers, Aaron raised his ·walking stick [staff] and struck the water in the Nile River. So all the water in the Nile changed into blood. 21The fish in the Nile died, and the river began to stink, so the Egyptians could not drink water from it. Blood was everywhere in the land of Egypt.

22Using their ·tricks [magic arts], the ·magicians [sorcerers] of Egypt did the same thing. So the ·king was stubborn [Lheart of Pharaoh was hardened] and refused to listen to Moses and Aaron, just as the LORD had said. 23·The king [LPharaoh] turned and went into his ·palace [house] and ·ignored what Moses and Aaron had done [Ldid not take this to heart]. 24The Egyptians could not drink the water from the Nile, so all of them dug along the bank of the river, looking for water to drink.

The Frogs

25Seven days passed after the LORD ·changed [Lstruck] the Nile River.

8 Then the LORD told Moses, "Go to the king of Egypt and tell him, 'This is what the LORD says: Let my people go to ·worship [serve] me. 2If you refuse, I will ·punish [plague] ·Egypt [Lyour boundaries] with frogs. 3The Nile River will ·be filled [swarm] with frogs. They will come up into your palace, into your bedroom, on your bed, into the houses of your officers, and onto your people. They will come into your ovens and into your baking pans. 4The frogs will ·jump all over [Lcome up on] you, your people, and your officers.' "

5Then the LORD said to Moses, "Tell Aaron to ·hold his walking stick [stretch out his stick/staff] in his hand over the rivers, canals, and ponds. Make frogs come up out of the water onto the land of Egypt."

6So Aaron ·held [extended] his hand over the waters of Egypt, and the frogs came up out of the water and covered the land of Egypt. 7The ·magicians [sorcerers] used their ·tricks [magic arts] to do the same thing, so even more frogs came up onto the land of Egypt.

8·The king [LPharaoh] called for Moses and Aaron and said, "·Pray to [Intreat; Intercede] the LORD to take the frogs away from me and my people. I will let your people go to offer sacrifices to the LORD."

9Moses said to ·the king [LPharaoh], "Please set the time when I should ·pray [intreat; intercede] for you, your people, and your officers. Then the frogs will ·leave [be removed/cut off from] you and your houses and will remain only in the Nile."

10The king answered, "Tomorrow."
Moses said, "·What you want will happen [LAccording to your word].
By this you will know that there is no one like the LORD our God. 11The
frogs will ·leave [be removed from] you, your houses, your officers, and
your people. They will remain only in the Nile."
12After Moses and Aaron ·left the king [went out from Pharaoh], Moses
·asked [cried out to] the LORD about the frogs he had ·sent to [Lset against]
·the king [LPharaoh]. 13And the LORD did as Moses asked. The frogs died
in the houses, in the ·yards [courtyards], and in the fields. 14The Egyptians
put them in piles, and the whole country began to stink. 15But when ·the
king [LPharaoh] saw that they were free of the frogs, he ·became stubborn
again [Lhardened his heart]. He did not listen to Moses and Aaron, just as
the LORD had said.

The Gnats

16Then the LORD said to Moses, "Tell Aaron to ·raise [extend] his ·walk-
ing stick [staff] and strike the dust on the ground. Then everywhere in
Egypt the dust will change into gnats." 17They did this, and when Aaron
·raised [extended] the ·walking stick [staff] that was in his hand and
struck the dust on the ground, everywhere in Egypt the dust changed into
gnats. The gnats got on the people and ·animals [cattle]. 18Using their
·tricks [magic arts], the ·magicians [sorcerers] tried to do the same thing,
but they could not make the dust change into gnats. The gnats remained
on the people and animals. 19So the ·magicians [sorcerers] told ·the king
[LPharaoh] that the ·power [Lfinger] of God had done this. But the ·king
was stubborn [Lheart of Pharaoh was hard] and refused to listen to them,
just as the LORD had said.

The Flies

20The LORD told Moses, "Get up early in the morning, and meet the
king of Egypt as he goes out to the ·river [Lwater]. Tell him, 'This is what
the LORD says: Let my people go so they can ·worship [serve] me. 21If you
don't let them go, I will send swarms of flies into your houses. The flies
will be on you, your officers, and your people. The houses of Egypt will be
full of flies, and they will be all over the ground, too. 22·But I will not treat
the Israelites the same as the Egyptian people [On that day I will separate
the land of Goshen where my people are; Clocated in the eastern part of
the Nile Delta; Gen. 45:10]. There will not be any flies ·in the land of
Goshen, where my people live [Lthere]. By this you will know that I, the
LORD, am in this land. 23I will ·treat my people differently from [*or* set
redemption between my people and] your people. This ·miracle [sign]
will happen tomorrow.' "
24So the LORD did as he had said, and great swarms of flies came into
·the king's [LPharaoh's] palace and his officers' houses. All over Egypt flies
were ·ruining [destroying] the land. 25·The king [LPharaoh] called for
Moses and Aaron and told them, "[LGo,] Offer sacrifices to your God here
in this ·country [land]."
26But Moses said, "It wouldn't be right to do that, ·because the
Egyptians hate the sacrifices we offer to the LORD our God [Lthe sacrifices
we offer to the LORD our God are an abomination to the Egyptians]. If they
see us offering sacrifices they ·hate [detest], ·they will throw stones at us
and kill us [Lwill they not stone us?]. 27Let us make a three-day journey
into the ·desert [wilderness]. We must offer sacrifices to the LORD our God
there, as he told us to do."
28·The king [LPharaoh] said, "I will let you go so that you may offer

sacrifices to the LORD your God in the ·desert [wilderness], but you must not go very far away. Now go and ·pray [intreat; intercede] for me."

29Moses said, "I will ·leave [go out] and ·pray [intreat; intercede] to the LORD, and he will take the flies away from you, your officers, and your people tomorrow. But do not ·try to trick [deal falsely with] us again. Do not stop the people from going to offer sacrifices to the LORD."

30So Moses ·left the king [Lwent out from Pharaoh] and ·prayed to [entreated; interceded with] the LORD, 31and the LORD did as he asked. He removed the flies from ·the king [LPharaoh], his officers, and his people so that not one fly was left. 32But ·the king became stubborn [LPharaoh hardened his heart] again and did not let the people go.

The Disease on the Farm Animals

9 Then the LORD told Moses, "Go to ·the king of Egypt [LPharaoh] and tell him, 'This is what the LORD, the God of the Hebrews, says: Let my people go to ·worship [serve] me. 2If you refuse to let them go and ·continue to hold [tighten your grip on] them, 3the ·LORD will punish you and will send [Lhand of the LORD will strike with] a terrible ·disease [pestilence] on your farm animals that are in the fields. He will cause your horses, donkeys, camels, cattle, goats, and sheep to become sick. 4But the LORD will ·treat Israel's animals differently from [make a distinction between the animals of Israel and] the animals of Egypt. None of the animals that belong to the Israelites will die. 5The LORD has set tomorrow as the [Lappointed] time he will do this in the land.'" 6The next day the LORD did as he promised. All the farm animals in Egypt died, but none of the animals belonging to Israelites died. 7·The king [LPharaoh] sent people to see what had happened to the animals of Israel, and they found that not one of them had died. But the ·king was still stubborn [Lheart of Pharaoh was hardened] and did not let the people go.

The Boils

8The LORD said to Moses and Aaron, "·Fill your hands with [Take handfuls of] ·ashes [soot] from a ·furnace [kiln]. Moses, throw the ashes into the air in front of ·the king of Egypt [LPharaoh]. 9The ·ashes [soot] will spread like dust through all the land of Egypt. They will cause boils to break out and become sores on the skin of people and animals everywhere in the land [Cperhaps skin anthrax]."

10So Moses and Aaron took ·ashes [soot] from a ·furnace [kiln] and went and stood before ·the king [LPharaoh]. Moses threw ·ashes [the soot; Lit] into the air, which caused boils to break out and become sores on people and animals. 11The ·magicians [sorcerers] could not stand before Moses, because all the Egyptians had boils, even the ·magicians [sorcerers]. 12But the LORD ·made the king stubborn [Lhardened the heart of Pharaoh], so he refused to listen to them, just as the LORD had said.

The Hail

13Then the LORD said to Moses, "Get up early in the morning and ·go to the king of Egypt [stand before Pharaoh]. Tell him, 'This is what the LORD, the God of the Hebrews, says: Let my people go to ·worship [serve] me. 14If you don't, this time I will ·punish you, your officers, and your people, with all my power [Lsend all my plagues against you, your officers, and your people]. Then you will know there is no one in the whole land like me. 15By now I could have ·used my power [Lstretched out my hand] and caused a terrible disease that would have destroyed you and your people from the earth. 16But I have let you live for this reason: to show you my power so that my ·name [fame; reputation] will

be ·talked about [recounted] in all the earth. 17You are still [Lexalting
yourself] against my people and do not want to let them go. 18So at this
time tomorrow, I will send a ·terrible [very heavy] hailstorm, the worst
in Egypt ·since it became a nation [Lfrom the day it was founded until
now]. 19Now send for your animals and whatever you have in the fields,
and bring them into a safe place. The hail will fall on every person or
animal that is still in the fields. If they have not been brought in, they
will die.' " 20Some of ·the king's [LPharaoh's] officers ·respected [Lfeared]
the word of the LORD and hurried to bring their slaves and animals
inside. 21But others ·ignored [Ldid not set their heart on] the LORD's
·message [word] and left their slaves and animals in the fields.

22The LORD told Moses, "·Raise [Stretch out] your hand toward the
·sky [heavens]. Then the hail will start falling in all the land of Egypt. It
will fall on people, animals, and on ·everything that grows [all the plants]
in the fields of Egypt." 23When Moses ·raised his walking stick [stretched
out his staff] toward the ·sky [heavens], the LORD sent thunder and hail,
and ·lightning [Lfire] ·flashed [Lcame] down to the earth. So he caused
hail to fall upon the land of Egypt. 24There was hail, and lightning flashed
as it hailed—the ·worst [most severe] hailstorm in Egypt since it had
become a nation. 25The hail ·destroyed [Lstruck] all the people and animals that were in the fields in all the land of Egypt. It also ·destroyed
[Lstruck] ·everything that grew [the plants] in the fields and broke all the
trees in the fields. 26The only place it did not hail was in the land of
Goshen [8:22], where the Israelites lived.

27·The king [LPharaoh] sent for Moses and Aaron and told them, "This
time I have sinned. The LORD is in the right, and I and my people are ·in
the wrong [guilty]. 28·Pray to [Entreat; Intercede with] the LORD. We have
had enough of God's thunder and hail. I will let you go; you do not have
to stay here any longer."

29Moses told ·the king [Lhim], "When I ·leave [Lgo out from] the city, I
will ·raise [Lspread] my hands to the LORD in prayer, and the thunder
[Lwill cease] and hail will ·stop [Lbe no more]. Then you will know that
the earth belongs to the LORD. 30But I know that you and your officers do
not yet fear the LORD God."

31The flax was in ·bloom [bud], and the barley ·had ripened [was in the
ear], so these crops were ·destroyed [ruined]. 32But ·both wheat crops
[Lthe wheat and the spelt] ripen later, so they were not ·destroyed [ruined].

33Moses left ·the king [LPharaoh] and went outside the city. He ·raised
[Lspread] his hands to the LORD, and the thunder and hail ·stopped
[Lceased]. The rain ·also stopped falling to [Lno longer poured on] the
ground. 34When ·the king [LPharaoh] saw that the rain, hail, and thunder
had ·stopped [Lceased], he sinned again, and he and his officers ·became
stubborn [Lhardened their hearts]. 35So ·the king [LPharaoh] ·became
stubborn [Lhardened his heart] and refused to let the Israelites go, just as
the LORD had said through [Lthe hand of] Moses.

The Locusts

10 The LORD said to Moses, "Go to ·the king of Egypt [LPharaoh].
I have ·made him and his officers stubborn [Lhardened his
heart and the hearts of his officers] so I could show them ·my powerful
miracles [Lthese signs of mine]. 2I also did this so you could ·tell
[Lrecount to] your children and your grandchildren how I ·was hard on
[*or* made sport of] the Egyptians. ·Tell [LRecount to] them about the

·miracles [L signs] I did among them so that all of you will know that I
am the LORD."
3So Moses and Aaron went to ·the king [L Pharaoh] and told him, "This
is what the LORD, the God of the Hebrews, says: 'How long will you refuse
to ·be sorry for what you have done [L humble yourself before me]? Let my
people go to ·worship [serve] me. 4If you refuse to let my people go,
tomorrow I will bring locusts into your ·country [land]. 5They will cover
the [L surface of the] land so that no one will be able to see the ·ground
[land]. They will eat ·anything that was [L the last remains] left from the
hailstorm and the leaves from every tree growing in the field. 6They will
fill your ·palaces [L houses] and all your officers' houses, as well as the
houses of all the Egyptians. There will be more locusts than your fathers
or ·ancestors [L the fathers of your fathers] have ever seen—more than
·there have been since people began living in Egypt [*or* the day they came
on the earth until now].'" Then Moses turned and walked away from ·the
king [L Pharaoh].
7·The king's [L Pharaoh's] officers asked him, "How long will this man
·make trouble for [L be a snare to] us? Let the ·Israelites [L men] go to ·wor-
ship [serve] the LORD their God. Don't you know [L yet] that Egypt is
·ruined [destroyed]?"
8So Moses and Aaron were brought back to ·the king [L Pharaoh]. He
said to them, "Go and ·worship [serve] the LORD your God. But tell me,
just who is going?"
9Moses answered, "We will go with our young and old people, our sons
and daughters, and our flocks and herds, because we are going to ·have a
feast [celebrate a festival; *or* make a pilgrimage] to honor the LORD."
10·The king [L He] said to them, "The LORD will really have to be with
you if ever I let you and all of your children leave Egypt. See, you are planning something evil! 11No! Only the men may go and ·worship [serve] the
LORD, which is what you have been asking for." Then ·the king forced
Moses and Aaron out of his palace [L he drove them from the presence of
Pharaoh].
12The LORD told Moses, "·Raise [Extend; Stretch] your hand over the
land of Egypt, and the locusts will come. They will ·spread all [L go up]
over the land of Egypt and will eat all the ·plants [vegetation] the hail ·did
not destroy [L left behind]."
13So Moses ·raised [extended; stretched] his ·walking stick [staff] over
the land of Egypt, and the LORD caused a strong east wind to blow across
the land all that day and night, and when morning came, the east wind
had brought the locusts. 14Swarms of locusts ·covered [L went up on] all
the land of Egypt and ·settled [rested] ·everywhere [L within all the borders of Egypt]. There were more locusts than ever before or after, 15and
they covered the [L surface of the] whole land so that it was ·black [dark-
ened]. They ate everything that was left after the hail—·every plant [L all
the vegetation] in the field and all the fruit on the trees. Nothing green
was left on any tree or plant anywhere in Egypt.
16·The king [L Pharaoh] quickly called for Moses and Aaron. He said, "I
have sinned against the LORD your God and against you. 17Now forgive
my sin this time. ·Pray to [Entreat; Intercede with] the LORD your God,
and ask him to ·stop [turn aside] this ·punishment that kills [deadly thing
from me]."
18Moses left ·the king [L Pharaoh] and ·prayed to [entreated; interceded

with] the LORD. [19]So the LORD ·changed [turned around; diverted] the wind. He made a very strong wind blow from the west, and it ·blew [Lcarried and drove] the locusts away into the ·Red [*or* Reed] Sea [Cprobably a body of water north of the Gulf of Suez]. Not one locust was left ·anywhere in [Lwithin the borders of] Egypt. [20]But the LORD ·caused the king to be stubborn again [Lhardened the heart of Pharaoh], and he did not let the ·Israelites [Lsons/Tchildren of Israel] go.

The Darkness

[21]Then the LORD told Moses, "·Raise [Stretch; Extend] your hand toward the ·sky [heavens], and darkness will ·cover [Lbe over] the land of Egypt. It will be so dark ·you will be able to feel it [*or* you will have to grope around]." [22]Moses ·raised [stretched; extended] his hand toward the ·sky [heavens], and ·total [dense; deep] darkness was everywhere in Egypt for three days. [23]No one could see ·anyone else [Lhis brother], and no one could go anywhere for three days. But the ·Israelites [Lsons/Tchildren of Israel] had light where they lived.

[24]Again ·the king of Egypt [LPharaoh] called for Moses. He said, "All of you may go and ·worship [serve] the LORD. You may take your ·women and children [Lchildren] with you, but you must leave your flocks and herds here."

[25]Moses said, "You must ·let us have animals to use as [Lgive into our hands] ·sacrifices [offerings] and burnt offerings [Lev. 1], ·because we have to offer them to [L…for] the LORD our God. [26]So we must take our animals with us; not a hoof will be left behind. We have to use some of the animals to ·worship [serve] the LORD our God. We won't know exactly what we will need to ·worship [serve] the LORD until we get there."

[27]But the LORD ·made the king stubborn again [Lhardened the heart of Pharaoh], so he ·refused [was unwilling] to let them go. [28]Then ·he [LPharaoh] told Moses, "Get ·out of here [Laway from me], ·and don't come again [Lwatch out that you don't see my face again]! ·The next time you see me, [LOn the day you see my face,] you will die."

[29]Then Moses ·told the king [Lsaid], "I'll do what you say. I will not ·come to see you [Lsee your face] again."

The Death of the Firstborn

11 Now the LORD had told Moses, "I have one more ·way to punish the king and the people of [Lplague to bring on Pharaoh and] Egypt. After this, ·the king [Lhe] will send all of you away from ·Egypt [Lthis place]. When he does, he will ·force you to leave completely [drive you away]. [2]Tell ·the men and women of Israel [Lin the hearing of the people] ·to ask their neighbors [that each man should ask his neighbor and each woman should ask her neighbor] for things made of silver and gold." [3]The LORD had caused the Egyptians to ·respect [show favor to] the Israelites, and both ·the king's [LPharaoh's] officers and the Egyptian people considered Moses to be a great man.

[4]So Moses said to ·the king [Lhim], "This is what the LORD says: 'About midnight tonight I will go through all Egypt. [5]Every firstborn son in the land of Egypt will die—from the firstborn son of ·the king [LPharaoh], who sits on his throne, to the firstborn of the slave girl ·grinding grain [Lwho is behind the handmill]. Also the firstborn farm animals will die. [6]There will be loud outcries everywhere in Egypt, worse than any time before or after this. [7]But not even a dog will ·bark [growl] at the ·Israelites [Lthe sons/Tchildren of Israel] or their animals.' Then you will know that the LORD ·treats Israel differently from [makes a distinction between Israel

and] Egypt. 8All your officers will come to me. They will bow facedown to the ground before me and say, 'Leave and take all your people ·with you [who follow you; Lwho are on your foot].' After that, I will leave." Then Moses very angrily left ·the king [LPharaoh].

9The LORD had told Moses, "·The king [LPharaoh] will not listen to ·you and Aaron [Lyou] so that I may do many ·miracles [wonders] in the land of Egypt." 10Moses and Aaron did all these great ·miracles [wonders] in front of ·the king [LPharaoh]. But the LORD ·made him stubborn [Lhardened the heart of Pharaoh], and the king would not let the ·Israelites [Lsons/Tchildren of Israel] leave his country.

The First Passover

12 The LORD spoke to Moses and Aaron in the land of Egypt: 2"This month will be the beginning of months, the first month [Cin terms of both the calendar and its importance] of the year for you. 3Tell the whole ·community [congregation; assembly] of Israel that on the tenth day of this month each man must get one lamb for [Leach family, a lamb for] ·the people in his house [Leach household]. 4If there are not enough people in his house to eat a whole lamb, he must share it with his closest neighbor, considering the number of people. There must be enough lamb for everyone to eat. 5The lamb must be a one-year-old male that has ·nothing wrong with it [no blemish]. This animal can be either a young sheep or a young goat. 6Take care of the animals until the fourteenth day of the month. On that day all the ·people of the community [assembly of the congregation] of Israel will ·kill [slaughter] them ·in the evening before dark [at twilight]. 7The people must take some of the blood and put it on the ·sides and tops of the doorframes [doorposts and lintels] of the houses where they eat the lambs. 8On this night they must roast the lamb over a fire. They must eat it with bitter herbs and ·bread made without yeast [unleavened bread]. 9Do not eat the lamb raw or boiled in water. Roast the whole lamb over a fire—with its head, legs, and inner organs. 10You must not leave any of it until morning, but if any of it is left over until morning, you must burn it with fire.

11"This is the way you must eat it: ·You must be fully dressed as if you were going on a trip [LWith your loins girded]. You must have your sandals on [Lyour feet] and your walking stick in your hand. You must eat it in a hurry; this is the LORD's Passover.

12"That night I will ·go [cross; pass] through the land of Egypt and ·kill [Lstrike] all the firstborn animals and [Lfirstborn] people in the land of Egypt. I will also ·punish [judge; have victory over] all the gods of Egypt [Cthe spiritual forces (demons) who spiritually empower Egypt]. I am the LORD. 13But the blood will be a sign on the houses where you are. When I see the blood, I will pass over you [Cthe verb is related to the Hebrew word for Passover]. ·Nothing terrible will hurt [LNo plague will destroy] you when I ·punish [Lstrike] the land of Egypt.

14"You are always to remember this day and celebrate it with a feast to the LORD. ·Your descendants are to honor the LORD with this feast from now on [LYou are to observe it throughout your generations as a perpetual statute/ordinance/requirement]. 15For this feast you must eat ·bread made without yeast [unleavened bread] for seven days. On the first day, you are to remove all the ·yeast [leaven] from your houses. No one should eat ·any yeast [anything leavened] from the first day until the seventh day, or that person will be cut off from Israel. 16You are to have ·holy meetings [sacred/

solemn convocation] on the first and last days of the feast. You must not
do any work on these days; the only work you may do is to prepare your
meals. 17You must ·celebrate [Lkeep; guard] the Feast of Unleavened
Bread, because on this very day I brought your ·divisions of people [hosts;
Ca military designation] out of Egypt. So all of your descendants must
celebrate this day. This is a ·law that will last from now on [Lperpetual
statute/ordinance/requirement throughout your generations]. 18In the
first month of the year you are to eat ·bread made without yeast [unleav-
ened bread], from the evening of the fourteenth day until the evening of
the twenty-first day [Cto commemorate their rapid departure; 12:39].
19For seven days there must not be any ·yeast [leaven] in your houses.
Anybody who eats ·yeast [something leavened] during this time, either an
·Israelite [Lnative citizen in the land] or ·non-Israelite [Lalien; sojourner],
must be cut off from the ·community [congregation; assembly] of Israel.
20During this feast you must not eat anything ·made with yeast [leav-
ened]. You must eat only ·bread made without yeast [unleavened bread]
wherever you live."

21Then Moses called all the elders of Israel together and told them,
"·Get the animals [LGo, select/separate lambs] for your families and ·kill
[slaughter] the lamb for the Passover. 22Take a ·branch of the hyssop plant
[La bunch of hyssop], dip it into the bowl filled with blood, and then ·wipe
[smear; Ltouch] the blood on the ·sides and tops of the doorframes [door-
posts and lintel]. No one may ·leave that [Lgo out of the door of his] house
until morning. 23When the LORD ·goes [passes; crosses] through Egypt to
·kill [strike down; Lplague] the Egyptians, he will see the blood on the
·sides and tops of the doorframes [doorposts and lintel], and he will ·pass
over [12:13] that house. He will not let the ·one who brings death
[destroyer] come into your houses and ·kill [strike; plague] you.

24"You must keep this ·command [word] as a ·law [statute; ordinance;
requirement] for you and your ·descendants [sons; children] ·from now
on [forever]. 25·Do this [LYou will keep/observe this ritual] when you go to
the land the LORD has promised to give you [23:14–15; Lev. 23:5–8; Num.
9:1–14; Deut. 16:1–8; Josh. 5:10–11]. 26When your ·children [sons] ask
you, '·Why are we doing these things [LWhat does this ritual mean]?' 27you
will say, 'This is the Passover sacrifice to honor the LORD. When we were
in Egypt, the LORD passed over the houses of ·Israel [Lthe sons/Tchildren
of Israel], and when he ·killed [struck down; plagued] the Egyptians, he
·saved [rescued; delivered] our homes.'" Then the people bowed down
and worshiped the LORD. 28They did just as the LORD commanded Moses
and Aaron.

29At midnight the LORD ·killed [struck] all the firstborn sons in the
land of Egypt—from the firstborn of ·the king [LPharaoh] who sat on the
throne to the firstborn of the prisoner in ·jail [dungeon; Lpit]. Also, all the
firstborn farm animals died. 30·The king [LPharaoh], his officers, and all
the Egyptians got up during the night because someone had died in every
house. So there was a loud outcry everywhere in Egypt.

Israel Leaves Egypt

31During the night ·the king [Lhe] called for Moses and Aaron and said,
"Get up and leave my people. You and ·your people [Lthe sons/Tchildren
of Israel] may do as you have asked; go and ·worship [serve] the LORD.
32Take all of your flocks and herds as you have asked, and go. And also
bless me." 33The Egyptians also ·asked [Lurged] the ·Israelites [Lpeople] to
hurry and leave, saying, "If you don't leave, we will all die!"

34So the people took their dough before the ·yeast [leaven] was added. They wrapped the ·bowls for making dough [Lkneading bowls] in clothing and carried them on their shoulders. 35The ·Israelites [Lsons/Tchildren of Israel] did what Moses told them to do and asked their Egyptian neighbors for things made of silver and gold and for clothing. 36The LORD caused the Egyptians to think ·well [favorably] of them, and the Egyptians gave the people everything they asked for. So ·the Israelites took rich gifts from them [Lthey plundered/picked clean the Egyptians].

37The ·Israelites [Lsons/Tchildren of Israel] traveled from Rameses to Succoth [Cboth were in the Nile Delta]. There were about six hundred thousand men ·walking [Lon foot], not including the ·women and children [Lchildren]. 38·Many other people who were not Israelites [LA mixed multiude] went with them, as well as a large number of sheep, goats, and cattle. 39·The Israelites [LThey] used the dough they had brought out of Egypt to bake loaves of ·bread without yeast [unleavened bread]. The dough ·had no yeast in it [was unleavened], because they had been ·rushed [driven] out of Egypt and had no time to get food ready for their trip.

40The people of Israel had lived in Egypt for four hundred thirty years; 41on the very day the four hundred thirty years ended, the LORD's ·divisions [hosts; 12:17] of people left Egypt. 42That night the LORD kept watch to bring them out of Egypt, and so on this same night the Israelites are to keep watch to honor the LORD ·from now on [Lthroughout their generations].

43The LORD told Moses and Aaron, "Here are the ·rules [statutes; ordinances; requirements] for Passover: No foreigner is to eat the Passover. 44If someone buys a slave and circumcises him, the slave may eat the Passover. 45But neither ·a person who lives for a short time in your country [Lalien; temporary resident] nor a hired worker may eat it.

46"The meal must be eaten inside a house; take none of the meat outside the house. Don't break any of the bones. 47The whole ·community [congregation; assembly] of Israel ·must take part in this feast [Lwill act thus]. 48A ·foreigner [sojourner; wanderer; resident alien] who ·lives [sojourns] with you may share in the LORD's Passover if all the males in his house become circumcised. Then, since he will be like a ·citizen [native] of Israel, he may share in the meal. But a man who is not circumcised may not eat the Passover meal. 49The same ·rules [laws; instructions] apply to ·an Israelite born in the country [the native] or to a ·foreigner [sojourner, wanderer; resident alien] living there."

50So all the ·Israelites [Lsons/Tchildren of Israel] did just as the LORD had commanded Moses and Aaron. 51On that same day the LORD led the ·Israelites [Lsons/Tchildren of Israel] out of Egypt by their ·divisions [hosts; 12:17].

The Law of the Firstborn

13 Then the LORD said to Moses, 2"·Give [Consecrate; Set apart] every firstborn male to me. ·Every firstborn male [LWhoever is first to open the womb] among the ·Israelites [Lsons/Tchildren of Israel] belongs to me, whether human or animal."

3Moses said to the people, "Remember this day, the day you left Egypt. ·You were slaves in that land [L...the house of slavery/bondage/service], but the LORD with his ·great power [Lstrong hand] brought you out of it. You must not eat ·bread made with yeast [unleavened bread]. 4Today, in the month of Abib [Cthe first month of the year, March–April; 12:18], you are ·leaving Egypt [Lcoming out]. 5The LORD will ·lead [*or* bring] you to the

land of the Canaanites, Hittites, Amorites, Hivites, and Jebusites [Cvarious
peoples who lived in the Promised Land]. This is the land he promised
your ancestors he would give you [Gen. 12:1–3], a ·fertile land [La land
flowing with milk and honey; 3:8]. There you must ·celebrate this feast
during the first month of every year [Lkeep this observance in this month].
6For seven days you must eat ·bread made without yeast [unleavened
bread], and on the seventh day there will be a feast to honor the LORD. 7So
for seven days you must not eat any ·bread made with yeast [unleavened
bread]. There must be no ·bread made with yeast [unleavened bread and
no leaven will be] anywhere ·in your land [Lwithin your borders]. 8On that
day you should tell your ·son [child]: '·We are having this feast [LIt is]
because of what the LORD did for me when I came out of Egypt.' 9This feast
will help you remember, like a ·mark [sign] on your hand or a reminder
·on your forehead [Lbetween your eyes]. This feast will remind you to
speak the LORD's ·teachings [law; instructions], because the LORD used his
·great power [Lstrong hand] to bring you out of Egypt. 10·So celebrate this
feast every year at the right time [LYou must observe/keep/guard this stat-
ute/ordinance/requirement as an appointed time for all time].

11"And when the LORD ·takes [brings] you into the land of the
Canaanites, the land he promised to give you and your ancestors [Gen.
12:1–3], 12you must ·give him [Lturn over to the LORD] ·every firstborn
male [Lall that first opens the womb]. Also every firstborn male animal
must be given to the LORD. 13·Buy back [Redeem; Ransom] every firstborn donkey by offering a lamb. But if you don't want to ·buy the
donkey back [redeem/ransom it], then break its neck. You must ·buy
back from the LORD [redeem; ransom] every firstborn of your sons.

14"·From now on [In the future; LTomorrow] when your son asks you,
'What does this mean?' you will answer, 'With his ·great power [strong
hand], the LORD brought us out from Egypt, ·the land where we were
slaves [Lfrom the house of bondage]. 15·The king of Egypt [LPharaoh]
was stubborn and refused to let us leave. But the LORD killed every firstborn male in Egypt, both human and animal. That is why I sacrifice
·every firstborn male animal [Levery male that first opens the womb] to
the LORD, and that is why I ·buy back [redeem; ransom] each of my firstborn sons from the LORD.' 16This feast is like a ·mark [sign] on your
hand and a ·reminder [phylactery; Clater a leather box containing
Scripture worn on arm and forehead, though here perhaps figurative]
·on your forehead [Lbetween your eyes] to help you remember that the
LORD brought us out of Egypt with his ·great power [Lmighty hand]."

The Way Out of Egypt

17When ·the king [LPharaoh] ·sent the people out of Egypt [Llet the
people go], God did not lead them on the road through the Philistine
country, though that was the shortest way. God said, "If they ·have to
fight [Lsee battle], they might change their minds and go back to Egypt."
18So God led them through the ·desert [wilderness] toward the ·Red [*or*
Reed; 10:19] Sea. The Israelites were ·dressed for fighting [prepared for
battle] when they left the land of Egypt.

19Moses carried the bones of Joseph with him, because before Joseph
died, he had made the ·Israelites [Lsons of Israel; Chere Joseph's brothers,
the sons of Israel (Jacob)] promise to do this [Gen. 50:22–26]. He had
said, "When God ·saves [shows concern toward; visits] you, remember to
carry my bones with you out of Egypt."

[20]The Israelites left Succoth and camped at Etham [[C]its exact location
is undetermined], on the edge of the ·desert [wilderness]. [21]The LORD
showed them the way; during the day he went ahead of them in a pillar of
cloud, and during the night he was in a pillar of fire to give them light. In
this way they could travel during the day or night. [22]The pillar of cloud
·was always with [[L]never withdrew from] them during the day, and the
pillar of fire ·was always with [[L]never withdrew from] them at night.

14 Then the LORD said to Moses, [2]"Tell the ·Israelites [[L]sons/
[T]children of Israel] to turn back to Pi Hahiroth and to camp
between Migdol and the ·Red [*or* Reed; 10:19] Sea. Camp ·across from
[opposite] Baal Zephon [[C]in the eastern Nile Delta; the exact locations of
these sites are unknown], ·on the shore of [[L]by] the sea. [3]·The king
[[L]Pharaoh] will think, 'The ·Israelites [[L]sons/[T]children of Israel] are ·lost
[wandering around], ·trapped [closed/shut in] by the ·desert [wilder-
ness].' [4]I will ·make the king stubborn [[L]harden the heart of Pharaoh]
again so he will ·chase after [pursue] them, but I will ·defeat the king
and his army, bringing honor to me [[L]gain glory over Pharaoh and over
his army], and the Egyptians will know that I am the LORD." ·The
Israelites [[L]They] did just as they were told.

The King Chases the Israelites

[5]When the king of Egypt was told that the ·Israelites [people] had ·left
[*or* fled], he and his officers changed their minds about them. They said,
"What have we done? We have ·lost [sent away] the Israelites who served
us!" [6]So ·the king [[L]he] ·prepared [harnessed] his war chariot and took
his army with him. [7]He took six hundred of his best chariots, together
with all the other chariots of Egypt, each with an officer in it. [8]The LORD
·made the king of Egypt stubborn [[L]hardened the heart of Pharaoh, king
of Egypt], so he ·chased [pursued] the ·Israelites [[L]sons/[T]children of
Israel], who were leaving ·victoriously [boldly; [L]with uplifted hand].
[9]The Egyptians—with all the king's horses, chariot drivers, and army—
·chased the Israelites [[L]pursued them]. They caught up with them while
they were camped by the ·Red Sea [[L]Sea; 10:19], near Pi Hahiroth and
Baal Zephon [14:1].
[10]When the ·Israelites [[L]sons/[T]children of Israel] saw ·the king and his
army [[L]Egypt] coming after them, they were very frightened and cried to
the LORD for help. [11]They said to Moses, "What have you done to us? Why
did you bring us out of Egypt to die in the ·desert [wilderness]? ·There
were [[L]Were there not…?] plenty of graves for us in Egypt. [12]·We told
[[L]Did we not tell…?] you in Egypt, 'Let us alone; we will stay and serve the
Egyptians.' Now we will die in the desert."
[13]But Moses answered, "Don't be afraid! Stand still and you will see
the LORD save you today. You will never see these Egyptians again after
today. [14]You only need to remain ·calm [*or* still]; the LORD will fight for
you [15:3]."
[15]Then the LORD said to Moses, "Why are you crying out to me?
Command the Israelites to ·start moving [get going; depart]. [16]Raise your
·walking stick [staff] and ·hold it [[L]extend/stretch your hand] over the sea
so that the sea will split and the ·people [[L]sons/[T]children of Israel] can
·cross it [[L]go in the midst of the sea] on dry land. [17]I will ·make the
Egyptians stubborn [[L]harden the hearts of the Egyptians] so they will
·chase the Israelites [[L]go after them], but I will be ·honored [glorified]
when I defeat ·the king [[L]Pharaoh] and all of his chariot drivers and

chariots. 18When I defeat ·the king [LPharaoh], his chariot drivers, and
chariots, the Egyptians will know that I am the LORD."
19Now the angel of God that usually traveled in front of ·Israel's army
[Lthem] moved behind them. Also, the pillar of cloud [13:21] moved from
in front of the people and stood behind them. 20So the cloud came
between the camp of the Egyptians and camp of the Israelites. This made
it dark for the Egyptians but gave light to the Israelites. So the cloud kept
·the two armies [Lthem] apart all night.
21Then Moses ·held [extended; stretched] his hand over the sea. All that
night the LORD drove back the sea with a strong east wind, making the sea
become dry ground. The water was split, 22and the ·Israelites [Lthe sons/
Tchildren of Israel] went through the sea on dry land, with a wall of water
on their right and on their left.
23Then all ·the king's [LPharaoh's] horses, chariots, and chariot drivers
·followed [pursued] them into the sea. 24·When morning came [LAt the
morning watch], the LORD looked down from the pillar of cloud and fire
at the Egyptian army and made them panic. 25He clogged their chariot
wheels,[n] making it hard to ·drive the chariots [Lturn]. The Egyptians
shouted, "Let's ·get away [flee] from the Israelites! The LORD is fighting
for them and against Egypt [15:3]."
26Then the LORD told Moses, "·Hold [Extend; Stretch] your hand over
the sea so that the water will come back over the Egyptians, their chariots,
and chariot drivers." 27So Moses ·raised [extended; stretched] his hand
over the sea, and at dawn the sea returned to its ·place [*or* normal depth].
The Egyptians tried to ·run [flee] from it, but the LORD ·swept them away
[tossed; overthrew them] into the sea. 28The water returned, covering the
chariots, chariot drivers, and all ·the king's [LPharaoh's] army that had
followed the Israelites into the sea. Not one of them ·survived [remained].
29But the ·Israelites [Lsons/Tchildren of Israel] crossed the sea on dry
land, with a wall of water on their right and on their left. 30So that day the
LORD saved the Israelites from the Egyptians, and the Israelites saw the
Egyptians lying dead on the seashore. 31When the Israelites saw ·the great
power the LORD had used [Lwhat God did with his strong hand] against
the Egyptians, the people feared the LORD, and they ·trusted [had confidence in] the LORD and his servant Moses.

The Song of Moses

15 Then Moses and the ·Israelites [Lsons/Tchildren of Israel]
sang this song to the LORD:

"I will sing to the LORD,
because he ·is worthy of great honor [is highly exalted; has
triumphed gloriously].
He has ·thrown the horse and its rider
into the sea.
2The LORD ·gives me strength and makes me sing [Lis my strength and
my song];
he ·has saved me [Lis my salvation].
He is my God,
and I will praise him.
He is the God of my ·ancestors [fathers],
and I will ·honor [exalt] him.

14:25 clogged their chariot wheels This phrase appears in some Greek copies. The Hebrew text has "misdirected their chariot wheels".

[3]The LORD is a ·warrior [[L]man of war];
·the LORD [[L]Yahweh; 3:14–17] is his name.
[4]The chariots and soldiers of ·the king of Egypt [[L]Pharaoh]
he has ·thrown [cast] into the sea.
·The king's [[L]His] ·best [handpicked; elite] officers
are drowned in the ·Red [*or* Reed; 10:19] Sea.
[5]The ·deep waters [floods] covered them,
and they sank ·to the bottom [[L]into the depths] like a ·rock [stone].
[6]Your right hand, LORD,
is ·amazingly [gloriously] strong.
LORD, your right hand
broke the enemy to pieces.
[7]In your great victory
you ·destroyed [demolished] those who ·were [[L]rose up] against you.
·Your anger destroyed them [[L]You sent out your anger],
·like fire burning straw [[L]it consumed them like chaff/stubble/straw].
[8]Just a blast of your ·breath [*or* anger],
and the waters piled up.
The moving water stood like a ·wall [*or* heap];
the ·deep waters [floods] ·became solid [congealed] in the ·middle [[L]heart] of the sea.

[9]"The enemy ·bragged [[L]said],
'I'll ·chase them [[L]pursue] and ·catch them [[L]overtake].
I'll ·take all their riches [[L]divide the plunder];
·I'll take all I want [[L]My desire/appetite will have my fill of them].
I'll ·pull out [draw] my sword,
and my hand will destroy them.'
[10]But you blew on them with your ·breath [*or* wind]
and covered them with the sea.
They sank like lead
in the ·raging water [mighty waters].

[11]"·Are there any gods like you [[L]Who is like you among the gods], LORD?
·There are no gods [[L]Who is…?] like you.
You are ·wonderfully holy [splendid/majestic in holiness],
·amazingly powerful [awesome in power],
·a worker of miracles [doing wonders].
[12]You ·reached out with [extend; stretch out] your right hand,
and the earth swallowed ·our enemies [[L]them].
[13]You ·keep your loving promise
and lead [[L]led by your covenant love] the people you have ·saved [[L]redeemed; ransomed].
With your strength you will guide them
to your holy ·place [abode; [C]the Promised Land].

[14]"The ·other nations [[L]peoples] will hear this and tremble with fear;
·terror [writhing; pangs] will take hold of the Philistines.
[15]The ·leaders of the tribes [chiefs] of Edom will be ·very frightened [scared];
the powerful men of Moab will ·shake with fear [be seized by shaking];
the people of Canaan will ·lose all their courage [[L]melt].

16 Terror and horror will fall on them.
·When they see your strength [LBy the power of your arm],
they will be as still as a ·rock [stone].
They will be still until your people pass by, LORD.
They will be still until the people you have ·taken as your own
[purchased; acquired; *or* created] pass by.
17 You will ·lead your people [Lbring them] and ·place [Lplant] them
on ·your very own mountain [Lthe mountain of your possession/
inheritance],
the place that you, LORD, made for ·yourself to live [your abode],
the ·temple [sanctuary], Lord, that your hands have ·made
[established].
18 The LORD will ·be king [reign] forever!"
19 The horses, chariot drivers, and chariots of ·the king of Egypt
[LPharaoh] went into the sea, and the LORD ·covered them with [Lreturned
on them the] water from the sea. But the Israelites walked through the sea
on dry land. 20 Then Aaron's sister Miriam, a prophetess, took a tambou-
rine in her hand. All the women followed her, playing tambourines and
dancing. 21 Miriam told them:
"Sing to the LORD,
because he ·is worthy of great honor [is highly exalted; *or* has
triumphed gloriously];
he has thrown the horse and its rider
into the sea."

Bitter Water Becomes Good

22 Moses led the Israelites away from the ·Red [*or* Reed; 10:19] Sea into
the ·Desert [Wilderness] of Shur. They traveled for three days in the ·desert
[wilderness] but found no water. 23 Then they came to Marah, where there
was water, but they could not drink it because it was too bitter. (That is why
the place was named Marah [CHebrew for "bitter"].) 24 The people ·grum-
bled [complained] to Moses and asked, "What will we drink?"
25 So Moses cried out to the LORD, and the LORD showed him a ·tree [*or*
piece of wood]. When Moses threw the ·tree [*or* piece of wood] into the
water, the water became ·good to drink [Lsweet].
There the LORD gave the people a ·rule [statute; ordinance; require-
ment] and a law to live by, and there he tested ·their loyalty to him
[Lthem]. 26 He said, "You must ·obey [*or* listen to the voice of] the LORD
your God and do what ·he says is right [Lis right in his eyes/sight]. If you
obey all his ·commands [statutes; ordinances; requirements] and keep his
rules, I will not bring on you any of the ·sicknesses [diseases] I brought on
the Egyptians. I am the LORD ·who heals you [your physician]."
27 Then the people traveled to Elim, where there were twelve springs of
water and seventy palm trees. So the people camped there near the water.

The People Demand Food

16 The whole ·Israelite community [Lcongregation/assembly of
the sons/Tchildren of Israel] left Elim and came to the ·Desert
[Wilderness] of Sin, which was between Elim and Sinai; they arrived
there on the fifteenth day of the second month after they had left Egypt.
2 Then the whole ·Israelite community [congregation; Lassembly of the
sons/Tchildren of Israel] ·grumbled [complained] to Moses and Aaron in
the ·desert [wilderness]. 3 ·They [LThe sons/Tchildren of Israel] said to
them, "It would have been better if the [Lhand of the] LORD had killed us
in the land of Egypt. There we ·had meat to eat and [Lsat by the fleshpots

and ate] all the ·food [bread] we wanted. But you have brought us into
this ·desert [wilderness] to starve ·us [Lall this assembly/crowd] to death."
4Then the LORD said to Moses, "I will cause ·food [bread] to fall like
rain from ·the sky [heaven] for all of you. Every day the people must go
out and gather what they need for that day. I want to ·see if the people will
do what I teach them [Ltest them to see if they will walk in my law/instruc-
tion or not]. 5On the sixth day of each week, they are to gather twice as
much as they gather on other days. Then they are to prepare it."
6So Moses and Aaron said to all the ·Israelites [Lsons/Tchildren of
Israel]: "This evening you will know that the LORD is the one who brought
you out of Egypt. 7Tomorrow morning you will see the glory of the LORD,
because he has heard you ·grumble [complain] against him. ·We are
nothing, so you are not grumbling against us, but against the LORD [LFor
what are we that you grumble/complain against us?]." 8And Moses said,
"Each evening the LORD will give you meat to eat, and every morning he
will give you all the bread you want, because he has heard you ·grumble
[complain] against him. You are not grumbling against ·Aaron and me,
because we are nothing; you are grumbling [Lus, but] against the LORD."
9Then Moses said to Aaron, "Speak to the whole ·community of the
Israelites [Lcongregation/assembly of the sons/Tchildren of Israel], and say
to them, '·Meet together in the presence of [LDraw near] the LORD, because
he has heard your ·grumblings [complaints].' "
10While Aaron was speaking to the whole ·community of the Israelites
[Lcongregation/assembly of the sons/Tchildren of Israel], they ·looked
[Lturned] toward the ·desert [wilderness]. There the glory of the LORD
appeared in a cloud.
11The LORD said to Moses, 12"I have heard the ·grumblings [complaints]
of the ·people [sons/Tchildren] of Israel. So tell them, 'At twilight you will
eat meat, and every morning you will eat all the bread you want. Then
you will know I am the LORD your God.' "
13That evening quail came and covered the camp, and in the morning
[La layer of] dew lay around the camp. 14When the [Llayer of] dew ·was
gone [evaporated; Lwent up], thin flakes like frost were on the ·desert [wil-
derness] ground. 15When the ·Israelites [Lsons/Tchildren of Israel] saw it,
they asked each other, "What is it?" because they did not know what it was.
So Moses told them, "This is the bread the LORD has given you to eat.
16The LORD has commanded, 'Each one of you must gather what he needs,
about ·two quarts [Lan omer] for every person in your ·family [Lown tent].' "
17So the ·people [Lsons; children] of Israel did this; some people gathered much, and some gathered little. 18Then they measured it [Lby omer].
The person who gathered more did not have too much, nor did the person who gathered less have too little. Each person gathered just as much
as he needed.
19Moses said to them, "Don't ·keep any of it to eat [Lleave any of it until]
the next day." 20But some of the people did not listen to Moses and kept
part of it to eat the next morning. It became full of worms and ·began to
stink [spoiled], so Moses was angry with those people.
21Every morning each person gathered as much food as he needed, but
when the sun became hot, it melted away.
22On the sixth day the people gathered twice as much food—·four
quarts [Ltwo omers] for every person. When all the leaders of the ·com-
munity [congregation; assembly] came and told this to Moses, 23he said

to them, "This is what the LORD ·commanded [Lsaid], because tomorrow is the Sabbath, the LORD's holy day of rest. Bake what you want to bake, and boil what you want to boil today. Save the rest of the food until tomorrow morning."

24So the people saved it until the next morning, as Moses had commanded, and none of it ·began to stink [spoiled] or have worms in it. 25Moses told the people, "Eat ·the food you gathered yesterday [Lit today]. Today is a Sabbath, ·the LORD's day of rest [L…of the LORD]; you will not find any out in the field today. 26You should gather ·the food [Lit] for six days, but the seventh day is a Sabbath day. On that day ·there will not be any food on the ground [Lit will not be on it]."

27On the seventh day some of the people went out to gather food, but they couldn't find any. 28Then the LORD said to Moses, "How long will you people refuse to ·obey [keep] my commands and ·teachings [instructions; laws]? 29Look, the LORD has ·made the Sabbath a day of rest for you [Lgiven to you the Sabbath]. So on the sixth day he will give you enough food for two days, but on the seventh day each of you must stay where you are. Do not go anywhere." 30So the people rested on the seventh day.

31The ·people [Lhouse] of Israel called the food manna [Cbased on the Hebrew phrase, "What is it?"; 16:15]. It was like ·small white seeds [Lcoriander seeds, white] and tasted like wafers made with honey.

32Then Moses said, "·The LORD said [LThis is the word/thing the LORD has commanded], '·Save [Keep; LFill] ·two quarts [Lan omer] of this food ·for your descendants [Lthroughout your generations]. Then they can see the food I gave you to eat in the ·desert [wilderness] when I brought you out of Egypt.' "

33Moses told Aaron, "Take a jar and fill it with ·two quarts [Lan omer] of manna. Then place it before the LORD, and ·save [keep] it ·for your descendants [Lthroughout your generations]." 34So Aaron did what the LORD had commanded Moses. He put ·the jar of manna [Lit] in front of the ·Agreement [LTestimony; Cthe Ark, named for the Ten Commandments placed in it] to keep it safe. 35The ·Israelites [Lsons/Tchildren of Israel] ate manna for forty years, until they came to the land where they settled—the edge of the land of Canaan [Josh. 5:12]. 36The measure they used for the manna was ·two quarts [Lan omer], or one-tenth of an ephah [Can ephah is about 20 quarts].

Water from a Rock

17 The whole ·Israelite community [congregation/assembly of the sons/Tchildren of Israel] left the ·Desert [Wilderness] of Sin and ·traveled from place to place [journeyed by stages], as the LORD commanded. They camped at Rephidim, but there was no water there for the people to drink. 2So the people ·quarreled with [accused; made a case against] Moses and said, "Give us water to drink."

Moses said to them, "Why do you ·quarrel with [accuse; make a case against] me? Why are you ·testing [putting on trial] the LORD?"

3But the people were very thirsty for water, so they ·grumbled [complained] against Moses. They said, "Why did you bring us out of Egypt? Was it to kill us, our children, and our farm animals with thirst?"

4So Moses cried to the LORD, "What can I do with these people? They are almost ready to stone me to death."

5The LORD said to Moses, "Go ahead of the people, and take some of the elders of Israel with you. Carry with you the ·walking stick [staff] that you used to strike the Nile River [14:21]. Now go! 6I will stand in front of you on a rock at ·Mount Sinai [LHoreb; Canother name for Sinai; 3:1]. ·Hit [Strike] that rock with the ·stick [staff], and water will come out of it so that the people can drink." Moses did these things as the elders of Israel watched. 7He named that place Massah [CHebrew for "test"], because the Israelites tested the LORD when they asked, "Is the LORD with us or not?" He also named it Meribah [CHebrew for "quarrel"], because they ·quarreled [accused; made a case].

The Amalekites Fight Israel

8At Rephidim the Amalekites came and fought the Israelites. 9So Moses said to Joshua, "·Choose [Select] some men and go and fight the Amalekites. Tomorrow I will stand on the top of the hill, ·holding [extending; stretching out] the ·walking stick [staff] of God in my hands."

10Joshua ·obeyed Moses [Ldid as Moses said] and went to fight the Amalekites, while Moses, Aaron, and Hur went to the top of the hill. 11As long as Moses ·held [raised] his hands up, the Israelites would ·win the fight [prevail], but when Moses put his hands down, the Amalekites ·would win [prevailed; Cthe staff represented the presence of God, who fought for Israel]. 12Later, when Moses' arms became ·tired [Lheavy], the men put a large rock under him, and he sat on it. Then Aaron and Hur held up Moses' hands—Aaron on one side and Hur on the other. They kept his hands steady until the sun went down. 13So Joshua defeated ·the Amalekites [LAmalek and his people] ·in this battle [Lwith the sword].

14Then the LORD said to Moses, "Write about this battle in a ·book [*or* scroll] ·so people will remember [Las a memorial]. And ·be sure to tell [Lplace this in the ear of] Joshua, because I will completely ·destroy [annihilate; blot out] the Amalekites from ·the earth [Lunder heaven; Deut. 25:17–19]."

15Then Moses built an altar and named it ·The LORD Is My Banner [LYahweh Nissi]. 16Moses said, "I lifted my hands toward the LORD's throne. The LORD will fight against the Amalekites forever."

Jethro Visits Moses

18 Jethro, Moses' father-in-law, was the priest of Midian [2:15]. He heard about everything that God had done for Moses and his people, the Israelites, and how the LORD had led the Israelites out of Egypt. 2Now Moses had sent [Laway] his wife Zipporah [2:21] to Jethro, his father-in-law [4:24–26], 3along with his two sons. The first son was named Gershom [Csounds like Hebrew for "stranger there"], because when he was born, Moses said, "I am a ·stranger [sojourner; wanderer; resident alien] in a foreign country." 4The other son was named Eliezer [Csounds like Hebrew for "my God is help"], because when he was born, Moses said, "The God of my father is my help. He saved me from ·the king of Egypt [Lthe sword of Pharaoh]."

5So Jethro, Moses' father-in-law, took Moses' wife and his two sons and went to Moses. He was camped in the ·desert [wilderness] near the mountain of God [CMount Sinai]. 6Jethro had sent a message ahead to Moses that said, "I, Jethro, your father-in-law, am coming to you with your wife and her two sons."

7So Moses went out to meet his father-in-law and bowed down and kissed him. After the two men asked about each other's ·health [well-being], they went into Moses' tent. 8Moses told his father-in-law everything the LORD had done to ·the king [LPharaoh] and the Egyptians to help Israel. He told about all the ·problems [hardship] they had faced along the way and how the LORD had saved them.

9Jethro ·was very happy to hear [rejoiced concerning] all the good
things the LORD had done for Israel when he had saved them from the
Egyptians. 10He said, "·Praise [Blessed be] the LORD. He has saved you
from the [Lhand of the] Egyptians and [Lthe hand of] ·their king
[LPharaoh], and he has saved the people from the ·power [Lhand] of the
Egyptians. 11Now I know the LORD is greater than all gods, because he did
this to those who ·looked down on Israel [treated Israel with insolence/
arrogance]." 12Then Jethro, Moses' father-in-law, gave a whole burnt
offering [Lev. 1:1–17] and other sacrifices to God. Aaron and all the elders
of Israel came to Moses' father-in-law to eat ·the holy meal [Lbread/food]
together before God.

13The next day Moses ·solved disagreements [decided cases; Lsat as
judge] among the people, and the people stood around him from morning
until night. 14When Moses' father-in-law saw all that Moses was doing for
the people, he asked, "What is all this you are doing for the people? Why
are you the only one ·to solve disagreements [Lsitting]? All the people are
standing ·around you [*or* in line] from morning until night!"

15Then Moses said to his father-in-law, "It is because the people come
to me ·for God's help in solving their disagreements [Lto seek/inquire of
God]. 16When people have a ·disagreement [Lmatter; case], they come to
me, and I ·decide who is right [judge between a person and his neighbor].
I tell them God's ·laws [statutes; ordinances; requirements] and ·teachings
[instructions; laws]."

17Moses' father-in-law said to him, "·You are not doing this right [LWhat
you are doing is not good]. 18You and the people who ·come to you [Lare
with you] will ·get too tired [wear out]. ·This is too much work for you
[LThe matter is too heavy for you]; you can't do it by yourself. 19Now listen
to me, and I will give you some advice. I want God to be with you. You
must speak to God for the people and tell him about their ·disagreements
[cases]. 20Warn them about the ·laws [statutes; ordinances; requirements]
and ·teachings [instructions; laws], and ·teach [make known to] them the
·right way to live [Lway they should go] and what they should do. 21But
choose some ·capable [virtuous; noble] men from among the people—
men who ·respect [fear] God [Prov. 1:7], who can be trusted, and who ·will
not change their decisions for money [Lhate dishonest profit]. Make these
men officers over the people, to rule over groups of thousands, hundreds,
fifties, and tens. 22Let these officers ·solve the disagreements [consider
cases; judge] among the people all the time. They can bring the ·hard [Lbig]
cases to you, but they can ·decide [judge] the ·simple [Lsmall] cases themselves. That will make it easier for you, because they will share the work
with you. 23If you do this as God commands you, then you will be able to
do your job, and all the people will go ·home [to their place] ·with their
disagreements solved [Lin peace]."

24So Moses listened to [Lthe voice of] his father-in-law and did everything he said. 25He ·chose [selected] ·capable [virtuous; noble] men from
all the Israelites and made them ·leaders [heads] over the people; they
were officers over groups of thousands, hundreds, fifties, and tens.
26These officers ·solved disagreements among [judged] the people all the
time. They brought the hard cases to Moses, but they ·decided [judged]
the ·simple [Lsmall] cases themselves.

27So Moses sent his father-in-law on his way, and Jethro went back to
his own ·home [Lland].

Israel Camps at Sinai

19 Exactly three months after the Israelites had left Egypt, ·they
[Lthe sons/Tchildren of Israel] ·reached [came to] the ·Desert
[Wilderness] of Sinai. 2When they left Rephidim, they came to the ·Desert
[Wilderness] of Sinai and camped in the ·desert [wilderness] in front of
the mountain. 3Then Moses went up on the mountain to God. The LORD
called to him from the mountain and said, "Say this to the ·family [Lhouse]
of Jacob, and tell the ·people [sons; children] of Israel: 4'Every one of you
has seen what I did to the people of Egypt. You saw how I carried you out
of Egypt, as if on eagle's wings [CGod protected and guided them; Deut.
32:11]. And I brought you here to me. 5So now if you ·obey me [Llisten to
my voice] and keep my ·agreement [covenant; treaty], you will be my own
possession [special treasure], chosen from all nations. Even though the
whole earth is mine, 6you will be my kingdom of priests and a holy nation
[Cset apart to serve God and bring others to him; Gen. 12:1–3].' You must
tell the ·Israelites [Lthe sons/Tchildren of Israel] these words."
7So Moses went down and called the elders of the people together. He
told them all the words the LORD had commanded him to say. 8All the people answered together, "We will do everything the LORD has said." Then
Moses took ·their answer [Lthe words of the people] back to the LORD.
9And the LORD said to Moses, "I will come to you in a ·thick [dense]
cloud and speak to you. The people will hear me speaking with you and
will always trust you." Then Moses told the LORD ·what the people had
said [Lthe words of the people].
10The LORD said to Moses, "Go to the people and have them ·spend
today and tomorrow preparing themselves [consecrate/sanctify themselves today and tomorrow]. They must wash their clothes 11and be ready
by the ·day after tomorrow [Lthird day]. On that day I, the LORD, will come
down on Mount Sinai, and all the people will see me. 12But you must set
a ·limit around the mountain that the people are not to cross [Lboundary
around the people]. ·Tell [Warn] them not to go up on the mountain and
not to touch the ·foot [edge] of it. Anyone who touches the mountain
must be put to death 13with stones or shot with arrows. No one is allowed
to touch him [Ctouching a dead body rendered a person ritually unclean;
Num. 5:2]. Whether it is a person or an animal, he will not live. But the
·trumpet [ram's horn] will make a long blast, and only then may the people go up on the mountain."
14After Moses went down from the mountain to the people, he made
them ·prepare themselves for service to God [consecrate/sanctify them-
selves], and they washed their clothes. 15Then Moses said to the people,
"Be ready in three days. Do not ·have sexual relations during this time
[Ltouch a woman; Can emission of semen rendered a man ritually unclean;
Lev. 15:16–18]."
16On the morning of the third day, there was thunder and lightning
with a thick cloud on the mountain. There was a very loud blast from a
·trumpet [ram's horn], ·and [*or* so that] all the people in the camp trembled. 17Then Moses ·led [brought] the people out of the camp to meet
God, and they stood at the foot of the mountain. 18Mount Sinai was covered with smoke, because the LORD came down on it in fire. The smoke
rose from the mountain like smoke from a ·furnace [kiln], and the whole
mountain ·shook wildly [trembled]. 19The ·sound [blast] from the ·trum-
pet [ram's horn] became louder. Then Moses spoke, and ·the voice of [*or*
in thunder] God answered him.

20When the LORD came down on top of Mount Sinai, he ·called [invited]
Moses to come up to the top of the mountain, and Moses went up. 21The
LORD said to Moses, "Go down and warn the people that they must not
·force their way [break] through to see me. If they do, many of them will
·die [Lfall]. 22Even the priests, who may ·come near [approach] me, must
first ·prepare [consecrate; sanctify] themselves. If they don't, I, the LORD,
will ·punish [Lbreak out against] them."
23Moses told the LORD, "The people cannot come up on Mount Sinai,
because you yourself ·told [warned] us, 'Set a ·limit [boundary] around
the mountain, and ·set it apart as holy [consecrate/sanctify it].' "
24The LORD said to him, "Go down and bring Aaron up with you, but
don't allow the priests or the people to ·force their way [break] through.
They must not come up to the LORD, or I will ·punish [Lbreak out
against] them."
25So Moses went down to the people and told them these things.

The Ten Commandments

20 Then God spoke all these words:
2"I am the LORD your God, who brought you out of the land
of Egypt ·where you were slaves [Lfrom the house of bondage].
3"You must not have any other gods ·except [*or* before] me.
4"You must not make for yourselves an idol that looks like anything in
the ·sky [heavens] above or on the earth below or in the water below the
·land [earth]. 5You must not worship or serve them, because I, the LORD
your God, am a jealous God. ·If you hate me, I will punish your children,
and even your grandchildren and great-grandchildren [LI will visit/punish
the guilt of the fathers on the sons/Tchildren until the third and fourth
generations of those who hate me]. 6But I show kindness to ·thousands [*or*
thousands of generations of those] who love me and obey my commands.
7"You must not ·use the name of the LORD your God thoughtlessly
[take/lift up the name of the LORD your God in vain]; the LORD will ·pun-
ish [Lnot hold/treat as innocent; not acquit] anyone who ·misuses [takes
in vain] his name.
8"Remember to ·keep the Sabbath holy [consecrate/sanctify the
Sabbath]. 9Work and get everything done during six days each week, 10but
the seventh day is a ·day of rest to honor [Sabbath to] the LORD your God.
On that day no one may do any work: not you, your son or daughter, your
male or female slaves, your animals, or the ·foreigners [sojourners; wanderers; resident aliens] living in your ·cities [Lgates]. 11The reason is that in
six days the LORD made everything—the ·sky [heavens], the earth, the sea,
and everything in them. On the seventh day he rested. So the LORD blessed
the Sabbath day and ·made it holy [consecrated/sanctified it].
12"Honor your father and your mother so that you will live ·a long time
[Lfor many days] in the land that the LORD your God is going to give you.
13"You must not murder anyone.
14"You must not ·be guilty of [commit] adultery.
15"You must not steal.
16"You must not ·tell lies about [bear false witness against] your
neighbor.
17"You must not ·want to take [covet] your neighbor's house. You must
not ·want [covet] his wife or his male or female slaves, or his ox or his
donkey, or anything that belongs to your neighbor [Cthis commandment
internalizes previous commandments]."

18When the people heard the thunder and the ·trumpet [ram's horn], and when they saw the lightning and the smoke rising from the mountain, they ·shook with fear [trembled] and stood far away from the mountain. 19Then they said to Moses, "Speak to us yourself, and we will listen. But don't let God speak to us, or we will die."

20Then Moses said to the people, "Don't be afraid, because God has come to test you. He wants ·you to respect him [Lto put the fear of him on you] so you will not sin."

21The people stood far away from the mountain while Moses went near the dark cloud where God was. 22Then the LORD told Moses to say these things to the ·Israelites [Lsons/Tchildren of Israel]: "You yourselves have seen that I talked with you from heaven. 23You must not use gold or silver to make idols for yourselves; do not worship these gods in addition to me.

24"Make an altar of dirt for me, and sacrifice on it your whole burnt offerings [Lev. 1] and ·fellowship [*or* peace; Lev. 3] offerings, your sheep and your cattle. Worship me in every place that I choose, and I will come and bless you. 25If you use stones to make an altar for me, don't use ·stones that you have shaped with tools [hewn/cut stones]. When you use any ·tools [chisel] on them, you ·make them unsuitable for use in worship [profane them]. 26And you must not go up to my altar on steps, or ·people will be able to see under your clothes [Lyour nakedness will be exposed on it; Cmeant to avoid a Canaanite-style fertility worship]."

Laws for Living

21 Then God said to Moses, "These are the ·laws for living [regulations] that you will ·give to the Israelites [Lset before them]:

2"·If [*or* When] you buy a Hebrew slave, he will serve you for six years. In the seventh year you are to set him free, ·and he will have to pay nothing [with no debt]. 3If he ·is not married when he becomes your slave [Lcame single/alone], he must leave ·without a wife [Lsingle; alone]. But if he ·is married when he becomes your slave [Lcomes in with a wife], he may ·take [Lgo out with] his wife with him. 4If the slave's master gives him a wife, and she gives birth to sons or daughters, the woman and her children will belong to the master. ·When the slave is set free, only he may leave [LHe will go out single/alone].

5"But if the slave says, 'I love my master, my wife and my children, and I don't want to go free,' 6then the slave's master must take him to ·God [Tthe judges; CHebrew: Elohim]. The master is to take him to a door or ·doorframe [doorpost] and ·punch a hole through [pierce] the slave's ear using ·a sharp tool [an awl]. Then the slave will serve that master all his life.

7"·If [*or* When] a man sells his daughter as a slave, ·the rules for setting her free are different from the rules for setting the male slaves free [Lshe will not go out like male slaves go out]. 8If ·the master wanted to marry her but then decided he was not pleased with her [Lshe does not please her master who designated her for himself], he must let ·one of her close relatives buy her back [Lher be redeemed]. He has no right to sell her to foreigners, because he has treated her unfairly. 9If the man ·who bought her promises to let the woman marry [Ldesignated her for] his son, he must ·treat her as [give her the rights of] a daughter. 10If ·the man who bought her marries another woman [he takes another wife], he must not ·keep his first wife from having [deprive her of] food or clothing or ·sexual relations [marital rights]. 11If he does not give her these

three things, she may go free, ·and she owes him no money [Lwith no debt; Lev. 25:39–43; Deut. 15:12–18].

Laws About Injuries

12“**Anyone who ·hits** [strikes] **a person and kills him must be put to death.** 13**But if a person kills someone ·accidentally** [without premeditation], **God allowed that to happen, so ·the person must go to a place I will choose** [LI will appoint for you a place to which the person may flee; Josh. 20:1–9]. 14**But if someone plans and murders another person on purpose, put him to death, even if he has run to my altar for safety.**

15“**Anyone who ·hits** [strikes] **his father or his mother must be put to death.**

16“**Anyone who kidnaps someone and either sells him as a slave or ·still has him when he is caught** [Lhe is found in his hand] **must be put to death.**

17“**Anyone who ·says cruel things to** [curses] **his father or mother must be put to death.**

18“**If two men ·argue** [quarrel; contend], **and one hits ·the other** [Lhis neighbor] **with a rock or with his ·fist** [*or* tool], **the one who is hurt but not killed might have to stay in bed.** 19**Later if he is able to get up and walk around outside with his ·walking stick** [staff], **the one who hit him ·is not to be punished** [has no liability]. **But he must pay the injured man for the loss of his time, and he must support the injured man until he is completely healed.**

20“**If a man ·beats** [strikes] **his male or female slave with a ·stick** [rod], **and the slave dies on the spot, the owner must be punished.** 21**But if the slave gets well after a day or two, the owner will not be punished since the slave belongs to him.**

22“**Suppose two men are fighting and ·hit** [injure] **a pregnant woman, causing ·the baby to come out** [*or* a miscarriage; Cthe Hebrew is not clear whether dead or alive]. **If there is no further ·injury** [harm], **the man who caused the accident must pay money—whatever amount the woman's husband says and the court allows.** 23**But if there is further ·injury** [harm], **then ·the punishment that must be paid is** [Lyou shall give] **life for life,** 24**eye for eye, tooth for tooth, hand for hand, foot for foot,** 25**burn for burn, wound for wound, and bruise for bruise** [Cto guard against excessive punishment].

26“**If a man ·hits** [strikes] **his male or female slave in the eye, and ·the eye is blinded** [Ldestroys it], **the man is to free the slave to pay for the eye.** 27**If a master knocks out a tooth of his male or female slave, the man is to free the slave to pay for the tooth.**

28“**If a man's ·bull** [ox] **kills a man or woman, you must kill that bull by ·throwing stones at** [stoning] **it, and you should not eat ·the bull** [Lits meat]. **But the owner of the bull is ·not guilty** [innocent]. 29**However, suppose the ·bull** [ox] **has ·hurt** [gored] **people in the past and the owner, though warned, did not ·keep it in a pen** [restrain/confine it]. **Then if it kills a man or woman, the ·bull** [ox] **must be stoned to death, and the owner must also be put to death.** 30**But if ·the family of the dead person accepts money** [La ransom is imposed on him], **the owner of the bull must pay whatever is demanded ·to buy back his life** [for his redemption]. 31**Use this same ·law** [rule] **if the ·bull** [ox] **·kills** [gores] **a person's son or daughter.** 32**If the ·bull** [ox] **·kills** [gores] **a male or female slave, the owner must pay the master ·the price for a new slave, or twelve ounces** [Lthirty shekels] **of silver, and the ·bull** [ox] **must also be stoned to death.**

33“If a man takes the cover off a pit, or digs a pit and does not cover it, and another man’s ox or donkey comes and falls into it, 34the owner of the pit must ·pay [compensate] the owner of the animal for the loss. The dead animal will belong to the one who pays.

35“If a man’s ·bull [ox] ·kills [gores] another man’s ·bull [ox] and it dies, they must sell the ·bull [ox] that is alive. Both men will get half of the money and half of the bull that was killed. 36But if a person’s ·bull [ox] has ·hurt [gored] other animals in the past and the owner did not ·keep it in a pen [restrain/confine it], that owner must pay bull for bull, and the dead animal is his.

Property Laws

22 “If a man steals a ·bull [ox] or a sheep and ·kills [slaughters] or sells it, he must ·pay back [compensate] five ·bulls [oxen] for the one bull he stole and four sheep for the one sheep he stole.

2-4“The robber who is caught must ·pay back what he stole [make restitution]. If he owns nothing, he must be sold as a slave to pay for what he stole. If the stolen animal is found alive with the robber, he must give the owner two animals for every animal he stole, whether it was a ·bull [ox], donkey, or sheep.

“If a thief is killed while breaking into a house at night, the one who killed him is not guilty of ·murder [bloodshed]. But if this happens ·during the day [Lafter the sun is risen], he is guilty of ·murder [bloodshed].

5“If a man lets his farm animal graze in his field or vineyard, and it wanders into another man’s field or vineyard, the owner of the animal must ·pay back the loss [make restitution] from the best of his ·crop [Lfield and from the best of his vineyard].

6“Suppose a man starts a fire that ·spreads through the thornbushes to his neighbor’s field [Lcatches in the thorns]. If the fire burns ·his neighbor’s growing [Lthe standing] grain or grain that has been stacked, or if it burns his whole field, the person who started the fire must pay ·for what was burned [full restitution].

7“Suppose a man gives his neighbor money or other things ·to keep for him [for safekeeping] and those things are stolen from the neighbor’s house. If the thief is caught, he must pay back twice as much as he stole. 8But if the thief is never ·found [caught], the owner of the house must ·make a promise [Lbe brought] before ·God [*or* the judges] that he has not ·stolen [Lsent out his hand toward] his neighbor’s things.

9“Suppose ·two men disagree about who owns something [Lthere is a matter/report of transgression]—whether ox, donkey, sheep, clothing, or something else that is lost. If each says, ‘This is mine,’ each man must bring his case ·to God [*or* before the judges]. ·God’s judges [LGod; TThe judges; CHebrew: Elohim] will decide who is guilty, and that person must pay the other man twice as much as the object is worth.

10“Suppose a man ·asks [Lgives] his neighbor to ·keep [safeguard] his donkey, ox, sheep, or some other animal for him, and that animal dies, gets ·hurt [injured; Lbroken], or is taken away, without anyone seeing what happened. 11·That neighbor must promise before the LORD [LAn oath before God will decide] that he did not ·harm or kill [Lsend his hand against] the other man’s animal, and the owner of the animal must accept ·his promise made before God [the oath]. The neighbor does not have to ·pay the owner for the animal [make restitution]. 12But if the animal was stolen from the neighbor, ·he must pay the owner for it [restitutiton must

be made to the owner]. 13If wild animals killed it, the neighbor must bring
·the body [Lit] as proof, and ·he will not have to pay for the animal that
was killed [Lrestitution will not be made for the torn-up remains].
14"If a man borrows an animal from his neighbor, and it gets ·hurt
[injured; Lbroken] or dies while the owner is not there, the one who borrowed it must pay [Lrestitution to] the owner for the animal. 15But if the
owner is with the animal, the one who borrowed it does not ·have to pay
[make restitution]. If the animal was ·rented [hired], the ·rental [hiring]
price covers the loss.

Laws and Relationships

16"Suppose a man finds a woman who is not ·pledged [engaged] to be
married and ·has never had sexual relations with a man [Lis a virgin]. If
he ·tricks [*or* seduces] her into having sexual relations with him, he must
give ·her family the payment to marry [Lthe bride-price for] her, and she
will become his wife. 17But if her father refuses to allow his daughter to
marry him, the man must still give the usual ·payment for a bride who
has never had sexual relations [bride-price for a virgin].
18"·Put to death any woman who does evil magic [LYou shall not let a
female sorceress live].
19"Put to death anyone who ·has sexual relations [Llies] with an animal.
20"·Destroy completely [Devote to destruction; Put under the ban] any
person who makes a sacrifice to any god except the LORD.
21"Do not ·cheat [wrong; maltreat] or ·hurt [oppress] a ·foreigner
[sojourner; resident alien], because you were ·foreigners [sojourners; resident aliens] in the land of Egypt.
22"Do not ·cheat [abuse; Lafflict] a widow or an orphan. 23If you ·do
[cheat; abuse; Lafflict], and they cry out to me for help, I certainly will
·hear [*or* act on] their cry. 24And I will be very angry and kill you ·in war
[Lwith the sword]. Then your wives will become widows, and your children will become orphans.
25"If you lend money to one of my people who is poor, do not treat him
as a ·moneylender [creditor] would. ·Charge him nothing for using your
money [LTake no interest; Lev. 25:36–37; Deut. 23:19; Ps. 15:5]. 26If your
neighbor gives you his coat as ·a promise for the money he owes you [col-
lateral], you must give it back to him by sunset, 27because his coat is the
only cover to keep his body warm. He has nothing else to sleep in. If he
cries out to me for help, I will ·hear [*or* act], because I am ·merciful [gra-
cious; compassionate].
28"You must not ·speak against [revile; trifle with; disrespect] God or
curse a leader of your people.
29"Do not hold back your offering from the first of your harvest and
the first wine that you make. Also, you must give me your firstborn sons.
30You must do the same with your ·bulls [oxen] and your sheep. Let the
firstborn males stay with their mothers for seven days, and on the eighth
day you must give them to me.
31"You are to be my ·holy [consecrated; sanctified; set-apart] people.
You must not eat the meat of any animal that has been ·killed [torn up]
by wild animals. Instead, ·give [Lthrow] it to the dogs.

Laws About Fairness

23 "You must not ·tell lies [Lgive a false report]. If you are a witness in court, ·don't help [Lyou shall not set hands with] a
wicked person ·by telling lies [with a false/violent/malicious witness].
2"You must not ·do wrong just because everyone else is doing it [follow

the crowd in evil]. ·If you are a witness in court, you must not ruin a fair trial. You must not tell lies just because everyone else is [LYou are not to give testimony in an accusation by siding with everyone else in order to distort justice]. 3·If a poor person is in court, you must not take his side just because he is poor [LYou must not be partial to a poor person in his dispute/lawsuit].

4"If you ·see [Lencounter] your enemy's ox or donkey wandering away, you must return it to him. 5If you see that ·your enemy's donkey [Lthe donkey of one who hates you] has fallen because its load is too heavy, do not leave it there. You must ·help your enemy get the donkey back on its feet [set it free; *or* rearrange its load].

6"You must not ·be unfair to [pervert the justice of] a poor person when he is in court. 7·You must not lie when you accuse someone in court [LKeep yourself far from a false charge/report]. Never allow an innocent or honest person to be put to death as punishment, because I will not ·treat guilty people as if they were innocent [acquit the guilty].

8"You must not accept ·money from a person who wants you to lie in court [La bribe], because ·such money will not let you see what is right [La bribe blinds officials; Prov. 15:27; 17:8; 18:16]. Such money ·makes good people tell lies [undermines the cause of the righteous].

9"You must not ·mistreat [oppress] a ·foreigner [sojourner; resident alien]. You know how it feels to be a ·foreigner [sojourner; resident alien], because you were ·foreigners [sojourners; resident aliens] in Egypt [22:21].

Laws for the Sabbath

10"For six years you are to ·plant [sow] and harvest crops on your land. 11Then during the seventh year, ·do not plow or plant your land [Lyou will let it lie fallow and untilled]. If any food grows there, allow the poor people to have it, and let the wild animals eat what is left. You should do the same with your vineyards and your orchards of olive trees [Lev. 25:1–7].

12"You should work six days a week, but on the seventh day you must ·rest [stop]. This lets your ox and your donkey rest, and it also lets the slave born in your house and the ·foreigner [sojourner; resident alien] be refreshed.

13"Be sure to do all that I have said to you. You must not ·even say [invoke; bring to mind] the names of other gods; those names must not ·come out of [Lbe heard from] your mouth.

Three Yearly Feasts

14"Three times each year you must ·hold a feast to honor me [hold a festival; *or* make a pilgrimage for me]. 15You must celebrate the ·Feast [Festival] of Unleavened Bread [34:18] in the way I commanded you. For seven days you must eat ·bread that is made without yeast [unleavened bread] at the set time during the month of Abib [13:4], the month when you came out of Egypt. No one is to ·come to worship [appear before] me ·without bringing an offering [empty-handed].

16"You must celebrate the ·Feast [Festival] of Harvest [Ccalled Feast of Weeks in 34:22; later called Pentecost]. Offer to God the first things you harvest from the crops you planted in your fields.

"You must celebrate the ·Feast [Festival] of Ingathering [Clater called Feast of Shelters or Booths; Lev. 23:33–36] in the fall, when you gather all the crops from your fields.

17"So three times during every year all your males must come ·to worship [Lbefore] the LORD God.

18“You must not offer ·animal blood [Lblood of a sacrifice] along with
anything ·that has yeast in it [leavened].
“You must not save any of the fat from the sacrifice for the next day.
19“You must bring the best of the firstfruits of your land to the ·Holy
Tent [LHouse; 25:9] of the LORD your God.
“You must not cook a young goat in its mother’s milk [Cprobably a
pagan ritual; Deut. 14:21].

God Will Help Israel

20“I am sending an angel ahead of you, who will ·protect [guard] you
·as you travel [Lon the way/path]. He will ·lead [bring] you to the place I
have prepared. 21Pay attention to him and ·obey him [Llisten to his voice].
Do not ·turn [rebel] against him; he will not forgive ·such turning against
him [Lit] because my ·power [Lname] is in him. 22If you listen carefully to
·all he says [Lhis voice] and do everything that I tell you, I will be an
enemy to your enemies. I will fight all who fight against you. 23My angel
will go ahead of you and take you into the land of the Amorites, Hittites,
Perizzites, Canaanites, Hivites, and Jebusites, and I will ·destroy them
[wipe/blot them out].
24“You must not bow down to their gods or ·worship [serve] them. You
must not live the way those people live. You must ·destroy their idols
[demolish them], breaking into pieces ·the stone pillars they use in worship [Ltheir pillars]. 25If you worship the LORD your God, ·I [Lhe] will bless
your bread and your water. I will take away sickness from you. 26None of
your women will miscarry or be ·unable to have children [barren]. I will
·allow you to live long lives [Lfill the number of your days].
27“I will ·make your enemies afraid of me [Lsend the dread of me before
you]. I will confuse any people ·you fight against [Lagainst whom you
come], and I will make all your enemies ·run away from [Lturn their backs
to] you. 28I will send ·terror [*or* pestilence; *or* the hornet] ahead of you
that will force the Hivites, Canaanites, and Hittites out of your way. 29But
I will not ·force all those people out [drive them out] in only one year. If
I did, the land would become ·a desert [desolate] and the wild animals
would become too many for you. 30Instead, I will ·force those people
[drive them] out ·slowly [little by little], until there are enough of you to
·take over [possess] the land.
31“I will give you the land from the ·Red [*or* Reed; 10:19] Sea to the
·Mediterranean [LPhilistine] Sea, and from the ·desert [wilderness] to the
·Euphrates River [LRiver]. I will give ·you power over [Linto your hand]
the people who now live in the land, and you will ·force [drive] them out
ahead of you. 32You must not ·make an agreement [Lcut a covenant] with
those people or with their gods. 33You must not let them live in your land,
or they will make you sin against me. If you ·worship [serve] their gods,
·you will be caught in a trap [Lthey will be a trap/snare to you].”

God Makes a Covenant with Israel

24 The LORD told Moses, “You, Aaron, Nadab, Abihu, and seventy of the elders of Israel must come up to me and ·worship
[bow down to] me from a distance. 2Then Moses alone must come near
me; the others must not come near. The rest of the people must not come
up the mountain with Moses.”
3Moses ·told [Lwent and recounted to] the people all the LORD’s words
and ·laws for living [regulations; judgments]. Then all of the people
answered out loud together, “We will do all the things the LORD has said.”
4So Moses wrote down all the words of the LORD. And he got up early the

next morning and built an altar near the bottom of the mountain. He set up twelve ·stones [[L]pillars], one ·stone [pillar] for each of the twelve tribes of Israel. [5]Then Moses sent ·young Israelite men [[L]youth of the sons/[T]children of Israel] to offer whole burnt offerings and to sacrifice young bulls as ·fellowship [*or* peace; Lev. 3] offerings to the LORD. [6]Moses put half of the blood of these animals in ·bowls [basins], and he ·sprinkled [*or* dashed] the other half of the blood on the altar. [7]Then he took the Book of the ·Agreement [Covenant; Treaty [C]referring to the laws found in 20:2–23:19] and read it so the people could hear him. And they said, "We will do everything that the LORD has said; we will obey."

[8]Then Moses took ·the blood from the bowls [[L]the blood] and ·sprinkled [dashed] it on the people, saying, "This is the blood ·that begins [[L]of] the ·Agreement [Covenant; Treaty], the ·Agreement [Covenant; Treaty] which the LORD ·has made [[L]cut] with you ·about [*or* in accord with] all these words."

[9]Moses, Aaron, Nadab, Abihu, and seventy of the elders of Israel went up the mountain [10]and saw the God of Israel. Under his feet was a ·surface [pavement] that looked as if it were paved with blue sapphire stones, and it was as clear as the ·sky [heavens]! [11]These ·leaders of the Israelites [[L]eminent men of the sons/[T]children of Israel] saw God, but ·God did not destroy them [[L]he did not send out his hand]. Then they ate and drank together [[C]meals often sealed covenant/treaty agreements].

God Promises Moses the Stone Tablets

[12]The LORD said to Moses, "Come up the mountain to me. Wait there, and I will give you two stone tablets [[C]perhaps two copies of the Ten Commandments]. On these are the ·teachings [laws; instructions] and the commands I have written to instruct the people."

[13]So Moses and his ·helper [assistant] Joshua ·set out [[L]got up], and Moses went up to ·Sinai, the mountain of God [[L]the mountain of God]. [14]Moses said to the elders, "Wait here for us until we come back to you. Aaron and Hur are with you, and anyone who ·has a disagreement with others [has many words/a dispute; [L]is a master of words] can take it to them."

Moses Meets with God

[15]When Moses went up on the mountain, the cloud [[C]representing God's presence] covered it. [16]The glory of the LORD [[C]representing his manifest presence] ·came down [[L]settled] on Mount Sinai, and the cloud covered it for six days. On the seventh day the LORD called to Moses from inside the cloud. [17]To the ·Israelites [[L]sons/[T]children of Israel] the glory of the LORD looked like a fire burning on top of the mountain. [18]Then Moses went into the cloud and went higher up the mountain. He was on the mountain for forty days and forty nights.

Gifts for the Lord

25 The LORD said to Moses, [2]"Tell the ·Israelites [[L]sons/[T]children of Israel] to bring me ·gifts [tribute]. Receive for me the ·gifts [tribute] ·each person wants [[L]from each one whose heart moves them] to give. [3]·These are the gifts [This is the tribute] that you should receive from them: gold, silver, bronze; [4]blue, purple, and ·red [scarlet] thread; fine linen, goat hair, [5]·sheepskins [*or* ramskins] that are dyed red; ·fine leather [*or* sea cow/porpoise hide]; acacia wood; [6]olive oil to burn in the lamps; spices for sweet-smelling incense, and the special olive oil ·poured on a person's head to make him a priest [[L]for anointing; Ps. 133]; [7]onyx stones, and other jewels to be put on the ·holy vest [ephod; 28:6–14] and the ·chest covering [breastpiece; 28:15–30].

8"The people must build a ·holy place [sanctuary] for me so that I can live among them. 9Build this ·Holy Tent [Tabernacle] and ·everything in it [all its furniture] by the ·plan [pattern] I will show you [Cevery detail reflects a heavenly reality].

The Ark of the Covenant

10"·Use acacia wood and build an Ark [LThey will make an Ark of acacia wood; Cthe Ark, considered the footstool of God's throne, was a powerful symbol of God's presence; 1 Sam. 4] ·forty-five inches [Ltwo and a half cubits] long, ·twenty-seven inches [La cubit and a half] wide, and ·twenty-seven inches [La cubit and a half] high. 11·Cover the Ark [LOverlay it] inside and out with pure gold, and put a gold ·strip [molding] all around it. 12·Make [Cast] four gold rings for the Ark and attach them to its four feet, two rings on ·each [one side and two rings on the other] side. 13Then make poles from acacia wood and ·cover [cast; overlay] them with gold. 14Put the poles through the rings on the sides of the Ark, and use these poles to carry it. 15These poles must always stay in the rings of the Ark. Do not take them out. 16Then put in the Ark the ·Agreement [Covenant; Treaty; LTestimony] which I will make with you [Ca reference to the tablets of the Ten Commandments].

17"Then make the ·lid of the Ark [mercy seat; atonement cover] of pure gold. Make it ·forty-five inches [Ltwo and a half cubits] long and ·twenty-seven inches [Lone and a half cubits] wide. 18·Then hammer gold to make two creatures with wings [Make two cherubim of hammered gold], and put one on each end of the ·lid [mercy seat; atonement cover]. 19Attach one ·creature [cherub] on one end of the ·lid [mercy seat; atonement cover] and the other ·creature [cherub] on the other end. Make them to be one piece with the ·lid [mercy seat; atonement cover] at the ends. 20The ·creatures' [cherubim's] wings should be spread upward, covering the ·lid [mercy seat; atonement cover], and the ·creatures [cherubim] are to face each other across the ·lid [mercy seat; atonement cover]. 21Put this ·lid [mercy seat; atonement cover] on top of the Ark, and put in the Ark the ·Agreement [Covenant; Treaty; LTestimony] which I will make with you. 22I will meet with you there, above the ·lid [mercy seat; atonement cover] between the two ·winged creatures [cherubim] on the Ark of the ·Agreement [Covenant; Treaty; LTestimony]. There I will give you all my commands for the ·Israelites [Lsons/Tchildren of Israel].

The Table

23"Make a table out of acacia wood, ·thirty-six inches [Ltwo cubits] long, ·eighteen inches [Lone cubit] wide, and ·twenty-seven inches [Lone and a half cubits] high. 24·Cover [Overlay] it with pure gold, and put a gold ·strip [molding] around it. 25Make a ·frame [rim] ·three inches [La handbreadth] high ·that stands up all around the edge, and put a gold ·strip [molding] around it. 26Then make four gold rings. Attach them to the four corners of the table where the four legs are. 27Put the rings close to the ·frame [rim] around the top of the table, because they will hold the poles for carrying it. 28Make the poles out of acacia wood, ·cover [overlay] them with gold, and carry the table with these poles. 29Make the plates and bowls for the table, as well as the jars and cups, out of pure gold. They will be used for pouring out the drink offerings [Ezra 1:9–11; Dan. 1:2; 5:1–4]. 30On this table put the ·bread that shows you are in my presence [Bread of Presence] so that it is always there in front of me.

The Lampstand

31"Hammer pure gold to make a ·lampstand [Lmenorah]. Its base, ·stand [shaft], flower-like cups, buds, and petals must all be joined together in one

piece [Cits tree shape suggests that the Tabernacle represented Eden where
God and humans lived in harmony]. 32The lampstand must have six
branches going out from its sides—three on one side and three on the
other. 33Each branch must have three cups shaped like almond flowers on
it. Each cup must have a bud and a petal. Each of the six branches going out
from the lampstand must be the same. 34And there must be four more cups
made like almond flowers on the lampstand itself. These cups must also
have buds and petals. 35Put a bud under each pair of branches that goes out
from the lampstand. Each of the six branches going out from the lampstand must be the same. 36The branches, buds, and lampstand must be
made of one piece, hammered out of pure gold.
37"Then make seven ·small oil lamps [Llamps for it] and put them on
the lampstand so that they give light to the area in front of it. 38The ·wick
trimmers [snuffers] and trays must be made of pure gold. 39Use ·seventy-
five pounds [Lone talent] of pure gold to make the lampstand and
everything with it. 40Be very careful to make them by the ·plan [pattern]
I showed you on the mountain [25:9].

The Holy Tent

26 "Make for the ·Holy Tent [Tabernacle] ten curtains of fine
linen and blue, purple, and ·red [scarlet] thread. Have a skilled
craftsman sew designs of ·creatures with wings [cherubim; 37:7] on the
pieces of cloth [Cthese deep blue curtains with cherubim represent heaven
on earth]. 2Make each curtain the same size—·forty-two feet [Ltwenty-
eight cubits] long and ·six feet [Lfour cubits] wide. 3·Sew [LJoin; Bind] five
curtains together for one set, and ·sew [join; bind] the other curtains
together for the second set. 4Make loops of blue cloth on the edge of the
end curtain of one set, and do the same for the end curtain of the other
set. 5Make fifty loops on the end curtain of the first set and fifty loops
on the end curtain of the second set. These loops must be opposite each
other. 6And make fifty gold ·hooks [clasps] to join the two sets of curtains so that the ·Holy Tent [Tabernacle] is one piece.
7"Then make another tent that will cover the ·Holy Tent [Tabernacle],
using eleven curtains made from goat hair. 8All these curtains must be
the same size—·forty-five feet [Lthirty cubits] long and ·six [Lfour cubits]
feet wide. 9·Sew [Join; Bind] five of the curtains together into one set.
Then ·sew [join; bind] the other six curtains together into the second set.
Fold the sixth curtain double over the front of the Tent. 10Make fifty loops
down the edge of the end curtain of one set, and do the same for the end
curtain of the other set. 11Then make fifty bronze ·hooks [clasps] and put
them in the loops to ·join [bind] the tent together so that the covering is
one piece. 12Let the extra half piece of cloth hang over the back of the
·Holy Tent [Tabernacle]. 13There will be ·eighteen inches [Lone cubit]
hanging over the sides of the ·Holy Tent [Tabernacle], to ·protect [cover]
it [Cthis is the innermost of the weatherproofing protecting the innermost
curtain]. 14Make a covering for the ·Holy Tent [Tabernacle] from ·sheep-
skins colored red [*or* tanned rams' skins; Cthe second weatherproof
covering], and over that make a covering from ·fine leather [*or* sea cow
hide; Cthe outermost covering used for weatherproofing].
15"Use acacia wood to make upright frames for the ·Holy Tent
[Tabernacle]. 16Each frame must be ·fifteen feet [Lten cubits] long and
·twenty-seven inches [La cubit and a half] wide, 17with two pegs side by
side. Every frame [Lof the Holy Tent/Tabernacle] must be made the same

way. 18Make twenty frames for the south side of the ·Holy Tent [Tabernacle]. 19Each frame must have two silver bases to go under it, a peg fitting into each base. You must make forty silver bases for the [Ltwenty] frames. 20Make twenty more frames for the [Lsecond side on the] north side of the ·Holy Tent [Tabernacle] 21and forty silver bases for them—two bases for each frame. 22You must make six frames for the rear or west end of the ·Holy Tent [Tabernacle] 23and two frames for each corner at the rear [Lof the Holy Tent/Tabernacle]. 24The two frames are to be doubled at the bottom and joined at the top with a metal ring. Both corner frames must be made this way. 25So there will be a total of eight frames at the rear of the Tent, and there will be sixteen silver bases—two bases under each frame.

26"Make crossbars of acacia wood to connect the upright frames of the ·Holy Tent [Tabernacle]. Make five crossbars to hold the frames together on one side 27and five to hold the frames together on the ·other [Lsecond] side. Also make five crossbars to hold the frames together on the west end, at the rear. 28The middle crossbar is to be set halfway up the frames, and it is to run along the entire length of each side and rear. 29Make gold rings on the sides of the frames to hold the crossbars, and ·cover [overlay] the frames and the crossbars with gold. 30Set up the ·Holy Tent [Tabernacle] by the ·plan [pattern] shown to you on the mountain [25:9].

31"Make a curtain of fine linen and blue, purple, and ·red [scarlet] thread, and have a skilled craftsman sew ·designs of creatures with wings [cherubim; 37:7] on it. 32·Hang [Place] the curtain by gold ·hooks [clasps] on four posts of acacia wood that are ·covered [overlaid] with gold, and set them in four silver bases. 33·Hang [Place] the curtain from the ·hooks [clasps] in the roof, and put the Ark of the ·Agreement [Covenant; Treaty; LTestimony; 25:10] containing the two stone tablets [24:12] behind it. This curtain will separate the ·Holy Place [Tabernacle] from the ·Most Holy Place [THoly of Holies; Cthe back third, the throne room of God]. 34Put the ·lid [mercy seat; atonement cover; 25:13–22] on the Ark of the ·Agreement [Covenant; Treaty; LTestimony; 25:10] in the Most Holy Place.

35"Outside the curtain, put the table [25:23–30] on the north side of the ·Holy Tent [Tabernacle]. Put the lampstand [25:31–40] on the south side of the ·Holy Tent [Tabernacle] across from the table.

The Entrance of the Holy Tent

36"Then, for the entrance of the Tent, make a ·curtain [Lscreen] with fine linen and blue, purple, and ·red [scarlet] thread. ·Someone who can sew well is to sew designs on it [L…embroidered with needlework]. 37Make five posts of acacia wood ·covered [overlaid] with gold. Make gold ·hooks [clasps] for them on which to hang the ·curtain [Lscreen], and make five bronze bases for them.

The Altar for Burnt Offerings

27 "Make an altar of acacia wood, ·four and one-half feet [Lthree cubits] high. It should be square—·seven and one-half feet [Lfive cubits] long and ·seven and one-half feet [Lfive cubits] wide. 2Make each of the four corners of the altar stick out like a horn [Csignificance uncertain, but refers to rounded projections on each corner of top; 29:10–12; Lev. 4:18–21; 1 Kin. 2:28–34], in such a way that the corners with their horns are all one piece. Then ·cover [overlay] the whole altar with bronze.

3"Use bronze to make all ·the tools and dishes that will be used on the altar [Lits utensils]: the pots to remove the ashes, the shovels, the ·bowls

for sprinkling blood [Lbasins], the meat forks, and the ·pans for carrying
the burning wood [firepans].
4“Make a large bronze screen to hold the burning wood, and put a
bronze ring at each of the four corners of it. 5Put the screen inside the
altar, under its ·rim [ledge], halfway up from the bottom [Lof the altar].
6“Make poles of acacia wood for the altar, and ·cover [overlay] them
with bronze. 7Put the poles through the rings on both sides of the altar to
carry it. 8Make the altar out of boards and leave the inside hollow. Make
it as you were shown on the mountain [25:9].

The Courtyard of the Holy Tent

9“Make ·a wall of curtains to form a courtyard around the Holy Tent
[Lthe court of the Tabernacle]. The south side should have a wall of fine
linen curtains ·one hundred fifty feet [Lone hundred cubits] long. 10Hang
the curtains with silver hooks and bands on twenty bronze ·posts [pillars]
with twenty bronze bases. 11The north side must also be ·one hundred fifty
feet [Lone hundred cubits] long. Hang its curtains on silver hooks and
bands on twenty bronze ·posts [pillars] with twenty bronze bases.
12“The west end of the courtyard must have a wall of curtains ·seventy-
five feet [Lfifty cubits] long, with ten ·posts [pillars] and ten bases on that
wall. 13The [Lfront on the] east end of the courtyard must also be ·sev-
enty-five feet [Lfifty cubits] long. 14On one side of the entry, there is to be
a wall of curtains ·twenty-two and one-half feet [Lfifteen cubits] long,
held up by three ·posts [pillars] on three bases. 15On the other side of the
entry, there is also to be a wall of curtains ·twenty-two and one-half feet
[Lfifteen cubits] long, held up by three ·posts [pillars] on three bases.
16“The ·entry [Lgate] to the courtyard is to be a ·curtain [screen] ·thirty
feet [Ltwenty cubits] wide, made of fine linen with blue, purple, and ·red
[scarlet] thread. ·Someone who can sew well is to sew designs on it [L…
embroidered with needlework]. It is to be held up by four ·posts [pillars]
on four bases. 17All the ·posts [pillars] around the courtyard must have
silver bands and hooks and bronze bases. 18The courtyard must be ·one
hundred fifty feet [Lone hundred cubits] long and ·seventy-five feet [Lfifty
cubits] wide, with a wall of curtains around it ·seven and one-half feet
[Lfive cubits] high, made of fine linen. The bases in which the ·posts [pil-
lars] are set must be bronze. 19All the ·things used in the Holy Tent
[utensils of the Tabernacle] and all the tent pegs for the ·Holy Tent
[Tabernacle] and the wall around the courtyard must be made of bronze.

Oil for the Lamp

20“Command the ·people [Lsons/Tchildren] of Israel to bring you pure
olive oil, made from ·pressed [*or* pounded] olives, to keep the lamps on
the lampstand burning [Lregularly; *or* continually]. 21Aaron and his sons
must keep the lamps burning before the LORD from evening till morning.
This will be in the Meeting Tent, outside the curtain which is in front of
the ·Ark [Covenant; Testimony; Treaty]. The Israelites and their descendants must obey this ·rule [statute; ordinance; requirement] ·from now
on [Lthroughout their generations].

Clothes for the Priests

28 “·Tell your brother Aaron to come [LBring near your brother
Aaron] to you, along with his sons Nadab, Abihu, Eleazar,
and Ithamar. ·Separate them from the other Israelites to [L…to] serve
me as priests. 2Make holy ·clothes [garments; vestments] for your
brother Aaron to give him ·honor [glory] and ·beauty [splendor]. 3Tell
all the ·skilled craftsmen to whom I have given wisdom [Lthe wise of

heart whom I have filled with the spirit of wisdom; [Cwisdom here is a practical knowledge, a skill] to make ·special clothes [garments; vestments] for Aaron—clothes to show that he ·belongs to me [is consecrated/ set apart/ holy] so that he may serve me as a priest. 4These are the clothes they must make: a ·chest covering [breastpiece], a ·holy vest [ephod], an outer robe, a ·woven inner [*or* checkered] robe, a turban, and a ·cloth belt [sash]. They must make these ·holy [sacred] clothes for your brother Aaron and his sons. Then they may serve me as priests. 5They must use gold and blue, purple and ·red [scarlet] thread, and fine linen.

The Holy Vest

6"Use gold and blue, purple and ·red [scarlet] thread, and fine linen to make the ·holy vest [ephod]; ·skilled craftsmen are to make it [skillfully worked]. 7At each top corner of it there will be a pair of shoulder straps tied together over each shoulder.

8"·The craftsmen will very carefully weave a belt [LThe embroidered waistband] on the ·holy vest that is [Lephod will be] made with the same materials—gold and blue, purple and ·red [scarlet] thread, and fine linen.

9"Take two onyx stones and write the names of the twelve sons of Israel on them, 10six on one stone and six on the other. Write the names in order, ·from the oldest son to the youngest [according to the order of their birth]. 11·Carve [Engrave] the names of the sons of Israel on these stones in the same way a person ·carves words and designs on a seal [engraves a seal/ signet]. Put gold [Lfiligree] around the stones to hold them on the ·holy vest [ephod]. 12Then put the two stones on the two straps of the ·holy vest [ephod] as reminders of the twelve sons of Israel. Aaron is to ·wear [bear] their names on his shoulders in the presence of the LORD as reminders of the sons of Israel. 13Make ·two gold pieces to hold the stones [settings of gold filigree] 14and two chains of pure gold, twisted together like a rope. Attach the chains to the ·two gold pieces that hold the stones [Lsettings].

The Chest Covering

15"Make a ·chest covering to help in making decisions [Lbreastpiece of judgment; Cso called because it contained the Urim and Thummim used to discern God's will; 28:30]. ·The craftsmen should make it as they made the holy vest [L...of skilled work like the ephod], using gold and blue, purple and ·red [scarlet] thread, and fine linen. 16It must be square—·nine inches [La span] long and ·nine inches [La span] wide—and ·folded double to make a pocket [Ldoubled]. 17Put four rows of ·beautiful gems [Lstones] on it: The first row must have a ·ruby [*or* carnelian], ·topaz [*or* chrysolite], and ·yellow quartz [*or* emerald]; 18the second must have turquoise, a ·sapphire [*or* lapis], and an ·emerald [*or* moonstone]; 19the third must have a jacinth, an agate, and an amethyst; 20the fourth must have a chrysolite [*or* beryl], an onyx, and a jasper [Cthe exact identity of some of these stones is unclear]. Put gold [Lfiligree] around these ·jewels [stones] to attach them to it. 21There must be twelve ·jewels on the chest covering [Lstones]—one ·jewel [stone] for each of the names of the sons of Israel. ·Carve [Engrave] the name of one of the twelve tribes on each of the stones as you would ·carve [engrave] a ·seal [signet].

22"Make chains of pure gold, twisted together like rope, for the ·chest covering [breastpiece]. 23Make two gold rings and put them on the two upper corners of the chest covering. 24Attach the two gold chains to the two rings at the upper corners of the ·chest covering [breastpiece]. 25Attach the other ends of the two chains to the two ·gold pieces [*or* settings] on the shoulder straps in the front of the ·holy vest [ephod].

26“Make two gold rings and put them at the two lower corners of the
·chest covering [breastpiece], on the inside edge next to the ·holy vest
[ephod]. 27Make two more gold rings and attach them to the bottom of
the shoulder straps in the front of the ·holy vest [ephod]. Put them close
to the seam above the ·woven belt [Lembroidered waistband] of the ·holy
vest [ephod]. 28Join the rings of the ·chest covering [breastpiece] to the
rings of the ·holy vest [ephod] with blue ·ribbon [cord], connecting it to
the ·woven belt [embroidered waistband] so the ·chest covering [breast-
piece] will not ·swing out [get loose] from the ·holy vest [ephod].

29“When Aaron enters the Holy Place, he will wear the names of the
sons of Israel over his heart, on the ·chest covering that helps in making
decisions [breastpiece of judgment; 28:15]. This will be a continual
reminder before the Lord. 30And put the Urim and Thummim [Cdevices,
probably lots, that were used to discern God’s will; the name means “light
and truth”] inside the ·chest covering [breastpiece] so that they will be on
Aaron’s heart when he goes before the Lord. They will help in making
decisions for the Israelites. So Aaron will always carry them with him
when he is before the Lord.

31“Make the outer robe ·to be worn under the holy vest [Lof the ephod],
·using only blue cloth [Lall of blue]. 32Make ·a hole [an opening] in the
center for ·Aaron’s [Lthe] head, with a woven collar ·with an oversewn
edge [Llike a coat of mail; Cthe Hebrew is obscure] around the ·hole [open-
ing] so it will not tear. 33Make balls like pomegranates of blue, purple,
and ·red [scarlet] thread, and hang them around the bottom of the outer
robe with gold bells between them. 34All around the bottom of the outer
robe there should be a gold bell and a pomegranate ball, a gold bell and a
pomegranate ball. 35Aaron must wear this robe when he ·serves as priest
[ministers]. ·The ringing of the bells [LTheir sound] will be heard when
he enters and leaves the Holy Place before the Lord so that he will not die.

36“Make a ·strip [rosette; medallion; plate; Lflower] of pure gold and
·carve [engrave] these words on it as you would ·carve [engrave] a ·seal
[signet]: ‘Holy to the Lord.’ 37Use blue ·ribbon [cord] to tie it to the turban; put it on the front of the turban. 38Aaron must wear this on his
forehead. In this way, he will ·be blamed [Lcarry/bear the guilt] if anything is wrong with the ·gifts [holy offerings] of the Israelites. ·Aaron
must always wear this on his head [LIt will always be on his forehead] so
the Lord will ·accept the gifts of the people [Lbe favorable toward them].

39“·Make [*or* Weave] the ·woven [*or* checkered] inner robe of fine linen,
and make the turban of fine linen also. Make the ·cloth belt [sash] ·with
designs sewn on it [embroidered with needlework]. 40Also make ·woven
[*or* checkered] inner robes, ·cloth belts [sashes], and ·headbands [head-
dresses] for Aaron’s sons, to give them honor [glory] and beauty
[splendor]. 41Put these clothes on your brother Aaron and his sons, and
·pour olive oil on their heads to appoint them as priests [Lanoint them].
·Make them belong to me [Ordain them; LFill their hand] so they may be
·set apart [consecrated] and serve me as priests.

42“Make for them linen underclothes to cover ·them [Ltheir naked
flesh] from the ·waist [hip] to the ·upper parts of the legs [thigh]. 43Aaron
and his sons must wear these underclothes when they enter the Meeting
Tent and anytime they come near the altar to ·serve as priests [Lminister]
in the Holy Place. ·If they do not wear these clothes, they will be guilty of
wrong, and they will [L...so they do not bear guilt and] die. This will be a

·law [statute; ordinance; requirement] that will last from now on for Aaron and all his ·descendants [Lseed].

Appointing the Priests

29 "This is what you must do to ·appoint Aaron and his sons [Lthem to consecrate them] to serve me as priests. Take one young bull and two ·male sheep [rams] ·that have nothing wrong with them [Lwithout blemish]. 2Use ·fine [choice] wheat flour ·without yeast to make bread [to make unleavened bread], cakes ·without yeast [unleavened] mixed with olive oil, and wafers ·without yeast [unleavened] brushed with olive oil. 3Put these in one basket, and bring them along with the bull and two ·male sheep [rams]. 4Bring Aaron and his sons to the entrance of the Meeting Tent and wash them with water. 5Take the clothes and dress Aaron in the inner robe [28:39–41] and the outer robe [28:31–35] of the ·holy vest [ephod; 28:6–14]. Then put on him the ·holy vest [ephod] and the ·chest covering [breastpiece; 28:15–28], and tie the ·holy vest [ephod] on him with its ·skillfully woven belt [embroidered waistband of the ephod]. 6Put the turban on his head, and put the holy ·crown [diadem] on the turban. 7Take the special olive oil and pour it on his head to ·make him a priest [Lanoint him].

8"Then bring his sons and put the inner robes on them. 9·Put [LGird them with] the ·headbands [headdresses] on their heads, and tie ·cloth belts around their waists [Lsashes on Aaron and his sons]. ·Aaron and his descendants [LThey] will be priests in Israel, according to a ·rule that will continue from now on [perpetual statute/ordinance/requirement]. This is how you will ·appoint Aaron and his sons as priests [ordain Aaron and his sons; Lfill the hand of Aaron and his sons].

10"Bring the bull to the front of the Meeting Tent, and Aaron and his sons must ·put [lay] their hands on the bull's head [Ca ritual of identification; the animal stood in the place of the offerer]. 11Then ·kill [slaughter] the bull before the Lord at the entrance to the Meeting Tent. 12Use your finger to put some of the bull's blood on the ·corners [Lhorns; 27:2] of the altar, and then pour the blood that is left at the ·bottom [base; foundation] of the altar. 13Take all the fat that covers the inner organs, as well as the ·best part [appendage] of the liver, both kidneys, and the fat around them, and ·burn them [Lturn them into smoke] on the altar. 14Take the bull's meat, skin, and ·intestines [*or* dung], and burn them outside the camp. This is an ·offering to take away sin [sin offering; Lev. 4:1–5:13].

15"Take one of the ·male sheep [rams], and have Aaron and his sons ·put [lay] their hands on its head. 16·Kill [Slaughter] it, and take its blood and ·sprinkle [dash] it on all four sides of the altar. 17Then cut the ram into pieces and wash its inner organs and its legs, putting them with its head and its other pieces. 18·Burn [LTurn into smoke] the whole sheep on the altar; it is a burnt offering made by fire [Lev. 1] to the Lord. Its smell is pleasing to the Lord.

19"Take the ·other male sheep [second ram], and have Aaron and his sons ·put [lay] their hands on its head [29:10]. 20·Kill [Slaughter] it and take some of its blood. Put the blood on the ·bottom [lobe] of the right ears of Aaron and his sons and on the thumbs of their right hands and on the big toes of their right feet [Lev. 14:14; Cthe significance is unclear]. Then sprinkle the rest of the blood ·against all four sides of [Lall around] the altar. 21Take some of the blood from the altar, and mix it with the ·special oil used in appointing priests [Lanointing oil]. Sprinkle this on Aaron and his clothes and on his sons and their clothes. ·This will show that Aaron [LThen he] and his sons and their clothes ·are given to my service [Lwill be holy/consecrated].

22"Then take the fat from the ·male sheep [ram], the fat tail, and the fat that covers the inner organs. In addition, take the best part of the liver, both kidneys, and the fat around them, and the right thigh. (This is the ·male sheep to be used in appointing priests [ordination ram].)

23"Then take the basket of ·bread that you made without yeast [unleavened bread], which you put before the LORD. From it take a loaf of bread, a cake made with olive oil, and a wafer. 24Put all of these in the hands of Aaron and his sons, and tell them to ·present them as an [Lwave them as a wave] offering to the LORD [Ca ritual whereby the offerer symbolically waves the offering before God but then uses it]. 25Then take them from their hands and ·burn them [Lturn them into smoke] on the altar with the whole burnt offering. This is an offering made by fire to the LORD; its smell is pleasing to the LORD. 26Then take the breast of the ·male sheep used to appoint Aaron as priest [ordination ram], and ·present it before the LORD as an offering [Lwave it as a wave offering before the LORD]. This part of the animal will be your ·share [portion]. 27·Set aside [Consecrate] the breast [Lthat was waved as a wave offering] and the thigh of the ·sheep that were used to appoint [Lordination ram that was elevated as an elevation offering for] Aaron and his sons as priests. These parts belong to them. 28They are to be the ·regular share [perpetual statute/ordinance/requirement] which the Israelites will always give to Aaron and his sons. It is the gift the Israelites must give to the LORD from their ·fellowship [*or* peace] offerings [Lev. 3].

29"The ·holy [sacred; consecrated] clothes made for Aaron will belong to his ·descendants [sons] so that they can wear these clothes when they are ·appointed as priests [Lanointed and ordained]. 30Aaron's son, who will become high priest after him, will come to the Meeting Tent to ·serve [minister] in the Holy Place. He is to wear these clothes for seven days.

31"Take the ·male sheep used to appoint priests [ordination ram] and boil its meat in a place that is holy. 32Then at the entrance of the Meeting Tent, Aaron and his sons must eat the meat of the ·sheep [ram] and the bread that is in the basket. 33They should eat these offerings that were used to ·remove their sins [atone] and to ·make them holy when they were made priests [ordain and consecrate]. But no ·stranger [outsider] is to eat them, because they are holy things. 34If any of the ·meat from that sheep [Lordination meat] or any of the bread is left the next morning, it must be burned. It must not be eaten, because it is holy.

35"Do all these things that I commanded you to do to Aaron and his sons, and spend seven days ·appointing [ordaining] them. 36Each day you are to offer a bull ·to remove the sins of [Las a sin offering of atonement for] Aaron and his sons so they will be given for service to the LORD. ·Make the altar ready for service to the LORD [LOffer a sin offering for the altar to make atonement for it], and also ·pour oil on it to make it holy [anoint it to consecrate it]. 37Spend seven days making ·the altar ready for service to God [Latonement for the altar] and ·making it holy [consecrate it]. Then the altar will become very holy, and anything that touches it must be holy.

The Daily Sacrifices

38"Every day ·from now on [regularly; continually], offer on the altar two lambs that are one year old. 39Offer one lamb in the morning and the ·other [second] in the evening ·before dark [at twilight]. 40·In the morning,

when you offer the [LFor the] first lamb, offer also ·two quarts [La tenth of
an ephah] of fine flour mixed with ·one quart [Lone fourth of a hin] of oil
from ·pressed [or pounded] olives. Pour out a ·quart [Lfourth of a hin] of
wine as a drink offering. 41Offer the second lamb ·in the evening [at twi-
light] with the same ·grain [or gift; tribute] offering [Lev. 3] and drink
offering as you did in the morning. This is an offering made by fire to the
LORD, and its smell is pleasing to him.
42"·You must burn these things as an offering [LIt is a burnt offering;
Lev. 1] to the LORD ·every day [regularly; continuously], ·from now on
[Lthroughout your generations], at the entrance of the Meeting Tent before
the LORD. ·When you make the offering, [L…where] I, the LORD, will meet
you there and speak to you. 43I will meet with the ·people [Lsons; children]
of Israel there, and that place will be holy because of my glory.
44"So I will make the Meeting Tent and the altar ·holy [consecrated]; I
will also make Aaron and his sons ·holy [consecrated] so they may serve
me as priests. 45I will ·live [dwell] with the ·people [Lsons; children] of
Israel and be their God. 46And they will know that I am the LORD their
God who ·led [brought] them out of Egypt so that I could ·live [dwell]
with them. I am the LORD their God.

The Altar for Burning Incense

30 "Make an altar out of acacia wood for burning incense.
2Make it square—·eighteen inches [La cubit] long and ·eigh-
teen inches [La cubit] wide—and make it ·thirty-six inches [Ltwo cubits]
high. The ·corners that stick out like horns [Lhorns; 27:2] must be one
piece with the altar. 3·Cover [LOverlay] its top, its sides, and its ·corners
[Lhorns] with pure gold, and put a gold ·strip [molding] all around the
altar. 4Make two gold rings beneath the gold ·strip [molding] on opposite sides of the altar, and slide poles through them to carry the altar.
5Make the poles from acacia wood and ·cover [overlay] them with gold.
6Put the altar of incense in front of the curtain that is ·near [or above]
the Ark of the ·Agreement [Covenant; Treaty; LTestimony; 25:10], in
front of the ·lid that covers that Ark [mercy seat; atonement cover; 25:17–
22]. There I will meet with you.
7"Aaron must burn sweet-smelling incense on the altar every morning
when he comes to ·take care of [trim; dress; put in good order] the oil
lamps. 8He must burn incense again ·in the evening [at twilight] when he
lights the lamps, so incense will burn before the LORD ·every day [regu-
larly; continually] ·from now on [Lthroughout your generations]. 9Do not
use this altar for offering ·any other [Lstrange; profane] incense [Lev.
10:1–7], or burnt offering [Lev. 1], or any kind of ·grain [or gift; tribute]
offering [Lev. 3], or drink offering. 10Once a year Aaron must make ·the
altar ready for service to God by putting blood on its corners [atonement
on its corners/horns]—the blood of the animal ·offered to remove sins
[as an atoning sin offering]. He is to do this once a year ·from now on
[Lthroughout your generations]. ·This altar belongs completely to the
LORD's service [LIt is most holy/Tthe holy of holies to the LORD]."

The Tax for the Meeting Tent

11The LORD said to Moses, 12"When you ·count [register] the ·people
[Lsons; children] of Israel, every person must ·buy back [ransom; atone
for] his life from the LORD so that no ·terrible things [disaster; plague] will
happen to the people when you ·number [register] them. 13Every person
who is ·counted [registered] must pay ·one-fifth of an ounce of silver [Lhalf
a shekel]. (·This is set by using one-half of the Holy Place measure, which

weighs two-fifths of an ounce [L...according to the shekel of the Holy Place which is twenty gerahs].) This amount is a ·gift [contribution] to the LORD. 14Every person who is ·counted [registered] and is twenty years old or older must give this ·amount [gift; contribution] to the LORD. 15A rich person must not give more than ·one-fifth of an ounce [La half shekel], and a poor person must not give less. You are ·paying this to the LORD to buy back your lives [giving a gift/contribution to the LORD as a ransom/atonement for your life]. 16·Gather [Take] from the ·people [Lsons; children] of Israel this ·money [silver] paid to ·buy back their lives [Latone; ransom], and ·spend [give] it on things for the ·service [work] in the Meeting Tent. This payment will remind the LORD that the ·Israelites' [Lsons/Tchildren of Israel's] lives have been ·bought back [ransomed; atoned]."

The Bronze Bowl

17The LORD said to Moses, 18"Make a bronze bowl, on a bronze stand, for washing. Put the bowl and stand between the Meeting Tent and the altar, and put water ·in the bowl [Lthere]. 19Aaron and his sons must wash their hands and feet with the water from this bowl. 20Each time they enter the Meeting Tent they must wash with water so they will not die. Whenever they approach the altar to ·serve as priests [minister] and offer a sacrifice to the LORD by fire, 21they must wash their hands and their feet so they will not die. This is a ·rule [statute; ordinance; requirement] for Aaron and his ·descendants [Lseed] ·from now on [Lthroughout their generations]."

Oil for Appointing

22Then the LORD said to Moses, 23"Take the finest spices: ·twelve pounds [Lfive hundred (shekels)] of liquid myrrh, half that amount (that is, ·six pounds [Ltwo hundred and fifty]) of sweet-smelling cinnamon, ·six pounds [Ltwo hundred and fifty] of sweet-smelling cane, 24and ·twelve pounds [Lfive hundred] of cassia. Weigh all these by the Holy Place ·measure [Lshekel]. Also take ·four quarts [La hin] of olive oil, 25and ·mix [blend; Lmake] all these things like a perfume to make a holy olive oil. ·This special oil must be put on people and things to make them ready for service to God [LIt is a holy anointing oil]. 26·Put this oil on [LAnoint] the Meeting Tent and the Ark of the ·Agreement [Covenant; Treaty; LTestimony], 27on the table and all its dishes, on the lampstand [25:31–40] and all its tools, and on the incense altar [30:1–6]. 28Also, ·put the oil on [anoint] the altar for burnt offerings [27:1–8] and on all its tools, as well as on the bowl [30:17–21] and the stand under the bowl. 29You will ·prepare all these things for service to God [consecrate/sanctify them], and they will be very holy. Anything that touches these things must be holy.

30"·Put the oil on [Anoint] Aaron and his sons to ·give them for service to me [consecrate; sanctify them], that they may serve me as priests. 31Tell the ·Israelites [Lsons/Tchildren of Israel], 'This is to be my holy olive oil ·from now on [Lthroughout your generations]. It is ·to be put on people and things to make them ready for service to God [Lfor anointing]. 32Do not pour it on the bodies of ordinary people, and do not make perfume the same way you make this oil. It is holy, and you must treat it as holy. 33If anyone makes perfume like it or puts it on someone who is ·not a priest [not qualified; Lstrange], that person must be cut off from his people.'"

Incense

34Then the LORD said to Moses, "Take these sweet-smelling spices: resin, onycha, galbanum [Csome identifications are uncertain], and pure frankincense. Be sure that you have equal amounts of each. 35Make incense as a person who makes perfume would do. Add salt to it to keep it pure and holy. [36]Beat some of the incense into a fine powder, and put it in front of the ·Ark of the Agreement [Covenant; Testimony; Treaty] in the Meeting Tent, where I will meet with you. ·You must use this incense powder only for its very special purpose [[L]It will be most holy to you]. [37]Do not make incense for yourselves the same way you make this incense. Treat it as holy to the LORD. [38]Whoever makes incense like this to use as perfume must be cut off from his people."

Bezalel and Oholiab Help

31 Then the LORD said to Moses, [2]"See, I have ·chosen [[L]called by name] Bezalel son of Uri from the tribe of Judah. (Uri was the son of Hur.) [3]I have filled Bezalel with the ·Spirit [*or* spirit] of God and have given him the ·skill [wisdom], ability, and knowledge to do all kinds of work. [4]He is able to ·design [plan] pieces to be made from gold, silver, and bronze, [5]to cut jewels and put them in metal, to ·carve [engrave] wood, and to do all kinds of work. [6]I have also ·chosen [[L]given him] Oholiab son of Ahisamach from the tribe of Dan to work with Bezalel. I have given ·skills [wisdom] to all the craftsmen, and they will be able to make all these things I have commanded you: [7]the Meeting Tent, the Ark of the ·Agreement [Covenant; Treaty; [L]Testimony], the ·lid that covers [mercy seat; atonement cover] the Ark, and ·everything in [all the utensils of] the Tent. [8]This includes the table and ·everything on it [all its utensils], the pure gold lampstand and ·everything with it [all its utensils], the altar of incense, [9]the altar for burnt offerings and ·everything used with it [all its utensils], and the bowl and the stand under it. [10]They will make the woven clothes and the ·holy [sacred] clothes for Aaron and the clothes for his sons to wear when they serve as priests. [11]They will also make the special olive oil used ·in appointing people and things to the service of the LORD [[L]for anointing], and the sweet-smelling incense for the Holy Place.

"These workers will make all these things just as I have commanded you."

The Day of Rest

[12]Then the LORD said to Moses, [13]"Tell the ·Israelites [[L]sons/[T]children of Israel], 'You must ·keep the rules about [[L]guard; keep] my Sabbaths, because they will be a sign [[C]reminders of the covenant; 9:13; 17:11] between you and me from now on. In this way you will know that I, the LORD, make you holy.

[14]" '·Make the Sabbath a holy day [[L]Keep/Guard the Sabbath for it is holy]. If anyone ·treats the Sabbath like any other day [profanes/desecrates the Sabbath] that person must be put to death; anyone who works on the Sabbath day must be cut off from his people [20:8–11]. [15]There are six days for working, but the seventh day is a day of rest, a day holy for the LORD. Anyone who works during the Sabbath day must be put to death. [16]The ·Israelites [[L]sons/[T]children of Israel] must ·remember [keep; guard] the Sabbath day as an ·agreement [covenant; treaty] between them and me ·that will continue from now on [[L]throughout their generations]. [17]The Sabbath day will be a sign between me and the ·Israelites [[L]sons/[T]children of Israel] forever, because in six days I, the LORD, made the ·sky [heavens] and the earth. On the seventh day I did not work; I rested [Gen. 2:1–3].' "

[18]When the LORD finished speaking to Moses on Mount Sinai, he gave him the two stone tablets with the ·Agreement [Covenant; Testimony; Treaty] written on them, written by the finger of God.

The People Make a Gold Calf

32 The people saw that ·a long time had passed and Moses had not [LMoses delayed to] come down from the mountain. So they ·gathered [assembled] ·around [*or* against] Aaron and said, "[LThis man] Moses ·led [brought] us out of Egypt, but we don't know what has happened to him. Make us ·gods [*or* a god; *or* an image of God] who will ·lead [Lgo before] us."

2Aaron said to ·the people [Lthem], "·Take [Pull] off the gold earrings that your wives, sons, and daughters are wearing, and bring them to me." 3So all the people ·took [pulled off] their gold earrings and brought them to Aaron. 4He took ·the gold [Lit] from ·the people [Ltheir hands] and formed it ·with a tool [*or* in a mold] and made a ·statue [image] of a calf. Then the people said, "Israel, ·these are your gods [*or* this is your God; Ceither an idol to a false god or an inappropriate image for a false worship of the true God] who brought you out of the land of Egypt [1 Kin. 12:28]!"

5When Aaron saw all this, he built an altar before the calf and announced, "Tomorrow there will be a ·special feast to honor [festival for] the LORD." 6The people got up early the next morning and offered whole burnt offerings [Lev. 1] and ·fellowship [*or* peace] offerings [Lev. 3]. They sat down to eat and drink, and then they ·got up and sinned sexually [got up and amused themselves; Trose up to play; Ca euphemism].

7Then the LORD said to Moses, "Go down from this mountain, because your people, the people you brought out of the land of Egypt, have ·ruined themselves [acted in a debauched/perverse manner]. 8They have quickly turned away from the ·things [path; way] I commanded them to do. They have made for themselves a calf ·covered with gold [Limage], and they have worshiped it and offered sacrifices to it. They have said, 'Israel, ·these are your gods [*or* this is the God; 32:4] who brought you out of Egypt.' "

9The LORD said to Moses, "I have seen these people, and I know that they are ·very stubborn [La stiff-necked people]. 10So now do not stop me. I am so angry with them that I am going to ·destroy [Lconsume] them. Then I will make ·you and your descendants [Lyou] a great nation [Cechoing the promise to Abraham; Gen. 12:1–3]."

11But Moses ·begged [tried to appease] the LORD his God and said, "LORD, ·don't let your anger destroy [Lwhy does your anger burn against…?] your people, whom you brought out of Egypt with your great power and ·strength [La mighty hand]. 12·Don't let [LWhy should…?] the people of Egypt say, 'The LORD brought the Israelites out of Egypt for an evil purpose. He planned to kill them in the mountains and ·destroy [Lwipe] them from the earth.' So ·stop being angry [change your mind; relent], and don't ·destroy [Lbring harm on] your people. 13Remember ·the men who served you [Lyour servants]—Abraham, Isaac, and Israel. You promised with an oath to them and said, 'I will make your ·descendants [seed] as many as the stars in the sky [Gen. 15:5; 22:17; 26:4]. I will give your descendants all this land that I have promised them, and ·it will be theirs [Lthey will inherit it] forever [Gen. 12:1–3].' " 14So the LORD ·changed his mind [relented] and did not ·destroy [Lbring harm on] the people as he had said he might.

15Then Moses went down the mountain, and in his hands he had the two stone tablets with the ·Agreement [Covenant; Testimony; Treaty] on them. The ·commands [Ltablets] were written on both sides of each stone, front and back. 16God himself had made the tablets, and God himself had ·written the commands on [Lengraved] the tablets.

17When Joshua heard the sound of the people shouting, he said to
Moses, "It sounds like war down in the camp."
18Moses answered:
"It is not a shout of victory;
it is not a cry of defeat.
It is the sound of singing that I hear."
19When Moses came close to the camp, he saw the gold calf and the
dancing, and he became very angry. He threw down the stone tablets that
he was carrying and broke them at the bottom of the mountain [Csignifying
the broken covenant]. 20Then he took the calf that they had made and
melted it in the fire. He ground it into powder. Then he ·threw [scattered]
the powder into the water and forced the Israelites to drink it [Cparalleling
an ancient Near Eastern ritual for destroying a statue of a god].
21Moses said to Aaron, "What did these people do to you? Why did you
·cause them to do [Lbring on them] such a terrible sin?"
22Aaron answered, "Don't be angry, ·master [sir]. You know that these
people are always ready to do wrong. 23They said to me, '[LThis man]
Moses ·led [brought] us out of Egypt, but we don't know what has happened to him. Make us ·gods [*or* a god; *or* an image of God] who will ·lead
[Lgo before] us.' 24So I told them. '·Take off your gold jewelry [LWhoever
has gold, pull it off].' When they gave it to me, I threw it into the fire and
out ·came [popped] this calf!"
25Moses saw that the people were ·acting wildly [out of control]. Aaron
had let them ·get out of control [act wildly] and become ·fools [the object
of slander] in front of their enemies. 26So Moses stood at the ·entrance
[Lgate] to the camp and said, "·Let anyone who wants to follow [LWhoever
is for] the LORD come to me." And all the ·people from the family of [Lsons
of] Levi gathered around Moses.
27Then Moses said to them, "The LORD, the God of Israel, says this:
'Every man must put on his sword and go through the camp from ·one
end to the other [Lgate to gate]. Each man must kill his brother, his friend,
and his neighbor.' " 28The ·people from the family [Lsons] of Levi obeyed
Moses, and that day about three thousand of the Israelites died. 29Then
Moses said, "Today you have been ·given for service [ordained; Cto the
priesthood] to the LORD. You were willing to kill your own sons and
brothers, and God has blessed you for this."
30The next day Moses told the people, "You have ·done [Lsinned] a terrible
sin. But now I will go up to the LORD. Maybe I can ·do something so your sins
will be removed [make atonement for your sin]." 31So Moses went back to
the LORD and said, "How terribly these people have sinned! They have made
for themselves ·gods [*or* a god; 32:4] from gold. 32Now, please forgive them
of this sin. If you will not, then ·erase [blot out] my name from the book in
which you have written the names of your people."
33But the LORD told Moses, "I will ·erase [blot out] from my book the
names of the people who sin against me. 34So now, go. Lead the people
where I have told you, and my ·angel [messenger] will ·lead [Lgo in front
of] you. When the time comes to punish, I will punish them for their sin."
35So the LORD ·caused terrible things to happen to [sent a plague on]
the people because of what they did with the calf Aaron had made.
33 Then the LORD said to Moses, "You and the people you
brought out of Egypt must ·leave [Lgo up from] this place. Go
to the land that I promised with an oath to give to Abraham, Isaac, and

Jacob when I said, 'I will give that land to your ·descendants [[L]seed; Gen. 12:1–3].' 2I will send an ·angel [*or* messenger] ·to lead [[L]before] you, and I will ·force [drive] these people out of the land: the Canaanites, Amorites, Hittites, Perizzites, Hivites, and Jebusites. 3Go up to a ·fertile land [[L]land flowing with milk and honey; 3:8]. But I will not go with you, because I might ·destroy [consume] you on the way, since you are such a ·stubborn people [stiff-necked people]."

4When the people heard this bad news, they ·became very sad [mourned], and none of them put on ·jewelry [ornaments; *or* festive dress]. 5This was because the LORD had said to Moses, "Tell the ·Israelites [[L]sons/[T]children of Israel], 'You are a ·stubborn [[L]stiff-necked] people. If I were to go with you even for a moment, I would destroy you. So take off all your ·jewelry [ornaments; *or* festive dress], and I will decide what to do with you.' " 6So the ·people [[L]sons; children] of Israel ·took [stripped] off their ·jewelry [ornaments; *or* festive dress] at Mount ·Sinai [[L]Horeb; 3:1].

The Meeting Tent

7Moses used to take a tent and ·set it up [pitch it] a long way outside the camp; he called it the "Meeting Tent." Anyone who wanted to ·ask [seek] the LORD about something would go to the Meeting Tent outside the camp. 8Whenever Moses went out to the Tent, all the people would rise and stand at the entrances of their tents, watching him until he entered the ·Meeting Tent [[L]Tent]. 9When Moses went into the Tent, the pillar of cloud [13:21–22] would always come down and stay at the entrance of the Tent while the LORD spoke with Moses. 10Whenever the people saw the pillar of cloud at the entrance of the Tent, they stood and worshiped, each person at the entrance of his own tent.

11The LORD spoke to Moses face to face as a man speaks with his friend [Num. 12:6–8]. Then Moses would return to the camp, but Moses' young ·helper [assistant], Joshua son of Nun, did not leave the Tent.

12Moses said to the LORD, "You have told me to ·lead [[L]bring up] these people, but you did not say whom you would send with me. You have said to me, 'I know you ·very well [[L]by name], and ·I am pleased with you [[L]you have found favor in my eyes].' 13If I have ·truly pleased you [[L]found favor in your eyes], show me your ·plans [path; way] so that I may know you and continue to ·please you [[L]find favor/grace in your eyes]. ·Remember [Consider] that this nation is your people."

14The LORD answered, "·I myself [[L]My presence] will go with you, and I will give you ·victory [*or* rest]."

15Then Moses said to him, "If ·you yourself don't [[L]your presence does not] go with us, then don't send us ·away [up] from this place. 16·If you don't go with us, no one will know [[L]How else will it be known…?] that ·you are pleased with me [[L]I have found favor in your eyes] and with your people. These people and I will be no different from any other people on earth."

17Then the LORD said to Moses, "I will do what you ask, because I know you ·very well [[L]by name], and ·I am pleased with you [[L]you have found favor/grace in my eyes]."

Moses Sees God's Glory

18Then Moses said, "Now, please show me your glory [[C]his manifest presence]."

19The LORD answered, "I will cause all my goodness to pass in front of you, and I will announce my name, the LORD, so you can hear it. I will show ·kindness [favor] to anyone to whom I want to show ·kindness [favor], and I will show ·mercy [compassion] to anyone to whom I want to show ·mercy [compassion]. 20But you cannot see my face, because no one can see me and live.

21"There is a place near me where you may stand on a rock. 22When my glory passes that place, I will put you in a large ·crack [fissure; Tcleft] in the rock and ·cover [screen] you with my hand until I have passed by. 23Then I will ·take away [remove] my hand, and you will see my back. But my face must not be seen."

Moses Gets New Stone Tablets

34 The LORD said to Moses, "·Cut [Hew out; Chisel] two more stone tablets like the ·first two [former], and I will write the same words on them that were on the ·first two [former] stones which you broke [32:15–16]. 2Be ready tomorrow morning, and then come up on Mount Sinai. Stand before me there on the top of the mountain. 3No one may come with you or even be seen any place on the mountain. Not even the flocks or herds may ·eat grass [graze] near that mountain."

4So Moses ·cut [hewed out] two stone tablets like the ·first ones [former]. Then early the next morning he went up Mount Sinai, just as the LORD had commanded him, carrying the two stone tablets with him. 5Then the LORD came down in the cloud and stood there with Moses, and the LORD called out his name: the LORD [LYahweh; 3:14].

6The LORD passed in front of Moses and said, "I am the LORD. The LORD is a God who shows ·mercy [compassion], who is ·kind [gracious], ·who doesn't become angry quickly [patient], who has great ·love [loyalty] and faithfulness 7and ·is kind [Lguards/preserves loyalty] to thousands of people. The LORD forgives people for ·evil [iniquity], for ·sin [transgression], and for ·turning against him [sin], but he does not ·forget to punish guilty people [Lclear]. He will punish not only the guilty people, but also their children, their grandchildren, ·their great-grandchildren, and their great-great-grandchildren [Lto the third and fourth generations; Num. 14:18; Neh. 9:17; Ps. 86:15; 103:8; 145:8; Nah. 1:3]."

8Then Moses quickly bowed to the ground and worshiped. 9He said, "Lord, if ·you are pleased with me [LI have found favor in your eyes], please, [LLord] go with us. I know that these are ·stubborn [Lstiff-necked] people, but forgive our ·evil [iniquity] and our sin. Take us as your ·own people [Linheritance; possession]."

10Then he said, "I am making this ·agreement [covenant; treaty] with you. I will do ·miracles [wonders] in front of all your people—things that have never before been done for any other nation on earth—and the people with you will see my work. I, the LORD, will do ·wonderful [awesome] things for you. 11·Obey [Observe] the things I command you today, and I will ·force [drive] out the Amorites, Canaanites, Hittites, Perizzites, Hivites, and Jebusites ahead of you. 12·Be careful [Watch/Guard yourself] that you don't ·make an agreement [Lcut a covenant/treaty] with the people who live in the land where you are going, because ·it will bring you trouble [Lthey will be a snare/trap in your midst]. 13·Destroy [Tear down] their altars, break their stone pillars, and cut down their Asherah ·idols [poles; Cobjects sacred to the Canaanite goddess of fertility]. 14Don't worship any other god, because I, the LORD, ·the Jealous One [Lwhose name is Jealous], am a jealous God [20:5].

15"Be careful that you don't ·make an agreement [Lcut a covenant] with the people who live in that land. When they ·worship [Lwhore after and sacrifice to] their gods, they will invite you to join them. Then you will eat

their sacrifices. 16If you ·choose [take] some of their daughters as wives
for your sons and those daughters ·worship [Lwhore after other] gods,
they will lead your sons to ·do the same thing [Lwhore after their gods].
17"Do not make gods of ·melted [cast] metal [20:4–6].
18"Celebrate the Feast of Unleavened Bread [12:17–20]. For seven days
you must eat ·bread made without yeast [unleavened bread] as I commanded you. Do this ·during the month I have chosen, [Lat the appointed
time in] the month of Abib [13:4], because in ·that month [Lthe month of
Abib] you came out of Egypt.
19"·The firstborn of every mother [LEverything that first opens the
womb] belongs to me, including every firstborn male animal that is born
in your flocks and herds. 20You may ·buy back [redeem; ransom] a donkey
·by paying for it with [Lwith] a lamb, but if you don't want to ·buy back a
donkey [Lredeem; ransom], you must break its neck. You must ·buy back
[redeem; ransom] all your firstborn sons [13:11–13].
"No one is to come before me ·without a gift [Lempty-handed].
21"You must work for six days, but on the seventh day you must rest—
even during the ·planting [plowing] season and the harvest season
[20:8–11].
22"Celebrate the Feast of Weeks when you gather the first grain of the
wheat harvest [23:16]. And celebrate the Feast of ·Shelters [LIngathering]
·in the fall [Lat the turn of the year; 23:17].
23"Three times each year all your males must ·come [Lappear] before
the Lord GOD, the God of Israel. 24I will ·force out [dispossess] nations
ahead of you and ·expand [enlarge] the borders of your land. You will go
before the LORD your God three times each year, and at that time no one
will ·try to take [Lcovet] your land from you.
25"Do not offer the blood of a sacrifice to me with ·anything containing yeast [leaven], and do not leave any of the sacrifice of the Feast of
Passover until the next morning [12:10].
26"Bring the ·best first crops [firstfruits; 23:19] that you harvest from
your ground to the ·Tent [Lhouse] of the LORD your God.
"You must not cook a young goat in its mother's milk [23:19]."
27Then the LORD said to Moses, "Write down these words, because with
these words I have ·made an agreement [Lcut a covenant] with you and
Israel."
28Moses stayed there with the LORD forty days and forty nights, and
during that time he did not eat food or drink water. And Moses wrote the
words of the ·Agreement [Covenant; Treaty]—the Ten ·Commandments
[LWords]—on the stone tablets.

The Face of Moses Shines

29Then Moses came down from Mount Sinai, carrying the two stone
tablets of the ·Agreement [Covenant; Testimony; Treaty] in his hands. But
he did not know that his face was shining because he had talked with the
LORD [Creflecting God's holiness and glory and demonstrating Moses'
authority]. 30When Aaron and all the ·people [Lsons; children] of Israel
saw that Moses' face was shining, they were afraid to go near him. 31But
Moses called to them, so Aaron and all the ·leaders of the people [Lmen of
the community/congregation/assembly] returned to Moses, and he talked
with them. 32After that, all the ·people [Lsons; children] of Israel came
near him, and he gave them all the commands that the LORD had given
him on Mount Sinai.

33When Moses finished speaking to the people, he put a ·covering [veil] over his face. 34Anytime Moses went before the LORD to speak with him, Moses took off the ·covering [veil] until he came out. Then Moses would come out and tell the Israelites what the LORD had commanded. 35They would see that Moses' face was shining. So he would ·cover [veil] his face again until the next time he went in to speak with the LORD [2 Cor. 3:12–18].

Rules About the Sabbath

35 Moses ·gathered [assembled] all the ·Israelite community [congregation/assembly of the sons/Tchildren of Israel] together and said to them, "·These are the things [LThis is the word/thing] the LORD has commanded you to do. 2You are to work for six days, but the seventh day will be a holy ·day [Sabbath], a Sabbath of rest to honor the LORD. Anyone who works on that day must be put to death. 3On the Sabbath day you must not ·light [burn] a fire in any of your ·houses [dwellings]."

4Moses said to all the ·Israelites [community/congregation/assembly of the sons/Tchildren of Israel], "This is ·what [Lthe word/thing] the LORD has commanded: 5From what you have, take ·an offering [tribute] for the LORD. Let everyone ·who is willing [whose heart moves them] bring this ·offering [tribute] to the LORD: gold, silver, bronze, 6blue, purple and ·red [scarlet] thread, and fine linen, goat hair 7and male sheepskins that are colored red. They may also bring ·fine leather [*or* sea cow/porpoise hides], acacia wood, 8olive oil for the lamps, spices for the special olive oil used for ·appointing priests [anointing] and for the sweet-smelling incense, 9onyx stones, and other jewels to be put on the ·holy vest [ephod; 28:6–14] and ·chest covering of the priests [breastpiece; 28:15–30].

10"Let all the ·skilled workers [Lwise of heart/mind] come and make everything the LORD commanded: 11the ·Holy Tent [Tabernacle], its outer tent and its covering, the ·hooks [clasps], frames, crossbars, ·posts [pillars], and bases; 12the ·Ark of the Agreement [LArk; 25:10], its poles, ·lid [mercy seat; atonement cover; 25:17–22], and the curtain ·in front of it [Lfor the screen]; 13the table [25:23–30], and its poles, all ·the things that go with the table [Lits tools/utensils], and the ·bread that shows we are in God's presence [LBread of the Presence]; 14the ·lampstand [LMenorah; 25:31–40] for the light and all ·the things that go with it [its tools/utensils], the lamps, and olive oil for the light; 15the altar of incense [30:1–6] and its poles, the ·special [Lanointing] oil and the sweet-smelling incense, the ·curtain [Lscreen for the entrance,] for the entrance of the Meeting Tent; 16the altar of burnt offering and its bronze ·screen [grating], its poles and all its ·tools [utensils], the bronze bowl and its base [30:17–21]; 17the curtains around the courtyard, their ·posts [pillars] and bases, and the ·curtain [screen] at the ·entry [Lgate] to the courtyard; 18the pegs of the ·Holy Tent [Tabernacle] and of the courtyard and their ropes; 19the ·special [elaborately sewn] clothes that the priest will wear in the Holy Place [28:1–43]. These are the holy clothes for Aaron the priest and his sons to wear when they ·serve [minister] as priests."

20Then all the ·people [Lcommunity; congregation; assembly] of ·Israel [Lthe sons/Tchildren of Israel] went ·away [out] from Moses. 21Everyone ·who wanted to give [Lwhose heart was favorable and whose spirit was willing] came and brought a ·gift [offering] to the LORD for making the Meeting Tent, all ·the things in the Tent [its service], and the ·special

[Lholy; sacred] clothes. 22All the men and women who wanted to give
brought gold jewelry of all kinds—pins, earrings, rings, and bracelets.
They all ·presented their [Lwaved a wave offering of] gold to the LORD.
23Everyone who had blue, purple, and ·red [scarlet] thread, and fine linen,
and anyone who had goat hair or male ·sheepskins [ramskins] colored
red or ·fine leather [*or* sea cow/porpoise hides] brought them to the LORD.
24Everyone who could give silver or bronze brought that as a ·gift [offer-
ing] to the LORD, and everyone who had acacia wood to be used in the
work brought it. 25Every ·skilled woman [Lwise of heart/mind] used her
hands to ·make [Lspin] the blue, purple, and ·red [scarlet] thread, and fine
linen, and they brought what they had ·made [Lspun]. 26All the women
who were ·skilled [wise] and ·wanted to help [Lwhose hearts were favor-
able] ·made thread of [Lspun] the goat hair. 27The leaders brought onyx
stones and other jewels ·to put on the holy vest [Lfor the ephod; 28:6–14]
and ·chest covering for the priest [breastpiece; 28:15–28]. 28They also
brought spices and olive oil for the sweet-smelling incense, the ·special
[Lanointing] oil, and the oil to burn in the lamps. 29All the men and
women of Israel ·who wanted [Lwhose hearts were favorable] to help
brought ·gifts [La free will offering] to the LORD for all the work the LORD
had commanded Moses and the people to do.

30Then Moses said to the Israelites, "Look, the LORD has ·chosen
[Lcalled by name] Bezalel son of Uri the son of Hur, from the tribe of
Judah. 31The LORD has filled Bezalel with the ·Spirit [*or* spirit] of God
and has given him the ·skill [wisdom], ability, and knowledge to do all
kinds of work. 32He is able to ·design [plan] pieces to be made of gold,
silver, and bronze, 33to cut stones and jewels and put them in metal,
to ·carve [engrave] wood, and to do all kinds of work. 34Also, the LORD
has ·given [Lplaced in the heart of] Bezalel and Oholiab, the son of
Ahisamach from the tribe of Dan, the ·ability [*or* desire] to teach others.
35The LORD has ·given them [Lfilled them with] the skill to do all kinds of
work. They are able to ·cut [engrave] designs in metal and stone. They
can plan and ·sew designs [embroider] in the fine linen with the blue,
purple, and ·red [scarlet] thread. And they are alsoable to weave things.

36 1So Bezalel, Oholiab, and every ·skilled [Lwise of heart/mind]
person will do the work the LORD has commanded, because he
gave them the wisdom and understanding to do all the skilled work
needed to build the Holy ·Tent [Place]."

2Then Moses called Bezalel, Oholiab, and all the other ·skilled [Lwise of
heart/mind] people to whom the LORD had given ·skills [Lwisdom in their
heart], and they came because ·they wanted [Ltheir hearts were favorable]
to help with the work. 3They received from Moses everything the ·people
[Lsons; children] of Israel had brought as ·gifts [offerings] ·to build the
Holy Tent [Lfor doing the work of the Holy Place]. The people continued
to bring ·gifts [Lfree will offerings] ·each morning because they wanted to
[morning after morning]. 4So all the ·skilled [wise] workers left the work
they were doing on the Holy ·Tent [LPlace], 5and they said to Moses, "The
people are bringing more than we need to do the work the LORD
commanded."

6Then Moses sent this command throughout the camp: "No man or
woman should make anything else as a ·gift for the Holy Tent [offering
for the Holy Place]." So the people were kept from giving more, 7because
what they had was already more than enough to do all the work.

The Holy Tent
(compare 26:1–37)

8Then the ·skilled workers [Lall the skilled/wise of heart] made the ·Holy
Tent [Tabernacle]. They made the ten curtains with linen and of blue, purple, and ·red [scarlet] cloth, and they sewed designs of ·creatures with
wings [Lcherubim] on the curtains [CThese deep blue curtains with cherubim represented heaven on earth]. 9Each curtain was the same
size—·forty-two feet [Ltwenty-eight cubits] long and ·six feet [Lfour cubits]
wide. 10Five of the curtains were ·fastened [bound; joined] together to
make one set, and the other five were ·fastened [bound; joined] together to
make another set. 11Then they made loops of blue cloth along the edge of
the end curtain on the first set of five, and they did the same thing with the
other set of five. 12There were fifty loops on one curtain and fifty loops on
the other curtain, with the loops opposite each other. 13They made fifty
gold ·hooks [clasps] to join the two curtains together so that the ·Holy
Tent [Tabernacle] was joined together as one piece.

14Then they made another tent of eleven curtains made of goat hair
[26:7], to put over the ·Holy Tent [Tabernacle]. 15All eleven curtains were
the same size—·forty-five feet [Lthirty cubits] long and ·six feet [Lfour
cubits] wide. 16The workers sewed [joined; bound] five curtains together
into one set and six together into another set. 17They made fifty loops
along the edge of the outside curtain of one set and fifty loops along the
edge of the outside curtain of the other set. 18Then they made fifty bronze
·rings [hooks; clasps] to ·join [bind] the two sets of cloth together and
make the tent one piece. 19They made two more coverings for the outer
tent—one made of ·male sheepskins colored red [*or* tanned rams' skins;
26:14] and the other made of ·fine leather [*or* sea cow hide; 26:14].

20Then they made upright frames of acacia wood for the ·Holy Tent
[Tabernacle]. 21Each frame was ·fifteen feet [Lten cubits] long and ·twenty-
seven inches [La cubit and a half] wide, 22and there were two pegs side by
side on each one. Every frame of the ·Holy Tent [Tabernacle] was made
this same way. 23They made twenty frames for the south side of the Tent,
24and they made forty silver bases that went under the twenty frames.
There were two bases for every frame—one for each peg of each frame.
25They also made twenty frames for the [Lsecond side of the] north side of
the ·Holy Tent [Tabernacle] 26and forty silver bases—two to go under
each frame. 27They made six frames for the rear or west end of the ·Holy
Tent [Tabernacle] 28and two frames for the corners at the rear of the ·Holy
Tent [Tabernacle]. 29These two frames were doubled at the bottom and
joined at the top with a metal ring. They did this for each of these corners.
30So there were eight frames and sixteen silver bases—two bases under
each frame.

31Then they made crossbars of acacia wood to connect the upright
frames of the ·Holy Tent [Tabernacle]. Five crossbars held the frames
together on one side of the Tent, 32and five held the frames together on
the other [Lsecond] side. Also, five crossbars held the frames together on
the west end, at the rear of the Tent. 33They made the middle crossbar run
along the entire length of each side and rear of the Tent. It was set halfway
up the frames. 34They made gold rings on the sides of the frames to hold
the crossbars, and they ·covered [overlaid] the frames and the crossbars
with gold.

35Then they made the curtain of blue, purple, and ·red [scarlet] thread,
and fine linen. A skilled craftsman sewed designs of ·creatures with wings
[cherubim; 37:7] on it. 36They made four posts of acacia wood for it and

·covered [overlaid] them with gold. Then they made gold ·hooks [clasps] for the posts, as well as four silver bases in which to set the posts. [37]For the entrance to the Tent, they made a ·curtain [[L]screen] of blue, purple, and ·red [scarlet] thread, and fine linen. ·A person who sewed well sewed designs on it [...embroidered with needlework]. [38]Then they made five posts and ·hooks [clasps] for it. They covered the tops of the posts and their bands with gold, and they made five bronze bases for the posts.

The Ark of the Covenant
(compare 25:10–22)

37 Bezalel made the Ark of acacia wood; it was ·forty-five inches [[L]two and a half cubits] long, ·twenty-seven inches [[L]one and a half cubits] wide, and twenty-seven inches [[L]one and a half cubits] high. [2]He ·covered [overlaid] it, both inside and out, with pure gold, and he put a gold ·strip [molding] around it. [3]He ·made [cast] four gold rings for it and attached them to its four feet, with two rings on ·each [one side and two rings on the other] side. [4]Then he made poles of acacia wood and ·covered [cast; overlay] them with gold. [5]He put the poles through the rings on each side of the Ark to carry it. [6]Then he made a ·lid [mercy seat; atonement cover] of pure gold that was ·forty-five inches [[L]two and a half cubits] long and ·twenty-seven inches [[L]one and a half cubits] wide. [7]Then Bezalel ·hammered gold to make two creatures with wings [[L]made two golden cherubim of hammered gold; [C]cherubim are powerful angelic creatures] and attached them to each end of the ·lid [cover; [C]the mercy seat]. [8]He made one ·creature [[L]cherubim] on one end of the lid and the ·other creature [[L]cherubim] on the other end. He attached them to the ·lid [mercy seat; atonement cover] so that it would be one piece. [9]The ·creatures' [[L]cherubim's] wings were spread upward, covering the ·lid [mercy seat; atonement cover], and the ·creatures [[L]cherubim] faced each other across the ·lid [mercy seat; atonement cover].

The Table
(compare 25:23–30)

[10]Then he made the table of acacia wood; it was ·thirty-six inches [[L]two cubits] long, ·eighteen inches [[L]one cubit] wide, and ·twenty-seven inches [[L]one and a half cubits] high. [11]He ·covered [overlaid] it with pure gold and put a gold ·strip [molding] around it. [12]He made a ·frame [rim] ·three inches [[L]a handbreadth] high ·that stood up all around the edge [all around it], and he put a gold ·strip [molding] around it. [13]Then he made four gold rings for the table and attached them to the four corners of the table where the four legs were. [14]The rings were put close to the ·frame [rim] around the top of the table, because they held the poles for carrying it. [15]The poles for carrying the table were made of acacia wood and were ·covered [overlaid] with gold. [16]He made of pure gold all the ·things [vessels] that were used on the table: the plates, bowls, cups, and jars used for pouring the drink offerings [Ezra 1:9–11; Dan. 1:2; 5:1–4].

The Lampstand
(compare 25:31–40)

[17]Then he made the ·lampstand [[L]Menorah] of pure gold, hammering out its base and ·stand [shaft]. Its flower-like cups, buds, and petals were joined together in one piece with the base and ·stand [shaft; 25:31]. [18]Six branches went out from the sides of the lampstand—three on one side and three on the other. [19]Each branch had three cups shaped like almond flowers, and each cup had a bud and a petal. Each of the six branches going out from the lampstand was the same. [20]There were four more cups shaped like almond flowers on the lampstand itself, each with its buds and petals.

21Three pairs of branches went out from the lampstand. A bud was under
the place where each pair was attached to the lampstand. Each of the six
branches going out from the lampstand was the same. 22The buds, branches,
and lampstand were all one piece of pure, hammered gold. 23He made seven
pure gold lamps for this lampstand, and he made pure gold ·wick trimmers
[snuffers] and trays. 24He used about ·seventy-five pounds [L one talent] of
pure gold to make the lampstand and all the things that go with it.

The Altar for Burning Incense
(compare 30:1–6)

25Then he made the altar of incense out of acacia wood. It was square—
·eighteen inches [L one cubit] long and ·eighteen inches [L one cubit]
wide—and it was ·thirty-six inches [L two cubits] high. Each ·corner that
stuck out like a horn [horn; 27:2] was joined into one piece with the altar.
26He ·covered [overlaid] the top and all the sides and the ·corners [horns]
with pure gold, and he put gold ·trim [molding] around the altar 27He
made two gold rings and put them below the ·trim [molding] on opposite
sides of it; these rings held the poles for carrying it. 28He made the poles
of acacia wood and ·covered [overlaid] them with gold.
29Then he made the holy olive oil for ·appointing the priests [anoint-
ing] and the pure, sweet-smelling incense. He made them like a person
who mixes perfumes.

The Altar for Burnt Offerings
(compare 27:1–8)36

38 Then he built the altar for burnt offerings [Lev. 1] out of acacia wood. The altar was square—·seven and one-half feet
[L five cubits] long and ·seven and one-half feet [L five cubits] wide—and
it was ·four and one-half feet [L three cubits] high. 2He made each corner
stick out like a horn [27:2] so that the horns and the altar were joined
together in one piece. Then he ·covered [overlaid] the altar with bronze.
3He made all the ·tools [utensils] of bronze to use on the altar: the pots,
shovels, ·bowls for sprinkling blood [L basins], meat forks, and ·pans for
carrying the fire [firepans]. 4He made a large bronze screen to hold the
burning wood for the altar and put it inside the altar, under its ·rim
[ledge], halfway up from the bottom. 5He made bronze rings to hold the
poles for carrying the altar, and he put them at the four corners of the
screen. 6Then he made poles of acacia wood and ·covered [overlaid] them
with bronze. 7He put the poles through the rings on both sides of the
altar, to carry it. He made the altar of boards and left the inside hollow.

The Bronze Bowl
(compare 30:17–21)

8He made the bronze ·bowl for washing [basin], and he built it on a
bronze stand. He used the bronze from mirrors that belonged to the
women who served at the entrance to the Meeting Tent.

The Courtyard of the Holy Tent
(compare 27:9–19)

9Then he made ·a wall of curtains to form a courtyard around the Holy
Tent [the court]. On the south side the curtains were ·one hundred fifty
feet [L one hundred cubits] long and were made of fine linen. 10The curtains hung on silver hooks and bands, placed on twenty bronze ·posts
[pillars] with twenty bronze bases. 11On the north side the wall of curtains was also ·one hundred fifty feet [L one hundred cubits] long, and it
hung on silver hooks and bands on twenty ·posts [pillars] with twenty
bronze bases.
12On the west side of the courtyard, the wall of curtains was ·seventy-
five feet [L fifty cubits] long. It was held up by silver hooks and bands on
ten ·posts [pillars] with ten bases. 13The [L front of the] east side was also
·seventy-five feet [L fifty cubits] long. 14On one side of the entry there was
a wall of curtains ·twenty-two and one-half feet [L fifteen cubits] long,

held up by three ·posts [pillars] and three bases. 15On the other side of the
entry there was also a wall of curtains ·twenty-two and one-half feet
[Lfifteen cubits] long, held up by three ·posts [pillars] and three bases.
16All the curtains around the courtyard were made of fine linen. 17The
bases for the ·posts [pillars] were made of bronze. The hooks and the
bands on the ·posts [pillars] were made of silver, and the tops of the ·posts
[pillars] were ·covered [overlaid] with silver also. All the ·posts [pillars] in
the courtyard had silver bands.

18The ·curtain [screen] for the ·entry [gate] of the courtyard was made
of blue, purple, and ·red [scarlet] thread, and fine linen, ·sewn by a person
who could sew well [embroidered with needlework]. The curtain was
·thirty feet [Ltwenty cubits] long and ·seven and one-half feet [Lfive cubits]
high, the same height as the curtains around the courtyard. 19It was held
up by four ·posts [pillars] and four bronze bases. The hooks and bands on
the posts were made of silver, and the tops on the ·posts [pillars] were
·covered [overlaid] with silver. 20All the tent pegs for the ·Holy Tent
[Tabernacle] and for the curtains around the courtyard were made of
bronze.

21This is a ·list of the materials used to make [inventory; record of] the
·Holy Tent [Tabernacle], the ·Holy Tent [LTabernacle] ·where the
Agreement was kept [Lof the Covenant/Testimony/Treaty; Creference to
the tablets of the Ten Commandments; ch. 20]. Moses ordered the Levites
to make this list, ·and Ithamar son of Aaron was in charge of keeping it
[Lby the hand of Ithama son of Aaron]. 22Bezalel son of Uri, the son of
Hur of the tribe of Judah, made everything the LORD commanded Moses.
23Oholiab son of Ahisamach of the tribe of Dan ·helped [Lwas with] him.
He ·could cut designs into metal and stone; he was a designer and also
skilled at sewing [Lwas an engraver, designer, and embroiderer of] the
blue, purple, and ·red [scarlet] thread, and fine linen.

24The total amount of gold used to build the Holy ·Tent [Place] was
·presented [Loffered as a wave offering] to the LORD. It weighed over ·2,000
pounds [L29 talents and 730 shekels], as set by the Holy Place measure.

25The silver was given by the ·members of the community [congrega-
tion; assembly] who were counted. It weighed ·7,550 pounds [L100 talents
and 1,775 shekels], as set by the Holy Place measure. 26All the men twenty
years old or older were counted. There were 603,550 men, and each ·man
[head] had to pay ·one-fifth of an ounce [La beka, that is half a shekel] of
silver, as set by the Holy Place measure. 27Of this silver, ·7,500 pounds
[L100 talents] were used to ·make [cast] the one hundred bases for the
Holy Tent and for the curtain—·75 pounds of silver [La talent] in each
base. 28They used ·50 pounds of silver [L1775 shekels] to make the hooks
for the ·posts [pillars] and to ·cover [overlay] the tops of the ·posts [pil-
lars] and to make the bands on them.

29The bronze which was ·presented [Loffered as a wave offering] to the
LORD weighed about ·5,000 pounds [70 talents and 2400 shekels]. 30They
used ·the bronze to make the bases at the entrance of the Meeting Tent, to
make the altar and the bronze ·screen [grating], and to make all the ·tools
[utensils] for the altar. 31·This bronze was also used to make [L...and the]
bases for the wall of curtains around the courtyard and bases for curtains
at the ·entry [Lgate] to the courtyard, as well as to make the tent pegs for
the ·Holy Tent [Tabernacle] and the pegs around the courtyard.

Clothes for the Priests

39 They used blue, purple, and ·red [scarlet] thread to make woven clothes for the priests to wear when they ·served [ministered] in the Holy Place. They made the holy clothes for Aaron as the LORD had commanded Moses.

2They made the ·holy vest [ephod] of gold, and blue, purple, and ·red [scarlet] thread, and fine linen [28:6–14]. 3They hammered the gold into sheets and then cut it into long, thin strips. They worked the gold into the blue, purple, and ·red [scarlet] thread, and fine linen. This was done ·by skilled craftsmen [*or* with a skilled design]. 4They made the shoulder straps for the ·holy vest [ephod], which were attached to the top corners of it and tied together over each shoulder. 5The skillfully ·woven belt [embroidered waistband] was made in the same way; it was joined to ·the holy vest [Lit] as one piece. It was made of gold, and blue, purple, and ·red [scarlet] thread, and fine linen, the way the LORD commanded Moses.

6They put gold [Lfiligree] around the onyx stones and then ·wrote [engraved] the names of the sons of Israel on these gems, ·as a person carves words and designs on a seal [like the engravings on a seal/signet]. 7Then they attached the gems on the shoulder straps of the ·holy vest [ephod], as reminders of the twelve sons of Israel. This was done just as the LORD had commanded Moses.

8·The skilled craftsmen [LThey] made the ·chest covering [breastpiece] like the ·holy vest [ephod]; it was made of gold, and blue, purple, and ·red [scarlet] thread, and fine linen. 9·The chest covering [LIt] was square—·nine inches [a span] long and ·nine inches [a span] wide—and it was ·folded double to make a pocket [Ldoubled]. 10Then they put four rows of ·beautiful jewels [Lstones] on it: In the first row there was a ·ruby [*or* carnelian], a ·topaz [*or* chrysolite], and a ·yellow quartz [*or* emerald]; 11in the second there was a turquoise, a ·sapphire [*or* lapis], and an ·emerald [*or* moonstone]; 12in the third there was a jacinth, an agate, and an amethyst; 13in the fourth there was a ·chrysolite [*or* beryl], an onyx, and a jasper [Cidentification is uncertain]. Gold [Lfiligree] was put around these ·jewels [stones] to attach them to the ·chest covering [breastpiece], 14and the names of the sons of Israel were ·carved [engraved] on these twelve ·jewels [stones] as a person ·carves [engraves] a ·seal [signet]. Each ·jewel [stone] had the name of one of the twelve tribes of Israel.

15They made chains of pure gold, twisted together like a rope, for the ·chest covering [breastpiece]. 16They made two gold pieces and two gold rings. They put the two gold rings on the two upper corners of the ·chest covering [breastpiece]. 17Then they put two gold chains in the two rings at the ends of the ·chest covering [breastpiece], 18and they fastened the other two ends of the chains to the two ·gold pieces [*or* settings]. They attached these gold pieces to the two shoulder straps in the front of the ·holy vest [ephod]. 19They made two gold rings and put them at the lower corners of the ·chest covering [breastpiece] on the inside edge next to the ·holy vest [ephod]. 20They made two more gold rings on the bottom of the shoulder straps in front of the ·holy vest [ephod], near the seam, just above the ·woven belt [embroidered waistband] of the ·holy vest [ephod]. 21They used a blue ·ribbon [cord] and tied the rings of the ·chest covering [breastpiece] to the rings of the ·holy vest [ephod], connecting it to the ·woven belt [Lembroidered waistband]. In this way the ·chest covering [breastpiece] would not ·swing out [get loose] from the ·holy vest [ephod]. They did all these things the way the LORD commanded.

22Then they made the outer robe ·to be worn under the holy vest [Lof
the ephod]. It was woven only of blue cloth. 23They made a ·hole [open-
ing] in the center of the outer robe, with a woven collar ·sewn around it
[Llike a coat of mail; Cthe Hebrew is obscure] so it would not tear. 24Then
they made balls like pomegranates of blue, purple, and ·red [scarlet]
thread, and fine linen and hung them around the bottom of the outer
robe. 25They also made bells of pure gold and hung these around the bottom of the outer robe between the balls. 26So around the bottom of the
outer robe there was a bell and a pomegranate ball, a bell and a pomegranate ball. The priest wore this outer robe when he ·served as priest
[ministered], just as the LORD had commanded Moses.

27They ·wove [Lmade] inner robes of fine linen for Aaron and his sons,
28and they made turbans, ·headbands [headdresses], and underclothes of
fine linen. 29Then they made the ·cloth belt [sash] of fine linen, and blue,
purple, and ·red [scarlet] thread·, and designs were sewn onto it [embroi-
dered with needlework], just as the LORD had commanded Moses.

30They made a ·strip [rosette; medallion; plate; Lflower] of pure gold,
which is the holy ·crown [diadem], and ·carved [engraved] these words in
the gold, as one might ·carve [engrave] on a ·seal [signet]: "Holy to the
LORD." 31Then they tied ·this flat piece [a blue cord to it to fasten it] to the
turban with a blue ribbon, as the LORD had commanded Moses.

32So all the work on the [LTabernacle of the] Meeting Tent was finished.
The ·Israelites [Lsons/Tchildren of Israel] did everything just as the LORD
had commanded Moses. 33Then they brought the ·Holy Tent [LTabernacle]
to Moses: the Tent and all its furniture, hooks, frames, crossbars, ·posts
[pillars], and bases; 34the covering made of male ·sheepskins [ramskins]
colored red, the covering made of ·fine leather [sea cow/porpoise hide],
and the curtain ·that covered the entrance to the Most Holy Place [Lfor the
screen]; 35the Ark of the ·Agreement [Covenant; Treaty; LTestimony; 25:10],
its poles and ·lid [the mercy seat/atonement cover; 25:17–22]; 36the table
[25:23–40], all its ·containers [utensils; tools], and the bread ·that showed
they were in God's presence [Lof presence]; 37the pure ·gold lampstand
[LMenorah; 25:31–40] with its lamps in a row, all its ·tools [utensils], and
the olive oil for the light; 38the gold altar [Cthe incense altar; 30:1–6], the
special olive oil used for ·appointing priests [anointing], the sweet-smelling incense, and the ·curtain that covered [screen at] the entrance to the
Tent; 39the bronze altar [27:1–8] and its ·screen [Lbronze grating], its poles
and all its ·tools [utensils], the bowl and its stand [30:17–21]; 40the curtains for the courtyard with their ·posts [pillars] and bases, the ·curtain
that covered the entry to [Lscreen for the gate of] the courtyard, the cords,
pegs, and all the ·things [Lutensils for service] in the Meeting Tent. 41They
brought the clothes for the priests to wear when they ·served [ministered]
in the Holy ·Tent [Place]—the ·holy [sacred] clothes for Aaron the priest
and the clothes for his sons, which they wore when they served as priests.

42The ·Israelites [Lsons/Tchildren of Israel] had done all this work just
as the LORD had commanded Moses. 43Moses looked closely at all the
work and saw they had done it just as the LORD had commanded. So
Moses blessed them.

Setting Up the Holy Tent

40 Then the LORD said to Moses: 2"On the first day of the first
month, set up the ·Holy Tent [Tabernacle], which is the
Meeting Tent. 3Put the Ark of the ·Agreement [Covenant; Treaty;

[L]Testimony; 25:10] in it and ·hang the curtain in front of the Ark [[L]screen
the Ark with a curtain]. [4]Bring in the table [25:23–30] and arrange
·everything on the table that should be there [[L]its setting]. Then bring in
the ·lampstand [[L]Menorah; 25:31–40] and set up its lamps. [5]Put the gold
altar for ·burning incense [[L]offering smoke; 30:1–6] in front of the Ark
of the ·Agreement [Covenant; Treaty; [L]Testimony], and put the ·curtain
[screen] at the entrance to the ·Holy Tent [Tabernacle].

[6]"Put the altar of burnt offerings [27:1–8] in front of the entrance of
the ·Holy Tent [Tabernacle], the Meeting Tent. [7]Put the bowl [30:17–21]
between the Meeting Tent and the altar, and put water in it. [8]Set up the
courtyard ·around the Holy Tent [[L]all around], and put the ·curtain
[screen] at the ·entry [[L]gate] to the courtyard.

[9]"Use the ·special [anointing] olive oil and ·pour it on [[L]anoint] the
·Holy Tent [Tabernacle] and everything in it, in order to ·give the Tent
and all that is in it for service to the Lord [sanctify/consecrate it and all its
utensils/tools]. They will be holy. [10]·Pour the special oil on [[L]Anoint] the
altar for burnt offerings and on all its ·tools [utensils]. ·Give the altar for
service to God [Consecrate/Sanctify the altar], and it will be ·very holy [[T]a
holy of holies]. [11]Then ·pour the special olive oil on [[L]anoint] the bowl
and the base under it so that they will be ·given for service to God [con-
secrated; sanctified].

[12]"Bring Aaron and his sons to the entrance of the Meeting Tent, and
wash them with water. [13]Then put the ·holy [sacred] clothes on Aaron.
·Pour the special oil on [[L]Anoint] him [Ps. 133], and ·give him for service
to God [[L]consecrate/sanctify him] so that he may serve me as a priest.
[14]Bring his sons and put the inner robes [28:39–41] on them. [15]·Pour the
special oil on [[L]Anoint] them in the same way that you ·appointed
[[L]anointed] their father as priest so that they may also serve me as priests.
·Pouring oil on [[L]Anointing] them will make them a family of priests,
they and their descendants ·from now on [[L]throughout their genera-
tions]." [16]Moses did everything that the Lord commanded him.

[17]So the ·Holy Tent [Tabernacle] was set up on the first day of the first
month during the second ·year after they left Egypt [[L]year]. [18]When
Moses set up the ·Holy Tent [Tabernacle], he put the bases in place, and
he put the frames on the bases. Next he put ·the crossbars through the
rings of the frames [[L]in the poles] and set up the ·posts [pillars]. [19]After
that, Moses spread ·the cloth over the Holy Tent [[L]the tent over the
Tabernacle] and put the covering over it, just as the Lord commanded.

[20]Moses put the ·stone tablets that had the Agreement written on them
[Covenant; Testimony; Treaty] into the Ark. He put the poles ·through the
rings of [[L]on] the Ark and put the ·lid [mercy seat; atonement cover] on
it. [21]Next he brought the Ark into the ·Tent [Tabernacle] and hung the
curtain to ·cover [screen] the Ark [[L]of the Testimony], just as the Lord
commanded him.

[22]Moses put the table in the Meeting Tent on the north side of the
·Holy Tent [Tabernacle] in front of the curtain. [23]Then he ·put [arranged]
the bread ·on the table [[L]in rows] before the Lord, just as the Lord commanded him. [24]Moses put the lampstand [[L]Menorah] in the Meeting Tent
on the south side of the ·Holy Tent [Tabernacle] across from the table.
[25]Then he put the lamps on the lampstand before the Lord, just as the
Lord commanded him.

[26]Moses put the gold altar for burning incense in the Meeting Tent in

front of the curtain. 27Then he ·burned [Lturned into smoke] sweet-smelling incense on it, just as the LORD commanded him. 28Then he hung the
·curtain [screen] at the entrance to the ·Holy Tent [LTabernacle].

29He put the altar for burnt offerings [Lev. 1] at the entrance to the
·Holy Tent [Tabernacle], the Meeting Tent, and offered a whole burnt
offering and ·grain [Lgift; tribute; Lev. 3] offerings on it, just as the LORD
commanded him. 30Moses put the bowl [30:17–21] between the Meeting
Tent and the altar for burnt offerings, and he put water in it for washing.
31Moses, Aaron, and Aaron's sons used this water to wash their hands and
feet [Ccleansing rituals]. 32They washed themselves every time they
entered the Meeting Tent and every time they went near the altar for
burnt offerings, just as the LORD commanded Moses.

33Then Moses set up the courtyard around the ·Holy Tent [Tabernacle]
and the altar, and he put up the ·curtain [screen] at the entry to the courtyard. So Moses finished the work.

The Cloud over the Holy Tent

34Then the cloud covered the Meeting Tent [Crepresenting God's pres-
ence], and the glory of the LORD filled the Holy Tent [Crepresenting his
manifest presence]. 35Moses could not enter the Meeting Tent, because
the cloud had settled on it, and the glory of the LORD filled the ·Holy Tent
[Tabernacle].

36When the cloud rose from the ·Holy Tent [Tabernacle], the Israelites
would begin to travel, 37but as long as the cloud ·stayed on the Holy Tent
[Ldid not rise], they did not travel. They stayed in that place until the
cloud rose. 38So the cloud of the LORD was over the ·Holy Tent [Tabernacle]
during the day, and there was a fire in the cloud at night. So all the
·Israelites [Lhouse of Israel] could see the cloud while they traveled.

LEVITICUS

The Burnt Offering

1 The LORD ·called to [summoned] Moses and spoke to him from
the Meeting Tent, saying, 2"'Tell the ·people [Lsons; children] of
Israel: 'When you bring an offering [Lof livestock] to the LORD, bring as
your offering an animal from the herd or flock.
3"'If the offering is a whole burnt offering from the herd, it must be
a male ·that has nothing wrong with it [without blemish/defect]. The
person must take the animal to the entrance of the Meeting Tent so
that the LORD will accept the offering. 4He must ·put [lay] his hand on
the animal's head [Cto identify with the animal that served as a substi-
tute], and ·the LORD will accept it to remove the person's sin so he will
belong to God [Lit will be acceptable as atonement/expiation for him].
5He must ·kill [slaughter] the young bull before the LORD, and Aaron's
sons, the priests, must bring its blood and ·sprinkle [dash] it on all sides
of the altar at the entrance to the Meeting Tent. 6After that he will skin
the ·animal [Lwhole burnt offering] and cut it into pieces. 7The [Lsons of
Aaron, the] priests, when they have ·put [arranged] wood and fire on the
altar, 8[Lthe sons of Aaron, the priests,] are to ·lay [arrange] the head, the
·fat [suet], and other pieces on the wood that is on the fire of the altar.
9The animal's inner organs and legs must be washed with water. Then
the priest must ·burn all the animal's parts [Lturn it into smoke] on the
altar. It is a whole burnt offering, an offering made by fire, and its smell
is pleasing to the LORD.
10"'If the ·burnt offering [Loffering; gift] is a sheep or a goat from
the flock [Cacceptable if the worshiper could not afford a bull], it must
be a male ·that has nothing wrong with it [without blemish/defect].
11The person must ·kill [slaughter] the animal on the north side of the
altar before the LORD, and Aaron's sons, the priests, must ·sprinkle
[dash] its blood on all sides of the altar. 12The person must cut the
animal into pieces, and the priest must ·lay [arrange] them, with the
head and ·fat [suet], on the wood that is on the fire of the altar. 13The
person must wash the animal's inner organs and legs with water, and
then the priest must ·burn all its parts [Lturn it into smoke] on the
altar. It is a whole burnt offering, an offering made by fire, and its
smell is pleasing to the LORD.
14"'If the ·whole burnt offering [offering; gift] for the LORD is a bird
[Cpresumably because the worshiper could not afford an animal from
the herd or flock], it must be a dove or a young pigeon. 15The priest will
bring it to the altar and ·pull [wring] off its head, which he will ·burn
[Lturn into smoke] on the altar; its blood must be drained out on the
side of the altar. 16The priest must remove the bird's crop [Ca part of its

digestive system] and its contents and throw them on the east side of the altar, where the ashes are. 17Then he must tear the bird open by its wings without dividing it into two parts. LThe priest must ·burn the bird [Lturn it into smoke] on the altar, on the wood which is on the fire. It is a whole burnt offering, an offering made by fire, and its smell is pleasing to the LORD.

The Grain Offering

2 "'When anyone offers a ·grain [Lgift; tribute; Cthis offering of grain, called a gift offering, was not considered an atonement for sin] offering to the LORD, that ·offering [gift] must be made from ·fine [choice] flour. The person must pour oil on it, put ·incense [frankincense] on it, 2and then take it to Aaron's sons, the priests. The priest must take a handful of the ·fine [choice] flour and oil and all the incense, and ·burn it [Lturn it into smoke] on the altar as a memorial portion. It is an offering made by fire, and its smell is pleasing to the LORD. 3The rest of the ·grain [Lgift; tribute] offering will belong to Aaron and the priests; it is a most ·holy [sacred] part of the offerings made by fire to the LORD.

4"'If you bring a ·grain [Lgift; tribute] offering that was baked in the oven, it must be made from ·fine [choice] flour. It may be ·loaves made without yeast [unleavened cakes] and mixed with oil, or it may be ·wafers made without yeast [unleavened wafers] that have oil ·poured [spread] over them. 5If your grain offering is cooked on a griddle, it must be made, ·without yeast [unleavened], of ·fine [choice] flour mixed with oil. 6·Crumble it [Break it in pieces] and pour oil over it; it is a ·grain [Lgift; tribute] offering. 7If your ·grain [Lgift; tribute] offering is cooked in a pan, it must be made from ·fine [choice] flour and oil. 8Bring the ·grain [Lgift; tribute] offering made ·of these things [*or* in any of these ways] to the LORD. Give it to the priest, and he will take it to the altar. 9He will take out the memorial portion [2:2] from the ·grain [Lgift; tribute] offering and ·burn it [Lturn it into smoke] on the altar, as an offering made by fire. Its smell is pleasing to the LORD. 10The rest of the ·grain [Lgift; tribute] offering belongs to Aaron and the priests. It is a most ·holy [sacred] part of the offerings made to the LORD by fire.

11"'Every ·grain [Lgift; tribute] offering you bring to the LORD must be made without ·yeast [Lleaven], because you must not ·burn [Lturn into smoke] any ·yeast [leaven] or honey [Cboth of them ferment in fire, a form of decay] in an offering made by fire to the LORD. 12You may bring yeast and honey to the LORD as ·an offering [gift] from the first harvest, but they must not be ·burned [Lraised up] on the altar as a pleasing smell. 13You must also put salt on all your ·grain [Lgift; tribute] offerings. Salt stands for your ·agreement [covenant; treaty] with God that will last forever; do not leave salt out of your ·grain [Lgift; tribute] offering. You must add salt to all your offerings [Csalt would endure the fire, thereby representing the eternal covenant].

14"'If you bring a ·grain [Lgift; tribute] offering from the first harvest to the LORD, bring crushed heads of new grain ·roasted [parched] in the fire. 15Put oil and ·incense [frankincense] on it; it is a ·grain [Lgift; tribute] offering. 16The priest will ·burn [Lturn into smoke] the memorial portion of the crushed grain and oil, with the ·incense [frankincense] on it. It is an offering by fire to the LORD.

The Fellowship Offering

3 "'If a person's ·fellowship [*or* peace; well-being] offering [Cdemonstrated fellowship because the meat was to be eaten by the worshipers] to the Lord is from the herd, it may be a male or female, but it must ·have nothing wrong with it [be unblemished]. 2The person must ·put [lay] his hand on the animal's head [1:4] and ·kill [slaughter] it at the entrance to the Meeting Tent. Then Aaron's sons, the priests, must ·sprinkle [dash] the blood on all sides of the altar. 3From the ·fellowship [*or* peace; well-being] offering he must make a sacrifice by fire to the Lord. He must offer the fat of the animal's inner organs (both the fat that is in them and that covers them), 4both kidneys with the fat that is on them near the ·lower back muscle [loins], and the ·best part [appendage] of the liver, which he will remove with the kidneys. 5Then the priests will ·burn these parts [Lturn these into smoke] on the altar, on the whole burnt offering that is on the wood of the fire. It is an offering made by fire, and its smell is pleasing to the Lord.

6"'If a person's ·fellowship [*or* peace; well-being] offering to the Lord is ·a lamb or a goat [Lfrom the flock], it may be a male or female, but it must ·have nothing wrong with it [be unblemished]. 7If he offers a lamb, he must bring it before the Lord 8and ·put [lay] his hand on its head [1:4]. Then he must ·kill [slaughter] the animal in front of the Meeting Tent, and the ·priests [Lsons of Aaron] must ·sprinkle [dash] its blood on all sides of the altar. 9From the ·fellowship [*or* peace; well-being] offering the person must make a sacrifice by fire to the Lord. He must bring the fat, the whole fat tail cut off close to the backbone, the fat of the inner organs (both the fat that is in them and that covers them), 10both kidneys with the fat that is on them, near the ·lower back muscle [loins], and the ·best part [appendage] of the liver, which he will remove with the kidneys. 11Then the priest will ·burn these parts [Lturn them into smoke] on the altar as food; it will be an offering made by fire to the Lord.

12"'If a person's ·offering [gift] is a goat, he must offer it before the Lord 13and ·put [lay] his hand on its head [1:4]. Then he must ·kill [slaughter] it in front of the Meeting Tent, and the priests must ·sprinkle [dash] its blood on all sides of the altar. 14From this ·offering [gift] the person must make a sacrifice by fire to the Lord. He must offer all the fat of the goat's inner organs (both the fat that is in them and that covers them), 15both kidneys with the fat that is on them near the ·lower back muscle [loins], and the ·best part [appendage] of the liver, which he will remove with the kidneys. 16The priest will ·burn these parts [Lturn them into smoke] on the altar as food. It is an offering made by fire, and its smell is pleasing to the Lord. All the fat belongs to the Lord [see v. 17].

17"'This ·law [statute; ordinance; requirement] will continue for people ·from now on [forever], ·wherever you live [Lin all your habitations/settlements]: You must not eat any fat [Cperhaps considered the location of an animal's strength; 7:22–25] or ·blood [Cthe source of life; 7:26–27; 17:10; 19:26; Gen. 9:4; Deut. 12:16, 23; 15:23].'"

The Sin Offering

4 The Lord said to Moses, 2"Tell the ·people [Lsons; children] of Israel this: 'When a person sins ·by accident [unintentionally; inadvertently; Cin contrast to a deliberate sin; Num. 15:22–31] ·and does some things the Lord has commanded not to be done [Lin any of the Lord's commandments/regulations], ·that person must do these things [Land does any one of them]:

3“ ‘If the ·appointed [Lanointed] priest sins so that he brings guilt on the people, then he must offer a young bull to the LORD, ·one that has nothing wrong with it [unblemished], as a ·sin [*or* purification; Cthe offering would purify the offerer of the effects of sin] offering for the sin he has done. 4He will bring the bull to the entrance of the Meeting Tent in front of the LORD, ·put [lay] his hand on its head [1:4], and ·kill [slaughter] it before the LORD. 5Then the ·appointed [Lanointed] priest must bring some of the bull’s blood into the Meeting Tent. 6The priest is to dip his finger into the blood and ·sprinkle [dash] it seven times before the LORD in front of the curtain of the ·Most Holy Place [sanctuary]. 7The priest must also put some of the blood on the ·corners [Lhorns; Ex. 27:2] of the altar of incense that stands before the LORD in the Meeting Tent. The rest of the blood he must pour out at the ·bottom [base; foundation] of the altar of burnt offering, which is at the entrance of the Meeting Tent. 8He must remove all the fat from the bull of the ·sin [*or* purification; 4:3] offering—the fat on and around the inner organs, 9both kidneys with the fat that is on them near the ·lower back muscle [loins], and the ·best part [appendage] of the liver which he will remove with the kidneys. 10(He must do this in the same way the fat is removed from the bull of the ·fellowship [peace; well-being] offering [3:3–4].) Then the priest must ·burn [Lturn into smoke] the animal parts on the altar of burnt offering. 11But the priest must carry off the skin of the bull and all its meat, along with the rest of the bull—its head, legs, intestines, and other inner organs. 12He must take it outside the camp to the special clean [Cin a ritual sense] place where the ashes are poured out. He must burn it on a wood fire on the pile of ashes.

13“ ‘If the whole ·nation [congregation; assembly] of Israel sins ·accidentally [inadvertently; unintentionally; 4:2] ·without knowing it [Land the matter is hidden from the eyes of the assembly/crowd] and does something the LORD has commanded not to be done, they are guilty. 14When they learn about the sin they have done, they must offer a young bull as a ·sin [*or* purification] offering [4:3] and bring it before the Meeting Tent. 15The elders of the ·group of people [congregation; assembly] must ·put [lay; 1:4] their hands on the bull’s head before the LORD, and it must be ·killed [slaughtered] before the LORD. 16Then the ·appointed [Lanointed] priest must bring some of the bull’s blood into the Meeting Tent. 17Dipping his finger in the blood, he must ·sprinkle [dash] it seven times before the LORD in front of the curtain. 18Then he must put some of the blood on the ·corners [horns; Ex. 27:2] of the altar that is before the LORD in the Meeting Tent. The priest must pour out the rest of the blood at the ·bottom [base; foundation] of the altar of burnt offering, which is at the entrance to the Meeting Tent. 19He must remove all the fat from the animal and ·burn it [Lturn it into smoke] on the altar; 20he will do the same thing with this bull that he did with the first bull of the ·sin [*or* purification] offering [4:3]. In this way the priest ·removes the sins of the people so they will belong to the LORD and [Latones for them and they will] be forgiven. 21Then the priest must carry the bull outside the camp and burn it, just as he did with the first bull. This is the ·sin [*or* purification] offering [4:3] for the whole ·community [assembly; crowd].

22“ ‘If a ·ruler [leader; prince] sins ·by accident [inadvertently; unintentionally; 4:2] and does something the LORD his God has commanded must not be done, he is guilty. 23When he learns about his sin, he must bring a male goat that ·has nothing wrong [is unblemished] with it as his ·offering [gift]. 24The ·ruler [leader; prince] must ·put [lay; 1:4] his hand on the goat's head and ·kill [slaughter] it in the place where they ·kill [slaughter] the whole burnt offering before the LORD; it is a ·sin [purification] offering [4:3]. 25The priest must take some of the blood of the ·sin [purification] offering [4:3] on his finger and put it on the ·corners [horns; Ex. 27:2] of the altar of burnt offering. He must pour out the rest of the blood at the ·bottom [base; foundation] of the altar of burnt offering. 26He must ·burn [Lturn into smoke] all the goat's fat on the altar in the same way he ·burns [Lturns into smoke] the fat of the ·fellowship [peace; well-being] offerings [3:3–4]. In this way the priest ·removes the ruler's sin so he belongs to the LORD, and the LORD will forgive him [Lmakes atonement for him and he is forgiven].

27" 'If any ·person in the community [ordinary/private/lay person; Lof the people of the land] sins ·by accident [inadvertently; unintentionally; 4:2] and does something which the LORD has commanded must not be done, he is guilty. 28When the person learns about his sin, he must bring a female goat ·that has nothing wrong with it [unblemished] as an ·offering [gift] for his sin. 29He must ·put [lay] his hand on the animal's head [1:4] and ·kill [slaughter] it at the place of the whole burnt offering. 30Then the priest must take some of the goat's blood on his finger and put it on the ·corners [horns; Ex. 27:2] of the altar of burnt offering. He must pour out the rest of the goat's blood at the ·bottom [base; foundation] of the altar. 31Then the priest must remove all the goat's fat in the same way the fat is removed from the ·fellowship [peace; well-being] offerings [3:3–4]. He must ·burn it [Lturn it into smoke] on the altar as a smell pleasing to the LORD. In this way the priest ·will remove that person's sin so he will belong to the LORD, and the LORD will forgive him [Lmakes atonement for him and he is forgiven].

32" 'If this person brings a lamb as his ·offering [gift] for sin, he must bring a female ·that has nothing wrong with it [unblemished]. 33He must ·put [lay] his hand on the animal's head [1:4] and ·kill [slaughter] it as a ·sin [*or* purification] offering [4:3] in the place where the whole burnt offering is ·killed [slaughtered]. 34The priest must take some of the blood from the sin offering on his finger and put it on the ·corners [horns; Ex. 27:2] of the altar of burnt offering. He must pour out the rest of the lamb's blood at the ·bottom [base; foundation] of the altar. 35Then the priest must remove all the lamb's fat in the same way that the lamb's fat is removed from the ·fellowship [peace; well-being] offerings [3:3–4]. He must ·burn the pieces on the altar [Lturn them into smoke] on top of the offerings made by fire for the LORD. In this way the priest ·will remove that person's sins so he will belong to the LORD, and the LORD will forgive him [Lmakes atonement for him and he is forgiven].

Special Types of Accidental Sins

5 " 'If a person ·is ordered to tell in court [Lhears a public oath and he has been a witness of] what he has seen or what he knows and he does not ·tell the court [Lmake it known], he is guilty of sin.

2" 'Or someone might touch something unclean, such as the dead body of an unclean wild animal or an unclean farm animal or an unclean crawling animal [11:24–28, 32–40]. Even if he does not know that he touched it, he will still be unclean and guilty of sin.

3" 'Someone might touch human uncleanness—anything that makes someone unclean—and not know it. But when he learns about it, he will be guilty.

4“ ‘Or someone might make a promise before the LORD ·without thinking [rashly]. It might be a [rash] promise to do something bad or something good; it might be about anything. Even if he forgets about it, when he remembers, he will be guilty [Deut. 23:22–23; Eccl. 5:4].

5“ ‘When anyone is guilty of any of these things, he must ·tell how he sinned [Lconfess his sin]. 6He must bring an offering to the LORD as a penalty for sin; it must be a female lamb or goat from the flock. The priest will ·perform the acts to remove that person's sin so he will belong to the LORD [Lmake atonement for his sin].

7“ ‘But if the person cannot afford a lamb, he must bring two ·doves [turtledoves] or two young pigeons to the LORD as the penalty for his sin. One bird must be for a ·sin [*or* purification] offering [4:3], and the other must be for a whole burnt offering [1:1–17]. 8He must bring them to the priest, who will first offer the one for the ·sin [*or* purification] offering [4:3]. He will ·pull [wring] the bird's head from its neck, but he will not ·pull it completely off [sever it]. 9He must ·sprinkle [dash] the blood from the ·sin [purification] offering [4:3] on the side of the altar, and then he must pour the rest of the blood at the ·bottom [base; foundation] of the altar; it is a ·sin [*or* purification] offering [4:3]. 10Then the priest must offer the second bird as a whole burnt offering, as the ·law [regulation] says [1:14–17]. In this way the priest ·will remove the person's sin so he will belong to the LORD, and the LORD will forgive him [Lmakes atonement for him and he is forgiven].

11“ ‘If the person cannot afford two ·doves [turtledoves] or two pigeons, he must bring about ·two quarts of [Lone-tenth of an ephah of] ·fine [choice] flour as an ·offering for sin [purification offering; 4:3]. He must not put oil or ·incense [frankincense] on the flour, because it is a ·sin [*or* purification] offering. 12He must bring the flour to the priest. The priest will take a handful of the flour as a memorial offering and burn it on the altar on top of the offerings made by fire to the LORD; it is a ·sin [*or* purification] offering [4:3]. 13In this way the priest ·will remove the person's sins so he will belong to the LORD, and the LORD will forgive him [Lmakes atonement for him and he will be forgiven]. What is left of the sin offering belongs to the priest, like the ·grain [Lgift; tribute] offering [2:10].’ ”

The Penalty Offering

14The LORD said to Moses, 15“If a person ·accidentally [inadvertently; unintentionally; 4:2] sins and ·does something against [is unfaithful/disloyal toward] the holy things of the LORD, he must bring from the flock a male sheep ·that has nothing wrong with it [unblemished]. This will be his ·penalty [guilt; reparation] offering to the LORD. Its value in silver must be correct as set by the Holy Place measure. It is a ·penalty [guilt; reparation] offering. 16That person must pay for the sin he did against the holy thing, adding one-fifth to its value. Then he must give it all to the priest. In this way the priest will ·remove the person's sin so he will belong to the LORD [make atonement for him], by using the male sheep as the ·penalty [guilt; reparation] offering. And ·the LORD will forgive the person [Lhe will be forgiven].

17“If a person sins and does something the LORD has commanded not to be done, even if he does not know it, he is still guilty. He is responsible for his sin. 18He must bring the priest a male sheep from the flock, one that ·has nothing wrong with it [is unblemished] and that is worth the correct amount. It will be a ·penalty [guilt; reparation] offering. Though the person sinned without knowing it, with this offering the priest will ·remove the sin so the person will belong to the LORD, and the LORD will forgive him [make atonement for him and he will be forgiven]. 19The person is guilty of doing wrong, so he must give the ·penalty [guilt; reparation] offering to the LORD."

6The LORD said to Moses, 2"A person might sin against the LORD ·by doing one of these sins [L and be unfaithful/disloyal]: He might lie about ·what happened to something he was taking care of for someone else [L a deposit], or ·he might lie about a promise he made [L a pledge]. He might steal something or cheat someone. 3He might find something that had been lost and then lie about it. He might make a promise before the LORD about something and not mean it, or he might do some other sin. 4If he does any of these things, he is guilty of sin. He must bring back whatever he stole or whatever he took by cheating. He must bring back the ·thing he took care of for someone else [deposit]. He must bring back what he found and lied about 5or what he made a false promise about. He must pay the full price plus an extra one-fifth of the value of what he took. He must give the money to the true owner on the day he brings his ·penalty [guilt; reparation] offering. 6He must bring his penalty to the priest—a male sheep from the flock, ·one that does not have anything wrong with it [unblemished] and that is worth the correct amount. It will be a ·penalty [guilt; reparation] offering to the LORD. 7Then the priest will ·perform the acts to remove that person's sin so he will belong to the LORD, and the LORD will forgive him [make atonement for him and he will be forgiven] for the sins that made him guilty."

The Whole Burnt Offering

8The LORD said to Moses, 9"Give this command to Aaron and ·the priests [L his sons]: 'These are the ·teachings [laws; instruction] about the whole burnt offering [1:1–17]: The burnt offering must stay on the [L hearth of the] altar all night until morning, and the altar's fire must be kept burning. 10The priest must put on his linen robe and linen underclothes next to his body. Then he will remove the ashes from the burnt offering on the altar and put them beside the altar. 11Then he must take off those clothes and put on others and carry the ashes outside the camp to a special clean [C in a ritual sense] place. 12But the fire must be kept burning on the altar; it must not be ·allowed to go out [extinguished]. The priest must put more firewood on the altar every morning, place the whole burnt offering on the fire, and ·burn [L turn into smoke] the fat of the ·fellowship [*or* peace; well-being] offerings [3:1]. 13The fire must be kept burning on the altar ·all the time [perpetually]; it must not ·go out [be extinguished].

The Grain Offering

14" 'These are the ·teachings [laws; instructions] about the ·grain [L gift; tribute] offering [2:1]: The ·priests [L sons of Aaron] must bring it to the LORD in front of the altar. 15The priest must take a handful of ·fine [choice] flour, with the oil and all of the ·incense [frankincense] on it, and ·burn the grain offering [L turn it into smoke] on the altar as a memorial offering to the LORD. Its smell is pleasing to him. 16Aaron and ·the priests [L his sons] may eat what is left, but it must be eaten ·without yeast [unleavened] in a holy place. They must eat it in the courtyard of the Meeting Tent. 17It must not be ·cooked [baked] with ·yeast [leaven]. I have given it

as their ·share [portion] of the offerings made to me by fire; it is most
holy, like the ·sin [*or* purification] offering [4:3] and the ·penalty [guilt;
reparation] offering [5:14–6:7]. 18Any male descendant of Aaron may eat
it as his ·share of the offerings [perpetual due; decree] made to the LORD
by fire, ·and this will continue from now on [Lthroughout your genera-
tions]. Whatever touches these offerings shall become holy.' "

19The LORD said to Moses, 20"This is the ·offering [gift] Aaron and ·the
priests [Lhis sons] must bring to the LORD on the day they ·appoint Aaron
as high priest [Lanoint him]: They must bring ·two quarts [Lone-tenth of
an ephah] of ·fine [choice] flour for a ·continual [perpetual] ·grain [Lgift;
tribute] offering [2:1], half of it in the morning and half in the evening.
21The ·fine [choice] flour must be mixed with oil and cooked on a griddle.
Bring it when it is well ·mixed [*or* soaked]. Present the ·grain [Lgift; tribute]
offering [2:1] that is ·broken into pieces [*or* partly baked; *or* folded], and it
will be a smell that is pleasing to the LORD. 22One of the priests ·appointed
[anointed] to take Aaron's place as high priest must make the ·grain [Lgift;
tribute] offering [2:1]. It is a ·rule [statute; ordinance; regulation] forever
that the ·grain [Lgift; tribute] offering [2:1] must be completely burned to
the LORD. 23Every grain offering made by a priest must be completely
·burned [Lturned into smoke]; it must not be eaten."

The Sin Offering

24The LORD said to Moses, 25"Tell Aaron and ·the priests [Lhis sons]:
'These are the ·teachings [laws; instructions] about the ·sin [*or* purification; 4:3] offering: The ·sin [*or* purification; 4:3] offering must be ·killed
[slaughtered] in front of the LORD in the same place the whole burnt
offering [ch. 1] is ·killed [slaughtered]; it is most holy. 26The priest who
offers the ·sin [*or* purification; 4:3] offering must eat it in a holy place, in
the courtyard of the Meeting Tent. 27Whatever touches the meat of the
·sin [*or* purification; 4:3] offering ·must be [*or* will become] ·holy [conse-
crated; set apart], and if the blood is ·sprinkled [spattered] on any clothes,
you must wash them in a holy place. 28The clay pot the meat is ·cooked
[boiled] in must be broken, or if a bronze pot is used, it must be scrubbed
and rinsed with water. 29Any male in a priest's family may eat the offering; it is most holy. 30But if the blood of the ·sin [*or* purification; 4:3]
offering is taken into the Meeting Tent and used to ·remove sin [make
atonement] in the Holy Place, that ·sin [*or* purification; 4:3] offering must
be burned with fire. It must not be eaten.

The Penalty Offering

7" 'These are the ·teachings [laws; instructions] about the ·penalty
[guilt; reparation] offering [5:14–6:7], which is most holy: 2The
·penalty [guilt; reparation] offering must be ·killed [slaughtered] where
the whole burnt offering is ·killed [slaughtered; ch. 1]. Then the priest
must ·sprinkle [dash] its blood on all sides of the altar. 3He must offer all
the fat from the ·penalty [guilt; reparation] offering—the fat tail, the fat
that covers the inner organs, 4both kidneys with the fat that is on them
near the ·lower back muscle [loins], and the ·best part [appendage] of the
liver, which is to be removed with the kidneys. 5The priest must ·burn
[Lturn into smoke] all these things on the altar as an offering made by fire
to the LORD. It is a ·penalty [guilt; reparation] offering. 6Any male in a
priest's family may eat it. It is most holy, so it must be eaten in a holy place.

7" 'The ·penalty [guilt; reparation] offering [5:14–6:7] is like the ·sin [*or*
purification] offering [4:3] in that the ·teachings [laws; instructions] are
the same for both. The priest who ·offers the sacrifice to remove sins

[makes atonement with it] will ·get the meat for food [Lhave it]. 8The priest
who offers the burnt offering [ch. 1] may also have the skin from it. 9Every
·grain [Lgift; tribute] offering [2:1] that is baked in an oven, cooked on a
griddle, or baked in a dish belongs to the priest who offers it. 10Every ·grain
[Lgift; tribute] offering [2:1], either dry or mixed with oil, belongs to the
priests, and ·all priests [Lsons of Aaron] will share alike.

The Fellowship Offering

11" 'These are the ·teachings [laws; instructions] about the ·fellowship
[*or* peace; well-being] offering [3:1] a person may offer to the LORD: 12If he
brings the ·fellowship [*or* peace; well-being] offering [3:1] to show his
thanks, he should also bring loaves of bread made without ·yeast [leaven]
that are mixed with oil, wafers made without ·yeast [leaven] that have oil
poured over them, and loaves of ·fine [choice] flour that are ·mixed [*or*
soaked] with oil. 13He must also offer loaves of bread made with ·yeast
[leaven] along with his ·fellowship [*or* peace; well-being] offering [3:1],
which he gives to show thanks. 14One of each kind of ·offering [gift] will
be for the LORD; it will be given to the priest who ·sprinkles [dashes] the
blood of the ·fellowship [*or* peace; well-being] offering. 15When the fellowship [*or* peace; well-being] offering [3:1] is given to thank the LORD,
the meat from it must be eaten the same day it is offered; none of it must
be left until morning.

16" 'If a person brings a ·fellowship [*or* peace; well-being] offering [3:1]
·just to give a gift to God [as a freewill offering] or because of a ·special
promise to him [votive offering; Cin fulfillment of a vow], the sacrifice
should be eaten the same day he offers it. If there is any left, it may be eaten
the next day. 17If any meat from this sacrifice is left on the third day, it
must be burned ·up [Lwith fire]. 18Any meat of the ·fellowship [*or* peace;
well-being] offering eaten on the third day will not be accepted, nor will
the sacrifice count for the person who offered it. It ·will become unclean
[is an abomination], and anyone who eats the meat will be guilty of sin.

19" 'People must not eat meat that touches anything unclean [Cin a
ritual sense]; they must burn this meat with fire. Anyone who is clean
may eat other meat. 20But if anyone is unclean and eats the meat from the
·fellowship [*or* peace; well-being] offering [3:1] that belongs to the LORD,
he must be cut off from his people.

21" 'If anyone touches something unclean [Cin a ritual sense]—uncleanness that comes from people, from an animal, or from some ·hated thing
[*or* swarming creature]—touching it will make him unclean. If he then
eats meat from the ·fellowship [*or* peace; well-being] offering [3:1] that
belongs to the LORD, he must be cut off from his people.' "

22The LORD said to Moses, 23"Tell the ·people [Lsons; children] of Israel:
'You must not eat any of the fat from cattle, sheep, or goats [3:17]. 24If an
animal is found dead or torn by wild animals, you may use its fat for other
things, but you must not eat it. 25If someone eats fat from an animal offering made by fire to the LORD, he must be cut off from his people. 26No
matter where you live, you must not eat blood from any bird or animal.
27Anyone who eats blood must be cut off from his people [3:17].' "

The Priests' Share

28The LORD said to Moses, 29"Tell the ·people [Lsons; children] of Israel:
'If someone brings a ·fellowship [*or* peace; well-being] offering [3:1] to
the LORD, he must give part of it as his sacrifice to the LORD. 30He must
carry that part of the gift in his own hands as an offering made by fire to
the LORD. He must bring the fat and the breast of the animal to the priest,

to be presented to the LORD as ·the priests' share [Lan elevation offering].
31Then the priest must ·burn [Lturn into smoke] the fat on the altar, but
the breast of the animal will belong to Aaron and ·the priests [Lhis sons].
32You must also give the right thigh from the ·fellowship [*or* peace; well-
being] offering [3:1] to the priest as a ·gift [Lelevation offering]; 33it will
belong to the ·priest [Lson of Aaron] who offers the blood and fat of the
·fellowship [*or* peace; well-being] offering. 34I have taken the breast and
the thigh from the ·fellowship [*or* peace; well-being] offerings [3:1] of the
·Israelites [Lsons/Tchildren of Israel], and I have given these parts to Aaron
and ·the priests [Lhis sons] as ·their share for all time [an eternal regula-
tion] from the ·Israelites [Lsons/Tchildren of Israel].' "

35This is the portion that belongs to Aaron and his sons from the offerings made by fire to the LORD. They were given this share on the day they
were presented to the LORD as priests. 36On the day ·the LORD appointed
the priests [Lhe anointed them], he commanded Israel to give this share to
them, and it is ·to be given to the priests as their share [Lan eternal regula-
tion] ·from now on [Lthroughout their generations].

37These are the ·teachings [laws; instructions] about the whole burnt
offering, the ·grain [gift; tribute] offering [2:1], the ·sin [*or* purification;
4:3] offering, the ·penalty [guilt; reparation] offering [5:14–6:7], the offering for ·the appointment of priests [ordination], and the ·fellowship [*or*
peace; well-being] offering [3:1]. 38The LORD ·gave these teachings to
[Lcommanded] Moses on Mount Sinai on the day he commanded the
·Israelites [Lsons/Tchildren of Israel] to bring their ·offerings [gifts] to the
LORD in the Sinai ·Desert [Wilderness].

Aaron and His Sons Appointed

8 The LORD said to Moses, 2"Bring Aaron and his sons and their
clothes, the special olive oil used ·in appointing people and things
to the service of the LORD [for anointing], the bull of the ·sin [*or* purification; 4:3] offering and the two male sheep, and the basket of bread made
without ·yeast [leaven]. 3Then gather the ·people [Lcommunity; congregation; assembly] together at the entrance to the Meeting Tent." 4Moses did
as the LORD commanded him, and the ·people [Lcommunity; congregation;
assembly] met together at the entrance to the Meeting Tent.

5Then Moses spoke to the ·people [Lcommunity; congregation; assem-
bly] and said, "This is what the LORD has commanded to be done."
6Bringing Aaron and his sons forward, Moses washed them with water.
7He put the inner robe [Ex. 28:39–41] on Aaron and tied the ·cloth belt
[sash] around him. Then Moses put the outer robe [Ex. 28:31–41] on him
and placed the ·holy vest [Lephod; Ex. 28:6–14] on him. He tied the ·skill-
fully woven belt [embroidered waist band] around him so that the ·holy
vest [Lephod; Ex. 28:6–14] was tied to Aaron. 8Then Moses put the ·chest
covering [breastpiece; Ex. 28:15–30] on him and put the Urim and the
Thummim [Cdevices, probably lots, that were used to discern God's will;
the name means "light and truth"; Ex. 28:30] in the chest covering. 9He
also put the turban on Aaron's head. He put the ·strip of gold [rosette;
medallion; plate; Lflower], the holy crown, on the front of the turban, as
the LORD commanded him to do [Ex. 28:36].

10Then Moses ·put the special oil on [Ltook the anointing oil and
anointed] the ·Holy Tent [Tabernacle] and everything in it, ·making them
holy for the LORD [consecrating/sanctifying them]. 11He sprinkled some
oil on the altar seven times, ·sprinkling [anointing] the altar [Ex. 27:1–8]

and all its tools and the large bowl [Ex. 30:17–21] and its base. In this way he ·made them holy for the LORD [consecrated/sanctified them]. 12He poured some of the ·special [anointing] oil on Aaron's head [Ps. 133] to ·make Aaron holy for the LORD [consecrate/sanctify him]. 13Then Moses brought Aaron's sons forward. He put the inner robes [Ex. 28:39–41] on them, tied ·cloth belts [sashes] around them, and put ·headbands [headdresses] on them, as the LORD had commanded him.

14Then Moses brought the bull for the ·sin [*or* purification; 4:3] offering, and Aaron and his sons ·put [lay] their hands on its head. 15Moses ·killed [slaughtered] the bull, took the blood, and with his finger put some of it on all the ·corners [horns; Ex. 27:2] of the altar, to ·make it pure [purify it]. Then he poured out the rest of the blood at the ·bottom [base] of the altar. In this way he ·made it holy [sanctified/consecrated it] and ·ready for service to God [Lmade atonement for it]. 16Moses took all the fat from the inner organs of the bull, the ·best part [appendage] of the liver, and both kidneys with the fat that is on them, and he ·burned them [Lturned them into smoke] on the altar. 17But he took the bull's skin, its meat, and its ·intestines [*or* dung] and burned them in a fire outside the camp, as the LORD had commanded him.

18Next Moses brought the ·male sheep [ram] of the burnt offering [1:1–17], and Aaron and his sons ·put [lay] their hands on its head. 19Then Moses ·killed [slaughtered] it and ·sprinkled [dashed] the blood on all sides of the altar. 20He cut the male sheep into pieces and ·burned [Lturned into smoke] the head, the pieces, and the fat. 21He washed the inner organs and legs with water and ·burned [Lturned into smoke] the whole ·sheep [ram] on the altar as a burnt offering [1:1–17] made by fire to the LORD; its smell was pleasing to the LORD. Moses did these things as the LORD had commanded him.

22Then Moses brought the other ·male sheep [ram], ·the one used in appointing Aaron and his sons as priests [Lof ordination], and Aaron and his sons ·put [lay] their hands on its head. 23Then Moses ·killed [slaughtered] the sheep and put some of its blood on the ·bottom [lobe] of Aaron's right ear, some on the thumb of Aaron's right hand, and some on the big toe of his right foot [Ex. 29:20]. 24Then Moses brought Aaron's sons close to the altar. He put some of the blood on the ·bottom [lobe] of their right ears, some on the thumbs of their right hands, and some on the big toes of their right feet. Then he ·sprinkled [dashed] blood on all sides of the altar. 25He took the fat, the fat tail, all the fat on the inner organs, the ·best part [appendage] of the liver, both kidneys with their fat, and the right thigh. 26From the basket of bread made without ·yeast [leaven] that is put before the LORD each day [Ex. 25:30], Moses took a loaf of bread, a loaf made with oil, and a wafer. He put these pieces of bread on the fat and right thigh of the ·male sheep [ram]. 27All these things he put in the hands of Aaron and his sons and ·presented [raised] them as an [Lelevation] offering before the LORD. 28Then Moses took them from their hands and ·burned them [Lturned them into smoke] on the altar on top of the burnt offering [1:1–17]. So this was the offering ·for appointing Aaron and his sons as priests [for ordination]. It was an offering made by fire to the LORD, and its smell was pleasing to him. 29Moses also took the breast and ·presented [raised] it as an [Lelevation] offering before the LORD. It was Moses' share of the ·male sheep used in appointing the priests [ram of ordination], as the LORD had commanded him.

30Moses took some of the ·special [anointing] oil and some of the blood which was on the altar, and he sprinkled them on Aaron and Aaron's clothes and on Aaron's sons and their clothes. In this way Moses made Aaron, his clothes, his sons, and their clothes ·holy for the LORD [consecrated; sanctified].

31Then Moses said to Aaron and his sons, "I gave you a command, saying, 'Aaron and his sons will eat these things.' So take the meat and basket of bread from the offering ·for appointing priests [of ordination]. Boil the meat at the door of the Meeting Tent, and eat it there with the bread. 32If any of the meat or bread is left, burn it [Lwith fire]. 33The time of ·appointing [ordination] will last seven days; you must not go outside the entrance of the Meeting Tent until that time is up. Stay there until the time of your ·appointing [ordination] is finished. 34The LORD commanded the things that were done today to ·remove your sins so you will belong to him [make atonement for you]. 35You must stay at the entrance of the Meeting Tent day and night for seven days. If you don't obey the LORD's commands, you will die. The LORD has given me ·these commands [this charge]."

36So Aaron and his sons did everything the LORD had commanded through Moses.

Aaron and His Sons Offer Sacrifices

9 On the eighth day after the time of appointing, Moses called for Aaron and his sons and for the elders of Israel. 2He said to Aaron, "Take a bull calf and a ·male sheep [ram] ·that have nothing wrong with them [unblemished], and offer them to the LORD. The calf will be a ·sin [*or* purification; 4:3] offering, and the male sheep will be a whole burnt offering [1:1–17]. 3Tell the ·people [Lsons; children] of Israel, 'Take a male goat for a ·sin [*or* purification; 4:3] offering and a calf and a lamb for a whole burnt offering [1:1–17]; each must be one year old, and it must ·have nothing wrong with it [be unblemished]. 4Also take a bull and a male sheep for ·fellowship [*or* peace; well-being] offerings [3:1], along with a ·grain [Lgift; tribute] offering [2:1] mixed with oil. Offer all these things to the LORD, because the LORD will appear to you today.' "

5So all the ·people [community; congregation; assembly] came to the front of the Meeting Tent, bringing the things Moses had commanded them to bring, and they stood before the LORD. 6Moses said, "You have done what the LORD commanded, so you will see the LORD's glory [Chis manifest presence]."

7Then Moses told Aaron, "Go to the altar and offer ·sin [*or* purification; 4:3] offerings and whole burnt offerings [1:1–17]. Do this to ·remove your sins and the people's sins so you will belong to God [make atonement for you and the people]. Offer the sacrifices for the people and ·perform the acts to remove their sins for them so they will belong to the LORD [make atonement for them] as the LORD has commanded."

8So Aaron went to the altar and ·killed [slaughtered] the bull calf as a ·sin [purification; 4:3] offering for himself. 9Then Aaron's sons brought the blood to him, and he dipped his finger in the blood and put it on the ·corners [horns; 27:2] of the altar. He poured out the rest of the blood at the ·bottom [base] of the altar. 10Aaron took the fat, the kidneys, and the ·best part [appendage] of the liver from the ·sin [*or* purification; 4:3] offering and ·burned them [Lturned them into smoke] on the altar, in the way the LORD had commanded Moses. 11The meat and skin he burned outside the camp.

12Then Aaron ·killed [slaughtered] the animal for the whole burnt

offering [1:1–17]. His sons brought the blood to him, and he ·sprinkled
[dashed] it on all sides of the altar. 13As they gave him the pieces and head
of the burnt offering [1:1–17], Aaron ·burned them [Lturned them into
smoke] on the altar. 14He also washed the inner organs and the legs of the
burnt offering [1:1–17] and ·burned them [Lturned them into smoke] on
top of the burnt offering [1:1–17] on the altar.
15Then Aaron brought the offering that was for the people. He took the
goat of the people's ·sin [*or* purification; 4:3] offering and ·killed [slaughtered] it and offered it for the sin [*or* purification; 4:3] offering, just as he
had done the first ·sin [*or* purification; 4:3] offering.
16Then Aaron brought the whole ·burnt offering [1:1–17] and offered it
·in the way that the LORD had commanded [Laccording to regulations]. 17He
also brought the ·grain [Lgift; tribute] offering [2:1] to the altar. He ·took a handful of the grain [Lfilled his hand with a portion] and ·burned it [Lturned it into smoke] on the altar, in addition to the morning's burnt offering.
18Aaron also ·killed [slaughtered] the bull and the ·male sheep [ram] as
the ·fellowship [*or* peace; well-being] offerings [3:1] for the people. His
sons brought him the blood, and he ·sprinkled [dashed] it on all sides of
the altar. 19Aaron's sons also brought to Aaron the fat of the bull and the
·male sheep [ram]—the fat tail, the fat covering the inner organs, the kidneys, and the ·best part [appendage] of the liver. 20Aaron's sons put them
on the breasts of the bull and the sheep. Then Aaron ·burned [Lturned
into smoke] these fat parts on the altar. 21He ·presented [raised] the
breasts and the right thigh before the LORD as ·the priests' share of the [an elevation] offering, as Moses had commanded.
22Then Aaron lifted his hands toward the people and blessed them.
When he had finished offering the ·sin [*or* purification; 4:3] offering, the burnt offering [1:1–17], and the ·fellowship [*or* peace; well-being] offering [3:1], he stepped down from the altar.
23Moses and Aaron went into the Meeting Tent. Then they came out
and blessed the people, and the LORD's glory [Chis manifest presence]
came to all the people. 24Fire came out from the LORD and burned up the
burnt offering [1:1–17] and fat on the altar. When the people saw this, they shouted with joy and bowed facedown on the ground.

God Destroys Nadab and Abihu

10 Aaron's sons Nadab and Abihu took their ·pans for burning incense [censers; firepans], put fire in them, and added incense; ·but they did not use the special fire Moses had commanded them to use in the presence of the LORD [Land they offered unholy/illicit/Lstrange fire such as he had not commanded them; Cthey failed, in some unknown way, to follow strict ritual protocol]. 2So fire came down from
the LORD and ·destroyed [consumed] Nadab and Abihu, and they died in
front of the LORD. 3Then Moses said to Aaron, "This is what the LORD was speaking about when he said,

'I ·must be respected as [*or* will show myself] holy
·by [*or* through] those who come near me;
before all the people
I must be ·given honor [glorified].'"

So Aaron did not say anything about the death of his sons.
4Aaron's uncle Uzziel had two sons named Mishael and Elzaphan. Moses
said to them, "Come here and pick up your cousins' bodies. Carry them
outside the camp away from the front of the ·Holy Place [sanctuary]." 5So

Mishael and Elzaphan obeyed Moses and carried the bodies of Nadab
and Abihu, still clothed in the special priest's inner robes [Ex. 28:39–43],
outside the camp.
[6]Then Moses said to Aaron and his other sons, Eleazar and Ithamar,
"Don't show sadness by tearing your clothes or leaving your hair
uncombed. If you do, you will die, and the Lord will be angry with all the
·people [community; congregation; assembly]. All the ·people [[L]house]
of Israel, your relatives, may cry loudly about the Lord burning Nadab
and Abihu, [7]but you must not even leave the Meeting Tent. If you go out
of the entrance, you will die, because the ·Lord has appointed you to his
service [[L]anointing oil of the Lord is on you]." So Aaron, Eleazar, and
Ithamar obeyed Moses.
[8]Then the Lord said to Aaron, [9]"You and your sons must not drink wine
or ·beer [[T]strong drink; [C]an alcoholic beverage made from grain] when you
go into the Meeting Tent. If you do, you will die. This ·law will continue [is
a perpetual/eternal regulation] ·from now on [[L]throughout your genera-
tions]. [10]You must keep what is holy separate from what is ·not holy
[common]; you must keep what is clean separate from what is unclean [[L]in
a ritual sense]. [11]You must teach the ·people [[L]sons/[T]children of Israel] all
the ·laws [regulations] that the Lord gave to them through Moses."
[12]Moses said to Aaron and his remaining sons, Eleazar and Ithamar,
"Eat the part of the ·grain [[L]gift; tribute] offering [2:1] that is left from
the sacrifices offered by fire to the Lord, but do not add ·yeast [leaven] to
it. Eat it near the altar because it is most holy. [13]You must eat it in a holy
place, because this part of the offerings made by fire to the Lord ·belongs
to you and [[L]is your due and the due of] your sons. I have been commanded to tell you this.
[14]"Also, you and your sons and daughters may eat the breast and thigh
of the ·fellowship [[L]elevation; [C]the offering was lifted to the Lord before it
was eaten] offering that was presented to the Lord. You must eat them in
a clean [[C]in a ritual sense] place; they are your ·share [due] of the ·fellow-
ship [peace; well-being] offerings [3:1] given by the ·Israelites [[L]sons/
[T]children of Israel]. [15]The people must bring the fat from their animals
that was part of the offering made by fire, and they must ·present it to the
Lord along with the thigh [[L]that is raised] and the breast of the ·fellow-
ship [[L]elevation—see v. 14] offering. They will be ·the regular share of the
offerings for you and [your due and the due of] your children, as the Lord
has commanded."
[16]Moses ·looked for [made inquiry about] the goat of the ·sin [*or* purification; 4:3] offering, but it had already been burned up. So he became
very angry with Eleazar and Ithamar, Aaron's remaining sons. He said,
[17]"Why didn't you eat ·that goat [[L]the sin/or purification offering] in a
holy place? It is most holy, and the Lord gave it to you to take away the
guilt of the people, to ·remove their sins so they will belong to [make
atonement for them before] the Lord. [18]You didn't bring the goat's blood
inside the Holy Place. You were supposed to eat the goat in a holy place,
as I commanded!"
[19]But Aaron said to Moses, "Today they brought their ·sin [*or* purifica-
tion] offering [4:3] and burnt offering [1:1–17] before the Lord, but these
terrible things have still happened to me! Do you think the Lord would
·be any happier [*or* think it right] if I ate the ·sin [*or* purification] offering
[4:3] today?" [20]When Moses heard this, he was satisfied.

Rules About What May Be Eaten

11 The LORD said to Moses and Aaron, 2“Tell the ·Israelites [Lsons/Tchildren of Israel] this: ‘From among the land animals, these are the creatures you may eat: 3You may eat any animal that has split hoofs completely divided and that chews the cud [Cconsidered a normal land animal].

4“ ‘Some animals only chew the cud or only have split hoofs, and you must not eat them. The camel chews the cud but does not have a split hoof; it is unclean [Cin a ritual sense] for you. 5The rock badger chews the cud but does not have a split hoof; it is unclean for you. 6The rabbit chews the cud but does not have a split hoof; it is unclean for you. 7Now the pig has a split hoof that is completely divided, but it does not chew the cud; it is unclean for you. 8You must not eat the meat from these animals or even touch their dead bodies; they are unclean for you.

9“ ‘Of the animals that live in the sea or in a river, if the animal has fins and scales, you may eat it [Cconsidered a normal aquatic creature]. 10But whatever lives in the sea or in a river and does not have fins and scales—including the things that ·fill [swarm] the water and all other things that live in it—·you should hate [Lthey are detestable/abominable]. 11You must not eat any meat from them or even touch their dead bodies, because ·you should hate them [Lthey are detestable/abominable to you]. 12·You must hate [Detestable/Abominable to you is] any animal in the water that does not have fins and scales.

13“ ‘Also, these are the birds you ·are to hate [should find detestable/abominable]. They are ·hateful [detestable; abominable] and should not be eaten. You must not eat eagles, vultures, black vultures, 14kites, any kind of falcon, 15any kind of raven, 16horned owls, screech owls, sea gulls, any kind of hawk, 17little owls, cormorants, great owls, 18white owls, desert owls, ospreys, 19storks, any kind of heron, hoopoes, or bats [Cexact identification is sometimes uncertain, but all eat prey or carcasses and/or live in desolate places].

20“ ‘Don’t eat insects that have wings and walk on all four feet; they also are ·to be hated [detestable/abominable to you; Ctheir way of moving makes them abnormal insects].

21“ ‘But you may eat certain insects that have wings and walk on four feet. You may eat those that have legs with joints above their feet so they can ·jump [leap]. 22These are the insects you may eat: all kinds of locusts, winged locusts, crickets, and grasshoppers [Cexact identification is uncertain]. 23But all other insects that have wings and walk on four feet ·you are to hate [are detestable/abominable to you]. 24Those insects will make you unclean [Cin a ritual sense], and anyone who touches the dead body of one of these insects will become unclean until evening. 25Anyone who picks up one of these dead insects must wash his clothes and be unclean until evening.

26“ ‘Some animals have split hoofs, but the hoofs are not completely divided; others do not chew the cud. They are unclean for you, and anyone who touches the dead body of one of these animals will become unclean [Cin a ritual sense]. 27Of all the animals that walk on four feet, the animals that walk on their paws are unclean for you. Anyone who touches the dead body of one of these animals will become unclean until evening.

28 Anyone who picks up their dead bodies must wash his clothes and be
unclean until evening; these animals are unclean for you.
29 " 'These ·crawling [swarming] animals [C animals that move close to
the ground] are unclean for you: moles, rats, all kinds of great lizards,
30 geckos, crocodiles, lizards, sand reptiles, and chameleons [C identification
of some of these animals is uncertain]. 31 These ·crawling [swarming] animals are unclean for you [C probably because they eat carrion or touch
dead bodies]; anyone who touches their dead bodies will be unclean [C in
a ritual sense] until evening.
32 " 'If an unclean animal dies and falls on something, that item will
also become unclean [C in a ritual sense]. This includes anything made
from wood, cloth, leather, or rough cloth, regardless of its use. Whatever
the animal falls on must be washed with water and be unclean until evening; then it will become clean again. 33 If the dead, unclean animal falls
into a clay bowl, anything in the bowl will become unclean, and you must
break the bowl. 34 If water from the unclean clay bowl gets on any food,
that food will become unclean. 35 If any dead, unclean animal falls on
something, it becomes unclean. If it is a clay oven or a clay baking pan, it
must be broken into pieces. These things will be unclean; they are unclean
for you.
36 " 'A spring or ·well that collects water [cistern] will stay clean [C in a
ritual sense], but anyone who touches the dead body of any unclean animal will become unclean. 37 If a dead, unclean animal falls on a seed to be
planted, that seed is still clean. 38 But if you put water on some seeds and
a dead, unclean animal falls on them, they are unclean for you.
39 " 'Also, if an animal which you use for food dies, anyone who touches
its body will be unclean [C in a ritual sense] until evening. 40 Anyone who
eats meat from this animal's dead body must wash his clothes and be
unclean until evening. Anyone who picks up the animal's dead body must
wash his clothes and be unclean until evening.
41 " 'Every animal that ·crawls [swarms] on the ground is ·to be hated
[detestable; abominable]; it must not be eaten. 42 You must not eat any of
the animals that ·crawl [L walk] on the ground, including those that ·crawl
[walk] on their stomachs, that walk on all four feet, or on many feet. They
are ·to be hated [detestable; abominable]. 43 Do not make yourself unclean
[C in a ritual sense] by these animals; you must not become unclean by
them. 44 I am the LORD your God. ·Keep yourselves holy for me [L Sanctify/
Consecrate yourselves and be holy] because I am holy. Don't ·make yourselves unclean [defile yourselves] with any of these ·crawling [swarming]
animals. 45 I am the LORD who brought you out of Egypt to be your God;
you must be holy because I am holy.
46 " 'These are the ·teachings [laws; instructions] about all of the cattle,
birds, and other animals on earth, as well as the animals ·in the sea [L that
moves in the water] and those that ·crawl [swarm] on the ground. 47 These
·teachings [laws; teachings] help people know the difference between
unclean animals and clean animals [C in a ritual sense]; they help people
know which animals may be eaten and which ones must not be eaten.' "

Rules for New Mothers

12 The LORD said to Moses, 2 "Tell the ·people [L sons; children]
of Israel this: 'If a woman [L conceives; becomes pregnant
and] gives birth to a son, she will become unclean [C in a ritual sense] for
seven days, as she is unclean during her ·monthly period [menstruation;

15:19]. 3On the eighth day the ·boy [Lflesh of his foreskin] must be circumcised [Gen. 17:10–14]. 4Then it will be thirty-three days before she becomes clean from her loss of blood. She must not touch anything that is holy or enter the ·Holy Tent [Lsanctuary] until her time of ·cleansing [purification] is finished. 5But if she gives birth to a daughter, the mother will be unclean for two weeks, as she is unclean during her ·monthly period [menstruation]. It will be sixty-six days before she becomes clean from her loss of blood.

6" 'After she has a son or daughter and her days of ·cleansing [purification] are over, the new mother must bring certain sacrifices to the Meeting Tent. She must give the priest at the entrance a year-old lamb for a burnt offering [1:1–17] and a dove or young pigeon for a ·sin [*or* purification; 4:3] offering. 7He will offer them before the LORD to make her clean [Cin a ritual sense] ·so she will belong to the LORD again [Lto make atonement for her]; then she will be clean from her ·loss [flow] of blood. These are the ·teachings [laws; instructions] for a woman who gives birth to a boy or girl.

8" 'If she cannot afford a lamb, she is to bring two doves or two young pigeons, one for a burnt offering [1:1–17] and one for a ·sin [*or* purification; 4:3] offering. In this way the priest will make her clean [Cin a ritual sense] ·so she will belong to the LORD again [Land make atonement for her], and she will be clean.' "

Rules About Skin Diseases

13 The LORD said to Moses and Aaron, 2"Someone might have on ·his skin [Lthe skin of his body; Cand so throughout the passage] a swelling or a ·rash [eruption] or a bright spot. If the sore looks like ·a harmful skin disease [Tleprosy; the term does not refer to modern leprosy (Hansen's disease), but to various skin disorders], the person must be brought to Aaron the priest or to one of Aaron's sons, the priests. 3The priest must ·look at [examine] the sore on the person's skin. If the hair in the sore has become white, and the sore seems deeper than the person's skin, it is a harmful skin disease [13:2]. When he has finished ·looking at [examining] the person, the priest must announce that the person is unclean [Cin a ritual sense; the principle of "wholeness" was disturbed by running sores or by a skin disease that partially covered the body; see 13:12–13].

4"If there is a white spot on a person's skin, but the spot does not seem deeper than the skin, and if the hair from the spot has not turned white, the priest must ·separate [confine; quarantine] that person from other people for seven days. 5On the seventh day the priest must ·look at [examine] the person again. If he sees that the sore has not changed and it has not spread on the skin, the priest must keep the person ·separated [confined; quarantined] for seven more days. 6On the seventh day the priest must ·look at [examine] the person again. If the sore has faded and has not spread on the skin, the priest must announce that the person is clean [Cin a ritual sense]. The sore is only a ·rash [eruption]. The person must wash his clothes, and he will become clean again.

7"But if the ·rash [eruption] spreads again after the priest has announced him clean [Cin a ritual sense], the person must come again to the priest. 8The priest must ·look at [examine] him, and if the ·rash [eruption] has spread on the skin, the priest must announce that the person is unclean; it is a harmful skin disease [13:2].

9"If a person has a harmful skin disease [13:2], he must be brought to
the priest, 10and the priest must ·look at [examine] him. If there is a white
swelling in the skin, and the hair has become white, and the skin looks
raw in the swelling, 11it is a harmful skin disease [13:2]. It is one he has
had for a long time. The priest must announce that the person is unclean
[Cin a ritual sense]. He will not need to ·separate [confine; quarantine]
that person from other people, because everyone already knows that the
person is unclean.

12"If the skin disease [13:2] spreads all over a person's body, covering
his skin from his head to his feet, as far as the priest can see, the priest
must ·look at [examine] the person's whole body. 13If the priest sees that
the disease covers the whole body and has turned all of the person's skin
white, he must announce that the person is clean [Cin a ritual sense; he
was clean because he was whole, uniformly covered by skin disease; 13:3].

14"But when the person has ·an open sore [raw flesh], he is unclean [Cin
a ritual sense; because there was a break in the surface of his body, he was
no longer whole]. 15When the priest sees the ·open sore [raw flesh], he
must announce that the person is unclean. The open sore is not clean; it
is a harmful skin disease [13:2]. 16If the ·open sore [raw flesh] becomes
white again, the person must come to the priest. 17The priest must ·look
at [examine] him, and if the ·sores have [raw flesh has] become white, the
priest must announce that the person with the ·sores [raw flesh] is clean.
Then he will be clean.

18"Someone may have a boil on his skin that is healed. 19If in the place
where the boil was, there is a white swelling or a bright red spot, this place
on the skin must be shown to the priest. 20And the priest must ·look at
[examine] it. If the spot seems deeper than the skin and the hair on it has
become white, the priest must announce that the person is unclean [Cin a
ritual sense]. The spot is a harmful skin disease [13:2] that has broken out
from inside the boil. 21But if the priest looks at the spot and there are no
white hairs in it and the spot is not deeper than the skin and it has faded,
the priest must ·separate [confine; quarantine] the person from other people for seven days. 22If the spot spreads on the skin, the priest must
announce that the person is unclean; it is a disease that will spread. 23But
if the bright spot does not spread or change, it is only the scar from the old
boil. Then the priest must announce that the person is clean.

24"When a person gets a burn on his skin, if the ·open sore [raw flesh]
becomes white or red, 25the priest must ·look at [examine] it. If the white
spot seems deeper than the skin and the hair at that spot has become
white, it is a harmful skin disease [13:2]. The disease has broken out in
the burn, and the priest must announce that the person is unclean [Cin a
ritual sense]. It is a harmful skin disease [13:2]. 26But if the priest ·looks
at [examines] the spot and there is no white hair in the bright spot, and
the spot is no deeper than the skin and has faded, the priest must ·sepa-
rate [confine; quarantine] the person from other people for seven days.
27On the seventh day the priest must ·look at [examine] him again. If the
spot has spread on the skin, the priest must announce that the person is
unclean. It is a harmful skin disease [13:2]. 28But if the bright spot has not
spread on the skin but has faded, it is the swelling from the burn. The
priest must announce that the person is clean, because the spot is only a
scar from the burn.

29"When a man or a woman gets a sore on the scalp or on the ·chin [*or* cheek; *or* beard], 30a priest must ·look at [examine] the sore. If it seems deeper than the skin and the hair around it is thin and yellow, the priest must announce that the person is unclean [Cin a ritual sense]. It is an ·itch [scaly patch; Cperhaps eczema or ringworm], a harmful skin disease [13:2] of the head or ·chin [*or* cheek; *or* beard]. 31But if the priest ·looks at [examines] it and it does not seem deeper than the skin and there is no black hair in it, the priest must ·separate [confine; quarantine] the person from other people for seven days. 32On the seventh day the priest must ·look at [examine] the ·sore [itch; scaly patch; 13:30]. If it has not spread, and there are no yellow hairs growing in it, and the ·sore [itch; scaly patch] does not seem deeper than the skin, 33the person must shave himself, but he must not shave the ·sore place [itch; scaly patch]. The priest must ·separate [confine; quarantine] that person from other people for seven more days. 34On the seventh day the priest must ·look at [examine] the ·sore [itch; scaly patch]. If it has not spread on the skin and it does not seem deeper than the skin, the priest must announce that the person is clean [Cin a ritual sense]. So the person must wash his clothes and become clean. 35But if the ·sore [itch; scaly patch] spreads on the skin after the person has become clean, 36the priest must ·look at [examine] him again. If the sore has spread on the skin, the priest doesn't need to look for the yellowish hair; the person is unclean. 37But if the priest thinks the sore has stopped spreading, and black hair is growing in it, the ·sore [itch; scaly patch; 13:30] has healed. The person is clean, and the priest must announce that he is clean.

38"When a man or a woman has white spots on the skin, 39a priest must ·look at [examine] them. If the spots on the skin are dull white, the disease is only a harmless rash. That person is clean [Cin a ritual sense].

40"When anyone loses hair from his head and is bald, he is clean [Cin a ritual sense]. 41If he loses hair from the front of his head and has a bald forehead, he is clean. 42But if there is a red-white sore on his bald head or forehead, it is a skin disease [13:2] breaking out in those places. 43A priest must ·look at [examine] that person. If the swelling of the sore on his bald head or forehead is red-white, like a skin disease that spreads, 44that person has a skin disease [13:2]. He is unclean. The priest must announce that the person is unclean because of the sore on his head.

45"If a person has a skin disease [13:2] that spreads, he must warn other people by shouting, 'Unclean, unclean [Cin a ritual sense]!' His clothes must be torn at the seams, he must let his hair stay uncombed, and he must cover his ·mouth [Lupper lip]. 46That person will be unclean the whole time he has the disease; he is unclean. He must live alone outside the camp.

Rules About Mildew

47"Clothing might have ·mildew [*or* mold; Cthe same Hebrew word as for "skin disease"; 13:2] on it. It might be clothing made of linen or wool 48(either woven or knitted), or of leather, or something made from leather. 49If the mildew [13:47] in the clothing, leather, or woven or knitted material is green or red, it is a spreading mildew. It must be shown to the priest. 50The priest must ·look at [examine] the mildew, and he must put that piece of clothing in a ·separate [confined; quarantined] place for seven days. 51On the seventh day he must ·look at [examine] the mildew [13:47] again. If the mildew has spread on the cloth (either woven or knitted) or the leather, no matter what the leather was used for, it is a mildew

[13:47] that destroys; it is unclean [Cin a ritual sense]. 52The priest must burn the clothing. It does not matter if it is woven or knitted, wool or linen, or made of leather, because the mildew is spreading. It must be burned.

53“If the priest sees that the mildew [13:47] has not spread in the cloth (either knitted or woven) or leather, 54he must order the people to wash that piece of leather or cloth. Then he must ·separate [confine; quarantine] the clothing for seven more days. 55After the piece with the mildew has been washed, the priest must ·look at [examine] it again. If the mildew [13:47] still looks the same, the piece is unclean, even if the mildew has not spread. You must burn it in fire; it does not matter if the mildew is on one side or the other.

56“But when the priest ·looks at [examines] that piece of leather or cloth, the mildew [13:47] might have faded after the piece has been washed. Then the priest must tear the mildew out of the piece of leather or cloth (either woven or knitted). 57But if the mildew comes back to that piece of leather or cloth (either woven or knitted), the mildew is spreading. And whatever has the mildew must be burned with fire. 58When the cloth (either woven or knitted) or the leather is washed and the mildew [13:47] is gone, it must be washed again; then it will be clean [Cin a ritual sense].

59“These are the ·teachings [laws; instructions] about mildew [13:47] on pieces of cloth (either woven or knitted) or leather, to decide if they are clean or unclean [Cin a ritual sense].”

Rules for Cleansing from Skin Diseases

14 The LORD said to Moses, 2“These are the ·teachings [instructions; laws] for the time at which people who had a harmful skin disease [13:2] are made clean [Cin a ritual sense].

“The person shall be brought to the priest, 3and the priest must go outside the camp and ·look at [examine] the one who had the skin disease. If the skin disease is healed, 4the priest will command that two living, clean birds, a piece of cedar wood, a piece of red string, and a hyssop plant [Ex. 12:22] be brought for cleansing the person with the skin disease.

5“The priest must order one bird to be ·killed [slaughtered] in a clay bowl containing fresh water. 6Then he will take the living bird, the piece of cedar wood, the red string, and the hyssop; all these he will dip into the blood of the bird that was ·killed [slaughtered] over the fresh water. 7The priest will sprinkle the blood seven times on the person being cleansed from the skin disease [13:2]. He must announce that the person is clean [Cin a ritual sense] and then go to an open field and let the living bird go free.

8“The person to be cleansed must wash his clothes, shave off all his hair, and bathe in water [Cperhaps representing complete decontamination]. Then he will be clean and may go into the camp, though he must stay outside his tent for the first seven days. 9On the seventh day he must shave off all his hair—the hair from his head, his beard, his eyebrows, and the rest of his hair. He must wash his clothes and bathe his body in water, and he will be clean [Cin a ritual sense].

10“On the eighth day the person who had the skin disease must take two male lambs that ·have nothing wrong with them [are unblemished] and a year-old female lamb that ·has nothing wrong with it [is unblemished]. He must also take six quarts of fine flour mixed with oil for a ·grain [Lgift;

tribute] offering [2:1] and ·two-thirds of a pint [Lthree-tenths of an ephah] of olive oil. 11The priest who is to announce that the person is clean [Cin a ritual sense] must bring him and his sacrifices before the LORD at the entrance of the Meeting Tent. 12The priest will take one of the male lambs and offer it with the olive oil as a ·penalty [guilt; reparation; 5:14–6:7] offering; he will present them before the LORD as an offering. 13Then he will ·kill [slaughter] the male lamb in the holy place, where the ·sin [*or* purification; 4:3] offering and the whole burnt offering are killed. The ·penalty [guilt; reparation] offering is like the ·sin [*or* purification; 4:3] offering—it belongs to the priest and it is most holy.

14"The priest will take some of the blood of the ·penalty [guilt; reparation; 5:14–6:7] offering and put it on the ·bottom [lobe] of the right ear of the person to be made clean. He will also put some of it on the thumb of the person's right hand and on the big toe of the person's right foot. 15Then the priest will take some of the [Llog of; Ca liquid measure] oil and pour it into his own left hand. 16He will dip a finger of his right hand into the oil that is in his left hand, and with his finger he will sprinkle some of the oil seven times before the LORD. 17The priest will put some oil from his hand on the ·bottom [lobe] of the right ear of the person to be made clean, some on the thumb of the person's right hand, and some on the big toe of the person's right foot. The oil will go on these places on top of the blood for the ·penalty [guilt; reparation] offering. 18He will put the rest of the oil that is in his left hand on the head of the person to be made clean [Cin a ritual sense]. In this way the priest will make that person clean ·so he can belong to [Land make atonement for that person before] the LORD again.

19"Next the priest will offer the ·sin [*or* purification; 4:3] offering to make that person clean ·so he can belong to the LORD again [Land make atonement]. After this the priest will ·kill [slaughter] the animal for the whole burnt offering [1:1–17], 20and he will offer the burnt offering and ·grain [Lgift; tribute] offering [2:1] on the altar. In this way he will make that person clean [Cin a ritual sense] ·so he can belong to the LORD again [Land make atonement for him].

21"But if the person is poor and unable to afford these offerings, he must take one male lamb for a ·penalty [guilt; reparation; 5:14–6:7] offering. It will be presented to the LORD to make him clean [Cin a ritual sense] ·so he can belong to the LORD again [Land make atonement for him]. The person must also take ·two quarts [Lone tenth of an ephah] of ·fine [choice] flour mixed with oil for a ·grain [Lgift; tribute] offering [2:1]. He must also take ·two-thirds of a pint [La log; Ca liquid measure] of olive oil 22and two doves or two young pigeons, which he can afford. One bird is for a ·sin [*or* purification; 4:3] offering and the other for a whole burnt offering [1:1–17]. 23On the eighth day the person will bring them for his cleansing to the priest at the entrance of the Meeting Tent, before the LORD. 24The priest will take the lamb for the ·penalty [guilt; reparation] offering and the oil, and he will present them as an offering before the LORD. 25Then he will ·kill [slaughter] the lamb of the ·penalty [guilt; reparation] offering, take some of its blood, and put it on the ·bottom [lobe] of the right ear of the person to be made clean [Cin a ritual sense]. The priest will put some of this blood on the thumb of the person's right hand and some on the big toe of the person's right foot. 26He will also pour some of the oil into his own left hand. 27Then with a finger of his right hand, he will sprinkle some of the oil from his left hand seven times before the LORD. 28The priest will take some of the oil

from his hand and put it on the ·bottom [lobe] of the right ear of the person to be made clean. He will also put some of it on the thumb of the
person's right hand and some on the big toe of the person's right foot. The
oil will go on these places on top of the blood from the ·penalty [guilt; repa-
ration] offering. 29The priest must put the rest of the oil that is in his hand
on the head of the person to be made clean, to make him clean ·so he can
belong to [Lto make atonement for him before] the LORD again. 30Then the
priest will offer one of the doves or young pigeons, which the person can
afford. 31He must offer one of the birds for a ·sin [*or* purification; 4:3] offering and the other for a whole burnt offering [1:1–17], along with the grain
[Lgift; tribute; 2:1] offering. In this way the priest will make the person clean
so he can ·belong to [make atonement before] the LORD again; he will
become clean.
32"These are the ·teachings [regulations; laws] for making a person
clean [Cin a ritual sense] after he has had a skin disease [13:2], if he cannot
afford the regular sacrifices for becoming clean."

Rules for Cleaning Mildew

33The LORD also said to Moses and Aaron, 34"I am giving the land of
Canaan to your people. When they enter that land [Lof your possession],
if I cause ·mildew [*or* mold; 13:47] to grow in someone's house in that
land [Lof your possession], 35the owner of that house must come and tell
the priest. He should say, 'I have seen something like ·mildew [*or* mold; La
disease] in my house.' 36Then the priest must order the people to empty
the house before he goes in to ·look at [examine] the ·mildew [*or* mold;
Ldisease]. This is so he will not have to say that everything in the house is
unclean [Cin a ritual sense]. After this, the priest will go in to ·look at
[examine] it. 37He will ·look at [examine] the ·mildew [*or* mold; Ldisease],
and if the ·mildew [*or* mold; Ldisease] on the walls of the house is green or
red and goes into the wall's surface, 38he must go out and close up the
house for seven days. 39On the seventh day the priest must come back and
check the house. If the ·mildew [*or* mold; Ldisease] has spread on the walls
of the house, 40the priest must order the people to tear out the stones with
the ·mildew [*or* mold; Ldisease] on them. They should throw them away,
at a certain unclean place outside the city. 41Then the priest must have all
the inside of the house scraped. The people must throw away the plaster
they scraped off the walls, at a certain unclean place outside the city.
42Then the owner must put new stones in the walls, and he must cover the
walls with new clay plaster.
43"Suppose a person has taken away the old stones and plaster and put
in new stones and plaster. If ·mildew [*or* mold; Ldisease] again appears in
his house, 44the priest must come back and check the house again. If the
·mildew [*or* mold; Ldisease] has spread in the house, it is a ·mildew [*or*
mold; 13:47] that destroys things; the house is unclean [Cin a ritual sense].
45Then the owner must tear down the house, remove all its stones, plaster,
and wood, and take them to the unclean place outside the city. 46Anyone
who goes into that house while it is closed up will be unclean until evening. 47Anyone who eats in that house or lies down there must wash his
clothes.
48"Suppose after new stones and plaster have been put in a house, the
priest checks it again and the ·mildew [*or* mold; Ldisease] has not spread.
Then the priest will announce that the house is clean [Cin a ritual sense],
because the ·mildew [*or* mold; Ldisease] is gone.

49“Then, to make the house clean [Cin a ritual sense], the priest must
take two birds, a piece of cedar wood, a piece of red string, and a hyssop
plant. 50He will ·kill [slaughter] one bird in a clay bowl containing fresh
water. 51Then he will take the bird that is still alive, the cedar wood, the
hyssop, and the red string, and he will dip them into the blood of the bird
that was ·killed [slaughtered] over the fresh water. The priest will sprinkle
the blood on the house seven times. 52He will use the bird’s blood, the
fresh water, the live bird, the cedar wood, the hyssop, and the red string to
make the house clean. 53He will then go to an open field outside the city
and let the living bird go free. This is how the priest makes the house
clean and ·ready for service to the Lord [makes atonement for the house].”

54These are the ·teachings [regulations; laws] about any kind of skin
disease [13:2], 55·mildew [*or* mold] on pieces of cloth or in a house,
56swellings, rashes, or bright spots on the skin; 57they help people decide
when things are unclean [Cin a ritual sense] and when they are clean.
These are the ·teachings [regulations; laws] about all these kinds of
diseases.

Rules About a Person’s Body

15 The Lord also said to Moses and Aaron, 2“Say to the ·people
[Lsons; children] of Israel: ‘When ·a fluid comes from a person’s body [Lany man has a discharge from his genitals/flesh], the ·fluid
is [discharge makes him] unclean [Cin a ritual sense]. 3It doesn’t matter
if the ·fluid [discharge] flows freely or if it is blocked from ·flowing [dis-
charging]; the ·fluid [discharge] will make him unclean. This is the way
the ·fluid [discharge] makes him unclean:

4“ ‘If the person ·who discharges the body fluid [with the discharge]
lies on a bed, that bed becomes unclean [Cin a ritual sense], and everything he sits on becomes unclean. 5Anyone who touches his bed must
wash his clothes and bathe in water, and the person will be unclean until
evening. 6Whoever sits on something that the person ·who discharges the
fluid [with the discharge] sat on must wash his clothes and bathe in water;
he will be unclean until evening. 7Anyone who touches the person ·who
discharges the body fluid [with the discharge] must wash his clothes and
bathe in water; he will be unclean until evening.

8“ ‘If the person ·who discharges the body fluid [with the discharge]
spits on someone who is clean [Cin a ritual sense], that person must wash
his clothes and bathe in water; he will be unclean until evening.
9Everything on which the person who is unclean sits when riding
[Cspecifically a saddle] will become unclean. 10Anyone who touches something that was under him will be unclean until evening. And anyone who
carries these things must wash his clothes and bathe in water; he will be
unclean until evening.

11“ ‘If the person ·who discharges a body fluid [with a discharge] has
not washed his hands in water and touches another person, that person
must wash his clothes and bathe in water; he will be unclean [Cin a ritual
sense] until evening.

12“ ‘If a person ·who discharges a body fluid [with a discharge] touches
a clay bowl, that bowl must be broken. If he touches a wooden bowl, that
bowl must be washed in water.

13“ ‘When a person ·who discharges a body fluid [with a discharge] is
made clean [Cin a ritual sense], he must count seven days for himself for
his cleansing. He must wash his clothes and bathe his body in fresh water,

and he will be clean. 14On the eighth day he must take two doves or two
young pigeons before the LORD at the entrance of the Meeting Tent. He
will give the two birds to the priest. 15The priest will offer the birds, one
for a sin [*or* purification; 4:3] offering and the other for a burnt offering
[1:1–17]. And the priest will make that person clean ·so he can belong to
the LORD again [Land make atonement for him].
16" 'If semen [Cconsidered holy due to its association with life] goes out
from a man, he must bathe in water; he will be unclean [Cin a ritual sense]
until evening [Ccontact with something holy also rendered a person
unclean]. 17If the fluid gets on any clothing or leather, it must be washed
with water; it will be unclean until evening.
18" 'If a man ·has sexual relations [Llies] with a woman [Cpresumably his
wife] and ·semen comes out [has an emission of semen], both people must
bathe in water; they will be unclean [Cin a ritual sense] until evening.

Rules About a Woman's Body

19" 'When a woman has ·her monthly period [La discharge of blood
from her genitals/body], she is unclean [Cin a ritual sense; the blood's
association with reproduction makes it holy; 15:16] for seven days; anyone who touches her will be unclean until evening. 20Anything she lies on
during this time will be unclean, and everything she sits on during this
time will be unclean. 21Anyone who touches her bed must wash his
clothes and bathe in water; that person will be unclean until evening.
22Anyone who touches something she has sat on must wash his clothes
and bathe in water; that person will be unclean until evening. 23It does
not matter if the person touched the woman's bed or something she sat
on; he will be unclean until evening.
24" 'If a man ·has sexual relations with a woman [lies with her] and her
·monthly period [discharge] touches him, he will be unclean [Cin a ritual
sense] for seven days; every bed he lies on will be unclean.
25" 'If a woman has a ·loss [discharge] of blood for many days and it is
not during her regular monthly period, or if she continues to have a ·loss
[discharge] of blood after her regular period, she will be unclean [Cin a
ritual sense], as she is during her monthly period. She will be unclean for
as long as she continues to bleed [Matt. 9:20; Mark 5:25; Luke 8:43]. 26Any
bed she lies on during all the time of her ·bleeding [discharge] will be like
her bed during her regular monthly period. Everything she sits on will be
unclean, as during her regular monthly period.
27" 'Whoever touches those things will be unclean [Cin a ritual sense] and
must wash his clothes and bathe in water; he will be unclean until evening.
28When the woman becomes clean from her ·bleeding [discharge], she
must ·wait [Lcount] seven days, and after this she will be clean. 29Then on
the eighth day she must take two doves or two young pigeons and bring
them to the priest at the entrance of the Meeting Tent. 30The priest must
offer one bird for a sin [*or* purification; 4:3] offering and the other for a
whole burnt offering [1:1–17]. In this way the priest will make her clean so
she can belong to the LORD again [Land make atonement for her].
31" 'So you must warn the ·people [Lsons; children] of Israel to stay
separated from things that make them unclean [Cin a ritual sense]. If you
don't warn the people, they might make my ·Holy Tent [Tabernacle]
unclean, and then they would have to die!' "
32These are the ·teachings [laws; instructions] for the person who ·dis-
charges a body fluid [has a discharge] and for the man who becomes

unclean [Cin a ritual sense] from ·semen coming out of his body [an emission of semen]. 33These are the ·teachings [laws; regulations] for the woman who becomes unclean from her monthly period, for a man or woman who has a discharge, and for a man who ·becomes unclean by having sexual relations [Llies] with a woman who is unclean.

The Day of Cleansing

16 Now two of Aaron's sons had died ·while offering incense to [Lwhen they drew near to/approached] the Lord, and after that time the Lord spoke to Moses. 2The Lord said to him, "Tell your brother Aaron that there are times when he cannot go ·behind [inside] the curtain ·into the Most Holy Place [Lbefore the mercy seat/atonement cover; Ex. 25:17–22] where the Ark is. If he goes in when I appear in a cloud over the ·lid on the Ark [mercy seat; atonement cover], he will die.

3"This is how Aaron may enter the Most Holy Place: Before he enters, he must offer a bull for a ·sin [*or* purification; 4:3] offering and a ·male sheep [ram] for a whole burnt offering [1:1–17]. 4He must put on the holy linen inner robe [Ex. 28:39–41], with the linen underclothes [Ex. 28:42–43] next to his body. His belt will be the cloth belt [sash], and he will wear the linen turban. These are holy clothes, so he must bathe his body in water before he puts them on.

5"Aaron must take from the ·people [Lsons; children] of Israel two male goats for a sin [*or* purification; 4:3] offering and one ·male sheep [ram] for a burnt offering [1:1–17]. 6Then he will offer the bull for the ·sin [*or* purification; 4:3] offering ·for himself to remove sins from him and his family so they will belong to the Lord [Lto make atonement for him and for his family/house].

7"Next Aaron will take the two goats and bring them before the Lord at the entrance to the Meeting Tent. 8He will throw lots for the two goats—one will be for the Lord and the other for ·the goat that removes sin [Tthe scapegoat; LAzazel; Cmeaning uncertain; perhaps a geographical name]. 9Then Aaron will take the goat that was chosen for the Lord by throwing the lot, and he will offer it as a ·sin [*or* purification; 4:3] offering. 10The other goat, which was chosen by lot ·to remove the sin [Tas the scapegoat; Lfor Azazel to make atonement], must be brought alive before the Lord. The priest will use it to perform the acts that remove Israel's sin so they will belong to the Lord. Then this goat will be sent out into the ·desert [wilderness] ·as a goat that removes sin [Tas the scapegoat; Lto Azazel].

11"Then Aaron will offer the bull as a ·sin [*or* purification; 4:3] offering for himself, ·to remove the sins from him and his family so they will belong to the Lord [Lto make atonement for himself and his family]; he will ·kill [slaughter] the bull for the ·sin [*or* purification; 4:3] offering for himself. 12Then he must take a pan full of burning coals from the altar before the Lord and two handfuls of sweet incense that has been ground into powder. He must bring it into the room ·behind [inside] the curtain. 13He must put the incense on the fire before the Lord so that the cloud of incense will cover the ·lid [mercy seat; atonement cover; Ex. 25:17–22] on the ·Ark [Covenant; Treaty; LTestimony; Ex. 25:10]. Then when Aaron comes in, he will not die. 14Also, he must take some of the blood from the bull and sprinkle it with his finger on the front of the ·lid [mercy seat; atonement cover]; with his finger he will sprinkle the blood seven times in front of the ·lid [mercy seat; atonement cover].

15"Then Aaron must ·kill [slaughter] the goat of the ·sin [*or* purification;

4:3] offering for the people and bring its blood into the room ·behind [inside] the curtain. He must do with the goat's blood as he did with the bull's blood, sprinkling it on the ·lid [mercy seat; atonement cover] and in front of the ·lid [mercy seat; atonement cover]. 16Because the ·people [Lsons; children] of Israel have been unclean [Cin a ritual sense], Aaron will ·perform the acts to make the Most Holy Place ready for service to the Lord [Lmake atonement for the sanctuary]. Then it will be clean from the sins and crimes of the ·Israelites [Lsons/Tchildren of Israel]. He must also do this for the Meeting Tent, because it stays in the middle of unclean people. 17When Aaron makes ·the Most Holy Place ready for service to the Lord [Latonement for the sanctuary], no one is allowed in the Meeting Tent until he comes out. So Aaron will ·perform the acts to remove sins from [make atonement for] himself, his family, and all the ·people [assembly; crowd] of Israel, so they will belong to the Lord. 18Afterward he will go out to the altar that is before the Lord and ·will make it ready for service to the Lord [make atonement for it]. Aaron will take some of the bull's blood and some of the goat's blood and put it on the ·corners [horns; Ex. 27:2] of the altar on all sides. 19Then, with his finger, he will sprinkle some of the blood on the altar seven times to make the altar holy for the Lord and clean from all the sins of the Israelites.

20"When Aaron has finished making ·the Most Holy Place, the Meeting Tent, and the altar ready for service to the Lord [Latonement for the Most Holy Place, the Meeting Tent, and the altar], he will offer the living goat. 21He will ·put [lay] both his hands on the head of the living goat [Ca sign of association of the offerer and the animal], and he will confess over it all the sins and crimes of Israel. In this way Aaron will put the people's sins on the goat's head. Then he will send the goat away into the ·desert [wilderness], and a man who has been appointed will lead the goat away. 22So the goat will carry on itself all the people's sins to a lonely place in the desert. The man who leads the goat will let it loose there.

23"Then Aaron will enter the Meeting Tent and take off the linen clothes he had put on before he went into the Most Holy Place; he must leave these clothes there. 24He will bathe his body in water in a holy place and put on his regular clothes [Chis more ornate priestly clothes]. Then he will come out and offer the whole burnt offering [1:1–17] for himself and for the people, to ·remove sins from himself and the people so they will belong to the Lord [Lmake atonement for himself and the people]. 25Then he will burn the fat of the sin offering on the altar.

26"The person who led the goat, ·the goat to remove sins [Tthe scapegoat; Lfor/to Azazel; 16:8], into the desert must wash his clothes and bathe his body in water. After that, he may come back into the camp.

27"The bull and the goat for the ·sin [*or* purification; 4:3] offerings, whose blood was brought into the Most Holy Place to make ·it ready for service to the Lord [atonement], must be taken outside the camp; the animals' skins, bodies, and intestines will be burned in the fire. 28Then the one who burns them must wash his clothes and bathe his body in water. After that, he may come back into the camp.

29"This ·law [statute; ordinance; requirement] will always continue for you: On the tenth day of the seventh month, you must deny yourself [Cperhaps a reference to fasting] and you must not do any work. The ·travelers [*or* citizens] or ·foreigners living with you [alien residents] must not work either. 30It is on this day that the priests will make you clean ·so you will belong to the LORD again [Land make atonement for you]. All your sins will be removed. 31This is a very important day of rest for you, and you must deny yourselves. This ·law [statute; ordinance; regulation] will continue forever.

32"The priest ·appointed to take his father's place, on whom the oil was poured [who is anointed and consecrated in his father's place], will ·perform the acts for making things ready for service to the LORD [Lmake atonement]. He must put on the holy linen clothes 33and make ·the Most Holy Place, the Meeting Tent, and the altar ready for service to the LORD [Latonement for the Most Holy Place, the Meeting Tent, and the altar]. He must ·also remove the sins of the priests and all the people of Israel so they will belong to the LORD [Lmake atonement for the priests and the people of Israel]. 34That ·law [statute; ordinance; requirement] for removing the sins of the Israelites ·so they will belong to the LORD [Land make atonement] will continue forever. You will do these things once a year."

So they did the things the LORD had commanded Moses.

Offering Sacrifices

17 The LORD said to Moses, 2"Speak to Aaron, his sons, and all the ·people [Lsons; children] of Israel. Tell them: 'This is what the LORD has commanded. 3If ·an Israelite [La person from the house of Israel] ·kills [slaughters] an ox, a lamb, or a goat either inside the camp or outside it, 4when he should have brought the animal to the entrance of the Meeting Tent as a ·gift [offering] to the LORD in front of the LORD's ·Holy Tent [sanctuary], he is guilty of ·killing [Lshedding blood]. He has ·killed [Lshed blood], and he must be cut off from the people. 5This rule is so ·people [Lthe sons/Tchildren of Israel] will bring their sacrifices, which they have been sacrificing in the open fields, to the LORD. They must bring those animals to the LORD at the entrance of the Meeting Tent; they must bring them to the priest and offer them as ·fellowship [*or* peace; well-being] offerings [3:1]. 6Then the priest will ·sprinkle [dash] the blood from those animals on the LORD's altar near the entrance of the Meeting Tent. And he will ·burn [Lturn into smoke] the fat from those animals on the altar [3:17], as a smell pleasing to the LORD. 7They must not offer any more sacrifices to their goat idols [Cgoat images representing demons; 2 Chr. 11:15; Is. 13:21; 34:14], which they have chased like prostitutes [Cspiritual infidelity is often likened to marital infidelity; Hos. 1:2]. These ·rules [statutes; ordinances; requirements] will continue for people ·from now on [Lthroughout their generations].'

8"Tell the people this: 'If ·any citizen [Lanyone from the house] of Israel or ·foreigner living with you [sojourner; wanderer; resident alien] offers a burnt offering [1:1–17] or sacrifice, 9that person must take his sacrifice to the entrance of the Meeting Tent to offer it to the LORD. If he does not do this, he must be cut off from the people.

10" 'I will be against ·any citizen [Lanyone from the house] of Israel or ·foreigner living with you [sojourner; wanderer; resident alien] who eats blood [3:17]. I will cut off that person from the people. 11This is because the life of the body is in the blood, and I have given you rules for pouring that blood on the altar ·to remove your sins so you will belong to the LORD [to make atonement]. It is the blood that ·removes the sins [makes atonement], because it is life. 12So I tell the ·people [Lsons; children] of Israel this: "None of you may eat blood, and no ·foreigner living among you [resident alien] may eat blood."

13“ ‘If any ·citizen [Lof the sons/Tchildren] of Israel or ·foreigner living
among you [resident alien] ·catches [hunts] a wild animal or bird that can
be eaten, that person must pour the blood on the ground and cover it
with dirt. 14If blood is still in the ·meat [flesh], the animal’s life is still in
it. So I give this command to the ·people [Lsons; children] of Israel: “Don’t
eat ·meat [flesh] that still has blood in it, because the animal’s life is in its
blood. Anyone who eats blood must be cut off [3:17].”
15“ ‘If a person, either a ·citizen [native] or a ·foreigner [resident
alien], eats an animal that died by itself or was killed by another animal, he must wash his clothes and bathe in water. He will be unclean
[Cin a ritual sense] until evening; then he will be clean. 16If he does not
wash his clothes and bathe his body, he will ·be guilty of sin [carry
their guilt].’ ”

Rules About Sexual Relations

18 The LORD said to Moses, 2“Tell the ·people [Lsons; children]
of Israel: ‘I am the LORD your God. 3In the past you lived in
Egypt, but you must not do what was done in that country. And you
must not do as they do in the land of Canaan, where I am bringing you.
Do not follow their ·customs [statutes; ordinances; requirements]. 4You
must obey my ·rules [regulations] and ·follow [guard; keep] ·them [Lmy
statutes/ordinances/requirements]. I am the LORD your God. 5·Obey
[Guard; Keep] my ·laws [statutes; ordinances; requirements] and ·rules
[regulations]; a person who obeys them will live because of them. I am
the LORD.
6“ ‘You must never ·have sexual relations with [Lexpose/uncover the
nakedness of] your close relatives. I am the LORD.
7“ ‘You must not ·shame [Lexpose/uncover the nakedness of] your
father by ·having sexual relations with [Lexposing/uncovering the nakedness of] your mother. She is your mother; do not ·have sexual relations
with her [Lexpose/uncover her nakedness]. 8You must not ·have sexual
relations with [Lexpose/uncover the nakedness of] your father’s wife; ·that
would shame [Lit is the nakedness of] your father.
9“ ‘You must not ·have sexual relations with [Lexpose/uncover the nakedness of] your sister, either the daughter of your father or your mother. It
doesn’t matter if she was born in your house or somewhere else.
10“ ‘You must not ·have sexual relations with [Lexpose/uncover the
nakedness of] your son’s daughter or your daughter’s daughter; ·that
would bring shame on you [Ltheir nakedness is your nakedness].
11“ ‘If your father and his wife have a daughter, she is your sister. You
must not ·have sexual relations with her [Lexpose/uncover her
nakedness].
12“ ‘You must not ·have sexual relations with [Lexpose/uncover the
nakedness of] your father’s sister; she is your father’s close relative.
13You must not ·have sexual relations with [Lexpose/uncover the nakedness of] your mother’s sister; she is your mother’s close relative. 14You
must not ·have sexual relations with [Lexpose/uncover the nakedness
of] the wife of your father’s brother, ·because this would shame him
[Lyou should not approach his wife]. She is your aunt.
15“ ‘You must not ·have sexual relations with [Lexpose/uncover the
nakedness of] your daughter-in-law; she is your son’s wife. ·Do not have
sexual relations with her [LYou must not expose/uncover her nakedness].
16“ ‘You must not ·have sexual relations with [Lexpose/uncover the

nakedness of] your brother's wife. ·That would shame [LIt is the nakedness of] your brother.

17" 'You must not ·have sexual relations with [Lexpose/uncover the nakedness of] both a woman and her daughter. And do not ·have sexual relations with [Lexpose/uncover the nakedness of] this woman's granddaughter, either the daughter of her son or her daughter; they are her close relatives. It is evil to do this.

18" 'While your wife is still living, you must not take her sister as ·another wife [La rival]. Do not ·have sexual relations with her [Lexpose/uncover her nakedness].

19" 'You must not go near a woman to ·have sexual relations with her [Lexpose/uncover her nakedness] during her monthly period, when she is unclean [Cin a ritual sense; 15:19–33].

20" 'You must not have ·sexual relations [intercourse] with your neighbor's wife and make yourself unclean with her.

21" 'You must not give any of your children to ·be sacrificed [Lpass them over; Can allusion to passing them through fire] to Molech [Cprobably an Ammonite god; 20:3–5; 2 Kin. 23:10; Jer. 32:35], ·because this would show that you do not respect [Land so profane the name of] your God. I am the Lord.

22" 'You must not ·have sexual relations [Llie] with a man as you would a woman. That is ·a hateful sin [an abomination].

23" 'You must not have ·sexual relations [intercourse] with an animal and make yourself unclean with it. Also a woman must not ·have sexual relations with an animal [Lstand in front of an animal for copulation]; it is ·not natural [perverted].

24" 'Don't make yourself unclean by any of these wrong things. I am forcing nations out of their countries because they did these sins, and I am giving their land to you. 25The land has become unclean [Cin a ritual sense], and I punished it for its sins, so the land is ·throwing [vomiting] out those people who live there.

26" 'You must ·obey [guard; keep] my ·laws [statutes; ordinances; requirements] and ·rules [regulations], and you must not do any of these ·hateful sins [abominations]. ·These rules [LThey] are for ·the citizens of Israel and for the people who live with you [natives and resident aliens]. 27The people who lived in the land before you did all these ·hateful [abominable] things and made the land unclean. 28If you do these things, you will also make the land unclean, and it will ·throw [vomit] you out as it ·threw [vomited] out the nations before you. 29Anyone who does these ·hateful sins [abominations] must be cut off from the people. 30·Keep [Guard] my command not to do these ·hateful sins [abominations] that were done by the people who lived in the land before you. Don't make yourself unclean by doing them. I am the Lord your God.' "

Other Laws

19 The Lord said to Moses, 2"Tell all the ·people [Lcongregation/community of the sons/Tchildren] of Israel: 'I am the Lord your God. You must be holy because I am holy.

3" 'You must ·respect [fear; revere] your mother and father [Ex. 20:12; Deut. 5:16], and you must keep my Sabbaths [Ex. 20:8–11; Deut. 5:12–15]. I am the Lord your God.

4" 'Do not ·worship [Lturn to] idols or make ·statues of gods [cast images] for yourselves [Ex. 20:4–6; Deut. 5:8–10]. I am the Lord your God.

5“ ‘When you sacrifice a ·fellowship [*or* peace; well-being] offering
[3:1] to the LORD, offer it in such a way that will be accepted. 6You may eat
it the same day you offer it or on the next day. But if any is left on the
third day, you must burn it ·up [Lwith fire]. 7If any of it is eaten on the
third day, it is unclean, and it will not be accepted. 8Anyone who eats it
then will ·be guilty of sin [bear iniquity], because he ·did not respect [pro-
faned] the holy things that belong to the LORD. He must be cut off from
the people.
9“ ‘When you harvest your crops on your land, do not harvest all the
way to the corners of your fields. If grain falls onto the ground, don't
gather it up. 10Don't pick all the grapes in your vineyards, and don't pick
up the grapes that fall to the ground. You must leave those things for poor
people and for ·people traveling through your country [resident aliens;
Deut. 24:19–22; Ruth 2]. I am the LORD your God.
11“ ‘You must not steal [Ex. 20:15; Deut. 5:19]. You must not cheat people, and you must not lie to each other [Ex. 20:16; Deut. 5:20]. 12You must
not make a false promise by my name, or you will ·show that you don't
respect [Lprofane the name of] your God. I am the LORD.
13“ ‘You must not ·cheat [Loppress] your neighbor or rob him. You
must not keep a hired worker's salary all night until morning [Deut.
24:14–15; Jer. 22:13]. 14You must not ·curse [*or* belittle] a deaf person or
put ·something [a stumbling block] in front of a blind person to make
him fall [Deut. 27:18]. But you must ·respect [fear; Prov. 1:7] your God. I
am the LORD.
15“ ‘·Be fair in your judging [LDo not render perverted judgment]. You
must not show ·special favor [partiality] to poor people or great people,
but ·be fair when you [Lwith righteousness] judge your ·neighbor [coun-
tryman; James 2:1, 9]. 16You must not spread ·false stories [slander]
against other people, and you must not do anything that would ·put your
neighbor's life in danger [Lstand against the blood of your neighbor]. I am
the LORD.
17“ ‘You must not hate your ·fellow citizen [brother] in your heart. ·If
your ·neighbor [countryman] does something wrong, tell him about it
[LYou must reprove your brother], or you will be partly to blame. 18·Forget
about the wrong things people do to you, and do not try to get even [You
should not seek revenge or bear a grudge against any of your people]. Love
your neighbor as you love yourself [Matt. 19:19; 22:39; Mark 12:31, 33;
Luke 10:27]. I am the LORD.
19“ ‘·Obey [Keep; Guard] my ·laws [Lstatutes; ordinances; requirements].
You must not ·mate [breed] two different kinds of ·cattle [animals] or sow
your field with two different kinds of seed. You must not wear clothing
made from two different kinds of material mixed together.
20“ ‘If a man ·has sexual relations [Llies] with a slave girl ·of [Lbetrothed
to] another man, but this slave girl has not been ·bought [ransomed] or
given her freedom, there must be ·punishment [Lan inquiry]. But they are
not to be put to death, because the woman was not free. 21The man must
bring a ·male sheep [ram] as his ·penalty [guilt; reparation; 5:14–6:7]
offering to the LORD at the entrance to the Meeting Tent. 22The priest will
offer the ·sheep [ram] as a ·penalty [guilt; reparation; 5:14–6:7] offering
before the LORD for the man's sin, ·to remove the sins of the man so he will
belong to the LORD [L…and make atonement for him]. Then he will be
forgiven for his sin.

23“ ‘In the future, when you enter your country, you will plant many kinds of trees for food. ·After planting a tree, wait three years before using its fruit [LYou should regard its fruit as uncircumcised for three years; do not eat it]. 24In the fourth year the fruit from the tree will be the LORD's, a holy offering of praise to him. 25Then in the fifth year, you may eat the fruit from the tree. The tree will then produce more fruit for you. I am the LORD your God.

26“ ‘You must not eat anything with the blood in it [3:17].

“ ‘You must not try to tell the future by signs or ·black magic [divination; Deut. 18:9–12].

27“ ‘You must not cut the hair on ·the sides of your heads [your temples] or cut the edges of your beard. 28You must not cut your body for the dead [Ca pagan sign of mourning; Deut. 14:1; Jer. 16:6; 41:5] or put tattoo marks on yourselves. I am the LORD.

29“ ‘Do not ·dishonor [profane] your daughter by making her become a prostitute. If you do this, the country will be ·filled [Lprostituted] with all kinds of sin.

30“ ‘·Obey [Keep; Guard] ·the laws about Sabbaths [Lmy Sabbaths], and ·respect [reverence] my ·Most Holy Place [sanctuary]. I am the LORD.

31“ ‘Do not ·go [Lturn] to mediums or ·fortune-tellers [wizards] ·for advice [Land do not seek them], or you will become unclean [Cin a ritual sense]. I am the LORD your God.

32“ ‘Show respect to old people; stand up in their presence [Prov. 16:31; 20:29]. ·Show respect also to [Fear] your God. I am the LORD.

33“ ‘Do not mistreat ·foreigners living [resident aliens] in your country, 34but treat them just as you treat your own ·citizens [natives]. Love ·foreigners [resident aliens] as you love yourselves, because you were ·foreigners [sojourners; wanderers; resident aliens; Ex. 22:21; Jer. 22:3] one time in Egypt. I am the LORD your God.

35“ ‘Do not ·cheat [do injustice] when you measure the length or weight or ·amount of something [quantity; capacity; Deut. 25:13–16; Prov. 11:1; Ezek. 45:10–12]. 36Your weights and balances should weigh ·correctly [honestly], with your weighing baskets the right size and your jars holding the right amount of liquid. I am the LORD your God. I brought you out of the land of Egypt.

37“ ‘·Remember [Keep; Guard] all my ·laws [statutes; regulations; requirements] and ·rules [regulations], and obey them. I am the LORD.’ ”

Warnings About Various Sins

20 The LORD said to Moses, 2“You must also tell the ·people [Lsons; children] of Israel these things: ‘If a person in your country gives one of his children to Molech [18:21], that person must be ·killed [put to death]. It doesn't matter if he is a ·citizen [Lson of Israel] or a ·foreigner living [Lresident alien sojourning] in Israel; you must ·throw stones at [stone] him and ·kill him [put him to death]. 3I will be against him and cut him off from his people, because he gave his children to Molech. He showed that he ·did not respect [profaned] my holy name, and he made my ·Holy Place [sanctuary] unclean. 4The people of the ·community [Lland] might ·ignore [close their eyes to; *or* connive with] that person and not kill the one who gave his children to Molech. 5But I will ·be [Lset my face] against him and his family, and I will cut him off from his people. I will do this to anyone who follows him in ·being unfaithful to me [Lprostituting himself] by worshiping Molech.

6“ ‘I will ·be [Lset my face] against anyone who ·goes [turns] to mediums and ·fortune-tellers [wizards] for advice, because that person is
·being unfaithful to [Lprostituting himself against] me. So I will cut him
off from his people.
7“ ‘Be my holy people. Be holy because I am the LORD your God.
8·Remember [Keep; Guard] and obey my ·laws [statutes; ordinances; require-
ments]. I am the LORD, and I have ·made you holy [consecrated you].
9“ ‘Anyone who curses his father or mother must be put to death. He
has cursed his father or mother, so he has brought his own ·death [Lblood]
on himself [Ex. 20:12; Deut. 5:16].

Punishments for Sexual Sins

10“ ‘If a man ·has sexual relations [commits adultery] with his neighbor’s wife, both the ·man and the woman are guilty of adultery and
[Ladulterer and the adulteress] must be put to death [18:20; Deut. 22:22].
11If a man ·has sexual relations [Llies] with his father’s wife, ·he has
shamed [Lexposing/revealing the nakedness of] his father, and both the
man and his father’s wife must be put to death. They have brought ·it
[Lblood] on themselves [18:8; Deut. 22:30].
12“ ‘If a man ·has sexual relations [Llies] with his daughter-in-law, both
of them must be put to death. What they have done is ·not natural [per-
verted]. They have brought ·their own deaths [Lblood] on themselves.
13“ ‘If a man ·has sexual relations [Llies] with another man as a man
does with a woman, these two men have ·done a hateful sin [committed
an abomination]. They must be put to death. They have brought ·it
[blood] on themselves [18:22].
14“ ‘If a man ·has sexual relations with [*or* marries; Ltakes] both a
woman and her mother, this is ·evil [lewd; depraved]. The people must
burn that man and the two women in fire so that your people will not be
·evil [lewd; depraved].
15“ ‘If a man has sexual relations with an animal, he must be put to
death. You must also kill the animal. 16If a woman approaches an animal
and has sexual relations with it, you must kill the woman and the animal. They must be put to death. They have brought ·it [blood] on
themselves [18:23; Ex. 22:19; Deut. 27:21].
17“ ‘It is shameful for a brother to ·marry [Ltake] his sister, the
daughter of either his father or his mother, and ·to have sexual relations with her [Lhe sees her nakedness, and she sees his nakedness]. In
front of everyone they must both be cut off from their people. The
man has ·shamed [Lexposed/revealed the nakedness of] his sister, and
he is guilty of sin [18:9].
18“ ‘If a man ·has sexual relations [Llies] with a woman during her
monthly period, both the woman and the man must be cut off from
their people. They sinned because ·they showed the source of her blood
[Lhe uncovered her fountain and she has revealed the fountain of her
blood; 18:19].
19“ ‘Do not ·have sexual relations with [Luncover the nakedness of]
your mother’s sister or your father’s sister, because that would ·shame a
close relative [Lexpose one’s own flesh]. Both of you are guilty of this sin
[18:12–13].
20“ ‘If a man ·has sexual relations [Llies] with his uncle’s wife, he has
·shamed [Lexposed/revealed the nakedness of] his uncle. That man and
his uncle’s wife will die without children; they are guilty of sin.

21“ ‘It is unclean [Cin a ritual sense] for a man to ·marry [Ltake] his
brother’s wife. That man has ·shamed [Lexposed/revealed the nakedness
of] his brother, and they will have no children [18:16].
22“ ‘·Remember [Keep; Guard] all my ·laws [statutes; ordinances;
requirements] and ·rules [regulations], and obey them. I am leading you
to your own land, and if you obey my laws and rules, that land will not
·throw [vomit] you out. 23I am ·forcing [driving] out ahead of you the
people who live there. Because they did all these sins, I have hated them.
Do not live ·the way those people lived [Laccording to the statutes/ordi-
nances/requirements of that nation].
24“ ‘I have told you that you will ·get [inherit] their land, which I will
give to you as your ·very own [possession]; it is a ·fertile land [Lland flowing with milk and honey; Ex. 3:8]. I am the Lord your God, and I have set
you apart from other people and made you my own. 25So you must treat
clean [Cin a ritual sense] animals and birds differently from unclean animals and birds. Do not make yourselves detestable by any of these unclean
birds or animals or things that crawl on the ground, which I have made
unclean for you [11:1–47]. 26So you must be holy to me because I, the
Lord, am holy, and I have set you apart from other people to be my own.
27“ ‘A man or woman who is a medium or a ·fortune-teller [wizard]
must be put to death. You must stone them to death; they have brought
·it [Lblood] on themselves [19:31; 20:6].’ ”

How Priests Must Behave

21 The Lord said to Moses, “Tell these things to Aaron’s sons,
the priests: ‘A priest must not make himself unclean [Cin a
ritual sense] ·by touching a dead person [Lfor a death among his people/
relatives]. 2·But if the dead person was one of his close relatives, he may
touch him [L…except for a close relative]. The priest may make himself
unclean if the dead person is his mother or father, son or daughter,
brother or 3·unmarried [Lvirgin] sister who is close to him because she
has no husband. The priest may make himself unclean for her if she dies.
4But a priest must not make himself unclean ·if the dead person was only
related to him by marriage [Las a husband among his people].
5“ ‘Priests must not shave their heads, or shave off the edges of their
beards, or cut their bodies [Cas pagan priests often did]. 6They must be
holy to their God and ·show respect for [Lnot defile] God’s name, because
they present the offerings made by fire to the Lord, which is the food of
their God. So they must be holy [19:27–28].
7“ ‘A priest must not marry ·a defiled prostitute [*or* a prostitute or a
defiled woman] or a divorced woman, because he is holy to his God.
8Treat him as holy, because he offers up the food of your God. Think of
him as holy; I am the Lord who ·makes you holy [consecrates/sanctifies
you], and I am holy.
9“ ‘If a priest’s daughter defiles herself by becoming a prostitute, she
·shames [defiles] her father. She must be burned with fire.
10“ ‘The high priest, who was ·chosen from among his brothers [Lexalted
among his brothers], had the ·special [Lanointing] olive oil poured on his
head. He was also ·appointed [consecrated] to wear the priestly clothes.
So he must not let his hair go uncombed or tear his clothes [Csigns of
mourning]. 11He must not go into a house where there is a dead body. He
must not make himself unclean [Cin a ritual sense], even if it is for his
own father or mother. 12The high priest must not go out of the ·Holy

Place [sanctuary], because if he does and becomes ·unclean [defiled], he
will make God's ·Holy Place [sanctuary] unclean. The ·special oil used in
appointing priests [Lanointing oil] was poured on his head to separate
him from the rest of the people. I am the LORD.
13" 'The high priest must marry a woman who is a virgin. 14He must
not marry a widow, a divorced woman, or ·a defiled prostitute [*or* a defiled
woman or a prostitute; v. 7]. He must marry a virgin from his own people
15so ·the people will respect his children as his own [he will not defile his
children]. I am the LORD. I have ·set the high priest apart for his special
job [sanctified/consecrated him].' "
16The LORD said to Moses, 17"Tell Aaron: 'If any of your descendants
have ·something wrong with them [a blemish], they must never come
near to offer the special food of their God. 18Anyone who has ·something
wrong with him [a blemish] must not come near: blind men, crippled
men, men with damaged faces, deformed men, 19men with a crippled foot
or hand, 20hunchbacks, dwarfs, men who have something wrong with
their eyes, men who have an itching disease or a skin disease, or men who
·have damaged testicles [are eunuchs; Acts 8:27].
21" 'If one of Aaron's descendants has ·something wrong with him [a
blemish], he cannot come near to make the offerings made by fire to the
LORD. He has ·something wrong with him [a blemish]; he cannot offer the
food of his God. 22He may eat the most holy food and also the holy food.
23But he may not go through the curtain into the ·Most Holy Place [sanc-
tuary], and he may not go near the altar, because he has ·something wrong
with him [a blemish]. He must not defile my ·Holy Place [sanctuary]. I
am the LORD who makes these places holy.' "
24So Moses told these things to Aaron, Aaron's sons, and all the people
of Israel.

22 The LORD said to Moses, 2"Tell Aaron and his sons: 'The
·people [Lsons; children] of Israel will give offerings to me.
These offerings are ·holy, and they are mine [Lconsecrated/sanctified to
me], so you must ·respect [be scrupulous with] them to show that you
·respect [Ldo not defile] my holy name. I am the LORD.' 3Say to them: 'If
any one of your descendants ·from now on [Lthroughout your genera-
tions] is unclean [Cin a ritual sense] and comes near the offerings that
the Israelites ·made holy for [consecrated/sanctified to] me, that person
must be cut off from appearing before me. I am the LORD.
4" 'If one of Aaron's descendants has a harmful skin disease [13:2], or
if he discharges a body fluid [15:1–18], he cannot eat the holy offerings
until he becomes clean [Cin a ritual sense]. He could also become unclean
from touching a dead body, from his own semen, 5from touching any
unclean crawling animal, or from touching an unclean person (no matter
what made the person unclean). 6Anyone who touches those things will
become unclean until evening. That person must not eat the holy offerings unless he washes with water. 7He will be clean only after the sun goes
down. Then he may eat the holy offerings; the offerings are his food.
8" 'If a priest finds an animal that died by itself or that was killed by
some other animal, he must not eat it. If he does, he will become unclean
[Cin a ritual sense]. I am the LORD [11:39–40; 17:15].
9" 'If the priests ·keep [guard] all the rules I have given, they will not
become guilty; ·if they are careful, they will not die [*or*...and die in it/the
sanctuary because they defiled it]. I am the LORD who has made them holy.

10·Only people in a priest's family [LNo stranger/layperson] may eat the holy offering. A visitor staying with the priest or a hired worker must not eat it. 11But if the priest buys a slave with his own money, that slave may eat the holy offerings; ·slaves [Lthose] who were born in his house may also eat his food. 12If a priest's daughter marries a ·person who is not a priest [layperson; Lstranger], she must not eat any of the holy offerings. 13But if the priest's daughter becomes widowed or divorced, with no children to support her, and if she goes back to her father's house where she lived as a child, she may eat some of her father's food. But ·only people from a priest's family [no layperson/Lstranger] may eat this food.

14" 'If someone eats some of the holy offering by mistake, that person must pay back the priest for that holy food, adding another one-fifth of the price of that food.

15" 'When the ·Israelites [Lsons/Tchildren of Israel] give their holy offerings to the Lord, ·the priest must not treat these holy things as though they were not holy [Lno one will profane them]. 16The priests must not allow those who are not priests to eat the holy offerings. If they do, they cause the ones who eat the holy offerings to become guilty, and they will have to ·pay for it [Loffer a penalty/guilt/reparation offering; 5:14–6:7]. I am the Lord, who makes them holy.' "

17The Lord said to Moses, 18"Tell Aaron and his sons and all the people of Israel: 'A ·citizen of [Lperson from the house of] Israel or a ·foreigner living [sojourner; wanderer; resident alien] in Israel might want to bring a whole burnt offering [1:1–17], either for ·some special promise he has made [a vow] or for a ·special gift he wants to give [freewill offering] to the Lord. 19If he does, he must bring a male animal that has ·nothing wrong with it [no blemish]—a bull, a sheep, or a goat—so it might be accepted for him. 20He must not bring an animal that has ·something wrong with it [a blemish], or it will not be accepted for him.

21" 'If someone brings a ·fellowship [*or* peace; well-being] offering [3:1] to the Lord, either as ·payment [fulfillment] for a ·special promise the person has made [vow] or as a ·special gift the person wants to give the Lord [freewill offering], it might be from the herd or from the flock. But it must be ·healthy [perfect], with ·nothing wrong with it [no blemish], so that it will be accepted. 22You must not offer to the Lord any animal that is blind, that has broken bones or is crippled, that has running sores or any sort of ·skin disease [Litch or scabs]. You must not offer any animals like these on the altar as an offering by fire to the Lord.

23" 'If an ox or lamb ·is smaller than normal [*or* has a short tail] or is not perfectly formed, you may give it as a ·special gift to the Lord [freewill offering]; it will be accepted. But it will not be accepted as payment for a ·special promise you have made [vow].

24" 'If an animal has bruised, crushed, torn, or cut testicles, you must not offer it to the Lord. You must not do this in your own land, 25and you must not ·take [get] such animals from foreigners as sacrifices to the Lord. Because the animals have been hurt in some way and have ·something wrong with them [blemishes], they will not be accepted for you.' "

26The Lord said to Moses, 27"When an ox, a sheep, or a goat is born, it must stay seven days with its mother. But from the eighth day on, this animal will be accepted as a sacrifice by fire to the Lord. 28But you must not ·kill [slaughter] the animal and its mother on the same day, either an ox or a sheep.

29“If you want to offer ·some special offering of thanks [a thank offer-
ing] to the Lord, you must do it in a way that pleases him. 30You must eat
the whole animal that same day and not leave any of the meat for the next
morning. I am the Lord.
31“·Remember [Keep; Guard] my commands and obey them; I am the
Lord. 32·Show respect for [LDo not defile] my holy name. ·You Israelites
must remember that I am holy [LI must be sanctified/considered holy
among the sons/Tchildren of Israel]; I am the Lord, who has ·made you
holy [consecrated/sanctified you]. 33I brought you out of Egypt to be your
God. I am the Lord.”

Special Holidays

23 The Lord said to Moses, 2“Tell the ·people [Lsons; children]
of Israel: ‘You will announce the Lord’s appointed ·feasts
[festivals] as holy ·meetings [convocations]. These are my special ·feasts
[festivals].

The Sabbath

3“ ‘There are six days for you to work, but the seventh day will be a
special day of rest. It is a day for a holy ·meeting [convocation]; you must
not do any work. It is a Sabbath to the Lord in all your homes [Ex. 20:8–
11; 31:12–17; 35:1–3; Num. 28:9–10; Deut. 5:12–15].

The Passover and Unleavened Bread

4“ ‘These are the Lord’s appointed ·feasts [festivals], the holy ·meetings
[convocations], which you will announce at the times set for them. 5The
Lord’s Passover is on the fourteenth day of the first month, beginning at
twilight. 6The ·Feast [Festival] of Unleavened Bread begins on the fifteenth day of the same month. You will eat bread made without ·yeast
[leaven] for seven days. 7On the first day of this ·feast [festival] you will
have a holy ·meeting [convocation], and you must not do any work. 8For
seven days you will bring an offering made by fire to the Lord. There will
be a holy ·meeting [convocation] on the seventh day, and on that day you
must not do any regular work [Ex. 12:1–13, 21–27; 23:15; Num. 28:16–25;
Deut. 16:1–8].’ ”

The First of the Harvest

9The Lord said to Moses, 10“Tell the ·people [Lsons; children] of Israel:
‘You will enter the land I will give you and gather its harvest. At that time
you must bring the first bundle of grain from your harvest to the priest.
11The priest will ·present [wave] the bundle before the Lord, and it will be
accepted for you; he will ·present [wave] the bundle on the day after the
Sabbath.
12“ ‘On the day when you ·present [wave; 23:15] the bundle of grain,
offer a male lamb, one year old, that ·has nothing wrong with it [is per-
fect], as a burnt offering [1:1–17] to the Lord. 13You must also offer a
·grain [Lgift; tribute] offering [2:1]—·four quarts [Ltwo tenths of an
ephah] of ·fine [choice] flour mixed with olive oil as an offering made by
fire to the Lord; its smell will be pleasing to him. You must also offer ·a
quart [Lone-fourth of a hin] of wine as a drink offering. 14Until the day
you bring your offering to your God, do not eat any new grain, roasted
grain, or bread made from new grain. This ·law [statute; ordinance;
requirement] will always continue ·for people from now on [Lthroughout
your generations], wherever you live [Ex. 23:16; Num. 28:26–31; Deut.
16:9–12].

The Feast of Weeks

15“ ‘Count seven full weeks from the morning after the Sabbath. (This
is the Sabbath that you bring the bundle of grain to ·present [wave] as an

offering [Ca ritual whereby the offerer symbolically waves the offering before God but then uses it].) 16On the fiftieth day, the first day after the seventh week, you will bring a new grain offering to the LORD. 17On that day bring two loaves of bread from your homes to be ·presented [waved] as an offering. Use yeast and ·four quarts [Ltwo-tenths of an ephah] of flour to make those loaves of bread; they will be your gift to the LORD from the first wheat of your harvest.

18" 'Offer with the bread one young bull, two male sheep, and seven male lambs that are one year old and have ·nothing wrong with them [no blemish]. Offer them with their ·grain [Lgift; tribute] offerings [2:1] and drink offerings, as a burnt offering [1:1–17] to the LORD. They will be an offering made by fire, and the smell will be pleasing to the LORD. 19You must also offer one male goat for a ·sin [*or* purification; 4:3] offering and two male, one-year-old lambs as a ·fellowship [*or* peace; well-being] offering [3:1].

20" 'The priest will ·present [wave; 23:15] the two lambs as an offering before the LORD, along with the bread from the first wheat of the harvest. They are holy to the LORD, and they will belong to the priest. 21On that same day you will call a holy ·meeting [convocation]; you must not do any work that day. This ·law [statute; ordinance; requirement] will continue for you ·from now on [Lthroughout your generations], wherever you live.

22" 'When you harvest your crops on your land, do not harvest all the way to the corners of your field. If grain falls onto the ground, don't gather it up. Leave it for poor people and ·foreigners in your country [resident aliens; 19:9–10; Deut. 24:19–22; Ruth 2]. I am the LORD your God.' "

The Feast of Trumpets

23Again the LORD said to Moses, 24"Tell the ·people [Lsons] of Israel: 'On the first day of the seventh month you must have a special day of rest, a holy ·meeting [convocation], when you blow the trumpet for a special time of remembering. 25Do not do any work, and bring an offering made by fire to the LORD [Num. 29:1–6].' "

The Day of Cleansing

26The LORD said to Moses, 27"The Day of ·Cleansing [Atonement] will be on the tenth day of the seventh month. There will be a holy ·meeting [convocation], and you will deny yourselves and bring an offering made by fire to the LORD. 28Do not do any work on that day, because it is the Day of ·Cleansing [Atonement]. On that day the priests will go before the LORD and ·perform the acts to make you clean from sin so you will belong to the LORD [make atonement for you].

29"Anyone who ·refuses to give up food [*or* does not deny himself] on this day must be cut off from the people. 30If anyone works on this day, I will destroy that person from among the people. 31You must not do any work at all; this ·law [statute; ordinance; requirement] will continue ·for people from now on [Lthroughout your generations] wherever you live. 32It will be a special day of rest for you, and you must ·deny yourselves [*or* fast]. You will start this special day of rest on the evening after the ninth day of the month, and it will continue from that evening until the next evening [ch. 16; Num. 9:7–11]."

The Feast of Shelters

33Again the LORD said to Moses, 34"Tell the ·people [Lsons; children] of Israel: 'On the fifteenth day of the seventh month is the ·Feast [Festival] of ·Shelters [Booths]. This ·feast [festival] to the LORD will continue for seven days. 35There will be a holy ·meeting [convocation] on the first day; do not do any work. 36You will bring an offering made by fire to the LORD each day for seven days. On the eighth day you will have another holy ·meeting [convocation], and you will bring an offering made by fire to the LORD. This will be a holy ·meeting [convocation]; do not do any work.

37(" 'These are the LORD's special ·feasts [festivals], when there will be holy ·meetings [convocations] and when you bring offerings made by fire to the LORD. You will bring whole burnt offerings [1:1–17], ·grain [Lgift; tribute] offerings [2:1], sacrifices, and drink offerings—each at the right time. 38These offerings are in addition to those for the LORD's Sabbath days, in addition to offerings you give as payment for ·special promises [vows], and in addition to ·special offerings you want to give to the LORD [freewill offerings].)

39" 'So on the fifteenth day of the seventh month, after you have gathered in the crops of the land, celebrate the LORD's ·festival [feast] for seven days. You must rest on the first day and the eighth day. 40On the first day you will take good fruit from the fruit trees, as well as branches from palm trees, poplars, and other leafy trees. You will celebrate before the LORD your God for seven days. 41Celebrate this ·festival [feast] to the LORD for seven days each year. This ·law [statute; ordinance; requirement] will continue ·from now on [Lthroughout your generations]; you will celebrate it in the seventh month. 42Live in ·shelters [booths] for seven days. All the people born in Israel must live in ·shelters [booths] 43so that all your descendants will know I made Israel live in ·shelters [booths] during the time I brought them out of Egypt. I am the LORD your God [Ex. 23:16–17; Num. 29:12–39; Deut. 16:13–15; 31:9–13].' "

44So Moses told the people of Israel about all of the LORD's appointed ·feast [festival] days.

The Lampstand and the Holy Bread

24 The LORD said to Moses, 2"Command the ·people [Lsons; children] of Israel to bring you pure oil from crushed olives. That oil is for the lamps so that these lamps may never go out. 3Aaron will keep the lamps burning in the Meeting Tent from evening until morning before the LORD; this is ·in front of [Loutside] the curtain of the ·Ark of the Agreement [Covenant; Treaty; LTestimony]. This ·law [statute; ordinance; regulation] will continue ·from now on [Lthroughout your generations]. 4Aaron must always keep the lamps burning on the ·lampstand of pure gold [Lpure lampstand/Menorah; Ex. 25:31–40] before the LORD.

5"Take ·fine [choice] flour and bake twelve loaves of bread with it, using ·four quarts [Ltwo-tenths of an ephah] of flour for each loaf. 6Put them in two rows on the ·golden [Lpure] table [Ex. 25:23–30] before the LORD, six loaves in each row. 7Put pure incense on each row as the memorial portion to take the place of the bread. It is an offering made by fire to the LORD. 8Every Sabbath day Aaron will put the bread in order before the LORD, as an ·agreement [covenant; treaty] with the people of Israel that will continue forever. 9That bread will belong to Aaron and his sons. They will eat it in a holy place, because it is a most holy part of the offerings made by fire to the LORD. That bread is their share forever."

The Man Who Cursed God

10Now there was a son of an Israelite woman and an Egyptian father who ·was walking [Lcame out] among the Israelites. A fight broke out in the camp between him and an Israelite. 11The son of the Israelite woman began cursing and ·speaking against the LORD [Lblaspheming the name], so the people took him to Moses. (The mother's name was Shelomith, the

daughter of Dibri from the family of Dan.) 12The people ·held him as a
prisoner [put him in custody] while they waited for the LORD's ·command
[decision; will] to be made clear to them.
13Then the LORD said to Moses, 14"Take the one who ·spoke against
[Lcursed; blasphemed] me outside the camp. Then all the people who
heard him must put their hands on his head, and all the ·people [com-
munity; assembly; congregation] must ·throw stones at him and kill
[stone] him. 15Tell the ·people [Lsons; children] of Israel this: 'If anyone
curses his God, he is guilty of sin [Ex. 20:7; Deut. 5:11]. 16Anyone who
·speaks against [Lcurses/blasphemes the name of] the LORD must be put to
death; all the ·people [community; assembly; congregation] must ·kill
him by throwing stones at [stone] him. ·Foreigners [Sojourners;
Wanderers; Resident aliens] must be punished just like ·the people born
in Israel [natives]; if they ·speak against the LORD [Lcurse/blaspheme the
name], they must be put to death.
17" 'Whoever ·kills [Lstrikes] another person must be put to death.
18Whoever ·kills [Lstrikes] an animal that belongs to another person must
give that person another animal to take its place. 19And whoever causes
an injury to a ·neighbor [countryman] must receive the same kind of
injury in return: 20Broken bone for broken bone, eye for eye, tooth for
tooth. Anyone who injures another person must be injured in the same
way in return [Ex. 21:24]. 21Whoever ·kills [Lstrikes] another person's animal must give that person another animal to take its place. But whoever
·kills [strikes] another person must be put to death.
22" 'The ·law [regulation; standard] will be the same for the ·foreigner
[sojouner; wanderer; resident alien] as for ·those from your own country
[the native]. I am the LORD your God.' "
23Then Moses spoke to the ·people [Lsons; children] of Israel, and they
took the person who had cursed outside the camp and ·killed him by
throwing stones at [stoned] him. So the ·people [Lsons; children] of Israel
did as the LORD had commanded Moses.

The Time of Rest for the Land

25 The LORD said to Moses at Mount Sinai, 2"Tell the people of
Israel this: 'When you enter the land I will give you, let it have
a ·special time of rest, to honor [Lsabbath to/for] the LORD. 3You may plant
seed in your field for six years, and you may trim your vineyards for six
years and bring in their fruits. 4But during the seventh year, you must let
the land ·rest [have a sabbath]. This will be a ·special time to honor
[Lsabbath to/for] the LORD. You must not plant seed in your field or ·trim
[prune] your vineyards. 5You must not cut the crops that grow by themselves after harvest, or gather the grapes from your vines that are not
·trimmed [pruned]. The land will have a ·year of rest [sabbath].
6" 'You may eat whatever the land produces during that ·year of rest
[sabbath]. It will be food for your men and women servants, for your
hired workers, and for the ·foreigners living in your country [sojourners;
wanderers; resident aliens]. 7It will also be food for your cattle and the
wild animals of your land. Whatever the land produces may be eaten.

The Year of Jubilee

8" 'Count off seven groups of seven years, [Lseven times seven years] or
forty-nine years. During that time there will be seven ·years of rest [sab-
batical years; 25:1–7] for the land. 9On the Day of ·Cleansing [Atonement;
16:1–34], you must blow the horn of a ·male sheep [ram]; this will be on
the tenth day of the seventh month. You must blow the horn through the

whole country. 10Make the fiftieth year a ·special [consecrated; holy] year, and announce ·freedom [liberty] for all the people living in your country. This time will be called Jubilee [C a word related to the Hebrew for "ram's horn"]. You will each go back to your own property, each to your own family and family group. 11The fiftieth year will be a special time for you to celebrate. Don't plant seeds, or harvest the crops that grow by themselves, or gather grapes from the vines that are not ·trimmed [pruned]. 12That year is Jubilee; it will be a holy time for you. You may eat only the crops that come from the field. 13In the year of Jubilee you each must go back to your own property.

14" 'If you sell your land to your ·neighbor [countryman], or if you buy land from your ·neighbor [countryman], don't ·cheat [mistreat; exploit] each other. 15If you want to buy your ·neighbor's [countryman's] land, count the number of years since the last Jubilee, and use that number to decide the right price. If your ·neighbor [countryman] sells the land to you, count the number of years left for harvesting crops, and use that number to decide the right price. 16If there are many years, the price will be high. But if there are only a few years, lower the price, because your neighbor is really selling only a few crops to you. 17You must not ·cheat [mistreat; exploit] ·each other [L your neighbor/countryman], but you must ·respect [fear] your God. I am the LORD your God.

18" '·Remember [L Observe] my ·laws [statutes; ordinances; requirements] and ·rules [regulations], and ·obey [keep; guard] them so that you will live ·safely [securely] in the land. 19The land will give ·good crops [its fruit] to you, and you will eat as much as you want and live ·safely [securely] in the land.

20" 'But you might ask, "If we don't plant seeds or gather crops, what will we eat the seventh year?" 21I will ·send [L command for] you such a great blessing during the sixth year that the land will produce enough crops for three years. 22When you plant in the eighth year, you will still be eating from the old crop; you will eat the old crop until the harvest of the ninth year.

Property Laws

23" 'The land really belongs to me, so you can't sell it ·for all time [in perpetuity]. You are only ·foreigners [sojourners; wanderers; resident aliens] and ·travelers living for a while on my land [L tenants with me]. 24·People might sell their land, but it must always be possible for the family to get its land back [L Throughout all the land of your possession, you must allow for redemption of the land]. 25If ·a person in your country [your brother/kinsman] becomes very poor and sells some land, then close relatives ·must [*or* can] come and ·buy it back [redeem what his brother/kinsman has sold]. 26If there is not a ·close relative to buy the land back [redeemer], but if the person ·makes enough money to be able to buy it back [prospers and he is able to redeem it], 27the years must be ·counted [calculated] since the land was sold. That number must be used to decide how much the first owner should pay back the one who bought it. Then the land will belong to the first owner again. 28But if there is not enough money to buy it back, the one who bought it will keep it until the year of Jubilee. During that celebration, the land will go back to the first owner's family.

29" 'If someone sells a home in a walled city, for a full year after it is sold, the person has the right to ·buy it back [redeem it]. 30But if the owner does

not ·buy back the house [redeem it] before a full year is over, it will belong
to the one who bought it ·and to his future sons [Lin perpetuity, throughout his generations]. The house will not go back to the first owner at
Jubilee. 31But houses in ·small towns [villages] without walls are like open
·country [fields]; they can be ·bought back [redeemed], and they must be
returned to their first owner at Jubilee.
32" 'The Levites may always ·buy back [redeem] their houses in the cities that belong to them. 33If someone buys a house from a Levite, that
house in the Levites' city will again belong to the Levites in the Jubilee.
This is because houses in Levite cities belong to the people of Levi; ·the
Israelites gave these cities to them [Lfor the houses of the cities of the
Levites are their possession in the midst of the sons/Tchildren of Israel;
Num. 35:1–8; Josh. 21:1–45]. 34Also the ·fields and pastures [Lopen land]
around the Levites' cities cannot be sold, because ·those fields belong to
the Levites [Lthat is their possession] forever.

Rules for Slave Owners

35" 'If ·anyone from your country [your brother/kinsman] becomes too
poor ·to support himself [*or* and dependent on you], ·help [support] him
to live among you as you would a ·stranger [sojourner/wanderer/resident
alien] or ·foreigner [*or* tenant]. 36Do not charge him any interest on
money ·you loan to him [Lor try to make a profit; Ex. 22:25; Deut. 23:19–
20], but ·respect [fear] your God; let ·the poor [Lyour brother/kinsman]
live among you. 37Don't lend him money for interest, and don't try to
make a profit from the food he buys. 38I am the LORD your God, who
brought you out of the land of Egypt to give the land of Canaan to you
and to become your God.
39" 'If ·anyone from your country [your brother/kinsman] becomes
very poor and sells himself as a slave to you, you must not make him
work like a slave [Ex. 21:2–6; Deut. 15:12–18]. 40He will be like a hired
worker and a ·visitor [*or* tenant] with you until the year of Jubilee. 41Then
he may leave you, take his children, and go back to his family and the land
of his ancestors. 42This is because the Israelites are my servants, and I
brought them out of slavery in Egypt. They must not become slaves
again. 43You must not ·rule this person [exercise dominion; Gen. 1:26]
cruelly, but you must ·respect [fear] your God.
44" 'Your men and women slaves must come from other nations around
you; from them you may buy slaves. 45Also you may buy as slaves children
from the families of ·strangers [sojourners/wanderers/resident aliens] or
·foreigners [*or* tenants] living in your land. ·These child slaves will belong
to you [LThose born in your land will be your property], 46and you may
even ·pass them on to your children after you die [will them to your chil-
dren]; you can make them slaves forever. But you must not ·rule [exercise
dominion] cruelly over your own ·people [brothers; kinsmen], the
·Israelites [Lsons/Tchildren of Israel].
47" 'Suppose a ·stranger [sojourner/wanderer/resident alien] or ·for-
eigner [*or* tenant] among you becomes rich. If ·someone in your country
[a brother/kinsman] becomes so poor that he has to sell himself as a slave
to the ·foreigner [sojourner; wanderer; resident alien] living among you
or to a member of the ·foreigner's [sojourner's; wanderer's; resident
alien's] family, 48·the poor person has the right to be bought back and
become free [Lafter he is sold he has the right of redemption]. One of his
relatives may ·buy him back [redeem him]: 49His uncle, his uncle's son, or

any one of his close relatives may ·buy him back [redeem him]. Or, if he
gets enough money, he may pay the money to ·free [redeem] himself.
50“ ‘He and the one who bought him must ·count [calculate] the time
from when he sold himself up to the next year of Jubilee. Use that number to decide the price, because the person really only hired himself out
for a certain number of years. 51If there are still many years before the
year of Jubilee, the person must ·pay back [redeem] a large part of the
price. 52If there are only a few years left until Jubilee, the person must pay
a small part of the first price. 53But he will live like a hired person with
·the foreigner [Lhim] every year; don’t let the ·foreigner [Lhim] ·rule
[exercise dominion] cruelly over him.
54“ ‘Even if no one ·buys him back [redeems him], at the year of Jubilee,
he and his children will ·become free [Lgo out]. 55This is because the ·peo-
ple [Lsons; children] of Israel are servants to me. They are my servants,
whom I brought out of Egypt. I am the LORD your God.

Rewards for Obeying God

26 “ ‘Don’t make idols for yourselves or set up ·statues [carved
images] or ·memorials [pillars]. Don’t put stone statues in
your land to bow down to, because I am the LORD your God [19:4; Ex.
20:4–6; Deut. 5:8–10].
2“ ‘·Remember [Keep; Guard] my Sabbaths, and ·respect [fear] my
·Holy Place [sanctuary; 19:3, 30; 23:3; Ex. 20:8–14; Deut. 5:12–15]. I am
the LORD.
3“ ‘If you ·remember [keep; guard] my ·laws [statutes; ordinances;
requirements] and commands and obey them, 4I will give you rains at the
right season [Deut. 11:14]; the land will produce crops, and the trees of
the field will produce their fruit. 5Your threshing will continue until the
grape harvest, and your grape harvest will continue until it is time to
plant. Then you will have plenty to eat and live ·safely [securely] in your
land. 6I will give peace to your country; you will lie down ·in peace, and
no one will make you afraid [Land not be afraid]. I will keep ·harmful
[dangerous] animals out of your country, and ·armies [Lthe sword] will
not pass through it.
7“ ‘You will ·chase [pursue] your enemies and ·defeat them, killing them
with your [Lthey will fall before you by the] sword. 8Five of you will ·chase
[pursue] a hundred men; a hundred of you will ·chase [pursue] ten thousand men [Deut. 32:30; Josh. 23:10; Is. 30:17]. ·You will defeat your enemies
and kill them with your [LThey will fall before you by the] sword.
9“ ‘Then I will ·show kindness to [Lturn toward] you and ·let you have
many children [LI will make you fruitful and multiply you]; I will ·keep
my agreement [establish my covenant/treaty] with you. 10You will ·have
enough crops to last for more than a year [old grain long stored]. When
you harvest the new crops, you will have to throw out the old ones to
make room for them. 11Also I will place my ·Holy Tent [sanctuary] among
you, and I will not ·turn away from [Labhor] you. 12I will walk with you
and be your God, and you will be my people. 13I am the LORD your God,
who brought you out of Egypt, where you were slaves. I broke the ·heavy
weights that were on your shoulders [bars of your yoke] and let you walk
·proudly [erect; standing tall] again.

Punishment for Not Obeying God

14“ ‘But if you do not ·obey [keep; guard] me and ·keep [obey] all my
commands, 15and if you ·turn away from [disdain] my ·rules [statutes;
ordinances; requirements] and ·hate [abhor] my ·laws [regulations],

refusing to obey all my commands, you have broken our ·agreement
[covenant; treaty]. 16As a result, I will do this to you: I will ·cause terrible
things to happen to [bring dread/terror on] you. I will cause you to have
disease and fever that will destroy your eyes and slowly kill you. You will
not have success when you plant your seed, and your enemy will eat your
crops. 17I will ·be [Lset my face] against you, and your enemies will defeat
you. These people who hate you will ·rule [exercise dominion] over you,
and you will run away even when no one is ·chasing [pursuing] you.

18" 'If after all this you still do not ·obey [listen to] me, I will ·punish
[discipline] you seven times more for your sins. 19I will break your great
pride, and I will make the sky like iron and the earth like bronze [Cthere
would be no rain]. 20·You will work hard, but it will not help [LYour
strength will be for no purpose]. Your land will not grow any crops, and
your trees will not give their fruit.

21" 'If you still turn against me and refuse to ·obey [listen to] me, I will
·beat [strike] you seven times harder. The more you sin, the more you will
be punished. 22I will send wild animals to attack you, and they will ·take
your children away from you and destroy [Lbereave you and cut off] your
cattle. They will make you so few in number the roads will be empty.

23" 'If you don't learn your lesson after all these things, and if you still
turn against me, 24I will also turn against you. I will ·punish [strike] you
seven more times for your sins. 25You broke my agreement, and I will
·punish [Lhave my revenge against] you. I will bring ·armies [Lthe sword]
against you, and if you go into your cities for safety, I will cause ·diseases
[plagues] to spread among you so that ·your enemy will defeat you [Lyou
will be given into the enemy's hand]. 26·There will be very little bread to
eat; [LWhen I break your staff of bread,] ten women will ·be able to cook
all [bake] your bread in one oven. They will measure [Lby weight] each
piece of bread, and you will eat, but you will ·still be hungry [Lnot be
satisfied].

27" 'If you still refuse to ·listen to [obey] me and still turn against me, 28I
will ·show [Lturn against you with] my great anger; I will ·punish [disci-
pline] you seven more times for your sins. 29You will eat the ·bodies [flesh]
of your sons and [Lthe flesh of your] daughters [Deut. 28:53–57; Is. 49:26;
Jer. 19:9; Ezek. 5:10]. 30I will destroy your ·places where gods are worshiped
[Lhigh places] and cut down your incense altars. I will pile your dead bodies on the lifeless forms of your idols [2 Kin. 23:14–16]. I will ·hate [abhor]
you. 31I will ·destroy your cities [make your cities a ruin] and make your
holy places ·empty [desolate], and I will not smell the pleasing smell of
your offerings. 32I will make the land ·empty [desolate] so that your enemies who come to live in it will be shocked at it. 33I will scatter you among
the nations, and I will pull out my sword and destroy you. Your land will
become empty, your cities a ·waste [ruin]. 34When you are taken to your
enemy's country, your land will finally get its ·rest [sabbath; 25:1–7]. It will
enjoy its ·time of rest [sabbath] all the time it lies empty. 35During the time
the land is empty, it will have the ·rest [sabbath] you should have given it
while you lived in it [2 Chr. 36:21].

36" 'Those of you who are left alive will ·lose their courage [Lplace
despondency in their hearts] in the land of their enemies. ·They will be
frightened by the sound of a leaf being blown by the wind [LThe sound of
a driven leaf will make them flee]. They will ·run [flee] as if someone were
chasing them with a sword, and they will fall even when no one is ·chasing

[pursuing] them. 37They will fall over ·each other [Ltheir brother/kinsman], as if ·someone were chasing them with [Lbefore] a sword, even though no one is ·chasing [pursuing] them. You will not be strong enough to stand up against your enemies. 38You will ·die [perish] among other nations and ·disappear in your enemies' countries [Lthe land of your enemies will consume you]. 39So those who are left alive will ·rot [*or* pine] away in their enemies' countries because of their sins. They will also ·rot [*or* pine] away because of their ·ancestors' [fathers'] sins.

There Is Always Hope

40" 'But maybe the people will confess their sins and the sins of their ·ancestors [fathers]; maybe they will admit they turned against me and ·sinned [committed treachery] against me, 41which made me turn against them and send them into the land of their enemies. If ·these disobedient people [Ltheir uncircumcised hearts; Deut. 10:16; 30:6; Jer. 4:4] are ·sorry for what they did [Lhumbled] and accept punishment for their sin, 42I will remember my ·agreement [covenant; treaty] with Jacob [Gen. 35:9–15], my ·agreement [covenant; treaty] with Isaac [Gen. 26:24], and my ·agreement [covenant; treaty] with Abraham [Gen 12:1–3; 15; 17], and I will remember the land. 43The land will be ·left empty by its people [Lforsaken/abandoned of them], and it will enjoy its ·time of rest [sabbath; 25:1–7] as it lies ·bare [desolate] without them. Then those who are left alive will accept the punishment for their sins. They will learn that they were punished because they ·hated [disdained] my ·laws [regulations] and ·refused to obey [abhorred] my ·rules [statutes; ordinances; requirements]. 44But even though this is true, I will not ·turn away from [disdain] them when they are in the land of their enemies. I will not ·hate [abhor] them so much that I completely destroy them and break my ·agreement [covenant; treaty] with them, because I am the LORD their God. 45For their good I will remember the ·agreement with their ancestors [Lformer covenant/treaty], whom I brought out of the land of Egypt [Cthe covenant with Moses; Ex. 19–24] so I could become their God; the other nations saw these things. I am the LORD.' "

46These are the ·laws [statutes; ordinances; requirements], ·rules [regulations], and ·teachings [laws; instructions] the LORD made between himself and the Israelites through Moses at Mount Sinai.

Promises Are Important

27 The LORD said to Moses, 2"Speak to the ·people [Lsons; children] of Israel and tell them: 'If someone makes a ·special promise [vow] ·to give a person as a servant to the LORD by paying a price that is the same value as that person [Lconcerning an equivalent for a person; Ca person, such as a child or a slave, could be given for God's service, or money paid instead to fulfill the vow], 3the ·price [equivalent] for a man twenty to sixty years old is about ·one and one-fourth pounds [Lfifty shekels] of silver. (You must use the measure as set by the ·Holy Place [sanctuary].) 4The ·price [equivalent] for a woman twenty to sixty years old is about ·twelve ounces [Lthirty shekels] of silver. 5The ·price [equivalent] for a man five to twenty years old is about ·eight ounces [Ltwenty shekels] of silver; for a woman it is about ·four ounces [Lten shekels] of silver. 6The ·price [equivalent] for a baby boy one month to five years old is about ·two ounces [Lfive shekels] of silver; for a baby girl the price is about ·one and one-half ounces [Lthree shekels] of silver. 7The ·price [equivalent] for a man sixty years old or older is about ·six ounces [Lfifteen shekels] of silver; for a woman it is about ·four ounces [Lten shekels] of silver.

8“ ‘If anyone is too poor to pay the ·price [equivalent], bring him to the
priest, and the priest will set the price. The priest will decide how much
money the person making the vow can afford to pay.

Gifts to the Lord

9“ ‘Some animals may be used as ·sacrifices [gifts] to the LORD. If someone ·promises to bring [Lgives] one of these to the LORD, it will become
holy. 10That person must not try to ·put another animal in its place
[Lsubstitute for it] or exchange it, a good animal for a bad one, or a bad
animal for a good one. If this happens, both animals will become holy.
11“ ‘Unclean [Cin a ritual sense] animals cannot be offered as ·sacrifices
[gifts] to the LORD, and if someone brings one of them to the LORD, that
animal must be brought to the priest. 12The priest will decide a ·price
[equivalent] for the animal, according to whether it is good or bad; as the
priest decides, that is the ·price [equivalent] for the animal. 13If the person wants to ·buy back [redeem] the animal, an additional one-fifth must
be added to the ·price [equivalent].

Value of a House

14“ ‘If a person ·gives [dedicates; consecrates] a house as holy to the
LORD, the priest must decide its ·value [equivalent], according to whether
the house is good or bad; as the priest decides, that is the ·price [equiva-
lent] for the house. 15But if the person who ·gives [dedicates; consecrates]
the house wants to ·buy it back [redeem it], an additional one-fifth must
be added to the ·price [equivalent]. Then the house will belong to that
person again.

Value of Land

16“ ‘If a person ·gives [dedicates; consecrates] some family property to
the LORD, the ·value [equivalent] of the fields will depend on how much
seed is needed to plant them. It will cost about ·one and one-fourth
pounds [Lfifty shekels] of silver for each ·six bushels [Lhomer] of barley
seed needed. 17If the person ·gives [dedicates; consecrates] a field at the
year of Jubilee [25:8–22], its value [equivalent] ·will stay at what the priest
has decided [Lwill stand]. 18But if the person ·gives [dedicates; conse-
crates] the field after the Jubilee, the priest must ·decide [calculate] the
exact ·price [equivalent] by counting the number of years to the next year
of Jubilee. Then he will subtract that number from its ·value [equivalent].
19If the person who ·gave [dedicated; consecrated] the field wants to ·buy
it back [redeem it], one-fifth must be added to that ·price [equivalent],
and the field will belong to the first owner again.
20“ ‘If the person does not ·buy back [redeem] the field, or if it is sold
to someone else, the first person cannot ever ·buy it back [redeem it].
21When the land is released at the year of Jubilee, it will become holy to
the LORD, like land ·specially given [devoted] to him. It will become the
property of the priests.
22“ ‘If someone ·gives [dedicates; consecrates] to the LORD a field he has
bought, which is not a part of his family land, 23the priest must ·count
[calculate] the years to the next Jubilee. He must decide the ·price [equiv-
alent] for the land, and the ·price [equivalent] must be paid on that day.
Then that land will be holy to the LORD. 24At the year of Jubilee, the land
will go back to its first owner, to the family who sold the land.
25“ ‘You must use the measure as set by the ·Holy Place [sanctuary] in
paying these ·prices [equivalents]; ·it weighs two-fifths of an ounce
[Ltwenty gerahs will make a shekel].

Value of Animals

26“ ‘If an animal is the first one born to its parent, it already belongs to

the Lord, so people may not ·give [dedicate; consecrate] it again. If it is a
·cow [[L]ox] or a sheep, it is the Lord's. 27If the animal is unclean [[C]in a ritual sense], the person must ·buy it back [ransom it] for the ·price set by
the priest [equivalent], and the person must add one-fifth to that price. If
it is not ·bought back [redeemed], the priest must sell it for ·the price he
had decided [its equivalent].

28" '·There is a special kind of gift that people set apart to give [[L]All
devoted things that are devoted…] to the Lord; it may be a person, animal, or field from the family property. That gift cannot be ·bought back
[redeemed] or sold. Every ·special kind of gift [devoted thing] is most
holy to the Lord.

29" '·If anyone is given for the purpose of being destroyed, he [[L]Everyone
who is devoted from among people] cannot be ·bought back [redeemed];
he must be put to death.

30" 'One-tenth of all crops belongs to the Lord, including the crops
from fields and the fruit from trees. That one-tenth is holy to the Lord.
31If a person wants to ·get back [redeem] that tenth, one-fifth must be
added to its price.

32" '·The priest will take every [[L]Every] tenth animal from a person's
herd or flock, ·and it [[L]a tenth of all that passes under the shepherd's rod,]
will be holy to the Lord. 33The owner should not ·pick out the good animals from the bad [inquire whether they are good or bad] or exchange
one animal for another. If that happens, both animals will become holy;
they cannot be ·bought back [redeemed].' "

34These are the commands the Lord ·gave to [commanded] Moses at
Mount Sinai for the ·people [[L]sons; children] of Israel.

NUMBERS

The People of Israel Are Counted

1 **The Lord spoke to Moses in the Meeting Tent** [Cthe Tabernacle; Ex. 25–31] **in the ·Desert** [Wilderness] **of Sinai. This was on the first day of the second month in the second year after the Israelites left Egypt** [Ex. 12:50–51; Cone year later]. **He said to Moses: 2"You and Aaron must ·count** [take a census of; Llift the head of] **all the ·people of Israel** [community/congregation/assembly of the sons/Tchildren of Israel] **by ·families** [clans] **and family groups, listing the name of each ·man** [male]. **3You and Aaron must count every man twenty years old or older who will serve in the army of Israel, and list them by their divisions** [Clike a military registration]. **4One man from each tribe, the leader of his family, will help you. 5These are the names of the men who will help you:**

from the tribe of Reuben—Elizur son of Shedeur;
6from the tribe of Simeon—Shelumiel son of Zurishaddai;
7from the tribe of Judah—Nahshon son of Amminadab;
8from the tribe of Issachar—Nethanel son of Zuar;
9from the tribe of Zebulun—Eliab son of Helon;
10from the tribe of Ephraim son of Joseph—Elishama son of Ammihud;
from the tribe of Manasseh son of Joseph—Gamaliel son of Pedahzur;
11from the tribe of Benjamin—Abidan son of Gideoni;
12from the tribe of Dan—Ahiezer son of Ammishaddai;
13from the tribe of Asher—Pagiel son of Ocran;
14from the tribe of Gad—Eliasaph son of Deuel;
15from the tribe of Naphtali—Ahira son of Enan."

16These were the men chosen from the ·people [community; congregation; assembly] **to be leaders of their tribes, the heads of Israel's family groups.**

17Moses and Aaron took these men ·who had been picked [Lwhose names had been designated] **18and ·called** [assembled] **all the ·people** [community; congregation; assembly] **of Israel together on the first day of the second month. Then the people ·were listed** [registered their genealogies] **by their ·families** [clans] **and family groups, and all the ·men** [males] **who were twenty years old or older were listed by name. 19Moses did exactly what the Lord had commanded and ·listed** [enrolled] **the people while they were in the ·Desert** [Wilderness] **of Sinai.**

20The ·tribe [Lsons; descendants] **of Reuben, the first son born to Israel** [CJacob; Gen. 35:23; 46:8; 49:3], **·was counted** [Laccording to their records/lineage]; **all the men twenty years old or older who were able to serve in the army were listed by name with their ·families** [clans] **and family groups. 21The tribe of Reuben totaled 46,500 men.**

22The ·tribe [Lsons; descendants] **of Simeon ·was counted** [Laccording to their records/lineage]**; all the men twenty years old or older who were able to serve in the army were listed by name with their ·families** [clans] **and family groups. 23The tribe of Simeon totaled 59,300 men.**

24The ·tribe [Lsons; descendants] **of Gad ·was counted** [Laccording to their records/lineage]**; all the men twenty years old or older who were able to serve in the army were listed by name with their ·families** [clans] **and family groups. 25The tribe of Gad totaled 45,650 men.**

26The ·tribe [Lsons; descendants] **of Judah ·was counted** [Laccording to their records/lineage]**; all the men twenty years old or older who were able to serve in the army were listed by name with their ·families** [clans] **and family groups. 27The tribe of Judah totaled 74,600 men.**

28The ·tribe [Lsons; descendants] **of Issachar ·was counted** [Laccording to their records/lineage]**; all the men twenty years old or older who were able to serve in the army were listed by name with their ·families** [clans] **and family groups. 29The tribe of Issachar totaled 54,400 men.**

30The ·tribe [Lsons; descendants] **of Zebulun ·was counted** [Laccording to their records/lineage]**; all the men twenty years old or older who were able to serve in the army were listed by name with their ·families** [clans] **and family groups. 31The tribe of Zebulun totaled 57,400 men.**

32The ·tribe [Lsons; descendants] **of Ephraim, a son of Joseph, ·was counted** [Laccording to their records/lineage]**; all the men twenty years old or older who were able to serve in the army were listed by name with their ·families** [clans] **and family groups. 33The tribe of Ephraim totaled 40,500 men.**

34The ·tribe [Lsons; descendants] **of Manasseh, also a son of Joseph, ·was counted** [Laccording to their records/lineage]**; all the men twenty years old or older who were able to serve in the army were listed by name with their ·families** [clans] **and family groups. 35The tribe of Manasseh totaled 32,200 men.**

36The ·tribe [Lsons; descendants] **of Benjamin ·was counted** [Laccording to their records/lineage]**; all the men twenty years old or older who were able to serve in the army were listed by name with their ·families** [clans] **and family groups. 37The tribe of Benjamin totaled 35,400 men.**

38The ·tribe [Lsons; descendants] **of Dan ·was counted** [Laccording to their records/lineage]**; all the men twenty years old or older who were able to serve in the army were listed by name with their ·families** [clans] **and family groups. 39The tribe of Dan totaled 62,700 men.**

40The ·tribe [Lsons; descendants] **of Asher ·was counted** [Laccording to their records/lineage]**; all the men twenty years old or older who were able to serve in the army were listed by name with their ·families** [clans] **and family groups. 41The tribe of Asher totaled 41,500 men.**

42The ·tribe [Lsons; descendants] **of Naphtali ·was counted** [Laccording to their records/lineage]**; all the men twenty years old or older who were able to serve in the army were listed by name with their ·families** [clans] **and family groups. 43The tribe of Naphtali totaled 53,400 men.**

44Moses, Aaron, and the twelve leaders of Israel, one from each of the family groups, counted these men. 45Every man of Israel twenty years old or older who was able to serve in the army was counted and listed with his family group. 46The total number of men was 603,550.

47The families groups from the tribe of Levi were not ·listed [counted] **with the others, because 48the LORD had told Moses: 49"Do not count the**

tribe of Levi or ·include [take a census of; Llift the head of] them with the other Israelites. 50Instead put the Levites in charge of the ·Holy Tent [Tabernacle] of the ·Agreement [Treaty; Covenant; LTestimony; Cthe Ten Commandments were in the Ark in the Tabernacle; Ex. 25:10] and everything that is with it [Ex. 32:26–29]. They must carry the ·Holy Tent [Tabernacle] and everything in it, and they must take care of it and make their camp around it. 51Any time the ·Holy Tent [Tabernacle] ·is moved [sets out], the Levites must take it down, and any time it is ·set up [pitched], the Levites must do it. Anyone else who goes near the ·Holy Tent [Tabernacle] will be put to death. 52The ·Israelites [Lsons/Tchildren of Israel] will make their camps in separate divisions, each family near its ·flag [standard]. 53But the Levites must make their camp around the ·Holy Tent [Tabernacle] of the ·Agreement [Testimony; Treaty; Covenant; 1:50] so that I will not be angry with the ·Israelites [community/ congregation/assembly of the sons/Tchildren of Israel]. The Levites will take care of the ·Holy Tent [Tabernacle] of the ·Agreement [Testimony; Treaty; Covenant; 1:50]."

54So the Israelites did everything just as the LORD commanded Moses.

The Camp Arrangement

2 The LORD said to Moses and Aaron: 2"The ·Israelites [Lsons/Tchildren of Israel] should make their camps around the Meeting Tent, but they should not camp too close to it. They should camp under their ·family flag [standard] and ·banners [ensign]."

3The camp of Judah will ·be [camp] on the east side, where the sun rises, and they will camp by divisions there under their ·flag [banner]. The leader of the ·people [Lsons; descendants] of Judah is Nahshon son of Amminadab. 4There are 74,600 men in his division.

5Next to them the tribe of Issachar will camp. The leader of the ·people [Lsons; descendants] of Issachar is Nethanel son of Zuar. 6There are 54,400 men in his division.

7Next is the tribe of Zebulun. The leader of the ·people [Lsons; descendants] of Zebulun is Eliab son of Helon. 8There are 57,400 men in his division.

9There are a total of 186,400 men in the camps of Judah and its neighbors, in all their divisions. They will be the first to march out of camp.

10The divisions of the camp of Reuben will be on the south side, where they will camp under their ·flag [banner]. The leader of the ·people [Lsons; descendants] of Reuben is Elizur son of Shedeur. 11There are 46,500 men in his division.

12Next to them the tribe of Simeon will camp. The leader of the ·people [Lsons; descendants] of Simeon is Shelumiel son of Zurishaddai. 13There are 59,300 men in his division.

14Next is the tribe of Gad. The leader of the ·people [Lsons; descendants] of Gad is Eliasaph son of Deuel. 15There are 45,650 men in his division.

16There are a total of 151,450 men in the camps of Reuben and its neighbors, in all their divisions. They will be the second group to march out of camp.

17When the camp of the Levites march out with the Meeting Tent, they will be in the middle of the other camps. The tribes will march out in the same order as they camp, each in its place under its ·flag [banner].

18The divisions of the camp of Ephraim will be on the west side, where they will camp under their ·flag [banner]. The leader of the ·people [Lsons;

descendants] of Ephraim is Elishama son of Ammihud. 19There are
40,500 men in his division.
20Next to them the tribe of Manasseh will camp. The leader of the ·peo-
ple [Lsons; descendants] of Manasseh is Gamaliel son of Pedahzur. 21There
are 32,200 men in his division.
22Next is the tribe of Benjamin. The leader of the ·people [Lsons;
descendants] of Benjamin is Abidan son of Gideoni. 23There are 35,400
men in his division.
24There are a total of 108,100 men in the camps of Ephraim and its
neighbors, in all their divisions. They will be the third group to march
out of camp.
25The divisions of the camp of Dan will be on the north side, where
they will camp under their ·flag [banner]. The leader of the ·people [Lsons;
descendants] of Dan is Ahiezer son of Ammishaddai. 26There are 62,700
men in his division.
27Next to them the tribe of Asher will camp. The leader of the ·people
[Lsons; descendants] of Asher is Pagiel son of Ocran. 28There are 41,500
men in his division.
29Next is the tribe of Naphtali. The leader of the ·people [Lsons;
descendants] of Naphtali is Ahira son of Enan. 30There are 53,400 men in
his division.
31There are 157,600 men in the camps of Dan and its neighbors. They
will be the last to march out of camp, and they will travel under their own
·flag [banner].
32These are the ·Israelites [Lsons/Tchildren of Israel] who were counted
by families groups. The total number in the camps, counted by divisions,
is 603,550. 33Moses obeyed the LORD and did not count the Levites among
the other ·people [Lsons; Tchildren] of Israel.
34So the ·Israelites [Lsons/Tchildren of Israel] obeyed everything the
LORD commanded Moses. They camped under their ·flags [banners] and
marched out by ·families [clans] and family groups.

Aaron's Family, the Priests

3 ·This is the family history [LThese are the generations; Gen. 2:4]
of Aaron and Moses at the time the LORD talked to Moses on
Mount Sinai.
2·Aaron had four sons [LThese are the names of the sons of Aaron]:
Nadab, the ·oldest [firstborn], Abihu, Eleazar, and Ithamar. 3These were
the names of Aaron's sons, who were appointed to serve as priests. 4But
Nadab and Abihu died in the presence of the LORD when they offered ·the
wrong kind of [Lstrange; Can inappropriate performance of a ritual] fire
before the LORD in the ·Desert [Wilderness] of Sinai [Lev. 10]. They had
no sons. So Eleazar and Ithamar served as priests during the lifetime of
their father Aaron.
5The LORD said to Moses, 6"Bring the tribe of Levi and ·present them
to [Lmake them stand before] Aaron the priest to ·help [minister to;
assist] him. 7They will ·help [take care of] him and all the ·Israelites
[community; assembly; congregation] at the Meeting Tent, doing the
work in the ·Holy Tent [Tabernacle]. 8The Levites must take care of
everything in the Meeting Tent and serve the people of Israel by doing
the work in the ·Holy Tent [Tabernacle]. 9Give the Levites to Aaron and
his sons; of all the ·Israelites [Lsons/Tchildren of Israel], the Levites are
given completely to him. 10Appoint Aaron and his sons to serve as

priests, but anyone else who comes near the holy things must be put to
death."
11The LORD also said to Moses, 12"I am ·choosing [taking] the Levites
from all the ·Israelites [Lsons/Tchildren of Israel] to take the place of all
the firstborn ·children [Lwho open the womb] of ·Israel [Lthe sons/
Tchildren of Israel]. The Levites will be mine, 13because the firstborn are
mine. When you were in Egypt, I ·killed [Lstruck] all the firstborn ·chil-
dren of the [Lin the land of the] Egyptians [Ex. 12:12–13] and took all the
firstborn of Israel to be mine [Ex. 13:2, 11–16; 22:29–30; 34:19–20], both
animals and children. They are mine. I am the LORD."
14The LORD again said to Moses in the ·Desert [Wilderness] of Sinai,
15"Count the ·Levites [Lsons/descendants of Levi] by ·families [clans] and
family groups. Count every male one month old or older." 16So Moses
obeyed the LORD and counted them all.
17Levi had three sons, whose names were Gershon, Kohath, and Merari.
18The Gershonite ·family groups [clans] were Libni and Shimei
[4:21–28].
19The ·Kohathite family groups [Lthe sons/descendants of Kohath by
their clans] were Amram, Izhar, Hebron, and Uzziel [4:1–20].
20The ·Merarite family groups [Lthe sons/descendants of Merari by
their clans] were Mahli and Mushi [4:29–33].
These were the ·family groups [clans according to the family groups] of
the Levites.
21The ·family groups [clans] of Libni and Shimei belonged to Gershon;
they were the Gershonite ·family groups [clans]. 22The number that was
counted was 7,500 males one month old or older. 23The Gershonite ·family
groups [clan] camped on the west side, behind the ·Holy Tent [Tabernacle].
24The leader of the ·families [family groups] of Gershon was Eliasaph son
of Lael. 25In the Meeting Tent the Gershonites were in charge of the ·Holy
Tent [Tabernacle], its covering [Ex. 26:1–6], the curtain at the entrance to
the Meeting Tent, 26the curtains in the courtyard, the curtain at the entry
to the courtyard around the ·Holy Tent [Tabernacle] and the altar, the
ropes, and all the work connected with these items.
27The ·family groups [clans] of Amram, Izhar, Hebron, and Uzziel
belonged to Kohath; they were the Kohathite ·family groups [clans].
28They had 8,600 males one month old or older, and they were responsible for taking care of the Holy Place. 29The Kohathite ·family groups
[clans] camped south of the ·Holy Tent [Tabernacle]. 30The leader of the
Kohathite families was Elizaphan son of Uzziel. 31They were responsible for the Ark [Ex. 25:10], the table [Ex. 25:23–30], the lampstand
[LMenorah; Ex. 25:31–40], the altars [Ex. 27:1–8], the tools of the Holy
Place which they were to use, the curtain, and all the work connected
with these items. 32The main leader of the Levites was Eleazar son of
Aaron, the priest, who was in charge of all those responsible for the
Holy Place.
33The ·family groups [clans] of Mahli and Mushi belonged to Merari;
they were the Merarite ·family groups [clans]. 34The number that was
counted was 6,200 males one month old or older. 35The leader of the
Merari families was Zuriel son of Abihail, and they were to camp north of
the ·Holy Tent [Tabernacle]. 36The Merarites were responsible for the
frames of the ·Holy Tent [Tabernacle], the ·braces [bars], the ·posts [pil-
lars], the bases, and all the work connected with these items. 37They were

also responsible for the ·posts [pillars] in the courtyard around the ·Holy Tent [Tabernacle] and their bases, tent pegs, and ropes.

38Moses, Aaron, and his sons camped east of the ·Holy Tent [Tabernacle], toward the sunrise, in front of the Meeting Tent. They were responsible for the Holy Place for the ·Israelites [Lsons/Tchildren of Israel]. Anyone else who came near the Holy Place was to be put to death.

39Moses and Aaron counted the Levite men by their ·families [clans], as the LORD commanded, and there were 22,000 males one month old or older.

Levites Take the Place of the Firstborn Sons

40The LORD said to Moses, "Count all the firstborn sons in Israel one month old or older, and list their names. 41Take the Levites for me instead of the firstborn sons of Israel; take the animals of the Levites instead of the firstborn animals from the ·rest [Lsons] of Israel. I am the LORD."

42So Moses did what the LORD commanded and counted all the firstborn sons of the Israelites. 43When he listed all the firstborn sons one month old or older, there were 22,273 names.

44The LORD also said to Moses, 45"Take the Levites instead of all the firstborn sons of the Israelites, and take the animals of the Levites instead of the animals of the other people. The Levites are mine. I am the LORD. 46Since there are 273 more firstborn sons than Levites, 47collect ·two ounces [Lfive shekels] of silver for each of the 273 sons. Use the ·measure as set by [Lshekel of] the Holy Place, which is ·two-fifths of an ounce [La shekel of twenty gerahs]. 48Give the silver to Aaron and his sons as the payment for the 273 Israelites."

49So Moses collected the money for the people the Levites could not ·replace [redeem]. 50From the firstborn of the Israelites, he collected ·thirty-five pounds [L1,365 shekels] of silver, using the ·measure set by [Lshekel of] the Holy Place. 51Moses obeyed the command of the LORD and gave the silver to Aaron and his sons.

The Jobs of the Kohath Family

4 The LORD said to Moses and Aaron, 2"·Count [Take a census of; LLift the head of] the Kohathites ·among [*or* separate from] the Levites by ·family groups [clans] and families. 3·Count [Take a census of; LLift the head of] the men from thirty to fifty years old, all who come to serve in the Meeting Tent.

4"The Kohathites are responsible for the most holy things in the Meeting Tent. 5When the ·Israelites are [Lcamp is] ready to move, Aaron and his sons must go into the ·Holy Tent [Tabernacle], take down the curtain, and cover the Ark of the ·Agreement [Covenant; Treaty; LTestimony; Ex. 25:10] with it. 6Over this they must put a covering made from ·fine leather [*or* sea cow hide; Ex. 26:14], then spread the solid blue cloth over that [Ex. 26:1–6], and put the poles in place.

7"Then they must spread a blue cloth over the table for the ·bread that shows a person is in God's presence [Bread of Presence; Ex. 25:30]. They must put the plates, pans, bowls, and the jars for drink offerings on the table; they must leave the bread that is always there on the table. 8Then they must put a ·red [crimson] cloth over all of these things, cover everything with ·fine leather [*or* sea cow hide; Ex. 26:14], and put the poles in place.

9"With a blue cloth they must cover the ·lampstand [LMenorah; Ex. 25:31–40], its lamps, its wick trimmers, its trays, and all the jars for the oil used in the lamps. 10Then they must wrap everything in ·fine leather [*or* sea cow hide; Ex. 26:14] and put all these things on a frame for carrying them.

11"They must spread a blue cloth over the gold altar [Cthe altar of incense; Ex. 30:1–6], cover it with ·fine leather [*or* sea cow hide; Ex. 26:14], and put the poles in place.

12"They must gather all the things used for serving in the Holy Place and wrap them in a blue cloth. Then they must cover that with ·fine leather [*or* sea cow hide; Ex. 26:14] and put these things on a frame for carrying them.

13"They must clean the ashes off the bronze altar [Ex. 27:1–8] and spread a purple cloth over it. 14They must gather all the things used for serving at the altar—the ·pans for carrying the fire [firepans], the meat forks, the shovels, and the ·bowls [basins]—and put them on the bronze altar. Then they must spread a covering of ·fine leather [*or* sea cow hide; Ex. 26:14] over it and put the poles in place.

15"When the ·Israelites are [Lcamp is] ready to move, and when Aaron and his sons have covered the ·holy furniture [*or* Holy Place] and all the holy things, the Kohathites may go in and carry them away. In this way they won't touch the holy things and die. It is the Kohathites' job to carry the things that are in the Meeting Tent.

16"Eleazar son of Aaron, the priest, will be responsible for the ·Holy Tent [Tabernacle] and for everything in it, for all the holy things it has: the oil for the lamp [Ex. 27:20–21], the sweet-smelling incense, the continual ·grain [Lgift; tribute] offering [Lev. 2:1], and the oil used to appoint priests [Ex. 30:22–38] and things to the LORD's service."

17The LORD said to Moses and Aaron, 18"Don't let the ·Kohathites [Lthe tribe of the clans of Kohath] be cut off from the Levites. 19Do this for the Kohathites so that they may go near the Most Holy Place and live and not die: Aaron and his sons must go in and show each Kohathite what to do and what to carry. 20The Kohathites must not enter and look at the holy things, even for a second, or they will die."

The Jobs of the Gershon Family

21The LORD said to Moses, 22"·Count [Take a census of; LLift the head of] the Gershonites by families and ·family groups [clans]. 23·Count [Take a census of; LLift the head of] the men from thirty to fifty years old, all who have a job to do in the Meeting Tent.

24"This is what the Gershonite ·family groups [clans] must do and what they must carry. 25They must carry the curtains of the ·Holy Tent [Tabernacle], the Meeting Tent, its covering, and its outer covering made from ·fine leather [*or* sea cow hide; Ex. 26:14]. They must also carry the ·curtains [screen] for the entrance to the Meeting Tent, 26the curtains of the courtyard [Ex. 27:9–19] that go around the ·Holy Tent [Tabernacle] and the altar [Ex. 27:1–8], the ·curtain [screen] for the entry to the courtyard, the ropes, and all the things used with the curtains. They must do everything connected with these things. 27Aaron and his sons are in charge of what the Gershonites do or carry; you tell them what they are responsible for carrying. 28This is the work of the ·Gershonite family group [Lclan of the sons of Gershon] at the Meeting Tent. Ithamar son of Aaron, the priest, will direct their work.

The Jobs of the Merari Family

29"·Count [Take a census of; LLift the head of] the ·Merarite families and [Lsons of Merari by] ·family groups [clans]. 30·Count [Take a census of; LLift the head of] the men from thirty to fifty years old, all who work at the Meeting Tent. 31It is their job to carry the following as they serve in the Meeting Tent: the frames of the ·Holy Tent [Tabernacle], the crossbars, the

·posts [pillars], and bases, 32in addition to the ·posts [pillars] that go around the courtyard, their bases, tent pegs, ropes, and everything that is used with the poles around the courtyard. Tell each man exactly what to carry. 33This is the work the Merarite ·family group [clan] will do for the Meeting Tent. Ithamar son of Aaron, the priest, will direct their work."

The Levite Families

34Moses, Aaron, and the leaders of ·Israel [Lthe community/congregation/assembly] counted the ·Kohathites [Lsons/descendants of Kohath] by families and ·family groups [clans], 35the men from thirty to fifty years old who were to work at the Meeting Tent. 36There were 2,750 men in the ·family groups [clans]. 37This was the total of the Kohath ·family groups [clans] who worked at the Meeting Tent, whom Moses and Aaron counted as the LORD had commanded Moses.

38Also, the ·Gershonites [Lthe sons/descendants of Gershon] were counted by families and ·family groups [clans], 39the men from thirty to fifty years old who were given work at the Meeting Tent. 40The families and family groups had 2,630 men. 41This was the total of the Gershon ·family groups [clans] who worked at the Meeting Tent, whom Moses and Aaron counted as the LORD had commanded.

42Also, the men in the families and ·family groups [clans] of the ·Merari family [Lsons/descendants of Merari] were counted, 43the men from thirty to fifty years old who were to work at the Meeting Tent. 44The family groups had 3,200 men. 45This was the total of the Merari ·family groups [clans], whom Moses and Aaron counted as the LORD had commanded Moses.

46So Moses, Aaron, and the leaders of Israel counted all the Levites by families and ·family groups [clans]. 47They counted the men from thirty to fifty who were given work at the Meeting Tent and who carried the Tent. 48The total number of these men was 8,580. 49Each man was counted as the LORD had commanded Moses; each man was given his work and told what to carry as the LORD had commanded Moses.

Rules About Cleanliness

5 The LORD said to Moses, 2"Command the ·Israelites [Lsons/Tchildren of Israel] to send away from camp anyone with ·a harmful skin disease [Tleprosy; Cthe term does not refer to modern leprosy (Hansen's disease), but to various skin disorders; Lev. 13:2]. Send away anyone who gives off body fluid [Lev. 15:2] or who has become unclean by touching a dead body [Lev. 5:2; 21:11]. 3Send both men and women outside the camp so that they won't spread the disease there, where I am living among you." 4So ·Israel [Lthe sons/Tchildren of Israel] obeyed the LORD's command and sent those people outside the camp. They did just as the LORD had told Moses.

Paying for Doing Wrong

5The LORD said to Moses, 6"Tell the ·Israelites [Lsons/Tchildren of Israel]: 'When a man or woman does something wrong to another person, that is really sinning against the LORD. That person is guilty 7and must ·admit [confess] the wrong that has been done. The person must fully pay for the wrong that has been done, adding one-fifth to it, and giving it to the person who was wronged. 8But if that person is dead and does not have any close relatives to receive the payment, the one who did wrong owes the LORD and must pay the priest. In addition, the priest must sacrifice a male sheep to remove the wrong so that the person will belong to the LORD. 9When an Israelite brings a holy gift, it should be given to the priest. 10No one has to give these holy gifts, but if someone does give them, they belong to the priest [Lev. 6:1–7].' "

Suspicious Husbands

11Then the LORD said to Moses, 12"Tell the ·Israelites [Lsons/Tchildren of Israel]: 'A man's wife might ·be unfaithful to him [Lgo astray and break faith with him] 13and have sexual relations with another man. Her sin might be kept hidden from her husband so that he does not know about the wrong she did. Perhaps ·no one saw it [there was no witness], and she wasn't caught. 14But if her husband has feelings of jealousy and suspects she has sinned—whether she has or not—15he should take her to the priest. The husband must also take an offering for her of ·two quarts [Lone tenth of an ephah] of barley flour. He must not pour oil or incense on it, because this is a ·grain [Lgift; tribute] offering for jealousy [Lev. 2:1], an offering of remembrance. It is to find out if she is guilty.

16" 'The priest will bring ·in [near] the woman and make her stand before the LORD. 17He will take some holy water in a clay jar, and he will put some ·dirt [dust] from the floor of the ·Holy Tent [Tabernacle] into the water. 18The priest will make the woman stand before the LORD, and he will loosen her hair [Cperhaps signifying ritual uncleanness; Lev. 13:45]. He will hand her the grain [Ltribute; gift] offering [Lev. 2:1] of remembrance, the ·grain [Ltribute; gift] offering [Lev. 2:1] for jealousy; he will hold the bitter water that brings a curse. 19The priest will make her take an oath and ask her, "Has another man had sexual relations with you? Have you been unfaithful to your husband? If you haven't, this bitter water that brings a curse won't hurt you. 20But if you have been unfaithful to your husband and have defiled yourself and had sexual relations with a man besides him"—21the priest will then put on her the curse that the oath will bring—"the LORD will make the people curse and reject you. He will make your ·stomach get big [uterus drop], and he will make your ·body unable to give birth to another baby [womb discharge; Lthigh waste away/wither; Ca euphemism for the womb]. 22This water that brings a curse will go inside you and make your ·stomach get big [*or* uterus drop] and make your ·body unable to give birth to another baby [womb discharge; Lyour thigh waste away/wither; 5:21]."

" 'The woman must say, "I agree."

23" 'The priest should write these curses on a scroll, wash the words off into the bitter water, 24and make the woman drink the bitter water that brings a curse. If she is guilty, the water will ·make her sick [cause bitter pain]. 25Then the priest will take the ·grain [Ltribute; gift] offering [Lev. 2:1] for jealousy from her. He will ·present [elevate] it before the LORD and bring it to the altar. 26He will take a handful of the grain, which is a memorial offering, and ·burn it [turn it into smoke] on the altar. After that he will make the woman drink the water 27to see if she ·is not pure [defiled herself] and if she has sinned against her husband. When it goes into her, if her ·stomach gets big [*or* uterus falls] and ·she is not able to have another baby [her thigh wastes away/withers; 5:21], her people will reject her. 28But if the woman has not sinned, she is pure. She is not guilty, and she will be able to have babies.

29" 'So this is the ·teaching [instruction; law] about jealousy. This is what to do when a woman does wrong and is unfaithful while she is married to her husband. 30It also should be done if the man gets jealous because he suspects his wife. The priest will have her stand before the

LORD, and he will do all these things, just as the ·teaching [instruction; law] commands. 31 In this way the husband can be proven correct, and the woman will suffer if she has done wrong.' "

Rules for the Nazirites

6 The LORD said to Moses, 2 "Tell the LORD ·Israelites [Lsons/Tchildren of Israel]: 'If men or women want to ·promise [make a special vow] to ·belong to the LORD in a special way [separate themselves to the LORD], they will be called Nazirites [Cpeople especially set apart in devotion to God; Samson and Samuel are examples]. 3 During this time, they must not drink wine or ·beer [Tstrong drink; Can alcoholic beverage made from grain], or vinegar made from wine or ·beer [Tstrong drink]. They must not even drink grape juice or eat grapes or raisins. 4 While they are Nazirites, they must not eat anything that comes from the grapevine, even the seeds or the skin.

5 " 'During the time they have ·promised [vowed] to ·belong to the [separate themselves to the] LORD, they must not cut their hair [Cavoiding contact with dead matter]. They must be holy until this special time is over. They must let their hair grow long. 6 During ·their special time of belonging [the time of their vow] to the LORD, Nazirites must not go near a dead body. 7 Even if their own father, mother, brother, or sister dies, they must not ·touch them, or they will become unclean [Ldefile themselves; Cin a ritual sense]. ·They must still keep their promise to belong to God in a special way [LThe consecration/separation to God is on their head]. 8 While they are Nazirites, they ·belong to the LORD in a special way [Lare holy to the LORD].

9 " 'If they are next to someone who dies suddenly, their hair, which was ·part of their promise [consecrated], has been ·made unclean [defiled; Cin a ritual sense]. So they must shave their head seven days later to be clean. 10 Then on the eighth day, they must bring two doves or two young pigeons to the priest at the entrance to the Meeting Tent. 11 The priest will offer one as a ·sin [*or* purification; Lev. 4:3] offering and the other as a burnt offering [Lev. 1:1–17]. This ·removes sin so they will belong to the LORD [makes atonement for them]. (They had sinned because they were near a dead body.) That same day they ·will again promise to let their hair grow [Lsanctify/consecrate the head] 12 and ·give themselves [separate themselves] to the LORD for ·another special time [Ltheir time as Nazirites]. They must bring a male lamb a year old as a ·penalty [guilt; reparation; Lev. 5:14—6:9] offering. The days of the special time before don't count, because ·they became unclean during their first special time [Lthe consecrated/sanctified head became defiled].

13 " 'This is the ·teaching [instruction; law] for the Nazirites. When the ·promised time [time of their consecration] is over, they must go to the entrance of the Meeting Tent 14 and give their offerings to the LORD. They must offer a year-old male lamb that ·has nothing wrong with it [is unblemished], as a burnt offering [Lev. 1:1–17], a year-old female lamb that ·has nothing wrong with it [is unblemished], as a ·sin [*or* purification; Lev. 4:3] offering, and a ·male sheep [ram] that ·has nothing wrong with it [is unblemished], for a ·fellowship [*or* peace; well-being] offering [Lev. 3:1]. 15 They must also bring the ·grain [Lgift; tribute] offerings [Lev. 2:1] and drink offerings that go with them. And they must bring a basket of bread made without ·yeast [leaven], loaves made with ·fine [choice] flour mixed with oil, and wafers made without ·yeast [leaven] spread with oil.

16“ ‘The priest will give these offerings to the LORD and make the ·sin
[*or* purification; Lev. 4:3] offering and the burnt offering [Lev. 1:1–17].
17Then he will ·kill [Loffer] the ·male sheep [ram] as a ·fellowship [*or*
peace; well-being] offering [Lev. 3:1] to the LORD; along with it, he will
present the basket of bread made without yeast [leaven], the ·grain [Lgift;
tribute] offering [Lev. 2:1], and the drink offering.
18“ ‘The Nazirites must go to the entrance of the Meeting Tent and
shave ·off their hair that they grew for their promise [Ltheir consecrated
head]. The hair will be put in the fire that is under the sacrifice of the ·fel-
lowship [*or* peace; well-being] offering [Lev. 3:1].
19“ ‘After the Nazirites ·cut off their hair [Lshave their consecrated
head], the priest will give them a boiled shoulder from the ·male sheep
[ram]. From the basket he will also give a loaf and a wafer, both made
without ·yeast [leaven]. 20Then the priest will ·present [elevate] them to
the LORD. They are ·holy and belong to [a holy portion for] the priest.
Also, he is to ·present [elevate] the breast and the thigh from the ·male
sheep [ram]. After that, the Nazirites may drink wine.
21“ ‘This is the ·teaching [instruction; law] for the Nazirites who ·make
a promise [take a vow]. Everyone who makes the Nazirite ·promise [vow]
must give all of these gifts to the LORD. If they promised to do more, they
must keep their ·promise [vow], according to the ·teaching [instruction;
law] of the Nazirites.’ ”

The Priests' Blessings

22The LORD said to Moses, 23“Tell Aaron and his sons, ‘This is how you
should bless the ·Israelites [Lsons/Tchildren of Israel]. Say to them:
24“May the LORD bless you and ·keep [guard] you.
25May the LORD ·show you his kindness [Lmake his face shine upon you]
and ·have mercy on [be gracious to] you.
26May the LORD ·watch over [Llift his face/presence/countenance upon]
you
and give you peace.” ’
27“So Aaron and his sons will ·bless the Israelites with my name [Lput
my name upon the sons/Tchildren of Israel], and I will bless them.”

The Holy Tent

7When Moses finished setting up the ·Holy Tent [Tabernacle], he
·gave it for service to the LORD [consecrated/sanctified it] by ·pour-
ing olive oil on the Tent [anointing it] and on everything used in it. He also
·poured oil on [anointed] the altar and all its tools to ·prepare them for
service to the LORD [consecrate/sanctify it]. 2Then the leaders of Israel made
offerings. These were the heads of the families, the leaders of each tribe
who counted the people. 3They brought to the LORD six covered ·carts [wag-
ons] and twelve oxen—each leader giving an ox, and every two leaders
giving a ·cart [wagon]. They brought these to the Holy Tent.
4The LORD said to Moses, 5“Accept these gifts from the leaders and use
them in the work of the Meeting Tent. Give them to the Levites as they
need them.”
6So Moses accepted the ·carts [wagons] and the oxen and gave them to
the Levites. 7He gave two ·carts [wagons] and four oxen to the ·Gershonites
[Lsons/descendants of Gershon], which they needed for their work. 8Then
Moses gave four ·carts [wagons] and eight oxen to the ·Merarites [Lsons/
descendants of Merari], which they needed for their work. Ithamar son of
Aaron, the priest, directed the work of all of them. 9Moses did not give
any oxen or ·carts [wagons] to the ·Kohathites [Lsons/descendants of

Kohath], because their job was to carry the holy things on their shoulders.

10When the ·oil was poured on the altar [altar was anointed], the leaders brought their offerings to it to ·give it to the LORD's service [dedicate it]; they presented them in front of the altar. 11The LORD told Moses, "Each day one leader must bring his gift ·to make the altar ready for service to me [for the dedication of the altar]."

12-83Each of the twelve leaders brought these gifts. Each leader brought one silver plate that weighed about ·three and one-fourth pounds [L130 shekels], and one silver bowl that weighed about ·one and three-fourths pounds [L70 shekels]. These weights were set by the Holy Place measure. The bowl and the plate were filled with ·fine [choice] flour mixed with oil for a ·grain [Lgift; tribute] offering [Lev. 2:1]. Each leader also brought a large gold dish that weighed about ·four ounces [L10 shekels] and was filled with incense.

In addition, each of the leaders brought one young bull, one ·male sheep [ram], and one male lamb a year old for a burnt offering [Lev. 1:1–17]; one male goat for a ·sin [*or* purification; Lev. 4:3] offering; and two oxen, five ·male sheep [rams], five male goats, and five male lambs a year old for a ·fellowship [*or* peace; well-being] offering [Lev. 3:1; Cthe Hebrew text repeats the preceding two paragraphs with each of the twelve leaders listed below].

On the first day Nahshon son of Amminadab brought his gifts. He was the leader of the tribe of Judah.

On the second day Nethanel son of Zuar brought his gifts. He was the leader of the tribe of Issachar.

On the third day Eliab son of Helon brought his gifts. He was the leader of the tribe of Zebulun.

On the fourth day Elizur son of Shedeur brought his gifts. He was the leader of the tribe of Reuben.

On the fifth day Shelumiel son of Zurishaddai brought his gifts. He was the leader of the tribe of Simeon.

On the sixth day Eliasaph son of Deuel brought his gifts. He was the leader of the tribe of Gad.

On the seventh day Elishama son of Ammihud brought his gifts. He was the leader of the tribe of Ephraim.

On the eighth day Gamaliel son of Pedahzur brought his gifts. He was the leader of the tribe of Manasseh.

On the ninth day Abidan son of Gideoni brought his gifts. He was the leader of the tribe of Benjamin.

On the tenth day Ahiezer son of Ammishaddai brought his gifts. He was the leader of the tribe of Dan.

On the eleventh day Pagiel son of Ocran brought his gifts. He was the leader of the tribe of Asher.

On the twelfth day Ahira son of Enan brought his gifts. He was the leader of the tribe of Naphtali.

84So these were the gifts from the Israelite leaders when ·oil was poured on the altar [the altar was anointed] ·and it was given for service to the LORD [to dedicate it]: twelve silver plates, twelve silver bowls, and twelve gold dishes. 85Each silver plate weighed about ·three and one-fourth pounds [L130 shekels], and each bowl weighed about ·one and three-fourths pounds [L70 shekels]. All the silver plates and silver bowls together weighed about

·sixty pounds [L2,400 shekels] according to a weight set by the Holy Place measure. 86The twelve gold dishes filled with incense weighed ·four ounces [L10 shekels] each, according to the weight set by the Holy Place measure. Together the gold dishes weighed about ·three pounds [L120 shekels]. 87The total number of animals for the burnt offering [Lev. 1:1–17] was twelve bulls, twelve ·male sheep [rams], and twelve male lambs a year old. There was also a ·grain [Lgift; tribute] offering [Lev. 2:1], and there were twelve male goats for a ·sin [*or* purification; Lev. 4:3] offering. 88The total number of animals for the ·fellowship [*or* peace; well-being] offering [Lev. 3:1] was twenty-four bulls, sixty ·male sheep [rams], sixty male goats, and sixty male lambs a year old. All these offerings were for ·giving the altar to the service of the LORD [the dedication of the altar] after ·the oil had been poured on it [it had been anointed].

89When Moses went into the Meeting Tent to speak with the LORD, he heard the LORD speaking to him. The voice was coming from between the two ·gold creatures with wings [cherubim; Ex. 37:7] that were above the ·lid [Mercy Seat/Cover; Ex. 25:17–22] of the Ark of the ·Agreement [Treaty; Covenant; LTestimony; 1:50]. In this way the LORD spoke with him.

The Lampstand

8 The LORD said to Moses, 2"Speak to Aaron and tell him, 'Put the seven lamps where they can light the area in front of the ·lampstand [LMenorah; Ex. 25:31–40].' "

3Aaron did this, putting the lamps so they lighted the area in front of the ·lampstand [LMenorah]; he obeyed the command the LORD gave Moses. 4The ·lampstand [LMenorah] was made from hammered gold, from its base to the flowers [Clike a flowering tree, reminding worshipers of Eden]. It was made exactly the way the LORD had showed Moses.

The Levites Are Given to God

5The LORD said to Moses, 6"Take the Levites away from the other ·Israelites [Lsons/Tchildren of Israel] and make them clean [Cin a ritual sense]. 7This is what you should do to make them clean: Sprinkle the cleansing water on them, and have them shave their bodies and wash their clothes so they will be clean. 8They must take a young bull and the grain offering of flour mixed with oil that goes with it. Then take a second young bull for a ·sin [*or* purification] offering [Lev. 4:3]. 9Bring the Levites to the front of the Meeting Tent, and gather all the ·Israelites [Lcommunity/congregation/assembly of the sons/Tchildren of Israel] around. 10When you bring the Levites before the LORD, the ·Israelites [Lsons/Tchildren of Israel] should put their hands on them [Ca ritual of identification, showing that the Israelites had a part in their consecration]. 11Aaron will present the Levites before the LORD as an offering presented from the ·Israelites [Lsons/Tchildren of Israel]. Then the Levites will be ready to do the work of the LORD.

12"The Levites will ·put [lay] their hands [8:10; Ex. 29:10] on the bulls' heads—one bull will be a ·sin [*or* purification] offering [Lev. 4:3] to the LORD, and the other will be a burnt offering [Lev. 1:1–17], to ·remove the sins of the Levites so they will belong to the LORD [make atonement for the Levites]. 13Make the Levites stand in front of Aaron and his sons and present the Levites as an elevation offering to the LORD. 14In this way you must ·set apart [separate] the Levites from the other ·Israelites [Lsons/Tchildren of Israel]; the Levites will be mine.

15"Make the Levites pure [Cin a ritual sense], and ·present [elevate] them as an offering so that they may come to work at the Meeting Tent.

16 They will be given completely to me from the ·Israelites [Lsons/
Tchildren of Israel]; I have taken them for myself instead of ·the firstborn of every Israelite woman [Lthose who open the womb, the firstborn
of all the sons/Tchildren of Israel]. 17 All the firstborn ·in Israel—people
or animals—[Lamong the sons/Tchildren of Israel and among people
and among animals] are mine. When I ·killed [Lstruck] all the firstborn
in Egypt [Ex. 12:12–13], I ·set the firstborn in Israel aside for myself
[Lconsecrated/sanctified them to me; Ex. 13:2, 11–16; 22:29–30; 34:19–
20]. 18 But I have taken the Levites instead of all the firstborn ·in Israel
[Lamong the sons/Tchildren of Israel]. 19 From all the ·Israelites [Lsons/
Tchildren of Israel] I have given the Levites to Aaron and his sons so that
they may serve the Israelites at the Meeting Tent. They will ·help remove
the Israelites' sins so they will belong to the LORD [Lmake atonement for
the sons/Tchildren of Israel] and so that no ·disaster [plague] will strike
the Israelites when they approach the ·Holy Place [Tabernacle]."

20 So Moses, Aaron, and all the ·Israelites [Lcommunity/congregation/
assembly of the sons/Tchildren of Israel] obeyed and did with the Levites
what the LORD commanded Moses. 21 The Levites made themselves clean
from sin and washed their clothes. Then Aaron ·presented [elevated] them
as an offering to the LORD. He also ·removed their sins [made atonement
for them] so they would be pure [Cin a ritual sense]. 22 After that, the Levites
came to the Meeting Tent to work, and Aaron and his sons told them what
to do. They did with the Levites what the LORD commanded Moses.

23 The LORD said to Moses, 24 "This command is for the Levites. Everyone
twenty-five years old or older must come to the Meeting Tent, because
they all have jobs to do there. 25 At the age of fifty, they must retire from
their jobs and not work again. 26 They may ·help [serve; minister to] their
fellow Levites with their work at the Meeting Tent, but they must not do
the work themselves. This is the way you are to give the Levites their jobs."

The Passover Is Celebrated

9 The LORD spoke to Moses in the ·Desert [Wilderness] of Sinai in
the first month of the second year after the Israelites left Egypt
[1:1]. He said, 2 "Tell the ·Israelites [Lsons/Tchildren of Israel] to celebrate
the Passover at the appointed time [Ex. 12:14–20; Ccommemorating the
departure from Egypt]. 3 That appointed time is the fourteenth day of this
month ·at twilight [Lbetween the two evenings]; they must obey all the
rules about it."

4 So Moses told the ·Israelites [Lsons/Tchildren of Israel] to celebrate the
Passover, 5 and they did; it was in the ·Desert [Wilderness] of Sinai ·at
twilight [Lbetween the two evenings] on the fourteenth day of the first
month. The ·Israelites [Lsons/Tchildren of Israel] did everything just as
the LORD commanded Moses.

6 But some of the people could not celebrate the Passover on that day
because they were unclean [Cin a ritual sense; 5:2] from touching a dead
body. So they went to Moses and Aaron that day and 7 said to Moses, "We
are unclean because of touching a dead body. But why should we be kept
from offering gifts to the LORD at this appointed time? Why can't we join
the other ·Israelites [Lsons/Tchildren of Israel]?"

8 Moses said to them, "Wait, and I will find out what the LORD says
about you."

9 Then the LORD said to Moses, 10 "Tell the ·Israelites [Lsons/Tchildren of
Israel] this: 'If you or your descendants become unclean [Cin a ritual

sense] because of a dead body, or if you are away on a trip during the
Passover, you must still celebrate the LORD's Passover. 11But celebrate it at
·twilight [Lbetween the two evenings] on the fourteenth day of the second
month. Eat the lamb with bitter herbs [Ex. 12:8] and bread made without
·yeast [leaven]. 12Don't leave any of it until the next morning or break any
of its bones [Ex. 12:46]. When you celebrate the Passover, follow all the
rules [2 Chr. 30:1–27]. 13Anyone who is clean and is not away on a trip but
does not eat the Passover must be cut off from the people. That person
did not give an offering to the LORD at the appointed time and must be
punished for the sin.

14" '·Foreigners [Resident aliens] among you may celebrate the LORD's
Passover, but they must follow all the rules. You must have the same rules for
·foreigners [resident aliens] as you have for ·yourselves [Lnatives; citizens].' "

The Cloud Above the Tent

15On the day the ·Holy Tent [Tabernacle], the Tent of the ·Agreement
[Testimony; Treaty; Covenant], was set up, a cloud covered it. From dusk
until dawn the cloud above the ·Tent [Tabernacle] looked like fire [Ex.
40:34–38]. 16The cloud stayed above the ·Tent [Tabernacle], and at night
it looked like fire. 17When the cloud moved from its place over the Tent,
the ·Israelites [Lsons/Tchildren of Israel] moved, and wherever the cloud
stopped, the ·Israelites [Lsons/Tchildren of Israel] camped. 18So the
·Israelites [Lsons/Tchildren of Israel] moved at the LORD's command, and
they camped at his command. While the cloud stayed over the ·Tent
[Tabernacle], they remained camped. 19Sometimes the cloud stayed over
the ·Tent [Tabernacle] for a long time, but the ·Israelites [Lsons/Tchildren
of Israel] obeyed the LORD and did not move. 20Sometimes the cloud was
over it only a few days. At the LORD's command the people camped, and
at his command they moved. 21Sometimes the cloud stayed only from
dusk until dawn; when the cloud lifted the next morning, the people
moved. When the cloud lifted, day or night, the people moved. 22The
cloud might stay over the ·Tent [Tabernacle] for two days, a month, or a
year. As long as it stayed, the people camped, but when it lifted, they
moved. 23At the LORD's command the people camped, and at his command they moved. They obeyed the LORD's order that he commanded
through Moses.

The Silver Trumpets

10 The LORD said to Moses, 2"Make two trumpets of hammered
silver, and use them to call the ·people [community; congregation; assembly] together and to march out of camp. 3When both
trumpets are blown, the ·people [community; congregation; assembly]
should gather before you at the entrance to the Meeting Tent. 4If you
blow only one trumpet, the leaders, the heads of the ·family groups
[clans] of Israel, should meet before you. 5When you loudly blow the
trumpets, the ·tribes [Lcamps] camping on the east should move. 6When
you loudly blow them again, the ·tribes [Lcamps] camping on the south
should move; the loud sound will tell them to move. 7When you want to
gather the people, blow the trumpets, but don't blow them as loudly.

8"Aaron's sons, the priests, should blow the trumpets. This is a ·law
[perpetual/eternal regulation] for you and your descendants ·from now on
[throughout your generations]. 9When you are fighting an enemy who
attacks you in your own land, blow the trumpets loudly. The LORD your
God will ·take notice of [remember] you and will save you from your enemies. 10Also blow your trumpets at happy times and during your feasts

and at New Moon festivals [29:6; 1 Sam. 20:5; 2 Kin. 4:23; Ezra 3:5; Ps. 81:3; Is. 1:13; Amos 8:5]. Blow them over your burnt offerings [Lev. 1:1–17] and ·fellowship [*or* peace; well-being] offerings [Lev. 3:1], because they will help you remember your God. I am the LORD your God."

The Israelites Move Camp

11The cloud lifted from the ·Tent [Tabernacle] of the ·Agreement [Testimony; Treaty; Covenant] on the twentieth day of the second month of the second year. 12So the ·Israelites [Lsons/Tchildren of Israel] moved from the ·Desert [Wilderness] of Sinai and continued until the cloud stopped in the ·Desert [Wilderness] of Paran. 13This was their first time to move, and they did it as the LORD had commanded Moses.

14The divisions from the camp of ·Judah [Lthe sons/descendants of Judah] moved first under their ·flag [banner]. Nahshon son of Amminadab was the commander. 15Nethanel son of Zuar was over the division of the tribe of ·Issachar [Lthe sons/descendants of Issachar]. 16Eliab son of Helon was over the division of the tribe of ·Zebulun [Lthe sons/descendants of Zebulun]. 17Then the ·Holy Tent [Tabernacle] was taken down, and the ·Gershonites [Lsons/descendants of Gershon; 3:18, 21–26; 4:21–28] and ·Merarites [Lsons/descendants of Merari; 3:20, 33–37; 4:29–33], who carried it, moved next.

18Then came the divisions from the camp of Reuben under their ·flag [banner], and Elizur son of Shedeur was the commander. 19Shelumiel son of Zurishaddai was over the division of the tribe of ·Simeon [Lthe sons/descendants of Simeon]. 20Eliasaph son of Deuel was over the division of the tribe of Gad. 21Then came the Kohathites [3:19, 27–32; 4:1–20], who carried the holy things; the ·Holy Tent [Tabernacle] was to be set up before they arrived.

22Next came the divisions from the camp of ·Ephraim [Lthe sons/descendants of Ephraim] under their ·flag [banner], and Elishama son of Ammihud was the commander. 23Gamaliel son of Pedahzur was over the division of the tribe of ·Manasseh [Lthe sons/descendants of Manasseh], 24and Abidan son of Gideoni was over the division of the tribe of ·Benjamin [Lthe sons/descendants of Benjamin].

25The last ones were the rear guard for all the tribes. These were the divisions from the camp of ·Dan [Lthe sons/descendants of Dan] under their flag, and Ahiezer son of Ammishaddai was the commander. 26Pagiel son of Ocran was over the division of the tribe of ·Asher [Lthe sons/descendants of Asher]; 27Ahira son of Enan was over the division of the tribe of ·Naphtali [Lthe sons/descendants of Naphtali]. 28This was the order the Israelite divisions marched in when they moved.

29Hobab was the son of Reuel the Midianite, who was Moses' father-in-law [Calso called Jethro; Ex. 2:16]. Moses said to Hobab, "We are moving to the land the LORD promised to give us. Come with us and we will be good to you, because the LORD has promised good things to Israel."

30But Hobab answered, "No, I will not go. I will go back to my own land where I was born."

31But Moses said, "Please don't ·leave [abandon; forsake] us. You know where we can camp in the ·desert [wilderness], and you can be our ·guide [Leyes]. 32Come with us. We will share with you all the good things the LORD gives us." 33So they left the mountain of the LORD [CMount Sinai] and traveled for three days. The Ark of the LORD's ·Agreement [Treaty; Covenant; Ex. 25:10] went in front of the people for those three days, as

they looked for a ·place to camp [resting place]. 34The LORD's cloud
[Csymbolic of God's presence] was over them during the day when they
left their camp.
35When the Ark left the camp, Moses said,
"Rise up, LORD!
Scatter your enemies:
make those who hate you run from you [Cthe wilderness journey was
seen as a march into battle]."
36And when the Ark ·was set down [came to rest], Moses said,
"Return, LORD,
to the thousands of people of Israel."

Fire from the Lord

11 Now the people complained ·to [Lin the ears of] the LORD
about their troubles, and when he heard them, he became
angry. Then fire from the LORD burned ·among the people at the edge
[Lon the outskirts] of the camp. 2The people cried out to Moses, and
when he prayed to the LORD, the fire stopped burning. 3So that place was
called Taberah [C"Burning"; Deut. 9:22], because the LORD's fire had
burned among them.

Seventy Elders Help Moses

4Some ·troublemakers [rabble; foreign elements] among them wanted
better food, and soon all the ·Israelites [Lsons/Tchildren of Israel] began
·complaining [Lweeping]. They said, "We want meat! 5We remember the
fish we ate for free in Egypt. We also had cucumbers, melons, leeks,
onions, and garlic. 6But now we have lost our ·appetite [*or* vitality;
strength]; we never see anything but this manna [Ex. 16:1–36]!"
7The manna was like ·small white seeds [Lcoriander seed and its color
was like bdellium/gum resin]. 8The people would go to gather it, and then
grind it in handmills, or crush it ·between stones [with mortars]. After
they ·cooked [*or* boiled] it in a pot or made cakes with it, it tasted like
·bread [cakes] baked with olive oil. 9When the dew fell on the camp each
night, so did the manna.
10Moses heard every ·family [clan] ·crying [weeping] as they stood in
the entrances of their tents. Then the LORD became very angry, and ·Moses
got upset [Lit was bad in the eyes of Moses]. 11He asked the LORD, "Why
have you brought me, your servant, this trouble? ·What have I done
wrong [LWhy have I not found favor in your eyes] that you ·made me
responsible [Lset the burden on me] for all these people? 12·I am not the
father of [LDid I conceive/Am I the mother of] all these people, and ·I
didn't [Ldid I…?] give birth to them. So why do you make me carry them
to the land you promised to our ancestors? Must I carry them in my ·arms
[Lbosom] as a nurse carries a baby? 13Where can I get meat for all these
people? They keep crying to me, 'We want meat!' 14I can't take care of all
these people alone. It is too ·much [difficult; Lheavy] for me. 15If you are
going to continue doing this to me, then kill me now. If ·you care about
me [LI have found favor in your eyes], put me to death, and ·then I won't
have [Ldo not let me see] any more troubles."
16The LORD said to Moses, "·Bring [LGather for] me seventy of Israel's
elders, men that you know are leaders among the people. Bring them to
the Meeting Tent, and have them stand there with you. 17I will come
down and speak with you there. I will take some of the Spirit [Cthat
enables Moses to do his work] that is in you, and I will ·give it to [*or* put
it on] them. They will ·help you care for the people [Lbear the burden of

the people with you] so that you will not have to ·care for them [Lbear it] alone.

18“Tell the people this: ‘·Make yourselves holy [Consecrate yourselves; Cin a ritual sense] for tomorrow, and you will eat meat. You cried ·to the [Lin the ears of the] LORD, “·We want meat [LIf only we had meat to eat]! We were better off in Egypt!” So now the LORD will give you meat to eat. 19You will eat it not for just one, two, five, ten, or even twenty days, 20but you will eat that meat for a whole month. You will eat it until it comes out your nose, and you will grow to ·hate [loathe] it. This is because you have rejected the LORD, who is with you. You have cried to him, saying, “Why did we ever leave Egypt?” ’ ”

21Moses said, “LORD, here are six hundred thousand people ·standing [Lon foot] around me, and you say, ‘I will give them enough meat to eat for a month!’ 22If we ·killed [slaughtered] all the flocks and herds, ·that would not be [Lwould there be…?] enough. If we caught all the fish in the sea, ·that would not be [Lwould there be…?] enough.”

23But the LORD said to Moses, “·Do you think I'm weak [LIs the hand of the LORD too short]? Now you will see if ·I can do what I say [Lthe words I spoke to you come true or not].”

24So Moses went out to the people and told them ·what the LORD had said [Lthe words of the LORD]. He gathered seventy of the elders together and had them stand around the Tent. 25Then the LORD came down in the cloud [Crepresenting God's presence] and spoke to Moses. The LORD took some of the Spirit Moses had, and he ·gave it to [*or* put it on] the seventy leaders. ·With the Spirit in [LWhen the Spirit rested on] them, they prophesied, but just that one time [Cas evidence that they had the Spirit; 1 Sam. 10:6–13; 19:18–24].

26Two men named Eldad and Medad were also ·listed as leaders [Lregistered; enrolled], but they did not go to the Tent. They stayed in the camp, but the Spirit was also ·given to [*or* rested on] them, and they prophesied in the camp. 27A young man ran to Moses and said, “Eldad and Medad are prophesying in the camp.”

28Joshua son of Nun said, “Moses, my ·master [lord], stop them!” (·Ever since he was a young boy [*or* One of his chosen men], Joshua ·had been [*or* was] Moses' assistant [Ex. 17:8; 24:13; 32:17; 33:7–11].)

29But Moses answered, “Are you jealous for me? I wish all the LORD's people could prophesy. I wish the LORD would give his Spirit to all of them [Joel 2:28–29; Acts 2:16–21; 1 Cor. 12:27–31; 14:1–5]!” 30Then Moses and the leaders of Israel went back to the camp.

The Lord Sends Quail

31·The LORD sent a strong wind [LThen a wind went out from the LORD] from the sea, and it blew quail into the area all around the camp. The quail were about ·three feet [Ltwo cubits] deep on the ground, and there were quail a day's walk in any direction [Ex. 16:13; Ps. 78:26–31]. 32The people went out and gathered quail all that day, that night, and the next day. Everyone gathered at least ·sixty bushels [Lten homers], and they spread them around the camp. 33But the LORD became very angry, and he ·gave the people a terrible sickness [Lstruck the people with a terrible plague] that came while the meat was still ·in their mouths [Lbetween their teeth]. 34So the people named that place Kibroth Hattaavah [CGraves of Wanting/Craving], because there they buried those who ·wanted [craved] other food.

35From Kibroth Hattaavah the people went to stay at Hazeroth.

Miriam and Aaron Speak Against Moses

12 Miriam [Ex. 15:20] **and Aaron** [CMoses' sister and brother] **began to talk against Moses because of his Cushite wife (he had married a Cushite** [Cperhaps Zipporah (Hab. 3:7), but more likely an Ethiopian]). 2**They said, "Is Moses the only one the LORD speaks through? Doesn't he also speak through us?" And the LORD heard this.**

3**(Now Moses was very** ·**humble** [*or* devout]. **He was the** ·**least proud** [Lmost humble; *or* most devout] **person on earth.)**

4**So the LORD suddenly spoke to Moses, Aaron, and Miriam and said, "All three of you come to the Meeting Tent." So they went.** 5**The LORD came down in a pillar of cloud** [Crepresenting his presence; Ex. 13:21] **and stood at the entrance to the Tent. He called to Aaron and Miriam, and they both came near.** 6**He said, "Listen to my words:**

When prophets are among you,
I, the LORD, ·**will show myself** [make myself known] **to them in visions;**
I will speak to them in dreams [Cindirectly].
7**But this is not true with my servant Moses.**
I trust him to lead all my ·**people** [Lhouse].
8**I speak face to face with him—**
clearly, not with hidden meanings [Cdirectly].
He has even seen the form of the LORD [Heb. 3:1–6].
·**You should be** [LWhy are you not…?] **afraid**
to speak against my servant Moses."

9**The LORD was very angry with them, and he left.**

10**When the cloud lifted from the Tent and Aaron turned toward Miriam, she was as white as snow; she had a skin disease** [Crendering her ritually unclean; Num. 5:2; Lev. 13:2]. 11**Aaron said to Moses, "Please, my** ·**master** [lord], ·**forgive us for our foolish sin** [do not punish us for our foolish sin; Ldo not lay sin on us that we foolishly committed]. 12**Don't let her be like a baby who is** ·**born dead** [stillborn]. **(Sometimes a baby is born with half of its flesh eaten away.)"**

13**So Moses cried out to the LORD, "God, please heal her!"**

14**The LORD answered Moses, "If her father had spit in her face,** ·**she would** [Lwould she not…?] **have been shamed for seven days, so** ·**put her** [she was shut] **outside the camp for seven days. After that, she may come back."** 15**So Miriam was** ·**put** [shut] **outside of the camp for seven days, and the people did not move on until she came back.**

16**After that, the people left Hazeroth and camped in the** ·**Desert** [Wilderness] **of Paran.**

The Spies Explore Canaan

13 **The LORD said to Moses,** 2**"Send men to** ·**explore** [spy on] **the land of Canaan, which I will give to the** ·**Israelites** [Lsons/Tchildren of Israel]. **Send one leader from each tribe** [Deut. 1:19–46]."

3**So Moses obeyed the LORD's command and sent the** ·**Israelite leaders** [Lleaders of the sons/Tchildren of Israel] **out from the** ·**Desert** [Wilderness] **of Paran.** 4**These are their names: from the tribe of Reuben, Shammua son of Zaccur;** 5**from the tribe of Simeon, Shaphat son of Hori;** 6**from the tribe of Judah, Caleb son of Jephunneh;** 7**from the tribe of Issachar, Igal son of Joseph;** 8**from the tribe of Ephraim, Hoshea son of Nun;** 9**from the tribe of Benjamin, Palti son of Raphu;** 10**from the tribe of Zebulun, Gaddiel son of Sodi;** 11**from the tribe of Manasseh (a tribe of Joseph), Gaddi son of Susi;** 12**from the tribe of Dan, Ammiel son of Gemalli;** 13**from** the tribe of Asher, Sethur son of Michael; 14from the tribe of Naphtali, Nahbi son of Vophsi; 15from the tribe of Gad, Geuel son of Maki.

16These are the names of the men Moses sent to explore the land. (Moses gave Hoshea son of Nun the new name Joshua.)

17Moses sent them to ·explore [spy on] Canaan and said, "Go through ·southern Canaan [the Negev] and then into the mountains. 18See what the land looks like. Are the people who live there strong or weak? Are there a few or many? 19What kind of land do they live in? Is it good or bad? What about the towns they live in—are they ·open like camps [unwalled], or do they have walls? 20What about the soil? Is it ·fertile [rich] or poor? ·Are there trees there [LDoes it have trees or not]? ·Try to [*or* Be courageous and] bring back some of the fruit from that land." (It was the season for the first grapes.)

21So they went up and ·explored [spied on] the land, from the ·Desert [Wilderness] of Zin all the way to Rehob by Lebo Hamath. 22They went through the ·southern area [Negev] to Hebron, where Ahiman, Sheshai, and Talmai [Josh. 15:14; Judg. 1:10; 1 Chr. 9:17], the descendants of Anak lived [Deut. 1:28; 2:10–11, 21; 9:2; Josh. 11:21–22]. (The city of Hebron had been built seven years before Zoan in Egypt.) 23In the Valley of Eshcol, they cut off a branch of a grapevine that had one bunch of grapes on it and carried that branch on a pole between two of them. They also got some pomegranates and figs. 24That place was called the Valley of Eshcol [C"Bunch"], because the ·Israelites [Lsons/Tchildren of Israel] cut off the bunch of grapes there. 25After forty days of ·exploring [spying on] the land, the men returned to the camp.

26They came back to Moses and Aaron and all the ·Israelites [Lcommunity/congregation/assembly of the sons/Tchildren of Israel] at Kadesh, in the ·Desert [Wilderness] of Paran. The men reported to them and showed ·everybody [Lall the community/congregation/assembly] the fruit from the land. 27They ·told [reported to] Moses, "We went to the land where you sent us, and it is a ·fertile land [Lland flowing with milk and honey; Ex. 3:8]! Here is some of its fruit. 28But the people who live there are strong. Their cities are walled and very large. We even saw some Anakites there. 29The Amalekites live in the ·southern area [Negev; Ex. 17:8–16]; the Hittites, Jebusites [Cinhabitants in and around Jerusalem], and Amorites live in the mountains; and the Canaanites live near the sea and along the Jordan River."

30Then Caleb told the people near Moses to be quiet, and he said, "We should certainly go up and take the land for ourselves. We can certainly do it."

31But the men who had gone with him said, "We can't attack those people; they are stronger than we are." 32And those men gave the ·Israelites [Lsons/Tchildren of Israel] a bad report about the land they ·explored [spied on], saying, "The land that we ·explored [spied on] ·is too large to conquer [Ldevours its inhabitants]. All the people we saw are very tall. 33We saw the Nephilim people there [Cperhaps named for the pre-flood people mentioned in Gen. 6:4]. (The Anakites come from the Nephilim people.) We felt like grasshoppers, and we looked like grasshoppers to them."

The People Complain Again

14 That night all the ·people [community; congregation; assembly] in the camp began crying loudly. 2All the ·Israelites [Lsons/Tchildren of Israel] ·complained [grumbled] against Moses and Aaron, and all the ·people [community; congregation; assembly] said to

them, "We wish we had died in Egypt or in this ·desert [wilderness]. 3Why is the LORD bringing us to this land to ·be killed with [Lmake us fall by] swords? Our wives and children will be ·taken away [war plunder]. We would be better off going back to Egypt." 4They said to each other, "Let's choose a leader and go back to Egypt."

5Then Moses and Aaron ·bowed [Lfell] facedown in front of all the ·Israelites [Lassembly/crowd of the community/congregation/assembly of the sons/Tchildren of Israel] gathered there. 6Joshua son of Nun and Caleb son of Jephunneh, who had ·explored [spied on] the land, tore their clothes [Critual of grief]. 7They said to all of the ·Israelites [Lcommunity/congregation/assembly of the sons/Tchildren of Israel], "The land we ·explored [spied on] is very good. 8If the LORD is pleased with us, he will lead us into that land and give us that ·fertile land [Lland flowing with milk and honey; Ex. 3:8]. 9Don't ·turn [rebel] against the LORD! Don't be afraid of the people in that land! We will chew them up. They have no protection, but the LORD is with us. So don't be afraid of them."

10Then all the ·people [community; congregation; assembly] talked about ·killing them with stones [stoning them]. But the glory of the LORD [Crepresenting his manifest presence] appeared at the Meeting Tent to all the ·Israelites [Lsons/Tchildren of Israel]. 11The LORD said to Moses, "How long will these people ·ignore [despise] me? How long will they not believe me in spite of the ·miracles [signs] I have done among them? 12I will ·give them a terrible sickness [Lstrike them with disease/pestilence] and ·get rid of [disinherit; dispossess] them. But I will make you into a great nation that will be stronger than they are [Ex. 32:10]."

13Then Moses said to the LORD, "The Egyptians will hear about it! You brought these people from there by your great power [Ex. 12–15], 14and the Egyptians will tell this to those who live in this land [CCanaan]. They have already heard about you, LORD. They know that you are with your people and that you were seen face to face. They know that your cloud [Crepresenting God's presence] stays over your people and that you lead your people with that cloud during the day and with fire at night [Ex. 13:20–22]. 15If you put these people to death all at once, the nations who have heard about your power will say, 16'The LORD was not able to bring them into the land he ·promised [swore to] them. So he ·killed [slaughtered] them in the ·desert [wilderness].'

17"So show your strength now, Lord. Do what you said: 18'The LORD ·doesn't become angry quickly [is slow to anger], but he has great ·love [covenant love; loyalty; Ex. 34:6; Neh. 9:17; Ps. 86:15; 103:8; 145:8; Nah. 1:3]. He forgives sin and ·law breaking [transgression]. But the LORD never forgets to punish guilty people. ·When parents sin, he will also punish [LHe visits the sin/iniquity/guilt of the fathers on] their children, their grandchildren, their great-grandchildren, and their great-great-grandchildren [Ex. 20:5–6].' 19By your great ·love [covenant love; loyalty], forgive these people's sin, just as you have forgiven them from the time they left Egypt until now."

20The LORD answered, "I have forgiven them as you asked. 21But, as surely as I live and as surely as my glory fills the whole earth, I make this promise: 22All these people saw my glory and the ·miracles [signs] I did in Egypt and in the ·desert [wilderness], but they ·disobeyed me [Ldid not listen to my voice] and tested me ten times [Csymbolic for many times]. 23So not one of them will see the land I ·promised [swore to give] to their ancestors. No one who ·rejected [despised] me will see that land. [24]But my servant Caleb ·thinks differently [Lhas a different spirit] and follows me completely. So I will bring him into the land he has already seen, and his ·children [seed] will ·own [possess] that land [Josh. 15:13–19; Judg. 1:9–15]. [25]Since the Amalekites and the Canaanites are living in the valleys, leave tomorrow and follow the ·desert [Wilderness] road toward the ·Red [*or* Reed; Ex. 10:19] Sea."

The Lord Punishes the People

[26]The LORD said to Moses and Aaron, [27]"How long will these evil ·people [community; congregation; assembly] ·complain [grumble] about me? I have heard the ·complaining [grumbling] of these ·Israelites [Lsons/Tchildren of Israel]. [28]So tell them, 'This is ·what the LORD says [Lthe utterance/decree of the LORD]. I heard what you said, and as surely as I live, I will do those very things to you: [29]·You will die [LYour dead bodies will fall] in this ·desert [wilderness]. Every one of you who is twenty years old or older [Cof military age] and who was counted with the people [1:1–54]—all of you who ·complained [grumbled] against me—will die. [30]Not one of you will enter the land where I ·promised [Llifted my hand; Cas when swearing an oath] you would live; only Caleb son of Jephunneh and Joshua son of Nun will go in. [31]You said that your children would be ·taken away [war plunder], but I will bring them into the land to enjoy what you refused. [32]As for you, ·you will die [Lyour bodies will fall] in this ·desert [wilderness]. [33]Your children will be shepherds here for forty years. Because you were ·not loyal [unfaithful; Cthe term suggests sexual unfaithfulness as a metaphor of spiritual unfaithfulness], they will suffer until ·you lie dead [the last of your bodies lie] in the ·desert [wilderness]. [34]For forty years you will suffer for your sins—a year for each of the forty days you ·explored [spied on] the land. You will know me as your enemy.' [35]I, the LORD, have spoken, and I will certainly do these things to all ·these evil people [this evil community/congregation/assembly] who have come together against me. So they will all die here in this ·desert [wilderness]."

[36]The men Moses had sent to ·explore [spy on] the land had returned and ·spread complaints [grumbled] among all the ·people [community; congregation; assembly]. They had given a bad report about the land. [37]The men who gave a very bad report died; the LORD killed them with a terrible ·sickness [plague]. [38]Only two of the men who ·explored [spied on] the land did not die—Joshua son of Nun and Caleb son of Jephunneh.

[39]When Moses told these things to all the ·Israelites [Lsons/Tchildren of Israel], they ·were very sad [mourned greatly]. [40]Early the next morning they started to go toward the top of the mountains, saying, "We have sinned. We will go where the LORD told us."

[41]But Moses said, "Why are you ·disobeying [transgressing] the LORD's command? You will not ·win [succeed]! [42]Don't go, because the LORD is not with you and you will be ·beaten [struck down] by your enemies. [43]You will run into the Amalekites and Canaanites, who will ·kill [Lfell] you with swords. You have turned away from the LORD, so the LORD will not be with you."

[44]But they were ·proud [presumptuous; reckless]. They went toward the top of the mountains, ·but [*or* even though] Moses and the Ark of the ·Agreement [Treaty; Covenant; Ex. 25:10] with the LORD did not leave the camp. [45]The Amalekites and the Canaanites who lived in those mountains came down and ·attacked the Israelites [Lstruck them down] and beat them back all the way to Hormah.

Rules About Sacrifices

15 The LORD said to Moses, 2“Speak to the ·Israelites [Lsons/
Tchildren of Israel] and say to them, ‘When you enter the land
that I am giving you as a home, 3give the LORD offerings made by fire.
These may be from your herds or flocks, as a smell pleasing to the LORD.
These may be burnt offerings [Lev. 1:1–17] or sacrifices for ·special promises [a vow], or as gifts to him, or as festival offerings. 4The one who brings
the offering shall also give the LORD a ·grain [Lgift; tribute] offering [Lev.
2:1]. It should be ·two quarts [Lone-tenth of an ephah] of ·fine [choice]
flour mixed with ·one quart [Lone-fourth of a hin] of olive oil. 5Each time
you offer a lamb as a burnt offering [Lev. 1:1–17] or sacrifice, also prepare
·one quart [Lone-fourth of a hin] of wine as a drink offering.
6“ ‘If you are giving a ·male sheep [ram], also prepare a ·grain [Lgift;
tribute] offering [Lev. 2:1] of ·four quarts [Ltwo-tenths of an ephah] of
·fine [choice] flour mixed with ·one and one-fourth quarts [Lone-third of
a hin] of olive oil. 7Also prepare ·one and one-fourth quarts [Lone-third of
a hin] of wine as a drink offering. Its smell will be pleasing to the LORD.
8“ ‘If you prepare a young bull as a burnt offering [Lev. 1:1–17] or sacrifice, whether it is for a ·special promise [vow] or a ·fellowship [*or* peace;
well-being] offering [Lev. 3:1] to the LORD, 9bring a ·grain [Lgift; tribute]
offering [Lev. 2:1] with the bull. It should be ·six quarts [Lthree-tenths of
an ephah] of ·fine [choice] flour mixed with ·two quarts [Lhalf a hin] of
olive oil. 10Also bring ·two quarts [Lhalf a hin] of wine as a drink offering.
This offering is made by fire, and its smell will be pleasing to the LORD.
11Prepare each bull or ·male sheep [ram], lamb or young goat this way.
12Do this for every one of the animals you bring.
13“ ‘All ·citizens [natives] must do these things in this way, and the smell
of their offerings by fire will be pleasing to the LORD. 14·From now on
[LThroughout your generations] if ·foreigners [resident aliens] who live
among you want to make offerings by fire so the smell will be pleasing to
the LORD, they must offer them the same way you do. 15As for the ·people
[community; congregation; assembly], the ·law [statute; ordinance;
requirement] is the same for you and for ·foreigners [resident aliens], and
it will be ·from now on [a perpetual requirement]; you and the ·foreigners
[resident aliens] are alike before the LORD. 16The ·teachings [instructions;
laws] and ·rules [regulations] are the same for you and for the ·foreigners
[resident aliens] among you.’ ”
17The LORD said to Moses, 18“Tell the ·Israelites [Lsons/Tchildren of
Israel]: ‘You are going to another land, where I am taking you. 19When
you eat the food there, ·offer [elevate] part of it to the LORD. 20·Offer
[Elevate] a loaf of bread from the first of your ·grain [*or* dough], which
will be your ·offering [elevation offering] from the threshing floor.
21·From now on [LThroughout your generations] ·offer [elevate] to the
LORD the first part of your ·grain [*or* dough].
22“ ‘Now what if you ·forget [unintentionally fail] to ·obey [do] any of
these commands the LORD gave Moses? 23These are the LORD’s commands
given to you through Moses, which began the day the LORD ·gave them to
[commanded] you and will continue ·from now on [Lthroughout your
generations]. 24If the ·people [community; congregation; assembly] ·for-
get [unintentionally fail] to ·obey [do] one of these commands, all the
·people [community; congregation; assembly] must offer a young bull as
a burnt offering [Lev. 1:1–17], a smell pleasing to the LORD. By law you
must also give the ·grain [Lgift; tribute] offering [Lev. 2:1] and the drink

offering with it, and you must bring a male goat as a ·sin [*or* purification;
Lev. 4:3] offering.
25“ ‘The priest will ·remove that sin for all the Israelites so they will
belong to the LORD [[L]atone for all the community/congregation/assembly
of the sons/[T]children of Israel]. They are forgiven, because they ·didn’t
know they were sinning [sinned unintentionally]. For the unintentional
wrong they did they brought offerings to the LORD, an offering by fire and
a ·sin [*or* purification; Lev. 4:3] offering. 26So all of the ·people [commu-
nity; congregation; assembly] of ·Israel [[L]the sons/[T]children of Israel] and
the ·foreigners [resident aliens] living among them will be forgiven. ·No
one meant to do wrong [They were all involved in unintentional sin].
27“ ‘If just one person sins ·without meaning to [unintentionally], a
year-old female goat must be brought for a ·sin [*or* purification; Lev. 4:3]
offering. 28The priest will ·remove [atone for] the sin of the person who
sinned ·accidentally [unintentionally]. He will ·remove it before the LORD
[atone for him]; and the person will be forgiven. 29The same ·teaching
[instruction; law] is for everyone who sins ·accidentally [unintention-
ally]—for those ·born Israelites [natives] and for ·foreigners [resident
aliens] living among you.
30“ ‘But anyone who sins ·on purpose [[L]with a high hand; [C]knowingly]
·is against [insults] the LORD and must be cut off from the people, whether
it is ·someone born among you [a native] or a ·foreigner [resident alien].
31That person has ·turned against [despised] the LORD’s word and has ·not
obeyed [broken] his commands. Such a person must surely be cut off
from the others. He is guilty.’ ”

A Man Worked on the Sabbath

32When the ·Israelites [[L]sons/[T]children of Israel] were still in the ·desert
[wilderness], they found a man gathering wood on the Sabbath day [Gen.
2:2–3; Ex. 20:8–11; 35:2; Deut. 5:13–15]. 33Those who found him gathering wood brought him to Moses and Aaron and all the people. 34They
held the man under guard, because they did not know what to do with
him. 35Then the LORD said to Moses, “The man must surely die. All the
·people [community; congregation; assembly] must kill him by ·throwing
stones at [stoning] him outside the camp.” 36So all the ·people [commu-
nity; congregation; assembly] took him outside the camp and stoned him
to death, as the LORD commanded Moses.

The Tassels

37The LORD said to Moses, 38“Speak to the ·Israelites [[L]sons/[T]children of
Israel] and tell them this: ‘·Tie several pieces of thread together and attach
them to [Make fringes/tassels on] the corners of your clothes. Put a blue
thread ·in each one of these tassels [[L]on the fringe/tassel of each corner].
Wear them ·from now on [[L]throughout your generations]. 39You will have
these ·tassels [fringes] to look at to remind you of all the LORD’s commands. Then you will obey them and not ·be disloyal by following what
your bodies and eyes want [[L]follow after your own heart or your own eyes
to be unfaithful/play the harlot after them]. 40Then you will remember to
obey all my commands, and you will be God’s holy people. 41I am the LORD
your God, who brought you out of Egypt to be your God [Ex. 12–15]. I am
the LORD your God.’ ”

Korah, Dathan, Abiram, and On

16 Korah, Dathan, Abiram, and On turned against Moses. (Korah
was the son of Izhar [26:9–11; 27:3; Ex. 6:21, 24], the son of
Kohath, the son of Levi; Dathan and Abiram were brothers [Deut. 11:6;

Ps. 106:17], **the sons of Eliab; and On was the son of Peleth; Dathan, Abiram, and On were from the tribe of Reuben** [Gen. 49:3–4].) **2These men gathered two hundred fifty other ·Israelite men** [Lmen of the sons/ Tchildren of Israel], **·well-known leaders** [Lmen of name/reputation] **chosen by the ·community** [congregation; assembly], **and ·challenged** [confronted] **Moses. 3They ·came as a group to speak to** [Lassembled against] **Moses and Aaron and said, "You have gone too far. All the ·people** [community; congregation; assembly] **are holy, every one of them, and the LORD is among them** [Ex. 19:6]. **So why do you put yourselves above all the ·people** [assembly; crowd] **of the LORD?"**

4When Moses heard this, he ·bowed facedown [Lfell on his face]. **5Then he said to Korah and all his ·followers** [community; congregation; assembly]: **"Tomorrow morning the LORD will show who belongs to him. He will bring the one who is holy near to him; he will bring to himself the person he chooses. 6So Korah, you and all your ·followers** [community; congregation; assembly] **do this: Get some ·pans for burning incense** [censers; firepans]. **7Tomorrow put fire and incense in them and take them before the LORD** [Lev. 10:1–2]. **He will choose the man who is holy. You ·Levites** [Lsons/descendants of Levi] **have gone too far."**

8Moses also said to Korah, "Listen, you ·Levites [Lsons of Levi]. **9The God of Israel has ·separated** [divided] **you from the rest of the ·Israelites** [Lcommunity/congregation/assembly of Israel]. **He brought you near to himself to do the work in the LORD's ·Holy Tent** [Tabernacle] **and to stand before all the ·Israelites** [community; congregation; assembly] **and ·serve** [minister to] **them** [8:14; Ex. 32:29; Lev. 8–9; Deut. 33:8–11]. **·Isn't that enough** [LIs it too little for you]? **10He has brought you and all your ·fellow** [brother] **·Levites** [Lsons of Levi] **near to himself, yet now you ·want to be priests** [Lseek the priesthood]. **11You and your ·followers** [community; congregation; assembly] **have joined together against the LORD. ·Your complaint is not against Aaron** [LWho is Aaron that you complain/grumble against him?]."

12Then Moses called Dathan and Abiram, the sons of Eliab, but they said, "We will not come! 13Is it too little that you have brought us out of a ·fertile land [Lland flowing with milk and honey; CEgypt] **to this ·desert** [wilderness] **to kill us? Now you want to ·order us around** [lord it over us]. **14You haven't brought us into a ·fertile land** [Lland flowing with milk and honey; Ex. 3:8]; **you haven't given us ·any land** [Lan inheritance] **with fields and vineyards. Will you put out the eyes of these men? No! We will not come!"**

15Then Moses became very angry and said to the LORD, "Don't accept their ·gifts [tribute]. **I have not taken anything from them, not even a donkey, and I have not done wrong to any of them."**

16Then Moses said to Korah, "You and all your ·followers [community; congregation; assembly] **must stand before the LORD tomorrow. And Aaron will stand there with you and them. 17Each of you must take your ·pan** [censer; firepan] **and put incense in it; present these two hundred fifty ·pans** [censers; firepans] **before the LORD. You and Aaron must also present your ·pans** [censers; firepans]." **18So each man got his ·pan** [censer; firepan] **and put burning incense in it and stood with Moses and Aaron at the entrance to the Meeting Tent. 19Korah ·gathered** [assembled] **all his ·followers** [community; congregation; assembly] **who were against Moses and Aaron, and they stood at the entrance to the Meeting Tent.**

Then the glory of the LORD [Crepresenting God's manifest presence, often in the form of fire and smoke] appeared to everyone.

20The LORD said to Moses and Aaron, 21"·Move away [Separate/Divide yourselves] from these men so I can destroy them quickly."

22But Moses and Aaron ·bowed facedown [Lfell on their faces] and cried out, "God, you are the God ·over [of] the spirits of all ·people [flesh; 27:16; Gen 2:7]. Please don't be angry with this whole ·group [community; congregation; assembly]. Only one man has really sinned."

23Then the LORD said to Moses, 24"Tell ·everyone [the community/congregation/assembly] to ·move away from [Lgo up from around] the ·tents [dwellings] of Korah, Dathan, and Abiram."

25Moses stood and went to Dathan and Abiram; the elders of Israel followed him. 26Moses warned the people, "·Move away [Turn aside] from the tents of these evil men! Don't touch anything of theirs, or you will be ·destroyed [swept away] because of their sins." 27So they ·moved away [went up] from the ·tents [dwellings] of Korah, Dathan, and Abiram. Dathan and Abiram were standing outside their tents with their wives, children, and little babies.

28Then Moses said, "Now you will know that the LORD has sent me to do all these things; it was not ·my idea [Lfrom my heart/mind]. 29If these men die a normal death—·the way men usually die [if a normal fate comes on them]—then the LORD did not really send me. 30But if the LORD ·does [Lcreates] something new, you will know they have ·insulted [despised] the LORD. The ground will open and swallow them. They will be buried alive and will go to ·the place of the dead [LSheol; Cthe grave or the underworld], and everything that belongs to them will go with them."

31When Moses finished saying these things, the ground under the men split open. 32The earth opened its mouth and swallowed them and all their families. All Korah's men and everything they owned went down. 33They were buried alive, going to ·the place of the dead [LSheol ;Cthe grave or the underworld], and everything they owned went with them. Then the earth covered them. They ·died and were gone [perished] from the ·community [assembly; crowd]. 34·The people of [LAll] Israel around them heard their screams and ran away, saying, "The earth will swallow us, too!"

35Then a fire came ·down [*or* out] from the LORD and ·destroyed [consumed] the two hundred fifty men who had presented the incense [Lev. 10:1–2].

36The LORD said to Moses, 37"Tell Eleazar son of Aaron, the priest, to take all the ·incense pans [censers; firepans] out of the ·fire [flames]. Have him scatter the ·coals [Lfire] a long distance away. But the ·incense pans [censers; firepans] are still holy. 38Take the ·pans [censers; firepans] of these men who sinned and lost their lives, and hammer them into flat sheets that will be used to cover the altar. They are holy, because they were presented to the LORD, and they will be a sign to the ·Israelites [Lsons/Tchildren of Israel]."

39So Eleazar the priest gathered all the bronze ·pans [censers; firepans] that had been brought by the men who were burned up. He had the ·pans [censers; firepans] hammered into flat sheets to put on the altar, 40as the LORD had commanded him through Moses. These sheets were to remind the Israelites that only ·descendants [Lthe seed] of Aaron should burn incense before the LORD. Anyone else would die like Korah and his ·followers [community; congregation; assembly].

Aaron Saves the People

41The next day all the ·Israelites [Lcommunity/congregation/assembly of the sons/Tchildren of Israel] ·complained [grumbled] against Moses and Aaron and said, "You have killed the LORD's people."

42When the ·people [community; congregation; assembly] ·gathered [assembled] to ·complain [grumble] against Moses and Aaron, they turned toward the Meeting Tent, and the cloud covered it. The glory of the LORD [Crepresenting his manifest presence] appeared. 43Then Moses and Aaron went in front of the Meeting Tent.

44The LORD said to Moses, 45"Move away from ·these people [this community/congregation/assembly] so I can ·destroy [consume] them quickly." So Moses and Aaron ·bowed facedown [Lfell on their faces].

46Then Moses said to Aaron, "Get your ·pan [censer; firepan], and put fire from the altar and incense in it. Hurry to the people and ·remove their sin [make atonement for them]. The LORD is angry with them; the ·sickness [plague; pestilence] has already started." 47So Aaron did as Moses said. He ran to the middle of the ·people [assembly; crowd], where the ·sickness [plague; pestilence] had already started among them. So Aaron offered the incense to ·remove their sin [make atonement for them]. 48He stood between the dead and the living, and the ·sickness [plague; pestilence] stopped there. 49But 14,700 people died from that ·sickness [plague; pestilence], in addition to those who died because of Korah. 50Then Aaron went back to Moses at the entrance to the Meeting Tent. The terrible ·sickness [plague; pestilence] had been stopped.

Aaron's Walking Stick Buds

17 The LORD said to Moses, 2"Speak to the ·people [Lsons; Tchildren] of Israel and get twelve ·walking sticks [staffs] from them—one from the leader of each ·tribe [family group; Lhouse of their fathers]. Write the name of each man on his ·stick [staff], and 3on the ·stick [staff] from Levi, write Aaron's name. There must be one ·stick [staff] for the head of each ·tribe [family; Lhouse of their fathers]. 4Put them in the Meeting Tent in front of the ·Ark of the Agreement [Treaty; Covenant; LTestimony; Ex. 25:10], where I meet with you. 5I will choose one man whose ·walking stick [staff] will begin to grow leaves [Cindicating God's affirmation]; in this way I will stop the ·Israelites [Lsons/Tchildren of Israel] from always ·complaining [grumbling] against you."

6So Moses spoke to the ·Israelites [Lsons/Tchildren of Israel]. Each of the twelve leaders gave him a ·walking stick [staff]—one from each ·tribe [family; Lhouse of their fathers]—and Aaron's ·walking stick [staff] was among them. 7Moses put them before the LORD in the Tent of the ·Agreement [Testimony; Treaty; Covenant].

8The next day, when Moses entered the Tent of the ·Agreement [Testimony; Treaty; Covenant], he saw that Aaron's ·stick [staff] (which stood for the family of Levi) had grown leaves. It had even budded, blossomed, and produced almonds. 9So Moses brought out to the ·Israelites [Lsons/Tchildren of Israel] all the ·walking sticks [staffs] from the LORD's presence. They all looked, and each man took back his ·stick [staff].

10Then the LORD said to Moses, "Put Aaron's ·walking stick [staff] back in front of the ·Ark of the Agreement [Treaty; Covenant; LTestimony; Ex. 25:10]. It will ·remind [Lserve as a sign to] these people who are always turning against me to stop their ·complaining [grumbling] against me so they won't die." 11So Moses obeyed what the LORD commanded him.

12The ·people [Lsons/Tchildren] of Israel said to Moses, "We ·are going to die [will perish]! We are ·destroyed [lost]. We are all ·destroyed [lost]! 13Anyone who even comes near the Holy Tent of the LORD will die. Will we all ·die [perish]?"

The Work of the Priests and Levites

18 The LORD said to Aaron, "You, your sons, and your ·family [father's house] are now responsible for any wrongs done against the Holy Place; you and your sons are responsible for any wrongs done against the priests. 2Bring with you your ·fellow [brother] Levites from your tribe, and they will ·help [join; Cthe name Levi means "joined"] you and your sons serve in the Tent of the ·Agreement [Testimony; Treaty; Covenant; Ex. 25:10]. 3They are under your control, to do all the work that needs to be done in the Tent. But they must not go near the things in the Holy Place or near the altar. If they do, both you and they will die. 4They will join you in taking care of the Meeting Tent. They must do the work at the Tent, and no ·one else [stranger; outsider] may come near you.

5"You must take care of the Holy Place and the altar so that I won't become angry with the ·Israelites [Lsons/Tchildren of Israel] again. 6I myself chose your ·fellow [brother] Levites from among the ·Israelites [Lsons/Tchildren of Israel] as a gift given for you to the LORD, to work at the Meeting Tent. 7But only you and your sons may ·serve as priests [Lguard the priesthood]. Only you may serve at the altar or go behind the curtain. I am giving you this gift of serving as a priest, and ·anyone else [any stranger/outsider] who comes near the Holy Place will be put to death."

8Then the LORD said to Aaron, "I myself make you responsible for the offerings given to me. All the holy offerings that the ·Israelites [Lsons/Tchildren of Israel] give to me, I give to you and your sons as your share, your ·continual [perpetual] portion. 9Your share of the ·holy offerings [Lholy of the holy things] is that part which is not burned. When the people bring me gifts as ·most holy offerings [Lholy of the holy things], whether they are ·grain [Lgift; tribute; Lev. 2:1] or ·sin [*or* purification; Lev. 4:3] or ·penalty [guilt; reparation; Lev. 5:14—6:7] offerings, they will be set apart for you and your sons. 10You must eat the offering in ·a most holy place [Lthe holy of holy places]. Any male may eat it, but you must respect it as holy.

11"I also give you the offerings the ·Israelites [Lsons/Tchildren of Israel] present to me. I give these to you and your sons and daughters as your ·continual [perpetual] share. Anyone in your ·family [Lhouse] who is clean [Cin a ritual sense] may eat it.

12"And I give you all the best olive oil and all the best new wine and grain. This is what ·the Israelites [Lthey] give to me, the LORD, from the first crops they harvest. 13When they bring to the LORD all the first things they harvest, they will be yours. Anyone in your ·family [Lhouse] who is clean [Cin a ritual sense] may eat these things.

14"Everything in Israel that is ·given to the LORD [devoted; Cset aside for God] is yours. 15The ·first one born [Lone that opens the womb] to any family, whether people or animals, will be offered to the LORD. And that will be yours. But you must ·make a payment for [ransom; redeem] every firstborn child and every firstborn animal that is unclean [Cin a ritual sense]. 16When they are one month old, you ·must make a payment for [ransom; redeem] them of ·two ounces [Lfive shekels, that is twenty gerahs] of silver, as set by the Holy Place measure [3:40–50; Ex. 13:2, 11–16].

17"But you must not ·make a payment for [ransom; redeem] the firstborn ox or sheep or goat. Those animals are holy. ·Sprinkle [Dash] their
blood on the altar and ·burn [turn into smoke] their fat as an offering
made by fire. The smell is pleasing to the LORD. 18But the meat will be
yours, just as the breast that is presented and the right thigh will be yours.
19Anything the ·Israelites [[L]sons/[T]children of Israel] present as holy gifts I,
the LORD, give to you, your sons and daughters as your ·continual [per-
petual] portion. This is a lasting ·agreement [treaty; covenant] of salt
[[C]representing perpetual agreement because salt can survive fire; Lev.
2:13] before the LORD for you and your children forever."

20The LORD also said to Aaron, "You will not inherit any of the land,
and you will not own any land among the other people [Gen. 49:5–7]. I
will be yours. Out of all the ·Israelites [[L]sons/[T]children of Israel], only you
will inherit me.

21"When the people of Israel give me a ·tenth [[T]tithe] of what they
make, I will give that tenth to the ·Levites [[L]sons of Levi; Lev. 27:30–32;
Deut. 12:17–19; 14:22–29]. This is their payment for the work they do
serving at the Meeting Tent. 22But the other ·Israelites [[L]sons/[T]children of
Israel] must never go near the Meeting Tent, or they will die for their sin.
23Only the Levites should work in the Meeting Tent and be responsible
for any sins against it. This is a ·rule from now on [perpetual statute/ordi-
nance/requirement throughout your generations]. The Levites will not
inherit any land among the other ·Israelites [[L]sons/[T]children of Israel],
24but when the ·Israelites [[L]sons/[T]children of Israel] give a ·tenth [[T]tithe]
of everything they make to me, I will give that ·tenth [[T]tithe] to the Levites
as a reward. That is why I said about the Levites: 'They will not inherit
any land among the ·Israelites [[L]sons/[T]children of Israel].' "

25The LORD said to Moses, 26"Speak to the Levites and tell them: 'You
will receive a ·tenth [[T]tithe] of everything the ·Israelites [[L]sons/[T]children
of Israel] make, which I will give to you. But you must give a ·tenth of that
[[L]tenth of a tenth; [T]tithe of a tithe] back to the LORD. 27I will accept your
offering just as much as I accept the offerings from others, who give ·new
grain [[L]the grain of the threshing floor] or ·new wine [[L]the fullness of the
winepress]. 28In this way you will present an offering to the LORD as the
other ·Israelites [[L]sons/[T]children of Israel] do. When you receive a ·tenth
[[T]tithe] from the ·Israelites [[L]sons/[T]children of Israel], you will give a
·tenth [tithe] of that to Aaron, the priest, as the LORD's share. 29Choose the
best and holiest part from what you are given as the portion you must
give to the LORD.'

30"Say to the Levites: 'When you present the best, it will be accepted as
much as the ·grain [[L]product of the threshing floor] and ·wine [[L]product
of the wine press] from the other people. 31You and your ·families [[L]house]
may eat all that is left anywhere, because it is your pay for your work in
the Meeting Tent. 32And if you always give the best part to the LORD, you
will never be guilty. If you do not ·sin against [profane] the holy offerings
of the ·Israelites [[L]sons/[T]children of Israel], you will not die.' "

The Offering for Cleansing

19 The LORD said to Moses and Aaron, 2"These are the ·teachings
[statutes; ordinances; requirements] that the LORD commanded.
Tell the ·Israelites [[L]sons/[T]children of Israel] to get a young red ·cow [[T]heifer]
that does not have ·anything wrong with it [[L]a defect and is without a blem-
ish] and that has never ·been worked [[L]worn a yoke]. 3Give the ·cow [[T]heifer]

to Eleazar the priest; he will take it outside the camp and ·kill [slaughter] it
in his presence. [4]Then Eleazar the priest must put some of its blood on his
finger and sprinkle it seven times toward the front of the Meeting Tent.
[5]The whole ·cow [[T]heifer] must be burned while he watches; the skin, the
meat, the blood, and ·the intestines [[L]its dung] must all be burned. [6]Then
the priest must take a cedar stick, a hyssop branch, and a red string [[C]the
redness of the heifer and these objects probably represent blood] and throw
them onto the burning ·cow [[T]heifer]. [7]After the priest has washed himself
and his clothes with water, he may come back into the camp, but he will be
unclean [[C]in a ritual sense] until evening. [8]The man who burns the ·cow
[[T]heifer] must wash himself and his clothes in water; he will be unclean
until evening.

[9]"Then someone who is clean [[C]in a ritual sense] will collect the ashes
from the ·cow [[T]heifer] and put them in a clean place outside the camp.
The ·Israelites [[L]community/congregation/assembly of the sons/[T]children
of Israel] will keep these ashes to use in the cleansing water, in a ·special
ceremony to cleanse away sin [[L]sin offering; *or* purification offering; Lev.
4:3]. [10]The man who collected the ·cow's [[T]heifer's] ashes must wash his
clothes and be unclean until evening. This is a lasting ·rule [statute; ordinance; requirement] ·for the Israelites [[L]in their midst] and for the
·foreigners [resident aliens] among them.

[11]"Those who touch a dead person's body will be unclean [[C]in a ritual
sense] for seven days. [12]They must ·wash themselves with the cleansing
[purify themselves with the] water on the third day and on the seventh
day; then they will be clean. But if they do not ·wash themselves [purify
themselves] on the third day and the seventh day, they cannot be clean.
[13]If those who touch a dead person's body ·stay unclean [do not purify
themselves] and go to the LORD's ·Holy Tent [Tabernacle], it becomes
unclean; they must be cut off from Israel. If the cleansing water is not
sprinkled on them, they are unclean and will stay unclean.

[14]"This is the ·teaching [instruction; law] about someone who dies in a
tent: Anyone in the tent or anyone who enters it will be unclean [[C]in a
ritual sense] for seven days. [15]And every open jar or pot without a cover
becomes unclean. [16]If anyone is ·outside [[L]in the open field] and touches
someone who was killed by a sword or who died [[C]a natural death], or if
anyone touches a human bone or a grave, that person will be unclean for
seven days.

[17]"So you must use the ashes from the burnt sin [*or* purification; Lev.
4:3] offering to make that person clean [[C]in a ritual sense] again. Pour
·fresh [running; [L]living] water over the ashes into a jar. [18]A clean person
must take a hyssop branch and dip it into the water, and then he must
sprinkle it over the tent and all its objects. He must also sprinkle the people who were there, as well as anyone who touched a bone, or the body of
someone who was killed, or a dead person, or a grave. [19]The person who is
clean must sprinkle this water on the unclean people on the third day and
on the seventh day. On the seventh day they will ·become clean [be puri-
fied]. They must wash their clothes and take a bath, and they will be clean
that evening. [20]If any who are unclean do not become ·clean [purified],
they must be cut off from the ·community [assembly; crowd]. Since they
were not sprinkled with the cleansing water, they stay unclean, and they
could make the LORD's ·Holy Tent [Tabernacle] unclean. [21]This is a lasting
·rule [statute; ordinance; requirement]. Those who sprinkle the cleansing

water must also wash their clothes, and anyone who touches the water will be unclean until evening. 22Anything an unclean person touches becomes unclean, and whoever touches it will be unclean until evening."

Moses Disobeys God

20 In the first month all the ·people [Lsons; Tchildren] of Israel, the community [congregation; assembly] arrived at the ·Desert [Wilderness] of Zin, and they stayed at Kadesh. There Miriam [CMoses' sister; Ex. 15:20–21; Num. 12:1–13] died and was buried. 2There was no water for the ·people [community; congregation; assembly], so they ·came together [assembled] against Moses and Aaron. 3They ·argued with [contended with; brought a case against] Moses and said, "We should have died in front of the LORD as our brothers did. 4Why did you bring the LORD's ·people [community; congregation; assembly] into this ·desert [wilderness]? Are we and our animals to die here? 5Why did you bring us from Egypt to this terrible place? It has no grain, figs, grapevines, or pomegranates, and there's no water to drink!"

6So Moses and Aaron left the ·people [community; congregation; assembly] and went to the entrance of the Meeting Tent. There they ·bowed facedown [Lfell on their faces], and the glory of the LORD [Chis manifest presence] appeared to them. 7The LORD said to Moses, 8"Take your ·walking stick [staff], and you and your brother Aaron should gather the ·people [community; congregation; assembly]. Speak to that rock in front of them so that its water will flow from it. When you bring the water out from that rock, give it to the ·people [community; congregation; assembly] and their animals."

9So Moses took the ·stick [staff] from in front of the LORD, as he had said. 10Moses and Aaron ·gathered [assembled] the ·people [community; congregation; assembly] in front of the rock, and Moses said, "Now listen to me, you ·who turn against God [Lrebels]! Do you want us [Crather than God] to bring water out of this rock?" 11Then Moses lifted his hand and hit the rock twice with his ·stick [staff; Che was supposed to speak to it, 20:8]. Water began pouring out, and the ·people [community; congregation; assembly] and their animals drank it.

12But the LORD said to Moses and Aaron, "Because you did not ·believe [trust] me, and because you did not ·honor me as holy [show my holiness] before the ·people [Lsons/Tchildren of Israel], you will not lead ·them [Lthis community; congregation; assembly] into the land I will give them [20:22–29; Deut. 34:1–12]."

13These are the waters of Meribah [C"Argument"], where the ·Israelites [Lsons/Tchildren of Israel] ·argued with [contended with; brought a case against] the LORD and where he showed them he was holy.

Edom Will Not Let Israel Pass

14From Kadesh, Moses sent messengers to the king of Edom. He said, "Your brothers, the Israelites, say to you: You know about all the ·troubles [hardship] we have had, 15how our ·ancestors [fathers] went down into Egypt and we lived there for many years. The people of Egypt ·were cruel to [oppressed] us and our ·ancestors [fathers], 16but when we cried out to the LORD, he heard ·us [Lour voice] and sent us an ·angel [messenger] to bring us out of Egypt.

"Now we are here at Kadesh, a town on the edge of your ·land [boundaries]. 17Please let us pass through your country. We will not ·touch [pass through] any fields of grain or vineyards, and will not drink water from the wells. We will travel only along the ·king's road [King's Highway; Ca

north-south international highway], not turning right or left until we
have passed through your ·country [boundaries]."
18But the king of Edom answered: "You may not pass through here. If
you try, I will come and meet you with swords."
19The ·Israelites [Lsons/Tchildren of Israel] answered: "We will go along
the ·main road [highway], and if we or our animals drink any of your
water, we will pay for it. We only want to walk through. That's all."
20But he answered: "You may not pass through here."
Then the Edomites went out to meet the Israelites with a large and
powerful army. 21The Edomites refused to let them pass through their
·country [boundaries], so the Israelites turned back.

Aaron Dies

22·All the Israelites [LThe sons/Tchildren of Israel, all the community/
assembly/congregation] moved from Kadesh to Mount Hor, 23near the
border of Edom. There the LORD said to Moses and Aaron, 24"Aaron will
·die [Lbe gathered to his people]. He will not enter the land that I'm giving
to the ·Israelites [Lsons/Tchildren of Israel], because you both ·acted
[rebelled] against my command at the waters of Meribah [20:1–13].
25Take Aaron and his son Eleazar up on Mount Hor, 26and take off Aaron's
special clothes and put them on his son Eleazar. Aaron will die there; he
will ·join his people [Lbe gathered]."
27Moses obeyed the LORD's command. They climbed up Mount Hor,
and all the ·people [community; assembly; congregation] saw them go.
28Moses took off Aaron's clothes and put them on Aaron's son Eleazar.
Then Aaron died there on top of the mountain. Moses and Eleazar came
back down the mountain, 29and when all the ·people [community; assembly; congregation] learned that Aaron was dead, ·everyone in [Lall the
house of] Israel cried for him for thirty days.

War with the Canaanites

21 The Canaanite king of Arad lived in the ·southern area
[Negev]. When he heard that the Israelites were coming on
the road to Atharim, he attacked them and captured some of them.
2Then the Israelites made ·this promise [a vow] to the LORD: "If you will
·help us defeat these people [Lgive this people into our hands], we will
·completely destroy [devote to the LORD] their cities." 3The LORD listened
to the Israelites, and he let them defeat the Canaanites. The Israelites
·completely destroyed [devoted to the LORD] the Canaanites and their
cities, so the place was named Hormah [C"Completely Destroyed";
"Devoted to the Lord"].

The Bronze Snake

4The Israelites left Mount Hor and went on the road toward the ·Red
[*or* Reed] Sea, in order to go around the country of Edom. But the people
became impatient on the way 5and ·grumbled at [Lspoke against] God
and Moses. They said, "Why did you bring us out of Egypt to die in this
·desert [wilderness]? There is no bread and no water, and we hate this terrible food!"
6So the LORD sent them ·poisonous [Lburning] snakes; they bit the people, and many of the ·Israelites [Lpeople from Israel] died. 7The people
came to Moses and said, "We sinned when we ·grumbled at [spoke
against] you and the LORD. Pray that the LORD will take away these snakes."
So Moses prayed for the people.
8The LORD said to Moses, "Make a bronze snake, and put it on a pole.
When anyone who is bitten looks at it, that person will live." 9So Moses

made a bronze snake and put it on a pole. Then when a snake bit anyone,
that person looked at the bronze snake and lived [2 Kin. 18:4; John 3:14].

The Journey to Moab

10The ·Israelites [Lsons/Tchildren of Israel] went and camped at Oboth.
11They went from Oboth to Iye Abarim, in the ·desert [wilderness] east of
Moab. 12From there they went and camped in the Zered ·Valley [Wadi].
13From there they went and camped across the Arnon, in the ·desert [wil-
derness] just inside the Amorite country. The Arnon is the border
between the Moabites and the Amorites. 14That is why the Book of the
Wars of the LORD [Ca source now lost] says:

"... and Waheb in Suphah, and the ·ravines [wadis],
the Arnon, 15and the slopes of the ·ravines [wadis]
that lead to the settlement of Ar.
These places are at the border of Moab."

16The Israelites went from there to Beer; a well is there where the LORD
said to Moses, "Gather the people and I will give them water."
17Then the Israelites sang this song:

"·Pour out water [Spring up], well!
Sing ·about [*or* to] it.
18Princes dug this well.
·Important men [Leaders of the people] made it.
With their scepters and poles, they dug it."

The people went from the ·desert [wilderness] to Mattanah. 19From
Mattanah they went to Nahaliel and on to Bamoth. 20From Bamoth they
went to the valley of Moab where the top of Mount Pisgah looks over the
·desert [wilderness].

Israel Kills Sihon and Og

21The Israelites sent messengers to Sihon, king of the Amorites, saying,
22"Let ·us [Lme] pass through your country. We will not go through any
fields of grain or vineyards, or drink water from the wells. We will travel
only along the ·king's road [King's Highway; 20:17] until we have passed
through your ·country [boundaries]."
23But King Sihon would not let the Israelites pass through his ·country
[boundaries]. He gathered his whole army together, and they marched out
to meet Israel in the ·desert [wilderness]. At Jahaz they fought the Israelites.
24Israel ·killed [Lstruck with the sword] the king and captured his land
from the Arnon River to the Jabbok River. They took the land as far as the
·Ammonite border [Lborder of the sons of Ammon], which was strongly
defended. 25Israel captured all the Amorite cities and lived in them, taking
Heshbon and all the towns around it. 26Heshbon was the city where Sihon,
the Amorite king, lived. In the past he had fought with the king of Moab
and had taken all the land from his hand as far as the Arnon.
27That is why the poets say:

"Come to Heshbon
and rebuild it;
·rebuild [establish] Sihon's city.
28A fire ·began in [Lwent out from] Heshbon;
flames came from Sihon's city.
It destroyed Ar in Moab,
and it ·burned [*or* swallowed] the Arnon highlands.
29·How terrible for [TWoe to] you, Moab!
The people of Chemosh are ruined.
His sons ran away

and his daughters were captured
by Sihon, king of the Amorites.
30But we defeated those Amorites.
We ruined their towns from Heshbon to Dibon,
and we destroyed them as far as Nophah, near Medeba."
31So Israel lived in the land of the Amorites.
32After Moses sent spies to the town of Jazer, they captured ·the towns
around it [its villages], forcing out the Amorites who lived there.
33Then the Israelites went up the road toward Bashan. Og king of
Bashan and his whole army marched out to meet the Israelites, and they
fought at Edrei.
34The LORD said to Moses, "Don't be afraid of him. I will hand him, his
whole army, and his land over to you. Do to him what you did to Sihon,
the Amorite king who lived in Heshbon."
35So the Israelites ·killed [Lstruck] Og and his sons and all his army; no
one was left alive. And they took his land [Deut. 1:4; 3:1–7; Ps. 135:11;
136:20].

Balak Sends for Balaam

22 Then the ·people [Lsons/Tchildren of] of Israel went to the
plains of Moab, and they camped near the Jordan River
across from Jericho.
2Balak son of Zippor saw everything the Israelites had done to the
Amorites. 3And Moab ·was scared of [dreaded] so many Israelites; truly,
Moab was terrified by them.
4The Moabites said to the elders of Midian, "·These people [LThis com-
munity/assembly/congregation] will ·take [lick up] everything around us
like an ox ·eating [licking] grass."
Balak son of Zippor was the king of Moab at this time. 5He sent messengers to Balaam son of Beor at Pethor, near the Euphrates River in ·his
native land [*or* the land of Amaw]. Balak said, "A nation has come out of
Egypt that covers the land. They have ·camped [Lsettled] next to me, 6and
they are too powerful for me. So come and put a curse on them. Maybe
then I can defeat them and ·make them leave [drive them from] the area.
I know that if you bless someone, the blessings happen, and if you put a
curse on someone, it happens."
7The elders of Moab and Midian went with ·payment [Lfee for divina-
tion] in their hands. When they found Balaam, they told him what Balak
had said.
8Balaam said to them, "Stay here for the night, and I will tell you what
the LORD tells me." So the Moabite leaders stayed with him.
9God came to Balaam and asked, "Who are these men with you?"
10Balaam said to God, "The king of Moab, Balak son of Zippor, sent
them to me with this message: 11'A ·nation [people] has come out of Egypt
that ·covers [spreads over] the land. So come and put a curse on them,
and maybe I can fight them and force them out of my land.'"
12But God said to Balaam, "Do not go with them. Don't put a curse on
those people, because I have blessed them."
13The next morning Balaam ·awoke [rose] and said to Balak's leaders, "Go
back to your own country; the LORD has refused to let me go with you."
14So the Moabite leaders went back to Balak and said, "Balaam refused
to come with us."
15So Balak sent other leaders—this time there were more of them, and

they were more ·important [distinguished]. 16They went to Balaam and said,
"Balak son of Zippor says this: Please don't let anything stop you from coming to me. 17I will ·pay you very well [make you wealthy; honor you], and I
will do what you say. Come and put a curse on these people for me."
18But Balaam answered Balak's servants, "King Balak could give me his
palace full of silver and gold, but I cannot ·disobey [transgress] the LORD
my God in anything, great or small. 19You stay here tonight as the other
men did, and I will find out what more the LORD tells me."
20That night God came to Balaam and said, "These men have come to
ask you to go with them. Go, but only do what I tell you."

Balaam's Donkey Speaks

21Balaam got up the next morning and put a saddle on his donkey.
Then he went with the Moabite leaders. 22But God became angry because
Balaam went, so the ·angel [messenger] of the LORD stood in the road to
·stop [challenge] Balaam. Balaam was riding his donkey, and he had two
servants with him. 23When the donkey saw the ·angel [messenger] of the
LORD standing in the road with a drawn sword in his hand, the donkey left
the road and went into the field. Balaam ·hit [struck] the donkey to force
her back on the road.
24Later, the ·angel [messenger] of the LORD stood on a narrow path
between two vineyards, with walls on both sides. 25Again the donkey saw
the angel of the LORD, and she walked close to one wall, ·crushing [squeez-
ing; scraping] Balaam's foot against it. So he ·hit [struck] her again.
26The ·angel [messenger] of the LORD went ahead again and stood at a
narrow place, too narrow to turn left or right. 27When the donkey saw the
·angel [messenger] of the LORD, she lay down under Balaam. This made
him so angry that he ·hit [struck] her with his stick. 28Then the LORD
made the donkey talk, and she said to Balaam, "What have I done to make
you ·hit [strike] me three times?"
29Balaam answered the donkey, "You have made me look foolish! I
wish I had a sword in my hand! I would kill you right now!"
30But the donkey said to Balaam, "·I am [LAm I not...?] your very own
donkey, which you have ridden for years. Have I ever done this to you
before?"
"No," Balaam said.
31Then the LORD opened the eyes of Balaam and let Balaam see the
·angel [messenger] of the LORD, who was standing in the road with his
sword drawn in his hand. Then Balaam bowed facedown on the ground.
32The ·angel [messenger] of the LORD asked Balaam, "Why have you
·hit [struck] your donkey three times? I have stood here to ·stop [chal-
lenge] you, because what you are doing is wrong. 33The donkey saw me
and turned away from me three times [Cit was more spiritually sensitive
than Balaam]. If she had not turned away, I would have killed you by now,
but I would have let her live."
34Then Balaam said to the ·angel [messenger] of the LORD, "I have
sinned; I did not know you were standing in the road to stop me. If I am
wrong, I will go back."
35The ·angel [messenger] of the LORD said to Balaam, "Go with these
men, but say only what I tell you." So Balaam went with Balak's leaders.
36When Balak heard that Balaam was coming, he went out to meet him
at Ar in Moab, which was beside the Arnon, at the edge of his ·country
[boundary]. 37Balak said to Balaam, "·I had asked you before [LDid I not

send for you...?] to come quickly. Why didn't you come to me? ·I am [LAm I not...?] able to ·reward you well [give you wealth]."

38But Balaam answered, "I have come to you now, but I can't say just anything. I can only say what God tells me to say."

39Then Balaam went with Balak to Kiriath Huzoth. 40Balak offered cattle and sheep as a sacrifice and gave some meat to Balaam and the leaders with him.

41The next morning Balak took Balaam to Bamoth Baal; from there he could see the edge of the ·Israelite camp [Lpeople].

Balaam's First Message

23 Balaam said to Balak, "Build me seven altars here, and prepare seven bulls and seven ·male sheep [rams] for me." 2Balak did what Balaam asked, and they offered a bull and a ·male sheep [ram] on each of the altars.

3Then Balaam said to Balak, "Stay here beside your burnt offering [Lev. 1:1–17] and I will go. If the LORD comes to me, I will tell you whatever he shows me." Then Balaam went to a ·higher place [*or* barren height].

4God came to Balaam there, and Balaam said to him, "I have prepared seven altars, and I have offered a bull and a ·male sheep [ram] on each altar."

5The LORD ·told Balaam what he should say [Lput a word in the mouth of Balaam]. Then the LORD said, "Go back to Balak and ·give him this message [Lthus you will speak]."

6So Balaam went back to Balak. Balak and all the leaders of Moab were still standing beside his burnt offering [Lev. 1:1–17] 7when Balaam gave them this ·message [*or* oracle; *or* poem]:

"Balak brought me here from Aram;
the king of Moab brought me from the eastern mountains.
Balak said, 'Come, put a curse on the people of Jacob for me.
Come, call down evil on the people of Israel.'
8But ·God has not cursed them,
so I cannot curse them [Lhow can I curse what God has not cursed?].
·The LORD has not called down evil on them,
so I cannot call down evil on them [LHow can I call down evil on/
denounce what the LORD has not called down evil/denouced?].
9I see them from the top of the ·mountains [cliffs];
I see them from the hills.
I see a people who live alone,
who think they are different from other nations [Ex. 19:5–6].
10No one can number the ·many people [Ldust; Gen. 13:16; 28:14] of Jacob,
and no one can count a ·fourth [*or* dust cloud] of Israel.
Let me die like ·good [virtuous; upright] people,
and let me end up like them!"

11Balak said to Balaam, "What have you done to me? I brought you here to curse my enemies, but you have only blessed them!"

12But Balaam answered, "·I must [LMust I not...?] say what the LORD ·tells me to say [Lput in my mouth]."

Balaam's Second Message

13Then Balak said to him, "Come with me to another place, where you can also see the people. But you can only see part of them, not all of them [Cperhaps he could curse a part of Israel]. Curse them for me from there."
14So Balak took Balaam to the field of Zophim, on top of Mount Pisgah. There Balak built seven altars and offered a bull and a ·male sheep [ram] on each altar.

[15]So Balaam said to Balak, "Stay here by your burnt offering [Lev. 1:1–17], and I will meet with God over there."

[16]So the LORD came to Balaam and ·told him what to say [[L]put a word in his mouth]. Then he said, "Go back to Balak and say ·such and such [[L]thus]."

[17]So Balaam went to Balak, where he and the leaders of Moab were standing beside his burnt offering [Lev. 1:1–17]. Balak asked him, "What did the LORD say?"

[18]Then Balaam gave this ·message [*or* oracle; *or* poem]:

"Stand up, Balak, and listen.
  Hear me, son of Zippor.
[19]God is not a human being, and he will not lie.
  He is not a human, and he does not change his mind.
What he says he will do, ·he does [[L]will he not do it?].
  What he promises, ·he makes come true [[L]will he not fulfill it/make it come true?].
[20]He ·told [commanded] me to bless them,
  so I cannot change the blessing.
[21]He ·has found [observes] no wrong in the people of Jacob;
  he saw no ·fault [trouble] in Israel.
The LORD their God is with them,
  and they praise their King.
[22]God brought them out of Egypt;
  they are ·as strong as [[L]like the horns of] a wild ox.
[23]No ·tricks [divination] will work on the people of Jacob,
  and no magic will work against Israel.
People now say about ·them [[L]Jacob],
  'Look what God has done for Israel!'
[24]The people rise up like a lioness;
  they get up like a lion.
Lions don't rest until they have eaten prey,
  until they have drunk ·their enemies' blood [[L]the blood of corpses]."

[25]Then Balak said to Balaam, "You haven't cursed these people, so at least don't bless them!"

[26]Balaam answered Balak, "·I told [[L]Did I not tell…?] you before that I can only do what the LORD tells me."

Balaam's Third Message

[27]Then Balak said to Balaam, "Come, I will take you to another place.
Maybe ·God will be pleased [[L]it will be right in the eyes/sight of God] to
let you curse them from there." [28]So Balak took Balaam to the top of Peor,
the mountain that looks over the ·desert [wasteland; *or* Jeshimon].

[29]Balaam told Balak, "Build me seven altars here and prepare for me
seven bulls and seven ·male sheep [rams]." [30]Balak did what Balaam
asked, and he offered a bull and a ·male sheep [ram] on each altar.

24 Balaam saw that ·the LORD wanted [[L]it was good in the eyes/sight of the LORD] to bless Israel, so he did not try to use any ·magic [divination] but looked toward the ·desert [wilderness]. [2]When
Balaam ·saw [[L]lifted his eyes and saw] the Israelites camped in their tribes, the Spirit of God ·took control of [[L]was on] him, [3]and he gave this
·message [*or* oracle; *or* poem]:

"This is the ·message [utterance] of Balaam son of Beor,
  the ·message [utterance] of a man ·who sees clearly [[L]whose eye is open];

[4]this is the ·message [utterance] of a man who hears the words of God.
I see a vision from the Almighty,
and my eyes are open as I fall before him.
[5]·Your tents are beautiful [LHow beautiful/fair are your tents], people of Jacob!
·So are your homes [LYour dwellings], Israel!
[6]Your tents spread out like ·valleys [wadis],
like gardens beside a river.
They are like ·spices [Laloes] planted by the LORD,
like cedar trees growing by the water.
[7]Israel's water buckets will always ·be full [*or* flow],
and their ·crops [Lseed] will have plenty of water.
Their king will be greater than Agag [Cperhaps a dynastic name of the Amalekites (Ex. 17:8–13); 1 Sam. 15:7–9, 32–33];
their kingdom will be very great.
[8]God brought them out of Egypt;
they are ·as strong as [Llike the horns of] a wild ox.
They will defeat their enemies
and break their enemies' bones;
they will ·shoot [Lstrike] them with arrows.
[9]Like a lion, they lie waiting to attack;
like a lioness, ·no one would be brave enough to wake [Lwho will rouse…?] them.
Anyone who blesses you will be blessed,
and anyone who curses you will be cursed [Gen. 12:3]."

[10]Then Balak was angry with Balaam, and he ·pounded his fist [*or*
struck his hands together]. He said to Balaam, "I called you here to curse
my enemies, but you have continued to bless them three times. [11]Now go
home! I said I would ·pay you well [make you wealthy], but the LORD has
·made you lose [denied you] your reward."

[12]Balaam said to Balak, "When you sent messengers to me, ·I told [Ldid
I not tell…?] them, [13]'Balak could give me his ·palace [Lhouse] filled with
silver and gold, but I still cannot ·go against [transgress] the LORD's commands. I could not do anything, good or bad, on my own, but I must say
what the LORD says.' [14]Now I am going back to my own people, but I will
·tell [Ladvise] you what these people will do to your people in the ·future
[Llater days]."

Balaam's Final Message

[15]Then Balaam gave this ·message [*or* oracle; *or* poem]:
"This is the ·message [utterance] of Balaam son of Beor,
the ·message [utterance] of a man ·who sees clearly [Lwhose eye is open];
[16]this is the ·message [utterance] of a man who hears the words of God.
I know well the Most High God.
I see a vision from the Almighty,
and my eyes are open as I fall before him.
[17]I see someone ·who will come someday [Lbut not now],
·someone who will come, but not soon [LI see him, but not near].
A star will come from Jacob;
a ·ruler [Lscepter] will rise from Israel [CSaul, then David and his descendants, including the Messiah].
He will crush the heads of the Moabites

and smash the skulls of the sons of Sheth [Cidentity uncertain].
18Edom will be conquered;
his enemy Edom will be conquered,
but Israel will grow ·wealthy [*or* valiant].
19A ruler will come from the descendants of Jacob
and will destroy those left in the city."
20Then Balaam saw Amalek and gave this message:
"Amalek was the most important nation,
but Amalek will be destroyed at last [Cthe book of Esther tells the story of the final destruction of Amalek; Haman is a descendant of Agag; 24:7]."
21Then Balaam saw the Kenites and gave this ·message [*or* oracle; *or* poem]:
"Your home is ·safe [enduring],
like a nest on a ·cliff [rock].
22But you Kenites will be burned up;
·Assyria will [LHow long will Assyria…?] keep you captive."
23Then Balaam gave this ·message [*or* oracle; *or* poem]:
"·No one [LWho…?] can live when God does this.
24 Ships will sail from the shores of ·Cyprus [Kittim]
and ·defeat [afflict] Assyria and Eber,
but they will also be destroyed."
25Then Balaam got up and returned home, and Balak also went on his way.

Israel Worships Baal at Peor

25 While the people of Israel were still camped at ·Acacia [LShittim], the men began ·sinning sexually [to prostitute themselves] with Moabite women [Con the advice of Balaam who found another way to get his money; 31:16]. 2The women invited them to their sacrifices to their gods, and the ·Israelites [Lpeople] ate food there and worshiped these gods. 3So the Israelites ·began to worship [Lyoked themselves to] Baal of Peor, and the LORD was very angry with them.

4The LORD said to Moses, "Get all the leaders of the people and ·kill [impale] them in open daylight in the presence of the LORD. Then the LORD will not be angry with the people of Israel."

5So Moses said to Israel's judges, "Each of you must ·put to death [kill] your people who have become ·worshipers of [Lyoked to] Baal of Peor."

6Moses and the Israelites were gathered at the entrance to the Meeting Tent, crying there. Then an ·Israelite man [Lman of the sons/Tchildren of Israel] brought a Midianite woman to his ·brothers [family] in plain sight of Moses and all the ·people [community; congregation; assembly]. 7Phinehas son of Eleazar, the son of Aaron, the priest, saw this, so he ·left the meeting [Lrose up from the community/congregation/assembly] and ·got [Ltook in his hand] his spear. 8He followed the Israelite into his ·tent [vaulted/newlywed tent] and drove his spear through the belly of both the Israelite man and the Midianite woman [Cwhile they were embracing]. Then the ·terrible sickness [plague] among the ·Israelites [Lsons/Tchildren of Israel] stopped.

9This ·sickness [plague] had killed twenty-four thousand people.

10The LORD said to Moses, 11"Phinehas son of Eleazar, the son of Aaron, the priest, has saved the ·Israelites [Lsons/Tchildren of Israel] from my anger. He hates sin as much as I do. ·Since he tried to save my honor among them [LBecause of his zeal in their midst], I will not kill them in my zeal. 12So tell Phinehas that I am making my ·peace agreement [covenant/treaty of peace] with him. 13He and his ·descendants [Lseed] will ·always be priests [Lhave a covenant/treaty of eternal/perpetual priesthood], because he had ·great concern for the honor of [Lpassion/zeal for] his God. He ·removed the sins of the Israelites so they would belong to God [Lprovided atonement for the sons/Tchildren of Israel]."

14The Israelite man who was ·killed [Lstruck] with the Midianite woman was named Zimri son of Salu. He was the leader of a ·family [ancestral clan] in the tribe of Simeon. 15And the name of the Midianite woman who was ·put to death [Lstruck] was Cozbi daughter of Zur, who was the chief of a Midianite ·family [ancestral clan].

16The LORD said to Moses, 17"·The Midianites are your enemies [Harrass the Midianites], and you should ·kill [Lstrike] them. 18They have already ·made you their enemies [harrassed you], because they tricked you at Peor and because of their sister Cozbi, the daughter of a Midianite leader. She was the woman who was killed when the ·sickness [plague] came because the people sinned at Peor."

The People Are Counted

26 After the ·great sickness [plague], the LORD said to Moses and Eleazar son of Aaron, the priest, 2"·Count [Take a census of; LLift the head of] all the ·people of Israel [Lcommunity/congregation of the sons/Tchildren of Israel] by ·families [clans], all the men who are twenty years old or older who will serve in the army of Israel [Clike a military registration; chapter 1 counts the generation that came out of Egypt; this counts the one that would enter the land]." 3Moses and Eleazar the priest spoke to the people on the plains of Moab near the Jordan River, across from Jericho. They said, 4"Count the men [Csupplied from v. 2] twenty years old or older, as the LORD commanded Moses."

Here are the ·Israelites [Lsons/Tchildren of Israel] who came out of Egypt:

5The ·tribe [Lsons; descendants] of Reuben, the first son born to Israel, was counted. From Hanoch came the Hanochite ·family group [clan]; from Pallu came the Palluite ·family group [clan]; 6from Hezron came the Hezronite ·family group [clan]; from Carmi came the Carmite ·family group [clan]. 7These were the ·family groups [clans] of Reuben, and the total number of men was 43,730.

8The son of Pallu was Eliab, 9and Eliab's sons were Nemuel, Dathan, and Abiram. Dathan and Abiram were the ·leaders [conveners of the community/congregation/assembly] who turned against Moses and Aaron and ·followed [Lwere in the assembly of] Korah when he ·turned [rebelled] against the LORD. 10The earth opened up and swallowed them and Korah; they died at the same time the fire burned up the 250 men [16:1–40]. This was a warning, 11but the children of Korah did not die.

12These were the ·family groups [clans] in the ·tribe [Lsons; descendants] of Simeon: From Nemuel came the Nemuelite ·family group [clan]; from Jamin came the Jaminite ·family group [clan]; from Jakin came the Jakinite ·family group [clan]; 13from Zerah came the Zerahite ·family group [clan]; from Shaul came the Shaulite ·family group [clan]. 14These were the ·family groups [clans] of Simeon, and the total number of men was 22,200.

15These were the ·family groups [clans] in the ·tribe [Lsons; descendants] of Gad: From Zephon came the Zephonite ·family group [clan];

from Haggi came the Haggite ·family group [clan]; from Shuni came the Shunite ·family group [clan]; 16from Ozni came the Oznite ·family group [clan]; from Eri came the Erite ·family group [clan]; 17from Arodi came the Arodite ·family group [clan]; from Areli came the Arelite ·family group [clan]. 18These were the ·family groups [clans] of Gad, and the total number of men was 40,500.

19Two of Judah's sons, Er and Onan, died in Canaan [Gen. 38:6–11].

20These were the ·family groups [clans] in the ·tribe [Lsons; descendants] of Judah: From Shelah came the Shelanite ·family group [clan]; from Perez came the Perezite ·family group [clan]; from Zerah came the Zerahite ·family group [clan]. 21These were the ·family groups [clans] from Perez: From Hezron came the Hezronite ·family group [clan]; from Hamul came the Hamulite ·family group [clan]. 22These were the ·family groups [clans] of Judah, and the total number of men was 76,500.

23These were the ·family groups [clans] in the ·tribe [Lsons; descendants] of Issachar: From Tola came the Tolaite ·family group [clan]; from Puah came the Puite ·family group [clan]; 24from Jashub came the Jashubite ·family group [clan]; from Shimron came the Shimronite ·family group [clan]. 25These were the ·family groups [clan] of Issachar, and the total number of men was 64,300.

26These were the ·family groups [clans] in the ·tribe [Lsons; descendants] of Zebulun: From Sered came the Seredite ·family group [clan]; from Elon came the Elonite ·family group [clan]; from Jahleel came the Jahleelite ·family group [clan]. 27These were the ·family groups [clans] of Zebulun, and the total number of men was 60,500.

28These were the ·family groups [clans] of Joseph through Manasseh and Ephraim.

29These were the ·family groups [clans] of [Lthe sons/descendants of] Manasseh: From Makir came the Makirite ·family group [clan] (Makir was the father of Gilead); from Gilead came the Gileadite ·family group [clan]. 30These were the ·family groups [clans] that came from Gilead: From Iezer came the Iezerite ·family group [clan]; from Helek came the Helekite ·family group [clan]; 31from Asriel came the Asrielite ·family group [clan]; from Shechem came the Shechemite ·family group [clan]; 32from Shemida came the Shemidaite ·family group [clan]; from Hepher came the Hepherite ·family group [clan]. 33(Zelophehad son of Hepher had no sons; he had only daughters, and their names were Mahlah, Noah, Hoglah, Milcah, and Tirzah [27:1–11; 36:1–13; Josh. 17:3–6].) 34These were the ·family groups [clans] of Manasseh, and the total number of men was 52,700.

35These were the ·family groups [clans] in the ·tribe [Lsons; descendants] of Ephraim: From Shuthelah came the Shuthelahite ·family group [clan]; from Beker came the Bekerite ·family group [clan]; from Tahan came the Tahanite ·family group [clan]. 36This was the ·family group [clan] from Shuthelah: From Eran came the Eranite ·family group [clan]. 37These were the ·family groups [clans] of [Lthe sons/descendants of] Ephraim, and the total number of men was 32,500. These are the ·family groups [clans] that came from Joseph.

38These were the ·family groups [clans] in the ·tribe [Lsons; descendants] of Benjamin: From Bela came the Belaite ·family group [clan]; from Ashbel came the Ashbelite ·family group [clan]; from Ahiram came the Ahiramite ·family group [clan]; 39from Shupham came the

Shuphamite ·family group [clan]; from Hupham came the Huphamite
·family group [clan]. 40These were the ·family groups [clans] from Bela
through Ard and Naaman: From Ard came the Ardite ·family group
[clan]; from Naaman came the Naamite ·family group [clan]. 41These
were the ·family groups [clans] of Benjamin, and the total number of
men was 45,600.

42This was the ·family group [clan] in the ·tribe [Lsons; descendants] of
Dan: From Shuham came the Shuhamite ·family group [clan]. That was
the ·family group [clan] of Dan, 43and the total number of men in the
Shuhamite ·family group [clan] of Dan was 64,400.

44These were the ·family groups [clans] in the ·tribe [Lsons; descen-
dants] of Asher: From Imnah came the Imnite ·family group [clan]; from
Ishvi came the Ishvite ·family group [clan]; from Beriah came the Beriite
·family group [clan]. 45These were the ·family groups [clans] that came
from Beriah: From Heber came the Heberite ·family group [clan]; from
Malkiel came the Malkielite ·family group [clan]. 46(Asher also had a
daughter named Serah.) 47These were the ·family groups [clans] of Asher,
and the total number of men was 53,400.

48These were the ·family groups [clans] in the ·tribe [Lsons; descen-
dants] of Naphtali: From Jahzeel came the Jahzeelite ·family group [clan];
from Guni came the Gunite ·family group [clan]; 49from Jezer came the
Jezerite ·family group [clan]; from Shillem came the Shillemite ·family
group [clan]. 50These were the ·family groups [clans] of Naphtali, and the
total number of men was 45,400.

51So the total number of the ·men [Lsons; Tchildren] of Israel was 601,730.

52The Lord said to Moses, 53"·Divide [Apportion] the land among
these people by the number of names. 54A large tribe will get more ·land
[Linheritance], and a small tribe will get less ·land [Linheritance]; the
amount of ·land each tribe gets [Linheritance] will depend on the number
of its people. 55·Divide [Apportion] the land by drawing lots, and the land
each tribe ·gets [Linherits] will be named for that tribe. 56·Divide
[Apportion] the land between large and small groups by drawing lots
[Josh. 14:2; 18:6, 8]."

57The tribe of Levi was also counted. These were the ·family groups
[clans] of Levi: From Gershon came the Gershonite ·family group [clan];
from Kohath came the Kohathite ·family group [clan]; from Merari came
the Merarite ·family group [clan]. 58These also were Levite ·family groups
[clans]: the Libnite ·family group [clan], the Hebronite ·family group
[clan], the Mahlite ·family group [clan], the Mushite ·family group [clan],
and the Korahite ·family group [clan]. (Kohath was the ancestor of
Amram, 59whose wife was named Jochebed. She was from the tribe of
Levi and she was born in Egypt. She and Amram had two sons, Aaron and
Moses, and their sister Miriam [Ex. 2:1–10]. 60Aaron was the father of
Nadab, Abihu, Eleazar, and Ithamar. 61But Nadab and Abihu died because
they made an offering before the Lord with ·the wrong kind of [Lstrange;
Cunauthorized by God] fire [Lev. 10:1–20].)

62The total number of male Levites one month old or older was 23,000.
But these men were not counted with the other ·Israelites [Lsons/Tchildren
of Israel], because they were not given any ·of the land [Linheritance]
among the other ·Israelites [Lsons/Tchildren of Israel].

63Moses and Eleazar the priest counted all these people. They counted
the ·Israelites [Lsons/Tchildren of Israel] on the plains of Moab across the

Jordan River from Jericho. 64Moses and Aaron the priest had counted the Israelites in the ·Desert [Wilderness] of Sinai [1:1–54], but no one Moses counted on the plains of Moab was in the first counting. 65The LORD had told the Israelites they would all die in the ·desert [wilderness], and the only two left were Caleb son of Jephunneh and Joshua son of Nun [14:20–25].

Zelophehad's Daughters

27 Then the daughters of Zelophehad came near. Zelophehad was the son of Hepher, the son of Gilead, the son of Makir, the son of Manasseh. Zelophehad's daughters belonged to the ·family groups [clans] of Manasseh son of Joseph [26:29–34]. The daughters' names were Mahlah, Noah, Hoglah, Milcah, and Tirzah. 2They went to the entrance of the Meeting Tent and stood before Moses, Eleazar the priest, the leaders, and all the ·people [community; congregation; assembly]. They said, 3"Our father died in the ·desert [wilderness]. He was not ·one of Korah's followers [Lin the community/congregation/assembly of Korah] who came together against the LORD [16:1–50], but he died because of his own sin, and he had no sons. 4·Our father's name will [LWhy should our father's name…?] die out because he had no sons. Give us ·property [a possession] among our father's relatives [36:1–13; Josh. 17:3–6]."

5So Moses brought their case to the LORD, 6and the LORD said to him, 7"The daughters of Zelophehad are right; they should certainly get ·what their father owned [La possession of the inheritance in the midst of the relatives of their father]. ·Give [LPass on to] them ·property among their father's relatives [Lthe inheritance of their father].

8"Tell the ·Israelites [Lsons/Tchildren of Israel], 'If a man dies and has no son, then ·everything he owned should go [Lpass on his inheritance] to his daughter. 9If he has no daughter, then ·everything he owned should go [Lyou should give his inheritance] to his brothers. 10If he has no brothers, then ·everything he owned should go [Lyou should give his inheritance] to his father's brothers. 11And if his father had no brothers, then ·everything he owned should go [Lyou should give his inheritance] to the nearest relative in his ·family group [clan]. This should be a ·rule [statute; ordinance; requirement] among the ·people [Lsons; Tchildren] of Israel, as the LORD has given this command to Moses.'"

Joshua Is the New Leader

12Then the LORD said to Moses, "Climb this mountain in the Abarim Mountains, and look at the land I have given to the ·Israelites [Lsons/Tchildren of Israel]. 13After you have seen it, you will ·die and join your ancestors [Lbe gathered to your people] as your brother Aaron ·did [Lwas gathered; 20:22–29], 14because you both ·acted [rebelled] against my command in the ·Desert [Wilderness] of Zin. You did not honor me as holy before the people at the waters of Meribah [20:1–13]." (This was at Meribah in Kadesh in the ·Desert [LWilderness] of Zin.)

15Moses said to the LORD, 16"The LORD is the God of the spirits of all ·people [Lflesh]. May he ·choose a leader for these people [Lappoint someone over the community/assembly/congregation], 17who will go in and out before them. He must lead them out like sheep and bring them in; the LORD's ·people [community; assembly; congregation] must not be like sheep without a shepherd."

18So the LORD said to Moses, "Take Joshua son of Nun, because my Spirit is in him. ·Put [Lay] your hand on him, 19and have him stand before Eleazar the priest and all the ·people [community; assembly; congregation]. Then give him his orders ·as they watch [Lbefore their eyes]. 20Let him share your honor so that all the ·Israelites [Lcommunity/assembly/congregation of the sons/Tchildren of Israel] will ·obey [listen to] him. 21He must stand before Eleazar the priest, and Eleazar will get advice from the LORD by using the Urim [Ex. 28:30]. At his command all the ·Israelites [Lsons/Tchildren of Israel, the whole community/assembly/congregation] will go out, and at his command they will all come in."

22Moses did what the LORD told him. He took Joshua and had him stand before Eleazar the priest and all the ·people [community; assembly; congregation], 23and he ·put [lay] his hands on him and gave him orders, just as the LORD had told him.

Daily Offerings

28

The LORD said to Moses, 2"Give this command to the ·Israelites [Lsons/Tchildren of Israel]. Tell them: 'Bring me food offerings made by fire, for a smell that is pleasing to me, and be sure to bring them at the ·right [appointed] time.' 3Say to them, 'These are the offerings you must bring to the LORD: two male lambs, a year old, as a burnt offering [Lev. 1:1–17] each day. They must have ·nothing wrong with them [no blemish]. 4Offer one lamb in the morning and the other lamb ·at twilight [Lbetween the two evenings]. 5Also bring a ·grain [Lgift; tribute] offering [Lev. 2:1] of ·two quarts [Lone-tenth of an ephah] of ·fine [choice] flour, mixed with ·one quart [Lone-fourth of a hin] of oil from pressed olives. 6This is the daily burnt offering [Lev. 1:1–17] which began at Mount Sinai; its smell is pleasing to the LORD. 7Offer ·one quart [Lone-fourth of a hin] of wine with each lamb as a drink offering; pour it out to the LORD at the Holy Place. 8Offer the second lamb at ·twilight [Lbetween the two evenings]. As in the morning, also give a ·grain [Lgift; tribute] offering [Lev. 2:1] and a drink offering. This offering is made by fire, and its smell is pleasing to the LORD [Ex. 29:38–43].

Sabbath Offerings

9" 'On the Sabbath day you must give two male lambs, a year old, that have ·nothing wrong with them [no blemish]. Also give a drink offering and a ·grain [Lgift; tribute] offering [Lev. 2:1]; the ·grain [Lgift; tribute] offering [Lev. 2:1] must be four quarts of fine flour mixed with olive oil. 10This is the burnt offering [Lev. 1:1–17] for every Sabbath, in addition to the daily burnt offering [Lev. 1:1–17] and drink offering.

Monthly Offerings

11" 'On the first day of each month bring a burnt offering [Lev. 1:1–17] to the LORD. This will be two young bulls, one ·male sheep [ram], and seven male lambs a year old, and they must have ·nothing wrong with them [no blemish]. 12Give a ·grain [Lgift; tribute] offering [Lev. 2:1] with each bull of ·six quarts [Lthree-tenths of an ephah] of ·fine [choice] flour mixed with olive oil. Also give a ·grain [Lgift; tribute] offering [Lev. 2:1] with the ·male sheep [ram]. It must be ·four quarts [Ltwo-tenths of an ephah] of ·fine [choice] flour mixed with olive oil. 13And give a ·grain [Lgift; tribute] offering [Lev. 2:1] with each lamb of ·two quarts [Lone-tenth of an ephah] of ·fine [choice] flour mixed with olive oil. This is a burnt offering [Lev. 1:1–17], and its smell is pleasing to the LORD. 14The drink offering with each bull will be ·two quarts [Lhalf a hin] of wine, with the ·male sheep [ram] it will be ·one and one-third quarts [Lone-third of a hin], and with each lamb it will be ·one quart [Lone-fourth of a hin] of wine. This is the burnt offering [Lev. 1:1–17] that must be offered each month of the year. 15Besides the daily burnt offerings [Lev. 1:1–17] and drink offerings, bring a ·sin [*or* purification] offering [Lev. 4:3] of one goat to the LORD.

The Passover

16"'The LORD's Passover will be on the fourteenth day of the first month [Ex. 12:1–20; Lev. 23:4–8; Deut. 16:1–8]. 17The Feast of Unleavened Bread begins on the fifteenth day of that month. For seven days, you may eat only bread made without ·yeast [leaven]. 18Have a ·holy meeting [sacred/solemn convocation] on the first day of the festival, and don't work that day. 19Bring to the LORD an offering made by fire, a burnt offering [Lev. 1:1–17] of two young bulls, one ·male sheep [ram], and seven male lambs a year old. They must have ·nothing wrong with them [no blemish]. 20With each bull give a ·grain [Lgift; tribute] offering [Lev. 2:1] of ·six quarts [Lthree-tenths of an ephah] of ·fine [choice] flour mixed with olive oil. With the ·male sheep [ram] it must be ·four quarts [Ltwo-tenths of an ephah] of ·fine [choice] flour mixed with oil. 21With each of the seven lambs, it must be ·two quarts [Lone-tenth of an ephah] of ·fine [choice] flour mixed with oil. 22Bring one goat as a ·sin [*or* purification] offering [Lev. 4:3], to ·remove your sins so you will belong to God [make atonement for yourself]. 23Bring these offerings in addition to the burnt offerings [Lev. 1:1–17] you give every morning. 24So bring food for the offering made by fire each day for seven days, for a smell that is pleasing to the LORD. Do it in addition to the daily burnt offering [Lev. 1:1–17] and its drink offering. 25On the seventh day have a holy meeting [sacred/solemn convocation], and don't work that day.

The Feast of Weeks

26"'On the day of firstfruits when you bring new grain to the LORD during the Feast of Weeks [Lev. 23:15–23], have a ·holy meeting [sacred/solemn convocation]. Don't work that day. 27Bring this burnt offering [Lev. 1:1–17] to the LORD: two young bulls, one ·male sheep [ram], and seven male lambs a year old. This smell is pleasing to the LORD. 28Also, with each bull give a ·grain [Lgift; tribute] offering [Lev. 2:1] of ·six quarts [Lthree-tenths of an ephah] of ·fine [choice] flour mixed with oil. With the ·male sheep [ram], it must be ·four quarts [Ltwo-tenths of an ephah] of flour, 29and with each of the seven lambs offer ·two quarts [Lone-tenth of an ephah] of flour. 30Offer one male goat to ·remove your sins so you will belong to God [make atonement for yourself]. 31Bring these offerings and their drink offerings in addition to the daily burnt offering [Lev. 1:1–17] and its ·grain [Lgift; tribute] offering [Lev. 2:1]. The animals must have ·nothing wrong with them [no blemish].

The Feast of Trumpets

29 "'Have a ·holy meeting [sacred/solemn convocation] on the first day of the seventh month, and don't work on that day. That is the day you blow the trumpets. 2Bring these burnt offerings [Lev. 1:1–17] as a smell pleasing to the LORD: one young bull, one ·male sheep [ram], and seven male lambs a year old. They must have ·nothing wrong with them [no blemish]. 3With the bull give a ·grain [Lgift; tribute] offering [Lev. 2:1] of ·six quarts [Lthree-tenths of an ephah] of ·fine [choice] flour mixed with oil. With the ·male sheep [ram] offer ·four quarts [Ltwo-tenths of an ephah], 4and with each of the seven lambs offer ·two quarts [Lone-tenth of an ephah]. 5Offer one male goat for a ·sin [*or* purification] offering [Lev. 4:3] to ·remove your sins so you will belong to God [make atonement for yourself]. 6These offerings are in addition to the monthly [28:11–15] and daily burnt offerings [28:1–8; Lev. 1:1–17].

Their ·grain [Lgift; tribute] offerings [Lev. 2:1] and drink offerings must be done as you have been told. These offerings are made by fire to the LORD, and their smell is pleasing to him.

The Day of Atonement

7“ ‘Have a ·holy meeting [sacred/solemn convocation] on the tenth day of the seventh month [Lev. 16; 23:26–32]. On that day do not eat and do not work. 8Bring these burnt offerings [Lev. 1:1–17] as a smell pleasing to the LORD: one young bull, one ·male sheep [ram], and seven male lambs a year old. They must have ·nothing wrong with them [no blemish]. 9With the bull give a ·grain [Lgift; tribute] offering [Lev. 2:1] of ·six quarts [Lthree-tenths of an ephah] of ·fine [choice] flour mixed with oil. With the ·male sheep [ram] it must be ·four quarts [Ltwo-tenths of an ephah], 10and with each of the seven lambs it must be ·two quarts [Lone-tenth of an ephah]. 11Offer one male goat as a ·sin [*or* purification] offering [Lev. 4:3]. This will be in addition to the sin [*or* purification] offering [Lev. 4:3] which ·removes your sins [makes atonement for you], the daily burnt offering [28:1–8; Lev. 1:1–17] with its ·grain [Lgift; tribute] offering [Lev. 2:1], and the drink offerings.

The Feast of Shelters

12“ ‘Have a ·holy meeting [sacred/solemn convocation] on the fifteenth day of the seventh month, and do not work on that day. Celebrate a festival to the LORD for seven days [Lev. 23:33–44]. 13Bring these burnt offerings [Lev. 1:1–17], made by fire, as a smell pleasing to the LORD: thirteen young bulls, two ·male sheep [rams], and fourteen male lambs a year old. They must have ·nothing wrong with them [no blemish]. 14With each of the thirteen bulls offer a ·grain [Lgift; tribute] offering [Lev. 2:1] of ·six quarts [Lthree-tenths of an ephah] of ·fine [choice] flour mixed with oil. With each of the two ·male sheep [rams] it must be ·four quarts [Ltwo-tenths of an ephah], 15and with each of the fourteen lambs it must be ·two quarts [Lone-tenth of an ephah]. 16Offer one male goat as a ·sin [*or* purification] offering [Lev. 4:3] in addition to the daily burnt offering [28:1–8; Lev. 1:1–17] with its ·grain [Lgift; tribute; Lev. 2:1] and drink offerings.

17“ ‘On the second day of this festival give an offering of twelve bulls, two ·male sheep [rams], and fourteen male lambs a year old. They must have ·nothing wrong with them [no blemish]. 18Bring the ·grain [Lgift; tribute; Lev. 2:1] and drink offerings for the bulls, sheep, and lambs, according to the number required. 19Offer one male goat as a ·sin [*or* purification] offering [Lev. 4:3], in addition to the daily burnt offering [28:1–8; Lev. 1:1–17] with its ·grain [Lgift; tribute; Lev. 2:1] and drink offerings.

20“ ‘On the third day offer eleven bulls, two ·male sheep [rams], and fourteen male lambs a year old. They must have ·nothing wrong with them [no blemish]. 21Bring the ·grain [Lgift; tribute; Lev. 2:1] and drink offerings for the bulls, sheep, and lambs, according to the number required. 22Offer one male goat as a ·sin [*or* purification] offering [Lev. 4:3], in addition to the daily burnt offering [28:1–8; Lev. 1:1–17] with its ·grain [Lgift; tribute; Lev. 2:1] and drink offerings.

23“ ‘On the fourth day offer ten bulls, two ·male sheep [rams], and fourteen male lambs a year old. They must have ·nothing wrong with them [no blemish]. 24Bring the ·grain [Lgift; tribute; Lev. 2:1] and drink offerings for the bulls, sheep, and lambs, according to the number required. 25Offer one male goat as a ·sin [*or* purification] offering [Lev. 4:3], in addition to the daily burnt offering [28:1–8] with its ·grain [Lgift; tribute; Lev. 2:1] and drink offerings.

26“ ‘On the fifth day offer nine bulls, two ·male sheep [rams], and fourteen male lambs a year old. They must have ·nothing wrong with them [no blemish]. 27Bring the ·grain [Lgift; tribute; Lev. 2:1] and drink offerings for the bulls, sheep, and lambs, according to the number required. 28Offer one male goat as a ·sin [*or* purification] offering [Lev. 4:3], in addition to the daily burnt offering [28:1–8; Lev. 1:1–17] with its ·grain [Lgift; tribute; Lev. 2:1] and drink offerings.

29“ ‘On the sixth day offer eight bulls, two ·male sheep [rams], and fourteen male lambs a year old. They must have ·nothing wrong with them [no blemish]. 30Bring the ·grain [Lgift; tribute; Lev. 2:1] and drink offerings for the bulls, sheep, and lambs, according to the number required. 31Offer one male goat as a ·sin [*or* purification] offering [Lev. 4:3], in addition to the daily burnt offering [28:1–8; Lev. 1:1–17] with its ·grain [Lgift; tribute; Lev. 2:1] and drink offerings.

32“ ‘On the seventh day offer seven bulls, two ·male sheep [rams], and fourteen male lambs a year old. They must have ·nothing wrong with them [no blemish]. 33Bring the ·grain [Lgift; tribute; Lev. 2:1] and drink offerings for the bulls, sheep, and lambs, according to the number required. 34Offer one male goat as a ·sin [*or* purification] offering [Lev. 4:3], in addition to the daily burnt offering [28:1–8; Lev. 1:1–17] with its ·grain [Lgift; tribute; Lev. 2:1] and drink offerings.

35“ ‘On the eighth day have a ·closing meeting [closing/festive assembly], and do not work on that day. 36Bring an offering made by fire, a burnt offering [Lev. 1:1–17], as a smell pleasing to the LORD. Offer one bull, one ·male sheep [ram], and seven male lambs a year old. They must have ·nothing wrong with them [no blemish]. 37Bring the ·grain [Lgift; tribute; Lev. 2:1] and drink offerings for the bull, the ·male sheep [ram], and the lambs, according to the number required. 38Offer one male goat as a ·sin [*or* purification; Lev. 4:3] offering, in addition to the daily burnt offering [28:1–8; Lev. 1:1–17] with its grain [Lgift; tribute; Lev. 2:1] and drink offerings.

39“ ‘At your ·festivals [sacred/solemn convocations] you should bring these to the LORD: your burnt offerings [1:1–17], ·grain [Lgift; tribute] offerings [Lev. 2:1], drink offerings and ·fellowship [*or* peace; well-being] offerings [Lev. 3:1]. These are in addition to other ·promised [votive] offerings and special gifts you want to give to the LORD.’ ”

40Moses told the ·Israelites [Lsons/Tchildren of Israel] everything the LORD had commanded him.

Rules About Special Promises

30 Moses spoke with the leaders of the ·Israelite tribes [Ltribes of the sons/Tchildren of Israel]. He told them these commands from the LORD.

2“If a man makes a ·promise [vow] to the LORD or ·says he will do something special [swears an oath to bind himself to an obligation], he must ·keep his promise [Lnot break his word]. He must do what he said [Deut. 23:21; Ps. 50:14; Eccl. 5:4–5; Matt. 5:33–37]. 3If a young woman still living at ·home [Lthe house of her father] makes a ·promise [vow] to the LORD or ·pledges to do something special [binds herself to an obligation], 4and if her father hears about the ·promise [vow] or ·pledge [obligation by which she has bound herself] and says nothing, ·she must do what she promised [Lall her vows stand]. ·She must keep her pledge [LAll her obligations to which she has bound herself will stand]. 5But if her father hears about the ·promise [vow] or ·pledge [obligation by which she has bound herself] and ·does not allow it [disapproves], then the ·promise [vow] or ·pledge [obligation] does not ·have to be kept [Lstand]. Her father ·would not allow it [disapproves], so the LORD will ·free her from her promise [Lforgive her].

6“If a woman ·makes a pledge [binds herself to an obligation] or speaks a ·careless [rash; thoughtless] ·promise [vow] and then gets married, 7and if her husband hears about it and says nothing, ·she must keep her promise [Lher vow stands] ·or the pledge she made [Land the obligation by which she bound herself will stand]. 8But if her husband hears about it and ·does not allow it [disapproves], he cancels her ·pledge [vow] or the ·careless [rash; thoughtless] ·promise [vow] ·she made [by which she bound herself]. The LORD will ·free her from keeping it [forgive her].

9“If a widow or divorced woman makes a ·promise [vow], ·she must do whatever she promised [Lall by which she bound herself stands].

10“If a woman makes a ·promise [vow] or ·pledge [Lbinds herself in an obligation] ·while she is married [Lin the house of her husband], 11and if her husband hears about it but says nothing and does not ·stop her [disapprove], ·she must keep her promise [all her vows stand] ·or pledge [Land all that to which she bound herself will stand]. 12But if her husband hears about it and cancels it, ·she does not have to do what she said [Lher vow and all that which she bound herself do not stand]. Her husband has canceled it, so the LORD will ·free her from it [forgive her]. 13A woman's husband may make her keep or cancel any ·promise [vow] or ·pledge [obligation] she has made to ·deny [mortify] herself. 14If he says nothing to her about it for several days, ·she must keep her promises [Lher vows stand]. If he hears about them and says nothing, ·she must keep her promises [Lthe obligations by which she bound herself will stand]. 15But if he cancels them long after he heard about them, he ·is responsible if she breaks her promise [Lwill bear her guilt].”

16These are ·commands [statutes; ordinances; requirements] that the LORD gave to Moses for husbands and wives, and for fathers with ·daughters living at home [Lhis daughters in her youth in the house of her father].

Israel Attacks the Midianites

31 The LORD spoke to Moses and said, 2“·Pay back [Avenge] the Midianites for what they did to the ·Israelites [Lsons/Tchildren of Israel; 25:6]; after that you will ·die [Lbe gathered to your people].”

3So Moses said to the people, “·Get some men ready [Arm some men] for war. The LORD will use them to ·pay back [avenge himself against] the Midianites. 4Send to war a thousand men from each of the tribes of Israel.” 5So twelve thousand men ·got ready for war [were armed], out of the thousands of Israel a thousand men from each tribe. 6Moses sent ·those men [La thousand from each tribe] to war; Phinehas son of Eleazar the priest was with them. He took with him the ·holy things [*or* vessels of the Holy Place] and the trumpets for giving the alarm. 7They fought the Midianites as the LORD had commanded Moses, and they killed every Midianite man. 8Among those they killed were Evi, Rekem, Zur, Hur, and Reba, who were the five kings of Midian. They also killed Balaam son of Beor with a sword [Num. 22–24; Deut. 23:4–5; Josh. 13:22; 24:10; Neh. 13:2; 2 Pet. 2:15; Jude 11; Rev. 2:14].

9The ·Israelites [Lsons of Israel] captured the Midianite women and children, and they took all their flocks, herds, and goods. 10They burned all the Midianite towns where they had settled and all their camps, 11but they took all the ·people and animals and goods [Lplunder and all the spoil, both people and animals]. 12Then they brought the captives, the ·animals, and the goods [Lspoil and the plunder] back to Moses and Eleazar the priest and all the ·Israelites [Lcommunity/assembly/congregation of the sons/Tchildren of Israel]. Their camp was on the plains of Moab near the Jordan River, across from Jericho.

13Moses, Eleazar the priest, and all the leaders of the ·people [community; assembly; congregation] went outside the camp to meet them. 14Moses was angry with the army officers, the commanders over a thousand men, and those over a hundred men, who returned from war.

15He asked them, "Why did you let the women live? 16They were the ones who followed Balaam's advice [Jude 11] and turned the ·Israelites [Lcommunity/assembly/congregation of Israel] from the LORD at Peor. Then a ·terrible sickness [plague] struck the LORD's people [Num. 25]. 17Kill all the Midianite boys, and kill all the Midianite women who have ·had sexual relations [Lknown a man by going to bed with him]. 18But save for yourselves the girls who have not ·had sexual relations with a man [Lknown a man by going to bed with him].

19"All you men who killed anyone or touched a dead body must stay outside the camp for seven days [19:11]. On the third and seventh days you and your captives must make yourselves clean [Cin a ritual sense]. 20You must clean all your clothes and anything made of leather, goat hair, or wood."

21Then Eleazar the priest said to the soldiers who had gone to war, "These are the ·teachings [Lstatutes/ordinances/requirements of the law/instruction] that the LORD gave to Moses: 22Put any gold, silver, bronze, iron, tin, or lead—23anything that will not burn—into the fire, and then it will be clean. But also purify those things with the cleansing water. Then they will be clean. If something cannot stand the fire, wash it with the water. 24On the seventh day wash your clothes, and you will be clean. After that you may come into the camp."

Dividing the Goods

25The LORD said to Moses, 26"You, Eleazar the priest, and the leaders of the ·family groups [clans of the community/assembly/congregation] should take a count of the ·goods [spoils], the men, and the animals that were taken. 27Then divide ·those possessions [the spoil] between the soldiers who went to war and the ·rest of the people [community; assembly; congregation]. 28From the soldiers who went to war, take a ·tax [tribute] for the LORD of one item out of every five hundred. This includes people, cattle, donkeys, or sheep. 29Take it from the soldiers' half, and give it to Eleazar the priest as the LORD's ·share [offering]. 30And from the ·people's half [Lhalf of the sons/Tchildren of Israel], take one item out of every fifty. This includes people, cattle, donkeys, sheep, or other animals. Give that to the Levites, who take care of the LORD's ·Holy Tent [Tabernacle]." 31So Moses and Eleazar did as the LORD commanded Moses.

32There remained from what the soldiers had taken 675,000 sheep, 3372,000 cattle, 3461,000 donkeys, 35and 32,000 women who had not ·had sexual relations with a man [Lknown a man by going to bed with him]. 36The soldiers who went to war got 337,500 sheep, 37and they gave 675 of them to the LORD. 38They got 36,000 cattle, and they gave 72 of them to the LORD. 39They got 30,500 donkeys, and they gave 61 of them to the

LORD. 40They got 16,000 people, and they gave 32 of them to the LORD. 41Moses gave the LORD's ·share [tribute] to Eleazar the priest, as the LORD had commanded him.

42Moses separated the ·people's [Lsons/Tchildren of Israel's] half from the soldiers' half. 43The people got 337,500 sheep, 4436,000 cattle, 4530,500 donkeys, 46and 16,000 people. 47From the ·people's [Lsons/Tchildren of Israel's] half Moses took one item out of every fifty for the LORD. This included the animals and the people. Then he gave them to the Levites, who took care of the LORD's ·Holy Tent [Tabernacle]. This was what the LORD had commanded Moses.

48Then the officers of the army, the commanders of a thousand men and commanders of a hundred men, came to Moses. 49They told Moses, "We, your servants, have ·counted [taken a census of; Llifted the head of] our soldiers ·under our command [Lin our hand], and not one of them is missing. 50So we have brought the LORD a ·gift [offering] of the gold things that each of us found: arm bands, bracelets, signet rings, earrings, and necklaces. These are to ·remove our sins so we will belong to [make atonement for ourselves before] the LORD."

51So Moses and Eleazar the priest took the gold from them, which had been made into all kinds of objects. 52The commanders of a thousand men and the commanders of a hundred men gave the LORD the gold, and all of it together weighed about ·420 pounds [L16,750 shekels]; 53each soldier had taken ·something [plunder] for himself. 54Moses and Eleazar the priest took the gold from the commanders of a thousand men and the commanders of a hundred men. Then they put it in the Meeting Tent as a memorial before the LORD for the ·people [Lsons; Tchildren] of Israel.

The Tribes East of the Jordan

32 The ·people [Lsons; descendants] of Reuben and ·Gad [Lthe sons/descendants of Gad] had large flocks and herds. When they saw that the lands of Jazer and Gilead were good for the animals, 2they came to Moses, Eleazar the priest, and the leaders of the ·people [community; assembly; congregation]. 3-4They said, "We, your servants, have flocks and herds. The LORD has ·captured [Lstruck] for the ·Israelites [Lthe community/assembly/congregation of Israel] a land that is good for animals—the land around Ataroth, Dibon, Jazer, Nimrah, Heshbon, Elealeh, Sebam, Nebo, and Beon. 5If ·it pleases you [Lwe have found grace in your eyes], we would like this land ·to be given to us [Las a possession for your servants]. Don't make us cross the Jordan River."

6Moses told the ·people of Gad [Lsons/descendants of Gad] and ·Reuben [Lthe sons/descendants of Reuben], "Shall your brothers go to war while you stay ·behind [Lhere]? 7·You will [LWhy should you…?] discourage the ·Israelites [Lsons/Tchildren of Israel] from going over to the land the LORD has given them. 8Your ·ancestors [fathers] did the same thing. I sent them from Kadesh Barnea to look at the land. 9They went as far as the ·Valley of [Wadi] Eshcol, and when they saw the land, they discouraged the hearts of the ·Israelites [Lsons/Tchildren of Israel] from going into the land the LORD had given them. 10The LORD became very angry that day and ·made this promise [swore]: 11'None of the people who came from Egypt and who are twenty years old or older will see the land that I promised to Abraham, Isaac, and Jacob. These people have not ·followed me [*or* been loyal to me] completely. 12Only Caleb son of Jephunneh the Kenizzite and Joshua son of Nun ·followed [*or* were loyal to] the LORD completely [chs. 13–14].'

13“The LORD was angry with Israel, so he made them wander in the
·desert [wilderness] for forty years. Finally all the ·people [generation]
who had ·sinned against [Ldone evil in the eyes/sight of] the LORD died,
14and now you ·are acting [Lhave risen up] just like your ·ancestors
[fathers]! You sinful people are making the LORD even more angry with
Israel. 15If you quit following him, it will add to their stay in the ·desert
[wilderness], and you will destroy all these people.”

16Then ·the Reubenites and Gadites [Lthey] came up to Moses and said,
“We will build ·pens for our animals [sheepfolds for our flocks] and cities
for our children here. 17Then our children will be in strong, walled cities,
safe from the people who live in this land. Then we will prepare for war. We
will help the other ·Israelites [Lsons/Tchildren of Israel] get their land, 18and
we will not return home until every Israelite has ·received his land [inher-
ited their inheritance]. 19We won’t ·take [inherit] any of the land west of the
Jordan River; our ·part of the land [inheritance] is east of the Jordan.”

20So Moses told them, “You must do these things. You must go before
the LORD into battle 21and cross the Jordan River armed, until the LORD
·forces out [dispossesses] the enemy. 22After the LORD helps us take the
land, you may return home. You will ·have done your duty to [be free of
your obligation; be innnocent before] the LORD and Israel, and you may
have this land as ·your own [La possession before the LORD].

23“But if you don’t do these things, you will be sinning against the LORD;
know for sure that ·you will be punished for your sin [Lyour sin will find
you]. 24Build cities for your children and ·pens for your animals [sheepfolds
for your flocks], but then you must do what you ·promised [said].”

25The ·Gadites [Lsons/descendants of Gad] and ·Reubenites [Lthe sons/
descendants of Reuben] said to Moses, “We are your servants, and we will
do what you, our ·master [lord], command. 26Our children, wives, and all
our cattle will stay in the cities of Gilead, 27but we, your servants, will
prepare for battle. We will go over and fight for the LORD, as you, our
·master [lord], have said.”

28So Moses gave orders about them to Eleazar the priest, to Joshua son
of Nun, and to the leaders of the clans of the tribes of ·Israel [Lsons/
Tchildren of Israel]. 29Moses said to them, “If the ·Gadites [Lsons/descen-
dants of Gad] and ·Reubenites [Lthe sons/descendants of Reuben] prepare
for battle and cross the Jordan River with you, to go before the LORD and
help you take the land, give them the land of Gilead ·for their own [Las a
possession]. 30But if they do not go over armed, they will not receive it;
their land will be in Canaan with you.”

31The ·Gadites [Lsons/descendants of Gad] and ·Reubenites [Lthe sons/
descendants of Reuben] answered, “We are your servants, and we will do
as the LORD said. 32We will cross over into Canaan and go before the LORD
ready for battle. But ·our land [Lthe possession of our inheritance] will be
·east of [beyond] the Jordan River.”

33So Moses gave that land to the tribes of ·Gad [Lthe sons/descendants
of Gad], ·Reuben [Lthe sons/descendants of Reuben], and ·East [Lthe half
tribe of] Manasseh. (Manasseh was Joseph’s son.) That land had been the
kingdom of Sihon, king of the Amorites, and the kingdom of Og, king of
Bashan, as well as all the cities and the land around them.

34The ·Gadites [Lsons/descendants of Gad] rebuilt the cities of Dibon,
Ataroth, Aroer, 35Atroth Shophan, Jazer, Jogbehah, 36Beth Nimrah, and Beth
Haran. These were strong, walled cities. And they built sheep ·pens [folds].

37The ·Reubenites [Lsons/descendants of Reuben] rebuilt Heshbon,
Elealeh, Kiriathaim, 38Nebo, Baal Meon, and Sibmah. They renamed
Nebo and Baal Meon when they rebuilt them.
39The ·descendants [sons] of Makir son of Manasseh went and captured Gilead and forced out the Amorites who were there. 40So Moses
gave Gilead to the family of Makir son of Manasseh, and they settled
there. 41Jair son of Manasseh went out and captured the ·small towns [vil-
lages] there, and he called them the ·Towns of Jair [*or* Villages of Jair; *or*
Havvoth-jair]. 42Nobah went and captured Kenath and the small towns
around it; then he named it Nobah after himself.

Israel's Journey from Egypt

33 These are the places the ·Israelites [Lsons/Tchildren of Israel]
went as Moses and Aaron led them out of Egypt in divisions
[Clike an army]. 2At the LORD's command Moses ·recorded [wrote down]
the places they went, and these are the places they went.
3On the fifteenth day of the first month, the day after the Passover [Ex.
12:1–30], the ·Israelites [Lsons/Tchildren of Israel] left Rameses and
marched out ·boldly [Lwith a high hand] in front of all the Egyptians [Ex.
12:31–42]. 4The Egyptians were burying their firstborn sons, whom the
LORD had ·killed [Lstruck]; the LORD ·showed that the gods of Egypt were
false [*or* even executed judgment against their gods; Ex. 12:12].
5The ·Israelites [Lsons/Tchildren of Israel] left Rameses and camped
at Succoth.
6They left Succoth and camped at Etham, at the edge of the ·desert
[wilderness; Ex. 13:20].
7They left Etham and went back to Pi Hahiroth, to the east of Baal
Zephon, and camped near Migdol [Ex. 14:2].
8They left Pi Hahiroth and walked through the sea into the ·desert
[wilderness; Ex. 14:1–31]. After going three days through the ·Desert
[Wilderness] of Etham, they camped at Marah [Ex. 15:23].
9They left Marah and went to Elim; there were twelve springs of water
and seventy palm trees where they camped [Ex. 15:27].
10They left Elim and camped near the ·Red [*or* Reed; Ex. 10:19] Sea.
11They left the ·Red [*or* Reed] Sea and camped in the ·Desert [Wilderness]
of Sin [Ex. 16:1].
12They left the ·Desert [Wilderness] of Sin and camped at Dophkah.
13They left Dophkah and camped at Alush.
14They left Alush and camped at Rephidim, where the people had no
water to drink [Ex. 17:1–7].
15They left Rephidim and camped in the ·Desert [Wilderness] of Sinai
[Ex. 19:1].
16They left the ·Desert [Wilderness] of Sinai and camped at Kibroth
Hattaavah [11:34–35].
17They left Kibroth Hattaavah and camped at Hazeroth [11:35; 12:16].
18They left Hazeroth and camped at Rithmah.
19They left Rithmah and camped at Rimmon Perez.
20They left Rimmon Perez and camped at Libnah.
21They left Libnah and camped at Rissah.
22They left Rissah and camped at Kehelathah.
23They left Kehelathah and camped at Mount Shepher.
24They left Mount Shepher and camped at Haradah.
25They left Haradah and camped at Makheloth.

[26]They left Makheloth and camped at Tahath.
[27]They left Tahath and camped at Terah.
[28]They left Terah and camped at Mithcah.
[29]They left Mithcah and camped at Hashmonah.
[30]They left Hashmonah and camped at Moseroth.
[31]They left Moseroth and camped at Bene Jaakan.
[32]They left Bene Jaakan and camped at Hor Haggidgad.
[33]They left Hor Haggidgad and camped at Jotbathah.
[34]They left Jotbathah and camped at Abronah.
[35]They left Abronah and camped at Ezion Geber.
[36]They left Ezion Geber and camped at Kadesh in the ·Desert [Wilderness] of Zin [20:1].
[37]They left Kadesh and camped at Mount Hor, on the border of Edom.
[38]Aaron the priest obeyed the LORD and went up Mount Hor. There he died on the first day of the fifth month in the fortieth year after the ·Israelites [Lsons/Tchildren of Israel] left Egypt [20:22–29]. [39]Aaron was 123 years old when he died on Mount Hor.
[40]The Canaanite king of Arad, who lived in the ·southern area of Canaan [Negev], heard that the ·Israelites [Lsons/Tchildren of Israel] were coming [21:1].
[41]The people left Mount Hor and camped at Zalmonah.
[42]They left Zalmonah and camped at Punon.
[43]They left Punon and camped at Oboth [21:10].
[44]They left Oboth and camped at Iye Abarim, on the border of Moab [21:11].
[45]They left Iye Abarim and camped at Dibon Gad.
[46]They left Dibon Gad and camped at Almon Diblathaim.
[47]They left Almon Diblathaim and camped in the mountains of Abarim, near Nebo [27:12].
[48]They left the mountains of Abarim and camped on the plains of Moab near the Jordan River across from Jericho. [49]They camped along the Jordan on the plains of Moab, and their camp went from Beth Jeshimoth to Abel Acacia [22:1].

[50]On the plains of Moab by the Jordan River across from Jericho, the LORD spoke to Moses. He said, [51]"Speak to the ·Israelites [Lsons/Tchildren of Israel] and tell them, 'When you cross the Jordan River and go into Canaan, [52]force out all the people who live there. Destroy all of their carved statues and metal idols. Wreck all of their ·places of worship [Lhigh places; Cworship sites that became associated with pagan worship or inappropriate worship of Yahweh; 1 Kin. 3:2]. [53]Take over the land and settle there, because I have given this land to you to own. [54]Throw lots [Cperhaps the Urim and Thummim; Ex. 28:30; Lev. 8:8] to ·divide up [apportion] the land by ·family groups [clans], giving larger portions to larger ·family groups [clans] and smaller portions to smaller ·family groups [clans]. The land will be given as the lots decide; each tribe will get its own land.

[55]" 'But if you don't force those people out of the land, they will bring you trouble. They will be like ·sharp hooks [barbs] in your eyes and thorns in your sides. They will bring trouble to the land where you live. [56]Then I will punish you as I had planned to punish them.' "

The Borders of Canaan

34 The Lord said to Moses, 2“Give this command to the ·people
[Lsons/Tchildren] of Israel: ‘You will soon enter Canaan and
·it will be yours. These shall be the borders [L…this is the land that will
fall to you as an inheritance, the land of Canaan according to its borders/
boundaries]: 3On the south you will get part of the ·Desert [Wilderness]
of Zin near the border of Edom. On the east side your southern border
will start at the south end of the ·Dead [LSalt] Sea, 4cross south of
·Scorpion Pass [*or* the Ascent of Akrabbim], and go through the ·Desert
[Wilderness] of Zin and south of Kadesh Barnea. Then it will go to Hazar
Addar and over to Azmon. 5From Azmon it will go to the ·brook [wadi]
of Egypt, and it will end at the ·Mediterranean Sea [LSea].

6“ ‘Your western border will be the ·Mediterranean [LGreat] Sea.

7“ ‘Your northern border will begin at the ·Mediterranean [LGreat]
Sea and ·go [Lmark/draw a line] to Mount Hor. 8From Mount Hor ·it will
go [Lmark/draw a line] to Lebo Hamath, and on to Zedad. 9Then the
border will go to Ziphron, and it will end at Hazar Enan. This will be
your northern border.

10“ ‘Your eastern border will begin at Hazar Enan and ·go [Lmark/draw
a line] to Shepham. 11From Shepham the border will go ·east of [Ldown
to] Ain to Riblah and ·along [Lgo down to] the hills east of ·Lake [Tthe Sea
of] ·Galilee [LKinnereth]. 12Then the border will go down along the
Jordan River and end at the ·Dead [LSalt] Sea.

“ ‘These are the borders around your country.’ ”

13So Moses gave this command to the Israelites: “This is the land you
will ·receive [Linherit]. Throw lots [Cperhaps the Urim and Thummim; Ex.
28:30; Lev. 8:8] to divide it among the nine and one-half tribes, because
the Lord commanded that it should be theirs. 14The tribes of ·Reuben
[Lthe sons/descendants of Reuben] by their families [clans], ·Gad [Lthe
sons/descendants of Gad] by their families [clans], and ·East [Lthe half-
tribe of] Manasseh have already ·received [Linherited] their land. 15These
two and one-half tribes received ·land [Ltheir inheritance] east of the
Jordan River, across from Jericho [32:1–42].”

16Then the Lord said to Moses, 17“These are the names of the men who
will ·divide [apportion] the land for inheritance: Eleazar the priest and
Joshua son of Nun. 18Also take one leader from each tribe to help ·divide
[apportion] the land for inheritance. 19These are the names of the leaders:
from the tribe of Judah, Caleb son of Jephunneh; 20from the tribe of
·Simeon [Lthe sons/descendants of Simeon], Shemuel son of Ammihud;
21from the tribe of Benjamin, Elidad son of Kislon; 22from the tribe of
·Dan [Lthe sons/descendants of Dan], Bukki son of Jogli; 23from the tribe
of ·Manasseh [Lthe sons/descendants of Manasseh] son of Joseph, Hanniel
son of Ephod; 24from the tribe of ·Ephraim [Lthe sons/descendants of
Ephraim] son of Joseph, Kemuel son of Shiphtan; 25from the tribe of
·Zebulun [Lthe sons/descendants of Zebulun], Elizaphan son of Parnach;
26from the tribe of ·Issachar [Lthe sons/descendants of Issachar], Paltiel
son of Azzan; 27from the tribe of ·Asher [Lthe sons/descendants of Asher],
Ahihud son of Shelomi; 28from the tribe of ·Naphtali [Lthe sons/descen-
dants of Naphtali], Pedahel son of Ammihud.”

29The Lord commanded these men to ·divide [apportion] for inheritance the land of Canaan among the ·Israelites [Lsons/Tchildren of Israel].

The Levites' Towns

35 The LORD spoke to Moses on the plains of Moab across from
Jericho by the Jordan River. He said, 2“Command the
·Israelites [Lsons/Tchildren of Israel] to give the Levites cities to live in
from the ·land [Lpossession] they ·receive [Linherit]. Also give the Levites
the pastureland around these cities. 3Then the Levites will have cities
where they may live and pastureland for their cattle, flocks, and other
animals. 4The pastureland you give the Levites will extend ·fifteen hundred feet [La thousand cubits] from the city wall. 5Also measure ·three
thousand feet [Ltwo thousand cubits] in each direction outside the city
wall—·three thousand feet [Ltwo thousand cubits] east of the city, ·three
thousand feet [Ltwo thousand cubits] south of the city, ·three thousand
feet [Ltwo thousand cubits] west of the city, and ·three thousand feet
[Ltwo thousand cubits] north of the city, with the city in the center. This
will be pastureland for the Levites' cities.

Cities of Safety

6“Six of the cities you give the Levites will be cities of ·safety [refuge].
A person who accidentally kills someone may run to one of those cities
for ·safety [refuge]. You must also give forty-two other cities to the
Levites; 7give the Levites a total of forty-eight cities and their pastures.
8The larger tribes of ·Israel [Lthe sons/Tchildren of Israel] must give more
cities, and the smaller tribes must give fewer cities. Each tribe must give
some of its cities to the Levites, but the number of cities they give will
depend on the size of their land.”

9Then the LORD said to Moses, 10“Tell the ·Israelites [Lsons/Tchildren of
Israel] these things: ‘When you cross the Jordan River and go into Canaan,
11you must choose cities to be cities of ·safety [refuge], so that a person
who ·accidentally [unintentionally] kills someone may run to them for
·safety [refuge]. 12There the person will be safe from the dead person's
·relative who has the duty of punishing the killer [avenger; near-kins-
man]. He will not die before he ·receives a fair trial in court [Lstands
before the community/assembly/congregation for judgment]. 13The six
cities you give will be cities of ·safety [refuge]. 14Give three cities ·east of
[Lbeyond] the Jordan River and three cities in Canaan as cities of ·safety
[refuge]. 15These six cities will be places of ·safety [refuge] for ·citizens
[Lsons; Tchildren] of Israel, as well as for ·foreigners [resident aliens] and
·other people living with you [tenants]. Any of these people who ·acci-
dentally [unintentionally] kills someone may run to one of these cities.

16“ ‘Anyone who uses an iron weapon to ·kill [Lstrike] someone is a
murderer. He must be put to death. 17Anyone who takes a rock and ·kills
[Lstrikes] a person with it is a murderer. He must be put to death. 18Anyone
who picks up a piece of wood and ·kills [Lstrikes] someone with it is a
murderer. He must be put to death. 19A ·relative of the dead person [near-
relative; avenger of blood] must put the murderer to death; when they
meet, the relative must kill the murderer. 20A person might shove someone out of hatred or throw something at someone while lying in wait and
cause death. 21Or a person might ·hit [Lstrike] someone with his hand and
cause death. If it were done from hate, the person is a murderer and must
be put to death. A ·relative of the dead person [near-relative; avenger of
blood] must kill the murderer when they meet.

22“ ‘But a person might suddenly shove someone, and not from hatred.
Or a person might ·accidentally [without lying in wait] throw something
and ·hit [Lstrike] someone. 23Or a person might drop a rock on someone

he couldn't see and kill that person. There was no plan to hurt anyone
and ·no hatred for the one who was killed [Lthey were not enemies]. 24If
that happens, the ·community [assembly; congregation] must judge
between the ·relative of the dead person [near-relative; avenger of blood]
and the ·killer [Lstriker], according to these rules. 25·They [LThe commu-
nity/assembly/congregation] must protect the killer from the ·dead
person's relative [near-relative; avenger of blood], sending the killer back
to the original city of ·safety [refuge], to stay there until the high priest
dies (the high priest ·had the holy oil poured on him [was anointed with
holy oil]).
26" 'Such a person must never go outside the limits of the city of ·safety
[refuge]. 27If a ·relative of the dead person [near-relative; avenger of
blood] finds the killer outside the city, the ·relative [near-relative; avenger
of blood] may kill that person and ·not be guilty of murder [Lthere will be
no bloodguilt]. 28The killer must stay in the city of ·safety [refuge] until
the high priest dies. After the high priest dies, the killer may ·go home
[Lreturn to the land of his possession].
29" 'These ·laws [Lstatutes/ordinances/requirements and judgments] are
for you ·from now on [Lthroughout your generations], wherever you live.
30" 'If anyone ·kills [Lstrikes] a person, the murderer may be put to
death only if there are witnesses. No one may be put to death with only
one witness.
31" 'Don't take ·money to spare the life of [ransom for] a murderer who
should be put to death. A murderer must be put to death.
32" 'If someone has run to a city of ·safety [refuge], don't take money to
let the person go back home before the high priest dies.
33" 'Don't let murder ·spoil [pollute; defile] your land. The only way to
·remove the sin [atone for] of killing an innocent person is for the murderer
to be put to death. 34I am the LORD, and I live among the Israelites. I live in
that land with you, so do not ·spoil [pollute; defile] it with murder.' "

Land for Zelophehad's Daughters

36 The leaders of ·Gilead's family group [Lthe clan of the sons/
descendants of Gilead] went to talk to Moses and the leaders of
the ·families [clans] of ·Israel [Lsons/Tchildren of Israel]. (Gilead was the
son of Makir, the son of Manasseh, the son of Joseph.) 2They said, "The
LORD commanded you, our ·master [lord], to give the land for inheritance
to the ·Israelites [Lsons/Tchildren of Israel] by throwing lots [Cperhaps the
Urim and Thummim; Ex. 28:30; Lev. 8:8], and the LORD commanded you,
our master [lord], to give for inheritance the land of Zelophehad, our
brother, to his daughters [27:1–11]. 3But if his daughters marry ·men
[Lsons] from other tribes of ·Israel [Lthe sons/Tchildren of Israel], then
·that land will leave our family [Ltheir inheritance will be taken from the
inheritance of our ancestors/fathers], and the people of the other tribes
will get that land. So ·we will lose some of our land [Lpart of our allotted
portion will be lost]. 4When the time of Jubilee [Cevery fiftieth year; Lev.
25:8–55] comes for the ·Israelites [Lsons/Tchildren of Israel], their land
will go to the tribes of the people they marry; ·their land will be taken
away from us, the land we received from our fathers [Lthe inheritance of
the tribe of our ancestors/fathers will be deprived of inheritance]."
5Then Moses gave the ·Israelites [Lthe sons/Tchildren of Israel] this
command from the LORD: "These men from the ·tribe [Lsons; descen-
dants] of Joseph are right. 6This is the LORD's command to Zelophehad's

daughters: You may marry anyone you wish, as long as the person is from ·your [La clan of your] **own tribe.** 7 **In this way the ·Israelites' land** [Linheritance of the sons/Tchildren of Israel] **will not pass from tribe to tribe, and each ·Israelite** [Lson/child of Israel] **will keep the land in the tribe that belonged to his ·ancestors** [fathers]. 8 **A woman who inherits her father's land may marry, but she must marry someone from ·her own** [La clan of her own] **tribe. In this way every ·Israelite** [Lson/child of Israel] **will keep the land that belonged to his ·ancestors** [fathers]. 9 **The ·land** [inheritance] **must not pass from tribe to tribe, and each ·Israelite tribe** [Ltribe of the sons/Tchildren of Israel] **will keep the land it ·received** [inherited] **from its ·ancestors** [fathers]."

10 **Zelophehad's daughters obeyed the LORD's command to Moses.**

11 **So Zelophehad's daughters—Mahlah, Tirzah, Hoglah, Milcah, and Noah—married ·their cousins, their father's relatives** [Lsons of their father's brothers]. 12 **Their husbands were from the ·tribe of** [Lclan of the sons of] **Manasseh son of Joseph, so their ·land** [inheritance] **stayed in their father's ·family group** [clan] **and tribe.**

13 **These were the laws and commands that the LORD gave to the ·Israelites** [Lsons/Tchildren of Israel] **through Moses on the plains of Moab by the Jordan River, across from Jericho.**

DEUTERONOMY

Moses Talks to the Israelites

1 ·This is the message [LThese are the words] Moses gave to all the people of Israel in the ·desert [wilderness] east of the Jordan River. They were in the ·desert [wilderness] area near Suph, between Paran and the towns of Tophel, Laban, Hazeroth, and Dizahab.

2(The trip from Mount Sinai to Kadesh Barnea on the Mount Seir road takes eleven days.) 3·Forty years after the Israelites had left Egypt [LIn the fortieth year], on the first day of the eleventh month, Moses told the ·people [Lsons; Tchildren] of Israel everything the LORD had commanded him to tell them. 4This was after the LORD had ·defeated [Lstruck] Sihon and Og. Sihon was king of the Amorite people and lived in Heshbon. Og was king of Bashan and lived in Ashteroth and Edrei [Num. 21:21–35].

5Now ·the Israelites [Lthey] were ·east of [Lbeyond] the Jordan River in the land of Moab, and there Moses began to ·explain [make clear] ·what God had commanded [Lthis law/instruction]. He said:

6The LORD our God spoke to us at ·Mount Sinai [LHoreb; Canother name for Sinai] and said, "You have stayed long enough at this mountain. 7·Get ready [LTurn face], and go to the mountain country of the Amorites, and to all the places around there—the ·Jordan Valley [LArabah], the mountains, the ·western hills [LShephelah], the ·southern area [LNegev], the seacoast, the land of Canaan, and Lebanon. Go as far as the great river, the Euphrates [Gen. 15:18–21]. 8See, I have given you this land, so go in and take it for yourselves. The LORD ·promised it [swore] to your ancestors—Abraham, Isaac, and Jacob and their descendants [Gen. 12:1–3; 15:17–20]."

Moses Appoints Leaders

9At that time I said, "I am not able to ·take care of you [Llift you up; bear you] by myself. 10The LORD your God has made you grow in number so that there are as many of you as there are stars in the ·sky [heavens; Gen. 15:5; 22:17; 26:41; Ex. 32:13]. 11I pray that the LORD, the God of your ·ancestors [fathers], will give you a thousand times more people and ·do all the wonderful things [Lbless you as] he promised. 12·But I cannot take care of [LHow can I lift up/bear…?] your problems, your troubles, and your arguments by myself. 13So choose some men from each tribe—wise men who have ·understanding [discernment] and experience—and I will make them leaders over you."

14And you said, "That's a good thing to do."

15So I took the wise and experienced leaders of your tribes, and I made them your leaders. I appointed commanders over a thousand people, over a hundred people, over fifty people, and over ten people and made them officers over your tribes. 16Then I told your ·leaders [judges], "Listen to the arguments between your people. Judge fairly between two ·Israelites [relatives; Lbrothers] or between an ·Israelite [Lrelative; brother] and a ·foreigner [resident alien]. 17When you judge, ·be fair to everyone [do not show favoritism]; don't act as if one person is more important than another, and don't be ·afraid of [intimidated by] anyone, because your decision comes from God. Bring the hard cases to me, and I will judge them." 18At that time I told you everything you must do [Ex. 18:13–23].

Spies Enter the Land

19Then, as the LORD our God commanded us, we left ·Mount Sinai [LHoreb; 1:6] and went toward the mountain country of the Amorite people. We went through that ·large [vast] and terrible ·desert [wilderness] you saw, and then we came to Kadesh Barnea. 20I said to you, "You have now come to the mountain country of the Amorites, to the land the LORD our God will give us. 21Look, here it is! Go up and ·take [possess] it. The LORD, the God of your ·ancestors [fathers], told you to do this, so don't be afraid and don't ·worry [be dismayed]."

22Then all of you came to me and said, "Let's send men before us to spy out the land. They can come back and ·tell us [bring back a report] about the way we should go and the cities we will find [Num. 13–14]."

23·I thought that was a good idea [LThe matter was good/right in my eyes], so I ·chose [took] twelve of your men, one for each tribe. 24They ·left [Lturned face] and went up to the mountains, and when they came to the ·Valley of [Wadi] Eshcol they ·explored [spied on] it. 25They took some of the fruit from that land and brought it down to us, ·saying [Land gave us a report, saying], "It is a good land that the LORD our God is giving us."

Israel Refuses to Enter

26But you refused to go. You ·would not obey [rebelled against] the command of the LORD your God, 27but grumbled in your tents, saying, "The LORD hates us. He brought us out of Egypt just to give us to the Amorites, who will destroy us. 28Where can we go now? ·The spies we sent have [LOur relatives/brothers] made ·us afraid [Lour hearts melt], because they said, 'The people there are stronger and taller than we are. The cities are big, with walls up to the ·sky [heavens]. And we saw the Anakites there [Num. 13:28–33]!' "

29Then I said to you, "Don't be frightened; don't be afraid of those people. 30The LORD your God will go ahead of you and fight for you as he did in Egypt; ·you saw him do it [Lbefore your eyes]. 31And in the ·desert [wilderness] you saw how the LORD your God carried you, like one carries a child [Ps. 131]. And he has brought you safely all the way to this place."

32But you still did not trust the LORD your God, even though 33he had always gone before you to find places for you to camp. In a fire at night and in a cloud during the day, he showed you which way to go.

34When the LORD heard what you said, he was angry and ·made an oath [swore], saying, 35"I promised a good land to your ·ancestors [fathers], but none of ·you evil people [this evil generation] will see it. 36Only Caleb son of Jephunneh will see it [Num. 14:24]. I will give him and his descendants the land he walked on, because he followed the LORD completely [Josh. 15:13–19; Judg. 1:9–15]."

37Because of you, the LORD was also angry with me and said, "You won't enter the land either [Num. 20:12], 38but ·your assistant [Lthe one who stands before you], Joshua son of Nun, will enter it. Encourage him, because he will lead Israel to take the land for their own.

39"Your little children that you said would be ·captured [plunder], who do not know right from wrong at this time, will go into the land. I will give the land to them, and they will ·take it for their own [possess it]. [40]But you must turn ·around [Lface] and follow the ·desert [wilderness] road toward the ·Red [*or* Reed] Sea [Ex. 10:19]."

[41]Then you said to me, "We have sinned against the LORD, but now we will go up and fight, as the LORD our God commanded us." Then all of you put on weapons, thinking it would be easy to go into the mountains.

[42]But the LORD said to me, "Tell the people, 'You must not go up there and fight. I will not be with you, and your enemies will defeat you.'"

[43]So I told you, but you would not listen. You ·would not obey [rebelled against] the LORD's command. You were ·proud [presumptuous], so you went on up into the mountains, [44]and the Amorites who lived in those mountains came out and fought you. They ·chased [swarmed over] you like bees and ·defeated [Lstruck] you from ·Edom [LSeir; Canother name for Edom] to Hormah [Num. 14:39–45]. [45]So you came back and cried before the LORD, but the LORD did not listen to you; he refused to pay attention to you. [46]So you stayed in Kadesh a long time.

Israel Wanders in the Desert

2 Then we turned ·around [Lface], and we traveled on the ·desert [wilderness] road toward the ·Red [*or* Reed] Sea [Ex. 10:19], as the LORD had told me to do. We traveled through the mountains of ·Edom [LSeir; 1:44] for many days.

[2]Then the LORD said to me, [3]"You have traveled through these mountains long enough. Turn north [4]and give the people this command: 'You will soon go through the land that belongs to your ·relatives [brothers], the ·descendants [sons] of Esau who live in ·Edom [LSeir; 1:44]. They will be afraid of you, but be very careful. [5]Do not go to war against them. I will not give you any of their land—not even a foot of it, because I have given the mountains of ·Edom [LSeir; 1:44] to Esau as his own. [6]You must pay them in silver for any food you eat or water you drink.'"

[7]The LORD your God has blessed everything you have done; he has protected you while you traveled through this ·great desert [vast wilderness]. The LORD your God has been with you for the past forty years, and you have had everything you needed.

[8]So we passed by our ·relatives [brothers], the ·descendants [sons] of Esau who lived in ·Edom [LSeir; 1:44]. We turned off the ·Jordan Valley [LArabah] road that comes from the towns of Elath and Ezion Geber and traveled along the ·desert [wilderness] road to Moab [Num. 20:14–21].

The Land of Ar

[9]Then the LORD said to me, "Don't ·bother [harrass] the people of Moab. Don't go to war against them, because I will not give you any of their land as your own; I have given Ar to the ·descendants [Lsons] of Lot as their own." [10](The Emites, who lived in ·Ar [Lit] before, were strong people, and there were many of them. They were very tall, like the Anakites. [11]The Emites were thought to be ·Rephaites [*or* Rephaim; 3:11, 13; Gen. 14:5], like the Anakites, but the Moabite people called them Emites. [12]The Horites also lived in ·Edom [LSeir; 1:44] before, but the ·descendants [Lsons] of Esau forced them out and destroyed them, taking their place as Israel did in the land the LORD gave them as their own.)

[13]And the LORD said to me, "Now get up and cross the Zered ·Valley [Wadi]." So we crossed the ·valley [wadi]. [14]It had been thirty-eight years from the time we left Kadesh Barnea until we crossed the Zered ·Valley [Wadi]. By then, all the fighting men ·from that time [Lof that generation] had died, as the LORD had ·promised [sworn] would happen

[Num. 14:20–23]. 15The [Lhand of the] LORD ·continued to work [Lwas]
against them to remove them from the camp until they were all dead.
16When the last of those fighting men had died, 17the LORD said to me,
18"Today you will pass by Ar, on the border of Moab. 19When you come
near the ·people [Lsons; descendants] of Ammon, don't ·bother [harrass]
them or go to war against them, because I will not give you any of their land
as your own. I have given it to the ·descendants [sons] of Lot for their own."
20(That land was also thought to be a land of the ·Rephaites [*or*
Rephaim; 2:11], because those people used to live there, but the
Ammonites called them Zamzummites. 21They were strong people, and
there were many of them; they were very tall, like the Anakites. The LORD
destroyed the Zamzummites, and the Ammonites forced them out of the
land and took their place. 22The LORD did the same thing for the ·descen-
dants [sons] of Esau, who lived in ·Edom [LSeir; 1:44], when he destroyed
the Horites. ·The Edomites [LThey] forced them out of the land and took
their place, and they live there to this day. 23The ·Cretan people
[LCaphtorim; Cbetter known as Philistines] came from ·Crete [LCaphtor]
and destroyed the Avvites, who lived in towns all the way to Gaza; the
·Cretans [LCaphtorim] destroyed them and took their place.)

Fighting the Amorites

24The LORD said, "Get up and cross the Arnon ·Ravine [Wadi]. See, I am
·giving you the power to defeat [Lputting in your hand] Sihon the Amorite,
king of Heshbon, and I am giving you his land [Num. 21:21–32]. So fight
against him and begin taking his land. 25Today I will begin to make all the
people ·in the world [Lunder heaven] afraid of you. When they hear reports
about you, they will shake with fear, and they will be terrified of you."
26I sent messengers from the ·desert [wilderness] of Kedemoth to
Sihon king of Heshbon. ·They offered him [L...with words/messages of]
peace, saying, 27"If you let us pass through your country, · we will stay on
the road and [LI will] not turn right or left. 28We will pay you in silver for
any food we eat or water we drink. We only want to walk through your
country. 29The ·descendants [sons] of Esau in ·Edom [LSeir; 1:44] let us go
through their land, and so did the Moabites in Ar. We want to cross the
Jordan River into the land the LORD our God has given us." 30But Sihon
king of Heshbon would not let us pass, because the LORD your God had
·made him stubborn [Lhardened his spirit and made his heart defiant].
The LORD wanted ·you to defeat Sihon, and now this has happened [Lto
give him into your hand as it is on this day].
31The LORD said to me, "See, I have begun to give Sihon and his country
to you. Begin taking the land as your own."
32Then Sihon and all his army came out and fought us at Jahaz, 33but
the LORD our God gave Sihon to us. We ·defeated [Lstruck] him, his sons,
and all his army. 34We captured all his cities at that time and ·completely
destroyed them [devoted them to the LORD; 20:15–20; Josh. 6:17], as well
as the men, women, and children. We left no one alive. 35But we kept the
cattle and ·valuable things [Lplunder] from the cities for ourselves. 36We
defeated Aroer on the edge of the Arnon ·Ravine [Wadi], and we defeated
the town in the ·ravine [wadi], and even as far as Gilead. No ·town was too
strong [*or* citadel was too high] for us; the LORD our God gave us all of
them. 37But you did not go near the land of the ·Ammonites [Lsons/
descendants of Ammon], on the shores of the Jabbok ·River [Wadi], or
the towns in the mountains, as the LORD our God had commanded.

11When you ·came [approached] and stood at the bottom of the mountain, it blazed with fire that reached to the sky, and black clouds made it
very dark [Ex. 19:16–20]. 12The LORD spoke to you from the fire. You
heard the sound of words, but you did not see ·him [La form]; there was
only a voice. 13The LORD told you about his ·Agreement [Covenant;
Treaty], the Ten ·Commandments [LWords]. He told you to obey them,
and he wrote them on two stone tablets. 14Then at that time the LORD
commanded me to teach you the ·laws [statutes; ordinances; require-
ments] and rules that you must obey in the land you will ·take [possess]
when you cross ·the Jordan River [Lthere].

Laws About Idols

15Since the LORD spoke to you from the fire at ·Mount Sinai [LHoreb;
4:10], but you did not see ·him [Lany form], watch yourselves carefully!
16Don't ·sin [ruin/destroy/spoil/corrupt yourselves] by making idols of
any kind, and don't make statues—of men or women, 17of animals on
earth or birds that fly in the air, 18of anything that ·crawls [swarms] on
the ground, or of fish in the water below. 19When you ·look up at [Llift
your eyes to] the ·sky [heavens], you see the sun, moon, and stars, and
·everything in the sky [all the host of heaven]. But don't bow down and
worship them [5:8–9; Ex. 20:4–5], because the LORD your God has ·made
these things [apportioned them] for all people everywhere [32:8]. 20But
the LORD brought you out of Egypt, ·which tested you like a furnace for
melting iron [Lthe iron-smelter; 1 Kin. 8:51; Jer. 11:4], and he made you
his ·very own people [Linheritance], as ·you are now [Lthis day].
21The LORD was angry with me because of you, and he swore that I
would not cross the Jordan River to go into the good land the LORD your
God is giving you as ·your own [Lan inheritance]. 22I will die here in this
land and not cross the Jordan [34:1–8], but you will soon go across and
take that good land. 23Be careful. Don't forget the ·Agreement [Covenant;
Treaty] of the LORD your God that he made with you, and don't make any
idols for yourselves, as the LORD your God has commanded you not to do.
24The LORD your God is a jealous God [5:9; 6:15; Ex. 20:5; 34:14; Josh.
24:19; Nah. 1:2], ·like a fire that burns things up [a consuming fire].
25Even after you have ·lived [grown old; *or* become complacent] in the
land a long time and have had children and grandchildren, don't ·do evil
things [ruin/destroy/spoil/corrupt yourselves]. Don't make any kind of
idol, and don't do what ·the LORD your God says is evil [Lwhat is evil/wrong
in the eyes of the LORD your God], because that will make him angry. 26If
you do, I ask heaven and earth to ·speak [witness] against you this day that
you will quickly be removed from this land that you are crossing the
Jordan River to ·take [possess]. You will not live there long after that, but
you will be completely destroyed. 27The LORD will scatter you among the
other nations. Only a few of you will be left alive, and those few will be in
other nations where the LORD will ·send [lead] you. 28There you will ·wor-
ship [serve] gods made by ·people [Lhuman hands], gods made of wood
and stone, that cannot see, hear, eat, or smell. 29But even there you can
look for the LORD your God, and you will find him if you look for him with
·your whole being [Lall your heart/mind and all your inner being]. 30It will
be ·hard [distressful] when all these things happen to you. But after that
you will come back to the LORD your God and ·obey [hear] him, 31because
the LORD your God is a merciful God [Ex. 34:6; 2 Chr. 30:9; Neh. 9:31; Ps.
111:4; Joel 2:3]. He will not ·leave [fail] you or ·destroy [ruin; spoil] you.

He will not forget the ·Agreement [Covenant; Treaty] with your ·ancestors [fathers], which he ·swore [promised] to them.

The Lord Is Great

32·Nothing like this has ever happened before! Look at the past [LAsk about the former days], long before ·you were even born [Lyou]. Go all the way back to when God ·made [created] humans on the earth [Gen. 1:26–27], and look from one end of heaven to the other. ·Nothing like this has ever [LHas anything as great as this…?] been heard of! 33·No [LWhat…?] other people have ever heard God speak from a fire and have still lived. But you have. 34·No [LWhat…?] other god has ever taken for himself one nation out of another. But the LORD your God did this for you in Egypt, right before your own eyes. He did it with tests, signs, miracles, war, and great sights, by his ·great power [Lstrong hand] and ·strength [Loutstretched arm].

35He ·showed you [revealed] things so you would know that the LORD is God, and there is no other God besides him. 36He spoke to you from heaven to ·teach [instruct; *or* discipline] you. He ·showed [revealed to] you his great fire on earth, and you heard him speak from the fire. 37Because the LORD loved your ·ancestors [fathers; Gen. 12:1–3], he chose you, their ·descendants [Lseed], and he brought you out of Egypt himself by his great strength. 38He ·forced [dispossessed] nations out of their land ahead of you, nations that were bigger and stronger than you were. The LORD did this so he could bring you into their land and give it to you as your ·own [Linheritance], ·and this land is yours today [Las it is this day].

39Know and ·believe [take to heart; bear in mind] today that the LORD is God. He is God in heaven above and on the earth below. There is no other god! 40Obey his ·laws [statutes; ordinances; requirements] and commands that I am giving you today so that things will go well for you and your children. Then you will live a long time in the land that the LORD your God is giving to you forever.

Cities of Safety

41Moses ·chose [set apart] three cities east ·of [beyond] the Jordan River, 42where a person who ·accidentally [unintentionally] killed someone could go [Num. 35:9–34]. If the person was not killed because of hatred, the murderer's life could be saved by running to one of these cities. 43These were the cities: Bezer in the ·desert [wilderness] high plain was for the Reubenites; Ramoth in Gilead was for the Gadites; and Golan in Bashan was for the Manassites.

The Laws Moses Gave

44These are the ·teachings [laws; instructions] Moses gave to the ·people [Lsons; Tchildren] of Israel. 45They are the rules, ·commands [statutes; ordinances; requirements], and laws he gave ·them [Lthe sons/Tchildren of Israel] when they came out of Egypt. 46They were in the ·valley [glen] near Beth Peor, ·east of [beyond] the Jordan River, in the land of Sihon. Sihon king of the Amorites ruled in Heshbon and was ·defeated [Lstruck] by Moses and the ·Israelites [Lsons/Tchildren of Israel] as they came out of Egypt [Num. 21:21–32]. 47·The Israelites [LThey] took his land and the land of Og king of Bashan [Num. 21:33–35], the two Amorite kings east ·of [beyond] the Jordan River. 48This land went from Aroer, on the edge of the Arnon ·Ravine [Wadi], to Mount Hermon. 49It included all the ·Jordan Valley [LArabah] ·east of [beyond] the Jordan River, and it went as far as the ·Dead [LSalt] Sea below Mount Pisgah.

The Ten Commandments

5 Moses called all the people of Israel together and said: Listen,
Israel, to the ·commands [statutes; requirements; ordinances] and
laws I am ·giving you [Lspeaking in your ears] today. Learn them and obey
them carefully. 2The LORD our God ·made [Lcut] an ·Agreement [Covenant;
Treaty] with us at ·Mount Sinai [LHoreb; 1:6]. 3He did not ·make [Lcut]
this ·Agreement [Covenant; Treaty] with our ·ancestors [fathers], but he
made it with us, with all of us who are alive here today. 4The LORD spoke
to you face to face from the fire on the mountain [Ex. 19]. 5(At that time
I stood between you and the LORD in order to tell you what the LORD said;
you were afraid of the fire, so you would not go up on the mountain.) The
LORD said:
6"I am the LORD your God; I brought you out of the land of Egypt
·where you were slaves [Lfrom the house of bondage].
7"You must not have any other gods ·except [*or* before] me.
8"You must not make for yourselves any idols or anything to worship
that looks like something in the ·sky [heavens] above or on the earth
below or in the water below the ·land [earth]. 9You must not worship or
serve ·any idol [Lthem], because I, the LORD your God, am a jealous God
[4:24]. ·If people sin against me and hate me, I will punish their children,
even their grandchildren and great-grandchildren [LI will visit/punish the
guilt of the fathers on the sons until the third and fourth generations of
those who hate me]. 10But I will be very kind for a thousand lifetimes to
those who love me and obey my commands.
11"You must not ·use the name of the LORD your God thoughtlessly
[take/lift up the name of the LORD your God in vain], because the LORD
will ·punish [Lnot hold/treat as innocent; not acquit] anyone who ·uses
[takes in vain] his name in this way.
12"·Keep [Observe] the Sabbath ·as a holy day [Lto consecrate/sanctify
it], as the LORD your God has commanded you. 13You may work and get
everything done during six days each week, 14but the seventh day is a ·day
of rest to honor [Sabbath to] the LORD your God. On that day no one may
do any work: not you, your son or daughter, your male or female slaves,
your ox, your donkey, or any of your animals, or the ·foreigners [resident
aliens] living in your cities. That way your servants may rest as you do.
15Remember that you were slaves in Egypt and that the LORD your God
brought you out of there by his ·great power [Lstrong hand] and ·strength
[Lextended arm]. So the LORD your God has commanded you to rest on
the Sabbath day.
16"Honor your father and your mother as the LORD your God has commanded you. Then you will live ·a long time [Lfor many days], and things
will go well for you in the land that the LORD your God is going to give you.
17"You must not murder anyone.
18"You must not ·be guilty of [commit] adultery.
19"You must not steal.
20"You must not ·tell lies about [bear false witness against] your
neighbor.
21"You must not ·want to take [covet] your neighbor's wife. You must
not ·want to take [covet] your neighbor's house or land, his male or
female slaves, his ox or his donkey, or anything that belongs to your
neighbor [Cthis final commandment indicates that the previous commandments also involve attitudes, not just actions]."
22The LORD spoke these ·commands [Lwords] to ·all of you [your whole

community/congregation/assembly] on the mountain in a loud voice out of the fire, the cloud, and the deep darkness; he did not say anything else. Then he wrote them on two stone tablets, and he gave them to me.

23When you heard the voice from the darkness, as the mountain was blazing with fire, all the leaders of your tribes and your elders ·came to [approached] me. 24And you said, "The LORD our God has shown us his glory [Chis manifest presence] and ·majesty [greatness], and we have heard his voice from the fire. Today we have seen that a person can live even if God speaks to him. 25But now, ·we will [Lwhy should we . . . ?] die! This great fire will burn us up, and we will die if we hear the LORD our God speak anymore. 26·No human being [LFor who of all flesh…?] has ever heard the living God speaking from a fire and still lived, but we have. 27Moses, you go near and listen to everything the LORD our God says. Then you tell us what the LORD our God tells you, and we will listen and obey."

28The LORD heard what you said to me, and he said to me, "I have heard what the people said to you. Everything they said was good. 29·I wish [LIf only] their ·hearts [minds] would always ·respect [fear] me and that they would always obey my commands so that things would go well for them and their children forever!

30"Go and tell the people to return to their tents, 31but you stay here with me so that I may give you all the commands, ·rules [statutes; ordinances; requirements], and laws that you must teach the people to obey in the land I am giving them as their ·own [possession]."

32So be careful to do what the LORD your God has commanded you, and ·follow the commands exactly [Ldo not turn aside to the right or to the left]. 33·Live the way [LWalk on the way/path that] the LORD your God has commanded you so that you may live and have what is good and have a long life in the land you will ·take [possess].

The Command to Love God

6 These are the commands, ·rules [statutes; ordinances; requirements], and laws that the LORD your God told me to teach you to obey in the land you are crossing the Jordan River to ·take [possess]. 2You, your children, and your grandchildren must ·respect [fear] the LORD your God ·as long as you live [Lall the days of your life]. Obey all his ·rules [statutes; ordinances; requirements] and commands I give you so that ·you will live a long time [Lyour days will be long]. 3Listen, Israel, and carefully obey these laws. Then all will go well for you, and you will become a great nation in a ·fertile land [Lland flowing with milk and honey; Ex. 3:8], just as the LORD, the God of your ·ancestors [fathers], has promised you [Gen. 12:1–3; 15:17–20].

4·Listen, people of [THear, O] Israel! The LORD our God is the ·only [*or* one] LORD. 5Love the LORD your God with all your heart, all your soul, and all your strength. 6Always ·remember [Lkeep in your heart] these commands I give you today. 7·Teach [Recite; Repeat] them to your children, and talk about them when you sit at home and walk along the road, when you lie down and when you get up. 8·Write them down and tie [LBind] them to your hands as a sign. Tie them ·on your forehead [Lbetween your eyes] ·to remind you [as an emblem/headband/frontlet], 9and write them on ·your doors [Lthe lintels/doorposts of your house] and gates.

10The LORD your God will bring you into the land he promised to your ·ancestors [fathers], to Abraham, Isaac, and Jacob, and he will give it to you [Gen. 12:1–3; 15:17–20]. The land has large, ·growing [Lgood; fine] cities you did not build, 11houses full of good things you did not ·buy [Lfill], ·wells [cisterns] you did not dig, and vineyards and olive trees you did not plant. You will eat as much as you want. 12But be careful! Do not forget the LORD, who brought you out of the land of Egypt ·where you were slaves [Lfrom the house of bondage].

13·Respect [Fear] the LORD your God. You must ·worship [serve] him and make your ·promises [oaths; vows] only in his name. 14Do not ·worship [Lgo after] other gods as the people around you do, 15because the LORD your God is a jealous God [4:24]. He is present with you, and if you worship other gods, he will become angry with you and destroy you from the earth. 16Do not test the LORD your God as you did at Massah [Ex. 17:1–7; Ps. 95:8; Matt. 4:7]. 17Be sure to obey the commands of the LORD your God and the ·rules [statutes; requirements; ordinances] and laws he has given you. 18Do what ·the LORD says is good and right [Lis good and right in the LORD's eyes] so that things will go well for you. Then you may go in and ·take [possess] the good land the LORD promised to your ·ancestors [fathers; Gen. 12:1–3; 15:17–20]. 19He will force all your enemies out as you go in, as the LORD has said.

20In the future when your children ask you, "What is the meaning of the laws, ·commands [statutes; ordinances; requirements], and rules the LORD our God gave us?" 21tell them, "We were slaves to the king of Egypt, but the LORD brought us out of Egypt ·by his great power [Lwith a strong hand]. 22The LORD showed us great and terrible signs and miracles, which he did to Egypt, the king, and his whole ·family [Lhouse]. 23The LORD brought us out of Egypt to lead us here and to give us the land he promised our ·ancestors [fathers; Gen. 12:1–3; 15:17–20]. 24The LORD ordered us to obey all these ·commands [statutes; ordinances; requirements] and to ·respect [fear] the LORD our God so that we will always do well and stay alive, as we are today. 25The right thing for us to do is this: Obey all these rules in the presence of the LORD our God, as he has commanded."

You Are God's People

7 The LORD your God will bring you into the land that you are entering and that you will ·have as your own [possess]. As you go in, he will ·force out [clear away/out] these nations: the Hittites, Girgashites, Amorites, Canaanites, Perizzites, Hivites, and Jebusites—seven nations that are stronger than you. 2The LORD your God will hand these nations over to you, and when you ·defeat [Lstrike] them, you must ·destroy them completely [devote them to the LORD; 20:15–18; Josh. 6:17]. Do not ·make [Lcut] a ·peace treaty [covenant] with them or show them any mercy. 3Do not marry any of them, or let your daughters marry their sons, or let your sons marry their daughters. 4If you do, those people will turn your children away from me, to begin serving other gods. Then the LORD will be very angry with you, and he will quickly destroy you. 5This is what you must do to those people: Tear down their altars, smash their holy stone pillars, cut down their ·Asherah idols [LAsherah; 7:5; Judg. 3:7], and burn their idols in the fire. 6You are holy people who belong to the LORD your God. He has chosen you from all the people on earth ·to be his very own [as his treasured/special possession; Ex. 19:5].

7The LORD did not ·care [have affection] for you and choose you because there were many of you—you are the smallest nation of all. 8But the LORD chose you because he loved you, and he kept his promise to your ·ancestors [fathers; Gen. 12:1–3; 15:17–20]. So he brought you out of

Egypt by his ·great power [Lstrong hand] and ·freed [ransomed; redeemed] you from the ·land of slavery [Lhouse of bondage], from the ·power [Lhand] of the king of Egypt. 9So know that the LORD your God is God, the faithful God. He will ·keep [guard] his ·agreement [covenant; treaty] of love for a thousand ·lifetimes for people [generations] who love him and obey his commands. 10But he will pay back those people who hate him. He will destroy them, and he will not be slow to pay back those who hate him. 11So be careful to obey the commands, ·rules [statutes; ordinances; requirements], and laws I give you today.

12If you pay attention to these laws and obey them carefully, the LORD your God will keep his ·agreement [covenant; treaty] and show his ·love [loyalty] to you, as he promised your ·ancestors [fathers]. 13He will love and bless you. He will ·make the number of your people grow; he will bless you with children [Lmultiply the fruit of your womb]. ·He will bless your fields with good crops and will give you grain, new wine, and oil [L…and the fruit of your land, your grain, new wine, and oil]. ·He will bless your herds with calves and your flocks with lambs [L…the increase of your cattle and the issue of your flocks] in the land he promised your ·ancestors [fathers] he would give you. 14You will be blessed more than any other people [Gen. 12:1–3]. ·Every husband and wife will have children, and all your cattle will have calves [LThere will be no barrenness or sterility among you or your livestock]. 15The LORD will take away all disease from you; ·you will not have [Lhe will not inflict you with] the terrible diseases that were in Egypt, but he will give them to all the people who hate you. 16You must ·destroy [devour] all the people the LORD your God hands over to you. Do not ·feel sorry for [pity] them, and do not ·worship [serve] their gods, or they will trap you.

17You might say ·to yourselves [Lin your hearts], "Because these nations are stronger than we are, ·we can't [Lhow can we…?] ·force them out [dispossess them]." 18But don't be afraid of them. Remember what the LORD your God did to all of Egypt and ·its king [LPharaoh]. 19·You [LYour eyes] saw for yourselves the troubles, signs, and miracles he did, how the LORD's ·great power [Lstrong hand] and ·strength [Loutstretched arm] brought you out of Egypt. The LORD your God will do the same thing to all the nations you now fear. 20The LORD your God will also send ·terror [*or* pestilence; *or* hornets] among them so that even those who are alive and hiding from you will die. 21Don't ·be afraid of [dread] them, because the LORD your God is with you; he is a great God and ·people are afraid of him [awesome]. 22When the LORD your God ·forces those nations out [clears away/out those nations] of the land, he will do it little by little ahead of you. You won't be able to destroy them all at once; otherwise, the wild animals will grow too many in number [Cbecause of the reduced population]. 23But the LORD your God will hand those nations over to you, ·confusing [panicking] them until they are destroyed. 24The LORD will ·help you defeat their kings [Lgive their kings into your hand], and ·the world will forget who they were [Lyou will destroy their name from under the heavens]. No one will be able to ·stop you [stand against you]; you will destroy them all. 25Burn up their idols in the fire. Do not ·wish for [covet] the silver and gold they have, and don't take it for yourselves, or you will be trapped by it. The LORD your God ·hates [despises] it. 26Do not bring one of those ·hateful [despised] things into your house, or you will be ·completely destroyed [devoted to the LORD; 20:15–18; Josh. 6:17] along with it. ·Hate [Detest] and reject those things; they must be ·completely destroyed [devoted to the LORD; 20:15–18; Josh. 6:17].

Remember the Lord

8 Carefully obey every command I give you today. Then you will live and ·grow in number [multiply], and you will enter and ·take [possess] the land the LORD promised your ·ancestors [fathers; Gen. 12:1–3; 15:17–20]. 2Remember ·how the LORD your God has led [all the way the LORD brought] you in the ·desert [wilderness] for these forty years, ·taking away your pride [humbling you] and testing you, because he wanted to know what was in your heart. He wanted to know if you would obey his commands. 3He ·took away your pride [humbled you] when he let you get hungry, and then he fed you with manna [Ex. 16:31–36], which neither you nor your ·ancestors [fathers] had ever seen. This was to teach you that a person does not live on bread alone, but by everything the LORD says [Matt. 4:4]. 4During these forty years, your clothes did not wear out, and your feet did not swell. 5Know in your heart that the LORD your God ·corrects [instructs; disciplines] you as a parent ·corrects [instructs; disciplines] a child.

6Obey the commands of the LORD your God, ·living as he has commanded you [Lgoing in his way] and ·respecting [fearing] him. 7The LORD your God is bringing you into a good land, a land with ·rivers [wadis] and pools of water, with ·springs [deeps; underground water] that flow in the valleys and hills, 8a land that has wheat and barley, vines, fig trees, pomegranates, olive oil, and honey. 9It is a land where you will have ·plenty of food [Lno scarcity of food/bread], where you will have everything you need, where the rocks are iron, and where you can ·dig [mine] copper out of the hills.

10When you ·have all you want to eat [Leat and are satisfied], then ·praise [bless] the LORD your God for giving you a good land. 11Be careful not to forget the LORD your God so that you ·fail to obey [do not keep] his commands, laws, and ·rules [statutes; ordinances; requirements] that I am giving to you today. 12When you eat ·all you want [Land are satisfied] and build nice houses and live in them, 13when your herds and flocks ·grow large [multiply] and your silver and gold ·increase [multiply], ·when you have more of everything [and all you have multiplies], 14then your heart will ·become proud [Lbe lifted up/exalted]. You will forget the LORD your God, who brought you out of the land of Egypt, ·where you were slaves [Lfrom the house of bondage]. 15He led you through the ·large [vast] and ·terrible [awesome] ·desert [wilderness] that was dry and had no water, and that had ·poisonous [Lburning] snakes and stinging insects. He gave you water from a ·solid [*or* flint] rock [Ex. 17:1–7] 16and manna to eat in the ·desert [wilderness; Ex. 16:31–36]. Manna was something your ·ancestors [fathers] had never seen. He did this to ·take away your pride [humble you] and to test you, so things would go well for you in the end. 17You might say ·to yourself [Lin your heart/mind], "I am rich because of ·my own power and strength [Lthe power and strength of my hand; Ps. 30:6–7]," 18but remember the LORD your God! It is he who gives you the power to become rich, keeping the ·agreement [covenant; treaty] he promised to your ·ancestors [fathers], as it is today.

19If you ever forget the LORD your God and ·follow [Lgo after] other gods and ·worship [serve] them and bow down to them, I ·warn you [testify/witness to you] today that you will be destroyed. 20Just as the LORD

destroyed the other nations for you, you can be destroyed if you do not ·obey [Llisten to the voice of] **the LORD your God.**

The Lord Will Be with Israel

9 Listen, Israel. You will soon cross the Jordan River to go in and ·force out [dispossess] **nations that are bigger and stronger than you. They have large cities with ·walls** [fortifications] **up to the ·sky** [heavens]. **2The people there are ·Anakites** [Lsons/descendants of the Anakim], **who are strong and tall** [1:28; Num. 13:28]. **You know about them, and you have heard it said: "·No one can stop** [LWho can stand up to…?] **the ·Anakites** [Lthe sons/descendants of Anak]." **3But today remember that the LORD your God goes in before you to destroy them like a ·fire that burns things up** [consuming fire]. **He will defeat ·them** [Land subdue them] **ahead of you, and you will force them out and destroy them quickly, just as the LORD has said.**

4After the LORD your God has forced those nations out ahead of you, don't say ·to yourself [Lin your heart/mind], **"The LORD brought me here to take this land because I am so ·good** [righteous]." **No! It is because these nations are evil that the LORD will ·force them out** [dispossess them] **ahead of you. 5You are going in to ·take** [possess] **the land, not because ·you are good and honest** [Lof your righteousness or the integrity/virtue of your heart/mind], **but because these nations are evil. That is why the LORD your God will ·force them out** [dispossess them] **ahead of you, to keep his promise to your ·ancestors** [fathers], **to Abraham, Isaac, and Jacob** [Gen. 12:1–3; 15:17–20]. **6The LORD your God is giving you this good land to ·take** [possess] **as your own. But know this: It is not because you are ·good** [righteous]; **you are a ·stubborn** [Lstiff-necked] **people.**

Remember the Lord's Anger

7Remember this and do not forget it: You made the LORD your God angry in the ·desert [wilderness]. **You ·would not obey** [rebelled against] **the LORD from the day you left Egypt until you arrived here. 8At ·Mount Sinai** [LHoreb; 1:6] **you made the LORD angry—angry enough to destroy you** [Ex. 32]. **9When I went up on the mountain to receive the stone tablets, the tablets with the ·Agreement** [Covenant; Treaty] **the LORD had ·made** [Lcut] **with you, I stayed on the mountain for forty days and forty nights; I did not eat bread or drink water. 10The LORD gave me two stone tablets, which God had written on with his own finger** [Cthe Ten Commandments; Ex. 20:2–17; 31:18]. **On them were all the commands that the LORD gave to you on the mountain out of the fire, on the day ·you were gathered there** [of the assembly].

11When the forty days and forty nights were over, the LORD gave me the two stone tablets, the tablets with the ·Agreement [Covenant; Treaty] **on them. 12Then the LORD told me, "Get up and go down quickly from here, because the people you brought out from Egypt are ·ruining** [corrupting] **themselves. They have quickly turned away from ·what** [Lthe way] **I commanded and have made an idol for themselves** [Ca golden calf; Ex. 32:3–4]."

13The LORD said to me, "I have watched these people, and they are very ·stubborn [Lstiff-necked]! **14Get away so that I may destroy them and ·make the whole world forget who they are** [Lblot off their name from under heaven]. **Then I will make another nation from you that will be bigger and stronger than they are."**

15So I turned and came down the mountain that was burning with fire, and the two stone tablets with the ·Agreement [Covenant; Treaty] **were in**

my hands. 16When I looked, I saw you had sinned against the LORD your
God and had made an idol in the shape of a calf. You had quickly turned
away from ·what [Lthe way] the LORD had ·told [commanded] you to do.
17So I took the two stone tablets and threw them down, breaking them
into pieces ·right in front of you [Lbefore your eyes; Ex. 32:19].
18Then I ·again [as before/formerly] bowed facedown on the ground
before the LORD for forty days and forty nights; I did not eat bread or drink
water. You had sinned by doing what the LORD said was evil, and you made
him angry. 19I was afraid of the LORD's anger and rage, because he was angry
enough with you to destroy you, but the LORD listened to me ·again [Lat that
time]. 20And the LORD was angry enough with Aaron to destroy him, but
then I prayed for Aaron, too. 21I took that sinful calf idol you had made and
burned it in the fire. I crushed it into a powder like dust and threw the dust
into a stream that flowed down the mountain [Ex. 32:20].
22You also made the LORD angry at Taberah [Num. 11:3], Massah [Ex.
17:7], and Kibroth Hattaavah [Num. 11:34].
23Then the LORD sent you away from Kadesh Barnea and said, "Go up
and ·take [possess] the land I have given you." But you ·rejected [rebelled
against] the command of the LORD your God. You did not trust him or
·obey him [Llisten to his voice; Num. 13–14]. 24You have ·refused to obey
[rebelled against] the LORD as long as I have[n] known you.
25The LORD had said he would destroy you, so I threw myself down in
front of him for those forty days and forty nights. 26I prayed to the LORD
and said, "Lord GOD, do not destroy your people, your ·own people
[Linheritance], whom you ·freed [ransomed; redeemed] and brought out
of Egypt by your great power and ·strength [Lstrong hand]. 27Remember
your servants Abraham, Isaac, and Jacob. Don't look at how ·stubborn
[hard] these people are, and don't look at their sin and evil. 28Otherwise,
·Egypt [Lthe land from which you brought us] will say, 'It was because the
LORD was not able to take his people into the land he promised them, and
it was because he hated them that he took them into the ·desert [wilder-
ness] to kill them.' 29But they are your people, LORD, your ·own people
[Linheritance], whom you brought out of Egypt with your great power
and ·strength [Loutstretched arm]."

New Stone Tablets

10 At that time the LORD said to me, "·Cut [Carve; Chisel] two
stone tablets like the first ones and come up to me on the
mountain. Also make a wooden Ark [Ex. 25:10]. 2I will write on the tablets the same words that were on the first tablets, which you broke, and
you will put the new tablets in the Ark [Ex. 34]."
3So I made the Ark out of acacia wood, and I ·cut [carved; chiseled] out
two stone tablets like the first ones. Then I went up on the mountain with
the two tablets in my hands. 4The LORD wrote the same things on these
tablets he had written before—the Ten ·Commandments [LWords; Ex.
20:2–27; 34] that he had told you on the mountain from the fire, on the
day ·you were gathered [of the assembly] there. And the LORD gave them
to me. 5Then I turned and came down the mountain; I put the tablets in
the Ark I had made, as the LORD had commanded, and they are still there.
6(The ·people [Lsons; children] of Israel went from ·the wells of the
Jaakanites [*or* Beeroth-bene-jaakan] to Moserah. Aaron died there and
was buried [Num. 20:22–29]; his son Eleazar became priest in his place.

9:24 I have Hebrew copies read "I have." Greek copies and the Samaritan Pentateuch have "he has."

7From Moserah they went to Gudgodah, and from Gudgodah they went to
Jotbathah [Num. 33:33], a place with ·streams [wadis] of water. 8At that
time the LORD ·chose [set apart] the tribe of Levi to carry the Ark of the
·Agreement [Treaty; Covenant; Ex. 25:10] with the LORD. They were to
·serve [minister to] the LORD and to bless the people in his name, which
they still do today [Num. 6:22–27]. 9That is why the Levites did not ·receive
any land of their own [Lhave an allotment and inheritance along with their
brothers]; instead, they ·received the LORD himself as their gift [Linherited
the LORD himself], as the LORD your God ·told [promised] them.)
10I stayed on the mountain forty days and forty nights just like the first
time, and the LORD listened to me this time also. He did not want to
destroy you. 11The LORD said to me, "Go and lead the people so that they
will go in and ·take [possess] the land I promised their ·ancestors [fathers;
Gen. 12:1–3; 15:17–20]."

What the Lord Wants You to Do

12Now, Israel, ·this is what [Lwhat is it that…?] the LORD your God
wants you to do: ·Respect [Fear] the LORD your God, and ·do what he has
told you to do [Lwalk on all his ways/paths]. Love him. Serve the LORD
your God with ·your whole being [Lall your heart/mind and all your soul],
13and obey the LORD's commands and ·laws [statutes; ordinances; require-
ments] that I am giving you today for your own good.
14The LORD owns the ·world [earth] and everything in it—the heavens,
even the ·highest heavens [Lheaven of heavens], are his. 15But the LORD
·cared for [stuck to] and loved your ·ancestors [fathers], and he chose you,
their ·descendants [Lseed], over all the other nations, just as it is today.
16·Give yourselves completely to serving him [LCircumcise the foreskin of
your heart], and do not be stubborn any longer. 17The LORD your God is
God of all gods and Lord of all lords. He is the great God, who is strong
and ·wonderful [awesome]. He does not ·take sides [show favoritism/par-
tiality], and he will not ·be talked into doing evil [take a bribe]. 18He ·helps
[grants justice to] orphans and widows, and he loves ·foreigners [resident
aliens] and gives them food and clothes. 19You also must love ·foreigners
[resident aliens], because you were ·foreigners [resident aliens] in Egypt.
20·Respect [Fear] the LORD your God and serve him. ·Be loyal [Cling] to
him and ·make your promises in [swear by] his name. 21He is the one you
should praise; he is your God, who has done great and ·wonderful [awe-
some] things for you, which you have seen with your own eyes. 22There
were only seventy of your ·ancestors [fathers] when they went down to
Egypt [Gen. 46:26; Ex. 1:5], and now the LORD your God has made you as
many as the stars in the sky [Gen. 15:5; 22:19].

Great Things Israel Saw

11 Love the LORD your God and always obey his orders, ·rules
[statutes; ordinances; requirements], laws, and commands.
2·Remember [LYou know] today it was not your children who saw and
·felt [experienced; knew] the ·correction [discipline] of the LORD your
God. They did not see his ·majesty [greatness], his ·power [Lstrong
hand], his ·strength [Loutstretched arm], 3or his signs and the things he
did in Egypt to Pharaoh, the king, and his whole country. 4They did not
see what he did to the Egyptian army, its horses and chariots, when he
drowned them in the ·Red [or Reed] Sea [Ex. 10:19] as they were chasing
you. The LORD ·ruined [destroyed] them forever. 5They did not see what
he did for you in the ·desert [wilderness] until you arrived here. 6They
did not see what he did to Dathan and Abiram, the sons of Eliab the

Reubenite, when the ground opened ·up [Lits mouth] and swallowed
them, their ·families [Lhouses], their tents, and everyone who stood
·with them in Israel [Lon their feet in all Israel; Num. 16]. 7It was ·you
who [Lyour eyes that] saw all these great things the LORD has done.

8So ·obey [keep] all the commands I am ·giving [commanding] you
today so that you will be strong and can go in and ·take [possess] the land
you are ·going to take as your own [Lcrossing over to possess]. 9Then you
will live a long time in the land that the LORD ·promised [swore] to give to
your ·ancestors [fathers] and their ·descendants [Lseed], a ·fertile land
[Lland flowing with milk and honey; Ex. 3:8]. 10The land you are going to
take is not like Egypt, where you were. There you had to plant your seed
and water it, like a vegetable garden, by using your feet. 11But the land that
you will soon cross ·the Jordan River [Lthere] to ·take [possess] is a land of
hills and valleys, ·a land that drinks [watered by] rain from heaven. 12It is
a land the LORD your God ·cares for [looks after]. His eyes are on it continually, and he watches it from the beginning of the year to the end.

13If you carefully ·obey [Llisten to] the commands I am ·giving [com-
manding] you today and love the LORD your God and serve him with
·your whole being [Lall your heart/mind and all your soul], 14then he[n] will
send rain on your land at the right time, in the ·fall [Learly rain] and
·spring [Llate rain], and you will be able to gather your grain, new wine,
and oil. 15He[n] will put grass in the fields for your cattle, and you will have
plenty to eat.

16Be careful, or you will be ·fooled [tricked; deceived; seduced] and will
turn away to serve and worship other gods. 17If you do, the LORD will
become angry with you and will ·shut [close up] the heavens so it will not
rain [1 Kin. 17:1]. Then the land will not ·grow [produce] crops, and you
will soon ·die [perish] in the good land the LORD is giving you.
18·Remember my words with your whole being [LPut these words of mine
on your hearts/minds and on your soul]. ·Write them down and tie
[LBind] them to your hands as a sign; tie them ·on your foreheads
[Lbetween your eyes] ·to remind you [as an emblem/headband/frontlet;
6:8]. 19Teach them well to your children, talking about them when you
sit at home and walk along the road, when you lie down and when you
get up. 20Write them on ·your doors [Lthe lintels/doorposts of your
house] and gates 21so that both you and your children will live a long
time in the land the LORD promised your ·ancestors [fathers], as long as
the ·skies [heavens] are above the earth.

22If you are careful to obey every command I am ·giving you to follow
[Lcommanding you to do], and love the LORD your God, and ·do what he
has told you to do [Lwalk on all his ways/paths], and ·are loyal [cling] to
him, 23then the LORD will ·force [dispossess] all those nations out of the
land ahead of you, and you will ·take [possess] the land from nations that
are bigger and stronger than you. 24Everywhere ·you step [Lthe heel of your
foot treads] will be yours. Your land will go from the ·desert [wilderness] to
Lebanon and from the Euphrates River to the ·Mediterranean [LGreat]
Sea. 25No one will be able to ·stop [stand against] you. The LORD your God
will ·do what he promised and will make the people afraid everywhere
you go [Lput the dread and fear of you on all the land on which you tread
as he promised].

11:14, 15 he Some Greek and Latin copies read "he." The Hebrew text has "I."

26See, today I am ·letting you choose [setting before you] a blessing or a curse. 27You will be blessed if you obey the commands of the LORD your God that I am ·giving [commanding] you today. 28But you will be cursed if you ·disobey [Ldo not listen to] the commands of the LORD your God. So do not ·disobey the commands [Lturn aside from the way] I am ·giving [commanding] you today, and do not ·worship [go after] other gods you do not know. 29When the LORD your God brings you into the land you will ·take as your own [possess], you are to announce the blessings from Mount Gerizim and the curses from Mount Ebal [27–28; Josh. 8:30–35]. 30(·These mountains are [LAre they not…?] ·on the other side of [beyond] the Jordan River, to the west, toward the sunset. They are near the great trees of Moreh [Gen. 12:6] in the land of the Canaanites who live in the ·Jordan Valley [LArabah] opposite Gilgal.) 31You will soon cross the Jordan River to enter and ·take [possess] the land the LORD your God is giving you. When you ·take it over [possess it] and live there, 32be careful to obey all the commands and ·laws [statutes; ordinances; requirements] I am giving you today.

The Place for Worship

12 These are the ·commands [statutes; ordinances; requirements] and laws you must carefully obey in the land the LORD, the God of your ·ancestors [fathers], is giving you to possess. Obey them as long as you live in the land. 2When you ·inherit [possess] the lands of these nations, you must completely destroy all the places where they serve their gods, on high mountains and hills and under every green tree. 3Tear down their altars, smash their holy stone pillars, and burn their ·Asherah idols [LAsherim; 7:5; Judg. 3:7] in the fire. Cut down their idols and destroy their names from those places.

4Don't ·worship [act for] the LORD your God that way, 5but look for the place the LORD your God will choose—·a place among your tribes where he is to be worshiped [Las his dwelling where he will place his name]. Go there, 6and bring to that place your burnt offerings [Lev. 1:1–17] and sacrifices; bring ·a tenth of what you gain [Tyour tithes] and your special gifts; bring what you have ·promised [vowed] and the special gifts you want to give the LORD, and bring the first animals born to your herds and flocks.

7There you and your families will eat in the presence of the LORD, and you will enjoy all ·the good things for which you have worked [your undertakings; Lall that is sent out from your hand], because the LORD your God has blessed you.

8Do not ·worship [act] the way we have been ·doing [acting] today, each person doing what ·he thinks is right [Lis right/virtuous in his own eyes]. 9You have not yet come to a resting place, to the ·land [Linheritance] the LORD your God will give you as your own. 10But soon you will cross the Jordan River to live in the land the LORD your God is ·giving you as your own [Lcausing you to inherit], where he will give you rest from all your enemies and you will live in safety [2 Sam. 7:1; CDavid would achieve rest from enemies; Solomon would build the temple in an era of peace]. 11Then the LORD your God will choose a place where he ·is to be worshiped [Lwill cause his name to dwell; CZion, where the Temple would be built]. To that place you must bring everything I ·tell [command] you: your burnt offerings [Lev. 1:1–17] and sacrifices, your ·offerings of a tenth of what you gain [Ttithes], your special gifts, and all your best things you ·promised [vowed] to the LORD. 12There rejoice before the LORD your

God. Everyone should rejoice: you, your sons and daughters, your male
and female servants, and the Levites ·from your towns [Lin your gates]
who have no ·land [allotment] of their own. 13Be careful that you don't
sacrifice your burnt offerings [Lev. 1:1–17] just anywhere you ·please
[Lsee]. 14Offer them only in the place the LORD will choose [CZion; v. 11].
He will choose a place in one of your tribes, and there you must do everything I am commanding you.

15But you may ·kill [slaughter] your animals in any of your ·towns
[Lgates] and eat ·as much of the meat as you want [Las much of the meat
as your soul desires; *or* when your soul desires], as if it were a deer or a
gazelle; this is the blessing the LORD your God is giving you. Anyone,
clean or unclean [Cin a ritual sense], may eat this meat, 16but do not eat
the blood [Gen. 9:4; Lev. 3:17; Acts 15:20, 29]. Pour it out on the ground
like water. 17Do not eat in your own ·towns [Lgates] what belongs to the
LORD: ·one-tenth [Ta tithe] of your grain, new wine, or oil; the first animals born to your herds or flocks; whatever you have ·promised to give
[vowed]; the special gifts you want to give to the LORD, or any other gifts.
18Eat these things when you are together with the LORD your God, in the
place the LORD your God chooses to be worshiped. Everyone must do this:
you, your sons and daughters, your male and female servants, and the
Levites from your ·towns [Lgates]. Rejoice in the LORD your God's presence about ·the things you have worked for [your undertakings; Lall that
is sent out from your hand]. 19Be careful not to ·forget [Labandon; for-
sake] the Levites as long ·as you live [Lall your days] in the land.

20When the LORD your God enlarges your ·country [borders] as he has
promised, and ·you want [Lyour soul desires] some meat so you say, "I
want some meat," you may eat ·as much meat as you want [Lwhat your
soul desires; *or* when your soul desires]. 21If the LORD your God chooses a
place where he ·is to be worshiped [Lputs his name] that is too far away
from you, you may ·kill [slaughter] animals from your herds and flocks,
which the LORD has given to you. I have commanded that you may do
this. You may eat ·as much of them as you want [Las much as your soul
desires; *or* when your soul desires] in your own ·towns [Lgates], 22as you
would eat gazelle or deer meat. Both clean and unclean people [Cin a ritual sense] may eat this meat, 23but be sure you don't eat the blood, because
the life is in the blood [Gen. 9:4; Lev. 3:17; Acts 15:20, 29]. Don't eat the
life with the meat. 24Don't eat the blood, but pour it out on the ground
like water. 25If you don't eat it, things will go well for you and your children, because you will be doing what ·the LORD says is right [Lis right/
virtuous in the eyes of the LORD].

26Take your holy ·things [gifts; donations] and ·the things you have
promised to give [Lyour vows that you have lifted up], and go to the place
the LORD will choose. 27Present your burnt offerings [Lev. 1:1–17] on the
altar of the LORD your God, both the meat and the blood. The blood of
your sacrifices should be poured beside the altar of the LORD your God,
but you may eat the meat. 28Be careful to ·obey [Llisten to] all the rules I
am ·giving [commanding] you so that things will always go well for you
and your children, and you will be doing what the LORD your God says is
good and ·right [virtuous in his eyes].

29You will enter the land and ·take it away from [dispossess] the nations
that the LORD your God will ·destroy [Lcut them off] ahead of you. When
you ·force them out [dispossess] and live in their land, 30they will be

destroyed for you, but be careful not to be ·trapped [snared] by asking about their gods. Don't say, "How do these nations ·worship [Lserve]? I will do the same." 31Don't ·worship [act toward] the LORD your God that way, because the LORD hates the ·evil [detestable; abhorrent; abominable] ways they ·worship [act toward] their gods. They even burn their sons and daughters as sacrifices to their gods!

32Be sure to do everything I have commanded you. Do not add anything to it, and do not take anything away from it.

False Prophets

13 Prophets or ·those who tell the future with dreams [Ldreamers of dreams] might come to you and ·say they will show [Lgive] you a sign or a ·miracle [wonder]. 2The sign or ·miracle [wonder] might even happen, and then they might say, "Let's serve other gods" (gods you have not known) "and let's ·worship [Lgo after] them." 3But you must not listen to those prophets or dreamers. The LORD your God is testing you, to ·find out [know] if you love him with ·your whole being [Lall your heart/mind and all your soul]. 4Serve only the LORD your God. ·Respect [Fear] him, keep his commands, and ·obey him [Llisten to his voice]. Serve him and ·be loyal [cling] to him. 5The prophets or dreamers must be killed, because they said you should turn against the LORD your God, who brought you out of Egypt and ·saved [ransomed; redeemed] you from the ·land where you were slaves [Lhouse of bondage]. They tried to turn you from ·doing what [Lthe way] the LORD your God commanded you to ·do [go]. You must ·get rid of [banish; purge] the evil among you.

6Someone might try to ·lead you to serve other gods [Lsecretly entice you]—it might be your brother, your son or daughter, the wife you ·love [embrace], or a ·close [intimate] friend. The person might say, "Let's go and worship other gods." (These are gods that neither you nor your ·ancestors [fathers] have known, 7gods of the people who live around you, either nearby or far away, from one end of the ·land [*or* earth] to the other.) 8Do not ·give in to [agree with; consent to] such people. Do not listen or ·feel sorry for [Llet your eyes look compassionately on] them, and do not ·let them go free [pity them] or ·protect [shield] them. 9You must ·put them to death [kill them]. ·You must be the first one to start [LYour own hand will be the first on them] to kill them, and then ·everyone else must join in [Lthe hand of all the people]. 10You must ·throw stones at them until they die [stone them to death], because they tried to turn you away from the LORD your God, who brought you out of the land of Egypt, ·where you were slaves [Lthe house of bondage]. 11Then everyone in Israel will hear about this and be afraid, and no one among you will ever do such an evil thing again.

Cities to Destroy

12The LORD your God is giving you cities in which to live, and you might hear something about one of them. Someone might say 13that ·evil people [worthless people; scoundrels] have moved in among you. And they might lead the people of that city away from God, saying, "Let's go and ·worship [Lserve] other gods." (These are gods you have not known.) 14Then you must ask about it, ·looking into [investigating] the matter and checking carefully whether it is true. If it is proved that a ·hateful [detestable; abhorrent; abominable] thing has happened among you, 15you must ·kill [Lstrike] with a sword everyone who lives in that city. ·Destroy the city completely and kill everyone in it [Devote that city to the LORD;

20:15–18; Josh. 6:17], as well as the animals, with a sword. [16]Gather up ·everything those people owned [Lall its plunder], and put it in the middle of the city square. Then completely burn the city and ·everything they owned [Lall its plunder] as a burnt offering [Lev. 1:1–17] to the LORD your God. That city should never be rebuilt; let it be ·ruined [a ruin heap] forever. [17]Don't ·keep for yourselves [Lgrasp in your hand] any of the ·things found in that city [Ldevoted things; 20:15–18; Josh. 6:17], so the LORD will not be angry anymore. He will give you ·mercy and feel sorry for you, and he [L…mercy/compassion, and his mercy/compassion] will make your nation grow larger, as he ·promised [swore] to your ·ancestors [fathers]. [18]You will have ·obeyed [Llistened to the voice of] the LORD your God by keeping all his commands that I am ·giving [commanding] to you today, and you will be doing what ·the LORD says is right [Lis right/virtuous in the eyes of the LORD].

God's Special People

14 You are the ·children [sons] of the LORD your God. When someone dies, do not ·cut [lacerate; gash] yourselves or ·shave your heads [Lset baldness between your eyes; Cto show sadness; mourning customs of the pagan Canaanites]. [2]You are holy people, who belong to the LORD your God. He has chosen you from all the people on earth ·to be his very own [as his special treasure; Ex. 19:5–6].

[3]Do not eat anything ·the LORD hates [Ldetestable; abominable; cf. Lev. 11]. [4]These are the animals you may eat: oxen, sheep, goats, [5]deer, gazelle, roe deer, wild goats, ibex, antelope, and mountain sheep. [6]You may eat any animal that has a split hoof and chews the cud [Cconsidered a normal land animal], [7]but you may not eat camels, rabbits, or rock badgers. These animals chew the cud, but they do not have split hoofs, so they are unclean [Cin a ritual sense] for you. [8]Pigs are also unclean for you; they have split hoofs, but they do not chew the cud. Do not eat their meat or touch their dead bodies.

[9]There are many things that live in the water. You may eat anything that has fins and scales [Cconsidered a normal aquatic creature], [10]but do not eat anything that does not have fins and scales. It is unclean [Cin a ritual sense] for you.

[11]You may eat any clean [Cin a ritual sense] bird. [12]But do not eat these birds: eagles, vultures, black vultures, [13]red kites, falcons, any kind of kite, [14]any kind of raven, [15]horned owls, screech owls, sea gulls, any kind of hawk, [16]little owls, great owls, white owls, [17]desert owls, ospreys, cormorants, [18]storks, any kind of heron, the hoopoes, or bats [Cthe exact identification of many of these birds is disputed, but they all eat prey or dead matter and/or live in desolate places].

[19]All insects with wings are unclean [Cin a ritual sense] for you; do not eat them. [20]Other things with wings are clean, and you may eat them.

[21]Do not eat anything you find that is already dead. You may give it to a ·foreigner living in your town [resident alien living within your gates], and he may eat it, or you may sell it to a foreigner. But you are holy people, who belong to the LORD your God.

Do not cook a baby goat in its mother's milk [Cprobably a pagan ritual; Ex. 23:19].

Giving a Tithe

[22]Be sure to ·save [set aside/apart] ·one-tenth [Ta tithe] of all ·your crops [Lthe produce/yield of your seed of the field] each year. [23]Eat it in the presence of the LORD your God in the place where he chooses to ·be worshiped [Lcause his name to dwell; CZion; 12:4–7]. Eat the ·tenth [tithe]

of your grain, new wine, and oil, and eat the animals born first to your
herds and flocks. Do this so that you will learn to ·respect [fear] the LORD
your God ·always [Levery day]. 24But if the place the LORD will choose to
·be worshiped [Lset his name there] is too far away and he has blessed you
so much you cannot carry a ·tenth [Ttithe], 25exchange your ·one-tenth
[Ttithe] for silver. Then ·take [Lgrasp in your hand] the silver with you to
the place the LORD your God shall choose. 26·Use [Spend; LGive] the silver
to buy anything you wish—cattle, sheep, wine, ·beer [Tstrong drink; Can
alcoholic beverage made from grain], or anything you wish. Then you
and your ·family [Lhouse] will eat and celebrate there before the LORD
your God. 27Do not ·forget [Labandon; forsake] the Levites in your ·town
[Lgates], because they have no land of their own among you.
28At the end of every third year, everyone should bring ·one-tenth [Ta
tithe] of that year's crop and store it in your ·towns [Lgates]. 29This is for
the Levites so they may eat and be full. (They have no ·land of their own
[Lallotment or inheritance] among you.) It is also for ·strangers [foreign-
ers; resident aliens], orphans, and widows who live in your ·towns [Lgates]
so that all of them may eat and be full. Then the LORD your God will bless
you and all the work ·you do [Lof your hands that you do].

The Special Seventh Year

15 At the end of every seven years, you must ·tell those who owe
you anything that they do not have to pay you back [grant
remission of debts; Ex. 23:10–11]. 2This is ·how you must do it [the manner of remission]: Everyone who has ·loaned money [a claim] must
·cancel [remit] the loan and not make a neighbor or ·relative [*or* countryman; Lbrother] pay it back. This is the LORD's time for ·canceling what
people owe [remitting debts]. 3You may make a foreigner pay what is
owed to you, but you must ·not collect [remit] what ·another Israelite [a
relative; *or* a countryman; La brother] owes you. 4But there should be no
·poor [needy] people among you, because the LORD your God will richly
bless you in the land he is giving you as your ·own [possession]. 5He will
bless you if you obey the LORD your God completely, but you must be
careful to obey all the commands I am ·giving [commanding] you today.
6The LORD your God will bless you as he promised, and you will lend to
other nations, but you will not need to borrow from them. You will rule
over many nations, but none will rule over you.
7If there are ·poor [needy] among ·you [your relatives; *or* your countrymen; Lyour brothers], in one of the ·towns [Lgates] of the land the LORD
your God is giving you, do not be ·selfish [Lhard-hearted] or ·greedy
[Ltight-fisted] toward them [Prov. 28:27; 29:7, 14]. 8But ·give freely [Lopen
your hand] to them, and freely lend them whatever they need. 9Beware of
·evil [useless] thoughts. Don't think, "The seventh year is near, the year
·to cancel what people owe [of remission]." ·You might be mean to [LYour
eye might be evil toward] ·the needy [your needy relative/*or* countryman/
Lbrother] and not give them anything. Then they will ·complain [call out]
to the LORD about you, and he will find you guilty of sin. 10Give freely to
the poor person, and do not ·wish that you didn't have to give [begrudge
him this matter]. The LORD your God will bless your work and everything
you ·touch [undertake; Lsend from your hand]. 11There will always be
poor people in the land, so I command you to ·give freely [Lopen your
hand] to your ·neighbors [*or* relatives; *or* countrymen; Lbrothers] and to
the poor and needy in your land.

Letting Slaves Go Free

12 If one of your own ·people [relatives; Lbrothers] ·sells himself [*or* is sold] to you as a slave, whether it is a Hebrew man or woman, that person will serve you for six years [Lev. 25:39; Neh. 5:4–5]. But in the seventh year you must let the slave go free. 13 When you let slaves go, don't send them away ·without anything [empty-handed]. 14 ·Give them [Provide/ Outfit them with] some of your flock, your grain, and your wine, giving to them as the LORD has ·given to [Lblessed] you. 15 Remember that you were slaves in Egypt, and the LORD your God ·saved [ransomed; redeemed] you. That is why I am commanding this to you today.

16 But if your slave says to you, "I don't want to leave you," because he loves you and your ·family [Lhouse] and has a good life with you, 17 stick an awl [Ca pointed tool for making holes] through his ·ear [earlobe] into the door; he will be your slave for life. Also do this to a female slave.

18 Do not think of it as a hard thing when you let your slaves go free. After all, they served you six years and did twice the work of a hired person. The LORD your God will bless you in everything you do [Ex. 21:2–6; Lev. 25:39–46].

Rules About Firstborn Animals

19 Save all the first male animals born to your herds and flocks [Ex. 13:2, 11–16; 22:29; Num. 18:15–18]. They are ·for [consecrated to] the LORD your God. Do not work the first calf born to your oxen, and do not cut off the wool from the first lamb born to your sheep. 20 Each year you and your ·family [Lhouse] are to eat these animals in the presence of the LORD your God, in the place he will choose to be worshiped [CZion; 12:4–7]. 21 If an animal is crippled or blind or has ·something else wrong [some blemish/defect], do not sacrifice it to the LORD your God. 22 But you may eat that animal in your own ·town [Lgate]. Both clean and unclean people [Cin a ritual sense] may eat it, as they would eat a gazelle or a deer. 23 But don't eat its blood; pour it out on the ground like water [12:24].

The Passover

16 Celebrate the Passover of the LORD your God during the month of Abib [CMarch-April], because it was during Abib that he brought you out of Egypt at night [Ex. 12:1–6; Lev. 23:5–8]. 2 As the sacrifice for the Passover to the LORD your God, offer an animal from your flock or herd at the place the LORD will choose to ·be worshiped [Lcause his name to dwell there; CZion; 12:4–7]. 3 Do not eat it with bread made with ·yeast [leaven]. But for seven days eat bread made without ·yeast [leaven], the bread of ·suffering [affliction], because you left Egypt in a hurry. So all your life you will remember the time you left Egypt. 4 There must be no ·yeast [leaven] anywhere in your land for seven days. Offer the sacrifice on the evening of the first day, and eat all the meat before morning; do not leave it overnight.

5 Do not offer the Passover sacrifice in just any ·town [Lgate] the LORD your God gives you, 6 but offer it in the place he will choose to ·be worshiped [Lcause his name to dwell there; 12:4–7]. Offer it in the evening as the sun goes down, which is when you left Egypt. 7 ·Roast the meat [Cook it] and eat it at the place the LORD your God will choose. The next morning go back to your tents. 8 Eat bread made without ·yeast [leaven] for six days. On the seventh day have a ·special meeting [festive assembly] for the LORD your God, and do not work that day.

The Feast of Weeks

9 Count seven weeks from the time you ·begin to harvest [Lput the sickle to] the grain, 10 and then celebrate the ·Feast [Festival] of Weeks for the

LORD your God [Ex. 23:16; 34:22; Lev. 23:9–21; Num. 28:26–31]. Bring an
offering as a special gift to him, giving to him just as he has blessed you.
11Rejoice before the LORD your God at the place he will choose to ·be worshiped [Lcause his name to dwell there; 12:4–7]. Everybody should rejoice:
you, your sons and daughters, your male and female servants, the Levites
in your ·town [Lgates], the ·strangers [resident aliens], orphans, and widows living among you. 12Remember that you were slaves in Egypt, and
carefully obey all these ·laws [statutes; ordinances; requirements].

The Feast of Shelters

13Celebrate the ·Feast [Festival] of ·Shelters [Booths; Tabernacles] for
seven days, after you have gathered your harvest from the threshing floor
and winepress [Ex. 23:16; 34:22; Lev. 23:33–36]. 14Everybody should
rejoice at your ·Feast [Festival]: you, your sons and daughters, your male
and female servants, the Levites, ·strangers [resident aliens], orphans, and
widows who live in your ·towns [Lgates]. 15Celebrate the ·Feast [Festival]
to the LORD your God for seven days at the place he will choose [v. 2;
12:4–7], because the LORD your God will bless all your ·harvest [yield;
produce] and all the work ·you do [Lof your hands], and you will be completely happy.

16All your men must ·come [Lappear] before the LORD three times a
year to the place he will choose [v. 2; 12:4–7]. They must come at these
times: the ·Feast [Festival] of Unleavened Bread [Canother name for
Passover], the ·Feast [Festival] of Weeks, and the ·Feast [Festival] of
·Shelters [Booths; Tabernacles]. No man should come before the LORD
·without a gift [empty-handed]. 17Each of you must bring a gift that will
show how much the LORD your God has blessed you.

Judges for the People

18Appoint judges and officers for your tribes in every ·town [Lgate] the
LORD your God is giving you; they must judge the people fairly. 19Do not
·judge unfairly [distort justice] or ·take sides [show partiality/favoritism].
Do not ·let people pay you to make wrong decisions [take bribes], because
·that kind of payment [bribes] makes wise people seem blind, and it
·changes the words of good people [undermines the cause of the innocent; Ex. 23:8; Ps. 5:5; Prov. 6:35; 17:8, 23; 21:14; Eccl. 7:7]. 20Do [pursue]
what is ·right [righteous] so that you will live and ·always have [possess]
the land the LORD your God is giving you.

God Hates Idols

21Do not set up a wooden ·Asherah idol [LAsherah; 7:5; Judg. 3:7] next
to the altar you build for the LORD your God, 22and do not set up holy
stone pillars. The LORD your God hates them.

17 If an ox or sheep has ·something wrong with it [La blemish/
defect, anything wrong with it; Lev. 22:17–25], do not offer it
as a sacrifice to the LORD your God. He would ·hate [detest] that.

2A man or woman in one of the ·towns [Lgates] the LORD gave you
might be found doing something evil in the ·sight [Leyes] of the LORD
your God and ·breaking [transgressing] the ·Agreement [Covenant;
Treaty]. 3That person may have served other gods and bowed down to
them or to the sun or moon or ·stars of the sky [any of the host of heaven],
which I have commanded should not be done [4:19]. 4If someone has
told you about it, you must look into the matter carefully. If it is true that
such a ·hateful [detestable; abhorrent; abominable] thing has happened
in Israel, 5take the man or woman who has done the evil thing to the city
gates and ·throw stones at [stone] that person until he dies. 6There must

be two or three witnesses that it is true before the person is put to death;
if there is only one witness, the person should not be put to death [Num.
35:30]. 7The hands of the witnesses must be the first to ·throw stones at
[stone] the person, and then everyone else will follow. You must get rid of
the evil among you.

Courts of Law

8Some cases that come before you, ·such as murder [between one kind
of bloodshed and another; Cintentional or unintentional], ·quarreling
[between one kind of right and another], or ·attack [Lbetween one kind of
assault and another; Ex. 21:18–21], may be too difficult to judge. Take
these cases to the place the LORD your God will choose [12:4–7]. 9Go to
the priests who are Levites and to the judge who is ·on duty at that time
[in office in those days]. ·Ask them about the case [Make inquiry], and
they will decide. 10You must follow the decision they give you at the place
the LORD your God will choose. Be careful to do everything they ·tell
[Lteach] you. 11Follow the ·teachings [laws; instructions] they give you,
and do whatever they decide, ·exactly as they tell you [Lyou must not turn
aside from the thing they tell you to the right or to the left]. 12The person
who ·does not show respect for [presumes not to listen to] the judge or
priest who is there serving the LORD your God must be put to death. You
must ·get rid of [banish; purge] that evil from Israel. 13Then everyone will
hear about this and will be afraid, and they will not ·show disrespect [be
presumptuous] anymore.

Choosing a King

14When you enter the land the LORD your God is giving you, taking it
as your ·own [possession] and living in it, you will say, "·Let's appoint [LI
will set] a king over ·us [Lme] like the nations all around us [1 Sam. 8:5,
20]." 15Be sure to ·appoint [set] over you the king the LORD your God
chooses. He must be one of your own ·people [relatives; Lbrothers]. Do
not ·appoint [set] as your king a foreigner who is not a ·fellow Israelite
[relative; Lbrother]. 16The king must not ·have too many [multiply] horses
for himself [Is. 2:7–9], and he must not send people to Egypt to get more
horses, because the LORD has told you, "Don't return that way again."
17The king must not ·have many [multiply for himself] wives, or his heart
will ·be led away [turn aside] from God [1 Kin. 11:1–13]. He must not
have too much silver and gold.

18When he ·becomes king [Lsits on the throne of his kingdom], he
should write a copy of ·the teachings [these laws/instructions] on a scroll
for himself, a copy taken from the priests and Levites. 19He should keep it
with him all the time and read from it every day of his life. Then he will
learn to ·respect [fear] the LORD his God, and he will obey all ·the teachings [these laws/instructions] and ·commands [statutes; ordinances;
requirements]. 20He should not ·think he is better than his fellow Israelites
[Lexalt his heart above his relatives/brothers], and he must not ·stop obeying [turn aside from] the law ·in any way [Lto the right or the left] so that
he and his ·descendants [sons] may rule the kingdom for a long time [2
Sam. 7:16].

Shares for Priests and Levites

18 The priests are from the tribe of Levi, and that tribe will not
·receive a share of the land [Lhave an allotment or inheri-
tance] with the Israelites. They will eat the offerings made to the LORD
by fire, which is their ·share [Linheritance]. 2They will not inherit any of
the land like their brothers [Num. 26:62; Josh. 13:14; 14:4–5; 21], but

they will inherit the LORD himself [10:9; Ex. 32:25–29; Josh. 18:7], as he has promised them.

3When you offer a bull or sheep as a sacrifice, you must share with the priests, giving them the shoulder, the ·cheeks [jowls], and the ·inner organs [stomach]. 4Give them the first of your grain, new wine, and oil, as well as the first wool you cut from your sheep. 5The LORD your God has chosen the priests and their ·descendants [sons] out of all your tribes to stand and serve ·the [Lin the name of the] LORD ·always [Lall their days; 33:8–11].

6If a Levite moves from one of your ·towns [Lgates] anywhere in Israel where he ·lives [resides; sojourns] and comes to the place the LORD will choose [12:4–7], because ·he wants [Lhis soul desires] to serve the LORD there, 7he may serve ·the [Lthe name of the] LORD his God. He will be like his ·fellow [Lbrother] Levites who ·serve [Lstand] there before the LORD. 8They all will have an equal share of the food. That is separate from what he has received from the sale of family possessions.

Do Not Follow Other Nations

9When you enter the land the LORD your God is giving you, don't learn to do the ·hateful [detestable; abhorrent; abominable] things the other nations do. 10Don't let anyone among you offer a son or daughter as a sacrifice in the fire [12:30–31]. Don't let anyone use ·magic [divination; Ex. 7:11; Ezek. 21:21] or witchcraft, or ·try to explain the meaning of signs [augury or sorcery]. 11Don't let anyone ·try to control others with magic [cast spells], and don't let them ·be mediums [consult/inquire of ghosts or spirits] or try to ·talk with the spirits of [consult] dead people [1 Sam. 28]. 12The LORD ·hates [detests] anyone who does these things. Because the other nations do these things, the LORD your God will ·force [dispossess] them out of the land ahead of you. 13But you must be ·innocent [blameless] in the presence of the LORD your God.

The Lord's Special Prophet

14The nations you will ·force out [dispossess] listen to people who use ·magic [divination] and witchcraft, but the LORD your God will not let you do those things. 15The LORD your God will ·give [Lraise up for] you a prophet like me, who is one of your own ·people [relatives; brothers; Cultimately Jesus]. Listen to him [Acts 3:25–26; 7:37]. 16This is what you asked the LORD your God to do when you were ·gathered [assembled] at ·Mount Sinai [Horeb; 1:6]. You said, "Don't make ·us [Lme] listen to the voice of the LORD ·our [Lmy] God again, and don't make ·us [Lme] look at this ·terrible [great] fire anymore, or ·we [LI] will die [5:23–27]."

17So the LORD said to me, "What they have said is good. 18So I will ·give [Lraise up for] them a prophet like you, who is one of their own ·people [relatives; brothers]. I will ·tell him what to say [Lput my words in his mouth], and he will tell them everything I command. 19This prophet will speak for me; anyone who does not listen when he speaks in my name will ·answer [be accountable] to me. 20But if a prophet ·says something I did not tell him to say as though he were speaking for me [Lspeaks presumptuously in my name a word I did not command him to speak], or if a prophet speaks in the name of other gods, that prophet must be killed [Jer. 28:15–17]."

21You might be ·thinking [Lsaying in your heart/mind], "How can we know if a message is not from the LORD?" 22If what a prophet says in the name of the LORD does not happen, it is not the LORD's message. That prophet was speaking ·his own ideas [presumptuously]. Don't be afraid of him.

Cities of Safety

19 When the LORD your God gives you land that belongs to the
other nations, nations that he will ·destroy [cut off], you will
·force them out [dispossess them] and live in their cities and houses.
2Then ·choose [set apart; separate] three cities in the middle of the land
the LORD your God is giving you as your ·own [possession]. 3·Build
roads to these cities [or Work out the distances], and divide the land the
LORD is giving you into three parts so that someone who kills another
person may run to ·these cities [Lthere].
4This is the rule for someone who kills another person and runs to one
of these cities in order to save his life [Ex. 21:13–14; Num. 35:6–34; Josh.
20]. But the person must have killed a neighbor ·without meaning to
[accidentally; unintentionally], not out of hatred. 5For example, suppose
someone goes into the forest with a neighbor to cut wood and swings an
ax to cut down a tree. If the ax head ·flies [slips] off the handle, ·hitting
and killing [Lfinds] the neighbor, the one who killed him may run to one
of these cities to save his life. 6Otherwise, the ·dead person's relative who
has the duty of punishing a murderer [near-kinsman; Lavenger of blood]
might be angry and chase him. If the city is far away, the relative might
·catch [Lpursue and overtake] and kill the person, even though he should
not be killed because there was no intent to kill his neighbor. 7This is why
I command you to ·choose [set apart; separate] these three cities.
8-9Carefully obey all these laws I'm ·giving [commanding] you today.
Love the LORD your God, and always do what he wants you to do. Then the
LORD your God will enlarge your ·land [boundaries] as he ·promised [Lswore
to] your ·ancestors [fathers], giving you the whole land he promised to
them. After that, ·choose three more cities of safety [Ladd three more cities
to these three] 10so that innocent ·people will not be killed [Lblood will not
be shed] in your land, the land that the LORD your God is giving you as your
·own [Linheritance]. ·By doing this you will not be guilty of allowing the
death of innocent people [L...bringing bloodguilt on you].
11But if a person hates his neighbor and, after ·hiding and waiting
[lying in wait], ·attacks [Lrises up] and ·kills [Lstrikes] him and then runs
to one of these cities for safety, 12the elders of his own city should send for
the murderer. They should bring the person back from the city of safety
and hand him over to the ·relative who has the duty of punishing the
murderer [near-kinsman; Lavenger of blood]. 13·Show no mercy [LDo not
let your eyes show compassion on him]. You must ·remove [banish; purge]
from Israel the ·guilt of murdering [Lblood of] innocent people so that
things will go well for you.
14Do not move the ·stone that marks the border [boundary marker] of
your neighbor's land, which people long ago set in place [27:17; Job 24:2–
4; Prov. 23:10–11; Hos. 5:10]. It marks what you inherit in the land the
LORD your God is giving you as your ·own [possession].

Rules About Witnesses

15One witness is not enough to accuse a person of a crime or sin. A case
must be proved by two or three witnesses [17:6; Num. 35:30].
16If a witness ·lies [is malicious/unjust] and accuses a person of a crime,
17the two people who are arguing must stand in the presence of the LORD
before the priests and judges who are ·on duty [in office in those days].
18The judges must check the matter carefully. The witness who is a liar,
lying about a ·fellow Israelite [relative; brother], 19must be punished. He
must be punished in the same way the ·other person [relative; brother]

would have been punished. You must ·get rid of [banish; purge] the evil
among you. 20The rest of the people will hear about this and be afraid,
and no one among you will ever do such an evil thing again. 21·Show no
mercy [LDo not let your eyes show compassion on him]. A life must be
paid for a life, an eye for an eye, a tooth for a tooth, a hand for a hand, a
foot for a foot [Ex. 21:24–25; Lev. 24:17–20].

Laws for War

20 When you go to war against your enemies and you see horses
and chariots and an army that is bigger than yours, don't be
afraid of them. The LORD your God, who brought you out of Egypt, will
be with you. 2The priest must ·come [approach] and speak to the army
before you ·go into [engage in] battle. 3He will say, "Listen, Israel! Today
you are going into battle against your enemies. Don't lose ·your courage
[Lheart] or be afraid. Don't panic or be ·frightened [in dread], 4because
the LORD your God goes with you, to fight for you against your enemies
and to ·save you [give you the victory]."
5The ·officers [or scribes] should say to the army, "·Has anyone [LWho
has] built a new house but not ·given it to God [dedicated it]? He may go
home, because he might die in battle and someone else would ·get to give
his house to God [dedicate it]. 6·Has anyone [LWho has] planted a vineyard and not begun to enjoy it? He may go home, because he might die in
battle and someone else would enjoy his vineyard. 7·Is any man [LWho is]
engaged to a woman and not yet married to her? He may go home,
because he might die in battle and someone else would marry her." 8Then
the ·officers [or scribes] should also say, "Is anyone here afraid? Has anyone lost ·his courage [Lheart]? He may go home so that he will not ·cause
others to lose their courage, too [Lmelt the hearts of his relatives/brothers
like his heart]." 9When the ·officers [scribes] finish speaking to the army,
they should appoint commanders to lead it.
10When you march up to attack a city, first make them an offer of
peace. 11If they accept your offer and open their gates to you, all the people of that city will ·become your slaves and work for you [serve you in
forced labor]. 12But if they do not make peace with you and fight you in
battle, you should ·surround [besiege] that city. 13The LORD your God will
give it ·to you [Linto your hands]. Then ·kill [Lstrike] all the men with your
swords, 14and you may take ·everything else [all the plunder] in the city
for yourselves. Take the women, children, and animals, and you may use
·these things [the plunder] the LORD your God gives you from your enemies. 15Do this to all the cities that are far away, that do not belong to the
nations nearby.
16But ·leave nothing alive [Ldo not let anything that breathes live] in the
cities of the land the LORD your God is giving you as an inheritance.
17·Completely destroy [Devote to the LORD; Josh. 6:17] these people: the
Hittites, Amorites, Canaanites, Perizzites, Hivites, and Jebusites, as the
LORD your God has commanded. 18Otherwise, they will teach you what
they do for their gods, and if you do these ·hateful [detestable; abhorrent;
abominable] things, you will sin against the LORD your God.
19If you ·surround [besiege] and attack a city for ·a long time [Lmany
days], trying to capture it, do not destroy its trees with an ax. You can eat
the fruit from the trees, but do not cut them down. ·These trees are not
the enemy, so don't make war against them [LAre these trees of the field
human that you should go against them in siege?]. 20But you may cut

down trees that you know are not fruit trees and use them to build devices to attack the city walls, until the city is captured.

A Person Found Murdered

21 Suppose ·someone is found murdered [La corpse], lying in a field in the land the LORD your God is giving you as your ·own [possession], and no one knows who ·killed [Lstruck] the person. 2Your elders and judges should go to where the ·body [Lcorpse] was found, and they should measure how far it is to the nearby cities. 3The elders of the city nearest the body must take a ·young cow [heifer] that has never worked or ·worn [Lpulled] a yoke, 4and they must lead her down to a ·valley [wadi] that has never been plowed or planted, with a ·stream [wadi] flowing through it. There they must break the ·young cow's [heifer's] neck. 5The priests, the sons of Levi, should come forward, because they have been chosen by the LORD your God to serve him and to give blessings in the LORD's name. They are the ones who decide cases of ·quarreling [accusation] and attacks. 6Then all the elders of the city nearest the ·murdered person [Lcorpse] should wash their hands over the ·young cow [heifer] whose neck was broken in the ·valley [wadi]. 7They should declare: "·We did not kill this person [LOur hands did not spill this blood], and ·we [Lour eyes] did not see it happen. 8LORD, ·remove this sin from [make atonement for] your people Israel, whom you have ·saved [redeemed; ransomed]. Don't ·blame your people, the Israelites, for the murder of this innocent person [Lplace the guilt of innocent blood in the midst of your people Israel]." And so the murder will be ·paid [atoned] for. 9Then you will have ·removed [banished; purged] from yourselves the guilt of ·murdering an innocent person [innocent blood], because you will be doing what ·the LORD says is right [Lis right/virtuous in the eyes of the LORD].

Captive Women as Wives

10When you go to war against your enemies, the LORD will ·help you defeat them [Lgive them into your hands] so you will take them captive. 11If you see a beautiful woman among the captives and ·are attracted to [desire; fall in love with] her, you may take her as your wife. 12Bring her into your home, where she must shave her head and cut her nails 13and change the clothes she was wearing when you captured her. After she has lived in your house and cried for her ·parents [Lfather and her mother] for a month, you may marry her. You will be her husband, and she will be your wife. 14But if you are not pleased with her, you must let her go anywhere she wants. You must not sell her for money or make her a slave, because you have ·taken away her honor [humiliated; exploited her].

The Oldest Son

15A man might have two wives, one he loves and one he ·doesn't [Lhates; dislikes]. Both wives might have sons by him. If the ·older son [firstborn] belongs to the wife he ·does not love [Lhates; dislikes], 16when that man wills his property to his sons he must not give the son of the wife he loves what belongs to the ·older [firstborn] son, the son of the wife he ·does not love [Lhates; dislikes]. 17He must agree to give the ·older son [firstborn] two shares of everything he owns, even though the ·older son [firstborn] is from the wife he does ·not love [Lhates; dislikes]. That son was the first ·to prove his father could have children [Lof his virility], so he has the rights that belong to the ·older son [firstborn].

Sons Who Refuse to Obey

18If someone has a son who is stubborn, who ·turns [rebels] against his father and mother and doesn't obey them or listen when they ·correct [discipline] him, 19his ·parents [Lmother and his father] must ·take [grab] him to the elders at the city gate [Ex. 21:15; Lev. 20:9]. 20They will say to the elders, "Our son is stubborn and ·turns [rebels] against us. He will not obey us. He ·eats too much [is a glutton], and he is ·always drunk [a drunk]." 21Then all the men in his town must ·throw stones at [stone] him until he dies. ·Get rid of [Banish; Purge] the evil among you, because then all the people of Israel will hear about this and be afraid.

Other Laws

22If someone is guilty of a sin worthy of death, he must be put to death and his body ·displayed [hung] on a tree. 23But don't leave his body hanging on the tree overnight; be sure to bury him that same day, because anyone whose body is displayed on a tree is cursed by God [Matt. 27:57–58; Gal. 3:13]. You must not ruin the land the LORD your God is giving you as your ·own [Linheritance].

22 If you see your ·fellow Israelite's [relative's; brother's] ox or sheep wandering away, don't ignore it. Take it back to ·its owner [your relative/brother; Ex. 23:4–5]. 2If ·the owner [your relative/brother] does not live close to you, or if you do not know who the owner is, take the animal home with you. Keep it until ·the owner [your relative/brother] comes looking for it; then give it back. 3Do the same thing if you find a donkey or ·coat [cloak; garment] or anything someone lost. Don't just ignore it.

4If you see your ·fellow Israelite's [relative's; brother's] donkey or ox fallen on the road, don't ignore it. Help the owner get it up.

5A woman must not wear men's ·clothes [apparel; items], and a man must not wear women's clothes. The LORD your God ·hates [detests] anyone who does that.

6If you find a bird's nest by the road, either in a tree or on the ground, and the mother bird is sitting on the young birds or eggs, do not take the mother bird with the young birds. 7You may take the young birds, but you must let the mother bird go free. Then things will go well for you, and you will live a long time.

8When you build a new house, build a ·low wall around the edge of [a fence/parapet on] the roof [Cthe flat roofs of Israelite houses were used for living space] so you will not ·be guilty [have bloodguilt] if someone falls off the roof [Cto avoid negligent homicide].

9Don't plant two different kinds of seeds in your vineyard. Otherwise, ·both crops will be ruined [Lthe fullness will be forfeit, both the seed that has been sown as well as the produce of the vineyard; Cto avoid unnatural combinations, perhaps as a reminder that Israelites were to be separate from Gentiles, see also vv. 10–11].

10Don't plow with an ox and a donkey tied together.

11Don't wear clothes made of wool and linen woven together.

12Tie several pieces of thread together; then put these tassels on the four corners of your coat [Cperhaps to weigh down the garment to avoid exposure].

Marriage Laws

13If a man marries a girl and has sexual relations with her but then decides he ·does not like [Lhates] her, 14he might ·talk badly about her [charge her with wanton behavior] and give her a bad name. He might say, "I married this woman, but when I ·had sexual relations with [approached] her, I did not find that she was a virgin." 15Then the girl's ·parents [Lfather and mother] must bring ·proof [evidence] that she was a virgin to the

elders at the city gate. 16The girl's father will say to the elders, "I gave my
daughter to this man to be his wife, but now he ·does not want [Lhates] her.
17This man has ·told lies about my daughter [charged my daughter with
wanton behavior]. He has said, 'I did not find your daughter to be a virgin,'
but here is the ·proof [evidence] that my daughter was a virgin." Then her
parents are to show the sheet [Cblood-stained, showing she had been a vir-
gin] to the elders of the city, 18and the elders must take the man and
·punish [discipline] him. 19They must make him pay about ·two and one-
half pounds [Lone hundred shekels] of silver to the girl's father, because
the man has given an Israelite virgin a bad name. The girl will continue to
be the man's wife, and he may not divorce her as long as he lives.
20But if ·the things the husband said about his wife are [Lthis word/
charge is] true, and there is no ·proof [evidence] that she was a virgin, 21the
girl must be brought to the door of her father's house. Then the men of the
town must put her to death by ·throwing stones at [stoning] her. She has
done a ·disgraceful [shameful] thing in Israel by ·having sexual relations
before she was married [Lacting like a prostitute in the house of her father].
You must ·get rid of [banish; purge] the evil among you.
22If a man is found ·having sexual relations [Llying] with another man's
wife, both the woman and the man who ·had sexual relations [Llay] with
her must die. ·Get rid of [Banish; Purge] this evil from Israel.
23If a man meets a virgin in a city and ·has sexual relations [Llies] with her,
but she is engaged to another man, 24you must take both of them to the city
gate and ·put them to death by throwing stones at [stone] them. Kill the girl,
because she was in a city and did not scream for help. And kill the man for
having sexual relations with ·another man's wife [the wife of his neighbor/
friend]. You must ·get rid of [banish; purge] the evil among you.
25But if a man meets an engaged girl out in the ·country [field] and
·forces her to have sexual relations with him [Lseizes her and lies with her],
only the man who ·had sexual relations [Llay] with her must be put to
death. 26Don't do anything to the girl, because she has not done a sin worthy of death. This is like the person who ·attacks [rises up] and murders a
neighbor; 27the man found the engaged girl in the ·country [field] and she
·screamed [yelled for help], but no one was there to ·save [rescue] her.
28If a man meets a virgin who is not engaged to be married and ·forces
her to have sexual relations with him [Lgrabs her and lies with her] and
·people find out about it [Lis discovered], 29the man who ·had sexual relations [Llay] with her must pay the girl's father about ·one and one-fourth
pounds [Lfifty shekels] of silver. He must also marry the girl, because he
has ·dishonored [humiliated; raped] her, and he may never divorce her
for as long as he lives [Ex. 22:16–17].
30A man must not marry his father's wife; he must not ·dishonor his
father in this way [Luncover his father's skirt; Lev. 18:7–8; 20:11].

The Lord's People

23 No man who has had ·part of his sex organ [Lhis testicles
crushed or his penis] cut off may come into the ·meeting to
worship [assembly of] the LORD [Acts 8:26–40].
2No one born ·to parents who were forbidden by law to marry [of a
forbidden marriage] may come into the ·meeting to worship [assembly of]
the LORD. The descendants for ten generations may not come in either.
3No Ammonite or Moabite may come into the ·meeting to worship
[assembly of] the LORD, and none of their descendants for ten generations

may come in. 4This is because the Ammonites and Moabites did not give you bread and water when you came out of Egypt. And they hired Balaam son of Beor, from Pethor in Northwest Mesopotamia, to put a curse on you [Num. 22–24]. 5But the LORD your God would not listen to Balaam. He ·turned [transformed; overturned] the curse into a blessing for you, because the LORD your God loves you. 6Don't ·wish for [seek] their peace or ·success [prosperity] as long as you live.

7Don't ·hate [detest] Edomites; they are your ·close relatives [brothers; Cdescendants of Esau the brother of Jacob/Israel]. Don't ·hate [detest] Egyptians, because you were ·foreigners [resident aliens] in their country [Cduring the time of Joseph, God's people survived a famine in Egypt; Gen. 41–42]. 8·The great-grandchildren of these two peoples [Ltheir children to the third generation] may come into the ·meeting to worship [assembly of] the LORD.

Keeping the Camp Clean

9When you are camped ·in time of war [Lagainst your enemies], keep away from ·unclean things [foulness; La bad/evil thing; Creferring to ritual uncleanness]. 10If a man becomes unclean during the night, he must go outside the camp and not come back [Creferring to an emission of semen; Lev. 15:16]. 11But when evening comes, he must wash himself, and at sunset he may come back into the camp.

12Choose a place outside the camp where people may go ·to relieve themselves [Loutside]. 13·Carry a tent peg with you [LAs part of your equipment have a tent peg/*or* trowel with you], and when you ·relieve yourself [squat; Lsit], dig a hole and cover up your ·dung [excrement]. 14The LORD your God ·moves [walks] around through your camp to protect you and to defeat your enemies for you, so the camp must be holy. He must not see anything ·unclean [indecent] among you so that he will not leave you.

Other Laws

15If an escaped slave comes to you, do not hand over the slave to his master. 16Let the slave live with you anywhere he likes, in any ·town [gate] he chooses. Do not ·mistreat [oppress; exploit] him.

17No Israelite ·man [Lson] or ·woman [Ldaughter] must ever become a ·temple [sacred] prostitute. 18Do not bring ·a male or female prostitute's pay [Lthe pay of a prostitute or the price of a "dog"; C"dog" is probably a reference to a male temple prostitute] to the ·Temple [Lhouse] of the LORD your God to pay what you have ·promised [vowed] to the LORD, because the LORD your God ·hates [detests] ·prostitution [Lboth of them; Cmale and female temple prostitution].

19If you loan your ·fellow Israelites [relatives; brothers] money or food or anything else, don't make them pay back ·more than you loaned them [interest; Ex. 22:25; Lev. 25:36–37]. 20You may charge foreigners, but not ·fellow Israelites [Lyour relatives/brothers]. Then the LORD your God will bless ·everything you do [your undertakings; Lall that is sent out from your hand] in the land you are entering to ·take as your own [possess].

21If you make a ·promise [vow] to give ·something [a vow] to the LORD your God [Lev. 7:16–17; Num. 30:2–17], do not ·be slow [delay] to pay it, because the LORD your God ·demands [will surely seek] it from you. Do not be guilty of sin. 22But if you do not make the ·promise [vow], you will not be guilty. 23You must do whatever ·you say you will do [Lcomes out of your lips], because you ·chose to make [Lfreely made with your own mouth] the ·promise [vow] to the LORD your God [Eccl. 5:4–5].

24If you go into your neighbor's vineyard, you may eat as many grapes

as you wish, but do not put any grapes into your basket. 25If you go into
your neighbor's grainfield, you may pick grain with your hands, but you
must not cut down your neighbor's grain with your sickle.

24 A man might marry a woman but later decide she doesn't
·please him [Lfind favor in his eyes] because he has found
something ·bad [indecent; objectionable] about her. He writes out
divorce papers for her, ·gives them to her [Lplaces them in her hand], and
sends her away from his house. 2After she leaves his house, she goes and
marries another man, 3but her second husband ·does not like her either
[hates her]. So he writes out divorce papers for her, ·gives them to her
[Lplaces them in her hand], and sends her away from his house. Or the
second husband might die. 4In either case, her first husband who
divorced her must not marry her again, because she has become ·unclean
[Cin a ritual sense]. The LORD would ·hate [detest] this. Don't bring this
sin into the land the LORD your God is giving you as your ·own
[Linheritance; Matt. 5:31–32; 19:3–9].

5A man who has just married must not be sent ·to war [Lwith the army]
or be given any other duty. He should be free to stay home for a year to
make his new wife happy [20:7].

6If someone owes you ·something [a pledge], do not take his two stones
for grinding grain—not even the upper one—·in place of what he owes
[as a pledge], ·because this is how the person makes a living [Lthat would
be taking a person's life as a pledge].

7If someone ·kidnaps a fellow Israelite [Lis found stealing one of his
brothers from among the sons/Tchildren of Israel], either to make him a
slave or sell him, the ·kidnapper [robber] must be killed. You must ·get rid
of [banish; purge] the evil among you [Ex. 21:16].

8Be careful when someone has a ·skin disease [Tleprosy; Cthe term does
not refer to modern leprosy (Hansen's disease), but to various skin disorders; Lev. 13:2]. Do exactly what the priests, the Levites, teach you, being
careful to do what I have commanded them. 9Remember what the LORD
your God did to Miriam on your way out of Egypt [Num. 12:10].

10When you make a loan to your neighbors, don't go into their homes
to get ·something in place of it [a pledge]. 11Stay outside and let them go
in and get what they ·promised [pledged to] you. 12If a poor person gives
you a ·coat to show he will pay the loan back [Lpledge], don't keep it
overnight. 13Give the ·coat [Lpledge] back at sunset, because your neighbor needs that coat to sleep in, and he will ·be grateful to [bless] you.
And the LORD your God will see that you have done a ·good [righteous]
thing.

14Don't ·cheat [oppress; exploit] hired servants who are poor and needy,
whether they are ·fellow Israelites [relatives; brothers] or ·foreigners [resi-
dent aliens] living in one of your ·towns [gates]. 15Pay them each day before
sunset, because they are poor and need the money. Otherwise, they may
·complain [cry out] to the LORD about you, and you will be guilty of sin.

16·Parents [Fathers] must not be put to death if their children do
wrong, and children must not be put to death if their ·parents [fathers] do
wrong. Each person must die for his own sin [Jer. 31:29–30; Ezek.
18:1–4].

17Do not be unfair to a ·foreigner [resident alien] or an orphan. Don't
take a widow's coat ·to make sure she pays you back [as a pledge; 24:10–
13]. 18Remember that you were slaves in Egypt, and the LORD your God

·saved [ransomed; redeemed] you from there. That is why I am commanding you to do this.
19When you are ·gathering [reaping] your harvest in the field and
·leave behind [Lforget] a bundle of grain, don't go back and get it. Leave it
there for ·foreigners [resident aliens], orphans, and widows so that the
Lord your God can bless everything you do [Ruth 2]. 20When you beat
your olive trees to knock the olives off, don't ·beat the trees a second time.
Leave [...strip] what is left for ·foreigners [resident aliens], orphans, and
widows. 21When you harvest the grapes in your vineyard, don't ·pick the
vines a second time [glean what is left]. Leave what is left for foreigners
[resident aliens], orphans, and widows. 22Remember that you were slaves
in Egypt; that is why I am commanding you to do this [Ex. 23:11; Lev.
19:9–10; 23:22].

25 If two people have an argument and go to court, the judges
will decide the case. They will ·declare one person right
[acquit the innocent] and ·the other [convict the] guilty. 2If the guilty
person has to be ·punished with a beating [struck; flogged], the judge
will make that person lie down and be ·beaten [struck; flogged] in front
of him. The number of lashes should match the crime. 3But don't ·hit
[strike] a person more than forty times, because more than that would
disgrace ·him [your relative/neighbor] before others [2 Cor. 11:24].
4When an ox is ·working in the grain [treading the grain], do not ·cover
its mouth to keep it from eating [muzzle it; 1 Cor. 9:9].
5If two brothers are living together, and one of them dies without having a son, his widow must not marry ·someone [a stranger] outside her
husband's family. Her husband's brother must marry her, which is his
duty to her as a brother-in-law. 6The first son she has ·counts as the son of
the dead [will raise up the name of his] brother so that his name will not
be ·forgotten [blotted/wiped out] in Israel [Gen. 38; Ruth 4].
7But if a man does not want to marry his brother's widow, she should
go to the elders at the town gate. She should say, "My brother-in-law will
not ·carry on [raise up] his brother's name in Israel. He refuses to do his
duty for me."
8Then the elders of the town must call for the man and talk to him. But
if he ·is stubborn [Lstands] and says, "I don't want to marry her," 9the
woman must go up to him in ·front of the leaders [the presence of the
elders]. She must take off one of his sandals and spit in his face and say,
"This is for the man who won't ·continue [Lbuild] his brother's ·family
[Lhouse]!" 10Then that man's ·family [Lhouse] shall be known in Israel as
the ·Family [LHouse] of the Unsandaled.
11If two men are fighting and one man's wife comes to ·save [protect]
her husband from his attacker, grabbing the attacker by his ·sex organs
[genitals], 12you must cut off her hand. ·Show her no mercy [LDo not let
your eyes show compassion on her].
13Don't carry two ·sets of weights [Lstones] ·with you [Lin your bag/
pouch], one heavy and one light. 14Don't have two different sets of measures in your house, one large and one small. 15You must have ·true [whole;
full] and ·honest [accurate] weights and measures so that you will live a
long time in the land the Lord your God is giving you. 16The Lord your
God ·hates [detests] anyone who ·is dishonest and uses dishonest measures [Ldoes such things—who acts crookedly/does bad things; Lev.
19:35–37; Prov. 11:1; Ezek. 45:10–12; Amos 8:5; Mic. 6:10–12].

17Remember what the Amalekites did to you when you came out of Egypt [Ex. 17:8–16]. 18When you were tired and worn out, they met you on the road and ·attacked [picked off] all ·those lagging behind [the stragglers]. They were not afraid of God. 19When the LORD your God gives you rest from all the enemies around you in the land he ·is giving you [Lmakes you inherit] as your ·own [possession], you shall ·destroy [blot/wipe out] any memory of the Amalekites ·on the earth [Lfrom under the heavens]. Do not forget [CSaul forgot (1 Sam. 15), but the Amalekites (called Agagites) come to an end in the book of Esther (Esth. 3:1)]!

The First Harvest

26 When you go into the land the LORD your God is giving you as your ·own [Linheritance], to ·take it over [possess it] and live in it, 2you must take some of the first harvest of crops that grow from the land the LORD your God is giving you. Put the food in a basket and go to the place where the LORD your God will choose to ·be worshiped [Lcause his name to dwell; CZion; 12:4–6]. 3Go and say to the priest ·on duty at that time [in office in those days], "Today I declare before the LORD your God that I have come into the land the LORD promised our ·ancestors [fathers] that he would give us [Gen. 12:1–3]." 4The priest will take your basket and set it down in front of the altar of the LORD your God. 5Then you shall announce before the LORD your God: "My father was a wandering Aramean [Clikely a reference to Jacob/Israel's stay in Paddan-Aram; Gen. 28–31]. He went down to Egypt and lived as a ·foreigner [resident alien] with only a few people, but they became a great, powerful, and large nation there [Gen. 12:1–3]. 6But the Egyptians were ·cruel [mean] to us, ·making us suffer [afflicting/humiliating us] and ·work very hard [giving us onerous work]. 7So we ·prayed [cried out] to the LORD, the God of our ·ancestors [fathers], and he heard us. When he saw our ·trouble [affliction; humiliation], hard work, and ·suffering [oppression; Ex. 2:23–25; 3:7, 9], 8the LORD brought us out of Egypt with his ·great power [Lstrong hand] and ·strength [Loutstretched arm], using great terrors, signs, and ·miracles [wonders]. 9Then he brought us to this place and gave us this ·fertile land [Lland flowing with milk and honey; Ex. 3:8]. 10Now I bring part of the first harvest from this land that you, LORD, have given me." Place the basket before the LORD your God and bow down before him. 11Then you and the Levites and ·foreigners [resident aliens] among you should rejoice, because the LORD your God has given good things to you and your ·family [Lhouse].

12·Bring [Finish paying] a ·tenth [Ttithe] of all your harvest the third year [14:28–29] (the year to give a ·tenth [Ttithe] of your harvest). Give it to the Levites, ·foreigners [resident aliens], orphans, and widows so that they may eat in your ·towns [Lgates] and be full. 13Then say to the LORD your God, "I have taken out of my house ·the part of my harvest that belongs to God [Lwhat is holy/consecrated/sacred], and I have given it to the Levites, ·foreigners [resident aliens], orphans, and widows. I have done everything you commanded me; I have not broken your commands, and I have not forgotten any of them. 14I have not eaten any of the holy part while I was in ·sorrow [mourning]. I have not removed any of it while I was unclean [Cin a ritual sense], and I have not offered it ·for [*or* to] dead people. I have obeyed you, the LORD my God, and have done everything you commanded me. 15So look down from heaven, your holy home. Bless your people Israel and bless the land you have given us,

which you ·promised [swore] **to our ·ancestors** [fathers]**—a ·fertile land** [Lland flowing with milk and honey; Ex. 3:8].**"**

Obey the Lord's Commands

16Today the LORD your God commands you to obey all these ·rules [statutes; ordinances; requirements] **and laws; be careful to obey them with ·your whole being** [Lall your heart/mind and all your soul]. **17Today you have said that the LORD is your God, and you ·have promised to do what he wants you to do** [Lwill walk on his way/path]**—to keep his ·rules** [statutes; ordinances; requirements]**, commands, and laws. You have said you will ·obey him** [listen to his voice]. **18And today the LORD has said that you are his ·very own people** [treasured/special possession; Ex. 19:5]**, as he has promised you. But you must obey his commands. 19He will ·make you greater** [set you higher] **than all the other nations he made. He will give you praise, fame, and honor, and you will be a holy people to the LORD your God, as he has said** [Ex. 19:6].

The Law Written on Stones

27 Then Moses, along with the elders of Israel, commanded the people, saying, "Keep all the commands I have ·given [commanded] **you today. 2Soon you will cross the Jordan River to go into the land the LORD your God is giving you. On that day set up some large stones and cover them with plaster. 3When you cross over, write all the words of these ·teachings** [laws; instructions] **on them. Then you may enter the land the LORD your God is giving you, a ·fertile land** [Lland flowing with milk and honey; Ex. 3:8]**, just as the LORD, the God of your ·ancestors** [fathers]**, promised. 4After you have crossed the Jordan River, set up these stones on Mount Ebal** [11:29; Josh. 8:30–35]**, as I command you today, and cover them with plaster. 5Build an altar of stones there to the LORD your God, but don't use any iron tool to cut the stones** [Ex. 20:25]; **6build the altar of the LORD your God with ·stones from the field** [uncut stones; Lwhole stones]. **Offer burnt offerings** [Lev. 1:1–17] **on it to the LORD your God, 7and offer ·fellowship** [*or* peace; well-being] **offerings** [Lev. 3:1] **there, and eat them and rejoice before the LORD your God. 8Then write clearly all the words of these ·teachings** [laws; instructions] **on the stones."**

Curses of the Law

9Then Moses and the Levites who were priests spoke to all Israel and said, "Be ·quiet [silent]**, Israel. Listen! Today you have become the people of the LORD your God. 10·Obey** [LListen to the voice of] **the LORD your God, and keep his commands and ·laws** [statutes; ordinances; requirements] **that I ·give** [command] **you today."**

11That day Moses also gave the people this command:

12When you cross the Jordan River, these tribes must stand on Mount Gerizim to bless the people: Simeon, Levi, Judah, Issachar, Joseph and Benjamin. 13And these tribes must stand on Mount Ebal to announce the curses: Reuben, Gad, Asher, Zebulun, Dan, and Naphtali [Cthese two mountains form a natural amphitheatre].

14The Levites will say to all the people of Israel in a loud voice:

15"Anyone will be cursed who makes an idol or statue and secretly sets it up, because the LORD ·hates [detests] **the ·idols people make** [Lthe work of the hand of an artisan; 5:8–10; Ex. 20:3–5; 34:17; Is. 44:9–20].**"**

Then all the people will say, "Amen!"

16"Anyone will be cursed who dishonors his father or mother [5:16; Ex. 20:12; 21:17; Lev. 20:9].**"**

Then all the people will say, “Amen!”
17 “Anyone will be cursed who moves ·the stone that marks a neighbor’s
border [La neighbor’s boundary marker; 19:14; Job 24:2–4; Prov. 23:10–11;
Hos. 5:10].”
Then all the people will say, “Amen!”
18 “Anyone will be cursed who ·sends [misleads] a blind person down
the wrong road [Lev. 19:14].”
Then all the people will say, “Amen!”
19 “Anyone will be cursed who is ·unfair [deprives justice] to ·foreigners
[resident aliens], orphans, or widows.”
Then all the people will say, “Amen!”
20 “A man will be cursed who ·has sexual relations [Llies] with his
father’s wife, because it ·is a dishonor to [Luncovers the skirt of; Lev. 18:7–
8; 20:11] his father.”
Then all the people will say, “Amen!”
21 “Anyone will be cursed who ·has sexual relations [Llies] with an animal [Ex. 22:19; Lev. 18:23; 20:15].”
Then all the people will say, “Amen!”
22 “A man will be cursed who ·has sexual relations [Llies] with his sister,
whether she is his father’s daughter or his mother’s daughter [Lev. 18:9,
11; 20:17].”
Then all the people will say, “Amen!”
23 “A man will be cursed who ·has sexual relations [Llies] with his
mother-in-law [Lev. 18:17; 20:14].”
Then all the people will say, “Amen!”
24 “Anyone will be cursed who ·kills [Lstrikes] a neighbor secretly.”
Then all the people will say, “Amen!”
25 “Anyone will be cursed who takes ·money [a bribe] to ·murder
[Lstrike] an innocent person [Ex. 23:8].”
Then all the people will say, “Amen!”
26 “Anyone will be cursed who does not ·agree with [confirm] the words
of these ·teachings [laws; instructions] and does not obey them.”
Then all the people will say, “Amen!”

Blessings for Obeying

28 You must completely ·obey [listen to the voice of] the LORD
your God, and you must carefully follow all his commands I
am ·giving [commanding] you today. Then the LORD your God will
·make you greater [set you higher] than any other nation on earth.
2 ·Obey [Listen to the voice of] the LORD your God so that all these blessings will come and ·stay with [overtake] you:
3 You will be blessed in the city and blessed in the ·country [field].
4 ·Your children [LThe fruit of your womb] will be blessed, as well as
·your crops [Lthe fruit of your land]; your ·herds [Lthe fruit of your live-
stock] will be blessed with calves and your flocks with lambs.
5 Your basket and your ·kitchen [Lkneading bowl] will be blessed.
6 You will be blessed when you come in and when you go out.
7 The LORD will help you defeat the enemies that ·come [Lrise against
you] to fight you. They will attack you from one direction, but they will
run from you in seven directions [Cas at Jericho; Josh. 6–7].
8 The LORD your God will bless you with full barns, and he will bless
·everything you do [all your undertakings; Lall that is sent out from your
hand]. He will bless the land he is giving you.

9The LORD will make you his holy people, as he ·promised [swore; Ex. 19:6]. But you must obey his commands and ·do what he wants you to do [Lyou must walk on his way/path]. 10Then everyone on earth will see that you are ·the LORD's people [Lcalled by the name of the LORD], and they will be afraid of you. 11The LORD will make you rich: ·You will have many children, your animals will have many young, and your land will give good crops [L...in the fruit of your womb, in the fruit of your livestock, and in the fruit of your land]. It is the land that the LORD ·promised [swore to] your ·ancestors [fathers] he would give to you [Gen. 12:1–3].

12The LORD will open up his heavenly storehouse so that the skies send rain on your land at the right time, and he will bless everything you do. You will lend to other nations, but you will not need to borrow from them. 13The LORD will make you like the head and not like the tail; you will be on top and not on bottom. But you must obey the commands of the LORD your God that I am ·giving [commanding] you today, being careful to keep them. 14Do not ·disobey [Lturn aside to the right or to the left from] anything I command you today. Do exactly as I command, and do not follow other gods or serve them.

Curses for Disobeying

15But if you do not ·obey [listen to the voice of] the LORD your God and carefully follow all his commands and ·laws [statutes; ordinances; requirements] I am ·giving [commanding] you today, all these curses will come upon you and ·stay [overtake you]:

16You will be cursed in the city and cursed in the ·country [field].

17Your basket and your ·kitchen [Lkneading bowl] will be cursed.

18·Your children [LThe fruit of your womb] will be cursed, as well as ·your crops [Lthe fruit of your land]; the calves of your herds and the lambs of your flocks will be cursed.

19You will be cursed when you go in and when you go out.

20The LORD will send you curses, confusion, and punishment in ·everything you do [all your undertakings; Lall that is sent out from your hand]. You will be destroyed and suddenly ruined because you did wrong when you ·left [abandoned; forsook] him. 21The LORD will ·give [make cling to] you ·terrible diseases [plagues] and destroy you from the land you are going to ·take [possess]. 22The LORD will ·punish [Lstrike] you with disease, fever, swelling, heat, lack of rain, plant diseases, and mildew until you ·die [perish]. 23The ·sky [heavens] above will be like bronze [Cgiving no rain], and the ground below will be like iron [1 Kin. 17:1]. 24The LORD will turn the rain into dust and sand, which will fall from the ·skies [heavens] until you are destroyed.

25The LORD will help your enemies defeat you [Cas at Ai; Josh. 8]. You will attack them from one direction, but you will run from them in seven directions. And you will become a thing of horror among all the kingdoms on earth. 26Your dead bodies will be food for all the birds of the ·sky [heavens] and wild animals, and there will be no one to scare them away. 27The LORD will ·punish [Lstrike] you with boils like those the Egyptians had. You will have ·bad growths [tumors; ulcers], sores, and itches that can't be ·cured [healed]. 28The LORD will ·give you [Lstrike you with] madness, blindness, and a confused mind. 29You will have to feel around ·in the daylight [at noon] like a blind person in darkness. You will ·fail in everything you do [Lnot succeed in your way]. People will ·hurt [oppress] you and steal from you every day, and no one will ·save [help] you.

30 You will be engaged to a woman, but another man will ·force her to
have sexual relations with him [have her]. You will build a house, but you
will not live in it. You will plant a vineyard, but you will not ·get its grapes
[Lenjoy it]. 31 Your ox will be ·killed [slaughtered; butchered] before your
eyes, but you will not eat any of it. Your donkey will be ·taken away [sto-
len] from you, and it will not be brought back. Your sheep will be given to
your enemies, and no one will ·save [help] you. 32 Your sons and daughters
will be given to another nation, and you will grow tired looking for them
every day, but there will be nothing you can do. 33 People you don't know
will eat the ·crops [Lfruit of] your land and hard work have produced. You
will be ·mistreated [oppressed] and ·abused [ill-treated] all your life.
34 The things ·you [Lyour eyes] see will ·cause you to go mad [drive you
crazy]. 35 The LORD will ·give you [Lstrike you with] ·sore [horrible] boils
on your knees and legs that cannot be cured, and they will go from the
soles of your feet to the tops of your heads.

36 The LORD will send you and the king whom you set over yourselves
away to a nation neither you nor your ·ancestors [fathers] know, where
you will serve other gods made of wood and stone. 37 You will become a
·hated thing [object of horror] to the nations where the LORD sends you;
·they will laugh at you and make fun of you [La proverb and a byword].

38 You will ·plant much seed in [carry out much seed to] your field, but
your harvest will be small, because locusts will ·eat the crop [consume it].
39 You will plant vineyards and work hard in them, but you will not ·pick
the grapes [harvest] or drink the wine, because the worms will eat them.
40 You will have olive trees in all your land, but you will not ·get any
[Lanoint yourself with] olive oil, because the olives will drop off the trees.
41 You will ·have [bear] sons and daughters, but you will not be able to
keep them, because they will be taken captive. 42 ·Locusts [*or* Crickets] will
·destroy [Ltake possession of] all your trees and crops.

43 The ·foreigners [resident aliens] who live among you will ·get stronger and stronger [go higher and higher], and you will ·get weaker and
weaker [go lower and lower]. 44 ·Foreigners [LThey] will lend money to
you, but you will not be able to lend to them. They will be like the head,
and you will be like the tail.

45 All these curses will come upon you. They will ·chase [pursue] you
and ·catch [overtake] you and destroy you, because you did not ·obey
[listen to the voice of] the LORD your God and keep the commands and
·laws [statutes; ordinances; requirements] he ·gave [commanded] you.
46 The curses will be signs and ·miracles [wonders] to you and your
·descendants [Lseed] forever. 47 You had plenty of everything, but you did
not serve the LORD your God with joy and a ·pure [*or* glad] heart, 48 so you
will serve the enemies the LORD sends against you. You will be hungry,
thirsty, naked, and poor, and the LORD will put a ·load on you [Lyoke of
bronze on your neck] until he has destroyed you [Jer. 28:14].

The Curse of an Enemy Nation

49 The LORD will bring a nation against you from far away, from the end
of the world, and it will swoop down like an eagle. You won't ·understand
their language [Lhear its tongue; Jer. 5:15–17], 50 and they will ·look mean
[be stern-faced]. They will not ·respect [show favoritism to] old people or
·feel sorry for [favor; have compassion for] the young. 51 They will eat the
·calves from your herds and the harvest of your field [Lfruit of your livestock and the fruit of your land], and you will be destroyed. They will not

leave you any grain, new wine or oil, or any calves from your herds or lambs from your flocks. You will ·be ruined [perish]. 52That nation will ·surround and attack [besiege] all your ·cities [Lgates]. You trust in your high, ·strong [fortified] walls, but they will fall down. That nation will ·surround [besiege] all your ·cities [gates] everywhere in the land the LORD your God is giving you.

53·Your enemy will surround you. Those people will make you starve so that [LIn the dire position that the siege of your enemies places you] you will eat ·your own babies [Lthe fruit of your womb], the ·bodies [Lflesh] of the sons and daughters the LORD your God gave you. 54Even the most gentle and kind man among you will ·become cruel [look threateningly] to his brother, his wife ·whom he loves [Lof his lap], and his children who ·are still alive [remain]. 55He will not even give them any of the flesh of his children he is eating, because it will be all he has left. ·Your enemy will surround you and make you starve [LIn the dire position that the siege of your enemies places you] in all your ·cities [Lgates]. 56The most gentle and kind woman among you, so gentle and kind she would hardly even walk on the ground, will ·be cruel [look threateningly] to her husband ·whom she loves [Lof her lap] and to her son and daughter. 57She will give birth to a baby, but she will plan to eat the baby and ·what comes after the birth itself [the afterbirth; Lthat which comes out between her feet]. She will eat them secretly ·while the enemy surrounds the city. Those people will make you starve in all your cities [L…in the dire position that the siege of your enemies places you; Lam. 2:20].

58Be careful to obey everything in these ·teachings [laws; instructions] that are written in this ·book [scroll]. You must respect the glorious and ·wonderful [awesome] name of the LORD your God, 59or the LORD will give terrible diseases to you and your ·descendants [Lseed]. You will have long and serious diseases, and long and miserable sicknesses. 60He will ·give [bring back to] you all the diseases of Egypt that you dread, and the diseases will ·stay with [cling to] you. 61The LORD will also give you every disease and sickness not written in this ·Book [Scroll] of the ·Teachings [Law; Instruction], until you are destroyed. 62You people may have outnumbered the stars [Gen. 15:5; 22:17; 26:41; Ex. 32:13], but only a few of you will be left, because you did not ·obey [listen to the voice of] the LORD your God. 63Just as the LORD was once ·happy [pleased; delighted] with you and gave you ·good things [prosperity] and made you grow in number, so then the LORD will be ·happy [pleased; delighted] to ruin and destroy you, and you will be removed from the land you are entering to take as your ·own [possession].

64Then the LORD will scatter you among the nations—from one end of the earth to the other [Jer. 9:16; 18:17; Ezek. 12:15]. There you will serve other gods of wood and stone, gods that neither you nor your ·ancestors [fathers] have known. 65You will have no rest among those nations and no place that is yours. The LORD will make your ·mind [*or* heart] ·worried [tremble], your ·sight weak [eyes fail], and your soul ·sad [languish; Cdepressed]. 66You will live ·with danger [in suspense] and be afraid night and day. You will not be sure that you will live. 67In the morning you will say, "·I wish [O that] it were evening," and in the evening you will say, "·I wish [O that] it were morning." ·Terror [Dread] will be in your heart, and the things you have seen will scare you. 68The LORD will send you back to Egypt in ships, even though ·I, Moses, [LI; Cpossibly a reference to God] said you would never go back to Egypt. And there you will try to sell yourselves as slaves to your enemies, but no one will buy you.

The Agreement in Moab

29 The LORD commanded Moses to ·make [Lcut] an ·agreement [covenant; treaty] with the ·Israelites [Lsons/Tchildren of Israel] in Moab in addition to the ·agreement [covenant; treaty] he had ·made [Lcut] with them at ·Mount Sinai [LHoreb; 1:6]. These are the words of that ·agreement [covenant; treaty].

2Moses called all the Israelites together and said to them:

You have seen everything the LORD did before your own eyes to ·the king of Egypt [LPharaoh] and to ·the king's [Lhis] leaders and to the whole country. 3With your own eyes you saw the great ·troubles [trials; tests], signs, and ·miracles [wonders]. 4But to this day the LORD has not given you a ·mind [heart] that understands; you don't really understand what you see with your eyes or hear with your ears. 5I led you through the ·desert [wilderness] for forty years, and during that time neither your clothes nor sandals wore out [8:4]. 6You ate no bread and drank no wine or ·beer [Tstrong drink; Calcoholic beverage made from grain]. This was so you would understand that I am the LORD your God.

7When you came to this place, Sihon king of Heshbon and Og king of Bashan came out to fight us, but we ·defeated [Lstruck] them [Num. 21:21–35]. 8We captured their land and gave it to the tribes of Reuben, Gad, and ·East [Lthe half-tribe of] Manasseh ·to be their own [Las an inheritance; Num. 32].

9You must carefully obey everything in this ·agreement [covenant; treaty] so that you will ·succeed [prosper] in everything you do. 10Today you are all standing here before the LORD your God—your leaders and important men, your elders, ·officers [scribes], and all the other men of Israel, 11your wives and children and the ·foreigners [resident aliens] who ·live among you [Lare in the midst of your camp], who chop your wood and carry your water. 12You are all here to enter into an ·agreement [covenant; treaty] ·and a promise with the LORD your God [sworn by an oath], an ·agreement [covenant; treaty] the LORD your God is ·making [Lcutting] with you today. 13This will make you today his own people. He will be your God, as he told you and as he ·promised [swore to] your ·ancestors [fathers] Abraham, Isaac, and Jacob [Gen. 12:1–3; 15:17–20]. 14But I am not just making this ·agreement [covenant; treaty] ·and its promises [sworn by an oath] with you 15who are standing here before the LORD your God today, but also with those who are not here today.

16You know how we lived in Egypt and how we passed through the countries when we came here. 17You saw their ·hateful idols [Ldetestable things, the filthy idols] made of wood, stone, silver, and gold. 18Make sure no man, woman, ·family group [clan], or tribe among you ·leaves [Lwhose heart turns away from] the LORD our God to go and serve the gods of those nations. They would be to you like a ·plant [Lroot] that grows bitter, poisonous fruit.

19These are the kind of people who hear ·these curses [*or* the words of this oath] but bless themselves ·internally [Lin their hearts/minds], thinking, "We will ·be safe [have peace] ·even though we continue doing what we want to do." Those people may destroy all of your land, both wet and dry [*or* if we act with determination so water may bring an end to the drought]. 20The LORD will ·not [be unwilling to] forgive them. His anger

will be like a burning fire against those people, and all the curses written
in this ·book [scroll] will come on them [chs. 27–28]. The LORD will
·destroy [blot out; wipe away] ·any memory of them on the earth [Ltheir
name from under the heavens]. 21He will separate them from all the tribes
of Israel for punishment. All the curses of the ·Agreement [Covenant;
Treaty] that are written in this ·Book [Scroll] of the ·Teachings [Laws;
Instructions] will happen to them.

22Your children, the generation that will come after you, as well as foreigners from faraway lands, will see the disasters that come to this land
and the diseases the LORD will send on it. They will say, 23"The land is
·nothing but burning cinders [burned by sulphur] and salt. Nothing is
planted, nothing grows, and nothing blooms. It is like Sodom and
Gomorrah [Gen. 19], and Admah and Zeboiim [Gen. 14:2; Hos. 11:8],
which the LORD ·destroyed [overturned] ·because he was very angry [Lin
his anger and his wrath]." 24All the other nations will ask, "Why has the
LORD done this to the land? Why is he so angry?"

25And the answer will be, "It is because the people broke the ·Agreement
[Covenant; Treaty] of the LORD, the God of their ·ancestors [fathers],
which he ·made [Lcut] with them when he brought them out of Egypt.
26They went and served other gods and bowed down to gods they did not
even know. The LORD did not ·allow [permit] that, 27so he became very
angry at the land and brought all the curses on it that are written in this
·book [scroll; chs. 27–28]. 28Since the LORD became angry, upset, and furious with them, he took them out of their land and put them in another
land where they are today."

29There are some things the LORD our God has kept secret, but there are
some things he has ·let us know [revealed]. These things belong to us and
our children forever so that we will do everything in these ·teachings
[laws; instructions].

The Israelites Will Return

30 When all these blessings and curses I have described happen
to you, and the LORD your God has ·sent [driven] you away to
other nations [2 Kin. 25:1–21; 2 Chr. 36:17–20; Jer. 39:1–10; 52:1–30],
·think about [call to mind; meditate on] these things. 2Then you and your
children will return to the LORD your God, and you will ·obey him [listen
to his voice] with ·your whole being [Lall your heart/mind and all your
soul] in everything I am commanding you today. 3Then the LORD your
God will ·give you back your freedom [restore your fortunes]. He will ·feel
sorry for [have mercy on] you, and he will bring you back again from the
nations where he scattered you [2 Chr. 36:22–23; Ezra 1:1—2:70]. 4He
may ·send [drive] you to the ends of the ·earth [Lheavens], but he will
gather you and bring you back from there, 5back to the land that
belonged to your ·ancestors [fathers]. It will be yours. He will give you
success, and there will be more of you than there were of your ·ancestors
[fathers]. 6The LORD your God will ·prepare you and your descendants
[Lcircumcise your heart and the heart of your seed] to love him with
·your whole being [Lall your heart/mind and all your soul] so that you
will live. 7The LORD your God will put all these curses on your enemies,
who hate you and ·are cruel to [persecute] you. 8And you will again
·obey [listen to the voice of] the LORD, keeping all his commands that I
·give [command] you today. 9The LORD your God will make you ·suc-
cessful [prosperous] in ·everything you do [Lall the work of your hands].

·You will have many children, your cattle will have many calves, and
your fields will produce good crops [L...in the fruit of your womb, in the
fruit of your livestock, and in the fruit of your land], because the LORD
will again be ·happy [pleased; delighted] with you, just as he was with
your ·ancestors [fathers]. 10But you must ·obey [listen to the voice of]
the LORD your God by keeping all his commands and ·rules [statutes;
ordinances; requirements] that are written in this ·Book [Scroll] of the
·Teachings [Laws; Instructions]. You must return to the LORD your God
with ·your whole being [Lall your heart/mind and all your soul].

Choose Life or Death

11This command I ·give [command] you today is not too hard for you;
it is not ·beyond what you can do [far away]. 12It is not up in heaven. You
do not have to ask, "Who will go up to heaven and get it for us so we can
obey it and keep it?" 13It is not on the other side of the sea. You do not
have to ask, "Who will go across the sea and get it? Who will tell it to us so
we can keep it?" 14No, the word is very near you. It is in your mouth and
in your heart so you may obey it [Rom. 10:6–8].
15Look, today I offer you life and ·success [prosperity; good things],
death and ·destruction [failure; bad things]. 16I command you today to
love the LORD your God, to ·do what he wants you to do [Lwalk in his
ways/paths], and to keep his commands, his ·rules [statutes; ordinances,
requirements], and his laws. Then you will live and ·grow in number
[multiply], and the LORD your God will bless you in the land you are
entering to take as your ·own [possession].
17But if you turn away from the LORD and do not ·obey [listen to] him,
if you are led to bow and serve other gods, 18I tell you today that you will
surely be destroyed. And you will not live long in the land you are crossing the Jordan River to enter and ·take as your own [possess].
19Today I ask heaven and earth to be witnesses. I am offering you life or
death, blessings or curses. Now, choose life! Then you and your ·children
[Lseed] may live. 20To choose life is to love the LORD your God, ·obey him
[listen to his voice], and ·stay close [cling] to him. He is your life, and he
will let you live many years in the land, the land he ·promised [swore] to
give your ·ancestors [fathers] Abraham, Isaac, and Jacob [Gen. 12:1–3;
15:17–20].

Joshua Takes Moses' Place

31 Then Moses went and spoke these words to all the Israelites:
2"I am now one hundred twenty years old, and I cannot lead
you anymore. The LORD told me I would not cross the Jordan River [Num.
20:12]; 3the LORD your God will lead you across himself. He will destroy
those nations for you, and you will take ·over [possession of] their land.
Joshua will also lead you across, as the LORD has said [1:37; Num. 27:18–
22; Josh. 1]. 4The LORD will do to those nations what he did to Sihon and
Og, the kings of the Amorites, when he destroyed them and their land
[Num. 21:21–35]. 5The LORD will give those nations to you; do to them
·everything [Laccording to all the commandments] I ·told [commanded]
you. 6Be strong and ·brave [courageous; Josh. 1:6–9]. Don't be afraid of
them and don't be frightened, because the LORD your God will go with
you. He will not ·leave [fail] you or ·forget [abandon; forsake] you."
7Then Moses called Joshua and said to him in front of the people, "Be
strong and ·brave [courageous], because you will lead these people into
the land the LORD ·promised [swore] to give their ·ancestors [fathers], and

help them take it as their own. 8The LORD himself will go before you. He will be with you; he will not ·leave [fail] you or ·forget [abandon; forsake] you. Don't be afraid and don't worry."

Moses Writes the Teachings

9So Moses wrote down these ·teachings [laws; instructions] and gave them to the priests and all the elders of Israel. (The priests are the sons of Levi, who carry the Ark of the ·Agreement [Treaty; Covenant; Ex. 25:10] with the LORD.) 10-11Then Moses commanded them: "Read these teachings for all Israel to hear at the end of every seven years, which is the year ·to cancel what people owe [of remission; 15:1–12]. Do it during the ·Feast [Festival] of ·Shelters [Booths; Tabernacles; Ex. 23:16; 34:22; Lev. 23:33–36], when all the Israelites will come to appear before the LORD your God and stand at the place he will choose [12:4–7]. 12·Gather [Assemble] all the people: the men, women, children, and ·foreigners [resident aliens] living in your ·towns [Lgates] so that they can listen and learn to ·respect [fear] the LORD your God and carefully obey everything in this ·law [teaching; instruction]. 13Since their children do not know ·this law [Lit], they must hear it. They must learn to ·respect [fear] the LORD your God for as long as they live in the land you are crossing the Jordan River to take ·for your own [as your possession]."

The Lord Calls Moses and Joshua

14The LORD said to Moses, "·Soon you will [LLook, the day is approaching for you to] die. ·Get [Call] Joshua and ·come [present him] to the Meeting Tent so that I may command him." So Moses and Joshua ·went to [presented themselves at] the Meeting Tent.

15The LORD appeared at the Meeting Tent in a pillar of cloud; the pillar of cloud stood over the entrance of the Tent [Crepresenting the presence of God; Ex. 13:21; 40:34–38]. 16And the LORD said to Moses, "You will soon ·die [Llie down/Tsleep with your fathers]. Then these people will ·not be loyal to me but will worship [Lprostitute themselves with] the foreign gods of the land they are entering. They will ·leave [abandon; forsake] me, breaking the ·Agreement [Covenant; Treaty] I ·made [Lcut] with them. 17·Then [LOn that day] I will become very angry at them, and I will ·leave [abandon; forsake] them. I will ·turn away [Lhide my face] from them, and they will be ·destroyed [devoured; consumed]. Many terrible things will happen to them. ·Then [LOn that day] they will say, '·It is [LIs it not…?] because God is not with us that these terrible things are happening.' 18I will surely ·turn away [Lhide my face] from them ·then [Lon that day], because they have done wrong and have turned to other gods.

19"Now write down this song and teach it to the ·Israelites [Lsons/Tchildren of Israel]. ·Then have them sing it [LPlace it in their mouth], because it will be my witness against ·them [Lthe sons/Tchildren of Israel]. 20When I bring them into the land I ·promised [swore] to their ·ancestors [fathers], a ·fertile land [Lland flowing with milk and honey; Ex. 3:8], they will eat as much as they want and get fat. Then they will turn to other gods and serve them. They will ·reject [despise] me and break my ·Agreement [Covenant; Treaty]. 21Then when many troubles and terrible things happen to them, this song will testify against them, because the song will not be forgotten by their ·descendants [Lseed]. I know what they ·plan [incline; Gen. 6:5; 8:21] to do, even before I take them into the land I ·promised [swore to] them." 22So Moses wrote down the song that day, and he taught it to the ·Israelites [Lsons/Tchildren of Israel].

23Then the LORD gave this command to Joshua son of Nun: "Be strong and ·brave [courageous; Josh. 1:6–9], because you will lead the people of Israel to the land I promised them, and I will be with you [Ex. 3:12]."

24After Moses finished writing all the words of the ·teachings [laws; instructions] in a ·book [scroll],
25he gave a command to the Levites, who carried the Ark of the ·Agreement [Treaty; Covenant; Ex. 25:10] with the LORD.
26He said, "Take this ·Book [Scroll] of the ·Teachings [Laws; Instructions] and put it beside the Ark of the ·Agreement [Treaty; Covenant; Ex. 25:10] with the LORD your God. It must stay there as a witness against you.
27I know how ·stubborn [Lstiff-necked] and ·disobedient [rebellious] you are. You have ·disobeyed [rebelled against] the LORD while I am alive and with you, and you will ·disobey [rebel against me] even more after I die!
28·Gather [Assemble] all the elders of your tribes and all your ·officers [scribes] to me so that I may say these things ·for them to hear [Lin their ears], and so that I may ask heaven and earth to ·testify [witness] against them [30:19].
29I know that after I die you will become completely ·evil [corrupt]. You will turn away from the ·commands I have given [Lway I commanded] you. Terrible things will happen to you in the future when you do what the LORD says is evil, and you will make him angry with the ·idols you have made [Lwork of your hands]."

Moses' Song

30And Moses spoke this whole song ·for all the people of Israel to hear [Lin the ears of the whole assembly of Israel]:

32 ·Hear [LGive ear], heavens, and I will speak.
Listen, earth, to ·what I say [Lthe words of my mouth].
2My teaching will drop like rain;
my words will ·fall [distill] like dew.
They will be like showers on the grass;
they will pour down like rain on young plants.
3I will announce the name of the LORD.
·Praise God because he is great [LAscribe greatness to our God]!
4He is like a rock; what he does is perfect,
and ·he is always [Lall his ways are] fair.
He is a faithful God who does no wrong,
who is ·right [righteous] and ·fair [virtuous].

5They ·have done evil against him [are corrupt].
·To their shame [*or* Their faults show] they are no longer his children [Is. 1:2–4; Hos. 1:9];
they are an ·evil [perverted] and ·lying [crooked] people.
6This is not the way to repay the LORD,
you foolish and unwise people.
·He is [LIs he not…?] your Father and Maker,
who made you and formed you.

7Remember the old days.
Think of the years already passed.
Ask your father and he will tell you;
ask your elders and they will inform you.
8God Most High gave ·the nations their lands [Leach nation its inheritance],
dividing up the ·human race [Lsons of man].
He set up borders for the people

·and even numbered the Israelites[n] [Laccording to the number of the sons/Tchildren of Israel].
9The LORD took his people as his ·share [portion],
the people of Jacob as his ·very own [Lspecial inheritance].

10He found them in a ·desert [wilderness],
a windy, ·empty [unformed; Gen. 1:2] land.
He surrounded them and brought them up,
guarding them as ·those he loved very much [Lthe apple/pupil of his eye].
11He was like an eagle ·building [watching; stirring up] its nest
that ·flutters [hovers] over its young.
It spreads its wings to catch them
and carries them on its feathers.
12The LORD alone led them,
and there was no foreign god ·helping [Lwith] him.

13The LORD ·brought them to [*or* made them ride over] the heights of the land
and fed them the fruit of the fields.
He ·gave them [suckled them with] honey from the rocks,
bringing oil from the ·solid [flint] rock.
14There were milk curds from the cows and milk from the flock;
there were fat sheep and goats.
There were sheep and goats from Bashan [Ca particularly fertile area east of the Sea of Galilee]
and the best of the wheat.
You drank the ·juice [Lfermenting/foaming blood] of grapes [Cwine].

15·Israel [LJeshurun; Ca name for Israel meaning "virtuous"; perhaps intended ironically; 33:5, 26; Is. 44:2] grew fat and kicked;
they were fat and ·full [bloated] and firm.
They ·left [abandoned] the God who made them
and ·rejected [dishonored] the Rock who saved them.
16They made God jealous with ·foreign [strange] gods [4:24]
and angry with ·hateful idols [Labominations].
17They made sacrifices to demons, not God,
to gods they had never known,
new gods from nearby,
gods your ·ancestors [fathers] did not fear.
18You left God who is the Rock, ·your Father [Lwho bore you; *or* who begot you],
and you forgot the God who gave you birth.

19The LORD saw this and ·rejected [spurned] them;
his sons and daughters had made him angry.
20He said, "I will turn ·away [Lmy face away] from them
and see what ·will happen to them [their end will be].
They are ·evil people [La perverted generation],
·unfaithful [untrustworthy] children.

32:8 Israelites Hebrew copies, including the Dead Sea Scrolls, read "sons of God." Some Greek copies read "angels of God."

[21]They used things that are not gods to make me jealous [4:24]
and ·worthless idols [vanities; vain idols] to make me angry.
So I will use those who are not a nation to make them jealous;
I will use a nation that ·does not understand [[L]is foolish] to make them angry.
[22]My anger has started a fire
that burns down to ·the place of the dead [[L]Sheol; [C]the grave or the underworld].
It will ·burn up [consume] the ·ground [*or* earth] and its ·crops [produce],
and it will set fire to the ·base [foundations] of the mountains.

[23]"I will pile ·troubles [disasters] upon them
and shoot my arrows at them.
[24]They will be starved and sick,
destroyed by terrible diseases.
I will send them ·vicious [[L]the teeth of] animals
·and gliding, poisonous snakes [[L]with the poison/venom of creatures that crawl in the dust].
[25]In the streets the sword will ·kill [bereave];
in their ·homes [bedrooms] there will be terror.
Young men and women will die,
and so will ·babies [sucklings] and gray-haired men.
[26]I will ·scatter them [*or* dash them to pieces] as I said,
and ·no one will remember them [[L]I will cause their memory to cease from among humans].
[27]But I didn't want ·their enemy to brag [*or* to provoke the enemy];
their enemy might misunderstand
and say, '·We have won [[L]Our hand is lifted up]!
The LORD has done none of this.'"

[28]·Israel [[L]They are a nation that] has no sense;
they do not understand.
[29]I wish they were wise and understood this;
I wish they could see ·what will happen to them [their end].
[30]·One person cannot [[L]How can one person…?] chase a thousand people,
and ·two people cannot [[L]two…?] fight ten thousand
unless their Rock has sold them,
unless the LORD has ·given them up [surrendered them; 28:25–27].
[31]The rock of these people is not like our Rock;
our enemies ·agree to that [[L]are judges].
[32]Their vine comes from Sodom,
and their fields are like Gomorrah [Gen. 19].
Their grapes are full of poison;
their bunches of grapes are bitter.
[33]Their wine is like ·snake poison [the venom of serpents],
like the ·deadly [cruel] poison of cobras.

[34]"·I have been saving this [[L]Is this not stored up with me…?],
and I have it ·locked [sealed] in my ·storehouses [treasuries].

[35]·I will punish those who do wrong [LVengeance is mine; Rom. 12:9];
I will repay them.
Soon their foot will slip,
because their day of ·trouble [disaster] is near,
and their ·punishment [doom] will come quickly."

[36]The LORD will ·defend [vindicate; judge] his people
and have mercy on his servants.
He will see that their ·strength [power; control; Lhand] is gone,
that nobody is left, slaves or free.
[37]Then he will say, "Where are their gods?
Where is the rock they ·trusted [took refuge in]?
[38]Who ate the fat from their sacrifices [Lev. 3:17],
and who drank the wine of their drink offerings?
Let those gods come to help you!
Let them protect you!

[39]"Now you will see that I am ·the one God [Lhe]!
There is no god but me.
I ·send death and life [kill and make alive];
I ·can hurt [wound], and I can heal.
No one can escape from ·me [Lmy hand].
[40]I raise my hand toward heaven [Cto make a promise]:
As surely as I live forever,
[41]I will sharpen my flashing sword,
and I will take it in my hand to judge [Ps. 7:12–13].
I will ·punish [bring vengeance on] my enemies
and pay back those who hate me.
[42]My arrows will be ·covered [Ldrunk] with their blood;
my sword will eat their flesh.
The blood will flow from those who are killed and the captives.
The ·heads of the enemy leaders [*or* long-haired enemy] will be cut off."

[43]·Be happy [Rejoice], nations, with his people,
because he will repay you for the blood of his servants.
He will ·punish [work vengeance on] his enemies,
and he will ·remove the sin of [provide atonement for] his land and people.

[44]Moses came with Joshua son of Nun, and they spoke all the words of
this song ·for the people to hear [Lin the ears of his people]. [45]When Moses
finished speaking these words to all Israel, [46]he said to them: "·Pay careful
attention to [LSet your heart on] all the words I ·have said [testify; give
witness] to you today, and command your children to obey carefully
everything in these ·teachings [laws; instructions]. [47]These should not be
unimportant words for you, but rather they mean life for you! By these
words you will live a long time in the land you are crossing the Jordan
River to take as your ·own [possession]."

Moses Goes Up to Mount Nebo

[48]The LORD spoke to Moses again that same day and said, [49]"Go up the
Abarim Mountains, to Mount Nebo in the country of Moab, across from
Jericho. Look at the land of Canaan that I am giving to the Israelites as

their ·own [possession; [C]one can look far into the Promised Land from
Nebo]. 50On that mountain that you climb, you will die and ·join [be
gathered to] your ·ancestors [fathers], just as your brother Aaron died on
Mount Hor and joined his ·ancestors [fathers; Num. 20:22–29]. 51You
both sinned against me at the waters of Meribah Kadesh in the Desert of
Zin, and you did not honor me as holy there among the ·Israelites [[L]sons/
[T]children of Israel; Num. 20:1–13]. 52So now you will only look at the land
from far away. You will not enter the land I am giving the ·people [[L]sons;
[T]children] of Israel."

Moses Blesses the People

33 Moses, the man of God, gave this blessing to the ·Israelites
[[L]sons/[T]children of Israel] before he died. 2He said:
"The LORD came from Mount Sinai
and ·rose like the sun [shone forth] from ·Edom [[L]Seir; [C]another name for Edom];
he ·showed his greatness [blazed forth] from Mount Paran.
He came with ·thousands of angels [myriads of holy ones]
·from the southern mountains [*or* marching at his right hand; Ex. 15:17; Judg. 5:4–5; Ps. 68:7–8, 17–18; Hab. 3:3–7].
3The LORD surely loves his people
and takes care of all ·those who belong to him [his holy/consecrated ones].
They ·bow down [submit; *or* followed] at his feet,
and they are taught by him.
4Moses ·gave us [commanded us with] the ·teachings [laws; instructions]
that ·belong to the people [[L]are the possession of the assembly] of Jacob.
5The LORD became king ·of Israel [[L]in Jeshurun; 32:15]
when the leaders of the people gathered,
when the tribes of Israel came together.

6"Let the people of Reuben live and not die,
but let ·the people [[L]his numbers] be few [2 Kin. 10:32–34]."

7Moses said this about the people of Judah:
"LORD, listen to Judah's ·prayer [[L]voice];
bring them back to their people.
They ·defend [contend for] themselves with their hands.
Help them fight their enemies!"

8Moses said this about the people of Levi:
"LORD, your Thummim and Urim [Ex. 28:30] belong
to ·Levi, whom you love [[L]your loyal one].
LORD, you tested him at Massah
and argued with him at the waters of Meribah [Ex. 17:1–7].
9He said about his father and mother,
'I don't care about them.'
He did not treat his brothers as favorites
or give special favors to his children,
but he protected your word
and guarded your ·agreement [covenant; treaty; Ex. 32:25–29].
10He teaches your ·laws [judgments] to the people of Jacob
and your ·teachings [laws; instructions] to the people of Israel.

He ·burns [places] incense before you
and makes whole burnt offerings [Lev. 1:1–17] on your altar.
11LORD, ·make them strong [Lbless his powers];
be pleased with the work ·they do [Lof their hand].
·Defeat those who attack them [LStrike the loins of those who rise against them],
and don't let ·their enemies [Lthose who hate them] rise up again."

12Moses said this about the people of Benjamin:
"The LORD's loved ones will lie down in safety,
because ·he [*or* the Most High] protects them all day long.
The ones he loves rest ·with him [Lbetween his shoulders]."

13Moses said this about the people of Joseph:
"May the LORD bless their land with ·wonderful [*or* the best fruits from the] dew from heaven,
·with water from the springs [and from the deeps] below,
14with the best fruits that the sun brings,
and with the best fruits ·that the moon brings [*or* of the months].
15Let the ·old [ancient] mountains give the finest crops,
and let the everlasting hills give the best fruits.
16Let the ·full earth [Learth and its fullness] give the best fruits,
and let the LORD who lived in ·the burning bush [the thorn bush; *or* Sinai; Ex. 3:2] be pleased.
May ·these blessings [Lthey] rest on the head of Joseph,
on the forehead of the ·one who was blessed [Lprince] among his brothers.
17Joseph has the majesty of a firstborn bull;
·he is as strong as [Lhis horns are the horns of] a wild ox [Ex. 27:2].
He will ·stab [gore] other nations with them,
even those ·nations far away [Lat the ends of the earth].
These are the ·ten thousands [myriads] of Ephraim,
and these are the thousands of Manasseh [Ctribes named after Joseph's sons]."

18Moses said this about the people of Zebulun:
"·Be happy [Rejoice] when you go out, Zebulun,
and ·be happy [rejoice] in your tents, Issachar.
19They will call the people to the mountain,
and there they will offer the ·right [righteous] sacrifices.
They will ·do well from all that is in [Lsuck the abundance of] the sea,
and from the treasures hidden in the sand on the shore."

20Moses said this about the people of Gad:
"·Praise God who gives Gad more land [LBlessed be the one who enlarges Gad]!
Gad lives there like a lion,
who tears off arms and heads.
21They chose the best land for themselves.
They received a large share, like that given to an officer.
When the leaders of the people ·gathered [*or* came],
the people of Gad did what the LORD said was ·right [righteous; just],

and they judged Israel fairly."

[22]Moses said this about the people of Dan:
"Dan is like a lion's cub,
who ·jumps out of [leaps forth from] Bashan [32:14]."

[23]Moses said this about the people of Naphtali:
"Naphtali ·enjoys special kindnesses [is deeply favored],
and they are full of the LORD's blessings.
·Take as your own [*or* It possesses] the west and south."

[24]Moses said this about the people of Asher:
"Asher is the most blessed of the sons;
let him be his brothers' favorite.
Let him ·bathe [dip] his feet in olive oil [[C]symbolizing comfort and luxury].
[25]Your ·gates will have locks of [[L]bolts/bars are] iron and bronze,
and ·you will be strong as long as you live [[L]your strength will be like your days].

[26]"There is no one like the God of ·Israel [[L]Jeshurun; 32:15],
who rides through the ·skies [heavens] to help you,
who rides on the clouds in his majesty [Ps. 18:7–15; 68:5–7; Dan. 7:13–14; Nah. 1:3; Matt. 24:30; Rev. 1:7].
[27]·The everlasting God is your place of safety [*or* He humbles the gods of old],
and ·his arms will hold you up forever [*or* humbles the ancient powers].
He will force your enemy out ahead of you,
saying, 'Destroy the enemy!'
[28]The people of Israel will ·lie down [reside; dwell] in safety.
Jacob's ·spring [*or* abode] is theirs alone.
Theirs is a land full of grain and new wine,
where the ·skies [heavens] drop their dew.
[29]Israel, you are blessed!
·No one else [[L]Who…?] is like you,
because you are a people saved by the LORD.
He is your shield and helper,
your glorious sword.
Your enemies will ·be afraid of you [come cringing to you],
and you will ·walk all over [trample] their ·holy places [[L]high places; *or* backs]."

Moses Dies

34 Then Moses climbed Mount Nebo from the plains of Moab to
the top of Mount Pisgah, across from Jericho. From there the
LORD showed him all the land from Gilead to Dan, [2]all of Naphtali and the
lands of Ephraim and Manasseh, all the land of Judah as far as the
·Mediterranean [[L]Western] Sea, [3]as well as the ·southern desert [[L]the
Negev] and the whole Valley of Jericho up to Zoar. (Jericho is called the city
of palm trees.) [4]Then the LORD said to Moses, "This is the land I ·promised
[swore] to Abraham, Isaac, and Jacob when I said to them, 'I will give this
land to your ·descendants [[L]seed; Gen. 12:1–13; 15:17–20].' ·I have let you
look at [[L]Your eyes have seen] it, Moses, but you will not cross over there."

5Then Moses, the servant of the LORD, died there in Moab, as the LORD
had said [Num. 20:12]. 6He buried Moses in Moab in the valley opposite
Beth Peor, but even today no one knows where his grave is. 7Moses was
one hundred twenty years old when he died. His eyes were not weak, and
·he was still strong [Lhis vigor had not left him]. 8The ·Israelites [Lsons/
Tchildren of Israel] cried for Moses for thirty days, staying in the plains of
Moab until the time of ·sadness [mourning] was over.

9Joshua son of Nun was then filled with the spirit of wisdom, because
Moses had ·put [laid] his hands on him. So the ·Israelites [Lsons/Tchildren
of Israel] listened to Joshua, and they did what the LORD had commanded
Moses.

10There has never been another prophet in Israel like Moses [Acts
3:22–23; Heb. 3:1–19]. The LORD knew Moses face to face [Num. 12:6–8]
11and sent him to do signs and ·miracles [wonders] in Egypt—to ·the king
[LPharaoh], to all his ·officers [Lservants], and to the whole land of Egypt.
12Moses had ·great power [La strong hand], and he did great and wonderful things for all the Israelites to see.

JOSHUA

God's Command to Joshua

1 After Moses, the servant of the ·LORD [*or* Yahweh; [C]"LORD" (capital letters) represents the divine name YHWH, usually pronounced "Yahweh"], died, the LORD spoke to Joshua son of Nun, Moses' ·assistant [aide; servant]. [2]The LORD said, "My servant Moses is dead. Now you and all these people ·go across [get ready to cross; [L]arise and cross] the Jordan River into the land I am giving to the ·Israelites [[L]sons/[T]children of Israel]. [3]I promised Moses I would give you this land [Deut. 11:24], so I will give you every place ·you go [[L]the sole of your foot walks/treads] in the land. [4]All the land from the ·desert in the south [[L]desert; wilderness] to ·Lebanon in the north [[L]Lebanon] will be yours. All the land from the great river, the ·Euphrates, in the east [[L]Euphrates], to the ·Mediterranean [[L]Great] Sea ·in the west [[L]toward the going down of the sun] will be yours, too, ·including [*or* which is all] the land of the Hittites [[C]Palestine was known as "Hatti-land" (or "Hittite country") by the Egyptians and Babylonians]. [5]No one will be able to ·defeat [resist; stand against] you all your life. Just as I was with Moses, so I will be with you. I will not ·leave [fail] you or ·forget [desert; forsake] you.

[6]"Joshua, be strong and ·brave [courageous; resolute]! You must lead these people ·so they can take [to possess/inherit] the land that I promised their fathers I would give them. [7]Be strong and ·brave [courageous; resolute]. Be ·sure [careful] to obey all the ·teachings [law] my servant Moses ·gave [commanded] you. If you ·follow them exactly [[L]do not turn from it to the right or to the left], you will be successful in everything you do. [8]·Always remember [[L]Do not let depart from your mouth] what is written in the Book of the ·Teachings [Law]. ·Study [Meditate on] it day and night to be ·sure [careful; diligent] to obey everything that is written there. If you do this, you will be ·wise [prudent; successful] and ·successful [prosperous] ·in everything [*or* along life's path; along the way]. [9]·Remember that I [[L]Have I not…?] commanded you to be strong and ·brave [courageous; resolute]. Don't be afraid or ·discouraged [dismayed], because the LORD your God will be with you ·everywhere you go [*or* in all you do]."

Joshua's Orders to the People

[10]Then Joshua gave orders to the ·officers [leaders] of the people: [11]"Go through the camp and ·tell [command] the people, 'Get your ·supplies [provisions] ready. ·Three days from now [*or* Within a few days] you will cross the Jordan River and take the land the LORD your God is ·giving you [[L]giving you to inherit/possess].'"

[12]Then Joshua said to the people of Reuben, Gad, and ·East [[L]the half-tribe of] Manasseh, [13]"Remember what Moses, the servant of the LORD, told you [Deut. 3:18–20]. He said the LORD your God would give you ·rest [a place of rest/security] and would give you this land. [14]Now your wives,

children, and animals may stay here in the land Moses has given you east of the Jordan River, but your fighting men must dress for war and cross the Jordan River ahead of your brothers to help them. [15]The LORD has given you a place ·to rest [of security] and will do the same for your brothers. But you must help them until they take the land the LORD their God is giving them. Then you may return to your own land east of the Jordan River, the land that Moses, the servant of the LORD, gave you [Deut. 3:18–20]."

[16]Then the people answered Joshua, "Anything you command us to do, we will do. Any place you send us, we will go. [17]Just as we fully obeyed Moses, we will obey you. ·We ask only that [*or* And may] the LORD your God be with you just as he was with Moses. [18]Whoever ·refuses to obey [rebels against] your commands or ·turns against [refuses to obey] you will be put to death. Just be strong and ·brave [courageous; resolute]!"

Spies Sent to Jericho

2 Joshua son of Nun secretly sent out two spies from ·Acacia [[L]Shittim; [C]a Hebrew word meaning "acacia"] and said to them, "Go and ·look at [check out] the land, particularly at the city of Jericho."

So the men went to Jericho and ·stayed [lodged] at the house of a prostitute named Rahab.

[2]Someone told the king of Jericho, "[[L]Look; [T]Behold] Some men from Israel have come here tonight to spy out the land."

[3]So the king of Jericho sent this message to Rahab: "Bring out the men who came to you and entered your house. They have come to spy out our whole land."

[4]But the woman had hidden the two men. She said, "They did come here, but I didn't know where they came from. [5]In the evening, when it was time to close the city gate, they left. I don't know where they went, but if you go quickly, maybe you can catch them." [6](The woman had taken the men up to the roof and had hidden them there under stalks of flax that she had spread out.) [7]So the king's men went out looking for the spies on the road that leads to the ·crossings [fords] of the Jordan River. The city gate was closed just after the king's men left the city.

[8]Before the spies went to sleep for the night, Rahab went up to the roof. [9]She said to them, "I know the LORD has given this land to your people. ·You frighten us very much [[L]A terror of you has fallen on us]. Everyone living in this land is ·terribly afraid of [[L]melting away before] you [10]because we have heard how the LORD dried up the ·Red Sea [*or* Sea of Reeds] when you came out of Egypt [Ex. 14:15–31]. We have heard how you ·destroyed [*or* devoted to the Lord for destruction; see 6:17; Deut. 20:15–18] Sihon and Og, two Amorite kings who lived ·east of [beyond] the Jordan. [11]When we heard this, ·we were very frightened [[L]our hearts melted]. ·Now our men are afraid to fight you [[L]And there rose up no spirit/breath in a man because of you] because the LORD your God ·rules [[L]is God in] the heavens above and the earth below! [12]So now, ·promise [swear to] me ·before [*or* by] the LORD that you will show ·kindness [loyalty] to my family just as I showed ·kindness [loyalty] to you. Give me ·some proof [a sure sign; a solemn pledge] that you will do this. [13]Allow my father, mother, brothers, sisters, and all of their families to live. ·Save [Rescue; Preserve] us from death."

[14]The men agreed and said, "It will be our lives for your lives if you don't tell anyone what we are doing. When the LORD gives us the land, we will be ·kind [loyal] and ·true [faithful] to you."

15The house Rahab lived in was built on the city wall, so she used a rope
to let the men down through a window. 16She said to them, "Go into the
hills so the ·king's men [Lpursuers] will not find you. Hide there for three
days. After the ·king's men [Lpursuers] return, you may go on your way."
17The men said to her, "You must do as we say. If not, we ·cannot be
responsible for keeping [will be free from] this oath you have made us
swear. 18When we return to this land, you must tie this ·red [scarlet] rope
in the window through which you let us down. Bring your father, mother,
brothers, and all your ·family [Lfather's house] into your house. 19If anyone leaves your house and is killed, ·it is his own fault [Lhis blood is on his
head]. We ·cannot be responsible for him [are innocent]. If anyone in
your house ·is hurt [Lhas a hand laid on them], ·we will be responsible [his
blood will be on our head]. 20But if you tell anyone about this, we will be
free from the oath you made us swear."
21Rahab answered, "·I agree to this [LLet it be according to your words]."
So she sent them away, and they left. Then she tied the ·red [scarlet] rope
in the window.
22The men left and went into the hills where they stayed for three days.
The ·king's men [pursuers] looked for them all along the road, but after
three days, they returned to the city without finding them. 23Then the
two men started back. They left the hills and crossed the river and came
to Joshua son of Nun and told him everything that had happened to
them. 24They said, "The LORD surely has given ·us all of the land [Lall the
land into our hand]. All the people in that land are ·terribly afraid of
[melting away before] us."

Crossing the Jordan

3 Early the next morning Joshua and all the ·Israelites [Lsons/
Tchildren of Israel] left ·Acacia [CHebrew: Shittim; 2:1]. They traveled to the Jordan River and camped there before crossing it. 2After three
days the ·officers [leaders] went through the camp 3and gave orders to the
people: "When you see the priests and Levites carrying the Ark of the
·Agreement with [Covenant/Treaty of] the LORD your God [Ex. 25:10–22],
leave where you are and follow it. 4That way you will know which way to
go since you have never ·been here [passed this way] before. But do not
·follow too closely [come near it]. Stay about ·a thousand yards [Ltwo
thousand cubits] behind the Ark."
5Then Joshua told the people, "·Make yourselves holy [Consecrate
yourselves], because tomorrow the LORD will do ·amazing [miraculous]
things among you."
6Joshua said to the priests, "Take the Ark of the ·Agreement [Covenant;
Treaty] and go ahead of the people." So the priests lifted the Ark and carried it ahead of the people.
7Then the LORD said to Joshua, "Today I will begin to ·make you great
[exalt/honor you] in the ·opinion [Leyes] of all the Israelites so the people
will know I am with you just as I was with Moses. 8·Tell [Command] the
priests who carry the Ark of the ·Agreement [Covenant; Treaty] to go to
the edge of the Jordan River and stand in the water."
9Then Joshua said to the ·Israelites [Lsons/Tchildren of Israel], "Come
here and listen to the words of the LORD your God. 10Here is proof that the
living God is ·with [among] you and that he will ·force [drive] out the
Canaanites, Hittites, Hivites, Perizzites, Girgashites, Amorites, and
Jebusites. 11[LLook; TBehold] The Ark of the ·Agreement with [Covenant/

Treaty of] the Lord of the whole world will go ahead of you into the Jordan
River. 12Now choose twelve men from among you, one from each of the
twelve tribes of Israel. 13The priests will carry the Ark of the Lord, the
·Master [Ruler; Lord] of the whole world [Ex. 9:29], into the Jordan ahead
of you. When they step into the water, it will stop. The ·river will stop flowing [Lwaters going down will be cut off from above] and will stand up in a
heap [Cthus reminding them of the crossing of the sea in Ex. 14]."
14So the people left ·the place where they had camped [their camp/
Ltents], and they followed the priests who carried the Ark of the
·Agreement [Covenant; Treaty] across the Jordan River. 15During harvest
the Jordan overflows its banks. When the priests carrying the Ark came
to the edge of the river and stepped into the water, 16the water ·upstream
[Lgoing down from above] stopped flowing. It stood up in a heap a great
distance away at Adam, a town near Zarethan. The water flowing down to
the Sea of Arabah (the ·Dead [LSalt] Sea) was completely cut off. So the
people crossed the river ·near [opposite; across from] Jericho. 17The
priests carried the Ark of the ·Agreement with [Covenant/Treaty of] the
Lord to the middle of the river and stood there on dry ground. They
waited there while ·all the people [the whole nation] of Israel walked
across the Jordan River on dry land.

Rocks to Remind the People

4After all the ·people [nation] had finished crossing the Jordan,
the Lord said to Joshua, 2"Choose twelve men from among the
people, one from each tribe. 3·Tell [Command; Instruct] them to get
twelve rocks from the middle of the river, from where the priests stood.
Carry the rocks and put them down where you ·stay [camp; lodge]
tonight."
4So Joshua ·chose [appointed] one man from each tribe. Then he called
the twelve men together 5and said to them, "Go out into the river where
the Ark of the Lord your God is. Each of you bring back one rock, one for
each tribe of Israel, and carry it on your shoulder. 6They will be a ·sign
[reminder; memorial] among you. In the future your children will ask
you, 'What do these rocks mean [Lto you]?' 7Tell them the water stopped
flowing in the Jordan when the Ark of the ·Agreement with [Covenant/
Treaty of] the Lord crossed the ·river [LJordan]. These rocks will always
remind the ·Israelites [Lsons/Tchildren of Israel] of this [Cstone memorials
are common in the OT; 7:26; 24:26–27; Gen. 28:18–22; 31:45–47]."
8So the ·Israelites [Lsons/Tchildren of Israel] obeyed Joshua and carried
twelve rocks from the middle of the Jordan River, one rock for each of the
twelve tribes of Israel, just as the Lord had commanded Joshua. They carried the rocks with them and put them down where they made their
camp. 9Joshua also put twelve rocks in the middle of the Jordan River
where the priests had stood while carrying the Ark of the ·Agreement
[Covenant; Treaty]. These rocks are still there today.
10The priests carrying the Ark continued standing in the middle of the
river until everything was done that the Lord had commanded Joshua to
tell the people, just as Moses had told Joshua. The people hurried across the
river. 11After they finished crossing the river, the priests carried the Ark of
the Lord to the other side as the people watched. 12The men from the tribes
of Reuben, Gad, and ·East [Lthe half-tribe of] Manasseh obeyed what Moses
had told them. They were dressed for war, and they crossed the river ahead
of the other people. 13About forty thousand soldiers prepared for war

passed before the Lord as they marched across the river, going toward the plains of Jericho.

14 That day the Lord ·made Joshua great [honored/exalted Joshua] **in the ·opinion** [Leyes] **of all the Israelites. They ·respected** [revered; stood in awe of] **Joshua all his life, just as they had ·respected** [revered; stood in awe of] **Moses.**

15 Then the Lord said to Joshua, 16 "Command the priests to bring the Ark of the ·Agreement [Covenant; Treaty; LTestimony] **out of the river."**

17 So Joshua commanded the priests, "Come up out of the Jordan."

18 Then the priests carried the Ark of the ·Agreement with [Covenant/Treaty of] **the Lord out of the river. As soon as their feet touched dry land, the water began flowing again. The river again overflowed its banks, just as it had before they crossed.**

19 The people ·crossed [Lcame up from] **the Jordan on the tenth day of the first month and camped at Gilgal, ·east** [on the eastern border] **of Jericho. 20 They carried with them the twelve rocks taken from the Jordan, and Joshua set them up at Gilgal. 21 Then he spoke to the ·Israelites** [Lsons/Tchildren of Israel]: **"In the future your children will ask you, 'What ·do these rocks mean** [Lare these stones]?' **22 Tell them, 'Israel crossed the Jordan River on dry land. 23 The Lord your God ·caused the water to stop flowing** [Ldried up the river before you] **until you finished crossing it, just as the Lord did to the ·Red Sea** [*or* Sea of Reeds; Ex. 14–15]. **He ·stopped the water** [Ldried it up] **until we crossed it. 24 The Lord did this so all ·people** [Lthe nations/people of the earth] **would know ·he has great power** [Lthat the hand of the Lord is powerful] **and so you would always ·respect** [revere; fear] **the Lord your God.'"**

5 All the kings of the Amorites west of the Jordan and the Canaanite kings living by the ·Mediterranean Sea [LSea] **heard that the Lord dried up the Jordan River until the ·Israelites** [Lsons/Tchildren of Israel] **had crossed it. ·After that they were scared** [LTheir hearts melted] **and ·too afraid to face** [Lthere was no breath/spirit in them because of] **the ·Israelites** [Lsons/Tchildren of Israel].

The Israelites Are Circumcised

2 At that time the Lord said to Joshua, "Make knives from flint stones and circumcise [Gen. 17:7–14] **the ·Israelites** [Lsons of Israel a second time]." **3 So Joshua made knives from flint stones and circumcised the ·Israelites** [Lsons/Tchildren of Israel] **at ·Gibeath Haaraloth** [CHebrew for "Hill of Foreskins"].

4 This is why Joshua circumcised the men: After the Israelites left Egypt, all the men old enough to serve in the army died in the desert on the ·way [journey] **·out of** [*or* after leaving] **Egypt. 5 The men who had come out of Egypt had been circumcised, but none of those who were born in the desert on the trip from Egypt had been circumcised. 6 The ·Israelites** [Lsons/Tchildren of Israel] **had moved about in the ·desert** [wilderness] **for forty years. During that time all the fighting men who had left Egypt had died because they had not obeyed the Lord** [Num. 13–14]. **So the Lord swore they would not see the land he had promised their ancestors to give them, a ·fertile land** [Lland flowing with milk and honey; Ca phrase describing the natural bounty of the land]. **7 Their sons ·took** [were raised up in] **their places. But none of the sons born on the trip from Egypt had been circumcised, so Joshua circumcised them. 8 After all the Israelites had been circumcised, they stayed in camp until they were healed.**

9 Then the LORD said to Joshua, "Today I have ·removed [rolled away] the shame [disgrace; reproach] of ·your slavery in Egypt [L Egypt]." So that place was named Gilgal [C sounds like Hebrew for "rolled away"; 4:19], which it is still named today.

10 The ·people [L sons/T children] of Israel were camped at Gilgal [4:19] on the plains of Jericho. It was there, on the evening of the fourteenth day of the month, they celebrated the Passover Feast [Ex. 12]. 11 The day after the Passover, the people ate food grown on that land: ·bread made without yeast [unleavened bread] and roasted grain. 12 The day they ate this food, the manna stopped coming [Ex. 16:35]. The ·Israelites [L sons/T children of Israel] no longer got the manna from heaven. They ate the food grown in the land of Canaan that year.

13 Joshua was near Jericho when he looked up and saw a man standing in front of him with a sword in his hand [Ex. 3:2—4:17; Judg. 6:11–23]. Joshua went to him and asked, "Are you ·a friend or an enemy [L for us or for our enemies/adversaries]?"

14 The man answered, "·I am neither [L No]. I have come as the commander of the LORD's army [C God himself who comes as a warrior; Ex. 15:3]."

Then Joshua bowed facedown on the ground and asked, "Does my ·master [lord] have a ·command [message] for me, his servant?"

15 The commander of the LORD's army answered, "Take off your sandals, because the place where you are standing is holy [Ex. 3:5]." So Joshua did.

The Fall of Jericho

6 The people of Jericho were afraid because the Israelites were near. They closed the city gates and guarded them [L Now Jericho was tightly shut because of the sons/T children of Israel]. No one went into the city, and no one came out.

2 Then the LORD said to Joshua, "Look, I have given ·you Jericho [L Jericho into your hands], its king, and all its fighting men. 3 March around the city with your ·army [L fighting men] once a day for six days. 4 Have seven priests carry trumpets made from ·horns of male sheep [rams' horns] and have them march in front of the Ark. On the seventh day march around the city seven times and have the priests blow the trumpets as they march. 5 They will make one long blast on the trumpets. When you hear that sound, have all the people give a loud shout. Then the walls of the city will ·fall [collapse] so the people can ·go [charge] straight into the city."

6 So Joshua son of Nun called the priests together and said to them, "Carry the Ark of the ·Agreement [Covenant; Treaty]. Tell seven priests to carry trumpets and march in front of it." 7 Then Joshua ordered the ·people [*or* army], "Now go! March around the city. The ·soldiers with weapons [armed troops; *or* royal guard] should march in front of the Ark of the ·Agreement with [Covenant/Treaty of] the LORD."

8 When Joshua finished speaking to the ·people [*or* army], the seven priests began marching before the LORD. They carried the seven trumpets and blew them as they marched. The priests carrying the Ark of the ·Agreement with [Covenant/Treaty of] the LORD followed them. 9 ·Soldiers with weapons [Armed troops; *or* The royal guard] marched in front of the priests, and ·armed men [the rear guard] walked behind the Ark. The priests were blowing their trumpets. 10 But Joshua had ·told [commanded] the people not to give ·a war cry [the shout]. He said, "Don't shout. Don't say a word until the day I tell you. Then shout." 11 So Joshua had the Ark

of the Lord carried around the city one time. Then they went back to camp for the night.

12 Early the next morning Joshua got up, and the priests carried the Ark of the Lord again. 13 The seven priests carried the seven trumpets and marched in front of the Ark of the Lord, blowing their trumpets. ·Soldiers with weapons [Armed troops *or* The royal guard] marched in front of them, and ·other soldiers [the rear guard] walked behind the Ark of the Lord. ·All this time the priests were blowing their trumpets [...while the trumpets kept blowing]. 14 So on the second day they marched around the city one time and then went back to camp. They did this every day for six days.

15 On the seventh day they got up at dawn and marched around the city, just as they had on the days before. But on that day they marched around the city seven times. 16 The seventh time around the priests blew their trumpets. Then Joshua gave the command: "Now, ·shout [give the battle cry]! The Lord has given you this city! 17 The city and everything in it are to be ·destroyed as an offering [Ldevoted; set apart; 2:10] to the Lord. Only Rahab the prostitute and everyone in her house should remain alive. They must not be killed, because Rahab hid the ·two spies [Lmessengers] we sent out [2:1–24]. 18 ·Don't take any of [Keep away from] the things that are ·to be destroyed as an offering [devoted; set apart] to the Lord. If you take them and bring them into ·our camp [Lthe camp of Israel], you yourselves will be ·destroyed [devoted/set apart for destruction], and you will bring trouble to all of Israel. 19 All the silver and gold and things made from bronze and iron belong to the Lord and must ·be saved for him [Lgo into the treasury of the Lord]."

20 When the priests blew the trumpets, the ·people [army] shouted. At the sound of the trumpets and the ·people's [army's] shout, the walls fell, and everyone ·ran [charged] straight into the city. So the Israelites ·defeated [captured; took] that city. 21 They ·completely destroyed [devoted to the Lord] with the ·sword [Ledge of the sword] every living thing in the city—men and women, young and old, cattle, sheep, and donkeys.

22 Joshua said to the two men who had spied out the land, "Go into the prostitute's house. Bring her out and bring out those who ·are with [belong to] her, because of the ·promise you made [oath you swore] to her." 23 So the ·two men [young men] went into the house and brought out Rahab, her father, mother, brothers, and all ·those with [who belonged to] her. They put all of her family in a safe place outside the camp of Israel.

24 Then Israel burned the whole city and everything in it, but they did not burn the things made from silver, gold, bronze, and iron. These were ·saved for [Lput in the treasury of the house of] the Lord. 25 Joshua saved Rahab the prostitute, her ·family [Lfather's household], and all who ·were with [belonged to] her, because Rahab had helped the men he had sent to spy out Jericho (Matt. 1:5; Heb. 11:31; James 2:25). Rahab still lives among the Israelites today.

26 Then Joshua ·made [*or* caused them to take] this oath:

"Anyone who tries to rebuild this city of Jericho
  will be cursed ·by [*or* before] the Lord.
The one who lays the foundation of this city
  will lose his ·oldest [firstborn] son,
and the one who sets up the gates
  will lose his youngest son [1 Kin. 16:34]."

27So the LORD was with Joshua, and Joshua became famous through all the land.

The Sin of Achan

7 But the ·Israelites [Lsons/Tchildren of Israel] ·did not obey the LORD [Lacted unfaithfully in regard to the devoted things; 6:17]. There was a man from the tribe of Judah named Achan. (He was the son of Carmi and grandson of Zabdi, who was the son of Zerah.) Because Achan kept some of the ·things that were to be given to the LORD [Ldevoted things], the ·LORD became very angry [LLORD's anger burned] at the Israelites.

2Joshua sent some men from Jericho to Ai [Cthe name means "dump," indicating that it should have been an easy military target], which was near Beth Aven, east of Bethel. He told them, "Go to Ai and spy out the area." So the men went to spy on Ai.

3Later they came back to Joshua and said, "There are ·only a few people [few soldiers] in Ai, so we will not need all our people to defeat them. Send only two or three thousand men to fight. ·There is no need to send [*or* Don't tire out] all of our people." 4So about three thousand men went up to Ai, but ·the people of Ai beat them badly [Lthey fled from the men of Ai]. 5The people of Ai killed about thirty-six Israelites and then chased the rest from the city gate all the way down to ·the canyon [*or* the stone quarries; *or* Shebarim], killing them as they went down the hill. When the Israelites saw this, ·they lost their courage [Lthe heart of the people melted and became like water].

6Then Joshua tore his ·clothes in sorrow [Lclothes]. He ·bowed [fell] facedown on the ground before the Ark of the LORD and stayed there until evening. The ·leaders [Lelders] of Israel did the same thing. They also threw ·dirt [dust] on their heads [Cto show their sorrow]. 7Then Joshua said, "·Lord GOD [*or* Sovereign LORD], why did you bring our people across the Jordan River ·and then let the Amorites destroy us [to give us into the hands of the Amorites]? ·We would have [LIf only we had] been happy to stay on the other side of the Jordan. 8Lord, ·there is nothing I can say now [what can I say now that…]. Israel has ·been beaten by [fled from; Lturned their back before] the enemy. 9The Canaanites and all the other people in this country will hear about this and will ·surround [encircle] and ·kill us all [Lcut off our name from the earth]! Then what will you do for your own great name?"

10The LORD said to Joshua, "Stand up! Why are you down on your face? 11The Israelites have sinned; they have broken the ·agreement [covenant; treaty] I commanded them to obey. They took some of the ·things I commanded them to destroy [devoted things]. They have stolen and lied and have ·taken those things for themselves [Lput them among their own belongings]. 12That is why the ·Israelites [Lsons/Tchildren of Israel] cannot ·face [stand before] their enemies. They ·turn away from the fight and run [fled/turned their backs before their enemies], because I have ·commanded that they be destroyed [devoted them for destruction]. I will not ·help [Lbe with] you anymore unless you destroy ·everything as I commanded [the things devoted for destruction from among] you.

13"Now go! ·Make the people holy [Consecrate the people]. Tell them, '·Set yourselves apart to the LORD [Consecrate yourselves] for tomorrow. The LORD, the God of Israel, says ·some of you are keeping things he commanded you to destroy [Lthere are devoted things among you, Israel!].

You will never ·defeat [Lstand before] your enemies until you ·throw away those things [Lremove the devoted things from among you].

14“ ‘Tomorrow morning you must be present with your tribes. The LORD will choose one tribe to stand alone before him. Then the LORD will choose ·one family group [clan] from that tribe to stand before him. Then the LORD will choose one family from that ·family group [clan] to stand before him, person by person. 15The one who is ·keeping what should have been destroyed [Lcaught with the devoted things] will himself be destroyed by fire. Everything ·he owns [that is his] will be destroyed with him. He has broken the ·agreement [covenant; treaty] with the LORD and has done a disgraceful thing ·among the people of [Lin] Israel!’ ”

16Early the next morning Joshua led all of Israel to present themselves in their tribes, and the LORD chose the tribe of Judah. 17So the ·family groups [clans] of Judah presented themselves, and the LORD then chose the ·family group [clan] of Zerah. When all the ·families [clan] of Zerah presented themselves, the family of Zabdi was chosen. 18And Joshua told all the men in that family to present themselves. The LORD chose Achan son of Carmi. (Carmi was the son of Zabdi, who was the son of Zerah.)

19Then Joshua said to Achan, “My son, ·tell the truth. Confess to the LORD, the God of Israel [LGive glory to the LORD God of Israel and give praise to him; Ca solemn charge to tell the truth and confess his sins to God]. Tell me what you did, and don’t try to hide anything from me.”

20Achan answered, “It is true! I have sinned against the LORD, the God of Israel. This is what I did: 21Among the things I saw was a beautiful ·coat [robe; cloak] from ·Babylonia [LShinar] and about ·five pounds [Ltwo hundred shekels] of silver and ·more than one and one-fourth pounds of gold [La gold bar weighing fifty shekels]. I wanted these things very much for myself, so I took them. You will find them buried in the ground under my tent, with the silver underneath.”

22So Joshua sent ·men [Lmessengers] who ran to the tent and ·found the things [Tbehold, it was] hidden there, with the silver underneath. 23The men brought them out of the tent, took them to Joshua and all the ·Israelites [Lsons/Tchildren of Israel], and spread them out on the ground before the LORD. 24Then Joshua and all the people led Achan son of Zerah to the Valley of ·Trouble [*or* Achor; Ca Hebrew word meaning “trouble” or “disaster”]. They also took the silver, the coat, the gold bar, Achan’s sons, daughters, cattle, donkeys, sheep, tent, and everything he owned. 25Joshua said, “·I don’t know why [LWhy have...?] you caused so much trouble [CHebrew *achor*] for us, but now the LORD will bring trouble [CHebrew *achor*] to you.” Then all the people threw stones at Achan and his family until they died [Ex. 19:13; Lev. 24:23; Num. 15:36]. Then the people burned them. 26They piled rocks over Achan’s body, and they are still there today. That is why it is called the Valley of ·Trouble [LAchor]. After this the LORD ·was no longer angry [Lturned from his burning anger].

Ai Is Destroyed

8 Then the LORD said to Joshua, “Don’t be afraid or ·give up [be discouraged/dismayed; 1:9; 10:25]. Lead ·all your fighting men [the whole army] to Ai. I ·will help you defeat [Lhave given into your hand] the king of Ai, his people, his city, and his land. 2You will do to Ai and its king what you did to Jericho and its king. Only this time you may ·take all the wealth [Lplunder its goods and livestock] and keep it for yourselves. Now ·tell some of your soldiers to set up [Lset] an ambush behind the city.”

[3]So Joshua ·led his whole army toward [[L]and all the people rose to go up against] Ai. Then he chose thirty thousand ·of his best fighting men [brave warriors] and sent them out at night. [4]Joshua gave them these orders: "·Listen carefully [Look; [T]Behold]. You must set up an ambush behind the city. Don't go far from it, but continue to watch and be ready. [5]I and the men who are with me will march toward the city, and the men in the city will come out to fight us, just as they did before. Then we will ·turn and run away from [[L]flee before] them. [6]They will chase us away from the city, thinking we are running away from them as we did before. When we run away, [7]come out from your ambush and take the city. The LORD your God will give ·you the power to win [[L]it into your hand]. [8]After you take the city, burn it. ·See to it [[L]Look; [T]Behold]! You have your orders."

[9]Then Joshua sent them to wait in ambush between Bethel and Ai, to the west of Ai. But Joshua stayed the night ·with his [among the] people.

[10]Early the next morning Joshua ·gathered his men together [mustered the army]. He and the ·older leaders [elders] of Israel led them up to Ai. [11]All of the soldiers who were with Joshua marched up to Ai and stopped in front of the city and made camp north of it. There was a valley between them and the city. [12]Then Joshua chose about five thousand men and set them in ambush in the area west of the city between Bethel and Ai. [13]So the people took their positions; the main camp was north of the city, and the ·other men [rear guard; ambush] were hiding to the west. That night Joshua went down into[n] the valley.

[14]Now when the king of Ai saw the army of Israel, he and his people got up early the next morning and hurried out to fight them. They went out to ·a place east of the city [*or* the meeting/appointed place near the Arabah/desert plain], but the king did not know soldiers were waiting in ambush behind the city. [15]Joshua and all the men of Israel ·let the army of Ai push them back [pretended to be defeated]. Then they ran toward the ·desert [wilderness]. [16]All the men in Ai were called to chase Joshua and his men, so they ·left the city and went after them [were lured away from the city]. [17]All the men of Ai and Bethel chased the army of Israel [[C]nearby Bethel must have been closely allied with Ai]. The city was left ·open [unguarded]; not a man ·stayed to protect it [[L]was left in Ai or Bethel].

[18]Then the LORD said to Joshua, "Hold ·your spear [[L]the spear/javelin that is in your hand] toward Ai, because I will give ·you that city [[L]it into your hand]." So Joshua held ·his spear [[L]the spear/javelin that was in his hand] toward the city of Ai. [19]When the Israelites who were in ambush saw this, they quickly came out of their hiding place and hurried toward the city. They entered the city, ·took control of [captured] it, and quickly set it on fire.

[20]When the men of Ai looked back, ·they saw [[L]look; [T]behold] smoke rising [[L]into the sky] from their city. At the same time the Israelites stopped running and turned against ·the men of Ai [[L]their pursuers], who could not escape in any direction. [21]When Joshua and all ·his men [[L]Israel] saw that the ·army [men in ambush] had taken control of the city and saw the smoke rising from it, they stopped running and turned to ·fight [strike down] the men of Ai. [22]The men who were in ambush also came out of the city to help with the fight. So the men of Ai were caught between the armies of Israel. None of the enemy escaped. The Israelites ·fought

8:13 went down into Some Hebrew copies read "spent the time in" instead of "went down into."

[struck them down] until not one of the men of Ai ·was left alive [Leither
survived or escaped], except 23the king of Ai, and they brought him to
Joshua.

A Review of the Fighting

24During the fighting the army of Israel chased the men of Ai into the
fields and ·desert [wilderness] and killed all of them. Then they went back
to Ai and killed everyone there. 25All the people of Ai died that day, twelve
thousand men and women. 26Joshua ·had held his spear toward Ai, as a
sign to destroy the city, and did not draw it back [Ldid not draw back the
hand that held his spear/javelin] until all the people of Ai were ·destroyed
[devoted to destruction; 2:10; 6:17]. 27The people of Israel kept for themselves the animals and the ·other things the people of Ai had owned
[plunder of the city], as the LORD had commanded Joshua to do.

28Then Joshua burned the city of Ai and made it [Lpermanently; for-
ever] a pile of ruins. And it is still like that today. 29Joshua hanged the
king of Ai on a tree and left him there until evening [Can act of humiliation and shame; Deut. 21:23]. At sunset Joshua told his men to take the
king's body down from the tree and to throw it down at the city gate.
Then they covered it with a pile of rocks [7:26], which is still there today.

30Joshua built an altar for the LORD, the God of Israel, on Mount Ebal,
as 31Moses, the LORD's servant, had commanded the ·Israelites [Lsons/
Tchildren of Israel]. Joshua built the altar as it was explained in the Book
of the ·Teachings [Law] of Moses. It was made from ·uncut [whole]
stones; no tool was ever used on them. On that altar the Israelites offered
burnt offerings [Lev. 1:1–17] to the LORD and ·fellowship [*or* peace; well-
being] offerings [Lev. 3:1]. 32There Joshua ·wrote [made a copy of] the
teachings of Moses on stones for all the ·people [Lsons; children] of Israel
to see. 33The elders, officers, judges, and all the Israelites were there;
·Israelites and non-Israelites [native-born and foreigners] were all standing around the Ark of the ·Agreement with [Covenant of] the LORD in
front of the priests, the Levites who had carried the Ark. Half of the people stood in front of Mount Ebal, and half stood in front of Mount
Gerizim. This was the way the LORD's servant Moses had earlier commanded the people to be blessed [Deut. 11:29; 27:11–26].

34Then Joshua read all the words of the ·teachings [law; instruction], the
blessings and the curses, exactly as they were written in the Book of the
·Teachings [Law]. 35All the Israelites were gathered together—men, women,
and children—along with the ·non-Israelites [foreigners] who lived among
them. Joshua read every ·command [word] that Moses had given.

The Gibeonite Trickery

9 All the kings ·west of [Lbeyond] the Jordan River heard about
these things: the kings of the Hittites, Amorites, Canaanites,
Perizzites, Hivites, and Jebusites. They lived in the ·mountains [hill coun-
try] and ·on the western foothills [*or* in the lowlands/LShephelah] and
along the whole ·Mediterranean [LGreat] Sea coast. 2So all these kings
gathered to fight Joshua and the Israelites.

3When the ·people [inhabitants] of Gibeon heard ·how Joshua had
defeated [Lwhat Joshua had done to] Jericho and Ai, 4they decided to trick
the Israelites. They gathered old sacks and old ·leather wine bags [wine-
skins] that were cracked and mended, and they put them on the backs of
their donkeys. 5They put ·old [Lworn and patched] sandals on their feet
and wore ·old [ragged] clothes, and they took some dry, ·moldy [*or* crum-
bling] bread. 6Then they went to Joshua in the camp near Gilgal [4:19].

The men said to Joshua and the ·Israelites [Lmen of Israel], "We have
traveled from a faraway country. Make a peace ·agreement [covenant;
treaty] with us."
7The ·Israelites [men of Israel] said to these Hivites, "Maybe you live
near us. How can we make a peace ·agreement [covenant; treaty] with you
[Deut. 20:10–18]?"
8The Hivites said to Joshua, "We are your servants."
But Joshua asked, "Who are you? Where do you come from?"
9The men answered, "We are your servants who have come from a far
country, because we heard of the ·fame [reputation; Lname] of the LORD
your God. We heard about what he has done and everything he did in
Egypt. 10We heard that he defeated the two kings of the Amorites ·from
the east side of [Lwho were beyond] the Jordan River—Sihon king of
Heshbon and Og king of Bashan who ·ruled [Lwas] in Ashtaroth. 11So our
elders and ·our people [Lall the inhabitants of our country] said to us,
'Take ·food [provisions] for your journey and go and meet ·the Israelites
[Lthem]. Tell them, "We are your servants. Make a peace ·agreement [cov-
enant; treaty] with us." '
12"Look at our bread. On the day we left home to come to you it was
warm and fresh, but now [Llook; Tbehold] it is dry and ·moldy [*or* crum-
bling]. 13Look at our ·leather wine bags [wineskins]. They were new and
filled with wine, but now they ·are cracked and old [are ripped; *or* have
burst]. Our clothes and sandals are worn out from the long journey."
14The men of Israel ·tasted [*or* examined; Ltook some of] the bread, but
they did not ·ask the LORD what to do [seek the LORD's guidance]. 15So
Joshua agreed to make peace with the Gibeonites and to let them live.
And the leaders of the Israelites ·swore an oath to keep the agreement
[Lswore to them].
16Three days after they had made the ·agreement [covenant; treaty],
the Israelites learned that the Gibeonites ·lived nearby [Lwere neighbors
and lived in their midst]. 17So the ·Israelites [Lsons/Tchildren of Israel]
went to where they lived and on the third day came to their cities: Gibeon,
Kephirah, Beeroth, and Kiriath Jearim. 18But the ·Israelites [Lsons/
Tchildren of Israel] did not attack those cities, because they had ·made a
promise [Lsworn] to them before the LORD, the God of Israel.
·All the Israelites [The whole assembly/congregation] grumbled
against the leaders. 19But [Lall] the leaders answered, "We ·have given our
promise [Lswore (an oath)] before the LORD, the God of Israel, so we cannot ·attack [Ltouch] them now. 20This is what we must do. We must let
them live. Otherwise, ·God's anger [Lwrath] will ·be against [come upon]
us for breaking the oath we swore to them. 21So let them live, but they will
cut wood and carry water for ·our people [the whole congregation]." ·So
the leaders kept their promise to them [*or*...as the leaders had decided].
22Joshua called for the Gibeonites and asked, "Why did you ·lie to
[deceive; trick] us? ·Your land was near our camp [LYou live among us],
but you told us you were from a far country. 23Now, you will be placed
under a curse to ·be our slaves [never cease being slaves/servants]. You will
have to cut wood and carry water for the house of my God."
24The Gibeonites answered Joshua, "We lied to you because we were
afraid you would kill us. ·We heard [LIt was clearly/with certainty reported
to your servants] that the LORD your God commanded his servant Moses
to give you all of this land and to ·kill [destroy] all the people who lived in

it [Deut. 20:15–18]. That is why we did this. 25Now [Llook; Tbehold] ·you can decide what [Lwe are in your hands] to do with us, whatever you think is right."

26So Joshua saved their lives by not allowing the ·Israelites [Lsons/Tchildren of Israel] to kill them, 27but he made the Gibeonites slaves. They cut wood and carried water for the Israelites, and they did it for the altar of the LORD—·wherever he chose it to be [Lat the place that he would choose; 1 Sam. 4:3; 1 Kin. 9:3]. They are still doing this today [2 Sam. 21:1–14].

The Sun Stands Still

10 At this time Adoni-Zedek king of Jerusalem heard that Joshua had ·defeated [captured] Ai and ·completely destroyed it [devoted it to destruction; 2:10; 6:17], doing to Ai and its king as he had also done to Jericho and its king. The king also learned that the Gibeonites had made a peace ·agreement [covenant; treaty] with Israel and that they ·lived nearby [were living among them; *or* had become allies]. 2Adoni-Zedek and his people were very afraid because of this. Gibeon was not a little town like Ai; it was a ·large [great; important] city, ·as big as a city that had a king [Llike one of the royal cities], and all its men were good fighters. 3So Adoni-Zedek king of Jerusalem sent a message to Hoham king of Hebron, Piram king of Jarmuth, Japhia king of Lachish, and Debir king of Eglon [Cfive major cities in the southern mountains]. He begged them, 4"Come with me and help me attack Gibeon, which has made a peace ·agreement [covenant; treaty] with Joshua and the Israelites."

5Then these five Amorite kings—the kings of Jerusalem, Hebron, Jarmuth, Lachish, and Eglon—gathered their armies, went to Gibeon, surrounded it, and attacked it.

6The Gibeonites sent this message to Joshua in his camp at Gilgal [4:19]: "Don't ·let us, your servants, be destroyed [abandon your servants]. Come quickly and help us! Save us! All the Amorite kings from the mountains have joined their armies and are fighting against us."

7So Joshua marched out of Gilgal with his whole army, including his best fighting men. 8The LORD said to Joshua, "Don't be afraid of those armies, because I will ·hand them over to you [Lgive them into your hand]. None of them will be able to stand against you."

9Joshua and his army marched all night from Gilgal for a surprise attack. 10The LORD ·confused those armies [threw them into a panic] when Israel attacked, so Israel defeated them in a great victory at Gibeon. They chased them along the road going up to Beth Horon and ·killed men [Lstruck them down] all the way to Azekah and Makkedah. 11As they chased the enemy down the Beth Horon Pass to Azekah, the LORD threw large hailstones on them from the ·sky [heavens] and killed them. More people were killed by the hailstones than by the Israelites' swords.

12On the day that the LORD gave up the Amorites to the ·Israelites [Lsons/Tchildren of Israel], Joshua stood before all the people of Israel and said to the LORD:

"Sun, stand still over Gibeon.
  Moon, stand still over the Valley of Aijalon."
13So the sun stood still,
  and the moon stopped
  until the ·people [nation] ·defeated [took vengeance on] their enemies.

·These words are [LIs this not…?] written in the ·Book [Scroll] of Jashar [Cmeaning "Upright One"; an extrabiblical account of Israel's wars, now lost; 2 Sam. 1:18].

The sun stopped in the middle of the sky and waited to go down for a full day. 14·That has never happened at any time [LThere has been no day like it] before that day or since. That was the day the LORD listened to a human being. Truly the LORD was fighting for Israel!

15After this, Joshua and his army went back to the camp at Gilgal.

16During the fight the five kings ran away and hid in a cave ·near [at] Makkedah, 17but someone found them hiding in the cave at Makkedah and told Joshua. 18So he said, "·Cover the opening of the cave with large rocks [LRoll large stones against the mouth of the cave]. Put some men there to guard it, 19but don't stay there yourselves. Continue chasing the enemy and attacking them from behind. Don't let them get to their cities, because the LORD your God will ·hand them over to you [Lgive them into your hand]."

20So Joshua and the ·Israelites [Lsons/Tchildren of Israel] ·killed the enemy [Lfinished slaying them with a very great slaughter], but a ·few [remnant; few survivors] were able to get back to their strong, walled cities. 21After the fighting, Joshua's men came back safely to him at Makkedah. No one ·was brave enough to say a word against [*or* suffered even a scratch on his tongue; Cthe Hebrew idiom "sharpened/scratched his tongue" may mean to threaten with words or to suffer a minor injury] the ·Israelites [Lsons/Tchildren of Israel].

22Joshua said, "Move the ·rocks that are covering the opening [Lmouth] of the cave and bring those five kings out to me." 23So Joshua's men brought the five kings out of the cave—the kings of Jerusalem, Hebron, Jarmuth, Lachish, and Eglon. 24When they brought the five kings out to Joshua, he called for all his men. He said to the commanders of his army, "Come here! Put your feet on the necks of these kings." So they came close and put their feet on their necks [Ca gesture of triumph and dominance; 2 Sam. 22:41; Ps. 18:41].

25Joshua said to his men, "Be strong and brave! Don't be afraid or ·discouraged [dismayed; 1:9; 8:1], because I will show you what the LORD will do to the enemies you will fight in the future." 26Then Joshua killed the five kings and hung their bodies on five trees [Can act of humiliation and shame; Deut. 21:23], where he left them until evening.

27At sunset Joshua ·told [commanded] his men to take the bodies down from the trees. Then they threw them into the same cave where they had been hiding and covered the opening of the cave with large rocks, which are still there today.

28That day Joshua ·defeated [Lcaptured] Makkedah. He killed the king and ·completely destroyed [devoted to destruction; 2:10; 6:17; 10:1] all the people in that city as an offering to the LORD; no one was left alive. He did the same thing to the king of Makkedah that he had done to the king of Jericho.

Defeating Southern Cities

29Joshua and all the Israelites traveled from Makkedah to Libnah and attacked it. 30The LORD handed over the city and its king. They ·killed [Lstruck with the edge of the sword] every person in the city; no one was left alive. And they did the same thing to that king that they had done to the king of Jericho.

31 Then Joshua and all the Israelites left Libnah and went to Lachish,
which they ·surrounded [took up positions against; besieged] and
attacked. 32 The LORD ·handed over Lachish [Lgave Lachish into their hand]
on the second day. The Israelites ·killed [Lstruck with the edge of the
sword] everyone in that city just as they had done to Libnah. 33 During
this same time Horam king of Gezer came to help Lachish, but Joshua
also defeated him and his army; no one was left alive.
34 Then Joshua and all the Israelites went from Lachish to Eglon. They
·surrounded [took up positions against; besieged] Eglon, attacked it, and
35 captured it the same day. They ·killed [Lstruck with the edge of the
sword] all its people and ·completely destroyed [devoted to destruction;
6:17; 10:28] everything in it as an offering to the LORD, just as they had
done to Lachish.
36 Then Joshua and the Israelites went from Eglon to Hebron and
attacked it, 37 capturing it and all the little towns near it. The Israelites
·killed [Lstruck with the edge of the sword] its king, its surrounding towns,
and everyone in Hebron; no one was left alive there. Just as they had done
to Eglon, they ·completely destroyed [devoted to destruction; 6:17; 10:28]
the city and all its people as an offering to the LORD.
38 Then Joshua and the Israelites went back to Debir and attacked it.
39 They captured that city, its king, and all the little towns near it, ·com-
pletely destroying [Lstriking with the edge of the sword and devoting to
destruction; 10:37] everyone in Debir as an offering to the LORD; no one
was left alive there. Israel did to Debir and its king just as they had done
to Libnah and its king, just as they had done to Hebron.
40 So Joshua ·defeated [Lstruck down] ·all the kings of the cities of these
areas [Lthe whole region/land]: the ·mountains [hill country], ·southern
Canaan [Lthe Negev], the ·western foothills [lowlands; LShephelah], and
the slopes [Land all their kings]. The LORD, the God of Israel, had ·told
[commanded] Joshua to ·completely destroy [devote to destruction; 2:10;
6:17] all ·the people [Lthat breathed] as an offering to the LORD, so he left
no one alive in those places. 41 Joshua captured all the cities from Kadesh
Barnea to Gaza, and from Goshen to Gibeon. 42 He captured all these cities and their kings ·on one trip [in one campaign; Lat one time], because
the LORD, the God of Israel, was fighting for Israel.
43 Then Joshua and all the Israelites returned to their camp at Gilgal
[4:19].

Defeating Northern Kings

11 When Jabin king of Hazor [Cthe largest and best fortified of
the Canaanite cities] heard about all that had happened, he
sent messages to Jobab king of Madon, to the king of Shimron, and to
the king of Acshaph. 2 He sent messages to the kings in the northern
·mountains [hill country] and also to the kings in the ·Jordan Valley [*or*
Arabah] south of ·Lake Galilee [LKinnereth] and in the ·western foothills [lowlands; LShephelah]. He sent a message to the king of ·Naphoth
[*or* the heights of] Dor in the west [Cthe coastal plain south of Mount
Carmel] 3 and to the kings of the Canaanites in the east and in the west.
He sent messages to the Amorites, Hittites, Perizzites, and Jebusites in
the ·mountains [hill country]. Jabin also sent one to the Hivites, who
lived below Mount Hermon in the area of Mizpah [Ca coalition of the
northern cities of Palestine]. 4 So the armies of all these kings came
together with their horses and chariots [Ca great challenge to the

Israelites, who only had foot soldiers]. There were as many soldiers as grains of sand on the seashore [Gen. 22:17].

5 All of these kings met together at the waters of Merom [Cprobably modern Meirun, eight miles northwest of the Sea of Galilee], joined their armies together into one camp, and made plans to fight against the Israelites.

6 Then the LORD said to Joshua, "Don't be afraid of them, because at this time tomorrow I will give them to you. You will ·cripple [hamstring] their horses and burn all their chariots."

7 So Joshua and his whole army surprised the enemy [10:9] by attacking them at the waters of Merom. 8 The LORD ·handed them over to [Lgave them into the hand of] Israel. They chased them to Greater Sidon, Misrephoth Maim, and the Valley of Mizpah in the east [Clocations north and west of the battle]. Israel fought until none of the enemy was left alive. 9 Joshua did what the LORD said to do; he ·crippled [hamstrung] their horses and burned their chariots [CIsrael did not take the horses and chariots to use themselves, in order to show their trust in God; Ps. 20:7].

10 Then Joshua went back and captured the city of Hazor and ·killed [Lstruck with the sword] its king. (Hazor had been the leader of all the kingdoms that fought against Israel.) 11 Israel ·killed [Lstruck with the sword] everyone in Hazor, ·completely destroying them [devoting them to destruction; 2:10; 6:21]; no one was left ·alive [Lthat breathed]. Then they burned Hazor itself.

12 Joshua captured all of these cities, ·killed [Lstruck with the edge of the sword] all of their kings, and ·completely destroyed [devoted to destruction; v. 11] everything in these cities. He did this just as Moses, the servant of the LORD, had commanded. 13 But the Israelites did not burn any cities that were built on their mounds [Cso Israel could immediately occupy these strategically important cities; Deut. 6:10–11], except Hazor; only that city was burned by Joshua. 14 The ·people [Lsons; children] of Israel kept for themselves ·everything [the plunder/spoil] they found in the cities, including all the animals. But they ·killed [Lstruck with the edge of the sword] all the people there; they left no one ·alive [Lthat breathed]. 15 Long ago the LORD had commanded his servant Moses to do this, and then Moses had commanded Joshua to do it [Deut. 7:1–6; 20:16–18]. Joshua ·did everything [Lleft nothing undone that] the LORD had commanded Moses.

16 So Joshua defeated all the people in the land [Ca general statement, since not every city was taken; 17:16; Judg. 1]. He had control of the mountains and ·the area of southern Canaan [Lall the Negev], all the areas of Goshen, the ·western foothills [lowlands; LShephelah], and the ·Jordan Valley [*or* Arabah]. He controlled the ·mountains [hill country] of Israel and ·all the hills near them [*or* its lowlands/LShephelah]. 17 ·Joshua controlled all the land from [L...from] Mount Halak near ·Edom [LSeir] to Baal Gad in the Valley of Lebanon, below Mount Hermon. Joshua also captured all the kings in the land and killed them. 18 He ·fought [waged war] against them for ·many years [a long time; Lmany days]. 19 The people of only one city in all the land had made a peace ·agreement [covenant; treaty] with Israel—the Hivites living in Gibeon. All the other cities were defeated in war. 20 The LORD ·made those people stubborn [Lhardened their hearts; Ex. 8:15] so they would fight against Israel and ·he could completely destroy them [would be devoted to destruction; 2:10; 6:17] without mercy. This is what the LORD had commanded Moses to do.

21 Now Joshua fought the Anakites [*or* Anakim; Num. 13:33] who lived

in the ·mountains [hill country] of Hebron, Debir, Anab, Judah, and Israel, and he completely destroyed them and their towns. [22]There were no Anakites left living in the land of the Israelites ·and only a few were left [*or* though some remained] in Gaza, Gath, and Ashdod. [23]Joshua took control of all the ·land of Israel [[L]land] as the LORD had ·told Moses to do [*or* promised Moses] long ago. He gave the land to Israel, ·because he had promised it to them [[L]as an inheritance]. ·Then Joshua divided the land among the tribes of Israel [[L]...according to their tribal divisions], and ·there was peace in the land [the land had rest from war].

Kings Defeated by Israel

12 The Israelites took control of the land east of the Jordan River from the Arnon ·Ravine [Gorge; Valley; [C]enters the middle of Dead Sea from the east] to Mount Hermon [[C]in the far north] and all the land along the eastern side of the ·Jordan Valley [*or* Arabah]. These ·lands belonged to the kings [were the kings of the land] whom the ·Israelites [[L]sons/[T]children of Israel] defeated.

[2]Sihon king of the Amorites [Num. 21:21–30; Deut. 1:4; 2:24–37; 29:7–8] ·lived in [*or* ruled] the city of Heshbon and ruled the land from Aroer ·at [*or* on the edge/rim of] the Arnon ·Ravine [Gorge; Valley] to the Jabbok River [[C]flows from the northeast into the Jordan about 20 miles north of the Dead Sea]. His land started in the middle of the ravine, which was their border with the Ammonites. Sihon ruled over half the land of Gilead [[C]the region east of the Jordan between Galilee and just north of the Dead Sea] [3]and over the eastern side of the ·Jordan Valley [*or* Arabah] from Lake ·Galilee [[L]Kinnereth] to the ·Dead Sea [[L]Sea of Arabah, the Salt Sea]. And he ruled from Beth Jeshimoth south to the slopes of Pisgah [Deut. 34:1].

[4]Og king of Bashan was one of the ·last [remnant] of the Rephaites. He ·ruled [*or* lived in] the land in Ashtaroth and Edrei [[C]cities east and southeast of Galilee]. [5]He ruled over Mount Hermon, Salecah, and all the area of Bashan [[C]east and northeast of Galilee] up to ·where the people of Geshur and Maacah lived [[L]the border of the Geshurites and the Maacathites]. Og also ruled half the land of Gilead up to the border of Sihon king of Heshbon.

[6]The LORD's servant Moses and the ·Israelites [[L]sons/[T]children of Israel] defeated all these kings, and Moses gave that land to the tribes of Reuben and Gad and to ·East [[L]the half-tribe of] Manasseh as their own [13:8–32; Deut. 3:12–13].

[7]Joshua and the ·Israelites [[L]sons/[T]children of Israel] also defeated kings in the land west of the Jordan River. He gave the people the land ·and divided it among the twelve tribes to be their own [[L]according to their tribal divisions]. It was between Baal Gad in the Valley of Lebanon [[C]the far north] and Mount Halak near ·Edom [[L]Seir; [C]the far south]. [8]This included the ·mountains [hill country], the ·western foothills [lowlands; [L]Shephelah], the ·Jordan Valley [[L]Arabah], the slopes, the ·desert [wilderness], and ·southern Canaan [[L]the Negev]. This was the land where the Hittites, Amorites, Canaanites, Perizzites, Hivites, and Jebusites had lived. The Israelites defeated the king of each of the following cities: [9]·Jericho [[L]the king of Jericho, one; [C]and so throughout the list], Ai (near Bethel), [10]Jerusalem, Hebron, [11]Jarmuth, Lachish, [12]Eglon, Gezer, [13]Debir, Geder, [14]Hormah, Arad, [15]Libnah, Adullam, [16]Makkedah, Bethel, [17]Tappuah, Hepher, [18]Aphek, Lasharon, [19]Madon, Hazor, [20]Shimron Meron, Acshaph,

21Taanach, Megiddo, 22Kedesh, Jokneam ·in [*or* near] Carmel, 23Dor (in
Naphoth Dor), Goyim in Gilgal, and 24Tirzah.
The total number of kings was thirty-one.

Land Still to Be Taken

13 When Joshua was very old, the LORD said to him, "Joshua, you
have grown old, but there is still much land for you to ·take
[possess; conquer]. 2This is what is left: the regions of Geshur and of the
Philistines [Cthe southern coastline along the Mediterranean Sea]; 3the
area from the Shihor River [CWadi el-Arish located below Gaza] ·at the
border [east; Lin front] of Egypt ·to [Lto the border of] Ekron in the north,
which ·belongs to the Canaanites [Lis regarded/counted as Canaanite];
the five Philistine ·leaders [rulers; lords] at Gaza, Ashdod, Ashkelon,
Gath, and Ekron; the Avvites, 4·who live south of the Canaanite land,
from Arah of the Sidonians [Cthe people of the northern coastal plains] to
Aphek, to the border of the Amorites; 5the ·Gebalites [Cinhabitants of the
city of Byblos, located north of modern Beirut], and the area of Lebanon
east of Baal Gad below Mount Hermon to Lebo Hamath.
6"The Sidonians are living in the hill country from Lebanon to
Misrephoth Maim, but I will ·force [drive] all of them out ahead of the
·Israelites [Lsons/Tchildren of Israel]. Be sure to ·remember this land when
you divide the land among the Israelites [Lallocate this land to Israel as an
inheritance], as I ·told [commanded] you.
7"Now divide the land ·among [Las an inheritance among] the nine
tribes and ·West [Lthe half-tribe of] Manasseh."

Dividing the Land

8·East Manasseh and [LWith it; Creferring to the other half-tribe of
Manasseh] the tribes of Reuben and Gad had received their ·land [inheri-
tance]. The LORD's servant Moses had given them the land east of the
Jordan River [Deut. 3:18–20]. 9·Their land started at [LFrom] Aroer at the
Arnon ·Ravine [Valley; 12:1] ·and continued to [*or* including] the town in
the middle of the ravine, and it included the whole ·plain [*or* plateau]
from Medeba to Dibon. 10All the towns ruled by Sihon king of the
Amorites, who ruled in the city of Heshbon, were in that land. The land
continued to the area where the Ammonites lived. 11Gilead [12:3] was
also there, as well as the area where the people of Geshur and Maacah
lived, and all of Mount Hermon and Bashan as far as Salecah. 12All the
kingdom of Og king of Bashan was in the land [12:4–5]. Og was ·one of
the last [Lfrom the remnant] of the Rephaites, and in the past he ruled in
Ashtaroth and Edrei. Moses had ·defeated [struck] them and had taken
their land. 13Because the ·Israelites [Lsons/Tchildren of Israel] did not
·force [drive] out the people of Geshur and Maacah, they still live among
the Israelites today.
14The tribe of Levi was the only one that ·did not get any land [Lhe gave
no inheritance]. Instead, they were given all the burned sacrifices [Ca portion of the food offerings] made to the LORD, the God of Israel, as he had
promised them [14:3–4; Num. 3:45; 35:1–8].
15Moses had given each ·family group [clan] from the tribe of Reuben
some land: 16Theirs was the land from Aroer near the Arnon ·Ravine
[Valley; 12:1] to the town of Medeba, including the whole plain and the
town in the middle of the ·ravine [valley]; 17Heshbon and all ·the [Lits]
towns on the plain: Dibon, Bamoth Baal, and Beth Baal Meon, 18Jahaz,
Kedemoth, Mephaath, 19Kiriathaim, Sibmah, Zereth Shahar on the hill in
the valley, 20Beth Peor, the ·hills [slopes] of Pisgah, and Beth Jeshimoth.

21So that land included all the towns on the plain and all the area that Sihon king of the Amorites had ruled from the town of Heshbon. Moses had defeated him along with the leaders of the Midianites, including Evi, Rekem, Zur, Hur, and Reba. All these ·leaders [princes] ·fought together with [*or* were subjects of] Sihon and lived in that country. 22The ·Israelites [Lsons/Tchildren of Israel] ·killed [Lslayed with the sword] many people during the fighting, including Balaam of Beor, who ·tried to use magic to tell the future [practiced divination; Num. 22–24]. 23The land given to Reuben stopped at the shore of the Jordan River. So the ·land [inheritance] given to the ·family groups [clans] of Reuben included all these towns and their villages.

24This is the land Moses gave to the tribe of Gad, to all its ·family groups [clans]: 25the land of Jazer and all the towns of Gilead; half the land of the Ammonites that went as far as Aroer near Rabbah; 26the area from Heshbon to Ramath Mizpah and Betonim; the area from Mahanaim to the land of Debir; 27in the valley, Beth Haram, Beth Nimrah, Succoth, and Zaphon, the ·other land [rest of the kingdom] Sihon king of Heshbon had ruled east of the Jordan River and continuing to the end of Lake ·Galilee [LKinnereth]. 28·All this land went to [LThis is the inheritance of] the ·family groups [clans] of Gad, including all these towns and their villages.

29This is the land Moses had given to ·East [Lthe half-tribe of] Manasseh. Half of all the ·family groups [clans] in the tribe of Manasseh were given this land: 30The land started at Mahanaim and included all of Bashan [12:4] and the land ruled by Og king of Bashan; all the towns of Jair in Bashan, sixty cities in all; 31half of Gilead, Ashtaroth, and Edrei, the cities where Og king of Bashan had ruled. All this went to the ·family [*or* descendants; Lchildren/sons] of Makir son of Manasseh, and half of all his ·sons [descendants] were given this land.

32Moses had given this land to these tribes on the plains of Moab across the Jordan River east of Jericho [Num. 32:32, 39–42]. 33But Moses had given no land to the tribe of Levi because the LORD, the God of Israel, promised that he himself would be the gift for the Levites [v. 14; 18:7; Num. 18:20; Deut. 18:1–8].

14 Eleazar the priest [the son of Aaron; Ex. 28:1; Num. 34:17], Joshua son of Nun, and the ·leaders [Lheads of the fathers] of all the tribes of Israel decided what land to give to the people in the land of Canaan. 2The LORD had commanded Moses long ago how he wanted the people to choose their land. The people of the nine-and-a-half tribes threw lots [Ccasting lots left the decision to God; the Urim and Thummim may have been used; Ex. 28:30; Num. 27:21] to decide which land they would receive. 3Moses had already given the two-and-a-half tribes their land east of the Jordan River. But the tribe of Levi was not given any ·land [inheritance] like the others. 4The sons of Joseph had ·divided into [Lbecome] two tribes—Manasseh and Ephraim. The tribe of Levi was not given any ·land [inheritance]. It was given only some towns in which to live and pastures for its ·animals [Lcattle and property]. 5The LORD had told Moses how to give the land to the tribes of Israel, and the ·Israelites [Lsons/Tchildren of Israel] divided the land.

Caleb's Land

6One day ·some men from the tribe of Judah [Lthe sons/descendants of Judah] went to Joshua at Gilgal [4:19]. Among them was Caleb son of Jephunneh the Kenizzite. He said to Joshua, "You remember what the

LORD said at Kadesh Barnea when he was speaking to ·the prophet Moses [LMoses, the man of God] about you and me [Num. 14:6–9, 24, 30]. 7Moses, the LORD's servant, sent me to ·look at [spy out] the land where we were going. I was forty years old then. When I came back, I ·told Moses what I thought about the land [brought back an honest report; Lbrought him word as it was in my heart; Num. 13:30]. 8The other men who went with me ·frightened the people [Lmade the heart of the people melt; Num. 13:27–29; 14:1–4], but I ·fully believed the LORD would allow us to take the land [*or* remained loyal to the LORD; Lfollowed the LORD]. 9So that day Moses ·promised [swore to; made an oath to] me, 'The land where ·you went [Lyour foot has trodden] will become your ·land [inheritance], and your children will own it forever. I will give you that land because you ·fully believed in [*or* remained loyal to; Lfollowed] the LORD, my God.'

10"Now then, [Llook; Tbehold] the LORD has kept his promise. He has kept me alive for forty-five years from the time he said this to Moses during the time ·we all [LIsrael] wandered in the ·desert [wilderness]. Now ·here [Llook; Tbehold] I am, eighty-five years old. 11I am still as strong today as I was the day Moses sent me out, ·and I am just as ready to fight now as I was then [Lmy strength then is like my strength now, for battle and for going out and coming in]. 12So give me the mountain country the LORD promised me that day long ago. Back then you heard that the ·Anakite people [Anakim] lived there and the cities were large and well protected. But now with the LORD helping me, I will ·force [drive] them out, just as the LORD said."

13Joshua blessed Caleb son of Jephunneh and gave him the city of Hebron [Csouthwest of Jerusalem in the Judean hills] as his ·own [Linheritance]. 14Hebron still ·belongs to [remains the inheritance of] the family of Caleb son of Jephunneh the Kenizzite because he ·had faith and obeyed [remained loyal to; Lwholly followed] the LORD, the God of Israel. 15(In the past Hebron was called Kiriath Arba, named for Arba, the greatest man among the Anakites.)

After this ·there was peace in the land [Lthe land had rest from war].

Land for Judah

15 The ·land that was given to [allotment for] the tribe of Judah was divided among all the ·family groups [clans]. It went all the way to the ·Desert [Wilderness] of Zin in the far south, at the border of Edom.

2The southern border of Judah's land started at the south end of the ·Dead [LSalt] Sea 3and went south of ·Scorpion Pass [*or* the ascent of Akrabbim] to Zin. From there it passed to the south of Kadesh Barnea and continued past Hezron to Addar. From Addar it turned and went to Karka. 4It continued to Azmon, the ·brook [stream; wadi] of Egypt, and then to the ·Mediterranean Sea [LSea]. This was the southern border.

5The eastern border was the shore of the ·Dead [LSalt] Sea, as far as the mouth of the Jordan River.

The northern border started at the bay of the sea at the mouth of the Jordan River. 6Then it went to Beth Hoglah and continued north of Beth Arabah to the stone of Bohan son of Reuben. 7Then ·the northern border went [Lthe border went up] through the Valley of Achor to Debir where it turned toward the north and went to Gilgal. Gilgal is ·across from the road that goes through [Lopposite] Adummim Pass, on the south side of

the ·ravine [valley; gorge]. The border continued to the waters of En
Shemesh and stopped at En Rogel. 8Then it went through the Valley of
·Ben [the Son of] Hinnom, next to the southern ·side [slope] of the
Jebusite city (·which is called [that is,] Jerusalem). There the border went
to the top of the hill on the west side of Hinnom Valley, at the northern
end of the Valley of ·Giants [LRaphaim]. 9From there it went to the spring
of the waters of Nephtoah and then it went to the cities near Mount
Ephron. There it turned and went toward Baalah, ·which is called [that
is,] Kiriath Jearim. 10At Baalah the border turned west and went toward
Mount Seir. It continued along the ·north side [northern slope] of Mount
Jearim (also called Kesalon) and ·came [*or* descended] to Beth Shemesh.
From there it ·went past [*or* crossed to] Timnah 11to the ·hill north [north-
ern slope] of Ekron. Then it turned toward Shikkeron and ·went past [*or*
crossed to] Mount Baalah and continued on to Jabneel, ending at the sea.
12The ·Mediterranean [Great] Sea was the western border. Inside these
borders lived the ·family groups [clans] of Judah.
13The LORD had commanded Joshua to give Caleb son of Jephunneh
·part of the land [a portion] in Judah, so he gave Caleb the town of Kiriath
Arba, ·also called [that is,] Hebron [14:13]. (Arba was the father of Anak.)
14Caleb ·forced [drove] out the three ·Anakite families [Lsons of Anak]
living in Hebron: Sheshai, Ahiman, and Talmai, the descendants of Anak.
15Then he left there and went to fight against the people living in Debir.
(In the past Debir had been called Kiriath Sepher.) 16Caleb said, "I will
give Acsah, my daughter, as a wife to the man who attacks and captures
the city of Kiriath Sepher." 17Othniel son of Kenaz, Caleb's brother, captured the city, so Caleb gave his daughter Acsah to Othniel to be his wife.
18When Acsah came to ·Othniel [Lhim; Ccould be Othniel or Caleb], she
·told him to ask [*or* asked] her father for a field.
So Acsah went to her father. When she got down from her donkey,
Caleb asked her, "What do you want?"
19Acsah answered, "·Do me a special favor [LGive me a blessing]. Since
you have given me land in ·southern Canaan [Lthe Negev], also give me
springs of water." So Caleb gave her the upper and lower springs.
20·The tribe of Judah got the land God had promised them [LThis is the
inheritance of the tribe of the sons of Judah]. ·Each family group got part
of the land [L...according to its clans].
21The tribe of Judah got all these towns in the ·southern part of Canaan
[extreme south; LNegev] near the border of Edom: Kabzeel, Eder, Jagur,
22Kinah, Dimonah, Adadah, 23Kedesh, Hazor, Ithnan, 24Ziph, Telem,
Bealoth, 25Hazor Hadattah, Kerioth Hezron (also called Hazor), 26Amam,
Shema, Moladah, 27Hazar Gaddah, Heshmon, Beth Pelet, 28Hazar Shual,
Beersheba, Biziothiah, 29Baalah, Iim, Ezem, 30Eltolad, Kesil, Hormah,
31Ziklag, Madmannah, Sansannah, 32Lebaoth, Shilhim, Ain, and Rimmon.
There were twenty-nine towns and their villages.
33The tribe of Judah got these towns in the ·western foothills [low-
lands]: Eshtaol, Zorah, Ashnah, 34Zanoah, En Gannim, Tappuah, Enam,
35Jarmuth, Adullam, Socoh, Azekah, 36Shaaraim, Adithaim, and Gederah
(also called Gederothaim). There were fourteen towns and their villages.
37Judah was also given Zenan, Hadashah, Migdal Gad, 38Dilean,
Mizpah, Joktheel, 39Lachish, Bozkath, Eglon, 40Cabbon, Lahmas, Kitlish,
41Gederoth, Beth Dagon, Naamah, and Makkedah. There were sixteen
towns and their villages.

42Judah was also given Libnah, Ether, Ashan, 43Iphtah, Ashnah, Nezib,
44Keilah, Aczib, and Mareshah. There were nine towns and their villages.
45Judah was also given Ekron and all the small towns and villages near
it; 46the area west of Ekron and all the villages and small towns near
Ashdod; 47Ashdod and the small towns and villages around it; the villages
and small towns around Gaza as far as the ·brook [stream; wadi] of Egypt
and along the coast of the ·Mediterranean [LGreat] Sea.
48Judah was also given these towns in the ·mountains [hill country]:
Shamir, Jattir, Socoh, 49Dannah, Kiriath Sannah (also called Debir),
50Anab, Eshtemoh, Anim, 51Goshen, Holon, and Giloh. There were eleven
towns and their villages.
52They were also given Arab, Dumah, Eshan, 53Janim, Beth Tappuah,
Aphekah, 54Humtah, Kiriath Arba (also called Hebron), and Zior. There
were nine towns and their villages.
55Judah was also given Maon, Carmel, Ziph, Juttah, 56Jezreel, Jokdeam,
Zanoah, 57Kain, Gibeah, and Timnah. There were ten towns and their
villages.
58They were also given Halhul, Beth Zur, Gedor, 59Maarath, Beth
Anoth, and Eltekon. There were six towns and their villages.
60They were also given the two towns of Rabbah and Kiriath Baal (also
called Kiriath Jearim) and their villages.
61Judah was given these towns in the ·desert [wilderness]: Beth Arabah,
Middin, Secacah, 62Nibshan, the City of Salt, and En Gedi. There were six
towns and all their villages.
63The ·army [people; Lsons] of Judah was not able to ·force [drive] out
the Jebusites living in Jerusalem, so the Jebusites still live among the people of Judah to this day.

Land for Ephraim and Manasseh

16 This is the ·land [allotment] the ·tribe [Lsons; descendants] of
Joseph received. It started at the Jordan River near Jericho
and continued to the ·waters [springs] of Jericho, just east of the city.
The border went up from Jericho to the ·mountains [hill country] of
Bethel [Clocated northwest of Jersusalem]. 2Then it continued from
Bethel ·(also called Luz) [or to Luz] ·to [crossing over to] the Arkite border at Ataroth. 3From there it went west to the ·border [Lterritory] of the
Japhletites and continued to the area of the Lower Beth Horon. Then it
went to Gezer and ended at the sea.
4So Manasseh and Ephraim, sons of Joseph, received their ·land
[inheritance].
5This is the land that was given to the ·family groups [clans] of
Ephraim: Their border [Lof their inheritance] started at Ataroth Addar in
the east, went to Upper Beth Horon, 6and then to the sea. From
Micmethath [Lon the north] it turned eastward toward Taanath Shiloh
and ·continued eastward [or passing by it on the east] to Janoah. 7Then it
went down from Janoah to Ataroth and to Naarah. It continued until it
touched Jericho and stopped at the Jordan River. 8The border went from
Tappuah west to Kanah ·Ravine [Valley; or Brook] and ended at the sea.
This is all the ·land [inheritance] that was given to each ·family group
[clan] in the tribe of the Ephraimites. 9·Many of the towns were actually
within Manasseh's borders, but the people of Ephraim got those towns
and their villages [L...and the cities set apart for the sons of Ephraim in
the midst of the inheritance of the sons of Manasseh, all the cities and

their villages]. 10The Ephraimites could not ·force the Canaanites to leave
[drive out the Canaanites living in] Gezer, so the Canaanites still live
among the Ephraimites today, but they became ·slaves [forced laborers]
of the Ephraimites.

17 Then land was ·given [allotted] to the tribe of Manasseh,
Joseph's ·first son [firstborn; Gen. 41:51]. Manasseh's ·first
son [firstborn] was Makir [Gen. 50:23], the ·father of Gilead [*or* ancestor
of the Gileadites]. ·Makir was a great soldier [*or* His descendants were
great solders], so the lands of Gilead and Bashan were given to his family. 2·Land [An allotment] was also given to the other ·family groups of
Manasseh [Lsons/descendants of Manasseh, by their clans]—[Lthe sons/
descendants of] Abiezer, Helek, Asriel, Shechem, Hepher, and Shemida.
These were ·all the other sons [the male descendants] of Manasseh son
of Joseph.

3Zelophehad was the son of Hepher, who was the son of Gilead, who
was the son of Makir, who was the son of Manasseh. Zelophehad had
no sons, but he had five daughters, named Mahlah, Noah, Hoglah,
Milcah, and Tirzah. 4They ·went to [presented themselves before]
Eleazar the priest [14:1; 19:51; 21:1] and to Joshua son of Nun and all
the leaders. They said, "The LORD told Moses to give us land ·like the
men received [Lamong/*or* along with our brothers; Num. 26:33; 27:1–
7]." So ·Eleazar [*or* Joshua; Lhe] obeyed the LORD and gave the daughters
·some land [an inheritance], ·just like [*or* among] the brothers of their
father. 5So the tribe of Manasseh had ten sections of land ·west of the
Jordan River and two more sections, [Lin addition to] Gilead and
Bashan [12:3–4], on the east side of the Jordan River. 6The daughters
of Manasseh received ·land just as the sons did [Lan inheritance among/
along with his sons]. Gilead was given to the rest of the ·families [sons;
descendants] of Manasseh.

7The ·lands [border] of Manasseh ·were in the area between Asher and
[Lran from Asher to] Micmethath, ·near [*or* east of] Shechem. The border
went south to the ·En Tappuah area [Linhabitants of En Tappuah], 8which
belonged to Manasseh, except for the town of Tappuah. It was along the
border of Manasseh's land and belonged to the ·sons [people; tribe] of
Ephraim. 9The border of Manasseh continued south to Kanah ·Ravine
[Valley; *or* Brook]. The cities in this area of Manasseh belonged to
Ephraim. Manasseh's border was on the north side of the ravine and went
to the sea. 10The land to the south belonged to Ephraim, and the land to
the north belonged to Manasseh. The ·Mediterranean Sea [Lsea] was the
western border. The border touched Asher's land on the north and
Issachar's land on the east.

11In the areas of Issachar and Asher, the people of Manasseh ·owned
[included; had] these towns: Beth ·Shan [*or* Shean] and its small towns;
Ibleam and its small towns; the people who lived in Dor and its small
towns; the people in ·Naphoth Dor [*or* Dor, that is, Naphoth; LDor…the
third is Naphoth] and its small towns; the people who lived in Taanach
and its small towns; the people in Megiddo and its small towns.
12·Manasseh [LThe sons/descendants of Manasseh] was not able to
defeat those cities, so the Canaanites ·continued [persisted; were deter-
mined] to live there. 13When the ·Israelites [Lsons/Tchildren of Israel]
grew strong, they forced the Canaanites to work for them, although

they did not ·force them to leave the land [drive them out completely; Judg. 1:27–28].

14The ·people from the tribes [sons/descendants] of Joseph said to Joshua, "You gave ·us [Lme] only one ·area of land [Lportion as an inheritance], but ·we are many [LI am a great] people. Why did you give us only one part of all the land the LORD gave his people?"

15And Joshua answered them, "If you have too many people, go up to the forest and ·make a place [clear out land] for yourselves to live there in the land of the Perizzites and the Rephaites. The ·mountain [hill] country of Ephraim is too small for you."

16The ·people [Lsons/descendants] of Joseph said, "It is true. The ·mountain [hill] country of Ephraim is not enough for us, but the Canaanites who live in the valley have ·strong armies [Liron chariots], both in Beth Shan and all the small towns in that area, and in the Valley of Jezreel."

17Then Joshua said to the ·people [Lhouse] of Joseph—to Ephraim and Manasseh, "There are many of you, and you have great power. You should be given more than one ·share of land [allotment]. 18You also will have the ·mountain [hill] country. It is a forest, but you can ·cut down the trees and make it a good place to live [Lclear it and possess its farthest border]. You will own all of it because you will ·force the Canaanites to leave the land [drive out the Canaanites] even though they have ·powerful weapons [Liron chariots] and are strong."

The Rest of the Land Divided

18 All of the Israelites [Lthe whole congregation of the sons/Tchildren of Israel] gathered together at Shiloh where they set up the Meeting Tent [Ex. 33:7–11]. The land was now under their control. 2But there were still seven tribes of Israel that had not yet received their ·land [inheritance].

3So Joshua said to the ·Israelites [Lsons/Tchildren of Israel]: "·Why do you wait so long [LHow long will you delay] to take your land? The LORD, the God of your ancestors, has given this land to you. 4Choose three men from each tribe, and I will send them out to study the land. They will ·describe in writing [*or* make a map of] the land their tribe wants as its ·share [inheritance], and then they will come back to me. 5They will divide the land into seven parts. Judah will keep their land in the south, and the ·people [house] of Joseph will keep their land in the north. 6You should ·describe [*or* map out] the seven parts of land in writing and bring what you have written to me. Then I will ·throw [cast] lots in the presence of the LORD our God. 7But the Levites do not ·get any part of these lands [have an allotment among you], because ·they are priests, and their work is to serve [Ltheir portion/inheritance is the priesthood of] the LORD. Gad, Reuben, and ·East [the half-tribe of] Manasseh have received the ·land [inheritance] promised to them, which is east of the Jordan River. Moses, the servant of the LORD, gave it to them [Deut. 3:18–20]."

8So the men who were chosen to map the land started out. Joshua told them, "Go and study the land and describe it in writing. Then come back to me, and I will ·throw [cast] lots in the presence of the LORD here in Shiloh." 9So the men left and ·went into [passed through] the land. They ·described [mapped out] in a scroll each town in the seven parts of the land. Then they came back to Joshua, who was still at the camp at Shiloh.

10There Joshua ·threw [cast] lots in the presence of the LORD to ·choose [apportion] the lands that should be given to each tribe.

Land for Benjamin

11The first ·part of the land [lot] was given to the tribe of Benjamin. Each ·family group [clan] received some land between the land of Judah and the land of Joseph. This is the land chosen for Benjamin: 12The northern border started at the Jordan River and went along the northern ·edge [slope] of Jericho, and then it went west into the ·mountains [hill country]. That boundary continued ·until it was just east [Lto the desert/wilderness] of Beth Aven. 13From there it ·went [crossed] south to Luz (also called Bethel) and then down to Ataroth Addar, which is on the hill south of Lower Beth Horon.

14At the hill to the south of Beth Horon, the border turned and went south near the western side of the hill. It went to Kiriath Baal (also called Kiriath Jearim), a town ·where people of Judah lived [Lof the sons/descendants of Judah]. This was the western border.

15The southern border started ·near [at the edge of] Kiriath Jearim and went west to the ·waters [spring] of Nephtoah. 16Then ·it [Lthe boundary] went down to the bottom of the hill, which was near the Valley of Ben Hinnom, on the north side of the Valley of Rephaim. The border continued down the Hinnom Valley just south of the Jebusite city to En Rogel. 17There it turned north and went to En Shemesh. It continued to Geliloth ·near [opposite] the Adummim Pass. Then it went down to the ·great Stone [LStone] of Bohan son of Reuben. 18The border continued to the northern ·part [slope] of Beth Arabah and went down into the ·Jordan Valley [*or* Arabah]. 19From there it went to the northern ·part [slope] of Beth Hoglah and ended at the north shore of the ·Dead [LSalt] Sea, ·where the Jordan River flows into the sea [Lat the mouth of the Jordan in the south]. This was the southern border.

20The Jordan River was the border on the eastern side. So this was the ·land [inheritance] given to the ·family groups [clans] of Benjamin with the borders on all sides.

21The ·family groups [clans] of Benjamin received these cities: Jericho, Beth Hoglah, Emek Keziz, 22Beth Arabah, Zemaraim, Bethel, 23Avvim, Parah, Ophrah, 24Kephar Ammoni, Ophni, and Geba. There were twelve towns and all their villages.

25The tribe of Benjamin also received Gibeon, Ramah, Beeroth, 26Mizpah, Kephirah, Mozah, 27Rekem, Irpeel, Taralah, 28Zelah, Haeleph, the Jebusite city (Jerusalem), Gibeah, and Kiriath. There were fourteen towns and their villages. All these areas are the lands the ·family groups [clans] of Benjamin were given.

Land for Simeon

19 The second ·part of the land [lot] was given to the tribe of Simeon. Each ·family group [clan] received some of the land ·inside the area [in the midst of the inheritance of the sons/descendants] of Judah. 2They received Beersheba (also called Sheba), Moladah, 3Hazar Shual, Balah, Ezem, 4Eltolad, Bethul, Hormah, 5Ziklag, Beth Marcaboth, Hazar Susah, 6Beth Lebaoth, and Sharuhen. There were thirteen towns and their villages.

7They received the towns of Ain, Rimmon, Ether, and Ashan, four towns and their villages. 8They also received all the villages around these towns as far as Baalath Beer (this is the same as Ramah in ·southern Canaan [Lthe Negev]). So ·these were the lands given to [this was the inheritance of] the

·family groups [clans] in the tribe of Simeon. 9The land of the Simeonites
was taken from part of the land of Judah. Since Judah had much more
land than they needed, the Simeonites received ·part of their land [Ltheir
inheritance in the midst of Judah's inheritance].

Land for Zebulun

10The third ·part of the land [lot] was given to the tribe of Zebulun [Cin
southwestern Galilee, north of West Manasseh and east of the coastal tribe
of Asher]. Each ·family group [clan] of Zebulun received some of the
land. The border of Zebulun went as far as Sarid. 11Then it went west to
Maralah and ·came near [touched] Dabbesheth and then ·near [Lthe
brook/valley in front of/east of] Jokneam. 12Then it turned ·to the east
[Leastward toward the sunrise]. It went from Sarid to the area of Kisloth
Tabor and on to Daberath and ·to [Lup to] Japhia. 13It continued eastward
to Gath Hepher and Eth Kazin, ending at Rimmon. There the border
turned and went toward Neah. 14At Neah it turned again and went to the
north to Hannathon and continued to the Valley of Iphtah El. 15Inside
this border were the cities of Kattath, Nahalal, Shimron, Idalah, and
Bethlehem. There were twelve towns and their villages.
16So these are the towns and the villages that were given to the ·family
groups [clans] of Zebulun.

Land for Issachar

17The fourth ·part of the land [lot] was given to the ·tribe [sons; descen-
dants] of Issachar [Cin southern Galilee, southeast of Zebulun and north
of East Manasseh]. Each ·family group [clan] of Issachar received some of
the land. 18Their land included Jezreel, Kesulloth, Shunem, 19Hapharaim,
Shion, Anaharath, 20Rabbith, Kishion, Ebez, 21Remeth, En Gannim, En
Haddah, and Beth Pazzez.
22The border of their land touched the area called Tabor, Shahazumah,
and Beth Shemesh and stopped at the Jordan River. There were sixteen
towns and their villages.
23These cities and towns were part of the ·land that was given to [inher-
itance of] the ·family groups [clans] of Issachar.

Land for Asher

24The fifth ·part of the land [lot] was given to the tribe of Asher [Calong
the Mediterranean coast north of East Manasseh]. Each ·family group
[clan] of Asher received some of the land. 25Their land included Helkath,
Hali, Beten, Acshaph, 26Allammelech, Amad, and Mishal.
The western border touched Mount Carmel and Shihor Libnath.
27Then it turned east and went to Beth Dagon, touching Zebulun and the
Valley of Iphtah El. Then it went north of Beth Emek and Neiel and
passed north to Cabul. 28From there it went to Abdon,[n] Rehob, Hammon,
and Kanah and continued to Greater Sidon. 29Then the border went back
south toward Ramah and continued to the ·strong, walled [fortified] city
of Tyre. There it turned and went toward Hosah, ending at the sea. This
was in the area of Aczib, 30Ummah, Aphek, and Rehob. There were twenty-
two towns and their villages.
31These cities and their villages were part of the ·land that was given to
[inheritance of] the ·family groups [clans] of [Lthe sons/descendants of]
Asher.

Land for Naphtali

32The sixth ·part of the land [lot] was given to the ·tribe [Lsons; descen-
dants] of Naphtali [Ceast and north of the Sea of Galilee]. Each ·family

19:28 Abdon Some Hebrew copies read "Ebron."

group [clan] of Naphtali received some of the land. 33The border of their land started at the ·large tree [Loak] in Zaanannim, ·which is near [*or* in] Heleph. Then it went through Adami Nekeb and Jabneel, as far as Lakkum, and ended at the Jordan River. 34Then it went to the west through Aznoth Tabor and ·stopped at [extended to] Hukkok. It ·went to the area of [touched] Zebulun on the south, Asher on the west, and Judah, at the Jordan River, on the east. 35The ·strong, walled [fortified] cities inside these borders were called Ziddim, Zer, Hammath, Rakkath, Kinnereth, 36Adamah, Ramah, Hazor, 37Kedesh, Edrei, En Hazor, 38·Iron [*or* Yirom], Migdal El, Horem, Beth Anath, and Beth Shemesh. There were nineteen towns and all their villages.

39The towns and the villages around them were ·in the land that was given to [the inheritance of] the ·family groups [clans] of [Lthe sons/descendants of] Naphtali.

Land for Dan

40The seventh ·part of the land [lot] was given to the ·tribe [Lsons; descendants] of Dan [Lbetween Ephraim and Judah along the Mediterranean coast]. Each ·family group [clan] of Dan received some of the land. 41·Their land [LThe territory of their inheritance] included Zorah, Eshtaol, Ir Shemesh, 42Shaalabbin, Aijalon, Ithlah, 43Elon, Timnah, Ekron, 44Eltekeh, Gibbethon, Baalath, 45Jehud, Bene Berak, Gath Rimmon, 46Me Jarkon, Rakkon, and the area ·near [*or* opposite] Joppa.

47(·But the Danites had trouble taking their land [LWhen the territory of the sons/descendants of Dan was lost to them...]. They went and fought against Leshem [*or* Laish; Cin the far north between Naphtali and West Manasseh], defeated it, and ·killed the people who lived there [Lstruck it with the edge of the sword]. So the Danites ·moved into [Ltook possession and settled in] the town of Leshem and changed its name to Dan, because he was the father of their tribe.) 48All of these towns and villages were given to the ·family groups [clans] of Dan.

Land for Joshua

49After ·the leaders [Lthey] finished dividing the land and giving it to the different tribes, the ·Israelites [Lsons/Tchildren of Israel] gave Joshua son of Nun ·his land [an inheritance] also. 50They gave Joshua the town he asked for, Timnath Serah in the ·mountains [hill country] of Ephraim, just as the LORD commanded. He built up the town and lived there.

51So these ·lands [inheritances] were given to the different tribes of Israel. Eleazar the priest, Joshua son of Nun, and the ·leaders [Lheads of the fathers] of each tribe divided up the land by lots at Shiloh. They met in the presence of the LORD at the entrance to the Meeting Tent [18:1]. Now they were finished dividing the land.

Cities of Safety

20 Then the LORD said to Joshua: 2"Tell the ·Israelites [Lsons/Tchildren of Israel] to ·choose [designate] the special cities of ·safety [refuge], as I had Moses command you to do [Num. 35:1–8]. 3If a person kills someone accidentally and without meaning to kill him, that person may go to a city of ·safety [refuge] to hide. There the killer will be safe from the ·relative who has the duty of punishing a murderer [near-relative; Lavenger of blood].

4"When the killer ·runs [flees] to one of those cities, he must stop at the entrance ·gate [Lof the city gate], stand there, and tell the ·leaders of the people [Lelders of that city] what happened [Cthe council of leaders met at the city gate and held trials there; Deut. 21:19; Ruth 4:1]. Then that person will be allowed to enter the city and will be given a place to live among them. 5But if the ·one who is chasing him [near-relative; Lavenger of blood] follows him to that city, ·the leaders of the city [Lthey] must not hand over the ·killer [manslayer]. It was an accident. He did not hate him beforehand or kill him on purpose. 6·The killer [LHe] must stay in the city until ·a court comes to a decision [Lhe stands before the congregation for judgment] and until the high priest dies [Num. 35:25–28; Cthe high priest's death may have marked a general amnesty]. Then he may go back home to the town from which he ran away."

7So the Israelites chose these cities to be cities of ·safety [refuge]: Kedesh in Galilee in the ·mountains [hill country] of Naphtali; Shechem in the ·mountains [hill country] of Ephraim; Kiriath Arba (also called Hebron) in the ·mountains [hill country] of Judah; 8Bezer ·on the east side of the Jordan River near [Lbeyond the Jordan east of] Jericho in the ·desert [wilderness plain] in the land of Reuben; Ramoth in Gilead in the land of Gad; and Golan in Bashan in the land of Manasseh. 9Any Israelite or ·anyone living among them [resident alien; sojourner] who killed someone accidentally was to be allowed to run to one of these cities of ·safety [refuge]. There he would not be killed, before he ·was judged [Lstood before the congregation], by the ·relative who had the duty of punishing a murderer [near-relative; Lavenger of blood].

Towns for the Levites

21 The heads of the ·Levite families [Lfathers of the Levites] went to talk to Eleazar the priest, to Joshua son of Nun, and to the heads of the ·families [fathers] of all the tribes of Israel. 2At Shiloh in the land of Canaan, they said to them, "The LORD commanded Moses that you give us towns where we may live and pastures for our animals." 3So the Israelites obeyed this command of the LORD and gave the Levite people these towns and pastures ·for their own land [Lfrom their own inheritance/possessions]: 4The Kohath ·family groups [clans] were part of the tribe of Levi [Cthe three sons of Levi were Kohath, Gershom, and Merari; Ex. 6:16; Num. 3:17]. Some of the Levites in the Kohath ·family groups [clans] were from the family of Aaron the priest. To these Levites were ·given [allotted; given by lot] thirteen towns in the areas of Judah, Simeon, and Benjamin. 5The ·other family groups [Lrest of the sons/descendants] of Kohath were given ten towns in the areas of Ephraim, Dan, and ·West [Lthe half-tribe of] Manasseh.

6The ·people from the Gershon family groups [Lsons/descendants of Gershom] were given thirteen towns ·in the land [Lfrom the clans of the tribe] of Issachar, Asher, Naphtali, and the East Manasseh in Bashan.

7The ·family groups [Lclans of the sons/descendants] of Merari were given twelve towns in the areas of Reuben, Gad, and Zebulun.

8So the ·Israelites [Lsons/Tchildren of Israel] gave the Levites these towns and the pastures around them, just as the LORD had commanded Moses.

9These are the names of the towns that came from the ·lands [Ltribe of the sons/descendants] of Judah and Simeon. 10The first ·choice of towns [Llot] was given to the Kohath ·family groups [clans] of the Levites. 11They gave them Kiriath Arba, also called Hebron, and all its pastures in the ·mountains [hill country] of Judah. (Arba was the father of Anak.) 12But the fields and the villages around Kiriath Arba had been given to Caleb son of Jephunneh [Las his possession].

13So they gave the city of Hebron to the descendants of Aaron (Hebron was a city of ·safety [Lrefuge for the killer/manslayer]). They also gave

them the towns of Libnah, [14]Jattir, Eshtemoa, [15]Holon, Debir, [16]Ain,
Juttah, and Beth Shemesh, and all the pastures around them. Nine towns
were given from these two tribes.
[17]·They also gave the people of Aaron these cities that belonged to
[[L]And from] the tribe of Benjamin: Gibeon, Geba, [18]Anathoth, and
Almon. They gave them these four towns and the pastures around them.
[19]So these thirteen towns with their pastures were given to the priests,
who were from the ·family [[L]sons; descendants] of Aaron.
[20]The other Kohathite ·family groups [clans] of the Levites were ·given
[allotted] these towns from the tribe of Ephraim: [21]Shechem in the mountains of Ephraim (which was a city of ·safety [[L]refuge for the killer/
manslayer]), Gezer, [22]Kibzaim, and Beth Horon. There were four towns
and their pastures.
[23]The tribe of Dan gave them Eltekeh, Gibbethon, [24]Aijalon, and Gath
Rimmon. There were four towns and their pastures.
[25]·West [[L]The half-tribe of] Manasseh gave them Taanach and Gath
Rimmon and the pastures around these two towns.
[26]So these ten towns and the pastures around them were given to the
rest of the Kohathite ·family groups [clans].
[27]The Gershonite ·family groups [clans] of the Levite tribe were given
these towns: ·East [[L]The half-tribe of] Manasseh gave them Golan in
Bashan, which was a city of ·safety [[L]refuge for the killer/manslayer], and
Be Eshtarah, and the pastures around these two towns.
[28]The tribe of Issachar gave them Kishion, Daberath, [29]Jarmuth, and
En Gannim, and the pastures around these four towns.
[30]The tribe of Asher gave them Mishal, Abdon, [31]Helkath, and Rehob,
and the pastures around these four towns.
[32]The tribe of Naphtali gave them Kedesh in Galilee (a city of ·safety
[refuge for the killer/manslayer]), Hammoth Dor, and Kartan, and the
pastures around these three towns.
[33]So the Gershonite ·family groups [clans] received thirteen towns and
the pastures around them.
[34]The Merarite ·family groups [clans] (the rest of the Levites) were
given these towns: The tribe of Zebulun gave them Jokneam, Kartah,
[35]Dimnah, and Nahalal, and the pastures around these four towns.
[36]The tribe of Reuben gave them Bezer, Jahaz, [37]Kedemoth, and
Mephaath, along with the pastures around these four towns.
[38]The tribe of Gad gave them Ramoth in Gilead (a city of ·safety
[[L]refuge for the killer/manslayer]), Mahanaim, [39]Heshbon, and Jazer, and
the pastures around these four towns.
[40]So the total number of towns given to the Merarite ·family groups
[clans] was twelve.
[41]A total of forty-eight towns with their pastures in the ·land [[L]midst of
the possession of the sons/[T]children of Israel] of Israel were given to the
Levites. [42]Each town had pastures around it [[L]this was true of all the cities].
[43]So the LORD gave ·the people [[L]Israel] all the land he had promised
their ancestors. The people took the land and lived there. [44]The LORD gave
them ·peace [rest] on all sides, as he had ·promised [sworn to] their ancestors. None of their enemies ·defeated [could resist] them; the LORD handed
all their enemies ·over to them [[L]into their hands]. [45]He kept every promise he had made to the Israelites; each one came true.

Three Tribes Go Home

22 Then Joshua called a meeting of the people from the tribes of
Reuben, Gad, and ·East [Lhalf-tribe of] Manasseh. 2He said
to them, "You have done everything Moses, the LORD's servant, told you
to do. You have also obeyed ·all my commands [Lmy voice in all I commanded you]. 3For a long time you have ·supported [Lnot abandoned/
forsaken] the other Israelites. You have been careful to ·obey the commands [*or* carry out the task] the LORD your God gave you [Deut.
3:18–20]. 4The LORD your God promised to give the Israelites ·peace
[rest], and he has kept his promise. Now you may go back to your homes,
to the land that Moses, the LORD's servant, gave you, ·on the east side of
[Lbeyond] the Jordan River. 5But be careful to obey the ·teachings [com-
mandment] and laws Moses, the LORD's servant, gave you: to love the
LORD your God and ·obey his commands [Lwalk in his paths], to ·con-
tinue to follow [Lhold fast to] him and serve him ·the very best you can
[Lwith all your heart and with all your soul]."
6Then Joshua ·said good-bye to [blessed] them, and ·they left and [Lsent
them away and they] went away to their ·homes [Ltents]. 7Moses had given
the land of Bashan to ·East [the half-tribe of] Manasseh. Joshua gave land
on the west side of the Jordan River to ·West Manasseh [Lthe other half].
And he sent them to their homes and he blessed them. 8He said, "Go back
to your homes with your riches. You have many animals, silver, gold,
bronze, and iron, and many beautiful clothes. Divide among ·yourselves
[Lyour brothers] the ·things [plunder] you have taken from your enemies.
9So the people from the tribes of Reuben, Gad, and ·East [the half-tribe
of] Manasseh left the other ·Israelites [Lsons/Tchildren of Israel] at Shiloh
in Canaan and went back to Gilead. It was their own land, given to them
by Moses as the LORD had commanded.
10The people of Reuben, Gad, and ·East [the half-tribe of] Manasseh
went to Geliloth, near the Jordan River in the land of Canaan. There they
built a ·beautiful [*or* imposing; impressive] altar. 11The ·other Israelites
still at Shiloh [Lsons/Tchildren of Israel] heard about the altar these three
tribes built at the border of Canaan at Geliloth, near the Jordan River on
Israel's side. 12All the ·Israelites [Lsons/Tchildren of Israel] became very
angry at these three tribes, so ·they [Lthe whole assembly/congregation]
met together and decided to ·fight [wage war against] them [Cbecause
they considered this idolatry; Deut. 13:12–18].
13The ·Israelites [Lsons/Tchildren of Israel] sent Phinehas son of Eleazar
the priest to Gilead to talk to the people of Reuben, Gad, and East
Manasseh. 14They also sent ·one leader [Lten leaders, one] from each of
the ten tribes at Shiloh. Each of them was a leader ·of his family group
[among the clans] of Israelites.
15These leaders went to Gilead to talk to the people of Reuben, Gad,
and ·East [Lthe half-tribe of] Manasseh. They said: 16"·All the Israelites
[LThe whole assembly/congregation of the LORD] ask you: 'Why did you
·turn against [break faith by turning away from] the God of Israel by
building an altar for yourselves? You know that this is ·against God's law
[Lrebellion this day against the LORD]. 17·Remember what happened at
Peor [LWasn't the sin of Peor enough; Num. 24]? We still ·suffer today
[Lhave not cleansed/purified ourselves] because of that sin, for which
·God made many Israelites very sick [La plague came against the congre-
gation/assembly of the LORD]. 18And now are you turning against the
LORD and refusing to follow him?

"'If you ·don't stop what you're doing [Lrebel against the Lord] today,
the Lord will be angry with ·everyone in Israel [the whole congregation/
assembly] tomorrow. 19If your land is ·unclean [Cin a ritual sense], come
over into our land where the Lord's ·Tent [TTabernacle] is. Share it with
us. But don't ·turn [rebel] against the Lord and us by building another
altar for the Lord our God. 20·Remember how [LIs it not true that…?]
Achan son of Zerah refused to obey the command about ·what must be
completely destroyed [Lthe devoted things; 7:1–26]. That one man broke
God's law, but ·all the Israelites [Lthe whole assembly/congregation] were
punished. ·Achan died because of his sin, but others also died [LAnd he
did not die alone for his sin].'"

21The people from Reuben, Gad, and ·East [the half-tribe of] Manasseh
answered [Lthe heads of the clans of Israel], 22"·The Lord is God of gods!
[or El, God, the Lord] ·The Lord is God of gods [or El, God, the Lord]!
God knows, and we want you to know also. If we have ·done something
wrong [Lrebelled or broken faith with the Lord], ·you may kill us [Ldo not
spare us today]. 23If we have built our own altar to turn away from the
Lord or to offer burnt offerings [1:1–17] or ·grain [Lgift; tribute; Lev. 2:1]
and ·fellowship [or peace; well-being] offerings [3:1], may the Lord himself punish us.

24"We did not build it for that reason. We feared that someday your
people would not accept us as part of your nation. Then they might say,
'·You cannot worship [LWhat do you have to do with…?] the Lord, the
God of Israel. 25The Lord made the Jordan River a border between us and
you people of Reuben and Gad. You ·cannot worship [Lhave no share/por-
tion in] the Lord.' So we feared that your children might make our
·children [descendants] stop ·worshiping [Lfearing] the Lord.

26"That is why we decided to build this altar. But it is not for burnt offerings [Lev. 1:1–17] and sacrifices. 27This altar is ·proof to [witness between]
you and us and to all our ·children [generations] who will come after us
that we ·worship the Lord [Ldo the service of the Lord before him] with our
whole burnt offerings, grain, and ·fellowship [or peace] offerings. This was
so your ·children [descendants] would not say to our ·children [descen-
dants], 'You ·are not the Lord's [Lhave no share/portion in the Lord].'

28"In the future if ·your children [Lthey] say that to us or our ·children
[generations], we can say, 'See the altar made by our ancestors. It is
·exactly like [a copy/model of] the Lord's altar, but we do not use it for
burnt offerings or sacrifices. It ·shows that we are part of Israel [Lis a witness between us and you].'

29"·Truly, we don't want to be [LFar be it from us to rebel] against the
Lord or to ·stop following [turn away from] him by building an altar for
burnt offerings [Lev. 1:1–17], grain [Lgift; tribute] offerings [Lev. 2:1], or
sacrifices. We know the only true altar to the Lord our God is in front of
the ·Holy Tent [TTabernacle]."

30When Phinehas the priest and the ·ten leaders [Lleaders of the congregation, the heads of the clans of the families of Israel,] heard the people
of Reuben, Gad, and East Manasseh, they were ·pleased [satisfied]. 31So
Phinehas, son of Eleazar the priest, said to the people of Reuben, Gad,
and Manasseh, "·Now [LToday] we know the Lord is ·with us [Lin our
midst] ·and that you didn't turn against [or because you have not broken
faith with] him. Now ·the Israelites will not be punished by [Lyou have
rescued the Israelites from the hand of] the Lord."

32Then Phinehas the son of Eleazar the priest, and the leaders left the
people of Reuben and Gad in Gilead and went back to Canaan where they
told the ·Israelites [Lsons/Tchildren of Israel] what had happened. 33They
were ·pleased [satisfied] and thanked God. So they ·decided not to fight
[Ltalked no more about going to war against] the people of Reuben and
Gad and destroy those lands.
34And the people of Reuben and Gad named the altar ·Proof That We
Believe the LORD Is God [LA Witness Between Us—That the LORD Is God; *or*
Witness, "For," they said, "it is a witness between us that the LORD is God"].

The Last Words of Joshua

23 The LORD gave Israel ·peace [rest] from their enemies around
them. Many years passed, and Joshua grew very old. 2He
called a meeting of ·all [Lall Israel:] the elders, heads of families, judges,
and officers of Israel. He said, "I am now very old. 3You have seen what
the LORD has done to ·our enemies [Lthese nations] to help us. The LORD
your God fought for you. 4·Remember that [See; TBehold] ·your people
have been given their [LI have alloted to you the] land between the Jordan
River and the ·Mediterranean [LGreat] Sea in the west, the land I promised to give you. 5The LORD your God will ·force [drive] out the people
living there. The LORD will push them out ahead of you. And you will
·own the [occupy/possess their] land, as he has promised you.
6"Be strong. You must be careful to obey everything ·commanded
[Lthat is written] in the Book of the ·Teachings [Law] of Moses. Do not
·stray [Lturn aside] from it either from the left or the right. 7Don't ·become
friends [associate; mix] with ·the people living among us who are not
Israelites [Lthese nations remaining among you]. Don't ·say [mention; *or*
invoke] the names of their gods or make anyone swear by them. Don't
serve or ·worship [bow down before] them. 8You must ·continue to follow
[Lhold fast to; cling to] the LORD your God, as you have done ·in the past
[Lto this day].
9"The LORD has ·forced to leave [driven out] many great and powerful
nations. No nation has been able to ·defeat [resist; stand before] you [Lto
this day]. 10With his help, one Israelite ·could defeat [routs] a thousand,
because the LORD your God fights for you, as he promised to do. 11So you
must be careful to love the LORD your God.
12"[LBut] If you turn away from the way of the LORD and ·become
friends with [ally yourselves with; cling to] ·these people who are not part
of Israel [the remnant of these nations who remain among you] and marry
them, 13the LORD your God will not ·help you defeat [drive out] your enemies. They will be like ·traps [La snare and a trap] for you, like whips on
your back and thorns in your eyes, ·and none of you will be left in [Luntil
you perish from] this good land the LORD your God has given you.
14"·It's almost time for me to die [LLook, today I am going the way of all
the earth]. You know ·and fully believe [Lin your hearts and souls] that the
LORD has not failed to keep a single one of the good promises he made. He
has fulfilled every one of them. Not one of them has failed. 15Every good
promise that the LORD your God made has come true, and in the same
way, his other promises will come true. He promised that evil will come
to you and that he will destroy you from this good land that he gave you.
16This will happen if you don't keep your ·agreement [covenant; treaty]
with the LORD your God. If you go and serve other gods and ·worship
[bow down before] them, the ·LORD will become very angry with you

[L anger of the LORD will burn against you]. Then ·none of you will be left
in [L you will quickly perish from] this good land he has given you."

24 Joshua gathered all the tribes of Israel together at Shechem.
He called the elders, heads of families, judges, and officers of
Israel to ·stand [present themselves] before God.
2 Then Joshua said to all the people, "Here's what the LORD, the God of
Israel, says to you: 'A long time ago your ancestors lived on the other side
of the Euphrates River. Terah, the father of Abraham and Nahor, worshiped other gods. 3 But I, the LORD, took your ancestor Abraham from the
other side of the river and led him through the land of Canaan [Gen.
12:1–3; 17:4–8]. And I ·gave him many children, including [*or* multiplied
his descendants, beginning with] his son Isaac [Gen. 21]. 4 I gave Isaac two
sons named Jacob and Esau [Gen. 25]. I gave the land around the ·moun-
tains [hill country] of ·Edom [C Hebrew: Seir] to Esau, but Jacob and his
sons went down to Egypt [Gen. 46]. 5 Then I sent Moses and Aaron to
Egypt, where I ·brought many disasters on the Egyptians [L plagued Egypt
by what I did in their midst; Ex. 1–11]. Afterwards I brought you out [Ex.
12]. 6 When I brought your ancestors out of Egypt, they came to the ·Red
Sea [L Sea], and the Egyptians chased them with chariots and men on
horses. 7 So the people called out to the LORD. And ·I [L he] brought darkness between you and the Egyptians and made the sea to cover them [Ex.
13–15]. ·You yourselves [L Your eyes] saw what I did ·to the army of [L in]
Egypt. After that, you lived in the ·desert [wilderness] for a long time.
8 " 'Then I brought you to the land of the Amorites, east of the Jordan
River. They fought against you, but I handed them over to you. I destroyed
them before you, and you took ·control [possession] of that land [Num.
21; Deut. 2–3]. 9 But the king of Moab, Balak son of Zippor, ·prepared to
fight [L arose and fought] against the Israelites. The king sent for Balaam
son of Beor to curse you [Num. 22–24], 10 but I refused to listen to Balaam.
So he ·asked for good things to happen to you [L kept blessing you]! I ·saved
you and brought you out of his power [L delivered you out of his hand].
11 " 'Then you crossed the Jordan River and came to Jericho, where the
·people [*or* leaders] of Jericho fought against you. Also, the Amorites,
Perizzites, Canaanites, Hittites, Girgashites, Hivites, and Jebusites fought
against you. But I ·handed them over to you [L gave them into your hand].
12 I sent ·terror [*or* the hornet; C the meaning of the Hebrew is uncertain]
ahead of you to ·force [drive] out two Amorite kings [2:10; Num. 21:21–
35]. ·You took the land without using swords and bows [L It was not by
your sword or by your bow]. 13 I gave you that land where you had not
worked. I gave you cities that you did not have to build. And now you live
in that land and in those cities, and you eat from vineyards and olive trees
that you did not plant.' "
14 Then Joshua said to the people, "Now ·respect [fear; be in awe of] the
LORD and serve him ·fully [faithfully; in truth] and sincerely. ·Throw [Put]
away the gods that your ancestors worshiped on the other side of the
·Euphrates River [L River] and in Egypt. Serve the LORD. 15 But if ·you don't
want [L it is undesirable/evil in your eyes] to serve the LORD, you must choose
for yourselves today whom you will serve. You may serve the gods that your
ancestors worshiped when they lived on the other side of the ·Euphrates
River [L River], or you may serve the gods of the Amorites who lived in this
land. As for me and my ·family [L house], we will serve the LORD."
16 Then the people answered, "·We will never stop following [L Far be it

from us to forsake] **the Lord to serve other gods! 17It was the Lord our God who brought ·our** [[L]us and our] **ancestors out of Egypt. ·We were slaves in that land, but** […[L]out of the house of slavery, and] **the Lord did great ·things** [[L]signs] **for us there. He brought us out and ·protected** [preserved] **us while we traveled through other lands. 18Then he ·forced** [drove] **out all the people living in these lands, even the Amorites. So we will serve the Lord, because he is our God."**

19Then Joshua said, "You are not able to serve the Lord, because he is a holy God [Lev. 19:2] **and a jealous God** [Ex. 20:5]**. If you ·turn against him** [rebel] **and sin, he will not forgive you. 20If you ·leave** [forsake; abandon] **the Lord and serve ·other** [foreign] **gods, he will ·send you great trouble** [bring disaster on you]**. The Lord may have been good to you, but if you turn against him, he will ·destroy** [consume] **you."**

21But the people said to Joshua, "No! We will serve the Lord."

22Then Joshua said, "You are your own witnesses that you have chosen to serve the Lord."

The people said, "Yes, we are."

23Then Joshua said, "Now throw away the [[L]foreign] **gods that ·you have** [are in your midst]**. ·Love the Lord, the God of Israel, with all your heart** [[L]Bend your heart toward the Lord, the God of Israel]**."**

24Then the people said to Joshua, "We will serve the Lord our God, and we will obey him."

25On that day at Shechem Joshua made an ·agreement [covenant; treaty] **for the people. He made ·rules** [statutes; ordinances; requirements] **and ·laws** [regulations] **for them to follow. 26Joshua wrote these things in the Book of the ·Teachings** [Law] **of God. Then he took a large stone and set it up under the oak tree near the Lord's ·Holy Tent** [sanctuary; shrine; holy place]**.**

27Joshua said to all the people, "·See [[T]Behold] **this stone! It will ·remind you of what we did today** [[L]be a witness against you]**. ·It was here the Lord spoke to us today** [[L]It has heard all the words the Lord said to us]**. It will ·remind you of what happened so you will not** [be a witness against you, lest you] **·turn against** [are untrue to; deal falsely with] **your God."**

Joshua Dies

28Then Joshua sent the people back ·to their land [[L]each to their own inheritance]**.**

29After that, Joshua son of Nun, the Lord's servant, died at the age of one hundred ten. 30They buried him in ·his own land [[L]the land of his inheritance] **at Timnath Serah, in the ·mountains** [hill country] **of Ephraim, north of Mount Gaash.**

31The Israelites served the Lord during the lifetime of Joshua and during the lifetimes of the elders who lived after Joshua who had ·seen [experienced; known] **what the Lord had done for Israel.**

Joseph Comes Home

32When the ·Israelites [[L]sons/[T]children of Israel] **left Egypt, they carried the bones of Joseph with them** [Gen. 50:25; Ex. 13:19; Heb. 11:22]**. They buried them at Shechem, in the ·land** [piece of ground] **Jacob had bought for a hundred pieces of silver from the sons of Hamor (Hamor was the father of Shechem)** [Gen. 33:19]**. This land ·now belonged to** [became the inheritance of] **Joseph's children.**

33And Eleazar son of Aaron died and was buried at Gibeah in the ·mountains [hill country] **of Ephraim, which had been given to Eleazar's son Phinehas.**

JUDGES

Judah Fights the Canaanites

1 After Joshua died, the ·Israelites [Lsons/Tchildren of Israel]
asked the ·LORD [or Yahweh; Cthe translation "LORD" (all caps)
represents the divine name YHWH, usually pronounced "Yahweh"],
"Who will ·be first to go and [lead the] fight for us against the
Canaanites?"
2The LORD said to them, "·The tribe of Judah [LJudah] will go. [LLook;
TBehold] I have ·handed the land over to them [Lgiven the land into his
hand]."
3·The men of Judah [LJudah] said to ·the men of Simeon, their relatives [Lhis brother Simeon], "Come and help us fight the Canaanites for
our ·land [allotment]. If you do, we will go and help you fight for your
·land [allotment]." So ·the men of Simeon [LSimeon] went with them
[CSimeon's land lay within Judah; Josh. 19:1].
4When Judah attacked, the LORD handed over the Canaanites and the
Perizzites to them, and they defeated ten thousand men at the city of
Bezek. 5·There [LAt Bezek] they found Adoni-Bezek [Cthe ruler of the
city], and fought him. The men of Judah defeated the Canaanites and the
Perizzites, 6but Adoni-Bezek ran away. The men of Judah chased him, and
when they caught him, they cut off his thumbs and big toes [Csuch mutilation was common in the ancient Near East, rendering a king unfit for
military service or priestly functions; Lev. 8:23–24].
7Adoni-Bezek said, "Seventy kings whose thumbs and big toes had
been cut off used to eat scraps that fell from my table. Now God has paid
me back for what I did to them." The men of Judah took Adoni-Bezek to
Jerusalem, and he died there.
8Then the ·men [Lsons] of Judah fought against Jerusalem and captured it. They ·attacked with their swords [Lstruck it with the edge of the
sword] and burned the city [Ca temporary conquest; David later captured
the city; 2 Sam. 5:7].
9Later, they went down to fight the Canaanites who lived in the mountains, in the ·dry [or hill] country ·to the south [Lin the Negev], and in the
·western hills [or lowland]. 10·The men of Judah [LJudah] went to fight
against the Canaanites in the city of Hebron (which used to be called
Kiriath Arba [Gen. 13:18; 23:2; Josh. 14:15]). And they defeated Sheshai,
Ahiman, and Talmai [Num. 13:22; Josh. 15:14].

Caleb and His Daughter

11Then they left there and went to fight against the people living in
Debir. (In the past Debir had been called Kiriath Sepher.) 12Before attacking the city, Caleb said, "I will give Acsah, my daughter, as a wife to the
man who attacks and captures the city of Kiriath Sepher." 13Othniel son
of Kenaz, Caleb's younger brother, captured the city, so Caleb gave his

daughter Acsah to Othniel to be his wife. 14When Acsah came to ·Othniel [Lhim; Ccould be Othniel or Caleb], **she ·told him to ask** [*or* asked] **her father for a field. When she got down from her donkey, Caleb asked her, "What do you want?"** [Josh. 15:16–18]

15Acsah answered him, "·Do me a special favor [LGive me a blessing]. **Since you have given me land in ·southern Canaan** [Lthe Negev], **also give me springs of water." So Caleb gave her the upper and lower springs** [Josh. 15:19].

Fights with the Canaanites

16The ·Kenite people, who were from the family of [Lsons/descendants of the Kenite] **Moses' father-in-law** [Ex. 2:16], **left the city of palm trees** [CJericho]. **They went with the men of Judah to the ·Desert** [Wilderness] **of Judah to live with them there in ·southern Judah** [Lthe Negev] **near the city of Arad.**

17The men of Judah and the men of Simeon [1:3], **their ·relatives** [brothers], **defeated the Canaanites who lived in Zephath. They ·completely destroyed the city** [devoted it to the LORD for destruction; see Josh. 2:10; 6:17–19], **so they called it Hormah** [Csounds like Hebrew for "total destruction"]. **18The men of Judah captured Gaza, Ashkelon, Ekron** [CPhilistine cities along the coast], **and the lands around them.**

19The LORD was with the men of Judah. They took the land in the ·mountains [hill country], **but they could not force out the people living on the plain, because they had iron chariots** [Cwooden chariots with iron fittings]. **20As Moses had promised, Hebron was given to Caleb, and Caleb forced out the three sons of Anak** [Num. 14:24; Deut. 1:36; Josh. 14:9-14]. **21But the people of Benjamin could not ·make the Jebusite people leave** [Ldrive out the Jebusites from] **Jerusalem. Since that time the Jebusites have lived with the ·Benjaminites** [Lsons of Benjamin] **in Jerusalem.**

22The ·men [Lhouse] **of Joseph went to fight against the city of Bethel, and the LORD was with them. 23They sent some spies to Bethel (which used to be called Luz). 24The spies saw a man coming out of the city and said to him, "Show us a way into the city, and we will ·be kind to** [have mercy on; *or* reward] **you." 25So the man showed them the way into the city. The men of Joseph ·attacked with swords the people in Bethel** [Lstruck the city with the edge of the sword], **but they let the man and his family go free. 26He went to the land where the Hittites lived** [Cin Syria, north of Israel] **and built a city. He named it Luz, which it is called even today.**

27The people of Manasseh did not ·force [drive] **out the inhabitants of the cities of Beth Shan, Taanach, Dor, Ibleam, Megiddo, nor the small towns around them, because the Canaanites were determined to stay there. 28Later, the Israelites grew strong and forced the Canaanites ·to work as slaves** [into forced labor], **but they did not ·make all the Canaanites leave their land** [Ldrive them out completely]. **29The people of Ephraim did not ·force** [drive] **out all of the Canaanites living in Gezer. So the Canaanites continued to live in Gezer with the people of Ephraim. 30The people of Zebulun did not force out the Canaanites living in the cities of Kitron and Nahalol. They stayed and lived with the people of Zebulun, but Zebulun ·made them work as slaves** [forced them into hard labor].

31The people of Asher did not ·force [drive out] **the Canaanites from the cities of Acco, Sidon, Ahlab, Aczib, Helbah, Aphek, and Rehob** [Ccities on the Mediterranean Sea north of Carmel and inland from the coast]. **32Since the people of Asher did not ·force** [drive] **them out, the Canaanites**

continued to live with them. 33The people of Naphtali did not ·force [drive] out the people of the cities of Beth Shemesh and Beth Anath [Cthe region east of Asher]. So they continued to live with the Canaanites in those cities, and the Canaanites ·worked as slaves [did forced labor]. 34The Amorites forced the Danites back into the ·mountains [hill country] and would not let them come down to live in the plain [Josh. 19:47–48; Judg. 18]. 35The Amorites were determined to stay in Mount Heres, Aijalon, and Shaalbim. But when the Israelites grew stronger, they made the Amorites ·work as slaves [do forced labor]. 36The land of the Amorites was from ·Scorpion [*or* Akrabbim; CHebrew for "scorpion"] ·Pass [*or* Ascent; Csouth of the Dead Sea] to Sela and beyond.

The Angel of the Lord at Bokim

2 The ·angel [messenger] of the Lord [Can angelic spokesperson for God, sometimes identified with the Lord himself; Gen. 16:7; Ex. 14:19; 23:20] went up from Gilgal to Bokim and said, "I brought you up from Egypt and led you to the land I promised to give your ancestors. I said, 'I will never break my ·agreement [covenant] with you [Gen. 17:7; Ex. 6:4]. 2But you must not make an ·agreement [covenant] with the people who live in this land [Ex. 23:32]. You must ·destroy [tear down] their altars [Deut. 7:2].' But you did not obey me. How could you do this [LWhat is this you have done]? 3·Now I tell you [*or* Then I told you; Num. 33:55; Josh. 23:12–13], 'I will not ·force [drive] out the people in this land. They will ·be your enemies [*or* ensnare you; *or* be thorns in your side], and their gods will be a ·trap [snare] for you.' "

4After the angel gave ·Israel [Lthe sons/Tchildren of Israel] this message from the Lord, they ·cried loudly [Llifted up their voices and wept]. 5So they named the place Bokim [C"weeping ones"]. There they offered sacrifices to the Lord.

Joshua Dies

6After Joshua ·dismissed [sent away] the people, the ·Israelites [Lsons/Tchildren of Israel] went to take possession of the land that they had been given. 7The people ·served [worshiped; remained faithful to] the Lord during the lifetime of Joshua and during the lifetimes of the elders who ·lived after [outlived] Joshua and who had seen what great things the Lord had done for Israel. 8Joshua son of Nun, the servant of the Lord, died at the age of one hundred ten. 9They buried him in ·his own land [the territory of his inheritance] at Timnath Heres [Calso known as Timnath Serah; Josh. 19:50; 24:30] in the ·mountains [hill country] of Ephraim, north of Mount Gaash.

The People Disobey

10After ·those people [Lthe whole generation] ·had died [Lwere gathered to their fathers/ancestors], ·their children [Lanother generation] grew up and did not know the Lord or what he had done for Israel. 11So ·they [Lthe sons/Tchildren of Israel] did ·what the Lord said was wrong [Levil in the eyes/sight of the Lord], and they worshiped the ·Baal idols [LBaals; CBaal was the main god of the Canaanites, but had many local manifestations]. 12They ·quit following [abandoned] the Lord, the God of their ancestors who had brought them out of Egypt. They began to worship the gods of the people who lived around them, and that made the Lord angry. 13The Israelites ·quit following [abandoned] the Lord and worshiped Baal and Ashtoreth. 14The Lord was angry with the people of Israel, so he ·handed them over to [gave them into the hand of] ·robbers [raiders; plunderers] who took their possessions. He ·let their enemies who lived around them defeat them [Lsold them into the hand of their enemies around them]; they could not ·protect themselves [resist/Lstand before them]. 15When the Israelites went out to fight, ·they always lost, because the LORD was not with them [Lthe hand of the LORD was against them for harm/evil]. The LORD had sworn to them this would happen. So the Israelites ·suffered very much [were in great distress].

God Chooses Judges

16Then the LORD ·chose leaders called [Lraised up] ·judges [leaders; Cnot courtroom judges, but leaders who guided the nation through difficult times, sometimes as military commanders], ·who saved the Israelites from [Lto deliver them from the hand of] the ·robbers [raiders; plunderers]. 17But the Israelites did not listen to their ·judges [leaders; v. 16]. They ·were not faithful to God but [Lprostituted themselves to and] worshiped other gods instead. Their ancestors had ·obeyed [Lwalked in the way/path of] the LORD's commands, but they quickly turned away and did not obey. 18Whenever the LORD sent ·judges [leaders] to save the Israelites from their enemies, he was with that ·judge [leader] and rescued the people during that ·judge's [leader's] lifetime. The LORD ·felt sorry for them [took pity on them; *or* relented] when they cried for help because of those who ·hurt [oppressed and afflicted] them. 19But when the ·judges [leaders; 2:16] died, the Israelites ·again sinned [returned to their corrupt ways] and worshiped other gods. They became worse than their ancestors. The Israelites were very stubborn and refused to change their evil ways.

20So the ·LORD became angry with [Langer of the LORD burned against] the Israelites. He said, "These people have ·broken [violated] the ·agreement [covenant] I made with their ancestors. They have not listened to me. 21I will no longer ·defeat [Ldrive out before them] the nations who were left when Joshua died. 22I will use them to test Israel, to see if Israel will keep ·the LORD's commands [Lthe way of the LORD to walk in it] as their ancestors did." 23In the past the LORD had permitted those nations to stay in the land. He did not quickly ·force [drive] them out or ·help Joshua's army defeat them [Lgive them into the hand of Joshua].

3 These are the nations the LORD did not force to leave. He wanted to test the Israelites who had not ·fought in [experienced; known] the wars of Canaan. 2(The only reason the LORD left those nations in the land was to teach the descendants of the Israelites who had not fought in those wars how to fight.) 3These are the nations: the five ·rulers [lords] of the Philistines, all the Canaanites, the people of Sidon, and the Hivites who lived in the Lebanon mountains from Mount Baal Hermon to Lebo Hamath. 4Those nations were in the land to test the Israelites—to see if they would obey the commands the LORD had given to their ancestors by [Lthe hand of] Moses.

5The people of Israel lived with the Canaanites, Hittites, Amorites, Perizzites, Hivites, and Jebusites. 6The Israelites ·began to marry [Ltook as wives] the daughters of those people, and they ·allowed their daughters to marry [Lgave their daughters to] the sons of those people. Israel also served their gods.

Othniel, the First Judge

7The ·Israelites [Lsons/Tchildren of Israel] did ·what the LORD said was wrong [Levil in the eyes/sight of the LORD]. They forgot about the LORD their God and served the ·idols of Baal [LBaals; 2:11] and ·Asherah [LAsherahs; Csacred trees or poles dedicated to the goddess Asherah; Deut. 16:21; Judg. 6:25]. 8So the LORD ·was angry with [Lburned in anger against]

Israel and allowed ·Cushan-Rishathaim [*or* Cushan, the Doubly Wicked] **king of ·northwest Mesopotamia** [*or* Aram Naharaim; CNaharaim means "two rivers," referring to Mesopotamia] **to rule over the ·Israelites** [Lsons/Tchildren of Israel] **for eight years. 9When Israel cried to the LORD, the LORD ·sent someone to save them** [Lraised up a deliverer]. **Othniel son of Kenaz, Caleb's younger brother, saved the Israelites. 10The Spirit of the LORD ·entered** [enpowered; came upon; was upon] **Othniel, and he became Israel's ·judge** [leader; 2:16]. **When he went to war, the LORD ·handed over to him** [Lgave into his hand] **·Cushan-Rishathaim** [*or* Cushan, the Doubly Wicked; v. 8] **king of ·northwest Mesopotamia** [*or* Aram Naharaim; v. 8]. **11So the land was at ·peace** [rest] **for forty years. Then Othniel son of Kenaz died.**

Ehud, the Judge

12Again the ·people [Lsons/Tchildren] **of Israel did ·what the LORD said was wrong** [Levil in the eyes/sight of the LORD]. **So the LORD gave Eglon king of Moab power to defeat Israel because of the evil Israel did. 13Eglon got the ·Ammonites and the Amalekites** [Lsons/descendants of Ammon and Amalek] **to join him. Then he attacked Israel and took the city of palm trees** [CJericho]. **14So the ·people** [Lsons; Tchildren] **of Israel were ·ruled by** [subject to] **Eglon king of Moab for eighteen years.**

15When the people cried to the LORD, he ·sent someone to save [Lraised up a rescuer/Tdeliverer for] **them. He was Ehud, son of Gera from the people of Benjamin, who was ·left-handed** [Lbound in the right hand]. **Israel sent Ehud to give Eglon king of Moab the ·payment** [tribute money] **he demanded. 16Ehud made himself a sword with two edges, ·about eighteen inches** [La cubit; Cthe distance between the elbow and the tip of the fingers] **long, and he tied it to his right hip under his clothes. 17Ehud gave Eglon king of Moab the ·payment** [tribute money] **he demanded. Now Eglon was a very fat man** [CEglon means "fat calf"]. **18After he had given Eglon the ·payment** [tribute money], **Ehud ·sent away** [dismissed] **the people who had carried it. 19When he passed the ·statues** [images; idols] **near Gilgal, he turned around** [CEhud returned to Eglon's palace and sought a private audience with the king] **and said to Eglon, "I have a secret message for you, King Eglon."**

The king said, "·Be quiet [Silence; *or* Give us privacy]**!" Then he sent all of his servants out of the room. 20Ehud went to King Eglon, as he was sitting alone in the ·room above his summer palace** [Lcool upper room; Cprobably a breezy roof-top room with lattice windows; perhaps a bathroom].

Ehud said, "I have a message from God for you." As the king stood up from his chair [Cperhaps an act of reverence to receive the divine oracle], **21Ehud reached with his left hand and took out the sword that was tied to his right hip** [Cthe unusual location on the right allowed concealment and caught the king by surprise]. **Then he stabbed the sword deep into the king's belly! 22Even the handle sank in, and ·the blade came out his back** [*or* his bowels discharged]. **The king's fat covered the whole sword, so Ehud left the sword in Eglon. 23Then he went out ·of the room** [*or* to the porch/vestibule; *or* through the latrine] **and closed and locked the doors behind him.**

24When the servants returned just after Ehud left, they found the doors to the room locked. So they thought the king was ·relieving himself [Lcovering his feet; Ca euphemism]. **25They waited for a long time. Finally they became ·worried** [anxious; *or* embarrassed] **because he still had not**

opened the doors. So they got the key and unlocked them and ·saw [[L]look;
[T]behold] their king lying dead on the floor!
[26]While the servants were waiting, Ehud had escaped. He passed by the
·statues [idols; images] and went to Seirah. [27]When he reached the ·moun-
tains [hill country] of Ephraim he blew the trumpet. The ·people [[L]sons;
[T]children] of Israel heard it and went down from the hills with Ehud leading them.
[28]He said to them, "Follow me! The LORD has ·helped you to defeat
[[L]given into your hand] your enemies, the Moabites." So Israel followed
Ehud and captured the ·crossings [fords] of the Jordan River ·across from
[*or* against] Moab. They did not allow the Moabites to cross the Jordan
River. [29]Israel killed about ten thousand strong and able men from Moab;
not one escaped. [30]So that day Moab was ·forced to be under the rule of
Israel [[L]subdued/made subject that day under the hand of Israel], and
there was ·peace [rest] in the land for eighty years.

Shamgar, the Judge

[31]After Ehud, Shamgar son of Anath saved Israel. Shamgar killed six
hundred Philistines with ·a sharp stick used to guide oxen [an oxgoad].

Deborah, the Woman Judge

4 After Ehud died, the ·Israelites [[L]sons/[T]children of Israel] again
did ·what the LORD said was wrong [[L]evil in the eyes/sight of the
LORD]. [2]So he ·let them be defeated by [[L]sold them into the hands of]
Jabin, a king of Canaan who ruled in the city of Hazor. Sisera, who lived
in Harosheth Haggoyim, was the commander of Jabin's army. [3]Because
he had nine hundred ·iron [iron-clad; iron-fitted; 1:19] chariots and ·was
very cruel to [harshly oppressed] the ·people [[L]sons; [T]children] of Israel
for twenty years, they cried to the LORD for help.
[4]A prophetess named Deborah, the wife of Lappidoth, was ·judging
[leading; 2:16] Israel at that time. [5]Deborah would sit under the Palm
Tree of Deborah, which was between the cities of Ramah and Bethel, in
the ·mountains [hill country] of Ephraim. And the ·people [[L]sons;
[T]children] of Israel would come to her ·to settle their arguments [[L]for
judgment].
[6]Deborah ·sent a message to [*or* sent for; summoned] Barak son of
Abinoam. Barak lived in ·the city of Kedesh, which is in the area of
Naphtali [[L]Kedesh-Naphtali]. Deborah said to Barak, "The LORD, the God
of Israel, commands you: 'Go and gather ten thousand ·men [[L]sons] of
Naphtali and Zebulun [[C]two tribes covering most of Israel's area north of
the Jezreel Valley] and lead them to Mount Tabor [[C]a cone-shaped mountain in Jezreel Valley southwest of Lake Galilee]. [7]I will ·make [[L]draw/pull
out] Sisera, the commander of Jabin's army, and his chariots, and his
army meet you at the Kishon River. I will ·hand Sisera over to you [[L]give
him into your hand].'"
[8]Then Barak said to Deborah, "I will go if you will go with me, but if
you won't go with me, I won't go."
[9]"·Of course [Certainly; [L]Going] I will go with you," Deborah answered,
"but you will not get ·credit [honor; glory; fame] ·for the victory [[L]in the
road/way/venture you are taking]. The LORD will ·let a woman defeat
Sisera [[L]sell Sisera into the hand of a woman]." So Deborah [[L]arose and]
went with Barak to Kedesh. [10]At Kedesh, Barak ·called [summoned] the
people of Zebulun and Naphtali together. ·From them, he gathered ten
thousand men to follow him [[L]Ten thousand men went up at his feet], and
Deborah went with him also.

11Now Heber the Kenite had ·left [separated/moved away from] the
other Kenites, the descendants of Hobab, Moses' ·brother-in-law [*or*
father-in-law]. Heber had put up his tent by the great tree in Zaanannim,
near Kedesh [Cthis verse introduces the family of Jael, the woman alluded
to by Deborah in v. 9; see v. 17].
12When Sisera was told that Barak son of Abinoam had gone to Mount
Tabor, 13Sisera gathered his nine hundred ·iron [iron-clad; iron-fitted; v.
3] chariots and all the men with him, from Harosheth Haggoyim to the
Kishon River.
14Then Deborah said to Barak, "Get up! Today is the day the LORD ·will
hand over Sisera [Lhas given Sisera into your hand]. The LORD has ·already
cleared the way for [Lgone out before] you." So Barak led ten thousand men
down Mount Tabor. 15As Barak approached, the LORD ·confused [caused to
panic; *or* routed] Sisera and his army and chariots. The LORD defeated them
with the [Ledge of the] sword, but Sisera ·left [jumped out of] his chariot
and ran away on foot. 16Barak and his men chased Sisera's chariots and
army to Harosheth Haggoyim. ·With their swords [LBy the edge of the
sword] they killed all of Sisera's men; not one of them was left alive.
17But Sisera himself ran away to the tent where Jael lived. She was the
wife of Heber, one of the Kenite family groups [v. 11]. ·Heber's family
[LThe house of Heber] ·was at peace [*or* had an alliance] with Jabin king
of Hazor. 18Jael went out to meet Sisera and said to him, "·Come into my
tent [LTurn aside], master! Come in. Don't be afraid." So Sisera went into
Jael's tent, and she covered him with a ·rug [*or* blanket].
19Sisera said to Jael, "I am thirsty. Please give me some water to drink."
So she opened a ·leather bag [goatskin] of milk and gave him a drink.
Then she covered him up.
20He said to her, "Go stand at the entrance to the tent. If anyone comes
and asks you, 'Is anyone here?' say, 'No.' "
21But Jael, the wife of Heber, took a tent peg and a hammer and ·quietly
[secretly] went to Sisera. Since he was very tired, he was in a deep sleep.
She hammered the tent peg through the side of Sisera's ·head [temple; *or*
mouth] and into the ground. And so Sisera died.
22·At that very moment [TAnd behold] Barak came by Jael's tent, chasing Sisera. Jael went out to meet him and said, "Come. I will show you the
man you are looking for." So Barak entered her tent, and there Sisera lay
dead, with the tent peg in his ·head [temple; *or* mouth].
23On that day God ·defeated [subdued; humiliated] Jabin king of
Canaan ·in the sight of [Lbefore the sons/Tchildren of] Israel.
24·Israel became stronger and stronger [LThe hand of sons/Tchildren of
Israel pressed harder and harder] against Jabin king of Canaan until
finally they destroyed him.

The Song of Deborah

5 On that day Deborah and Barak son of Abinoam sang this song:
2"·The leaders led Israel [*or* When locks of hair grow in Israel;
Creferring to the keeping of a Nazirite vow (Num. 6:5); the Hebrew
here is obscure].
The ·people [nation] ·volunteered to go to battle [answered the call;
offered themselves willingly].
·Praise [Bless] the LORD!
3Listen, kings.
Pay attention, rulers!

I ·myself [even I] will sing to the LORD.
I will ·make music [*or* sing praises] to the LORD, the God of Israel.

4"LORD, when you came from Seir [Canother name for Edom],
when you marched from the ·land [*or* fields] of Edom,
the earth shook,
the ·skies [heavens] ·rained [poured; dropped],
and the clouds ·dropped [poured] water.
5The mountains ·shook [quaked] before the LORD, the God of Mount Sinai,
before the LORD, the God of Israel!

6"In the days of Shamgar son of Anath [3:31],
in the days of Jael, the ·main roads were empty [highways were deserted; *or* caravans were no more].
Travelers went on ·the back roads [winding paths; Cbecause of Canaanite robbers on the highways].
7·There were no warriors in Israel [*or* The villagers/peasants would not fight; *or* The villagers deserted their villages]
until ·I [*or* you], Deborah, arose,
until ·I [*or* you] arose to be a mother to Israel.
8At that time ·they chose to follow new gods [*or* God chose new leaders/warriors].
Because of this, ·enemies fought us at our [war came to the] city gates.
·No one could find a shield or a spear [LA shield, it could not be seen, nor a spear]
among the forty thousand people of Israel.
9My heart is with the ·commanders [leaders; princes] of Israel.
·They volunteered freely [*or* And with those who volunteered freely] from among the people.
·Praise [Bless] the LORD!

10"You who ride on white [Lfemale] donkeys
and sit on ·saddle blankets [*or* rich carpets],
and you who walk along the road, ·listen [ponder this; *or* tell of this]!
11Listen to the sound of the ·singers [village musicians; *or* those who distribute the water; *or* those who divide the sheep]
at the watering holes.
There they tell about the ·victories [*or* righteous deeds/triumphs] of the LORD,
the ·victories [*or* righteous deeds/triumphs] of the LORD's ·warriors [*or* villagers; peasantry] in Israel.
Then the LORD's people went down to the city gates.

12"Wake up, wake up, Deborah!
Wake up, wake up, sing a song!
Get up, Barak!
·Go capture your enemies [LTake captive your captives], son of Abinoam!

13"Then ·those who were left [the remnant/survivors] ·came down to the important leaders [*or* of the nobles/leaders came down].

The LORD's people came down to me ·with strong men [*or* against the mighty].
[14]They came from Ephraim ·in the mountains of [*or* whose roots were in; *or* who uprooted] Amalek.
·Benjamin was among the people who followed you [*or* They follow you, Benjamin, with your people/soldiers].
From ·the family group of Makir [LMakir], the commanders came down.
And from Zebulun came those who ·lead [Lcarry the officer's/commander's staff].
[15]The princes of Issachar were with Deborah.
The people of Issachar were loyal to Barak
and ·followed him [were sent under his command; Lwere sent at his feet] into the valley.
·The Reubenites [LAmong the clans of Reuben they] ·thought hard about what they would do [greatly searched their hearts; *or* had great indecision].
[16]Why did you stay by the sheepfold?
Was it to hear the ·music played [whistling] for your ·sheep [flocks]?
·The Reubenites [LAmong the clans of Reuben they] ·thought hard about what they would do [greatly searched their hearts; *or* had great indecision].
[17]·The people of Gilead [LGilead; Cthe grandson of Manasseh, though the term is used for the tribe of Gad and the half-tribe of Manasseh east of the Jordan] stayed east of the Jordan River.
·People of Dan [LDan; 1:34], why did you stay by the ships [CDan remained on the Mediterranean coast rather than help in the battle]?
The people of Asher stayed at the seashore,
at their ·safe harbors [coves; landings].
[18]But the people of Zebulun ·risked their lives [Ldespised their lives even to death],
as did the people of Naphtali on the ·battlefield [Lheights of the field].

[19]"The kings came, and they fought.
At that time the kings of Canaan fought
at Taanach, by the waters of Megiddo.
But they took away no ·silver or possessions of Israel [plunder of silver].
[20]The stars fought from heaven [Cpersonified as God's army];
from their ·paths [courses], they fought Sisera.
[21]The Kishon River swept Sisera's men away,
that ·old river [ancient torrent], the Kishon ·River [torrent; Ca rainstorm sent from God swelled the river].
March on, my soul, with strength!
[22]Then the horses' hoofs ·beat [pounded] the ground.
Galloping, galloping go Sisera's ·mighty horses [stallions; steeds; Lmighty ones].
[23]'·May the town of Meroz be cursed [LCurse Meroz],' said the angel of the LORD.
'·Bitterly curse [Utterly curse; LCurse a curse upon] its ·people [inhabitants],
because they did not come to help the LORD.

·They did not fight the strong enemy [To help the LORD against the warriors/mighty ones].'

24"Most blessed among women is Jael, the wife of Heber the Kenite,
May she be blessed above all women who live in tents.
25Sisera asked for water,
but Jael gave him milk.
In a bowl fit for a ·ruler [noble; king],
she brought him ·cream [*or* curds].
26Jael reached out her hand and took the tent peg.
Her right hand reached for the workman's hammer.
She ·hit [struck] Sisera! She ·smashed [crushed] his head!
She ·crushed [shattered] and pierced ·the side of his head [his temple/*or* mouth]!
27·At [*or* Between] Jael's feet he ·sank [bowed].
He fell, and he lay there.
·At [*or* Between] her feet he ·sank [bowed]. He fell.
Where Sisera ·sank [bowed], there he fell, dead!

28"Sisera's mother looked out through the window.
She looked through the ·curtains [lattice] and cried out,
'Why is Sisera's chariot so late in coming?
Why are ·sounds of his chariots' horses [Lthe chariots' hoofbeats] delayed?'
29The wisest of her ·servant ladies [*or* princesses] answer her,
·and [indeed] Sisera's mother says to herself,
30'Surely they are ·robbing the people they defeated and dividing those things among themselves [Lfinding and dividing the spoil]!
Each soldier is given a ·girl [Lwomb; Cslang for women] or two.
·Maybe Sisera is taking [LFor Sisera a plunder of] ·pieces of dyed cloth [*or* colorful garments].
·Maybe they are even taking [LFor spoil/plunder]
pieces of dyed, embroidered cloth for the necks of the ·victors [plunderers]!'

31"·Let [May] all your enemies ·die [perish] this way, LORD!
But ·let [may] all the people who love you
be ·as strong as the rising sun [Llike the sun rising in its strength]!"

Then there was ·peace [rest] in the land for forty years.

The Midianites Attack Israel

6 Again the ·Israelites [Lsons/Tchildren of Israel] did ·what the LORD
said was wrong [Levil in the eyes/sight of the LORD]. So for seven
years the LORD ·handed them over to [Lgave them into the hand of] Midian.
2Because the ·Midianites were very powerful and were cruel to [Lhand of
Midian was so strong/oppressive against] Israel, the Israelites made ·hiding
places [shelters; dens] in the mountains, in caves, and in ·safe places
[strongholds]. 3Whenever the Israelites planted crops, the Midianites,
Amalekites, and other ·peoples [Lsons] from the east would come and
attack them. 4They ·camped in the land [Lencamped against them] and
destroyed the crops that the Israelites had planted as far away as Gaza.
They left ·nothing [no sustenance/living thing] for Israel to eat, and no

sheep, cattle, or donkeys. 5The Midianites came with their tents and their
·animals [livestock] **·like swarms of** [as numerous as] **locusts to ·ruin** [rav-
age; lay waste] **the land. There were so many people and camels they could**
not be counted. 6Israel ·became very poor [*or* was weakened; Lwas brought
low] **because of the Midianites, so they cried out to the LORD.**
7When the ·Israelites [Lsons/Tchildren of Israel] **cried out to the LORD**
·against [*or* because of] **the Midianites, 8the LORD sent a prophet to them.**
He said, "This is what the LORD, the God of Israel, says: I brought you out
of Egypt, the ·land [Lhouse] **of slavery. 9I ·saved** [rescued; Tdelivered] **you**
from the [Lhand of the] **Egyptians and from all those who ·were against**
[oppressed] **you. I ·forced** [drove] **·the Canaanites** [Lthem] **out of their**
land and gave it to you. 10Then I said to you, 'I am the LORD your God. Do
not ·worship [fear; reverence] **the gods of the Amorites, in whose land**
you now live.' But you did not ·obey me [Llisten to my voice]**."**

The Angel of the Lord Visits Gideon

11The angel of the LORD [Cangelic spokesperson for God, sometimes
identified with the LORD himself; 2:1; Gen. 16:7; Ex. 14:19; 23:20] **came**
and sat down under the oak tree at Ophrah that belonged to Joash, ·one
of the Abiezrite people [Lthe Abiezrite]**. Gideon, Joash's son, was ·separat-**
ing some wheat from the chaff [threshing/Lbeating out wheat] **in a**
winepress to keep the wheat from the Midianites [Cin a pit hidden from
sight]**. 12The angel of the LORD appeared to Gideon and said, "The LORD is**
with you, ·mighty [courageous] **warrior!"**
13Then Gideon said, "·Sir [My lord]**, if the LORD is with us, why ·are we**
having so much trouble [Lhas all this happened to us]**? Where are the**
·miracles [wonderful deeds] **our ancestors told us about? They said,**
"Didn't the LORD bring us up out of Egypt? But now the LORD has ·left
[abandoned] **us and has ·handed us over to the Midianites** [Lgiven us into
the hand of Midian]**."**
14The LORD turned to Gideon and said, "Go with your strength and
·save [rescue; Tdeliver] **Israel from the ·Midianites** [Lhand of Midian]**. ·I**
am the one who is sending you. [LAm I not sending you?]**"**
15But Gideon answered, "Lord, how can I ·save [rescue; Tdeliver] **Israel?**
My ·family group [clan] **is the weakest in Manasseh, and I am the ·least**
important [*or* youngest] **member of my family."**
16The LORD answered him, "I will be with you. ·It will seem as if the
Midianites you are fighting are only one man [*or* You will strike down the
whole Midian army; LYou will strike/defeat Midian as one man]**."**
17Then Gideon said to the LORD, "If ·you are pleased with me [LI have
found favor in your eyes]**, give me ·proof** [a sign] **that it is really you talk-**
ing with me. 18Please ·wait here [Ldo not leave] **until I come back to you.**
Let me bring my offering and set it in front of you."
And the LORD said, "I will ·wait [stay] **until you return."**
19So Gideon went in and ·cooked [prepared] **a young goat, and with**
·twenty quarts [Lan ephah] **of flour, made ·bread without yeast** [unleav-
ened bread]**. Then he put the meat into a basket and the broth into a pot.**
He brought them out and ·gave [presented; offered] **them to ·the angel**
[Lhim] **under the oak tree.**
20The angel of God [6:11] **said to Gideon, "Put the meat and the ·bread**
without yeast [unleavened bread] **on that rock over there. Then pour the**
broth on them." And Gideon did as he was told. 21The angel of the LORD
touched the meat and the bread with the end of ·the stick that was in his

hand [[L]his staff]. Then fire jumped up from the rock and completely burned up the meat and the bread! And the angel of the LORD disappeared! 22 Then Gideon ·understood [realized; saw] he had been talking to the angel of the LORD. So Gideon cried out, "[Oh no; Alas; [L]Aha] ·Lord GOD [Sovereign LORD]! I have seen the angel of the LORD face to face!"

23 But the LORD said to Gideon, "·Calm down [[L]Peace to you]! Don't be afraid! You will not die!"

24 So Gideon built an altar there to the LORD and named it The LORD Is Peace. ·It still [[L]To this day it] stands at Ophrah, ·where the Abiezrites live [[L]of the Abiezrite].

Gideon Tears Down the Altar of Baal

25 That same night the LORD said to Gideon, "Take the bull that belongs to your father and a second bull seven years old. Pull down your father's altar to Baal, and cut down the ·Asherah idol [*or* Asherah pole; [L]Asherah; [C]a Canaanite fertility goddess; 3:7] beside it. 26 Then build an altar to the LORD your God ·with its stones in the right order [*or* in the proper manner] on this ·high ground [stronghold]. ·Kill and burn a [Sacrifice as a burnt offering the] second bull on this altar, using the wood from the Asherah idol."

27 So Gideon got ten of his servants and did what the LORD had told him to do. But Gideon was afraid that his family and the men of the city might see him, so he did it at night, not in the daytime.

28 When the men of the city got up the next morning, ·they saw that [[L]look; [T]behold] the altar for Baal ·had been destroyed [[L]was cut down] and that the ·Asherah idol [Asherah pole; [L]Asherah; v. 25] beside it had been cut down! They also saw the altar Gideon had built and the second bull that had been sacrificed on it. 29 The men of the city asked each other, "Who did this?"

After they ·asked many questions [made a careful investigation], someone told them, "Gideon son of Joash did this."

30 So the men of the city said to Joash, "Bring your son out. He has pulled down the altar of Baal and cut down the ·Asherah idol [Asherah pole; [L]Asherah] beside it. He must die!"

31 But Joash said to ·the angry crowd around [[L]all those who stood against] him, "·Are you going to take Baal's side [*or* Are you pleading Baal's case; *or* Does Baal need you to defend him]? Are you going to ·defend [save; rescue; [T]deliver] him? Anyone who ·takes Baal's side [*or* pleads his case; *or* thinks Baal needs defending] will be killed by morning! If Baal is a god, let him fight for himself. It's his altar that has been pulled down." 32 So on that day Gideon got the name Jerub-Baal, which means "let Baal ·fight against him [*or* plead his own case; *or* defend himself]," because Gideon pulled down Baal's altar.

Gideon Defeats Midian

33 All the Midianites, the Amalekites, and other ·peoples from [[L]sons of] the east ·joined together [assembled; formed an alliance] and came across the Jordan River and camped in the Valley of Jezreel. 34 But the Spirit of the LORD ·entered [empowered; came upon; clothed] Gideon, and he blew a trumpet to call the Abiezrites to follow him. 35 He sent messengers to all of Manasseh, calling them to follow him. He also sent messengers to the people of Asher, Zebulun, and Naphtali. So they also went up to meet Gideon and his men.

36 Then Gideon said to God, "·You said you would help me save Israel [[L]If you are about to deliver Israel by my hand, as you said…]. 37 [[L]Look;

[T]Behold] I will put ·some wool [a wool fleece] on the threshing floor. If
there is dew only on the ·wool [fleece] but all of the ground is dry, then I
will know that you will ·use me to save Israel [[L]save Israel by my hand], as
you said." 38And that is just what happened. When Gideon got up early
the next morning and squeezed the ·wool [fleece], he got a full bowl of
water from it.
39Then Gideon said to God, "Don't ·be angry with [[L]let your anger
burn against] me if I ask just one more thing. Please let me make one
more test. Let only the ·wool [fleece] be dry while the ground around it
gets wet with dew." 40That night God did that very thing. Just the ·wool
[fleece] was dry, but the ground around it was wet with dew.
7 Early in the morning Jerub-Baal (also called Gideon) and all his
men set up their camp at the spring of Harod [[C]at the foot of
Mount Gilboa]. The Midianites were camped north of them in the valley
[[C]of Jezreel] at the bottom of the hill called Moreh. 2Then the LORD said to
Gideon, "You have too many men ·to defeat the Midianites [[L]for me to
give Midian into your hand]. I don't want the Israelites to brag ·that they
saved themselves [[L]saying, "My own hand has saved/[T]delivered me"]. 3So
now, ·announce to [[L]call into the ears of] the ·people [nation; army],
'Anyone who is ·afraid [[L]fearful and trembling] may leave Mount Gilead
[[C]probably another name for Gilboa] and go back home.'" So twenty-two
thousand men returned home, but ten thousand remained.
4Then the LORD said to Gideon, "There are still too many men. Take the
men down to the water, and I will ·test [sort; sift out] them for you there.
If I say, 'This man will go with you,' he will go. But if I say, 'That one will
not go with you,' he will not go."
5So Gideon led the men down to the water. There the LORD said to him,
"Separate them into those who drink water by lapping it up like a dog
[[C]with cupped hand making a bowl] and those who ·bend down [kneel]
to drink [[C]with faces in the water]." 6There were three hundred men who
used their hands to bring water to their mouths, ·lapping it as a dog does
[[L]lapping]. All the rest ·got down on their knees [kneeled] to drink.
7Then the LORD said to Gideon, "Using the three hundred men who
lapped the water, I will save you and ·hand Midian over to you [[L]give the
Midianites into your hand]. Let all the others go home." 8So Gideon sent
the rest of Israel ·to their homes [[L]each to his tent]. But he kept three
hundred men and took the ·jars [provisions] and the trumpets of those
who left.
Now the camp of Midian was in the valley below Gideon. 9That night
the LORD said to Gideon, "Get up. Go down and attack the camp of the
Midianites, because I will give ·them to you [[L]it into your hands]. 10But if
you are afraid to go down, take your servant Purah with you. 11When you
come to the camp of Midian, you will hear what they are saying. Then ·you
will not be afraid [[L]your hands will be strengthened] to attack the camp."

Gideon Is Encouraged

So Gideon and his servant Purah went down to the ·edge [outposts;
guardposts] of the enemy camp. 12The Midianites, the Amalekites, and all
the ·peoples from [[L]sons of] the east were camped in that valley. ·There
were so many of them they seemed like locusts [[L]...like locusts in num-
bers/greatness]. Their camels could not be counted because they were as
many as the grains of sand on the seashore!
13When Gideon came to the enemy camp, he heard a man telling his

friend about a dream. He was saying, "[LLook; TBehold] I dreamed that a
loaf of barley bread rolled into the camp of Midian. It hit the tent so hard
that the tent turned over and fell flat!"
14The man's friend said, "·Your dream is about [LThis can be nothing
except] the sword of Gideon son of Joash, a man of Israel. God ·will hand
[Lhas given into his hand] Midian and the whole army over to him!"
15When Gideon heard about the dream and what it meant, he ·wor-
shiped God [Lbowed in worship]. Then Gideon went back to the camp of
Israel and called out to them, "Get up! The LORD has handed the army of
Midian ·over to you [Linto your hand]!" 16Gideon divided the three hundred men into three ·groups [companies; divisions]. He gave each man a
trumpet and an empty jar with a burning torch inside.
17Gideon told the men, "Watch me and do what I do. When I get to the
edge of the camp, do what I do. 18Surround the enemy camp. When I and
everyone with me blow our trumpets, you blow your trumpets, too. Then
shout, 'For the LORD and for Gideon!' "

Midian Is Defeated

19So Gideon and the one hundred men with him came to the edge of
the enemy camp at the beginning of the middle watch of the night, just
after they had ·changed guards [posted sentries; set the watch]. Then
Gideon and his men blew their trumpets and smashed their jars. 20All
three groups of Gideon's men blew their trumpets and smashed their
jars. They held the torches in their left hands and the trumpets in their
right hands. Then they shouted, "A sword for the LORD and for Gideon!"
21Each of Gideon's men ·stayed [stood] in his place around the camp, but
the Midianites began shouting and running to escape.
22When Gideon's three hundred men blew their trumpets, the LORD
·made all the Midianites fight each other with their swords [Lset the sword
of a man against his companion]! The enemy army ran away to the city of
Beth Shittah toward Zererah. They ran as far as the border of Abel
Meholah, near the city of Tabbath [Ctoward the southeast]. 23Then men of
Israel from Naphtali, Asher, and all of Manasseh were called out to chase
the Midianites. 24Gideon sent messengers through all the ·mountains
[hill country] of Ephraim, saying, "Come down and attack the Midianites.
Take control of the ·Jordan River [Lwaters; Cthe shallow crossing points] as
far as Beth Barah before the Midianites can get to it."
So they called out all the men of Ephraim, who took control of the
·Jordan River [waters of the Jordan ahead of them; 3:28] as far as Beth
Barah. 25The men of Ephraim captured two ·princes [leaders; command-
ers] of Midian named Oreb and Zeeb. They killed Oreb at the rock of
Oreb and Zeeb at the winepress of Zeeb, and they continued chasing the
Midianites. They brought the heads of Oreb and Zeeb to Gideon, ·who
was east of [*or* who was beside/across; Lfrom beyond] the Jordan River.

8 The men of Ephraim asked Gideon, "·Why did you treat us this
way [LWhat is this thing you have done to us]? Why didn't you call
us when you went to fight against Midian?" They argued ·angrily [fiercely;
greatly] with Gideon.
2But he answered them, "·I have not done as well as you! [LWhat have I
done compared to you?] The ·small part you did [Lthe gleanings of
Ephraim; Cpicking up the leftover grapes after harvest] was better than ·all
that my people of Abiezer did [Lthe vintage/grape harvest of Abiezer].
3God ·let you capture [Lgave into your hand] Oreb and Zeeb, the ·princes

[leaders; commanders] of Midian. ·How can I compare what I did with what you did [LWhat did I do in comparison]?" When the men of Ephraim heard Gideon's answer, ·they were not as angry anymore [they calmed down; Ltheir spirit declined/subsided].

Gideon Captures Two Kings

4When Gideon and his three hundred men came to the Jordan River, they were ·tired [exhausted], but they chased the enemy across to the other side. 5Gideon said to the men of Succoth, "Please give my soldiers some loaves of bread because they are ·very tired [exhausted]. I am chasing Zebah and Zalmunna, the kings of Midian."

6But the ·leaders [princes; officials] of Succoth said, "Why should we give your soldiers bread? ·You haven't caught Zebah and Zalmunna yet [LAre the hands of Zebah and Zalmunna in your hand?]."

7Then Gideon said, "·The LORD will surrender [LWhen the LORD surrenders] Zebah and Zalmunna to me. After that, I will ·whip [beat; tear; Lthresh] your skin with thorns and briers from the ·desert [wilderness]."

8Gideon left Succoth and went up to the city of Peniel and ·asked them for food [Lspoke this to them]. But the people of Peniel gave him the same answer as the people of Succoth. 9So Gideon said to the men of Peniel, "·After I win the victory [LWhen I return in peace], I will return and pull down this tower."

10Zebah and Zalmunna and their army were in the city of Karkor. About fifteen thousand men were left of the armies of the ·peoples [Lsons] of the east. Already one hundred twenty thousand ·soldiers [Lmen who draw the sword] had ·been killed [fallen in battle]. 11Gideon went up the road of those who live in tents [Cthe route taken by caravans or nomads] east of Nobah and Jogbehah, and he attacked the ·enemy army [camp] ·when they did not expect it [in a surprise attack; Lwhile they were secure]. 12Zebah and Zalmunna, the kings of Midian, ran away, but Gideon chased and captured them and ·frightened away [routed; caused to panic] their army.

13Then Gideon son of Joash returned from the battle by the ·Pass [*or* Ascent] of Heres. 14Gideon captured a young man from Succoth and ·asked him some questions [interrogated him]. So the young man wrote down for Gideon the names of seventy-seven ·officers [princes; leaders] and elders of Succoth.

Gideon Punishes Succoth

15When Gideon came to Succoth, he said to the people of that city, "·Here are [LLook!; TBehold!] Zebah and Zalmunna. You ·made fun of [taunted; insulted] me by saying, 'Why should we give bread to your tired men? ·You have not caught Zebah and Zalmunna yet [LAre the hands of Zebah and Zalmunna in your hand?].'" 16So Gideon took the elders of the city and ·punished them [taught them a lesson] with thorns and briers from the ·desert [wilderness]. 17He also pulled down the tower of Peniel and killed the people in that city.

18Gideon asked Zebah and Zalmunna, "What were the men like that you killed on Mount Tabor?"

They answered, "They were like you. Each one of them looked like ·a prince [Lsons of a king]."

19Gideon said, "Those were my brothers, my mother's sons. As surely as the LORD lives, I would not kill you if you had spared them." 20Then Gideon said to Jether, his oldest son, "Kill them." But Jether was only a boy and was afraid, so he did not draw his sword.

21Then Zebah and Zalmunna said to Gideon, "Come on. ·Kill us [LDo it] yourself. As the saying goes, '·It takes a man to do a man's job [LAs is a man, so is his strength; Cit was honorable to be killed by a great warrior, but humiliating to be killed by a boy].'" So Gideon got up and killed Zebah and Zalmunna and took the ·decorations [Lcrescent-shaped ornaments] off their camels' necks.

Gideon Makes an Idol

22 The people of Israel said to Gideon, "You ·saved [rescued; Tdelivered] us from the Midianites. Now, we want you and your son and your grandson to rule over us [Cto establish a royal dynasty]."

23 But Gideon told them, "I will not rule over you, nor will my son rule over you. The Lord will be your ruler." 24 He said, "I want you to do this one thing for me. I want each of you to give me a gold earring from ·the things you took in the fighting [Lhis plunder]." (The Ishmaelites [Crelated to the Midianites, and sometimes identified with them; Gen. 37:25–28] wore gold earrings.)

25 They said, "We will ·gladly [indeed] give you what you want." So they spread out a ·coat [cloak; garment], and everyone threw down an earring from ·what he had taken [his plunder]. 26 The gold earrings weighed ·about forty-three pounds [L1,700 shekels of gold]. This did not count the ·decorations [Lcrescent-shaped ornaments], ·necklaces [pendants], and purple robes worn by the kings of Midian, nor the chains from the camels' necks. 27 Gideon used the gold to make a ·holy vest [ephod; Cperhaps in imitation of the high priest and used to discern God's will; Ex. 29:2–5], which he put in his hometown of Ophrah. But all the Israelites ·were unfaithful to God [Lprostituted themselves] and worshiped it, so it became a ·trap [snare; cause of sin] for Gideon and his family.

The Death of Gideon

28 So Midian was ·under the rule of [subdued before] ·Israel [Lthe sons/Tchildren of Israel]; they did not ·cause trouble anymore [Lraise its head again]. And the land had ·peace [rest] for forty years, ·as long as Gideon was alive [Lin the days of Gideon].

29 Jerub-Baal [Canother name for Gideon; 6:32] son of Joash went to his home to live. 30 He had seventy sons ·of his own [Lwho went out from his loins], because he had many wives. 31 He had a ·slave woman [concubine; Ca secondary wife, of lower status than a primary wife but higher than a common servant] who lived in Shechem, and he had a son by her, whom he named Abimelech [C"My father is king"]. 32 So Gideon son of Joash died at a good old age. He was buried in the tomb of Joash, his father, in Ophrah, ·where the Abiezrites live [Lof the Abiezrites].

33 As soon as Gideon died, the ·people [Lsons; Tchildren] of Israel ·were again unfaithful to God and followed [Lprostituted themselves to] the Baals. They made Baal-Berith their god. 34 The ·Israelites [Lsons/Tchildren of Israel] did not remember the Lord their God, who had ·saved [rescued; Tdelivered] them from all their enemies living all around them. 35 And they were not ·kind [loyal; faithful] to the family of Jerub-Baal, also called Gideon, for all the good he had done for Israel.

Abimelech Becomes King

9 Abimelech [8:31] son of Jerub-Baal [CGideon; 6:32] went to his ·uncles [Lmother's brothers] in the city of Shechem. He said to ·his uncles [Lthem] and all of his mother's ·family group [clan], 2 "·Ask [*or* Whisper to; LSpeak in the ears of] the ·leaders [leading citizens; lords] of Shechem, 'Is it better for the seventy sons of Gideon to rule over you or for one man to rule?' Remember, I am your ·relative [Lbone and your flesh]."

3Abimelech's ·uncles [mother's brothers] ·spoke to [*or* whispered to; Lspoke in the ears of] all the ·leaders [leading citizens; lords] of Shechem about this [Lfor him; on his behalf]. And ·they decided [they were inclined; Ltheir heart was stretched] to follow Abimelech, because they said, "He is our ·relative [brother]." 4So the leaders of Shechem gave Abimelech about ·one and three-quarter pounds [Lseventy pieces/coins] of silver from the temple of the god Baal-Berith [8:33]. Abimelech used the silver to hire some worthless, reckless men, who ·followed him wherever he went [Lwent after him]. 5He went to Ophrah, the hometown of his father, and murdered his seventy brothers, the sons of Jerub-Baal [CGideon; 6:32]. He killed them all on one stone. But Jerub-Baal's youngest son, Jotham, hid from Abimelech and ·escaped [survived; was left]. 6Then all of the leaders of Shechem and Beth Millo [C"house of the fill"; probably the earthen structure on which the Tower of Shechem (v. 46) was built] gathered beside the ·great tree [oak] by the pillar [Clikely an object of pagan worship] in Shechem. There they made Abimelech their king.

Jotham's Story

7When Jotham heard this, he went and stood on the top of Mount Gerizim. He shouted to the people: "Listen to me, you ·leaders [leading citizens; lords] of Shechem, so that God will listen to you! 8One day the trees decided to ·appoint [Lanoint] a king to rule over them. They said to the olive tree, '·You be king [Rule; Reign] over us!'

9"But the olive tree said, 'Men and gods are honored by my oil. Should I ·stop making it [Lcease my fatness/abundance] and go and sway over the other trees?' [CAncient kings were sometimes compared to trees, providing shelter and protection for their subjects.]

10"Then the trees said to the fig tree, 'Come and ·be king [rule; reign] over us!'

11"But the fig tree answered, 'Should I stop making my sweet and good fruit and go and sway over the other trees?'

12"Then the trees said to the vine, 'Come and ·be king [rule; reign] over us!'

13"But the vine answered, 'My new wine makes men and gods happy. Should I stop making it and go and sway over the trees?'

14"Then all the trees said to the thornbush, 'Come and ·be king [rule; reign] over us.'

15"But the thornbush said to the trees, 'If you really want to ·appoint [Lanoint] me king over you, come and ·find shelter [take refuge] in my shade! But if not, let fire come out of the thornbush and ·burn up [consume; devour] the cedars of Lebanon!' [CA worthless thornbush provides no shelter and burns hot and quick (Ps. 58:9), igniting the great cedars of Lebanon (the most valuable trees in the ancient Near East); see v. 20.]

16"Now, ·were you completely honest and sincere [Lif you acted in truth and integrity/blamelessness] when you made Abimelech king? ·Have you [LAnd if you have] been fair to Jerub-Baal [CGideon; 6:32] and his ·family [Lhouse]? ·Have [LAnd if] you treated him as ·you should [Lhis hands deserved]? 17Remember, my father fought for you and risked his life to ·save [rescue; Tdeliver] you from the ·power of the Midianites [Lhand of Midian]. 18But now you have ·turned [revolted; risen up] against my father's ·family [Lhouse] and have killed his seventy sons on one stone [v. 5]. You have made Abimelech, the son of my father's ·slave girl [maidservant], king over the ·leaders [leading citizens; lords] of Shechem just

because he is your ·relative [brother]! 19So then, if you have ·been honest
and sincere [acted in truth and integrity/blamelessness] to Jerub-Baal
[CGideon; 6:32] and his ·family [Lhouse] today, ·be happy with [rejoice in]
Abimelech as your king. And may he ·be happy with [rejoice in] you! 20But
if not, may fire come out of Abimelech and completely burn you ·leaders
[leading citizens; lords] of Shechem and Beth Millo [Cthe cedars of Lebanon
in the allegory; v. 15]! Also may fire come out of the ·leaders [leading citizens; lords] of Shechem and Beth Millo and burn up Abimelech!"
21Then Jotham ran away and escaped to the city of Beer [Cmeaning
"well"]. He lived there because he was afraid of his brother Abimelech.

Abimelech Fights Against Shechem

22Abimelech ruled Israel for three years. 23Then God sent an evil spirit
to make trouble between Abimelech and the ·leaders [leading citizens;
lords] of Shechem so that they ·turned [revolted; acted treacherously]
against him. 24God did this to repay [avenge] the violence done to the
seventy sons of Jerub-Baal [CGideon; 6:32] and to make their brother
Abimelech pay for their spilled blood, together with the ·leaders [leading
citizens; lords] of Shechem who ·helped him murder [Lstrengthened his
hand to kill] his brothers. 25The ·leaders [leading citizens; lords] of
Shechem were against Abimelech then and put men on the hilltops in
ambush to rob everyone going by. And Abimelech was told.
26A man named Gaal son of Ebed and his brothers ·moved into [came
to] Shechem, and the ·leaders [leading citizens; lords] of Shechem ·trusted
[*or* gave their allegiance to] him. 27They went out to the vineyards to pick
grapes, and they ·squeezed [stomped/trod on] the grapes. Then they had
a feast in the temple of their god, where they ate and drank and cursed
Abimelech. 28Gaal son of Ebed said, "·We are the men of Shechem. Who
is Abimelech [LWho is Abimelech and who is Shechem] that we should
serve him? Isn't he one of Jerub-Baal's [CGideon's] sons, and isn't Zebul
his ·officer [deputy; lieutenant]? ·We should serve [LServe…!] the men of
Hamor, Shechem's father. Why should we serve Abimelech? 29If you made
me commander of these people, I would get rid of Abimelech. I would say
to him, '·Get your army ready [Muster your troops; Strengthen your
army] and come out to battle.' "
30Now when Zebul, the ·ruler [governor] of ·Shechem [Lthe city], heard
what Gaal son of Ebed said, ·he was very angry [Lhis anger burned]. 31He
sent messengers to Abimelech ·secretly [deceptively; *or* in Arumah], saying, "Gaal son of Ebed and Gaal's brothers have come to Shechem, and
they are ·turning [inciting; stirring up] the city against you! 32You and
your men should get up during the night and ·hide [lie in wait; set an
ambush] in the fields outside the city. 33As soon as the sun comes up in
the morning, ·attack [raid; rush upon] the city. When Gaal and his men
come out to fight you, do what ·you can to them [Lyour hand finds to do]."
34So Abimelech and all his soldiers got up during the night and ·hid
near [lay in wait outside; set an ambush against] Shechem in four groups.
35Gaal son of Ebed went out and was standing at the entrance to the city
gate. As he was standing there, Abimelech and his soldiers came out of
their ·hiding places [ambush].
36When Gaal saw the soldiers, he said to Zebul, "Look! There are people coming down from the mountains!"
But Zebul said, "You are seeing the shadows of the mountains. The
shadows just look like people."

37But again Gaal said, "Look, there are people coming down from the ·center of the land [*or* navel of the earth; Ezek. 38:12], and there is a group coming from the ·fortune-tellers' tree [diviner's oak; Ca place where fortunes were told; ironically, Gaal's fortune had been sealed]!"

38Zebul said to Gaal, "Where is your ·bragging [Lmouth] now? You said, 'Who is Abimelech that we should serve him?' ·You made fun of [Didn't you mock/insult/despise…?] these men. Now go out and fight them."

39So Gaal led the ·men [leading citizens; lords] of Shechem out to fight Abimelech. 40Abimelech ·and his men chased them [Lchased him], and many of Gaal's men ·were killed [*or* fell wounded] before they could get back to the city gate. 41While Abimelech stayed at Arumah, Zebul forced Gaal and his brothers to leave Shechem.

42The next day the people of Shechem went out to the fields. When Abimelech was told about it, 43he separated his men into three groups and ·hid them [set an ambush; lay in wait] in the fields. When he saw the people coming out of the city, he jumped up and ·attacked [struck; slew] them. 44Abimelech and his ·group [force; company] ran to the entrance gate to the city. The other two groups ran out to the people in the fields and struck them down. 45Abimelech and his men fought the city of Shechem all day until they captured it and killed its people. Then he ·tore it down [razed/leveled the city] and ·threw salt over the ruins [Lsowed it with salt; Cto symbolize destruction and desolation; Deut. 29:23; Ps. 107:34].

The Tower of Shechem Burns

46When the ·leaders [leading citizens; lords] who were in the Tower of Shechem [Ceither a nearby town or a structure within Shechem; v. 6] heard what had happened to Shechem, they gathered in the ·safest room [stronghold; inner chamber] of the temple of El Berith [9:4]. 47Abimelech heard that all the ·leaders [leading citizens; lords] of the Tower of Shechem had gathered there. 48So he and all his men went up Mount Zalmon [Cnear Shechem]. Abimelech took an ax and cut some ·branches [brushwood] and put them on his shoulders. He said to all those with him, "Hurry! Do what I have done!" 49So all those men cut ·branches [brushwood] and followed Abimelech and piled them against the ·safest room [stronghold; inner chamber] of the temple. Then they set them on fire and burned ·the people inside [Lthe stronghold over them]. So all the people who were at the Tower of Shechem also died—about a thousand men and women.

Abimelech's Death

50Then Abimelech went to the city of Thebez. He ·surrounded the city, attacked it, [Lbesieged/encamped against Thebez] and captured it. 51But inside the city was a strong ·tower [*or* fortress], so all the men, women, and ·leaders [leading citizens; lords] of that city ran to the tower. When they got inside, they locked the door behind them. Then they climbed up to the roof of the tower [Cto fight back and avoid the fate of the people of Shechem; v. 49]. 52Abimelech came to the tower to attack it. He approached the door of the tower to set it on fire, 53but as he came near, a woman dropped a ·grinding stone [Lupper millstone; Cthe smaller stone (about 10 inches long) that was rolled by hand over the top of the larger lower millstone; Deut. 24:6] on his head, crushing his skull.

54He quickly called to the officer who carried his armor and said, "Draw your sword and kill me. I don't want people to say, 'A woman killed Abimelech [Ca humiliation for a warrior; 4:17–24; 1 Sam. 31:4].'" So ·the officer [his servant; *or* the young man] stabbed Abimelech, and he died.

55When the people of Israel saw Abimelech was dead, they all returned
·home [Leach man to his place].
56In that way God ·punished [repaid; returned to] Abimelech for all the
evil he had done to his father by killing his seventy brothers. 57God also
·punished [repaid; Lreturned on the heads of] the men of Shechem for the
evil they had done. So the curse spoken by Jotham, the son of Jerub-Baal
[CGideon], came ·true [Lon them].

Tola, the Judge

10 ·After Abimelech died [LAfter Abimelech], another ·judge
[leader; 2:16] ·came [arose] to save Israel. He was Tola son of
Puah, the son of Dodo. Tola was from the people of Issachar and lived in
the city of Shamir in the ·mountains [hill country] of Ephraim. 2Tola
·judged [led; 2:16] Israel for twenty-three years. Then he died and was
buried in Shamir.

Jair, the Judge

3After ·Tola died [Lhim], Jair ·from the region of Gilead [Lthe Gileadite]
·judged [led; 2:16] Israel for twenty-two years. 4Jair had thirty sons, who
rode thirty donkeys [12:14]. These thirty sons controlled thirty towns in
Gilead, which are called the ·Towns [LHavvoth; CHebrew for "towns" or
"tent-villages"] of Jair to this day. 5Jair died and was buried in the city of
Kamon.

The Ammonites Trouble Israel

6Again the ·Israelites [Lsons/Tchildren of Israel] did ·what the LORD said
was wrong [Levil in the eyes/sight of the LORD]. They ·worshiped [served]
·Baal and Ashtoreth [Lthe Baals and Ashtoreths; 2:11–13; Creferring to the
idols of these gods found throughout Israel], the gods of Aram [Cthese
included Hadad, Mot, Anath, and Rimon], Sidon [CBaal and Ashtoreth],
Moab [CChemosh; Num. 21:29], and Ammon [CMolech; 1 Kin. 11:7], and
the gods of the Philistines [CDagon; 16:23]. The Israelites ·left [aban-
doned; forsook] the LORD and stopped serving him. 7So the LORD ·was
angry with [Lburned with anger against] them and ·handed them over to
[Lgave them into the hand of] the Philistines and the Ammonites. 8In the
same year those people ·destroyed [Lshattered and crushed; Cfrom two
Hebrew words that sound similar] the ·Israelites [Lsons/Tchildren of
Israel] who lived east of the Jordan River in the region of Gilead, where
the Amorites lived. So the Israelites suffered for eighteen years. 9The
Ammonites then crossed the Jordan River to fight the people of Judah,
Benjamin, and Ephraim, causing much ·trouble [distress] to the people of
Israel. 10So the ·Israelites [Lsons/Tchildren of Israel] cried out to the LORD,
"We have sinned against you. We ·left [abandoned; forsook] our God and
·worshiped [served] the ·Baal idols [LBaals]."
11The LORD answered the ·Israelites [Lsons/Tchildren of Israel], "When
the Egyptians, Amorites, Ammonites, Philistines, 12Sidonians, Amalekites,
and Maonites ·were cruel to [oppressed] you, you cried out to me, and ·I
saved [Ldid I not save/rescue/Tdeliver…?] you [Lfrom their hand]. 13But
now you have ·left [abandoned; forsaken] me again and have ·worshiped
[served] other gods. So I ·refuse to [will no longer] save you again. 14You
have chosen those gods. So go ·call [cry out] to them for help. Let them
·save [rescue; Tdeliver] you when you are in ·trouble [distress]."
15But the ·people [Lsons; Tchildren] of Israel said to the LORD, "We have
sinned. Do to us whatever ·you want [you see fit; Lis good in your eyes],
but please ·save [rescue; Tdeliver] us today!" 16Then the Israelites threw
away the foreign gods among them, and they worshiped the LORD again.

So ·he felt sorry for them [*or* he could no longer bear it; *or* he grew impatient; Lhis spirit grew short] **when he saw their suffering.**

17**The ·Ammonites** [Lsons/descendants of Ammon] **·gathered for war** [were called to arms] **and camped in Gilead. The Israelites gathered and camped at Mizpah.** 18**The leaders of the people of Gilead said, "Who will lead us to attack the ·Ammonites** [Lsons/descendants of Ammon]**? He will become the head of all those who live in Gilead."**

Jephthah Is Chosen as Leader

11 **Jephthah was a ·strong soldier** [mighty warrior] **from Gilead** [Ca region east of the Jordan]. **His father was named Gilead, and his mother was a prostitute.** 2**Gilead's wife had several sons. When they grew up, they forced Jephthah to leave his home, saying to him, "You will not get any of our father's ·property** [inheritance], **because you are the son of another woman."** 3**So Jephthah ran away from his brothers and lived in the land of Tob** [Cregion northeast of Gilead; 2 Sam. 10:6, 8]. **There some ·worthless** [good-for-nothing; trouble-making] **men began to ·follow** [*or* travel with] **him.**

4**After a time the ·Ammonites** [Lsons/descendants of Ammon] **fought against Israel.** 5**When the ·Ammonites** [Lsons/descendants of Ammon] **made war against Israel, the elders of Gilead went to Jephthah to bring him back from Tob.** 6**They said to him, "Come and ·lead our army** [Lbe our commander/ruler] **so we can fight the ·Ammonites** [Lsons/descendants of Ammon]."

7**But Jephthah said to them, "Didn't you hate me? You forced me to leave my father's house. Why are you coming to me now that you are in trouble?"**

8**The elders of Gilead said to Jephthah, "·It is because of those troubles that** [For that reason; *or* Despite that; Nevertheless][n] **we come to you now. Please come with us and fight against the ·Ammonites** [Lsons/descendants of Ammon]. **You will be the ·ruler** [leader; head] **over everyone who lives in Gilead."**

9**Then Jephthah answered, "If you take me back to Gilead to fight the ·Ammonites** [Lsons/descendants of Ammon] **and the LORD helps me win, ·I will be your ruler** [*or* will I really be your ruler/leader/head?]."

10**The elders of Gilead said to him, "The LORD ·is listening to everything we are saying** [is our witness; *or* will mediate for us; Lwill hear between us; Can oath formula]. **·We promise to do all that you tell us to do** [*or*...if we do not do as you say]." 11**So Jephthah went with the elders of Gilead, and the people made him their ·leader** [head; ruler] **and ·commander of their army** [*or* chief; leader]. **Jephthah repeated all of his words in front of the LORD at Mizpah** [Ceither to further ratify them or to confirm God's direction].

Jephthah Sends Messengers to the Ammonite King

12**Jephthah sent messengers to the king of the ·Ammonites** [Lsons/descendants of Ammon], **asking, "What ·have you got against Israel** [Lto me and to you]**? ·Why have you** [L...that you have] **come to attack our land?"**

13**The king of the ·Ammonites** [Lsons/descendants of Ammon] **answered the messengers of Jephthah, "We are fighting Israel because you took our land when you came up from Egypt. You took our land from the Arnon River to the Jabbok River to the Jordan River. Now give our land back to us peacefully."**

11:8 For that reason Some Greek copies read "Not so."

14Jephthah sent the messengers to the Ammonite king again. 15They said: "This is what Jephthah says: Israel did not take the land of Moab or Ammon. 16When the Israelites came up out of Egypt, they went through the ·desert [wilderness] to the Red Sea and then to Kadesh. 17Israel sent messengers to the king of Edom, saying, 'Please let ·the people of Israel [Lus] ·go across [pass through] your land [Num. 20:14–17].' But the king of Edom ·refused [Lwould not listen]. They sent the same message to the king of Moab, but he also refused. So the Israelites stayed at Kadesh.

18"Then the Israelites went through the ·desert [wilderness] around the borders of the lands of Edom and Moab. Israel went east of the land of Moab and camped on the other side of the Arnon River [Cthe border of Moab]. They did not cross it to go into the land of Moab.

19"Then Israel sent messengers to Sihon king of the Amorites, king of the city of Heshbon, asking, 'Let the people of Israel pass through your land to go to our ·land [place].' 20But Sihon did not trust the Israelites to cross his land. So he ·gathered all of his people [mobilized his army] and camped at Jahaz and fought with Israel.

21"But the LORD, the God of Israel, handed Sihon and his army ·over to [Linto the hand of] Israel. All ·the land [*or* that territory] of the Amorites became the property of Israel. 22So Israel took all the ·land [territory] of the Amorites from the Arnon River to the Jabbok River, from the desert to the Jordan River [Num. 21:21–30].

23"It was the LORD, the God of Israel, who ·forced [drove] out the Amorites ahead of his people Israel. So do you think you can ·make them leave [take possession of it]? 24·Take [LWill you not possess…?] the land that your god Chemosh [Cthe chief god of the Moabites, which the Amorites were evidently also worshiping] has given you. We will live in the land the LORD our God has ·given [Ldispossessed before] us!

25"Are you any better than Balak son of Zippor, king of Moab [Num. 22–24]? Did he ever quarrel or fight with the people of Israel? 26For three hundred years the Israelites have lived in Heshbon and Aroer and the towns around them and in all the cities along the Arnon River. Why have you not taken these cities back in all that time? 27I have not sinned against you, but you are sinning against me by making war on me. May the LORD, the Judge, decide today whether the ·Israelites [Lsons/Tchildren of Israel] or the Ammonites [Lsons/descendants of Ammon] are right."

28But the king of the ·Ammonites [Lsons/descendants of Ammon] ·ignored [would not listen to] this message from Jephthah.

Jephthah's Promise

29Then the Spirit of the LORD ·entered [empowered; came/was upon; 3:10; 6:34] Jephthah. Jephthah passed through Gilead and Manasseh and the city of Mizpah in Gilead to the land of the ·Ammonites [Lsons/descendants of Ammon]. 30Jephthah made a ·promise [vow] to the LORD, saying, "If you will ·hand over the Ammonites to me [Lgive the sons of Ammon into my hand], 31I will ·give you [offer; sacrifice] as a burnt offering [Lev. 1:1–17] the first thing that comes out of the door of my house to meet me when I return ·from the victory [Lin peace]. It will be the LORD's."

32Then Jephthah went over to fight the ·Ammonites [Lsons/descendants of Ammon], and the LORD ·handed them over to him [Lgave them into his hand]. 33Jephthah ·struck them down [crushed/defeated them with a great slaughter] from the city of Aroer to the area of Minnith, twenty cities in all, and as far as the city of Abel Keramim. So the

·Ammonites [[L]sons/descendants of Ammon] were ·defeated [subdued] by
the ·Israelites [[L]sons/[T]children of Israel].
34When Jephthah returned to his home in Mizpah, [[L]look; [T]behold] his
daughter was the first one to come out to meet him, ·playing a tambou-
rine [[L]with tambourines] and dancing [Ex. 15:20]. She was his only child;
he had no other sons or daughters. 35When Jephthah saw his daughter, he
tore his clothes [[C]to show his sorrow] and said, "[[L]Ah!] My daughter! You
have ·made me so sad [devastated me; brought me to my knees]. You have
brought me disaster! I ·made a promise [have given my word; [L]opened my
mouth] to the LORD, and I cannot ·break it [recant; [L]return]!"
36Then his daughter said, "Father, you ·made a promise [gave your
word; [L]opened your mouth] to the LORD. So do to me just what ·you
promised [[L]came out of your mouth], because the LORD ·helped you
defeat [avenged you of; *or* vindicated you before] your enemies, the
·Ammonites [[L]sons/descendants of Ammon]." 37She also said, "But let me
do one thing. Let me be alone for two months to go ·to [[L]down and up in]
the mountains. Let me and my friends go and ·cry together since I will
never marry [[L]weep for my virginity]."
38Jephthah said, "Go." So he sent her away for two months. She and her
friends ·stayed [walked] in the mountains and ·cried for her because she
would never marry [[L]wept for her virginity]. 39After two months she
returned to her father, and Jephthah did to her what he had ·promised
[vowed; v. 31]. Jephthah's daughter ·never had a husband [*or* died a virgin; [L]never knew a man; [C]some claim Jephthah committed her to lifelong
service as a virgin at the sanctuary (Ex. 38:8); more likely, he literally fulfilled his rash vow (see next verse)].
From this came a custom in Israel that 40every year the young women
of Israel would go out for four days to ·remember [commemorate] the
daughter of Jephthah from Gilead.

Jephthah and Ephraim

12 The men of Ephraim called all their soldiers together and
crossed the river to the town of Zaphon. They said to
Jephthah, "Why didn't you call us to help you fight the ·Ammonites
[[L]sons/descendants of Ammon]? We will burn your house down ·with
you in it [over you]."
2Jephthah answered them, "My people and I fought a great battle
against the ·Ammonites [[L]sons/descendants of Ammon]. I called you,
but you didn't ·come to help me [[L]save/rescue/[T]deliver me from their
hand]. 3When I saw that you would not help me, I risked my own life
and went against the Ammonites. The LORD ·handed them over to me
[[L]gave them into my hand]. So why have you come to fight against me
today?"
4Then Jephthah called the men of Gilead together and fought the men
of Ephraim. The men of Gilead struck them down because the
Ephraimites had said, "You men of Gilead are ·nothing but deserters [*or*
fugitives; *or* renegades] from Ephraim—living ·between [*or* in the territory of] Ephraim and Manasseh." 5The men of Gilead captured the
·crossings [fords; 3:28] of the Jordan River ·that led to the country of
[opposite] Ephraim. A person from Ephraim trying to escape would say,
"Let me cross the river." Then the men of Gilead would ask him, "Are you
from Ephraim?" If he replied no, 6they would say to him, "Say the word
'Shibboleth [the word means "flood" or "stream" in Hebrew].'" The men

of Ephraim could not say that word correctly [Cthe difference in accent
gave them away (cf. Matt. 26:73)]. So if the person from Ephraim said,
"Sibboleth," the men of Gilead would kill him at the ·crossing [ford]. So
forty-two thousand people from Ephraim were killed at that time.
7Jephthah ·judged [led; 2:16] Israel for six years. Then Jephthah, the
man from Gilead, died and was buried in a town in Gilead.

Ibzan, the Judge

8After Jephthah died, Ibzan from Bethlehem ·judged [led; 2:16] Israel.
9He had thirty sons and thirty daughters. He ·let his daughters marry
[Lgave them in marriage to] men who were not in his ·family group [clan],
and he brought thirty women who were not in his tribe to be wives for his
sons. Ibzan ·judged [led] Israel for seven years. 10Then he died and was
buried in Bethlehem.

Elon, the Judge

11After Ibzan died, Elon from the tribe of Zebulun ·judged [led; 2:16]
Israel. He ·judged [led] Israel for ten years. 12Then Elon, the man of
Zebulun, died and was buried in the city of Aijalon in the land of Zebulun.

Abdon, the Judge

13After Elon died, Abdon son of Hillel from the city of Pirathon ·judged
[led; 2:16] Israel. 14He had forty sons and thirty grandsons, who rode on
seventy donkeys [10:4]. He ·judged [led] Israel for eight years. 15Then
Abdon son of Hillel died and was buried in Pirathon in the land of
Ephraim, in the ·mountains [hill country] where the Amalekites lived.

The Birth of Samson

13 Again the ·people [Lsons; Tchildren] of Israel did ·what the
LORD said was wrong [Levil in the eyes/sight of the LORD]. So
he ·handed them over to [Lgave them into the hand of] the Philistines for
forty years.
2There was a man named Manoah from the tribe of Dan, who lived in
the city of Zorah [Cfifteen miles west of Jerusalem; v. 25]. He had a wife,
but she [Lwas barren/infertile and] could not have children [Ca cause of
both sadness and shame; Gen. 11:30; 29:31]. 3The ·angel [messenger] of
the LORD [Cangelic spokesperson for God, sometimes identified with the
LORD himself; 2:1; 6:11; Gen. 16:7; Ex. 14:19; 23:20] appeared to Manoah's
wife and said, "·You [LLook/TBehold, you are barren and] have not been
able to have children, but you will ·become pregnant [conceive] and give
birth to a son. 4Be careful not to drink wine or ·beer [*or* other fermented
drink; Tstrong drink; Can alcoholic beverage made from grain] or eat anything that is unclean [Cin a ritual sense], 5because you will ·become
pregnant [conceive] and have a son. You must never cut his hair, because
he will be a Nazirite [Num. 6:1–12], given to God from ·birth [Lthe
womb]. He will begin to ·save [rescue; Tdeliver] Israel from the ·power
[hand] of the Philistines."
6Then Manoah's wife went to him and told him what had happened.
She said, "A man from God came to me. He looked like an angel from
God; ·his appearance was frightening [very terrifying/awesome]. I didn't
ask him where he was from, and he didn't tell me his name. 7But he said
to me, 'You will ·become pregnant [conceive] and will have a son. Don't
drink wine or ·beer [*or* other fermented drink; Tstrong drink; v. 4] or eat
anything that is unclean, because the boy will be a Nazirite [v. 5] to God
from his birth until the day of his death.'"
8Then Manoah prayed to the LORD: "Lord, I beg you to let the man of
God come to us again. Let him teach us what we should do for the boy
who will be born to us."

9God heard Manoah's prayer, and the ·angel [messenger] of God came
to Manoah's wife again while she was sitting in the field. But her husband
Manoah was not with her. 10So she ran to tell him, "·He is here [LLook;
TBehold]! The man who ·appeared [came] to me the other day is here!"
11Manoah got up and followed his wife. When he came to the man, he
said, "Are you the man who spoke to my wife?"
The man said, "I am."
12So Manoah asked, "When what you say happens, what kind of life
should the boy live? What ·should he do [is his mission/vocation]?"
13The ·angel [messenger] of the LORD said, "Your wife must be careful
to do everything I told her to do. 14She must not eat anything that grows
on a grapevine, or drink any wine or ·beer [*or* other fermented drink;
Tstrong drink; v. 4], or eat anything that is unclean [Cin a ritual sense]. She
must do everything I have commanded her."
15Manoah said to the ·angel [messenger] of the LORD, "We would like
you to stay awhile so we can cook a young goat for you."
16The ·angel [messenger] of the LORD answered, "Even if I stay awhile, I
would not eat your food. But if you want to prepare something, offer a
burnt offering [Lev. 1:1–17] to the LORD." (Manoah did not understand
that the man was really the ·angel [messenger] of the LORD.)
17Then Manoah asked the ·angel [messenger] of the LORD, "What is your
name? Then we will honor you when what you have said really happens."
18The ·angel [messenger] of the LORD said, "Why do you ask my name?
It is ·too amazing for you to understand [beyond comprehension; wonderful; Is. 9:6]." 19So Manoah sacrificed a young goat on a rock and offered
·some grain as a gift [a grain/gift/tribute offering; Lev. 2:1] to the LORD.
Then ·an amazing thing happened [*or* the LORD did an amazing thing] as
Manoah and his wife watched. 20As the flames went up to ·the sky [heaven]
from the altar, the ·angel [messenger] of the LORD ·went up [ascended] in
the flame. When Manoah and his wife saw that, they bowed facedown on
the ground. 21The ·angel [messenger] of the LORD did not appear to them
again. Then Manoah ·understood [realized; knew] that the man was
really the ·angel [messenger] of the LORD. 22Manoah said, "We have seen
·God [*or* a divine being; CHebrew: *Elohim*; v. 3], so we will surely die [6:23;
Gen. 16:13]."
23But his wife said to him, "If the LORD wanted to kill us, he would not
have accepted our burnt offering [Lev. 1:1–17] or ·grain [Lgift; tribute]
offering [Lev. 2:1]. He would not have shown us all these things or told us
all this."
24So the woman gave birth to a boy and named him Samson [Crelated
to the Hebrew word for "sun"; perhaps "sun-like" or "light from God";
Mal. 4:2]. He grew, and the LORD blessed him. 25The Spirit of the LORD
began to ·work in Samson [move/stir/empower him] while he was in the
city of Mahaneh Dan, between the cities of Zorah and Eshtaol.

Samson's First Marriage

14 Samson went down to the city of Timnah where he saw ·a
Philistine woman [Lone of the daughters of the Philistines].
2When he returned home, he said to his father and mother, "I saw ·a
Philistine woman [Lone of the daughters of the Philistines] in Timnah. I
want you to get her for me so I can marry her."
3His father and mother answered, "·Surely there is [LIs there not...?] a
woman from ·Israel [Lthe daughters of your brothers/relatives] you can

marry. Do you have to marry a woman from the uncircumcised Philistines [Deut. 7:1–3]?"

But Samson said, "Get that woman for me! She is ·the one I want [Lright in my eyes]!" 4(Samson's parents did not know that ·the LORD wanted this to happen [this was from the LORD] because he was looking for a ·way [opportunity] to challenge the Philistines, who were ruling over Israel at this time.) 5Samson went down with his father and mother to Timnah, as far as the vineyard near there. ·Suddenly [TAnd behold], a young lion came roaring toward Samson! 6The Spirit of the LORD ·entered Samson with great power [empowered/came upon/rushed upon him; 3:10; 6:34; 11:29], and he tore the lion apart with his bare hands. ·For him it was as easy as tearing apart [L…as one tears] a young goat. But Samson did not tell his father or mother what he had done. 7Then he went down to the city and talked to the Philistine woman, and ·he liked her [Lshe was right in Samson's eyes].

8Several days later Samson went back to ·marry [get; take] her. On his way he went over to look at the body of the dead lion and ·found [Tbehold, there was] a swarm of bees and honey in it. 9Samson ·got [scooped; scraped] some of the honey with his hands and walked along eating it. When he came to his parents, he gave some to them. They ate it, too, but Samson did not tell them he had ·taken [scooped; scraped] the honey from the body of the dead lion [Ctouching the carcass violated Samson's Nazirite vow; 13:5, 7; Num. 6:6].

10Samson's father went down to see the Philistine woman. And Samson gave a feast, as was the custom for the ·bridegroom [Lyoung men]. 11When the people saw him, they sent thirty ·friends [companions; groomsmen] to be with him.

Samson's Riddle

12Samson said to them, "Let me tell you a riddle. Try to find the answer during the seven days of the feast. If you can, I will give you thirty linen ·shirts [garments] and thirty changes of clothes. 13But if you can't, you must give me thirty linen ·shirts [garments] and thirty changes of clothes."

So they said, "Tell us your riddle so we can hear it."

14Samson said,

"Out of the eater comes something to eat.
Out of the strong comes something sweet."

After three days, they had not ·found the answer [solved the riddle].

15On the fourth[n] day they said to Samson's wife, "Did you invite us here to make us poor? ·Trick [Entice; Coax] your husband into telling us the answer to the riddle. If you don't, we will burn you and everyone in your father's house."

16So Samson's wife went to him, crying, and said, "You hate me! You don't really love me! You told ·my people [Lthe sons of my people] a riddle, but you won't tell me the answer."

Samson said, "I haven't even told my father or mother. Why should I tell you?"

17Samson's wife cried for the rest of the seven days of the feast. So he finally gave her the answer on the seventh day, because she kept ·bothering [nagging; pressing] him. Then she told ·her [Lthe sons of her] people the answer to the riddle.

14:15 fourth The Hebrew text has "seven." Some old translations read "fourth," which fits the order of events better.

18 Before sunset on the seventh day of the feast, the Philistine men had
the answer. They came to Samson and said,

"What is sweeter than honey?
What is stronger than a lion?"

Then Samson said to them,

"If you had not plowed with my ·young cow [heifer; C referring to his
wife],
you would not have solved my riddle!"

19 Then the Spirit of the LORD ·entered Samson and gave him great
power [empowered/came upon/rushed upon him; v. 6]. Samson went
down to the city of Ashkelon [C a Philistine capital] and killed thirty of its
men and took all that they had and gave the clothes to the men who had
answered his riddle. Then he went to his father's house very angry. 20 And
Samson's wife was given to his best man [C one of those companions who
had attended the feast].

Samson Troubles the Philistines

15 At the time of the wheat harvest [C late May or early June],
Samson went to visit his wife, taking a young goat with him
[C as a gift]. He said, "I'm going to my wife's room," but her father would
not let him go in.

2 He said to Samson, "I thought you really hated your wife, so I gave her
to your ·best man [companion; 14:20]. ·Her younger sister is [L Is not her
younger sister…?] more beautiful. Take her instead."

3 But Samson said to them, "This time ·no one will blame me [I am
justified/blameless/innocent] for hurting you Philistines!" 4 So Samson
went out and caught three hundred ·foxes [*or* jackals]. He took two at a
time, tied their tails together, and then tied a torch to the tails of each pair
of ·foxes [*or* jackals]. 5 After he lit the torches, he let the ·foxes [*or* jackals]
loose in the grainfields of the Philistines so that he burned up their standing grain, the ·piles [heaps; shocks] of grain, their vineyards, and their
olive trees.

6 The Philistines asked, "Who did this?"

Someone told them, "Samson, the son-in-law of the ·man from Timnah
[L Timnite], did because his father-in-law gave his wife to his ·best man
[companion]."

So the Philistines burned Samson's wife and her father to death. 7 Then
Samson said to the Philistines, "Since you did this, I won't stop until I
·pay you back [get revenge on you]!" 8 Samson ·attacked the Philistines
and killed many of them [L struck them down calf on thigh with a great
slaughter]. Then he went down and stayed in a cave in the rock of Etam.

9 The Philistines went up and camped in the land of Judah, ·near a place
named [spreading out near; *or* overrunning/raiding] Lehi. 10 The men of
Judah asked them, "Why have you come here to fight us?"

They answered, "We have come to make Samson our prisoner, to ·pay
him back for what he did to our people [L do to him as he did to us]."

11 Then three thousand men of Judah went to the ·cave [cleft] in the
rock of Etam and said to Samson, "What have you done to us? Don't you
know that the Philistines rule over us?"

Samson answered, "I only ·paid them back for [L did to them] what they
did to me."

12 Then they said to him, "We have come to ·tie you up [bind you] and
to hand you over to the Philistines."

Samson said to them, "Promise me you will not ·hurt [attack; come
against] me yourselves."
13The men from Judah said, "·We agree [LNo; Cmeaning they wouldn't
hurt him]. We will just ·tie you up [bind you] and give you to the Philistines.
We will not kill you." So they tied Samson with two new ropes and led him
up from the cave in the rock. 14When Samson came to the Lehi, the
Philistines came to meet him, ·shouting for joy [*or* with shouts of triumph;
Lshouting]. Then the Spirit of the LORD ·entered Samson and gave him great
power [came upon/rushed upon/empowered him; 14:19]. The ropes on
him weakened like burned ·strings [flax] and [Lhis bonds] fell off his hands!
15Samson found the ·jawbone [Lfresh jawbone; Cnot yet decayed] of a ·dead
donkey [Tass], took it, and ·killed [Lstruck down] a thousand men with it!
16Then Samson said,

"With a donkey's jawbone
I ·made donkeys out of them [*or* have piled them in heaps].
With a donkey's jawbone
I ·killed [Lstruck down] a thousand men!"

17When he finished speaking, he threw away the jawbone. So that place
was named Ramath Lehi [CJawbone Hill].
18Samson was very thirsty, so he cried out to the LORD, "You gave me,
your servant, this great victory. Do I have to die of thirst now? Do I have
to be captured by ·people who are not circumcised [*or* these pagans; Lthe
uncircumcised]?" 19Then God ·opened up a hole in the ground [Lsplit
open the basin/hollow place] at Lehi, and water came out. When Samson
drank, his strength returned and he ·felt better [revived]. So he named
that spring ·Caller's Spring [*or* Spring of the One Who Cries Out; LEn
Hakkore], which is still in Lehi.
20Samson ·judged [led] Israel for twenty years in the days of the Philistines.

Samson Goes to the City of Gaza

16 One day Samson went to Gaza and saw a prostitute there. He
went in ·to spend the night with her [Lto her; Ca euphemism
for sexual relations]. 2When the people of Gaza heard, "Samson has
come here!" they surrounded the place and ·waited for him [set an
ambush; lay in wait] near the city gate all night. They whispered to each
other, "·When dawn comes [At the morning light], we will kill Samson!"
3But Samson only stayed with the prostitute until midnight. Then he
got up and took hold of the doors and the two posts of the city gate and
tore them loose, along with the bar. He put them on his shoulders and
carried them to the top of the hill that faces the city of Hebron.

Samson and Delilah

4After this, Samson fell in love with a woman named Delilah, who lived
in the Valley of Sorek. 5The Philistine ·rulers [lords] went to Delilah and
said, "Find out what makes Samson so strong. ·Trick [Seduce; Entice] him
into telling you how we can overpower him and tie him up and ·capture
[subdue] him. If you do this, each one of us will give you ·twenty-eight
pounds [Leleven hundred pieces] of silver."
6So Delilah said to Samson, "Tell me why you are so strong. How can
someone tie you up and ·capture [subdue] you?"
7Samson answered, "Someone would have to tie me up with seven ·new
[fresh] bowstrings that have not been dried. Then I would be as weak as
any other man."
8The Philistine ·rulers [lords] brought Delilah seven ·new [fresh] bowstrings that had not been dried, and she tied Samson with them. 9Some

men were ·hiding [lying in wait] in ·another [an inner; *or* their] room.
Delilah said to him, "Samson, the Philistines are here!" But Samson broke
the bowstrings like pieces of burned ·string [flax]. So the Philistines did
not find out the secret of Samson's strength.
10Then Delilah said to Samson, "You ·made a fool of [mocked; *or*
deceived] me. You lied to me. Now tell me how someone can ·tie you up
[subdue you]."
11Samson said, "They would have to tie me with new ropes that have
not been used before. Then I would become as weak as any other man."
12So Delilah took new ropes and tied Samson. Some men were hiding
in ·another [an inner; *or* their] room. She called out to him, "Samson, the
Philistines are here!" But he broke the ropes from his arms as easily as if
they were threads.
13Then Delilah said to Samson, "·Again [LUntil now] you have ·made a
fool of [mocked; *or* deceived] me. You lied to me. Tell me how someone
can tie you up."
He said, "Using the loom, weave the seven braids of my hair into the
·cloth [woven fabric; web], and tighten it with a pin. Then I will be as
weak as any other man."
While Samson slept, Delilah wove the seven braids of his hair into the
·cloth [woven fabric; web]. 14Then she fastened it with a pin.
Again she said to him, "Samson, the Philistines are here!" Samson woke
up and pulled out the pin and the loom with the ·cloth [woven fabric; web].
15Then Delilah said to him, "How can you say, 'I love you,' when ·you
don't even trust me [Lyour heart is not with me]? This is the third time
you have ·made a fool of [mocked; *or* deceived] me. You haven't told me
the secret of your great strength." 16She ·kept bothering [nagged; pressed]
Samson about his secret day after day until ·he felt he was going to die
[Lhis soul was annoyed to death]!
17So he told her ·everything [Lall his heart]. He said, "·I have never had
my hair cut [LA razor has never come upon my head], because I have been
set apart to God as a Nazirite ·since I was born [Lfrom my mother's womb;
13:5, 7; Num. 6:1–12]. If someone shaved my head, I would lose my
strength and be as weak as any other man."
18When Delilah saw that he had told her ·everything sincerely [Lall his
heart], she sent a message to the Philistine ·rulers [lords]. She said, "Come
back one more time, because he has told me ·everything [Lall that is in his
heart]." So the Philistine rulers came back to Delilah and brought the
silver ·with them [Lin their hands]. 19Delilah got Samson to sleep, lying in
her lap. Then she called in a man to shave off the seven braids of Samson's
hair. In this way she began to ·make him weak [subdue him; make him
vulnerable], and his strength left him.
20Then she said, "Samson, the Philistines are here!"
He woke up and thought, "I'll leave as I did before and shake myself
free." But he did not know that the LORD had left him.
21Then the Philistines captured Samson and ·tore [gouged] out his
eyes. They took him down to Gaza, where they put bronze ·chains [shack-
les] on him and made him grind grain in the prison. 22But his hair began
to grow again after it was shaved off.

Samson Dies

23The Philistine ·rulers [lords] gathered to celebrate and to offer a
great sacrifice to their god Dagon. They said, "Our god has handed

Samson our enemy ·over to us [into our hand]." 24When the people saw him, they praised their god, saying,

"This man ·destroyed [laid waste; ravaged] our country.
He ·killed many of us [Lmultiplied our dead]!
But our god handed over
our enemy to us."

25·While the people were enjoying the celebration [When they were in high spirits; LWhen their heart was good], they said, "Bring Samson out to ·perform for [entertain; amuse] us." So they brought Samson from the prison, and he ·performed for [entertained; amused] them. They made him stand between the pillars. 26Samson said to the ·servant [youth; young man] holding his hand, "Let me feel the pillars that hold up the ·temple [house] so I can lean against them." 27Now the ·temple [house] was full of men and women. All the Philistine ·rulers [lords] were there, and about three thousand men and women were on the roof watching Samson perform. 28Then Samson prayed to the Lord, "·Lord God [Sovereign Lord], remember me. God, please give me strength one more time so I ·can pay these Philistines back [avenge the Philistines] for putting out my two eyes!" 29Then Samson ·turned to [grasped] the two center pillars ·that supported the whole temple [Lon which the house rested]. He braced himself between the two pillars, with his right hand on one and his left hand on the other. 30Samson said, "Let me die with these Philistines!" Then he pushed ·as hard as he could [with all his strength], causing the temple to fall on the ·rulers [lords] and all the people in it. So Samson killed more of the Philistines when he died than ·when he was alive [during his lifetime].

31Samson's brothers and ·his whole family [Lall the house of his father] went down to get his body. They brought him back and buried him in the tomb of Manoah, his father, between the cities of Zorah and Eshtaol. Samson had ·judged [led; 2:16] Israel for twenty years.

Micah's Idols

17 There was a man named Micah who lived in the ·mountains [hill country] of Ephraim. 2He said to his mother, "I heard you speak a curse [Cuttered against the thief] about the ·twenty-eight pounds [Leleven hundred pieces] of silver that were taken from you. I have the silver with me; I took it."

His mother said, "The Lord bless you, my son [Cfor confessing the crime]!"

3Micah gave the ·twenty-eight pounds [Leleven hundred pieces] of silver to his mother. Then she said, "I will ·give [dedicate] this silver [Lfrom my hand] to the Lord. ·I will have my son make [*or* For the benefit of my son I will make] ·an idol and a statue [a carved image and a cast-metal image; *or* a carved image overlaid with silver]. So I will give the silver back to you."

4When he gave the silver back to his mother, she took about ·five pounds [Ltwo hundred pieces of silver] and gave it to a ·silversmith [*or* idol-maker; Acts 19:24]. With it he made an ·idol and a statue [*or* carved image overlaid with silver; Can abomination and violation of the law; Deut. 27:15], which stood in Micah's house. 5Micah had a ·special holy place [shrine], and he made a ·holy vest [ephod] and some ·household idols [Lteraphim; Gen. 31:19]. Then Micah ·chose [ordained; installed; *or* paid; Lfilled the hand of] one of his sons to be his priest. 6At that time Israel did not have a king, so

everyone did what seemed right in their own eyes [Cthe common refrain
through the rest of Judges, referring both to the lack of a human king and
the rejection of God's sovereignty; 18:1; 19:1; 21:25].
7There was a young man who was a Levite [Cthe priestly tribe of Israel;
Num. 1:47–53] from the city of Bethlehem in Judah who was ·from [*or*
living among] the people of Judah. 8He left Bethlehem to look for another
place to live, and ·on his way [*or* to carry on his vocation] he came to
Micah's house in the ·mountains [hill country] of Ephraim. 9Micah asked
him, "Where are you from?"
He answered, "I'm a Levite from Bethlehem in Judah. I'm looking for a
place to live."
10Micah said to him, "Live with me and be my father [Cmeaning an
advisor or counselor; Gen. 45:8] and my priest. I will give you ·four ounces
[Lten pieces] of silver each year and clothes and food." So the Levite went
in. 11He agreed to live with Micah and became like one of Micah's own
sons. 12Micah ·made him [installed/ordained him as; *or* paid him to be;
Lfilled his hand to be] a priest, and he lived in Micah's house. 13Then
Micah said, "Now I know the LORD will ·be good to [prosper] me, because
I have a Levite as my priest."

The Tribe of Dan Captures Laish

18 At that time Israel did not have a king [17:6]. And at that time
the tribe of Dan was still ·looking for a land [Lseeking an
inheritance] where they could live, a land of their own. The Danites had
not yet ·been given their own land [moved into their land; received their
allotment] among the tribes of Israel. 2So, from their family groups,
they chose five ·soldiers [valiant men; Lmen, sons of strength] from the
cities of Zorah and Eshtaol to spy out and explore the land. They were
told, "Go, explore the land."
They came to the ·mountains [hill country] of Ephraim, to Micah's
house, where they spent the night. 3When they came near Micah's house,
they recognized the ·voice [*or* accent] of the young Levite [17:7]. So they
stopped there and asked him, "Who brought you here? What are you
doing here? ·Why are you here [What is your business here]?"
4He told them what Micah had done for him, saying, "He hired me. I
am his priest."
5They said to him, "Please ask God if ·our journey [our mission; Lthe
way we are going] will be successful."
6The priest said to them, "Go in peace. The LORD ·is pleased with
[approves of; watches over] your journey."
7So the five men left. When they came to the city of Laish, they saw that
the people there lived in safety, ·like [Laccording to the custom of] the people
of Sidon. They ·thought they were safe [were quiet and secure/unsuspecting]
and ·had plenty of everything [*or* no ruler was humiliating them]. They lived
a long way from the Sidonians and had no dealings with anyone else.
8When the five men returned to Zorah and Eshtaol, their ·relatives
[brothers] asked them, "What did you find?"
9They answered, "We have seen the land, and it is very good. ·We should
attack [LArise, let us go up against] them. ·Aren't you going to do something
[Are you just going to sit there]? Don't ·wait [hesitate; *or* be lazy]! Let's go
and take that land! 10When you go, you will see there is ·plenty of [a wide/
spacious] land—·plenty of everything [lacking nothing]! The people are
not expecting an attack. Surely God has handed that land over to us!"

11So six hundred Danites left Zorah and Eshtaol ·ready for [armed with weapons of] war. 12On their way they set up camp near the city of Kiriath Jearim in Judah. That is why the place west of Kiriath Jearim is named Mahaneh Dan [C"Camp of Dan"] to this day. 13From there they traveled on to the ·mountains [hill country] of Ephraim. Then they came to Micah's house.

14The five men who had explored the land around Laish said to their ·relatives [Lbrothers], "Do you know in one of these houses there are a ·holy vest [ephod; Ex. 28:6–14], household gods [17:5], an ·idol, and a statue [*or* image overlaid with silver; 17:3]? ·You know [*or* Decide now] what to do." 15So they stopped at the Levite's house, which was also Micah's house, and ·greeted the Levite [*or* asked how he was doing]. 16The six hundred ·Danites [Lmen who were of the sons/descendants of Dan] stood at the entrance gate, wearing their weapons of war. 17The five spies went into the house and took the ·idol [carved image], the ·holy vest [ephod], the household idols, and the ·statue [cast-metal image]. The priest and the six hundred men armed ·for [Lwith weapons of] war stood by the entrance gate.

18When the spies went into Micah's house and took the [carved] image, the ·holy vest [ephod], the household idols, and the ·statue [cast-metal image], the priest asked them, "What are you doing?"

19They answered, "Be quiet! ·Don't say a word [LPut your hand over your mouth]. Come with us and be our father [Cmeaning an advisor or counselor; 17:10; Gen. 45:8] and priest. Is it better for you to be a priest for one man's house or for a tribe and ·family group [clan] in Israel?" 20This ·made the priest happy [Lpleased the heart of the priest]. So he took the ·holy vest [ephod], the household idols [17:5], and the ·idol [carved image] and went with the ·Danites [people]. 21They left Micah's house, putting their little children, their animals, and everything they owned in front of them [Cfor protection in case of attack; Gen. 33:2–3].

22When they had gone a little way from Micah's house, the men who lived near Micah ·were called out [assembled] and caught up with them. 23The men with Micah shouted at the ·Danites [Lsons/descendants of Dan], who turned around and said to Micah, "What's the matter with you? Why have you ·been called out to [assembled for a] fight?"

24Micah answered, "You took my gods that I made and my priest. What do I have left? How can you ask me, 'What's the matter?' "

25The ·Danites [Lsons/descendants of Dan] answered, "·You should not argue with [*or* Don't say another word to; LDon't let your voice be heard among] us. Some of our ·angry [bitter] men might attack you, ·killing you [and you will lose your life] and your ·family [Lhousehold]." 26Then the ·Danites [Lsons/descendants of Dan] went on their way. Micah knew they were too strong for him, so he turned and went back home.

27Then the Danites took what Micah had made and his priest and went on to Laish. They attacked those ·peaceful [quiet] and ·unsuspecting [secure] people and killed them with their swords and then burned the city. 28There was no one to ·save [rescue; Tdeliver] the people of Laish. They lived too far from Sidon, and they had no dealings with anyone else. Laish was in a valley near Beth Rehob.

The people of Dan rebuilt the city and lived there. 29They named the city Dan after their ancestor Dan, one of the sons of Israel; the city's original name was Laish.

30The ·people [Lsons; descendants] of Dan set up the ·idol [carved image] in the city of Dan. Jonathan son of Gershom, Moses' son, and his sons served as priests for the tribe of Dan until the ·land was captured [captivity of the land; time of the exile]. 31The people of Dan set up the ·idols [carved images] Micah had made as long as the ·Holy Tent [Tabernacle; LHouse] of God was in Shiloh.

A Levite and His Servant

19 At that time Israel did not have a king [17:6].

There was a Levite who lived in the ·faraway [remote] ·mountains [hill country] of Ephraim. He had taken a ·slave woman [concubine; 8:31] from the city of Bethlehem in the land of Judah to live with him, 2but she ·was unfaithful to [*or* became angry with] him. She left him and went back to her father's house in Bethlehem in Judah and stayed there for four months. 3Then her husband went to ·ask her [persuade her; Lspeak to her heart] to come back to him, taking with him his servant and two donkeys. When the Levite came to her father's house, she invited him to come in, and her father was happy to ·see [welcome; meet] him. 4The father-in-law, the young woman's father, ·asked [urged; persuaded] him to stay. So he stayed for three days and ate, drank, and slept there [Chospitality was (and is) a very high cultural value in the Middle East].

5On the fourth day they got up early in the morning. The Levite was getting ready to leave, but the woman's father said to his son-in-law, "·Refresh [Strengthen] yourself by eating something. Then go." 6So the two men sat down to eat and drink together. After that, the father said to him, "Please stay tonight. Relax and enjoy yourself." 7When the man got up to go, his father-in-law ·asked [urged; persuaded] him to stay. So he stayed again that night. 8On the fifth day the man got up early in the morning to leave. The woman's father said, "·Refresh [Strengthen] yourself. Wait until this afternoon." So the two men ate together.

9When the Levite, his ·slave woman [concubine; v. 1], and his servant got up to leave, the father-in-law, the young woman's father, said, "It's almost night. The day is almost gone. Spend the night here and enjoy yourself. Tomorrow morning you can get up early and go home." 10But the Levite did not want to stay another night. So he took his two saddled donkeys and his ·slave woman [concubine] and ·traveled toward [Larose and went and came opposite] the city of Jebus (also called Jerusalem).

11As the day was almost over, they came near Jebus. So the servant said to his master, "Let's stop at this city of the Jebusites, and spend the night here."

12But his master said, "No. We won't go inside a foreign city. Those people are not ·Israelites [Lof the sons/Tchildren of Israel]. We will go on to the city of Gibeah." 13He said, "Come on. Let's try to make it to Gibeah or Ramah so we can spend the night in one of those cities." 14So they went on. The sun went down as they came near Gibeah, which belongs to the tribe of Benjamin. 15They stopped there to spend the night. They came to the public square [Can open area inside the city gate, the hub for business, government, and social interaction] of the city and sat down, but no one invited them home to spend the night [Ca mark of shame for the city, since hospitality was of great importance; contrast this with vv. 3–9].

16Finally, in the evening an old man came in from his work in the fields. His home was in the ·mountains [hill country] of Ephraim, but now he was ·living [residing; staying] in Gibeah. (The people of Gibeah were from the tribe of Benjamin.) 17He saw the traveler in the public square and asked, "Where are you going? Where did you come from?"

18The Levite answered, "We are traveling from Bethlehem in Judah to my home in a remote area of the ·mountains [hill country] of Ephraim. I have been to Bethlehem in Judah, but now I am going to the ·Holy Tent [LHouse] of the LORD [Cprobably the shrine at Shiloh; 18:31; Josh. 18:1].ⁿ No one has invited me to stay in his house. 19We already have straw and food for our donkeys and bread and wine for me, ·the young woman [Lyour maidservant], and my ·servant [Lthe young man with your servants; Cpolitely referring to himself and his servants as the old man's servants]. We don't need anything."

20The old man said, "You are welcome to stay at my house. Let me give you anything you need, but don't spend the night in the public square." 21So the old man took the Levite into his house, and he fed their donkeys. They washed their feet and had something to eat and drink.

22While they were enjoying themselves, [Llook; Tbehold] some ·wicked [worthless; troublemaking] men of the city surrounded the house and beat on the door. They shouted to the old man who owned the house, "Bring out the man who came to your house. We want to ·have sexual relations with [Lknow; Ca euphemism for sex] him." [CThe Benjamites had become as evil as the men of Sodom; Gen. 19:1–11.]

23The owner of the house went outside and said to them, "No, my ·friends [brothers]. Don't be so evil. This man is a guest in my house. Don't do this ·terrible [outrageous; disgraceful; vile] thing! 24Look, here are my ·daughter, who has never had sexual relations before [Lvirgin daughter], and the man's ·slave woman [concubine; v. 1]. I will bring them out to you now. You can ·abuse [violate] them and do ·anything you want [Lwhat is good in your eyes] with them, but don't do such a ·terrible [outrageous; disgraceful; vile] thing to this man."

25But the men would not listen to him. So the Levite took his ·slave woman [concubine; v. 1] and sent her outside to them. They ·forced her to have sexual relations with them [raped her], and they abused her all night long. Then, at dawn, they let her go. 26She came back to the house where her master was staying and fell down at the door and lay there until daylight.

27In the morning when the Levite got up, he opened the door of the house and went outside to go on his way. But his slave woman was lying at the doorway of the house, with her hands on the ·doorsill [threshold]. 28The Levite said to her, "Get up; let's go." But she did not answer. So he put her on his donkey and went home.

29When the Levite got home, he took a knife and cut his ·slave woman [concubine; v. 1] into twelve parts, limb by limb. Then he sent a part to each area of Israel. 30Everyone who saw this said, "Nothing like this has ever happened before, not since the ·people [Lsons; Tchildren] of Israel came out of Egypt. Think about it [Consider this; *or* Just imagine!]. Discuss it [Take counsel; *or* Make a plan]. Tell us what to do [*or* Speak out against this!]."

The War Between Israel and Benjamin

20 So all the ·Israelites [Lsons/Tchildren of Israel] from Dan to Beersheba [Cfrom the farthest north to the farthest south], including the land of Gilead [Con the east side of the Jordan River], ·joined together [assembled] before the LORD in the city of Mizpah. 2The

19:18 going to the Holy Tent of the LORD Some Greek copies read "going home."

·leaders [Lcornerstones; Is. 19:13] of all the tribes of Israel took their places in the ·meeting [assembly] of the people of God. There were 400,000 soldiers ·with swords [Lwho drew the sword]. 3(The ·people [Lsons; descendants] of Benjamin heard that the ·Israelites [Lsons/Tchildren of Israel] had gone up to Mizpah.) Then the ·Israelites [Lsons/Tchildren of Israel] said to the Levite, "Tell us how this evil thing happened."

4So the husband of the murdered woman answered, "My ·slave woman [concubine; 8:31] and I came to Gibeah in Benjamin to spend the night. 5During the night the ·men [leaders; lords] of Gibeah came after me. They surrounded the house and wanted to kill me. They ·forced my slave woman to have sexual relations [abused/raped my concubine] and she died. 6I took her and cut her into parts and sent ·one part [Lher] to ·each area [every region of the inheritance] of Israel because the people of Benjamin did this ·wicked [lewd; abominable] and ·terrible [outrageous; shameful] thing in Israel. 7Now, all you ·Israelites [Lsons/Tchildren of Israel], speak up. What is your decision?"

8Then all the people stood up at the same time, saying, "None of us will go ·home [Lto his tent]. Not one of us will go back to his house! 9Now this is what we will do to Gibeah. We will ·throw lots [Lgo against it by lot]. 10That way we will choose ten men from every hundred men from all the tribes of Israel, and we will choose a hundred men from every thousand, and a thousand men from every ten thousand. These will find ·supplies [provisions; food] for the army. Then the army will go to the city of Gibeah of Benjamin to ·repay [punish] them for the ·terrible [outrageous; shameful] thing they have done in Israel." 11So all the men of Israel were united and gathered against the city.

12The tribes of Israel sent men throughout the tribe of Benjamin demanding, "What is this ·evil [wicked; terrible] thing ·some of your men have done [that has taken place among you]? 13Hand over the ·wicked [worthless; troublemaking] men in Gibeah so that we can put them to death. We must ·remove [purge] this evil from Israel."

But the ·Benjaminites [Lsons of Benjamin] would not listen to their ·fellow Israelites [Lbrothers, the sons of Israel]. 14The ·Benjaminites [Lsons of Benjamin] left their own cities and met at Gibeah to fight the Israelites. 15In only one day the ·Benjaminites [Lsons of Benjamin] ·got [mobilized; mustered] 26,000 soldiers together who ·were trained with swords [Ldrew the sword]. They also had 700 ·chosen [elite; well-trained] men from Gibeah. 16Among all these trained soldiers, seven hundred were left-handed [3:15], each of whom could sling a stone at a hair and not miss [1 Sam. 17:49]!

17The Israelites, except for the Benjaminites, gathered 400,000 ·soldiers with swords [men who drew the sword, all of them men of war].

18The ·Israelites [Lsons/Tchildren of Israel] went up to the ·city of Bethel [*or* house of God; Cthe meaning of the name "Bethel"] and asked God, "·Which tribe [LWho] shall be first to attack the Benjaminites?"

The LORD answered, "Judah shall go first."

19The next morning the ·Israelites [Lsons/Tchildren of Israel] got up and ·made a camp near [*or* encamped against] Gibeah. 20The men of Israel went out to fight the Benjaminites and took their battle position at Gibeah. 21Then the ·Benjaminites [Lsons/descendants of Benjamin] came out of Gibeah and killed 22,000 Israelites during the battle that day. 22-23The ·Israelites [Lsons/Tchildren of Israel] went before the LORD and cried until evening. They asked the LORD, "Shall we go to fight ·our relatives, the Benjaminites [Lthe sons of my brother Benjamin], again?"

The LORD answered, "Go up and fight them." The men of Israel encouraged each other. So they took the same battle positions they had taken the first day.

24The ·Israelites [Lsons/Tchildren of Israel] ·came to fight [Ldrew near to] the ·Benjaminites [Lsons/descendants of Benjamin] the second day. 25The Benjaminites came out of Gibeah to attack the Israelites. This time, the Benjaminites killed 18,000 ·Israelites [Lmen of the sons/Tchildren of Israel], all of whom ·carried swords [drew the sword].

26Then all the ·Israelites [Lsons/Tchildren of Israel], the whole army, went up to Bethel [v. 18]. There they sat down and cried to the LORD and fasted all day until evening. They also brought burnt offerings and ·fellowship [*or* peace] offerings to the LORD. 27The ·Israelites [Lsons/Tchildren of Israel] asked the LORD a question. (In those days the Ark of the ·Agreement with God [Covenant; Treaty] was there. 28A priest named Phinehas son of Eleazar, the son of Aaron, served before ·the Ark of the Agreement [Lit].) They asked, "Shall ·we [LI] go to fight ·our relatives [Lmy brother], the Benjaminites, again, or shall we stop fighting?"

The LORD answered, "Go, because tomorrow I will ·hand them over to you [give them into your hand]."

29Then the Israelites set up ambushes all around Gibeah. 30They went to fight against the Benjaminites at Gibeah on the third day, getting into position for battle as they had done before. 31When the Benjaminites came out to fight them, the ·Israelites [Lpeople] backed up and drew them away from the city. The ·Benjaminites [Lsons/descendants of Benjamin] began to kill some of the ·Israelites [Lpeople] as they had done before. About thirty Israelites were killed—some in the fields and some on the roads leading to Bethel and to Gibeah.

32The ·Benjaminites [Lsons/descendants of Benjamin] said, "We are winning as before!"

But the ·Israelites [Lsons/Tchildren of Israel] said, "Let's ·run [retreat; flee]. Let's ·trick them into going farther away [Ldraw/lure them away] from their city and onto the roads."

33All the Israelites moved from their places and got into battle positions at a place named Baal Tamar. Then the Israelites ·ran out [charged; jumped up] from their hiding places ·west of Gibeah [*or* from Maareh-geba]. 34Ten thousand of the ·best trained [elite; chosen] soldiers from all of Israel attacked Gibeah. The battle was very hard. The Benjaminites did not know disaster was ·about to come to them [close at hand; Ltouching against them]. 35The LORD ·used the Israelites to defeat the Benjaminites [Lstruck Benjamin in front of Israel]. On that day the ·Israelites [Lsons/Tchildren of Israel] killed 25,100 Benjaminites, ·all armed with swords [Lwho drew the sword]. 36Then the ·Benjaminites [Lsons/descendants of Benjamin] saw that they were defeated.

The Israelites had ·moved back [retreated] because they were depending on the ·surprise attack [ambush] they had set up near Gibeah [Cverses 36b–45 now detail the account summarized in verses 29–36a)]. 37The men in ·hiding [ambush] rushed into Gibeah, spread out, and killed everyone in the city with ·their swords [Lthe edge of the sword]. 38Now the Israelites had set up a signal with the men in hiding. The men in the ·surprise attack [ambush] were to send up a cloud of smoke from the city. 39Then the army of Israel ·turned around in the battle [counterattacked; Ca similar strategy was used against Ai; Josh. 8].

The Benjaminites had killed about thirty Israelites. They were saying, "·We are winning [They are defeated], as in the first battle!" 40But then a cloud of smoke began to rise from the city. The Benjaminites turned around and ·saw that [Llook; Tbehold] the whole city was going up ·in smoke [Linto the sky/heavens]. 41Then the Israelites turned and began to fight. The Benjaminites were terrified because they knew that disaster was ·coming to them [close at hand; Ltouching against them]. 42So the Benjaminites ran away from the Israelites toward the ·desert [wilderness], but ·they could not escape the battle [the battle pursued/overtook them]. And the Israelites who came out of the cities ·killed [struck; destroyed] them. 43They surrounded the Benjaminites and chased them and ·caught [overtook; stomped on] them in the area east of ·Gibeah [*or* Geba]. 44So 18,000 ·brave [valiant; capable] Benjaminite fighters were killed. 45The Benjaminites ·ran [fled; retreated] toward the ·desert [wilderness] to the rock of Rimmon, but the Israelites ·killed [cut down; Lgleaned] 5,000 Benjaminites along the roads. They chased them as far as Gidom and ·killed [struck down] 2,000 more Benjaminites there.

46On that day 25,000 Benjaminites were killed, ·all of whom had fought bravely with swords [Lvaliant/capable men who drew the sword]. 47But 600 Benjaminites ran to the rock of Rimmon in the ·desert [wilderness], where they stayed for four months. 48Then the Israelites went back to the ·land [Lsons] of Benjamin and killed the people in every city and also the animals and everything they could find. And they burned every city they ·found [came to].

Wives for the Men of Benjamin

21 At Mizpah the men of Israel had sworn, "Not one of us will let his daughter marry a man from the tribe of Benjamin."

2The people went to the city of Bethel and sat before God until evening, ·crying loudly [Llifting their voices weeping greatly]. 3They said, "LORD, God of Israel, why has this terrible thing happened to us so that one tribe ·of Israel is missing [has disappeared from Israel] today?"

4Early the next day the people built an altar and put burnt offerings [Lev. 1:1–17] and ·fellowship [*or* peace; well-being] offerings [Lev. 3:1] to God on it.

5Then the ·Israelites [Lsons/Tchildren of Israel] asked, "Did any tribe of Israel not ·come here to meet [assemble] with us ·in the presence of [before] the LORD?" They asked this question because they had ·sworn [taken a solemn oath] that anyone who did not meet with them at Mizpah would be ·killed [put to death].

6The ·Israelites [Lsons/Tchildren of Israel] felt sorry for ·their relatives, the Benjaminites [LBenjamin, their brother]. They said, "Today one tribe has been cut off from Israel. 7We swore before the LORD that we would not ·allow our daughters to marry a Benjaminite [give our daughters to them for wives]. How can we make sure that the remaining men of Benjamin will have wives?" 8Then they asked, "Which one of the tribes of Israel did not ·meet with us [assemble] ·in the presence of [before] the LORD at Mizpah?" ·They found that [LAnd look/Tbehold] no one from the city of Jabesh Gilead had come. 9The people of Israel counted everyone, but there was no one from Jabesh Gilead.

10So the ·whole group of Israelites [assembly; congregation] sent twelve thousand ·soldiers [Lmen, sons of strength] to Jabesh Gilead to kill the people with ·their swords [the edge of the sword], even the women and children.

11“This is what you must do: Kill every man in Jabesh Gilead and every ·married woman [Lwoman who has known the bed of a male].”[n] 12The soldiers found four hundred young ·unmarried women [virgins; Num. 31:17–18] among the residents of Jabesh Gilead, so they brought them to the camp at Shiloh in the land of Canaan.

13Then the whole ·group of Israelites [assembly; congregation] sent a message to the ·men [Lsons; descendants] of Benjamin, who were at the rock of Rimmon, ·offering to make peace with [Lcalling/proclaiming peace to] them. 14So the men of Benjamin came back at that time. The Israelites gave them the women from Jabesh Gilead who had ·not been killed [been spared/kept alive], but there were not enough women.

15The people of Israel ·felt sorry [had compassion; grieved] for the Benjaminites because the Lord had ·separated [made a gap/breach in] the tribes of Israel. 16The elders of the ·Israelites [Lassembly; congregation] said, “The women of Benjamin have been ·killed [destroyed; wiped out]. ·Where can we get wives [LWhat shall we do] for the men of Benjamin who are still alive? 17·These men must have children to continue their families [LThe survivors of Benjamin must have heirs/an inheritance] so a tribe in Israel will not ·die [be wiped/blotted] out. 18But we cannot allow our daughters to marry them, because ·we swore [Lthe sons/Tchildren of Israel had sworn], ‘Anyone who gives a wife to ·a man of Benjamin [LBenjamin] is cursed.’ 19·We have an idea [LLook; TBehold]! There is a yearly festival of the Lord at Shiloh, which is north of the city of Bethel, east of the road that goes from Bethel to Shechem, and south of the city of Lebonah.”

20So ·the elders [Lthey] told the men of Benjamin, “Go and ·hide [lie in wait/ambush] in the vineyards. 21Watch for the young women from Shiloh to come out to join the dancing. Then run out from the vineyards and ·take [seize; catch] ·one of the young Shiloh women [Leach man his wife from the daughters of Shiloh] and return to the land of Benjamin. 22·If [*or* When] their fathers or brothers come to us and complain, we will say: ‘·Be kind to the men of Benjamin [*or* Do us a favor], because we did not get wives for Benjamin during the war. And you are not guilty [Cof breaking your oath; v. 18] because you did not [Cvoluntarily] give the women to the men from Benjamin.’ ”

23So that is what the ·Benjaminites [Lsons/descendants of Benjamin] did. While the young women were dancing, each man caught one of them [Laccording to their number], ·took her away, and married her [Land carried her off]. Then they went back to ·the land God had given them [their inheritance] and rebuilt their cities and lived there.

24Then the ·Israelites [Lsons/Tchildren of Israel] went home to their own tribes and ·family groups [clans], to their own ·land that God had given them [inheritance].

25In those days Israel did not have a king. All the people did whatever seemed right in their own eyes [17:6; 18:1; 19:1].

21:11 married woman Greek copies continue “But spare any who are virgins. This they did.”

RUTH

1 Long ago when the ·judges [leaders; Cnot courtroom judges, but
leaders who guided the nation through difficult times; Judg.
2:16; a very dark time in Israel's history] ruled Israel, there was a ·short-
age of food [famine] in the land. So a man from the town of Bethlehem
in Judah left to ·live [sojourn; reside as a resident alien] in the ·country
[region] of Moab [Ceast of the Jordan River and the Dead Sea; Gen.
19:37] with his wife and his two sons. 2The man's name was Elimelech,
his wife was named Naomi, and his two sons were named Mahlon and
Kilion. They were Ephrathahites from Bethlehem in Judah. When they
came to Moab, they settled there.
3Then Naomi's husband, Elimelech, died, and she was left with her two
sons. 4These sons married women from Moab. One was named Orpah,
and the other was named Ruth. Naomi and her sons had lived in Moab
about ten years 5when Mahlon and Kilion also died. So Naomi was left
alone without her husband or her two ·sons [offspring; 4:16].
6While Naomi was in Moab, she heard that the LORD had ·come to help
[Lvisited] his people and had given them food again. So she and her
daughters-in-law ·got ready [Larose] to leave Moab and return home.
7Naomi and her daughters-in-law left the place where they had lived and
·started back [set off on the road to return] to the land of Judah. 8But
Naomi said to her two daughters-in-law, "Go back home, each of you to
your own mother's house. May the LORD ·be as kind [show mercy/loving-
kindness] to you as you have been to me and ·my sons who are now dead
[Lwith the dead]. 9May the LORD give you ·another happy home and a new
[Lto find rest/security, each in the house of her] husband."
When Naomi kissed the women good-bye, they ·began to cry out loud
[Lraised their voices and wept]. 10They said to her, "No, we ·want to go
[will return] with you to your people."
11But Naomi said, "My daughters, ·return to your own homes [Lreturn].
Why ·do you want to [should you] go with me? ·I cannot give birth to
more sons [LDo I have sons in my womb...?] to give you new husbands;
12go back, my daughters, to your own homes. [L...because] I am too old
to have another husband. Even if I told myself, 'I still have hope' and had
another husband tonight, and even if I had more sons, 13·should [*or*
would] you wait until they were grown into men [Deut. 25:5–10]? ·Should
[*or* Would] you ·live for so many years without husbands [remain unmar-
ried]? Don't do that, my daughters. ·My life is much too sad for you to
share [*or* It is more bitter for me than for you], because the LORD has been
against me!"
14The women ·cried together out loud [Lraised their voices and wept]

again. Then Orpah kissed her mother-in-law Naomi good-bye, but Ruth
·held on [clung] to her tightly.
15Naomi said to Ruth, "Look, your sister-in-law is going back to her
own people and her own ·gods [*or* god; CChemosh was the chief god of the
Moabites; 1 Kin. 11:33]. Go back with her."

Ruth Stays with Naomi

16But Ruth said, "Don't ·beg [urge] me to ·leave [abandon] you or to
·stop following [Lturn back from] you. Where you go, I will go. Where you
live, I will live. Your people will be my people, and your God will be my
God. 17And where you die, I will die, and there I will be buried. May the
LORD ·punish me terribly [Ldo to me and even more] if I do not keep this
promise: ·Not even [*or* Nothing but] death will separate us."
18When Naomi saw that Ruth ·had firmly made up her mind [was
resolved/determined] to go with her, she stopped ·arguing with [urging;
talking to] her. 19So Naomi and Ruth went on until they came to the town
of Bethlehem. When they entered Bethlehem, ·all the people became very
excited [the whole town was abuzz/stirred up]. The women of the town
said, "Is this really Naomi?"
20Naomi answered the people, "Don't call me Naomi [C"pleasant" or
"happy"]. Call me Mara [C"bitter" or "sad"], because ·the Almighty
[LShaddai] has ·made my life very sad [dealt bitterly/harshly with me].
21·When I left, I had all I wanted [LI went out full], but now, the LORD has
brought me home ·with nothing [empty]. Why should you call me Naomi
when the LORD has ·spoken against [testified against; *or* afflicted; opposed]
me and the Almighty [1:20] has ·given me so much trouble [brought
calamity/misfortune/evil on me]?"
22So Naomi and her daughter-in-law Ruth, the Moabite, returned from
the land of Moab and arrived at Bethlehem at the beginning of the barley
harvest [CApril or May].

Ruth Meets Boaz

2 Now Naomi had a ·rich [*or* influential; Lman of great wealth/
standing] relative named Boaz, from Elimelech's ·family [clan].
2One day Ruth, the Moabite, said to Naomi, "[LPlease] Let me go to the
fields. Maybe someone ·will be kind enough to [Lin whose eyes/sight I find
grace/favor will] let me ·gather the grain he leaves behind [Lglean among
the sheaves/bundles; Deut. 24:21–22]."
Naomi said, "Go, my daughter."
3So Ruth went ·to the fields and gathered the grain that the workers
cutting the grain had left behind [Land gleaned in the field behind the
reapers/harvesters]. It just so happened that the field belonged to Boaz,
from Elimelech's ·family [clan; Ca chance event from Ruth's perspective,
but part of God's plan].
4·Soon [*or* Just then; LAnd look/Tbehold] Boaz came from Bethlehem
and greeted his ·workers [reapers; harvesters], "The LORD be with you!"
And the workers answered, "May the LORD bless you!"
5Then Boaz asked his ·servant [young man; foreman] in charge of the
·workers [reapers; harvesters], "·Whose girl is that [To whom does that
young woman belong; Creferring, in this patriarchal culture, to her husband or father]?"
6The ·servant [young man; foreman] answered, "She is the young
Moabite woman who came back with Naomi from the ·country [land] of
Moab. 7She said, 'Please let me follow the ·workers cutting grain [reapers;
harvesters] and ·gather what they leave behind [Lglean among the sheaves/

bundles].' She came and has remained here, from morning until just now.
She ·has stopped only a few moments [*or* just now stopped for a moment]
to rest in the ·shelter [hut; house]."

8Then Boaz said to Ruth, "·Listen [LHave you not heard…?], my daughter. Don't go to ·gather grain for yourself [glean] in another field. Don't
even leave this field at all, but ·continue following closely behind [stay close
to; cling to] my ·women workers [servant girls; young women]. 9Watch to
see into which fields ·they [the men reaping; Cthe Hebrew pronoun is
masculine] go to ·cut grain [reap] and follow ·them [the women gathering; Cthe Hebrew pronoun is feminine]. I ·have warned [*or* will warn] the
young men not to ·bother [harass; touch] you. When you are thirsty, you
may go and drink from the water jugs that the young men have ·filled
[Ldrawn (from the well)]."

10Then Ruth bowed low with her face to the ground and said to him, "I
am ·not an Israelite [La foreigner]. Why have ·you been so kind to notice
me [LI found favor/grace in your eyes]?"

11Boaz answered her, "I ·know [have been fully informed] about all ·the
help you have given [that you have done for] your mother-in-law after
your husband died. You left your father and mother and your ·own country [native land] to come to a ·nation [people] where you did not know
anyone. 12May the LORD reward you for all you have done. May your
wages be paid in full by the LORD, the God of Israel, under whose wings
you have come for shelter [Clike a protective mother bird]."

13Then Ruth said, "·I hope I can continue to please you [May I continue
to find grace/favor in your eyes; *or* I have found favor/grace in your eyes],
·sir [my lord]. [LBecause] You have ·said kind and encouraging words to
[Lcomforted and spoken to the heart of] me, your servant, though I am
not one of your servants."

14At mealtime Boaz told Ruth, "Come here. Eat some of our bread and
dip it in ·our sauce [the vinegar/wine-vinegar]."

So Ruth sat down beside the ·workers [reapers; harvesters]. Boaz
·handed [offered; served] her some roasted grain, and she ate until she
was ·full [satisfied]; she even had some food left over. 15When Ruth rose
and went back to work, Boaz commanded his ·workers [young men], "Let
her ·gather [glean] even around the ·piles of cut grain [sheaves]. Don't
·tell her to go away [reprimand/insult/humiliate her]. 16In fact, pull out
some full heads of grain for her from the bundles and let her gather them.
Don't ·tell her to stop [rebuke/scold her]."

17So Ruth gathered grain in the field until evening. Then she ·separated
the grain from the chaff [threshed/beat out what she had gleaned], and
there was about ·one-half bushel [Lan ephah; Cabout 30 pounds] of barley.
18Ruth carried the grain into town, and her mother-in-law saw how much
she had ·gathered [gleaned]. Ruth also took out the food that was left over
·from lunch [Lafter she was full/satisfied] and gave it to Naomi.

19·Naomi [LHer mother-in-law] asked her, "Where did you ·gather all
this grain [glean] today? Where did you work? Blessed be whoever noticed
you!"

Ruth told her mother-in-law in whose field she had worked. She said,
"The man I worked with today is named Boaz."

20Naomi told her daughter-in-law, "The LORD bless him! ·He continues
to be kind to us—both [L…who has not abandoned] the living and the
dead!" Then Naomi told Ruth, "Boaz is one of our close relatives, one

·who should take care of us [of our guardians/[T]kinsmen-redeemers; [C]a relative who would care for a bereaved family in various ways: looking after
destitute members (Lev. 25:35); avenging a murdered relative (Num. 35:19);
marrying a sister-in-law to raise up children for her deceased husband (Deut.
25:5–10; called "levirate" marriage); buying back family land (Lev. 25:25) or
redeeming family members who had been sold as slaves (Lev. 25:47–49)]."
21Then Ruth, the Moabite, said, "Boaz ·also [even] told me, 'Keep close
to my ·workers [young men] until they have finished my whole harvest.' "
22But Naomi said to her daughter-in-law Ruth, "It is better for you to
continue working with his ·women workers [female servants; young
women]. If you work in another field, someone might ·hurt [harm; *or*
harass] you." 23So Ruth continued working closely with the ·workers
[female workers; young women] of Boaz, gathering grain until the barley
harvest [[C]March-April] and the wheat harvest [[C]April-May] were finished. And she continued to live with Naomi, her mother-in-law.

Naomi's Plan

3 Then Naomi, Ruth's mother-in-law, said to her, "My daughter, ·I
must [[L]Should I not…?] find ·a suitable home [[L]rest; [C]a husband
and a home to provide security] for you, ·one that will be good for you [*or*
so you will be secure; [L]that it will go/be well for you]. 2Now Boaz, whose
·young women [female servants] you worked with, is our close relative
[[C]and so an appropriate guardian/kinsman-redeemer to marry Ruth;
2:20]. [[L]Look; [T]Behold] Tonight he will be ·working [[L]winnowing barley]
at the threshing floor. 3Wash yourself, put on perfume, ·change your
clothes [*or* get dressed up; *or* put on your cloak], and go down to the
threshing floor. But don't let him know you're there until he has finished
·his dinner [[L]eating and drinking]. 4Watch him so you will know where he
lies down to sleep. When he lies down, go and ·lift the cover off [uncover]
his ·feet [*or* legs; [C]evidently an appeal for marriage] and lie down. He will
tell you what you should do."
5Then Ruth answered, "I will do everything you say."
6So Ruth went down to the threshing floor and did all her mother-in-
law ·told [instructed; commanded] her to do. 7After ·his evening meal
[[L]he had eaten and drunk], ·Boaz felt good [[L]his heart was good/pleased]
and went to sleep lying ·beside [at the end of] the pile of grain. Ruth went
to him quietly and lifted the cover from his feet and lay down.
8About midnight Boaz ·was startled [*or* shuddered] and rolled over.
[[L]And look/[T]behold] There was a woman lying near his feet! 9Boaz asked,
"Who are you?"
She said, "I am Ruth, your servant girl. Spread ·your cover [*or* the corner of your garment; *or* your wings; 2:12] over me [[C]a request for the
provision and protection of marriage], because you are a ·relative who is
supposed to take care of me [guardian; kinsman-redeemer; 2:20]."
10Then Boaz said, "The LORD bless you, my daughter. This [second;
[L]last] act of kindness is greater than the ·kindness you showed to Naomi
in the beginning [[L]first]. You didn't look for a young man to marry, either
rich or poor. 11Now, my daughter, don't be afraid. I will do everything you
ask, because all the people in our town know you are a ·good [worthy;
noble] woman [Prov. 31:10]. 12It is true that I am a ·relative who is to take
care of you [guardian; kinsmen-redeemer; 2:20], but you have a closer
relative than I. 13Stay here tonight, and in the morning we will see if he
will ·take care of [be a guardian for; redeem] you. If he decides to ·take

care of [be a guardian for; redeem] you, that is fine. But if he refuses, I will
·take care of [be a guardian for; redeem] you myself, as surely as the LORD
lives. So ·stay here [[L]lie down] until morning."
14So Ruth stayed near his feet until morning but got up while it was
still too dark to recognize anyone. Boaz thought, "People in town must
not know that the woman came here to the threshing floor." 15So Boaz
said to Ruth, "Bring me your ·shawl [cloak] and hold it open."
So Ruth held her ·shawl [cloak] open, and Boaz poured six portions of
barley into it. Boaz then put it on ·her head [*or* her back; [L]her] and
went[n] back to the city.
16When Ruth went back to her mother-in-law, Naomi asked, "How did
·you do [things go], my daughter?"
Ruth told Naomi everything that ·Boaz [[L]the man] did for her. 17She
said, "Boaz gave me these six portions of barley, saying, 'You must not go
home ·without a gift for [[L]empty to] your mother-in-law.'"
18Naomi answered, "·Wait [Stay here; *or* Be patient], my daughter, until
you see what happens. ·Boaz [[L]The man] will not rest until he has finished doing what he should do today."

Boaz Marries Ruth

4 Boaz went to the city gate [[C]the hub of the town for judicial, business, and social interaction] and sat there until the ·close relative
[guardian; kinsman-redeemer; 2:20] he had mentioned passed by. Boaz
called to him, "·Come here [[L]Turn aside], ·friend [*or* so-and-so; [C]the man
is not named, perhaps ironically because he refused to preserve Naomi's
family name], and sit down." So the man ·came over [turned aside] and
sat down. 2Boaz gathered ten of the elders of the city and told them, "Sit
down here!" So they sat down.
3Then Boaz said to the ·close relative [guardian; kinsman-redeemer],
"Naomi, who has come back from the country of Moab, ·wants to sell [is
selling] the piece of land that belonged to our relative Elimelech [[C]it was
important in Israel to keep property in the family]. 4So I ·decided [*or*
thought it my obligation] to tell you about it: If you want to ·buy back the
land [redeem it], then ·buy it [redeem] in front of the people who are sitting here and in front of the elders of my people. But if you don't want to
buy it, tell me, because you are the ·only one [*or* first in line] who can buy
it, and I am next after you."
The close relative answered, "I will ·buy back the land [redeem it]."
5Then Boaz explained, "When you ·buy [acquire] the land from [[L]the
hand of] Naomi, you must also ·marry [acquire] Ruth, the Moabite, the
dead man's wife. ·That way, the land will stay in the dead man's name [[L]…
to raise up a name for the dead man upon his inheritance]."
6The ·close relative [guardian; kinsman-redeemer] answered, "I can't
·buy back the land [redeem it]. If I did, I might ·harm [destroy; endanger;
put in jeopardy] ·what I can pass on to my own sons [my inheritance]. I
cannot ·buy the land back [redeem it], so ·buy it [redeem it for] yourself."
7Long ago in Israel ·when people traded or bought back [for the
redemption and transfer of] something, one person took off his sandal
and gave it to the other person. This was the ·proof of ownership [*or* vali-
dation of the transaction] in Israel.
8So the ·close relative [guardian; kinsman-redeemer] said to Boaz,
"Buy the land yourself," and he took off his sandal.

3:15 went Some Greek copies read "she went."

9Then Boaz said to the elders and to all the people, "You are witnesses
today. I ·am buying [have bought] from Naomi everything that belonged
to Elimelech and Kilion and Mahlon. 10I ·am also taking [have also
acquired] Ruth, the Moabite, who was the wife of Mahlon, as my wife. ·I
am doing this so her dead husband's property will stay in his name and
his name will not be separated [L...so that his name will not be cut off]
from his ·family [Lbrothers] and ·his hometown [Lthe gate of his place].
You are witnesses today."

11So all the people and elders who were at the city gate said, "We are
witnesses. May the LORD make this woman, who is coming into your
home, like Rachel and Leah, who together built up the ·people [Lhouse] of
Israel [Cthe twelve sons of Israel were born to Leah, Rachel and their servant girls; Gen. 29:31—30:24]. May you become ·powerful [*or* wealthy; *or*
renowned] in the district of Ephrathah and ·famous [renowned] in
Bethlehem. 12As Tamar gave birth to Judah's son Perez [Can ancestor of
Boaz (v. 18) whose birth resulted from a levirate union (2:20; Gen. 38:27–
30; Deut. 25:5–10) and so was parallel to this situation], may the LORD give
you many children through Ruth. May your family be great like his."

13So Boaz took Ruth home as his wife and ·had sexual relations with
[Lwent in to] her. The LORD let her become pregnant, and she gave birth
to a son. 14The women told Naomi, "·Praise [Blessed be] the LORD who
·gave you this grandson [Lhas not left you today without a guardian/kins-
man-redeemer]. May ·he [Lhis name] become ·famous [renowned] in
Israel. 15He will ·give you new [restore/renew your] life and will take care
of you in your old age because of your daughter-in-law who loves you.
She is better for you than seven sons, because she has given birth to ·your
grandson [Lhim]."

16Naomi took the boy, ·held him in her arms [*or* put him on her lap; *or*
took him to her breast], and ·cared for him [*or* became his nurse/care-
giver]. 17The neighbors gave the boy his name, saying, "·This boy was [LA
son has been] born for Naomi." They named him Obed [C"servant"].
Obed was the father of Jesse, and Jesse was the father of David [CIsrael's
greatest king, through whom the Messiah would come; 2 Sam. 7:11–17;
Matt. 1:1, 5–6; Luke 3:32].

18This is the family history of Perez, the father of Hezron. 19Hezron
was the father of Ram, who was the father of Amminadab. 20Amminadab
was the father of Nahshon, who was the father of Salmon. 21Salmon was
the father of Boaz, who was the father of Obed. 22Obed was the father of
Jesse, and Jesse was the father of David [Matt. 1:3–6; Luke 3:31–33].

1 SAMUEL

Samuel's Birth

1 **There was a** [certain] **man named Elkanah son of Jeroham from ·Ramathaim** [Ramah; Cjust north of Jerusalem] **in the ·mountains** [hill country] **of Ephraim. Elkanah was from the ·family** [*or* region] **of Zuph. (Jeroham was Elihu's son. Elihu was Tohu's son, and Tohu was the son of Zuph ·from the family group of Ephraim** [an Ephraimite]**.)** **2Elkanah had two wives named Hannah and Peninnah. Peninnah had children, but Hannah had none** [Cchildlessness carried a serious social stigma].

3Every year Elkanah left his town of Ramah and ·went up [traveled] **to Shiloh** [Cthe central worship place at that time, 30 miles north of Jerusalem, where the tabernacle was located] **to worship the LORD ·All-Powerful** [Almighty; of Heaven's Armies; of Hosts] **and to offer sacrifices to him. Shiloh was where Hophni and Phinehas, the sons of Eli, served as priests of the LORD.** **4·When** [LOn the day] **Elkanah offered sacrifices, he always gave ·a share of the meat** [portions] **to his wife Peninnah and to all her sons and daughters.** **5But Elkanah always gave Hannah ·a double portion of the meat because he loved her and the LORD had kept her from having children** [*or* only one portion of the meat even though he loved her, because the LORD had kept her from having children; Conly one portion would be needed since there was no child to feed]. **6·Peninnah** [LHer rival/foe] **would ·tease** [taunt] **Hannah and ·upset** [provoke; irritate; make fun of] **her, because the LORD had ·made her unable to have children** [Lclosed her womb]. **7This happened ·every year** [Lyear after year] **·when** [whenever] **they went up to the house of the LORD at Shiloh** [1:3]. **Peninnah would ·upset** [taunt; provoke] **Hannah until Hannah would cry and not eat anything.** **8Her husband Elkanah would say to her, "Hannah, why are you crying and why won't you eat? Why are you ·sad** [downhearted]**? ·Don't I mean more** [*or* Am I not better] **to you than ten sons?"**

9Once, after ·they had eaten their meal [Leating and drinking] **in Shiloh** [1:3], **Hannah got up. Now Eli the priest was sitting on ·a chair** [the seat] **·near the entrance to** [by the doorpost of] **the LORD's ·house** [temple; Tabernacle]. **10Hannah was so ·sad** [anguished; deeply distressed; Lbitter] **that she cried bitterly ·and** [as she] **prayed to the LORD.** **11She made this ·promise** [vow], **saying, "LORD ·All-Powerful** [Almighty; of Heaven's Armies; of Hosts], **if you will look on the ·sorrow** [affliction; misery; humiliation] **of your maidservant, and will ·remember** [Lremember and not forget] **me, and will give ·me** [Lyour maidservant] **a son, I will give him back to ·you** [Lthe LORD] **all the days of his life, and no one will ever ·cut his hair** [Ltouch his head] **with a razor** [Cindicating consecration to the Lord as a Nazirite; Num. 6:1–5]**."**

12While Hannah kept praying [Lbefore the LORD], Eli watched her mouth. 13Hannah was praying ·in her heart [silently]; her lips moved, but her voice was not heard. So Eli thought she was drunk 14and said to her, "·Stop getting [LHow long are you going to stay…?] drunk! ·Throw away [Get rid of; Put away] your wine!"

15Hannah answered [Land said], "No, sir, I have not drunk any wine or ·beer [Tstrong drink; Can alcoholic beverage made of grain]. I am ·a deeply troubled woman [very discouraged; oppressed in spirit], and I was ·telling the LORD about all my problems [Lpouring out my heart/soul to/before the LORD]. 16Don't think ·I am [your maidservant is] an ·evil [worthless] woman. I have been praying all this time ·because I have many troubles and am very sad [Lout of great anguish/anxiety and sorrow/resentment]."

17Eli answered, "·Go! I wish you well [Go in peace!]. May the God of Israel ·give you what [Lgrant the request/petition] you asked of him."

18Hannah said, "May ·I always please you [your servant find favor in your sight]." So she left and ate something, and ·she [Lher face/countenance] was not sad anymore.

19Early the next morning they got up and worshiped [Lbefore] the LORD. Then they went back home to Ramah. Elkanah ·had sexual relations with [Lknew] his wife Hannah, and the LORD remembered her. 20So Hannah ·became pregnant [Lconceived], and in time she gave birth to a son. She named him Samuel [Csounds like "God heard" in Hebrew], saying, "His name is Samuel because I asked the LORD for him."

Hannah Gives Samuel to God

21·Every [*or* The next] year Elkanah went with his whole family to Shiloh [1:3] to offer sacrifices and to keep the ·promise [vow] he had made to ·God [Lthe LORD]. 22·But one time [LBut] Hannah did not go with him. She told her husband, "When the boy is ·old enough to eat solid food [weaned], I will take him to Shiloh [1:3]. Then I will give him to [… and present him before] the LORD, and he will ·always live there [stay there permanently/forever]."

23Elkanah, Hannah's husband, said to her, "Do what you think is best. ·You may stay home until the boy is old enough to eat [Stay until you have weaned him]. May the LORD ·do what you have said [bring about his promise; Lconfirm/establish his word]." So Hannah stayed at home to nurse her son until he was ·old enough to eat [weaned].

24When Samuel was ·old enough to eat [weaned], [Lthough still very young,] Hannah took him to the house of the LORD at Shiloh [1:3], along with a three-year-old bull, ·one-half bushel [Lan ephah] of flour, and a ·leather bag filled with [skin of] wine. 25After they had ·killed the bull for the sacrifice [Lslaughtered the bull], they brought Samuel to Eli. 26Hannah said to Eli, "As surely as you live, sir, I am the same woman who stood ·near [beside] you praying to the LORD. 27I prayed for this child, and the LORD answered my ·prayer [request; petition] and gave him to me. 28Now I ·give him back [dedicate him; Llend him] to the LORD. He ·will belong [is dedicated/given over/lent] to the LORD all his life." And ·he [*or* they] worshiped the LORD there.

Hannah Gives Thanks

2 Hannah prayed [Land said; CHannah's prayer is similar to Psalm 113 and Mary's song in Luke 1:46–55]:

"·The LORD has filled my heart with joy [LMy heart rejoices/exults in the LORD];
·I feel very strong in the LORD [My strength/Lhorn is exalted/lifted up

in the LORD; [C]a lifted horn symbolizes strength, based on an animal lifting its head triumphantly]
·I can laugh at [[L]My mouth mocks/derides] **my enemies;**
I ·am glad [rejoice/delight] **because you have ·helped** [saved; rescued; delivered] **me!**

2"**There is no one ·holy** [set apart] **like the LORD.**
There is no ·God but [one besides] **you;**
there is no Rock like our God.

3"**·Don't continue bragging** [Talk/Boast no more so proudly/ haughtily],
·don't speak proud words [don't let such arrogance come out of your mouth].
The LORD is a God who ·knows everything [is wise],
and he ·judges [weighs] **what people do.**

4"**The bows of ·warriors** [the mighty] **·break** [are shattered],
but ·weak people [[L]those who stumbled/tottered] **·become strong** [[L]gird on strength].
5**Those who ·once had plenty of food** [were well fed] **now ·must work** [hire themselves out] **for ·food** [bread],
but people who were hungry ·are hungry no more [grow fat].
The woman who ·could not have children [was barren] **now ·has** [[L]gives birth to] **seven,**
but the woman who had many children now ·is sad [[L]wastes away; languishes].

6"**The LORD ·sends death** [kills],
and he ·brings to [gives] **life.**
He ·sends people to the grave [brings down to Sheol; [C]the grave or the place of the dead],
and he raises ·them to life again [[L]up].
7**The LORD makes some people poor,**
and others he makes rich.
He ·makes some people humble [brings low/down],
and others he ·makes great [lifts up; exalts].
8**The LORD ·raises** [lifts] **the poor up from the dust,**
and he lifts the needy from the ·ashes [garbage heap].
He ·lets the poor sit [sets/seats the poor] **with princes**
and ·receive [[L]they inherit] **a throne of honor.**

"**The ·foundations** [pillars] **of the earth belong to the LORD,**
and the LORD ·set [poised] **the world upon them.**
9**He ·protects** [[L]guards the feet/steps of] **those who are ·loyal** [faithful] **to him,**
but ·evil people [the wicked] **will ·be silenced** [disappear] **in darkness.**
·Power is not the key to success [[L]For no one succeeds/prevails by strength alone].
10**The LORD ·destroys** [shatters] **·his enemies** [those who oppose/fight against him];

he will thunder ·in [from] heaven against them.
The LORD will judge ·all [throughout; Lthe ends of] the earth.
He will give ·power [strength] to his king
and ·make his appointed king strong [Lexalt the horn of his anointed/anointed one; 2:1]."

Eli's Evil Sons

11 Then Elkanah went home to Ramah [1:1], but the boy ·continued to serve [ministered to/before] the LORD ·under [in the presence of] Eli the priest.

12 Now Eli's sons were ·evil men [scoundrels; good-for-nothings]; they did not ·care about [know; respect; regard] the LORD. 13 ·This is what the priests would normally do to [... nor about their duties as priests for] the people: Every time someone ·brought [offered] a sacrifice, the meat would be ·cooked [Lboiled] in a pot. The priest's servant would then come carrying a fork that had three prongs. 14 He would plunge the fork into the pot or the kettle or cauldron or pan. Whatever the fork brought out of the pot belonged to the priest. But this is how they treated all the Israelites who came to Shiloh [1:3] to offer sacrifices. 15 Even before the fat was burned, the priest's servant would come to the person offering sacrifices and say, "Give the priest some meat to roast. He won't accept boiled meat from you, only raw meat."

16 If the one who offered the sacrifice said, "Let the fat be burned up first as usual, and then take anything you want," the priest's servant would answer, "No, give me the meat now. If you don't, I'll take it by force."

17 ·The LORD saw that [In the LORD's sight] the sin of the servants was very ·great [serious] because they ·did not show respect for [treated with contempt; despised] the offerings ·made to [Lof] the LORD.

Samuel Grows Up

18 But Samuel ·obeyed [Lserved; ministered before] the LORD. As a boy he wore a linen ·holy vest [ephod; Ca special garment worn only by priests; Ex. 28:6–14]. 19 Every year his mother made a little ·coat [robe] for him and took it to him when she went with her husband to Shiloh [1:3] for the [annual] sacrifice. 20 When Eli blessed Elkanah and his wife, he would say, "May the LORD ·repay you with [*or* give you] ·children [an heir; Lseed] through Hannah ·to take the place of [in exchange for] the boy Hannah ·prayed for and gave back [dedicated] to the LORD." Then Elkanah and Hannah would go home. 21 The LORD was ·kind to [gracious to; *or* visited] Hannah, so she ·became the mother of [Lconceived and bore] three sons and two daughters. And the boy Samuel grew up ·serving [in the presence of; before] the LORD.

22 Now Eli was very old. He heard about everything his sons were doing to all ·the Israelites [Israel] and how his sons ·had sexual relations [lay] with the women who served at the ·entrance [doorway] to the Meeting Tent. 23 Eli said to them, "Why do you do these evil things that the people tell me about? 24 No, my sons. The LORD's people are spreading a bad report about you. 25 If you sin against someone, God can ·help [intercede/mediate/arbitrate for] you. But if you sin against the LORD himself, ·no one [who...?] can ·help [intercede/mediate/arbitrate for] you!" But Eli's sons would not listen to ·him [Lthe voice/words/rebuke of their father], because the LORD ·had decided [desired; wanted] to put them to death.

26 The boy Samuel grew ·physically and pleased [in stature and in favor with] the LORD and the people.

27 A man of God [Ca prophet] came to Eli and said, "·This is what the

LORD says [TThus says the LORD]: '·I [LDid I not...?] clearly showed myself to the ·family [Lhouse] of your ·ancestor Aaron [father] when in Egypt they were slaves to ·the king of Egypt [LPharaoh's house]. 28·I chose [LDid I not choose...?] them from all the tribes of Israel to be my priests. I wanted them to go up to my altar, to burn incense, and to wear the ·holy vest [Lephod in my presence/before me]. ·I [LDid I not...?] also let the ·family [Lhouse] of your ·ancestor [father] have ·part of all [all] the offerings by fire sacrificed by the Israelites. 29So why ·don't you respect [do you scorn/trample/look greedily at; Lkick at] the sacrifices and ·gifts [offerings that I have commanded/prescribed]? You honor your sons ·more than [above] me. You ·grow fat [fatten yourselves] on the ·best [choicest] parts of the meat the Israelites bring to me.'

30"So the LORD, the God of Israel, says: 'I promised that your ·family [Lhouse] and your ·ancestor's family [father's house] would ·serve [minister/walk before] me always.' But now the LORD says: '·This must stop [Far be it from me]! I will honor those who honor me, but I will ·dishonor [despise; have contempt for] those who ·ignore [disdain] me. 31The ·time [day] is coming when I will ·destroy [Lbreak/cut off the strength of] the ·descendants [Lseed] of both you and your ·ancestors [Lfather's house]. No ·man [one] will ·grow old [reach old age] in your family. 32You will ·see trouble in my house. No matter what good things happen to Israel, [*or* watch with envy/distress/greedy eyes on all the prosperity I pour out on Israel. But] there will never be an old ·man [person] in your family [22:11–23]. 33I will ·not totally cut off your family from my altar. But [... keep one of you alive at my altar so that] your eyes will cry and your heart be sad, because all your descendants will die.

34" '·I will give you a [This will be your] sign. Both your sons, Hophni and Phinehas, will die on the same day [4:1–22]. 35Then I will ·choose [Lraise up] a loyal priest ·for myself [*or* myself] who will ·listen to me and do what I want [act according to what is in my heart and soul/mind]. I will ·make his family continue [build him an enduring family/house], and he will always ·serve before [walk/go in and out before] my ·appointed king [anointed one; 1 Kin. 2:26–27]. 36Then everyone left in your ·family [Lhouse] will come and bow down before him. They will beg for a ·little money [piece of silver] or a ·little food [loaf of bread] and say, "Please give me ·a job as priest [some priestly duty/work] so I can ·have food to eat [eat a morsel of bread]." ' "

God Calls Samuel

3 The boy Samuel ·served [ministered before] the LORD under Eli. In those days ·the LORD did not speak directly to people very often [Lthe word from the LORD was rare]; there were very few visions.

2Eli's eyes were so ·weak [dim] he ·was almost blind [Lcould not see]. One night he was lying in ·bed [his usual place]. 3Samuel was ·also in bed [Llying down] in the LORD's ·house [sanctuary; temple], where the Ark of God [Canother name for the Ark of the Covenant; 4:3] was. God's lamp [Cprobably the Menorah] ·was still burning [had not yet gone out].

4Then the LORD called Samuel, and he answered, "I am here!" 5He ran to Eli and said, "I am here. You called me."

But Eli said, "I didn't call you. Go back ·to bed [and lie down]." So Samuel went back ·to bed [and lay down].

6The LORD called again, "Samuel!"

Samuel again went to Eli and said, "I am here. You called me."

Again Eli said, "I didn't call you. Go back ·to bed [and lie down]."
7Samuel did not yet know the LORD, and ·the LORD had not spoken
directly to him yet [Lthe word of the LORD had not been revealed to him
before].
8The LORD called Samuel for the third time. Samuel got up and went to
Eli and said, "I am here. You called me."
Then Eli ·realized [understood; perceived; discerned that] the LORD was
calling the boy. 9So he told Samuel, "Go ·to bed [lie down]. If he calls you
again, say, 'Speak, LORD. ·I am your servant and I am [...for your servant
is] listening.'" So Samuel went and lay down in ·bed [his place].
10The LORD came and stood there and called as he had before, "Samuel,
Samuel!"
Samuel said, "·Speak, LORD. I am your servant and I am [LSpeak, for
your servant is] listening."
11The LORD said to Samuel, "Watch, I am going to do something in
Israel that will ·shock [Lmake the ears ring/tingle of] those who hear
about it. 12·At that time [LIn that day] I will ·do to [carry out against] Eli
and his ·family [Lhouse] everything I ·promised [threatened; spoke], from
beginning to end. 13I told Eli I would ·punish [judge] his ·family always
[Lhouse forever], because ·he knew his sons were evil [of the sin/iniquity
he knew of]. They ·cursed God[n] [blasphemed], but he did not ·stop [cor-
rect; discipline; rebuke] them. 14So I swore to Eli's ·family [Lhouse], 'Your
·guilt [sins; iniquity] will never be ·removed [forgiven; atoned for; expi-
ated] by sacrifice or offering.'"
15Samuel lay down until morning. Then he opened the doors of the
·house [temple] of the LORD. He was afraid to tell Eli about the vision,
16but Eli called to him, "Samuel, my son!"
Samuel answered, "I am here."
17Eli asked, "·What did the LORD say [What word/message did he speak/
give] to you? Don't hide it from me. May God ·punish you terribly [Ldo so
to you, and more also,] if you hide from me anything he said to you." 18So
Samuel told Eli everything and did not hide anything from him. Then Eli
said, "He [*or* It] is the LORD. Let him do what he thinks ·is best [good]."
19The LORD was with Samuel as he grew up; he did not let any of
Samuel's ·messages [words] ·fail to come true [Lfall to the ground]. 20Then
all Israel, from Dan to Beersheba [Cfrom the extreme north to the extreme
south], knew Samuel was ·a true [confirmed/attested as a] prophet of the
LORD [Deut. 13:1–5; 18:14–22]. 21And the LORD continued to ·show himself [appear; manifest himself] at Shiloh [1:3], and he ·showed [revealed]
himself to Samuel through his word.

4 So, ·news about Samuel [*or* Samuel's words] spread through all of
Israel.

The Philistines Capture the Ark of the Agreement

At that time the Israelites went out to fight the Philistines [Ca rival
nation occupying the southwest coast of Israel]. The Israelites camped at
Ebenezer [Csomewhere near Aphek; means "stone of help"] and the
Philistines [Lcamped] at Aphek [Con the plain of Sharon, northeast of
Joppa]. 2The Philistines ·went [deployed; drew up in battlelines] to meet
the Israelites in battle. And ·as the battle spread [*or* when battle was
joined], they defeated the Israelites, killing about four thousand soldiers

3:13 cursed God Some Greek copies read "cursed God." The Hebrew text has "brought a curse on themselves."

on the battlefield. 3When ·some Israelite soldiers [Lthe troops] **went back to their camp, the elders of Israel asked, "Why did the LORD ·let the Philistines defeat us** [*or* defeat/rout us before the Philistines]**? Let's bring the Ark of the ·Agreement** [Covenant; Treaty] **·with** [*or* of] **the LORD** [Cthe Ark represented the presence of God; Ex. 25:10–22] **here from Shiloh** [1:3] **and take it with us into battle. Then ·God** [*or* it] **will save us from the ·power** [Lhand] **of our enemies."**

4So the ·people [*or* troops] **sent men to Shiloh** [1:3]**. They brought back the Ark of the ·Agreement** [Covenant; Treaty] **·with** [*or* of] **the LORD** [4:3] **·All-Powerful** [Almighty; of Heaven's Armies; of Hosts]**, who sits ·between** [on] **the ·gold creatures with wings** [Lcherubim; Cpowerful angelic creatures]**. Eli's two sons, Hophni and Phinehas, were there with the Ark** [Lof the covenant of God]**.**

5When the Ark of the ·Agreement [Covenant; Treaty] **·with** [*or* of] **the LORD came into the camp, all the Israelites ·gave a great shout of joy** [shouted with a great shout] **that made the ground shake. 6When the Philistines heard Israel's shout, they asked, "What's all this shouting in the Hebrew camp?"**

Then the Philistines ·found out [realized; understood] **that the Ark of the LORD had come into the Hebrew camp. 7They were afraid and said, "·A god** [*or* The gods; *or* God] **has come into the Hebrew camp! ·We're in trouble** [LWoe to us; Disaster]**! This has never happened before! 8·How terrible it will be for** [LWoe to] **us! Who can ·save** [rescue; deliver] **us from these powerful gods? ·They are the ones** [These are the gods] **who ·struck** [Tsmote] **the Egyptians with ·all kinds of disasters** [plagues] **in the ·desert** [wilderness; Ex. 7–12]**. 9Be brave, Philistines! Fight like men! In the past they were ·our** [your] **slaves. So fight like men, or ·we** [you] **will become their slaves."**

10So the Philistines fought hard and defeated the Israelites, and every ·Israelite soldier ran away to his own home [man fled to his tent]**. It was a great ·defeat** [slaughter] **for Israel, because thirty thousand Israelite** [foot] **soldiers ·were killed** [Lfell]**. 11The Ark of God was ·taken** [captured] **by the Philistines, and Eli's two sons, Hophni and Phinehas, died.**

12That same day a man ·from the tribe of [Lof] **Benjamin ran from the battle. He tore his clothes and put dust on his head** [Cto indicate mourning]**. 13When he arrived in Shiloh** [1:3]**, Eli was by the side of the road. He was sitting there in a chair, watching** [Leagerly; anxiously]**, because ·he was worried about** [Lhis heart trembled/feared for] **the Ark of God. When the Benjaminite entered Shiloh** [1:3]**, he told ·the bad news** [what had happened]**. Then all the ·people in town** [city; towns] **cried loudly. 14Eli heard the crying and asked, "What's all this ·noise** [commotion]**?"**

The Benjaminite ran to Eli and told him what had happened. 15Eli was now ninety-eight years old, and ·he was blind [Lhis gaze was fixed, so he could not see] **. 16The Benjaminite told him, "I have come from the battle. I ·ran all the way here** [escaped/fled from the battle line] **today."**

Eli asked, "What happened, my son?"

17The ·Benjaminite [Lmessenger] **answered, "Israel ·ran away** [fled] **from the Philistines, and the ·Israelite army has lost many soldiers** [people/troops have been slaughtered]**. Your two sons are both dead, and the Philistines have ·taken** [captured] **the Ark of God."**

18When he mentioned the Ark of God [4:3]**, Eli fell backward off his chair. He fell beside the gate, broke his neck, and died, because he was old and ·fat** [heavy]**. He had ·led** [judged; been judge of] **Israel for forty years.**

The Glory Is Gone

19Eli's daughter-in-law, the wife of Phinehas, was pregnant and was
about to give birth. When she heard the news that the Ark of God had
been taken and that Eli, her father-in-law, and Phinehas, her husband,
were both dead, she ·began to give [went into labor/crouched down and
gave] birth to her child. The child was born, but ·the mother had much
trouble in giving birth [her labor pains overwhelmed her]. 20As she was
dying, the women who helped her said, "Don't ·worry [be afraid]! You've
given birth to a son!" But she did not answer or pay attention. 21She
named the baby Ichabod [Cmeaning "No Glory"], saying, "Israel's glory
·is gone [has departed]." She said this because the Ark of God had been
·taken [captured] and her father-in-law and husband were dead. 22She
said, "Israel's glory is ·gone [departed], because the Ark of God has been
·taken away [captured]."

Trouble for the Philistines

5 After the Philistines [4:1] had captured the Ark of God [4:3], they
took it from Ebenezer [4:1] to Ashdod [Cone of the five chief cities
of the Philistines]. 2They carried it into Dagon's [Ca major Philistine god,
perhaps a storm god] temple and put it next to Dagon [Cto symbolize that
Israel's god was now on the side of Dagon]. 3When the people of Ashdod
rose early the next morning, they found that Dagon had fallen on his face
on the ground before the Ark of the LORD [Cas if in worship]. So they put
Dagon back in his place. 4The next morning when they rose, they again
found Dagon fallen face-down on the ground before the Ark of the LORD.
His head and hands had broken off and were lying ·in the doorway [on
the threshold; Cthe treatment given corpses of enemy soldiers]. Only his
·body [trunk] was ·still in one piece [intact; left to him]. 5So, ·even today
[to this day], Dagon's priests and others who enter his temple at Ashdod
refuse to step on the ·doorsill [threshold of Dagon].
6The ·LORD was hard [Lhand of the LORD was heavy] on the people of
Ashdod and ·their neighbors [its environs]. He ·caused them to suffer [ravaged/terrified them] and ·gave them [struck/afflicted them with] ·growths
on their skin [tumors; *or* hemorrhoids]. 7When the people of Ashdod saw
what was happening, they said, "The Ark of the God of Israel can't stay with
us. ·God is punishing [LHis hand is heavy on] us and Dagon our god." 8The
people of Ashdod called all five Philistine ·kings [rulers] together and asked
them, "What should we do with the Ark of the God of Israel?"

The rulers answered, "Move the Ark of the God of Israel to Gath
[Canother major city of the Philistines to the southeast of Ashdod]." So the
Philistines moved it to Gath.
9But after they moved it to Gath, there was a great panic. The ·LORD was
hard [Lhand of the LORD was heavy] on that city also, and he ·gave [struck;
afflicted] both old and young people in Gath ·growths on their skin [with
an outbreak of tumors/*or* hemorrhoids]. 10Then the Philistines sent the
Ark of God to Ekron [Ca third major city of the Philistines north of Gath].

But when it came into Ekron, the people of Ekron ·yelled [cried out],
"Why are you bringing the Ark of the God of Israel to our city? Do you
want to kill us and our people?" 11So they called all the ·kings [rulers] of
the Philistines together and said, "Send the Ark of the God of Israel back
to its own place ·before it kills [or it will kill] us and our people!" All the
people in the city were struck with ·terror [deadly panic] because ·God
was so hard [LGod's hand was so heavy] on them there. 12The people who
did not die were ·troubled [struck; afflicted] with ·growths on their skin

[tumors; *or* hemorrhoids]. So the people of Ekron ·cried [wailed] loudly to heaven.

The Ark of God Is Sent Home

6 The Philistines kept the ·Ark of God [4:3] in their ·land [territory; country] seven months. 2Then the Philistines [4:1] called for their priests and ·magicians [diviners] and said, "What should we do with the Ark of the LORD? Tell us how to send it back ·home [to its place]!"

3They answered, "If you send back the Ark of the God of Israel, don't send it back ·empty [without a gift]. ·You must give [Return it to him with] a ·penalty [guilt] offering. If you are then healed, you will know that it was ·because of the Ark that you had such trouble [Lhis hand that has been lifted from you]."

4The Philistines asked, "What kind of ·penalty [guilt] offering should we send to ·Israel's God [Lhim]?"

They answered, "Make five gold ·models [likenesses; images] of the ·growths on your skin [tumors] and five gold ·models [likenesses; images] of ·rats [*or* mice]. ·The number of ·models [likenesses; images] must match the number of Philistine ·kings [rulers; lords], because the same ·sickness [plague] has ·come on [struck; afflicted] you and your ·kings [rulers; lords]. 5Make ·models [likenesses; images] of the ·growths [tumors] and the ·rats [*or* mice] that are ·ruining [destroying; ravaging] the ·country [land], and give ·honor [glory] to Israel's God. Then maybe he will ·stop being so hard on [Llift his hand from] you, your gods, and your ·land [country]. 6·Don't be stubborn [LWhy do you harden your hearts…?] like the ·king [LPharaoh] of Egypt and the Egyptians [Ex. 7:13; 8:15; 9:34]. After God ·punished them terribly [brought disaster on; *or* made fools of them], ·they let the Israelites leave Egypt [Ldid they not send the Israelites out, and they departed?].

7"You must ·build [prepare] a new cart and get two cows that have just had calves. These must be cows that have never had yokes on their necks. Hitch the cows to the cart, and take the calves ·home, away from their mothers [away from them and put them in a pen]. 8Put the Ark of the LORD [4:3] on the cart and the gold ·models [likenesses; objects] you are sending him for the ·penalty [guilt] offering in a ·box [chest] beside the Ark. Then send the cart ·straight on its way [to go its own way]. 9Watch the cart. If it goes toward Beth Shemesh [Ca town on the border with Philistia about 24 miles west of Jerusalem] in ·Israel's own land [its own territory], [then] the LORD has ·given us this great sickness [brought this great disaster/harm on us]. But if it doesn't, we will know that ·Israel's God has not punished us [it was not God's hand that struck us]. It just happened by chance."

10·The Philistines did what the priests and magicians said [LThe men did so]. They took two cows that had just had calves and hitched them to the cart, but they kept their calves ·at home [in a pen]. 11They put the Ark of the LORD and the ·box [chest] with the gold rats and ·models [likenesses; images] of ·growths [tumors] on the cart. 12Then the cows went straight toward Beth Shemesh. They stayed on the road, ·mooing [lowing] all the way, and did not turn right or left. The Philistine ·kings [rulers; lords] followed the cows as far as the border of Beth Shemesh.

13Now the people of Beth Shemesh were ·harvesting [reaping] their wheat in the valley. When they ·looked up [Lraised their eyes] and saw the Ark of the LORD, they were ·very happy [joyful to see it]. 14The cart came to the field belonging to Joshua of Beth Shemesh and stopped near a large rock. The people of Beth Shemesh chopped up the wood of the cart. Then they ·sacrificed [offered] the cows as burnt offerings to the LORD. 15The Levites took down the Ark of the LORD and the ·box [chest] that had the gold ·models [likenesses; images], and they put both on the large rock. That day the people of Beth Shemesh offered whole burnt offerings and made sacrifices to the LORD. 16After the five Philistine ·kings [rulers; lords] saw this, they went back to Ekron [5:10] the same day.

17The Philistines had sent these gold ·models [likenesses; images] of the ·growths [tumors] as ·penalty [guilt] offerings to the LORD. They sent one ·model [likeness; image] for each Philistine town: Ashdod, Gaza, Ashkelon, Gath, and Ekron [Cthe five chief cities of Philistia]. 18And the Philistines also sent gold ·models [likenesses; images] of ·rats [*or* mice]. The number of ·rats [*or* mice] matched the number of towns belonging to the Philistine ·kings [rulers; lords], including both ·strong, walled [fortified] cities and country villages. The large rock on which they put the Ark of the LORD is still there [as a witness] in the field of Joshua of Beth Shemesh.

19But some of the men of Beth Shemesh looked into the Ark of the LORD. So God killed seventy of them. The people of Beth Shemesh ·cried [mourned] because the LORD had struck them ·down [so heavily; with a great slaughter]. 20·They [LThe men of Beth Shemesh] said, "Who can stand ·before [in the presence of] the LORD, this holy God? ·Whom will he strike next [*or* To whom shall he/it go next]?"

21Then they sent messengers to the people of Kiriath Jearim [Ca town nine miles north of Jerusalem], saying, "The Philistines have ·brought back [returned] the Ark of the LORD. Come down and take it to your city."

7 The men of Kiriath Jearim [6:21] came and took the Ark of the LORD [4:3] to Abinadab's house on a hill. There they made Abinadab's son Eleazar ·holy [consecrated; Cset him apart] for the LORD so he could ·guard [have charge of] the Ark of the LORD.

The Lord Saves the Israelites

2The Ark stayed at Kiriath Jearim a long time—twenty years in all. And the people of Israel ·began to follow [lamented; longed for] the LORD again. 3Samuel spoke to ·the whole group [Lall the people/house] of Israel, saying, "If you're turning back to the LORD with all your hearts, you must ·remove [get rid of; banish] your foreign gods and your idols of Ashtoreth. You must ·give yourselves [commit; direct your hearts] fully to the LORD and serve only him. Then he will ·save [rescue; deliver] you from the Philistines."

4So the Israelites [Lsons/Tchildren of Israel] ·put away [got rid of; banished] their idols of Baal and Ashtoreth, and they served only the LORD.

5Samuel said, "·All Israel must meet [Gather/Assemble all of Israel] at Mizpah [Cjust north of Jerusalem within the tribe of Benjamin], and I will ·pray to [plead to; intercede with] the LORD for you." 6So the Israelites ·met together [gathered; assembled] at Mizpah. They drew water from the ground and poured it out before the LORD [Ca ritual not commonly found in the OT] and fasted that day. They confessed, "We have sinned against the LORD." And Samuel ·served as judge of [judged] Israel at Mizpah.

7The Philistines heard the Israelites were ·meeting [gathered; assembled] at Mizpah, so the Philistine ·kings [rulers; lords] came up to attack them. When ·the Israelites [sons/Tchildren of Israel] heard they were coming, they were afraid. 8They said to Samuel, "Don't stop ·praying

[pleading; interceding; crying out] to the LORD our God for us! Ask him to
·save [rescue; deliver] us from the [Lhand of the] Philistines!" 9Then
Samuel took a ·baby [suckling] lamb and offered it to the LORD as a whole
burnt offering [Can atonement sacrifice; Lev. 1]. He ·called to [pleaded/
interceded with; cried out to] the LORD for Israel's sake, and the LORD
·answered [heard] him.
10While Samuel was ·burning [sacrificing] the [Lburnt] offering, the
Philistines came near to attack Israel. But [Lon that day] the LORD thundered against them with ·loud thunder [a loud voice]. They were ·so
frightened they became confused. So [… thrown into such a panic that]
the Israelites ·defeated [routed] the Philistines in battle. 11The men of
Israel ·ran [rushed; Lwent] out of Mizpah and ·chased [pursued] the
Philistines almost to Beth Car [Cexact location is unknown], ·killing the
Philistines [slaughtering them] along the way.

Peace Comes to Israel

12After this happened Samuel took a stone and set it up between
Mizpah and Shen.ⁿ He named the stone Ebenezer [C"Stone of help"], saying, "The LORD has helped us ·to this point [this far]." 13So the Philistines
were ·defeated [subdued; humbled] and did not enter the Israelites' ·land
[borders] again.
The [Lhand of the] LORD was against the Philistines all Samuel's life.
14Earlier the Philistines had taken towns from the Israelites, but ·the
Israelites won them back [they were restored to Israel], from Ekron [5:10]
to Gath [5:8]. They also took back from the [Lhand of the] Philistines the
·lands [territory] near these towns. There was peace also between Israel
and the Amorites.
15Samuel ·continued as judge of [judged] Israel all [Lthe days of] his
life. 16Every year he went [Lon circuit] from Bethel [Cnorth of Jerusalem,
near Ai in the central hill country] to Gilgal [Cnear Jericho] to Mizpah and
judged the Israelites in all these towns. 17But he always went back to
Ramah [1:1], where his home was. There he judged Israel and built an
altar to the LORD.

Israel Asks for a King

8 When Samuel was old, he ·made [appointed] his sons judges ·for
[over] Israel. 2His first son was named Joel, and his second son was
named Abijah. Joel and Abijah were judges in Beersheba [Cin the Negev to
the extreme south]. 3But Samuel's sons did not ·live as he did [Lwalk/follow
in his ways]. They ·tried to get money dishonestly [were greedy; wandered
after money], and they accepted ·money secretly [bribes] ·to make wrong
judgments [and perverted justice/made biased decisions].
4So all the elders ·came together [assembled] and met Samuel at Ramah
[1:1]. 5They said to him, "You're old, and your sons don't ·live as you do
[Lwalk/follow in your ways]. Give us a king to ·rule over [judge] us like all
the other nations [Deut. 17:14]."
6When the elders said, "Give us [Appoint; LNow, set for us] a king to
·rule over [judge] us," ·Samuel was not pleased [Lit was evil/wrong in the
eyes of Samuel]. So he prayed to the LORD, 7and the LORD told Samuel,
"Listen to ·whatever [Lthe voice of] the people [Lregarding what they] say
to you. They have not rejected you. They have rejected me from being
their king. 8They are doing as they have always done. When I ·took them
out of [brought them up from] Egypt, they ·left [abandoned; deserted;

7:12 Shen Hebrew copies read "Shen." Some Greek copies have "Jeshenah."

forsook] me and ·served [followed] other gods. They are doing the same
to you. 9Now ·listen to the people [listen to their voice; do as they ask], but
[Lsolemnly] warn them ·what the king who rules over them will do [about
the way/manner/custom in which he will rule/reign over them]."
10So Samuel told those who had asked him for a king ·what [every-
thing; Lall the words] the LORD had said. 11Samuel said, "If you have a king
·ruling [reigning] over you, ·this is what he will do [he will act this way;
Lthis will be the way/manner/custom in which he will rule/reign over you]:
He will ·take [draft] your sons and make them serve with his chariots and
his ·horses [*or* charioteers; horsemen], and they will run in front of the
king's chariot. 12He will make some of your sons commanders over thousands or over fifties. He will make some of your other sons plow his
·ground [fields] and ·reap his harvest [harvest his crops]. He will take others to make weapons of war and equipment for his chariots. 13He will take
your daughters to make perfume and cook and bake for him. 14He will
take your best fields, vineyards, and olive groves and give them to his
·servants [officials; attendants]. 15He will take ·one-tenth [a tithe] of your
·grain [crops; seed] and ·grapes [vineyards] and give it to his officers and
·servants [officials; attendants]. 16He will take your male and female servants, your best cattle, and your donkeys and use them all for his own
work. 17He will take ·one-tenth [a tithe] of your flocks, and you yourselves will become his ·slaves [servants]. 18·When that time comes [LIn
that day], you will cry out because of the king you ·chose [selected]. But
the LORD will not ·answer [help] you then."
19But the people ·would not [Lrefused to] listen to [Lthe voice of] Samuel.
They said, "No! We ·want [are determined to have] a king to rule over us.
20Then we will be the same as all the other nations. Our king will ·judge for
[govern; rule over] us and go ·with [before] us and fight our battles."
21After Samuel ·heard [listened to] all that the people said, he repeated
their words ·to the LORD [Lin the LORD's hearing/ears]. 22The LORD
answered, "You must ·listen to them [do as they say]. ·Give [Appoint]
them a king."
Then Samuel told the people of Israel, "Go back [Leach of you] to your
·towns [own town/city]."

Saul Looks for His Father's Donkeys

9 Kish, son of Abiel from the tribe of Benjamin, was an ·important
man [man of wealth/rank/standing/valor]. (Abiel was the son of
Zeror, who was the son of Becorath, who was the son of Aphiah of
Benjamin.) 2Kish had a son named Saul, who was a ·fine [handsome]
young man. There was no Israelite ·better [more handsome] than he. Saul
stood ·a head [head and shoulders] taller than any other man in Israel.
3Now the donkeys of Saul's father, Kish, were lost. So Kish said to Saul,
his son, "Take one of the servants, and go and look for the donkeys." 4Saul
went through the ·mountains [hill country] of Ephraim and the ·land
[area; territory] of Shalisha, but he and the servant could not find the
donkeys. They went into the ·land [area; territory] of Shaalim, but the
donkeys were not there. They went through the ·land [area; territory] of
Benjamin, but they still did not find them. 5When they arrived in the area
of Zuph, Saul said to his servant, "Let's go back or my father will stop
thinking about the donkeys and will start worrying about us."
6But the servant answered, "A man of God [Ca title for a prophet] is in
this town. People ·respect [honor] him because everything he says comes

true. Let's go ·into the town now [Lthere]. Maybe he can tell us ·something
about the journey we have taken [*or* what way to go]."
[7]Saul said to his servant, "If we go into the town, what can we give him?
The ·food [bread] in our bags is gone. We have no gift to give him. ·Do we
have anything [What do we have]?"
[8]Again the servant answered Saul. "Look, I have ·one-tenth of an ounce
[La quarter of a shekel] of silver. ·Give [*or* I will give] it to the man of God.
Then he will tell us ·about our journey [Lwhat to do/way to go]." [9](In ·the
past [Lthose days], if someone in Israel wanted to ·ask something from
[inquire of] God, he would say, "Let's go to the seer." We call the person a
prophet today, but in ·the past [Lthose days] he was called a seer.)
[10]Saul said to his servant, "·That's a good idea [Well said]. Come, let's
go." So they went toward the town where the man of God was.
[11]As Saul and the servant were going up the hill to the town, they met
some young women coming out to ·get [draw] water. Saul and the servant
asked them, "Is the seer here?"
[12]The young women answered, "Yes, he's here. He's ahead of you.
Hurry now. He has just come to our town today, because the people will
offer a sacrifice at the ·place of worship [high place]. [13]As soon as you
enter the town, you ·will [can] find him before he goes up to the ·place of
worship [high place] to eat. The people will not begin eating until the seer
comes, because he must bless the sacrifice. After that, the guests will eat.
Go now, and you should find him [Lquickly; at once]."

Saul Meets Samuel

[14]Saul and the servant went up to the town. Just as they ·entered it
[Larrived in the midst of the town], they saw Samuel coming toward them
on his way up to the ·place of worship [high place].
[15]The day before Saul came, the LORD had ·told [revealed this to] Samuel:
[16]"About this time tomorrow I will send you a man from the ·land [terri-
tory] of Benjamin. ·Appoint [Anoint] him ·to lead [Lruler/prince over] my
people Israel. He will ·save [rescue; deliver] my people from the [Lhand of
the] Philistines. I have seen ·the suffering of my people, and I have listened
to their cry [Lmy people because their cry has reached me]."
[17]When Samuel first saw Saul, the LORD said to Samuel, "This is the
man I told you about. He will ·organize [rule over; govern] my people."
[18]Saul approached Samuel at the gate and said, "Please tell me where
the seer's house is."
[19]Samuel answered, "I am the seer. Go ·with [ahead of] me to the ·place
of worship [high place]. Today you and your servant are to eat with me.
Tomorrow morning I will ·answer all your questions [Ltell you all that is
in your heart/mind] and send you home. [20]Don't worry about the donkeys you lost three days ago, because they have been found. Soon all the
·wealth [desires] of Israel will ·belong to [be focused/fixed on; turn to]
you and your family."
[21]Saul answered, "·But I am [LAm I not…?] from the tribe of Benjamin,
the smallest tribe in Israel. And ·my family group is [Lis not my family/
clan…?] the ·smallest [least] in the tribe of Benjamin. Why are you ·say-
ing such things [talking this way to me]?"
[22]Then Samuel took Saul and his servant into ·a large room [the hall]
and ·gave them a choice place at [placed them at the head of] the table.
About thirty guests were there. [23]Samuel said to the cook, "Bring the meat
I gave you, the portion I told you to set aside."

24So the cook took the thigh and put it on the table in front of Saul. Samuel said, "This is the meat saved for you. Eat it, because it was set aside for you for this ·special [appointed] time. ·As I said, 'I had invited the people.' [or ... even before I invited these others]." So Saul ate with Samuel that day.

25After they finished eating, they came down from the ·place of worship [high place] and went to the town. Then Samuel ·talked with [or prepared a bed for] Saul on the roof of his house [Cthe flat roofs of Israelite houses served as living space]. 26At dawn they got up, and Samuel called to Saul on the roof. He said, "Get up, and I will send you on your way." So Saul got up and went out of the house with Samuel. 27As Saul, his servant, and Samuel were getting near the edge of the city, Samuel said to Saul, "Tell the servant to go on ahead of us, but you stay, ·because I have a message from [so I may give/proclaim the word of] God for you."

Samuel Appoints Saul

10 Samuel took a ·jar [flask; vial] of olive oil and poured it on Saul's head. He kissed Saul and said, "The LORD has ·appointed [anointed] you ·to lead [ruler; prince over] his ·people[n] [special possession; inheritance]. 2After you leave me today, you will meet two men near Rachel's tomb on the border of Benjamin at Zelzah [Gen. 35:19]. They will say to you, 'The donkeys you were looking for have been found. But now your father has stopped thinking about his donkeys and is ·worrying [anxious] about you. He is asking, "What will I do about my son?" '

3"Then you will go on until you reach the ·big [Loak] tree at Tabor. Three men ·on their way to worship [Lgoing up to] God at Bethel will meet you there. One man will be carrying three ·goats [kids]. Another will be carrying three loaves of bread. And the third will have a ·leather bag [skin] full of wine. 4They will greet you and offer you two loaves of bread, which you must accept. 5Then you will go to ·Gibeah [or the hill] of God, where a Philistine ·camp [garrison] is. When you approach this town, a group of prophets will come down from the ·place of worship [high place]. They will be playing harps, tambourines, flutes, and lyres, and they will be prophesying. 6Then the Spirit of the LORD will ·rush upon [come on; seize; possess] you with power. You will prophesy with them, and you will be changed into a different man. 7After these signs happen, do ·whatever you find to do [what must be done; what you see fit to do; Lwhat your hand finds to do], because God ·will help [is with] you [CSaul was supposed to attack the garrison, but he did not do so].

8"Go ahead of me to Gilgal. I will come down to you to offer whole burnt offerings [Lev. 1] and to sacrifice ·fellowship [peace; well-being] offerings [Lev. 3:1]. But you must wait seven days. Then I will come and ·tell [show; reveal to] you what to do [CSaul did not do this either]."

Saul Made King

9When Saul turned to leave Samuel, God ·changed Saul's [gave Saul a new/another] heart. All these signs ·came true [were fulfilled; occurred] that day. 10When they arrived at Gibeah, Saul met a ·group [band; procession] of prophets. The Spirit of God ·rushed upon [overwhelmed; seized; possessed] him, and he prophesied with the prophets. 11When people who had known Saul before saw him prophesying with the prophets, they asked each other, "What has happened to Kish's son? Is even Saul ·one of [among] the prophets?"

10:1 people Some Greek copies add "You will reign over the LORD's people and will save them from the enemies around them. And this will be the sign to you that the LORD has appointed you to lead his people."

12 A man who lived there ·said [answered; retorted], "Who is the father of these prophets [CSaul's prophesying amazed and confused him]?" So this became a ·famous saying [proverb]: "Is ·even Saul one of [Saul also among] the prophets?" 13 When Saul finished prophesying, he ·entered the place of worship [came/went to the high place].

14 Saul's uncle asked him and his servant, "Where have you been?"

Saul said, "We were looking for the donkeys. When we couldn't find them, we went to talk to Samuel."

15 Saul's uncle asked, "Please tell me. What did Samuel say to you?"

16 Saul answered, "He told us the donkeys had already been found." But Saul did not tell his uncle what Samuel had said about ·his becoming king [the kingdom; CSaul should have announced publicly that he was king].

17 Samuel called all the people of Israel ·to meet with [to] the LORD at Mizpah [7:5–11, 15–17]. 18 He said [Lto the sons of Israel], "This is what the LORD, the God of Israel, says: 'I ·led [brought up] Israel out of Egypt. I ·saved [rescued; delivered] you from Egypt's ·control [Lhand] and from [Lthe hand of] other kingdoms that were ·troubling [oppressing] you.' 19 But ·now [today] you have rejected your God. He ·saves [rescues; delivers] you from all your ·troubles [calamities; disasters; miseries] and ·problems [distresses], but you said, 'No! ·We want [Appoint; Set] a king to rule over us.' Now come, ·stand [present yourselves] before the LORD in your tribes and ·family groups [clans]."

20 When Samuel ·gathered [brought forward] ·all [each of] the tribes of Israel, the tribe of Benjamin was ·picked [chosen/taken by lot]. 21 Samuel had ·them [the tribe of Benjamin] pass by in ·family groups [clans], and Matri's family was ·picked [chosen/taken by lot]. Then he had each man of Matri's family pass by, and Saul son of Kish was ·picked [chosen/taken by lot]. But when they looked for Saul, ·they could not find him [he had disappeared]. 22 They ·asked [inquired further of] the LORD, "Has ·Saul [Lthe man] come here yet?"

The LORD said, "Yes. He's hiding ·behind [among] the baggage."

23 So they ran and brought him out. When Saul stood among the people, he was ·a head [head and shoulders] taller than anyone else. 24 Then Samuel said to the people, "See the man the LORD has chosen. ·There is no one like him [He has no equal] among all the people."

Then the people shouted, "Long live the king!"

25 Samuel explained the ·rights and duties [ordinances; customs] of the king and then wrote them ·in a book [on a scroll] and put it before the LORD. Then he told the people to go to their homes.

26 Saul also went to his home in Gibeah. ·God touched the hearts of certain brave men who went along with him [...accompanied by warriors/valiant men whose hearts God had touched]. 27 But some ·troublemakers [scoundrels; worthless men] said, "How can this man ·save [rescue; deliver] us?" They ·disapproved of [scorned; despised] Saul and refused to bring gifts to him. But Saul kept ·quiet[n] [silent; held his peace; ignored them].

10:27 quiet The Dead Sea Scrolls add an additional paragraph here, which reads, "Nahash, king of the Ammonites, had been terribly oppressing the people of Gad and Reuben who lived east of the Jordan River. He gouged out the right eye of each of the Israelites living there, and he didn't allow anyone to save them. There were no Israelites east of the Jordan whose right eye Nahash had not gouged out. But there were 7,000 men who had escaped from the Ammonites, and they had settled in Jabesh Gilead."

Nahash Troubles Jabesh Gilead

11 About a month later[n] Nahash the Ammonite and his army
·surrounded [attacked and besieged] the city of Jabesh in
Gilead. All the people of Jabesh said to Nahash, "·Make [LCut] a ·treaty
[covenant] with us, and we will ·serve [be subject to] you."

2But Nahash the Ammonite answered, "I will ·make a treaty [Lcut] with
you only if I'm allowed to ·poke [gouge] out the right eye of each of you.
Then all Israel will be ·ashamed [disgraced]!"

3The elders of Jabesh said to Nahash, "Give us seven days to send messengers through all [Lthe borders/territories of] Israel. If no one comes to
·help [rescue; deliver] us, we will ·give ourselves up [surrender] to you."

4When the messengers came to Gibeah where Saul lived and told the
people the news, they ·cried loudly [Lraised their voices and wept]. 5Saul
was coming home from plowing the fields with his oxen when he heard
the people crying. He asked, "What's wrong with the people that they are
crying?" Then they told Saul what the ·messengers [Lmen] from Jabesh
had said. 6When Saul heard their words, God's Spirit ·rushed upon him
with power [came mightily/powerfully on Saul], and he ·became very
angry [burned with anger]. 7So he took a pair of oxen and cut them into
pieces. Then he gave the pieces of the oxen to messengers and ordered
them to carry them through all the land of Israel [Ca ritual to curse an
enemy].

The messengers said, "This is what will happen to the oxen of anyone
who does not ·follow [march with; Cinto battle] Saul and Samuel." So the
·people became very afraid of the LORD [Lterror/dread of the LORD fell on
the people]. They all ·came together [marched out] as if they were one
person. 8Saul ·gathered [mobilized; mustered] the people together at
Bezek. There were three hundred thousand men from Israel and thirty[n]
thousand men from Judah.

9They said to the messengers who had come, "Tell the people at Jabesh
Gilead this: '·Before the day warms up tomorrow [By the time the sun is
hot], you will be ·saved [rescued; delivered].'" So the messengers went
and reported this to the people at Jabesh, and they were ·very happy
[elated; overjoyed]. 10The people said to Nahash the Ammonite,
"Tomorrow we will ·come out to meet [surrender to] you. Then you can
do ·anything you want to us [to us whatever seems good to you]."

11The next morning Saul divided his soldiers into three ·groups [com-
panies; divisions]. At dawn they entered the Ammonite camp and defeated
them ·before [until] the heat of the day. The Ammonites who ·escaped
[survived] were scattered; no two of them were still together.

12Then the people said to Samuel, "Who ·didn't want Saul as king [was
it that questioned, 'Will Saul rule/reign over us]?' Bring them here and we
will kill them!"

13But Saul said, "No! No one will be put to death today. Today the LORD
has ·saved [rescued; delivered] Israel!"

14Then Samuel said to the people, "Come, let's go to Gilgal. There we
will ·again promise to obey the king [renew the kingdom]." 15So all the
people went to Gilgal, and there, before the LORD, the people made Saul
king. They offered ·fellowship [peace; communion] offerings to the LORD,
and Saul and all the Israelites ·had a great celebration [rejoiced greatly].

11:1 About a month later This phrase is lacking in Hebrew copies, but appears in some Greek copies. **11:8 thirty** Some ancient copies read "seventy."

Samuel's Farewell Speech

12 Samuel said to all Israel, "I have ·done everything you wanted me to do [listened to everything you said] and have ·put [appointed] a king over you. 2Now you have a king ·to lead [walking before/in front of] you. I am old and gray, and my sons are here with you. I have ·been your leader [walked before/in front of you] since I was young [L until this day]. 3Here I am. ·If I have done anything wrong, you must testify [Bear witness] against me before the LORD and his ·appointed king [anointed]. Did I steal anyone's ox or donkey? Did I ·hurt [oppress] or cheat anyone? Did I ever secretly accept a bribe to ·look the other way [L close my eyes]? If I did any of these things, I will make ·it right [amends]."

4The Israelites answered, "You have not cheated us, or ·hurt [oppressed] us, or taken anything ·unfairly from anyone [from anyone's hand]."

5Samuel said to them, "The LORD is a witness ·to what you have said [against you]. His ·appointed [anointed] king is also a witness today that you did not find anything ·wrong in me [L in my hand]."

"He is our witness," they said.

6Then Samuel said to the people, "It is the LORD who ·chose [appointed; L made] Moses and Aaron and brought your ·ancestors [fathers] out of Egypt. 7Now, ·stand there [*or* take your stand], and I will ·remind you of [plead with you/confront you concerning] all the ·good things [righteous/saving acts] the LORD did for you and your ·ancestors [fathers].

8"After Jacob [C the Israelites] ·entered [went to; arrived in] Egypt, ·his descendants [they] cried to the LORD for help. So the LORD sent Moses and Aaron, who took your ·ancestors [fathers] out of Egypt and ·brought them to live [settled them] in this place.

9"But they forgot the LORD their God. So he ·handed them over as slaves [sold them] to Sisera [Judg. 4–5], the commander of the army of Hazor, and ·as slaves to [into the hand of] the Philistines [Judg. 13–16] and the king of Moab. ·They all [...all of whom had] fought against your ·ancestors [fathers]. 10Then your ancestors cried to the LORD and said, 'We have sinned. We have ·left [turned away from; forsaken] the LORD and served the Baals and the Ashtoreths [C gods and goddesses of the Canaanites]. But now ·save [rescue; deliver] us from [L the hand of] our enemies, and we will ·serve [worship] you.' 11So the LORD sent ·Gideon [L Jerubbaal; C another name for Gideon; Judg. 6:32], ·Barak [L Bedan; Judg. 4:6], Jephthah [Judg. 11–12], and Samuel. He ·saved [rescued; delivered] you from [L the hands of] your enemies around you, and you lived in ·safety [security]. 12But when you saw Nahash king of the ·Ammonites [L sons of Ammon] ·coming [marching] against you, you said, 'No! We want a king to ·rule [reign] over us!'—even though the LORD your God was your king. 13·Now [All right; So] here is the king you chose, the one you asked for. The LORD has ·put [set; appointed] him over you. 14·You must [If you...] ·honor [fear] the LORD and ·serve [worship] him. You must ·obey [listen to] his ·word [voice] and not ·turn [rebel] against ·his commands [L the mouth of the LORD]. Both you and the king ·ruling [reigning] over you must follow the LORD your God. If you do, it will be well with you. 15But if you don't ·obey [listen to the voice of] the LORD, and if you ·turn [rebel] against ·his commands [L the mouth of the LORD], ·he [the hand of the LORD] will be ·against [heavy on] you. ·He will do to you what he did to [...as it was on] your ·ancestors [fathers].

16“Now stand ·still [where you are] and see the ·great thing [wonder;
Lthing] the LORD will do before your eyes. 17·It is [Is it not…?] now the
time of the wheat harvest [Cthe dry season]. I will pray for the LORD to
send thunder and rain [Cthe rain would destroy the wheat harvest]. Then
you will know what an ·evil [wicked] thing you did ·against [in the eyes/
sight of] the LORD when you ·asked for [demanded] a king.”
18Then Samuel ·prayed [called] to the LORD, and that same day the
LORD sent thunder and rain. So the people were ·very afraid [in awe] of
the LORD and Samuel. 19·They [LAll the people] said to Samuel, “Pray to
the LORD your God for us, your servants! Don’t let us die! We’ve added to
all our sins the evil of ·asking for [demanding] a king.”
20Samuel answered [Lthe people], “Don’t be afraid. It’s true that you
did ·wrong [evil], but don’t turn away from the LORD. ·Serve [Worship]
the LORD with all your heart. 21·Idols [Futile things] are of no use, so don’t
worship them. They can’t help you or ·save [rescue; deliver] you. They are
·useless [futile]! 22For his own [Lname’s] sake, the LORD won’t ·leave [aban-
don; reject; desert] his people. ·Instead, [For; Because] he was pleased to
make you his own people. 23 [LAs for me,] ·I will surely not [Far be it from
me to] stop praying for you, because that would be sinning against the
LORD. I will ·teach [instruct] you ·what [in the way that] is good and right.
24·You must honor [Fear only] the LORD and ·truly serve [worship] him
with all your heart. ·Remember [Keep in mind; Consider] the ·wonderful
[great] things he did for you! 25But if you ·are stubborn and do [persist in
doing] evil, he will sweep you and your king away.”

13 Saul was thirty years old when he ·became king [began to reign/
rule], and he ·was king [reigned; ruled] over Israel forty-two
years.[n] 2Saul chose three thousand men from Israel. Two thousand men
stayed with him at Micmash in the ·mountains [hill country] of Bethel,
and one thousand men stayed with Jonathan at Gibeah in Benjamin. Saul
sent the other men in the army back ·home [Lto their tents].
3Jonathan ·attacked [Lstruck] the Philistine ·camp [garrison] in Geba,
and the other Philistines heard about it. Saul said, “Let the Hebrews hear
what happened.” So he told the men to blow ·trumpets [ram’s horns]
through all the land of Israel. 4All the Israelites heard the news. The men
said, “Saul has ·defeated [struck] the Philistine camp [garrison; CSaul
receives credit for Jonathan’s victory]. Now ·the Philistines will really hate
us [LIsrael will stink among the Philistines]!” Then the Israelites were
called to join Saul at Gilgal.
5The Philistines gathered to fight Israel with three thousand[n] chariots
and six thousand ·men to ride in them [horsemen; charioteers]. Their
soldiers were as many as the grains of sand on the seashore. The Philistines
went and camped at Micmash, which is east of Beth Aven. 6When the
Israelites saw that they were in ·trouble [a tight spot; desperate straits],
they went to hide in caves and ·bushes [thickets; *or* holes], among the
·rocks [cliffs; crevices], and in ·pits [cellars; tombs; vaults] and ·wells [cis-
terns]. 7Some Hebrews even went across the Jordan River to the land of
Gad and Gilead.
But Saul stayed at Gilgal, and all the men in his army were ·shaking
with fear [trembling; quaking]. 8Saul waited seven days, ·because Samuel

13:1 Saul… years This is how the verse is worded in some early Greek copies. The Hebrew is not clear here. **13:5 three thousand** Some Greek copies read “three thousand.” Hebrew copies say “thirty thousand.”

had said he would meet him then [Lthe period/time Samuel had set; Cas a
priest, Samuel had to offer sacrifices before battle]. **But Samuel did not
come to Gilgal, and the soldiers began to ·leave** [scatter; slip away].
9**So Saul said, "Bring me the whole burnt offering and the ·fellowship**
[peace; communion] **offerings." Then Saul ·offered** [sacrificed] **the whole
burnt offering.** 10**Just as he finished, Samuel arrived, and Saul went to
greet him.**
11**Samuel asked, "What have you ·done** [been doing]**?"**
Saul answered, "I saw the soldiers ·leaving [scattering from] **me, and
you were not here ·when you said you would be** [at the set/appointed
time]. **The Philistines were gathering at Micmash.** 12**Then I thought, 'The
Philistines will come against me at Gilgal, and I haven't asked for the
LORD's ·approval** [help; favor]**.' So I ·forced myself** [felt compelled/it nec-
essary] **to offer the whole burnt offering."**
13**Samuel said, "You acted foolishly** [Conly priests could legitimately
offer sacrifices]**! You haven't ·obeyed** [kept] **the command of the LORD
your God** [Cfrightened troops should have been allowed to leave; Deut.
20:8–9]. **If you had obeyed him, the LORD would have ·made your kingdom continue** [established your kingdom] **·in** [over] **Israel always** [CSaul
rather than David would have had a dynasty], 14**but now your kingdom
will not ·continue** [last; endure]. **The LORD has ·looked for the kind of
man he wants** [Lsought a man after his own heart; 16:6–13]. **He has
appointed him to ·rule** [Lbe prince over] **his people, because you haven't
·obeyed his** [kept the LORD's] **command."**
15**Then Samuel left Gilgal and went to Gibeah in Benjamin. Saul
counted the men who were still with him, and there were about six
hundred.**

Hard Times for Israel

16**Saul and his son Jonathan and the soldiers with him stayed in Gibeah
in the land of Benjamin. The Philistines made their camp at Micmash.**
17**Three ·groups** [raiding parties] **went out from the Philistine camp to
make raids. One ·group** [company] **went on the Ophrah road in the land
of Shual.** 18**The second group went on the Beth Horon road. The third
group went on the border road that overlooks the Valley of Zeboim
toward the ·desert** [wilderness].
19**The whole land of Israel had no blacksmith because the Philistines
had said, "The Hebrews ·might** [Lmust not] **make swords and spears."**
20**So all the Israelites had to go down to the Philistines to have their plows,
hoes, axes, and sickles sharpened.** 21**The Philistine blacksmiths charged
·about one-fourth of an ounce of silver** [Ltwo-thirds of a shekel] **for
sharpening plows and hoes. And they charged ·one-eighth of an ounce of
silver** [Lone-third of a shekel] **for sharpening picks, axes, and the ·sticks
used to guide oxen** [goads].
22**So when the battle came, the ·soldiers** [people] **with Saul and
Jonathan had no swords or spears** [Lin their hands]. **Only Saul and his son
Jonathan had them.**

23**A ·group from** [unit/detachment of] **the Philistine army had gone
out to the pass at Micmash.**

Israel Defeats the Philistines

14 **One day Jonathan, Saul's son, said to ·the officer who carried
his armor** [his armor bearer], **"Come, let's go over to the
Philistine ·camp** [outpost] **on the other side." But Jonathan did not tell
his father.**

2 Saul was sitting under a pomegranate tree at ·the threshing floor [*or* Migron] **near Gibeah. He had about six hundred men with him. 3 One man was Ahijah who was wearing the ·holy vest** [ephod; Ex. 28:6–14]. **(Ahijah was a son of Ichabod's brother Ahitub. Ichabod was the son of Phinehas, the son of Eli, the LORD's priest in Shiloh.) No one knew Jonathan had left.**

4 There was a ·steep slope [rocky crag/cliff] **on each side of the pass that Jonathan planned to go through to reach the Philistine ·camp** [outpost]. **The cliff on one side was named Bozez, and the cliff on the other side was named Seneh. 5 One ·cliff** [crag] **faced north toward Micmash. The other faced south toward Geba.**

6 Jonathan said to his ·officer who carried his armor [armor bearer], **"Come. Let's go to the ·camp** [outpost] **of those men who are not circumcised** [CPhilistines were among the few Near Eastern people of the day who did not practice circumcision; it had special significance in Israel; Gen. 17:9–14]. **Maybe the LORD will ·help** [act/work something for] **us. The LORD ·can give us victory if** [is able to save/rescue whether] **we have many people, or just a few."**

7 ·The officer who carried Jonathan's armor [His armor bearer] **said to him, "Do whatever you think is best. Go ahead. ·I'm with you** [Our hearts/minds are one]."

8 Jonathan said, "Then come. We will cross over to the Philistines and let them see us. 9 If they say to us, 'Stay there until we come to you [Cin order to kill them],' **we will stay where we are. We won't go up to them. 10 But if they say, 'Come up to us** [Cin order to fight],' **we will climb up, and the LORD will ·let us defeat them** [Lgive them into our hands]. **This will be the sign for us."**

11 When they both let the Philistines see them, the Philistines said, "Look! The Hebrews are crawling out of the holes they were hiding in!" 12 The Philistines in the ·camp [outpost] **shouted to Jonathan and his officer, "Come up to us. ·We'll teach you a lesson** [*or* We have something to tell/show you]!"

Jonathan said to his ·officer [armor bearer], **"Climb up behind me, because the LORD has given the Philistines ·to** [Linto the hands of] **Israel!" 13 So Jonathan climbed up, using his hands and feet, and his ·officer** [armor bearer] **climbed just behind him. ·Jonathan struck down the Philistines** [LAnd they fell before Jonathan] **as he went, and his ·officer** [armor bearer] **killed ·them as he followed** [those who came from] **behind him. 14 In that first ·fight** [attack; slaughter] **Jonathan and his officer killed about twenty Philistines over a ·half acre** [Lyoke] **of ground.**

15 All the Philistine soldiers panicked—those in the ·camp [outpost] **and those in the raiding party. ·The ground itself shook** [An earthquake struck]! **God had caused the panic.**

16 Saul's ·guards [watchmen] **were at Gibeah in the land of Benjamin when they saw the ·Philistine soldiers** [Lvast army; multitude] **·running in every direction** [Lmelting away, here and there]. **17 Saul said to his army, "·Check to see who has left our camp** [Call the roll and see who has left us]." **When they ·checked** [called the roll], **they learned that Jonathan and his ·officer** [armor bearer] **were gone.**

18 So Saul said to Ahijah the priest, "Bring the ·Ark of God[n] [*or* ephod; Csee text note; both are means of discerning God's will]." **(At that time ·it was with**

14:18 Ark of God Some Greek copies read "ephod."

[*or* he was wearing it in front of] the Israelites.) 19While Saul was talking to the priest, the confusion in the Philistine camp was growing. Then Saul said to Ahijah, "Put your hand down! [Cto stop the inquiry of God]"

20Then Saul ·gathered his army [assembled; gathered] and entered the battle. They found the Philistines [Ltotally; greatly] confused, striking each other with their swords! 21Earlier, there were Hebrews who had ·served [defected/gone over to] the Philistines and had stayed in their camp, but now they ·joined [went over to] the Israelites with Saul and Jonathan. 22When all the Israelites hidden in the ·mountains [hill country] of Ephraim heard that the Philistine soldiers were running away, they also joined the battle ·and chased the Philistines [in hot pursuit]. 23So the LORD ·saved [rescued; delivered] the Israelites that day, and the battle ·moved on past [spread beyond] Beth Aven.

Saul Makes Another Mistake

24The men of Israel were ·miserable [exhausted; hard pressed] that day because Saul had ·made an oath for all of them [put them under an oath]. He had said, "No one should eat food before evening and before I ·finish defeating [have had revenge on] my enemies. If he does, he will be cursed!" So no Israelite soldier ate food.

25Now ·the whole army [Lall the land] went into the woods, where there was some honey on the ground. 26·They came upon some ·honey [honeycomb], but no one ·took any [Lput his hand to his mouth] because they were afraid of the oath. 27[But] Jonathan had not heard ·the oath Saul had put on the army [that Saul had bound the people with a vow], so he dipped the end of his ·stick [staff] into the honey and lifted some out and ·ate it [Lput his hand to his mouth]. Then ·he felt better [his eyes brightened]. 28Then one of the soldiers told Jonathan, "Your father ·made an oath for all the soldiers [bound the people with a strict oath/vow]. He said any man who eats today will be cursed! That's why they are so ·weak [weary; faint]."

29Jonathan said, "My father has made trouble for the land! See how ·much better I feel [Lmy eyes have brightened] after just tasting a little of this honey! 30It would have been much better for the men to eat the ·food [plunder; spoil] they took from their enemies today. We could have ·killed [slaughtered] many more Philistines!"

31That day the Israelites ·defeated [attacked; struck down] the Philistines from Micmash to Aijalon. After that, they were very ·tired [weary; faint]. 32They ·had taken [rushed to the plunder, taking] sheep, ·cattle [oxen], and calves from the Philistines. Now they were so hungry they ·killed [butchered] the animals on the ground and ate them, ·without draining the blood from them [with the blood]! 33Someone said to Saul, "Look! The men are sinning against the LORD. ·They're eating meat without draining the blood from it [...by eating with the blood; Gen. 9:4; Deut. 12:23]!"

Saul said, "You ·have sinned [acted treacherously; broken faith]! Roll a large stone over here now!" 34Then he said, "·Go [Disperse yourselves] ·to [among] the men and tell them that each person must bring his ox and sheep to me and ·kill [slaughter] it here and eat it. Don't sin against the LORD by eating ·meat without draining the blood from it [with the blood]."

That night everyone brought his ·animals [oxen] and ·killed [slaughtered] them there. 35Then Saul built an altar to the LORD. It was the first altar he had built to the LORD.

36Saul said, "Let's go after the Philistines ·tonight [after dark] and ·rob [plunder; despoil] **them. We won't ·let any of them live** [leave one of them]**!"**

The men answered, "Do whatever you think is best."

But the priest said, "Let's ·ask [approach; draw near to] **God** [Cby making inquiry through the sacred lots or ephod]**."**

37 **So Saul asked God, "Should I ·chase** [Lgo down after] **the Philistines? Will you ·let us defeat them** [Lgive them into Israel's hand]**?" But God did not answer Saul ·at that time** [that day]. 38 **·Then** [So] **Saul said to all the ·leaders** [commanders] **of his army, "Come here. Let's find out what sin has been ·done** [committed] **today** [CSaul believed God had not answered him because of a sin]. 39 **As surely as the LORD lives who has ·saved** [rescued; delivered] **Israel, even if my son Jonathan did the sin, he must die." But no one ·in the army** [of all the people] **spoke.**

40 **Then Saul said to all the Israelites, "You stand on this side. I and my son Jonathan will stand on the other side."**

The men answered, "Do whatever you think is best."

41 **Then Saul prayed to the LORD, the God of Israel, "·Give me the right answer** [Let the sacred lots reveal the answer; LGive Thummim; CSaul is making inquiry through the sacred lots (the Urim and Thummim) as to who sinned; Ex. 28:29–30]**."**

And Saul and Jonathan were picked; the ·other men went free [people were cleared/went free/escaped blame]. 42 **Saul said, "Now ·let us discover if it is I or Jonathan my son who is guilty** [cast sacred lots between me and Jonathan]**." And Jonathan was ·picked** [taken].

43 **Saul said to Jonathan, "Tell me what you have done."**

So Jonathan told Saul, "I only tasted a little honey from the end of my ·stick [staff]. **·And must I die now** [Does that deserve death; *or* I am ready to die.]**?"**

44 **Saul said, "Jonathan, if you don't die, may God ·punish me terribly** [do the same to me, and even more]**."**

45 **But the ·soldiers** [people] **said to Saul, "Must Jonathan die? Never! He is responsible for ·saving** [rescuing; delivering; Lthis great victory in] **Israel today! As surely as the LORD lives, not even a hair of his head will fall to the ground! ·Today Jonathan fought against the Philistines with God's help** […for he has worked with God today]**!" So the ·army** [people] **·saved** [rescued; redeemed] **Jonathan, and he did not die.**

46 **Then Saul stopped chasing the Philistines, and they** [Cthe Philistines] **went back to their own ·land** [territory; Lplace].

Saul Fights Israel's Enemies

47 **When Saul ·became king** [had secured/consolidated his rule/kingship] **over Israel, he fought against Israel's enemies ·all around** [on every side]. **He fought Moab, the Ammonites, Edom, the ·king** [*or* kings] **of Zobah, and the Philistines. Everywhere Saul ·went** [Lturned] **he ·defeated** [punished; routed] **Israel's enemies.** 48 **He ·fought bravely** [performed valiantly] **and ·defeated** [struck] **the Amalekites. He ·saved** [rescued; delivered] **the Israelites from ·their enemies who had robbed** [Lthe hand of those who plundered/pillaged] **them.**

49 **Saul's sons were Jonathan, Ishvi, and Malki-Shua. His ·older** [firstborn] **daughter was named Merab, and his younger daughter was named Michal.** 50 **Saul's wife was Ahinoam daughter of Ahimaaz. The commander of his army was Abner son of Ner, Saul's uncle.** 51 **Saul's father Kish and Abner's father Ner were sons of Abiel.**

52All Saul's life ·he fought hard against [there was bitter/fierce warfare with] the Philistines. When he saw strong or brave men, he ·took [drafted] them into his ·army [service; 8:11].

Saul Rejected as King

15 Samuel said to Saul, "The LORD sent me to ·appoint [anoint] you king over [Lhis people] Israel. Now listen to ·his message [Lthe words of the LORD]. 2This is what the LORD ·All-Powerful [Almighty; of Heaven's Armies; of hosts] says: 'When the Israelites came out of Egypt, the Amalekites ·tried to stop them from going to Canaan [opposed/laid a trap for them; Ex. 17:8–16]. So I will ·punish [settle accounts with] them [Deut. 25:17–19]. 3Now go, ·attack [crush; Lstrike] the Amalekites and ·completely destroy everything they own as an offering devoted to the LORD [devote to destruction; CIsrael was commanded to kill all the inhabitants of the land; Deut. 20:15–18]. Don't ·let anything live [spare anything]. Put to death men and women, children and small babies, ·cattle [ox] and sheep, camels and donkeys.' "

4So Saul ·called [mobilized] the army together at Telaim and ·counted [reviewed] them. There were two hundred thousand foot soldiers and ten thousand men from Judah. 5Then Saul went to the city of Amalek and set up an ambush in the ·ravine [valley]. 6He said to the Kenites [Gen. 15:19; Num. 24:21–22; Judg. 4:11; 5:24], "·Go [Move] away. Leave the Amalekites ·so that I won't [or I will] destroy you with them, because you showed ·kindness [lovingkindness; treaty faithfulness] to the Israelites when they came out of Egypt." So the Kenites moved away from the Amalekites.

7Then Saul ·defeated [Lstruck] the Amalekites. He fought them all the way from Havilah to Shur, ·at the border [east] of Egypt. 8He ·took [captured] King Agag of the Amalekites alive, but he ·killed all of Agag's army [totally destroyed all the people; 15:3] with the sword. 9Saul and the ·army let Agag live [people spared Agag], along with the best sheep, [Loxen,] fat cattle, and lambs. They let every ·good [valuable] animal live, because they did not want to ·destroy them [devote them to destruction; 15:3]. But when they found an animal that was ·weak [despised] or useless, they ·killed it [devoted it to destruction].

10Then the LORD spoke his word to Samuel: 11"I ·am sorry [regret] I made Saul king, because he has ·stopped [turned away from] following me and has not ·obeyed [carried out] my commands." Samuel was ·upset [distressed; angry; deeply moved], and he cried out to the LORD all night long.

12Early the next morning Samuel got up and went to ·meet [find] Saul. But the people told Samuel, "Saul has gone to Carmel, where he has put up a monument ·in his own honor [to himself]. Now he has gone down to Gilgal."

13When Samuel came to Saul, Saul said, "May the LORD bless you! I have ·obeyed [carried out; upheld] the LORD's commands."

14But Samuel said, "Then why do I hear ·cattle mooing [oxen lowing] and sheep bleating?"

15Saul answered, "The ·soldiers [people] took them from the Amalekites. They saved the best sheep and cattle to offer as sacrifices to the LORD your God, but we ·destroyed [devoted to destruction; 15:3] all the other animals."

16Samuel said to Saul, "·Stop [Enough]! Let me tell you what the LORD said to me last night."

Saul answered, "·Tell me [Speak]."

17 Samuel said, "·Once [Although] you ·didn't think much of yourself
[L are/were little/small in your own eyes], but now you have become the
·leader [head] of the tribes of Israel. The LORD ·appointed [anointed] you to
be king over Israel. 18 And he sent you on a mission. He said, 'Go and ·destroy
[devote to destruction; 15:3] those ·evil people [L sinners], the Amalekites.
Make war on them until all of them are ·dead [wiped out; exterminated;
consumed].' 19 Why didn't you obey the [L the voice of the] LORD? Why did
you ·take the best things [L rush for/pounce on the plunder/spoils]? Why did
you do what ·the LORD said was wrong [L was evil in the LORD's sight/eyes]?"
20 Saul said [L to Samuel], "But I did obey [L the voice of] the LORD. I ·did
what the LORD told [went on the mission the LORD gave] me to do. I
·destroyed [devoted to destruction; 15:3] all the Amalekites, and I brought
back Agag their king. 21 The ·soldiers [people] took [L from the plunder/
spoil] the best sheep and cattle to sacrifice to the LORD your God at Gilgal."
22 But Samuel answered,

"What pleases the LORD more:
burnt offerings and sacrifices
or obedience to his voice?
·It is better to obey [Obedience is better] than ·to sacrifice [sacrifice].
·It is better to listen to God than to offer [Submission/Heeding is better than] the fat of ·sheep [rams].
23 ·Disobedience [Rebellion] is as bad as the sin of ·sorcery [witchcraft; divination].
·Pride [Stubbornness; Arrogance; Presumption; Insubordination] is as bad as ·the sin of worshiping idols [idolatry].
You have rejected the LORD's ·command [word].
Now he rejects you as king."

24 Then Saul said to Samuel, "I have sinned. I ·didn't obey [broke; violated; transgressed] the LORD's commands and your ·words [instructions].
I was afraid of the people, and I ·did what they said [L listened to their
voice]. 25 Now, I beg you, ·forgive [pardon] my sin. Come back with me so
I may worship the LORD."
26 But Samuel said to Saul, "I won't go back with you. You rejected the
LORD's ·command [word], and now he rejects you as king of Israel."
27 As Samuel turned to leave, Saul ·caught [grabbed] his robe, and it
tore. 28 Samuel said to him, "The LORD has torn the kingdom of Israel
from you today and has given it to one of your neighbors [C David; 16:13]
who is better than you. 29 The LORD is the ·Eternal One [*or* Glory] of Israel.
He does not lie or change his mind. He is not a ·human being [mortal], so
he does not change his mind."
30 Saul answered, "I have sinned. But please ·honor [respect] me in
front of the elders of my people and in front of the Israelites. Come back
with me so that I can worship the LORD your God." 31 So Samuel went back
with Saul, and Saul worshiped the LORD.
32 Then Samuel said, "Bring me King Agag of the Amalekites."
Agag came to Samuel ·in chains [*or* cheerfully; hopefully; *or* haltingly],
but Agag thought, "Surely the ·threat [bitterness] of death has passed. [*or*
Surely, death is bitter]."
33 Samuel said to him, "Your sword made other mothers ·lose their children [childless]. Now your mother will ·have no children [be childless]."
And Samuel ·cut Agag to pieces [butchered Agag] before the LORD at Gilgal.
34 Then Samuel left and went to Ramah, but Saul went up to his home in

Gibeah [Lof Saul]. 35And Samuel never saw Saul again ·the rest of his life
[Luntil the day of his death], but he ·was sad [mourned; grieved] for Saul.
And the LORD ·was very sorry [regretted] he had made Saul king of Israel.

Samuel Goes to Bethlehem

16 The LORD said to Samuel, "How long will you ·continue to feel
sorry [mourn; grieve] for Saul? I have rejected him as king of
Israel. Fill your ·container [flask; Lhorn] with olive oil and go. I am
sending you to Jesse who lives in Bethlehem, because I have ·chosen
[selected; found myself] one of his sons to be king."
2But Samuel said, "·If [LHow can…?] I go, Saul will hear the news and
will try to kill me."
The LORD said, "Take a ·young calf [heifer] with you. Say, 'I have come
to offer a sacrifice to the LORD.' 3Invite Jesse to the sacrifice. Then I will tell
you what to do. You must ·appoint [anoint] the one I ·show you [indicate;
designate; name; Ltell you]."
4Samuel did what the LORD told him to do. When he arrived at
Bethlehem, the elders of Bethlehem ·shook with fear [trembled]. They
met him and asked, "Are you coming in peace?"
5Samuel answered, "Yes, I come in peace. I have come to make a sacrifice to the LORD. ·Set yourselves apart to the LORD [Consecrate/Purify/
Sanctify yourselves] and come to the sacrifice with me." Then he ·set Jesse
and his sons apart to the LORD, [consecrated/purified/sanctified Jesse and
his sons] and he invited them to come to the sacrifice.
6When they arrived, Samuel saw Eliab, and he thought, "Surely, here
stands before me the LORD's ·appointed [anointed]."
7But the LORD said to Samuel, "Don't look at ·how handsome Eliab is
[his appearance] or ·how tall he is [his height], because I have ·not chosen
[rejected] him. God does not see ·the same way [as] people see. People
look at ·the outside of a person [appearances; the outward appearance],
but the LORD looks ·at [on] the heart."
8Then Jesse called Abinadab and told him to ·pass by [walk in front of]
Samuel. But Samuel said, "The LORD has not chosen this man either."
9Then Jesse had Shammah pass by. But Samuel said, "No, the LORD has
not chosen this one." 10Jesse had seven of his sons ·pass by [presented to]
Samuel. But Samuel said to him, "The LORD has not chosen any of these."
11Then he asked Jesse, "Are these all the sons you have?"
Jesse answered, "I still have the youngest son. He is out taking care of
the sheep."
Samuel said, "Send for him. We will not sit down to eat until he arrives."
12So Jesse sent and had his youngest son brought in. He was ·a fine boy,
tanned [dark; ruddy], [Lwith beautiful eyes] and handsome.
The LORD said to Samuel, "·Go [Rise], ·appoint [anoint] him, because
he is the one."
13So Samuel took the ·container [flask; Lhorn] of olive oil and ·poured
it on Jesse's youngest son to appoint [anointed] him in front of his brothers. From that day on, the LORD's Spirit ·worked in [came powerfully
upon] David. Samuel then went back to Ramah.

David Serves Saul

14But the LORD's Spirit ·had left [departed from] Saul, and an ·evil [tor-
menting] spirit from the LORD ·troubled [terrorized; afflicted] him.
15Saul's servants said to him, "See, an ·evil [tormenting] spirit from
God is ·troubling [terrorizing; afflicting] you. 16Give ·us [Lyour servants]
the command to look for someone who can play the ·harp [lyre]. When

the ·evil [tormenting] spirit from God ·troubles [terrorizes; afflicts] you,
he will play, and you will ·feel better [be well].”
17So Saul said to his servants, “Find someone who can play well and
bring him to me.”
18One of the servants said, “I have seen a son of Jesse of Bethlehem play
the ·harp [lyre]. He is brave and ·courageous [a warrior]. He ·is a good
speaker [*or* has good judgment] and handsome, and the LORD is with
him.”
19Then Saul sent messengers to Jesse, saying, “Send me your son David,
·who is with the sheep [the shepherd].” 20So Jesse loaded a donkey with
bread, a ·leather bag [wineskin] full of wine, and a young goat, and he
sent them with his son David to Saul.
21When David came to Saul, he ·began to serve him [entered his service; Lstood before him]. Saul ·liked David [loved David very much] and
made him ·the officer who carried his armor [his armor bearer]. 22Saul
sent a message to Jesse, saying, “Let David ·stay and serve me [remain in
my service] because ·I like him [I am pleased with him; Lhe has found
grace/favor in my sight].”
23When the ·evil [tormenting] spirit from God ·troubled [terrorized;
afflicted] Saul, David would take his ·harp [lyre] and play. Then the ·evil
[tormenting] spirit would leave him, and Saul would feel ·better
[refreshed; soothed].

David and Goliath

17 The Philistines ·gathered [assembled; mustered] their armies
for ·war [battle]. They ·met [gathered; assembled; mustered]
at Socoh in Judah and camped at Ephes Dammim between Socoh and
Azekah. 2Saul and the Israelites ·gathered [assembled; mustered] in the
Valley of Elah and camped there and ·took their positions [drew up their
battle line] to fight the Philistines. 3The Philistines ·controlled [occu-
pied; stood on] one hill while the Israelites ·controlled [occupied; stood
on] another. The valley was between them.
4The Philistines had a champion fighter from Gath named Goliath. He
was ·about nine feet, four inches tall [Lsix cubits and a span].[n] He came
out of the Philistine camp 5with a bronze helmet on his head and a coat
of bronze ·armor [mail; scale-armor] that weighed ·about one hundred
twenty-five pounds [Lfive thousand shekels]. 6He wore bronze ·protectors
[greaves] on his legs, and he had a bronze spear ·on his back [across his
shoulders]. 7The wooden part of his larger spear was like a weaver’s ·rod
[beam], and its ·blade [head] weighed ·about fifteen pounds [Lsix hundred shekels of iron]. The ·officer who carried his shield [shield bearer]
walked in front of him.
8Goliath stood and shouted to the ·Israelite soldiers [Lranks of Israel],
“Why have you ·taken positions [lined up] for battle? ·I am [LAm I not...?]
a Philistine, and you are Saul’s servants! Choose a man and send him to
fight me. 9If he can fight and kill me, we will be your ·servants [slaves].
But if I can kill him, you will be our ·servants [slaves] [Land serve us].”
10Then he said, “Today I stand and ·dare [defy; challenge] the ·army
[ranks] of Israel! ·Send one of your men [LGive me a man] to fight me!”
11When Saul and the Israelites heard the Philistine’s words, they were
·very scared [dismayed and terrified].

17:4 six cubits and a span Hebrew copies read “six cubits and a span.” Some Greek copies and one Dead Sea Scroll copy read “four cubits and a span” (about six feet, nine inches).

12Now David was the son of Jesse, an Ephrathite from Bethlehem in Judah. Jesse had eight sons. In Saul's time Jesse was an old man [16:1–13]. 13His three oldest sons followed Saul to the war. The ·first [Lfirstborn] son was Eliab, the second was Abinadab, and the third was Shammah. 14David was the youngest. Jesse's three oldest sons ·followed [remained with] Saul, 15but David went back and forth from Saul to Bethlehem, where he took care of his father's sheep.

16For forty days the Philistine came out every morning and evening and ·stood before the Israelite army [Ltook his stand].

17Jesse said to his son David, "Take [Lquickly] this ·half bushel [Lepah] of ·cooked [roasted] grain and ten loaves of bread to your brothers in the camp. 18Also take ten ·pieces [cuts] of cheese to the commander [Lof thousands]. See how your brothers are and bring back some ·proof to show me that they are all right [news/token/assurance of them]. 19They are with Saul and the Israelite army in the Valley of Elah, fighting against the Philistines."

20Early in the morning David left the sheep with ·another shepherd [La keeper]. He took the food and left as Jesse had ·told [directed; ordered] him. When David arrived at the camp, the army was going out to their battle positions, shouting their war cry. 21The Israelites and Philistines were lining up their men ·to face each other in battle [army against army]. 22David left ·the food [his baggage/bundle/things] with the man who kept the supplies and ran to the battle line to ·talk to [greet; Linquire about the welfare of] his brothers. 23While he was talking with them, Goliath, the Philistine champion from Gath, came out [Lfrom the Philistine ranks]. He shouted things against Israel as usual, and David heard him. 24When the Israelites saw Goliath, they were very much afraid and ·ran away [fled].

25They said, "·Look at [LHave you seen…?] this man! He keeps coming out to ·challenge [defy] Israel. The king will give ·much money [a great reward; great wealth] to whoever kills him. He will also let whoever kills him marry his daughter. And his father's family will ·not have to pay taxes [be made free] in Israel."

26David asked the men who stood near him, "What will be done to reward the man who kills this Philistine and takes away ·the shame [this disgrace/reproach] from Israel? Who does this ·uncircumcised [pagan] Philistine think he is? Does he think he can ·speak against [taunt; defy; challenge] the armies of the living God?"

27The Israelites told David what would be done for the man who would kill Goliath.

28When David's oldest brother Eliab heard David talking with the ·soldiers [men], ·he was angry with [Lhis anger burned against] David. He asked David, "Why did you come here? Who's taking care of those few sheep of yours in the ·desert [wilderness]? I know you are ·proud [insolent; impudent] and ·wicked at heart [deceitful]. You came down here just to watch the battle."

29David asked, "Now what have I done wrong? Can't I even ·talk [ask a question]?" 30When he turned [away] to other people and asked the same questions, they gave him the same answer as before. 31·Yet [Then] what David said was told to Saul, and he sent for David.

32David said to Saul, "Don't let anyone ·be discouraged [lose heart because of him]. I, your servant, will go and fight this Philistine!"

33Saul answered, "You can't go out against this Philistine and fight him.

You're only a ·boy [youth]. Goliath has been a warrior since ·he was a
young man [his youth]."
34But David said to Saul, "I, your servant, have been keeping my
father's sheep. When a lion or bear came and ·took [carried off; stole] a
·sheep [lamb] from the flock, 35I would chase it. I would ·attack [Lstrike]
it and ·save [rescue] the sheep from its ·mouth [jaws]. ·When [If] it
·attacked [turned on] me, I caught it by its ·fur [*or* jaw] and hit [Lstruck]
it and killed it. 36I, your servant, have ·killed [Lstruck] both ·a [the] lion
and ·a [the] bear! This ·uncircumcised [pagan] Philistine will be like
them, because he has ·spoken against [taunted; defied; challenged] the
armies of the living God. 37The LORD who ·saved [rescued; delivered] me
from a lion and a bear will ·save [rescue; deliver] me from this Philistine."
Saul said to David, "Go, and may the LORD be with you." 38Saul put his
own ·clothes [tunic] on David. He put a bronze helmet on his head and
dressed him in ·armor [mail; a breastplate]. 39David put on Saul's sword
[Lover it] and tried to walk around, but he was not used to all the armor
Saul had put on him.

He said to Saul, "I can't go in this, because I'm not used to ·it [them]."
Then David took it all off. 40He took his ·stick [staff] in his hand and
chose five smooth stones from a ·stream [wadi]. He put them in his shepherd's bag and grabbed his sling. Then he ·went to meet [walked toward;
approached] the Philistine.
41At the same time, the Philistine was ·coming closer to [approaching]
David. ·The man who held his shield [His shield bearer] walked in front of
him. 42When Goliath looked at David and saw that he was only a ·boy [youth],
·tanned [ruddy] and handsome, he looked down on David with ·disgust
[contempt; scorn; disdain]. 43The Philistine said to David, "·Do you think I
am [Am I] a dog, that you come at me with a ·stick [staff]?" He used his gods'
names to curse David. 44He said to David, "Come here. I'll ·feed your body
[Lgive your flesh] to the birds of the air and the wild animals [Lof the field]!"
45But David said to ·him [the Philistine], "You come to me using a
sword ·and two spears [a spear and a javelin]. But I come to you in the
name of the LORD ·All-Powerful [Almighty; of Heaven's Armies; of hosts],
the God of the armies of Israel! You have ·spoken against [taunted; defied;
challenged] him. 46Today the LORD will ·hand you over to me [deliver you
into my hands], and I'll ·kill you [Lstrike you down] and cut off your head.
Today I'll feed the bodies of the Philistine soldiers to the birds of the air
and the wild animals. Then all the ·world [earth] will know there is a God
in Israel! 47Everyone ·gathered here [in this assembly/crowd] will know
the LORD does not need swords or spears to ·save [rescue; deliver] people
[Ps. 46:9]. The battle ·belongs to him [is the LORD's], and he will ·hand you
over to us [give you into our hands]."
48As ·Goliath [Lthe Philistine] came ·near [closer] to attack him, David
ran quickly [Ltoward the battle line] to meet him. 49He took a stone from
his bag, put it into his sling, and slung it. The stone hit the Philistine and
went deep into his forehead, and Goliath fell facedown on the ground.
50So David ·defeated [triumphed/prevailed over] the Philistine with
only a sling and a stone. He hit him and killed him. He did not even have
a sword in his hand. 51Then David ran and stood ·beside [over] him. He
took Goliath's sword out of its ·holder [sheath] and killed him ·by cutting
[*or* and then cut] off his head.

When the Philistines saw that their champion was dead, they turned

and ·ran [fled]. 52The men of Israel and Judah ·shouted [surged forward
with a shout] and chased the Philistines all the way to the entrance of the
city of Gath and to the gates of Ekron.
The Philistines' bodies lay on the Shaaraim road as far as Gath and
Ekron. 53The ·Israelites [Lsons/Tchildren of Israel] returned after chasing
the Philistines and ·robbed [sacked; plundered] their camp. 54David took
Goliath's head to Jerusalem and put Goliath's weapons in his own tent.
55When Saul saw David go out to ·meet [fight] Goliath, Saul asked
Abner, commander of the army, "Abner, ·who is that young man's father
[whose son is that young boy]?"
Abner answered, "·As surely as you live [LBy your life/soul], my king, I
don't know."
56The king said, "Find out whose son ·he [the lad/youth] is."
57When David came back from ·killing [striking] ·Goliath [the
Philistine], Abner brought him to Saul. David was still holding ·Goliath's
[the Philistine's] head.
58Saul asked him, "Young man, ·who is your father [whose son are
you]?"
David answered, "I am the son of your servant Jesse of Bethlehem."

Saul Fears David

18 When David finished talking with Saul, ·Jonathan felt very
close to David [Lthe life/soul of Jonathan was knit/bound to
the life/soul of David]. He loved David as much as ·he loved himself [Lhis
own life/soul]. 2Saul kept David with him from that day on and did not
let him go home to his father's house. 3Jonathan made an ·agreement
[covenant; solemn pact; treaty] with David, because he loved David as
much as ·himself [Lhis own life/soul]. 4He took off his ·coat [robe;
Cperhaps a royal robe] and gave it to David, along with his ·armor [tunic],
including his sword, bow, and belt [Can expression of loyalty to David
and perhaps even giving him the future kingship].
5 [LWherever] Saul sent David ·to fight in different battles, and David
[out, he] was very successful. Then Saul put David ·over [in command of]
the soldiers, which pleased Saul's ·officers [servants] and all the other
people.
6After David had ·killed [Lstruck] the Philistine, he and the men
returned home. Women came out from all the towns of Israel to meet
King Saul. They sang songs of joy, danced, and played tambourines and
·stringed [musical] instruments. 7As they played, they sang,

"Saul has ·killed thousands of his enemies [Tslain his thousands],
·but [and] David has ·killed [Tslain his] tens of thousands."

8The women's ·song upset [refrain/saying displeased/Lwas evil in the
eyes/sight of] Saul, and he became very angry. He thought, "The women
·say David has killed [credit/ascribe to David] tens of thousands, but they
·say I have killed [credit/ascribe to me] only thousands. The only thing
left for him to have is the kingdom!" 9So Saul watched David closely from
then on, because he was jealous.
10The next day an ·evil [tormenting] spirit from God ·rushed upon
[overwhelmed; seized; possessed] Saul, and he ·prophesied [*or* raved
madly] in his house. David was playing the harp as he usually did, but
Saul had a spear in his hand. 11Saul threw the spear, thinking, "I'll pin
David to the wall." But David ·escaped from [eluded] him twice.
12The LORD was with David but had ·left [departed/withdrawn/turned

away from] Saul. So Saul was afraid of David. 13He sent David away and made him commander of a thousand soldiers. So David led them ·in battle [Lout and back in]. 14He ·had great success [prospered] in everything he did because the LORD was with him. 15When Saul saw that David ·was very successful [greatly prospered], he ·feared [dreaded; was in awe of] David even more. 16But all the people of Israel and Judah loved David because he led them ·well in battle [Lout and back in].

Saul's Daughter Marries David

17Saul said to David, "Here is my older daughter Merab. I will ·let you marry her [Lgive her to you as a wife]. ·All I ask is that you remain [*or* But first you must show yourself] brave [Lfor me] and fight the LORD's battles." Saul thought, "I won't ·have to kill David [Lraise a hand against him]. The Philistines will do that."

18But David answered Saul, saying, "Who am I? ·My family is not important enough [What is my father's family in Israel…?] for me to become the king's son-in-law." 19So, when the time ·came [should have come] for Saul's daughter Merab to marry David, Saul gave her instead to Adriel of Meholah [Las a wife].

20Now Saul's other daughter, Michal, loved David. When they told Saul, ·he was pleased [Lthe matter was right in his eyes]. 21He thought, "I will ·let her marry [Lgive her to] David. ·Then […so that] she will be a ·trap [snare] for him, and the ·Philistines will defeat him [Lhand of the Philistines will be against him]." So Saul said to David ·a second time, "You may [You have a second chance to] become my son-in-law."

22And Saul ordered his servants to talk with David ·in private [secretly] and say, "Look, the king ·likes [is delighted with] you. His servants love you. You should ·be [become] his son-in-law."

23Saul's servants said these words ·to [Lin the ears of] David, but David answered, "Do you think it is ·easy [La small/trivial thing] to become the king's son-in-law? I am poor and ·unimportant [have no position/reputation; CDavid cannot afford to pay the expected dowry]."

24When Saul's servants told him what David had said, 25Saul said, "Tell David, 'The king doesn't want ·money [La dowry/bride price] for the bride. All he wants is a hundred Philistine foreskins to get ·even with [revenge on] his enemies.'" Saul planned to let ·the Philistines kill David [LDavid fall at the hands of the Philistines].

26When Saul's servants told this to David, ·he was pleased [he was happy/delighted; Lthe thing was right in the eyes of David] to become the king's son-in-law. [LSo before the days were expired/fulfilled…] 27He and his men went out and killed two hundred Philistines. David brought all their foreskins [Land counted them out] to ·Saul [the king] so he could be the king's son-in-law. Then Saul gave him his daughter Michal for his wife. 28Saul ·saw [realized; Lsaw and knew] that the LORD was with David and that his daughter Michal loved David. 29So he grew even more afraid of David, and he was David's enemy ·all his life [from then on; Lall the days].

30The Philistine commanders continued to go out to fight the Israelites, but every time, David was more ·skillful [successful; wise] than Saul's officers. So he became ·famous [highly esteemed; Lhis name became extremely valuable].

Saul Tries to Kill David

19 Saul told his son Jonathan and all his servants to kill David, but Jonathan ·liked [delighted in] David very much. 2So he warned David, "My father Saul is ·looking for a chance [Lseeking] to kill

you. ·Watch out [Be on guard] in the morning. Hide in a secret place. 3I
will go out and stand with my father in the field where you are hiding,
and I'll talk to him about you. Then I'll let you know what I find out."

4When Jonathan talked to Saul his father, he ·said good things about
[spoke well of] David. Jonathan said, "The king should ·do no wrong to
[not harm/sin against] your servant David since he has ·done nothing
wrong to [not harmed/sinned against] you. What he has done has ·helped
[benefited; served] you greatly. 5·David risked his life [LHe took his life in
his hand] when he ·killed Goliath the Philistine [Lstruck the Philistine],
and the LORD won a great victory for all Israel. You saw it and ·were happy
[rejoiced]. Why would you ·do wrong against David? He's innocent [L…
sin against innocent blood?]. There's no reason to kill him!"

6Saul listened to Jonathan and then ·made this promise [vowed; swore]:
"As surely as the LORD lives, David won't be put to death."

7·So [Afterward] Jonathan called to David and told him everything
that had been said. He brought David to Saul, and David ·was with
[served] Saul as before.

8When war broke out again, David went out to ·fight [Lstrike] the
Philistines. He ·defeated them [attacked them with great force], and they
ran away from him.

9But once again an ·evil [tormenting] spirit from the LORD ·rushed
upon [overwhelmed; seized; possessed] Saul as he was sitting in his house
with his spear in his hand. David was playing the ·harp [lyre]. 10Saul tried
to pin David to the wall with his spear, but David ·jumped out of the way
[slipped away; eluded him]. So Saul's spear ·went into [stuck in] the wall,
and David ·ran away [escaped] that night.

11Saul sent ·messengers [agents; soldiers] to David's house to watch it
and to kill him in the morning. But Michal, David's wife, warned him,
saying, "Tonight you must ·run for [save] your life. If you don't, you will
be dead in the morning." 12So she let David down out of a window, and he
·ran away [fled] and escaped. 13Then Michal took an ·idol [household
image; Lteraphim; Cprobably household gods; Gen. 31:19], laid it on the
bed, covered it with ·clothes [blankets], and put goats' hair at its head.

14Saul sent ·messengers [agents; soldiers] to take David prisoner, but
Michal said, "He is sick."

15Saul sent ·them [Lmessengers; agents; soldiers] back to see David, saying, "Bring him to me on his bed so I can kill him."

16When the ·messengers [agents; soldiers] entered David's house, they
found just an ·idol [household image; 19:13] on the bed with goats' hair
on its head.

17Saul said to Michal, "Why did ·you trick [deceive; betray] me this
way? You let my enemy go so he could ·run away [escape]!"

Michal answered Saul, "David told me ·if I did not help him escape, he
would kill me [L"Let me go. Why should I kill you?]."

18After David had [Lfled and] escaped from Saul, he went to Samuel at
Ramah and told him everything Saul had done to him. Then David and
Samuel went to Naioth and stayed there. 19Saul heard that David was in
Naioth at Ramah. 20So he sent ·messengers [agents; soldiers] to capture
him. But they met a group of prophets ·prophesying [in a frenzy], with
Samuel standing there ·leading [in charge of] them. So the Spirit of God
·entered [came upon] Saul's men, and they also ·prophesied [fell into a
frenzy].

21When Saul heard the news, he sent more ·messengers [agents; soldiers], but they also ·prophesied [fell into a frenzy]. Then he sent ·messengers [agents; soldiers] a third time, but they also ·prophesied [fell into a frenzy]. 22Finally, Saul himself went to Ramah, to the [large; great] well at Secu. He asked, "Where are Samuel and David?"

The people answered, "In Naioth at Ramah."

23When Saul went to Naioth at Ramah, the Spirit of God also ·rushed upon [overwhelmed; seized; possessed] him. And he walked on, ·prophesying [in a frenzy,] until he came to Naioth at Ramah. 24He ·took [tore; stripped] off his ·robes [clothes] and prophesied in front of Samuel. He lay ·that way [[L]naked] all day and all night. That is why people ask, "Is ·even [also] Saul one of the prophets?"

Jonathan Helps David

20 Then David ·ran away [fled] from Naioth in Ramah. He went to Jonathan and asked, "What have I done? What is my ·crime [guilt; iniquity]? How did I ·sin against [offend; wrong] your father? Why is he ·trying to kill me [[L]seeking my life]?"

2Jonathan answered, "·No [Never; Far from it]! You won't die! See, my father doesn't do anything ·great or small [important or unimportant] without first ·telling [confiding in] me. Why would he ·keep [hide] this from me? It's not true!"

3But David ·took an oath [vowed; swore], saying, "Your father knows very well that ·you like me [[L]I have found favor in your sight]. He says to himself, 'Jonathan must not know about it, or he will be ·upset [hurt; grieved].' As surely as the LORD lives and as you live, I am only a step away from death!"

4Jonathan said to David, "I'll do ·anything you want me to do [[L]for you whatever you say]."

5So David said, "Look, tomorrow is the New Moon festival [Num. 29:6; 2 Chr. 8:13; Ezra 3:5; Col. 2:16]. I am supposed to eat with the king, but let me hide in the field until the ·third evening [[L]evening of the third day]. 6If your father notices I am gone, tell him, 'David begged ·me to let him go [[L]to hurry/run] to his hometown of Bethlehem. Every year at this time his ·family group [whole clan] offers a sacrifice.' 7If your father says, '·Fine [Very well; Good],' ·I am safe [[L]your servant is well]. But if he becomes angry, you will know that he ·wants to hurt me [is determined to harm me; has an evil plan]. 8Jonathan, ·be loyal [show kindness/faithful love] to me, your servant. You have made an ·agreement [covenant; solemn pact] with me before the LORD. If I ·am guilty [have sinned], you may kill me yourself! Why ·hand me over [betray me] to your father?"

9Jonathan answered, "·No, never [[L]Far be it from you]! If I learn that my father ·plans to hurt you [[L]decided on evil], ·I will warn you [wouldn't I tell you?]!"

10David asked, "Who will let me know if your father answers you ·unkindly [harshly]?"

11Then Jonathan said [[L]to David], "Come, let's go out into the field." So the two of them went out into the field.

12Jonathan said to David, "·I promise this before [[L]By] the LORD, the God of Israel: ·At [By] this same time ·the day after tomorrow [*or* tomorrow or the next day], I will ·find out how my father feels [sound out my father]. If he feels good toward you, I will send word to you and let you know. 13But if my father plans to ·hurt [harm; kill] you, I will let you

know and send you away safely. May the LORD ·punish me terribly [Ldeal severely with me, and worse,] **if I don't do this. And may the LORD be with you as he ·has been** [used to be] **with my father. 14·But show me the kindness of the LORD as long as I live so that I may not die** [*or* If I am still alive, show me the faithful love/loyalty of the LORD. But if I die…]. **15You must never ·stop showing** [Lcut off] **your ·kindness** [faithful love/loyalty] **to my ·family** [Lhouse], **even when the LORD has ·destroyed** [exterminated; Lcut off] **all your enemies from the** [Lface of the] **earth."**

16So Jonathan ·made [Lcut] **an ·agreement** [covenant; solemn pact] **with David. He said, "May the LORD ·hold David's enemies responsible** [*or* destroy David's enemies]." **17And Jonathan asked David to repeat his ·promise** [vow; oath] **of love for him, because he loved David as much as he loved ·himself** [Lhis own life/soul].

18Jonathan said to David, "Tomorrow is the New Moon festival [20:5]. **Your ·seat** [place] **will be empty, so my father will miss you. 19·On the third day** [The day after tomorrow] **go to the place where you hid when this trouble began. Wait by the ·rock Ezel** [stone pile; mound of rock]. **20I will shoot three arrows to the side of the rock as if I am shooting at a target. 21Then I will send a boy to find the arrows. If I say to him, 'The arrows are ·near you** [Lon this side]; **bring them here,' you may come out of hiding. You are safe. As the LORD lives, there is no ·danger** [trouble; harm]. **22But if I say to the ·boy** [youngster], **'Look, the arrows are ·beyond you** [further on],**' you must go, because the LORD is sending you away. 23Remember ·what we talked about** [the promise we made]. **The LORD is a witness between you and me forever."**

24So David hid in the field. When the New Moon festival [20:5] **came, the king sat down to eat. 25He sat where he ·always** [usually; customarily] **sat, near the wall. Jonathan sat ·across from** [facing] **him, and Abner sat next to Saul, but David's place was empty. 26That day Saul said nothing. He thought, "Maybe something has happened to David so that he is unclean.** [LYes, surely he is unclean; Critually unclean so he could not participate in a religious ceremony; Lev. 11–15] **27But the next day was the second day of the month, and David's place was still empty. So Saul said to Jonathan, "Why hasn't the son of Jesse come to the ·feast** [meal] **yesterday or today?"**

28Jonathan answered [LSaul], **"David begged me to let him go to Bethlehem. 29He said, 'Let me go, because our ·family** [whole clan] **has a sacrifice in the town, and my brother has ·ordered** [commanded] **me to be there. Now if I ·am your friend** [Lhave found favor in your sight/eyes], **please let me go to see my brothers.' That is why he has not come to the king's table."**

30Then Saul ·became very angry with [Lburned with anger against] **Jonathan. He said, "You son of a ·wicked, worthless woman** [whore; rebellious slut]! **·I** [LDo I not…?] **know you are on the side of David son of Jesse! ·You bring shame on yourself and on your mother who gave birth to you** [L…to your own shame and the shame of your mother's nakedness]. **31As long as Jesse's son lives** [Lon this earth], **·you will never be king or have a kingdom** [Lneither you nor your kingdom will be established]. **Now send for David and bring him to me. He ·must** [deserves to] **die!"**

32Jonathan asked his father, "Why should David be killed? What wrong has he done?" 33Then Saul threw his spear at Jonathan, ·trying to kill [Lto strike] **him. So Jonathan knew that his father ·really wanted** [was

determined] to kill David. 34Jonathan ·was very angry [rose in fierce
anger] **and left the table. That second day of the ·month** [*or* New Moon
festival] **he refused to eat. He ·was ashamed of his father and upset over
David** [grieved at his father's shameful treatment of David; *or* grieved for
David and because his father had disgraced/insulted/dishonored him].
**35The next morning Jonathan went out to the field to meet David as
they had agreed. He had a young boy with him. 36Jonathan said to the
boy, "Run and find the arrows I shoot." When he ran, Jonathan shot an
arrow beyond him. 37The boy ran to the place where Jonathan's arrow
fell, but Jonathan called, "The arrow is ·beyond** [further ahead of] **you!"
38Then he shouted** [Lto the boy], **"Hurry! Go quickly! Don't ·stop** [stay;
linger]**!" The boy picked up the arrow and brought it back to his master.
39(The boy ·knew nothing about what this meant** [suspected nothing];
only Jonathan and David ·knew [understood].**) 40Then Jonathan gave his
weapons to the boy and told him, "Go** [Lbring them] **back to town."**
**41When the boy left, David came out from the south side of the rock.
He bowed facedown on the ground ·before Jonathan three** [three] **times.
Then David and Jonathan kissed each other and cried together, but David
cried the more.**
42Jonathan said to David, "Go in ·peace [safety]. **We have ·promised**
[vowed; sworn] **by the** [Lname of the] **LORD ·that we will be friends** [to
each other]. **We said, 'The LORD will ·be a witness** [Lbe] **between you and
me, and between our descendants always.'" Then ·David** [Lhe got up and]
left, and Jonathan went back to town.

David Goes to See Ahimelech

**21 David went to Nob to see Ahimelech the priest. Ahimelech
·shook with fear** [trembled; Cperhaps rumors of Saul's displea-
sure were circulating] **when he saw David, and he asked, "Why are you
alone? Why is no one with you?"**
2David answered him, "The king ·gave me a special order [sent me on
a mission; commissioned me]. **He told me, 'No one must know ·what I am
sending you to do or what I told you to do** [about the mission I am sending you on]**.' I told my** [Lyoung] **men ·where to meet me** [to meet me at a
certain place]. **3Now, what ·food do you have with you** [Lis at hand]**? Give
me five loaves of bread or anything you find."**
4The priest said to David, "I don't have any ·plain [ordinary; regular]
bread here, but I do have some ·holy [consecrated; holy] **bread** [Cfrom the
Table of Presence; Ex. 25:23–30]. **You may eat it if your men have ·kept
themselves from** [not recently slept with] **women** [Csexual relations rendered a man ritually unclean; Lev. 15:16–18]**."**
5David answered [Lthe priest and said to him], **"No women have been
near us ·for days** [*or* as usual on a campaign]. **My men always keep ·them-
selves** [their bodies/Lvessels] **holy, even ·when we do ordinary work** [on an
ordinary/common journey]. **And this is especially true when the ·work**
[journey] **is holy."**
6So the priest gave David the ·holy [consecrated] **bread ·from the presence of God** [—the bread of the Presence—] **because there was no other.
Each day the holy bread was replaced with ·hot** [fresh] **bread.**
**7One of Saul's servants happened to be there that day. He had been
·held there** [detained] **before the LORD** [Cfor some unspecified ritual pur-
pose]. **He was Doeg the Edomite, the chief of Saul's shepherds.**
8David asked Ahimelech, "Do you have a spear or sword here? The

king's business was very ·important [urgent], so I ·left without [brought
neither…nor] my sword or any other weapon."
9The priest answered, "The sword of Goliath the Philistine, the one
you ·killed [Lstruck] in the Valley of Elah [ch. 17], is here. It is wrapped in
a cloth behind the ·holy vest [ephod; Ex. 28:6–14]. If you want it, you may
take it. There's no other sword here but that one."
David said, "There is ·no other sword [none] like it. Give it to me."

David Goes to Gath

10That day David ·ran away [Lfled] from Saul and went to Achish king
of Gath [Ca major Philistine town]. 11But the servants of Achish said to
him, "·This is [LIsn't this…?] David, the king of the ·Israelites [Lland].
·He's [LIsn't he…?] the man they dance and sing about, saying:
'Saul has ·killed thousands of his enemies [Tslain his thousands],
·but [and] David has ·killed [Tslain his] tens of thousands [18:7].'"
12David ·paid attention to [Ltook to heart] these words and was very
much afraid of Achish king of Gath. 13So he ·pretended to be crazy in
front of Achish and his servants [Lchanged his behavior in their eyes/pres-
ence]. ·While he was with them [LIn their hands], he acted like a madman
and ·clawed [scratched; scribbled] on the doors of the gate and ·let spit
run [drooled] down his beard.
14Achish said to his servants, "Look at the man! He's crazy! Why do
you bring him to me? 15 ·I [Don't I…?] have enough madmen. I don't
need you to bring him here to act like this in front of me! ·Don't let him
in [Must this one come into…?] my house!"

David at Adullam and Mizpah

22 David ·left Gath [Lwent from there] and ·escaped to [took refuge in] the cave of Adullam [Cin the lowlands of Judah,
southwest of Jerusalem]. When his brothers and ·other relatives [Lhis
father's household] heard that he was there, they went to ·see him [join
him; Lhim]. 2Everyone who was in ·trouble [distress], or ·who owed
money [in debt], or who was ·unsatisfied [discontented; had a grievance]
gathered around David, and he became their ·leader [captain; com-
mander]. About four hundred men were with him.
3From there David went to Mizpah in Moab and spoke to the king of
Moab. He said, "Please let my father and mother come and stay with you
until I learn what God ·is going [intends] to do for me." 4So he left them
with the king of Moab, and they stayed with him as long as David was
hiding in the stronghold.
5But the prophet Gad said to David, "Don't stay in the stronghold. ·Go
[Return] to the land of Judah." So David left and went to the forest of Hereth.

Saul Destroys Ahimelech's Family

6Saul heard that David and his men had been ·seen [discovered; located].
Saul was sitting under the tamarisk tree on the hill at Gibeah, and all his
officers were standing around him. He had a spear in his hand. 7Saul said
to them, "·Listen [Hear now], men of Benjamin! Do you think the son of
Jesse will give all of you fields and vineyards? Will David make you commanders over thousands of men or hundreds of men? 8·You have all made
plans [LIs that why you have all conspired…?] against me! No one tells me
when my son makes an ·agreement [covenant; solemn pact; treaty] with
the son of Jesse! No one ·cares about [feels sorry/pity for] me! No one tells
me when my son has ·encouraged [stirred up; incited] my servant to
·ambush [lie in wait for] me this very day!"
9Doeg the Edomite, who was standing there with Saul's ·officers [officials;

servants], said, "I saw the son of Jesse. He came to see Ahimelech son of Ahitub at Nob. 10Ahimelech ·prayed to [consulted; inquired of] the LORD for David and gave him ·food [provisions] and gave him the sword of Goliath the Philistine."

11Then the king sent for the priest Ahimelech son of Ahitub and for all of ·Ahimelech's relatives [Lhis father's household] who were priests at Nob. And they all came to the king. 12Saul said to Ahimelech, "Listen now, son of Ahitub."

Ahimelech answered, "·Yes, master [LHere I am, my lord/king]."

13Saul said, "Why ·are [have] you and Jesse's son [Lconspired] against me? You gave him bread and a sword! You ·prayed to [consulted; inquired of] God for him. David has ·turned [rebelled; conspired; Lrisen up] against me and is ·waiting [lying in wait/ambush] ·to attack [for] me even now!"

14Ahimelech answered [Lthe king], "·You have no other servant who [LWho of all your servants…?] is as ·loyal [faithful] as David, your own son-in-law and captain of your bodyguards. Everyone in your house ·respects [honors] him. 15·That was not [LWas today…?] the first time I ·prayed to [consulted; inquired of] God for David. Don't ·blame [accuse; charge] me or any of my relatives. I, your servant, know nothing about ·what is going on [all this; this whole affair]."

16But the king said, "Ahimelech, you and all your ·relatives [Lfather's household] ·must [will surely] die!" 17Then he told the ·guards [*or* bodyguard] at his side, "·Go [Turn; Forward] and kill the priests of the LORD, because ·they are on David's side [Ltheir hand is with David]. They knew he was running away, but they didn't ·tell [warn] me."

But the king's ·officers [Lservants] refused to ·kill [attack; raise a hand against] the priests of the LORD.

18Then the king ordered Doeg, "·Go [Turn; Forward] and ·kill [attack; strike] the priests." So Doeg the Edomite ·went [turned] and ·killed [attacked; struck] the priests. That day he killed eighty-five men who wore the linen ·holy vest [ephod; Ca distinctively priestly garment; Ex. 28:6–14]. 19He also ·killed [struck; put to the sword] the people of Nob, the city of the priests. With the sword he killed men, women, children, babies, ·cattle [oxen], donkeys, and sheep.

20But Abiathar, a son of Ahimelech, who was the son of Ahitub, escaped. He ·ran away [fled] and joined David. 21He told David that Saul had killed the LORD's priests. 22Then David told him, "Doeg the Edomite was there at Nob that day. I knew he would surely tell Saul. So I ·am responsible for [caused] the death of all your father's ·family [household]. 23Stay with me. Don't be afraid. The man who ·wants to kill you [Lseeks your life] also ·wants to kill me [Lseeks my life]. You will be safe with me."

David Saves the People of Keilah

23 ·Someone told [News came to; LThey told] David, "Look, the Philistines are fighting ·against [at] Keilah and ·stealing grain from [Lrobbing; plundering; looting] the threshing floors."

2David ·asked [inquired of] the LORD, "Should I go and ·fight [attack; Lstrike] these Philistines?"

The LORD answered him, "Go. ·Attack [LStrike] the Philistines, and ·save [rescue; deliver] Keilah."

3But David's men said to him, "We're afraid here in Judah. We will be more afraid if we go to Keilah ·where the Philistine army is [Lagainst the ranks of the Philistines]."

4David ·again asked [inquired again of] the LORD, and the LORD [Lagain]
answered, "Go down to Keilah. I will ·help you defeat [Lgive into your
hand] the Philistines." 5So David and his men went to Keilah and fought
the Philistines and took their cattle. David ·killed [slaughtered] many
Philistines and ·saved [rescued; delivered] the people of Keilah. 6(Now
Abiathar son of Ahimelech had brought the ·holy vest [ephod] ·with him
[Lin his hand] when he came to David at Keilah [Cthe ephod probably held
the Urim and Thummim used to determine God's will; Ex. 28:30].)

Saul Chases David

7Someone told Saul that David was now at Keilah. Saul said, "God has
·handed David over to me [Lmade a stranger of him into my hand; Cthe
Hebrew is obscure]! He has ·trapped [imprisoned] himself, because he
has entered a town with gates and bars [CSaul could lay siege to such a
town]." 8Saul called all his army together for battle, and they prepared to
go down to Keilah to ·attack [Lbesiege] David and his men.
9David learned Saul was ·making evil plans [plotting evil] against him.
So he said to Abiathar the priest, "Bring the ·holy vest [ephod]." 10David
prayed, "LORD, God of Israel, ·I have [Lyour servant has] heard that Saul
plans to come to Keilah to destroy the town because ·of me [I am here].
11Will the ·leaders [citizens; men] of Keilah ·hand me over [surrender/
betray me] to Saul? Will Saul come down to Keilah, as I heard? LORD, God
of Israel, tell me, your servant!"
The LORD answered, "Saul will come down."
12Again David asked, "Will the ·leaders [citizens; men] of Keilah ·hand
[surrender; betray] me and my men over to Saul?"
The LORD answered, "They will [Lsurrender/betray you]."
13So David and his six hundred men left Keilah and ·kept moving from
place to place [Lwent/roamed wherever they could]. When Saul found out
that David had escaped from Keilah, he ·did not go there [gave up pur-
suit/the campaign].
14David stayed in the ·desert [wilderness] ·hideouts [strongholds] and
in the hills of the ·Desert [Wilderness] of Ziph. Every day Saul looked for
David, but the LORD did not ·surrender David to him [Lgive David into his
hand].
15While David was at Horesh in the ·Desert [Wilderness] of Ziph, he
learned that Saul was coming to kill him. 16But Saul's son Jonathan went
to David at Horesh and ·strengthened his faith [encouraged him;
Lstrengthened his hand] in God. 17Jonathan told him, "Don't be afraid,
because [Lthe hand of] my father Saul won't ·touch [Lfind] you. You will
be king of Israel, and I will be ·second [next] to you. Even my father Saul
knows this." 18The two of them ·made [Lcut] an ·agreement [covenant;
solemn pact] before the LORD. Then Jonathan went home, but David
stayed at Horesh.
19The people from Ziph went to Saul at Gibeah and told him, "David is
hiding in our land. He's at the ·hideouts [strongholds] of Horesh, on the
hill of Hakilah, ·south of [in the southern part of] Jeshimon. 20Now, our
king, come down ·anytime you want [whenever you're ready]. It's our
duty to hand David over to you."
21Saul answered, "The LORD bless you for ·helping [Lshowing concern
for; having compassion on] me. 22Go and ·learn more about him [make
sure]. ·Find out [Investigate] where he is staying and who has seen him
there. I have heard that he is ·clever [very cunning/crafty]. 23Find all the

hiding places he uses, and come back ·and tell me everything [when you are sure; with definite information]. Then I'll go with you. If David is in the ·area [land], I will ·track him down [search him out] among all the ·families [clans; *or* thousands] in Judah."

24 So they went back to Ziph ahead of Saul. Now David and his men were in the ·Desert [Wilderness] of Maon[n] in the ·desert [wilderness] area south of Jeshimon. 25 Saul and his men went to look for David, but David heard about it and went down to ·a [the great] rock and stayed in the ·Desert [Wilderness] of Maon. When Saul heard that, he ·followed [pursued] David into the ·Desert [Wilderness] of Maon.

26 Saul was going along one side of the mountain, and David and his men were on the other side. They were hurrying to get away from Saul, because Saul and his men were ·closing in on [surrounding] them. 27 But a messenger came to Saul, saying, "Come quickly! The Philistines are ·attacking [raiding] our land!" 28 So Saul stopped chasing David and went to ·challenge [meet; oppose] the Philistines. That is why people call this place Rock of ·Parting [Escape; *or* Separations]. 29 David also left the ·Desert [Wilderness] of Maon and stayed in the ·hideouts [strongholds] of En Gedi.

David Shames Saul

24 After Saul returned from chasing the Philistines, he was told, "David is in the ·Desert [Wilderness] of En Gedi." 2 So he took three thousand ·chosen men [elite soldiers] from all Israel and began looking for David and his men near the ·Rocks [Crags] of the ·Wild [Mountain] Goats.

3 Saul came to the sheep ·pens [folds] ·beside the road [along the way]. A cave was there, and he went in to ·relieve himself [Lcover his feet]. Now David and his men were hiding ·far back in [in the inner recesses of] the cave. 4 The men said to David, "Today is the day the LORD spoke of when he said, 'I will give your enemy ·over to you [Linto your hand]. ·Do anything you want with him [Deal with him as you wish/as is good in your eyes].'"

Then David crept up to Saul and ·quietly [secretly; stealthily] cut off ·a corner [the border/edge/hem] of Saul's robe. 5 Later ·David felt guilty [David's conscience bothered him; Lthe heart/mind of David struck him] because he had cut off a corner of Saul's robe. 6 He said to his men, "May the LORD ·keep [forbid; preserve] me from doing such a thing to my master! Saul is the LORD's ·appointed king [anointed]. I should not ·do anything [raise/Lsend my hand] against him, because he is the LORD's ·appointed king [anointed]!" 7 David used these words to ·stop [restrain; persuade; rebuke; scold] his men; he did not let them attack Saul. Then Saul left the cave and went his way.

8 When David came out of the cave, he ·shouted [called] to Saul, "My ·master [lord] ·and [the] king!" Saul looked back, and David bowed ·facedown [prostrate] on the ground. 9 He said to Saul, "Why do you listen when people say, 'David wants to harm you'? 10 You have seen ·something with [with] your own eyes today. ·The [...how the] LORD ·put you in my power [Lgave you into my hand] in the cave. ·They [Some] said I should kill you, but I ·was merciful [pitied/spared you]. I said, 'I won't ·harm [raise/Lsend my hand against] my master, because he is the LORD's ·appointed king [anointed].' 11 My father, look at this ·piece [border; edge; hem] of your robe in my hand! I cut off the ·corner [border; edge; hem] of your robe, but I didn't kill you. ·Now understand and know [This

23:24 Maon Some early Greek copies read "Maon." Hebrew copies read "Paran."

proves] ·I am not planning any evil [there is no wrong or rebellion/treason] against you. I ·did nothing wrong to [have not sinned against] you, but you are hunting me to ·kill me [Ltake my life]. 12May the LORD judge between us, and may he ·punish [avenge me on] you for the wrong you have done to me! But I ·am not against you [will not harm you/lay a hand on you]. 13There is an old ·saying [proverb]: 'Evil ·things [deeds] come ·from [out of] evil people.' ·But [So] I ·am not [will not harm/raise my hand] against you. 14Whom is the king of Israel ·coming out against [attacking]? Whom are you ·chasing [pursuing]? ·It's as if you are chasing a [A…?] dead dog or a flea. 15May the LORD be our judge and decide ·between you and me [which of us is right]. May he ·support me [consider/see me] and ·show that I am right [uphold/plead my cause]. May he ·save [rescue; deliver] me from ·you [Lyour hand/power]!"

16When David finished saying these words, Saul asked, "Is that your voice, David my son?" And he cried loudly. 17He said, "You are ·a better man [more righteous] than I am. You have ·been good [behaved well; Lrepaid good] to me, but I have ·done wrong [behaved badly; Lrepaid evil] to you. 18You [Lhave just] told me what good things you did [Lto me]. The LORD handed me over to you, but you did not kill me. 19·People don't normally let an enemy get away like this, do they [LFor who has found his enemy and sends him on his way safely]? May the LORD reward you ·because you were good to [*or* with good for what you have done for] me today. 20I [Lnow] know you will surely be king, and ·you will rule [in your hand will be established] the kingdom of Israel. 21Now swear to me by the LORD that you will not ·kill [Lcut off] my ·descendants [Lseed] and that you won't wipe out my name from my father's ·family [household; Cby killing all Saul's children]."

22So David ·made the promise [swore] to Saul. Then Saul went back home, and David and his men went up to their ·hideout [stronghold].

Nabal Insults David

25 Now Samuel died, and all the Israelites ·met [Lgathered; assembled] and ·had a time of sadness [mourned] for him. Then they buried him at his home in Ramah.

David moved to the ·Desert [Wilderness] of Maon.*n* 2A man in Maon who had ·land [business] at Carmel was very rich. He had three thousand sheep and a thousand goats. He was ·cutting the wool off his sheep [having his sheep shorn] at Carmel. 3His name was Nabal [Cmeaning "Fool" in Hebrew], and he was a descendant of Caleb [Num. 13:6, 30; 14:6, 24, 30; Josh. 14:6; 15:14; Judg. 1:12–20]. His wife was named Abigail. She was ·wise [intelligent; clever; sensible] and beautiful, but Nabal was ·cruel [harsh; crude; surly] and mean. He was a Calebite.

4While David was in the ·desert [wilderness], he heard that Nabal was ·cutting the wool from [shearing] his sheep. 5So he sent ten young men and told them, "Go to Nabal at Carmel, and greet him ·for me [Lin my name]. 6Say to Nabal, 'May you and your ·family [Lhouse] and all who belong to you have ·good health [long life; peace; prosperity]! 7I have heard that you are ·cutting the wool from [shearing] your sheep. When your shepherds were with us, we did not ·harm [mistreat] them. All the time your shepherds were at Carmel, ·we stole nothing from them [they missed/lost nothing]. 8Ask your ·servants [Lyoung men], and they will tell you. We come at a ·happy time [feast day; festive time], so ·be kind [show

25:1 Maon Some early Greek copies read "Maon." Hebrew copies read "Paran."

favor] to my young men. Please give anything [C provisions] you ·can find
[have at hand] for them and for your son David.'"
9 When David's men arrived, they gave the message to Nabal [L in
David's name], ·but Nabal insulted them [L and then waited]. 10 He
answered them, "Who is David? Who is this son of Jesse? Many ·slaves
[servants] are running away from their masters ·today [these days]! 11 I
have bread and water, and I have meat that I ·killed [slaughtered] for my
·servants who cut the wool [shearers]. ·But I won't give it to men I don't
know [L Why should I give it to men from who knows where?]."
12 David's men went back and told him all Nabal had said. 13 Then David
said to them, "·Put [Strap; Buckle; T Gird] on your swords!" So they ·put
[strapped; buckled; T girded] on their swords, and David put [strapped;
buckled; T girded] on his also. About four hundred men went with David,
but two hundred men stayed with the ·supplies [equipment; baggage].
14 One of Nabal's ·servants [young men] said to Abigail, Nabal's wife,
"David sent messengers from the ·desert [wilderness] to greet our master,
but Nabal ·insulted [scorned] them. 15 These men were very good to us.
They did not ·harm [mistreat] us. ·They stole nothing from us [Nothing
was missing] during all the time we were out in the field with them.
16 Night and day they ·protected us. They were [...were] like a wall around
us while we were with them ·caring for [tending; minding] the sheep.
17 Now ·think about it [make up your mind], and ·decide [consider] what
you ·can [should] do. ·Terrible trouble is coming to [Disaster is certain for;
Evil is fated for] our master and all his ·family [household]. Nabal is such a
·wicked [ill-tempered; quarrelsome] man that no one can even talk to him."
18 Abigail hurried. She took two hundred loaves of bread, two ·leather
bags [wineskins] full of wine, five ·cooked [prepared; slaughtered] sheep, ·a
bushel [five measures/L seahs] of ·cooked [roasted] grain, a hundred ·cakes
[clusters] of raisins, and two hundred cakes of pressed figs and ·put
[loaded] all these on donkeys. 19 Then she told her ·servants [L young men],
"Go on [L ahead]. I'll follow you." But she did not tell her husband Nabal.
20 Abigail rode her donkey and came down toward ·the [a] mountain
·hideout [ravine]. There she met David and his men coming down toward
her.
21 David had just said, "·It's been useless! [In vain have] I ·watched over
[guarded; protected] Nabal's property in the ·desert [wilderness]. I made
sure ·none of his sheep was missing [nothing was stolen]. I did good to
him, but he has paid me back with evil. 22 May God punish ·me [L David][n]
even more than my enemies if I leave even one of Nabal's ·men [L one who
urinates against a wall] alive until morning.
23 When Abigail saw David, she quickly got off her donkey and ·bowed
facedown on the ground [prostrated herself] before him. 24 She fell at
David's feet and said, "My ·master [lord], let the ·blame [guilt] be on me!
Please let ·me [L your maidservant] talk to you. Listen to what ·I [L your
maidservant has to] say. 25 My ·master [lord], [L please] don't ·pay attention
to [L set your heart/mind on] this worthless man Nabal. He is like his name.
His name means ·'fool' ['brute'], and he is truly a ·fool [brute]. But I, your
servant, didn't see the men you sent. 26 The LORD has kept you from killing
and ·punishing anyone [taking revenge/vengeance by your own hand]. As
surely as the LORD lives and as surely as you live, may your enemies [L and

25:22 David Some Greek copies read "David." Hebrew copies read "the enemies of David."

those who seek to harm my lord] become like Nabal! 27·I [LYour maidser-
vant] have brought a gift to you for the men who follow you. 28Please
forgive ·my [Lyour maidservant's] ·wrong [offense; transgression]. The LORD
will certainly ·let your family have many kings [make a lasting/enduring
dynasty/house for my lord; 2 Sam. 7], because you fight ·his [Lthe LORD's]
battles. As long as you live, ·may you do nothing bad [Lno evil/wrong will be
found in you]. 29Should someone try to chase you to ·kill you [Lseek your
life], the LORD your God will ·keep you alive [Lwrap/bind you up with the
living]. He will ·throw [sling; hurl; fling] away your enemies' lives as ·he
would throw a stone from [Lthe pocket of] a sling. 30When the LORD has
done all the good he promised, he will make you ·leader [ruler; prince] over
Israel. 31Then you won't feel ·guilty [grieved; anxious] or ·troubled
[remorse] because you ·killed innocent people and punished them [Lshed
blood without cause and avenged yourself]. Please remember ·me [Lyour
maidservant] when the LORD ·brings you success [has done well by you]."

32David answered Abigail, "·Praise [Blessed be] the LORD, the God of
Israel, who sent you to meet me today. 33May you be blessed for your
·wisdom [good sense/judgment; discernment]. You have kept me from
·killing [bloodshed] or ·punishing people [Lavenging myself with my own
hand] today. 34As surely as the LORD, the God of Israel, lives, he has kept
me from ·hurting [harming] you. If you hadn't come quickly to meet me,
not one of Nabal's ·men [Lthose who urinate against a wall] would ·have
lived until [still be alive in the] morning."

35Then David ·accepted Abigail's gifts [Lreceived from her hand that which
she had brought]. He told her, "Go home in peace. I have heard your words,
and ·I will do what you have asked [granted your request/petition]."

Nabal's Death

36When Abigail went back to Nabal, he was in the house, ·eating [feast-
ing; drinking] like a king. He was very drunk and in ·a good mood [high
spirits]. So she told him nothing until ·the next morning [daybreak; dawn].
37In the morning when ·he was not drunk [Lthe wine had left him], his wife
told him everything. ·His heart stopped [He had a stroke], and he became
like stone. 38About ten days later the LORD struck Nabal and he died.

39When David heard that Nabal was dead, he said, "·Praise [Blessed be]
the LORD! Nabal insulted me, but the LORD has ·supported me [avenged
me; pleaded/judged my case; upheld my cause]! He has kept ·me [Lhis ser-
vant] from doing ·wrong [evil]. The LORD has ·punished Nabal for his
wrong [Lreturned Nabal's evildoing on his own head]."

Then David sent a ·message [proposal] to Abigail, asking her to be his
wife. 40His servants went to Carmel and said to Abigail, "David sent us to
take you so you can become his wife."

41Abigail ·bowed facedown [prostrated herself] on the ground and
said, "·I am [LYour maidservant is] your ·servant [slave]. I'm ready to
serve you and to wash the feet of my ·master's [lord's] servants." 42Abigail
quickly got on a donkey and went with David's messengers, with her five
·maids [servant-girls] following her. And she became David's wife.

43David also had married Ahinoam of Jezreel. So they were both
David's wives. 44Saul's daughter Michal was also David's wife [18:20–29],
but Saul had given her to Paltiel son of Laish, who was from Gallim.

David Shames Saul Again

26 The people of Ziph went to Saul at Gibeah and said to him,
"David is hiding on the hill of Hakilah ·opposite [overlook-
ing; facing] ·Jeshimon [or the wasteland]."

2So Saul went down to the ·Desert [Wilderness] **of Ziph with three**
thousand ·chosen men [elite soldiers] **of Israel to look for David ·there**
[Lin the Desert/Wilderness of Ziph]. **3Saul made his camp beside the road**
on the hill of Hakilah ·opposite [overlooking; facing] **·Jeshimon** [*or* the
wasteland], **but David stayed in the ·desert** [wilderness]. **When he heard**
Saul had followed him [Linto the desert/wilderness], **4he sent out ·spies**
[scouts] **and learned for certain that Saul had come to Hakilah.**
5Then David went to the place where Saul had camped. He saw where
Saul and Abner son of Ner, the commander of Saul's army, were sleeping.
Saul was sleeping ·in [within] **the ·middle** [circle; ring] **of the camp with**
all the army around him.
6David asked Ahimelech the Hittite and Abishai son of Zeruiah, Joab's
brother, "Who will go down into Saul's camp with me?"
Abishai answered, "I'll go with you."
7So that night David and Abishai went ·into Saul's camp [Lamidst the
army]. **Saul was asleep ·in** [within] **the ·middle** [circle; ring] **of the camp**
with his spear stuck in the ground near his head. Abner and the army
were sleeping around Saul. 8Abishai said to David, "Today God has
·handed [delivered] **your enemy ·over to you** [Linto your hand]. **Let me**
pin Saul to the ground with my spear. I'll only have to do it once. I won't
need to ·hit [Lstrike] **him twice."**
9But David said to Abishai, "Don't ·kill [Ldestroy] **Saul! ·No one**
[Who…?] **can ·harm** [raise a hand against] **the LORD's ·appointed king**
[anointed] **and still be ·innocent** [without guilt]! **10As surely as the LORD**
lives, the LORD himself will ·punish Saul [strike him]. **·Maybe Saul will die**
naturally [LHis day to die will come], **or maybe he will go into battle and**
be killed. 11But may the LORD ·keep me from [forbid my] **·harming** [rais-
ing my hand against] **his ·appointed king** [anointed]! **Take the spear and**
water jug that are near Saul's head. Then let's go."
12So David took the spear and water jug that were near Saul's head, and
they left. No one saw them or knew about it or woke up, because ·the LORD
had put them sound asleep [La deep sleep from the LORD had fallen on
them].
13David crossed over to the other side of the hill and stood on top of
the mountain far from Saul's camp. They were a long way away from each
other. 14David ·shouted [called] **to the army and to Abner son of Ner,**
"Won't you answer me, Abner?"
Abner answered, "Who is calling for the king? Who are you [Lthat calls
on the king]?**"**
15David said, "You're ·the greatest man [La man unlike any] **in Israel.**
Isn't that true? Why didn't you ·guard [protect] **your ·master** [lord] **the**
king? Someone came into your camp to kill your ·master [lord] **the king!**
16·You have not done well [LThis thing you've done is not good]. **As surely**
as the LORD lives, you and your men ·should [must] **die. You haven't**
guarded your ·master [lord], **the LORD's ·appointed king** [anointed].
Look! Where are the king's spear and water jug that were near his head?"
17Saul ·knew [recognized] **David's voice. He said, "Is that your voice,**
David my son?"
David answered, "Yes, it is [Lmy voice], **my ·master** [lord] **and king."**
18David also said, "Why are you ·chasing me [pursuing your servant], **my**
·master [lord]**? What wrong have I done? What ·evil** [crime] **·am I guilty**
of [Lis in my hand]? **19My ·master** [lord] **and king, listen to me. If the LORD**

·made you angry with [Lstirred you up/incited you against] me, let him
accept an offering. But if people did it, may the LORD curse them! They
have ·made me leave [driven me out today from] ·the land the LORD gave
me [Lmy share in the LORD's inheritance/heritage]. They have told me, 'Go
and ·serve [worship] other gods.' 20Now don't let ·me die [Lmy blood fall
to the ground so] far away from the LORD's presence. The king of Israel
has come out looking for a [Lsingle] flea! You're just hunting a ·bird
[Lpartridge] in the mountains!"
21Then Saul said, "I have sinned. Come back, David my son. Today you
·respected [valued; considered precious] my life, so I will not try to hurt
you. I have been very ·stupid [wrong; mistaken] and foolish."
22David answered, "·Here is [TBehold] your spear [LO king]. Let one of
your young men come here and get it. 23The LORD ·rewards us for the
things we do right [repays each one for his righteousness] and for our
·loyalty [faithfulness] to him. The LORD ·handed you over to me [Lplaced
you in my hand] today, but I wouldn't ·harm [raise a hand against] the
LORD's ·appointed king [anointed]. 24As I ·respected [valued; considered
precious] your life today, may the LORD also ·respect [value; consider pre-
cious] my life and ·save [rescue; deliver] me from all ·trouble
[tribulation]."
25Then Saul said to David, "·You are [May you be] blessed, my son
David. You will do great things and ·succeed [surely prevail/triumph]."
So David went on his way, and Saul went back home.

David Lives with the Philistines

27 But David ·thought to himself [Lsaid in his heart], "·Saul will
catch me someday [LEventually I will die/perish at Saul's
hands]. The best thing I can do is escape to the land of the Philistines.
Then he will give up looking for me in Israel, and I can ·get away from
him [Lescape from his hand]."
2So David and his six hundred men ·left Israel and went [Lcrossed over]
to Achish son of Maoch, king of Gath. 3David, his men, and their ·families
[households] made their home in Gath with Achish. David had his two
wives with him—Ahinoam of Jezreel [25:43] and Abigail of Carmel, the
widow of Nabal [25:1–42]. 4When Saul heard that David had run away to
Gath, he stopped ·looking [searching; hunting] for him.
5Then David said to Achish, "If ·you are pleased with me [LI have found
favor in your eyes/sight], give me a place in one of the country towns
where I can live. ·I don't need to [LWhy should your servant…?] live in the
royal city with you."
6That day Achish gave David the town of Ziklag, and Ziklag has
belonged to the kings of Judah ·ever since [to this day]. 7David lived in the
Philistine land a year and four months.
8David and his men raided the people of Geshur, Girzi, and Amalek.
(These people had lived ·for a long time [since ancient times] in the land
·that reached to [near] Shur ·in the direction of [*or* as far as] Egypt.)
9When David ·fought [attacked; Lstruck] them, he ·killed [Ldid not let live]
all the men and women and took their sheep, cattle, donkeys, camels, and
clothes. Then he returned to Achish.
10Achish would ask David, "Where did you go raiding today?" And
David would tell him ·that he had gone to the southern part [against the
Negev] of Judah, or [against the Negev of] Jerahmeel, or ·to the land
[against the Negev] of the Kenites. 11David never brought a man or

**woman alive to Gath. He thought, "If we bring people alive, they may tell
Achish, 'This is what David really did.'" David did this all the time he
lived in the Philistine land. 12So Achish trusted David and said to himself,
"·David's own people, the Israelites, now hate him very much** [LHe has
made himself detested/abhorrent/odious to his people Israel]. **He will
·serve me** [Lbe my servant] **forever."**

Saul and the Medium of Endor

28 **·Later** [LIn those days], **the Philistines ·gathered** [mobilized;
mustered] **their armies** [for war] **to fight against Israel.
Achish said to David, "You understand that you and your men must
·join** [go out with; accompany] **my army."**
2**David answered, "You will see for yourself what I, your servant, can do!"**
Achish said, "Fine, I'll make you my ·permanent [lifelong] **·bodyguard**
[Lprotector/guard of my head]."
3**Now Samuel was dead, and all the Israelites had ·shown their sadness**
[mourned; lamented] **for him. They had buried Samuel in his hometown
of Ramah.**
And Saul had ·forced out [removed; banned] **the mediums and ·for-
tune-tellers** [wizards; spiritists] **from the land** [Lev. 19:31; 20:6].
4**The Philistines ·came together** [assembled; mobilized] **and made
camp at Shunem. Saul gathered all the Israelites and made camp at
Gilboa. 5When he saw the Philistine army, he was afraid, and his heart
·pounded with fear** [trembled violently]. 6**He ·prayed to** [inquired of] **the
LORD, but the LORD did not answer him through dreams, Urim** [Cdevices
carried by the High Priest to inquire of God; Ex. 28:30], **or prophets.
7Then Saul said to his ·servants** [advisers; attendants], **"Find me a woman
who ·is a medium** [is a necromancer; Thas a familiar spirit] **so I may go
and ·ask her what will happen** [inquire of/consult her]."
His servants answered, "There is a ·medium [a necromancer; Twoman
with a familiar spirit] **in Endor."**
8**Then Saul put on other clothes to disguise himself, and at night he
and two of his men went to see the woman. Saul said to her, "·Talk to**
[Consult] **a spirit for me. ·Bring** [Conjure] **up the person I name."**
9**But the woman said to him, "Surely you know what Saul has done. He
has ·forced** [outlawed; Lcut off] **the mediums and ·fortune-tellers** [wiz-
ards; spiritists] **from the land. ·You are** [Why are you…?] **trying to trap
me and get me killed."**
10**Saul made a ·promise** [vow; oath] **to the woman in the name of the
LORD. He said, "As surely as the LORD lives, you won't be ·punished**
[blamed] **for this."**
11**The woman asked, "Whom do you want me to ·bring up** [conjure]?"
He answered, "·Bring [Conjure] **up Samuel."**
12**When the woman saw Samuel, she screamed. She said, "Why have
you ·tricked** [deceived] **me? You are Saul!"**
13**The king said to the woman, "Don't be afraid! What do you see?"**
The woman said, "I see a ·spirit [ghost; god; divine being] **coming up
out of the ·ground** [earth]."
14**Saul asked, "What ·does he look like** [is his appearance/form]?"
The woman answered, "An old man wearing a ·coat [robe; cloak] **is
coming up."**
Then Saul knew it was Samuel, and he ·bowed facedown [prostrated
himself] **on the ground** [and paid homage/did obeisance].

15 Samuel asked Saul, "Why have you disturbed me by ·bringing [con-
juring] me up?"
Saul said, "I am ·greatly troubled [Lin great trouble/distress]. The
Philistines are fighting against me, and God has ·left [abandoned;
departed/turned away from] me. He won't answer me anymore, either by
prophets or in dreams. That's why I ·called for [summoned] you. Tell me
what to do."
16 Samuel said, "The LORD has ·left [abandoned; departed/turned away
from] you and has become your enemy. So why do you ·call on [ask; con-
sult] me? 17 He has done what he ·said he would do [predicted;
foretold]—the things he said ·through me [Lby my hand; 15:27–29]. He
has torn the kingdom out of your hands and given it to one of your
neighbors, David [16:1–13]. 18 You did not obey the [Lvoice of the] LORD;
you did not ·show the Amalekites how angry he was with them [carry
out/execute his fierce anger/wrath on Amalek; 15:10–23]. That's why he
has done this to you today. 19 The LORD will hand over both Israel and you
·to [Linto the hands of] the Philistines. Tomorrow you and your sons will
be with me. The LORD will hand over the army of Israel to the Philistines."
20 Saul ·quickly [immediately] fell flat on the ground and was ·afraid
[terrified] of what Samuel had said. ·He was also very weak [And his
strength was gone] because he had eaten nothing all that day and night.
21 Then the woman came to Saul and saw that he was really ·frightened
[terrified; shaken; distraught]. She said, "Look, I, your servant, have
obeyed you. I have ·risked my life [Ltaken my life in my hands] and ·done
[listened to] what you told me to do. 22 Now please also listen to me. Let
me give you some ·food [bread] so you may eat and have enough strength
to go on your way."
23 But Saul refused, saying, "I won't eat."
His servants joined the woman in ·asking [urging] him to eat, and he
listened to them. So he got up from the ground and sat on the ·bed
[couch].
24 At the house the woman had a fat calf, which she quickly ·killed
[slaughtered]. She took some flour and kneaded dough with her hands.
Then she baked some ·bread without yeast [unleavened bread]. 25 She put
the food before Saul and his servants, and they ate. That same night they
got up and left.

David Goes Back to Ziklag

29 The Philistines ·gathered [mobilized; mustered] all their soldiers at Aphek. Israel camped by the spring at Jezreel. 2 The
Philistine ·kings [rulers; lords] were marching with their groups of ·a
hundred [hundreds] and ·a thousand men [thousands]. David and his
men were marching ·behind [*or* at the rear with] Achish. 3 The Philistine
commanders asked, "What are these Hebrews doing here?"
Achish told them, "·This is David. He [LIs this not David who…?]
served Saul king of Israel, but he has been with me for ·over a year now
[Ldays and years]. I have found nothing wrong in David since the time he
·left Saul [Ldeserted until today]."
4 But the Philistine commanders were angry with Achish and said,
"Send David back to the ·city you gave him [place you assigned him]. He
cannot go with us into battle. If he does, ·we'll have an enemy in our own
camp [Lhe may become an adversary to us]. He could ·please [make himself acceptable to/reconcile himself to] his king ·by killing our own [with

the heads of these] men. 5·David is [LIs not David…?] the one the Israelites dance and sing about, saying:

"'Saul has ·killed thousands of his enemies [Tslain his thousands],
·but [and] David has ·killed [Tslain his] tens of thousands [18:7].'"

6So Achish called David and said to him, "As surely as the LORD lives, you ·are loyal [have been trustworthy/reliable/honest]. I would be pleased to have you ·serve in my army [march into battle]. Since the day you came to me [Luntil the present], I have found no ·wrong [fault; evil] in you. But the other ·kings [rulers; lords] don't ·trust [approve of] you. 7Go back in peace. Don't do anything ·to displease [Levil in the eyes/sight of] the Philistine ·kings [rulers; lords]."

8David asked, "What ·wrong have [have] I done? What ·evil have [have] you found in ·me [Lyour servant] from the day I came to you until now? Why can't I go fight your enemies, my lord ·and [the] king?"

9Achish answered, "I know you are as ·good [pleasing to me] as an angel from God. But the Philistine commanders have said, 'David must not go with us into battle.' 10Early in the morning you and your master's servants should leave. Get up as soon as it is light and go."

11So David and his men got up early in the morning and went back to the country of the Philistines. And the Philistines went up to Jezreel.

David's War with the Amalekites

30 ·On the third day [Three days later], when David and his men arrived at Ziklag, he found that the Amalekites had raided ·southern Judah [the Negev] and Ziklag, ·attacking [crushing; sacking; Lstriking] Ziklag and burning it. 2They captured the women and everyone, ·young and old [Lsmall and great], but they had not killed anyone. They had only ·taken [carried] them away.

3When David and his men came to Ziklag, they found the town had been burned and their wives, sons, and daughters had been taken ·as prisoners [captive]. 4Then David and his ·army [people] cried loudly until they were too weak to cry anymore. 5David's two wives had also been taken—Ahinoam of Jezreel [25:43] and Abigail the widow of Nabal from Carmel [25:1–42]. 6The men in the army ·were threatening to kill David with stones [talked of stoning him], which greatly ·upset [endangered] David. Each man was ·sad and angry [embittered] because his sons and daughters had been captured, but David found ·strength [courage] in the LORD his God. 7David said to Abiathar the priest [Lthe son of Ahimelech], "Bring me the ·holy vest [ephod; Ex. 28:6–14]." So Abiathar brought the ephod [Cthe ephod contained the means to inquiry of God; 23:6].

8Then David asked the LORD, "Should I ·chase the people who took our families [Lpursue them]? Will I ·catch [overtake] them?"

The LORD answered, "·Chase [Pursue] them. You will catch them, and you will ·succeed in saving your families [certainly rescue them all]."

9David and the six hundred men with him came to the Besor ·Ravine [Valley; Wadi; Brook], where some of the men stayed [Lbehind]. 10David and four hundred men kept up the chase. The other two hundred men stayed behind because they were too ·tired [exhausted] to cross the ·ravine [valley].

11They found an Egyptian in a field and brought him to David. They gave the Egyptian some water to drink and some ·food [bread] to eat. 12And they gave him a piece of a fig cake and two clusters of raisins. Then ·he felt better [he revived; Lhis spirit returned to him], because he had not eaten any ·food [bread] or drunk any water for three days and nights.

13 David asked him, "Who ·is your master [do you belong to]? Where do you come from?"

He answered, "I'm an [Lyoung] Egyptian, the ·slave [servant] of an Amalekite. Three days ago my master ·left [abandoned] me, because I was sick. 14 We had raided the ·southern area [Negev] of the Kerethites, the ·land [territory] of Judah, and the ·southern area [Negev] of Caleb. We burned Ziklag, as well."

15 David asked him, "Can you lead me to ·the people who took our families [Lthis band of raiders]?"

He answered, "·Yes, if you promise me [Swear; Take an oath] before God that you won't kill me or ·give [hand] me back to my master. Then I will take you to ·them [Lthis band of raiders]."

16 So the Egyptian led David to the Amalekites. They were ·lying around [Lspread out] on the ground, eating and drinking and ·celebrating [dancing] with the ·things [great plunder/spoil] they had taken from the land of the Philistines and from Judah. 17 David ·fought [slaughtered; Lstruck] them from ·sunset [twilight; dusk] until the evening of the next day. None of them escaped, except four hundred young men who rode off on their camels. 18 David ·got his two wives back [rescued his two wives] and [recovered] everything the Amalekites had taken. 19 Nothing was missing. David brought back everyone, ·young and old [Lgreat and small], sons and daughters. He ·recovered [brought back] the ·valuable things [plunder; spoil] and everything the Amalekites had taken. 20 David took all the sheep and cattle, and his men made these animals go in front, saying, "They are David's ·prize [plunder; spoil]."

21 Then David came to the two hundred men who had been too ·tired [exhausted] to follow him, who had stayed at the Besor ·Ravine [Valley; Wadi; Brook]. They came out to meet David and the people with him. When he came near, David greeted the men at the ravine.

22 But the ·evil men [rogues; corrupt] and ·troublemakers [scoundrels; worthless] among those who followed David said, "Since these two hundred men didn't go with us, we shouldn't give them any of the ·things we recovered [plunder; spoil]. Just let each man take his wife and children and ·go [be off/gone]."

23 David answered, "No, my brothers. Don't do that after what the LORD has given us. He has ·protected [preserved; kept] us and ·given [handed over to] us the ·enemy [raiders] who attacked us. 24 Who will listen ·to what you say [when you speak this way]? The share will be the same for the one who stayed with the ·supplies [equipment; baggage] as for the one who went into battle. All will share alike." 25 David made this an ·order [statute; ordinance; requirement] and ·rule [regulation] for Israel, which continues even today.

26 When David arrived in Ziklag, he sent some of the ·things he had taken from the Amalekites [plunder; spoil] to his friends, the ·leaders [elders] of Judah. He said, "Here is a ·present [gift] for you from the ·things [plunder; spoil] we took from the LORD's enemies."

27 David also sent some things to the leaders in Bethel, Ramoth in the ·southern part of Judah [Negev], Jattir, 28 Aroer, Siphmoth, Eshtemoa, 29 Racal, the cities of the Jerahmeelites and the Kenites, 30 Hormah, Bor Ashan, Athach, 31 Hebron, and to the people in all the other places where he and his men had ·been [roamed; visited].

The Death of Saul

(31:1–13; 1 Chr. 10:1–14)

31 The Philistines fought against Israel, and the ·Israelites [Lmen of Israel] ·ran away from [fled before] them. Many Israelites ·were killed [Lfell slain] on Mount Gilboa. 2The Philistines ·fought hard against [overtook; closed in/bore down on] Saul and his sons, killing his sons Jonathan, Abinadab, and Malki-Shua. 3The fighting was ·heavy [fierce] around Saul. The archers ·shot [Lfound] him, and he was ·badly [severely; critically] wounded. 4He said to ·the officer who carried his armor [his armor bearer], "·Pull out [Draw] your sword and ·kill me [run me through]. Then those ·uncircumcised men [pagans] won't ·make fun of [taunt; abuse] me and ·kill me [run me through]." But Saul's ·officer [armor bearer] refused, because he was ·afraid [terrified]. So Saul took his own sword and ·threw himself [Lfell] on it. 5When ·the officer [his armor bearer] saw that Saul was dead, he ·threw himself [Lfell] on his own sword, and he died with Saul. 6So Saul, his three sons, ·and the officer who carried his armor [his armor bearer] and all his men died together that day.

7When the Israelites who lived across the Jezreel Valley and those who lived across the Jordan River saw how the Israelite army had ·run away [fled], and that Saul and his sons were dead, they ·left [abandoned] their cities and ran away. Then the Philistines came and ·lived there [occupied them].

8The next day when the Philistines came to ·take all the valuable things from the dead soldiers [Lstrip the dead/corpses], they found Saul and his three sons ·dead [fallen; lying] on Mount Gilboa. 9They cut off Saul's head and ·took [stripped] off his armor. Then they sent messengers through all the land of the Philistines to tell the [Lgood] news in the ·temple [Lhouses] of their idols and to their people. 10They put Saul's armor in the ·temple [Lhouse] of the Ashtoreths [*or* Astarte; Ca pagan deity] and ·hung [fastened] his body on the wall of Beth Shan.

11When the people living in Jabesh Gilead heard what the Philistines had done to Saul, 12the ·brave men [valiant/mighty warriors] of Jabesh ·marched [walked; traveled] all night and came to Beth Shan. They ·removed [took] the bodies of Saul and his sons from the wall of Beth Shan and brought them to Jabesh. There they burned the bodies. 13They took their bones and buried them under the tamarisk tree in Jabesh. Then the people of Jabesh fasted for seven days.

2 SAMUEL

David Learns About Saul's Death

1 Now Saul was dead. After David had ·defeated [slaughtered; been victorious over] the Amalekites, he returned to Ziklag and stayed there two days. 2On the third day a young man from Saul's camp came to Ziklag. ·To show his sadness, [L...and] his clothes were torn and he had dirt on his head. He came and ·bowed facedown on the ground [Lfell to the ground and prostrated himself] before David.

3David asked him, "Where did you come from?"

The man answered, "I escaped from the Israelite camp."

4David asked him, "·What happened [How did things go]? Please tell me!"

The man answered, "The ·people [army; men] have ·run away [fled] from the battle, and many of them have fallen and are dead. Saul and his son Jonathan are dead also."

5David asked him, "How do you know Saul and his son Jonathan are dead?"

6The young man answered, "I happened to be on Mount Gilboa. There I saw Saul leaning on his spear. The Philistine chariots and the ·men riding in them [charioteers; *or* horsemen; cavalry] were ·coming closer to Saul [closing in on him]. 7When he looked back and saw me, he called to me. I answered him, 'Here I am!'

8"Then Saul asked me, 'Who are you?'

"I told him, 'I am an Amalekite.'

9"Then Saul said to me, 'Please come here and ·kill me [put me out of my misery]. I am ·badly hurt [in the throes of death; Lconvulsions have seized me] and ·am almost dead already [yet my life still lingers].'

10"So I ·went over [Lstood beside/over him] and killed him. He had ·been hurt so badly [Lfallen and] I knew he couldn't live. Then I took the crown from his head and the ·bracelet [band] from his arm, and I have brought them here to you, my ·master [lord]."

11Then David tore his clothes [Ca sign of mourning or distress] and all the men with him did also. 12They ·were very sad [mourned] and cried and fasted until evening. They cried for Saul and his son Jonathan and for all the people of the LORD and for all the ·Israelites [Lhouse of Israel] who had ·died in the battle [Lhad fallen by the sword].

David Orders the Amalekite Killed

13David asked the young man who brought the report, "Where are you from?"

The young man answered, "I am the son of a ·foreigner [resident alien], an Amalekite."

14David asked him, "Why were you not afraid to ·kill [lift your hand and destroy] the LORD's ·appointed king [anointed]?"

15 Then David called one of his [Lyoung] men and told him, "·Go! Kill
the Amalekite [LCome, strike him down]!" So the Israelite ·killed him
[Lstruck him down and he died]. 16 David had said to the Amalekite, "·You
are responsible for your own death [LYour blood is/be on your own head].
·You confessed [LYour own mouth has testified against you] by saying, 'I
have killed the LORD's ·appointed king [anointed].' "

David's Song About Saul and Jonathan

17 David ·sang [chanted; intoned; *or* composed] a ·funeral song [lament]
·about [over] Saul and his son Jonathan, 18 and he ordered that the people
of Judah be taught this song. It is called "The Bow," and it is written in the
Book of Jashar [Can ancient record of heroic deeds, now lost; Josh. 10:13]:

19 "Israel, your ·leaders [glorious/beautiful/proud ones; *or* gazelle; Ca metaphor for a leader] have been killed on ·the hills [your heights].
How the mighty have ·fallen in battle [Lfallen]!
20 Don't ·tell [announce; speak of] it in Gath.
Don't ·announce [proclaim; broadcast] it in the streets of Ashkelon.
If you do, the Philistine ·women [Ldaughters] will ·be happy [rejoice].
The daughters of the ·Philistines [pagans; Luncircumcised] will ·rejoice [gloat; exult].

21 "May there be no dew or rain on the mountains of Gilboa,
and may their fields produce no [Lofferings of] grain,
because there the mighty warrior's shield was ·dishonored [defiled; despised].
Saul's shield will no longer be ·rubbed [anointed] with oil.
22 Jonathan's bow did not ·fail [turn back]
·to kill many soldiers [Lfrom shedding the blood of the slain].
Saul's sword did not ·fail [return empty]
·to wound many strong men [Lfrom the fat/bodies of the mighty].

23 "We loved Saul and Jonathan
and ·enjoyed [admired] them ·while they lived [in life].
They ·are together [were not parted] even in death.
They were ·faster [swifter] than eagles.
They were stronger than lions.

24 "You daughters of Israel, ·cry for [weep over] Saul.
Saul clothed you with ·red dresses [luxurious scarlet/crimson]
and put gold ·decorations [ornaments/jewelry] on them.

25 "How the mighty have fallen in battle!
Jonathan ·is dead [lies slain] on Gilboa's ·hills [heights].
26 I ·cry [grieve; am desolate/distressed] for you, my brother Jonathan.
·I enjoyed your friendship so much [You were greatly loved by me].
Your love to me was wonderful,
·better than [surpassing; deeper than] the love of women.

27 "How the mighty have fallen!
·The weapons of war are gone [Stripped of their weapons of war]."

David Is Made King of Judah

2 Later, David ·prayed to [consulted; inquired of] the LORD, saying,
"Should I ·go up [move back; return] to any of the ·cities [*or*
towns] of Judah?"
The LORD said to David, "·Go [Move back; Return]."
David asked, "·Where [To which town] should I go?"
The LORD answered, "To Hebron [Cin the heartland of Judah, David's
tribe]."
2So David went up to Hebron with his two wives: Ahinoam from
Jezreel [1 Sam. 25:43] and Abigail, the widow of Nabal from Carmel [1
Sam. 25:39–42]. 3David also brought his men and their ·families [house-
holds], and they all ·made their homes in the cities of [settled in the
villages near] Hebron. 4Then the men of Judah came to Hebron and
·appointed [anointed] David king over [the people/house of] Judah.
They told David that the men of Jabesh Gilead had buried Saul [1 Sam.
31:11–13]. 5So David sent messengers to the men of Jabesh Gilead and
said to them, "The LORD bless you. You have shown ·loyalty [kindness;
faithful love] to your master Saul by burying him. 6May the LORD now ·be
loyal [show kindness/faithful love] and ·true [faithfulness] to you. I will
also ·treat you well [show this goodness to you; reward you] because you
have done this. 7Now ·be [Llet your hands be] strong and ·brave [valiant].
Saul your ·master [lord] is dead, and the ·people [Lhouse] of Judah have
appointed me their king."

War Between Judah and Israel

8Abner son of Ner was the commander of Saul's army [1 Sam. 14:50–
51; 17:55–57; 26:14–15]. Abner took Saul's son Ish-Bosheth [C"man of
shame"] to Mahanaim 9and ·made [proclaimed] him king of Gilead,
Ashuri, Jezreel, Ephraim, Benjamin, and all Israel. 10Saul's son Ish-
Bosheth was forty years old when he became king over Israel, and he
·ruled [reigned] two years. But the ·people [Lhouse] of Judah followed
David. 11David was king in Hebron for seven years and six months.
12Abner son of Ner and the ·servants [soldiers; men] of Ish-Bosheth
son of Saul left Mahanaim and went to Gibeon. 13Joab son of Zeruiah
[CDavid's general] and David's men also went there and met Abner and
Ish-Bosheth's men at the pool of Gibeon. Abner's group sat on one side of
the pool; Joab's group sat on the other.
14Abner said to Joab, "Let the young men ·have a contest [perform;
sport; Lplay] ·here [before us]."
Joab said, "Yes, let them ·have a contest [Lcome forward]."
15Then the men got up and were counted—twelve from the people of
Benjamin for Ish-Bosheth son of Saul, and twelve from David's men.
16Each man grabbed the one opposite him by the ·head [hair] and stabbed
him in the side with a ·knife [dagger; sword]. So the men fell down together.
For that reason, that place in Gibeon is called the Field of ·Knives [Daggers;
Swords; *or* Sides]. 17That day there was a ·terrible [fierce] battle, and
David's ·men [Lservants] defeated Abner and the Israelites.

Abner Kills Asahel

18Zeruiah's three sons, Joab, Abishai, and Asahel, were there. Now Asahel
was ·a fast runner, as fast as a deer [Las fleet-footed as a gazelle] in the field.
19Asahel chased Abner, ·going straight toward him [Lturning neither to the
right or left]. 20Abner looked back and asked, "Is that you, Asahel?"
Asahel said, "Yes, it is."
21Then Abner said to Asahel, "·Turn to your right or left [Go elsewhere]
and catch one of the young men and ·take his armor [strip him of his

weapons; [L]take his spoil].” But Asahel refused to ·stop [[L]turn away from] chasing him.

22 Abner again said to Asahel, “·Stop chasing me [[L]Turn another way]! ·If you don’t stop, I’ll have to kill you! [[L]Why should I strike you down?] Then ·I won’t be able to [[L]how could I…?] face your brother Joab again!”

23 But Asahel refused to ·stop chasing Abner [[L]turn aside/back]. So using the ·back [butt] end of his spear, Abner ·stabbed [struck] Asahel in the stomach, and the spear came out of his back. Asahel [[L]fell/stumbled and] died right there, and everyone ·stopped [stood still] when they came to the place where Asahel’s body lay.

24 But Joab and Abishai ·continued chasing [took up the pursuit of] Abner. As the sun was going down, they arrived at the hill of Ammah, ·near [in front of] Giah on the way to the ·desert [wilderness] near Gibeon. 25 The men of Benjamin [[C]part of Abner’s troops] came to Abner, and ·all stood together [regrouped; reunited] at the top of the hill.

26 Abner shouted to Joab, “Must the sword ·kill [[L]devour] forever? Surely you must know this will only end in ·sadness [bitterness]! ·Tell [[L]How long before you tell…?] the people to stop chasing their own brothers!”

27 Then Joab said, “As surely as God lives, if you had not said anything, the people would have chased their brothers until morning.” 28 Then Joab blew a ·trumpet [ram’s horn], and his people stopped chasing ·the Israelites [[L]Israel]. They did not fight them anymore.

29 Abner and his men marched all night through the ·Jordan Valley [Arabah]. They crossed the Jordan River, and after marching all ·day [morning], arrived at Mahanaim.

30 After he had stopped chasing Abner, Joab came back and gathered the people together. Asahel and nineteen of David’s ·men [soldiers; [L]servants] were missing. 31 But David’s ·men [[L]servants] had ·killed [[L]struck] three hundred sixty Benjaminites who had followed Abner. 32 David’s men took Asahel and buried him in the tomb of his father at Bethlehem. Then Joab and his men marched all night. ·The sun came up as [At daybreak] they reached Hebron.

3 There was a long war between the ·people who supported Saul’s family [[L]the house of Saul] and ·those who supported David’s family [[L]the house of David]. ·The supporters of David’s family [[L]David] became stronger and stronger, but the ·supporters of Saul’s family [[L]house of Saul] became weaker and weaker.

David’s Sons

(3:2–5; 1 Chr. 3:1–4)

2 Sons were born to David at Hebron. The first was Amnon [13:1–22], whose mother was Ahinoam from Jezreel [1 Sam. 25:43]. 3 The second son was Kileab, whose mother was Abigail, the widow of Nabal from Carmel [1 Sam. 25:39–42]. The third son was Absalom [13:23—18:33], whose mother was Maacah daughter of Talmai, the king of Geshur. 4 The fourth son was Adonijah [1 Kin. 1:5–27], whose mother was Haggith. The fifth son was Shephatiah, whose mother was Abital. 5 The sixth son was Ithream, whose mother was Eglah, David’s wife. These sons were born to David at Hebron.

Abner Joins David

6 During the war between the ·supporters of Saul’s family [[L]house of Saul] and the ·supporters of David’s family [[L]house of David], Abner made himself ·a main leader [strong] ·among the supporters [[L]in the house] of Saul.

7 Saul once had a ·slave woman [concubine; [C]a secondary wife of lower

status than a primary wife, but higher than a common servant] named
Rizpah, who was the daughter of Aiah. Ish-Bosheth said to Abner, "Why
·did you have sexual relations with [Lhave you gone in to] my father's
·slave woman [concubine]?"
8Abner was ·very angry [furious; in a rage] because of what Ish-Bosheth
said, and he replied, "I have ·been loyal [shown kindness/faithful love] to
[Lthe house of your father] Saul and his ·family [Lbrothers] and friends! I
didn't hand you over to David. ·I am not a traitor working for Judah!
[LAm I a Judean dog/dog's head for Judah?] But now you are ·saying I did
something wrong with [finding fault with me/charging me with wrong
regarding] this woman! 9May God ·help [deal severely with] me if I don't
·join David! I will make sure that what the LORD promised does happen
[L...accomplish for David everything the LORD has promised him]! 10I will
·take [transfer] the kingdom from the ·family [Lthe house] of Saul and
·make David king of [Lestablish the throne of David over] Israel and
Judah, from Dan to Beersheba [Cin the far north and south of Israel]!"
11Ish-Bosheth ·couldn't [dared not] say anything to Abner, because he
was afraid of him.
12Then Abner sent messengers to ask David [Lon his own behalf; *or* at
his place], "·Who is going to rule the land [LWhose land is it]? Make an
·agreement [treaty; covenant] with me, and ·I will help you unite [Lmy
hand will be with you to bring over to you] all Israel."
13David answered, "Good! I will make an ·agreement [treaty; covenant]
with you, but I ·ask [demand/require of] you one thing. I will not ·meet
with you [Lallow you to see my face/in my presence] unless you bring
Saul's daughter Michal to me [Lwhen you come; Cto strengthen his claim
to the throne; 1 Sam. 18:26–29]." 14Then David sent messengers to Saul's
son Ish-Bosheth, saying, "Give me my wife Michal. She was ·promised
[engaged; betrothed] to me, ·and I killed a hundred Philistines to get her
[Lfor one hundred Philistine foreskins]."
15So Ish-Bosheth sent men to take Michal from her husband Paltiel son
of Laish. 16Michal's husband went with her, crying as he followed her ·to
[as far as] Bahurim. But Abner said to Paltiel, "Go back home." So he went
home.
17Abner ·sent this message to [consulted/conferred with] the elders of
Israel: "[LFor some time now] You have been wanting to make David your
king. 18Now do it! The LORD said of David, '·Through [LBy the hand of]
my servant David, I will ·save [rescue; Tdeliver] my people Israel from the
[Lhand of the] Philistines and all their enemies.' "
19Abner also said these things to the people of Benjamin. He then went
to Hebron to tell David what the Benjaminites and Israel ·wanted [agreed]
to do. 20Abner came with twenty men to David at Hebron. There David
prepared a ·feast [banquet] for them. 21Abner said to David, "·I will [Let
me] go and ·bring all the Israelites [Lgather all Israel] to my ·master [lord]
and king. Then they will make an ·agreement [treaty; covenant] with you
so you will rule over all ·Israel as you wanted [Lthat your soul desires]." So
David let Abner go, and he left in peace.

Abner's Death

22Just then Joab and David's ·men [Lservants] came from a ·battle
[raid], bringing ·many valuable things they had taken from the enemy
[Lmuch plunder/spoil with them]. David had let Abner leave in peace, so
he was not with David at Hebron. 23When Joab and all his army arrived

at Hebron, the army said to Joab, "Abner son of Ner came to King David,
and David let him leave in peace."
24Joab came to the king and said, "What have you done? Abner came to
you. Why did you let him go? Now he's gone. 25You know Abner son of
Ner! He came to ·trick [deceive] you! He came to learn about [Lyour
movements/coming and going and] everything you are doing!"
26After Joab left David, he sent messengers after Abner, and they
brought him back from the ·well [cistern] of Sirah. But David did not
know this. 27When Abner arrived at Hebron, Joab took him aside into
·the gateway [an inner chamber]. He acted as though he wanted to talk
with Abner in private, but Joab stabbed him in the stomach, and Abner
died. ·Abner had killed Joab's brother Asahel, so Joab killed Abner to pay
him back [L...on account of/to revenge the blood/killing of Asahel his
brother].
28Later when David heard the news, he said, "My kingdom and I are
innocent before the LORD forever of the ·death [Lblood] of Abner son of
Ner. 29·Joab and his family are responsible for this. [LMay it/the guilt fall
on the head of Joab and on all his father's house.] May his family always
have someone with [running] sores or ·with a skin disease [Tleprosy; Cthe
term covers a variety of skin diseases that would render a person ritually
unclean; Lev. 13–14]. May they always have someone who must lean on a
crutch. May ·some of his family be killed in war [Lsomeone always fall by
the sword]. May they always have someone without food to eat."
30(Joab and his brother Abishai killed Abner, because he had killed
their brother Asahel in the battle at Gibeon [2:18–32].)
31Then David said to Joab and to all the people with Joab, "Tear your
clothes and put on ·rough cloth [sackcloth; burlap; Ca sign of mourning or
distress]. ·Cry [...lament; mourn] for Abner." King David himself followed the ·body of Abner [Lbier]. 32They buried Abner in Hebron, and
David and all the people cried at Abner's grave.
33King David ·sang [chanted; intoned; *or* composed] this ·funeral song
[lament] for Abner.

"·Did [Should] Abner ·die [have died] like a fool?
34 ·His [LYour] hands were not tied.
·His [LYour] feet were not ·in chains [fettered].
·He [LYou] fell ·at the hands of [as one falls before] evil men."

Then all the people cried again for Abner. 35They came to ·encourage
[persuade] David to eat while it was still day. But he made a ·promise
[vow], saying, "May God ·punish me terribly [deal severely with me] if I
·eat [taste] bread or anything else before the sun sets!"
36All the people ·saw what happened [took note], and ·they agreed with
what the king was doing [it pleased them; Lit was good in their eyes], just
as they ·agreed [were pleased] with everything ·he [Lthe king] did. 37That
day all the ·people of Judah [Lpeople; Clikely a reference to the people of
Judah] and Israel understood that David ·did not order [had no part in]
the killing of Abner son of Ner.
38David said to his ·officers [Lservants], "[LDon't...?] You know that a
[Lprince and a] great man died today in Israel. 39Even though I am the
·appointed [anointed] king, I ·feel empty [am weak/powerless]. These
sons of Zeruiah are too ·much [strong; difficult] for me. May the LORD
·give them the punishment they should have [Lrepay the evildoer as his
evil deserves]."

Ish-Bosheth's Death

4 When Ish-Bosheth son of Saul heard that Abner had died at Hebron, ·he was shocked [he lost his courage; Lhis hands grew limp] and all Israel ·became frightened [was alarmed/dismayed]. 2·Two men who were captains in Saul's army came to Ish-Bosheth [Saul's son had two leaders of raiding parties]. One was named Baanah, and the other was named Recab. They were the sons of Rimmon of Beeroth, who was a Benjaminite. (The town Beeroth belonged to the tribe of Benjamin. 3The people of Beeroth ran away to Gittaim, and they still live there as ·foreigners [resident aliens] today.)

4(Saul's son Jonathan had a son named Mephibosheth, who was ·crippled [lame] in both feet. He was five years old when the ·news [report] came from Jezreel ·that Saul and Jonathan were dead [about Saul and Jonathan]. Mephibosheth's nurse had picked him up and run away. But as she hurried to leave, she dropped him, and now he was lame.)

5Recab and Baanah, sons of Rimmon from Beeroth, went to Ish-Bosheth's house in the ·afternoon [Lheat of the day] while he was taking ·a nap [his midday rest]. 6-7They went into the middle of the house as if to get some wheat. Ish-Bosheth was lying on his bed in his bedroom. Then Recab and Baanah ·stabbed [Lstruck] him in the stomach, killed him, cut off his head, and took it with them. They escaped and traveled all night through the ·Jordan Valley [LArabah]. 8When they arrived at Hebron, they ·gave [brought] his head to David and said to the king, "Here is the head of Ish-Bosheth son of Saul, your enemy. He ·tried to kill you [sought your life]! Today the LORD has ·paid back [given my lord the king revenge on] Saul and his ·family [offspring; descendants; Lseed] for what they did to you!"

9David answered Recab and his brother Baanah, the sons of Rimmon of Beeroth, "As surely as the LORD lives, he has ·saved [Lransomed; redeemed] me from all ·trouble [danger; adversity; *or* my enemies]! 10Once a man thought he was bringing me good news. When he told me, 'Saul is dead!' I seized him and killed him at Ziklag. That was the reward I gave him for his news [1:1–16]! 11·So even more I must [LHow much more must I…?] put you evil men to death because you have killed an ·innocent [righteous] man on his own bed in his own house!"

12So David commanded his men to kill Recab and Baanah. They cut off the hands and feet of Recab and Baanah and hung ·them [their bodies] ·over [beside] the pool of Hebron. Then they took Ish-Bosheth's head and buried it in Abner's ·tomb [grave] at Hebron.

David Is Made King of Israel

*(5:1–5; 1 Chr. 11:1–3)*4

5 Then all the tribes of Israel came to David at Hebron and said to him, "Look, we are your own ·family [flesh and blood; Lbone and flesh]. 2·Even [In the past] when Saul was [Lour] king, you were the one who led Israel ·in battle [Lout and in]. The LORD said to you, 'You will be a shepherd for my people Israel. You will be their ·leader [ruler].' "

3So all the elders of Israel came to King David at Hebron, and he ·made [Lcut] an ·agreement [treaty; covenant] with them in Hebron in the presence of the LORD. Then they ·poured oil on [anointed] David to make him king ·over [of] Israel.

4David was thirty years old when he became king, and he ·ruled [reigned] forty years. 5He was king over Judah ·in [at; from] Hebron for seven years and six months, and he was king over all Israel and Judah ·in [at; from] Jerusalem for thirty-three years.

David Captures Jerusalem

(5:6–10; 1 Chr. 11:4–9)

6When the king and his men went to Jerusalem to attack the Jebusites

who lived there, the Jebusites said to David, "You can't ·get inside our city [Lcome in here]. **Even the blind and the ·crippled can stop you** [Llame can hold you off/turn you away]." **They thought David could not enter their city.** 7**But David did ·take the city of Jerusalem with its strong walls** [capture the stronghold/fortress of Zion], **and it ·became** [is] **the City of David** [Cit did not belong to a specific tribe; David made it the national capital].

8**That day David said to his men, "To ·defeat** [Lstrike] **the Jebusites you must go through the water tunnel. ·Then you can reach** [*or* David hates] **those ·'crippled'** [lame] **and 'blind' enemies. This is why people say, 'The blind and the ·crippled** [lame] **may not enter the ·palace** [Lhouse; *or* Temple].'"

9**So David lived in the ·strong, walled city** [stronghold; fortress] **and called it the City of David. David built more buildings around it, ·beginning where the land was filled in. He also built more buildings inside the city** [L…from the Millo/terraces inward; CMillo may refer to earth-filled terraces that allowed the expansion of the city]. 10**He became ·stronger and stronger** [more and more powerful/great], **because the LORD God ·All-Powerful** [of Heaven's Armies; Tof hosts] **was with him.**

David Consolidates His Kingdom
(5:11–25; 1 Chr. 14:1–17)

11**Hiram king of the city of Tyre sent messengers to David, along with cedar logs, carpenters, and ·stonecutters** [stonemasons]. **They built a ·palace** [Lhouse] **for David.** 12**Then David ·knew** [realized] **that the LORD really had ·made** [confirmed; established] **him king ·of** [over] **Israel and that the LORD had ·made his kingdom great** [blessed/exalted his kingdom] **·because the LORD loved** [for the sake of] **his people Israel.**

13**After he came from Hebron, David took for himself more ·slave women** [concubines; Ca secondary wife; 3:7] **and wives in Jerusalem. More sons and daughters were born to David.** 14**These are the names of the sons born to David in Jerusalem: Shammua, Shobab, Nathan, Solomon,** 15**Ibhar, Elishua, Nepheg, Japhia,** 16**Elishama, Eliada, and Eliphelet.**

David Defeats the Philistines

17**When the Philistines heard that David had been ·made** [anointed] **king over Israel, all the Philistines went to ·look for** [seek; search for] **him. But when David heard the news, he went down to the stronghold.** 18**The Philistines ·came** [arrived] **and ·camped** [Lspread out] **in the Valley of Rephaim.** 19**David ·asked** [consulted; inquired of] **the LORD** [Cthrough the Urim and Thummim; Ex. 28:30; 1 Sam. 23:1–6], **"Should I ·attack** [Lgo up against] **the Philistines? Will you hand them over to me?"**

The LORD said to David, "Go [Lup]! **I will ·certainly** [surely] **hand them over to you."**

20**So David went to Baal Perazim and ·defeated** [Lstruck] **the Philistines there. David said, "Like a flood of water, the LORD has broken through my enemies in front of me." So David named the place Baal Perazim** [C"the Lord breaks through"]. 21**The Philistines ·left their idols behind** [abandoned their idols] **at Baal Perazim, so David and his men carried them away.**

22**Once again the Philistines came and ·camped at** [Lspread out in] **the Valley of Rephaim.** 23**When David ·prayed to** [consulted; inquired of] **the LORD, he answered, "Don't ·attack the Philistines from the front** [go up]. **Instead, go around and attack them ·in front of** [across from; near] **the balsam trees.** 24**When you hear the sound of marching in the tops of the balsam trees, ·act quickly** [be alert]. **I, the LORD, will have gone ahead of you to ·defeat** [Lstrike] **the Philistine army."** 25**So David did what the LORD**

commanded. He ·defeated the Philistines and chased them [Lstruck the
Philistines] all the way from ·Gibeon [Giba] to Gezer.

The Ark Is Brought to Jerusalem

(6:1–11; 1 Chr. 13:1–14)

6 David again gathered all the ·chosen men [elite troops] of Israel—
thirty thousand of them. 2Then he and all his people went to
Baalah in Judah [Canother name for Kiriath Jearim] to bring back the Ark
of God [Ex. 25:10; 1 Sam. 7:2–3]. The Ark is called by the Name, the name
of the LORD ·All-Powerful [of Heaven's Armies; Tof hosts], ·whose throne
is [Lwho is enthroned] ·between [*or* above; *or* on] the ·gold creatures with
wings [Lcherubim; Ex. 25:18–22]. 3They put the Ark of God on a new cart
and brought it out of Abinadab's house on the hill. Uzzah and Ahio, sons
of Abinadab, ·led [guided; drove] the new cart 4which had the Ark of God
on it. Ahio was walking in front of it. 5David and all the Israelites were
celebrating in the presence of the LORD. They were playing wooden
instruments: lyres, harps, tambourines, ·rattles [castanets], and cymbals.
6When David's men came to the threshing floor of Nacon, the oxen
·stumbled [*or* made it tilt]. So Uzzah reached out ·to steady [Land took
hold of] the Ark of God. 7The ·LORD was angry with [LLORD's anger burned
against] Uzzah and [Lhe] ·killed him [Lstruck him down there] because of
what he did. So Uzzah died there beside the Ark of God. 8David ·was
angry because the LORD had killed [Lresented the LORD's outburst of anger
against] Uzzah. ·Now [LTo this day] that place is called ·the Punishment of
Uzzah [Outburst upon/against Uzzah; LPerez-uzzah].
9David was afraid of the LORD that day, and he said, "How can the Ark
of the LORD come ·to me [into my care] now?" 10So David ·would not
[Lwas unwilling to] move the Ark of the LORD to be with him in ·Jerusalem
[Lthe City of David]. Instead, he took it to the house of Obed-Edom, ·a
man from Gath [the Gittite]. 11The Ark of the LORD stayed in Obed-
Edom's house for three months, and the LORD blessed Obed-Edom and all
his ·family [household].
12The people told David, "The LORD has blessed the ·family [house-
hold] of Obed-Edom and all that belongs to him, because the Ark of God
is there." So David went and brought it up from Obed-Edom's house to
Jerusalem with ·joy [gladness; a great celebration]. 13When the men carrying the Ark of the LORD had walked six steps, David sacrificed a bull
and a ·fat calf [fat sheep; Lfatling]. 14Then David danced with all his might
before the LORD. He had on a holy linen ·vest [ephod; Ex. 28:6–14].
15David and all the Israelites shouted with joy and blew the ·trumpets
[ram's horns] as they brought the Ark of the LORD to the city.
16As the Ark of the LORD came into the city [Lof David], Saul's daughter
Michal looked out the window. When she saw David ·jumping [leaping]
and ·dancing [whirling] in the presence of the LORD, she ·hated him
[Ldespised/had contempt for him in her heart].
17David put up a tent for the Ark of the LORD, and then the Israelites
put it in its place inside the tent. David offered whole burnt offerings and
·fellowship [*or* peace; well-being] offerings [Lev. 3:1] before the LORD.
18When David finished offering the whole burnt offerings and the ·fel-
lowship [peace; well-being] offerings [Lev. 3:1], he blessed the people in
the name of the LORD ·All-Powerful [of Heaven's Armies; Tof hosts].
19David gave a loaf of bread, a ·cake [cluster] of dates, and a ·cake [cluster]
of raisins to ·every Israelite [Lthe whole multitude/crowd of Israel], both
men and women. Then all the people went home.

20 David went back to bless ·the people in his home [his household/fam-
ily], but Saul's daughter Michal came out to meet him. She said, "·With
what honor [How] the king of Israel ·acted [distinguished himself] today!
You ·took off your clothes [exposed/uncovered/displayed yourself] in
front of the servant girls of your officers like ·one who takes off his clothes
without shame [any vulgar/foolish/shameless fellow might do]!"
21 Then David said to Michal, "I did it ·in the presence of [before] the
LORD. The LORD chose me, ·not [over; above] your father ·or anyone from
Saul's family [and all his house]. The LORD appointed me ·to be [ruler;
leader; prince] over Israel. So I will celebrate ·in the presence of [before]
the LORD. 22 Maybe I will ·lose even more honor [become even more lightly
esteemed/contemptible/undignified], and maybe I will be ·brought down
in my own opinion [humbled in my own eyes], but the ·girls [maids; servant girls] you talk about will honor me!"
23 And Saul's daughter Michal had no children to the day she died.

David Wants to Build a Temple

(7:1–29; 1 Chr. 17:1–27)

7 King David was living in his ·palace [Lhouse], and the LORD had
given him ·peace [Lrest] from all his enemies ·around [Lsur-
rounding] him [Deut. 12:10; Capparently a sign that the conquest of
Canaan was complete and the Temple should be built]. 2 Then David said
to Nathan the prophet, "Look, I am living in a ·palace [Lhouse] made of
cedar wood, but the Ark of God ·is [stays; dwells] in a tent!"
3 Nathan said to the king, "Go and do what you ·really want to do [Lhave
in your mind/heart], because the LORD is with you."
4 But that night the ·LORD spoke his word [Lword of the LORD came] to
Nathan, 5 "Go and tell my servant David, '·This is what the LORD says: ·Will
you [Are you the one to] build a house for me to ·live [dwell] in? 6 From the
time I brought the Israelites out of Egypt until ·now [Lthis day] I have not
·lived [dwelt] in a house. I have been moving around all this time with a
tent ·as my home [*or* and a tabernacle]. 7 As I have moved with the Israelites,
·I have never [Lhave I ever] said to ·the tribes [any of the tribal leaders],
whom I commanded to ·take care of [shepherd] my people Israel, "Why
haven't you built me a house of cedar?"'
8 "You must tell my servant David, 'This is what the LORD ·All-Powerful
[of Heaven's Armies; Tof hosts] says: I took you from the pasture and
from ·tending [following] the sheep and made you ·leader [ruler; prince]
of my people Israel. 9 I have been with you everywhere you have gone and
have ·defeated [destroyed; Lcut off] your enemies for you. I will make ·you
as famous [Lfor you a name as great] as any of the great people on the
earth. 10 Also I will ·choose [appoint; provide] a place for my people Israel,
and I will plant them ·so they can live in their own homes [Lto dwell in
their own place]. They will not be bothered anymore. Wicked people will
no longer ·bother [afflict; oppress] them as they have in the past 11 when I
·chose [appointed; commanded; instituted] judges for my people Israel.
But I will give you ·peace [Lrest] from all your enemies. ·I also tell you
[LThe LORD also declares] that ·I [Lthe LORD] will ·make your descendants
kings of Israel after [Lestablish a house/dynasty for] you.
12 "'When ·you die [Lyour days are complete/fulfilled/over] and ·join
[you lie down/are buried with] your ancestors, I will ·make one of your
sons the next king [Lraise up your descendant/offspring after you;
CSolomon; 1 Kin. 1–2], and I will ·set up [establish] his kingdom. 13 He will
build a house [Cthe Temple; 1 Kin. 6–7] for ·me [Lmy name], and I will ·let

his kingdom rule always [Lestablish the throne of his kingdom forever]. 14I
will be his father, and he will be my son [Ps. 2:7]. When he ·sins [does
wrong], I ·will use other people to punish him. They will be my whips
[L...correct/discipline him with the rod of/used by men and the whip-
pings/blows used by humans]. 15I took away my ·love [favor; faithful love]
from Saul, whom I removed before you, but I will never stop loving your
son. 16But your ·family [Lhouse] and your kingdom will ·continue
[endure] always before me. Your throne will ·last [Lbe established/secure]
forever.' "

17Nathan told David ·everything God had said in [all these words of]
this vision.

David Prays to God

18Then King David went in and sat ·in front of [before; in the presence
of] the LORD. David said, "Lord GOD, who am I? What is my ·family
[Lhouse]? Why did you bring me ·to this point [this far]? 19But even this
·is not enough for you [Lwas a small thing in your eyes], Lord GOD. You
have also ·made promises about my future family [spoken about the
future of my house]. ·This is extraordinary [So it is with humanity; *or*
This is a decree/instruction/charter for the people/humanity], Lord GOD.
20"What more can I say to you, Lord GOD, since you know me, your
servant, so well! 21You have done ·this great thing [Lall this greatness]
·because you said you would [Lfor the sake of your word/promise] and
·because you wanted to [Laccording to your will/heart], and you have ·let
me know about it [made it known to your servant]. 22This is why you are
great, Lord GOD! There is no one like you. There is no God except you.
·We have heard all this ourselves [...that we have ever heard of]! 23·There
is no nation like [LWhat other nation/people is like...?] your people Israel.
·They are the only [LWhat other...?] people on earth ·that God chose [did
God choose] to be his own [Gen. 12:1–3]. ·You made your name well
known. You did great and wonderful miracles for them [...to make a
name for himself by doing great and awesome things/miracles/wonders
on their behalf?]. You went ahead of them and ·forced [drove] other
nations and their gods out of the land. You ·freed [redeemed; ransomed]
your people from ·slavery in Egypt [Egypt]. 24You ·made [established] the
people of Israel your very own people forever, and, LORD, you ·are [have
become] their God.

25"Now, LORD God, keep the ·promise forever that you made [word you
have spoken] about my ·family [Lhouse] and me, your servant. Do what
you have said [promised]. 26Then ·you [Lyour name] will be ·honored
[magnified] ·always [forever], ·and people will say [...by people saying],
'The LORD ·All-Powerful [of Heaven's Armies; Tof hosts] is God over
Israel!' And ·the family [Lmay the house] of your servant David will ·con-
tinue [be established/secure] before you.

27"LORD ·All-Powerful [of Heaven's Armies; Tof hosts], the God of
Israel, you have ·said to me [revealed this to me, saying], 'I will ·make your
family great [Lbuild a house/dynasty for you].' So I, your servant, am
·brave [bold; courageous] enough to pray to you. 28Lord GOD, you are
God, and your words are ·true [truth; trustworthy]. And you have promised these good things to me, your servant. 29Please, bless ·my family [Lthe
house of your servant]. Let it ·continue [remain] before you always. Lord
GOD, you have ·said so [spoken]. With your blessing let ·my family [Lthe
house of your servant] always be blessed."

David Wins Many Battles
(8:1–18; 1 Chr. 18:1–17)

8 **Later, David ·defeated** [Lstruck] **the Philistines, ·conquered** [sub-
dued] **them, and took ·the city of Metheg Ammah** [*or* a city of
importance; Cperhaps a reference to Gath (1 Chr. 18:1)].
2**He also ·defeated** [Lstruck] **the people of Moab. He made them lie on
the ground, and then he used a rope to measure them. ·Those who were
measured within two rope lengths were killed, but those who were within
the next rope length were allowed to live** [He put to death two measured
groups for every one measured group he allowed to live]. **So the people of
Moab became ·servants** [subjects] **of David and ·gave him the payment
he demanded** [paid/brought him tribute].
3**David also ·defeated** [Lstruck] **Hadadezer son of Rehob, king of Zobah,
as he went to ·take control again at** [extend his power/rule/Lhand over; *or*
restore his monument at] **the Euphrates River.** 4**David captured ·one
thousand chariots, seven thousand men who rode in chariots** [*or* 1,700
charioteers], **and twenty thousand foot soldiers. He ·crippled** [ham-
strung] **all but a hundred of the chariot horses.**
5**·Arameans** [Syrians] **from Damascus came to help Hadadezer king of
Zobah, but David ·killed** [Lstruck] **twenty-two thousand of them.** 6**Then
David put ·groups** [garrisons] **of soldiers in Damascus in Aram. The
·Arameans** [Syrians] **became David's ·servants** [subjects] **and ·gave him
the payment he demanded** [paid/brought him tribute]. **The LORD gave
David victory everywhere he went.**
7**David took the shields of gold that had belonged to Hadadezer's ·offi-
cers** [Lservants] **and brought them to Jerusalem.** 8**David also took many
things made of bronze from Tebah and Berothai, which had been cities
under Hadadezer's control.**
9**Toi king of Hamath heard that David had ·defeated** [Lstruck] **all the
army of Hadadezer.** 10**So Toi sent his son Joram to greet and ·congratulate**
[bless] **King David for defeating Hadadezer. (Hadadezer had been at war
with Toi.) Joram brought ·items** [objects; articles] **made of silver, gold,
and bronze.** 11**King David ·gave** [dedicated; consecrated] **them to the
LORD, along with the silver and gold he had taken from the other nations
he had ·defeated** [subdued; subjugated]. 12**These nations were ·Edom**
[LAram; Cthe Hebrew has Aram (Syria), but the context suggests Edom],
**Moab, Ammon, Philistia, and Amalek. David also gave the LORD ·what he
had taken from** [the spoil/plunder of] **Hadadezer son of Rehob, king of
Zobah.**
13**David ·was famous** [Lmade a name for himself] **after he returned
from ·defeating** [*or* killing; Lstriking] **eighteen thousand ·Arameans** [*or*
Edomites; 1 Chr. 18:12; Ps. 60 title] **in the Valley of Salt.** 14**He put ·groups**
[garrisons] **of soldiers all over Edom, and all the Edomites became his
·servants** [subjects]. **The LORD gave David victory everywhere he went.**
15**David ·was king** [reigned] **over all Israel, and he did what was ·fair**
[just] **and ·right** [equitable] **for all his people.** 16**Joab son of Zeruiah was
commander over the army. Jehoshaphat son of Ahilud was the ·recorder**
[royal historian]. 17**Zadok son of Ahitub and Abiathar son of Ahimelech
were priests. Seraiah was the royal secretary.** 18**Benaiah son of Jehoiada
was over the Kerethites and Pelethites** [Cforeign mercenaries who served
as the king's bodyguards]. **And David's sons were ·priests** [*or* important
officials; C"priests" is the more likely reading, but uncertain because only
Levites were supposed to be priests].

David Helps Saul's Family
(9:1–13; 1 Chr. 19:1–19)

9 David asked, "Is anyone still left in Saul's ·family [Lhouse]? I want
to show ·kindness [loyalty] to that person for Jonathan's sake [1
Sam. 20:13–15]!"
2Now there was a servant named Ziba from Saul's ·family [Lhouse]. So
David's servants ·called [summoned] Ziba to him. King David said to
him, "Are you Ziba?"
He answered, "·Yes, I am your servant [At your service]."
3The king asked, "Is anyone left in Saul's ·family [Lhouse]? I want to
show God's kindness to that person."
Ziba answered the king, "Jonathan has a son still living who is ·crip-
pled [lame] in both feet."
4The king asked Ziba, "Where is this son?"
Ziba answered, "He is at the house of Makir son of Ammiel in Lo
Debar."
5Then King David had servants bring Jonathan's son from the house of
Makir son of Ammiel in Lo Debar. 6Mephibosheth, Jonathan's son, came
before David and bowed facedown ·on the floor [and prostrated
himself].
David said, "Mephibosheth!"
Mephibosheth said, "·I am your servant [At your service]."
7David said to him, "Don't be afraid. I will be kind to you for your
father Jonathan's sake. I will ·give you back [restore to you] all the ·land
[property] of your grandfather Saul, and you will always eat at my table
[Cthe king will provide for his provisions]."
8Mephibosheth ·bowed [prostrated himself] to David again and said,
"·You are being very kind to me, your servant! And I am no better than a
dead dog! [LWhat is your servant, that you should show kindness/favor to
a dead dog like me?]"
9Then King David called Saul's servant Ziba. David said to him, "I have
given your master's grandson everything that belonged to Saul and his
·family [Lhouse]. 10You, your sons, and your servants will farm the land
and harvest the crops. ·Then your family [...so your master's household]
will have food to eat. But Mephibosheth, your master's grandson, will
always eat at my table."
(Now Ziba had fifteen sons and twenty servants.) 11Ziba said to King
David, "I, your servant, will do everything my ·master [lord], the king,
commands me."
So Mephibosheth ate at David's table as if he were one of the king's
sons. 12Mephibosheth had a young son named Mica. Everyone in Ziba's
·family [household] became Mephibosheth's servants. 13Mephibosheth
lived in Jerusalem, because he always ate at the king's table. And he was
·crippled [lame] in both feet.

War with the Ammonites and Arameans

10 When Nahash king of the ·Ammonites [Lsons/descendants of
Ammon] died, his son Hanun became king after him. 2David
said, "Nahash ·was loyal [showed kindness; Ckept treaty obligations] to
me, so I will ·be loyal [show kindness] to his son Hanun." So David sent
his ·messengers [Lservants] to ·comfort [console; express sympathy/con-
dolences to] Hanun about his father's death.
David's ·officers [Lservants] went to the land of the ·Ammonites [Lsons/
descendants of Ammon]. 3But the ·Ammonite leaders [Lprinces/com-
manders of the sons/descendants of Ammon] said to Hanun, their master,

"Do you think David wants to honor your father by sending men to
·comfort [console; sympathize with] you? No! David sent them to ·study
[explore; search] the city and spy it out and ·capture [overthrow] it!" [4]So
Hanun ·arrested [seized] David's ·officers [[L]servants]. To shame them he
shaved off half their beards and cut off their clothes at the ·hips
[[L]buttocks]. Then he sent them away.

[5]When the people told David, he sent messengers to meet ·his officers
[[L]the men] because they were ·very ashamed [humiliated]. King David said,
"Stay in Jericho until your beards have grown back. Then come home."

[6]·The Ammonites knew that they had insulted David. So [[L]When the
sons/descendants of Ammon realized they had become odious to/greatly
offended David,] they hired twenty thousand Aramean foot soldiers from
Beth Rehob and Zobah. They also hired the king of Maacah with a thousand men and twelve thousand men from Tob.

[7]When David heard about this, he sent Joab with the whole army
[[L]with all its warriors]. [8]The ·Ammonites [[L]sons/descendants of Ammon]
came out and ·prepared for battle [drew up in battle formations] at the
city gate. The ·Arameans [Syrians] from Zobah and Rehob and the men
from Tob and Maacah were out in the field by themselves.

[9]Joab saw that there were ·enemies [battle lines] both in front of him
and behind him. So he chose some of the ·best soldiers [elite troops] of
Israel and ·sent them out to fight [deployed them against] the ·Arameans
[Syrians]. [10]Joab put the rest of the army under the command of Abishai,
his brother. Then he ·sent them out to fight [deployed them against] the
·Ammonites [[L]sons/descendants of Ammon]. [11]Joab said to Abishai, "If
the ·Arameans [Syrians] are too strong for me, you must help me. Or, if
the ·Ammonites [[L]sons/descendants of Ammon] are too strong for you, I
will help you. [12]Be strong. ·We must fight bravely [Let us show ourselves
courageous] for our people and the cities of our God. ·The LORD will [May
the LORD] do what he thinks is right."

[13]Then Joab and the army with him ·went [advanced] to attack the
·Arameans [Syrians], and the ·Arameans [Syrians] ·ran away [fled before
him]. [14]When the ·Ammonites [[L]sons/descendants of Ammon] saw that
the ·Arameans [Syrians] were ·running away [fleeing], they also ·ran away
[fled] from Abishai and ·went back [retreated] to their city. So Joab
returned from the battle with the ·Ammonites [[L]sons/descendants of
Ammon] and came to Jerusalem.

[15]When the ·Arameans [Syrians] saw that Israel had defeated them,
they came together into one big army. [16]Hadadezer sent messengers to
bring the ·Arameans [Syrians] from ·east of the Euphrates River [[L]beyond
the river], and they went to Helam. Their leader was Shobach, the commander of Hadadezer's army.

[17]When David heard about this, he gathered all the Israelites together.
They crossed over the Jordan River and went to Helam. There the
·Arameans [Syrians] ·prepared for battle [drew up in battle formations]
and attacked him. [18]But the ·Arameans [Syrians] ·ran away [fled] from
the Israelites. David killed seven hundred Aramean chariot drivers and
forty thousand Aramean ·horsemen [*or* foot soldiers]. He also killed
Shobach, the commander of the Aramean army.

[19]When the kings who ·served [were allied with; [L]were the servants of]
Hadadezer saw that the Israelites had defeated them, they ·made peace
with [surrendered to] the Israelites and served them. And the ·Arameans

[Syrians] were afraid to help the ·Ammonites [Lsons/descendants of
Ammon] again.

David Sins with Bathsheba

11 In the spring, when the kings normally went out to war, David
sent out Joab, his ·servants [officers; army], and all the
Israelites. They ·destroyed [massacred; ravaged] the Ammonites and
·attacked [besieged] the city of Rabbah. But David stayed in Jerusalem.
2One ·evening [afternoon] David got up from his ·bed [midday rest] and
walked around on the roof [Cthe flat roofs of Israelite houses were used
for living space] of ·his palace [Lthe king's house]. While he was on the
roof, he saw a woman bathing. She was very beautiful. 3So David sent his
servants to find out who she was. A servant answered, "That woman is
Bathsheba daughter of Eliam. She is the wife of Uriah the Hittite
[CHittites were foreigners, but he joined the Israelite cause]." 4So David
sent messengers to bring Bathsheba to him. When she came to him, he
·had sexual relations [Llay] with her. (Now Bathsheba had purified herself from her ·monthly period [Luncleanness; Lev. 15:19–24].) Then she
went back to her house. 5But Bathsheba ·became pregnant [conceived]
and sent word to David, saying, "I am pregnant."

6So David sent a message to Joab: "Send Uriah the Hittite to me." And
Joab sent Uriah to David. 7When Uriah came to him, David asked him
how Joab was, how the soldiers were, and how the war was going. 8Then
David said to Uriah, "Go home and ·rest [Lwash your feet; Cperhaps a
euphemism for sex]."

So Uriah left the ·palace [Lking's house], and the king sent a gift to him.
9But Uriah did not go home. Instead, he slept outside the door of the
palace as all the king's ·officers [guard; Lservants] did.

10The officers told David, "Uriah did not go home."

Then David said to Uriah, "You came from a long trip. Why didn't you
go home?"

11Uriah said to him, "The Ark and the soldiers of Israel and Judah are
staying in ·tents [booths; Ctemporary shelters]. My ·master [lord; com-
mander] Joab and his officers are camping out in the fields. ·It isn't right
for me to [LHow can I…?] go home to eat and drink and ·have sexual relations [Llie] with my wife [Cthus rendering himself ritually unclean and
unable to go into the presence of the Ark; Lev. 15:16–18]!"

12David said to Uriah, "Stay here today. Tomorrow I'll send you back to
the battle." So Uriah stayed in Jerusalem that day and the next. 13Then
David called Uriah to come to see him, so Uriah ate and drank with
David. David made Uriah drunk, but he still did not go home. That evening Uriah again slept with the king's ·officers [guard; Lservants].

14The next morning David wrote a letter to Joab and sent it by Uriah.
15In the letter David wrote, "Put Uriah on the front lines where the fighting is ·worst [fiercest; hardest] and ·leave him there alone [then pull back/
withdraw]. Let him be ·killed in battle [Lstruck down and die]."

16Joab ·watched [*or* besieged] the city and saw where its ·strongest
defenders [valiant men] were and put Uriah there. 17When the men of the
city came out to fight against Joab, some of David's men ·were killed
[Lfell]. And Uriah the Hittite was one of them.

18Then Joab sent David a complete ·account [report] of the ·war [bat-
tle; fighting]. 19Joab told the messenger, "Tell King David what happened
in the ·war [battle; fighting]. 20After you finish, the king may be angry and

ask, 'Why did you go so near the city to fight? Didn't you know they would shoot arrows from the city wall? 21Do you remember who killed Abimelech son of Jerub-Besheth [Canother name for Gideon]? It was a woman on the city wall. She threw a large stone for grinding grain on Abimelech and killed him there in Thebez [Judg. 9:50–57]. Why did you go so near the wall?' If King David asks that, tell him, 'Your servant Uriah the Hittite also died.' "

22The messenger left and went to David and told him everything Joab had told him to say. 23The messenger told David, "The men of Ammon were ·winning [gaining an advantage over us]. They came out and attacked us in the field, but we ·fought [drove; chased] them back to the city gate. 24The archers on the city wall shot at your servants, and some of ·your men [Lthe king's servants] were killed. Your servant Uriah the Hittite also died."

25David said to the messenger, "Say this to Joab: 'Don't be ·upset [discouraged; troubled] about this. The sword ·kills everyone the same [Ldevours first one and then another]. ·Make a stronger attack [Fight harder; Press your attack] against the city and capture it.' Encourage Joab with these words."

26When ·Bathsheba [Lthe wife of Uriah] heard that her husband was dead, she ·cried [mourned] for him. 27After she finished her time of ·sadness [mourning], David sent servants to bring her to his house. She became David's wife and gave birth to his son, but the LORD was displeased with what David had done.

David's Son Dies

12 The LORD sent Nathan [Ca prophet who was in the king's court; 7:2–17] to David. When he came to David, he said, "There were two men in a city. One was rich, but the other was poor. 2The rich man had many ·sheep [flocks] and ·cattle [herds]. 3But the poor man had nothing except one little ·female [ewe] lamb he had bought. The poor man fed the lamb, and it grew up with him and his children. It ·shared his food [Late from his plate] and drank from his cup and slept in his ·arms [Lbosom]. The lamb was like a daughter to him.

4"Then a traveler stopped to visit the rich man. The rich man wanted to feed the traveler, but he ·didn't want [was unwilling/loath] to take one ·of his own sheep or cattle [from his own flock or herd]. Instead, he took the lamb from the poor man and ·cooked [Lprepared] it for his visitor."

5David ·became very angry at [Lburned with anger against] the rich man. He said to Nathan, "As surely as the LORD lives, the man who did this ·should [deserves to] die! 6He must ·pay for the lamb four times [repay four lambs] for doing such a thing [Ex. 22:1]. He had no ·mercy [pity; compassion]!"

7Then Nathan said to David, "You are ·the [that] man! This is what the LORD, the God of Israel, says: 'I ·appointed [anointed] you king of Israel and [LI] ·saved [rescued; delivered] you from [Lthe hand of] Saul. 8I gave you ·his kingdom [Lyour master's house] and his wives [Linto your arms/bosom]. And I ·made you king [Lgave you the house] of Israel and Judah. And if that had not been enough, I would have given you ·even [much] more. 9So why did you ·ignore the LORD's command [Ldespise the word of the LORD]? Why did you do what ·he says is wrong [Lis evil in his sight/eyes]? You ·killed [Lstruck down] Uriah the Hittite with the sword of the Ammonites and took his wife to be your wife! 10·Now [Therefore] ·there will always be people in your family who will die by a sword [Lthe sword will never depart from your house], because you ·did not respect [Lhave despised] me; you took the wife of Uriah the Hittite for yourself!'

11"This is what the LORD says: 'I am ·bringing trouble to [Lraising up evil against] you from your own ·family [Lhouse]. ·While you watch [LBefore your eyes], I will take your wives from you and give them to ·someone who is very close to you [Lyour neighbor]. He will ·have sexual relations [Llie] with your wives, ·and everyone will know it [in broad daylight]. 12You ·had sexual relations with Bathsheba [Ldid it] in secret, but I will do this ·so all the people of Israel can see it [Lbefore all Israel in broad daylight; 16:21–22].' "

13Then David said to Nathan, "I have sinned against the LORD." Nathan answered, "The LORD has ·taken away [forgiven] your sin. You will not die [Ps. 51]. 14But what you did ·caused the LORD's enemies to lose all respect for him [*or* has shown utter contempt/scorn for the LORD]. For this reason the ·son [child] who was born to you will die."

15Then Nathan went home. And the LORD ·caused the son [Lstruck the child] of David and Bathsheba, Uriah's widow, ·to be [and he became] very sick. 16David ·prayed to [pleaded with; begged; Linquired of] God for the baby. David fasted and went into his house and stayed there, lying on the ground all night. 17The elders of David's ·family [Lhouse] ·came to [stood around] him and tried to pull him up from the ground, but he refused to get up or to eat food with them.

18On the seventh day the baby died. David's ·servants [advisers] were afraid to tell him that the baby was dead. They said, "Look, we tried to talk to David while the baby was alive, but he refused to listen to ·us [reason]. If we tell him the baby is dead, he may do ·something awful [something desperate; himself harm]."

19When David saw his ·servants [advisers] whispering, he knew that the baby was dead. So he asked them, "Is the ·baby [child] dead?"

They answered, "Yes, he is dead."

20Then David got up from the ·floor [ground], washed himself, ·put lotions on [anointed himself], and changed his clothes. Then he went into ·the LORD's house [the Tabernacle; Lhis house] to worship. After that, he went home and asked for something to eat. His servants gave him some food, and he ate.

21David's ·servants [advisers] said to him, "Why are you ·doing [behaving like] this? When the ·baby [child] was still alive, you fasted and you cried. Now that the ·baby [child] is dead, you get up and eat food."

22David said, "While the ·baby [child] was still alive, I fasted, and I cried. I thought, 'Who knows? Maybe the LORD will ·feel sorry for [Lbe gracious to] me and let the ·baby [child] live.' 23But now that the ·baby [child] is dead, why should I fast? ·I can't [LCan I...?] bring him back to life. Someday I will go to him, but he cannot come back to me."

24Then David ·comforted [consoled] Bathsheba his wife. He ·slept with [Lwent in to] her and ·had sexual relations [Llay] with her. She ·became pregnant again [conceived] and ·had another [Lgave birth to a] son, whom ·David [*or* she; they] named Solomon. The LORD loved Solomon. 25The LORD sent word through Nathan the prophet to name the baby Jedidiah [C"loved by the LORD"], ·because the LORD loved the child [Lfor the LORD's sake].

David Captures Rabbah
(11:1; 12:26–31; 1 Chr. 20:1–3)

26Joab fought against Rabbah, a royal city of the Ammonites, and he was about to capture it. 27Joab sent messengers to David and said, "I have fought against Rabbah and have captured ·its water supply [*or* the City of

Waters]. 28Now bring the ·other soldiers [Lrest of the army] together and
attack this city. Capture it before I capture it myself and it is ·called by my
name [named after me]!"
29So David gathered all the army and went to Rabbah and ·fought
against [attacked] it and captured it. 30David took the crown ·off their
king's [*or* of Milcom from his] head [CMilcom was their main god] and
had it placed on his own head. That gold crown weighed ·about seventy-
five pounds [La talent], and ·it had valuable gems in it [was set with precious
stones]. And David took ·many valuable things [great amounts of plunder/
spoil] from the city. 31He also brought out the people of the city and forced
them to work with saws, iron picks, and axes. He also ·made them build
with bricks [sent them to the brick kilns]. David did this to all the
Ammonite cities. Then David and all his army returned to Jerusalem.

Amnon and Tamar

13 [LSometime later; After this] David had a son named Absalom
and a son named Amnon. Absalom had a beautiful sister
named Tamar, and Amnon loved her. 2Tamar was a virgin. Amnon made
himself sick ·just thinking about her [by his obsession/frustration with
her], because ·he could not find any chance to be alone with her [it
seemed impossible for him to do anything to her; it appeared he could
never have her].
3Amnon had a friend named Jonadab son of Shimeah, David's brother.
Jonadab was a very ·clever [shrewd; crafty; wise] man. 4He asked Amnon,
"Son of the king, why do you look so ·sad [depressed; dejected] ·day after
day [Lmorning after morning]? Tell me what's wrong!"
Amnon told him, "I love Tamar, the sister of my ·half-brother [Lbrother]
Absalom."
5Jonadab said to Amnon, "Go to bed and ·act as if you are [pretend to
be] sick. ·Then [When…] your father will come to see you. Tell him,
'Please let my sister Tamar come in and give me food to eat. Let her make
the food in front of me so I can watch and eat it from her hand.'"
6So Amnon went to bed and acted sick. When King David came in to
see him, Amnon said to him, "Please let my sister Tamar come in. Let her
make ·two of her special cakes [some special bread] for me while I watch.
Then I will eat them from her hands."
7David sent for Tamar in the palace, saying, "Go to your brother
Amnon's house and make some food for him." 8So Tamar went to her
brother Amnon's house, and he was ·in bed [Llying down]. Tamar took
some dough and ·pressed it together with her hands [kneaded it]. She
made some special ·cakes [bread] while Amnon watched. Then she baked
them. 9Next she took the pan and ·served him [Ldished/poured them out
before him], but he refused to eat.
He said to his servants, "·All of you, leave me alone [Everyone get out of
here]!" So they all ·left him alone [got out]. 10Amnon said to Tamar, "Bring
the food into the ·bedroom [inner room] so I may eat from your hand."
Tamar took the ·cakes [bread] she had made and brought them to her
brother Amnon in the ·bedroom [inner room]. 11She went to him so he
could eat from her hands, but Amnon grabbed her. He said, "Sister, come
and ·have sexual relations [Llie] with me."
12Tamar said to him, "No, [Lmy] brother! Don't ·force [violate; rape;
Lhumiliate] me! This ·should never be [isn't] done in Israel! Don't do this
·shameful [disgraceful; wicked; vile] thing! 13·I could never [LWhere could

I...?] get rid of my shame! And you will be ·like the shameful [one of the
greatest] ·fools [scoundrels] in Israel! Please talk with the king, and he
will ·let you marry [Lnot refuse your marrying] me."
14But Amnon refused to listen to her. He was stronger than she was, so
he ·forced her to have sexual relations with him [raped/Lhumiliated her
and lay with her]. 15After that, Amnon hated Tamar [Lintensely; with a
great hatred]. He hated her more than he had loved her before. Amnon
said to her, "Get ·up and leave [out]!"
16Tamar said to him, "No! Sending me away would be ·worse [a greater
wrong] than what you've already done [Lto me]!"
But he refused to listen to her. 17He called his young ·servant [Lman]
back in and said, "Get this woman out of here and away from me! Lock
the door ·after [behind] her." 18So his servant led her out of the room and
bolted the door ·after [behind] her.
Tamar was wearing a special robe with long sleeves, because the king's
virgin daughters wore this kind of robe. 19Tamar put ashes on her head and
tore her special robe [Ca sign of mourning or distress]. ·Putting her hand on
her head [*or* with her face in her hands], she went away, crying loudly.
20Absalom, Tamar's brother, said to her, "Has Amnon, your brother,
·forced you to have sexual relations with him [Lbeen with you]? For now,
sister, ·be quiet [keep silent]. He is your half-brother. Don't ·let this upset
you so much [worry about this; Ltake this to heart]!" So Tamar lived in
her brother Absalom's house and was ·sad and lonely [desolate and
inconsolable].
21When King David heard the news, he was very angry. 22Absalom did
not say a word, good or bad, to Amnon. But he hated Amnon for ·disgrac-
ing [violating; raping; Lhumiliating] his sister Tamar.

Absalom's Revenge

23Two years later Absalom had some men come to Baal Hazor, near
Ephraim, to cut the wool from his sheep. Absalom invited all the king's
sons to come also [Cfor a feast]. 24Absalom went to the king and said, "I
have men coming to cut the wool. Please come with your ·officers [atten-
dants; Lservants] and join ·me [Lyour servant]."
25King David said to Absalom, "No, my son. We won't all go, because it
would be too much ·trouble [of a burden] for you." Although Absalom
·begged [urged; pressed] David, he would not go, but he did give his
blessing.
26Absalom said, "If you don't want to come, then please let my brother
Amnon come with us."
King David asked, "Why should he go with you?"
27Absalom kept ·begging [urging; pressing] David until he let Amnon
and all the king's sons go with Absalom.
28Then Absalom instructed his ·servants [Lmen], "Watch Amnon.
When ·he is drunk [he's in high spirits; Lhis heart is merry with wine], I
will tell you, '·Kill [LStrike] Amnon.' Right then, kill him! Don't be afraid,
because I have ·commanded [ordered] you! Be ·strong [courageous] and
·brave [valiant]!" 29So Absalom's ·young men [servants] killed Amnon as
Absalom ·commanded [ordered], ·but [then] all of David's other sons got
on their mules and ·escaped [fled].
30While the king's sons were on their way [Cback to Jerusalem], the news
came to David, "Absalom has ·killed [Lstruck down] all of the king's sons!
Not one of them is left alive!" 31King David [Lgot up,] tore his clothes [Ca

sign of mourning or distress] and ·lay [threw himself] on the ground. All
his ·servants [officers; attendants] standing nearby tore their clothes also.
32 Jonadab son of Shimeah, David's brother, said to David, "Don't
·think [believe; suppose] all the young men, your sons, are killed. No, only
Amnon is dead! Absalom has ·planned [plotted; been determined to do]
this ever since Amnon ·forced his sister Tamar to have sexual relations
with him [raped/violated/Lhumiliated his sister Tamar]. 33 My ·master and
[lord the] king, don't ·think [imagine; Ltake to heart] that all of the king's
sons are dead. Only Amnon is dead!"
34 In the meantime Absalom had run away.
A ·guard [watchman] standing on the city wall saw many people coming [Lon the road] from the other side of the hill. 35 So Jonadab said to
King David, "Look, ·I was right [Ljust as your servant said]! The king's
sons are coming!"
36 As soon as Jonadab had said this, the king's sons arrived, ·crying
[wailing] loudly. David and all his servants began ·crying [wailing] also.
37 David ·cried [mourned] for his son ·every day [many days].
But Absalom ran away to Talmai [Chis grandfather] son of Ammihud,
the king of Geshur. 38 After Absalom ran away to Geshur, he stayed there
for three years. 39 When King David ·got over [was reconciled to/com-
forted about/consoled over] Amnon's death, he ·missed [longed/yearned
for] Absalom greatly.

Joab Sends a Wise Woman to David

14 Joab son of Zeruiah knew that ·King David missed Absalom
very much [LDavid's heart longed for/mind was on Absalom].
2 So Joab sent messengers to Tekoa to bring a wise woman from there. He
said to her, "Pretend ·to be very sad [Lyou are in mourning]. Put on
·funeral [mourning] clothes and don't put ·lotion [perfume; anointing
oil] on yourself. Act like a woman who has been ·crying [mourning]
many days for someone who died. 3 Then go to the king and say these
words." Then Joab ·told her what to say [Lput the words in her mouth].
4 ·So [When…] the woman from Tekoa spoke to the king. She bowed
facedown on the ground ·to show respect [Land prostrated herself] and
said, "My king, help me!"
5 King David asked her, "What is ·the matter [troubling you]?"
The woman said, "I am a widow; my husband is dead. 6 I had two sons.
They were out in the field fighting, and no one was there to ·stop [sepa-
rate] them. So one ·son [Lstruck and] killed the other son. 7 Now ·all the
family group [the whole family/clan] ·is [Lhas risen] against me. They said
to me, '·Bring [Hand over; Give up] the son who ·killed [Lstruck] his
brother so we may ·kill [execute] him for ·killing [murdering; taking the
life of] his brother. That way we will ·also get rid of the one who would
receive what belonged to his father [destroy the heir as well; Cso he doesn't
profit from his crime].' ·My son is like the last spark of a fire. He is all
[LThey want to extinguish/quench the only coal/ember] I have left. ·If they
kill him, my [LMy] husband's name and ·property [*or* family; descen-
dents; Lremnant] will be gone from the ·earth [Lface of the earth]."
8 Then the king said to the woman, "Go home. I will ·take care of this
for [Lgive orders concerning] you."
9 The woman of Tekoa said to him, "Let the ·blame [guilt] be on me and
my father's family. My ·master and [lord the] king, you and your throne
are ·innocent [guiltless]."

10King David said, "Bring me anyone who ·says anything bad to
[threatens; criticizes] you. Then he won't ·bother [[L]touch] you again."
11The woman said, "Please ·promise in the name of [swear by; remember; keep in mind] the LORD your God. Then ·my relative who has the
duty of punishing a murderer [my near-relative; [L]the avenger of blood; [C]a
relative obligated to execute the murderer; Num. 35:12, 19–21] won't ·add
to [continue] the destruction by killing my son."
David said, "As surely as the LORD lives, ·no one will hurt your son [[L]not
one hair from his head will fall to the ground]."
12The woman said, "Let me say something to you, my ·master and [lord
the] king."
The king said, "Speak."
13Then the woman said, "Why have you ·decided this way against [acted/
[L]planned to the harm/detriment of] the people of God? When you ·judge
[decide; [L]speak] this way, you ·show that you are guilty [convict yourself]
for not bringing back your son who was ·forced to leave home [banished].
14We will all die someday. We're like water spilled on the ground; no one
can ·gather it back [collect it together]. But God doesn't ·take away [discard]
life. Instead, he plans ways that ·those who have been sent away will not
have to stay away from him [will bring back/home the banished]! 15My
·master and [lord the] king, I came to say this to you because the people
have ·made me afraid [threatened/intimidated me]! I thought, 'Let me talk
to the king. Maybe he will ·do [grant] what I ask. 16Maybe he will listen.
Perhaps he will ·save [rescue; deliver] me from ·those who want to keep
both me and my son from getting what God gave us [[L]the hand of the man
who would cut me and my son from God's inheritance/heritage].'
17"Now I say, 'May the words of my ·master [lord] the king give me ·rest
[comfort; peace]. Like an angel of God, you ·know [discern; understand]
what is good and what is ·bad [evil]. May the LORD your God be with you!' "
18Then King David said, "Do not ·hide [evade] the truth. Answer me
one question."
The woman said, "My ·master [lord] the king, please ·ask your question [speak]."
19The king said, "·Did Joab tell you to say [[L]Is Joab's hand with you in]
all these things?"
The woman answered, "As you live, my ·master [lord] the king, no one
·could avoid that question [can fool/mislead you; [L]turn to the right or left
concerning what you've said]. You are right. Your servant Joab ·did tell me
to say these things [[L]commanded me and put all these words in my
mouth]. 20Joab did it ·so you would see things differently [to change the
look of things]. My ·master [lord], you are wise like an angel of God who
knows ·everything that happens [all things] on earth."

Absalom Returns to Jerusalem

21The king said to Joab, "Look, I ·will do what I promised [grant this
request]. Bring back the young man Absalom."
22Joab bowed facedown on the ground [[L]and prostrated himself] and
blessed the king. Then he said, "Today I know ·you are pleased with me [[L]I
have found favor in your sight/eyes], because you have done what I asked."
23Then Joab got up and went to Geshur and brought Absalom back to
Jerusalem. 24But King David said, "Absalom must go to his own house. He
may not ·come to see me [[L]see my face]." So Absalom went to his own
house and did not ·go to see the king [[L]see the king's face].

25 Absalom was greatly praised for his ·handsome appearance [beauty]. No man in Israel was as handsome as he. No ·blemish [flaw; defect] was on him from his head to his foot. 26 At the end of every year, Absalom would cut his hair, because it became too heavy. When he weighed it, it would weigh ·about five pounds by the royal measure [L200 shekels by the king's standard].

27 Absalom had three sons and one daughter. His daughter's name was also Tamar, and she was a beautiful woman.

28 Absalom lived in Jerusalem for two full years without seeing ·King David [Lthe king's face]. 29 Then Absalom sent for Joab so he could send him to the king [Cto intercede for him], but Joab would not come. Absalom sent a message a second time, but Joab still refused to come. 30 Then Absalom said to his servants, "Look, Joab's field is next to mine, and he has barley growing there. Go burn it." So Absalom's servants set fire to Joab's field.

31 Then Joab went to Absalom's house and said to him, "Why did your servants burn my field?"

32 Absalom said to Joab, "I sent a message to you, asking you to come here. I wanted to send you to the king to ask him why ·he brought me home [LI have come] from Geshur. It would have been better for me to stay there! Now let me see the ·king [Lking's face]. If I have ·sinned [guilt/iniquity in me], he can put me to death!"

33 So Joab went to the king and told him Absalom's words. Then the king called for Absalom. Absalom came and ·bowed facedown [prostrated himself] on the ground before the king, and the king kissed him.

Absalom Plans to Take David's Kingdom

15 After this, Absalom got a chariot and horses for himself and fifty men to run before him [Cto signal his power and claim of heir to the throne]. 2 Absalom would get up early and stand near the city gate [Cthe hub of the town for judicial, business, and social interaction]. Anyone who had a ·problem [suit; petition; case] for the king to ·settle [judge] would come here. When someone came, Absalom would call out and say, "What city are you from?"

The person would answer, "·I'm [LYour servant is] from one of the tribes of Israel."

3 Then Absalom would say, "Look, your claims are ·right [sound/valid and just], but the king has no ·one [representative; deputy] to listen to you." 4 Absalom would also say, "I wish someone would ·make [appoint] me judge in this land! Then people with ·problems [any suit/complaint/case or cause] could come to me, and I ·could help them get [would give them] justice."

5 People would come near Absalom to ·bow to [prostrate themselves before] him. When they did, Absalom would reach out his hand and take hold of them and kiss them [Cto show he treated them as his equals]. 6 Absalom did that to all the Israelites who came to King David for ·decisions [judgment]. In this way, Absalom stole the hearts of all Israel.

7 After four[n] years Absalom said to King David, "Please let me go to Hebron. I want to carry out my ·promise [vow] that I made to the LORD 8 while ·I [Lyour servant] was living in Geshur in Aram. I said, 'If the LORD takes me back to Jerusalem, I will ·worship [offer devotion/a sacrifice to] him in Hebron.' "

15:7 four Some Greek copies read "four." Hebrew copies read "forty."

[9]The king said, "Go in peace."

So Absalom went to Hebron. [10]But he sent ·secret messengers [spies; *or* runners] through all the tribes of Israel. They told the people, "When you hear the trumpets, say this: 'Absalom is the king ·at [in] Hebron!' "

[11]Absalom ·had invited [took] two hundred men to go with him. So they went from Jerusalem with him [Linnocently], ·but they didn't know [not knowing] what he was planning. [12]While Absalom was offering sacrifices, he sent for Ahithophel, ·one of the people who advised David [David's counselor], to come from his hometown of Giloh. So ·Absalom's plans were working very well [the conspiracy grew stronger]. More and more people began to support him.

[13]A messenger came to David, saying, "The ·Israelites are giving their loyalty to [Lhearts of the people/Israelites are with] Absalom."

[14]Then David said to all his ·officers [officials; Lservants] who were with him in Jerusalem, "We must ·leave [flee] quickly! If we don't, we won't be able to ·get away from [escape] Absalom. We must hurry before he ·catches [overtakes] us and ·destroys us and kills the people of Jerusalem [Lbrings disaster and puts the city to the sword]."

[15]The king's ·officers [officials; Lservants] said to him, "We will do anything you ·say [decide; Lchoose]."

[16]The king set out with everyone in his house, but he left ten ·slave women [Lconcubines; Csecondary wives; 3:7] to take care of the palace.
[17]The king left [Lon foot] with all his people following him, and they stopped at ·a house far away [the last house]. [18]All the king's ·servants [men; officers; officials] passed by him—the Kerethites and Pelethites [Cforeign mercenaries who served as the king's bodyguards], ·all those from Gath, and the six hundred men who had followed him [*or* and the six hundred men from Gath].

[19]The king said to Ittai, a man from Gath, "Why are you also going with us? Turn back and stay with ·King Absalom [Lthe king] because you are a foreigner. ·This is not [L...—an exile from] your homeland. [20]You joined me only ·a short time ago [Lyesterday]. Should I make you wander with us when I don't even know where I'm going? Turn back and take your ·brothers [kinsmen; people] with you. May ·kindness [faithful love] and ·loyalty [faithfulness; truth] be shown to you."

[21]But Ittai said to the king, "As surely as the LORD lives and as ·you live [Lmy lord the king lives], I will ·stay with you [Lgo wherever my lord the king goes], whether it means life or death."

[22]David said to Ittai, "Go, march on." So Ittai from Gath and all his people with their ·children [families] marched on. [23]All the people ·cried loudly [wept out loud] as ·everyone [the people] passed by. King David crossed the Kidron Valley, and then all the people went on to the ·desert [wilderness]. [24]Zadok and all the Levites with him carried the Ark of the ·Agreement with God [Covenant/Treaty of God]. They set it down, and Abiathar offered sacrifices until all the people had ·left [marched out of] the city.

[25]The king said to Zadok, "Take the Ark of God back into the city. If ·the LORD is pleased with me [LI find favor in the LORD's sight/eyes], he will bring me back and will let me see both it and ·Jerusalem [Lits dwelling place/tent/Tabernacle] again. [26]But if the LORD says ·he is not pleased with me [L"I take no delight in you"], ·I am ready [here I am]. He can do ·what he wants with me [Lto me what is good in his sight/eyes]."

[27]The king also said to Zadok the priest, "·Aren't you a seer [*or* Do you

understand]? Go back to the city ·in peace [quietly] and take your son Ahimaaz and Abiathar's son Jonathan with you. [28]I will wait near the ·crossings into the desert [fords in the wilderness; Cshallow crossing points of the Jordan River] until I hear from you." [29]So Zadok and Abiathar took the Ark of God back to Jerusalem and stayed there.

[30]David went up the ·Mount [LAscent] of Olives, crying as he went. He covered his head and went barefoot [Csigns of mourning]. All the people with David covered their heads also and cried as they went. [31]Someone told David, "Ahithophel is one of the ·people with Absalom who made secret plans against you [conspirators with Absalom]."

So David prayed, "LORD, please ·make [turn] Ahithophel's ·advice foolish [counsel into foolishness]."

[32]When David reached the top of the mountain where people ·used to worship [worshiped] God, Hushai the Arkite came to meet him. Hushai's coat was torn, and there was dirt on his head [Ca sign of mourning or distress]. [33]David said to Hushai, "If you go with me, you will be ·just one more person for me to take care of [La burden]. [34]But if you return to the city, you can ·make Ahithophel's advice useless [thwart/frustrate/counter Ahithophel's counsel]. Tell Absalom, 'I am your servant, my king. In the past I served your father, but now I will serve you.' [35]The priests Zadok and Abiathar will [Lthey not…?] be with you. Tell them everything you hear in the royal palace. [36]Zadok's son Ahimaaz and Abiathar's son Jonathan are with them. Send them to tell me everything you hear." [37]So David's friend Hushai ·entered [returned to] Jerusalem just as Absalom arrived.

Ziba Meets David

16 When David had passed a short way ·over the top of the Mount of Olives [Lbeyond the summit], Ziba, Mephibosheth's [CJonathan's son and Saul's grandson; 4:4] servant, met him. Ziba had a ·row [string; *or* couple] of donkeys loaded with two hundred loaves of bread, one hundred ·cakes [*or* clusters] of raisins, one hundred ·cakes of figs [Lbunches of summer fruits], and ·leather bags full [skins] of wine. [2]The king asked Ziba, "What are these things for?"

Ziba answered, "The donkeys are for your ·family [household] to ride. The bread and ·cakes of figs [Lsummer fruit] are for the ·servants [men; soldiers] to eat. And the wine is for anyone to drink who might become ·weak [exhausted; faint] in the ·desert [wilderness]."

[3]The king asked, "Where is ·Mephibosheth [Lyour master's son/grandson]?"

Ziba answered him, "Mephibosheth is staying in Jerusalem because he thinks, 'Today the Israelites will ·give [Lrestore] my father's kingdom back to me!' "

[4]Then the king said to Ziba, "All right. Everything that belonged to Mephibosheth, I now give to you!"

Ziba said, "I ·bow to you [prostrate myself]. ·I hope I will always be able to please you [LMay I find favor in your sight/eyes, my lord the king]."

Shimei Curses David

[5]As King David came to Bahurim, a man came out ·and cursed him [cursing at them]. He was from ·Saul's family group [Lthe clan of the house of Saul], and his name was Shimei son of Gera. [6]He threw stones at David and his ·officers [officials; Lservants], but the people and soldiers gathered ·all around David [Lto his right and left]. [7]Shimei cursed David, saying, "Get out, get out, you ·murderer [Lman of blood], you ·troublemaker [scoundrel]. [8]The LORD is ·punishing [repaying] you for ·the people

in Saul's family you killed [Lall the bloodshed of the house of Saul]! You
·took [reigned in] Saul's place as king, but now the LORD has given the
kingdom to your son Absalom! Now you are ·ruined [caught in your own
evil] because you are a ·murderer [Lman of blood]!"
9Abishai son of Zeruiah said to the king, "Why should this dead dog
curse you, the king? Let me go over and cut off his head!"
10But the king answered, "·This does not concern you [LWhat have I to
do with you], sons of Zeruiah! If ·he is cursing me because the LORD told
him to [Lthe LORD has told him, "Curse David"] , who can ·question him
[Lsay, "Why have you done so"]?"
11David also said to Abishai and all his ·officers [officials; Lservants],
"My own ·son [flesh and blood] is trying to kill me! ·This man is a
Benjaminite and has more right to kill me [LHow much more reason has
this Benjaminite; Cas a member of Saul's clan]! Leave him alone and let
him ·curse me [Lcurse], ·because [*or* if] the LORD told him to do this.
12Maybe the LORD will see ·my misery [my affliction/distress; *or* that I am
being wronged] and repay me with ·something good [blessing] for
Shimei's curses today!"
13So David and his men went on down the road, ·but [while] Shimei
·followed [went along] on the nearby hillside. He kept cursing David and
throwing stones and ·dirt [flinging dust] at him. 14When the king and all
his people arrived at the Jordan, they were very tired, so they rested there.
15Meanwhile, Absalom, Ahithophel, and all the ·Israelites [Lpeople/
army of Israel] arrived at Jerusalem. 16David's friend Hushai the Arkite
came to Absalom and said to him, "Long live the king! Long live the king!"
17Absalom asked, "·Why are you not loyal [LIs this the love/loyalty you
show] to your friend David? Why didn't you leave Jerusalem with your
friend?"
18Hushai said, "I belong to the one chosen by the LORD and by these
people and everyone in Israel. I will stay with ·you [Lhim]. 19In the past I
served your father. So whom should I serve now? David's son! I will serve
you as I served him."

Ahithophel's Advice

20Absalom said to Ahithophel, "·Tell [LAdvise; Counsel] us what we
should do."
21Ahithophel said, "Your father left behind some of his ·slave women
[Lconcubines; Csecondary wives; 3:7] to take care of the palace. ·Have sexual
relations with [Sleep with; LGo into] them. Then all Israel will hear that
·your father is your enemy [Lyou have gravely insulted/made yourself odious to your father], and all ·your people [Israel; *or* those who support you]
will be ·encouraged to give you more [stronger in their] support." 22So they
put up a tent for Absalom on the roof [Cthe flat roofs of Israelite houses
were used for living space] of ·his palace [Lthe king's house] where everyone
in Israel could see it. And Absalom ·had sexual relations with [slept with;
Lwent in to] his father's ·slave women [concubines].
23At that time people thought Ahithophel's advice was as ·reliable as
God's own word [Lif one consulted a word/message/oracle from God].
Both David and Absalom thought ·it was that reliable [so].
17 Ahithophel said to Absalom, "Let me choose twelve thousand
men and chase David tonight. 2I'll catch him while he is tired
and ·weak [discouraged], and I'll ·frighten [terrorize] him so all his ·peo-
ple [troops] will run away. But I'll ·kill [strike down] only King David.

3Then I'll bring everyone back to you [Las a bride returns to her husband]." ·If the man you are looking for is dead [Since you seek the life of only one man], everyone else will ·return safely [be at peace]." 4This plan ·seemed good to [pleased] Absalom and to all the ·leaders [elders] of Israel.

5But Absalom said, "Now call Hushai the Arkite, so I can hear what he says." 6When Hushai came to Absalom, Absalom said to him, "This is the plan Ahithophel gave. Should we follow it? If not, ·tell us [give us your view]."

7Hushai said to Absalom, "Ahithophel's advice is not good this time." 8Hushai added, "You know your father and his men are ·strong [Lmighty fighters/warriors]. They are as ·angry [fierce] as a bear that is robbed of its cubs. Your father is a ·skilled [experienced; expert] ·fighter [in war]. He won't stay all night with the ·army [troops]. 9He is probably already hiding in a cave or ·some other place [Lpit; hollow]. ·If the first attack fails [LWhen some of our men fall at the first attack], people will hear the news and think, 'Absalom's followers are ·losing [being slaughtered]!' 10Then even the men who are ·as brave as lions [Lvaliant, with the heart of a lion] will ·be frightened [Lmelt/be paralyzed with fear], because all the Israelites know your father is a ·fighter [Lmighty warrior]. They know his men are brave!

11"This is what I ·suggest [advise; counsel]: Gather all the Israelites from Dan to Beersheba [Cin the far north and south of Israel]. There will be as many people as grains of sand by the sea. Then you ·yourself must go [personally lead them] into the battle. 12We will ·go to [attack; come at] David wherever he is hiding. We will fall on him as dew falls on the ground. ·We will kill him and all of his men so that no one [LNeither he nor any of his men] will be left alive. 13If David ·escapes [withdraws] into a city, all the Israelites will bring ropes to that city and pull it into the valley. Not ·a stone will be left [a pebble will be found there]!"

14Absalom and all the Israelites said, "The ·advice [counsel] of Hushai the Arkite is better than ·that [the counsel] of Ahithophel." (The LORD had ·planned [determined; resolved; ordained] to ·destroy [thwart; defeat; frustrate] the good ·advice [counsel] of Ahithophel so the LORD could bring ·disaster [calamity; ruin] on Absalom.)

15Hushai told Zadok and Abiathar, the priests, what Ahithophel had ·suggested [advised; counseled] to Absalom and the elders of Israel. He also reported to them what he himself had ·suggested [advised; counseled]. Hushai said, 16"Quickly! Send a message to David. Tell him not to stay tonight at the ·crossings into the desert [fords in the wilderness] but to cross over the Jordan River at once. ·If he crosses the river, he and all his people won't be destroyed [LOtherwise the king and everyone with him will be swallowed up]."

17Jonathan and Ahimaaz were waiting at En Rogel. They did not want to ·be [risk being] seen going into the city, so a servant girl would go out to them and give them messages. Then Jonathan and Ahimaaz would go and tell King David.

18But a ·boy [lad; young man] saw Jonathan and Ahimaaz and told Absalom. So Jonathan and Ahimaaz left quickly and went to a man's house in Bahurim. He had a well in his courtyard, and they climbed down into it. 19The man's wife spread a ·sheet [covering] over the opening of the well and ·covered [scattered] it with grain. ·No one could tell that anyone was hiding there [LNothing was known].

17:3 as a bride returns to her husband Some Greek copies read "as a bride returns to her husband." Hebrew copies read "like the return of the whole is the man you seek."

20 Absalom's ·servants [men] came to the woman at the house and
asked, "Where are Ahimaaz and Jonathan?"
She said to them, "They have already crossed the brook."
Absalom's ·servants [men] then went to ·look [search] for Jonathan
and Ahimaaz, but they could not find them. So they went back to
Jerusalem.
21 After ·Absalom's servants [they] left, Jonathan and Ahimaaz climbed
out of the well and went to tell King David. They said, "Hurry, cross over
the ·river [water]! Ahithophel has ·said [advised; counseled] these things
against you!" 22 So David and all his people crossed the Jordan River. By
dawn, everyone had crossed the Jordan.
23 When Ahithophel saw that the Israelites did not ·accept his advice
[follow his counsel], he saddled his donkey and went to his hometown.
He ·left orders for his family and property [set his affairs/house in order],
and then he hanged himself. He died and was buried in his father's tomb.

War Between David and Absalom

24 David arrived at Mahanaim. And Absalom and all ·his Israelites [Lthe
men/army of Israel] crossed over the Jordan River. 25 Absalom had made
Amasa ·captain [commander; head] of the army instead of Joab. Amasa
was the son of a man named ·Jether [*or* Ithra] the Ishmaelite.[n] Amasa's
mother was Abigail daughter of Nahash and sister of Zeruiah, Joab's
mother. 26 Absalom and the Israelites camped in the land of Gilead.
27 Shobi, Makir, and Barzillai were at Mahanaim when David arrived.
Shobi son of Nahash was from the Ammonite town of Rabbah. Makir son
of Ammiel was from Lo Debar, and Barzillai was from Rogelim in Gilead.
28 They brought beds, bowls, clay pots, wheat, barley, flour, roasted grain,
beans, ·small peas [lentils], 29 honey, milk curds, sheep, and cheese made
from ·cows' milk [Lthe herd] for David and his people. They said, "The
people are hungry and tired and thirsty in the ·desert [wilderness]."

18 David ·counted [mustered; reviewed] his men and placed
over them commanders of thousands and commanders of
hundreds. 2 He sent the troops out in three groups. Joab commanded
one-third of the men. Joab's brother Abishai son of Zeruiah commanded
another third. And Ittai from Gath commanded the last third. King
David said to them, "I will also go with you."
3 But the men said, "You must not go ·with us [out]! If we ·run away in the
battle [flee], Absalom's men won't care. Even if half of us are killed, Absalom's
men won't care. But you're worth ten thousand of us! ·You can help us most
by staying in the city [It is better that you support us from the city]."
4 The king said to his people, "I will do what ·you think is best [Lis good
in your sight/eyes]." So the king stood at the side of the gate as the army
went out in groups of a hundred and a thousand.
5 The king commanded Joab, Abishai, and Ittai, "Be gentle with young
Absalom for my sake." Everyone heard the king's orders to the commanders about Absalom.
6 David's army went out into the field against ·Absalom's Israelites
[Israel], and they fought in the forest of Ephraim. 7 There David's army
defeated the Israelites. ·Many died [LThe slaughter was/casualties were
great] that day—twenty thousand men. 8 The battle spread through all
the ·country [countryside], but that day more men ·died [Lwere devoured/
swallowed up] in the forest than ·in the fighting [Lby the sword].

17:25 Ishmaelite This is in agreement with 1 Chr. 2:17. Hebrew copies read "Israelite."

Absalom Dies

9Then Absalom happened to ·meet [run into; come upon] David's
·troops [Lservants]. As Absalom was riding his mule, it went under the
thick branches of a large oak tree. Absalom's head got caught in the tree,
and his mule ran out from under him. So Absalom was left hanging
·above the ground [Lbetween heaven and earth].
10When one of the men saw it happen, he told Joab, "I saw Absalom
·hanging [dangling] in an oak tree!"
11Joab said to him, "You saw him? Why didn't you ·kill him and let him
fall to [Lstrike him to] the ground? I would have given you a belt and ·four
ounces [Lten pieces] of silver!"
12The man answered, "I wouldn't ·touch [Lraise my hand against] the
king's son even if ·you gave me [LI felt in my hand the weight of] ·twenty-five
pounds [La thousand pieces] of silver. We heard the king command you,
Abishai, and Ittai, '·Be careful not to hurt [For my sake protect/spare] young
Absalom.' 13If I had ·killed him [betrayed the king by killing his son], ·the
king would have found out [and there is nothing hidden from the king], and
you would ·not have protected [have kept your distance/aloof from] me!"
14Joab said, "I won't waste time here with you!" Absalom was still alive in
the oak tree, so Joab took three spears and stabbed him in the heart. 15Ten
young men who carried Joab's armor also gathered around Absalom and
struck him and killed him.
16Then Joab blew the trumpet, so the troops ·stopped [returned from]
chasing the Israelites. 17Then Joab's men took Absalom's body and threw it
into a ·large [deep] pit in the forest and ·filled the pit with [Lpiled over him]
many stones. All the Israelites ·ran away [fled] to their homes.
18When Absalom was alive, he had ·set up a pillar for [built a monument
to] himself in the King's Valley. He said, "I have no son to keep my name
alive." So he named the ·pillar [monument] after himself, and it is called
Absalom's Monument even today.
19Ahimaaz son of Zadok said to Joab, "Let me run and take the news to
King David. I'll tell him the LORD has ·saved [rescued; Tdelivered] him from
his enemies."
20Joab answered Ahimaaz, "No, you are not the one to take the news
today. You may do it another time, but do not take it today, because the
king's son is dead."
21Then Joab said to a man from Cush, "Go, tell the king what you have
seen." The Cushite bowed to Joab and ran to tell David.
22But Ahimaaz son of Zadok begged Joab again, "No matter what happens, please let me ·go along [run] with the Cushite!"
Joab said, "Son, why do you want to ·carry the news [run]? You won't get
any reward."
23Ahimaaz answered, "No matter what happens, I will run."
So Joab said to Ahimaaz, "Run!" Then Ahimaaz ran by way of the ·Jordan
Valley [plain] and ·passed [outran] the Cushite.
24David was sitting between the inner and outer gates of the city. The
watchman went up to the roof of the gate by the walls, and as he looked up,
he saw a man running alone. 25He shouted the news to the king.
The king said, "If he is alone, he ·is bringing good news [has news to
give/Lin his mouth]!"
The man came nearer and nearer to the city. 26Then the watchman saw
another man running, and he called to the gatekeeper, "Look! Another
man is running alone!"

The king said, "He is also bringing ·good news [news]!"
27 The watchman said, "I think the first man runs like Ahimaaz son of
Zadok."
The king said, "Ahimaaz is a good man. He must be bringing good
news!"
28 Then Ahimaaz called a greeting to the king. He ·bowed facedown on
the ground [prostrated himself] before the king and said, "·Praise [Blessed
be] the LORD your God! The LORD has ·defeated [handed over] those who
·were [Lraised their hand] against ·you, my [Lmy lord the] king."
29 The king asked, "Is young Absalom ·all right [well]?"
Ahimaaz answered, "When Joab sent me, I saw some great ·excitement
[commotion; confusion], but I don't know what it was."
30 The king said, "Step over here and wait." So Ahimaaz stepped aside
and stood there.
31 Then the Cushite arrived. He said, "·Master and [My Lord the] king,
hear the good news! Today the LORD has ·punished [rescued/Tdelivered
you from] those who ·were [rebelled; Lrose up] against you!"
32 The king asked the Cushite, "Is young Absalom ·all right [well]?"
The Cushite answered, "May your enemies and all who ·come to hurt
you [Lrise up to do you harm] ·be like [share the fate of] that young man!"
33 Then the king was ·very upset [overcome with emotion], and he went
to the room over the city gate and cried. As he went, he cried out, "My son
Absalom, my son Absalom! ·I wish [Would that] I had died and not you.
Absalom, my son, my son!"

Joab Scolds David

19 People told Joab, "Look, the king is ·sad [mourning] and crying ·because of [for] Absalom." 2 David's army had won the
battle that day. But ·it became a very sad day for all the people [Lthe victory that day turned to mourning], because they heard that the king was
·very sad [grieving] for his son. 3 The ·people [men; soldiers] ·came into
the city quietly [Lstole/crept into the city] that day. They were like an
army that had been ·defeated in battle and had run away [Lshamed for
fleeing in battle]. 4 The king covered his face and cried loudly, "My son
Absalom! Absalom, my son, my son!"
5 Joab went into the king's house and said, "Today you have ·shamed
[humiliated] all your men. They ·saved [rescued; Tdelivered] your life and
the lives of your sons, daughters, wives, and ·slave women [Lconcubines;
Csecondary wives; 3:7]. 6 You have shamed them because you love those
who hate you, and you hate those who love you. Today you have made it
clear that your commanders and men mean nothing to you. What if
Absalom had lived and all of us were dead? I can see you would be ·pleased
[content]. 7 Now go out and ·encourage [reassure; speak kindly to] your
servants. I swear by the LORD that if you don't go out, ·no man will be left
with you by tonight [Lnot one man will stay with you tonight]! That will
be worse than ·all the troubles [any disaster/evil] you have had from your
youth until today."
8 So the king went to the city gate [Ca place where public meetings and
court cases were held; 15:2]. When the news spread that the king was at
the gate, ·everyone [all the soldiers] came to see him.

David Goes Back to Jerusalem

·All the Israelites who had followed Absalom [LIsrael] had run away to
their ·homes [Ltents]. 9 People in all the tribes of Israel began to argue,
saying, "The king ·saved [rescued; Tdelivered] us from the Philistines and

our other enemies, but he ·left [fled] the country because of Absalom. 10We ·appointed [anointed] Absalom to rule us, but now he has died in battle. ·We should make [LWhy do you say nothing about making…?] David the king again."

11King David sent a message to Zadok and Abiathar, the priests, that said, "Speak to the elders of Judah. Say, 'Even in my house ·I have heard what all the Israelites are saying [the talk of Israel has reached the king]. So why are you the last tribe to bring the king back to his ·palace [Lhouse; Ceven David's own tribe was wavering in their support]? 12You are my ·brothers [relatives; kin], my own ·family [Lbone and flesh]. Why are you the last tribe to ·bring [welcome] back the king?' 13And say to Amasa, '·You are part of my own family [LAre you not my bone and flesh?]. May God punish me terribly if I don't make you commander of the army [Lfrom now on; for life] in Joab's place!' "

14·David [*or* Amasa; LHe] ·touched [turned; swayed] the hearts of all the people of Judah ·at once [as one]. They sent a message to the king that said, "Return with all ·your men [Lwho serve you]." 15Then the king returned as far as the Jordan River. The men of Judah came to Gilgal to meet him and to ·bring [escort] him across the Jordan.

16Shimei son of Gera, a Benjaminite who lived in Bahurim, hurried down with the men of Judah to meet King David. 17With Shimei came a thousand Benjaminites. Ziba, the servant from Saul's family, also came, bringing his fifteen sons and twenty servants with him. They all hurried to the Jordan River ·to meet [arriving before] the king. 18The people went across the ·Jordan [Lford] to help ·bring [escort] the king's family back to Judah and to do whatever the king wanted. As the king was crossing the river, Shimei son of Gera came to him and ·bowed facedown on the ground [prostrated himself] in front of the king. 19He said to the king, "My master, don't hold me guilty. ·Don't remember [Forget] the wrong ·I [Lyour servant] did when you left Jerusalem! ·Don't hold it against me [Put it out of your mind]. 20I know I have sinned. That is why I am the first person from Joseph's ·family [Lhouse; Cthat is, the first Israelite] to come down and meet you today, my master and king!"

21But Abishai son of Zeruiah said, "·Shimei should die [LShould not Shimei die…?] because he cursed you, the LORD's ·appointed king [anointed; 16:5–14]!"

22David said, "·This does not concern [LWhat does this have to do with…?] you, sons of Zeruiah! Today you're ·against me [my adversary]! No one will be put to death in Israel today. Today I know I am king over Israel!" 23Then the king ·promised [vowed to] Shimei, "You won't die [1 Kin. 2:8–9, 41–46]."

24Mephibosheth, Saul's grandson, also went down to meet King David. Mephibosheth had not cared for his feet, cut his beard, or washed his clothes from the time the king had left Jerusalem until he returned ·safely [in peace; Cdemonstrating his concern for David's welfare]. 25When Mephibosheth came from Jerusalem to meet the king, the king asked him, "Mephibosheth, why didn't you go with me?"

26He answered, "My master, my servant [CZiba] tricked me! I am crippled, so ·I [Lyour servant] said to ·Ziba [Lhim], 'Saddle a donkey. Then I will ride it so I can go with the king.' 27But he ·lied about [slandered] ·me [Lyour servant] to you [16:1–4]. You, my master and king, are like an angel from God. Do what ·you think is good [Lis right in your eyes]. 28·You could have killed all my grandfather's family [LMy father's household were doomed to death/as good as dead before my lord the king]. ·Instead [Yet], you put ·me [Lyour servant] with those people who eat at your own table. So I don't have a right to ask anything more from the king!"

29The king said to him, "Don't say anything more. I have decided that you and Ziba will divide the land."

30Mephibosheth said to the king, "Let Ziba take ·all the land [everything] now that my master the king has arrived safely home."

31Barzillai of Gilead came down from Rogelim to cross the Jordan
River with the king. 32Barzillai was a very old man, eighty years old. He had ·taken care of [provided food for] the king when David was staying at
Mahanaim, because Barzillai was a very rich man [17:27–29]. 33David
said to Barzillai, "Cross the river with me. Come with me to Jerusalem, and I will ·take care of [provide for] you."

34But Barzillai answered the king, "·Do you know how old I am [LHow
long do I have to live]? Do you think I can go with you to Jerusalem? 35I am
eighty years old! Can your servant tell the difference between what is ·good [pleasant] and ·bad [unpleasant]? ·I am too old to [LCan I…?] taste what I eat or drink. ·I am too old to [LCan I …?] hear the voices of men and women singers. Why should you be ·bothered [burdened] with ·me [Lyour servant]?
36·I am not worthy of a reward from you, but I will cross [LWhy should the king reward me for merely going across…?] the Jordan River with you.
37·Then [Please] let ·me [Lyour servant] go back so I may die in my own city near the grave of my father and mother. But here is Kimham, your servant. Let him go with you, my master and king. Do with him whatever ·you want [seems good to you/Lin your eyes; 1 Kin. 2:7]."

38The king answered, "Kimham will go with me. I will do for him anything ·you wish [that seems good to you/Lin your eyes], and I will do anything
for you that you wish." 39The king kissed Barzillai and blessed him. Then
Barzillai returned home, and the king and all the people crossed the Jordan.

40When the king crossed over to Gilgal, Kimham went with him. All the ·troops [people] of Judah and half the ·troops [people] of Israel ·led [escorted; accompanied] David across [Cthe river Jordan].

41Soon all the Israelites came to the king and said to him, "Why did our ·relatives [brothers], the people of Judah, steal you away? Why did they bring you and your family across the Jordan River ·with [along with all] your men?"

42All the people of Judah answered the Israelites, "We did this because the king is our ·close relative [kin]. Why are you angry about it? ·We have not [LHave we…?] eaten food at the king's expense or ·taken anything [received any favors/gifts] for ourselves!"

43The Israelites answered the people of Judah, "We have ten ·tribes [Lshares] in the ·kingdom [Lking], so we have more ·right to [claim on] David than you do! ·But you ignored us! [LWhy did you treat us with contempt?] ·We were [LWeren't we…?] the first ones to talk about bringing our king back!"

But the people of Judah spoke even more ·unkindly [harshly; fiercely] than the people of Israel.

Sheba Leads Israel Away from David

20 It happened that a ·troublemaker [scoundrel; worthless fellow] named Sheba son of Bicri from the tribe of Benjamin was there. He blew the ·trumpet [ram's horn] and said:

"We have no ·share [interest; portion] in David!
We have no ·part [inheritance; heritage] in the son of Jesse!
People of Israel, ·let's go home [Leveryone to your tents]!"
2So all the Israelites ·left [deserted; withdrew from] David and followed
Sheba son of Bicri. But the people of Judah ·stayed with [faithfully followed; clung to] their king all the way from the Jordan River to Jerusalem.
3David came back to his ·palace [Lhouse] in Jerusalem. He had left ten
of his ·slave women [Lconcubines; Csecondary wives; 3:7] there to take
care of the ·palace [Lhouse; 16:21–22]. Now he put them in a ·locked
[guarded] house. He ·gave them food [provided for them], but he did not
·have sexual relations with [Lgo in to] them. So they [Lwere shut up/con-
fined and] lived like widows until they died.
4The king said to Amasa, "·Tell the men [Mobilize the army] of Judah
to meet with me ·in [within] three days, and you must also be here." 5So
Amasa went to ·call [summon] the men of Judah together, but he ·took
more time [delayed longer] than the king had said.
6David said to Abishai, "Sheba son of Bicri ·is more dangerous to us
than Absalom was [Lwill do us more harm than Absalom]. Take ·my men
[Lthe servants of your master] and chase him before he finds ·walled [forti-
fied] cities and escapes from ·us [Lour sight]." 7So Joab's men, the Kerethites
and the Pelethites [Cforeign mercenaries who served as the king's body-
guards], and all the ·soldiers [mighty warriors] went with Abishai. They
went out from Jerusalem to ·chase [pursue] Sheba son of Bicri.
8When Joab and the army came to the great rock at Gibeon, Amasa
came out to meet them. Joab was wearing his ·uniform [military tunic],
and at his waist he wore a belt that held his ·sword [dagger] in its ·case
[sheath]. As Joab stepped forward, his ·sword [dagger] fell out of its ·case
[sheath]. 9Joab asked Amasa, "·Brother [Cterm of endearment, but Amasa
is also his cousin], is everything all right with you?" Then with his right
hand he took Amasa by the beard to kiss him. 10Amasa ·was not watching
[did not notice; wasn't on guard against] the ·sword [dagger] in Joab's
hand. So Joab ·pushed the sword into Amasa's [Lstruck him in the] stomach, causing Amasa's insides to ·spill [pour; gush] onto the ground. Joab
did not have to stab Amasa again; he was already dead. Then Joab and his
brother Abishai continued to ·chase [pursue] Sheba son of Bicri.
11One of Joab's young men stood by Amasa's body and ·said [shouted],
"Everyone who ·is for [Lfavors] Joab and [Lis for] David should follow
Joab!" 12Amasa lay in the middle of the road, ·covered with [wallowing in]
his own blood. When the young man saw that everyone was ·stopping to
look at the body [stopping], he dragged it from the road, laid it in a field,
and put a ·cloth [cloak; garment] over it. 13After Amasa's body was taken off
the road, all the men followed Joab to ·chase [pursue] Sheba son of Bicri.
14Sheba ·went [traveled; passed] through all the tribes of Israel to Abel
Beth Maacah [Ca town in the extreme north of Israel]. All the ·Berites [*or*
Bicrites; CSheba's own tribe] also came together and followed him. 15So
Joab and his men came to Abel Beth Maacah and ·surrounded [besieged]
it. They ·piled dirt up [built a siege ramp] against the city wall, and they
began ·hacking at [battering; undermining] the walls to bring them down.
16But a wise woman shouted out from the city, "Listen! Listen! Tell
Joab to come here. I want to talk to him!"
17So Joab came near her. She asked him, "Are you Joab?"
He answered, "Yes, I am."

Then she said, "Listen to ·what I say [Lthe words of your maidservant]."

Joab said, "I'm listening."

18Then the woman said, "In the past people would say, '·Ask for advice [Let them inquire] at Abel,' and the problem would be solved. 19I am one of the peaceful, ·loyal [faithful] people of Israel. You are trying to destroy ·an important city of [La city that is a mother in] Israel. Why must you ·destroy what belongs to [Ldevour/swallow up the inheritance/heritage of] the LORD?"

20Joab answered, "I would prefer not to ·destroy [Ldevour; swallow up] or ruin anything! 21That is not ·what I want [Lthe case]. But there is a man here from the ·mountains [hill country] of Ephraim, who is named Sheba son of Bicri. He has ·turned [Llifted his hand] against King David. If you ·bring him to me [hand him over], I will leave the city alone."

The woman said to Joab, "His head will be thrown over the wall to you."

22Then the woman spoke very wisely to all the people of the city. They cut off the head of Sheba son of Bicri and threw it over the wall to Joab. So he blew the ·trumpet [ram's horn], and the army left the city. Every man returned ·home [Lto his tent], and Joab went back to the king in Jerusalem.

23Joab was commander of all the army of Israel. Benaiah son of Jehoiada led the Kerethites and Pelethites [20:7]. 24Adoniram was in charge of the ·men who were forced to do hard work [forced/slave labor; *or* labor force]. Jehoshaphat son of Ahilud was the ·recorder [royal historian]. 25Sheba was the royal ·secretary [scribe]. Zadok and Abiathar were the priests, 26and Ira the Jairite was David's priest.

The Gibeonites Punish Saul's Family

21 During the time David was king, there was a ·shortage of food [famine] that lasted for three years. So David ·prayed to [inquired of; consulted; Lsought the face/presence of] the LORD.

The LORD answered, "Saul and his ·family of murderers [Lbloody house] are the reason for this shortage, because he ·killed [murdered] the Gibeonites." 2(Now the Gibeonites were not Israelites; they were ·a group of Amorites who were left alive [Lthe remnant of the Amorites]. The Israelites had ·promised [sworn; vowed; Josh. 9:14–15] not to hurt the Gibeonites, but Saul had tried to ·kill [annihilate; exterminate] them, because ·he was eager to help [of his zeal for] the people of Israel and Judah.)

King David called the Gibeonites together and spoke to them. 3He asked, "What can I do for you? How can I make ·up [amends; expiation; atonement] for the harm done so you can bless the LORD's ·people [Linheritance]?"

4The Gibeonites said to David, "We cannot ·demand [settle this with] silver or gold from Saul or his ·family [Lhouse]. And ·we don't have the right [Lit's not for us] to kill anyone in Israel."

Then David asked, "·What do you want me to do for you [Tell me what to do and I will do it]?"

5The Gibeonites said, "·Saul [LThe man] ·made plans against [destroyed; consumed] us and ·tried to destroy [planned to annihilate/exterminate] all our people ·who are [so we would have no place] left in the land of Israel. 6So bring seven of his sons to us. Then we will ·kill them and hang them on stakes [impale/execute them] in the presence of the LORD at Gibeah, the hometown of Saul, the LORD's chosen king."

The king said, "I will give them to you." 7But the king ·protected

[spared] Mephibosheth, the son of Jonathan, the son of Saul, because of
the ·promise [oath] he had made to Jonathan in the LORD's name [1 Sam.
20:14–17]. 8The king did take Armoni and Mephibosheth [Cnot Jonathan's
son, but another person with the same name], sons of Rizpah and Saul
[3:7]. (Rizpah was the daughter of Aiah.) And the king took the five sons
of Saul's daughter Merab [1 Sam. 14:49; 18:17–19]. (Adriel son of Barzillai
the Meholathite was the father of Merab's five sons.) 9David gave these
seven sons to the Gibeonites. Then the Gibeonites ·killed them and hung
them on stakes on a hill [impaled/executed them] in the presence of the
LORD. All seven sons ·died [fell] together. They were put to death during
the first days of the harvest season at the beginning of barley harvest.

10Aiah's daughter Rizpah took ·the rough cloth [burlap; sackcloth; Ca
sign of mourning or distress] and put it on a rock for herself. She stayed
there from the beginning of the harvest until the rain fell on ·her sons'
bodies [Lthem from the heavens/sky]. During the day she did not let the
·birds of the sky [scavenger birds] touch her sons' bodies, and during the
night she did not let the wild animals touch them.

11People told David what Aiah's daughter Rizpah, Saul's ·slave woman
[Lconcubine; Ca secondary wife; 3:7], was doing. 12Then David took the
bones of Saul and Jonathan from the men of Jabesh Gilead. (The Philistines
had hung the bodies of Saul and Jonathan in the public square of Beth
Shan after they had killed Saul at Gilboa. Later the men of Jabesh Gilead
·had secretly taken [stole] them from there [1 Sam. 31:8–13].) 13David
brought the bones of Saul and his son Jonathan from Gilead. Then the
people gathered the ·bodies of Saul's seven sons who were hanged on stakes
[bones of those who had been impaled/executed]. 14The people buried the
bones of Saul and his son Jonathan at Zela in Benjamin in the tomb of
Saul's father Kish. The people did everything the king commanded.

Then God ·answered the prayers for [took pity on] the land.

Wars with the Philistines
(21:15–22; 1 Chr. 20:4–8)

15Again there was war between the Philistines and Israel. David and his
·men [servants] went out to fight the Philistines, ·but [and] David
·became tired [grew weary/exhausted]. 16Ishbi-Benob, one of the ·sons of
Rapha [*or* descendants of the giants], had a bronze ·spearhead [spear]
weighing ·about seven and one-half pounds [Lthree hundred shekels] and
[Lwas armed with] a new sword. He ·planned [was about] to kill David,
17but Abishai son of Zeruiah ·killed the Philistine and saved David's life
[Lcame to help him and struck down the Philistine].

Then David's men ·made a promise [swore; vowed] to him, saying,
"Never again will you go out with us to battle. ·If you were killed, Israel
would lose its greatest leader [L...so that you do not extinguish the lamp/
light of Israel]."

18Later, at Gob, there was another battle with the Philistines. Sibbecai
the Hushathite killed Saph, another ·one of the sons of Rapha [*or* descendant of the giants].

19Later, there was another battle at Gob with the Philistines. Elhanan
son of Jaare-Oregim from Bethlehem killed Goliath from Gath [Csee 1
Chr. 20:5 where he is called Lahmi, the brother of Goliath]. His spear was
as large as a weaver's ·rod [beam].

20At Gath another battle took place. A huge man was there; he had six
fingers on each hand and six toes on each foot—twenty-four fingers and
toes in all. This man also was ·one of the sons of Rapha [*or* descended

from the giants]. [21]When he ·challenged [defied; taunted] Israel, Jonathan
son of Shimeah, David's brother, killed him.
[22]These four ·sons of Rapha [*or* descendants of giants] from Gath were
killed by David and his ·men [[L]servants].

David's Song of Praise
(22:1–51; Ps. 18:1–50)

22 David sang [[L]the words of] this song [[C]see the close parallel to
the following song in Psalm 18] to the LORD when the LORD
·saved [rescued; [T]delivered] him from Saul and all his other enemies.
[2]He said:

"The LORD is my rock, my fortress, my ·Savior [rescuer; [T]deliverer].
[3]My God is my rock.
·I can run to him for safety [[L]In whom I find protection/take refuge].
He is my shield and ·my saving strength [[L]the horn of my salvation; [C]symbolizes strength based on an animal lifting its head triumphantly],
my ·defender [stronghold] and my ·place of safety [refuge].
The LORD saves me from ·those who want to harm me [[L]violence].
[4]I ·will call to [call upon] the LORD, who is worthy of praise,
and I ·will be [*or* am] saved from my enemies.

[5]"The waves of death ·came around [swirled about; encompassed] me;
the ·deadly rivers [floods/torrents of destruction] overwhelmed me.
[6]The ·ropes of death [cords of the grave/Sheol] ·wrapped around [entangled; coiled around] me.
The ·traps [snares] of death ·were before [confronted; lay ahead of] me.
[7]In my ·trouble [distress; anguish] I ·called [cried out] to the LORD;
I ·cried out [called] to my God.
From his ·temple [sanctuary] he heard my voice;
my ·call for help [cry] reached his ears.

[8]"The earth ·trembled [reeled; quaked] and ·shook [rocked].
The foundations of heaven began to ·shake [shudder].
They ·trembled [reeled; quaked] because the LORD was angry.
[9]Smoke ·came out of his nose [poured/rose from his nostrils],
and ·burning [devouring] fire came out of his mouth.
Burning coals ·went before [blazed/flamed out from] him.
[10]He ·tore open [parted; bowed] the ·sky [heavens] and came down
with ·dark clouds [storm clouds; thick darkness] under his feet.
[11]He rode a ·creature with wings [cherub; [C]a mighty spiritual being/angel; Ezek. 1] and flew.
·He raced [...soaring] on the wings of the wind.
[12]He made darkness his ·shelter [canopy, shroud]
surrounded by ·fog and [thick rain] clouds.
[13]Out of the brightness ·of his presence [before him]
·came [blazed; flamed] ·flashes of lightning [[L]fiery coals].
[14]The LORD thundered from heaven;
the ·Most High raised his voice [voice of the Most High resounded].
[15]He shot his arrows and scattered his enemies.
His bolts of lightning ·confused them with fear [routed them].
[16]·The wind blew from his nose [[L]At the blast of breath from his nostrils...] when he spoke.

Then the ·valleys [floor; channels] of the sea ·appeared [were exposed],
and the foundations of the earth were ·seen [laid bare].

17"The Lord reached down from ·above [heaven; on high] and ·took [rescued] me;
he ·pulled me from the deep water [drew me out of mighty waters].
18He ·saved [rescued; [T]delivered] me from my powerful enemies,
from those who hated me, because they were too strong for me.
19They ·attacked [confronted] me ·at my time of trouble [[L]in the day of my distress/calamity/disaster],
but the Lord ·supported me [was my stay].
20He took me to a ·safe [spacious; open; [L]broad] place.
Because he delights in me, he ·saved [rescued; [T]delivered] me.

21"The Lord ·spared [rewarded] me ·because I did what was right [[L]according to my righteousness].
Because ·I have not done evil [of my innocence; [L]of the cleanness of my hands], he has ·rewarded [[L]restored] me.
22I have ·followed [obeyed; kept; [L]guarded] the ways of the Lord;
I have not done evil by turning from my God.
23I ·remember [follow; [L]have before me] all his ·laws [regulations]
and have not ·broken [abandoned; [L]turned from] his ·rules [statutes; ordinances; requirements].
24I am ·innocent [blameless] before him;
I have kept myself from ·doing evil [sin; guilt; iniquity].
25The Lord ·rewarded [repaid] me ·because I did what was right [[L]according to my righteousness],
·because I did what the Lord said was right [[L]according to my cleanness/purity in his sight].

26"Lord, you ·are [show yourself] ·loyal [faithful; kind] to those who are loyal [faithful; kind],
and you are good to those who are good.
27You ·are [show yourself] ·pure [sincere] to those who are pure [sincere],
but you ·are [show yourself] ·against [hostile/shrewd/cunning/perverse to] those who are ·evil [perverse; devious; crooked].
28You ·save [rescue; [T]deliver] the ·humble [afflicted],
but you ·bring down [watch and humiliate] ·those who are proud [the haughty].
29Lord, you ·give light to [[L]are] my lamp.
The Lord ·brightens the darkness around me [lights up/illuminates my darkness].
30With your help I can ·attack [crush] an army.
With God's help I can ·jump over [scale] a wall.

31"The ·ways [way; path] of God are ·without fault [blameless; perfect];
the Lord's ·words [promises] are ·pure [tested; flawless; proven true].
He is a shield to those who ·trust [seek protection/take refuge in] him.
32Who is God? Only the Lord.
Who is the Rock? Only our God.

33God ·is my protection [is my strong fortress; *or* girds me with strength].
He makes my way ·free from fault [perfect; secure; a wide path].
34He makes ·me [Lmy feet] like a deer [Csurefooted];
he ·helps me stand [sets me] on the ·steep mountains [heights].
35He trains my hands for battle
so my arms can bend a bronze bow.
36You ·protect me with your saving shield [Lhave given me the shield of your salvation/victory].
·You have stooped to make [Your help makes] me great.
37You ·give me a better way to live [broaden my path; Lwiden my steps beneath me]
so ·I live as you want me to [my feet do not slip/Lankles do not weaken].
38I ·chased [pursued] my enemies and ·destroyed [exterminated] them.
I did not ·quit [turn back] till they were ·destroyed [annihilated; consumed].
39I ·destroyed [devoured; consumed] and ·crushed them [shattered them; struck them down]
so they couldn't ·rise [get] up again.
They fell beneath my feet.
40You ·gave me [Larmed/girded me with] strength ·in [for] battle.
You ·made my enemies bow [humbled/subdued my enemies] ·before me [under my feet].
41You made my enemies ·turn back [turn their backs; retreat],
and I destroyed ·those who hated me [my foes].
42They ·called for help [looked around],
but no one came to ·save [rescue] them.
They ·called [looked] to the LORD,
but he did not answer them.
43I ·beat my enemies into pieces [ground/pulverized them],
like dust ·on the ground [of the earth].
I ·poured them out and walked [crushed and stamped] on them
like ·mud [mire] in the streets.

44"You ·saved [rescued; Tdelivered] me when my people ·attacked me [quarreled; fought].
You kept me as the ·leader [ruler; head] of nations.
People I never knew serve me.
45Foreigners ·obey [cower/Lcringe before] me.
As soon as they hear ·me [of me], they obey me.
46They all ·become afraid [lose heart/their courage]
and ·tremble in [come trembling from] their ·hiding places [fortresses; strongholds].

47"The LORD lives!
May my Rock be ·praised [blessed]!
Praise God, the Rock, ·who saves me […of my salvation]!
48God gives me ·victory [revenge; vengeance] over my enemies
and brings ·people [the nations] under ·my rule [me].
49He frees me from my enemies.

"You ·set me over those who hate me [exalt/lift me above my enemies].

You ·saved [rescued; [T]delivered] me from violent people.
50So I will ·praise [extol] you, LORD, among the nations.
I will sing praises to your name.
51The LORD ·gives great victories [is a tower of salvation] to his king.
He ·is loyal [shows kindness/faithful love] to his ·appointed king [anointed],
to David and his descendants forever."

David's Last Words

23 These are the last words of David.
This is the ·message [declaration; oracle; inspired words] of David son of Jesse.
The man ·made great by the Most High God [raised high/exalted by God] speaks.
He is the ·appointed king of [anointed by] the God of Jacob;
he is the sweet ·singer [psalmist; *or* hero] of Israel:

2"The LORD's Spirit spoke through me,
and his word was on my tongue.
3The God of Israel spoke;
the Rock of Israel said to me:
'Whoever rules ·fairly [justly; righteously] over people,
who rules ·with respect for [in fear of] God [Prov. 1:7],
4is like the morning light at ·dawn [sunrise],
like a morning without clouds.
He is like sunshine after a rain
that makes the grass ·sprout from the ground [[L]of the earth sparkle/gleam].'

5"·This is how God has cared for my family [[L]Is it not so with my house and God?].
God made a lasting ·agreement [treaty; covenant] with me [7:1–17],
·right [ordered; arranged] and ·sure [secured; guaranteed; assured] in ·every way [all things].
·He will [[L]Will he not…?] ·accomplish [ensure] my ·salvation [safety]
and ·satisfy [fufill; bring about/to fruition] all my desires.
6"But all ·evil [worthless; godless] people will be thrown away like thorns
that cannot be held in a hand.
7No one can touch them
except with a tool of iron or ·wood [[L]the shaft of a spear].
They will be ·thrown in [consumed by] the fire and burned where they lie."

David's Army
(23:8–39; 1 Chr. 11:10–47)

8These are the names of David's warriors:
Josheb-Basshebeth, the Tahkemonite, was ·head of the Three [chief of
the captains; [C]David's most prestigious soldiers; 1 Chr. 11:11]. He ·used
[wielded; brandished] his spear and killed eight hundred men at one time.
9Next was Eleazar son of Dodai the Ahohite. Eleazar was one of the
three ·soldiers [warriors; champions; mighty men] who were with David
when they ·challenged [defied; taunted] the Philistines. The Philistines
were gathered for battle, and the Israelites ·drew back [had fled/disbanded].
10But Eleazar ·stayed where he was [stood his ground] and
·fought [killed; [L]struck] the Philistines until ·he was so tired his hand [[L]his

hand was so stiff that it] stuck to his sword. The LORD ·gave [brought about] a great victory for the Israelites that day. The troops came back after Eleazar had won the battle, but only to ·take weapons and armor from the enemy [plunder].

11Next there was Shammah son of Agee the Hararite. The Philistines came together to fight in a ·vegetable [lentil] field. Israel's troops ·ran away [fled] from the Philistines, 12but Shammah stood in the middle of the field and ·fought for [defended] it and ·killed [Lstruck] the Philistines. And the LORD ·gave [brought about] a great victory.

13Once, three of the Thirty, David's chief ·soldiers [warriors], came down to him at the cave of Adullam during harvest. The Philistine army had camped in the Valley of Rephaim. 14At that time David was in the stronghold, and ·some [La detachment/garrison] of the Philistines were in Bethlehem.

15David had a ·strong desire for some water [Lcraving; longing]. He said, "·Oh, I wish [If only] someone would get me water from the well near the city gate of Bethlehem!" 16So the three warriors broke through the Philistine ·army [lines; camp] and ·took [drew] water from the well near the city gate of Bethlehem. Then they brought it to David, but he refused to drink it. He poured it out before [Cas an offering to] the LORD, 17saying, "·May the LORD keep me from drinking this water [LThe LORD forbid that I should do this]! It would be like drinking the blood of the men who risked their lives!" So David refused to drink it. ·These [Such] were the ·brave things [exploits; deeds] that the three ·warriors [champions] did.

18Abishai, brother of Joab son of Zeruiah, was ·captain [leader; chief] of the Three. Abishai fought three hundred soldiers with his spear and killed them. He ·became as famous as [won/earned a name among] the Three 19and was ·more honored than the Three [*or* the most honored of the Thirty; Cthe Hebrew text has "Three"; the Syriac text has "Thirty" and fits the context better]. He became their commander even though he was not one of ·them [Lthe Three].

20Benaiah son of Jehoiada was a ·brave [valiant] fighter from Kabzeel who ·did mighty things [performed great/heroic exploits]. He killed two ·of the best warriors [*or* sons of Ariel] from Moab. He also went down into a ·pit [storage well] and killed a lion on a snowy day. 21Benaiah killed a ·large [impressive; *or* handsome] Egyptian who had a spear in his hand. Benaiah had a club, but he grabbed the spear from the Egyptian's hand and killed him with his own spear. 22These were the things Benaiah son of Jehoiada did. He ·was as famous as [Lhad a name among] the Three. 23He ·received more honor than [was honored among] the Thirty, but ·he did not become a member of [was not equal to] the Three. David ·made him leader [put him in charge/command] of his bodyguards.

The Thirty Chief Soldiers

24The following men were among the Thirty:
Asahel brother of Joab;
Elhanan son of Dodo from Bethlehem;
25Shammah the Harodite;
Elika the Harodite;
26Helez the Paltite;
Ira son of Ikkesh from Tekoa;
27Abiezer the Anathothite;
Mebunnai the Hushathite;

28Zalmon the Ahohite;
Maharai the Netophathite;
29·Heled [*or* Heleb] son of Baanah the Netophathite;
Ithai son of Ribai from Gibeah in Benjamin;
30Benaiah the Pirathonite;
Hiddai from the ravines of Gaash;
31Abi-Albon the Arbathite;
Azmaveth the Barhumite;
32Eliahba the Shaalbonite;
the sons of Jashen;
Jonathan 33son of Shammah the Hararite;
Ahiam son of Sharar the Hararite;
34Eliphelet son of Ahasbai the Maacathite;
Eliam son of Ahithophel the Gilonite;
35Hezro the Carmelite;
Paarai the Arbite;
36Igal son of Nathan of Zobah;
the son of Hagri;
37Zelek the Ammonite;
Naharai the Beerothite, who carried the armor of Joab son of Zeruiah;
38Ira the Ithrite;
Gareb the Ithrite,
39and Uriah the Hittite.

There were thirty-seven in all.

David Counts His Army
(24:1–25; 1 Chr. 21:1–22:1)

24 The ·LORD was angry with [Langer of the LORD burned against;
Ccompare 1 Chr. 21:1] Israel again, and he ·caused [incited]
David to turn against the Israelites. He said, "Go, ·count [number; take
a census of] the people of Israel and Judah."
2So King David said to Joab, the commander of the army, "Go through
all the tribes of Israel, from Dan to Beersheba [Cthe far north and south
of Israel], and ·count [take a census of; register; number] the people. Then
I will know how many there are."
3But Joab said to the king, "May the LORD your God give you a hundred
times more ·people [soldiers], and may my master the king live to see this
happen. ·Why do you [LBut why does my lord the king] want to do this?"
4But the ·king commanded [Lking's word overruled/prevailed against]
Joab and the commanders of the army, so they left the king to ·count
[take a census of; register; number] the Israelites [Ctaking the census indicates David's ungodly dependence on the number of his troops].
5After crossing the Jordan River, they camped near Aroer on the south
side of the city in the ·ravine [valley]. They went through Gad and on to
Jazer. 6Then they went to Gilead and the land of Tahtim Hodshi and to
Dan Jaan and around to Sidon. 7They went to the ·strong, walled city
[fortress] of Tyre and to all the cities of the Hivites and Canaanites.
Finally, they went to ·southern [Lthe Negev of] Judah, to Beersheba. 8After
nine months and twenty days, they had gone through all the land. Then
they came back to Jerusalem.
9Joab ·gave the list of the people [reported the number of soldiers] to
the king. There were eight hundred thousand men in Israel who could
·use [draw; handle] the sword and five hundred thousand men in Judah.
10·David felt ashamed [LDavid's heart/conscience troubled him] after

he had ·counted [taken a census of; registered; numbered] **the people. He**
said to the Lord, "I have sinned greatly by what I have done. Lord, I beg
you to ·forgive me, [Ltake away the guilt/iniquity of] **your servant, because**
I have been very foolish."
11**When David got up in the morning, the ·Lord spoke his word** [Lword
of the Lord came] **to Gad, who was a prophet and David's seer.** 12**The**
Lord told Gad, "Go and tell David, 'This is what the Lord says: I offer you
three ·choices [options; things]. **Choose one of them and I will ·do it to**
[inflict it on] **you.'"**
13**So Gad** [1 Sam. 22:5] **went to David and said to him, "Should ·three**
[Cso 1 Chr. 21:12; the Hebrew text has "seven"] **years of ·hunger** [famine]
come to you and your land? Or should ·your enemies chase you [Lyou flee
from your pursuing enemies] **for three months? Or should there be three**
days of ·disease [epidemics; pestilence; plagues] **in your land? Think**
about it. Then decide ·which of these things [what answer] **I should ·tell**
[give] **the Lord who sent me."**
14**David said to Gad, "I am in ·great** [deep] **·trouble** [distress]. **Let ·the**
Lord punish us [Lus fall into the hands of the Lord], **because ·the Lord is**
very merciful [Lhis mercy is great]. **Don't let ·my punishment come from**
human beings [Lme fall into human hands]**!"**
15**So the Lord sent a ·terrible disease** [epidemic; pestilence; plague] **on**
Israel. It began in the morning and continued until the ·chosen time to
stop [appointed time]. **From Dan to Beersheba** [Cfrom the far north and
the far south of Israel] **seventy thousand people died.** 16**When the angel**
raised his ·arm [Lhand] **toward Jerusalem to destroy it, the Lord ·felt very**
sorry about the terrible things that had happened [relented about the
calamity/disaster]. **He said to the angel who was ·destroying** [afflicting]
the people, "That is enough! ·Put down [Stay; Withdraw] **your ·arm**
[Lhand]**!" The angel of the Lord was ·then** [at that moment] **by the thresh-**
ing floor of Araunah the Jebusite.
17**When David saw the angel that ·killed** [Lwas striking down/ravaging]
the people, he said to the Lord, "I am the one who sinned and did wrong.
·These people only followed me like sheep. They did nothing wrong
[LWhat have these sheep done?]. **Please ·punish me and my family** [Llet
your hand fall on me and my father's house]**."**
18**That day Gad came to David and said, "Go and build an altar to the**
Lord on the threshing floor of Araunah the Jebusite." 19**So David did**
what Gad told him to do, just as the Lord commanded.
20**Araunah looked and saw the king and his servants coming to him. So**
he went out and ·bowed facedown [prostrated himself] **on the ground**
before the king. 21**He said, "Why has my ·master** [lord] **the king come to**
·me [Lhis servant]**?"**
David answered, "To buy the threshing floor from you so I can build
an altar to the Lord. Then the ·terrible disease [epidemic; pestilence;
plague] **will ·stop** [be averted/lifted/withheld from the people]**."**
22**Araunah said to David, "My ·master** [lord] **and king, you may take**
anything you want for a ·sacrifice [offering]. **Here are some oxen for the**
whole burnt offering and the threshing ·boards [sledges] **and the yokes**
for the wood. 23**My king, I give ·everything** [all this] **to you." Araunah also**
said to the king, "May the Lord your God ·be pleased with [respond
favorably to; accept] **you."**
24**But the king answered Araunah, "No, I ·will pay you for** [insist on

buying] the land. I won't ·offer [sacrifice] **to the LORD my God burnt offerings that cost me nothing."**

So David bought the threshing floor and the oxen for ·one and one-fourth pounds [Lfifty shekels] **of silver. 25He built an altar to the LORD there and ·offered** [sacrificed] **whole burnt offerings and ·fellowship** [*or* peace; well-being; Lev. 3:1] **offerings** [Cthis site is the later location of the temple; 1 Chr. 22:1]. **Then the LORD ·answered his** [was moved by/felt pity from this] **prayer for the country, and the ·disease** [epidemic; pestilence; plague] **in Israel ·stopped** [was averted/lifted/withheld].

1 KINGS

Adonijah Tries to Become King

1 At this time King David was ·very old [[L]old and advanced in
years], and although his servants covered him with ·blankets
[bedclothes], he could not keep warm. 2They said to him, "·We will look
for [Let us find] a young woman to ·care for you [[L]serve/wait on my lord
the king]. She will lie ·close to you [[L]in your bosom] and keep you
warm." 3After searching everywhere in Israel for a beautiful young
woman, they found a girl named Abishag from Shunam and brought
her to the king. 4The girl was very beautiful, and she cared for the king
and served him. But the king did not have sexual relations with her.
5Adonijah was the son of King David and Haggith, and he ·was very
proud [began boasting; [L]exalted himself]. "I will be the king," he said. So
he got chariots and ·horses [*or* horsemen; charioteers] for himself and
fifty men ·for his personal bodyguard [[L]to run ahead of him]. 6Now David
had never ·interfered with [disciplined; crossed; rebuked] Adonijah by
·questioning what he did [[L]asking, "Why are you doing that?"]. Born next
after Absalom, Adonijah was a very handsome man.
7Adonijah ·spoke [conferred] with Joab son of Zeruiah and Abiathar
the priest, and they agreed to ·help [support] him. 8But Zadok the priest,
Benaiah son of Jehoiada, Nathan the prophet, Shimei, Rei, and King
David's ·special guard [[L]mighty men] did not join Adonijah.
9Then Adonijah killed some sheep, ·cows [oxen], and fat calves for sacrifices at the Stone of Zoheleth near the spring of Rogel. He invited all his
brothers, the other sons of King David, to come, as well as all the men of
Judah. 10But Adonijah did not invite Nathan the prophet, Benaiah, ·his
father's special guard [[L]the mighty men], or his brother Solomon.
11When Nathan heard about this, he went to Bathsheba, Solomon's
mother. "Have you heard that Adonijah, Haggith's son, has ·made himself
[become] king?" Nathan asked. "Our ·real king, [lord] David, does not
know it. 12Now I will give you advice on how to save yourself and your
son Solomon. 13Go to King David and tell him, 'My master and king, ·you
promised [[L]didn't you promise/vow/swear…?] that my son Solomon
would be king and would rule on your throne after you. Why then has
Adonijah become king?' 14While you are still talking to the king, I will
come in and ·tell him that what you have said about Adonijah is true
[confirm your words]."
15So Bathsheba went in to see the aged king in his bedroom, where
Abishag, the girl from Shunam, was caring for him. 16Bathsheba bowed
and knelt before the king. He asked, "What do you ·want [wish]?"
17She answered, "My master, you ·made a promise [vowed; swore] to
me in the name of the LORD your God. You said, 'Your son Solomon will

surely become king after me, and he will ·rule [sit] on my throne.' 18But
now, unknown to you, Adonijah ·has become [is] king. 19He has killed
many ·cows [oxen], fat calves, and sheep for sacrifices. And he has invited
all your sons, as well as Abiathar the priest and Joab the commander of
the army, but he did not invite Solomon, who serves you. 20My master
and king, ·all the Israelites are watching you [Lthe eyes of Israel are on
you], waiting for you to decide who will ·be [Lsit on the throne of my lord
the] king after you. 21Otherwise, as soon as ·you die [Lmy lord the king
sleeps with his fathers/ancestors], Solomon and I will be treated as ·criminals [offenders]."

22While Bathsheba was still talking with the king, Nathan the prophet
arrived. 23The servants told the king, "Nathan the prophet is here." So
Nathan went to the king and ·bowed facedown [prostrated himself] on
the ground before him.

24Nathan said, "My ·master and [lord the] king, have you ·said [decreed]
that Adonijah will be the king after you and that he will ·rule [sit] on your
throne? 25Today he has sacrificed many ·cows [oxen], fat calves, and sheep,
and he has invited all ·your other [the king's] sons, the commanders of
the army, and Abiathar the priest. Right now they are eating and drinking
with him. They are saying, 'Long live King Adonijah!' 26But he did not
invite me, your own servant, or Zadok the priest, or Benaiah son of
Jehoiada, or your ·son [Lservant] Solomon. 27Did ·you [the lord my king]
do this? Since we are your servants, why didn't you tell us who should ·be
[Lsit on the throne of the lord my] king after you?"

David Makes Solomon King

28Then the king said, "Tell Bathsheba to come in!" So she came in and
stood before the king.

29Then the king ·made this promise [vowed; swore this oath], "The
LORD has ·saved [rescued; delivered] me from all ·trouble [adversity; danger; distress]. As surely as he lives, 30I will do today what I have ·promised
[vowed/sworn to] you ·in the name of [by] the LORD, the God of Israel. I
·promised [vowed/swore to] that your son Solomon would be king after
me and ·rule [sit] on my throne in my place."

31Then Bathsheba ·bowed facedown [prostrated herself] on the ground
and knelt before the king and said, "·Long live [Live forever] my ·master
[lord] King David!"

32Then King David said, "Tell Zadok the priest, Nathan the prophet,
and Benaiah son of Jehoiada to come in." When they came before the
king, 33he said to them, "Take my servants with you and put my son
Solomon on my own mule. Take him down to ·the spring called Gihon
[Gihon]. 34There Zadok the priest and Nathan the prophet should ·pour
olive oil on [Lanoint] him and make him king over Israel. Blow the ·trumpet [ram's horn] and shout, 'Long live King Solomon!' 35Then come back
up here with him. He will sit on my throne and ·rule [be king] in my
place, because he is the one I have ·chosen [appointed] to be the ruler
over Israel and Judah."

36Benaiah son of Jehoiada answered the king, "·Amen [So be it]! This is
what the LORD, the God of my ·master [lord], has ·declared [decreed;
ordained]! 37The LORD has always ·helped [been with] you, our king. May
he also ·help [be with] Solomon and make King Solomon's throne an
even greater throne than ·yours [Lthe throne of my lord King David]."

38So Zadok the priest, Nathan the prophet, and Benaiah son of Jehoiada left with the Kerethites and Pelethites [Cking's bodyguard]. They put Solomon on King David's mule and took him to the spring called Gihon. [39]Zadok the priest took the ·container [flask; horn] of olive oil from the ·Holy Tent [sacred tent; Ltent] and ·poured the oil on Solomon's head to show he was the king [Lanointed Solomon]. Then they blew the ·trumpet [ram's horn], and all the people shouted, "Long live King Solomon!" [40]All the people followed Solomon into the city. Playing flutes and ·shouting for joy [Lrejoicing with great joy], they made so much noise the ·ground [earth] shook.

[41]At this time Adonijah and all the guests with him ·were [heard it while] finishing their meal. When he heard the sound from the ·trumpet [ram's horn], Joab asked, "·What does all that noise from the city mean [Why is the city in such an uproar]?"

[42]While Joab was speaking, Jonathan son of Abiathar the priest arrived. Adonijah said, "Come in! You are an ·important [worthy; honest; valiant] man, so you must be bringing good news."

[43]But Jonathan answered, "No! Our master King David has made Solomon the new king. [44]King David sent Zadok the priest, Nathan the prophet, Benaiah son of Jehoiada, and all the Kerethites and Pelethites [Cking's bodyguard] with him, and they have put Solomon on the king's own mule. [45]Then Zadok the priest and Nathan the prophet ·poured olive oil on [Lanointed] Solomon at Gihon to make him king. After that they went into the city, shouting with joy. Now the whole city is ·excited [celebrating; in an uproar], and that is the noise you hear. [46]Solomon has now ·become the king [Ltaken his seat on the royal throne]. [47]All the ·king's officers [royal officials/servants] have come to ·tell King David that he has done a good thing [congratulate/bless our lord King David]. They are saying, 'May your God make ·Solomon [LSolomon's name] even more famous than ·you [Lyour name] and ·an even greater king than you [Lhis throne/reign greater than your throne/reign].'" Jonathan continued, "And King David bowed down on his ·bed to worship God [bed], [48]saying, 'Bless the LORD, the God of Israel. Today he has ·made one of my sons the king [Lgranted one to sit on my throne] and allowed me to see it.'"

[49]Then all of Adonijah's guests were ·afraid [terrified; panicked], and they left quickly and scattered. [50]Adonijah was also afraid of Solomon, so he went and took hold of the ·corners [Lhorns; Ex. 27:2] of the altar [Cin hopes that he would not be killed in a sacred place]. [51]Then someone told Solomon, "Adonijah is afraid of you, so he is at the altar, holding on to its ·corners [Lhorns]. He says, 'Tell King Solomon to promise me today that he will not ·kill me [Lput his servant to death with the sword].'"

[52]So Solomon answered, "·Adonijah must show that he is a man of honor. If he does that, I promise [If he is loyal/honorable/worthy,] he will not lose even a single hair from his head. But if ·he does anything wrong [he makes trouble; Levil is found in him], he will die." [53]Then King Solomon sent some men to get Adonijah. When he was brought from the altar, he came before King Solomon and ·bowed down [prostrated himself]. Solomon told him, "Go home."

The Death of David
(2:10–12; 1 Chr. 29:21–30)

2 ·Since it was almost time [As the time approached] for David to die, he gave ·his son Solomon his last commands [this charge to Solomon]. [2]David said, "·My time to die is near [LI am going the way of all the earth]. Be ·a good and strong leader [Lstrong and show yourself a

man].3·Obey [Observe the injunctions/requirements of] the LORD your God. ·Follow him [Walk in his ways] by obeying his demands, his ·commands [statutes; ordinances; requirements], his laws, and his ·rules [regulations] that are written in the ·teachings [Law; LTorah] of Moses. If you do these things, you will ·be successful [prosper] in all you do and wherever you ·go [turn]. 4And if you obey the LORD, he will ·keep the promise he made to [fulfill the word he spoke concerning] me. He said: 'If your descendants ·live as I tell them [Lare careful of their way] and ·have complete faith in me [Lwalk in truth/faith before me], ·a man from your family will always be king over the people [Lthey will never fail to have a man on the throne] of Israel.'

5"Also, you remember what Joab son of Zeruiah did to me. He killed the two commanders of Israel's armies: Abner son of Ner [2 Sam. 3:22–39] and Amasa son of Jether [2 Sam. 20:8–10]. ·He did this as if he and they were at war, although it was a time of peace [*or*…retaliating in time of peace for blood that had been shed in war]. He ·put their blood on [stained with their blood] the belt around his waist and the sandals on his feet. 6·Punish him in [LAct] the way you think is wisest, but do not let him ·die peacefully of old age [go to Sheol/the grave in peace; Cthe place of the dead].

7"·Be kind [Show love] to the children of Barzillai of Gilead, and allow them to eat at your table. They ·welcomed [cared for; stood by] me when I ·ran away [fled] from your brother Absalom.

8"And remember, Shimei son of Gera, the Benjaminite, is here with you. He cursed ·me [Lme violently/with a terrible curse] the day I went to Mahanaim [2 Sam. 16:5–19]. But when he came down to meet me at the Jordan River, I ·promised [vowed/swore to] him before the Lord, 'Shimei, I will not ·kill you [Lput you to death by the sword; 2 Sam 19:16–23].' 9But you should not ·leave him unpunished [consider him innocent/guiltless]. You are a wise man, and you will know what to do to him, ·but you must be sure he is killed [Land will bring his bloody gray head to Sheol/the grave; 2:6]."

10Then David ·died [Llay down/Tslept with his fathers/ancestors] and was buried with his ancestors in the City of David [CJerusalem]. 11He had ·ruled [reigned] over Israel forty years—seven years in Hebron and thirty-three years in Jerusalem.

12Solomon ·became king after [Lsat on the throne of] David, his father, and ·he was in firm control of [firmly established] his ·kingdom [rule].

Solomon's Reign Begins

13At this time Adonijah son of Haggith went to Bathsheba, Solomon's mother. "Do you come in peace?" Bathsheba asked.

"Yes, ·this is a peaceful visit [Lin peace]," Adonijah answered. 14"I have something to say to you."

"You may speak," she said.

15"You ·remember [know] that at one time the kingdom was mine," Adonijah said. "All the people of Israel ·recognized [wanted; looked to; expected] me as their king, but ·things have changed [Lthe kingdom has turned]. Now my brother is the king, because ·the LORD chose him [Lit was his from the LORD]. 16Now I have one ·thing [request; favor] to ask you; please do not refuse me."

Bathsheba answered, "What do you want?"

17"I know King Solomon will ·do anything you ask him [not refuse you]," Adonijah continued. "Please ask him to give me Abishag the Shunammite [1 Kin. 1:3–4] to be my wife."

18“Very well,” she answered. “I will speak to the king for you.”
19So Bathsheba went to King Solomon to speak to him for Adonijah.
When Solomon saw her, he stood up to meet her, then bowed down, and
sat on the throne. He told some servants to bring another throne for his
mother. Then she sat down at his right ·side [hand].
20Bathsheba said, “I have one small thing to ask you. Please do not
·refuse me [turn me down].”
“Ask, mother,” the king answered. “I will not ·refuse you [turn you
down].”
21So she said, “Allow Abishag the Shunammite to ·marry [be given to]
your brother Adonijah.”
22King Solomon answered his mother, “Why do you ask me to give him
Abishag? ·Why don’t you also [You may as well] ask for him to become
the king since he is my older brother? Abiathar the priest and Joab son of
Zeruiah ·would support him [are on his side]!”
23Then King Solomon ·swore [vowed; promised] by the name of the
LORD, saying, “May God ·punish me terribly [deal severely with me, and
worse; Ldo to me, and even more] if ·this doesn’t cost Adonijah [Adonijah
doesn’t pay for this request/word with] his life! 24By the LORD who has
·given me [established/confirmed me on] the throne that belonged to my
father David and who has kept his promise and ·given the kingdom to me
and my people [established my dynasty; Lmade me a house; 2 Sam. 7],
Adonijah will die today!” 25Then King Solomon gave orders to Benaiah
son of Jehoiada, and he went and ·killed [struck down] Adonijah.
26King Solomon said to Abiathar the priest, “·I should kill you too [You
deserve to die], but ·I will allow you to go back [go] to your fields in
Anathoth. I will not kill you at this time, because you helped carry the
Ark of the Lord GOD ·while marching with [for; before] my father David.
And I know you shared in all the hard times with him.” 27Then Solomon
·removed [dismissed; banished] Abiathar from being the LORD’s priest.
·This happened as the LORD had said it would […in order to fulfill the
word of the LORD], when he was speaking in Shiloh about the priest Eli
and his ·descendants [Lhouse; 1 Sam. 2:34–36].
28When Joab heard about what had happened, he was afraid. He had
supported Adonijah but not Absalom. So Joab ·ran [fled] to the Tent of
the LORD [Cin which the Ark was kept] and took hold of the ·corners
[horns; 1:50] of the altar. 29Someone told King Solomon that Joab had
run to the Tent of the LORD and was beside the altar. Then Solomon
ordered Benaiah to go and kill him.
30Benaiah went into the Tent of the LORD and said to Joab, “The king
says, ‘Come out!’ ”
But Joab answered, “No, I will die here.”
So Benaiah went back to the king and told him what Joab had said.
31Then the king ordered Benaiah, “Do as he says! Kill him there and bury
him. Then my ·family [Lfather’s house] and I will ·be free of the guilt of
Joab, who has killed innocent people [Lhave taken away the blood Joab
shed without cause]. 32Without my father knowing it, he killed two men
who were ·much [more righteous and] better than he was—Abner son of
Ner, the commander of Israel’s army [2 Sam. 3:22–39], and Amasa son of
Jether, the commander of Judah’s army [2 Sam. 20:8–10]. So the LORD will
·pay him back [Lbring his blood on his own head] for those deaths. 33Joab
and his ·family [descendants] will ·be forever guilty for their deaths [Lhave

their blood on their heads forever], but there will be peace from the LORD for David, his descendants, his ·family [Lhouse], and his throne forever."

34 So Benaiah son of Jehoiada killed Joab, and he was buried near his home in the ·desert [wilderness]. 35 The king then ·made [appointed] Benaiah son of Jehoiada commander of the army in Joab's place. He also ·made [appointed] Zadok the new high priest in Abiathar's place.

36 Next the king sent for Shimei. Solomon said to him, "Build a house for yourself in Jerusalem and live there. Don't leave the city. 37 The very day you leave and cross the Kidron Valley [Cbordering Jerusalem], ·someone will kill you [Lyou will surely die], and ·it will be your own fault [Lyour blood will be on your own head]."

38 So Shimei answered the king, "·I agree with what you say [Your sentence/demand/word is fair]. I will do what you say, my master and king." So Shimei lived in Jerusalem ·for a long time [Lmany days].

39 But three years later two of Shimei's ·slaves [servants] ran away to Achish king of Gath, who was the son of Maacah. Shimei heard that his ·slaves [servants] were in Gath, 40 so he put his saddle on his donkey and went to Achish at Gath to find them. Then he brought them back from Gath.

41 Someone told Solomon that Shimei had gone from Jerusalem to Gath and had returned. 42 So Solomon sent for Shimei and said, "I made you ·promise [vow; swear] in the name of the LORD not to leave Jerusalem. I warned you ·if you went out anywhere you would [Lthat on the day you left you would surely] die, and you ·agreed to what I said [said, "The sentence/demand/word is fair"]. 43 Why did you break your ·promise [vow; oath] to the LORD and disobey my command?" 44 The king also said, "You know the ·many wrong [evil; wicked] things you did to my father David, so now the LORD will ·punish you for those wrongs [Lreturn your evil on your own head]. 45 But the LORD will bless ·me [LKing Solomon] and ·make the rule of David safe [establish/secure the throne of David] before the LORD forever."

46 Then the king ordered Benaiah to kill Shimei, and he did. Now ·Solomon was in full control of his kingdom [Lthe kingdom was established/secured in Solomon's hands].

Solomon Asks for Wisdom
(3:1–15; 2 Chr. 1)

3 Solomon made an ·agreement [alliance] with Pharaoh, the king of Egypt, by marrying his daughter and bringing her to the City of David [CJerusalem]. At this time Solomon was still building his ·palace [Lhouse] and the ·Temple [Lhouse] of the LORD, as well as a wall around Jerusalem. 2 The ·Temple [Lhouse] for the ·worship [Lname] of the LORD had not yet been finished, so people were still sacrificing at ·altars in many places of worship [Lthe high places; Cworship sites that became associated with pagan worship or inappropriate worship of God]. 3 Solomon showed he loved the LORD by following the commands his father David had given him, except ·many other places of worship were still used to offer sacrifices and to burn incense [Lhe sacrificed and burned incense at the high places; 3:2].

4 King Solomon went to Gibeon to offer a sacrifice, because it was the most important ·place of worship [high place; 3:2]. He offered a thousand burnt offerings [Lev. 1:1–17] on that altar. 5 While he was at Gibeon, the LORD appeared to him in a dream during the night. God said, "Ask for whatever you want me to give you."

6 Solomon answered, "You ·were very kind [showed faithful love/great

lovingkindness] to your servant, my father David. He ·obeyed you, and he
was honest and lived right [walked before you in truth/faithfulness and
righteousness and integrity of heart]. You showed ·great kindness [faith-
ful love; lovingkindness] to him when you allowed his son to ·be king [Lsit
on his throne] after him. 7LORD my God, now you have made me, your
servant, king in place of my father David. But I am like a little child; I
don't know how to ·do what must be done [Lgo out or come in]. 8I, your
servant, am here among your chosen people, and there are too many of
them to count. 9I ask that you give me a heart that ·understands [discerns;
Llistens], so I can ·rule [govern] the people in the right way and will ·know
the difference between right and wrong [discern between good and evil].
·Otherwise, it is impossible to rule this great people of yours [LFor who is
capable of governing this great people?]."
10The Lord was pleased that Solomon had asked this. 11So God said to
him, "You did not ask for a long life, or riches for yourself, or the ·death
[Llife] of your enemies. Since you asked for ·wisdom to make the right
decisions [understanding to discern what is right/just], 12I will do what you
asked. I will give you ·wisdom and understanding [a wise and discerning/
Llistening heart] that ·is greater than anyone has had in the past or will
have in [will make you unlike anyone in the past or in] the future. 13I will
also give you what you did not ask for: riches and ·honor [fame]. During
your life no other king will be as great as you. 14If you ·follow me [Lwalk in
my ways] and obey my ·laws [statutes; ordinances; requirements] and
commands, as your father David did, I will also give you a long life."
15After Solomon woke up ·from the [and realized it had been a] dream,
he went to Jerusalem. He stood before the Ark of the ·Agreement [Treaty;
Covenant; Ex. 25:10] with the LORD, where he made burnt offerings [Lev.
1:1–17] and ·fellowship [*or* peace; well-being] offerings [Lev. 3:1]. After
that, he gave a ·feast [banquet] for all his ·leaders and officers [Lservants].

Solomon Makes a Wise Decision

16One day two women who were ·prostitutes [Tharlots] came to Solomon.
As they stood before him, 17one of the women said, "My master, this
woman and I live in the same house. I gave birth to a baby while she was
there with me. 18Three days later this woman also gave birth to a baby. No
one else was in the house with us; it was just the two of us. 19One night
this woman ·rolled over [lay] on her baby, and he died. 20So she took my
son from my bed during the night while ·I [Lyour servant] was asleep, and
she ·carried him to her bed [Llaid him at her breast]. Then she ·put the
dead baby in my bed [Llaid her dead son at my breast]. 21The next morning when I got up to ·feed my baby [nurse my son], I saw that he was dead!
When I looked at him more ·closely [carefully in the morning light], I
realized he was not my son."
22"No!" the other woman cried. "The living baby is my son, and the
dead baby is yours!"
But the first woman said, "No! The dead baby is yours, and the living
·one [son] is mine!" So the two women argued before the king.
23Then King Solomon said, "One of you says, 'My son is alive and your
son is dead.' Then the other one says, 'No! Your son is dead and my son is
alive.' "
24The king sent his servants to get a sword. When they brought it to
him, 25he said, "·Cut [Divide] the living baby into two pieces, and give
each woman half."

26The real mother of the living child was ·full of love [filled with compassion; deeply moved] for her son. So she said to the king, "Please, my
·master [lord], don't kill him! Give the baby to her!"
But the other woman said, "Neither of us will have him. ·Cut him into
two pieces [Divide him]!"
27Then King Solomon said, "Don't kill him. Give the baby to the first
woman, because she is the real mother."
28When the people of Israel heard about King Solomon's ·decision
[judgment; verdict], they ·respected him very much [Lwere in awe of/
feared the king]. They saw he had wisdom from God to ·make the right
decisions [render/administer justice].

Solomon's Officers

4 King Solomon ·ruled [was king] over all Israel. 2These are the
names of his ·leading officers [chief officials]:
Azariah son of Zadok was the priest;
3Elihoreph and Ahijah, sons of Shisha, ·recorded what happened in the
courts [were court secretaries];
Jehoshaphat son of Ahilud ·recorded the history of the people [was
recorder/royal historian];
4Benaiah son of Jehoiada was commander of the army;
Zadok and Abiathar were priests;
5Azariah son of Nathan was in charge of the district governors;
Zabud son of Nathan was a priest and ·adviser [Lfriend] to the king;
6Ahishar was ·responsible for everything in the palace [manager of the
household];
Adoniram son of Abda was in charge of ·the labor force [*or* forced
labor].
7Solomon placed twelve ·governors [deputies; administrators] over the
districts of Israel, who gathered ·food from their districts [provisions] for
the king and his ·family [household]. Each ·governor [deputy; adminis-
trator] was responsible for bringing food to the king one month of each
year. 8These are the names of the twelve ·governors [deputies;
administrators]:
Ben-Hur was ·governor [deputy; administrator] of the ·mountain [hill]
country of Ephraim.
9Ben-Deker was ·governor [deputy; administrator] of Makaz, Shaalbim,
Beth Shemesh, and Elon Bethhanan.
10Ben-Hesed was ·governor [deputy; administrator] of Arubboth,
Socoh, and all the land of Hepher.
11Ben-Abinadab was ·governor [deputy; administrator] of Naphoth
Dor. (He was married to Taphath, Solomon's daughter.)
12Baana son of Ahilud was ·governor [deputy; administrator] of
Taanach, Megiddo, and all of Beth Shan next to ·Zarethan. This was below
Jezreel [Zarethan below Jezreel, and] from Beth Shan to Abel Meholah
·across from [and over to] Jokmeam.
13Ben-Geber was ·governor [deputy; administrator] of Ramoth in
Gilead. (He was ·governor [deputy; administrator] of all the towns of Jair
in Gilead. Jair was the son of Manasseh. Ben-Geber was also over the district of Argob in Bashan, which had sixty large, walled cities with bronze
bars on their gates.)
14Ahinadab son of Iddo was ·governor [deputy; administrator] of
Mahanaim.

15 Ahimaaz was ·governor [deputy; administrator] of Naphtali. (He was
married to Basemath, Solomon's daughter.)
16 Baana son of Hushai was ·governor [deputy; administrator] of Asher
and Aloth.
17 Jehoshaphat son of Paruah was ·governor [deputy; administrator] of
Issachar.
18 Shimei son of Ela was ·governor [deputy; administrator] of Benjamin.
19 Geber son of Uri was ·governor [deputy; administrator] of Gilead.
Gilead had been the country of Sihon king of the Amorites and Og king
of Bashan. ·But Geber was the only governor over this district [In addition, there was one governor/deputy/adminstrator over the land of Judah].

Solomon's Kingdom
(4:20–21; 2 Chr. 9:26)

20 There were as many people in Judah and Israel as grains of sand on
the seashore [Gen. 22:17; 32:12]. The people ate, drank, and were ·happy
[content; rejoicing]. 21 Solomon ruled over all the kingdoms from the
Euphrates River to the land of the Philistines, as far as the border of
Egypt. These countries brought Solomon ·the payments he demanded
[tribute], and they ·were under his control [served him] all his life.
22 ·Solomon needed much food each day to feed himself and all the people who ate at his table: Solomon's daily provisions were one hundred
ninety-five bushels [Lthirty cors] of fine flour, three hundred ninety bushels [Lsixty cors] of ·grain [meal], 23 ten ·cows that were fed on good grain
[fat oxen], twenty ·cows [oxen] that were raised in the fields, one hundred
sheep, deer, gazelles, and roe deer, and ·fattened birds [choice poultry].
24 Solomon ·controlled [ruled; had dominion over] all the countries
west of the ·Euphrates River [LRiver]—the land from Tiphsah to Gaza.
And he had peace on all ·sides of his kingdom [his borders/frontiers].
25 During Solomon's life Judah and Israel, from Dan to Beersheba [Cthe
extreme north to the extreme south], also lived in ·peace [safety]; all of his
people were able to sit under their own fig trees and grapevines.
26 Solomon had four[n] thousand stalls for his chariot horses and twelve
thousand ·horses [or horsemen; cavalry]. 27 Each month one of the ·dis-
trict governors [deputies; administrators] ·gave King Solomon all the
food he needed [provided for King Solomon]—enough for every person
who ate at the king's table. The ·governors [deputies; administrators]
made sure ·he had everything he needed [that nothing was lacking].
28 They also brought enough barley and straw for Solomon's ·chariot
[Lswift steeds] and work horses; each person ·brought this grain to the
right place [according to his duty/charge].

Solomon's Wisdom

29 God gave Solomon great wisdom ·so he could understand many
things [Land great discernment/understanding]. His [Lbreadth/width of]
·wisdom [mind; heart] was ·as hard to measure as [*or* as vast as; Llike] the
grains of sand on the seashore. 30 His wisdom was greater than any wisdom of the East, or any wisdom in Egypt. 31 He was wiser than ·anyone on
earth [Lall mankind]. He was even wiser than Ethan the Ezrahite [Csee Ps.
89 title], as well as Heman [Csee Ps. 88 title], Calcol, and Darda—the three
sons of Mahol. King Solomon became famous in all the surrounding
·countries [nations]. 32 During his life he spoke three thousand ·wise sayings [proverbs] and also wrote one thousand five songs. 33 He taught
about many kinds of plants—everything from the great cedar trees of

4:26 four Some Greek copies read "four." Hebrew copies read "forty."

Lebanon to the ·weeds [hyssop] that grow out of the walls. He also taught about animals, birds, ·crawling things [reptiles], and fish. 34People from all nations came to listen to King Solomon's wisdom. The kings of all nations sent them to him, ·because they had heard of [*or* to listen to] Solomon's wisdom.

Preparing to Build the Temple
(5:1–18, 7:13–14; 2 Chr. 2:1–18)

5 Hiram, the king of Tyre, had always been David's friend. When Hiram heard that Solomon had been ·made [Lanointed] king in ·David's [Lhis father's] place, he sent his ·messengers [ambassadors; servants] to Solomon. 2Solomon sent this message back to King Hiram: 3"You ·remember [Lknow] my father David had to fight many wars with ·the countries around [enemies surrounding] him, so he was never able to build a ·temple for worshiping [Lhouse for the name of] the LORD his God. David was waiting until the LORD ·allowed him to defeat all his enemies [Lput them under the soles of his feet]. 4But now the LORD my God has given me ·peace [rest] on all sides of my country. I have no enemies now, and no ·danger threatens my people [adversity; calamity; misfortune].

5"The LORD ·promised [Ltold] my father David, 'I will ·make your son king after you [Lput your son on the throne in your place], and he will build ·a temple for worshiping me [Lthe house/temple for my name].' Now, I plan to build ·that temple for worshiping [La house for the name of] the LORD my God. 6So ·send your men [command them] to cut down cedar trees for me from Lebanon. My servants will work with yours, and I will pay them whatever wages you decide. We don't have anyone who can cut down ·trees [timber] as well as the people of Sidon."

7When Hiram heard what Solomon asked, he ·was very happy [rejoiced greatly]. He said, "·Praise [Blessed be] the LORD today! He has given David a wise son to rule over this great ·nation [people]!" 8Then Hiram sent back this message to Solomon: "I ·received [heard] the message you sent, and I will ·give you [supply] all the cedar and ·pine trees [cypress; juniper] you ·want [need]. 9My servants will bring them down from Lebanon to the sea. There I will ·tie them together [Lmake them into rafts] and ·float them along the shore [go by sea] to the place you choose. Then I will separate the logs there, and you can take them away. ·In return it is my wish that you give [And you shall meet my needs/desire by providing] food to ·all those who live with me [Lmy household]." 10So Hiram gave Solomon as much cedar and ·pine [cypress; juniper] as he wanted. 11And Solomon gave Hiram about ·one hundred twenty-five thousand bushels [Ltwenty thousand cors] of wheat each year ·to feed the people who lived with him [Lfor his household]. Solomon also gave him ·about one hundred fifteen thousand gallons [Ltwenty cors] of pure olive oil every year.

12The LORD gave Solomon wisdom as he had promised. And there was peace between Hiram and Solomon; these two kings made a ·treaty between themselves [covenant; alliance].

13King Solomon ·forced [conscripted] thirty thousand men of Israel to help in this work. 14He sent ·a group [shifts; relays] of ten thousand men each month to Lebanon. Each group worked in Lebanon one month, then went home for two months. A man named Adoniram was in ·charge [charge of the forced labor/*or* this labor force]. 15Solomon ·forced [had] eighty thousand men to work in the hill country, cutting stone, and he had seventy thousand ·men to carry the stones [common laborers]. 16There were also thirty-three hundred ·men who directed the workers [foremen;

overseers]. 17King Solomon commanded them to cut large blocks of ·fine [costly; high-quality] stone to ·be used for the foundation of the Temple [lay the foundation of the house with dressed/cut stone]. 18Solomon's and Hiram's builders and the ·men from Byblos [LGebalites; CGebal was a Phoenician city the Greeks called Byblos] carved the stones and prepared the stones and the ·logs [timber] for building the ·Temple [Lhouse].

Solomon Builds the Temple

(6:1–38; 2 Chr. 3:1–14)

6 Solomon began to build the ·Temple [Lhouse of the LORD] four hundred eighty years after the people of Israel ·had left [Lcame out of the land of] Egypt. This was during the fourth year of King Solomon's ·rule [reign] over Israel. It was the second month, the month of Ziv [Cmidspring]. 2The ·Temple [Lhouse that Solomon built for the LORD] was ·ninety feet [Lsixty cubits] long, ·thirty feet [Ltwenty cubits] wide, and ·forty-five feet [Lthirty cubits] high. 3The ·porch [entry room; portico; vestibule] in front of the ·main room [main hall; nave] of the ·Temple [Lhouse] was ·fifteen feet [Lten cubits] deep and ·thirty feet [Ltwenty cubits] wide. This room ·ran along [projected from] the front of the ·Temple [Lhouse] itself. Its width was equal to that of the ·Temple [Lhouse]. 4The ·Temple [Lhouse] also had ·windows that opened and closed [narrow, recessed windows]. 5Solomon also built ·some [a complex of] side ·rooms [chambers] against the walls of the ·main room [main hall; nave] and the inner room of the ·Temple [Lhouse]. He built rooms all around. 6The rooms on the bottom floor were ·seven and one-half feet [Lfive cubits] wide. Those on the middle floor were ·nine feet [Lsix cubits] wide, and the rooms above them were ·ten and one-half feet [Lseven cubits] wide. The ·Temple [Lhouse] wall that formed the side of each room ·was thinner than the wall in the room below [had offset ledges]. These rooms were pushed against the ·Temple wall [Lhouse], but they did not have their ·main [support] beams built into this wall.

7The stones used to build the ·Temple [Lhouse] were ·prepared [finished; shaped] at the quarry. So there was no noise of hammers, axes, or any other iron tools at the ·Temple [Lhouse].

8The entrance to the lower rooms beside the ·Temple [Lhouse] was on the south side. From there, [winding] stairs went up to the second-floor rooms. And from there, stairs went on to the third-floor rooms. 9Solomon put a ·roof [ceiling] made from beams and cedar boards on the ·Temple [Lhouse]. So he finished building the Temple [Lhouse] 10as well as the bottom floor that was beside the ·Temple [Lhouse]. This bottom floor was ·seven and one-half feet [Lfive cubits] high and was attached to the ·Temple [Lhouse] by cedar beams.

11The ·LORD said [Lword of the LORD came] to Solomon: 12"If you ·obey [follow; walk in] all my laws and commands, I will ·do for you [fulfill] what I promised your father David. 13I will ·live [dwell; make my home] among the Israelites in this Temple, and I will never ·leave [abandon; forsake] my people Israel."

14So Solomon finished building the ·Temple [Lhouse]. 15The inside walls were ·covered [paneled] from floor to ceiling with cedar boards. The floor was made from ·pine [cypress; juniper] boards. 16A room ·thirty feet [Ltwenty cubits] long was built in the back part of the ·Temple [Lhouse]. This room, called the ·Most Holy Place [THoly of Holies], was an inner ·room [Lsanctuary] ·separated from the rest of the Temple by [*or* paneled with] cedar boards which reached from floor to ·ceiling [rafters]. 17The ·main room [main hall;

nave], the one in front of ·the Most Holy Place [Lit], was ·sixty feet [Lforty
cubits] long. 18Everything inside the ·Temple [Lhouse] was covered with
cedar, which was carved with pictures of flowers and ·plants [open flowers].
A person could not see the stones of the wall, only the cedar.

19Solomon prepared the inner ·room [sanctuary] ·at the back of
[within] the ·Temple [Lhouse] to keep the Ark of the ·Agreement [Treaty;
Covenant; Ex. 25:10] with the LORD. 20This inner ·room [sanctuary] was
·thirty feet [Ltwenty cubits] long, ·thirty feet [Ltwenty cubits] wide, and
·thirty feet [Ltwenty cubits] high. He covered this ·room [sanctuary] with
pure gold, and he also covered the altar of cedar. 22So all the inside of the
·Temple [Lhouse], as well as the altar of the ·Most Holy Place [Linner sanc-
tuary], was covered with gold.

23Solomon made two ·creatures [cherubim; Cparticularly powerful
spiritual beings] from olive wood and placed them in the ·Most Holy
Place [Linner sanctuary]. ·Each creature [LThe cherub] was ·fifteen feet
[Lten cubits] tall 24and had two wings. Each wing was ·seven and one-half
feet [Lfive cubits] long, so it was ·fifteen feet [Lten cubits] from the end of
one wing to the end of the other. 25·The creatures [LThe other cherub also
measured ten cubits; both cherubim] were the same size and shape; 26each
was ·fifteen feet [Lten cubits] tall. 27These ·creatures [Lcherubim; 6:23]
were put beside each other in the ·Most Holy Place [Linner house] with
their wings spread out. One creature's wing touched one wall, and the
other creature's wing touched the other wall with their wings touching
each other in the middle of the room. 28These two creatures were ·covered
[overlaid] with gold.

29All the walls around the ·Temple [Lhouse] were carved with ·pictures
[engravings] of ·creatures with wings [cherubim; 6:23], as well as palm
trees and open flowers. ·This was true for both the main room and the
inner room [L...both the inner and the outer (rooms)]. 30The floors of
both rooms were ·covered [overlaid] with gold.

31Doors made from olive wood were placed at the entrance to the
·Most Holy Place [Linner sanctuary]. These doors had five-sided ·frames
[doorposts]. 32·Creatures with wings [Cherubim; 6:23], as well as palm
trees and open flowers, were also carved on the two olive wood doors that
were ·covered [overlaid] with gold. The ·creatures [cherubim; 6:23] and
the palm trees on the doors were ·covered [overlaid] with gold as well.
33At the entrance to the ·main room [main hall; nave] there ·was a square
door frame [were four-sided doorposts] made of olive wood. 34Two doors
were made from ·pine [cypress; juniper]. Each door had two parts so the
doors ·folded [turned on pivots]. 35The doors were ·covered with pictures
of creatures with wings [Lcarved with cherubim; 6:23], as well as palm
trees and open flowers. All of the carvings were covered with gold, which
was evenly ·spread [hammered; applied] over them.

36The inner courtyard was enclosed by walls, which were made of three
rows of ·cut [finished; dressed] stones ·and one [for each] row of cedar
·boards [beams].

37·Work began on [LThe foundation was laid of] the ·Temple [Lhouse of
the LORD] in Ziv, the second month, during the fourth ·year Solomon was
king over Israel [Lyear]. 38The ·Temple [Lhouse] was finished during the
eleventh ·year he was king [Lyear], in the eighth month, the month of Bul.
It was ·built exactly as it was planned [Lfinished according to all its parts
and according to all its plans]. Solomon had spent seven years building it.

Solomon's Palace

7 King Solomon also built a ·palace [Lhouse] for himself; it took
him thirteen years to finish it. 2·Built of cedars from [He built the
House/Palace of] the Forest of Lebanon, it was ·one hundred fifty feet
[Lone hundred cubits] long, ·seventy-five feet [Lfifty cubits] wide, and
·forty-five feet [Lthirty cubits] high. It had four rows of cedar columns
which supported the cedar beams. 3There were forty-five beams on the
roof, with fifteen beams in each row, and the ceiling was ·covered [pan-
eled] with cedar above the beams. 4Windows were placed in three rows
facing each other. 5All the doors ·were square [had rectangular frames],
and the three ·doors [*or* windows] at each end faced each other.

6Solomon also built the ·porch that had pillars [Hall of Pillars;
Colonnade]. This porch was ·seventy-five feet [Lfifty cubits] long and
·forty-five feet [Lthirty cubits] wide. Along the front of the porch was a
·roof [cornice; canopy] supported by pillars.

7Solomon also built a throne room where he ·judged people [dispensed
justice/judgment; decided legal matters], called the Hall of ·Justice [*or*
Judgment]. This room was ·covered [paneled] with cedar from floor to
·ceiling [beams; rafters; *or* floor]. 8The ·palace [Lhouse] where Solomon
lived was built like the Hall of Justice, and it was behind this hall. Solomon
also built the same kind of ·palace [Lhouse] for his wife, who was the
daughter of ·the king of Egypt [LPharaoh].

9All these buildings were made with blocks of ·fine [costly, high-grade]
stone. First they were ·carefully cut [cut to measure/size]. Then they were
trimmed with a saw in the front and back. These fine stones went from
the foundations of the buildings to the ·top of the walls [eaves; coping].
·Even the courtyard was made with blocks of stone [...and all the way to
the courtyard]. 10The foundations were made with large blocks of ·fine
[costly; high-grade] stone, some as long as ·fifteen feet [Lten cubits].
Others were ·twelve feet [Leight cubits] long. 11On top of these foundation
stones were other blocks of ·fine [costly; high-grade] stone and cedar
beams [cut to measure/size]. 12The ·palace courtyard [great court], the
courtyard inside the ·Temple [Lhouse], and the porch of the ·Temple
[Lhouse] were surrounded by walls. All of these walls had three ·rows [lay-
ers] of stone blocks ·and one row [for each layer] of cedar beams.

The Temple Is Completed Inside

(7:13–51; 2 Chr. 2:13–14, 3:15–5:1)

13King Solomon sent to Tyre and had ·Huram [LHiram; Ca variant
spelling of Huram (2 Chr. 2:13; 4:11); this craftsman is to be distinguished
from the king of the same name (5:1)] brought to him. 14·Huram's mother
was [LHe was the son of] a widow from the tribe of Naphtali. His father
was from Tyre and had been ·skilled in making things from [a craftsman/
artisan in] bronze. ·Huram [LHe] was also very skilled and ·experienced
[knowledgeable; wise] in bronze work. So he came to King Solomon and
did all ·the bronze [his] work.

15He made two bronze pillars, each one ·twenty-seven feet [Leighteen
cubits] tall and ·eighteen feet [Ltwelve cubits] ·around [in circumference].
16He also made two bronze capitals that were ·seven and one-half feet
[Lfive cubits] tall, and he put them on top of the pillars. 17Then he made a
net of seven ·chains [sets of filigree/latticework] for each capital, which
covered the capitals on top of the two pillars. 18He made two rows of
bronze pomegranates to go ·on [around] the nets. These covered the capitals at the top of the pillars. 19The capitals on top of the pillars in the
porch were shaped like lilies, and they were ·six feet [Lfour cubits] tall.

[20]The capitals were on top of both pillars, above the ·bowl-shaped [round]
section and next to the nets. At that place there were two hundred pomegranates in rows all around the capitals. [21]·Huram [LHe] put these two
bronze pillars at the ·porch [portico; entrance] of the ·Temple [Lhouse].
He named the ·south [right-hand] pillar ·He Establishes [LJachin] and the
·north [left-hand] pillar ·In Him Is Strength [LBoaz]. [22]The capitals on
top of the pillars were shaped like lilies. So the work on the pillars was
finished [Cpillars represent establishment].

[23]Then ·Huram [Lhe] made from bronze a large round bowl, which was
called the Sea [Csymbol of chaos subdued]. It was ·forty-five feet [Lthirty
cubits] around, ·fifteen feet [Lten cubits] across, and ·seven and one-half
feet [Lfive cubits] deep. [24]Around the outer edge of the bowl was a rim.
Under this rim were two rows of ·bronze plants [gourds] which surrounded the ·bowl [Sea]. There were ten ·plants [gourds] every ·eighteen
inches [Lcubit], and these ·plants [gourds] were made in one piece with
the bowl. [25]The ·bowl [Sea] rested on the backs of twelve ·bronze bulls
[oxen] that faced outward from the center of the bowl. Three bulls faced
north, three faced west, three faced south, and three faced east. [26]The
sides of the bowl were ·four inches [La hand's breadth] thick, and it held
·about eleven thousand gallons [Ltwo thousand baths]. The rim of the
bowl was like the rim of a cup or like a lily blossom.

[27]Then ·Huram [Lhe] made ten bronze ·stands [water carts], each one
·six feet [Lfour cubits] long, ·six feet [Lfour cubits] wide, and ·four and
one-half feet [Lthree cubits] high. [28]The ·stands [water carts] were made
from ·square sides, which were put on frames [*or* side panels braced with
crossbars/uprights]. [29]On the sides were bronze lions, ·bulls [oxen], and
·creatures with wings [Lcherubim]. On the ·frames [panels] above and
below the lions and ·bulls [oxen] were ·designs of flowers [wreaths] hammered into the bronze. [30]Each stand had four bronze wheels with bronze
axles. At the corners there were bronze supports for a ·large bowl [basin],
and the supports had ·designs of flowers [wreaths]. [31]There was a frame
on top of the bowls, ·eighteen inches [Lone cubit] high above the bowls.
The opening of the bowl was round, ·twenty-seven inches [Lone and one-
half cubits] deep. ·Designs [Engravings] were carved into the bronze on
the frame, which was square, not round. [32]The four wheels, placed under
the frame, were ·twenty-seven inches [Lone and one-half cubits] high. The
axles between the wheels were ·made as one piece with [within; attached
to] the stand. [33]The wheels were like a chariot's wheels. Everything on the
wheels—the axles, rims, spokes, and hubs—were ·made [cast] of bronze.

[34]The four supports were on the four corners of each stand. They were
made as one piece with the stand. [35]A ·strip of bronze [rim; band] around
the top of each stand was ·nine inches [Lone-half cubit] deep. ·It was [The
corner supports were] also made as one piece with the stand. [36]·Wherever
there was room [LAccording to the space of each], the sides of the stand
and the frames were ·covered with carvings of [engraved with] ·creatures
with wings [cherubim; 6:23], as well as lions, palm trees, and ·flowers
[wreaths]. [37]This is the way ·Huram [Lhe; v. 13] made the ten ·stands
[water carts]. ·The bronze for each stand [LEach] was melted and poured
into a mold, ·so all the stands were [Lall] the same size and shape.

[38]·Huram [LHe] also made ten bronze ·bowls [basins], one ·bowl [basin]
for each of the ten ·stands [water carts]. Each bowl was ·six feet [Lfour
cubits] across and could hold ·about two hundred thirty gallons [Lforty

baths]. 39·Huram [Hiram] put five stands on the ·south [right] side of the
·Temple [Lhouse] and five on the ·north [left] side. He put the ·large bowl
[Sea on the right] in the southeast corner of the ·Temple [Lhouse].
40·Huram [Hiram] also made ·bowls [washbasins; pots], shovels, and
small bowls.

So ·Huram [LHiram; v. 13] finished all his work for King Solomon on
the ·Temple [Lhouse] of the LORD:

41two pillars;
two ·large bowls for the [bowl-shaped] capitals on top of the pillars;
two ·nets [sets of latticework/filigree] to cover the two large bowls for
the capitals on top of the pillars;
42four hundred pomegranates for the two ·nets [sets of latticework/
filigree] (there were two rows of pomegranates for each ·net [set
of latticework/filigree] covering the bowls for the capitals on top
of the pillars);
43ten ·stands [water carts] with a ·bowl [basin] on each ·stand [one];
44the ·large bowl [Sea] with twelve ·bulls [oxen] under it;
45the ·pots [pails; ash buckets], shovels, small bowls, and all the utensils
for the ·Temple [Lhouse] of the LORD.

·Huram [LHiram] made everything King Solomon wanted from ·pol-
ished [burnished] bronze. 46The king had these things ·poured [cast] into
clay molds that were made in the plain of the Jordan River between
Succoth and Zarethan. 47Solomon never weighed the bronze used to
make these things, because there ·was too much to weigh [were so many].
So the total weight of all the bronze was never ·known [calculated].

48Solomon also made all the items for the ·Temple [Lhouse] of the LORD:
the golden altar;
the golden table which held the bread ·that shows God's people are in
his presence [of the Presence];
49the lampstands of pure gold (five on the right side and five on the left
side in front of the inner ·room [Lhouse], the ·Most Holy Place
[THoly of Holies]);
the flowers, lamps, and tongs—all of gold;
50the pure gold bowls, wick ·trimmers [snuffers], small bowls, pans, and
·dishes used to carry coals [firepans; incense burners];
the gold hinges for the doors of the inner ·room [Lhouse], the ·Most
Holy Place [THoly of Holies] and the ·main room [main hall;
nave] of the ·Temple [Lhouse].

51·Finally [Thus] the work King Solomon did for the ·Temple [Lhouse]
of the LORD was finished. Solomon brought in everything his father
David had ·set apart [dedicated; consecrated] for the ·Temple [Lhouse]—
silver, gold, and ·other articles [the various utensils]. He put everything in
the treasuries of the ·Temple [Lhouse] of the LORD.

The Ark Is Brought into the Temple
(8:1–66; 2 Chr. 5:2–7:10; Ps. 132:8–10)

8 King Solomon ·called for [assembled; summoned] the elders of
Israel, the heads of the tribes, and the leaders of the ·families
[ancestral houses] to come to him in Jerusalem. He wanted them to bring
the Ark of the ·Agreement [Treaty; Covenant; Ex. 25:10] with the LORD
from the ·older part of the city [Lcity of David, also known as Zion]. 2So
all the Israelites ·came together with [assembled before] King Solomon
during the festival in the month of Ethanim, the seventh month.

3When all the elders of Israel arrived, the priests ·lifted [picked; took]

up the Ark. 4They ·carried [brought] the Ark of the LORD, the Meeting
Tent, and the holy ·utensils [vessels; items]; the priests and the Levites
brought them up. 5King Solomon and all the ·Israelites [congregation/
community/assembly of Israel] gathered before the Ark and sacrificed so
many sheep and ·cattle [oxen] no one could count or number them all.
6Then the priests ·put [brought; carried] the Ark of the ·Agreement
[Treaty; Covenant; Ex. 25:10] with the LORD ·in [to] its place inside the
inner ·room [Lsanctuary] in the ·Temple [Lhouse], the ·Most Holy Place
[THoly of Holies], under the wings of the ·golden creatures [cherubim;
6:23]. 7The wings of ·these creatures [the cherubim] were spread out over
the place ·for [of] the Ark, ·covering [forming a canopy over] it and its
carrying poles. 8The carrying poles were so long that anyone standing in
the Holy Place in front of the ·Most Holy Place [Linner sanctuary] could
see the ends of the poles, but no one could see them from outside the
Holy Place. The poles are still there today. 9The only things inside the Ark
were two stone tablets [Con which were the Ten Commandments] that
Moses had put in the Ark at ·Mount Sinai [Horeb; Ex. 40:20]. That was
where the LORD made his ·agreement [covenant; treaty] with the Israelites
after they came out of [Lthe land of] Egypt.

10When the priests ·left [came/withdrew from] the Holy Place, a cloud
filled the ·Temple [Lhouse] of the LORD. 11The priests could not continue
their ·work [service; duties], because the ·Temple [Lhouse] was filled with
the glory of the LORD.

Solomon Speaks to the People

12Then Solomon said, "The LORD said he would live in a ·dark [thick;
dense] cloud. 13LORD, I have truly built a ·wonderful [exalted; glorious; mag-
nificent] ·Temple [Lhouse] for you—a place for you to ·live [dwell] forever."

14While all the ·Israelites [congregation/community/assembly of Israel]
were standing there, King Solomon turned to them and blessed them.

15Then he said, "·Praise [Blessed be] the LORD, the God of Israel. He has
·done [fulfilled] what he promised [Lwith his mouth] to my father David.
The LORD said, 16'Since the ·time [Lday] I brought my people Israel out of
Egypt, I have not chosen a city in any tribe of Israel where a ·temple
[Lhouse] will be built ·for me [to honor my name; Lfor my name to be
there]. But I have chosen David to ·lead [rule over] my people Israel.'

17"My father David ·wanted [Lhad it in his heart/mind] to build a ·tem-
ple [Lhouse] for the LORD, the God of Israel. 18But the LORD said to my
father David, 'It was good that you ·wanted [Lhad it in your heart/mind]
to build a ·temple [Lhouse] for me. 19But you are not the one to build it.
Your son, who ·comes from your own body [will be born from you], is the
one who will build my ·temple [Lhouse] ·for my name [to honor my name;
2 Sam. 7:13].'

20"Now the LORD has ·kept [fulfilled] his promise. I ·am the king now
[Lhave risen] in place of David my father. Now I ·rule [Lsit on the throne
of] Israel as the LORD promised, and I have built the ·Temple [Lhouse] ·for
[to honor; Lfor the name of] the LORD, the God of Israel. 21I have ·made
[prepared; provided] a place there for the Ark, in which is the ·Agreement
[Covenant; Treaty; Ex. 25:10] the LORD made with our ancestors when he
brought them out of Egypt."

Solomon's Prayer

22Then Solomon stood ·facing [before] the LORD's altar, and all the
·Israelites [Lcongregation/community/assembly of Israel] were standing
behind him. He spread out his hands toward the sky 23and said:

"LORD, God of Israel, there is no god like you in heaven above or on
earth below. You keep your ·agreement [treaty; covenant] ·of love [and
steadfast love/lovingkindness] with your servants who ·truly follow you
[Lwalk before you with all their heart]. 24You have kept the ·promise [cov-
enant; solemn pact] you made to your servant David, my father. You
spoke it with your own mouth and ·finished [fulfilled] it with your hands
today. 25Now LORD, God of Israel, keep the promise you made to your
servant David, my father. You said, 'If your sons are careful to ·obey
[Lwalk before] me as you have ·obeyed me [Lwalked], ·there will always be
someone from your family [Lyou will never lack a man] ·ruling [to sit on
the throne of] Israel [2 Sam. 7:16].' 26Now, God of Israel, ·please continue
to keep that promise [confirm the word] you made to your servant David,
my father.
27"But, God, ·can [will] you really ·live [dwell] here on the earth?
[LLook; TBehold] ·The sky [Even heaven] and the highest ·place in heaven
[heavens] cannot contain you. Surely this ·house [Temple] which I have
built cannot contain you. 28But please ·listen to [regard] my prayer and
my ·request [plea; supplication], because I am your servant. LORD my
God, hear this prayer your servant prays to you today. 29Night and day
please watch over this ·Temple [Lhouse] where you have said, '·I will be
worshiped [LMy name will be] there.' Hear the prayer I pray facing this
·Temple [Lhouse]. 30Hear my ·prayers [pleas; supplications] and the
prayers of your people Israel when we pray ·facing [toward] this place.
Hear from your home in heaven, and when you hear, forgive us.
31"If someone ·wrongs another person [sins against a neighbor], he
will be brought to the altar in this ·Temple [Lhouse]. If he swears an oath
that he is not guilty, 32then hear in heaven. ·Judge the case [Act and judge
between your servants], ·punish [condemn] the guilty ·as they deserve
[Lby bringing his conduct on his own head], but ·declare that the innocent
person is not guilty [acquit/vindicate the righteous/innocent in accordance with their righteousness/innocence].
33"When your people, the Israelites, sin against you, their enemies will
defeat them. But if they ·come back [turn] to you and ·praise you [Lconfess
your name] and pray and ·plead [make supplication] to you in this
·Temple [Lhouse], 34then hear them in heaven. Forgive the ·sins [*or* sin] of
your people Israel, and bring them back to the land you gave to their
ancestors.
35"When they sin against you, ·you will stop the rain from falling on
their land [Lthe heavens will be shut and there will be no rain]. Then they
will pray, facing this place and ·praising you [Lconfess your name]; they
will stop sinning when you ·make them suffer [afflict them]. 36·When this
happens [Then], please hear their prayer in heaven, and forgive the ·sins
[*or* sin] of your servants, ·the Israelites [Lyour people Israel]. Teach them
·to do what is right [Lthe good way they should walk]. Then please send
rain to this land you have given ·particularly to them [Lyour people for an
inheritence].
37"·At times the land will become so dry that no food will grow [If
there is a famine in the land], or ·a great sickness will spread among the
people [pestilence]. ·Sometimes all the crops will be destroyed by [...or
blight or mildew or] locusts or grasshoppers. ·Your people will be attacked
in [...or the people are besieged in the land of] their cities by their enemy
or ·will become sick [struck by plague or sickness...]. 38When any of these

things happen, ·the people will become truly sorry [^{L}each will know the affliction of his own heart]. ·If your people spread their hands in prayer [^{L}…and spread his hands] toward this ·Temple [^{L}house], 39 then hear their prayers from your ·home [dwelling place] in heaven. Forgive and ·treat [^{L}act and give to] each person ·as he should be treated [^{L}according to his ways/conduct] because you know what is in a person's heart. Only you know what is in everyone's heart. 40 Then your people will ·respect [fear] you ·as long as [^{L}all the days] they live in this land you gave to our ancestors.

41-42 "People who are not Israelites, ·foreigners [resident aliens] from other lands, will hear about your ·greatness and power [^{L}great name and mighty hand and outstretched arm]. They will come from far away [^{L}because of your name] to pray ·at [*or* toward] this ·Temple [^{L}house]. 43 Then hear from your ·home [dwelling place] in heaven, and do ·whatever they ask you [all they call for to you]. Then people everywhere will know you and ·respect [fear] you, just as your people in Israel do. Then everyone will know I built this ·Temple [^{L}house] as a place ·to worship you [^{L}that bears your name].

44 "When your people go out to fight their enemies ·along some [by whatever] road on which you send them, your people will pray to you, facing the city which you have chosen and the ·Temple [^{L}house] I have built for ·you [^{L}your name]. 45 Then hear in heaven their prayer and their ·plea [supplication], and ·do what is right [uphold/maintain their cause].

46 "When ·your people [^{L}they] sin against you (for there is no one who does not sin), you will become angry with them and ·hand them over [abandon/give them] to their enemies. Their enemies will capture them and take them away to their countries far or near. 47 But if they ·become sorry for their sins [*or* come to their senses; *or* have a change of heart; ^{L}return to their heart] and ·are sorry [repent] and ·pray [plead; make supplications] to you in the land ·where they are held as prisoners [of their captors], saying, 'We have sinned; we have ·done wrong [committed iniquity] and acted wickedly.' 48 If they ·truly turn back to you [^{L}repent with all their heart and all their soul] in the land of their enemies who have taken them captive and pray to you, ·facing this [toward their] land you gave their ancestors, this city you have chosen, and the ·Temple [^{L}house] I have built for ·you [^{L}your name], 49 then hear their prayers and their ·requests [pleas; supplications] from your ·home [dwelling place] in heaven, and ·do what is right [act with justice/judgment; *or* uphold/maintain their cause].

50 Forgive your people of all their sins and for ·turning [^{L}all their transgressions/offenses they have committed] against you. Make those who have captured them show them ·mercy [compassion]. 51 Remember, they are your ·special people [^{L}inheritance]. You brought them out of Egypt, ·as if you were pulling them out of a blazing [^{L}from the midst of the iron-smelting] furnace.

52 "·Give your attention to my prayers and [^{L}May your eyes be open to] the ·prayers [pleas; requests; supplications] of your people Israel. Listen to them anytime they ·ask you for help [call/cry out to you]. 53 You ·chose them [set them apart; separated them; singled them out] from all the ·nations [peoples] on earth to be your ·very own people [inheritance]. This is what you ·promised [spoke] through Moses your servant when you brought our ancestors out of Egypt, Lord God."

54 Solomon prayed this prayer and ·plea [request; supplication] to the

LORD, kneeling in front of the altar with his ·arms raised [hands spread] toward heaven. When he finished praying, he got up. [55]Then, in a loud voice, he stood and blessed ·all the people [[L]the whole assembly/congregation] of Israel, saying: [56]"·Praise [Blessed be] the LORD! He promised he would give rest to his people Israel, and he has given us rest. ·The LORD has kept [Not one word has failed/[L]fallen of] all the ·good [wonderful] promises he gave through his servant Moses. [57]May the LORD our God be with us as he was with our ancestors. May he never leave or ·abandon [forsake] us, [58]and may he ·turn us [[L]incline/stretch out our hearts/desires] to himself so we will ·follow him [[L]walk in his ways]. Let us obey all the ·laws [commandments], ·rules [statutes; decrees] and ·commands [regulations; judgments] he gave our ancestors. [59]May the LORD our God ·remember [[L]keep near] ·this prayer [these words of mine that I have prayed/pleaded] day and night and ·do what is right [act with justice/judgment; *or* uphold/maintain their cause] for his servant and his people Israel ·day by day [according to the needs of each day]. [60]Then all the people of the ·world [earth] will know the LORD is ·the only true God [[L]God and there is no one else]. [61]·You must fully obey [Devote your heart completely to] the LORD our God and ·follow all his laws [walk in his statutes/decrees] and [[L]keep his] commands. ·Continue to obey in the future as you do now [[L]…as to this day]."

Sacrifices Are Offered

[62]Then King Solomon and all Israel with him offered sacrifices to the LORD. [63]Solomon killed twenty-two thousand ·cattle [oxen] and one hundred twenty thousand sheep as ·fellowship [*or* peace; well-being] offerings [Lev. 3:1]. So the king and all the people ·gave [dedicated] the ·Temple [[L]house] to the LORD.

[64]On that day King Solomon ·made holy [consecrated] the middle part of the courtyard which is in front of the ·Temple [[L]house] of the LORD. There he offered whole burnt offerings [Lev. 1:1–17], grain [[L]gift; tribute] offerings [Lev. 2:1], and the fat of the ·fellowship [peace; well-being] offerings [Lev. 3:1]. He offered them in the courtyard, because the bronze altar before the LORD was too small to hold all the burnt offerings, the grain offerings, and the fat of the ·fellowship [peace] offerings.

[65]Solomon and all the Israelites ·celebrated the other festival [observed the feast; [C]the Feast of Shelters;] that came at that time. People came from as far away as Lebo Hamath [[C]in the north] and the brook of Egypt [[C]in the south]. A great many people celebrated before the LORD for seven days, then seven more days, for a total of fourteen days. [66]On the ·following [[L]eighth] day Solomon sent the people home. They blessed the king as they went, happy because of all the ·good things [goodness] the LORD had ·done [shown] for his servant David and his people Israel.

The Lord Appears to Solomon Again

(9:1–9; 2 Chr. 7:11–22)

9 Solomon finished building the ·Temple [[L]house] of the LORD and ·his royal palace [[L]the king's house] and everything he wanted to build. [2]Then the LORD appeared to him ·again [[L]a second time] just as he had done before, in Gibeon. [3]The LORD said to him: "I have heard your prayer and ·what you have asked me to do [[L]pleas/requests/supplications that you made before me]. I have ·made this Temple holy [[L]consecrated this house] that you built, and I ·will be worshiped there [[L]have put my name there] forever. ·I will watch over it and protect it always [[L]My eyes and my heart will be there all the days].

[4]"But you must ·serve [walk before; follow] me as your father David

did; ·he was fair and sincere [...with integrity of heart and godliness/
uprightness]. You must obey all I have commanded and keep my ·laws
[statutes; decrees] and ·rules [regulations; judgments]. 5 If you do, I will
·make your kingdom strong [Lestablish the throne of your kingdom]. This
is the promise I made to your father David—·that someone from his family would always rule [you will never lack a man/successor on the throne
of] Israel [2 Sam. 7:16].
6 "But if you and your children do not follow me and obey the laws and
·commands [decrees] I have given you, and if you serve ·or [and] worship
other gods, 7 I will ·force Israel to leave [banish/Lcut off Israel from] the
land I have given them, and I will ·leave [reject; disown; remove from my
sight] this ·Temple [Lhouse] that I have ·made holy [Lconsecrated for my
name]. ·All the nations will make fun of Israel and speak evil about them
[LIsrael will become a byword/proverb among the nations/peoples]. 8 If the
·Temple is destroyed [Lhouse becomes a heap of rubble], everyone who
passes by will be ·shocked [astonished; appalled]. They will ·make fun of
you [scoff; hiss] and ask, 'Why did the LORD do this terrible thing to this
land and this ·Temple [Lhouse]?' 9 People will answer, 'This happened
because they ·left [abandoned; deserted; forsook] the LORD their God.
This was the God who brought their ancestors out of Egypt, but they
·decided to follow [embraced; adopted] other gods. They worshiped and
served those gods, so the LORD brought all this ·disaster [adversity; calam-
ity] on them.'"

Solomon's Other Achievements
(9:10–28; 2 Chr. 8:1–18)

10 By the end of twenty years, King Solomon had built two buildings—
the ·Temple [Lhouse] of the LORD and the ·royal palace [Lking's house].
11 At that time King Solomon gave twenty towns in Galilee to Hiram king
of Tyre, because Hiram had helped with the buildings. Hiram had given
Solomon all the cedar, ·pine [juniper; cypress timber], and gold he wanted.
12 So Hiram traveled from Tyre to see the towns Solomon had given him,
but when he saw them, he was not pleased. 13 He asked, "What ·good are
these towns [kinds of towns have] you have given me, my brother?" So he
named them the Land of ·Cabul [Cmeaning "worthless"], and they are still
called that today. 14 Hiram had sent Solomon ·about nine thousand
pounds [L120 talents] of gold.
15 This is the account of the forced labor Solomon ·used [conscripted]
to build the ·Temple [Lhouse] and ·the palace [Lhis own house]. He had
them fill in the ·land [terraces; Lthe Millo; Ca fortification of uncertain
type] and build the ·wall [fortifications] around Jerusalem. He also had
them rebuild the cities of Hazor, Megiddo, and Gezer. 16 (In the past
Pharaoh, king of Egypt had attacked and captured Gezer. After burning
it, he killed the Canaanites who lived there. Then he gave it as a ·wedding
present [dowry] to his daughter, who married Solomon. 17 So Solomon
rebuilt it.) He also built the cities of Lower Beth Horon 18 and Baalath, as
well as Tadmor, which is in the ·desert [wilderness]. 19 King Solomon also
built ·cities for storing grain and supplies [supply centers/cities/towns]
and ·cities for [towns to station] his chariots and horses. He built whatever he wanted in Jerusalem, Lebanon, and everywhere he ruled.
20 There were other people in the land who were not ·Israelites [Lsons/
Tchildren of Israel]—Amorites, Hittites, Perizzites, Hivites, and Jebusites.
21 They were descendants of people that the ·Israelites [Lsons/Tchildren of
Israel] had ·not destroyed [been unable to completely exterminate].

Solomon ·forced them to work for him as slaves [conscripted them for forced/slave labor], **as is still true today.** 22**But Solomon did not ·make slaves of** [conscript] **the Israelites. They were his soldiers, government ·leaders** [officials], **officers, captains, chariot commanders, and ·drivers** [charioteers].

23**These were his ·most important officers** [chief officials] **over the work. There were five hundred fifty supervisors over the people who did the work on Solomon's projects.**

24**The daughter of ·the king of Egypt** [LPharaoh] **moved from the old part of the City of David** [CJerusalem] **to the ·palace** [Lhouse] **that Solomon had built for her. Then Solomon ·filled in the surrounding land** [built the terraces/Millo; 9:15].

25**Three times each year Solomon offered whole burnt offerings and ·fellowship** [*or* peace; well-being] **offerings** [Lev. 3:1] **on the altar he had built for the LORD. He also burned incense before the LORD. So he finished the ·work on the Temple** [Lhouse].

26**King Solomon also built ships at Ezion Geber, a town near Elath on the shore of the ·Red Sea** [*or* Sea of Reeds; Ex. 10:19], **in the land of Edom.** 27**Hiram sent ·skilled sailors** [Lseamen who knew the sea] **to serve in these ships with Solomon's ·men** [servants]. 28**The ships sailed to Ophir and brought back ·about thirty-two thousand pounds** [L420 talents] **of gold to King Solomon.**

The Queen of Sheba Visits Solomon

(10:1–13; 2 Chr. 9:1–12)

10 When the queen of Sheba heard ·about [the reports about; *or* the fame of] **Solomon ·because of** [Lfor; to] **the ·reputation** [name] **of the LORD, she came to test him with ·hard questions** [riddles]. 2**She traveled to Jerusalem with a ·large group of servants** [caravan; retinue] **and camels carrying spices, ·jewels** [precious stones], **and ·much** [immense quantities of] **gold. When she came to Solomon, she talked with him about all she had in ·mind** [Lher heart], 3**and Solomon answered all her questions. Nothing was ·too hard for** [hidden from; too obscure for] **him to explain to her.** 4**The queen of Sheba ·learned** [perceived; observed; realized] **that Solomon was very wise. She saw the ·palace** [Lhouse] **he had built,** 5**the food on his table, the ·accommodations** [seating; organization] **of his many ·officers** [officials; servants], **the ·palace** [attending of his] **servants, and their ·good clothes** [robes]. **She saw ·the servants who served him at feasts** [his cupbearers] **and the whole burnt offerings** [Lev. 1:1–17] **he made in the ·Temple** [Lhouse] **of the LORD. All these things ·amazed** [overwhelmed; Ltook the spirit from] **her.**

6**So she said to King Solomon, "What I heard in my own country about your ·achievements** [*or* words] **and wisdom is true.** 7**I could not believe it then, but now I have come and seen it with my own eyes. I was not told even half of it! Your wisdom and wealth are much greater than I had heard.** 8**Your ·men and officers** [*or* wives and servants] **are very ·lucky** [blessed; happy], **because in always ·serving** [standing before] **you, they ·are able to hear** [listen to] **your wisdom.** 9**·Praise** [Blessed be] **the LORD your God, who ·was pleased to make you king** [delighted in you and set you on the throne] **of Israel. The LORD has ·constant** [eternal; everlasting] **love for Israel, so he made you king to ·keep** [maintain; execute; administer] **justice and ·to rule fairly** [righteousness]."

10**Then she gave the king ·about nine thousand pounds** [Lone hundred and twenty talents] **of gold and many spices and ·jewels** [precious stones].

No one since that time has brought more spices than the queen of Sheba
gave to King Solomon.
11(Moreover, Hiram's ships brought gold from Ophir, as well as much
·juniper wood [almug; red sandalwood] and ·jewels [precious stones].
12Solomon used the ·juniper wood [almug; red sandalwood] to build supports for the ·Temple [Lhouse] of the LORD and the ·palace [Lking's house],
and to make harps and lyres for the ·musicians [singers]. Such fine ·juni-
per wood [almug; red sandalwood] has not been brought in or been seen
since that time.)
13King Solomon gave the queen of Sheba everything she wanted and
asked for, in addition to what he had already given her ·of his wealth
[according to his royal bounty; *or* out of his royal treasury]. Then she and
her ·servants [attendants; retinue] returned to her own country.

Solomon's Wealth
(10:14–29, 4:21; 2 Chr. 1:14–17, 9:13–28)

14·Every [*or* In one] year King Solomon received ·about fifty thousand
pounds [L666 talents] of gold. 15Besides that, he also received gold from
the traders and merchants, as well as from the kings of Arabia and governors of the ·land [territories; provinces].
16King Solomon made two hundred large shields of ·hammered
[beaten] gold, each of which contained ·about seven and one-half pounds
[Lsix hundred shekels] of gold. 17He also made three hundred smaller
shields of ·hammered [beaten] gold, each of which contained ·about four
pounds [Lthree minas] of gold. The king put them in the ·Palace [LHouse]
of the Forest of Lebanon.
18The king built a large throne ·of [decorated with] ivory and covered
it with fine gold. 19The throne had six steps on it, and its back was round
at the top. There were armrests on both sides of the chair, and each armrest had a lion beside it. 20Twelve lions stood on the six steps, one lion at
each end of each step. Nothing like this had ever been made for any other
kingdom. 21All of Solomon's drinking ·cups [goblets; vessels], as well as
the ·dishes [utensils; vessels] in the Palace of the Forest of Lebanon, were
made of pure gold. Nothing was made from silver, because silver was ·not
valuable [considered worthless/nothing] in Solomon's time.
22King Solomon also had ·many trading ships [La fleet of ships of
Tarshish] at sea, along with Hiram's ships. Every three years the ·ships
[Lfleet of Tarshish] returned, bringing back gold, silver, ivory, apes, and
·baboons [*or* peacocks].
23So Solomon had more riches and wisdom than all the other kings on
earth. 24·People everywhere wanted [The whole earth sought] to see King
Solomon and listen to the wisdom God had ·given him [Lput into his heart/
mind]. 25Every ·year [*or* one of] those who came brought gifts of silver and
gold, ·clothes [robes; garments], weapons, spices, horses, and mules.
26Solomon had fourteen hundred chariots and twelve thousand ·horses
[*or* horsemen; charioteers]. He ·kept [stationed] some in special cities for
the chariots, and others he kept with him in Jerusalem. 27In Jerusalem
Solomon made silver as common as stones and cedar trees as ·common
[plentiful] as the ·fig [sycamore] trees on the ·western hills [*or* lowlands].
28He imported horses from Egypt and ·Kue [Cilicia]. His traders bought
them in Kue. 29A chariot from Egypt cost ·about fifteen pounds [Lsix hundred shekels] of silver, and a horse cost ·nearly four pounds [L150 pieces]
of silver. Solomon's traders also ·sold [exported] horses and chariots to
all the kings of the Hittites and the Arameans.

Solomon's Many Wives

11 King Solomon loved many ·women who were not from Israel [Lforeign women]. He loved the daughter of ·the king of Egypt [LPharaoh], as well as women of the Moabites, Ammonites, Edomites, Sidonians, and Hittites [Prov. 5–7]. 2The LORD had told the ·Israelites [Lsons/Tchildren of Israel], "You must not ·marry people of other nations [*or* associate with them; Lcome into them, and they must not come into you]. If you do, they will cause you to ·follow [Lturn your hearts to] their gods." But Solomon ·fell in love with these women [Lclung/held fast to them in love]. 3He had seven hundred wives who were from royal families and three hundred ·slave women who gave birth to his children [concubines; Ca secondary wife of lower status than a primary wife, but higher than a common servant]. His wives ·caused him to turn away from God [led him astray; Lturned his heart away]. 4As Solomon grew old, his wives ·caused him to follow [led him astray after; Lturned his heart away after] other gods. ·He did not follow the LORD completely [LHis heart was not wholly devoted/faithful to the LORD his God] as ·his father David had done [the heart of his father David had been]. 5Solomon ·worshiped [followed; went after] Ashtoreth, the goddess of the people of Sidon, and ·Molech [LMilcom], the ·hated [detestable] god of the Ammonites. 6So Solomon did ·what the LORD said was wrong [Levil in the eyes/sight of the LORD] and ·did not [refused to] follow the LORD completely as his father David had done.

7On a hill east of Jerusalem [Cthe Mount of Olives], Solomon built two ·places for worship [Lhigh places; 3:2]. One was a place to worship Chemosh, the ·hated [detestable] god of the Moabites, and the other was a place to worship Molech, the ·hated [detestable] god of the Ammonites. 8Solomon did the same thing for all his foreign wives so they could burn incense and offer sacrifices to their gods.

9The LORD had appeared to Solomon twice, but the ·king [Lhis heart had] turned away from following the LORD, the God of Israel. The LORD was angry with Solomon, 10because he had ·commanded [warned] Solomon not to follow other gods. But Solomon did not ·obey [observe; keep] the LORD's command. 11So the LORD said to Solomon, "Because you have chosen to break your ·agreement [covenant; treaty] with me and have not obeyed my commands, I will tear your kingdom away from you and give it to one of your ·officers [Lservants]. 12But I will not take it away ·while you are alive [Lin your days] ·because of my love for [for the sake of] your father David. I will tear it away from [Lthe hand of] your son. 13I will not tear away all the kingdom from him, but I will ·leave [give] him one tribe to rule. I will do this ·because [for the sake] of David, my servant, and ·because [for the sake] of Jerusalem, the city I have chosen."

Solomon's Enemies

14The LORD ·caused [Lraised up] Hadad the Edomite, a member of the royal family of Edom, to become Solomon's ·enemy [adversary]. 15Earlier, David had defeated Edom. When Joab, the commander of David's army, went into Edom to bury the dead [CIsraelite soldiers], he ·killed [slaughtered] all the males. 16Joab and all the Israelites stayed in Edom for six months and ·killed [exterminated; eliminated] every male in Edom. 17At that time Hadad was only a young boy, so he ·ran away [fled; escaped] to Egypt with some of his father's ·officers [servants]. 18They ·left [set out from] Midian and went ·to Paran, where they were joined by other men [*or* with men from Paran]. Then they all went to Egypt to see Pharaoh the king, who ·gave [assigned] Hadad a house, some food, and some land.

19·The king liked Hadad so much [Hadad became such a great favorite of Pharaoh that] he gave Hadad a wife—the sister of Tahpenes, the king's wife. 20·They had [LShe bore for him] a son named Genubath. Queen Tahpenes ·brought him up [raised; *or* weaned him] in the royal palace with ·the king's [LPharaoh's] own ·children [*or* sons].

21While he was in Egypt, Hadad heard that David ·had died [Llay down/Tslept with his fathers/ancestors] and that Joab, the commander of the army, was dead also. So Hadad said to the king, "Let me go; I will return to my own country."

22"Why do you want to go back to your own country?" the king asked. "What ·haven't I given you here [Ldo you lack with me]?"

"Nothing," Hadad answered, "but please, let me go."

23God also caused another man to be Solomon's ·enemy [adversary]—Rezon son of Eliada. Rezon had ·run away [fled] from his master, Hadadezer king of Zobah. 24After David ·defeated [slaughtered; massacred] the army of Zobah, Rezon gathered some men and became the leader of a ·small army [marauding band; gang of rebels]. They went to Damascus and settled there, and Rezon ·became king of [took control of] Damascus. 25Rezon ruled Aram, and he ·hated [abhorred; despised; was hostile to] Israel. So he was an ·enemy [adversary] of Israel all the ·time Solomon was alive [Ldays of Solomon]. Both Rezon and Hadad made trouble for Israel.

26Jeroboam son of Nebat was one of Solomon's ·officers [Lservants]. He was an Ephraimite from the town of Zeredah, and he was the son of a widow named Zeruah. Jeroboam ·turned [rebelled] against the king.

27This is the ·story [account] of how Jeroboam turned against the king. Solomon was ·filling in the land [building the terraces/Millo; 9:15] and ·repairing [Lclosed the gap/breach in] the wall of Jerusalem, the city of David, his father. 28Jeroboam was a ·capable [energetic] man, and Solomon saw that this young man was ·a good worker [industrious]. So Solomon put him over all the ·workers [labor force; *or* forced labor] from the tribes of Ephraim and Manasseh.

29One day as Jeroboam was leaving Jerusalem, Ahijah, the prophet from Shiloh, who was wearing a new ·coat [cloak], met him on the road. The two men were alone out in ·the country [a field]. 30Ahijah took his new ·coat [cloak] and tore it into twelve pieces [Crepresenting the original twelve tribes of Israel]. 31Then he said to Jeroboam, "Take ten pieces of this coat for yourself. The LORD, the God of Israel, says: 'I will tear the kingdom away from ·Solomon [LSolomon's hand] and give you ten tribes. 32But ·I will allow him to control [Lhe will have] one tribe. I will do this for the sake of my servant David and for Jerusalem, the city I have chosen from all the tribes of Israel. 33I will do this because ·Solomon has [Lthey have][n] stopped following me and has worshiped the Sidonian goddess Ashtoreth, the Moabite god Chemosh, and the Ammonite god ·Molech [LMilcom]. Solomon has not ·obeyed me [walked in my ways] by doing what ·I said is right [Lis right in my sight/eyes] and obeying my laws and commands, as his father David did.

34" 'But I will not take all the kingdom away from ·Solomon [Lhis hand]. I will let him rule all ·his life [Lthe days of his life] ·because [for the sake of] of my servant David, whom I chose, who ·obeyed [observed;

11:33 they have Greek, Latin, and Syriac copies read "he has."

kept] all my commands and laws. 35But I will take the kingdom away from
his ·son [Lson's hand], and I will ·allow you to rule over [give you] the ten
tribes. 36I will ·allow Solomon's son to continue to rule over [Lgive to his
son] one tribe so that David, my servant will always have a ·descendant
[Llamp before me; Cpossibly a metaphor for the reign of a king] in
Jerusalem, the city where I chose to ·be worshiped [Lput my name]. 37But
I will make you ·rule [reign] over everything you ·want [desire]. You will
·rule [be king] over all of Israel, 38and I will always be with you if you ·do
what I say [Lwalk in my ways/paths and do what] is right. You must obey
all my commands. If you obey my laws and commands as David did, I
will be with you. I will ·make your family a lasting family of kings [build
you an enduring house/dynasty], as I did for David, and give Israel to you.
39I will ·punish [afflict; humble] David's children because of this, but I
will not ·punish [afflict; humble] them forever.' "

Solomon's Death
(11:40–43; 2 Chr. 9:29–31)

40Solomon tried to kill Jeroboam, but he ·ran away [fled] to Egypt, to
Shishak king of Egypt, where he stayed until Solomon died.
41Everything else King Solomon did, and the wisdom he showed, ·is [Lis
it not . . . ?] written in the book of the ·history [acts] of Solomon. 42Solomon
ruled in Jerusalem over all Israel for forty years. 43Then he ·died [Llay
down/Tslept with his fathers/ancestors] and was buried in the City of
David [CJerusalem], his father. And his son Rehoboam ·became king
[reigned] in his place.

Israel Turns Against Rehoboam
(12:1–24; 2 Chr. 10:1–11:4)

12 Rehoboam went to Shechem, where all the Israelites had ·gone
[gathered] to make him king. 2Jeroboam son of Nebat was still
in Egypt, where he had ·gone to escape [fled] from Solomon. When
Jeroboam heard about Rehoboam being made king, he was living in
Egypt. 3After ·the people [*or* the leaders; Lthey] sent for him, he and ·the
people [Lall the assembly/crowd of Israel] went to Rehoboam and said to
him, 4"Your father ·forced us to work [Lmade our yoke] very hard. Now,
·make it easier for us [lighten the harsh labor], and ·don't make us work
as hard as he did [Lthe heavy yoke he put on us]. Then we will serve you."
5Rehoboam answered, "Go away for three days, and then come back to
me." So the people left.
6King Rehoboam asked the elders who had ·advised [served; attended]
Solomon during his lifetime, "How do you ·think I should [advise/coun-
sel me to] answer these people?"
7They said, "You should be like a servant to them today. If you serve
them and ·give them a kind answer [Lspeak good words], they will serve
you always."
8But Rehoboam ·rejected this advice [Ldisregarded/forsook the counsel
given by the elders]. Instead, he asked the young men who had grown up
with him and who served ·as his advisers [Lhim]. 9Rehoboam asked them,
"What is your ·advice [counsel]? How should we answer these people
who said, '·Don't make us work as hard as your father did' [LLighten the
yoke that your father put on us]?"
10The young men who had grown up with him answered, "Those people said to you, 'Your father ·forced us to work very hard [Lmade our yoke
heavy]. Now make our work ·easier [lighter].' You should tell them, 'My
little finger is ·bigger [thicker] than my father's ·legs [Lloins; Cmore
manly]. 11·He forced you to work hard [LMy father loaded/burdened you
with a heavy yoke], but I will ·make you work even harder [Ladd to your

yoke]. My father ·beat [scourged; disciplined; controlled] you with whips, but I will ·beat [scourge; discipline; control] you with ·whips that have sharp points [*or* scorpions].' "

12 After three days Jeroboam and all the people returned to Rehoboam as the king had ordered. 13 King Rehoboam spoke ·cruel [harsh] words to them, because he had ·rejected the advice [disregarded the counsel] the elders had given him. 14 He followed the ·advice [counsel] of the young men and said to the people, "My father ·forced you to work hard [Lloaded/burdened you with a heavy yoke], but I will ·make you work even harder [Ladd to your yoke]. My father ·beat [scourged; disciplined; controlled] you with whips, but I will ·beat [scourge; discipline; control] you with ·whips that have sharp points [*or* scorpions]." 15 So the king did not listen to the people. The LORD caused this ·to happen [Lturn (of events)] to ·keep the promise [Lfulfill/establish the word/message] he had made to Jeroboam son of Nebat through Ahijah, a prophet from Shiloh [11:11–12, 29–31].

16 When all ·the Israelites [LIsrael] saw that the new king refused to listen to them, they said to the king,

"·We have no share [LWhat portion do we have…?] in David!
We have no ·part [Linheritance] in the son of Jesse!
·People of Israel, let's go to our own homes [LTo your tents, Israel]!
·Let David's son rule his own people [LLook out for your own house, David]!"

So the Israelites went ·home [Lto their tents]. 17 But Rehoboam still ruled over the Israelites who lived in the towns of Judah.

18 ·Adoniram[n] [CHebrew: Adoram] was in charge of the ·forced labor [*or* labor force; 2 Sam. 20:24; 1 Kin. 4:6]. When Rehoboam sent him to the people of Israel, they ·threw stones at him until he died [stoned him to death]. But King Rehoboam ran to his chariot and ·escaped [fled] to Jerusalem. 19 Since then, Israel has ·been against [refused to be ruled by; been in rebellion against] the family of David.

20 When all ·the Israelites [LIsrael] heard that Jeroboam had returned, they called ·him to a meeting [an assembly] and made him king over all Israel. Only the tribe of Judah ·continued to follow [stayed loyal to] the ·family [Lhouse] of David.

21 When Rehoboam arrived in Jerusalem, he ·gathered [mobilized; assembled] one hundred eighty thousand of the ·best [elite; select] soldiers from the tribes of Judah and Benjamin. As son of Solomon, Rehoboam wanted to fight the ·people [Lhouse] of Israel to ·take back [restore] his kingdom.

22 But ·God spoke his word [Lthe word of God came] to Shemaiah, ·a [*or* the] man of God [Ca prophet], saying, 23 "·Speak [Say] to Solomon's son Rehoboam, the king of Judah, and to all the ·people [Lhouse] of Judah and Benjamin and the rest of the people. Say to them, 24 '·The LORD says [TThus says the LORD,] you must not go to war against your ·brothers [relatives], the ·Israelites [Lsons/Tchildren of Israel]. Every one of you should go home, because ·I made all these things happen [this has come from me; this is my doing].' " So they ·obeyed the LORD's command [Llistened to the word of the LORD] and went home ·as the LORD had commanded [in accordance with his word].

25 Then Jeroboam ·built up [fortified] Shechem in the mountains of

12:18 Adoniram Hebrew copies read Adoram. Some Greek and Syriac copies read Adoniram.

Ephraim, and he lived there. He also went out and ·built up [fortified] the city of Peniel.

Jeroboam Builds Golden Calves

26Jeroboam said ·to himself [Lin his heart], "The kingdom will probably ·go back [revert] to David's ·family [Lhouse]. 27If the people continue going to the ·Temple [Lhouse] of the LORD in Jerusalem to offer sacrifices, ·they will want to be ruled again by [Lthe heart of the people will return to] Rehoboam king of Judah. Then they will kill me and ·follow [return to] Rehoboam king of Judah."

28King Jeroboam asked for advice. Then he made two golden calves [Con the model of Aaron's calf; Ex. 32]. "It is too ·long a journey [much] for you to go to Jerusalem [Cto worship]," he said to the people. "Israel, here are your gods [*or* this is your God; Cit is possible that the image was associated with the false worship of the true God] who brought you out of Egypt." 29Jeroboam put one golden calf in the city of Bethel and the other in the city of Dan [Cat opposite ends of his kingdom]. 30This became a very great sin, because the people traveled as far as Dan*n* [Cin the north] to worship the calf there.

31Jeroboam built ·temples [Lhouses] on the ·places of worship [Lhigh places; 3:2]. He also chose priests from all the people, not just from the tribe of Levi [Ca violation of God's command; cf. Num. 3:10]. 32And he started a new festival on the fifteenth day of the eighth month, just like the festival in Judah [Cthe Feast of Shelters; he was trying to imitate Israel's way of worship]. During that time the king ·offered sacrifices on [went up to] the altar, along with sacrifices to the calves in Bethel he had made. He also chose priests in Bethel to serve at the ·places of worship [Lhigh places; 3:2] he had made. 33So Jeroboam ·chose his own time [devised in his own heart the month] for a festival for the Israelites—the fifteenth day of the eighth month. During that time he offered sacrifices on the altar he had built in Bethel. He ·set up [instituted] a festival for the Israelites and ·offered sacrifices [burned incense] on the altar.

The Man of God Speaks Against Bethel

13 ·The LORD commanded [LBy the word of the LORD] a man of God from Judah ·to go [went up] to Bethel. When he arrived, Jeroboam was standing by the altar to ·offer a sacrifice [burn incense]. 2·The LORD had commanded [LBy the word of the LORD] the man of God ·to speak [spoke] against the altar. The man said, "Altar, altar, the LORD says to you: 'David's ·family [Lhouse] will ·have [have born] a son named Josiah. The priests ·for the places of worship [Lof the high places; 3:2] now ·make their sacrifices [burn incense] on you, but Josiah will sacrifice those priests on you. Human bones will be burned on you.' " 3That same day the man of God gave ·proof [a sign] that these things would happen. "This is the LORD's sign that this will happen," he said. "This altar will break apart, and the ashes on it will ·fall to the ground [spill; be poured out; 2 Kin. 23:15–16]."

4When King Jeroboam heard what the man of God said ·about [against] the altar in Bethel, the king raised his hand from the altar and pointed at the man. "·Take [Seize] him!" he said. But when the king said this, his ·arm [*or* hand] ·was paralyzed [withered; dried up], and he could not ·move it [pull it back]. 5The altar also broke into pieces, and its ashes ·fell to the ground [spilled; poured out]. This was the sign the ·LORD had told the man of God to give [Lman had given by the word of the LORD].

12:30 as far as Dan The original Hebrew text may have read, "to Bethel and as far as Dan."

6Then the king said to the man of God, "Please ·pray to [intercede with;
entreat] the LORD your God for me, and ask him to ·heal my arm [*or*
restore my hand]."

So the man of God ·prayed to [interceded with; entreated] the LORD, and
the king's ·arm was healed [*or* hand was restored], becoming as it was before.
7Then the king said to the man of God, "Please come home and ·eat
with me [refresh yourself], and I will give you a gift."
8But the man of God answered the king, "Even if you gave me half of
your ·kingdom [possessions; Lhouse], I would not go with you. I will not
·eat or drink [Leat bread or drink water] in this place. 9The ·LORD [Lword of
the LORD] commanded me not to ·eat or drink [Leat bread or drink water]
nor to return on the same road by which I came." 10So he took a different
road and did not return on the same road by which he had come to Bethel.
11Now an old prophet was living in Bethel. His sons came and told him
what the man of God had done there that day. They also told their father
what he had said to King Jeroboam. 12The father asked, "Which road did
he use when he left?" So his sons showed him the road the man of God
from Judah had taken. 13Then the prophet told his sons to put a saddle on
his donkey. So they saddled the donkey, and he ·left [mounted it].
14He went after the man of God and found him sitting under an oak
tree. The prophet asked, "Are you the man of God who came from Judah?"
The man answered, "Yes, I am."
15The prophet said, "Please come home and ·eat [Leat bread] with me."
16"I can't go home with you," the man of God answered. "I can't ·eat or
drink [Leat bread or drink water] with you in this place. 17The LORD said
to me, 'Don't ·eat or drink [Leat bread or drink water] there or return on
the same road by which you came.' "
18Then the old prophet said, "But I also am a prophet, like you." Then
he lied. "An angel from the LORD came to me and told me to bring you to
my home. He said you should ·eat and drink [Leat bread and drink water]
with me." 19So the man of God went to the old prophet's house, and he ate
·and drank [Lbread and drank water] with him there.
20While they were sitting at the table, the LORD spoke his word to the
·old prophet [Lprophet who had brought him back]. 21·The old prophet
[LHe] cried out to the man of God from Judah, "·The LORD said [TThus
says the LORD,] you ·did not obey him! He said you did not do what the
LORD your God commanded you [...have defied the LORD's command].
22The LORD commanded you not to ·eat or drink [Leat bread or drink
water] in this place, but you came back and ·ate and drank [Late bread and
drank water]. So your body will not ·be buried in your family grave
[Lcome to the grave/tomb of your ancestors]."
23After the man of God finished eating [Lbread] and drinking, the
prophet put a saddle on his donkey [Cpossibly the old prophet's own don-
key] for him, and the man left. 24As he was traveling home, a lion ·attacked
[Lmet] and killed him. His body lay on the road, with the donkey and the
lion standing nearby. 25Some men who were traveling by saw the body on
the road and the lion standing nearby. So they went to the city [CBethel]
where the old prophet lived and told what they had seen.
26The old prophet who had brought back the man of God heard what
had happened. "It is the man of God who did not obey the LORD's command," he said. "So the LORD sent a lion to kill him, ·just as he said he
would [Laccording to the word of the LORD]."

27 Then the prophet said to his sons, "Put a saddle on my donkey," and
they saddled it. 28 The old prophet went out and found the body lying on
the road, with the donkey and the lion still standing nearby. The lion had
not eaten the body or ·hurt [attacked; mauled] the donkey. 29 The prophet
put the body on his donkey and carried it back to the city to ·have a time
of sadness for him [mourn] and to bury him. 30 The prophet ·buried [laid]
the body in his own family ·grave [tomb], and they ·were sad for [mourned
over] the man of God and said, "·Oh [Alas; Woe], my brother."
31 After the prophet buried the body, he said to his sons, "When I die,
bury me in ·this same grave [Lthe grave in which the man of God is bur-
ied]. ·Put [Lay] my bones next to his. 32 Through him the LORD ·spoke
[cried; proclaimed] against the altar at Bethel and against the ·places of
worship [shrines/Lhouses of the high places; 3:2] in the towns of Samaria.
What the LORD spoke through him will certainly come ·true [to pass]."
33 After this ·incident [event] King Jeroboam did not ·stop [turn from]
doing evil. He continued to choose priests for the ·places of worship
[Lhigh places; 3:2] from among all the people [12:31]. Anyone who wanted
to be a priest for the ·places of worship [Lhigh places] ·was allowed [he
appointed/ordained] to be one. 34 In this way the ·family [Lhouse] of
Jeroboam sinned, and this sin caused its ·ruin [downfall] and destruction
from the face of the earth.

Jeroboam's Son Dies

14 At that time Jeroboam's son Abijah became very sick. 2 So
Jeroboam said to his wife, "Go to Shiloh to see the prophet
Ahijah. He is the one who said I would become king of Israel. But ·dress
[disguise] yourself so people won't know you are my wife. 3 Take the
prophet ten loaves of bread, some cakes, and a jar of honey. He will tell
you what will happen to the boy." 4 So the king's wife did as he said and
went to Ahijah's home in Shiloh.
Now Ahijah was very old and ·blind [Lhis eyes were dim]. 5 The LORD
said to him, "Jeroboam's son is sick, and Jeroboam's wife is coming to ask
you about him. When she arrives, she will pretend to be ·someone else
[another woman]." Then the LORD told Ahijah ·what to say [to say such
and such/thus and thus].
6 When Ahijah heard her walking to the door, he said, "Come in, wife of
Jeroboam. Why are you pretending to be ·someone else [another woman]?
I have ·bad [heavy] news for you. 7 Go back and tell Jeroboam ·that this is
what [Tthus says] the LORD, the God of Israel, says: 'Jeroboam, I ·chose
[exalted; raised; promoted] you from among all the people and made you
the leader of my people Israel. 8 I ·tore [ripped] the kingdom away from
David's ·family [Lhouse], and I gave it to you. But you ·are not [have not
been] like my servant David, who always obeyed my commands and followed me with all his heart. He did only what ·I said was right [Lwhat was
right in my eyes/sight]. 9 But you have done more evil than ·anyone who
ruled [all who were] before you. You have ·quit following me [turned your
back on me; Lthrown me behind your back] and have made other gods
and idols of metal. This has ·made me very angry [provoked/aroused my
anger], 10 so I will soon bring ·disaster [calamity] to ·your family [Lthe
house of Jeroboam]. I will ·kill [Lcut off] all the men ·in your family [Lfrom
Jeroboam], both ·slaves [bond] and free men. I will ·destroy [*or* sweep
away] your family as ·completely as fire burns up [*or* one sweeps away]
·manure [dung]. 11 Anyone from your family who dies in the city will be

eaten by dogs, and those who die in the ·fields [country] will be eaten by the ·birds [vultures; Lbirds of the air/sky]. The LORD has spoken.'"

12Then Ahijah said to Jeroboam's wife, "Go home now. As soon as you enter your city, ·your son [the child/boy] will die, 13and all Israel will ·be sad [mourn] for him and bury him. He is the only one of Jeroboam's family who will ·be buried [have a proper burial; Lcome to the grave], because he is the only one in ·the king's family [LJeroboam's house] ·who pleased the LORD, the God of Israel [in whom the LORD, the God of Israel, found something good].

14"The LORD will ·put [raise up] a new king over Israel, who will ·destroy [Lcut off] Jeroboam's ·family [Lhouse], ·and this will happen soon [from this day on; Lthis day, what, even now?; Cthe meaning of the Hebrew is uncertain]. 15Then the LORD will ·punish [shake; Lstrike] Israel, which will be like reeds ·swaying [shaking] in the water. The LORD will ·pull up [uproot] Israel from this good land, the land he gave their ancestors. He will scatter Israel beyond the Euphrates River, because he is angry with the people. They ·made the LORD angry [aroused/provoked the LORD to anger] when they set up ·idols to worship Asherah [LAsherahs; Csacred trees or poles dedicated to the goddess Asherah]. 16Jeroboam sinned, and then he made the people of Israel sin. So the LORD will ·let the people of Israel be defeated [abandon/give up Israel]."

17Then Jeroboam's wife left and returned to Tirzah. As ·soon as she entered [Lshe crossed the threshold of] her home, the boy died. 18After they buried him, all Israel ·had a time of sadness [mourned] for him, ·just as the LORD had said [according to the word of the LORD, which he spoke] ·through [Lby the hand of] his servant, the prophet Ahijah.

19Everything else Jeroboam did, his wars and how he ruled, ·is [Lis it not…?] written in the book of the ·history [chronicles; annals] of the kings of Israel [Ca history book now lost]. 20He served [reigned] as king for twenty-two years. Then he ·died [Llay down/Tslept with his fathers/ancestors], and his son Nadab ·became king [reigned] in his place.

The Death of Rehoboam

(14:21–31; 2 Chr. 12:1–16)

21Solomon's son Rehoboam was forty-one years old when he became king of Judah. His mother was Naamah from Ammon. Rehoboam ·ruled [reigned] in Jerusalem for seventeen years. (The LORD had chosen that city from all the ·land [Ltribes] of Israel ·as the place where he would be worshiped [Lin which to put his name].)

22The people of Judah did ·what the LORD said was wrong [Levil in the eyes/sight of the LORD]. Their sins ·made the LORD very angry, even more angry than he had been at what [provoked/aroused his resentment/jealousy more than anything] their ancestors had done. 23The people built ·places to worship gods [Lhigh places; 3:2] and pillars and Asherah ·idols [poles; 14:15] on every high hill and under every ·green [luxuriant; spreading] tree. 24There were even male prostitutes [Cassociated with pagan cults] in the land. They ·acted like [imitated/committed the detestable acts/abominations of] the people God had ·driven out of [dispossessed from] the land before the ·Israelites [Lsons/Tchildren of Israel].

25During the fifth year Rehoboam was king, Shishak king of Egypt [Cruler of Egypt 935–914 BC] ·attacked [came against] Jerusalem. 26He took the treasures from the ·Temple [Lhouse] of the LORD and the king's ·palace [Lhouse]. He took everything, even the gold shields Solomon had made. 27So King Rehoboam made bronze shields to put in their place and

·gave [entrusted; committed] **them to the commanders of the guards for the ·palace gates** [Ldoorway/entrance of the king's house]. **28Whenever the king went to the ·Temple** [Lhouse] **of the LORD, the guards carried the shields. Later, they would put them back in the guardroom.**

29·Everything [LIs not everything…?] **else King Rehoboam did is written in the book of the ·history** [chronicles; annals; 14:19] **of the kings of Judah. 30There was war between Rehoboam and Jeroboam ·the whole time** [continually; constantly]. **31Rehoboam, son of Naamah from Ammon, ·died** [Llay down/Tslept with his fathers/ancestors] **and was buried with his ·ancestors** [fathers] **in the City of David** [CJerusalem], **and his son Abijam**[n] [Ca pejorative name for Abijah; see 15:1] **became king in his place.**

Abijam King of Judah
(15:1–24; 2 Chr. 13:1–2; 13:22–14:5; 15:16–19; 16:1–17:1)

15 Abijam [C"My father is the Sea" (symbol of chaos); compare Abijah ("My father is the Lord") in 2 Chr. 13:1] **became king of Judah during the eighteenth year Jeroboam son of Nebat was king of Israel. 2Abijam ruled in Jerusalem for three years. His mother was Maacah daughter of Abishalom** [CDavid's son Absalom]. **3He ·did** [committed; Lwalked in] **all the same sins his father before him had ·done** [committed]. **·Abijam was not faithful** [LHis heart was not fully/wholly devoted] **to the LORD his God as David, his ·great-grandfather** [Lfather; Cin the sense of ancestor], **had been. 4·Because the LORD loved David** [For David's sake], **the LORD gave him a ·kingdom** [Llamp; Cpossibly a metaphor for the reign of a king] **in Jerusalem and allowed him to have a son to be king after him. The LORD also ·kept Jerusalem safe** [strengthened/established Jerusalem]. **5David did what ·the LORD said was right** [Lwas right in the eyes/sight of the LORD] **and ·obeyed** [Lhad not turned aside from] **his commands all his ·life** [Ldays], **except ·the one time when David sinned ·against** [in the case/matter of] **Uriah the Hittite** [2 Sam. 11–12].

6There was war between ·Abijam[n] **and Jeroboam during Abijam's lifetime. 7Everything else Abijam did is written in the book of the ·history** [chronicles; annals; 14:19] **of the kings of Judah. There was war between Abijam and Jeroboam. 8Abijam ·died** [Llay down/Tslept with his fathers/ancestors] **and was buried in the City of David** [CJerusalem], **and his son Asa became king in his place.**

Asa King of Judah

9During the twentieth year Jeroboam was king of Israel, Asa became king of Judah. 10His ·grandmother's [mother's; Cin the sense of ancestor] **name was Maacah, the daughter of Abishalom** [15:2]. **Asa ruled in Jerusalem for forty-one years.**

11Asa did what ·the LORD said was right [Lwas right in the eyes/sight of the LORD], **as his ·ancestor** [Lfather] **David had done. 12He ·forced the male prostitutes at the worship places to leave the country** [expelled/banished the male cult prostitutes from the land; 14:24]. **He also took away the idols that his ·ancestors** [fathers] **had made. 13His ·grandmother** [mother; ancestor] **Maacah had made a ·terrible** [obscene; repulsive; abominable] **Asherah ·idol** [pole; 14:15], **so Asa removed her from being queen mother. He cut down ·that idol** [her obscene/repulsive/abominable image/pole] **and burned it in the Kidron Valley. 14The ·places of worship to gods** [Lhigh places; 3:2] **were not removed. Even so, Asa was ·faithful** [devoted; true] **to the LORD all his life. 15Asa brought into the ·Temple** [Lhouse] **of the LORD**

14:31 Abijam Some Hebrew and Greek copies read "Abijah." **15:6 Abijam** Some Hebrew and Syriac copies read "Abijam." Most Hebrew copies read "Rehoboam."

the gifts he and his father had ·given [dedicated]: gold, silver, and utensils.

16There was war between Asa and Baasha king of Israel all ·the time they were kings [their days]. 17Baasha ·attacked [invaded; Lwent up against] Judah, and he ·made the town of Ramah strong [fortified Ramah] so he could keep people from leaving or entering ·Judah, Asa's country [LAsa, king of Judah].

18Asa took the rest of the silver and gold from the treasuries of the ·Temple [Lhouse] of the LORD and ·his own palace [Lthe treasuries of the king's house] and gave it to his ·officers [officials; servants]. Then he sent them to Ben-Hadad son of Tabrimmon, who was the son of Hezion. Ben-Hadad was the king of Aram and ·ruled [lived] in the city of Damascus. Asa said, 19"Let there be a treaty between you and me as there was between my father and your father. I am sending you a gift of silver and gold. Break your treaty with Baasha king of Israel so he will ·leave my land [withdraw from me]."

20Ben-Hadad ·agreed with [listened to] King Asa, so he sent the commanders of his armies ·to attack [against] the towns of Israel. They defeated the towns of Ijon, Dan, and Abel Beth Maacah, as well as all ·Galilee [LKinnereth] and the area of Naphtali. 21When Baasha heard about these attacks, he stopped ·building up [fortifying] Ramah and ·returned [withdrew] to Tirzah. 22Then King Asa gave an ·order [proclamation] to all the people of Judah; everyone had to help carry away all the stones and ·wood [timber] Baasha had used in building Ramah, and they used them to build up Geba and Mizpah in the land of Benjamin.

23Everything else Asa did—his ·victories [power] and the cities he built—·is [Lare they not…?] written in the book of the ·history [chronicles; annals; 14:19] of the kings of Judah. When he became old, he got a disease in his feet. 24After Asa ·died [Llay down/Tslept with his fathers/ancestors], he was buried with his ·ancestors [fathers] in the City of David [CJerusalem], his ·ancestor [father]. Then Jehoshaphat, Asa's son, ·became king [reigned] in his place.

Nadab King of Israel

25Nadab son of Jeroboam became king of Israel during the second year Asa was king of Judah. Nadab ·was king of [reigned over] Israel for two years, 26and he did ·what the LORD said was wrong [Levil in the eyes/sight of the LORD]. Jeroboam had led the people of Israel to sin, and Nadab ·sinned in the same way as his father Jeroboam [Lwalked in the way/path of his father and in his sin].

27Baasha son of Ahijah, from the ·tribe [Lhouse] of Issachar, ·made plans to kill Nadab [plotted/conspired against him]. Nadab and all Israel were ·attacking [laying siege to] the Philistine town of Gibbethon, so Baasha killed Nadab there. 28·This happened [Baasha killed him] during Asa's third year as king of Judah, and ·Baasha became the next king of Israel [reigned in his place].

Baasha King of Israel

29As soon as Baasha became king, he killed all of Jeroboam's ·family [Lhouse], leaving no one in Jeroboam's ·family [Lhouse] alive. He destroyed them all ·as the LORD had said would happen [Laccording to the word which the LORD spoke] ·through [Lby the hand of] his servant Ahijah from Shiloh. 30All this was because King Jeroboam had sinned very much and had led the people of Israel to sin, ·provoking [arousing] the LORD, the God of Israel, to anger.

31 Everything else Nadab did ·is [Lis it not…?]written in the book of the
·history [chronicles; annals; 14:19] of the kings of Israel. 32 There was war
between Asa [Cking of Judah] and Baasha king of Israel all ·the time they
ruled [their days].
33 Baasha son of Ahijah became king of Israel during Asa's third year as
king of Judah. Baasha ruled in Tirzah for twenty-four years, 34 and he did
·what the LORD said was wrong [Levil in the eyes/sight of the LORD].
Jeroboam had led the people of Israel to sin, and Baasha ·sinned in the
same way as [Lwalked in the way of] Jeroboam.

16 Jehu son of Hanani spoke the word of the LORD against King
Baasha. 2 The LORD said, "·You were nothing, but I took you [LI
raised/exalted you from the dust] and made you ·a leader [ruler] over my
people Israel. But you have ·followed [Lwalked in] the ·ways [paths] of
Jeroboam and have led my people Israel to sin. Their sins have ·made me
angry [provoked/aroused me to anger], 3 so, Baasha, I will soon ·destroy
[consume; wipe out] you and your ·family [Lhouse]. I will do to you
what I did to the ·family [Lhouse] of Jeroboam son of Nebat. 4 Anyone
·from your family [Lof Baasha] who dies in the city will be eaten by dogs,
and anyone from your ·family [Lhouse] who dies in the ·fields [country]
will be eaten by ·birds [vultures; Lbirds of the air/sky]."
5 Everything else Baasha did and all his victories ·are [Lare they not…?]
written down in the book of the ·history [chronicles; annals; 14:19] of the
kings of Israel. 6 So Baasha ·died [Llay down/Tslept with his fathers/ances-
tors] and was buried in Tirzah, and his son Elah became king in his place.
7 The LORD spoke his word against Baasha and his ·family [Lhouse]
through the prophet Jehu son of Hanani. Baasha had done ·many things
the LORD said were wrong [Levil in the eyes/sight of the LORD], ·which made
the LORD very angry [Lprovoking/arousing him to anger with the works of
his hand]. He did the same evil deeds that Jeroboam's ·family [Lhouse] had
done before him. ·The LORD also spoke against Baasha because he killed all
of [And Baasha had also destroyed/struck] Jeroboam's ·family [Lhouse].

Elah King of Israel

8 Elah son of Baasha became king of Israel during Asa's twenty-sixth
year as king of Judah, and Elah ruled in Tirzah for two years.
9 Zimri, one of Elah's ·officers [officials; Lservants], commanded half of
Elah's chariots. Zimri ·made plans [plotted; conspired] against Elah while
the king was in Tirzah, getting drunk at Arza's home. (Arza was ·in charge
of the palace [Lover the household] at Tirzah.) 10 Zimri went into Arza's
house and ·killed [Lstruck down and killed] Elah during Asa's twenty-seventh year as king of Judah. Then Zimri became king of Israel in Elah's place.

Zimri King of Israel

11 As soon as Zimri became king, he killed all of Baasha's ·family
[Lhouse], not allowing ·any of Baasha's family [Lany male/one who urinates against the wall, of his relatives] or friends to live. 12 So Zimri
destroyed all of Baasha's ·family [Lhouse] ·just as the LORD had said it
would happen [Laccording to the word of the LORD as spoken] through the
prophet Jehu. 13 Baasha and his son Elah sinned and led the people of
Israel to sin, ·provoking [arousing] the LORD, the God of Israel, to anger
because of their worthless idols.
14 Everything else Elah did ·is [Lis it not…?] written in the book of the
·history [chronicles; annals; 14:19] of the kings of Israel.
15 So during Asa's twenty-seventh year as king of Judah, Zimri became
king of Israel and ruled in Tirzah seven days.

The ·army of Israel [people] was camped near Gibbethon, a Philistine
town. 16The men in the camp heard that Zimri had ·made secret plans
[plotted; conspired] against King Elah and had killed him. So that day in
the camp ·they [Lall Israel] made Omri, the commander of the army, king
over Israel. 17So Omri and all the Israelite army left Gibbethon and
·attacked [besieged] Tirzah. 18When Zimri saw that the city had been captured, he went into the ·palace [Lcitadel of the king's house] and set it on
fire, burning the palace and himself with it. 19So Zimri died because he
had sinned by doing ·what the LORD said was wrong [Levil in the eyes/sight
of the LORD]. Jeroboam had led the people of Israel to sin, and Zimri
·sinned in the same way as [Lwalked in the way/path of] Jeroboam.

20Everything else Zimri did and ·the story of how he turned [his con-
spiracy] against King Elah ·are [Lare they not…?] written down in the
book of the ·history [chronicles; annals; 14:19] of the kings of Israel.

Omri King of Israel

21The people of Israel were divided into two ·groups [factions; parts].
Half of the people ·wanted [followed; supported] Tibni son of Ginath to
be king, while the other half ·wanted [followed; supported] Omri.
22Omri's followers ·were stronger than [prevailed over; overcame] the followers of Tibni son of Ginath, so Tibni died, and Omri became king.

23Omri became king of Israel during the thirty-first year Asa was king of
Judah. Omri ruled Israel for twelve years, six of those years in the city of
Tirzah. 24He bought the hill of Samaria from Shemer for ·about one hundred fifty pounds [Ltwo talents] of silver. Omri built a ·city [fortified city]
on that hill and called it Samaria after the name of its earlier owner, Shemer.

25But Omri did ·what the LORD said was wrong [Levil in the eyes/sight
of the LORD]; he did more evil than all the kings who came before him.
26Jeroboam son of Nebat had led the people of Israel to sin, and Omri
·sinned in the same way as [Lwalked in the way/path of] Jeroboam. The
Israelites ·provoked [aroused] the LORD, the God of Israel, to anger
·because they worshiped [with their] worthless idols.

27Everything else Omri did and all his successes ·are [Lare they not…?]
written in the book of the ·history [chronicles; annals; 14:19] of the kings
of Israel. 28So Omri ·died [Llay down/Tslept with his fathers/ancestors] and
was buried in Samaria, and his son Ahab became king in his place.

Ahab King of Israel

29Ahab son of Omri became king of Israel during Asa's thirty-eighth
year as king of Judah, and Ahab ·ruled [reigned over] Israel in the city of
Samaria for twenty-two years. 30More than any king before him, Ahab
son of Omri did ·many things the LORD said were wrong [Levil in the eyes/
sight of the LORD]. 31He ·sinned in the same ways as [Lwalked in the ways/
paths of] Jeroboam son of Nebat, ·but he did even worse things [Las
though it were a light/trivial thing]. He married Jezebel daughter of
Ethbaal, the king of Sidon. Then Ahab began to serve Baal and worship
him. 32He built a ·temple [Lhouse] in Samaria for worshiping Baal and
put an altar there for Baal. 33Ahab also ·made an idol for worshiping
Asherah [set up an Asherah pole; 14:15]. He did more things to ·provoke
[arouse] the LORD, the God of Israel, to anger than all the other kings
before him.

34During the time of Ahab, Hiel from Bethel rebuilt the city of Jericho.
·It cost Hiel the life of Abiram, his oldest son, to begin work on the city
[LWith Abiram, his firstborn, he laid its foundation], and ·it cost the life of
Segub, his youngest son, to build [Lwith Segub, his youngest, he set up]

the city gates. This happened ·just as the LORD, speaking [Laccording to
the word of the LORD spoken] ·through [Lby the hand of] Joshua son of
Nun [Josh. 6:26].

Elijah Stops the Rain

17 Now Elijah the Tishbite was a prophet from the settlers in
Gilead. "I ·serve [Lstand before] the LORD, the God of Israel,"
Elijah said to Ahab. "As surely as the LORD lives, no dew or rain will fall
during the next few years ·unless I command it [except by my word; Cthe
people were worshiping the false god Baal whom they believed brought
rain]."
2 Then the ·LORD spoke his word [word of the LORD came] to Elijah:
3 "Leave this place and go east and hide near Kerith ·Ravine [Brook; Wadi]
east of the Jordan River. 4 Drink from the stream, and I have ·commanded
[ordered] ravens to bring you food there." 5 So Elijah did ·what the LORD
said [Laccording to the word of the LORD]; he went to Kerith ·Ravine
[Brook; Wadi], east of the Jordan, and lived there. 6 The ·birds [ravens]
brought Elijah bread and meat every morning and evening, and he drank
water from the stream.
7 After a while the stream dried up because there was no rain in the
land. 8 Then the ·LORD spoke his word to Elijah [Lword of the LORD came to
him], 9 "Go to Zarephath in Sidon and live there. I have commanded a
widow there to ·take care of [provide for; feed] you."
10 So Elijah went to Zarephath. When he reached the town gate, he saw
a widow gathering ·wood for a fire [sticks]. Elijah asked her, "·Would you
[Please] bring me a little water in a ·cup [jar; pitcher] so I may have a
drink?" 11 As she was going to get his water, Elijah said, "Please bring me a
·piece [scrap] of bread [Lin your hand]."
12 The woman answered, "As surely as the LORD your God lives, I have
no bread. I have only a handful of flour in a ·jar [bowl] and only a little
olive oil in a jug. I came here to gather some wood so I could go home and
cook our last meal. My son and I will eat it and then die [Cof hunger]."
13 "Don't ·worry [be afraid]," Elijah said to her. "Go home and cook
your food as you have said. But first make a small loaf of bread from the
flour you have, and bring it to me. Then cook something for yourself and
your son. 14 The LORD, the God of Israel, says, 'That jar of flour will never
be ·empty [spent; used up], and the jug will ·always have oil in it [not run
dry/fail/be empty], until the day the LORD sends rain to the land.' "
15 So the woman went home and did what Elijah told her to do. And the
woman and her ·son and Elijah [family; Lhousehold] had enough food
·every day [Lfor many days]. 16 The ·jar [bowl] of flour and the jug of oil
were never empty, ·just as the LORD, through Elijah, had promised
[Laccording to the word of the LORD, spoken through Elijah].

Elijah Brings a Boy Back to Life

17 ·Some time later [LAfter these things] the son of the woman who
owned the house became sick. He grew worse and worse and finally
·stopped breathing [died; Lthere remained no breath in him]. 18 The
woman said to Elijah, "Man of God, what ·have you done to me [do you
have against me; Lto me and to you]? Did you come here to ·remind me of
[reveal; point out] my sin and to kill my son?"
19 Elijah said to her, "Give me your son." Elijah took the boy from ·her
[her arms/lap/Lbosom], carried him upstairs, and laid him on the bed in
the room where he was staying. 20 Then he prayed to the LORD: "LORD my
God, this widow is letting me stay in her house. Why have you ·done this

terrible thing [brought tragedy/calamity] to her and caused her son to die?" 21Then Elijah ·lay on top of [stretched himself on] the boy three times. He prayed to the LORD, "LORD my God, let this ·boy live again [boy's life/breath/soul return to him]!"

22The LORD ·answered [heard] Elijah's ·prayer [cry; Lvoice]; the ·boy began breathing again [boy's life/breath/soul returned to him] and ·was alive [revived]. 23Elijah carried the boy downstairs and gave him to his mother and said, "See! Your son is alive!"

24"Now I know you really are a man from God," the woman said to Elijah. "I know that the ·LORD truly speaks through you [Lword of the LORD in your mouth is true]!"

Elijah Kills the Prophets of Baal

18 During the third year without rain, the ·LORD spoke his word [Lword of the LORD came] to Elijah: "Go and ·meet [present/show yourself to] King Ahab, and I will soon send rain." 2So Elijah went to ·meet [present/show himself to] Ahab.

By this time ·there was no food [the famine was severe] in Samaria. 3King Ahab sent for Obadiah, who was in charge of the ·king's palace [household]. (Obadiah ·was a true follower of [Lgreatly revered/feared] the LORD. 4When Jezebel was killing the LORD's prophets, Obadiah hid a hundred of them in two caves, fifty in one cave and fifty in another. He also ·brought [provided] them food and water.) 5Ahab said to Obadiah, "·Let's [Go] check every spring and valley in the land. Maybe we can find enough grass to keep our horses and mules alive and not have to kill our animals." 6So ·each one chose a part of the country to search [they divided the land between them]; Ahab ·went in one direction [Lwalked one way by himself] and Obadiah ·in another [Lwalked one way by himself].

7While Obadiah was on his way, Elijah met him. Obadiah recognized Elijah, so he ·bowed down to the ground [Lfell on his face] and said, "Elijah? Is it really you, ·master [my lord]?"

8"Yes," Elijah answered. "Go tell your master that I am here."

9Then Obadiah said, "What ·wrong [sin] have I done for you to hand me over to Ahab like this? He will put me to death. 10As surely as the LORD your God lives, the king has sent people to every ·country [nation and kingdom] to search for you. If the ruler said you were not there, Ahab ·forced the ruler to swear [required an oath that] you could not be found in his country. 11Now you want me to go to my master and tell him, 'Elijah is here'? 12The Spirit of the LORD may carry you to some ·other [unknown] place after I leave. If I go tell King Ahab you are here, and he comes and doesn't find you, he will kill me! ·I [Even though/Yet I] have ·followed [Lrevered; feared] the LORD since I was a boy. 13Haven't you been told what I did? When Jezebel was killing the LORD's prophets, I hid a hundred of them, fifty in one cave and fifty in another. I ·brought [provided] them food and water. 14Now you want me to go and tell my master, 'Elijah is here'? He will kill me!"

15Elijah answered, "As surely as the LORD ·All-Powerful [of Heaven's Armies; of hosts] lives, whom I serve, I will ·be seen by [present/show myself to] Ahab today."

16So Obadiah went to Ahab and told him. Then Ahab went to meet Elijah.

17When he saw Elijah, he asked, "Is it you—·the biggest troublemaker in [Lyou troubler of] Israel?"

18 Elijah answered, "I have not made trouble in Israel. You and your
father's ·family [Lhouse] have made all this trouble by ·not obeying [forsak-
ing; abandoning] the LORD's commands. You have ·gone after [followed;
worshiped] the Baals. 19 Now ·tell [summon; assemble] all Israel to meet me
at Mount Carmel. Also bring the four hundred fifty prophets of Baal and
the four hundred prophets of Asherah [14:15], who eat at Jezebel's table."
20 So Ahab ·called [summoned; assembled] all the ·Israelites [Lsons/
Tchildren of Israel] and those prophets to Mount Carmel. 21 Elijah
approached the people and said, "How long will you ·not decide between
two choices [Llimp/hobble/waver between two opinions]? If the LORD is
·the true God [LGod], follow him, but if ·Baal is the true God [LBaal], follow him!" But the people ·said nothing [Ldid not answer a word].
22 Elijah said, "I am the only prophet of the LORD ·here [left], but there
are four hundred fifty prophets of Baal. 23 Bring two ·bulls [oxen]. Let the
prophets of Baal choose one bull and kill it and cut it into pieces. Then let
them put the meat on the wood, but they are not to set fire to it. I will
prepare the other ·bull [ox], putting the meat on the wood but not setting
fire to it. 24 You prophets of Baal, ·pray to [Lcall on the name of] your god,
and I will ·pray to [Lcall on the name of] the LORD. The god who answers
by ·setting fire to his wood is the true [fire—he is] God [CBaal, the storm
god, threw lightening from the sky]."
All the people agreed that this was a good idea.
25 Then Elijah said to the prophets of Baal, "There are many of you, so
you go first. Choose a ·bull [ox] and prepare it. ·Pray to [LCall on the
name of] your god, but don't start the fire."
26 So they took the ·bull [ox] that was given to them and prepared it.
They ·prayed to [Lcalled on the name of] Baal from morning until noon,
shouting "Baal, answer us!" But there was no ·sound [voice; response],
and no one answered. They ·danced [leaped; *or* limped; C"limped" may
suggest that Israel had hobbled itself by worshiping both God and Baal]
around the altar they had built.
27 At noon Elijah began to ·make fun of [mock; taunt] them. "·Pray
[Call; Shout] louder!" he said. "·If Baal really is [Since he is surely] a god,
maybe he is ·thinking [preoccupied; daydreaming], or ·busy [has wandered away], or ·traveling [is on a trip/journey]! Maybe he is sleeping so
you will have to wake him!" 28 The prophets ·prayed [called; shouted]
louder, cutting themselves with swords and ·spears [lances] until their
blood flowed, ·which was the way they worshiped [as was their custom; Ca
ritual performed when they thought Baal had temporarily gone to the
underworld]. 29 The afternoon passed, and the prophets ·continued to act
like this [raved; ranted] until it was time for the evening sacrifice. But no
voice was heard; Baal did not answer, and no one paid attention.
30 Then Elijah said to all the people, "Now come ·to [near/closer to]
me." So they gathered around him, and Elijah ·rebuilt [repaired] the altar
of the LORD, which had been torn down [Cthe remains of a previous altar
to God]. 31 He took twelve stones, one stone for each of the twelve tribes
[Csymbolizing a previously unified Israel; cf Josh. 4:2–20], the number of
Jacob's sons. (·The LORD changed Jacob's name to Israel […to whom the
word of the LORD had come, saying "Israel will be your name"; Gen. 32:22–
32].) 32 Elijah used these stones to ·rebuild the [build an] altar in ·honor
[Lthe name] of the LORD. Then he dug a ·ditch [trench] around the altar
that was big enough to hold ·about thirteen quarts [Ltwo measures/seahs]

of seed. 33Elijah ·put [piled; arranged] the wood on the altar, cut the ·bull
[ox] into pieces, and laid the pieces on the wood. 34Then he said, "Fill four
·jars [pitchers] with water, and pour it on the ·meat [Lburnt offering; Lev.
1:1–17] and on the wood." Then Elijah said, "Do it ·again [a second time],"
and they did it ·again [a second time]. Then he said, "Do it a third time,"
and they did it the third time. 35So the water ran ·off [all around] the altar
and filled the ·ditch [trench].

36At the time for the evening sacrifice, the prophet Elijah went near the
altar. "LORD, you are the God of Abraham, Isaac, and Israel," he ·prayed
[said]. "·Prove [LLet it be known this day] that you are the God ·of [in]
Israel and that I am your servant. Show these people that ·you commanded me to do all these things [LI have done all these things at your
word]. 37Answer me, LORD, answer ·my prayer [Lme,] so these people will
know that you, LORD, are God and that you ·will change their minds
[Lhave turned their hearts back again]."

38Then fire from the LORD came down and ·burned the sacrifice [con-
sumed the burnt offering; Lev. 1:1–17], the wood, the stones, and the
·ground [dust] around the altar. It also ·dried [Llicked] up the water in the
·ditch [trench]. 39When all the people saw this, they fell ·down to the
ground [on their faces], crying, "·The LORD is God [LThe LORD—he is
God]! ·The LORD is God [LThe LORD—he is God]!"

40Then Elijah said, "·Capture [Seize] the prophets of Baal! Don't let
·any [a single one] of them ·run away [escape]!" The people ·captured
[seized] all the prophets. Then Elijah led them down to the Kishon ·Valley
[Brook], where he ·killed [slaughtered] them.

The Rain Comes Again

41Then Elijah said to Ahab, "Now, go, eat, and drink, ·because a heavy
rain is coming [Lfor there is the sound of rushing rain]." 42So King Ahab
went to eat and drink. At the same time Elijah climbed to the top of
Mount Carmel, where he bent down to the ground with his ·head [Lface]
between his knees.

43Then Elijah said to his servant, "Go and look toward the sea."

The servant went and looked. "I see nothing," he said.

Elijah told him to go and look again. This happened seven times. 44The
seventh time, the servant said, "I see a small cloud, the size of a ·human
fist [man's hand], ·coming [rising] from the sea."

Elijah told the servant, "Go to Ahab and tell him to get his chariot
ready and go ·home [Ldown] now. Otherwise, the rain will stop him."

45After a short time the sky ·was covered with dark [grew black with]
clouds. The wind began to blow, and soon a ·heavy [torrential] rain began
to fall [Cshowing that it was the Lord, not Baal, that supplied the rain].
Ahab got in his chariot and started back to Jezreel. 46·The LORD gave his
power to [LThe hand of the LORD was on] Elijah, who ·tightened his
clothes around him [Tgirded up his loins] and ·ran ahead of King [out-
ran] Ahab all the way to Jezreel.

Elijah Runs Away

19 King Ahab told Jezebel every thing Elijah had done and how
Elijah had killed all the prophets with a sword. 2So Jezebel
sent a messenger to Elijah, saying, "May the gods ·punish me terribly
[deal severely with me, and worse; Ldo to me, and even more] if by this
time tomorrow I don't ·kill you just as you killed those prophets [Lmake
your life like the life of one of them]."

3Elijah was afraid and ran for his life, taking his servant with him.

When they came to Beersheba in Judah, Elijah left his servant there. 4Then Elijah ·walked [journeyed] for a whole day into the ·desert [wilderness]. He sat down under a ·bush [juniper/broom tree] and asked to die. "I have had enough, LORD," he prayed. "·Let me die [LTake my life]. I am no better than my ·ancestors [fathers; Cthat is, he is as good as dead, as they already are]." 5Then he lay down under the tree and slept.

Suddenly an ·angel [messenger] came to him and touched him. "Get up and eat," the angel said. 6Elijah saw near his head a loaf baked over ·coals [hot stones] and a jar of water, so he ate and drank. Then he ·went back to sleep [Llay down again].

7The LORD's ·angel [messenger] came to him a second time. The angel touched him and said, "Get up and eat. If you don't, the journey will be too ·hard [much] for you." 8So Elijah got up and ate and drank. The food made him strong enough to walk for forty days and nights to Mount ·Sinai [LHoreb; Ex. 3:1, 17:6; 19:18], the mountain of God. 9There Elijah went into a cave and stayed all night.

Then the ·LORD spoke his word to [word of the LORD came to] him: "Elijah! ·Why are you [What are you doing] here?"

10He answered, "LORD God ·All-Powerful [of Heaven's Armies; Tof hosts], I have ·always served you as well as I could [been very zealous for you]. But the ·people [Lsons; Tchildren] of Israel have ·broken [abandoned; forsaken] their ·agreement [covenant; solemn pact] with you, ·destroyed [torn down] your altars, and killed your prophets with swords. I ·am the only prophet [alone am] left, and now they ·are trying to kill me [seek my life], too."

11The LORD said to Elijah, "Go, stand ·in front of [before] me on the mountain, ·and I will pass by you [for the LORD is about to pass by]." Then a very strong wind ·blew until it caused the mountains to fall apart and large rocks to break in front of [tore apart the mountain and shattered the rocks before] the LORD. But the LORD was not in the wind. After the wind, there was an earthquake, but the LORD was not in the earthquake. 12After the earthquake, there was a fire, but the LORD was not in the fire. After the fire, there was ·a quiet, gentle sound [the sound of a gentle whisper/blowing/wind; *or* a brief sound of silence; Ta still small voice]. 13When Elijah heard it, he covered his face with his coat and went out and stood at the entrance to the cave.

Then a voice said to him, "Elijah! ·Why are you [What are you doing] here?"

14He answered, "LORD God ·All-Powerful [of Heaven's Armies; Tof hosts], I have ·always served you as well as I could [been very zealous for you]. But the ·people [Lsons; Tchildren] of Israel have ·broken [abandoned; forsaken] their ·agreement [covenant; treaty] with you, ·destroyed [torn down] your altars, and killed your prophets with swords. I ·am the only prophet [alone am] left, and now they ·are trying to kill me [seek my life], too."

15The LORD said to him, "Go back on the road that leads to the ·desert [wilderness] around Damascus. Enter that city, and ·pour olive oil on [Lanoint] Hazael to make him king over Aram [2 Kin. 8:7–15]. 16Then ·pour oil on [Lanoint] Jehu son of Nimshi to make him king over Israel [2 Kin. 9:1–13]. Next, ·pour oil on [Lanoint] Elisha son of Shaphat from Abel Meholah to ·make him a prophet in your place [succeed you as prophet; 2 Kin. 2:1–18]. 17Jehu will kill anyone who escapes from Hazael's sword,

and Elisha will kill anyone who escapes from Jehu's sword. [18]I ·have left
[*or* will preserve/spare/leave] seven thousand people in Israel who have
never bowed down before Baal and whose mouths have never kissed ·his
idol [[L]him]."

Elisha Becomes a Prophet

[19]So Elijah left that place and found Elisha son of Shaphat plowing a
field with ·a team of oxen. He owned twelve teams of oxen and was plowing with the twelfth team [*or* twelve teams of oxen, and he with the twelfth].
Elijah came up to Elisha, took off his ·coat [[T]mantle], and put it on Elisha.
[20]Then Elisha left his oxen and ran to follow Elijah. "Let me kiss my father
and my mother good-bye," Elisha said. "Then I will go with you."

Elijah answered, "Go back. ·It does not matter to me [For what have I
done to you?; *or* But consider what I have done to you]."

[21]So Elisha went back and took his pair of oxen and ·killed [slaugh-
tered; sacrificed] them. He used ·their wooden yoke [the plowing gear] for
a fire [[C]symbolizing his turning from farming to a new calling as a
prophet]. Then he cooked the meat and gave it to the people. After they
ate it, Elisha left and followed Elijah and became his ·helper [servant;
assistant].

Ben-Hadad and Ahab Go to War

20 Ben-Hadad king of Aram ·gathered together [mobilized;
mustered] all his army. There were thirty-two kings with
their horses and chariots who went with him and ·surrounded [besieged]
Samaria and attacked it. [2]The king sent messengers into the city to Ahab
king of Israel.

This was his message: "Ben-Hadad says, [3]'Your silver and gold ·belong
to me [are mine], as well as the best of your wives and children.' "

[4]Ahab king of Israel answered, "My ·master [lord] and king, ·I agree to
what you say [[L]it is as you say/according to your word]. I and everything I
have ·belong to you [are yours]."

[5]Then the messengers came to Ahab again. They said, "Ben-Hadad
says, 'I told you before that you must give me your silver and gold, your
wives and your children. [6]About this time tomorrow I will send my ·men
[officials; servants], who will search everywhere in your ·palace [[L]house]
and in the homes of your ·officers [officials; servants]. Whatever ·they
want [*or* you value] they will take and carry off.' "

[7]Then Ahab called a meeting of all the elders of his country. He said,
"Ben-Hadad is looking for trouble. First he said I had to give him my
wives, my children, my silver, and my gold, and I have not refused him."

[8]The elders and all the people said, "Don't listen to him or ·agree to this
[consent]."

[9]So Ahab said to Ben-Hadad's messengers, "Tell my ·master [lord] the
king: 'I will do what you said at first, but ·I cannot allow this second command [this thing I cannot do].' " And King Ben-Hadad's men carried the
message back to him.

[10]Then Ben-Hadad sent another message to Ahab: "May the gods ·pun-
ish me terribly [deal severely with me, and worse; [L]do to me, and even
more] if I don't completely destroy Samaria. There won't be enough left
for each of my men to get a handful of dust!"

[11]Ahab answered, "Tell Ben-Hadad, '·The man who puts on his armor
should not brag. It's the man who lives to take it off who has the right to
brag [[L]Let not him who puts on boast like him who takes off; [C]that is,
boast only after victory in battle, not before].' "

12Ben-Hadad was drinking in his tent with the ·other rulers [kings]
when the message came from Ahab. Ben-Hadad commanded his men to
prepare to attack the city, and they ·moved into place for battle [took
their positions].
13At the same time a prophet came to Ahab king of Israel. The prophet
said, "Ahab, ·the LORD says to you [[T]thus says the LORD], 'Do you see that
·big army [[L]great multitude]? I will hand it over to you today so you will
know I am the LORD.' "
14Ahab asked, "·Who will you use to defeat them [By what means; [L]By
whom]?"
The prophet answered, "·The LORD says [[T]Thus says the LORD], 'The
young officers of the ·district governors [provincial commanders] will
defeat them.' "
Then the king asked, "Who will ·command the main army [*or* attack
first; begin the battle]?"
The prophet answered, "You will."
15So Ahab ·gathered [summoned; mustered] the young officers of the
·district governors [provincial commanders], two hundred thirty-two of
them. Then he called together the ·army [[L]sons] of Israel, about seven
thousand people in all.
16They marched out at noon, while Ben-Hadad and the thirty-two ·rul-
ers [kings] helping him were getting drunk in their tents. 17The young
officers of the ·district governors [provincial commanders] attacked first.
Ben-Hadad sent out scouts who told him that soldiers were coming from
Samaria. 18Ben-Hadad said, "They may be coming to fight, or they may
be coming to ask for peace. In either case capture them alive."
19The young officers of the ·district governors [provincial command-
ers] ·led the attack [went out from the city], followed by the army of
Israel. 20Each officer of Israel killed the man who came against him. The
men from Aram ran away as Israel chased them, but Ben-Hadad king of
Aram escaped on a horse with some of his ·horsemen [cavalry; chario-
teers]. 21Ahab king of Israel ·led the army [[L]went out] and destroyed the
horses and chariots and slaughtered the Arameans.
22Then the prophet went to Ahab king of Israel and said, "The king of
Aram will attack you again ·next spring [[L]at the turn of the year]. So go
home now and strengthen ·your army [[L]yourself] and see what you need
to do."
23Meanwhile the officers of Ben-Hadad king of Aram said to him, "The
gods of Israel are mountain gods, so they were stronger. Let's fight them
on the ·flat land [plain], and then we will ·win [be stronger]. 24This is what
you should do. ·Don't allow the thirty-two rulers to command the armies,
but [[L]Remove the kings from their place/commands, and] put other commanders in their places. 25·Gather [Recruit; Raise; Muster] an army like
the one ·that was destroyed and as many horses and chariots as before
[[L]you lost, horse for horse and chariot for chariot]. We will fight the
Israelites on ·flat land [the plain], and then we will ·win [be stronger]."
Ben-Hadad ·agreed with their advice [[L]heeded their voice] and did what
they said.
26·The next spring [[L]At the turn of the year] Ben-Hadad ·gathered
[mustered] the army of Aram and went up to Aphek to fight against
Israel.
27The ·Israelites [[L]sons/[T]children of Israel] also had ·prepared for war

[mustered and gathered provisions]. They marched out to meet the Arameans and camped opposite them. The Israelites looked like two small flocks of goats, but the Arameans covered the ·area [countryside].

28 A man of God came to the king of Israel with this message: "·The LORD says [TThus says the LORD], 'The people of Aram say that I, the LORD, am a god of the mountains, not a god of the ·valleys [plains]. So I will ·allow you to defeat this huge army [Lgive this great multitude into your hands], and then you will know I am the LORD.' "

29 The armies were camped across from each other for seven days. On the seventh day the battle began. The ·Israelites [Lsons of Israel] ·killed [slaughtered] one hundred thousand Aramean soldiers in one day. 30 The rest of them ran away to the city of Aphek, where a city wall fell on twenty-seven thousand of them. Ben-Hadad also ran away to the city and hid in a room.

31 His ·officers [officials; Lservants] said to him, "We have heard that the kings of Israel are ·trustworthy [merciful]. Let's dress in ·rough cloth [sackcloth; burlap; Cindicating sorrow], and wear ropes on our heads. Then we will go to the king of Israel, and perhaps he will ·let you live [spare your life]."

32 So they dressed in ·rough cloth [sackcloth; burlap] and wore ropes on their heads and went to the king of Israel. They said, "Your servant Ben-Hadad says, 'Please ·let me live [spare my life].' "

Ahab answered, "Is he still alive? He is my brother."

33 Ben-Hadad's men ·had wanted a sign from Ahab [took this as a good sign]. They quickly ·caught [picked up on] his word, "Yes! Ben-Hadad is your brother."

Ahab said, "Bring him to me." When Ben-Hadad came, Ahab asked him to join him in the chariot.

34 Ben-Hadad said to him, "Ahab, I will ·give you back [restore] the cities my father took from your father. And you may ·put shops [establish bazaars/markets/trading areas] in Damascus, as my father did in Samaria."

Ahab said, "If you ·agree [covenant] to this, I will allow you to go free." So the two kings made a ·peace agreement [covenant; treaty]. Then Ahab let Ben-Hadad go free.

A Prophet Speaks Against Ahab

35 One ·prophet from one of the groups of prophets [Lof the sons of the prophets] told another, "Hit me!" He said this ·because the LORD had commanded it [by the word of the LORD], but the other man refused. 36 The prophet said, "You did not obey the ·LORD's command [Lvoice of the LORD], so a lion will kill you as soon as you leave me." When the man left, a lion found him and killed him.

37 The prophet went to another man and said, "Hit me, please!" So the man hit him and hurt him. 38 The prophet ·wrapped his face in a cloth [placed a bandage over his eyes; Cto disguise himself]. Then he went and waited by the road for the king. 39 As Ahab king of Israel passed by, the prophet called out to him. "I went to fight in the battle," the prophet said. "One of our men brought an ·enemy soldier [Lman] to me. Our man said, 'Guard this man. If he ·runs away [is missing], ·you will have to give your life in his place [Lit will be your life for his life]. Or, you will have to pay a ·fine of seventy-five pounds [Ltalent] of silver.' 40 But I was busy doing other things, so the man ran away."

The king of Israel answered, "That is your ·sentence [judgment]. You have ·already said what the punishment is [pronounced it yourself]."

41Then the prophet quickly took the ·cloth from his face [bandage from
his eyes]. When the king of Israel saw him, he knew he was one of the
prophets. 42The prophet said to the king, "·This is what the LORD says
[TThus says the LORD]: 'You freed the man I ·said should die [Lhad devoted
to destruction], so your life will be ·taken instead of his [for his life]. ·The
lives of your people will also be taken instead of the lives of [...and your
people for] his people.' "
43Then King Ahab went back to his palace in Samaria, ·angry and upset
[resentful and sullen].

Ahab Takes Naboth's Vineyard

21 After these things had happened, this is what followed. A
man named Naboth owned a vineyard in Jezreel, near the
palace of Ahab king of Israel. 2One day Ahab said to Naboth, "Give me
your vineyard. It is near my palace, and I want to make it into a vegetable garden. I will give you a better vineyard in its place, or, if you prefer,
I will pay you what it is worth."
3Naboth answered, "·May the LORD keep me from ever giving my land
to you. It belongs to my family [LThe LORD forbid that I should give you
the inheritance of my fathers/ancestors]."
4Ahab went home ·angry and upset [resentful and sullen], because he
did not like what Naboth from Jezreel had said. (Naboth had said, "I will
not give you ·my family's land [Lthe inheritance of my fathers/ancestors].")
Ahab lay down on his bed, turned his face to the wall, and refused to eat.
5His wife, Jezebel, came in and asked him, "Why are you so ·upset [sul-
len; depressed] that you refuse to eat?"
6Ahab answered, "I talked to Naboth, the man from Jezreel. I said, 'Sell
me your vineyard, or, if you prefer, I will give you another vineyard for it.'
But Naboth refused."
7Jezebel answered, "Is this how you ·rule as king [reign] over Israel?
Get up, eat something, and cheer up. I will get Naboth's vineyard for you."
8So Jezebel wrote some letters, signed Ahab's name to them, and used
his own seal to seal them. Then she sent them to the elders and ·impor-
tant men [nobles] who lived in Naboth's town. 9The letter she wrote said:
"Declare a day during which the people are to fast. Call the people
together, and give Naboth a place of honor among them. 10Seat two ·trou-
blemakers [scoundrels] across from him, and have them say ·they heard
Naboth speak against ["You cursed..."] God and the king. Then take
Naboth out of the city and ·kill him with stones [stone him to death]."
11The elders and important men of Jezreel obeyed Jezebel's command,
just as she wrote in the letters. 12They declared a ·special day on which the
people were to fast [fast]. And they put Naboth in a place of honor before
the people. 13Two ·troublemakers [scoundrels] sat across from Naboth
and said in front of everybody ·that they had heard him speak against
["You cursed..."] God and the king. So the people carried Naboth out of
the city and ·killed him with stones [stoned him to death]. 14Then the
leaders sent a message to Jezebel, saying, "Naboth has been ·killed [Lstoned
and is dead]."
15When Jezebel heard that Naboth had been ·killed [Lstoned and was
dead], she told Ahab, "Naboth of Jezreel is no longer alive; he's dead. Now
you may go and take for yourself the vineyard he would not sell to you."
16When Ahab heard that Naboth of Jezreel was dead, he got up and went
to the vineyard to take ·it for his own [possession of it].

17 At this time the ·LORD spoke his word [Lword of the LORD came] to the prophet Elijah the Tishbite. The LORD said, 18 "Go to Ahab king of Israel in Samaria. He is at Naboth's vineyard, where he has gone to take ·it as his own [possession of it]. 19 Tell Ahab that I, the LORD, say to him, '·You have [LHave you not…?] murdered Naboth and taken his land. So I tell you this: In the same place the dogs licked up Naboth's blood, they will also lick up your blood [1 Kin. 22:37–38]!' "

20 When Ahab saw Elijah, he said, "So you have found me, my enemy!"

Elijah answered, "Yes, I have found you. You ·have always chosen to do what the LORD says is wrong [Lsold yourself to do evil in the eyes/sight of the LORD]. 21 So the LORD says to you, 'I will ·soon destroy you [bring evil/disaster on you]. I will ·kill you [sweep you away] and ·every [Lcut off every] ·male [Lone who urinates against the wall] in your ·family [Lhouse], both slave and free. 22 Your ·family [Lhouse] will be like the ·family [Lhouse] of King Jeroboam son of Nebat and like the ·family [Lhouse] of King Baasha son of Ahijah. I will destroy you, because you have ·made me angry [provoked/aroused me to anger] and have led the people of Israel to sin.'

23 "And the LORD also says, 'Dogs will eat the body of Jezebel in the ·city [fields; boundaries] of Jezreel [2 Kin. 9:30–37].'

24 "Anyone in Ahab's ·family [Lhouse] who dies in the city will be eaten by dogs, and anyone who dies in the ·fields [country] will be eaten by ·birds [vultures; Lbirds of the air/sky; 16:4]."

25 There was no one like Ahab who ·had chosen so often [Lsold himself] to do ·what the LORD said was wrong [Levil in the eyes/sight of the LORD], ·because his wife Jezebel influenced him to do evil [urged on by his wife Jezebel]. 26 Ahab ·sinned terribly [acted most detestably/abominably] by ·worshiping [following; going after] idols, just as the Amorites did. And the LORD had ·taken away their land and given it to [driven them out before] the people of Israel.

27 After Elijah finished speaking, Ahab tore his clothes. He put on ·rough cloth [sackcloth; burlap; Cindicating sorrow and contrition] and fasted, and even slept in ·the rough cloth [sackcloth; burlap] and walked about ·dejectedly [despondently; with slow steps].

28 The ·LORD spoke his word [Lword of the LORD came] to Elijah the Tishbite: 29 "·I see that [LHave you seen how…?] Ahab ·is now sorry for what he has done [has now humbled himself before me]. So I will not ·cause the trouble to come to him during his life [Lbring this evil/disaster on him during his days], but I will wait until his son is king. Then I will bring this ·trouble [evil; disaster] to Ahab's ·family [Lhouse]."

The Death of Ahab

(22:1–40; 2 Chr. 18:1–34)

22 For three years there was ·peace [Lno war] between Israel and Aram. 2 During the third year Jehoshaphat king of Judah went to visit Ahab king of Israel.

3 At that time Ahab asked his ·officers [officials; Lservants], "Do you ·remember [realize; know] that the king of Aram took Ramoth in Gilead from us? Why have we done nothing to get it back?" 4 So Ahab asked King Jehoshaphat, "Will you go with me to fight at Ramoth in Gilead [CJehoshaphat was a subordinate treaty partner with Ahab]?"

"I will go with you," Jehoshaphat answered. "My ·soldiers are yours [Lpeople are your people], and my horses are ·yours [Lyour horses]." 5 Jehoshaphat also said to Ahab, "But first we should ·ask if this is the LORD's will [Linquire for the word of the LORD]."

[6]Ahab called about four hundred prophets together and asked them, "Should I go to war against Ramoth in Gilead or ·not [hold back]?"

They answered, "Go, because the Lord will hand them over to you."

[7]But Jehoshaphat asked, "Isn't there a prophet of the LORD here [Cindicating skepticism about their reliability]? Let's ask him what we should do."

[8]Then King Ahab said to Jehoshaphat, "There is one other prophet. We could ask the LORD through him, but I hate him. He never prophesies anything good about me, ·but something bad [only evil]. He is Micaiah son of Imlah."

Jehoshaphat said, "King Ahab, you shouldn't say that!"

[9]So Ahab king of Israel told one of his officers to bring Micaiah son of Imlah to him at once.

[10]Ahab king of Israel and Jehoshaphat king of Judah had on their royal robes and were sitting on their thrones at the threshing floor, near the entrance to the gate of Samaria. All the prophets were standing before them, ·speaking their messages [prophesying]. [11]Zedekiah son of Kenaanah had made some iron horns. He said to Ahab, "·This is what the LORD says [TThus says the LORD], 'You will use these horns to ·fight [gore] the Arameans until they are destroyed.' "

[12]All the other prophets said the same thing. "Attack Ramoth in Gilead and ·win [triumph; prosper], because the LORD will hand the Arameans over to you."

[13]The messenger who had gone to get Micaiah said to him, "All the ·other prophets are saying King Ahab will succeed [words of the prophets are favorable to the king]. ·You should agree with them and give the king a good answer [Let your word be like theirs and speak favorably]."

[14]But Micaiah answered, "As surely as the LORD lives, I ·can tell him [will say] only what the LORD tells me."

[15]When Micaiah came to Ahab, the king asked him, "Micaiah, should we attack Ramoth in Gilead or ·not [hold back]?"

Micaiah answered, "Attack and ·win [triumph; prosper]! The LORD will hand them over to you [CMicaiah must have spoken sarcastically]."

[16]But Ahab said to Micaiah, "How many times ·do I have to tell you [must I make you swear] to speak only the truth to me in the name of the LORD?"

[17]So Micaiah answered, "I saw ·the army of [all] Israel scattered over the ·hills [mountains] like sheep without a shepherd. The LORD said, 'They have no ·leaders [master; Cforeshadowing Ahab's death]. They should go home ·and not fight [Lin peace].' "

[18]Then Ahab king of Israel said to Jehoshaphat, "I told you! He never prophesies anything good about me, but only ·bad [evil]."

[19]But Micaiah said, "Hear the ·message from [Lword of] the LORD: I saw the LORD sitting on his throne with his heavenly ·army [hosts] standing near him on his right and on his left. [20]The LORD said, 'Who will ·trick [entice; deceive] Ahab into attacking Ramoth in Gilead where he will ·be killed [fall]?'

"Some ·said [suggested; answered] one thing; some ·said [suggested; answered] another. [21]Then one spirit came and stood before the LORD and said, 'I will ·trick [entice; deceive] him.'

[22]"The LORD asked, 'How will you do it?'

"The spirit answered, 'I will go to Ahab's prophets and ·make them tell lies [Lbe a lying/deceiving spirit in their mouths].'

"So the LORD said, 'You will succeed in ·tricking [enticing; deceiving]
him. Go and do it.' "
23Micaiah said, "Ahab, the LORD has ·made your prophets lie to you
[Lput a deceiving/lying spirit in the mouth of your prophets], and the
LORD has ·decided [pronounced; proclaimed; decreed] that disaster
·should come to [for; on] you."
24Then Zedekiah son of Kenaanah went up to Micaiah and slapped
him in the ·face [cheek]. Zedekiah said, "·Has [How did] the LORD's spirit
·left [pass from] me to speak through you?"
25Micaiah answered, "You will find out on the day you go to hide in an
·inside [secret] room [Cwhen the prophesied disaster strikes]."
26Then Ahab king of Israel ordered, "Take Micaiah and ·send [return]
him to Amon, the governor of the city, and to Joash, the king's son. 27Tell
them I said to put this man in prison and ·give [feed] him only bread and
water until I return safely [Cfrom the upcoming battle]."
28Micaiah said, "Ahab, if you come back safely, the LORD has not spoken
through me. ·Remember [Mark; Listen to] my words, all you people!"
29So Ahab king of Israel and Jehoshaphat king of Judah ·went to
[marched on] Ramoth in Gilead. 30King Ahab said to Jehoshaphat, "When
I go into battle, I will ·wear other clothes [disguise myself] so no one will
recognize me. But you wear your royal clothes." So Ahab ·wore other
clothes [disguised himself] and went into battle [22:15].
31The king of Aram had ordered his thirty-two chariot commanders,
"Don't fight with anyone—·important or unimportant [Lsmall or
great]—except the king of Israel." 32When these chariot commanders saw
Jehoshaphat, they thought he was certainly the king of Israel, so they
turned to attack him. But when Jehoshaphat began shouting, 33they saw
he was not King Ahab, and they stopped chasing him.
34By chance, a soldier shot an arrow and hit Ahab king of Israel ·between
the pieces [in a gap/joint] of his armor. King Ahab said to his chariot
driver, "Turn around and get me out of the battle, because I am ·hurt
[badly wounded]!" 35The battle ·continued [raged] all day. King Ahab was
·held [propped] up in his chariot and faced the Arameans. His blood from
the wound flowed down to the bottom of the chariot. That evening he
died. 36Near sunset a cry went out through the army of Israel: "Each man
go back to his own city and land [Can indication of panic and defeat]."
37In that way King Ahab ·died [Llay down/Tslept with his fathers/ances-
tors]. His body was carried to Samaria and buried there. 38The men
cleaned Ahab's chariot at a pool in Samaria ·where prostitutes bathed [*or*
and the prostitutes bathed in his blood], and the dogs licked his blood
from the chariot. These things happened as the ·LORD had said they would
[word of the LORD had spoken].
39Everything else Ahab did ·is [Lis it not…?] written in the book of the
·history [chronicles; annals; 14:19] of the kings of Israel. It tells about the
·palace Ahab built and decorated with ivory [Livory house] and the cities
he built. 40So Ahab ·died [Llay down/Tslept with his fathers/ancestors], and
his son Ahaziah became king in his place.

Jehoshaphat King of Judah
(22:41–50; 2 Chr. 20:31–21:1)

41Jehoshaphat son of Asa became king of Judah during Ahab's fourth
year as king of Israel. 42Jehoshaphat was thirty-five years old when he
became king, and he ·ruled [reigned] in Jerusalem for twenty-five years.
His mother's name was Azubah daughter of Shilhi. 43Jehoshaphat ·was

**good, like [Lwalked/followed in the way/path of] his father Asa, and he did
·what the Lord said was right [Lright in the eyes/sight of the Lord]. But
Jehoshaphat did not destroy the ·places where gods were worshiped
[Lhigh places; 3:2], so the people continued offering sacrifices and burning incense there. [44]Jehoshaphat was at peace with the king of Israel.
[45]·Jehoshaphat fought many wars, and these wars and his successes are
[LConcerning the rest of the acts of Jehoshaphat and his power and the
wars he waged, are they not…?] written in the book of the ·history
[chronicles; annals; 14:19] of the kings of Judah. [46]There were male prostitutes still in the places of worship from the days of his father, Asa
[14:24]. So Jehoshaphat ·forced them to leave [banished/expelled/*or*
exterminated them].**

**[47]During this time the land of Edom had no king; it was ruled by a
·governor [deputy].**

**[48]King Jehoshaphat built ·trading ships [ships of Tarshish] to sail to
Ophir for gold. But the ships were wrecked at Ezion Geber, so they never
set sail. [49]Ahaziah son of Ahab went to help Jehoshaphat, offering to give
Jehoshaphat some men to sail with his men, but Jehoshaphat refused.**

**[50]Jehoshaphat ·died [Llay down/Tslept with his fathers/ancestors] and
was buried with his ancestors in the City of David [CJerusalem], his
·ancestor [father]. Then his son Jehoram became king in his place.**

Ahaziah King of Israel

**[51]Ahaziah son of Ahab became king of Israel in Samaria during
Jehoshaphat's seventeenth year as king over Judah. Ahaziah ·ruled
[reigned] Israel for two years, [52]and he did ·what the Lord said was wrong
[Levil in the eyes/sight of the Lord]. He ·did the same evil as [Lwalked in
the way/path of his] his father Ahab, his mother Jezebel, and Jeroboam
son of Nebat. All these rulers led the people of Israel into more sin.
[53]Ahaziah worshiped and served the god Baal, and this ·made the Lord,
the God of Israel, very angry [provoked/aroused the Lord, the God of
Israel to anger], just as his father had done.**

2 KINGS

Elijah and King Ahaziah

1 After Ahab died, Moab ·broke away from Israel's rule [rebelled against Israel]. 2Ahaziah fell down through the ·wooden bars in [lattice of] his upstairs room in Samaria and was badly hurt. He sent messengers and told them, "Go, ask Baal-Zebub, god of Ekron, if I will recover from my ·injuries [illness]."

3But the LORD's ·angel [messenger] said to Elijah the Tishbite, "Go up and ·meet [confront; intercept] the messengers sent by the king of Samaria. Ask them, 'Why are you going to ·ask questions of [consult with; inquire of] Baal-Zebub, god of Ekron? Is it because there is no God in Israel?' 4This is what the LORD says: 'You will never get up from the bed you are lying on; you will surely die.' " Then Elijah ·left [set out; departed].

5When the messengers returned to Ahaziah, he asked them, "Why have you returned [Cso soon after being sent]?"

6They said, "A man came to meet us. He said, 'Go back to the king who sent you and tell him ·what the LORD says [TThus says the LORD]: 'Why are you going to ·ask questions of [consult with; inquire of] Baal-Zebub, god of Ekron? Is it because there is no God in Israel?' You will never get up from the bed you are lying on; you will surely die.' ' "

7Ahaziah asked them, "What ·did the man look like who [kind of man] met you and told you this?"

8They answered, "He ·was a hairy man [*or* wore a hairy cloak] and wore a leather belt around his waist."

Ahaziah said, "It was Elijah the Tishbite."

9Then he sent a captain with his fifty men to Elijah. The captain went to Elijah, who was sitting on top of the hill, and said to him, "Man of God [Ca prophet], the king says, 'Come down!' "

10Elijah answered the captain, "If I am a man of God, let fire come down from heaven and ·burn up [consume; destroy] you and your fifty men." Then fire came down from heaven and ·burned up [consumed; destroyed] the captain and his fifty men.

11Ahaziah sent another captain and fifty men to Elijah. The captain said to him, "Man of God, this is what the king says: 'Come down ·quickly [at once]!' "

12Elijah answered, "If I am a man of God, let fire come down from heaven and ·burn up [consume; destroy] you and your fifty men!" Then fire came down from heaven and ·burned up [consumed; destroyed] the captain and his fifty men.

13Ahaziah then sent a third captain with his fifty men. The third captain came and fell down on his knees before Elijah and ·begged [pleaded], "Man of God, please ·respect [value; consider precious] my life and the lives of your fifty servants. 14·See [[T]Behold], fire came down from heaven and ·burned up [consumed; destroyed] the first two captains of fifty with all their men. But now, ·respect [value; consider precious] my life."

15The LORD's ·angel [messenger] said to Elijah, "Go down with him and don't be afraid of him." So Elijah got up and went down with him to see the king.

16Elijah told Ahaziah, "This is what the LORD says: 'You have sent messengers to ·ask questions of [consult with; inquire of] Baal-Zebub, god of Ekron. Is it because there is no God in Israel to ask? Because of this, you will never get up from your bed; you will surely die.' " 17So Ahaziah died, ·just as the LORD, through Elijah, had said he would [[L]in accordance with the word of the LORD which Elijah had spoken].

Because Ahaziah had no son to take his place, Joram[n] became king in Ahaziah's place during the second year Jehoram son of Jehoshaphat was king of Judah. 18The other things Ahaziah did ·are [[L]are they not…?] written in the book of the ·history [chronicles; annals] of the kings of Israel [[C]a history book now lost].

Elijah Is Taken to Heaven

2 When the LORD was about to take Elijah by a whirlwind up into heaven, Elijah and Elisha were leaving Gilgal. 2Elijah said to Elisha, "Please stay here. The LORD has ·told me to go to [[L]sent me as far as] Bethel."

But Elisha said, "As the LORD lives, and as you live, I won't leave you." So they went down to Bethel. 3The ·groups [company; brotherhood; [L]sons] of prophets at Bethel came out to Elisha and said to him, "Do you know the LORD will take your ·master [lord] away from you today?"

Elisha said, "Yes, I know, ·but don't talk about it [be quiet/still]."

4Elijah said to him, "Stay here, Elisha, because the LORD has sent me to Jericho."

But Elisha said, "As the LORD lives, and as you live, I won't leave you."

So they went to Jericho. 5The ·groups [company; brotherhood; [L]sons] of prophets at Jericho came to Elisha and said, "Do you know that the LORD will take your ·master [lord] away from you today?"

Elisha answered, "Yes, I know, ·but don't talk about it [be quiet/still]."

6Elijah said to Elisha, "Stay here. The LORD has sent me to the Jordan River."

Elisha answered, "As the LORD lives, and as you live, I won't leave you."

So the two of them went on. 7Fifty men of the ·groups [company; brotherhood; [L]sons] of prophets came and stood ·far [at a distance] from where Elijah and Elisha were standing by the Jordan. 8Elijah took off his ·coat [cloak; [T]mantle], ·rolled [folded] it up, and hit the water. The water divided to ·the right and to the left [[L]one side and the other], and Elijah and Elisha crossed over on dry ground [[C]reminiscent of the crossing of the Sea; Ex. 14].

9After they had crossed over, Elijah said to Elisha, "What can I do for you before I am taken from you?"

Elisha said, "Leave me a double ·share [portion] of your spirit [[C]like a firstborn heir (Deut. 21:17), he asks for double the blessing of other followers of Elijah, not twice as much as Elijah]."

10Elijah said, "You have asked a ·hard [difficult] thing. But if you see me

1:17 Joram Hebrew copies read "Jehoram."

when I am taken from you, it will be ·yours [as you request]. If you don't, it won't happen."

11 As they were walking along and talking, a chariot of fire and horses of fire appeared and ·separated [drove between] Elijah from Elisha. Then Elijah ·went up [ascended] to heaven in a whirlwind. 12 Elisha saw it and shouted, "My father! My father! The chariots of Israel and ·their horsemen [its charioteers/*or* horses]!" And Elisha did not see him anymore. Then Elisha grabbed his own clothes and tore them in two [[C]a sign of mourning or distress].

13 He picked up Elijah's ·coat [cloak; [T]mantle] that had fallen from him. Then he returned and stood on the bank of the Jordan. 14 Elisha hit the water with Elijah's ·coat [cloak; [T]mantle] and said, "Where is the LORD, the God of Elijah?" When he hit the water, it divided to ·the right and to the left [[L]one side and the other], and Elisha crossed over [2:8].

15 The ·groups [company; brotherhood; [L]sons] of prophets at Jericho were watching from a distance and said, "·Elisha now has the spirit Elijah had [[L]Elijah's spirit now rests on Elisha]." And they came to meet him, bowing down to the ground before him. 16 They said to him, "There are fifty ·strong [able] men with us. Please let them go and look for your ·master [lord]. Maybe the Spirit of the LORD has taken Elijah up and set him down on some mountain or in some valley."

But Elisha answered, "No, don't send them."

17 When the ·groups [company; brotherhood; [L]sons] of prophets had begged Elisha until he ·couldn't refuse them anymore [was too embarrassed/ashamed to refuse], he said, "Send them." So they sent fifty men who looked for three days, but they could not find him. 18 Then they came back to Elisha at Jericho where he was staying. He said to them, "I told you not to go, didn't I?"

Elisha Makes the Water of Jericho Pure

19 The people of the city said to Elisha, "Look, ·master [lord], this city is ·a nice place to live [well/pleasantly situated/located] as you can see. But the water is so bad the land ·cannot grow crops [is unproductive/unfruitful]."

20 Elisha said, "Bring me a new bowl and put salt in it." So they brought it to him.

21 Then he went out to the ·spring [water source] and threw the salt in it. He said, "·This is what the LORD says [[T]Thus says the LORD]: 'I have ·healed [purified; made wholesome] this water. From now on it won't cause death, ·and it won't keep the land from growing crops [or unfruitfulness/unproductiveness/*or* miscarriage].'" 22 So the water has been ·healed [purified; made wholesome] to this day just as Elisha had said.

Boys Make Fun of Elisha

23 From there Elisha went up to Bethel. On the way some boys came out of the city and ·made fun of [mocked; jeered at; Ps. 1:1; Prov. 1:22; 3:34; 13:1; Gal. 6:7] him. They said to him, "Go ·up too, you baldhead [away, baldy]! Go ·up too, you baldhead [away, baldy]!" 24 Elisha turned around, looked at them, and put a curse on them in the name of the LORD. Then two mother bears came out of the woods and ·tore [mauled] forty-two of the boys to pieces. 25 Elisha went to Mount Carmel and from there he returned to Samaria.

War Between Israel and Moab

3 Joram son of Ahab became king over Israel at Samaria in Jehoshaphat's eighteenth year as king of Judah. And Joram ·ruled [reigned] twelve years. 2 He did ·what the LORD said was wrong [[L]evil in the

eyes/sight of the LORD], but ·he was not like [not to same extent as] his
father and mother; he removed the stone pillars his father had made for
Baal. 3But he ·continued to sin like [Lclung to the sin of] Jeroboam son of
Nebat who had led Israel to sin. Joram did not ·stop doing these same sins
[depart/Lturn away from it].
4Mesha king of Moab ·raised [bred] sheep. He ·paid [delivered to] the
king of Israel one hundred thousand lambs and the wool of one hundred
thousand sheep [Cas annual tribute]. 5But when Ahab died, the king of
Moab turned against the king of Israel. 6So King Joram went out from
Samaria and ·gathered [mobilized; mustered] ·Israel's army [Lall Israel].
7He also sent messengers to Jehoshaphat king of Judah. "The king of
Moab has ·turned [rebelled] against me," he said. "Will you go with me to
fight against Moab?"
Jehoshaphat replied, "I will go with you. My ·soldiers [Lsoldiers are
your soldiers] and my horses are ·yours [Lyour horses]."
8Jehoshaphat asked, "Which ·way should we attack [route should we
take]?"
Joram answered, "Through the ·Desert [Wilderness] of Edom."
9So the king of Israel went with the king of Judah, joined by the king of
Edom. After a ·roundabout [circuitous] march for seven days, there was
no more water for the army or for their animals that were with them.
10The king of Israel said, "·This is terrible [TAlas]! The LORD has called us
three kings together to hand us over to the Moabites!"
11But Jehoshaphat asked, "Is there ·a [Lno] prophet of the LORD here?
We can ·ask [inquire of] the LORD through him."
An officer of the king of Israel answered, "Elisha son of Shaphat is
here. He ·was Elijah's servant [Lused to pour water on the hands of Elijah]."
12Jehoshaphat said, "·He speaks the LORD's truth [The word of the LORD
is with him]." So the king of Israel and Jehoshaphat and the king of Edom
went down to see Elisha.
13Elisha said to the king of Israel, "·I have nothing [LWhat have I…?] to
do with you. Go to the prophets of your father and to the prophets of
your mother [Cthat is, to the prophets of their false gods]!"
The king of Israel said to Elisha, "No, the LORD has called us three kings
together to hand us over to the Moabites."
14Elisha said, "As surely as the LORD ·All-Powerful [Almighty; of
Heaven's Armies; Tof hosts] lives, ·whom I serve [Lbefore whom I stand], I
wouldn't even look at you or notice you if Jehoshaphat king of Judah
were not here. I ·respect [have regard for] him. 15Now bring me someone
who plays the ·harp [lyre]."
While the ·harp [lyre] was being played, the ·LORD gave Elisha power
[Lhand of the LORD came upon him]. 16Then Elisha said, "·The LORD says
to [TThus says the LORD:] ·dig holes in the valley [make trenches in this
valley; *or* I will fill this valley full of pools]. 17The LORD says you won't see
wind or rain, but the valley will be filled with water. Then you, your cattle, and your other animals can drink. 18This is ·easy for the LORD to do [a
slight/simple thing in the eyes/sight of the LORD]; he will also hand Moab
over to you. 19You will destroy every ·strong, walled [fortified] city and
every important town. You will cut down every good tree and stop up all
springs. You will ruin every good field with rocks."
20The next morning, about the time the sacrifice was offered, water
·came [flowed] from the direction of Edom and filled the valley.

21All the Moabites heard that the kings had come up to fight against them. So they ·gathered [mobilized; called up] everyone old enough to put on armor and ·waited [they took up positions] at the border. 22But when the Moabites got up early in the morning, the sun was shining on the water. They saw the water across from them, and it looked as red as blood. 23Then they said, "This is blood! The kings must have fought and killed each other! Come, Moabites, ·let's take the valuables from the dead bodies [let's plunder them; Lto the spoil]!"

24When the Moabites came to the camp of Israel, the Israelites came out and fought them until they ran away. Then the Israelites ·went on into [invaded] the land, ·killing [slaughtering] the Moabites. 25They ·tore down [destroyed; overturned] the cities and threw rocks all over every good field. They stopped up all the springs and cut down all the good trees. Kir Hareseth was the only city ·with its stones still in place [still standing], but the men with ·slingshots [slings] surrounded it and ·conquered [attacked] it, too.

26When the king of Moab saw that the battle was ·too much for him [going against him], he took seven hundred men with swords to try to break through ·to [near to; across from] the king of Edom. But they could not break through. 27Then the king of Moab took his oldest son, who would have been king after him, and ·offered [sacrificed] him as a burnt offering on the wall. ·So there was great anger against the Israelites, who [*or* Alarmed at this, the Israelites] left and went back to their own land.

A Widow Asks Elisha for Help

4 The wife of a man from the ·groups [company; brotherhood; Lsons] of prophets said to Elisha, "Your servant, my husband, is dead. You know he ·honored [revered; feared] the LORD. But now ·the man he owes money to [a creditor] is coming to take my two boys as his slaves!"

2Elisha answered, "How can I help you? Tell me, what do you have in your house?"

The woman said, "I don't have anything there except a ·pot [jar; flask] of oil."

3Then Elisha said, "Go and get empty jars from all your neighbors. Don't ask for just a few. 4Then go into your house and shut the door behind you and your sons. Pour oil into all the jars, and set the full ones aside."

5So she left Elisha and shut the door behind her and her sons. As they brought the jars to her, she poured out the oil. 6When the jars were all full, she said to her son, "Bring me another jar."

But he said, "There are no more jars." Then the oil stopped flowing.

7She went and told Elisha. And the prophet said to her, "Go, sell the oil and pay ·what you owe [your debts]. You and your sons can live on what is left."

The Shunammite Woman

8One day Elisha went to Shunem, where an ·important [prominent; wealthy] woman lived. She ·begged [urged; pressed] Elisha to stay and eat. So every time Elisha passed by, he stopped there to eat. 9The woman said to her husband, "I ·know that [am sure] this is a holy man of God who passes by our house ·all the time [often]. 10Let's make a small walled room on the roof [Croofs were flat and served as an extra room] and put a bed in the room for him. We can put a table, a chair, and a lampstand there. Then when he comes by, he can stay there."

11One day Elisha came to the woman's house. After he went to ·his [the upper] room and rested, 12he said to his servant Gehazi, "Call the Shunammite woman."

When the servant had called her, she stood in front of him. 13Elisha had told his servant, "Now say to her, 'You have gone to all this trouble for us. What can I do for you? Do you want me to speak to the king or the commander of the army for you?' "

She answered, "I live among my own people [Ca way of saying she is content and has no pressing needs]."

14Elisha said to Gehazi, "But what can we do for her?"

He answered, "She has no son, and her husband is old."

15Then Elisha said to Gehazi, "Call her." When he called her, she stood in the doorway. 16Then Elisha said, "This ·time [season] next year, you will hold a son in your arms."

The woman said, "No, ·master [lord], man of God, don't ·lie to [deceive; mislead] me, your servant!"

17But the woman ·became pregnant [conceived] and gave birth to a son at that ·time [season] the next year, just as Elisha had told her.

18The boy grew up and one day went out to his father, who was with the ·grain harvesters [reapers]. 19The boy said to his father, "My head! My head!"

The father said to his servant, "·Take [Carry] him to his mother!" 20The servant ·took [carried] him to his mother, and he lay on his mother's lap until noon. Then he died. 21So she took him up and laid him on ·Elisha's bed [Lthe bed of the man of God]. Then she shut the door and left.

22She called to her husband, "Send me one of the servants and one of the donkeys. Then I can go quickly to the man of God and return."

23The husband said, "Why do you want to go to him today? It isn't the New Moon or the Sabbath day."

She said, "It will be all right."

24Then she saddled the donkey and said to her servant, "Lead on. Don't slow down for me unless I tell you." 25So she went to Elisha, the man of God, at Mount Carmel.

When he saw her coming ·from far away [in the distance], he said to his servant Gehazi, "Look, there's the Shunammite woman! 26Run to meet her and ask, 'Are you ·all right [well]? Is your husband ·all right [well]? Is the boy ·all right [well]?' "

She answered, "Everything is ·all right [well]."

27Then she came to Elisha at the hill and grabbed his feet. Gehazi came near to pull her away, but Elisha said to him, "Leave her alone. She's ·very upset [Lin bitter distress in her soul], and the Lord has not told me about it. He has hidden it from me."

28She said, "·Master [My lord], did I ask you for a son? Didn't I tell you not to ·lie to [deceive; mislead] me?"

29Then Elisha said to Gehazi, "·Get ready [Tuck in your cloak; LGird up your loins; Cpulling up the back of the cloak between the legs and tucking it in the belt allowed freer movement]. Take my ·walking stick [staff] in your hand and go quickly. If you meet anyone, don't ·say hello [greet him]. If anyone greets you, don't ·respond [answer]. Lay my ·walking stick [staff] on the boy's face."

30The boy's mother said, "As surely as the Lord lives and as you live, I won't leave you [Cto return home]!" So Elisha got up and followed her.

31Gehazi went on ahead and laid the ·walking stick [staff] on the boy's

face, but the boy did not talk or ·move [respond]. Then Gehazi went back
to meet Elisha. "The boy has not awakened," he said.
32When Elisha came into the house, the boy was lying dead on ·his
[Elisha's] bed. 33Elisha entered the room and shut the door on the two of
them. Then he prayed to the LORD. 34He went to the bed and lay on the
boy, putting his mouth on the boy's mouth, his eyes on the boy's eyes, and
his hands on the boy's hands. He stretched himself out on top of the boy.
Soon the boy's ·skin [body; Lflesh] became warm. 35Elisha ·turned away
[got up] and walked ·around [back and forth once across] the room. Then
he went back and ·put himself [stretched out] on the boy again. The boy
sneezed seven times and opened his eyes.
36Elisha called Gehazi and said, "Call the Shunammite!" So he did.
When she came, Elisha said, "·Pick up [Take] your son." 37She came in and
fell at Elisha's feet, bowing facedown to the floor. Then she ·picked up
[took] her son and went out.

Elisha and the Stew

38When Elisha returned to Gilgal, there was a ·shortage of food [fam-
ine] in the land. While the ·groups [company; brotherhood; Lsons] of
prophets were sitting in front of him, he said to his servant, "Put the large
pot on the fire, and boil some stew for ·these men [this company/brother-
hood/Lsons of prophets]."
39One of them went out into the field to gather ·plants [herbs]. Finding
a wild vine, he ·picked fruit from the vine and filled his robe with it [gath-
ered a lapful of wild gourds]. ·Then he came and cut up the fruit into the
pot. But they didn't know what kind of fruit it was. [He returned and
sliced them into a pot of stew, not knowing what they were.] 40They
·poured out [served] the stew for the others to eat. When they began to
eat it, they shouted, "Man of God, there's death [Cpoison] in the pot!"
And they could not eat it.
41Elisha told them to bring some ·flour [meal]. He threw it into the pot
and said, "·Pour it out for [Serve it to] the people to eat." Then there was
nothing harmful in the pot.

Elisha Feeds the People

42A man from Baal Shalishah came to Elisha, bringing him twenty
loaves of barley bread from the first ·harvest [fruits]. He also brought
fresh grain in his sack. Elisha said, "Give it to the people to eat."
43Elisha's servant asked, "How can I ·feed a hundred people with so
little [Lset this before a hundred people]?"
"Give the bread to the people to eat," Elisha ·said [repeated]. "·This is
what the LORD says [TThus says the LORD]: 'They will eat and will have
food left over.' " 44After he gave it to them, the people ate and had food left
over, ·as the LORD had said [Lin accordance with the word of the LORD].

Naaman Is Healed

5 Naaman was commander of the army of the king of Aram. He
was ·honored [held in great favor] by his master and much
respected, because the LORD used him to give victory to Aram. He was a
·mighty and brave man [valiant soldier], but he had ·a skin disease
[Tleprosy; Crefers to a variety of skin diseases; Lev. 13:2].
2The Arameans had gone out to raid the Israelites and had taken a little
girl as a captive. This little girl served Naaman's wife. 3She said to her
mistress, "I wish my ·master [lord] would meet the prophet who lives in
Samaria. He would cure him of his ·disease [Tleprosy; 5:1]."
4Naaman went to the king and told him ·what the girl from Israel had

said [Laccording to this and according to that the girl said]. 5The king of Aram said, "Go ahead, and I will send a letter to the king of Israel." So Naaman left and took with him ·about seven hundred fifty pounds [Lten talents] of silver, as well as ·one hundred fifty pounds [Lsix thousand shekels] of gold and ten ·changes of clothes [sets of festal/formal robes]. 6He brought the letter to the king of Israel, which read, "I am sending my servant Naaman to you so you can heal him of his ·skin disease [Tleprosy; 5:1]."

7When the king of Israel read the letter, he tore his clothes [Ca sign of mourning or distress]. He said, "·I'm not God! I can't kill and make alive again! [LAm I God, to give life or take it away?] Why does this man send someone with ·a skin disease [Tleprosy; 5:1] for me to heal? You can see that the king of Aram is trying to ·start trouble [pick a fight/quarrel] with me."

8When Elisha, the man of God, heard that the king of Israel had torn his clothes, he sent the king this message: "Why have you torn your clothes? Let Naaman come to me. Then he will ·know [learn] there is a prophet in Israel." 9So Naaman went with his horses and chariots to Elisha's house and stood outside the door.

10Elisha sent Naaman a messenger who said, "Go and wash in the Jordan River seven times. Then your ·skin will be healed [Lflesh will be restored], and you will be ·clean [cleansed]."

11Naaman ·became angry [was provoked/aroused to anger] and left. He said, "I thought Elisha would surely come out and stand before me and call on the name of the Lord his God. I thought he would wave his hand over the place and heal the ·disease [Tleprosy; 5:1]. 12·The [Are not the…?] Abana and the Pharpar, the rivers of Damascus, are better than all the waters of Israel. Why can't I wash in them and ·become clean [be cleansed; Cboth physically healed and ritually clean]?" So Naaman went away ·very angry [in a rage].

13Naaman's servants came near and said to him, "My father, if the prophet had told you to do some ·great [very difficult] thing, wouldn't you have done it? All the more reason then when he simply says, 'Wash, and you will be clean [v. 12].'" 14So Naaman went down and dipped in the Jordan seven times, ·just as Elisha had said [Lin accordance with the word of the man of God]. Then his skin ·became new again [was restored], like the skin of a child. And he was clean.

15Naaman and all his ·group [company; brotherhood] returned to Elisha. He stood before Elisha and said, "Look, I now know there is no God in all the earth except in Israel. Now please accept a gift from me."

16But Elisha said, "As surely as the Lord lives ·whom I serve [Lbefore whom I stand], I won't accept anything." Naaman urged him to take the gift, but he refused.

17Then Naaman said, "If you won't take the gift, then please give me some soil—as much as two of my mules can carry. From now on I'll not offer any burnt offering [Lev. 1:1–17] or sacrifice to any other gods but the Lord. 18But let the Lord pardon me for this: When my ·master [lord] goes into the ·temple [Lhouse] of Rimmon [Ca pagan deity] to worship, he leans on my arm. Then I must bow in that ·temple [Lhouse]. May the Lord pardon me when I do that."

19Elisha said to him, "Go in peace."

Naaman had left Elisha and gone a short way 20when Gehazi, the servant of Elisha the man of God, thought, "My ·master [lord] has ·gone easy on [spared] this Naaman the Aramean by not taking what he brought. As

surely as the LORD lives, I'll run after him and get something from him."
21So Gehazi ·went after [pursued; ran after] Naaman.

When Naaman saw someone running after him, he got off the chariot to meet Gehazi. He asked, "Is ·everything all right [all well]?"

22Gehazi said, "Everything is ·all right [well]. My ·master [lord] has sent me. He said, 'Two young men from the ·groups [company; brotherhood; Lsons] of prophets in the ·mountains [hill country] of Ephraim just came to me. Please give them ·seventy-five pounds [La talent] of silver and two changes of clothes.' "

23Naaman said, "Please take ·one hundred fifty pounds [Ltwo talents]," and he urged Gehazi to take it. He tied ·one hundred fifty pounds [Ltwo talents] of silver in two bags with two changes of clothes. Then he gave them to two of his servants to carry for Gehazi. 24When they came to the hill, Gehazi took these things from Naaman's servants and ·put [hid; stored] them in the house. Then he let Naaman's servants go, and they left.

25When he came in and stood before his ·master [lord], Elisha said to him, "Where have you been, Gehazi?"

"I didn't go anywhere," he answered.

26But Elisha said to him, "·My spirit was [LDid not my heart/spirit go…?] with you. I knew when the man ·turned [stepped down] from his chariot to meet you. ·This isn't [Is this…?] a time to take money, clothes, ·olives, grapes [olive groves and vineyards], sheep, oxen, male servants, or female servants. 27So Naaman's ·skin disease [Tleprosy; 5:1] will ·come on [cling to] you and your ·children [descendants] forever." When Gehazi left Elisha, he ·had the disease [Twas a leper; 5:1] and was as white as snow.

An Axhead Floats

6 The ·groups [company; brotherhood; Lsons] of prophets said to Elisha, "The place where we ·meet [*or* are living] with you is too small for us. 2Let's go to the Jordan River. There everyone can get a ·log [beam; pole], and let's build a place there to ·live [meet]."

Elisha said, "Go."

3One of them said, "Please go with us."

Elisha answered, "I will go," 4so he went with them. When they arrived at the Jordan, they cut down some trees. 5As one man was cutting down a tree, the head of his ax fell into the water. He yelled, "·Oh no [TAlas], my ·master [lord]! I borrowed that ax!"

6·Elisha [LThe man of God] asked, "Where did it fall?" The man showed him the place. Then Elisha cut down a stick and threw it into the water, and it made the iron head float. 7Elisha said, "Pick up the axhead." Then the man reached out and took it.

Elisha and the Blinded Arameans

8The king of Aram was at war with Israel. He ·had [would have] a council meeting with his officers and ·said [say], "I will set up my camp in ·this [such and such a] place."

9Elisha, the man of God, ·sent [would send] a message to the king of Israel, saying, "·Be careful [Beware]! Don't pass that place, because the Arameans are going ·down [to attack/gather] there!"

10The king of Israel ·checked [would send word to] the place about which Elisha had warned him. Elisha warned him several times, so the king ·protected himself [was on his guard] there.

11The king of Aram was ·angry [greatly disturbed] about this. He called his officers together and demanded, "Tell me who of us is ·working for [siding with; Che suspects a traitor] the king of Israel."

[12]One of the officers said, "No one, my ·master [lord] and king. It's Elisha, the prophet from Israel. He can tell ·you [Lthe king of Israel] what you speak in your bedroom."

[13]The king said, "Go and find him so I can send men and ·catch [capture; seize] him."

The report came back, "He is in Dothan."

[14]Then the king sent horses, chariots, and many troops to Dothan. They arrived at night and surrounded the city.

[15]·Elisha's [LThe man of God's] servant got up early, and when he went out, he saw an army with horses and chariots all around the city. The servant said to Elisha, "·Oh no [TAlas], my ·master [lord], what ·can [will] we do?"

[16]Elisha said, "Don't be afraid. ·The army that fights for us is larger than the one against us [LThose with us are more than those with them]."

[17]Then Elisha prayed, "LORD, open my servant's eyes, and let him see."

The LORD opened the eyes of the young man, and he saw that the ·mountain [hillside] was full of horses and chariots of fire all around Elisha.

[18]As the enemy came down toward Elisha, he prayed to the LORD, "·Make [Strike] these people blind." So he made the Aramean army blind, ·as Elisha had asked [Lin accordance with the word of Elisha].

[19]Elisha said to them, "This is not the ·right road [way] or the ·right city [city]. Follow me and I'll take you to the man you are looking for." Then Elisha led them to Samaria [Cthe city, not the region].

[20]After they entered Samaria, Elisha said, "LORD, open these men's eyes so they can see." So the LORD opened their eyes, and the Aramean army saw that they were inside the city of Samaria!

[21]When the king of Israel saw the Aramean army, he said to Elisha, "My father, should I kill them? Should I kill them?"

[22]Elisha answered, "Don't kill them. ·You wouldn't [LWould you…?] kill people whom you captured with your sword and bow. Give them food and water, and let them eat and drink and then go home to their ·master [lord]." [23]So he prepared a great feast for the Aramean army. After they ate and drank, the king sent them away, and they went home to their ·master [lord]. The ·soldiers [raiders] of Aram did not come anymore into the land of Israel.

A Great Famine

[24]Later, Ben-Hadad king of Aram gathered his whole army and ·surrounded and attacked [besieged] Samaria. [25]There was a ·shortage of food [great famine] in Samaria. ·It was so bad [*or* The siege lasted so long] that a donkey's head sold for ·about two pounds [Leighty shekels/*or* pieces] of silver, and ·half of a pint [La fourth of a kab] of dove's dung sold for ·about two ounces [Lfive shekels/*or* pieces] of silver. [26]As the king of Israel was passing by on the wall, a woman yelled out to him, "Help me, my ·master [lord] and king!"

[27]The king said, "If the LORD doesn't help you, how can I? Can I get help from the threshing floor or from the winepress [Che has neither food nor drink to offer]?" [28]Then the king said to her, "What is your ·trouble [complaint]?"

She answered, "This woman said to me, 'Give up your son so we can eat him today. Then we will eat my son tomorrow.' [29]So we ·boiled [cooked] my son and ate him. Then the next day I said to her, 'Give up your son so we can eat him.' But she has hidden him."

[30]When the king heard the woman's words, he tore his clothes [Ca sign

of mourning or distress]. As he walked along the wall, the people looked
and saw he had on ·rough cloth [sackcloth; burlap] under his clothes
[Calso a sign of mourning]. 31He said, "May God ·punish me terribly [deal
severely with me, and worse; Ldo to me, and even more] if the head of
Elisha son of Shaphat ·isn't cut off from his body [Lremains on his shoul-
ders] today [Cthe king blames Elisha for the situation]!"
32The king sent a messenger to Elisha, who was sitting in his house
with the elders [Can indication that Elisha is more powerful than the king].
But before the messenger arrived, Elisha said to them, "See, this murderer
is sending men to ·cut off [Ltake away] my head. When the messenger
arrives, shut the door and hold it; don't let him in. ·The [LIs not the…?]
sound of his ·master's [lord's] feet is behind him."
33Elisha was still talking with the leaders when the messenger arrived.
The king said, "This ·trouble [misery; Levil] has come from the LORD. Why
should I wait for the LORD any longer?"

7 Elisha said, "Listen to the LORD's word. ·This is what the LORD says
[TThus says the LORD]: 'About this time tomorrow ·seven quarts [a
measure/Lseah; Cthe exact quantity of a seah is debated] of ·fine [choice]
flour will be sold for ·two-fifths of an ounce of silver [La shekel], and ·thir-
teen quarts [two measures/Lseahs] of barley will be sold for ·two-fifths of an
ounce of silver [La shekel; Cfood would be readily available]. This will happen at the gate of Samaria [Cthe common location of the marketplace].'"
2Then the officer ·who was close to the king [Lon whose arm the king
was leaning] answered Elisha, "Even if the LORD opened windows in the
sky [Cresulting in rain], that couldn't happen."
Elisha said, "You will see it with your own eyes, but you will not eat any
of it."
3There were four men with ·a skin disease [Tleprosy; 5:1] at the entrance
to the city gate. They said to each other, "Why ·do [should] we sit here
until we die? 4There is ·no food [famine] in the city. So if we go into the
city, we will die there. If we stay here, we will die. So let's go to the Aramean
camp. If they ·let us live [spare us], we will live. If they kill us, we die."
5So they got up at ·twilight [dusk] and went to the Aramean camp, but
when they arrived at the edge of the camp, no one was there. 6The Lord
had caused the Aramean army to hear the sound of chariots, horses, and
a large army. They had said to each other, "The king of Israel has hired
the Hittite and Egyptian kings to attack us!" 7So they got up and ran away
in the ·twilight [dusk], ·leaving [abandoning] their tents, horses, and
donkeys. They left the camp ·standing [just as it was] and ·ran [fled] for
their lives.
8When the ·men with the skin disease [Tlepers; 5:1] came to the edge of
the camp, they went into one of the tents and ate and drank. They carried
silver, gold, and clothes out of the camp and hid them. Then they came
back and entered another tent. They carried things from this tent and hid
them, also. 9Then they said to each other, "We're ·doing wrong [Lnot
doing right]. ·Today we have [This is a day of] good news, but we are
·silent [keeping it to ourselves; holding our tongues]. If we wait until the
sun comes up, we'll be ·discovered [punished; found guilty]. Let's go right
now and tell the people in the king's ·palace [Lhousehold]."
10So they went and called to the gatekeepers of the city. They said, "We
went to the Aramean camp, but no one is there; we didn't hear anyone.

The horses and donkeys were still tied up, and the tents ·were still standing [as they were].” [11]Then the gatekeepers shouted out and told the ·people in the palace [Lking's household].

[12]The king got up in the night and said to his officers, “I'll tell you what the Arameans are doing to us. They know we are starving. They have gone out of the camp to hide in the field. They're saying, ‘When the Israelites come out of the city, we'll capture them alive. Then we'll enter the city.’ ”

[13]One of his officers answered, “Let some men take five of the horses that are still left in the city. These men are like all the Israelites who are left; they, like a multitude of Israelites who have already perished, are about to die. Let's send them to see what has happened.”

[14]So the men took two chariots with horses. The king sent them after the Aramean army, saying, “Go and see what has happened.” [15]The men followed the Aramean army as far as the Jordan River. The road was full of clothes and equipment that the Arameans had thrown away as they had hurriedly left. So the messengers returned and told the king. [16]Then the people went out and ·took valuables from [plundered; ransacked] the Aramean camp. So ·seven quarts [a measure/Lseah] of fine flour were sold for ·two-fifths of an ounce of silver [La shekel], and ·thirteen quarts [two measures/Lseahs; 7:1] of barley were sold for ·two-fifths of an ounce of silver [La shekel], ·just as the LORD had said [Lin accordance with the word of the LORD].

[17]The king ·chose [appointed] the officer ·who was close to him [Lon whose arm he leaned] to guard the gate, but the people trampled the officer to death. This happened just as ·Elisha [the man of God] had told the king when the king came to his house. [18]He had said, “·Thirteen quarts [Two measures/Lseahs] of barley and ·seven quarts [a measure/Lseah]of fine flour will each sell for ·two-fifths of an ounce of silver [a shekel] about this time tomorrow at the gate of Samaria.”

[19]But the officer had answered, “Even if the LORD opened windows in the sky, that couldn't happen.” And Elisha had told him, “You will see it with your own eyes, but you won't eat any of it.” [20]It happened to the officer just that way. The people trampled him in the gateway, and he died.

The Shunammite Regains Her Land

8 Elisha spoke to the woman whose son he had ·brought back [restored] to life. He said, “Get up and go with your ·family [Lhousehold]. ·Stay [Settle; Live; TSojourn] any place you can, because the LORD has called for a ·time without food [famine] that will last seven years.” [2]So the woman got up and did as the man of God had said. She left with her ·family [Lhousehold], and they ·stayed [settled; lived; Tsojourned] in the land of the Philistines for seven years. [3]After seven years she returned from the land of the Philistines and went to ·beg [appeal to] the king for her house and land. [4]The king was talking with Gehazi, the servant of the man of God. The king had said, “Please tell me all the great things Elisha has done.” [5]Gehazi was telling the king how Elisha had ·brought [restored] a dead boy back to life. Just then the woman whose son Elisha had ·brought back [restored] to life came and ·begged [appealed to] the king for her house and land.

Gehazi said, “My ·master [lord] and king, this is the woman, and this is the son Elisha ·brought back [restored] to life.”

[6]The king ·asked [questioned] the woman, and she told him about it.

Then the king ·chose [appointed] an officer to help her. "·Give [Restore
to] the woman everything that is hers," the king said. "Give her all the
·money made [revenue] from her land from the day she left until now."

Ben-Hadad Is Killed

7Then Elisha went to Damascus, where Ben-Hadad king of Aram was
sick. Someone told him, "The man of God has ·arrived [come all this way]."
8The king said to Hazael, "Take a gift in your hand and go meet him.
·Ask [Inquire of] the LORD through him if I will recover from my
sickness."
9So Hazael went to meet Elisha, taking with him a gift of forty camels
loaded with ·every good thing [the finest wares] in Damascus. He came
and stood before Elisha and said, "Your son [Ca term of respect, not lit-
eral] Ben-Hadad king of Aram sent me to you. He asks if he will recover
from his sickness."
10Elisha said to Hazael, "Go and tell Ben-Hadad, 'You will surely
recover,' but the LORD has told me he will really die [Cperhaps indicating
that Elisha knew that the king would soon die, but not from illness]."
11·Hazael stared at Elisha [*or* Elisha stared at Hazael; LHe stared at him]
until he felt ·ashamed [uneasy]. Then Elisha cried.
12Hazael asked, "Why are you crying, my ·master [lord]?"
Elisha answered, "Because I know what ·evil [harm; terrible things]
you will do to the ·Israelites [Lsons/Tchildren of Israel]. You will burn their
·strong, walled [fortified] cities with fire and kill their young men with
the sword. You will ·throw [dash] their babies ·to the ground [*or* in pieces]
and ·split [rip] open their pregnant women."
13Hazael said, "·Am I a dog? How could I [*or* How could I, a mere dog,]
·do such things [*or* accomplish such great things]?"
Elisha answered, "The LORD has shown me that you will be king over
Aram."
14Then Hazael left Elisha and ·came [returned] to his ·master [lord].
Ben-Hadad said to him, "What did Elisha say to you?"
Hazael answered, "He told me that you will ·surely [certainly] recover."
15But the next day Hazael took a blanket and ·dipped [soaked] it in water.
Then he ·put [spread; held] it over Ben-Hadad's face, and he died. So
Hazael became king in Ben-Hadad's place.

Jehoram King of Judah

(8:16–29; 2 Chr. 21:2–10, 18–20; 22:1–6)

16While Jehoshaphat was king in Judah, Jehoram son of Jehoshaphat
became king of Judah. This was during the fifth year Joram son of Ahab
was king of Israel. 17Jehoram was thirty-two years old when he ·began to
rule [became king], and he ·ruled [reigned] eight years in Jerusalem. 18He
·followed [Lwalked in] the ways of the kings of Israel, just as the ·family
[Lhouse] of Ahab had done, because he married Ahab's daughter. Jehoram
did ·what the LORD said was wrong [Levil in the eyes/sight of the LORD].
19But the LORD ·would not [was unwilling to] destroy Judah ·because [for
the sake] of his servant David. The LORD had promised ·that one of
David's descendants would always rule [Lto give a lamp to him and his
descendants forever; Ca metaphor for the reign of a king; 2 Sam. 7:12; 1
Kin. 11:36; 2 Chr. 21:7].
20In Jehoram's time Edom ·broke away from [revolted against] Judah's
·rule [Lhand] and ·chose [set up] their own king. 21So Jehoram and all his
chariots ·went [crossed over] to Zair. The Edomites surrounded him and
his chariot commanders. Jehoram got up and attacked the Edomites at
night, but his army ran away to their ·tents [homes]. 22From then until now

Edom has ·fought [been in revolt/rebellion] against the rule of Judah. At the
same time Libnah also ·broke away from Judah's rule [revolted; rebelled].
23The other acts of Jehoram and all the things he did ·are [[L]are they
not…?] written in the book of the ·history [chronicles; annals; 1:18] of
the kings of Judah. 24Jehoram ·died [[L]lay down/[T]slept with his fathers/
ancestors] and was buried with his ·ancestors [fathers] in the City of
David [[C]Jerusalem], and Jehoram's son Ahaziah ·ruled [became king] in
his place.
25Ahaziah son of Jehoram ·became king of [began to reign/rule over]
Judah during the twelfth year Joram son of Ahab was king of Israel.
26Ahaziah was twenty-two years old when he became king, and he ·ruled
[reigned] one year in Jerusalem. His mother's name was Athaliah, a
granddaughter of Omri king of Israel. 27Ahaziah ·followed [[L]walked in]
the ways of Ahab's ·family [[L]house]. He did ·what the LORD said was wrong
[[L]evil in the eyes/sight of the LORD], as Ahab's ·family [[L]house] had done,
because he was a son-in-law to the house of Ahab.
28Ahaziah went with Joram son of Ahab to Ramoth in Gilead, where
they fought against Hazael king of Aram. The Arameans wounded Joram.
29So King Joram returned to Jezreel to ·heal [recover] from the wound he
had received from the Arameans at Ramoth when he fought Hazael king
of Aram. Ahaziah son of Jehoram king of Judah went down to visit Joram
son of Ahab at Jezreel, because he ·had been wounded [was ailing/ill].

Jehu Is Chosen King

9 At the same time, Elisha the prophet called a man from the
·groups [company; brotherhood; [L]sons] of prophets. Elisha said,
"·Get ready [[L]Gird up your loins; 4:29], and take this ·small bottle [flask]
of olive oil in your hand. Go to Ramoth in Gilead. 2When you arrive, find
Jehu son of Jehoshaphat, the son of Nimshi. Go in and make Jehu get up
from among his ·brothers [companions], and take him to an ·inner [pri-
vate] room. 3Then take the ·bottle [flask] and pour the oil on Jehu's head
and say, '·This is what the LORD says [[T]Thus says the LORD]: I have
·appointed [anointed] you king over Israel.' Then open the door and ·run
away [flee]. Don't wait!"
4So the young man, the young prophet, went to Ramoth in Gilead.
5When he arrived, he saw the officers of the army sitting together. He
said, "Commander, I have a message for you."
Jehu asked, "For which one of us?"
The young man said, "For you, commander."
6Jehu got up and went into the house. Then the young prophet poured
the olive oil on Jehu's head and said to him, "This is what the LORD, the
God of Israel says: 'I have ·appointed [anointed] you king over the LORD's
people Israel. 7You must ·destroy [strike down] the ·family [[L]house] of
Ahab your ·master [lord]. I will ·punish [have vengeance against] Jezebel
for the ·deaths [[L]blood] of my servants the prophets and ·for [[L]for the
blood of] all the LORD's servants. 8All of Ahab's ·family [[L]house] must die.
I will ·destroy [[L]cut off] every ·male [[L]one who urinates against the wall]
child in Ahab's ·family [[L]house] in Israel, whether slave or free. 9I will
make Ahab's ·family [[L]house] like the ·family [[L]house] of Jeroboam son of
Nebat and like the ·family [[L]house] of Baasha son of Ahijah. 10The dogs
will ·eat [devour] Jezebel at Jezreel, and no one will bury her.'"
Then the young prophet opened the door and ·ran away [fled].
11When Jehu went back to his ·master's [lord's] officers, one of them

said to Jehu, "Is everything all right? Why did this ·crazy man [madman]
come to you?"
Jehu answered, "You know ·the [that kind of] man and how he ·talks
[babbles]."
12They answered, "·That's not true [Liar]. Tell us."
Jehu said, "He said to me, 'This is what the LORD says: I have ·appointed
[anointed] you to be king over Israel.' "
13Then the officers hurried, and each man took off his own coat and
put it on the stairs for Jehu [[C]signifying submission]. They blew the trumpet and shouted, "Jehu is king!"

Joram and Ahaziah Are Killed

(9:14–29; 2 Chr. 22:7, 9)

14So Jehu son of Jehoshaphat, the son of Nimshi, ·made plans [con-
spired; plotted] against Joram. Now Joram and all Israel had been
defending Ramoth in Gilead from Hazael king of Aram. 15But King Joram
had to return to Jezreel to ·heal [recover] from the ·injuries [wounds] the
Arameans had given him when he fought against Hazael king of Aram.
Jehu said, "If you ·agree with this [want me to be king], don't let anyone leave the city to tell the news in Jezreel." 16Then he got into his chariot
and set out for Jezreel, where Joram was resting. Ahaziah king of Judah
had gone down to see him.
17The lookout was standing on the watchtower in Jezreel when he saw
Jehu's troops coming. He said, "I see ·some [a company of] soldiers!"
Joram said, "Take a horseman and send him to meet them. Tell him to
ask, '·Is all in order [Do you come in peace; [L]Is it peace]?' "
18The horseman rode out to meet Jehu, and he said, "This is what the
king says: '·Is all in order [Do you come in peace; [L]Is it peace]?' "
Jehu said, "·Why bother yourself with order [What is peace to you]?
·Come along [Fall in] behind me."
The lookout reported, "The messenger reached them, but he is not
coming back."
19Then Joram sent out a second horseman. This rider came to Jehu's
group and said, "This is what the king says: '·Is all in order [Do you come
in peace; [L]Is it peace]?' "
Jehu answered, "·Why bother yourself with order [What is peace to
you]? ·Come along [Fall in] behind me."
20The lookout reported, "He reached them, but he is not coming back.
The man in the chariot is driving like Jehu son of Nimshi. He drives ·as if
he were crazy [like a madman/maniac]!"
21Joram said, "Get my chariot ready." Then the servant got Joram's
chariot ready. Joram king of Israel and Ahaziah king of Judah went out,
each in his own chariot, and met Jehu at the ·property of [plot of ground
belonging to] Naboth the Jezreelite [1 Kin. 21:1–19].
22When Joram saw Jehu, he said, "·Is all in order [Do you come in
peace; [L]Is it peace], Jehu?"
Jehu answered, "There will never be any ·order [peace] as long as your
mother ·Jezebel worships idols and uses witchcraft [Jezebel's prostitu-
tions/harlotries and witchcraft/sorceries abound]."
23Joram turned the horses to run away and yelled to Ahaziah, "·It's a
trick [Treason; Treachery], Ahaziah!"
24Then Jehu drew his bow with all his strength and shot Joram between
his shoulders. The arrow ·went through [pierced] Joram's heart, and he
·fell [sank; slumped] down in his chariot.

25Jehu ordered Bidkar, his chariot officer, "Pick up Joram's body, and
throw it into the field of Naboth the Jezreelite. Remember when you and
I rode together ·with [behind] Joram's father Ahab. The LORD ·made this
prophecy [pronounced this oracle; 1 Kin. 19:17, 21:19–29] against him:
26'Yesterday I saw the blood of Naboth and his sons, says the LORD, so I
will ·punish [repay] Ahab in his field, says the LORD.' Take Joram's body
and throw it into the field, ·as the LORD has said [Lin accordance with the
word of the LORD]."
27When Ahaziah king of Judah saw this, he ·ran away [fled] toward Beth
Haggan. Jehu chased him, saying, "Shoot Ahaziah, too!" Ahaziah was
wounded in his chariot ·on the way up to [at the Ascent of] Gur near
Ibleam. He got as far as Megiddo but died there. 28Ahaziah's servants carried his body in a chariot to Jerusalem and buried him with his ·ancestors
[fathers] in his tomb in the City of David [CJerusalem]. 29(Ahaziah had
become king over Judah in the eleventh year Joram son of Ahab was king.)

Death of Jezebel

30When Jehu came to Jezreel, Jezebel heard about it. She ·put on her
eye makeup [painted her eyes] and ·fixed her hair [adorned her head].
Then she ·looked out [appeared/sat at] the window. 31When Jehu entered
the city gate, Jezebel said, "·Have you come in peace [LIs it peace], ·you
Zimri [LZimri; Ca sarcastic reference to a previous king who had assassinated his predecessor; 1 Kin. 16:8–12], you who ·killed [murdered] your
·master [lord]?"
32Jehu looked up at the window and said, "Who is on my side? Who?"
Two or three ·servants [officials] looked ·out the window [down] at Jehu.
33He said to them, "Throw her down." So they threw Jezebel down, and
the horses ·ran over [trampled] her. Some of her blood ·splashed [spat-
tered] on the wall and on the horses.
34Jehu went into the house and ate and drank. Then he said, "Now see
about this cursed woman. Bury her, because she is a king's daughter."
35The men went to bury Jezebel, but they found only her skull, feet,
and the palms of her hands. 36When they came back and told Jehu, he
said, "The ·LORD [word of the LORD] said this through his servant Elijah
the Tishbite: 'The dogs will eat Jezebel's flesh at Jezreel [1 Kin. 21:23; 2
Kin. 9:7–10]. 37Her body will be like ·manure [dung] on the field in the
land at Jezreel. No one will be able to say that this is Jezebel.' "

Families of Ahab and Ahaziah Killed

10 Ahab had seventy sons in Samaria [Cthe city, not the region].
Jehu wrote letters and sent them to Samaria—to the officers
of the city[n] and elders—and to the guardians of the sons of Ahab. Jehu
said, 2"You have your ·master's [lord's] sons with you, and you have
chariots, horses, a ·city with strong walls [fortified city], and weapons.
When you get this letter, 3choose the best and most worthy person
among your ·master's [lord's] sons, and make him king. Then fight for
your ·master's [lord's] ·family [Lhouse]."
4But the officers and leaders of Jezreel were ·frightened [utterly terri-
fied]. They said, "Two kings could not ·stand up to [resist] Jehu, so how can
we?"
5The ·palace manager [steward of the house], the city ·governor
[administrator], the ·leaders [elders], and the guardians sent a message to
Jehu. "We are your servants," they said. "We will do everything you tell us

10:1 the city Greek copies read "the city." Hebrew copies read "Jezreel."

to do. We won't make any man king, so do whatever ·you think is best [Lis good in your eyes/sight]."

6Then Jehu wrote a second letter, saying, "If you are on my side and will obey me, cut off the heads of your ·master's [lord's] sons and come to me at Jezreel tomorrow about this time."

Now the seventy sons of the king's ·family [Lhouse] were with the leading men of the city who were ·their guardians [raising them]. 7When the leaders received the letter, they took the king's sons and ·killed [slaughtered] all seventy of them. They put their heads in baskets and sent them to Jehu at Jezreel. 8The messenger came to Jehu and told him, "They have brought the heads of the king's sons."

Then Jehu said, "·Lay [Pile] the heads in two ·piles [heaps] at the city gate until morning."

9In the morning, Jehu went out and stood before the people and said to them, "You are innocent. Look, I ·made plans [conspired; plotted] against my ·master [lord] and killed him. But who killed all these [CJehu might have been blaming the Samaritan officials, or perhaps was implying that God ordered the killing]? 10You should know that ·everything [Lnothing] the Lord said about Ahab's ·family [Lhouse] will ·come true [Lfall to the ground/earth]. The Lord ·has spoken [spoke his word] through his servant Elijah, and the Lord has done what he said." 11So Jehu killed everyone of Ahab's ·family [Lhouse] in Jezreel who was still alive. He also killed all Ahab's ·leading men [important officials], ·close [personal] friends, and priests. ·No one who had helped Ahab was left alive [He left no one to survive him].

The Killing of Ahaziah's Relatives

(10:12–14; 2 Chr. 22:8)

12Then Jehu left and went to Samaria by way of the road to Beth Eked of the Shepherds. 13There Jehu met some relatives of Ahaziah king of Judah. Jehu asked, "Who are you?"

They answered, "We are relatives of Ahaziah. We have come down to ·get revenge for [*or* greet; visit] the families of the king and the king's mother."

14Then Jehu said, "Take them alive!" So they captured Ahaziah's relatives alive and killed them at the ·well [pit] near Beth Eked—forty-two of them. Jehu ·did not leave anyone alive [spared no one].

15After Jehu left there, he met Jehonadab son of Recab [Jer. 35], who was also on his way to meet Jehu. Jehu greeted him and said, "·Are you as good a friend to me as I am to you [Are you as loyal to me as I am to you; LIs your heart right, as my heart is with your heart]?"

Jehonadab answered, "·Yes, I am [LIt is]."

Jehu said, "If you are, then give me your hand." So Jehonadab gave him his hand, and Jehu pulled him into the chariot. 16"Come with me," Jehu said. "You can see ·how strong my feelings are [my zeal/devotion] for the Lord." So Jehu had Jehonadab ride in his chariot.

17When Jehu came to Samaria, he killed all of Ahab's ·family [Lhouse] in Samaria. He destroyed all those who were left, ·just as the Lord had told Elijah it would happen [Lin accordance with the word of the Lord spoken to Elijah].

Baal Worshipers Killed

18Then Jehu gathered all the people together and said to them, "Ahab served Baal a little, but Jehu will serve Baal ·much [greatly]. 19Now ·call for me [summon; assemble] all Baal's prophets and priests and all the people who ·worship [serve] Baal. Don't let anyone miss this meeting, because I have a great sacrifice for Baal. Anyone who is not there will not live." But Jehu was ·tricking them [deceiving them; Lacting cunningly] so he could destroy ·the worshipers of [those who served] Baal. 20He said, "Prepare a ·holy [sacred; solemn] meeting for Baal." So they ·announced [proclaimed] the meeting. 21Then Jehu sent word through all Israel, and all ·the worshipers of [who served] Baal came; not one stayed ·home [behind]. They came into the ·temple [Lhouse] of Baal, and the ·temple [Lhouse] was filled from one side to the other.

22Jehu said to the man who kept the robes, "Bring out ·robes [garments; vestments] for all ·the worshipers of [those who serve] Baal." After he brought out ·robes [garments; vestments] for them, 23Jehu and Jehonadab son of Recab went into the ·temple [Lhouse] of Baal. Jehu said to ·the worshipers of [those who served] Baal, "Look around, and make sure there are no servants of the LORD with you. Be sure there are only ·worshipers of [those who serve] Baal." 24Then they went in to offer sacrifices and burnt offerings.

Jehu had eighty men waiting outside. He had told them, "·Don't let anyone escape. If you do, you [The one who allows any of these men who I have put in your hands to escape] must ·pay with [exchange] your own life."

25As soon as Jehu finished offering the burnt offering, he ordered the guards and the ·captains [officers], "Go in and kill ·the worshipers of [those who serve] Baal. Don't let anyone ·come out [escape]." So the guards and ·captains [officers] killed ·the worshipers of [those who served] Baal with the sword and threw their bodies out. Then they went to the inner rooms of the ·temple [Lhouse of Baal] 26and brought out the ·pillars [sacred poles/stone; Cused in worship] of the ·temple [Lhouse] of Baal and burned them. 27They ·tore down [smashed] the stone pillar of Baal, as well as the ·temple [Lhouse] of Baal. And they made it into a ·sewage pit [public toilet; latrine], as it is today.

28So Jehu destroyed Baal worship in Israel, 29but he did not ·stop doing [turn/depart from] the sins Jeroboam son of Nebat had done. Jeroboam had led Israel to sin by worshiping the golden calves at Bethel and Dan.

30The LORD said to Jehu, "You have done well in ·obeying what I said was right [Ldoing what was right in my eyes/sight]. You have done to the ·family [Lhouse] of Ahab ·as I wanted [Lall that was in my heart/mind]. Because of this, your ·descendants as far as your great-great-grandchildren [sons to the fourth generation] will ·be kings [Lsit on the throne] of Israel." 31But Jehu was not careful to follow the ·teachings [law; Ltorah] of the LORD, the God of Israel, with all his heart. He did not ·stop doing [turn/depart from] the same sins Jeroboam had done, by which he had led Israel to sin.

32At that time the LORD began to ·make Israel smaller [cut/trim off parts of Israel]. Hazael defeated the Israelites ·in all the land [throughout the territory] of Israel, 33taking all the land east of the Jordan known as the land of Gilead. (It was the region of Gad, Reuben, and Manasseh.) He took land from Aroer by the Arnon Ravine through Gilead to Bashan.

34The other things Jehu did—everything he did and all his ·victories [achievements; power]—are [Lare they not…?] recorded in the book of the ·history [chronicles; annals; 1:18] of the kings of Israel. 35Jehu ·died [Llay down/Tslept with his fathers/ancestors] and was buried in Samaria, and his son Jehoahaz became king in his place. 36Jehu ·was king [reigned] over Israel in Samaria for twenty-eight years.

Athaliah and Joash
(11:1–20; 2 Chr. 22:10–23:21)

11 When Ahaziah's mother, Athaliah, ·saw [learned] that her son was dead, she ·killed [destroyed] all the royal ·family [offspring; Cin order to claim power herself; she was a granddaughter of Omri, king of Israel; 8:26]. 2But Jehosheba, King Jehoram's daughter and Ahaziah's sister, took Joash [Cabout a year old], Ahaziah's son [CJoash was also known as Jehoash]. She stole him away from among the other sons of the king who were about to be murdered. She put Joash and his nurse in a bedroom to hide him from Athaliah, so he was not ·killed [murdered]. 3He hid with her in the ·Temple [Lhouse] of the Lord for six years. During that time Athaliah ·ruled [reigned over] the land.

4In the seventh year Jehoiada sent for the ·commanders [captains] of groups of a hundred men, as well as the Carites [Cmercenaries, probably a palace guard like the Kerethites and the Pelethites; 2 Sam. 8:18; 20:23]. He brought them together in the ·Temple [Lhouse] of the Lord and ·made [Lcut] an ·agreement [covenant; treaty] with them. There, in the ·Temple [Lhouse] of the Lord, he ·made them promise loyalty [put them under oath], and then he showed them the king's son. 5He commanded them, "This is what you must do. A third of you who go on duty on the Sabbath will guard the king's ·palace [Lhouse]. 6A third of you will be at the Sur Gate, and another third will be at the gate behind the guard. This way you will guard the ·Temple [Lhouse]. 7The two groups who go off duty on the Sabbath must ·protect [stand guard/watch over] the ·Temple [Lhouse] of the Lord for the king. 8·All of you must stand around [Surround] the king, with weapons in hand. Kill anyone who ·comes near [tries to break your ranks]. Stay ·close to [with] the king when he goes out and when he comes in."

9The ·commanders [captains] over a hundred men ·obeyed [did] everything Jehoiada the priest had commanded. Each one took his men who came on duty on the Sabbath and those who went off duty on the Sabbath, and they came to Jehoiada the priest. 10He gave the commanders the spears and shields that had belonged to King David and that were kept in the ·Temple [Lhouse] of the Lord.

Joash Becomes King

11Then each guard took his place with his weapons in his hand. ·There were guards [They stretched] from the ·south [Lright] side of the ·Temple [Lhouse] to the ·north [Lleft] side. They stood by the altar and the ·Temple [Lhouse] and around the king. 12Jehoiada brought out the king's son and put the crown on him and gave him a copy of the ·agreement [covenant; testimony]. They ·appointed him king and poured olive oil on [anointed] him. Then they clapped their hands and ·said [shouted], "Long live the king!"

13When Athaliah heard the noise of the guards and the people, she went to them at the ·Temple [Lhouse] of the Lord. 14She looked, and there was the king, standing by the pillar [Ca symbol of authority], as the custom was. The ·officers [commanders; captains] and trumpeters were standing beside him, and all the people of the land were ·very happy [rejoicing] and were blowing trumpets. Then Athaliah tore her clothes [Ca sign of mourning or distress] and screamed, "·Traitors! Traitors! [Treason! Treason!]"

15Jehoiada the priest gave orders to the ·commanders [captains] of a hundred men, who led the army. He said, "·Surround her with soldiers [Take her out under guard; LBring her out between the ranks] and kill with a sword anyone who follows her." For he had said, "Don't put

Athaliah to death in the ·Temple [Lhouse] of the LORD." 16So they ·caught
[seized] her ·when she came [and took her] to the horses' entrance near
the ·palace [Lking's house]. There she was put to death.
17Then Jehoiada ·made [Lcut] an ·agreement [covenant; treaty] between
the LORD and the king and the people that they would be the LORD's people. He also made an ·agreement [covenant; treaty] between the king and
the people. 18All the people of the land went to the ·temple [Lhouse] of
Baal and tore it down, smashing the altars and idols. They also killed
Mattan, the priest of Baal, in front of the altars.
Then Jehoiada the priest ·placed [stationed; posted] guards at the
·Temple [Lhouse] of the LORD. 19He took with him the ·commanders [cap-
tains] of a hundred men and the ·Carites [Cmercenaries; v. 4], the royal
bodyguards, as well as the guards and all the people of the land. Together
they ·took [brought; escorted] the king out of the ·Temple [Lhouse] of the
LORD and went into the ·palace [king's house] through the gate of the
guards. Then the king sat on the ·royal throne [throne of the kings]. 20So
all the people of the land ·were very happy [rejoiced], and Jerusalem ·had
peace [was quiet/calm], because Athaliah had been put to death with the
sword at the ·palace [Lking's house].

Joash's Reign
(11:21–12:16; 2 Chr. 24:1–14)

21Joash was seven years old when he became king.
12 Joash became king of Judah in Jehu's seventh year as king of
Israel, and he ·ruled [reigned] for forty years in Jerusalem.
His mother's name was Zibiah, and she was from Beersheba. 2Joash did
·what the LORD said was right [Lright in the sight of the LORD] as long as
Jehoiada the priest ·taught [instructed] him. 3But the ·places where gods
were worshiped [Lhigh places; Cworship sites that became associated with
pagan worship or inappropriate worship of God] were not removed; the
people still made sacrifices and burned incense there.

Joash Repairs the Temple

4Joash said to the priests, "Take all the money brought as offerings to
the ·Temple [Lhouse] of the LORD. This includes the money each person
·owes in taxes [is assessed] and the money ·each person promises [from
personal vows] or ·brings freely [money brought voluntarily] to the LORD.
5Each priest will take the money from ·the people he serves [donors; *or*
acquaintances; *or* the treasurers]. Then the priests must ·repair [restore]
any damage they find in the ·Temple [Lhouse]."
6But by the twenty-third year Joash was king, the priests still had not
·repaired [restored] the ·Temple [Lhouse]. 7So King Joash called for
Jehoiada the priest and the other priests and said to them, "Why aren't you
·repairing the damage of [restoring] the ·Temple [Lhouse]? Don't take any
more money from ·the people you serve [donors; *or* acquaintances; *or* the
treasurers], but hand over the money for the ·repair [restoration] of the
·Temple [Lhouse]." 8The priests agreed not to take any more money from
the people and not to ·repair [restore] the ·Temple [Lhouse] themselves.
9Jehoiada the priest took a box and made a hole in the ·top of it [lid].
Then he put it by the altar, on the right side as the people came into the
·Temple [Lhouse] of the LORD. The priests guarding the ·doorway
[entrance; threshold] put all the money brought to the ·Temple [Lhouse]
of the LORD into the box.
10Each time the priests saw that the box was full of money, the king's
royal secretary and the high priest came. They counted the money that
had been brought to the ·Temple [Lhouse] of the LORD, and they put it

into bags. 11Next they weighed the money and gave it to the people in
charge of the work on the ·Temple [Lhouse]. With it they paid the carpenters and the builders who worked on the ·Temple [Lhouse] of the LORD,
12as well as the ·bricklayers [masons] and stonecutters. They also used the
money to buy timber and cut stone to ·repair the damage of [restore] the
·Temple [Lhouse] of the LORD. It paid for ·everything [anything else that
was used].
13The money brought into the ·Temple [Lhouse] of the LORD was not
used to make silver cups, ·wick trimmers [snuffers], bowls, trumpets, or
gold or silver vessels. 14They paid the money to the workers, who used it
to ·repair [restore] the ·Temple [Lhouse] of the LORD. 15They did not
·demand to know how the money was spent [require an accounting],
because the workers were honest. 16The money from the ·penalty [guilt]
offerings and sin offerings was not brought into the ·Temple [Lhouse] of
the LORD, because it belonged to the priests.

Joash Saves Jerusalem
(12:17–21; 2 Chr. 24:23–27)

17About this time Hazael king of Aram attacked Gath and captured it.
Then he ·went [Lset his face] to attack Jerusalem. 18Joash king of Judah
took all the ·holy things [sacred objects; votive gifts] ·given [dedicated] by
his ·ancestors [fathers], the kings of Judah—Jehoshaphat, Jehoram, and
Ahaziah. He also took his own ·holy things [sacred objects; votive gifts] as
well as the gold that was found in the treasuries of the ·Temple [Lhouse]
of the LORD and the gold from the ·palace [Lking's house]. Joash sent all
this treasure to Hazael king of Aram, who ·turned away [withdrew] from
Jerusalem.
19Everything else Joash did ·is [Lis it not…?] written in the book of the
·history [chronicles; annals; 1:18] of the kings of Judah. 20His officers
·made plans [conspired; plotted] against him and ·killed [assassinated]
him at Beth Millo on the road down to Silla. 21The officers who ·killed
[assassinated] him were Jozabad son of Shimeath and Jehozabad son of
Shomer. Joash was buried with his ·ancestors [fathers] in the City of
David [CJerusalem], and Amaziah, his son, became king in his place.

Jehoahaz King of Israel

13 Jehoahaz son of Jehu became king over Israel in Samaria during the twenty-third year Joash son of Ahaziah was king of
Judah. Jehoahaz ·ruled [reigned] seventeen years, 2and he did ·what the
LORD said was wrong [Levil in the eyes/sight of the LORD]. Jehoahaz ·did
[followed] the same sins Jeroboam son of Nebat had done. Jeroboam
had led Israel to sin, and Jehoahaz did not ·stop doing these same sins
[depart/turn away from them]. 3So the ·LORD was angry with [LLORD's
anger burned/kindled against] Israel and handed them over to Hazael
king of Aram and his son Ben-Hadad ·for a long time [*or* repeatedly].
4Then Jehoahaz ·begged [entreated; prayed to; sought the favor of] the
LORD, and the LORD listened to him. The LORD had seen the ·troubles [oppres-
sion] of Israel; he saw how ·terribly [severely] the king of Aram was ·treating
[oppressing] them. 5He gave Israel a ·man to save them [rescuer; savior;
Tdeliverer], and they escaped from the ·hand [grip; power] of the Arameans.
The ·Israelites [Lsons/Tchildren of Israel] then lived in their own ·homes
[Ltents] as they had before, 6but they still did not ·stop doing [depart/turn
away from] these same sins that the ·family [Lhouse] of Jeroboam had done.
He had led Israel to sin, and they ·continued doing those sins [Lwalked in
them]. The Asherah ·idol [pole; Ca sacred tree or pole dedicated to the god-
dess Asherah; 1 Kin. 14:15] also was left standing in Samaria.

[7]Nothing was left of Jehoahaz's army except fifty horsemen, ten chariots, and ten thousand foot soldiers. The king of Aram had destroyed
them and made them like ·chaff [[L]dust at threshing time].
[8]Everything else Jehoahaz did and all his ·victories [achievements;
power] ·are [[L]are they not...?] written in the book of the ·history [chron-
icles; annals; 1:18] of the kings of Israel. [9]Jehoahaz ·died [[L]lay down/[T]slept
with his fathers/ancestors] and was buried in Samaria, and his son Jehoash
became king in his place.

Jehoash King of Israel

[10]Jehoash son of Jehoahaz became king of Israel in Samaria during
Joash's thirty-seventh year as king of Judah. Jehoash ·ruled [reigned] sixteen years, [11]and he did ·what the LORD said was wrong [[L]evil in the eyes/
sight of the LORD]. He did not ·stop doing [depart/turn away from] the
same sins Jeroboam son of Nebat had done. Jeroboam had led Israel to
sin, and Jehoash continued to do the same thing. [12]Everything else he did
and all his ·victories [achievements; power], including his war against
Amaziah king of Judah, ·are [[L]are they not...?] written in the book of the
·history [chronicles; annals; 1:18] of the kings of Israel. [13]Jehoash ·died
[[L]lay down/[T]slept with his fathers/ancestors], and Jeroboam took his place
on the throne. Jehoash was buried in Samaria with the kings of Israel.

The Death of Elisha

[14]At this time Elisha became sick. ·Before he died [*or* ...with the illness
of which he would die], Jehoash king of Israel went to Elisha and cried
·for [over] him. Jehoash said, "My father, my father! ·The chariots [*or*
Chariot; [C]a reference to Elisha as Israel's defender; cf. 2:12] of Israel and
·their [its] horsemen!"
[15]Elisha said to Jehoash, "Take a bow and arrows." So he took a bow
and arrows. [16]Then Elisha said to him, "Put your hand on the bow." So
Jehoash put his hand on the bow. Then Elisha put his hands on the king's
hands. [17]Elisha said, "Open the east window." So Jehoash opened the window. Then Elisha said, "Shoot," and Jehoash shot. Elisha said, "The LORD's
arrow of victory, the arrow of victory over Aram! You will defeat the
Arameans at Aphek until you ·destroy [make an end of] them."
[18]Elisha said, "Take the arrows." So Jehoash took them. Then Elisha
said to him, "Strike the ground." So Jehoash struck the ground three
times and stopped. [19]The man of God was ·angry [aroused/provoked to
anger] with him. "You should have struck five or six times!" Elisha said.
"Then you would have struck Aram until you had completely destroyed
it. But now you will ·defeat it [[L]strike down Aram] only three times."
[20]Then Elisha died and was buried.
At that time ·groups [bands] of Moabites would rob the land in the
springtime. [21]Once as some Israelites were burying a man, suddenly they
saw a ·group [band] of Moabites coming. The Israelites threw the dead
man into Elisha's ·grave [tomb]. When the man touched Elisha's bones,
the man ·came back to life [revived] and stood on his feet.

War with Aram

[22]During all the days Jehoahaz was king, Hazael king of Aram ·trou-
bled [oppressed] Israel. [23]But the LORD was ·kind [gracious] to the
Israelites; he had ·mercy [compassion; pity] on them and helped them
because of his ·agreement [covenant; treaty] with Abraham, Isaac, and
Jacob. To this day he has ·never wanted [been unwilling] to destroy them
or ·reject them [banish/cast them from his presence].
[24]When Hazael king of Aram died, his son Ben-Hadad became king in

his place. 25During a war Hazael had taken some cities from Jehoahaz,
Jehoash's father. Now Jehoash took back those cities from Hazael's son
Ben-Hadad. He defeated Ben-Hadad three times and ·took back [recov-
ered] the cities of Israel.

Amaziah King of Judah

(14:1–20; 2 Chr. 25:1–28)

14 Amaziah son of Joash became king of Judah during the second year Jehoash son of Jehoahaz was king of Israel. 2Amaziah
was twenty-five years old when he became king, and he ·ruled [reigned]
twenty-nine years in Jerusalem. His mother was named Jehoaddin, and
she was from Jerusalem. 3Amaziah did ·what the LORD said was right
[Lright in the eyes/sight of the LORD]. He did everything his father Joash
had done, but he did not do as his ·ancestor [father] David had done.
4The ·places where gods were worshiped [Lhigh places; 12:3] were not
removed, so the people still sacrificed and burned incense there.
5As soon as Amaziah took control of the kingdom, he executed the ·offi-
cers [officials] who had ·murdered [assassinated] his father the king. 6But
he did not put to death the ·children [sons] of the ·murderers [assassins]
because of the rule written in the Book of the ·Teachings [Law; Ltorah] of
Moses. The LORD had commanded: "·Parents [Fathers] must not be put to
death ·when their children do wrong [Lfor their sons], and ·children [sons]
must not be put to death ·when their parents do wrong [Lfor their fathers].
Each must ·die [put to death] for his own sins [Deut. 24:16]."
7In battle Amaziah killed ten thousand Edomites in the Valley of Salt.
He also took the city of Sela. He called it Joktheel, as it is still called today.
8Amaziah sent messengers to Jehoash son of Jehoahaz, the son of
Jehu, king of Israel. They said, "Come, let's meet face to face [Ceither a
call for negotiations or a challenge to battle, but taken by Jehoash as the
latter]."
9Then Jehoash king of Israel answered Amaziah king of Judah, "A
thornbush in Lebanon sent a message to a cedar tree in Lebanon. It said,
'Let your daughter marry my son.' But then a wild ·animal [beast] from
Lebanon came by, ·walking [trampling] on and crushing the thornbush.
10You have defeated Edom, ·but [and now] you have become ·proud
[arrogant]. Stay at home and ·brag [*or* enjoy your victory/glory]. Don't
·ask for [stir up] trouble, or you and Judah will ·be defeated [fall]."
11But Amaziah would not listen, so Jehoash king of Israel went ·to attack
[Lup]. He and Amaziah king of Judah faced each other in battle at Beth
Shemesh in Judah. 12Israel ·defeated [routed] Judah, and every man of
Judah ·ran away [fled] to his ·home [Ltent]. 13At Beth Shemesh Jehoash
king of Israel captured Amaziah king of Judah. (Amaziah was the son of
Joash, who was the son of Ahaziah.) Jehoash went up to Jerusalem and
·broke down [demolished] the wall of Jerusalem from the Gate of Ephraim
to the Corner Gate, which was about ·six hundred feet [Lfour hundred
cubits]. 14He took all the gold and silver and all the utensils found in the
·Temple [Lhouse] of the LORD, and he took the treasures of the ·palace
[Lking's house] and some hostages. Then he returned to Samaria.
15The other acts of Jehoash and his ·victories [achievements; power],
including his war against Amaziah king of Judah, ·are [Lare they not…?]
written in the book of the ·history [chronicles; annals; 1:18] of the kings
of Israel. 16Jehoash ·died [Llay down/Tslept with his fathers/ancestors] and
was buried in Samaria with the kings of Israel, and his son Jeroboam
became king in his place.

17Amaziah son of Joash, the king of Judah, lived fifteen years after the
death of Jehoash son of Jehoahaz, the king of Israel. 18The other things
Amaziah did ·are [Lare they not…?] written in the book of the ·history
[chronicles; annals; 1:18] of the kings of Judah. 19The people in Jerusalem
·made plans [conspired; plotted] against him. So he ·ran away [fled] to the
town of Lachish, but they sent men after him to Lachish and killed him.
20They brought his body back on horses, and he was buried with his
·ancestors [fathers] in Jerusalem, in the city of David.

Uzziah Becomes King
(14:21–22; 2 Chr. 26: 1–2)

21Then all the people of Judah made Uzziah [Calso called Azariah] king
in place of his father Amaziah. Uzziah was sixteen years old. 22He rebuilt
the town of Elath and ·made it part of [restored it to] Judah again after
Amaziah ·died [Llay down/Tslept with his fathers/ancestors].

Jeroboam King of Israel

23Jeroboam son of Jehoash became king of Israel in Samaria during the
fifteenth year Amaziah was king of Judah. (Amaziah was the son of
Joash.) Jeroboam ·ruled [reigned] forty-one years, 24and he did ·what the
LORD said was wrong [Levil in the eyes/sight of the LORD]. Jeroboam son of
Nebat had led Israel to sin, and Jeroboam son of Jehoash did not ·stop
doing [depart/turn away from] the same sins. 25Jeroboam ·won back
[restored] Israel's border from Lebo Hamath to the ·Dead Sea [LSea of
Arabah]. This happened ·as [Lin accordance with the word of] the LORD,
the God of Israel, ·had said [spoken] through his servant Jonah son of
Amittai, the prophet from Gath Hepher. 26The LORD had seen how the
Israelites suffered bitterly, and no one, slave or free, could help them.
27The LORD had not said he would ·completely destroy [blot out; eradi-
cate] Israel from the world, so he ·saved [rescued; Tdelivered] the Israelites
through Jeroboam son of Jehoash.
28Everything else Jeroboam did—all his ·victories [achievements;
power] and how he ·won back [recovered] from Judah the towns of
Damascus and Hamath for Israel—·is [LIs not all this…?] written in the
book of the ·history [chronicles; annals; 1:18] of the kings of Israel.
29Jeroboam ·died and was buried with his ancestors [Llay down/Tslept
with his fathers/ancestors], the kings of Israel. Jeroboam's son Zechariah
became king in his place.

Uzziah King of Judah
(15:1–7; 2 Chr. 26:3–5, 16–23)

15 Uzziah son of Amaziah became king of Judah during
Jeroboam's twenty-seventh year as king of Israel. 2Uzziah was
sixteen years old when he became king, and he ·ruled [reigned] fifty-two
years in Jerusalem. His mother was named Jecoliah, and she was from
Jerusalem. 3He did ·what the LORD said was right [Lright in the eyes/sight
of the LORD], just as his father Amaziah had done. 4But the ·places where
gods were worshiped [Lhigh places; 12:3] were not removed, so the people still made sacrifices and burned incense there.
5The LORD struck Uzziah with ·a skin disease [Tleprosy; 5:1], which he
had until the day he died. So he had to live in a separate house. Jotham,
the king's son, was in charge of the ·palace [Lking's house], and he ·gov-
erned [judged] the people of the land.
6All the other things Uzziah did ·are [Lare they not…?] written in the
book of the ·history [chronicles; annals; 1:18] of the kings of Judah.
7Uzziah ·died [Llay down/Tslept with his fathers/ancestors] and was buried
·near his ancestors [with his ancestors/fathers] in the City of David
[CJerusalem], and his son Jotham became king in his place.

Zechariah King of Israel

8Zechariah son of Jeroboam was king over Israel in Samaria. He ·ruled [reigned] for six months during Uzziah's [Calso called Azariah] thirty-eighth year as king of Judah. 9Zechariah did ·what the LORD said was wrong [Levil in the eyes/sight of the LORD], just as his ·ancestors [fathers] had done. Jeroboam son of Nebat had led the people of Israel to sin, and Zechariah did not ·stop doing [depart/turn away from] the same sins.

10Shallum son of Jabesh ·made plans [conspired; plotted] against Zechariah and ·killed [assassinated] him in front of the people. Then Shallum became king in his place. 11The other acts of Zechariah ·are [Lare they not…?] written in the book of the ·history [chronicles; annals; 1:18] of the kings of Israel. 12The LORD had told Jehu: "Your sons down to ·your great-great-grandchildren [the fourth generation; 10:30] will be kings of Israel," and ·the LORD's word came true [so it was/happened].

Shallum King of Israel

13Shallum son of Jabesh became king during Uzziah's thirty-ninth year as king of Judah. Shallum ·ruled [reigned] for a month in Samaria. 14Then Menahem son of Gadi came up from Tirzah to Samaria and attacked Shallum son of Jabesh in Samaria. He ·killed [assassinated] him and became king in Shallum's place.

15The other acts of Shallum and his ·secret plans [conspiracy; plot] ·are [Lare they not…?] written in the book of the ·history [chronicles; annals; 1:18] of the kings of Israel.

Menahem King of Israel

16Menahem ·started out from Tirzah and attacked Tiphsah, destroying the city and the area nearby [*or* destroyed Tiphsah and everyone in it and the surrounding region/countryside as far as Tirzah]. This was because the people had refused to open the city gate for him. He defeated them and ripped open all their pregnant women.

17Menahem son of Gadi became king over Israel during Uzziah's thirty-ninth year as king of Judah. Menahem ·ruled [reigned] ten years in Samaria, 18and he did ·what the LORD said was wrong [Levil in the eyes/sight of the LORD]. Jeroboam son of Nebat had led Israel to sin, and all the time Menahem was king, he did not ·stop doing [depart/turn away from] the same sins.

19Pul [Canother name for Tiglath-pileser] king of Assyria ·came to attack [invaded] the land. Menahem gave him ·about seventy-four thousand pounds [La thousand talents] of silver so Pul would support him ·and make his hold on the kingdom stronger [in tightening his grip/hold on royal power/the kingdom]. 20Menahem ·taxed [exacted/extorted the money from] the rich in Israel to pay ·about one and one-fourth pounds [Lfifty shekels] of silver for each soldier to the king of Assyria. So the king left and did not stay in the land.

21Everything else Menahem did ·is [Lis it not…?] written in the book of the ·history [chronicles; annals; 1:18] of the kings of Israel. 22Then Menahem ·died [Llay down/Tslept with his fathers/ancestors], and his son Pekahiah became king in his place.

Pekahiah King of Israel

23Pekahiah son of Menahem became king over Israel in Samaria during Uzziah's [Calso called Azariah] fiftieth year as king of Judah. Pekahiah ·ruled [reigned] two years, 24and he did ·what the LORD said was wrong [Levil in the eyes/sight of the LORD]. Jeroboam son of Nebat had led Israel to sin, and Pekahiah did not ·stop doing [depart/turn away from] the same sins.

[25]Pekah son of Remaliah was one of Pekahiah's captains, and he ·made plans [conspired; plotted] against Pekahiah. He took fifty men of Gilead with him and ·killed [assassinated] Pekahiah, as well as Argob and Arieh, in the ·palace [king's house] at Samaria. Then Pekah became king in Pekahiah's place.

[26]Everything else Pekahiah did ·is [is it not…?] written in the book of the ·history [chronicles; annals; 1:18] of the kings of Israel.

Pekah King of Israel

[27]Pekah son of Remaliah became king over Israel in Samaria during Uzziah's [Calso called Azariah] fifty-second year as king of Judah. Pekah ·ruled [reigned] twenty years, [28]and he did ·what the LORD said was wrong [Levil in the eyes/sight of the LORD]. Jeroboam son of Nebat had led Israel to sin, and Pekah did not ·stop doing [depart/turn away from] the same sins.

[29]Tiglath-pileser [Calso called Pul; 15:19] was king of Assyria. He attacked while Pekah was king of Israel, capturing the cities of Ijon, Abel Beth Maacah, Janoah, Kedesh, and Hazor. He also captured Gilead and Galilee and all the land of Naphtali and carried the people away to Assyria as captives. [30]Then Hoshea son of Elah ·made plans [conspired; plotted] against Pekah son of Remaliah and attacked and ·killed [assassinated] him. Then Hoshea became king in Pekah's place during the twentieth year Jotham son of Uzziah was king.

[31]Everything else Pekah did ·is [Lis it not…?] written in the book of the ·history [chronicles; annals; 1:18] of the kings of Israel.

Jotham King of Judah
(15:32–38; 2 Chr. 27:1–9)

[32]Jotham son of Uzziah became king of Judah during the second year Pekah son of Remaliah was king of Israel. [33]Jotham was twenty-five years old when he became king, and he ·ruled [reigned] sixteen years in Jerusalem. His mother's name was Jerusha daughter of Zadok. [34]Jotham did ·what the LORD said was right [Lright in the eyes/sight of the LORD], just as his father Uzziah had done. [35]But the ·places where gods were worshiped [Lhigh places; 12:3] were not removed, and the people still made sacrifices and burned incense there. Jotham rebuilt the Upper Gate of the ·Temple [Lhouse] of the LORD.

[36]The other things Jotham did while he was king ·are [Lare they not…?] written in the book of the ·history [chronicles; annals; 1:18] of the kings of Judah. [37]At that time the LORD began to send Rezin king of Aram and Pekah son of Remaliah against Judah. [38]Jotham ·died [Llay down/Tslept with his fathers/ancestors] and was buried with his ·ancestors [fathers] in the City of David [CJerusalem], his ·ancestor [father]. Then Jotham's son Ahaz became king in his place.

Ahaz King of Judah
(16:1–20; 2 Chr. 28:1–7, 16–27)

16 Ahaz was the son of Jotham king of Judah. Ahaz became king of Judah in the seventeenth year Pekah son of Remaliah was king of Israel. [2]Ahaz was twenty years old when he became king, and he ·ruled [reigned] sixteen years in Jerusalem. Unlike his ·ancestor [father] David, he did not do ·what the LORD his God said was right [right in the eyes/sight of the LORD his God]. [3]Ahaz ·did the same things the kings of Israel had done [Lwalked in the way/path of the kings of Israel]. He even ·made his son pass through fire [sacrificed his son in the fire; Ca reference to human sacrifice]. He did the same ·hateful sins [detestable/abominable practices] as the nations had done whom the LORD had ·forced [driven] out of the land ahead of the ·Israelites [Lsons/Tchildren

of Israel]. 4Ahaz offered sacrifices and burned incense at the ·places
where gods were worshiped [Lhigh places: 12:3], on the hills, and under
every ·green [spreading] tree.
5Rezin king of Aram and Pekah son of Remaliah, the king of Israel,
came up to attack Jerusalem. They ·surrounded [besieged] Ahaz but
could not ·defeat [conquer; overpower] him. 6At that time Rezin king of
Aram ·took back [recovered] the city of Elath for Aram, and he forced out
all the people of Judah. Then ·Edomites [Arameans] moved into Elath,
and they still live there today.
7Ahaz sent messengers to Tiglath-pileser king of Assyria, saying, "I am
your servant and your ·friend [vassal; Lson]. Come and ·save [rescue;
Tdeliver] me from the hand of the king of Aram and the king of Israel,
who are attacking me." 8Ahaz took the silver and gold that was in the
·Temple [Lhouse] of the Lord and in the treasuries of the ·palace [Lking's
house], and he sent these as a gift to the king of Assyria. 9So the king of
Assyria listened to Ahaz. He attacked Damascus and captured it and ·sent
all [exiled; deported] its people away to Kir. And he killed Rezin.
10Then King Ahaz went to Damascus to meet Tiglath-pileser king of
Assyria. Ahaz saw an altar at Damascus, and he sent ·plans [a model] and
a ·pattern [detailed plan] of this altar to Uriah the priest. 11So Uriah the
priest built an altar, just like the plans King Ahaz had sent him from
Damascus. Uriah finished the altar before King Ahaz came back from
Damascus. 12When the king arrived from Damascus, he saw the altar and
went ·near [up to it/onto it] and offered sacrifices on it [Cthe building of
this altar was an act of apostasy]. 13He ·burned [offered; presented] his
burnt offerings and grain offerings and poured out his drink offering. He
also sprinkled the blood of his ·fellowship [*or* peace; well-being] offerings
[Lev. 3:1] on the altar.
14Ahaz moved the bronze altar that was previously before the Lord at
the front of the ·Temple [Lhouse]. It was between Ahaz's altar [Cthe new
one] and the ·Temple [Lhouse] of the Lord [Cthe Temple entrance], but he
put it on the north side of his altar. 15King Ahaz commanded Uriah the
priest, "On the ·large [great; Cthe new one] altar ·burn [offer; present] the
morning burnt offering [Lev. 1:1–17], the evening grain offering, the
king's burnt offering and ·grain [Lgift; tribute] offering [Lev. 2:1], and the
whole burnt offering, the ·grain [Lgift; tribute] offering, and the drink
offering for all the people of the land. Sprinkle on the altar all the blood
of the burnt offering and of the sacrifice. But I will use the bronze altar to
·ask questions [inquire] of God." 16So Uriah the priest did everything as
King Ahaz commanded him.
17Then King Ahaz ·took [cut] off the side panels from the bases and
removed the ·washing bowls [basins] from the top of the ·bases [movable
stands; portable water carts]. He also took the large bowl, which was
called the Sea, off the bronze ·bulls [oxen] that held it up, and he put it on
·a [the] stone ·base [pavement; pediment]. 18Ahaz took away the ·plat-
form [dais; *or* canopy; covered portal] for the royal throne, which had
been built at the ·Temple [Lhouse] of the Lord. He also took away the
outside entrance for the king. He did these things because of the king of
Assyria [Cto show deference and submission].
19The other things Ahaz did as king ·are [Lare they not...?] written in
the book of the ·history [chronicles; annals; 1:18] of the kings of Judah.
20Ahaz ·died [Llay down/Tslept with his fathers/ancestors] and was buried

with his ·ancestors [fathers] in the City of David [CJerusalem], and Ahaz's son Hezekiah ·became king [reigned] in his place.

Hoshea, Last King of Israel

17 Hoshea son of Elah became king over Israel during Ahaz's twelfth year as king of Judah. Hoshea ·ruled [reigned] in Samaria nine years. 2He did ·what the LORD said was wrong [Levil in the eyes/sight of the LORD], but ·he was not as bad as [not like] the kings of Israel who had ·ruled [reigned] before him.

3Shalmaneser king of Assyria came to attack Hoshea. Hoshea had been Shalmaneser's ·servant [vassal] and had ·made the payments to Shalmaneser that he had demanded [paid him tribute]. 4But the king of Assyria found that Hoshea had betrayed him. Hoshea had ·made plans [conspired; plotted] against him by sending messengers to So, the king of Egypt. Hoshea had also ·stopped giving Shalmaneser the payments [offered no tribute to the king of Assyria], which he had paid every year in the past. For that, the king of Assyria put Hoshea in prison. 5Then the king of Assyria ·came and attacked [invaded] all the land of Israel. He ·surrounded [besieged] Samaria for three years. 6He ·defeated [captured] Samaria in the ninth year Hoshea was king, and he ·took [carried; exiled; deported] the Israelites away to Assyria. He settled them in Halah, in Gozan on the Habor River, and in the cities of the Medes.

Israelites Punished for Sin

7All these things happened because the ·Israelites [Lsons/Tchildren of Israel] had sinned against the LORD their God. He had brought them out of Egypt and had rescued them from the ·power [Lhand] of Pharaoh the king of Egypt [Ex. 20:2], but ·the Israelites [Lthey] had ·honored [revered; feared] other gods [Deut. 29:26]. 8They ·lived like [followed/Lwalked in the practices of] the nations the LORD had ·forced [driven] out of the land ahead of them. They lived as their evil kings had shown them, 9secretly ·sinning [doing things that were not right] against the LORD their God. They ·built [set up] ·places to worship gods [Lhigh places; 12:3] in all their cities, from the watchtower to the ·strong, walled [fortified] city. 10They put up ·stone [sacred] pillars to gods and Asherah ·idols [poles; Ca sacred tree or pole dedicated to the goddess Asherah; 13:6; 1 Kin. 14:15] on every high hill and under every ·green [spreading] tree. 11The Israelites burned incense ·everywhere gods were worshiped [Lon all the high places; 12:3], just as the nations who lived there before them had done, whom the LORD had ·forced [driven] out of the land. The Israelites did ·wicked [evil] things that ·made the LORD angry [aroused/provoked the LORD's anger]. 12They served idols when the LORD had said, "You must not do this." 13The LORD used every prophet and seer to warn Israel and Judah. He said, "·Stop [Turn from] your evil ways and ·obey [keep; observe] my commands and laws. Follow all the ·teachings [law; Ltorah] that I commanded your ·ancestors [fathers], the ·teachings [law; Ltorah] that I gave you through my servants the prophets."

14But the people would not listen. They were ·stubborn [Lstiff-necked], just as their ·ancestors [fathers] had been who did not ·believe [trust; have faith] in the LORD their God. 15They rejected the LORD's laws and the ·agreement [covenant; treaty] he had ·made [Lcut] with their ·ancestors [fathers]. And they refused to listen to his warnings [Deut. 12:30–31]. They worshiped ·useless [worthless; futile; vain] idols and became ·useless [worthless; futile; vain] themselves [1 Sam. 12:21]. They did what the nations around them did, which the LORD had ·warned [commanded; ordered] them not to do [Lev. 18:3, 24–28].

16The people ·rejected [forsook] all the commands of the LORD their God. They molded ·statues [cast images] of two calves [1 Kin. 12:28–30], and they made an Asherah ·idol [pole; ^{C}a sacred tree or pole dedicated to the goddess Asherah; 13:6; Deut. 16:21]. They worshiped all the ·stars of the sky [forces/hosts of heaven; Deut. 4:19] and served Baal. 17They ·made their sons and daughters pass through [sacrificed their sons and daughters in the] fire [16:3; 21:6; Deut. 12:31] and tried to find out the future by magic and witchcraft [1 Sam 15:23]. They always chose to do ·what the LORD said was wrong [evil in the eyes/sight of the LORD], which ·made him angry [aroused/provoked him to anger]. 18Because he was very angry with the people of Israel, he removed them from his ·presence [sight]. Only the tribe of Judah was left.

Judah Is Also Guilty

19·But even [Also] Judah did not ·obey [keep; observe] the commands of the LORD their God. They ·did what [followed/^{L}walked in the practices] the Israelites had done, 20so the LORD rejected all the ·people [descendants] of Israel. He ·punished [afflicted] them and ·let others destroy them [handed them over to plunderers/marauders]; he ·threw [banished; thrust] them out of his ·presence [sight]. 21When the LORD ·separated [tore; ripped] them from the ·family [^{L}house] of David, the Israelites made Jeroboam son of Nebat their king. Jeroboam ·led [drew; enticed] the Israelites away from the LORD and led them to sin greatly [1 Kin. 13:33–34]. 22So they ·continued to do [persisted; ^{L}walked in] all the sins Jeroboam did. They did not ·stop doing [depart/turn away from] these sins 23until the LORD removed the Israelites from his ·presence [sight], just as he had ·said [warned; 14:15–16; 1 Kin. 9:7] through all his servants the prophets. So the Israelites were ·taken out of [carried into exile/deported from] their land to Assyria, and they have been there to this day.

The Beginning of the Samaritan People

24The king of Assyria brought people from Babylon, Cuthah, Avva, Hamath, and Sepharvaim and ·put [settled] them in the cities of Samaria to replace the ·Israelites [^{L}sons/^{T}children of Israel]. These people took ·over [possession of] Samaria and lived in the cities. 25At first they did not ·worship [revere; fear] the LORD, so he sent lions among them which killed some of them. 26The king of Assyria was told, "You ·sent foreigners [deported/exiled/carried nations] into the cities of Samaria who do not know the ·law [custom] of the god of the land. This is why he has sent lions among them. The lions are killing them because they don't know ·what the god wants [^{L}the law/custom of the god of the land]."

27Then the king of Assyria commanded, "Send back one of the priests you ·took away [carried into exile; deported]. Let him live there and teach the people ·what the god wants [^{L}the law/custom of the god of the land]." 28So one of the priests who had been carried ·away [into exile] from Samaria returned to live ·in [at] Bethel. And he taught the people how to ·honor [revere; fear] the LORD.

29But each nation made gods of its own and put them in the cities where they lived and in the ·temples [^{L}houses] ·where gods were worshiped [^{L}of the high places; 12:3]. These ·temples [^{L}houses] had been built by the Samaritans. 30The people from Babylon made Succoth Benoth their god. The people from Cuthah ·worshiped [made] Nergal. The people of Hamath ·worshiped [made] Ashima. 31The Avvites ·worshiped [made] Nibhaz and Tartak. The Sepharvites burned their children in the fire, sacrificing them to Adrammelech and Anammelech, the gods of

Sepharvaim. 32They also ·honored [revered; feared] the LORD, but they
chose priests for the ·places where gods were worshiped [Lhigh places;
12:3]. The priests were chosen from among themselves, and they ·made
sacrifices [Lofficiated at the temple/houses of the high places] for the people. 33The people ·honored [revered; feared] the LORD but also ·served
[followed] their own gods, ·just as [Lin accordance with the customs of]
the nations ·did from which they had been brought [from which they had
been exiled]. 34Even today they ·do as they did in the past [practice their
former customs]. They do not ·worship [revere; fear] the LORD nor obey
his ·rules [statutes; ordinances; requirements] and commands. They do
not ·obey [worship nor observe] the ·teachings [law; Ltorah] or the commands of the LORD, which he gave to the ·children [descendants] of Jacob,
whom he had named Israel [Gen. 32:28]. 35The LORD had made an ·agree-
ment [covenant; treaty] with them and had commanded them, "Do not
·honor [revere; fear] other gods. Do not bow down to them or ·worship
[serve] them or offer sacrifices to them. 36·Worship [Revere; Fear] the
LORD who brought you up out of the land of Egypt with great power and
·strength [Lan outstretched arm]. Bow down to him and offer sacrifices to
him. 37Always obey the rules, orders, ·teachings [law; Ltorah], and commands he wrote for you. Do not ·honor [revere; fear] other gods. 38Do not
forget the ·agreement [covenant; treaty] I made with you, and do not
·honor [revere; fear] other gods. 39Instead ·worship [revere; fear] the LORD
your God, who will ·save [rescue; Tdeliver] you from all your enemies."

40But the Israelites did not listen. They ·kept on doing the same things
they had done before [continued in their former practices/custom]. 41So
these nations ·honored [revered; feared] the LORD but also ·worshiped
[served] their idols, and their children and grandchildren still do as their
·ancestors [fathers] did.

Hezekiah King of Judah
(18:1–8; 2 Chr. 29:1–2, 31:1)

18 Hezekiah son of Ahaz king of Judah became king during the
third year Hoshea son of Elah was king of Israel. 2Hezekiah
was twenty-five years old when he became king, and he ·ruled [reigned]
twenty-nine years in Jerusalem. His mother's name was ·Abijah [LAbi; in
2 Chr. 29:1 she is called Abijah] daughter of Zechariah. 3Hezekiah did
·what the LORD said was right [Lright in the eyes/sight of the LORD], just
as his ·ancestor [father] David had done. 4He removed the ·places where
gods were worshiped [Lhigh places; 12:3]. He smashed the stone pillars
and ·cut down [smashed; broke] the Asherah ·idols [poles; Ca sacred tree
or pole dedicated to the goddess Asherah; 13:6]. Also the ·Israelites
[Lsons/Tchildren of Israel] had been burning incense to Nehushtan, the
bronze ·snake [serpent] Moses had made [Num. 21:9]. But Hezekiah
broke it into pieces.

5Hezekiah trusted in the LORD, the God of Israel. There was no one like
him among all the kings of Judah, either before him or after him.
6Hezekiah ·was loyal [clung; held fast; remained faithful/devoted] to the
LORD and did not ·stop [depart from] following him; he ·obeyed [kept]
the commands the LORD had given Moses. 7And the LORD was with
Hezekiah, so he ·had success [prospered] in everything he did. He ·turned
[rebelled] against the king of Assyria and stopped serving him [Cstopped
paying tribute]. 8Hezekiah defeated the Philistines ·all the way to [as far
as] Gaza and its ·borders [territory], ·including [from] the watchtowers
and the ·strong, walled [fortified] cities.

The Assyrians Capture Samaria
(18:9–12; 17:5–6)

[9]Shalmaneser king of Assyria surrounded Samaria and ·attacked [besieged] it in the fourth year Hezekiah was king. This was the seventh year Hoshea son of Elah was king of Israel. [10]After three years the Assyrians captured Samaria. This was in the sixth year Hezekiah was king, which was Hoshea's ninth year as king of Israel. [11]The king of Assyria ·took [carried] the Israelites away to Assyria and settled them in Halah, in Gozan on the Habor River, and in the cities of the Medes. [12]This happened because they did not obey the voice of the Lord their God. They broke his ·agreement [covenant; treaty] and did not obey all that Moses, the Lord's servant, had commanded. They would not listen to the commands or do them.

Assyria Attacks Judah
(18:13–37; 2 Chr. 32:1–19; Is. 36:1–22)

[13]During Hezekiah's fourteenth year as king, Sennacherib king of Assyria attacked all the ·strong, walled [fortified] cities of Judah and captured them. [14]Then Hezekiah king of Judah sent a message to the king of Assyria at Lachish. He said, "I have done wrong. ·Leave me alone [Withdraw from me], and I will ·pay [bear] anything you ·ask [impose]." So the king of Assyria made Hezekiah pay ·about twenty-two thousand pounds [Lthree hundred talents] of silver and ·two thousand pounds [Lthirty talents] of gold. [15]Hezekiah gave him all the silver that was in the ·Temple [Lhouse] of the Lord and in the ·palace [Lking's house] treasuries. [16]Hezekiah stripped all the gold that covered the doors and doorposts of the ·Temple [Lhouse] of the Lord. Hezekiah had ·put [overlaid] gold on these doors himself, but he gave it all to the king of Assyria.

[17]The king of Assyria sent out his supreme commander, his chief officer, and his field commander. They went with a large army from Lachish to King Hezekiah in Jerusalem. When they came near the ·waterway [aqueduct; conduit] from the upper pool on the road ·where people do their laundry [to the Fuller's Field], they stopped. [18]They called for the king, so the king sent Eliakim, Shebna, and Joah out to meet them. Eliakim son of Hilkiah was the ·palace [Lking's house] manager, Shebna was the royal secretary, and Joah son of Asaph was the ·recorder [royal historian].

[19]The field commander said to them, "Tell Hezekiah this:

" 'The great king, the king of Assyria, says: ·What can you trust in now [On what do you base your confidence; Where does this confidence come from]? [20]You say you have ·battle plans [strategy; counsel] and ·power [strength] for war, but your words ·mean nothing [are empty]. Whom are you ·trusting [relying/counting on] for help so that you ·turn [rebel] against me? [21]Look, you are depending on Egypt to help you, but Egypt is like a ·splintered [broken] ·walking stick [reed]. If you lean on it for help, it will stab your hand and ·hurt [pierce] you. So it will be with the king of Egypt for all those who depend on him. [22]You might say, "We are depending on the Lord our God," but ·Hezekiah [Ldid not Hezekiah…?] destroyed the Lord's altars and ·the places of worship [Lhigh places; 12:3]. Hezekiah told Judah and Jerusalem, "You must worship only at this one altar in Jerusalem."

[23]" 'Now make an ·agreement [covenant; treaty] with my ·master [lord], the king of Assyria: I will give you two thousand horses if you can find enough men to ride them [Ca taunt that Judah's army was small]. [24]You cannot ·defeat [repel] one of my ·master's [lord's] least important officers, so why do you depend on Egypt to give you chariots and ·horsemen [charioteers]? [25]·I have not [LDo you think I have…?] come to attack and

destroy this place without ·an order from the LORD [Lthe LORD]. The LORD himself told me to come ·to [against] this country and destroy it.' "

26 Then Eliakim son of Hilkiah, Shebna, and Joah said to the field commander, "Please speak to us in the Aramaic language. We understand it. Don't speak to us in ·Hebrew [Judean], because the people on the city wall can hear you."

27 "No," the commander said, "my ·master [lord] did not send me to tell these ·things [words] only to your ·master [lord] and you. He sent me to speak also to those people sitting on the wall who, like you, will have to eat their own dung and drink their own urine."

28 Then the commander stood and shouted loudly in ·the Hebrew language [Judean], "·Listen to what [LHear the word of] the great king, the king of Assyria, says! 29 The king says you should not let Hezekiah ·fool [deceive; delude] you, because he can't ·save [rescue; Tdeliver] you from my ·power [Lhand]. 30 Don't let Hezekiah ·talk [persuade] you into trusting the LORD by saying, 'The LORD will surely ·save [rescue; Tdeliver] us. This city won't be handed over to the king of Assyria.'

31 "Don't listen to Hezekiah. The king of Assyria says, 'Make peace with me, and come out of the city to me. Then everyone will be free to eat the fruit from his own grapevine and fig tree and to drink water from his own well. 32 After that I will come and take you to a land like your own—a land with grain and new wine, bread and vineyards, olives, and honey. Choose to live and not to die [Ca promise that if they gave up, their resettlement would be pleasant]!'

"Don't listen to Hezekiah. He is ·fooling [misleading] you when he says, 'The LORD will ·save [rescue; Tdeliver] us.' 33 Has a god of any other nation ·saved [rescued; Tdelivered] his people from the ·power [Lhand] of the king of Assyria? 34 Where are the gods of Hamath and Arpad? Where are the gods of Sepharvaim, Hena, and Ivvah? They did not ·save [rescue; Tdeliver] Samaria from my power. 35 Not one of all the gods of these countries has ·saved [rescued; Tdelivered] his people from me. Neither can the LORD ·save [rescue; Tdeliver] Jerusalem from my ·power [Lhand]."

36 The people were silent. They didn't answer the commander at all, because King Hezekiah had ordered, "Don't answer him."

37 Then Eliakim, Shebna, and Joah tore their clothes [Ca sign of mourning or distress]. (Eliakim son of Hilkiah was the ·palace [king's house] manager, Shebna was the royal secretary, and Joah son of Asaph was the ·recorder [royal historian].) The three men went to Hezekiah and told him what the field commander had said.

Jerusalem Will Be Saved
(19:1–34; 2 Chr. 32:20; Is. 37:1–35)

19 When King Hezekiah heard the message, he tore his clothes [Ca sign of mourning or distress] and put on ·rough cloth [sackcloth; burlap; Calso a sign of mourning]. Then he went into the ·Temple [Lhouse] of the LORD. 2 Hezekiah sent Eliakim, the ·palace [Lking's house] manager, and Shebna, the royal secretary, and the ·older [*or* elders of the] priests to Isaiah. They were all wearing ·rough cloth [sackcloth; burlap] when they came to Isaiah the prophet, the son of Amoz. 3 They told Isaiah, "This is what Hezekiah says: Today is a day of ·sorrow [distress; trouble] and ·punishment [insults, rebuke] and ·disgrace [rejection], as when a child ·should [is ready to] be born, but the mother is not strong enough to give birth to it. 4 The king of Assyria sent his field commander to ·make fun of [defy; ridicule; insult] the living God. Maybe the LORD your God

will hear what the commander said and will ·punish [rebuke] him for it.
So pray for the ·few of us who are left alive [remnant that is left]."
5When Hezekiah's ·officers [officials] came to Isaiah, 6he said to them,
"Tell your ·master [lord] this: ·The LORD says [TThus says the LORD], 'Don't
be afraid of what you have heard. Don't be frightened by the words the
servants of the king of Assyria have ·spoken [used to blaspheme] against
me. 7Listen! I am going to put a spirit in the king of Assyria. He will hear
a ·report [rumor; message] that will make him return to his own country,
and I will cause him to ·die [Lfall] by the sword there.' "
8The field commander heard that the king of Assyria had left Lachish.
When he went back, he found the king fighting against the city of Libnah.
9The king received a report that Tirhakah, the Cushite king of ·Egypt
[LCush; Cpresent-day Ethiopia], was coming to attack him. When the king
of Assyria heard this, he sent messengers to Hezekiah, saying, 10"Tell
Hezekiah king of Judah: Don't be ·fooled [deceived; deluded] by the god
you trust. Don't believe him when he says Jerusalem will not be handed
over to the king of Assyria. 11You ·have heard [know] what the kings of
Assyria have done. They have completely defeated every country, so do ·not
[Lyou…?] think you will be ·saved [rescued; Tdelivered]. 12Did the gods of
those ·people [nations] ·save [rescue; Tdeliver] them? My ·ancestors [fathers]
destroyed them, defeating the cities of Gozan, Haran, and Rezeph, and the
people of Eden living in Tel Assar. 13Where are the kings of Hamath and
Arpad? Where are the kings of Sepharvaim, Hena, and Ivvah?"

Hezekiah Prays to the Lord

14·When [After] Hezekiah received the letter from the messengers and
read it, he went up to the ·Temple [Lhouse] of the LORD. He spread the letter out before the LORD 15and prayed ·to [before] the LORD: "LORD, God of
Israel, whose throne is ·between [above] the ·gold creatures with wings
[Lcherubim; Ex. 37:7], ·only you [you alone] are God of all the kingdoms
of the earth. You made the heavens and the earth. 16·Hear [LExtend/Incline
your ear], LORD, and listen. Open your eyes, LORD, and see. Listen to the
words Sennacherib has said to ·insult [defy; ridicule; mock] the living
God. 17It is true, LORD, that the kings of Assyria have ·destroyed [devas-
tated; laid waste to] these ·countries [nations] and their lands. 18They
have thrown the gods of these nations into the fire, ·but [for] they were
not gods at all but only wood and rock statues that people made. So the
kings have destroyed them. 19Now, LORD our God, ·save [rescue; Tdeliver]
us from the king's ·power [Lhand] so that all the kingdoms of the earth
will know that you, LORD, ·are the only [alone are] God."

God Answers Hezekiah

20Then Isaiah son of Amoz sent a message to Hezekiah that said, "This
is what the LORD, the God of Israel, says: I have heard your prayer to me
about Sennacherib king of Assyria. 21This is ·what [Lthe word] the LORD
has said against Sennacherib:

'The ·people of Jerusalem [Lvirgin daughter of Zion]
·hate you [despises] and ·make fun of [mocks; scorns] you.
The ·people [Ldaughter] of Jerusalem
·laugh at you [Ltosses her head] ·as you run away [as you flee; *or*
behind your back].
22·You have insulted me and spoken against me [Whom have you defied/
ridiculed/mocked?];
·you have raised your voice against me [Against whom have you
raised your voice…].

·You have a proud look on your face [and arrogantly lifted your eyes/
gaze?]!
Against the Holy One of Israel!
23You have sent your messengers to ·insult [defy; ridicule; mock] the
Lord.
You have said, "With my many chariots
I have gone to the tops of the mountains,
to the ·highest [*or* remotest] mountains of Lebanon.
I have cut down its tallest cedars
and its best ·pine [cypress] trees.
I have gone to its farthest places
and to its ·best [densest] forests.
24I have dug wells in foreign ·countries [lands]
and drunk water there.
By the soles of my feet,
I have ·dried [stopped] up all the rivers of Egypt."

25" 'King of Assyria, ·surely you have [Lhave you not...?] heard.
Long ago I, the LORD, ·planned [determined; ordained] these things.
·Long ago [In ancient times/days of old] I ·designed them [planned it],
and now I have ·made them happen [brought them to pass].
I allowed you to turn those ·strong, walled [fortified] cities
into piles of ·rocks [rubble; ruins].
26The people in those cities were ·weak [powerless; drained of strength];
they were ·frightened [dismayed] and ·put to shame [confused;
confounded].
They were like grass in the field,
like tender, young ·grass [shoots],
like grass on the housetop
that is ·burned [scorched] by the wind before it can grow.

27" 'I know ·when you rest [when you stand or sit; *or* where you are],
when you come and go,
and how you ·rage [rave] against me.
28Because you ·rage [rave] against me,
and because I have heard your ·proud [arrogant] words,
I will put my hook in your nose
and my bit in your mouth.
Then I will ·force you to leave my country [turn you back; make you
retreat]
the ·same way [road] you came.'

29"Then the LORD said, 'Hezekiah, I will give you this sign:
This year you will eat the grain that grows ·wild [Lof itself],
and the second year you will eat what ·grows [springs] from that.
But in the third year, ·plant grain [sow] and ·harvest it [reap].
Plant vineyards and eat their fruit.
30·Some of the people in [A remnant of] the ·family [Lhouse] of Judah
will ·escape [survive].
·Like plants that take root [They will put down roots below],
·they will grow strong and have many children [and will bear fruit
above].

[31]A ·few people will come out of Jerusalem alive [remnant will spread
out from Jerusalem];
·a few from Mount Zion will live [and survivors out from Mount Zion].
The ·strong love [zeal] of the LORD All-Powerful
will ·make this happen [accomplish this].'

[32]"So this is what the LORD says about the king of Assyria:
'He will not enter this city
or even shoot an arrow here.
He will not fight against it with shields
or build a ramp to ·attack the city walls [lay siege to it].
[33]He will ·return to his country [retreat] the same ·way [road] he came,
and he will not enter this city,'
says the LORD.
[34]'I will defend and ·save [rescue; [T]deliver] this city
for my sake and for the sake of David, my servant.'"

The Angel of Death
(19:35–37; 2 Chr. 32:21–23; Is. 37:36–38)

[35]That night the ·angel [messenger] of the LORD went out and killed one
hundred eighty-five thousand men in the Assyrian camp. When the people
got up early the next morning, they saw all the dead bodies. [36]So Sennacherib
king of Assyria left and went back to Nineveh and stayed there.
[37]One day as Sennacherib was worshiping in the ·temple [[L]house] of
his god Nisroch, his sons Adrammelech and Sharezer killed him with a
sword. Then they escaped to the land of Ararat. So Sennacherib's son
Esarhaddon became king of Assyria.

Hezekiah's Illness
(20:1–11; 2 Chr. 32:24–26; Is. 38:1–8, 21–22)

20 At that time Hezekiah became so sick he ·almost died [was
about to die]. The prophet Isaiah son of Amoz went to see
him and told him, "·This is what the LORD says [[T]Thus says the LORD]:
·Make arrangements [[L]Set your house in order] because you are going to
die. You will not recover."
[2]Hezekiah turned toward the wall and prayed to the LORD, [3]"LORD,
please remember that I have always ·obeyed [[L]walked before] you. I have
·given myself completely to you [served you wholeheartedly] and have
done ·what you said was right [[L]right in the eyes/sight of the LORD]." Then
Hezekiah ·cried loudly [wept bitterly].
[4]Before Isaiah had left the middle courtyard, the LORD spoke his word
to Isaiah: [5]"Go back and tell Hezekiah, the ·leader [ruler; prince] of my
people: 'This is what the LORD, the God of your ·ancestor [father] David,
says: I have heard your prayer and seen your tears, so I will heal you.
Three days from now you will go up to the ·Temple [[L]house] of the LORD.
[6]I will add fifteen years to your life. I will ·save [rescue; [T]deliver] you and
this city from [[L]the hand of] the king of Assyria; I will ·protect [defend]
the city for my sake and for the sake of my servant David.'"
[7]Then Isaiah said, "Make a ·paste [ointment; poultice] from figs." So
they made it and put it on Hezekiah's boil, and he got well.
[8]Hezekiah had asked Isaiah, "What will be the sign that the LORD will
heal me and that I will go up to the ·Temple [[L]house] of the LORD on the
third day?"
[9]Isaiah said, "The LORD will do what he ·says [promises]. This is the
sign from the LORD to show you: Do you want the shadow to go forward
ten steps or back ten steps?"

10Hezekiah answered, "It's ·easy [normal] for the shadow to ·go forward [lengthen] ten steps. Instead, let it go back ten steps."
11Then Isaiah the prophet called to the LORD, and the LORD brought the
shadow ten steps back up the ·stairway [*or* dial; Cthe shadows moved
either on outside stairs or on a sundial] of Ahaz that it had gone down.

Messengers from Babylon
(20:12–21; 2 Chr. 32:31–33; Is. 39:1–8)

12At that time Merodach-baladan son of Baladan was king of Babylon.
He sent ·letters [greetings] and a gift to Hezekiah, because he had heard
that Hezekiah ·was [had been] sick. 13Hezekiah ·listened to [received] the
messengers, ·so [and] he showed them what was in his storehouses: the
silver, gold, spices, ·expensive perfumes [precious oils], his ·swords and
shields [armory], and all his ·wealth [treasures]. He showed them everything in his ·palace [Lhouse] and his kingdom.
14Then Isaiah the prophet went to King Hezekiah and asked him,
"What did these men say? Where did they come from?"
Hezekiah said, "They came from a faraway country—from Babylon."
15So Isaiah asked him, "What did they see in your ·palace [Lhouse]?"
Hezekiah said, "They saw everything in my ·palace [Lhouse]. I showed
them all my ·wealth [Ltreasuries; store houses]."
16Then Isaiah said to Hezekiah, "Listen to the words of the LORD: 17'·In
the future to you [The time/day is coming when] everything in your ·pal-
ace [Lhouse] and everything your ·ancestors [fathers] have stored up until
this day will be ·taken away [carried off] to Babylon. Nothing will be left,'
says the LORD. 18'Some of your own ·children [sons], those ·who will be
born to you [you will father], will be taken away. And they will become
·servants [eunuchs] in the palace of the king of Babylon.' "
19Hezekiah told Isaiah, "These words from the LORD that you have spoken are good." He said this because he thought, "Why not? There will be
peace and security in my lifetime."
20Everything else Hezekiah did—all his ·victories [achievements; power],
his work on the pool, his work on the tunnel to bring water into the city—
·is [Lis it not…?] written in the book of the ·history [chronicles; annals;
1:18] of the kings of Judah. 21Then Hezekiah ·died [Llay down/Tslept with
his fathers/ancestors], and his son Manasseh became king in his place.

Manasseh King of Judah
(21:1–18; 2 Chr. 33:1–20)

21 Manasseh was twelve years old when he became king, and he
·was king [reigned] fifty-five years in Jerusalem. His mother's
name was Hephzibah. 2He did ·what the LORD said was wrong [Levil in
the eyes/sight of the LORD]. He did the ·hateful things [detestable/abom-
inable practices] the other nations had done—the nations that the LORD
had ·forced [driven] out of the land ahead of the ·Israelites [Lsons/
Tchildren of Israel]. 3Manasseh's father, Hezekiah, had destroyed the
·places where gods were worshiped [Lhigh places; 12:3], but Manasseh
rebuilt them. He built altars for Baal, and he made an Asherah ·idol
[pole; Ca sacred tree or pole dedicated to the goddess Asherah; 13:6] as
Ahab king of Israel had done. Manasseh also worshiped all the ·stars of
the sky [hosts of heaven] and served them. 4The LORD had said about the
·Temple [Lhouse], "I will ·be worshiped [Lput my name] in Jerusalem,"
but Manasseh built altars [Cpagan] in the ·Temple [Lhouse] of the LORD.
5He built altars to worship the ·stars [hosts of heaven] in the two courtyards of the ·Temple [Lhouse] of the LORD. 6He ·made his own son pass
through fire [sacrificed his son in the fire; 16:3]. He practiced ·magic
[sorcery; soothsaying] and ·told the future by explaining signs and

dreams [divination], and he ·got advice from [consulted] mediums and
·fortune-tellers [psychics; spiritualists]. He did ·many things the LORD
said were wrong [[L]much evil in the eyes/sight of the LORD], which ·made
the LORD angry [aroused/provoked the LORD to anger].
7 Manasseh carved an Asherah ·idol [pole; [C]a sacred tree or pole dedicated to the goddess Asherah; 13:6] and put it in the ·Temple [[L]house].
The LORD had said to David and his son Solomon about the ·Temple
[[L]house], "I will ·be worshiped [[L]put my name] forever in this ·Temple
[[L]house] and in Jerusalem, which I have chosen from all the tribes of
Israel. 8 I will never again make the ·Israelites [[L]feet of Israel to] wander
out of the land I gave their ·ancestors [fathers]. But they must ·obey
[observe; do] everything I have commanded them and all the ·teachings
[law; [L]torah] my servant Moses gave them." 9 But the people did not listen.
Manasseh led them to do more evil than the nations the LORD had
destroyed ahead of the ·Israelites [[L]sons/[T]children of Israel].
10 The LORD said through his servants the prophets, 11 "Manasseh king
of Judah has done these ·hateful things [detestable/abominable practices].
He has done more ·evil [wickedness] than the Amorites before him. He
also has led Judah to sin with his idols. 12 So this is what the LORD, the God
of Israel, says: 'I will bring ·so much trouble [such disaster/calamity] on
Jerusalem and Judah that anyone who hears about it will ·be shocked
[[L]have tingling ears]. 13 I will stretch over Jerusalem the measuring line
used for Samaria , and the plumb line used against Ahab's ·family [[L]house]
will be used on Jerusalem. I will wipe out Jerusalem as a person wipes a
dish and turns it upside down. 14 I will ·throw away the rest of my people
who are left [abandon/forsake/reject the remnant of my inheritance/heri-
tage]. I will ·give them [hand them over; deliver them] to their enemies,
and they will be ·robbed by all [the plunder and spoil of] their enemies,
15 because my people did ·what I said was wrong [[L]evil in my eyes/sight].
They have ·made me angry [aroused/provoked my anger] from the day
their ·ancestors [fathers] left Egypt until ·now [today].'"
16 Manasseh also ·killed [murdered] many innocent people, filling
Jerusalem from one end to the other with their blood. This was besides
the sin he led Judah to do; he led Judah to do ·what the LORD said was
wrong [[L]evil in the eyes/sight of the LORD].
17 The other things Manasseh did as king, even the sin he did, ·are [[L]are
they not…?] written in the book of the ·history [chronicles; annals; 1:18]
of the kings of Judah. 18 Manasseh ·died [[L]lay down/[T]slept with his fathers/
ancestors] and was buried in the garden of his own ·palace [[L]house], the
garden of Uzza. Then Manasseh's son Amon became king in his place.

Amon King of Judah
(21:19–26; 2 Chr. 33:21–25)

19 Amon was twenty-two years old when he became king, and he was
king for two years in Jerusalem. His mother's name was Meshullemeth
daughter of Haruz, who was from Jotbah. 20 Amon did ·what the LORD
said was wrong [[L]evil in the eyes/sight of the LORD], as his father Manasseh
had done. 21 He ·lived [followed; [L]walked] in the same way his father had
·lived [followed; [L]walked]: he ·worshiped [served] the idols his father had
·worshiped [served], and he ·bowed down before [worshiped] them.
22 Amon ·rejected [abandoned; forsook] the LORD, the God of his ·ances-
tors [fathers], and did not ·follow [walk in] the ways of the LORD.
23 Amon's officers ·made plans [conspired; plotted] against him and
killed him in his ·palace [[L]house]. 24 Then the people of the land killed all

those who had ·made plans [conspired; plotted] to kill King Amon, and
they made his son Josiah king in his place.
25Everything else Amon did ·is [Lis it not…?] written in the book of the
·history [chronicles; annals; 1:18] of the kings of Judah. 26He was buried in
his grave in the garden of Uzza, and his son Josiah became king in his place.

Josiah King of Judah
(22:1–20; 2 Chr. 34:1–3, 8–28)

22 Josiah was eight years old when he became king, and he
·ruled [reigned] thirty-one years in Jerusalem. His mother's
name was Jedidah daughter of Adaiah, who was from Bozkath. 2Josiah
did ·what the LORD said was right [Lright in the eyes/sight of the LORD].
He ·lived [Lwalked] as his ·ancestor [father] David had ·lived [Lwalked],
and he did not ·stop doing what was right [turn aside/deviate to the right
or to the left].
3In Josiah's eighteenth year as king, he sent Shaphan to the ·Temple
[Lhouse] of the LORD. Shaphan son of Azaliah, the son of Meshullam, was
the royal secretary. Josiah said, 4"Go up to Hilkiah the high priest, and
have him ·empty [count] out the money the ·gatekeepers [doorkeepers]
have ·gathered [collected] from the people. This is the money they have
brought into the ·Temple [Lhouse] of the LORD. 5Have him ·give [entrust]
the money to the supervisors of the work on the ·Temple [Lhouse] of the
LORD. They must pay the workers who ·repair [restore] the ·Temple
[Lhouse] of the LORD—6the carpenters, builders, and ·bricklayers
[masons]. Also use the money to buy timber and ·cut [finished; dressed]
stone to ·repair [restore] the ·Temple [Lhouse]. 7They do not need to
·report [account for] how they use the money given to them, because they
are working ·honestly [faithfully; conscientiously; 12:15]."

The Book of the Teachings Is Found

8Hilkiah the high priest said to Shaphan the royal secretary, "I've found
the Book of the ·Teachings [Law; Ltorah] in the ·Temple [Lhouse] of the
LORD." He gave it to Shaphan, who read it.
9Then Shaphan the royal secretary went to the king and reported to
Josiah, "Your ·officers [officials] have ·paid [emptied] out the money that
was in the ·Temple [Lhouse] of the LORD. They have ·given [entrusted] it
to the workers and supervisors at the ·Temple [Lhouse]." 10Then Shaphan
the royal secretary told the king, "Hilkiah the priest has given me a ·book
[scroll]." And Shaphan read from the ·book [scroll] to the king.
11When the king heard the words of the Book of the ·Teachings [Law;
Ltorah], he tore his clothes [Ca sign of mourning or distress]. 12He gave
orders to Hilkiah the priest, Ahikam son of Shaphan, Acbor son of
Micaiah, Shaphan the royal secretary, and Asaiah the king's servant.
These were the orders: 13"Go and ·ask [inquire of] the LORD about the
words in the ·book [scroll] that was found. Ask for me, for all the people,
and for all Judah. The LORD's anger is burning ·greatly [fiercely] against
us, because our ·ancestors [fathers] did not ·obey [listen to] the words of
this ·book [scroll]; they did not do all the things written ·for us to do
[concerning us]."
14So Hilkiah the priest, Ahikam, Acbor, Shaphan, and Asaiah went to
talk to Huldah the prophetess. She was the wife of Shallum son of Tikvah,
the son of Harhas, who took care of the king's ·clothes [wardrobe].
Huldah lived in Jerusalem, in the ·new area [New Quarter] of the city.
15She said to them, "·This is what the LORD, the God of Israel, says
[TThus says the LORD, the God of Israel]: Tell the man who sent you to me,
16'This is what the LORD says: I will bring ·trouble to [disaster/evil on] this

place and to the people living here, ·as it is written [Lin accordance with the words] in the ·book [scroll] which the king of Judah has read. 17The people of Judah have ·left [abandoned; forsaken] me and have burned incense to other gods. They have ·made me angry [aroused/provoked me to anger] by all that they have done. My anger burns against this place, and it will not be ·put out [quenched].' 18Tell the king of Judah, who sent you to ·ask [seek; inquire of] the LORD, 'This is what the LORD, the God of Israel, says about the words you heard: 19When you heard ·my words [what I spoke] against this place and its people, ·you became sorry for what you had done [your heart was touched/responsive/penitent/tender] and humbled yourself before me. I said they would be cursed and ·would be destroyed [desolated]. You tore your clothes [Ca sign of mourning or distress], and you ·cried in my presence [wept before me]. This is why I have heard you, says the LORD. 20So I will ·let you die [Lgather you to your fathers/ancestors], and you will be ·buried [Lgathered to your grave] in peace. You won't see all the ·trouble [disaster; evil] I will bring to this place.'"

So they took her message back to the king.

The People Hear the Agreement

(23:1–20; 2 Chr. 34:4–7, 29–33)

23 Then the king ·gathered [summoned] all the elders of Judah and Jerusalem together. 2He went up to the ·Temple [Lhouse] of the LORD, and all the people from Judah and Jerusalem went with him. The priests, prophets, and all the people—·from the least important to the most important [both small/low and great/high]—went with him. He read to them all the words of the Book of the ·Agreement [Treaty; Covenant] that was found in the ·Temple [Lhouse] of the LORD. 3The king stood by the pillar and made an ·agreement [covenant; treaty] ·in the presence of [before] the LORD to follow the LORD and obey his commands, rules, and laws with his whole being, and to obey the words of the ·agreement [covenant; treaty] written in this ·book [scroll]. Then all the people ·promised to obey [pledged themselves to; entered into] the ·agreement [covenant; treaty].

Josiah Destroys the Places for Idol Worship

4The king commanded Hilkiah the high priest and the priests of the ·next rank [second order] and the ·gatekeepers [doorkeepers] to bring out of the ·Temple [Lhouse] of the LORD ·everything [all the vessels/articles] made for Baal, Asherah, and all the ·stars of the sky [powers/hosts of heaven]. Then Josiah burned them outside Jerusalem in the ·open country [fields; terraces] of the Kidron Valley and carried their ashes to Bethel. 5The kings of Judah had ·chosen [appointed] priests for these gods. These priests burned incense in the ·places where gods were worshiped [Lhigh places; 12:3] in the cities of Judah and the ·towns [area] around Jerusalem. They burned incense to Baal, the sun, the moon, the ·planets [constellations], and all the ·stars of the sky [hosts/powers of heaven]. But Josiah ·took those priests away [did away with/*or* exterminated those priests]. 6He removed the Asherah ·idol [pole; Ca sacred tree or pole dedicated to the goddess Asherah; 13:6] from the ·Temple [Lhouse] of the LORD and took it outside Jerusalem to the Kidron Valley, where he burned it and ·beat [ground] it into dust. Then he threw the dust on the graves of the common people. 7He also tore down the houses of the male prostitutes [1 Kin. 14:24] who were in the ·Temple [Lhouse] of the LORD, where the women ·did weaving [wove hangings/coverings/veils] for Asherah.

8King Josiah brought all the false priests from the cities of Judah. He ·ruined [desecrated; defiled] the ·places where gods were worshiped

[Lhigh places; 12:3], where the priests had burned incense, from Geba to
Beersheba. He destroyed the ·places of worship [Lhigh places; 12:3] at the
entrance to the Gate of Joshua, the ·ruler [governor] of the city, on the left
side of the city gate. 9The priests at the ·places where gods were worshiped
[Lhigh places; 12:3] were not allowed to ·serve [officiate; Lgo up] at the
LORD's altar in Jerusalem. But they could eat ·bread made without yeast
[unleaven bread] with their ·brothers [fellow priests].

10Josiah ·ruined [desecrated; defiled] Topheth, in the Valley of Ben
Hinnom, so no one could ·sacrifice [Lpass through the fire] his son or daughter to Molech. 11Judah's kings had ·placed [dedicated] horses to the sun at
the front door of the ·Temple [Lhouse] of the LORD in the courtyard near the
room of Nathan-Melech, an ·officer [official]. Josiah removed them and
burned the chariots that were ·for sun worship also [dedicated to the sun].

12The kings of Judah had built altars on the ·roof [Croofs were flat and
served as an extra room] of the ·upstairs [upper] room of Ahaz. Josiah
·broke down [destroyed] these altars and the altars Manasseh had made
in the two courtyards of the ·Temple [Lhouse] of the LORD. Josiah smashed
them to pieces and threw their ·dust [rubble] into the Kidron Valley.
13King Josiah ·ruined [desecrated; defiled] the ·places where gods were
worshiped [Lhigh places; 12:3] east of Jerusalem, south of the Mount of
·Olives [*or* Corruption; *or* Destruction; Cso called because of the pagan
sites]. Solomon king of Israel had built these places. One was for
Ashtoreth, the ·hated goddess [detestable thing; Tabomination] of the
Sidonians. One was for Chemosh, the ·hated god [detestable thing;
Tabomination] of Moab. And one was for Molech, the ·hated god [detest-
able thing; Tabomination] of the Ammonites. 14Josiah smashed to pieces
the ·stone [sacred] pillars they worshiped, and he cut down the Asherah
·idols [poles; Ca sacred tree or pole dedicated to the goddess Asherah;
13:6]. Then he covered the places with human bones.

15Josiah also ·broke down [demolished] the altar at Bethel—the ·place
of worship [high place; 12:3] made by Jeroboam son of Nebat, who had
led Israel to sin. Josiah burned that place, broke the stones of the altar
into pieces, then ·beat [ground] them into dust. He also burned the
Asherah ·idol [pole; 13:6]. 16When he turned around, he saw the ·graves
[tombs] on the ·mountain [hillside]. He had the bones taken from the
graves, and he burned them on the altar to ·ruin [desecrate; defile] it. This
happened ·as the LORD had said it would [Lin accordance with the word of
the LORD proclaimed] through the man of God [1 Kin. 13:1–3].

17Josiah asked, "What is that monument I see?"

The people of the city answered, "It's the grave of the man of God who
came from Judah. This prophet announced the things you have done
against the altar ·of [at] Bethel."

18Josiah said, "Leave the grave alone. No one may ·move [disturb] this
man's bones." So they left his bones and the bones of the prophet who
had come from Samaria.

19The kings of Israel had built ·temples for worshiping gods [shrines/
Lhouses at the high places; 12:3] in the cities of Samaria, which had ·caused
the LORD to be angry [aroused/provoked the LORD to anger]. Josiah
removed all those ·temples [shrines; Lhouses] and did the same things as
he had done at Bethel. 20He ·killed [slaughtered] all the priests of ·those
places of worship [the high places; 12:3]; he killed them on the altars and
burned human bones on the altars. Then he went back to Jerusalem.

Josiah Celebrates the Passover
(23:21–30; 2 Chr. 35:1–27)

21The king commanded all the people, "·Celebrate [Observe] the Passover to the LORD your God as it is written in this Book of the ·Agreement [Treaty; Covenant; Ex. 12]." 22The Passover had not been ·celebrated [observed] like this since the judges ·led [ruled; judged] Israel. Nor had one like it happened ·while there were [in all the days/years of the] kings of Israel and kings of Judah. 23This Passover was ·celebrated [observed] to the LORD in Jerusalem in the eighteenth year of King Josiah's rule.

24Josiah ·destroyed [removed; got rid of] the mediums, ·fortune-tellers [spiritualists], house gods, and idols. He also ·destroyed [removed; got rid of] all the ·hated gods [detestable/abominable practices] seen in the land of Judah and Jerusalem. This was to ·obey [fulfill; confirm] the words of the ·teachings [law; Ltorah] written in the ·book [scroll] Hilkiah the priest had found in the ·Temple [Lhouse] of the LORD.

25There was no king like Josiah before or after him. He ·obeyed [Lturned to] the LORD with all his heart, soul, and strength [cf. Mark 12:30, 33; Luke 10:27], following all the ·Teachings [Law; Ltorah] of Moses.

26Even so, the LORD did not ·stop [Lturn from] ·his strong and terrible [Lthe heat of his great] anger. His anger burned against Judah because of all Manasseh had done to ·make him angry [provoke/arouse him to anger]. 27The LORD said, "I will ·send [remove] Judah out of my sight, as I have ·sent Israel away [removed Israel]. I will ·reject [cast away] Jerusalem, which I chose. And I will take away the ·Temple [Lhouse] about which I said, '·I will be worshiped [LMy name will be] there.' "

28Everything else Josiah did ·is [Lis it not…?] written in the book of the ·history [chronicles; annals; 1:18] of the kings of Judah.

29While Josiah was king, Pharaoh Neco king of Egypt went to help the king of Assyria at the Euphrates River. King Josiah marched out to fight against Neco, but at Megiddo, Neco ·faced [met] him and killed him. 30Josiah's ·servants [officers] carried his body in a chariot from Megiddo to Jerusalem and buried him in his own ·grave [tomb]. Then the people of Judah ·chose [took] Josiah's son Jehoahaz and ·poured olive oil on [anointed] him to make him king in his father's place.

Jehoahaz King of Judah
(23:30–24:7; 2 Chr. 36:1–8)

31Jehoahaz was twenty-three years old when he became king, and he ·was king [reigned] in Jerusalem for three months. His mother's name was Hamutal, who was the daughter of Jeremiah from Libnah. 32Jehoahaz did ·what the LORD said was wrong [Levil in the eyes/sight of the LORD], just as his ·ancestors [fathers] had done.

33·King [LPharaoh] Neco took Jehoahaz prisoner at Riblah in the land of Hamath so that Jehoahaz could not ·rule [reign] in Jerusalem. Neco ·made the people of Judah pay about [imposed a tribute of] ·seventy-five hundred pounds [Lone hundred talents] of silver and ·about seventy-five pounds [La talent] of gold.

34·King [LPharaoh] Neco made Josiah's son Eliakim the king in place of Josiah his father. Then Neco changed Eliakim's name to Jehoiakim [CEliakim means "God has established"; Jehoiakim means "Yahweh has established"; changing Eliakim's name was a way Pharaoh asserted his authority over him]. But Neco took Jehoahaz to Egypt, where he died. 35Jehoiakim gave ·King Neco [LPharaoh] the silver and gold he demanded. Jehoiakim taxed the land and took silver and gold from the people of the land to give to ·King [LPharaoh] Neco. Each person had to pay ·his share [according to his wealth/assessment].

Jehoiakim King of Judah

36Jehoiakim was twenty-five years old when he became king, and he
was king in Jerusalem for eleven years. His mother's name was Zebidah
daughter of Pedaiah, who was from Rumah. 37Jehoiakim did ·what the
LORD said was wrong [Levil in the eyes/sight of the LORD], just as his ·ances-
tors [fathers] had done.

24 While Jehoiakim was king, Nebuchadnezzar king of Babylon
attacked the land of Judah. So Jehoiakim became Nebuchadnezzar's ·servant [vassal] for three years. Then he turned against
Nebuchadnezzar and ·broke away from his rule [rebelled]. 2The LORD sent
raiding ·parties [bands] from Babylon, Aram, Moab, and Ammon against
Jehoiakim to destroy Judah. This happened ·as the LORD had said it
would [Lin accordance with the word of the LORD spoken] through his
servants the prophets.
3The LORD commanded this to happen to the people of Judah, to
remove them from his ·presence [sight], because of all the sins of
Manasseh. 4He had killed many innocent people and had filled Jerusalem
with their blood. And the LORD would not forgive these sins.
5The other things that happened while Jehoiakim was king and all he
did ·are [Lare they not…?] written in the book of the ·history [chronicles;
annals; 1:18] of the kings of Judah. 6Jehoiakim ·died [Llay down/Tslept with
his fathers/ancestors], and his son Jehoiachin became king in his place.
7The king of Egypt did not ·leave [march/venture out from] his land
again, because the king of Babylon had captured all that belonged to the
king of Egypt, from the brook of Egypt to the Euphrates River.

Jehoiachin King of Judah

(24:8–17; 2 Chr. 36:9–10)

8Jehoiachin was eighteen years old when he became king, and he ·was
king [reigned] three months in Jerusalem. His mother's name was
Nehushta daughter of Elnathan from Jerusalem. 9Jehoiachin did ·what
the LORD said was wrong [Levil in the eyes/sight of the LORD], just as his
father had done.
10At that time the officers of Nebuchadnezzar king of Babylon came up
to Jerusalem. When they reached the city, they ·attacked [besieged] it.
11Nebuchadnezzar himself came to the city while his officers were ·attack-
ing [besieging] it. 12Jehoiachin king of Judah surrendered to the king of
Babylon, along with Jehoiachin's mother, servants, nobles, and ·officers
[officials]. So Nebuchadnezzar made Jehoiachin a prisoner in the eighth
year he was king of Babylon. 13Nebuchadnezzar ·took [carried off] all the
treasures from the ·Temple [Lhouse] of the LORD and from the ·palace
[Lking's house]. He ·cut up [stripped away] all the gold ·objects [vessels;
articles] Solomon king of Israel had made for the ·Temple [Lhouse] of the
LORD. This happened as the LORD had said it would. 14Nebuchadnezzar
took ·away [into exile] all the people of Jerusalem, including all the ·lead-
ers [commanders], all the ·wealthy people [nobles; *or* warriors], and all
the craftsmen and ·metal workers [artisans]. There were ten thousand
·prisoners [captives] in all. Only the poorest people in the land were left.
15Nebuchadnezzar carried away Jehoiachin to Babylon, as well as the
king's mother and his wives, the ·officers [officials], and the ·leading men
[elite] of the land. They were taken ·captive [into exile] from Jerusalem to
Babylon. 16The king of Babylon also ·took [exiled] all seven thousand
·soldiers [Lmen of valor], who were strong and ·able to fight in [fit for]
war, and about a thousand craftsmen and ·metal workers [artisans].
Nebuchadnezzar ·took [exiled] them as ·prisoners [captives] to Babylon.

17 Then he made Mattaniah, Jehoiachin's uncle, king in Jehoiachin's place. He also changed Mattaniah's name to Zedekiah.

Zedekiah King of Judah

(24:18–20; 2 Chr. 36:11–21; Jer. 52:1–3)

18 Zedekiah was twenty-one years old when he became king, and he ·was king [reigned] in Jerusalem for eleven years. His mother's name was Hamutal daughter of Jeremiah [Cnot the prophet Jeremiah] from Libnah. 19 Zedekiah did ·what the LORD said was wrong [Levil in the eyes/sight of the LORD], just as Jehoiakim had done. 20 All this happened in Jerusalem and Judah because the LORD was angry with them. Finally, he ·threw [banished; cast] them out of his presence.

Zedekiah ·turned [rebelled] against the king of Babylon.

The Fall of Jerusalem

(25:1–17; Jer. 39:1–10, 42:4–23)

25 Nebuchadnezzar king of Babylon marched against Jerusalem with his whole army during Zedekiah's ninth year as king, on the tenth day of the tenth month [CJanuary 15, 588 BC]. He made a camp around the city and ·piled dirt against the city walls to attack it [built siege walls all around it]. 2 The city was under ·attack [siege] until Zedekiah's eleventh year as king. 3 By ·the ninth day of the fourth month [CJuly 18, 586 BC], the ·hunger [famine] was ·terrible [severe] in the city. There was no food for the people to eat. 4 Then the wall of the city was breached, and the whole army ran away at night through the gate between the two walls by the king's garden. ·While [Though] the Babylonians were still surrounding the city, Zedekiah and his men ran away toward the ·Jordan Valley [LArabah; Ca plain near Jericho, east of Jerusalem]. 5 But the Babylonian army chased King Zedekiah and caught up with him in the plains of Jericho. All of his army ·was scattered from [deserted] him, 6 so they captured Zedekiah and took him to the king of Babylon at Riblah. There he passed sentence on Zedekiah. 7 They ·killed [slaughtered] Zedekiah's sons as he watched. Then they ·put [gouged] out his eyes and put bronze ·chains [shackles] on him and took him to Babylon.

8 Nebuzaradan was the commander of the king's special guards. This officer of the king of Babylon came to Jerusalem on ·the seventh day of the fifth month [CAugust 14, 586 BC], in Nebuchadnezzar's nineteenth year as king of Babylon. 9 Nebuzaradan ·set fire to [burned down] the ·Temple [Lhouse] of the LORD and the ·palace [Lking's house] and all the houses of Jerusalem. Every important building was burned.

10 The whole Babylonian army, led by the commander of the king's special guards, ·broke down [demolished] the walls around Jerusalem. 11 Nebuzaradan, the commander of the guards, ·captured [carried into exile] the people left in Jerusalem, those who had ·surrendered [deserted] to the king of Babylon, and the rest of the people. 12 But the commander of the guard left behind some of the poorest people of the land to ·take care of [work] the vineyards and fields.

13 The Babylonians broke up the bronze pillars, the bronze stands, and the large bronze ·bowl [basin] called the Sea [1 Kin. 7:23–45] in the ·Temple [Lhouse] of the LORD. Then they carried the bronze to Babylon. 14 They also took the pots, shovels, ·wick trimmers [snuffers], dishes, and all the bronze objects used to serve in the ·Temple [Lhouse]. 15 The commander of the king's special guards took away the ·pans for carrying hot coals [censers], the ·bowls [basins], and everything made of ·pure [fine] gold or silver. 16 There were two pillars and the large bronze Sea and the ·movable stands [water carts] which Solomon had made for the ·Temple [Lhouse] of the LORD. There was so much bronze that it could not be

weighed. 17Each pillar was ·about twenty-seven feet [Leighteen cubits; 1 Kin. 7:15–20] high. The bronze capital on top of the pillar was ·about four and one-half feet [Lthree cubits] high. It was decorated with a ·net design and [latticework/network of] bronze pomegranates all around it. The other pillar also had a ·net design [latticework; network] and was like the first pillar.

Judah Is Taken Prisoner
(25:18–21; Jer. 52:24–27)

18The commander of the guards took some ·prisoners [captives]—Seraiah the chief priest, Zephaniah the priest next in rank, and the three ·doorkeepers [gatekeepers]. 19Of the people who were still in the city, he took the officer in charge of the ·fighting men [soldiers], as well as five advisors to the king. He took the royal secretary who ·selected [conscripted] people for the army and sixty other men who were in the city. 20Nebuzaradan, the commander, took all these people and brought them to the king of Babylon at Riblah. 21There at Riblah, in the land of Hamath, the king had them killed. So the people of Judah were ·led away from their country as captives [sent into exile from their land].

Gedaliah Becomes Governor
(25:22–26; Jer. 52:28–30)

22Nebuchadnezzar king of Babylon left some people in the land of Judah. He appointed Gedaliah son of Ahikam, the son of Shaphan, as governor.

23The army captains and their men heard that the king of Babylon had made Gedaliah governor, so they came to Gedaliah at Mizpah. They were Ishmael son of Nethaniah, Johanan son of Kareah, Seraiah son of Tanhumeth the Netophathite, Jaazaniah son of the Maacathite, and their men. 24Then Gedaliah ·promised [vowed/swore to] these army captains and their men, "Don't be afraid of the Babylonian ·officers [officials]. Live in the land and serve the king of Babylon, and everything will go well for you."

25In ·the seventh month [mid-autumn] Ishmael son of Nethaniah, son of Elishama from the king's family, came with ten men and ·killed [assassinated; murdered] Gedaliah. They also killed the men of Judah and Babylon who were with Gedaliah at Mizpah. 26Then all the people, ·from the least important to the most important [both great/high and small/low], along with the army leaders, ran away to Egypt, because they were afraid of the Babylonians.

Jehoiachin Is Set Free
(25:27–30; Jer. 52:31–34)

27Jehoiachin king of Judah was ·held [exiled] in Babylon for thirty-seven years. In the thirty-seventh year Evil-Merodach became king of Babylon, and he let Jehoiachin out of prison on ·the twenty-seventh day of the twelfth month [CApril 2]. 28Evil-Merodach spoke kindly to Jehoiachin and gave him a seat of honor above the seats of the other kings who were with him in Babylon. 29So Jehoiachin put ·away [aside] his prison clothes. For ·the rest [Lall the days] of his life, he ate ·at [in] the king's ·table [presence]. 30Every day, for as long as Jehoiachin lived, the king gave him an allowance.

1 CHRONICLES

From Adam to Abraham

1 Adam was the father of Seth [C“was the father of” is added in
verses 1–4; the Hebrew simply lists names; “father” can also
mean “ancestor”]. Seth was the father of Enosh. Enosh was the father
of Kenan. 2Kenan was the father of Mahalalel. Mahalalel was the father
of Jared. Jared was the father of Enoch. 3Enoch was the father of
Methuselah. Methuselah was the father of Lamech, and Lamech was
the father of Noah.

4The sons of Noah were Shem, Ham, and Japheth.

5Japheth’s sons were Gomer, Magog, Madai, Javan, Tubal, Meshech,
and Tiras.

6Gomer’s sons were Ashkenaz, ·Riphath [*or* Diphath; Gen. 10:3], and
Togarmah.

7Javan’s sons were Elishah, Tarshish, Kittim [Chis descendants were the
people of Cyprus], and ·Rodanim [*or* Dodanim; Gen. 10:4].

8Ham’s sons were Cush, Mizraim [Canother name for Egypt], Put, and
Canaan.

9Cush’s sons were Seba, Havilah, Sabta, Raamah, and Sabteca.

Raamah’s sons were Sheba and Dedan.

10Cush was the father of Nimrod, who ·grew up [was the first] to
become a mighty warrior on the earth [Gen. 10:8–12].

11Mizraim was the father of the Ludites, Anamites, Lehabites, and
Naphtuhites,

12Pathrusites, Casluhites, and Caphtorites. (The Philistines came from
the Casluhites.)

13Canaan’s first child was Sidon. He was also the father of the Hittites,
14Jebusites, Amorites, Girgashites, 15Hivites, Arkites, Sinites, 16Arvadites,
Zemarites, and Hamathites.

17Shem’s sons were Elam, Asshur, Arphaxad, Lud, and Aram.

Aram’s sons were Uz, Hul, Gether, and ·Meshech [*or* Mash; Gen. 10:23].

18·Arpachshad [*or* Arphaxad] was the father of Shelah, who was the
father of Eber.

19Eber had two sons. One son was named Peleg [C“divided”], because
the people on the earth were divided [Cinto different language groups or
districts] during his ·life [Ldays]. Peleg’s brother was named Joktan.

20Joktan was the father of Almodad, Sheleph, Hazarmaveth, Jerah,
21Hadoram, Uzal, Diklah, 22·Obal [*or* Ebal; Gen. 10:28], Abimael, Sheba,
23Ophir, Havilah, and Jobab. All these were Joktan’s sons. 24The ·family
[clan] line included Shem, ·Arphaxad [*or* Arpachshad], Shelah, 25Eber,
Peleg, Reu, 26Serug, Nahor, Terah, 27and Abram, who was called [Clater]
Abraham [Gen. 17:5–6].

Abraham's Family

28 Abraham's sons were Isaac and Ishmael. 29 These ·were the sons [are
the descendants/genealogies] of Isaac and Ishmael. Ishmael's ·first son
[firstborn] was Nebaioth. His other sons were Kedar, Adbeel, Mibsam,
30 Mishma, Dumah, Massa, Hadad, Tema, 31 Jetur, Naphish, and Kedemah.
These were Ishmael's sons. 32 Keturah, Abraham's ·slave woman [concu-
bine; C a secondary wife], gave birth to Zimran, Jokshan, Medan, Midian,
Ishbak, and Shuah.

Jokshan's sons were Sheba and Dedan.

33 Midian's sons were Ephah, Epher, Hanoch, Abida, and Eldaah. All
these were descendants of Keturah [Gen. 25:1–4].

34 Abraham was the father of Isaac, and Isaac's sons were Esau and Israel.

35 Esau's sons were Eliphaz, Reuel, Jeush, Jalam, and Korah.

36 Eliphaz's sons were Teman, Omar, ·Zephi [*or* Zepho; Gen. 36:11],
Gatam, Kenaz, Timna, and Amalek.

37 Reuel's sons were Nahath, Zerah, Shammah, and Mizzah.

The Edomites from Seir

38 Seir's sons were Lotan, Shobal, Zibeon, Anah, Dishon, Ezer, and
Dishan.

39 Lotan's sons were Hori and Homam, and his sister was Timna.

40 Shobal's sons were ·Alian [*or* Alvan; Gen. 36:23], Manahath, Ebal,
·Shepho [*or* Shephi; Gen. 36:23], and Onam.

Zibeon's sons were Aiah and Anah.

41 Anah's son was Dishon.

Dishon's sons were ·Hemdan [*or* Hamran; Gen. 36:26], Eshban, Ithran,
and Keran.

42 Ezer's sons were Bilhan, Zaavan, and ·Akan [*or* Jaakan; Gen. 36:27].

Dishan's sons were Uz and Aran.

The Kings of Edom

43 These kings ·ruled [reigned] in Edom before there were kings in
Israel [Gen. 36:31–39]. Bela son of Beor was king of Edom, and his city
was named Dinhabah.

44 When Bela died, Jobab son of Zerah became king. He was from Bozrah.

45 When Jobab died, Husham became king. He was from the land of the
Temanites.

46 When Husham died, Hadad son of Bedad became king, and his city
was named Avith. Hadad defeated Midian in the ·country [land; plains;
field] of Moab.

47 When Hadad died, Samlah became king. He was from Masrekah.

48 When Samlah died, Shaul became king. He was from Rehoboth ·by
[on; near] the river [C perhaps the Euphrates River].

49 When Shaul died, Baal-Hanan son of Acbor became king.

50 When Baal-Hanan died, Hadad became king, and his city was named
·Pau [Pai]. Hadad's wife was named Mehetabel, and she was the daughter
of Matred, who was the daughter of Me-Zahab. 51 Then Hadad died.

The ·leaders of the family groups [clan/tribal leaders; chiefs] of Edom
were Timna, Alvah, Jetheth, 52 Oholibamah, Elah, Pinon, 53 Kenaz, ·Teman
[*or* Temam; Gen. 36:42], Mibzar, 54 Magdiel, and Iram. These were the
·leaders [clan/tribal leaders; chiefs] of Edom.

Israel's Family

2 The sons of Israel [C another name for Jacob] were Reuben,
Simeon, Levi, Judah, Issachar, Zebulun, 2 Dan, Joseph, Benjamin,
Naphtali, Gad, and Asher.

Judah's Family

3 Judah's sons were Er, Onan, and Shelah. A Canaanite woman, ·the
daughter of Shua [*or* Bath-shua], was their mother. Judah's ·first son
[firstborn], Er, did ·what the LORD said was wicked [L evil in the LORD's
sight/eyes], so the LORD ·put him to death [killed him]. 4 Judah's daughter-
in-law Tamar gave birth to Perez and Zerah, giving Judah five sons in all
[Gen. 38].
5 Perez's sons were Hezron and Hamul.
6 Zerah had five sons: Zimri, Ethan, Heman, Calcol, and ·Darda [*or*
Dara; 1 Kin. 4:31].
7 Carmi's son was ·Achan [*or* Achar; C "disaster"; Josh. 7:1], ·who caused
trouble for [the troubler of] Israel because he ·took [stole] ·things [plun-
der] that had been ·given to the LORD to be destroyed [set apart/devoted
to the LORD; Josh. 7:16–26].
8 Ethan's son was Azariah.
9 Hezron's sons were Jerahmeel, Ram, and ·Caleb [Chelubai; v. 18].
10 Ram was Amminadab's father, and Amminadab was Nahshon's
father. Nahshon was the leader of the ·people [L sons] of Judah. 11 Nahshon
was the father of ·Salmon [*or* Salma; Ruth 4:21], who was the father of
Boaz. 12 Boaz was the father of Obed, and Obed was the father of Jesse.
13 Jesse's ·first son [firstborn] was Eliab. His second son was Abinadab,
his third was Shimea, 14 his fourth was Nethanel, his fifth was Raddai,
15 his sixth was Ozem, and his seventh son was David. 16 Their sisters were
Zeruiah and Abigail. Zeruiah's three sons were ·Abishai [*or* Abshai; 2 Sam.
2:18], Joab, and Asahel. 17 Abigail ·was the mother of [L gave birth to]
Amasa, and his father was Jether, an Ishmaelite.

Caleb's Family

18 Caleb son of Hezron ·had [fathered] children by his wife Azubah and
by Jerioth [C possibly two names for the same woman]. Caleb and Azubah's
sons were Jesher, Shobab, and Ardon. 19 When Azubah died, Caleb married Ephrath. They ·had [L gave birth to] a son named Hur, 20 who was the
father of Uri, who was the father of Bezalel.
21 Later, when Hezron was sixty years old, he married the daughter of
Makir, Gilead's father. Hezron ·had sexual relations with [L went in to]
Makir's daughter, and she ·had [L gave birth to] a son named Segub.
22 Segub was the father of Jair. Jair ·controlled [held; owned; ruled] twenty-
three cities in the ·country [land; territory] of Gilead. 23 (But Geshur and
Aram ·captured [took] the Towns of Jair, as well as Kenath and the ·small
towns [villages] around it—sixty towns in all.) All these were descendants of Makir, the father of Gilead.
24 After Hezron died ·in Caleb Ephrathah, his wife Abijah [*or* Caleb had
sexual relations with Ephrath, his father Hezron's wife, and she] ·had [L gave
birth to] his son, named Ashhur. Ashhur became the father of Tekoa.

Jerahmeel's Family

25 Hezron's ·first son [firstborn] was Jerahmeel. Jerahmeel's sons were
Ram, Bunah, Oren, Ozem, and Ahijah. Ram was Jerahmeel's ·first son
[firstborn]. 26 Jerahmeel had another wife, named Atarah. She was the
mother of Onam.
27 Jerahmeel's ·first son [firstborn], Ram, had sons. They were Maaz,
Jamin, and Eker.
28 Onam's sons were Shammai and Jada.
Shammai's sons were Nadab and Abishur.
29 Abishur's wife was named Abihail, and ·their sons were [L she gave
birth to] Ahban and Molid.

30Nadab's sons were Seled and Appaim. Seled died without having
children.
31Appaim's son was Ishi, who became the father of Sheshan.
Sheshan was the father of Ahlai.
32Jada was Shammai's brother, and Jada's sons were Jether and
Jonathan. Jether died without having children.
33Jonathan's sons were Peleth and Zaza.
These were Jerahmeel's descendants.
34Sheshan did not have any sons, only daughters. He had a ·servant
[slave] from Egypt named Jarha. 35Sheshan let his daughter marry his
·servant [slave] Jarha, and she ·had [Lgave birth to] a son named Attai.
36Attai was the father of Nathan. Nathan was the father of Zabad.
37Zabad was the father of Ephlal. Ephlal was the father of Obed. 38Obed
was the father of Jehu. Jehu was the father of Azariah. 39Azariah was the
father of Helez. Helez was the father of Eleasah. 40Eleasah was the father
of Sismai. Sismai was the father of Shallum. 41Shallum was the father of
Jekamiah, and Jekamiah was the father of Elishama.

Caleb's Family

42Caleb was Jerahmeel's brother. Caleb's ·first son [firstborn] was Mesha.
Mesha was the father of Ziph, and his son Mareshah was the father of
Hebron.
43Hebron's sons were Korah, Tappuah, Rekem, and Shema. 44Shema
was the father of Raham, who was the father of Jorkeam. Rekem was the
father of Shammai. 45Shammai was the father of Maon, and Maon was
the father of Beth Zur. 46Caleb's ·slave woman [concubine; Ca secondary
wife] was named Ephah, and she ·was the mother of [Lgave birth to]
Haran, Moza, and Gazez. Haran was the father of Gazez.
47Jahdai's sons were Regem, Jotham, Geshan, Pelet, Ephah, and Shaaph.
48Caleb had another ·slave woman [concubine; Ca secondary wife]
named Maacah. She ·was the mother of [Lgave birth to] Sheber, Tirhanah,
49Shaaph, and Sheva. Shaaph was the father of Madmannah. Sheva was
the father of Macbenah and Gibea. Caleb's daughter was Acsah.
50-51These were Caleb's descendants: Caleb's son Hur was the ·first son
[firstborn] of his mother Ephrathah [Ccalled Ephrath in v. 19]. Hur's sons
were Shobal, Salma, and Hareph. Shobal was the father of Kiriath Jearim.
Salma was the father of Bethlehem. And Hareph was the father of Beth
Gader.
52Shobal was the father of Kiriath Jearim. Shobal's descendants were
Haroeh, half the Manahathites, 53and the ·family groups [clans] of Kiriath
Jearim: the Ithrites, Puthites, Shumathites, and Mishraites. The Zorathites
and the Eshtaolites ·came [descended; Lwent forth] from the Mishraite
people.
54Salma's descendants were Bethlehem, the Netophathites, Atroth Beth
Joab, half the Manahathites, and the Zorites. 55His descendants included
the families who lived at Jabez, who ·wrote and copied important papers
[were scribes]. They were called the Tirathites, Shimeathites, and
Sucathites and were from the Kenite ·family group [clan] who came from
Hammath. He was the father of the ·people living in [Lhouse of] Recab.

David's Family

(3:1–4; 2 Sam. 3:1–5)

3 These are David's sons who were born in Hebron. The first was
Amnon [2 Sam. 13], whose mother was Ahinoam from Jezreel.
The second son was Daniel, whose mother was Abigail from Carmel. 2The
third son was Absalom, whose mother was Maacah daughter of Talmai,

the king of Geshur. The fourth son was Adonijah [1 Kin. 1:5–27], whose mother was Haggith. 3The fifth son was Shephatiah, whose mother was Abital. The sixth son was Ithream, whose mother was Eglah. 4These six sons of David were born to him in Hebron, where David ruled for seven and one-half years.

David ruled in Jerusalem thirty-three years. 5These were his children who were born in Jerusalem: ·Shammua [*or* Shimea; 2 Sam. 5:14], Shobab, Nathan, and Solomon—the four children of David and ·Bathsheba [*or* Bathshua; 2 Sam. 12:24], Ammiel's daughter. 6-8David's other nine children were Ibhar, ·Elishua [*or* Elishama; [C]apparently not the same son as later in the list; 2 Sam. 5:16], ·Eliphelet [*or* Elpelet, 2 Sam. 5:16]; [C]apparently not the same son as at the end of this list], Nogah, Nepheg, Japhia, Elishama, Eliada, and Eliphelet. 9These were all of David's sons, except for those born to his ·slave women [concubines; [C]secondary wives]. Tamar was their sister.

The Kings of Judah

10Solomon's son was Rehoboam. Rehoboam's son was Abijah. Abijah's son was Asa. Asa's son was Jehoshaphat. 11Jehoshaphat's son was ·Jehoram [*or* Joram; [C]a variant of the same name]. ·Jehoram's [*or* Joram's] son was Ahaziah. Ahaziah's son was Joash. 12Joash's son was Amaziah. Amaziah's son was Azariah. Azariah's son was Jotham. 13Jotham's son was Ahaz. Ahaz's son was Hezekiah. Hezekiah's son was Manasseh. 14Manasseh's son was Amon, and Amon's son was Josiah.

15These were Josiah's sons: His ·first son [firstborn] was Johanan, his second was Jehoiakim, his third was Zedekiah, and his fourth was Shallum.

16Jehoiakim was ·followed [succeeded] by ·Jehoiachin [*or* Jeconiah], and he was ·followed by [succeeded by his son] Zedekiah.

David's Descendants After the Babylonian Captivity

17·Jehoiachin [*or* Jeconiah] was taken as a prisoner [2 Chr. 36:10]. His sons were Shealtiel, 18Malkiram, Pedaiah, Shenazzar, Jekamiah, Hoshama, and Nedabiah.

19Pedaiah's sons were Zerubbabel and Shimei.

Zerubbabel's sons were Meshullam and Hananiah, and their sister was Shelomith. 20Zerubbabel also had five other sons: Hashubah, Ohel, Berekiah, Hasadiah, and Jushab-Hesed.

21Hananiah's descendants were Pelatiah and ·Jeshaiah, and the sons of Rephaiah, Arnan, Obadiah, and Shecaniah [*or* his son Jeshaiah, and Jeshaiah's son Rephaiah, and Rephaiah's son Arnan, and Arnan's son Obadiah, and Obadiah's son Shecaniah].

22Shecaniah's son was Shemaiah. Shemaiah's sons were Hattush, Igal, Bariah, Neariah, and Shaphat. There were six in all.

23Neariah had three sons: Elioenai, Hizkiah, and Azrikam.

24Elioenai had seven sons: Hodaviah, Eliashib, Pelaiah, Akkub, Johanan, Delaiah, and Anani.

Other Family Groups of Judah

4 Judah's descendants were Perez, Hezron, Carmi, Hur, and Shobal. 2Reaiah was Shobal's son. Reaiah was the father of Jahath, and Jahath was the father of Ahumai and Lahad. They were the ·family groups [clans] of the Zorathite people.

3-4Hur was the ·oldest son [[L]firstborn] of Caleb and his wife Ephrathah. Hur was the ·leader [[L]father] of Bethlehem. His three sons were Etam, Penuel, and Ezer. Etam's sons were Jezreel, Ishma, and Idbash. They had a sister named Hazzelelponi. Penuel was the father of Gedor, and Ezer was the father of Hushah.

5Tekoa's father was Ashhur. Ashhur had two wives named Helah and Naarah.

6Naarah gave birth to Ahuzzam, Hepher, Temeni, and Haahashtari. These were the descendants of Naarah.

7Helah's sons were Zereth, Zohar, Ethnan, 8and Koz. Koz was the father of Anub, Hazzobebah, and the Aharhel ·family group [clan]. Aharhel was the son of Harum.

9There was a man named Jabez, who was more ·respected [honorable; honored; known] than his brothers. His mother named him Jabez [Csounds like the word for "pain"] because she said, "I was in much pain when I gave birth to him." 10Jabez ·prayed [called/cried out] to the God of Israel, "·Please [Oh that/If only you would] ·do good things for me [bless me] and ·give me more land [enlarge/extend/expand my territory/border]. ·Stay [Keep your hand] with me, and ·don't let anyone hurt me [keep me from harm/trouble]. ·Then [...so that] I ·won't have any [will be free from/not have to endure] pain." And God ·did what Jabez had asked [granted/answered his request/prayer].

11Kelub, Shuhah's brother, was the father of Mehir. Mehir was the father of Eshton. 12Eshton was the father of Beth Rapha, Paseah, and Tehinnah. Tehinnah was the father of the people from the town of Nahash. These ·people were [are the men/descendants] from Recah.

13The sons of Kenaz were Othniel and Seraiah.

Othniel's sons were Hathath and Meonothai. 14Meonothai was the father of Ophrah.

Seraiah was the father of Joab. Joab was the ·ancestor of the people from [father/founder of] ·Craftsmen's Valley [LGeharashim], named that because they were ·craftsmen [artisans].

15Caleb was Jephunneh's son. Caleb's sons were Iru, Elah, and Naam. Elah's son was Kenaz.

16Jehallelel's sons were Ziph, Ziphah, Tiria, and Asarel.

17-18Ezrah's sons were Jether, Mered, Epher, and Jalon. Mered married Bithiah, the daughter of the king of Egypt. The children of Mered and Bithiah were Miriam, Shammai, and Ishbah. Ishbah was the father of Eshtemoa. Mered also had a wife from Judah, who gave birth to Jered, Heber, and Jekuthiel. Jered became the father of Gedor. Heber became the father of Soco. And Jekuthiel became the father of Zanoah.

19Hodiah's wife was Naham's sister. The sons of Hodiah's wife were Eshtemoa and the father of Keilah. Keilah was from the Garmite people, and Eshtemoa was from the Maacathite people.

20Shimon's sons were Amnon, Rinnah, Ben-Hanan, and Tilon.

Ishi's sons were Zoheth and Ben-Zoheth.

21-22Shelah was Judah's son. Shelah's sons were Er, Laadah, Jokim, the men from Cozeba, Joash, and Saraph. Er was the father of Lecah. Laadah was the father of Mareshah and the ·family groups [clans] of linen workers at Beth Ashbea. Joash and Saraph ·ruled [*or* married] in Moab ·and Jashubi [*or* but returned to] Lehem. ·The writings about this family are very old [This is from the ancient records/traditions]. 23These sons of Shelah were potters. They lived in Netaim and Gederah and worked for the king.

Simeon's Children

24Simeon's sons were Nemuel, Jamin, Jarib, Zerah, and Shaul. 25Shaul's son was Shallum. Shallum's son was Mibsam. Mibsam's son was Mishma.

26Mishma's son was Hammuel. Hammuel's son was Zaccur. Zaccur's
son was Shimei. 27Shimei had sixteen sons and six daughters, but his
brothers did not have many children, so ·there were not as many people
in their family group as there were in [Ltheir clan did not grow large/mul-
tiply like the sons of] Judah.
28·Shimei's children [LThey] lived in Beersheba, Moladah, Hazar Shual,
29Bilhah, Ezem, Tolad, 30Bethuel, Hormah, Ziklag, 31Beth Marcaboth,
Hazar Susim, Beth Biri, and Shaaraim. They lived in these cities until
·David became king [David's reign]. 32The five villages near these cities
were Etam, Ain, Rimmon, Token, and Ashan. 33There were also other villages as far away as ·Baalath [Baal]. ·This is where they lived [These were
their settlements]. And they ·wrote the history of their family [kept genealogical records].
34-38The men in this list were leaders of their ·family groups [clans]:
Meshobab, Jamlech, Joshah son of Amaziah, Joel, Jehu son of Joshibiah
(Joshibiah was the son of Seraiah, who was the son of Asiel), Elioenai,
Jaakobah, Jeshohaiah, Asaiah, Adiel, Jesimiel, Benaiah, and Ziza. (Ziza
was the son of Shiphi, who was the son of Allon. Allon was the son of
Jedaiah, who was the son of Shimri. And Shimri was the son of Shemaiah.)
·These families [LTheir father's houses] grew very large. 39They went
·outside [to the entrance/outskirts of] the city of Gedor to the east side of
the valley to look for pasture for their flocks. 40They found ·rich [fertile]
and ·good [lush] pasture, and the land was ·open country [broad] and
·peaceful [undisturbed; untroubled] and quiet. Ham's descendants had
lived there ·in the past [formerly].
41These men ·who were [whose names are] listed came to Gedor while
Hezekiah was king of Judah. They ·fought against [attacked] the Hamites,
destroying their tents, and also ·against [attacked] the Meunites who
lived there, and ·completely destroyed them [*or* put them under a curse of
destruction]. So there are no Meunites there even today. Then these men
·began to live there [lived there in their place], because there was pasture
for their flocks. 42Ishi's sons, Pelatiah, Neariah, Rephaiah, and Uzziel, led
five hundred of the Simeonites and attacked ·the people living in the
mountains of Edom [Lthe hill country of Seir; *or* Mount Seir]. 43They
·killed [destroyed; defeated] the few Amalekites who were still alive. From
that time until now these Simeonites have lived in Edom.

Reuben's Children

5 Reuben was Israel's [CJacob's] ·first son [firstborn]. Reuben ·should
have received the special privileges of the oldest son [was the
firstborn], but he ·had sexual relations with his father's slave woman
[Ldefiled his father's bed; Gen. 35:22]. So ·those special privileges [that
birthright] were given to Joseph's sons. (Joseph was a son of Israel
[CJacob].) In the ·family history Reuben's name [genealogical record he]
is not listed as ·the first son [having the right of the firstborn]. 2Judah
became ·stronger than [predominant/prominent over] his brothers, and a
leader came from his family [Clikely referring to David]. But ·Joseph's
family received the privileges that belonged to the oldest son [the birthright belonged to Joseph]. 3Reuben was Israel's ·first son [firstborn].
Reuben's sons were Hanoch, Pallu, Hezron, and Carmi.
4These were the children of Joel: Shemaiah was Joel's son. Gog was
Shemaiah's son. Shimei was Gog's son. 5Micah was Shimei's son. Reaiah
was Micah's son. Baal was Reaiah's son. 6Beerah was Baal's son. Beerah

was a leader of the tribe of Reuben. Tiglath-pileser king of Assyria captured him and took him ·away [Linto exile/captivity].
7Joel's ·brothers [relatives; kinsmen] and all his ·family groups [clans]
are listed ·just as they are written in their family histories [according to
their genealogical records]: Jeiel was the ·first [leader; chief], then
Zechariah, 8and Bela. (Bela was the son of Azaz. Azaz was the son of
Shema, and Shema was the son of Joel.) They lived in the area ·of [that
stretches from] Aroer all the way to Nebo and Baal Meon. 9Bela's people
lived to the east—as far as the edge of the ·desert [wilderness], ·which is
beside [that stretches to] the Euphrates River—because they had ·too [so]
many cattle ·for [in] the land of Gilead.
10When Saul was king, Bela's people fought a war against the Hagrite
people ·and defeated them [Lwho fell by their hand]. Then Bela's people
lived in the ·tents [settlements] that had belonged to the Hagrites in all
the area east of Gilead.

Gad's Children

11The ·people from the tribe [Lsons] of Gad lived ·near [beside] the
Reubenites. The Gadites lived in the area of Bashan all the way to Salecah.
12Joel was the ·main leader [chief], Shapham was second, and then Janai
and Shaphat were leaders in Bashan.
13The seven ·relatives [brothers] in their ·families [clans] were Michael,
Meshullam, Sheba, Jorai, Jacan, Zia, and Eber. 14They were the descendants of Abihail. Abihail was Huri's son. Huri was Jaroah's son. Jaroah
was Gilead's son. Gilead was Michael's son. Michael was Jeshishai's son.
Jeshishai was Jahdo's son, and Jahdo was the son of Buz. 15Ahi was Abdiel's
son, and Abdiel was Guni's son. Ahi was the leader of their ·family [clans].
16The Gadites lived in Gilead, Bashan and the small towns around it, and
on all the pasturelands in the Plain of Sharon all the way to the borders.
17All these names were written in the ·family history [genealogical
records] of Gad during the time Jotham was king of Judah and Jeroboam
was king of Israel.

Soldiers Skilled in War

18There were forty-four thousand seven hundred sixty ·soldiers [able-
bodied/valiant men] from the tribes of Reuben and Gad and ·East [Lthe
half-tribe of] Manasseh who carried shields and swords and bows. They
were ·skilled in war [trained for battle]. 19They ·started [waged] a war
against the Hagrites and the people of Jetur, Naphish, and Nodab. 20The
men from the tribes of Manasseh, Reuben, and Gad ·prayed [cried out] to
God during the ·war [battle], asking him to help them. So he helped them
because they trusted him. He handed over to them the Hagrites and all
those who were with them. 21They took the animals that belonged to the
Hagrites: fifty thousand camels, two hundred fifty thousand sheep, and
two thousand donkeys. They also captured one hundred thousand people. 22Many Hagrites were killed because God helped the people of
Reuben, Gad, and Manasseh. Then they ·lived there [occupied their land/
territory] until ·Babylon captured them and took them away [Lthe exile/
captivity; 2 Chr. 36:17–21].

East Manasseh

23The many people of ·East [Lthe half-tribe of] Manasseh lived in the
area of Bashan all the way to Baal Hermon, Senir, and Mount Hermon.
24These were the ·family [clan] leaders: Epher, Ishi, Eliel, Azriel, Jeremiah,
Hodaviah, and Jahdiel. They were ·all strong, brave [mighty warriors/men of
valor], and ·famous men [men of reputation], and ·leaders in their families

[head of their clans]. [25]**But they ·sinned against** [were unfaithful to] **the God ·that their ancestors had worshiped** [Lof their fathers]. **They ·began worshiping** [Lprostituted themselves to] **the gods of the people in that land, ·and those were the people God was destroying** [whom God had destroyed before them]. [26]**So the God of Israel ·made Pul king of Assyria want to go to war** [Lstirred up the spirit of Pul king of Assyria]. **(Pul was also called Tiglath-pileser** [Cruled 744–727 BC].**) He ·captured** [carried into exile] **the people of Reuben, Gad, and ·East** [Lthe half-tribe of] **Manasseh, and he took them away to Halah, Habor, Hara, and near the Gozan River. They have lived there from that time until this day.**

Levi's Children

6 Levi's sons were Gershon, Kohath, and Merari.

[2]**Kohath's sons were Amram, Izhar, Hebron, and Uzziel.**

[3]**Amram's children were Aaron, Moses, and Miriam.**

Aaron's sons were Nadab, Abihu, Eleazar, and Ithamar [Ex. 6:23; Lev. 10:1]. [4]**Eleazar was the father of Phinehas** [Num. 25:7, 11; 31:6; Ps. 106:30]. **Phinehas was the father of Abishua.** [5]**Abishua was the father of Bukki. Bukki was the father of Uzzi.** [6]**Uzzi was the father of Zerahiah. Zerahiah was the father of Meraioth.** [7]**Meraioth was the father of Amariah. Amariah was the father of Ahitub.** [8]**Ahitub was the father of Zadok. Zadok was the father of Ahimaaz.** [9]**Ahimaaz was the father of Azariah. Azariah was the father of Johanan.** [10]**Johanan was the father of Azariah. (Azariah was a priest in the ·Temple** [Lhouse] **Solomon built in Jerusalem.)** [11]**Azariah was the father of Amariah. Amariah was the father of Ahitub.** [12]**Ahitub was the father of Zadok. Zadok was the father of Shallum.** [13]**Shallum was the father of Hilkiah. Hilkiah was the father of Azariah.** [14]**Azariah was the father of Seraiah, and Seraiah was the father of Jehozadak.**

[15]**Jehozadak ·was forced to leave his home** [went into exile] **when the LORD sent Judah and Jerusalem into ·captivity** [exile] **under Nebuchadnezzar** [2 Kin. 25:1–21; 2 Chr. 36:17–21].

[16]**Levi's sons were ·Gershon** [*or* Gershom; v. 1], **Kohath, and Merari.**

[17]**The names of ·Gershon's** [*or* Gershom's] **sons were Libni and Shimei.**

[18]**Kohath's sons were Amram, Izhar, Hebron, and Uzziel.**

[19]**Merari's sons were Mahli and Mushi.**

This is a list of the ·family groups [clans] **of Levi, ·listed by the name of the father of each group** [Lby their fathers].

[20]**·Gershon's** [*or* Gershom's; v. 16] **son was Libni. Libni's son was Jehath. Jehath's son was Zimmah.** [21]**Zimmah's son was Joah. Joah's son was Iddo. Iddo's son was Zerah. And Zerah's son was Jeatherai.**

[22]**Kohath's ·son** [descendant; Cthe list differs from v. 18] **was Amminadab. Amminadab's son was Korah. Korah's son was Assir.** [23]**Assir's son was Elkanah. Elkanah's son was Ebiasaph. Ebiasaph's son was Assir.** [24]**Assir's son was Tahath. Tahath's son was Uriel. Uriel's son was Uzziah, and Uzziah's son was Shaul.**

[25]**Elkanah's sons were Amasai and Ahimoth.** [26]**Ahimoth's son was Elkanah. Elkanah's son was Zophai. Zophai's son was Nahath.** [27]**Nahath's son was Eliab. Eliab's son was Jeroham. Jeroham's son was Elkanah, and Elkanah's son was Samuel.**

[28]**Samuel's sons were Joel, the ·first son** [firstborn], **and Abijah, the second son** [1 Sam. 8:1–3].

[29]**Merari's son was Mahli. Mahli's son was Libni. Libni's son was Shimei. Shimei's son was Uzzah.** [30]**Uzzah's son was Shimea. Shimea's son was Haggiah, and Haggiah's son was Asaiah.**

The Temple Musicians

31David ·chose [appointed; assigned] some people to be in charge of the music in the house of the LORD. They began their work after the ·Ark of the Agreement [LArk] was put there. 32They ·served by making music [ministered with song] at the ·Holy Tent [Tabernacle] (also called the Meeting Tent), and they served until Solomon built the ·Temple [Lhouse] of the LORD in Jerusalem. They ·followed the rules for their work [served according to the regulations].

33These are ·the musicians [Lthose who served] and their sons:

From ·Kohath's family [Lthe sons of the Kohathites] there was Heman the ·singer [musician]. Heman was Joel's son. Joel was Samuel's son. 34Samuel was Elkanah's son. Elkanah was Jeroham's son. Jeroham was Eliel's son. Eliel was Toah's son. 35Toah was Zuph's son. Zuph was Elkanah's son. Elkanah was Mahath's son. Mahath was Amasai's son. 36Amasai was Elkanah's son. Elkanah was Joel's son. Joel was Azariah's son. Azariah was Zephaniah's son. 37Zephaniah was Tahath's son. Tahath was Assir's son. Assir was Ebiasaph's son. Ebiasaph was Korah's son. 38Korah was Izhar's son. Izhar was Kohath's son. Kohath was Levi's son. Levi was Israel's son.

39There was Heman's ·helper [assistant; *or* kinsman; Lbrother] Asaph, whose group stood by Heman's right side. Asaph was Berekiah's son. Berekiah was Shimea's son. 40Shimea was Michael's son. Michael was ·Baaseiah's[n] son. Baaseiah was Malkijah's son. 41Malkijah was Ethni's son. Ethni was Zerah's son. Zerah was Adaiah's son. 42Adaiah was Ethan's son. Ethan was Zimmah's son. Zimmah was Shimei's son. 43Shimei was Jahath's son. Jahath was ·Gershon's [Gershom's; v. 16] son, and Gershon was Levi's son.

44Merari's ·family [clan] were the ·helpers [assistants; *or* kinsmen; Lbrothers;] of Heman and Asaph, and they stood by Heman's left side. In this group was Ethan son of Kishi. Kishi was Abdi's son. Abdi was Malluch's son. 45Malluch was Hashabiah's son. Hashabiah was Amaziah's son. Amaziah was Hilkiah's son. 46Hilkiah was Amzi's son. Amzi was Bani's son. Bani was Shemer's son. 47Shemer was Mahli's son. Mahli was Mushi's son. Mushi was Merari's son, and Merari was Levi's son.

48·The other [LTheir brothers/kinsmen the] Levites ·served by doing their own special work [were appointed/assigned to other tasks/duties/service] in the ·Holy Tent [Tabernacle], the house of God. 49Aaron and his descendants offered the sacrifices on the altar of burnt offering [Lev. 1:1–17] and burned the incense on the altar of incense [Ex. 30:1–6]. They offered the sacrifices that ·removed [made atonement for] the Israelites' sins. They did all the work in the Most Holy Place ·and followed all the laws [according to all] that Moses, God's servant, had commanded.

50These were Aaron's sons: Eleazar was Aaron's son. Phinehas was Eleazar's son. Abishua was Phinehas' son. 51Bukki was Abishua's son. Uzzi was Bukki's son. Zerahiah was Uzzi's son. 52Meraioth was Zerahiah's son. Amariah was Meraioth's son. Ahitub was Amariah's son. 53Zadok was Ahitub's son, and Ahimaaz was Zadok's son.

Land for the Levites

54These are the ·places [settlements; areas] where Aaron's descendants lived. His descendants from the Kohath ·family group [clan] received the first ·share of the land [*or* territory by means of sacred lots].

55They were given the city of Hebron in Judah and the pastures around it, 56but the fields farther from the city and the villages near Hebron were

6:40 Baaseiah's Some Hebrew, Greek and Syriac copies read "Masseiah."

given to Caleb son of Jephunneh. [57]So the descendants of Aaron were given Hebron, one of the cities of ·safety [refuge]. They also received the towns and pastures of Libnah, Jattir, Eshtemoa, [58]·Hilen [*or* Hilez; Josh. 21:15], Debir, [59]·Ashan [*or* Ain; Josh. 21:16], Juttah, and Beth Shemesh. [60]They also received these towns and pastures from the tribe of Benjamin: Gibeon, Geba, Alemeth, and Anathoth.

The Kohath ·family groups [clans; CAaron's descendants] received a total of thirteen towns.

[61]The rest of the ·Kohath family group [Lsons of Kohath] was given ten towns from the ·family groups of West [Lthe half-tribe of] Manasseh. The towns were chosen by ·throwing [sacred] lots.

[62]The Gershon ·family group [clan] received thirteen towns from the tribes of Issachar, Asher, Naphtali, and the part of Manasseh living in Bashan.

[63]The ·Merari family group [Lsons/descendants of Merari] received twelve towns from the tribes of Reuben, Gad, and Zebulun. Those towns were chosen by ·throwing [sacred] lots.

[64]So the Israelites gave these towns and their pastures to the Levites. [65]The towns from the tribes of Judah, Simeon, and Benjamin, ·which were named [previously mentioned], were chosen by ·throwing [sacred] lots.

[66]Some of the Kohath ·family groups [clans] received ·towns and pastures [territory] from the tribe of Ephraim. [67]They received Shechem, one of the cities of ·safety [refuge; Csomeone who accidentally killed another person could receive protection from those seeking revenge; Num. 35:9–34; Josh. 20:1–9], with its pastures in the ·mountains [hill country] of Ephraim. They also received the towns and pastures of Gezer, [68]Jokmeam, Beth Horon, [69]Aijalon, and Gath Rimmon.

[70]The rest of the people in the Kohath ·family group [clan] received the towns of Aner and Bileam and their pastures from ·West [Lthe half-tribe of] Manasseh.

[71]From ·East [Lthe half-tribe of] Manasseh, the ·Gershon [*or* Gershom; v. 16] ·family [clan] received the towns and pastures of Golan in Bashan and Ashtaroth.

[72-73]From the tribe of Issachar, the ·Gershon [*or* Gershom] family received the towns and pastures of Kedesh, Daberath, Ramoth, and Anem.

[74-75]From the tribe of Asher, the ·Gershon [*or* Gershom] ·family [clan] received the towns and pastures of Mashal, Abdon, Hukok, and Rehob.

[76]From the tribe of Naphtali, the ·Gershon [*or* Gershom] ·family [clan] received the towns and pastures of Kedesh in Galilee, Hammon, and Kiriathaim.

[77]The rest of the Levites, the people from the Merari ·family [clan], received from the tribe of Zebulun the towns and pastures of Jokneam, Kartah, Rimmono, and Tabor.

[78-79]From the tribe of Reuben, the Merari ·family [clan] received the towns and pastures of Bezer in the desert, Jahzah, Kedemoth, and Mephaath. (The tribe of Reuben lived east of the Jordan River, across from Jericho.)

[80-81]From the tribe of Gad, ·the Merari family [they] received the towns and pastures of Ramoth in Gilead, Mahanaim, Heshbon, and Jazer.

Issachar's Children

7 Issachar had four sons: Tola, Puah, Jashub, and Shimron. 2Tola's sons were Uzzi, Rephaiah, Jeriel, Jahmai, Ibsam, and Samuel, and they were leaders of their ·families [clans]. In the ·family [clan] ·history [genealogy] of Tola's descendants, twenty-two thousand six hundred men were listed as ·fighting men [warriors; Lmighty men of valor] during the time ·David was king [Lof David].

3Uzzi's son was Izrahiah.

Izrahiah's sons were Michael, Obadiah, Joel, and Isshiah. All five of them were ·leaders [chiefs]. 4Their ·family [clan] ·history [genealogy] shows they had thirty-six thousand ·men [troops] ready to ·serve in [go to war with] the army, because they had many wives and children.

5The ·records [genealogy] of the ·family groups [clans] of Issachar show there were eighty-seven thousand ·fighting men [warriors; Lmighty men of valor].

Benjamin's Children

6Benjamin had three sons: Bela, Beker, and Jediael.

7Bela had five sons: Ezbon, Uzzi, Uzziel, Jerimoth, and Iri, and they were leaders of their ·families [clans]. Their ·family [clan] ·history [genealogy] shows they had twenty-two thousand thirty-four ·fighting men [warriors; Lmighty men of valor].

8Beker's sons were Zemirah, Joash, Eliezer, Elioenai, Omri, Jeremoth, Abijah, Anathoth, and Alemeth. They all were Beker's sons. 9Their ·family [clan] ·history [genealogy] listed the ·family [clan] ·leaders [chiefs] and twenty thousand two hundred ·fighting men [warriors; Lmighty men of valor].

10Jediael's son was Bilhan.

Bilhan's sons were Jeush, Benjamin, Ehud, Kenaanah, Zethan, Tarshish, and Ahishahar. 11All these sons of Jediael were leaders of their ·families [clans]. They had seventeen thousand two hundred ·fighting men [warriors; Lmighty men of valor] ready to ·serve in [go to war with] the army.

12The Shuppites and Huppites were descendants of Ir, and the Hushites were descendants of ·Aher [Ahiram; Num. 26:38].

Naphtali's Children

13Naphtali's sons were ·Jahziel [*or* Jahzeel; Gen. 46:24], Guni, Jezer, and ·Shillem [Shallum; Gen. 46:24, Num. 26:49]. They were Bilhah's ·grandsons [descendants; CBilhah was Jacob's concubine].

Manasseh's Children

14These are Manasseh's descendants. Manasseh had an Aramean ·slave woman [concubine; Ca secondary wife], who ·was the mother of [Lgave birth to] Asriel and Makir. Makir was Gilead's father. 15Makir took a wife from the Huppites and Shuppites. His sister was named Maacah. His second son was named Zelophehad, and he had only daughters. 16Makir's wife Maacah ·had [Lgave birth to] a son whom she named Peresh. Peresh's brother was named Sheresh. Sheresh's sons were Ulam and Rakem.

17Ulam's son was Bedan.

These were the sons of Gilead, who was the son of Makir. Makir was Manasseh's son. 18Makir's sister Hammoleketh gave birth to Ishhod, Abiezer, and Mahlah.

19The sons of Shemida were Ahian, Shechem, Likhi, and Aniam.

Ephraim's Children

20These are the names of Ephraim's descendants. Ephraim's son was Shuthelah. Shuthelah's son was Bered. Bered's son was Tahath. Tahath's son was Eleadah. Eleadah's son was Tahath. 21Tahath's son was Zabad. Zabad's son was Shuthelah.

Ezer and Elead went to Gath to steal ·cows and sheep [cattle; livestock;
[C]the term "cattle" can refer to various domesticated animals] and were
killed by some men who grew up in that city. [22]Their father Ephraim
·cried [mourned] for them many days, and his ·family [relatives; broth-
ers] came to ·comfort [console] him. [23]Then he ·had sexual relations with
[slept with; [L]went in to] his wife again. She became pregnant and gave
birth to a son whom Ephraim named Beriah [[C]sounds like "trouble"]
because of the ·trouble [disaster; tragedy] that had ·happened to his family [come upon his house]. [24]Ephraim's daughter was Sheerah. She built
Lower Beth Horon, Upper Beth Horon, and Uzzen Sheerah.
[25]Rephah was Ephraim's son. Resheph was Rephah's son. Telah was
Resheph's son. Tahan was Telah's son. [26]Ladan was Tahan's son. Ammihud
was Ladan's son. Elishama was Ammihud's son. [27]Nun was Elishama's
son, and Joshua was the son of ·Nun [*or* Non; Ex. 33:11].
[28]Ephraim's descendants lived in these lands and towns: Bethel and the
villages near it, Naaran on the east, Gezer and the villages near it on the
west, and Shechem and the villages near it all the way to Ayyah and its
villages. [29]Along the borders of Manasseh's land were the towns of Beth
Shan, Taanach, Megiddo, and Dor, and the villages near them. The
descendants of Joseph son of Israel [[C]Jacob] lived in these towns.

Asher's Children

[30]Asher's sons were Imnah, Ishvah, Ishvi, and Beriah. Their sister was
Serah.
[31]Beriah's sons were Heber and Malkiel. Malkiel was Birzaith's father.
[32]Heber was the father of Japhlet, Shomer, Hotham, and their sister
Shua.
[33]Japhlet's sons were Pasach, Bimhal, and Ashvath. They were Japhlet's
children.
[34]Japhlet's brother was ·Shemer [*or* Shomer; v. 32]. Shemer's sons were
Rohgah, ·Hubbah [*or* Jachbah; [C]the text says Jachbah; the marginal reading has Hubbah], and Aram.
[35]Shemer's brother was ·Helem [*or* Hotham; v. 32]. Helem's sons were
Zophah, Imna, Shelesh, and Amal.
[36]Zophah's sons were Suah, Harnepher, Shual, Beri, Imrah, [37]Bezer,
Hod, Shamma, Shilshah, Ithran [[C]perhaps another name for Jether; v. 38],
and Beera.
[38]Jether's sons were Jephunneh, Pispah, and Ara.
[39]Ulla's sons were Arah, Hanniel, and Rizia.
[40]All these men were descendants of Asher and leaders of their ·fami-
lies [clans]. They were ·powerful warriors [[L]mighty men of valor] and
·outstanding leaders [chief of princes]. Their ·family history [genealogi-
cal record] lists that they had twenty-six thousand soldiers ready to ·serve
in [go to war with] the army.

The Family History of King Saul

8 Benjamin was the father of Bela, his ·first son [firstborn]. Ashbel
was his second son, Aharah was his third, [2]Nohah was his fourth,
and Rapha was his fifth son.
[3]Bela's sons were Addar, Gera, Abihud, [4]Abishua, Naaman, Ahoah,
[5]Gera, Shephuphan, and Huram.
[6]These were the descendants of Ehud and leaders of their ·families
[clans] in Geba. They were ·forced to move [exiled; deported] to Manahath.
[7]Ehud's descendants were Naaman, Ahijah, and ·Gera [*or* Geba]. ·Gera [*or*

Geba] ·forced them to leave [led them into exile]. He was the father of Uzza and Ahihud.

8-11 Shaharaim and his wife Hushim had sons named Abitub and Elpaal. In Moab, Shaharaim ·divorced [Lsent away] his wives Hushim and Baara. Shaharaim and his wife Hodesh had these sons: Jobab, Zibia, Mesha, Malcam, Jeuz, Sakia, and Mirmah. They were leaders of their ·families [clans].

12-13 Elpaal's sons were Eber, Misham, Shemed, Beriah, and Shema. Shemed built the towns of Ono and Lod and the villages around them. Beriah and Shema were leaders of the ·families [clans] living in Aijalon, and they ·forced out [drove out; routed] the people who lived in Gath.

14 Beriah's sons were Ahio, Shashak, Jeremoth, 15 Zebadiah, Arad, Eder, 16 Michael, Ishpah, and Joha.

17 Elpaal's sons were Zebadiah, Meshullam, Hizki, Heber, 18 Ishmerai, Izliah, and Jobab.

19 Shimei's sons were Jakim, Zicri, Zabdi, 20 Elienai, Zillethai, Eliel, 21 Adaiah, Beraiah, and Shimrath.

22 Shashak's sons were Ishpan, Eber, Eliel, 23 Abdon, Zicri, Hanan, 24 Hananiah, Elam, Anthothijah, 25 Iphdeiah, and Penuel.

26 Jeroham's sons were Shamsherai, Shehariah, Athaliah, 27 Jaareshiah, Elijah, and Zicri.

28 The ·family histories [genealogical records] show that all these men were leaders of their ·families [clans] and lived in Jerusalem.

29 Jeiel lived in the town of Gibeon, where he was the leader. His wife was named Maacah. 30 Jeiel's ·first son [firstborn] was Abdon. His other sons were Zur, Kish, Baal, Ner, Nadab, 31 Gedor, Ahio, Zeker, 32 and Mikloth. Mikloth was the father of Shimeah. These sons also lived ·near [with; across from] their relatives in Jerusalem.

33 Ner was the father of Kish. Kish was the father of Saul, and Saul was the father of Jonathan, Malki-Shua, Abinadab, and Esh-Baal [CIshbosheth; 2 Sam. 2:8].

34 Jonathan's son was Merib-Baal [CMephibosheth; 2 Sam. 4:4], who was the father of Micah.

35 Micah's sons were Pithon, Melech, Tarea, and Ahaz. 36 Ahaz was the father of Jehoaddah. Jehoaddah was the father of Alemeth, Azmaveth, and Zimri. Zimri was the father of Moza. 37 Moza was the father of Binea. Raphah was Binea's son. Eleasah was Raphah's son, and Azel was Eleasah's son.

38 Azel had six sons: Azrikam, ·Bokeru [*or* the firstborn], Ishmael, Sheariah, Obadiah, and Hanan. All these were Azel's sons.

39 Azel's brother was Eshek. Eshek's ·first son [firstborn] was Ulam, his second was Jeush, and Eliphelet was his third. 40 Ulam's sons were mighty ·warriors [Lmen of valor] and good archers. They had many sons and grandsons—one hundred fifty of them in all.

All these men were Benjamin's descendants.

9 The names of all the people of Israel were listed in their ·family histories [genealogical records], and those ·family histories [genealogical records] were put in the ·book [scroll] of the kings of Israel.

The People in Jerusalem

The people of Judah were captured and ·forced to go [exiled] to Babylon [2 Kin. 25:1–21; 2 Chr. 36:17–21], because ·they were not faithful to God [of their unfaithfulness/infidelity]. 2 The first people to come back

and live in their own lands and towns were some Israelites, priests,
Levites, and ·Temple [Lhouse] servants.

3People from the tribes of Judah, Benjamin, Ephraim, and Manasseh
lived in Jerusalem. This is a list of those people.

4There was Uthai son of Ammihud. (Ammihud was Omri's son. Omri
was Imri's son. Imri was Bani's son. Bani was a descendant of Perez, and
Perez was Judah's son.)

5Of the Shilonite people there were Asaiah and his sons. Asaiah was the
·oldest son [firstborn] in his family.

6Of the Zerahite people there were Jeuel and other relatives of Zerah.
There were six hundred ninety ·of them [*or* families] in all.

7From the ·tribe [Lsons] of Benjamin there was Sallu son of Meshullam.
(Meshullam was Hodaviah's son, and Hodaviah was Hassenuah's son.)
8There was also Ibneiah son of Jeroham and Elah son of Uzzi. (Uzzi was
Micri's son.) And there was Meshullam son of Shephatiah. (Shephatiah
was Reuel's son, and Reuel was Ibnijah's son.) 9The ·family history [genea-
logical record] of Benjamin lists nine hundred fifty-six ·people [*or* families]
living in Jerusalem, and all these were leaders of their ·families [clans].

10Of the priests there were Jedaiah, Jehoiarib, Jakin, and 11Azariah son
of Hilkiah. (Hilkiah was Meshullam's son. Meshullam was Zadok's son.
Zadok was Meraioth's son. Meraioth was Ahitub's son. Ahitub was the
officer ·responsible for [in charge of] the ·Temple [Lhouse] of God.) 12Also
there was Adaiah son of Jeroham. (Jeroham was Pashhur's son, and
Pashhur was Malkijah's son.) And there was Maasai son of Adiel. (Adiel
was Jahzerah's son. Jahzerah was Meshullam's son. Meshullam was
Meshillemith's son, and Meshillemith was Immer's son.) 13There were
one thousand seven hundred sixty priests. They were leaders of their
·families [clans], and they were ·responsible [capable] for serving in the
·Temple [Lhouse] of God.

14Of the Levites there was Shemaiah son of Hasshub. (Hasshub was
Azrikam's son, and Azrikam was Hashabiah's son. Hashabiah was ·from
the family [a descendant; Lof the sons of] of Merari.) 15There were also
Bakbakkar, Heresh, Galal, and Mattaniah son of Mica. (Mica was Zicri's
son, and Zicri was Asaph's son.) 16There was also Obadiah son of
Shemaiah. (Shemaiah was Galal's son, and Galal was Jeduthun's son.)
And there was Berekiah son of Asa. (Asa was the son of Elkanah, who
lived in the ·villages [area] of the Netophathites.)

17Of the gatekeepers there were Shallum, Akkub, Talmon, Ahiman, and
their relatives. Shallum was ·their leader [the chief]. 18These gatekeepers
·from [for] the ·tribe [camp] of Levi ·still stand [*or* previously stood] next
to the King's Gate on the east side of the city. 19Shallum was Kore's son.
Kore was Ebiasaph's son, and Ebiasaph was Korah's son. Shallum and his
relatives from the ·family [clan] of Korah were gatekeepers and were
·responsible for [in charge of] guarding the ·gates of the Temple
[Lthreshold of the tent/sanctuary/Tabernacle]. Their ancestors had also
been ·responsible for [in charge of] guarding the entrance to the ·Temple
[camp; dwelling] of the LORD. 20In the past Phinehas, Eleazar's son, was
·in charge of the [the leader of the] gatekeepers, and the LORD was with
Phinehas. 21Zechariah son of Meshelemiah was the gatekeeper at the
entrance to the ·Temple [tent of meeting; Tabernacle].

22In all, two hundred twelve men were chosen ·to guard the gates [Las
gatekeepers at the thresholds], and their names were written in their

·family histories [genalogical records] in their villages. David and Samuel the ·seer [prophet] chose these men because they were ·dependable [trustworthy]. 23The gatekeepers and their descendants ·had to guard [were in charge of] the gates of the ·Temple [Lhouse] of the LORD when it was a tent. 24There were gatekeepers on all four sides of the ·Temple [Lhouse]: east, west, north, and south. 25The gatekeepers' relatives who lived in the villages had to come and help them at times. ·Each time they came they helped the gatekeepers for [*or* They came in every] seven days. 26Because they were ·dependable [trustworthy], four gatekeepers were made the leaders of all the gatekeepers. They were Levites, and they were ·responsible for [in charge of] the ·rooms [storerooms] and ·treasures [treasuries] in the ·Temple [Lhouse] of God. 27They stayed up all night guarding the ·Temple [Lhouse] of God because that was their responsibility, and they opened it every morning.

28Some of the gatekeepers were ·responsible for [in charge of] the utensils ·used in the Temple services [Lof service]. They counted these utensils when people took them out and when they brought them back. 29Other gatekeepers were chosen to take care of the furniture and utensils in the ·Holy Place [sanctuary]. They also took care of the flour, wine, oil, ·incense [frankincense], and spices, 30but ·some of [Lsons of] the priests took care of ·mixing [blending] the spices. 31There was a Levite named Mattithiah who was ·dependable and had the job of [entrusted with] baking the ·bread used for the offerings [flat/unleaven bread; Ex. 25:30; Lev. 24:5–6]. He was the ·first son [firstborn] of Shallum, ·who was from the family of Korah [the Korahite]. 32Some of ·the gatekeepers [their relatives] from the Kohath ·family [clan] had the job of preparing the ·special bread that was put on the table [Tshowbread] every Sabbath day.

33Some of the Levites were ·musicians in the Temple [singers]. The leaders of these ·families [clans] stayed in the ·rooms of the Temple [chambers]. Since they were on duty day and night, they did not do other ·work in the Temple [service].

34These are the leaders of the Levite ·families [clans]. Their names were listed in their ·family histories [genealogical records], and they lived in Jerusalem.

The Family History of King Saul

35Jeiel lived in the town of Gibeon. His wife was named Maacah. 36Jeiel's ·first son [firstborn] was Abdon. His other sons were Zur, Kish, Baal, Ner, Nadab, 37Gedor, Ahio, Zechariah, and Mikloth. 38Mikloth was Shimeam's father. Jeiel's family lived near their relatives in Jerusalem.

39Ner was Kish's father. Kish was Saul's father. Saul was the father of Jonathan, Malki-Shua, Abinadab, and ·Esh-Baal [*or* Ishbosheth; 2 Sam. 2:8].

40Jonathan's son was ·Merib-Baal [*or* Mephibosheth; 2 Sam. 4:4], who was the father of Micah.

41Micah's sons were Pithon, Melech, Tahrea, and Ahaz. 42Ahaz was Jadah's[n] father. Jadah was the father of Alemeth, Azmaveth, and Zimri. Zimri was Moza's father. 43Moza was Binea's father. Rephaiah was Binea's son. Eleasah was Rephaiah's son, and Azel was Eleasah's son.

44Azel had six sons: Azrikam, ·Bokeru [*or* the firstborn], Ishmael, Sheariah, Obadiah, and Hanan. They were Azel's sons.

9:42 Jadah's Some Hebrew and Greek copies read "Jadah." Other Hebrew copies read "Jarah."

The Death of King Saul
(10:1–14; 1 Sam. 31:1–13)

10 The Philistines ·fought against [attacked] Israel, and the
Israelites ran away from them. Many Israelites ·were killed
[were slaughtered; Lfell dead] on Mount Gilboa. 2The Philistines ·fought
hard against [hotly pursued; closed in on] Saul and his sons, killing his
sons Jonathan, Abinadab, and Malki-Shua. 3The fighting was ·heavy
[fierce] around Saul, and the archers ·shot him with their arrows [Lfound
him] and wounded him.
4Then Saul said to ·the officer who carried his armor [his armor bearer],
"·Pull out [Draw; Take] your sword and ·stab me [run me through]. If you
don't, these Philistines who are not circumcised will come and ·hurt
[abuse] me." But Saul's ·officer [armor bearer] refused, because he was
·afraid [terrified]. So Saul took his own sword and ·threw himself [fell] on
it. 5When the officer saw that Saul was dead, he ·threw himself [fell] on his
own sword and died. 6So Saul and three of his sons died; all his ·family
[Lhouse] died together.
7When the Israelites living in the valley saw that their army had ·run
away [fled] and that Saul and his sons were dead, they ·left [abandoned]
their towns and ·ran away [fled]. Then the Philistines came and ·settled in
[occupied] them.
8The next day when the Philistines came to strip the dead soldiers, they
found Saul and his sons ·dead [fallen] on Mount Gilboa. 9The Philistines
stripped Saul's body and took his head and his armor. Then they sent
messengers through ·all their country [the land of the Philistines] to tell
the good news to their idols and to their people. 10The Philistines put
Saul's armor in the ·temple [Lhouse] of their ·idols [Lgods] and hung his
head in the ·temple [Lhouse] of Dagon.
11All the people in Jabesh Gilead heard what the Philistines had done
to Saul. 12So the ·brave [valiant] men of Jabesh went and got the bodies of
Saul and his sons and brought them to Jabesh. They buried their bones
under the oak tree in Jabesh [Cevidently a major landmark]. Then the
people of Jabesh fasted for seven days.
13Saul died because he was not faithful to the LORD and ·did not obey
[Lacted unfaithfully against the word of] the LORD. He even went to a
medium and asked her for ·advice [counsel] 14instead of asking the LORD.
This is why the LORD put Saul to death and ·gave [turned over] the kingdom to Jesse's son David.

David Becomes King
(11:1–3; 2 Sam. 5:1–5)

11 Then the people of Israel ·came to [gathered before; joined]
David at the town of Hebron and said, "Look, we are your
own ·family [Lbone and flesh]. 2In the past, even when Saul was king,
you were the one who led Israel ·in battle [Lout and brought it in]. The
LORD your God said to you, 'You will be the shepherd for my people
Israel. You will be their leader.'"
3So all the elders of Israel came to King David at Hebron. He made an
·agreement [covenant; treaty] with them in Hebron ·in the presence of
[before] the LORD. Then they ·poured oil on [anointed] David to make him
king over Israel. ·The LORD had promised through Samuel that this would
happen [This was according to the word of the LORD through Samuel].

David Captures Jerusalem
(11:4–9; 2 Sam. 5:6–10)

4David and all the Israelites went to the city of Jerusalem. ·At that time
Jerusalem was called [L...that is,] Jebus, and the people living there were
named Jebusites. 5They said to David, "You can't ·get inside our city
[Lenter here]." But David ·did take the city of Jerusalem with its strong

walls [Lcaptured the stronghold/fortress of Zion], **and it became the City of David.**

6**David had said, "The person who ·leads the** [*or* is the first to] **·attack against** [kill one of] **the Jebusites will become ·the commander over all my army** [commander-in-chief]." **Joab son of Zeruiah ·led the attack** [went up first], **so he became ·the commander of the army** [chief].

7**Then David made his home in the ·strong, walled city** [stronghold; fortress], **which is why it ·was named** [is called] **the City of David.** 8**David rebuilt the city, beginning ·where the land was filled in** [with the terraces; Lthe Millo] **and going to the ·wall that was around the city** [surrounding area/walls]. **Joab ·repaired** [restored; rebuilt] **the other parts of the city.** 9**David became ·stronger and stronger** [Lgreater and greater], **and the LORD ·All-Powerful** [of Heaven's Armies; Tof hosts] **was with him.**

David's Mighty Warriors
(11:10–47; 2 Sam. 23:8–39)

10**·This is a list of the leaders** [These are the chiefs/heads] **over David's ·warriors** [Tmighty men] **who ·helped make David's kingdom strong** [*or* strongly supported his kingdom]. **All the people of Israel also supported David's kingdom, ·just as the LORD had promised** [Laccording to the word of the LORD].

11**This is a ·list** [record; account; roll] **of David's ·warriors** [Tmighty men]:

Jashobeam was from the Hacmonite people. He was the head of the ·Three [*or* Thirty; *or* officers; CDavid's most elite soldiers; 11:26–47; 2 Sam. 23:8–39]. **He used his spear to fight three hundred men at one time, and he killed them all.**

12**Next was Eleazar, one of the Three. Eleazar was Dodai's son from the Ahohite people.** 13**Eleazar was with David at Pas Dammim when the Philistines came there to fight. There was a field of barley at that place. The Israelites ·ran away** [fled] **from the Philistines,** 14**but they ·stopped** [took a stand; held their ground] **in the middle of that field and ·fought for** [defended] **it and killed the Philistines. The LORD ·gave them** [rescued/saved them with] **a great victory.**

15**Once, three of the Thirty, David's chief soldiers, came down to him at the ·rock** [cliff face] **by the cave near Adullam. At the same time the Philistine army had camped in the Valley of Rephaim.**

16**At that time David was in a stronghold, and ·some of the Philistines** [a Philistine detachment/garrison] **were in Bethlehem.** 17**David had a ·strong desire** [craving; longing] **for some water. He said, "Oh, I wish someone would get me water from the well near the city gate of Bethlehem!"** 18**So the Three broke through the Philistine ·army** [camp; lines] **and took water from the well near the city gate in Bethlehem. Then they brought it to David, but he refused to drink it. He poured it out ·before** [as an offering to] **the LORD,** 19**saying, "·May God keep me from drinking** [God forbid that I drink] **this water! ·It would be like drinking** [LShould I drink…?] **the blood of the men who risked their lives to bring it to me!" So David refused to drink it.**

These were the ·brave things [kind of things] **that the three warriors did.**

20**Abishai brother of Joab was the ·captain** [leader; chief] **of the Three. Abishai fought three hundred soldiers with his spear and killed them. He ·became as famous as** [Lhad a name as did] **the ·Three** [*or* Thirty; *or* officers; v. 11] 21**and was more honored than the ·Three** [*or* Thirty]. **He**

became their commander even though he was not ·one of [*or* equal to]
them.
22 Benaiah son of Jehoiada was a brave fighter from Kabzeel who did
mighty things. He killed ·two of the best warriors [*or* the two sons of
Ariel] from Moab. He also went down into a pit and killed a lion on a
snowy day. 23 Benaiah killed an Egyptian who was ·about seven and one-
half feet [Lfive cubits] tall and had a spear ·as large as [Llike] a weaver's
·rod [beam]. Benaiah had a ·club [staff], but he ·grabbed [wrenched] the
spear from the Egyptian's hand and killed him with his own spear.
24 ·These [Such] were the things Benaiah son of Jehoiada did. He ·was as
famous as [Lhad a name as well as] the Three. 25 He received more honor
than the Thirty, but he did not become a member of the Three. David
·made [appointed] him ·leader [captain] of his bodyguards.

The Thirty Chief Soldiers

26 These were also mighty warriors:
Asahel brother of Joab;
Elhanan son of Dodo from Bethlehem;
27 ·Shammoth [*or* Shammah; 2 Sam. 23:25] the Harorite;
Helez the ·Pelonite [*or* Paltite; 2 Sam. 23:26];
28 Ira son of Ikkesh from Tekoa;
Abiezer the Anathothite;
29 ·Sibbecai [*or* Mebunnai; 2 Sam. 23:27] the Hushathite;
·Ilai [*or* Zalmon; 2 Sam. 23:28] the Ahohite;
30 Maharai the Netophathite;
Heled son of Baanah the Netophathite;
31 Ithai son of Ribai from Gibeah in Benjamin;
Benaiah the Pirathonite;
32 ·Hurai [*or* Hiddai; 2 Sam. 23:30] from the ·ravines [valleys; *or* brooks] of Gaash;
·Abiel [*or* Abi-Albon; 2 Sam. 23:31] the Arbathite;
33 Azmaveth the ·Baharumite [*or* Barhumite; 2 Sam. 23:31];
Eliahba the Shaalbonite;
34 the sons of ·Hashem [*or* Jashen; cf. 2 Sam. 23:32] the Gizonite;
Jonathan son of ·Shagee [*or* Shammah; 2 Sam. 23:33] the Hararite;
35 Ahiam son of ·Sacar [*or* Sharar; 2 Sam. 23:33] the Hararite;
·Eliphal son of Ur [*or* Eliphelet son of Ahasbai the Maacathite; 2 Sam. 23:34];
36 Hepher the Mekerathite;
Ahijah the Pelonite;
37 ·Hezro [*or* Hezrai; 2 Sam. 23:35] the Carmelite;
Naarai son of Ezbai;
38 Joel brother of ·Nathan [*or* Igal son of Nathan from Zobah, 2 Sam. 23:36];
Mibhar son of Hagri;
39 Zelek the Ammonite;
Naharai the Berothite, the ·officer who carried the armor [armor bearer] for Joab son of Zeruiah;
40 Ira the Ithrite;
Gareb the Ithrite;
41 Uriah the Hittite;
Zabad son of Ahlai;
42 Adina son of Shiza the Reubenite, who was the ·leader [chief] of the Reubenites, and his thirty soldiers;

43 Hanan son of Maacah;
Joshaphat the Mithnite;
44 Uzzia the Ashterathite;
Shama and Jeiel sons of Hotham the Aroerite;
45 Jediael son of Shimri;
Joha, Jediael's brother, the Tizite;
46 Eliel the Mahavite;
Jeribai and Joshaviah, Elnaam's sons;
Ithmah the Moabite;
47 Eliel, Obed, and Jaasiel the Mezobaites.

Warriors Join David

12 These were the men who came to David at Ziklag when David
was ·hiding [banished; kept away] from Saul son of Kish. They
were among the ·warriors [champions] who helped David in battle. 2 They
·came [were armed/equipped] with bows for weapons and could use
either their right or left hands to shoot arrows or to sling rocks. They
were Saul's relatives from the tribe of Benjamin. 3 Ahiezer was their
·leader [chief], and there was Joash. (Ahiezer and Joash were sons of
Shemaah, who was from the town of Gibeah.) There were also Jeziel and
Pelet, the sons of Azmaveth. There were Beracah and Jehu from the town
of Anathoth. 4 And there was Ishmaiah from the town of Gibeon; he was
one of the Thirty. In fact, he was the leader of the Thirty. There were
Jeremiah, Jahaziel, Johanan, and Jozabad from Gederah. 5 There were
Eluzai, Jerimoth, Bealiah, and Shemariah. There was Shephatiah from
Haruph. 6 There were Elkanah, Isshiah, Azarel, Joezer, and Jashobeam
from the ·family group of Korah [LKorahites]. 7 And there were Joelah
and Zebadiah, the sons of Jeroham, from the town of Gedor.

8 Part of the people of Gad joined David at his stronghold in the ·desert
[wilderness]. They were ·brave warriors [Lmighty men of valor] trained
for war and ·skilled [expert] with shields and spears. They ·were as fierce
as [Lhad faces of] lions and as ·fast [swift; *or* nimble] as gazelles over the
hills.

9 Ezer was the leader of Gad's army, and Obadiah was second in command. Eliab was third, 10 Mishmannah was fourth, Jeremiah was fifth,
11 Attai was sixth, Eliel was seventh, 12 Johanan was eighth, Elzabad was
ninth, 13 Jeremiah was tenth, and Macbannai was eleventh in command.

14 They were the ·commanders [leaders; captains] of the army from
Gad. The least of these leaders ·was in charge of [*or* was a match for; could
take on; Lwas equal to] a hundred soldiers, and the greatest ·was in charge
of [*or* was a match for; could take on; Lwas equal to] a thousand. 15 They
crossed the Jordan River and ·chased away [drove out; put to flight] the
people living in the ·valleys [lowlands], to the east and to the west. This
happened in the first month of the year when the Jordan ·floods the valley [was overflowing its banks].

16 ·Other people from the tribes [LSome of the sons] of Benjamin and
Judah also came to David at his stronghold. 17 David went out to meet
them and said to them, "If you have come peacefully to help me, ·I welcome you. Join me. [...I am your friend; *or* we will make an alliance; Lmy
heart will be united with you]. But if you have come to ·turn me over to
my enemies [betray me to my adversaries], even though I have ·done
nothing wrong [Lno violence in my hands], the God of our ·ancestors
[Lfathers] will see this and ·punish you [Ljudge/decide]."

18Then the Spirit ·entered [came upon; Lclothed] Amasai, the ·leader [chief] of the Thirty, and he said:

"We ·belong to you [are yours], David.
We are with you, son of Jesse.
·Success, success [Peace and prosperity] to you.
·Success [Peace] to those who help you,
because your God helps you."

So David ·welcomed [received] these men and made them ·leaders [captains] of his ·army [fighters; raiders].

19Some of the men from Manasseh also ·joined [defected/deserted to] David when he went with the Philistines to fight Saul. But David and his men did not really help the Philistines. After ·talking about it [consultation], the Philistine leaders decided to send David away. They said, "If David ·goes [defects; deserts] back to his master Saul, ·we will be killed [Lit will be our heads]." 20These are the men from Manasseh who ·joined [defected/deserted to] David when he went to Ziklag: Adnah, Jozabad, Jediael, Michael, Jozabad, Elihu, and Zillethai. Each of them was a ·leader [captain; chief] of a thousand men from Manasseh. 21All these men of Manasseh were ·brave soldiers [Lmighty men of valor], and they helped David fight against ·groups of men who went around the country robbing people [raiding bands]. These soldiers became ·commanders [captains] in David's army. 22Every day more men ·joined [came to help] David, and his army became ·large [great], like the army of God.

Others Join David at Hebron

23These are the numbers of the soldiers ·ready [armed] for battle who ·joined [came to] David at Hebron. They came to help turn the kingdom of Saul over to David, ·just as the LORD had said [Laccording to the word of the LORD].

24There were sixty-eight hundred armed ·men from [Ldescendants/sons of] Judah, carrying shields and spears.

25There were seventy-one hundred men from Simeon. They were ·warriors [Lmighty men of valor] ready for war.

26There were forty-six hundred ·men from [Ldescendants/sons of] Levi. 27Jehoiada, a leader from Aaron's family, was in that group. There were thirty-seven hundred with him. 28Zadok was also in that group. He was a ·strong [brave] young warrior, and with him came twenty-two leaders from his ·family [Lfather's house].

29There were three thousand men from Benjamin, who were Saul's ·relatives [kinsmen; Lbrothers]. Most of them had ·remained loyal [kept their allegiance] to Saul's ·family [Lhouse] until then.

30There were twenty thousand eight hundred ·men from [Lsons of] Ephraim. They were brave warriors and were famous men in their ·own family groups [clans].

31There were eighteen thousand men from ·West [Lthe half-tribe of] Manasseh. Each one was ·especially chosen [Ldesignated by name] to make David king.

32There were two hundred leaders from Issachar. They knew what Israel should do, and they ·knew the right time to do it [*or* understood the times]. Their ·relatives [kinsmen; Lbrothers] were with them and under their command.

33There were fifty thousand men from Zebulun. They were ·trained [skilled] soldiers and ·knew how to use [equipped with] every kind of weapon of war. They followed David ·completely [with undivided loyalty/heart].

[34]There were one thousand ·officers [commanders; captains] from Naphtali. They had thirty-seven thousand soldiers with them who carried shields and spears.

[35]There were twenty-eight thousand six hundred men from Dan, who were ready for ·war [battle].

[36]There were forty thousand trained soldiers from Asher, who were ready for ·war [battle].

[37]There were one hundred twenty thousand soldiers from the east side of the Jordan River from the people of Reuben, Gad, and ·East [Lthe half-tribe of] Manasseh. They had every kind of weapon.

[38]All these fighting men were ready to go to war. They came to Hebron
·fully agreed [determined; Lwith a complete/perfect heart] to make David
king of all Israel. All the other Israelites also ·agreed [Lwere of one mind]
to make David king. [39]They spent three days there with David, eating and
drinking, because their ·relatives [kinsmen; Lbrothers] had prepared food
for them. [40]Also, their neighbors came from as far away as Issachar,
Zebulun, and Naphtali, bringing food on donkeys, camels, mules, and
oxen. They brought much flour, fig cakes, raisins, wine, oil, ·cows [oxen;
cattle], and sheep, because ·the people of Israel were very happy [there
was great joy in Israel].

Bringing Back the Ark
(13:1–14; 2 Sam. 6:1–11)

13 David ·talked with [consulted] all the officers of his army, the
·commanders [captains; leaders] of a hundred men and the
·commanders [captains; leaders] of a thousand men. [2]Then David ·called
the people of Israel together and said [Lsaid to the whole assembly of
Israel], "If you ·think it is a good idea [approve], and if it is ·what the
LORD our God wants [the will of/from the LORD our God], let's send a
message. Let's tell our ·fellow Israelites [kinsmen; brothers] in all the
·areas [land] of Israel and the priests and Levites living with them in
their towns and pastures to come and ·join [meet] us. [3]Let's bring the
Ark of our God back to us. We did not ·use it to ask God for help [inquire
of it] while Saul was king." [4]All the people agreed ·with David [to do so],
because they all thought it was the right thing to do.

[5]So David ·gathered [summoned; assembled] all the Israelites, from
the Shihor River in Egypt to ·Lebo [*or* The Entrance/Pass of] Hamath, to
bring the Ark of God back from the town of Kiriath Jearim. [6]David and
all the Israelites with him went to Baalah of Judah, which is Kiriath
Jearim, to get the Ark of God the LORD. God's throne is ·between [above;
on] the ·golden, winged creatures on the Ark [Lcherubim], and the Ark is
called by his name.

[7]The people carried the Ark of God from Abinadab's house on a new
cart, and Uzzah and Ahio guided it. [8]David and all the Israelites were
celebrating ·in the presence of [before] God. With all their ·strength
[might] they were singing and playing lyres, harps, ·tambourines [timbrels], cymbals, and trumpets.

[9]When David's men came to the threshing floor of Kidon, the oxen
stumbled, and Uzzah reached out his hand to ·steady [hold] the Ark.
[10]The ·LORD was angry with [Lthe LORD's anger burned against] Uzzah and
·killed him [struck him dead], because he had touched the Ark. So Uzzah
died there ·in the presence of [before] God.

11David was angry because the ·LORD had punished Uzzah in his anger [LORD's anger had Lburst/broken out against Uzzah]. Now that place is called Perez-uzzah [C"the outburst against Uzzah"].

12David was afraid of God that day and asked, "How can I bring the Ark of God home to me?" 13So David did not take the Ark with him to the City of David [CJerusalem]. Instead, he took it to the house of Obed-Edom who was from Gath. 14The Ark of God stayed with Obed-Edom's ·family [household] in his house for three months, and the LORD blessed Obed-Edom's ·family [household] and everything he owned.

David's Kingdom Grows
(14:1–17; 2 Sam. 5:11–25)

14 Hiram king of the city of Tyre sent messengers to David. He also sent cedar logs, bricklayers, and carpenters to build a ·palace [Lhouse] for David. 2Then David ·knew [understood; realized] that the LORD really had ·made [confirmed; established] him king of Israel and that he had made his kingdom ·great [highly exalted]. The LORD did this ·because he loved [for the sake of] his people Israel.

3David ·married more women [took more wives] in Jerusalem and ·had [fathered] more sons and daughters. 4These are the names of David's children born in Jerusalem: Shammua, Shobab, Nathan, Solomon, 5Ibhar, Elishua, Elpelet, 6Nogah, Nepheg, Japhia, 7Elishama, Beeliada, and Eliphelet.

David Defeats the Philistines

8When the Philistines heard that David had been ·made [anointed] king of all Israel, they went ·to look [in full force to search] for him. But David heard about it and went out ·to fight [against] them. 9The Philistines had ·attacked and robbed the people in [raided] the Valley of Rephaim. 10David ·asked [inquired of; Cperhaps by means of the Urim and Thummim; Ex. 28:30] God, "Should I go ·and attack [against] the Philistines? Will you hand them over to me?"

The LORD answered him, "Go, I will hand them over to you."

11So David and his men went up to the town of Baal Perazim and defeated the Philistines. David said, "Like a flood of water, God has used me to break through my enemies." So that place was named Baal Perazim [C"Lord who bursts through"]. 12The Philistines had ·left [abandoned] their idols there, so David ordered his men to burn them.

13Soon the Philistines ·attacked the people in [raided] the valley again. 14David ·prayed to [inquired of] God again [v. 10], and God answered him, saying, "Don't attack the Philistines ·from the front [straight on; directly]. Instead, ·go [circle] around them and attack them ·in front of the balsam [*or* near the poplar] trees. 15When you hear the sound of marching in the tops of the ·balsam [*or* poplar] trees, then attack. I, God, will have gone out before you to ·defeat [strike down] the Philistine army." 16David did as God commanded, and he and his men ·defeated [struck down] the Philistine army all the way from Gibeon to Gezer.

17So David became famous in ·all the countries [every land], and the LORD made all nations afraid of him.

The Ark Is Brought to Jerusalem
(15:1–16:3; 2 Sam. 6:12–19)

15 David built ·houses [buildings] for himself in the City of David [CJerusalem]. Then he prepared a place for the Ark of God, and he set up a tent for it. 2David said, "Only the Levites may carry the Ark of God. The LORD chose them to carry the Ark of the LORD and to ·serve [minister to/for] him forever."

3David ·called [summoned; assembled] all the people of Israel to come

to Jerusalem. He wanted to bring the Ark of the LORD to the place he had
·made [prepared] for it. 4David called together the descendants of Aaron
and the Levites. 5There were one hundred twenty ·people from [Lsons of]
Kohath's ·family group [clan], with Uriel as their ·leader [chief]. 6There
were two hundred twenty ·people from [Lsons of] Merari's ·family group
[clan], with Asaiah as their ·leader [chief]. 7There were one hundred
thirty ·people from [Lsons of] ·Gershon's [*or* Gersom's; 6:1] ·family group
[clan], with Joel as their ·leader [chief]. 8There were two hundred ·people
from [Lsons of] Elizaphan's ·family group [clan], with Shemaiah as their
·leader [chief]. 9There were eighty ·people from [Lsons of] Hebron's ·fam-
ily group [clan], with Eliel as their ·leader [chief]. 10And there were one
hundred twelve ·people from [Lsons of] Uzziel's ·family group [clan],
with Amminadab as their ·leader [chief].

11Then David ·asked [called for; summoned] the priests Zadok and
Abiathar and these Levites to come to him: Uriel, Asaiah, Joel, Shemaiah,
Eliel, and Amminadab. 12David said to them, "You are the leaders of the
·families [clans] of Levi. You and the other Levites must ·give yourselves
for service [consecrate/purify/sanctify yourselves] to the LORD, so that you
can bring up the Ark of the LORD, the God of Israel, to the place I have
·made [prepared] for it. 13The first time we did not ask the LORD ·how [the
proper/lawful way] to carry it. You Levites didn't carry it, so the LORD our
God ·punished [Lburst/broke out against] us."

14Then the priests and Levites ·prepared themselves for service to the
LORD [consecrated/purified/sanctified themselves] so they could ·carry
[bring up] the Ark of the LORD, the God of Israel. 15The Levites used special poles to carry the Ark of God on their shoulders, as Moses had
·commanded [ordered; instructed], ·just as the LORD had said they should
[Laccording to the word of the LORD].

16David ·told [commanded; ordered] the ·leaders [chiefs] of the Levites
to appoint their ·relatives [kinsmen; Lbrothers] as ·singers [musicians] to
play their lyres, harps, and cymbals and to ·sing happy songs [play/sing
joyfully].

17So the Levites appointed Heman and his ·relatives [kinsmen;
Lbrothers] Asaph and Ethan. Heman was Joel's son. Asaph was Berekiah's
son. And Ethan, from the Merari ·family group [clan], was Kushaiah's
son. 18There was also a second ·group [rank; Cpossibly assistants] of
Levites: Zechariah, Jaaziel, Shemiramoth, Jehiel, Unni, Eliab, Benaiah,
Maaseiah, Mattithiah, Eliphelehu, Mikneiah, Obed-Edom, and Jeiel.
They were the Levite ·guards [gatekeepers].

19The ·singers [musicians] Heman, Asaph, and Ethan played bronze
cymbals. 20Zechariah, Jaaziel, Shemiramoth, Jehiel, Unni, Eliab, Maaseiah,
and Benaiah played ·the lyres [harps] according to alamoth [Cpossibly
indicating to be sung by a soprano; Ps. 46:title]. 21Mattithiah, Eliphelehu,
Mikneiah, Obed-Edom, Jeiel, and Azaziah played the ·harps [lyres]
according to ·sheminith [Leighth; Ca reference to an eight-stringed instrument or perhaps to the manner of singing; Ps. 12:title; Ps. 16:title]. 22The
Levite leader Kenaniah was in charge of the singing, because he was ·very
good at it [highly skilled; very knowledgeable].

23Berekiah and Elkanah were two of the ·guards [gatekeepers] for the Ark.
24The priests Shebaniah, Joshaphat, Nethanel, Amasai, Zechariah, Benaiah,
and Eliezer had the job of blowing trumpets ·in front of [before] the Ark of
God. Obed-Edom and Jehiah were also ·guards [gatekeepers] for the Ark.

25David, the ·leaders [elders] of Israel, and the ·commanders [captains] of a thousand soldiers went to ·get [bring up] the Ark of the ·Agreement [Treaty; Covenant] with the LORD. They all went to bring the Ark from Obed-Edom's house with great ·joy [celebration]. 26Because God helped the Levites who carried the Ark of the ·Agreement [Testimony; Treaty; Covenant] with the LORD, they sacrificed seven bulls and seven ·male sheep [rams]. 27All the Levites who carried the Ark, and Kenaniah, the man in charge of the singing, and all the singers wore robes of fine linen. David also wore a robe of fine linen and a ·holy vest of fine linen [Lephod; Ex. 28:6–14]. 28So all the people of Israel brought up the Ark of the ·Agreement [Testimony; Treaty; Covenant] with the LORD. They shouted, blew horns and trumpets, and played cymbals, lyres, and harps.

29As the Ark of the ·Agreement [Testimony; Treaty; Covenant] with the LORD entered the City of David [CJerusalem], Saul's daughter Michal watched from a window. When she saw King David ·dancing [leaping] and celebrating, she hated him in her heart.

16 They brought the Ark of God and put it ·inside [in the middle of] the tent that David had set up for it. Then they offered burnt offerings [Lev. 1:1–17] and ·fellowship [*or* peace; well-being] offerings [Lev. 3:1] to God. 2When David had finished ·giving [sacrificing; offering] the burnt offerings [Lev. 1:1–17] and ·fellowship [*or* peace; well-being] offerings [Lev. 3:1], he blessed the people in the name of the LORD. 3He gave a loaf of bread, some ·dates [*or* meat], and raisins to every Israelite man and woman.

The Ministry of the Levites
(16:4–42; Ps. 96:1–13; 105:1–15; 106:1, 47–48)

4Then David appointed some of the Levites to ·serve [minister] before the Ark of the LORD. They had the job of ·leading the worship [celebrating; extolling; invoking; offering prayers] and giving thanks and praising the LORD, the God of Israel. 5Asaph, who played the cymbals, was the ·leader [chief]. Zechariah was second to him. The other Levites were Jaaziel, Shemiramoth, Jehiel, Mattithiah, Eliab, Benaiah, Obed-Edom, and Jeiel. They played the lyres and harps. 6Benaiah and Jahaziel were priests who ·blew [played] the trumpets regularly before the Ark of the ·Agreement [Testimony; Treaty; Covenant] ·with [of] God. 7That day David first ·gave [assigned; appointed] Asaph and his ·relatives [kinsmen; Lbrothers] ·the job of singing praises [this song of thanksgiving; vv. 8–22 correspond to Ps. 105:1–15] to the LORD.

David's Song of Thanks

8Give thanks to the LORD and ·pray to him [Lcall upon his name].
·Tell [Make known among; Proclaim to] the ·nations [world; peoples]
·what he has done [his deeds/accomplishments].
9Sing to him; ·sing praises [make music] to him.
Tell about all his ·miracles [wonders; wonderful acts/works].
10·Be glad that you are his [Glory/Exult/Take pride in his holy name];
let the hearts of those who seek the LORD ·be happy [rejoice].
11·Depend on [Search for] the LORD and his strength;
·always go to him for help [seek his presence/Lface continually].
12Remember the ·miracles [wonders; wonderful acts/works] he has ·done [performed],
his ·marvels [miracles; mighty acts], and his ·decisions [judgments he pronounced/Lfrom his mouth].
13You are the ·descendants [Lseed] of his servant, Israel;
you are the ·children [Lsons] of Jacob, his chosen ·people [Lones].

[14]He is the LORD our God.
His ·laws [judgments; justice] are ·for [*or* in; throughout] all the
·world [earth; land].
[15]·He will keep [*or* Remember] his ·agreement [treaty; covenant] forever;
·he will keep his promises always [the commitment/promise/word he
made/commanded for a thousand generations].
[16]He will keep the ·agreement [covenant; treaty] he made with Abraham
and the ·promise he made [oath/vow he swore] to Isaac.
[17]He made it a law ·for the people of [to] Jacob;
he made it an ·agreement [treaty; covenant] with Israel to last
forever.
[18]He said, "I will give the land of Canaan to you,
·to belong to you [as the portion you will inherit]."

[19]Then God's people were few in number, very few,
and they were strangers in the land.
[20]They ·went [wandered] from one nation to another,
from one kingdom to another.
[21]But he did not let anyone ·hurt [oppress] them;
he ·warned kings not to harm them [rebuked/admonished kings].
[22]He said, "Don't touch my ·chosen people [[L]anointed ones],
and don't harm my prophets."

[23]Sing to the LORD, all the earth.
Every day ·tell [proclaim] ·how he saves us [his salvation].
[24]·Tell [Declare to] the nations about his glory [[C]his manifest presence];
tell all ·peoples [the nations] the ·miracles [wonders; wonderful acts/
works] he does.
[25]The LORD is great; ·he should be praised [most worthy of praise; [T]and
greatly to be praised].
He should be ·respected more than [feared above] all gods.
[26]All the gods of the ·nations [peoples] are only idols,
but the LORD made the ·skies [heavens].
[27]·He has glory and majesty [Splendor/Honor and majesty surround/[L]are
before him];
·he has power and joy in [strength and joy are in/fill] his ·Temple
[[L]place].

[28]·Praise [Recognize; Give what's due to; [T]Ascribe to] the LORD, all
nations on earth.
·Praise [Recognize; Give what's due to; [T]Ascribe to] the LORD's glory
and ·power [strength];
[29] ·praise [recognize; give what's due to; [T]ascribe to] the glory of the
LORD's name.
Bring an offering and come ·to him [before him; into his presence].
Worship the LORD ·because he is holy [in his holy splendor].
[30]Tremble before him, ·everyone on [all the] earth.
The earth is ·set [firmly established], and it cannot be moved.
[31]Let the ·skies [heavens] rejoice and the earth be glad.
Let ·people [the nations] everywhere say, "The LORD ·is king
[reigns]!"
[32]Let the sea and everything in it ·shout [roar; thunder];

let the fields and everything in them ·rejoice [exult; celebrate; be jubilant].
[33]Then the trees of the forest will ·sing [shout; cry out]
for joy before the LORD.
·They will sing because [For] he is coming to judge the ·world [earth].

[34]Thank the LORD because he is good.
His ·love [steadfast love; lovingkindness] ·continues [endures] forever.
[35]Say to him, "Save us, God ·our Savior [of our salvation],
and ·bring us back and save [gather and rescue] us from ·other [the] nations.
Then we will thank ·you [your holy name]
and ·will gladly praise you [glory in your praise]."
[36]·Praise [Blessed be] the LORD, the God of Israel.
·He always was and always will be [... from everlasting to everlasting].
All the people said "Amen" and praised the LORD.

[37]Then David left Asaph and ·the other Levites [his relatives/kinsmen/
[L]brothers] there ·in front of [before] the Ark of the ·Agreement [Testimony;
Treaty; Covenant] ·with [of] the LORD. They were to ·serve [minister]
there ·every day [as each day's work required]. [38]David also left Obed-
Edom and sixty-eight ·other Levites [relatives; kinsmen; [L]brothers] to
serve with them. Hosah and Obed-Edom son of Jeduthun were ·guards
[gatekeepers].

[39]David left Zadok the priest and ·the other priests who served with
him in front of [his relatives/kinsmen/[L]brothers before] the ·Tent
[Tabernacle] of the LORD at the ·place of worship [[L]high place] in Gibeon.
[40]Every morning and evening they offered burnt offerings [Lev. 1:1–17]
to the LORD on the altar of burnt offerings, ·following [according to] ·the
rules written in the Teachings [[L]everything written in the Law] of the
LORD, which he had ·given [commanded] Israel. [41]With them were Heman
and Jeduthun and the rest chosen by name to ·sing praises [give thanks]
to the LORD because his ·love [steadfast love; lovingkindness] ·continues
[endures] forever. [42]Heman and Jeduthun ·also had the job of playing the
[*or* had with them] trumpets and cymbals and other musical instruments
·when songs were sung to God [for sacred songs]. Jeduthun's sons guarded
the gates.

[43]Then all the people left for their homes, and David also went home to
bless ·the people in his home [his household].

God's Promise to David
(17:1–27; 2 Sam. 7:1–29)

17 When David ·moved [had settled] into his ·palace [[L]house],
he said to Nathan the prophet, "·Look [[T]Behold], I am living
in a ·palace [[L]house] made of cedar, but the Ark of the ·Agreement
[Testimony; Treaty; Covenant] with the LORD ·sits in [is under] a tent."

[2]Nathan said to David, "Do ·what you want to do [whatever you have
in mind], because God is with you."

[3]But that night God spoke his word to Nathan, saying, [4]"Go and tell
David my servant, '·This is what the LORD says [[T]Thus says the LORD]: You
are not the person to build a house for me to live in. [5]From the time I
brought Israel ·out of [[L]up from] Egypt until now I have not lived in a

house. I have moved from one tent site to another and ·from one place to another [*or* lived in a Tabernacle]. 6As I have ·moved [walked] with the Israelites to different places, ·I have never [Lhave I ever…?] said to the ·leaders [Ljudges of Israel], whom I commanded to ·take care of [shepherd] my people, "Why haven't you built me a house of cedar?" '

7"Now, tell my servant David: 'This is what the LORD ·All-Powerful [of Heaven's Armies; Tof hosts] says: I took you from the pasture and from ·tending [following] the sheep and made you ·king [ruler; leader] of my people Israel. 8I have been with you everywhere you have gone. I have ·defeated [destroyed; Lcut off] your enemies for you. I will make you ·as famous as any of [La name like the name of] the great people on the earth. 9I will ·choose [provide; appoint] a place for my people Israel, and I will plant them so they can live in their own homes. They will not be ·bothered [disturbed; moved] anymore. ·Wicked [Evil] people will no longer ·hurt [oppress] them as they have in the past 10·when I chose [beginning when I appointed] judges for my people Israel. I will ·defeat [subdue] all your enemies.

" 'I tell you that the LORD will ·make your descendants kings of Israel after [Lbuild a house for] you. 11When ·you die [your days are over/ Tfulfilled] and join your ·ancestors [fathers], I will ·make [Lraise up] one of your descendants—one of your sons [CSolomon]—the new king, and I will ·set up [establish; secure] his kingdom. 12He will build a house [Cthe Temple] for me, and I will ·let his kingdom rule always [establish/secure his throne forever]. 13I will be his father, and he will be my son [2 Sam. 7:14; Ps. 2:7]. I took away my ·love [steadfast love; lovingkindness] from Saul, who ruled before you, but I will never ·stop loving your son [take it away from him]. 14I will ·put him in charge of [confirm him in] my house and kingdom forever. His ·family [Lthrone] will ·rule [be established/ secure] forever.' "

15Nathan told David ·everything God had said in this vision [all the words revealed to him].

David Prays to God

16Then King David went in and sat ·in front of [before] the LORD. David said, "LORD God, who am I? What is my ·family [Lhouse] that you have brought me ·to this point [this far]? 17But that was ·not enough for you [La small thing in your eyes], God. You have ·also made promises about my future family [spoken about your servant's house in the distant future]. LORD God, you have treated me like a ·very important [great; exalted] person.

18"What more can ·I [LDavid] say to you for honoring me, your servant? You know me so well. 19LORD, you have done this wonderful thing for ·my [Lyour servant's] sake ·and because you wanted to [according to your will/heart]. You have done all these great things and made them known.

20"There is ·no one [Tnone] like you, LORD. There is no God except you. ·We have heard all this ourselves [...as all that we've heard with our own ears confirms]! 21·There is no nation [LAnd is there another nation…?] like your people Israel. ·They are the only people on earth that [LWhat other nation on earth did…?] God chose to be his own. You made ·your name well known [a name for yourself] by the great and ·wonderful [awesome; terrible] things you did for them. You went ahead of them and ·forced other [drove out] nations. You ·freed [redeemed] your people

from slavery in Egypt. 22You made the people of Israel your very own
people forever, and, Lord, you ·are [became; have become] their God.
23"Lord, ·keep the promise [Llet the word be established/secure] forever
that you ·made [spoke] about my ·family [Lhouse] and me, your servant.
Do what you have ·said [spoken]. 24·Then you will be honored always
[May your name be established and honored/exalted/magnified forever],
and people will say, 'The Lord ·All-Powerful [of Heaven's Armies; Tof
hosts], the God over Israel, is Israel's God!' And the ·family [Lhouse] of
your servant David will ·continue [be established/secure] before you.
25"My God, you have told me that you ·would make my family great
[Lbuild for your servant a house]. So I, your servant, ·am brave enough
[have found courage] to pray to you. 26Lord, you are God, and you have
promised these good things to me, your servant. 27·You have chosen [It
has pleased you] to bless my ·family [Lhouse]. Let it continue before you
always. Lord, you have blessed ·my family [Lit], ·so it will [let it] ·always
[forever] be blessed."

David Defeats Nations
(18:1–17; 2 Sam. 8:1–18)

18 Later, David defeated the Philistines, ·conquered [subdued]
them, and took the city of Gath and the surrounding towns
from the Philistines.
2He also defeated the people of Moab. So the people of Moab became
·servants [subjects] of David and ·gave him the payment he demanded
[paid tribute money].
3David also defeated Hadadezer king of Zobah all the way to the town
of Hamath as he ·tried to spread his kingdom to [extended his authority/
rule to; *or* set up his boundary marker at; Lextended his hand; Cthe Hebrew
word can mean control or, less often, monument] the Euphrates River.
4David captured one thousand of his chariots, seven thousand ·chario-
teers [horsemen], and twenty thousand foot soldiers. He ·crippled
[hamstrung] all but a hundred of the chariot horses.
5Arameans from Damascus came to help Hadadezer king of Zobah, but
David killed twenty-two thousand of them. 6Then David put ·groups of
soldiers [garrisons] in Damascus in Aram. The Arameans became David's
·servants [subjects] and ·gave him the payments he demanded [brought
him tribute]. So the Lord gave David victory everywhere he went.
7David took the shields of gold that had belonged to Hadadezer's ·offi-
cers [guards; servants] and brought them to Jerusalem. 8David also took
many things made of bronze from Tebah and Cun, which had been cities
under Hadadezer's control. Later, Solomon used this bronze to make
things for the ·Temple [Lhouse]: the large bronze bowl, which was called
the Sea [1 Kin. 7:23–26], the pillars [1 Kin. 7:15–22], and other bronze
utensils.
9·Toi [Tou] king of Hamath heard that David had ·defeated all the
[destroyed the entire] army of Hadadezer king of Zobah. 10So Toi sent his
son ·Hadoram [Joram, 2 Sam. 8:10) to greet and congratulate King David
for defeating Hadadezer. (Hadadezer had been at war with Toi.) Hadoram
brought items made of gold, silver, and bronze. 11King David ·gave [dedi-
cated] them to the Lord, along with the silver and gold he had taken from
these nations: ·Edom [Aram, 2 Sam. 8:12, 14], Moab, the Ammonites, the
Philistines, and Amalek.
12Abishai son of Zeruiah killed eighteen thousand Edomites in the
Valley of Salt [Cthis victory is attributed to David in 2 Sam. 8:13]. 13David

put ·groups of soldiers [garrsions] in Edom, and all the Edomites became his ·servants [subjects]. The LORD gave David victory everywhere he went.

David's Important Officers

14David ·was king [reigned] over all of Israel, and he did what was ·fair [just] and ·right [righteous] for all his people. 15Joab son of Zeruiah was commander over the army. Jehoshaphat son of Ahilud was the ·recorder [secretary; royal historian]. 16Zadok son of Ahitub and Abiathar son of Ahimelech were priests. ·Shavsha [*or* Seriah; 2 Sam. 8:17] was the royal ·secretary [scribe]. 17Benaiah son of Jehoiada was over the Kerethites and Pelethites [C foreign mercenaries who served as the king's bodyguards]. And David's sons were ·important officers who served [chief officials/assistants] at his side.

War with the Ammonites and Arameans
(19:1–19; 2 Sam. 10:1–19)

19 When Nahash king of the Ammonites died, his son became king after him. 2David said, "Nahash ·was loyal [showed kindness] to me, so I will ·be loyal [show kindness] to his son Hanun." So David sent messengers to ·comfort [express sympathy to] Hanun about his father's death.

David's officers went to the land of the Ammonites to ·comfort [express sympathy to] Hanun. 3But the Ammonite ·leaders [officials; commanders] said to Hanun, "Do you think David wants to honor your father by sending men to ·comfort you [express sympathy]? No! David sent them to ·study [search; explore] the land and ·capture [conquer; overthrow] it and spy it out." 4So Hanun ·arrested [seized] David's officers. He shaved their beards and cut off their clothes at the ·hips [buttocks; C both intended to shame them]. Then he sent them away.

5When the people told David what had happened to ·his officers [the men], he sent messengers to meet them, because they were ·very ashamed [greatly humiliated]. King David said, "Stay in Jericho until your beards have grown back. Then come home."

6·The Ammonites knew that they had insulted [When the Ammonites realized they had become disgusting/L a stench to] David. So Hanun and the Ammonites sent ·about seventy-four thousand pounds [L one thousand talents] of silver to hire chariots and chariot drivers from ·northwest Mesopotamia [L Aram-naharaim], Aram Maacah, and Zobah. 7The Ammonites hired thirty-two thousand chariots and the king of Maacah and his ·army [people]. So they came and set up camp near the town of Medeba. The Ammonites themselves ·came out of [assembled/mustered from] their towns and got ready for battle.

8When David heard about this, he sent Joab with the ·whole army [entire army of warriors/mighty men]. 9The Ammonites came out and ·prepared for battle [drew up in battle lines] at the city ·gate [entrance]. The kings who had come to help were out in the ·field [open country] by themselves.

10Joab saw that there were enemies both in front of him and behind him. So he chose some of the ·best [elite] soldiers of Israel and ·sent them out to fight [deployed/arrayed them against] the ·Arameans [*or* Ammonites, 2 Sam. 10:10]. 11Joab put the rest of the army under the command of Abishai, his brother. ·Then they went out to fight the Ammonites [*or* …who was to attack the Ammonites; C possibly Joab attacked the Arameans and Abishai attacked the Ammonites]. 12Joab said to Abishai, "If the Arameans are too strong for me, you must help me. Or, if the Ammonites are too strong for you, I will help you. 13Be ·strong [brave;

courageous]. We must fight bravely for our people and the cities of our God. The LORD will do what ·he thinks is right [Lis good in his sight]."

14Then Joab and the army with him went to attack the Arameans, and the Arameans ·ran away [fled before him]. 15When the Ammonites saw that the Arameans were ·running away [fleeing], they also ·ran away [fled] from Joab's brother Abishai and ·went back [retreated] to their city. So Joab went back to Jerusalem.

16When the Arameans saw that Israel had defeated them, they sent messengers to bring other Arameans from ·east of the Euphrates [Lbeyond the] River. Their leader was ·Shophach [*or* Shobach; 2 Sam. 10:18], the commander of Hadadezer's army.

17When David heard about this, he ·gathered [mobilized; mustered] all the Israelites, and they crossed over the Jordan River. He ·prepared [positioned; deployed] them for battle, facing the Arameans. The Arameans fought with him, 18but they ·ran away [fled] from the Israelites. David killed seven thousand [Cseven hundred in 2 Sam. 10:18] Aramean chariot drivers and forty thousand Aramean foot soldiers. He also killed ·Shophach [*or* Shobach, 2 Sam. 10:18], the commander of the Aramean army.

19When ·those who served [the subjects/vassals of] Hadadezer saw that the Israelites had defeated them, they made peace with David and ·served him [became his subjects]. So the Arameans ·refused [were unwilling] to help the Ammonites again.

Joab Destroys the Ammonites

(20:1-3; 2 Sam. 11:1; 12:26-31)

20 In the ·spring [Lturning of the year], the time of year when kings normally went out to ·battle [war], Joab led out the army of Israel. But David stayed in Jerusalem. The army of Israel ·destroyed [ravaged; laid waste] the land of Ammon and went to the city of Rabbah and ·attacked it [lay siege to it; tore it down]. 2David took the crown off the head of ·their king [*or* Milcom; Cthe god of the Ammonites], and had it placed on his own head. That gold crown weighed ·about seventy-five pounds [Lone talent], and it ·had valuable gems in it [was set with precious stones]. And David took ·many valuable things [a great amount of plunder/spoil] from the city. 3He also brought out the people of the city and forced them to work [Censlaved them] with saws, iron picks, and axes. David did this to all the Ammonite cities. Then David and all his army returned to Jerusalem.

Philistine Giants Are Killed

(20:4-8; 2 Sam. 21:15-22)

4Later, at Gezer [CGob in 2 Sam. 21:18], war broke out with the Philistines. Sibbecai the Hushathite killed ·Sippai [*or* Saph; 2 Sam. 21:18], who was one of the descendants of the Rephaites. So those Philistines were ·defeated [subdued; subjugated].

5Later, there was another battle with the Philistines. Elhanan son of Jair killed Lahmi, the brother of Goliath, who was from the town of Gath. His spear was as ·large [thick] as a weaver's ·rod [beam; 2 Sam. 21:19].

6At Gath another battle took place. A huge man was there; he had six fingers on each hand and six toes on each foot—twenty-four fingers and toes in all. This man also was ·one of the sons of Rapha [*or* a descendant of the giants]. 7When he ·spoke against [taunted; defied] Israel, Jonathan son of Shimea, David's brother, killed him.

8These descendants ·of Rapha [from the giants] from Gath were killed by David and his ·men [warriors].

David Counts the Israelites
(21:1–22:1; 2 Sam. 24:1–25)

21 ·Satan was against [*or* An adversary opposed] Israel, and he ·caused [incited] David to ·count [take a census of; Cdoing so implied trust in themselves rather than in God] the people of Israel. 2So David said to Joab and the commanders of the troops, "Go and ·count [take a census of] all the Israelites from Beersheba to Dan [Cthe whole expanse of Israel from south to north]. Then tell me so I will know how many there are."

3But Joab said, "May the LORD give the ·nation [*or* army] a hundred times more people. My ·master [lord] the king, ·all the Israelites are [Lare they not all…?] your servants. Why do you want to do this, my master? ·You will make Israel guilty of sin [Why should you bring guilt/judgment to Israel?]."

4But the ·king commanded [king's word/edict prevailed despite] Joab, so Joab left and went through all Israel. Then he returned to Jerusalem. 5Joab gave the ·list [number] of the ·people [soldiers; warriors] to David. There were one million one hundred thousand men in all of Israel who could use the sword, and there were four hundred seventy thousand men in Judah who could use the sword. 6But Joab did not count the tribes of Levi and Benjamin, because he ·didn't like [was repulsed/disgusted/distressed by] King David's order. 7David had done something ·God had said was wrong [that displeased/offended God], so God ·punished [attacked; struck] Israel [Ctaking a census of the army indicated confidence in military strength].

8Then David said to God, "I have sinned greatly by what I have done! Now, I beg you to ·forgive me, [take away the guilt/iniquity of] your servant, because I have been very foolish."

9The LORD said to Gad, who was David's ·seer [prophet], 10"Go and tell David, '·This is what the LORD says [TThus says the LORD]: I offer you three ·choices [Lthings]. Choose one of them and I will ·do it [inflict it on you].'"

11So Gad went to David and said to him, "·This is what the LORD says [TThus says the LORD]: '·Choose for yourself [Take your choice:] 12three years of ·hunger [famine]. Or choose three months of ·running from [being swept away by] your enemies as they ·chase [overtake] you with their swords. Or choose three days of ·punishment from [Lthe sword of] the LORD, in which a ·terrible disease [plague; pestilence] will spread through the ·country [land]. The angel of the LORD will go through Israel ·destroying [ravaging] the people.' Now, David, decide ·which of these things [what answer] I should ·tell [give] the LORD who sent me."

13David said to Gad, "I am in ·great trouble [deep distress; a desperate situation]. Let ·the LORD punish me [Lme fall into the hand of the LORD], because the LORD is very merciful. Don't let ·my punishment come from [Lme fall into the hand of] human beings."

14So the LORD sent a ·terrible disease [plague; pestilence] on Israel, and seventy thousand people died. 15God sent an angel to destroy Jerusalem, but when the angel ·started [was about/preparing] to destroy it, the LORD saw it and ·felt very sorry about the terrible things that had happened [Lrelented regarding the disaster/calamity]. So he said to the angel who was destroying, "That is enough! ·Put down your arm [LWithhold your hand]!" The angel of the LORD was then standing at the threshing floor of ·Araunah [*or* Ornan; *or* Aravna; 2 Sam. 24:16] the Jebusite.

16David looked up and saw the angel of the LORD ·in the sky [Lstanding

between earth and heaven], with his drawn sword in this hand ·pointing
toward [extended over] Jerusalem. Then David and the ·elders [leaders]
bowed facedown on the ground. They were wearing ·rough cloth [sack-
cloth; burlap; Ca sign of grief or repentance]. 17David said to God, "·I am
[LAm not I…?] the one who sinned and did wrong. I gave the order for
the ·people to be counted [census]. ·These people only followed me like
sheep. They did nothing wrong. [LThese sheep—what have they done?]
LORD my God, please ·punish [Llet your hand fall on] me and my ·family
[Lfather's house], but ·stop the terrible disease that is killing [lift the
plague from] your people."
18Then the angel of the LORD ·told [ordered; commanded] Gad to tell
David that he should build an altar to the LORD on the threshing floor of
·Araunah [or Ornan; or Aravna; 2 Sam. 24:16] the Jebusite. 19So David
·did what Gad told him to do, [went up as Gad had spoken/instructed/
commanded] in the name of the LORD.
20·Araunah [or Ornan; or Aravna; 2 Sam. 24:16] was ·separating the
wheat from the straw [threshing wheat]. When he turned around, he saw
the angel. Araunah's four sons who were with him hid themselves. 21David
came to Araunah, and when Araunah saw him, he left the threshing floor
and bowed facedown on the ground before David.
22David said to him, "·Sell me [Let me have] your threshing floor so I
can build an altar to the LORD here. Then the ·terrible disease will stop
[plague will be lifted from the people]. ·Sell it to me for the full price [I'll
pay top price; LFull silver]."
23·Araunah [or Ornan; or Aravna; v. 18] said to David, "Take this
threshing floor. My master the king, do ·anything you want [Lwhatever is
good in your eyes]. Look, I will also give you oxen for the whole burnt
offerings [Lev. 1:1–17], the threshing ·boards [sledges; sleds] for the
wood, and wheat for the ·grain [Lgift; tribute] offering [Lev. 2:1]. I give
everything to you."
24But King David answered Araunah, "No, I ·will pay [insist on paying]
the full price for the land. I won't take anything that is yours and give it to
the LORD. I won't offer a burnt offering [Lev. 1:1–17] that costs me
nothing."
25So David paid ·Araunah [or Ornan; or Aravna; v. 18] ·about fifteen
pounds [Lsix hundred shekels] of gold for the place. 26David built an altar
to the LORD there [Cthe site of the future Temple; 2 Chr. 3:1] and offered
whole burnt offerings [Lev. 1:1–17] and ·fellowship [or peace; well-being]
offerings [Lev. 3:1]. David ·prayed to [called on] the LORD, and he
answered him by sending down fire from heaven on the altar of burnt
offering. 27Then the LORD commanded the angel to put his sword back
into its ·holder [sheath].
28When David saw that the LORD had answered him on the threshing
floor of ·Araunah [or Ornan; or Aravna; v. 18], he offered sacrifices
there. 29The ·Holy Tent [Tabernacle] that Moses made while the
Israelites were in the ·desert [wilderness] and the altar of burnt offerings [Lev. 1:1–17] were in Gibeon at the ·place of worship [Lhigh place].
30But David could not go ·to the Holy Tent to speak with [before it to
inquire of] God, because he was ·afraid [terrified] of the sword of the
angel of the LORD.

22 David said, "The ·Temple [Lhouse] of the LORD God and the
altar for Israel's burnt offerings [Lev. 1:1–17] will be here."

David Makes Plans for the Temple

2 So David ordered all ·foreigners [sojourners; resident aliens] living in
Israel to gather together. From that group David ·chose [appointed;
assigned] stonecutters to cut stones to be used in building the ·Temple
[Lhouse] of God. 3 David supplied a large amount of iron to be used for
making nails and ·hinges [clamps; braces; fittings] for the gate doors. He
also supplied more bronze than could be weighed, 4 and he supplied more
cedar logs than could be counted. ·Much of the [Great quantities of]
cedar had been brought to David by the people from Sidon and Tyre.
5 David said, "We should build a ·great [exceedingly magnificent]
·Temple [Lhouse] for the LORD, which will be famous everywhere for its
·greatness and beauty [splendor; gloriousness]. But my son Solomon is
young and ·inexperienced [Ltender], so I will make preparations for it."
So David got many of the materials ready before he died.
6 Then David called for his son Solomon and ·told [commanded;
charged] him to build the ·Temple [Lhouse] for the LORD, the God of
Israel. 7 David said to him, "My son, I ·wanted [intended; planned; Lhad
my heart set] to build a ·temple [Lhouse] ·for worshiping [Lto the name
of] the LORD my God. 8 But the LORD spoke his word to me, 'David, you
have ·killed many people [shed much blood]. You have fought ·many
[great] wars. You cannot build a ·temple [Lhouse] ·for worship to me [to
my name], because you have ·killed many people [shed so much blood on
the earth in my sight; Che completed the conquest of Canaan]. 9 But, you
will have a son, a man of ·peace [Lrest]. I will give him rest from all his
enemies around him. His name will be Solomon [Ca name derived from
shalom, "peace"], and I will give Israel peace and quiet ·while he is king
[Lin his days]. 10 Solomon will build a ·temple [Lhouse] for ·worship to me
[my name]. He will be my son, and I will be his father [2 Sam. 7:14; Ps.
2:7]. I will ·make his kingdom strong; someone from his family will rule
[establish/secure his throne over] Israel forever.' "
11 David said, "Now, my son, may the LORD be with you and give you
success. May you build a ·temple [Lhouse] for the LORD your God, as he
·said [announced; promised] you would. 12 When he makes you the king
of Israel, may the LORD give you ·wisdom [discretion] and understanding
so you will be able to ·obey [keep; observe] the ·teachings [law; instruc-
tions] of the LORD your God. 13 Be careful to obey the ·rules [statutes;
ordinances; requirements] and laws the LORD ·gave [commanded] Moses
for Israel. If you obey them, you will ·have success [prosper]. Be strong
and brave. Don't be afraid or ·discouraged [dismayed].
14 "Solomon, I have ·worked hard getting many of the materials [taken
great pains to provide] for building the ·Temple [Lhouse] of the LORD. I
have supplied ·about seven and one-half million pounds [Lone hundred
thousand talents] of gold, ·about seventy-five million pounds [Lone million talents] of silver, so much bronze and iron it cannot be weighed, and
wood and stone. You may add to them. 15 You have many workmen—
stonecutters, ·bricklayers [stonemasons], carpenters, and ·people skilled
[craftsmen; artisans] in every kind of work. 16 They are skilled in working
with gold, silver, bronze, and iron. You have more craftsmen than can be
counted. ·Now begin the [Set to] work, and may the LORD be with you."
17 Then David ·ordered [commanded] all the leaders of Israel to help
his son Solomon. 18 David said to them, "The LORD your God is with you.
He has given you ·rest from our enemies [peace on every side; Deut. 12:2].
He has handed over to me the people living around us. The LORD and his

people ·are in control of [have subdued] this land. [19]Now ·give yourselves completely to obeying [devote your heart/mind and soul to seeking] the LORD your God. Build the ·holy place [sanctuary] of the LORD God; build the ·Temple [Lhouse] ·for worship to the LORD [to honor the LORD's name]. Then bring the Ark of the ·Agreement [Testimony; Treaty; Covenant] with the LORD and the holy ·items [vessels; articles] that belong to God into the ·Temple [Lhouse]."

The Levites

23 After David ·had lived long [Lwas full of years] and was old, he made his son Solomon the new king of Israel. [2]David gathered all the leaders of Israel, along with the priests and Levites. [3]He counted the Levites who were thirty years old and older, and they totaled thirty-eight thousand. [4]David said, "Of these, twenty-four thousand Levites will ·direct [oversee; supervise] the work of the ·Temple [Lhouse] of the LORD, six thousand Levites will be ·officers [officials] and judges, [5]four thousand Levites will be gatekeepers, and four thousand Levites will praise the LORD with musical instruments I made for ·giving praise [worship]."

[6]David separated the Levites into three groups that were led by Levi's three sons: Gershon, Kohath, and Merari.

The People of Gershon

[7]From the people of Gershon [6:1], there were Ladan and Shimei. [8]Ladan had three sons. His first son was Jehiel, and his other sons were Zetham and Joel.

[9]Shimei's sons were Shelomoth, Haziel, and Haran. These three sons were leaders of Ladan's ·families [clans]. [10]Shimei had four sons: Jahath, Ziza,[n] Jeush, and Beriah. [11]Jahath was the ·first son [eldest; chief; family leader], and Ziza was the second son. But Jeush and Beriah did not have many children, so they were counted as if they were one family, with one ·assignment [responsibility].

The People of Kohath

[12]Kohath had four sons: Amram, Izhar, Hebron, and Uzziel.

[13]Amram's sons were Aaron and Moses. Aaron and his descendants were ·chosen to be special [set apart] forever. They were chosen to ·prepare [dedicate; sanctify] the holy things, to ·offer sacrifices [burn incense] before the LORD, and to ·serve [minister to] him. They were to ·give [pronounce] blessings in his name forever.

[14]Moses was the man of God, and his sons were counted as part of the tribe of Levi. [15]Moses' sons were Gershom [Judg. 18:30] and Eliezer. [16]Gershom's ·first [oldest; chief] son was Shubael. [17]Eliezer's ·first [oldest; chief] son was Rehabiah. Eliezer had no other sons, but Rehabiah had many sons.

[18]Izhar's ·first [oldest; chief] son was Shelomith.

[19]Hebron's ·first [oldest; chief] son was Jeriah, his second was Amariah, his third was Jahaziel, and his fourth was Jekameam.

[20]Uzziel's ·first [oldest; chief] son was Micah and his second was Isshiah.

The People of Merari

[21]Merari's sons were Mahli and Mushi. Mahli's sons were Eleazar and Kish. [22]Eleazar died without sons; he had only daughters. Eleazar's daughters married their cousins, the sons of Kish. [23]Mushi's three sons were Mahli, Eder, and Jerimoth.

23:10 Ziza Some Hebrew, Greek and Latin copies read "Ziza." Other Hebrew copies read "Zina."

The Levites' Work

24These were Levi's descendants listed by ·their families [clans]. They
were the leaders of families. Each person who was twenty years old or
older was ·listed [counted]. They served in the LORD's ·Temple [Lhouse].
25David had said, "The LORD, the God of Israel, has given ·rest [peace]
to his people. He ·has come to live [dwells] in Jerusalem forever. 26So the
Levites don't need to carry the ·Holy Tent [Tabernacle] or any of the
·things [articles; objects] used in its services anymore." 27David's ·last
[final] instructions were to count the Levites who were twenty years old
and older.
28The Levites had the ·job [duty; office] of ·helping [assisting] Aaron's
descendants in the service of the ·Temple [Lhouse] of the LORD. They
cared for the ·Temple [Lhouse] ·courtyard [courts] and side rooms, and
they ·made all the holy things pure [ceremonially purified all holy/sacred
things]. Their job was to serve in the ·Temple [Lhouse] of God. 29They
were ·responsible for [in charge of] putting the ·holy bread [Tshowbread]
on the table, for the choice flour in the grain offerings, for the ·bread
made without yeast [unleaven bread/wafers], for the ·baking and mixing
[*or* the round cakes], and for the measuring of quantity or size. 30The
Levites also stood every morning and gave thanks and praise to the LORD.
They also did this every evening. 31The Levites offered all the burnt offerings [Lev. 1:1–17] to the LORD on the ·special days of rest [sabbaths], at the
New Moon festivals [Num. 10:10; 29:6; 1 Sam. 20:5; 2 Kin. 4:23; Ezra 3:5;
Ps. 81:3; Is. 1:13; Amos 8:5], and at all appointed feasts. They served
before the LORD ·every day [continually]. They were to follow the rules for
how many Levites should serve each time. 32So the Levites ·took care
[were in charge] of the ·Meeting Tent [Tabernacle] and the ·Holy Place
[sanctuary]. And they helped their relatives, Aaron's descendants, with
the services at the ·Temple [Lhouse] of the LORD.

The Groups of the Priests

24 These were the ·groups [divisions; orders] of Aaron's sons:
Aaron's sons were Nadab, Abihu, Eleazar, and Ithamar. 2But
Nadab and Abihu died before their father did [Lev. 10:1–2], and they
had no sons. So Eleazar and Ithamar served as the priests. 3David, with
the help of Zadok, a descendant of Eleazar, and Ahimelech, ·a descendant of Ithamar, separated their [CAaron's] ·family groups [descendants]
into two different groups according to their ·various duties [assigned
responsibilities/offices]. 4There were more ·leaders [chiefs] from
Eleazar's ·family [descendants] than from Ithamar's—sixteen ·leaders
[heads of their clans] from Eleazar's ·family [descendants] and eight
·leaders [heads of their clans] from Ithamar's ·family [descendants].
5Men were ·chosen [divided; allocated; organized] ·impartially [*or* simi-
larly] from Eleazar's and Ithamar's ·families [descendants] by throwing
lots. Some men ·from each family were chosen to be in charge [were offi-
cials] of the ·Holy Place [sanctuary], and some were ·chosen to serve as
priests [officials of God].
6Shemaiah son of Nethanel, ·from the tribe [son] of Levi, was the ·secre-
tary [recorder; scribe]. He recorded the names of those descendants in
·front [the presence] of King David, the ·officers [officials; leaders], Zadok
the priest, Ahimelech son of Abiathar, and the leaders of the ·families
[clans] of the priests and Levites. The work was divided by lots among the
·families [clans] of Eleazar and Ithamar. 7The first ·one chosen was [lot fell
to] Jehoiarib. The second was Jedaiah. 8The third was Harim. The fourth

was Seorim. 9The fifth was Malkijah. The sixth was Mijamin. 10The seventh was Hakkoz. The eighth was Abijah. 11The ninth was Jeshua. The tenth was Shecaniah. 12The eleventh was Eliashib. The twelfth was Jakim. 13The thirteenth was Huppah. The fourteenth was Jeshebeab. 14The fifteenth was Bilgah. The sixteenth was Immer. 15The seventeenth was Hezir. The eighteenth was Happizzez. 16The nineteenth was Pethahiah. The twentieth was Jehezkel. 17The twenty-first was Jakin. The twenty-second was Gamul. 18The twenty-third was Delaiah. The twenty-fourth was Maaziah.

19These were ·the groups chosen to serve [*or* their appointed duties; Lthe order of their serving] in the ·Temple [Lhouse] of the LORD. They obeyed the ·rules [procedures; regulations] given them by Aaron, just as the LORD, the God of Israel, had commanded him.

The Other Levites

20These are the names of the rest of Levi's descendants:

Shubael was a descendant of Amram, and Jehdeiah was a descendant of Shubael.

21Isshiah was the ·first [firstborn; chief] son of Rehabiah.

22From the Izhar ·family group [clan], there was Shelomoth, and Jahath was a descendant of Shelomoth.

23Hebron's ·first son was [descendants included] Jeriah, Amariah was his second, Jahaziel was his third, and Jekameam was his fourth.

24Uzziel's ·son was [descendants included] Micah. Micah's son was Shamir. 25Micah's brother was Isshiah, and Isshiah's ·son was [descendants included] Zechariah.

26Merari's descendants were Mahli and Mushi. Merari's son was Jaaziah. 27Jaaziah ·son [descendant] of Merari had ·sons [descendants] named Shoham, Zaccur, and Ibri. 28Mahli's ·son [descendant] was Eleazar, but Eleazar did not have any sons.

29Kish's ·son [descendant] was Jerahmeel.

30Mushi's ·sons were [descendants included] Mahli, Eder, and Jerimoth.

These are the Levites, listed by their ·families [clans]. 31They ·were chosen for special jobs by throwing [cast] lots in front of King David, Zadok, Ahimelech, the leaders of the ·families [clans] of the priests, and the Levites. They did this just as their relatives, Aaron's descendants, had done. The families of the oldest brother and the youngest brother were treated the same.

The Music Groups

25 David and the ·commanders [officers] of the army chose some of the sons of Asaph, Heman, and Jeduthun to ·preach [proclaim; prophesy] and play harps, lyres, and cymbals. Here is a list of the men who ·served in this way [performed/were assigned these services]:

2Asaph's sons who served were Zaccur, Joseph, Nethaniah, and Asarelah. King David ·chose [directed] Asaph to ·preach [proclaim; prophesy], and Asaph directed his sons.

3Jeduthun's sons who served were Gedaliah, ·Zeri [*or* Izri; v. 11], Jeshaiah, Shimei [Cname not included in most manuscripts], Hashabiah, and Mattithiah. There were six of them, and Jeduthun directed them. He ·preached [proclaimed; prophesied] and used a harp to give thanks and praise to the LORD.

4Heman's sons who served were Bukkiah, Mattaniah, Uzziel, Shubael, Jerimoth, Hananiah, Hanani, Eliathah, Giddalti, Romamti-Ezer, Joshbekashah, Mallothi, Hothir, and Mahazioth. 5All these were sons of Heman,

David's ·seer [prophet]. God promised to ·make Heman strong, so Heman had [exalt/honor him with] many sons. God gave him fourteen sons and three daughters. 6Heman directed all his sons in ·making music [singing] for the ·Temple [Lhouse] of the LORD with cymbals, lyres, and harps; that was their way of serving in the ·Temple [Lhouse] of God. King David ·was in charge of [directed; supervised] Asaph, Jeduthun, and Heman. 7These men and their relatives were trained and skilled in ·making music for [singing to] the LORD. There were two hundred eighty-eight ·of them [with these skills; experts]. 8Everyone threw lots ·to choose the time his family was to serve at the Temple [for their duties]. The ·young [small] and the ·old [great], the teacher and the student, had to throw lots.

9First, the lot fell to Joseph, from the ·family [clan] of Asaph [Cthe number twelve needs to be understood here, as in the following verses, to make the total come to the stated 288].

Second, twelve men were chosen from Gedaliah, his sons and ·relatives [kinsmen; Lbrothers].

10Third, twelve men were chosen from Zaccur, his sons and ·relatives [kinsmen; Lbrothers].

11Fourth, twelve men were chosen from ·Izri [*or* Zeri; v. 3], his sons and ·relatives [kinsmen; Lbrothers].

12Fifth, twelve men were chosen from Nethaniah, his sons and ·relatives [kinsmen; Lbrothers].

13Sixth, twelve men were chosen from Bukkiah, his sons and ·relatives [kinsmen; Lbrothers].

14Seventh, twelve men were chosen from ·Jesarelah [*or* Asarelah; 25:2], his sons and ·relatives [kinsmen; Lbrothers].

15Eighth, twelve men were chosen from Jeshaiah, his sons and ·relatives [kinsmen; Lbrothers].

16Ninth, twelve men were chosen from Mattaniah, his sons and ·relatives [kinsmen; Lbrothers].

17Tenth, twelve men were chosen from Shimei, his sons and ·relatives [kinsmen; Lbrothers].

18Eleventh, twelve men were chosen from ·Azarel [*or* Uzziel; 25:4], his sons and ·relatives [kinsmen; Lbrothers].

19Twelfth, twelve men were chosen from Hashabiah, his sons and ·relatives [kinsmen; Lbrothers].

20Thirteenth, twelve men were chosen from Shubael, his sons and·relatives [kinsmen; Lbrothers].

21Fourteenth, twelve men were chosen from Mattithiah, his sons and ·relatives [kinsmen; Lbrothers].

22Fifteenth, twelve men were chosen from Jerimoth, his sons and ·relatives [kinsmen; Lbrothers].

23Sixteenth, twelve men were chosen from Hananiah, his sons and ·relatives [kinsmen; Lbrothers].

24Seventeenth, twelve men were chosen from Joshbekashah, his sons and ·relatives [kinsmen; Lbrothers].

25Eighteenth, twelve men were chosen from Hanani, his sons and ·relatives [kinsmen; Lbrothers].

26Nineteenth, twelve men were chosen from Mallothi, his sons and ·relatives [kinsmen; Lbrothers].

27Twentieth, twelve men were chosen from Eliathah, his sons and ·relatives [kinsmen; Lbrothers].

28Twenty-first, twelve men were chosen from Hothir, his sons and ·rel-
atives [kinsmen; [L]brothers].
29Twenty-second, twelve men were chosen from Giddalti, his sons and
·relatives [kinsmen; [L]brothers].
30Twenty-third, twelve men were chosen from Mahazioth, his sons and
·relatives [kinsmen; [L]brothers].
31Twenty-fourth, twelve men were chosen from Romamti-Ezer, his
sons and ·relatives [kinsmen; [L]brothers].

The Gatekeepers

26 These are the ·groups [divisions; orders] of the gatekeepers.
From the ·family [clan] of Korah, there was Meshelemiah
son of Kore, who was from Asaph's ·family [descendants]. 2Meshelemiah
had sons. Zechariah was his ·first son [firstborn], Jediael was second,
Zebadiah was third, Jathniel was fourth, 3Elam was fifth, Jehohanan
was sixth, and Eliehoenai was seventh.
4Obed-Edom had sons. Shemaiah was his ·first son [firstborn],
Jehozabad was second, Joah was third, Sacar was fourth, Nethanel was
fifth, 5Ammiel was sixth, Issachar was seventh, and Peullethai was eighth.
God indeed blessed Obed-Edom.
6Obed-Edom's son Shemaiah also had sons. They ·were leaders in
[ruled over] their father's ·family [[L]house] because they were ·capable
men [highly respected; [L]mighty men of valor]. 7Shemaiah's sons were
Othni, Rephael, Obed and Elzabad, whose ·brothers [relatives] Elihu and
Semakiah were ·skilled workers [*or* valiant men; *or* also respected]. 8All
these were Obed-Edom's descendants. They and their sons and ·relatives
[brothers; grandsons] were capable men and ·strong [well-qualified]
workers. Obed-Edom had sixty-two ·descendants [relatives] in all.
9Meshelemiah had sons and ·relatives [brothers] who were ·skilled
workers [capable/respected men]. In all, there were eighteen.
10From the Merari ·family [clan], Hosah had sons. Shimri, although
not the oldest son, was chosen by his father to be in charge. 11Hilkiah was
his second son, Tabaliah was third, and Zechariah was fourth. In all,
Hosah had thirteen sons and ·relatives [brothers].
12These were the leaders of the ·groups [divisions; orders] of gatekeepers, and they served in the ·Temple [[L]house] of the LORD, as did their
·relatives [brothers]. 13By throwing lots, each ·family [clan] chose a gate
to guard. ·Young [Small] and ·old [great] threw lots.
14·Meshelemiah [*or* Shelemiah; v. 2] was chosen by lot to guard the East
Gate. Then lots were ·thrown [cast] for Meshelemiah's son Zechariah. He
was a ·wise counselor [prudent advisor] and was chosen for the North
Gate. 15Obed-Edom was ·chosen for [allotted] the South Gate, and Obed-
Edom's sons were ·chosen to guard [allotted] the storehouse. 16Shuppim
and Hosah were chosen for the West Gate and the Shalleketh Gate on the
·upper [ascending] road [[C]to the Temple].
·Guards stood side by side with guards [*or* Guard duty was evenly
divided; [L]A guard alongside a guard]. 17Six Levites stood guard every day
at the East Gate; four stood guard every day at the North Gate; four stood
guard every day at the South Gate; and two at a time guarded the storehouse. 18There were two guards at the ·western court [colonnade; Parbar;
[C]the gateway leading up to the Temple] and four guards on the road.
19These were the ·groups [divisions; orders] of the gatekeepers from
the ·families [clans; [L]sons] of Korah and Merari.

Other Leaders

20·Other [Their fellow/brother] Levites were ·responsible for guarding [in charge of] the treasuries of the ·Temple [Lhouse] of God and for the ·places where the holy items were kept [treasuries of dedicated/consecrated gifts].

21·Ladan [*or* Libni] was Gershon's son and the ancestor of several ·family groups [clans]. ·Jehiel [*or* Jehieli; 23:8] was a ·leader [chief] of one of the ·family groups [clans]. 22His sons were Zetham and Joel his brother, and they were ·responsible for [in charge of] the treasuries of the ·Temple [Lhouse] of the LORD.

23Other leaders were chosen from the ·family groups [clans] of Amram, Izhar, Hebron, and Uzziel. 24Shubael,*n* the descendant of Gershom, who was Moses' son, was the ·leader [chief] ·responsible for [in charge of] the treasuries. 25These were Shubael's relatives from Eliezer: Eliezer's son Rehabiah, Rehabiah's son Jeshaiah, Jeshaiah's son Joram, Joram's son Zicri, and Zicri's son Shelomith. 26Shelomith and his relatives were ·responsible for [in charge of] ·everything that had been collected for the Temple [the treasuries of dedicated/consecrated gifts collected] by King David, by the heads of ·families [clans], by the commanders of a thousand men and of a hundred men, and by other army ·commanders [officers]. 27They also ·gave [dedicated] some of the ·things they had [plunder; spoil] taken in wars to be used in repairing the ·Temple [Lhouse] of the LORD. 28Shelomith and his relatives took care of all the ·holy items [dedicated/consecrated gifts]. Some had been given by Samuel the ·seer [prophet], Saul son of Kish, Abner son of Ner, and Joab son of Zeruiah.

29Kenaniah was from the Izhar ·family [clan]. He and his sons worked outside the ·Temple [Lhouse] as officers and judges in Israel.

30Hashabiah was from the Hebron ·family [clan]. He and his relatives were ·responsible for [in charge of] the LORD's work and ·the king's business [served the king] in Israel west of the Jordan River. There were seventeen hundred ·skilled [capable; respected] men in Hashabiah's group. 31The ·history [genealogy] of the Hebron ·family [clan] shows that Jeriah was their ·leader [chief]. In David's fortieth year ·as king [of reign], the ·records [genealogies] were searched, and some ·capable [skilled; respected] men of the Hebron ·family [clan] were found living at Jazer in Gilead. 32Jeriah had twenty-seven hundred relatives who were ·capable [skilled; respected] men and leaders of families. King David ·gave them the responsibility of directing [put them in charge of] the tribes of Reuben, Gad, and ·East [Lthe half-tribe of] Manasseh in God's work and the king's ·business [service].

Army Divisions

27 This is the list of the Israelites who served the king in the army. Each division was on duty one month each year. There were leaders of ·families [clans], commanders of a thousand men, commanders of a hundred men, and other officers. Each division had twenty-four thousand men.

2Jashobeam son of Zabdiel was in charge of the first division for the first month. There were twenty-four thousand men in his division. 3Jashobeam, one of the descendants of Perez, was ·leader [chief; commander] of all the army officers for the first month.

4Dodai, from the Ahohites, was in charge of the division for the second

26:24 Shubael Some Greek and Latin copies read "Shubael." Hebrew copies read "Shebuel."

month. Mikloth was a ·leader [chief; commander] in the division. There
were twenty-four thousand men in Dodai's division.
5The third commander, for the third month, was Benaiah son of
Jehoiada the priest. There were twenty-four thousand men in his division. 6He was the Benaiah who was one of the Thirty [11:11]. Benaiah was
a ·brave [mighty] warrior who led those men. Benaiah's son Ammizabad
was in charge of Benaiah's division.
7The fourth commander, for the fourth month, was Asahel, the brother
of Joab. Later, Asahel's son Zebadiah ·took his place as commander [suc-
ceeded him]. There were twenty-four thousand men in his division.
8The fifth commander, for the fifth month, was Shamhuth, from Izrah's
·family [clan]. There were twenty-four thousand men in his division.
9The sixth commander, for the sixth month, was Ira son of Ikkesh from
the town of Tekoa. There were twenty-four thousand men in his
division.
10The seventh commander, for the seventh month, was Helez. He was
from the Pelonites and a descendant of Ephraim. There were twenty-four
thousand men in his division.
11The eighth commander, for the eighth month, was Sibbecai. He was
from Hushah and was from Zerah's ·family [clan]. There were twenty-
four thousand men in his division.
12The ninth commander, for the ninth month, was Abiezer. He was
from Anathoth in Benjamin. There were twenty-four thousand men in
his division.
13The tenth commander, for the tenth month, was Maharai. He was
from Netophah and was from Zerah's ·family [clan]. There were twenty-
four thousand men in his division.
14The eleventh commander, for the eleventh month, was Benaiah. He
was from Pirathon in Ephraim. There were twenty-four thousand men in
his division.
15The twelfth commander, for the twelfth month, was Heldai. He was
from Netophah and was from Othniel's ·family [clan]. There were twenty-
four thousand men in his division.

Leaders of the Tribes

16These were ·the leaders [in charge] of the tribes of Israel. Eliezer son
of Zicri was over the tribe of Reuben. Shephatiah son of Maacah was over
the tribe of Simeon. 17Hashabiah son of Kemuel was over the tribe of
Levi. Zadok was over the people of Aaron. 18Elihu, one of David's brothers, was over the tribe of Judah. Omri son of Michael was over the tribe
of Issachar. 19Ishmaiah son of Obadiah was over the tribe of Zebulun.
Jerimoth son of Azriel was over the tribe of Naphtali. 20Hoshea son of
Azaziah was over the tribe of Ephraim. Joel son of Pedaiah was over ·West
[Lthe half-tribe of] Manasseh. 21Iddo son of Zechariah was over ·East
Manasseh [Lthe half-tribe of Manasseh in Gilead]. Jaasiel son of Abner
was over the tribe of Benjamin. 22Azarel son of Jeroham was over the
tribe of Dan.
These were the ·leaders [chiefs; commanders] of the tribes of Israel.
23The LORD had promised to make the Israelites as ·many [numerous]
as the stars ·in the sky [of heaven; Gen. 22:17; 26:4; Ex. 32:13]. So David
did not count those younger than twenty years old. 24Joab son of Zeruiah
began ·to count [the census of] the people, but he did not finish. ·God
became angry with [LWrath came upon] Israel for counting the people, so

the number of the people was not put in the ·history book about [chron-
icles/annals of] King David.

The King's Directors

25 Azmaveth son of Adiel was in charge of the royal ·storehouses
[treasuries].
Jonathan son of Uzziah was in charge of the ·storehouses [treasuries]
in the country, towns, villages, and ·towers [fortresses].
26 Ezri son of Kelub was in charge of the field workers who ·farmed
[tilled] the land.
27 Shimei, from the town of Ramah, was in charge of the vineyards.
Zabdi, from Shapham, was in charge of storing the wine that came
from the vineyards.
28 Baal-Hanan, from Geder, was in charge of the olive trees and sycamore trees in the ·western hills [LShephelah].
Joash was in charge of storing the olive oil.
29 Shitrai, from Sharon, was in charge of the herds that ·fed [grazed] in
the Plain of Sharon.
Shaphat son of Adlai was in charge of the ·herds [cattle] in the valleys.
30 Obil, an Ishmaelite, was in charge of the camels.
Jehdeiah, from Meronoth, was in charge of the donkeys.
31 Jaziz, from the Hagrites, was in charge of the flocks.
All these men were the ·officers who took care [officials/overseers in
charge] of King David's property.
32 Jonathan was David's uncle, and he ·advised [counseled] David.
Jonathan was a ·wise man [man of understanding/insight] and a ·teacher
of the law [scribe]. Jehiel son of Hacmoni ·took care of [taught; tutored]
the king's sons. 33 Ahithophel ·advised [counseled] the king. Hushai, from
the Arkite people, was the king's ·friend [confidant]. 34 Jehoiada and
Abiathar later took Ahithophel's place in ·advising [counseling] the king.
Jehoiada was Benaiah's son. Joab was the commander of the king's army.

David's Plans for the Temple

28 David ·commanded [summoned] all the ·leaders [officials]
of Israel to come to Jerusalem. There were the ·leaders [offi-
cials; commanders; chiefs] of the tribes, ·commanders [officers] of the
army divisions serving the king, commanders of a thousand men and of
a hundred men, ·leaders [officials; overseers] who took care of the property and animals that belonged to the king and his sons, ·men over the
palace [palace officials], the ·powerful [mighty] men, and all the ·brave
[valiant] warriors.
2 King David stood up and said, "Listen to me, my ·relatives [brothers]
and my people. I ·wanted [intended; planned; had my heart set] to build a
place to keep the Ark of the ·Agreement [Testimony; Treaty; Covenant]
with the LORD. I wanted it to be God's footstool. So I made ·plans [prepa-
rations] to build ·a temple [it]. 3 But God said to me, 'You must not build
a ·temple [Lhouse] for ·worshiping me [my name/Name], because you are
a ·soldier [man of war] and have ·killed many people [shed blood; Che
completed the conquest of Canaan].'
4 "·But [Yet; Nevertheless] the LORD, the God of Israel, chose me from
my whole ·family [clan; father's house] to be king of Israel forever. He
chose the tribe of Judah to ·lead [rule], and from the ·people [house] of
Judah, he chose my father's ·family [clan; Lhouse]. From ·that family [Lmy
father's sons] God was pleased to make me king ·of [over all] Israel. 5 The
LORD has given me many sons, and from those sons he has chosen

Solomon to ·be the new king [Lsit on the throne] **of Israel. Israel is the**
LORD's kingdom. 6The LORD said to me, 'Your son Solomon will build my
·Temple [Lhouse] **and ·its courtyards** [my courts]**. I have chosen Solomon**
to be my son, and I will be his father. 7He is obeying my laws and com-
mands now. If he continues ·to obey them [resolutely; unswervingly]**, I**
will ·make his kingdom strong [establish/secure his kingdom] **forever.' "**
8David said, "Now, in ·front [the sight] **of all Israel, the assembly of the**
LORD, and in the hearing of God, I tell you these things: Be careful to
·obey [observe; follow] **all the commands of the LORD your God. Then**
you will ·keep [possess] **this good land and ·pass it on** [Lleave it as an
inheritance] **to your ·descendants** [children] **forever.**
9"And you, my son Solomon, ·accept [acknowledge; Lknow] **the God of**
your father. Serve him ·completely and willingly [Lwith your whole heart
and a willing mind/spirit]**, because the LORD ·knows what is in everyone's**
mind [Lsearches every heart]**. He understands ·everything you think**
[every desire/motive and thought]**. If you ·go to him for help** [seek him]**,**
·you will get an answer [you will find him; *or* he will let you find him]**. But**
if you ·turn away from [abandon; forsake] **him, he will ·leave** [reject] **you**
forever. 10Solomon, ·you must understand this [see now]**. The LORD has**
chosen you to build ·the Temple [La house] **as his ·holy place** [sanctuary]**.**
Be strong and ·finish the job [do it; go to work]**."**
11Then David gave his son Solomon the plans for ·building the Temple
[the porch/portico]**. They included its buildings, its storerooms, its upper**
rooms, its inside rooms, and the ·place where the people's sins were
removed [room for atonement/Tthe mercy seat]**. 12David gave him plans**
for everything he had in mind: the courtyards around the LORD's ·Temple
[Lhouse] **and all the rooms around it, the ·Temple treasuries** [storehouses
of God's house]**, and the ·treasuries** [storehouse] **of the ·holy items used**
in the Temple [dedicated/consecrated things/gifts]**. 13David gave Solomon**
directions for the ·groups [divisions; orders] **of the priests and Levites,**
and for all the work of serving in the ·Temple [Lhouse] **of the LORD, and**
about the ·items [utensils] **to be used for service in the ·Temple** [Lhouse]
of the LORD 14that were made of gold or silver. David told Solomon ·how
much [the weight of] **gold or silver to use to make each thing. 15David**
told him ·how much [the weight of] **gold to use for each gold lampstand**
and its lamps and ·how much [the weight of] **silver to use for each silver**
lampstand and its lamps according to how the lampstands were to be
used . 16David told ·how much [the weight of] **gold to use for each table**
that held the ·holy [Tshow] **bread and ·how much** [the weight of] **silver to**
use for the silver tables. 17He told ·how much [the weight of] **pure gold to**
use to make the forks, ·bowls [basins]**, and pitchers and ·how much** [the
weight of] **gold to use to make each gold ·dish** [bowl]**. He told ·how much**
[the weight of] **silver to use to make each silver ·dish** [bowl] **18and ·how**
much [the weight of] **pure gold to use for the altar of incense. He also**
gave Solomon the plans for the ·chariot [*or* seat] **of the ·golden creatures**
[cherubim] **that spread their wings over the Ark of the ·Agreement**
[Testimony; Treaty; Covenant] **with the LORD.**
19David said, "All these plans were written with the LORD ·guiding
[directing] **me. He ·helped me understand** [made clear to me; gave me
insight into/understanding of] **everything in the plans."**
20David also said to his son Solomon, "Be strong and brave, and do the
work. Don't be afraid or discouraged, because the LORD God, my God, is

with you. He will not fail you or ·leave [abandon; forsake] you until all the work for the service of the ·Temple [Lhouse] of the LORD is finished. 21The ·groups [divisions; orders] of the priests and Levites are ready for all the ·work on [service of] the ·Temple [Lhouse] of God. Every skilled worker is ready to help you with all the work. The ·leaders [officials] and all the ·people [nation] will ·obey every command you give [be at your command]."

Gifts for Building the Temple

29 King David said to ·all the Israelites who were gathered [the entire assembly], "God chose my son Solomon, who is young and ·hasn't yet learned what he needs to know [inexperienced], ·but [and] the ·work is important [task is great/huge]. This ·palace [temple] is not for ·people [mortals]; it is for the LORD God. 2I have ·done my best [made every effort; Laccording to all my strength] to prepare for building the ·Temple [Lhouse] of my God. I have given gold for the things made of gold and silver for the things made of silver. I have given bronze for the things made of bronze and iron for the things made of iron. I have given wood for the things made of wood and onyx for the settings. I have given turquoise gems of many different colors, ·valuable [precious] stones, and ·white marble [alabaster]. I have given all these things in ·abundance [great quantities]. 3I have already given this for the ·Temple [Lhouse], but because of my ·devotion to [commitment to; delight in] the ·Temple [Lhouse] of my God, I am also giving my own treasures of gold and silver. 4I am giving ·about two hundred twenty thousand pounds [Lthree thousand talents] of gold from Ophir and ·about five hundred twenty thousand pounds [Lseven thousand talents] of ·pure [refined] silver. They will be used to ·cover [overlay] the walls of the buildings 5and for all the gold and silver work to be done by the craftsmen. Now, who is ·ready [willing] to ·give himself [consecrate/devote yourself] to the service of the LORD today [Cby also making an offering]?"

6The ·family [clan] leaders and the ·leaders [chiefs; heads] of the tribes of Israel, the commanders of a thousand men and of a hundred men, and the ·leaders [officials; overseers] ·responsible for [in charge of] the king's work gave willingly. 7They donated ·about three hundred eighty thousand pounds [Lfive thousand talents] of gold, ·about seven hundred fifty thousand pounds [Lten thousand darics] of silver, ·about one million three hundred fifty thousand pounds [Leighteen thousand talents] of bronze, and ·about seven million five hundred thousand pounds [Lone hundred thousand talents] of iron to the ·Temple [Lhouse] of God. 8People who had ·valuable gems [precious stones] gave them to the treasury of the ·Temple [Lhouse] of the LORD, under the care of Jehiel, from the Gershon ·family [clan]. 9The leaders gave ·willingly and completely [freely and wholeheartedly] to the LORD. The people rejoiced to see their leaders give so gladly, and King David was also ·very happy [filled with joy].

David's Prayer

10David ·praised [blessed] the LORD in ·front [the presence] of all the ·people who were gathered [assembly]. He said:

"We ·praise [bless] you, LORD,
God of our father Israel,
forever and ever.
11LORD, ·you are great and powerful [yours is the greatness and power].

You have glory, victory, and ·honor [majesty; splendor].
Everything in heaven and on earth belongs to you.
·The kingdom [Sovereignty; Dominion] belongs to you, LORD;
you are ·the ruler [head; exalted] over everything.
12 ·Riches [Wealth] and honor come from you.
You rule everything.
·You have the [LIn your hand is] power and ·strength [might]
to make ·anyone [everyone] great and strong.
13 Now, our God, we thank you
and praise your glorious name.

14 "·These things did not really come from me and my people. [LBut who am I and who are my people that we have this much to give?]
Everything comes from you;
we have given you back what ·you [Lyour hand] gave us.
15 We are like ·foreigners [aliens; Tsojourners] and ·strangers [transients; nomads],
as our ·ancestors [fathers] were.
Our ·time [Ldays] on earth is like a shadow.
There is no ·hope [*or* security].
16 LORD our God, we have gathered all this abundance
to build your ·Temple [Lhouse] for ·worship to you [Lyour holy name/ Name].
But everything has come from ·you [Lyour hand];
everything belongs to you.
17 I know, my God, that you ·test [examine; search] people's hearts.
You ·are happy when people do what is right [Ldelight/rejoice in integrity/Tuprightness].
I ·was happy to [willingly; freely] give all these things,
and I gave with ·an honest heart [pure motives].
Your people gathered here ·are happy to [willingly] give to you,
and I rejoice to see their giving.
18 LORD, you are the God of our ·ancestors [fathers],
the God of Abraham, Isaac, and ·Jacob [Israel].
·Make your people want to serve you always [Keep these motives always in their heart],
and ·make them want to obey you [direct their heart toward you].
19 Give my son Solomon a ·desire to serve you [perfect heart; undivided mind; Lwhole heart].
Help him always obey your commands, laws, and rules.
Help him build ·the Temple [this temple/palace]
for which I have ·prepared [provided]."

20 Then David said to all the ·people who were gathered [assembly], "·Praise [Bless] the LORD your God." So they all ·praised [blessed] the LORD, the God of their ·ancestors [fathers], and they bowed to the ground ·to give honor to [and prostrated themselves before] the LORD and the king.

Solomon Becomes King
(29:22–25; 1 Kin. 2:10–12)

21 The next day the people sacrificed to the LORD. They offered burnt
offerings [Lev. 1:1–17] to him of a thousand bulls, a thousand ·male sheep
[rams], and a thousand male lambs. They also brought ·drink offerings
[libations]. Many sacrifices were made for all the people of Israel. 22 That

day the people ·ate and drank [feasted] with much joy, ·and the LORD was
with them [Lbefore the LORD].

And they ·made [designated; acknowledged] David's son Solomon
king for the second time. They ·poured olive oil on Solomon to appoint
[anointed] him king ·in the presence of [before] the LORD. And they
·poured oil on Zadok to appoint him [anointed Zadok] as priest. 23Then
Solomon sat on the LORD's throne as king and took his father David's
place. Solomon ·was very successful [prospered], and all the people of
Israel obeyed him. 24All the ·leaders [officials; chiefs] and ·soldiers [mighty
warriors] and King David's sons ·accepted Solomon as king and promised to obey him [pledged their allegiance to King Solomon]. 25The LORD
·made Solomon great before [exalted Solomon in the sight of] all the
Israelites and gave him greater royal ·splendor [majesty] than any king
before him in Israel.

David's Death

26David son of Jesse was king over all Israel. 27He had ·ruled [reigned]
over Israel forty years—seven years in Hebron and thirty-three years in
Jerusalem. 28David died when he was old. He had lived a good, long life
·and had received many [full of] riches and honors. His son Solomon
·became king after him [reigned in his place].
29·Everything David did as king [The acts/events of King David], from
·beginning to end [first to last], is ·recorded [written] in the ·records [chron-
icles; annals] of Samuel the ·seer [prophet], the ·records [chronicles; annals]
of Nathan the prophet, and the ·records [chronicles; annals] of Gad the
·seer [prophet]. 30Those writings tell what David did ·as king of Israel [dur-
ing his reign]. They tell about his power and what happened to him and to
Israel and to all the kingdoms ·around them [of the earth/land].

2 CHRONICLES

Solomon Asks for Wisdom

(1:1–13; 1 Kin. 2:46–3:15)

1 Solomon, David's son, ·became a powerful king [solidified/
secured/established his kingdom/royal authority; Lstrengthened
himself over his kingdom], because the LORD his God was with him and
·made him very great [exalted/magnified/empowered him].
2Solomon spoke to all the people of Israel—the ·commanders [offi-
cers] of thousands of men and of hundreds of men, the judges, every
leader in all Israel, and the ·leaders [Lheads] of the ·families [clans].
3Then Solomon and all the ·people [assembly] with him went to the
·place of worship [Lhigh place] at the town of Gibeon. God's ·Meeting
Tent [Tabernacle], which Moses the LORD's servant had made in the ·des-
ert [wilderness], was there. 4David had brought the Ark of God from
Kiriath Jearim to Jerusalem, where he had ·made [prepared] a place for it
and had set up a tent for it [1 Sam. 6:1–15]. 5But the bronze altar that
Bezalel son of Uri, who was the son of Hur, had made was in Gibeon in
front of the ·Holy Tent [Tabernacle]. So Solomon and the ·people [assem-
bly] worshiped there. 6Solomon went up to the bronze altar ·in the
presence of [before] the LORD at the ·Meeting Tent [Tabernacle] and
·offered [sacrificed] a thousand burnt offerings on it.
7That night God appeared to Solomon and said to him, "Ask for whatever you want me to give you."
8Solomon answered, "You have ·been very kind [shown/demonstrated
loyalty/unfailing love] to my father David, and you have made me king in
his place. 9Now, LORD God, ·may your promise to my father David come
true [*or* your promise to my father David has been fulfilled]. You have
made me king of a ·people [nation] ·who are as many [as numerous] as
the dust of the earth [Gen. 1:16]. 10Now give me wisdom and knowledge
so I can lead these people, ·because no one can rule them without your
help [for who can rule/govern this great people/nation of yours?]."
11God said to Solomon, "You have not asked for wealth or riches or
·honor [fame], or for the ·death of your enemies [Llife of those who hate
you], or for a long life. ·But since [Because] you have asked for wisdom
and knowledge to ·lead [rule; govern] my people, over whom I have made
you king, 12I will give you wisdom and knowledge. I will also give you
more wealth, riches, and ·honor [fame] than any king who has lived
before you or any who will live after you."
13Then Solomon left the ·place of worship [Lhigh place], the ·Meeting
Tent [Tabernacle], at Gibeon and went back to Jerusalem. There King
Solomon ·ruled [reigned] over Israel.

Solomon's Wealth

(1:14–17; 1 Kin. 4:21; 10:14–29)

14Solomon ·had [gathered; amassed; accumulated] fourteen hundred
chariots and twelve thousand horses. He kept some in ·special cities for
the chariots [chariot cities], and others he kept with him in Jerusalem.

15 In Jerusalem Solomon made silver and gold as ·plentiful [common] as
stones and cedar trees as ·plentiful [common] as the ·fig [sycamore-fig]
trees on the ·western hills [LShephelah]. 16 He imported horses from Egypt
and ·Kue [Cilicia; Cpresent-day southern Turkey]; his traders bought
them in ·Kue [Cilicia] for the ·prevailing [usual; standard] price. 17 They
imported chariots from Egypt for ·about fifteen pounds [Lsix hundred
shekels] of silver apiece, and horses cost ·nearly four pounds of silver
[Lone hundred fifty] apiece. Then they ·sold [exported] the horses and
chariots to all the kings of the Hittites and the Arameans.

Solomon Prepares for the Temple

(2:1–18;
1 Kin. 5:1–18; 7:13–51)

2 Solomon decided to build a ·temple [Lhouse] ·as a place to worship [Lfor the name of] the Lord and also a ·palace [Lroyal house]
for himself. 2 He ·chose [assigned; conscripted] seventy thousand men ·to
carry loads [as common laborers], eighty thousand men to ·cut [quarry]
stone in the hill country, and thirty-six hundred men to ·direct the workers [supervise/oversee them].
3 Solomon sent this message to ·Hiram [*or* Huram; Cvariants of the
same name; 1 Chr. 14:1 calls him Hiram; the Hebrew text here reads
Huram] king of the city of Tyre: "·Help me as you helped [Do as you did
for] my father David by sending him cedar logs so he could build himself
a ·palace [Lhouse] to live in. 4 I ·will [am about to] build a ·temple [Lhouse]
for ·worshiping [Lthe name of] the Lord my God, and I will ·give [dedi-
cate] this ·temple [Lhouse] to him. There we will ·burn sweet-smelling
spices [offer fragrant incense] ·in his presence [before him]. We will continually set out the ·holy bread [Tshowbread] in God's presence. And we
will burn sacrifices every morning and evening, on Sabbath days and
New Moons, and on the other feast days ·commanded [appointed; pre-
scribed] by the Lord our God. This ·is a rule for Israel to obey forever
[Lpermanently in/upon Israel].
5 "The ·temple [Lhouse] I ·build [am about to build] will be great,
because our God is greater than all gods. 6 But ·no one can really [Lwho is
able to…?] build a house for our God. Not even the highest of heavens
can ·hold [contain] him. ·How then can I [So who am I to] build a ·temple
[Lhouse] for him except as a place to burn ·sacrifices [*or* incense; Cwhat is
being burned is not indicated] to him?
7 "Now send me a man skilled in working with gold, silver, bronze, and
iron, and with purple, ·red [crimson], and ·blue thread [violet cloth]. He
must also know how to make engravings. He will work with my skilled
craftsmen in Judah and Jerusalem, whom my father David ·chose
[provided].
8 "Also send me cedar, ·pine [cypress; juniper; evergreens], and ·juniper
logs [sandalwood/algum timber] from Lebanon. I know your servants are
·experienced [skilled; adept] at cutting down the trees in Lebanon, and
my servants will help them. 9 Send me a ·lot [vast amount] of wood,
because the ·temple [Lhouse] I am going to build will be large and ·won-
derful [magnificent]. 10 I will give your servants who cut the wood ·one
hundred twenty-five thousand bushels [Ltwenty thousand kors] of wheat,
·one hundred twenty-five thousand bushels [Ltwenty thousand kors] of
barley, ·one hundred fifteen thousand gallons [Ltwenty thousand baths]
of wine, and ·one hundred fifteen thousand gallons [Ltwenty thousand
baths] of oil."
11 Then ·Hiram [*or* Huram; v. 3] king of Tyre answered Solomon with

this letter: "Solomon, because the LORD loves his people, he ·chose [made]
you to be their king." 12 ·Hiram [*or* Huram; v. 3] also said: "·Praise [Blessed
be] the LORD, the God of Israel, who made ·heaven [the sky] and earth! He
has given King David a wise son, ·one [endowed; gifted] with ·wisdom
[discernment; intelligence; discretion] and ·understanding [insight], who
will build a ·temple [Lhouse] for the LORD and a ·palace [Lhouse] for
himself.

13 "I will send you a skilled and ·wise [talented; capable] man named
Huram-Abi. 14 His mother was from the people of Dan, and his father was
from Tyre. Huram-Abi is ·skilled [trained; knowledgeable] in working
with gold, silver, bronze, iron, stone, and wood, and with purple, ·blue
[violet], and ·red thread [crimson cloth/yarn], and ·expensive [fine] linen.
He is skilled in making engravings and can ·make [execute] any design
·you show [given to] him. He will help your ·craftsmen [artisans] and the
craftsmen of your father David.

15 "Now my lord send ·my [Lto his] servants the wheat, barley, oil, and
wine you ·promised [spoke of]. 16 We will cut as much wood from Lebanon
as you need and will bring it on rafts by sea to Joppa. Then you may
·carry [haul; transport] it to Jerusalem."

17 Solomon ·counted [numbered; took a census of] all the foreigners
living in Israel. (This was after the time his father David had counted the
people [2 Sam. 24; 1 Chr. 21].) There were one hundred fifty-three thousand six hundred foreigners. 18 Solomon ·chose [assigned; conscripted]
seventy thousand of them ·to carry loads [as common laborers], eighty
thousand of them to ·cut [quarry] stone in the mountains, and thirty-six
hundred of them to ·direct [supervise; oversee] the workers and to keep
the people working.

Solomon Builds the Temple
(3:1–14; 1 Kin. 6:1–38)

3 Then Solomon began to build the ·Temple [Lhouse] of the LORD in
Jerusalem on Mount Moriah [Gen. 22:2]. This was where the
LORD had appeared to David, Solomon's father. Solomon built the ·Temple
[Lhouse] on the place David had prepared on the threshing floor of
·Araunah [*or* Ornan; 1 Chr. 21:15, 18–28] the Jebusite. 2 Solomon began
building in the ·second month [*or* second day of the second month;
Cmidspring] of the fourth year ·he ruled Israel [of his reign].

3 Solomon used ·these measurements [*or* this foundation] for building
the ·Temple [Lhouse] of God. It was ·ninety feet [Lsixty cubits] long and
·thirty feet [Ltwenty cubits] wide, using the old ·measurement [standard].
4 The ·porch [portico; vestibule; entry room] in front of the main ·room
[hall] of the ·Temple [Lhouse] was ·thirty feet [Ltwenty cubits] long and
·thirty feet [Ltwenty cubits; *or* Lone hundred twenty cubits] high.

He ·covered [overlaid] the ·inside of the porch [main hall; nave] with
·pure [fine] gold. 5 He put panels of ·pine [cypress; juniper; evergreens] on
the walls of the ·main room [main hall; nave] and ·covered [overlaid]
them with ·pure [fine] gold. Then he ·put [decorated/ornamented it with]
designs of palm trees and chains in the gold. 6 He ·decorated [adorned]
the ·Temple [Lhouse] with ·gems [precious stones] and gold from Parvaim.
7 He ·put [overlaid] gold on the ·Temple's [Lhouse's] ceiling beams, ·door-
posts [thresholds], walls, and doors, and he carved ·creatures with wings
[cherubim] on the walls.

8 Then he made the ·Most Holy Place [THoly of Holies]. It was ·thirty
feet [Ltwenty cubits] long and ·thirty feet [Ltwenty cubits] wide, ·as wide

as [corresponding to the width of] the ·Temple [Lhouse]. He ·covered
[overlaid] its walls with ·about forty-six thousand pounds [Lsix hundred
talents] of ·pure [fine] gold. 9The gold nails weighed ·over a pound [Lfifty
shekels]. He also ·covered [overlaid] the upper rooms with gold.
10He ·made [sculpted; modeled] two ·creatures with wings [cherubim] for
the ·Most Holy Place [THoly of Holies] and ·covered [overlaid] them with
gold. 11The wings of the ·gold creatures [cherubim] were ·thirty feet [Ltwenty
cubits] across. One wing of one creature was ·seven and one-half feet [Lfive
cubits] long and touched the ·Temple [Lhouse] wall. The creature's other
wing was also ·seven and one-half feet [Lfive cubits] long, and it touched a
wing of the second ·creature [cherub]. 12One wing of the second creature
touched the other side of the room and was also ·seven and one-half feet
[Lfive cubits] long. The second creature's other wing touched the first creature's wing, and it was also ·seven and one-half feet [Lfive cubits] long.
13Together, the creatures' wings were ·thirty feet [Ltwenty cubits] across. The
creatures stood on their feet, facing the ·main room [main hall; nave].
14He made the ·curtain [veil] of ·blue [violet], purple, and ·red thread
[crimson cloth/yarn], and ·expensive [fine] linen, and he ·put [worked;
embroidered] designs of ·creatures with wings [cherubim] in it.

The Pillars and Furnishings for the Temple
(3:15–5:1; 1 Kin. 7:13–51)

15He made two pillars to stand in front of the ·Temple [Lhouse]. They
were ·about fifty-two feet [Lthirty-five cubits; Cpossibly the combined
length of the two] tall, and the capital on top of each pillar was over ·seven
feet [Lfive cubits] tall. 16He made ·a net of [interwoven] chains and put
them on the tops of the pillars. He made a hundred pomegranates and
put them on the chains. 17Then he put the pillars up in front of the
Temple. One pillar stood on the ·south [Lright] side, the other on the
·north [Lleft]. He named the ·south [Lright] pillar Jachin [C"he establishes"] and the ·north [Lleft] pillar Boaz [C"in him is strength"].

4 He made a bronze altar ·thirty feet [Ltwenty cubits] long, ·thirty
feet [Ltwenty cubits] wide, and ·fifteen feet [Lten cubits] tall. 2Then
he made from ·bronze [cast metal] a large round ·bowl [basin], which was
called the Sea [Csymbol of chaos subdued; 1 Kin. 7:23]. It was ·forty-five
feet [Lthirty cubits] ·around [in circumference], ·fifteen feet [Lten cubits]
·across [from rim to rim], and ·seven and one-half feet [Lfive cubits] ·deep
[high]. 3There were ·carvings [figures; images] of ·bulls [oxen] under the
rim of the bowl—ten ·bulls [oxen] every ·eighteen inches [Lcubit]. They
were in two rows and were ·made [cast] in one piece with the bowl.
4The bowl rested on the backs of twelve bronze ·bulls [oxen] ·that faced
outward from the center of the bowl [Lall their hindquarters were toward
the inside]. Three ·bulls [oxen] faced north, three faced west, three faced
south, and three faced east. 5The sides of the bowl were ·four inches [four
fingers; La handbreadth] thick, and it held ·about seventeen thousand five
hundred gallons [Lthree thousand baths]. The rim of the bowl was like the
rim of a cup ·or like [and resembled] a lily blossom.
6He made ten ·smaller bowls [basins] and put five on the ·south [Lright]
side and five on the ·north [Lleft]. They were for ·washing [rinsing] the
·animals [*or* utensils; Lthings] for the burnt offerings [Lev. 1:1–17], but
the ·large bowl [LSea; v. 2] was for the priests to wash in.
7He ·made [cast] ten lampstands of gold, ·following the plans [accord-
ing to the specifications]. He put them in the Temple, five on the ·south
[Lright] side and five on the ·north [Lleft].

8He made ten tables and put them in the Temple, five on the ·south
[Lright] side and five on the ·north [Lleft]. And he used gold to ·make
[mold] a hundred other ·bowls [basins].

9He also made the priests' courtyard and the large courtyard. He made
the doors that opened to the courtyard and ·covered [overlaid] them with
bronze. 10Then he put the large ·bowl [basin; Cthe Sea] on the right side
toward the southeast corner.

11Huram also made ·bowls [pots; pails; washbasins], shovels, and ·small
[*or* sprinkling] bowls. So he finished his work for King Solomon on the
·Temple [Lhouse] of God:
12two pillars;
two ·large bowls for the [bowl-shaped] capitals on top of the pillars;
two ·nets [networks of interwoven chains] to cover the two ·large bowls
for the [bowl-shaped] capitals on top of the pillars;
13four hundred pomegranates for the ·two nets [chains] (there were two
rows of pomegranates for each ·net [chain] covering the ·bowls
for the [bowl-shaped] capitals on top of the pillars);
14the ·stands [water carts] with a ·bowl [basin] on each stand;
15the large ·bowl [basin] with twelve ·bulls [oxen] under it;
16the ·pots [pails; ash buckets], shovels, ·forks [meat hooks], and all the
·things to go with them [related articles/utensils].

All the things that Huram-Abi made for King Solomon for the ·Temple
[Lhouse] of the LORD were made of ·polished [burnished] bronze. 17The
king had these things ·poured [cast] into clay molds that were made in
the plain of the Jordan River between Succoth and Zarethan. 18Solomon
had so many things made that the total weight of all the bronze ·was
never known [could not be/was not calculated].

19Solomon also made all the ·things [furnishings] for God's ·Temple
[Lhouse]: the golden altar; tables which held the bread ·that shows God's
people are in his presence [Lof Presence; Ex. 25:23–30]; 20the lampstands
and their lamps of ·pure [solid] gold, to burn in front of the ·Most Holy
Place [inner sanctuary] as ·planned [prescribed; specified]; 21the flowers,
lamps, and tongs of pure gold; 22the pure gold ·wick trimmers [lamp
snuffers], small bowls, pans, and dishes ·used to carry coals [and incense
burners/censers], the gold doors for the ·Temple [Lhouse], and the inside
doors of the ·Most Holy Place [THoly of Holies] and of the ·main room
[main hall; nave].

5 Finally all the work Solomon did for the ·Temple [Lhouse] of the
LORD was finished. He brought in everything his father David had
·set apart [dedicated] for the ·Temple [Lhouse]—all the silver and gold
and other ·articles [utensils]. And he ·put [stored] everything in the treasuries of God's ·Temple [Lhouse].

The Ark Is Brought into the Temple
(5:2–7:10; 1 Kin. 8:1–66; Ps. 136:1; 132:1, 8–10)

2Solomon ·called for [summoned; assembled; convened] the elders of
Israel, the heads of the tribes, and the ·leaders [chiefs] of the ·families
[clans] to come to him in Jerusalem. He wanted them to bring the Ark of
the ·Agreement [Covenant; Treaty; LTestimony] with the LORD from ·the
older part of the city [Lthe city of David, that is, Zion]. 3So all the Israelites
came together with the king during the festival in the seventh month
[Cthe Festival of Shelters or Tabernacles or Booths held in early autumn].
4When all the ·elders [men] of Israel arrived, the Levites ·lifted [picked;
took] up the Ark. 5They ·carried [brought up] the ·Ark of the Agreement

[Lark; Ex. 25:10], the ·Meeting Tent [Tabernacle], and the ·holy utensils
[sacred furnishings] in it; the ·priests and the Levites [Levitical priests]
brought them up. 6King Solomon and all the ·Israelites [Lcongregation/
community of Israel) gathered before the ·Ark of the Agreement [Lark]
and sacrificed so many sheep and ·bulls [oxen] no one could count or
record them.
7Then the priests put the Ark of the ·Agreement [covenant; treaty;
LTestimony] with the LORD in its place inside the inner sanctuary of the
·Temple [Lhouse], the ·Most Holy Place [THoly of Holies], under the wings
of the ·golden creatures [Lcherubim]. 8The wings of ·these creatures
[Lcherubim] were spread out over the place for the Ark, ·covering [form-
ing a canopy over] it and its carrying poles. 9The carrying poles were so
long that anyone standing in the ·Holy Place [inner sanctuary] in front of
the ·Most Holy Place [THoly of Holies] could see the ends of the poles.
But no one could see them from outside the Holy Place. The poles are still
there today. 10The only things inside the Ark were two stone tablets
[Cinscribed with the Ten Commandments] that Moses had put in the Ark
at ·Mount Sinai [LHoreb]. That was where the LORD made his ·agreement
[covenant; treaty] with the Israelites after they came out of Egypt.
11Then all the priests ·left [came out of; withdrew from] the Holy Place.
(All the priests ·from each group [regardless of their divisions/orders; *or*
whether they were serving that day or not] had ·made themselves ready to
serve the LORD [consecrated/purified/sanctified themselves].) 12All the
Levite ·musicians [singers]—Asaph, Heman, Jeduthun [Call associated
with certain psalms; see titles of Ps. 50, 73–83 (Asaph), 88 (Heman), 39,
62, 77 (Jeduthun)], and all their sons and ·relatives [kinsmen; Lbrothers]—
stood on the east side of the altar. They were dressed in ·white [fine] linen
and played cymbals, harps, and lyres. ·With [Accompanying] them were
one hundred twenty priests who blew trumpets. 13Those who blew the
trumpets and those who sang ·together sounded like one person [per-
formed in unison] as they praised and thanked the LORD. They sang ·as
others played their [accompanied by] trumpets, cymbals, and other
instruments. They praised the LORD with this song:

"He is good;
his ·love [unfailing love; lovingkindness; loyalty] ·continues [endures]
forever [Ps. 136:1]."

Then the ·Temple [Lhouse] of the LORD was filled with a cloud. 14The
priests could not continue their ·work [service] because of the cloud,
because the LORD's ·glory [splendor] filled the ·Temple [Lhouse] of God.

Solomon Speaks to the People

6 Then Solomon said, "The LORD said he would live in the ·dark
cloud [thick cloud; thick cloud of darkness]. 2LORD, I have built a
·wonderful [magnificent; glorious; lofty] ·Temple [Lhouse] for you—a
place for you to ·live [dwell] forever."
3While all the ·Israelites [Lcommunity of Israel] were standing there,
King Solomon turned to them and blessed them. 4Then he said, "·Praise
[Bless] the LORD, the God of Israel. He has ·done [Lfulfilled with his hand]
what he ·promised [spoke] to my father David [2 Sam. 7:1–16]. The LORD
said, 5'Since the ·time [Lday] I brought my people out of Egypt, I have not
chosen a city in any tribe of Israel where a ·Temple [Lhouse] will be built
for ·me [Lmy name to be there]. I did not choose a man to ·lead [rule] my
people Israel. 6But now I have chosen Jerusalem ·as the place I am to be

worshiped [Lfor my name to be], and I have chosen David to ·lead [rule]
my people Israel.’
7“My father David wanted to build a ·Temple [Lhouse] for ·the [Lthe
name of the] LORD, the God of Israel. 8But the LORD said to my father
David, ‘·It was good that you [You did well to have] wanted to build a
·Temple [Lhouse] for me. 9But you are not the one to build it. Your son,
who ·comes from your own body [will be born to you], is the one who will
build ·my Temple [Lthe house for my name].’
10“Now the LORD has ·kept his promise [Lestablished the word he
spoke]. I am the king now in place of David my father. Now I ·rule [Lsit on
the throne of] Israel as the LORD promised, and I have built the ·Temple
[Lhouse] for ·the [Lthe name of the] LORD, the God of Israel. 11There I have
put the Ark, in which is the ·Agreement [covenant; treaty] the LORD made
with the ·Israelites [people of Israel].”

Solomon’s Prayer

12Then Solomon stood ·facing [Lbefore] the LORD’s altar, ·and all the
Israelites were standing behind him [Lin the presence of the assembly/
community of Israel]. He ·spread out [lifted] his hands. 13He had made a
bronze platform ·seven and one-half feet [Lfive cubits] long, ·seven and
one-half feet [Lfive cubits] wide, and ·seven and one-half feet [Lfive cubits]
high, and he had placed it in the middle of the outer courtyard. Solomon
stood on the platform. Then he kneeled in front of all the ·people
[Lassembly; community] of Israel gathered there, and he spread out his
hands toward ·the sky [heaven]. 14He said, “LORD, God of Israel, there is
no god [Cno true God] like you in heaven or on earth. You keep your
·agreement of love with [covenant/treaty and show unfailing love/loyalty
to] your servants who ·truly follow [wholeheartedly/devotedly walk
before] you. 15You have kept the promise you made to your servant David,
my father. You spoke it with your own mouth and finished it with your
hands today.
16“Now, LORD, God of Israel, keep the promise you made to your servant David, my father. You said, ‘If your sons ·are careful [guard their
steps] ·to obey my teachings [Land walk in my laws] as you have ·obeyed
[Lwalked], ·there will always be someone from your family [you will never
fail to have someone] ·ruling [Lsitting on the throne of] Israel.’ 17Now,
LORD, God of Israel, ·please continue to keep that promise you made [ful-
fill this word you have spoken] to your servant.
18“But, ·God, can you [will God] really live here on the earth with ·peo-
ple [mortals]? The ·sky and the highest place in heaven [heavens, even the
highest heavens,] cannot contain you. ·Surely this house which I have
built cannot contain you [How much less this temple/Lhouse I have built].
19But ·please listen [listen favorably; attend] to my prayer and my request,
because I am your servant. LORD my God, hear this ·prayer [cry] your
servant prays to you. 20Day and night please watch over this ·Temple
[Lhouse] where you have said you would ·be worshiped [Lput your name].
Hear the prayer I pray facing this place. 21Hear ·my prayers and the
prayers of [Lthe pleas/entreaties/Tsupplications of your servant and] your
people Israel when we pray facing this place. Hear from your home in
heaven, and when you hear, forgive us.
22“If someone ·wrongs another person [sins against his neighbor], he
will be brought to the altar in this ·Temple [Lhouse]. If he swears an oath
[Cthat he is innocent], 23then hear in heaven and act. Judge ·the case

[Lbetween your servants; Cthe accuser and the accused], ·punish [condemn;
repay] the guilty, but ·declare that [justify; acquit] the ·innocent person is
not guilty [righteous because of their innocence/righteousness].
24"·When [If] your people, the Israelites, sin against you, their enemies
will defeat them. But if they ·come back [return] to you and ·praise you
[acknowledge/confess your name] and pray and ·appeal [Tmake supplica-
tion] to you in this ·Temple [Lhouse], 25then ·listen [hear] from heaven.
Forgive the sin of your people Israel, and bring them back to the land you
gave to them and their ·ancestors [fathers].
26"When they sin against you, you will ·stop the rain from falling on
their land [shut up the heavens/sky and stop the rain]. Then they will
pray, facing this place and ·praising you [acknowledge/confess your
name]; they will stop sinning ·when [because] you ·make them suffer
[punish/afflict them]. 27When this happens, hear their prayer in heaven,
and forgive the sins of your servants, the Israelites. Teach them ·to do
what is right [the right way to live; Lthe good way in which they should
walk]. Then please send rain to ·this [Lyour] land you have given ·particu-
larly to them [Lto your people as an inheritance/special possession].
28"·At times the land will get so dry that no food will grow [LIf there is
famine in the land…], or ·a great sickness will spread among the people
[a plague; pestilence…]. ·Sometimes [L…or if…] the crops will be
destroyed by blight, mildew, locusts, or grasshoppers. ·Your [L…or if…]
people will be attacked in their cities by their enemies, or will become
sick. 29·When any of these things [—whatever plague/disaster or disease]
happens, ·the [L…and if the…] people will ·become truly sorry [pray
about their troubles/affliction and pain/sorrows…]. ·If [L…and] your
people spread their hands in prayer toward this ·Temple [Lhouse], 30then
hear their prayers from your home in heaven. Forgive and ·treat [deal
with] each person as he ·should be treated [deserves] because you know
what is in a person's heart. Only you know ·what is in people's hearts [the
human heart]. 31Then the people will ·respect [fear; revere; honor] and
·obey you [Lwalk in your ways] as long as they live in this land you gave
our ·ancestors [fathers].
32"People who are not Israelites, foreigners from other lands, will hear
about your ·greatness [Lgreat name] and ·power [Lmighty hand and outstretched arm]. They will come from far away to pray ·at this Temple
[Ltoward this house]. 33Then hear from your home in heaven, and ·do
[grant; answer] whatever they ask you. Then ·people everywhere [Lall the
peoples of the earth] will know ·you [Lyour name] and ·respect [fear;
revere; acknowledge] you, just as your people Israel do. Then everyone
will know that I built this ·Temple [Lhouse] as a place to ·worship you
[Lbear your name].
34"When your people go out to fight their enemies ·along some road
on which [by whichever way] you send them, your people will pray to
you, ·facing [toward] this city which you have chosen and the ·Temple
[Lhouse] I have built for ·you [Lyour name]. 35Then hear in heaven their
prayers and their ·plea [Tsupplication], and ·do what is right [uphold their
cause; vindicate them].
36"·Everyone sins, so your people will also sin against you [When/If
your people sin against you—for there is no one who does not sin—…].
You will become angry with them and will ·hand them over [deliver
them] to their enemies. Their enemies will capture them and take them

away to a country far or near. 37·Your people will be sorry for their sins [If
they stop and think/come to their senses…] **when they are held as ·pris-
oners** [captives] **in another country. ·They will be sorry** […and they
repent…] **and ·pray** [plead; make supplication] **to you in the land ·where
they are held as prisoners** [of their captivity], **saying, 'We have sinned. We
have done ·wrong** [evil] **and acted wickedly.' 38·They will truly turn back
to you** […and they return to you with all their heart and soul/being] **in
the land where they are captives. ·They will** […and they] **pray, ·facing this**
[toward the] **land you gave their ·ancestors** [fathers], **this city you have
chosen, and the ·Temple** [Lhouse] **I have built for ·you** [Lyour name…].
39**Then hear their prayers and their ·plea** [Tsupplication] **from your home
in heaven, and ·do what is right** [uphold their cause; vindicate them].
Forgive your people who have sinned against you.
40"**Now, my God, ·look at us. Listen** [L…may your eyes be open and
your ears attentive] **to the prayers we pray in this place.**
41**Now, ·rise** [ascend], **LORD God, and ·come to** [enter] **your resting place.**
Come with the ·Ark of the Agreement that shows your strength [Lark
of your might/power].
Let your priests ·receive [Lbe clothed with] **your salvation, LORD God,**
and may your ·holy people [godly/faithful ones] **·be happy because
of your goodness** [rejoice in what is good].
42**LORD God, do not ·reject** [turn away from] **your ·appointed** [anointed]
·one [*or* ones].
Remember your ·love [unfailing love; lovingkindness; loyalty] **for
your servant David** [Ps. 132:1, 8–10]."

The Temple Is Given to the Lord

7 When Solomon finished praying, fire came down from ·the sky
[heaven] **and ·burned up** [consumed] **the burnt offering and the
sacrifices. The LORD's ·glory** [splendor] **filled the ·Temple** [Lhouse]. 2**The
priests could not enter the ·Temple** [Lhouse] **of the LORD, because the
LORD's ·glory** [splendor] **filled it. 3When all the people of Israel saw the
fire come down and the LORD's ·glory** [splendor] **on the ·Temple** [Lhouse],
**they bowed down on the pavement with their faces to the ground. They
worshiped and ·thanked** [praised] **the LORD, saying,**
"He is good;
his ·love [unfailing love; lovingkindness; loyalty] **·continues** [endures]
forever [Ps. 136]."
4**Then King Solomon and all the people ·offered** [sacrificed] **sacrifices to
the LORD. 5King Solomon ·offered** [sacrificed] **a sacrifice of twenty-two
thousand ·cattle** [oxen] **and one hundred twenty thousand sheep. So the
king and all the people ·gave** [dedicated] **the ·Temple** [Lhouse] **to God.**
6**The priests stood ·ready to do their work** [in their places/positions/
posts]. **The Levites also stood with the instruments of the LORD's music
that King David had made for praising the LORD. The priests and Levites
were ·saying** [singing], **"His ·love** [unfailing love; lovingkindness; loyalty]
·continues [endures] **forever** [Ps. 136]." **The priests, who stood across
from the Levites, blew their trumpets, and all the Israelites were
standing.**
7**Solomon ·made holy** [consecrated] **the middle part of the courtyard,
which is in front of the ·Temple** [Lhouse] **of the LORD. There he ·offered**
[sacrificed] **whole burnt offerings and the fat of the ·fellowship** [peace]
offerings. He ·offered [sacrificed] **them in the courtyard, because the**

bronze altar he had made could not hold the burnt offerings [Lev. 1:1–17], ·grain [Lgift; tribute] offerings [Lev. 2:1], and fat [Lev. 3:16].
8Solomon and all the Israelites ·celebrated [kept; observed] the festival [Cof Shelters/Tabernacles/Booths] for seven days. There ·were many people [Lwas a great assembly/congregation], and they came from as far away as Lebo Hamath [Cin the north] and the brook of Egypt [Cin the south].
9For seven days they celebrated ·giving [the dedication of] the altar. Then they ·celebrated [kept; observed] the festival for seven days. On the eighth day they had a ·meeting [solemn assembly; closing ceremony]. 10On the twenty-third day of the seventh month Solomon sent the people home, full of joy. They were ·happy [content; glad; Lgood of heart] because the LORD had been so good to David, Solomon, and his people Israel.

The Lord Appears to Solomon
(7:11–22; 1 Kin. 9:1–9)

11Solomon finished the ·Temple [Lhouse] of the LORD and his royal ·palace [Lhouse]. He had success in ·doing [completing; accomplishing] everything he planned in the ·Temple [Lhouse] of the LORD and his own ·palace [Lhouse]. 12Then the LORD appeared to Solomon at night and said to him, "I have heard your prayer and have chosen this place for myself to be a ·Temple [Lhouse] ·for [of] sacrifices.
13"·I may [LIf I…] ·stop the sky [shut the heavens] from sending rain. ·I may [L…or if I…] command the locusts to ·destroy [devour] the land. ·I may [L…or if I…] send ·sicknesses [plague; pestilence] to my people.
14Then if my people, who ·are called by my name [belong to me], will humble themselves, if they will pray and seek ·me [Lmy face] and stop their evil ways, I will hear them from heaven. I will forgive their sin, and I will ·heal [restore] their land. 15Now ·I will see them, and I will listen [my eyes will be open and my ears attentive; 6:40] to the prayers prayed in this place. 16I have chosen this ·Temple [Lhouse] and ·made it holy [consecrated/purified/sanctified it]. So ·I will be worshiped [Lmy name will be] there forever. Yes, ·I will always watch over it and love it [Lmy eyes and my heart will be there forever].
17"But you must ·serve [Lwalk before] me as your father David did. You must ·obey [do] all I have commanded and keep my laws and rules. 18If you do, I will ·make your kingdom strong [secure/establish your throne/dynasty]. This is the ·agreement [covenant; treaty] I made with your father David, saying, '·Someone from your family will always [You will not fail to have a successor to] rule in Israel [17:10–14; 2 Sam. 7:11–16].'
19"But ·you must follow me and obey the [if any of you turn away from me and abandon/forsake my…] laws and commands I have given you, and you must not serve or worship other gods. 20If you do, I will ·take the Israelites out of [Luproot you from] my land, the land I have given ·you [Lthem], and I will ·leave [reject; disown; abandon] this ·Temple [Lhouse] that I have ·made holy [Lconsecrated/purified/sanctified for my name]. All the nations will ·make fun of [mock] it and ·speak evil about [ridicule] it. 21This ·Temple [Lhouse] is ·honored [exalted] now, but then, everyone who passes by will be ·shocked [appalled]. They will ask, 'Why did the LORD do this terrible thing to this land and this ·Temple [Lhouse]?'
22People will answer, 'This happened because they ·left [abandoned; forsook] the LORD, the God of their ·ancestors [fathers], the God who brought them out of Egypt. They ·decided to follow [embraced; adopted] other gods and worshiped and served them, so he brought all this ·disaster [calamity] on them.'"

Solomon's Other Achievements
(8:1–18; 1 Kin. 9:10–28)

8 By the end of twenty years, Solomon had built the ·Temple [Lhouse] of the LORD and the royal ·palace [Lhouse]. 2Solomon then rebuilt the towns that ·Hiram [*or* Huram; 2:3] had given him, and Solomon sent Israelites to live in them. 3Then he went to Hamath Zobah and captured it. 4Solomon also built the town of Tadmor in the ·desert [wilderness], and he built all the towns in Hamath as ·towns for storing grain and supplies [supply centers; storage cities]. 5He rebuilt the towns of Upper Beth Horon and Lower Beth Horon, ·protecting [fortifying] them with strong walls, gates, and bars in the gates. 6He also rebuilt the town of Baalath. And he built all the other ·towns for storage [supply centers; storage cities] and all the cities for his chariots and horses. He built all he ·wanted [desired] in Jerusalem, Lebanon, and ·everywhere he ruled [throughout his kingdom/realm].

7·There were other people [Others survived] in the land who were not Israelites—the Hittites, Amorites, Perizzites, Hivites, and Jebusites. 8They were descendants of the ·people [nations] that the Israelites had not destroyed. Solomon ·forced [conscripted] them to be ·slave workers [forced labor], as is still true today. 9But Solomon did not ·make slaves of [impose forced labor on] the Israelites. They were his soldiers, ·chief captains [officers], commanders of his chariots, and his ·chariot drivers [*or* cavalry]. 10These were his most important officers. There were two hundred fifty of them to ·direct [supervise; be in charge of] the people.

11Solomon brought the daughter of the king of Egypt from the ·older part of Jerusalem [LCity of David] to the ·palace [Lhouse] he had built for her. Solomon said, "My wife must not live in King David's ·palace [house], because the places where the Ark of the ·Agreement [LLORD] has ·been [entered] are ·holy [consecrated; purified; sanctified]."

12Then Solomon ·offered [sacrificed] burnt offerings [Lev. 1:1–17] to the LORD on the altar he had built for the LORD in front of the ·Temple [Lhouse] ·porch [portico; vestibule; entry room]. 13He ·offered [sacrificed] sacrifices ·every day [according to the daily requirements/rule] as Moses had commanded. They were ·offered [sacrificed] on the Sabbath days, New Moons, and the three yearly feasts—the ·Feast [Festival] of Unleavened Bread, the ·Feast [Festival] of Weeks, and the ·Feast [Festival] of ·Shelters [Tabernacles; Booths]. 14Solomon followed his father David's instructions and ·chose [appointed] the ·groups [divisions; orders] of priests for their service and the Levites ·to lead the [for their duties/offices of] praise and to help the priests do their daily work. And he ·chose [appointed] the gatekeepers by their ·groups [divisions] to serve at each gate, as David, the man of God, had commanded. 15They ·obeyed all of [Ldid not deviate from] Solomon's commands to the priests and Levites, as well as his commands about the ·treasuries [storehouses].

16All Solomon's work was done as he had ·said [ordered] from the day the foundation of the ·Temple [Lhouse] of the LORD was begun, until it was finished. So the ·Temple [Lhouse] was ·finished [completed].

17Then Solomon went to the towns of Ezion Geber and Elath near the ·Red Sea [Lcoast] in the land of Edom. 18·Hiram [*or* Huram; 2:3] sent ships to Solomon that were commanded by his own men, who ·were skilled sailors [Lknew the sea]. ·Hiram's [*or* Huram's] men went with Solomon's men to Ophir and brought back ·about thirty-four thousand pounds [L450 talents] of gold to King Solomon.

The Queen of Sheba Visits
(9:1–12; 1 Kin. 10:1–13)

9 When the queen of Sheba heard about Solomon's fame, she came
to Jerusalem to ·test [challenge] him with ·hard questions [diffi-
cult riddles]. She ·had a large group of servants with her [Lcame with very
great strength; Cpossibly referring to her large retinue or great wealth] and
camels carrying spices, ·jewels [precious stones], and much gold. When
she came to Solomon, she talked with him about all she had ·in mind [Lon
her heart/mind], 2and Solomon answered all her questions. Nothing was
·too hard for him to [hidden from him that he could not] explain to her.
3The queen of Sheba ·saw [realized; observed] that Solomon was very
wise. She saw the ·palace [Lhouse] he had built, 4the food on his table, ·his
many officers [the organization/attendance of his officials], the palace
servants and their ·good [fine; splendid] clothes, the ·servants who served
Solomon his wine [cupbearers] and their ·good [fine; splendid] clothes.
She saw the whole burnt offerings [Lev. 1:1–17] he made in the ·Temple
[Lhouse] of the LORD. All these things ·amazed her [overwhelmed her;
took her breath away].
5So she said to King Solomon, "What I heard in my own country about
your ·achievements [wise sayings; Lwords] and wisdom is true. 6I did not
believe it then, but now I have come and seen it with my own eyes. I was
not told even half of your great wisdom! You ·are much greater than [sur-
pass/exceed what] I had heard. 7Your people and officials are very ·lucky
[happy; fortunate; blessed], because in ·always serving [continually standing before] you, they are able to hear your wisdom. 8·Praise [Blessed be]
the LORD your God who ·was pleased to make you king [delights in you].
He has put you on his throne to ·rule [reign] for the LORD your God,
because your God loves the people of Israel and ·supports [upholds;
secures; establishes] them forever. He has made you king over them to
·keep justice and to rule fairly [rule/act with justice and righteousness]."
9Then she gave the king ·about nine thousand pounds [L120 talents] of
gold and many spices and ·jewels [precious stones]. No one had ever given
such spices as the queen of Sheba gave to King Solomon.
10·Hiram's [*or* Huram's; 2:3] men and Solomon's men brought gold
from Ophir [Cperhaps a region in southern Arabia], ·juniper wood [san-
dalwood; algum], and ·jewels [precious stones]. 11King Solomon used the
·juniper wood [sandalwood; algum] to build steps for the ·Temple
[Lhouse] of the LORD and the ·palace [Lhouse] and to make lyres and harps
for the ·musicians [singers]. No one in Judah had ever seen ·such beautiful things as these [anything like them].
12King Solomon gave the queen of Sheba everything she ·wanted
[desired] and asked for, even more than she had brought to him. Then she
and her servants returned to her own country.

Solomon's Wealth
(9:13–28; 1 Kin. 4:21; 10:14–29)

13Every year King Solomon received ·about fifty thousand pounds
[L666 talents] of gold. 14Besides that, he also received gold from traders
and merchants. All the kings of Arabia and the governors of the land also
brought gold and silver to Solomon.
15King Solomon made two hundred large shields of hammered gold,
each of which contained ·about seven and one-half pounds [Lsix hundred
shekels] of hammered gold. 16He also made three hundred smaller shields
of hammered gold, each of which contained ·about four pounds [Lthree
hundred shekels] of gold. The king put them in the ·Palace [Lhouse] of the
Forest of Lebanon [1 Kin. 7:2; 10:17, 21].

[17]The king built a large throne of ivory and ·covered [overlaid] it with pure gold. [18]The throne had six steps on it and an attached gold footstool. There were armrests on both sides of the ·chair [seat], and each armrest had a lion beside it. [19]Twelve lions stood on the six steps, one lion at each end of each step. Nothing like this had ever been made for any other kingdom. [20]All of Solomon's drinking cups, as well as the ·dishes [vessels; utensils] in the ·Palace [[L]house] of the Forest of Lebanon, were made of pure gold. In Solomon's time ·people did not think silver was valuable [silver was considered worthless].

[21]King Solomon had many ships that ·he sent out to trade [[L]went to Tarshish; [C]in present-day Spain, hence a large, seagoing trading ship], with ·Hiram's [*or* Huram's; 2:3] men as the crews. Every three years the ships returned, bringing back gold, silver, ivory, apes, and ·baboons [*or* peacocks].

[22]King Solomon had more riches and wisdom than all the other kings on earth. [23]All the kings of the earth ·wanted to see [sought audience with; came to consult] Solomon and listen to the wisdom God had given him. [24]Year after year everyone who came brought gifts of silver and gold, ·clothes [robes], weapons, spices, horses, and mules.

[25]Solomon had four thousand stalls for horses and chariots, and he had twelve thousand ·horses [*or* horsemen; cavalry]. He kept some in ·special cities for the chariots [chariot cities], and others he kept with him in Jerusalem. [26]Solomon ·ruled [reigned] over all the ·kingdoms [[L]kings] from the Euphrates River to the land of the Philistines, as far as the border of Egypt [1 Kin. 4:20–21]. [27]In Jerusalem the king made silver as common as stones and cedar trees as plentiful as the ·fig [sycamore-fig] trees ·on the western hills [[L]in the Shephelah]. [28]Solomon imported horses from Egypt and all other countries.

Solomon's Death
(9:29–31; 1 Kin. 11:41–43)

[29]·Everything else Solomon did [The rest of the events/acts/history of Solomon's reign], from ·the beginning to the end [first to last], ·is [are they not…?] written in the ·records [history; annals] of Nathan the prophet, and in the prophecy of Ahijah the Shilonite, and in the visions of Iddo the ·seer [prophet], who wrote about Jeroboam, Nebat's son [[C]some consider these titles of writings]. [30]Solomon ·ruled [reigned] in Jerusalem over all Israel for forty years. [31]Then Solomon ·died [[L]lay down/[T]slept with his fathers/ancestors] and was buried in the city of David [[C]Jerusalem], his father. And Solomon's son Rehoboam became king in his place.

Israel Turns Against Rehoboam
(10:1–11:4; 1 Kin. 12:1–24)

10 Rehoboam went to Shechem, where all the Israelites had gone to make him king. [2]Jeroboam son of Nebat was in Egypt, where he had ·gone to escape [fled] from King Solomon. When Jeroboam heard about Rehoboam being made king, he returned from Egypt. [3]After the people ·sent for [summoned; [L]sent and called for] him, he and the people went to Rehoboam and said to him, [4]"Your father ·forced us to work very hard [[L]made our yoke heavy]. Now, ·make it easier for us, and don't make us work as he did [[L]lighten the hard labor and heavy yoke of your father]. Then we will serve you."

[5]Rehoboam answered, "Come back to me in three days." So the people left.

[6]King Rehoboam ·asked [consulted] the elders who had advised Solomon during his lifetime, "How do you ·think I should [advise/counsel me to] answer these people?"

7They answered, "·Be kind [LIf you are fair] to these people. If you
please them and give them a ·kind [cordial] answer, they will serve you
always."
8But Rehoboam rejected ·this advice [Lthe advice/counsel of the elders].
Instead, he ·asked [consulted] the young men who had grown up with
him and who ·served as his advisers [served/attended him]. 9Rehoboam
asked them, "What is your ·advice [counsel]? How should we answer
these people who said to me, '·Don't make us work as hard as your father
did' [LLighten the yoke your father put on us]?"
10The young men who had grown up with him answered, "The people
said to you, 'Your father ·forced us to work very hard [Lmade our yoke
heavy]. Now make our work ·easier [lighter].' You should tell them, 'My
little ·finger [Lone] is ·bigger than my father's legs [Lthicker than my
father's loins/waist]. 11·He forced you to work hard [LMy father laid a
heavy yoke on you], but I will ·make you work even harder [Ladd to your
yoke]. My father ·beat [scourged; disciplined] you with whips, but I will
·beat [scourge; discipline] you with ·whips that have sharp points
[Lscorpions; Ceither a metaphor or an especially painful kind of whip].'"
12Rehoboam had told the people, "Come back to me in three days." So
after three days Jeroboam and all the people returned to Rehoboam.
13King Rehoboam spoke ·cruel words [harshly] to them, because he had
rejected the ·advice [counsel] of the elders. 14He followed the ·advice
[counsel] of the young men and said, "My father ·forced you to work hard
[Llaid a heavy yoke on you], but I will ·make you work even harder [Ladd
to your yoke]. My father beat you with whips, but I will ·beat [scourge;
discipline] you with ·whips that have sharp points [Lscorpions; v. 11]."
15So the king ·did not [refused to] listen to the people. God caused this
·to happen [turn of events] so that the LORD could ·keep the promise he
had made [fulfill/establish the word he spoke] to Jeroboam son of Nebat
through Ahijah, a prophet from Shiloh.
16When all the Israelites saw that the king refused to listen to them,
they said to the king,

"·We have no share [LWhat share/part/Tportion have we…?] in David
[Cin David's dynasty]!
We have no ·part [inheritance; interest; heritage] in the son of Jesse!
People of Israel, ·let's go to our own homes [Leach one to your tents]!
Let David's son ·rule his own people [Llook after your own house;
Cthat is, the tribe of Judah]."

So all the Israelites ·went home [Lleft for their tents]. 17But Rehoboam ·still
ruled [continued to reign] over the Israelites who lived in the towns of Judah.
18·Adoniram [*or* Hadoram] was in charge of the ·forced labor [labor
force]. When Rehoboam sent him to the people, they ·threw stones at him
until he died [stoned him to death]. But King Rehoboam ·ran to his [hur-
riedly jumped into his] chariot and ·escaped [fled] to Jerusalem. 19Since
then, Israel has been in rebellion against the ·family [dynasty; Lhouse] of
David.

11 When Rehoboam arrived in Jerusalem, he ·gathered [sum-
moned; mobilized; mustered] one hundred eighty thousand
·of the best [skilled; select] ·soldiers [warriors] from Judah and Benjamin.
He wanted to fight Israel to ·take back [restore] his kingdom. 2But the
LORD spoke his word to Shemaiah, a man of God, saying, 3"Speak to
Solomon's son Rehoboam, the king of Judah, and to all the Israelites liv-

ing in Judah and Benjamin. Say to them, 4"The LORD says you must not
·go to war against your brothers [fight against your relatives/kinsmen].
Every one of you should go home, because ·I made all these things happen [Lthis thing is from me].'" So they ·obeyed [listened to; heeded] the
LORD's ·command [words] and turned back and did not attack Jeroboam.

Rehoboam Makes Judah Strong

5Rehoboam lived in Jerusalem and built ·strong [fortified] cities in
Judah for defense. 6He built up the cities of Bethlehem, Etam, Tekoa, 7Beth
Zur, Soco, Adullam, 8Gath, Mareshah, Ziph, 9Adoraim, Lachish, Azekah,
10Zorah, Aijalon, and Hebron. These were ·strong, walled [fortified] cities
in Judah and Benjamin. 11When Rehoboam ·made those cities strong
[strengthened the fortresses/their defenses], he put ·commanders [officers]
and ·supplies [stores] of food, oil, and wine in them. 12Also, Rehoboam put
shields and spears in all the cities and made them very strong. Rehoboam
kept the people of Judah and Benjamin under his control.

13The priests and the Levites from all over Israel ·joined [stood/sided
with] Rehoboam. 14The Levites even ·left [abandoned] their pasturelands
and property and came to Judah and Jerusalem, because Jeroboam and
his sons ·refused to let them serve [rejected/excluded them from serving]
as priests to the LORD. 15Jeroboam ·chose [appointed] his own priests for
the ·places of worship [Lhigh places; Cworship sites associated with pagan
worship or inappropriate worship of God] and for the ·goat [goat-demon;
satyr] and calf idols he had made. 16There were people from all the tribes
of Israel who ·wanted to obey [Lset their hearts to seek] the LORD, the God
of Israel. So they went to Jerusalem with the Levites to sacrifice to the
LORD, the God of their ·ancestors [fathers]. 17These people made the kingdom of Judah strong, and they supported Solomon's son Rehoboam for
three years. During this time they ·lived [Lwalked in] the way ·David and
Solomon had lived [of David and Solomon].

Rehoboam's Family

18Rehoboam married Mahalath, the daughter of Jerimoth and Abihail.
Jerimoth was David's son, and Abihail was the daughter of Eliab, Jesse's
son. 19Mahalath ·gave [Tbore] Rehoboam these sons: Jeush, Shemariah,
and Zaham. 20Then Rehoboam married Absalom's daughter Maacah, and
she ·gave [Tbore] Rehoboam these children: Abijah, Attai, Ziza, and
Shelomith. 21Rehoboam loved Maacah more than his other wives and
·slave women [concubines; Csecondary wives]. Rehoboam had eighteen
wives and sixty ·slave women [concubines] and was the father of twenty-
eight sons and sixty daughters.

22Rehoboam ·chose [appointed] Abijah son of Maacah to be ·the leader
[head; Ccrown prince] of his own brothers, because he planned to make
Abijah king [Chis successor]. 23Rehoboam acted wisely. He spread his sons
through all the areas of Judah and Benjamin [Cboth giving them responsibilities and dispersing/diluting their power], sending them to every
·strong, walled [fortified] city. He gave plenty of supplies to his sons, and
he also ·found wives [sought/acquired many wives] for them.

Shishak Attacks Jerusalem
(12:1–16; 1 Kin. 14:21–31)

12 After Rehoboam's kingdom was ·set up [secure; consolidated;
established] and he became strong, he and the people of
Judah ·stopped obeying [abandoned; forsook] the ·teachings [instruc-
tions; laws] of the LORD. 2During the fifth year Rehoboam was king,
Shishak king of Egypt attacked Jerusalem, because Rehoboam and the
people were unfaithful to the LORD. 3Shishak had twelve hundred

chariots and sixty thousand ·horsemen [*or* horses]**. He brought troops of ·Libyans** [Lubim]**, Sukkites, and Cushites** [CEthiopians] **from Egypt with him, so many they couldn't be counted.** [4]**Shishak captured the ·strong, walled** [fortified] **cities of Judah and ·came as far as** [advanced on/to] **Jerusalem.**

[5]**Then Shemaiah the prophet came to Rehoboam and the ·leaders** [officers; officials] **of Judah who had gathered in Jerusalem because they were afraid of Shishak. Shemaiah said to them, "This is what the LORD says: 'You have ·left** [abandoned; forsaken] **me, so now I will ·leave you to face Shishak alone** [abandon/forsake you to Shishak]**.'"**

[6]**Then the ·leaders** [officers; officials] **of ·Judah** [LIsrael; Csometimes the name Israel refers specifically to Judah] **and King Rehoboam ·were sorry for what they had done** [humbled themselves]**. They said, "The LORD ·does what is right** [is just/fair/righteous]**."**

[7]**When the LORD saw they ·were sorry for what they had done** [humbled themselves]**, the LORD spoke his word to Shemaiah, saying, "·The king and the leaders are sorry** [They have humbled themselves]**. So I will not destroy them but will ·save** [rescue; Tdeliver] **them soon. I will not use Shishak to ·punish Jerusalem in** [pour out on Jerusalem] **my anger.** [8]**But the people of Jerusalem will become Shishak's ·servants** [subjects; slaves] **so they may learn the difference between serving me and serving the ·kings** [kingdoms] **of other nations."**

[9]**Shishak king of Egypt attacked Jerusalem and took the treasures from the ·Temple** [Lhouse] **of the LORD and the king's ·palace** [Lhouse]**. He took everything, even the gold shields Solomon had made.** [10]**So King Rehoboam made bronze shields to take their place and ·gave** [entrusted] **them to the ·commanders** [officers] **of the guards for the ·palace gates** [doors of the king's house]**.** [11]**Whenever the king went to the ·Temple** [Lhouse] **of the LORD, the guards went with him, carrying the shields. Later, they would put them back in the guardroom.**

[12]**When Rehoboam ·was sorry for what he had done** [humbled himself]**, the LORD held his anger back and did not ·fully** [completely] **destroy Rehoboam. ·There was some** [*or* Conditions/Things were] **good in Judah.**

[13]**King Rehoboam ·made himself a strong king** [strengthened/established himself] **in Jerusalem. He was forty-one years old when he became king, and he ·was king** [reigned] **in Jerusalem for seventeen years. Jerusalem is the city that the LORD chose from all the tribes of Israel in which ·he was to be worshiped** [Lto put his name]**. Rehoboam's mother was Naamah from the country of Ammon.** [14]**Rehoboam did evil because he did not ·want to obey** [Lset/commit his heart to seek] **the LORD.**

[15]**The ·things Rehoboam did as king** [events/acts/history of Rehoboam]**, from ·the beginning to the end** [first to last]**, ·are** [Lare they not…?] **written in the ·records** [annals] **of Shemaiah the prophet and Iddo the ·seer** [prophet]**, in the ·family histories** [genealogical records]**. There were continual wars between Rehoboam and Jeroboam.** [16]**Rehoboam ·died** [Llay down/Tslept with his fathers/ancestors] **and was buried in the City of David** [CJerusalem]**, and his son Abijah became king in his place.**

Abijah King of Judah
(13:1–21; 1 Kin. 15:1–8)

13 Abijah became the king of Judah during the eighteenth year Jeroboam was king of Israel. [2]**Abijah ·ruled** [reigned] **in Jerusalem for three years. His mother was Maacah daughter of Uriel from the town of Gibeah.**

And there was war between Abijah and Jeroboam. 3Abijah led an army of four hundred thousand ·capable [skilled; valiant] soldiers into battle, and Jeroboam prepared to fight him with eight hundred thousand ·capable [skilled; valiant] soldiers.

4Abijah stood on Mount Zemaraim in the mountains of Ephraim and said, "Jeroboam and all Israel, listen to me! 5·You should know [LDo you not know/realize…?] that the LORD, the God of Israel, gave David and his sons the right to ·rule [reign over] Israel forever by an ·agreement [covenant; treaty] of salt [Lev. 2:13; Num. 18:19]. 6But Jeroboam son of Nebat, one of the ·officers [officials] of Solomon, David's son, ·turned [rebelled] against his master. 7Then ·worthless [Lempty], ·evil men [scoundrels] joined Jeroboam against Rehoboam, Solomon's son. He was young and ·didn't know what to do [inexperienced; indecisive], so he could not ·stop [resist; stand up to] them.

8"Now you ·people are making plans against [propose to resist/stand against] the LORD's kingdom, which belongs to David's sons. ·There are many of you [You are a vast army], and you have the gold calves Jeroboam made for you as gods. 9·You have [Have you not…?] thrown out the Levites and the LORD's priests, Aaron's sons. You have ·chosen [appointed] your own priests [Crather than God appointing them] as people in other ·countries [lands; nations] do. Anyone who comes with a young bull and seven ·male sheep [rams] can become a priest of idols that are not gods [Cthat is, they buy or bribe their way into the priesthood].

10"But as for us, the LORD is our God; we have not ·left [abandoned; forsaken] him. The priests who serve the LORD are Aaron's ·sons [descendants], and the Levites ·help [assist; attend] them. 11They ·offered [sacrificed] burnt offerings and ·sweet-smelling [fragrant] incense to the LORD every morning and evening. They put the ·bread [Tshowbread] on the ·special [holy; ritually clean] table [Cin the Temple]. And they light the lamps on the gold lampstand every evening. We obey the command of the LORD our God, but you have ·left [abandoned; forsaken] him. 12God himself is with us as our ·ruler [head]. His priests blow the trumpet to ·call us to war [sound the alarm] against you. Men of Israel, don't fight against the LORD, the God of your ·ancestors [fathers], because you won't succeed."

13But Jeroboam had sent some troops to ·sneak behind Judah's army [ambush from behind]. So while Jeroboam was ·in front of [confronting] Judah's army, ·Jeroboam's soldiers [the ambushers] were behind them. 14When the soldiers of Judah turned around, they saw Jeroboam's army attacking both in front and back. So they cried out to the LORD, and the priests blew the trumpets. 15Then the men of Judah ·gave [shouted out] a battle cry. When they shouted, God ·caused Jeroboam and the army of Israel to run away from [routed/defeated Jeroboam and all Israel before] Abijah and the army of Judah. 16When the army of Israel ·ran away from the men of [fled before] Judah, God handed them over to Judah. 17Abijah's army ·struck [inflicted a great slaughter on] Israel so that five hundred thousand of Israel's ·best [select] men were killed. 18So at that time the people of Israel were ·defeated [subdued]. And the people of Judah ·won [conquered; prevailed], because they ·depended on [trusted] the LORD, the God of their ·ancestors [fathers].

19Abijah's army chased Jeroboam's army and captured from him the towns of Bethel, Jeshanah, and Ephron, and the small villages near them.

20 Jeroboam never ·became strong [regained his power] again while Abijah
was alive. The LORD struck Jeroboam, and he died.
21 But Abijah ·became strong [grew more powerful]. He married fourteen women and was the father of twenty-two sons and sixteen daughters.
22 ·Everything else Abijah did [The rest of the events/acts/history of
Abijah]—what he said and what he did—is recorded in the ·writings
[commentary; treatise] of the prophet Iddo.

14 Abijah ·died [Llay down/Tslept with his fathers/ancestors] and
was buried in the City of David [CJerusalem]. His son Asa
became king in his place, and there was ·peace in the country [rest in the
land] for ten years during Asa's time.

Asa King of Judah
(14:2–15; 1 Kin. 15:9–12)

2 Asa did what the LORD his God ·said was good and right [desired and
approved]. 3 He removed the foreign altars and the ·places where gods
were worshiped [Lhigh places; 11:15]. He smashed the ·stone pillars that
honored other gods [Lpillars], and he ·tore [cut] down the Asherah [Ca
Canaanite fertility goddess] ·idols [poles; Deut. 7:5; 12:3; 16:21; Judg. 6:25,
28, 30; 2 Kin. 18:4]. 4 Asa commanded the people of Judah to ·follow [seek]
the LORD, the God of their ·ancestors [fathers], and to obey his ·teachings
[instructions; laws] and commandments. 5 He also removed the ·places
where gods were worshiped [Lhigh places; 11:15] and the incense altars
from every town in Judah. So the kingdom ·had peace [was undisturbed]
while Asa was king. 6 Asa built ·strong, walled [fortified] cities in Judah
·during the time of peace [while the land was undisturbed]. He had no
war in these years, because the LORD gave him ·peace [rest].
7 Asa said to the people of Judah, "Let's ·build up [fortify] these towns
and put walls around them. Let's make towers, gates, and bars in the gates.
This country is still ours, because we have ·obeyed [sought] the LORD our
God. We have ·followed [sought] him, and he has given us ·peace all
around [rest on every side]." So they built and ·had success [prospered].
8 Asa had an army of three hundred thousand men from Judah and two
hundred eighty thousand men from Benjamin. The men from Judah carried large shields and spears. The men from Benjamin carried small shields
and bows. All of them were ·brave fighting men [valiant/skilled warriors].
9 Then Zerah from ·Cush [Ethiopia] came out to fight them with an
·enormous army [army of one million men; La thousand thousands] and
three hundred chariots. They ·came as far as [advanced to] the town of
Mareshah. 10 So Asa went out to fight Zerah and ·prepared for battle [took
battle positions] in the Valley of Zephathah at Mareshah.
11 Asa called out to the LORD his God, saying, "LORD, only you can help
·weak people [the powerless] against the ·strong [mighty; many]. Help us,
LORD our God, because we ·depend on [trust in; rely on] you. We fight
against this ·enormous army [multitude] in your name. LORD, you are our
God. Don't let ·anyone [man; mortals] ·win [prevail] against you."
12 So the LORD ·defeated [routed; struck down] the ·Cushites [Ethiopians]
·when Asa's army from Judah attacked them [before Asa and Judah], and
the Cushites ·ran away [fled]. 13 Asa's army chased them as far as the town
of Gerar. So many ·Cushites [Ethiopians] were killed that ·the army could
not fight again [they could not recover]; they were ·crushed [shattered;
destroyed] by the LORD and his army. Asa and his army carried ·many valuable things away from the enemy [off a great amount of plunder]. 14 They
destroyed all the towns ·near [around] Gerar, because the ·people living in

these towns were afraid of the Lord [Lterror/dread of the Lord came upon
them]. Since these towns had ·many valuable things [a lot of loot/plunder],
Asa's army ·took them away [looted/plundered/despoiled them]. 15Asa's
army also attacked the ·camps where the shepherds lived [herdsmen] and
took many ·sheep [Lflocks] and camels. Then they returned to Jerusalem.

Asa's Changes

15 The Spirit of God ·entered [came upon] Azariah son of Oded.
2Azariah went to meet Asa and said, "Listen to me, Asa and
all you people of Judah and Benjamin. The Lord ·is [will be] with you
when you are with him. If you ·obey [seek] him, you will find him, but if
you ·leave [abandon; forsake] him, he will ·leave [abandon; forsake] you.
3For a long time Israel was without the true God and without a priest to
·teach [instruct] them and without the ·teachings [instructions; laws].
4But ·when they were in trouble [in their distress], they turned to the
Lord, the God of Israel. They ·looked for [sought] him and found him.
5In those days no one could travel safely. There was ·much trouble [tur-
moil; total chaos] in ·all the nations [every land]. 6One nation would
·destroy [crush] another nation, and one city would ·destroy [crush]
another city, because God ·troubled [confused] them with all kinds of
distress. 7But you should be strong. Don't ·give up [be discouraged],
because you will be rewarded for your good work."
8Asa ·felt brave [was encouraged] when he heard these words and the
·message [prophecy] from Azariah son of Oded the prophet. So he removed
the ·hateful [detestable; abominable] idols from all the land of Judah and
Benjamin and from the towns he had captured in the hills of Ephraim. He
·repaired [restored] the Lord's altar that was in front of the ·porch [portico;
vestibule; entry room] of the ·Temple [Lhouse] of the Lord.
9Then Asa gathered all the people from Judah and Benjamin and from
the tribes of Ephraim, Manasseh, and Simeon who were living in Judah.
Many people ·came [defected; deserted] to Asa even from Israel, ·because
[when] they saw that the Lord, Asa's God, was with him.
10Asa and these people ·gathered [assembled] in Jerusalem in the third
month [Clate spring] of the fifteenth year of Asa's ·rule [reign]. 11·At that
time [LOn that day] they sacrificed to the Lord seven hundred ·bulls [oxen]
and seven thousand sheep and goats from the ·valuable things Asa's army
had taken from their enemies [plunder/spoil they had brought back].
12Then they made an ·agreement [covenant; treaty] to ·obey [seek] the
Lord, the God of their ·ancestors [fathers], with their whole ·being [Lheart
and soul]. 13Anyone who refused to ·obey [seek] the Lord, the God of Israel,
was to be ·killed [executed; put to death]. It did not matter if that person
was ·important [great] or ·unimportant [small], a man or woman. 14Then
Asa and the people ·made a promise before [swore allegiance/an oath/a vow
to] the Lord, shouting with a loud voice and blowing trumpets and sheep's
horns. 15All the people of Judah ·were happy about [rejoiced over] the
·promise [vow; oath], because they had ·promised [vowed; sworn] with all
their heart. They ·looked for [earnestly sought] God and found him. So the
Lord gave them ·peace [rest] ·in all the country [on every side].

The Removal of Maacah
(15:16–19; 1 Kin. 15:13–15)

16King Asa also removed Maacah, his ·grandmother [Lmother], from
being queen mother, because she had made a ·terrible [obscene; repulsive;
loathsome; abominable] Asherah ·idol [pole; 14:3]. Asa cut down that
idol, ·smashed it into pieces, [and crushed] and burned it in the Kidron

Valley. [17]But the ·places of worship to gods [Lhigh places; 11:15] were not
removed from ·Judah [LIsrael; 12:6]. Even so, Asa was ·faithful [whole-
heartedly loyal/devoted] all his life.
[18]Asa brought into the ·Temple [Lhouse] of God the ·gifts [dedicated/holy
things] he and his father had given: silver, gold, and ·utensils [articles].
[19]There was no more war until the thirty-fifth year of Asa's ·rule
[reign].

Asa's Last Years
(16:1–17:1;
1 Kin. 15:16–24)

16 In the thirty-sixth year of Asa's ·rule [reign], Baasha king of
Israel ·attacked [invaded] Judah. He ·made the town of
Ramah strong [fortified Ramah] so he could keep people from leaving
or entering Judah, Asa's ·country [territory].
[2]Asa took silver and gold from the treasuries of the ·Temple [Lhouse] of
the LORD and out of his own ·palace [Lhouse]. Then he sent it with ·mes-
sengers [this message] to Ben-Hadad king of Aram, who lived in
Damascus. Asa said, [3]"Let there be a ·treaty [alliance] between you and
me as there was between my father and your father. I am sending you
silver and gold. Break your treaty with Baasha king of Israel so he will
·leave [withdraw from] my land."
[4]Ben-Hadad ·agreed with [Llistened to] King Asa and sent the ·com-
manders [officers] of his armies ·to attack [against] the towns of Israel.
They ·defeated the towns of [conquered] Ijon, Dan, and Abel Beth
Maacah, and all the ·towns in Naphtali where treasures were stored [stor-
age/supply cities of Naphtali]. [5]When Baasha heard about this, he stopped
·building up [fortifying] Ramah and ·left [abandoned; ceased] his work.
[6]Then King Asa brought all the people of Judah to Ramah, and they carried away the ·rocks [stones] and ·wood [timber] that Baasha had used.
And they used them to ·build up [fortify] Geba and Mizpah.
[7]At that time Hanani the ·seer [prophet] came to Asa king of Judah and
said to him, "You ·depended on [trusted; relied on] the king of Aram to
help you and not on the LORD your God. So the king of Aram's army
escaped from you. [8]·The Cushites and Libyans had [LDid not the
Ethiopians and Lubim have…?] a large and powerful army and many
chariots and horsemen. But you ·depended on [trusted; relied on] the
LORD to help you, so he handed them over to you. [9]·The LORD searches
[LThe eyes of the LORD search] ·all [throughout] the earth for people ·who
have given themselves completely to him [whose hearts are completely
his/committed to him]. He wants to strengthen them. Asa, you did a foolish thing, so from now on you will have wars."
[10]Asa was angry with Hanani the ·seer [prophet] because of what he
had said; he was so ·angry [enraged] that he put Hanani in prison. And
Asa ·was cruel to [oppressed] some of the people at the same time.
[11]·Everything Asa did as king [The events/acts/history of Asa's reign],
from ·the beginning to the end [first to last], is written in the ·book [scroll]
of the kings of Judah and Israel. [12]In the thirty-ninth year of his ·rule [reign],
Asa got a disease in his feet. Though his disease was very bad, he did not ·ask
for help from [seek] the LORD, but only ·from the doctors [the physicians].
[13]Then Asa was buried [Llay down; Trested] with his ·ancestors [fathers], having died in the forty-first year of his ·rule [reign]. [14]The people buried Asa in
the tomb he had ·made [Lcarved out] for himself in Jerusalem. They laid him
on a ·bed filled [bier covered] with spices and ·different kinds of [assorted]
mixed perfumes, and they made a large funeral fire to honor him.

Jehoshaphat King of Judah

17 Jehoshaphat, Asa's son, became king of Judah in his place.
Jehoshaphat ·made Judah strong so they could fight [strength-
ened himself] against Israel. 2He put ·troops [garrisons] in all the
·strong, walled [fortified] cities of Judah, in the land of Judah, and in the
towns of Ephraim that his father Asa had captured.
3The LORD was with Jehoshaphat, because he ·lived as his ancestor
David had lived when he first became king [followed the earlier example/
ways of his ancestor/father David]. Jehoshaphat did not ·ask for help from
[seek; consult] the Baal idols, 4but ·from [sought; consulted] the God of
his father. He ·obeyed [Lwalked in] God's commands and did not ·live as
the people of Israel lived [behave like Israel]. 5The LORD ·made Jehoshaphat
a strong king over Judah [secured/established the kingdom under his con-
trol/Lhand]. All the people of Judah brought ·gifts [tribute] to Jehoshaphat,
so he had much wealth and ·honor [esteem]. 6·He wanted very much to
obey [LHis heart was devoted/committed to the ways of] the LORD. He also
removed the ·places for worshiping gods [Lhigh places; 11:15] and the
Asherah ·idols [poles; 14:3] from Judah.
7During the third year of his ·rule [reign], Jehoshaphat sent his ·offi-
cers [officials] to teach in the towns of Judah. These ·officers [officials]
were Ben-Hail, Obadiah, Zechariah, Nethanel, and Micaiah. 8Jehoshaphat
sent with them these Levites: Shemaiah, Nethaniah, Zebadiah, Asahel,
Shemiramoth, Jehonathan, Adonijah, Tobijah, and Tob-Adonijah. He
also sent the priests Elishama and Jehoram. 9·These leaders, Levites, and
priests [LThey] taught the people in Judah. They took the ·Book [scroll]
of the ·Teachings [instructions; laws] of the LORD and went through all
the towns of Judah and taught the people.
10The ·nations near Judah were afraid of the LORD [Lfear/dread of the
LORD was on/seized the surrounding kingdoms], so they did not start a
war against Jehoshaphat. 11Some of the Philistines brought ·gifts [trib-
ute] and silver to Jehoshaphat. Some Arabs brought him flocks:
seventy-seven hundred sheep and seventy-seven hundred goats.
12Jehoshaphat grew more and more powerful. He built ·strong, walled
cities [fortresses] and ·towns for storing supplies [storage cities] in Judah.
13He kept many supplies in the towns of Judah, and he kept ·trained soldiers [skilled warriors] in Jerusalem. 14These soldiers were ·listed
[enrolled; divided] by ·families [clans]. From the ·families [clans] of
Judah, these were the ·commanders [officers] of groups of a thousand
men: Adnah was the commander of three hundred thousand skilled soldiers; 15Jehohanan was the commander of two hundred eighty thousand
skilled soldiers; 16Amasiah was the commander of two hundred thousand
skilled soldiers. Amasiah son of Zicri had volunteered to serve the LORD.
17These were the ·commanders [officers] from the ·families [clans] of
Benjamin: Eliada, a brave soldier, had two hundred thousand soldiers
·who used [armed/equipped with] bows and shields. 18And Jehozabad
had one hundred eighty thousand men ·armed [equipped] for war.
19All these soldiers served King Jehoshaphat. The king also put other
men in the ·strong, walled [fortified] cities through all of Judah.

Micaiah Warns King Ahab

(18:1–34; 1 Kin. 22:1–40)

18 Jehoshaphat had much wealth and ·honor [esteem], and he
made an ·agreement [alliance] with King Ahab through marriage [Chis son married Athaliah, Ahab's daughter; 21:6]. 2A few years
later Jehoshaphat went to visit Ahab in Samaria. Ahab ·sacrificed

[slaughtered] many sheep and ·cattle [oxen] ·as a great feast to honor
Jehoshaphat [Lfor him] and the ·people [officials] with him. He ·encour-
aged [enticed; persuaded; induced] Jehoshaphat to attack Ramoth in
Gilead. 3Ahab king of Israel asked Jehoshaphat king of Judah, "Will you
go with me to attack Ramoth in Gilead?"
Jehoshaphat answered, "I ·will go [Lam one] with you, and my ·soldiers
[people] are ·yours [your people]. We will join you in the battle."
4Jehoshaphat also said to Ahab, "But first we should ·ask if this is the
LORD's will [Lseek/inquire about the word/counsel of the LORD]."
5So ·King Ahab [Lthe king of Israel] ·called [assembled; summoned]
four hundred prophets together and asked them, "Should we go to war
against Ramoth in Gilead or ·not [hold back]?"
They answered, "Go, because God will hand them over to you."
6But Jehoshaphat asked, "Isn't there still a prophet of the LORD here?
Let's ·ask [inquire of] him."
7Then King Ahab said to Jehoshaphat, "There is one other prophet. We
could ·ask [inquire of] the LORD through him, but I hate him. He never
prophesies anything good about me, but always ·something bad [evil;
disaster]. He is Micaiah son of Imlah."
Jehoshaphat said, "King Ahab, you shouldn't say ·that [such things]!"
8So Ahab king of Israel told one of his ·officers [officials] to bring
Micaiah to him at once.
9Ahab king of Israel and Jehoshaphat king of Judah ·had on [were
arrayed/dressed in] their royal robes and were sitting on their thrones at
the threshing floor, near the entrance to the gate of Samaria. All the prophets were ·standing before them speaking their messages [prophesying
before them]. 10Zedekiah son of Kenaanah had made some iron horns. He
said to Ahab, "·This is what the LORD says [TThus says the LORD]: 'You will
use these horns to ·fight [gore] the Arameans until they are destroyed.'"
11All the other prophets ·said [prophesied] the same thing, "Attack
Ramoth in Gilead and ·win [triumph; be victorious], because the LORD
will hand the Arameans over to you."
12The messenger who had gone to ·get [summon] Micaiah said to him,
"All the other prophets are ·saying King Ahab will win [speaking favorably with one voice for the king]. ·You should agree with them and give
the king a good answer [LLet your word be like theirs and speak
favorably]."
13But Micaiah answered, "As surely as the LORD lives, I ·can tell him
[will speak] only what my God says."
14When Micaiah came to Ahab, the king asked him, "Micaiah, should
we attack Ramoth in Gilead or ·not [hold back]?"
Micaiah answered, "Attack and win! They will be handed over to you
[CHe was keeping his vow to speak what God said because this lie was what
God wanted him to say to Ahab]."
15But Ahab said to Micaiah, "How many times ·do I have to tell you
[must I make you swear] to speak only the truth to me in the name of the
LORD?" [CMicaiah's tone was likely sarcastic.]
16So Micaiah answered, "I saw ·the army of [Lall] Israel scattered over
the hills like sheep without a shepherd. The LORD said, 'They have no
·leaders [master; Cimplying that their king had been killed]. They should
go home ·and not fight [Lin peace].'"
17Then Ahab king of Israel said to Jehoshaphat, "·I told [LDidn't I

tell…?] you! He never prophesies anything good about me, but only ·bad [evil; disaster]."

18But Micaiah said, "Hear the ·message from [Lword of] the LORD: I saw the LORD sitting on his throne with ·his heavenly army standing [Lall the host of heaven] on his right and on his left. 19The LORD said, 'Who will ·trick [entice; deceive] King Ahab of Israel into attacking Ramoth in Gilead where he will ·be killed [Lfall]?'

"Some ·said [suggested] one thing; some ·said [suggested] another. 20Then one spirit came and stood before the LORD and said, 'I will ·trick [entice; deceive] him.'

"The LORD asked, 'How will you do it?'

21"The spirit answered, 'I will go ·to Ahab's prophets and make them tell lies [Land be a lying/deceiving spirit in the mouths of all his prophets].'

"So the LORD said, 'You will succeed in ·tricking [enticing; deceiving] him. Go and do it.' "

22Micaiah said, "Ahab, the LORD has ·made your prophets lie to you [Lput a lying/deceiving spirit in the mouths of your prophets], and the LORD has ·decided that disaster should come to you [pronounced your doom]."

23Then Zedekiah son of Kenaanah went up to Micaiah and slapped him ·in the face [Lon the cheek]. Zedekiah said, "·Has [How is it that] the LORD's Spirit left me to speak through you?"

24Micaiah answered, "You will find out on the day you go to hide in an ·inside [secret] room [Cwhen the predicted disaster would strike]."

25Then Ahab king of Israel ordered, "Take Micaiah and ·send [return] him to Amon, the governor of the city, and to Joash, the king's son. 26Tell them I said to put this man in prison and give him only bread and water until I return ·safely [Lin peace] from the battle."

27Micaiah said, "Ahab, if you come back safely from the battle, the LORD has not spoken through me. ·Remember my words [LListen], all you people!"

Ahab Is Killed

28So Ahab king of Israel and Jehoshaphat king of Judah ·went to [attacked] Ramoth in Gilead. 29King Ahab said to Jehoshaphat, "I will go into battle, but I will ·wear other clothes so no one will recognize me [disguise myself]. But you wear your royal ·clothes [robes]." So Ahab ·wore other clothes [disguised himself], and they went into battle.

30The king of Aram ordered his chariot ·commanders [officers], "Don't fight with anyone—·important [great] or ·unimportant [small]—·except [but only with] the king of Israel." 31When these ·commanders [officers] saw Jehoshaphat, they ·thought he was [said, "There is…"] the king of Israel, so they turned to attack him. But Jehoshaphat ·began shouting [cried/called out; Ceither for help or with his war cry], and the LORD ·helped [saved] him. God ·turned [drew; lured; diverted] the chariot ·commanders [officers] away from Jehoshaphat. 32When they saw he was not King Ahab of Israel, they stopped chasing him.

33·By chance [Randomly; LIn innocence], a soldier shot an arrow which hit Ahab king of Israel between the ·pieces [joints; plates] of his armor. King Ahab said to his chariot driver, "Turn around and get me out of the battle, because I am ·hurt [badly wounded]!" 34The battle ·continued [raged] all day. King Ahab ·held [propped] himself up in his chariot and faced the Arameans until evening. Then he died at sunset.

19 Jehoshaphat king of Judah came back safely to his ·palace [Lhouse] in Jerusalem. 2Jehu son of Hanani, a ·seer [prophet], went out to meet him and said to the king, "·Why did [Should] you help evil people? ·Why do [Should] you love those who hate the LORD [Ca reference to his ill-advised alliance with Ahab]? That is the reason the ·LORD is angry with [wrath of the LORD is on] you. 3But there is some good in you. You took the Asherah ·idols [poles; 14:3] out of this ·country [land], and you have ·tried to obey [Lyour heart set on seeking] God."

Jehoshaphat Chooses Judges

4Jehoshaphat lived in Jerusalem. He went out again ·to be with [among] the people, from Beersheba to the mountains of Ephraim, and he ·turned [brought] them back to the LORD, the God of their ·ancestors [fathers]. 5Jehoshaphat appointed judges in all the land, in each of the ·strong, walled [fortified] cities of Judah. 6Jehoshaphat said to them, "·Watch [Consider; Think carefully about] what you do, because you are not judging ·for [for the sake of] people but for the LORD. He will be with you when you ·make a decision [give a verdict; pronounce judgment]. 7Now let each of you ·fear [respect] the LORD [Prov. 1:7] ·Watch what you do [Judge/Decide carefully/with integrity], because the LORD our God ·wants people to be fair [does not tolerate injustice/unrighteousness…]. ·He wants all people to be treated the same […or partiality], ·and he doesn't want decisions influenced by money […or taking of bribes]."

8And in Jerusalem Jehoshaphat appointed some of the Levites, priests, and ·leaders [heads] of Israelite ·families [clans] to be judges. They were to ·decide [judge] cases about the law of the LORD and settle ·problems [disputes] between the people who lived in Jerusalem. 9Jehoshaphat ·commanded [instructed; charged] them, "You must ·always serve the LORD completely [act faithfully and wholeheartedly], and you must fear him. 10Your ·people [kinsmen; brothers] living in the cities will bring you cases about ·killing [murder; violent crime; Lbetween blood pertaining to blood], about the ·teachings [laws], commands, rules, or some other ·law [regulation]. In all these cases you must warn the people not to sin against the LORD. If you don't, ·he will be angry with [wrath will come on] you and your ·people [kinsmen; brothers]. But if you warn them, you won't ·be guilty [sin].

11"Amariah, the ·leading [chief; high] priest, will be over you in all cases about the LORD [Cin matters of God's law]. Zebadiah son of Ishmael, a leader in the ·tribe [Lhouse] of Judah, will be over you in all cases about the king [Ccivil cases]. Also, the Levites will serve as ·officers [officials; Cof the court] for you. Have ·courage [confidence]. May the LORD be with those who do what is right."

Jehoshaphat Faces War

20 Later the Moabites, Ammonites, and some Meunites came to start a war with Jehoshaphat. 2Messengers came and told Jehoshaphat, "A ·large army [vast horde; Tgreat multitude] is coming against you from ·Edom [Lbeyond the sea; Cthe Dead Sea]. They are already in Hazazon Tamar (that is, En Gedi)!" 3Jehoshaphat was ·afraid [alarmed], so he decided to ·ask the LORD what to do [seek the LORD]. He announced that everyone in Judah should fast. 4The people of Judah ·came together [assembled] to ·ask the LORD for help [seek the LORD]; they came from every town in Judah.

5The ·people [assembly] of Judah and Jerusalem met in front of the new courtyard in the ·Temple [Lhouse] of the LORD. Then Jehoshaphat stood up, 6and he said, "LORD, God of our ·ancestors [fathers], ·you are the [Lare you not…?] God in heaven. ·You [LDo you not…?] rule over all the kingdoms of the nations. You have power and strength in your hand, so no one can ·stand against [withstand; resist] you. 7Our God, ·you forced [Ldid you not drive…?] out the people who lived in this land ·as your people Israel moved in [before your people Israel]. And you gave this land forever to the descendants of your friend Abraham. 8They lived in this land and built a ·Temple [sanctuary here] for ·you [Lyour name]. They said, 9'If ·trouble [disaster; evil] comes upon us, or ·war [Lthe sword], ·punishment [judgment; Cthis term should perhaps be combined with the previous one to read "the sword of judgment"], ·sickness [plague; pestilence], or ·hunger [famine], we will stand before you and before this ·Temple [Lhouse] ·where you have chosen to be worshiped [for your name is in this house]. We will cry out to you ·when we are in trouble [in our distress]. Then you will hear and ·save [rescue; Tdeliver] us.'

10"But now here are men from Ammon, Moab, and ·Edom [LMount Seir]. You wouldn't let the Israelites ·enter [invade] their lands when the Israelites came from Egypt. So the Israelites ·turned away [bypassed/went around them] and did not destroy them. 11But see how they repay us! They have come to force us out of your ·land [possession], which you gave us as our ·own [inheritance]. 12Our God, ·punish those people [will you not judge them?]. We have no power against this ·large army [vast horde; Tgreat multitude] that is attacking us. We don't know what to do, so ·we look to you for help [Lour eyes are on you]."

13All the men of Judah stood before the LORD with their babies, wives, and children. 14Then the Spirit of the LORD ·entered [came on] Jahaziel. (Jahaziel was Zechariah's son. Zechariah was Benaiah's son. Benaiah was Jeiel's son, and Jeiel was Mattaniah's son.) Jahaziel, a Levite and a descendant of Asaph, stood up in the ·meeting [assembly]. 15He said, "Listen to me, King Jehoshaphat and all you people living in Judah and Jerusalem. ·The LORD says this [TThus says the LORD] to you: 'Don't be afraid or ·discouraged [dismayed] because of this ·large army [vast horde; Tgreat multitude]. The battle is not your battle, it is God's. 16Tomorrow go down ·there and fight those people [Lagainst them]. They will come up through the ·Pass [ascent] of Ziz. You will find them at the end of the ·ravine [valley] that ·leads [opens] to the ·Desert [wilderness] of Jeruel. 17You won't need to fight in this battle. Just ·stand strong in your places [take your positions], and you will see the ·LORD save you [salvation/deliverance/rescue of the LORD]. Judah and Jerusalem, don't be afraid or ·discouraged [dismayed], because the LORD is with you. So go out ·against those people [to face them] tomorrow.' "

18Jehoshaphat bowed facedown on the ground. All the people of Judah and Jerusalem bowed down before the LORD and worshiped him. 19Then some Levites from the Kohathite and Korahite people stood up and praised the LORD, the God of Israel, with very loud ·voices [shouts].

20Jehoshaphat's army went out into the ·Desert [wilderness] of Tekoa early in the morning. As they were starting out, Jehoshaphat stood and said, "Listen to me, people of Judah and Jerusalem. ·Have faith [Trust; Believe] in the LORD your God, and you will ·stand strong [be secure/safe/Testablished]. ·Have faith [Trust; Believe] in his prophets, and you will succeed." 21Jehoshaphat ·listened to the advice of [consulted/conferred with] the people. Then he ·chose [appointed] men to be singers to the

LORD, to praise him ·because he is holy and wonderful [for his holy splendor;
or in their holy/sacred vestments/robes]. As they ·marched in front [went
ahead] of the army, they said,

"·Thank [Give thanks to; Praise] the LORD,
because his ·love [unfailing love; lovingkindness; loyalty] ·continues
[endures] forever [Ps. 136]."

22 As they began to sing and praise God, the LORD set ambushes for the
people of Ammon, Moab, and ·Edom [LMount Seir] who had come to
attack Judah. And they were ·defeated [routed]. 23 The Ammonites and
Moabites attacked ·the Edomites [Lthose from Mount Seir], ·destroying
[annihilating] them completely. After they had ·killed [finished off] the
Edomites, they killed each other.

24 When the men from Judah came to ·a place where they could see [the
lookout point in] the ·desert [wilderness], they looked ·at the enemy's
large army [toward the vast horde; Tgreat multitude]. But they only saw
·dead bodies [corpses] lying on the ground; no one had escaped. 25 When
Jehoshaphat and his army came to ·take [gather; carry off] their ·valu-
ables [plunder; spoil; booty], they found many supplies, much clothing,
and other valuable things. There was more than they could carry away;
there was so much it took three days to gather it all. 26 On the fourth day
Jehoshaphat and his army met in the Valley of Beracah [C"blessing"] and
·praised [blessed] the LORD. That is why that place has been called the
Valley of Beracah [C"blessing"] to this day.

27 Then Jehoshaphat led all the men from Judah and Jerusalem back to
Jerusalem. The LORD had ·made them happy because their enemies were
defeated [given them cause to rejoice over their enemies]. 28 They entered
Jerusalem with harps, lyres, and trumpets and went to the ·Temple
[Lhouse] of the LORD.

29 When all the kingdoms of the lands around them heard how the
LORD had fought Israel's enemies, ·they feared God [Lthe terror/dread of
God came upon them]. 30 So Jehoshaphat's kingdom was at ·peace [rest].
His God gave him ·peace from all the countries around him [Lrest on
every side].

Jehoshaphat's Rule Ends
(20:31–21:1; 1 Kin. 22:41–50)

31 Jehoshaphat ·ruled [reigned] over the country of Judah. He was
thirty-five years old when he became king, and he ·ruled [reigned] in
Jerusalem for twenty-five years. His mother's name was Azubah daughter
of Shilhi. 32 Jehoshaphat ·was good like [Lwalked in the way of] his father
Asa, and he did what ·the LORD said was right [Lwas right/pleasing in the
eyes/sight of the LORD]. 33 But the ·places where gods were worshiped
[Lhigh places; 11:15] were not removed, and the people ·did not really
want to follow [had not committed/devoted themselves to; had not set
their hearts on] the God of their ·ancestors [fathers].

34 The other things Jehoshaphat did as king, from ·the beginning to the
end [first to last], ·are [are they not…?] written in the records of Jehu son
of Hanani, which are in the ·book [scroll] of the kings of Israel.

35 Later, Jehoshaphat king of Judah made a ·treaty [alliance] with
Ahaziah king of Israel, which was a ·wrong [wicked; evil] thing to do.
36 Jehoshaphat agreed with Ahaziah to build ·trading ships [Lships to go to
Tarshish; Cin present-day Spain, hence a large, seagoing trading ship],
which they built in the town of Ezion Geber. 37 Then Eliezer son of
Dodavahu from the town of Mareshah ·spoke [prophesied] against

Jehoshaphat. He said, "Jehoshaphat, because you ·joined [allied] with
Ahaziah, the LORD will destroy what you have made." The ships were
wrecked so they could not sail out to trade.

21 Jehoshaphat ·died [Llay down/Tslept with his fathers/ances-
tors] and was buried with his ·ancestors [fathers] in the City
of David [CJerusalem]. Then his son Jehoram became king in his place.
2Jehoram's brothers were Azariah, Jehiel, Zechariah, Azariahu, Michael,
and Shephatiah. They were the sons of Jehoshaphat king of ·Judah
[LIsrael; 12:6]. 3Jehoshaphat gave his sons many gifts of silver, gold, and
·valuable [precious] things, and he gave them ·strong, walled [fortified]
cities in Judah. But Jehoshaphat gave the kingdom to Jehoram, because
he was the ·first son [firstborn].

Jehoram King of Judah
(21:2–10; 2 Kin. 8:16–22)

4When Jehoram took control of his father's kingdom and ·made himself
secure [established himself], he killed all his brothers with the sword and
also killed some of the ·leaders [officials] of Judah. 5He was thirty-two years
old when he began to ·rule [reign], and he ·ruled [reigned] eight years in
Jerusalem. 6He ·followed [Lwalked] in the ways of the kings of Israel, just as
the ·family [Lhouse] of Ahab had done, because he married Ahab's daughter. Jehoram did ·what the LORD said was wrong [Levil in the LORD's sight/
eyes]. 7But the LORD would not destroy David's ·family [Lhouse] because of
the ·agreement [covenant; treaty] he had made with David. He had promised ·that one of David's descendants would always rule [Lto give a lamp to
David and his descendants/sons forever; Chere a lamp symbolizes a dynasty].
8In Jehoram's time, Edom ·broke away from [revolted/rebelled against]
Judah's ·rule [reign] and ·chose [set up] their own king. 9So Jehoram went
to Edom with all his ·commanders [officers] and chariots. The Edomites
surrounded him and his chariot ·commanders [officers], but Jehoram got
up and attacked the Edomites at night [Cthe implication is that Jehoram is
victorious, but the next verse suggests otherwise; see 2 Kin. 8:21]. 10From
then until now the country of Edom has ·fought against [been free from]
the ·rule [reign] of Judah. At the same time the people of Libnah also
·broke away from [rebelled/revolted against] Jehoram because Jehoram
·left [abandoned; forsook] the LORD, the God of his ·ancestors [fathers].
11Jehoram also built ·places to worship gods [Lhigh places; 11:15] on
the hills in Judah. He led the people of Jerusalem to ·sin [commit adultery; Lplay the harlot], and he led the people of Judah ·away from the LORD
[astray]. 12Then Jehoram received this letter from Elijah the prophet:

> ·This is what the LORD says [TThus says the LORD], the God of
> your ·ancestor [father] David, "Jehoram, you have not ·lived as
> [Lwalked in the ways of] your father Jehoshaphat and Asa king of
> Judah. 13But you have ·lived as the kings of Israel lived [Lwalked in
> the way of the kings of Israel], leading the people of Judah and
> Jerusalem to ·sin against God [commit adultery; Lplay the harlot],
> as Ahab and his ·family [Lhouse] did. You have killed your broth-
> ers, your own family, and they were better than you. 14So now the
> LORD is about to ·punish [severely strike] your people, your chil-
> dren, your wives, and everything you own. 15You will have a
> terrible disease in your ·intestines [bowels] that will become
> worse every day until your intestines ·come out [protrude]."

16The Lord caused the Philistines and the Arabs who lived near the ·Cushites [Ethiopians] to be ·angry with [Lstirred in their spirits against] Jehoram. 17So the Philistines and Arabs attacked and invaded Judah and carried away all the wealth of Jehoram's ·palace [Lhouse], as well as his sons and wives. Only Jehoram's youngest son, Ahaziah, was left.

Jehoram Dies

(21:18–20; 2 Kin. 8:23–24)

18After these things happened, the Lord ·gave Jehoram [struck/afflicted/Tsmote him with] a disease in his ·intestines [bowels] that could not be cured. 19After he was sick for two years, Jehoram's ·intestines [bowels] ·came out [protruded] because of the disease, and he died in ·terrible pain [agony]. The people did not make a funeral fire to honor Jehoram as they had done for his ·ancestors [fathers].

20Jehoram was thirty-two years old when he became king, and he ·ruled [reigned] eight years in Jerusalem. No one ·was sad [regretted] when he died. He was buried in the City of David [CJerusalem], but not in the ·graves for [tombs of] the kings.

Ahaziah King of Judah

(22:1–6; 2 Kin. 8:24–29)

22 The people of Jerusalem ·chose [made] Ahaziah, Jehoram's youngest son, to be king in his place. The ·robbers [raiders; marauders] who had come with the Arabs to attack Jehoram's camp had killed all of Jehoram's older sons. So Ahaziah began to ·rule [reign over] Judah. 2Ahaziah was twenty-two years old when he became king, and he ·ruled [reigned] one year in Jerusalem. His mother's name was Athaliah, a granddaughter of Omri. 3Ahaziah ·followed [Lwalked in] the ways of Ahab's ·family [Lhouse], because his mother ·encouraged [counseled; advised] him to do ·wrong [evil]. 4Ahaziah did ·what the Lord said was wrong [Levil in the Lord's sight/eyes], as Ahab's ·family [Lhouse] had done. They ·gave advice to Ahaziah [were his counselors] after his father died, ·and their bad advice led to his death [leading to his destruction]. 5Following their ·advice [counsel], Ahaziah went with Joram son of Ahab to Ramoth in Gilead, where they fought against Hazael king of Aram. The Arameans wounded Joram. 6So Joram returned to Jezreel to heal from the wounds he received at Ramoth when he fought Hazael king of Aram.

Ahaziah son of Jehoram and king of Judah went down to visit Joram son of Ahab at Jezreel because he had been ·wounded [sick].

Ahaziah Dies

[22:7, 9; 2 Kin. 9:14–29]

7God caused Ahaziah's ·death [downfall] when he went to visit Joram. Ahaziah arrived and went out with Joram to ·meet [fight] Jehu son of Nimshi, whom the Lord had ·appointed [Lanointed] to destroy Ahab's ·family [Lhouse]. 8While Jehu was ·punishing [executing judgment against] Ahab's ·family [Lhouse], he found the ·leaders [officials] of Judah and the sons of Ahaziah's ·relatives [brothers] who served Ahaziah, and Jehu killed them all [2 Kin. 10:12–14]. 9Then Jehu ·looked [searched] for Ahaziah. Jehu's men caught him hiding in Samaria, so they brought him to Jehu. Then they killed and buried him. They said, "Ahaziah is a descendant of Jehoshaphat, and Jehoshaphat ·obeyed [sought] the Lord with all his heart." No one in Ahaziah's ·family [Lhouse] ·had the power [was strong enough] to take control of the kingdom of Judah.

Athaliah and Joash

(22:10–23:21; 2 Kin. 11:1–20)

10When Ahaziah's mother, Athaliah, saw that her son was dead, she ·killed [destroyed] all the royal ·family [line] of the house of Judah. 11But Jehosheba, King Jehoram's daughter, took Joash, Ahaziah's son. She stole him from among the other sons of the king who were going to be ·murdered [executed] and put him and his nurse in a bedroom. So Jehosheba,

who was King Jehoram's daughter and Ahaziah's sister and the wife of
Jehoiada the priest, hid Joash so Athaliah could not ·kill [execute] him.
12He hid with them in the ·Temple [Lhouse] of God for six years. During
that time Athaliah ·ruled [reigned over] the land.

23 In the seventh year Jehoiada ·decided to do something [summoned his courage/strength]. He made an ·agreement
[covenant; pact] with the ·commanders [officers] of the groups of a hundred men: Azariah son of Jeroham, Ishmael son of Jehohanan, Azariah
son of Obed, Maaseiah son of Adaiah, and Elishaphat son of Zicri. 2They
went throughout Judah and ·gathered [summoned; assembled] the
Levites from all the towns, and they gathered the ·leaders [heads] of the
·families [clans] of ·Judah [LIsrael; 12:6]. Then they went to Jerusalem.
3All the people together made an ·agreement [covenant; pact] with the
king in the ·Temple [Lhouse] of God.

Jehoiada said to them, "The king's son will ·rule [reign], as the LORD
·promised [has spoken] about David's ·descendants [sons]. 4Now this is
what you must do: You priests and Levites ·go [*or* who go…] on duty on
the Sabbath. A third of you will ·guard the doors [be gatekeepers]. 5A
third of you will be at the king's ·palace [Lhouse], and a third of you will
be at the Foundation Gate. All the other people will stay in the courtyards
of the ·Temple [Lhouse] of the LORD. 6Don't let anyone ·come into [enter]
the ·Temple [Lhouse] of the LORD except the priests and Levites ·who serve
[on duty]. They may come because they ·have been made ready to serve
the LORD [are holy/consecrated/set apart], but all the others must ·do the
job the LORD has given them [obey the LORD's instructions]. 7The Levites
must ·stay near [surround] the king, each man with his weapon in his
hand. If anyone tries to enter the ·Temple [Lhouse], kill him. Stay close to
the king when he goes in and when he goes out."

Joash Becomes King

8The Levites and all the people of Judah obeyed everything Jehoiada the
priest ·had commanded [ordered]. He did not ·excuse [dismiss; release]
anyone from the ·groups [divisions] of the priests. So each commander
took his men who came on duty on the Sabbath ·with [as well as] those
who went off duty on the Sabbath. 9Jehoiada gave the ·commanders [officers] of a hundred men the spears and the large and small shields that had
belonged to King David and that were kept in the ·Temple [Lhouse] of
God. 10Then Jehoiada ·told the soldiers where to stand [stationed/positioned all the people] with weapon in hand. There were guards from the
·south [Lright] side of the ·Temple [Lhouse] to the ·north [Lleft] side. They
stood by the altar and the ·Temple [Lhouse] and around the king.

11Jehoiada and his sons brought out the king's son and put the crown
on him and gave him a copy of the ·agreement [covenant; treaty]. Then
they ·appointed [anointed] him king and shouted, "Long live the king!"

12When Athaliah heard the noise of the people running and ·praising
[cheering] the king, she ·went to them [joined the crowd] at the ·Temple
[Lhouse] of the LORD. 13She looked, and there was the king standing by his
pillar at the entrance [Ca symbolic place of authority]. The ·officers [commanders] and the trumpeters were standing beside him, and all the
people of the land were ·happy [rejoicing] and blowing trumpets. The
singers were playing musical instruments and leading the ·praises [celebration]. Then Athaliah tore her clothes [Ca sign of mourning or distress]
and screamed, "·Traitors! Traitors! [Treason! Treason!]"

14Jehoiada the priest sent out the ·commanders [officers] of a hundred men, who ·led [were in charge of] the army. He said, "Surround her with soldiers and take her out of the ·Temple [Lhouse] area. Kill with a sword anyone who follows her." He had said, "Don't put Athaliah to death in the ·Temple [Lhouse] of the LORD." 15So they ·caught [seized] her ·when she came [*or* and took her] to the entrance of the Horse Gate near the ·palace [Lhouse]. There they put her to death.

16Then Jehoiada made an ·agreement [covenant; treaty] with the people and the king that they would be ·the LORD's special people [La people for the LORD]. 17All the people went to the ·Temple [Lhouse] of Baal and tore it down, ·smashing [demolishing] the altars and ·idols [images]. They killed Mattan, the priest of Baal, in front of the altars.

18Then Jehoiada chose the priests, who were Levites, to be ·responsible for [in charge of] the ·Temple [Lhouse] of the LORD. David had ·given [assigned] them duties in the ·Temple [Lhouse] of the LORD. They were to ·offer [sacrifice] the burnt offerings [Lev. 1:1–17] to the LORD as the ·Teachings [law] of Moses commanded, and they were to ·offer [sacrifice] them with much joy and singing as David had ·commanded [ordered; instructed]. 19Jehoiada ·put [stationed; positioned] guards at the gates of the ·Temple [Lhouse] of the LORD so that anyone who was ·unclean [defiled; Critually] in any way could not enter.

20Jehoiada took with him the ·commanders [officers] of a hundred men, the ·important men [nobles], the rulers of the people, and all the people of the land to ·take [lead; escort] the king out of the ·Temple [Lhouse] of the LORD. They went through the Upper Gate into the ·palace [Lhouse], and then they seated the king on the throne. 21So all the people of the land ·were very happy [rejoiced], and Jerusalem ·had peace [was quiet], because Athaliah had been put to death with the sword.

Joash Repairs the Temple
(24:1–14; 2 Kin. 11:21–12:16)

24 Joash was seven years old when he became king, and he ·ruled [reigned] forty years in Jerusalem. His mother's name was Zibiah, and she was from Beersheba. 2Joash did what ·the LORD said was right [was pleasing/proper in the eyes/sight of the LORD] ·as long as Jehoiada the priest was alive [Lall the days of Jehoiada the priest]. 3Jehoiada chose two wives for Joash, and Joash ·had [fathered] sons and daughters.

4Later, Joash decided to ·repair [restore] the ·Temple [Lhouse] of the LORD. 5He ·called [assembled; summoned] the priests and the Levites together and said to them, "Go to the towns of Judah and gather the annual offering. Use it to repair the ·Temple [Lhouse] of your God. Do this ·now [quickly; immediately]." But the Levites ·did not hurry [delayed].

6So King Joash ·called for [summoned] Jehoiada the leading priest and said to him, "Why haven't you made the Levites bring in from Judah and Jerusalem the tax money that Moses, the LORD's servant, and the people of Israel used for the ·Holy Tent [Ltent/tabernacle of the testimony/covenant]?"

7In the past the sons of wicked Athaliah had broken into the ·Temple [Lhouse] of God and used its ·holy things [sacred/dedicated objects] for worshiping the Baal idols.

8King Joash commanded that a ·box for contributions [chest] be made. They put it outside, at the gate of the ·Temple [Lhouse] of the LORD. 9Then the Levites made an ·announcement [proclamation; edict] in Judah and

Jerusalem, telling people to bring to the LORD the ·tax money [levy] Moses, the servant of God, had made the Israelites give while they were in the ·desert [wilderness]. 10 All the ·officers [leaders; officials] and people ·were happy to bring [rejoiced and brought] their ·money [levies; contributions], and they put it in the box until the box was full. 11 When the Levites would take the box to the king's ·officers [officials; accountants], they would see that ·it was full [there was a lot] of money. Then the king's ·royal secretary [scribe] and the ·leading [chief; high] priest's officer would come and ·take out the money [empty the chest] and return ·the box [Lit] to its place. They did this ·often [Lday after day] and gathered much money. 12 King Joash and Jehoiada gave the money to the people who worked on the ·Temple [Lhouse] of the LORD. And they hired ·stoneworkers [masons] and carpenters to ·repair [restore] the ·Temple [Lhouse] of the LORD. They also hired people to work with iron and bronze to ·repair [restore] the ·Temple [Lhouse].

13 The people worked hard, and the work to ·repair [restore] the ·Temple [Lhouse] ·went well [progressed]. They ·rebuilt [restored] the ·Temple [Lhouse] of God ·to be as it was before [according to its original design/specifications], but even stronger. 14 When the workers finished, they brought the money that was left to King Joash and Jehoiada. They used that money to make ·utensils [articles] for the ·Temple [Lhouse] of the LORD, ·utensils [articles] for the service in the ·Temple [Lhouse] and for the burnt offerings [Lev. 1:1–17], and ·bowls [pans; ladles] and other ·utensils [articles] from gold and silver. Burnt offerings [Lev. 1:1–17] were ·given every day [offered/sacrificed continually] in the ·Temple [Lhouse] of the LORD ·while Jehoiada was alive [Lall the days of Jehoiada].

15 Jehoiada grew old and ·lived many years [Lfull of days]. Then he died when he was one hundred thirty years old. 16 Jehoiada was buried in the City of David [CJerusalem] with the kings, because he had done much good in Judah for God and his ·Temple [Lhouse].

Joash Does Evil

17 After Jehoiada died, the ·officers [officials] of Judah came and bowed down to King Joash, and he listened to ·them [their advice]. 18 The king and these leaders ·stopped worshiping in [abandoned] the ·Temple [Lhouse] of the LORD, the God of their ·ancestors [fathers]. Instead, they began to ·worship [serve] the Asherah ·idols [poles; 14:3] and other idols. Because ·they did wrong [of their sin/guilt], ·God was angry with [Lwrath came upon] the people of Judah and Jerusalem. 19 Even though the LORD sent prophets to the people to turn them back to him and even though the prophets ·warned [testified against] them, they refused to listen.

20 Then the Spirit of God ·entered [came upon] Zechariah son of Jehoiada the priest. Zechariah stood before the people and said, "·This is what God says [TThus says God]: 'Why do you ·disobey [violate; transgress] the LORD's commands? You will not ·be successful [prosper; succeed]. Because you have ·left [abandoned; forsaken] the LORD, he has also ·left [abandoned; forsaken] you.'"

21 But ·the king and his officers made plans [they conspired; plotted] against Zechariah. At the king's command they ·threw stones at [stoned] him in the courtyard of the ·Temple [Lhouse] of the LORD until he died. 22 King Joash did not remember Jehoiada's ·kindness [loyalty; devotion] to him, so Joash ·killed [murdered] Zechariah, Jehoiada's son. ·Before [As] Zechariah died, he said, "May the LORD ·see what you are doing and punish you [see and avenge]."

Aramea Attacks Judah

(24:23–27; 2 Kin. 12:17–21)

23 At the ·end [Lturning; Cspring] of the year, the Aramean army came against Joash. They attacked Judah and Jerusalem, killed all the ·leaders [officials] of the people, and sent all the ·valuable things [plunder; spoil; booty] to their king in Damascus. 24 The Aramean army came with only a small group of men, but the LORD handed over to them a very large army from Judah, because the people of Judah had ·left [abandoned; forsaken] the LORD, the God of their ·ancestors [fathers]. So Joash was ·punished [judged]. 25 When the Arameans left, Joash was badly wounded. His own ·officers [officials] made plans against him because ·he had killed [Lof the shed blood of] Zechariah son of Jehoiada the priest. So they ·killed [murdered] Joash in his own bed. He died and was buried in the City of David [CJerusalem] but not in the ·graves [tombs] of the kings.

26 The ·officers who made plans [conspirators; plotters] against Joash were Jozabad and Jehozabad. Jozabad was the son of Shimeath, a woman from Ammon. And Jehozabad was the son of Shimrith, a woman from Moab. 27 The story of Joash's sons, the ·great [*or* many] ·prophecies [oracles] against him, and how he ·repaired [restored] the ·Temple [Lhouse] of God ·are [Lare they not…?] written in the ·book [scroll] of the kings. Joash's son Amaziah became king in his place.

Amaziah King of Judah

(25:1–28; 2 Kin. 14:1–20)

25 Amaziah was twenty-five years old when he became king, and he ·ruled [reigned] for twenty-nine years in Jerusalem. His mother's name was Jehoaddin, and she was from Jerusalem. 2 Amaziah did what ·the LORD said was right [Lwas pleasing/proper in the eyes/sight of the LORD], but ·he did not really want to obey him [not wholeheartedly]. 3 As soon as Amaziah ·took strong [secured; established] control of the kingdom, he executed the officers who had ·murdered [assassinated] his father the king. 4 But Amaziah did not put to death their children. He obeyed what was written in the law in the ·Book [scroll] of Moses, where the LORD commanded, "·Parents [Fathers] must not be put to death ·when their children do wrong [for sons], and ·children [sons] must not be put to death ·when their parents do wrong [for fathers]. Each must die for his own sins [Deut. 24:16]."

5 Amaziah ·gathered [summoned; assembled] the people of Judah together. He ·grouped [assigned] all the people of Judah and Benjamin by ·families [clans], and he put commanders over groups of a thousand and over groups of a hundred. He ·counted [took a census of] the men who were twenty years old and older. In all there were three hundred thousand soldiers ready to fight and ·skilled [trained] with spears and shields. 6 Amaziah also hired one hundred thousand skilled soldiers from Israel for ·about seventy-five hundred pounds [Lone hundred talents] of silver. 7 But a man of God [Cprophet] came to Amaziah and said, "My king, don't let the army of Israel go with you. The LORD is not with Israel or any of the people from the tribe of Ephraim. 8 You can ·make yourself strong for war [fight bravely/well], but God will ·defeat you [Lcause you to stumble before the enemy]. He has the power to help you or to ·defeat you [Lcause you to stumble]."

9 Amaziah said to the man of God, "But what about the ·seventy-five hundred pounds [Lone hundred talents] of silver I paid to the Israelite army?"

The man of God answered, "The LORD can give you much more than that."

10So Amaziah ·sent the Israelite [discharged/dismissed the] army back
home to Ephraim. ·They were very angry with [LTheir anger burned
against] the people of Judah and went home ·angry [incensed; in a rage].
11Then Amaziah ·became very brave [summoned his courage] and led
his army to the Valley of Salt in the country of Edom. There Amaziah's
army killed ten thousand ·Edomites [Lsons of Seir]. 12The army of Judah
also captured ten thousand alive and took them to the top of a cliff and
threw them off so that they ·split open [were dashed to pieces].
13At the same time the Israelite troops that Amaziah had not let fight
in the war ·were robbing [raided] towns in Judah. From Samaria to Beth
Horon they killed three thousand people and took ·many valuable things
[much plunder/spoil/booty].
14When Amaziah came home after ·defeating [slaughtering] the
Edomites, he brought back the ·idols they worshiped [Lgods of the sons of
Seir] and ·started to worship them himself [set them up as his own gods].
He bowed down to them and ·offered sacrifices [burned incense] to them.
15The ·LORD was very angry with [LLORD's anger burned against] Amaziah,
·so [and] he sent a prophet to him who said, "Why have you asked their
gods for help? They could not even ·save [rescue; Tdeliver] their own people from ·you [Lyour hand]!"
16As the prophet spoke, Amaziah said to him, "·We never gave you the
job of advising the king [LWho made you the royal counselor?]. Stop, or
you will be killed."
The prophet stopped speaking except to say, "I know that God has
·decided [advised/counseled himself; Ca play on words since the king had
rejected God's counsel through the prophet] to destroy you because you
have done this. You did not listen to my ·advice [counsel]."
17Amaziah king of Judah ·talked with those who advised him [took
counsel; sought advice]. Then he sent a message to Jehoash son of
Jehoahaz, who was the son of Jehu king of Israel. Amaziah said to Jehoash,
"Come, let's meet face to face [Cpossibly a call to negotiate, but more likely
a challenge to battle]."
18Then Jehoash king of Israel answered Amaziah king of Judah, "A
·thornbush [thistle] in Lebanon sent a message to a cedar tree in Lebanon.
It said, 'Let your daughter marry my son.' But then a wild animal from
Lebanon came by, ·walking on and crushing [trampling] the ·thornbush
[thistle]. 19You say to yourself that you have defeated Edom, but ·you have
become proud [Lyour heart is lifted up], and you brag. But you stay at
home! Don't ask for trouble, or you and Judah will ·be defeated [Lfall]."
20But Amaziah would not listen. God caused this to happen so that
Jehoash would defeat Judah, because Judah ·asked for help from [sought;
followed] the gods of Edom. 21So Jehoash king of Israel went to attack. He
and Amaziah king of Judah faced each other at Beth Shemesh in Judah.
22Israel defeated Judah, and every man of Judah ran away to his ·home
[Ltent]. 23At Beth Shemesh Jehoash king of Israel captured Amaziah king
of Judah. (Amaziah was the son of Joash, who was the son of Ahaziah.)
Then Jehoash brought him to Jerusalem. Jehoash broke down the wall of
Jerusalem, from the Gate of Ephraim to the Corner Gate, ·about six hundred feet [Lfour hundred cubits]. 24He took all the gold and silver and all
the ·utensils [articles] from the ·Temple [Lhouse] of God that Obed-Edom
had taken care of. He also took the treasures from the ·palace [Lhouse]
and some hostages. Then he returned to Samaria.

[25]Amaziah son of Joash, the king of Judah, lived fifteen years after the death of Jehoash son of Jehoahaz, the king of Israel. [26]The ·other things Amaziah did as king [rest of the events/acts/history of Amaziah], from ·the beginning to the end [first to last], ·are [[L]are they not…?] written in the ·book [scroll] of the kings of Judah and Israel. [27]When Amaziah ·stopped obeying [turned away from] the LORD, the people in Jerusalem ·made plans [conspired; plotted] against him. So he ·ran away [fled] to the town of Lachish, but they sent men after him to Lachish and killed him there. [28]They brought his body back on horses, and he was buried with his ·ancestors [fathers] in the city of ·Judah [*or* David; [C]see 2 Kin. 14:20].

Uzziah King of Judah

(26:1–5; 2 Kin. 14:21–22; 15:1–3)

26 Then all the people of Judah made Uzziah [[C]also called Azariah] king in place of his father Amaziah. Uzziah was sixteen years old. [2]He rebuilt the town of Elath and made it part of Judah again after Amaziah ·died [[L]lay down/[T]slept with his fathers/ancestors].

[3]Uzziah was sixteen years old when he became king, and he ·ruled [reigned] fifty-two years in Jerusalem. His mother's name was Jecoliah, and she was from Jerusalem. [4]He did what ·the LORD said was right [[L]was pleasing/proper in the eyes/sight of the LORD], just as his father Amaziah had done [[C]in the beginning]. [5]Uzziah ·obeyed [sought] God while Zechariah was alive, because he taught Uzziah how to ·respect and obey [fear] God [Prov. 1:7]. And as long as Uzziah ·obeyed [sought] the LORD, God ·gave him success [made him prosper].

[6]Uzziah fought a war against the Philistines. He tore down the walls around their towns of Gath, Jabneh, and Ashdod and built new towns near Ashdod and in other places among the Philistines. [7]God helped Uzziah ·fight [[L]against] the Philistines, the Arabs living in Gur Baal, and the Meunites. [8]Also, the Ammonites ·made the payments Uzziah demanded [paid tribute to Uzziah]. He was very powerful, so his ·name became famous all the way [fame spread/extended] to the border of Egypt.

[9]Uzziah built towers in Jerusalem at the Corner Gate, the Valley Gate, and ·where the wall turned [at the angle of the wall], and he ·made them strong [fortified them]. [10]He also built towers in the ·desert [wilderness] and dug many ·wells [cisterns], because he had many cattle ·on the western hills [[L]in the Shephelah] and in the plains. He had people who worked his fields and vineyards in the hills and in ·the fertile lands [*or* Carmel], because he loved the ·land [soil].

[11]Uzziah had an army of trained soldiers. They were counted and put in ·groups [divisions; units] by Jeiel the ·royal secretary [scribe] and Maaseiah the ·officer [official]. Hananiah, one of the king's ·commanders [officers], ·was their leader [directed them]. [12]There were twenty-six hundred ·leaders [family/clan heads] over the soldiers. [13]They ·were in charge of [commanded] an army of three hundred seven thousand five hundred men who ·fought with great power [*or* were a powerful force] to help the king against the enemy. [14]Uzziah gave his army shields, spears, helmets, armor, bows, and stones for their slings. [15]In Jerusalem Uzziah made ·cleverly [expertly; carefully] designed ·devices [machines]. These ·devices [machines] on the towers and corners of the city walls were used to shoot arrows and large rocks. So Uzziah became famous in faraway places, because he ·had much help until he became [was marvelously/tremendously helped to become] powerful.

Uzziah's Downfall
(26:16–23; 2 Kin. 15:4–7)

16 But when Uzziah became powerful, his pride led to his ·ruin [downfall]. He was unfaithful to the LORD his God; he went into the ·Temple [Lhouse] of the LORD to burn incense on the altar for incense [Cwhich only priests should do]. 17 Azariah and eighty other brave priests who served the LORD followed Uzziah into the ·Temple [Lhouse]. 18 They ·told him he was wrong [confronted the king] and said to him, "·You don't have the right [It is not for you, Uzziah,] to burn incense to the LORD. Only the priests, Aaron's descendants, should burn the incense, because they have been ·made holy [consecrated; set apart]. ·Leave this holy place [Get out of the sanctuary]. You have ·been unfaithful [sinned; disobeyed], and the LORD God will not honor you for this."

19 Uzziah was standing beside the altar for incense in the ·Temple [Lhouse] of the LORD, and in his hand was a ·pan for burning incense [censer]. He was ·very angry [furious] with the priests. As he was standing in front of the priests, ·a skin disease [Tleprosy; Cthe term does not refer to modern leprosy (Hansen's disease), but to various skin disorders; Lev. 13:2] broke out on his forehead. 20 Azariah, the leading priest, and all the other priests looked at him and saw the ·skin disease [Tleprosy] on his forehead. So they hurried him out of the ·Temple [Lhouse]. Uzziah also rushed to get out, because the LORD ·was punishing [had struck/afflicted] him. 21 So King Uzziah had ·the skin disease [Tleprosy] until the day he died. He had to live in a separate house and could not enter the ·Temple [Lhouse] of the LORD. His son Jotham was in charge of the ·palace [Lhouse], and he ·governed [ruled over; judged] the people of the land.

22 The ·other things Uzziah did as king [rest of the events/acts/history of Uzziah's reign], from ·beginning to end [first to last], were written down by the prophet Isaiah son of Amoz. 23 Uzziah ·died [Llay down/Tslept with his fathers/ancestors] and was buried near his ·ancestors [fathers] in a ·graveyard [burial field] that belonged to the kings. This was because people said, "He ·had a skin disease [Twas a leper; v. 19]." And his son Jotham became king in his place.

Jotham King of Judah
(27:1–9; 2 Kin. 15:32–38)

27 Jotham was twenty-five years old when he became king, and he ·ruled [reigned] sixteen years in Jerusalem. His mother's name was Jerusha daughter of Zadok. 2 Jotham did what ·the LORD said was right [Lwas pleasing/proper in the eyes/sight of the LORD], just as his father Uzziah had done. But Jotham did not enter the ·Temple [Lhouse] of the LORD [Ca reference to Uzziah's sin, 26:16–21]. But the people continued ·doing wrong [sinning; in their corrupt practices]. 3 Jotham rebuilt the Upper Gate of the ·Temple [Lhouse] of the LORD, and he added greatly to the wall at Ophel. 4 He also built towns in the hill country of Judah, as well as ·walled cities [fortresses] and towers in the forests.

5 Jotham also fought the king of the Ammonites and ·defeated [conquered] them. So each year for three years they ·gave [paid] Jotham ·about seventy-five hundred pounds [Lone hundred talents] of silver, ·about sixty-two thousand bushels [Lten thousand kors] of wheat, and ·about sixty-two thousand bushels [Lten thousand kors] of barley. 6 Jotham became powerful, because he ·always obeyed [walked purposefully before; Lordered his ways before] the LORD his God.

7 The ·other things Jotham did while he was king [rest of the events/acts/history of Jotham's reign] and all his wars ·are [Lare they not…?] written in the ·book [scroll] of the kings of Israel and Judah. 8 Jotham was

twenty-five years old when he became king, and he ·ruled [reigned] sixteen years in Jerusalem. 9Jotham ·died [Llay down/Tslept with his fathers/ancestors] and was buried in the City of David [CJerusalem]. Then Jotham's son Ahaz became king in his place.

Ahaz King of Judah

(28:1-7; 2 Kin. 16:1-5)

28 Ahaz was twenty years old when he became king, and he ·ruled [reigned] sixteen years in Jerusalem. Unlike his ·ancestor [father] David, he did not do what ·the LORD said was right [Lwas pleasing/proper in the eyes/sight of the LORD]. 2Ahaz ·did the same things as [Lwalked in the ways of] the kings of Israel. He made ·metal [cast; molten] ·idols [images] to worship Baal. 3He ·burned incense [offered sacrifices] in the Valley of Ben Hinnom and ·made [sacrificed] his children ·pass through [in] the fire. He ·did [followed] the ·same hateful sins [detestable/abominable practices] as the nations had done whom the LORD had ·forced [driven] out of the land ahead of the Israelites. 4Ahaz ·offered [sacrificed] sacrifices and burned incense at the ·places where gods were worshiped [Lhigh places; 11:15], and on the hills, and under every green tree.

5So the LORD his God handed over Ahaz to the king of Aram. The Arameans defeated Ahaz and ·took [deported] many people of Judah as ·prisoners [captives] to Damascus.

He also handed over Ahaz to Pekah king of Israel, ·and Pekah's army killed many soldiers of Ahaz [who inflicted heavy casualties on him]. 6Pekah son of Remaliah killed one hundred twenty thousand ·brave [skilled] soldiers from Judah in one day. Pekah defeated them because they had ·left [abandoned; forsaken] the LORD, the God of their ·ancestors [fathers]. 7Zicri, a mighty warrior from Ephraim, killed King Ahaz's son Maaseiah. He also killed Azrikam, the ·officer [commander] in charge of the ·palace [Lhouse], and Elkanah, who was second in command to the king. 8The Israelite army captured two hundred thousand of their own relatives. They took women, sons and daughters, and ·many valuable things [much plunder/spoil/booty] from Judah and carried ·them [it] back to Samaria. 9But a prophet of the LORD named Oded was there. He met the Israelite army when it returned to Samaria and said to them, "The LORD, the God of your ·ancestors [fathers], handed Judah over to you, because he was angry with them. But ·God has seen the cruel way you killed them [you slaughtered them in a rage that has reached to heaven]. 10Now you plan to make the people of Judah and Jerusalem your slaves, but ·you also have sinned [Lwhat about your own sins/transgressions…?] against the LORD your God. 11Now listen to me. Send back ·your brothers and sisters whom you captured [the captives you have taken from your brothers], because the ·LORD is very angry with you [Lfierce anger of the LORD burns against you]."

12Then some of the ·leaders [officials] in Ephraim—Azariah son of Jehohanan, Berekiah son of Meshillemoth, Jehizkiah son of Shallum, and Amasa son of Hadlai—·met [confronted; Lrose against] the Israelite soldiers coming home from ·war [battle]. 13They warned the soldiers, "Don't bring the ·prisoners [captives] from Judah here. If you do, we will ·be guilty of sin against the LORD, and that will make our sin and guilt even worse [add to our sins and guilt before the LORD]. Our guilt is already so great that ·he is angry with [Lhis fierce anger is burning against] Israel."

14So the soldiers left the ·prisoners [captives] and ·valuable things [plunder; spoil; booty] in front of the ·officers [officials] and ·people there [the entire assembly]. 15The ·leaders [men] who were named took the ·prisoners [captives] and gave those who were naked clothes from ·what the Israelite army had taken [the plunder/spoil/booty]. They gave the ·prisoners [captives] clothes, sandals, food, drink, and ·medicine [oil for their wounds; Lanointed them]. They put the weak on donkeys and took them back to their ·families [brothers] in Jericho, the city of palm trees. Then they returned home to Samaria.

More Attacks
(28:16–27; 2 Kin. 16:6–20)

16-17At that time the Edomites came again and attacked Judah and carried away ·prisoners [captives]. So King Ahaz sent to the king of Assyria for help. 18The Philistines also ·robbed [raided; invaded] the towns in the ·western hills [LShephelah] and in ·southern [Lthe Negev of] Judah. They captured the towns of Beth Shemesh, Aijalon, Gederoth, Soco, Timnah, and Gimzo, and the villages around them. Then the Philistines ·lived [settled] in those towns. 19The LORD ·brought trouble on [humbled; humiliated; *or* subdued] Judah because Ahaz their king ·led the people of Judah to sin [acted without restraint/irresponsibly], and he was ·very [completely; utterly] unfaithful to the LORD. 20Tiglath-pileser king of Assyria came to Ahaz, but he ·gave Ahaz trouble instead of help [oppressed him rather than helped him]. 21Ahaz ·took some valuable things from [plundered] the ·Temple [Lhouse] of the LORD, from the ·palace [Lhouse], and from the ·princes [officials], and he gave them to the king of Assyria, but it did not help.

22During Ahaz's ·troubles [Ltime of distress] he was even more unfaithful to the LORD. 23He ·offered [sacrificed] sacrifices to the gods of the people of Damascus, who had defeated him. He thought, "The gods of the kings of Aram helped them. If I ·offer [sacrifice] sacrifices to them, they ·will [may] help me also." But this brought ·ruin to [the downfall of] Ahaz and all Israel.

24Ahaz gathered the ·things [articles; utensils] from the ·Temple [Lhouse] of God and ·broke [cut] them into pieces. Then he closed the doors of the ·Temple [Lhouse] of the LORD. He made himself altars [Cto pagan gods] and put them on every street corner in Jerusalem. 25In every town in Judah, Ahaz made ·places [Lhigh places; 11:15] for burning sacrifices to other gods. So he ·made [provoked] the LORD, the God of his ·ancestors [fathers], ·very angry [to anger].

26The ·other things Ahaz did as king [rest of the events/acts/history of Ahaz's reign], from ·beginning to end [first to last], are written in the ·book [scroll] of the kings of Judah and Israel. 27Ahaz ·died [Llay down/ Tslept with his fathers/ancestors] and was buried in the City of David [CJerusalem], but not in the ·graves [tombs] of the kings of Israel. Ahaz's son Hezekiah became king in his place.

Hezekiah Purifies the Temple
(29:1–2; 2 Kin. 18:1–3)

29 Hezekiah was twenty-five years old when he became king, and he ·ruled [reigned] twenty-nine years in Jerusalem. His mother's name was Abijah daughter of Zechariah. 2Hezekiah did what ·the LORD said was right [Lwas pleasing/proper in the eyes/sight of the LORD], just as his ·ancestor [father] David had done.

3Hezekiah opened the doors of the ·Temple [Lhouse] of the LORD and ·repaired [restored] them in the first month of the first year he was king. 4Hezekiah brought in the priests and Levites and gathered them in the

·courtyard [square] on the east side of the ·Temple [Lhouse]. 5Hezekiah
said, "Listen to me, Levites. ·Make yourselves ready for the LORD's service
[Consecrate/Purify/Sanctify yourselves], and ·make holy [consecrate/
purify/sanctify] the ·Temple [Lhouse] of the LORD, the God of your ·ances-
tors [fathers]. Remove from the ·Temple [Lhouse] everything that makes
it ·impure [defiled; ritually unclean]. 6Our ·ancestors [fathers] were
unfaithful to God and did ·what the LORD said was wrong [Levil in the
LORD's sight/eyes]. They ·left [abandoned; forsook] the LORD and ·stopped
worshiping at [Lturned their faces away from] the ·Temple [Lhouse] where
he lives. They ·rejected [Lturned their backs on] him. 7They shut the doors
of the ·porch [portico; vestibule; entry room] of the ·Temple [Lhouse],
and ·they let the fire go out in [put/snuffed out] the lamps. They stopped
burning incense and offering burnt offerings in the ·holy place to [sanc-
tuary of] the God of Israel. 8So the LORD became very angry with the
people of Judah and Jerusalem, and he ·punished them. Other people are
frightened and shocked by what he did to them. So they ·insult the people
of Judah. You know these things are true […made them an object of
dread/terror, horror, and ridicule/Lhissing, as you can see with your own
eyes]. 9That is why our ·ancestors [fathers] ·were killed in battle [Lhave
fallen by the sword] and our sons, daughters, and wives ·were [are] taken
captive. 10Now I, Hezekiah, ·have decided [intend] to make an ·agreement
[covenant; treaty] with the LORD, the God of Israel, so ·he will not be
angry with us anymore [Lhis burning anger will turn away from us]. 11My
sons, don't ·waste any more time [be negligent now]. The LORD chose you
to stand ·before him [in his presence], to ·serve [minister to] him, to be
his ·servants [ministers], and to burn incense to him."

12·These are [Then] the Levites ·who started to work [Lrose]. From the
Kohathite ·family [clan] there were Mahath son of Amasai and Joel son of
Azariah. From the Merarite ·family [clan] there were Kish son of Abdi
and Azariah son of Jehallelel. From the Gershonite ·family [clan] there
were Joah son of Zimmah and Eden son of Joah. 13From Elizaphan's ·fam-
ily [clan] there were Shimri and Jeiel. From Asaph's ·family [clan] there
were Zechariah and Mattaniah. 14From Heman's ·family [clan] there were
Jehiel and Shimei. From Jeduthun's ·family [clan] there were Shemaiah
and Uzziel [5:12].

15These Levites gathered their brothers together and ·made themselves
holy [consecrated/purified/sanctified themselves]. Then they went into
the ·Temple [Lhouse] of the LORD to purify it. They obeyed the king's command that had come from the LORD. 16When the priests went into the
·Temple [Lhouse] of the LORD to ·purify [cleanse] it, they took out all the
·unclean [defiled; Critually] things they found in the ·Temple [Lhouse] of
the LORD and put them in the ·Temple [Lhouse] courtyard. Then the
Levites took these things out to the Kidron Valley. 17Beginning on the
first day of the first month, they ·made holy [consecrated; purified; sanc-
tified] the ·Temple [Lhouse]. On the eighth day of the month, they came
to the ·porch [portico; vestibule; entry room] of the ·Temple [Lhouse], and
for eight more days they ·made holy [consecrated; purified; sanctified]
the ·Temple [Lhouse] of the LORD. So they finished on the sixteenth day of
the first month.

18Then they went to King Hezekiah and said, "We have ·purified
[cleansed] the entire ·Temple [Lhouse] of the LORD, the altar for burnt
offerings and its ·utensils [equipment], and the table for the ·holy bread

[Tshowbread] and all its ·utensils [equipment]. 19When Ahaz was king, he was unfaithful to God and ·removed some things [discarded some utensils/equipment]. But we have ·put them back [prepared] and ·made them holy [consecrated/purified/sanctified them] for the LORD. They are now in front of the LORD's altar."

20Early the next morning King Hezekiah ·gathered [assembled] the ·leaders [officials] of the city and went up to the ·Temple [Lhouse] of the LORD. 21They brought seven ·bulls [oxen], seven ·male sheep [rams], seven lambs, and seven male goats. These animals were an ·offering to remove the sin of the people and [sin offering for] the kingdom ·of [*or* and for] Judah and ·to make [for] the ·Temple [sanctuary]. King Hezekiah commanded the priests, the descendants of Aaron, to ·offer [sacrifice] these animals on the LORD's altar. 22So the priests ·killed [slaughtered] the ·bulls [oxen] and sprinkled their blood on the altar. They ·killed [slaughtered] the ·sheep [rams] and sprinkled their blood on the altar. Then they ·killed [slaughtered] the lambs and sprinkled their blood on the altar. 23Then the priests brought the male goats for the sin offering before the king and the people there. After the king and the people ·put [laid] their hands on the goats, 24the priests ·killed [slaughtered] them. They ·made an offering [sprinkled/presented their blood] on the altar to ·remove the sins of the Israelites [atone for all Israel]. The king had said that the burnt offering [Lev. 1:1–17] and ·sin [*or* purification] offering [Lev. 4:3] should be made for all Israel.

25King Hezekiah ·put [stationed; positioned] the Levites in the ·Temple [Lhouse] of the LORD with cymbals, harps, and lyres, as David, Gad, and Nathan had commanded. (Gad was the king's ·seer [prophet], and Nathan was a prophet.) This command came from the LORD through his prophets. 26So the Levites stood ready with David's musical instruments, and the priests with their trumpets.

27Then Hezekiah gave the order to ·sacrifice [offer] the burnt offering [Lev. 1:1–17] on the altar. When the burnt offering [Lev. 1:1–17] began, the singing to the LORD also began. The trumpets were blown, and the musical instruments of David king of Israel were played. 28·All the people [The entire assembly] worshiped, the singers sang, and the trumpeters ·blew their trumpets [sounded] until the burnt offering [Lev. 1:1–17] was finished.

29When the sacrifices were completed, King Hezekiah and everyone with him bowed down and worshiped. 30King Hezekiah and his ·officers [officials] ordered the Levites to ·praise [sing praises to] the LORD, using the words David and Asaph the ·seer [prophet] had used. So they praised God with ·joy [gladness] and bowed down and worshiped.

31Then Hezekiah said, "Now that you people of Judah have ·given [consecrated; dedicated] yourselves to the LORD, come near to the ·Temple [Lhouse] of the LORD. Bring sacrifices and ·offerings, to show thanks to him [*or* thank offerings]." So the people brought sacrifices and thank offerings, and anyone who was willing also brought burnt offerings [Lev. 1:1–17]. 32For burnt offerings [Lev. 1:1–17] they brought a total of seventy ·bulls [oxen], one hundred ·male sheep [rams], and two hundred lambs; all these animals were sacrificed as burnt offerings to the LORD. 33The ·holy [consecrated] offerings totaled six hundred ·bulls [oxen] and three thousand sheep and goats. 34There were not enough priests to skin all the animals for the burnt offerings. So their ·relatives [brothers] the Levites helped them until the work was finished and other priests could be ·made holy [consecrated; purified; sanctified]. The Levites had been more careful to ·make themselves holy [consecrate/purify/sanctify themselves] than the priests. 35There were many burnt offerings [Lev. 1:1–17] along with the fat of ·fellowship [*or* peace; well-being] offerings [Lev. 3:1] and drink offerings. So the service in the ·Temple [Lhouse] of the LORD ·began again [was established/restored]. 36And Hezekiah and the people ·were very happy [rejoiced] that God had made it happen so quickly for his people.

The Passover Celebration

30 King Hezekiah sent messages to all the people of Israel and Judah, and he wrote letters to the people of Ephraim and Manasseh. Hezekiah invited all these people to come to the ·Temple [Lhouse] of the LORD in Jerusalem to ·celebrate [keep; observe] the Passover for the LORD, the God of Israel [Ex. 12]. 2King Hezekiah, his ·officers [officials], and all the ·people [community; assembly] in Jerusalem ·agreed [decided] to ·celebrate [keep; observe] the Passover in the second month. 3They could not ·celebrate [keep; observe] it at the ·normal [prescribed] time, because not enough priests had ·made themselves ready to serve the LORD [consecrated/purified/sanctified themselves], and the people had not yet ·gathered [assembled] in Jerusalem. 4This plan ·satisfied [seemed right to] King Hezekiah and all the ·people [community; assembled]. 5So they ·made an announcement [sent a proclamation/edict] everywhere in Israel, from Beersheba [Cin the south] to Dan [Cin the north; that is, all the people in Israel], telling the people to come to Jerusalem to ·celebrate [keep; observe] the Passover for the LORD, the God of Israel. The people had not ·celebrated [kept; observed] the Passover as the law commanded ·for a long time [*or* in great numbers]. 6At the king's command, ·the messengers [couriers; Lrunners] took letters from him and his ·officers [officials] all through Israel and Judah. This is what the letters said:

> People of Israel, return to the LORD, the God of Abraham, Isaac, and Israel. Then God will return to the ·few [remnant] of you who have ·escaped [been spared] from the kings of Assyria. 7Don't be like your ·ancestors [fathers] or your ·relatives [brothers]. They ·turned against [were unfaithful to] the LORD, the God of their ·ancestors [fathers], so he ·caused other people to be disgusted with them. You know this is true [...made them an object of horror/derision, as you see]. 8Don't be ·stubborn [Lstiff-necked] as your ·ancestors [fathers] were, but ·obey the LORD willingly [submit/yield to the LORD]. Come to the ·Temple [sanctuary], which he has ·made holy [consecrated; Lset apart] forever. Serve the LORD your God so ·he will not be angry with [his fierce anger will turn away from] you. 9Come back to the LORD. Then the people who captured your ·relatives [brothers] and ·children [sons] will be ·kind [merciful; compassionate] to them and will let them return to this land. The LORD your God is ·kind [gracious] and ·merciful [compassionate]. He will not turn ·away [Lhis face] from you if you return to him.

10The ·messengers [couriers; Lrunners] went to every town in Ephraim and Manasseh, and all the way to Zebulun, but the people ·laughed at

[scorned] them and ·made fun of [mocked; ridiculed] them. 11But some
men from Asher, Manasseh, and Zebulun ·were sorry for what they had
done [humbled themselves] and went to Jerusalem. 12And ·God united all
the people of [LGod's hand was on] Judah ·in obeying [Lgiving them one
heart to do the commands of] King Hezekiah and his ·officers [officials],
because their command ·had come from [Lwas the word of] the LORD.
13In the second month a very large crowd came together in Jerusalem
to ·celebrate [keep; observe] the ·Feast [Festival] of Unleavened Bread.
14The people removed the altars and incense altars [Cto pagan gods] in
Jerusalem and threw them into the Kidron Valley.
15They ·killed [slaughtered] the Passover lamb on the fourteenth day of
the second month. The priests and the Levites were ashamed [Cbecause
others are doing what they should be doing], so they ·made themselves
holy [consecrated/purified/sanctified themselves] and brought burnt
offerings into the ·Temple [Lhouse] of the LORD. 16They took their ·regular
places [stations; posts] in the ·Temple [Lhouse] as the ·Teachings [law] of
Moses, the man of God, ·commanded [prescribed]. The Levites gave the
blood [Cfrom the sacrifices] to the priests, who sprinkled it [Con the altar].
17Since many people in the crowd had not ·made themselves holy [conse-
crated/purified/sanctified themselves], the Levites ·killed [slaughtered]
the Passover lambs for everyone who was ·not clean [defiled; ritually
unclean]. The Levites ·made each lamb holy [consecrated/purified/sancti-
fied them] for the LORD. 18–19Although many people from Ephraim,
Manasseh, Issachar, and Zebulun had not ·purified [consecrated; sanctified; cleansed] themselves, they ate the Passover even though it was
·against the law [Lwithout what is written]. So Hezekiah prayed for them,
saying, "LORD, you are good. You are the LORD, the God of our ·ancestors
[fathers]. Please ·forgive [pardon] all those who ·try to obey you [Lset
their heart on seeking God] even if they did not ·make themselves clean
[purify themselves] as the rules of the ·Temple [sanctuary] command."
20The LORD listened to Hezekiah's prayer, and he healed the people. 21The
Israelites in Jerusalem ·celebrated [kept; observed] the ·Feast [Festival] of
Unleavened Bread for seven days with great joy. The Levites and priests
praised the LORD every day with loud ·music [instruments]. 22Hezekiah
encouraged all the Levites who showed ·they understood well how to do
[*or* good skill in] their service for the LORD. The people ate the feast for
seven days, ·offered [sacrificed] ·fellowship [*or* peace; well-being] offerings [Lev. 3:1], and ·praised [gave thanks to] the LORD, the God of their
·ancestors [fathers].
23Then all the people agreed to stay seven more days, so they celebrated
with joy for seven more days. 24Hezekiah king of Judah gave one thousand
·bulls [oxen] and seven thousand sheep to the ·people [assembly]. The
·officers [officials] gave one thousand ·bulls [oxen] and ten thousand
sheep to the ·people [assembly]. Many priests ·made themselves holy
[consecrated/purified/sanctified themselves]. 25All the ·people [assembly]
of Judah, the priests, the Levites, those who came from Israel, the ·foreign-
ers [sojourners; wanderers; resident aliens] from Israel, and the ·foreigners
[sojourners; wanderers; resident aliens] living in Judah ·were very happy
[rejoiced]. 26There was much joy in Jerusalem, because there had not been
a celebration like this since the time of Solomon son of David and king of
Israel. 27The priests and Levites stood up and blessed the people, and God
heard them ·because their prayer reached [from] heaven, his holy home.

The Collection for the Priests

(31:1; 2 Kin. 18:4–8)

31 When the Passover celebration was finished, all the Israelites
in Jerusalem went out to the towns of Judah. There they
smashed the ·stone [sacred] pillars [Cused in pagan worship]. They cut
down the Asherah ·idols [poles; 14:3] and destroyed the altars and
·places for worshiping gods [Lhigh places; 11:15] in all of Judah,
Benjamin, Ephraim, and Manasseh. After they had destroyed all of
them, the Israelites returned to their own towns and ·homes
[properties].
2King Hezekiah ·appointed [organized; assigned] ·groups [divisions] of
priests and Levites for their special duties. They were to ·offer [sacrifice]
burnt offerings [Lev. 1:1–17] and ·fellowship [*or* peace; well-being] offerings [Lev. 3:1], to ·worship [serve], and to give thanks and praise at the
gates of the LORD's ·house [Lcamp]. 3Hezekiah gave some of his own animals for the burnt offerings [Lev. 1:1–17], which were given every morning
and evening, on Sabbath days, during New Moons, and at other feasts
·commanded [prescribed] in the LORD's ·Teachings [instructions; laws].
4Hezekiah commanded the people living in Jerusalem to give the
priests and Levites the portion ·that belonged to [prescribed for] them.
Then the priests and Levites could ·give all their time [devote themselves]
to the LORD's ·Teachings [instructions; laws]. 5As soon as the king's command went out to the Israelites, they gave ·freely of the [generously/
abundantly from the] first ·portion [fruits; harvest] of their grain, new
wine, oil, honey, and ·everything they grew [all the produce] in their
fields. They brought a large amount, ·one-tenth [a tithe] of everything.
6The people of Israel and Judah who lived in Judah also brought ·one-
tenth [a tithe] of their cattle and sheep and ·one-tenth [a tithe] of the
·holy things [sacred/consecrated/dedicated things] that were given to the
LORD their God, and they put all of them in ·piles [heaps]. 7The people
began the ·piles [heaps] in the third month [Clate spring] and finished in
the seventh month [Cearly autumn]. 8When Hezekiah and his ·officers
[officials] came and saw the ·piles [heaps], they ·praised [blessed; thanked]
the LORD and his people Israel. 9Hezekiah asked the priests and Levites
about the ·piles [heaps]. 10Azariah, the leading priest from Zadok's ·fam-
ily [clan; Lhouse], answered Hezekiah, "Since the people began to bring
their ·offerings [contributions; gifts] to the ·Temple [Lhouse] of the LORD,
we have had plenty to eat and plenty left over, because the LORD has
blessed his people. So we have all this left over."
11Then Hezekiah commanded the priests to prepare the storerooms in
the ·Temple [Lhouse] of the LORD. So this was done. 12Then the priests
brought in the ·offerings [contributions] and the ·things given to the
LORD [consecrated/purified/sanctified things] and ·one-tenth of everything the people had given [the tithes]. Conaniah the Levite was the
officer in charge of these things, and his brother Shimei was ·second to
him [his assistant]. 13Conaniah and his brother Shimei were over these
supervisors: Jehiel, Azaziah, Nahath, Asahel, Jerimoth, Jozabad, Eliel,
Ismakiah, Mahath, and Benaiah. King Hezekiah and Azariah the officer
in charge of the ·Temple [Lhouse] of God had ·chosen [appointed] them.
14Kore son of Imnah the Levite was in charge of the ·special gifts the
people wanted to give [voluntary/free will offerings] to God. He was
responsible for ·giving out [distributing] the contributions made to the
LORD and the ·holy [consecrated; dedicated] gifts. Kore was the guard at
the East Gate. 15Eden, Miniamin, Jeshua, Shemaiah, Amariah, and

Shecaniah helped Kore in the towns where the priests lived. They gave from what was collected to ·the other groups of priests [their brothers by divisions], both ·old [great] and ·young [small].

[16]They also gave to the males three years old and older who had their names in the ·Levite family [genealogical] ·histories [records]. ·They were to enter [...all who entered] the ·Temple [Lhouse] of the LORD for their daily ·service [duties], ·each group having its own responsibilities [according to their divisions]. [17]The priests were given their part of the collection, by ·families [ancestral houses], as listed in the ·family [genealogical] ·histories [records]. The Levites twenty years old and older were given their part of the collection, based on their ·responsibilities [duties] and their ·groups [divisions]. [18]The Levites' babies, wives, sons, and daughters also got part of the collection. This was done for all the Levites who were ·listed [enrolled] in the ·family histories [genealogical records], because they ·always kept themselves ready to serve the LORD [faithfully consecrated/purified themselves].

[19]Some of Aaron's descendants, the priests, lived on the farmlands near the towns or in the towns. Men were ·chosen [appointed; designated] by name to ·give [distribute] part of the collection to these priests. All the males and those ·named [listed] in the ·family histories [genealogical records] of the Levites received part of the collection.

[20]This is what King Hezekiah did ·in [throughout] Judah. He did what was good and right and ·obedient [faithful; true; pleasing] before the LORD his God. [21]Hezekiah tried to ·obey [seek] God in his service of the ·Temple [Lhouse] of God, and in following his ·teachings [instructions; laws] and commands. He ·gave himself fully to his work for God [did so wholeheartedly] and therefore ·had success [prospered].

Assyria Attacks Judah

(32:1–19; 2 Kin. 13:3–7; Is. 36:1–22)

32 After Hezekiah ·did all these things to serve the LORD [accomplished these faithful acts], Sennacherib king of Assyria ·came and attacked [invaded] Judah. He and his army ·surrounded and attacked [besieged] the ·strong, walled [fortified] cities, ·hoping [intending] to take them for himself. [2]Hezekiah ·knew [realized] that Sennacherib had come to Jerusalem to attack it. [3]So Hezekiah and his ·officers [officials] and army ·commanders [officers] decided to ·cut off [stop the flow of] the water from the springs outside the city. So they helped Hezekiah. [4]Many people ·came [gathered] and ·cut off [stopped up] all the springs and the stream that flowed through the land. They said, "Why should the king of Assyria come and find ·plenty of [abundant] water?" [5]Then Hezekiah ·made Jerusalem stronger. He [...took courage/*or* worked hard/Lstrengthened himself and] rebuilt all the broken parts of the wall and ·put [erected; raised] towers on it. He also built another wall outside the first one and strengthened the ·area that was filled in on the east side [LMillo; Cpossibly fortified terraces] of the City of David [CJerusalem]. He also made many weapons and shields.

[6]Hezekiah ·put [appointed] army ·commanders [officers] over the ·people [*or* army] and met with them ·at the open place near [in the square at] the city gate. Hezekiah encouraged them, saying, [7]"Be strong and ·brave [courageous]. Don't be afraid or ·worried [panic] because of the king of Assyria or ·his large army [all his horde]. There is a greater ·power [one] with us than with him. [8]He only has ·men [human strength; Lan arm of flesh], but we have the LORD our God to help us and to fight

our battles." The people were encouraged by the words of Hezekiah king
of Judah.
9After this King Sennacherib of Assyria and all his army ·surrounded
and attacked [besieged] Lachish. Then he sent his ·officers [officials; ser-
vants] to Jerusalem with this message for King Hezekiah of Judah and all
the people of Judah in Jerusalem:

> 10Sennacherib king of Assyria says this: "·You have nothing to
> trust in [LOn what are you trusting…?] to help you. ·It is no use
> for you to [LWhy do you…?] stay in Jerusalem under ·attack
> [siege]. 11Hezekiah says to you, 'The LORD our God will ·save
> [rescue; Tdeliver] us from the hand of the king of Assyria,' but he
> is ·fooling [misleading; deceiving] you, condemning you to death
> from hunger and thirst. 12·Hezekiah [LDid not Hezekiah…?]
> himself removed your LORD's ·places of worship [Lhigh places;
> 11:15] and altars. He told you people of Judah and Jerusalem
> that you must worship and burn incense on only one altar [Cin
> the Temple at Jerusalem].
> 13"·You know [LDo you not realize…?] what my ·ancestors
> [fathers] and I have done to all the people ·in other nations [of
> the lands]. ·The gods of those nations could not [LWere the gods
> of those lands able to…?] ·save [rescue] their people from my
> ·power [Lhand]. 14My ·ancestors [fathers] destroyed those nations.
> ·None [LWhich…?] of their gods could save them from ·me [Lmy
> hand]. ·So your god cannot [LWhy suppose your god/God can…?]
> ·save [rescue; Tdeliver] you from my ·power [Lhand]. 15Do not let
> Hezekiah ·fool [deceive] you or ·trick [mislead] you, and do not
> believe him. No god of any nation or kingdom has been able to
> ·save [rescue; Tdeliver] his people from me or my ·ancestors
> [fathers]. ·Your god is even less [LHow much less will your god/
> God be…?] able to ·save [rescue; Tdeliver] you from me."

16Sennacherib's ·officers [officials] ·said worse things against [further
insulted/mocked] the LORD God and his servant Hezekiah. 17King
Sennacherib also wrote letters ·insulting [mocking] the LORD, the God of
Israel. They spoke against him, saying, "The gods of the other nations
could not ·save [rescue; Tdeliver] their people from me. In the same way
Hezekiah's ·god [God] won't be able to ·save [rescue; Tdeliver] his people
from me." 18Then the king's ·officers [officials] shouted in ·Hebrew [Lthe
language of Judah], calling out to the people of Jerusalem who were on
the city wall. The ·officers [officials] wanted to ·scare [frighten and ter-
rify] the people so they could capture Jerusalem. 19They spoke about the
God of Jerusalem as though he were like the gods the people of the ·world
[earth] worshiped, which are made by human hands.

God Rescues Judah
(32:20–23; 2 Kin. 19:1–37; Is. 36:1–37:35)

20King Hezekiah and the prophet Isaiah son of Amoz ·prayed [cried
out to] to heaven about this. 21Then the LORD sent an angel who ·killed
[destroyed; annihilated] all the soldiers, ·leaders [commanders], and officers in the ·camp [army] of the king of Assyria. So the king went back to
his own country in ·disgrace [shame; humiliation]. When he went into
the ·temple [Lhouse] of his god, some of his own ·sons [children] killed
him with a sword.

22So the LORD ·saved [rescued; Tdelivered] Hezekiah and the people in Jerusalem from [Lthe hand of] Sennacherib king of Assyria and from all other people. He ·took care of [guided; *or* gave rest to] them on every side. 23Many people brought ·gifts [offerings] for the LORD to Jerusalem, and they also brought ·valuable gifts [precious things] to King Hezekiah of Judah. From then on all the nations ·respected [looked up to; exalted] Hezekiah.

Hezekiah Dies
(32:24–26; 2 Kin. 20:1–11; Is. 38:1–8, 21–22)

24At that time Hezekiah became so sick he almost died. When he prayed to the LORD, the LORD spoke to him and gave him a ·sign [miraculous sign; CGod gave him a sign that he would live for another fifteen years; Is. 38:1–8]. 25But Hezekiah ·did not thank God for his kindness [did not respond to/was not grateful for the kindness shown him], because he was so proud. So ·the LORD was angry with [Lwrath came upon] him and the people of Judah and Jerusalem. 26·But later [Then] Hezekiah and the people of Jerusalem ·were sorry and stopped being proud [humbled themselves], so ·the LORD did not punish [Lthe wrath of the LORD did not come on] them while Hezekiah was alive.

27Hezekiah had ·many riches [great wealth] and much honor. He made treasuries for his silver, gold, ·gems [precious stones], spices, shields, and other valuable things. 28He built ·storage buildings [storehouses] for grain, new wine, and olive oil and stalls for all the cattle and pens for the sheep. 29He also built many towns. He had ·many [vast] flocks and herds, because God had given Hezekiah much wealth.

30It was Hezekiah who ·cut off [blocked; stopped; dammed] the upper pool of the Gihon spring and ·made those waters flow [channeled/directed the water] straight down to the west side of the City of David [CJerusalem]. And Hezekiah ·was successful [prospered] in everything he did. 31But one time the ·leaders [officials] of Babylon sent messengers to Hezekiah, asking him about a ·strange [miraculous] sign that had happened in the land [2 Kin. 20:12–19; Is. 39:1–8]. When they came, God left Hezekiah ·alone [to himself] to test him so he could know everything that was in Hezekiah's heart.

Hezekiah Dies
(32:32–33; 2 Kin. 20:20–21)

32Hezekiah's ·love for God [acts of devotion] and the ·other things [rest of the events/acts] he did as king are written in the vision of the prophet Isaiah son of Amoz. This is in the ·book [scroll] of the kings of Judah and Israel. 33Hezekiah ·died [Llay down/Tslept with his fathers/ancestors] and was buried on a hill, where the ·graves [tombs] of David's ·ancestors [descendants] are. All the people of Judah and Jerusalem honored Hezekiah when he died, and his son Manasseh became king in his place.

Manasseh King of Judah
(33:1–20; 2 Kin. 21:1–18)

33 Manasseh was twelve years old when he became king, and he ·was king [reigned] for fifty-five years in Jerusalem. 2He did ·what the LORD said was wrong [Levil in the LORD's sight/eyes]. He did the ·hateful [detestable; abominable] things the nations had done—the nations that the LORD had ·forced [driven] out of the land ahead of the Israelites. 3Manasseh's father, Hezekiah, had torn down ·places where gods were worshiped [Lthe high places; 11:15], but Manasseh rebuilt them. He also built altars for the Baal gods, and he made Asherah ·idols [poles; 14:3] and worshiped all the ·stars of the sky [powers/hosts of heaven] and ·served [worshiped] them. 4The LORD had said about the ·Temple [Lhouse], "·I will be worshiped [LMy name will be] in Jerusalem

forever," but Manasseh built altars in the ·Temple [Lhouse] of the LORD.
[5]He built altars to worship the ·stars [Lpowers/hosts of heaven] in the
two courtyards of the ·Temple [Lhouse] of the LORD. [6]He ·made his children pass through [sacrificed his children in the] fire in the Valley of
Ben Hinnom. He practiced magic and witchcraft and ·told the future by
explaining signs and dreams [divination; augery]. He ·got advice from
[dealt with] mediums and ·fortune-tellers [spiritualists; spiritists; Deut.
18:9–13]. He did ·many things the LORD said were wrong [Lmuch evil in
the LORD's sight/eyes], which made the LORD angry.

[7]Manasseh carved an idol and put it in the ·Temple [Lhouse] of God.
God had said to David and his son Solomon about the ·Temple [Lhouse],
"I will ·be worshiped [Lput my name] forever in this ·Temple [Lhouse] and
in Jerusalem, which I have chosen from all the tribes of Israel. [8]I will
never again make the ·Israelites [Lfeet of Israel] ·leave [wander from; Cinto
exile] the land I ·gave to [appointed for] their ·ancestors [fathers]. But
they must ·obey [be careful to do] everything I have commanded them in
all the ·teachings [instructions; laws], ·rules [statutes; ordinances; require-
ments], and ·commands [judgments] I gave them through Moses." [9]But
Manasseh led the people of Judah and Jerusalem ·to do wrong [astray].
They did more evil than the nations the LORD had destroyed ahead of the
Israelites.

[10]The LORD spoke to Manasseh and his people, but they ·did not listen
[paid no attention]. [11]So the LORD brought the king of Assyria's army
commanders to attack Judah. They captured Manasseh, put hooks in him
[Cin his nose], ·placed bronze chains on his hands [bound him with
bronze chains], and took him to Babylon. [12]·As Manasseh suffered [LWhen
he was in distress], he ·begged [entreated; Lsought] the LORD his God for
help and humbled himself greatly before the God of his ·ancestors
[fathers]. [13]When Manasseh prayed, the LORD heard ·him [Lhis plea] and
·had pity on him [was moved]. So the LORD ·let him return [brought him
back] to Jerusalem and to his kingdom. Then Manasseh knew that the
LORD is the true God.

[14]After that happened, Manasseh rebuilt the outer wall of the City of
David [CJerusalem] and made it higher. It was in the valley on the west
side of the Gihon spring and went to the entrance of the Fish Gate and
around the hill of Ophel. Then he ·put [stationed] ·commanders [offi-
cers] in all the ·strong, walled [fortified] cities in Judah.

[15]Manasseh removed the ·idols of other nations [foreign gods], including the idol in the ·Temple [Lhouse] of the LORD. He removed all the altars
he had built on the hill of the ·Temple [Lhouse] of the LORD and in
Jerusalem and threw them out of the city. [16]Then he ·set up [restored] the
LORD's altar and ·sacrificed [offered] on it ·fellowship [*or* peace; well-
being] offerings [Lev. 3:1] and ·offerings to show thanks to God [thank/
thanksgiving offerings]. Manasseh commanded all the people of Judah to
serve the LORD, the God of Israel. [17]The people continued to offer sacrifices at the ·places of worship [Lhigh places], but their sacrifices were only
to the LORD their God. [18]The ·other things Manasseh did as king [rest of
the events/acts/history of Manasseh], his prayer to his God, and what the
·seers [prophets] said to him in the name of the LORD, the God of Israel—
all are recorded in the ·book [scroll] of the ·history [annals; records] of
the kings of Israel. [19]Manasseh's prayer and ·God's pity for him [how God
responded to his plea/entreaty], his sins, his unfaithfulness, the ·places

[sites on which] he built ·for worshiping gods [Lhigh places; 11:15] and the Asherah ·idols [poles; 14:3] before he humbled himself—all are written in the ·book [scroll] of the ·seers [prophets]. 20 Manasseh ·died [Llay down/Tslept with his fathers/ancestors] and was buried in his ·palace [Lhouse]. Then Manasseh's son Amon became king in his place.

Amon King of Judah

(33:21–25; 2 Kin. 21:19–26)

21 Amon was twenty-two years old when he became king, and he ·was king [reigned] for two years in Jerusalem. 22 He did ·what the LORD said was wrong [Levil in the LORD's sight/eyes], as his father Manasseh had done. Amon ·worshiped [served] and ·offered [sacrificed] sacrifices to all the carved ·idols [images] Manasseh had made. 23 Amon did not humble himself before the LORD as his father Manasseh had done. Instead, Amon ·sinned even more [Lmultiplied guilt].

24 King Amon's ·officers [officials; servants] ·made plans [conspired; plotted] against him and killed him in his ·palace [Lhouse]. 25 Then the people of the land ·killed [executed] all those who had ·made plans [conspired; plotted] to kill King Amon, and they made his son Josiah king in his place.

Josiah King of Judah

(34:1–33; 2 Kin. 22:1–20; 23:1–20)

34

Josiah was eight years old when he became king, and he ·ruled [reigned] thirty-one years in Jerusalem. 2 He did what ·the LORD said was right [Lwas pleasing/proper in the eyes/sight of the LORD]. He lived as his ·ancestor [father] David had lived, and he did not ·stop doing what was right [Lturn aside/deviate to the right or the left].

3 In his eighth year as king while he was still young, Josiah began to ·obey [seek] the God of his ·ancestor [father] David. In his twelfth year as king, Josiah began to ·remove [purge; rid] from Judah and Jerusalem the ·places for worshiping gods [Lhigh places; 11:15], the Asherah ·idols [poles; 14:3], and the ·wooden [carved] and ·metal [cast; molten] ·idols [images]. 4 The people tore down the altars for the Baal gods ·as Josiah directed [*or* in his presence]. Then Josiah cut down the incense altars that were above them. He broke up the Asherah ·idols [poles; 14:3] and the wooden and ·metal [cast; molten] idols and ·beat [ground; crushed] them into powder. Then he sprinkled the powder on the ·graves [tombs] of the people who had ·offered [sacrificed] sacrifices to these gods. 5 He burned the bones of their priests on their own altars. So Josiah ·removed idol worship from [purged; purified] Judah and Jerusalem, 6 and from the towns in the areas of Manasseh, Ephraim, and Simeon all the way to Naphtali, and in the ·ruins [*or* regions] near these towns. 7 Josiah broke down the altars and Asherah ·idols [poles; 14:3] and ·beat [ground; crushed] the ·idols [carved images] into powder. He ·cut down [chopped up; smashed] all the incense altars in all of Israel. Then he went back to Jerusalem.

8 In Josiah's eighteenth year ·as king [of reigning], ·he made [he continued to make; *or* after he had made…] ·Judah [Lthe land] and the ·Temple [Lhouse] pure. He sent Shaphan son of Azaliah, Maaseiah the city ·leader [official; governor], and Joah son of Joahaz the ·recorder [royal historian] to ·repair [restore] the ·Temple [Lhouse] of the LORD, the God of Josiah. 9 These men went to Hilkiah the high priest and ·gave him [delivered] the money the Levite gatekeepers had gathered from the people of Manasseh, Ephraim, and all the ·Israelites who were left alive [Lremnant of Israel], and also from all the people of Judah, Benjamin, and Jerusalem. This is the money they had brought into the ·Temple [Lhouse] of God. 10 Then

the Levites gave it to the ·supervisors [overseers; foremen] of the work on
the ·Temple [Lhouse] of the LORD, and they paid the workers who ·rebuilt
[restored] and repaired the ·Temple [Lhouse]. 11They gave money to carpenters and builders to buy ·cut [quarried; finished] stone and ·wood
[timber]. The ·wood [timber] was used ·to rebuild [for rafters/joists/
braces for] the buildings and to make beams for them, because the kings
of Judah had let the buildings fall into ruin. 12The men did their work
·well [faithfully]. Their ·supervisors [overseers; foremen] were Jahath and
Obadiah, who were Levites from the ·family [clan] of Merari, and
Zechariah and Meshullam, who were from the ·family [clan] of Kohath.
·These [*or* Other] Levites were all skilled musicians. 13They were also ·in
charge [supervisors; overseers; foremen] of the ·workers who carried
loads [burden bearers; laborers] and all the other workers. Some Levites
worked as ·secretaries [scribes], ·officers [officials], and gatekeepers.

The Book of the Teachings Is Found

14The Levites brought out the money that was in the ·Temple [Lhouse]
of the LORD. As they were doing this, Hilkiah the priest found the ·Book
[scroll] of the LORD's ·Teachings [instructions; laws] that had been given
through Moses. 15Hilkiah said to Shaphan the royal ·secretary [scribe] ,
"I've found the ·Book [scroll] of the ·Teachings [instructions; laws] in the
·Temple [Lhouse] of the LORD!" Then he gave it to Shaphan.
16Shaphan took the ·book [scroll] to the king and reported to Josiah,
"Your ·officers [officials] are doing everything you ·told [assigned;
entrusted] them to do. 17They have paid out the ·money [silver] that was
in the ·Temple [Lhouse] of the LORD and have ·given [delivered; entrusted]
it to the ·supervisors [overseers] and the workers." 18Then Shaphan the
royal ·secretary [scribe] told the king, "Hilkiah the priest has given me a
·book [scroll]." And Shaphan read from the ·book [scroll] to the king.
19When the king heard the words of the ·Teachings [instructions; laws],
he tore his clothes [Ca sign of mourning or distress]. 20He gave orders to
Hilkiah, Ahikam son of Shaphan, Acbor son of Micaiah, Shaphan the
royal ·secretary [scribe], and Asaiah, the king's servant. These were the
orders: 21"Go and ·ask [inquire of] the LORD about the words in the ·book
[scroll] that was found. Ask for me and for the ·people who are left alive
in [remnant of] Israel and Judah. The LORD is ·very angry with [Lpouring
out/igniting his wrath on] us, because our ·ancestors [fathers] did not
·obey [seek] the LORD's word; they did not ·do [act in accordance with]
everything this ·book [scroll] says to do."
22So Hilkiah and those the king sent with him went to talk to Huldah
the prophetess. She was the wife of Shallum son of Tikvah, the son of
Harhas, ·who took care of the king's clothes [keeper of the wardrobe].
Huldah lived in Jerusalem, in the ·new area of the city [second quarter].
23She said to them, "·This is what the LORD, the God of Israel, says
[TThus says the LORD, the God of Israel]: Tell the man who sent you to me,
24'This is what the LORD says: I will bring ·trouble to [disaster/Levil on]
this place and ·to [on] the people living here. I will bring all the curses
that are written in the ·book [scroll] that was read to the king of Judah
[Deut. 27–28]. 25The people of Judah have ·left [abandoned; forsaken] me
and have burned incense to other gods. They have ·made me angry
[Lprovoked/aroused me to anger] by all the evil things [Cidols] they have
made. So ·I will punish them in my anger [Lmy wrath will be poured out
on this place], which will not be ·put out [quenched; extinguished].' 26Tell

the king of Judah, who sent you to ·ask [inquire of] the LORD, 'This is what
the LORD, the God of Israel, says about the ·words [message] you heard:
27When you heard my words against this place and its people, ·you
became sorry for what you had done [your heart was tender/responsive/
sensitive] and you humbled yourself before me. You tore your clothes [Ca
sign of mourning or distress], and you cried in my presence. This is why I
have heard you, says the LORD. 28So I will ·let you die and be buried
[Lgather you to your ancestors/fathers and to your grave/tomb] in peace.
You won't see all the ·trouble [disaster; Levil] I will bring to this place and
the people living here.' "

So they took her ·message [response; answer] back to the king.

29Then the king ·gathered [summoned] all the elders of Judah and
Jerusalem together. 30He went up to the ·Temple [Lhouse] of the LORD,
and all the people from Judah and from Jerusalem went with him. The
priests, the Levites, and all the people—·from the most important to the
least important [both great and small; *or* from the oldest to the young-
est]—went with him. He read to them all the words in the ·Book [scroll]
of the ·Agreement [covenant; treaty] that was found in the ·Temple
[Lhouse] of the LORD. 31The king stood by his pillar [Ca place of authority]
and made an ·agreement [covenant; treaty] ·in the presence of [before]
the LORD to follow the LORD and ·obey [keep] his commands, rules, and
laws with ·his whole being [all his heart] and to obey the words of the
·agreement [covenant; treaty] written in this ·book [scroll]. 32Then Josiah
·made [required] all the people in Jerusalem and Benjamin ·promise to
accept [stand with him regarding] the ·agreement [covenant; treaty]. So
the people of Jerusalem ·obeyed [acted in accordance with] the ·agree-
ment [covenant; treaty] of God, the God of their ·ancestors [fathers].

33And Josiah threw out the [detestable; abominable] idols from all the
land that belonged to the Israelites. He ·led [forced; caused] everyone in
Israel to serve the LORD their God. While Josiah lived, the people ·obeyed
[did not turn from] the LORD, the God of their ·ancestors [fathers].

Josiah Celebrates the Passover

(35:1–19; 2 Kin. 23:21–27)

35 King Josiah ·celebrated [kept; observed] the Passover to the
LORD in Jerusalem. The Passover lamb was ·killed [slaugh-
tered] on the fourteenth day of the first month. 2Josiah ·chose [appointed;
assigned] the priests to ·do their duties [fulfill their offices], and he
encouraged them as they served in the ·Temple [Lhouse] of the LORD.
3The Levites taught the Israelites and were ·made holy [set apart] for
service to the LORD. Josiah said to them, "Put the Holy Ark in the ·Temple
[Lhouse] that David's son Solomon, the king of Israel, built. Do not carry
it from place to place on your shoulders anymore. Now serve the LORD
your God and his people Israel. 4Prepare yourselves by your family
·groups [divisions] for service, and do the jobs that King David and his
son Solomon ·gave [wrote down for] you to do.

5"Stand in the ·holy place [sanctuary] with a ·group [division] of the
Levites for each family group of the people. 6·Kill [Slaughter] the Passover
lambs, and ·make yourselves holy [consecrate/purify/sanctify yourselves]
to the LORD. Prepare for your relatives, the people of Israel, to do as the
LORD through Moses commanded."

7Josiah ·gave [provided] the Israelites thirty thousand sheep and goats
to ·kill [slaughter] for the Passover sacrifices, and he gave them three
thousand cattle. They were all his own ·animals [property].

[8]Josiah's ·officers [officials] also gave willingly to the people, the priests,
and the Levites. Hilkiah, Zechariah, and Jehiel, the ·officers [officials] in
charge of the ·Temple [Lhouse], gave the priests twenty-six hundred
lambs and goats and three hundred cattle for Passover ·sacrifices [offer-
ings]. [9]Conaniah, his brothers Shemaiah and Nethanel, and Hashabiah,
Jeiel, and Jozabad gave the Levites five thousand sheep and goats and five
hundred cattle for Passover sacrifices. These men were ·leaders [officials]
of the Levites.

[10]When everything was ready for the Passover service, the priests and
Levites in their divisions went to their ·places [stations], as the king had
commanded. [11]The Passover lambs were ·killed [slaughtered]. Then the
Levites skinned the animals and gave the blood to the priests, who ·sprin-
kled [splashed] it on the altar. [12]Then they ·gave [divided; set aside] the
animals for the burnt offerings to the different family ·groups [divisions]
so the burnt offerings [Lev. 1:1–17] could be ·offered [sacrificed] to the
LORD as was written in the ·book [scroll] of Moses. They also did this with
the cattle. [13]The Levites roasted the Passover sacrifices over the fire as
·they were commanded [prescribed], and they boiled the ·holy [conse-
crated] offerings in pots, kettles, and pans. Then they quickly ·gave
[served] the meat to the people. [14]After this was finished, the Levites prepared meat for themselves and for the priests, the descendants of Aaron.
The priests worked until night, offering the burnt offerings [Lev. 1:1–17]
and burning the fat of the sacrifices.

[15]The Levite singers ·from Asaph's family [descended from Asaph]
stood in ·the places chosen for them by [their stations as prescribed by]
King David, Asaph, Heman, and Jeduthun [5:12], the king's ·seer
[prophet]. The gatekeepers at each gate did not have to leave their ·places
[posts], because their fellow Levites had prepared ·everything for them
for the Passover [Lfor them].

[16]So everything was ·done [completed] that day for the ·worship [ser-
vice] of the LORD, as King Josiah commanded. The Passover was
·celebrated [kept; observed], and the burnt offerings were ·offered [sacri-
ficed] on the LORD's altar. [17]The Israelites who were there ·celebrated
[kept; observed] the Passover and the ·Feast [Festival] of Unleavened
Bread for seven days. [18]The Passover had not been ·celebrated [observed;
kept] like this in Israel since the prophet Samuel was alive [Cover four
hundred years earlier]. None of the kings of Israel had ever ·celebrated
[kept; observed] a Passover like the one ·celebrated [kept; observed] by
King Josiah, the priests, the Levites, the people of Judah and Israel who
were there, and the people of Jerusalem. [19]This Passover was ·celebrated
[kept; observed] in the eighteenth year Josiah ·was king [reigned].

The Death of Josiah
(35:20–27; 2 Kin. 23:28–30)

[20]After Josiah ·did all this for [restored; set in order] the ·Temple
[Lhouse], Neco king of Egypt led an army to ·attack [fight/do battle at]
Carchemish, a town on the Euphrates River. And Josiah marched out to
fight against Neco. [21]But Neco sent messengers to Josiah, saying, "King
Josiah, ·there should not be war between us [what have we to do with each
other? Lwhat to me and to you]. I did not come to fight you, but ·my enemies [the kingdom/Lhouse with which I am at war]. God told me to hurry,
and he is on my side. So ·don't fight [stop opposing] God, ·or he will [so
he will not] destroy you."

[22]But Josiah did not ·go [Lturn his face] away. He ·wore different clothes

[disguised himself] ·so no one would know who he was [in order to fight him]. Refusing to listen to ·what Neco said at God's command [Lthe words Neco received from God's mouth], Josiah went to fight on the plain of Megiddo. 23In the battle King Josiah was shot by archers. He told his servants, "Take me away because I am badly wounded." 24So they took him out of his chariot and put him in another chariot and carried him to Jerusalem. There he died and was buried in the ·graves [tombs] where his ·ancestors [fathers] were buried. All the people of Judah and Jerusalem ·were very sad because he was dead [mourned for him].

25Jeremiah ·wrote some sad songs about [composed a lament for] Josiah. Even to this day all the men and women singers ·remember and honor [lament; mourn] Josiah with these songs. It became a ·custom [tradition] in Israel to sing these songs that are written in ·the collection of sad songs [*The Book of Laments*].

26The ·other things Josiah did as king [rest of the acts/events/history of Josiah] and his acts of devotion in obedience to what was was written in the LORD's ·Teachings [instructions; laws], 27from ·beginning to end [first to last], ·are [Lare they not…?] written in the ·book [scroll] of the kings of Israel and Judah.

Jehoahaz King of Judah
(36:1–4; 2 Kin. 23:30–34)

36 The people of ·Judah [Lthe land] ·chose [Ltook] Josiah's son Jehoahaz and made him king in Jerusalem in his father's place.

2Jehoahaz was twenty-three years old when he became king, and he ·was king [reigned] in Jerusalem for three months. 3Then King Neco of Egypt ·removed Jehoahaz from being king [dethroned/deposed him] in Jerusalem. Neco made the people of Judah pay a ·tax [*or* fine] of ·about seventy-five hundred pounds [Lone hundred talents] of silver and ·about seventy-five pounds [Lone talent] of gold. 4The king of Egypt made Jehoahaz's brother Eliakim the king of Judah and Jerusalem and changed his name to Jehoiakim. But Neco took his brother Jehoahaz to Egypt [Cas a prisoner].

Jehoiakim King of Judah
(36:5–8; 2 Kin. 23:35–24:7)

5Jehoiakim was twenty-five years old when he became king, and he ·was king [reigned] in Jerusalem for eleven years. He did ·what the LORD said was wrong [evil in the LORD's sight/eyes]. 6King Nebuchadnezzar of Babylon attacked ·Judah [Lhim], ·captured Jehoiakim [bound him], put bronze chains on him, and ·took him [carried him away] to Babylon. 7Nebuchadnezzar removed some of the ·things [articles; vessels] from the ·Temple [Lhouse] of the LORD, took them to Babylon, and put them in his own ·palace [*or* temple; Lhouse].

8The ·other things Jehoiakim did as king [rest of the events/acts/history of Jehoiakim], the ·hateful [detestable; abominable] things he did, and everything ·he was guilty of doing [found against him], ·are [Lare they not…?] written in the ·book [scroll] of the kings of Israel and Judah. And Jehoiakim's son Jehoiachin became king in his place.

Jehoiachin King of Judah
(36:9–10; 2 Kin. 24:8–17)

9Jehoiachin was ·eight [*or* eighteen; 2 Kin. 24:8] years old when he became king of Judah, and he ·was king [reigned] in Jerusalem for three months and ten days. He did ·what the LORD said was wrong [Levil in the LORD's sight/eyes]. 10·In the spring [LAt the turn of the year] King Nebuchadnezzar sent for Jehoiachin and brought him and some valuable ·treasures [articles; vessels] from the ·Temple [Lhouse] of the LORD to

Babylon. Then Nebuchadnezzar made Jehoiachin's ·uncle [relative; Lbrother] **Zedekiah the king of Judah and Jerusalem.**

Zedekiah King of Judah
(36:11–21; 2 Kin. 24:18–20; Jer. 52:1–3)

11**Zedekiah was twenty-one years old when he became king of Judah, and he ·was king** [reigned] **in Jerusalem for eleven years.** 12**Zedekiah did ·what the LORD said was wrong** [Levil in the LORD's sight/eyes]. **The prophet Jeremiah spoke ·messages from** [Lfrom the mouth of] **the LORD, but Zedekiah did not ·obey** [Lhumble himself]. 13**Zedekiah turned against King Nebuchadnezzar, who had forced him to ·swear** [vow; take an oath] **in God's name to be loyal to him. But Zedekiah ·became stubborn** [Lstiffened his neck] **and ·refused to obey** [Lhardened his heart against seeking] **the LORD, the God of Israel.** 14**Also, all the ·leaders** [officials] **of the priests and the people of Judah became more ·wicked** [unfaithful], **following the ·evil example** [detestable/abominable practices] **of the other nations. The LORD had ·made holy** [consecrated; sanctified] **the ·Temple** [Lhouse] **in Jerusalem, but the leaders ·made it unholy** [defiled/polluted it].

The Fall of Jerusalem

15**The LORD, the God of their ·ancestors** [fathers], **sent ·prophets** [Lmessengers] **again and again to warn his people, because he had ·pity** [compassion] **on them and on his ·Temple** [dwelling place]. 16**But they ·made fun of** [mocked] **God's ·prophets** [Lmessengers] **and hated God's ·messages** [Lwords]. **They ·refused to listen to the** [ridiculed/scoffed at his] **prophets until, finally, the LORD became so angry with his people that ·he could not be stopped** [there was no remedy/Lhealer]. 17**So God brought the king of ·Babylon** [the Chaldeans] **to attack them. The king ·killed** [slaughtered; Lkilled with the sword] **the young men even when they were in the ·Temple** [Lhouse of their sanctuary]. **He had no ·mercy** [pity; compassion] **on the young men or women, the old men or those who were ·sick** [infirm]. **God handed all of them over to Nebuchadnezzar.** 18**Nebuchadnezzar carried away to Babylon all the ·things** [articles; vessels] **from the ·Temple** [Lhouse] **of God, both large and small, and all the treasures from the ·Temple** [Lhouse] **of the LORD and from the king and his ·officers** [officials]. 19**Nebuchadnezzar and his army ·set fire to** [burned down] **God's ·Temple** [Lhouse] **and broke down Jerusalem's wall and burned all the ·palaces** [*or* fortifications; Lhouses]. **They destroyed every valuable thing in Jerusalem.**

20**Nebuchadnezzar took ·captive** [into exile] **to Babylon the people who ·were left alive** [Lescaped the sword], **and he forced them to be ·slaves** [servants] **for him and his descendants. They remained there as ·slaves** [servants] **until the Persian kingdom ·defeated Babylon** [Lcame/rose to power]. 21**And so ·what the LORD had told Israel through the prophet Jeremiah happened** [Lthe word of the LORD through the mouth of Jeremiah was fulfilled; Che prophesied the fall of Jerusalem]: **The country ·was an empty wasteland** [lay desolate/fallow] **for seventy years ·to make up for the years of Sabbath rest** [Lev. 25:1–7] **that the people had not kept** [*or* enjoying its sabbath rest; Ca bitter observation that the land experienced an ironic "rest" while the Israelites were in exile; Lev. 25:4, 26:33–35].

The Return from Exile
(36:22–23; Ezra 1:1–4)

22**In the first year Cyrus was king of Persia** [539–38 BC], **the LORD ·had Cyrus** [Lstirred the heart/spirit of Cyrus to] **send an ·announcement to** [decree/proclamation throughout] **his whole kingdom. This happened ·so the LORD's message spoken by Jeremiah would come true** [to fulfill the word of the LORD in the mouth of Jeremiah]. **He wrote:**

[23]·This is what Cyrus king of Persia says [[T]Thus says Cyrus king of Persia]:

> **The Lord, the God of ·heaven [the heavens], has given me all the kingdoms of the earth, and he has appointed me to build a ·Temple [[L]house] for him at Jerusalem in Judah. Now may the Lord your God ·be with [accompany; fill] all of you who are his people. You are free to go [[C]back to Jerusalem at the end of the exile; Ezra 1].**

EZRA

Cyrus Helps the Captives Return

1 In the first year Cyrus was king of Persia [C539 BC], the LORD ·caused [Lstirred up the spirit of] Cyrus to send an announcement to his whole kingdom and to put it in writing. This happened so the LORD's ·message [prophecy; Lword] ·spoken by [Lby the mouth of] Jeremiah would ·come true [be fulfilled]. He wrote:
2 This is what Cyrus king of Persia says:

> The LORD, the God of heaven, has given all the kingdoms of the earth to me, and he has ·appointed [instructed; charged] me to build a ·Temple [Lhouse] for him at Jerusalem in Judah. 3 May God be with all ·of [among] you who are his people. You ·are free to [may] go to Jerusalem in Judah and ·build [*or* rebuild] the ·Temple [Lhouse] of the LORD, the God of Israel, [Lhe is the God] who is in Jerusalem. 4 Those who ·stay behind [Lsurvive], ·wherever they live [in those places; Creferring to the Jews remaining in exile, to the Jewish remnant who remained in Israel during the exile, or to their non-Jewish neighbors], ·should [must] ·support [help; assist; provide for] those who want to go. Give them silver and gold, ·supplies [goods] and ·cattle [livestock], and ·special gifts [voluntary/freewill offerings] for the ·Temple [Lhouse] of God in Jerusalem.

5 Then the ·family [clan] leaders of Judah and Benjamin and the priests and Levites ·got ready [Larose] to go to Jerusalem—everyone ·God had caused to want [Lwhose spirit/heart/mind God had stirred] to go to Jerusalem to ·build [*or* rebuild] the ·Temple [Lhouse] of the LORD. 6 All their neighbors ·helped them [encouraged/assisted/aided them; Lstrengthened their hands], giving them things made of silver and gold, along with ·supplies [goods], ·cattle [livestock], valuable gifts, and ·special gifts [voluntary/freewill offerings]. 7 Also, King Cyrus brought out the ·bowls and pans [Larticles] that belonged in the ·Temple [Lhouse] of the LORD, which Nebuchadnezzar had ·taken [carried away] from Jerusalem and put in the ·temple [Lhouse] of his own ·god [gods; Dan. 1:2; 5:1–4]. 8 Cyrus king of Persia had Mithredath the treasurer bring them and count them out ·for [to] Sheshbazzar, the ·prince [leader of the exiles] of Judah.

9 He listed thirty gold dishes, one thousand silver dishes, twenty-nine ·pans [*or* knives; *or* utensils], 10 thirty gold bowls, four hundred ten matching silver bowls, and one thousand other pieces.

11 There was a total of fifty-four hundred ·pieces [articles; vessels] of

gold and silver. Sheshbazzar brought all these things along when the ·captives [exiles] went from Babylon to Jerusalem.

The Captives Who Returned

2 These are the people of the ·area [province] who ·returned [were returning/on their way back] from ·captivity [exile], whom Nebuchadnezzar king of Babylon had ·taken [carried] away to Babylon [2 Kin. 25:11–12]. They returned to Jerusalem and Judah, each going back to his own town. 2These people returned with Zerubbabel [3:2], Jeshua [3:2], Nehemiah, Seraiah, Reelaiah, Mordecai, Bilshan, Mispar, Bigvai, Rehum, and Baanah.

·These are [This is the number/list of] the people from Israel: 3the ·descendants [sons; Cand so throughout the list] of Parosh—2,172; 4the descendants of Shephatiah—372; 5the descendants of Arah—775; 6the descendants of Pahath-Moab (through the ·family [line] of Jeshua and Joab)—2,812; 7the descendants of Elam—1,254; 8the descendants of Zattu—945; 9the descendants of Zaccai—760; 10the descendants of Bani—642; 11the descendants of Bebai—623; 12the descendants of Azgad—1,222; 13the descendants of Adonikam—666; 14the descendants of Bigvai—2,056; 15the descendants of Adin—454; 16the descendants of Ater (through the ·family [line] of Hezekiah)—98; 17the descendants of Bezai—323; 18the descendants of Jorah—112; 19the descendants of Hashum—223; 20the descendants of Gibbar—95.

21These are the people from the towns: of Bethlehem—123; 22of Netophah—56; 23of Anathoth—128; 24of Azmaveth—42; 25of Kiriath Jearim, Kephirah, and Beeroth—743; 26of Ramah and Geba—621; 27of Micmash—122; 28of Bethel and Ai—223; 29of Nebo—52; 30of Magbish—156; 31of the other town of Elam—1,254; 32of Harim—320; 33of Lod, Hadid and Ono—725; 34of Jericho—345; 35of Senaah—3,630.

36These are the priests: the ·descendants [sons; Cand so on throughout the list] of Jedaiah (through the ·family [line; Lhouse] of Jeshua)—973; 37the descendants of Immer—1,052; 38the descendants of Pashhur—1,247; 39the descendants of Harim—1,017.

40These are the Levites: the descendants of Jeshua and Kadmiel (through the ·family [line] of Hodaviah)—74.

41These are the ·singers [musicians]: the descendants of Asaph—128.

42These are the gatekeepers of the ·Temple [Lhouse]: the descendants of Shallum, Ater, Talmon, Akkub, Hatita, and Shobai—139.

43These are the Temple servants: the ·descendants [sons; Cand so throughout the list] of Ziha, Hasupha, Tabbaoth, 44Keros, Siaha, Padon, 45Lebanah, Hagabah, Akkub, 46Hagab, Shalmai, Hanan, 47Giddel, Gahar, Reaiah, 48Rezin, Nekoda, Gazzam, 49Uzza, Paseah, Besai, 50Asnah, Meunim, Nephussim, 51Bakbuk, Hakupha, Harhur, 52Bazluth, Mehida, Harsha, 53Barkos, Sisera, Temah, 54Neziah, and Hatipha.

55These are the descendants of the servants of Solomon: the descendants of Sotai, Hassophereth, Peruda, 56Jaala, Darkon, Giddel, 57Shephatiah, Hattil, Pokereth-Hazzebaim, and Ami.

58The Temple servants and the descendants of the servants of Solomon numbered 392.

59·Some [The following; Another group of] people came to Jerusalem from the towns of Tel Melah, Tel Harsha, Kerub, Addon, and Immer, but they could not prove that their ·ancestors [families; Lhouse of their fathers and their seed] came from Israel. 60They were the descendants of Delaiah, Tobiah, and Nekoda—652.

61 Also these priests: the descendants of Hobaiah, Hakkoz, and Barzillai,
who had ·married a daughter [Ltaken a wife from the daughters] of
Barzillai from Gilead and was called by her family name.
62 These people searched ·for their family [*or* in the genealogical]
records but could not find them. So they could not be priests, because
they were ·thought to be unclean [disqualified; Ldesecrated]. 63 The governor ordered them not to eat any of the ·food offered to God [sacred food;
Lmost holy things] until a priest ·had settled this matter by using [Lstood
up with] the Urim and Thummim [Ex. 28:30].
64 The total number of ·those who returned [the company/assembly/
group] was 42,360. 65 This is not counting their 7,337 male and female
servants and the 200 male and female singers they had with them. 66 They
had 736 horses, 245 mules, 67 435 camels, and 6,720 donkeys.
68 When they arrived at the ·Temple [Lhouse] of the LORD in Jerusalem,
some of the ·leaders of families [Lheads of the fathers] ·gave [made volun-
tary] offerings to rebuild the ·Temple [Lhouse] of God on the same site as
before. 69 They gave as much as they could to the treasury ·to rebuild the
Temple [for this work]—·about 1,100 pounds [L61,000 drachmas] of
gold, ·about 6,000 pounds [L5,000 minas] of silver, and 100 ·pieces of
clothing for the priests [priestly garments/robes].
70 All the Israelites settled in their hometowns. The priests, Levites,
·singers [musicians], gatekeepers, and Temple servants, along with some
of the other people, settled in their own towns as well.

Rebuilding the Altar

3 In the seventh month, after the Israelites were settled in their
hometowns, they ·met together [assembled in unity/with one
accord; Las one man] in Jerusalem. 2 Then Jeshua son of Jozadak [Zech.
3:1–9] and his ·fellow [Lbrothers the] priests joined Zerubbabel son of
Shealtiel [and his brothers/colleagues; v. 8; 4:2–3; 5:2; Neh. 7:7; Hag. 1:1,
12, 14; 2:2, 4, 21, 23; Zech. 4:6–10; Matt. 1:12–13; Luke 3:27] and began to
build the altar of the God of Israel where they could offer burnt offerings,
just as ·it is written [instructed; required] in the ·Teachings [Law; LTorah]
of Moses, the man of God. 3 ·Even though [*or* Because] they were afraid of
the people living around them, they ·built [set up; established] the altar
where it had been before. And they ·offered [sacrificed] burnt offerings
[Lev. 1:1–17] on it to the LORD morning and evening. 4 Then, to obey what
was ·written [instructed; required], they celebrated the Feast of ·Shelters
[Booths; Tabernacles; Ex. 23:16; Lev. 23:33–36]. They offered the ·right
[specified; proper; fixed] number of sacrifices ·for [according to the ordi-
nance/requirement for] each day. 5 After the Feast of Shelters, they had
·regular [continual] ·sacrifices [burnt offerings; Lev. 1:1–17], as well as
sacrifices for the New Moon and all the festivals ·commanded by [of] the
LORD. Also there were ·special [freewill; voluntary] offerings to the LORD.
6 On the first day of the seventh month [Cfifteen days before the beginning
of the festival] they began to ·bring [offer; sacrifice] burnt offerings to the
LORD, ·but [though] the foundation of the LORD's ·Temple [Lhouse] had
not yet been laid.

Rebuilding the Temple

7 Then they gave money to the ·bricklayers [masons] and carpenters.
They also gave food, ·wine [drink], and olive oil to the cities of Sidon and
Tyre so they would ·float [bring] cedar logs from Lebanon to the seacoast
town of Joppa. Cyrus king of Persia had given permission for this.
8 In the second month [Cmidspring] of the second year after their

arrival at the ·Temple [Lhouse] of God in Jerusalem, Zerubbabel son of Shealtiel [v. 2], Jeshua son of Jozadak, their fellow priests and Levites, and all who had returned from ·captivity [exile] to Jerusalem began to work. They ·chose [appointed] Levites twenty years old and older to ·be in charge of [supervise] the building of the ·Temple [Lhouse] of the LORD. 9The workers building the ·Temple [Lhouse] of God were supervised by Jeshua and his sons and brothers [3:2], together with Kadmiel and his sons who were the descendants of Hodaviah, and the sons of Henadad and their sons and brothers. They were all Levites.

10The builders finished laying the foundation of the Temple of the LORD. Then the priests, dressed in their ·robes [vestments], stood with their ·trumpets [clarions; Ca long, metallic instrument, not a ram's horn], and the Levites, the sons of Asaph, stood with their cymbals. They all took their places and praised the LORD just as David king of Israel had ·said to do [instructed; prescribed]. 11With praise and thanksgiving, they ·sang [Lanswered; Csang antiphonally] to the LORD:

"He is good;
his ·love [loyalty] for Israel ·continues [endures; lasts; is] forever."

And then all the people shouted loudly, "Praise the LORD! The foundation of his ·Temple [Lhouse] has been laid." 12But many of the older priests, Levites, and ·family leaders [Lheads of fathers] who had seen the first ·Temple [Lhouse] cried loudly when they saw the foundation of this Temple. ·Most of the other people [Many others] were shouting with joy. 13The people made so much noise it could be heard far away, and no one could tell the difference between the joyful shouting and the sad crying.

Enemies of the Rebuilding

4 When the enemies of the people of Judah and Benjamin heard that the returned ·captives [exiles] were building a Temple for the LORD, the God of Israel, 2they came to Zerubbabel [Ca descendant of David; 1 Chr. 3:19] and the ·leaders of the families [Lheads of the fathers]. The enemies said, "Let us help you build, because we are like you and ·want to worship [Lseek] your God. We have been offering sacrifices to him since the time of Esarhaddon king of Assyria [C680–669 BC], who brought us here."

3But Zerubbabel, Jeshua [3:2], and the ·leaders [Lheads of the fathers] of Israel answered, "You will ·not help us build [have no part in building] a ·Temple [Lhouse] to our God. We will build it ·ourselves [alone] for the LORD, the God of Israel, as King Cyrus, the king of Persia, commanded us to do [1:2–4]."

4Then the people around them tried to discourage the people of Judah by making them afraid to build. 5Their enemies ·hired others [bribed officials] to ·delay [frustrate] the building plans ·during [throughout] the time Cyrus was king of Persia. And it continued to the time Darius was king of Persia [C522–486 BC].

More Problems for the Builders

6When ·Xerxes [LAhasuerus; Cruled 486–465 BC; Esth. 1:1] first became king, those enemies ·wrote [filed; lodged] a ·letter [Laccusation] against the people of Judah and Jerusalem.

7When Artaxerxes [Cruled about 465–425 B.C.] became king of Persia, Bishlam, Mithredath, Tabeel, and those with them wrote a letter to Artaxerxes. It was written in the Aramaic language and translated.

8Rehum the ·governor [commander] and Shimshai the governor's

·secretary [scribe] and those with them wrote a letter against Jerusalem to Artaxerxes the king. It said:

9This letter is from Rehum the ·governor [commander], Shimshai the ·secretary [scribe], and their ·fellow workers [colleagues]—the judges and important officers over the men who came from Tripolis, Persia, Erech, and Babylon, the Elamite people of Susa, 10and those whom the great and honorable Ashurbanipal [LOsnappar; Cruled 668–627 BC] ·forced out of their countries [deported] and settled in the city of Samaria and in other places of the Trans-Euphrates [Cprovinces west of the Euphrates River].

11(This is a copy of the letter they sent to Artaxerxes.)

To King Artaxerxes.
From your servants who live in Trans-Euphrates [v. 10].

12King Artaxerxes, you should know that the Jews who came to us from you have gone to Jerusalem to rebuild that evil ·city that refuses to obey [and rebellious city]. They are ·fixing [restoring; rebuilding; finishing] the walls and repairing the foundations of the buildings.
13Now, King Artaxerxes, ·you should know [Llet it be known] that if Jerusalem is ·built [rebuilt] and its walls are ·fixed [completed; restored], Jerusalem will not pay ·taxes of any kind [Ltribute, custom, or toll]. Then the ·amount of money your government collects [king's/royal treasury/revenue] will ·be less [suffer]. 14Since we ·must be loyal to the government [Leat the palace's salt], ·we don't want [it is not proper] to see the king ·dishonored [damaged]. So we ·are writing to let the king know [Lsend and inform the king]. 15·We suggest you [...so that you may] search the ·records [annals; archives] of ·the kings who ruled before you [Lyour fathers/ancestors]. You will find out that the city of Jerusalem ·refuses to obey [Lis a rebellious city] and ·makes trouble for kings and areas controlled by Persia [troublesome for kings and provinces]. ·Since long ago it has been a place where disobedience has started [It has a long history of revolts/sedition]. That is why it was destroyed. 16We want you to know, King Artaxerxes, that if this city is rebuilt and its walls ·fixed [completed; restored], you will be left with ·nothing [no possessions] in Trans-Euphrates [Cprovinces west of the Euphrates River].

17King Artaxerxes sent this answer:

To Rehum the ·governor [commander] and Shimshai the ·secretary [scribe], to all their ·fellow workers [colleagues] living in Samaria [Cnorthern Israel], and to those ·in other places in [throughout] Trans-Euphrates [v. 10].

·Greetings [Peace].
18The ·letter [document] you sent to us has been translated

and read ·to me [Lin my presence]. 19I ordered ·the records to be
searched [La search], and it was done. We found that ·Jerusalem
[Lthe city] has a history of ·disobedience to [rising against] kings
and has been a place of ·problems and trouble [rebellion and
revolt/sedition]. 20Jerusalem has had powerful kings who have
ruled over the whole area of Trans-Euphrates [v. 10], and ·taxes
of all kinds [Ltribute, custom, and toll] have been paid to them.
21Now, ·give an order [issue a decree] for those men to stop work.
The city of Jerusalem will not be rebuilt until I ·say so [issue a
decree]. 22·Make sure you do this [Do not neglect this matter],
·because if they continue, it will hurt the government [—why
should the danger/damage grow and harm the king?].

23As soon as a copy of the ·letter [document] that King Artaxerxes sent
was read to Rehum and Shimshai the ·secretary [scribe] and ·the others
[their colleagues], they went to the Jews in Jerusalem and ·forced them [*or*
compelled them by force of arms] to stop building.
24So the work on the ·Temple [Lhouse] of God in Jerusalem ·stopped
[came to a standstill] until the second year Darius was king of Persia.

Tattenai's Letter to Darius

5 The prophets Haggai and Zechariah, a descendant of Iddo [Ca
grandson; Zech. 1:1], prophesied to the Jews in Judah and
Jerusalem in the name of the God of Israel, who was over them. 2Then
Zerubbabel son of Shealtiel [3:2] and Jeshua son of Jozadak [3:2] started
working again to rebuild the ·Temple [Lhouse] of God in Jerusalem. And
the prophets of God were there, ·helping [supporting] them.
3At that time Tattenai, the governor of Trans-Euphrates [Cprovinces
west of the Euphrates River], and Shethar-Bozenai, and their ·fellow
workers [colleagues] went to ·the Jews [Lthem] and asked, "Who gave you
·permission [authority; a decree] to rebuild this ·Temple [Lhouse] and ·fix
these walls [complete this structure]?" 4They also asked, "What are the
names of the men working on this building?" 5But their God was watching over the elders of the Jews. The builders were not stopped until a
report could go to King Darius [C522–486 BC] and his ·written answer
[reply; decision] could be received.
6This is a copy of the ·letter [document] that was sent to King Darius
by Tattenai, the governor of Trans-Euphrates [Cprovinces west of the
Euphrates River], Shethar-Bozenai, and the other important officers of
Trans-Euphrates. 7This is what was ·said [written] in the report they sent
to him:

To King Darius.

·Greetings. May you have peace [LAll peace].
8King Darius, ·you should know [may it be known] that we
went to the ·district [province] of Judah where the ·Temple
[Lhouse] of the great God is. The people are building that
·Temple [Lhouse] with ·large [prepared; cut; Lstones of rolling]
stones, and they are putting ·timbers [beams] in the walls. They
are working ·very hard [energetically; diligently] and ·are building very fast [successfully; are prospering].
9We asked their elders, "Who gave you ·permission [authority;

a decree] to rebuild this ·Temple [Lhouse] and ·these walls [this
structure]?" 10We also asked for their names, and we wrote down
the names of their leaders so ·you would know who they are [as
to inform you].
11This is the answer they gave to us: "We are the servants of
the God of heaven and earth. We are rebuilding the ·Temple
[Lhouse] that a great king of Israel [CSolomon] built and finished
many years ago [Ctenth century BC; 1 Kin. 7–8]. 12But our ·ances-
tors [fathers] made the God of heaven angry, so he handed them
over to Nebuchadnezzar king of Babylon, the Chaldean [Cthe
leading tribe of Babylon], who destroyed this ·Temple [Lhouse]
and ·took [deported] the people to Babylon ·as captives [into
exile].
13"Later, in the first year Cyrus was king of Babylon [Che was
a Persian king but had multiple titles, including this one], he
·gave a special order [issued a decree] for this ·Temple [Lhouse]
of God to be rebuilt. 14Cyrus brought out from the temple in
Babylon the gold and silver ·bowls and pans [vessels; utensils]
that came from the Temple of God. Nebuchadnezzar had taken
them from the Temple in Jerusalem and had ·put them in
[brought them to] the temple in Babylon.
"Then King Cyrus gave them to Sheshbazzar, his appointed
governor [Cof Judah; 1:8]. 15Cyrus said to him, 'Take these gold
and silver ·bowls and pans [vessels; utensils; 1:7], and ·put
[deposit] them back in the Temple in Jerusalem and rebuild the
·Temple [Lhouse] of God ·where it was [on its original site].' 16So
Sheshbazzar came and laid the foundations of the ·Temple
[Lhouse] of God in Jerusalem. From that day until now the work
has been going on, but it is not yet finished."
17Now, if the king wishes, let a search be made in the royal
·records [archives; Ltreasure house] of Babylon. See if King Cyrus
gave an order to rebuild this ·Temple [Lhouse] in Jerusalem.
Then let the king write us and tell us what he has decided concerning this matter.

The Order of Darius

6 So King Darius ·gave an order [issued a decree] to search the
·records [archives] kept in the treasury in Babylon. 2A scroll was
found in Ecbatana, ·the capital city [*or* a fortress in the province] of Media
[Ca major component of the Persian empire in the Zagros mountains,
south of the Caspian Sea]. This is what was written on it:

·Note [Memorandum]:

3King Cyrus ·gave an order [issued a decree] about the ·Temple
[Lhouse] of God in Jerusalem in the first year he was king [1:2–
4]. This was the order:
"Let the ·Temple [Lhouse] be rebuilt as a place to ·present
[offer] sacrifices. Let its foundations be ·laid [*or* retained]; it
should be ·ninety feet [L60 cubits] high and ·ninety feet [L60
cubits] wide. 4It must have three layers of large stones ·and then
one [for every] layer of timbers. The costs should be paid from
the king's treasury. 5The gold and silver ·utensils [articles; vessels]

from the ·Temple [Lhouse] of God should be returned and put
back in their places. Nebuchadnezzar took them from the Temple
in Jerusalem and brought them to Babylon [Dan. 1:1–3], but they
are to be put back in the ·Temple [Lhouse] of God in Jerusalem."
6Now then, Tattenai, governor of Trans-Euphrates [Cprovinces
west of the Euphrates River], Shethar-Bozenai, and ·all the officers of that area [their colleagues and officials of the
Trans-Euphrates], stay away from there. 7·Do not bother [LLeave
alone] the work on that ·Temple [Lhouse] of God. Let the governor of the Jews and the Jewish elders rebuild this ·Temple
[Lhouse] where it was before.
8Also, I ·order you [issue a decree] to do this for those elders
of the Jews who are ·building [rebuilding] this ·Temple [Lhouse]
of God: The cost of the building is to be fully paid from the royal
treasury, from ·taxes [tribute] collected from Trans-Euphrates.
Do this ·so the work will not stop [*or* without delay]. 9Give those
people anything they need—young bulls, ·male sheep [rams], or
lambs for burnt offerings [Lev. 1:1–17] to the God of heaven, or
wheat, salt, wine, or olive oil. Give the priests in Jerusalem anything they ·ask for [require] every day without fail. 10Then they
may offer sacrifices ·pleasing [acceptable] to the God of heaven,
and they may pray for the ·life [*or* welfare] of the king and his
·sons [family].
11Also, I ·give this order [issue this decree]: If anyone ·changes
[defies; violates] this ·order [decree], a wood beam is to be pulled
from his house and ·driven through his body [*or* he will be
hanged from/flogged on it]. Because of his crime, make his house
a ·pile of ruins [*or* rubbish heap; dung hill]. 12God has ·chosen
Jerusalem as the place he is to be worshiped [Lcaused his name to
reside there]. May he punish any king or ·person [*or* nation;
Lpeople] who ·tries [Lreaches out his hand] to ·change [defy; vio-
late] this ·order [decree] and destroy this ·Temple [Lhouse] of
God.

I, Darius, have ·given this order [issued this decree]. Let it be
·obeyed quickly and carefully [carried out with all diligence].

Completion of the Temple

13So, Tattenai, the governor of Trans-Euphrates [Cprovinces west of the
Euphrates River], Shethar-Bozenai, and their ·fellow workers [colleagues]
carried out King Darius' ·order [decree] ·quickly and carefully [with all dili-
gence]. 14The Jewish elders continued to build and ·were successful
[prospered] because of the ·preaching [prophesying] of Haggai the prophet
and Zechariah, a ·descendant [son; 5:1] of Iddo [Csee the biblical books
named for them]. They finished building the ·Temple [Lhouse] as the God
of Israel had commanded and as kings Cyrus [Cruled 559–529 BC, though
539 BC was the first year of his reign over the empire that included Babylon],
Darius [Cruled 522–486 BC], and Artaxerxes of Persia [Cruled 485–465 BC]
had ·ordered [decreed]. 15The ·Temple [Lhouse] was finished on the third
day of the month of Adar [CMarch 12] in the sixth year Darius was king.
16Then the people of Israel celebrated and ·gave [dedicated] the ·Temple
[Lhouse] to God to honor him. Everybody was happy: the priests, the
Levites, and the rest of the ·Jews who had returned from captivity [exiles;
Lsons/people of the exile]. 17They ·gave [dedicated] the ·Temple [Lhouse] to

God by offering a hundred bulls, two hundred ·male sheep [rams], and
four hundred lambs as sacrifices. And as an ·offering to forgive the sins of
[sin offering for *or* purification offering for; Lev. 4:3] all Israel, they offered
twelve male goats, ·one goat for each tribe in [corresponding to the number of tribes of] Israel. 18Then they ·put [installed; divided; appointed] the
priests and the Levites into their ·separate groups [various divisions] to
serve God at Jerusalem, as it is written in the Book of Moses.

The Passover Is Celebrated

19The ·Jews who returned from captivity [Lsons/people of the exile]
·celebrated [observed] the Passover on the fourteenth day of the first
month [CApril 21; Ex. 12:1–30, 43–51; Lev. 23:4–8; Num. 28:16–25; Deut.
16:1–18]. 20The priests and Levites had ·made themselves clean [purified
themselves]. Then the Levites ·killed [slaughtered; sacrified] the Passover
lambs for all the ·people who had returned from captivity [exiles], for
their ·relatives the [*or* fellow; Lbrothers the] priests, and for themselves.
21So all the ·people [sons] of Israel who returned from ·captivity [exile]
·ate the Passover lamb [Late]. So did the people who had ·given up the
unclean ways of their non-Jewish neighbors [separated themselves from
the impurity/pollution of the nations] in order to ·worship [seek] the
LORD, the God of Israel. 22For seven days they celebrated with joy the
Feast of Unleavened Bread [Ex. 12:17–20; 34:18]. The LORD had made
them ·happy [rejoice] by ·changing the mind [turning the heart] of the
king of Assyria [Ca deliberate anachronism, since Assyria had fallen earlier
in 612 BC] so that he helped them in the work on the ·Temple [Lhouse] of
the God of Israel.

Ezra Comes to Jerusalem

7After these things, during the rule of Artaxerxes king of Persia,
Ezra came up [CEzra's coming is not actually stated until v. 6] from
Babylon [Cif this refers to Artaxerxes I, then chapter seven takes place
around 458 BC, about fifty-eight years after chapter six, but some date the
events differently] as the son of Seraiah, the son of Azariah, the son of
Hilkiah, 2the son of Shallum, the son of Zadok, the son of Ahitub, 3the
son of Amariah, the son of Azariah, the son of Meraioth, 4the son of
Zerahiah, the son of Uzzi, the son of Bukki, 5the son of Abishua, the son
of Phinehas, the son of Eleazar, the son of Aaron the ·high [chief] priest.
6This Ezra came ·to Jerusalem [Lup] from Babylon. He was a ·teacher and
knew well [scribe skilled/well versed in] the ·Teachings [Law; LTorah] of
Moses that had been given by the LORD, the God of Israel. Ezra received
everything he asked for from the king, because the [Lhand of the] LORD
his God was ·helping [on] him. 7In the seventh year of King Artaxerxes
more ·Israelites [sons/people of Israel] came to Jerusalem. Among them
were priests, Levites, singers, gatekeepers, and Temple servants.

8Ezra arrived in Jerusalem in the fifth month of Artaxerxes' seventh
year as king. 9Ezra had left Babylon on the first day of the first month
[CApril 8], and he arrived in Jerusalem on the first day of the fifth month
[CAugust 4], because [the good/gracious hand of] God was ·helping [on]
him. 10Ezra had ·worked hard [dedicated/devoted himself; Lset his heart]
to ·know [study] and ·obey [practice; do; observe] the ·Teachings [Law;
LTorah] of the LORD and to teach his rules and commands to the Israelites.

Artaxerxes' Letter to Ezra

11King Artaxerxes had given a ·letter [document] to Ezra, a priest and
·teacher [scribe] ·who taught about [learned in] the commands and laws
the LORD gave Israel. This is a copy of the ·letter [document]:

12From Artaxerxes, king of kings, to Ezra the priest, a ·teacher
[scribe] of the Law of the God of heaven.

·Greetings [Peace].

13Now I ·give [issue] this ·order [decree]: Any Israelite in my
kingdom who wishes may go with you to Jerusalem, including
priests and Levites. 14Ezra, you are ·sent [authorized] by the king
and ·the [his] seven ·advisors [counselors] to ·ask [inquire] concerning Judah and Jerusalem in regards to the Law of your God
[Cwhether they were obeying it], which ·you are carrying with
you [Lis in your hand]. 15Also take with you the silver and gold
that the king and his ·advisors [counselors] have ·given [offered]
freely to the God of Israel, ·whose Temple is [whose dwelling is;
who lives] in Jerusalem. 16Also take the silver and gold you
·receive [collect; obtain] from the ·area [province] of Babylon.
Take the ·voluntary [freewill] offerings the Israelites and their
priests have given as gifts for the ·Temple [Lhouse] of your God
in Jerusalem. 17With this money be sure to buy bulls, ·male sheep
[rams], and lambs, and the appropriate grain offerings and
·drink offerings [liquid offerings; libations]. Then ·sacrifice
[offer] them on the altar in the ·Temple [Lhouse] of your God in
Jerusalem.

18You and your ·fellow Jews [colleagues; Lbrothers] may ·spend
[use] the silver and gold ·left over [remaining] as you want ·and
as God wishes [in keeping/accordance with God's will]. 19·Take
[Deliver] to the God of Jerusalem all the ·utensils [articles; ves-
sels] for ·worship [service] in the ·Temple [Lhouse] of your God.
20Use the royal treasury to ·pay for [provide; supply] anything
else you need for the ·Temple [Lhouse] of your God.

21Now I, King Artaxerxes, ·give this order [issue this decree] to
all the ·men in charge of the treasury [treasurers] of Trans-
Euphrates [Cprovinces west of the Euphrates River]: Give
[Ldiligently to] Ezra, a priest and ·a teacher [the scribe] of the
Law of the God of heaven, whatever he asks for. 22Give him up to
·seventy-five hundred pounds [Lone hundred talents] of silver,
·six hundred bushels [Lone hundred kors] of wheat, ·six hundred
gallons [Lone hundred baths] of wine, and ·six hundred gallons
[Lone hundred baths] of olive oil. And give him ·as much salt as
he wants [unlimited salt]. 23·Carefully [LZealously] give him
whatever the God of heaven ·wants [demands; commands] for
the ·Temple [Lhouse] of the God of heaven. ·We do not want God
to [LWhy should God …?] be angry with the [the kingdom/
empire of the] king and his sons. 24Remember, you ·must not
[have no authority to] make these people pay taxes of any kind:
priests, Levites, singers, gatekeepers, Temple servants, and other
workers in this ·Temple [Lhouse] of God.

25And you, Ezra, ·use [in accordance with] the wisdom you have
from your God ·to choose [appoint] judges and lawmakers to ·rule
[govern; arbitrate for] the ·Jews [people] of Trans-Euphrates
[Cprovinces west of the Euphrates River]. They know the laws of
your God, and you may teach anyone who does not know them.
26Whoever does not ·obey [observe] the law of your God or of the

king must be ·punished [judged quickly/immediately]. He will be
killed, or ·sent away [banished], or have his property ·taken away
[confiscated], or ·be put in jail [imprisoned].

27·Praise [Blessed be] the LORD, the God of our ·ancestors [fathers]. He
·caused the king [Lput in the king's heart] to want to ·honor [beautify;
adorn; glorify] the ·Temple [Lhouse] of the LORD in Jerusalem. 28The LORD
has shown me [CEzra], his ·love [loyalty] ·in the presence of [before] the
king, ·those who advise the king [his counselors/advisers], and ·the royal
officers [his mighty nobles/officials]. Because the LORD my God was helping me, I ·had courage [was strengthened], and I gathered the ·leaders
[Lheads of the fathers] of Israel to ·return [Lgo up] with me.

Leaders Who Returned with Ezra

8 These are the ·leaders [heads] of the family groups and ·those
who were listed with them [the genealogies of those] who ·came
back [Lwent up] with me from Babylon during the ·rule [reign] of King
Artaxerxes [Cruled 464–425 BC].
2From the ·descendants [family; sons; Cand so on throughout the list]
of Phinehas [Num. 25:7, 11]: Gershom.
From the descendants of Ithamar: Daniel.
From the descendants of David: Hattush 3of the descendants of
Shecaniah.
From the descendants of Parosh: Zechariah, with one hundred fifty
registered men.
4From the descendants of Pahath-Moab: Eliehoenai son of Zerahiah,
with two hundred men.
5From the descendants of Zattu: Shecaniah son of Jahaziel, with three
hundred men.
6From the descendants of Adin: Ebed son of Jonathan, with fifty men.
7From the descendants of Elam: Jeshaiah son of Athaliah, with seventy
men.
8From the descendants of Shephatiah: Zebadiah son of Michael, with
eighty men.
9From the descendants of Joab: Obadiah son of Jehiel, with two hundred eighteen men.
10From the descendants of Bani: Shelomith son of Josiphiah, with one
hundred sixty men.
11From the descendants of Bebai: Zechariah son of Bebai, with twenty-
eight men.
12From the descendants of Azgad: Johanan son of Hakkatan, with one
hundred ten men.
13From the descendants of Adonikam, these were the last ones:
Eliphelet, Jeuel, and Shemaiah, with sixty men.
14From the descendants of Bigvai: Uthai and Zaccur, with seventy men.

The Return to Jerusalem

15I ·called [assembled; gathered] all those people together [Che lists
1,513 males, probably over 5,000 total with women and children] at the
·canal [river] that flows toward Ahava, where we camped for three days. I
·checked [reviewed; observed] all the people and the priests, but I did not
find any Levites [Cneeded for service at a rebuilt Temple]. 16So I called
these leaders: Eliezer, Ariel, Shemaiah, Elnathan, Jarib, Elnathan, Nathan,
Zechariah, and Meshullam. And I called Joiarib and Elnathan, who were
·teachers [wise; judicious; men of learning/discernment]. 17I sent these

men to Iddo, the leader [[C]of the Levites] at Casiphia, and told them what to say to Iddo and his ·relatives [*or* collegues; [L]brothers], who are the Temple servants in Casiphia. I sent them to bring ·servants [ministers; attendants] to us for the ·Temple [[L]house] of our God. [18]The ·good [gracious] hand of our God was ·helping [[L]on] us, so ·Iddo's relatives [[L]they] ·gave [brought; sent] us Sherebiah, a ·wise [skilled; capable; astute] man from the ·descendants [sons] of Mahli ·son [descendant] of Levi, who was the son of Israel. And they brought Sherebiah's sons and brothers, for a total of eighteen men. [19]And they brought to us Hashabiah and Jeshaiah from the ·descendants [sons] of Merari, and his brothers and ·nephews [their sons]. In all there were twenty men. [20]They also brought two hundred twenty of the Temple servants, a group David and ·the officers [his officials] had ·set up [established; instituted] to ·help [assist; serve] the Levites. All of those men were ·listed [designated] by name.

[21]There by the Ahava ·Canal [River], I announced we would all fast and ·deny [humble] ourselves before our God. We would ask God for a safe ·trip [journey] for ourselves, our children, and all our possessions. [22]I was ashamed to ask the king for soldiers and ·horsemen [cavalry] to protect us from enemies on the ·road [way]. We had said to the king, "The hand of our God ·helps [[L]is on] everyone who ·obeys [seeks] him, but ·he is very angry with [his power and anger are against] all who reject him." [23]So we fasted and ·prayed to [petitioned; pleaded with; [T]sought] our God about our trip, and he ·answered [heard; listened to] our prayers.

[24]Then I ·chose [appointed; set apart] twelve of the priests who were leaders, Sherebiah, Hashabiah, and ten of their ·relatives [colleagues; [L]brothers]. [25]I weighed the offering of silver and gold and the ·utensils [articles; vessels] given for the ·Temple [[L]house] of our God, and I gave them to the twelve priests I had chosen. The king, ·the people who advised him [his counselors], his ·officers [officials], and all the Israelites there with us had given these things. [26]I weighed out ·and gave them [L][into their hands] ·about fifty thousand pounds [[L]650 talents] of silver, ·about seventy-five hundred pounds [[L]100 talents] of silver objects, and ·about seventy-five hundred pounds [[L]100 talents] of gold. [27]I gave them twenty gold bowls ·that weighed [*or* worth] ·about nineteen pounds [[L]1,000 darics] and two fine pieces of polished bronze that were as ·valuable [precious] as gold.

[28]Then I said to the priests, "You and these utensils ·belong [are set apart/holy] to the Lord. The silver and gold are ·gifts [a freewill/voluntary offering] to the Lord, the God of your ·ancestors [fathers]. [29]·Guard [Watch] these things carefully. In Jerusalem, weigh them in front of the ·leading [chief] priests, Levites, and the ·leaders [heads] of the family groups of Israel in the ·rooms [chambers; storerooms] of the ·Temple [[L]house] of the Lord." [30]So the priests and Levites accepted the silver, the gold, and the ·utensils [articles; vessels] that had been weighed to take them to the ·Temple [[L]house] of our God in Jerusalem.

[31]On the twelfth day of the first month [[C]April 19] we left the Ahava ·Canal [River] ·and started toward [to travel/journey to] Jerusalem. The hand of our God ·helped us [was over us] and ·protected [saved; [T]delivered] us from enemies and ·robbers [ambushes] along the way. [32]Finally we arrived in Jerusalem where we ·rested [stayed] three days.

[33]On the fourth day we weighed out the silver, the gold, and the ·utensils [articles; vessels] in the ·Temple [[L]house] of our God. We handed them to the priest Meremoth son of Uriah. Eleazar son of Phinehas was

with him, as were the Levites Jozabad son of Jeshua and Noadiah son of Binnui. 34We checked everything by number and by weight, and the total weight was ·written down [recorded].

35Then the ·captives [exiles] who returned from captivity made burnt offerings [Lev. 1:1–17] to the God of Israel. They sacrificed twelve bulls for all Israel, ninety-six ·male sheep [rams], and seventy-seven lambs. For a ·sin [*or* purification] offering [Lev. 4:3] there were twelve male goats. All this was a burnt offering [Lev. 1:1–17] to the Lord. 36They ·took [delivered] King Artaxerxes' ·orders [decrees] to the royal officers and to the governors of Trans-Euphrates [Cprovinces west of the Euphrates River]. Then these men gave help to the people and the ·Temple [Lhouse] of God.

Ezra's Prayer

9 After these things had been ·done [completed], the ·leaders [officials] came to me and said, "Ezra, the Israelites, including the priests and Levites, have not kept themselves separate from the people ·around us [Lof the land]. Those neighbors ·do [practice] ·evil [detestable; abominable] things, as the Canaanites, Hittites, Perizzites, Jebusites, Ammonites, Moabites, Egyptians, and Amorites did. 2·The Israelite men and their sons [LThey] have ·married [Ltaken] these women. They have ·mixed [intermingled] the ·people who belong to God [Lholy race] with the people ·around them [Lof the land]. The leaders and ·officers of Israel [officials] have led the rest of the Israelites to do this unfaithful thing."

3When I heard this, I angrily tore my ·robe [tunic; clothes] and ·coat [cloak; mantle], pulled hair from my head and beard, and sat down ·in shock [devastated; appalled; in horror]. 4Everyone who trembled at the words of the God of Israel gathered around me because of the unfaithfulness of the ·captives [exiles] who had returned. I sat there ·in shock [devastated; appalled; in horror] until the evening ·sacrifice [offering].

5At the evening ·sacrifice [offering] I got up from ·where I had shown my shame [my humiliation/self-abasement]. My ·robe [tunic; clothes] and ·coat [cloak; mantle] were torn, and I fell on my knees with my hands ·spread [stretched] out to the Lord my God. 6I prayed,

"My God, I am too ashamed and ·embarrassed [disgraced] to lift up my face to you, my God, because our ·sins [iniquities] are so many. They are higher than our heads. Our guilt even ·reaches up [extends] to the ·sky [heavens]. 7From the days of our ·ancestors [fathers] until now, our guilt has been great. Because of our ·sins [iniquities], we, our kings, and our priests have been ·punished by [Lgiven into the hands of the kings of the land, to] the sword and ·captivity [exile]. Foreign kings have ·taken away our things [plundered; pillaged] and ·shamed [humiliated] us, even as ·it [the case] is today.

8"But now, for a short time, the Lord our God has been ·kind [gracious; merciful] to us. He has let ·some of us [a remnant] ·come back from [escape; *or* survive] ·captivity [exile] and has ·let us live in safety [Lgiven us a peg; Ca tent peg symbolizing pitching a tent after travel] in his holy place. And so our God ·gives us hope [Lcauses our eyes to shine; Cthat is, revives] and a little relief ·from [in] our ·slavery [bondage]. 9Even though we ·are [were] slaves, our God in his ·unfailing love [loyalty] ·has not left [did not abandon/forsake] us. He caused the kings of Persia to ·be kind to [look kindly on] us and has ·given us new life [revived us]. We can rebuild the ·Temple [Lhouse] of our God and ·repair [restore] its ruins. And he has given us a wall [Cof protection] in Judah and Jerusalem.

10“But now, our God, what can we say after you have done all this? We
have ·disobeyed [abandoned; forsaken] your commands 11that you ·gave
[commanded] through your servants the prophets. You said, ‘The land
you are entering to ·own [possess] is ·ruined [defiled; polluted; unclean];
the people living there have ·spoiled it [defiled it; polluted it; made it
unclean] by ·the evil they do [their detestable/abominable practices].
Their evil filled the land with ·uncleanness [corruption; filth; impurity]
from one end to the other. 12So do not ·let your daughters marry [Lgive
your daughters to] their sons, and do not ·let their daughters marry [Ltake
their daughters for] your sons. Do not wish for their peace or ·success
[prosperity; welfare]. Then you will be strong and eat the good things of
the land. Then you can leave ·this land [Lit as an inheritance] to your
·descendants [sons] forever.’
13“What has happened to us is a result of our evil deeds and our great
guilt. But you, our God, have punished us less than ·we [our sin/iniqui-
ties] deserve; you have left a ·few of us alive [remnant such as this]. 14·We
should not [LShould we…?] again break your commands by ·allowing
marriages [intermarrying] with these ·wicked [detestable; abominable]
people. ·If we did, you would get angry [LWould not your anger be…?]
enough to destroy us, ·and none of us would be left alive [without remnant or survivor]. 15Lord, God of Israel, by your ·goodness [righteousness]
a ·few of us [remnant] are left alive today. We ·admit that we are guilty
[stand/come before you in our guilt] ·and [although] ·none of us should
be allowed to [no one can truly] stand before you.”

The People Confess Sin

10 As Ezra was praying and confessing and crying and throwing
himself down in front of the ·Temple [Lhouse], a large group
of Israelite men, women, and children gathered around him who were
also crying loudly. 2Then Shecaniah son of Jehiel the Elamite said to
Ezra, “We have been unfaithful to our God by marrying women from
the peoples around us. But even so, there is still hope for Israel. 3Now let
us make an ·agreement [covenant; treaty] before our God. We will send
away all these women and their children as you and those who ·respect
[Ltremble at] the commands of our God advise. Let it be done to obey
God’s ·Teachings [Law; LTorah]. 4Get up, Ezra. You are in charge, and we
will support you. Have courage and do it.”
5So Ezra got up and made the priests, Levites, and all the people of
Israel promise to do what was suggested; and they promised. 6Then Ezra
left the ·Temple [Lhouse] and went to the room of Jehohanan son of
Eliashib. While Ezra was there, he did not eat or drink, because he was still
sad about the unfaithfulness of the ·captives [exiles] who had returned.
7They sent an order in Judah and Jerusalem for all the ·captives [exiles]
who had returned to meet together in Jerusalem. 8Whoever did not come
to Jerusalem within three days would lose his property and would no
longer be a member of the community of the returned ·captives [exiles].
That was the decision of the officers and elders.
9So within three days all the men of Judah and Benjamin gathered in
Jerusalem. It was the twentieth day of the ninth month. All the men were
sitting in the open place in front of the ·Temple [Lhouse] and were upset
because of the meeting and because it was raining. 10Ezra the priest stood
up and said to them, “You have been unfaithful and have married ·non-
Jewish [Lforeign] women. You have made Israel more guilty. 11Now,

confess it to the LORD, the God of your ·ancestors [fathers]. Do his will and separate yourselves from the people living around you and from your ·non-Jewish [Lforeign] wives."

12 Then the whole group answered Ezra with a loud voice, "Ezra, you're right! We must do what you say. 13 But there are many people here, and it's the rainy season. We can't stand outside, and this problem can't be solved in a day or two, because we have sinned badly. 14 Let our officers make a decision for the whole group. Then let everyone in our towns who has married a non-Jewish woman meet with the elders and judges of each town at a planned time, until the hot anger of our God turns away from us." 15 Only Jonathan son of Asahel, Jahzeiah son of Tikvah, Meshullam, and Shabbethai the Levite were against the plan.

16 So the returned ·captives [exiles] did what was suggested. Ezra the priest chose men who were leaders of the family groups and named one from each family division. On the first day of the tenth month they sat down to study each case. 17 By the first day of the first month, they had finished with all the men who had married non-Jewish women.

Those Guilty of Marrying Non-Jewish Women

18 These are the ·descendants [sons; Cand so throughout this section] of the priests who had married foreign women:

From the descendants of Jeshua son of Jozadak [3:2] and Jeshua's brothers: Maaseiah, Eliezer, Jarib, and Gedaliah. 19 (They all promised to ·divorce [send away; Lput out] their wives, and each one brought a male sheep from the flock as a ·penalty [guilt; reparation] offering [Lev. 5:14—6:7].)

20 From the descendants of Immer: Hanani and Zebadiah.

21 From the descendants of Harim: Maaseiah, Elijah, Shemaiah, Jehiel, and Uzziah.

22 From the descendants of Pashhur: Elioenai, Maaseiah, Ishmael, Nethanel, Jozabad, and Elasah.

23 Among the Levites: Jozabad, Shimei, Kelaiah (also called Kelita), Pethahiah, Judah, and Eliezer.

24 Among the singers: Eliashib.

Among the gatekeepers: Shallum, Telem, and Uri.

25 And among the other Israelites, these married ·non-Jewish [Lforeign] women:

From the descendants of Parosh: Ramiah, Izziah, Malkijah, Mijamin, Eleazar, Malkijah, and Benaiah.

26 From the descendants of Elam: Mattaniah, Zechariah, Jehiel, Abdi, Jeremoth, and Elijah.

27 From the descendants of Zattu: Elioenai, Eliashib, Mattaniah, Jeremoth, Zabad, and Aziza.

28 From the descendants of Bebai: Jehohanan, Hananiah, Zabbai, and Athlai.

29 From the descendants of Bani: Meshullam, Malluch, Adaiah, Jashub, Sheal, and Jeremoth.

30 From the descendants of Pahath-Moab: Adna, Kelal, Benaiah, Maaseiah, Mattaniah, Bezalel, Binnui, and Manasseh.

31 From the descendants of Harim: Eliezer, Ishijah, Malkijah, Shemaiah, Shimeon, 32 Benjamin, Malluch, and Shemariah.

33 From the descendants of Hashum: Mattenai, Mattattah, Zabad, Eliphelet, Jeremai, Manasseh, and Shimei.

[34]From the descendants of Bani: Maadai, Amram, Uel, [35]Benaiah,
Bedeiah, Keluhi, [36]Vaniah, Meremoth, Eliashib, [37]Mattaniah, Mattenai,
and Jaasu.

[38]From the descendants of Binnui: Shimei, [39]Shelemiah, Nathan,
Adaiah, [40]Macnadebai, Shashai, Sharai, [41]Azarel, Shelemiah, Shemariah,
[42]Shallum, Amariah, and Joseph.

[43]From the descendants of Nebo: Jeiel, Mattithiah, Zabad, Zebina,
Jaddai, Joel, and Benaiah.

[44]All these men had married ·non-Jewish [[L]foreign] women, and some
of them had children by these wives.

NEHEMIAH

Nehemiah's Prayer

1 These are the ·words [memoirs] of Nehemiah son of Hacaliah.
In the month of Kislev [[C]late autumn] in the twentieth year
[[C]of the reign of King Artaxerxes I; 445 BC], I, Nehemiah, was in the
·capital city [*or* fortress; [C]the winter residence of Persian kings, separate
from the city] of Susa. [2]One of my ·brothers [relatives] named Hanani
came with some other men from Judah. I asked them about Jerusalem
and the Jewish people who ·lived through [had escaped and survived]
the ·captivity [exile].
[3]They answered me, "·Those who are left [The survivors/remnant
there in the province; [C]of Judah] from the ·captivity [exile] are in much
·trouble [distress; misery] and ·are full of shame [disgrace; humiliation].
The wall around Jerusalem is ·broken down [ruined; breached], and its
gates have been burned [[C]either at the time of the Babylonian destruction
of Jerusalem (2 Kin. 25:10) or later]."
[4]When I heard these things, I sat down and ·cried [wept] for several
days. I ·was sad [mourned] and fasted. I prayed to the God of heaven,
[5]"Lord, God of heaven, you are the great ·God who is to be respected [and
awesome God]. You ·are loyal, and you keep your agreement [keep your
loving covenant/treaty; keep your covenant/treaty of unfailing love] with
those who love you and ·obey [keep] your commands. [6]·Look and listen
carefully [Let your ears be attentive and eyes open]. Hear the prayer that
I, your servant, am praying to you day and night ·for [on behalf of] your
servants, the Israelites. I confess the sins ·we Israelites [the people/sons of
Israel] have ·done [[L]sinned] against you. My father's ·family [[L]house] and
I have sinned against you. [7]We have ·been wicked toward [acted corruptly
against] you and have not obeyed the commands, ·rules [statutes; ordinances; requirements], and ·laws [judgments] you ·gave [commanded]
your servant Moses [Ex. 19—24].
[8]"Remember ·what you taught [the word you commanded] your servant Moses, saying, 'If you are unfaithful, I will scatter you among the
·nations [[L]peoples]. [9]But if you return to me and obey my commands
[[L]and do/live by them], I will gather your people from the far ends of the
·earth [[L]heavens; sky; [C]a reference to the Babylonian exile]. And I will
bring them from there to ·where [the place] I have chosen ·to be worshiped [[L]for my name to dwell; Deut. 4:25–31; 30:1–10].'
[10]"They are your servants and your people, whom you have ·saved
[redeemed; rescued] with your great strength and ·power [[L]strong hand].
[11]Lord, ·listen carefully [[L]may your ear be attentive] to the prayer of your
servant and the prayers of your servants who ·love to honor you [take
pleasure in revering/[L]fearing your name]. ·Give [Grant] me, your servant,
success today; allow this king to show ·kindness [compassion] to me."
I was the ·one who served wine to the king [king's cupbearer].

Nehemiah Is Sent to Jerusalem

2 It was the month of Nisan [Cearly spring] in the twentieth year Artaxerxes was king [C445 BC]. Wine was brought ·for him [*or* to me]. I took some and gave it to the king. I had not been sad in his presence before. [2]So the king said, "Why does your face look sad even though you are not sick? ·Your heart must be sad [You must be very troubled]."

Then I was very afraid. [3]I said to the king, "May the king live forever! ·My face is sad because [LWhy should my face not look sad/dejected when...?] the city ·where my ancestors are buried [of my fathers' tombs] lies in ruins, and its gates have been ·destroyed [Ldevoured] by fire."

[4]Then the king said to me, "What do you ·want [seek; request]?"

·First [Then; So] I prayed to the God of heaven. [5]Then I answered the king, "If ·you are willing [it pleases/is good to you] and if I have ·pleased you [found favor in your sight], send me to Judah, to the city ·where my ancestors are buried [of my fathers' tombs; CJerusalem] so I can rebuild it."

[6]The queen was sitting next to the king. He asked me, "How long will your ·trip [journey] take, and when will you get back?" It ·pleased [Lwas good to] the king to send me, so I set a time.

[7]I also said to him, "If ·you are willing [it pleases/is good to you], give me letters for the governors of ·Trans-Euphrates [Cprovinces west of the Euphrates River]. Tell them to let me pass safely through their lands ·on my way to [until I reach] Judah. [8]And may I have a letter for Asaph, the keeper of the king's forest, telling him to give me timber? I will need it to make ·boards [beams] for the gates of the ·palace [*or* fortress], which is by the ·Temple [Lhouse], and for the city wall, and for the house in which I will live." So the king ·gave [granted] me the letters, because ·God was showing kindness to me [Lthe gracious/good hand of God was on me]. [9]Then I went to the governors of ·Trans-Euphrates [Cprovinces west of the Euphrates River] and gave them the king's letters. The king had also sent army officers and ·horsemen [cavalry] with me.

[10]When Sanballat the Horonite and Tobiah the Ammonite ·officer [official] heard about this, they were ·upset [very displeased] that someone had come to ·help [promote/seek the welfare of] the Israelites.

Nehemiah Inspects Jerusalem

[11]I went to Jerusalem and ·stayed there three days [*or* after three days...]. [12]Then at night I started out with a few men. I had not told anyone what God had ·caused me [put in my mind/heart] to do for Jerusalem. There were no animals with me except the one I was riding.

[13]I went out at night through the Valley Gate. I rode toward the Dragon Well and the ·Trash [Garbage; Refuse; TDung] Gate, inspecting the walls of Jerusalem that had been broken down and the gates that had been ·destroyed [devoured] by fire. [14]Then I rode on toward the Fountain Gate and the King's Pool, but there was not enough room for the animal I was riding to pass through. [15]So I went up the ·valley [ravine; Clikely the Kidron Valley; many of these walls no longer exist] at night, inspecting the wall. Finally, I turned and went back in through the Valley Gate. [16]The ·guards [officials] did not know where I had gone or what I was doing. I had not yet said anything to the Jewish people, the priests, the ·important men [nobles], the ·officers [officials], or any of the others who would do the work.

[17]Then I said to them, "You can see the trouble we ·have here [are in]. Jerusalem is ·a pile of ruins [desolate], and its gates have been burned. Come, let's rebuild the wall of Jerusalem so we won't be ·full of shame [disgraced; humiliated] any longer." [18]I also told them how ·God had been

kind to [the gracious hand of God had been on] me and what the king
had said to me.
Then they answered, "Let's start rebuilding." So they ·began to work
hard [Lstrengthened their hands for this good work].
19But when Sanballat the Horonite, Tobiah the Ammonite officer, and
Geshem the Arab heard about it, they ·made fun of us and laughed at
[mocked and ridiculed/jeered at] us. They said, "What are you doing? Are
you ·turning [rebelling] against the king?"
20But I answered them, "The God of heaven will ·give us success [pros-
per us]. We, his servants, will start rebuilding, but you have no share,
claim, or ·memorial [historic/ancient right] in Jerusalem."

Builders of the Wall

3 Eliashib the high priest and his ·fellow priests [Lbrothers] went to
work and rebuilt the Sheep Gate. They ·gave it to the Lord's service [dedicated/consecrated it] and set its doors in place. They worked as
far as the Tower of the Hundred and ·gave it to the Lord's service
[Ldedicated/consecrated it]. Then they went on to the Tower of Hananel.
2Next to them, the people of Jericho built part of the wall, and Zaccur son
of Imri built next to them.
3The sons of Hassenaah rebuilt the Fish Gate, laying its ·boards
[beams] and setting its doors, bolts, and bars in place. 4Meremoth son of
Uriah, the son of Hakkoz, made repairs next to them. Meshullam son of
Berekiah, the son of Meshezabel, made repairs next to Meremoth. And
Zadok son of Baana made repairs next to Meshullam. 5The people from
Tekoa [La town ten miles south of Jerusalem] made repairs next to them,
but the ·leading men of Tekoa [nobles] would not work under ·their
supervisors [*or* their lords; *or* their Lord; Cor possibly a reference to
Nehemiah].
6Joiada son of Paseah and Meshullam son of Besodeiah repaired the
Old Gate. They laid its ·boards [beams] and set its doors, bolts, and bars
in place. 7Next to them, Melatiah from Gibeon, other men from Gibeon
and Mizpah, and Jadon from Meronoth made repairs. These places were
·ruled by [under the jurisdiction of] the governor of ·Trans-Euphrates
[Cprovinces west of the Euphrates River]. 8Next to them, Uzziel son of
Harhaiah, a goldsmith, made repairs. And next to him, Hananiah, a perfume maker, made repairs. These men rebuilt Jerusalem as far as the
Broad Wall. 9The next part of the wall was repaired by Rephaiah son of
Hur, the ·ruler [official; head] of half of the district of Jerusalem. 10Next
to him, Jedaiah son of Harumaph made repairs ·opposite [across from]
his own house. And next to him, Hattush son of Hashabneiah made
repairs. 11Malkijah son of Harim and Hasshub son of Pahath-Moab
repaired another part of the wall and the Tower of the ·Ovens [Furnaces;
Fire Pots; Cpossibly the bakery district]. 12Next to them Shallum son of
Hallohesh, the ·ruler [official; head] of half of the district of Jerusalem,
and his daughters made repairs.
13Hanun and the people of Zanoah repaired the Valley Gate, rebuilding it and setting its doors, bolts, and bars in place. They also repaired the
·five hundred yards [Lone thousand cubits] of the wall to the ·Trash
[Garbage; Refuse; TDung] Gate.
14Malkijah son of Recab, the ·ruler [official; head] of the district of
Beth Hakkerem, repaired the ·Trash [Garbage; Refuse; TDung] Gate. He
rebuilt that gate and set its doors, bolts, and bars in place.

15Shallun son of Col-Hozeh, the ·ruler [official; head] **of the district of Mizpah, repaired the Fountain Gate. He rebuilt it, ·put a roof over** [covered] **it, and set its doors, bolts, and bars in place. He also repaired the wall of the Pool of ·Siloam** [*or* Shelah] **next to the King's Garden all the way to the steps that went down from the ·older part of the city** [LCity of David]. **16Next to Shallun was Nehemiah** [Cnot the governor] **son of Azbuk, ·the ruler** [official; head] **of half of the district of Beth Zur. He made repairs ·opposite** [across from] **the tombs of David and as far as the ·man-made** [artificial] **pool and the House of the ·Heroes** [Champions; Warriors; TMighty Men].

17Next to him, the Levites made repairs, working under Rehum son of Bani. Next to him, Hashabiah, the ·ruler [official; head] **of half of the district of Keilah, for his district. 18Next to him, ·Binnui** [*or* Bavvai] **son of Henadad and his ·relatives** [kinsmen; Lbrothers] **made repairs. ·Binnui** [*or* Bavvai] **was the ·ruler** [official; head] **of the other half of the district of Keilah. 19Next to them, Ezer son of Jeshua, the ·ruler** [official; head] **of Mizpah, repaired another part of the wall. He worked across from the way up to the armory, as far as the ·bend** [angle; buttress]. **20Next to him, Baruch son of Zabbai worked ·hard** [zealously] **on the wall that went from the ·bend** [angle; buttress] **to the ·entrance to** [door of] **the house of Eliashib, the high priest. 21Next to him, Meremoth son of Uriah, the son of Hakkoz, repaired the wall that went from the ·entrance to** [door of] **Eliashib's house to the far end of it.**

22Next to him worked the priests from the ·surrounding area [nearby district]. **23Next to them, Benjamin and Hasshub made repairs ·in front of** [across from] **their own house. Next to them, Azariah son of Maaseiah, the son of Ananiah, made repairs ·beside** [near] **his own house. 24Next to him, Binnui son of Henadad repaired ·the wall** [another section] **that went from Azariah's house to the ·bend** [angle; buttress] **and on to the corner. 25Palal son of Uzai worked across from the ·bend** [angle; buttress] **and by the tower on the upper ·palace** [Lhouse of the king], **which is near the courtyard of the guard. Next to Palal, Pedaiah son of Parosh made repairs. 26The Temple servants who lived on the hill of Ophel made repairs as far as a point ·opposite** [across from] **the Water Gate. They worked toward the east and the ·tower that extends from the palace** [projecting/protruding tower]. **27Next to them, the people of Tekoa** [v. 5] **repaired ·the wall** [another section] **from the great ·tower that extends from the palace** [projecting/protruding tower] **to the wall of Ophel.**

28The priests made repairs above the Horse Gate, each working ·in front of [across from] **his own house. 29Next to them, Zadok son of Immer made repairs across from his own house. Next to him, Shemaiah son of Shecaniah, the guard of the East Gate, made repairs. 30Next to him, Hananiah son of Shelemiah, and Hanun, the sixth son of Zalaph, made repairs on another ·part of the wall** [section]. **Next to them, Meshullam son of Berekiah made repairs across from ·where he lived** [his quarters]. **31Next to him, Malkijah, one of the goldsmiths, made repairs. He worked as far as the house of the Temple servants and the ·traders** [merchants], **which is across from the Inspection Gate, and as far as the ·room above the corner of the wall** [upper room at the corner]. **32The goldsmiths and the traders made repairs between the ·room above the corner of the wall** [upper room at the corner] **and the Sheep Gate.**

Those Against the Rebuilding

4 When Sanballat heard we were rebuilding the wall, he was very
angry, even furious. He ·made fun of [mocked; ridiculed] the
Jewish people. 2He said to his ·friends [colleagues; Lbrothers] and ·those
with power in [*or* the army/aristocracy of] Samaria, "What are these
·weak [feeble; pathetic] Jews doing? Will they ·rebuild the wall [*or* leave it
all to God]? Will they offer sacrifices? Can they finish it in one day? Can
they ·bring stones back to life from piles of trash and ashes [revive stones
from piles of rubble—burnt stones at that]?"

3Tobiah the Ammonite, who was ·next to Sanballat [Lbeside him], said,
"If a fox climbed up on the stone wall they are building, it would break it
down."

4I prayed, "Hear us, our God. We are ·hated [despised]. Turn the ·insults
[taunts; sneers] of Sanballat and Tobiah back on their own heads. ·Let
them be captured and stolen like valuables [Send them as plunder to a
land of exile]. 5Do not ·hide [cover; ignore] their guilt or ·take away [blot
out] their sins so that you can't see them, because they have ·insulted
[deeply offended; *or* demoralized] the builders."

6So we rebuilt [Land connected/joined together] the wall to half its
height, because the people were ·willing to [enthusiastic in their; Lhad a
heart to] work.

7But Sanballat, Tobiah, the Arabs, the Ammonites, and the people
from Ashdod were very angry when they heard that the repairs to
Jerusalem's walls were continuing and that the ·holes [gaps; breaches] in
the wall were being closed. 8So they all made plans to come to Jerusalem
and fight and ·stir up trouble [cause confusion/a disturbance]. 9But we
prayed to our God and appointed guards ·to watch for [Lagainst] them
day and night.

10The people of Judah said, "The ·workers are getting tired [strength of
the laborers is failing]. There is so much ·trash [debris; rubble] we cannot
rebuild the wall."

11And our enemies said, "·The Jews [LThey] won't know or see anything until we come among them and kill them and stop the work."

12Then the Jewish people who lived near our enemies came and ·told
[warned] us repeatedly [Lten times], "·Everywhere you turn [From every
direction], the enemy will attack us." 13So I ·put [stationed] people behind
the lowest places along the wall—the ·open [exposed] places—and I ·put
families together [stationed people by families] with their swords, spears,
and bows. 14·Then I looked around and [After an inspection, I] stood up
and said to the ·important men [nobles], the ·leaders [officials], and the
rest of the people: "Don't be afraid of them. Remember the Lord, who is
great and ·powerful [awesome; glorious]. Fight for your brothers, your
sons and daughters, your wives, and your homes."

15Then our enemies heard that we knew about their plans and that
God had ·ruined [frustrated; thwarted] their plans. So we all went back to
the wall, each to his own work.

16From that day on, half my people worked on the wall. The other half
was ready with spears, shields, bows, and armor. The ·officers [leaders]
stood in back of the ·people [Lhouse] of Judah 17who were building the
wall. Those who carried ·materials [loads] did their work with one hand
and carried a weapon with the other. 18Each builder wore his sword at his
side as he ·worked [built]. The trumpeter [Cto signal an attack] stayed
next to me.

19Then I said to the ·important people [nobles], the ·leaders [officials],
and everyone else, "This is ·a very big job [demanding work]. We are
spread out along the wall so that we are far apart. 20Wherever you hear
the sound of the trumpet, ·assemble there [rally to us here]. Our God will
fight for us."
21So we continued to work with half the men holding spears from ·sun-
rise [dawn] till the stars came out. 22At that time I also said to the people,
"Let every man and his ·helper [servant] stay inside Jerusalem at night.
They can be our guards at night and workmen during the day." 23Neither
I, my ·brothers [colleagues], my ·workers [servants], nor the guards with
me ever ·took off [changed] our clothes. Each person carried his weapon
even when he went for water.

Nehemiah Helps Poor People

5 The men and their wives ·complained [cried out] loudly against
their ·fellow Jews [LJewish brothers]. 2Some of them were saying,
"We have many sons and daughters in our families. To eat and stay alive,
we need grain [CThis group may have owned no land that could provide
them food.]."
3Others were saying, "We are ·borrowing money [mortgaging; Cfrom
their fellow Jews, which increased their frustration] against our fields,
vineyards, and homes to get grain ·because there is not much food [dur-
ing the famine]."
4And still others were saying, "We are borrowing money to pay the
king's tax on our fields and vineyards. 5·We are just like our fellow Jews
[LOur flesh is like our brothers' flesh], and our ·sons [children] are like
their ·sons [children]. But we have to sell our sons and daughters ·as
slaves [into bondage/slavery; Can often temporary servitude to satisfy
debts; Ex. 21:2–11]. Some of our daughters have already been ·sold
[enslaved]. But ·there is nothing we can do [we are powerless/helpless],
because our fields and vineyards already belong to other people."
6When I heard their ·complaints about these things [Loutcry and these
words], I was very angry. 7After ·I thought about [reflecting on] it, I
·accused [reprimanded] the ·important people [nobles] and ·leaders
[officials], "You are ·charging your own ·brothers [kinsmen] interest
[committing usury; Cin these situations, lenders were not to make a profit;
Deut. 24:10; Prov. 22:26]." So I called a ·large meeting to deal with [great
assembly against] them. 8I said to them, "·As much as possible [To the best
of our ability], we have ·bought freedom for [redeemed] our fellow Jews
who had been sold to ·foreigners [Lthe Gentiles]. Now you are selling your
fellow Jews to us [Cthe creditors were selling their fellow Jews into slavery,
requiring Nehemiah and others to buy them back]!" ·The leaders [LThey]
were ·quiet [silent] and ·had nothing [Lcouldn't find a word] to say.
9Then I said, "What you are doing is not ·right [good]. ·Don't you fear
[LShould you not walk in fear of] God [Prov. 1:7]? Don't let our ·foreign
[Gentile] enemies shame us. 10I, my ·brothers [colleagues], and my ·men
[servants] are lending money and grain to the people. But stop charging
them ·for this [interest]. 11Give back their fields, vineyards, olive trees,
and houses ·right now [Lthis very day]. Also give back the ·extra amount
[interest] you charged—·the hundredth part [one percent] of the money,
grain, new wine, and oil."
12They said, "We will give it back and not demand anything more from
them. We will do as you say."

Then I called for the priests, and I made the ·important people [nobles]
and ·leaders [officials] ·take an oath [swear; vow] to do what they had
·said [promised]. 13Also I shook out the folds of my ·robe [Lbosom] and
said, "In this way may God shake out everyone who does not ·keep his
[fulfill/Lcause to stand this] promise. May God shake him out of his house
and ·out of the things that are his [his possessions/property]. Let that person be shaken out and emptied!"

Then the whole ·group [assembly] said, "Amen," and they praised the
LORD. So the people did what they had ·promised [sworn; vowed].

14I was appointed governor in the land of Judah in the twentieth year
of King Artaxerxes' rule [C445 BC]. I was governor of Judah for twelve
years, until his thirty-second year. During that time neither my ·brothers
[colleagues; relatives; *or* officials] nor I ate the food that was allowed for a
governor [CNehemiah is demonstrating his own selflessness during this
time]. 15But the governors before me [Cin contrast] had placed a heavy
·load [burden] on the people. They took ·about one pound [Lforty shek-
els] of silver from each person, along with food and wine. ·The governors'
helpers before me [Their associates/assistants] also ·controlled [oppressed;
dominated] the people, but I did not do that, because I feared God [Prov.
1:7]. 16I ·worked [devoted myself to working] on the wall, as did all my
·men [servants] who were ·gathered [assembled] there. We did not buy
any ·fields [land].

17·Also [Furthermore], I fed one hundred fifty Jewish people and ·offi-
cers [officials] at my table, as well as those who came from the nations
around us. 18This is what was prepared every day: one ox, six ·good
[choice] sheep, and birds. And every ten days there were all kinds of wine
[in abundance]. But I never demanded the food that was due a governor,
because the people were already ·working very hard [carrying a great
burden].

19Remember ·to be kind to me [Lfor my good], my God, for all I have
done for these people.

More Problems for Nehemiah

6Then Sanballat, Tobiah, Geshem the Arab, and our other enemies
heard that I had rebuilt the wall and that there was not one ·gap
[breach] in it. But I had not yet set the doors in the gates. 2So Sanballat
and Geshem sent me this message: "Come, Nehemiah, let's meet together
in ·Kephirim [*or* one of the villages] on the plain of Ono."

But they were ·planning [plotting; scheming] to harm me. 3So I sent
messengers to them with this answer: "I am ·doing [engaged in] a great
work, and I can't come down. ·I don't want the work to [LWhy should the
work...?] stop while I leave to meet you." 4Sanballat and Geshem sent the
same message to me four times, and each time I sent back the same
answer.

5The fifth time Sanballat sent his ·helper [servant; assistant] to me, and
in his hand was an ·unsealed [open] letter. 6This is what was written:

> A report is going around to all the nations, and ·Geshem
> [Gashmu; Cthe same person as in 2:19] says it is true, that you
> and the Jewish people are planning to ·turn against the king
> [rebel; revolt] and ·that [therefore] you are rebuilding the wall.
> They say you are ·going [intending; planning; wishing] to be
> their king 7and that you have ·appointed [anointed; established]

prophets to ·announce [proclaim] in Jerusalem: "There is a king
of Judah!" The king will hear about ·this [these reports/rumors].
So come, let's ·discuss this [confer; take counsel] together.

8So I sent him back this answer: "·Nothing you are saying is really happening. [We are not doing what you are saying.] You are just ·making it up
[inventing/imagining them] in your own ·mind [Lheart]."
9Our enemies were trying to ·scare [intimidate; terrorize] us, thinking,
"They will get too ·weak [discouraged; Ltheir hands will grow slack] to
work. Then the wall will not be finished."
·But I prayed [So now], "God, ·make me strong [Lstrengthen my hands]."
10·One day [Then] I went to the house of Shemaiah son of Delaiah, the
son of Mehetabel. Shemaiah ·had to stay at [was confined to his; Cperhaps
related to a vow or to ritual uncleanness] home. He said, "Nehemiah, let's
meet in the ·Temple [Lhouse] of God. Let's go inside the Temple and ·close
[bar] the doors, because men are coming at night to kill you."
11But I said, "Should a man like me [Cin his position] run away? Should
I run ·for [to save] my life into the Temple [Cto seek asylum; Ex. 21:13–14;
1 Kin. 1:50–53; 2:28–34; 2 Chr. 26:16–20; 27:2]? I will not go." 12I ·knew
[realized; perceived; recognized] that God had not sent him but that
Tobiah and Sanballat had ·paid [hired] him to prophesy against me.
13They ·paid [hired] him to ·frighten [intimidate; terrorize] me so I would
do this and sin. Then they could ·give me a bad name to shame [accuse
and discredit/blame] me.
14I prayed, "My God, remember Tobiah and Sanballat and what they
have done. Also remember the prophetess Noadiah and the other prophets who have been trying to ·frighten [intimidate; terrorize] me."

The Wall Is Finished

15The wall of Jerusalem was completed on the twenty-fifth day of the
month of Elul [COctober 2, 515 BC]. It took fifty-two days to rebuild.
16When all our enemies heard about it and all the nations around us saw
it, they were ·shamed [disheartened; *or* amazed]. They ·understood [rec-
ognized; realized] that the work had been ·done [accomplished] with the
help of our God.
17Also in those days the ·important people [nobles] of Judah sent many
letters to Tobiah, and he answered them. 18Many ·Jewish people [Lin
Judah] ·had promised to be faithful [were under oath; had sworn alle-
giance] to Tobiah, because he was the son-in-law of Shecaniah son of
Arah. And Tobiah's son Jehohanan had married the daughter of
Meshullam son of Berekiah. 19·These important people [LThey] kept telling me about the good ·things [deeds] Tobiah was doing, and then they
would tell Tobiah ·what I said about him [Lmy words]. So Tobiah sent letters to ·frighten [intimidate; terrorize] me.

7 After the wall had been rebuilt and I had set the doors in ·place
[the gates], the gatekeepers, ·singers [musicians], and Levites
were chosen. 2I put my brother Hanani, along with Hananiah, the commander of the ·palace [fortress; citadel], ·in charge of [to administer]
Jerusalem. Hananiah was ·honest [La faithful man] and feared God more
than ·most [many] people. 3I said to them, "The gates of Jerusalem should
not be opened ·until [*or* while] the sun is hot [Ceither don't open until
later in the day, or shut them at midday while people are resting from the
heat]. ·While [Even while] the gatekeepers are still on duty, have them

shut and bolt the doors. Appoint people who live in Jerusalem as guards,
and put some at guard posts and some near their own houses."

The Captives Who Returned

4The city was large and ·roomy [spacious; spread out; Lwide of two
hands], but there were few people in it, and the houses had not yet been
rebuilt. 5Then my God ·caused me [Lput it in my heart/mind] to ·gather
[assemble] the ·important people [nobles], ·leaders [officials], and the
common people so I could ·register [enroll] them by ·families [geneal-
ogy]. I found the ·family history [genealogical records] of those who had
returned first. This is what I found written there:
6These are the people of the ·area [province] who returned from ·cap-
tivity [exile], whom Nebuchadnezzar king of Babylon had ·taken [carried]
·away [into exile]. They returned to Jerusalem and Judah, each to his own
town. 7These people returned with Zerubbabel, Jeshua, Nehemiah,
Azariah, Raamiah, Nahamani, Mordecai, Bilshan, Mispereth, Bigvai,
Nehum, and Baanah.
These are the [Lmen from the; Cthe following numbers likely reflect
only males] people from Israel: 8the ·descendants [sons; Cand so throughout the following list] of Parosh—2,172; 9the descendants of
Shephatiah—372; 10the descendants of Arah—652; 11the descendants of
Pahath-Moab (through the ·family [line; sons] of Jeshua and Joab)—
2,818; 12the descendants of Elam—1,254; 13the descendants of Zattu—845;
14the descendants of Zaccai—760; 15the descendants of Binnui—648;
16the descendants of Bebai—628; 17the descendants of Azgad—2,322;
18the descendants of Adonikam—667; 19the descendants of Bigvai—2,067;
20the descendants of Adin—655; 21the descendants of Ater (through
Hezekiah)—98; 22the descendants of Hashum—328; 23the descendants of
Bezai—324; 24the descendants of Hariph—112; 25the descendants of
Gibeon—95.
26These are the ·people [*or* men] from the towns of Bethlehem and
Netophah—188; 27of Anathoth—128; 28of Beth Azmaveth—42; 29of
Kiriath Jearim, Kephirah, and Beeroth—743; 30of Ramah and Geba—
621; 31of Micmash—122; 32of Bethel and Ai—123; 33of the other
Nebo—52; 34of the other Elam—1,254; 35of Harim—320; 36of
Jericho—345; 37of Lod, Hadid, and Ono—721; 38of Senaah—3,930.
39These are the priests: the descendants of Jedaiah (through the ·family
[Lhouse] of Jeshua)—973; 40the descendants of Immer—1,052; 41the
descendants of Pashhur—1,247; 42the descendants of Harim—1,017.
43These are the Levites: the descendants of Jeshua (through Kadmiel
through the ·family [line; sons] of Hodaviah)—74.
44These are the singers: the descendants of Asaph—148.
45These are the gatekeepers: the descendants of Shallum, Ater, Talmon,
Akkub, Hatita, and Shobai—138.
46These are the Temple servants: the descendants of Ziha, Hasupha,
Tabbaoth, 47Keros, Sia, Padon, 48 [Lthe descendants/sons of] Lebana,
Hagaba, Shalmai, 49 [Lthe descendants/sons of] Hanan, Giddel, Gahar,
50[Lthe descendants/sons of] Reaiah, Rezin, Nekoda, 51 [Lthe descendants/
sons of] Gazzam, Uzza, Paseah, 52 [Lthe descendants/sons of] Besai,
Meunim, Nephussim, 53 [Lthe descendants/sons of] Bakbuk, Hakupha,
Harhur, 54Bazluth, Mehida, Harsha, 55 [Lthe descendants/sons of] Barkos,
Sisera, Temah, 56 [Lthe descendants/sons of] Neziah, and Hatipha.
57These are the descendants of the servants of Solomon: the descendants

of Sotai, Sophereth, Perida, 58[Lthe descendants/sons of] Jaala, Darkon, Giddel, 59[Lthe descendants/sons of] Shephatiah, Hattil, Pokereth-Haz zebaim, and Amon.

60The Temple servants and the descendants of the servants of Solomon totaled 392 people.

61Some people came to Jerusalem from the towns of Tel Melah, Tel Harsha, Kerub, Addon, and Immer, but they could not prove that ·their ancestors [Lthe house of their fathers] came from Israel. They were as follows: 62the descendants of Delaiah, Tobiah, and Nekoda—642.

63And these priests were in that group: the descendants of Hobaiah, Hakkoz, and Barzillai. (He had married a daughter of Barzillai from Gilead and ·was called by [adopted; took] her family name.)

64These people searched ·for [in] their ·family [genealogical] records, but they could not find ·them [themselves there]. So they ·could not be priests [were excluded/disqualified from the priesthood], because they were ·thought to be unclean [Ldesecrated]. 65The governor ordered them not to eat any of the ·holy [sacred; Lmost holy; Lev. 2:3; 7:21–36] food until a priest settled this matter by using the Urim and Thummim [Csacred lots used to determine God's will; Ex. 28:30].

66The total ·number of those who returned was [assembly/group numbered] 42,360. 67This is not counting their 7,337 male and female servants and the 245 male and female singers with them. 68They had 736 horses, 245 mules, 69435 camels, and 6,720 donkeys.

70Some of the ·family leaders [Lheads of the fathers] ·gave [contributed] to the work. The governor gave to the treasury ·about 19 pounds [L1,000 drachmas/*or* darics] of gold, 50 ·bowls [basins], and 530 ·pieces of clothing [robes; garments] for the priests. 71Some of the family ·leaders [heads] gave ·about 375 pounds [20,000 drachmas/*or* darics] of gold and ·about 2,660 pounds [2,200 minas] of silver to the treasury for the work. 72The total of what the other people gave was ·about 375 pounds [2,000 drachmas/*or* darics] of gold, about ·2,250 pounds [2,000 minas] of silver, and 67 ·pieces of clothing [robes; garments] for the priests. 73So these people all settled in their own towns: the priests, the Levites, the gatekeepers, the singers, the Temple servants, and all the other people of Israel.

Ezra Reads the Teachings

By the seventh month [COctober-November 445 BC] the Israelites were settled in their own towns.

8 All the people of Israel ·gathered [assembled] ·together [Llike one man/person] in the square ·by [in front of] the Water Gate. They asked Ezra the ·teacher [scribe] to bring out the ·Book [scroll] of the ·Teachings [Law; LTorah] of Moses, which the LORD had ·given to [commanded/prescribed for] Israel.

2So on the first day of the seventh month [COctober 8], Ezra the priest brought out the ·Teachings [Laws; Instructions; LTorah] for the ·crowd [assembly]. Men, women, and all who could ·listen and understand [understand what they heard; Cpresumably older children] had ·gathered [assembled]. 3At the square by the Water Gate Ezra read the ·Teachings [Laws; Instructions; LTorah] out loud from early morning until noon to the men, women, and everyone who could ·listen and understand [understand what they heard; Cpresumably older children]. All the people listened ·carefully [attentively; eagerly] to the ·Book [scroll] of the ·Teachings [Laws; Instructions; LTorah].

4 Ezra the ·teacher [scribe] stood on a high ·wooden platform [dais; Ltower of wood; 2 Chr. 6:13] that had been built just for this ·time [occasion; purpose]. On his right were Mattithiah, Shema, Anaiah, Uriah, Hilkiah, and Maaseiah. And on his left were Pedaiah, Mishael, Malkijah, Hashum, Hashbaddanah, Zechariah, and Meshullam.

5 Ezra opened the ·book [scroll] ·in full view [Lto the eyes] of everyone, because he was above them. As he opened it, all the people stood up [Ca sign of respect; Judg. 3:20; Job 29:8; Ezek. 2:1). 6 Ezra ·praised [blessed] the LORD, the great God, and all the people ·held up [lifted] their hands [Ezra 9:5; Ps. 28:2; 134:2] and said, "Amen! Amen!" Then they bowed ·down [low] and worshiped the LORD with their faces to the ground.

7 These Levites ·explained [instructed regarding; 2 Chr. 17:7–9] the ·Teachings [Laws; Instructions; LTorah] to the people as they ·stood there [remained in place]: Jeshua, Bani, Sherebiah, Jamin, Akkub, Shabbethai, Hodiah, Maaseiah, Kelita, Azariah, Jozabad, Hanan, and Pelaiah. 8 They read from the ·Book [scroll] of the ·Teachings [Laws; Instructions; LTorah] of God and ·explained [clarified; *or* translated] what it meant so the people understood what was being read.

9 Then Nehemiah the governor, Ezra the priest and ·teacher [scribe], and the Levites who were ·teaching [instructing; interpreting] said to all the people, "This is a ·holy [sacred] day to the LORD your God. Don't ·be sad [mourn] or ·cry [weep]." All the people had been ·crying [weeping] as they listened to the words of the ·Teachings [Laws; Instructions; LTorah].

10 Nehemiah said, "Go and ·enjoy good food [Leat of the fat] and sweet drinks [Lev. 3; 2 Sam. 6:19; 1 Chr. 12:40–41; 29:22; 2 Chr. 7:8–10; 30:21–26]. Send ·some [portions] to people who have ·none [nothing prepared], because today is a ·holy [sacred] day to the Lord. Don't ·be sad [grieve; mourn], because the joy of the LORD ·will make you strong [is your strength]."

11 The Levites helped calm the people, saying, "Be ·quiet [still], because this is a ·holy [sacred] day. Don't ·be sad [grieve; mourn]."

12 Then all the people went away to eat and drink, to ·send some of their food to others [share; send portions], and to ·celebrate with [Lmake] great joy. They finally understood ·what they had been taught [the words/matters that had been made known to them].

13 On the second day of the month [October 9, 445 BC], the ·leaders [heads] of all the families, the priests, and the Levites met with Ezra the ·teacher [scribe]. They ·gathered [assembled] to ·study [consider; gain insight into] the words of the ·Teachings [Laws; Instructions; LTorah]. 14 This is what they found written in the ·Teachings [Laws; Instructions; LTorah]: The LORD commanded through Moses that the people of Israel were to live in ·shelters [Tbooths; Ctemporary dwellings; Ex. 23:33; Deut. 16:13–15] during the feast of the seventh month. 15 The people ·were supposed to [should] ·preach this message [make/issue a proclamation] and ·spread [disseminate] it through all their towns and in Jerusalem: "Go out into the ·mountains [hills], and bring back branches from olive and wild olive trees, myrtle trees, palms, and ·shade [other leafy] trees. Make ·shelters [booths] with them, as it is written [Cprescribed in the Law of Moses]."

16 So the people went out and got tree branches. They built ·shelters [Tbooths] on their roofs [Croofs were living space], in their courtyards, in the courtyards of the ·Temple [Lhouse] of God, in the square by the Water Gate, and in the square next to the Gate of Ephraim. 17 The whole ·group

[assembly] that had come back from ·captivity [exile] built ·shelters [Tbooths] and lived in them. The Israelites had not done this since the ·time [days] of Joshua son of Nun. And ·they were very happy [there was great rejoicing].

18Ezra read to them every day from the ·Book [scroll] of the ·Teachings [Laws; Instructions; LTorah] of God, from the first day to the last [Cof the festival]. The people of Israel celebrated the feast for seven days, and then on the eighth day the people ·gathered [held a solemn assembly] ·as the law said [Laccording to the judgment].

Israel Confesses Sins

9 On the twenty-fourth day of that same month [October 31], the people of Israel ·gathered [assembled]. They fasted, and they wore ·rough cloth [sackcloth] and put dust on their heads [Csigns of grief or repentance]. 2·Those people whose ancestors were from Israel [LThe seed of Israel] had separated themselves from all foreigners. They stood and confessed their sins and their ancestors' ·sins [iniquities]. 3For a fourth of the day [Cthree hours] they stood where they were and read from the ·Book [scroll] of the ·Teachings [Laws; Instructions; LTorah] of the LORD their God. For another fourth of the day they confessed their sins and worshiped the LORD their God. 4These Levites were standing on the stairs: Jeshua, Bani, Kadmiel, Shebaniah, Bunni, Sherebiah, Bani, and Kenani. They called out to the LORD their God with loud voices. 5Then these Levites spoke: Jeshua, Kadmiel, Bani, Hashabneiah, Sherebiah, Hodiah, Shebaniah, and Pethahiah. They said, "Stand up and praise the LORD your God, who lives ·forever and ever [from age to age/everlasting to everlasting]."

The People's Prayer

[compare Ps. 78, 105, 135, 136]

"Blessed be your ·wonderful [glorious] name.
·It is more wonderful than [May it be exalted above] all blessing and praise.
6You ·are the only [alone are the] LORD.
You made the ·heavens [sky], even the ·highest [Lheavens of the] heavens,
with all ·the stars [Ltheir hosts].
You made the earth and everything on it,
the seas and everything in them;
you give life to everything.
The heavenly ·army [host] worships you.

7"You are the ·LORD,
the God [*or* LORD God,] who chose Abram
and brought him ·out of [forth from] Ur ·in Babylonia [Lof the Chaldeans; Gen. 12:1–3]
and named [Crenamed] him Abraham [Gen. 17:5].
8You found ·him [Lhis heart] faithful to you,
so you made an ·agreement [covenant; treaty] with him
to give his ·descendants [Lseed] the land of the Canaanites,
Hittites, Amorites,
Perizzites, Jebusites, and Girgashites.
You have ·kept [fulfilled] your ·promise [word],
because you ·do what is right [are righteous].

9"You saw our ·ancestors [fathers] ·suffering [miserable; afflicted; in distress] in Egypt
and heard them cry out ·at [beside] the ·Red Sea [LSea of Reeds; Ex. 14–15].
10You ·did [performed; displayed] signs and ·miracles [wonders] against ·the king of Egypt [LPharaoh],
and against all his ·officers [officials; servants] and all the people of his land,
because you knew how ·proud [arrogant; insolent] they were to them [CIsrael's ancestors].
You ·became as famous [Lmade a name for yourself] ·as you are today [which remains to this day].
11You ·divided [split; opened] the sea in front of ·our ancestors [Lthem];
they ·walked [passed] through the sea on dry ground [Ex. 14–15].
But you threw ·the people chasing them into the deep water [their pursuers into the depths],
like a stone thrown into ·mighty [raging; surging] waters.
12You ·led [guided] ·our ancestors [Lthem] with a ·pillar [column] of cloud by day
and with a ·pillar [column] of fire at night [Ex. 13:21].
It lit the way
they were supposed to go.
13You came down ·to [on; at] Mount Sinai
and spoke from heaven to ·our ancestors [Lthem].
You gave them ·fair [just] ·rules [judgments] and true ·teachings [laws; instructions; LTorah],
good ·orders [statutes; ordinances; requirements] and commands.
14You ·told [revealed; made known to] them about your holy Sabbath [Ex. 20:8–11; Deut. 5:12–15]
and gave them commands, ·orders [statutes; ordinances; requirements], and ·teachings [laws; instructions; LTorah]
through your servant Moses.
15When they were hungry, you gave them bread from heaven [Cthe manna; Ex. 16:31].
When they were thirsty, you brought them water from ·the [a] rock [Ex. 17:1–7; Num. 20:1–13].
You told them to enter and ·take over [possess]
the land you had ·promised [sworn; Lraised your hand] to give them.

16"But ·our ancestors [Lthey, our fathers,] were ·proud [arrogant; insolent] and ·stubborn [rebellious; Lstiff-necked]
and did not ·obey [listen/pay attention to] your commands.
17They refused to ·listen [obey];
they ·forgot [Ldid not remember/recall] the ·miracles [wonders] you ·did [performed] ·for [among] them.
So they became ·stubborn [rebellious; Lstiff-necked],
·choosing [appointing] a leader to take them back to slavery in Egypt."
But you are a forgiving God.
You are ·kind [gracious] and ·full of mercy [compassionate].

9:17 in Egypt Greek copies read "in Egypt." Hebrew copies read "in their rebellion." See Num. 14:4.

You ·do not become angry quickly [Tare slow to anger], **and ·you have great** [abounding in unfailing/steadfast] **love** [compare Ex. 34:6; Num. 14:18; Ps. 86:15, 145:8; Joel 2:13]
So you did not ·leave [abandon; desert; forsake] **them.**
18 **·Our ancestors** [LThey] **even ·made** [cast] **a calf** [Cas an idol] **for themselves.**
They said, 'This is your god
who brought you up out of Egypt [Ex. 32].'
They ·spoke against you [Lcommitted great blasphemies].

19 **"You have great ·mercy** [compassion],
so you did not ·leave [abandon; desert; forsake] **them in the ·desert** [wilderness].
The pillar of cloud ·guided them by day [Ldid not turn from them by day in guiding them in the path],
·and the pillar of fire led them at night,
lighting the way they were to go [nor did the pillar of fire stop illuminating for them by night the path on which they should travel].
20 **You ·gave** [sent; imparted] **your good Spirit to ·teach** [instruct] **them.**
You ·gave them manna to eat [Ldid not withhold manna from their mouth]
and gave them water when they were thirsty.
21 **You ·took care of** [sustained; provided for] **them for forty years in the ·desert** [wilderness];
they ·needed [lacked] **nothing.**
Their clothes did not wear out,
and their feet did not swell.

22 **"You gave them kingdoms and ·nations** [peoples; Cto conquer];
you ·gave them more land [put them in every corner; Lallotted/allocated to them every corner/frontier].
They ·took over [took possession of; inherited] **the country of Sihon king of Heshbon**
and the country of Og king of Bashan [Num. 21:21–33].
23 **You made their ·children** [descendants; sons] **as ·many** [numerous] **as the stars ·in the sky** [of heaven; Gen. 15:5; 22:17; 26:4],
and you brought them into the land
that you told their ·ancestors [fathers] **to enter and ·take over** [possess].
24 **So their ·children** [descendants; sons] **went into the land and took ·over** [possession].
The Canaanites lived there, but you ·defeated them for [subdued them before] **our ancestors.**
You handed over to them the Canaanites, their kings, and the ·people [peoples] **of the land.**
·Our ancestors [LThey] **could ·do what they wanted with them** [deal with them as they pleased].
25 **They captured ·strong, walled** [fortified] **cities and fertile land.**
They took over houses full of good things,
·wells [cisterns] **that were already dug,**
vineyards, olive ·trees [groves], **and ·many** [abundant] **fruit trees.**

They ate until they were full and grew fat;
they ·enjoyed [reveled; delighted themselves in] **your great goodness.**

[26]**"But they were disobedient and ·turned** [rebelled] **against you**
and ·ignored [turned their backs on] **your ·teachings** [laws; instructions; [L]Torah].
Your prophets ·warned [admonished] **them to come back to you,**
but they killed those prophets
and ·spoke against you [[L]committed great blasphemies].
[27]**So you handed them over to their ·enemies** [oppressors],
and their ·enemies treated them badly [oppressors oppressed them].
But in this time of ·trouble [distress; suffering; misery] **·our ancestors** [[L]they] **cried out to you,**
and you heard from heaven.
You had great ·mercy [compassion]
and gave them ·saviors [liberators; [T]deliverers] **who ·saved** [rescued] **them from the ·power** [hand] **of their ·enemies** [oppressors].
[28]**But as soon as they had ·rest** [peace],
they again ·did what was [committed] **evil.**
So you ·left [abandoned; deserted; forsook] **them to** [[L]the hand of] **their ·enemies** [oppressors]
who ·ruled over [conquered; oppressed] **them.**
When they cried out to you again,
you heard from heaven.
Because of your ·mercy [compassion], **you ·saved them again** [rescued them time] **and again.**
[29]**You ·warned** [admonished] **them to return to your ·teachings** [laws; instructions; [L]Torah],
but they were ·proud [arrogant; insolent] **and did not ·obey** [listen to] **your commands.**
If someone ·obeys [observes] **your ·laws** [judgments], **he will live,**
but they sinned against ·your laws [[L]them].
They ·were stubborn [[L]turned a stubborn shoulder], **·unwilling** [rebellious; [L]stiff-necked], **and ·disobedient** [rebellious].
[30]**You ·were patient** [[T]bore] **with them for many years**
and ·warned [admonished] **them by your Spirit through ·the** [your] **prophets,**
but they did not ·pay attention [[L]give ear].
So you handed them over to ·other countries [[L]the peoples of the lands].
[31]**But because your ·mercy** [compassion] **is great, you did not ·kill** [destroy; [L]make an end of] **them all or ·leave** [abandon; desert; forsake] **them.**
You are a ·kind [gracious] **and ·merciful** [compassionate] **God.**

[32]**"And so, our God, you are the great and ·mighty** [powerful] **and ·wonderful** [awesome] **God.**
You keep your ·agreement [covenant/treaty] **of ·love** [faithful/steadfast/unfailing love; lovingkindness].
Do not let all our ·trouble [hardship] **seem ·unimportant** [inconsequential; [L]small] **·to you** [[L]in your sight].
This trouble has come to us, to our kings and our ·leaders [officials],

to our priests and prophets,
to our ·ancestors [fathers] and all your people
from the days of the kings of Assyria ·until today [to this very day].
33You have been ·fair [just; righteous] in everything that has happened to us;
you have ·been loyal [been faithful; Ldone truth], but we have ·been wicked [acted wickedly/wrongly].
34Our kings, ·leaders [officials], priests, and ·ancestors [fathers] did not obey your ·teachings [laws; instructions; LTorah];
they did not pay attention to the commands and ·warnings [decrees; testimonies] you gave them.
35Even when ·our ancestors [Lthey] were living in their kingdom,
·enjoying [benefiting from] all the good things you ·had given [lavished/bestowed on] them,
·enjoying [benefiting from] the land that was ·fertile and full of room [rich and spacious],
they did not ·stop [serve you and turn from] their evil ·ways [deeds; practices].

36"·Look [TBehold], we are slaves today
in the land you gave our ·ancestors [fathers].
·They were to enjoy [L...to eat] its fruit and its good things,
but ·look [Tbehold], we are slaves here.
37The land's ·great [abundant] ·harvest [produce] belongs to the kings you have ·put [set; placed] over us
because of our sins.
Those kings rule over ·us [Lour bodies] and our cattle as they please,
so we are in ·much trouble [great distress/misery].

The People's Covenant

38"Because of all this, we are making an ·agreement [covenant; treaty] in writing, and our ·leaders [officials], Levites, and priests are putting their seals on it."

10 These are the men who sealed the ·agreement [covenant; treaty]:
Nehemiah the governor, son of Hacaliah.
Zedekiah, 2Seraiah, Azariah, Jeremiah, 3Pashhur, Amariah, Malkijah,
4Hattush, Shebaniah, Malluch, 5Harim, Meremoth, Obadiah, 6Daniel,
Ginnethon, Baruch, 7Meshullam, Abijah, Mijamin, 8Maaziah, Bilgai, and
Shemaiah. These are the priests.
9These are the Levites who sealed it: Jeshua son of Azaniah, Binnui of
the sons of Henadad, Kadmiel, 10and their ·fellow Levites [colleagues;
Lbrothers]: Shebaniah, Hodiah, Kelita, Pelaiah, Hanan, 11Mica, Rehob,
Hashabiah, 12Zaccur, Sherebiah, Shebaniah, 13Hodiah, Bani, and Beninu.
14These are the ·leaders [officials] of the people who sealed the ·agreement [covenant]: Parosh, Pahath-Moab, Elam, Zattu, Bani, 15Bunni,
Azgad, Bebai, 16Adonijah, Bigvai, Adin, 17Ater, Hezekiah, Azzur, 18Hodiah,
Hashum, Bezai, 19Hariph, Anathoth, Nebai, 20Magpiash, Meshullam,
Hezir, 21Meshezabel, Zadok, Jaddua, 22Pelatiah, Hanan, Anaiah, 23Hoshea,
Hananiah, Hasshub, 24Hallohesh, Pilha, Shobek, 25Rehum, Hashabnah,
Maaseiah, 26Ahiah, Hanan, Anan, 27Malluch, Harim, and Baanah.
28The rest of the people ·took an oath [made a vow; swore]. They were
the priests, Levites, gatekeepers, singers, Temple servants, all those who

separated themselves from ·foreigners [Lthe peoples of the lands] to keep
the ·Teachings [Laws; Instructions; LTorah] of God, and also their wives
and their sons and daughters who ·could [were able to; Cwere old enough]
understand. 29 They joined their ·fellow Israelites [kinsmen] and their
·leading men [nobles] in taking an ·oath with a curse [Lcurse and an oath/
vow; Cthe curse followed if they broke the oath]. They ·promised to follow
[Lwere to walk in] the ·Teachings [Laws; Instructions; LTorah] of God,
which they had been given through Moses the servant of God, and to
·obey [keep; observe] all the commands, ·rules [judgments], and ·laws
[statutes; ordinances; requirements] of the LORD our God.
30 They said:

We promise not to ·let [give] our daughters ·marry foreigners
[to the peoples of the land] nor to let our sons ·marry [take] their
daughters. 31 When ·foreigners [Lthe peoples of the land] bring
goods or grain to sell on the Sabbath, we will not buy on the
Sabbath or any holy day. Every seventh year we will not plant,
and that year we will ·forget all that people owe us [cancel every
debt/loan; Ex. 21:2–6; 23:10–11; Deut. 15:1–2].

32 We ·will be responsible for [accept the obligation of] the
commands to pay for the service of the ·Temple [Lhouse] of our
God. We will give ·an eighth of an ounce [Lone third of a shekel]
of silver each year. 33 It is for the ·bread that is set out on the table
[Bread of Presence; Tshowbread; Ex. 25:30; Cbread continually on
a table in the Temple as an offering to God]; the regular grain
[Lgift; tribute] offerings [Lev. 2:1] and burnt offerings [Lev. 1:1–
17]; the offerings on the Sabbaths, New Moon festivals, and
·special feasts [appointed festivals]; the ·holy [sacred] offerings;
the ·sin [or purification] offerings [Lev. 4:3] to make ·Israel right
with God [atonement for Israel]; and for the ·work [duties] of
the ·Temple [Lhouse] of our God.

34 We, the priests, the Levites, and the people, have ·thrown
[cast] lots to decide at what time of year each family must ·bring
[offer; supply] wood to the ·Temple [Lhouse]. The wood is for
burning on the altar of the LORD our God, and we will do this as
it is written in the ·Teachings [Laws; Instructions; LTorah].

35 We also will bring the firstfruits from our ·crops [Lland] and
the firstfruits of every tree to the ·Temple [Lhouse] of the LORD
each year.

36 We will bring to the ·Temple [Lhouse] of our God our firstborn sons and cattle and the firstborn of our herds and flocks, as
it is written in the ·Teachings [Laws; Instructions; LTorah; Ex.
13:1–3]. We will bring them to the priests who ·are serving [min-
ister] in the ·Temple [Lhouse] of our God.

37 We will bring to the priests at the storerooms of the ·Temple
[Lhouse] of our God the first of our ·ground meal [flour; *or*
dough], our ·offerings [contributions], the fruit from all our
trees, and our new wine and oil. And we will bring a ·tenth [tithe]
of our ·crops [Lground] to the Levites, who will collect these
things in all the rural towns where we work. 38 A priest of Aaron's
·family [line] must be with the Levites when they receive the
·tenth of the people's crops [tithe]. The Levites must bring a

·tenth [tithe] of ·all they receive [the tithes] to the ·Temple
[Lhouse] of our God to put in the storerooms of the treasury.
39The people of Israel and the Levites are to bring to the storerooms the ·gifts [contributions; offerings] of grain, new wine,
and oil. That is where the ·utensils [vessels] for the ·Temple
[sanctuary] are kept and where the priests who are ·serving
[ministering], the gatekeepers, and singers stay.
We will not ·ignore [neglect] the ·Temple [Lhouse] of our God.

New People Move into Jerusalem

11 The leaders of Israel ·lived [settled] in Jerusalem. The rest of
the people ·threw [cast] lots to choose one person out of every
ten to come and live in Jerusalem, the holy city. The other nine could
stay in their own cities. 2The people ·blessed [praised; commended]
those who volunteered to live in Jerusalem [Cat this point in the rebuilding, Jerusalem was dangerous and perhaps uncomfortable].
3These are the ·area [provincial] ·leaders [officials] who lived in
Jerusalem. (·Some [Other; Most] people lived on their own ·land [prop-
erty] in the cities of Judah. These included Israelites, priests, Levites,
Temple servants, and ·descendants [sons] of Solomon's servants. 4Others
from the ·families [sons] of Judah and Benjamin lived in Jerusalem.)
These are the ·descendants [sons] of Judah who ·moved into [settled
in] Jerusalem. There was Athaiah son of Uzziah. (Uzziah was the son of
Zechariah, the son of Amariah. Amariah was the son of Shephatiah, the
son of Mahalalel. Mahalalel was a ·descendant [son] of Perez.) 5There was
also Maaseiah son of Baruch. (Baruch was the son of Col-Hozeh, the son
of Hazaiah. Hazaiah was the son of Adaiah, the son of Joiarib. Joiarib was
the son of Zechariah, a ·descendant [son] of Shelah.) 6All the ·descen-
dants [sons] of Perez who ·lived [settled] in Jerusalem totaled 468 men.
They were ·soldiers [capable/outstanding/exceptional men].
7These are ·descendants [sons] of Benjamin who ·moved into [settled
in] Jerusalem. There was Sallu son of Meshullam. (Meshullam was the
son of Joed, the son of Pedaiah. Pedaiah was the son of Kolaiah, the son
of Maaseiah. Maaseiah was the son of Ithiel, the son of Jeshaiah.)
8·Following him [*or* His brothers] were Gabbai and Sallai, for a total of
928 men. 9Joel son of Zicri was ·appointed over them [their chief/supervi-
sor], and Judah son of Hassenuah was second in ·charge [command] of
the ·new area of the city [Lcity].
10These are the priests who moved into Jerusalem. There was Jedaiah
son of Joiarib, Jakin, 11and Seraiah son of Hilkiah, the ·supervisor [leader]
in the ·Temple [Lhouse] of God. (Hilkiah was the son of Meshullam, the
son of Zadok. Zadok was the son of Meraioth, the son of Ahitub.) 12And
there were ·others [colleagues; Lbrothers] with them who ·did [performed]
the work for the ·Temple [Lhouse]. All together there were 822 men. Also
there was Adaiah son of Jeroham. (Jeroham was the son of Pelaliah, the
son of Amzi. Amzi was the son of Zechariah, the son of Pashhur. Pashhur
was the son of Malkijah.) 13And there were family heads with him. All
together there were 242 men. Also there was Amashsai son of Azarel.
(Azarel was the son of Ahzai, the son of Meshillemoth. Meshillemoth was
the son of Immer.) 14And there were ·brave [capable; outstanding; excep-
tional] men with Amashsai. All together there were 128 men. Zabdiel son
of Haggedolim was ·appointed over them [their chief/supervisor].
15These are the Levites who moved into Jerusalem. There was Shemaiah

son of Hasshub. (Hasshub was the son of Azrikam, the son of Hashabiah. Hashabiah was the son of Bunni.) 16And there were Shabbethai and Jozabad, two of the leaders of the Levites who were in charge of the work outside the ·Temple [Lhouse] of God. 17There was Mattaniah son of Mica. (Mica was the son of Zabdi, the son of Asaph.) Mattaniah was the ·director who led the people [leader] in thanksgiving and prayer. There was Bakbukiah, who was second in charge over his ·fellow Levites [colleagues; Lbrothers]. And there was Abda son of Shammua. (Shammua was the son of Galal, the son of Jeduthun.) 18All together 284 Levites lived in the holy city.

19The gatekeepers who moved into Jerusalem were Akkub, Talmon, and others with them. There was a total of 172 men who ·guarded [kept watch at] the city gates.

20The other Israelites, priests, and Levites lived on their own ·land [property] in all the cities of Judah.

21The Temple servants lived on the hill of Ophel, and Ziha and Gishpa ·were in charge of [supervised] them.

22Uzzi son of Bani was ·appointed over [chief officer/supervisor of] the Levites in Jerusalem. (Bani was the son of Hashabiah, the son of Mattaniah. Mattaniah was the son of Mica.) Uzzi was one of Asaph's ·descendants [sons], who were the singers responsible for the service of the ·Temple [Lhouse] of God. 23The singers were under the king's ·orders [commandment], which regulated them day by day.

24Pethahiah son of Meshezabel was the king's ·spokesman [representative; adviser] in all matters concerning the people. (Meshezabel was a descendant of Zerah, the son of Judah.)

25Some of the people of Judah lived in ·villages [settlements] with their surrounding fields. They lived in Kiriath Arba and its ·surroundings [towns], in Dibon and its ·surroundings [towns], in Jekabzeel and its ·surroundings [settlements], 26in Jeshua, Moladah, Beth Pelet, 27Hazar Shual, Beersheba and its ·surroundings [towns], 28in Ziklag and Meconah and its ·surroundings [towns], 29in En Rimmon, Zorah, Jarmuth, 30Zanoah, Adullam and their ·villages [settlements], in Lachish and the fields around it, and in Azekah and its ·surroundings [towns]. So they ·settled [lived; Lcamped] from Beersheba all the way to the Valley of Hinnom.

31The ·descendants [sons] of the Benjaminites from Geba lived in Micmash, Aija, Bethel and its ·surroundings [towns], 32in Anathoth, Nob, Ananiah, 33Hazor, Ramah, Gittaim, 34Hadid, Zeboim, Neballat, 35Lod, Ono, and in the ·Valley of the Craftsmen [Ge-harashim].

36Some groups of the Levites from Judah settled in the land of Benjamin.

Priests and Levites

12 These are the priests and Levites who ·returned [Lwent up] with Zerubbabel son of Shealtiel and with Jeshua [Ezra 1—2]. There were Seraiah, Jeremiah, Ezra, 2Amariah, Malluch, Hattush, 3Shecaniah, Rehum, Meremoth, 4Iddo, Ginnethon, Abijah, 5Mijamin, Moadiah, Bilgah, 6Shemaiah, Joiarib, Jedaiah, 7Sallu, Amok, Hilkiah, and Jedaiah. They were the leaders of the priests and their ·relatives [colleagues; kinsmen; Lbrothers] in the days of Jeshua.

8The Levites were Jeshua, Binnui, Kadmiel, Sherebiah, Judah, and Mattaniah. Mattaniah and his ·relatives [colleagues; kinsmen; Lbrothers] were in charge of the songs of thanksgiving. 9Bakbukiah and Unni, their

·relatives [colleagues; kinsmen; [L]brothers], stood ·across from [opposite; [L]as an antiphonal choir; v. 24] them in the services.

[10]Jeshua was the father of Joiakim. Joiakim was the father of Eliashib. Eliashib was the father of Joiada. [11]Joiada was the father of Jonathan, and Jonathan was the father of Jaddua.

[12]In the days of Joiakim, these priests were the ·leaders [heads] of the families of priests: Meraiah, from Seraiah's family; Hananiah, from Jeremiah's family; [13]Meshullam, from Ezra's family; Jehohanan, from Amariah's family; [14]Jonathan, from Malluch's family; Joseph, from Shecaniah's family; [15]Adna, from Harim's family; Helkai, from Meremoth's family; [16]Zechariah, from Iddo's family; Meshullam, from Ginnethon's family; [17]Zicri, from Abijah's family; Piltai, from Miniamin's and Moadiah's families; [18]Shammua, from Bilgah's family; Jehonathan, from Shemaiah's family; [19]Mattenai, from Joiarib's family; Uzzi, from Jedaiah's family; [20]Kallai, from Sallu's family; Eber, from Amok's family; [21]Hashabiah, from Hilkiah's family; and Nethanel, from Jedaiah's family.

[22]The ·leaders [heads] of the families of the Levites and the priests were written down in the days of Eliashib, Joiada, Johanan, and Jaddua, while Darius the Persian was king. [23]The family ·leaders [heads] among the Levites were written down in the ·history book [Book/Scroll of the Chronicles/Annals/History] up to the time of Johanan son of Eliashib. [24]The ·leaders [heads] of the Levites were Hashabiah, Sherebiah, Jeshua son of Kadmiel, and their ·relatives [colleagues; kinsmen; [L]brothers]. Their ·relatives [colleagues; kinsmen; [L]brothers] stood ·across from [opposite] them and ·gave [offered] praise and thanksgiving. One group ·answered the [responded to the; [C]antiphonally] other group, as David, the man of God, had ·commanded [prescribed].

[25]These were the gatekeepers who ·guarded [kept watch at] the storerooms next to the gates: Mattaniah, Bakbukiah, Obadiah, Meshullam, Talmon, and Akkub. [26]They served in the days of Joiakim son of Jeshua, the son of Jozadak. They also served in the days of Nehemiah the governor and Ezra the priest and ·teacher [scribe].

The Wall of Jerusalem

[27]When the wall of Jerusalem was ·offered as a gift to God [[L]dedicated], they asked the Levites to come from wherever they lived to Jerusalem to celebrate with joy the ·gift of the wall [[L]dedication]. They were to celebrate with ·songs [hymns] of thanksgiving and with the music of cymbals, harps, and lyres. [28]They also brought together ·singers [[L]sons of singers] from all around Jerusalem, from the Netophathite ·villages [settlements], [29]from Beth Gilgal, and from the areas of Geba and Azmaveth. The singers had built ·villages [settlements] for themselves around Jerusalem. [30]The priests and Levites made themselves pure, and they also made the people, the gates, and the wall of Jerusalem pure.

[31]I had the leaders of Judah go up on top of the wall, and I appointed two large ·choruses [choirs] to give thanks. One ·chorus [choir] went to the right on top of the wall, toward the ·Trash [Garbage; Refuse; [T]Dung] Gate. [32]Behind them went Hoshaiah and half the leaders of Judah. [33]Azariah, Ezra, Meshullam, [34]Judah, Benjamin, Shemaiah, and Jeremiah also went. [35]Some ·priests [[L]sons of priests] with trumpets also went, along with Zechariah son of Jonathan. (Jonathan was the son of Shemaiah, the son of Mattaniah. Mattaniah was the son of Micaiah, the son of Zaccur. Zaccur was the son of Asaph.) [36]Zechariah's

·relatives [colleagues; kinsmen; Lbrothers] also went. They were
Shemaiah, Azarel, Milalai, Gilalai, Maai, Nethanel, Judah, and Hanani.
These men played the musical instruments of David, the man of God,
and Ezra the ·teacher [scribe] ·walked in front of [led] them. 37They
went from the Fountain Gate straight up the steps ·to the highest part
of the wall by the older part of the city [Lof the City of David]. They
·went on [passed] above the ·house [palace] of David to the Water Gate
on the east.
38The second ·chorus [choir] ·went to the left [proceeded in the opposite direction], while I followed them on top of the wall with half the
people. We went from the Tower of the ·Ovens [Furnaces; Firepots] to the
Broad Wall, 39·over [above] the Gate of Ephraim to the ·Old [LJeshanah]
Gate and the Fish Gate, to the Tower of Hananel and the Tower of the
Hundred. We went as far as the Sheep Gate and ·stopped [Lstood] at the
Gate of the Guard.
40The two ·choruses [choirs] ·took their places [Lstood] at the ·Temple
[Lhouse] of God. Half of the ·leaders [officials] and I did also. 41These
priests were there with their trumpets: Eliakim, Maaseiah, Miniamin,
Micaiah, Elioenai, Zechariah, and Hananiah. 42These people were also
there: Maaseiah, Shemaiah, Eleazar, Uzzi, Jehohanan, Malkijah, Elam,
and Ezer. The ·choruses [choirs] sang loudly, ·led [directed] by Jezrahiah.
43The people offered ·many [great] sacrifices that day and ·were happy
[rejoiced] because God had given them great joy. The women and children ·were happy [rejoiced]. The ·sound of happiness in [joy of; rejoicing
in] Jerusalem could be heard far away.
44At that time men were appointed to be in charge of the storerooms.
These rooms were for the ·gifts [contributions; offerings], the firstfruits
[Cof the harvest], and the ·ten percent that the people brought [tithes].
The ·Teachings [Laws; Instructions; LTorah] said they should bring a
share for the priests and Levites from the fields around the towns. The
people of Judah were ·happy [delighted] to do this for the priests and
Levites who ·served [Lstood]. 45They performed the service of their God
·in making things pure [*or* and the service of purification]. The singers
and gatekeepers also did their jobs, as David had commanded [*or* and]
his son Solomon. 46·Earlier [Long ago], in the ·time [days] of David and
Asaph, there was a ·leader [head; director] of the singers and of the songs
of praise and [Lhymns of] thanksgiving to God. 47So it was in the days of
Zerubbabel and Nehemiah. All the people of Israel gave ·something [the
daily portions] to the singers and gatekeepers, and they also ·set aside
[dedicated] part for the Levites. Then the Levites ·set aside [dedicated]
part for the ·descendants [sons] of Aaron.

Foreign People Are Sent Away

13 On that day they read aloud the ·Book [scroll] of Moses ·to
[Lin the ears/hearing of] the people, and they found that it
said no Ammonite or Moabite should ever ·be allowed in the meeting to
worship [enter the assembly of God; Deut. 23:3–6; CTobiah's ancestry, v.
4, was Ammonite; 2:10]. 2The Ammonites and Moabites had not ·wel-
comed [Lmet] the Israelites with ·food [Lbread] and water. Instead, they
had hired Balaam to put a curse on Israel [Num. 22–24]. (But our God
turned the curse into a blessing.) 3When the people heard this ·teaching
[law; instruction; LTorah], they ·separated [excluded; removed] all foreigners [Cincluding people of mixed ancestry] from Israel.

Nehemiah Returns to Jerusalem

4Before that happened, Eliashib the priest, who was ·in charge of
[appointed over] the ·Temple [Lhouse] storerooms, was ·friendly with [*or*
a relative of] Tobiah. 5Eliashib let Tobiah use one of the large storerooms.
Earlier it had been used for ·grain [Lgift; tribute] offerings [Lev. 2:3],
incense, the ·utensils [vessels], and the ·tenth offerings [tithes] of grain,
new wine, and olive oil ·that belonged to [commanded/prescribed for]
the Levites, singers, and gatekeepers. It had also been used for ·gifts [con-
tributions; offerings] for the priests.
6I was not in Jerusalem ·when this happened [at that time]. I had gone
back to Artaxerxes king of Babylon in the thirty-second year he was king
[C433 BC]. ·Finally [Later; After some time] I asked the king to let me
leave. 7When I returned to Jerusalem, I found out the evil Eliashib had
done by letting Tobiah have a room in the ·Temple [Lhouse] courtyard. 8I
was very ·upset [displeased; angry] at this, so I threw all of Tobiah's ·goods
[belongings; possessions] out of the room. 9I ordered the rooms to be
·purified [cleansed; Critually], and I brought back the ·utensils [vessels]
for God's ·Temple [Lhouse], the ·grain [Lgift; tribute] offerings [Lev. 2:3],
and the incense.
10Then I found out the people were not giving the Levites their ·shares
[portions]. So the Levites and singers who served had gone back to their
·own farms [fields]. 11I ·argued with [reprimanded; confronted] the officers, saying, "Why ·haven't you taken care of [have you neglected/
abandoned/forsaken] the ·Temple [Lhouse] of God?" Then I ·gathered
[assembled] the Levites and singers and ·put them back at [restored them
to] their ·places [posts; stations].
12All the people of Judah then brought to the storerooms a ·tenth
[tithe] of their ·crops [grain], new wine, and olive oil. 13I ·put [appointed]
these men ·in charge of [over] the storerooms: Shelemiah the priest,
Zadok the ·teacher [scribe], and Pedaiah a Levite. I made Hanan son of
Zaccur, the son of Mattaniah, their helper. Everyone knew they were
·honest [reliable; trustworthy]. ·They gave out the portions that went
[Their job/responsibility was to distribute] to their ·relatives [colleagues;
kinsmen; Lbrothers].
14Remember me, my God, for this. Do not ·ignore [forget; wipe/blot
out] my ·love [loyal/faithful deeds] for the ·Temple [Lhouse] of my God
and its services.
15In those days I saw people in Judah ·working in the [Ltreading] winepresses on the Sabbath day. They were bringing in grain and loading it on
donkeys. And they were bringing loads of wine, grapes, and figs and other
things into Jerusalem on the Sabbath day. So I ·warned [admonished;
rebuked] them about selling food on that day. 16People from the city of
Tyre who were living in Jerusalem ·brought in [imported] fish and other
·things [merchandise] and sold them there on the Sabbath day to the
people of Judah—in Jerusalem itself! 17I ·argued with [reprimanded; con-
fronted] the ·important men [nobles] of Judah and said to them, "What
is this evil thing you are doing? You are ·ruining [desecrating; profaning]
the Sabbath day [Ex. 20:8–11; 31:12–17; Deut. 5:8–10]. 18·This is [LIsn't
this...?] just what your ·ancestors [fathers] did. So our God ·did terrible
things to us and [brought on us all this trouble/calamity and on] this city.
Now you are ·making him even more angry at [bringing even more wrath
on] Israel by ·ruining [desecrating; profaning] the Sabbath day."
19So I ordered that the ·doors [Lgates of Jerusalem] be shut at ·sunset

[Ldark] before the Sabbath and not be opened until the Sabbath was over. I ·put [Lstood] my servants at the gates so no load could come in on the Sabbath. 20Once or twice traders and ·sellers [merchants] of all kinds of ·goods [merchandise] spent the night outside Jerusalem. 21So I ·warned [admonished; rebuked] them, "Why are you spending the night ·by [in front of] the wall? If you do it again, I will ·force you away [arrest/forcibly remove you; Lsend a hand on you]." After that, they did not come back on the Sabbath. 22Then I ordered the Levites to purify themselves and to guard the city gates to make sure the Sabbath remained holy.

Remember me, my God, for this. Have ·mercy [compassion] on me because of your ·great [great and steadfast/unfailing] love.

23In those days I saw men of Judah who had married women from Ashdod, Ammon, and Moab. 24Half their children were speaking the language of Ashdod or some other place, and they couldn't speak the language of Judah. 25I ·argued with [reprimanded; confronted] those people, put curses on them, ·hit [beat] some of them, and pulled out their hair. I ·forced them to make a promise [made them vow/swear/take an oath] to God, saying, "Do not ·let your daughters marry the sons of foreigners [give your daughters to their sons], and do not take ·the daughters of foreigners as wives [their daughters] for your sons or yourselves. 26·Foreign women [LWas it not things like this that…?] made King Solomon of Israel sin. There was never a king like him in any of the nations. God loved Solomon and made him king over all Israel, but foreign ·women [wives] made even him sin [1 Kin. 11:1–13]. 27And now ·you are not obedient when [Lmust we hear how…?] you do this evil thing. You are unfaithful to our God when you ·marry [Lgive a dwelling to] foreign ·wives [women]."

28Joiada was the son of Eliashib the high priest. One of Joiada's sons married a daughter of Sanballat the Horonite, so I ·sent [drove; banished] him away from ·me [my sight].

29Remember them, my God, because they ·made the priesthood unclean [defiled the priesthood] and the ·agreement [covenant; treaty] of the priests and Levites.

30So I ·purified [purged; cleansed] them of everything that was foreign. I ·appointed [assigned] duties for the priests and Levites, giving each man his own ·job [tasks; work; duties]. 31I also ·made sure wood was brought for the altar [provided for the wood offering] at ·regular [designated; proper] times and that the firstfruits [Cof the harvest] were brought.

Remember me, my God; ·be kind to me [for good; with favor].

ESTHER

Queen Vashti Disobeys the King

1 This is what happened during the ·time [days] of ·King Xerxes
[LAhasuerus; Cthe Persian king who reigned about 486–465
BC], the ·king [LAhasuerus] who ruled the one hundred twenty-seven
·states [provinces] from India to Cush [Cin present-day Sudan and
Ethiopia]. 2 In those days King ·Xerxes [LAhasuerus] ·ruled from his
[Lsat on his royal throne in the] ·capital city [*or* fortress; citadel; Cthe
winter residence of Persian kings, separate from the city] of Susa. 3 In
the third year of his ·rule [reign; Cabout 483 BC], he gave a banquet for
all his ·important men [nobles] and ·royal officers [ministers; officials].
The ·army [military] leaders from Persia and Media and the ·important
men [nobles] from all ·Xerxes' empire [Lhis provinces] were there.
4 The ·banquet [celebration] lasted one hundred eighty days. All during
that time King ·Xerxes [LAhasuerus] ·was showing off [displayed] the
·great wealth of his kingdom [riches of his royal glory] and ·his own great
riches and glory [splendor of his great majesty]. 5 When the one hundred
eighty days were ·over [completed], the king gave another banquet [Cthese
celebrations may have been in preparation for the Persian invasion of
Greece in 480 BC]. It was held in the courtyard of the palace garden for
seven days, and it was for everybody in the ·palace [citadel; fortress] at
Susa, from the greatest to the least. 6 The courtyard had fine white ·cur-
tains [linen hangings] and ·purple [blue; violet] drapes that were tied to
silver rings on marble pillars by white and purple cords. And there were
gold and silver couches on a floor set with ·tiles [mosaics] of ·white [por-
phyry] ·marble [alabaster], ·shells [mother-of-pearl], and ·gems [precious
stones]. 7 ·Wine [Drinks] was served in gold ·cups [goblets] of various
kinds. And there was ·plenty [an abundance] of the king's wine, ·because
he was very generous [in keeping with his generosity/liberality]. 8 ·The
king commanded that the guests be permitted to drink as much as they
wished [LThe drinking was according to law/edict without compulsion].
He told the ·wine servers [staff] to serve each man what he wanted.
9 Queen Vashti also gave a banquet for the women in the royal ·palace
[Lhouse] of King ·Xerxes [LAhasuerus].
10 On the seventh day of the banquet, King ·Xerxes [LAhasuerus] was
·very happy [in high spirits], because of the wine. He gave a command to
the seven eunuchs who served him—Mehuman, Biztha, Harbona, Bigtha,
Abagtha, Zethar, and Carcas. 11 He commanded them to bring him Queen
Vashti, wearing her royal crown. She was to come to ·show [display] her
beauty to the people and ·important men [nobles] because she was very
beautiful. 12 The eunuchs told Queen Vashti about the king's ·command
[Lword], but she refused to come [Cpossibly because she felt it would be
humiliating; a dangerous decision]. Then the king became very angry; his

anger ·was like a burning fire [Lburned in him; Cbecause it undermined
his authority].
13It was customary for the king to ·ask advice from [confer with]
·experts [wise men] about law and ·order [justice; custom; Ljudgment]. So
King ·Xerxes [LAhasuerus] spoke with ·the wise men who would know the
right thing to do [Lthose who understood the times]. 14The wise men ·the
king usually talked to [closest to the king] were Carshena, Shethar,
Admatha, Tarshish, Meres, Marsena, and Memucan, seven of the ·impor-
tant men [nobles] of Persia and Media. These seven had ·special privileges
to see [access to] the king and had the highest ·rank [offices] in the kingdom. 15The king asked them, "What does the law say must be done to
Queen Vashti? She has not obeyed the command of King ·Xerxes
[LAhasuerus], which the eunuchs took to her."
16Then Memucan said to the king and the other ·important men
[nobles], "Queen Vashti has not done wrong to the king alone. She has
also done wrong to all the ·important men [nobles] and all the people in
all the ·empire [Lprovinces] of King ·Xerxes [LAhasuerus]. 17All the wives
of the ·important men [nobles] of Persia and Media will hear about the
queen's ·actions [conduct]. Then they will ·no longer honor [be contemp-
tuous of; despise] their husbands. They will say, 'King ·Xerxes [LAhasuerus]
commanded Queen Vashti to be brought to him, but she refused to come.'
18Today the ·wives [noble ladies] of the ·important men [nobles] of Persia
and Media have heard about the queen's actions. So they will speak in the
same way to ·their husbands [the king's nobles], and there will be no end
to ·disrespect [contempt] and anger.
19"So, our king, if it pleases you, give a royal ·order [edict; decree], and
let it be written in the laws of Persia and Media, which cannot be ·changed
[repealed; revoked; 8:8; Dan. 6:8, 12, 15]. The law should say Vashti [Cat
this point, the title "queen" is symbolically dropped from before her name]
is never again to enter the presence of King ·Xerxes [LAhasuerus]. Also let
the king give her place as queen to someone who is ·better [more worthy/
deserving] than she is. 20And let the king's ·order [edict; decree] be
·announced [spread] everywhere in his ·enormous [great] kingdom.
Then all the women will ·respect [honor] their husbands, from the greatest to the least."
21The king and his ·important men [nobles] were ·happy [pleased]
with this advice, so King ·Xerxes [LAhasuerus] did as Memucan ·sug-
gested [advised; proposed]. 22He sent ·letters [dispatches; scrolls] to all the
·states [provinces] of the kingdom in the ·writing [script] of each ·state
[province] and in the language of each group of people. These ·letters
[dispatches; scrolls] announced that each man was to be the ·ruler [mas-
ter] ·of [over] his own family.

Esther Is Made Queen

2 Later, when King ·Xerxes [LAhasuerus] was not so angry, he
remembered Vashti and what she had done and his ·order [decree;
edict] about her. 2Then the king's personal ·servants [attendants] suggested, "Let a search be made for ·beautiful young girls [Lyoung women,
virgins, good of form] for the king. 3Let the king choose ·supervisors
[commissioners] in every ·state [province] of his kingdom to bring ·beau-
tiful young girls [Lyoung women, virgins, good of form] to the ·palace
[citadel; fortress; 1:2] at Susa. They should be taken to the ·women's quarters [harem; Lhouse of the women] and put under the ·care [custody;

authority] of Hegai, the king's eunuch in charge of the ·women [harem]. And let ·beauty treatments [cosmetics; Lointments] be given to them. 4Then let the ·girl [young woman] who ·most pleases [Lis good in the eyes of] the king become queen in place of Vashti." The king ·liked [was pleased/delighted by] this idea, so he did as they said.

5Now there was a Jew in the ·palace [citadel; fortress; 1:2] of Susa whose name was Mordecai son of Jair. Jair was the son of Shimei, the son of Kish [Cthese are relatives of Saul, showing that Mordecai was his descendant; 1 Sam. 9:1–3; 2 Sam. 16:5]. Mordecai was from the tribe of Benjamin, 6which had been taken ·captive [into exile] from Jerusalem by Nebuchadnezzar king of Babylon. They were part of the group taken into ·captivity [exile] with Jehoiachin king of Judah [C597 BC; 2 Kin. 24:8–17]. 7Mordecai had a cousin named Hadassah, who had no father or mother, so Mordecai ·took care of her [was her guardian; brought her up]. Hadassah was also called Esther, and she ·had a very pretty figure and face [Lwas beautiful of form]. Mordecai had ·adopted [raised; taken] her as his own daughter when her father and mother died.

8When the king's command and ·order [decree; edict] had been ·heard [proclaimed], many ·girls [young women] had been brought to the ·palace [citadel; fortress; 1:2] in Susa and put under the ·care [custody; authority] of Hegai. Esther was also taken to the king's ·palace [Lhouse] and put under the ·care [custody; authority] of Hegai, who was in charge of the women. 9Esther ·pleased [impressed; Lwas good in his eyes] Hegai, and ·he liked her [Lfound favor with him]. So Hegai quickly began giving Esther her ·beauty treatments [cosmetics; Lointments] and special food. He gave her seven ·servant girls [maids; attendants] chosen from the king's ·palace [Lhouse]. Then he ·moved [transferred] her and her ·seven servant girls [maids; attendants] to the best part of the ·women's quarters [harem; Lhouse of the women].

10Esther did not tell anyone about her ·family [people; nationality] or ·who her people were [her kindred/lineage], because Mordecai had ·told [instructed] her not to. 11Every day Mordecai walked back and forth ·near [in front of] the courtyard ·where the king's women lived [of the harem] to find out how Esther was and what was happening to her.

12Before a girl could take her turn ·with [to go to] King ·Xerxes [LAhasuerus], she had to complete twelve months of beauty treatments ·that were ordered [prescribed; required] for the women. For six months she was treated with oil ·and [*or* of] myrrh and for six months with ·perfumes [spices] and ·cosmetics [ointments]. 13Then she ·was ready to go [would go in this way] to the king. Anything she ·asked for [desired] was given to her to take with her from the ·women's quarters [harem; Lhouse of the women] to the king's ·palace [Lhouse]. 14In the evening she would go to the king's ·palace [Lhouse], and in the morning she would return ·to another part of the [*or* to a second; *or* again to the] ·women's quarters [harem; Lhouse of the women]. There she would be placed under the ·care [custody; authority] of Shaashgaz, the king's eunuch in charge of the ·slave women [concubines; Csecondary wives]. The girl would not go back to the king again unless he was pleased with her and ·asked for [summoned; requested] her by name.

15The ·time [Lturn] came for Esther daughter of Abihail, Mordecai's uncle [CEsther was Mordecai's younger cousin, v. 7], who had been raised [taken] by Mordecai as his own daughter, to go to the king. She asked for

only what Hegai ·suggested [advised; recommended] she should take.
(Hegai was the king's eunuch who ·was in charge of [supervised] the
women.) Everyone who saw Esther ·liked [favored] her. 16So Esther was
taken to King ·Xerxes [LAhasuerus] in the royal ·palace [Lhouse] in the
tenth month [Cearly winter], the month of Tebeth, during ·Xerxes'
[LAhasuerus's] seventh year ·as king [of his reign].
17And the king ·was pleased with [loved] Esther more than with any of
the other ·virgins [young women]. He liked her more than any of the
·others [other virgins], so he put a royal crown on her head and ·made
[proclaimed; declared] her queen in place of Vashti. 18Then the king gave
a great banquet for Esther and invited all his ·important men [nobles;
officials] and ·royal officers [ministers; servants]. He announced a holiday
for all the ·empire [Lprovinces] and ·had the government give away gifts
[gave gifts with royal liberality/generosity].

Mordecai Discovers an Evil Plan

19Now Mordecai was sitting at the king's gate [Can indication he was
likely a government official] when the girls were ·gathered the second time
[*or* transferred to the second harem; *or* gathered again]. 20Esther still had
not told anyone about ·who her people were [her kindred/lineage] or
her ·family [people; nationality], just as Mordecai had ·commanded
[instructed] her. She ·obeyed Mordecai [followed Mordecai's instructions]
just as she had done when ·she was under his care [he was raising her].
21Now Bigthana and Teresh were two of the king's eunuchs who guarded
the ·doorway [entrance; Lthreshold]. While Mordecai was sitting at the
king's gate, they became angry and ·began to make plans [plotted; con-
spired] to ·kill [assassinate; Lsend a hand against] King ·Xerxes [LAhasuerus].
22But Mordecai found out about their ·plans [plot] and told Queen Esther.
Then Esther told the king ·how Mordecai had discovered the evil plan [Lin
Mordecai's name]. 23When the report was investigated, it was found to be
·true [so], and ·the two officers who had planned to kill the king [Lthey
both] were ·hanged [impaled; Con a stake or sharpened pole, a common
form of execution]. All this was written down in the ·daily court record
[book of the annals/chronicles] in the king's presence.

Haman Plans to Destroy the Jews

3 After these ·things happened [events], King ·Xerxes [LAhasuerus]
·honored [promoted; Lmade great] Haman son of Hammedatha
the Agagite [Ca descendant of King Agag of the Amalekites, the hated enemies of Israel (which Saul failed to eradicate; 1 Sam. 15); Ex. 17:8–15;
Deut. 23:3–6]. He ·gave him a new rank that was [exalted/elevated him]
·higher than [above] all the ·important men [nobles; officials]. 2All the
·royal officers [king's ministers; officials] at the king's gate would bow
down and ·kneel before [pay homage to] Haman, as the king had ·ordered
[commanded]. But Mordecai would not bow down or ·show him honor
[pay him homage; Cbecause he was a hated Amalekite].
3Then the ·royal officers [ministers; officials] at the king's gate asked
Mordecai, "Why don't you obey the king's command?" 4And they said
this to him every day. When he did not listen to them, they told Haman.
They wanted to see if Haman would ·accept [tolerate; Llet stand]
Mordecai's behavior because Mordecai had told them he was a Jew.
5When Haman saw that Mordecai would not bow down to him or ·honor
[pay homage to] him, he became ·very angry [enraged]. 6He ·thought of
himself as too important [disdained; thought it beneath him] to ·try to kill
[lay hands on] only Mordecai. He had been told who the people of Mordecai

were, so he looked for a way to destroy all of Mordecai's people, the Jews, in
all of ·Xerxes' [LAhasuerus's] ·kingdom [empire].
7It was in the first month [CApril] of the twelfth year [Cabout 474 BC;
approximately a year later] of King ·Xerxes' [LAhasuerus's] ·rule [reign]—
the month of Nisan. Pur (that is, the lot [Cdice-like objects]) was thrown
before Haman to choose a day and a month. ·So [...and; ...until] the
twelfth month, the month of Adar, was chosen.
8Then Haman said to King ·Xerxes [LAhasuerus], "There is ·a certain
group of [Lone] people ·scattered [dispersed and spread] among the
·other people [nations; Lpeoples] in all the ·states [provinces] of your
·kingdom [empire]. Their ·customs [laws] are different from those of all
the other ·people [nations; Lpeoples], and they do not ·obey [observe;
keep] the king's laws. It is not ·right for you [in the king's interest] to allow
them to ·continue living in your kingdom [remain; Lcause them to rest].
9If it ·pleases [Lis good to] the king, let ·an order be given [it be decreed]
to destroy those people. Then I will pay ·seven hundred fifty thousand
pounds [Lten thousand talents] of silver to ·those who do the king's [the
officials who carry out this] business, and they will put it into the royal
treasury."
10So the king took his signet ring off his hand and gave it to Haman son
of Hammedatha, the Agagite, the ·enemy [persecutor; oppressor] of the
Jews. 11Then the king said to Haman, "The ·money [Lsilver] and the people are yours [Cperhaps telling Haman to keep his money, or that he could
have the Jews' money, or that he could spend his money this way if he
wished; see 4:7]. Do with them as ·you please [Lis good in your eyes]."
12On the thirteenth day of the first month [CApril 17], the royal ·secre-
taries [scribes] were called, and they wrote out all of Haman's ·orders
[commands]. They wrote to the king's governors and to the ·captains of
the soldiers [high officials] in each ·state [province] and to the ·important
men [nobles] of each ·group of people [nation]. The ·orders [edicts;
decrees] were written in the ·writing [script] of each ·state [province] and
in the language of each people. They were written in the name of King
·Xerxes [LAhasuerus] and sealed with his signet ring. 13·Letters [Dispatches;
Scrolls] were sent by ·messengers [couriers] to all the king's ·empire
[Lprovinces] ordering them to destroy, kill, and ·completely wipe out
[annihilate] all the Jews, young and old, including women and little children. It was to happen on a single day—the thirteenth day of the twelfth
month [CMarch 7, about twelve months later], which was Adar. And they
could ·take [plunder; confiscate] ·everything the Jewish people owned
[Ltheir possessions]. 14A copy of the ·order [edict; decree] was given out as
a law in every ·state [province] so all the ·people [nations; Lpeoples] would
be ready for that day.
15The ·messengers [couriers] set out, ·hurried [spurred on; impelled]
by the king's command, as soon as the ·order [edict; decree] was given in
the ·palace [citadel; fortress] at Susa. The king and Haman sat down to
drink, but the city of Susa was ·in confusion [bewildered; in an uproar].

Mordecai Asks Esther to Help

4 When Mordecai ·heard [learned] about all that had been done, he
tore his clothes, put on ·rough cloth [burlap; sackcloth] and ashes
[Csigns of grief or repentance], and went out into the city ·crying [wail-
ing] loudly and ·painfully [bitterly]. 2But Mordecai went only as far as the
king's gate, because no one was allowed to enter that gate dressed in

·rough cloth [burlap; sackcloth]. 3As the king's ·order [edict; decree]
reached every area, there was great ·sadness and loud crying [mourning]
among the Jews. They fasted and ·cried out loud [wept and wailed], and
many of them lay down on ·rough cloth [burlap; sackcloth] and ashes
[Csigns of grief or repentance].
4When Esther's ·servant girls [maids; attendants] and eunuchs came to
her and told her about Mordecai, she was ·very upset and afraid [deeply
distressed; overcome with anguish]. She sent clothes for Mordecai to put
on instead of the ·rough cloth [burlap; sackcloth], but he would not ·wear
[accept] them. 5Then Esther called for Hathach, one of the king's eunuchs
chosen by the king to serve her. Esther ordered him to find out what was
bothering Mordecai and why.
6So Hathach went to Mordecai, who was in the city square in front of the
king's gate. 7Mordecai told Hathach everything that had happened to him,
and he told Hathach about the exact amount of money Haman had promised to pay into the king's treasury for the ·killing [destruction] of the Jews.
8Mordecai also gave him a copy of the ·order [edict; decree] to ·kill [destroy]
the Jews, which had been ·given [issued] in Susa. He wanted Hathach to
show it to Esther and to ·tell her about [explain] it. And Mordecai told him
to ·order [direct; instruct] Esther to go into the king's presence to beg for
mercy and to ·plead with [petition] him for her people.
9Hathach went back and reported to Esther everything Mordecai had
·said [instructed]. 10Then Esther told Hathach to tell Mordecai, 11"All the
·royal officers [ministers; officials] and people of the ·royal [king's] ·states
[provinces] know that no man or woman may ·go [come] to the king in
the inner courtyard ·without being called [uninvited]. ·There is [He has]
only one law about this: Anyone who enters must be put to death unless
the king holds out his gold scepter. Then that person may live. And I have
not been ·called [summoned; invited] to go to the king for thirty days."
12Esther's ·message [Lwords] was given to Mordecai. 13Then Mordecai
sent back ·word [this answer/reply] to Esther: "Just because you ·live in
[are part of] the king's ·palace [Lhouse], don't ·think [imagine] that out of
all the Jews you alone will escape. 14If you keep ·quiet [silent] at this time,
·someone else will help and save the Jews [liberation/relief and protec-
tion/deliverance for the Jews will arise/appear from another place], but
you and your ·father's family [relatives] will all die. And who knows, you
may have ·been chosen queen [come to your royal position; Lcome to the
kingdom] for just such a time as this."
15Then Esther sent this answer to Mordecai: 16"Go and ·get [assemble]
all the Jews in Susa together. ·For my sake [On my behalf], fast; do not eat
or drink for three days, night ·and [or] day. I and my ·servant girls [maids;
attendants] will also fast. Then I will go to the king, even though it is
against the law, and if I die, I die."
17So Mordecai went away and did everything Esther had ·told [com-
manded; instructed] him to do.

Esther Speaks to the King

5 On the third day Esther put on her royal robes and stood in the
inner courtyard of the king's ·palace [Lhouse], ·facing [in front of;
across from] the king's ·hall [quarters; Lhouse]. The king was sitting on his
royal throne in the hall, ·facing the doorway [across from the entrance].
2When the king saw Queen Esther standing in the courtyard, ·he was
pleased [Lshe obtained grace in his eyes]. He ·held out [extended] to her

the gold scepter that was in his hand, so Esther ·went forward [approached;
came near] and touched the ·end [tip] of it.
3The king asked, "What is it, Queen Esther? What ·do you want to ask
me [is your request]? I will give you as much as half of my kingdom."
4Esther answered, "My king, if it pleases ·you [Lthe king], come today
with Haman to a banquet that I have prepared for ·you [Lhim]."
5Then the king said, "·Bring [Find] Haman quickly so we may do what
Esther ·asks [desires]."
So the king and Haman went to the banquet Esther had prepared. 6As
they were drinking wine, the king said to Esther, "Now, what ·are you asking for [is your petition]? I will ·give it to you [grant it]. What is ·it you
want [your request]? ·I will give you [Ask for] as much as half of my kingdom and it shall be done."
7Esther answered, "This is ·what I want [my request] and ·what I ask for
[my petition]. 8My king, if ·you are pleased with me [LI have found favor in
the king's sight] and if it ·pleases [seems good to] you, ·give me what I ask
for [grant my petition] and do what I ·want [request]. Come with Haman
tomorrow to the banquet I will prepare for you. Then I will ·answer your
question about what I want [do as the king says/wishes]."

Haman's Plans Against Mordecai

9Haman left the king's ·palace [Lhouse] that day happy and ·content
[Lgood of heart]. But when he saw Mordecai at the king's gate and saw
that Mordecai did not ·stand up [rise] or tremble ·with fear before him
[in his presence], Haman ·became very angry with [was filled with rage
against] Mordecai. 10But he ·controlled his anger [restrained himself] and
went home.
Then Haman called together his friends and his wife, Zeresh. 11He ·told
[boasted/recounted to] them ·how wealthy he was [Lof the glory of his
riches] and how many sons he had [Cten; 9:10]. He also told them all the
ways the king had ·honored [Lmagnified] him and how the king had
·placed him higher than [exalted him over] his ·important men [nobles]
and his ·royal officers [ministers; officials]. 12He also said, "I'm the only
person Queen Esther ·invited [Lcaused] to come with the king to the banquet she gave. And tomorrow also the queen has asked me to be her guest
with the king. 13But all this does not ·really make me happy [satisfy me]
·when [as long as] I see that Jew Mordecai sitting at the king's gate."
14Then Haman's wife, Zeresh, and all his friends said, "Have a ·seventy-
five-foot [Lfifty cubits] ·platform [gallows; pole] built, and in the morning
ask the king to have Mordecai ·hanged [impaled] on it. Then go to the
banquet with the king and be ·happy [content; joyful]." Haman ·liked [was
pleased/delighted by] this suggestion, so he ordered the ·platform [gal-
lows; pole] to be built.

Mordecai Is Honored

6 That same night the ·king could not sleep [Lking's sleep fled]. So
he gave an order for the ·daily court record [book of history/
remembrances, the annals/chronicles] to be brought in and read to him.
2It was found recorded that Mordecai had warned the king about Bigthana
and Teresh, two of the king's ·officers [eunuchs] who guarded the doorway and who had ·planned [plotted] to ·kill [assassinate] the king.
3The king asked, "What honor and ·reward [recognition; distinction;
Lgreatness] have been given to Mordecai for this?"
The king's ·personal servants [attendants] answered, "Nothing has
been done for Mordecai."

4The king said, "Who is in the courtyard?" Now Haman had just entered the outer court of the king's ·palace [Lhouse]. He had come to ask the king about ·hanging [impaling] Mordecai on the ·platform [pole] he had prepared.

5The king's ·personal servants [attendants] said, "Haman is standing in the courtyard."

The king said, "Bring him in."

6So Haman came in. And the king asked him, "What should be done for a man whom the king ·wants very much [delights] to honor?"

And Haman thought to himself, "Whom would the king want to honor more than me?" 7So he answered the king, "Do this for the man you ·want very much [delight] to honor. 8Have them bring a royal robe that the king himself has worn. And also bring a horse with a royal ·crown [crest; emblem; insignia] on its head, a horse that the king himself has ridden. 9Let the robe and the horse be given to one of the king's most ·important [noble] ·men [officials]. Let ·them [*or* him] ·put the robe on [clothe; array; robe] the man the king ·wants [delights] to honor, and let ·them [*or* him] lead him on the horse through the city ·streets [square]. Let ·them [*or* him] announce: 'This is what is done for the man whom the king ·wants [delights] to honor!' "

10The king commanded Haman, "Go quickly. Take the robe and the horse just as you have said, and do all this for Mordecai the Jew who sits at the king's gate. Do not ·leave out [neglect; Llet fall] anything you have ·suggested [recommended]."

11So Haman took the robe and the horse, and he ·put the robe on [clothed; arrayed; robed] Mordecai. Then he led him on horseback through the city ·streets [square], announcing before Mordecai: "This is what is done for the man whom the king ·wants [delights] to honor!"

12Then Mordecai returned to the king's gate, but Haman hurried home with his head covered in ·mourning [humiliation]. 13He told his wife, Zeresh, and all his friends everything that had happened to him.

Haman's wife and ·advisers [wise friends] said, "You are ·starting to lose power to [Lbeginning to fall before] Mordecai. ·Since [*or* If] he is ·a Jew [Lfrom the seed of the Jews], you cannot ·win [prevail; stand] against him. You will surely ·be ruined [fall before him]." 14While they were still talking, the king's eunuchs came to Haman's house and hurried him to the banquet Esther had prepared.

Haman Is Hanged

7 So the king and Haman went in to ·eat [Ldrink; Ca reference to elaborate feasting] with Queen Esther. 2As they were drinking wine on ·the second day [*or* this second occasion; 5:4–6], the king asked Esther again, "What ·are you asking for [is your petition]? I will ·give it to you [grant it]. What is ·it you want [your request]? ·I will give you [Ask for] as much as half of my kingdom and it shall be done."

3Then Queen Esther answered, "My king, if ·you are pleased with me [LI have found favor in the king's sight] and if it ·pleases [seems good to] you, let me live. This is ·what I ask [my petition]. And let my people live, too. This is ·what I want [my request]. 4My people and I have been sold to be destroyed, ·killed [slaughtered] and ·completely wiped out [annihilated]. If we had ·merely [only; simply] been sold as male and female slaves, I would have ·kept quiet [remained silent], because that would not ·be enough of a problem to bother [have justified/been sufficent for troubling] the king."

5Then King ·Xerxes [LAhasuerus] asked Queen Esther, "Who is he, and where is he? Who has ·done [dared; presumed to do] such a thing?"

6Esther said, "Our ·enemy [oppressor; adversary] and foe is this ·wicked [evil] Haman!"

Then Haman was filled with terror before the king and queen. 7The king was ·very angry [filled with rage], got up, left his wine, and went out into the ·palace [Lhouse] garden. But Haman stayed inside to beg Queen Esther ·to save [for] his life. He could see that the king had already decided ·to kill [Lon calamity/disaster for] him.

8When the king returned from the ·palace [Lhouse] garden to the banquet hall, he saw Haman falling on the couch where Esther was ·lying [reclining]. The king said, "Will he even ·attack [assault; molest] the queen while I am in the house?"

As soon as the king said that, servants came in and covered Haman's face [Csignaling his doom]. 9Harbona, one of the eunuchs there serving the king, said, "Look, a ·seventy-five-foot [Lfifty cubits high] ·platform [gallows; pole] stands near Haman's house. This is the one Haman had prepared for Mordecai, who ·gave the warning that saved [spoke out on behalf of] the king."

The king said, "·Hang [Impale] Haman on it!" 10So they ·hanged [impaled] Haman on the ·platform [gallows; pole] he had prepared for Mordecai. Then the king's anger subsided.

The King Helps the Jews

8 That same day King ·Xerxes [LAhasuerus] gave Queen Esther ·everything belonging to [the estate of; Lthe house of] Haman, the enemy of the Jews. And Mordecai came in to see the king, because Esther had ·told [disclosed/revealed to] the king how he was related to her. 2Then the king took off his signet ring that he had taken back from Haman, and he gave it to Mordecai. Esther put Mordecai ·in charge of everything belonging to [Lover the house of] Haman.

3Once again Esther spoke to the king. She fell at the king's feet and ·cried [wept] and ·begged [implored] him to stop the evil ·plan [plot] that Haman the Agagite had ·planned [devised] against the Jews [CEsther wisely did not implicate the king in the plan]. 4The king ·held out [extended] the gold scepter to Esther. So Esther got up and stood in front of him.

5She said, "My king, if ·you are pleased with me [LI have found favor in the king's sight], and if it ·pleases [seems good to] you to do this, if you think it is the right thing to do, and if ·you are happy with me [I am pleasing/attractive to you], let an ·order [edict; decree] be written to ·cancel [revoke; rescind] the ·letters [dispatches; scrolls] Haman the son of Hammedatha the Agagite ·wrote [devised] to destroy the Jews in all of your ·kingdom [Lprovinces]. 6 ·I could not stand [LHow could I endure…?] to see that ·terrible thing [calamity; disaster] ·happen to [Lfall on] my people. ·I could not stand [LHow could I endure…?] to see my ·family [relatives; Lkindred] ·killed [destroyed]."

7King ·Xerxes [LAhasuerus] answered Queen Esther and Mordecai the Jew, "Because Haman was against the Jews, I have given his ·things [estate; property] to Esther, and my soldiers have ·hanged [impaled] him on the ·platform [gallows; pole]. 8Now, in the king's name, write another ·order [edict; decree] ·to [concerning] the Jews as seems ·best [appropriate] to you. Then seal the ·order [edict; decree] with the king's signet ring,

because no ·letter [dispatch] written in the king's name and sealed with
his signet ring can be ·canceled [revoked; rescinded]."
9At that time the king's ·secretaries [scribes] were called. This was the
twenty-third day of the third month [CJune 25], which is Sivan. The sec-
retaries wrote out all of Mordecai's ·orders [commands] ·to [concerning]
the Jews, to the governors, to the ·captains of the soldiers [high officials]
in each ·state [province], and to the ·important men [nobles] of the one
hundred twenty-seven ·states [provinces] that reached from India to
Cush [1:1]. They wrote in the ·writing [script] of each ·state [province]
and in the language of each people. They also wrote to the Jews in their
own ·writing [script] and language. 10Mordecai wrote ·orders [edicts;
decrees] in the name of King ·Xerxes [LAhasuerus] and sealed the ·letters
[dispatches; scrolls] with the king's signet ring. Then he sent the king's
·orders [edicts; decrees] by ·messengers [couriers] on fast horses, horses
that were ·raised [bred] ·just [especially] for the king.
11These were the king's ·orders [edicts; decrees]: The Jews in every city
have the right to ·gather together [assemble] to ·protect themselves
[defend their lives]. They may destroy, kill, and ·completely wipe out
[annihilate] the army of any ·state [province] or ·people [nation] who
attack them [Cthe king could not cancel his previous unalterable decree,
but he could allow the Jews to defend themselves and attack], including
their women and children. They may also ·take by force [plunder; confis-
cate] the property of their enemies. 12The one day set for the Jews to do
this in all the ·empire [provinces] of King ·Xerxes [LAhasuerus] was the
thirteenth day of the twelfth month [CMarch 7, about twelve months after
Haman devised his plot], the month of Adar. 13A copy of the king's ·order
[edict; decree] was to be ·sent out [issued; presented] as a law in every
·state [province]. It was to be made known to ·the people of every nation
living in the kingdom [Lall the peoples] so the Jews would be ready on
that set day to ·strike back at [avenge themselves on] their enemies.
14The ·messengers [couriers] hurried out, riding on the royal horses,
urged on by the king's command. And the ·order [edict; decree] was also
given in the ·palace [citadel; fortress; 1:2] at Susa.
15Mordecai left the king's presence wearing royal ·clothes [garments] of
blue and white and a large gold crown. He also had a purple ·robe [mantle]
made of the best linen. And the people of Susa shouted for joy. 16It was a
time of ·happiness [Llight], joy, gladness, and honor for the Jews. 17As the
king's ·order [edict; decree] went to every ·state [province] and city, there
was joy and gladness among the Jews. In every ·state [province] and city to
which the king's ·order [edict; decree] went, they were having ·feasts [ban-
quets] and ·celebrating [holidays]. And many ·people through all the empire
[Lpeoples of the land] ·became [professed/pretended to be] Jews, because
·they were afraid of the Jews [Ldread of the Jews had fallen on them].

Victory for the Jews

9 The ·order [edict; decree] the king had commanded was to be
·done [executed; carried out] on the thirteenth day of the twelfth
month [CMarch 7], the month of Adar. That was the day the enemies of
the Jews had hoped to ·defeat [overpower] them, but ·that was changed
[the opposite happened]. So the Jews themselves ·defeated [overpowered]
·those who hated them [their enemies]. 2The Jews ·met [assembled] in
their cities in all the ·empire [Lprovinces] of King ·Xerxes [LAhasuerus] in
order to ·attack [strike; Llay hands on] those who wanted to ·harm

[destroy] them. No one ·was strong enough to fight [Lcould stand] against
them, because ·all the other people living in the empire were afraid of
them [Ldread of them fell on all the peoples]. 3All the ·important men
[nobles] of the ·states [provinces], the governors, ·captains of the soldiers
[high officials], and the king's officers helped the Jews, because they were
afraid of Mordecai. 4Mordecai was ·very important [Lgreat] in the king's
·palace [Lhouse]. He was famous in all the ·empire [Lprovinces], because
he was becoming ·a leader of more and more people [more and more
powerful/influential].

5And, with their swords, the Jews ·defeated [Lstruck] all their enemies,
·killing [slaughtering] and destroying them. And they did ·what they wanted
[as they pleased] with those people who hated them. 6In the ·palace [citadel;
fortress; 1:2] at Susa, they ·killed [slaughtered] and destroyed five hundred
men. 7They also killed: Parshandatha, Dalphon, Aspatha, 8Poratha, Adalia,
Aridatha, 9Parmashta, Arisai, Aridai, and Vaizatha, 10the ten sons of Haman,
son of Hammedatha, the enemy of the Jews. But the Jews did not ·take
[plunder; confiscate] their ·belongings [property; Cthis shows they attacked
out of self-defense, not for material gain; 8:11; Gen. 14:23].

11On that day the number killed in the ·palace [citadel; fortress; 1:2] at
Susa was reported to the king. 12The king said to Queen Esther, "The Jews
have ·killed [slaughtered] and destroyed five hundred people in the ·pal-
ace [citadel; fortress; 1:2] at Susa, as well as Haman's ten sons. What then
have they done in the rest of the king's ·empire [provinces]! Now what
·else are you asking [Lis your petition]? I will do it! What ·else [more] do
you want? It will be ·done [granted]!"

13Esther answered, "If it pleases the king, give the Jews who are in Susa
permission to do again tomorrow what the king ·ordered [decreed] for
today. And let the bodies of Haman's ten sons be ·hanged [impaled] on
the ·platform [gallows; pole]."

14So the king ·ordered [decreed] that it be done. A ·law [edict; decree]
was given in Susa, and the bodies of the ten sons of Haman were ·hanged
[impaled]. 15The Jews in Susa ·came together [assembled] on the fourteenth day of the month of Adar [CMarch 8]. They ·killed [slaughtered]
three hundred people in Susa, but they did not ·take [plunder; confiscate]
their ·belongings [property; 9:10].

16At that same time, all the Jews in the king's ·empire [Lprovinces] also
·met [assembled] to ·protect themselves [defend their lives] and get rid of
their enemies. They ·killed [slaughtered] seventy-five thousand of those
who hated them, but they did not ·take [plunder; confiscate] their ·belong-
ings [property; 9:10]. 17This happened on the thirteenth day of the month
of Adar [CMarch 7]. On the fourteenth day they rested and made it a day
of joyful ·feasting [banqueting].

The Feast of Purim

18But the Jews in Susa ·met [assembled] on the thirteenth and fourteenth days of the month of Adar [Cand killed their enemies]. Then they
rested on the fifteenth day and made it a day of joyful feasting
[banqueting].

19This is why the Jews who live in the country and small villages celebrate on the fourteenth day of the month of Adar [CMarch 8]. It is a ·day
[holiday] of joyful ·feasting [banqueting] and a day for exchanging ·gifts
[gifts of food].

20Mordecai ·wrote down [recorded] everything that had happened.

Then he sent ·letters [dispatches; scrolls] to all the Jews in all the ·empire
[provinces] of King ·Xerxes [LAhasuerus], far and near. 21He ·told [called
on] them to celebrate every year on the fourteenth and fifteenth days of
the month of Adar, 22because that was when the Jews got rid of their enemies [Ca descendant of Saul (2:5–6) had overcome an Amalekite and
descendant of King Agag (3:1), thus completing God's mandate (Deut.
23:3–6) that Saul failed to accomplish (1 Sam. 15)]. They were also to
celebrate it as the month their ·sadness [sorrow] was turned to ·joy [glad-
ness] and their ·crying for the dead [mourning] was turned into
·celebration [a holiday]. He told them to celebrate those days as days of
joyful ·feasting [banqueting] and as a time for giving [presents of] food to
each other and ·presents [gifts] to the poor [CPurim thus became an
annual festival still celebrated by the Jewish people today].

23So the Jews agreed to do what Mordecai had written to them, and
·they agreed to hold the celebration every year [Lto continue what they
had begun]. 24Haman son of Hammedatha, the Agagite, was the enemy of
all the Jews. He had ·made [devised] an evil ·plan [plot] against the Jews
to destroy them, and he had thrown the Pur (that is, the lot [Cdice-like
objects]) to choose a day to ·ruin [crush; afflict] and destroy them. 25But
when the king learned of the evil ·plan [plot], he sent out written ·orders
[edicts; decrees] that the evil ·plans [plot] Haman had made against the
Jews would ·be used against him [Lfall/return on his own head]. And those
·orders [edicts; decrees] said that Haman and his sons should be ·hanged
[impaled] on the ·platform [gallows; pole]. 26So these days were called
Purim, which comes from the word "Pur" (the lot [Cdice-like objects]).
Because of everything written in this ·letter [dispatch] and what they had
seen and what happened to them, 27the Jews set up this ·custom [tradi-
tion]. They and their descendants and all those who join them are ·always
[Lwithout fail] to ·celebrate [observe; keep] these two days every year.
They should do it ·in the right way [Las it is written] and at the time
Mordecai had ·ordered [decreed]. 28These two days should be remembered and ·celebrated [observed; kept] ·from now on [Lthrough every
generation] in every family, in every ·state [province], and in every city.
These days of Purim should ·always [Lnot fail to] be ·celebrated [observed;
kept] ·by [among] the Jews, and their memory never fade among their
descendants.

29So Queen Esther daughter of Abihail, along with Mordecai the Jew,
wrote with full authority to confirm this second ·letter [dispatch] about
Purim. 30And Mordecai sent ·letters [dispatches; scrolls] to all the Jews in
the one hundred twenty-seven ·states [provinces] of the kingdom of ·Xerxes
[LAhasuerus], writing them ·a message [Lwords] of peace and ·truth [*or*
security; assurance]. 31He wrote to ·set up [establish] these days of Purim at
the ·chosen [proper; appointed] times. Mordecai the Jew and Queen Esther
had sent out the ·order [edict; decree] for the Jews, just as they had ·set up
[established] for themselves and their descendants instruction concerning
fasting and ·loud weeping [lamentations]. 32Esther's ·letter [command] ·set
up [established] the rules for Purim, and they were written down in the
records.

The Greatness of Mordecai

10 King ·Xerxes [LAhasuerus] demanded ·taxes everywhere,
even from the cities [tribute on the land and] on the seacoast.
2And all the great ·things [achievements] ·Xerxes [LAhasuerus] did by

**his ·power [authority] and strength ·are [Lare they not…?] written in the
·record books [chronicles; annals] of the kings of Media and Persia. Also
written in those record books are all the things done by Mordecai, whom
the king made great. 3Mordecai the Jew was second in importance to
King ·Xerxes [LAhasuerus], and he was ·the most important man [great;
powerful; preeminent] among the Jews. His fellow Jews ·respected
[admired; esteemed] him very much, because he ·worked for [Lsought]
the good of his people and ·spoke up [interceded; advocated] for the
·safety [welfare; Lpeace] of all the Jews.**

JOB

Job, the Good Man

1 A man named Job lived in the land of Uz [Ceast of Israel in Edom (present-day Jordan); Lam. 4:21]. He was an ·honest [innocent; blameless; Prov. 2:7, 21] and ·innocent [virtuous; Prov. 1:3] man; he ·honored [feared; respected] God [28:28; Prov. 1:7] and stayed away from evil [Cthese terms are used to describe the wise in Proverbs]. 2Job had seven sons and three daughters [Cindicating a large and complete family]. 3He owned seven thousand sheep, three thousand camels, five hundred teams of oxen, and five hundred female donkeys. He also had a large number of servants. He was the ·greatest [*or* richest] man among all the people of the East [Cthe expected reward of wisdom].

4Job's sons took turns holding feasts [Lon their day; Cperhaps birthday celebrations] in their homes and invited their sisters to eat and drink with them. 5After a feast was over, Job would send and have them ·made clean [consecrated; made holy]. Early in the morning Job would offer a burnt offering [Can atonement offering; Lev. 1:1–17] for each of them, because he thought, "My children may have sinned and ·cursed [Lblessed; Ca euphemism for "cursed"] God in their hearts." Job did this every time.

Satan Appears Before the Lord

6One day the ·angels [Lsons of God] came to ·show themselves [stand] before the LORD, and ·Satan [Lthe Satan; Cmeans "the Accuser" or "the Adversary"; either the Devil or a member of God's heavenly court] was with them. 7The LORD said to Satan, "Where have you come from?"

Satan [1:6] answered the LORD, "I have been ·wandering around [roaming] the earth, ·going back and forth in [patrolling] it."

8Then the LORD said to Satan, "Have you noticed [considered; Lset your heart on] my servant Job? No one else on earth is like him. He is an honest and innocent man, honoring God and staying away from evil [1:1]."

9But Satan [1:6] answered the LORD, "·Job honors God for a good reason [LDoes Job honor/fear/respect God for no good reason?]. 10·You have [LDon't you…?] put a ·wall [hedge; Cto protect from danger] around him, his family, and everything he owns. You have blessed ·the things he has done [Lall the works of his hands]. His flocks and herds ·are so large they almost cover [Lburst forth on] the land. 11But ·reach out [stretch forth] your hand and ·destroy [afflict] everything he has, and [Lsee if] he will curse you to your face."

12The LORD said to Satan [1:6], "All right, then. Everything Job has is in your ·power [Lhand], but ·you must not touch Job himself [Lbut don't send your hand against him]." Then Satan [1:6] left the LORD's presence.

13One day Job's sons and daughters were ·eating and drinking wine [feasting; celebrating] together at the ·oldest [Lfirstborn] brother's house.

14A messenger came to Job and said, "The oxen were plowing and the donkeys were eating grass nearby, 15when the Sabeans [Ca people from southern Arabia] attacked and carried them away. They killed the servants with swords, and I am the only one who escaped to tell you!"

16The messenger was still speaking when another messenger arrived and said, "·Lightning [LFire] from God fell from ·the sky [heaven]. It burned up the sheep and the servants, and I am the only one who escaped to tell you!"

17The second messenger was still speaking when another messenger arrived and said, "The ·Babylonians [LChaldeans; Ca people located in present-day southern Iraq] sent three ·groups of attackers [raiding parties] that swept down and stole your camels and killed the servants [Lwith the sword]. I am the only one who escaped to tell you!"

18The third messenger was still speaking when another messenger arrived and said, "Your sons and daughters were ·eating and drinking wine [feasting; celebrating] together at the ·oldest [Lfirstborn] brother's house. 19Suddenly a ·great [strong; mighty] wind came from the desert, hitting all four corners of the house at once. The house fell in on the young people, and they are all dead. I am the only one who escaped to tell you!"

20When Job heard this, he got up and tore his robe and shaved his head [Cancient mourning customs]. Then he bowed down to the ground to worship God. 21He said:

"I was naked when I ·was born [Lcame from my mother's womb],
  and I will be naked when I ·die [Lreturn there].
The LORD gave these things to me,
  and he has taken them away.
  ·Praise [Blessed be] the name of the LORD."

22In all this Job did not sin or blame God.

Satan Appears Before the Lord Again

2 ·On another day [*or* One day] the ·angels [Lthe sons of God] came to ·show themselves [Lstand] before the LORD, and Satan [1:6] was with them again. 2The LORD said to Satan, "Where have you come from?"

Satan answered the LORD, "I have been ·wandering around [roaming] the earth, ·going back and forth in [patrolling] it."

3Then the LORD said to Satan, "Have you noticed my servant Job [1:8]? No one else on earth is like him. He is an honest and innocent man, honoring God and staying away from evil [1:1]. You ·caused [*or* enticed] me to ·ruin [injure] him for no good reason, but he ·continues to be without blame [*or* maintains his innocence]."

4"One skin for another [LSkin for skin; Ca proverb meaning that people only react if they are affected directly]!" Satan [1:6] answered. "A man will give all he has to save his own life. 5But reach out your hand and ·destroy [afflict; Ltouch] his bones and flesh, and he will ·curse [Lbless; Ca euphemism for "curse"; 1:5] you to your face."

6The LORD said to Satan [1:6], "All right, then. Job is in your ·power [Lhand], but you ·may not take [Lmust preserve] his life."

7So Satan [1:6] left the LORD's presence. He put ·painful sores [horrible boils] on Job's body, from the top of his head to the soles of his feet. 8Job took a ·piece of broken [shard of] pottery to scrape himself, and he sat in ashes in misery.

9Job's wife said to him, "Why are you ·trying to stay innocent [maintaining your innocence]? Curse [2:5] God and die!"

[10]Job answered, "You are talking like a foolish woman. Should we take
only good things from God and not ·trouble [*or* evil]?" In spite of all this
Job did not sin ·in what he said [Lwith his lips].

Job's Three Friends Come to Help

[11]Now Job had three friends: Eliphaz the Temanite [Cfrom Tema, a town
in Edom (1:1)], Bildad the Shuhite, and Zophar the Naamathite. When
these friends heard about Job's troubles, they agreed to meet and visit him.
They wanted to ·show their concern [mourn] and to comfort him. [12]They
·saw Job [Llifted their eyes] from far away, but he looked so different they
almost didn't recognize him. They began to cry loudly and tore their robes
and put ·dirt [dust] on their heads [Cancient mourning customs]. [13]Then
they sat on the ground with Job seven days and seven nights. No one said a
word to him because they saw how much he was ·suffering [in pain].

Job Curses His Birth

3 ·After seven days [LAfterward] Job ·cried out [Lopened his mouth]
and cursed ·the day he had been born [Lhis day; Jer. 20:14–18],
[2]saying:

[3]"Let the day I was born be destroyed,
and the night it was said, 'A boy is ·born [Lconceived]!'
[4]Let that day turn to darkness [Ccontrast Gen. 1:3].
Don't let God ·care about [Lseek] it.
Don't let light shine on it.
[5]Let darkness and gloom ·have that day [Lredeem it].
Let a cloud ·hide [Lsettle over] it.
Let thick darkness ·cover its light [overwhelm the day].
[6]Let thick darkness capture that night.
Don't count it among the days of the year
or put it in any of the months.
[7]Let that night be ·empty [barren],
with no shout of joy ·to be heard [Lentering it].
[8]Let those who curse ·days [*or* the Sea; Ca symbol of chaos] curse that
day [CBalaam (Num. 22–24) is an example of a professional
curser].
Let them prepare to wake up the sea monster Leviathan [Ca creature
in ancient Near Eastern texts that represents chaos; 41:1, 12; Ps.
74:14; 104:26; Is. 27:1].
[9]Let that day's morning stars ·never appear [Lbecome dark];
let it ·wait [hope] for daylight that never comes.
Don't let it see the first light of dawn,
[10]because it ·allowed me to be born [Ldid not shut the doors of my
(mother's) womb]
and did not hide trouble from my eyes.

[11]"Why didn't I die as soon as I ·was born [Lcame out of the womb]?
Why didn't I die when I came out of the ·womb [Lbelly; Eccl. 6:3–5]?
[12]Why did my mother's knees receive me,
and ·my mother's breasts feed me [Lwhy were there breasts that I
could suck]?
[13]If they had not been there,
I would be lying dead in peace;
I would be asleep and at rest
[14]with kings and wise men of the earth
who built places for themselves that are now ruined.

[15]I would be asleep with rulers
who filled their houses with gold and silver.
[16]Why was I not ·buried [[L]hidden] like a ·child born dead [stillborn],
like a baby who never saw the light of day?
[17]In the grave the wicked ·stop making trouble [*or* cease their agitation],
and the weary workers are at rest.
[18]In the grave there is rest for the ·captives [prisoners]
who no longer hear the ·shout [[L]voice] of the ·slave driver [taskmaster].
[19]People great and small are ·in the grave [[L]there],
and the ·slave [servant] is freed from his master.

[20]"Why is light given to those in misery?
Why is life given to those who are ·so unhappy [depressed]?
[21]They want to die, but death does not come.
They search for death more than for hidden treasure.
[22]They are very happy
[[L]they celebrate] when they get to the grave.
[23]They cannot see where they are going.
God has ·hidden the road ahead [[L]placed a hedge around him].
[24]I ·make sad sounds [sigh] as I eat;
my groans pour out like water.
[25]·Everything I feared and dreaded
has happened to me.
[*or* For the dread I dreaded has come to me,
and what I feared has come to me.]
[26]I have no peace or quietness.
I have no rest, only ·trouble [agitation]."

Eliphaz Speaks

4 Then Eliphaz the Temanite answered:
[2]"If someone tried to speak with you, would you be ·upset [*or* discouraged]?
I cannot keep from speaking.
[3]Think about the many people you have taught
and the weak hands you have made strong.
[4]Your words have ·comforted [[L]lifted up] those who ·fell [stumbled],
and you have strengthened those ·who could not stand [[L]with weak knees].
[5]But now trouble comes to you, and you are discouraged;
·trouble hits [[L]it touches] you, and you are ·terrified [disturbed].
[6]·You should have [Shouldn't you have…?] confidence because you ·respect [fear; have awe for] God;
·you should [should you not…?] have hope because ·you are innocent [[L]of your innocent ways].

[7]"Remember ·that the innocent will not die [[L]who being innocent/blameless has perished…?];
·honest people will never be [[L]when were the honest/virtuous…?] destroyed.
[8]I have ·noticed [seen] that people who plow ·evil [wickedness]
and plant trouble, harvest it.
[9]God's breath destroys them,
and a blast of his anger ·kills [finishes] them.

10Lions may roar and lion cubs growl,
but when the teeth of a strong lion are broken,
11that lion dies ·of hunger [Lwithout prey].
The cubs of the mother lion are scattered [Cthe wicked may briefly prosper but will ultimately perish].

12"A word ·was brought to me in secret [Lstole over me],
and my ears heard a whisper of it [CEliphaz claims a supernatural revelation that supports his teaching].
13It was during ·a nightmare [Lanxious thoughts of a night vision]
when people are in deep sleep.
14I was trembling with fear;
all my bones were shaking.
15A spirit glided past my face,
and the hair on my ·body [Lskin] stood on end.
16The spirit stopped,
but I could not see what it was.
A shape stood before my eyes,
and I heard a quiet voice.
17It said, 'Can a human be more right than God?
Can a person be pure before his maker? [Cthe implied answer is no]
18God does not trust his ·angels [Lservants];
he blames ·them [Langels] for mistakes.
19So ·he puts even more blame on [Lwhat about…?] people who live in clay houses [Cphysical bodies],
whose foundations are made of dust [Gen. 2:7],
who can be crushed like a moth.
20Between ·dawn and sunset [Lmorning and evening] many people are broken to pieces;
without being noticed, they die and are gone forever.
21The ropes of their tents are pulled up,
and they die without wisdom.'

5 "Call if you want to, Job, ·but no one [Lis there anyone who…?] will answer you.
·You can't [LCan you…?] turn to any of the holy ones [Cangels].
2·Anger [Irritation] kills the fool,
and jealousy slays the ·stupid [or naïve; simpleminded; Cthese emotions can lead to death; Prov. 14:30; 27:4].
3I have seen a fool ·succeed [Ltaking root],
but I cursed his ·home [household; pasturage] ·immediately [suddenly].
4His children are far from safety
and are crushed in court with no ·defense [or rescuer].
5The hungry eat his harvest,
even taking what grew among the thorns,
and thirsty people ·want [Lpant after] his wealth.
6·Hard times do [Misery does] not come up from the ·ground [dust],
and trouble does not ·grow [sprout] from the earth [Cthey come from anger and jealousy].
7People ·produce [Lare born for] trouble
as surely as sparks fly upward.

8"But if I were you, I would ·call on [Lseek] God
and ·bring my problem [Lcommit my thoughts/cause] before him
[Cargues that Job needs to repent].
9God does wonders that cannot be understood;
he does so many ·miracles [marvelous acts] they cannot be counted.
10He gives rain to the earth
and sends water on the fields.
11He makes the ·humble [lowly] person important [Ps. 113]
and lifts ·the sad [mourners] to places of safety.
12He ruins the ·plans [pretensions; strategies] of those who ·trick others
[are crafty]
so ·they [Ltheir hands] have no success.
13He catches the ·wise [crafty; clever] in their own ·clever traps
[craftiness]
and ·sweeps away [ends; finishes off] the ·plans [advice; schemes] of
those who ·try to trick others [are wily].
14Darkness ·covers them up [*or* encounters them] in the daytime;
even at noon they ·feel [grope] around in the dark.
15God saves the needy from their lies
and from the harm done by powerful people.
16So the poor have hope,
while those who are ·unfair [unjust] ·are silenced [Lshut their mouth].

17"The one whom God ·corrects [reproves] is ·happy [blessed],
so do not ·hate being corrected by [Lreject/despise the instruction of]
the Almighty [Prov. 3:11–12].
18God ·hurts [wounds], but he also bandages up;
he ·injures [strikes], but his hands also heal.
19He will ·save [rescue] you from six ·troubles [dangers];
even seven ·troubles [*or* evils] will not ·harm [Ltouch] you [C"six…
seven" is a poetic way of saying "all troubles"].
20God will ·buy you back [redeem/ransom you] from death in times of
·hunger [famine],
and in ·battle [war] he will save you from the sword.
21You will be ·protected [hidden] from the ·tongue that strikes like a
whip [lash of the tongue],
and you will not be afraid when destruction comes.
22You will laugh at destruction and hunger [Ps. 112:7],
and you will not fear the wild animals,
23because you will have an ·agreement [treaty; alliance; covenant] with
the stones in the field,
and the wild animals will be at peace with you [Cdescribes a peaceful
relationship with all nature].
24You will know that your tent is safe,
because you will ·check [visit] ·the things you own [your pasturage/
home] and find nothing missing.
25You will know that you will have many ·children [descendants],
and your ·descendants [offspring] will be like the grass on the earth.
26You will come to the grave ·with all your strength [*or* at a ripe old age],
like bundles of grain gathered at the right time.

27"We have ·checked [examined] this, and it is true,
so hear it and ·decide what it means to you [know it yourself]."

Job Answers Eliphaz

6 Then Job answered [Land said]:
2"·I wish [*or* If only] my ·suffering [anguish; irritation] could be weighed
and my misery put on scales.
3·My sadness [LIt] would be heavier than the sand of the seas.
No wonder my words ·seem careless [blurt out; are wild/rash].
4[LFor] The arrows of ·the Almighty [LShaddai] are in me;
my spirit drinks in their poison;
God's terrors ·are gathered [are ranged; enter into battle] against me.
5·A wild donkey does not bray when it has grass to eat [LDoes not a wild donkey bray for grass?],
·and an ox is quiet when it has feed [LDoes not an ox bellow for fodder?; CJob's complaints are as natural as the sounds animals make when hungry].
6·Tasteless food is not [LWould tasteless food be…?] eaten without salt,
and ·there is no [Lis there…?] flavor in the ·white of an egg [*or* juice of a weed; CJob's "food" (his lot in life) is inedible].
7I refuse to touch it;
such food makes me sick [Ca word connected to menstruation and therefore ritual uncleanness; Lev. 15:19–30].

8"How I wish that I might have what I ask for
and that God would give me what I hope for.
9How I wish God would crush me
and reach out his hand to ·destroy me [cut me off].
10Then I would have this ·comfort [consolation]
and be glad even in this unending pain,
because I would know I did not reject the words of the Holy One.

11"·I do not have the [LWhat is my…?] strength to wait.
·There is nothing to hope for,
so why should I be patient [LWhat is my end that I should arrange my life]?
12·I do not [LDo I…?] have the strength of stone;
·my flesh is not [Lis my flesh…?] bronze.
13·I have no power to help myself [LIs there no help for me?],
because ·success [resourcefulness] has been ·taken away [driven] from me.

14"They say, '·A person's friends should be kind to him when he is in trouble,
even if he stops fearing the Almighty [*or* Those who withhold loyalty from their friend do not fear the Almighty/Shaddai; CJob here criticizes his friends' attitude toward him].'
15But my ·brothers [CJob's three friends] cannot be counted on.
They are like ·streams that do not always flow [Lwadis; Cseasonal riverbeds that are dry in the summer],
streams that sometimes run over.
16They are made dark by melting ice

and rise with melting snow.
17But they ·stop flowing [Lare silent] in the dry season;
they disappear when it is hot.
18·Travelers [*or* Caravans] turn away from their paths
and go into the desert and die.
19The groups of travelers from Tema [Can oasis in north Arabia] look for
water,
and the traders of Sheba [Cin south Arabia; both places were well
known for their trade through the desert] look for it hopefully.
20They are ·upset [Lashamed] because they had been sure;
when they arrive, they are ·disappointed [dismayed].
21You ·also have been no help [Lbecome like this to me].
You see something terrible, and you are afraid.
22·I have never said [LDid I ever say...?], 'Give me a gift.
Use your wealth to ·pay my debt [*or* make a bribe for me].
23·Save [Rescue] me from the enemy's power.
·Buy me back [Redeem me] from the clutches of ·cruel [violent] people.'

24"Teach me, and I will be quiet.
·Show me [LHelp me understand] where I have been wrong.
25·Honest [Virtuous; CJob speaks sarcastically] words are painful,
but your ·arguments [reproofs] prove nothing.
26Do you mean to correct what I say?
Will you treat the words of a ·troubled [despairing] man as if they
were only wind [Cthat is, empty]?
27You would even ·gamble [cast lots] for orphans
and would ·trade away [sell] your friend.

28"But now please look at me.
I would not lie to your face.
29·Change your mind [LReturn now]; do not be unfair;
·think [return] again, because my ·innocence [righteousness] is being
questioned.
30What I am saying is not wicked;
I can ·tell [Ltaste] ·the difference between right and wrong [*or* tragedy].

7 "·People have [LDo not people have...?] a hard ·task [service] on
earth,
and their days are like those of a [Lhired] laborer [Chard work with
little profit].
2They are like a ·slave [servant] ·wishing [Lpanting] for the evening
shadows,
like a [Lhired] laborer waiting to be paid.
3But I ·am given [Linherit] months that are ·empty [vain; futile],
and nights of ·misery [*or* toil] have been ·given [Lallotted] to me.
4When I lie down, I think, 'How long until I get up?'
The night is long, and I toss until dawn.
5My body is covered with worms and ·scabs [Lclods of dust/dirt],
and my skin ·is broken and full of sores [Lcrusts over and oozes].

6"My days go by faster than a weaver's ·tool [shuttle],
and they come to an end without hope.

7Remember, God, that my life is only a breath.
My eyes will never see happy times again.
8·Those who [LThe eyes that] see me now will see me no more;
you will look for me, but I will ·be gone [Lbe no more; not exist].
9As a cloud ·disappears [fades] and is gone,
people go to ·the grave [LSheol; Cthe grave or the underworld] and never return.
10They will never come back to their houses again,
and their places will not know them anymore.

11"So I will not ·stay quiet [Lrestrain my mouth];
I will speak out in the ·suffering [distress; Lpinch] of my spirit.
I will ·complain [groan] ·because I am so unhappy [Lin the bitterness of my soul].
12·I am not [LAm I…?] ·the sea [LYam] or ·the sea monster [LTannin; CYam and Tannin are legendary sea monsters representing chaos].
·So why have you […that you] set a guard over me?
13Sometimes I think my bed will comfort me
or that my couch will ·stop my complaint [ease my groans].
14Then you ·frighten [terrorize] me with dreams
and ·terrify [scare] me with visions.
15My throat prefers to be choked;
my bones welcome death.
16I ·hate [Lreject] my life; I don't want to live forever.
Leave me alone, because my days have no meaning.

17"Why do you make people so important
and ·give them so much attention [Lset your heart on them; Ccontrast Ps. 8:4]?
18You ·examine [visit] them every morning
and test them ·every moment [all the time].
19Will you never look away from me
or leave me alone even long enough to swallow [Lmy saliva]?
20If I have sinned, what have I done to you,
you watcher of humans?
Why have you made me your target?
Have I become a ·heavy load [burden] for you?
21Why don't you ·pardon [forgive] my ·wrongs [transgressions]
and ·forgive my sins [carry away my guilt]?
I will soon lie down in the dust of death.
Then you will ·search [look] for me, but I will be no more."

Bildad Speaks to Job

8 Then Bildad the Shuhite answered:
2"How long will you [Lcontinue to] say such things?
Your words are ·no more than [La strong] wind [Che accuses Job of passion without substance].
3God does not ·twist [pervert] justice;
·the Almighty [Shaddai] does not ·make wrong [twist; pervert] ·what is right [righteousness].
4[LIf] Your children sinned against God,
and he ·punished them for their sins [Lsent them into the power of their transgression].

[5]·But [[L]If] you ·should ask God for help [[L]look for God]
and ·pray [plead] to ·the Almighty [Shaddai] for ·mercy [grace].
[6]If you are ·good [pure] and ·honest [virtuous; 1:1, 8; 2:3],
he will ·stand up [[L]immediately rouse himself] for you
and ·bring you back [restore you] ·where you belong [to your right/
righteous pasture/place/home].
[7]·Where you began will seem unimportant [[L]Though your start was small],
·because your future will be so successful [[L]your end will be exalted].

[8]"Ask ·old people [[L]the previous generation];
·find out [reflect on] what their ancestors learned,
[9]because we were only born yesterday and know nothing.
Our days on earth are only a shadow.
[10]Those people will teach you and tell you
and speak about what they know.
[11]·Papyrus plants cannot [[L]Do papyrus plants…?] grow where there is
no swamp,
·and reeds cannot [[L]or reeds…?] grow tall without water.
[12]While they are still growing and not yet cut,
they will dry up quicker than grass [Ps. 37:2; 102:4, 11; 129:6].
[13]That is ·what will happen to [[L]the path of] those who forget God;
the hope of the ·wicked [godless] will ·be gone [perish].
[14]·What they hope in is easily broken [[L]Their confidence is gossamer
thread];
what they trust is like a spider's web [[C]without substance].
[15]They lean on ·the spider's web [[L]its house], but it ·breaks [[L]does not
stand].
They grab it, but it does not hold up.
[16]They are like well-watered plants in the sunshine
that spread their roots all through the garden.
[17]They wrap their roots around a pile of rocks
and look for a place among the stones.
[18]But if a plant is torn from its place,
then that place rejects it and says, 'I never saw you.'
[19]Now ·joy has gone away [*or* it (the plant) dissolves on the way];
other plants grow up from the same dirt.

[20]"Surely God does not reject the innocent
or ·give strength to [*or* grasp the hand of] those who do evil.
[21]God will yet fill your mouth with laughter
and your lips with shouts of joy.
[22]·Your enemies [[L]Those who hate you] will be covered with shame,
and the tents of the wicked will be gone."

Job Answers Bildad

9 Then Job answered:
[2]"·Yes [Truly], I know that this [[C]Zophar's point that God
punishes the wicked] is ·true [correct],
but how can anyone be ·right [righteous; vindicated] in the presence
of God?
[3]Someone might want to ·argue with God [take God to court],
but no one could answer God,
not one time out of a thousand.

[4]·God's wisdom is deep [[L]He is wise of heart], and his power is great;
no one can ·fight [[L]press] him ·without getting hurt [and come out whole/unscathed].
[5]He moves mountains [[C]an earthquake] without anyone knowing it
and turns them over when he is angry.
[6]He shakes the earth out of its place
and makes its ·foundations [pillars] ·tremble [shudder].
[7]He ·commands the sun not to [[L]speaks to the sun and it does not] shine
and ·shuts off the light of [[L]seals up] the stars.
[8]He alone stretches out the ·skies [heavens]
and ·walks [treads] on the ·waves [[L]high places] of the sea.
[9]It is God who made the Bear, Orion, and the Pleiades [[C]well-known constellations]
and the ·groups of stars in the southern sky [[L]chambers of the south].
[10]He does ·wonders [great things] that cannot be understood;
he does so many ·miracles [*or* marvelous things] they cannot be counted.
[11]·When [*or* If] he passes me, I cannot see him;
·when [*or* if] he goes by me, I do not ·recognize [perceive] him.
[12]If he snatches ·something [*or* someone] away, no one can ·stop him [*or* bring them back]
or say to him, 'What are you doing?'
[13]God will not ·hold back [relent from] his anger.
Even the ·helpers [allies] of the monster Rahab [[C]a sea monster; Ps. 89:10] ·lie at his feet in fear [[L]cower under him].
[14]So how can I ·argue with [[L]answer] God,
or even ·find words to argue [[L]choose words] with him?
[15]Even if I were ·right [righteous], I could not answer him;
I could only ·beg God [plead], my Judge, for mercy.
[16]If I ·called to [summoned] him and he answered,
I still don't believe he would ·listen to me [[L]hear my voice].
[17]He would crush me with a ·storm [whirlwind; 38:1]
and multiply my ·wounds [bruises] ·for no reason [without cause].
[18]He would not let me ·catch [regain] my breath
but would ·overwhelm [satiate] me with ·misery [bitterness].
[19]·When [*or* If] it comes to ·strength [power], God is stronger than I;
·when [*or* if] it comes to ·justice [*or* judgment], no one can ·accuse [testify against] him.
[20]·Even if I were [*or* Though I am] ·right [righteous], my own mouth would ·say I was wrong [condemn me];
·if I were [*or* I am] innocent, ·my mouth would say I was [*or* he declares me] guilty.

[21]"I am innocent,
but I don't ·care about myself [*or* know for sure].
I ·hate [loathe] my own life.
[22]It is all the same. That is why I say,
'God destroys both the innocent and the ·guilty [wicked].'
[23]If ·the whip [*or* disaster] brings sudden death,
God will ·laugh [ridicule] ·at the suffering [*or* the despair] of the innocent.

[24]When the ·land [earth] ·falls [Lis given] into the ·hands [power] of evil
people,
he covers the judges' faces so they can't see it.
If it is not God who does this, then who is it?

[25]"My days go by faster than a runner;
they ·fly away without my seeing any joy [Lare swift but not good].
[26]They ·glide past [pass by] like ·paper [Lreed] boats.
They ·attack [*or* go fast] like eagles swooping down to feed.
[27]·Even though [*or* If] I say, 'I will forget my ·complaint [sighs];
I will ·change the look on my face [Labandon my countenance] and
·smile [be cheerful],'
[28]I still dread all my ·suffering [distress].
I know you will ·hold me guilty [Lnot find me innocent].
[29]I have already been ·found guilty [declared wicked],
so why should I ·struggle [Lexhaust myself] for no reason?
[30][LEven if] I might wash myself with ·soap [*or* snow]
and ·scrub [cleanse] my hands with ·strong soap [lye],
[31]but you would ·push [plunge] me into a dirty pit,
and even my clothes would ·hate [abhor] me.

[32]"[LFor] God is not human like me, ·so I cannot [Lthat I could] answer
him.
·We cannot meet each other in court [L...that we could go together
into judgment].
[33]·I wish there were someone to make peace [LThere is no umpire]
between us,
·someone to decide our case [Lwho would set his hand on both of us].
[34]Maybe he could remove ·God's punishment [Lhis rod from me]
so his terror would no longer frighten me.
[35]Then I could speak without being afraid [Lof him],
but I am not able to do that.

10 "I ·hate [am disgusted with] my life,
so I will ·complain without holding back [Labandon myself to
my sighs];
I will speak ·because I am so unhappy [Lin my bitterness].
[2]I will say to God: Do not ·hold [declare] me guilty,
but tell me ·what you have against [why you accuse] me.
[3]·Does it make you happy [*or* Is it right for you] to ·trouble [oppress] me?
·Don't you care about [LMust you despise] me, the work of your
hands?
·Are you happy with [*or* Do you favor] the plans of evil people?
[4]Do you have ·human eyes [Leyes of flesh]
that see ·as we see [Lwith human vision]?
[5]Are your days like the days of humans,
and your years like our years?
[6][LFor] You ·look for the evil I have done [Linvestigate my transgression]
and search for my sin.
[7]You know I am not guilty,
but no one can ·save [rescue] me from your ·power [Lhand].

8"Your hands shaped and made me.
Do you now turn around and ·destroy [Lswallow] me?
9Remember that you molded me like a piece of clay.
Will you now turn me back into dust [Gen. 2:7; Eccl. 12:7]?
10·You formed me inside my mother
like cheese formed from milk [LDo you not pour me out like milk, curdle me like cheese?].
11You dressed me with skin and flesh;
you ·sewed [knit] me together with bones and ·muscles [sinews].
12You gave me life and showed me ·kindness [loyalty],
and in your care you ·watched over my life [Lset a watch over me].

13"But in your heart you hid ·other plans [Lthese things].
I know this was in your mind.
14If I sinned, you would watch me
and would not ·let my sin go unpunished [Ldeclare me innocent of my transgression].
15·How terrible it will be for [LWoe to] me if I am guilty!
Even if I am ·right [righteous], I cannot lift my head.
I am full of shame
and ·experience [Llook on] only ·pain [affliction].
16·If I hold up my head, you hunt me like a lion [*or* Proud like a lion you hunt me]
and again show your terrible power against me.
17You bring new witnesses against me
and increase your anger against me.
Your armies come against me.

18"So why did you ·allow me to be born [Lbring me out of the womb]?
·I wish I had died [LWhy did I not die...?] before ·anyone [Lany eye] saw me.
19I wish I had never lived,
but had been carried straight from ·birth [Lwomb] to the grave.
20The few days of my life are almost over.
Leave me alone so I can have a moment of joy [Eccl. 2:24–26; 3:12–14, 22; 8:15; 5:19–20; 9:7–10].
21Soon I will leave; I will not return
from the land of darkness and gloom,
22the land of ·darkest night [*or* dimness and blackness],
from the land of gloom and ·confusion [chaos],
where even the light is darkness."

Zophar Speaks to Job

11 Then Zophar the Naamathite answered:
2"Should ·these [Lsuch a large number of] words go unanswered?
·Is this talker in the right [*or* Should a talkative man be declared righteous]?
3Your ·lies [Lempty words] do not make people quiet;
people should ·correct [Lshame] you when you ·make fun of God [Lmock].
4You ·say [claim], 'My teachings are ·right [Lpure],
and I am clean in ·God's sight [Lyour eyes].'

5I wish God would speak
and open his ·lips [Lmouth] against you
6and tell you the secrets of wisdom,
because ·wisdom [resourcefulness] has ·two [*or* many] sides.
Know this: God has even forgotten some of your sin [Che has been tolerant of Job's sin].
7"Can you ·understand [Ldiscover] the ·secrets [Ldeep things] of God?
Can you ·search [Ldiscover] the limits of ·the Almighty [Shaddai]?
8His limits are higher than the heavens; ·you cannot reach them [Lwhat can you do]!
They are deeper than ·the grave [LSheol]; you cannot understand them!
9His limits are longer than the earth
and wider than the sea.

10"If God ·comes along [Lpasses by] and puts you in prison
or ·calls you into court [Lassembles for judgment], ·no one can stop him [Lwho can turn him back?].
11God knows who is ·evil [worthless],
and when he sees ·evil [*or* an evil person], ·he takes [Ldoes he not take...?] note of it.
12A ·fool [Lempty-headed person] cannot ·become wise [get understanding]
any more than a wild donkey can ·be born tame [*or* give birth to a human; CZophar insults Job's wisdom].

13"You must ·give your whole heart to him [focus your heart]
and ·hold [spread] out your hands to him for help.
14·Put away [Remove] the sin that is in your hand;
let no ·evil [iniquity] ·remain [Ltake up residence] in your tent [CZophar urges Job to repent].
15Then you can lift up your face without ·shame [Lblemish],
and you can ·stand strong [Lbe secure] without fear.
16You will forget your trouble
and remember it only as water ·gone by [running away].
17Your life will be ·as bright as [brighter than] the noonday sun,
and darkness will seem like morning.
18You will ·feel safe [be secure] because there is hope;
you will ·look around [explore] and ·rest [Llie down] in safety.
19You will lie down, and ·no one will scare you [Lnot tremble with fear].
Many people will want favors from you.
20But the ·wicked will not be able to see [Leyes of the wicked will fail],
so ·they will not escape [Ltheir escape route will be lost to them].
Their only ·hope [expectation] will be to die."

Job Answers Zophar

12 Then Job answered:
2"You ·really [truly] think you are the ·only wise people [Lpeople]
and that when you die, wisdom will die with you [CJob attacks the friends' confidence in their wisdom]!
3But my ·mind [Lheart; Cthe heart was considered the location of thought] is as good as yours;
·you are not better than I am [LI am not inferior to you].

·Everyone knows all these things [LWho is not like these?; Cprobably a reference to the three friends and their intelligence].
4·My friends all laugh at me [LI am a joke to my friends],
I who called on God and he answered me [Ca reference to his earlier days, which the friends now think are a joke];
they laugh at me even though I am right and innocent!
5Those who are ·comfortable [at ease] ·don't care that [Lhave contempt when] others have trouble;
they think it right that those people ·should have troubles [Lhave shaky/unstable feet].
6The tents of ·robbers [marauders] ·are not bothered [Lhave peace and quiet],
and those who make God angry are ·safe [confident].
They have their god in their ·pocket [control; Lhand].

7"But ask the ·animals [beasts; cattle], and they will teach you [Cthat God is unjust],
or ask the birds of the ·air [sky], and they will ·tell [inform] you.
8Speak to the plants of the earth, and they will teach you,
or let the fish of the sea ·tell [recount it to] you.
9·Every one of these knows [LWho does not know…?]
that the hand of the LORD has done this.
10The ·life [Lbreath] of ·every creature [all living things]
and the ·breath [*or* spirit] of all people are in God's hand.
11·The ear tests [Does not the ear test…?] words
as the ·tongue [palate] tastes food.
12Older people are wise,
and long life brings understanding.

13"But only God has wisdom and power,
·good advice [Ladvice] and understanding.
14What he tears down cannot be rebuilt;
anyone he ·puts in prison [Lshuts up] cannot be let out.
15If God holds back the waters, ·there is no rain [Lthey dry up];
if he lets the waters go, they flood the land.
16He is strong and ·victorious [successful; *or* resourceful];
both the one who ·fools others [deceives] and the one who is ·fooled [deceived] belong to him.
17God leads ·the wise away [counselors] ·as captives [plundered]
and ·turns judges into fools [Lrenders judges deluded].
18He ·takes off chains that kings put on [*or* loosens the sash of kings]
and ·puts a garment on their bodies [*or* tightens the waistcloth around their hips; Che undermines their royal prerogatives and powers and causes them pain].
19He leads priests away ·naked [Lplundered]
and destroys the ·powerful [Llong-established].
20He makes trusted people be silent
and takes away the ·wisdom [discernment] of elders.
21He brings disgrace on ·important people [princes]
and ·takes away the weapons [Lloosens the belt] of the strong.
22He uncovers the deep things ·of [Lfrom the] darkness

and brings dark shadows ·into [*or* to overshadow] **the light** [Ccan mean either that God lightens the dark or darkens the light].
23**He makes nations great and then destroys them;**
he makes nations large and then scatters them.
24**He takes ·understanding** [Lheart] **away from the leaders of the earth**
and makes them wander through a ·pathless desert [chaos/wasteland without a path].
25**They ·feel around** [grope] **in darkness with no light;**
he makes them ·stumble [Lwander around] **like drunks.**

13 "·**Now** [Look,] **my eyes have seen all this;**
my ears have heard and understood it [CJob claims to be as wise as the three friends].
2**What you know, I also know.**
·You are not better than I am [LI am not inferior to you; 12:3].
3**But I want to speak to ·the Almighty** [Shaddai]
and [LI would love] **to ·argue my case with** [reprove] **God.**
4**But you smear me with lies** [Cgood doctors would smear their patients with healing lotions].
You are worthless ·doctors [physicians], **all of you!**
5**I wish you would just ·stop talking** [shut up];
then you would really be wise [Prov. 17:28]!
6**Listen to my ·argument** [reproof],
and ·hear [Lpay attention to] **the ·pleading** [Laccusation] **of my lips.**
7**·You should not speak evil in the name of** [LWill you speak unjustly for…?] **God;**
·you cannot speak God's truth by telling lies [Lwill you speak deceitful things about him?].
8**·You should not unfairly choose his side against mine** [LWill you favor him…?];
·you should not argue the case [Lif you make an accusation] **for God.**
9**·You will not do** [Will it go…?] **well if he examines you;**
you cannot ·fool [deceive] **God as you might ·fool** [deceive] **humans.**
10**God would surely ·scold** [reprimand; reprove] **you**
if you ·unfairly [*or* secretly] **took one person's side.**
11[LDoes not…?] **His ·bright glory** [majesty] **would scare you,**
and ·you would be very much afraid of him [Lhis fear fall on you].
12**Your ·wise sayings** [Lproclamations] **are ·worth no more than ashes** [Lare made of dust],
and your ·arguments [responses] **are ·as weak as** [Lmade of] **clay.**

13"**Be quiet and let me speak.**
Let things happen to me as they will.
14**·Why should I** [*or* I will…] **·put myself in danger** [Ltake my flesh in my teeth; Ca metaphor for risk-taking]
and take my life in my own ·hands [Lpalm]?
15**·Even if God kills me, I have hope in him** [*or* See, he will kill me; I have no hope];
I will ·still defend [reprove him concerning] **my ways to his face.**
16**This is my salvation.**
The wicked cannot come ·before him [into his presence].

17“Listen ·carefully [closely] to my words;
let your ears hear what I say.
18See, I have prepared ·my case [for the judgment],
and I know I ·will be proved right [*or* am righteous].
19·No one can accuse [LWho is it that accuses…?] me of doing wrong.
If someone can, I will be quiet and die.

20“God, please just give me these two things,
and then I will not hide from you:
21Take your ·punishment [Lpalm] away from me,
and stop frightening me with your terrors.
22Then call me, and I will answer,
or let me speak, and you answer.
23·How many [*or* What are the] ·evil things [faults] and sins have I done?
·Show [Make known to] me my ·wrong [transgressions] and my sin.
24·Don’t [LWhy do you…?] hide your face from me;
don’t ·think of me as [consider me] your enemy [Ps. 30:6–7].
25·Don’t punish [LWill you frighten…?] a leaf that is blown by the wind;
·don’t [Land] chase after straw.
26You write down ·cruel [bitter] things against me
and make me ·suffer for [inherit] my boyhood sins.
27You put my feet in ·chains [stocks]
and ·keep close watch wherever I go [Lguard all my paths].
You even ·mark [incise; cut] the soles of my feet [Cto leave a
distinctive footprint easily followed].

28“Everyone wears out like something rotten,
like clothing eaten by moths.

14 “·All of us [LHuman beings; TMan] born ·to women [Tof woman]
·live only a few [Lare short of] days and ·have lots [full] of trouble.
2·We [LThey] grow up like flowers and then ·dry up and die [Lwither].
·We are like a passing [L…and flee like a] shadow that does not last.
3Lord, do you need to watch me like this?
Must you bring me before you to be judged?
4No one can bring something clean [Cin a ritual sense] from something
unclean.
5·Our [LIf their] time is limited.
You have given ·us [Lthem] only so many months to live
and have set limits ·we [Lthey] cannot go beyond.
6So look away from us and ·leave us alone [stop; desist]
until we put in our time like a laborer [Cuntil death].

7“If a tree is cut down,
there is hope that it will grow again
and will send out new ·branches [shoots].
8Even if its roots grow old in the ground,
and its stump dies in the ·dirt [dust],
9at the ·smell [scent] of water it will bud
and put out new ·shoots [boughs] like a plant.
10But ·we [Lmortals] die, and ·our bodies are laid in the ground
[Ldwindle away];

·we take our last breath [Lhumans expire] and are ·gone [Lno more; Cunlike trees, humans do not come back to life].
11Water disappears from a ·lake [sea],
and a river ·loses its water and dries up [Ldries up and withers away].
12In the same way, ·we [Lhumans] lie down and do not rise again;
·we [Lthey] will not get up or be awakened
until the heavens disappear [Cthat is, never].

13"I wish you would hide me in ·the grave [LSheol; Cthe grave or the underworld];
·hide [conceal] me until your anger is gone.
I wish you would set a ·time [limit]
and then remember me!
14Will the dead live again [Cthe implied answer is no]?
All my days are ·a struggle [Lhard service];
I will wait until my ·change [Lrelease] comes.
15You ·will call [Lwould summon me], and I ·will [*or* would] answer you;
you ·will [*or* would] desire the ·creature your hands have made [Lwork of your hands].
16·Then [*or* Now] you ·will count [count] my steps [Cmeaning God would focus negatively on Job's sin],
but you ·will [*or* would] not keep track of my sin [Cin a hypothetical future].
17My wrongs ·will [*or* would] be closed up in a bag,
and you ·will [*or* would] cover up my sin.

18"A mountain ·washes [Lfalls] away and crumbles;
and a rock can be moved from its place.
19Water ·washes over stones and wears them down [Lgrinds down the stones],
and ·rushing waters [*or* violent storms] wash away the ·dirt [dust].
In the same way, you destroy hope.
20You ·defeat [overpower] people forever, and they are gone;
you change their appearance [Cfrom joy to despair] and send them away.
21Their children are honored, but they do not know it [Cbecause they, the parents, are dead or dying];
their children are ·disgraced [lowered], but they [Cthe parents] do not see it.
22They [Cthe parents] only feel the pain of their ·body [Lflesh]
and ·feel sorry [mourn] for themselves."

Eliphaz Answers Job

15 Then Eliphaz the Temanite answered:
2"·A wise person would not [LShould a wise person…?]
answer with ·empty [Lwindy] words
or fill his stomach with the hot east wind.
3·He would not [LShould he…?] ·argue [reprimand; reprove] with useless words
or make speeches that have no value.
4But you even ·destroy [invalidate] ·respect for God [Lfear]
and limit the worship of him.
5Your ·sin [iniquity] teaches your mouth what to say;

you ·use words to trick others [Lchoose the tongue of the crafty].
6 It is your own mouth, not mine, that ·shows you are wicked [condemns];
your own lips testify against you.

7 "·You are not [LAre you…?] the first man ever born [Cperhaps a reference to Adam; Ezek. 28:12–13];
·you are not [Lare you…?] older than the hills [Ceither a reference to the wisdom of the elders or to wisdom personified as a woman; Prov. 8:22–25].
8 ·You did not [LDid you…?] listen in on God's secret council [Clike a prophet].
But you limit wisdom to yourself.
9 ·You don't [LDo you…?] know any more than we know.
·You don't [LDo you…?] understand any more than we understand.
10 Old people with gray hair are on our side;
they are even older than your father.
11 Is the ·comfort [consolation] God gives you not enough for you,
even when words are spoken gently to you?
12 Has your heart ·carried you away from God [Ltaken you away; Cperhaps suggesting that Job has lost control of his emotions]?
Why do your eyes ·flash with anger [*or* wink]?
13 Why do you ·speak out your anger [Lturn your spirit] against God?
Why do these words pour out of your mouth?

14 "How can anyone be pure?
How can someone born to a woman be ·good [righteous]?
15 God places no trust in his holy ones [Cangels],
and even the heavens are not pure in his eyes.
16 How much less pure is one who is ·terrible [abominable] and ·rotten [corrupt]
and drinks up ·evil [injustice] as if it were water [Prov. 4:17–19]!

17 "Listen to me, and I will tell you about it;
I will ·tell [recount to] you what I have seen.
18 These are things wise men have told;
their ancestors told them, and they have hidden nothing.
19 (The land was given to their fathers only,
and no ·foreigner [stranger] lived among them [Csuggesting wisdom untainted by foreign influence].)
20 The wicked suffer pain all their lives;
the cruel suffer during all the years saved up for them.
21 Terrible sounds ·fill [reach; Lare in] their ears,
and when things ·seem to be going well [are at peace], ·robbers [*or* destroyers] attack them.
22 Evil people ·give up trying [Lcannot hope] to ·escape [Lreturn] from the darkness;
it has been decided that they will die by the sword.
23 They wander around ·and will become food for vultures [*or* for food, saying "Where is it?"].
They know [La day of] darkness ·will soon come [Lis prepared for them].
24 ·Worry [Distress] and ·suffering [hardship] terrify them;

they overwhelm them, like a king ready to attack,
25because they ·shake their fists at [Lstretched their hands against; Ex. 6:6; Deut. 4:34] God
and ·try to get their own way against [defy] ·the Almighty [Shaddai].
26They ·stubbornly [defiantly] charge at God
with ·thick, strong [Lthick-bossed; Cthe boss is the convex centerpiece] shields.

27"Although the faces of the wicked are thick with fat [Ca sign of prosperity, but here the result of ill-gotten gain],
and their ·bellies [*or* loins] are fat with ·flesh [blubber],
28they will live in towns that are ruined,
in houses where no one lives,
·which are crumbling into ruins [Ldestined to become a ruin heap].
29The wicked will no longer ·get [*or* be] rich,
and the riches they have will not last [Ps. 73; Prov. 11:18; 13:11; 21:6; 22:16]
the things they own will no longer spread over the land.
30They will not ·escape [Lturn aside from] the darkness.
A flame will dry up their ·branches [shoots];
God's breath will carry the wicked away."
31The wicked should not fool themselves by trusting what is useless.
If they do, they will get nothing in return [C"useless" and "nothing" are the same Hebrew word].
32Their branches will dry up ·before they finish growing [Lout of season]
and will never turn green.
33They will be like a vine whose grapes ·are pulled [shake] off before they are ripe,
like an olive tree that ·loses [throws off] its blossoms.
34·People without God [LThe assembly of the godless] ·can produce nothing [Lare barren].
Fire will ·destroy [consume] the tents of those who take ·money to do evil [Lbribes],
35who ·plan [Lconceive] trouble and give birth to evil,
whose ·hearts [Lwomb] plan ways to ·trick [Ldefraud; Ps. 7:14; Is. 59:4] others."

Job Answers Eliphaz

16 Then Job answered:
2"I have heard many things like these.
You are all ·painful [*or* troublesome] comforters!
3Will your ·long-winded speeches [Lwindy words] never end?
What ·makes [Lprovokes] you keep on ·arguing [Lresponding]?
4I also could speak as you do
if you were in my place.
I could ·make great speeches [Ljoin words] against you
and shake my head at you [Clike wagging a finger at someone].
5But, instead, I would ·encourage you [Lstrengthen you with my mouth],
and ·my words [Lthe words of my lips] would bring you ·relief [comfort].

15:30 God's breath will carry the wicked away Some Greek copies read "their blossom will be carried off by the wind."

6 “Even if I speak, my pain is not less,
and if I don’t speak, it still does not go away.
7 ·God, you have [[L]He has] surely ·taken away my strength [worn me out]
and ·destroyed [*or* stunned] ·my whole family [*or* everyone around me; [L]my assembly].
8 You have ·made me thin and weak [shriveled me up; *or* bound me],
·and this shows I have done wrong [[L]as a witness against me].
9 God ·attacks me and tears me with anger [[L]preys on me and hates me];
he ·grinds [gnashes] his teeth at me;
my enemy ·stares at me with his angry eyes [[L]sharpens his eyes at me].
10 People open their mouths ·to make fun of [[L]wide at] me
and hit my cheeks to ·insult [*or* reproach] me.
They ·join [congregate; assemble] together against me.
11 God has turned me over to evil people
and has ·handed [thrown] me over to the wicked.
12 ·Everything was fine with me [[L]I was at ease],
but God ·broke me into pieces [shattered me];
he ·held [grabbed; seized] me by the neck and ·crushed [mauled] me.
He has ·made me [set me up as] his target;
13 his archers surround me.
He ·stabs [[L]splits open] my kidneys without mercy;
he spills my ·blood [[L]gall] on the ground.
14 ·Again and again God attacks me [[L]He breaches me, breach after breach];
he runs at me like a soldier.

15 “I have sewed ·rough cloth over my skin to show my sadness [sackcloth over my skin; [C]traditional mourning clothes]
and have buried my ·face [[L]horn] in the dust [[C]a sign of grief; like an animal lowering its horn].
16 My face is red from crying;
I have ·dark circles [deep darkness] around my eyes.
17 Yet my hands have never done anything ·cruel [violent],
and my prayer is pure.

18 “Earth, please do not cover up my blood.
Don’t let my cry ever ·stop being heard [find a place of rest]!
19 Even now I have ·one who speaks for me [[L]a witness] in heaven;
the one who ·is on my side [[L]testifies for me] is high above.
20 ·The one who speaks for me is my friend [*or* My friends scorn me].
My eyes pour out tears to God.
21 He ·begs God [negotiates/arbitrates with God] on behalf of a human
as a person ·begs for [negotiates/arbitrates with] his friend.
22 “Only a few years will pass
before I go on the journey of no return [[C]at his death].

17 My spirit is broken;
the days of my life are ·almost gone [extinguished].
The grave is ·waiting [ready] for me.
2 Those who ·laugh [mock; scoff] at me surround me;
·I watch them insult me [[L]My eye dwells/lodges on their obstinate behavior].

3 “·God, make me a promise [[L]Make a pledge for me with yourself].

·No one will make a pledge for me [[L]Who else will clap hands with me; [C]a gesture that seals an agreement].
[4]**You have closed their minds to understanding.**
·Do not let them win over me [[L]You will not let them triumph].
[5]**People might ·speak against** [denounce] **their friends for ·money** [[L]a share; a piece of property],
but if they do, the eyes of their children ·go blind [[L]will fade].

[6]**"God has made my name a ·curse word** [[L]proverb; byword; 1 Kin. 9:7; 2 Chr. 7:20; Ps. 44:14; Jer. 24:9; Ezek. 14:8; Joel 2:17];
people spit in my face.
[7]**My sight has grown ·weak** [dim] **because of my ·sadness** [grief],
and my ·body [whole frame] **is ·as thin as** [[L]like] **a shadow.**
[8]**·Honest** [Virtuous] **people are ·upset** [depressed; desolated] **about this;**
·innocent [blameless] **people are ·upset with** [*or* aroused against] **those who ·do wrong** [*or* are godless].
[9]**But ·those who do right** [the righteous] **will ·continue to do right** [[L]hold on to their way],
and those whose hands are ·not dirty with sin [[L]clean; [C]in a ritual sense] **will grow stronger.**

[10]**"But, all of you, come ·and try again** [[L]back now]!
I ·do [*or* will] **not find a wise person among you.**
[11]**My days are gone, and my plans have been ·destroyed** [[L]torn away],
along with the desires of my heart.
[12]**·These men think night is** [[L]They make night into] **day;**
·when it is dark, they say, 'Light is near [[L]light is near the darkness].'
[13]**If the only home I hope for is ·the grave** [[L]Sheol; [C]the place of the dead],
if I spread out my bed in darkness,
[14]**if I say to the ·grave** [[L]pit], **'You are my father,'**
and to the worm, 'You are my mother' or 'You are my sister,'
[15]**where, then, is my hope?**
Who can see any hope for me?
[16]**Will hope go down to the gates of ·death** [[L]Sheol; 17:13]?
Will we go down together into the dust?"

Bildad Answers Job

18 **Then Bildad the Shuhite answered:**
[2]**"·When will you stop these speeches** [[L]How long before you stop these words]?
·Be sensible [*or* Reflect], **and then we can talk** [Prov. 15:28; 18:13; 29:20].
[3]**·You think of** [[L]Why do you consider/count] **us as cattle,**
as ·if we are stupid [[L]stupid in your eyes/estimation].
[4]**You tear ·yourself** [your life] **to pieces in your anger.**
Should the earth be vacant ·just for [*or* because of] **you?**
Should the rocks move from their places [14:18]?

[5]**"The lamp of the wicked will be put out,**
and the flame in their lamps will stop burning.
[6]**The light in their tents will grow dark,**
and the lamps ·by their sides [*or* above them] **will go out.**
[7]**Their ·strong steps** [vigorous gait] **will grow ·weak** [cramped; restricted];

·they will fall into their own evil traps [*or* their own schemes/advice
will throw them down].
8Their feet will be caught in a net [Prov. 28:9]
when they walk into ·its web [a snare].
9A trap will catch them by the heel [Prov. 22:5]
and [La noose] hold them tight.
10A ·trap for them [Lrope] is hidden on the ground,
right in their path.
11·Terrible things [LTerrors] startle them from every side
and ·chase [*or* disperse] them at ·every step [Ltheir feet].
12·Hunger takes away their strength [*or* Calamity is hungry for them],
and disaster is ·at their side [*or* prepared for them when they
stumble].
13Disease eats away ·parts of their skin [*or* their fleshy limbs];
·death [Lthe firstborn of Death; Cdeath is personified] ·gnaws at
[consumes] their ·arms and legs [Llimbs].
14They are torn from the ·safety [confidence] of their tents
and ·dragged off to Death, the King of Terrors [Lterrors march them
off to their king].
15·Their tents are set on fire [*or* Nothing of theirs will remain in their
tents],
and sulfur is scattered over their ·homes [*or* pastures].
16Their roots dry up below ground,
and their branches die above ground [Cthe wicked are like a dead tree].
17People on earth will not remember them;
their names will be forgotten in the land.
18They will be driven from light into darkness
and ·chased [driven] out of the world [Cthey will die].
19They have no children or descendants among their people,
and no one will be left alive where they once lived.
20People ·of the west [*or* who come after] will be ·shocked [desolated] ·at
what has happened to them [by their end/fate],
and people ·of the east [*or* who came before] will be ·very frightened
[seized with horror].
21Surely this is ·what will happen to [Lthe dwelling of] the wicked;
such is the place of one who does not know God."

Job Answers Bildad

19 Then Job answered:
2"How long will you ·hurt [torment] me
and crush me with your words?
3You have ·insulted [disgraced; shamed] me ten times ·now [over]
and ·attacked me without shame [*or* are you not shamed to wrong
me?].
4Even if I have ·sinned [erred; made a mistake],
·it is my worry alone [Lmy sin/mistake lodges within me].
5If you want to make yourselves ·look better than I [*or* powerful against
me],
you can ·blame me for my suffering [make my shame/disgrace an
argument against me].
6Then know that God has ·wronged [*or* a distorted view of; unjustly
blamed] me
and ·pulled [thrown] his net around me [Clike a hunter].

7"I shout, '·I have been wronged [[L]Violence]!'
But I get no answer.
I scream for help
but I get no justice.
8God has ·blocked [walled up] my way so I cannot pass;
he has covered my paths with darkness [Prov. 4:19].
9He has ·taken away [stripped off] my ·honor [glory]
and removed the crown from my head.
10He beats me down on every side until I am gone;
he ·destroys [uproots] my hope like a fallen tree.
11·His anger burns [[L]He kindles his anger] against me,
and he ·treats [*or* considers] me like an ·enemy [foe].
12His ·armies [troops] gather;
they ·prepare to attack [[L]build up a road against; [C]a siege ramp] me.
They camp around my tent.

13"God has ·made my brothers my enemies [[L]moved my brothers far from me],
and my friends have become strangers.
14·My relatives [[L]Those near me] have ·gone away [*or* failed me],
and my ·friends [acquaintances] have forgotten me.
15My guests and my ·female servants [[T]maidservants] ·treat [*or* consider] me like a stranger;
they look at me as if I were a foreigner.
16I call for my servant, but he does not answer,
even when I ·beg him with my own mouth [ask him for a personal favor].
17My wife ·can't stand [abhors] my breath,
and my own family ·dislikes me [finds me repulsive].
18Even the little boys ·hate [[L]reject] me
and talk ·about [*or* against] me when I leave.
19All my close friends ·hate [[L]detest] me;
even those I love have turned against me.
20·I am nothing but skin and bones [[L]My bones cling to my skin and my flesh];
I have escaped by the skin of my teeth.
21Pity me, my friends, pity me,
because the hand of God has ·hit [touched; struck] me.
22Why do you ·chase [pursue; persecute] me as God does?
·Haven't you hurt me enough [[L]Aren't you satisfied with my flesh]?

23"How I wish my words were written down,
·written [[L]inscribed] on a scroll.
24I wish they were carved with an iron pen ·into [[L]and] lead,
or carved into stone ·forever [*or* as a witness; [C]Job wants the following statement to last].
25I know that my ·Defender [Redeemer; *or* defender; redeemer; [C]likely referring to God himself] lives,
and ·in the end [*or* at last] he will ·stand upon [rise up on] the earth [[L]dust].
26Even after my skin has been ·destroyed [*or* peeled off],
·in [from; *or* without] my flesh I will see God.

27I will see him myself;
I ·myself [Land not a stranger] will see him with my very own eyes.
How my heart ·wants that to happen [Lfades/faints within me]!

28"·If [*or* When] you say, '·We will continue to trouble Job [LHow should we pursue/persecute him?],
because the ·problem [Lroot of the matter] lies with him,'
29you should be afraid of the sword yourselves.
·God's anger [LWrath] will bring punishment by the sword.
Then you will know there is judgment."

Zophar Answers

20 Then Zophar the Naamathite answered:
2"My ·troubled thoughts [distress; worries] cause me to ·answer [respond],
because ·I am very upset [Lof the agitation within me].
3You ·correct [instruct] me and I am ·insulted [shamed],
but ·I understand how to answer you [*or* a spirit beyond my understanding gives me an answer].

4"·You [LDo you not…?] know how it has been ·for a long time [since time immemorial],
ever since ·people were first put [*or* he put people] on the earth.
5The ·happiness [luxuriance; enjoyment] of evil people is brief,
and the joy of the ·wicked [Lgodless] lasts only a moment.
6·Their pride may be [LThey may go] as high as the heavens,
and their heads may touch the clouds,
7but they will ·be gone [perish] forever, like their own dung.
People who ·knew [Lsaw] them will say, 'Where are they?'
8They will fly away like a dream
and not be found again;
they will be ·chased away [put to flight] like a vision in the night.
9·Those who [LThe eye that] saw them will not see them again;
the places where they lived will see them no more.
10Their children will ·have to pay back [*or* run after] the poor,
and ·they will have to give up [Ltheir hand will return] their wealth.
11They had the strength of their youth in their bones,
but it will lie with them in the dust of death.

12"Evil may taste sweet in their mouths,
and they may hide it under their tongues.
13They ·cannot stand to [Lfight/linger over it and do not] let go of it;
they ·keep it in their mouths [Lhide it under their tongues].
14But their food ·will turn sour [Lturns over] in their stomachs,
like the poison of a ·snake [asp] inside them.
15They have swallowed riches, but they will ·spit [vomit] them out;
God will make them ·vomit [disgorge] ·their riches up [Lit from their bellies; Prov. 11:4; 21:6].
16They will suck the poison of ·snakes [asps],
and the ·snake's fangs [Lviper's tongue] will kill them.
17They will not ·admire [Llook at] ·the sparkling streams [*or* streams of oil]
or the rivers flowing with honey and ·cream [*or* butter; *or* curds].

[18]They must give back ·what they worked for [their gains] ·without eating it [unswallowed];
they will not enjoy the ·money they made from their trading [*or* benefit of their reward],
[19]because they ·troubled the poor and left them with nothing [[L]crushed and abandoned the poor].
They have ·taken [stolen] houses they did not build [Prov. 28:27; 29:7].

[20]"Evil people never ·lack an appetite [[L]experience ease/comfort in their bellies],
and nothing ·escapes their selfishness [[L]they covet escapes them].
[21]But nothing will be left ·for them to eat [*or* after they eat];
their riches will not continue.
[22]When they still have plenty, ·trouble will catch up to them [[L]they will have distress],
and ·great misery [[L]all the force/hand of trouble] will come down on them.
[23]When the wicked fill their stomachs,
God will send his burning anger against them,
·and blows of punishment will fall on them like rain [*or* raining it on them like their food].
[24]The wicked may run away from an iron weapon,
but a bronze ·arrow [[L]bow] will ·stab [pierce] them.
[25]They will pull the arrows out of their backs
and pull the points out of their ·livers [[L]gall bladders].
·Terrors [Dread] will come over them;
[26] total darkness ·waits for their treasure [*or* is stored up for them].
A fire not fanned by people [[C]perhaps lightning] will ·destroy [[L]consume] them
and ·burn up [[L]horrible things will happen to] ·what is left of [*or* the survivors in] their tents.
[27]The heavens will ·show [reveal] their guilt,
and the earth will rise up against them.
[28]·A flood will carry their houses away [*or* The possessions of their house will be taken away],
·swept away [[L]like the torrents] on the day of God's anger.
[29]This is ·what God plans for evil [[L]the lot/fate of guilty] people;
·this is what he has decided they will receive [[L]the inheritance decreed by God]."

Job Answers Zophar

21 Then Job answered:
[2]"Listen carefully to my words [[C]Job feels that his previous speeches have not been heard],
and let this be ·the way you comfort me [[L]your consolation].
[3]·Be patient [Bear with me] while I speak.
After I have finished, you may ·continue to make fun of [ridicule; mock] me.

[4]"My complaint is not just against people;
I have reason to be impatient.
[5]Look at me and be ·shocked [desolated];
put your hand over your mouth in shock.

[6]When I think about this [Cthe success of the wicked], I am terribly afraid
and ·my body shakes [Ltrembling seizes my flesh].
[7]Why ·do evil people live a long time [Lare evil people allowed to live]?
They grow old and ·become more powerful [increase in strength].
[8]They see their children ·around [Lestablished before] them;
they watch them grow up.
[9]Their homes are safe and without fear;
·God does not punish them [LGod's rod is not on them].
[10]Their bulls never fail to mate;
their cows ·have healthy calves [Lcalve and have no miscarriages].
[11]They send out their ·children [infants] like a flock [Cthey will have many children, a sign of blessing];
their ·little ones [children] dance about.
[12]They sing to the music of tambourines and ·harps [lyres],
and the sound of the flute makes them ·happy [rejoice].
[13]Evil people ·enjoy successful lives [Llive out their days in prosperity]
and then go ·peacefully [in tranquility] to ·the grave [LSheol].
[14]They say to God, '·Leave us alone [Get away from me]!
We don't ·want [desire] to know your ways.
[15]Who is ·the Almighty [Shaddai] that we should serve him?
What would we gain by ·praying to [interceding with] him?'
[16]·The success of the wicked is not their own doing [*or* Is not the success/prosperity of the wicked in their control/hand?].
Their ·way of thinking [plan; counsel] is ·different [far] from ·mine [*or* his; Cthat is, God's].
[17]Yet how often are the lamps of evil people ·turned off [extinguished; Cthe implied answer is not often; Job questions the type of teaching found in Proverbs; Prov. 24:19–20]?
How often does ·trouble [calamity] come to them [Prov. 24:21–22]?
How often ·do they suffer God's angry punishment [Ldoes he deal out pain in his anger]?
[18]·How often are they [*or* Let them be] like straw in the wind
or like chaff that is blown away by a storm [Ps. 1:4]?
[19]It is said [Cdefenders of the idea that the wicked suffer for their sins],
'God ·saves [stores] up a person's ·punishment [guilt] for his children.'
But God should ·punish [pay back] the wicked themselves so they will know it.
[20]Their eyes should see their own destruction,
and they should ·suffer [Ldrink from the] the anger of ·the Almighty [Shaddai].
[21]They do not care about the families they leave behind
when their lives have come to an end.

[22]"·No one [LWho…?] can teach knowledge to God;
he is the one who judges even the most ·important [exalted] people [CJob wants to teach God to punish the wicked but thinks his attempt will be futile].
[23]One person dies ·while he still has all his strength [Lin perfect vigor],
feeling completely safe and ·comfortable [untroubled].
[24]His ·body [*or* pail] was ·well fed [Lfull of milk],

and ·his bones were strong and healthy [Lthe marrow of his bones were well lubricated].
25**But another person dies ·with an unhappy heart** [Lin bitterness],
never enjoying ·any happiness [*or* the good life].
26**They ·are buried next to each other** [Llie down together in the dust],
and worms cover them both.

27**"I know very well your thoughts**
and your ·plans [schemes] **to ·wrong** [hurt; do violence to] **me.**
28**You** [Cthe friends] **ask, 'Where is this ·great man's** [Lprince's] **house?**
Where are the tents where the wicked live [Cthey don't agree with Job that the wicked are rich and successful]**?'**
29**Have you never asked those who ·travel** [Lpass by on the road]**?**
Have you ·never listened to their stories [Lnot recognized their signs]**?**
30**On the day of ·God's anger and punishment** [Lcalamity; disaster],
it is the wicked who are spared.
31**Who will accuse them to their faces?**
Who will pay them back for the evil they have done?
32**They are carried to their graves,**
and someone keeps watch over their tombs [Ca sign of a peaceful death and burial].
33**The dirt in the valley seems sweet to them.**
Everybody follows after them,
and many people go before them.

34**"So how can you comfort me with this ·nonsense** [empty/meaningless drivel]**?**
Your answers are ·only lies [*or* disloyal]**!"**

Eliphaz Answers

22 Then Eliphaz the Temanite answered:
2**"Can anyone ·be of real use to** [benefit] **God?**
Can even a ·wise [skilled] **person ·do him good** [benefit him]**?**
3**Does it ·help** [delight; give pleasure to] **·the Almighty** [Shaddai] **for you to be ·good** [righteous]**?**
·Does he gain anything [What profit is it to him] **if you are ·innocent** [blameless]**?**
4**Does God ·punish** [reprimand; reprove] **you for ·respecting him** [Lyour fear; Cin the sense of piety]**?**
Does he ·bring you into court for this [Lenter into judgment with you]**?**
5**No! It is because your evil is ·without limits** [Labundant]
and your ·sins have [guilt has] **no end.**
6**You ·took your brothers' things for a debt they didn't owe** [Lexacted pledges from your brothers for no reason; Ex. 21:25–27];
you took clothes from people and left them naked.
7**You did not give water to ·tired** [weary] **people,**
and you kept food from the ·hungry [famished; starving].
8**·You were a powerful man who** [LThe powerful] **owned land;**
·you were honored and [Lthe favored] **lived in the land.**
9**But you sent widows away empty-handed,**
and you ·mistreated [Lcrushed the arms/strength of the] **orphans.**
10**That is why traps are all around you**
and sudden danger frightens you.

[11]That is why it is so dark you cannot see
and a flood of water covers you.

[12]"·God is [LIs not God…?] in the highest part of heaven.
See how high the highest stars are [CGod is even higher]!
[13]But you ask, 'What does God know?
Can he judge us through the ·dark clouds [thick darkness]?
[14]Thick clouds ·cover [hide] him so he cannot see us
as he ·walks [wanders] around ·high up in the sky [Lthe vault/dome of heaven; CEliphaz suspects Job denies God knows what is going on in human affairs].'
[15]Are you going to ·stay on [guard] the ·old [ancient] path
where ·evil [guilty] people ·walk [tread]?
[16]They were ·carried away [*or* bound up] before their time was up,
and their foundations were washed away by a ·flood [Lriver].
[17]They said to God, '·Leave us alone [Get away from us; 21:14]!
·The Almighty can do nothing [LWhat can the Almighty/Shaddai do…?] to us.'
[18]But ·it was God [Lwas it not he…?] who filled their houses with good things.
Their ·way of thinking [plan; counsel] is ·different [far] from mine [21:16].

[19]"·Good [Righteous] people can watch and be glad;
the innocent can ·laugh at [mock; ridicule] them and say,
[20]'Surely our enemies are destroyed,
and fire burns up ·their wealth [*or* what is left of theirs].'

[21]"·Obey God [LGet along with him] and be at peace with him;
this is the way to ·happiness [*or* prosperity; CEliphaz calls on Job to repent].
[22]Accept ·teaching [instruction] from his mouth,
and ·keep [put] his words in your heart.
[23]If you return to ·the Almighty [Shaddai], you will be ·blessed again [Lrestored].
So remove ·evil [iniquity] from your ·house [Ltent].
[24]·Throw [Put] your gold nuggets into the dust
and ·your fine gold [LOphir; Creferring to the fine gold of the region of Ophir, perhaps southern Arabia] among the rocks in the ·ravines [wadis].
[25]Then ·the Almighty [Shaddai] will be your gold
and the ·best [choice] silver for you.
[26]You will ·find pleasure [delight] in ·the Almighty [Shaddai],
and you will ·look up [show favor] to him.
[27]You will ·pray to [entreat] him, and he will hear you,
and you will keep your ·promises [vows; Cmade in anticipation of answered prayer] to him.
[28]Anything you decide will be done,
and light will ·shine on [illuminate] your ways.
[29]When people are made humble and you say, '·Have courage [*or* It is pride],'
then ·the humble [Lthose with downcast eyes] will be saved.

30·Even a guilty person will escape [*or* He rescues the innocent]
and ·be saved [*or* and saves you] because your hands are ·clean [pure]."

Job Answers

23 Then Job answered:
2"My ·complaint [*or* speech] is still ·bitter [*or* rebellious] today.
·I groan because God's heavy hand is on me [*or* My hand is heavy with groaning].
3I wish I knew where to find God
so I could go to ·where he lives [Lhis place].
4I would present my case before him
and fill my mouth with ·arguments [*or* reprimands; reproofs].
5I would learn ·how [Lthe words by which] he would answer me
and would think about what he would say.
6Would he not ·argue [present his case] ·strongly [Lwith great power] against me?
No, he would really listen to me.
7·Then [LThere] an ·honest [virtuous] person could ·present his case to God [reprimand/reprove him],
and I would ·be saved [escape] forever ·by [*or* from] my judge.

8"If I go to the east, God is not there;
if I go to the west, I do not ·see [perceive] him.
9When he ·is at work [acts] in the north, I catch no ·sight [glimpse] of him;
when he ·turns to [Lwraps himself up in] the south, I cannot see him.
10But God knows the way that I take,
and when he has tested me, I will come out like gold [Ps. 139:23–24].
11My feet have ·closely followed [Lheld fast to] his steps;
I have stayed in his ·way [path; Prov. 4:10–11];
I did not turn aside.
12I have never ·left [departed from] the commands ·he has spoken [Lof his lips];
I have ·treasured his words more than my own [Lstored up in my bosom the speeches of his mouth].

13"But he is ·the only God [unique].
Who can ·come against him [Lturn him back]?
He does anything he wants.
14He will do to me what he ·said he would do [has designated for me],
and he ·has [*or* may have] many plans like this.
15That is why I am ·frightened [terrified] of ·him [Lhis presence];
when I ·think of [reflect on] this, I am ·afraid [in dread] of him.
16God has made ·me afraid [Lmy heart timid];
·the Almighty [LShaddai] terrifies me.
17But I am not ·hidden [silenced] by the darkness,
by the thick darkness that covers my face [Cthough afraid, Job still seeks to set God straight].

24 "·I wish the Almighty would set a time for judging [LWhy are times not kept by the Almighty/Shaddai?].
·Those who know God do [LWhy do those who know God …?] not see such a day.

2·Wicked people [[L]They] ·take other people's land [[L]move boundaries;
[C]move boundary markers];
they steal flocks and ·take them to new pastures [[L]pasture them].
3They chase away the orphan's donkey
and take the widow's ox ·when she has no money [[L]as a pledge; Deut. 24:6, 10–13, 17].
4They push needy people off the path;
all the poor of the land hide from them.
5The poor become like wild donkeys in the ·desert [wilderness]
who go about their ·job of finding food [[L]work].
·The desert gives them [[L]In the desert they forage for] food for their children.
6They ·gather hay and straw in the fields [[L]reap in fields not their own]
and ·pick up leftover grapes [[L]glean] from the vineyard of the wicked.
7They spend the night naked, because they have no clothes,
nothing to cover themselves in the cold.
8They are soaked from mountain ·rains [storms]
and ·stay near [hug; embrace] the ·large rocks [cliffs] because they have no shelter.
9The ·fatherless child [orphan] is grabbed from its mother's breast;
they take a poor mother's baby ·to pay for what she owes [[L]as a pledge; 24:3].
10So the poor ·go [wander] around naked without any clothes;
they carry bundles of grain but still go hungry;
11they crush olives to get oil
and grapes to get wine, but they still go thirsty.
12Dying people groan in the city,
and the ·injured [*or* living dead] cry out for help,
but God ·accuses no one of doing wrong [*or* does not hear/react to their prayers].

13"Those who ·fight [rebel] against the light
do not ·know [recognize] God's ways
or stay in his paths.
14·When the day is over [*or* At the light], the murderers get up
to ·kill [slay] the poor and needy.
At night they go about like thieves [Ex. 22:2].
15·Those who are guilty of adultery [[L]The eyes of the adulterer] watch for the ·night [dusk],
thinking, 'No ·one [[L]eye] will see us,'
and they keep their faces covered [Prov. 7:6–9].
16In the dark, evil people break into houses [v. 14].
In the daytime they ·shut [seal] themselves up in their own houses,
because they ·want nothing to do with [[L]do not know] the light.
17Darkness is like morning to all these evil people
who ·make friends with [[L]recognize] the terrors of darkness.

18"·They [The wicked] are ·like foam floating [*or* like scum; [L]quick] on the water.
Their ·part of the land [lot; portion] is cursed;
no one ·uses the road that goes by [[L]turns toward] their vineyards.

[CThis seems to contradict Job's contention that the wicked escape judgment. Perhaps these are his opponents' views, or his wish.]

19As ·heat and dryness [the desert and heat] ·quickly melt the snow
[Lsteal away the snow waters],
so ·the grave [LSheol] quickly takes away the sinners.
20·Their mothers [LThe womb] forget them,
and worms ·will eat their bodies [Lthink they are sweet].
They will not be remembered,
so wickedness is broken in pieces like a ·stick [Ltree; Cperhaps by wind or lightening; Ps. 29:5–6; Ezek. 17:24].
21These evil people ·abuse women who cannot have children [*or* associate with barren women]
·and show no kindness to widows [*or* which is not favorable to their widow].
22But God drags away the strong by his power.
Even though they ·seem strong [Lrise up], they ·do not know how long they will live [Lcan have no confidence in life].
23God may ·let these evil people feel safe [give them security they can lean on],
but ·he is watching [Lhis eyes are on] their ways.
24For a little while they are ·important [exalted], and then ·they die [Lare no more];
they ·are laid low [*or* give in] and ·buried [Lare gathered/drawn in] like everyone else;
they ·are cut off [*or* wither] like the heads of grain.
25If this is not true, who can prove I am ·wrong [La liar]?
Who can show that my words are worth nothing?"

Bildad Answers

25 Then Bildad the Shuhite answered:
2"·God rules and he must be honored [LRule/Dominion and dread are with him];
he ·set up order [establishes peace] in his high heaven.
3·No one can count God's armies [LIs there a number to his troops?].
·His light shines on all people [LUpon whom does his light not rise?].
4·So no one can be good [What mortal can be righteous…?] in the presence of God,
and ·no one [who…?] born to a woman can be pure.
5Even the moon is not bright
and the stars are not pure in his eyes.
6People are much less! They are like ·insects [Lmaggots].
They are only worms!"

Job Answers Bildad

26 Then Job answered:
2"You are no help to the ·helpless [powerless]!
You have not ·aided [rescued] the ·weak [Lweak armed]!
3·Your advice lacks wisdom [*or* You have brought no counsel to those without wisdom]!
You have shown little understanding!
4·Who has helped you say these words [LWhose words do you speak]?
And ·where did you get these ideas [Lwhose breath comes from you]?

5"The ·spirits of the dead [shades; LRephaim; Cdeparted ancestors] tremble,

·those who are beneath and in the waters [[L]the waters and their inhabitants are terrified; [C]symbol for the forces of evil].
[6]**·Death** [[L]The grave; Sheol] **·is naked** [lies exposed] **before God;**
·destruction [Abaddon; [C]the underworld] **is uncovered before him** [[C]God is in control of them].
[7]**God stretches ·the northern sky** [*or* Zaphon; [C]a reference to Baal's mountain; indicating God's control over it] **out over empty space**
and hangs the earth on nothing.
[8]**He wraps up the waters in his thick clouds,**
but the clouds do not ·break under their weight [[L]burst under them].
[9]**He covers the face of the ·moon** [*or* throne],
spreading his clouds over it.
[10]**He draws the horizon like a circle on the water**
at the place where light and darkness meet.
[11]**·Heaven's foundations** [[L]The pillars of heavens; [C]perhaps mountains] **·shake** [quake]
·when he thunders at them [[L]astounded by his rebuke/blast].
[12]**With his power he ·quiets** [stills] **the ·sea** [*or* Sea; [C]the powers of chaos];
by his ·wisdom [understanding] **he ·destroys** [struck] **Rahab, the sea monster** [9:13].
[13]**He breathes, and ·the sky clears** [[L]he makes the heavens beautiful].
His hand ·stabs [slays] **the fleeing ·snake** [serpent; [C]Leviathan, another sea monster representing chaos; 3:8; Is. 27:1].
[14]**And these are ·only a small part of God's works** [[L]fringes of his way].
We only hear a small whisper of him.
Who could understand God's thundering power?"

27 **And Job continued ·speaking** [[L]his discourse]:
[2]**"·As surely as God lives** [By the living God], **who has ·taken away** [turned aside] **my rights,**
·the Almighty [Shaddai], **who has made me ·unhappy** [bitter],
[3]**as long as ·I am alive** [my breath is in me]
and God's ·breath of life [[L]spirit; breath; Gen. 2:7; Eccl. 12:7] **is in my nose,**
[4]**my lips will not speak ·evil** [*or* falsehood],
and my tongue will not ·tell [[L]mutter] **·a lie** [deceit].
[5]**·I will never** [Far be it from me to] **·agree** [concede] **you are right;**
until I ·die [expire], **I will never ·stop saying I am innocent** [[L]turn aside my innocence].
[6]**I will ·insist that I am right** [[L]embrace my righteousness]; **I will not ·back down** [weaken].
·My conscience will never bother me [[L]My heart will not reproach my days].

[7]**"Let my enemies be like evil people,**
·my foes [those who rise up against me] **like ·those who are wrong** [the guilty].
[8]**What hope do the wicked have when they ·die** [[L]are cut off],
when God ·takes their life away [requires their life]?
[9]**God will not listen to their cries**
when trouble comes to them.

10·They will not [Will they…?] find joy in ·the Almighty [Shaddai],
·even though [or will…?] they call out to God all the time.

11"I will ·teach [instruct] you about the ·power [[L]hand] of God
and will not ·hide [conceal] ·the ways of [[L]that which is with] ·the
Almighty [Shaddai].
12You have all seen this yourselves.
·So why are we having all this talk that means nothing [[L]Why have
you become so meaningless/vaporous/vain]?

13"Here is ·what God has planned for evil people [[L]the lot of evil people
with God],
and ·that the Almighty will give to cruel people [[L]the inheritance that
the cruel receive from the Almighty/Shaddai]:
14They may have many children, but the sword will kill them.
Their ·children [[L]offspring] will never have enough ·to eat [[L]bread;
food].
15Then those who are left will die of disease and be buried,
and the widows will not even cry for them.
16·The wicked [[L]They] may heap up silver like ·piles of dirt [dust]
and ·have so many clothes they are like piles of clay [pile up clothes
like mounds of earth/clay].
17But ·good people [the righteous] will wear ·what evil people have
gathered [[L]them],
and the innocent will ·divide up [distribute among themselves] their
silver.
18·The houses the wicked build are [[L]They will build their houses] like a
·spider's web [*or* moth's cocoon],
like a ·hut [booth; shelter] that a guard builds.
19·The wicked are rich when they go to bed [[L]They may lie down
wealthy],
but ·they are rich for the last time [[L]not again];
when they open their eyes, everything is gone.
20·Fears [Terrors] ·come over [overtake] them like ·a flood [waters],
and a storm snatches them away in the night.
21The east wind will ·carry them away [[L]lift them up], and then they are
gone,
because it sweeps them out of their place.
22·The wind [*or* God; [L]He; It] will hit them without mercy
as they ·try to run away [flee] from ·its power [*or* his power/hand].
23It will be as if ·the wind [*or* God; [L]he; it] is clapping ·its [*or* his] hands;
·it [*or* he] will ·whistle [*or* hiss] at them as they run from their place
[[C]clapping and hissing are gestures of contempt].

28 "There are mines where people dig silver
and places where gold is ·made pure [refined].
2Iron is taken from the ·ground [dust],
and copper is ·melted out of [poured from the] rocks.
3·Miners [[L]They] ·bring lights [[L]put an end to darkness]
and ·search deep into the mines [[L]investigate every limit]
for ore in thick darkness.
4They ·dig a tunnel [sink a shaft] far from where people live,

·where no one has ever walked [[L]a place forgotten by human feet];
they work far from people, ·swinging and swaying from ropes [[L]they sway suspended].
[5]·Food grows on top of the earth [[L]Bread/Food comes out of the earth],
but below ground things are ·changed [overturned] as if by fire.
[6]·Sapphires [*or* Lapis lazuli] are found in rocks,
and gold dust is also found there.
[7]No ·hawk [bird of prey] knows that path;
the ·falcon [*or* black kite] has not seen it.
[8]Proud animals have not walked there,
and no lions cross over it.
[9]·Miners [[L]They] ·hit [[L]put their hands to] the rocks of flint
·and dig away at the bottom of the mountains [upturning the mountains from their root].
[10]They cut tunnels through the rock
and see all the ·treasures [precious things] there.
[11]They ·search for places where rivers begin [*or* dam up the sources of the rivers]
and bring things hidden out into the light.

[12]"But where can wisdom be found,
and where ·does understanding live [is understanding]?
[13]People do not understand ·the value of wisdom [[L]its price];
it cannot be found ·among those who are alive [[L]in the land of the living].
[14]The ·deep ocean [*or* Deep] says, 'It's not in me;'
the ·sea [*or* Sea; [C]the Deep and Sea may represent the forces of chaos] says, 'It's not in me.'
[15]Wisdom cannot be bought with gold,
and its cost cannot be weighed in silver.
[16]Wisdom cannot be bought with ·fine gold [[L]the gold of Ophir; 22:24]
or with ·valuable [precious] onyx or ·sapphire gems [*or* lapis lazuli].
[17]Gold and ·crystal [*or* glass] ·are not as valuable as wisdom [[L]cannot match it],
and you cannot buy it with jewels of gold.
[18]Coral and ·jasper [*or* crystal; [C]the identification of gems is often uncertain] are not worth talking about,
and the price of wisdom is much greater than ·rubies [*or* pearls].
[19]The ·topaz [*or* chrysolite] from ·Cush [Ethiopia] cannot compare to wisdom;
it cannot be bought with the purest gold.
[20]"So where does wisdom come from,
and where does understanding live?
[21]It is hidden from the eyes of every living thing,
[[L]concealed] even from the birds of ·the air [[L]the sky; heaven].
[22]·The places of destruction [[L]Abaddon] and ·death [*or* Death; [C]the forces of the underworld] say,
'We have heard reports about it.'
[23]Only God understands the way to wisdom,
and he alone knows ·where it lives [[L]its place],
[24]because he looks to the ·farthest parts [ends] of the earth
and sees everything under ·the sky [*or* heaven].

25When God gave ·power [substance; [L]weight] to the wind
and measured the water,
26when he made ·rules [*or* limits] for the rain
and set a path for a thunderstorm to follow,
27then he looked at ·wisdom [[L]it] and ·decided its worth [[L]declared it];
he ·set wisdom up [[L]established it] and ·tested [*or* investigated] it.
28Then he said to humans,
'The fear of the Lord is wisdom [Prov. 1:7];
to ·stay [*or* turn] away from evil is understanding [Prov. 3:7].'"

Job Continues

29 Job continued ·to speak [[L]his discourse; 27:1]:
2"How I wish for the months ·that have passed [of old]
and the days when God ·watched over [protected; guarded] me.
3God's lamp shined ·on [*or* over] my head,
and I walked ·through [in] darkness by his light.
4I wish for the days when I was ·strong [in the prime of my life],
when God's close friendship ·blessed my house [[L]was over my tent].
5·The Almighty [Shaddai] was still with me,
and my children were all around me.
6It was as if my ·path [*or* steps] were covered with ·cream [*or* butter]
and the rocks poured out olive oil for me [[C]representing his earlier prosperity; 1:1–5].
7I would go to the city gate
and sit in the public square [[C]indicating Job was a city leader/elder].
8When the young men saw me, they would ·step aside [*or* hide],
and the old men would stand up in respect.
9The ·leading men [princes] ·stopped speaking [[L]grew silent]
and covered their mouths with their hands.
10The voices of the ·important men [nobles] ·were quiet [grew silent],
as if their tongues stuck to the roof of their mouths.
11·Anyone [[L]Any ear] who heard me ·spoke well of [[L]blessed] me,
and ·those who [[L]the eye that] saw me ·praised [[L]bore testimony to] me,
12because I ·saved [rescued] the poor who ·called out [[L]cried for help]
and the orphan who had no one to help.
13The ·dying [[L]perishing] person blessed me,
and I made the widow's heart ·sing [[L]shout for joy].
14I ·put on right living as if it were clothing [[L]clothed myself with righteousness and it clothed me];
I wore ·fairness [justice] like a robe and a turban.
15I was eyes for the blind
and feet for the lame.
16I was like a father to needy people,
and I ·took the side of [examined the cause of] ·strangers who were in trouble [[L]strangers; those I did not know].
17I broke the ·fangs [*or* jaw] of evil people
and snatched the ·captives [[L]prey; [C]the wicked are predators] from their teeth.

18"I thought, 'I will ·live for as many days as there are grains of [[L]multiply my days like] sand,
and I will die in my ·own house [[L]nest].

19My roots ·will reach down [opened] to the water.
The dew ·will lie [lodged] on the branches all night.
20·New honors will come to me continually [My honor/*or* liver/heart was new],
and ·I will always have great strength [Lmy bow was renewed within my hand].'

21"People listened to me carefully
and waited ·quietly [silently] for my advice.
22After I finished speaking, they spoke no more.
My words ·fell [Ldripped] very gently on their ears.
23They waited for me as they would for rain
and ·drank in my words like [Lopened their mouth for] spring rain.
24I smiled at them when they ·doubted [Lhad no confidence],
and ·my approval was important to them [Lthey did not frown at the light of my countenance].
25I chose the way for them and ·was their leader [Lsat as their chief].
I lived like a king among his army,
like a person who comforts ·sad [mourning] people.

30 "But now those who are younger than I
·make fun of [laugh at] me.
I would ·not have even [Lhave disdained to] let their fathers
sit with my sheep dogs.
2What use did I have for their strength
since they had lost their ·strength [vigor] to work [Cvv. 2–8 describe the young men who torment Job]?
3They were thin from hunger
and ·wandered the dry and ruined land at night [*or* they gnawed the desert on the brink of desolation and destruction].
4They ·gathered desert plants [plucked mallow] among the brush
and ·ate [*or* warmed themselves on] the root of the broom tree.
5They were ·forced to live away [driven out] from people;
people shouted at them as if they were thieves.
6They lived ·in dried-up streambeds [on the slopes of the wadis],
in ·caves, and among the rocks [dusty and rocky holes].
7They howled like animals among the bushes
and huddled together ·in [*or* under] the brush.
8They are ·worthless people without names [disreputable children of fools]
and were ·forced to leave the land [Lwhipped off the land/earth].

9"Now ·they make fun of me with songs [I am the object of their melodious taunts];
my name is a ·joke [byword] among them.
10They hate me and ·stay far away [keep their distance] from me,
but they do not mind spitting in my face.
11God has ·taken away my strength [Lloosened my bowstring] and ·made me suffer [humiliated me],
so they ·attack me with all their anger [Lhave removed all restraint before me].

12On my right side they rise up like a mob.
They ·lay traps for my feet [Ltake my feet out from under me]
and ·prepare to attack me [Lbuild up paths for my calamity].
13They ·break [tear] **up my road**
and ·work to destroy me [*or* they profit from my ruin],
and ·no one helps me [*or* they need no help].
14They come at me as if through a ·hole in the wall [wide breech],
and they roll in among the ruins.
15Great fears ·overwhelm [*or* transform] **me.**
They blow my honor away as if by a great wind,
and my ·safety [*or* hope of rescue] **disappears like a cloud.**

16"Now my life is ·almost over [Lpoured out in me];
my days are full of suffering.
17At night my bones ache;
gnawing pains ·never stop [*or* do not let me lie down to sleep].
18In his great power ·God [Lhe] **grabs hold of my clothing**
and ·chokes me with [*or* seizes me by] **the collar of my coat.**
19He throws me into the mud,
and I become like dirt and ashes.

20"I cry out to you, God, but you do not answer;
I stand up, but you just look at me.
21You have turned on me ·without mercy [with cruelty];
with your powerful hand you ·attacked [Lhate] **me.**
22You snatched me up and ·threw me into [Lmade me ride] **the wind**
and ·tossed me about [made me reel] **in the storm.**
23I know you will bring me down to death,
to the ·place where all living people must go [Lhouse appointed for all the living].

24"Surely no one would hurt [*or* Should not one send his hand out to help…?] **those who are ruined**
when they cry for help in their time of trouble.
25·I cried [LDo I not cry…?] **for those ·who were in trouble** [whose day was hard];
·I have been very sad [Ldon't I have pity…?] **for ·poor** [needy] **people.**
26But when I hoped for ·good [*or* the best], **only ·evil** [*or* the worst] **came to me;**
when I ·looked [waited] **for light, darkness came.**
27·I never stop being upset [LMy insides are brought to a boil and not stilled];
days of ·suffering [affliction] **are ahead of me.**
28·I have turned black, but not by the sun [*or* I walk around mourning, without passion].
I stand up in public and cry for help.
29I have become a brother to ·wild dogs [jackals]
and a friend to ·ostriches [*or* eagle owls; Canimals that live in the desolate wilderness].
30My skin has become black and peels off,
as my ·body [Lbones] **burns with ·fever** [heat].
31My ·harp [lyre] **is tuned to sing a sad song,**
and my ·flute [reed pipe] **is tuned to moaning.**

31 **"But I ·made an agreement** [[L]cut a covenant] **with my eyes**
not to ·look with desire [leer] **at a ·girl** [[L]virgin].
2**What ·has God above promised for people** [[L]would be my portion with God above]?
What ·has the Almighty planned from [would be my inheritance/heritage with the Almighty/Shaddai] **on high?**
3**·It is ruin** [[L]Isn't calamity reserved…?] **for evil people**
and ·disaster [misfortune] **for those who do wrong.**
4**·God sees** [[L]Does he not see…?] **my ways**
and counts every step I take.

5**"If I have ·been dishonest** [[L]walked with falsehood]
or ·lied to others [[L]my feet hasten to fraud],
6**then let God weigh me on ·honest** [just] **scales** [Prov. 11:1].
Then he will know I ·have done nothing wrong [am blameless/innocent].
7**If ·I have turned away from doing what is right** [[L]my feet have wandered off the path; Prov. 2:20],
or my heart has ·been led by my eyes to do wrong [[L]followed my eyes],
or ·my hands have been made unclean [[L]blemish has clung to my hand],
8**then let ·other people eat what I have planted** [[L]me sow and not eat],
and let my crops be ·plowed up [uprooted].
9**"If ·I have desired** [[L]my heart has been enticed/seduced by] **another woman** [Prov. 5–7]
or have waited at my ·neighbor's [*or* friend's] **door for his wife,**
10**then let my wife grind ·another man's grain** [[L]another man; [C]a euphemism for sexual intercourse],
and let other men ·have sexual relations with [[L]kneel over] **her.**
11**That would be ·shameful** [a foul deed],
a ·sin to be punished [a criminal offense; [L]a guilty thing before the judges].
12**It is like a fire that burns ·and destroys** [[L]down to Abaddon; 26:6; 28:22];
all I have done would be ·plowed up [[L]burned to the root].

13**"If I ·have been unfair to** [[L]reject proper judgment for] **my male and female slaves**
when they had a ·complaint [case] **against me,**
14**·how could I tell God what I did** [*or* what would I do when God rises against me]?
What will I answer when he asks me to explain what I've done?
15**God made me in my mother's womb, and he also made them;**
the same God formed both of us in our mothers' wombs.

16**"I have never ·refused the appeals of the poor** [*or* deprived the poor of some pleasure]
or ·let widows give up hope while looking for help [[L]caused the eyes of the widow to fail].
17**I have not ·kept my food to myself** [eaten my morsel alone]
·but have given it to the orphans [[L]or not let orphans eat it].
18**Since I was young, ·I have been like a father to the orphans** [[L]I have raised them like a father; *or* he (God) raised me like a father].
From ·my birth [[L]the womb of my mother] **I guided the widows.**

19 I have not let anyone ·die [Lperish] for lack of clothes
or let a needy person go without ·a coat [Lcovering].
20 That person's ·heart [Lloins] blessed me,
because I warmed him with the ·wool [fleece] of my sheep.
21 I have never ·hurt [Lraised my hand threateningly against] an orphan
even when I knew I ·could win in court [Lhad allies in the gate; Cthe city gate was where court was held].
22 If I have, then let my ·arm [Lshoulder blade] fall off my shoulder
and [Lmy arm] be broken at the ·joint [socket].
23 I fear ·destruction [calamity] from God,
and I fear his ·majesty [ruin], so I could not do such things.

24 "I have not put my trust in gold
or said to pure gold, 'You are my security.'
25 I have not ·celebrated [exulted in] my great wealth
or the ·riches [substance] my hands had gained.
26 I have not thought about worshiping the sun in its brightness
nor admired the moon moving in glory
27 so that my heart was ·pulled away from God [Lenticed in secret].
My hand has never ·offered the sun and moon a kiss of worship [Lpassed a kiss from my mouth].
28 If I had, these also would have been ·sins to be punished [a criminal offense; La guilty thing before the judges],
because I would have ·been unfaithful to [deceived; defrauded] God [Labove].

29 "I have not been happy ·when my enemies fell [Lin the disaster of those who hate me]
or ·laughed when they had trouble [Lbecome excited when evil found them out].
30 I have not let my mouth sin
by cursing my enemies' life.
31 The servants of my house have always said,
'All have eaten what they want of Job's food.'
32 No stranger ever had to ·spend the night [lodge] in the street,
because I ·always let travelers stay in my home [Lopened the door to the traveler; Chospitality was highly valued in the ancient Near East].
33 I have not hidden my ·sin [transgression] ·as others do [*or* like Adam did; Gen. 3],
·secretly keeping my guilt to myself [Lconcealing my guilt in my bosom].
34 I was not so afraid of the crowd [large multitude]
that I kept quiet and ·stayed inside [Ldid not go out the door]
because I feared being ·hated [held in contempt] by other families.

35 ("How I wish ·a court would hear my case [Lsomeone would listen to me]!
Here ·I sign my name to show I have told the truth [is my signature].
Now let ·the Almighty [Shaddai] answer me;
let the one who accuses me write ·it [an indictment/writ] down.
36 I would wear ·the writing [Lit] on my shoulder;
I would ·put [Lbind] it on like a crown.

37I would ·explain to God [Lgive him an account of] every step I took,
and I would ·come near to [approach] him like a prince.)

38"If my land cries out against me
and its ·plowed rows [furrows] ·are wet with tears [Lhave wept together],
39if I have taken the land's harvest without paying
or have broken the spirit of those who ·worked [*or* own] the land,
40then let ·thorns [brambles] come up instead of wheat,
and let ·weeds [stinkweed] come up instead of barley."
The words of Job are ·finished [ended].

Elihu Speaks

32 These three men stopped trying to answer Job, because he
was ·so sure he was right [right/righteous in his own eyes].
2But Elihu son of Barakel the Buzite, from the family of Ram, became
very angry with Job, because Job ·claimed he was right instead of [*or* he
was more right/righteous than] God. 3Elihu was also angry with Job's
three friends who had no answer to show that Job was wrong, yet
continued to ·blame him [treat him as wrong]. 4Elihu had waited
before speaking to Job, because the three friends were older than he
was. 5But when Elihu saw that the three men had nothing more to say,
he became very angry.

6So Elihu son of Barakel the Buzite said this:
"I am young,
and you are ·old [aged].
That is why I was ·afraid [Ltimid and afraid]
to tell you ·what I know [my opinion].
7I thought, '·Older people should [LLet days] speak,
and those who have lived many years should ·teach [make known;
reveal] wisdom.'
8But it is the spirit in a person,
the breath of ·the Almighty [Shaddai], that gives understanding.
9It is not just ·older people [Lthe many] who are wise;
·they [Lthe elders] are not the only ones who understand ·what is
right [justice].
10So I say, listen to me.
I too will ·tell [show] you ·what I know [my opinion].
11I waited ·while you three spoke [Lfor your words],
and ·listened [bent an ear] to your ·explanations [*or* arguments].
While you ·looked for words to use,
12 I paid close attention to you.
But not one of you has proved Job wrong;
none of you has answered his arguments.
13Don't say, 'We have found wisdom;
only God will show Job to be wrong, not people.'
14Job has not spoken his words against me,
so I will not use your arguments to answer Job.

15"·These three friends [LThey] are ·defeated [dismayed; discouraged]
and ·have no more to say [cannot answer];
words have failed them.
16Now they are standing there with no answers for Job.
·Now that they are quiet [LIf they don't speak], must I wait to speak?

17No, I too will speak
and ·tell what I know [share my opinion].
18I am full of words,
and the spirit in me ·causes me to speak [compels me].
19I am like wine that has ·been bottled up [no vent/opening];
I am ready to burst like a new leather wine bag.
20I must speak so I will feel relief;
I must open my ·mouth [Llips] and answer.
21I will ·be fair to everyone [Lnot favor anyone]
and not flatter anyone.
22I don't know how to flatter,
and if I did, my Maker would quickly take me away.

33 "Now, Job, ·listen to [hear] my words.
Pay attention to ·everything I say [Lall my words].
2I open my mouth
and ·am ready to speak [Lthe tongue in my mouth speaks].
3My words come from an ·honest [virtuous] heart,
and ·I am sincere in saying what I know [Lwhat my lips know they speak with sincerity].
4The Spirit of God ·created [has made] me,
and the breath of ·the Almighty [Shaddai] gave me life.
5Answer me if you can;
get yourself ready and stand before me.
6I am just like you before God;
I too ·am made [was formed] out of clay.
7·Don't be afraid of me [LDread of me should not scare you];
·I will not be hard on you [LMy pressure will not be too heavy on you].

8"But ·I heard what you have said [Lyou have spoken in my ear];
I heard ·every word [Lthe sound of your words].
9You said, 'I am pure and without ·sin [transgression];
I am ·innocent [Lclean] and free from guilt.
10But God has found ·fault [reason to be upset] with me;
he ·considers me [thinks I am] his enemy.
11He ·locks [places] my feet in ·chains [shackles]
and ·closely watches everywhere I go [Lguards all my paths].'

12"But I tell you, you are not ·right in saying this [Lcorrect],
I will answer you, for God is greater than ·we are [Lany human being].
13Why do you ·accuse [contend with] God
·of not answering anyone [*or* for no one can answer all his words]?
14God does speak—sometimes ·one way and sometimes another [*or* once and sometimes twice]—
even though people may not ·understand [perceive] it.
15He speaks in a dream or a vision of the night
when people are in a deep sleep,
lying on their beds in slumber.
16He ·speaks in [Lopens] their ears
and frightens them with warnings

17to turn them away from doing wrong
and to keep them from being proud.
18God does this to ·save people [Lkeep them] from ·death [Lthe Pit; Ca reference to the grave and the underworld],
to keep them from ·dying [Lthe water channel; Canother reference to the grave and the underworld].
19People may be ·corrected [reprimanded; reproved] while in bed in great pain;
they may have continual pain in their very bones.
20·They may be in such pain that they even hate [LTheir lives loathe] food,
even ·the very best meal [choice food].
21·Their body becomes so thin [LTheir flesh wastes away so that] ·there is almost nothing left of it [Lit cannot be seen],
and their bones that were hidden now stick out.
22·They are [LTheir souls draw] near ·death [Lthe Pit; 33:18],
and their life ·is almost over [Lcomes near those who bring death].

23"·But there may be [LIf there is] an angel to speak for him,
one out of a thousand, ·who will tell him what to do [a mediator who declares a person virtuous].
24The angel will ·beg for mercy [*or* be gracious to him] and say:
'·Save [Redeem] him from ·death [Lgoing down to the Pit; 33:18].
I have found a ·way to pay for his life [ransom].'
25Then his body is made new like a ·child's [youth's].
It will return to the way it was when he was ·young [vigorous].
26That person will pray to God, and God will ·listen to [Laccept] him.
He will see God's face and will shout with happiness.
And ·God will set things right for him again [*or* he will repeat to others that he has been vindicated].
27Then he will ·say [Lsing] to others,
'I sinned and ·twisted what was right [perverted/sullied virtue],
but I did not receive the punishment I should have received.
28God ·bought [redeemed] my life ·back from death [Lfrom crossing over to the Pit; 33:18],
and ·I will continue to enjoy life [Lmy life will yet see the light].'

29"God does all these things to a person
two or even three times
30·so he won't die as punishment for his sins [Lto bring back his life from the Pit; 33:18]
and so he may ·still enjoy life [Lbe illuminated with the light of life].

31"Job, pay attention and listen to me;
be quiet, and I will speak.
32If you have anything to say, answer me;
speak up, because I want to ·prove you right [vindicate you].
33But if you have nothing to say, then listen to me;
be quiet, and I will teach you wisdom."

34 Then Elihu answered:
2"Hear my words, you wise men;

listen to me, you who know a lot.
[3]**The ear tests words**
as the ·tongue [[L]palate] **tastes food.**
[4]**Let's ·decide** [choose] **for ourselves what is ·right** [just],
and let's learn together what is good.

[5]**"Job says, 'I am ·not guilty** [right/righteous],
and God has ·refused me a fair trial [[L]turned justice away from me].
[6]**·Instead of getting a fair trial** [concerning my case],
I am ·called [considered] **a liar.**
·I have been seriously hurt [An arrow has given me an incurable wound; [L]My arrow is incurable],
even though I have not sinned.'
[7]**·There is no other** [[L]Who is a…?] **man like Job;**
he ·takes [*or* receives] **·insults** [ridicule; scoffing] **as if he were drinking water.**
[8]**He ·keeps company** [travels] **with those who do evil**
and ·spends time [[L]goes] **with wicked men,**
[9]**because he says, 'It is no use**
to try to please God.'

[10]**"So listen to me, you who ·can understand** [*or* are sensible].
God can never do wrong!
It is impossible for the Almighty to do evil.
[11]**God pays people back for what they have done**
and ·gives them what their actions deserve [[L]finds them out according to their ways].
[12]**Truly God will never do wrong;**
the Almighty will never ·twist [pervert] **·what is right** [justice].
[13]**·No one** [[L]Who…?] **chose God to rule over the earth**
or put him in charge of the whole world.
[14]**If God should ·decide** [[L]set his mind/heart to himself]
to take away ·life [[L]spirit] **and breath,**
[15]**then ·everyone** [[L]all flesh] **would ·die** [expire] **together**
and turn back into dust.

[16]**"If you can understand, hear this;**
·listen to what I have to say [[L]give ear to my words].
[17]**Can anyone govern who hates what is right?**
How can you ·blame God [[L]condemn one] **who is both ·fair** [righteous] **and powerful?**
[18]**·God** [[L]Who…?] **is the one who says to kings, 'You are worthless,'**
or to important people, 'You are evil.'
[19]**He ·is not nicer to princes than other people** [[L]shows no favoritism to princes],
nor ·kinder [[L]gives more recognition] **to ·rich people** [nobles] **than poor people,**
because he made them all with his own hands [Prov. 14:31; 17:5; 22:2].
[20]**They can die in a moment, in the middle of the night.**
·They are struck down [[L]The people are shaken], **and then they pass away;**

powerful people ·die [are taken away] ·without help [*or* not by
human hand].
21“·God watches where people go [LHis eyes are on the path of people];
he sees every step they take.
22There is no dark place or deep shadow
where those who do evil can hide from him.
23He does not set a time
for people to come before him for judging.
24Without ·asking questions [investigation; inquiry], God breaks
powerful people into pieces
and puts others in their place.
25Because God knows what people do,
he ·defeats [overturns] them in the night, and they are crushed.
26He ·punishes [slaps] them for the evil they do
so that everyone else can watch,
27because they ·stopped [turned away from] following God
and did not care about any of his ways.
28The cry of the poor comes to God;
he hears the cry of the ·needy [afflicted].
29But if God keeps quiet, who can blame him?
If he hides his face, who among nations or people can see him?
30 He keeps the wicked from ruling
and from trapping others.

31“But suppose someone says to God,
‘I ·am guilty, but [*or* have endured punishment, so] I will not sin
anymore.
32Teach me what I cannot see.
If I have done wrong, I will not do it again.’
33So, Job, should God ·reward [*or* make peace with] you as you want
·when [*or* since] you refuse to change?
You must ·decide [choose], not I,
so tell me what you know.

34“Those ·who understand [with sense] speak,
and the wise who hear me say,
35‘Job speaks without knowing what is true;
his words show he ·does not understand [has no insight].’
36I wish Job would be ·tested completely [examined forever],
because he answered like an evil man!
37Job now adds to his sin ·by turning against God [with
transgression].
He ·claps his hands in protest [Lclaps among us; Cclapping is a sign of
protest or contempt],
speaking more and more against God.”

35 Then Elihu answered:
2“Do you think this is ·fair [just]?
You say, ‘·God will show that I am right [*or* I am more right than God],’
3but you also ask, ‘What’s the use?
·I don’t gain [LHow have I gained…?] anything by not sinning.’

4"I will answer you
and your friends who are with you.
5Look up at the ·sky [Lheavens and see]
and observe the clouds so high above you.
6If you sin, it does nothing to ·God [Lhim];
even if your ·sins [transgressions] are many, they do nothing to him.
7If you are ·good [right; righteous], ·you give nothing [Lwhat would you give...?] to God;
·he receives nothing [Lwhat would he receive...?] from your hand.
8Your ·evil ways [wickedness] only ·hurt [*or* influence] others like yourself,
and ·the good you do [your righteousness] only ·helps [*or* influences] other human beings.

9"·People [LThey] cry out ·when they are in trouble [due to their many oppressions];
they ·beg for relief [shout for help] ·from powerful people [Lbecause of the arm of the strong].
10But no one asks, 'Where is God, my Maker,
who gives us ·songs [*or* strength] in the night,
11who ·makes us smarter [*or* teaches us more] than the animals of the earth
and wiser than the birds of the ·air [heavens]?'
12He does not answer evil people when they cry out,
because the wicked are proud.
13God does not listen to their useless begging;
the Almighty pays no attention to them.
14·He will listen to you even [LHow much] less
when you say that you do not see him,
that your case is before him,
that you must wait for him,
15 that his anger never punishes,
and that he doesn't notice evil.
16So Job is only speaking ·nonsense [meaningless things],
saying many words ·without knowing what is true [ignorantly]."

Elihu's Speech Continues

36 Elihu continued:
2"·Listen to [*or* Be patient with] me a little longer, and I will ·show [inform] you
that there is more to be said for God.
3What I know comes from far away.
I will ·show that my Maker is right [ascribe righteousness to my Maker].
4You can be sure that my words are not false;
·one who really knows is with you [Lperfect knowledge is with me].

5"God is powerful, but he does not ·hate [disdain; reject] people;
he is strong and ·sure of what he wants to do [Lpowerful in understanding/heart].
6He will not keep evil people alive,
but he gives the ·poor [afflicted] their rights.
7He ·always watches over [Ldoes not withhold his eye from] those who do right;
he sets them on thrones with kings
and they are ·honored [exalted] forever.

8If people are bound in chains,
or if ·trouble [affliction], like ropes, ties them up,
9God tells them what they have done,
that they have sinned in their pride.
10He ·makes them listen [Lopens their ear] to his ·warning [instruction; discipline]
and commands them to change from doing evil.
11If they ·obey [*or* listen] and serve him,
·the rest of their lives will be successful [Ltheir days will finish happily],
and the rest of their years will be ·happy [pleasant].
12But if they do not listen,
they will ·die by the sword [*or* pass through the water channel; Creference to death],
and they will die ·without knowing why [in ignorance].

13"Those who have ·wicked [Lgodless] hearts hold on to anger.
Even when ·God punishes [Lhe imprisons] them, they do not cry for help.
14They die while they are still young,
and their lives end ·in disgrace [Lamong male prostitutes].
15But God saves those who ·suffer [are afflicted] ·through [*or* by means of] their ·suffering [affliction];
he ·gets them to listen [Lopens their ear] ·through [*or* by means of] their pain.

16"God ·is gently calling [has wooed/enticed] you from the jaws of ·trouble [distress]
to an ·open place of freedom [Lbroad place with no constraints]
where he has set your table full of ·the best food [Lfatness].
17But now you are ·being punished like [obsessed/filled with the case of] the wicked;
·you are getting justice [Ljudgment and justice hold on tight to you].
18Be careful! ·Don't be led away from God by riches [L…lest anger seduce you by abundance];
don't let ·much money [a big ransom/bribe] turn you away.
19Neither your wealth nor all your great strength
will keep you out of trouble.
20Don't ·wish [pant; long] for the night
when people are taken from their homes.
21Be careful not to turn to evil,
which you ·seem to want more [have chosen rather] than ·suffering [affliction].
22"God is ·great [exulted] and powerful;
·no other teacher is [Lwho is a teacher…?] like him.
23·No one [LWho…?] has ·planned [prescribed] his ways for him;
·no one can say to God [Lwho says to him…?], 'You have done wrong.'
24Remember to ·praise [extol] his work,
about which people have sung.
25Everybody has seen it;
people look at it from far off.

26**God is so ·great, greater than we can understand** [exalted and we do not understand]**!**
·No one knows how old he is [LThe number of his years is unknown].

27"**He ·evaporates** [*or* holds in check] **the drops of water from the earth**
and ·turns them into rain [filters rain for his streams/*or* mists; Gen. 2:6].
28**The rain then pours down from the clouds,**
and ·showers fall [Ldrops abundantly] **on people.**
29**·No one understands** [LWho can understand...?] **·how God spreads out the** [Lthe spreading] **clouds**
or how he sends thunder from ·where he lives [Lhis booth/pavilion].
30**Watch how God ·scatters** [spreads] **his lightning around him,**
·lighting up the deepest parts [Lcovering the roots] **of the sea.**
31**This is the way God ·governs** [*or* sustains] **the nations;**
this is how he gives us ·enough [plenty; abundant] **food.**
32**God ·fills** [Lcovers] **his hands with lightning**
and commands it to strike its target.
33**His thunder announces ·the coming storm** [Labout him/it; Cthunder announces either the coming storm or the coming of God],
and ·even the cattle know it is near [*or* the storm announces his coming wrath; *or* the passion of his anger is against inquity].

37 "**At ·the sound of his thunder** [Lthis], **my heart ·pounds** [trembles]
as if it will ·jump [leap; *or* drop] **out of ·my chest** [Lits place].
2**Listen! Listen to the ·thunder** [Lshaking] **of God's voice**
and to the rumbling that comes from his mouth.
3**He turns his lightning loose under the whole ·sky** [heavens]
and sends it to the farthest parts of the earth.
4**After that you can hear the roar**
when he thunders with a ·great sound [exalted voice].
He does not hold back the flashing
when his voice is heard.
5**God's voice thunders in wonderful ways;**
he does great things we cannot understand.
6**He says to the snow, 'Fall on the earth,'**
and to the shower, 'Be a heavy rain.'
7**With it, he ·stops everyone from working** [Lputs a seal on the hand of all people]
so everyone knows it is ·the work of God [Lhis work].
8**The animals ·take cover from the rain** [Lenter their hiding place/lair]
and stay in their dens.
9**The storm comes from ·where it was stored** [Lits chamber];
the cold comes with the ·strong winds [*or* north wind].
10**The breath of God makes ice,**
and the wide waters become frozen.
11**He ·fills** [loads] **the clouds with ·water** [moisture]
and scatters his lightning through them.
12**At his ·command** [Lguidance] **they swirl around**
over the ·whole [Linhabited] **earth,**
doing whatever he commands.
13**·He uses the clouds to punish people** [LWhether for correction/the rod]
or ·to water his [Lfor the] **earth and ·show his love** [*or* loyalty].

14"Job, ·listen [give ear] to this:
Stop and notice God's ·miracles [wonders].
15Do you know how God ·controls the clouds [appoints their tasks]
and makes his lightning ·flash [Lshine in the clouds]?
16Do you know how the clouds ·hang [*or* spread] in the sky?
Do you know the ·miracles [wonders] of God, ·who knows
everything [Lthe one perfect in knowledge]?
17You ·suffer [Lswelter] in your clothes
when the land is silenced by the hot, south wind.
18You cannot stretch out the sky ·like God [Lwith him]
and make it look as hard as ·polished bronze [La cast mirror].
19·Tell [LTeach] us what we should say to him;
we cannot get our arguments ·ready [Lin order] because ·we do not
have enough understanding [Lof the darkness].
20Should God be told ·that I want to [*or* when I] speak?
Would a person ask to be swallowed up?
21No one can look at the ·sun [Llight]
when it is bright in the sky
after the wind ·has blown all the clouds away [Lpasses by and clears it].
22·God comes out of the north in golden light [LGold comes from the
north],
·in overwhelming greatness [Lan awesome splendor is all around God].
23·The Almighty [LShaddai]·is too high for us to reach [L—we cannot
find him].
He ·has great [is exalted in] strength;
he ·is always right and never punishes unfairly [Lwill not violate
justice and abundant righteousness].
24That is why people ·honor [fear] him;
·he does not respect those who say they are wise [*or* all the wise of
heart fear him]."

The Lord Questions Job

38 Then the LORD answered Job from the ·storm [whirlwind; 9:17]. He said:
2"Who is this that makes my ·purpose [Lcounsel; advice] ·unclear
[Ldark]
·by saying things that are not true [Lwith ignorant words]?
3·Be strong [Brace yourself; LGird your loins] like a man!
I will ask you questions,
and you must ·answer [inform] me.
4Where were you when I made the earth's foundation?
Tell me, if you understand.
5Who marked off ·how big it should be [Lits measurements]? Surely you
know!
Who stretched a ·ruler [line; Csurveyor's instrument] across it?
6What were the earth's foundations ·set on [Lsunk in],
or who put its cornerstone in place
7while the morning stars sang together
and all the ·angels [Lsons of god] shouted with joy?

8"Who shut the doors to keep the sea in
when it broke through ·and was born [Lcoming out of the womb],
9when I made the clouds like a coat for the sea

and ·wrapped [swaddled] it in dark clouds,
[10]when I ·put [prescribed] ·limits [boundaries] on the sea
and put its doors and bars in place,
[11]when I said to the sea, 'You may come this far, but no farther;
this is where your proud waves must stop'?

[12]"Have you ever ordered the morning to begin,
or ·shown [informed] the dawn where its place was
[13]in order to ·take hold of [grasp] the earth by its edges [[C]the horizon]
and shake evil people out of it [[C]the light exposes the wicked]?
[14]At dawn the earth changes like clay being pressed by a seal;
·the hills and valleys [[L]They] stand out like ·folds in a coat [[L]a garment].
[15]Light is ·not given to [held back from] evil people;
their arm is raised to do harm, but it is broken.

[16]"Have you ever gone to ·where the sea begins [[L]the sources of the sea]
or walked in the ·valleys under the sea [[L]depths of the deep]?
[17]Have the gates of death been ·opened [*or* revealed] to you?
Have you seen the gates of the deep darkness?
[18]Do you understand how wide the earth is?
Tell me, if you know all these things.

[19]"What is the path to light's home,
and where does darkness live?
[20]Can you take them to their places?
Do you know the ·way [path] to their homes?
[21]Surely you know, if you were already born when all this happened!
Have you lived that many years?

[22]"Have you ever gone into the storehouse of the snow
or seen the storehouses for hail,
[23]which I save for times of trouble,
for days of war and battle?
[24]Where is the place from which light ·comes [[L]is distributed]?
Where is the place from which the east winds ·blow [scatter] over the
earth?
[25]Who cuts a waterway for the heavy rains
and sets a path for the thunderstorm?
[26]Who waters the land where no one lives,
the ·desert [wilderness] that has no one in it?
[27]Who sends rain to satisfy the ·empty [[L]ruined and desolate] land
so the grass begins to grow?
[28]Does the rain have a father?
Who ·is father [[L]has given birth] to the drops of dew?
[29]·Who is the mother of the ice [[L]From whose womb did the ice come out]?
Who gives birth to the frost from the ·sky [heavens]
[30]when the water becomes hard as stone,
and even the surface of the ·ocean [deep] is frozen?

[31]"Can you tie up the ·stars [[L]chains] of the Pleiades
or ·loosen [open] the ·ropes of the stars in [[L]fetters of] Orion?
[32]Can you bring out ·the stars [[L]Mazzeroth; [C]probably the name of a

specific constellation] on time
or lead out the stars of the Bear with its cubs?
33Do you know the laws of the ·sky [heavens]
and ·understand [*or* set] their rule over the earth?

34"Can you ·shout an order [Lraise your voice] to the clouds
·and [*or* so that you] cover yourself with a flood of water?
35Can you send lightning bolts on their way?
Do they come to you and say, 'Here we are'?
36Who put wisdom ·inside the mind [*or* in the ibis; Can animal associated with wisdom and representing Thoth, the Egyptian god of wisdom]
or understanding ·in the heart [*or* to the rooster]?
37Who has the wisdom to count the clouds?
Who can ·pour water from the jars [Ltilt the wineskins] of the ·sky [heavens]
38when the dust becomes hard
and the clumps of dirt stick together?

39"Do you hunt food for the lioness
to satisfy the hunger of the young lions
40while they ·lie [crouch] in their dens
or hide in the bushes waiting to attack?
41Who gives food to the ·birds [Lraven]
when their young cry out to God
and wander about without food?

39 "Do you know when the mountain goats give birth?
Do you watch ·when the deer gives birth to her fawn [Lthe birth pangs of the deer]?
2Do you count the months until they ·give birth [are fulfilled]
and know the right time for them to give birth?
3They lie down, their young are born,
and ·then the pain of giving birth is over [Ldeliver their fetuses].
4Their young ones grow big and strong in the wild country.
Then they leave their homes and do not return.

5"Who let the ·wild donkey [*or* onager; Ca donkey-like animal also known as the Asian wild ass; Gen. 16:12] go free?
Who untied ·its ropes [Lthe Arabian onager from its bonds; Canother Hebrew word for a wild donkey]?
6I am the one who gave ·the donkey [Lit] the ·desert [steppe] as its home;
I gave it the ·desert [Lsalt] lands as a place to live.
7·The wild donkey [LIt] ·laughs [scoffs] at the ·confusion [tumult; noise] in the city,
and it does not hear the drivers shout.
8It ·roams [scouts out] the ·hills [mountains] looking for pasture,
looking for anything green to eat.

9"Will the wild ox agree to serve you
and stay by your ·feeding box [stable] at night?
10Can you hold it to the ·plowed row [furrow] with a ·harness [rope]

so it will ·plow [harrow] the valleys for you?
11 Will you depend on the wild ox for its great strength
and ·leave [hand over] your heavy work for it to do?
12 Can you trust the ox to bring in your grain
and gather it to your threshing floor?

13 "The wings of the ostrich flap happily,
but ·they are not like the feathers of the stork [*or* its pinions lack plumage].
14 The ostrich lays its eggs on the ground
and lets them warm in the ·sand [dust].
15 It ·does not stop to think [forgets] that a foot might step on them and crush them;
·it does not care that some animal [Lor a wild animal] might ·walk on [trample] them.
16 The ostrich ·is cruel to [treats harshly] its young, as if they were not even its own.
It does not care that its work is for nothing,
17 because God ·did not give the ostrich [*or* made her forget] wisdom;
God did not give it a share of ·good sense [understanding].
18 But when ·the ostrich gets up to run, it is so fast
that [*or* it flaps its wings aloft and] it laughs at the horse and its rider.

19 "Job, are you the one who gives the horse its strength
or puts a flowing mane on its neck?
20 Do you make the horse ·jump like a locust [*or* quiver like locust wings]?
It scares people with its ·proud [splendid] snorting.
21 It paws ·wildly [*or* the dirt of the valley], enjoying its strength,
and ·charges into battle [Lgoes out to encounter the weapons].
22 It laughs at ·fear [*or* danger] and is afraid of nothing;
it does not run away from the sword.
23 The ·bag of arrows [quiver] rattles against the horse's side,
along with the flashing ·spears and swords [*or* javelins and spears].
24 With ·great excitement [Ltrembling and shaking], the horse ·races over [Lswallows up] the ground;
and it cannot stand still when it hears the ·trumpet [ram's horn].
25 When the ·trumpet [ram's horn] blows, the horse snorts, 'Aha!'
It ·smells [senses] the battle from far away;
·it hears the shouts [Lthe thunder] of commanders and the battle cry.

26 "Is it through your ·wisdom [understanding] that the ·hawk [*or* falcon] ·flies [soars]
and spreads its wings toward the south?
27 Are you the one that commands the eagle to fly
and build its nest so high?
28 It lives on a high cliff and stays there at night;
the ·rocky [sharp] peak is its ·protected place [fortress].
29 From there it ·looks [scouts] for its food;
its eyes can see it from far away.
30 Its young ·eat [suck; gorge on] blood,
and where ·there is something dead [the slain are], the eagle is there."

40 The LORD answered and said to Job:
2"Will the person who ·argues [contends] with the Almighty
correct him?
Let the person who ·accuses [reproves] God answer him."

3Then Job answered the LORD:
4"I am ·not worthy [small]; I cannot answer you anything,
so I will put my hand over my mouth [Cto indicate no more
talking].
5I spoke one time, but I will not answer again;
I even spoke two times, but I will ·say [add] nothing more."

6Then the LORD spoke to Job from the ·storm [whirlwind]:
7"·Be strong [Brace yourself; LGird your loins], like a man!
I will ask you questions,
and you must ·answer [inform] me [38:3].
8Would you ·say that I am unfair [discredit my justice]?
Would you ·blame [condemn] me to make yourself look ·right
[righteous]?
9·Are you [LIs your arm] as strong as God?
Can your voice thunder like his?
10If so, then decorate yourself with ·glory [loftiness] and ·beauty
[pride];
dress in ·honor [splendor] and ·greatness [majesty] as if they were
clothing.
11Let your great anger ·punish [Lloose];
look at the proud and bring them down.
12Look at the proud and make them ·humble [submit].
Crush the wicked wherever they ·are [stand].
13·Bury [LHide] them all in the ·dirt [dust] together;
·cover [hide] their faces in the ·grave [Lhidden place].
14If you can do that, then I myself will ·praise [acknowledge] you,
because ·you are strong enough to save yourself [Lyour right hand
has given you the victory].

15"Look at Behemoth, [Ca large land animal or monster],
which I made just as I made you.
It eats grass like an ox.
16Look at the strength it has in its ·body [Lloins];
the muscles of its stomach are powerful.
17Its tail ·is [stiffens] like a cedar tree;
the ·muscles [sinews] of its thighs are woven together.
18Its bones are like tubes of bronze;
its legs are like bars of iron.
19It is one of the first of God's works,
but its Maker can ·destroy it [Lapproach it with a sword].
20The hills, where the wild animals play,
provide food for it.
21It ·lies [lives] under the lotus plants,
hidden by the ·tall grass in the swamp [reeds of the marsh].
22The lotus plants ·hide [cover] it in their shadow;
the poplar trees by the ·streams [wadis] surround it.

23If the river ·floods [grows turbulent], it will not ·be afraid [*or* hurry away];
it is ·safe [confident; secure] even if the Jordan River rushes to its mouth.
24Can anyone ·blind its eyes and capture it [*or* take it with a hook]?
Can anyone ·put hooks in its nose [pierce its nose with a snare]?

41 "Can you catch Leviathan [Ca large sea creature or monster; 3:8] on a fishhook
or tie its tongue down with a rope?
2Can you put a cord through its nose
or ·a hook in its jaw [Lpierce its jaw/cheek with a hook]?
3Will it keep begging you for mercy
and speak to you with ·gentle [soft; kind; tender] words?
4Will it ·make [Lcut] an ·agreement [covenant; treaty] with you
and let you take it as your slave ·for life [Lforever]?
5Can you ·make a pet of Leviathan [Lplay with it] as you would a bird
or put it on a leash for your girls?
6Will ·traders [the fishing guild] try to ·bargain [haggle] with you for it?
Will they divide it up among the merchants?
7Can you stick ·darts [harpoons] all over its skin
or fill its head with fishing spears?
8If you put one hand on it,
you will ·never forget [Lremember] the battle,
and you will never do it again!
9·There is no hope of defeating it [Any hope of defeating/subduing it will prove a lie];
just seeing it ·overwhelms people [Lthrows people down].
10No one is ·brave [fierce] enough to ·make it angry [arouse it; stir it up],
so who would be able to stand up against ·me [*or* it]?
11·No one [LWho…?] has ever ·given me anything that I must pay back [*or* confronted it and come out whole/safe],
·because everything under the sky belongs to me [*or* who—under the entire heavens?].

12"I will ·speak [Lnot keep quiet] about Leviathan's ·arms and legs [limbs],
its great strength and ·well-formed body [Lgrace of form].
13·No one [LWho…?] can ·tear off [Lexpose] its outer ·hide [Lgarment]
or ·poke [enter] through its double armor.
14·No one [LWho…?] can force open ·its great jaws [Lthe doors of its face];
they are filled with frightening teeth.
15It has rows of shields on its back
that are tightly sealed together.
16Each ·shield is so close to the next one [Ldraws near the other, so]
that no air can go between them.
17·They are joined strongly to one another [LEach clings to its neighbor];
they hold on to each other and cannot be ·separated [broken off].
18When it ·snorts [sneezes], flashes of light are thrown out,
and its eyes look like the light at dawn.

[19]Flames blaze from its mouth;
sparks of fire shoot out.
[20]Smoke pours out of its nose,
as if coming from a large pot over a hot fire.
[21]Its breath sets coals on fire,
and flames come out of its mouth.
[22]There is great strength in its neck.
·People are afraid and run away [*or* Violence leaps before it].
[23]The folds of its skin are tightly joined;
they are set and cannot be moved.
[24]Its ·chest [[L]heart] is as hard as a rock,
even as hard as a ·grinding stone [lower millstone].
[25]The ·powerful [mighty; *or* gods] fear ·its terrible looks [[L]when it lifts itself up]
and ·draw back in fear as it moves [*or* the waves miss their mark/ retreat].
[26]The sword that ·hits [approaches] it does not hurt it,
nor the arrows, darts, and spears.
[27]It ·treats [considers] iron as if it were straw
and bronze metal as if it were rotten wood.
[28]It does not run away from arrows;
stones from slings are like chaff to it.
[29]Clubs feel like ·pieces of straw [chaff] to it,
and it laughs when they ·shake [rattle] a spear at it.
[30]The underside of its body is like ·broken [*or* sharp] pieces of pottery.
It leaves a trail in the mud like a threshing board.
[31]It makes the deep sea ·bubble like a boiling [[L]boil like a] pot;
it ·stirs up the sea like a pot of oil [[L]makes the sea like ointment].
[32]·When it swims [[L]After it], it leaves a shining path in the water
that makes the sea look as if it had white hair.
[33]Nothing else on earth is equal to it;
it is a creature without fear.
[34]It looks down on all those who are ·too proud [proud; lofty];
it is king over all proud creatures."

Job Answers the Lord

42 Then Job answered the LORD [[L]and said]:
[2]"I know that you can do all things
and that no plan of yours ·can be ruined [is impossible; can be hindered].
[3]You asked, 'Who is this that made my ·purpose [[L]counsel; advice] ·unclear [hidden] by ·saying things that are not true [[L]ignorance; 38:2]?'
Surely I spoke of things I did not understand;
I talked of things too wonderful for me to know.
[4]You said, 'Listen now, and I will speak.
I will ask you questions,
and you must ·answer [inform] me.'
[5]My ears had heard of you before,
but now my eyes have seen you.
[6]So now I ·hate [despise] myself;
I will ·change my heart and life [[L]repent], ·and will sit in [[L]...in] dust and ashes [[C]for his questioning of God, not for anything that led to his suffering]."

End of the Story

7After the LORD had said these things to Job, he said to Eliphaz the Temanite, "·I am angry with [LMy anger burns against] you and your two friends, because you have not said what is ·right [correct] about me, as my servant Job did. 8Now take seven bulls and seven male sheep, and go to my servant Job, and offer a burnt offering [Lev. 1:1–7] for yourselves [Cfor atonement]. My servant Job will ·pray [intercede] for you, and I will ·listen to [accept] his prayer. Then I will not ·punish you for being foolish [Ltreat you according to your foolishness]. You have not said what is ·right [correct] about me, as my servant Job did." 9So Eliphaz the Temanite, Bildad the Shuhite, and Zophar the Naamathite did as the LORD said, and the LORD ·listened to [accepted] Job's prayer.

10After Job had ·prayed [interceded] for his friends, the LORD ·gave him success again [restored his fortunes]. The LORD gave Job twice as much as he had owned before. 11Job's brothers and sisters came to his house, along with everyone who had known him before, and they all ate with him there. They ·comforted him and made him feel better about the trouble [commiserated with him concerning the trouble/evil] the LORD had brought on him, and each one gave Job a piece of silver and a gold ring.

12The LORD blessed the last part of Job's life even more than the first part. Job had fourteen thousand sheep, six thousand camels, a thousand teams of oxen, and a thousand female donkeys. 13Job also had seven sons and three daughters. 14He named the first daughter Jemimah [C"turtledove"], the second daughter Keziah [C"cassia," a spice], and the third daughter Keren-Happuch [C"a horn (jar) of eye paint"]. 15There were no other women in all the ·land [*or* earth] as beautiful as Job's daughters. And their father Job gave them land to own along with their brothers.

16After this, Job lived one hundred forty years. He lived to see his children, grandchildren, great-grandchildren, and great-great-grandchildren. 17Then Job died; he was old and ·had lived many years [Lfull of days].

PSALMS

Book 1: Psalms 1–41

Two Ways to Live

1 ·Happy [Blessed] are those who don't ·listen to [Lwalk in the counsel of] the wicked,
who don't ·go where sinners go [Lstand in the way of sinners],
who don't ·do what evil people do [Lsit in the seat of mockers].
2They ·love [delight in] the LORD's ·teachings [laws; instructions],
and they ·think about [meditate on] those ·teachings [laws; instructions] day and night.
3They are like a tree planted by ·a river [Lstreams of water; Cfull of life, strong, vibrant].
The tree produces fruit in season,
and its leaves don't ·die [wither].
Everything they do will ·succeed [prosper].

4But wicked people are not like that.
They are like chaff that the wind blows away [Cdead, unstable].
5So the wicked will not ·escape God's punishment [Lstand in the judgment].
Sinners will not ·worship with God's people [Lbe in the assembly of the righteous].
6This is because the LORD ·takes care of his people [Lknows the way of the righteous],
but the way of the wicked will be destroyed.

The Lord's Chosen King

2 Why ·are the nations so angry [do the nations rage/*or* conspire]?
Why ·are the people making useless plans [do the people plot in vain]?
2The kings of the earth ·prepare to fight [Ltake their stand],
and their leaders ·make plans [plot] together
against the LORD
and his ·appointed one [anointed; Messiah; Cthe king, ultimately Jesus; Acts 4:25–28].
3They say, "Let's break ·the chains that hold us back [Ltheir chains/bonds]
and throw off ·the ropes that tie us down [Ltheir ropes/cords from us]."

4But the one who sits in heaven [CGod] laughs;
the Lord ·makes fun of [ridicules; derides] them.
5Then the LORD ·warns them [Lspeaks to them in anger]
and frightens them with his ·anger [fury].

[6]He says, "I have ·appointed [installed; set] my own king
over my holy mountain, Zion [[C]the location of the Temple in
Jerusalem; 9:11; 48:2, 11; 50:2; 1 Kin. 8:1]."

[7]Now I will ·tell [recount to] you what the LORD has ·declared [decreed]:
He said to me, "You are my son.
Today I have become your father [2 Sam. 7:14; Matt. 3:17; Mark 1:11;
Luke 3:22; Acts 13:32–33; Heb. 1:5].
[8]·If you ask me [[L]Ask of me], I will give you the nations as your
inheritance;
all the ·people on [[L]ends of the] earth will be ·yours [[L]your
possession].
[9]You will rule over them with an iron ·rod [scepter; [C]a symbol of royal
authority; Rev. 12:5; 19:15].
You will ·break [dash] them into pieces like pottery."

[10]·So [Now], kings, be wise;
·rulers [[L]rulers/judges of the earth], ·learn this lesson [be warned].
[11]·Obey [Serve] the LORD with great fear.
·Be happy [Rejoice], ·but tremble [[L]with trembling].
[12]·Show that you are loyal to his [[L]Kiss the] son,
or ·you will be destroyed by his anger [[L]he will be angry and you will
perish on the way],
because he can quickly become angry.
But ·happy [blessed] are those who ·trust him for protection [find
refuge in him].

A Morning Prayer

David sang this when he ran away from his son
Absalom [2 Sam. 15–19].

3 LORD, ·I have many enemies [[L]how many are my foes?]!
·Many people [[L]How many…?] have ·turned [[L]risen] against me.
[2]Many are saying about me,
"·God won't rescue him [[L]There is no salvation for him in God]."
·Selah [Interlude]

[3]But, LORD, you are my shield [[C]protector],
my ·wonderful God [[L]glory] who ·gives me courage [[L]lifts up my
head].
[4]I will ·pray [[L]lift my voice] to the LORD,
and he will answer me from his holy mountain [[C]Zion, the location
of the Temple]. *·Selah* [Interlude]

[5]I can lie down and go to sleep,
and I will wake up again,
because the LORD ·gives me strength [sustains/upholds me].
[6]Thousands of troops may ·surround me [[L]set themselves around me],
but I am not afraid.

[7]LORD, rise up!
My God, come ·save [rescue; [T]deliver] me!
You have struck my enemies on the cheek;
you have broken the teeth of the wicked.

8·The LORD can save his people [LSalvation/Rescue/Deliverance belongs
to the LORD].
·Bless your people [LMay your blessing be on your people].
·*Selah* [Interlude]

An Evening Prayer

For the director of music. With stringed instruments.
A psalm of David.

4 Answer me when I ·pray [Lcall] to you,
my God who ·does what is right [is righteous; *or* who vindicates me].
·Make things easier for me [Give me room; Widen my way] when I am
in trouble.
Have mercy on me and hear my prayer.

2People, how long will you turn my ·honor [glory] into shame?
How long will you love what is ·false [empty] and ·look for [seek] lies
[Cpossibly referring to false gods]? ·*Selah* [Interlude]
3You know that the LORD has ·chosen [set apart; distinguished] for
himself those who are loyal to him [Cin covenant relationship with
him].
The LORD listens when I ·pray [call] to him.
4When you ·are angry [are disturbed; Ltremble], do not sin.
·Think about these things [Meditate; LSpeak to your heart] quietly
·as you go to bed [Lon your bed]. ·*Selah* [Interlude]
5·Do what is right as a sacrifice to the LORD [LSacrifice right/righteous
sacrifices]
and trust the LORD.

6Many people ask,
"Who will ·give us [Lmake us see] anything good?"
LORD, ·be kind to us [Llet the light of your face shine on us; Num.
6:24–26].
7But you have ·made me very happy [Lgiven joy to my heart],
happier than they are,
even with all their grain and new wine.
8I ·go to bed [Llie down] and sleep in peace,
because, LORD, only you ·keep me safe [make me secure].

A Morning Prayer for Protection

For the director of music. For flutes. A psalm of David.

5 LORD, ·listen [Lgive ear] to my words.
Understand my ·sadness [Lmoans; sighs].
2·Listen [Pay attention] to my cry for help, my King and my God,
because I pray to you.
3LORD, every morning you hear my voice.
Every morning, I ·tell you what I need [*or* prepare a sacrifice for you;
Lstretch out/arrange before you],
and I ·wait for your answer [Lwatch].

4You are not a God who ·is pleased with the wicked [takes delight in evil];
·you do not live with those who do evil [Levil does not sojourn with you].
5Those people who ·make fun of you [*or* boast] cannot stand before ·you
[Lyour eyes].
You hate all those who do evil.

6You destroy ·liars [Lthose who speak lies];
the Lord ·hates [despises] those ·who kill and trick others [Lwith bloodguilt and deceit].

7Because of your great ·love [loyalty; covenant love],
I ·can [*or* will] come into your ·Temple [Lhouse].
Because I ·fear you [hold you in awe],
I can ·worship [bow down] ·in [*or* toward] your holy Temple.
8Lord, since I have many enemies,
·show me the right thing to do [Llead/guide me in your righteousness].
·Show me clearly how you want me to live [LMake your way straight before me].

9My enemies' mouths do not tell the truth;
·in their hearts they want to destroy others [Ltheir innards are destruction].
Their throats are like open graves [Rom. 3:13];
they use their tongues for ·telling lies [flattery].
10God, ·declare them guilty [Lmake them bear their iniquity]!
Let them fall ·into their own traps [*or* by their own advice].
·Send [Cast] them away because their ·sins [transgressions] are many;
they have ·turned [rebelled] against you.

11But let everyone who ·trusts [finds refuge in] you ·be happy [rejoice];
let them sing glad songs forever.
·Protect [LSpread your protection on] those who love you
and ·who are happy because of you [Llet those who love your name rejoice in you].
12Lord, you bless those who ·do what is right [are righteous];
you ·protect them [Lsurround them with favor] like a shield.

A Prayer for Mercy in Troubled Times

For the director of music. With stringed instruments. Upon the ·sheminith [Leighth; Ca reference to an eight-stringed instrument or possibly the manner of singing]. A psalm of David.

6 Lord, don't ·correct [rebuke; reprove] me when you are angry;
don't ·punish [discipline] me when you are ·very angry [enraged].
2Lord, ·have mercy on [be gracious to] me because I ·am weak [languish; faint].
Heal me, Lord, because my bones ·ache [are in agony].
3I ·am very upset [ache; am in agony].
Lord, how long will it be?

4Lord, return and save me;
·save [rescue; Tdeliver] me because of your ·kindness [loyalty; covenant love].
5Dead people don't remember you;
those in ·the grave [*or* the underworld; LSheol] don't praise you.

6I am ·tired [weary] ·of crying to you [Lbecause of my moaning].
Every night ·my bed is wet [LI flood my pillow] with tears;

my bed is soaked from my crying.
[7]**My eyes are weak ·from so much crying** [[L]because of my grief];
they are weak ·from crying about [[L]because of] **my enemies.**

[8]**Get away from me, all you who do evil,**
because the LORD has heard my ·crying [supplication].
[9]**The LORD has heard my cry for help;**
the LORD will ·answer [accept] **my prayer.**
[10]**All my enemies will be ashamed and ·troubled** [in agony; vv. 2–3].
They will turn and suddenly leave in shame.

A Prayer for Fairness

A shiggaion [[C]a musical or literary term of uncertain meaning] of **David which he sang to the LORD about Cush, from the tribe of Benjamin** [[C]an unknown person, but the tribe of Benjamin, Saul's tribe, resisted David's kingship at first; 2 Sam. 3–4].

7 **LORD my God, I ·trust in you for protection** [find refuge in you].
·Save [Rescue; [T]Deliver] **me and rescue me**
from those who are ·chasing [pursuing] **me.**
[2]**Otherwise, like a lion they will tear me apart.**
They will ·rip me to pieces [*or* drag me away], **and no one can ·save** [rescue; [T]deliver] **me.**

[3]**LORD my God, what have I done?**
Have my hands done something ·wrong [to make me guilty]?
[4]**Have I done wrong to ·my friend** [[L]the one at peace with me]
or stolen without reason from my enemy?
[5]**If I have, let my enemy ·chase** [pursue] **me and ·capture** [overtake] **me.**
Let him trample ·me [[L]my life] **into the ·dust** [earth]
and ·bury me [[L]lay my honor] **in the ground.** ·*Selah* [Interlude]

[6]**LORD, rise up in your anger;**
·stand up [[L]lift yourself up] **against my enemies' ·anger** [fury].
·Get up [Wake up], **·my God** [*or* for me], **and ·demand fairness** [insist on/[L]command judgment].
[7]**Gather the ·nations** [[L]assembly/congregations of the peoples] **around you**
and ·rule [*or* take a seat over; [L]return] **them from ·above** [on high].
[8]**LORD, judge the people.**
LORD, ·defend [judge] **me ·because I am right** [according to my righteousness],
·because I have done no wrong [according to my innocence].
[9]**God, you ·do what is right** [are righteous].
You ·know [[L]test] **our ·thoughts** [[L]hearts/minds] **and ·feelings** [[L]kidneys; [C]the seat of emotions in Hebrew thought].
Stop those wicked actions done by evil people,
and ·help [establish] **those who ·do what is right** [are righteous].

[10]**God ·protects me like a** [is my] **shield;**
he saves those whose hearts ·are right [have integrity].
[11]**God ·judges by what is right** [is a righteous judge],
and God is ·always ready to punish the wicked [[L]angry every day].
[12]**If they do not ·change their lives** [repent],

God will sharpen his sword;
he will string his bow and take aim.
13He has prepared his deadly weapons;
he has made his flaming arrows.

14There are people who ·think up [Lconceive] evil
and ·plan [Lare pregnant with] ·trouble [malice] and ·tell [Lgive birth to] lies.
15They dig a ·hole [pit] ·to trap others [Land dig it deep],
but they will fall into it themselves.
16·They will get themselves into trouble [LTheir trouble/malice will return to their head];
the violence they cause will ·hurt only themselves [Lcome down on their heads; Prov. 26:27; Matt. 26:52].

17I praise the LORD ·because he does what is right [according to his righteousness].
I sing praises to the LORD Most High.

The Lord's Greatness

For the director of music. On the gittith [Cperhaps a musical term or instrument]. A psalm of David.

8 LORD our Lord,
·Your name is the most wonderful name [LHow majestic is your name] in all the earth [Ex. 3:14–15]!
·It brings you praise [LYou have set your splendor/glory] in heaven above [Rom. 1:20].
2·You have taught children and babies
to sing praises to you [LOut of the mouth of babies and infants you have established/founded strength]
because of your enemies.
And so you silence your enemies
and those who try to get ·even [revenge].

3I look at your heavens,
·which you made with [Lthe work of] your fingers.
I see the moon and stars,
which you ·created [Lestablished; Gen. 1:17–18].
4·But why are people even important to you [LWhat are people that you remember them]?
Why do you take care of ·human beings [Lthe son of man]?
5You made them a little lower than ·the angels [*or* God]
and crowned them with glory and honor [Gen. 1:26–27].
6You ·put them in charge of [give them rule over] ·everything you made [Lthe work of your hands].
You put all things under their ·control [Lfeet; Heb. 2:6–8]:
7all the sheep, the cattle,
and the ·wild animals [Lbeasts of the field],
8the birds in the ·sky [heavens],
the fish in the sea,
and everything that ·lives under water [Lpasses/travels on the paths of the sea; Gen. 1:28; 9:1–3].

9LORD our Lord,
·your name is the most wonderful [Lhow majestic is your] name in all the earth!

Thanksgiving for Victory

For the director of music. To the tune of "The Death of the Son." A psalm of David.

9 I will ·praise [*or* give thanks to] you, LORD, with all my heart.
I will ·tell [recount] all ·the miracles you have done [your wonderful deeds].
2I will be happy and rejoice because of you;
God Most High, I will sing praises to your name.

3My enemies turn back;
they ·are overwhelmed [Lstumble] and ·die [perish] ·because of [*or* before] you.
4You have ·heard [upheld; maintained] my ·complaint [just cause; *or* right and my cause];
you sat on your throne and judged ·by what was right [righteously].
5You ·spoke strongly against the [rebuked; reproved] foreign nations and destroyed the wicked;
you ·wiped out [blotted out; erased] their names forever and ever.
6The enemy is ·gone [done; a ruin] forever.
You ·destroyed [uprooted] their cities;
·no one even remembers them [Ltheir memory perishes].

7But the LORD ·rules [is enthroned; Lsits] forever.
He ·sits on his throne to judge [Lhas established his throne for justice/judgment],
8and he will judge the world ·in fairness [with righteousness];
he will decide what is fair for the ·nations [peoples; 96:10; 98:9].
9The LORD ·defends [Lis a refuge for] those who ·suffer [are oppressed/exploited];
·he defends them [La refuge] in times of ·trouble [distress].
10Those who know ·the LORD [Lyour name] trust ·him [Lyou],
because ·he [Lyou] will not ·leave [abandon; forsake] those who ·come to him [Lseek you; Deut. 31:6, 8; Matt. 28:20; Heb. 13:5].

11Sing praises to the LORD who ·is king on Mount [Ldwells on] Zion [Cthe location of the Temple].
Tell ·the nations [Lamong the peoples] what he has done.
12·He remembers who the murderers are [*or* The one who avenges blood remembers them; CGod];
he will not forget the cries of those who suffer.
13LORD, ·have mercy on [be gracious toward] me.
See how ·my enemies [Lthose who hate me] ·hurt [afflict; persecute] me.
·Do not let me go through [LLift me up from] the gates of death.
14Then, at the gates of ·Jerusalem [the daughter of Zion; Ca name of Jerusalem], I will ·praise you [Ldeclare your praises];
I will rejoice ·because you saved me [Lin your salvation].

15The nations have ·fallen [Lsunk] into the pit they ·dug [Lmade].
Their feet are caught in the nets they ·laid [Lhid].

[16]The LORD has made himself known by ·his fair decisions [[L]the judgments he has made];
the wicked get trapped by ·what they do [[L]the deeds of their palms/ hands]. ·*Higgaion* [[C]a musical notation]. ·*Selah* [Interlude]

[17]Wicked people will ·go [[L]return] to the ·grave [*or* underworld; [L]Sheol],
and so will all ·those who [[L]the nations that] forget God.
[18]But those who ·have troubles [are afflicted] will not always be forgotten.
The hopes of the ·poor [oppressed; exploited] will never ·die [perish].

[19]LORD, rise up and don't let people ·think they are strong [[L]prevail].
Judge the nations in your presence.
[20]·Teach them to fear you [*or* Strike them with terror; Deut. 4:34; 28:8; 34:12], LORD.
The nations must learn that they are ·only human [mere mortals].
·*Selah* [Interlude]

A Complaint About Evil People

10 LORD, why ·are you [[L]do you stand] so far away?
Why do you hide ·when there is [[L]in times of] ·trouble [distress]?
[2]Proudly the wicked ·chase down [hunt down; persecute] ·those who suffer [*or* the poor].
Let them be caught in ·their own traps [[L]the schemes they have thought up].
[3]They ·brag [boast] about the ·things they want [[L]cravings/desires of their soul].
·They bless the greedy but [*or* The greedy curse and] ·hate [reject] the LORD.
[4]The wicked people are too proud.
They do not ·look for [pursue; seek] God;
there is no room for God in their thoughts.
[5]·They always succeed [[L]Their ways are always successful/prosperous].
·They are far from keeping your laws [[L]Your judgments are above their grasp];
they ·make fun of [sneer/scoff at] their enemies.
[6]They say ·to themselves [[L]in their hearts], "·Nothing bad will ever happen to me [[L]I will never be moved/shaken];
I will never ·be ruined [have trouble/be harmed]."
[7]Their mouths are full of curses, ·lies [deceit], and ·threats [violence];
·they use their tongues for [[L]under their tongues is] ·sin [trouble] and evil [Rom. 3:14].
[8]They ·hide [[L]lie in ambush] near the villages.
They ·look for innocent people to kill [murder the innocent; Prov. 1:11];
·they watch in secret [[L]their eyes look intently] for the helpless.
[9]They ·wait in hiding [[L]lie in ambush in a covert/cover] like a lion.
They ·wait [[L]lie] to catch poor people;
they catch the poor in nets and drag them off.
[10]The poor are crushed and thrown down;
they ·are defeated [[L]fall] ·because the others are stronger [[L]by their might].
[11]The wicked ·think [[L]say in their hearts], "God has forgotten us.

He ·doesn't see what is happening [Lhas hidden his face and does not see anything]."

12LORD, rise up and ·punish the wicked [Lraise your hand, God].
Don't forget those who ·need help [are oppressed].
13Why do wicked people ·hate [despise] God?
They say ·to themselves [Lin their hearts], "·God won't punish us [LYou will not pursue]."
14LORD, surely you see these ·cruel [troublesome] and ·evil [grievous] things;
look at them and ·do something [Lput it in your hands].
·People in trouble [LThe helpless] ·look to you for help [entrust/abandon themselves to your hands].
You are the one who helps the orphans.
15Break the ·power [Lhand] of wicked and evil people.
·Punish them for the evil they have done [LYou will seek out their wickedness until you find none].

16The LORD is King forever and ever.
·Destroy from your land those nations [LThe nations will perish from his land].
17LORD, you have heard ·what the poor people want [the desires of the poor].
·Do what they ask [LYou will strengthen their heart], and ·listen to them [Lyou will cause your ear to pay attention].
18·Protect [LBring justice to] the orphans and ·put an end to suffering [Lthe oppressed]
so ·they will no longer be afraid of evil people [Lthose from the earth may terrify no more].

Trust in the Lord

For the director of music. Of David.

11 I ·trust in the LORD for protection [find refuge in the LORD].
So why do you say to me,
"·Fly [LFlee] like a bird to your mountain.
2For, look, the wicked ·string [bend] their bows;
they set their arrows on the bowstrings.
They shoot from dark places
at those who are ·honest [Lupright/virtuous in heart].
3When the foundations [Ca stable society] collapse,
what can ·good [righteous] people do?"

4The LORD is in his holy Temple;
the LORD sits on his throne in heaven.
·He sees what people do [LHis eyes watch];
·he keeps his eye on them [Lhis gaze examines/tests people].
5The LORD ·tests [examines] ·those who do right and those who do wrong [the righteous and the wicked],
but he hates those who love ·to hurt others [violence].
6He will ·send [Lrain] hot coals and burning sulfur on the wicked.
A ·whirlwind [scorching wind] is ·what they will get [Lthe portion of their cup; Can image of judgment; Is. 51:17, 22; Ezek. 23:31–33; Matt. 26:39].

[7]The LORD ·does what is right [is righteous], and he loves ·justice [righteousness],
so ·honest people [the upright/virtuous] will see his face.

A Prayer Against Liars

For the director of music. Upon the ·sheminith [[L]eighth; [C]a reference to an eight-stringed instrument or possibly the manner of singing]. A psalm of David.

12 Save me, LORD, because the ·good [faithful; godly; covenantal; loyal] people are all gone;
·no true believers are left on earth [[L]the faithful have vanished among humanity].
[2]Everyone ·lies [[L]speaks falsehood] to his neighbors;
they ·say one thing and mean another [speak with flattering lips and with a double heart/[L]heart and heart].
[3]The LORD will ·stop [[L]cut off] those flattering lips
and those bragging tongues.
[4]They say, "Our tongues will ·help us win [prevail].
·We can say what we wish [[L]Our lips belong to us]; ·no one [[L]who…?] is our master."

[5]But the LORD says,
"I will now rise up,
because the ·poor [weak] are ·being hurt [destroyed; plundered; oppressed].
Because of the ·moans [groans; sighs] of the ·helpless [needy],
I will give them the ·help [victory] they ·want [long for]."
[6]The LORD's ·words [*or* promises] are ·pure [flawless],
like silver ·purified [refined] ·by fire [*or* in a furnace],
·purified [refined] seven times over [18:30; 119:140].

[7]LORD, you will ·keep us safe [[L]guard/protect them];
you will always ·protect [guard] us from such ·people [a generation].
[8]But the wicked ·are [[L]walk] all around us;
·everyone loves what is wrong [[L]what is vile is lifted up among the sons of man/humanity].

A Prayer for God to Be Near

For the director of music. A psalm of David.

13 How long will you forget me, LORD? Forever?
How long will you hide your face from me?
[2]How long must I ·worry [*or* bear pain; [L]hold counsels]
and ·feel sad [hold sorrow] in my heart all day?
How long will my enemy ·win [rise up] over me?

[3]LORD, look at me.
Answer me, my God;
·tell me [[L]light up my eyes], or I will ·die [[L]sleep the sleep of death].
[4]Otherwise my enemy will say, "I have ·won [finished him off]!"
·Those against me [My foes] will rejoice that I've been ·defeated [shaken; moved].

[5]I ·trust [have confidence] in your ·love [loyalty; covenant love].

My heart ·is happy [rejoices] because ·you saved me [of your victory/
salvation].
6I sing to the LORD
because he has ·taken care of [been good to] me.

The Unbelieving Fool

For the director of music. Of David.

14 Fools say ·to themselves [Lin their hearts],
"There is no God [CPsalm 53 largely parallels this psalm]."
·Fools are evil [LThey are corrupt] and do ·terrible [detestable] things
[Deut. 32:5];
there is no one who does anything good.

2The LORD looked down from heaven on all people
to see if anyone ·understood [Lwas wise/insightful],
if anyone was ·looking to God for help [seeking God].
3But all have ·turned [wandered] away.
Together, everyone has become ·evil [perverse].
There is no one who does anything good,
not even one [Rom. 3:10–12].

4Don't ·the wicked [Lthose who do evil] ·understand [know]?
They ·destroy [consume; Leat] my people as if they were ·eating
[consuming] bread.
They do not ·ask the LORD for help [call on the LORD].
5But the wicked are ·filled [terrified] with terror,
because God is with ·those who do what is right [the company of the
righteous].
6The wicked ·upset [confuse; frustrate] the plans of the poor,
but the LORD ·will protect them [is their refuge].

7I pray that ·victory [salvation] will come to Israel from Mount Zion
[Cthe location of the Temple]!
May the LORD ·bring them back [restore the fortunes of his people;
Cperhaps at the end of the exile].
Then the people of Jacob will rejoice,
and the people of Israel will be glad.

What the Lord Demands

A psalm of David.

15 LORD, who may ·enter [dwell/abide/sojourn in] your Holy Tent
[Cthe Tabernacle]?
Who may live on your holy mountain [CMount Zion]?

2Only those who ·are innocent [walk innocently]
and who do ·what is right [righteousness; 1:1; Job 1:1].
Such people speak the truth from their hearts
3 and do not ·tell lies about others [slander with their tongue].
They do no ·wrong [evil] to their neighbors
and do not ·gossip [Lraise a reproachful matter with their associates].
4·They do not respect hateful people [LThe wicked are despised in their eyes]
but honor those who ·honor [Lfear] the LORD.
They keep their promises to their neighbors,
even when it hurts.

5 They do not charge interest on money they lend [Ex. 22:25–27; Lev. 25:35–36; Deut. 23:19]
and do not take ·money [a bribe] to hurt innocent people [Ex. 23:8; Deut. 16:19].

Whoever does all these things will never be ·destroyed [Lmoved].

The Lord Takes Care of His People

A miktam [Cperhaps "inscription"] of David.

16 ·Protect [Guard] me, God,
because I ·trust [take refuge] in you.
2 I said to the Lord, "You are my Lord.
·Every good thing I have comes from you [I have no good apart from you]."
3 As for the ·godly people [holy ones; saints] in the ·world [*or* land],
they are the ·wonderful [noble] ones I ·enjoy [take pleasure in].
4 But those who ·turn to [run/hurry after] ·idols [other gods]
·will have much [multiply] pain.
I will not ·offer [pour out offerings of] blood to those idols
or even ·speak [Ltake on my lips] their names.

5 No, the Lord is ·all I need [Lmy portion and my cup].
·He takes care of me [LYou hold my lot; Ca device like the Urim and Thummim whereby God reveals one's future; Ex. 28:30].
6 ·My share in life has been pleasant [LThe boundary lines fall for me in pleasant places];
my ·part [inheritance] has been beautiful.

7 I ·praise [bless] the Lord because he advises me.
Even at night, ·I feel his leading [Lmy innards instruct me].
8 I keep the Lord before me always.
Because he is ·close by my side [Lat my right hand],
I will not be ·hurt [Lmoved; Acts 2:25].
9 So ·I rejoice and am glad [Lmy heart exults and my glory/soul/*or* innards is glad].
Even my body ·has hope [dwells securely; Acts 2:26],
10 because you will not ·leave [abandon] me in ·the grave [*or* the underworld; LSheol].
You will not let your ·holy one [saint; loyal one] ·rot [Lsee the Pit; Cthe grave; Acts 2:27; 13:35].
11 You will teach me ·how to live a holy [Lthe path of] life.
·Being with you will fill me with joy [LIn your face/presence is the fullness of joy; Acts 2:28];
at your right hand I will find pleasure forever.

A Prayer for Protection

A prayer of David.

17 Lord, hear ·me begging for fairness [a just cause];
·listen [pay attention] to my cry for help.
·Pay attention [Bend your ear] to my prayer,
because ·I speak the truth [Lmy lips are not deceitful].
2 ·You will judge that I am right [LMy judgment/vindication will come from before you];
your eyes can see what is ·true [virtuous].

[3]You have examined my heart;
you have ·tested me all [*or* visited me at] **night.**
You ·questioned [tested] **me without finding anything wrong;**
·I have not sinned with my mouth [[L]my mouth has not transgressed].
[4]·I have obeyed your commands [[L]As for the deeds of people, by the word of your lips],
·so I have not done what evil people do [I have kept away from the ways of the violent].
[5]·I have done what you told me [[L]My steps have held fast to your paths];
·I have not failed [[L]My feet have not slipped].

[6]I call to you,
·and [[L]for] **you answer me, O God.**
·Listen [[L]Extend your ear] **to me now,**
and hear what I say.
[7]Your ·love [loyalty; covenant love] **is wonderful.**
·By your power [[L]At your right hand] **you save those who ·trust** [find their refuge in] **you**
from ·their enemies [those who rise up against them].
[8]Protect me as ·you would protect your own [*or* the apple/[L]pupil of your] **eye.**
Hide me under the shadow of your wings.
[9]Keep me from the wicked who ·attack [mistreat] **me,**
from my enemies who surround me.
[10]They ·are selfish [close their callous hearts]
and ·brag about themselves [[L]their mouths speak proudly].
[11]They have ·chased [tracked] **me until they have surrounded me.**
They ·plan [[L]set their eyes] **to throw me to the ground.**
[12]They are like lions ready to ·kill [tear up prey];
like lions, they sit in ·hiding [ambush; cover].

[13]LORD, rise up, ·face [confront] **the enemy, and ·throw them down** [subdue them].
·Save [Rescue; [T]Deliver] **me from the wicked with your sword.**
[14]LORD, save me by your ·power [[L]hand] **from mortals,**
from mortals whose ·reward [portion] **in the world is in this life.**
·They have plenty of food [[L]Your stores have filled their bellies].
·They have many sons [*or* Their sons have plenty]
and leave ·much money [[L]their surplus] **to their children.**

[15]·Because I have lived right [In righteousness], **I will see your face.**
When I wake up, I will see your likeness and be satisfied.

A Song of Victory

For the director of music. By the LORD's servant, David. David sang this song to the LORD ·when [[L]on the day] **the LORD had ·saved** [rescued; [T]delivered] **him from Saul and all his other enemies** [[C]the occasion is unknown; 2 Sam. 22 parallels this psalm]. **He said:**

18

I love you, LORD. You are my strength.

[2]The LORD is my rock, my ·protection [[L]fortress], **my ·Savior** [rescuer; [T]deliverer].
My God is my rock.

·I can run to him for safety [L...in whom I find protection/take refuge].
He is my shield and ·my saving strength [Lthe horn of my salvation; Csymbolizing strength based on an animal lifting its head triumphantly], my ·defender [stronghold].
3I ·will call to [call upon] the LORD, who is worthy of praise,
and I ·will be [*or* am] saved from my enemies.

4The ·ropes [cords] of death ·came around [swirled about; encompassed] me;
the ·deadly rivers [floods/torrents of destruction] overwhelmed me.
5The ·ropes [cords] of death ·wrapped around [entangled; coiled around] me.
The ·traps [snares] of death ·were before [confronted; lay ahead of] me.
6In my ·trouble [distress; anguish] I ·called [cried out] to the LORD.
I ·cried out [called] to my God for help.
From his ·Temple [sanctuary] he heard my voice;
my ·call for help [cry] reached his ears.

7The earth ·trembled [reeled; quaked] and ·shook [rocked].
The foundations of the mountains began to ·shake [shudder].
They ·trembled [reeled; quaked] because the LORD was angry.
8Smoke ·came out of his nose [poured/rose from his nostrils],
and ·burning [devouring] fire came out of his mouth.
Burning coals ·went before [blazed/flamed out from] him.
9He ·tore open [parted] the ·sky [heavens] and came down
with ·dark clouds [storm clouds; thick darkness] under his feet.
10He rode a ·creature with wings [Lcherub; Ca mighty spiritual being/angel; Ezek. 1] and flew.
·He raced [...soaring] on the wings of the wind.
11He made darkness his covering, his ·shelter [canopy; shroud] around him,
surrounded by ·fog [thick rain] and clouds.
12Out of the brightness ·of his presence [before him] came clouds
with hail and ·lightning [Lfiery coals].
13The LORD thundered from heaven;
the ·Most High raised his voice [voice of the Most High resounded],
and there was hail and ·lightning [Lfiery coals].
14He shot his arrows and scattered his enemies.
His many bolts of lightning ·confused them with fear [routed them].
15·LORD, you spoke strongly [LAt your rebuke, O LORD...].
·The wind blew from your nose [L...at the blast of breath from your nostrils...].
Then the ·valleys [floor; channels] of the sea ·appeared [were exposed],
and the foundations of the earth were ·seen [laid bare].

16The LORD reached down from ·above [heaven; on high] and ·took [rescued] me;
he ·pulled me from the deep water [drew me out of mighty waters].
17He ·saved [rescued; Tdelivered] me from my powerful enemies,
from those who hated me, because they were too strong for me.

18 **They ·attacked** [confronted] **me ·at my time of trouble** [[L]in the day of
my distress/calamity/disaster],
but the LORD ·supported me [was my stay].
19 **He took me to a ·safe** [spacious; open; [L]broad] **place.**
Because he delights in me, he ·saved [rescued; [T]delivered] **me.**

20 **The LORD ·spared** [rewarded] **me ·because I did what was right**
[[L]according to my righteousness].
Because ·I have not done evil [of my innocence; [L]of the cleanness of
my hands], **he has ·rewarded** [restored] **me.**
21 **I have ·followed** [obeyed; kept; [L]guarded] **the ways of the LORD;**
I have not done evil by turning away from my God.
22 **I ·remember** [follow; [L]have before me] **all his ·laws** [regulations]
and have not ·broken [abandoned; [L]turned aside from] **his ·rules**
[statutes; ordinances; requirements].
23 **I am ·innocent** [blameless] **before him;**
I have kept myself from ·doing evil [sin; guilt; iniquity].
24 **The LORD ·rewarded** [repaid] **me ·because I did what was right**
[[L]according to my righteousness],
·because I did what the LORD said was right [[L]according to my
cleanness/purity in his sight].

25 **LORD, you ·are** [show yourself] **·loyal** [faithful; kind] **to those who are
·loyal** [faithful; kind],
and you are good to those who are good.
26 **You ·are** [show yourself] **·pure** [sincere] **to those who are ·pure** [sincere],
but you ·are [show yourself] **·against** [hostile/shrewd/cunning/
perverse to] **those who are ·bad** [perverse; devious; crooked].
27 **You ·save** [rescue; [T]deliver] **the ·humble** [afflicted],
but you ·bring down [watch and humiliate] **·those who are proud**
[the haughty].
28 **LORD, you give light to my lamp.**
My God ·brightens the darkness around me [lights up/illuminates
my darkness].
29 **With your help I can ·attack** [crush] **an army.**
With God's help I can ·jump over [scale] **a wall.**

30 **The ·ways** [way; path] **of God are ·without fault** [blameless; perfect].
The LORD's ·words [promises] **are ·pure** [tested; flawless; proven true].
He is a shield to those who ·trust [seek protection/take refuge in] **him.**
31 **Who is God? Only the LORD.**
Who is the Rock? Only our God.
32 **God ·is my protection** [is my strong fortress; *or* girds me with strength].
He makes my way ·free from fault [perfect; secure; a wide path].
33 **He makes ·me** [[L]my feet] **like a deer that does not stumble** [[C]sure-
footed];
he ·helps me stand [sets me] **on the ·steep mountains** [heights].
34 **He trains my hands for battle**
so my arms can bend a bronze bow.
35 **You ·protect me with your saving shield** [[L]have given me the shield of
your salvation/victory].
You support me with your right hand.

·You have stooped to make [Your help makes] **me great.**
36**You ·give me a better way to live** [broaden my path; [L]widen my steps
beneath me],
so ·I live as you want me to [my feet do not slip; [L]my ankles do not
weaken].
37**I ·chased** [pursued] **my enemies and ·caught** [exterminated] **them.**
I did not ·quit [turn back] **until they were ·destroyed** [annihilated;
consumed].
38**I ·crushed them** [shattered them; struck them down] **so they couldn't
·rise** [get] **up again.**
They fell beneath my feet.
39**You ·gave me** [[L]armed/girded me with] **strength ·in** [for] **battle.**
You ·made my enemies bow [humbled/subdued my enemies] **·before
me** [*or* under my feet].
40**You made my enemies ·turn back** [turn their backs; retreat],
and I destroyed ·those who hated me [my foes].
41**They ·called for help** [looked around],
but no one came to ·save [rescue; [T]deliver] **them.**
They ·called [looked] **to the LORD,**
but he did not answer them.
42**I ·beat my enemies into pieces** [ground/pulverized them], **like dust in
the wind.**
I poured them out like ·mud [mire] **in the streets.**

43**You ·saved** [rescued; [T]delivered] **me when the people ·attacked me**
[quarreled; fought].
You made me the ·leader [ruler; head] **of nations.**
People I never knew serve me.
44**As soon as they hear ·me** [*or* of me], **they obey me.**
Foreigners ·obey [cower/cringe before] **me.**
45**They all ·become afraid** [lose heart/their courage]
and ·tremble in [come trembling from] **their ·hiding places**
[fortresses; strongholds].

46**The LORD lives!**
May my Rock be ·praised [blessed].
Praise the God ·who saves me [...of my salvation]!
47**God gives me ·victory** [revenge; vengeance] **over my enemies**
and brings ·people [nations] **under ·my rule** [me].
48**He ·saves** [rescues; [T]delivers] **me from my enemies.**

You ·set me over those who hate me [exalt/lift me above my
enemies].
You ·saved [rescued; [T]delivered] **me from violent people.**
49**So I will ·praise** [extol] **you, LORD, among the nations.**
I will sing praises to your name.
50**The LORD ·gives great victories** [is a tower of salvation] **to his king.**
He ·is loyal [shows kindness/faithful love] **to his ·appointed king**
[anointed],
to David and his descendants forever.

For the director of music. A psalm of David.

God's Works and Word

19 The heavens ·declare [recount; narrate] the glory [[C]the manifest presence] of God,
and the ·skies [firmament; dome; Gen. 1:6] ·announce [speak out] ·what his hands have made [[L]the works of his hands].
2 Day after day they ·tell the story [[L]bubble/pour forth speech];
night after night they ·tell it again [[L]declare knowledge].
3 They have no speech or words;
they have no voice to be heard.
4 But their ·message [[L]line] goes out through all the world;
their words go ·everywhere on [[L]to the ends of the] earth.
·The sky [Heaven; [L]In them] is like a ·home [[L]tent] for the sun.
5 The sun comes out like a bridegroom from his ·bedroom [[L]wedding chamber].
It rejoices like an ·athlete [strong man] eager to run a race.
6 The sun rises at one end of the ·sky [heavens]
and ·follows its path [[L]its circuit is] to the other end.
Nothing hides from its heat.

7 The ·teachings [laws; instructions] of the LORD are perfect;
they ·give new strength [[T]revive the soul].
The ·rules [testimonies] of the LORD ·can be trusted [are faithful/sure];
they make ·plain [simpleminded; immature] people wise [Prov. 1:4].
8 The orders of the LORD are ·right [virtuous];
·they make people happy [[L]rejoicing the heart].
The commands of the LORD are pure;
·they light up the way [[L]giving light to the eyes].
9 ·Respect [Fear] for the LORD [Prov. 1:7] is ·good [pure];
it will ·last [endure] forever.
The judgments of the LORD are true;
they are ·completely [altogether] ·right [righteous].
10 They are ·worth [desired; coveted] more than gold,
even ·the purest [fine] gold.
They are sweeter than honey,
even the ·finest honey [[L]droppings of the honeycomb].
11 By them your servant is warned.
·Keeping [Observing] them brings great reward.

12 ·People cannot [[L]Who can…?] ·see [detect; [L]understand] their own ·mistakes [errors].
·Forgive [Clear] me for my ·secret [hidden] sins.
13 ·Keep me [[L]Restrain your servant] from ·the sins of pride [proud thoughts];
don't let them ·rule [dominate] me.
Then I can be pure
and innocent of the greatest of sins.

14 ·I hope my ·words [[L]The words of my mouth] and ·thoughts [meditations of my heart] ·please [[L]be before] you.
LORD, you are my Rock, ·the one who saves me [[L]and my redeemer].

A Prayer for the King

For the director of music. A psalm of David.

20 **May the LORD answer you in ·times** [Lthe day] **of ·trouble** [distress].
May the name of the God of Jacob ·protect [defend; provide refuge for] **you** [Num. 6:24].
2**May he send you help from ·his Temple** [Lthe sanctuary]
and support you from Mount Zion [Clocation of the Temple].
3**May he remember all your ·offerings** [gifts; tributes; grain offerings; Lev. 2]
and ·accept [look with favor on] **all your ·sacrifices** [Lwhole burnt offerings; Lev. 1]. *·Selah* [Interlude]
4**May he give you ·what you want** [Lall your heart]
and ·make all your plans succeed [Lfulfill all your plans],
5**and we will shout for joy when you ·succeed** [are victorious; Cas in battle],
and we will raise a ·flag [banner] **in the name of our God.**
May the LORD ·give you [fulfill] **all that you ask for.**

6**Now I know the LORD ·helps** [saves; gives victory to] **his ·appointed king** [anointed].
He answers him from his holy heaven
and ·saves him [gives him victory] **with his strong right hand.**
7**Some ·trust in** [boast in; rely on] **chariots, others in horses,**
but we ·trust [boast in; rely on] **the name of the LORD our God** [Is. 20:7].
8**They ·are overwhelmed and defeated** [collapse and fall],
but we ·march forward and win [Lrise and stand erect].
9**LORD, ·save** [give victory to] **the king!**
Answer us when we call for help.

Thanksgiving for the King

For the director of music. A psalm of David.

21 **LORD, the king rejoices because of your strength;**
he is so happy when you ·save him [give him victory/help]!
2**You gave the king ·what he wanted** [Lthe desire of his heart]
and did not ·refuse [withhold] **·what he asked for** [Lthe request of his lips]. *·Selah* [Interlude]

3**You put ·good things** [rich blessings] **before him**
and placed a gold crown on his head.
4**He asked you for life,**
and you gave it to him,
·so his years go on and on [Llength of days forever and ever].
5**He has great glory because you gave him ·victories** [help];
you gave him ·honor [splendor] **and ·praise** [majesty].
6**You ·always** [forever] **gave him blessings;**
you made him glad because ·you were with him [Lof the joy of your presence].
7**The king truly ·trusts** [has confidence in] **the LORD.**
Because God Most High always ·loves [is loyal toward] **him,**
he will not be ·overwhelmed [moved].
8**Your hand ·is against** [Lwill find out] **all your enemies;**
·those who hate you will feel your power [Lyour right hand will find out those who hate you].

[9]When ·you [[L]the LORD] appear,
you will burn them as in a furnace.
In your anger you will swallow them up,
and fire will burn them up.
[10]You will destroy their ·families [offspring] from the earth;
their ·children [[L]seed] will not live.
[11]They made evil plans against you,
but ·their traps [[L]the schemes they devise] won't ·work [succeed].
[12]You will make them turn their backs
when you aim your arrows at ·them [[L]their faces].
[13]Be ·supreme [exalted], LORD, in your power.
We sing and praise your ·greatness [strength].

The Prayer of a Suffering Man

For the director of music. To the tune of "The Doe of Dawn."
A psalm of David.

22 My God, my God, why have you ·abandoned [forsaken] me
[Matt. 27:46; Mark 15:34]?
You seem far from ·saving [helping] me,
far away from my groans.
[2]My God, I call to you during the day,
but you do not answer.
I call at night;
I ·am not silent [*or* get no rest].

[3]You ·sit as the Holy One [[L]are holy].
·The praises of Israel are your throne [[L]You are enthroned on the
praises of Israel].
[4]Our ·ancestors [fathers] ·trusted [had confidence in] you;
they ·trusted [had confidence], and you ·saved [rescued; [T]delivered]
them.
[5]They ·called [cried out] to you for help
and were rescued.
They ·trusted [had confidence in] you
and were not ·disappointed [shamed; humiliated].

[6]But I am like a worm instead of ·a man [human].
People ·make fun of [scorn; reproach] me and ·hate [despise] me.
[7]Those who look at me ·laugh [ridicule/mock me].
They ·stick out their tongues [throw insults; [L]open lips] and shake
their heads.
[8]They say, "·Turn to the LORD for help [[L]Trust the LORD].
Maybe he will ·save [rescue; [T]deliver] you.
If he ·likes [delights/takes pleasure in] you,
maybe he will ·rescue [save; [T]deliver] you."

[9]You ·had my mother give birth to me [[L]brought me out of the womb].
You made me ·trust [have confidence in] you
while I was ·just a baby [[L]at the breasts of my mother].
[10]·I have leaned on you since the day I was born [[L]On you I was cast
from the womb];
you have been ·my God [[L]mine] ·since my mother gave me birth
[[L]from the womb of my mother].

11So don't be far away from me.
Now ·trouble [distress] is near,
and there is no one to help.
12People have surrounded me like ·angry [Lmany] bulls.
Like the strong bulls of Bashan [Deut. 32:14; Mic. 7:14], they ·are on every side [encircle me].
13Like ·hungry [rending; Ltearing their prey], roaring lions
they open their mouths at me.
14My strength is gone,
like water poured out onto the ground,
and my bones are out of joint.
My heart is like wax [Cweak, formless];
it has melted inside me.
15My strength has dried up like a ·clay pot [potsherd],
and my tongue sticks to the top of my mouth.
You laid me in the dust of death.
16Evil people have surrounded me;
like dogs ·they [a group of evil people] have trapped me.
They have ·bitten [pierced; *or* shriveled] my ·arms [hands] and ·legs [feet].
17I can count all my bones;
people look and stare at me.
18They divided my clothes among them,
and they ·threw [cast] lots for my clothing.

19But, Lord, don't be far away.
You are my ·strength [*or* help]; hurry to help me.
20·Save [Rescue; TDeliver] me from the sword;
save my life from the dogs.
21·Rescue [Save; TDeliver] me from the lion's mouth;
·save [Lanswer] me from the horns of the bulls.

22Then I will ·tell my brothers and sisters about you [Lrecount your name/reputation to my brothers];
I will praise you in the ·public meeting [assembly; congregation].
23Praise the Lord, all you who ·respect [fear] him [Prov. 1:7].
All you ·descendants [seed] of Jacob [CIsraelites], ·honor [glorify] him;
·fear [revere] him, all you Israelites.
24He does not ·ignore [despise or disdain] ·those in trouble [Lthe suffering of the afflicted].
He doesn't hide his face from them
but listens when they ·call out to him [cry to him for help].
25Lord, ·I praise you [Lfrom you comes my praise] in the great ·meeting of your people [assembly];
these ·worshipers [Lwho fear him] will see me ·do what I promised [Lfulfill my vows].
26·Poor [*or* Afflicted] people will eat ·until they are full [and be satisfied];
those who ·look to the Lord [Lseek him] will praise him.
May your hearts live forever!
27·People everywhere [LAll the ends of the earth] will remember
and will turn to the Lord.
All the families of the nations
will worship him

[28]because ·the LORD is King [rule belongs to the LORD],
and he rules the nations.

[29]All the ·powerful people [[L]fat ones] on earth will eat and worship.
Everyone will ·bow down to [kneel before] him,
all who will ·one day die [[L]go down to the dust and cannot keep themselves alive].
[30]The ·people in the future [posterity; seed] will serve him;
they will always be told about the Lord.
[31]They will ·tell that he does what is right [recount his righteousness].
People who are not yet born
will hear what God has done.

The Lord the Shepherd

A psalm of David.

23 The LORD is my shepherd;
I ·have everything I need [[L]will lack nothing].
[2]He ·lets me rest [makes me lie down] in green pastures.
He leads me to ·calm [quiet] water.
[3]He ·gives me new strength [[T]renews my soul].
He leads me on paths that are ·right [righteous; *or* straight]
for the ·good [sake] of his ·name [reputation].
[4]Even if I walk through ·a very dark valley [*or* the shadow of death],
I will ·not be afraid [[T]fear no evil],
because you are with me.
Your rod and your shepherd's staff comfort me.

[5]You prepare a ·meal [[L]table] for me
in ·front [the presence] of my enemies.
You ·pour oil of blessing on my head [anoint my head with oil; [C]oil was a means of refreshment in a hot, dry environment];
you ·fill my cup to overflowing [[L]make my cup overflow; [C]a cup of blessing].
[6]Surely your goodness and ·love [loyalty; [T]mercy] will ·be with [pursue; [T]follow] me
all my life,
and I will live in the house of the LORD ·forever [[L]for length of days].

A Welcome for God into the Temple

A psalm of David.

24 The earth belongs to the LORD, and ·everything in it [[L]its fullness]—
the world and all its ·people [inhabitants].
[2]He ·built [founded] it on the waters
and ·set [established] it on the rivers [Gen. 1:9–10; Is. 45:18].

[3]Who may go up on the mountain of the LORD [[C]Zion, the location of the Temple]?
Who may stand in his holy ·Temple [[L]place]?
[4]Only those with clean hands and pure hearts [[C]innocent in actions and thoughts],
who have not ·worshiped idols [[L]lifted their souls to false things],
who have not made promises ·in the name of a false god [*or* deceitfully].

[5]They will receive a blessing from the LORD;
the God who ·saves [rescues; [T]delivers] them will ·declare them right [vindicate them].
[6]·They try to follow God [[L]This is the generation/people of those who seek him];
they ·look to the God of Jacob for help [[L]search for your face, O God of Jacob]. ·*Selah* [Interlude]

[7]·Open up [[L]Lift up your heads], you gates.
·Open wide [[L]Be lifted up], you ·aged [ancient] doors
and the ·glorious King [King of glory] will come in.
[8]Who is this ·glorious King [King of glory]?
The LORD, strong and mighty.
The LORD, ·the powerful warrior [mighty in battle].
[9]·Open up [[L]Lift up your heads], you gates.
·Open wide [[L]Be lifted up], you ·aged [ancient] doors
and the ·glorious King [King of glory] will come in.
[10]Who is this ·glorious King [King of glory]?
The LORD ·All-Powerful [of Heaven's Armies/[T]Hosts]—
he is the ·glorious King [King of glory]. ·*Selah* [Interlude]

A Prayer for God to Guide

Of David.

25 LORD, I ·give myself [[L]lift my soul] to you;
[2] my God, I ·trust [have confidence in] you.
Do not let me be ·disgraced [shamed];
do not let my enemies ·laugh at [triumph/exult over] me.
[3]No one who ·trusts [hopes in; waits on] you will be ·disgraced [shamed],
but those who ·sin [betray; are treacherous] without excuse will be ·disgraced [shamed].

[4]LORD, ·tell me [make me know] your ways.
·Show [[L]Teach] me ·how to live [[L]your paths].
[5]·Guide [Lead] me in your truth,
and teach me, my God, my ·Savior [Helper; Victor].
I ·trust [hope in; wait on] you all day long.
[6]LORD, remember your ·mercy [compassion] and ·love [loyalty; covenant love]
that you have shown since long ago.
[7]Do not remember the sins
and ·wrong things I did when I was young [transgressions of my youth].
But remember ·to love me [[L]according to your love/loyalty/covenant love] always
·because you are good [on account of your goodness], LORD.

[8]The LORD is good and ·right [upright; virtuous];
he ·points [instructs] sinners to the right way.
[9]He shows those who are humble how to do right,
and he teaches them his ways.
[10]All the LORD's ·ways [paths] are ·loving [loyal] and ·true [reliable]
for those who ·follow [keep; guard] the demands of his ·agreement [covenant].

[11]For the sake of your ·name [reputation], LORD,
forgive my many sins.
[12]·Are there [[L]Who are…?] those who ·respect [fear] the LORD [Prov. 1:7]?
He will ·point [teach] them ·to the best way [[L]the way they should choose].
[13]·They will enjoy a good life [[L]Their soul will dwell/lodge in goodness],
and their ·children [[L]seed] will inherit the ·land [*or* earth].
[14]The LORD ·tells his secrets to [confides in; *or* makes friends with] those who ·respect [fear] him;
he ·tells them about [makes known to them] his ·agreement [covenant].
[15]My eyes are always ·looking to the LORD for help [[L]toward the LORD].
He will ·keep me [[L]remove my feet] from any traps.
[16]Turn to me and ·have mercy on [[L]be gracious to] me,
because I am lonely and hurting.
[17]·My troubles have [[L]The distress of my heart has] ·grown larger [widened];
·free me from [bring me out of] my ·problems [anguish; distress].
[18]Look at my ·suffering [affliction] and troubles,
and ·take away [forgive] all my sins.
[19]Look at how many enemies I have!
See how ·much [[L]violently] they hate me!
[20]Protect me and ·save [rescue; [T]deliver] me.
I ·trust [find refuge in] you, so do not let me be ·disgraced [shamed].
[21]My hope is in you,
so may ·goodness [blamelessness; innocence] and ·honesty [virtue] guard me.
[22]God, ·save [redeem; ransom] Israel from all their ·troubles [distress]!

The Prayer of an Innocent Believer

Of David.

26 LORD, ·defend [vindicate] me because I have ·lived an innocent life [[L]walked in innocence; Job 1:1].
I have ·trusted [confidence in] the LORD and never ·doubted [wavered; faltered].
[2]LORD, try me and test me;
look closely into my ·heart and mind [[L]kidneys and heart; [C]the seat of emotions and mind in Hebrew thought].
[3]·I see your love [[L]Your loyalty/covenant love is before my eyes],
and I ·live by your truth [walk in your truth/faithfulness].
[4]I do not ·spend time [[L]sit] with ·liars [*or* worthless people],
nor do I ·make friends [[L]go] with ·those who hide their sin [hypocrites].
[5]I hate the ·company [assembly] of evil people,
and I won't sit with the wicked.
[6]I wash my hands ·to show I am innocent [[L]in innocence],
and I ·come to [[L]go around] your altar, LORD.
[7]I raise my voice in ·praise [*or* thanks]
and tell of all the ·miracles [wonderful things] you have done.
[8]LORD, I love the ·Temple [[L]house] where you live,
where your glory [[C]manifest presence] ·is [dwells].
[9]Do not ·kill me [take me away] with those sinners
or take my life with ·those murderers [the bloodthirsty; [L]men of blood].

10·Evil is [Schemes are] in their hands,
and ·they do wrong for money [Ltheir right hand is full of bribes].
11But I have ·lived an innocent life [Lwalked in innocence; v. 1],
so ·save [redeem; ransom] me and have mercy on me.
12·I stand in a safe place [LMy feet stand on level ground].
Lord, I ·praise [bless] you in the great ·meeting [assembly].

A Song of Trust in God

Of David.

27 The Lord is my light [18:28; 43:3; Is. 9:2; John 1:4, 9; 8:12; 1 John 1:5] and ·the one who saves me [my salvation].
·So why should I fear anyone [LWhom should I fear]?
The Lord ·protects [Lis the stronghold/refuge of] my life.
·So why [LOf whom] should I be afraid?
2Evil people may try to ·destroy my body [Lapproach me and devour/consume my flesh].
My enemies and those who hate me ·are overwhelmed and defeated [Lstumble and fall].
3If an army ·surrounds [Lcamps around] me,
·I [Lmy heart] will not be afraid.
If war ·breaks out [rises against me],
I will ·trust [have confidence in] ·the Lord [Lin this; Rom. 8:31–39].

4I ask only one thing from the Lord.
This is what I ·want [Lseek after]:
Let me ·live [dwell] in the Lord's house [Cthe sanctuary]
all the days of my life.
Let me see the Lord's beauty
and ·look with my own eyes [Lmake inquiry; Cdiscover God's will] at his Temple.
5·During danger [LIn the day of trouble] he will ·keep me safe [Lhide me] in his shelter.
He will ·hide [conceal] me in his Holy Tent,
or he will ·keep me safe [Lset me high] on a ·high mountain [Lrock].
6My head is higher than my enemies around me.
I will offer joyful sacrifices in his Holy Tent [Cthe Tabernacle].
I will sing and praise the Lord.

7Lord, hear ·me [Lmy voice] when I ·call [pray];
have mercy and answer me.
8My heart said of you, "Go, ·worship him [Lseek his face]."
So I ·come to worship you [Lseek your face], Lord.
9Do not ·turn away [Lhide your face] from me.
Do not turn your servant away in anger;
you have helped me.
Do not push me away or ·leave me alone [abandon me],
God, my Savior.
10If my father and mother ·leave [abandon] me,
the Lord will take me in.
11Lord, teach me your ways,
and guide me ·to do what is right [Lon a straight/right path]
because ·I have [Lof my] enemies.
12Do not hand me over to my enemies,

because ·they tell lies about [Lfalse witnesses rise up against] me
[Ex. 20:16]
and ·say they will hurt me [Lthey breathe out violence].

13I truly believe
I will see the LORD's goodness ·during my life [Lin the land of the
living].
14·Wait for [Hope in] the LORD's help.
Be strong and let your heart be brave,
and ·wait for [hope in] the LORD's help.

A Prayer in Troubled Times

Of David.

28 LORD, my Rock [Cproviding protection], I ·call out to you for
help [pray].
Do not be ·deaf [silent] to me.
If you are silent,
I will be like those ·in the grave [Lwho go down to the Pit; 16:10].
2Hear the sound of my ·prayer [supplication],
when I cry out to you for help.
I raise my hands
toward your Most Holy Place [Cthe place where God made his
presence known, the sanctuary].
3Don't drag me away with the wicked,
with those who do evil.
They say "Peace" to their neighbors,
but evil is in their hearts.
4Pay them back for what they have done,
for their evil deeds.
Pay them back for ·what they have done [Lthe work of their hands];
give them their reward.
5They don't understand what the LORD has done
or ·what he has made [Lthe work of his hands].
So he will ·knock [tear] them down
and not ·lift [Lbuild] them up.

6·Praise [LBlessed be] the LORD,
because he heard ·my prayer for help [Lthe sound of my
supplication].
7The LORD is my strength [Ex. 15:2] and shield.
·I trust [My heart has confidence in] him, and he helps me.
·I am [LMy heart is] very happy,
and I ·praise [give thanks to] him with my song.
8The LORD is powerful;
he ·gives victory [is a saving refuge] to his ·chosen one [anointed].
9·Save [LGive victory to] your people
and bless ·those who are your own [Lyour inheritance].
Be their shepherd and carry them forever.

God in the Thunderstorm

A psalm of David.

29 ·Praise [TAscribe to] the LORD, you ·angels [Lsons of God; CGod's
council];
·Praise the LORD's [TAscribe to the LORD] glory and power.

[2]·Praise the LORD for [TAscribe to the LORD] the glory of his name;
worship the LORD ·because he is holy [Lin the splendor of his holiness].

[3]The LORD's voice [Cthunder] is heard over the ·sea [Lwaters; Ca symbol of chaos].
The glorious God thunders;
the LORD thunders over the ·ocean [Lmany/mighty waters].
[4]The LORD's voice is powerful;
the LORD's voice is ·majestic [splendid; awesome].
[5]The LORD's voice breaks the ·trees [Lcedars];
the LORD breaks the cedars of Lebanon [Cthe most famous cedar forests].
[6]He makes the land of Lebanon dance like a calf
and ·Mount Hermon [LSirion] jump like a baby bull.
[7]The LORD's voice ·makes the lightning flash [strikes with flashes of lightning].
[8]The LORD's voice shakes the ·desert [wilderness];
the LORD shakes the ·Desert [Wilderness] of Kadesh.
[9]The LORD's voice ·shakes the oaks [*or* makes the deer give birth]
and strips the ·leaves off the trees [Lforests bare].
In his Temple everyone says, "Glory!"

[10]The LORD ·controls [Lis enthroned over] the flood [Ccontrols chaos].
The LORD ·will be [Lis enthroned as] King forever.
[11]The LORD gives strength to his people;
the LORD blesses his people with peace.

Thanksgiving for Escaping Death

A psalm of David. A song for ·giving the Temple to the LORD [Lthe dedication of the Temple; Cperhaps written by David in anticipation of the dedication of the Temple under Solomon; the connection with healing is uncertain].

30 I will ·praise [Lexalt] you, LORD,
because you ·rescued me [Lbrought me up].
You did not let my enemies ·laugh at [rejoice over] me.
[2]LORD, my God, I ·prayed to you [cried to you for help],
and you healed me.
[3]You lifted me out of ·the grave [*or* the underworld; LSheol];
you spared me from going down to the ·place of the dead [LPit; 16:10].

[4]Sing praises to the LORD, you ·who belong to him [loyal ones; saints];
·praise [give thanks to] his holy name.
[5]His anger lasts only a moment,
but his ·kindness [favor] lasts for a lifetime.
Crying may last for a night,
but joy comes in the morning.

[6]When I ·felt safe [*or* was prosperous], I said,
"I will never ·fear [Lbe moved]."
[7]LORD, in your ·kindness [favor] you made my mountain ·safe [Lstand; CGod made him prosperous and safe].

But when you ·turned away [[L]hid your face; [C]because he became
self-reliant, v. 6], I was ·frightened [terrified; *or* discouraged].

8I ·called [prayed] to you, LORD,
and ·asked you to have mercy on me [made supplication].
9I said, "What ·good will it do if I die [profit is there for you in my
blood]
or if I go down to ·the grave [corruption; destruction]?
·Dust cannot [[L]Will the dust…?; Gen. 2:7; Eccl. 12:7] ·praise [thank]
you;
·it cannot [[L]will it…?] speak about your ·truth [faithfulness].
10LORD, hear me and have mercy on me.
LORD, help me."

11You changed my ·sorrow [mourning] into dancing.
You took away my ·clothes of sadness [sackcloth],
and clothed me in ·happiness [joy].
12I will sing to you and not be silent.
LORD, my God, I will ·praise you [give you thanks] forever.

A Prayer of Faith in Troubled Times

For the director of music. A psalm of David.

31 LORD, I ·trust [seek refuge] in you;
let me never be ·disgraced [shamed].
·Save [Rescue; [T]Deliver] me ·because you do what is right [in your
righteousness].
2·Listen [[L]Incline your ear] to me
and ·save [rescue; [T]deliver] me quickly.
Be my rock of ·protection [refuge],
a strong ·city [fortress] to save me.
3You are my rock and my ·protection [fortress].
For the ·good [sake] of your name, lead me and guide me.
4Set me free from the ·trap [snare; net] they ·set [hid] for me,
because you are my ·protection [refuge].
5·I give you my life [[L]Into your hand I commend my spirit; Luke 23:46].
·Save [Redeem; *or* You have redeemed] me, LORD, ·God of truth [*or*
faithful God].

6I hate those who ·worship [serve; have concern for] ·false [worthless]
gods.
I ·trust [have confidence] only in the LORD.
7I will be glad and rejoice in your ·love [loyalty; covenant love],
because you saw my ·suffering [affliction];
you knew ·my troubles [the distress of my soul].
8You have not handed me over to my enemies
but have ·set me in a safe place [[L]made my feet stand in a broad place].

9LORD, ·have mercy [be gracious], because I am in ·misery [distress;
trouble].
My eyes ·are weak [waste away; are dim] from so much crying,
·and my whole being is tired [[L]as is my soul and my body] from grief.
10My life is ending in ·sadness [sorrow],
and my years are spent ·in crying [[L]with sighs/moans].

My ·troubles are using up my strength [Lstrength stumbles in my affliction/misery],
and my bones ·are getting weaker [waste away].
11Because of all my ·troubles [distress], my enemies ·hate [scorn] me,
and even my neighbors look down on me.
When my ·friends [acquaintances] see me in public,
they are afraid and ·run [flee].
12I am like a piece of a broken pot.
I am forgotten as if I were dead.
13I have heard many ·insults [threats].
Terror is all around me.
They make plans against me
and ·want [plot] to kill me.

14LORD, I ·trust [have confidence in] you.
I have said, "You are my God."
15My ·life is [times/fortunes are] in your hands.
·Save [Rescue; TDeliver] me from my enemies
and from those who are ·chasing [pursuing] me.
16·Show your kindness to me, [Shine your face on] your servant [Num. 6:25].
Save me because of your ·love [loyalty; covenant love].
17LORD, I ·called [prayed] to you,
so do not let me be ·disgraced [shamed].
Let the wicked be ·disgraced [shamed]
and lie silent in ·the grave [*or* the underworld; LSheol].
18With pride and hatred
they speak against ·those who do right [the righteous].
So silence their lying lips.

19How great is your goodness
that you have stored up for those who fear you,
that you have ·given to [Laccomplished for] those who ·trust [have confidence in] you.
·You do this for all to see [L...before humanity].
20You ·protect [hide] them ·by your [Lin the shelter of your] presence
from what people plan against them.
You ·shelter them [Lstore them in shelter] from ·evil words [contentious/accusing tongues].
21·Praise [Blessed be] the LORD.
His ·love [loyalty; covenant love] to me was wonderful
when ·my city was attacked [*or* I was like a city under siege].
22In my ·distress [alarm], I said,
"·God cannot see me [LI am cut off from your eyes]!"
But you heard my ·prayer [supplication]
when I cried out to you for help.
23Love the LORD, all you ·who belong to him [loyal ones; saints].
The LORD protects those who ·truly believe [are faithful],
but he ·punishes [repays] ·the proud as much as they have sinned [Lthose who act with pride].
24All you who ·put your hope in [wait for] the LORD
be strong and ·brave [Llet your heart be courageous].

A ·maskil [skillful psalm; meditation] **of David.**

It Is Better to Confess Sin

32 **·Happy** [Blessed] **is the person**
whose ·sins [transgressions] **are forgiven,**
whose ·wrongs [sins] **are ·pardoned** [Lcovered].
2**·Happy** [Blessed] **is the person**
whom the LORD ·does not consider guilty [imputes no guilt to]
and in ·whom [Lwhose spirit] **there is nothing ·false** [deceptive].

3**When I kept ·things to myself** [silent],
·I felt weak deep inside me [Lmy bones wasted away].
I ·moaned [sighed] **all day long.**
4**Day and night ·you punished me** [Lyour hand was heavy on me].
My strength was ·gone [dried up; sapped] **as in the summer heat.**
·*Selah* [Interlude]
5**Then I ·confessed** [made known; disclosed] **my sins to you**
and didn't ·hide [cover up] **my guilt.**
I said, "I will confess my ·sins [transgressions] **to the LORD,"**
and you forgave ·my guilt [Lthe guilt of my sin]. **·*Selah*** [Interlude]

6**For this reason, all ·who obey you** [your saints/holy ones]
should pray to you while ·they still can [*or* you may be found; Lat a time of finding only; Prov. 1:24–27].
When troubles rise like a flood,
they will not reach them.
7**You are my hiding place.**
You protect me from ·my troubles [distress]
and ·fill [Lsurround] **me with ·songs** [loud cries] **of ·salvation** [rescue; Tdeliverance]. **·*Selah*** [Interlude]

8**The LORD says, "I will ·make you wise** [instruct you] **and ·show** [teach] **you ·where to** [Lthe way you should] **go.**
I will ·guide [counsel] **you and ·watch over** [Lmy eye will be on] **you.**
9**So don't be like a horse or donkey,**
that doesn't understand.
·They must be led [L…whose temper/*or* gallop must be restrained]
with bits and reins,
or they will not come near you."

10**Wicked people have many ·troubles** [pains; torments; woes],
but the LORD's ·love [loyalty; covenant love] **surrounds those who ·trust** [have confidence in] **him.**
11**·Good** [Righteous] **people, rejoice and be happy in the LORD.**
·Sing [Shout joyfully] **all you whose hearts are ·right** [upright; virtuous].

Praise God Who Creates and Saves

33 **·Sing** [Shout for joy] **to the LORD, you ·who do what is right** [righteous ones];
·honest people should praise him [Lpraise is fitting from the upright/virtuous].
2**·Praise** [Give thanks to] **the LORD on the harp;**
make music for him on a ten-stringed lyre.
3**Sing a new song** [Ccelebrating victory; 40:3; 96:1; 98:1; 144:9; 149:1; Is. 42:10; Rev. 5:9; 14:3] **to him;**
play well ·and joyfully [with a loud/a victory shout].

4God's word is ·true [upright; virtuous],
and everything he does is ·right [faithful].
5He loves what is right and ·fair [just];
the LORD's ·love [loyalty; covenant love] fills the earth.

6The ·sky was [heavens were] made at the LORD's ·command [word; Gen. 1:8].
By the breath from his mouth, he made all ·the stars [Lits hosts; Gen. 1:16].
7He gathered the water of the sea into ·a heap [*or* jars; bottles].
He ·made the great ocean stay in its place [Lplaced the deeps in a storehouse; Job 38:8–11].
8All the earth should ·worship [fear; hold in awe] the LORD [Prov. 1:7];
·the whole [Lall the inhabitants of the] world should ·fear him [hold him in awe].
9He spoke, and it happened.
He commanded, and it ·appeared [Lstood; Heb. 11:3].
10The LORD ·upsets [frustrates] the ·plans [counsels] of nations;
he ·ruins [foils] ·all their plans [Lthe plans of the peoples].
11But the LORD's ·plans [counsels] will ·stand [endure] forever;
·his ideas [Lthe plans of his heart] will last from now on.
12·Happy [Blessed] is the nation whose God is the LORD,
the people he chose for his ·very own [Linheritance; Ex. 19:5].
13The LORD looks down from heaven
and sees every person.
14From his throne he watches
all who live on earth.
15He ·made [fashions all] their hearts
and understands everything they do.
16No king is saved by his ·great [large] army.
No warrior ·escapes [is rescued/Tdelivered] by his great strength.
17Horses ·can't bring [are a vain hope for] victory;
they can't save by their strength.
18But the ·LORD looks after [Leye of the LORD is on] those who fear him,
those who ·put their hope [wait on him] in his ·love [loyalty; covenant love].
19He ·saves [rescues; Tdelivers] ·them [their soul] from death
and ·spares their lives in times of hunger [revives them in famine].
20So our hope is in the LORD.
He is our help, our shield to protect us.
21·We [LOur hearts] rejoice in him,
because we ·trust [have confidence in] his holy name.
22LORD, ·show your love to us [Llet your loyalty/covenant love be on us]
as we ·put our hope in [wait for] you.

Praise God Who Judges and Saves

David's song from the time he ·acted crazy [acted mad/insane; Lchanged his mind/discernment] so Abimelech [Cperhaps another name for Achish] would ·send [drive] him away, and David did leave [1 Sam. 21:10–15].

34 I will ·praise [bless] the LORD at all times;
his praise is always ·on my lips [Lin my mouth].
2My ·whole being [soul] praises the LORD.

The ·poor [humble] will hear and be glad.
3·Glorify [Praise; Magnify] the LORD with me,
and let us ·praise [Lextol] his name together.

4I ·asked the LORD for help [sought the LORD], and he answered me.
He ·saved [rescued; Tdelivered] me from all that I feared.
5Those who ·go [Llook] to him for help are ·happy [radiant],
and ·they [Ltheir faces] are never ·disgraced [shamed].
6This ·poor [afflicted] man [Csomeone in the congregation or the psalmist himself] ·called [prayed], and the LORD heard him
and ·saved him from [gave him victory over] all his ·troubles [distress].
7The angel of the LORD [91:11; Gen. 32:1–2; 2 Kin. 6:17; Matt. 4:5–6] camps around those who fear God [Prov. 1:7],
and he saves them.

8·Examine [LTaste] and see how good the LORD is.
·Happy [Blessed] is the person who ·trusts [finds refuge in] him.
9You ·who belong to the LORD [holy ones], fear him [Prov. 1:7]!
Those who fear him will ·have everything they need [not lack anything; 23:1].
10Even lions [Cthe most noble wild beast] may get weak and hungry,
but those who ·look to [seek] the LORD ·will have every [Ldo not lack any] good thing.
11Children, come and listen to me.
I will teach you ·to worship [Lthe fear of] the LORD.
12·You must do these things
to enjoy life and have many happy days [LWho of you takes pleasure in life and loves days to experience good?].
13You must ·not say evil things [Lguard/keep your tongue from evil],
and ·you must not tell lies [Lyour lips from deception].
14·Stop doing [LTurn aside from] evil and do good.
·Look for [Seek] peace and ·work for [pursue] it.

15·The LORD sees the [LThe eyes of the LORD are on] ·good [righteous] people
and ·listens to their prayers [Lhis ears attend to their cries for help].
16But the ·LORD is [Lface of the LORD is] against those who do evil;
he ·makes the world forget them [Lcuts memory of them off the earth].
17·The LORD hears good people when they [LThey] cry out to him,
and he saves them from all their ·troubles [distress].
18The LORD is close to the brokenhearted,
and he saves those whose spirits have been crushed.

19People who ·do what is right may [are righteous] have many ·problems [afflictions],
but the LORD ·will solve them [Lsaves them from them] all.
20He will protect their very bones;
not one of them will be broken.
21Evil will kill the wicked;
those who hate ·good [righteous] people will be judged guilty.

22But the LORD ·saves [redeems; ransoms] his servants' lives;
no one who ·trusts [finds refuge in] him will be judged guilty.

A Prayer for Help

Of David.

35 LORD, ·battle with [contend with; accuse; bring a charge against]
those who ·battle with [contend with; accuse; bring a charge against] me.
Fight against those who fight against me.
2Pick up the ·shield and armor [Lsmall shield and large shield].
Rise up and help me.
3Lift up your ·spears [javelins], both large and small,
against those who ·chase [pursue] me.
Tell ·me [Lmy soul], "I ·will save you [am your salvation/victory]."

4Make those who ·want to kill me [Lseek my life/soul]
be ashamed and ·disgraced [humiliated].
Make those who ·plan to harm me [plot evil against me]
turn back and ·run away [be dismayed].
5Make them like chaff [Cthe worthless leftovers from threshing grain] blown by the wind
as the angel of the LORD ·forces [drives] them away.
6Let their road be dark and slippery
as the angel of the LORD chases them.
7For no reason they ·spread out [Lhid] their ·net [Lpit] to trap me;
for no reason they dug a pit for me.
8So let ruin strike them ·suddenly [*or* without their awareness].
Let them be caught in their own nets;
let them fall into the pit and ·die [be ruined].
9Then ·I [my soul] will rejoice in the LORD;
I will be happy when he ·saves me [provides victory for me].
10Even my bones will say,
"LORD, who is like you?
You ·save [rescue; Tdeliver] the ·weak [afflicted; *or* poor] from the strong,
the ·weak [afflicted; *or* poor] and poor from robbers."

11·Men without mercy stand up to testify [LViolent witnesses rise up].
They ask me things I do not know.
12They repay me with evil for the good I have done,
and ·they make me very sad [my soul is bereaved].
13Yet when they were sick, I put on ·clothes of sadness [sackcloth; burlap]
and showed my sorrow by fasting.
But my prayers ·were not answered [Lturned back on my bosom].
14 I acted as if they were my ·friends [*or* neighbors] or brothers.
I ·bowed in sadness as if I were crying [went around as if mourning] for my mother.
15But when I ·was in trouble [stumbled], they gathered and laughed;
they gathered to attack before I knew it.
They ·insulted [tore at] me without stopping.
16They made fun of me and were cruel to me
and ·ground [gnashed] their teeth at me in anger.

[17]Lord, how long will you watch this happen?
Save my life from their attacks;
·save me from these people who are like [[L]my life from the] **lions.**
[18]I will ·praise [thank] **you in the great ·meeting** [assembly].
I will praise you among ·crowds of people [the mighty crowd/throng].
[19]Do not let my enemies ·laugh at [rejoice over] **me;**
they hate me for no reason.
Do not let them ·make fun of me [[L]wink their eye at me; [C]a reference to secretive plans or magic; Prov. 6:12–13];
they have no cause to hate me.
[20]Their words are not ·friendly [peaceful]
but are lies ·about [*or* against] **·peace-loving people** [[L]the quiet in the land].
[21]They ·speak against me [[L]open their mouths]
and say, "Aha! ·We saw what you did [Our eyes have seen it]!"

[22]LORD, you have been watching. Do not keep quiet.
Lord, do not ·leave me alone [[L]be far from me].
[23]Wake up! ·Come [Arouse yourself] **and ·defend** [vindicate; show justice to] **me!**
My God and Lord, ·fight [contend] **for me!**
[24]LORD my God, ·defend [vindicate] **me with your justice.**
Don't let them ·laugh at [rejoice over] **me.**
[25]Don't let them ·think [[L]say in their hearts], **"Aha! We got what we wanted!"**
Don't let them say, "We ·destroyed [[L]swallowed] **him."**
[26]Let them be ashamed and ·embarrassed [humiliated],
because they ·were happy [rejoiced] **when I hurt.**
·Cover [[L]Clothe] **them with shame and disgrace,**
because they thought they were better than I was.
[27]May ·my friends [[L]those who want my vindication] **sing and shout for joy.**
May they always say, "Praise the greatness of the LORD,
who ·loves [delights; takes pleasure] **to see ·his servants do well** [[L]the peace/prosperity of his servant]."
[28]·I [[L]My tongue] **will tell of your goodness**
and will praise you every day.

Wicked People and a Good God

For the director of music. Of David, the servant of the LORD.

36 **·Sin speaks to the wicked in their hearts** [[L]Oracle/Decree of transgression to the wicked in the midst of their heart].
They have no ·fear [terror] **of God** [Prov. 1:7; Rom. 3:18].
[2]They ·think too much of themselves [[L]flatter themselves in their own eyes]
so they don't ·see [discover; find] **their sin and ·hate** [*or* change] **it.**
[3]·Their words [[L]The words of their mouth] **are ·wicked lies** [mischief and deceit];
they ·are no longer wise or good [[L]have stopped being wise/insightful in order to do good].
[4]·At night [[L]In their bed] **they make evil plans;**
·what they do leads to nothing [[L]they are set on a way that does no] **good.**
They don't ·refuse [reject] **things that are evil.**

[5]**LORD, your ·love** [loyalty; covenant love] **·reaches** [extends] **to the heavens,**
your ·loyalty [faithfulness] **to the skies.**
[6]**Your ·goodness** [righteousness] **is like the mighty mountains** [[C]majestic].
Your ·justice [judgment] **is like the great ocean** [[C]deep].
LORD, you ·protect [save] **both people and animals.**
[7]**God, ·your love is so precious** [[L]how precious is your loyalty/covenant love?]!
You ·protect [provide refuge for] **people in the shadow of your wings.**
[8]**They ·eat** [feast on; are filled with] **·the rich food** [[L]from the fat/abundance] **in your house,**
and you let them drink from your river of ·pleasure [delights].
[9]**You are the ·giver** [[L]fountain] **of life.**
·Your light lets us enjoy life [[L]In your light we see light].

[10]**Continue to ·love** [show loyalty/covenant love to] **those who know you**
and ·to do good [[L]your good/righteousness] **to those who are ·good** [upright/virtuous in heart].
[11]**Don't let ·proud people attack me** [[L]the foot of the arrogant come near me]
·and the wicked [[L]or the hand of the wicked] **·force** [drive] **me away.**
[12]**Those who do evil ·have been defeated** [[L]fall there].
They are overwhelmed;
they cannot ·do evil any longer [[L]arise again].

God Will Reward Fairly

Of David.

37 **Don't be ·upset** [worried; angry] **because of evil people.**
Don't be jealous of those who do wrong [Prov. 24:1, 19],
[2]**because like the grass, they will ·soon** [quickly] **·dry up** [wither].
Like green plants, they will soon ·die [fade] **away.**

[3]**·Trust** [[L]Have confidence in] **the LORD** [Prov. 3:5] **and do good.**
·Live [Reside; Settle] **in the land and ·feed on truth** [*or* find reliable pastureland].
[4]**Enjoy serving the LORD,**
and he will give you ·what you want [[L]the requests of your heart].
[5]**·Depend on** [[L]Commit your way to] **the LORD;**
·trust [have confidence in] **him, and he will take care of you** [Prov. 16:3; 1 Pet. 5:7].
[6]**Then your ·goodness** [righteousness] **will shine like the ·sun** [[L]light],
and your ·fairness [justice] **like the noonday sun.**

[7]**·Wait** [[L]Be quiet before] **and ·trust** [[L]wait for] **the LORD.**
Don't be ·upset [worried; angry] **·when others get rich** [[L]with the prosperity/success of their way]
or when ·someone else's plans succeed [*or* they do evil deeds].
[8]**·Don't get angry** [[L]Hold back from anger; Abandon wrath].
Don't be ·upset [worried; angry]**; it only leads to ·trouble** [*or* evil].
[9]**Evil people will be ·sent away** [[L]cut off],
but those who ·trust [wait/pin their hope on] **the LORD will inherit the land.**

[10]In a little while the wicked will be no more.
You may look for them, but they will be ·gone [*or* no more].
[11]·People who are not proud [[L]The humble/meek] will inherit the land [Matt. 5:5]
and will enjoy ·complete peace [*or* much prosperity].

[12]The wicked make evil plans against ·good [righteous] people.
They ·grind [gnash] their teeth at them [[C]in anger].
[13]But the LORD laughs at the wicked,
because he sees that their day [[C]of judgment] is coming.
[14]The wicked draw their swords
and ·bend [string] their bows
to ·kill [[L]fell] the poor and helpless,
to ·kill [slaughter] those ·who are honest [[L]whose way is straight].
[15]But their swords will ·stab [[L]enter] their own hearts,
and their bows will break.

[16]It is better to have little and be ·right [*or* righteous]
than to have much and be ·wrong [*or* wicked; Prov. 15:16; 16:8, 19].
[17]The ·power [[L]arm] of the wicked will be broken,
but the LORD ·supports [upholds] those who ·do right [are righteous].
[18]The LORD ·watches over [[L]knows] the ·lives [[L]days] of the ·innocent [blameless],
and their ·reward [inheritance] will last forever.
[19]They will not be ashamed ·when trouble comes [[L]in the day of evil/trouble].
They will be ·full [satisfied; satiated] in times of ·hunger [famine].
[20]But the wicked will ·die [perish].
The LORD's enemies will be like the ·beauty [best] of the ·fields [[L]pastures; [C]flowers or animals];
·they will disappear [[L]vanishing, they will vanish] ·like [*or* in] smoke.
[21]The wicked borrow and don't pay back,
but ·those who do right [the righteous] give freely to others.
[22]Those whom ·the LORD [[L]he] blesses will inherit the land,
but those he curses will be ·sent away [[L]cut off].

[23]When people's steps ·follow [[L]are made firm/established by] the LORD [Prov. 24:16],
God ·is pleased with [delights in] their ways.
[24]If they stumble, they will not fall,
because the LORD ·holds [upholds] their hand.

[25]I was young, and now I am old,
but I have never seen ·good [righteous] people ·left helpless [abandoned; forsaken; Gen. 28:15; Matt. 28:20]
or their ·children [seed] ·begging for [seeking] food [Prov. 10:3].
[26]Good people always lend freely to others,
and their ·children [seed] are a blessing.

[27]·Stop doing [Turn aside from] evil and do good,
so you will ·live [dwell] forever.
[28]The LORD loves ·justice [judgment]

and will not ·leave [abandon; forsake] ·those who worship him [his loyal ones/saints].
He will always ·protect [keep; guard] them,
but the ·children [seed] of the wicked will ·die [Lbe cut off].
29·Good [Righteous] people will inherit the land
and will ·live [dwell] in it forever.

30·Good people speak with [LThe mouth of the righteous mutters] wisdom,
and ·they say what is fair [Ltheir tongue speaks justice/judgment].
31The ·teachings [instructions; laws] of their God are in their heart [Jer. 31:33],
so ·they do not fail to keep them [Ltheir steps do not slip/slide/totter].
32The wicked watch for ·good [righteous] people
·so that they may [Lto seek to] kill them [Prov. 1:8–19].
33But the LORD will not ·take away his protection [Labandon/forsake them to their hand/power/control]
or let ·good people be judged guilty [them be condemned when brought to trial].

34·Wait for [Hope in] the LORD
and ·follow him [Lkeep/guard his way].
He will ·honor [exalt] you and ·give you [you will inherit] the land,
and you will see the wicked ·sent away [*or* destroyed].

35I saw a wicked and ·cruel [oppressive] man
who ·looked [flourished] like a luxurious cedar tree [Cstrong and healthy].
36But he ·died [passed on] and was ·gone [no more];
I ·looked for [sought] him, but he couldn't be found.

37·Think of [Observe] the ·innocent [blameless] person,
and watch the ·honest [upright; virtuous] one.
The man who has peace
will have ·children to live after him [posterity].
38But sinners will be destroyed;
·in the end [*or* the posterity of] the wicked will ·die [Lbe cut off].

39The LORD ·saves [rescues; Tdelivers] ·good [righteous] people;
he is their strength in times of ·trouble [distress].
40The LORD helps them and ·saves [rescues; Tdelivers] them;
he ·saves [rescues; Tdelivers] them from the wicked,
because they ·trust [take refuge] in him for protection.

A Prayer in Time of Sickness

A psalm of David ·to remember [*or* for the memorial offering].

38 LORD, don't ·correct [rebuke; reprove] me when you are angry.
Don't ·punish [discipline] me when you are ·furious [enraged; 6:1].
2Your arrows have ·wounded [pierced] me,
and your hand has come down on me.
3My ·body [flesh] is ·sick [Lnot sound] from your ·punishment [Lindignation].

Even my bones are not healthy because of my sin.
4My guilt has ·overwhelmed me [Lpassed over my head];
like a ·load [burden] it ·weighs me down [is too heavy for me].

5My sores stink and become infected
because I was foolish.
6I am bent over and bowed down;
I ·am sad [Lwalk around mourning] all day long.
7·I am burning with fever [LMy loins are burned with fever],
and my ·whole body [flesh] is ·sore [Lnot sound].
8I am weak and ·faint [Lcompletely crushed].
I ·moan [groan] from the ·pain I feel [Languish of my heart].

9LORD, you know everything I ·want [desire; long for];
my ·cries [sighs] are not hidden from you.
10My heart pounds, and my strength ·is gone [abandons/forsakes me].
·I am losing my sight [LThe light of my eyes is not with me].
11Because of my wounds, ·my friends [Lthose who love me] and
neighbors ·avoid [Lstand away from] me,
and my relatives ·stay [Lstand] far away.
12·Some people set traps to kill me [LThose who seek my life set
traps for me].
Those who ·want [seek] to ·hurt [harm; trouble] me plan trouble;
all day long they ·think up [meditate on] ·lies [deception].

13I am like the deaf; I cannot hear.
Like the mute, I cannot ·speak [open my mouth].
14I am like those who do not hear,
who have no ·answer [reproof] ·to give [Lin their mouth].
15I ·trust [hope in; wait for] you, LORD.
You will answer, my Lord and God.
16I said, "Don't let them ·laugh at [rejoice in] me
or ·brag [boast] when ·I am defeated [Lmy foot totters/slips]."
17I am ·about to die [Lready to stumble],
and ·I cannot forget my pain [Lmy pain is constantly with me].
18I confess my guilt;
I am troubled by my sin.
19My ·enemies are strong and [Lliving enemies are] healthy,
and many hate me for no reason.
20They repay me with evil for the good I did.
They ·lie about me [Lare my accusers/adversaries] because I ·try to do
[Lpursued] good.

21LORD, don't ·leave [abandon; forsake] me;
my God, don't ·go away [be far from me].
22Quickly come and help me,
my Lord and Savior.

Life Is Short

For the director of music. For Jeduthun [CLevitical musician; 1 Chr. 16:41–42; 25:1, 6; 2 Chr. 5:12]. A psalm of David.

39 I said, "I will ·be careful how I act [Lguard my way]
and will not sin ·by what I say [Lwith my tongue].

I will ·be careful what I say [[L]keep a muzzle on my mouth]
around wicked people."
2So I kept ·very quiet [silent and still].
I didn't even say anything good,
but ·I became even more upset [[L]my agony/sorrow got worse].
3·I became very angry inside [[L]My heart grew hot within me],
and as I ·thought [meditated] about it, ·my anger [[L]a fire] burned.
So I ·spoke [[L]said with my tongue]:
4"LORD, ·tell [inform; reveal to] me when ·the end [*or* my end] will come
and how long ·I will live [[L]will be my days].
Let me know how ·long I have [[L]fleeting I am; 90:1–12].
5You have given ·me only a short life [[L]my days a handbreadth; [C]about four inches];
my lifetime is like nothing to you.
Everyone's life is only ·a breath [vapor; Eccl. 1:2]. ·*Selah* [Interlude]
6People are like shadows moving about.
All their ·work [*or* wealth; *or* turmoil] is ·for nothing [a breath/vapor; Luke 12:13–21; James 4:3–17];
they ·collect things [accumulate riches/wealth] but don't know who will ·get [gather] them.

7"So, Lord, what ·hope do I have [do I wait for]?
You are my hope.
8Save me from all my ·sins [transgressions].
Don't ·let wicked fools make fun of me [[L]set the scorn of fools on me].
9I am quiet; I do not open my mouth,
because you are the one who has done this.
10·Quit punishing me [[L]Turn your blows/scourge away from me];
·your beating is about to kill me [[L]I am exhausted/finished from the hostility/beatings of your hand].
11You correct and punish people for their sins;
like a moth, you destroy what they ·love [covet; desire].
Everyone's life is only a ·breath [vapor; Eccl. 1:2]. ·*Selah* [Interlude]

12"LORD, hear my prayer,
and listen to my cry.
Do not ignore my tears.
I am like a ·visitor [sojourner; wanderer; resident alien] with you.
Like my ·ancestors [fathers], I'm only ·here a short time [a temporary resident].
13Leave me alone so I can be happy
before I leave and am no more."

Praise and Prayer for Help

For the director of music. A psalm of David.

40 I waited patiently for the LORD.
He ·turned [bent down; inclined; stooped] to me and heard my cry.
2He ·lifted [drew] me out of the pit of ·destruction [*or* desolation],
out of the ·sticky mud [miry/muddy pit/bog/swamp].
He ·stood me [[L]placed my feet] on a rock
and made my ·feet [[L]step] steady.

[3]He put a new song [[C]celebrating victory; 33:3; 96:1; 98:1; 144:9; 149:1; Is. 42:10; Rev. 5:9; 14:3] **in my mouth,**
a song of praise to our God.
Many people will see this and ·worship [fear] **him.**
Then they will ·trust [find refuge in] **the LORD.**

[4]·**Happy** [Blessed] **is the person**
who ·trusts [finds refuge in] **the LORD,**
who doesn't turn to those who are proud
or to those who ·worship [go astray to] **·false gods** [[L]a lie].
[5]**LORD my God, you have done many ·miracles** [wonders; great acts].
Your plans for us are many.
If I tried to tell them all,
there would be too many to count [104:24; 139:17–18; John 21:25].

[6]**You do not want sacrifices and ·offerings** [grain offerings; *or* gifts; tribute; Lev. 2:1].
But you have ·made a hole in [*or* pierced; [L]dug] **my ear** [[C]to make him hear better or perhaps a reference to the ritual that made one a slave forever; Ex. 21:6; Heb. 10:5–7].
You do not ask for burnt offerings [Lev. 1:1–17]
and ·sin [*or* purification] **offerings** [Lev. 4:3].
[7]**Then I said, "Look, I have come.**
It is written about me in the ·book [scroll].
[8]**My God, I ·want** [delight; take pleasure] **to do ·what you want** [your pleasure].
Your ·teachings [instructions; laws] **are in my heart."**

[9]**I will tell ·about your goodness** [the good news] **in the great ·meeting of your people** [assembly].
LORD, you know ·my lips are not silent [[L]I have not restrained my lips].
[10]**I do not hide your ·goodness** [righteousness] **in my heart;**
I speak about your ·loyalty [faithfulness] **and ·salvation** [victory].
I do not hide your ·love [loyalty] **and ·truth** [faithfulness]
from the people in the great ·meeting [assembly].

[11]**LORD, do not ·hold back** [restrain] **your ·mercy** [compassion] **from me;**
let your ·love [loyalty] **and ·truth** [faithfulness] **always protect me.**
[12]·**Troubles** [Evils] **have surrounded me;**
·there are too many to count [[L]without number].
My ·sins [iniquities] **have ·caught** [overtaken] **me**
so that I cannot see [[C]a way to escape].
I have more ·sins [iniquities] **than hairs on my head,**
and ·I have lost my courage [[L]my heart fails/abandons/forsakes me].
[13]·**Please** [[L]Be pleased], **LORD, ·save** [rescue; [T]deliver] **me.**
Hurry, LORD, to help me.
[14]**People are ·trying to kill me** [[L]seeking my life].
Shame them and disgrace them.
People want to hurt me.
Let them ·run away [be turned back] **in disgrace.**
[15]**People are ·making fun of me** [[L]saying to me, "Aha! Aha!"].
Let them be ·shamed into silence [[L]devastated by their own shame].

16 But let those who ·follow [[L]seek] you
be happy and glad.
They love you for ·saving [delivering] them.
May they always say, "·Praise [Magnify; Great is] the Lord!"

17 Lord, because I am poor and ·helpless [needy],
please ·remember [[L]think of; consider] me.
You are my helper and ·savior [rescuer; [T]deliverer].
My God, do not ·wait [delay].

A Prayer in Time of Sickness

For the director of music. A psalm of David.

41 ·Happy [Blessed] are those who ·think about [*or* care for] the poor [James 1:27].
·When trouble comes [[L]In the day of trouble/evil], the Lord will ·save [rescue; [T]deliver] them.
2 The Lord will ·protect [guard; keep] them and ·spare their life [keep them alive]
and will ·bless them [make them happy] in the land.
He will not ·let their enemies take them [[L]give their lives to their enemy; *or* give them over to the desire of their enemy].
3 The Lord will give them strength when they are ·sick [[L]on their sickbed],
and he will ·make them well again [[L]restore them from their bed of illness].

4 I said, "Lord, have ·mercy [compassion] on me.
Heal me, because I have sinned against you."
5 My enemies are saying evil things about me.
They say, "When will he die and ·be forgotten [[L]his name/reputation perish]?"
6 Some people come to see me,
but ·they lie [[L]speak deceptive/vain things].
·They just come to get bad news [[L]Their hearts collect iniquities].
Then they go ·and gossip [[L]out and speak].
7 All ·my enemies [[L]those who hate me] whisper about me
and ·think [imagine] ·the worst [trouble; evil] about me.
8 They say, "·He has a terrible disease [*or* An evil spell has been cast on him].
He ·will never get out of bed again [[L]lies down and will not get up]."
9 ·My best and truest friend [[L]A man of peace in whom I trust/find support], who ate at my table,
has ·even turned against me [[L]lifted his heel against me; [C]an act of treachery; 55:12–14; Matt. 26:23; Mark 14:18; Luke 22:21; John 13:18].

10 Lord, have ·mercy [compassion] on me.
·Give me strength [[L]Raise me up] so I can pay them back.
11 Because my enemies do not ·defeat [triumph over; *or* make fun of] me,
I know you are ·pleased [delighted] with me.
12 Because I am ·innocent [blameless], you support me
and will ·let me be with you [[L]set me in your presence] forever.

13·Praise [Blessed be] the LORD, the God of Israel.
·He has always been [L...from everlasting to everlasting],
and he will always be.
Amen and amen [Cverse 13 is a doxology that closes Book 1].

Book 2: Psalms 42–72

Wishing to Be Near God

For the director of music. A ·maskil [skillful psalm; meditation] of the sons of Korah [Cdescendants of Kohath, son of Levi, who served as Temple musicians; 1 Chr. 6:22].

42 As a deer ·thirsts [longs; Tpants] for streams of water,
so ·I [Tmy soul] ·thirst [Llongs] for you, God.
2·I [TMy soul] thirst for the living God.
When can I go to ·meet with [Lsee] ·him [Lthe face of God]?
3Day and night, my tears have been my food.
People are always saying,
"Where is your God?"
4When I remember these things,
I ·speak with a broken heart [Lpour out my soul].
I used to walk with the ·crowd [throng]
and lead them to ·God's Temple [Lthe house of God]
with ·songs of praise [Lthe sound of praise and thanks, a crowd in procession].

5Why ·am I so sad [Lare you cast down, my soul]?
Why ·am I so upset [Lare you groaning/in an uproar]?
I ·should [*or* will] ·put my hope in [wait for] God
and ·keep praising [*or* will again praise] him,
my ·Savior [Victor] and 6my God.

·I am very sad [My soul is cast down].
So I remember you ·where the Jordan River begins [Lfrom the land of Jordan],
·near the peaks of [Land from] Hermon and Mount Mizar [Cfar from the Temple where God made his presence known].
7·Troubles have come again and again [LDeep calls to deep], ·sounding like waterfalls [Lat the sound of your torrents; Cwaters represent distress; 69:1–2].
Your waves and your breakers ·are crashing all around [Lpass over] me.
8The LORD ·shows [commands] his ·true love [loyalty; covenant love] every day.
At night I have a song,
and I pray to my living God.
9I say to God, my Rock,
"Why have you forgotten me?
Why am I ·sad [Lgoing around in mourning]
and ·troubled [oppressed] by my enemies?"
10My enemies' ·insults [scorn] make me feel
as if my bones were ·broken [Lmurdered].
They are always saying,
"Where is your God?"

[11]Why ·am I so sad [[L]are you cast down, my soul]?
Why ·am I so upset [are you groaning/in an uproar]?
I ·should [*or* will] ·put my hope in [wait for] God
and ·keep praising [*or* will again praise] him,
my ·Savior [Victor] and my God.

A Prayer for Protection

43 God, defend me.
·Argue my case [[L]Vindicate me, O God, and contend for/defend me] against ·those who don't follow you [[L]a godless nation].
·Save [Rescue; [T]Deliver] me from ·liars [deceivers] and those who ·do evil [are unjust].
[2]God, you are my ·strength [[L]refuge].
Why have you rejected me?
Why am I ·sad [[L]going around in mourning]
and ·troubled [oppressed] by my enemies?
[3]Send me your light and ·truth [faithfulness]
to ·guide [lead] me.
Let them ·lead [bring] me to your holy mountain [[C]Zion, the location of the Temple],
to ·where you live [your dwelling].
[4]Then I will go to the altar of God,
to God who is my joy and happiness.
I will praise you with a ·harp [lyre],
God, my God.

[5]Why ·am I so sad [[L]are you downcast, my soul]?
Why ·am I so upset [are you groaning/in an uproar]?
I ·should [*or* will] ·put my hope in [wait for] God
and ·keep praising [*or* will again praise] him,
my ·Savior [Victor] and my God.

A Prayer for Help

For the director of music. A ·maskil [skillful psalm; meditation] of the sons of Korah [[C]descendants of Kohath, son of Levi, who served as Temple musicians; 1 Chr. 6:22].

44 God, we have heard ·about you [[L]with our ears; 78:3].
Our ·ancestors [fathers] ·told [recited to] us
what you did in their days,
in days long ago.
[2]With your ·power [[L]hand] you ·forced [dispossessed] the nations out of the land
and ·placed [[L]planted] our ancestors here.
You ·destroyed [troubled] ·those other nations [[L]the peoples],
but you ·made our ancestors grow strong [set them free].
[3]It wasn't their swords that ·took [possessed] the land.
It wasn't their ·power [[L]arm] that gave them victory.
But it was your ·great power [[L]arm] and ·strength [[L]right hand].
·You were with them [[L]...and the light of your face] because you ·loved [delighted in] them.

[4]My God, you are my King.
·Your commands led Jacob's people to victory [*or* You command victory for Jacob; [C]Jacob is another name for Israel].
[5]With your help we pushed ·back [down] our enemies.

In your name we trampled those who ·**came** [rose up] **against us.**
[6]**I don't trust my bow to help me,**
and my sword can't ·**save me** [give me victory].
[7]**You** ·**saved us from** [gave us victory over] **our foes,**
and you made ·**our enemies** [[L]those who hate us] **ashamed.**
[8]**We will praise God every day;**
we will ·**praise** [give thanks to] **your name forever.** ·*Selah* [Interlude]

[9]**But you have rejected us and** ·**shamed** [humiliated] **us.**
You don't ·**march** [[L]go out] **with our armies anymore** [Ex. 15:3; 2 Chr. 20:20–21].
[10]**You let our enemies push us back,**
and those who hate us have ·**taken our wealth** [plundered us].
[11]**You** ·**gave us away** [made us] **like sheep** ·**to be eaten** [for slaughter]
and have scattered us among the nations.
[12]**You sold your people for nothing**
and made no profit on the sale.

[13]**You made us a** ·**joke** [reproach] **to our neighbors;**
those around us ·**laugh** [ridicule] **and make fun of us.**
[14]**You made us a** ·**joke** [byword; proverb] **to the other nations;**
people shake their heads.
[15]**I am always in disgrace,**
and ·**I am** [[L]my face is] **covered with shame.**
[16]**My enemy is getting** ·**even** [revenge]
with ·**insults** [taunts] **and curses.**

[17]**All these things have happened to us,**
but we have not forgotten you
or ·**failed to keep** [been false to; betrayed] **our** ·**agreement** [covenant; treaty] **with you** [[C]perhaps a reference to the covenant with Moses; Ex. 19–24].
[18]**Our hearts haven't turned** ·**away** [back] **from you,**
and ·**we haven't stopped following you** [[L]our steps have not departed from your way].
[19]**But you crushed us in this place where** ·**wild dogs** [jackals] **live** [[C]desolate areas],
and you covered us with ·**deep darkness** [*or* the shadow of death; Nah. 1:8].

[20]**If we had forgotten the name of our God**
or ·**lifted** [[L]spread] **our hands in prayer to** ·**foreign** [[L]strange] **gods,**
[21]·**God would have known** [[L]Would not God discover this…?],
because he knows ·**what is in** [[L]the secrets of] **our hearts.**
[22]**But for you we are** ·**in danger of death** [[L]killed] **all the time.**
People think we are worth no more than sheep to be ·**killed** [slaughtered; Is. 53:7].

[23]**Wake up, Lord! Why are you sleeping?**
Get up! Don't reject us forever [Lam. 5:22].
[24]**Why do you hide your face from us?**
Have you forgotten our ·**pain** [affliction] **and** ·**troubles** [oppression]**?**

25We have ·been pushed down [sunk down] into the ·dirt [dust];
·we are flat on the ground [Lour stomachs cleave to the earth].
26·Get [Rise] up and help us.
Because of your ·love [loyalty], ·save [redeem; ransom] us.

A Song for the King's Wedding

For the director of music. To the tune of "Lilies." A ·maskil [skillful psalm; meditation]. A love song of the sons of Korah [Cdescendants of Kohath, son of Levi, who served as Temple musicians; 1 Chr. 6:22].

45 ·Beautiful words fill my mind [LMy heart is stirred with a good word].
I ·am speaking of royal things [*or* address my work to the king].
My tongue is like the pen of a skilled writer [Ezra 7:6].

2You are more ·handsome [*or* excellent] than anyone,
and ·you are an excellent speaker [Lgrace flows from your lips; Prov. 22:11],
so God has blessed you forever.
3Put on your sword ·at your side [Lon your thigh], powerful warrior.
Show your ·glory [splendor] and majesty.
4In your majesty ·win [Lride forth for] the victory
for what is ·true [faithful] and ·right [righteous].
Your ·power [Lright hand] ·will do [Lteaches you] amazing things.
5Your sharp arrows will ·enter [pierce]
the hearts of the king's enemies.
·Nations [Peoples] will ·be defeated before [Lfall beneath] you.
6·God, your throne will last [*or* Your throne is a throne of God] forever and ever.
·You will rule your kingdom with fairness [LA scepter of virtue will be the scepter of your kingdom].
7You love ·right [righteousness] and hate ·evil [wickedness],
so God has ·chosen [anointed] you from among your ·friends [companions];
·he has set you apart with much joy [L...with the oil of joy; Ckings were anointed with oil at their coronation; 1 Sam. 10:1; 16:13; Heb. 1:8–9].
8Your clothes smell like myrrh, aloes, and cassia.
From palaces of ivory
·music [stringed instruments] comes to make you happy.
9Kings' daughters are among your honored women.
Your ·bride [queen; consort] stands at your right side
wearing gold from Ophir [Cperhaps a region in southern Arabia].

10Listen to me, daughter; look and ·pay attention [Lincline your ear].
Forget your people and your father's ·family [Lhouse; Gen. 2:24].
11The king ·loves [Ldesires; longs for] your beauty.
Because he is your ·master [lord], you should ·obey [Lbow yourself before] him.
12·People from the city [LThe daughter] of Tyre have brought ·a gift [tribute].
Wealthy people ·will want to meet you [seek your favor].

13The ·princess [Ldaughter of the king] is ·very beautiful [Lall glorious within].

Her gown is woven with gold.
14In her ·beautiful [embroidered] clothes she is brought to the king.
·Her bridesmaids [Virgins] follow behind her,
and ·they are also brought to him [Lher friends follow].
15They come with happiness and joy;
they enter the king's palace.

16You will have sons to replace your fathers [Caddressed to the king].
You will make them ·rulers [princes] through all the land.
17I will make your name famous from now on,
so people will praise you forever and ever.

God Protects His People

For the director of music. By ·alamoth [maidens; young women; Cperhaps for soprano voices]. A psalm of the sons of Korah [Cdescendants of Kohath, son of Levi, who served as Temple musicians; 1 Chr. 6:22].

46 God is our ·protection [refuge] and our strength.
He ·always helps [is an ever present/timely help] in times of ·trouble [distress].
2So we will not be afraid even if the earth ·shakes [quakes],
or the mountains ·fall [reel; totter] into the heart of the sea,
3even if the ·oceans [Lwaters] roar and foam,
or the mountains ·shake [tremble] at ·the raging sea [Lits surging].
·*Selah* [Interlude]

4There is a river ·that [Lwhose channels/streams] brings joy to the city of God,
the holy place where God Most High lives.
5God is in that city, and so it will not ·be shaken [reel; totter].
God will help her at dawn.
6Nations ·tremble [roar] and kingdoms ·shake [reel; totter].
God ·shouts [Lgives forth his voice] and the earth ·crumbles [melts].

7The Lord ·All-Powerful [Almighty; of Heaven's Armies; Tof hosts] is with us;
the God of Jacob is our ·defender [refuge; fortress]. ·*Selah* [Interlude]

8Come and see what the Lord has done,
·the amazing things he has done [*or* the desolations he has brought] on the earth.
9He stops wars ·everywhere on [Lto the ends of] the earth.
He breaks all bows and shatters spears
and burns up the ·chariots [*or* shields] with fire.
10God says, "Be still and know that I am God.
I will be ·praised [exalted] in all the nations;
I will be ·praised [exalted] throughout the earth."

11The Lord ·All-Powerful [Almighty; of Heaven's Armies; Tof hosts] is with us;
the God of Jacob is our ·defender [refuge; fortress].
·*Selah* [Interlude]

God, the King of the World

For the director of music. A psalm of the sons of Korah [[C]descendants of Kohath, son of Levi, who served as Temple musicians; 1 Chr. 6:22].

47 Clap your hands, all you people.
Shout to God with ·joy [jubilant shouts/cries/[L]sound].
[2]The LORD Most High is ·wonderful [awesome].
He is the great King over all the earth!
[3]He ·defeated [subdues] ·nations [*or* armies] ·for [[L]under] us
and ·put them under our control [[L]peoples under our feet].
[4]He chose ·the land we would inherit [[L]for us our heritage/inheritance].
We are the ·children [[L]pride] of Jacob, whom he loved.
·*Selah* [Interlude]

[5]God has risen with a shout of joy;
the LORD has risen ·as the trumpets sounded [[L]with the sound of the ram's horn].
[6]Sing praises to God. Sing praises.
Sing praises to our King. Sing praises.
[7]God is King of all the earth,
so sing a ·song of praise [psalm; a skillful psalm; meditation; [L]maskil] to him.
[8]God is King over the nations.
God sits on his holy throne.
[9]The ·leaders [princes] of the ·nations [*or* armies] ·meet [[L]gather together]
with the ·people [*or* army] of the God of Abraham,
because the ·leaders [[L]shields; [C]military leaders] of the earth belong to God.
He is ·supreme [highly exalted].

Jerusalem, the City of God

A psalm of the sons of Korah [[C]descendants of Kohath, son of Levi, who served as Temple musicians; 1 Chr. 6:22].

48 The LORD is great; ·he should [[L]and greatly to] be praised
in the city of our God, on his holy mountain [[C]Mount Zion, the location of the Temple].
[2]It is ·high and beautiful [beautiful in elevation]
·and brings joy to [[L]the joy of] the whole world [Lam. 2:15].
Mount Zion ·is like the high mountains [[L]on the sides] of ·the north [*or* Zaphon; [C]comparing Yahweh's mountain with the mountain of Baal];
it is the city of the Great King.
[3]God is within its ·palaces [citadels];
he is known as its defender.
[4]Kings joined together
and came ·to attack the city [[L]on together; 2:1].
[5]But when they saw it, they were ·amazed [astonished].
They ran away in ·fear [panic].
[6]·Fear [[L]Trembling] ·took hold of [seized] them;
they ·hurt [were in pain] like a woman ·having a baby [in labor].
[7]You ·destroyed [broke up] the ·large trading ships [[L]ships of Tarshish; [C]large trading vessels capable of going to distant ports; Tarshish may have been in Spain (Tartessus) or an island in the eastern Mediterranean; Is. 2:16; Jon. 1:3]
with an east wind.

[8]First we heard
and now we have seen
that God ·will always keep his city safe [establishes forever].
It is the city of the LORD ·All-Powerful [Almighty; of Heaven's
Armies; [T]of hosts],
the city of our God. *·Selah* [Interlude]

[9]God, we come into your Temple
to ·think [ponder; meditate] about your ·love [loyalty].
[10]God, your name is known everywhere;
·all over the earth people [[L]the ends of the earth] praise you.
Your right hand is full of ·goodness [righteousness; *or* victory].
[11]Mount Zion is happy
and ·all the towns [[L]the daughters] of Judah rejoice,
because ·your decisions are fair [*or* of your judgments].

[12]Walk around Jerusalem
and count its towers.
[13]·Notice how strong they are [[L]Set your heart on its ramparts].
Look at the ·palaces [citadels].
Then you can ·tell [recount it to] ·your children about them [[L]a later
generation].
[14]This God is our God forever and ever.
He will guide us from now on.

Trusting Money Is Foolish

For the director of music. A psalm of the sons of Korah [[C]descendants of Kohath, son of Levi, who served as Temple musicians; 1 Chr. 6:22].

49 Listen to this, all you ·nations [peoples];
·listen [[L]give ear], all you who live on earth.
[2]Listen, both ·great [high] and ·small [low],
rich and poor together.
[3]·What I say is wise [[L]My mouth speaks wisdom],
and ·my heart speaks with [[L]the meditation of my heart is]
understanding.
[4]I will ·pay attention [extend my ear] to a ·wise saying [proverb];
I will ·explain [solve] my riddle on the ·harp [lyre].

[5]Why should I ·be afraid of [fear] ·bad [evil] days?
·Why should I fear when evil people [...when the guilt of deceivers/
the treacherous] surround me?
[6]They ·trust [find refuge] in their ·money [wealth]
and ·brag [boast] about their riches.
[7]No one can ·buy back [ransom; redeem] the life of ·another [*or* a brother].
No one can ·pay [[L]give a ransom to] God for his own life,
[8]because the ·price [ransom; redemption] of a life is ·high [precious].
No payment is ever enough.
[9]Do people live forever?
Don't they all ·face death [[L]see the Pit; 16:10]?

[10]See, even wise people die.
Fools and stupid people also ·die [perish; Eccl. 2:12–16]
and ·leave [abandon; forsake] their wealth to others.

11Their graves will ·always [forever] be their homes.
·They will live there from now on [L…their dwelling to all generations],
even though they named places after themselves.
12Even rich people do not ·live forever [abide];
like the animals, people ·die [perish; Eccl. 3:19].

13This is ·what will happen to [Lthe way/path for] those who trust in themselves
and ·to their followers [*or* the end of those; Lafter them] who ·believe them [Lare pleased with their mouth]. ·*Selah* [Interlude]
14Like sheep, they ·must die [Lhead to Sheol; Cthe grave or the underworld],
and death will be their shepherd.
·Honest [Virtuous; Upright] people will ·rule [have dominion] over them in the morning,
and their bodies will ·rot in a grave [waste away in Sheol] far from ·home [their grand homes].
15But God will ·save [ransom; redeem] my life
and will take me from ·the grave [*or* the underworld; LSheol; v. 14].
·*Selah* [Interlude]

16Don't be afraid of ·rich [wealthy] people
because their houses are more ·beautiful [*or* substantial].
17They don't take anything ·to the grave [when they die];
their ·wealth [substance] won't go down with them.
18Even though they were ·praised [blessed] when they were alive—
and people may praise you when you ·succeed [do well]—
19they will go to where their ancestors are [Cthe grave].
They will never see light again.
20Rich people with no understanding
are just like animals that ·die [perish].

God Wants True Worship

A psalm of Asaph [Ca Levitical musician, a descendant of Gershon, at the time of David; 1 Chr. 6:39; 15:17; 2 Chr. 5:12].

50 The God of gods, the LORD, speaks.
He ·calls [proclaims to; summons] the earth from the rising to the setting sun.
2God shines from ·Jerusalem [LZion; Cthe location of the Temple],
·whose beauty is perfect [Lthe perfection of beauty; 48:2; Lam. 2:15].
3Our God comes, and he will not be silent.
A fire ·burns [consumes] in front of him [Heb. 12:29],
and a ·powerful storm [whirlwind; tempest] surrounds him [Is. 66:15].
4He ·calls to [summons] the ·sky [heavens] above and to the earth
that he might judge his people.
5He says, "Gather around, you ·who worship me [holy ones; saints],
who have made an ·agreement [covenant; treaty] with me, using a sacrifice [Ex. 24:5–8]."
6God is the judge,
and even the ·skies say he is right [heavens proclaim his righteousness]. ·*Selah* [Interlude]

7God says, "My people, listen to me;
Israel, I will ·testify [witness] against you.
I am God, your God.
8I do not ·scold [reprimand; rebuke] you for your sacrifices.
You always bring me your burnt offerings [Lev. 1:1–17].
9But I do not ·need [*or* accept] bulls from your ·stalls [Lhouse]
or goats from your ·pens [folds],
10because every animal of the forest is already mine.
The cattle on a thousand hills are mine.
11I know every bird on the mountains,
and every living thing in the fields is mine.
12If I were hungry, I would not tell you,
because the earth and ·everything in it [Lits fullness] are mine.
13·I don't [LDo I…?] eat the meat of bulls
or drink the blood of goats.
14Give an ·offering to show thanks [thank offering] to God [Lev. 7:12; 22:29; Heb. 13:15].
Give God Most High what you have ·promised [vowed].
15Call to me in times of ·trouble [distress].
I will ·save [rescue; Tdeliver] you, and you will ·honor [glorify] me."

16But God says to the wicked,
"Why do you ·talk about [recount] my ·laws [statutes; ordinances; requirements]?
Why do you ·mention [Llift up on your mouth] my ·agreement [covenant; treaty]?
17You hate my ·teachings [instruction; discipline; Prov. 1:7]
and turn your back on what I say.
18When you see a thief, you ·join [delight in; *or* run with] him.
·You take part in adultery [Your lot/portion is with adulterers].
19You ·don't stop your mouth from speaking evil [Lsend your mouth into evil],
and your tongue ·makes up lies [Lis yoked to deception].
20You sit around and speak against your brother
and ·lie [Lgive a stain/fault] about your mother's son.
21I have kept quiet while you did these things,
so you thought I was just like you.
But I will ·scold [reprimand; reprove] you
and ·accuse [indict] you ·to your face [Lbefore your eyes].

22"·Think about [Understand] this, you who forget God.
Otherwise, I will tear you apart,
and no one will ·save [protect] you.
23Those people ·honor [glorify] me
who bring me ·offerings to show thanks [thank offerings; v. 14].
And I, God, will save those who ·do that [Lgo on my way/path]."

A Prayer for Forgiveness

For the director of music. A psalm of David when the prophet Nathan came to David after ·David's sin with Bathsheba [he committed adultery with/[L]had gone to Bathsheba; 2 Sam. 11:1—12:25].

51 God, be ·merciful [gracious] to me
·because you are loving [according to your love/loyalty].
·Because you are always ready to be merciful [According to your abundant compassion],
·wipe [blot] out all my ·wrongs [transgressions].
2 Wash ·away [[L]me thoroughly from] all my guilt
and make me clean ·again [[L]from my sin].

3 I know about my ·wrongs [transgressions],
and ·I can't forget my sin [[L]my sin is continually before me].
4 You ·are the only one [alone] I have sinned against;
I have done ·what you say is wrong [[L]evil in your eyes].
You are ·right [vindicated] when you speak
and ·fair [pure; blameless] when you judge.
5 I was ·brought into this world [born] in ·sin [guilt].
In sin my mother ·gave birth to [conceived] me [Rom. 3:9–20; 7:18].

6 You ·want me to be completely truthful [[L]desire truth/faithfulness in my inward parts],
·so teach me wisdom [[L]and secretly you make me know wisdom].
7 ·Take away my sin [[L]Remove my sin with hyssop; Ex. 12:22; [C]a plant used in purification rituals; Lev. 14:4, 6, 49–51; Num. 19:18], and I will be clean.
Wash me, and I will be whiter than snow [Is. 1:18].
8 Make me hear sounds of joy and gladness;
let the bones you crushed ·be happy [rejoice] again.
9 ·Turn [[L]Hide] your face from my sins
and ·wipe [blot] out all my guilt.

10 Create in me a ·pure [clean] heart, God,
and ·make my spirit right again [[L]renew a right/steadfast spirit in me].
11 Do not send me away from you
or take your ·Holy Spirit [*or* holy spirit] away from me.
12 ·Give me back [Restore to me] the joy of your ·salvation [rescue].
·Keep me strong by giving [Sustain in] me a willing spirit.
13 Then I will teach your ways to ·those who do wrong [transgressors],
and sinners will turn back to you.

14 God, save me from ·the guilt of murder [bloodshed],
God of my ·salvation [rescue],
and ·I will sing about your goodness [[L]let my tongue sing for joy of your righteousness].
15 Lord, let ·me speak [[L]my lips open]
so ·I may praise you [[L]my mouth may speak your praise].
16 You are not pleased by sacrifices, or I would give them.
You don't want burnt offerings [Lev. 1:1–17].
17 The sacrifice God wants is a broken spirit.
God, you will not ·reject [despise] a heart that is broken and ·sorry for sin [contrite; Is. 57:15; 66:2; Mic. 6:6–8].

18Do whatever good you wish for ·Jerusalem [LZion; Cthe location of the
Temple].
Rebuild the walls of Jerusalem.
19Then you will be pleased with right sacrifices and whole burnt
offerings [Lev. 1:1–17],
and bulls will be offered on your altar.

God Will Punish the Proud

For the director of music. A ·maskil [skillful psalm; meditation] of David. When Doeg the Edomite came to Saul and ·said [reported] to him, "David ·is in [Lhas come to/entered] Ahimelech's house [1 Sam. 21:7; 22:7–23]."

52 Mighty warrior, why do you ·brag [boast] about the evil you do?
God's ·love [loyalty] will continue ·forever [Leveryday; all day].
2You think up ·evil plans [Ldestruction].
Your tongue is like a sharp razor [Prov. 18:21],
making up ·lies [deception].
3You love ·wrong [evil] more than ·right [good]
and ·lies [falsehood] more than speaking the truth. ·*Selah* [Interlude]
4You love words that ·bite [destroy; Lswallow up]
and ·tongues that lie [deceptive tongues; James 3:1–12].

5But God will ·ruin you [Lbreak you down] forever.
He will grab you and ·throw [tear] you out of your tent;
he will ·tear you away [uproot you] from the land of the living.
·*Selah* [Interlude]
6Those who ·do right [are righteous] will see this and ·fear God [Lfear;
Prov. 1:7].
They will laugh at you and say,
7"·Look what happened to [TBehold] the man
who did not ·depend on God [Lmake God his refuge]
but ·depended on [trusted/put his confidence in] ·his money [Lthe
abundance of his wealth].
He grew strong by his ·evil [destructive] plans."

8But I am like ·an olive tree
growing [La green olive tree] in God's ·Temple [Lhouse; 1:3; 92:12–13;
Jer. 11:16].
I ·trust [have confidence in] God's ·love [loyalty]
forever and ever.
9God, I will ·thank [praise] you forever for what you have done.
With ·those who worship you [his loyal ones/saints], I will ·trust [put
my confidence in] you because you are good.

The Unbelieving Fool

For the director of music. By mahalath [Cperhaps "sickness"]. A ·maskil [skillful psalm; meditation] of David.

53 Fools say ·to themselves [Lin their hearts],
"There is no God [CPsalm 14 largely parallels this psalm]."
·Fools are evil [LThey are corrupt] and do ·terrible [detestable] things
[Deut. 32:5];
none of them does anything good.

2God looked down from heaven on all people

to see if anyone was ·wise [insightful],
if anyone was ·looking to God for help [seeking God].
3But all have ·turned [wandered] away.
Together, everyone has become ·evil [perverse];
none of them does anything good.
Not a single person [Rom. 3:10–12].

4Don't ·the wicked [Lthose who do evil] ·understand [know]?
They ·destroy [consume; Leat] my people as if they were ·eating [consuming] bread.
They do not ·ask God for help [call on God].
5The wicked are ·filled [terrified] with terror
where there ·had been nothing to [Lwas no] fear.
God will scatter the bones of ·your enemies [the godless].
You will ·defeat [shame; humiliate] them,
because God has rejected them.

6I pray that ·victory [salvation] will come to Israel from Mount Zion [Cthe location of the Temple, the house of God]!
May God ·bring them back [restore the fortunes of his people; Cperhaps at the end of the exile].
Then the people of Jacob will rejoice,
and the people of Israel will be glad.

A Prayer for Help

For the director of music. With stringed instruments. A ·maskil [skillful psalm; meditation] of David when the Ziphites went to Saul and said, "·We think David is [LIs not David…?] hiding among ·our people [Lus; 1 Sam. 23:13–29; 26:1]."

54 God, ·save [give victory to] me ·because of who you are [Lby your name].
By your ·strength [Lname] ·show that I am innocent [contend for me].
2Hear my prayer, God;
·listen [Lgive ear] to ·what I say [Lthe speech of my mouth].
3Strangers ·turn [Lrise up] against me,
and ·cruel people want to kill me [Lviolent people seek my life].
They do not ·care about God [think about God; Lset God before them]. *·Selah* [Interlude]

4·See [TBehold], God ·will help me [Lis my helper];
the Lord ·will support me [Lis with/*or* among those who uphold me].
5Let ·my enemies be punished with their own evil [Levil return to my enemies].
·Destroy [Put an end to] them because ·you are loyal to me [Lof your faithfulness].

6I will ·offer a sacrifice as a special gift [sacrifice a freewill offering] to you.
I will ·thank [praise] ·you [Lyour name], LORD, because you are good.
7You have ·saved [rescued] me from all my ·troubles [distress],
and ·I have seen my enemies defeated [Lmy eyes have looked on my enemies].

For the director of music. With stringed instruments.
A ·maskil [skillful psalm; meditation] **of David.**

A Prayer About a False Friend

55 **God, ·listen** [[L]give ear] **to my prayer**
and do not ·ignore [hide from] **my ·cry for help**
[supplication].
[2]**Pay attention to me and answer me.**
·I am troubled and [My cares give me no peace and I am]
upset
[3]**by ·what the enemy says** [[L]the voice/sound of my enemy]
and ·how the wicked look at me [before the stares/*or* because
of the afflictions of my enemy].
They bring troubles down on me,
and in anger they ·attack [persecute; *or* hate] **me.**

[4]**·I am frightened inside** [[L]My heart writhes inside me];
the terror of death has ·attacked [[L]fallen on] **me.**
[5]**·I am scared and shaking** [Fear and trembling come on me],
and ·terror [shuddering] **·grips** [overwhelms] **me.**
[6]**I said, "·I wish** [O that] **I had wings like a dove.**
Then I would fly away and rest.
[7]**I would ·wander** [flee] **far away**
and stay in the ·desert [wilderness]. ·*Selah* [Interlude]
[8]**I would hurry to my place of escape,**
far away from the raging wind and ·storm [tempest]."

[9]**Lord, ·destroy** [*or* frustrate; *or* check; *or* confuse; [L]swallow] **and**
·confuse [confound; [L]divide] **their ·words** [speech; *or* plans;
[L]tongues; Gen. 11:1–9],
because I see violence and ·fighting [strife; contention; accusation] **in**
the city.
[10]**Day and night they are all around its walls,**
and evil and trouble are everywhere inside.
[11]**Destruction is ·everywhere in the city** [[L]in its midst];
·trouble [oppression] **and ·lying** [deception] **never leave its ·streets**
[public square].

[12]**It was not an enemy ·insulting** [scorning; reproaching] **me.**
I could ·stand [bear] **that.**
It was not someone who hated me who insulted me.
I could hide from him.
[13]**But it is you, a person like me,**
my companion and good friend.
[14]**We had ·a good friendship** [sweet fellowship together]
and walked ·together [*or* noisily; *or* quietly; *or* with the crowd]
to God's ·Temple [[L]house].

[15]**Let death ·take away** [[L]rise up on] **·my enemies** [[L]them].
Let them ·die while they are still young [[L]go down to the grave/
underworld/Sheol while they are living]
because evil ·lives with them [[L]is their home within them].
[16]**But I will call to God for help,**
and the LORD will ·save me [give me victory].

[17]Morning, noon, and ·night [[L]evening] I ·am troubled and upset [sigh and moan],
but he will listen to ·me [[L]my voice].
[18]Many are against me,
but he ·keeps me safe [[L]redeems/ransoms me whole/in peace] in battle.
[19]God who ·lives forever [*or* is enthroned from of old]
will hear me and ·punish [[L]humble] them. ·*Selah* [Interlude]
But they will not change;
they do not fear God [Prov. 1:7].

[20]·The one who was my friend attacks his friends [[L]He sends his hand against his friend]
and ·breaks [violates; profanes] his ·promises [covenant; treaty].
[21]His words are ·slippery like [[L]smoother than] butter,
but war is in his heart.
His words are ·smoother [softer] than oil,
but they cut like ·knives [unsheathed swords; Prov. 5:3–4].

[22]·Give [[L]Cast; Throw] your ·worries [burden; [L]that which he has given you] to the LORD,
and he will ·take care of [sustain] you.
He will never let ·good [righteous] people ·down [[L]be moved].
[23]But, God, you will bring down
the wicked to the ·grave [deepest pit; [L]pit of corruption].
Murderers and ·liars [deceivers] will ·live
only half a lifetime [[L]not live half their days].
But I will ·trust [have confidence] in you.

Trusting God for Help

For the director of music. To the tune of "The Dove in the Distant Oak." A miktam [[C]perhaps "inscription"] of David when the Philistines ·captured [seized] him in Gath [[C]referring to the episode in 1 Sam. 21:10–15 or to an unrecorded event].

56 God, be ·merciful [gracious] to me because people are ·chasing [trampling; hounding; snapping at] me;
the battle has ·pressed [harrassed] me all day long.
[2]My enemies have ·chased [trampled on; hounded; snapped at] me all day;
there are many proud people fighting me.
[3]When I am afraid,
I will ·trust [have confidence in] you.
[4]I praise God for his word.
I ·trust [have confidence in] God, so I am not afraid.
What can ·human beings [[L]flesh] do to me?

[5]All day long they ·twist [find fault with] my words;
all their evil ·plans [*or* thoughts] are against me.
[6]They ·wait [*or* attack; *or* strive]. They hide.
They watch my ·steps [[L]heels],
hoping to kill me.
[7]God, do not let them escape;
·punish [[L]bring down] the ·foreign nations [peoples] in your anger.

[8]You have ·recorded [recounted] my ·troubles [wanderings].
You have ·kept a list of my tears [[L]put my tears in your bottle].
Aren't they in your records?

[9]On the day I call for help, my enemies will ·be defeated [[L]turn back].
I know that God is on my side.
[10]I praise God for his word to me;
I praise the LORD for his word.
[11]I ·trust [have confidence] in God. I will not be afraid.
What can people do to me?

[12]God, I must keep my ·promises [vows] to you.
I will give you my ·offerings to thank you [thank offerings],
[13]because you have ·saved [protected] me from death.
You have kept ·me from being defeated [[L]my feet from falling].
So I will walk ·with [[L]in the presence of] God
in light ·among [of] the living.

A Prayer in Troubled Times

For the director of music. To the tune of "Do Not Destroy." A miktam [[C]perhaps "inscription"] of David when he ·escaped [fled] from Saul in the cave [[C]likely a reference to 1 Sam. 22:1–5, but possibly 1 Sam. 24].

57 Be ·merciful [gracious] to me, God; be ·merciful [gracious] to me
because I ·come to you for protection [[L]seek refuge].
Let me ·hide [be protected; [L]seek refuge] under the shadow of your
wings [Ruth 2:12; Matt. 23:37]
until the ·trouble [destruction] has passed.

[2]I cry out to God Most High,
to the God who ·does everything for [fulfills his purpose for; *or* avenges] me.
[3]He sends help from heaven and ·saves me [gives me victory].
He ·punishes [reproaches; scorns] those who ·chase [trample on; hound; snap at] me. ·*Selah* [Interlude]
God sends me his ·love [loyalty] and ·truth [faithfulness].

[4]I lie down among lions [[C]his enemies];
who are aflame for human prey.
Their teeth are like spears and arrows,
their tongues as sharp as swords.

[5]God is ·supreme [exalted] over the ·skies [heavens];
his ·majesty [glory; [C]his manifest presence] ·covers [[L]is over] the earth.

[6]They set a ·trap [net] for ·me [[L]my feet].
I am ·very worried [bowed down].
They dug a pit ·in my path [[L]before me],
but they fell into it themselves. ·*Selah* [Interlude]

[7]My heart is ·steady [steadfast; ready], God; my heart is ·steady [steadfast; ready].
I will sing and ·praise [play a psalm for] you.
[8]Wake up, my ·soul [*or* glory].

Wake up, harp and lyre!
I will wake up the dawn.
9Lord, I will ·praise [thank] you among the ·nations [peoples];
I will ·sing songs of praise about [play a psalm for] you to all the nations.
10Your ·love [loyalty] ·reaches to [is greater than] the ·skies [heavens],
your ·truth [faithfulness] to the clouds.
11God, you are ·supreme [exalted] above the ·skies [heavens].
Let your glory [Cmanifest presence] be over all the earth.

Unfair Judges

For the director of music. To the tune of "Do Not Destroy."
A miktam [Cperhaps "inscription"] of David.

58 Do you ·rulers [*or* silent ones; *or* gods; Csometimes spiritual
beings such as angels are called "gods" in the OT; 82:1] really
say what is ·right [righteous]?
Do you judge people ·fairly [with integrity]?
2No, in your heart you plan evil;
you ·think up [dispense] ·violent crimes [violence] in the land.
3From ·birth [Lthe womb], evil people ·turn away [go astray] from God;
they wander off and tell lies ·as soon as they are born [Lfrom the
belly; Canother word for the womb; 51:5].
4They ·are [Lhave poison/venom] like ·poisonous [venomous] snakes,
like deaf cobras that ·stop [plug] up their ears
5so they cannot hear the music of the snake charmer
no matter how ·well he plays [wisely/skillfully he enchants].

6God, break the teeth in their mouths!
·Tear out [Uproot] the fangs of those lions, Lord!
7Let them ·disappear [vanish] like water that flows away.
Let them ·be cut short like a broken arrow [Ldraw their arrows like
they are cut off].
8Let them be like ·snails [slugs] that ·melt [dissolve] as they move
[Csnails leave a slime as they move].
Let them be like a ·child born dead [stillborn] who never saw the sun.
9His anger will blow them away alive
faster than burning thorns can heat a pot [Clikely a reference to quick
retribution].
10·Good [Righteous] people will be glad when they see ·him get even
[vengeance].
They will wash their feet in the blood of the wicked [Is. 63:1–6; Rev.
14:19–20; 19:13–14].
11Then people will say,
"There really are ·rewards [fruits] for ·doing what is right [the
righteous].
There really is a God who judges the ·world [earth; land]."

A Prayer for Protection

For the director of music. To the tune of "Do Not Destroy." A miktam
[Cperhaps "inscription"] of David when Saul sent men to ·watch
David's house [Lthe house] to kill him [1 Sam. 19:11–17].

59 God, ·save [protect] me from my enemies.
·Protect me [Give me refuge] from those who ·come [rise]
against me.
2·Save [Protect] me from those who do evil

and ·save me from [give me victory over] **·murderers** [the bloodthirsty].

[3]**Look, they are waiting to ambush ·me** [my life; Prov. 1:11].
·Cruel [Defiant; Strong] **people attack me,**
but I have not sinned or ·done wrong [transgressed], **LORD.**
[4]**I have done nothing wrong, but they ·are ready to attack me** [[L]run and get ready].
Wake up to ·help [meet] **me, and look.**
[5]**You are the LORD God ·All-Powerful** [Almighty; of Heaven's Armies; [T]of hosts], **the God of Israel.**
·Arise [[L]Awake] **and ·punish** [visit] **·those people** [[L]all the nations].
Do not give those traitors any ·mercy [grace]. ***·Selah*** [Interlude]

[6]**They come back at ·night** [evening].
Like dogs they ·growl [make a commotion] **and ·roam around** [surround] **the city.**
[7]**Notice what ·comes** [bubbles up] **from their mouths.**
·Insults [[L]Swords] **come from their lips,**
because they say, "Who's listening?"
[8]**But, LORD, you laugh at them** [2:4];
you ·make fun of [ridicule] **all ·of them** [[L]the nations].

[9]**God, my strength, I ·am looking to** [keep watch for] **you,**
because God is my ·defender [refuge].
[10]**My God ·loves** [is loyal to] **me, and he goes in front of me.**
He will help me ·defeat [[L]look on] **my enemies.**
[11]**Lord, our ·protector** [[L]shield], **do not kill them, or my people will forget.**
With your power ·scatter them [make them wander] **and ·defeat them** [[L]bring them down].
[12]**They sin by what they say;**
they sin with their ·words [[L]lips].
They curse and tell lies,
so let their pride ·trap [capture] **them.**
[13]**·Destroy** [Annihilate] **them in your anger;**
·destroy [annihilate] **them ·completely** [[L]so they will be no more]!
Then they will know
that God rules over ·Israel [[L]Jacob]
and to the ends of the earth. ***·Selah*** [Interlude]

[14]**They come back at ·night** [evening].
Like dogs they ·growl [make a commotion]
and ·roam around [surround] **the city.**
[15]**They wander about looking for food,**
and they ·howl [grumble] **if they ·do not find enough** [are not satisfied].
[16]**But I will sing about your strength.**
In the morning I will sing about your ·love [loyalty].
You are my ·defender [refuge],
my place of safety in ·times of trouble [[L]the day of distress].
[17]**God, my strength, I will sing ·praises** [a psalm] **to you.**
God, my ·defender [refuge], **you are the God who ·loves** [is loyal to] **me.**

A Prayer After a Defeat

For the director of music. To the tune of "Lily of the ·Agreement [Testimony]." A miktam [Cperhaps "inscription"] of David. For teaching. When David fought the Arameans of ·northwest Mesopotamia [Naharaim; Lthe Two Rivers] and Zobah, and when Joab returned and ·defeated [Lstruck] twelve thousand ·Edomites at the Valley of Salt [2 Sam. 8; 1 Chr. 18].

60 God, you have rejected us and ·scattered us [broken us down; burst forth on us].
You have been angry, but please ·come back to [restore] us.
2 You made the earth shake and ·crack [split open].
Heal its ·breaks [cracks; fractures] because it ·is shaking [totters].
3 You have ·given your people [Lmade your people see] ·trouble [hardship].
You made us ·unable to walk straight, like people drunk with wine [Ldrink wine that makes us reel; Cthe cup of God's wrath; Jer. 25:15–29; Nah. 3:11; Matt. 26:39].
4 You have raised a banner to gather those who fear you.
Now they can ·stand up against the enemy [Lescape/flee from the bow]. *·Selah* [Interlude]

5 Answer us and ·save us [give us victory] by your ·power [Lhand]
so ·the people you love [your beloved] will be rescued.

6 God has said ·from his Temple [from his Holy Place; *or* in his holiness],
"·When I win [*or* With joy], I will ·divide [parcel up] Shechem
and measure off the Valley of Succoth [Gen. 33:17–20].
7 Gilead and Manasseh are mine.
Ephraim is like my helmet.
Judah holds my royal scepter [Gen. 49:10; Cthey are agents of God's power].
8 Moab is like my washbowl.
I throw my sandals at Edom [Cshowing contempt].
I shout [Cin triumph] at Philistia [Cenemies of Israel]."

9 Who will bring me to the ·strong, walled [fortified] city?
Who will lead me to Edom?
10 God, ·surely you have rejected [Lhave you not rejected…?] us;
you do not go out with our armies.
11 ·Help us fight the enemy [LGive us help against the foe].
Human ·help [deliverance] is useless,
12 but we can ·win [fight bravely] with God's help.
He will ·defeat [tread on] our ·enemies [foes].

A Prayer for Protection

For the director of music. With stringed instruments. Of David.

61 God, hear my cry;
·listen [pay attention] to my prayer.
2 I call to you from the ends of the earth [Cfar from the Temple]
when ·I am afraid [Lmy heart grows faint].
·Carry [Lead] me away to ·a high mountain [Lthe rock that is higher than I am; Ca place of refuge, perhaps referring to God as the rock; 18:2, 46; 19:14; 62:2].
3 You have been my ·protection [refuge],
like a strong tower against my enemies.

[4]**Let me ·live** [sojourn] **in your ·Holy Tent** [[L]tent; [C]the sanctuary] **forever.**
Let me find ·safety [refuge] **in the shelter of your wings** [[C]an image of compassion, or perhaps referring to the cherubim whose wings cover the Ark of the Covenant; Ex. 25:20]. *·Selah* [Interlude]

[5]**God, you have heard my ·promises** [vows].
You have given me what belongs to those who fear ·you [[L]your name].

[6]**·Give the king a long life** [[L]Add days to the days of the king];
let ·him live many years [[L]his years be forever and ever].
[7]**Let him ·rule** [reign] **in the presence of God forever.**
Protect him with your ·love [loyalty] **and ·truth** [faithfulness].
[8]**Then I will ·praise** [sing a psalm to] **your name forever,**
and every day I will ·keep my promises [fulfill my vows].

Trust Only in God

For the director of music. For Jeduthun [[C]a Levitical musician; 1 Chr. 16:41–42; 25:1, 6; 2 Chr. 5:12]. **A psalm of David.**

62 **I ·find rest** [wait quietly] **in God;**
only he can ·save me [give me victory].
[2]**He is my rock** [61:2] **and my ·salvation** [victory].
He is my ·defender [fortress];
I will not be ·defeated [shaken].

[3]**How long will you ·attack** [assault] **someone?**
Will all of you ·kill [murder] **that person?**
Who is like a leaning wall, like a fence ·ready to fall [that totters; [C]the wicked take advantage of the weak]?
[4]**They are planning to make that person ·fall** [totter].
They enjoy telling lies.
With their mouths they bless,
but in their ·hearts [[L]innards] **they curse.** *·Selah* [Interlude]

[5]**I ·find rest** [wait quietly] **in God;**
·only he gives me hope [[L]for my hope is in him].
[6]**He is my rock** [61:2] **and my ·salvation** [victory].
He is my ·defender [fortress];
I will not be ·defeated [shaken].
[7]**My ·honor** [glory] **and ·salvation** [victory] **come from God.**
He is my ·mighty [strong] **rock and my ·protection** [refuge].

[8]**People, ·trust** [have confidence in] **God all the time.**
·Tell him all your problems [[L]Pour out your heart before him],
because God is our ·protection [refuge]. *·Selah* [Interlude]

[9]**The least of people are only a ·breath** [vapor; bubble; vanity],
and even the greatest are just a ·lie [delusion].
On the scales, they ·weigh nothing [[L]go up];
together they are only a ·breath [vapor; bubble; vanity].
[10]**Do not ·trust** [have confidence] **in ·force** [oppression; extortion].
Stealing is ·of no use [meaningless].
Even if you gain more riches,
don't ·put your trust in [[L]set your heart on] **them.**

[11]God has said this once,
and I have heard it ·over and over [[L]twice]:
God is strong.
[12]The Lord is ·loving [loyal].
You ·reward [repay] people for what they have done [1 Pet. 1:17; Rev. 20:12–13; 22:12].

Wishing to Be Near God

A psalm of David when he was in the ·desert [wilderness] of Judah [[C]fleeing from a jealous Saul; 1 Sam. 21–31].

63 God, you are my God.
I ·search for [am intent on] you.
I thirst for you [42:1–2]
·like someone [*or* my flesh yearns for you] in a dry, ·empty [exhausted; weary] land
where there is no water.
[2]I have seen you in ·the Temple [[L]the Holy Place; *or* holiness]
and have seen your strength and glory.
[3]Because your ·love [loyalty] is better than life,
·I [[L]My lips] will praise you.
[4]I will ·praise [bless] you ·as long as I live [[L]with my life].
I will lift up my hands in your name [[C]in prayer].
[5]I will be ·content as if I had eaten the best foods [[L]satisfied as with fat and fatness].
My lips will sing, and my mouth will praise you.

[6]I remember you while I'm lying in bed;
I ·think about [meditate on] you through the watches of the night [[C]the night was divided into four watches of three hours each].
[7]You are my help.
·Because of your protection [[L]In the shadow of your wings; [C]an image of compassion or perhaps a reference to the cherubim whose wings covered the Ark of the Covenant; Ex. 25:20], I sing.
[8]I ·stay close [cling] to you;
·you support me with your right hand [[L]your right hand sustains me].

[9]·Some people are trying to kill me [[L]They seek my life for ruin],
but they will go down to the ·grave [[L]underbelly of the earth].
[10]They will be ·killed with swords [[L]handed over to the sword]
and ·eaten by wild dogs [[L]be the prey of jackals].
[11]But the king will rejoice in his God.
All who ·make promises in his name [[L]swear by him] will praise him,
but the mouths of liars will be shut.

A Prayer Against Enemies

For the director of music. A psalm of David.

64 God, listen to my complaint.
·I am afraid of my enemies;
protect my life from them [[L]Protect my life from the dread of my enemies].
[2]Hide me from ·those who plan wicked things [[L]the secret plans/conspiracy of the wicked],
from that ·gang [mob; restless group] who does evil [Prov. 1:8–19].

[3]They sharpen their tongues like swords
and ·shoot [aim] bitter words like arrows.
[4]From their hiding places they shoot at ·innocent [blameless] people;
they shoot suddenly and are not afraid.
[5]They encourage each other to do wrong.
They talk about setting traps,
·thinking [*or* saying] ·no one will [[L]who can…?] see them.
[6]They plan wicked things and say,
"We have a perfect plan."
The ·mind [[L]insides and the heart/mind] of human beings is ·hard to understand [[L]deep].

[7]But God will shoot them with arrows;
they will suddenly be struck down.
[8]Their own ·words [tongues] will ·be used against them [[L]make them stumble].
All who see them will shake their heads [[C]in amazement at their downfall].
[9]Then everyone will fear God [Prov. 1:7].
They will tell what God has done,
and they will ·learn from [reflect on] what he has done.
[10]·Good [Righteous] people will be happy in the LORD
and will find ·protection [refuge] in him.
Let everyone who is ·honest [virtuous in heart] praise the LORD.

A Hymn of Thanksgiving

For the director of music. A psalm of David. A song.

65 God, ·you will be praised in Jerusalem [[L]praise is due/proper/fitting to you in Zion; [C]the location of the Temple].
We will ·keep our promises [fulfill our vows] to you.
[2]You ·hear [*or* answer] our prayers.
All ·people [[L]flesh] will come to you.
[3]Our guilt ·overwhelms [overpowers] us,
but you ·forgive [wipe/blot out; make atonement for] our ·sins [transgressions].
[4]·Happy [Blessed] are the people you choose
and ·invite [[L]bring near] to stay in your court.
We are ·filled [satisfied] with good things in your house,
your holy Temple.

[5]You answer us in amazing ways with ·vindication [victory; righteousness],
God our ·Savior [Victor].
People ·everywhere on [[L]of all the ends of] the earth
and ·beyond the sea [[L]the farthest seas] ·trust [have confidence in] you.
[6]You ·made [established] the mountains by your strength;
you are ·dressed [girded; armed] in power.
[7]You ·stopped [silence; calm] the roaring seas,
the roaring waves [[C]representing chaos],
and the ·uproar [tumult] of the ·nations [peoples].
[8]Even those people at the ends of the earth fear your ·miracles [signs].
You are praised from ·where the sun rises [the east; [L]the gateways of the morning] to ·where it sets [the west; [L]evening].

9You ·take care of [visit] the land and water it;
you make it very ·fertile [rich].
The ·rivers [channels] of God are full of water.
Grain grows because you make it grow.
10You send rain to the plowed fields;
you ·fill the rows with water [level its ridges].
You soften the ground with rain,
and then you bless ·it with crops [its growth].
11You ·give [Lcrown] the year ·a good harvest [Lwith your goodness/bounty],
and ·you load the wagons with many crops [Lyour wagon tracks/ruts drip with plenty].
12The ·desert [wilderness] ·is covered [drips] with ·grass [pasturage]
and the hills with happiness.
13The ·pastures [meadows] are ·full of [Lclothed with] flocks,
and the valleys are ·covered [wrapped] with grain.
Everything shouts and sings for joy.

Praise God for What He Has Done

For the director of music. A song. A psalm.

66 Everything on earth, shout with joy to God!
2·Sing [Make a psalm] about ·his glory [Lthe glory of his name]!
Make his praise glorious!
3Say to God, "Your works are ·amazing [majestic]!
Because your power is great,
your enemies ·fall [cringe; cower] before you.
4All the earth ·worships [bows down to] you
and ·sings praises to [makes a psalm for] you.
They ·sing praises to [make a psalm for] your name [Phil. 2:10–12]."
·*Selah* [Interlude]

5Come and see what God has done,
the ·amazing [majestic] things he has done for people.
6He turned the sea into dry land [Ex. 14–15].
The people crossed the river on foot [Josh. 3].
So let us rejoice because of what he did.
7He rules forever with his power.
·He keeps his eye [LHis eyes keep watch] on the nations,
so ·people should not turn [the rebellious might not rise] against him.
·*Selah* [Interlude]

8You people, ·praise [bless] our God;
·loudly sing his praise [Llet the sound of his praise be heard].
9He ·protects our lives [Lsets our lives among the living]
and does not let ·us be defeated [Lour feet be moved].
10God, you have ·tested [examined] us;
you have ·purified [refined] us like silver [Cremoving the dross].
11You ·let us be trapped [brought us into the net]
and put ·a heavy load on us [Lmisery on our backs].
12You let our enemies ·walk on [Lride over] our heads.
We went through fire and ·flood [Lwater],
but you brought us to a place with ·good things [abundance].

[13]I will come to your ·Temple [[L]house] with burnt offerings [Lev. 1:1–17].
I will ·give you what I promised [repay my vows],
[14] ·things I promised when I was in trouble [[L]which my lips poured out and my mouth said when I was in distress].
[15]I will bring you burnt offerings [Lev. 1:1–17] of fat animals,
and ·I will offer sheep, bulls, and goats [[L]with the smoke of rams, I will offer bulls and goats]. ·*Selah* [Interlude]

[16]All of you who fear God [Prov. 1:7], come and listen,
and I will tell you what he has done for me.
[17]I ·cried out [called] to him with my mouth
and ·praised [exalted] him with my tongue.
[18]If I had ·known of [[L]seen] any sin in my heart,
the Lord would not have listened to me.
[19]But God has listened;
he has ·heard [[L]paid attention to the sound of] my prayer.
[20]·Praise [Blessed be] God,
who did not ·ignore [turn aside from] my prayer
or hold back his ·love [loyalty] from me.

Everyone Should Praise God

For the director of music. With stringed instruments. A psalm. A song.

67 God, ·have mercy on [be gracious to] us and bless us
and ·show us your kindness [[L]make your face shine on us; Num. 6:24–26] ·*Selah* [Interlude]
[2]so the world will ·learn [know] your ways,
and all nations ·will learn that you can save [[L]your salvation/victory].

[3]God, the people should ·praise [thank] you;
all people should ·praise [thank] you.
[4]The ·nations [peoples] should be glad and sing
because you judge people fairly.
You ·guide [lead] all the ·nations [peoples] on earth.
·*Selah* [Interlude]

[5]God, the people should ·praise [thank] you;
all people should ·praise [thank] you.

[6]The land has given its ·crops [bounty].
God, our God, blesses us.
[7]God blesses us
so people all over the earth will fear him [Prov. 1:7].

Praise God Who Saved the Nation

For the director of music. A psalm of David. A song.

68 Let God rise up and scatter his enemies;
let those who hate him ·run away [flee] from him.
[2]Blow them away as smoke
is ·driven [blown] away by the wind [Hos. 13:3].
As wax melts before a fire,
let the wicked ·be destroyed [perish] before God [Mic. 1:4].
[3]But ·those who do right [the righteous] should be glad
and should rejoice before God;
they should be happy and glad.

4Sing to God; ·sing praises [make a psalm] to his name.
Prepare the way for him
who rides ·through the desert [on the clouds; Cas on a chariot; 18:10–19; 104:3; Is. 19:1; Dan. 7:13–14; Luke 21:27; Rev. 1:7],
whose name is the LORD.
Rejoice before him.
5God is in his holy ·Temple [Labode].
He is a father to orphans [10:14; 146:9],
and he defends the widows [146:9].
6God gives the lonely a home.
He leads prisoners out ·with joy [with singing; *or* to prosperity],
but ·those who turn against God [Lthe rebellious] will live in a dry land.

7God, you led your people out
when you marched through the ·desert [wasteland; wilderness].
·*Selah* [Interlude]

8The ·ground [earth; land] shook
and the ·sky [heavens] poured down rain
before God, the God of Mount Sinai [Ex. 19],
before God, the God of Israel.
9God, you sent much rain;
you ·refreshed [restored] your ·tired [withering] ·land [Linheritance].
10Your people settled there.
God, in your goodness
you took care of the poor.

11The Lord gave the command,
and a great ·army [*or* company of women] told the news:
12"Kings and their ·armies [hosts] ·run away [Lflee].
·In camp they [LThe abode of the house; Cmay indicate the women] divide the ·wealth taken in war [plunder].
13Those who stayed ·by the campfires [Lbetween the saddlebags/*or* sheepfolds]
will share the ·riches taken in battle [Lwings of a dove covered with silver and its feathers with green gold; Cspecific precious items among the plunder]."
14The Almighty scattered kings
like snow on Mount Zalmon [Cperhaps near Shechem; Judg. 9:48].

15The mountains of Bashan [Cin the Golan heights, east of the Sea of Galilee] are ·high [mighty];
the mountains of Bashan have many peaks.
16Why do you mountains with many peaks look with ·envy [*or* hostility]
on the mountain that God ·chose [Ldesired] for his home [CZion, the location of the Temple]?
The LORD will live there forever.
17God comes with ·millions [Ltwice ten thousand, thousands of thousands] of chariots;
the Lord ·comes from Mount Sinai to his holy place [Lis among them Sinai in holiness].

[18]When you went up to the heights,
you led a parade of captives.
You received gifts from the people,
even from those who ·turned [rebelled] **against you** [2 Cor. 2:14; Eph. 4:8].
And the LORD God will live there.

[19]·Praise [Blessed be] **the Lord, God our ·Savior** [Victor],
who ·helps us [[L]bears our burdens] **every day.** ·*Selah* [Interlude]
[20]Our God is a God who ·saves us [gives us victory];
the LORD God ·saves us [[L]brings us out] **from death.**

[21]God will ·crush [shatter] **his enemies' heads,**
the hairy ·skulls [pates; [C]tops of their heads] **of those who continue to ·sin** [[L]walk in their guilt].
[22]The Lord said, "I will bring ·the enemy [[L]them] **back from Bashan** [v. 15];
I will bring them back from the depths of the sea [[C]representing chaos].
[23]Then you can ·stick [bathe; *or* shatter] **your feet in their blood,**
and ·your dogs can lick [[L]the tongues of your dogs can have] **their share."**

[24]God, people have seen your victory ·march [procession];
God my King marched into the holy place [[C]the Tabernacle].
[25]The singers are in front and the ·instruments [musicians] **are behind.**
In the middle are the girls with the tambourines.
[26]·Praise [Bless] **God in the ·meeting place** [assembly];
·praise [bless] **the LORD ·in the gathering** [*or* the fountain] **of Israel.**
[27]There is the smallest tribe, Benjamin, ·leading them [[L]bringing them down].
And there are the ·leaders [princes] **of Judah with their group.**
There also are the ·leaders [princes] **of Zebulun and of Naphtali.**

[28]God, ·order up [command] **your power;**
show the mighty power you have used for us before.
[29]Kings will bring their ·wealth [[L]presents; gifts] **to you,**
·to [*or* because of] **your Temple in Jerusalem.**
[30]·Punish [Reprimand; Rebuke] **the beast in the ·tall grass along the river** [[L]reed; [C]crocodile or hippopotamus representing Egypt].
·Punish [Reprimand; Rebuke] **·those bulls among the cows** [[L]the herd of bulls among the calves of the peoples; [C]leaders of other nations].
·Defeated [Trampled], **they will bring you their silver.**
Scatter those ·nations [peoples] **that ·love** [delight in] **war.**
[31]Messengers will come from Egypt;
the people of ·Cush [Ethiopia] **will ·pray** [[L]stretch their hands] **to God.**

[32]Kingdoms of the earth, sing to God;
·sing praises [make a psalm] **to the Lord.** ·*Selah* [Interlude]
[33]Sing to the one who rides through the ·skies [heavens], **·which are from long ago** [the ancient heavens; v. 4].
He ·speaks with a thundering voice [[L]puts forth his voice, his strong voice].

[34]·Announce [Ascribe] that God is ·powerful [strong].
·He rules [[L]His majesty is] over Israel,
and his power is in the ·skies [clouds].
[35]God, you are ·wonderful [awesome] in your ·Temple [sanctuary; [L]Holy Place].
The God of Israel gives his people strength and power.

·Praise [Bless] God!

A Cry for Help

For the director of music. To the tune of "Lilies." A psalm of David.

69 God, ·save me [give me victory],
because the water has risen to my neck [[C]the waters of chaos].
[2]I'm sinking down into the ·mud [mire],
and there is nothing to stand on.
I ·am in deep water [have come into the depths of the waters],
and the flood ·covers [overwhelms] me.
[3]I am ·tired [exhausted] from calling for help;
my throat is ·sore [dry].
My eyes are ·tired [worn out] from ·waiting [hoping]
for God to help me.
[4]There are more people who hate me for no reason than hairs on my head;
·powerful [*or* many] enemies want to destroy me for no reason.
They make me ·pay back [return]
what I did not steal.

[5]God, you know ·what I have done wrong [my foolishness];
I cannot hide my guilt from you.
[6]Lord God ·All-Powerful [Almighty; of Heaven's Armies; [T]of hosts],
do not let those who ·hope in [wait for] you be ashamed because of me.
God of Israel,
do not let ·your worshipers [[L]those who seek you] be disgraced because of me.
[7]For you, I carry this ·shame [reproach; scorn],
and my face is covered with disgrace.
[8]I am like a stranger to my closest relatives
and a foreigner to my mother's children.
[9]My ·strong love [jealousy; passion; zeal] for your ·Temple [[L]house] ·completely controls [[L]consumes] me [John 2:17].
·When people insult you, it hurts me [[L]The reproaches/scorn of those who reproach/scorn you fall on me; Rom. 15:3].
[10]When I ·cry [weep] and fast,
they ·make fun of [reproach; scorn] me.
[11]When I wear ·rough cloth [sackcloth; burlap; [C]a sign of grief],
·they joke about me [[L]I am a byword/proverb/joke to them].
[12]·They make fun of me in public places [[L]Those who sit in the gate complain about me],
and the drunkards make up songs about me.

[13]But I pray to you, Lord, ·for favor [*or* at an appropriate time].
God, because of your great ·love [loyalty], answer me.
You are ·truly able [faithful] to ·save [give victory].

14·Pull [Protect] me from the ·mud [mire],
and do not let me sink.
·Save [Protect] me from those who hate me
and from the deep water.
15Do not let the flood ·drown [overwhelm] me
or the deep water swallow me
or the ·grave [Lpit] close its mouth over me.
16LORD, answer me because your ·love [loyalty] is so good.
Because of your ·great kindness [abundant compassion], turn to me.
17Do not hide your face from me, your servant.
I am in ·trouble [distress]. Hurry to ·help [Lanswer] me!
18Come near and ·save [ransom] me;
·rescue [redeem] me from my enemies.

19You ·see [know] my ·shame [reproach; scorn] and disgrace.
·You know all my enemies and what they have said [LThe humiliation
of all my foes is before you].
20·Insults [Reproach; Scorn] have broken my heart
and ·left me weak [I am depressed].
I ·looked [hoped; waited] for ·sympathy [pity; consolation], but there
was none;
I found no one to comfort me.
21They ·put [Lgave me] poison in my food
and gave me vinegar to drink for my thirst [Matt. 27:48; Mark 15:23,
36; Luke 23:36; John 19:29].

22Let their ·own feasts cause their ruin [Ltable be a snare before them];
·let their feasts trap them and pay them back [*or* a trap for their friends].
23Let their eyes be ·closed [Ldarkened] so they cannot see
and their ·backs [Lloins] ·be forever weak from troubles [Ltremble all
the time].
24Pour your ·anger [wrath] out on them;
let your anger ·catch up with [overtake] them.
25May their ·place [camp] be ·empty [desolate];
leave no one to live in their tents.
26They ·chase after [persecute; pursue] those you have ·hurt [struck],
and they talk about the pain of those you have wounded.
27Charge them with ·crime after crime [Lguilt on guilt],
and do not ·let them have anything good [vindicate them].
28·Wipe [Blot] their names from the book of life [Ckill them],
and do not ·list them [write them down] with those who ·do what is
right [are righteous].

29I am ·sad [afflicted] and ·hurting [in pain].
God, ·save me [give me victory] and ·protect me [give me refuge].

30I will praise ·God [Lthe name of God] in a song
and will ·honor [magnify] him by giving thanks.
31That will please the LORD more than ·offering him cattle [Lan ox],
more than sacrificing a bull with horns and hoofs.
32Poor people will see this and be glad [Coffering an ox or bull is
expensive].

·Be encouraged, you who worship God [The hearts of those who seek
God will be enlivened].
33The LORD listens to those in need
and does not ·look down on [despise] ·captives [prisoners].

34Heaven and earth should praise him,
the seas and ·everything in them [Lall that swarms in them].
35God will ·save Jerusalem [Lgive Zion victory; Cthe location of the Temple]
and rebuild the cities of Judah.
Then people will live there and own the land.
36 The ·descendants [Lseed] of his servants will inherit that land,
and those who love ·him [Lhis name] will live there.

A Cry for God to Help Quickly

For the director of music. A psalm of David. ·To help people remember [For remembrance; *or* For a memorial offering].

70 God, ·come quickly and save [Lprotect] me.
LORD, hurry to help me.
2Let those who are ·trying to kill me [Lseeking my life]
be ashamed and ·disgraced [scorned; reproached].
Let those who want to hurt me
·run away [Lturn back] in disgrace.
3Let those who ·make fun of me [Lsay, "Aha, Aha!"]
·stop [withdraw] because of their shame.
4But let all those who ·worship [Lseek] you
rejoice and be glad.
Let those who love your ·salvation [victory]
always say, "·Praise the greatness of [Magnify] God."
5I am poor and ·helpless [needy];
God, hurry to me.
You ·help me and save me [Lare my helper and my rescuer].
LORD, do not ·wait [delay].

An Old Person's Prayer

71 In you, LORD, ·is my protection [LI find refuge].
Never let me be ashamed.
2Because you ·do what is right [are righteous], ·save [protect] and
rescue me;
·listen [Lextend your ear] to me and ·save me [give me victory].
3Be my ·place of safety [Lrock of refuge]
where I can always come.
Give the command to ·save me [give me victory],
because you are my rock and my ·strong, walled city [fortress].
4My God, ·save [rescue] me from the ·power [Lhand] of the wicked
and from the ·hold [grasp; Lpalm] of evil and cruel people.
5LORD, you are my hope.
LORD, I have ·trusted [had confidence in] you since I was young.
6I have ·depended [Lleaned] on you ·since I was born [Lfrom the belly;
Cthe womb];
you ·helped me even on the day of my birth [brought me forth/cut
off my umbilical cord from my mother's innards].
I will always praise you.

7I am an ·example [portent] to many people,
because you are my strong ·protection [refuge].

8·I am always praising you [LMy mouth is filled with your praise];
all day long I ·honor [glorify] you.
9Do not ·reject me [cast me off] when I am old;
do not ·leave [abandon; forsake] me when my strength is ·gone [exhausted].
10My enemies ·make plans [speak] against me,
and they ·meet [take counsel] together to kill me.
11They say, "God has ·left [abandoned; forsaken] him.
·Go after [Pursue; Persecute] him and ·take [capture] him,
because no one will ·save [protect] him."

12God, don't be far off.
My God, hurry to help me.
13Let those who accuse me
be ashamed and ·destroyed [annihilated].
Let those who are ·trying [seeking] to hurt me
be covered with shame and disgrace.
14But I will always have hope
and will praise you more and more.
15·I will tell how you do what is right [LMy mouth will recount your righteousness].
I will tell about your ·salvation [victory] all day long,
even though ·it is more than I can tell [LI do not know the number].
16I will come and tell about your powerful works, Lord God.
I will remind people ·that only you do what is right [Lthat you alone are righteous].

17God, you have taught me since I was young.
To this day I tell ·about the miracles you do [of your wonderful works].
18Even though I am old and gray,
do not ·leave [abandon; forsake] me, God.
I will tell ·the children [La generation, to all that come] about your ·power [Larm];
I will tell of your might.

19God, your ·justice [righteousness] reaches to the ·skies [Lhigh heavens].
You have done great things;
God, there is no one like you.
20You have ·given [Lshown] me ·many troubles [much distress] and bad times,
but you will give me life again.
·When I am almost dead [LFrom the depths of the earth],
you ·will keep me alive [Lagain bring me up].
21You will make me greater than ever,
and you will comfort me again.

22I will ·praise [thank] you with the harp.
·I trust you […for your faithfulness], my God.
I will ·sing to [make a psalm for] you with the lyre,
Holy One of Israel.
23·I will [LMy lips] shout for joy when I ·sing praises to [make a psalm for] you.

You have ·saved [redeemed] me.
24·I [LMy tongue] will tell about your ·justice [righteousness] all day long.
And those who ·want [seek] to hurt me
will be ·ashamed [scorned and reproached] and disgraced.

A Prayer for the King

Of Solomon.

72 God, give the king your good judgment
and the king's son your ·goodness [righteousness].
2Help him judge your people ·fairly [rightly]
and decide what is ·right [just] for the poor.
3Let there be ·peace [or prosperity] on the mountains
and ·goodness [righteousness] on the hills for the people.
4Help him be ·fair [just] to the poor
and ·save [give victory to] the ·needy [or children of the needy]
and ·punish [crush] those who ·hurt [oppress; exploit] them.

5May they ·respect [fear] you as long as the sun
and as long as the moon, throughout the generations.
6Let him ·be [Lcome down] like rain on the mown grass,
like showers that water the earth.
7Let ·goodness [righteousness] ·be plentiful [bloom forth] while he lives.
Let ·peace [or prosperity] continue ·as long as there is a [Luntil there is no] moon.

8·Let his kingdom go [LMay he have dominion/rule] from sea to sea,
and from the ·Euphrates River [Lriver] to the ends of the earth.
9Let the people of the ·desert [wilderness] ·bow down to [cringe/cower before] him,
and make his enemies lick the dust.
10Let the kings of Tarshish [48:7] and the ·faraway lands [Lislands]
bring him ·gifts [tribute].
Let the kings of Sheba [Can unknown location, perhaps present-day Yemen, Eritrea, or Ethiopia; see 1 Kin. 10:1–13] and Seba [Ceither in southern Egypt or further south; Gen. 10:7; Is. 43:3; 45:14]
bring their ·presents [tribute] to him.
11Let all kings ·bow down [bend the knee] to him
and all nations serve him [Ps. 2].

12He will ·help [protect] the poor when they cry out
and the needy when no one else will help.
13He will ·be kind to [take pity on] the poor and the needy,
and he will ·save their lives [give victory to the needy].
14He will ·save [redeem] them from ·cruel people who try to hurt them [Lviolence and oppression],
because their ·lives [Lblood] are precious to ·him [Lhis eyes].

15Long live the king!
Let him receive gold from Sheba [v. 10].
Let people always pray for him
and ·bless [praise] him all day long.
16Let ·the fields grow plenty of grain [Lthere be much grain in the land/earth]

and ·the hills be covered with crops [Llet there be abundance on the top of the mountains; *or* let it wave on the top of the mountains].
·Let the land be as fertile as Lebanon [LMay its fruit be like that of Lebanon],
and let the cities grow like the grass in a field.
17**Let ·the king be famous** [Lhis name/fame be] **forever;**
let ·him be remembered as long as the sun shines [Lhis name/fame continue as long as the sun].
Let the nations be ·blessed [praised] **because of him,**
and may they all ·bless [praise] **him** [Gen. 12:3].

18**·Praise** [Blessed be] **the Lord God, the God of Israel,**
who alone does such ·miracles [wonderful things].
19**Praise his glorious name forever.**
Let his glory [Cmanifest presence] **fill the whole world.**
Amen and amen.

20**This ends the prayers of David son of Jesse** [Cat one time it did, but see other Davidic psalms at Ps. 101, 103, 108–110, and others].

Book 3: Psalms 73–89

Should the Wicked Be Rich?

A psalm of Asaph [Ca Levitical musician, a descendant of Gershon, at the time of David; 1 Chr. 6:39; 15:17; 2 Chr. 5:12].

73 **·God is truly** [Surely God is] **good to ·Israel** [*or* those with integrity/virtue],
to those who have pure hearts.
2**But ·I had almost stopped believing** [Las for me, my feet almost stumbled];
·I had almost lost my faith [my steps almost slipped]
3**because I was ·jealous** [envious] **of ·proud people** [braggers; boasters].
I saw wicked people ·doing well [prospering].

4**They are not ·suffering** [struggling; in pain];
·they [their bodies] **are ·healthy** [perfect] **and strong.**
5**They don't have ·troubles** [toils] **like the rest of us;**
they ·don't have problems [are not plagued] **like other people** [Gen. 3:17–19].
6**They wear pride like a necklace**
and ·put on violence as their clothing [Ladorn themselves with garments of violence].
7**·They are looking for profits** [LTheir eyes bulge with fat]
and ·do not control their selfish desires [cunning overflows from their hearts/minds].
8**They ·make fun of others** [scoff] **and speak ·evil** [harm];
·proudly [from high] **they speak of ·hurting** [oppressing; exploiting] **others.**
9**They ·brag to the sky** [Lset their mouth against heaven].
·They say that they own [LTheir tongue wanders] **the earth.**
10**So their people turn to them**
and ·give them whatever they want [Lthey drink up water in abundance].
11**They say, "How can God know?**
What does God Most High know?"

[12]These people are wicked,
always ·at ease [carefree], and getting richer.
[13]·So why have I kept my heart pure [[L]In vain, I kept my heart pure…]?
·Why have I kept my hands from doing wrong [[L]…and washed my hands in innocence; Matt. 27:24]?
[14]I ·have suffered [am plagued] all day long;
I have been ·punished [corrected] every morning.

[15]God, if I had ·decided to talk like this [[L]said, "I will recount this,"],
I would have ·let your people down [[L]betrayed the generation/race of your children].
[16]I ·tried [thought how] to understand all this,
but it was too ·hard [wearisome] ·for me to see [[L]in my eyes]
[17]until I went to the ·Temple [sanctuary; Holy Place] of God.
Then I understood ·what will happen to them [[L]their fate/end].
[18]You have put them in ·danger [[L]slippery places];
you cause them to ·be destroyed [[L]fall into disaster].
[19]They are destroyed in a moment;
they are swept away by terrors.
[20]It will be like waking from a dream.
Lord, when you ·rise up [awake; arouse yourself], ·they will disappear [[L]you despise their shadows].

[21]When my heart was ·sad [bitter]
and ·I was angry [[L]my innards felt stabbed],
[22]I was senseless and stupid.
I acted like an ·animal [brute beast] toward you.
[23]But I am always with you [[C]in covenant relationship];
you have held my ·hand [[L]right hand; [C]guiding him].
[24]You guide me with your advice,
and later you will receive me in ·honor [glory; [C]perhaps in the afterlife].
[25]·I have no one [[L]Whom do I have…?] in heaven but you;
I ·want [desire] nothing on earth besides you.
[26]My body and my ·mind [heart] may become weak,
but God is ·my strength [[L]the rock of my heart].
He is ·mine [[L]my portion] forever.

[27]Those who are far from ·God [[L]you] will ·die [perish];
you ·destroy [bring to an end] those who ·are unfaithful [prostitute themselves spiritually].
[28]But I am close to God, and that is good.
The Lord God ·is [I have made] my ·protection [refuge].
I will ·tell [recount] all that you have done.

A Nation in Trouble Prays

A ·maskil [skillful psalm; meditation] of Asaph [[C]a Levitical musician, a descendant of Gershon, at the time of David; 1 Chr. 6:39; 15:17; 2 Chr. 5:12].

74 God, why have you rejected us ·for so long [forever]?
Why ·are you angry with us, [[L]does your anger smoke against] the sheep of your pasture [100:3]?
[2]Remember the ·people [assembly; congregation] you ·bought [acquired] long ago.

You ·saved [redeemed] us, and we are ·your very own [Lthe tribe of your inheritance].
After all, you live on Mount Zion.
3·Make your way [Direct your steps] through ·these old [*or* the utter] ruins;
the enemy ·wrecked [destroyed] everything in the ·Temple [sanctuary; Holy Place; Cperhaps a reference to the Babylonian destruction of the Temple; 2 Kin. 25:8–21; 2 Chr. 36:17–21; Lam. 2:6].

4Those who were against you ·shouted [roared] in your meeting place
and ·raised their flags [Lset their signs as signs] there.
5·They came with axes raised [*or* They hacked at the upper entrances]
as if to cut down a forest of trees.
6They ·smashed [beat to pieces] the ·carved [engraved] panels
with their axes and ·hatchets [crowbars].
7They ·burned your Temple to the ground [Lset your sanctuary/Holy Place on fire];
they have made the ·place where you live [Lresidence of your name] ·unclean [profane].
8They ·thought [Lsaid in their hearts], "We will completely crush them!"
They burned ·every place where God was worshiped [Lall the meeting places of God] in the land.
9We do not see any signs.
There are no more prophets [Cwho can tell them what will happen],
and no one knows how long this will last.
10God, how much longer will the enemy ·make fun of [scorn] you?
Will they ·insult [revile] ·you [Lyour name] forever?
11Why do you ·hold back your power [Lreturn your hand]?
·Bring your power out in the open [LTake your right hand out of your bosom] and ·destroy [annihilate] them!

12God, you have been our king ·for a long time [of old; Ex. 15:18].
You bring ·salvation [victory] to the earth.
13You split open the sea by your power
and broke the heads of the sea monster [Can ancient Near Eastern symbol of chaos].
14You ·smashed [crushed in pieces] the heads of the monster Leviathan [Ca sea monster and symbol of chaos; 104:26; Job 3:8; 41:1; Is. 27:1]
and gave it to the ·desert [wilderness] creatures as food.
15You ·opened up [split] the springs and ·streams [wadis]
and made the flowing rivers run dry.
16Both the day and the night are yours;
you made the sun and the moon [Gen. 1:14–18].
17You set all the ·limits [borders] on the earth;
you ·created [formed] summer and winter [104:19–23; Gen. 8:22].

18Lord, remember how the enemy ·insulted [scorned] you.
Remember how those foolish people ·made fun of you [Lreviled your name].
19Do not give us, your doves, to those wild animals.
Never forget your poor people.

[20]·Remember [Regard] the ·agreement [covenant] you made with us,
because violence fills every dark corner of this land.
[21]Do not let your ·suffering [crushed] people be ·disgraced [humiliated].
Let the poor and ·helpless [needy] praise ·you [Lyour name].

[22]God, arise and ·defend [contend for] yourself.
Remember the ·insults [scorn] that come from those foolish people
all day long.
[23]Don't forget what your enemies said;
don't forget their roar as they rise against you always.

God the Judge

For the director of music. To the tune of "Do Not Destroy." A psalm of Asaph [Ca Levitical musician, a descendant of Gershon, at the time of David; 1 Chr. 6:39; 15:17; 2 Chr. 5:12]. A song.

75 God, we ·thank [praise] you;
we ·thank [praise] you because ·you [Lyour name] are near.
We tell about the ·miracles [wonders] you do.

[2]You say, "I set ·the time for trial [Lan appointed time],
and I will judge ·fairly [with integrity].
[3]The earth with all its people may ·shake [totter],
but I ·am the one who holds it steady [Lset/establish its pillars; Cthe
idea was that the earth was supported by pillars]. ·*Selah* [Interlude]
[4]I say to those who ·are proud [brag; boast], 'Don't ·be proud [brag; boast],'
and to the wicked, 'Don't ·show your power [Lexalt your horn;
Ca horn is a symbol of strength].
[5]Don't ·try to use your power [Lexalt your horn] against ·heaven [Lthe
heights; *or* on high].
Don't ·be stubborn [Lspeak with an insolent neck].'"

[6]No one from the east or the west
or the ·desert [wilderness] ·can judge you [comes exalting].
[7]God is the judge;
he ·judges one person as guilty [Lputs one down] and ·another as
innocent [Lraises another up].
[8]The Lord holds a cup in his hand;
it is ·full of wine mixed with [foaming wine full of] spices [Cthe cup
of God's wrath; 60:3; Jer. 25:15–29; Nah. 3:11; Matt. 26:39].
He pours it out ·even to the last drop [until its dregs drain out],
and the wicked drink it all.

[9]I will tell about this forever;
I will ·sing praise [make a psalm] to the God of Jacob.
[10]·He will take all power away from [LI will cut off all the horns of] the
wicked [v. 4],
but the ·power [Lhorn] of ·good [righteous] people will ·grow [be
exalted].

The God Who Always Wins

For the director of music. With stringed instruments. A psalm of Asaph [Ca Levitical musician, a descendant of Gershon, at the time of David; 1 Chr. 6:39; 15:17; 2 Chr. 5:12]. A song.

76 ·People in Judah know God [LGod is known in Judah];
his ·fame [name] is great in Israel.

[2]His Tent is in ·Jerusalem [[L]Salem; [C]shortened name of Jerusalem];
his ·home [abode] is on Mount Zion [Ps. 48].
[3]There God broke the flaming arrows,
the shields, the swords, and the weapons of war. ·*Selah* [Interlude]

[4]God, how ·wonderful [glorious; awesome; *or* radiant] you are!
You are more ·splendid [majestic] than the ·hills full of animals [hills full of prey; *or* everlasting mountains].
[5]The ·brave soldiers [[L]strong of heart] were ·stripped [plundered]
as they ·lay asleep in death [sleep their last sleep].
Not one ·warrior [valiant person]
·had the strength to stop it [[L]could lift their hand].
[6]God of Jacob, ·when you spoke strongly [[L]at your rebuke/reprimand],
horses and riders ·fell dead [[L]were in deep sleep; *or* lay stupefied].
[7]You are ·feared [awesome];
·no one [[L]who…?] can stand against you when you are angry.
[8]From heaven you ·gave the decision [made your judgment heard],
and the earth was afraid and silent.
[9]God, you ·stood [rose] up to judge
and to ·save [give victory to] the needy people of the earth. ·*Selah* [Interlude]
[10]·People praise you for your anger against evil [*or* Human anger praises you].
·Those who live through your anger are stopped from doing more evil [Those who survive your wrath are restrained; [L]You gird the remains of wrath on you].

[11]Make and keep your ·promises [vows] to the LORD your God.
From all around, gifts should come to the God ·we worship [[L]who is awesome].
[12]God ·breaks [cuts off] the spirits of ·great leaders [princes];
the kings on earth fear him.

Remembering God's Help

For the director of music. For Jeduthun [[C]a Levitical musician; 1 Chr. 16:41–42; 25:1, 6; 2 Chr. 5:12]. A psalm of Asaph [[C]a Levitical musician, a descendant of Gershon, at the time of David; 1 Chr. 6:39; 15:17; 2 Chr. 5:12].

77 I cry out to God;
I call to God, and he ·will hear [*or* heard] me.
[2]I ·look [sought] for the Lord on the day of ·trouble [[L]my distress].
All night long I ·reach out my untiring hands [[L]flow forth my hand and it does not grow weak],
but I ·cannot [refuse to] be comforted.
[3]When I remember God, I ·become upset [moan];
when I ·think [reflect; meditate], ·I become afraid [my soul faints]. ·*Selah* [Interlude]

[4]You ·keep my eyes from closing [[L]grab the eyelids of my eyes].
I am too ·upset [disturbed] to say anything.
[5]I keep thinking about the old days,
the years of long ago [[C]when things were going well].
[6]At night I remember my songs.

I ·think [meditate] and ·I ask myself [[L]my spirit inquires]:
[7]"Will the Lord reject us forever?
Will he never be ·kind [favorable] to us again?
[8]Is his ·love [loyalty] gone forever?
Has he stopped speaking for all time [[C]he questions God's commitment to the covenant]?
[9]Has God forgotten ·mercy [compassion]?
Is he too angry to ·pity [have mercy on] us?" ·*Selah* [Interlude]
[10]Then I say, "This is what makes me sad:
·For years the power of God Most High was with us [[L]The right hand of the God Most High has changed]."

[11]I remember what the Lord did;
I remember the ·miracles [wonderful acts] you did long ago.
[12]I ·think [mused] about all the things you did
and ·consider [meditated on] your deeds.

[13]God, your ways are holy.
·No god [[L]What god…?] is as great as our God.
[14]You are the God who does ·miracles [wonders];
you have ·shown [made known to] people your power.
[15]By your ·power [[L]arm] you have ·saved [redeemed] your people,
the descendants of Jacob and Joseph. ·*Selah* [Interlude]

[16]God, the waters saw you;
they saw you and ·became afraid [[L]writhed];
the deep waters shook with fear.
[17]The clouds poured down their rain.
The ·sky [clouds] ·thundered [[L]gave forth a sound].
Your lightning flashed back and forth like arrows.
[18]Your thunder sounded in the whirlwind.
Lightning lit up the world.
The earth trembled and ·shook [quaked].
[19]You made a way through the sea
and paths through the ·deep [[L]many] waters,
but your footprints were not ·seen [revealed].
[20]You led your people like a flock
by ·using [[L]the hand of] Moses and Aaron [Ex. 14–15].

God Saved Israel from Egypt

A ·maskil [skillful psalm; meditation] of Asaph [[C]a Levitical musician, a descendant of Gershon, at the time of David; 1 Chr. 6:39; 15:17; 2 Chr. 5:12].

78 My people, ·listen [give ear] to my ·teaching [instruction; law];
·listen [[L]incline your ear] to ·what I say [[L]the words of my mouth].
[2]I will ·speak [[L]open my mouth] ·using stories [[L]with a proverb/parable];
I will ·tell [expound] ·secret things [[L]riddles] from long ago [[C]the past contains lessons for the present generation].
[3]We have heard them and known them
by what our ·ancestors [fathers] have ·told [recounted to] us.
[4]We will not ·keep [hide] them from our children;
we will ·tell [recount them to] ·those who come later [a later generation]
about the praises of the Lord.

We will tell about his power
and the ·miracles [wonderful acts] he has done.

5 The LORD ·made an agreement [established a decree/testimony] with Jacob
and gave the ·teachings [instructions; laws] to Israel [Ex. 19–24],
which he commanded our ·ancestors [fathers]
to ·teach [make known] to their children [Deut. 6:6–9, 20–22].
6 Then ·their children [Lthe later generation] would know them,
even their children not yet born.
And they would ·tell [Lrise up and recount them to] their children.
7 So they would ·all trust [Lplace their trust/confidence in] God
and would not forget what he had done
but would ·obey [protect] his commands.
8 They would not be like their ·ancestors [fathers]
who were ·stubborn and disobedient [La stubborn and rebellious generation].
Their hearts were not ·loyal [steadfast; Lset] to God,
and they were not ·true [faithful] to him [Deut. 9:6–7, 13, 24; 31:27; 32:5; Acts 2:40].

9 The men of Ephraim ·had bows for weapons [Lwere armed for shooting the bow],
but they ·ran away [turned back] on the day of battle [Cperhaps 1 Sam. 4:1–4 or 1 Sam. 28–31].
10 They didn't ·keep [observe; guard] their ·agreement [covenant; treaty] with God
and refused to ·live [Lwalk] by his ·teachings [instructions; laws].
11 They forgot what he had done
and the ·miracles [wonderful acts] he had shown them.
12 He did ·miracles [wonderful acts] while their ·ancestors [fathers] watched,
in the fields of Zoan [Ca city in the Nile Delta also known as Tanis] in Egypt [Cthe plagues; Ex. 7–12].
13 He divided the ·Red Sea [LSea; Cprobably a lake north of the Gulf of Suez] and led them through [Ex. 14–15].
He made the water stand up like a ·wall [*or* heap; Ex. 15:8].
14 He led them with a cloud by day
and by the light of a fire by night [105:39; Ex. 13:21; Num. 10:34].
15 He split the rocks in the ·desert [wilderness]
and gave them more ·than enough water, as if from the deep ocean [Lwater, as much as the deeps].
16 He brought streams out of the rock
and caused water to flow down like rivers [Ex. 17:6; Num. 20:8; 1 Cor. 10:4].

17 But the people continued to sin against him;
in the ·desert [wasteland; wilderness] they ·turned [rebelled] against God Most High.
18 They ·decided to test God [Ltested God in their hearts]
by asking for the food ·they wanted [Lfor their appetite].
19 Then they spoke against God,
saying, "Can God prepare ·food [La table] in the ·desert [wilderness]?

20When he ·hit [Lstruck] the rock, water ·poured out [gushed]
and rivers flowed down.
But can he give us bread also?
Will he provide his people with meat [Ex. 16]?"
21When the LORD heard them, he was very angry.
·His anger was like fire to the people of [LA fire was ignited against] Jacob;
his anger ·grew against the people of [Lrose up against] Israel [Num. 11].
22They had not ·believed [trusted; been faithful to] God
and had not ·trusted [put confidence in] him to ·save them [give them victory].
23But he gave a command to the clouds above
and opened the doors of heaven.
24He rained manna down on them to eat;
he gave them grain from heaven.
25So they ate the bread of ·angels [Lstrong ones].
He sent them all the food they could eat.
26He sent the east wind from heaven
and ·led [guided] the south wind by his power.
27He rained meat on them like dust.
The birds were as many as the sand of the sea.
28He made the birds fall inside the camp,
all around the ·tents [Lresidences].
29So the people ate and became very ·full [satisfied; satiated].
God had given them what they ·wanted [desired].
30While ·they were still eating [Ltheir desire had not turned aside],
and while the food was still in their mouths,
31·God became angry with them [Lthe anger of God came up on them].
He killed some of the ·healthiest [most robust; sturdiest] of them;
he ·struck down [laid low] the best young men of Israel.

32But they kept on sinning;
they did not believe even with the ·miracles [wonderful acts].
33So he ended their days without ·meaning [purpose; Eccl. 1:2]
and their years in terror.
34Anytime he killed them, they would ·look to him for help [seek him];
they would ·come back to God [repent] and ·follow [be intent on] him.
35They would remember that God was their Rock [Cthe one who protected them],
that God Most High had ·saved [redeemed] them.
36But ·their words were false [Lthey deceived/*or* flattered him with their mouths],
and with their tongues they lied to him.
37Their hearts were not really ·loyal to [steadfast toward] God;
they ·did not keep [were not faithful to] his ·agreement [covenant].
38Still God was ·merciful [compassionate].
He ·forgave their sins [made atonement for their guilt]
and did not destroy them.
Many times he held back his anger
and did not stir up all his ·anger [wrath].

[39]**He remembered that they were ·only human** [flesh; 38:3; 56:4; 103:14–15; Gen. 6:3; Is. 2:22],
like a wind that blows and does not come back.

[40]**They ·turned** [rebelled] **against God so often in the ·desert** [wilderness]
and grieved him ·there [Lin the wasteland].
[41]**Again and again they tested God**
and ·brought pain to [provoked] **the Holy One of Israel.**
[42]**They did not remember his ·power** [Lhand]
or the ·time [Lday] **he ·saved** [ransomed] **them from the ·enemy** [foe].
[43]**They forgot the signs he did in Egypt**
and his wonders in the fields of Zoan [v. 12].
[44]**He turned their rivers to blood**
so no one could drink ·the water [Lfrom their streams; 105:29; Ex. 7:17–20; Rev. 16:4].
[45]**He sent flies that ·bit** [Lconsumed] **the people** [Ex. 8:20–32].
He sent frogs that destroyed them [Ex. 7:25—8:15].
[46]**He gave their crops to grasshoppers**
and ·what they worked for [Ltheir labor] **to locusts** [Ex. 10:1–20].
[47]**He ·destroyed** [Lkilled] **their vines with hail**
and their ·sycamore [*or* fig] **trees with ·sleet** [*or* frost; *or* floods; Ex. 9:13–35].
[48]**He ·killed their animals with** [Lhanded over their beasts to the] **hail**
and their cattle with lightning [Ex. 9:1–7].
[49]**He ·showed** [Lsent against] **them his hot anger.**
He sent his strong anger against them,
his ·destroying angels [*or* messengers of evil/harm].
[50]**He ·found a way to show** [Lmade a path for] **his anger.**
He did not ·keep them from dying [Lhold back their lives from death]
but ·let them die by a terrible disease [Lhanded their lives over to plague].
[51]**God ·killed** [Lstruck] **all the firstborn sons in Egypt** [Ex.12],
the ·oldest son of each family [Lfirst of their virility in the tents] **of Ham** [Cthe ancestor of the Egyptians; Gen. 10:6].
[52]**But God led his people out like sheep**
and he guided them like a flock through the ·desert [wilderness].
[53]**He led them to safety so they had nothing to fear,**
but ·their enemies drowned in the sea [Lthe sea covered their enemies].
[54]**So God brought them to his holy ·land** [Lboundary],
to the mountain country ·he took with his own power [Lhis hand acquired].
[55]**He ·forced out** [dispossessed before them] **the other nations,**
and he ·had his people inherit the land [Lalloted the land as an inheritance].
He let the tribes of Israel settle there in tents.

[56]**But they tested God**
and ·turned [rebelled] **against God Most High;**
they did not ·keep [observe; guard] **his ·rules** [decrees; testimonies].
[57]**They ·turned away** [recoiled] **and were disloyal just like their ·ancestors** [fathers].

They ·were like [turned into] **a ·crooked bow that does not shoot straight** [slack bow; [C]unreliable and ineffective].
58**They made God angry ·by building places to worship gods** [[L]with their high places; [C]worship sites associated with pagan worship or inappropriate worship of God; Deut. 12:2–3];
they made him jealous with their idols.
59**When God heard them, he became very angry**
and rejected the people of Israel completely.
60**He ·left** [cast off] **his dwelling at Shiloh,**
the Tent where he lived among the people.
61**He let his ·Power** [Strength; [C]the Ark] **be captured;**
he let his ·glory [beauty; [C]the Ark] **be taken by ·enemies** [[L]the hand of the foe; 1 Sam. 4–5].
62**He ·let his people be killed** [[L]handed his people over to the sword];
he was very angry with his ·children [[L]inheritance].
63**The young men ·died** [[L]were consumed] **by fire,**
and the young women ·had no one to marry [had no wedding songs; *or* could not sing a lament for them].
64**Their priests fell by the sword** [1 Sam. 4:12–22],
but their widows were not allowed to cry.

65**Then the Lord ·got up** [awoke] **as if he had been asleep;**
·he awoke like a man [[L]like a soldier] **who had been ·drunk with** [shouting/singing because of] **wine.**
66**He struck ·down** [[L]back] **his enemies**
and ·disgraced them forever [[L]placed on them eternal scorn/reproach].
67**But God rejected the ·family** [[L]tent] **of Joseph** [[C]the tribe of Ephraim];
he did not choose the tribe of Ephraim [[C]the most important northern tribe, here representing the house of Saul].
68**Instead, he chose the tribe of Judah**
and Mount Zion [[C]the location of the Temple], **which he loves.**
69**And he built his ·Temple** [sanctuary; Holy Place] **·high like the mountains** [*or* like the high heavens].
Like the earth, ·he built it to last [[L]its foundations are] **forever.**
70**He chose David to be his servant**
and took him from the sheep pens.
71**He brought him from tending the ·sheep** [[L]ewes]
so he could ·lead the flock, [shepherd] **the people of Jacob,**
his ·own people [inheritance], **the people of Israel.**
72**And David ·led** [shepherded] **them with an ·innocent** [blameless] **heart**
and guided them with skillful hands.

The Nation Cries for Jerusalem

A psalm of Asaph [[C]a Levitical musician, a descendant of Gershon, at the time of David; 1 Chr. 6:39; 15:17; 2 Chr. 5:12].

79

God, nations have come against your ·chosen people [[L]inheritance].
They have ·ruined [profaned] **your holy Temple.**
They have turned Jerusalem into ·ruins [a dump; 2 Kin. 25:9–10].
2**They have given the bodies of your servants as food to the ·wild birds** [[L]birds of the sky/heavens].
They have given the ·bodies [[L]flesh] **of ·those who worship you** [your faithful ones; saints] **to the wild animals** [Jer. 34:20].

[3]They have spilled blood like water all around Jerusalem.
No one was left to bury the dead.
[4]We are a ·joke [reproach; scorn] to the ·other nations [[L]residents];
·they [[L]the people around us] ·laugh [ridicule] and make fun of us.

[5]LORD, how long?
Will you be angry forever?
How long will your jealousy burn like a fire?
[6]·Be angry with [[L]Pour out your wrath on] the nations that do not know you
and ·with [*or* on] the kingdoms that do not ·honor you [[L]call on your name].
[7]They have ·gobbled up [devoured] the people of Jacob
and ·destroyed [desolated] their ·land [pasturage].
[8]Don't ·punish us for our past sins [[L]remember our former guilt].
Show your ·mercy [compassion] to us soon,
because we are ·helpless [very low]!
[9]God our ·Savior [Victor], help us
·so people will praise you [[L]for the glory of your name].
·Save [Protect] us and ·forgive [atone for] our sins
·so people will honor you [[L]for your name].
[10]Why should the nations say,
"Where is their God?"
·Tell [Inform] the other nations ·in our presence [[L]before our eyes]
that you ·punish [avenge] ·those who kill your servants [[L]the blood of your servants that has been poured out].
[11]·Hear the moans of the prisoners [Let the groans of the prisoner come before you].
Use your great ·power [[L]arm]
to save those ·sentenced [doomed] to die.

[12]Repay ·those around [[L]into the bosom of those around] us seven times over
for their ·insults to [reproach/scorn of] you, Lord.
[13]We are your people, the sheep of your ·flock [pasture].
We will ·thank [praise] you always;
·forever and ever [from generation to generation] we ·will praise you [[L]recount your praise].

A Prayer to Bring Israel Back

For the director of music. To the tune of "Lilies of the Agreement." A psalm of Asaph [[C]a Levitical musician, a descendant of Gershon, at the time of David; 1 Chr. 6:39; 15:17; 2 Chr. 5:12].

80 Shepherd of Israel, ·listen to us [give ear].
You ·lead [guide] the people of Joseph [[C]the northern empire of Israel] like a flock.
You sit on your throne between the ·gold creatures with wings [[L]cherubim; Ex. 25:18–22; 1 Kin. 8:7].
·Show your greatness [[L]Shine forth] [2]to the people of Ephraim, Benjamin, and Manasseh.
·Use [Arouse] your strength,
and come to ·save us [give us victory].

[3]God, ·take us back [restore us].
·Show us your kindness [LMake your face shine on us; 31:16; 67:1; Num. 6:24–26] so we can ·be saved [have victory].

[4]Lord God ·All-Powerful [Almighty; of Heaven's Armies; Tof hosts],
how long will you ·be angry [Lsmoke/fume at us]
at the prayers of your people?
[5]You have fed your people ·with tears [Lthe bread/food of tears];
you have made them drink ·many tears [tears by measure/Lthe third].
[6]You made ·those around us fight over us [Lus the strife of our neighbors],
and our enemies ·make fun of [ridicule] us.

[7]God ·All-Powerful [Almighty; of Heaven's Armies; Tof hosts], ·take us back [restore us].
·Show us your kindness [LMake your face shine on us; 31:16; 67:1; Num. 6:24–26] so we can ·be saved [have victory].

[8]You brought ·us out of Egypt as if we were a vine [La vine out of Egypt; Gen. 49:22; Is. 5:1–7; 27:2–6; Jer. 2:21; 12:10; Ezek. 15:1–8; 19:10–14; Hos. 10:1].
You ·forced out [dispossessed] other nations and planted us in the land.
[9]You cleared the ground for us.
We took root and filled the land.
[10]We covered the mountains with our shade.
We had branches like the mighty cedar tree.
[11]Our branches reached the Mediterranean Sea,
and our shoots went to the Euphrates River.

[12]So why did you ·pull [break] down our walls?
Now everyone who passes by ·steals from us [picks our fruit].
[13]Like ·wild pigs [Lboars of the forest] they ·walk over us [ravage us; gobble us up];
like ·wild animals [Lcreatures of the field] they feed on us.

[14]God ·All-Powerful [Almighty; of Heaven's Armies; Tof hosts], ·come back [restore us].
Look down from heaven and see.
Take care of us, your vine.
[15] You planted this ·shoot [root] with your own hands
and strengthened this child [Cthe king].
[16]Now it is cut down and burned with fire;
you destroyed us by ·your angry looks [Lthe rebuke of your face].
[17]·With your hand,
strengthen the one you have chosen for yourself [LLet your hand be on the man of your right hand; Cthe king].
[18]Then we will not ·turn away from [deviate from; be disloyal to] you.
Give us life again, and we will call ·to you for help [Lon your name].

[19]Lord God ·All-Powerful [Almighty; of Heaven's Armies; Tof hosts],
·take us back [restore us].

·Show us your kindness [LMake your face shine on us; 31:16; 67:1;
Num. 6:24–26] so we can ·be saved [have victory].

A Song for a Holiday

For the director of music. By the gittith [Cperhaps a musical term or instrument]. A psalm of Asaph [Ca Levitical musician, a descendant of Gershon, at the time of David; 1 Chr. 6:39; 15:17; 2 Chr. 5:12].

81 Sing for joy to God, our strength;
shout out loud to the God of Jacob [Canother name for Israel].
2·Begin the music [Lift up a psalm]. ·Play [Sound; LGive] the
tambourines [68:25; 149:3; 150:4; Ex. 15:20].
·Play pleasant music on the harps [L…the pleasant/sweet harps] and
lyres.
3Blow the ·trumpet [ram's horn] at ·the time of the New Moon [Lthe
month; Ca monthly religious festival],
when the moon is full, when our feast begins.
4This is the ·law [statute; ordinance; requirement] for Israel;
it is the ·command [judgment] of the God of Jacob [v. 1].
5He ·gave [set] this ·rule [decree; testimony] to the people of Joseph
[Creference to the northern tribes]
when they went out of the land of Egypt [Cthe exodus; Ex. 12–15].

I heard a ·language [Ltongue] I did not know, saying [CGod now speaks]:
6"I ·took the load off [removed the burden from] their shoulders;
·I let them put down their baskets [LTheir hands were removed from
the baskets].
7When you were in ·trouble [distress], you called, and I ·saved [rescued]
you.
I answered you ·with thunder [Lin the secret place of thunder; Ex.
19:18–19].
I tested you at the waters of Meribah [95:8; 106:32; Ex. 17:1–17;
Num. 20:1–13]. ·*Selah* [Interlude]
8My people, listen. I ·am warning [bear testimony/witness against] you.
Israel, please listen to me!
9You must not have ·foreign [strange] gods;
you must not worship any ·false [foreign] god.
10I, the LORD, am your God,
who brought you out of Egypt.
·Open [LWiden] your mouth and I will feed you [Deut. 29:6; 32:10–14].

11"But my people did not listen to ·me [Lmy voice];
Israel did not ·want [accept] me.
12So I ·let them go their stubborn way [Lthrew them away because of
their stubborn hearts]
and ·follow [walk according to] their own advice.
13I wish my people would listen to me;
I wish Israel would ·live [Lwalk on] my way.
14Then I would quickly ·defeat [subdue; quell] their enemies
and turn my hand against their foes.
15Those who hate the LORD would ·bow [cringe; cower] before him.
Their ·punishment [doom] would continue forever.
16But I would give you the finest wheat [Deut. 32:14]
and fill you with honey from the rocks [Deut. 32:13]."

A Cry for Justice

A psalm of Asaph [Ca Levitical musician, a descendant of Gershon, at the time of David; 1 Chr. 6:39; 15:17; 2 Chr. 5:12].

82 **God ·is in charge of the great meeting** [Ltakes his place/presides in the great assembly/*or* the assembly of the gods/divine council; Cthe angels (powers and authorities; Eph. 6:12) are here called "gods"];
he judges among the "gods" [John 10:35–36].
2**He says, "How long will you ·defend evil people** [*or* judge unfairly]?
How long will you show ·greater kindness [favor; preference] **to the wicked?** ·*Selah* [Interlude]
3**·Defend** [Judge] **the ·weak** [*or* poor] **and the orphans;**
·defend the rights of [vindicate] **the poor and ·suffering** [needy].
4**·Save** [Rescue] **the ·weak** [*or* poor] **and helpless;**
·free [protect] **them from the ·power** [Lhand] **of the wicked.**

5**"You know nothing. You don't understand.**
You walk in the dark,
while the ·world is falling apart [Lfoundations of the earth are tottering].
6**I said, 'You are "gods."**
You are all sons of God Most High.'
7**But you will die like any other person;**
you will fall like all the ·leaders [princes; CGod will punish these evil angels]."

8**God, ·come** [rise up] **and judge the earth,**
because you ·own [inherit] **all the nations.**

A Prayer Against the Enemies

A song. A psalm of Asaph [Ca Levitical musician, a descendant of Gershon, at the time of David; 1 Chr. 6:39; 15:17; 2 Chr. 5:12].

83 **God, do not keep quiet;**
God, do not be silent or still.
2**Your enemies are ·making noises** [in tumult];
those who hate you ·are getting ready to attack [Lraise up their head; 2:1].
3**They are making secret ·plans** [plots] **against your people;**
they plot against those you ·love [cherish; treasure].
4**They say, "Come, let's ·destroy them** [wipe them out] **as a nation.**
Then no one will ever remember the name 'Israel.'"
5**They ·are united in their plan** [Lplot with one mind/heart].
These have ·made an agreement [Lcut a covenant/treaty] **against you:**
6**the ·families** [Ltents] **of Edom and the Ishmaelites,**
Moab and the Hagrites,
7**the people of Byblos, Ammon, Amalek,**
Philistia, and inhabitants of Tyre.
8**Even Assyria has joined them**
to ·help Ammon and Moab, the [Lbe the arm of the] **descendants of Lot** [Ca list of traditional enemies of Israel]. ·*Selah* [Interlude]

9**God, do to them what you did to Midian,**
what you did to Sisera and Jabin at the Kishon ·River [Wadi; Judg. 4–5].
10**They ·died** [were destroyed] **at Endor,**
·and their bodies rotted [Llike dung/manure] **on the ground.**

[11]Do to their ·important leaders [princes; nobles] what you did to Oreb
and Zeeb [Judg. 7:25].
Do to their princes what you did to Zebah and Zalmunna [Judg. 8:21].
[12]They said, "Let's take for ourselves
the pasturelands that belong to God."
[13]My God, make them like tumbleweed,
like chaff blown ·away by [before] the wind [[C]rootless and landless; 1:4].
[14]Be like a fire that burns a forest
or like flames that blaze through the ·hills [mountains].
[15]·Chase [Pursue] them with your ·storm [tempest],
and ·frighten [terrify] them with your ·wind [hurricane].
[16]·Cover [[L]Fill] them with shame.
Then people will ·look for you [[L]seek your name], LORD.
[17]Make them afraid and ashamed forever.
·Disgrace [Humiliate] them and destroy them.
[18]Then they will know that ·you are the LORD [[L]the LORD is your name],
that only you are God Most High over all the earth.

Wishing to Be in the Temple

For the director of music. On the gittith [[C]perhaps a musical term or instrument]. A psalm of the sons of Korah [[C]descendants of Kohath, son of Levi, who served as temple musicians; 1 Chr. 6:22].

84 LORD ·All-Powerful [Almighty; of Heaven's Armies; [T]of hosts],
how lovely is your ·Temple [[L]residence; dwelling place]!
[2]I ·want more than anything
to be in [[L]long, even faint for] the courtyards of the ·LORD's Temple
[[L]LORD].
My ·whole being wants
to be with [[L]heart/mind and flesh sing for joy to] the living God.
[3]The sparrows have found a home,
and the swallows have nests.
They raise their young near your altars,
LORD ·All-Powerful [Almighty; of Heaven's Armies; [T]of hosts], my
King and my God.
[4]·Happy [Blessed] are the people who live at your ·Temple [[L]house];
they are always praising you. ·*Selah* [Interlude]

[5]·Happy [Blessed] are those whose strength comes from you,
·who want to travel to Jerusalem [[L]in whose hearts are highways;
[C]they want to make pilgrimage to Jerusalem to celebrate religious
festivals].
[6]As they pass through the Valley of Baca [[C]"weeping," location unknown],
they make it ·like [[L]a place with] a spring.
The ·autumn [early] rains ·fill [wrap; cover] it with ·pools of water
[*or* blessings].
[7]The people ·get stronger as they go [[L]go from strength to strength],
and everyone ·meets with [[L]sees] ·God [[L]the God of gods] in
·Jerusalem [[L]Zion; [C]the location of the Temple].

[8]LORD God ·All-Powerful [Almighty; of Heaven's Armies; [T]of hosts],
hear my prayer;
God of Jacob [[C]another name for Israel], ·listen to me [give ear].
·*Selah* [Interlude]

9 God, look at our shield [[C]the king];
be kind to your ·appointed king [anointed; Messiah; [C]the king,
ultimately Jesus; Acts 4:25–28].

10 One day in your courtyards is better
than a thousand days anywhere else.
I would rather be a doorkeeper in the Temple of my God
than live in the ·homes [[L]tents] of the wicked.
11 The LORD God is like a sun and shield;
the LORD gives us ·kindness [mercy; grace] and ·honor [glory].
He does not hold back anything good
from those ·whose lives are innocent [[L]who walk in innocence/
blamelessness].
12 LORD ·All-Powerful [Almighty; of Heaven's Armies; [T]of hosts],
·happy [blessed] are the people who ·trust [have confidence in] you!

A Prayer for the Nation

For the director of music. A psalm of the sons of Korah [[C]descendants
of Kohath, son of Levi, who served as temple musicians; 1 Chr. 6:22].

85

LORD, you ·have been kind to [delight in] your land;
you ·brought back [restored the fortunes of; [C]perhaps at the end
of the exile] the people of Jacob [[C]another name for Israel].
2 You forgave the guilt of the people
and covered all their sins. ·*Selah* [Interlude]
3 You ·stopped [drew back from] all your anger;
you turned back from your ·strong [burning] anger.

4 God our Savior, ·bring us back again [restore us again].
Stop being angry with us.
5 Will you be angry with us forever?
Will you ·stay angry [draw out your anger against us] from now on?
6 Won't you give us life again?
Your people would rejoice in you.
7 LORD, show us your ·love [loyalty],
and ·save us [[L]give to us your salvation/victory].

8 I will listen to what God the LORD says.
He has ·ordered [spoken; promised] ·peace [prosperity] for ·those
who worship him [[L]his people, his saints/loyal ones].
Don't let them go back to foolishness.
9 ·God will soon save those who respect him [[L]His salvation/victory is
near to those who fear him; Prov. 1:7],
and his glory will ·be seen [[L]dwell] in our land.
10 ·Love [Loyalty] and ·truth [faithfulness] ·belong to God's people
[[L]meet];
·goodness [righteousness] and ·peace [prosperity] ·will be theirs
[[L]kiss].
11 ·On earth people will be loyal to God [Faithfulness sprouts/blooms
from the earth/land],
and ·God's goodness [righteousness] will ·shine [look] down from
heaven.
12 The LORD will give his ·goodness [*or* good gifts],
and the land will give its crops.

[13]·Goodness [Righteousness] will go before ·God [[L]him]
and prepare the way for ·him [[L]his steps].

A prayer of David.

A Cry for Help

86 LORD, ·listen to me [[L]incline your ear] and answer me.
I am poor and ·helpless [needy].
[2]·Protect [Guard] me, because I ·worship you [am loyal/holy/a saint].
My God, ·save me [give me victory], your servant who ·trusts [has confidence] in you.
[3]Lord, ·have mercy on [be gracious to] me,
because I have called to you all day.
[4]Give ·happiness [joy] to me, your servant,
because I ·give [lift up] my life to you, Lord.
[5]Lord, you are ·kind [good] and forgiving
and have great ·love [loyalty] for those who call to you [Ex. 34:7].
[6]LORD, ·hear [[L]give ear to] my prayer,
and ·listen [pay attention] ·when I ask for mercy [[L]to the sound of my supplication].
[7]I call to you in ·times of trouble [[L]the day of my distress],
because you will answer me.

[8]Lord, there is ·no god like you [[L]none like you among the gods; Ex. 15:11; 20:3]
and no works like yours.
[9]Lord, all the nations you have made
will come and ·worship [bow down before] you.
They will ·honor you [[L]glorify your name].
[10]You are great and you do ·miracles [wonderful acts].
Only you are God.
[11]LORD, teach me ·what you want me to do [[L]your way],
and I will ·live [walk] ·by your truth [in your faithfulness].
·Teach me to respect you completely [[L]Give me an undivided heart to fear your name].
[12]Lord, my God, I will ·praise [thank] you with all my heart,
and I will ·honor [glorify] your name forever.
[13]You have great ·love [loyalty] for me.
You have ·saved [[T]delivered] me from ·death [[L]Sheol down below; [C]the grave or the underworld].

[14]God, ·proud [arrogant] people ·are attacking [rise up against] me;
a ·gang [assembly] of ·cruel [violent] people ·is trying to kill me [seek my life].
They do not ·respect you [[L]set you before them].
[15]But, Lord, you are a God who shows ·mercy [compassion] and is ·kind [merciful; compassionate].
You ·don't become angry quickly [are patient/longsuffering].
You have great ·love [loyalty] and ·faithfulness [truth; Ex. 34:6–7].
[16]Turn to me and ·have mercy [be gracious].
Give me, your servant, strength.
·Save [Give victory to] me, the son of your female servant.
[17]·Show [[L]Give] me a sign of your goodness.
When my enemies look, they will be ashamed.
You, LORD, have helped me and comforted me.

God Loves Jerusalem

A song. A psalm of the sons of Korah [Cdescendants of Kohath, son of Levi, who served as temple musicians; 1 Chr. 6:22].

87 **·The Lord built Jerusalem** [LIts foundations are] **on the holy mountain** [CZion, the location of the Temple].
2**·He** [LThe Lord] **loves ·its gates** [Lthe gates of Zion] **more than any other place in ·Israel** [LJacob].
3**City of God,**
·wonderful [glorious] **things are said about you** [46; 48; Is. 2:2–4; 26:1–2; 60:15–22; 61:1–7]. ***·Selah*** [Interlude]

4**God says, "I will ·put Egypt and Babylonia**
on the list of nations that know me [Lmention Rahab and Babylonia as those who know me].
People from Philistia, Tyre, and Cush [CEthiopia]
will be born there."
5**They will say about ·Jerusalem** [LZion; Cthe location of the Temple],
"This one and that one were born there.
God Most High will ·strengthen [establish] **her."**
6**The Lord will keep a list of the nations.**
He will note, "This person was born there." ***·Selah*** [Interlude]

7**They will dance and sing,**
"All ·good things come from Jerusalem [Lmy fountains are in you; 46:4; Jer. 2:13; Ezek. 47; Rev. 22:1–5]."

A Sad Complaint

A song. A psalm of the sons of Korah [Cdescendants of Kohath, son of Levi, who served as temple musicians; 1 Chr. 6:22]. **For the director of music. By the ·mahalath** [Cperhaps "sickness"; Ps. 53] **·leannoth** [Cperhaps related to a word for "affliction" or a word for "chant"]. **A ·maskil** [skillful psalm; meditation] **of Heman the Ezrahite** [Cperhaps a wise man (1 Kin. 4:31) or a Levitical singer (1 Chr. 6:16, 33, 39, 43–44; 15:17, 19)].

88 **Lord, you are the God who ·saves me** [gives me victory].
I cry out to you day and night.
2**Receive my prayer,**
and ·listen [Lextend your ear] **to my cry.**

3**My life is full of ·troubles** [hurt; harm],
and ·I am nearly dead [Lmy life approaches/touches Sheol; Cthe grave or the underworld].
4**They think I am ·on the way to my grave** [Llike someone who goes down into the Pit].
I am like a man with no strength.
5**I have been ·left as dead** [Lfreed among the dead],
like a ·body [corpse] **lying in a grave**
whom you don't remember anymore,
cut off from your ·care [Lhand].
6**You have ·brought me close to death** [Lset me in a Pit below];
·I am almost in the dark place of the dead [L…in the deepest darkness].
7**You have ·been very angry with** [Lput your wrath on] **me;**
·all your waves crush me [Lyou have afflicted me with all your breakers]. ***·Selah*** [Interlude]

8You have ·taken [moved] my friends away from me
and have made ·them hate me [me an abomination to them].
I am ·trapped [imprisoned] and cannot ·escape [get out].
9 My eyes ·are weak [waste away] from ·crying [affliction].
LORD, I have ·prayed [called] to you every day;
I have ·lifted [spread out] my hands to you [Cin prayer].

10Do you ·show [Ldo] your ·miracles [wonderful acts] for the dead?
Do their ·spirits [shades; departed] rise up and ·praise [thank] you?
·*Selah* [Interlude]

11Will your ·love [loyalty] be ·told [recounted] in the grave?
Will your ·loyalty [faithfulness] be told in ·the place of death
[LAbaddon/Destruction]?
12Will your ·miracles [wonderful acts] be known in the ·dark grave
[Ldarkness]?
Will your ·goodness [righteousness] be known in the land of
forgetfulness?

13But, LORD, I have called out to you for help;
every morning ·I pray to you [Lmy prayer comes before you].
14LORD, why do you reject me?
Why do you hide your face from me?
15I have been ·weak [afflicted] and dying since I was young.
I suffer from your terrors, and I am ·helpless [*or* depressed].
16·You have been angry with me [LYour wrath has passed over me],
and your terrors have ·destroyed [*or* silenced] me.
17They surround me daily like ·a flood [water; Crepresenting chaos];
they ·are [go] all around me.
18You have ·taken away [removed me from] my loved ones and friends.
Darkness is my only friend.

A Song About God's Loyalty

A ·maskil [skillful psalm; meditation] of Ethan the Ezrahite
[Ca wise man; 1 Kin. 4:31].

89 I will always sing about the LORD's ·love [loyalty];
I will ·tell of [Lmake known with my mouth] his ·loyalty
[faithfulness] ·from now on [for generations].
2I will say, "Your ·love [loyalty] ·continues [Lis built] forever;
your ·loyalty [faithfulness] ·goes on and on [is established] like the
·sky [heavens]."
3You said, "I ·made an agreement [Lcut a covenant/treaty] with the man
of my choice;
I made a promise to my servant David.
4I told him, 'I will ·make your family continue [Lestablish your seed]
forever.
·Your kingdom will go on and on [LI will build your throne for
generations; 2; 72; 78:70–72; 2 Sam. 7:11–16; 1 Chr. 17:10–14].' "
·*Selah* [Interlude]

5LORD, the heavens praise you for your ·miracles [wonderful acts]
and for your ·loyalty [faithfulness] in the ·meeting [assembly] of
your holy ones.

[6]Who in ·heaven [the skies] ·is equal to [ranks with] the Lord?
None of the ·angels [gods; divine council/assembly; [L]sons of God; 82:1] is like the Lord.
[7]When the ·holy ones [[L]council of holy ones] meet, it is God they fear.
He is more ·frightening [awesome] than all who surround him.
[8]Lord God ·All-Powerful [Almighty; of Heaven's Armies; [T]of hosts], who is like you?
Lord, you are powerful and completely ·trustworthy [faithful].
[9]You rule the ·mighty [raging; surging] sea
and ·calm [still] the ·stormy [rising] waves.
[10]You crushed the Rahab [[C]a sea monster, representing chaos (Job 26:12; Is. 51:9) and in some contexts Egypt defeated at the Sea (87:4; Is. 30:7; Ezek. 29:3; 32:3)] like a corpse;
by your ·power [[L]strong arm] you scattered your enemies.

[11]The ·skies [heavens] and the earth belong to you.
You ·made [founded] the world and ·everything in it [[L]its fullness].
[12]You created the north and the south.
Mount Tabor and Mount Hermon [[C]majestic mountains] sing for joy at your name.
[13]Your arm has great power.
Your hand is strong; your right hand is lifted up.
[14]Your ·kingdom [[L]throne] is ·built [established] on ·what is right and fair [righteousness and judgment/justice].
·Love [Loyalty] and ·truth [faithfulness] are ·in all you do [[L]before your face].

[15]·Happy [Blessed] are the people who know how to ·praise [shout to] you.
Lord, let them ·live [[L]walk] in the light of your ·presence [[L]face].
[16]In your name they rejoice
and continually ·praise [exalt] your ·goodness [righteousness].
[17]You are their ·glorious [beautiful] strength,
and in your ·kindness [favor] you ·honor our king [[L]lift up our horn; [C]symbol of power and here of the king].
[18]Our shield [[C]the king] belongs to the Lord,
our king to the Holy One of Israel.

[19]·Once [Then], in a vision [2 Sam. 7:4], you spoke
to ·those who worship you [your faithful ones/saints].
You said, "I have ·given strength to [[L]set help on] a warrior;
I have raised up a ·young man [chosen one] from my people [1 Sam. 13:14; Acts 13:22].
[20]I have found my servant David;
I ·appointed him by pouring [[L]have anointed him with] holy oil on him [1 Sam. 16:1–13].
[21]I will steady him with my hand
and strengthen him with my arm.
[22]No enemy will ·make him give forced payments [make him pay tribute; *or* prevail over/*or* outwit him],
and wicked people will not ·defeat [afflict; humble] him.
[23]I will ·crush [pound] his enemies in front of him;
I will ·defeat [strike down] those who hate him.

[24]My ·loyalty [faithfulness] and ·love [loyalty] will be with him.
Through ·me [Lmy name] ·he will be strong [Lhis horn will be raised up; v. 17].
[25]I will ·give him power [Lset his hand] over the sea
·and control [Lhis right hand] over the rivers [Cthe waters represent chaos].
[26]He will ·say [proclaim] to me, 'You are my father,
my God, the Rock, my ·Savior [Victor].'
[27]I will make him my firstborn son,
the ·greatest [highest] king on earth [2:7; 2 Sam. 7:14].
[28]My ·love [loyalty] will ·watch over [keep; guard] him forever,
and my ·agreement [covenant; treaty] with him will ·never end [be faithful].
[29]I will ·make his family continue [Lset his seed forever],
and his ·kingdom [Lthrone] ·will last as long as the skies [Llike the days of the skies/heavens].

[30]"If his descendants ·reject [leave; abandon] my ·teachings [instructions; laws]
and do not ·follow [Lwalk in] my ·laws [judgments],
[31]if they ·ignore [profane] my ·demands [statutes; ordinances; requirements]
and ·disobey [Ldo not keep/guard] my commands,
[32]then I will punish their ·sins [transgressions] with a rod
and their ·wrongs [guilt] with ·a whip [lashes].
[33]But I will not ·hold back [break; invalidate] my ·love [loyalty] from ·David [Lhim],
nor will I ·stop being loyal [Ldeal falsely with my faithfulness].
[34]I will not ·break [profane; violate] my ·agreement [covenant; treaty]
nor ·change [alter] what ·I have said [Lcame out of my lips].
[35]Once and for all I have ·promised [sworn] by my holiness,
I will not lie to David.
[36]His ·family [Lseed] will go on forever.
His ·kingdom [Lthrone] will last before me like the sun.
[37]It will ·continue [be established] forever, like the moon,
like a ·dependable [reliable; faithful] witness in the sky."
·*Selah* [Interlude]

[38]But now you have ·refused [spurned] and rejected him.
You have been angry with your ·appointed king [Lanointed; v. 20].
[39]You have ·abandoned [disavowed] the ·agreement [covenant; treaty] with your servant
and ·thrown [profaned; defiled] his crown ·to [*or* in] the ground [Jer. 13:18–19].
[40]You have ·torn down [broken up] all his city walls;
you have turned his strong cities into ruins.
[41]Everyone who passes by ·steals from [plunders] him.
·His neighbors insult him [LHe is scorned by/a reproach to his neighbors].
[42]You have ·given strength of [Lexalted the right hand of] his ·enemies [foes]
and have made ·them all [Lall his enemies] happy.

[43]You have ·made his sword useless [turned back the blade/[L]rock of his sword];
you did not help him stand in battle.
[44]You have ·kept him from winning [*or* put aside his purity]
and have thrown his throne to the ground.
[45]You have cut ·his life [[L]the days of his youth] short
and ·covered [wrapped] him with shame. ·*Selah* [Interlude]

[46]LORD, how long will this go on?
Will you ·ignore [hide from] us forever?
How long will your anger burn like a fire?
[47]Remember how ·short [fleeting] my life is.
Why did you create us? For ·nothing [futility; vanity; no purpose]?
[48]What person alive will not ·die [[L]see death]?
Who can escape ·the grave [[L]from the hand/power of Sheol; [C]the grave or the underworld]? ·*Selah* [Interlude]

[49]Lord, where is your ·love [loyalty] from times past,
which in your ·loyalty [faithfulness] you ·promised [swore] to David [2 Sam. 7:11–14]?
[50]Lord, remember ·how they insulted [[L]the reproach/scorn of] your servant;
remember how I ·have suffered the insults of the nations [[L]carry in my bosom all of the many peoples].
[51]LORD, remember how your enemies ·insulted [reproached; scorned] you
and how they ·insulted [reproached; scorned] ·your appointed king wherever he went [[L]the footsteps of your anointed; v. 20].

[52]·Praise [Blessed be] the LORD forever!
Amen and amen.

Book 4: Psalms 90–106

God Is Eternal, and We Are Not

A prayer of Moses, the man of God.

90 Lord, you have been our ·home [dwelling place; Deut. 33:27]
·since the beginning [[L]from all generations].
[2]Before the mountains were born
and before you ·created [brought forth] the earth and the world,
you are God [Prov. 8:22–31].
You have always been, and you will always be.

[3]You turn people back into ·dust [[L]what is crushed; Gen. 2:7; 3:19; Eccl. 12:7].
You say, "·Go back into dust [[L]Return; Turn back], human beings."
[4]·To you [[L]In your eyes], a thousand years
is like the passing of a day [2 Pet. 3:8],
or ·like a few hours [[L]a watch; [C]the night was divided into four watches of three hours each] in the night.
[5]While people sleep, you ·take [put an end to] their lives.
They are like grass that ·grows up [is new] in the morning.
[6]In the morning they ·are fresh and new [blossom and are renewed],
but by evening they ·dry up [fade] and ·die [wither].

7We are ·destroyed [annihilated] by your anger;
we are terrified by your hot anger.
8You have ·put [set] ·the evil we have done [our guilt/iniquity] right in front of you;
·you clearly see our secret sins [Lour hidden/secret sins in the light of your face].
9All our days pass while you are angry.
Our years end with a ·moan [sigh].
10·Our lifetime is [LThe days of our years are] seventy years
or, if we are strong, eighty years.
But ·the years are full of [Ltheir pride are] ·hard work [toil] and ·pain [trouble; Eccl. 1:2].
They pass quickly, and then we ·are gone [Lfly away].

11Who knows the ·full power [strength] of your anger?
Your anger is as great as our fear of you should be.
12·Teach us [Make us know] ·how short our lives really are [Lto count our days]
so that we ·may be wise [Lgain a wise heart].

13Lord, how long before you ·return [turn]
and show ·kindness [compassion] to your servants?
14·Fill [Satisfy] us with your ·love [loyalty] every morning.
Then we will sing and rejoice all our ·lives [Ldays].
15We have seen years of ·trouble [harm; hurt].
Now give us as ·much [Lmany days of] joy as you gave us ·sorrow [affliction].
16Show your servants ·the wonderful things you do [your miracles];
·show your greatness [your splendor/beauty] to their children.
17Lord our God, ·treat us well [favor us].
·Give us success in what we do [LEstablish the work of our hands for us];
·yes, give us success in what we do [Lestablish the work of our hands].

Safe in the Lord

91 Those who ·go to God Most High for safety [Ldwell/sit in the shelter of God Most High]
will ·be protected by [lodge in the shade/shadow of] the Almighty.
2I will say to the Lord, "You are my ·place of safety [refuge] and ·protection [fortress].
You are my God and I ·trust [have confidence in] you."

3God will ·save [protect] you from ·hidden traps [Lthe snare of the fowler]
and from deadly ·diseases [pestilence].
4He will cover you with his feathers,
and under his wings you ·can hide [will find refuge; Deut. 32:11; Is. 31:5; Matt. 23:37; Luke 13:34].
His ·truth [faithfulness] will be your shield and ·protection [buckler; Ca small shield].
5You will not fear any ·danger by [terror at] night
or an arrow that flies during the day.
6·You will not be afraid of diseases [L...or the pestilence] that ·come [walks; stalks] in the dark
or ·sickness [Lstings] that ·strikes [devastates; overpowers] at noon.

[7]At your side one thousand people may ·die [Lfall],
or even ten thousand ·right beside you [Lat your right hand],
but ·you will not be hurt [Lit will not touch you].
[8]You will only ·watch [Llook with your eyes]
and see the wicked ·punished [recompensed].

[9]·The LORD is your protection [LFor you, LORD, are my refuge];
you have made God Most High your ·place of safety [dwelling place].
[10]Nothing ·bad [evil; harmful] will ·happen to [befall] you;
no ·disaster [blow; *or* plague] will ·come to [approach] your ·home [Ltent].
[11]He has ·put his angels in charge of [Lcommanded his angels/
messengers concerning] you
to ·watch over [keep; guard] ·you wherever you go [Lall your ways].
[12]They will ·catch you [lift you up] in their hands
so that you will not hit your foot on a rock [Matt. 4:6; Luke 4:10–11].
[13]You will ·walk [tread] on lions and cobras;
you will ·step on [trample] strong lions and snakes.

[14]The LORD says, "Whoever ·loves [desires] me, I will ·save [rescue].
I will ·protect [lift to safety] those who know ·me [Lmy name].
[15]They will call to me, and I will answer them.
I will be with them in ·trouble [distress];
I will rescue them and ·honor [glorify] them.
[16]I will ·give them a long, full life [Lsatisfy them with length of days],
and ·they will see how I can save [Lshow them my salvation/victory]."

Thanksgiving for God's Goodness

A psalm. A song for the Sabbath day [Ex. 20:8–11; Deut. 5:12–15].

92 It is good to ·praise [thank] you, LORD,
to ·sing praises to [Lmake a psalm to the name of] God Most
High.
[2]It is good to ·tell of [proclaim] your ·love [loyalty] in the morning
and of your ·loyalty [faithfulness] at night.
[3]It is good to praise you with the ten-stringed lyre
and ·with the soft-sounding [melody of the] harp.

[4]LORD, you have made me ·happy [rejoice] by what you have done;
I will ·sing [shout] for joy about ·what your hands have done [Lthe
works of your hand].
[5]LORD, ·you have done such great things [Lhow great are your works]!
How deep are your thoughts [Is. 55:8; Rom. 11:33–34]!
[6]·Stupid [Senseless; Dull-witted] people don't know these things,
and fools don't understand.
[7]Wicked people ·grow [may sprout] like the grass.
Evil people ·seem to do well [may blossom/flourish],
but they will be ·destroyed [doomed] forever.
[8]But, LORD, you will be ·honored [exalted] forever.

[9]LORD, surely your enemies,
surely your enemies will ·be destroyed [perish],
and all who do evil will be scattered.
[10]But you have ·made me as strong as [exalted my horn like; Csymbol of
strength] an ox.

You have poured ·fine [rich; fresh] oils on me [Ca gesture of
hospitality].
11When ·I [Lmy eyes] looked, I saw my enemies;
I heard the cries of those who ·are against me [Lrose against me with
evil; Che sees and hears the defeat of his enemies].

12But ·good [righteous] people will ·grow [sprout] like palm trees [1:3;
52:8];
they will ·be tall [grow great] like the cedars of Lebanon [Ctrees that
are strong, majestic, and long-lived].
13Like trees planted in the ·Temple [Lhouse] of the LORD,
they will ·grow strong [sprout] in the courtyards of our God.
14When they are old, they will still produce fruit;
they will be healthy and ·fresh [green; verdant].
15They will ·say [proclaim] that the LORD is ·good [virtuous; full of
integrity; upright].
He is my Rock [28:1; 42:9; 62:2; Deut. 32:4], and there is no wrong in
him.

The Majesty of the Lord

93 The LORD ·is king [reigns; 47:2; 96:10; 97:1; 98:6; 99:1; Rev. 19:6].
He is ·clothed [robed] in majesty.
The LORD is ·clothed [robed] in majesty
and ·armed [girded] with strength.
The world is ·set [established],
and it ·cannot be moved [will not totter].
2LORD, your ·kingdom [Lthrone] was ·set up [established] long ago;
you are everlasting.

3LORD, the ·seas [Lrivers; Cperhaps referring to currents within the sea] raise,
the ·seas [Lrivers] raise their voice.
The ·seas [Lrivers] raise up their pounding waves [Crepresenting
chaos].
4The sound of the water is loud;
the ·ocean waves [Lbreakers of the sea] are ·powerful [majestic],
but the LORD above is much ·greater [more powerful/majestic; CGod
is in control of chaos].

5LORD, your ·laws [decrees; testimonies] ·will stand forever [are very
faithful/true].
·Your Temple will be holy forevermore [LAt your house holiness is
fitting/appropriate and will be for length of days].

God Will Pay Back His Enemies

94 The LORD is a God ·who punishes [of vengeance; Deut. 32:35;
Is. 34:8; Ezek. 24:8; 25:14–17; Nah. 1:2; Rom. 12:19; 1 Thess. 4:6].
·God, show your greatness and punish [LGod of vengeance, shine
forth]!
2Rise up, Judge of the earth,
and give the ·proud [arrogant] ·what they deserve [their due].
3How long will the wicked be ·happy [joyful]?
How long, LORD?

4They ·are full of [Lbubble forth, speaking] ·proud [insolent] words;
those who do evil ·brag about what they have done [Ltalk a lot].

[5]**LORD, they crush your people**
and ·make your children suffer [[L]afflict your inheritance].
[6]**They kill widows and ·foreigners** [sojourners; wanderers]
and murder orphans [Ex. 22:21–24].
[7]**They say, "The LORD doesn't see;**
the God of Jacob [[C]another name for Israel] **doesn't ·notice** [understand]."

[8]**You ·stupid** [senseless; dull witted] **ones among the people, ·pay attention** [[L]understand].
You fools, when will you ·understand [get insight]?
[9]**Can't the ·creator** [[L]planter] **of ears hear?**
Can't the ·maker [former; shaper] **of eyes see?**
[10]**Won't the one who ·corrects** [instructs; disciplines] **nations ·punish** [reprimand; reprove] **you?**
Doesn't the teacher of people know everything?
[11]**The LORD knows ·what people think** [[L]the thoughts of humans].
He knows their thoughts are ·just a puff of wind [a bubble/vapor/meaningless/futile; Eccl. 1:2].

[12]**LORD, those you ·correct** [instruct; discipline] **are ·happy** [blessed];
you teach them from your ·law [instruction; teaching].
[13]**You give them ·rest** [peace; quiet] **from ·times** [[L]days] **of ·trouble** [harm; evil]
until a pit is dug for the wicked [Prov. 26:7; Eccl. 10:8].
[14]**The LORD won't ·leave** [abandon; cast off] **his people**
nor ·give up [abandon; forsake] **his ·children** [[L]inheritance].
[15]**Judgment will again be ·fair** [just; righteous],
and all who are ·honest [[L]upright/virtuous of heart] **will follow it.**

[16]**Who will ·help me fight** [[L]rise up with me] **against the wicked?**
Who will stand with me against those who do evil?
[17]**If the LORD had not helped me,**
I would have ·died in a minute [[L]quickly dwelled in silence].
[18]**I said, "·I am about to fall** [[L]My feet totter],"
but, LORD, your ·love [loyalty] **·kept me safe** [steadied/supported me].
[19]**·I was very worried** [[L]In my many disquieting thoughts in my insides],
but you comforted me and ·made me happy [cheered me up].

[20]**·Crooked leaders** [[L]Ruinous thrones] **cannot be your ·friends** [allies].
They use the ·law [statute; ordinance; requirement] **to cause ·suffering** [distress].
[21]**They ·join forces** [band together] **against ·people who do right** [righteous people]
and ·sentence [condemn] **to death the innocent.**
[22]**But the LORD is my ·defender** [stronghold; fortress];
my God is the rock [28:1; 42:9; 62:2; Deut. 32:4] **of my ·protection** [refuge].
[23]**God will pay them back for their ·sins** [guilt; iniquity]
and will destroy them for their evil.
The LORD our God will destroy them.

A Call to Praise and Obedience

95 Come, let's sing for joy to the LORD.
Let's shout praises to the Rock [28:1; 42:9; 62:2; Deut. 32:4] who ·saves us [gives us victory].
2 Let's ·come [present ourselves] to him with ·thanksgiving [praise].
Let's ·sing songs [shout psalms] to him,
3 because the LORD is the great God,
the great King over all gods [Ex. 15:11].
4 The deepest places on earth are ·his [Lin his hand],
and the ·highest [peaks of the] mountains belong to him.
5 The sea is his because he made it,
and he created the ·land [dry ground] with his own hands.

6 Come, let's ·worship him [bow down] and ·bow down [bend the knee].
Let's kneel before the LORD who made us,
7 because he is our God
and we are the people ·he takes care of [Lof his pasture],
the sheep ·that he tends [Lof his hand; 74:1; 79:13; 100:3; John 10:11–14].

Today listen to ·what he says [Lhis voice]:
8 "Do not ·be stubborn [Lharden your heart], as at Meribah [C"contending"; 81:7; 106:32; Ex. 17:1–17; Num. 20:1–13],
as that day at Massah [C"testing"] in the ·desert [wilderness; Heb. 4:7].
9 There your ·ancestors [fathers] tested me
and tried me even though they saw what I did.
10 I ·was angry with [felt disgust for] ·those people [Lthat generation] for forty years.
I said, 'They are ·not loyal to me [La people whose hearts wander/go astray]
and have not understood my ways.'
11 I was angry and made a promise,
'They will never enter my rest.'"

Praise for the Lord's Glory

96 Sing to the LORD a new song [Ccelebrating victory; 33:3; 40:3; 98:1; 144:9; 149:1; Is. 42:10; Rev. 5:9; 14:3];
sing to the LORD, all the earth.
2 Sing to the LORD and ·praise [bless] his name;
every day ·tell [announce the good news] ·how he saves us [Lof his salvation/victory].
3 Tell the nations of his glory [Chis manifest presence];
tell all peoples the ·miracles [wonderful acts] he does,

4 because the LORD is great; he should be praised ·at all times [*or* with vigor].
He ·should be honored [is awesome; should be feared] more than all the gods,
5 because all the gods of the nations are ·only idols [*or* worthless],
but the LORD made the heavens [Gen. 1].
6 The LORD has ·glory [splendor] and majesty;
he has power and beauty in his ·Temple [sanctuary; LHoly Place].

7 ·Praise [LAscribe to] the LORD, all ·nations on earth [Lfamilies of peoples];
·praise the LORD's [Lascribe to the LORD] glory and power.

[8]·Praise the glory of the LORD's [[L]Ascribe to the LORD the glory of his] name.
Bring an ·offering [grain/gift/tribute sacrifice; Lev. 2:1] and come into his Temple courtyards.
[9]·Worship [Bow down to] the LORD ·because he is holy [[L]in the splendor of his holiness].
Tremble before him, everyone on earth.
[10]Tell the nations, "The LORD ·is king [reigns; 47:2; 93:1; 97:1; 98:6; 99:1; Rev. 19:6]."
The earth is ·set [established], and it cannot be moved.
He will judge the people fairly.
[11]Let the ·skies [heavens] rejoice and the earth be glad;
let the sea and everything in it ·shout [thunder; roar].
12 Let the fields and everything in them rejoice.
Then all the trees of the forest will sing for joy
13 before the LORD, because he is coming.
He is coming to judge the world;
he will judge the world with ·fairness [righteousness]
and the peoples with ·truth [faithfulness; 98:9].

A Hymn About the Lord's Power

97 The LORD ·is king [reigns; 47:2; 93:1; 96:10; 98:6; 99:1; Rev. 19:6].
Let the earth rejoice;
·faraway lands [*or* islands; *or* coastlands] should be glad.
[2]Thick, dark clouds surround him.
His ·kingdom [[L]throne] is ·built [established] on ·what is right [righteousness] and ·fair [justice].
[3]A fire goes before him
and ·burns up [flames] his enemies all around.
[4]His lightning ·lights up [illuminates] the world;
when the ·people [earth] see it, they ·tremble [writhe].
[5]The mountains melt like wax before the LORD,
before the Lord of all the earth.
[6]The heavens ·tell about [declare] his ·goodness [righteousness],
and all the people see his glory [[C]his manifest presence].

[7]Those who ·worship [serve] idols should be ·ashamed [embarrassed; Is. 42:17; 45:16];
they brag about their ·gods [worthless things].
All the gods should ·worship [bow down to] the LORD.
[8]When ·Jerusalem [[L]Zion; [C]the location of the Temple] hears this, she is glad,
and the ·towns [[L]daughters] of Judah rejoice.
They are happy because of your judgments, LORD.
[9]You are the LORD Most High over all the earth;
you are ·supreme [exalted] over all gods.

[10]People who love the LORD hate evil.
The LORD ·watches over [keeps; guards] ·those who follow him [his loyal ones/saints]
and ·frees [rescues] them from the ·power [[L]hand] of the wicked.
[11]Light ·shines [[L]is sown] on ·those who do right [the righteous];
joy belongs to those who are ·honest [[L]virtuous/upright in heart].

12Rejoice in the LORD, you who ·do right [are righteous].
Praise his ·holy name [*or* unforgettable holiness].

A psalm.

The Lord of Power and Justice

98 Sing to the LORD a new song [Ccelebrating victory; 33:3; 40:3; 96:1; 144:9; 149:1; Is. 42:10; Rev. 5:9; 14:3],
because he has done ·miracles [wonderful acts].
By his right hand and holy arm
he has won the victory.
2The LORD has made known his ·power to save [salvation; victory];
he has ·shown [revealed to] ·the other [Lbefore the eyes of the] nations his ·victory for his people [righteousness].
3He has remembered his ·love [loyalty]
and his ·loyalty [faithfulness] to the ·people [Lhouse] of Israel.
All the ends of the earth have seen
God's ·power to save [salvation; victory].

4Shout with joy to the LORD, all the earth;
·burst into songs [Lbreak forth and sing for joy] and make ·music [a psalm].
5Make music to the LORD with harps,
with harps and the sound of singing.
6Blow the trumpets and the ·sheep's [ram's] horns;
shout for joy to the LORD the King [47:2; 93:1; 96:10; 97:1; 99:1; Rev. 19:6].

7Let the sea and ·everything in it [its fullness] ·shout [thunder];
let the world and everyone in it sing.
8Let the rivers clap their hands;
let the mountains sing together for joy.
9Let them sing before the LORD,
because he is coming to judge the world.
He will judge the world ·fairly [with righteousness];
he will judge the peoples with fairness [96:13].

The Lord, the Fair and Holy King

99 The LORD ·is king [reigns; 47:2; 93:1; 96:10; 97:1; 98:6; Rev. 19:6].
Let the peoples ·shake [tremble; Cwith fear].
He sits between the ·gold creatures with wings [Lcherubim; Cabove the Ark of the Covenant; Ex. 25:17–22; 1 Kin. 8:7].
Let the earth shake.
2The LORD in ·Jerusalem [LZion; Cthe location of the Temple] is great;
he is ·supreme [exalted] over all the peoples.
3Let them ·praise [thank] your name;
it is great, holy and ·to be feared [awesome].

4The King is ·powerful [strong] and loves justice.
LORD, you ·made [established] things fair;
you have done what is ·fair [righteous] and ·right [just]
for the people of Jacob [Canother name for Israel].
5·Praise [Exalt] the LORD our God,
and ·worship [bow down] at the footstool of his feet [Cthe Ark located in the Temple].
He is holy.

[6]Moses and Aaron were among his priests,
and Samuel was among ·his worshipers [Lthose who called on his name].
They called to the LORD,
and he answered them [Ex. 32:11–13, 30–32; Num. 12:13; 14:13–19;
1 Sam. 7:5, 8–9; 12:16–18; Jer. 15:1].
[7]He spoke to them from the pillar of cloud [Ex. 13:21].
They ·kept [observed; guarded] the ·rules [statutes; ordinances;
requirements] and ·laws [decrees; testimonies] he gave them.

[8]LORD our God, you answered them.
You showed them that you are a forgiving God,
but you ·punished them [are an avenger] for their wrongs [Deut. 32:35;
Is. 34:8; Ezek. 24:8; 25:14–17; Nah. 1:2; Rom. 12:19; 1 Thess. 4:6].
[9]·Praise [Exalt] the LORD our God,
and ·worship [bow down] at his holy mountain,
because the LORD our God is holy.

A Call to Praise the Lord

A psalm of thanks.

100 Shout to the LORD, all the earth.
[2] Serve the LORD with joy;
come before him with singing.
[3]Know that the LORD is God.
He made us [Gen. 1–2], and ·we belong to him [*or* not ourselves];
we are his people, the sheep ·he tends [Lof his pasture; 74:1; 79:13;
John 10:11–14].

[4]Come into his ·city [Lgates] with songs of thanksgiving
and into his courtyards with songs of praise.
·Thank [Praise] him and ·praise [bless] his name.
[5]The LORD is good. His ·love [loyalty] is forever,
and his ·loyalty [faithfulness] ·goes on and on [Lfor all generations].

A Promise to Rule Well

A psalm of David.

101 I will sing of your ·love [loyalty] and ·fairness [justice; judgment];
LORD, I will ·sing praises [make a psalm] to you.
[2]I will ·be careful to live [lead; *or* study] ·an innocent life [the way that is
blameless].
When will ·you [*or* it; Cthe "way that is blameless"] come to me?

I will ·live [go; walk] ·an innocent life [Lin the blamelessness of my
heart] in my house.
[3] I will not ·look at [Lset before my eyes] anything ·wicked [vile].
I hate those who ·turn against you [are crooked/transgressors];
they will not ·be found near [cling to] me.
[4]Let those who ·want to do wrong [Lhave a perverse heart] stay away
from me;
I ·will have nothing to do with [Ldo not know] evil.
[5]If anyone secretly ·says things against [slanders] his neighbor,
I will ·stop [destroy; silence] him.
I will not allow people
to ·be proud [Lhave broad hearts] and ·look down on others
[Lhaughty eyes; 131:1].

[6]·I will look for trustworthy people [[L]My eyes are on the faithful of the land]
so ·I can live with them [[L]they may dwell with me].
Only those who ·live innocent lives [[L]walk in the way of blamelessness]
will ·be my servants [[L]serve me].
[7]No one who ·is dishonest [deceives] will live in my house;
no ·liars [[L]one who speaks falsehoods] will ·stay around me [[L]be established before my eyes].
[8]Every morning I will ·destroy [silence] all the wicked in the land.
I will ·rid [cut off] the LORD's city [[C]Jerusalem; 46:4] of people who do evil.

A Cry for Help

A prayer of a person who is suffering when he is ·discouraged [faint; disturbed] and ·tells the LORD his complaints [[L]pours out his concerns before the LORD].

102 LORD, listen to my prayer;
let my cry for help come to you.
[2]Do not hide your ·presence [[L]face] from me
in my time of ·trouble [distress].
·Pay attention [[L]Extend your ear] to me.
·When I cry for help [[L]On the day I call], answer me quickly.
[3]My ·life [[L]days] is ·passing away [vanishing] like smoke,
and my bones are burned up ·with fire [[L]like a furnace/oven/*or* glowing embers].
[4]My heart is like grass
that has been ·cut [stricken] and dried.
I forget to eat my ·food [*or* bread].
[5]Because of ·my grief [[L]the sounds of my groans],
my ·skin hangs on my bones [[L]bones cling to my flesh].
[6]I am like a ·desert [wilderness] owl,
like an owl living among the ·ruins [wastelands; Is. 34:10–15; Zeph. 2:13–15].
[7]I ·lie awake [*or* keep watch].
I am like a lonely bird on a ·housetop [roof].
[8]All day long enemies ·insult [scorn; reproach] me;
those who ·make fun of [mock] me use my name as a curse.
[9]I eat ashes for ·food [*or* bread],
and my tears ·fall into [mingle with] my drinks.
[10]Because of your ·great anger [[L]wrath and indignation],
you have picked me up and thrown me away.
[11]My days are like a passing shadow;
I am like dried grass.

[12]But, LORD, you ·rule [[L]are enthroned] forever,
and your ·fame [memory] ·goes on and on [[L]throughout the generations].
[13]You will ·come [[L]rise up] and have ·mercy [compassion] on ·Jerusalem [[L]Zion; [C]the location of the Temple],
because the time has now come to be ·kind [gracious] to her;
the ·right [appointed] time has come.
[14]Your servants ·love even [are pleased/delighted with] her stones;
they even ·care about [[L]have pity/compassion for] her dust.

[15]Nations will fear the name of the LORD,
and all the kings on earth ·will honor you [[L]your glory; [C]God's manifest presence].
[16]The LORD will rebuild ·Jerusalem [[L]Zion; [C]the location of the Temple];
there his glory [[C]manifest presence] will be seen.
[17]He will answer the prayers of the ·needy [lowly; [L]naked];
he will not ·reject [despise] their prayers.

[18]Write these things for ·the future [[L]a future generation]
so that people who are not yet ·born [created] will praise the LORD.
[19]The LORD looked down from his holy place above;
from heaven he ·looked [gazed] down at the earth.
[20]He heard the ·moans [groans] of the prisoners,
and he ·freed [released] those sentenced to die.
[21]The name of the LORD will be ·heard [recounted] in ·Jerusalem [[L]Zion; [C]the location of the Temple];
his praise ·will be heard there [[L]in Jerusalem].
[22]People will ·come [gather] together,
and kingdoms will serve the LORD.

[23]·God has made me tired of living [He broke my strength in midcourse/[L]the way];
he has cut short my ·life [[L]days].
[24]So I said, "My God, do not take me in the middle of my ·life [[L]days].
Your years ·go on and on [endure for generations].
[25]In the beginning you ·made [founded] the earth,
and ·your hands made the skies [[L]the heavens are the work of your hands; Gen. 1].
[26]They will be destroyed, but you will ·remain [endure].
They will all wear out like ·clothes [garments].
And, like clothes, you will change them
and throw them away.
[27]But you ·never change [are the same/[L]he],
and your ·life [[L]years] will never end.
[28]·Our children [[L]The children of your servants] will live in your presence,
and their ·children [offspring; [L]seed] will remain with you."

Praise to the Lord of Love

Of David.

103

·All that I am [[T]O my soul], ·praise [bless] the LORD;
·everything in me [[L]all my inward parts], ·praise [bless] his holy name.
[2]·My whole being [[T]O my soul], ·praise [bless] the LORD
and do not forget all his ·kindnesses [gifts; benefits].
[3]He forgives all ·my [*or* your] ·sins [iniquity]
and heals all ·my [*or* your] ·diseases [ills].
[4]He ·saves [redeems] ·my [*or* your] life from the ·grave [[L]pit]
and ·loads [*or* crowns] ·me [*or* you] with ·love [loyalty] and ·mercy [compassion].
[5]He satisfies ·me [*or* you] with good things [[L]as long as you live; *or* according to your desires]

and ·makes me young again [Lrenews your youth], like the eagle
[Is. 40:31].

6The Lord does what is ·right [righteous] and ·fair [just]
for all who are ·wronged by others [oppressed; exploited].
7He ·showed [revealed] his ways to Moses [Ex. 34:5–7]
and his deeds to the ·people [sons] of Israel.
8The Lord shows ·mercy [compassion] and ·is kind [grace].
He ·does not become angry quickly [is slow to anger], and he has
great ·love [loyalty; 86:15; 145:8–9; Ex. 34:6–7; Neh. 9:17. 31;
Joel 2:13; Jon. 4:2].
9He will not always ·accuse [charge; contend with] us,
and he will not ·be angry forever [Lkeep watch forever].
10He ·has not punished us as our sins should be punished [Ldoes not act
toward us according to our sins];
he has not repaid us ·for the evil we have done [Laccording to our
iniquity].
11As high as the ·sky [heaven] is above the earth,
so great is his ·love [loyalty] for those who ·respect [fear] him [Prov. 1:7].
12He has taken our ·sins [transgressions] away from us
as far as the east is from west.
13The Lord has ·mercy [compassion] on those who ·respect [fear] him
[Prov. 1:7],
as a father has ·mercy [compassion] on his children.
14He knows how we were ·made [formed];
he remembers that we are dust [Gen. 2:7; 3:19; Job 4:19; 10:9; 34:15;
Eccl. 3:20; 12:7].

15Human ·life [Ldays] is like grass [90:5–6; Is. 51:12];
we ·grow [sprout; flourish] like a flower in the field [Job 14:2; Is.
40:6–7].
16After the wind ·blows [passes by], ·the flower [Lit] is gone,
and ·there is no sign of where it was [Lno one can recognize its place].
17But the Lord's ·love [loyalty] for those who ·respect [fear] him [Prov. 1:7]
continues forever and ever,
and his ·goodness [righteousness] continues to their ·grandchildren
[Lchildren's children]
18and to those who ·keep [observe; guard] his ·agreement [covenant;
treaty; Ex. 19–24]
and who remember to ·obey [Ldo] his ·orders [precepts].

19The Lord has ·set [established] his throne in heaven,
and his kingdom rules over everything [93:1; 96:10; 99:1].
20You who are his ·angels [*or* messengers], ·praise [bless] the Lord.
You are the mighty warriors who do what he says
and who ·obey [listen to] his voice.
21You, his ·armies [hosts; Cperhaps the angelic army], ·praise [bless] the
Lord;
you are his ·servants [ministers] who do what he ·wants [desires].
22Everything the Lord has made
should ·praise [bless] him in all the places he rules.
·My whole being [TO my soul], ·praise [bless] the Lord.

Praise to God Who Made the World

104 ·My whole being [TO my soul], ·praise [bless] the LORD.
LORD my God, you are very great.
You are clothed with ·glory [splendor] and ·majesty [beauty];
2 you ·wear [Lwrap yourself in] light like a robe [Hab. 3:4; 1 John 1:5].
You stretch out the ·skies [heavens] like a tent [Is. 40:22].
3 You ·build your room above the clouds [Lset the beams of your upper room on the waters].
You make the clouds your chariot [18:10–19; 68:4; Is. 19:1; Dan. 7:13–14; Luke 21:27; Rev. 1:7],
and you ride on the wings of the wind.
4 You make the winds your messengers,
and flames of fire are your ·servants [ministers; Heb. 1:7].

5 You ·built [founded] the earth on its foundations
so it can never be moved.
6 You covered the earth with ·oceans [Lthe deeps];
the water ·was above [Lstood over] the mountains.
7 But at your ·command [reprimand; rebuke], the water ·rushed away [fled].
·When you thundered your orders [LAt the sound of your thunder],
it hurried away.
8 The mountains rose; the valleys sank.
The water went to the places you ·made [founded] for it.
9 You set borders for the seas that they cannot ·cross [pass],
so water will never cover the earth again [Cas before the third day creation or during the Flood; Gen. 1:9–10; 9:9–17; Job 38:8–11; Prov. 8:29].

10 You make springs pour into the ·ravines [wadis];
they flow between the mountains.
11 They water all the ·wild animals [Lcreatures of the field];
the wild donkeys ·come there to drink [Lquench their thirst].
12 ·Wild birds [Birds of the sky/heavens] ·make nests by the water [Ldwell by them];
they ·sing [Lgive voice] among the tree branches.
13 You water the mountains from ·above [Lyour high dwelling].
The earth is ·full of [*or* satisfied by] ·the things you made [Lthe fruit of your works].
14 You make the grass grow for cattle
and ·vegetables [plants] for the people to ·use [cultivate].
You make ·food [*or* bread] ·grow [Lcome out] from the earth.
15 You give us wine that ·makes happy hearts [rejoices the hearts of people; John 2:1–12]
and olive oil that makes our faces shine [Csoothing skin in a dry climate; Luke 7:46].
You give us bread that gives us ·strength [sustenance].
16 The LORD's trees ·have plenty of water [flourish];
they are the cedars of Lebanon [Cthe most majestic trees known],
which he planted.
17 The birds make their nests there;
the stork's home is in the fir trees.
18 The high mountains belong to the wild goats.
The rocks are ·hiding places [refuge] for the badgers.

[19]You made the moon ·to mark the seasons [for appointed times; Gen. 1:14; Lev. 23:2, 4, 37, 44],
and the sun always knows when to set.
[20]You make it dark, and it becomes night.
Then all the ·wild animals [[L]creatures of the forest] ·creep [swarm] around.
[21]The lions roar ·as they attack [[L]for prey].
They ·look to [seek] God for food.
[22]When the sun rises, they leave
and go back to their dens to lie down.
[23]Then people go to work
and ·work [labor] until evening.

[24]LORD, ·you have made many things;
with your wisdom you made them all [Prov. 8:22–31].
The earth is full of your ·riches [*or* creatures].
[25]Look at the sea, so big and wide,
with creatures large and small, ·creeping [swarming] things that cannot be counted.
[26]Ships travel over the ocean,
and there is Leviathan [[C]a sea monster and symbol of chaos; 74:14; Job 3:8; 41:1; Is. 27:1],
which you made to play there.

[27]All these things ·depend [hope; wait] on you
to give them their food at the right time.
[28]When you give it to them,
they gather it up.
When you open your hand,
they are ·filled [satisfied] with good food.
[29]When you ·turn away [[L]hide your face] from them,
they ·become frightened [are terrified].
When you take away their breath,
they ·die [expire] and turn to dust [Gen. 2:7; Eccl. 12:7].
[30]When you ·breathe [[L]send your breath/*or* Spirit] on them,
they are created [Gen. 2:7],
and you make the land new again.

[31]May the glory of the LORD [[C]his manifest presence] be forever.
May the LORD ·enjoy [rejoice in] what he has made.
[32]He just looks at the earth, and it ·shakes [trembles].
He touches the mountains, and they smoke.

[33]I will sing to the LORD all my life;
I will ·sing praises [make a psalm] to my God as long as I live.
[34]May my ·thoughts [meditations] please him;
I ·am happy [will rejoice] in the LORD.
[35]Let sinners be ·destroyed [obliterated] from the earth,
and let the wicked live no longer.

·My whole being [[T]O my soul], ·praise [bless] the LORD.
Praise the LORD.

God's Love for Israel

105 **Give thanks to the** **LORD** **and ·pray to him** [Lcall on his name].
·Tell [LMake known among] **the nations what he has done.**
[2]**Sing to him; ·sing praises** [make a psalm] **to him.**
Tell about all his ·miracles [wonderful acts].
[3]**·Be glad that you are his** [LExult/Glory in his holy name];
let ·those [Lthe heart of those] **who seek the** **LORD** **·be happy** [rejoice].
[4]**·Depend on** [Seek] **the** **LORD** **and his strength;**
always ·go to him for help [Lseek his face].
[5]**Remember the ·miracles** [wonderful acts] **he has done;**
remember his ·wonders [signs] **and ·his decisions** [Lthe judgments of his mouth].
[6]**You are ·descendants** [Lseed] **of his servant Abraham** [Gen. 12:1–3],
the children of Jacob, his chosen people.
[7]**He is the** **LORD** **our God.**
His ·laws [justice; judgments] **are for all the world.**

[8]**He will ·keep** [Lremember] **his ·agreement** [covenant; treaty] **forever;**
·he will keep his promises always [Lthe word which he commanded, for a thousand generations].
[9]**He will keep the ·agreement** [covenant; treaty] **he ·made** [Lcut] **with Abraham** [Gen. 12:1–3; 17:23]
and the ·promise [oath] **he made to Isaac** [Gen. 26:3–5].
[10]**He made it a ·law** [statute; ordinance; requirement] **for the people of Jacob;**
he made it an ·agreement [covenant; agreement] **with Israel to last forever.**
[11]**The** **LORD** **said, "I will give you the land of Canaan** [Gen. 15:18],
·and it will belong to you [Las a portion of your inheritance]."

[12]**Then ·God's people** [Lthey] **were few in number.**
They were ·strangers [sojourners; wanderers; resident aliens] **in the land.**
[13]**They went from one nation to another,**
from one kingdom to another.
[14]**But the** **LORD** **did not let anyone ·hurt** [exploit; oppress] **them;**
he warned kings ·not to harm them [Lconcerning them].
[15]**He said, "Don't touch my ·chosen** [anointed] **people,**
and don't harm my prophets."

[16]**·God** [He] **·ordered** [proclaimed] **a ·time of hunger** [famine] **in the land,**
and he ·destroyed all the food [Lbroke every staff of bread; Gen. 41:54].
[17]**Then he sent a man ahead of them—**
Joseph, who was sold as a slave [Gen. 37; 45:5; 50:20].
[18]**They ·put chains around his feet** [Lafflicted his feet with chain]
and an iron ·ring [collar] **around his neck.**
[19]**·Then the time he had spoken of came,**
and the **LORD's** **words proved that Joseph was right** [*or* Until the time he had spoken of came, the words of the LORD kept testing him].
[20]**The king** [Cof Egypt] **sent for Joseph and ·freed** [released] **him;**
the ruler of the people set him free [Gen. 41:14, 40].

[21]He made him the ·master [lord] of his house;
Joseph was in charge of his riches [Acts 7:10].
[22]He could ·order [bind] the princes as he wished.
He taught the older men to be wise.
[23]Then Israel [Canother name for Jacob, Joseph's father] came to Egypt;
Jacob lived in the land of Ham [CEgypt; Gen. 46:1–7].
[24]The LORD made his people ·grow in number [fruitful; Ex. 1:7],
and he ·made them stronger than [strengthened them against] their ·enemies [foes].
[25]He ·caused the Egyptians [Lturned their hearts] to hate his people
and to ·make plans [Lact deceptively] against his servants [Ex. 1:8].
[26]Then he sent his servant Moses,
and Aaron, whom he had chosen [Ex. 3:1—4:17].
[27]They did many signs among the Egyptians
and worked ·wonders [miracles; Cthe plagues; Ex. 7–12] in the land of Ham [CEgypt; Gen. 46:1–7].
[28]The LORD sent darkness and made the land dark,
but the Egyptians ·turned against what he said [rebelled against his word; Ex. 10:21–29].
[29]He changed their water into blood
and made their fish die [Ex. 7:14–25].
[30]Then their country ·was filled [swarmed] with frogs,
even in the bedrooms of their ·rulers [Lkings; Ex. 8:1–17].
[31]The LORD spoke and flies came [Ex. 8:20–32],
and gnats were everywhere in the country [Ex. 8:16–19].
[32]He made hail fall like rain
and sent lightning through their land.
[33]He struck down their grapevines and fig trees,
and he ·destroyed [shattered] every tree in the country [Ex. 9:13–35].
[34]He spoke and ·grasshoppers [locusts] came;
the ·locusts [young locusts] ·were too many to count [Lwithout number].
[35]They ate all the ·plants [vegetation] in the land
and ·everything the earth produced [Lthe fruit of the ground; Ex. 10:1–20].
[36]·The LORD [LHe] also ·killed [Lstruck] all the firstborn sons in the land,
the oldest son of each family [Lthe first of their virility; Ex. 11:1—12:30].

[37]Then he brought them out with silver and gold [Ex. 12:35–36].
·Not one of his people stumbled [LThere was no stumbling among the tribe].
[38]The Egyptians ·were glad [rejoiced] when they left,
because ·the Egyptians were afraid of them [Ldread of them fell on them; Cbecause of the plagues].
[39]·The LORD covered them with a cloud [LHe spread out a cloud as a covering]
and ·lit up the night with fire [La fire to illuminate the night; Ex. 13:21–22].
[40]When they asked, he brought them quail
and filled them with bread from heaven [Ex. 16].

[41]God ·split [[L]opened] the rock, and water flowed out;
it ran like a river through the ·desert [wasteland; Ex. 17:1–7].
[42]He remembered his holy ·promise [word]
to his servant Abraham [Gen. 12:1–3].

[43]So God brought his people out with joy,
his chosen ones with singing.
[44]He gave them lands of other nations,
so they received ·what others had worked for [[L]the labors of peoples].
[45]This was so they would ·keep [observe; guard] his ·orders [statutes; ordinances; requirements]
and ·obey [protect] his ·teachings [instructions; laws].

Praise the LORD!

Israel's Failure to Trust God

106 Praise the LORD!
Thank the LORD because he is good.
His ·love [loyalty] continues forever.
[2]·No one [[L]Who…?] can tell all the mighty things the LORD has done;
·no one [[L]who…?] can ·speak [declare] all his praise.
[3]·Happy [Blessed] are those who ·do [keep; observe; guard] ·right [justice],
who do what is ·fair [righteous] at all times.

[4]LORD, remember me when you ·are kind [show favor] to your people;
·help [come to] me when you ·save them [give them victory].
[5]Let me see the ·good things you do for [prosperity of] your chosen people.
Let me ·be happy [rejoice] along with your ·happy [rejoicing] nation;
let me join your ·own people [inheritance] in praising you.

[6]We have sinned just as our ·ancestors [fathers] did.
We have done wrong; we have done evil.
[7]Our ·ancestors [fathers] in Egypt
did not ·learn [grow in wisdom] from your ·miracles [wonderful acts].
They did not remember all your ·kindnesses [loyalty],
so they ·turned [rebelled] against you at the ·Red [*or* Reed] Sea [78:13; Ex. 14–15].
[8]But the LORD ·saved them [gave them victory] ·for his own sake [[L]because of his name],
to ·show [reveal] his great power.
[9]He ·commanded [reprimanded; rebuked] the ·Red [*or* Reed] Sea [v. 7], and it dried up.
He led them through the deep sea as if it were a ·desert [wilderness].
[10]He ·saved them [gave them victory over] from those who hated them.
He ·saved [redeemed] them from the ·power [hand] of their enemies,
[11]and the water covered their foes.
Not one of them ·escaped [[L]was left].
[12]Then the people ·believed what the LORD said [[L]had faith in his word],
and they sang praises to him.

13But they quickly forgot what he had done;
they did not wait for his ·advice [counsel].
14They ·became greedy for food [developed deep cravings] in the ·desert [wilderness; Num. 11],
and they tested God ·there [Lin desolate places; Ex. 17:7].
15So he gave them what they ·wanted [asked for],
but he also sent ·a terrible disease [a wasting sickness; emaciation] among them [Num. 11:33–35].

16The people in the camp were jealous of Moses
and of Aaron, the holy ·priest [one] of the LORD.
17Then the ground opened up and swallowed Dathan
and closed over Abiram's ·group [assembly].
18A fire burned among their ·followers [congregation],
and flames burned up the wicked [Num. 16].

19The people made a gold calf at ·Mount Sinai [LHoreb; Canother name for Sinai]
and ·worshiped [bowed down to] a metal statue [Ex. 32; Deut. 9:7–17].
20They exchanged their ·glorious God [Lglory; CGod's manifest presence]
for ·a statue [the image] of a bull that eats grass.
21They forgot the God who ·saved them [had given them victory],
who had done great things in Egypt,
22who had done miracles in the land of Ham [CEgypt]
and amazing things by the ·Red [*or* Reed] Sea [v. 7].
23So God said he would destroy them.
But Moses, his chosen one, stood ·before him [Lin the breech before him]
and ·stopped God's anger from destroying them [calmed his destructive wrath; Ex. 32:30—33:23; Deut. 9:18–21].

24Then they refused to go into the ·beautiful land of Canaan [desired/coveted land];
they did not ·believe what God promised [Ltrust his word; Num. 14:1–12].
25They ·grumbled [complained] in their tents [Deut. 1:27; 1 Cor. 10:10]
and did not ·obey [Llisten to] the LORD.
26So he ·swore [Llifted his hand; Can oath-taking gesture] to them
that ·they would die [Lhe would make them fall] in the ·desert [wilderness].
27He ·said their children would be killed by [Lwould make their seed fall to] other nations
and that they would be scattered among other countries [Cas happened in the exile; Num. 14:27–35].

28They ·joined in worshiping [Lyoked themselves to] Baal at Peor
and ate ·meat that had been sacrificed to lifeless statues [Lsacrifices to the dead; Num. 25].
29They ·made the LORD angry [Lprovoked him] by what they did,
so ·many people became sick with a terrible disease [plague broke out among them].

30 **But Phinehas ·prayed to the LORD** [Lstood and prayed],
and the ·disease [plague] **·stopped** [was restrained; Num. 25:6–9].
31 **·Phinehas did what was right** [LIt was counted/credited to him as righteousness],
·and it will be remembered from now on [Lthroughout the generations, forever; Num. 25:10–13; Mal. 2:4–6].

32 **The people also made the LORD angry at Meribah** [81:7; 95:8],
and Moses was in trouble because of them.
33 **The people ·turned** [rebelled] **against ·the Spirit of God** [Lhis Spirit/spirit],
so Moses ·spoke without stopping to think [Lchattered with his lips; Num. 20:10–11].

34 **The people did not destroy the other nations**
as the LORD had told them to do [Deut. 7:16; 20:17–18].
35 **Instead, they mixed with the other nations**
and learned their ·customs [deeds; Judg. 3:5–6].
36 **They ·worshiped** [Lserved] **other nations' idols** [Judg. 2:19]
and were ·trapped by them [La snare to them].
37 **They even killed their sons and daughters**
as sacrifices to demons [Lev. 18:21; Deut. 12:31; 2 Kin. 16:1; 21:6; 23:10; Jer. 7:31; Ezek. 16:20–21; 20:31; 1 Cor. 10:20].
38 **They ·killed** [Lspilled the blood of] **innocent people,**
their own sons and daughters,
as sacrifices to the idols of Canaan [Jer. 19:4].
So the land was ·made unholy [polluted] **by their blood.**
39 **The people became ·unholy** [unclean; Critually] **by their ·sins** [Lacts];
they ·were unfaithful to God in [prostituted themselves by] **what they did.**

40 **So the LORD became angry with his people**
and ·hated [was disgusted with] **his own ·children** [Linheritance].
41 **He ·handed them over to** [Lgave them over to the hand/power of] **other nations**
and let ·their enemies [Lthose who hated them] **·rule over** [dominate] **them.**
42 **Their enemies ·were cruel to** [oppressed] **them**
and ·kept them [they were brought into subjection] **under their ·power** [Lhand].
43 **The LORD ·saved** [rescued] **his people many times,**
but they continued to ·turn [rebel] **against him.**
So they ·became even more wicked [Lwere brought low by their iniquity].

44 **But God saw their ·misery** [distress]
when he heard their cry.
45 **He remembered his ·agreement** [treaty; covenant] **with them,**
and he felt ·sorry [compassion] **for them because of his great ·love** [loyalty].
46 **He caused them to be ·pitied** [shown mercy/compassion]
by those who held them captive.

34He made ·fertile [fruitful] land salty
because the people there did evil [Gen. 19].
35He ·changed [turned; [L]set] the ·desert [wilderness] into pools of water
and ·dry [parched] ground into springs of water.
36He had the hungry settle there
so they could ·build [establish] a city in which to live.
37They ·planted seeds in the fields and vineyards [[L]sowed fields and planted vineyards],
and they had a ·good harvest [fruitful crop].
38God blessed them, and they ·grew in number [multiplied greatly].
Their cattle did not ·become fewer [diminish].

39Because of ·disaster [oppression], ·troubles [evil], and sadness,
·their families [[L]they] ·grew smaller [diminished] and ·weaker [were brought low].
40He ·showed he was displeased with [[L]poured contempt on] their ·leaders [princes]
and made them wander in a pathless ·desert [waste].
41But he lifted the ·poor [needy] out of their suffering
and ·made their families grow [[L]set their clans] like flocks of sheep.
42·Good people [The upright/virtuous] see this and are happy,
but the wicked ·say nothing [[L]shuts their mouths].

43Whoever is wise will ·remember [keep; guard] these things
and will ·think about [consider] the ·love [loyalty] of the LORD.

A song. A psalm of David.

A Prayer for Victory

108 God, my heart is ·steady [steadfast; ready].
I will sing and ·praise [play a psalm for] you ·with all my being [[L]as will my soul/*or* glory].
2Wake up, harp and lyre!
I will wake up the dawn.
3LORD, I will ·praise [thank] you among the ·nations [peoples];
I will sing ·songs of praise [psalms] about you to all the nations.
4Your great ·love [loyalty] ·reaches to [is greater than] the ·skies [heavens],
your ·truth [faithfulness] to the heavens.
5God, you are ·supreme [exalted] above the ·skies [heavens].
Let your glory [[C]manifest presence] be over all the earth [57:5–11].

6Answer us and ·save us [give us victory] by your ·power [[L]right hand]
so ·the people you love [your beloved] will be rescued.
7God has said ·from his Temple [[L]from his Holy Place; *or* in his holiness],
"·When I win [*or* With joy], I will ·divide [parcel up] Shechem
and measure off the Valley of Succoth [Gen. 33:17–20].
8Gilead and Manasseh are mine.
Ephraim is like my helmet.
Judah holds my royal scepter [Gen. 49:10; [C]they are agents of God's power].
9Moab is like my washbowl.
I throw my sandals at Edom [[C]showing contempt].
I shout [[C]in triumph] at Philistia [[C]enemies of Israel]."

·Then make people forget about them completely [[L]Let memory of them be cut off from the land].

[16]"He did not remember to be ·loving [loyal].
He ·hurt [persecuted; [L]pursued] the poor, the needy, and those who were ·sad [depressed; [L]brokenhearted]
·until they were nearly dead [[L]to their death].
[17]He loved to put curses on others,
so let those same curses ·fall on [[L]come to] him.
He did not like to bless others,
so ·do not let good things happen to him [[L]let them (blessings) be far from him].
[18]He ·cursed others as often as he wore clothes [[L]wore curses like a coat].
·Cursing others filled his body and his life,
like drinking water and using olive oil [[L]Let them come like water in his innards and like oil in his bones].
[19]So let curses ·cover [wrap] him like ·clothes [a garment]
and ·wrap around him like a belt [[L]continually gird him]."
[20]May the LORD do these things to those who ·accuse [charge] me,
to those who speak evil against me.

[21]But you, Lord GOD,
·be kind to me so others will know you are good [[L]act on my behalf for the sake of your name].
Because your ·love [loyalty] is good, ·save [protect] me.
[22]I am poor and helpless
and ·very sad [[L]my heart is pierced/wounded in me].
[23]I am ·dying [[L]gone] like an evening shadow;
I am shaken off like a locust.
[24]My knees ·are weak [buckle; stumble] from fasting,
and ·I have grown thin [[L]my flesh is lean of fat].
[25]·My enemies insult me [[L]I am a reproach to them];
they look at me and shake their heads [[C]in scorn].

[26]LORD my God, help me;
because you are ·loving [loyal], ·save me [give me victory].
[27]Then they will know that ·your power has done this [[L]this is your hand];
they will know that you have done it, LORD.
[28]They may curse me, but you bless me.
They may ·attack [[L]rise against] me, but they will be ·disgraced [embarrassed].
Then I, your servant, will be glad.
[29]Let those who ·accuse [charge; attack] me be ·disgraced [[L]clothed with disgrace]
and ·covered [wrapped up] with shame like a coat.

[30]I will ·thank [praise] the LORD very much [[L]with my mouth];
I will praise him in ·front [the midst] of many people.
[31]He ·defends [[L]stands at the right hand of] the helpless
and ·saves them from [gives them victory over] those who ·accuse [judge] them.

The Lord Appoints a King

A psalm of David.

110

·The LORD said [LUtterance/Oracle of the LORD] to my Lord,
"Sit at my right ·side [Lhand]
until I put your enemies under your ·control [Lfeet; Matt. 22:44; 26:64; Mark 12:36; 16:19; Luke 20:42–44; 22:59; Acts 2:34–35; Rom. 8:34; 1 Cor. 15:25; Eph. 1:20; Col. 3:1; Heb. 1:3, 13; 8:1; 10:12–13; 12:2]."
2 The LORD will ·enlarge [Lsend] ·your kingdom [Lthe scepter of your strength; Csymbol of royal power] beyond ·Jerusalem [LZion; Clocation of the Temple],
and ·you will rule over [Lgive you dominion in the midst of] your enemies.
3 Your people will ·join [freely offer themselves to] you on ·your day of battle [Lthe day of your power/army].
You have been dressed in ·holiness [splendor of holiness] from ·birth [Lthe womb of dawn];
you have the ·freshness of a child [Ldew of your youth].

4 The LORD has made a promise
and will not ·change his mind [waver].
He said, "You are a priest forever,
a priest like Melchizedek [Cin reference to an ancient priest-king in Jerusalem; ultimately fulfilled in Christ; Gen. 14:18; Heb. 5:6; 7:17, 21]."

5 The Lord is ·beside you to help you [Lby your right hand].
·When he becomes angry [LIn the day of his anger], he will ·crush [shatter] kings.
6 He will judge those nations, filling them with ·dead bodies [corpses];
he will ·defeat rulers [Lcrush/shatter heads] ·all over the [Lthroughout the wide] world.
7 ·The king [*or* The Lord; LHe] will drink from the brook on the way.
Then he will ·be strengthened [Llift up his head].

Praise the Lord's Goodness

111

Praise the LORD!
I will ·thank [praise] the LORD with all my heart
in the ·meeting of his good people [council of the upright/virtuous, in the assembly].
2 The ·LORD does great things [Ldeeds of the LORD are great];
those who enjoy them ·seek [study] them.
3 ·What he does is [LHis deeds are] ·glorious [beautiful] and ·splendid [majestic],
and his ·goodness [righteousness] ·continues [stands] forever.
4 His ·miracles [wonderful acts] are ·unforgettable [remembered; well-known].
The LORD is ·kind [gracious] and ·merciful [compassionate].
5 He gives ·food [Lprey] to those who fear him [Prov. 1:7].
He remembers his ·agreement [covenant; treaty] forever.
6 He has ·shown [proclaimed to] his people ·his power [Lthe power/strength of his deeds]

when he gave them the ·lands [[L]inheritance] **of other nations** [[C]the conquest; Josh. 1–12].

[7]**·Everything he does is** [[L]The deeds of his hands are] **·good** [faithful; true] **and ·fair** [just];
all his ·orders [precepts] **·can be trusted** [are faithful/true/reliable].
[8]**They will ·continue** [endure; be unshakeable] **forever.**
They were made ·true [faithful] **and ·right** [virtuous; with integrity].
[9]**He ·sets his people free** [[L]sent redemption to his people].
He ·made his agreement everlasting [[L]commanded his covenant/ treaty forever].
·He [[L]His name] **is holy and ·wonderful** [awesome].

[10]**·Wisdom begins with respect for** [[L]The beginning/foundation of wisdom is fear of] **the LORD** [Prov. 1:7];
those who ·obey [[L]do] **·his orders** [[L]them] **have good ·understanding** [insight].
He ·should be praised [endures; [L]stands] **forever.**

Honest People Are Blessed

112 Praise the LORD!
·Happy [Blessed] **are those who ·respect** [fear] **the LORD** [Prov. 1:7; 31:30],
who ·want [take great delight in] **·what he** [[L]his] **commands.**
[2]**Their ·descendants** [[L]seed] **will be ·powerful** [strong] **in the land;**
the ·children [generation] **of ·honest** [virtuous] **people will be blessed.**
[3]**Their houses will be full of wealth and riches,**
and their ·goodness [righteousness] **will ·continue** [endure; [L]stand] **forever.**
[4]**A light shines in the dark for ·honest** [virtuous] **people,**
for those who are ·merciful [gracious] **and ·kind** [compassionate] **and ·good** [merciful].
[5]**It is good to be ·merciful** [gracious] **and ·generous** [to lend].
Those who ·are fair in their business [conduct their affairs justly]
[6]**will never be ·defeated** [moved].
·Good [Righteous] **people will always be remembered.**
[7]**They ·won't be afraid of** [do not fear] **·bad news** [to hear evil; Prov. 30:25];
their hearts are ·steady [steadfast; established; prepared] **because they ·trust** [have confidence in] **the LORD.**
[8]**They ·are confident** [endure; are unshakeable; 111:8] **and will not ·be afraid** [fear];
they will look down on their ·enemies [foes].
[9]**They ·give freely** [[L]distribute/scatter, they give] **to the ·poor** [needy].
·The things they do are right and [Their righteousness] **will ·continue** [endure] **forever** [2 Cor. 9:9].
·They will be given great honor [[L]Their horn is exalted in glory; [C]an animal's horn symbolizes strength].

[10]**The wicked will see this and become angry;**
they will ·grind [gnash] **their teeth** [[C]in anger] **and then ·disappear** [melt away].

The ·wishes [cravings; desires] of the wicked will ·come to nothing
[perish].

Praise for the Lord's Kindness

113 Praise the LORD!
Praise him, you servants of the LORD;
praise the name of the LORD.
2The LORD's name ·should [is to] be ·praised [blessed]
now and forever.
3The LORD's name ·should [is to] be praised
from where the sun rises to where it sets.
4The LORD is ·supreme [exalted] over all the nations [99:2];
his glory [CGod's manifest presence] ·reaches to the skies [is over the
heavens].

5·No one [LWho…?] is like the LORD our God,
who ·rules [Lis seated/enthroned] ·from heaven [on high],
6who ·bends [stoops] down to look
at the ·skies [heavens] and the earth.
7The LORD ·lifts [raises] the poor from the ·dirt [dust]
and ·takes [exalts] the ·helpless [needy] from the ashes.
8He ·seats [enthrones] them with princes,
the princes of his people [1 Sam. 2:8; Luke 1:52].
9He gives ·children to the woman who has none [Lthe barren woman a
home]
and makes her ·a happy mother [Ljoyful with children].

Praise the LORD!

God Brought Israel from Egypt

114 When ·the Israelites [Israel] went out of Egypt,
the ·people [Lhouse] of Jacob left ·that foreign country [La
people of incomprehensible language].
2Then Judah became God's holy place [Ex. 19:6];
Israel became ·the land he ruled [his dominion].

3The Sea [CRed (or Reed) Sea; Ex. 14–15] looked and ·ran away [fled];
the Jordan River turned back [Josh. 3].
4The mountains ·danced [skipped] like ·sheep [rams]
and the hills like little lambs.
5Sea, why did you ·run away [flee]?
Jordan, why did you turn back?
6Mountains, why did you ·dance [skip] like ·sheep [rams]?
Hills, why did you ·dance [skip] like little lambs?

7Earth, ·shake with fear [writhe; tremble] before the Lord,
before the God of Jacob.
8He turned a rock into a pool of water,
a hard ·rock [flint] into a spring of water [Ex. 17:1–7;
Num. 20:1–13].

The One True God

115 ·It does not belong [LNot to us, not] to us, LORD.
The glory belongs to ·you [Lyour name]
because of your ·love [loyalty] and ·loyalty [faithfulness].

[2]Why do the nations ask,
"Where is their God?"
[3]Our God is in heaven.
He does what he pleases.
[4]Their idols are made of silver and gold,
the work of human hands.
[5]They have mouths, but they cannot speak.
They have eyes, but they cannot see.
[6]They have ears, but they cannot hear.
They have noses, but they cannot smell.
[7]They have hands, but they cannot feel.
They have feet, but they cannot walk.
No sounds come from their throats.
[8]People who make ·idols [[L]them] **·will be** [*or* are] **like them,**
and so will those who ·trust [have confidence in] **them** [135:15–18; Is. 44:9–20; 46:6–7; Jer. 10:1–9; Hab. 2:18–19].

[9]·Family of [[L]O] **Israel, ·trust** [have confidence in] **the LORD;**
he is your helper and your ·protection [[L]shield].
[10]·Family [[L]House] **of Aaron** [[C]the priests], **·trust** [have confidence in] **the LORD;**
he is your helper and your ·protection [[L]shield].
[11]You who ·respect [fear] **the LORD** [Prov. 1:7] **should ·trust** [have confidence in] **him;**
he is your helper and your ·protection [[L]shield].

[12]The LORD remembers us and will bless us.
He will bless the ·family [[L]house] **of Israel;**
he will bless the ·family [[L]house] **of Aaron** [[C]the priests].
[13]The LORD will bless those who ·respect [fear] **him** [Prov. 1:7],
from the ·smallest [*or* least] **to the greatest.**

[14]May the LORD ·give you success [make you increase],
and may he give you and your children ·success [increase].
[15]May you be blessed by the LORD,
who made heaven and earth [Gen. 1].

[16]Heaven belongs to the LORD,
but he gave the earth to people.
[17]Dead people do not praise the LORD;
those ·in the grave are silent [[L]who go down in silence].
[18]But we will praise the LORD
now and forever.

Praise the LORD!

Thanksgiving for Escaping Death

116

I love the LORD,
because he ·listens to my prayers for help [[L]hears/*or* heard my voice, my prayer of supplication].
[2]He ·paid attention [[L]extends his ear] **to me,**
so I will ·call to him for help [call; pray] **·as long as I live** [[L]in my days].

[3]The ·ropes [cords] of death ·bound [encompass] me,
and the ·fear [hardship; distress] of ·the grave [LSheol; Cthe grave or the underworld] ·took hold of [reached; found] me.
I ·was troubled and sad [Lfound distress and sadness].
[4]Then I ·called out [prayed in] the name of the LORD.
I said, "Please, LORD, ·save [rescue] me!"

[5]The LORD is ·kind [gracious] and ·does what is right [righteous];
our God is ·merciful [compassionate; Ex. 34:6–7].
[6]The LORD ·watches over [keeps; guards] the ·foolish [immature; simpleminded];
when I was ·helpless [brought low], he ·saved me [gave me victory].
[7]I said to myself, "·Relax [LReturn, my soul/life to your rest],
because the LORD ·takes care of you [treats you well]."
[8]LORD, you ·saved [rescued] me from death.
·You stopped my eyes from crying [L…and my eyes from tears];
·you kept me from being defeated [L…my feet from stumbling].
[9]So I will walk ·with [before; in the presence of] the LORD
in the land of the living [Cas opposed to the grave].
[10]I ·believed [trusted], so I said,
"I am ·completely ruined [afflicted greatly; 2 Cor. 4:13]."
[11]In my ·distress [worry] I said,
"All people are liars [Rom. 3:4]."

[12]What can I ·give [Lreturn to] the LORD
for all the ·good things [benefits] he has given to me?
[13]I will lift up the cup of salvation,
and I will pray ·to [Lin the name of] the LORD.
[14]I will ·give the LORD what I promised [pay my vow to the LORD]
in front of all his people.

[15]The death of ·one that belongs to the LORD [his loyal ones/saints]
is precious in his ·sight [Leyes].
[16]LORD, I am your servant;
I am your servant and the son of your female servant.
You have ·freed me from [loosened] my chains.
[17]I will give you ·an offering to show thanks to you [a thanksgiving offering],
and I will pray ·to [Lin the name of] the LORD.
[18]I will ·give the LORD what I promised [pay my vow to the LORD]
in front of all his people,
[19]in the ·Temple courtyards [Lcourtyards of the house of the LORD]
in your midst, Jerusalem.

Praise the LORD!

A Hymn of Praise

117 All you nations, praise the LORD.
All you people, ·praise [extol] him
[2]because ·the LORD loves us very much [Lgreat is his loyalty/love toward us],
and his ·truth [faithfulness] is everlasting.

Praise the LORD!

Thanksgiving for Victory

118 ·Thank [Praise] the LORD because he is good.
His ·love [loyalty] ·continues [endures] forever.
2Let Israel say,
"His ·love [loyalty] ·continues [endures] forever."
3Let the ·family [Lhouse] of Aaron [Cthe priests] say,
"His ·love [loyalty] ·continues [endures] forever."
4Let those who ·respect [fear] the LORD [Prov. 1:7] say,
"His ·love [loyalty] ·continues [endures] forever."

5I was in ·trouble [distress], so I ·called [prayed] to the LORD.
The LORD answered me and set me ·free [Lin a broad place].
6I will not ·be afraid [fear], because the LORD is with me [Rom. 8:31].
·People can't do anything [LWhat can people do...?] to me
[Heb. 13:6].
7The LORD is with me to help me,
so I will ·see my enemies defeated [Llook on my enemy; Cin triumph].
8It is better to ·trust [find refuge in] the LORD
than to ·trust [have confidence in] people.
9It is better to ·trust [find refuge in] the LORD
than to ·trust [have confidence in] princes.

10All the nations surrounded me,
but I ·defeated them [warded them off] in the name of the LORD.
11They surrounded me; they surrounded me on every side,
but ·with the LORD's power [Lin the name of the LORD] I ·defeated
them [warded them off].
12They surrounded me like a swarm of bees,
but they ·died [Lwere extinguished] as quickly as thorns burn.
·By the LORD's power [LIn the name of the LORD], I ·defeated them
[warded them off].
13They [*or* You] ·chased me [pushed me hard] until I ·was almost
defeated [almost fell],
but the LORD helped me.
14The LORD ·gives me strength and a song [Lis my strength and song/*or*
might].
He has ·saved me [given me victory].

15Shouts of joy and victory
come from the tents of ·those who do right [the righteous]:
"The right hand of the LORD has done powerful things."
16The ·power [Lright hand] of the LORD ·has won the victory [is exalted];
with his ·power [Lright hand] the LORD has done powerful things.

17I will not die, but live,
and I will ·tell [recount] what the LORD has done.
18The LORD has ·taught me a hard lesson [Lsurely disciplined/instructed
me],
but he did not ·let me die [Lgive me over to death].

19Open for me the ·Temple gates [Lgates of righteousness].
Then I will come in and ·thank [praise] the LORD.
20This is the LORD's gate;

only ·those who are good [the righteous] may enter through it
[15; 24:3–6].
21LORD, I ·thank [praise] you for answering me.
You have ·saved me [given me victory].

22The stone that the builders rejected
became the chief cornerstone [Luke 20:17; Acts 4:11; Eph. 2:20;
1 Pet. 2:7].
23·The LORD did this [LThis is from the LORD],
and it is wonderful ·to us [Lin our eyes; Matt. 21:42; Mark 12:10–11].
24This is the day that the LORD has made.
Let us rejoice and be glad ·today [Lin it]!

25Please, LORD, ·save us [give us victory];
please, LORD, give us ·success [prosperity].
26·God bless [Blessed be] the one who comes in the name of the LORD.
We bless all of you from the ·Temple [Lhouse] of the LORD [Mark
11:9; Luke 13:35; 19:38].
27The LORD is God,
and he has ·shown kindness to [illuminated; given light to] us.
·With branches in your hands, join the feast [LBind the feast/
procession with branches].
Come to the ·corners [Lhorns; Ex. 27:2] of the altar.

28You are my God, and I will ·thank [praise] you;
you are my God, and I will ·praise your greatness [Lexalt you].

29·Thank [Praise] the LORD because he is good.
His ·love [loyalty] ·continues [endures] forever.

The Word of God

119 ·Happy [Blessed] are those ·who live pure lives [Lwhose way
is blameless],
who follow the LORD's ·teachings [instructions; law].
2Happy are those who keep his ·rules [decrees; testimonies],
who ·try to obey [Lseek] him with their whole heart.
3They don't do what is wrong;
they follow his ways.
4LORD, you ·gave [commanded] your ·orders [precepts]
to be obeyed completely.
5·I wish I [LO that my ways] were more ·loyal [steadfast; established; set]
in obeying your ·demands [statutes; ordinances; requirements].
6Then I would not be ashamed
·when I study [staring/gazing at] your commands.
7When I learned that your ·laws [judgments] are fair,
I ·praised [thanked] you with an ·honest [upright] heart.
8I will obey your ·demands [statutes; ordinances; requirements],
so please don't ever ·leave [abandon; forsake] me.

9How can a young person ·live a pure life [Lkeep his way pure]?
By ·obeying [guarding; keeping] your word.
10With all my heart I ·try to obey [seek] you.
Don't let me ·break [stray from] your commands.

11 I have ·taken your words to heart [treasured/stored your words in my heart]
so I would not sin against you.
12 LORD, you ·should be praised [are blessed].
Teach me your ·demands [statutes; ordinances; requirements].
13 My lips will ·tell about [recount]
all the ·laws you have spoken [Ljudgments of your mouth].
14 I enjoy ·living by your rules [the way of your decrees/testimonies]
as people enjoy great riches.
15 I ·think about [meditate on] your ·orders [precepts]
and ·study [look at] your ways.
16 I enjoy ·obeying your demands [your statutes/ordinances/requirements],
and I will not forget your word.

17 ·Do good [Grant this] to me, your servant, so I can live,
so I can ·obey [keep; guard] your word.
18 Open my eyes to see
the ·miracles [wonders] in your ·teachings [instructions; law].
19 I am a ·stranger [sojourner; alien resident] ·on earth [*or* in the land].
Do not hide your commands from me.
20 ·I wear myself out [My soul pines away] with ·desire [longing]
for your ·laws [judgments] all the time.
21 You ·scold [rebuke; reprimand] ·proud [arrogant] people;
those who ·ignore [wander from] your commands are cursed.
22 ·Don't let me be insulted and hated [LTake away insult and contempt]
because I keep your ·rules [decrees; testimonies].
23 Even if princes sit around and speak against me,
I, your servant, will ·think [meditate] about your ·demands [statutes; ordinances; requirements].
24 Your ·rules [statutes; ordinances; requirements] give me pleasure;
they ·give me good advice [Lare my advisors/counselors].

25 ·I am about to die [LMy soul clings to the dust].
Give me life, as you have promised.
26 I ·told you about my life [Lrecounted my way], and you answered me.
Teach me your ·demands [statutes; ordinances; requirements].
27 Help me understand your ·orders [Lthe way of your precepts].
Then I will ·think [meditate] about your ·miracles [wonders].
28 ·I am sad and tired [LMy soul is weary/melts with sorrow affliction].
Make me ·strong [Lrise up] again as you have promised.
29 ·Don't let me be dishonest [LTurn me away from a false way];
·have mercy on me by helping me obey your teachings [graciously teach me your instructions/laws].
30 I have chosen the way of ·truth [faithfulness];
I have ·obeyed [placed before me] your ·laws [judgments].
31 I ·hold on [cling] to your ·rules [decrees; testimonies].
LORD, do not let me be ·disgraced [shamed].
32 I will ·quickly obey [Lrun the way of] your commands,
because you have ·made me happy [Lenlarged my heart/mind].

[33]LORD, teach me ·your demands [[L]the way of your demands/statutes/ ordinances/requirements],
and I will ·keep [observe] them until the end.
[34]Help me understand, so I can ·keep [protect] your ·teachings [instructions; laws],
·obeying [guarding] them with all my heart.
[35]Lead me in the path of your commands,
because ·that makes me happy [[L]I take pleasure in them].
[36]Make me want to keep your ·rules [decrees; testimonies]
·instead of wishing for riches [[L]not to gain/profit].
[37]·Keep me [[L]Turn my eyes] from looking at ·worthless [false; vain] things.
Let me live ·by your word [[L]in your path].
[38]·Keep your promise [Confirm your word] to me, your servant,
so you will be ·respected [feared; Prov. 1:7].
[39]Take away ·the shame [my scorn/humiliation] I fear,
because your ·laws [judgments] are good.
[40]How I ·want to follow [long for] your ·orders [precepts].
Give me life because of your ·goodness [righteousness].

[41]LORD, ·show [[L]bring] me your ·love [loyalty],
and ·save me [give me victory] as you have ·promised [said].
[42]I have an answer for people who ·insult [scorn] me,
because I ·trust [find refuge in] what you say.
[43]Never ·keep me from speaking your truth [[L]take the word of truth from my mouth],
because I ·depend [pin my hopes] on your ·fair laws [judgments].
[44]I will ·obey [keep; guard] your ·teachings [instructions; laws]
forever and ever.
[45]So I will live in ·freedom [liberty],
because I ·want to follow [[L]seek] your ·orders [precepts].
[46]I will discuss your ·rules [decrees; testimonies] with kings
and will not be ashamed.
[47]I ·enjoy obeying [[L]delight in] your commands,
which I love.
[48]I ·praise [[L]lift my palms/hands to] your commands, which I love,
and I ·think [meditate] about your ·demands [statutes; ordinances; requirements].

[49]Remember your promise to me, your servant;
it gives me hope.
[50]When I suffer, this comforts me:
Your promise gives me life.
[51]·Proud [Arrogant] people always ·make fun of [mock] me,
but I do not ·reject [stray from] your ·teachings [instructions; laws].
[52]I remember your ·laws [judgments] from long ago,
and they comfort me, LORD.
[53]·I become angry with wicked people [[L]Indignation seizes me because of the wicked]
who ·do not keep [abandon; forsake] your ·teachings [instructions; laws].
[54]I sing about your ·demands [statutes; ordinances; requirements]
·wherever I live [[L]in the house of my dwelling].

55**LORD, I remember ·you** [Lyour name] **at night,**
and I will ·obey [keep; guard] **your ·teachings** [instructions; laws].
56**This is what I do:**
I ·follow [protect] **your ·orders** [precepts].

57**LORD, you are my ·share in life** [portion; lot];
I have promised to ·obey [keep; guard] **your words.**
58**I ·prayed to** [entreat; implore] **you with all my heart.**
·Have mercy on [Be gracious to] **me as you have promised.**
59**I ·thought about** [considered] **my ·life** [Lpath],
and I ·decided to follow [Lturned my feet to] **your ·rules** [decrees; testimonies].
60**I hurried and did not wait**
to ·obey [keep; obey] **your commands.**
61**Wicked people have ·tied me up** [ensnared me],
but I have not forgotten your ·teachings [instructions; laws].
62**In the middle of the night, I get up to ·thank** [praise] **you**
because your ·laws [judgments] **are ·right** [righteous].
63**I am a ·friend** [companion] **to everyone who fears you,**
to anyone who ·obeys [keeps; guards] **your ·orders** [precepts].
64**LORD, your ·love** [loyalty] **fills the earth.**
Teach me your ·demands [statutes; ordinances; requirements].

65**You have done good things for your servant,**
as you have promised, LORD.
66**Teach me ·wisdom** [Lgood judgment] **and knowledge**
because I ·trust [believe] **your commands.**
67**Before I ·suffered** [was humbled], **I ·did wrong** [wandered],
but now I ·obey [keep; guard] **your word.**
68**You are good, and you do what is good.**
Teach me your ·demands [statutes; ordinances; requirements].
69**·Proud** [Arrogant] **people ·have made up lies about me** [smear me with lies],
but I will ·follow [keep; protect] **your ·orders** [precepts] **with all my heart.**
70**·Those people have no feelings** [LTheir hearts are gross and fat],
but I ·love [delight in] **your ·teachings** [instructions; laws].
71**It was good for me to ·suffer** [be humbled]
so I would learn your ·demands [statutes; ordinances; requirements].
72**·Your teachings** [LThe instructions/laws of your mouth] **are ·worth more to** [better for] **me**
than thousands of pieces of gold and silver.

73**You made me and ·formed** [fashioned; *or* established] **me with your hands.**
Give me understanding so I can learn your commands.
74**Let those who ·respect** [fear; Prov. 1:7] **you rejoice when they see me,**
because I put my hope in your word.
75**LORD, I know that your ·laws** [judgments] **are ·right** [righteous]
and that it was ·right [faithful] **for you to ·punish** [humble] **me.**
76**Comfort me with your ·love** [loyalty],
as you promised me, your servant.

77·Have mercy [LLet your mercy/compassion come] **on me so that I may live.**
I ·love [delight in] **your ·teachings** [laws; instructions].
78**Make ·proud** [arrogant] **people ashamed because they ·lied about me** [perverted me with lies].
But I will ·think about [meditate on] **your ·orders** [precepts].
79**Let those who ·respect** [fear; Prov. 1:7] **you return to me,**
those who know your ·rules [decrees; testimonies].
80**·Let me obey your demands perfectly** [LMay my heart be blameless in regard to your statutes/ordinances/requirements]
so I will not be ashamed.

81**I ·am weak from waiting for you to save me** [grow weak for your salvation/victory],
but I hope in your word.
82**My eyes ·are tired from looking** [grow weak] **for your promise.**
I ask, "When will you comfort me?"
83**Even though I am like a wine bag in smoke** [Cshrunken and dried out],
I do not forget your ·demands [statutes; ordinances; requirements].
84**·How long will I live** [LLike what are the days of your servant]?
When will you ·judge [perform judgment on] **those who are ·hurting** [pursuing] **me?**
85**·Proud** [Arrogant] **people have dug pits** [Cto trap him].
They ·have nothing to do with your teachings [Lare not according to your teachings/instructions/laws].
86**All of your commands ·can be trusted** [are reliable].
Liars are ·hurting [pursuing] **me. Help me!**
87**They have almost put me in the ·grave** [Learth],
but I have not ·rejected [abandoned; forsaken] **your ·orders** [precepts].
88**Give me life ·by your love** [Laccording to your loyalty]
so I can ·obey [keep; guard] **your ·rules** [decrees; testimonies].

89**·LORD, your word is everlasting** [*or* The LORD is everlasting];
·it [Lyour word] **·continues forever** [Lis firm] **in heaven.**
90**Your ·loyalty** [faithfulness; truth] **will go on and on;**
you ·made [established] **the earth, and it ·still stands** [endures].
91**All things ·continue** [endure] **to this day because of your ·laws** [judgments],
because all things ·serve you [Lare your servants].
92**If I had not ·loved** [delighted in] **your ·teachings** [instructions; laws],
I would have ·died [perished] **·from my sufferings** [in my afflictions].
93**I will never forget your ·orders** [precepts],
because you have given me life by them.
94**I am yours. ·Save me** [Give me victory].
I ·want to obey [seek] **your ·orders** [precepts].
95**Wicked people ·are waiting** [hope] **to ·destroy me** [make me perish],
but I will ·think about [consider] **your ·rules** [decrees; testimonies].
96**Everything I see has its limits,**
but your commands ·have none [Lare very broad].

97**How I love your ·teachings** [instructions; laws]!
I ·think about [ponder; meditate on] **them all day long.**

98Your commands make me wiser than my enemies,
because they are mine forever.
99I am ·wiser [more insightful] than all my teachers,
because I ·think about [ponder; meditate on] your ·rules [decrees; testimonies].
100I have more understanding than the elders,
because I ·follow [protect] your ·orders [precepts].
101I have ·avoided [Lkept my feet from] every evil way
so I could ·obey [keep; guard] your word.
102I haven't ·walked [turned] away from your ·laws [judgments],
because you yourself are my teacher.
103·Your promises are sweet to me [LHow sweet your words slip/slide down my palate],
sweeter than honey in my mouth!
104Your ·orders [precepts] give me understanding,
so I hate lying ways.

105Your word is like a lamp for my feet
and a light for my path [Cit shows how life should be lived].
106I ·will do what I have promised [Lhave sworn and confirmed it]
and ·obey [keep; guard] your ·fair [righteous] ·laws [judgments].
107I have suffered ·for a long time [*or* greatly].
LORD, ·give me [spare my] life by your word.
108LORD, accept my ·willing [offering of] praise
and teach me your ·laws [judgments].
109My life is always in ·danger [Lmy hand],
but I haven't forgotten your ·teachings [instructions; laws].
110Wicked people have set a trap for me,
but I haven't ·strayed [wandered] from your ·orders [precepts].
111·I will follow your rules forever [LYour rules/decrees/precepts are my inheritance forever],
because they make ·me [Lmy heart] happy.
112I will ·try [Lincline my heart] to do ·what you demand [Lyour statutes/ordinances]
forever, until the end.

113I hate ·disloyal [*or* double-minded] people,
but I love your ·teachings [instructions; laws].
114You are my hiding place and my shield;
I hope in your word.
115Get away from me, you who do evil,
so I can ·keep [protect] my God's commands.
116·Support [Uphold] me as you promised so I can live.
Don't let me be embarrassed because of my hopes.
117·Help [Strengthen] me, and I will ·be saved [have victory].
I will always ·respect [care about] your ·demands [statutes; ordinances; requirements].
118You ·reject [treat as worthless] those who ·ignore [go astray from] your ·demands [statutes; ordinances; requirements],
because their lies ·mislead them [leave them in the lurch].
119You throw away the wicked of the world like ·trash [dross].
So I will love your ·rules [decrees; testimonies].

120·I [LMy flesh] ·shake [shudder] in ·fear [dread] of you;
I ·respect [fear] your ·laws [judgments].

121I have done what is ·fair [just] and ·right [righteous].
Don't leave me to ·those who wrong me [my oppressors/exploiters].
122·Promise that you will help me, [LStand as security for/Guarantee
good for] your servant.
Don't let ·proud [arrogant] people ·wrong [oppress; exploit] me.
123My eyes ·are tired from looking [fail; grow weak] for your ·salvation
[victory]
and for your good promise.
124·Show your love to me, your servant [Deal with your servant
according to your love/loyalty],
and teach me your ·demands [statutes; ordinances; requirements].
125I am your servant. ·Give me wisdom [Make me understand]
so I can ·understand [know] your ·rules [decrees; testimonies].
126LORD, it is time for you to do something,
because ·people have disobeyed your teachings [Lyour teachings/
instructions/laws have been broken].
127I love your commands
more than ·the purest gold [Lgold, the finest gold].
128I ·respect [*or* follow] all your ·orders [precepts],
so I hate ·lying [false] ways.

129Your ·rules [decrees; testimonies] are wonderful.
That is why I ·keep [protect] them.
130·Learning [LOpening] your words ·gives wisdom [illuminates; gives
light]
and understanding for the ·foolish [immature; simpleminded].
131·I am nearly out of breath [LI crack/open my mouth and pant].
I ·really want to learn [Llong for] your commands.
132·Look at [LTurn to] me and have ·mercy [compassion] on me
·as you do [Las is your custom] for those who love ·you [Lyour name].
133·Guide my steps [LSteady my feet] as you promised;
don't let any ·sin [guilt] ·control [dominate] me.
134·Save [Redeem] me from ·harmful [Loppressive; exploitative] people
so I can ·obey [keep; guard] your ·orders [precepts].
135·Show your kindness to [LMake your face shine on] me, your servant
[Num. 6:24–26].
Teach me your ·demands [statutes; ordinances; requirements].
136·Tears stream [LStreams of water come down] from my eyes,
because people do not ·obey [keep; guard] your ·teachings
[instructions; laws].

137LORD, you ·do what is right [are righteous],
and your ·laws [judgments] are ·fair [virtuous; upright].
138·The rules [LYour decrees/testimonies] you commanded are ·right
[righteous]
and completely ·trustworthy [true; faithful].
139·I am so upset I am worn out [LMy passion/zeal consumes; *or* silences
me],
because my ·enemies [foes] have forgotten your words.

140Your promises are ·proven [refined],
so I, your servant, love them.
141I am ·unimportant [small] and ·hated [despised],
but I have not forgotten your ·orders [precepts].
142Your ·goodness continues forever [righteousness is an everlasting righteousness],
and your ·teachings [instructions; laws] are ·true [faithful].
143·I have had troubles and misery [LDistress and pressure have found me],
but I ·love [delight in] your commands.
144Your ·rules [decrees; testimonies] are always ·good [righteous].
·Help [Make] me understand so I can live.

145I call to you with all my heart.
Answer me, Lord, and I will ·keep [protect] your ·demands [statutes; ordinances; requirements].
146I call to you.
·Save me [Give me victory] so I can ·obey [keep; guard] your ·rules [decrees; testimonies].
147I ·wake up early in the morning [get up before dawn] and cry out.
I hope in your word.
148·I stay awake all night [LMy eyes awake in the watches of the night]
so I can ·think about [meditate on] your promises.
149·Listen to me [LHear my voice] because of your ·love [loyalty];
Lord, ·give me [spare my] life by your ·laws [judgments].
150Those who ·love evil [Lpursue/persecute me with an evil plan] are near,
but they are far from your ·teachings [instructions; laws].
151But, Lord, you are also near,
and all your commands are ·true [faithful].
152Long ago I learned from your ·rules [decrees; testimonies]
that you made them ·to continue [foundational] forever.

153See my ·suffering [affliction] and rescue me,
because I have not forgotten your ·teachings [instructions; laws].
154Argue my case and ·save [redeem] me.
·Let me live [Spare my life] by your promises.
155·Wicked people are far from being saved [LSalvation/Victory is far from the wicked],
because they do not ·want [seek] your ·demands [statutes; ordinances; requirements].
156Lord, ·you are very kind [Lyour compassion/mercies are abundant];
give me life by your ·laws [judgments].
157Many ·enemies [foes] ·are after [pursue; persecute] me,
but I have not ·rejected [swerved from] your ·rules [decrees; testimonies].
158I see those traitors, and I ·hate [loathe; am disgusted by] them,
because they do not ·obey [keep; guard] what you say.
159See how I love your ·orders [precepts].
Lord, give me life by your ·love [loyalty].
160·Your words are true from the start [LThe head of your word is true/faithful],
and all your ·laws [judgments] will be ·fair [righteous] forever.

161Leaders ·attack [pursue] me for no reason,
but ·I fear your law in my heart [Lmy heart fears your words].
162I ·am as happy over [delight in] your promises
as if I had found ·a great treasure [much plunder].
163I hate and ·despise [loathe] lies,
but I love your ·teachings [instructions; laws].
164Seven times a day I praise you
for your ·fair laws [righteous judgments].
165Those who love your ·teachings [instructions; laws] will find ·true peace [*or* much prosperity],
and nothing will ·defeat them [make them stumble].
166I am ·waiting [hoping] for ·you to save me [Lyour salvation/victory], LORD.
I will ·obey [Ldo] your commands.
167I ·obey [keep; guard] your ·rules [decrees; testimonies],
and I love them very much.
168I ·obey [keep; guard] your ·orders [precepts] and ·rules [decrees; testimonies],
because ·you know everything I do [Lall my ways are before you].

169·Hear my cry to you [LLet my shout of joy come near you], LORD.
Let your word help me understand.
170Listen to my ·prayer [supplication];
·save [protect] me as you promised.
171Let ·me [Lmy lips] ·speak [bubble forth] your praise,
because you have taught me your ·demands [statutes; ordinances; requirements].
172Let ·me [Lmy tongue] sing about your promises,
because all your commands are ·fair [righteous].
173Give me your helping hand,
because I have chosen your ·commands [precepts].
174I ·want you to save me [Ldesire your salvation/victory], LORD.
I ·love [delight in] your ·teachings [instructions; laws].
175Let me live so I can praise you,
and let your ·laws [judgments] help me.
176I have ·wandered [gone astray] like a lost sheep.
·Look for [Seek] your servant, because I have not forgotten your commands.

A Prayer of Someone Far from Home

A psalm ·for going up to worship [of ascents; Cperhaps sung while traveling to Jerusalem to celebrate an annual religious festival like Passover].

120

When I was in ·trouble [distress], I called to the LORD,
and he answered me.
2LORD, ·save [protect] me from ·liars [Lfalse lips]
and from ·those who plan evil [La deceptive tongue].

3·You who plan evil [LO deceptive tongue], what will ·God do [Lhe give] to you?
·How will he punish [LWhat will he add to] you?
4·He will punish you with the sharp arrows of a warrior
and with burning coals of wood [LThe sharp arrows of a warrior and

the burning coals of a broom tree; [C]the broom tree produces excellent charcoal].

5·How terrible it is for [LWoe to] me to ·live in the land of [Lsojourn/wander in] Meshech [Cby the Black Sea in Asia Minor; Gen. 10:2; Ezek. 38:2],
to ·live [dwell; reside] among the ·people [Ltents] of Kedar [Cin the Arabian desert; Is. 21:16–17; Jer. 2:10; 49:28; Ezek. 27:21].
6I have ·lived [dwelt; resided] too long
with people who hate peace.
7When I talk peace,
they want war.

The Lord Guards His People

A song ·for going up to worship [of ascents; Cperhaps sung while traveling to Jerusalem to celebrate an annual religious festival like Passover].

121 I ·look up [Lraise my eyes] to the hills [Cthe hills surrounding Zion, the location of the Temple],
but where does my help come from?
2My help comes from the LORD,
who made heaven and earth [Gen. 1].

3He will not let ·you be defeated [Lyour feet be moved/slip].
He who ·guards [watches] you never sleeps.
4He who ·guards [watches] Israel
never ·rests [sleeps] or ·sleeps [slumbers].
5The LORD ·guards [watches] you.
The LORD is the shade ·that protects you from the sun [Lat your hand, your right hand; 91:1].
6The sun cannot ·hurt [Lstrike] you during the day,
and the moon cannot ·hurt [Lstrike] you at night.
7The LORD will ·protect [guard; watch] you from all ·dangers [trouble; evil];
he will ·guard [watch] your life.
8The LORD will ·guard [watch] you as you come and go,
both now and forever.

Happy People in Jerusalem

A song ·for going up to worship [of ascents; Cperhaps sung while traveling to Jerusalem to celebrate an annual religious festival like Passover]. Of David.

122 I ·was happy [rejoiced] when they said to me,
"Let's ·go [walk] to the ·Temple [Lhouse] of the LORD."
2Jerusalem, ·we [Lour feet] are standing
at your gates.

3Jerusalem is built as a city
·with the buildings close together [Lthat is closely tied together].
4The tribes [Cthe twelve tribes of Israel] go up there,
the tribes who belong to the LORD.
It is the ·rule [decree; testimony] in Israel
to ·praise [Lthank the name of] the LORD at Jerusalem.

5There ·are set thrones to judge the people [Ldwell thrones of judgment],
the thrones of the ·descendants [dynasty; Lhouse] of David.

6·Pray [LAsk] for peace in Jerusalem:
"May those who love her ·be safe [prosper].
7May there be peace within her ·walls [ramparts]
and ·safety [security] within her strong towers."
8To help my ·relatives [brothers] and ·friends [neighbors],
I say, "Let ·Jerusalem have peace [Lpeace be within you]."
9For the sake of the ·Temple [Lhouse] of the LORD our God,
I ·wish [Lseek] ·good [prosperity] for her.

A Prayer for Mercy

A song ·for going up to worship [of ascents; Cperhaps sung while traveling to Jerusalem to celebrate an annual religious festival like Passover].

123 LORD, I ·look upward [Llift up my eyes] to you,
you who ·live [are enthroned; Lsit] in heaven.
2·Slaves depend on their masters [LLike the eyes of servants/slaves to the hand of their master],
and ·a female servant depends on her mistress [Llike the eyes of a maidservant to the hand of her mistress].
·In the same way, we depend on the LORD our God [L…thus our eyes are to the LORD our God as…];
we wait for him to show us ·mercy [grace].

3·Have mercy on [Be gracious to] us, LORD. ·Have mercy on [Be gracious to] us,
because we have been insulted.
4We ·have suffered [are filled with the] ·many insults [much ridicule] from ·lazy [untroubled; unworried] people
and much ·cruelty [scorn] from the proud.

The Lord Saves His People

A song ·for going up to worship [of ascents; Cperhaps sung while traveling to Jerusalem to celebrate an annual religious festival like Passover]. Of David.

124 What if the LORD had not been on our side?
(Let Israel ·repeat this [Lsay].)
2What if the LORD had not been on our side
when ·we were attacked [Lpeople rose against us]?
3When they were angry with us,
they would have swallowed us alive.
4They would have been like ·a flood [Lwater] ·drowning [overflowing] us;
they would have ·poured [passed] over us like a ·river [torrent].
5 They would have ·swept us away [passed over us] like ·a mighty stream [raging waters].

6·Praise [Blessed be] the LORD,
who did not ·let them chew us up [Lgive us as prey to their teeth].
7We escaped like a bird
from the ·hunter's [fowler's] trap.
The trap broke,
and we escaped.

[8]Our help ·comes from [[L]is in the name of] the LORD,
who made heaven and earth [Gen. 1].

God Protects Those Who Trust Him

A song ·for going up to worship [of ascents; [C]perhaps sung while traveling to Jerusalem to celebrate an annual religious festival like Passover].

125 Those who ·trust [have confidence in] the LORD are like
Mount Zion [[C]the location of the Temple],
which sits unmoved forever.
[2]As the mountains surround Jerusalem,
the LORD surrounds his people
now and forever.
[3]The ·wicked will not rule
over [[L]scepter of the wicked will not rest on; [C]the scepter is a symbol of rule] ·those who do right [[L]the allotment of the righteous].
·If they did, the people who do right
might use their power to do evil [[L]…so the righteous do not send forth their hands in evil].

[4]LORD, ·be [*or* do] good to those who are good,
whose hearts are ·honest [virtuous; filled with integrity].
[5]But, LORD, when you ·remove [turn aside] those who ·do evil [are twisted/perverted],
also ·remove [[L]make go away] those who ·stop following you [[L]do evil].

Let there be peace in Israel.

Lord, Bring Your People Back

A song ·for going up to worship [of ascents; [C]perhaps sung while traveling to Jerusalem to celebrate an annual religious festival like Passover].

126 When the LORD ·brought the prisoners back to [brought back those who returned to; *or* restored the fortunes of]
Jerusalem [[L]Zion; [C]probably the return from the exile; 2 Chr. 36:22–23; Ezra 1],
it seemed as if we were dreaming [[C]so surprised and happy that it did not seem real].
[2]Then ·we [[L]our mouths] were filled with laughter,
and ·we [[L]our tongues] ·sang happy songs [shouted joyfully].
Then the other nations said,
"The LORD has done great things for them."
[3]The LORD has done great things for us,
and we ·are very glad [rejoice].

[4]LORD, ·return our prisoners [bring back those who return; *or* restore our fortunes] again,
as you bring streams to the ·desert [[L]Negev; [C]an arid area in the south of Israel].
[5]Those who cry as they ·plant crops [sow; plant seed]
will ·sing [shout for joy] at harvest time.
[6]Those who ·cry [[L]go out weeping]
as they carry out the ·seeds [[L]bag with seeds]
will return singing
and carrying ·bundles of grain [sheaves].

All Good Things Come from God

A song ·for going up to worship [of ascents; [C]perhaps sung while traveling to Jerusalem to celebrate an annual religious festival like Passover]. Of Solomon.

127 If the LORD doesn't build the house,
the builders are working ·for nothing [in vain;
without purpose].
If the LORD doesn't guard the city,
the guards are watching ·for nothing [in vain; without purpose].
2 It is ·no use [in vain; without purpose] for you to get up early
and stay up late,
·working for a living [[L]eating the bread of hardship/pain].
The LORD ·gives sleep to those he loves [*or* provides for those he loves
while they sleep].
3 Children are ·a gift [an inheritance] from the LORD;
·babies [[L]the fruit of the womb] are a reward.
4 Children ·who are born to a young man [[L]of one's youth]
are like arrows in the hand of a warrior [[C]they help in the challenges
and conflicts of life].
5 ·Happy [Blessed] is the man
who has his ·bag [quiver] full of ·arrows [[L]them].
They will not be ·defeated [[L]humiliated]
when they ·fight [[L]speak to] their enemies at the city gate [[C]the
central place of commerce and government].

The Happy Home

A song ·for going up to worship [of ascents; [C]perhaps sung while traveling to Jerusalem to celebrate an annual religious festival like Passover].

128 ·Happy [Blessed] are those who ·respect [fear] the LORD
[Prov. 1:7] and ·obey him [[L]walk in his ways].
2 You will ·enjoy what you work for [[L]eat the labor of your hands],
and you will be ·blessed [happy] with ·good things [prosperity].
3 Your wife will be like a fruitful vine [[C]produce many children] in your
house [Prov. 31:10–31].
Your children will be like olive branches [[C]bringing much good]
around your table [Mic. 4:4; Zech. 3:10].
4 This is how the man who ·respects [fears] the LORD [Prov. 1:7]
will be blessed.
5 May the LORD bless you from Mount Zion [[C]the location of the Temple];
may you ·enjoy [experience; [L]see] the ·good things [prosperity] of
Jerusalem all the days of your life.
6 May you see your grandchildren.

Let there be peace in Israel.

A Prayer Against the Enemies

A song ·for going up to worship [of ascents; [C]perhaps sung while traveling to Jerusalem to celebrate an annual religious festival like Passover].

129 ·They have treated me badly all my life [[L]Many are my
foes from my youth].
(Let Israel ·repeat this [[L]say].)
2 ·They have treated me badly all my life [[L]Many are my foes from my
youth],
but they have not ·defeated [overcome; prevailed over] me.

3 ·Like farmers plowing, they plowed over my back [LThe plowers
plowed my back],
making ·long wounds [Ltheir furrows long].
4 But the LORD does what is right;
he has ·set me free from those [Lcut the cords of] wicked people.

5 Let those who hate ·Jerusalem [LZion; Cthe location of the Temple]
be ·turned back in shame [Lhumiliated and turn back].
6 Let them be like the grass on the roof
that dries up before it has grown.
7 There is not enough of it ·to [Lfor the harvester to] fill a hand
or ·to make into a bundle [those who bind sheaves] to fill one's arms.
8 Let those who pass by them not say,
"May the LORD bless you.
We bless you by the ·power [Lname] of the LORD."

A Prayer for Mercy

A song ·for going up to worship [of ascents; Cperhaps sung while traveling to Jerusalem to celebrate an annual religious festival like Passover].

130 LORD, ·I am in great trouble [Lfrom the depths],
so I ·call out [pray] to you.
2 Lord, hear my voice;
·listen to my prayer for help [Llet your ear pay attention to the sound
of my supplication].
3 LORD, if you ·punished people for all their sins [Lobserved/watched/
guarded against iniquity],
·no one would be left [Lwho could stand…?], Lord.
4 But you forgive ·us [Lyour people],
so you are ·respected [feared; Prov. 1:7].

5 I ·wait [hope] for the LORD ·to help me [Lmy soul hopes],
and I ·trust [hope in] his word.
6 I ·wait for the Lord to help me [hope for the Lord]
more than night watchmen wait for the ·dawn [morning],
more than night watchmen wait for the ·dawn [morning].

7 People of Israel, put your hope in the LORD
because he is ·loving [loyal]
and ·able to save [Lwith him is abundant redemption].
8 He will ·save [redeem] Israel
from all their ·sins [iniquities].

Childlike Trust in the Lord

A song ·for going up to worship [of ascents; Cperhaps sung while traveling to Jerusalem to celebrate an annual religious festival like Passover]. Of David.

131 LORD, my heart is not proud;
·I don't look down on others [Lmy eyes are not
haughty/lifted up].
I don't ·do [consider doing] great things,
and I ·can't do [don't consider doing] ·miracles [wonderful acts].
2 But I ·am calm and quiet [Lhave stilled and quieted my soul]
like a ·baby [Lweaned child] with its mother,

like a ·baby [Lweaned child] with its mother [Ca relationship with God is like that of a mother with her weaned child resting comfortably in her arms].

3People of Israel, put your hope in the LORD
now and forever.

In Praise of the Temple

A song ·for going up to worship [of ascents; Cperhaps sung while traveling to Jerusalem to celebrate an annual religious festival like Passover].

132 LORD, remember David
and all his ·suffering [afflictions].
2He ·made an oath [swore] to the LORD,
a ·promise [vow] to the Mighty God of Jacob [Gen. 49:24].
3He said, "I will not ·go home to my house [Lenter into the tent of my house],
or ·lie down on my bed [Lgo up to the couch of my bed],
4or ·close [Lgive sleep to] my eyes,
or ·let myself sleep [Lslumber to my pupils]
5until I find a place for the LORD.
I want to provide a home for the Mighty God of Jacob [Gen. 49:24]."

6We heard about it [Cthe Ark] in ·Bethlehem [LEphrathah].
We found it in the fields of Jearim [CKiriath Jearim; 1 Sam 6:21—7:2].
7Let's go to ·the LORD's house [Lhis dwelling].
Let's worship at his footstool [Cthe Ark].
8Rise, LORD, and come to your resting place;
come with the Ark that shows your strength.
9May your priests ·do what is right [Lbe clothed with righteousness].
May your ·people [saints; loyal ones] sing for joy.

10For the sake of your servant David,
do not ·reject [Lturn from the face of] your ·appointed [anointed] king.
11The LORD ·made a promise [swore] to David,
a sure promise that he will not take back [2 Sam. 7:12–16, 28].
He promised, "I will ·make one of your descendants
rule as king after you [Lset on your throne from the fruit of your womb; Acts 2:30].
12If your sons ·keep [observe; guard] my ·agreement [covenant; treaty]
and the ·rules [decrees; testimonies] that I teach them,
then their sons after them will ·rule [Lsit]
on your throne forever and ever."

13The LORD has chosen ·Jerusalem [LZion; Cthe location of the Temple];
he ·wants [desires] it for his home.
14He says, "This is my resting place forever.
Here is where I ·want to stay [Lwill sit/reside because I desire it].
15I will bless her with ·plenty [provisions];
I will ·fill [satisfy] her poor with ·food [bread].
16I will ·cover [Lclothe] her priests with ·salvation [victory],
and ·those who worship me [Lher saints/loyal ones] will really sing for joy.

17"I will ·make a king come from the family of [Lcause a horn to sprout
up for; Can animal's horn symbolizes strength] David [Luke
1:69–70].
I will ·provide my appointed one descendants to rule after him
[Lprepare a lamp for my anointed king; 2 Sam. 21:17].
18I will ·cover [Lclothe] his enemies with shame,
but his crown will shine."

The Love of God's People

A song ·for going up to worship [of ascents; Cperhaps sung while traveling to Jerusalem to celebrate an annual religious festival like Passover]. Of David.

133 ·It is [LHow] good and pleasant
when ·God's people [Lbrothers] live together [Cin unity]!
2It is like ·perfumed [fine] oil on the head
and running down his beard [Ex. 30:22–33].
It ran down Aaron's beard
and on to the collar of his robes.
3It is like the dew of Mount Hermon [Cin the extreme north of Israel]
falling on the hills of ·Jerusalem [LZion; Cthe location of the Temple].
There the LORD ·gives [Lcommanded] his blessing
of life forever.

Temple Guards, Praise the Lord

A song ·for going up to worship [of ascents; Cperhaps sung while traveling to Jerusalem to celebrate an annual religious festival like Passover].

134 ·Praise [LBless] the LORD, all you servants of the LORD,
you who ·serve [Lstand] at night in the ·Temple [Lhouse]
of the LORD.
2Raise your hands in the ·Temple [Lholy place]
and ·praise [bless] the LORD.

3May the LORD bless you from Mount Zion [Lthe location of the Temple],
he who made heaven and earth [Gen. 1].

The Lord Saves, Idols Do Not

135 Praise the LORD!
Praise the name of the LORD;
praise him, you servants of the LORD,
2you who stand in the LORD's ·Temple [Lhouse]
and in the ·Temple courtyards [Lcourtyards of the house of our God].
3Praise the LORD, because the LORD is good;
·sing praises [make a psalm] to him, because it is pleasant.

4The LORD has chosen the people of Jacob for himself;
he has chosen the people of Israel ·for his very own [as his special
possession/treasure; Ex. 19:5–6; Deut. 7:6; 14:2; Mal. 3:17].
5I know that the LORD is great.
Our Lord is greater than all the gods.
6The LORD does what he pleases,
in heaven and on earth,
in the seas and the deep oceans.
7He brings the clouds from the ends of the earth.
He ·sends [Lmakes] the lightning with the rain.
He brings out the wind from his storehouses [Job 38:22–23].

[8]He ·destroyed [Lstruck] the firstborn sons in Egypt
the firstborn of both people and animals [Ex. 12].
[9]He ·did [Lsent] many signs and ·miracles [wonders] in Egypt
against ·the king [LPharaoh] and all his servants [Lthe plagues;
Ex. 7–12].
[10]He ·defeated [Lstruck] many nations
and killed ·powerful [strong] kings:
[11]Sihon king of the Amorites,
Og king of Bashan [Num. 21:21–35],
and all the kings of Canaan [Num. 21:1–3; Josh. 1–12].
[12]Then he gave their land as a ·gift [Linheritance],
a ·gift [Linheritance] to his people, the Israelites [Josh. 13–24].

[13]LORD, your name is everlasting;
LORD, you will be remembered forever.
[14]The LORD ·defends [vindicates] his people
and ·has mercy on [shows grace to] his servants.

[15]The idols of other nations are made of silver and gold,
the work of human hands.
[16]They have mouths, but they cannot speak.
They have eyes, but they cannot see.
[17]They have ears, but they cannot hear.
They have no breath in their mouths.
[18]People who make idols will be like them,
and so will those who ·trust [have confidence in] them [115:4–8;
Is. 44:9–20; 46:6–7; Jer. 10:1–9; Hab. 2:18–19].

[19]·Family [LHouse] of Israel, ·praise [bless] the LORD.
·Family [LHouse] of Aaron [Cthe priests], ·praise [bless] the LORD.
[20]·Family [LHouse] of Levi [Cassistants to the priests], ·praise [bless]
the LORD.
You who ·respect [fear] the LORD [Prov. 1:7] should ·praise [bless]
him.
[21]You ·people of [Lwho live in] Jerusalem, ·praise [bless] the LORD on
Mount Zion [Cthe location of the Temple].
Praise the LORD!

God's Love Continues Forever

136 ·Give thanks to [Praise] the LORD because he is good.
His ·love [loyalty] continues forever.
[2]·Give thanks to [Praise] the God of gods.
His ·love [loyalty] continues forever.
[3]·Give thanks to [Praise] the Lord of lords.
His ·love [loyalty] continues forever.

[4]Only he can do ·great miracles [great and wonderful acts].
His ·love [loyalty] continues forever.
[5]With his ·wisdom [Lunderstanding; 104:24; Prov. 3:19; Jer. 10:12] he
made the ·skies [heavens; Gen. 1:6–7].
His ·love [loyalty] continues forever.
[6]He spread out the earth on the ·seas [waters; Gen. 1:9–10].
His ·love [loyalty] continues forever.

7He made the ·sun and the moon [Lgreat lights; Gen. 1:14–15].
His ·love [loyalty] continues forever.
8He made the sun to rule the day [Gen. 1:16–18].
His ·love [loyalty] continues forever.
9He made the moon and stars to rule the night [Gen. 1:16–18].
His ·love [loyalty] continues forever.

10He ·killed [Lstruck] the firstborn sons of the Egyptians [Ex. 11].
His ·love [loyalty] continues forever.
11He brought the people of Israel out of ·Egypt [Ltheir midst; Ex. 12:31–51].
His ·love [loyalty] continues forever.
12He did it with his ·great power [Lstrong hand] and ·strength [Loutstretched arm].
His ·love [loyalty] continues forever.
13He parted the water of the ·Red [*or* Reed] Sea [78:13; Ex. 14–15].
His ·love [loyalty] continues forever.
14He brought the Israelites through the middle of it.
His ·love [loyalty] continues forever.
15But ·the king of Egypt [LPharaoh] and his army ·drowned in [were swept into] the ·Red [Reed] Sea [v. 13].
His ·love [loyalty] continues forever.

16He led his people through the ·desert [wilderness; Deut. 8:15; Jer. 2:6].
His ·love [loyalty] continues forever.
17He ·defeated [Lstruck] great kings.
His ·love [loyalty] continues forever.
18He killed ·powerful [mighty] kings.
His ·love [loyalty] continues forever.
19He defeated Sihon king of the Amorites [Num. 21:21–32].
His ·love [loyalty] continues forever.
20He defeated Og king of Bashan [Num. 21:32–35].
His ·love [loyalty] continues forever.
21He gave their land as a ·gift [inheritance].
His ·love [loyalty] continues forever.
22It was a ·gift [inheritance] to his servants, the Israelites.
His ·love [loyalty] continues forever.

23He remembered us ·when we were in trouble [Lin our low condition].
His ·love [loyalty] continues forever.
24He ·freed us from [pulled us away from] our ·enemies [foes].
His ·love [loyalty] continues forever.
25He gives ·food [bread] to ·every living creature [Lall flesh].
His ·love [loyalty] continues forever.

26·Give thanks to [Praise] the God of heaven.
His ·love [loyalty] continues forever.

Israelites in Captivity

137 By the rivers in Babylon we sat and ·cried [wept; Cduring the Babylonian exile]
when we remembered ·Jerusalem [LZion; Cthe location of the Temple].

[2]On the ·poplar [*or* willow] **trees nearby**
we hung our harps.
[3]·**Those who captured us** [Our captors] **asked us to sing;**
our ·enemies [oppressors] **wanted happy songs.**
They said, "Sing us a song about ·Jerusalem [[L]Zion; [C]the location of the Temple]**!"**

[4]**But we cannot sing songs about the LORD**
while we are in this foreign ·country [land]**!**
[5]**Jerusalem, if I forget you,**
let my right hand ·lose its skill [[L]forget; [C]its skill of playing a musical instrument].
[6]**Let my tongue stick to the roof of my mouth**
if I do not remember you,
if I do not ·think about Jerusalem
as my greatest joy [*or* go up to Jerusalem with joy on my head].

[7]**LORD, remember ·what the Edomites did** [[L]the sons of Edom]
on the day ·Jerusalem fell [[L]of Jerusalem; Lam. 4:21; Ezek. 25:12–14; 35:5–15; Obad. 11–14].
They said, "Tear it down!
Tear it down to its foundations!"

[8]·**People** [[L]Daughter] **of Babylon, you will be destroyed.**
The people who pay you back for what you did to us will be ·happy [blessed].
[9]**They will grab your ·babies** [little ones]
and throw them against the rocks.

A Hymn of Thanksgiving

A psalm of David.

138 **LORD, I will ·thank** [praise] **you with all my heart;**
I will ·sing [make a psalm] **to you before the gods.**
[2]**I will bow down facing your holy Temple,**
and I will ·thank [praise] **·you** [[L]your name] **for your ·love** [loyalty] **and ·loyalty** [faithfulness].
You have ·made your name and your word
greater than anything [[L]exalted your word above all your name].
[3]**On the day I ·called** [prayed] **to you, you answered me.**
You ·made me strong and brave [[L]have emboldened/encouraged my soul with strength].

[4]**LORD, let all the kings of the earth ·praise** [thank] **you**
when they hear the words ·you speak [[L]of your mouth].
[5]**They will sing about ·what the LORD has done** [[L]the way of the LORD],
because the LORD's glory [[C]his manifest presence] **is great.**

[6]**Though the LORD is ·supreme** [exalted],
he ·takes care of [looks on] **·those who are humble** [the lowly],
but he ·stays away from the proud [[L]perceives the proud from far away].
[7]**LORD, ·even when I have trouble all around me** [[L]if I walk in the midst of distress],
you will keep me alive.

When my enemies are angry,
you will ·reach down [Lsend out your hand] and save me by your ·power [Lright hand].
8LORD, you ·do everything [fulfill/accomplish your plan] for me.
LORD, your ·love [loyalty] continues forever.
Do not ·leave [abandon; forsake] us, ·whom you made [Lthe work of your hands].

For the director of music. A psalm of David.

God Knows Everything

139 LORD, you have ·examined [investigated; searched] me
and know all about me.
2You know when I sit down and when I ·get up [rise].
You ·know [understand] my thoughts ·before I think them [Lfrom afar].
3You ·know [Lmeasure] ·where I go [Lmy path] and ·where I lie down [Lmy lying down].
You ·know [are familiar with] ·everything I do [Lall my path].
4LORD, even ·before I say a word [Lwhen no word is on my tongue],
you already know ·it [Lall of it].
5You ·are all around me [Lhem me in]—in front and in back—
and have put your hand on me.
6Your knowledge is ·amazing [wonderful; *or* overwhelming] to me;
it is ·more than I can understand [too high/unattainable. I am not able to grasp it; Rom. 11:33].

7Where can I go to get away from your Spirit?
Where can I ·run [flee] from you?
8If I ·go [climb] up to the heavens, you are there.
If I ·lie down [spread out; make my bed] in ·the grave [LSheol; Cthe grave or the underworld], you are there.
9If I rise with the ·sun in the east [Lwings of the dawn]
and settle in the ·west beyond [Lback of] the sea,
10even there ·you [Lyour hand] would guide me.
With your right hand you would ·hold [grab; seize] me.

11I could say, "The darkness will ·hide [cover] me.
Let the light around me turn into night."
12But even the darkness is not dark to you.
The night ·is as light as [shines like] the day;
darkness and light are the same to you.

13You ·made [created] my ·whole being [inward parts];
you ·formed [knitted] me in my mother's ·body [belly; womb].
14I ·praise [thank] you because you made me in an ·amazing [awesome] and wonderful way.
What you have done is wonderful.
I know this very well.
15·You saw my bones being formed [LMy bones were not hidden from you]
as I ·took shape [was made] in ·my mother's body [Lsecret].
When I was ·put together [Lwoven] ·there [Lin the depths of the earth],
16 ·you [Lyour eyes] saw my ·body as it was formed [Lembyro].

All the days ·planned [[L]formed] for me
were written in your book
·before I was one day old [not one of them existed].

[17]God, your thoughts are precious to me.
·They are so many [[L]How vast are their sum; Job 42:3]!
[18]If I could count them,
they would be more than all the grains of sand.
When I ·wake up [*or* come to the end],
I am still with you.

[19]God, I wish you would kill the wicked!
Get away from me, you ·murderers [[L]people of blood]!
[20]They ·say evil things about [make evil plans against] you.
Your enemies ·use your name thoughtlessly [[L]lift in vain; Ex. 20:7].
[21]Lord, ·I hate [[L]Do I not hate…?] those who hate you;
·I hate [[L]Do I not abhor…?] those who rise up against you.
[22]I ·feel only hate for them [[L]hate them with a perfect/complete hatred];
they are my enemies.

[23]God, ·examine [investigate; search; v. 1] me and know my heart;
test me and know my anxious thoughts.
[24]See if there is any ·bad thing [hurtful way] in me.
Lead me on the ·road to everlasting life [[L]everlasting/*or* ancient way].

A Prayer for Protection

For the director of music. A psalm of David.

140 Lord, rescue me from evil people;
protect me from ·cruel [violent] people
[2]who ·make evil plans [[L]consider evil in their hearts],
who ·always start fights [[L]every day stir up war; Prov. 15:18; 29:22].
[3]They make their tongues sharp as a snake's;
·their words are like snake poison [[L]the venom of vipers is under
their lips; Rom. 3:13]. ·*Selah* [Interlude]

[4]Lord, ·guard [keep] me from the ·power [[L]hand] of wicked people;
protect me from ·cruel [violent] people
who plan ·to trip me up [my downfall].
[5]The ·proud [arrogant] hid a trap for me.
They spread out a net [[L]with cords] beside the road;
they set ·traps [snares] for me. ·*Selah* [Interlude]

[6]I said to the Lord, "You are my God."
Lord, ·listen [[L]give ear] to my prayer ·for help [of supplication].
[7]Lord God, my ·mighty [strong] ·savior [victor],
you ·protect me in [[L]cover my head in the day of] battle.
[8]Lord, do not give the wicked what they ·want [desire].
Don't let their plans succeed,
or they will become ·proud [exalted]. ·*Selah* [Interlude]

[9]Those around me have ·planned trouble [[L]uplifted heads].
Now let ·it [[L]the trouble of their lips] come to them.
[10]Let burning coals ·fall [rain] on them.

·Throw them [Let them fall] into the fire
or into pits from which they cannot ·escape [get up].
11Don't let ·liars [La tongue-man] ·settle [be established] in the land.
Let evil ·quickly [*or* with blows] hunt down ·cruel [violent] people.

12I know the LORD will get justice for the poor
and will defend the needy in court.
13·Good [Righteous] people will ·praise [thank] his name;
·honest [virtuous] people will live in his presence.

A Prayer Not to Sin

A psalm of David.

141 LORD, I ·call [pray] to you. Come quickly to me.
·Listen to me [LGive ear to my voice] when I ·call [pray] to you.
2Let my prayer be like incense placed before you [Ex. 30:7–8; Rev. 5:8],
and ·my praise [Lthe lifting of my hands] like the evening sacrifice.

3LORD, ·help me control my tongue [Lset a guard on my mouth];
·help me be careful about what I say [Lkeep watch on the door of my mouth; Prov. 13:3; 21:23; James 3:1–12].
4·Take away my desire to do evil [LDon't incline my heart to an evil matter]
or to join others in doing wrong.
Don't let me eat tasty food
with those who do evil.

5If a ·good [righteous] person ·punished [Lhit] me, that would be ·kind [an act of loyalty].
If he corrected me, that would be like perfumed oil on my head.
·I [LMy head] shouldn't refuse it.
But I pray against those who do evil.
6 Let their ·leaders [judges] be thrown down the cliffs.
Then people will ·know that I have spoken correctly [Llisten to my words for they are pleasant]:
7"·The ground [*or* The rock; LLike it] is plowed and broken up.
In the same way, our bones have been scattered at the ·grave [Lmouth of Sheol; Cthe grave or the underworld]."

8GOD, ·I look to you for help [Lmy eyes are to you].
I ·trust [find refuge] in you, LORD. Don't let ·me die [Lmy life pour out].
9·Protect [Guard; Keep] me from the traps they set for me
and from the net that evil people have spread.
10Let the wicked fall into their own nets,
but let me pass by safely.

A Prayer for Safety

A ·maskil [skillful psalm; meditation] of David when he was in the cave [Cat Adullam (1 Sam. 22:1, 4) or En-Gedi (1 Sam. 24:1–22)]. A prayer.

142 I cry out to the LORD;
I ·pray [cry out] to the LORD for ·mercy [grace].
2I pour out my ·problems [complaint] to him;
I tell him my ·troubles [distress].
3When ·I am afraid [I am depressed; Lmy spirit is faint],
you, LORD, know ·the way out [Lmy way].

In the path where I walk,
·a trap is hidden [Lthey have hidden a trap] for me.
4Look ·around me [Lat/on my right hand] and see.
No one cares about me.
·I have no place of safety [LA place of refuge perishes from me];
no one ·cares if I live [Lseeks for my soul].

5Lord, I cry out to you.
I say, "You are my ·protection [refuge].
·You are all I want in this life [L...my portion in the land of the living]."
6·Listen [Pay attention] to my cry,
because I am ·helpless [brought very low].
·Save [Protect] me from those who are ·chasing [pursuing; persecuting] me,
because they are too strong for me.
7·Free me [LBring me out] from my prison,
and then I will ·praise [thank] your name.
Then ·good [righteous] people will surround me,
because you have ·taken care of me [given me my reward].

A Prayer Not to Be Killed

A psalm of David.

143 Lord, hear my prayer;
·listen [Lgive ear] to my ·cry for mercy [prayer of supplication].
Answer me
because you are ·loyal [faithful] and ·good [righteous].
2Don't ·judge me [Lbring me into judgment], your servant,
because no one alive is ·right [righteous] before you [Rom. 3:22; Gal. 2:16].
3My enemies are ·chasing [pursuing; persecuting] me;
they crushed me to the ground.
They made me ·live [sit] in darkness
like those long dead [Lam. 3:6].
4·I am afraid [I am depressed; Lmy spirit is faint; 142:3];
my ·courage is gone [Lheart within me is desolated].

5I remember ·what happened long ago [Lthe former days];
I ·consider [meditated on] everything you have done.
I ·think [considered] ·about all you have made [Lthe work of your hands].
6I ·lift my hands to you in prayer [Lspread out my hands to you].
·As a dry land needs rain, I thirst [LMy life/soul is like a thirsty/parched land] for you. ·*Selah* [Interlude]

7Lord, answer me quickly,
because ·I am getting weak [Lmy spirit languishes].
Don't ·turn away [Lhide your face] from me,
or I will be like those who ·are dead [Lgo down to the pit].
8·Tell me [Make me hear] in the morning about your ·love [loyalty],
because I ·trust [have confidence in] you.
·Show me what I should do [LMake me know the way I should walk],
because ·my prayers go up [LI lift up my soul] to you.

[9]LORD, ·save [protect] me from my enemies;
I hide in you.
[10]Teach me to do ·what you want [your will],
because you are my God.
Let your good Spirit [*or* spirit]
·lead [guide] me on level ground.

[11]LORD, let me live
·so people will praise you [Lfor the sake of your name].
In your ·goodness [righteousness]
·save me [Lbring me out] from my ·troubles [distress].
[12]In your ·love [loyalty] ·defeat [destroy] my enemies.
·Destroy [LMake perish] all those who ·trouble [distress] me,
because I am your servant.

Of David.

A Prayer for Victory

144 ·Praise [Blessed be] the LORD, my Rock [61:2],
who trains ·me [Lmy hands] for war,
who trains ·me [Lmy fingers] for battle.
[2]·He protects me like a strong, walled city, and he loves me [LHe is my loyal one and my fortress].
He is my ·defender [stronghold] and my ·Savior [rescuer],
my shield ·and my protection [Lin whom I find refuge].
He ·helps me keep my people under control [Lsubdues my people under me].

[3]LORD, ·why are people important to you [Lwhat are people that you care about them]?
·Why do you even think about human beings [LWhat are human beings that you think about them; 8:4]?
[4]People are like ·a breath [vapor; 39:5, 11; 62:9; Eccl. 1:2];
their ·lives [Ldays] are like passing shadows [102:11; 109:23; Eccl. 6:12].

[5]LORD, ·tear open [bend] the ·sky [heavens] and come down.
Touch the mountains so they will smoke [18:9; Ex. 19:11, 18–19].
[6]Send the lightning and scatter ·my enemies [Lthem].
Shoot your arrows and ·force them away [rout them; 18:14].
[7]·Reach down [LSend forth your hand] from above.
·Save me [Set me free] and ·rescue [protect] me ·out of this sea of enemies [Lfrom the mighty waters; Csymbolizing chaos],
from ·these [Lthe hand/power of] foreigners.
[8]·They are liars [LTheir mouths speak vanities/falsehood];
·they are dishonest [Ltheir right hand is a false right hand].

[9]God, I will sing a new song [Ccelebrating victory; 33:3; 40:3; 96:1; 98:1; 149:1; Is. 42:10; Rev. 5:9; 14:3] to you;
I will ·play [make a psalm] to you on the ten-stringed harp.
[10]You give ·victory [salvation] to kings.
You ·save [set free] your servant David from ·cruel [evil] swords.
[11]·Save me [Set me free], ·rescue [protect] me from ·these [Lthe hand/power of the] foreigners.

·They are liars [LTheir mouths speak vanities/falsehood]; ·they are dishonest [Ltheir right hand is a false right hand].

12Let our sons in their youth
·grow like plants [*or* be like full-grown plants; Crobust and vital; 128:3].
Let our daughters be
like the ·decorated [cut] ·stones [*or* pillars] in the ·Temple [*or* palace; Cstately and beautiful].
13Let our barns be filled
with crops of all kinds.
Let our sheep in the fields have
thousands and tens of thousands of lambs.
14 Let our cattle be ·strong [well fed; *or* heavy with young].
Let ·no one break in [Lthere be no breach; *or* no miscarriage; Cin the city walls].
Let there be no ·war [Lgoing out; Cin war or exile, or perhaps referring to premature birth],
no screams in our ·streets [public areas].

15·Happy [Blessed] are ·those [Lthe people] who are like this;
·happy [blessed] are the people whose God is the LORD.

Praise to God the King

A psalm of praise. Of David.

145 I ·praise your greatness [exalt you], my God the King;
I will ·praise [bless] ·you [Lyour name] forever and ever.
2I will ·praise [bless] you every day;
I will praise ·you [Lyour name] forever and ever.
3The LORD is great and ·worthy of our praise [greatly to be praised; 48:1];
·no one can understand how great he is [Lthere is no searching out/limit to his greatness].

4·Parents [LA generation] will ·tell their children [Lpraise to a generation] what you have done.
They will ·retell [proclaim] your mighty acts,
5·wonderful majesty, and glory [Land the majestic glory of your splendor; CGod's manifest presence].
And I will ·think about [meditate on] your ·miracles [wonderful works].
6They will tell about the ·amazing things you do [Lmight of your awesomeness],
and I will ·tell [recount] how great you are.
7They will ·remember [bubble forth with] ·your great goodness [Lthe remembrance of your goodness]
and will sing about your ·fairness [righteousness].

8The LORD is ·kind [gracious] and ·shows mercy [compassionate].
He ·does not become angry quickly [is slow to anger] but ·is full of love [has great loyalty].
9The LORD is good to everyone;
he is ·merciful [compassionate] to all he has made [86:15; 103:8; Ex. 34:6–7; Neh. 9:17, 31; Joel 2:13; Jon. 4:2].
10LORD, everything you have made will ·praise [bless] you;
·those who belong to you [your saints/loyal ones] will bless you.

11They will tell about the glory of your kingdom
and will speak about your ·power [strength].
12Then everyone will know the mighty things you do
and the glory and ·majesty [splendor] of your kingdom.
13Your kingdom ·will go on and on [Lis an eternal kingdom],
and you will rule ·forever [Lfrom generation to generation; Dan. 4:3].

The LORD ·will keep all his promises [Lis faithful/true in all his words];
he is loyal to all he has made.n
14The LORD ·helps [supports] those who have ·been defeated [Lfallen]
and ·takes care of [Llifts up] those who are ·in trouble [bowed down].
15·All living things look to you for food [LThe eyes of all look to you],
and you give ·it [Ltheir food] to them at the right time.
16You open your hand,
and you satisfy the desire of all living things [Matt. 6:25–27].

17·Everything the LORD does is right [LThe LORD is righteous in all his ways].
He is loyal ·to all he has made [*or* in all his deeds].
18The LORD is ·close [near] to everyone who ·prays to [calls on] him,
to all who ·truly pray to him [call on him in truth/faithfulness].
19He ·gives those who respect him what they want [Laccomplishes the
desire of all who fear him; Prov. 1:7].
He listens when they cry, and he ·saves them [gives them victory].
20The LORD ·protects [guards; keeps] everyone who loves him,
but he will destroy the wicked.

21·I will praise [LMy mouth will speak the praise of] the LORD.
Let ·everyone [Lall flesh] ·praise [bless] his holy name forever.

Praise God Who Helps the Weak

146 Praise the LORD!
My ·whole being [soul; life], praise the LORD.
2I will praise the LORD ·all [Lwith] my life;
I will ·sing praises [make a psalm] to my God as long as I live.

3Do not put your ·trust [confidence] in princes
or other people, who cannot ·save you [give you victory; 118:8–9].
4·When people die [LTheir spirit goes out], they ·are buried [Lreturn to
the ground].
·Then all of [LOn that day] their plans ·come to an end [perish].
5·Happy [Blessed] are those who are helped by the God of Jacob
[Canother name for Israel].
Their hope is in the LORD their God.
6He made heaven and earth,
the sea and everything in it [Gen. 1].
He ·remains [keeps; observes; guards] ·loyal [faithfulness; truth] forever.
7He does ·what is fair [justice] for those who have been ·wronged
[oppressed; exploited].
He gives food to the hungry.
The LORD sets the prisoners free.
8 The LORD ·gives sight to [opens the eyes of] the blind.

145:13 made These last two cola do not appear in some Hebrew copies, but are found in the Dead Sea Scrolls and some Greek copies.

The LORD lifts up people who are ·in trouble [bowed down; 145:14].
The LORD loves ·those who do right [the righteous].
9The LORD ·protects [guards] the ·foreigners [sojourners].
He ·defends [supports] the orphans and widows [Cthe socially vulnerable],
but he ·blocks [frustrates] the way of the wicked.

10The LORD will ·be King [reign] forever [47:2; 93:1; 96:10; 97:1; 98:6; 99:1; Rev. 19:6].
·Jerusalem [LZion; Cthe location of the Temple], your God is everlasting.

Praise the LORD!

Praise God Who Helps His People

147 Praise the LORD!

It is good to ·sing praises [make a psalm] to our God;
it is pleasant and ·good [Lfitting] to praise him.
2The LORD rebuilds Jerusalem [51:18; 102:16; Is. 64:8–12];
he ·brings back [gathers; assembles] the ·captured [scattered; dispersed] Israelites [Cperhaps a reference to those who returned after the Babylonian exile; Deut. 30:1–4; Is. 11:12].
3He heals the brokenhearted
and ·bandages [binds up] their wounds.

4He ·counts [Lmeasures the number of] the stars
and ·names [Lassigns names to] each one [Is. 40:26].
5Our Lord is great and very powerful.
There is no limit to ·what he knows [Lhis understanding].
6The LORD ·defends [supports] the ·humble [needy],
but he throws the wicked to the ground.

7Sing ·praises [thanksgiving] to the LORD;
·praise [make a psalm to] our God with harps.
8He ·fills [covers] the ·sky [heavens] with clouds
and ·sends [sets; establishes] rain to the earth
and makes grass ·grow [sprout] on the ·hills [mountains].
9He gives food to cattle
and to the ·little birds [Lyoung ravens] that call.

10He ·is not impressed with [does not delight in] the strength of a horse,
nor does he take pleasure in ·human might [Lthe thighs of a person].
11The LORD ·is pleased with [takes pleasure in] those who ·respect [fear] him [Prov. 1:7],
with those who ·trust [wait for; hope in] his ·love [loyalty].

12Jerusalem, ·praise [celebrate] the LORD;
·Jerusalem [LZion; Cthe location of the Temple], praise your God.
13He ·makes your city gates strong [Lstrengthens the bars of your gates]
and blesses your children ·inside [Lwithin you].
14He ·brings [sets] peace to your ·country [Lboundaries]
and ·fills [satisfies; satiates] you with the finest ·grain [wheat].

15He ·gives a command [Lsends forth his word] to the earth,
and ·it quickly obeys him [Lhis word quickly runs].
16He ·spreads [Lgives] the snow like wool
and scatters the frost like ashes.
17He throws down hail like ·rocks [Lmorsels; bits; pieces].
No one can stand ·the cold he sends [Lbefore his cold].
18Then he ·gives a command [Lsends forth his word], and it melts.
He sends the breezes, and the waters flow.

19He ·gave [announced] his word to Jacob [Canother name for Israel],
his laws [statutes; requirements; ordinances] and ·demands
[judgments] to Israel [Ex. 19–24].
20He didn't do this for ·any other [Lall the] nation.
They don't know his ·laws [judgments].

Praise the LORD!

The World Should Praise the Lord

148 Praise the LORD!

Praise the LORD from the ·skies [heavens].
Praise him ·high above the earth [in the heights].
2Praise him, all you ·angels [messengers].
Praise him, all ·you armies of heaven [his hosts; Cthe angelic army].
3Praise him, sun and moon.
Praise him, all you ·shining stars [Lstars of light].
4Praise him, ·highest heavens [Lheaven of heavens]
and you waters above the ·sky [heavens].
5Let them praise the name of the LORD,
because ·they were created by his command [Lhe commands and they
were created; Gen. 1].
6He ·put them in place [Lmade them stand] forever and ever;
he made a ·law [statute; requirement; ordinance] that will never
·change [pass].

7Praise the LORD from the earth,
you large sea ·animals [monsters; Clike Leviathan; 74:12–17; 104:26;
Gen. 1:21; Job 3:8; 41; Is. 27:1] and all the ·oceans [deeps],
8·lightning [Lfire] and hail, snow and ·mist [cloud; *or* smoke],
and stormy winds that ·obey him [Ldo his word],
9mountains and all hills,
fruit trees and all cedars,
10wild animals and all cattle,
crawling animals and birds,
11kings of the earth and all ·nations [peoples],
princes and all ·rulers [judges] of the earth,
12young men and women,
old people and ·children [youth].

13Praise the name of the LORD,
because ·he [Lhis name] alone is ·great [exalted].
·He is more wonderful than [LHis splendor is over] heaven and earth.
14God has ·given his people a king [exalted/raised a horn over his people;
Can animal's horn symbolizes power].

He should be praised by all ·who belong to him [his saints/loyal ones];
he should be praised by the ·Israelites [Lsons/Tchildren of Israel], the people ·closest to his heart [Lnearest to him].

Praise the LORD!

Praise the God of Israel

149 Praise the LORD!

Sing a new song [Ccelebrating victory; 33:3; 40:3; 96:1; 98:1; 144:9; Is. 42:10; Rev. 5:9; 14:3] to the LORD;
sing his praise in the ·meeting [assembly; congregation] of his ·people [saints; loyal ones].

2Let the Israelites ·be happy [rejoice] because of God, [Lin] their Maker.
Let the ·people of Jerusalem [Lsons of Zion; Clocation of the Temple] rejoice ·because [Lin] of their King.
3They should praise him with dancing.
They should ·sing praises [make a psalm] to him with tambourines and harps.
4The LORD is pleased with his people;
he ·saves [Lendows with salvation/victory] the ·humble [needy].
5Let ·those who worship him [the saints/loyal ones] rejoice in his glory [CGod's manifest presence].
Let them sing for joy even in bed!

6Let them ·shout his praise [Lexalt God with their throats]
with their two-edged swords in their hands.
7They will ·punish [execute vengeance against] the nations
and ·defeat [punish] the people.
8They will put those kings in chains
and ·those important men [honored men] in iron bands.
9They will ·punish them as God has written [Laccomplish a written judgment].
God is honored by ·all who worship him [his saints/loyal ones].

Praise the LORD!

Praise the Lord with Music

150 Praise the LORD!

Praise God in his ·Temple [Lholy place; *or* holiness];
praise him in his ·mighty heaven [Lstrong firmament; Gen. 1:7].
2Praise him for his strength;
praise him for his [Labundant] greatness.
3Praise him with trumpet blasts;
praise him with harps and lyres.
4Praise him with tambourines and dancing;
praise him with stringed instruments and flutes.
5Praise him with loud cymbals;
praise him with crashing cymbals.
6Let everything that breathes praise the LORD.

Praise the LORD!

PROVERBS

The Importance of Proverbs

1 These are the ·wise words [proverbs] of Solomon son of David, king of Israel.
[2]They teach wisdom and ·self-control [discipline; instruction];
they will help you understand ·wise words [insightful sayings].
[3]They will teach you how to be ·wise [insightful] and ·self-controlled [disciplined]
and will teach you to do what is ·honest [righteous] and ·fair [just] and ·right [virtuous].
[4]They make the ·uneducated [simpleminded; immature; naive] ·wise [prudent]
and give knowledge and ·sense [discretion] to the young.
[5]Wise people can also listen and ·learn [add/increase teaching];
even ·they [Lthose with understanding] can find good ·advice in these words [guidance].
[6]Then ·anyone [Lthey] can understand ·wise words [proverbs] and ·stories [*or* difficult sayings],
the words of the wise and their ·riddles [difficulties].

[7]Knowledge begins with ·respect [fear; awe] for the LORD,
but fools ·hate [despise] wisdom and ·discipline [self-control; instruction].

Warnings Against Evil

[8]My ·child [Lson], listen to your father's ·teaching [instruction; discipline]
and do not ·forget [neglect] your mother's ·advice [instruction].
[9][LFor] ·Their teaching [LIt] will be like ·flowers in your hair [La gracious garland on your head]
or ·a necklace [Lbeads] around your neck.

[10]My ·child [Lson], if sinners try to ·lead [seduce; entice] you into sin,
do not follow them.
[11]They will say, "Come with us.
Let's ambush and kill someone;
let's attack some innocent people just for fun.
[12]Let's swallow them alive, ·as death does [like the grave/LSheol];
let's swallow them whole, ·as the grave does [Llike those who go down into the pit].
[13]We will ·take [Lfind] all kinds of ·valuable things [Lprecious wealth]
and fill our houses with ·stolen goods [plunder].
[14]·Come join us [LThrow in your lot with us],
and we will share ·with you stolen goods [La single bag (of loot)]."

[15]My ·child [Lson], do not go ·along with them [Lon their path];
·do not do what they do [Lkeep your foot from their way/path].
[16]·They are eager to do evil [LFor their feet run toward evil]
and are quick to ·kill [Lshed blood].
[17]It is useless to spread out a net
right where the birds can see it.
[18]But sinners will ·fall into their own traps [Lset up a deadly ambush];
they ·will only catch [Llie in wait for] themselves!
[19]All greedy people end up this way;
·greed kills selfish people [Lthey take their own lives].

Wisdom Speaks

[20]Wisdom [Cthe personification of God's wisdom; 8:1–36; 9:1–6] ·is like a woman shouting [Lshouts] in the street;
she ·raises her voice [yells out] in the city squares [Cthe hub for business, government, and social interaction].
[21]She cries out ·in the noisy street [Lat the top of the noisy throng]
and shouts at the [Lentrances of] city gates:
[22]"You ·fools [simpletons; immature ones], how long will you be ·foolish [immature]?
How long will you make ·fun of wisdom [mocking so dear to you]
and hate knowledge?
[23]If only you had ·listened [responded] when I corrected you,
I would have ·told you what's in my heart [Lpoured forth my spirit to you];
I would have ·told you what I am thinking [Lrevealed my words to you].
[24]I called, but you ·refused to listen [rejected me];
I held out my hand, but you paid no attention.
[25]You ·did not follow [ignored] my advice
and did not ·listen when I corrected [want me to correct] you.
[26]So I will laugh ·when you are in trouble [Lat your calamity].
I will ·make fun [ridicule you] when disaster strikes you,
[27]when ·disaster [dread] comes over you like a ·storm [tempest],
when trouble strikes you like a whirlwind,
when ·pain [distress] and ·trouble [oppression] overwhelm you.

[28]"Then you will call to me,
but I will not answer.
You will ·look for [seek] me,
but you will not find me.
[29]It is because you ·rejected [hated] knowledge
and did not choose to ·respect [fear; hold in awe] the LORD.
[30]You did not ·accept [want] my advice,
and you rejected my correction.
[31]So you will ·get what you deserve [Leat from the fruit of your path];
you will ·get what you planned for others [*or* be satisfied with your own counsel].
[32]·Fools [The simple/immature] will die because they ·refuse to listen [Lturn away];
·they [Lfools] will be destroyed because ·they do not care [of complacency].
[33]But those who ·listen to [obey] me will live in safety
·and be at peace, without fear of injury [untroubled by the dread of harm]."

Rewards of Wisdom

2 **My ·child** [*or* son], **·listen to** [grasp] **what I say**
and ·remember [Lstore up] **what I command you.**
2**·Listen carefully** [LBend your ear] **to wisdom;**
·set your mind on [Lstretch your heart to] **understanding.**
3**Cry out for wisdom,**
and ·beg [shout out loud] **for understanding.**
4**·Search** [Seek] **for it like silver,**
and ·hunt [search] **for it like hidden treasure.**
5**Then you will understand ·respect** [fear; awe; 1:7] **for the LORD,**
and you will find ·that you know God [the knowledge of God].
6**Only the LORD gives wisdom;**
·he gives [Lfrom his mouth comes] **knowledge and understanding.**
7**He stores up ·wisdom** [resourcefulness] **for those who ·are honest** [have integrity].
Like a shield he protects the innocent.
8**He ·makes sure that justice is done** [Lguards the path of justice],
and he protects those who are loyal to him.

9**Then you will understand what is ·honest** [righteous] **and ·fair** [just]
and what is ·the good and right thing to do [Lvirtuous, every good course/path].
10**Wisdom will ·come into your mind** [penetrate your heart],
and knowledge will be ·pleasing [attractive] **to you.**
11**·Good sense** [Discretion] **will protect you;**
understanding will guard you.
12**It will keep you from the ·wicked** [Levil path],
from those whose words are ·bad [perverted; twisted],
13**who ·don't do what is right** [Labandoned the road of integrity]
but ·what is evil [Lgo on dark paths].
14**They enjoy doing wrong**
and are happy ·to do what is crooked and [Lwith their twisted] **evil.**
15**What they do is ·wrong** [confused],
and ·their ways are dishonest [Lthey go on wrong courses].

16**It** [CWisdom] **will save you from the ·unfaithful wife** [Lstrange woman]
·who tries to lead you into adultery [Lfrom the foreign woman] **with ·pleasing words** [flattery; compliments].
17**She leaves ·the husband she married when she was young** [Lthe intimate relationship of her youth].
She ·ignores [forgets] **·the promise she made before** [Lher covenant with] **God.**
18**Her house ·is on the way** [Lsinks down] **to death;**
·those who took that path are now all dead [*or* her paths come down to her dead ancestors].
19**No one who goes to her comes back**
or walks the path of life again.

20**·But wisdom will help you be good** [*or* Stay on the path of good people]
and ·do what is right [guard the road of the righteous].
21**Those who ·are honest** [have integrity/virtue] **will live in the land,**
and those who are ·innocent [blameless] **will remain in it.**

[22]But the wicked will be ·removed [Lcut off] from the land,
and the unfaithful will be ·thrown out of [Luprooted from] it.

Advice to Children

3 My ·child [Lson], do not forget my ·teaching [instruction; law],
but ·keep my commands in mind [Llet your heart/mind protect my commands].
[2]Then ·you will live a long time,
and your life will be successful [Llength of days and years of life and peace will be added to you].

[3]Don't ·ever forget kindness and truth [Llet loyalty and faithfulness abandon you].
·Wear [Bind] them ·like a necklace [Lon your neck].
Write them on your heart as if on a tablet.
[4]Then you will ·be respected [find favor]
and will please both God and people.

[5]Trust the LORD with all your heart,
and don't ·depend [rely] on your own understanding.
[6]·Remember the LORD [LKnow him] ·in all you do [Lon all your paths],
and he will ·give you success [Lkeep your roads straight].

[7]Don't ·depend on your own wisdom [Lbe wise in your own eyes].
·Respect [Fear; Hold in awe] the LORD and ·refuse to do wrong [Lturn away from evil].
[8]Then your body will be healthy,
and your bones will be ·strong [refreshed].

[9]Honor the LORD with your wealth
and the firstfruits from all your crops.
[10]Then your barns will be full,
and your wine barrels will ·overflow [burst] with new wine.

[11]My ·child [Lson], do not reject the LORD's discipline,
and don't ·get angry [loathe] when he corrects you.
[12]The LORD corrects those he loves,
just as ·parents [Lfathers] correct the child they delight in.

[13]·Happy [Blessed] is the person who finds wisdom,
the one who ·gets [gains] understanding.
[14]·Wisdom [LHer profit] is worth more than silver;
·it brings more profit [Lher yield more] than gold.
[15]Wisdom is more precious than ·rubies [*or* pearls];
nothing you could want is equal to it.
[16]·With [In] her right hand ·wisdom offers you a long life [Lare length of days],
and ·with [in] her left hand ·she gives you [are] riches and honor.
[17]·Wisdom will make your life [LHer paths are] pleasant
and ·will bring you [Lher trails are] peace.
[18]As a tree produces fruit, wisdom gives life to those who use it,
and everyone who uses it will be happy.

[19]The LORD ·made [[L]laid the foundations of] the earth, ·using his wisdom
[*or* with Wisdom; 8:22–31].
He set the ·sky [heavens] in place, using his ·understanding
[competence].
[20]With his knowledge, ·he made springs flow into rivers [[L]the deeps
burst open]
and the clouds drop ·rain on the earth [[L]dew].

[21]My ·child [[L]son], ·hold on to [protect] ·wisdom [resourcefulness] and
·good sense [discretion].
Don't let them ·out of your sight [[L]slip from your eyes].
[22]They will give you life
and ·beauty like a necklace [[L]an ornament] around your neck.
[23]Then you will ·go your way [walk on your path; [C]of life] in safety,
and ·you will not get hurt [[L]your foot will not stumble].
[24]When you lie down, you won't be afraid;
when you lie down, you will sleep in peace.
[25]You won't be afraid of sudden ·trouble [terror];
you won't fear the ruin that comes to the wicked,
[26]because the LORD will ·keep you safe [be your confidence].
He will ·keep you from being trapped [guard your feet from capture].

[27]Whenever you are able,
·do [[L]do not withhold] good to people who ·need help [*or* deserve it].
[28]If you have what your neighbor asks for,
don't say, "Come back later.
I will give it to you tomorrow."
[29]Don't ·make plans to hurt [intend evil toward] your neighbor
who lives nearby and trusts you.
[30]Don't accuse a person for no good reason;
don't accuse someone who has not harmed you.

[31]Don't be jealous of those who use violence,
and don't ·choose to be like them [[L]prefer their path; [C]of life].
[32]·The LORD hates those who do wrong [[L]The devious are an
abomination to the LORD],
but he is a ·friend [confidant] to those who are ·honest [virtuous].
[33]The LORD will curse the evil person's house,
but he will bless the home of ·those who do right [the righteous].
[34]The LORD ·laughs at [mocks] those who ·laugh at [mock] him,
but he ·gives grace [shows favor] to ·those who are not proud [the
humble].
[35]Wise people ·will receive honor [possess glory],
but fools ·will be disgraced [give off/exude shame].

Wisdom Is Important

4 My ·children [[L]sons], listen to your father's ·teaching [discipline;
instruction];
pay attention ·so you will understand [[L]to the knowledge of
understanding].
[2]·What I am telling you is good [[L]I will give you good teaching],
so do not ·forget [[L]abandon; forsake] ·what I teach you [[L]my
instruction].

[3]When I was a ·young boy in my father's house [Lson to my father]
·and like an only child to [Ltender, and the only one of] my mother,
[4]my father taught me and said,
"Hold on to my words with all your heart.
·Keep [Guard] my commands and you will live.
[5]·Get [Acquire] wisdom and ·get [acquire] understanding.
Don't forget or ·ignore [turn away from] ·my words [Lthe speeches of my mouth].
[6]·Hold on to wisdom [LDon't abandon her; CWisdom is here personified as a woman; 1:20–33; 8:1—9:6], and it [*or* she] will ·take care of [guard] you.
Love ·it [*or* her], and ·it [*or* she] will ·keep you safe [protect you].
[7]·Wisdom is the most important thing; so get wisdom [LThe beginning of wisdom is: Get/Acquire wisdom].
·If it costs everything you have [LAbove all your acquisitions], ·get [acquire] understanding.
[8]·Treasure wisdom [Highly esteem her], and ·it [*or* she] will ·make you great [exalt you];
·hold on to it [*or* embrace her], and ·it [*or* she] will bring you honor.
[9]·It will be like flowers in your hair [LShe will place on your head a graceful garland;]
·and like a beautiful crown on your head [she will bestow on you a crown of glory]."

[10]My ·child [Lson], listen and ·accept what I say [Ltake in my speech].
Then ·you will have a long life [Lyour years will be multiplied].
[11]I am ·guiding [Lteaching] you in the way of wisdom,
and I am leading you on the ·right [*or* straight] path.
[12]·Nothing will hold you back [LWhen you walk, your step will not be hindered];
·you will not be overwhelmed [Lwhen you run, you will not stumble].
[13]·Always remember what you have been taught [LBe determined/resolute in our instruction],
and don't ·let go of it [slack off].
·Keep all that you have learned [LProtect it];
it is ·the most important thing in [Lyour] life.
[14]Don't ·follow the ways [go in the way] of the wicked;
don't ·do what evil people do [Lwalk straight on to the path of evil people].
[15]Avoid their ways, and don't ·follow [cross over to] them.
Stay away from them and keep on going,
[16]because they cannot sleep until they do evil.
·They cannot rest until they harm someone [LThey are robbed of sleep unless they cause people to stumble].
[17]They feast on wickedness as if they were eating bread.
They drink violence as if they were drinking wine.

[18]The way of the ·good [righteous] person is like the ·light of dawn [Lshining light],
growing brighter and brighter until full daylight.

19But the ·wicked walk around in the dark [Lpath of the wicked is like
deep darkness];
they ·can't even see what makes them [Ldon't know where they will]
stumble.

20My ·child [Lson], pay attention to my words;
·listen closely to what I say [Lbend your ear to my speech].
21Don't ·ever forget my words [Llet your eyes slip];
·keep them always in mind [Lguard them in your heart].
22They are ·the key to life [Llife] for those who find them;
they bring health to the whole body.
23·Be careful what you think [LAbove all that you guard, protect your
heart],
because ·your thoughts run your life [Llife flows from it].
24·Don't use your mouth to tell lies [LHave nothing to do with a perverse
mouth];
·don't ever say things that are not true [Lkeep loose lips far from you].
25Keep your eyes focused on what is ·right [*or* straight ahead],
and ·look straight ahead to what is good [Lyour eyelids on what is in
front].
26·Be careful what you do [LWatch your feet on the way],
and ·always do what is right [Lall your paths will be secure/sure].
27Don't turn off ·the road of goodness [Lto the right or to the left];
·keep away [Lturn your feet] from evil paths.

Warning About Adultery

5 My son, pay attention to my wisdom;
·listen [Lbend your ear] to my words of understanding.
2·Be careful to use good sense [*or* So you might keep discrete]
and ·watch what you say [Lyour lips might protect knowledge].
3The ·words of another man's wife [lips of an immoral/Lstrange woman]
may ·seem sweet as [Ldrip like] honey;
·they [Lher tongue/palette] may be as smooth as olive oil.
4But in the end she ·will bring you sorrow [Lis bitter like wormwood],
·causing you pain [Lsharp] like a two-edged sword.
5·She is on the way [LHer feet go down] to death;
her steps ·are headed straight [*or* grab on] to ·the grave [LSheol].
6She gives little thought to the path of life.
·She doesn't even know that her ways are wrong [LHer paths wander
and she does not even realize it].

7Now, my sons, listen to me,
and don't ·ignore what I say [Lturn aside from the speeches of my
mouth].
8·Stay away from such a woman [LKeep your path far from her].
Don't even go near the ·door [entrance] of her house,
9or you will give your ·riches [honor; *or* vitality; vigor] to others,
and the best years of your life will be given to someone cruel.
10Strangers will ·enjoy your wealth [*or* sap your strength],
and what you worked so hard for will ·go to someone else [Lend up
in the house of a foreigner].
11You will groan at the end of your life
when your ·health is gone [Lbody and flesh are exhausted].

[12]Then you will say, "I hated ·being told what to do [instruction; discipline]!
·I would not listen to [[L]My heart despised] correction!
[13]I would not listen to my teachers
or ·pay attention [extend my heart] to my instructors.
[14]I ·came [*or* am] close to being completely ruined
in front of ·a whole group of people [[L]the assembled congregation]."

[15]·Be faithful to your own wife [[L]Drink water from your own well; Song 4:10–15],
·just as you drink [[L]gushing] water from your own ·well [cistern].
[16]Don't ·pour your water in the streets [[L]let your fountains burst forth outside];
·don't give your love to just any woman [[L]streams of water in the public squares].
[17]These things are yours alone
and shouldn't be shared with strangers.
[18]·Be happy with the wife you married when you were young [[L]Rejoice in the wife of your youth].
·She gives you joy, as your fountain gives you water [[L]May your spring be blessed].
[19]She is a lovely deer and a graceful doe.
Let her ·love [*or* breasts] always make you happy;
let her love always ·hold you captive [intoxicate/inebriate you; Song 4:10].
[20]My son, ·don't be held captive [[L]why should you be intoxicated/inebriated…?] by a ·woman who takes part in adultery [[L]stranger].
Don't fondle the bosom of a ·woman who is not your wife [[L]foreigner].
[21]The ·LORD sees everything you do [[L]eyes of the LORD are on the path of every person],
and he watches ·where you go [[L]all their ways].
[22]An evil man will be ·caught [captured] in his wicked ways;
the ropes of his sins will tie him up.
[23]He will die ·because he does not control himself [[L]without discipline/instruction],
and he will be ·held captive [*or* intoxicated; inebriated] by his ·foolishness [stupidity].

Dangers of Being Foolish

6 My ·child [[L]son], ·be careful about giving [[L]if you make] a guarantee for ·somebody else's loan [[L]your neighbor/friend],
·about promising to pay what someone else owes [[L]shaking hands with a stranger in agreement; 11:15; 17:18; 20:16; 22:26; 27:13].
[2]You ·might [*or* will] get trapped by what you say;
you ·might [*or* will] be caught by ·your own words [*or* what you say].
[3]My ·child [[L]son], if you have done this and are under your ·neighbor's [*or* friend's] control,
here is how to ·get free [extricate yourself].
·Don't be proud [[L]Humble yourself]. Go to your ·neighbor [*or* friend]
and ·beg to be free from your promise [[L]press/urge your neighbor/friend].

[4]Don't ·go to [[L]let your eyes] sleep
or ·even rest your eyes [[L]let your eyelids/pupils slumber],
[5]but ·free [extricate] yourself like a ·deer [gazelle] running from ·a hunter [[L]his hand],
like a bird flying away from a ·trapper [fowler].

[6]Go watch the ants, you lazy person.
Watch ·what they do [[L]its paths] and ·be [*or* become] wise.
[7]Ants have no commander,
no leader or ruler,
[8]but they ·store up [get their] food in the summer
and gather their ·supplies [provisions] at harvest.
[9]How long will you lie there, you lazy person?
When will you get up from sleeping?
[10]·You sleep a little; you take a nap [[L]"A little sleep, a little slumber"].
·You fold your hands and [[L]"A little folding of the arms to…"] lie down to rest.
[11]So ·you will be as poor as if you had been robbed [[L]poverty will come on you like a robber];
·you will have as little as if you had been held up [[L]deprivation like a shielded warrior].

[12]Some people are ·wicked and no good [worthless and guilty].
They go around ·telling lies [[L]with crooked mouths],
[13]winking with their eyes, ·tapping with [*or* scraping] their feet,
and ·making signs [pointing; gesturing] with their fingers [[C]a reference to secretive plans or even magic].
[14]They ·make evil plans in their hearts [[L]are perverse in their hearts and determined to do evil]
and are always starting ·arguments [conflicts].
[15]So ·trouble [disaster] will strike them in an instant;
suddenly they will be so ·hurt [[L]broken] no one can ·help [[L]heal] them.

[16]There are six things the LORD hates.
There are seven things ·he cannot stand [[L]that are an abomination to his soul]:
[17] ·a proud look [haughty eyes],
a lying tongue,
hands that ·kill [[L]spill the blood of] innocent people,
[18] a ·mind [heart] that thinks up evil plans,
feet that are quick to ·do [[L]run to] evil,
[19] a witness who lies,
and someone who starts ·arguments [conflicts; fights] among ·families [brothers; Ps. 133].

Warning About Adultery

[20]My son, ·keep [protect] your father's commands,
and don't ·forget [[L]abandon; forsake] your mother's ·teaching [instruction].
[21]·Keep their words in mind [[L]Bind them to your heart] forever
·as though you had them tied [fasten them] around your neck.
[22]They will ·guide [lead] you when you walk.
They will ·guard [protect] you when you sleep.
They will ·speak to you [*or* occupy your attention] when you are awake.

[23]These commands are like a lamp;
this ·teaching [instruction] is like a light [[C]making things clear].
And ·the correction that comes from them [[L]disciplined correction]
·will help you have [[L]is the path of] life.
[24]They will ·keep [guard] you from ·sinful women [the evil woman]
and from the ·pleasing words [[L]flattering tongue] of ·another man's unfaithful wife [[L]the foreign woman].
[25]Don't desire her because she is beautiful.
Don't let her capture you by ·the way she looks at you [[L]her eyelashes].
[26]A prostitute will ·treat you like [*or* cost you] a loaf of bread,
·and [*or* but] a ·woman who takes part in adultery [married woman] ·may cost you [[L]hunts; stalks] your life.
[27]You cannot ·carry [*or* scoop] hot coals ·against your chest [*or* into your lap]
without burning your clothes,
[28]and you cannot walk on hot coals
without burning your feet.
[29]The same is true if you ·have sexual relations with [[L]go to] ·another man's wife [[L]the wife of a neighbor/friend].
·Anyone who does so will be punished [[L]All who touch her will not go unpunished].

[30]People don't ·hate [despise] a thief
when he steals because he is hungry.
[31]But if he is caught, he must pay back ·seven times what he stole [[L]sevenfold],
and ·it may cost him everything he owns [[L]he must give the riches of his house].
[32]A man who takes part in adultery ·has no sense [[L]lacks heart];
he will destroy himself.
[33]He will ·be beaten up and disgraced [[L]find affliction and scorn],
and his ·shame [reproach] will never ·go away [[L]be blotted out].
[34]Jealousy makes a husband very angry,
and he will ·have no pity [not forgive] when he gets revenge.
[35]He will accept no payment for the wrong;
he will ·take no amount of money [not take a bribe no matter how large].

The Woman of Adultery

7 My son, ·remember what I say [guard my speech], and ·treasure [store/hide in you] my commands.
[2]·Obey [Guard] my commands, and you will live.
Guard my ·teachings [instructions] ·as you would your own [[L]like the apple of your] eyes.
[3]·Remind yourself of them [[L]Bind them on your fingers];
write them on your heart as if on a tablet.
[4]·Treat wisdom as a sister [[L]Say to Wisdom, "You are my sister"; 1:20–33; 8:1—9:6],
and ·make understanding your closest friend [[L]call Understanding "Friend"].
[5]·Wisdom and understanding [[L]She] will ·keep you away [guard you] from ·adultery [[L]the strange woman],
away from the ·unfaithful wife [[L]foreign woman] and her ·pleasing [flattering] words.

6 Once while I was at the window of my house
I looked out through the ·shutters [lattice; curtains]
7 and saw some ·foolish [simpleminded; immature; naive], young men.
I noticed one of them ·had no wisdom [had no sense; Llacked heart].
8 He was ·walking down [crossing] the street near the corner
on the road leading to her house.
9 It was the twilight of the evening;
the darkness of the night was just beginning.
10 Then the woman ·approached [*or* propositioned] him,
dressed like a prostitute
and ·planning to trick him [Lwith a guarded heart].
11 She was ·loud [boisterous; noisy] and ·stubborn [defiant]
and ·never stayed at [Lher feet do not rest in her own] home.
12 ·She was always out [LA foot] in the streets ·or in [La foot in] the city
squares,
·waiting around [lurking] on the corners of the streets.
13 She grabbed him and kissed him.
·Without shame [LHer face was brazen as] she said to him,
14 "I made my fellowship offering [Lev. 3; 7:11–21; Cthe offerer ate the
meat of the offering].
Today I have ·kept [paid back] my ·special promises [vows].
15 So I have come out to meet you;
I have been ·looking for you [Lseeking your face] and have found you.
16 I have ·covered [ornamented] my bed
with colored sheets from Egypt.
17 I have ·made my bed smell sweet [Lsprinkled my bed]
with myrrh, aloes, and cinnamon.
18 Come, let's ·make [be intoxicated with] love until morning.
Let's ·enjoy each other's [rejoice in] love.
19 My husband is not home;
he has gone on a ·long [faraway] trip.
20 He took a ·lot of money with him [Lpouch of money in his hand]
and won't be home ·for weeks [Luntil the new moon]."
21 By her clever words she ·made him give in [seduces him];
by ·her pleasing words [Lthe flattery of her lips] she ·led him into
doing wrong [persuades/compels him].
22 All at once he followed her,
like an ox led to the ·butcher [slaughter],
like a ·deer caught in a trap [*or* fool to the stocks]
23 ·and shot through the liver with an arrow [until an arrow pierces his
liver].
Like a bird ·caught in [Lhurrying to] a trap,
he didn't know ·what he did would kill him [it would cost him his
life].

24 Now, my sons, listen to me;
pay attention to ·what I say [Lthe speech of my mouth].
25 Don't ·let yourself be tricked by such a woman [Lturn your heart to her
paths];
don't ·go where she leads you [wander onto her paths].
26 She has ·ruined many good men [Lcaused many corpses to fall],
and many ·have died because of her [are those she has killed].

27 **Her house is on the ·road** [path] **to ·death** [LSheol; Cthe grave or the
underworld],
·the road that leads down to the grave [Lgoing down to the chambers
of death].

Listen to Wisdom

8 **·Wisdom calls to you like someone shouting** [LDoes not Wisdom
call out?];
·understanding raises [Does not Understanding raise…?] **her voice.**
2 **On the ·hilltops** [Ltop of the high places] **along the road**
and at the crossroads, she ·stands calling [takes her stand].
3 **Beside the city gates,**
at the entrances into the city, she calls out:
4 **"Listen, ·everyone** [men], **I'm calling out to you;**
·I am shouting [my voice goes out] **to all ·people** [Lthe sons of
humanity].
5 **You who are ·uneducated** [simpleminded; immature; naive], **·seek
wisdom** [understand prudence].
You who are foolish, ·get understanding [Ltake this to heart].
6 **Listen, because I have ·important** [noble] **things to say,**
and what I tell you is ·right [virtuous].
7 **·What I say is true** [LMy mouth utters the truth],
·I refuse to speak evil [Lmy lips despise wickedness].
8 **·Everything I say is honest** [LAll the speeches of my mouth are
righteous];
nothing I say is ·crooked [twisted] **or ·false** [perverse].
9 **People ·with good sense** [who understand] **know what I say is ·true**
[straightforward];
and those ·with [Lwho seek] **knowledge know my words are ·right**
[virtuous].
10 **·Choose** [Take] **my ·teachings** [instructions; discipline] **instead of
silver,**
and knowledge rather than ·the finest [choice] **gold.**
11 **Wisdom is more precious than ·rubies** [*or* pearls].
Nothing ·you could want is equal to [is more delightful than] **it.**

12 **"I am Wisdom, and I ·have good judgment** [dwell with prudence].
I also have knowledge and ·good sense [discretion].
13 **·If you respect the LORD, you will also** [LThose who fear/have awe for
the LORD] **hate evil.**
I hate pride and ·bragging [arrogance],
·evil ways [Lthe path of evil] **and ·lies** [La perverse mouth].
14 **I have advice and ·good sense** [resourcefulness; ability],
and I have understanding and ·power [strength].
15 **·I help kings to govern** [LBy me kings reign]
and ·rulers [princes] **·to make fair laws** [issue just decrees].
16 **·Princes use me to lead** [LBy me rulers rule],
and ·so do all important people who [nobles] **judge fairly** [Deut.
34:9; 1 Kin. 3:1–15; Ezra 7:25; Col. 1:16].
17 **I love those who love me,**
and those who seek me find me.
18 **Riches and honor are mine to give.**
So are lasting wealth and ·success [*or* righteousness].

19What I give is better than gold, even the finest gold,
my ·results [yield] better than the purest silver.
20I ·do what is right [Lwalk on the way of righteousness]
·and follow [Lin the midst of] the path of justice.
21I ·give wealth to those who love me [Lcause those who love me to inherit substance],
filling their houses with treasures.

22"The LORD ·begot [*or* acquired; possessed] me ·when he began his work [Lat the beginning of his path],
long before he made anything else.
23I was ·created [formed; woven; *or* appointed] in the very beginning,
even before the world began.
24I was ·born [brought forth] ·before there were oceans [Lwhen there were no deeps],
or springs ·overflowing [heavy] with water,
25before the hills were ·there [Lsettled],
before the mountains I was ·born [brought forth].
26God had not made the earth or ·fields [open country],
not even the first ·dust [mud clods; soil] of the earth.
27I was there when God ·put the skies in place [established the heavens],
when he ·stretched [decreed] the horizon over the ·oceans [deep],
28when he ·made [thickened; strengthened] the clouds above
and put the deep underground springs in place.
29I was there when he ·ordered [decreed] the sea
not to go beyond the borders he had set.
I was there when he ·laid [decreed] the earth's foundation.
30 I was like a ·child [nursling; *or* craftsman; architect] by his side.
I was ·delighted [playing] every day,
·enjoying [laughing in] his presence all the time,
31·enjoying [laughing with the inhabitants of] the whole world,
and ·delighted [playing] with all its people [John 1:1–3; Col. 1:15; CJesus is associated with personified Wisdom in that both were present with God during creation].

32"Now, my ·children [Lsons], listen to me,
because those who ·follow my ways [guard my path] are happy.
33Listen to my ·teaching [instruction], and you will be wise;
do not ·ignore [avoid] it.
34Happy are those who listen to me,
watching at my door every day,
·waiting at my open doorway [Lguarding my doorposts].
35Those who find me find life,
and ·the LORD will be pleased with them [they gain favor from the LORD].
36Those who ·do not find [miss; *or* offend] me hurt themselves.
Those who hate me love death."

Being Wise or Foolish

9 Wisdom has built her house;
she has made its seven ·columns [pillars; Ca large house].
2She has ·prepared her food [Lslaughtered her slaughter] and prepared [mixed] her wine;
she has set her table.

³She has sent out her servant girls,
and she calls out from the highest place in the city [ᶜthe location of the Temple, indicating she symbolizes God].
⁴She says to those who are ·uneducated [naive; immature; simpleminded],
"·Come in [Turn aside] here, you ·foolish people [who lack sense]!
⁵Come and eat my food
and drink the wine I have ·prepared [mixed].
⁶Stop your ·foolish [naive; immature; simpleminded] ways, and you will live;
take the road of understanding.

⁷"If you ·correct [instruct; discipline] ·someone who makes fun of wisdom [a mocker], you will be insulted.
If you correct an evil person, you will ·get hurt [ᴸbe blemished].
⁸Do not correct ·those who make fun of wisdom [mockers], or they will hate you.
But correct the wise, and they will love you.
⁹·Teach [ᴸGive to] the wise, and they will become even wiser;
·teach [inform] ·good people [the righteous], and they will ·learn even more [ᴸadd to their learning].

¹⁰"Wisdom begins with ·respect [fear; awe] for the LORD,
and understanding begins with knowing the Holy One.
¹¹·If you live wisely [ᴸThrough/By me], you will live a long time;
wisdom will add years to your life.
¹²The wise person is rewarded by wisdom,
but ·whoever makes fun of wisdom will suffer for it [ᴸmockers will bear it alone]."

¹³·Foolishness is like a loud woman [Woman Folly is boisterous/noisy];
she ·does not have wisdom or knowledge [ᴸis ignorant and does not even know it].
¹⁴She sits at the door of her house
at the highest place in the city [9:3; ᶜher house is built on the highest point of the city, indicating she symbolizes false gods].
¹⁵She ·calls out to [invites] those who are passing by,
who are going along, minding their own business.
¹⁶She says to those who ·are uneducated [lack sense/heart],
"·Come in [Turn aside] here, you ·foolish [naive; immature; simpleminded] people!
¹⁷Stolen water is sweeter,
and food eaten in secret tastes better."
¹⁸But these people don't know that ·everyone who goes there dies [the dead/departed/shades are there],
that her guests ·end up deep in the grave [ᴸare in the depths of Sheol].

The Wise Words of Solomon

10 These are the ·wise words [proverbs] of Solomon:
Wise ·children [sons] make their father happy,
but foolish ·children [sons] make their mother sad.

²·Riches gotten by doing wrong [ᴸThe treasures of the wicked] have no value,
but ·right living [righteousness] will save you from death.

[3]The LORD does not let ·good [righteous] people ·go hungry [starve],
but he keeps evil people from getting what they want.

[4]A ·lazy person will end up [Lslack palm makes a person] poor,
but a ·hard worker will become [Ldetermined hand makes a person] rich.

[5]Those who gather crops ·on time [Lin the summer] are wise,
but those who sleep through the harvest are a disgrace.

[6]·Good [Righteous] people will have rich blessings,
but the mouth of the wicked ·will be overwhelmed by [*or* conceals] violence.

[7]·Good [Righteous] people will be remembered as a blessing,
but the name of evil people will soon ·be forgotten [Lrot].

[8]The wise of heart ·do what they are told [Lgrasps commands],
but ·a talkative fool [Lthe lips of a fool] will be ruined.

[9]·The honest person will live [LThose who walk in innocence walk] in safety,
but ·the dishonest [Lthose who twist their path] will be ·caught [found out].

[10]A wink may ·get you into [*or* cause] trouble,
and foolish talk will lead to your ruin.

[11]The ·words [Lmouth] of a ·good [righteous] person ·give life, like a fountain of water [Lis a fountain of life],
but the ·words [Lmouth] of the wicked ·contain nothing but [conceals] violence.

[12]Hatred stirs up ·trouble [conflict; fights],
but love ·forgives [covers] all wrongs.

[13]·Wise people speak with understanding [LWisdom is found on understanding lips],
but ·people without wisdom should be punished [La rod is for the backs of those who lack sense/heart].

[14]The wise ·don't tell [store up; treasure] everything they know,
but the ·foolish talk too much and are ruined [Lmouth of a fool means imminent ruin].

[15]·Having lots of money protects the rich [LThe wealth of the rich is their strong city],
but having no money ·destroys [is the ruin of] the poor.

[16]·Good [Righteous] people are rewarded with life,
but evil people are paid with punishment.

17Whoever ·accepts correction [guards instruction/discipline] **is on the way to life,**
but whoever ·ignores [abandons] **correction ·will lead others away from life** [Lwanders aimlessly].

18Whoever ·hides [conceals] **hate is a liar.**
Whoever ·tells lies [spreads slander] **is a fool.**

19·If you talk a lot [LIn an abundance of words], **·you are sure to sin** [Lwickedness does not cease];
if you are wise, you will ·keep quiet [Lrestrain your lips].

20The ·words [Ltongue] **of a ·good** [righteous] **person ·are like pure** [is choice] **silver,**
but an evil person's ·thoughts are [Lheart is] **worth very little.**
21·Good [Righteous] **people's ·words** [Llips] **·will help** [Lnourish] **many others,**
but fools will die because they ·don't have wisdom [lack sense/heart].

22The LORD's blessing brings wealth,
and no ·sorrow [trouble] **comes with it.**

23A foolish person ·enjoys [makes a sport of] **doing wrong,**
but a person with understanding enjoys doing what is wise.

24Evil people will get what they fear most,
but ·good [righteous] **people will get what they want most.**

25A ·storm [whirlwind] **will blow the evil person away,**
but a ·good [righteous] **person will always ·be safe** [Lhave a firm foundation].

26A lazy person affects the one ·he works for [Lwho sends him]
like vinegar on the teeth or smoke in the eyes [Cirritating].

27Whoever ·respects [fears] **the LORD will ·have a long life** [Lincrease his days],
but the ·life [Lyears] **of an evil person will be cut short.**

28A ·good [righteous] **person can look forward to happiness,**
but ·an evil person can expect nothing [Lthe hope of an evil person will perish].

29The path of the LORD ·will protect good people [Lis a refuge for the innocent]
but ruin for those who do evil.

30·Good [Righteous] **people will ·always be safe** [Lnever be shaken],
but evil people will not ·remain [dwell] **in the land.**

31·A good person says wise things [LThe mouth of a righteous person flows with wisdom],
but a ·liar's [perverse person's] **tongue will be ·stopped** [Lcut off].

32**·Good people** [LThe lips of the wise] **know the right thing to say,**
but [Lthe mouth of] **evil people only tell ·lies** [perversities].

11

The Lord ·hates [detests] **·dishonest** [fraudulent] **scales,**
but he is pleased with ·honest [accurate] **weights** [16:11; Lev. 19:35–37; Deut. 25:13–15; Ezek. 45:10; Hos. 12:7–8].

2**·Pride** [Insolence] **leads only to shame;**
it is wise to be humble.

3**·Good people** [People with integrity] **will be guided by ·honesty** [innocence];
dishonesty will ·destroy [devastate] **those who are not trustworthy.**

4**Riches will not help ·when it's time to die** [Lon the day of anger],
but ·right living [righteousness] **will save you from death.**

5**The ·goodness** [righteousness] **of the innocent makes ·life easier** [Ltheir path straight],
but the wicked will ·be destroyed [Lfall] **by their wickedness.**

6**·Doing right** [Righteousness] **brings freedom to ·honest people** [people with integrity],
but those who are not trustworthy will be caught by their own desires.

7**When the wicked die, hope ·dies with them** [perishes];
their hope in riches ·will come to nothing [perishes].

8**The ·good** [righteous] **person is saved from ·trouble** [distress];
it comes to the wicked instead.

9**With ·words** [Ltheir mouth] **an ·evil** [godless] **person can destroy a neighbor,**
but a ·good [righteous] **person will escape by ·being resourceful** [Ltheir knowledge].

10**When ·good** [righteous] **people ·succeed** [flourish], **the city is happy.**
When evil people ·die [perish], **there are shouts of joy.**

11**·Good** [Righteous] **people bless and build up their city,**
but the wicked can ·destroy [demolish] **it with their ·words** [Lmouth].

12**People ·without good sense** [who lack sense/heart] **·find fault with** [despise; belittle] **their neighbors,**
but those with understanding keep quiet.

13**Gossips ·can't keep** [Lgo/walk around revealing] **secrets,**
but a trustworthy person ·can [keeps a confidence; Lcovers up a word].

14**Without ·leadership** [guidance] **a ·nation** [people] **falls,**
but ·lots of good advice [Lan abundance of counselors] **will ·save it** [bring victory; Eccl. 9:13–15].

[15]Whoever guarantees to pay somebody else's loan will suffer.
It is safer to avoid such promises.

[16]A ·kind [gracious] woman gets ·respect [honor],
but ·cruel [violent] men get only wealth.

[17]·Kind [*or* Loyal] people ·do themselves a favor [benefit themselves],
but cruel people ·bring trouble on themselves [[L]harm their own bodies].

[18]An evil person ·really earns nothing [gets false/deceptive wages],
but a ·good [righteous] person will surely be rewarded.

[19]Those who are ·truly good [righteous] will live,
but those who chase after evil will die.

[20]The LORD ·hates [detests] those with ·evil [crooked] hearts
but is pleased with those who are innocent on the path.

[21]Evil people will certainly be punished,
but ·those who do right [[L]the children of the righteous] will be set free.

[22]A beautiful woman without ·good sense [discretion]
is like a gold ring in a pig's snout.

[23]Those who do right only wish for good,
but the wicked can ·expect to be defeated by God's [[L]hope only for] anger.

[24]Some people give much but get back even more.
Others don't give what they should and end up poor.
[25]Whoever ·gives to others will get richer [*or* blesses others will be refreshed];
those who ·help [satisfy] others will themselves be ·helped [satisfied].

[26]People curse those who keep all the grain,
but they bless the one who is willing to sell it.

[27]Whoever looks for good will find ·kindness [favor],
but whoever looks for evil will find trouble.

[28]Those who trust in riches will ·be ruined [[L]fall],
but a good person will ·be healthy [flourish] like a green leaf.

[29]Whoever brings trouble to his family
will ·be left with nothing but the [[L]inherit the] wind.
A fool will be a servant to the wise of heart.

[30]·A good person gives life to others [[L]The fruit of the righteous is the tree of life];
the wise person ·teaches others how to live [gathers lives/souls].

[31]If ·good [righteous] people will get their due on earth,
How much more the wicked and the sinners.

12 Anyone who loves ·learning [knowledge] ·accepts [[L]loves] ·correction [instruction; discipline],
but a person who hates being corrected is stupid.

[2]The LORD ·is pleased with [favors] a good person,
but he will ·punish [condemn] ·anyone who plans evil [schemers].

[3]Doing evil brings no safety at all,
but ·a good person has safety and security [[L]the root of the righteous will not be disturbed].

[4]A ·good [noble] wife is like a crown for her husband,
but a disgraceful wife is like ·a disease [rot] in his bones.

[5]The plans that ·good [righteous] people make are ·fair [just],
but the ·advice [guidance] of the wicked will ·trick [deceive; defraud] you.

[6]The ·wicked talk about killing people [[L]words of the wicked are a murderous ambush/ambush of blood],
but the ·words [mouth] of ·good [righteous] people will save them.

[7]Wicked people ·die [are overturned] and they are no more,
but a ·good [righteous] person's ·family [[L]house] ·continues [endures].

[8]The ·wisdom [insight] of the wise wins praise,
but there is ·no respect [shame] for the ·stupid [warped; distressed mind/heart].

[9]A person who is ·not important [belittled; of low regard; ordinary] but has a servant is better off
than someone who ·acts [*or* is thought] ·important [honorable] but has no food.

[10]·Good [Righteous] people ·take care [[L]know the desires] of their animals,
but even the ·kindest [most compassionate] acts of the wicked are cruel.

[11]Those who work their land will have plenty of food,
but the one who chases ·empty dreams [emptiness] ·is not wise [lacks sense/heart].

[12]The wicked ·want [covet; desire] ·what other evil people have stolen [*or* the catch/prey of the evil],
but ·good [[L]the root of righteous] people ·want to give what they have to others [*or* endures].

[13]Evil people are trapped by their ·evil [offensive] talk,
but ·good [righteous] people ·stay out of trouble [escape from distress].

[14]People will be rewarded for ·what they say [Lthe fruit of their mouth],
and they will also be rewarded for ·what they do [Lthe work of their hands].

[15]·Fools think they are doing right [LThe path of fools is virtuous/right in their own eyes],
but the wise listen to advice.

[16]Fools quickly show that they are upset,
but the ·wise [prudent] ·ignore [conceal; hide] ·insults [contempt].

[17]An honest witness tells the truth,
but a dishonest witness tells lies.

[18]·Careless [Chattering] words stab like a sword,
but ·wise words bring [La wise tongue brings] healing.

[19]·Truth [LTruthful lips] will continue forever,
but ·lies are [La lying tongue lasts] only for a moment.

[20]Those who plan evil are full of ·lies [deceit],
but those who ·plan [advise] peace are happy.

[21]No harm comes to a ·good [righteous] person,
but an evil person's life is full of trouble.

[22]The LORD ·hates [detests] ·those who tell lies [false lips]
but ·is pleased with [favors] those who ·keep their promises [do what is true].

[23]·Wise [Prudent] people ·keep what they know to themselves [Lconceal/hide their knowledge],
but ·fools can't keep from showing how foolish they are [Lthe heart of fools proclaim their stupidity].

[24]Hard workers will ·become leaders [be in charge],
but those who are lazy will be ·slaves [put to forced labor].

[25]·Worry [Anxiety] ·is a heavy load [leads to depression],
but a ·kind [good] word cheers you up.

[26]·Good [Righteous] people ·take advice from their friends [*or* show the way to their friends/neighbors],
but ·an evil person is easily led to do wrong [*or* the path of the evil person makes them wander].

[27]The lazy ·catch no food to cook [Ldo not roast their prey],
but a hard worker will have great wealth.

[28]Doing what is right is the way to life,
but there is another way that leads to death.

13 Wise ·children take their parents' advice [[L]sons listen to their father's discipline/instruction],
but ·whoever makes fun of wisdom [mockers] won't listen to ·correction [a rebuke].

2 People will ·be rewarded for what they say [[L]eat well from the fruit of their mouth],
but ·those who can't be trusted [the faithless] ·want only [[L]have an appetite for] violence.

3 Those who ·are careful about what they say [[L]watch/guard their mouth] protect their lives,
but whoever ·speaks without thinking [[L]spreads their lips wide] will be ruined.

4 The desire of the lazy is strong, but they get nothing,
but desire of those who work hard will be satisfied.

5 ·Good [Righteous] people hate what is false,
but the wicked do shameful and disgraceful things.

6 ·Doing what is right [Righteousness] protects the honest person on the path,
but doing evil ·ruins [*or* misleads] the sinner.

7 Some people pretend to be rich but really have nothing.
Others pretend to be poor but really are wealthy.

8 The rich may have to pay a ransom for their lives,
but the poor will face no ·such danger [threats].

9 ·Good people can look forward to a bright future [[L]The light of the righteous rejoices],
but the ·future of the wicked is like a flame going [[L]lamp of the wicked goes] out.

10 Pride only leads to arguments [*or* The empty-headed cause arguments out of pride],
but those who take advice are wise.

11 Money that comes easily disappears quickly,
but money that is gathered little by little will grow.

12 ·It is sad not to get what you hoped for [[L]Hope delayed makes the heart sick].
But ·wishes that come true are like eating fruit from [longing fulfilled is] the tree of life.

13 Those who ·reject what they are taught [despise a word] will pay for it,
but those who ·obey what they are told [respect/fear the commandment] will be rewarded.

14 The teaching of a wise person ·gives life [Lis a fountain of life]
·and can save people from death [Lturning people aside from death traps/snares].

15 People with good ·understanding [insight; sense] will ·be well liked [receive favor],
but the ·lives of those who are not trustworthy are [Lway of the faithless is] hard.

16 Every ·wise [prudent] person acts ·with good sense [knowledgeably],
but fools ·show how foolish they are [display stupidity].

17 A wicked messenger ·brings nothing but trouble [*or* will fall into evil],
but a ·trustworthy [reliable] ·one [envoy] ·makes everything right [Lbrings healing].

18 A person who ·refuses [neglects] ·correction [instruction; discipline] will end up poor and disgraced,
but the one who ·accepts [Lguards] correction will be honored.

19 ·It is so good when wishes come true [LA realized longing/desire is pleasant],
but fools ·hate [detest] ·to stop doing [turning from] evil.

20 ·Spend time [LWalk; Go] with the wise and you will become wise,
but the friends of fools will ·suffer [*or* get into trouble].

21 Trouble ·always comes to [Lpursues] sinners,
but ·good [righteous] people ·enjoy success [get a good reward].

22 Good people leave their wealth to their grandchildren,
but a sinner's wealth is stored up for ·good [righteous] people.

23 A poor person's ·field [soil] might produce plenty of food,
but ·others often steal it away [Lit is unjustly swept away].

24 If you ·do not punish your children [Lwithhold/Tspare the rod], you ·don't love them [hate your children/son],
but if you love your children, you will ·correct [discipline] them.

25 ·Good [Righteous] people ·have enough to eat [eat till they are full/satisfied],
but the ·wicked will go hungry [Lstomachs of the wicked will be empty].

14 A wise woman ·strengthens her family [builds her house],
but a foolish woman ·destroys hers by what she does [tears hers down with her own hands].

2 People who ·live good lives [walk in virtue/integrity] ·respect [fear] the Lord,
but those who ·live evil lives don't [Lgo the wrong way on their paths despise him].

[3]·**Fools will be punished for their proud words** [The talk of fools is a rod for their back; *or* In the mouth of fools is a sprig of pride],
but the ·words [[L]lips] **of the wise will protect them.**

[4]**When there are no oxen, ·no food is in the barn** [*or* the barn is empty].
But with a strong ox, much grain can be grown.

[5]**A truthful witness does not lie,**
but a false witness tells nothing but lies.

[6]·**Those who make fun of wisdom look for it** [Mockers seek wisdom] **and do not find it,**
but knowledge comes ·easily [*or* quickly] **to those with understanding.**

[7]**Stay away from fools,**
because they ·can't teach you anything [[L]don't have knowledgeable lips].

[8]**The wisdom of a ·wise** [prudent] **person will understand ·what to do** [[L]his path],
but the folly of a foolish person is ·dishonest [deceptive].

[9]**Fools ·don't care if they sin** [[L]mock a penalty/guilt/reparation offering; Lev. 5:14—6:7],
but ·honest people work at being right [those with integrity/virtue are favored].

[10]·**No one else can know your sadness** [[L]A heart knows its emotional distress],
and strangers cannot share your joy.

[11]**The wicked person's house will be ·destroyed** [annihilated],
but a good person's tent will ·still be standing [flourish].

[12]·**Some people think they are doing right** [[L]There is a path that seems straight to a person],
but in the end it ·leads [[L]is the path] **to death.**

[13]·**Someone who is laughing may be sad inside** [[L]Even in laughter the heart may feel pain],
and joy may end in sadness.

[14]·**Evil people** [[L]Rebellious hearts] **will be paid back for their evil ·ways** [paths],
and good people will be rewarded for their ·good ones [deeds].

[15]·**Fools** [The naive] **will believe anything,**
but the ·wise [prudent] **·think about what they do** [understand their steps].

[16]**Wise people ·are careful** [fear] **and stay ·out of trouble** [away from evil],
but fools ·are careless [*or* get mad] **and ·quick to act** [*or* feel safe].

[17]**Someone with a quick temper ·does foolish things** [makes stupid mistakes],
but ·someone with understanding remains calm [*or* schemers are hated].

[18]**·Fools** [Naive people] **·are rewarded with nothing but more foolishness** [[L]inherit stupidity],
but the wise ·are rewarded with knowledge [[L]wear knowledge as an ornament].

[19]**Evil people will bow down to those who are good;**
the wicked will bow down at the ·door of those who do right [[L]gates of the righteous].

[20]**The poor are ·rejected** [hated], **even by their neighbors,**
but the rich have many friends [[C]perhaps an ironic reference to fair-weather friends].

[21]**It is a sin to ·hate** [despise] **your neighbor,**
but being ·kind [gracious] **to the needy brings ·happiness** [a blessing].

[22]**·Those** [[L]Do not those…?] **who make evil plans ·will be ruined** [[L]wander aimlessly],
but those who plan to do good will ·be loved and trusted [receive loyalty and faithfulness].

[23]**Those who work hard make a profit,**
but ·those who only talk will be poor [[L]the word of the lips leads only to lack].

[24]**Wise people are ·rewarded** [crowned] **with wealth,**
but fools only get more foolishness.

[25]**A truthful witness saves lives,**
but a ·false witness is a traitor [deceptive person proclaims lies].

[26]**Those who ·respect** [fear] **the LORD will have ·security** [*or* confidence],
and their children will ·be protected [have a refuge].

[27]**·Respect for** [Fear of] **the LORD ·gives life** [[L]is a fountain of life]
·and can save people from death [[L]turning people aside from death traps/snares].

[28]**A king is honored when he has many people to rule,**
but a prince is ruined if he has none.

[29]**·Patient people have great** [Patience leads to] **understanding,**
but ·people with quick tempers show their foolishness [impatience leads to stupid mistakes].

[30]**·Peace of mind** [[L]A healthy mind/heart] **means a healthy body,**
but jealousy will rot your bones.

31Whoever ·mistreats [oppresses] the poor insults their Maker,
but whoever ·is kind [shows grace] to the needy honors God.

32The wicked are ·ruined [thrown down] by their own evil,
but those who ·do right [are righteous] ·are protected [find refuge] even in death.

33Wisdom lives in ·those with understanding [an understanding heart/mind],
and ·even fools recognize it [*or* it is not known in the innards of a fool].

34·Doing what is right [Righteousness] makes a nation great,
but sin will ·bring disgrace to any [diminish a] people.

35A king is pleased with a ·wise [insightful] servant,
but he will become angry with one who causes him shame.

15 A ·gentle [soft; tender] answer ·will calm a person's anger [[L]turns back/[T]away wrath],
but an ·unkind [painful; sharp] answer ·will cause more [raises] anger.

2Wise people use knowledge when they speak,
but fools ·pour out [bubble forth with] foolishness.

3The LORD's eyes ·see everything [[L]are everywhere];
he watches both evil and good people.

4·As a tree gives fruit, healing words give life [[L]A healthy/healing tongue is a tree of life],
but ·dishonest [deceitful; perverse] words crush the spirit.

5Fools ·reject [disdain] their ·parents' [father's] ·correction [discipline],
but anyone who ·accepts [guards] correction is wise.

6Much ·wealth [treasure] is in the houses of ·good [righteous] people,
but evil people get nothing but trouble.

7Wise people use their ·words [[L]lips] to ·spread [scatter; disperse] knowledge,
but there is no knowledge in the ·thoughts [hearts; minds] of fools.

8The LORD ·hates [detests] the sacrifice that the wicked offer,
but he ·likes [favors] the prayers of ·honest people [people with integrity].

9The LORD ·hates [detests] ·what evil people do [[L]the path of the wicked],
but he ·loves [favors] those who ·do what is right [pursue righteousness].

10The person who ·quits doing what is right [[L]abandons the way] will be punished,
and the one who hates to be corrected will die.

11·The LORD knows what is happening in the world of the dead [LSheol and Abaddon/Destruction are before the LORD],
so he surely knows the ·thoughts of the living [Lhuman heart].

12·Those who make fun of wisdom [LMockers] don't like to be corrected;
they will not ·ask the wise for advice [Lgo to the wise].

13·Happiness makes a person smile [LA joyful heart brightens one's face],
but ·sadness [La troubled heart] can break a person's spirit.

14·People with understanding want more [LUnderstanding hearts seek] knowledge,
but fools ·just want more [Lfeed on] foolishness.

15Every day is hard for ·those who suffer [*or* the poor],
but a happy heart is like a continual feast.

16It is better to ·be poor [have little] and ·respect [fear] the LORD
than to ·be wealthy [have great treasure] and ·have much trouble [turmoil].

17It is better to eat vegetables with those who love you
than ·to eat meat [Lan ox of the stall] with those who hate you.

18People with quick tempers cause ·trouble [conflict],
but ·those who control their tempers [patient people] stop ·a quarrel [accusations].

19A lazy person's ·life [Lpath] is like a patch of thorns,
but an ·honest [virtuous] person's ·life [path] is like a smooth highway.

20Wise ·children [sons] make their father happy,
but foolish ·children [Lpeople] disrespect their mother.

21A person without ·wisdom [sense/heart] enjoys being foolish,
but someone with understanding ·does what is right [walks straight ahead].

22Plans fail without good advice,
but they succeed with the advice of many others.

23People enjoy giving ·good advice [La right reply].
Saying the right word at the right time is so pleasing.

24·Wise [Insightful] people's ·lives [Lway] ·get better and better [move upward].
They ·avoid whatever would cause their death [Lturn aside from Sheol/the grave below].

25The LORD will ·tear down [uproot] the proud person's house,
but he will ·protect [establish] the widow's ·property [boundaries].

26The LORD ·hates [detests] evil ·thoughts [*or* plans]
but ·is pleased with kind words [Lpleasing words are pure].

27·Greedy people [LThose who get unjust gain] bring trouble to their ·families [Lhouse],
but the person who ·can't be paid to do wrong [Lhates gifts/bribes] will live.

28·Good people [LThe heart/mind of the righteous] ·think [reflect; meditate] before they answer,
but the wicked simply ·pour [blurt] out evil.

29The LORD ·does not listen to [Lis far from] the wicked,
but he hears the prayers of ·those who do right [the righteous].

30Good news ·makes you feel better [Lrefreshes the bone].
·Your happiness will show in your eyes [LThe light of the eyes give joy to the heart].

31·If you listen to correction to improve your life,
you [LThe ear that listens to correction] will ·live [lodge] among the wise.

32Those who ·refuse [neglect] ·correction [discipline] hate themselves,
but those who ·accept [listen to] correction ·gain understanding [Lacquire heart/mind].

33·Respect [Fear] for the LORD ·will teach you wisdom [is wise instruction/discipline].
·If you want to be honored, you must be humble [LHumility comes before glory].

16 People may make plans in their ·minds [hearts],
but ·only the LORD can make them come true [Lfrom the LORD comes a responding tongue].

2·You may believe you are doing right [LAll paths of people are pure in their eyes],
but the LORD will ·judge your reasons [measure your motives; Lweigh the spirits].

3·Depend on the LORD in whatever you do [Commit your acts/deeds to the LORD],
and your plans will ·succeed [be established].

4The LORD makes everything ·go as he pleases [for a purpose].
He has even prepared a day of ·disaster [evil; harm; trouble] for evil people.

5The LORD ·hates [detests] those who are proud.
They will surely be punished.

[6]·Love [Loyalty] and ·truth [faithfulness] bring ·forgiveness of sin [atonement for guilt].
By ·respecting [fearing] the LORD you will avoid evil.

[7]When ·people live so that they please the LORD [[L]people's paths draw the LORD's favor]
even their enemies will make peace with them.

[8]It is better to ·be poor [have little] and ·right [righteousness]
than ·to be wealthy [much gain] and ·dishonest [injustice].

[9]·People may make plans in their minds [[L]Human hearts plan their path],
but the LORD ·decides what they will do [[L]establishes their step].

[10]The words of a king are like a ·message from God [oracle],
so ·his decisions should be fair [[L]he should not betray justice with his mouth].

[11]The LORD wants honest balances and scales;
·all the weights are his work [[L]he concerns himself with the weights in the pouch].

[12]Kings ·hate [detest] those who do wrong,
because ·governments only continue if they are fair [[L]in righteousness the throne is established].

[13]Kings ·like [favor] ·honest people [[L]righteous lips];
they ·value [love] ·someone who speaks the truth [[L]those who speak with integrity].

[14]An angry king ·can put someone to [[L]is a messenger of] death,
so a wise person will ·try to make him happy [appease/calm him].

[15]·A smiling king can give people [[L]In the light of the face of the king there is] life;
his ·kindness [favor] is like a ·spring shower [[L]cloud that brings late rain].

[16]It is better to get wisdom than gold,
and to choose understanding rather than silver!

[17]·Good people stay [[L]The highway of those with integrity turns] away from evil.
By ·watching what they do [protecting their path], they ·protect [guard] their lives.

[18]Pride ·leads to destruction [comes before a disaster];
·a proud attitude brings ruin [[T]pride comes before a fall].

[19]It is better to be humble and ·be with those who suffer [with the needy]
than ·to share stolen property [dividing plunder/spoil] with the proud.

[20]**Whoever ·listens to what is taught** [has insight] **will ·succeed** [prosper],
and whoever trusts the LORD will be ·happy [blessed].

[21]**The wise of heart ·are known for their** [[L]will be called] **understanding.**
Their ·pleasant [sweet] **words ·make them better teachers** [enhance their teaching].

[22]**·Understanding is like a fountain which gives life to those who use it** [[L]One who possesses insight is a fountain of life],
but ·foolishness brings punishment to fools [*or* the instruction of foolish people is folly].

[23]**Wise people's ·minds** [hearts] **·tell them what to say** [[L]provide insight to their mouth],
and that ·helps them be better teachers [enhances their teaching].

[24]**Pleasant words are like ·a honeycomb** [liquid honey],
·making people happy and healthy [[L]sweet to the taste and healing to the bones].

[25]**·Some people think they are doing right** [[L]There is a path that is straight before a person/[T]seems right to a man],
but in the end it ·leads [[L]is the path] **to death.**

[26]**The workers' hunger ·helps** [[L]works for] **them,**
·because their desire to eat makes them work [[L]and their mouths press/urge them on].

[27]**·Useless** [Worthless] **people ·make evil plans** [[L]dig up evil],
and their ·words [[L]lips] **are like a burning fire.**

[28]**A ·useless** [perverse] **person causes ·trouble** [conflicts],
and a gossip ruins close friendships.

[29]**·Cruel** [Violent] **people ·trick** [entice] **their neighbors**
and ·lead them to do wrong [[L]make them walk on a path that is not good].

[30]**Someone who winks their eye is planning ·evil** [perverse things],
and the one who ·grins [[L]purses/narrows their lips] **is ·planning something wrong** [concealing evil].

[31]**Gray hair is like a crown of honor;**
it is ·earned by living a good life [[L]found on the path of righteousness].

[32]**Patience is better than strength** [*or* A patient person is better than a warrior].
Controlling your temper is better than capturing a city.

[33]**People throw lots ·to make a decision** [[L]into the lap],
but the ·answer [decision] **comes from the LORD.**

17 It is better to eat a dry crust of bread in ·peace [quiet]
than to have a feast where there is ·quarreling [strife; contention].

2 A ·wise [insightful] servant will rule over the master's disgraceful child
and will even ·inherit a share of what the master leaves his children [Ldivide an inheritance with the brothers/relatives].

3 A crucible ·tests [*or* refines] silver and a furnace gold,
but the LORD ·tests [*or* refines] hearts.

4 Evil people listen to ·evil words [Lguilty lips].
Liars pay attention to ·cruel words [La destructive tongue].

5 Whoever ·mistreats [ridicules; mocks] the poor insults their Maker;
whoever enjoys someone's trouble will ·be punished [Lnot go unpunished].

6 ·Old people are proud of their grandchildren [LGrandchildren are the crown of the elderly],
and ·children are proud of [Lthe glory/splendor of children are] their parents.

7 ·Fools should not be proud [*or* It is not right for fools to be good speakers],
and ·rulers [honorable people] should not ·be liars [Lhave lying lips].

8 ·Some people think they can pay others to do anything they ask [LA bribe is a magic stone in the eyes of those who give it].
·They think it will work every time [LIt grants success to all who use it].

9 ·Whoever forgives someone's sin makes a friend [LOne who seeks love conceals an offense],
but ·gossiping about the sin [repeating a thing] breaks up friendships.

10 A wise person will learn more from a ·warning [rebuke]
than a fool will learn from a hundred lashings.

11 Disobedient ·people look only for trouble [Lseek only rebellion],
so a cruel messenger will be sent against them.

12 It is ·better [safer] to meet a bear robbed of her cubs
than to meet a fool doing foolish things.

13 Whoever gives evil in return for good
will always have trouble at home.

14 Starting a quarrel is like ·a leak in a dam [Lletting out water],
so ·stop it [hold back an accusation] before a fight breaks out.

15 The LORD hates both of these things:
·freeing the guilty and punishing the innocent [Ljudging the righteous wicked and the wicked righteous].

16 **It won't do a fool any good to try to buy wisdom,**
because he doesn't have the ability to be wise.

17 **A friend loves you all the time,**
and a brother ·**helps in** [Lis born for a] **time of trouble.**

18 ·**It is not wise to promise**
to pay what your neighbor owes [LA person lacks sense/heart who shakes hands in agreement, who secures a loan for a friend/neighbor].

19 **Whoever loves to argue loves to sin.**
Whoever ·**brags a lot is asking for trouble** [Lbuilds a high doorway is seeking a collapse].

20 **A person with an** ·**evil** [crooked] **heart will find no success,**
and the person ·**whose words are evil** [Lwho twists matters with their tongue] **will get into trouble.**

21 **It is sad to have a foolish child;**
there is no joy in being the parent of a fool.

22 **A happy heart** ·**is like good medicine** [Lbrings healing],
but a broken spirit ·**drains your strength** [Ldries up bone].

23 **When the wicked** ·**accept money to do wrong** [take a secret bribe/Lbribe from the chest/bosom]
·**there can be no** [it stretches] **justice.**

24 **The person with understanding is always** ·**looking for** [focused on] **wisdom,**
but the mind of a fool wanders ·**everywhere** [Lto the ends of the earth].

25 **Foolish children make their father sad**
and cause their mother great ·**sorrow** [bitterness].

26 **It is not good to punish the** ·**innocent** [righteous]
or to beat leaders for being honest.

27 **The wise** ·**say very little** [restrain/hold back their talk],
and those with understanding stay ·**calm** [coolheaded].

28 **Even fools seem to be wise if they keep quiet;**
if they ·**don't speak** [Lkeep their lips shut], **they appear to understand.**

18 ·Unfriendly [Antisocial; Lonely] **people** ·**are selfish** [Lseek their own longings/desires]
and ·**hate** [Lbreak out against] **all good sense.**

2 **Fools do not** ·**want to understand anything** [Ldelight in understanding].
They only want to ·**tell others what they think** [Lreveal/disclose their heart].

He will take away the ·shame [disgrace] of his people from the earth.
The LORD has spoken.

9·At that time [LIn that day] people will say,
"·Our God is doing this [LLook/TBehold, this is our God]!
We have waited for him, and he has come to save us.
This is the LORD. We waited for him,
·so we will [let us] rejoice and ·be happy [be glad; celebrate] ·when he saves us [Lin his salvation]."
10The ·LORD will protect Jerusalem [Lhand of the LORD will rest on this mountain],
·but he will crush our enemy Moab [LMoab will be trampled under him]
like straw that is trampled down in the manure.
11They [LHe; CMoab] will spread their arms in it
like a person who is swimming.
But God will bring down their pride,
·and all the clever things they have made will mean nothing [Ltogether with the trickery of their hands].
12He will ·destroy [bring down] ·Moab's [Lyour] high, fortified walls,
·leveling them to the ground [laying them low].
He will throw them down to the ground,
even to the dust.

A Song of Praise to God

26 ·At that time [LIn that day] this song will be sung in Judah:
We have a strong city.
·God protects us with [LHis salvation/deliverance is] its strong walls and defenses.
2Open the gates,
and the ·good people [righteous nation] will enter,
those who ·follow God [remain faithful].
3You, LORD, ·give [preserve/keep in] ·true peace [complete peace; Lpeace, peace]
·to those who depend on you [Twhose mind is stayed on you; Lwhose purpose is firm],
because they trust you.
4So, trust the LORD always,
because ·he [Lin Yah, the LORD/Yahweh; CYah is a shorter version of Yahweh] is our ·Rock forever [eternal rock].
5He will ·destroy [humble; bring down] ·the people of that proud city [Lthose who dwell on a high place],
He will bring that ·high [lofty; arrogant] city down to the ground
and throw it down into the dust.
6·Then those who were hurt by the city will walk on its ruins [LThe foot tramples it down, the feet of the oppressed];
·those who were made poor by the city will trample it under their feet [Lthe footsteps of the poor (will trample it)].

7The ·path [way] of life is level for ·those who are right with God [the righteous];
·LORD [*or* Upright One], you make the way of life ·smooth [straight; level] for those people.

8But, LORD, we are waiting
·for your [*or* in the] ·way of justice [*or* path/way of your judgments].
Our souls ·want to remember [*or* desire; *or* wish to see glorified]
·you [your renown; your remembrance] and your name.
9My soul ·wants to be with [longs/yearns for] you at night,
and my spirit ·wants to be with [seeks; longs for] you ·at the dawn of every day [in the morning].
When your ·way of justice [judgment] comes to the ·land [earth],
·people [the inhabitants] of the world will learn ·the right way of living [righteousness; justice].
10Evil people will not learn ·to do good [righteousness; justice]
even if you show them ·kindness [mercy; grace].
They will continue ·doing evil [acting unjustly], even if they live in a ·good world [land of uprightness];
they never see the LORD's ·greatness [majesty].
11LORD, ·you are ready to punish those people [[L]your hand is lifted up; [C]ready to strike],
but they do not see that.
·Show them your strong love for your people [[L]They will see your zeal for your people; *or* They will see your zealous judgment against mankind].
·Then those who are evil [[L]…and they] will be ashamed.
·Burn [Consume] them in the fire
·you have prepared for [[L]of] your ·enemies [adversaries].
12LORD, all our ·success is [accomplishments/works are] because of what you have done,
·so give us peace [*or* and you give us peace/security].
13LORD, our God, other masters besides you have ruled us,
but we ·honor [praise; remember] only ·you [[L]your name].
14·Those masters are now dead [[L]They are dead, never to live];
their ·ghosts [spirits] will not rise from death.
You punished and destroyed them
and erased any memory of them.
15LORD, you ·multiplied the number of your people [enlarged/made great the nation];
you ·multiplied them [enlarged/made great the nation] and brought ·honor [glory] to yourself.
You ·widened [enlarged; extended] the borders of the land.
16LORD, people ·remember [seek; come to] you when they are in trouble;
they ·say quiet prayers to you [*or* utter incantations] when you punish them.
17LORD, ·when we are with you [*or* because of you],
we are like a woman giving birth to a baby;
she cries and has pain from the birth.
18·In the same way [[L]We were pregnant/conceived], we ·had pain [writhed; strained].
We gave birth, but only to wind.
We ·don't bring [*or* can't bring; haven't brought] salvation to the ·land [earth]
·or given birth to new people for the world [[L]nor have the inhabitants of the earth fallen]

[19]Your dead will live again;
their bodies will rise from death.
You who ·lie in the ground [[L]dwell in the dust],
wake up and ·be happy [shout joyfully]!
·The dew covering you [[L]Your dew] is ·like the dew of a new day [[L]a dew of lights];
the ·ground [earth] will give birth to the dead.

Judgment: Reward or Punishment

[20]My people, go into your ·rooms [chambers; inner rooms]
and shut your doors behind you.
Hide in your rooms for a short time
until God's anger ·is finished [has passed by].
[21] [[L]For look/[T]behold] The LORD ·will leave [is coming out of] his place
to punish the ·people [inhabitants] of the world for their sins.
The earth will ·show [reveal; disclose] ·the blood of the people who have been killed [[L]its blood];
it will not cover ·the dead [its slain] any longer.

27 ·At that time [[L]In that day] the LORD will punish Leviathan [[C]a sea creature in ancient Near Eastern texts that represents chaos; Job 3:8; 41:1, 12; Ps. 74:14; 104:26], the ·gliding [*or* swift-moving; *or* fleeing] ·snake [serpent].
He will punish Leviathan, the ·coiled [writhing; twisting] ·snake [serpent],
with his great and hard and powerful sword.
He will kill the ·monster [dragon] in the sea.
[2]·At that time [[L]In that day]
sing about the ·pleasant [beautiful; *or* fruitful] vineyard [[C]God's people; 5:1–7].
[3]"I, the LORD, will ·care for [watch over] that vineyard;
I will water it ·at the right time [regularly; continually].
No one will hurt it,
because I will guard it day and night.
[4]I am not ·angry [wrathful].
If ·anyone builds a wall of thornbushes in war [*or* only there were briers and thorns against me!],
I will march ·to it [against it in battle] and burn it.
[5]But if anyone comes to me for ·safety [refuge; protection]
and wants to make peace with me,
·he should come and [let him] make peace with me."
[6]In the days to come, ·the people of Jacob [[L]Jacob] will ·be like a plant with good roots [take root];
Israel will ·grow like a plant beginning to bloom [[L]blossom and bud].
·Then the world will be filled with their children [[L]…and fill all the world with fruit].

The Lord Will Send Israel Away

[7]·The LORD has not hurt [[L]Has the LORD struck down…?] his people as he ·hurt their enemies [[L]struck down those who struck them];
·his people have not [[L]have they…?] been killed like those who tried to kill them.
[8]He will ·settle his argument with Israel [*or* oppose her; contend with her] by sending her far away.
·Like a hot desert wind [[L]With his fierce breath in the day of the east wind; [C]the east wind came from the desert], he will drive her away.

9 This is how ·Israel's [[L]Jacob's] guilt will be forgiven;
this is how its sins will be taken away:
·Israel [[L]He] will crush the rocks of the altar [[C]pagan altars] to dust,
and no ·Asherah idols [[L]Asherahs; [C]sacred trees or poles dedicated to the goddess Asherah] or ·altars [incense altars] will be left standing.
10 ·At that time [[L]In that day] the ·strong, walled [fortified] city will be ·empty [desolate]
an abandoned settlement, empty like a ·desert [wilderness; 17:9; 32:14, 19].
Calves will eat grass there.
They will lie down there
and ·eat leaves from [strip bare] the branches.
11 The limbs will become dry and break off,
so women will use them for firewood.
The people ·refuse to understand [lack understanding/discernment],
so ·their Creator [the one who made them] will not comfort them;
·their Maker [the one who formed them] will not ·be kind [show favor] to them.

12 ·At that time [[L]In that day] the LORD will begin gathering ·his people
[[L]you, sons/children of Israel] one by one from the ·Euphrates River
[[L]flowing River] to the brook of Egypt. He will ·separate them from others
as grain is separated from chaff [thresh/[L]beat them out]. 13 ·At that time [In
that day] a great trumpet will be blown. Then those who are ·lost [*or* perish-
ing] in Assyria and those who ·have run away [were exiled/driven out] to
Egypt will come and worship the LORD on that holy mountain in Jerusalem.

Warnings to Israel

28 ·How terrible it will be for [[L]Woe to] Samaria [[C]the capital of the northern kingdom of Israel], the pride of ·Israel's [[L]Ephraim's] drunken people!
That beautiful ·crown [wreath; garland] of flowers is ·just a dying plant [fading]
set on ·a hill above [[L]the head of] a rich valley ·where drunkards live [of those overcome with wine].
2 Look, the Lord has someone who is strong and powerful.
Like a storm of hail and ·strong [destructive] wind,
like a sudden flood of water pouring over the country,
he will throw Samaria down to the ground [[L]with his hand].
3 That city, the pride of ·Israel's [[L]Ephraim's] drunken people,
will be trampled underfoot.
4 That beautiful ·crown [wreath; garland] of flowers is ·just a dying plant [fading]
set on ·a hill above [[L]the head of] a rich valley.
That city will be like the first ripe fig of summer.
Anyone who sees it
quickly ·picks it [takes it in hand] and ·eats [swallows] it.

5 ·At that time [[L]In that day] the LORD ·All-Powerful [Almighty; of Heaven's Armies; [T]of hosts]
·will be like [[L]will be] a beautiful crown,
·like a wonderful [a beautiful] ·crown of flowers [wreath; garland; diadem]
for ·his people who are left alive [the remnant of his people].

[6]Then he will give ·wisdom [a spirit of justice/judgment] to ·the judges
who must decide cases [[L]those who sit in judgment]
and strength to those who battle at the city gate.
[7]But now those leaders ·are drunk [reel] with wine;
they ·stumble [stagger] from drinking too much ·beer [[L]strong drink; [C]alcoholic beverage made from grain].
The priests and prophets ·are drunk [stagger] with ·beer [[T]strong drink]
and are ·filled with [swallowed by; *or* confused because of] wine.
They stumble from too much ·beer [[T]strong drink].
·The prophets [[L]They] ·are drunk [stagger] when they see their visions;
·the judges [they] stumble ·when they make their decisions [in judgment].
[8]Every table is covered with vomit,
so there is not a clean place anywhere.

[9]·The LORD is trying to teach the people a lesson [[L]Who is he teaching knowledge?];
·he is trying to make them understand his teachings [[L]To whom is he explaining the message?].
·But the people are like babies too old for breast milk [Those weaned from milk?],
·like those who no longer nurse at their mother's breast [Those taken from the breast?].
[10]So ·they make fun of the LORD's prophet and say [*or* the LORD must repeat himself again and again; [L]For it is]:
"·A command here, a command there [[T]Precept upon precept, precept upon precept].
·A rule here, a rule there [[T]Line upon line, line upon line; [C]Hebrew: *tsav latsav tsav latsav / kav lakav kav lakav;* it may be the people mocking the words of the prophets as nonsense; or it may refer to God repeating himself because the people will not listen].
A little lesson here, a little lesson there [[L]A little there, a little there]."
[11]So the LORD will use ·strange words [mocking/stammering lips] and foreign ·languages [tongues]
to speak to these people.
[12]God said to them,
"Here is a place of rest;
let the ·tired people [weary] come and rest.
This is the place of peace."
But the people would not listen.
[13]So the words of the LORD will be,
"·A command here, a command there [[T]Precept upon precept, precept upon precept].
·A rule here, a rule there [[T]Line upon line, line upon line].
·A little lesson here, a little lesson there [[L]A little there, a little there; [C]see v. 10; God now uses the same words to mimic the foreign language of the Assyrian invaders]."
They will fall back and be ·defeated [broken];
they will be ·trapped and captured [snared and taken].

14So listen to the LORD's message, you who ·brag [mock; scoff; Prov. 1:22; 9:7, 8, 12; 13:1],
you ·leaders [Lwho rule this people] in Jerusalem.
15You say, "We have made an ·agreement [treaty; covenant] with death;
we have a ·contract [agreement; pact] with ·death [or the grave; LSheol].
When ·terrible punishment [an overwhelming scourge/flood] passes by,
it won't ·hurt [touch; reach] us.
Our lies ·will keep us safe [Lare our refuge],
and ·our tricks [falsehood] ·will hide us [is our refuge/shelter]."
16Because of these things, this is what the Lord GOD says:
"I will ·put [lay; establish] a stone in the ground in ·Jerusalem [LZion; Cthe location of the Temple],
a tested stone.
·Everything will be built on this important and precious rock [L…a precious cornerstone for a firm foundation].
Anyone who trusts in it will never ·be disappointed [*or* panic; waver; be shaken; Rom. 9:33; 1 Pet. 2:6].
17I will use justice as a measuring line
and ·goodness [righteousness] as the ·standard [plumb line].
The lies you ·hide behind [take refuge in] will be ·destroyed [swept away] as if by hail.
·They [Your hiding place/shelter] will be washed away as if in a flood.
18Your ·agreement [covenant; treaty] with death will be ·erased [annulled];
your contract with ·death [*or* the grave; LSheol] will not ·help you [stand; last].
When ·terrible punishment [overwhelming scourge/flood] comes,
you will be ·crushed [beaten down] by it.
19Whenever ·punishment [Lit] comes, it will take you away.
It will come morning after morning;
it will ·defeat you [sweep through] by day and by night.
Those who understand this punishment will be terrified."
20·You will be like the person who tried to sleep
on a bed that was too short [LFor the bed is too short to stretch out on]
and ·with a blanket that [Lthe blanket] was too narrow
to wrap around himself.
21The LORD will ·fight [Lrise up] as he did at Mount Perazim [2 Sam. 5:20].
He will be ·angry [rouse himself] as he was in the Valley of Gibeon [Josh. 10:10–14].
He will do his work, his ·strange [peculiar] work.
He will finish his job, his ·strange [unusual] job.
22Now, ·you must not make fun of these things [do not mock; *or* stop your mocking],
or the ·ropes [*or* chains; bonds] around you will become ·tighter [*or* heavier].
The Lord GOD ·All-Powerful [Almighty; of Heaven's Armies; Tof hosts] has ·told me [decreed to me]
how the whole ·earth [land] will be destroyed.

The Lord Punishes Fairly

23Listen closely to ·what I tell you [my voice];
·listen carefully to [pay attention to; heed] what I say.
24·A farmer does not [LDoes the plower…?] plow his field all the time;
·he does not [Ldoes he…?] go on working the soil.
25·He makes [Does he not make…?] the ground flat and smooth.
Then he plants the dill and scatters the cumin.
·He plants [Does he not plant…?] the wheat in rows,
the barley in its special place,
and other wheat as a border around the field.
26His God ·teaches [instructs] him
and ·shows [teaches] him the right way.
27A farmer doesn't use ·heavy boards to crush [a sledge to thresh] dill;
he doesn't use a wagon wheel to crush cumin.
He uses a small stick to break open the dill,
and with a ·stick [rod; flail] he opens the cumin.
28The grain is ground to make bread.
People do not ruin it by ·crushing [threshing] it forever.
The farmer separates the wheat from the chaff with his cart,
but he does not let his horses ·grind [crush] it.
29This lesson [Cthat the Lord's punishment fits the sin] also comes from
the LORD ·All-Powerful [Almighty; of Heaven's Armies; Tof hosts],
who gives wonderful ·advice [counsel; 9:6], who ·is very wise [*or* gives
excellent/great wisdom].

Warnings to Jerusalem

29 ·How terrible it will be for [LWoe to] you, Ariel [Canother
name for Jerusalem, perhaps meaning either "lion" or "altar
hearth"; v. 2],
the city where David ·camped [lived; settled; *or* besieged; CDavid first
conquered, then lived in the city; 2 Sam. 5:6–9].
Your festivals have continued
year after year.
2I will ·attack [threaten; bring distress to] ·Jerusalem [LAriel; v. 1],
and that city will be filled with ·sadness [mourning] and ·crying
[lamentation].
It will be like an ·altar [*or* altar hearth; Cthe Hebrew word sounds like
Ariel, perhaps indicating that Jerusalem will burn like an altar] to me.
3I will ·put armies all around you [encamp against/besiege you; Csame
word as in v. 1];
I will surround you with towers
and with ·devices to attack [siege works against] you.
4You will be pulled down and will speak from the ground;
I will hear your voice rising from the ·ground [*or* underworld].
It will sound like the voice of a ghost;
your words will come like a whisper from the ·dirt [dust].

5Your ·many [multitude of] enemies will become like fine dust;
the many ·cruel people [ruthless hordes] will be like chaff that is
blown away.
·Everything will happen very quickly [LSuddenly, in an instant…; Cthis
phrase may go with what comes before or after].
6 The LORD ·All-Powerful [Almighty; of Heaven's Armies; Tof hosts]
will come

with thunder, earthquakes, and great noises,
with ·storms [whirlwind], ·strong winds [tempest], and a fire that ·destroys [devours].
7Then all the nations that fight against ·Jerusalem [LAriel; v. 1]
will be like a dream;
all the nations that ·attack [besiege; bring distress to] her
will be like a vision in the night.
8They will be like a hungry man who dreams he is eating,
but when he awakens, he is still hungry.
They will be like a thirsty man who dreams he is drinking,
but when he awakens, he is still weak and thirsty.
It will be the same way with ·all the [the multitude of] nations
who fight against Mount Zion.

9·Be surprised and amazed [Shock yourselves and be shocked].
Blind yourselves ·so that you cannot see [and be blind].
Become drunk, but not from wine.
Trip and fall, but not from ·beer [Tstrong drink; Calcoholic beverage made from grain].
10The Lord has ·made you go into [Lpoured out on you] a deep sleep.
He has closed your eyes. (The prophets are your eyes.)
He has covered your heads. (The seers [Canother name for prophets] are your heads.)
11This vision is like the words of a ·book [scroll] that is closed and
sealed. You may give the book to someone who can read and tell that
person to read it. But he will say, "I can't read the book, because it is
sealed." 12Or you may give the book to someone who cannot read and tell
him to read it. But he will say, "I don't know how to read."
13The Lord says:
"These people ·worship me [Lcome near to me] with their mouths,
and honor me with their lips,
but their hearts are far from me.
Their ·worship [awe; fear] is based on
nothing but human ·rules [Lcommandments that have been taught].
14So [Llook; Tbehold] I will continue to ·amaze [astound] these people
by doing more and more ·miracles [wonders].
·Their wise men will lose their wisdom [LThe wisdom of the wise will perish];
·their wise men will not be able to understand [Lthe discernment of the discerning will disappear; 1 Cor. 1:19]."

Warnings About Other Nations

15·How terrible it will be for [LWoe to] those who ·try
to hide [deeply hide; *or* hide too deep to see] ·things [plans; counsel] from the Lord
and who do their work in darkness.
They ·think no one will see them or know what they do [Lsay, "Who sees us? Who knows us?"].
16You ·are confused [Lturn things upside down!].
You think the clay is equal to the potter.
·You think that an object can [*or* Should the thing formed…?] tell the one who made it,
"You didn't make me [10:15; Rom. 9:20]."

This is like a pot telling ·its maker [the potter],
"You don't ·know anything [understand]."

A Better Time Is Coming

17In a very short time, Lebanon will become ·rich farmland [a fertile/fruitful field],
and the ·rich farmland [fertile/fruitful field] will seem like a forest.
18·At that time [LIn that day] the deaf will hear the words in a ·book [scroll].
·Instead of having [LFrom; Out of] darkness and gloom, the blind will see.
19The LORD will make the ·poor people [humble; lowly; meek] ·happy [rejoice];
·they [Lthe poor/needy] will ·rejoice [delight; exult] in the Holy One of Israel [1:4].
20Then the ·people without mercy [ruthless; tyrants] will come to an end;
·those who do not respect God [the scoffer/mocker/arrogant] will disappear.
Those who ·enjoy [are intent on; have an eye for] doing evil will be ·gone [cut off/down]:
21those who ·lie about others in court [bear false testimony; Lmake a person a sinner with a word],
those who trap ·people in court [Lthe arbiter at the city gate],
those who ·lie and [with false charges/testimony] take justice from innocent people in court.
22This is what the LORD who ·set free [redeemed; rescued] Abraham
says to the ·family [Lhouse] of Jacob:
"Now ·the people of Jacob [LJacob] will not be ashamed
or ·disgraced [Ltheir faces turn pale] any longer.
23When they see all their children,
the children I made with my hands,
they will ·say my name is holy [honor/sanctify my name].
They will ·agree [recognize; acknowledge] that the Holy One of Jacob [1:4] is holy,
and they will ·respect [stand in awe of; fear] the God of Israel.
24People who ·do wrong [wander/err in spirit] will now understand.
Those who complain will accept ·being taught [insight; instruction]."

Warnings to the Stubborn Nation

30 The LORD said
"·How terrible it will be for [LWoe to] these ·stubborn [rebellious] children.
They ·make plans [take counsel], but ·they don't ask me to help them [Lnot of/from me].
They make ·agreements with other nations [alliances], ·without asking [not of/from] my Spirit.
They are adding ·more and more sins to themselves [Lsin upon sin].
2They go down to Egypt for help
without asking me about it first.
They ·hope they will be saved by [Lseek protection in the strength of] ·the king of Egypt [LPharaoh];
they ·want Egypt to protect them [Lseek refuge in the shade of Egypt].
3But ·hiding in Egypt [Lthe protection of Pharaoh] will bring you only shame;
Egypt's ·protection [Lshade] will only disappoint you.

4 Your officers have gone to Zoan [Cin northern Egypt; 19:11],
and your messengers have gone to Hanes [Cin southern Egypt],
5 but they will be put to shame,
because Egypt is useless to them.
It will give no help and will be of no ·use [benefit; advantage];
it will cause them only shame and ·embarrassment [disgrace]."

God's Message to Judah

6 This is a ·message [prophecy; oracle; burden] about the ·animals [beasts]
in ·southern Judah [the South; Lthe Negev]:
·Southern Judah is a dangerous place [LThough a land of trouble and distress]
full of lions and lionesses,
·poisonous snakes [adders] and ·darting [*or* flying, fiery] ·snakes [serpents].
·The messengers travel through there with their wealth [LThey carry their riches] on the backs of donkeys
and their treasure on the ·backs [humps] of camels.
They carry them to a nation that cannot help them,
7 to Egypt whose help is ·useless [Lworthless and futile].
So I call that country Rahab [Cmythical sea monster symbolic of chaos; 51:9; Ps. 89:10] the ·Do-Nothing [Harmless; Silenced].

8 Now write this on a ·sign [tablet] for the people,
·write this [inscribe it] on a scroll,
so that for the days to come
this will be a witness forever.
9 These people are ·like children who lie and refuse to obey [La rebellious nation, lying children];
children who refuse to listen to the LORD's ·teachings [law; instruction; LTorah].
10 They tell the seers [Canother name for prophets],
"Don't see any more visions!"
They say to the prophets,
"Don't tell us ·the truth [what is right]!
Say ·things that will make us feel good [pleasant/smooth things];
·see only good things for us [Lprophesy illusions].
11 Stop blocking our path.
Get out of our way.
·Stop telling us about [*or* Rid us of]
the Holy One of Israel [1:4]."
12 So this is what the Holy One of Israel says:
"You people have ·refused to accept [rejected; despise] this message
and have depended on ·cruelty [oppression] and ·lies [deceit] to help you.
13 You are guilty of these things.
So you will be like a high wall ·with cracks in it [cracked and bulging]
that falls suddenly and ·breaks into small pieces [*or* in a flash/instant].
14 You will be like a clay jar that breaks,
smashed into many pieces.
Those pieces will be too small
to take coals from the fire
or to get water from a ·well [cistern]."

[15]This is what the Lord God, the Holy One of Israel [1:4], says:
"If you ·come back to me [repent] and ·trust [rest in] me, you will be saved.
If you will be calm and trust me, you will be strong."
But you ·don't want to do that [refused; would not].
[16]You say, "No, we need horses to ·run away on [flee]."
So you will ·run away on horses [Lflee].
You say, "We will ride away on fast horses."
So those who chase you will be fast.
[17]One enemy will make threats,
and a thousand of your men will ·run away [flee; Deut. 32:30].
Five enemies will make threats,
and all of you will run from them.
You will be left alone like a flagpole on a hilltop,
like a ·banner [standard; signal flag] on a hill.
[18]The LORD ·wants [is waiting] to ·show his mercy [be gracious] to you.
He ·wants to rise and [*or* is exalted and wants to] ·comfort [show compassion to] you.
The LORD is a ·fair [just] God,
and everyone who waits for ·his help [Lhim] will be ·happy [blessed].

The Lord Will Help His People

[19]You people who live on Mount Zion in Jerusalem will not ·cry [weep]
anymore. The LORD will hear your crying, and he will ·comfort [be gracious to] you. When he hears you, he will ·help [answer] you. [20]The Lord
has given you ·sorrow and hurt like the bread and water you ate every day
[Lthe bread of adversity and the water of affliction]. ·He is your teacher; he
will not continue to hide [*or* But your teachers will no longer be hidden]
from you, but you will see your ·teacher [*or* teachers] with your own eyes.
[21]If you go the wrong way—to the right or to the left—you will hear a
voice behind you saying, "This is the right way. ·You should go this way
[LWalk in it]." [22]Then you will ·ruin [destroy; desecrate] your statues covered with silver and gold. You will throw them away like ·filthy rags
[unclean things; a menstrual cloth; Lev. 15:19–24] and say, "Go away!"
[23]·At that time [LIn that day] the LORD will send rain for the seeds you
·plant [sow] in the ground, and the ground will grow food for you. The
harvest will be ·rich [fat] and ·great [plentiful], and ·you will have plenty
of food in the fields for your animals [Lyour cattle will graze in large pas-
tures]. [24]Your oxen and donkeys that work the soil will have ·all the food
they need [the best grain; seasoned feed]. ·You will have to use shovels and
pitchforks to spread all their food […winnowed with fork and shovel].
[25]Every mountain and hill will have streams flowing with water. ·These
things will happen after many people are killed and [L…in the day of
great slaughter when] the towers are pulled down. [26]·At that time [LIn that
day] the light from the moon will be bright like the sun, and the light
from the sun will be seven times brighter than now, like the light of seven
days. These things will happen when the LORD ·bandages his broken
[binds up the broken limbs of his] people and heals the ·hurts he gave
them [wounds he inflicted].
[27]Look! The ·LORD [Lthe name of the LORD; Cthe name represents the person] comes from far away.
His anger is like a fire with thick clouds of smoke.

His ·mouth is [lips are] filled with anger,
and his tongue is like a ·burning [consuming; devouring] fire.
28His breath is like a rushing river,
which rises to the ·throat [neck].
He will ·judge [Lsift; shake] the nations as if he is sifting them through the strainer of destruction.
He will place in their mouths a bit that will lead them ·the wrong way [astray].
29You will ·sing happy songs [Lhave a song]
as on the nights you begin a festival.
You will be happy like people ·listening to [*or* playing; Lgoing with] flutes
as they come to the mountain of the LORD,
to the Rock of Israel.
30The LORD will cause all people to hear his ·great [majestic; glorious] voice
and to see his powerful arm come down with anger,
like a ·great fire that burns everything [consuming/devouring fire],
like a great storm with much rain and hail.
31Assyria will be ·afraid [terrorized; *or* shattered] when it hears the voice of the LORD,
because he will strike Assyria with a rod.
32·When the LORD punishes Assyria with a rod [LEvery stroke he lays on them with his punishing club/rod],
he will beat them to the music of tambourines and harps;
he will fight against them with his mighty weapons.
33·Topheth [*or* The burning place; Cperhaps located in the Valley of Hinnom (Gehenna); Jer. 7:31–32] has been made ready for a long time;
it is ready for the king.
It was made deep and wide
with much wood and fire.
And the LORD's breath will come
like a stream of ·burning sulfur [Tbrimstone] and set it on fire.

Warnings About Relying on Egypt

31 ·How terrible it will be for [LWoe to] those people who go down to Egypt for help.
·They think horses will save them [L...who rely on horses].
·They think [L...who trust in] their many chariots
and strong horsemen will save them [Ps. 20:7].
But they don't trust God, the Holy One of Israel [1:4],
or ask the LORD for help.
2But he is wise and can bring them disaster.
He does not ·change his warnings [take back his words].
He will rise up and fight against the ·evil people [Lhouse of evildoers]
and against those who try to help ·evil people [sinners; workers of iniquity].
3The Egyptians are only people and are not God.
Their horses are ·only animals [Lflesh] and are not spirit.
The LORD will stretch out his arm,
and the one who helps will stumble,
and the people who wanted help will fall.

All of them will ·be destroyed [perish] together.
[4]The LORD says this to me:
"When a lion or a ·lion's cub [young lion],
stands over ·the dead animal it has killed [its prey] and roars.
A band of shepherds
may be assembled against it,
but the lion will not be afraid of their yelling
or upset by their noise.
So the LORD ·All-Powerful [Almighty; of Heaven's Armies; [T]of hosts]
will come down
to fight on Mount Zion and on its hill.
[5]The LORD ·All-Powerful [Almighty; of Heaven's Armies; [T]of hosts] will
·defend [protect] Jerusalem
like birds flying over their nests.
He will ·defend [protect] and save it;
he will 'pass over' and save Jerusalem."

[6]You children of Israel, come back to the God you ·fought [rebelled;
revolted] against. [7]·The time is coming when [[L]For in that day] each of you
will ·stop worshiping [throw/cast away] idols of gold and silver, which ·you
sinned by making [your sinful hands have made].

[8]"Assyria will ·be defeated [fall] by a sword, but not ·the sword of a
person [of man];
Assyria will be ·destroyed [devoured], but not by a person's sword.
Assyria will run away from the ·sword of God [[L]sword],
but its young men will be caught and made slaves.
[9]·They will panic, and [From terror] their ·protection [*or* strong ones;
rock] will be destroyed.
Their ·commanders [officers; princes] will be terrified when they see
·God's battle flag [[L]the standard/flag],"
says the LORD,
whose fire is in ·Jerusalem [[L]Zion; 1:27]
and whose furnace is in Jerusalem.

A Good Kingdom Is Coming

32 A king will rule in ·a way that brings justice [righteousness;
justice],
and ·leaders [rulers; princes] will ·make fair decisions [rule in
justice].
[2]Then each ruler will be like a shelter from the wind,
like a ·safe place [refuge] in a storm,
like streams of water in a dry land,
like a cool shadow from a large rock in a ·hot [thirsty; weary] land.

[3]Then the eyes of those who see will ·see the truth [not be closed],
and the ears of those who hear will listen.
[4]·People who are now worried [*or* Those who are reckless; [L]The heart of
the hasty] will be able to understand.
·Those who cannot speak clearly now [The stuttering/stammering
tongue] will then be able to speak clearly and quickly.
[5]Fools will not be called ·great [noble; honorable],
and people will not respect the ·wicked [scoundrel; deceiver].
[6]A fool says foolish things,
and in his ·mind [heart] he ·plans evil [*or* commits sin].

A fool ·does things that are wicked [practices ungodliness],
and he ·says wrong things [spreads error] about the LORD.
A fool does not feed the hungry
or let thirsty people drink water.
7The ·wicked person [scoundrel] uses evil ·like a tool [*or* schemes; methods].
He plans ·ways [wicked schemes] to take everything from the poor.
He destroys the poor with lies,
even when the ·poor person [needy] ·is in the right [Lspeak justice].
8But a ·good leader plans to do good [honorable/noble man plans honorable/noble things],
and those ·good [honorable; noble] things make him ·a good leader [*or* stand firm].

Hard Times Are Coming

9You women who are ·calm [complacent] now,
·stand [rise] up and listen to ·me [Lmy voice].
You ·women [Ldaughters] who feel ·safe [secure; self-confident] now,
hear what I say.
10You women feel ·safe [secure; self-confident] now,
but ·after one year [Lin a year and some days] you will ·be afraid [shudder; tremble].
There will be no grape harvest
and no summer fruit to gather.
11Women, you are ·calm [complacent] now, but you should shake with fear.
Women, you feel ·safe [secure; self-confident] now, but you should tremble.
·Take [Strip] off your nice clothes
and put ·rough cloth [burlap; sackcloth] around your waist [Ca sign of sorrow or despair].
12Beat your breasts [Ca sign of mourning or grief], ·because the fields that were pleasant are now empty [Lfor the pleasant fields].
·Cry, because the vines that once had fruit now have no more grapes [L…for the fruitful vine].
13·Cry for [L…for] the land of my people,
in which only thorns and weeds now grow [Gen. 3:18].
·Cry for [L…for] the city that once was happy
and for all the houses that once were filled with joy.
14The ·palace [*or* fortress] will be ·empty [abandoned; deserted];
the ·noisy [bustling; populous] city will be abandoned.
·Strong cities and towers [*or* The citadel and the watchtower] will be empty.
Wild donkeys will love to live there, and sheep will go there to eat.

Things Will Get Better

15This will continue until ·God pours his Spirit [Lthe Spirit is poured] from ·above [heaven; Ton high] upon us.
Then the desert will be like ·rich farmland [a fertile/fruitful field]
and the ·rich farmland [fertile/fruitful field] like a forest [29:17; 35:1, 2].
16Justice will ·be found [Ldwell] even in the desert,
and fairness will be found in the ·rich farmland [fertile/fruitful field].
17That fairness will bring peace,
and it will bring ·calm [quietness] and ·safety [trust; confidence] forever.

[18]My people will live in peaceful places
and in ·safe [secure] homes
and in ·calm [quiet] places of rest.
[19]Hail will destroy the forest,
and the city will be ·completely destroyed [brought down; laid low].
[20]But you will be happy [blessed] as you plant seeds near every stream
and as you let [Lthe feet of] your cattle and donkeys wander freely.

Warnings to Assyria and Promises to God's People

33 ·How terrible it will be for [LWoe to] you who destroy others
but have not been destroyed yet.
·How terrible it will be for [LWoe to] you, traitor,
whom no one has ·turned against yet [betrayed].
When you stop destroying,
others will destroy you.
When you stop ·turning against others [betraying],
they will ·turn against [betray] you.

[2]Lord, be ·kind [gracious; merciful] to us.
We have waited for your help.
·Give us strength [LBe our arm] every morning.
·Save us [L…our salvation] ·when we are in [Lin times of] trouble.
[3]·Your powerful voice makes [*or* At the sound of tumult] ·people [the peoples/nations] run away;
your ·greatness [majesty; *or* rising up] causes the nations to run away.
[4]Like ·locusts [*or* the caterpillar], your enemies will ·take away [gather; harvest] ·the things you stole in war [your plunder].
Like locusts ·rushing about [swarming], they will take your wealth.
[5]The Lord is ·very great [exalted], and he ·lives in a high place [Tdwells on high].
He fills ·Jerusalem [LZion; 1:27] with ·fairness [justice; judgment] and ·justice [righteousness].
[6]He will ·always be your safety [be the foundation/stability of your time].
He is ·full [a rich store/abundance] of salvation, wisdom, and knowledge.
·Respect for [The fear of] the Lord is the greatest treasure [Prov. 1:7].

[7]See, ·brave people [heroes; valiant ones] are crying out in the streets;
·those who tried to bring [envoys/ambassadors of] peace are weeping ·loudly [bitterly].
[8]·There is no one on the roads [LHighways lie desolate/deserted],
no ·one walking [travelers] in the ·paths [roads; way].
People have broken the ·agreements [treaties; covenants] they made.
They ·refuse to believe the proof from [Ldespise its] witnesses.
No one ·respects [cares about; regards] other people.
[9]The land ·is sick and dying [dries up and withers; *or* mourns and languishes];
Lebanon is ashamed and ·dying [shrivels; withers].
Sharon [Ca fertile plain along the Mediterranean coast] is like the desert,
and ·the trees of Bashan and Carmel are dying [LBashan and Carmel shake off; Ctheir leaves; these places were known for their lush trees and vegetation; 2:13; 35:2].

[10]The LORD says, "Now, I will ·stand [rise] up
and ·show my greatness [[L]be exalted].
Now, I will ·become important to the people [[L]be lifted up].
[11]You people ·do useless things [produce nothing; [L]conceive chaff/straw]
·that are like hay and straw [[L]you give birth to straw/stubble].
·A destructive wind [*or* Your breath] will ·burn [consume; devour]
you like fire.
[12]·People [*or* The nations] will be burned ·until their bones become like
lime [to ashes/lime];
they will burn quickly like ·dry [cut] thornbushes."

[13]You people in faraway lands, hear what I have done.
You people who are near me, ·learn about [*or* acknowledge] my
·power [might].
[14]The sinners in ·Jerusalem [[L]Zion; 1:27] are afraid;
those who are ·separated from God [godless] shake with fear.
They say, "·Can any of us [[L]Who can] live through this fire that
·destroys [consumes; devours]?
Who can live near this ·fire that burns on and on [unquenchable/
everlasting burning]?"
[15]A person who ·does what is right [walks righteously; Ps. 15]
and speaks ·what is right [truthfully; uprightly],
who ·refuses to take [rejects; despises] ·money unfairly [profit from
oppression/extortion],
who ·refuses to take money to hurt others [[L]shakes off his hands
from grabbing a bribe],
who ·does not listen [closes his ears] to plans of murder,
who ·refuses to think about [closes his eyes to looking on] evil—
[16]this is the kind of person who will ·be safe [[L]dwell on high/the heights].
He will ·be protected as he would be [find refuge] in a ·high, walled
city [rock stronghold/fortress].
He will always have ·bread [food],
and he will not run out of water.
[17]Your eyes will see the king in his ·beauty [splendor].
You will see the land that stretches far away.
[18]·You [[L]Your heart] will ·think about the terror of the past [[L]meditate on
terror]:
"Where is that ·officer [scribe; taxation officer; [L]counter]?
Where is the ·one who collected the taxes [[L]weigher]?
Where is the ·officer in charge of our defense towers [one who counts
the towers; [C]for taxation purposes]?"
[19]No longer will you see those ·proud [defiant; *or* fierce; *or* barbaric] people,
whose ·strange [obscure] ·language [speech; lip] you don't know
[[C]the Assyrians].
whose stammering ·speech [tongue] you cannot understand.

God Will Protect Jerusalem

[20]Look at ·Jerusalem [[L]Zion], the city of our festivals.
·Look at [[L]Your eyes will see] Jerusalem, that ·beautiful place of rest
[quiet dwelling].
It is like a tent that will never be moved;
·the pegs that hold her in place [[L]its stakes] will never be pulled up,
and her ropes will never be broken.

[21]There the LORD will be our Mighty One.
That land is a place with streams and wide rivers,
·but there will be no enemy boats on those rivers [Lno galley with oars will go];
no ·powerful [majestic] ship will sail on them.
[22]This is because the LORD is our judge.
The LORD ·makes our laws [is our lawgiver].
The LORD is our king.
He will ·save [rescue; Tdeliver] us.
[23]The ·ropes on your boats [Lropes; cords] hang loose [Cperhaps referring to the enemy ships or metaphorically to Judah].
The mast is not held firm.
The sails are not spread open.
Then ·your great wealth [an abundance of plunder] will be divided.
·There will be so much wealth that even the crippled people will carry off a share [LEven the lame will take the prey].
[24]No one living in ·Jerusalem [LZion; 1:27] will say, "I am sick."
The people who live there will have their sins forgiven.

God Will Punish His Enemies

34 All you nations, come near and listen.
Pay attention, you peoples!
The earth and ·everything in it [all it contains] should listen,
the world and all ·the people in it [its offspring].
[2]The LORD is angry with all the nations;
he is ·angry [furious] with their armies.
He will ·destroy them [devote them to destruction; Josh. 6:21] and ·kill them all [turn them over for slaughter].
[3]Their bodies will be thrown outside.
The ·stink [stench] will rise from the ·bodies [corpses],
and the blood will flow down the mountains.
[4]·The sun, moon, and stars [LAll the hosts/armies of heaven] will dissolve [Joel 2:31; Matt. 24:29; Acts 2:20; Rev. 6:13–14],
and the ·sky [heavens] will be rolled up like a scroll.
·The stars [LAll their hosts] will fall
like dead leaves from a vine
or dried-up figs from a fig tree.
[5]The LORD's sword in the ·sky [heavens] ·is covered with [has drunk its fill of] blood.
It will ·cut through [Ldescend upon] Edom
and ·destroy those people as an offering to the LORD [on the people who are devoted to destruction for judgment; v. 2; Josh. 6:21].
[6]The LORD's sword will be covered with blood;
it will be covered with fat,
with the blood from lambs and goats,
with the fat from the kidneys of ·sheep [rams].
This is because the LORD ·decided there will be [Lhas] a sacrifice in Bozrah [Cthe capital of Edom]
and ·much killing [a great slaughter] in the land of Edom.
[7]The wild oxen will ·be killed [Lfall with them],
and the ·cattle [*or* young bulls] and the strong ·bulls [Lones; Cperhaps referring to Edom's leaders].

The land will ·be filled with [drink its fill of] their blood,
and the dirt will be covered with their fat.

8The LORD has chosen a time for punishment.
He has chosen a year ·when people must pay [of retribution/recompense] for the ·wrongs they did to [*or* the cause of] ·Jerusalem [LZion; Cthe location of the Temple].
9Edom's rivers will be like ·hot tar [pitch].
Its ·dirt [dust] will be like ·burning sulfur [Tbrimstone].
Its land will be like burning ·tar [pitch].
10The fires will ·burn [Lnot be quenched] night and day;
the smoke will rise from Edom forever.
·Year after year [LFrom generation to generation] that land will be ·empty [desolate];
no one will ever ·travel [pass] through that land again.
11·Birds [Desert owls; *or* Pelicans] and ·small animals [screech owl; *or* porcupine] will own that land,
and owls and ravens will live there.
·God [LHe] will ·make it an empty wasteland [Lstretch over it a measuring line of confusion/chaos];
·it will have nothing left in it [Land the plumb line of desolation; Clike a careful craftsman, God has planned Edom's judgment].
12The ·important people [nobles] will have ·no one left to rule them [*or* nothing to call a kingdom];
the ·leaders [officials; princes] will ·all be gone [*or* be nothing].
13Thorns will ·take over [overrun] the ·strong towers [strongholds; citadels],
and wild bushes will grow in the ·walled cities [fortresses].
It will be a home for ·wild dogs [jackals]
and a place for ·owls [*or* ostriches] to live.
14Desert animals will live with the hyenas,
and wild goats will call to their friends.
Night animals will live there
and find a place of rest.
15Owls will nest there and lay eggs.
When they hatch open, the owls will gather their young under their ·wings [Lshadow].
Hawks will gather
with ·their own kind [*or* its mate].
16·Look at [LSearch] the LORD's scroll and read what is written there:
None of these will be missing;
none will be without its mate.
·God [LFor his mouth] has given the command,
so his Spirit will gather them together.
17God has ·divided the land among [*or* cast the lot for] them,
and he has ·given [measured to] them each their portion.
So they will ·own [possess] that land forever
and will live there ·year after year [from generation to generation].

God Will Comfort His People

35 The ·desert [wilderness] and dry land will ·become happy [rejoice];
the ·desert [arid plain; *or* Arabah] will be glad and will ·produce flowers [blossom; bloom].

Like a ·flower [lily; crocus], 2 it will have many blooms.
It will ·show its happiness [joyfully rejoice], as if it were ·shouting [*or* singing] with joy.
It will be ·beautiful like the forest [Lgiven the glory] of Lebanon,
·as beautiful as Mount Carmel and the Plain of Sharon [Lthe splendor of Carmel and Sharon; 33:9].
·Everyone [LThey] will see the glory of the LORD [Chis manifest presence]
and the splendor of our God.
3 Make the weak hands strong
and the weak knees steady.
4 Say to people who are ·frightened [anxious; Lhasty of heart],
"Be strong. Don't be afraid.
Look, your God will come,
·and he will punish your enemies [L...with vengeance].
·He will make them pay for the wrongs they did [...with the retribution of God],
but he will save you."

5 Then the blind ·people [Leyes] will see again,
and the ·deaf [Ldeaf ears] will hear [Matt. 11:5; Luke 7:22].
6 ·Crippled people [Then the lame] will ·jump [leap] like deer,
and ·those who can't talk now [Lthe tongue of the mute] will shout with joy.
Water will ·flow [burst forth] in the ·desert [wilderness],
and streams will flow in the ·dry land [arid plain; *or* Arabah].
7 The ·burning desert [scorched ground; parched earth] will have pools of water,
and the ·dry [parched; thirsty] ground will have springs.
Where ·wild dogs [jackals] once ·lived [lived and laid down],
grass and ·water plants [reeds and rushes/papyrus] will grow.
8 A road will be there;
this highway will be called "The ·Road to Being Holy [LWay/Highway of Holiness]."
·Evil people [The unclean; Critually] will not be allowed to walk on that road;
only good people [Cthose who walk in the Way of Holiness] will walk on it.
No fools [Cthe morally corrupt who disregard God] will go on it.
9 No lions will be there,
nor will ·dangerous animals [ravenous/violent beasts] be on that road.
They will not be found there.
That road will be for the ·people God saves [redeemed];
10 the people the LORD has ·freed [ransomed] will return there.
They will enter ·Jerusalem [LZion; Cthe location of the Temple] with ·joy [*or* singing; shouting],
and ·their happiness will last forever [Leternal joy will be upon their head; Cas a crown].
Their gladness and joy will ·fill them completely [overtake/come upon them],
and sorrow and ·sadness [sighing] will ·go far [flee] away.

The Assyrians Invade Judah

(36:1–22; 2 Kin. 18:13–37; 2 Chr. 32:1–19)

36 During Hezekiah's fourteenth year as king [C701 BC], Sennacherib king of Assyria attacked all the ·strong, walled [fortified] cities of Judah and captured them. 2The king of Assyria sent out ·his field commander [*or* chief advisor; *or* the Rabshakeh] with a large army from Lachish to King Hezekiah in Jerusalem [2 Chr. 32:9]. When the commander came near the ·waterway [aqueduct; conduit] from the upper pool on the road ·where people do their laundry [*or* to the Launderer's/TFuller's Field], he stopped. 3Eliakim son of Hilkiah [22:20], ·the palace manager [Lwho was over the house], Shebna [22:15], the ·royal secretary [scribe], and Joah son of Asaph, the ·recorder [royal historian] went out to meet him.

4The ·field commander [chief advisor; *or* Rabshakeh] said to them, "Tell Hezekiah this:

" 'The great king, the king of Assyria, says: ·What can you trust in now [On what do you base your confidence; Where does this confidence come from]? 5You say you have ·battle plans [strategy; counsel] and ·power [strength] for war, but your words ·mean nothing [are empty]. Whom are you ·trusting [relying/counting on] for help so that you ·turn [rebel] against me? 6Look, you are depending on Egypt to help you, but Egypt is like a ·splintered [broken] ·walking stick [reed]. If you lean on it for help, it will stab your hand and ·hurt [pierce] you. So it will be with the king of Egypt for all those who depend on him. 7You might say, "We are depending on the LORD our God," but ·Hezekiah destroyed [Ldid not Hezekiah destroy…?] the LORD's altars and ·the places of worship [Lhigh places; 2 Kin. 18:4; 2 Chr. 30:14; 31:1]. Hezekiah told Judah and Jerusalem, "You must worship only at this one altar [Cat the temple in Jerusalem; the Assyrian official wrongly assumes that the other altars and high places were dedicated to the Lord and that restricting worship to Jerusalem would offend him; Deut. 12]."

8" 'Now make an ·agreement [pledge; deal] with my ·master [lord], the king of Assyria: I will give you two thousand horses if you can find enough men to ride them [Ca taunt that Judah's army is too small even if Assyria were to supply it]. 9You cannot ·defeat [repel] one of my ·master's [lord's] least important officers, so why do you depend on Egypt to give you chariots and ·horsemen [charioteers]? 10·I have not [LDo you think I have…?] come to attack and destroy this country without ·an order from the LORD [Lthe LORD]. The LORD himself told me to come ·to [against] this country and destroy it [Cechoing Isaiah's prophecy that this is judgment from the Lord].' "

11Then Eliakim [22:20], Shebna [22:15], and Joah said to the ·field commander [chief advisor; *or* Rabshakeh], "Please speak to ·us [Lyour servants] in the Aramaic language [Cthe language of trade and diplomacy]. We understand it. Don't speak to us in ·Hebrew [LJudean], because the people on the city wall can hear you."

12But the commander said, "My master did not send me to tell these ·things [words] only to you and your ·king [Lmaster; lord]. He sent me to speak also to those people sitting on the wall who will have to eat their own ·dung [excrement] and drink their own urine like you [Cbecause of shortages caused by the upcoming siege]."

13Then the commander stood and shouted loudly in ·the Hebrew language [LJudean], "·Listen to what [LHear the word of] the great king, the king of Assyria, says. 14The king says you should not let Hezekiah ·fool [deceive; delude] you, because he can't ·save [rescue; Tdeliver] you. 15 Don't let Hezekiah talk you into trusting the LORD by saying, 'The LORD will surely ·save [rescue; Tdeliver] us. This city won't be handed over to the king of Assyria.'

16 "Don't listen to Hezekiah. The king of Assyria says, 'Make peace with me, and come out of the city to me. Then everyone will be free to eat the fruit from his own grapevine and fig tree and to drink water from his own ·well [cistern; Csymbols of freedom and prosperity]. 17 ·After that [L… until] I will come and take you to a land like your own—a land with grain and new wine, bread and vineyards.'

18 "Don't let Hezekiah ·fool [mislead] you, saying, 'The LORD will save us.' Has a god of any other nation saved his people from the ·power [Lhand] of the king of Assyria? 19 Where are the gods of Hamath and Arpad [Ccities conquered by Assyria; 10:9]? Where are the gods of Sepharvaim [Ccity in northern Syria conquered by Assyria]? They did not save Samaria from my ·power [Lhand]. 20 ·Not one [LWhich…?] of all the gods of these countries has ·saved [rescued; Tdelivered] his people from me. Neither can the LORD ·save [rescue; Tdeliver] Jerusalem from my ·power [Lhand]."

21 ·The people [LThey] were silent. They didn't answer the commander at all, because King Hezekiah had ordered, "Don't answer him."

22 Then Eliakim son of Hilkiah [22:20], ·the palace manager [Lwho was over the house], Shebna [22:15], the ·royal secretary [scribe], and Joah son of Asaph, the ·recorder [royal historian], went to Hezekiah. They tore their clothes [Ca sign of grief, anguish or despair] and went in and told him what the field commander had said.

Hezekiah Asks God to Help
(37:1–35; 2 Kin. 19:1–34; 2 Chr. 32:20)

37 When King Hezekiah heard the message, he tore his clothes [Ca sign of mourning or distress; 36:22] and put on ·rough cloth [burlap; sackcloth; Calso a sign of mourning]. Then he went into the ·Temple [Lhouse] of the LORD. 2 Hezekiah sent Eliakim [22:20], ·the palace manager [Lwho was over the house], and Shebna [22:15], the ·royal secretary [scribe], and the ·older [*or* senior; leading; Lelders of the] priests to Isaiah. They were all wearing ·rough cloth [burlap; sackcloth] when they came to Isaiah the prophet, the son of Amoz. 3 They told Isaiah, "This is what Hezekiah says: Today is a day of ·sorrow [distress; trouble] and ·punishment [insults; rebuke] and ·disgrace [rejection], as when a child ·should [is ready to] be born, but the mother is not strong enough to give birth to it. 4 The king of Assyria sent his ·field commander [chief advisor; *or* Rabshakeh] to ·make fun of [defy; ridicule; insult] the living God. Maybe the LORD your God will hear what the commander said and will ·punish [rebuke] him for it. So pray for the ·few of us who are left alive [remnant that is left]."

5 When Hezekiah's ·officers [officials] came to Isaiah, 6 he said to them, "Tell your ·master [lord] this: ·The LORD says [TThus says the LORD], 'Don't be afraid of what you have heard. Don't be frightened by the words the ·servants [subordinates; young men] of the king of Assyria have ·spoken [used to blaspheme] against me. 7 ·Listen [Look; TBehold]! I am going to put a spirit [Ceither an evil spirit or an inclination] in the king of Assyria. He will hear a report that will make him return to his own country, and I will cause him to ·die [Lfall] by the sword there.'"

8 The ·field commander [chief advisor; *or* Rabshakeh] heard that the

king of Assyria had left Lachish. When he went back, he found the king
fighting against the city of Libnah.
9The king received a report that Tirhakah, the ·Cushite king of Egypt
[Lking of Cush; Cruled 689–664 BC], was coming to attack him. When the
king of Assyria heard this, he sent messengers to Hezekiah, saying, 10"Tell
Hezekiah king of Judah: Don't be ·fooled [deceived; deluded] by the god
you trust. Don't believe him when he says Jerusalem will not be handed
over to the king of Assyria. 11You ·have heard [know] what the kings of
Assyria have done. They have completely defeated every country, so do ·not
[Lyou…?] think you will be ·saved [rescued; Tdelivered]. 12Did the gods of
·those people [the nations] ·save [rescue; Tdeliver] them? My ·ancestors
[predecessors; fathers] destroyed them, defeating the cities of Gozan,
Haran, and Rezeph, and the people of Eden living in Tel Assar [Ccities in
Mesopotamia]. 13Where are the kings of Hamath and Arpad [10:9; 36:19]?
Where are the kings of Sepharvaim [36:19], Hena, and Ivvah?"

Hezekiah Prays to the Lord

14When Hezekiah received the letter from the messengers and read it,
he went up to the ·Temple [Lhouse] of the LORD. He spread the letter out
before the LORD 15and prayed ·to [before] the LORD: 16"LORD ·All-Powerful
[Almighty; of Heaven's Armies; Tof hosts], you are the God of Israel,
whose throne is ·between [above] the ·gold creatures with wings
[Lcherubim; Ex. 25:18–22; Ezek. 10:1], only you are God of all the kingdoms of the earth. You made the heavens and the earth [Gen. 1]. 17·Hear
[LExtend/Incline your ear], LORD, and listen. Open your eyes, LORD, and
see. Listen to all the words Sennacherib has said to ·insult [defy; ridicule;
mock] the living God.
18"It is true, LORD, that the kings of Assyria have ·destroyed [devas-
tated; laid waste to] all these ·countries [nations] and their lands. 19They
have thrown the gods of these nations into the fire, ·but [for] they were
only wood and rock statues ·that people made [Lthe work of human
hands]. So they have destroyed them. 20Now, LORD our God, ·save [rescue;
Tdeliver] us from the king's ·power [Lhand] so that all the kingdoms of the
earth will know that you, ·LORD, are the only God [L…alone are LORD;
2 Kin. 19:19]."

The Lord Answers Hezekiah

21Then Isaiah son of Amoz sent a message to Hezekiah that said, "This
is what the LORD, the God of Israel, says: 'You prayed to me about
Sennacherib king of Assyria [Cfrom 704–681 BC]. 22So this is what the
LORD has said against Sennacherib:
The ·people of Jerusalem [Lvirgin daughter of Zion]
·hate you [despise] and ·make fun of [mock; scorn] you;
the ·people [Ldaughter] of Jerusalem
·laugh at you [Ltosses her head] ·as you run away [as you flee; *or*
behind your back].
23·You have insulted me and spoken against me [LWhom have you
defied/ridiculed/mocked?];
·you have raised your voice against me [Lagainst whom have you
raised your voice?].
·You have a proud look on your face [L…and arrogantly lifted your
eyes/gaze…?],
which is against me, the Holy One of Israel [1:4]!
24You have sent your messengers to ·insult [defy; ridicule; mock] the Lord.
You have said, "With my many chariots

I have gone to the tops of the mountains,
to the ·highest [*or* remotest] mountains of Lebanon.
I have cut down its tallest cedars
and its best ·pine [cypress] trees.
I have gone to its greatest heights
and its ·best [densest] forests.
25 I have dug wells in foreign ·countries [lands]
and drunk water there.
By the soles of my feet,
I have ·dried [stopped] up all the rivers of Egypt."

26 "'King of Assyria, ·surely you have [Lhave you not…?] heard.
Long ago I, the LORD, ·planned [determined; ordained] these things.
·Long ago [In ancient times/days of old] I ·designed them [planned it],
and now I have ·made them happen [brought them to pass].
I allowed you to turn those ·strong, walled [fortified] cities
into piles of ·rocks [rubble; ruins].
27 The people in those cities were ·weak [powerless; drained of strength];
they were ·frightened [dismayed] and ·put to shame [confused; confounded].
They were like grass in the field,
like tender, young ·grass [shoots],
like grass on the housetop
that is ·burned [scorched] by the wind before it can grow.

28 "'I know ·when you rest [when you stand or sit; *or* where you are],
when you come and go,
and how you ·rage [rave] against me.
29 Because you ·rage [rave] against me,
and because I have heard your ·proud [arrogant] words,
I will put my hook in your nose
and my bit in your mouth.
Then I will ·force you to leave my country [turn you back; make you retreat]
the ·same way [road] you came.'

30 "Then the LORD said, 'Hezekiah, I will give you this sign:
This year you will eat the grain that grows ·wild [Lof itself],
and the second year you will eat what ·grows [springs] from that.
But in the third year, ·plant grain [sow] and ·harvest it [reap].
Plant vineyards and eat their fruit.
31 ·Some of the people in [A remnant of] the ·family [Lhouse] of Judah
will ·escape [survive].
·Like plants that take root [They will put down roots below],
·they will grow strong and have many children [and will bear fruit above].
32 A ·few people will come out of Jerusalem alive [remnant will spread out from Jerusalem];
·a few from Mount Zion will live […and survivors out from Mount Zion].
The ·strong love [zeal] of the LORD ·All-Powerful [Almighty; of Heaven's Armies; Tof hosts]
will ·make this happen [accomplish this].'

[33]"So this is what the LORD says about the king of Assyria:
'He will not enter this city
or even shoot an arrow here.
He will not fight against it with shields
or build a ramp to ·attack the city walls [lay siege to it].
[34]He will ·return to his country [retreat] the same ·way [road] he came,
and he will not enter this city,'
says the LORD.
[35]'I will defend and ·save [rescue; [T]deliver] this city
for my sake and for David, my servant.'"

The Angel of Death
(37:36–38; 2 Kin. 19:35–37; 2 Chr. 32:21–23)

[36]Then the ·angel [messenger] of the LORD went out and killed one
hundred eighty-five thousand men in the Assyrian camp. When the people got up early the next morning, they saw all the dead bodies. [37]So
Sennacherib king of Assyria left and went back to Nineveh and stayed
there.
[38]One day as Sennacherib was worshiping in the ·temple [[L]house] of
his god Nisroch, his sons Adrammelech and Sharezer killed him with a
sword. Then they escaped to the land of Ararat. So Sennacherib's son
Esarhaddon became king of Assyria.

Hezekiah's Illness
(38:1–22; 2 Kin. 20:1–11; 2 Chr. 32:24–26)

38 At that time Hezekiah became so sick he ·almost died [was
about to die]. The prophet Isaiah son of Amoz went to see
him and told him, "·This is what the LORD says [[T]Thus says the LORD]:
·Make arrangements [[L]Set your house in order], because you are going to
die. You will not recover."
[2]Hezekiah turned toward the wall and prayed to the LORD, [3]"LORD,
please remember that I have always ·obeyed [[L]walked before] you. I have
·given myself completely to you [served you wholeheartedly] and have
done ·what you said was right [[L]right in the eyes/sight of the LORD]." Then
Hezekiah ·cried loudly [wept bitterly].
[4]Then the LORD spoke his word to Isaiah: [5]"Go to Hezekiah and tell
him: 'This is what the LORD, the God of your ·ancestor [father] David,
says: I have heard your prayer and seen your tears. So I will add fifteen
years to your life. [6]I will ·save [rescue] you and this city from [[L]the hand
of] the king of Assyria; I will defend this city.
[7]" 'The LORD will do what he ·says [promises]. This is the sign from the
LORD to show you: [8]The sun has made a shadow go down the stairway of
Ahaz, but I will make it go back ten steps.'" So the shadow made by the
sun went back up the ten steps it had gone down.
[9]After Hezekiah king of Judah got well, he wrote this ·song [*or* poem;
[L]writing]:
[10]I said, "I am in the ·middle [prime] of my life.
Do I have to go through the gates of ·death [*or* the grave; [L]Sheol]?
Will I have the rest of my life ·taken away [deprived; robbed] from me?"
[11]I said, "I will not see ·the LORD [the LORD, the LORD; [L]Yah, Yah; 26:4]
in the land of the living again.
I will not again see ·the people [a human being]
who live on the earth.
[12]Like a shepherd's tent,
my home has been pulled down and taken from me.
I am like the cloth a weaver rolls up and cuts from the loom.
·In one day [[L]From day to night] you brought me to this end.

13·All night I cried loudly [*or* I waited patiently till morning].
Like a lion, he ·crushed [breaks] all my bones.
·In one day [[L]From day to night] you brought me to this end.
14I ·cried [twitter; chatter] like a ·bird [[L]swallow or a crane]
and moaned like a dove.
My eyes ·became tired as I looked [grew weary from looking] to the
·heavens [heights].
Lord, I ·have troubles [am oppressed]. ·Please help me [Be my security]."

15What can I say?
·The Lord told me what would happen and then made it happen
[[L]He spoke to me and he did it].
I will ·be humble [wander about; shuffle along; walk slowly] all my ·life
[years]
because of ·these troubles in [the bitterness of] my soul.
16Lord, because of ·you [[L]these things], people live.
Because of ·you [[L]them], my spirit also lives;
you ·made me well [restored me] and let me live.
17It was for my own ·good [welfare; peace; [C]Hebrew *shalom*]
that I had such ·troubles [anguish; bitterness].
Because you love me very much,
you ·did not let me die [delivered my soul from the pit of
destruction/corruption]
but threw my sins
·far away [[L]behind your back].
18·People in the place of the dead [*or* For the grave; [L]For Sheol] cannot
·praise [thank] you;
·those who have died [[L]death] cannot ·sing praises [praise] to you;
those who ·die [[L]go down to the pit] ·don't trust you
to help them [[L]cannot hope for your faithfulness].
19·The people who are alive [[L]The living, the living] are the ones who
·praise [thank] you.
They praise you as I praise you today.
A father should tell his children
·that you provide help [[L]about your faithfulness].
20The LORD ·saved me [*or* will save; *or* is ready to save],
so we will play songs on stringed instruments
in the ·Temple [[L]house] of the LORD
all the days of our lives.

21Then Isaiah said, "·Make a paste from [*or* Take a cake of] figs and put
it on Hezekiah's boil. Then he will get well." 22Hezekiah ·then [*or* had]
asked Isaiah, "What will be the sign? What will show that I will go up to
the ·Temple [[L]house] of the LORD?"

Messengers from Babylon
(39:1–8; 2 Kin. 20:12–21; 2 Chr. 32:31–33)

39 At that time Merodach-Baladan son of Baladan was king of
Babylon [[C]ruled 722–710 and 703–702 BC]. He sent ·letters
[greetings] and a gift to Hezekiah, because he had heard that Hezekiah
had been sick and was now well. 2Hezekiah was pleased and showed the
messengers what was in his storehouses: the silver, gold, spices, ·expen-
sive perfumes [precious oils], his ·swords and shields [armory], and all
his ·wealth [treasures]. He showed them everything in his ·palace
[[L]house] and in his kingdom.

[3]Then Isaiah the prophet went to King Hezekiah and asked him, "What
did these men say? Where did they come from?"
Hezekiah said, "They came from a faraway country—from Babylon."
[4]So Isaiah asked him, "What did they see in your ·palace [[L]house]?"
Hezekiah said, "They saw everything in my ·palace [[L]house]. I showed
them all my ·wealth [[L]treasuries; store houses]."
[5]Then Isaiah said to Hezekiah: "Listen to the words of the LORD ·All-
Powerful [Almighty; of Heaven's Armies; [T]of hosts]: [6]'·In the future to you
[The time/day is coming when] everything in your palace and everything
your ·ancestors [fathers] have stored up until this day will be ·taken away
[carried off] to Babylon. Nothing will be left,' says the LORD. [7]Some of
your own ·children [sons], those ·who will be born to you [you will
father], will be taken away, and they will become ·servants [eunuchs] in
the palace of the king of Babylon."
[8]Hezekiah told Isaiah, "These words from the LORD are good." He said
this because he thought, "There will be peace and security in my lifetime."

Israel's Punishment Will End

40 Your God says,
"Comfort, comfort my people.
[2]Speak kindly to ·the people of Jerusalem [[L]Jerusalem]
and tell them
that their time of ·service [*or* warfare] is finished,
that ·they have paid for their sins [*or* her sins are pardoned],
that ·the LORD has punished Jerusalem [[L]she has received from the LORD]
·twice [double] for every sin they did."
[3]This is the voice of one who calls out:
"Prepare in the ·desert [wilderness]
the way for the LORD.
Make a straight road in the ·dry lands [arid plain]
for our God.
[4]Every valley will be ·raised up [elevated],
and every mountain and hill will be made ·flat [level; low].
The rough ground will be ·made level [smoothed out],
and the rugged ground will be made ·smooth [into a plain].
[5]Then the glory of the LORD [[C]his manifest presence] will be ·shown
[revealed],
and all ·people [flesh] together will see it.
·The LORD himself said these things [[L]For the mouth of the LORD has
spoken]."

[6]A voice says, "Cry out!"
Then I[n] said, "What shall I cry out?"

"Say all ·people [flesh] are like the grass,
and all their glory[n] is like the flowers of the field.
[7]The grass ·dies [withers] and the flowers fall
when the breath of the LORD blows on them.
Surely the people are like grass.
[8]The grass ·dies [withers] and the flowers fall,
but the word of our God will ·live [endure; stand] forever."

40:6 I The Dead Sea Scrolls and come Greek copies read "I." Some Hebrew copies read "he," meaning a second voice responds to the first. **glory** Some Greek copies read "glory." Hebrew copies read "loyalty."

9·Jerusalem [LZion], ·you have good news to tell [herald of good news].
Go up on a high mountain.
Jerusalem, ·you have good news to tell [herald of good news].
Shout out loud the good news.
Shout it out and don't be afraid.
Say to the towns of Judah,
"Here is your God."
10Look, the Lord God is coming with power
·to rule all the people [Lhis arm rules for him].
Look, ·he will bring reward for his people [Lhis reward is with him];
·he will have their payment with him [Lhis payment/prize is before him].
11He ·takes care of his people [Ltends his flock] like a shepherd.
He gathers them like lambs in his arms
and carries them ·close to him [on his chest/bosom].
He gently leads the mothers of the lambs.

God Is Supreme

12Who has measured the ·oceans [Lwaters] in the ·palm [hollow] of his hand?
Who has used ·his hand [La span; Cthe distance between the extended thumb and little finger] to measure the ·sky [heavens]?
Who has used a bowl to measure all the dust of the earth
and ·scales to weigh the mountains and [La balance (to weigh) the] hills?
13Who has ·known [comprehended; *or* directed; *or* measured] the ·mind [*or* Spirit] of the Lord
or been able to ·give him advice [instruct him as counselor; Job 38:2; Rom. 11:34]?
14Whom did he ·ask for help [take counsel from]?
Who taught him the ·right way [path/way of justice/judgment]?
Who taught him knowledge
and showed him the way to understanding?

15[LLook; TBehold] The nations are like one small drop in a bucket;
they are ·no more than [regarded as] the dust on his measuring scales.
·To him the islands are no more than fine dust on his scales [LHe weighs/*or* lifts the coastlands/islands like fine dust].
16·All the trees in Lebanon are not enough [LLebanon is not sufficient] for the altar fires,
and all the animals in Lebanon are not enough for burnt offerings.
17·Compared to the Lord [LBefore him] all the nations are worth nothing;
to him they are ·less than nothing [Lnothing and void/empty].

18To whom can you compare God?
To what image can you compare him?
19An idol is ·formed [cast] by a craftsman,
and a goldsmith ·covers [overlays] it with gold
and ·makes [forms; refines] silver chains for it.
20A poor person cannot ·buy those expensive statues [make such an offering],
so he finds a tree that will not rot.

Then he finds a skilled craftsman
to make it into an idol that will not fall over.

21·Surely you [LDo you not…?] know. ·Surely you have [LHave you not…?] heard.
·Surely [LHas not…?] from the beginning someone told you.
·Surely you [LDo you not…?] understand ·how the earth was created [*or* from the foundations of the earth].
22·God sits on his throne [LHe sits] above the ·circle [horizon] of the earth,
and ·compared to him, [Lits] people are like grasshoppers.
He stretches out the ·skies [heavens] like a ·piece of cloth [canopy; curtain]
and spreads them out like a tent to ·sit under [*or* live in].
23He makes rulers ·unimportant [nothing]
and the judges of this world ·worth nothing [insignificant; useless].
24·They are like plants that are placed in the ground [LIndeed, they are barely planted],
·like seeds that are planted [Lindeed, they are barely sown].
·As soon as they begin to grow strong [LIndeed, they barely take root],
he blows on them and they ·die [wither],
and the ·wind [storm; whirlwind] blows them away like ·chaff [straw].

25The Holy One [1:4], says, "To whom can you compare me?
Is anyone equal to me?"
26Look up to the ·skies [heavens].
Who created ·all these stars [Lthese]?
He leads out the ·army [hosts] of heaven one by one
and calls ·all the stars [Lthem all] by name.
Because ·he is strong and powerful [Lof his great strength and mighty power],
not one of them is missing.

27·People of Jacob [LJacob], why do you complain?
·People of Israel [LIsrael], why do you say,
"The Lord does not see ·what happens to me [Lmy way/path];
he ·does not care if I am treated fairly [disregards my cause]"?
28·Surely you [LDo you not…?] know.
·Surely you have [LHave you not…?] heard.
The Lord is the ·God who lives forever [everlasting God],
who created ·all [Lthe ends of] the ·world [earth].
He does not become tired or ·need to rest [weary].
No one can ·understand [fathom; comprehend] how great his ·wisdom [knowledge] is.
29He gives strength to those who are tired
and more power to those who are weak.
30Even ·children [youths; young people] become tired and ·need to rest [weary],
and young ·people [men] ·trip and fall [fall in exhaustion].
31But the people who ·trust [hope in; wait on] the Lord will become strong again.
They will rise up ·as an eagle in the sky [Lwith wings like eagles];

they will run and not ·need rest [grow weary];
they will walk and not ·become tired [Tfaint].

The Lord Will Help Israel

41 The LORD says, "·Faraway countries [*or* Coastlands; *or* Islands], listen to me.
Let the nations ·become strong [renew their strength].
·Come to me [Approach] and speak;
·we will [*or* let us] meet together ·to decide who is right [for judgment/*or* debate].

2"Who ·caused the one to come [stirs up one] from the east [Cthe Persian king Cyrus the Great; 44:28—45:6; 46:11; 48:14–16]?
Who ·gives him victories everywhere he goes [*or* calls him in righteousness to his service/Lfoot]?
He [Cthe Lord] gives nations over to him
and ·defeats [subdues] kings.
He uses his sword, and kings become like dust.
He uses his bow, and they are blown away like ·chaff [straw].
3He chases them and ·is never hurt [Lpasses by in peace],
·going places he has never been before [Lby a path his feet have not gone].
4Who caused this to happen?
·Who has controlled history [L...calling generations] since the beginning?
I, the LORD, am the one. ·I was here at the beginning,
and I will be here when all things are finished [*or*...the First and the Last; *or*...with them at the first and the last; Lfirst and with them at the last]."

5All you ·faraway places [*or* islands; *or* coastlands], look and be afraid;
all you ·places far away on [ends of] the earth, shake with fear.
Come close and ·listen to [approach] me.
6 ·The workers help each other [A man helps his companion/neighbor]
and say to ·each other [his brother], "Be strong!"
7The ·craftsman [engraver; metal worker] encourages the goldsmith,
and the workman who smooths the metal with a hammer
encourages the one who ·shapes the metal [strikes the anvil].
He says, "This ·metal work [welding; soldering] is ·good [sound; well crafted]."
He nails the statue to a base so it can't fall over [Cthe nations find false hope and baseless courage in their idols; vv. 28–29].

Only the Lord Can Save Us

8·The LORD says, "People of Israel, you are my servants [L"You Israel, my servant].
·People of Jacob, I chose you [LJacob, whom I have chosen; 44:1].
You are ·from the family [descendants; offspring; seed] of my friend Abraham [Gen. 12:1–3].
9I took you from ·places far away on [Lthe ends of] the earth
and called you from ·a faraway country [its farthest parts].
I said, 'You are my ·servants [Lservant].'
I have chosen you and have not ·turned against [rejected; thrown away] you.
10So don't ·worry [fear], because I am with you.
Don't be ·afraid [dismayed], because I am your God.

I will ·make you strong [strengthen you] **and will help you;**
I will ·support [uphold] **you with my ·right hand that saves you** [*or* righteous right hand; [C]a symbol of power to save and protect; Ex. 15:6; Ps. 63:8].

11"[[L]Look; [T]Behold] **All those people who ·are angry with** [seethe/rage against] **you**
will be ashamed and disgraced.
Those who ·are [strive] **against you**
will ·disappear [become nothing] **and ·be lost** [perish].
12**You will look for your enemies,**
but you will not find them.
Those who ·fought [wage war] **against you**
will ·vanish completely [be as nothing].
13[[L]For; Because] **I am the LORD your God,**
who holds your right hand,
and I tell you, 'Don't be afraid.
I will help you.'
14**Do not be afraid ·even though you are weak as a worm** [[L]you worm, Jacob],
you ·few people of Israel who are left [*or* people of Israel; *or* maggot, Israel].
I myself will help you," says the LORD.
"**·The one who saves you** [Your redeemer/protector] **is the Holy One of Israel** [1:4].
15**Look, I ·have made** [*or* will make] **you like a new threshing ·board** [sledge]
with many sharp teeth.
So you will ·walk on [thresh the] **mountains and crush them;**
you will make the hills like ·chaff [straw].
16**You will ·throw them into the air** [winnow them], **and the wind will carry them away;**
a ·windstorm [gale; tempest] **will scatter them.**
Then you will ·be happy [rejoice] **in the LORD;**
you will ·be proud of [boast in] **the Holy One of Israel** [1:4].

17"**The poor and needy people look for water,**
but ·they can't find any [there is none].
Their tongues are ·dry [parched] **with thirst.**
But I, the LORD, will answer ·their prayers [[L]them];
I, the God of Israel, will not ·leave them to die [[L]abandon/forsake them].
18**I will ·make rivers flow** [[L]open rivers] **on the ·dry hills** [barren heights]
and springs flow through the valleys.
I will change the ·desert [wilderness] **into ·a lake** [pools] **of water**
and the ·dry [arid; parched] **land into ·fountains** [springs] **of water.**
19**I will ·make trees grow** [plant; put] **in the ·desert** [wilderness]—
cedars, acacia, myrtle, and olive trees.
I will put pine, fir, and cypress trees
growing together in the desert.
20[[L]...so that] **People will see these things and ·understand** [know];
they will ·think carefully about these things [consider] **and ·learn** [comprehend]

that the LORD's ·power [Lhand] did this,
that the Holy One of Israel [1:4] ·made these things [created it]."

The Lord Challenges False Gods

21The LORD says, "Present your case."
The King of Jacob says, "·Tell me [Produce; Bring forth] your
·arguments [evidence; Lstrong words].
22·Bring in your idols [LLet them come forward] to tell us
what is going to happen.
Have them tell us ·what happened in the beginning [the former
things].
Then we will ·think about [consider] these things,
and we will know ·how they will turn out [their outcome; how they
were fulfilled].
Or tell us ·what will happen in the future [things to come].
23 Tell us what is coming next
so we will ·believe [know] that you are gods.
Do something, whether it is good or bad,
and make us ·afraid [*or* dismayed and afraid].
24[LLook; TBehold] ·You gods [LYou] are less than nothing;
you can't do anything.
Those who ·worship [Lchoose] you ·should be hated [are detestable/
an abomination].

25"I have ·brought [stirred up] someone to come out of the north
[CCyrus, king of Persia; 41:2; 44:28—45:6; 46:11; 48:14–16].
·I have called him by name from the east [*or*...one from the east/
rising sun who calls on my name].
He ·walks on kings [tramples on rulers] as if they were ·mud [mortar],
just as a potter ·walks [treads] on the clay.
26Who ·told us about [declared; decreed] this ·before it happened [Lfrom
the beginning]?
Who told us ahead of time so we could say, 'He was right'?
·None of you [LIndeed no one] told us anything;
·none of you [Lindeed no one] told us before it happened;
·no one [Lindeed no one] heard you tell about it.
27I, the LORD, was the first one to tell ·Jerusalem [LZion] ·that the people
were coming home [*or* "Look, help is coming!"; L"Look, here
they are!"].
I sent a messenger to Jerusalem with the good news.
28I ·look at the idols [Llook], but there is ·not one that can answer [Lno
one/man].
None of them can give ·advice [counsel];
none of them can answer my questions.
29Look, all these idols are ·false [a deception/delusion; *or* foolish;
worthless].
They cannot do anything;
their images are ·worth nothing [wind and confusion/chaos; *or*
empty wind].

The Lord's Special Servant

42 "Here is my servant [41:8; 43:10; 52:13; 53:11], the one I ·support
[strengthen; uphold; Cthe first of four "servant songs" in Isaiah,
concerning Israel, and applied to the mission and suffering of the
Messiah; 42:1–7; 49:1–13; 50:4–11; 52:13—53:12].

He is ·the one I chose [my chosen], and ·I am pleased with [my soul delights in] him [Matt. 3:17; 17:5; Luke 9:35].
I have put my Spirit upon him [11:1–9],
and he will bring justice to the nations [Matt. 12:18–20].
2He will not cry out or yell
or speak loudly in the streets.
3He will not break a ·crushed blade of grass [bruised reed]
or ·put out [extinguish] even a ·weak flame [dim/smoldering wick; [C]symbols of care for the weak and oppressed].
He will ·truly [faithfully] bring justice;
4 he will not ·lose hope [falter; *or* grow dim] or ·give up [be discouraged; *or* be bruised/crushed]
until he brings justice to the world.
And ·people far away [*or* the islands; *or* the coastlands] will ·trust [wait/put hope in] his ·teachings [instruction; law; [L]Torah]."

5God, the LORD, said these things.
He created the ·skies [heavens] and stretched them out.
He spread out the earth and ·everything on it [[L]its offspring].
He gives breath to all people on earth,
and life to everyone who walks on the earth.
6The LORD says, "I, the LORD, called you ·to do right [*or* to demonstrate my righteousness/justice; *or* by my righteous decree; [L]in righteousness],
and I will hold your hand
and ·protect [keep; guard] you.
·You will be the sign of my agreement with [[L]I will give/establish you as a covenant/treaty for] the people,
a light to shine for ·all people [the nations/Gentiles; 49:6; Luke 2:32; Acts 13:47].
7You will ·help the blind to see [[L]open blind eyes].
You will free those who are in prison,
and you will lead those who live in darkness out of their prison [35:5; 49:9; 61:1; Luke 4:18].

8"I am the LORD. That is my name.
I will not ·give [share; yield] my glory to another;
I will not let idols take ·the praise that should be mine [[L]my praise].
9[[L]Look; [T]Behold] The ·things I said would happen [[L]former things] have happened,
and now I ·tell you about [declare/announce] new things.
Before those things ·happen [spring forth; sprout],
I tell you about them."

A Song of Praise to the Lord

10Sing a ·new song [[C]celebrating victory; Ps. 33:3; 40:3; 96:1; 98:1; 144:9; 149:1; Rev. 5:9; 14:3] to the LORD;
sing his praise ·everywhere on [[L]from the end of] the earth.
Praise him, you people who ·sail on [go down to] the seas and ·you animals who live in them [[L]its fullness].
Praise him, you people living in ·faraway places [*or* islands; *or* coastlands].
11The ·deserts [wilderness] and their ·cities [towns] should ·praise him [shout; raise their voices].

The settlements of Kedar [Cdesert nomads, descended from Ishmael; Gen. 25:13] should praise him.
The people living in Sela [Can Edomite city; 16:1] should sing for joy;
they should shout from the mountaintops.
12They should give glory to the LORD.
People in ·faraway lands [*or* the islands; *or* the coastlands] should praise him.
13The LORD will march out like a ·strong soldier [mighty man/hero];
he will ·be excited [arouse/stir up zeal] like a man ready to fight a war.
He ·will shout out the battle cry [Lshouts, indeed he cries out]
and ·defeat [prevails/triumphs over] his enemies.

14The LORD says, "For a long time I have ·said nothing [kept silent/still];
I have been ·quiet [still] and held myself back.
But now I will cry out
and ·strain [pant and gasp] like a woman giving birth to a child.
15I will ·destroy [level; lay waste] the hills and mountains
and dry up all their plants.
I will make the rivers become ·dry land [Lislands; *or* coastlands]
and dry up the pools of water.
16Then I will lead the blind along a way they never knew;
I will guide them along paths they have not known.
I will make the darkness become light for them,
and the rough ground smooth.
These are the things I will do;
I will not ·leave [abandon; forsake] my people.
17But those who trust in idols,
who say to their ·statues [idols; carved images],
'You are our gods'
will be ·rejected [turned away/back] in ·disgrace [shame; humiliations].

Israel Refused to Listen to the Lord

18"You who are deaf, hear me.
You who are blind, look and see.
19·No one [LWho…?] is more blind than my servant Israel
or more deaf than the messenger I send.
·No one [LWho…?] is more blind than ·the person I own [*or* my covenant people]
or more blind than the servant of the LORD.
20Israel, you have seen much, but you have not ·obeyed [kept/guarded them].
·You hear [Your ears are open], but you refuse to listen."
21The LORD ·made his teachings wonderful [Lmagnified and made glorious his instruction/law/Torah],
because ·he is good [*or* of his righteousness].
22These people have been ·defeated and robbed [plundered and looted].
They are trapped in pits
or ·locked up [hidden] in prison.
·Like robbers, enemies have taken them away [LThey have become plunder],
and there is no one to ·save [rescue] them.

·Enemies carried them off [LThey have become loot],
and no one said, "Bring them back."

23Will any of you listen to this?
Will you ·listen carefully [pay attention] in the future?
24Who ·let [gave up; handed over] ·the people of Jacob [LJacob] ·be carried off [to the looter; for plunder]?
Who let ·robbers [plunderers] take Israel away?
·The LORD [LWas it not the LORD who…?] allowed this to happen,
because we sinned against him.
We did not ·live the way he wanted us to live [Lwalk in his ways]
and did not obey his ·teaching [law; instruction; LTorah].
25So he ·became very angry with us [Lpoured out on him his burning anger; Con Jacob/Israel]
and brought ·terrible wars [the violence/Lpower of war] against ·us [Lhim].
It ·was as if the people of Israel had fire all around them [Lenveloped him in flame],
but they didn't ·know what was happening [understand].
It ·was as if they were burning [Lburned him up],
but they didn't ·pay any attention [lay/take it to heart].

God Is Always with His People

43 Now this is what the LORD says.
He created you, ·people of Jacob [LJacob];
he formed you, ·people of Israel [LIsrael].
He says, "Don't be afraid, because I have ·saved [ransomed; redeemed] you.
I have called you by name, and you are mine.
2When you pass through the waters, I will be with you [Cas at the Red/ *or* Reed Sea; Ex. 13–14].
When you cross rivers, ·you will not drown [Lthey will not overflow you; Cas when Israel crossed the Jordan River into the Promised Land; Josh. 3–4].
When you walk through fire, you will not be burned [Dan. 3:25–27],
nor will the flames hurt you.
3This is because I, the LORD, am your God,
the Holy One of Israel [1:4], your Savior.
I gave Egypt ·to pay for you [for your ransom],
and I gave ·Cush [Ethiopia] and Seba ·to make you mine [in place of you].
4Because you are precious ·to me [Lin my eyes],
because I give you honor and love you,
I will give other people in your place;
I will give other nations ·to save [in exchange for] your life.
5Don't be afraid, because I am with you.
I will bring your ·children [descendants; offspring; seed] from the east
and gather you from the west.
6I will tell the north: Give my people to me.
I will tell the south: Don't ·keep my people in prison [*or* hold them back; restrain them].
Bring my sons from far away
and my daughters from ·faraway places [Lthe end of the earth].

[7]Bring to me all the people who are ·mine [[L]called by my name],
whom I ·made [created] for my glory,
whom I formed and made."

Judah Is God's Witness

[8]Bring out the people who have eyes but ·don't see [are blind]
and those who have ears but ·don't hear [are deaf; 42:19].
[9]All the nations gather together,
and all the people ·come together [assemble].
·Which of their gods [[L]Who among them] said this would happen?
·Which of their gods can tell what happened in the beginning [[L]…
and caused us to hear former things]?
Let them bring their witnesses to prove they were right.
Then others will say, "It is true."
[10]The LORD says, "You are my witnesses
and the servant I chose [42:1].
I chose you so you would know and believe me,
so you would understand that I am ·the true God [[L]he].
There was no God ·created [formed] before me,
and there will be ·no God [none] after me.
[11]I myself am the LORD;
I am the only Savior.
[12]I myself have ·spoken [made known] to you, saved you, and ·told
[proclaimed to] you these things.
It was not some foreign god among you.
You are my witnesses, and I am God,"
says the LORD.
[13] "·I have always been God [[L]Indeed from the day, I am he; [C]"day" may
mean the first day of creation or from this day forward].
No one can save people from my ·power [[L]hand];
when I do something, no one can ·change [undo; reverse] it."

[14]This is what the LORD, ·who saves you [your protector/redeemer;
41:14],
the Holy One of Israel [1:4], says:
"I will ·send armies [[L]send] to Babylon for you,
and I will ·knock down all its locked gates [*or* bring them down as
fugitives].
The ·Babylonians [[L]Chaldeans] will ·shout their cries of sorrow [*or* flee
in the ships they take such pride in].
[15]I am the LORD, your Holy One [1:4],
the Creator of Israel, your King."

God Will Save His People Again

[16]This is what the LORD says.
He is the one who made a road through the sea [v. 2]
and a path through ·rough [strong; mighty] waters.
[17]He is the one who ·defeated [[L]led out] the chariots and horses
and the mighty armies [Ex. 14:4–9].
They ·fell together [lay down] and will never rise again.
They were ·destroyed [extinguished] as a ·flame [[L]wick] is put out.
[18]The LORD says, "Forget what happened before,
and do not ·think about [consider; dwell on] the past.
[19]Look at the new thing I am going to do.
It is already ·happening [[L]sprouting/springing up]. Don't you see it?

I will make a ·road [path; way] in the ·desert [wilderness; [C]the return
from Babylon is portrayed as a new Exodus]
and ·rivers[n] [streams] in the ·dry land [desert; wasteland].
20 Even the wild animals will ·be thankful to [honor] me—
the ·wild dogs [jackals] and ·owls [*or* ostriches].
They will honor me when I put water in the ·desert [wilderness]
and ·rivers [streams] in the ·dry land [desert; wasteland]
to give ·water [drink] to my people, ·the ones I chose [my chosen; 42:1].
21 The people I ·made [[L]formed for myself]
will ·sing songs to praise me [[L]declare/proclaim my praise].

22 "People of Jacob, you have not ·called to me [called upon me; asked for
my help];
people of Israel, you have ·become tired of [*or* not wearied yourself
for] me.
23 You have not brought me your ·sacrifices [burnt offerings; Lev. 1:1–17]
of sheep
nor honored me with your sacrifices.
I did not ·weigh you down [burden you] with ·sacrifices to offer [grain/
or gift; tribute offering; Lev. 2:1]
or make you tired with incense to burn.
24 So you did not buy ·incense [fragrant calamus; aromatic cane]
for me;
you did not ·freely bring me [saturate/lavish me with] fat from your
sacrifices.
Instead you have ·weighed me down [burdened me] with your many sins;
you have made me tired of your ·many wrongs [iniquities].

25 "I, I am the One who ·erases [blots out] all your ·sins [transgressions],
for my sake;
I will not remember your sins.
26 But you should ·remind [*or* review with] me.
Let's ·meet and decide what is right [argue/contend together].
Tell what you have done and show ·you are right [your innocence].
27 Your first father sinned [[C]probably Jacob (58:14; 63:16), though
possibly Abraham (51:2)],
and your ·leaders [mediators; spokesmen] have ·turned
[transgressed] against me.
28 So I will make your ·holy rulers [*or* princes of the sanctuary; [C]either
rulers or priests] ·unholy [defiled; disgraced].
I will ·bring destruction on [devote to destruction; Josh. 2:10] ·the
people of Jacob [[L]Jacob],
and I will let Israel be ·insulted [reviled; scorned]."

The Lord Is the Only God

44 The LORD says, "·People of Jacob, you are my servants [[L]Jacob, my
servant]. Listen to me!
·People of Israel, I chose you [[L]Israel, my chosen; 41:8]."
2 This is what the LORD says, who made you,
who formed you in ·your mother's body [[L]the womb],
who will help you:

43:19 rivers A Dead Sea Scroll copy has "paths."

"·People of Jacob, my servants [LJacob, my servant], don't be afraid.
·Israel [LJeshurun; Cthe location of the Temple; Deut. 32:15; 33:5, 26],
I chose you.
3I will pour out water for the thirsty land
and make streams flow on dry land.
I will pour out my Spirit ·into your children [on your descendants/
offspring/seed]
and my blessing on your ·descendants [offspring].
4·Your children [LThey] will ·grow [sprout up] like a tree in the grass,
like ·poplar trees [*or* willows] growing beside streams of water.
5One person will say, 'I belong to the LORD,'
and another will use the name Jacob.
Another will ·sign his name [*or* write on his hand] 'I am the LORD's,'
and another will ·use [call himself by] the name Israel."

6The LORD, the king of Israel,
is the LORD ·All-Powerful [Almighty; of Heaven's Armies; Tof hosts],
who saves Israel.
This is what he says: "I am the ·beginning and the end [Lfirst and the
last].
·I am the only God [There is no god but me].
7Who is like me?
Let him ·come and prove [proclaim; claim] it.
Let him tell and explain all that has happened since I ·set up
[established] my ancient people.
He should also tell what will happen in the future.
8Don't be afraid! Don't ·worry [fear]!
·I have always told you what will happen [Have I not proclaimed it
long ago?].
You are my witnesses.
·There is no other [LIs there another…?] God but me.
I know of no other Rock; I am the only One."

Idols Are Useless

9Some people make idols, but they are ·worth nothing [nothing;
void].
People treasure them, but they are ·useless [worthless].
Those people are witnesses for the statues, but those people cannot
see.
They know nothing, so they will be ·ashamed [put to shame;
Cidolmakers are as ignorant as their idols].
10Who makes a god or ·shapes [casts; molds] an idol
that can do nothing for him?
11[LLook; TBehold] ·The workmen who made them [LAll his
compansions] will be ·ashamed [put to shame],
because ·they [Lthe craftsmen] are only human.
If they all would come together to stand against me,
they would all be ·afraid [terrified] and ·ashamed [put to shame].

12One ·workman [blacksmith] uses tools to heat iron,
and he works over hot coals.
With his hammer he beats the metal and makes a statue,
using his powerful arms.

But when he becomes hungry, he loses his ·power [strength].
If he does not drink water, he becomes tired.

[13]**·Another workman** [A carpenter/craftsman] **·uses a line and a compass** [[L]stretches a line]
to draw on the wood.
Then he uses his chisels to cut a statue
and his ·calipers [compass] **to measure the statue.**
In this way, the workman makes the wood ·look exactly like a person [like the pattern of a man],
and this statue of a person ·sits [*or* dwells] **in ·the house** [*or* a shrine].
[14]**He cuts down cedars**
or cypress or oak trees.
·Those trees grew by their own power in [*or* He secures it for himself from] **the forest.**
Or he plants a pine tree, and the rain makes it grow.
[15]**Then he burns the tree.**
He uses some of the wood for a fire to keep himself warm.
He also starts a fire to bake his bread.
But he uses part of the wood to make a god, and then he worships it!
He makes the idol and bows down to it [[C]showing the absurdity of worshiping an idol made from the same material he burns]**!**
[16]**The man burns half of the wood in the fire.**
He uses the fire to cook his meat,
and he eats the meat until he is full.
He also burns the wood to keep himself warm. He says,
"Good! Now I am warm. ·I can see because of the fire's light [*or* ...as I watch the fire; [L]I have seen the fire]**."**
[17]**But he makes a statue from the wood that is left and calls it his god.**
He bows down to it and worships it.
He prays to it and says,
"You are my god. ·Save [Rescue] **me!"**
[18]**Those people ·don't know what they are doing** [*or* know nothing].
They ·don't understand [are ignorant]**!**
·It is as if their eyes are covered [*or* They shut their eyes] **so they can't see.**
Their minds don't understand.
[19]**·They have not thought about these things** [No one considers];
they don't understand.
They have never thought to themselves,
"I burned half of the wood in the fire
and used the hot coals to bake my bread.
I cooked and ate my meat.
·And I used the wood that [*or* Should I use what...?] **was left to make this ·hateful** [abominable; detestable] **thing.**
·I am worshiping [*or* Should I bow down to...?] **a block of wood!"**
[20]**He ·doesn't know what he is doing** [[L]feeds on ashes; *or* eats on a pile of ashes];
his ·confused mind [deluded/deceived heart] **leads him ·the wrong way** [astray].
He cannot ·save [rescue; [T]deliver] **himself**
or say, "·This statue I am holding is a false god [[L]Is there not a lie in my right hand?]**."**

The Lord Is the True God

21"·People of Jacob [LJacob], remember these things!
·People of Israel [LIsrael], remember you are my servants.
I ·made [shaped; formed] you, and you are my servants.
So Israel, I will not forget you.
22I have ·swept away [removed; *or* blotted out] your ·sins [offenses; transgressions] like a big cloud;
I have removed your sins like a ·cloud that disappears into the air [mist].
Come back to me because I ·saved [redeemed] you."

23·Skies [*or* Heavens], sing for joy because the LORD ·did great things [*or* acts; intervenes; Lhas done this]!
Earth, shout for joy, even in your deepest parts!
·Sing [Break into song], you mountains, with thanks to God.
Sing, too, you forests and all your trees!
The LORD ·saved [redeemed] ·the people of Jacob [LJacob]!
He ·showed his glory when he saved [Lis glorified in] Israel.
24This is what the LORD ·who saved you [your redeemer] says,
the one who formed you in ·your mother's body [Lthe womb]:
"I, the LORD, made everything,
stretching out the skies by myself
and spreading out the earth all alone.
25I ·show that the signs of the lying prophets are false [Lfrustrate the signs of babblers/*or* empty talkers];
I make fools of ·those who do magic [diviners].
I ·confuse even [reverse what is said by] the wise;
they think they know much, but I make ·them look foolish [their knowledge into foolishness].
26I ·make the messages of my servants come true [confirm my servants' words];
I make the ·advice [*or* prophecies] of my messengers come true.
I say to Jerusalem,
'·People will live in you again [LIt will be inhabited]!'
I say to the towns of Judah,
'You will be built again!'
I say to Jerusalem's ruins,
'I will ·repair you [raise you up].'
27I tell the deep waters, 'Become dry!
I will make your streams become dry!'
28I say of Cyrus [Cthe Persian king (ruled 550–530 BC) who allowed Israel to return from exile; 41:2; 44:28—45:6; 46:11; 48:14–16], 'He is my shepherd
and will ·do [fulfill] all that I want him to do.
He will say to Jerusalem, "You will be built again!"
He will tell the Temple, "Your foundations will be rebuilt." ' "

God Chooses Cyrus to Free Israel

45 This is what the LORD says to Cyrus [44:28], his ·appointed king [anointed one; messiah]:
"I hold your right hand
and will help you ·defeat [subdue] nations
and ·take away other kings' power [*or* remove kings' armor; Lopen the loins of kings].

I will open doors for you
so city gates will not ·stop you [be shut].
2I will go before you
and ·make the mountains flat [level mountains; 40:4].
I will ·break down [shatter; smash] the bronze gates of the cities
and cut through their iron bars.
3I will give you the ·wealth that is stored away [Ltreasures of darkness]
and the ·hidden riches [hoards in secret places]
so you will know I am the LORD,
the God of Israel, who calls you by name.
4I do these things for ·my servants, the people of Jacob [Lthe sake of Jacob my servant],
and for ·my chosen people, the Israelites [Israel, my chosen].
·Cyrus, I call [LI call] you by name,
and I give you a title of honor even though you don't know me.
5I am the LORD. There is no other God;
I am the only God.
I will ·make you strong [*or* arm you for battle; Lgird you],
even though you don't know me,
6so that everyone will know
there is ·no other God [none besides me].
From the ·east [rising of the sun] to ·the west [its setting] they will know
I alone am the LORD.
7I make the light
and create the darkness.
I bring ·peace [prosperity; wholeness; CHebrew *shalom*], and I ·cause [create] ·troubles [disaster; calamity].
I, the LORD, do all these things.

8"·Sky [Heavens] above, make ·victory [*or* righteousness] fall like rain;
clouds, pour down ·victory [*or* righteousness].
Let the earth ·receive it [open up],
and let salvation grow,
and let ·victory [*or* righteousness] grow with it.
I, the LORD, have created it.

9"·How terrible it will be for [LWoe to] those who argue with ·the God who made them [their Maker].
·They are like a piece of broken pottery [LA potsherd] among ·many pieces [Lpotsherds of the earth].
·The clay does not [LDoes the clay…?] ask the potter [64:8; Rom. 9:20],
'What are you doing?'
The thing that is made doesn't say to its maker,
'You have no ·hands [*or* skill].'
10·How terrible it will be for [LWoe to] the child who says to his father,
'·Why are you giving me life [*or* What have you fathered]?'
·How terrible it will be for [LWoe to] the child who says to his mother,
'·Why are you giving birth to me [*or* What have you given birth to]?' "

11This is what the LORD,
the Holy One of Israel [1:4], and its Maker, says:

"You ask me about what will happen.
·You [*or* Do you...?; *or* How dare you...!] question me about my children.
·You [*or* Do you...?; *or* How dare you...!] give me orders about ·what I have made [the work of my hands].
12 I made the earth
and all the people living on it.
With my own hands I stretched out the ·skies [heavens],
and I commanded all ·the armies in the sky [*or* the stars in the sky; [T]their host].
13 I will ·bring [raise/stir up] ·Cyrus [[L]him; 44:28] ·to do good things [*or* for my righteous purpose; in my righteousness],
and I will make his ·work easy [ways/paths straight].
He will rebuild my city
and set my ·people [[L]exiles] free
without any payment or ·reward [gift; *or* bribe].
The LORD ·All-Powerful [Almighty; of Heaven's Armies; [T]of hosts] says this."

14 The LORD says,
"The ·goods made in [[L]labor of] Egypt and the ·products [merchandise; *or* revenue] of ·Cush [Ethiopia]
and the tall people of Seba [43:3]
will ·come to [*or* be brought to] you
and will become yours.
·The Sabeans [[L]They] will walk behind you,
coming along in chains [[C]Israel is depicted as a great empire, receiving tribute from other nations].
They will bow down before you
and pray to you [[C]because they recognize Israel as God's representative], saying,
'God is with you,
and there is no other God.' "

15 God and Savior of Israel,
·you are [*or* how, then, can you be...?] a God ·that people cannot see [[L]who hides himself].
16 All the people who make idols will be put to great shame;
they will go off together in ·disgrace [humiliation; *or* confusion].
17 But Israel will be saved by the LORD,
and that salvation will continue forever.
Never again will Israel be ·put to shame [shamed; disgraced].

18 The LORD created the heavens.
He is the God who formed the earth and made it.
He did not ·want [create] it to be ·empty [*or* formless; chaotic; Gen. 1:2],
but he ·wanted life on the earth [[L]formed it to be inhabited].
This is what the LORD says:
"I am the LORD. There is no other God.
19 I did not speak in secret
or hide my words in some dark place.

I did not tell the ·family [descendants; offspring; seed] of Jacob
to ·look for me in empty places [*or* seek me in vain].
I am the LORD, and I speak the truth;
I say what is right.

20"You ·people who have escaped [fugitives; refugees] from other nations,
gather together and come before me;
come near together.
People who carry idols of wood ·don't know what they are doing [know nothing; *or* are fools].
They pray to a god who cannot save them.
21·Tell these people to come to me [*or* Declare and bring your case].
Let them ·talk about these things [take counsel] together.
Who told you long ago that this would happen?
Who told about it long ago?
I, the LORD, said these things.
There is no other God besides me.
I am the only good God. I am the Savior.
There is no other God.

22"All ·people everywhere [the ends of the earth],
·follow [turn] and be saved.
I am God. There is no other God.
23I ·will make a promise by my own power [[L]have sworn by myself],
and ·my promise is true [[L]a righteous/right/true word goes out of my mouth];
what I say will not ·be changed [be revoked; [L]return].
·I promise that everyone will bow before me [[L]For to me every knee will bow]
and ·will promise to follow me [[L]every tongue will swear; [C]allegiance; Rom. 14:11; Phil. 2:10].
24People will say about me, '·Goodness [Righteousness; *or* Deliverance] and ·power [strength]
come only from the LORD.' "
Everyone who has been angry with him
will come to him and be ashamed.
25But with the LORD's help, the ·people [descendants; offspring; seed] of Israel
will be ·found to be good [justified; vindicated; *or* victorious],
and they will ·praise [boast/glory in] him.

False Gods Are Useless

46 Bel bows down and Nebo bends low [[C]important gods of Babylon].
Their ·idols [images] ·are carried by animals [[L]belong to beasts and cattle].
The statues are only heavy loads
carried by tired animals.
2·These gods will all ·bow [stoop and bow] down.
They cannot save themselves
but will all be carried away ·like prisoners [into captivity].

3"·Family [LHouse] of Jacob, listen to me!
All ·you people from Israel who are still alive [the remnant of the house of Israel], listen!
I have carried you since you were born;
I have taken care of you from ·your birth [Lthe womb].
4Even when you are old, I ·will be the same [Lam he].
Even when your hair has turned gray, I will ·take care of [sustain; carry] you.
I made you and will carry you.
I will ·take care of [sustain; carry] and ·save [rescue] you.

5"To whom can you compare me?
·No one [Who…?] is equal to me or ·like [comparable to] me.
6Some people ·are rich with gold [Lpour out gold from their bags]
and weigh their silver on the scales.
They hire a goldsmith, and he makes it into a god.
Then they bow down and worship it.
7They put it on their shoulders and carry it.
They set it in its place, and there it stands;
it cannot move from its place.
People may ·yell at [*or* cry out to] it, but it cannot answer.
It cannot save them from their troubles.

8"Remember this, and ·do not forget it [be firm/steadfast]!
Think about these things, you ·who turn against God [rebels; transgressors].
9Remember ·what happened long ago [Lthe former things of antiquity].
Remember that I am God, and there is no other God.
I am God, and there is no one like me.
10From the beginning I told you what would happen in the end.
·A long time ago [From ancient times] I told you things that have not yet happened.
·When I plan something, it happens [L…saying, "My counsel will stand"].
What I want to do, I will do.
11I am calling a man from the east to carry out my plan;
he will come like a ·hawk [bird of prey; eagle] from a country far away.
I will make what I have said come true;
I will do what I have planned.
12Listen to me, you stubborn ·people [hearted],
who are far from ·what is right [righteousness].
13I ·will soon do the things that are right [Lam bringing my righteousness near].
·I will bring salvation soon[LIt is not far away].
I will save ·Jerusalem [LZion; Cthe location of the Temple]
·and bring glory to Israel [LIsrael, my splendor/glory]."

God Will Destroy Babylon

47 The LORD says, "·City of [LVirgin daughter] Babylon, go down and sit in the ·dirt [dust].
·People of Babylon [LDaughter of the Chaldeans], sit on the ground.
·You are no longer the ruler [L…without a throne].
You will no longer be called

tender or ·beautiful [delicate; pampered].
2 Take millstones and grind grain into flour.
Remove your veil and ·take [strip] off your nice skirts.
Uncover your legs and cross the rivers [Cactions of a servant, not a queen].
3People will see your nakedness;
they will see your shame [Cprobably a euphemism for sexual organs].
I will ·punish you [take vengeance];
I will ·punish every one of you [spare no one]."

4Our ·Savior [Redeemer] is named the LORD ·All-Powerful [Almighty; of Heaven's Armies; Tof hosts];
he is the Holy One of Israel [1:4].

5"·Babylon [LDaughter of the Chaldeans], sit in ·darkness and say nothing [Lsilence and go into darkness].
You will no longer be called the queen of kingdoms.
6I was angry with my people,
so I ·rejected [defiled; desecrated; profaned] ·those who belonged to me [my inheritance/possession].
I gave them ·to you [Linto your hand],
but you showed them no mercy.
You even ·made the old people
work very hard [Llaid a very heavy yoke on the aged].
7You said, 'I will ·live [reign; be] forever as the queen.'
But you did not think about these things
or consider ·what would happen [the outcome/end].

8"Now, listen, you lover of pleasure.
You ·think you are safe [who dwell in security].
You tell yourself,
'·I am the only one [LI am], and there is no other [Zeph. 2:15].
I will never be a widow
or ·lose [Lknow the loss of] my children.'
9Two things will happen to you suddenly, in a single day.
You will lose your children and ·your husband [Lbecome a widow].
These things will ·truly happen to [*or* overwhelm; Lcome in abundance upon] you,
in spite of all your ·magic [sorceries],
in spite of your powerful ·tricks [spells; enchantments].
10You ·do evil things, but you feel safe [Ltrusted/felt secure in your evil/wickedness]
and say, 'No one sees ·what I do [Lme].'
Your wisdom and knowledge
have ·fooled [mislead] you.
You say to yourself,
'·I am the only one [LI am], and there is no other [v. 8].'
11But ·troubles [disaster; evil] will come ·to [upon] you,
and you will not know how to ·stop them [conjure/charm it away].
·Disaster [Calamity; Destruction] will fall on you,
and you will not be able to ·keep it away [appease it; make atonement/pay ransom for it].

A catastrophe will strike ·quickly [suddenly];
you will not even ·see it coming [[L]know].

12"Keep on using your ·tricks [magic spells; enchantments]
and doing all your ·magic [sorceries]
that you have ·used [practiced; labored at] since you were young.
Maybe ·they will help you [you will succeed/profit];
maybe you will be able to ·scare someone [provoke terror]
13You are tired of the ·advice [counsel] you have received.
So let ·those who study the sky [the astrologers; [L]those who divide the heavens]—
those who ·tell the future by looking at the stars and the new moons [[L]gaze at the stars to know the months]—
let them save you from what is about to happen to you.
14But they are like straw;
fire will quickly burn them up.
They cannot save themselves
from the power of the fire.
They are not like coals that give warmth
nor like a fire that you may sit beside.
15You have ·worked [labored] with these people,
and they have ·been [*or* done business] with you since you were young,
but they will not be able to help you.
Everyone will ·go [*or* wander off] his own way,
and there will be no one left to save you."

God Controls the Future

48 The LORD says, "·Family [[L]House] of Jacob, listen to me.
You are called [[L]by the name of] Israel,
and you come from the ·family [[L]waters; wellsprings] of Judah.
You ·swear [take oaths] by the LORD's name
and ·praise [confess; call on] the God of Israel,
but ·you are not honest or sincere [[L]not in truth or in righteousness].
2You call yourselves ·people of [*or* by the name of; [L]from] the holy city,
and you ·depend on [trust in] the God of Israel,
who is named the LORD ·All-Powerful [Almighty; of Heaven's Armies; [T]of hosts].
3Long ago I told you ·what would happen [[L]the former things].
·I said these things and [[L]They went out from my mouth and I] made them known;
suddenly I acted, and these things happened.
4I knew you were stubborn;
your neck was like an iron muscle,
and your ·head [forehead; brow] was like bronze.
5So a long time ago I told you about these things;
I told you about them before they happened
so you couldn't say, 'My idols did this,
and my ·wooden [carved images] and metal statues ·made these things happen [decreed/ordained/commanded them].'

6"You heard and saw everything that happened,
·so you should [[L]will you not…?] tell this news to others.

·Now [From this time on] **I will tell you about new things,**
hidden things that you don't know yet.
7·**These things are happening** [LThey are created] **now, not long ago;**
you have not heard about them before today.
So you cannot say, '[LLook; *or* Yes; TBehold] **We already knew about that.'**
8**But you have not heard; you have not understood.**
Even long ago ·you did not listen [Lyour ear has not been opened].
I knew you would surely ·turn [act treacherously] **against me;**
you ·have fought against me [Lwere called a rebel] **·since you were born** [Lfrom the womb].
9**But for my ·own** [Lname's] **sake I will ·be patient** [Lhold back my anger].
·People will praise me because [LFor the sake of my praise] **I did not become angry**
and ·destroy you [cut you off].
10**I have ·made you pure** [refined you], **but not by fire, as silver is made pure.**
I have purified you ·by giving you troubles [Lin the furnace of affliction/suffering].
11**I do this for myself, for my own sake.**
·I will not [LHow could I…?] **let ·people speak evil against me** [Lmy name be defiled/profaned],
and I will not ·let some god take my glory [Lgive/share my glory with another].

Israel Will Be Free

12"**·People of Jacob** [LJacob], **listen to me.**
·People of Israel [LIsrael], **·I have called you to be my people** [Lwhom I called].
I am ·God [Lhe; the one];
I am the ·beginning and the end [Lfirst and I am the last; 41:4; 44:5].
13**I ·made** [Llaid the foundation of] **the earth with my own hands.**
With my right hand I spread out the skies.
When I call them,
they ·come [stand] **together before me."**

14**All of you, come together and listen.**
·None of the gods [LWho among them…?] **said these things would happen.**
The Lord ·has chosen someone [has an ally; *or* loves him; Ca reference to Cyrus, king of Persia; see 41:2; 44:28–45:6; 46:11; 48:14–16]
to carry out his ·wishes [desire; purpose] **against Babylon,**
·to attack [Lhis arm will be against] **the Babylonians;**

15"**I have spoken; I have called him.**
I have brought him, and I will make him successful.
16**Come to me and listen to this.**
From the ·beginning [first] **I have ·spoken openly** [Lnot spoken in secret].
From the time it ·began [happened], **I was there."**

Now, the Lord God
·has sent me with his Spirit [*or* and his Spirit have sent me; CCyrus is probably speaking here; vv. 14–15].

[17]This is what the LORD, ·who saves you [your Redeemer],
the Holy One of Israel [1:4], says:
"I am the LORD your God,
who teaches you ·to do what is good [what is best; *or* how to succeed],
who leads you in the way you should go.
[18]If you had obeyed my commands,
you would have had peace like a river [Cabundant and overflowing; 66:12].
·Good things [Your righteousness] would have flowed to you like the waves of the sea.
[19]·Your ·children [descendants] would have been ·as numerous as [Llike] ·sand in the sea [Lsand]
and your ·descendants [offspring/seed of your body] like grains of sand [10:22; Gen. 15:5; 22:17; Hos. 1:10].
·They [LTheir name] would never have ·died out [been cut off]
nor been destroyed."

[20]·My people, leave [LGo out from] Babylon!
Run from the ·Babylonians [LChaldeans]!
Tell this news with shouts of joy to the people;
spread it ·everywhere on [Lto the end of] earth.
Say, "The LORD has ·saved [redeemed] his ·servants, the people of Jacob [Lservant Jacob]."
[21]They did not become thirsty when he led them through the deserts.
He made water flow from a rock for them.
He split the rock,
and water flowed out [43:19; Ex. 17:6; Num. 20:11].

[22]"There is no peace for ·evil people [the wicked]," says the LORD.

God Calls His Special Servant

49 All of you ·people in faraway places [*or* islands; *or* coastlands], listen to me.
·Listen [Pay attention], all you nations far away.
·Before I was born [LFrom the womb], the LORD called me to serve him.
The LORD named me while I was still in my mother's womb [Cthis passage (49:1–13) is the second of four "servant songs" in Isaiah; 42:1].
[2]He made my ·tongue [mouth] like a sharp sword [Chis words enact judgment; 11:4; Heb. 4:12; Rev. 1:16].
He hid me in the shadow of his hand.
He made me like a ·sharp [*or* polished] arrow.
He hid me in ·the holder for his arrows [his quiver].
[3]He told me, "Israel, you are my servant.
I will show my glory ·through [in] you."
[4]But I said, "I have worked hard ·for nothing [in vain];
I have used all my power, ·but I did nothing useful [for nothing; in futility].
But ·the LORD will decide what my work is worth [Lmy judgment/vindication is the LORD's];
God will decide my reward."

5The LORD made me in the ·body [womb] of my mother
to be his servant,
to lead ·the people of Jacob [LJacob] back to him
so that Israel might be gathered to him.
·The LORD will honor me [LI am honored in the eyes of the LORD],
and ·I will get my strength from my God [LGod will be my strength].
6Now he told me,
"·You are an important servant to me [It is too small a thing; *or* Is it
too small a thing...?]
to ·bring back [restore; raise up] the tribes of Jacob,
to bring back the ·people of Israel who are left alive [remnant/
preserved ones of Israel].
I will make you a light for the nations [42:6; Luke 2:32; Acts 13:47]
so that my salvation will reach ·people all over the world [Lthe end of
the earth]."

7The LORD ·who saves you [the Redeemer], the Holy One of Israel [1:4].
says to the one who is ·hated [Ldespised and abhorred] by the ·people
[*or* nation; *or* nations],
to the servant of rulers.
This is what he says: "Kings will see you and ·stand [rise; Cto honor
him];
·great leaders [princes] will bow down before you,
because the LORD ·can be trusted [is faithful].
He is the Holy One of Israel [1:4], who has chosen you."

The Day of Salvation

8This is what the LORD says:
"At the ·right time [time of favor] I will ·hear your prayers [answer
you].
On the day of salvation I will help you [2 Cor. 6:2].
I will protect you,
and ·you will be the sign of my agreement with [LI will give/establish
you as a covenant for] the people [42:6].
·You will bring back the people to the land [L...to restore/rebuild the
land]
and ·give the land that is now ruined back to its owners [Lbequeath
its desolate inheritances].
9You will tell the prisoners, '·Come out [42:7].'
You will tell those in darkness, '·Come into the light [Show
yourselves; Appear].'
·The people [LThey] will ·eat [feed; graze] beside the roads [Cthe people
are symbolically pictured as sheep],
and they will find ·food [pasture] even on bare hills.
10They will not be hungry or thirsty.
Neither the ·desert wind [Lheat] nor the hot sun will ·hurt [strike]
them.
The God who comforts them will lead them
and guide them by springs of water.
11I will make my mountains into roads,
and the ·roads [highways] will be raised up [Cto make a level road;
40:4].
12Look, people are coming to me from far away,

from the north and from the west,
from ·Aswan in southern Egypt [Lthe land of Sinim]."

13Heavens, shout with joy;
earth, be happy;
mountains, burst into song,
because the LORD comforts his people
and will have ·pity [compassion] on ·those who suffer [the oppressed].

Jerusalem and Her Children

14But ·Jerusalem [LZion; Cthe location of the Temple] said, "The LORD has ·left [abandoned; forsaken] me;
the Lord has forgotten me."

15The LORD answers, "Can a woman forget the baby she nurses?
Can she feel no kindness for the child ·to which she gave birth [of her womb]?
Even if she could forget her children,
I will not forget you.
16See, I have ·written [engraved; inscribed] your name on my ·hand [palms].
·Jerusalem, I always think about your walls [LYour walls are always before me; Cdestroyed by the Babylonians].
17Your children ·will soon return to you [Lhurry; hasten],
and the people who defeated you and destroyed you will leave.
18·Look up [LLift up your eyes] and look around you.
All your children are gathering to return to you."
The LORD says, "As surely as I live,
·your children will be [Lyou will wear them all] like ·jewels [*or* ornaments]
·that a bride wears proudly [Lyou will put them on like a bride].

19"You were destroyed and defeated,
and your land was made ·useless [desolate].
But now you will have more people than the land can hold,
and those people who ·destroyed [devoured] you will be far away.
20The children ·born to you while you were sad [Lof your bereavement] will say to you,
'This place is too small for us.
Give us a bigger place to live.'
21Then you will say ·to yourself [Lin your heart],
'Who ·gave me all these children [bore me these]?
I was ·sad [bereaved] and ·lonely [barren],
·defeated [rejected] and ·separated from my people [exiled].
So who reared these children?
I was left all alone.
Where did all these children come from?'"

22This is what the Lord GOD says:
"See, I will lift my hand ·to signal [Lto] the nations;
I will raise my banner for all the people to see.
Then they will bring your sons back to you in their ·arms [Lbosom; lap],

and they will carry your daughters on their shoulders [CJews returning from exile are pictured as children returning to their parents].
23Kings will ·teach your children [be guardians/foster parents],
and ·daughters of kings [princesses; *or* queens] will take care of them.
They will bow down before you with their faces to the ground
and ·kiss the dirt [lick the dust] at your feet.
Then you will know I am the LORD.
Anyone who ·trusts in [hopes in; waits on] me will not be ·disappointed [*or* ashamed]."

24Can ·the wealth a soldier wins in war [spoils; plunder] be taken away from ·him [a warrior; a strong man]?
Can a prisoner be freed from a ·powerful soldier [tyrant]ⁿ?
25This is what the LORD says:
"The ·prisoners [captives] will be taken from the ·strong soldiers [mighty one].
·What the soldiers have taken will be saved [L...and spoils/plunder rescued from the tyrant].
I will fight ·your enemies [Lthose who fight with you],
and I will save your children.
26I will force ·those who trouble you [your enemies/oppressors] to eat their own flesh.
Their own blood will be the wine that makes them drunk.
Then ·everyone [all flesh] will know
I, the LORD, am the One who saves you;
I am the Powerful One of Jacob ·who saves you [your redeemer]."

Israel Was Punished for Its Sin

50 This is what the LORD says:
"People of Israel, you say I ·divorced [Lsent away] your mother.
Then where is the certificate of divorce that proves it?
Or ·do you think I sold you to pay a debt [Lto which of my creditors did I sell you]?
Because of ·the evil things you did [your sins/iniquities], I sold you.
Because of ·the times she turned against me [your transgressions], your mother was sent away.
2·I came home and found [LWhy, when I came, did I find...?] no one there;
I called, but no one answered.
·Do you think I am not able [LIs my hand too short] to ·save [redeem] you [59:1]?
Do I not have the power to save you?
·Look [TBehold], ·I need only to shout and [LWith my rebuke] the sea becomes dry [Ex. 14:21].
I change rivers into a desert [Josh. 3:16],
and their fish rot because there is no water;
they die of thirst.
3I can ·make the skies dark [Lclothe the skies/heavens in darkness; Rev. 6:12];
I can make ·them black like clothes of sadness [Lsackcloth their covering]."

49:24 tyrant The Dead Sea Scrolls read "tyrant." Some Hebrew copies have "righteous one."

God's Servant Obeys

[4]The Lord GOD gave me the ·ability to teach [[L]tongue of a student/
learned one]
so that I know what to say to make the ·weak [weary] strong.
Every morning he wakes me.
He ·teaches me [[L]awakens my ear] to listen like a student [[C]this passage
(50:4–11) is the third of four "servant songs" in Isaiah; see 42:1].
[5]The Lord GOD ·helps me learn [*or* speaks clearly to me; [L]has opened my
ear],
and I have not ·turned against him [rebelled]
nor ·stopped following him [turned away/back].
[6]I offered my back to those who beat me.
I offered my cheeks to those who ·pulled [ripped out] my beard.
I ·won't [*or* did not] hide my face from them
when they ·make fun of [mocked; insulted; shamed] me and spit at
me [53:5; Matt. 26:67; 27:26; Mark 15:19; Luke 22:63].
[7]The Lord GOD helps me,
so I will not be ·ashamed [disgraced].
I ·will be determined [[L]have set my face like flint; Ezek. 3:8–9],
and I know I will not be ·disgraced [put to shame].
[8]He ·shows that I am innocent [vindicates], and he is ·close to me [near].
So who can ·accuse me [bring charges against me; Rom. 8:33–34]?
If there is someone, let us ·go to court [[L]stand up] together.
·If someone wants to prove I have done wrong [[L]Who are my
accusers?],
he should ·come and tell [challenge; [L]come near] me.
[9]Look! It is the Lord GOD who helps me.
So who can ·prove me guilty [condemn me]?
Look! All those who try will ·become useless like old clothes [wear out
like a garment];
moths will eat them.

[10]Who among you fears the LORD
and obeys his servant?
The person who walks in the dark without light
should trust in the [[L]name of the] LORD and depend on his God.
[11]·But instead [*or* Look; Behold], ·some of you want to [[L]all of you who]
light your own fires
and make your own light.
So, go, walk in the light of your fires,
and trust ·your own light to guide you [the torches you have ignited].
But this is what you will receive from ·me [my hand]:
You will lie down in ·a place of pain [torment; [C]could refer to physical
pain in the present world or to the torment of hell].

Jerusalem Will Be Saved

51 The LORD says, "Listen to me,
those of you who ·try to live right [[L]pursue righteousness] and
·follow [seek] the LORD.
Look ·at [*or* to] the rock from which you were cut;
look ·at [*or* to] the stone quarry from which you were dug [[C]referring
to their ancestors Abraham and Sarah; see v. 2].
[2]Look at Abraham, your ·ancestor [father],
and Sarah, who gave birth to ·your ancestors [[L]you].

Abraham ·had no children [was just one person; [L]was one] when I
called him [Gen. 12:1–3],
but I blessed him and ·gave him many descendants [[L]made him many].
3So the LORD will comfort ·Jerusalem [[L]Zion; [C]the location of the
Temple];
he will ·show mercy to [comfort] ·those who live in [[L]all] her ruins.
He will change her ·deserts [wilderness] into ·a garden like Eden
[[L]Eden];
he will make her ·empty lands [desert; arid plains] like the garden of
the LORD.
·People there will be very happy [[L]Joy and gladness will be found in her];
·they will give thanks and sing songs [[L]thanksgiving and the voice of
song].

4"My people, listen to me;
my nation, pay attention to me.
·I will give the people my teachings [[L]Law/Instruction/Torah will go
out from me],
and my ·decisions [justice] will be like a light to the ·people
[nations].
5·I will soon show that I do what is right [[L]My righteousness/justice
draws near].
·I will soon save you [[L]My salvation goes out].
·I will use my power and [[L]My arms will] judge the nations.
The ·faraway places [*or* islands; *or* coastlands] are ·waiting for [looking
to; hoping in] me;
they wait for my ·power to help them [[L]arm].
6·Look up [[L]Lift your eyes] to the heavens [40:26].
Look at the earth below.
The skies will disappear like clouds of smoke.
The earth will ·become useless [wear out] like old clothes [Ps. 102:26],
and its people will die like flies.
But my salvation will continue forever,
and my ·goodness [righteousness] will never end.

7"You people who know ·what is right [righteousness] should listen to
me;
you people who ·follow my teachings [have my law/[L]Torah in your
heart] should hear what I say.
Don't be afraid of the ·evil things people say [[L]reproach/scorn of
people],
and don't be ·upset [discouraged; dismayed] by their insults.
8Moths will eat those people as if they were clothes,
and worms will eat them as if they were wool.
But my goodness will continue forever,
and my salvation ·will continue from now on [[L]from generation to
generation]."

9Wake up, wake up, and ·use your [clothe yourself with] strength,
·powerful [[L]arm of the] LORD.
Wake up as you did in the ·old times [ancient days],
as you did ·a long time ago [[L]in generations everlasting].

·With your own power, you [LWere you not the one who…?] cut Rahab
[Ca mythical sea monster symbolizing chaos; 30:7; Ps. 89:10] into pieces
and ·killed [pierced] that ·sea monster [serpent; dragon; 27:1; Ps. 74:13–14].
10·You dried [LDid you not dry…?] up the sea
and the waters of the deep ocean.
You made a road through the deepest parts of the sea
for your ·people to cross over and be saved [or redeemed people to cross over; 43:16; Ex. 14:21; Ps. 106:9].
11The people the Lord has ·freed [rescued; ransomed] will return
and enter ·Jerusalem [LZion; v. 3] with ·joy [singing].
·Their happiness will last forever [LEverlasting joy will crown them/ be on their head].
They will ·have [be overwhelmed/overtaken with] joy and gladness,
and all sadness and sorrow will ·be gone far [flee] away [35:10].

12The Lord says, "·I [LI, even I] am the one who ·comforts you [40:1].
So why should you be afraid of people, who die?
·Why should you fear people [L…or the son of man; Chuman beings] who ·die [Lis given up] like the grass [40:6]?
13Have you forgotten the Lord who made you,
who stretched out the ·skies [heavens]
and ·made [Llaid the foundations of] the earth [48:13]?
Why are you always afraid
of ·those angry people who trouble you [the anger/wrath of the oppressor]
and who ·want [seek; plan] to destroy?
But where ·are those angry people [is the anger/wrath of the oppressor] now?
14 ·People in prison [LThose who are burdened/stooped over] will soon be set free;
they will not die in prison,
and they will ·have enough food [not lack bread].
15I am the Lord your God,
who stirs the sea and makes the waves roar.
My name is the Lord ·All-Powerful [Almighty; of Heaven's Armies; Tof hosts].
16I will ·give you the words I want you to say [Lput my words in your mouth].
I will cover you with ·my hands and protect you [Lthe shadow of my hand].
I ·made [established] the heavens and [Llaid the foundation of] the earth,
and I say to ·Jerusalem [LZion; v. 3], 'You are my people.' "

God Punished Israel

17Awake! Awake!
Get up, Jerusalem.
·The Lord was very angry with you;
your punishment was like wine in a cup.
The Lord made you drink that wine [LYou have drunk from the hand of the Lord the cup of his wrath];

you ·drank the whole cup [Ldrained the goblet to its dregs] until you
stumbled.
18·Though Jerusalem had many people [LAmong all the children she bore],
there was not one to lead her.
Of all the people ·who grew up there [she raised],
no one was there to ·guide her [Ltake her by the hand].
19·Troubles [Calamities] came to you two by two,
but no one will ·feel sorry for [*or* console] you.
There was ruin and ·disaster [destruction], ·great hunger [famine] and
·fighting [Lsword].
·No one [LBut who…?] can comfort you.
20Your ·people [Lchildren; sons] have ·become weak [fainted].
They fall down and lie ·on every street corner [Lat the head of every
street],
like ·animals [Lantelope] caught in a net.
They ·have felt the full anger [*or* are filled with the wrath] of the LORD
and have heard God's ·angry shout [rebuke].

21So listen to me, ·poor Jerusalem [Loppressed/afflicted one],
you who are drunk but not from wine.
22Your God will ·defend [plead the case of] his people.
This is what the LORD your God says:
"·The punishment I gave you is like a cup of wine.
You drank it and could not walk straight.
But I am taking that cup of my anger away from you, [LLook/TBehold,
I have taken from your hand the cup of staggering,
the dregs of the cup of my wrath]
and you will never ·be punished by my anger [Ldrink from it] again.
23I will now give that cup of punishment to ·those who gave you pain
[your tormentors; Jer. 25:17, 26, 28],
who told you,
'Bow down so we can walk over you.'
·They [LYou] made your back like dirt for them to walk on;
you were like a street for them to travel on."

Jerusalem Will Be Saved

52 Wake up, wake up, ·Jerusalem [LZion; Cthe location of the Temple]!
·Become strong [LClothe yourself with/Put on strength]!
·Be beautiful again [LPut on beautiful/glorious clothes],
holy city of Jerusalem.
The ·people who do not worship God and who are not pure
[Luncircumcised and defiled/unclean]
will not enter you again.
2Jerusalem, ·you once were a prisoner [*or* be enthroned/seated].
Now shake off the dust and ·stand up [arise].
·Jerusalem, you once were a prisoner [LCaptive daughter of Zion,].
Now free yourself from the chains around your neck.
3This is what the LORD says:
"You were ·not sold for a price [Lsold for nothing],
so you will be ·saved [redeemed] without cost."
4This is what the Lord GOD says:
"First my people went down to Egypt to live.
Later Assyria ·made them slaves [oppressed them].

5"Now ·see what has happened [what do I have here…?]," says the LORD.
"Another nation has taken away my people for nothing.
Those who rule them ·make fun of me [mock; taunt]ⁿ," says the LORD.
"All day long they ·speak against [slander; blaspheme] me.
6This has happened so my people will know ·who I am [Lmy name],
and so, ·on that future [Lin that] day, they will know
that I am the one speaking to them.
·It will really be me [LLook/TBehold, I]."

7·How beautiful [*or* How beautiful on the mountains] ·is the person [Lare the feet of him]
who ·comes over the mountains to bring [*or* brings] good news,
who announces peace
and brings good news,
who announces salvation [Nah. 1:15]
and says to ·Jerusalem [LZion; v. 1],
"Your God ·is King [*or* reigns]."
8Listen! Your ·guards [watchmen] ·are shouting [raise their voices].
They are all shouting [Ltogether] for joy!
They all will see ·with their own eyes [right in front of their eyes; Leye in eye]
when the LORD returns to ·Jerusalem [LZion; v. 1].
9·Jerusalem, although your buildings are destroyed now [LYou ruins of Jerusalem],
shout and rejoice together,
because the LORD has comforted his people.
He has ·saved [redeemed] Jerusalem.
10The LORD ·will show his holy power [flexes his holy muscles; Lbared his holy arm]
·to [Lto the eyes of] all the nations.
Then ·everyone on [Lall the ends of the] earth
will see the salvation of our God.

11You people, leave, leave; get out ·of Babylon [Lfrom there]!
Touch nothing that is ·unclean [defiled].
You who carry the ·LORD's things used in worship [articles/vessels of the LORD],
leave there and make yourselves pure.
12You will not ·be forced to leave Babylon quickly [leave in haste];
you will not be forced to run away,
because the LORD will go before you,
and the God of Israel will ·guard you from behind [be your rear guard].

The Lord's Suffering Servant

13The LORD says, "See, my servant will ·act wisely [*or* have success].
·People will greatly honor and respect him [He will be raised and exalted; C52:13—53:12 is the fourth of four "servant songs" in Isaiah; see 42:1].
14Many people were ·shocked [astonished; appalled] when they saw him.
His appearance was so ·damaged [disfigured; marred] he did not look like a man;

52:5 taunt The Dead Sea Scrolls read "wail."

his form ·was so changed they could barely tell he was human
[Lbeyond the sons of man/children of humanity].
15**But now he will ·surprise** [startle; *or* sprinkle; Cas the blood of a
sacrifice sprinkled on the altar; Lev. 4:6, 17] **many nations.**
Kings will ·be amazed [Lshut their mouths because of him].
They will see things they had not been ·told about him [Ltold],
and they will understand things they had not heard."

53 **Who ·would have** [*or* has] **believed ·what we heard** [*or* our
message; John 12:38; Rom. 10:16]**?**
·Who saw the LORD's power in this [LAnd to whom has the arm of the
LORD been revealed]?
2**He grew up like a ·small plant** [young plant; tender shoot; 11:1] **before**
·the LORD [Lhim],
like a root growing in a ·dry land [parched soil].
He had no special beauty or ·form [majesty] **to make us notice him;**
there was nothing in his appearance to make us desire him.
3**He was ·hated** [despised] **and rejected by people.**
·He had much pain [LA man of pain/suffering/Tsorrows] **and**
·suffering [one who knew/was acquainted with pain/grief].
People ·would not even look at [turned their backs on; Lhid their faces
from] **him.**
He was ·hated [despised], **and we ·didn't even notice him** [*or* did not
esteem him].

4**But he ·took** [bore] **our suffering on him**
and ·felt our pain for us [carried our sorrows/sickness].
·We saw his suffering
and thought God was punishing him [L…stricken and afflicted by
him; CGod].
5**But he was wounded for ·the wrong we did** [Tour transgressions];
he was crushed for ·the evil we did [Tour iniquities].
The punishment, which ·made us well [brought us wholeness/peace],
was given to him,
and we are healed because of his ·wounds [lacerations; Tstripes;
1 Pet. 2:24].
6**We all have ·wandered away** [Tgone astray] **like sheep;**
each of us has gone his own way [1 Pet. 2:25].
But the LORD has put on him ·the punishment
for all the evil we have done [Lall of our sins/iniquity].

7**He was ·beaten down** [oppressed] **and ·punished** [treated harshly;
Tafflicted],
but he didn't ·say a word [Lopen his mouth].
He was like a lamb being led to be ·killed [slaughtered].
He was quiet, as a sheep is quiet ·while its wool is being cut [Lbefore its
shearers; Acts 8:32; Matt. 26:63; Mark 14:61; John 19:9; 1 Pet. 2:23];
he never opened his mouth.
8**Men took him away ·roughly and unfairly** [*or* after unjustly
condemning him; Lfrom oppression and judgment].
·He died without children to continue his family [*or* Yet no one of his
generation objected; Land his generation, who considers/speaks of it?].
He was ·put to death [Lcut off from the land of the living];

he was ·punished [struck down] for the ·sins [transgressions] of my people.
9He was ·buried [assigned his grave] with ·wicked men [criminals],
and ·he died with the rich [*or* he was put in a rich man's tomb; [L]with the rich in his death; Matt. 27:57, 60].
He had done ·nothing wrong [[L]no violence],
and he had ·never lied [[L]no deceit in his mouth; 1 Pet. 2:22].

10But it was the ·LORD who decided [LORD's will]
to crush him and make him suffer.
The LORD made his life a ·penalty [sin] offering,
but he will still see his ·descendants [offspring; seed] and ·live a long life [[L]extend his days].
·He will complete the things the LORD wants him to do [[L]The pleasure/will/purpose of the LORD will prosper in his hands].
11"After his soul suffers many things,
he will see ·life[n] [*or* light; *or* the light of life] and be satisfied.
[By his knowledge/experience] My ·good [righteous] servant will ·make many people right with God [justify many];
he will carry away their ·sins [iniquities].
12For this reason I will ·make him a great man among people [*or* give him a portion with the great ones],
and he will ·share in all things [divide the spoils] with those who are strong,
because he ·willingly gave [laid bare; [T]poured out] his life
and was ·treated like a criminal [[L]numbered/counted with rebels/ trangressors].
But he ·carried away [bore] the sins of many people
and ·asked forgiveness [made intercession] for ·those who sinned [rebels; transgressors]."

People Will Return to Jerusalem

54 The LORD says, "Sing, ·Jerusalem [[L]barren one; Gal. 4:27].
·You are like a woman who [[L]...who] never gave birth to children.
Start singing and shout for joy.
You never ·felt the pain of giving birth [were in labor],
·but you will have more children [[L]for more are the children of the desolate one]
than the woman who has a husband.
2Make your tent bigger;
stretch ·it [[L]your tent curtains] out and make it wider.
Do not hold back.
Make the ·ropes [cords] longer
and its stakes stronger,
3because you will spread out to the right and to the left.
Your ·children [descendants; offspring; seed] will take ·over [possession of] other nations,
and they will ·again live in [resettle] cities that once were ·destroyed [ruined; desolate].

4"Don't be afraid, because you will not be ashamed.

53:11 see life The Dead Sea Scrolls and the Septuagint read "see light" (meaning "see life" or "live"). Some Hebrew copies have "see."

Don't be ·embarrassed [discouraged]**, because you will not be disgraced.**
You will forget the shame ·you felt earlier [[L]of your youth];
you will not remember the ·shame [disgrace; reproach] **·you felt when you lost your husband** [of your widowhood; *or* of your abandonment].
5·**The God who made you is like** [[L]For your Maker is] **your husband.**
His name is the LORD ·All-Powerful [Almighty; of Heaven's Armies; [T]of hosts].
The Holy One of Israel [1:4] **is ·the one who saves you** [your redeemer].
He is called the God of all the earth.
6**You were like a woman ·whose husband left her** [deserted; abandoned],
·and you were very sad [[L]grieved/distressed in spirit].
You were like a wife who married young
and then ·her husband left her [was rejected].
But the LORD ·called you to be his [*or* will call you back],"
says your God.
7**God says, "I left you for a ·short time** [moment],
but with great ·kindness [mercy; compassion] **I will bring you back again.**
8**I ·became very angry** [had a surge/burst of anger]
and hid from you for a ·time [moment],
but I will show you ·mercy [compassion] **with ·kindness** [lovingkindness; loyalty; covenant love] **forever,"**
says the LORD ·who saves you [your redeemer].

9**The LORD says, "This day is like the ·time** [days] **of Noah to me** [Gen. 6–9].
I ·promised [swore] **then that ·I** [[L]the waters of Noah] **would never ·flood** [cover] **the world again** [Gen. 9:11].
In the same way, I ·promise [swore] **I will not be angry with you**
or ·punish [rebuke] **you again.**
10**The mountains may ·disappear** [move; be shaken],
and the hills may ·come to an end [be removed; disappear],
but my ·love [lovingkindness; loyalty; covenant love] **will never ·disappear** [be moved/shaken];
my ·promise [covenant; treaty] **of peace will not ·come to an end** [be removed; disappear],"
says the LORD who ·shows mercy to [has compassion for] **you.**

11**"·You poor city** [[L]Afflicted one]. **Storms have ·hurt** [battered; tossed] **you,**
and you have not been comforted.
But I will rebuild you with ·turquoise stones [gems],
and I will build your foundations with ·sapphires [*or* lapis lazuli].
12**I will use ·rubies** [*or* agate; *or* jasper] **to build your ·walls** [towers; battlements; pinnacles]
and ·shining jewels [*or* beryl; *or* garnet; *or* crystal] **for the gates**
and precious jewels for all your outer walls.
13**All your children will be taught by the LORD,**
and they will have much ·peace [prosperity; wholeness; [C]Hebrew: *shalom*].
14**I will ·build** [establish] **you ·using fairness** [in righteousness].

·You will be safe from those who would hurt you [LTyranny/oppression will be far from you],
·so you will have nothing to fear [terror will be far away].
Nothing will come to make you afraid.
15·I will not send anyone to attack you [LIf anyone attacks, it is not from me],
and you will defeat those who do attack you.

16"See, I made the blacksmith.
He fans the fire to make it hotter,
and he ·makes the kind of tool he wants [forges a weapon for his purpose].
In the same way I have made the destroyer to destroy.
17 So no weapon ·that is used [forged] against you will ·defeat you [succeed].
You will ·show that those who speak against you are wrong [refute every accusation against you; Lrefute every tongue that rises against you in judgment].
These are the ·good things [heritage] my servants receive.
Their ·victory [vindication; righteousness] comes from me," says the LORD.

God Gives What Is Good

55 The LORD says, "All you who are thirsty,
come ·and drink [Lto the waters; John 7:37].
Those of you who do not have money,
come, buy and eat [Prov. 9:5]!
Come buy wine and milk
without money and without cost.
2Why spend your money on something that is not ·real food [bread]?
Why work for something that doesn't really satisfy you?
Listen closely to me, and you will eat what is good;
your soul will ·enjoy [delight in] the ·rich food that satisfies [Lfat].
3Come to me and ·listen [extend your ear];
listen to me so you may live.
I will make an ·agreement with you that will last forever [everlasting covenant/treaty with you].
I will give you the ·blessings [covenant love; loyalty; lovingkindness; Tsure mercies] I promised to David [2 Sam. 7:11–14; Ps. 89:33–35; Acts 13:34].
4[LLook; TBehold] I made David a witness ·of my power for all [Lto the] nations,
a ruler and commander of many nations.
5[LLook; TBehold] You will call for nations that you don't yet know.
And these nations that do not know you will run to you
because of the LORD your God,
because of the Holy One of Israel [1:4] who ·honors [has glorified] you."

6·So you should look for [LSeek] the LORD ·before it is too late [while he may be found];
you should call to him while he is near.
7The wicked should ·stop doing wrong [abandon/forsake their ways],
and ·they [Lthe unrighteous person] should stop their evil thoughts.

They should return to the LORD so he may have ·mercy [compassion]
on them.
They should come to our God, because he will freely forgive them
[Deut. 4:25–31; 30:1–10; 1 Kin. 8:46–53].

8The LORD says, "My thoughts are not like your thoughts.
Your ways are not like my ways.
9Just as the heavens are higher than the earth,
so are my ways higher than your ways
and my thoughts higher than your thoughts [Ps. 103:11].
10Rain and snow fall from the sky
and don't return without watering the ground.
They cause the plants to sprout and grow,
making seeds for the ·farmer [sower]
and bread for the ·people [Leater].
11The same thing is true of the words ·I speak [Lthat go out of my mouth].
They will not return to me empty.
They ·make the things happen that I want to happen [accomplish what
I desire/purpose],
and they succeed in doing what I send them to do.

12"So you will go out with joy [Creturning from the Babylonian exile]
and be led out in peace.
The mountains and hills will burst into song before you,
and all the trees in the fields will clap their hands [Cthe earth rejoices
at God's restoration of creation].
13·Large cypress [*or* Juniper; Evergreen] trees will grow where
thornbushes were.
Myrtle trees will grow where ·weeds [briers] were.
These things will be ·a reminder of the LORD's promise [*or* for the
LORD's honor/renown; Lto the LORD for a name],
·and this reminder will never be destroyed [Lfor an eternal sign that
will not be cut off]."

All Nations Will Obey the Lord

56 This is what the LORD says:
"·Give justice to all people [Promote justice],
and ·do what is right [practice righteousness],
because my salvation ·will come to you soon [draws near].
Soon ·everyone will know that I do what is right [my righteousness
will be revealed].
2The person who ·obeys the law about [keeps from defiling] the Sabbath
will be blessed,
and the ·person [Lson of man] who ·does no [keeps his hand from
doing] evil
will be blessed."

3Foreigners who have ·joined [committed to] the LORD should not say,
"The LORD will ·not accept me with [Lexclude/separate me from] his
people [14:1]."
The eunuch should not say,
"·Because I cannot have children, the LORD will not accept me
[LLook, I am a dry tree]."

[4]This is what the LORD says:
"This is for the eunuchs who ·obey the law about the Sabbath [keep my Sabbaths]
and ·do what I want [choose what pleases me]
and ·keep [hold firmly to] my ·agreement [covenant]:
[5]I will ·make their names remembered [[L]set up a memorial/monument and a name]
within my ·Temple [[L]house] and its walls.
It will be better for them than ·children [[L]sons and daughters].
I will give them a name that will last forever,
that will ·never be forgotten [[L]not be cut off].
[6]As for the foreigners who ·join [commit themselves to] the LORD
to ·worship [minister to] him and love ·him [[L]his name],
to serve him,
to ·obey the law about [keep from defiling] the Sabbath,
and to ·keep [hold firmly to] my ·agreement [covenant]:
[7]I will bring these people to my holy mountain
and give them joy in my house of prayer.
The offerings and sacrifices
they place on my altar will ·please me [be accepted],
because my Temple will be called
a house for prayer for people from all nations [Matt. 21:13; Mark 11:17; Luke 19:46]."
[8]The Lord GOD says—
he who gathers the ·Israelites that were forced to leave their country [outcasts/exiles of Israel]:
"I will ·bring together [gather] other people
to join those who are already gathered."

Israel's Leaders Are Evil

[9]All you ·animals [beasts] of the field,
all you animals of the forest, come to ·eat [devour].
[10]·The leaders who are to guard the people [[L]His watchmen; 62:6] are blind;
they ·don't know what they are doing [lack knowledge; are ignorant].
All of them are like ·quiet [mute; *or* muzzled] dogs
that ·don't know how to [cannot] bark.
They lie down and dream
and love to sleep.
[11]They are like ·hungry [greedy; ravenous] dogs
that are never satisfied.
They are like shepherds
who ·don't know what they are doing [lack understanding; are ignorant; Ezek. 34:2–3].
They all have gone their own way;
·all they want to do is satisfy themselves [each seeks their own gain/profit].
[12]They say, "Come, let's drink some wine;
let's ·drink all the [fill ourselves with] ·beer [[T]strong drink; [C]alcoholic beverage made from grain] we want.
And tomorrow ·we will do this again [will be like today],
·or, maybe we will have an even better time [even better; *or* it will be very great indeed; [L]very much abundantly great]."

Israel Does Not Follow God

57 ·Those who are right with God [The righteous] ·may die [perish; pass away],
but no one ·pays attention [cares; [L]sets/takes it to heart].
·Good people [The devout; People of lovingkindness/loyalty/covenant love] are taken away [[C]by death],
but no one understands.
·Those who do right [The righteous] are being taken away ·from [to be spared from; *or* by the power of] evil
2 and are given peace.
Those who ·live [walk] ·as God wants [uprightly]
·find rest in death [[L]rest on their beds].

3 "Come here, you ·magicians [[L]sons/children of a sorceress]!
Come here, you ·children [offspring; seed] of prostitutes and adulterers!
4 Of whom are you ·making fun [mocking; ridiculing]?
Whom are you ·insulting [sneering at; [L]opening your mouth at]?
At whom do you stick out your tongue?
You ·turn against God [[L]are children of rebellion],
and you are ·liars [[L]the offspring/seed of liars].
5 You ·have sexual relations [burn with lust; [L]inflame yourselves]
beneath the oaks and under every green tree [[C]a reference to pagan fertility rites].
You ·kill [slaughter] children in the ·ravines [valleys]
and ·sacrifice them in the rocky places [[L]under the rocky clefts; [C]child sacrifices, like those associated with the Phoenician god Molech; Lev. 18:21; 2 Kin. 23:19; Jer. 32:35].
6 You take the smooth rocks from the ·ravines [valleys]
as your portion.
·To them you are devoted [[L]They, they are your lot].
You pour drink offerings ·on them to worship them [[L]out to them],
and you give grain [[L]gift; tribute] offerings [Lev. 2:1] to them.
·Do you think this makes me want to show you mercy [Should I relent because of these things; *or* Should I be happy about these things]?
7 You make your bed on every hill and mountain,
and there you offer sacrifices.
8 You have hidden your ·idols [signs; pagan symbols; memorials]
behind your doors and doorposts.
You have ·left [deserted] me, and you have uncovered ·yourself [*or* your bed].
You have ·pulled back the covers [opened it] and climbed into bed.
You have made an ·agreement [pact; covenant] with those whose beds you love,
and you have looked at their nakedness [[C]euphemisms for sexual relations, here referring to pagan worship].
9 You ·use your oils and perfumes
to look nice for [[L]went with oil and increased your perfumes for] ·Molech [*or* the king].
You have sent your messengers to faraway lands;
you even tried to send them to ·the place of the dead [or the grave; [L]Sheol].

[10]You were tired from doing these things,
but you never ·gave up [[L]said, "It is hopeless"].
You found ·new strength [[L]the life of your hand],
so you did not ·quit [faint; grow weary].

[11]"Whom ·were you so afraid of [[L]did you fear or dread]
that you lied to me?
You have not remembered me
or even ·thought about me [[L]set/taken it to heart].
·I [*or* Is It because I...?] have been quiet for a long time.
Is that why you are not afraid of me?
[12]I will tell about your '·goodness [righteousness]' and ·what you do
[your works],
and those things will ·do you no good [not profit/help you].
[13]When you cry out for help,
let ·the gods you have gathered [your collection of idols] ·help [save;
rescue] you.
The wind will blow them all away;
just a ·puff of wind [breath] will take them away.
But the person who depends on me will ·receive [inherit] the land
and ·own [possess] my holy mountain."

The Lord Will Save His People

[14]Someone will say, "Build ·a road [up; *or* it]! Build ·a road [up; *or* it]!
Prepare the way [40:3; 62:10]!
·Make the way clear [Remove the obstacles] for my people."
[15]And this is the reason: God lives forever and is holy.
He is high and ·lifted up [exalted].
He says, "I live in a high and holy place,
but I also live with people who are ·sad [contrite] and ·humble [lowly
in spirit].
I ·give new life to [revive the spirit of] those who are ·humble [lowly]
and to those whose hearts are ·broken [contrite; repentant].
[16]I will not ·accuse [*or* contend/fight against them] forever,
nor will I always be angry,
because then ·human life [the spirit] would grow weak.
·Human beings [[L]The breath], whom I created, would die.
[17]I was angry because ·they were dishonest in order to make money [of
their sinful greed].
I punished them and ·turned away from them [[L]hid my face] in anger,
but they ·continued to do evil [[L]turned away in the way of their
heart].
[18]I have seen ·what they have done [their ways], but I will heal them.
I will guide them and comfort them and those who ·felt sad for them
[mourn].
·They will all praise me [I will create praise on their lips; [L]...creating
fruit of lips].
[19]·I will give peace, real peace [[L]Peace, peace], to those far and near,
and I will heal them," says the LORD.
[20]But ·evil people [the wicked] are like the ·angry [surging; tossing] sea,
which cannot rest,
whose waves toss up ·waste [mire; muck] and mud.
[21]"There is no peace for ·evil people [the wicked]," says my God.

How to Honor God

58 The LORD says, "Shout out loud. Don't hold back.
·Shout out loud [[L]Raise/lift up your voice] like a trumpet.
Tell my people ·what they have done against their God [their transgression];
tell ·the family of Jacob about [[L]Jacob] their sins.
2They ·still come looking for [seek] me ·every day [day to day]
and ·want [delight] to learn my ways.
They act just like a nation that does ·what is right [righteousness],
that ·obeys [[L]did not forsake/reject] the ·commands [judgments] of its God.
They ask me ·to judge them fairly [for righteous judgment].
They ·want [delight] to ·be near [draw near to] God.
3They say, '·To honor you we had special days when [[L]Why have…?] we fasted,
but you didn't see.
·We humbled ourselves to honor you [[L]Why have we afflicted our souls/selves…?],
but you didn't notice.'"

But the LORD says, "[[L]Look; [T]Behold] You ·do what pleases [satisfy; seek pleasure for] yourselves on these fast days,
and you ·are unfair to [exploit; oppress] your workers.
4Even when you fast, you argue and fight
and ·hit each other with your [[L]hit with wicked/sinful] fists.
You cannot do these things as you do now
and ·believe your prayers are [expect to be] heard ·in heaven [on high].
5·This kind of special day is not what [Is this the fast that…?] I ·want [have chosen].
·This is not the way I want people to be sorry for what they have done [[L]Do I want a day when people afflict/mortify themselves?].
I don't want people just to bow their heads like a ·plant [reed]
·and wear rough cloth and lie in ashes to show their sadness [[L]stretching out on sackcloth and ashes].
Is this what you call a fast?
·Do you really think this pleases [[L]…a day acceptable to] the LORD?

6"I will tell you the kind of fast I ·want [have chosen]:
·Free the people you have put in prison unfairly [[L]Release the chains/bonds of wickedness]
and ·undo their chains [*or* untie the ropes from the yoke].
Free ·those to whom you are unfair [the oppressed]
and ·stop their hard labor [[L]break every yoke].
7Share your food with the hungry
and bring poor, homeless people into your own homes.
When you see someone who has no clothes, ·give him yours [clothe him],
and don't ·refuse to help [[L]conceal yourself from] your ·own relatives [flesh].
8Then your light will shine like the dawn,
and your wounds will quickly heal.
Your ·God [[L]righteousness] will walk before you,
and the glory of the LORD [[C]his manifest presence] will ·protect you from behind [be your rear guard].

[9]Then you will call out, and the LORD will answer.
You will cry out, and he will say, 'Here I am.'

"If you ·stop making trouble for others [Ltake away the yoke from your midst],
if you stop ·using cruel words [speaking wickedness] and pointing your finger at others,
[10]if you ·feed [Loffer your soul/selves to] those who are hungry
and ·take care of [satisfy] the needs of ·those who are troubled [the afflicted/oppressed],
then your light will ·shine [Lrise] in the darkness,
and ·you will be bright like sunshine at [Lyour darkness/gloom like] noon.
[11]The LORD will always lead you.
He will satisfy your ·needs [soul] in dry lands
and give strength to your bones.
You will be like a garden that is well-watered,
like a spring ·that never runs dry [whose waters never fail].
[12]Your people will rebuild the ·old cities that are now in [Lancient] ruins;
you will rebuild their ancient foundations.
You will be ·known for repairing [called the repairer of] the broken walls
and ·for rebuilding [the restorer of] the roads and houses.

[13]"·You must obey God's law about [LIf you turn your foot away from…; Cavoiding Sabbath journeys] the Sabbath
and not do what pleases yourselves on that holy day.
·You should [L…and if you…] call the Sabbath a ·joyful day [delight]
and honor it as the LORD's holy day.
·You should [L…and if you…] honor it by not ·doing whatever you please [Lgoing your own way]
nor saying ·whatever you please [idle words] on that day.
[14]·Then [L…then] you will find ·joy [delight] in the LORD,
and I will ·carry you to [*or* cause you to ride on] the high places above the earth.
I will ·let you eat the crops of the land [Lfeed you with the inheritance] of your ancestor Jacob."
The ·LORD has said these things [Lmouth of the LORD has spoken].

The Evil That People Do

59 Surely the LORD's ·power [Lhand] is ·enough [Lnot too short] to save you.
·He can hear you when you ask him for help [L…nor his ear too heavy to hear].
[2]It is your ·evil [iniquity] that has separated
you from your God.
Your sins cause him to ·turn away [Lhide his face] from you,
so he does not hear you.
[3]·With your hands you have killed others [LFor your hands are defiled with blood],
and ·with your fingers you have done wrong [Lyour fingers with sin/iniquity].
With your lips you have lied,
and with your tongue you ·say [utter; mutter] evil things.

4·People take each other to court unfairly [LNo one sues with cause; *or* No one calls for justice],
and no one tells the truth in ·arguing [setting forth; pleading] his case.
They ·accuse each other falsely [*or* rely on empty arguments] and tell lies.
They ·cause [Lconceive] trouble and ·create more [Lgive birth to] evil.
5They hatch ·evil like eggs [Leggs] from ·poisonous snakes [vipers].
If you eat one of those eggs, you will die,
and if you break one open, a poisonous snake comes out.
People ·tell lies as they would spin [Lspin] a spider's web.
6 The webs they make cannot be used for clothes;
you can't cover yourself with ·those webs [Lwhat they make].
The things they do are evil,
and ·they use their hands to hurt others [La deed of violence is in their hands].
7·They eagerly [LTheir feet] run to do evil [Prov. 1:16; Rom. 3:15–17],
and they are always ready to ·kill innocent people [Lshed innocent blood].
They ·think evil thoughts [*or* devise evil schemes].
·They cause ruin and destruction everywhere they go [Ruin and destruction are in their paths/roads].
8They don't know ·how to live in [Lthe path/way of] peace,
and there is no ·fairness [justice] in their ·lives [paths].
They ·are dishonest [act deceitfully; Lhave made their paths/ways crooked].
Anyone who ·lives as they live [walks on them] will never ·have [know] peace.

Israel's Sin Brings Trouble

9·Fairness [Justice] has gone far away;
·goodness [righteousness] ·is nowhere to be found [Ldoes not reach/overtake us].
We ·wait [hope] for the light, but ·there is only darkness now [Llook/Tbehold, darkness].
We ·hope [wait] for a bright light, but ·all we have is darkness [Lwe walk in gloom/shadows/darkness].
10We are like the blind ·feeling our way [groping] along a wall.
We ·feel our way [grope] as if we had no eyes.
·In the brightness of day [At midday/noon] we ·trip [stumble] as if it were ·night [evening; twilight].
We are like dead men ·among the strong [*or* in desolate places].
11All of us growl like the bears.
We ·call out sadly [moan/coo mournfully] like the doves.
We ·look [hope; wait] for justice, but there isn't any.
We ·want to be saved [hope/wait for salvation], but salvation is far away.
12·We have done many wrong things [LFor our sins/transgressions are many] ·against our God [Lbefore you];
our sins ·show we are wrong [Ltestify against us].
·We know we have turned against God [LOur transgressions are with us];
we know the ·evil things [iniquities] we have done:

13·sinning [transgressing; rebelling] and ·rejecting [Llying against] the LORD,
turning ·away from [our backs to] our God,
·planning to hurt others and to disobey God [Lspeaking oppression and revolt],
·planning [conceiving] and speaking lies.
14So we have driven away justice,
and ·we have kept away from what is right [Lrighteousness stands far off].
Truth ·is not spoken [stumbles] in the ·streets [public squares];
what is honest ·is not allowed to enter the city [Lcannot enter].
15Truth ·cannot be found anywhere [is lost/gone; *or* fails],
and people who refuse to do evil ·are attacked [become prey].

The LORD looked and could not find any justice,
and he was displeased.
16He ·could not find anyone to help the people [Lsaw there was no one],
and he was ·surprised [shocked; appalled] that there was no one to ·help [intervene].
So ·he used his own power to save the people [Lhis own arm brought him salvation];
his own ·goodness [righteousness] gave him strength.
17He ·covered himself with goodness [put on righteousness] like ·armor [a breastplate].
He put the helmet of salvation on his head [1 Thess. 5:8; Eph. 6:13–17].
He put on ·his clothes for punishing [garments of vengeance]
and wrapped himself in ·the coat of his strong love [zeal/jealousy as a cloak].
18The LORD will ·pay back his enemies [Lrepay] ·for what they have done [according to their deeds].
He will show his ·anger [wrath] to ·those who were against him [his adversaries]
and will ·punish [repay] his ·enemies [foes];
he will ·punish [repay] the ·people in faraway places [*or* islands; *or* coastlands] as they deserve.
19Then people from the west will fear the [Lname of the] LORD,
and people from the ·east [rising of the sun] will fear his glory.
·The LORD [LFor he] will come quickly like a ·fast-flowing [*or* pent up] river,
driven by the ·breath [*or* wind; *or* Spirit] of the LORD.

20"Then a Savior will come to ·Jerusalem [LZion; Cthe location of the Temple]
and to the people of Jacob who have turned from ·sin [transgressions],"
says the LORD [Rom. 11:26–27].

21The LORD says, "This is my ·agreement [promise; covenant] with these people: My Spirit and my words that I ·give you [have put in your mouth] will ·never leave you [not depart from your mouth] or [Lthe mouth of] your ·children [descendants; seed] or [Lthe mouth of] your ·grandchildren [descendants' descendants; Lseed's seed], now and forever [Jer. 31:31; Heb. 8:10; 10:16]."

Jerusalem Will Be Great

60 "Jerusalem, ·get up [arise] and shine, because your light
has come,
and the glory of the LORD shines on you.
2 [[L]Look; [T]Behold] Darkness ·now covers [*or* will cover] the earth;
deep darkness covers ·her people [the nations].
But the LORD shines on you,
and people see his glory [[C]his manifest presence] ·around [upon]
you.
3 Nations will come to your light;
kings will come to ·the brightness of your sunrise [*or* your radiance].

4 "[[L]Lift up your eyes and] Look around you.
People are gathering and coming to you.
Your sons are coming from far away,
and your daughters are ·coming with them [*or* carried on the hip; *or*
nursed at their side; *or* escorted by guardians].
5 When you see them, you will ·shine with happiness [[L]shine; be radiant];
you will be excited and ·full of joy [[L]your heart will swell/enlarge],
because the wealth of the nations across the seas will be given
to you;
the riches of the nations will come to you.
6 ·Herds [*or* Caravans; [L]An abundance of] of camels will cover your land,
young camels from Midian and Ephah.
·People [[L]All] will come from Sheba [[C]unknown location, perhaps
present-day Yemen, Eritrea, or Ethiopia; see 1 Kin. 10:1–13]
bringing gold and ·incense [*or* frankincense],
and they will sing praises to the LORD.
7 All the sheep from Kedar will be ·given [gathered] to you;
the ·sheep [rams] from Nebaioth [Gen. 25:13] will ·be brought to
[serve; minister to; [C]perhaps for sacrifices] you.
They will be ·pleasing [acceptable] sacrifices on my altar,
and I will ·make my beautiful Temple more beautiful [glorify/adorn
my glorious Temple].

8 "·The people are returning to you [[L]Who are these who fly…?] like
clouds,
like doves flying to their ·nests [shelters; [L]windows].
9 ·People in faraway lands [[L]For the coastlands/*or* islands] ·are waiting
[*or* look] for me.
The ·great trading ships [[L]ships of Tarshish; 2:16] will come first,
bringing your children from ·faraway lands [afar],
and with them silver and gold.
·This will honor [[L]…for the name of] the LORD your God,
the Holy One of Israel [1:4],
·who does wonderful things for you [[L]because he has glorified/
beautified you].

10 "Jerusalem, foreigners will rebuild your walls,
and their kings will serve you.
·When I was angry [[L]In my wrath], I ·hurt [struck] you,
but now ·I want to be kind to you and comfort you [[L]in grace/favor I
will have compassion/mercy on you].

[11]Your gates will always be open;
they will not be closed day or night
so the nations can bring their wealth to you,
and their kings ·will be led to you [*or* leading the way; [C]either as captives or leading the procession of gifts].
[12]The nation or kingdom that doesn't serve you will ·be destroyed [perish];
it will be completely ruined.

[13]"The ·great trees [[L]glory] of Lebanon will ·be given [come] to you [35:2]:
its ·pine [juniper], fir, and cypress trees together.
You will use them to make ·my Temple [[L]the place of my sanctuary] beautiful,
and I will ·give much honor to [glorify] ·this place where I rest [[L]the place of] my feet [Ezek. 43:7].
[14]The ·people who have hurt you [[L]children/sons of your oppressors] will bow down to you;
those who ·hated [despised] you will bow down at your feet.
They will call you The City of the LORD,
·Jerusalem, city [[L]Zion; 59:20] of the Holy One of Israel [1:4].

[15]"You have been ·hated [despised] and ·left empty [abandoned; forsaken]
with no one passing through.
But I will make you great from now on;
you will be a place of ·happiness [pride; majesty] ·forever and ever [for generations to come].
[16]You will ·be given what you need from [[L]drink the milk of] the nations,
like a child ·drinking milk from its mother [nursing at royal breasts].
Then you will know that it is I, the LORD, ·who saves you [your savior].
You will know that the Powerful One of Jacob ·protects [redeems] you.
[17]I will bring you gold in place of bronze,
silver in place of iron,
bronze in place of wood,
iron in place of rocks.
I will ·change your punishment into peace [*or* make peace your governor/leader],
and ·you will be ruled by what is right [righteousness will be your ruler].
[18]There will be no more violence [[L]heard] in your country,
no more ·ruin [devastation; havoc] or destruction within your borders.
You will name your walls Salvation
and your gates Praise.
[19]The sun will no longer be your light during the day
nor will the brightness from the moon be your light,
because the LORD will be your ·light forever [everlasting light],
and your God will be your glory [Zech. 14:6–7; Rev. 21:23; 22:5].
[20]Your sun will never set again,
and your moon will ·never be dark [not wane/disappear],

because the LORD will be your ·light forever [everlasting light],
and your ·time of sadness [days of mourning] will end.
[21]All of your people will ·do what is right [be righteous].
They will ·receive [possess; inherit] the earth forever.
They are the ·plant [branch; shoot] I have planted,
the work of my own hands
to show my ·greatness [glory; Cmanifest presence].
[22]The ·smallest family will grow to [Lleast of you will become] a
thousand.
The ·least important [smallest] of you will become a powerful
nation.
I am the LORD,
and ·when it is [Lin its] time, I will ·make these things happen quickly
[hasten it]."

The Lord's Message of Freedom

61 The Lord GOD has put his Spirit in me,
because the LORD has ·appointed [anointed] me to ·tell [bring]
the good news to the poor.
He has sent me to ·comfort [bind up] those whose hearts are broken,
to tell the captives they are free,
and to tell the prisoners they are released.
[2]He has sent me to announce the ·time when the LORD will show his
kindness [year of the LORD's favor; Can allusion to the Year of
Jubilee; Lev. 25:10; Luke 4:18–19]
and the ·time when our God will punish evil people [Lday of
vengeance of our God].
He has sent me to comfort all those who ·are sad [mourn]
3 and to help the ·sorrowing [mourning] people of ·Jerusalem [LZion;
Clocation of the Temple; 59:20].
I will give them a ·crown [garland; headdress] to replace their ashes,
and the oil of ·gladness [joy] to replace their ·sorrow [mourning],
and ·clothes [a garment] of praise to replace their ·spirit of sadness
[discouragement; heavy heart].
Then they will be called ·Trees of Goodness [or Oaks of
Righteousness],
trees planted by the LORD to show his ·greatness [glory; Cmanifest
presence].

[4]They will rebuild the ·old [ancient] ruins
and restore the places destroyed long ago [58:12].
They will repair the ruined cities
that were destroyed for ·so long [generations].

[5]·Foreigners [Strangers] will come to tend your sheep.
·People from other countries [Foreigners] will ·tend [plow] your
fields and vineyards.
[6]You will be called priests of the LORD;
you will be named the ·servants [ministers] of our God.
You will ·have riches from all the nations on earth [Leat the wealth of
nations],
and ·you will take pride in them [Lin their glory you will boast].
[7]Instead of ·being ashamed [your shame], you will receive ·twice as
much wealth [a double portion].

Instead of being ·disgraced [dishonored; humiliated], **they will ·be happy because of what they receive** [[L]rejoice over their portion].
They will receive a double share of the land,
so ·their happiness will continue forever [[L]everlasting joy will be theirs].
8"**I, the LORD, love justice.**
I hate ·stealing [robbery] **and ·everything that is wrong** [wrongdoing].
·I will be fair and give my people what they should have [[L]I will reward/give wages in truth/faithfulness],
and I will make an ·agreement [covenant; treaty] **with them that will continue forever.**
9**·Everyone in all nations will know the children of my people** [[L]Their descendants/seed will be known among the nations/Gentiles],
and their ·children [offspring] **will be known among the ·nations** [peoples].
Anyone who sees them will know
that they are ·people [descendants; seed] **the LORD has blessed."**

10**I will ·rejoice** [delight] **greatly in the LORD;**
·all that I am [my soul] **·rejoices** [exults] **in my God.**
He has covered me with ·clothes [garments] **of salvation**
and wrapped me with a ·coat [robe] **of ·goodness** [righteousness],
like a bridegroom ·dressed for his wedding [*or* who adorns himself with a headdress like a priest],
like a bride ·dressed in [adorns herself with] **jewels.**
11[[L]For as] **The earth causes plants to grow,**
and a garden causes the seeds planted in it to grow.
In the same way the Lord GOD will make ·goodness [righteousness] **and praise**
·come [sprout; spring up] **·from** [*or* before; in front of] **all the nations.**

New Jerusalem

62 **·Because I love Jerusalem** [[L]For Zion's sake], **I will ·continue to speak for her** [not be silent];
for Jerusalem's sake I will not ·stop speaking [be silent]
until her ·goodness [vindication; righteousness] **shines like ·a bright light** [brightness],
until her salvation burns bright like a ·flame [torch].
2**Jerusalem, the nations will see your ·goodness** [righteousness; vindication],
and all kings will see your glory.
Then you will ·have [[L]be called by] **a new name,**
which the [[L]mouth of the] **LORD himself will ·give you** [name].
3**You will be like a ·beautiful crown** [crown of majesty/glory] **in the LORD's hand,**
like a ·king's crown [royal diadem] **in your God's hand.**
4**You will never again be called ·the People that God Left** [[L]Abandoned; Deserted],
nor your land ·the Land that God Destroyed [Desolate].
You will be called ·the People God Loves [[L]My Delight Is In Her; [T]Hephzibah; [C]a proper name],

and your land will be called ·the Bride of God [LMarried; TBeulah; Ca
proper name],
because the LORD ·loves you [takes delight in you].
And your land will ·belong to him as a bride belongs to her husband
[be married].
5As a young man marries a ·woman [young woman; virgin],
so your ·children [*or* builder] will marry ·your land [Lyou].
As a ·man [Lbridegroom] rejoices over ·his new wife [the bride],
so your God will rejoice over you.

6Jerusalem, I ·have put guards [post watchmen] on your walls.
They ·must not [*or* will never] be silent day or night.
You people who ·remind the LORD of your needs in prayer [*or* call on
the LORD]
should ·never be quiet [take no rest].
7You should ·not stop praying to him [Lgive him no rest] until he builds
up Jerusalem
and makes it a city ·all people will praise [of praise/pride in the
earth].

8The LORD ·has made a promise [Lswears by his right hand],
and by his ·power he will keep his promise [Lmighty arm].
He said, "I will never again give your grain
as food to your enemies.
I will not let ·your enemies [foreigners] drink the new wine
that you have worked to make.
9Those who ·gather food [gather/harvest it] will eat it,
and they will praise the LORD.
Those who gather the grapes will drink the wine
in the courts of my ·Temple [sanctuary; holy place]."

10Go through, go through the gates!
Make the way ready for the people.
Build up, build up the ·road [highway]!
Move all the stones off the road.
Raise ·the banner as a sign [a standard/signal flag] for the ·people
[nations].

11The LORD ·is speaking [announces]
to ·all the faraway lands [Lthe end of the earth]:
"·Tell the people of Jerusalem [LSay to the daughter of Zion; Zech. 9:9],
'Look, your Savior is coming.
He is bringing ·your reward to you [Lhis reward with him];
·he is bringing his payment [his recompense/reward is] with him.' "
12·His people [LThey] will be called the Holy People,
the ·Saved People [Redeemed] of the LORD,
and Jerusalem will be called ·the City God Wants [LSought After],
the City ·God Has Not Rejected [*or* Not Abandoned; Deserted].

The Lord Judges His People

63 Who is this coming from Edom [34:5],
from the city of Bozrah, ·dressed in red [*or* in crimson-stained
garments; CEdom means "red"]?

Who is this dressed in ·fine clothes [honorable clothing; *or* royal
garments]
and marching forward with his great power?

He says, "I, the LORD, speak ·what is right [in righteousness].
I ·have the power [am mighty] to save you."

2Someone asks, "Why are your clothes bright red
as if you had ·walked [stomped; trodden] on the grapes to make
wine?"

3The LORD answers, "I have ·walked [stomped; trodden] in the
winepress alone,
and no one among the nations ·helped [Lwas with] me.
I was angry and ·walked [stomped; trod] on the nations
and crushed them because of my anger.
Blood splashed on my clothes,
and I stained all my clothing.
4·I chose a time to punish people [L...for the day of vengeance was in
my heart],
and the ·time [year] has come for me to ·save [redeem].
5I looked around, but I saw no one to help me.
I was ·surprised [shocked; appalled] that no one supported me
[59:16].
So ·I used my own power to save my people [Lmy own arm
accomplished salvation/victory];
my own ·anger [wrath] ·supported [sustained; upheld] me.
6While I was angry, I ·walked on the [trampled] nations.
In my ·anger [wrath] I ·punished them [made them drunk; 49:26;
51:23]
and poured their ·blood [Ljuice] on the ·ground [earth]."

The Lord's Kindness to His People

7I will tell about the LORD's ·kindness [lovingkindness; loyalty; covenant
love]
and praise him for everything he has done.
I will praise the LORD for the many good things he has given us
and for his goodness to the ·people [Lhouse] of Israel.
·He has shown great mercy to us [...according to his compassion]
and ·has been very kind to us [according to his great lovingkindness/
loyalty/covenant love].
8He said, "[LSurely] These are my people;
my children will not ·lie to [deal falsely with; betray] me."
So he saved them.
9When they ·suffered [were distressed/afflicted], he ·suffered [was
distressed/afflicted] also.
·He sent his own angel to save them [LThe angel/messenger of his
presence/face saved them; Ex. 14:19].
Because of his love and kindness, he saved them.
·Since long ago [LAll the days of old] he has ·picked [lifted] them up
and carried them [Deut. 32:10–12].
10But they ·turned [rebelled] against him [Ex. 15:24; Num. 14:11;
Ps. 78:17]

and ·made his Holy Spirit very sad [grieved his Holy Spirit; Ps. 78:40].
So he became their enemy,
and he fought against them.
11But then his people remembered ·what happened long ago [Lthe days of old],
in the days of Moses and the Israelites with him.
Where is the LORD who brought the people ·through [up out of] the sea [Ex. 14:19–22],
with the ·leaders of his people [Lshepherds of the flock; Cprobably Moses, Aaron and the tribal leaders]?
Where is the one
who put his ·Holy Spirit [*or* holy spirit] among them,
12who led Moses by the right hand
with his ·wonderful power [Lglorious arm],
who divided the water before them [Ex. 14:21]
to make ·his name famous [a reputation/name for himself] forever,
13who led the people through the ·deep waters [depths]?
Like a horse walking ·through a desert [in the wilderness],
the people did not stumble.
14Like cattle that go down to the valley,
the Spirit of the LORD gave ·the people a place to rest [them rest].
LORD, that is the way you led your people,
and by this you ·won [made] for yourself ·wonderful fame [a glorious reputation/name].

A Prayer for Help

15LORD, look down from the heavens and see;
look at us from your ·wonderful [glorious] and holy ·home [abode] in heaven.
Where is your ·strong love [zeal] and power?
Why are you ·keeping [holding back] your ·love [tenderness] and ·mercy [compassion] from us?
16You are our father.
[L…though] Abraham doesn't know ·we are his children [Lus],
and Israel doesn't recognize us.
LORD, you are our father.
·You are called [*or* Your name is] "·the one who has always saved us [our redeemer from of old]."
17LORD, why are you making us wander from your ways?
Why do you make ·us stubborn [Lour hearts hard] so that we don't ·honor [fear] you?
For our sake come back to us,
your servants, ·who belong to you [Lthe tribes of your inheritance].
18Your ·people [*or* holy people] had ·your Temple [possession of your holy place; *or* possession of a land] for a while,
but now our enemies have ·walked on your holy place and crushed it [trampled down your sanctuary].
19We have become like people you never ruled over,
like those who have never ·worn [been called by] your name.

64 If only you would tear open the ·skies [heavens] and come down to earth
so that the mountains would ·tremble [shake] before you.

[2]Like a fire that ·burns [kindles; ignites] ·twigs [dry wood],
like a fire that makes water boil,
let your ·enemies [adversaries] know ·who you are [[L]your name].
Then all nations will shake with fear ·when they see you [before you].
[3]You have done amazing things ·we did not expect [beyond our expectations].
You came down, and the mountains trembled before you.
[4]From ·long ago [ancient times; of old] no ·one [[L]ear] has ever heard of a God like you.
No ·one [[L]eye] has ever seen a God besides you,
who ·helps [acts on behalf of] the people who ·trust [wait for] you.
[5]You help those who ·enjoy doing good [joyfully act righteously],
who remember ·how you want them to live [[L]your ways/paths].
·But [[L]Look; [T]Behold] you were angry because we sinned.
For a long time we disobeyed,
so how can we be saved?
[6]All of us ·are dirty with sin [became like an unclean/defiled thing].
All ·the right things we have done [our righteous deeds] are like ·filthy pieces of cloth [filthy garments/rags; *or* a menstrual cloth; 30:22].
All of us ·are [fade; shrivel] like dead leaves,
and our ·sins [iniquities], like the wind, have carried us away.
[7]No one ·worships you [[L]calls on your name]
or ·even asks you to help us [[L]rouses himself to lay hold of you].
That is because you have ·turned away [hidden your face] from us
and have ·let our sins destroy us [given us over to our sins].[n]

[8]But LORD, you are our father.
We are like clay, and you are the potter;
your hands made us all.
[9]LORD, don't continue to be angry with us;
don't remember our sins forever.
Please, look at us,
because we are your people.
[10]Your holy cities ·are empty like the desert [have become a wilderness/wasteland].
·Jerusalem [[L]Zion; [C]the location of the Temple] is like a ·desert [wilderness; wasteland];
it is ·destroyed [a desolation].
[11]Our ancestors worshiped you
in our holy and wonderful Temple,
but now it has been burned with fire,
and all our ·precious [treasured; pleasant] things have ·been destroyed [become ruins].
[12]·When you see these things [After this], will you hold yourself back from helping us, LORD?
Will you be silent and punish us beyond ·what we can stand [measure]?

All People Will Learn About God

65 The LORD says, "I ·made myself known to people [[L]allowed myself to be sought by those] who were not looking for me.
I was found by those who were not asking me for help.

64:7 let our sins destroy us Greek, Syriac, and Aramaic copies read "given us over to our sins." Hebrew copies read "caused us to melt in the hand of our sin."

I said, 'Here I am. Here I am,'
to a nation that ·was not praying to me [did not call on my name; *or* called by my name].
2All day long I ·stood ready to accept [Lstretched out my hands to a]
people who ·turned [rebelled] against me,
but the way they continue to ·live [walk] is not good;
·they do anything they want to do [following their own thoughts/ schemes].
3·Right in front of me [To my face]
they continue to do things that make me angry.
They offer sacrifices to their gods in their gardens [1:29],
and they burn incense on altars of brick.
4They sit among the graves
and spend their nights ·waiting to get messages from the dead [*or* keeping vigil; *or* in secret places].
They eat the ·meat [flesh] of pigs [Cunclean animal; Lev. 11:7; Deut. 14:8],
and their pots are full of soup made from ·meat that is wrong to eat [defiled/polluted things].
5But they tell others, 'Stay away, and don't come near me.
I am too holy for you.'
These ·people [*or* practices] are like smoke in my ·nose [nostrils].
Like a fire that burns all ·the time [day long; Ctheir sin never ceases and God's anger grows].

6"Look, it is written here before me.
I will not ·be quiet [keep silent]; instead, I will repay you in full.
I will ·punish you for what you have done [Lpay it back into their laps/bosom].
7I will punish you for your sins and your ·ancestors' [fathers'] sins,"
says the LORD.
"They burned incense ·to gods on [Lon] the mountains
and ·shamed [insulted; defied] me on those hills.
So I will ·punish them as they should be punished
for what they did [Lmeasure into their laps/bosoms payment for their former deeds]."

8This is what the LORD says:
"When there is ·juice left [new wine; *or* good grapes] in a bunch of grapes,
people say, "Don't destroy it,
because there is ·good left [Lblessing] in it."
So I will do the same thing to my servants—
I will not destroy them all.
9I will ·leave some of the children of [produce/bring forth offspring/ seed from] Jacob,
and some of the people of Judah will ·receive [possess; inherit] my mountain.
·I will choose the people who [My chosen ones] will ·live there [possess/inherit it];
my servants will live there.
10Then ·the Plain of Sharon [LSharon; Ca fertile plain in western Israel; 33:9] will be a field for flocks,

and the Valley of Achor [Clocated in eastern Israel, near Jericho] will
be a place for herds to rest.
They will be for the people who ·want to follow [have sought] me.

11"But as for you who ·left [abandoned; forsook] the LORD,
who forgot about my holy mountain,
who ·worship the god Luck [Lspread a table for Fortune/Luck; CHebrew
Gad, a pagan god],
·who hold religious feasts for the god Fate [Lfill bowls of mixed wine
for Fate; CHebrew *Meni*, a pagan god],
12I ·decide your fate, and I will punish you with my sword [Ldestine/
number you for the sword].
You will all ·be killed [fall in the slaughter; *or* bow to the executioner],
because I called you, but you refused to answer.
I spoke to you, but you wouldn't listen.
You did ·the things I said were evil [Levil before my eyes]
and chose to do things ·that displease me [LI did not delight in]."
13So this is what the Lord GOD says:
"My servants will eat,
but ·you evil people [Lyou] will be hungry.
My servants will drink,
but ·you evil people [Lyou] will be thirsty.
My servants will ·be happy [rejoice],
but ·you evil people [Lyou] will be shamed.
14My servants will shout for joy
because of the ·goodness [joy] of their hearts,
but ·you evil people [Lyou] will ·cry [shout; cry out],
·because you will be sad [from an anguished heart].
You will ·cry loudly [wail; lament], because your spirits will be
broken.
15Your names will be ·like curses to [*or* used as a curse by; Lleft as a curse
to] my ·servants [Lchosen ones],
and the Lord GOD will put you to death.
But he will call his servants by another name.
16People in the land who ask for blessings
will ·ask for them from [*or* be blessed by] the faithful God.
And people in the land who ·make a promise [swear an oath]
will ·promise [swear] ·in the name of the faithful God [*or* by the one
true God],
because the troubles of the past will be forgotten.
·I will make those troubles go away [L...and are hidden from my
eyes].

A New Time Is Coming

17"·Look [TBehold], I will ·make [create] new heavens and a new earth,
and people will not remember the ·past [former things]
or ·think about those things [bring them to heart/mind].
18My people will be happy and joyful forever
because of the things I will ·make [create].
I will make a Jerusalem that is full of joy,
and I will make her people a delight.
19Then I will rejoice over Jerusalem
and be delighted with my people.

There will never again be heard in that city
the sounds of ·crying [weeping] and ·sadness [crying].
20There will never be a ·baby [infant] from that city
who lives only a few days.
And there will never be an older person
who doesn't ·have a long life [Llive out his days].
A person who ·lives a hundred years will be called young [*or* dies at a hundred years will still be considered a child],
and a person who dies before he is a hundred will be thought of as a ·sinner [*or* accursed].
21In that city those who build houses will live there.
Those who plant vineyards will get to eat their grapes [Cas opposed to times of conquest, when homes are confiscated and crops are stolen].
22No more will one person ·build a house and someone else live there [Lbuild and another inhabit].
One person will not ·plant a garden and someone else eat its fruit [Lplant and another eat].
·My people will live a long time,
as trees live long [LFor like the days of a tree
shall be the days of my people].
My chosen people will live there
and enjoy the ·things they make [Lwork of their hands].
23They will ·never again work for nothing [not labor in vain].
They will never again give birth to children ·who die young [Ldoomed for misfortune/disaster].
All my people will be blessed by the LORD;
they and their ·children [descendants; seed] will be blessed.
24I will ·provide for their needs [Lanswer] before they ·ask [call],
and I will ·help them [Lhear] while they are still ·asking for help [Lspeaking].
25The wolf and the lamb will ·eat together in peace [feed/graze together].
The lion will eat hay like an ox,
and ·a snake on the ground will not hurt anyone [the serpent's food will be dust; Gen. 3:14].
They will not hurt or destroy each other
on all my holy mountain,"
says the LORD.

The Lord Will Judge All Nations

66 This is what the LORD says:
"Heaven is my throne,
and the earth is my footstool.
So ·do you think you can build a house for me [Lwhere is this house you would build for me]?
·Do I need a place to rest [Where is my resting place]?
2[LHasn't…?] My hand made all things.
All things are here because I made them,"
says the LORD.

"These are the people ·I am pleased with [Lupon whom I look]:
those who are ·not proud or stubborn [humble and contrite in spirit]
and who ·fear [tremble at] my word.

[3]But those people who kill bulls as a sacrifice to me
are like those who kill people.
Those who kill sheep as a sacrifice
are like those who break the necks of dogs.
Those who give me ·grain [[L]gift; tribute] offerings [Lev. 2:1]
are like those who offer me the blood of pigs [[C]dogs and pigs were ritually unclean animals and were forbidden as sacrifices].
Those who burn incense
are like those who worship idols [[C]their rituals were no better than pagan worship because their hearts were not right with God].
These people choose their own ways, not mine,
and they ·love [delight in] ·the terrible things they do [their abominations].
[4]So I will choose ·their punishments [harsh treatment for them],
and I will punish them with what they fear most.
This is because I called to them, but they did not listen.
I spoke to them, but they did not hear me.
They did things I said were evil;
they chose to do things I did not ·like [delight in]."

[5]You people who ·obey the words of the LORD [[L]tremble at his word],
listen to what he says:
"Your brothers hated you
and ·turned against [excluded; cast out] you because ·you followed me [[L]of my name].
Your brothers said, 'Let the LORD be ·honored [glorified]
so we may see ·you rejoice [your joy],'
but they will be ·punished [[L]put to shame].
[6]·Listen to the loud noise coming [[L]A sound of uproar…!] from the city;
hear the ·noise [*or* voice] from the Temple.
It is the [[L]voice/sound of the] LORD ·punishing [repaying] his enemies,
giving them the punishment they deserve.

[7]"·A woman does not give birth [[L]She gives birth; [C]alluding to Jerusalem/Zion; v. 8] before she ·feels the pain [goes into labor];
she ·does not give birth to a son [delivers a son/child] before the pain starts.
[8]·No one has ever [[L]Who has…?] heard of that happening;
·no one has ever [[L]Who has…?] seen that happen.
·In the same way no one ever saw [[L]Can…?] a country ·begin [be born] in one day;
·no one has ever heard of a new nation beginning [[L]can a nation be brought forth…?] in one moment.
But ·Jerusalem [[L]Zion; [C]the location of the Temple] will give birth to her children
just as soon as she feels the birth pains [[C]the rebirth of the nation will be sudden and unexpected].
[9]·In the same way I will not cause pain [[L]Will I bring one to the moment of birth…?]
without allowing something new to be born," says the LORD.
"If I cause you ·the pain [to deliver],
·I will not stop you from giving birth to your new nation [[L]will I (now) close the womb?]," says your God.

[10]"·Jerusalem, rejoice [*or* Rejoice with Jerusalem].
All you people who love Jerusalem, be ·happy [glad for/with her].
Those of you who ·felt sad [mourned] for Jerusalem
should now ·feel happy [[L]rejoice with joy] with her.
[11]You will ·take comfort from her [[L]nurse] and be satisfied,
·as a child is nursed by its mother [[L]at her comforting breasts].
You will ·receive her good things [[L]drink deeply]
·and enjoy her wealth [from her glorious abundance]."
[12]This is what the LORD says:
"I will give her peace that will flow to her like a river.
The ·wealth [glory] of the nations will come to her like a ·river overflowing its banks [flood].
·Like babies you will [[L]You will] be nursed and held in ·my [[L]her] arms
and bounced on ·my [[L]her] knees.
[13]I will comfort you
as a mother comforts her child.
You will be comforted in Jerusalem."

[14]When you see these things, ·you [[L]your heart] will ·be happy [rejoice],
and ·you [*or* your bones] will ·grow [flourish] like the grass.
The LORD's servants will see his ·power [[L]hand],
but his enemies will see his ·anger [wrath].
[15]Look, the LORD is coming with fire
and his ·armies [[L]chariots] with ·clouds of dust [a whirlwind].
He will ·punish those people with his anger [[L]satisfy/render his anger with fury/wrath];
he will ·punish them [[L]satisfy/render his rebuke] with flames of fire.
[16]The LORD will judge the people with fire,
and he will ·destroy many people [judge all people] with his sword;
·he will kill many people [[L]many will be slain by the LORD].

[17]"These people ·make themselves holy and pure [sanctify/consecrate
and purify themselves] to go ·to worship their gods in their [[L]into] gardens
[[C]pagan worship sites; 1:29]. Following ·each other [*or* their leader; [L]one],
they eat the meat of pigs and rats and other ·hateful [detestable; abomina-
ble] things. But they will ·all be destroyed [perish] together," says the LORD.
[18]"I know ·they have evil thoughts and do evil things [[L]their deeds and
thoughts], so I am ·coming to punish them [[L]coming]. I will gather all
nations and all ·people [[L]languages; tongues], and they will come together
and see my glory.
[19]"I will put a ·mark [sign] ·on some of the people [[L]among them], and
I will send ·some of these saved people [*or* those who survive] to the
nations: to Tarshish [2:16], ·Libya [[L]Pul], Lud (·the land of archers [[L]who
draw the bow]), Tubal, ·Greece [[L]Javan], and all the faraway ·lands [*or*
islands; *or* coastlands]. These people have never heard about ·what I have
done [my fame] nor seen my glory. So ·the saved people [[L]they] will tell the
nations about my glory. [20]And they will bring all your ·fellow Israelites
[[L]brothers] from all nations to my holy mountain in Jerusalem as an offering to the LORD. ·Your fellow Israelites [[L]They] will come on horses, donkeys,
and camels and in chariots and wagons. They will be like the grain offerings
that the people bring in ·clean [pure; undefiled] ·containers [vessels] to the
Temple," says the LORD. [21]"And I will ·choose [take] even some of these
people to be priests and Levites," says the LORD.

22“I will make new heavens and the new earth, which will ·last forever
[endure before me],” says the LORD. “In the same way, your name and
your ·children [descendants; offspring; seed] will ·always be with me
[remain; endure]. 23All ·people [flesh] will come to worship me every
Sabbath and every New Moon,” says the LORD. 24“They will go out and see
the dead bodies of the people who ·sinned [rebelled] against me. The
worms that eat them will never die, and the fires that burn them will
never ·stop [be quenched], and ·everyone will hate to see those bodies
[Lthey will be a horror/abhorrence to all flesh].”

JEREMIAH

1 These are the words of Jeremiah son of Hilkiah [Cperhaps the person who discovered the lost book of the law; 2 Kin. 22:4, 8–14]. ·He belonged to the family of [L…from the] priests who lived in Anathoth [Ca town given to the Levites a few miles northeast of Jerusalem; Josh. 21:18; 1 Kin. 2:26] in the land of Benjamin. 2The LORD spoke his word to Jeremiah during the thirteenth year that Josiah son of Amon was king of Judah [C627–626 BC; a good king who returned Israel to true worship; 2 Kin. 22:1—23:31; 2 Chr. 34–35]. 3The LORD also spoke to Jeremiah while Jehoiakim [2 Kin. 23:34–37; 2 Chr. 36:4–8] son of Josiah was king of Judah and during the eleven years that Zedekiah [2 Kin. 24:18–20; 2 Chr. 36:11–16] son of Josiah was king of Judah. In the fifth month of his last year [C586 BC], the people of Jerusalem were taken away as ·captives [exiles; 2 Kin. 25:1–21; 2 Chr. 36:4–8].

The Lord Calls Jeremiah

4The LORD spoke his word to me, saying:

5"Before I ·made [formed] you in your mother's womb, I ·chose
[Lknew] you.
Before you ·were born [Lcame out of the womb], I ·set you apart for a
special work [consecrated you].
I appointed you as a prophet to the nations."

6Then I said, "But Lord GOD, I don't know how to speak. I am only a ·boy [child; youth]."

7But the LORD said to me, "Don't say, 'I am only a ·boy [child; youth].' You must go everywhere I send you, and you must say everything I ·tell you to say [Lcommand you]. 8Don't be afraid of anyone, because I am with you to protect you," says the LORD.

9Then the LORD ·reached [Lsent] out his hand and touched my mouth [Cto consecrate it; Is. 6:7]. He said to me, "See, I am putting my words in your mouth. 10Today I have ·put you in charge of [Lappointed you over] nations and kingdoms. You will ·pull [pluck] up and ·tear [pull] down, destroy and overthrow, build up and plant [Che will announce judgment and salvation]."

Jeremiah Sees Two Visions

11The LORD spoke his word to me, saying: "Jeremiah, what do you see?"

I answered, "I see a ·stick [branch] of almond ·wood [tree]."

12The LORD said to me, "You have seen correctly, because I am watching to make sure my words come true [C"to watch" (*shaqad*) sounds like "almond tree" (*shoqed*)]."

13The LORD spoke his word to me ·again [*or* a second time]: "What do you see?"

I answered, "I see a pot of boiling water, tipping over from the north."

[14]The LORD said to me, "Disaster will ·come [let loose; open up] from
the north and strike all the people who live in this country [[C]the
Babylonians would attack from the north]. [15]In a short time I will call all
of the ·people [clans] in the northern kingdoms," said the LORD.

"Those kings will come and set up their thrones
near the entrance of the gates of Jerusalem.
They will attack all the city walls around Jerusalem
and all the cities in Judah.
[16]And I will announce my judgments against my people
because of their evil in ·turning away from [abandoning; forsaking] me.
They ·offered sacrifices [*or* burned incense] to other gods
and ·worshiped [bowed down to] ·idols they had made with [[L]the
works of] their own hands.

[17]"Jeremiah, ·get ready [brace yourself; [L]gird up your loins]. Stand up
and tell them everything I command you to say. Don't be afraid of the
people, or I will give you good reason to be afraid of them. [18]Today I am
going to make you a ·strong [fortified] city, an iron pillar, a bronze wall.
You will be able to stand against everyone in the land: Judah's kings, officers, priests, and the people of the land. [19]They will fight against you, but
they will not ·defeat [prevail over] you, because I am with you to protect
you!" says the LORD.

Israel Turns from God

2 The LORD spoke his word to me, saying: [2]"Go and ·speak to the
people of Jerusalem [[L]announce/proclaim in the ears of Jerusalem],
saying: This is what the LORD says:

'I remember ·how faithful you were to me when you were a young
nation [[L]your loyalty/devotion as a youth/girl/child].
You loved me like a young bride.
You ·followed [[L]went after] me through the ·desert [wilderness; [C]as
they traveled from Egypt to the Promised Land],
a land that had never been ·planted [sown].
[3]The people of Israel were holy to the LORD,
like the firstfruits from his harvest [[C]both belonged to God; Ex.
23:19; Lev. 23:10–14; Num. 18:12–13; Deut. 26:1–11].
Those who tried to ·hurt Israel [[L]consume it] were judged guilty.
·Disasters [Troubles] ·struck [[L]came to] them,'" says the LORD.

[4]Hear the word of the LORD, ·family [[L]house] of Jacob,
all you ·family groups [[L]clans of the house] of Israel.
[5]This is what the LORD says:
"·I was fair to your ancestors,
so why did they turn away from me? [[L]What wrong did your
ancestors/fathers find in me
that they removed themselves from me?]
Your ·ancestors [fathers] ·worshiped [[L]went after] ·useless idols
[worthless/meaningless things]
and became ·useless [worthless; meaningless] themselves.
[6]Your ·ancestors [fathers] didn't say,
'Where is the LORD who brought us out of Egypt?
He led us through the ·desert [wilderness],
through a ·dry [barren] and ·rocky [broken] land,
through a dangerous [parched] and dark land.
He led us where no one ·travels [passes through] or lives.'

[7]I brought you into a ·fertile land [orchard; land of plenty]
so you could eat its fruit and produce.
But you came and made my land unclean [Cin a ritual sense];
you made ·it [Lmy inheritance] a ·hateful place [abomination].
[8]The priests didn't ask,
'Where is the LORD?'
The people who ·know [handle; deal with] the ·teachings [laws; instructions; LTorah] didn't know me.
The ·leaders [Lshepherds] turned against me.
The prophets prophesied in the name of Baal [Deut. 13:1–5]
and ·worshiped useless idols [Lwent after unprofitable things].

[9]"So now I will ·again tell what I have against [accuse; charge] you," says the LORD.
"And I will ·tell what I have against [accuse; charge] ·your grandchildren [Lthe sons of your sons].
[10]·Go across the sea [LCross over] to the ·island [*or* coasts] of Cyprus [Cto the west] and see.
Send someone to the land of Kedar [Ceastern desert nomads; Gen. 25:13; Jer. 49:28–29; Song 1:5] to look closely.
See if there has ever been anything like this.
[11]Has a nation ever exchanged its gods?
(·Of course, its gods are not really gods at all [LAnd they are not gods].)
But my people have exchanged their glory [CGod]
for ·idols worth nothing [Lunprofitable things].
[12]·Skies [Heavens], be shocked at the things that have happened
and ·shake [shudder] with great fear!" says the LORD.
[13]"My people have done two evils:
They have ·turned away from [abandoned; forsaken] me,
the ·spring [fountain] of living water [17:13].
And they have dug their own ·wells [cisterns],
which are broken ·wells [cisterns] that cannot hold water [Cthe idols, like the wells, are useless].
[14]Have the people of Israel become slaves?
Have they become like ·someone who was born a slave [a home-born servant; Ex. 21:4]?
Why ·were they taken captive [Lhave they become plunder]?
[15]·Enemies have roared like lions at Israel [LThe lions roar against him];
they have ·growled at Israel [Lgiven forth their voice].
They have ·destroyed [Lmade a desolation of] the land of Israel.
The cities of Israel lie in ruins,
·and all the people have left [and there are no inhabitants].
[16]The ·men from the cities [Lsons] of ·Memphis [LNoph] and Tahpanhes [Ctwo important Egyptian cities]
have ·shaved [*or* broken] the top of your head [Cdisgracing them; Israel embarrassed itself by entering into alliances with Egypt; 41:5; 48:37; 2 Sam. 10:4; Is. 7:20; Ezek. 44:20].
[17]·Haven't you brought this on yourselves [LDid you not do this to yourself]
by ·turning away from [abandoning; forsaking] the LORD your God
when he was leading you in the ·right way [*or* path]?

18·It did not help to go to [LWhy would you go on the path to…?] Egypt
and drink from the Shihor River [Cthe Nile or one of its tributaries].
·It did not help to [LWhy would you…?] go to Assyria
and drink from the River [Cthe Euphrates].
19Your evil will ·bring punishment to [instruct; discipline] you,
and ·the wrong you have done [your apostasy/infidelity] will ·teach
you a lesson [reprove/convict/rebuke you].
·Think about it and understand [LKnow and see]
that it is ·a terrible evil [Levil and bitter] to ·turn away from [abandon;
forsake] the LORD your God.
It is wrong not to fear me,"
says the Lord GOD ·All-Powerful [Almighty; of Heaven's Armies; Tof
hosts].

20"Long ago you broke your yoke [Cabandoning God].
You snapped off your ropes [Crejecting their dependence on God]
and said, 'I will not serve you!'
In fact, on every high hill
and under every green tree
you lay down as a prostitute [Cworshiping at pagan altars in the hills;
Deut. 12:2; 1 Kin. 14:13; 2 Kin. 17:10; Is. 57:5; 65:7; Ezek. 6:12;
20:28; Hos. 4:13].
21But I planted you as a ·special [choice] vine [Is. 5:1–7],
·as a very good seed [from good stock].
How then did you turn
into a wild vine [Cgrowing bad fruit]?
22Although you wash yourself with ·cleanser [lye]
and use much soap [Mal. 3:2],
I can still see the stain of your guilt," says the Lord GOD.
23"How can you say to me, 'I am not ·guilty [Ldefiled].
I have not ·worshiped [Lgone after] the Baals [Cidols]'?
Look at ·the things you did [Lyour way/path] in the valley.
·Think about [Know] what you have done.
You are like a she-camel
that runs from place to place [Cas if in heat].
24You are like a wild donkey that lives in the ·desert [wilderness]
and sniffs the wind ·at mating time [when in heat].
At that time who can hold ·her back [back her lust]?
None who ·chase [seek] her ·will easily catch her [Lneed to exert
themselves];
·at mating time [Lin her month], it is easy to find her.
25Stop before your feet are bare
or your throat is dry [Cfrom running after her].
But you say, 'It's no use!
I love those strangers [Cother gods],
and I must ·chase [Lgo after] them!'

26"A thief is ·ashamed [humiliated] when someone ·catches [discovers]
him.
In the same way, the ·family [Lhouse] of Israel is ·ashamed
[humiliated]—
they, their kings, their ·officers [princes],
their priests, and their prophets.

27They say to ·things of wood [La tree], 'You are my father,'
and to a stone, 'You gave birth to me [Cidols were made out of wood and stone].'
Those people have turned their backs to me,
not their faces.
But when they get into trouble, they say,
'·Come [LRise up] and ·save [rescue] us!'
28Where are the gods you made for yourselves [Cidols]?
Let them ·come [Lrise up] and ·save [rescue] you
when you are in trouble [Deut. 32:37–38; Is. 43:8–13; 44:6–23]!
People of Judah, you have as many gods [Cidols]
as you have towns!

29"Why do you ·complain to [charge; accuse] me?
All of you have ·turned [rebelled; transgressed] against me," says the LORD.
30"I ·punished [Lstruck] your ·people [Lchildren], ·but it did not help [Lin vain].
They didn't ·come back when they were punished [Laccept instruction/discipline].
With your swords you ·killed [devoured] your prophets
like a ·hungry [ravenous] lion [Ps. 7:2; 10:9; Is. 5:29].
31"·People of Judah [LOh generation], ·pay attention [Llook] to the
word of the LORD:
Have I been a ·desert [wilderness] to the people of Israel
or a dark land [Cuseless or even dangerous]?
Why do my people say, 'We are ·free to wander [our own masters].
We won't come to you anymore'?
32·A young woman does not [LDoes a virgin…?] forget her ·jewelry [ornaments],
and ·a bride does not [Ldoes a bride…?] forget the decorations for her dress.
But my people have forgotten me
for more days than can be counted.
33·You really know how to chase after love [LHow well you know the path to seek lovers!].
Even ·the worst [evil] women can learn ·evil ways from you [Lyour ways/paths].
34Even on your clothes you have the blood
of poor and innocent people,
but ·they weren't thieves you caught breaking in [Lyou did not find them breaking in; Cin which case they could have killed them in self-defense; Ex. 22:2].
You do all these things,
35 but you say, 'I am innocent.
·God is not angry with me [LHis anger has turned from me].'
But I will judge you [Cguilty of lying],
because you say, 'I have not sinned.'
36It is so easy for you to change your ·mind [Lway; path].
Even Egypt will ·let you down [Lshame/embarrass you],
as Assyria ·let you down [Lshamed/embarrassed you].
37You will eventually ·leave that place [Lgo out]
with your hands on your head [Clike captives].

·You trusted those countries [^LFor the LORD has rejected these in whom you had confidence],
and you will not ·be helped by [find success with] **them.**

Judah Is Unfaithful

3 **"If a man ·divorces** [^Lsends away] **his wife**
and she leaves him and marries another man,
should her first husband come back to her again?
If he went back to her, wouldn't the land become completely ·unclean [defiled; polluted; ^Cin a ritual sense; such a thing was forbidden by the Law; Deut. 24:1–4]**?**
But you have acted like a prostitute with many lovers,
and now you want to come back to me?" says the LORD [Hos. 2:7]**;**
2"**·Look up** [^LLift up your eyes and look] **to the bare hilltops, Judah.**
Is there any place where ·you have not been a prostitute [^Lyou have not been lain with; ^Cthe hill country contained many pagan altars]**?**
You have sat by the road waiting for lovers,
like an Arab in the ·desert [wilderness]**.**
You made the land ·unclean [defiled; polluted; ^Cin a ritual sense]**,**
because you did evil and were like a prostitute.
3**So the rain has ·not come** [^Lbeen withheld]**,**
and there have not been any spring rains [1 Kin. 17:1]**.**
But ·your face still looks like the face [^Lyou have the forehead] **of a prostitute** [^Cunembarrassed]**.**
You refuse even to be ashamed of what you did.
4**·Now you are** [^LAre you not now...?] **calling to me,**
'My father, you have been my friend since I was young.
5**Will you always be angry at me?**
Will your anger last ·forever [^Lto the end]**?'**
Judah, you said this,
but you did as much evil as you could!"

Judah and Israel Are like Sisters

6**·When** [^LIn the days when] **Josiah** [^CJeremiah began his work in
Josiah's thirteenth year (626 BC) and continued until Josiah's death (609
BC) and beyond; 1:1–3] **was ·ruling Judah** [^Lking], **the LORD said to me,**
"Did you see what unfaithful Israel did? She was like a prostitute with
her idols on every hill and under every green tree [2:20]. 7**I said to myself,**
'Israel will come back to me after she does this evil,' but she didn't come
back. And Israel's ·wicked [traitorous; treacherous] **sister Judah saw what**
she did [Ezek. 13; 26]. 8**Judah saw that I ·divorced** [^Lsent away with a certificate of divorce] **unfaithful Israel because of her adultery** [^Cin the
Assyrian exile of 722 BC], **but that didn't make Israel's ·wicked** [traitor-
ous; treacherous] **sister Judah afraid. She also went out and acted like a**
prostitute! 9**And she didn't care that she was acting like a prostitute. So**
she made her country ·unclean [defiled; polluted; ^Cin a ritual sense] **and**
was guilty of adultery with stone and wood [^Cby worshiping idols made
of these materials]. 10**Israel's ·wicked** [traitorous; treacherous] **sister,**
Judah, didn't even come back to me with her whole heart, but only pre-
tended," says the LORD.

11**The LORD said to me, "·Unfaithful** [Apostate] **Israel ·had a better**
excuse [^Lis more righteous] **than ·wicked** [traitorous; treacherous] **Judah.**
12**Go and speak ·this message** [^Lthese words] **toward the north:**
'·Come back [Return], **·unfaithful** [apostate] **people of Israel,' says the LORD.**

'I will ·stop being angry [no longer frown; [L]make my face fall] at you,
because I am ·full of mercy [loyal],' says the LORD.
'I will not be angry with you forever.
13·All you have to do is admit your sin—[[L]Acknowledge your guilt]
that you ·turned [rebelled; transgressed] against the LORD your God
and ·worshiped gods [[L]scattered your ways to strangers] under every
green tree [2:20]
and didn't ·obey me [[L]listen to my voice],' " says the LORD.

14"·Come back [Return] to me, you ·unfaithful [apostate] children,"
says the LORD, "because I am your master. I will take one person from
every city and two from every ·family group [clan], and I will bring you to
·Jerusalem [[L]Zion; [C]the location of the Temple]. 15Then I will give you ·new
rulers [[L]shepherds] ·who will be faithful to me [[L]according to my heart],
who will ·lead [shepherd] you with knowledge and ·understanding
[insight]. 16In those days ·there will be many of you [[L]you will multiply and
be fruitful] in the land," says the LORD. "At that time people will no longer
say, 'The Ark of the ·Agreement [[L]Covenant; Testimony; Treaty; Ex. 25:10].'
They won't remember it or miss it or make another one. 17At that time
people will call Jerusalem The Throne of the LORD [[C]due to God's pres-
ence], and all nations will ·come together [gather] in Jerusalem to ·show
respect to [[L]the name of] the LORD [12:15–16; 16:19; Is. 2:2–4; 56:6–7; Mic.
4:1–3; Zech. 2:11; 8:2–23; 14:16–17]. They will not ·follow [[L]go after] their
stubborn, evil hearts anymore. 18In those days the ·family [[L]house] of
Judah will join the ·family [[L]house] of Israel. They will come together from
a land in the north to the land I ·gave their ancestors [[L]caused their ances-
tors/fathers to inherit; [C]the future return from exile].

19"I, the LORD, said,
'How ·happy I would be to treat you as [[L]I would set you among] my
own children
and give you a ·pleasant [favored; coveted; desired] land,
a ·land [inheritance] more beautiful than that of any other nation
[Ex. 3:8, 17; Lam. 2:15; Ezek. 20:6; Dan. 11:16, 41].'
I thought you would call me 'My Father'
and not turn away from me.
20But like a woman who is ·unfaithful [a traitor; treacherous] to her husband,
·family [[L]house] of Israel, you have been unfaithful [a traitor;
treacherous] to me," says the LORD.

21You can hear ·crying [[L]a voice] on the bare hilltops [3:2].
It is the people of Israel crying and ·praying for mercy [supplicating].
They have ·become very evil [[L]wandered off their path]
and have forgotten the LORD their God.

22"Come back to me, you ·unfaithful [apostate] children,
and I will ·forgive [[L]heal] you for being ·unfaithful [apostate]."

"Yes, we will come to you,
because you are the LORD our God.
23·It was foolish to worship idols on [[L]Deception/Illusions come from]
the hills
and ·orgies [[L]a tumult] on the mountains.
Surely the salvation of Israel
comes from the LORD our God.

24 **Since our youth, shameful things** [Cfalse gods] **have eaten up**
everything our ·ancestors [fathers] **worked for—**
their flocks and herds,
their sons and daughters.
25 **Let us lie down in our ·shame** [humiliation],
and let our disgrace cover us.
We have sinned against the LORD our God,
both we and our ·ancestors [fathers].
From our youth until now,
we have not ·obeyed [Llistened to the voice of] **the LORD our God."**

4 **"If you ·will** [want to] **return, Israel,**
then return to me," says the LORD.
"If you will ·throw away [turn from] **your abominations** [Cthe idols],
then ·don't wander away from me [no longer go astray].
2 **If you say when you ·make a promise** [swear],
'As surely as the LORD lives,'
and you can say it in a truthful, ·honest [just], **and ·right** [righteous] **way,**
then the nations will be blessed by him,
and they will ·praise him for what he has done [boast in him]."
3 **This is what the LORD says to the people of Judah and to Jerusalem:**
"Plow your unplowed fields [Ca metaphor for changing their spiritual condition],
and don't ·plant seeds [sow] **among thorns.**
4 **·Give yourselves to the service of** [LCircumcise yourself to] **the LORD** [Ca metaphor for obedience],
and ·decide to obey him [Lremove the foreskin of your heart; 9:25; Deut. 10:16],
people of Judah and ·people [Linhabitants] **of Jerusalem.**
If you don't, my anger will ·spread among you [flare/blaze up] **like a fire,**
and no one will be able to ·put it out [quench it],
because of the evil you have done.

Trouble from the North

5 **"·Announce this message** [Declare; Shout; LLet it be heard] **in Judah**
and ·say [proclaim] **it in Jerusalem:**
'Blow the ·trumpet [ram's horn] **throughout the ·country** [land]!'
Shout out loud and say,
'·Come [LGather] **together!**
Let's all ·escape [Lgo] **to the ·strong, walled** [fortified] **cities!'**
6 **Raise the ·signal flag** [banner; Cmilitary insignia] **toward ·Jerusalem** [LZion; Cthe location of the Temple]!
·Run for your lives [Take refuge/shelter], **and don't ·wait** [delay],
because I am bringing ·disaster [trouble] **from the north** [Cthe Babylonians; 1:13–14]
There will be terrible destruction."

7 **A lion has come out of his ·den** [lair; thicket; 2:15];
a destroyer of nations has begun to march.
He has left his ·home [Lplace]
to ·destroy [Lset destruction in] **your land.**
Your towns will be ·destroyed [devastated]
with no one left to live in them.

[8]So put on ·rough cloth [sackcloth; burlap; [C]mourning clothes],
·show how sad you are [lament; mourn], and ·cry loudly [wail].
The ·terrible [fierce] anger of the LORD
has not turned away from us.

[9]"·When this happens [[L]In that day]," says the LORD,
"the ·king and officers will lose their courage [[L]heart of king and
officers/princes will fail].
The priests will be ·terribly afraid [desolate],
and the prophets will be ·shocked [stunned; appalled]!"
[10]Then I said, "[[L]Aha,] Lord GOD, you have ·tricked [deceived] ·the
people of Judah [[L]this people] and Jerusalem. You said, 'You will have
peace,' but now the sword ·is pointing at [[L]touches] our ·throats [*or* very
lives]!"
[11]At that time ·this message will be given [[L]it will be said] to Judah and
Jerusalem: "A hot wind blows from the bare hilltops [3:2] of the ·desert
[wilderness] toward the ·LORD's [[L]daughter of my] people. ·It is not a gentle wind to separate grain from chaff [[L]...not for winnowing or for
cleansing]. [12]I feel a stronger wind than that. Now even I will announce
judgments against ·the people of Judah [[L]them]."
[13]Look! ·The enemy [[L]He] rises up like a cloud,
and his chariots come like a ·tornado [whirlwind].
His horses are faster than eagles.
·How terrible it will be for [Woe to] us! We are ·ruined [devastated]!
[14]People of Jerusalem, ·clean [wash] the evil from your hearts so that
you can be ·saved [rescued; 2:22; Ps. 51:7].
·Don't continue making [[L]How long will you lodge in your heart/
mind] evil plans.
[15]A voice from Dan makes an announcement
and ·brings bad news [[L]proclaims disaster/trouble] from the
mountains of Ephraim.
[16]"Report this to the nations.
·Spread this news [[L]Make it heard] in Jerusalem:
'Invaders are coming from a faraway country [[C]Babylon],
shouting [[C]war cries] against the cities of Judah.
[17]The enemy has surrounded Jerusalem as men guard a field,
because Judah ·turned [rebelled; transgressed] against me,'" says the
LORD.
[18]"·The way you have lived and acted [[L]Your path/way and your deeds]
has brought this trouble to you.
This is your ·punishment [trouble; disaster].
How ·terrible [bitter] it is!
·The pain stabs [[L]It reaches] your heart!"

Jeremiah's Cry

[19]Oh, ·how I hurt [my pain/anguish/[L]innards]! ·How I hurt [My pain/
anguish/[L]innards]!
·I am bent over in pain [[L]My heart writhes].
Oh, the ·torture in [[L]walls of] my heart!
My heart is pounding inside me.
I cannot keep quiet,
because I have heard the sound of the ·trumpet [ram's horn].
I have heard the shouts of war.

[20]Disaster after disaster is reported;
the whole country has been ·destroyed [devastated].
My tents are ·destroyed [devastated] ·in only a moment [suddenly].
My curtains are torn down quickly.
[21]How long must I look at the war flag?
How long must I listen to the ·war trumpet [Lsound of the ram's horn]?

[22]The LORD says, "My people are ·foolish [stupid].
They do not know me.
They are stupid children;
they don't understand.
They are ·skillful [wise] at doing evil,
but they don't know how to do good."

Disaster Is Coming

[23]I looked at the earth,
and it ·had no form and was empty [was a formless void; Gen. 1:2].
I looked at the ·sky [Lheavens],
and ·its light was gone [Lthere was no light].
[24]I looked at the mountains,
and they were shaking.
All the hills were ·trembling [rocking; reeling].
[25]I looked, and there were no people.
Every bird in the ·sky [heavens] had ·flown away [Lfled].
[26]I looked, and the good, ·rich land [fertile land; land of plenty;
orchards] had become a ·desert [wilderness].
All its towns had been destroyed
by the LORD and his great anger.
[27]This is what the LORD says:
"All the land will be ruined,
but I will not ·completely destroy it [Lmake a complete end].
[28]So the people in the land will ·cry loudly [mourn; wail],
and the ·sky [Lheavens above] will grow dark [Is. 13:10; 34:4;
Zech. 14:6; Mark 13:24–25],
because I have spoken and made a decision.
I will not change my mind; I will not turn back."

[29]At the sound of the horsemen and the archers,
all the people in the towns ·run away [flee].
They ·hide [Lgo] in the thick bushes
and climb up into the rocks.
All of the cities of Judah are ·empty [abandoned; forsaken];
no one lives in them.
[30]You destroyed nation [CJudah], what are you doing?
Why do you put on ·scarlet [purple; Can expensive dress]
and decorate yourself with gold jewelry?
Why do you ·put color around your eyes [Lenlarge your eyes with black
eye paint]?
You make yourself beautiful, ·but it is all useless [in vain; without
purpose].
Your lovers ·hate [despise; reject] you;
they ·want to kill you [Lseek your life].

[31]I hear a cry like a woman ·having a baby [writhing in labor],
·distress [trouble] like a woman having her first child.
It is the sound of ·Jerusalem [[L]the daughter of Zion; [C]the location of the Temple] gasping for breath.
She ·lifts [[L]spreads] her hands in prayer and says,
"·Oh! I am about to [Woe to me, for I am] faint
before my murderers!"

No One Is Right

5 The LORD says, "·Walk [*or* Run] up and down the streets of Jerusalem.
Look around and ·discover [know] these things.
Search the public squares of the city.
If you can find one person who does ·honest [just] things,
who ·searches for the truth [*or* seeks to be faithful],
I will forgive this city.
[2]Although the people say, 'As surely as the LORD lives!'
they ·don't really mean it [[L]swear/take an oath falsely]."

[3]LORD, ·don't you [[L]do your eyes] look for ·truth [faithfulness] in people?
You struck ·the people of Judah [[L]them],
but they didn't feel any ·pain [anguish].
You ·crushed [consumed] them,
but they refused to ·learn what is right [[L]take your correction/instruction].
·They became more stubborn [[L]Their faces became harder] than a rock;
they refused to ·turn back to God [[L]return; repent].
[4]But I thought,
"These are only the poor, ·foolish people [[L]they have no sense].
They ·have not learned [[L]do not know] the ·way [path] of the LORD
and ·what their God wants them to do [[L]the ordinances/judgments of their God].
[5]So I will go to the ·leaders [great; *or* rich]
and talk to them.
Surely they ·understand [[L]know] the ·way [path] of the LORD
and ·know what God wants them to do [[L]the ordinances/judgments of their God]."
But even ·the leaders [[L]they] had all joined together to break their yoke [[C]abandoning God];
they had snapped off their ropes [[C]rejecting their dependence on God; 2:20].
[6]So a lion from the forest will ·attack [[L]strike] them.
A wolf from the desert will ·kill [destroy] them.
A leopard is ·waiting for [[L]watching] them near their towns.
It will ·tear to pieces [make prey of] anyone who comes out of the city,
because the people of Judah have ·sinned [rebelled; transgressed] greatly.
·They have wandered away from the LORD many times [Their apostasies are great].

[7]The LORD said, "·Tell me why I should [[L]How can I...?] forgive you.
Your children have ·left [abandoned; forsaken] me
and have ·made promises [[L]sworn] to those who are not gods at all [[C]idols].

I ·gave your children everything they needed [Lsatisfied/sated them],
but they still ·were like an unfaithful wife to me [committed adultery].
They ·spent much time in [frequented; trooped to] houses of prostitutes.
8They are like well-fed horses filled with ·sexual desire [lust];
each one ·wants [Lneighs after] another man's wife [3:6–10].
9Shouldn't I punish them [Cthe people of Judah] for doing these things?" says the LORD.
"Shouldn't I ·give a nation such as this the punishment [Lget revenge on a nation as] it deserves?

10"Go along and ·cut down [destroy] her [CJudah's] ·vineyards [rows of vines; Is. 5:1–7],
but do not ·completely destroy them [Lmake a complete end; 4:27].
Cut off its branches [Crepresenting the people],
because they do not belong to the LORD.
11The ·families [Lhouses] of Israel and Judah
have been completely ·unfaithful [traitorous; treasonous] to me,"
says the LORD.

12Those people have lied about the LORD
and said, "He will not do anything to us!
·Nothing bad [No evil/trouble/harm] will happen to us!
We will never see ·war [Lsword] or ·hunger [famine]!
13The prophets are wind [Cempty];
the word [Cof God] is not in them.
Let the bad things they say happen to them."
14So this is what the LORD God ·All-Powerful [Almighty; of Heaven's
Armies; Tof hosts] says:
"Because they have spoken this word [Cthat God would not punish them],
the words I ·give you [Lplace in your mouth] will be like fire,
and these people will be like wood that it ·burns up [consumes; devours].
15Listen, ·family [Lhouse] of Israel," says the LORD,
"I will soon bring a nation from far away ·to attack [Lagainst] you.
It is an ·old [ancient] nation that has ·lasted [endured] a long time [CBabylon].
·The people there speak a language [Its language/Ltongue] you do not know [CAramaic or Akkadian];
you cannot ·understand [Lhear] what they say.
16Their ·arrows bring death [Lquiver is like an open grave].
All their people are strong warriors.
17They will ·eat [consume; devour] your crops and your food.
They will ·eat [consume; devour] your sons and daughters.
They will ·eat [consume; devour] your flocks and herds.
They will ·eat [consume; devour] your ·grapes [Lvines] and ·figs [Lfig trees].
They will destroy with their swords
the ·strong, walled [fortified] cities you ·trust [have confidence in].

18"Yet even ·then [Lin those days]," says the LORD, "I will not ·destroy
you completely [Lmake a complete end; v. 10; 4:27]. 19When the people
[Cof Judah] ask, 'Why has the LORD our God done all these things to us
[Chis acts of judgment]?' then give them this answer: 'You have ·left [aban-
doned; forsaken] the LORD and served foreign gods [Cidols] in your own
land. So now you will serve ·foreigners [Lstrangers] in a land that does not
belong to you.'

20"·Announce this message [Proclaim this] to the ·family [Lhouse] of
Jacob [CIsrael],
and ·tell it to the nation of [Lmake this heard in] Judah:
21Hear this message, you foolish people who have no ·sense [Lheart].
They have eyes, but they don't really see.
They have ears, but they don't really listen [CGod's people are like the
idols they worship; Ps. 115:6; 135:17].
22·Surely you are afraid of me [LDo you not fear me?]," says the LORD.
"·You should shake with fear [LDo you not tremble…?] in my
presence.
I am the one who ·made the beaches [Lset sand] to be a border for the
sea,
a ·border [limit] the water can never go past.
·The waves may pound the beach [LThey may rise and fall], but they
can't win over it.
·They [LThe waves] may roar, but they cannot go beyond it.
23But this people [Cof Judah] ·are stubborn and have turned against me
[Lhave a stubborn and rebellious heart].
They have turned aside and gone away from me.
24They do not say ·to themselves [Lin their hearts],
'We should fear the LORD our God [Prov. 1:7],
who gives us ·autumn [early] and ·spring [late] rains in their seasons,
who ·makes sure we have the harvest at the right time [brings us
unfailingly the weeks appointed for harvests].'
25But your ·evil [iniquities] has kept these [Crain and harvest] away.
Your sins have kept you from enjoying good things.
26There ·are wicked men [Lwicked are found] among my people.
Like ·those who make nets for catching birds [fowlers],
they set their traps to catch people.
27Like cages full of birds,
their houses are full of ·lies [deceit].
They have become ·powerful [great] and rich.
28 They have grown fat and sleek.
There is no end to the evil things they do.
They do not judge justly.
They won't plead the case of the orphan [Ex. 22:22–24; Deut. 10:18;
24:17, 19–21; 27:19]
or help the poor be judged fairly [Ex. 22:25–27; 23:6, 11; Deut. 15:11].
29Shouldn't I punish them [Cthe people of Judah] for doing these
things?" says the LORD.
"Shouldn't I ·give a nation such as this the punishment [Lget revenge
on a nation as] it deserves [v. 9]?

30"A terrible and shocking thing
has happened in the land [Cof Judah]:

31The prophets ·speak lies [[L]prophesy falsely; Deut. 18:14–22],
and the priests ·take power [rule] ·into their own hands [*or* by their
hand/control],
and my people love it this way.
But what will you do when the end comes?

Jerusalem Is Surrounded

6 "·Run for your lives [Take refuge/shelter], ·people [[L]sons] of Benjamin!
·Run away [Take refuge/shelter] from Jerusalem!
Blow the ·war trumpet [ram's horn] in the town of Tekoa [[C]about ten
miles southeast of Jerusalem]!
Raise the warning flag over the town of Beth Hakkerem [[C]"House of
Vineyards," of uncertain location]!
·Disaster [Evil] is coming from the north [[C]Babylon];
terrible destruction is coming to you.
2·Jerusalem [[L]Daughter of Zion; [C]the location of the Temple], I ·will
destroy you,
you who are fragile and gentle [*or* compare you to a delightful pasture].
3Shepherds [[C]leaders of the attacking army] with their flocks will come
against it [[C]Jerusalem].
They will set up their tents all around her,
each shepherd taking care of his own section."
4They say, "·Get ready to fight [[L]Consecrate yourselves for war; [C]against
Jerusalem; ancient Near Eastern peoples performed religious
rituals before battle]!
Get up! We will attack at noon!
·But it is already getting late [[L]Woe to us, for the day declines];
the evening shadows are growing long.
5So get up! We will attack at night.
We will destroy ·the strong towers [[L]its palaces]!"
6This is what the LORD ·All-Powerful [Almighty; of Heaven's Armies;
[T]of hosts] says:
"Cut down the trees [[C]around Jerusalem],
and ·build an attack ramp to the top of its walls [throw up a siege
ramp].
This city must be punished.
Inside it is nothing but ·slavery [oppression]
7Jerusalem ·pours out her evil [keeps its wickedness fresh]
as a well ·pours out its water [keeps its water fresh]
The sounds of violence and destruction are heard within her.
I can see the sickness and hurts ·of Jerusalem [always before me].
8·Listen to this warning [[L]Be instructed], Jerusalem,
or I will turn my back on you
and make your land an ·empty desert [[L]desolation]
where no one can live."
9This is what the LORD ·All-Powerful [Almighty; of Heaven's Armies;
[T]of hosts] says:
"·Gather [[L]Glean] the ·few people of Israel who are left alive [[L]remnant
of Israel],
as ·you would gather the last grapes on a grapevine [[L]a vine; [C]Israel is
often compared to a vine; Gen. 49:11–12, 22; Ps. 80:9–10; Is. 5:1–2].
·Check each vine again [[L]Return your hand over it again],
like ·someone who gathers grapes."

10To whom can I speak? Whom can I warn?
Who will listen to me?
·The people of Israel have closed ears [LYour ears have a foreskin; Care uncircumcised; a metaphor for not listening to God],
so they cannot ·hear my warnings [Lpay attention].
·They don't like the word of the LORD [LThe word of the LORD is a reproach to them];
they ·don't want to listen to it [Ltake no pleasure in it]!
11But I am full of the anger of the LORD,
and I am ·tired [weary] of holding it in.

"Pour ·out my anger [Lit out] on the children who play in the street
and on the young men gathered together.
A husband and his wife will both be caught in his anger,
as will the very old and ·aged [Lfull of years].
12Their houses will be turned over to others,
along with their fields and wives,
because I will ·raise [Lstretch out] my hand
·and punish [Lagainst] the people of Judah," says the LORD.
13"Everyone, from the least important to the greatest,
is greedy for ·money [unjust gain].
Even the prophets and priests
all ·tell lies [act falsely; are deceptive].
14They tried to heal my people's ·serious injuries [fracture]
as if they were small wounds.
They said, '·It's all right, it's all right [LPeace, peace].'
But ·really, it is not all right [Lthere is no peace].
15They should be ashamed of the ·terrible way they act [abominations they do],
but they are not ashamed at all.
They don't even know how to blush [Cabout their sins].
So they will fall, along with ·everyone else [Lthose who fall].
They will ·be thrown to the ground [stumble] ·when [Lat the time] I punish them," says the LORD.
16This is what the LORD says:
"Stand ·where the roads cross [at the crossroads] and look.
Ask where the ·old [eternal; enduring] way is [Deut. 32:7],
where the good way is, and walk on it.
If you do, you will find rest for ·yourselves [souls].
But they have said, 'We will not ·walk on the good way [follow it].'
17I set watchmen [Cprophets] over you
and told you, '·Listen for [Pay attention to] the sound of the ·war trumpet [ram's horn]!'
But they said, 'We will not ·listen [pay attention].'
18So listen, all you nations,
and ·pay attention [Lknow], you ·witnesses [assembly].
Watch what I will do to them [Cthe people of Judah].
19Hear this, people of the earth:
I am going to bring ·disaster [trouble; evil] to this people [Cof Judah]
because of the ·evil they plan [Lthe fruit of their plots].
They have not ·listened [paid attention] to my ·messages [words]
and have rejected my ·teachings [laws; instructions].

20Why do you bring me offerings of ·incense [frankincense] from the land of Sheba [Cunknown location, perhaps present-day Yemen, Eritrea, or Ethiopia; see 1 Kin. 10:1–13]?
Why do you bring me sweet-smelling cane from a faraway land?
Your burnt offerings [Lev. 1:1–7] will not be accepted;
your sacrifices do not please me [Ps. 40:6–8; Mic. 6:6–8]."
21So this is what the LORD says:
"I will put stumbling blocks [Cproblems] in front of this people [CJudah].
Fathers and sons will stumble over them together.
Neighbors and friends will ·die [perish]."
22This is what the LORD says:
"Look, an ·army [people] is coming
from the land of the north [CBabylon];
a great nation is ·coming [Lstirred up]
from the far sides of the earth.
23·The soldiers carry [LThey grasp/seize] bows and ·spears [javelins].
They are ·cruel [fierce] and show no ·mercy [compassion].
They sound like the roaring ·ocean [sea; Csymbol of chaos]
when they ride their horses.
That army is ·coming lined up [*or* equipped] for battle,
ready to attack you, ·Jerusalem [Ldaughter of Zion; Cthe location of the Temple]."

24We have heard the news about ·that army [Lthem]
and ·are helpless from fear [Lour hands grow limp].
We are gripped by our ·pain [distress],
like a woman ·having a baby [writhing in childbirth].
25Don't go out into the fields
or walk down the ·roads [paths],
because the enemy has swords.
There is terror on every side.
26·My people [LDaughter of my people], put on ·rough cloth [sackcloth; burlap]
and roll in the ashes [Cmourning rituals].
·Cry loudly for those who are dead,
as if your only son were dead [LMake mourning/Wail for your only son, a bitter lamentation],
because the destroyer
will ·soon [*or* suddenly] come against us.

27"I have made you [CJeremiah] like a ·worker who tests metal [Ltester and refiner/*or* fortress] among people [Cwho are like the ore].
You must ·observe [know] their ways
and test them.
28All my people have ·turned [rebelled] against me and are stubborn.
They go around ·telling lies about others [slandering].
They are like bronze and iron [Crusted, not refined]
that act dishonestly.
29The ·fire is fanned to make it hotter [bellows blow],
but the lead ·does not melt [is consumed by the fire].
·The pure metal does not come out [LThe refining is in vain];
the evil is not removed from my people.

30My people will be called rejected silver,
because the LORD has rejected them [Ezek. 22:17–22].”

Jeremiah's Temple Message

7 This is the word that the LORD spoke to Jeremiah: 2“Stand at the
gate of the ·Temple [Lhouse of God] and ·preach [proclaim] this
·message [Lword] there:
“ ‘Hear the word of the LORD, all you people of the nation of Judah! All
you who come through these gates to ·worship [bow down to] the LORD,
listen to this message! 3This is what the LORD ·All-Powerful [Almighty; of
Heaven's Armies; Tof hosts], the God of Israel, says: ·Change your lives
and do what is right [LReform/Amend your ways/paths and your deeds]!
Then I will ·let you live [*or* live with you] in this place. 4Don't ·trust [put
confidence in] ·the lies of people who say [Lfalse words], “This is the
Temple of the LORD. This is the Temple of the LORD. This is the Temple of
the LORD [Cpresumptuously thinking that God will not destroy the city as
long as his house is there]!” 5You must ·change your lives and do what is
right [Lreform/amend your ways/paths and your deeds]. Be fair to each
other. 6You must not ·be hard on [oppress] ·strangers [resident aliens],
orphans, and widows [Deut. 10:18]. Don't ·kill [Lspill the blood of] innocent people in this place! Don't ·follow [Lgo after] other gods, or they will
·ruin [harm; hurt] your lives. 7If you do these things, I will ·let you live [*or*
live with you] in this land that I gave to your ·ancestors [fathers] ·to keep
forever [Lforever and ever].
8“ ‘But look, you ·are trusting [have confidence in] ·lies [Lfalse words],
which is useless. 9Will you steal and murder and be guilty of adultery?
Will you falsely ·accuse other people [take oaths; swear]? Will you ·burn
incense [make offerings] to the god Baal and ·follow [Lgo after] other gods
you have not known? 10If you do that, do you think you can come before
me and stand in this ·place [Lhouse] ·where I have chosen to be worshiped
[Lwhich is called by my name]? Do you think you can say, “We are safe!”
when you do all these ·hateful things [abominations]? 11This ·place
[Lhouse] ·where I have chosen to be worshiped [Lthat is called by my
name] is nothing more to you than a ·hideout [den] for robbers [Mark
11:17; Luke 19:46]. I have been watching you, says the LORD.
12“ ‘You people of Judah, go now to the town of Shiloh, where I ·first
[formerly] made ·a place to be worshiped [Lmy name dwell]. See what I
did to it because of the evil things the people of Israel had done. 13You
[Cthe people of Judah] have done all these evil things too, says the LORD. I
spoke to you again and again, but you did not listen to me. I called you,
but you did not answer. 14So I will destroy the ·place [Lhouse] ·where I
have chosen to be worshiped in Jerusalem [which is called by my name].
You ·trust [have confidence] in that place, which I gave to you and your
·ancestors [fathers], but I will destroy it just as I destroyed Shiloh [1 Sam.
4:1–22; Ps. 78:60–64]. 15I will ·push you [throw you] away from me just as
I ·pushed [threw] away your ·relatives [Lbrothers], the people of Israel
[Lall the seed of Ephraim; Cthe dominant tribe of the northern kingdom of
Israel, exiled by the Assyrians in 722 BC]!’
16“As for you [CJeremiah], don't pray for these people. Don't cry out for
them or ask anything for them or ·beg me to help them [intercede with
me], because I will not listen to you. 17Don't you see what they are doing
in the towns of Judah and in the streets of Jerusalem? 18The children
gather wood, and the fathers use the wood to make a fire. The women

·make [knead] the dough for cakes of bread, and they offer them to the
Queen ·Goddess [Lof Heaven; Cprobably Ishtar or Asherah, important
goddesses of the surrounding cultures; 44:17–18]. They pour out drink
offerings to other gods to make me angry. 19But ·I am not the one [Lis it I
whom…?] the people of Judah are really hurting, says the LORD. ·They are
[LAre they not…?] only hurting themselves and bringing ·shame [humili-
ation] upon themselves.
20" 'So this is what the Lord GOD says: I will pour out my anger and
wrath on this place, on people and animals, on the trees in the field and
the ·crops in the [Lfruit of the] ground. My anger will not be ·put out
[extinguished; Clike a fire].

Obedience Is More than Sacrifice

21" 'This is what the LORD ·All-Powerful [Almighty; of Heaven's Armies;
Tof hosts], the God of Israel, says: ·Offer [LAdd your] burnt offerings [Lev.
1:1–17] along with your other sacrifices, and eat the ·meat [Lflesh] yourselves [Cit was forbidden to eat the meat of the burnt offering]! 22When I
brought your ·ancestors [fathers] out of Egypt, I did not speak to them
and give them commands only about burnt offerings [Lev. 1:1–17] and
sacrifices. 23I also ·gave them this command [Lcommanded this word]:
·Obey me [LListen to my voice], and I will be your God and you will be my
people. ·Do all that I command [LWalk in my way/path] so that ·good
things will happen to you [things might be well with you]. 24But your
·ancestors [fathers] did not listen or ·pay attention [Lbend their ear] to
me. They were stubborn in their evil hearts and ·did whatever they
wanted [Lwalked in their own counsels]. They went backward, not forward. 25Since the day your ·ancestors [fathers] left Egypt until today, I
have sent my servants, the prophets, again and again to you. 26But your
·ancestors [fathers] did not listen or ·pay attention [Lbend the ear] to me.
·They were very stubborn [LTheir necks were stiff] and they did more evil
than their ·ancestors [fathers].'
27"You [CJeremiah] will tell all these ·things [words] to them [Cthe people of Judah], but they will not listen to you. You will ·call [preach;
proclaim] to them, but they will not answer you. 28So say to them, 'This is
the nation that has not ·obeyed [Llistened to the voice of] the LORD its
God. These people do ·nothing when I correct them [Lnot accept the dis-
cipline/instruction]. ·They do not tell the truth [LThe truth perishes]; it
·has disappeared from their lips [Lis cut off from their mouths].

The Valley of Killing

29" 'Cut off your hair [Cthe Hebrew phrase suggests a Nazirite vow and
thus consecrated hair; Num. 6:5] and throw it away. Go up to the bare hilltop [3:2] and ·cry out [lament], because the LORD has rejected these people.
He has turned his back on ·them, and in his anger will punish them [Lthe
generation that enrages him]. 30The ·people [descendants; sons] of Judah
have done ·what I said was evil [Levil in my eyes], says the LORD. They have
set up their ·hateful [loathsome; abominable] idols in the ·place where I
have chosen to be worshiped [Lhouse that is called by my name] and have
made it ·unclean [defiled; Cin a ritual sense]. 31The people of Judah have
built ·places of worship [Lhigh places; Csites associated with pagan worship
or inappropriate worship of God; Deut. 12] at Topheth in the Valley of Ben
Hinnom [2 Kin. 23:10–11]. There they burned their own sons and daughters as sacrifices, something I never commanded. It never even entered my
·mind [Lheart; Lev. 18:21; Deut. 12:31; 18:10]. 32So, I warn you. The days are
coming, says the LORD, when people will not call this place Topheth [C"Spit"]

or the Valley of Ben Hinnom anymore. They will call it the Valley of ·Killing
[Slaughter]. They will bury the dead in Topheth until there is no room to
bury anyone else [19:1–15]. 33Then the ·bodies of the dead [corpses] will
become food for the birds of the ·sky [heavens] and for the ·wild animals
[Lanimals of the earth]. There will be no one ·left alive to chase [Lto frighten]
them away. 34I will end the happy sounds of the bride and bridegroom.
There will be no happy sounds in the cities of Judah or in the streets of
Jerusalem, because the land will become an empty desert!

8 " 'The LORD says: At that time they will ·remove [Lbring out] from
their tombs the bones of Judah's kings and ·officers [princes],
priests and prophets, and the ·people [inhabitants] of Jerusalem. 2The
bones will be spread on the ground under the sun, moon, and ·stars [Lthe
hosts of heaven] that the people loved and served and went after and
searched for and ·worshiped [bowed down to]. No one will gather up the
bones and bury them. So they will be like dung on the ground. 3·I will
force the people of Judah to leave their homes and their land. Those of
this evil family who are not dead will wish they were [LDeath will be pre-
ferred to life by all the remnant of those who remain from this evil clan in
all the places where I have driven them], says the LORD ·All-Powerful
[Almighty; of Heaven's Armies; Tof hosts].'

Sin and Punishment

4"Say to them [Cthe people of Judah]: 'This is what the LORD says:
When people fall down, don't they get up again?
And when someone goes the wrong way, doesn't he turn back?
5Why, then, have the people of Jerusalem gone the wrong way
and not turned back?
They ·believe their own lies [persisted in deceit/treachery]
and refuse to turn back.
6I have ·listened to them very carefully [paid attention and listened],
but they do not say what is ·right [honest].
They do not ·feel sorry about their wicked ways [Lrepent of evil],
saying, "What have I done?"
Each person ·goes his own way [runs his course],
like a horse ·charging [plunging] into a battle.
7Even the storks in the ·sky [heavens]
know ·the right times to do things [their appointed times].
The ·doves [turtledoves], ·swifts [*or* swallows], and ·thrushes [*or* cranes]
·know [observe] when it is time to ·migrate [return].
But my people don't know
·what the LORD wants them to do [Lthe ordinances/judgments of the
LORD].

8" '·You keep saying [LHow can you say…?], "We are wise,
·because we have the teachings of the LORD [Land the teachings/laws/
instructions of the LORD are with us]."
But actually, ·those who explain the Scriptures
have written lies with their pens [Lthe false pens of the scribes have
made it a lie].
9These wise teachers ·refused to listen to [Lrejected] the word of the LORD,
so ·they are not really wise at all [Lwhat wisdom is in them?].
They will be ·ashamed [humiliated].
They will be ·shocked [stunned; astonished] and trapped.

10So I will give their wives to other men
and their fields to ·new owners [*or* conquerors].
Everyone, from the least important to the greatest,
is greedy for ·money [unjust gain].
Even the prophets and priests
all ·tell lies [act falsely; are deceptive; 6:13].
11They tried to heal my people's ·serious injuries [fracture]
as if they were small wounds.
They said, "·It's all right, it's all right [LPeace, peace]."
But ·really, it is not all right [Lthere is no peace; 6:14].
12They should be ashamed of the ·terrible way they act [abominations
they do],
but they are not ashamed at all.
They don't even know how to blush [Cabout their sins].
So they will fall, along with ·everyone else [Lthose who fall].
They will ·be thrown to the ground [stumble] ·when [Lat the time] I
punish them, says the LORD [6:15].

13" 'I will ·take away their crops [Lgather them; *or* bring an end to them],
says the LORD.
There will be no grapes on the vine
and no figs on the fig tree.
Even the leaves will dry up.
I will take away what I gave them.' "

14"Why are we just sitting here?
Let's ·get [gather] together!
We have sinned against the LORD,
so he has given us poisoned water to drink.
Come, let's ·run [Lgo] to the ·strong, walled [fortified] cities.
The LORD our God has ·decided that we must die [doomed us],
so let's ·die [meet our doom] there.
15We hoped to have peace,
but ·nothing good has come [Lthere is none].
We hoped for a time when he would heal us,
but only terror has come.
16From the land of Dan [Cin the far north of Israel, the direction from
which the Babylonians attacked],
the snorting of its [Cthe enemy's] horses is heard.
The ·ground [earth] shakes from the neighing of their ·large horses
[stallions].
They have come and ·destroyed [Lconsumed]
the land and everything in it,
the city and all ·who live there [its inhabitants]."

17"Look! I am sending poisonous snakes [Cto attack you].
These ·snakes [vipers] cannot be charmed,
and they will bite you," says the LORD.

Jeremiah's Sadness

18God, ·you are my comfort when I am very sad [Lmy cheerfulness is
gone; grief has come on me]
and ·when I am afraid [Lmy heart is sick].

[19]Listen to the ·sound [Lcry of distress] of ·my people [Lthe daughter of
my people].
They cry from a faraway land:
"Isn't the LORD still in ·Jerusalem [LZion; Cthe location of the
Temple]?
Isn't ·Jerusalem's [Lits] king still there?"

But God says, "Why did the people make me angry ·by worshiping
idols [Lwith their images],
useless foreign idols?"

[20]And the people say, "Harvest time is over;
summer has ended,
and we have not been ·saved [rescued]."

[21]Because my people are ·crushed [broken; fractured], I am ·crushed
[broken; fractured].
I ·cry loudly [mourn; lament; wail] and ·am afraid for them [Lhorror
has seized me].
[22]Isn't there balm [Cthe resin of the storax tree used as medicine] in the
land of Gilead [Csouthern section of the Transjordan region]?
Isn't there a doctor there?
So why ·aren't the hurts of my people healed [Lis there no new skin
on the wound of the daughter of my people]?

9 ·I wish [Oh that] my head were like a spring of water
and my eyes like a fountain of tears!
Then I could cry day and night
for ·my people who have been killed [Lthe corpses of the daughter of
my people].
[2]·I wish [Oh that] I had a place in the ·desert [wilderness]—
a house where travelers spend the night—
so I could ·leave [abandon; forsake] my people.
I could go away from them,
because they are all adulterers [Cunfaithful to God; 2:20, 23–24; 3:1–5;
Hos. 7:4];
·they are all turning against him [La band of traitors].

Judah's Failures

[3]"They ·use [Lbend] their tongues like a bow [Cshooting lies from their
mouths like arrows; Ps. 64:3–4].
Lies, not truth,
have grown strong in the land.
They go from one evil thing to another.
They do not know ·who I am [Lme]," says the LORD.
[4]"·Watch out [Be on guard] for your ·friends [*or* neighbors],
and don't ·trust [have confidence in] your own ·relatives
[Lbrothers],
because every ·relative [Lbrother] is a ·cheater [LJacob, who supplants;
Gen. 25:19—35:29],
and every ·friend [*or* neighbor] ·tells lies about [Lgoes around
slandering] you.
[5]Everyone ·lies to [deceives] his ·friend [*or* neighbor],
and no one speaks ·the truth [honestly].

They [Cthe people of Judah] have taught their tongues to ·lie [Ltell
falsehoods].
They have become tired from ·sinning [their iniquity].
6You [CJeremiah] live in the middle of lies.
The people refuse to know me," says the LORD.
7So this is what the LORD ·All-Powerful [Almighty; of Heaven's Armies;
Tof hosts] says:
"I will test them [Cthe people of Judah] as a person ·tests [refines]
metal in a fire [6:27–30].
·I have no other choice [LFor what else can I do…],
because ·my people have sinned [Lof the daughter of my people?].
8Their tongues are like ·sharp [Ldeadly] arrows.
Their mouths speak ·lies [deceit].
Everyone speaks ·nicely [peace] to his ·neighbor [*or* friend],
but he ·is secretly planning to attack him [Lsets his ambush in his
innards/inwardly].
9Shouldn't I punish the people [Cof Judah] for doing this?" says the
LORD.
"Shouldn't I ·give a nation like this the punishment [Lget revenge on
a nation as] it deserves?"

10I [CJeremiah] will ·cry loudly [Ltake up crying and wailing] for the
mountains
and sing a ·funeral song [lamentation] for the ·empty fields
[Lpastures of the wilderness].
They are ·empty [scorched], and no one passes through.
The ·mooing [Lsound] of cattle cannot be heard.
The birds of the ·air [heavens]
and the animals have fled and are gone.

11"I, the LORD, will make the city of Jerusalem a heap of ruins,
a home for wild dogs.
I will destroy the cities of Judah
so no one can live there."
12What person is wise enough to understand these things? Is there
someone who has been ·taught [Lspoken to] by the LORD who can explain
them [Hos. 14:9]? Why was the land ·ruined [scorched]? Why has it been
made like an empty desert where no one goes?
13The LORD answered, "It is because Judah ·quit following [abandoned;
forsook] my ·teachings [laws; instructions] that I gave them. They have
not ·obeyed me [Llistened to my voice] or ·done what I told them to do
[Lwalked in it]. 14Instead, they ·were stubborn [Lwalked after their stubborn hearts] and ·followed [Lwalked after] the Baals, as their ·ancestors
[fathers] taught them to do." 15So this is what the LORD ·All-Powerful
[Almighty; of Heaven's Armies; Tof hosts], the God of Israel, says: "I will
soon make the people of Judah eat ·bitter food [Lwormwood; Cthe bitter
tasting leaves of a shrub] and drink poisoned water. 16I will scatter them
through other nations that they and their ·ancestors [fathers] never knew
about. I will ·chase [pursue; Lsend after] them [Cthe people of Judah] with
the sword until they are all ·killed [consumed; finished]."
17This is what the LORD ·All-Powerful [Almighty; of Heaven's Armies;
Tof hosts] says:
"Now, ·think about these things [Lreflect; consider]!

Call for the women who ·cry at funerals [mourn; [C]professional
mourners] to come.
Send for those women who are ·good at that job [skilled; wise].
18Let them come quickly
and ·cry loudly [wail; [L]raise a lament] for us.
Then our eyes will ·fill [flow] with tears,
and ·streams of water will flow from our eyelids [[L]eyelids will run
with water].
19The sound of ·loud crying [lamentation] is heard from ·Jerusalem
[[L]Zion; [C]the location of the Temple]:
'We are ·truly ruined [devastated; desolated]!
We are truly ·ashamed [humiliated]!
We must ·leave [abandon; forsake] our land,
because our ·houses [residences] are ·in ruins [[L]thrown down].'"

20Now, women [[C]of Judah], listen to the word of the LORD;
·open your ears to hear [[L]let your ears take in] the words of his mouth.
Teach your daughters ·how to cry loudly [a lament].
Teach ·one another [[L]each her neighbor] a ·funeral song [dirge].
21Death has climbed in through our windows
and has entered our ·strong cities [palaces].
·Death has taken away [[L]...to cut off] our children who play in the streets
and the young men ·who meet in [[L]from] the city squares.
22Say, "This is what the LORD says:
'The ·dead bodies [corpses] of people will ·lie [[L]fall]
in the open field like dung.
They will lie like grain ·a farmer has cut [[L]after the harvester/reaper],
but there will be no one to gather them.'"
23This is what the LORD says:
"The wise must not ·brag [boast] about their wisdom.
The strong must not ·brag [boast] about their strength.
The rich must not ·brag [boast] about their ·money [riches].
24But if people want to ·brag [boast], let them ·brag [boast]
that they understand and know me.
Let them ·brag [boast] that I am the LORD,
and that I am ·kind [loyal] and ·fair [just],
and ·that I do things that are right [righteous] on earth.
·This kind of bragging pleases me [[L]In this I am pleased]," says the
LORD [1 Cor. 1:31; 2 Cor. 10:17; James 1:9–10].
25The LORD says, "The ·time is [[L]days are] coming when I will punish all
those who are circumcised only in the ·flesh [[L]foreskin; [C]observing external rituals (Gen. 17:9–14), but not from the heart; 4:4; 6:10]: 26the people
of Egypt, Judah, Edom, ·Ammon [[L]the sons of Ammon], Moab, and the
·desert [wilderness] people who ·cut their hair short [[L]shave their temples;
Deut. 14:1]. ·The men in all those countries [[L]All these nations] are not
circumcised. And the ·whole family [[L]house] of Israel ·does not give itself
to serving me [[L]is uncircumcised in/of heart]."

The Lord and the Idols

10 ·Family [[L]House] of Israel, ·listen to what [[L]hear the word
that] the LORD says to you. 2This is what he says:
"Don't ·live like the people from [[L]learn the way/path of] other nations,
and don't be ·afraid of [terrified by] special signs in the ·sky
[heavens; [C]astrology],
even though the other nations are ·afraid [terrified] of them.

[3]The ·customs [statutes; ordinances; requirements] of other people are
·worth nothing [meaningless; useless; [L]a breath].
·Their idols are just wood cut from the forest [[L]A tree from the forest
is cut down],
shaped by a ·worker [craftsman] with his ·chisel [*or* ax; *or* adze; *or* blade].
[4]They decorate their idols with silver and gold.
With hammers and nails they fasten them down
so they ·won't fall over [can't move].
[5]Their idols are like scarecrows in ·melon [*or* cucumber] fields;
they cannot talk.
Since they cannot walk,
they must be carried.
Do not be afraid of those idols,
because they can't hurt you,
and they ·can't help you either [have no power to do good;
Is. 40:18–20; 41:7, 29; 44:6–23; 46:5–7]."

[6]LORD, there is no one like you.
You are great,
and your name is great and powerful.
[7]·Everyone should respect [[L]Who does not fear…?] you, King of the
nations;
·you deserve respect [for it is your due].
Of all the wise people among the nations
and in all the kingdoms,
·none of them is as wise as you [[L]there is none like you].
[8]Those wise people are stupid and foolish.
Their ·teachings [instructions] come from ·worthless [meaningless;
useless] ·wooden idols [[L]pieces of wood].
[9]Hammered silver is brought from Tarshish [[C]Tarshish may have been in
Spain (Tartessus) or an island in the eastern Mediterranean; Jonah 1:3]
and gold from Uphaz [[C]high quality],
so the idols are made by craftsmen and ·goldsmiths [smelters].
They put blue and purple clothes on the idols.
All these things are made by skilled workers.
[10]But the LORD is the only true God.
He is the only living God, the King forever.
The earth ·shakes [trembles] when he is angry,
and the nations cannot ·stand up to [endure] his anger.
[11]"Tell them this message: 'These gods did not make heaven and earth;
they will ·be destroyed and disappear [perish] from heaven and earth
[[C]this verse is in Aramaic, indicating it was a well known saying].'"
[12]God made the earth by his power.
He used his wisdom to ·build [[L]establish] the world
and his understanding to stretch out the ·skies [heavens].
[13]When he ·thunders [[L]gives forth his voice], the waters in the ·skies
[heavens] ·roar [are in tumult].
He makes ·clouds [*or* mist] rise ·in the sky all over the earth [[L]from
the ends of the earth].
He sends lightning with the rain
and brings out the wind from his storehouses.

[14]People are so stupid and know so little.
·Goldsmiths [Smelters] are ·made ashamed [humiliated] by their idols,
because those ·statues are only false gods [[L]images are false].
They have no breath in them.
[15]They are ·worth nothing [useless; meaningless; [L]a breath]; ·people make fun of them [laughable; a derision].
When they are judged, they will ·be destroyed [perish].
[16]But Jacob's [[C]another name for Israel] Portion [[C]referring to the Lord; God gives himself to Israel] is not like ·the idols [[L]these].
He ·made [[L]formed] everything,
and ·he chose Israel to be his special people [[L]Israel is the tribe of his inheritance].
The LORD ·All-Powerful [Almighty; of Heaven's Armies; [T]of hosts] is his name.

Destruction Is Coming

[17]·Get everything you own [[L]Gather your goods] ·and prepare to leave [*or* from the ground],
you people who are ·trapped by your enemies [[L]under siege].
[18]This is what the LORD says:
"At this time I will ·throw [[L]sling] out the people who live in this land.
I will bring ·trouble [distress] to them
so that they may be ·captured [[L]squeezed]."

[19]·How terrible it will be for me [Woe to me] because of my ·injury [fracture].
My wound ·cannot be healed [is severe].
Yet I told myself,
"This is my ·sickness [*or* punishment]; I must ·suffer through [endure] it."
[20]My tent is ·ruined [destroyed; desolated],
and all its ropes are broken.
My children have gone away and left me.
No one is left to ·put up [stretch out] my tent again
or to set up ·a shelter for me [[L]my curtains].
[21]The shepherds are stupid
and don't ·ask the LORD for advice [[L]seek the LORD].
So they do not have success,
and all their flocks are scattered.
[22]Listen! The news is coming.
A ·loud noise [great commotion] comes from the north [[C]the Babylonian army]
to make the towns of Judah an ·empty desert [desolation]
and a ·home [haunt] for wild dogs [jackals]!

Jeremiah's Prayer

[23]LORD, I know that ·our lives don't really belong to us [[L]his way/path does not belong to people].
·We can't control our own lives [[L]People as they walk cannot establish their steps].
[24]LORD, ·correct [teach; instruct] me, but be ·fair [just].
Don't punish me in your anger,
or you will ·destroy me [[L]make me dwindle].

25Pour out your anger on other nations
that do not know you
and do not pray to you.
Those nations have ·destroyed [consumed] the people of Jacob.
They have ·eaten [consumed] them up completely
and ·destroyed [desolated] their homeland.

The Agreement Is Broken

11 These are the words that the LORD spoke to Jeremiah: 2"Listen
to the words of this ·agreement [covenant; treaty] and tell
them to the people of Judah and those living in Jerusalem. 3Tell them this
is what the LORD, the God of Israel, says: 'Cursed is the person who does
not ·obey [listen to] the words of this ·agreement [covenant; treaty] 4that
I ·made with [Lcommanded] your ·ancestors [fathers] when I brought
them out of Egypt [Ex. 19–24]. Egypt was like a furnace for melting iron!'
I told them, '·Obey me [LListen to my voice] and do everything I command you. Then you will be my people, and I will be your God. 5Then I
will ·keep [confirm] the ·promise [oath] I made to your ·ancestors
[fathers] to give them a ·fertile land [Lland flowing with milk and honey;
Ex. 3:8].' ·And you are living in that country today [L...as it is today]."
I answered, "·Amen [So be it], LORD."
6The LORD said to me, "·Announce [Proclaim] ·this message [Lall these
words] in the towns of Judah and in the streets of Jerusalem: 'Listen to the
words of this ·agreement [covenant; treaty] and ·obey [Ldo] them. 7I
warned your ·ancestors [fathers] to obey me when I brought them out of
Egypt [Ex. 12–15]. I have warned them again and again to this very day:
"·Obey me [LListen to my voice]!" 8But your ·ancestors [fathers] did not
·listen [obey] or ·pay attention [Lbend their ear] to me. They ·were stubborn and did what their own evil hearts wanted [Lwalked in the stubborness
of their evil hearts]. So I made all the ·curses [Lwords] of this ·agreement
[covenant; treaty] come upon them [Deut. 28:15–68]. I commanded them
to obey the ·agreement [covenant; agreement], but they did not.'"
9Then the LORD said to me, "I know the people of Judah and those living in Jerusalem have made ·secret plans [a conspiracy]. 10They have
·gone back [returned] to the ·same sins their ancestors did [iniquity of
their fathers of old]. ·Their ancestors [LThey] refused to listen to my ·mes-
sage [Lwords] and ·followed and worshiped [Lwent after and served] other
gods instead [Ex. 20:3]. The ·families [Lhouse] of Israel and [Lthe house
of] Judah have broken the ·agreement [covenant; treaty] I ·made [Lcut]
with their ·ancestors [fathers]. 11So this is what the LORD says: 'I will soon
bring ·a disaster [harm; evil] on them [Cthe people of Judah] which they
will not be able to escape. They will cry to me for help, but I will not listen
to them. 12The ·people living in the towns [Ltowns] of Judah and the ·city
[Linhabitants] of Jerusalem will ·pray [Lcry for help] to ·their idols [Lthe
gods] to whom they burn incense. But ·those idols [Lthey] will not be able
to ·help [save them] when ·disaster [harm; evil] comes. 13Look, people of
Judah, you have as many ·idols [Lgods] as there are towns in Judah. You
have built as many altars to burn incense to that shameful god Baal as
there are streets in Jerusalem.'
14"As for you [CJeremiah], don't pray for these people or cry out for
them or ask anything for them. I will not listen when they call to me in
the time of their ·trouble [disaster; harm; evil].

15"What is my beloved [CJudah; 12:7; Deut. 33:12; Ps. 60:5; 108:6; 127:2; Is. 5:1] doing in my ·Temple [Lhouse]
when she makes many evil plans [Ctheir idolatry cancels their right to be there]?
Do you think ·animal sacrifices [Lsacred meat] will stop your ·punishment [disaster; harm; evil]?
Can you then be happy?"
16The LORD called you "a ·leafy [green] olive tree,
with beautiful fruit and shape [Hos. 14:6]."
But with the roar of a ·strong storm [tempest]
he will set that tree on fire,
and its branches will be burned up.
17The LORD ·All-Powerful [Almighty; of Heaven's Armies; Tof hosts],
who planted you, has announced that ·disaster [harm; evil] will come to
you. This is because the ·families [Lhouses] of Israel and Judah have done
evil and have made him angry by burning incense to Baal.

Evil Plans Against Jeremiah

18The LORD ·showed [Lmade known to] me that people were making
plans against me. Because he showed me what they were doing [Ctheir evil
deeds], I knew they were against me. 19Before this, I was like a gentle lamb
waiting to be ·butchered [slaughtered; Is. 53:7; John 1:29, 36]. I did not
know they had made plans against me, saying:
"Let us destroy the tree and its fruit.
Let's ·kill him [Lcut him off from the land of the living] so ·people will forget him [Lhis name will no longer be remembered]."
20But, LORD ·All-Powerful [Almighty; of Heaven's Armies; Tof hosts], you ·are a fair judge [judge righteously].
You know how to test peoples' ·hearts and minds [motives and thoughts].
I have ·told you what I have against them [committed my cause to you].
So let me see you give them the ·punishment [revenge] they deserve.
21So the LORD speaks about the people from Anathoth [CJeremiah's
hometown; 1:1; 12:6] who ·plan to kill Jeremiah [Lseek your life] and say,
"Don't prophesy in the name of the LORD, or ·we will kill you [Lyou will
die by our hand]!" 22So this is what the LORD ·All-Powerful [Almighty; of
Heaven's Armies; Tof hosts] says: "I will soon punish the men [Cfrom
Anathoth]. Their young men will die ·in war [Lby the sword]. Their sons
and daughters will die from ·hunger [famine]. 23·No one from the city of
Anathoth will be left alive [LThey will have no remnant], because I will
cause ·a disaster [harm; evil] to happen to them that year."

Jeremiah's First Complaint

12 LORD, when I bring ·my case to [charges against] you,
you are ·always right [righteous].
But I want to ·ask you about the justice you give [put my case to you].
Why ·are evil people [Lis the way/path of the wicked] successful?
Why do ·dishonest [treasonous; treacherous] people ·have such easy lives [thrive; Job; Ps. 73; Eccl. 7:15–18; 8:10–12]?
2You ·have put the evil people here
like plants with strong roots [Lplant them; they take root].
They grow and produce fruit [17:7–8].
·With their mouths they speak well of you [LYou are near in their mouths],
but ·their hearts are really far away from you [Lfar from their hearts/thoughts].

3But you know ·my heart [Lme], LORD.
You see me and test my ·thoughts [Lheart] about you [1:5; Ps. 139].
Drag the evil people away like sheep to be ·butchered [slaughtered].
·Set them aside [CConsecrate them] for the day of killing.
4How much longer will the land ·stay dried up [Lmourn]
and the grass in every field be ·dead [dry]?
The animals and birds in the land ·have died [Lare swept away],
because the people are evil.
Yes, they are even saying,
"God does not see what happens to us."

The Lord's Answer to Jeremiah

5"If you ·get tired while racing against people [Lraced with foot-runners and got tired],
how can you ·race against [compete with] horses?
·If you stumble in a country that is safe, [*or* You feel confident in a country that is safe, but…]
what will you do in the thick thornbushes along the Jordan River?
6Even your own brothers and ·members of your own family [Lthe house of your father]
are ·making plans against [betraying] you.
They are crying out against you.
Don't trust them,
even when they say nice things to you!

7"I have ·left [abandoned; forsaken] ·Israel [Lmy house; Ezek. 8:1—11:25];
I have ·left [cast off] my ·people [Linheritance].
I have given the people I love [CJudah]
·over to [Linto the palm of] their enemies.
8My ·people [Linheritance] have become to me
like a lion in the forest.
They ·roar [Lgive forth their voice] at me,
so I hate them.
9My people have become to me
like a ·speckled bird [*or* hyena's lair] attacked on all sides by ·hawks [birds of prey].
Go, gather the ·wild animals [Lbeasts of the field].
Bring them to get something to eat.
10Many shepherds [Cthe leaders of Judah] have ruined my vineyards
and trampled ·the plants in my field [Lmy portion].
They have turned my ·beautiful [precious; coveted; treasured] ·field [Lportion]
into an empty ·desert [wilderness].
11They have turned ·my field [Lit] into ·a desert [desolation]
that is ·wilted [desolate] and ·dead [Lmourns].
The whole country is ·an empty desert [desolate],
because no one ·who lives there cares [Lsets it on heart].
12·Many soldiers [LDestroyers] have marched over those barren hills.
·The LORD is using the armies to punish that land [LThe sword of the LORD devours]
from one end to the other.
·No one is safe [LThere is no peace for all flesh].

13 The people have planted wheat,
but they have harvested only thorns.
They have worked hard until they were very tired,
but they have nothing for all their work.
They are ashamed of their poor harvest,
because the LORD's terrible anger has caused this."

14 This is what the LORD said to me: "Here is what I will do to all my wicked neighbors [Clike Edom; Ps. 137:7; Obad. 10–14] who ·take [Ltouch] the ·land [Linheritance] I ·gave my people Israel [Lmade my people Israel inherit]. I will ·pull them up and throw them out of [Luproot them from] their land. And I will ·pull up [uproot] the ·people [Lhouse] of Judah from among them. 15 But after I ·pull them up [uproot them; 1:10], I will ·feel sorry for [have compassion on] them again. I will ·bring [restore] each person back to his own ·property [inheritance] and to his own land. 16 I want them to learn their lessons well. In the past they taught my people to swear by Baal's name. But if they will now learn to swear by my name, saying, 'As surely as the LORD lives...' I will ·allow them to rebuild [build them up] among my people. 17 But if a nation will not listen to my message, I will ·pull it up [uproot] completely and destroy it," says the LORD.

Jeremiah's Linen Belt

13 This is what the LORD said to me: "Go and buy a linen ·belt [loincloth; underwear; Cpriests like Jeremiah wore linen undergarments; Ex. 28:39; 39:27–29; Ezek. 44:17–18] and put it around your ·waist [loins]. Don't let the ·belt [loincloth; underwear] ·get wet [be washed; be brought into water]."

2 So I bought a ·linen belt [loincloth; underwear], just as the LORD told me, and put it around my ·waist [loins]. 3 Then the LORD spoke his word to me a second time: 4 "Take the ·belt [loincloth; underwear] you bought and ·are wearing [Lis on your loins], and go to Perath [Cthe name of the Euphrates River or a town near Jerusalem with a similar name (Josh. 18:23)]. Hide the ·belt [loincloth; underwear] there in a crack in the rocks." 5 So I went to Perath and hid the ·belt [loincloth; underwear] there, just as the LORD ·told [commanded] me.

6 ·Many days later [LAt the end of many days] the LORD said to me, "Now go to Perath [v. 4] and get the ·belt [loincloth; underwear] I ·told [commanded] you to hide there." 7 So I went to Perath and dug up the ·belt [loincloth; underwear] and took it from where I had hidden it. But now it was ruined; it was good for nothing.

8 Then the LORD spoke his word to me. 9 This is what the LORD said: "In the same way I will ·ruin [destroy; rot away] the pride of the people of Judah and the great pride of Jerusalem. 10 These evil people refuse to listen to my ·warnings [Lwords]. They ·stubbornly do only what they want to do [Lfollow/go after their stubborn hearts], and they ·follow [Lgo after] other gods to serve and ·worship [bow down to] them. So they will become like this ·linen belt [loincloth; underwear]—good for nothing. 11 As a ·belt [loincloth; underwear] ·is wrapped tightly around [clings to] a person's ·waist [loins], I ·wrapped the families of Israel and Judah around [Lcaused all the house of Israel and all the house of Judah to cling to] me," says the LORD. "I did that so they would be my people and bring fame, praise, and ·honor [splendor] to me. But my people would not listen.

Warnings About Leather Wine Bags

[12]"Say to them: 'This is what the LORD, the God of Israel, says: All
·leather bags for holding wine [wineskins] should be filled with wine.'
People will say to you: '·Of course, we know [LDo we not know that…?] all
wine bags should be filled with wine.' [13]Then you will say to them, 'This is
what the LORD says: I will ·make everyone in this land like a drunken person [Lfill with drunkenness all who live in this land; Cthey will drink from
the "cup of God's wrath" (25:15–18)]—the kings who sit on David's
throne, the priests and the prophets, and all the people who live in
Jerusalem. [14]I will make them smash against one another, fathers and
sons alike, says the LORD. I will not feel sorry or have pity on them or
show ·mercy [compassion] that would stop me from destroying them.'"

Threat of Slavery

[15]Listen and ·pay attention [Lgive ear].
Don't ·be too proud [exalt yourself],
because the LORD has spoken to you.
[16]Give glory to the LORD your God
before he brings darkness
and before ·you slip and fall [Lyour feet stumble]
on the dark hills.
You hope for light,
but he will turn it into thick darkness;
he will change it into deep gloom [Amos 5:18–20].
[17]If you don't listen to him,
I will cry secretly
because of your pride.
I will cry painfully,
and my eyes will ·overflow [run down] with tears,
because the ·LORD's people [Lthe flock of the LORD] will be ·captured [exiled].

[18]Tell this to the king and the queen mother [Lperhaps Jehoiachin and his mother Nehushta who went into exile in 597 BC (22:26; 29:2; 2 Kin. 24:8–17)]
"Come down from your thrones,
because your ·beautiful [splendid; glorious] crowns
·have fallen [*or* will fall] from your heads."
[19]The cities of ·southern Judah [Lthe Negev] are ·locked [shut] up,
and no one can open them.
All Judah will be ·taken as captives to a foreign land [exiled; Cto Babylon];
they will ·be carried away [exiled] completely [Cthe exile in 597 BC was a precursor to the more complete one in 586 BC].

[20]Look up and see [Caddressed to queen mother]
the people coming from the north [Cthe Babylonian army].
Where is the flock ·God gave you to care for [Lgiven to you],
·the flock you bragged about [Lyour splendid flock; Cthe people of Judah]?
[21]What will you say when ·they [*or* God] appoint as your ·heads [rulers]
those you had thought were your ·friends [allies]?
Won't ·you have much pain and trouble [Lpain seize you],
like a woman giving birth to a baby [4:31; 6:24; 22:23; 30:6; 48:41; 49:22, 24; 50:43]?

22You might ·ask yourself [Lsay in your heart],
"Why has this happened to me?"
It happened because of your many ·sins [iniquities].
Because of your ·sins [iniquities], your skirt was torn off
and your ·body [Lheel; Ceuphemism for genitals] has been ·treated badly [violated].
23Can a person from ·Cush [Ethiopia] change ·his skin [Lits color]?
Can a leopard change his spots?
In the same way, you [CJerusalem] cannot change and do good,
because you are accustomed to doing evil.

24"I will scatter you like chaff that is ·blown away [driven] by the ·desert [wilderness] wind.
25This is ·what will happen to you [Lyour lot];
·this is your part in my plans [Lthe portion decreed for you]," says the LORD.
"Because you forgot me
and ·trusted [had confidence] in ·false gods [falsehood; lies],
26I will pull your skirts up over your face
so everyone will see your ·shame [humiliation; Nah. 3:6].
27I have seen the terrible things you have done:
your acts of adultery and your ·snorting [neighing; Clike a horse in heat],
your prostitution,
your ·hateful [abominable; detestable] acts
on the hills and in the fields [Cwhere they had shrines to false gods].
·How terrible it will be for [Woe to] you, Jerusalem.
How long will you continue being unclean?"

A Time Without Rain

14 These are the words that the LORD spoke to Jeremiah ·about the
time when there was no rain [concerning the drought; Coften a
punishment from God; Lev. 26:18–20; Deut. 28:22–24; 1 Kin. 17:1]:
2"The nation of Judah ·cries as if someone has died [mourns],
and her ·cities [Lgates] ·are very sad [languish].
They ·are distressed [wail] over the land.
A cry goes up [Cto God] from Jerusalem.
3The ·important men [nobles] send their ·servants [Lyoung/little ones] to get water.
They go to the ·wells [cisterns],
but they find no water.
So they return with empty jars.
They are ·ashamed [humiliated] and embarrassed
and ·cover [veil] their heads [Cin shame].
4The ground is cracked open,
because no rain falls on the land.
The farmers are ·upset and sad [Lashamed],
so they ·cover [veil] their heads.
5Even the mother deer in the field
·leaves her newborn fawn to die [Lgives birth and leaves],
because there is no ·grass [vegetation].
6Wild donkeys stand on the bare hills
and ·sniff the wind [pant] like ·wild dogs [jackals].
But their eyes go blind,
because there is no ·food [pasture]."

7We know that we suffer because of our sins.
LORD, ·do something to help us for the good of your name [Lact on
behalf of your name/reputation].
·We have left you many times [LMany are our apostasies/infidelities];
we have sinned against you.
8The Hope of Israel [CGod],
you have ·saved [rescued] it [CIsrael] in times of ·trouble [distress].
Why are you like a ·stranger [alien resident] in the land,
or like a traveler who only stays one night?
9Why are you like someone who has been attacked by surprise,
like a warrior who is not able to ·save anyone [be victorious]?
But you are among us, LORD,
and we are called by your name
so don't ·leave us without help [forsake us]!
10This is what the LORD says about this people [Cof Judah]:
"They really love to wander from me;
they don't ·stop themselves from leaving me [Lrestrain their feet].
So now the LORD will not ·accept [be pleased with] them.
He will now remember ·the evil they do [their iniquity]
and will punish them for their sins."
11Then the LORD said, "Don't pray for good things to happen to the
people [Cof Judah]. 12Even if they fast, I will not listen to their ·prayers
[cry; Prov. 1:28]. Even if they offer burnt offerings [Lev. 1:1–17] and
·grain [Lgift; tribute] offerings [Lev. 2:1] to me, I will not ·accept [be
pleased with] them. Instead, I will ·destroy [finish] them [Cthe people of
Judah] with ·war [sword], ·hunger [famine], and ·terrible diseases
[plagues; pestilence]."
13But I said, "Oh, Lord GOD, the prophets keep telling the people, '·You
will not suffer from an enemy's [LDo not fear] sword or from ·hunger
[famine]. I, the LORD, will give you ·lasting [reliable; true] peace in this
land.'"
14Then the LORD said to me, "Those prophets are prophesying lies in
my name. I did not send them or ·appoint [command] them or speak to
them. They have been prophesying false visions, idolatries, worthless
·magic [divination], and ·their own wishful thinking [Lthe deceit of their
hearts; Deut. 13:1–5; 18:14–22]. 15So this is what I say about the prophets
who are prophesying in my name. I did not send them. They say, '·No
enemy will attack this country with swords. There will never be hunger
[LSword and famine will not be] in this land.' So those prophets will ·die
from [Lbe finished off by] ·hunger [famine] and from ·an enemy's sword
[Lsword]. 16And the people to whom the prophets speak will be thrown
into the streets of Jerusalem. There they will die from ·hunger [famine]
and from ·an enemy's sword [Lsword]. And no one will be there to bury
them, or their wives, or their sons, or their daughters. I will ·punish them
[Lpour out on them harm/disaster/evil].
17"Speak [Caddressed to Jeremiah] this ·message [word] to them [Cthe
people of Judah]:
'Let my eyes ·be filled [flow] with tears
night and day, without stopping.
·My people [LThe virgin daughter of my people] have received a
·terrible blow [Lgreat fracture];
they have been ·hurt [wounded] badly.

18 If I go into the ·country [Lfield],
I see people killed by swords.
If I go into the city,
I see ·much sickness, because the people have no food [Lthe sickness of famine].
Both the priests and the prophets
·have been taken to a foreign land [Lwander/*or* ply their trade in a land they do not know].' "

19 LORD, have you completely rejected the nation of Judah?
Do you ·hate [Labhor] ·Jerusalem [LZion; Cthe location of the Temple]?
Why have you ·hurt us so badly [Lstruck us]
·that we cannot be made well again [Land not healed us]?
We hoped for peace,
but nothing good has come.
We looked for a time of healing,
but only terror came.
20 LORD, we ·admit that we are wicked [Lknow our wickedness]
and ·that our ancestors did evil things [Lthe iniquity of our fathers].
We have sinned against you.
21 For ·your sake [Lthe sake of your name/fame/reputation], do not ·hate [despise] us [Lev. 26:11, 30, 44].
Do not ·take away the honor from [Ltreat disdainfully] your glorious throne.
Remember your ·agreement [covenant; treaty] with us,
and do not break it.
22 Do ·foreign idols [Lfutile/useless/meaningless things] have the power to bring rain?
Does the ·sky [heaven] itself have the power to send down showers?
·No, it is you [LIs it not you…?], LORD our God.
You are our only hope,
because you are the one who made all these things.

15 Then the LORD said to me: "Even if Moses and Samuel ·prayed
for them [Lstood before me], ·I [Lmy soul] would not ·feel
sorry for the people of Judah [Lturn toward this people; CMoses and
Samuel interceded on behalf of their sinful generations; Ex. 32:11–14,
30–34; Num. 14:13–19; 1 Sam. 7:5–11; 12:17–23]. Send them away from
me! Tell them to go! 2 When they ask you, 'Where will we go?' tell them:
'This is what the LORD says:
Those who are ·meant to die [Lfor death]
·will die [Lto death].
Those who are meant ·to die in war [Lfor the sword]
·will die in war [Lto the sword].
Those who are meant ·to die from hunger [Lfor famine]
·will die from hunger [Lto famine].
Those who are meant ·to be taken captive [Lfor exile]
·will be taken captive [Lto exile].'

3 "I will ·send [appoint] four kinds of destroyers against them," says the
LORD. "I will send ·war [Lthe sword] to kill, dogs to drag the bodies away,
and the birds of the ·air [sky; heavens] and ·wild animals [Lbeasts of the
land] to eat and destroy the bodies. 4 I will make them [Cthe people of

Judah] ·hated by [a horror to] everyone on earth because of what
Manasseh did in Jerusalem. (Manasseh son of Hezekiah was king of the
nation of Judah [Cfrom 698–642 BC; he was a particularly wicked king;
2 Kin. 21:1–18; 23:26–27].)
5 “Who will ·feel sorry for [have pity on] you, Jerusalem?
Who will ·be sad and cry [grieve] for you?
Who will go out of his way to ask how you are [Nah. 3:7]?
6 You [CJerusalem] have ·left me [cast me off],” says the LORD.
“You keep going ·farther and farther away [backward],
so I have ·taken hold of you [Lstretched out my hand] and destroyed you.
I was tired of ·holding back my anger [relenting].
7 I have ·separated [winnowed] them [Cthe people of Judah] with my
·pitchfork [winnowing fork] in the gates of the land.
My people haven’t changed their ways.
So I have destroyed ·them [Lmy people]
and ·taken away their children [bereaved them].
8 There are more widows than grains of sand in the sea [Can ironic
reference to Gen. 22:17; 32:12; 41:49].
I brought a destroyer at noontime
against the mothers of the young men of Judah.
I suddenly ·brought pain and fear
on the people of Judah [Lmade anguish and fear fall on them].
9 A woman with seven sons ·felt faint [languishes; Cbecause they would all die].
She ·became weak and unable to breathe [Lswoons].
Her ·bright day became dark from sadness [Lsun went down while it
was still day].
She felt ·shame [humiliation] and disgrace.
And ·everyone else left alive in Judah [Lthe rest of them]
I will hand over to the sword of their enemies, too!” says the LORD.

Jeremiah’s Second Complaint

10 Mother, ·I am sorry [woe to me] that you gave birth to me
·since I must accuse and criticize [La man of strife and contention to]
the whole land.
I have not loaned or borrowed anything,
but everyone curses me.
11 The LORD said,
“·I have [LHave I not…?] ·saved [*or* intervened for] you for a good reason.
·I have made your enemies beg you [*or* Will I not bring the enemy
against you…?]
in times of ·disaster [harm; evil] and ·trouble [distress].
12 ·No one can smash a piece of iron or bronze
that comes from the north [LCan iron break the iron of the north and
the bronze?; Cthe iron is Babylon (1:13–15; 4:6) and the bronze is
Jeremiah (15:20)].
13 Your wealth and treasures
I will give ·to others free of charge [Las plunder without price/charge],
because of all your [Cthe people of Judah] sins
throughout the country.
14 I will make you ·slaves to [serve] your enemies
in a land you have never known.
My anger ·is [Lkindles] like a hot fire,
and it will burn against you.”

15 LORD, you ·understand [Lknow].
Remember me and take care of me.
·Punish for me [Avenge me on] those who are ·hurting [persecuting; pursuing] me.
Don't ·destroy [snatch] me while you remain patient with them.
Think about the ·shame [reproaches] I ·suffer [endure] for you.
16 Your words ·came to me [Lwere found], and I ·listened carefully to [Late] them.
Your words made me very happy
and were the delight of my heart,
because I am called by your name,
LORD God ·All-Powerful [Almighty; of Heaven's Armies; Tof hosts].
17 I never sat with the ·crowd
as they laughed [Lcrowd of merrymakers/revelers] and ·had fun [LI did not rejoice].
I sat by ·myself [alone], ·because you were there [Lfrom before your hand/power],
and you filled me with anger [Cat the evil people around him].
18 ·I don't understand why my pain has [LWhy does my pain have...?] no end.
·I don't understand why my injury is not cured or healed [LMy wound is uncurable and refuses to be healed].
Will you be like a ·brook that goes dry [Ldeceitful brook]?
Will you be like a ·spring that stops flowing [Lunreliable spring]?
19 So this is what the LORD says:
"If you ·change your heart and return to me [Lreturn/repent], I will ·take you back [Lreturn to you].
Then you may ·serve me [Lstand before me].
And if you [CJeremiah] speak things that ·have worth [are precious], not useless words,
then you may ·speak for me [Lbe like my mouth].
Let them [Cthe people of Judah] turn to you,
but you must not ·change and be like them [Lturn to them].
20 I will make you as strong as a wall to this people,
·as strong [fortified] as a wall of bronze [v. 12].
They will fight against you,
but they will not ·defeat [prevail over] you,
because I am with you.
I will ·save [have victory for] you and ·rescue [protect] you," says the LORD.
21 "I will ·rescue [protect] you from ·these wicked people [Lthe hand/control of evil people]
and redeem you from ·these cruel people [Lthe hand of the violent]."

The Day of Disaster

16 Then the LORD spoke his word to me: 2 "You must not ·get married [Ltake a wife for yourself] or have sons or daughters in this place."
3 The LORD says this about the sons and daughters born in this ·land [Lplace] and their mothers who bear them and fathers who ·father [Lbeget] them in this land: 4 "They will die of ·terrible diseases [plagues; pestilence], and no one will ·cry for them [mourn] or bury them. Their bodies will lie on the ground like dung. They will ·die [perish] ·in war [Lby sword], or ·they will

starve to death [[L]by famine]. ·Their bodies [[L]They] will be food for the birds of the ·sky [air; heavens] and for the ·wild animals [[L]beasts of the land]."

5So this is what the LORD says [[C]addressed to Jeremiah]: "Do not go into a house where there is a funeral ·meal [feast; [C]a pagan mourning festival; Amos 6:7]. Do not go there to ·cry for the dead [lament] or to ·show your sorrow for [bemoan] them, because I have taken back my ·blessing [peace; welfare], my ·love [loyalty], and my ·pity [compassion] from these people," says the LORD. 6"·Important people and common people [[L]Great and small] will die in this land [[C]of Judah]. No one will bury them or ·cry [lament] for them or ·cut [gash] himself or shave his head for them [[C]pagan rituals of mourning; Lev. 19:27–28; 21:5; Deut. 14:1]. 7No one will ·bring food [break bread; [L]break] to comfort those who are crying for the dead. No one will offer a ·drink [[L]cup] to comfort someone whose mother or father has died.

8"Do not go into a ·house where the people are having a feast [banquet house; [L]drinking house] to sit down to eat and drink, 9because this is what the LORD ·All-Powerful [Almighty; of Heaven's Armies; [T]of hosts], the God of Israel, says: I will soon stop the sounds of joy and gladness and the happy sounds of brides and bridegrooms in this place. This will happen ·during your lifetime [[L]in your days and before your eyes].

10"When you tell this people [[C]of Judah] these things, they will ask you, 'Why has the LORD said these ·terrible [evil; harmful] things to us? What ·have we done wrong [[L]is our iniquity]? What sin have we done against the LORD our God?'

11"Then say to them: 'This is because your ·ancestors [fathers] ·quit following [abandoned; left; forsook] me,' says the LORD. 'And they ·followed [went after] other gods and served and ·worshiped [bowed down to] them. Your ·ancestors [fathers] ·left [abandoned; forsook] me and ·quit obeying [[L]did not keep/guard] my ·teaching [law; instruction]. 12But you have done even more ·evil [harm] than your ·ancestors [fathers]. You are ·very stubborn and do only what you want to do [[L]going after your stubborn heart]; you have not ·obeyed [listened to] me. 13So I will ·throw [hurl] you out of this ·country [land] and send you into a land that you and your ·ancestors [fathers] never knew. There you can ·serve [worship] other gods day and night, because I will not show you any favors.'

14"Therefore the ·time [[L]days] is coming," says the LORD, when it will no longer be said, 'As surely as the LORD lives, who brought the ·people [[L]sons] of Israel out of Egypt.' 15They will say instead, 'As surely as the LORD lives, who brought the ·Israelites [[L]sons of Israel] from the northern land [[C]Babylon] and from all the countries where he had ·sent [driven] them…' And I will ·bring them back [restore them] to the land I gave to their ·ancestors [fathers; [C]a second Exodus; Is. 40:1–11; 52:10; Hos. 2:14–15].

16"I will soon send for many fishermen," says the LORD. "And they will catch them [[C]the people of Judah]. After that, I will send for many hunters. And they will hunt them on every mountain and hill and in the ·cracks [clefts] of the rocks. 17·I see everything they do [[L]My eyes are on all their ways]. They ·cannot hide from me the things they do [[L]are not hidden from me]; their ·sin [iniquity] is not ·hidden [concealed] from my eyes. 18I will first pay them back twice for ·every one of their sins [[L]their iniquities and their sins], because they have made my land unclean [[C]in a ritual sense] with their lifeless idols. They have filled my ·country [inheritance] with their ·hateful idols [[L]abominations]."

19 LORD, you are my strength and my ·protection [stronghold],
my ·safe place [refuge] in times of ·trouble [distress].
The nations will come to you from ·all over [Lthe ends of] the world
and say, "Our ·ancestors [fathers] ·had [Lhave inherited] only ·false gods [Llies],
·useless [meaningless] idols that didn't ·help [profit] them.
20 Can people make gods for themselves?
They will not really be gods!"
21 The LORD says, "So I will teach those who make idols.
This time I will teach them
about my ·power [Lhand] and my strength.
Then they will know
that my name is the LORD.

Judah's Guilty Heart

17 "The sin of Judah is written with an iron ·tool [Lpen].
Their sins were cut with a ·hard [Ldiamond] point into the ·stone that is [Ltablet of] their hearts.
Their sins were cut into the ·corners [Lhorns] of their altars [Ex. 27:2].
2 Even their children remember
their altars [Cto idols] and their ·Asherah idols [sacred poles; LAsherim]
beside the green trees
and on the high hills [2:20].
3 My mountain in the open country
and your wealth and treasures
I will give ·away to other people [Las plunder].
I will give away the places of worship in your country,
because you sinned by worshiping there.
4 You will ·lose [drop] the ·land [Linheritance] I gave you,
and it is your own fault.
I will ·let your enemies take you as their slaves [Lmake you serve your enemies]
to a land you have never known.
This is because you ·have made my anger burn like a hot fire [Lkindled a fire in my anger],
and it will burn forever [15:11–14]."

Trusting in Humans or God

5 This is what the LORD says:
"·A curse is placed on [LCursed are] those who ·trust [have confidence in] other people,
who ·depend on humans for [Lmake flesh their] strength,
who have ·stopped trusting [Lturned their heart from] the LORD.
6 They are like a ·bush [shrub; *or* juniper] in a ·desert [steppe]
that ·grows in a land where no one lives [Llives in a salt land where no one lives],
a ·hot and dry land with bad soil [Lparched land in the wilderness].
They don't ·know about the good things God can give [Lsee when good comes].

7 "But the person who ·trusts [has confidence] in the LORD will be blessed.
·The LORD will show him that he can be trusted [L...whose trust/confidence is in him].

[8]He will be like a tree planted near water [[C]vital and strong]
that sends its roots by a stream [Ps. 1:3].
It is not afraid when the ·days are hot [[L]heat comes];
its leaves are always green.
It ·does not worry [is not anxious] in a year ·when no rain comes [of drought];
it always produces fruit.

[9]"·More than anything else [[T]Above all things], ·a person's mind is evil [[T]the heart is deceitful; [L]the heart is devious/crooked]
and ·cannot be healed [[T]desperately wicked; [L]it is perverse/sick].
Who can ·understand [know] it?
[10]But I, the LORD, ·look into a person's [investigate/test the] heart
and test the ·mind [[L]kidneys].
·So I can decide what each one deserves [[L]…to give to each according to his way/path];
I can give each one the right payment for what he does."

[11]Like a ·bird [[L]partridge] hatching an egg it did not lay,
so are the people who get rich ·by cheating [unjustly].
When their ·lives [[L]days] are half finished, ·they will lose their riches [[L]it will leave/abandon them].
At the end of their lives, it will be clear they were fools.

[12]From the beginning, our ·Temple [[L]sanctuary] has been ·honored [[L]exalted]
as a glorious throne [[C]for God; Is. 6:1–3; Ezek. 1:26–28; 43:2–5].
[13]LORD, hope of Israel,
those who ·leave [abandon; forsake] you will be ·shamed [humiliated].
People who ·quit following the LORD [[L]turn away from you] will be ·written [recorded] in the ·dust [*or* underworld],
because they have ·left [abandoned; forsaken] the LORD, the spring of living water [2:13].

Jeremiah's Third Complaint

[14]LORD, heal me, and I will truly be healed.
·Save [Rescue] me, and I will truly be ·saved [rescued].
You are ·the one I praise [[L]my praise].
[15]The people of Judah keep asking me,
"Where is the word from the LORD?
·Let's see that message come true [[L]Let it come]!"

[16]LORD, I didn't ·run away from [*or* insist on] being the shepherd ·you wanted [[L]after you].
I didn't want the ·terrible day [*or* day of despair] to come.
You know ·everything I have said [[L]what comes out of my lips];
·you see all that is happening [[L]it was before your face].
[17]Don't be a terror to me.
·I run to you for safety [[L]You are my refuge] in ·times [[L]days] of ·trouble [disaster; evil].
[18]Make those who are ·hurting [persecuting; pursuing] me be ·ashamed [humiliated],
but don't bring ·shame to [humiliation on] me.

Let them be terrified,
 but keep me from terror.
Bring the day of ·disaster [evil; trouble] on them [Cmy enemies].
 Destroy them, ·and destroy them again [Lwith double destruction].

Keeping the Sabbath Holy

19 This is what the LORD said to me: "Go and stand at the People's Gate [Cof Jerusalem], where the kings of Judah go in and out. And then go to all the other gates of Jerusalem. 20 Say to them there: 'Hear the word of the LORD, kings of Judah, all you people of Judah, and all who live in Jerusalem, who come through these gates into the city. 21 This is what the LORD says: Be careful not to ·carry [lift] a ·load [burden] on the Sabbath day or bring it through the gates of Jerusalem. 22 Don't take a ·load [burden] out of your houses on the Sabbath or do any work on that day. But keep the Sabbath as a holy day, as I commanded your ·ancestors [fathers; Ex. 20:8–11; 31:12–18; Deut. 5:12–15]. 23 But your ·ancestors [fathers] did not listen or ·pay attention [Lincline their ear] to me. They ·were very stubborn [Lstiffened their necks] and did not listen. ·I punished them, but it didn't do any good [LThey did not take instruction/discipline]. 24 But you must ·be careful to obey [listen to] me, says the LORD. You must not bring a ·load [burden] through the gates of this city [CJerusalem] on the Sabbath, but you must keep the Sabbath as a holy day and not do any work on that day.

25 " 'If you obey this command, kings who sit on David's throne [2 Sam. 7:11–16] will come through the gates of ·Jerusalem [Lthis city] with their officers. They will come riding in chariots and on horses, along with the people of Judah and Jerusalem. And ·the city of Jerusalem [Lthis city] will have people living in it forever. 26 People will come [Cto Jerusalem] from the villages around it, from the towns of Judah, from the land of Benjamin, from the ·western hills [LShephelah], from the mountains, and from ·southern Judah [Lthe Negev]. They will all bring to the ·Temple [Lhouse] of the LORD burnt offerings [Lev. 1:1–17], sacrifices, ·grain [Lgift; tribute] offerings [Lev. 2:1], incense, and ·offerings to show thanks to God [thank offerings]. 27 But you must obey me and keep the Sabbath day as a holy day. You must not carry any loads into Jerusalem on the Sabbath. If you don't ·obey [listen to] me, to keep the Sabbath day as a holy day, I will ·start [kindle] a fire at its gates [Cof Jerusalem], and it will ·burn until it burns even [Lconsume; devour] the ·strong towers [palaces]. And it will not be put out.' "

The Potter and the Clay

18 This is the word the LORD spoke to Jeremiah: 2 "Get up and go down to the potter's house, and I will ·give you my message there [Lmake you hear my words]." 3 So I went down to the potter's house and saw him working at the potter's wheel. 4 He was using his hands to make a pot from clay, but something went wrong with it. So he used that clay to make another pot the way he wanted it to be.

5 Then the LORD spoke his word to me: 6 " '·Family [LHouse] of Israel, can't I do the same thing with you?" says the LORD. "You are in my hands like the clay in the potter's hands. 7 There may come a time when I will ·speak about [declare concerning] a nation or a kingdom that I will ·pull [pluck] up by its roots or that I will ·pull [tear] down to destroy it [1:10]. 8 But if the people of that nation ·stop doing the evil they have done [turn back/repent from its evil concerning which I have spoken], I will ·change my mind [repent] and not carry out my plans to bring ·disaster to [evil on] them. 9 There may come another time when I will ·speak about a

[declare concerning that] **nation that I will build up and plant.** [10]**But if ·I see it doing evil** [Lit does evil in my eyes] **by not ·obeying** [listening to] **me, I will ·change my mind** [repent] **and not carry out my plans to do good for them.**

[11]**"·So** [Now], **say this to the people of Judah and those who live in Jerusalem: 'This is what the LORD says: I am ·preparing** [shaping] **·disaster** [evil] **for you and making plans against you. ·So stop doing evil** [LTurn away from your evil way/path]. **·Change** [Improve/Amend] **your ·ways** [paths] **and ·do what is right** [Lyour actions].' [12]**But they** [Cthe people of Judah] **will answer, 'It won't do any good to try! We will ·continue to do what we want** [Lgo after our plans]. **Each of us will do what his stubborn, evil heart wants!' "**

[13]**So this is what the LORD says:**
"Ask ·the people in other nations this question [Lamong the nations]:
'·Have you ever [LWho has] **heard anything like this?'**
The ·people [Lvirgin daughter] **of Israel have done a horrible thing.**
[14]**·The** [LDoes the…?] **snow of Lebanon**
·never melts from [ever leave the] **the rocks of ·the fields** [L*or* Sirion; Canother name for Mount Hermon].
Its cool, ·flowing [Lforeign; strange] **streams**
do not ·dry up [Lget plucked up].
[15]**But my people have forgotten me.**
They burn incense to ·worthless [useless; meaningless] **idols**
and ·have stumbled [Lthey make them stumble] **in ·what they do** [Ltheir ways/paths]
and in the ·old ways of their ancestors [Lancient ways].
They walk along back roads
·and on poor [Lways/paths that are not] **highways.**
[16]**So ·Judah's country** [Ltheir land] **will become an ·empty desert** [wasteland; desolation].
People will not stop ·making fun of [Lhissing at] **it.**
They will shake their heads as they pass by;
they will be shocked at how the country was destroyed.
[17]**Like a strong east wind,**
I will scatter them [Cthe people of Judah] **before their enemies.**
·At that awful time [LIn the day of their calamity] **·they will not see me coming to help them;**
they will see me leaving [LI will show them my back and not my face]."

Jeremiah's Fourth Complaint

[18]**Then the people said, "Come, let's make plans against Jeremiah. Surely the ·teaching of the law** [instruction] **by the priest will not ·be lost** [perish]. **We will still have the ·advice** [counsel] **from the wise teachers and the words of the prophets. So let's ·ruin him by telling lies about him** [bring charges against him; Lstrike him with the tongue]. **We won't pay attention to ·anything he says** [Lhis words]."
[19]**LORD, ·listen** [pay attention] **to me.**
Listen to what my ·accusers [adversaries] **are saying!**
[20]**·Good should not** [LShould good…?] **be paid back with evil,**
but they have dug a pit ·in order to kill me [Lfor my life].
Remember that I stood before you
and asked you to do good things for these people
and to turn your anger away from them.

21So now, ·let their children starve [Lgive their children to starvation],
and ·let their enemies kill them with swords [Lgive them over to the
power of the sword].
Let their wives ·lose their children and husbands [Lbe childless and
widows].
Let the men [Cfrom Judah] be ·put to death [slain by pestilence]
and the young men be killed with swords in battle.
22Let them cry out in their houses
when you bring ·an enemy [plunderers; marauders] against them
suddenly.
Let all this happen, because my enemies have dug
a pit to capture me and have hidden traps for my feet.
23LORD, you know
about all their plans to kill me.
Don't forgive their ·crimes [iniquity]
or ·erase [wipe away; blot out] their sins from ·your mind
[Lbefore you].
Make them ·fall [stumble] ·from their places [Lbefore you];
·punish [Ldeal with] them while you are angry.

Judah Is like a Broken Jar

19 This is what the LORD said to me: "Go and buy a clay ·jar [jug]
from a potter. 2Take some of the elders of the people and the
·priests [Lelders of the priests], and go out to the Valley of Ben Hinnom,
near the front of the Potsherd Gate. There speak [proclaim] the words I
tell you. 3Say, 'Kings of Judah and ·people [Linhabitants] of Jerusalem,
listen to this ·message [Lword] from the LORD. This is what the LORD ·All-
Powerful [Almighty; of Heaven's Armies; Tof hosts], the God of Israel,
says: I will soon bring ·a disaster [evil; trouble] on this place [CJudah
and Jerusalem] that will ·amaze and frighten [Ltingle the ears of] everyone who hears about it. 4They [Cthe people of Judah] have ·quit following
[abandoned; forsaken] me. They have made this a place for foreign gods.
They have burned sacrifices to other gods that neither they, nor their
·ancestors [fathers], nor the kings of Judah had ever known before. They
filled this place with the blood of innocent people. 5They have built
·places on hilltops to worship [Lhigh places to; Csites associated with
pagan worship or inappropriate worship of God] Baal [CGod of the
Canaanites], where they burn their children in the fire to Baal. That is
something I did not command or speak about; it never even ·entered my
mind [Lcame up in my heart; Lev. 18:21; Deut. 12:31; 18:10]. 6Now people
call this place the Valley of Ben Hinnom [2 Kin. 23:10–11] or Topheth
[C"Spit"], but the days are coming, says the LORD, when people will call
it the Valley of Killing [Slaughter; 7:30–34].
7" 'At this place I will ·ruin [make void] the plans of the people of Judah
and Jerusalem. The enemy will chase them, and I will ·have them killed
with swords [Lmake them fall by the sword before their enemies and by the
hand of those who seek their life]. I will make their ·dead bodies [corpses]
food for the birds of the ·sky [heavens] and ·wild animals [Lbeasts of the
land/country]. 8I will ·completely destroy this city [make this city a deso-
lation]. People will ·make fun of [hiss at] it and shake their heads when
they pass by. They will ·be shocked [hiss] when they see how the city was
destroyed. 9An enemy army will ·surround [besiege] the city and will not
let anyone go out to get food. I will make the people so hungry that they

will eat the ·bodies [flesh] of their own sons and daughters, and then they
will begin to eat ·each other [their neighbors].’
10“While the people with you are watching, break that ·jar [jug]. 11Then
say this: ‘The LORD ·All-Powerful [Almighty; of Heaven’s Armies; Tof
hosts] says: I will break this ·nation [people] and this city just as someone
breaks a clay ·jar [jug] that cannot be ·put back together [mended;
repaired] again. The dead people will be buried here in Topheth [C“Spit”;
v. 6; 7:32], because there is no other place for them. 12This is what I will
do to these ·people [inhabitants] and to this place, says the LORD. I will
make this city like Topheth. 13The houses in Jerusalem and the king’s palaces will become as unclean [Cin a ritual sense] as this place, Topheth,
because the people worshiped gods on the roofs of their houses [Cflat
roofs were living space]. They ·worshiped the stars and burned incense to
honor them [Lburned incense to the whole host of heaven] and gave drink
offerings to gods.’ ”
14When Jeremiah left Topheth [v. 11] where the LORD had sent him to
prophesy, he went to the LORD’s ·Temple [Lhouse], stood in the courtyard,
and said to all the people: 15“This is what the LORD ·All-Powerful
[Almighty; of Heaven’s Armies; Tof hosts], the God of Israel, says: ‘I will
soon bring ·disaster [evil; trouble] to ·Jerusalem [Lthis city] and the villages around it, as I said I would. This will happen because ·the people are
very stubborn [Lthey stiffened their necks] and do not listen at all to ·what
I say [Lmy words].’ ”

Pashhur Will Be Captured

20 Pashhur son of Immer was a priest and the ·highest [chief]
officer in the ·Temple [Lhouse] of the LORD. When he heard
Jeremiah prophesying these things, 2he had Jeremiah the prophet
beaten. And he ·locked [put] Jeremiah in stocks [Cwooden restraints] at
the Upper Gate of Benjamin of the LORD’s Temple. 3The next day when
Pashhur ·took [released] Jeremiah ·out of the blocks of wood [from the
stocks], Jeremiah said to him, “The LORD’s name for you is not Pashhur.
Now his name for you is Magor-Missabib [C“Terror on Every Side”].
4This is what the LORD says: ‘I will soon make you a terror to yourself
and to all your friends. You will watch enemies ·killing [Lmake fall] your
friends with swords. And I will give all the people of Judah to the king of
Babylon, who will ·take them away as captives [exile them] to Babylon
and then will ·kill [Lstrike] them with swords. 5I will give all the wealth
of this city to its enemies—its goods, its valuables, and the treasures of
the kings of Judah. ·The enemies will carry all those valuables off to
Babylon [L…into the hands of their enemies who will plunder them, take
them and bring them to Babylon]. 6And Pashhur, you and everyone in
your house will ·be taken captive [go into exile]. You will be forced to go
to Babylon, where you will die and be buried, you and your friends to
whom you have prophesied lies.’ ”

Jeremiah’s Fifth Complaint

7LORD, you ·tricked [enticed; seduced] me, and I was ·fooled [tricked;
enticed; seduced].
You ·are stronger than I am [overpowered me], so you won.
I have become a ·joke [laughing-stock];
everyone ·makes fun of [ridicules] me all day long.
8Every time I speak, I shout.
·I am always shouting about violence and destruction [LI call out
“Violence” and “Destruction”].

·I tell the people about the message I received from the LORD [L…for
the word of the LORD is with me],
·but this only brings me insults
and mockery [Lfor reproach and derision are with me] all day long.
9Sometimes I say to myself,
"I will ·forget about the LORD [Lnot remember him],
I will not speak anymore in his name."
But then his message becomes like a burning fire ·inside me [Lin my
heart],
·deep within [Lshut in] my bones.
I get tired of trying to hold it inside of me,
and finally, I cannot hold it in.
10I hear many people whispering about me:
"Terror on every side!
Tell on him! Let's tell [Cthe rulers] about him."
My friends are all just waiting for me to make ·some mistake [a false
step].
They are saying,
"Maybe we can ·trick [entice; seduce] him
so we can defeat him
and ·pay him back [take revenge against him]."

11But the LORD is with me like a ·strong [*or* fearful] warrior,
so those who are ·chasing [persecuting] me will trip and ·fall [stumble];
they will not defeat me.
They will be ·ashamed [humiliated] because they have failed,
and their shame will never be forgotten.

12LORD ·All-Powerful [Almighty; of Heaven's Armies; Tof hosts], you test
·good [righteous] people;
you look deeply into the ·heart [Lkidneys] and ·mind [Lheart] of a
person.
I have ·told [committed/revealed to] you my ·arguments [case] against
these people,
so let me see ·you give them the punishment they deserve [your
vengeance against them].

13Sing to the LORD!
Praise the LORD!
He ·saves [protects; rescues] the life of the ·poor [needy]
from the ·power [hand] of the wicked.

Jeremiah's Sixth Complaint

14·Let there be a curse on [Cursed be] the day I was born;
let there be no blessing on the day when my mother gave birth to me.
15·Let there be a curse on [Cursed be] the man
who brought my father the news:
"You have a son!"
This made my father very glad.
16Let that man be like the towns
the LORD ·destroyed [overturned] without ·pity [mercy; Gen. 18].
Let him hear loud crying in the morning
and battle cries at noon,

17because he did not kill me ·before I was born [Lin the womb; 1:5].
Then my mother would have been my grave;
she would have stayed pregnant forever.
18Why did I have to come out of ·my mother's body [the womb]?
All I have known is trouble and sorrow,
and my ·life [days] will end in ·shame [humiliation; Job 3].

God Rejects King Zedekiah's Request

21 This is the word that the LORD spoke to Jeremiah. It came
when Zedekiah king of Judah [Cruled 597–586 BC] sent
Pashhur son of Malkijah [Cnot the same man as in 20:1; 38:1; 1 Chr.
9:12] and the priest Zephaniah son of Maaseiah [29:25, 29; 37:3; 52:24;
2 Kin. 25:18] to Jeremiah. 2They said, "·Ask [Inquire of; LSeek] the LORD
for us what will happen, because Nebuchadnezzar king of Babylon is
·attacking [fighting against] us. Maybe the LORD will do ·miracles [won-
derful works] for us as he did in the past so ·Nebuchadnezzar will stop
attacking us and leave [he will go up from us]."
3But Jeremiah answered them, "Tell King Zedekiah this: 4'Here is what
the LORD, the God of Israel, says: You have weapons of war in your hands
to defend yourselves against the king of Babylon and the ·Babylonians
[LChaldeans], who are all around the city wall. But I will ·make those
weapons useless [turn them against you]. Soon I will ·bring [assemble]
them [Cthe weapons] into the center of this city. 5In my anger, my ·very
great anger [fury and great wrath], I myself will fight against you with my
·great power [outstretched hand] and ·strength [strong arm]. 6I will ·kill
[strike] ·everything living in Jerusalem [Lthe inhabitants of this city]—
both people and animals. They will die from ·terrible diseases [plagues;
pestilence]. 7Then, says the LORD, I'll hand over Zedekiah king of Judah,
his officers, and the people in Jerusalem who do not die from the ·terrible
diseases [plagues; pestilence] or ·battle [Lsword] or ·hunger [famine], ·to
[Linto the hands of] Nebuchadnezzar king of Babylon [Land into the
hands of their enemies]. ·I will let those win who want to kill the people
of Judah [L…and into the hands of those who seek their lives], so ·the
people of Judah and Jerusalem will be killed in war [Lhe will strike them
with the edge of the sword]. Nebuchadnezzar will not show any mercy or
pity or ·feel sorry [compassion] for them!'
8"Also tell this to this people [Cof Jerusalem]: 'This is what the LORD
says: I ·will let you choose to live or die [Lplace before you the way of life
and the way of death; Deut. 30:11–20]. 9Anyone who ·stays [resides] in
Jerusalem will die ·in war [Lby sword] or from ·hunger [famine] or from a
·terrible disease [plague; pestilence]. But anyone who goes out [Cof
Jerusalem] and ·surrenders to [Lfalls before] the ·Babylonians [LChaldeans]
who are ·attacking [Lbesieging] you will live. Anyone who leaves the city
will save his life as if it were ·a prize won [Lplunder] in war. 10I have
·decided to make trouble for [Lset my face against] this city and not ·to
help it [Lfor good], says the LORD. I will give it to the king of Babylon, and
he will burn it with fire.'
11"Say to ·Judah's royal family [Lthe house of the king of Judah]: 'Hear the
word of the LORD. 12·Family [LHouse] of David, this is what the LORD says:
You must judge people ·fairly [with justice] every morning.
·Save [Protect; Rescue] the person who has been robbed
from the ·power [Lhand] of his ·attacker [oppressor].
If you don't, ·I will become very angry [Lmy wrath will come out like fire].

·My anger will be like a fire that no one can put out [[L]It will burn and no one can extinguish; 2 Kin. 25:9],
because you have done evil things.

13“ ‘I am against you [[C]Jerusalem],
you who live ·on top of the mountain
over this valley [[L]in the valley, the rock of the plain], says the LORD.
You say, “·No one can attack [[L]Who can come down against…?] us
or come into our ·strong city [refuge].”
14But I will give you the punishment you deserve, says the LORD.
I will ·start [kindle] a fire in your forests
that will ·burn up [[L]devour] everything around you!’ ”

Judgment Against Evil Kings

22 This is what the LORD says: “Go down to the ·palace [[L]house]
of the king of Judah and ·prophesy this message [[L]say this
word] there: 2‘Hear the word of the LORD, king of Judah, who ·rules from
[[L]sits on] David’s throne. You and your officers, and your people who
come through these gates, listen! 3This is what the LORD says: Do ·what
is fair and right [[L]justice and righteousness]. ·Save [Protect; Rescue] the
one who has been robbed from the ·power [[L]hand] of his ·attacker
[[L]oppressor]. Don’t mistreat or ·hurt [do violence to] the ·foreigners
[resident aliens; Ex. 23:21; Lev. 19:33], orphans, or widows [Ex. 22:22;
Deut. 10:18; 27:19]. Don’t ·kill innocent people [[L]spill innocent blood;
Deut. 19:10; 27:25] here. 4If you carefully ·obey these commands [perform this word], kings who sit on David’s throne will come through the
gates of this ·palace [[L]house] with their officers and people, riding in
chariots and on horses. 5But if you don’t ·obey these commands [[L]listen
to these words], says the LORD, I swear by my ·own name [[L]myself] that
this ·king’s palace [[L]house] will become a ruin.’ ”
6This is what the LORD says about the ·palace where the king of Judah
lives [[L]house of the king of Judah]:

“You are like Gilead to me,
like the ·mountaintops [summit] of ·Lebanon [[C]lush; the palace was built with the cedars of Lebanon; 1 Kin. 7:2].
But I will truly make you into a ·desert [wilderness],
into towns where no one lives.
7I will ·send [[L]consecrate; set apart] ·men to destroy the palace [destroyers],
each with his weapons.
They will cut up your ·strong, beautiful cedar beams [[L]choice cedars]
and throw them into the fire.

8“People from many nations will pass by this city and ask each other,
‘Why has the LORD done such a terrible thing to Jerusalem, this great city?’
9And the answer will be: ‘Because they [[C]the people of Judah] ·quit following [abandoned; forsook] the ·agreement [covenant; treaty] with the LORD
their God. They ·worshiped [bowed down to] and served other gods.’ ”

Judgment Against Jehoahaz

10Don’t cry for the dead one [[C]the king] or ·be sad about [bemoan] him.
But cry ·painfully for the king who is being taken [[L]for the one who goes] away [[C]into exile],
because he will never return
or see ·his homeland [[L]the land of his birth] again.

[11]This is what the LORD says about Jehoahaz [LShallum; Cruled 597 BC;
2 Kin. 23:31–33] son of Josiah who became king of Judah after his father
left this place [Cdied]: "He will never return. [12]He will die where he has
been taken ·captive [into exile], and he will not see this land again."

Judgment Against Jehoiakim

[13]"·How terrible it will be for one [Woe to the one; CKing Jehoiakim (605–597 BC), placed on the throne by the Egyptian pharaoh to replace his brother Jehoahaz; 2 Kin. 23:34] who builds his ·palace [Lhouse] by ·doing evil [Lunrighteousness],
·who cheats people so he can build its upper rooms [his upper rooms without justice].
He makes his ·own people [Lneighbors] work for nothing
and does not pay them.
[14]He says, 'I will build a ·great palace [Lspacious house] for myself
with large upper rooms.'
So he ·builds it with [cuts out] large windows
and uses cedar wood for the ·walls [panels],
which he paints ·red [vermilion].

[15]"Does having a lot of cedar [Cin your house]
make you a great king?
·Your father was satisfied to [LDid not your father…?; CJosiah, a godly king] have food and drink.
He did what was right and fair,
so everything went well for him.
[16]He ·helped [Ljudged the cause of] those who were poor and needy,
so everything went well for him.
·That is what it [LIs this not what it…?] means to know ·God [Lme],"
says the LORD.
[17]"But ·you only look for and think about [Lyour eyes and your heart are on]
what you can get dishonestly.
You are even willing to ·kill innocent people [Lpour out innocent blood] to get it.
You feel free to ·hurt [oppress] people and to steal from them."
[18]So this is what the LORD says to Jehoiakim son of Josiah king of Judah:
"They [Cthe people of Judah] will not cry [mourn] ·when Jehoiakim dies [Lfor him],
saying: '·Oh [Woe], my brother,' or '·Oh [Woe], my sister.'
They will not ·cry [mourn] for him, saying:
'·Oh [Woe], master,' or '·Oh [Woe], my king.'
[19]They will bury him like a donkey,
dragging and throwing his body away
outside the gates of Jerusalem.

[20]"Judah, go up to Lebanon and cry out.
Let your voice be heard in Bashan.
Cry out from Abarim,
because all your friends are destroyed!
[21]When you [CJudah] were ·successful [prosperous], I warned you,
but you said, 'I won't listen.'
·You have acted like this [LThis is your way/path] since you were young;
you have not ·obeyed me [Llistened to my voice].

22·Like a storm, my punishment will blow all your shepherds away [LThe wind will shepherd all your shepherds away]
and send your ·friends [*or* lovers] into ·captivity [exile; 2 Kin. 23:36—24:7].
Then you will really be ashamed and ·disgraced [humiliated]
because of all the ·wicked things [evil] you did.
23You [CKing Jehoiakim] live in Lebanon [Cthe palace was made of cedar from Lebanon],
·cozy [nestled] in your rooms of cedar.
But when your ·punishment [Lpangs] comes, how you will groan
like a woman ·giving birth to a baby [in labor]!

Judgment upon Jehoiachin

24"As surely as I live," says the LORD, "·Jehoiachin [LConiah; Cruled 597
BC; 2 Kin. 24:8–17; 2 Chr. 36:9–10] son of Jehoiakim king of Judah, even
if you were a signet ring on my right hand, I would still ·pull [tear] you
off. 25I will ·hand you over to Nebuchadnezzar king of Babylon and to the
·Babylonians [LChaldeans]—those people you fear because they ·want to
kill you [Lseek your life]. 26I will ·throw [hurl] you and your mother who
bore you into another country [CBabylon]. Neither of you was born there,
but both of you will die there. 27They will want to come back, but they
will never be able to return."
28·Jehoiachin is like a broken pot someone threw away [LIs this man Jehoiachin a despised broken pot...?];
·he is like something [La vessel...?] no one wants.
Why will Jehoiachin and his children be ·thrown out [hurled away]
and ·sent [thrown] into a ·foreign land [country they do not know; Cexiled to Babylon]?
29Land, land, land [Cof Judah],
hear the word of the LORD!
30This is what the LORD says:
"Write this down ·in the record about [Labout this man; CJehoiachin]:
He is a man without children,
a man who will not be successful in his ·lifetime [Ldays].
And none of his descendants will be successful;
none will sit on the throne of David
or rule in Judah."

The Evil Leaders of Judah

23 "·How terrible it will be for [Woe to] ·those [Lthe shepherds;
Cthe leaders of Judah] who are scattering and destroying ·my
people [Lthe sheep of my pasture]," says the LORD.
2They are ·responsible for the people [Lthe shepherds who shepherd my
people; Num. 27:7; Ps. 78:70–72; Ezek. 34], so the LORD, the God of Israel,
says to them: "You have scattered my ·people [flock] and forced them
away and not taken care of them. So I will ·punish [take care of] you for
the evil things you have done," says the LORD. 3"But I will gather ·those
who are left alive [Lthe remnant of my flock] from all the lands where I
have driven them and bring them back to their own ·country [flock].
Then they will ·have many children and grow in number [be fruitful and
multiply]. 4I will ·place [raise up] ·new leaders over my people, who will
take care of them [Lshepherds who will shepherd them]. And my people
will not be afraid or terrified again, and none of them will be lost," says
the LORD.

The Good Branch Will Come

5"The days are coming," says the LORD,
"when I will raise up a ·good [righteous] branch ·in David's family [Lfor David; Is. 4:2; Zech. 3:8; 6:12].
He will be a king who will rule in a wise way;
he will do ·what is fair and right [justice and righteousness] in the land.
6In his time Judah will be ·saved [rescued],
and Israel will live ·in safety [with confidence].
This will be his name:
The LORD ·Does What Is Right [LOur Righteousness].
7"So the days are coming," says the LORD, "when people will not say again:
'As surely as the LORD lives, who brought Israel out of Egypt....' 8But people will say something new: 'As surely as the LORD lives, who brought the
·descendants of Israel [Lseed of the house of Israel] from the land of the
north [CBabylon] and from all the countries where he had ·sent [driven]
them away....' Then the people of Israel will live in their own land
[16:14–15]."

False Prophets Will Be Punished

9A message to the prophets:
My heart is ·broken [Lshattered within me].
All my bones shake.
I'm like someone who is drunk,
like someone who has been ·overcome [inebriated] with wine.
This is because of the LORD
and his holy words.
10The land [Cof Judah] is full of people who are guilty of adultery.
Because of the curse the land ·is sad [mourns],
and the pastures of the ·desert [wilderness] have dried up.
The people [Their lives/Lcourses] are evil
and ·they use their power in the wrong way [Ltheir power is not right].

11"Both the prophets and the priests are ungodly.
I have found even in my own ·Temple [Lhouse]," says the LORD.
12"So their ·lives [Lways; paths] will be slippery and dark [Cthey will be in danger].
They will ·be defeated [Lfall].
I will bring ·disaster [evil; trouble] on them
in the year I punish them," says the LORD.

13"I saw the prophets of Samaria [Ccapital of the northern kingdom destroyed in 722 BC]
do something ·wrong [disgusting].
Those prophets prophesied by Baal
and led my people Israel away [Deut. 13:1–5].
14And I have seen the prophets of Jerusalem
do ·terrible [shocking] things.
They are guilty of adultery
and ·live [walk] by lies.
They ·encourage [strengthen] ·evil people to keep on doing evil [Lthe hands of evildoers],
so the people don't ·stop sinning [Lturn back from their evil].
All of those people are like the city of Sodom.

The people of Jerusalem are like the city of Gomorrah to me [Csinful and soon to be punished; Gen. 18–19]!"

15So this is what the LORD ·All-Powerful [Almighty; of Heaven's Armies; Tof hosts] says about the prophets:

"I will make those prophets eat ·bitter food [Lwormwood; Cthe bitter tasting leaves of a shrub; 9:15]
and drink poisoned water,
because the prophets of Jerusalem spread ·wickedness [godlessness]
through the whole country."

16This is what the LORD ·All-Powerful [Almighty; of Heaven's Armies; Tof hosts] says:

"Don't ·pay attention [listen] to what those prophets are ·saying [prophesying] to you.
They are trying to ·fool [delude] you.
They talk about visions their own ·minds [Lhearts] made up,
not ·about visions from me [Lfrom the mouth of the LORD].
17They say to those who ·hate [despise] me:
'The LORD says: You will have peace.'
They say to all those who ·are stubborn and do as they please [Lwalk in the stubbornness of their heart]:
'Nothing ·bad [evil; disastrous] will happen to you.'
18·But none of these prophets has stood in the meeting of angels [LWho has stood in the assembly/council of the LORD…?; 1 Kin. 22:19–23; Job 1—2; 15:8; Ps. 82; Is. 6:1–3]
to see or hear the message of the LORD.
·None of them [LWho…?] has paid close attention to his message.
19Look, the ·storm [whirlwind] of the LORD!
His anger will pour forth like a ·hurricane [storm; whirlwind].
It will come swirling down on the heads of those wicked people [30:23].
20The LORD's anger will not ·stop [turn back]
until he finishes what he plans to do.
When that day is over,
you will understand this clearly [30:24].
21I did not send those prophets,
but they ran [Cto tell their message].
I did not speak to them,
but they prophesied anyway.
22But if they had stood in ·the meeting of angels [Lmy assembly/council],
they would have told my message to my people.
They would have turned the people from their evil ways
and from doing evil.

23"·I am [LAm I only…?] a God who is near," says the LORD.
"·I am [LAnd not…?] also a God who is far away.
24·No one [LWho…?] can hide
where I cannot see him," says the LORD.
"·I [LDo I not…?] fill all of heaven and earth," says the LORD.

25"I have heard the prophets who prophesy lies in my name. They say,
'I have had a dream! I have had a dream!' 26How long will this continue in
the ·minds [Lhearts] of these lying prophets? They prophesy from their
own ·wishful thinking [Ldeceitful hearts]. 27They are trying to make the

people of Judah forget ·me [Lmy name] by telling each other these dreams.
In the same way, their ·ancestors [fathers] forgot ·me [Lmy name] ·and
worshiped [Lfor] Baal. 28·Is straw the same thing as [LWhat has straw in
common with] wheat?" says the LORD. "If a prophet wants to tell about his
dreams, let him! But let the person who hears my message speak it truthfully! 29Isn't my message like a fire?" says the LORD. "Isn't it like a hammer
that smashes a rock?

30"So I am against the prophets [Cfalse prophets]," says the LORD. "They
keep stealing words from each other [Cand say they are from God]. 31I am
against the prophets [Cfalse prophets]," says the LORD. "They use their
own ·words [Ltongues] and ·pretend it is a message from me [Lsay, 'Says
the LORD']. 32I am against the prophets who prophesy false dreams," says
the LORD. "They mislead my people with their lies and ·false teachings
[recklessness]! I did not send them or command them to do anything for
me. They can't help the people of Judah at all," says the LORD.

The Sad Message from the Lord

33"Suppose this people [Cof Judah], a prophet, or a priest asks you
[CJeremiah]: 'What is the ·message [oracle; burden] from the LORD?' You
will answer them and say, 'You are a heavy ·load [burden] to the LORD, and
I will throw you down, says the LORD.' 34A prophet or a priest or one of the
people might say, 'This is a ·message [oracle; burden] from the LORD.' I
will punish him [Cfor lying that he has a message from God] and his whole
family. 35This is what you will say to each other: 'What did the LORD
answer?' or 'What did the LORD say?' 36But you will never again ·say [men-
tion; remember], 'The ·message [oracle; burden] of the LORD,' because the
only ·message [oracle; burden] you speak is your own words. You have
·changed [overturned; perverted] the words of our God, the living God,
the LORD ·All-Powerful [Almighty; of Heaven's Armies; Tof hosts]. 37This
is how you should speak to the prophets: 'What answer did the LORD give
you?' or 'What did the LORD say?' 38But don't say, 'The ·message [oracle;
burden] from the LORD.' If you use these words, this is what the LORD says:
Because you called it a '·message [oracle; burden] from the LORD,' though
I told you not to use those words, 39I will pick you up and ·throw [cast]
you away from me, along with the city [CJerusalem], which I gave to your
·ancestors [fathers] and to you. 40And I will ·make a disgrace of [give
shame to] you forever; your shame will never be forgotten."

The Good and Bad Figs

24 Nebuchadnezzar of Babylon ·captured [exiled] ·Jehoiachin
[Jeconiah] son of Jehoiakim and king of Judah, his officers,
and all the craftsmen and metalworkers of Judah [C597 BC]. He took
them away from Jerusalem and brought them to Babylon. It was then
that the LORD showed me two baskets of figs [Ca symbol of fruitfulness
(Hos. 9:11) and shelter (Mic. 4:4; Zech. 3:10)] arranged in front of the
Temple of the LORD. 2One of the baskets had very good figs in it, like figs
that ripen ·early in the season [first]. But the other basket had figs too
rotten to eat.

3The LORD said to me, "What do you see, Jeremiah?"

I answered, "I see figs. The good figs are very good, but the rotten figs
are too rotten to eat."

4Then the LORD spoke his word to me: 5"This is what the LORD, the God
of Israel, says: 'I sent the people of Judah out of their country to live in the
country of Babylon. I ·think of [regard] those people as good, like these
good figs. 6I will ·look after them [Lset my eyes on them for good] and

·bring them back [return them] to this land [Cof Judah]. I will not tear
them down, but I will build them up. I will not pull them up, but I will
plant them [Cso they can grow]. 7I will ·make them want [Lgive them a
heart] to know me, that I am the Lord. They will be my people, and I will
be their God, because they will return to me with their whole hearts.
8" 'But the bad figs are too rotten to eat.' So this is what the Lord says:
'Zedekiah king of Judah [Cruled 597–586 BC], his officers, and all the people from Jerusalem who are left alive, even those who live in Egypt, will be
like those rotten figs. 9I will make those people ·hated [a horror; abhor-
rent] as an evil people by all the kingdoms of the earth. ·People will make
fun of them and tell jokes about them and point fingers at them and curse
them [L...a reproach, a proverb/byword, a taunt, a curse] everywhere I
·scatter [drive] them. 10I will send ·war [sword], ·hunger [famine], and
·disease [pestilence] against them. ·I will attack them until they have all
been killed. Then they will no longer be in [L...until they have been anni-
hilated from] the land I gave to them and their ·ancestors [fathers].' "

A Summary of Jeremiah's Preaching

25 This is the message that came to Jeremiah concerning all the
people of Judah. It came in the fourth year that Jehoiakim
son of Josiah was king of Judah and the first year Nebuchadnezzar was
king of Babylon. 2This is the message Jeremiah the prophet spoke to all
the people of Judah and Jerusalem:
3The Lord has spoken his word to me again and again for these past
twenty-three years. I have been a prophet since the thirteenth year of
Josiah son of Amon king of Judah. I have spoken messages from the Lord
to you from that time until today, but you have not listened.
4The Lord has sent all his servants the prophets [7:25; 2 Kin. 17:13] to
you over and over again, but you have not listened or ·paid any attention
[Linclined/bent your ear] to them. 5Those prophets have said, "·Stop [Turn
from/Repent of] your evil ways. ·Stop doing [Turn from/Repent of] what is
wrong so you can stay in the land that the Lord gave to you and your ·ances-
tors [fathers] to live in forever. 6Don't ·follow [Lgo after] other gods to serve
them or to ·worship [bow down to] them. Don't make me, the Lord, angry
by the work of your own hands [Cidols], or I will ·punish [harm] you."
7"But you [Cpeople of Judah] did not listen to me," says the Lord. "You
made me angry by the work of your own hands [Cidols], so I ·punished
[harmed] you."
8So this is what the Lord ·All-Powerful [Almighty; of Heaven's Armies;
Tof hosts] says: "Since you have not listened to my messages, 9I will send
for all the ·peoples [clans; families] of the north [CBabylon]," says the
Lord, "along with my servant Nebuchadnezzar king of Babylon. I will
bring them all against Judah, those who live there, and all the nations
around you, too. I will ·completely destroy [annihilate] all those countries and leave them ·in ruins [desolate] forever. ·People will be shocked
when they see how badly I have destroyed those countries [LI will make
them a horror and a hissing and an everlasting reproach]. 10I will ·bring an
end to [banish; cause to perish] the sounds of joy and happiness, the
sounds of brides and bridegrooms [7:34; 16:9], and the sound of ·people
grinding meal [Lthe millstone]. And I will take away the light of the lamp.
11That whole ·area [Lland] will be an ·empty desert [ruin and desolate],
and these nations will ·be slaves of [serve] the king of Babylon
[CNebuchadnezzar] for seventy years [Cthe exile].

12“But when the seventy years ·have passed [are completed], I will punish the king of Babylon and his entire nation, the land of the Chaldeans, for their ·evil [iniquity],” says the Lord. “I will make that land a ·desert [desolation] forever. 13I will ·make happen [Lbring on this land] all the ·terrible things [Lwords] I said about it [CBabylonia]—everything Jeremiah prophesied about all those foreign nations, the warnings written in this book [chs. 46–51]. 14Even they [CBabylonians] will have to serve many nations and many great kings. I will ·give them the punishment they deserve for all their own hands have done [Lrepay them according to their deeds and according to the work of their hands].”

Judgment on the Nations

15The Lord, the God of Israel, said this to me: “Take the cup of the wine of my wrath [49:12; 51:7] from my hand and make all the nations, to whom I am sending you, drink from this cup. 16They will drink and ·stumble about [stagger; *or* vomit] and act like madmen because of the ·war [Lsword] I am going to send among them.”

17So I took the cup from the Lord’s hand and went to those nations where he sent me and made them drink from it. 18I served this wine to the people of Jerusalem and the towns of Judah, and the kings and officers of Judah, so they would become a ruin. Then people would be shocked and would ·insult them [hiss] and ·speak evil of [curse] them. And so it has been to this day. 19I also made these people drink of the Lord’s anger: Pharaoh the king of Egypt, his servants, his officers, all his people, 20and all the ·foreigners there [mixed crowd]; all the kings of the land of Uz; all the kings of the Philistines (the kings of the cities of Ashkelon, Gaza, Ekron, and the people left at Ashdod); 21the people of Edom, Moab, and ·Ammon [Lthe sons of Ammon]; 22all the kings of Tyre and Sidon; all the kings of the coastal countries ·to the west [*or* across the sea]; 23the people of Dedan and Tema and Buz; all who ·cut their hair short [Lshave their temples; Deut. 14:1]; 24all the kings of Arabia; and the kings of the ·people [Lmixed crowd] who live in the ·desert [wilderness]; 25all the kings of Zimri, Elam, and Media; 26and all the kings of the north, near and far, one after the other. I made all the kingdoms on earth drink [Cfrom the cup of wrath] of the Lord’s anger, but the king of ·Babylon [LSheshak; Ca coded reference to Babylon] will drink from this cup after all the others.

27“Then say to them, ‘This is what the Lord ·All-Powerful [Almighty; of Heaven’s Armies; Tof hosts], the God of Israel, says: Drink ·this cup [Cof my anger]. Get drunk from it and vomit. Fall down and don’t get up because of the ·war [Lsword] I am sending among you!’

28“If they refuse to take the cup from your hand and drink, say to them, ‘The Lord ·All-Powerful [Almighty; of Heaven’s Armies; Tof hosts] says this: You must drink [Cfrom this cup]. 29Look! I am ·already bringing [beginning to bring] ·disaster [harm; trouble] on this city that is called by my name [CJerusalem]. Do you think you will not be punished? You will ·be punished [Lnot go unpunished]! I am ·sending [Lcalling for] ·war [La sword] on all the people of the earth, says the Lord ·All-Powerful [Almighty; of Heaven’s Armies; Tof hosts].’

30“You [CJeremiah] will prophesy against them with all these words. Say to them:

‘The Lord will roar [Clike a lion] from heaven [Amos 1:2]
and will ·shout [Lgive forth] from his holy lair [Cthe Temple].
He will roar loudly against his ·land [Lsheepfold].

He will shout like people who walk on grapes [Is. 63:2–6; Rev. 19:15];
he will shout against all who live on the earth.
31The ·noise [clamor] will spread all over the earth,
because the LORD will accuse all the nations.
He will ·judge and tell what is wrong with [bring an indictment against]
all ·people [Lflesh],
and he will kill the evil people with a sword,' " says the LORD.

32This is what the LORD ·All-Powerful [Almighty; of Heaven's Armies; Tof hosts] says:
"Disasters will soon ·spread [Lgo out]
from nation to nation.
They will come like a powerful storm
from the faraway places on earth."
33At that time those killed by the LORD will reach from one end of the
earth to the other. No one will ·cry [mourn] for them or gather up their
bodies and bury them. They will be left lying on the ground like dung
[8:2; 9:22; 16:4].
34Cry, you ·leaders [Lshepherds]! Cry out loud!
Roll around in the ·dust [ashes], ·leaders of the people [Lnobles of the flock]!
·It is now time for you to be killed [LYour days are filled for slaughter].
You will fall and be scattered,
like ·pieces of a broken [La choice/precious] jar.
35There will be no place for the ·leaders [Lshepherds] to ·hide [Lflee];
·they [Lthe nobles of the flock] will not escape.
36I hear the sound of the ·leaders [Lshepherds] shouting.
I hear the ·leaders of the people [Lnobles of the flock] crying loudly,
because the LORD is destroying their ·land [Lpastureland].
37Those peaceful pastures will be ·like an empty desert [Ldevastated],
because the LORD is very angry.
38Like a lion, he has left his den.
Their land has been ·destroyed [desolated]
because of the terrible ·war [Lsword] he brought,
because of his fierce anger.

Jeremiah's Lesson at the Temple

26 This message came from the LORD ·soon after Jehoiakim son of
Josiah became [Lat the beginning of the reign of Jehoiakim]
king of Judah [Cruled 605–597 BC]. 2This is what the LORD said: "Jeremiah,
stand in the courtyard of the ·Temple [Lhouse] of the LORD. ·Give this message [LSay] to all the people of the towns of Judah who are coming to
·worship [bow down] at the ·Temple [Lhouse] of the LORD. Tell them everything I tell you to say; don't leave out a word. 3Maybe they will listen and
·stop [return/repent from] their evil ways. If they will, I will ·change my
mind [relent] about bringing on them the ·disaster [evil; trouble] that I
am planning because of the evil they have done. 4Say to them: 'This is
what the LORD says: You must ·obey [listen to] me and follow my ·teachings [instructions; laws] that I gave you. 5You must listen to what my
servants the prophets [25:4] say to you. I have sent them to you again and
again, but you did not ·listen [obey]. 6If you don't obey me, I will ·destroy
my Temple in Jerusalem as I destroyed my Holy Tent at [Lmake this house
like] Shiloh [7:12–14; 1 Sam. 4:1–22; Ps. 78:60–64]. When I do, ·people all
over the world will curse Jerusalem [LI will make this city a curse].' "

7The priests, the prophets, and all the people heard Jeremiah speaking these words in the ·Temple [Lhouse] of the LORD. 8When Jeremiah finished speaking ·everything [Lall the words] the LORD had commanded him to say, the priests, prophets, and all the people ·grabbed [seized] Jeremiah. They said, "You must die! 9·How dare [LWhy do…?] you prophesy in the name of the LORD that this ·Temple [Lhouse] will be like the one at Shiloh [Cdestroyed]! ·How dare [LWhy do…?] you say that this city [CJerusalem] will become a ·desert [ruin] without anyone to live in it!" And all the people ·crowded [assembled] around Jeremiah in the ·Temple [Lhouse] of the LORD.

10Now when the officers of Judah heard ·about what was happening [Lthese things/words], they came out of the king's ·palace [Lhouse] and went up to the ·Temple [Lhouse] of the LORD and took their places at the entrance of the New Gate. 11Then the priests and prophets said to the officers and all the other people, "·Jeremiah [LThis man] ·should be killed [Ldeserves the death sentence]. He prophesied against this city [CJerusalem], and you heard him ·yourselves [Lwith your ears]."

12Then Jeremiah spoke these words to all the officers of Judah and all the other people: "The LORD sent me to ·say [Lprophesy] ·everything [Lall these words] you have heard about this ·Temple [Lhouse] and this city. 13Now ·change [improve; mend] your ·lives and start doing good [Lways and your deeds] and ·obey [Llisten to the voice of] the LORD your God. Then he will ·change his mind and not bring on you [relent of] the ·disaster [evil; trouble] he has told you about. 14As for me, I am in your ·power [Lhand]. Do to me what you think is good and right in your eyes. 15But be sure of one thing. If you kill me, you will be ·guilty of killing an innocent person [Lplacing innocent blood on yourselves; Ex. 23:7; Deut. 19:10, 13]. ·You will make this city and everyone who lives in it guilty, too [L…and on this city and everyone who lives in it]! The LORD truly sent me to ·you to give you this message [Lspeak this word in your ears]."

16Then the officers and all the people said to the priests and the prophets, "·Jeremiah must not be killed [LThis man does not deserve the death penalty]. ·What he told us comes from [LHe has spoken to us in the name of] the LORD our God."

17Then some of the elders of the land [Cof Judah] stood up and said to all the people, 18"Micah, from the city of Moresheth [Micah 1:1, 14], was a prophet during the ·time Hezekiah was [Ldays of Hezekiah] king of Judah. Micah said to all the people of Judah, 'This is what the LORD ·All-Powerful [Almighty; of Heaven's Armies; Tof hosts] says:

·Jerusalem [LZion; Cthe location of the Temple] will be plowed like a field.
·It [LJerusalem] will become a ·pile of rocks [a heap of ruins],
and the ·hill [Lmountain] where the ·Temple [Lhouse] stands will be
·covered with bushes [La forested high place; Mic. 3:12].'

19"·Hezekiah king of Judah and the people of Judah did not [LDid Hezekiah king of Judah and people of Judah try to…?] kill Micah. ·You know [LDo you not know…?] that Hezekiah feared the LORD [Prov. 1:7] and ·tried to please [sought the favor of] the LORD. So the LORD ·changed his mind [relented] and did not bring on Judah the ·disaster [evil; harm] he had promised. We will bring a terrible ·disaster [evil; harm] on ourselves [Cby hurting Jeremiah]!"

20(Now there was another man who prophesied in the name of the LORD. His name was Uriah son of Shemaiah from the city of Kiriath

Jearim. He ·preached [Lprophesied] the same things against this city
[CJerusalem] and this land [CJudah] that Jeremiah did. 21When King
Jehoiakim, all his army officers, and all the leaders of Judah heard ·Uriah
preach [Lhis words], King Jehoiakim ·wanted [sought] to kill Uriah. But
Uriah heard about it and was afraid. So he escaped to Egypt. 22Then King
Jehoiakim sent Elnathan son of Acbor and some other men to Egypt,
23and they brought Uriah back from Egypt. Then they took him to King
Jehoiakim, who had Uriah ·killed [Lstruck] with a sword. His body was
thrown into the burial place where ·poor [common] people are buried.)
24·Ahikam son of Shaphan supported [LThe hand of Ahikam son of
Shaphan was with] Jeremiah [2 Kin. 22:3, 8–10]. So Ahikam did not hand
Jeremiah over to be killed by the people.

Nebuchadnezzar Is Made Ruler

27 The LORD spoke his word to Jeremiah soon after ·Zedekiah
[*or* Jehoiakim] son of Josiah was made king of Judah. 2This is
what the LORD said to me: "Make a yoke out of straps and poles, and put
it on the back of your neck. 3Then send messages to the kings of Edom,
Moab, ·Ammon [Lthe sons of Ammon], Tyre, and Sidon by their messengers who have come to Jerusalem to see Zedekiah king of Judah. 4Tell
them to give this message to their masters: 'The LORD ·All-Powerful
[Almighty; of Heaven's Armies; Tof hosts], the God of Israel, says: "Tell
your masters: 5I made the earth, its people, and all its animals with my
great power and ·strength [Loutstretched hand]. I can give the earth to
anyone ·I want [Lthat is right in my eyes]. 6Now I have given all these
lands to Nebuchadnezzar king of Babylon, my servant. I will make even
the wild animals ·obey [Lserve] him. 7All nations will serve
Nebuchadnezzar and his son and grandson. Then the time will come for
Babylon to be defeated, and many nations and great kings will make
Babylon their ·servant [*or* slave].
8" ' "But if some nations or kingdoms refuse to serve Nebuchadnezzar
king of Babylon and refuse to ·be under his control [Lput their necks under
the yoke of the king of Babylon], I will punish them with ·war [Lthe sword],
·hunger [famine], and ·terrible diseases [plague; pestilence], says the LORD.
·I will use Nebuchadnezzar to destroy them [L...until I have completed its
destruction by its hand]. 9So don't listen to your prophets, ·those who use
magic to tell the future [your diviners], ·those who explain dreams [your
dreamers], the mediums, or magicians. They all tell you, '·You will not be
slaves to [LDo not serve] the king of Babylon.' 10They are ·telling
[Lprophesying to] you lies that will cause you to be taken far from your
homeland. I will ·force you to leave [drive you from] your homes, and you
will ·die in another land [perish]. 11But the nations who ·put themselves
under the control [Lbring their necks under the yoke] of the king of
Babylon and serve him I will let stay in their own country, says the LORD.
The people from those nations will live in their own land and farm it." ' "
12I gave the same message to Zedekiah king of Judah. I said, "Put yourself under the ·control [Lyoke] of the king of Babylon and serve him, and
you will live. 13Why should you and your people die from ·war [Lsword],
·hunger [famine], or ·disease [pestilence], as the LORD said would happen to
those who do not serve the king of Babylon? 14But the prophets [Cfalse
prophets] are saying, 'You will ·never be slaves to [Lnot serve] the king of
Babylon.' Don't listen to them because they are prophesying lies to you! 15'I
did not send them,' says the LORD. 'They are prophesying lies ·and saying

the message is from me [Lin my name]. So I will ·send you away [drive you out; Csaid to Judah]. And you and those prophets who prophesy to you will ·die [perish; Deut. 18:21–22].' "

16Then I [CJeremiah] said to the priests and all this people, "This is what the Lord says: Those false prophets are saying, 'The ·Babylonians will soon return what they took from the Temple of the Lord [Lvessels of the house of the Lord will be returned from Babylon; 2 Kin. 24:13; Dan. 1:2].' Don't listen to them! They are prophesying lies to you. 17Don't listen to those prophets. But serve the king of Babylon, and you will live. ·There is no reason for you to cause Jerusalem to [LWhy should this city…?] become a ruin. 18If they are prophets and have the ·message from [word of] the Lord, let them ·pray to [Lintercede with] the Lord ·All-Powerful [Almighty; of Heaven's Armies; Tof hosts]. Let them ask that the ·items [vessels] which ·are still [Lremain] in the ·Temple [Lhouse] of the Lord and in the king's ·palace [Lhouse] and in Jerusalem not ·be taken away [Lgo] to Babylon.

19"This is what the Lord ·All-Powerful [Almighty; of Heaven's Armies; Tof hosts] says about those ·items [vessels] left in this city [CJerusalem]: the pillars [1 Kin. 7:15–22], the Sea [1 Kin. 7:23–26], the stands [1 Kin. 7:27–37] and other things [Cbronze basins, various altars, lampstands, and more]. 20Nebuchadnezzar king of Babylon did not take these away when he ·took as captives [exiled] Jehoiachin [LJeconiah] son of Jehoiakim king of Judah and all the ·other important people [nobles] from Judah and Jerusalem to Babylon. 21This is what the Lord ·All-Powerful [Almighty; of Heaven's Armies; Tof hosts], the God of Israel, says about the ·items [vessels] left in the ·Temple [Lhouse] of the Lord and in the king's ·palace [Lhouse] and in Jerusalem: 22'·All of them will also be taken [LThey will be brought] to Babylon. And they will stay there until the day I ·go to get [attend to] them,' says the Lord. 'Then I will bring them back and return them to this place.' "

The False Prophet Hananiah

28 It was in that same year, in the fifth month of Zedekiah's fourth year as king of Judah [C593 BC], soon after he began to rule. The prophet Hananiah son of Azzur, from the town of Gibeon, spoke to me in the ·Temple [Lhouse] of the Lord ·in front [Lbefore the eyes] of the priests and all the people. He said: 2"The Lord ·All-Powerful [Almighty; of Heaven's Armies; Tof hosts], the God of Israel, says: 'I have broken the yoke of the king of Babylon. 3Before two years are over, I will ·bring back [restore] ·everything [Lall the vessels] that Nebuchadnezzar king of Babylon took to Babylon from the Lord's ·Temple [Lhouse]. 4I will also ·bring back [restore] ·Jehoiachin [LJeconiah] son of Jehoiakim king of Judah and all the other ·captives [exiles] from Judah who went to Babylon,' says the Lord. 'So I will break the yoke of the king of Babylon.' "

5Then the prophet Jeremiah spoke to the prophet Hananiah ·in front [Lbefore the eyes] of the priests and all the people who were standing in the ·Temple [Lhouse] of the Lord. 6He said, "Amen! Let the Lord really do that! May the Lord ·make the message you prophesy come true [Lconfirm your word which you prophesied]. May he ·bring back here [Lrestore] ·everything [Lthe vessels] the Lord's ·Temple [Lhouse] and all the ·people who were taken as captives [exiles] to Babylon.

7"But listen to ·what I am going to say to you and [Lthis word which I am speaking in your ears and the ears of] all the people. 8There were

prophets long before we became prophets, Hananiah. They prophesied
that war, ·hunger [famine; *or* disaster; calamity], and ·terrible diseases
[plague; pestilence] would come to many countries and great kingdoms.
9But if a prophet prophesies that we will have peace and that message
comes true, he can be recognized as one truly sent by the LORD [Cprophets
usually came announcing judgment not peace]."
10Then the prophet Hananiah took the yoke off Jeremiah's neck and
·broke [shattered] it. 11Hananiah said ·in front [Lbefore the eyes] of all the
people, "This is what the LORD says: 'In the same way I will break the yoke
of Nebuchadnezzar king of Babylon. He put that yoke on all the nations
of the world, but I will break it before two years are over.' " After Hananiah
had said that, Jeremiah ·left the Temple [Lwent on his way].
12The LORD spoke his word to Jeremiah after the prophet Hananiah
had broken the yoke off of the prophet Jeremiah's neck. 13The LORD said,
"Go and tell Hananiah, 'This is what the LORD says: You have broken a
wooden yoke, but I will make a yoke of iron in its place! 14The LORD ·All-
Powerful [Almighty; of Heaven's Armies; Tof hosts], the God of Israel,
says: I will put a yoke of iron on the necks of all these nations to make
them serve Nebuchadnezzar king of Babylon, and they will be slaves to
him. I will even give Nebuchadnezzar ·control over the wild animals [Lthe
beasts of the field].' "
15Then the prophet Jeremiah said to the prophet Hananiah, "Listen,
Hananiah! The LORD did not send you, and you have made the people of
Judah ·trust [have confidence] in lies. 16So this is what the LORD says:
'Soon I will ·remove you from [Lsend you off the face of] the earth. You
will die this year, because you taught ·the people to turn [rebellion]
against the LORD [Deut. 18:20].' "
17Hananiah died in the seventh month of that same year.

A Letter to the Captives in Babylon

29 This is the ·letter [Lwords of the scroll] that Jeremiah the
prophet sent from Jerusalem to the remaining elders who
were among the ·captives [exiles], the priests, and the prophets. He sent
it to all the other people Nebuchadnezzar had taken as ·captives [exiles]
from Jerusalem to Babylon [Cin 597 BC; 2 Kin. 24:12–17; 2 Chr. 36:6–8].
2(This ·letter [Lscroll] was sent after all these people were taken away:
Jehoiachin [LJeconiah] the king and the queen mother [CNehushta;
13:18]; the ·officers [servants; Leunuchs] and leaders of Judah and
Jerusalem; and the craftsmen and metalworkers from Jerusalem.)
3Zedekiah king of Judah sent Elasah son of Shaphan [Cperhaps the court
secretary under Josiah; 2 Kin. 22:3, 8–9] and Gemariah son of Hilkiah
[Cperhaps the high priest under Josiah; 2 Kin. 22:8] to Babylon to
Nebuchadnezzar king of Babylon. So Jeremiah gave them this ·letter
[Lscroll] to carry to Babylon:

4This is what the LORD ·All-Powerful [Almighty; of Heaven's
Armies; Tof hosts], the God of Israel, says to all those ·people I
sent away [exiles] from Jerusalem as ·captives [exiles] to Babylon:
5"Build houses and settle ·in the land [down]. Plant gardens and
eat ·the food they grow [Ltheir fruit]. 6·Get married [LTake wives]
and have sons and daughters. ·Find [LTake] wives for your sons,
and let your daughters be married so they also may have sons
and daughters. ·Have many children in Babylon [LMultiply

there]; don't become fewer in number. 7·Also do good things for [LSeek the peace/security of] the city where I ·sent you as captives [exiled you]. Pray to the LORD for the city where you are living, because ·if good things happen in the city, good things will happen to you also [Lin its peace/security you will have peace/security]." 8The LORD ·All-Powerful [Almighty; of Heaven's Armies; Tof hosts], the God of Israel, says: "Don't let the prophets among you and the ·people who do magic [Ldiviners] ·fool [deceive] you. Don't listen to ·their dreams [their/*or* your dreams that they/*or* you dream]. 9They are prophesying ·lies [falsehoods] to you, ·saying that their message is from me [L...in my name]. But I did not send them," says the LORD.

10This is what the LORD says: "·Babylon will be powerful for seventy years. After that time I will come to [LOnly after the seventy years of Babylon are filled will I visit; 25:11] you, and I will ·keep my promise [Lconfirm my good word] to ·bring [restore] you back to ·Jerusalem [Lthis place]. 11I say this because I know ·what [Lthe plans] I am planning for you," says the LORD. "I have ·good plans for you [Lplans for your peace/security], not plans ·to hurt you [Lfor your harm]. I will give you hope and a good future. 12Then you will call ·my name [Lme]. You will come to me and pray to me, and I will listen to you. 13You will search for me. And when you search for me with all your heart, you will find me [Dan. 9:4–19]! 14I will let you find me," says the LORD. "And I will ·bring you back from your captivity [restore your fortunes]. I ·forced you to leave [drove you from] this place, but I will gather you from all the nations, from the places I have ·sent you as captives [exiled you]," says the LORD. "And I will ·bring you back [restore you] to this place."

15You might say, "The LORD has ·given [raised up/established/confirmed for; Deut. 18:18] us prophets here in Babylon."

16But the LORD says this about the king who is sitting on David's throne now and all the other people still in this city [CJerusalem], your ·relatives [Lbrothers] who did not go ·as captives to Babylon [Lout as exiles] with you. 17The LORD ·All-Powerful [Almighty; of Heaven's Armies; Tof hosts] says: "I will soon send ·war [Lsword], ·hunger [famine], and ·terrible diseases [plague; pestilence; Cagainst those still in Jerusalem]. I will make them like bad figs that are too rotten to eat [24:1–10]. 18I will ·chase [pursue] them with ·war [Lsword], ·hunger [famine], and ·terrible diseases [plague; pestilence]. I will make them ·hated by [a horror to] all the kingdoms of the earth. ·People will curse them and be shocked and will use them as a shameful example [L...an object of cursing, shock, hissing and reproach] ·wherever I make them go [Lamong the nations where I have driven them]. 19This is because they have not listened to my message," says the LORD. "I sent my ·message [word] to them again and again through my servants, the prophets, but they did not listen," says the LORD.

20You ·captives [exiles], whom I ·forced to leave [sent from] Jerusalem ·and go to [Lto] Babylon, listen to the message from the LORD. 21The LORD ·All-Powerful [Almighty; of Heaven's

Armies; Tof hosts], the God of Israel, says this about Ahab son of
Kolaiah and Zedekiah son of Maaseiah: "These two men have
been prophesying ·lies [falsehood] to you, ·saying that their message is from me [Lin my name]. But soon I will ·hand over those
two prophets to [Lgive them into the hand of] Nebuchadnezzar
king of Babylon, and he will ·kill [Lstrike] them ·in front of you
[Lbefore your eyes]. 22Because of them, all the ·captives [exiles]
from Judah in Babylon will use this curse: 'May the LORD ·treat
[make] you like Zedekiah and Ahab, whom the king of Babylon
·burned [roasted] in the fire.' 23They have done evil things among
the people of Israel. They are guilty of adultery with their neighbors' wives. They have also spoken ·lies and said those lies were
a message from me [Lfalsehoods in my name; Deut. 18:14–21]. I
did not ·tell [Lcommand] them to do that. I know what they have
done; I am a witness to it," says the LORD.

24Also give a message to Shemaiah from the Nehelamite family. 25The
LORD ·All-Powerful [Almighty; of Heaven's Armies; Tof hosts], the God of
Israel, says: "Shemaiah, you sent ·letters [scrolls] in your name to all the
people in Jerusalem, to the priest Zephaniah son of Maaseiah, and to all
the priests. 26You said to Zephaniah, 'The LORD has made you priest in
place of Jehoiada. You are to be in charge of the ·Temple [Lhouse] of the
LORD. You should arrest any ·madman [crazy person] who acts like a
prophet. Place him in stocks [Cwooden restraints] and put an iron collar
around his neck. 27Now Jeremiah from Anathoth is acting like a prophet.
So why haven't you ·arrested [Lrebuked] him? 28He [CJeremiah] has sent
[Cthis message] to us in Babylon: You will be there for a long time, so
build houses and settle down. Plant gardens and eat ·what they grow
[Ltheir fruit].' "

29Zephaniah the priest read ·the letter to [Lthis scroll in the ear of]
Jeremiah the prophet. 30Then the LORD spoke his word to Jeremiah:
31"Send this message to all the ·captives in Babylon [exiles]: 'This is what
the LORD says about Shemaiah the Nehelamite: Shemaiah has prophesied
to you, but I did not send him. He has made you ·believe [trust; have confidence in] a lie. 32So the LORD says, I will soon punish Shemaiah the
Nehelamite and his ·family [Lseed]. He will not see the good things I will
do for my people, says the LORD. None of his family will be left alive among
the people, because he has taught the people to ·turn [rebel] against me.' "

Promises of Hope

30 These are the words that the LORD spoke to Jeremiah. 2The
LORD, the God of Israel, said: "Jeremiah, write in a ·book
[scroll] all the words I have spoken to you. 3The days will come when I
will ·bring Israel and Judah back from captivity [restore the fortunes of
my people of Israel and Judah]," says the LORD. "I will ·return [restore]
them to the land I gave their ancestors, and they will ·own [possess] it!"
says the LORD."

4The LORD spoke this message about the people of Israel and Judah:
5This is what the LORD said:

"We hear ·people crying from [Lthe voice/sound of] fear.
·They are afraid; there [L...and of dread, and there] is no peace.
6Ask this question, and ·consider it [Lsee]:
·A man cannot [LCan a man...?] have a baby.

So why do I see every strong man
·holding his stomach in pain [Lwith his hands on his side/loins] like a woman ·having a baby [in labor; 13:21; 22:23; 49:24; 50:43; Is. 21:2–3; 26:16–21; 66:7–14]?
Why is everyone's face turning white [Clike a dead or frightened person's face]?
7This will be a ·terrible [Lgreat] day!
There will never be another time like this.
This is a time of ·great trouble [distress] for the people of Jacob,
but they will be ·saved [rescued] from it."

8The LORD ·All-Powerful [Almighty; of Heaven's Armies; Tof hosts] says,
"·At that time [LIn that day]
I will break the yoke from ·their [*or* your] necks
and ·tear [snap] off the ropes that hold ·them [*or* you].
·Foreign people [LStrangers] will never again make my people slaves.
9They will serve the LORD their God
and David their king,
whom I will ·send to [Lraise up for] them.

10"So people of Jacob, my servants, don't be afraid.
Israel, don't be ·frightened [terrified]," says the LORD.
"I will soon ·save [rescue] you from that faraway place.
I will ·save [rescue] your ·family [Lseed] from that land of your captivity.
The people of Jacob will be at rest again;
no one will frighten them.
11I am with you and will ·save [rescue] you,"
says the LORD.
"I will ·completely destroy [bring to an end] all those nations
where I scattered you,
but I will not ·completely destroy you [bring you to an end].
I will ·punish [discipline] you ·fairly [with justice],
but I will ·still punish you [Lnot leave you unpunished; 46:27–28]."
12This is what the LORD said:
"Your wound cannot be cured;
your injury will not heal [8:22; 10:19; Mic. 1:9; Nah. 3:19].
13There is no one to ·argue your case [uphold your cause]
and no ·cure [medicine] for your sores.
So you will not be healed.
14All your lovers [Callied nations] have forgotten you.
They don't ·care about [Lseek] you.
I have ·hurt you [struck you a blow] as an enemy would.
I ·punished [disciplined] you ·very hard [harshly],
because your ·guilt [iniquity] was so great
and your sins were so many.
15Why are you crying out about your injury?
There is no cure for your pain.
I did these things to you because of your great ·guilt [iniquity],
because of your many sins.
16But all those ·nations that destroyed you will now be destroyed [Lwho consumed/devoured you will be consumed/devoured].

All your ·enemies [foes] will become ·captives in other lands [exiles].
Those who ·stole from [Lplunder] you will ·have their own things stolen [Lbe plundered].
Those who took things from you in war will have their own things taken.
17I will bring back your health
and heal your injuries," says the LORD,
"because ·other people forced you away [Lthey called you 'driven out'/'an outcast'].
They said about you, 'No one ·cares about [Lseeks] ·Jerusalem [LZion; Cthe location of the Temple]!' "
18This is what the LORD said:
"I ·will soon make the tents of Jacob's people as they used to be [Lam restoring the fortunes of the tents of Jacob],
and I will have ·pity [compassion] on their houses.
The city will be rebuilt on its ·hill of ruins [mound],
and the king's palace will stand in its ·proper [traditional] place.
19·People in those places will sing songs of praise [LPraise/Thanks will go out from them; Ps. 126].
There will be the sound of laughter.
I will ·give them many children [Lmultiply them]
so ·their number will not be small [Lthey will not diminish; Gen. 12:1–3; 22:17; 32:12; 41:49].
I will bring ·honor [glory] to them
so no one will ·look down on [belittle] them.
20Their ·descendants [children] will be as they were in the old days.
·I will set them up as a strong people [LTheir congregation will be established] before me,
and I will punish ·the nations who have hurt them [their oppressors].
21·One of their own people will lead them [LTheir noble one will be of them];
their ruler will come from among them [Deut. 17:14–20].
·He will come near to me when I invite him [LI will bring him near and he will approach me].
Who would dare to ·come to [approach] me uninvited?" says the LORD.
22"So you will be my people,
and I will be your God [Cthey will be in a covenant relationship; Hos. 2:23]."

23Look! It is a ·storm [whirlwind] from the LORD!
·He is angry and has gone out to punish the people [LWrath has gone out].
·Punishment will come like a storm [LA whirling storm/tempest comes]
·crashing down on the evil people [Lswirling around the heads of the wicked; 23:19].
24The LORD will stay angry
until he performs and accomplishes
the ·intentions [plans] of his ·heart [mind].
·When that day comes [LIn future days],
you will understand this.

The New Israel

31 The LORD says, "At that time I will be God of all Israel's ·family groups [clans], and they will be my people [30:22]."
²This is what the LORD says:
"The people who ·were not killed by the enemy's [ᴸsurvived the] sword
found ·help [grace; favor] in the ·desert [wilderness; ᶜas during the exodus from Egypt].
I came to give rest to Israel."
³And from far away the LORD appeared to his people and said,
"I love you people
with a ·love that will last forever [eternal love].
That is why I have continued
showing you ·kindness [loyalty].
⁴·People [ᴸVirgin daughter] of Israel, I will build you up again,
and you will be rebuilt.
You will pick up your tambourines again
and dance with those who are joyful.
⁵You will plant vineyards again
on the hills around Samaria [ᶜin northern Israel].
The ·farmers [ᴸplanters] will plant them
and enjoy their fruit.
⁶There will be a time when ·watchmen [sentinels; guards] in the mountains of Ephraim [ᶜnorthern Israel] ·shout this message [ᴸproclaim]:
'·Come [ᴸGet up], let's go up to ·Jerusalem [ᴸZion; ᶜthe location of the Temple] to the LORD our God [ᶜto worship]!' "
⁷This is what the LORD says:
"·Be happy and sing [ᴸSing with joy] for the people of Jacob.
Shout for Israel, the ·greatest [head; foremost] of the nations.
·Sing your praises and shout this [ᴸMake yourself heard, praise, and say]:
'LORD, ·save [rescue] your people,
·those who are left alive from the nation [ᴸthe remnant] of Israel!'
⁸Look, I will soon bring them [ᶜthe remnant of Israel] from the country in the north [ᶜBabylon],
and I will gather them from the faraway places on earth.
Some of the people are blind and ·crippled [lame; Is. 35:5–6; Mic. 4:6–8].
Some of the women are pregnant, and some are ready to give birth.
A great ·many people [assembly] will ·come back [return].
⁹They will be crying as they come,
·but they will pray as [ᴸwith supplications] I ·bring [lead] them back.
I will lead those people by streams of water [Ps. 23]
on an ·even road [straight way] where they will not stumble.
I am Israel's father,
and ·Israel [ᴸEphraim; ᶜthe dominant tribe of the northern kingdom of Israel] is my firstborn son.

¹⁰"Nations, listen to the ·message from [ᴸword of] the LORD.
Tell this message in the faraway ·lands by the sea [coastlands]:
'The one who scattered the people of Israel will ·bring them back [gather them],
and he will ·watch over [keep; guard] his people like a shepherd of a flock. [Num. 27:17; 2 Sam. 7:7; Ps. 78:70–72; Ezek. 34].'

11 The LORD will ·pay for [ransom] the people of Jacob
and will ·buy them back [redeem them] from ·people [La hand/
power] stronger than they were.
12 They [Cpeople of Israel] will come to the high points of Jerusalem
and shout for joy.
·Their faces will shine with happiness [LThey will be radiant] about all
the good things from the LORD:
the grain, new wine, oil, young sheep, and young cows.
They will be like a garden that has plenty of water,
and they will not ·be troubled [languish] anymore.
13 Then ·young women [*or* virgins; Cof Israel] will be happy and dance,
the young men and old men also.
I will change their ·sadness [mourning] into ·happiness [joy];
I will give them comfort and joy instead of ·sadness [lament;
Ps. 30:11–12; 126].
14 The priests will have ·more than enough sacrifices [Ltheir fill of fatness],
and my people will be ·filled [satisfied; sated] with the good things I
give them!" says the LORD.
15 This is what the LORD says:
"A voice was heard in Ramah [Ca place from which God's people were
deported into exile; 40:1; Matt. 2:18]
of ·painful crying [lamentation] and ·deep sadness [Lbitter weeping]:
Rachel crying for her children [Cthe Israelites].
She refused to be comforted,
because her children are ·dead [Lno more]!"
16 But this is what the LORD says:
"·Stop crying [LRefrain your voice from weeping];
·don't let your eyes fill with tears [Lyour eyes from tears].
You will be rewarded for your work!" says the LORD.
"The people will return from their enemy's land.
17 So there is hope for you in the future," says the LORD.
"Your children will return to their own ·land [borders].

18 "I have heard ·Israel [LEphraim] ·moaning [pleading]:
'LORD, you ·punished [disciplined; instructed] me, and I ·have
learned my lesson [was disciplined/instructed].
I was like a calf that had never been trained [Hos. 10:11].
Take me back so that I may come back.
You truly are the LORD my God.
19 LORD, after I ·wandered away [turned away] from you,
I ·changed my heart and life [Lrepented].
After I understood,
I beat my ·breast [Lthigh; Cshowing sorrow].
I was ashamed and ·disgraced [humiliated],
because I ·suffered for the foolish things I did when I was young
[Lcarried the reproach of my youth].'

20 "·You know that Israel is my dear son [LDo you know how precious
Ephraim is to me…?],
The child I ·love [delight in].
Yes, I often speak against him [CIsrael],
but I still remember him.

·I love him very much [LMy innards roil/churn toward him],
and I want to ·comfort [be compassionate toward] him," says the LORD.

21"·Fix [LPut up; Erect] the road ·signs [markers].
·Put up signs to show you the way home [LMake guideposts].
·Watch the road [LSet your heart toward the highway].
Pay attention to the road on which you travel.
·People [LVirgin daughter; Young woman] of Israel, ·come home
[Lreturn; repent],
·come back to [Lreturn to these] your towns.
22You are an unfaithful daughter.
How long will you ·wander before you come home [Lwaver]?
The LORD has ·made [created] something new happen in the land:
A woman will ·go seeking [*or* protect; *or* embrace; Lsurround] a man."
23The LORD ·All-Powerful [Almighty; of Heaven's Armies; Tof hosts], the
God of Israel, says: "I will again do good things for the people of Judah. At
that time the people in the land of Judah and its towns will again use these
words: 'May the LORD bless you, ·home of what is good [Labode of righ-
teousness], holy mountain.' 24People in all the towns of Judah will live
together [Cin peace]. Farmers and those who ·move around [wander] with
their flocks will live together [Cin peace]. 25I will ·give rest [satisfy] and
·strength to [replenish] those who ·are weak [languish] and ·tired [faint]."
26After hearing that, I [CJeremiah], woke up and looked around. My
sleep had been very pleasant.
27The LORD says, "The ·time is [Ldays are] coming when I will ·help
[Lsow] the ·families [Lhouses] of Israel and Judah ·and their children
[Lwith the seed of humans] and ·animals to grow [Lseed of animals]. 28In
the past I watched over them [CIsrael and Judah; 1:12], to ·pull [pluck]
them up and ·tear [pull] them down, to destroy them and bring them
·disaster [harm; trouble]. But now I will watch over them to build them
up and ·make them strong [to plant them; 1:10]," says the LORD.
29"·At that time [LIn those days] people will no longer say:
'The ·parents [fathers] have eaten sour grapes,
and that caused the children to ·grind their teeth from the sour taste
[Lbe set on edge].'
30Instead, each person will die for his own ·sin [iniquity]; the person who
eats sour grapes ·will grind his own teeth [Lhis teeth are set on edge; Lam. 5:7;
Ezek. 18:2].

The New Agreement

31"Look, the ·time is [Ldays are] coming," says the LORD,
"when I will ·make [Lcut] a new ·agreement [covenant; treaty]
with the ·people [Lhouse] of Israel
and the ·people [Lhouse] of Judah.
32It will not be like the ·agreement [covenant; treaty]
I ·made [Lcut] with their ·ancestors [fathers]
when I took them by the hand
to bring them out of Egypt [Cthe Mosaic Covenant; Ex. 19–24].
I was a ·husband [*or* master] to them [2:2],
but they broke ·that agreement [my covenant/treaty]," says the LORD.
33"This is the ·agreement [covenant; treaty] I will ·make [Lcut]
with the ·people [Lhouse] of Israel ·at that time [Lafter those days],"
says the LORD:

"I will put my ·teachings [laws; instructions] in their ·minds [Linnards]
and write them on their hearts [Joel 2:28–29].
I will be their God,
and they will be my people [Ex. 6:6–8].
34People will no longer have to teach their neighbors and ·relatives
[brothers]
to know the LORD,
because all people will know me,
from the least to the most important," says the LORD.
"I will forgive them for ·the wicked things they did [Ltheir iniquities],
and I will not remember their sins anymore [32:37–44; 50:4–5;
Ezek. 37:15–28; Luke 22:20; 1 Cor. 11:25; 2 Cor. 3:5–14; Heb. 8:8–12;
10:16–17]."

The Lord Will Never Leave Israel

35The LORD ·makes [Lgives] the sun to ·shine in [Llight] the day
and [Lregulates; fixes the order of] the moon and stars to ·shine at
[Llight the] night [Gen. 1:14–18].
He stirs up the sea so that its waves ·crash on the shore [Lroar].
The LORD ·All-Powerful [Almighty; of Heaven's Armies; Tof hosts] is
his name.
This is what the LORD says:
36"Only if these ·laws [statutes; ordinances; requirements; Cthat uphold
the natural order] should ever ·fail [give way; Gen. 8:22; 9:8–17],"
says the LORD,
"will Israel's ·descendants [Lseed] ever ·stop [cease]
being a nation before me ·forever [Lfor all days]."
37This is what the LORD says:
"Only if people can measure the ·sky [heavens] above
and ·learn [investigate] the ·secrets [Lfoundations] of the earth below,
will I reject all the ·descendants [Lseed] of Israel
because of what they have done," says the LORD.

The New Jerusalem

38The LORD says, "The ·time is [Ldays are] coming when this city
[CJerusalem] will be rebuilt for me—everything from the Tower of
Hananel [Neh. 3:1; 12:39; Zech. 14:10] to the Corner Gate [2 Kin. 14:13; 2
Chr. 25:23; 26:9; Zech. 14:10]. 39The measuring line will stretch from ·the
Corner Gate [Lbefore it] straight to the hill of Gareb. Then it will turn to
the place named Goah. 40The whole valley where dead bodies and ashes
are thrown [Cthe Hinnom; ch. 19], and all the terraces out to the Kidron
Valley on the east as far as the corner of the Horse Gate [2 Chr. 23:15;
Neh. 3:28]—all that area will be holy to the LORD. It [CJerusalem] will
never again be torn down or destroyed [1:10]."

Jeremiah Buys a Field

32 This is the word the LORD spoke to Jeremiah in the tenth year
Zedekiah was king of Judah, which was the eighteenth year of
Nebuchadnezzar [C587 BC; 52:4–5]. 2At that time the army of the king
of Babylon was ·surrounding [besieging] Jerusalem. Jeremiah the
prophet was ·under arrest [imprisoned; confined] in the courtyard of
the guard, which was at the ·palace [Lhouse] of the king of Judah.
3Zedekiah king of Judah had ·put Jeremiah in prison there [confined;
imprisoned him]. Zedekiah had asked, "Why have you prophesied the
things you have?" (Jeremiah had said, "This is what the LORD says: 'I will
soon hand this city [CJerusalem] over to the king of Babylon, and he will

capture it. 4Zedekiah king of Judah will not ·escape [be rescued] from the
·Babylonian [LChaldean] army, but he will surely be handed over to the
king of Babylon. And he will speak to him [Cthe king of Babylon] face to
face and see him with his own eyes. 5The king will take Zedekiah to
Babylon, where he will stay until I have punished him,' says the LORD. 'If
you fight against the Babylonians, you will not succeed.' ")

6Jeremiah said [Cwhile still in prison], "The LORD spoke this word to
me: 7Hanamel, son of your uncle Shallum, will come to you soon.
Hanamel will say to you, 'Buy my field near the town of Anathoth
[CJeremiah's hometown; 1:1]. It is your right and your duty to buy that
field [Cbecause he is a near relative; Lev. 25:23–25].'

8"Then it happened just as the LORD had said. ·My cousin [LThe son of
my uncle] Hanamel came to me in the courtyard of the guard and said to
me, 'Buy for yourself my field near Anathoth in the land of Benjamin. It
is your right and duty to buy it and own it.' So I knew this was a ·message
[Lword] from the LORD.

9"I bought the field at Anathoth from ·my cousin [Lthe son of my uncle]
Hanamel, weighing out ·seven ounces [Lseventeen shekels] of silver for
him. 10I ·signed the record [Lwrote in a scroll] and sealed it and had some
people witness it. I also weighed out the silver on the scales. 11Then I took
both copies of the ·record [scroll] of ·ownership [purchase]—the one that
was sealed that had the demands and ·limits of ownership [terms], and the
one that was ·not sealed [Lexposed]. 12And I gave them to Baruch son of
Neriah, the son of Mahseiah [36; 43:3, 6; 45:1–2]. My cousin Hanamel, the
other witnesses who signed the ·record [scroll] of ·ownership [purchase],
and many ·Jews [LJudeans] sitting in the courtyard of the guard saw me
give the ·record [scroll] of ·ownership [purchase] to Baruch.

13"·With all the people watching [LBefore their eyes], I ·told
[Lcommanded] Baruch, 14"This is what the LORD ·All-Powerful [Almighty;
of Heaven's Armies; Tof hosts], the God of Israel, says: Take both copies of
the ·record [scroll] of ·ownership [purchase]—the sealed copy and the
copy that was ·not sealed [Lexposed]—and put them in a clay jar so they
will ·last [endure; stand] ·a long time [Lfor many days]. 15This is what the
LORD ·All-Powerful [Almighty; of Heaven's Armies; Tof hosts], the God of
Israel, says: In the future my people will once again buy houses and fields
and vineyards in this land [CIsrael].'

16"After I gave the ·record [scroll] of ·ownership [purchase] to Baruch
son of Neriah, I prayed to the LORD, 17Oh, Lord GOD, you made the ·skies
[heavens] and the earth with your very great power [Gen. 1] and ·strength
[Loutstretched arm]. There is nothing too hard for you to do [Ex. 3:20; Job
9:10; 37:5; Mic. 7:15]. 18You show ·love and kindness [loyalty] to thousands of people, but you also ·bring punishment to children for their
parents' sins [Lrepay the iniquities of the fathers to the laps of their children after them; Ex. 34:7; Deut. 5:9–10]. Great and powerful God, your
name is the LORD ·All-Powerful [Almighty; of Heaven's Armies; Tof hosts].
19You ·plan [are great in counsel] and ·do great things [mighty in deeds].
·You see everything that people do [LYour eyes are open to all the ways/
paths of people], and you ·reward people for the way they live and for
what they do [Lgive to each according to his way and according to the fruit
of his deeds]. 20You did ·miracles [signs] and wonderful things in the land
of Egypt [Ex. 7–15]. You have continued doing them in Israel and among
the other nations even until today. So you have ·become well known

[Lmade yourself a name]. 21You brought your people, the Israelites, out of
Egypt using signs and miracles and your ·great power [Lstrong hand] and
·strength [Loutstretched arm]. You brought great terror on everyone.
22You gave them this land that you promised to their ·ancestors [fathers]
long ago, a ·fertile land [land flowing with milk and honey; Gen. 12:1–3].
23They came into this land and ·took it for their own [possessed it], but
they did not ·obey you [Llisten to your voice] or follow your ·teachings
[laws; instructions]. They did not do everything you commanded. So you
made all these terrible things happen to them.
24"Look! The ·enemy has surrounded the city and has built roads to
the top of the walls [Lsiege ramps have come to the city] to capture it.
Because of ·war [Lsword], ·hunger [famine], and ·terrible diseases [plague;
pestilence], the city will be handed over to the ·Babylonians [LChaldeans]
who are attacking it. You said this would happen, and now you see it is
happening. 25But now, Lord God, you tell me, 'Buy the field with silver
and call in witnesses.' You tell me this while the ·Babylonian army is ready
to capture the city [Lcity is given into the hands of the Chaldeans]."
26Then the Lord spoke this word to Jeremiah: 27"I am the Lord, the God
of ·every person on the earth [Lall flesh]. ·Nothing is impossible [LIs anything too hard…?] for me. 28So this is what the Lord says: I ·will soon hand
over the city of Jerusalem to [Lam giving this city into the hand of] the
·Babylonian army [LChaldeans] and ·to [Linto the hand of] Nebuchadnezzar
king of Babylon, who will capture it. 29The ·Babylonian army [LChaldeans]
is already attacking this city [CJerusalem]. They will soon enter it and start
a fire to burn down the city and its houses. The people of Jerusalem
·offered sacrifices [*or* burned incense] to Baal [Cthe chief God of the
Canaanites] on the roofs [Cflat roofs were living space] of those same
houses and poured out drink offerings to other idols to make me angry.
30From their youth, the ·people [Lsons] of Israel and Judah have done only
·the things I said were wrong [Levil] in my eyes. They have made me angry
by ·worshiping idols made with [Lthe works of] their own hands," says the
Lord. 31"From the day this city was built until now, this city has made me
angry, so angry that I must remove it from ·my sight [before me]. 32I will
destroy it, because of all the evil the ·people [Lsons] of Israel and Judah
have done. The people, their kings and officers, their priests and prophets,
all the people of Judah, and the people of Jerusalem have made me angry.
33They turned their backs to me, not their faces. I tried to teach them again
and again, but they wouldn't listen or ·learn [Lreceive instruction/disci-
pline]. 34They put their ·hateful idols [abominations] in the ·place where I
have chosen to be worshiped [Lhouse called by my name], so they made it
unclean [Cin a ritual sense]. 35In the Valley of Ben Hinnom they built
·places to worship [Lhigh places of; Csites associated with pagan worship or
inappropriate worship of God] Baal so they could ·burn their sons and
daughters as sacrifices [Lmake their sons and daughters pass through (the
fire)] to Molech. But I never commanded them to do such a ·hateful thing
[abomination]. It never entered my ·mind [heart] that they would do such
a thing and cause Judah to sin [7:30–34; 19:1–6].
36"You are saying, 'Because of ·war [Lsword], ·hunger [famine], and
·terrible diseases [plague; pestilence], the city will be handed over to the
king of Babylon.' But the Lord, the God of Israel, says about this city
[CJerusalem]: 37I ·forced them [drove them out] from their land, because
I was furious and very angry with them. But soon I will gather them from

all the lands where I ·forced them to go [drove them out], and I will ·bring
them back [restore them] to this place, where they may live in ·safety
[confidence]. 38 They [Cpeople of Israel and Judah] will be my people, and
I will be their God. 39 I will ·make them truly want to be one people with
one goal [Lgive them one heart and one way/path]. They will truly want to
·worship [Lfear] me all their ·lives [Ldays], for their own good and for the
good of their children after them.
40 "I will ·make [Lcut] an ·agreement with them that will last forever
[Leternal covenant with them; 31:31–34; Is. 55:3; 61:8; Ezek. 16:60; 37:27].
I will never turn away from them; I will always do good to them. I will
·make them want to respect me [Lplace my fear in their hearts] so they will
never ·turn away [depart] from me. 41 I will enjoy doing good to them.
And with ·my whole being [Lall my heart and all my soul] I will ·surely [Lin
faithfulness] plant them in this land."
42 This is what the LORD says: "I have brought this great ·disaster [harm;
trouble] to this people [Cthe people of Israel and Judah]. In the same way
I will bring the good things that I promise to do for them. 43 You are saying, 'This land is an ·empty desert [desolation], without people or animals.
It has been handed over to the ·Babylonians [LChaldeans].' But in the
future, people will again buy fields in this land. 44 They will use their
·money [silver] to buy fields. They will ·sign [Lwrite] and seal their ·agree-
ments [scrolls] and call in witnesses. They will again buy fields in the land
of Benjamin, in the area around Jerusalem, in the towns of Judah and in
the mountains, in the ·western hills [LShephelah], and in ·southern Judah
[Lthe Negev]. I will ·make everything as good for them as it once was
[restore their fortunes]," says the LORD.

The Promise of the Lord

33 While Jeremiah was still ·locked up [confined; imprisoned]
in the courtyard of the guards, the LORD spoke his word to
him a second time: 2 "These are the words of the LORD, who made it [Cthe
earth; Gen. 1], ·shaped [formed; Clike a potter] it, and ·gave it order
[established it], whose name is the LORD: 3 'Pray [LCall] to me, and I will
answer you. I will tell you ·important secrets [Lgreat and hidden things]
you have never ·heard [Lknown] before.' 4 This is what the LORD, the God
of Israel, says about the houses in this city [CJerusalem] and the ·royal
palaces [Lhouses of the king] of Judah that have been torn down ·to be
used in defense of the attack by the Babylonian army [Lagainst the siege
ramps and against the sword]: 5 'Some people will come to fight against
the ·Babylonians [LChaldeans]. They will fill them [Cthe houses] with
·the bodies of people [corpses] I ·killed [struck] in my ·hot anger [Langer
and my wrath]. I have ·turned away [Lhidden my face] from this city
because of all the evil its people have done.
6 " 'But then I will bring ·health [recovery] and healing to the people
there. I will heal them and ·let them enjoy [Lreveal to them] ·great [an
abundance of] peace and ·safety [security]. 7 I will ·bring Judah and Israel
back from captivity [restore the fortunes of Judah and Israel] and ·make
them strong countries [Lrebuild them] as in the past. 8 They sinned against
me, but I will ·wash away [cleanse them from] that sin. They did ·evil
[iniquity] and ·turned away from [transgressed against] me, but I will forgive them. 9 Then it [CJerusalem] will be to me a name that brings joy! And
people from all nations of the earth will praise [Land glorify] it when they
hear about the good things I am doing there. They will ·be surprised

[fear] and ·shocked [tremble] at all the good things and the ·peace [*or* prosperity] I will bring to it.'

10"You are saying, 'Our country is an ·empty desert [ruin], without people or animals.' But this is what the LORD says: It is now quiet in the streets of Jerusalem and in the towns of Judah, without people or animals, but ·it will be noisy there soon [Lthere will once more be heard…]! 11·There will be [L…the] sounds of joy and gladness and the happy sounds of brides and bridegrooms. There will be the sounds of people bringing to the ·Temple [Lhouse] of the LORD their offerings of thanks to the LORD. They will say,

'Praise the LORD ·All-Powerful [Almighty; of Heaven's Armies; Tof hosts],
because the LORD is good!
His ·love [loyalty] continues forever!'

They will say this because I will ·again do good things for Judah [restore the fortunes of the land], as I did in the beginning," says the LORD.

12This is what the LORD ·All-Powerful [Almighty; of Heaven's Armies; Tof hosts] says: "This place is ·empty [a ruin] now, without people or animals. But there will be shepherds in this place [CJudah] and pastures where they let their flocks rest. 13·Shepherds will again count their sheep as the sheep walk in front of them [LFlocks will again pass under the hand of those who count them]. They will count them in the mountains and in the ·western hills [LShephelah], in ·southern Judah [Lthe Negev] and the land of Benjamin, and around Jerusalem and the other towns of Judah!" says the LORD.

The Good Branch

14The LORD says, "The ·time is [Ldays are] coming when I will do the good thing I promised to the people of Israel and Judah.

15In those days and at that time,
I will make a ·good [righteous] branch sprout from David's family [Is. 11:1; Zech. 3:8; 6:12].
He will do ·what is fair [justice] and ·right [righteousness] in the land.
16·At that time [LIn those days] Judah will be ·saved [rescued],
and the people of Jerusalem will live ·in safety [with confidence].
·The branch will be named [LThis one will be called by this]:
The LORD ·Does What Is Right [Our Righteousness]."

17This is what the LORD says: "·Someone from David's family will always sit on the throne of the family [LDavid will never lack a man who will sit on the throne of the house] of Israel [2 Sam. 7:11–16]. 18And there will always be priests from the family of Levi. They will always stand before me to offer burnt offerings [Lev. 1:1–17] and grain [Lgift; tribute] offerings [Lev. 2:1] and sacrifices to me [Num. 25:13]."

19The LORD spoke his word to Jeremiah, saying: 20"This is what the LORD says: I have an ·agreement [covenant; treaty] with day and night that they will always come at the right times [Cthe covenant with Noah; Gen. 9:8–17]. If you could ·change [Lbreak] that ·agreement [covenant; treaty], 21only then could you ·change [Lbreak] my ·agreement [covenant; treaty] with David and Levi. Only then would my servant David not have a descendant ruling on his throne. And only then would the family of Levi not be serving me [Cin the Temple]. 22But I will give many ·descendants [Lseed] to my servant David and to the family group of Levi who serve me. They will be as many as the stars in the sky that no one can count. They will be as many as the grains of sand on the seashore that no one can measure [Gen. 15:5; 22:17; 26:4]."

23The LORD spoke his word to Jeremiah, saying: 24"Have you [CJeremiah]
heard what the people are saying? They say: 'The LORD ·turned away from
[rejected] the two ·families [kingdoms; Cof Israel and Judah] that he
chose.' Now they [Lhold my people in such contempt that they] don't
think of them as a nation anymore!"
25This is what the LORD says: "If I had not made my ·agreement [cove-
nant; treaty] with day and night [v. 20], and if I had not made the ·laws
[statutes; ordinances; requirements] for the ·sky [heavens] and earth,
26only then would I ·turn away from [reject] Jacob's ·descendants [Lseed].
And only then would I not let the ·descendants [Lseed] of David my servant rule over the ·descendants [Lseed] of Abraham, Isaac, and Jacob. But
I will be ·kind [compassionate] to them and ·cause good things to happen
to them [restore their fortunes] again."

A Warning to Zedekiah

34 The LORD spoke his word to Jeremiah when Nebuchadnezzar
king of Babylon was fighting against Jerusalem and all the
towns around it. Nebuchadnezzar had with him all his army and the
armies of all the kingdoms and peoples ·he ruled [under his hand]. 2This
is what the LORD, the God of Israel, said: "Jeremiah, go to Zedekiah king
of Judah and tell him: 'This is what the LORD says: I will soon hand this
city [CJerusalem] over to the king of Babylon, and he will burn it ·down
[Lwith fire]! 3You will not escape from ·the king of Babylon [Lhis hand];
you will surely be captured and handed over to him. You will see the
king of Babylon ·with your own eyes [eye to eye], and he will talk to you
face to face. And you will go to Babylon. 4But, Zedekiah king of Judah,
listen to the promise of the LORD. This is what the LORD says about you:
You will not be killed with a sword. 5You will die in a peaceful way. As
people ·made funeral fires [*or* burn spices; Lburn] to honor your ·ances-
tors [fathers], the kings who ruled before you, so people will ·make a
funeral fire [*or* burn spices; Lburn] to honor you. They will ·cry for you
and sadly [mourn for you and] say, "Ah, master!" I myself make this
promise to you, says the LORD [52:8–11].'"
6So Jeremiah the prophet gave this message to Zedekiah in Jerusalem.
7This was while the army of the king of Babylon was fighting against
Jerusalem and the cities of Judah that ·had not yet been taken [remained]
—Lachish and Azekah [Cfortress cities to the west of Jerusalem]. These
were the only ·strong, walled [fortified] cities left in the land of Judah.

Slaves Are Mistreated

8The LORD spoke his word to Jeremiah. This was after King Zedekiah
had ·made [Lcut] an ·agreement [covenant; treaty] with all the people in
Jerusalem to ·free all the Hebrew slaves [Lproclaim liberty/emancipation;
Ex. 21:1–11; Lev. 25:39–46; Deut. 15:12–18]. 9Everyone was supposed to
free his Hebrew slaves, both male and female. No one was to keep a fellow
·Jew [LJudean] as a slave. 10All the officers and all the people ·accepted
[obeyed] this agreement; they agreed to free their male and female slaves
and no longer keep them as slaves. So all the slaves were set free. 11But
after that, they [Cthe people who owned slaves] ·changed their minds
[Lturned back]. So they took back the people they had set free and made
them slaves again.
12Then the LORD spoke his word to Jeremiah: 13"This is what the LORD,
the God of Israel, says: I brought your ·ancestors [fathers] out of Egypt
·where they were slaves [Lthe house of bondage/slavery] and ·made [Lcut]
an ·agreement [covenant; treaty] with them. 14I said to your ·ancestors

[fathers]: 'At the end of every seven years, each one of you must set his
Hebrew slaves free. If a fellow Hebrew has sold himself to you, you must
let him go free after he has served you for six years.' But your ·ancestors
[fathers] did not listen or ·pay attention [Lincline their ear] to me. 15A
short time ago you ·changed your hearts [repented] and did what ·I say is
right [Lwas right in my eyes]. ·Each of you gave freedom [L…to proclaim
liberty/emancipation] to his fellow Hebrews who were slaves. And you
even ·made [Lcut] an ·agreement [covenant; treaty] before me in the place
·where I have chosen to be worshiped [Lcalled by my name]. 16But now
you have ·changed your minds [turned around]. You have ·shown you do
not honor [profaned; dishonored] me. Each of you has taken back the
male and female slaves you had set free, and you have forced them to
become your slaves again.

17"So this is what the LORD says: You have not ·obeyed [listened to] me.
You have not ·given freedom [proclaimed liberty/emancipation] to your
fellow Hebrews, neither ·relatives [brothers] nor ·friends [neighbors]. But
now I will ·give freedom [proclaim liberty/emancipation to you], says the
LORD, to ·war [Lthe sword], to ·terrible diseases [plague; pestilence], and to
·hunger [famine]. I will make you ·hated by [a horror to] all the kingdoms
of the earth. 18I will hand over the men who ·broke [transgressed] my
·agreement [covenant; treaty], who have not kept the ·promises [Lterms of
the covenant/treaty] they made before me. They cut a calf into two pieces
before me and ·walked between [Lpassed through] the pieces [Can ancient
oath ritual saying that if one broke the agreement they would die like the
calf; Gen. 15:9–20]. 19These people made the ·agreement [covenant; treaty]
before me by ·walking between [Lpassing through] the pieces of the calf:
the leaders of Judah and Jerusalem, the ·officers of the court [*or* eunuchs],
the priests, and all the people of the land. 20So I will hand them over to
their enemies and to everyone who ·wants to kill them [Lseeks their life].
Their ·bodies [corpses] will become food for the birds of the ·air [heavens]
and for the wild animals of the earth. 21I will hand Zedekiah king of Judah
and his officers over to their enemies, and to everyone who ·wants to kill
them [Lseeks their life], and to the army of the king of Babylon, even
though they have ·left Jerusalem [Lgone up from you]. 22I will give the
order, says the LORD, to ·bring the Babylonian army back to Jerusalem
[Lreturn them to this city]. It will fight against it, capture it, set it on fire,
and burn it down. I will ·destroy the towns in Judah so that they become
ruins [Lmake the towns of Judah a desolation] where no one lives!"

The Recabite Family Obeys God

35 When Jehoiakim son of Josiah was king of Judah [Cruled
609–597 BC], the LORD spoke his word to Jeremiah, saying:
2"Go to the ·family [Lhouse] of Recab. Invite them to come to one of the
·side rooms [chambers] of the ·Temple [Lhouse] of the LORD, and offer
them wine to drink."

3So I went to get Jaazaniah son of Jeremiah [Cnot the prophet, but a
man with the same name], the son of Habazziniah. And I gathered all of
Jaazaniah's brothers and sons and the whole ·family [Lhouse] of the
Recabites together. 4Then I brought them into the ·Temple [Lhouse] of
the LORD. We went into the ·room [chamber] of the sons of Hanan son of
Igdaliah, who was a man of God. The ·room [chamber] was next to the
one where the officers stay and above the ·room [chamber] of Maaseiah
son of Shallum, the ·doorkeeper in the Temple [Lguard/keeper of the

threshold]. 5Then I put some ·bowls [pitchers] full of wine and some cups
before the men of the Recabite ·family [Lhouse]. And I said to them,
"Drink some wine."

6But the Recabite men answered, "We never drink wine. Our ·ancestor
[father] Jonadab son of Recab [2 Kin. 10:15–17] gave us this command:
'You and your descendants must never drink wine. 7Also you must never
build houses, ·plant [Lsow] seeds, or plant vineyards, or do any of those
things. You must live only in tents all your days. Then you will live ·a long
time [Lmany days] in the land where you are ·wanderers [sojourners; resident aliens].' 8So we Recabites ·have obeyed everything [Llistened to the
voice of] Jonadab our ·ancestor [father] commanded us. Neither we nor
our wives, sons, or daughters ever drink wine. 9We never build houses in
which to live, or own fields or vineyards, or ·plant crops [Lseed]. 10We
have lived in tents and have obeyed everything our ancestor Jonadab
commanded us. 11But when Nebuchadnezzar king of Babylon ·attacked
Judah [Lcame up to the land], we said to each other, 'Come, we must enter
Jerusalem ·so we can escape [Lfrom before] the ·Babylonian [LChaldean]
army and the Aramean army.' So we have stayed [lived] in Jerusalem
[Cthough they may not be living in houses, in conformity to their ancestor's command]."

12Then the LORD spoke his word to Jeremiah: 13"This is what the LORD
·All-Powerful [Almighty; of Heaven's Armies; Tof hosts], the God of Israel,
says: Jeremiah, go and tell the men of Judah and the people of Jerusalem:
'·You should [LCan you not…?] learn a lesson and obey my message,' says
the LORD. 14'Jonadab son of Recab ordered his descendants not to drink
wine, and that command has been obeyed. Until today they have obeyed
their ·ancestor's [father's] command; they do not drink wine. But I, the
LORD, have given you messages again and again, but you did not ·obey
[listen to] me. 15I sent all my servants the prophets to you again and
again, saying, "Each of you must ·stop doing evil [Lturn from his evil way/
path]. You must change and be good. Do not ·follow [Lgo after] other gods
to serve them. If you obey me, you will live in the land I have given to you
and your ·ancestors [fathers]." But you have not ·listened [Linclined your
ear] to me or paid attention to my message. 16The descendants of Jonadab
son of Recab obeyed the commands their ancestor gave them, but the
people of Judah have not obeyed me [Cthe Recabites carefully observe the
law of a human while Israel rejects divine law].'

17"So the LORD God ·All-Powerful [Almighty; of Heaven's Armies; Tof
hosts], the God of Israel, says: 'I will soon bring every ·disaster [trouble;
evil] I said would come to Judah and to everyone living in Jerusalem. I
spoke to those people, but they refused to listen. I called out to them, but
they did not answer me.'"

18Then Jeremiah said to the [Lhouse of the] Recabites, "This is what the
LORD ·All-Powerful [Almighty; of Heaven's Armies; Tof hosts], the God of
Israel, says: 'You have ·obeyed [listened to] the commands of your ·ances-
tor [father] Jonadab and have ·followed all of his teachings [kept/guarded
all his commands]; you have done everything he commanded.' 19So this is
what the LORD ·All-Powerful [Almighty; of Heaven's Armies; Tof hosts],
the God of Israel, says: '·There will always be a descendant of Jonadab son
of Recab to serve me [LJonadab son of Recab will not lack a descendant to
stand before me for all days].'"

Jehoiakim Burns Jeremiah's Scroll

36 The LORD spoke this word to Jeremiah during the fourth year
that Jehoiakim son of Josiah was king of Judah [C605 BC]:
2“Get a scroll. Write on it all the words I have spoken to you about Israel
and Judah and all the nations. Write everything from when I first spoke
to you, when Josiah was king, until now [Chis prophecies began in the
thirteenth year of this king, 626 BC; 1:1–3]. 3Maybe the ·family [Lhouse]
of Judah will hear what ·disasters [evil; troubles] I am planning to ·bring
on [Ldo to] them and will ·stop doing wicked things [Lturn back from his
evil ways/paths]. Then I would forgive them for ·the sins and the evil
things they have done [Ltheir iniquities and their sins].”
4So Jeremiah called for Baruch son of Neriah [32:12; 43:3, 6; 45:1–2].
·Jeremiah spoke the messages the LORD had given him, and Baruch wrote
those messages [LBaruch wrote from the mouth of Jeremiah all the words
of the LORD which he spoke to him] on the scroll. 5Then Jeremiah commanded Baruch, “I cannot go to the ·Temple [Lhouse] of the LORD. I ·must
stay here [Lam confined/restricted/imprisoned]. 6So I want you to go to the
·Temple [Lhouse] of the LORD on a day when the people are fasting. Read
from the scroll ·to [Lin the ears of] all the people of Judah who come into
Jerusalem from their towns. Read the messages from the LORD, which are
the words you wrote on the scroll ·as I spoke them to you [Lfrom my
mouth]. 7Perhaps ·they will ask the LORD to help them [Ltheir supplications
will fall before the LORD]. Perhaps each one will ·stop doing wicked things
[Lturn from their evil ways], because the LORD has announced that he is
very angry with them.” 8So Baruch son of Neriah did everything Jeremiah
the prophet ·told [Lcommanded] him to do. In the LORD's ·Temple [Lhouse]
he read aloud the scroll that had the LORD's messages written on it.
9In the ninth month of the fifth year that Jehoiakim son of Josiah was
king [C604 BC], a fast was announced. All the people of Jerusalem and everyone who had come into Jerusalem from the towns of Judah were supposed
to ·give up eating to honor [Lfast before] the LORD. 10At that time Baruch
read to all the people there the scroll containing Jeremiah's words. He read
the scroll in the ·Temple [Lhouse] of the LORD in the room of Gemariah son
of Shaphan, a ·royal secretary [scribe]. That ·room [chamber] was in the
upper courtyard at the entrance of the New Gate of the Temple.
11Micaiah son of Gemariah, the son of Shaphan, heard all the messages
from the LORD that were on the scroll. 12Micaiah went down to the ·royal
secretary's [scribe's] room in the king's ·palace [Lhouse] where all of the
officers were sitting: Elishama the ·royal secretary [scribe]; Delaiah son of
Shemaiah; Elnathan son of Acbor [2 Kin. 22:8–10]; Gemariah son of
Shaphan; Zedekiah son of Hananiah; and all the other officers. 13Micaiah
told those officers everything he had heard Baruch read to the people
from the scroll.
14Then the officers sent a man named Jehudi son of Nethaniah to
Baruch. (Nethaniah was the son of Shelemiah, who was the son of Cushi.)
Jehudi said to Baruch, “·Bring [LTake in your hand] the scroll that you
read ·to [Lin the ears of] the people and come with me.”

So Baruch son of Neriah took in his hand the scroll and went with
Jehudi to the officers. 15Then the officers said to Baruch, “Please sit down
and read the scroll ·to us [Lin our ears].”

So Baruch read the scroll ·to them [Lin their ears] . 16When the officers
heard all the words, they became afraid and looked at each other. They said
to Baruch, “We must certainly tell the king about these words.” 17Then the

officers asked Baruch, “Tell us, please, ·where did you get all these words
you wrote on the scroll [Lhow did you write all these words]? ·Did you write
down what Jeremiah said to you [At his dictation; LFrom his mouth]?”
18“Yes,” Baruch answered. “Jeremiah spoke them ·all to me [Lfrom his
mouth], and I wrote them down with ink on this scroll.”
19Then the officers said to Baruch, “You and Jeremiah must go and
hide, and ·don’t tell anyone [Lno one must know] where you are.”
20The officers put the scroll in the room of Elishama the ·royal secretary [scribe]. Then they went to the king in the courtyard and told ·him
all about the scroll [Lall these words in the ear of the king]. 21So King
Jehoiakim sent Jehudi to get the scroll. Jehudi brought the scroll from the
room of Elishama the ·royal secretary [scribe] and read it ·to [Lin the ears
of] the king and ·to [Lin the ears of] all the officers who stood around the
king. 22It was the ninth month of the year [Clate autumn], so King
Jehoiakim was sitting in the winter apartment. There was a fire burning
in a ·small firepot [brazier] in front of him. 23After Jehudi had read three
or four columns, ·the king [Lhe] cut those columns off of the scroll with a
penknife and threw them into the ·firepot [brazier]. Finally, the whole
scroll was burned in the fire. 24King Jehoiakim and his servants heard
·everything that was said [Lall these words], but they were not frightened!
They did not tear their clothes [Cto show their sorrow]. 25Elnathan,
Delaiah, and Gemariah ·even tried to talk [beseeched] King Jehoiakim
out of burning the scroll, but he would not listen to them. 26Instead, the
king ordered Jerahmeel son of the king, Seraiah son of Azriel, and
Shelemiah son of Abdeel to arrest Baruch the ·secretary [scribe] and
Jeremiah the prophet. But the LORD had hidden them.
27So King Jehoiakim burned the scroll where Baruch had written ·all
the words Jeremiah had spoken to him [Lfrom the mouth of Jeremiah].
Then the LORD spoke his word to Jeremiah: 28“Get another scroll. Write
all the words on it that were on the first scroll that Jehoiakim king of
Judah burned up. 29Also say this to Jehoiakim king of Judah: ‘This is what
the LORD says: You burned up that scroll and said, “Why, Jeremiah, did
you write on it ‘the king of Babylon will surely come and destroy this land
and the people and animals in it’?” 30So this is what the LORD says about
Jehoiakim king of Judah: Jehoiakim’s descendants will not sit on David’s
throne. When Jehoiakim dies, his body will be thrown out on the ground.
It will be left out in the heat of the day and in the frost of the night. 31I will
punish Jehoiakim and his ·children [Lseed] and his servants, because
·they have done evil things [of their guilt/iniquity]. I will bring ·disasters
[evil; trouble] upon them and upon all the people in Jerusalem and
Judah—everything I promised but which they refused to hear.’ ”
32So Jeremiah took another scroll and gave it to Baruch son of Neriah,
his ·secretary [scribe]. ·As Jeremiah spoke [LFrom the mouth of Jeremiah],
Baruch wrote on the scroll the same words that were on the scroll
Jehoiakim king of Judah had burned in the fire. And many similar words
were added to the second scroll.

Jeremiah in Prison

37 Nebuchadnezzar king of Babylon had ·appointed [made king]
Zedekiah son of Josiah to be king of Judah [Cin 597 BC; he
ruled until 586 BC]. Zedekiah took the place of ·Jehoiachin [LConiah] son
of Jehoiakim. 2But Zedekiah, his servants, and the people of Judah did not
listen to the words the LORD had spoken through Jeremiah the prophet.

3Now King Zedekiah sent Jehucal son of Shelemiah and the priest
Zephaniah son of Maaseiah [21:1; 29:25, 29; 52:24] with a message to
Jeremiah the prophet. This was the message: "Jeremiah, please pray to the
LORD our God for us."
4At that time Jeremiah had not yet been put into ·prison [Lthe house of
confinement]. So he ·was free to go anywhere he wanted [Lcame and went
among the people]. 5The army of the ·king of Egypt [LPharaoh] had
marched from Egypt [Ctoward Judah]. Now the ·Babylonian army
[LChaldeans] had ·surrounded [besieged] the city of Jerusalem. When
they heard about the Egyptian army marching toward them, the
Babylonian army left Jerusalem.
6The LORD spoke his word to Jeremiah the prophet: 7"This is what the
LORD, the God of Israel, says: Jehucal and Zephaniah, I know Zedekiah
king of Judah sent you to seek me [Cto get his help]. Tell this to King
Zedekiah: 'The army of the king of Egypt came here to help you, but they
will ·go back [return] to Egypt. 8After that, the ·Babylonian army
[LChaldeans] will return and ·attack [fight] this city [CJerusalem] and
capture it and burn it ·down [Lwith fire].'
9"This is what the LORD says: People of Jerusalem, do not ·fool [deceive]
yourselves. Don't say, 'The ·Babylonian army [LChaldeans] will surely
·leave us alone [Lgo away from us].' They will not! 10Even if you ·defeated
[Lstruck] all of the ·Babylonian army [LChaldeans] that is ·attacking
[fighting] you and there were only a few injured men left in their tents,
they would ·come from their tents [Lrise up] and burn ·down Jerusalem
[Lthis city with fire]!"
11So the ·Babylonian [LChaldean] army left Jerusalem to fight the army
of ·the king of Egypt [LPharaoh]. 12Now Jeremiah tried to travel from
Jerusalem to the land of Benjamin to get his share of the property ·that
belonged to his family [Lamong the people; 32:1–15]. 13When Jeremiah
got to the Benjamin Gate [38:7; Ezek. 48:32; Zech 14:10] of Jerusalem, the
captain in charge of the guards arrested him. The captain's name was
Irijah son of Shelemiah son of Hananiah. Irijah said, "You are ·leaving us
to join the Babylonians [deserting/defecting/Lfalling to the Chaldeans]!"
14But Jeremiah said to Irijah, "·That's not true [False; Lies]! I am not
·leaving to join the Babylonians [deserting/defecting/Lfalling to the
Chaldeans]." Irijah refused to listen to Jeremiah, so he arrested Jeremiah
and took him to the officers of Jerusalem. 15Those ·rulers [Lofficers] were
very angry with Jeremiah and ·beat [Lstruck] him. Then they put him in
·jail [Lhouse of confinement] in the house of Jonathan the ·royal secretary
[scribe], which had been made into a prison [Lhouse of confinement].
16So those people put Jeremiah into a cell in a ·dungeon [Lhouse of the pit/
cistern], and Jeremiah was there for ·a long time [Lmany days].
17Then King Zedekiah sent for Jeremiah and had him brought to the
palace. Zedekiah asked him in ·private [secret], "Is there any message
from the LORD?"
Jeremiah answered, "Yes, there is. Zedekiah, you will be handed over to
the king of Babylon." 18Then Jeremiah said to King Zedekiah, "What ·crime
[sin] have I done against you or your officers or the people of Jerusalem?
Why have you ·thrown [placed] me into ·prison [Lthe house of confine-
ment]? 19Where are your prophets that prophesied this message to you: 'The
king of Babylon will not attack you or this land' [CJudah]? 20But now, my
master, king [Cof Judah], please listen to me, and please ·do what I ask of [Llet

my pleas for help/supplications fall before] you. Do not send me back to the house of Jonathan the ·royal secretary [scribe], or I will die there!"

21So King Zedekiah gave orders for Jeremiah to be put under guard in the courtyard of the guard and to be given bread each day from the street of the bakers until there was no more bread in the city. So he stayed under guard in the courtyard of the guard.

Jeremiah Is Thrown into a Well

38 Shephatiah son of Mattan, Gedaliah son of Pashhur, ·Jehucal [LJucal; 37:3] son of Shelemiah, and Pashhur son of Malkijah [21:1] heard what Jeremiah was telling all the people. He said: 2"This is what the LORD says: 'Everyone who stays in this city [CJerusalem] will die ·from war [Lby sword], or ·hunger [famine], or ·terrible diseases [plague; pestilence]. But everyone who ·surrenders [Lgoes out] to the ·Babylonian army [LChaldeans] will live; ·they will escape with their lives and [Ltheir lives will be plunder and they will] live.' 3And this is what the LORD says: 'This city will surely be handed over to the army of the king of Babylon. He will capture this city!' "

4Then the officers said to the king, "This man [CJeremiah] must be put to death! He is ·discouraging [demoralizing; Lweakening the hands of] the soldiers who are still in the city, and all the people, by what he is saying to them. He ·does not want good to happen to us [Lis not seeking our welfare/peace]; ·he wants to ruin us [L...only harm/trouble/evil]."

5King Zedekiah said to them, "·Jeremiah is in your control [LHe is in your hands]. ·I cannot do anything [LThe king is powerless] to stop you."

6So they [Cthe officers] took Jeremiah and put him into the ·well [cistern; pit] of Malkijah, the king's son, which was in the courtyard of the guards. The officers used ropes to lower Jeremiah into the ·well [cistern; pit], which did not have any water in it, only mud. And Jeremiah sank down into the mud.

7But Ebed-Melech, a Cushite [Can Ethiopian] and a ·servant [*or* eunuch] in the ·palace [Lhouse of the king], heard that the officers had put Jeremiah into the ·well [cistern; pit]. As King Zedekiah was sitting at the Benjamin Gate, 8Ebed-Melech left the ·palace [Lhouse of the king] and went to the king. Ebed-Melech said to him, 9"My master and king, these rulers have acted in an evil way. They have treated Jeremiah the prophet badly. They have thrown him into a ·well [cistern; pit] and left him there to die! ·When there [*or* There] is no more bread in the city, he will starve to death."

10Then King Zedekiah commanded Ebed-Melech the Cushite, "Take thirty men from the palace and lift Jeremiah the prophet out of the ·well [cistern; pit] before he dies."

11So Ebed-Melech took the men with him and went to a room under the storeroom in the palace. He took some ·old rags [tattered] and worn-out clothes from that room. Then he let those rags down with some ropes to Jeremiah in the ·well [cistern; well]. 12Ebed-Melech the Cushite said to Jeremiah, "Put these ·old rags [tattered] and worn-out clothes under your arms to be pads for the ropes." So Jeremiah did as Ebed-Melech said. 13The men pulled Jeremiah up with the ropes and lifted him out of the ·well [cistern; pit; Ps. 30:1–3]. And Jeremiah stayed under guard in the courtyard of the guard [39:15–18].

Zedekiah Questions Jeremiah

14Then King Zedekiah sent someone to get Jeremiah the prophet and bring him to the third entrance to the ·Temple [Lhouse] of the LORD. The king said to Jeremiah, "I am going to ask you something. Do not hide anything from me, but tell me everything honestly [37:16–21]."

15 Jeremiah said to Zedekiah, "If I give you an answer, ·you will surely [Lwon't you…?] kill me. And even if I give you advice, you will not listen to me."

16 But King Zedekiah ·made a secret promise [Lswore in secret] to Jeremiah, "As surely as the LORD lives who has given us breath and life, I will not kill you. And I promise not to hand you over to these men [Cthe officers] who ·want to kill you [Lseek your life]."

17 Then Jeremiah said to Zedekiah, "This is what the LORD God ·All-Powerful [Almighty; of Heaven's Armies; Tof hosts], the God of Israel, says: 'If you ·surrender [Lgo out] to the officers of the king of Babylon, your life will be saved. This city [CJerusalem] will not be burned ·down [Lwith fire], and you and your ·family [Lhouse] will live. 18 But if you refuse to ·surrender [Lgo out] to the officers of the king of Babylon, this city will be handed over to the ·Babylonian army [LChaldeans], and they will burn it ·down [Lwith fire]. And you yourself will not escape from ·them [Ltheir hand].'"

19 Then King Zedekiah said to Jeremiah, "I'm afraid of some ·Jews [LJudeans] who have already ·gone over to the side of [Ldeserted/defected/Lfallen to] the ·Babylonian army [LChaldeans]. If they [Cthe Babylonians] hand me over to them, they will ·treat me badly [abuse me]."

20 But Jeremiah answered, "·The Babylonians will not hand you over to the Jews [LYou will not be given up]. ·Obey [LListen to the voice of] the LORD by doing what I tell you. Then things will go well for you, and your life will be saved. 21 But if you refuse to ·surrender [Lgo out] to the Babylonians, the LORD has shown me what will happen. 22 All the women left in the ·palace [Lhouse] of the king of Judah will be brought out and taken to the important officers of the king of Babylon. Your women will ·make fun of you with this song [Lsay]:

'Your good friends ·misled [deceived; seduced; enticed] you
  and ·were stronger than [overpowered] you.
While your feet ·were stuck [sank down] in the mud,
  they ·left [turned their back on] you.'

23 "All your wives and children will be brought out and given to the Babylonian army. You yourself will not even escape from them. You will be ·taken prisoner [captured] by the king of Babylon, and this city [CJerusalem] will be burned ·down [Lwith fire]."

24 Then Zedekiah said to Jeremiah, "Do not tell anyone that I have been talking to you, or you will die. 25 If the officers find out I talked to you, they will come to you and say, 'Tell us what you said to King Zedekiah and what he said to you. Don't ·keep any secrets from us [conceal anything from us]. If you don't tell us everything, we will kill you.' 26 If they ask you, tell them, 'I was ·begging [Lmaking my pleas for help/supplications/falling before] the king not to ·send [return] me back to Jonathan's house to die.'"

27 All the officers did come to question Jeremiah. So he told them everything the king had ordered him to say. Then the officers said no more to Jeremiah, because no one had heard what Jeremiah and the king had discussed.

28 So Jeremiah stayed under guard in the courtyard of the guard until the day Jerusalem was captured.

The Fall of Jerusalem

39 This is how Jerusalem was captured: Nebuchadnezzar king of Babylon marched against Jerusalem with his whole army and ·surrounded the city to attack it [Lbesieged it]. This was during the tenth month of the ninth year Zedekiah was king of Judah [CJanuary 588 BC;

52:4]. 2This lasted until the ninth day of the fourth month in Zedekiah's eleventh year [CJuly 18, 586 BC]. Then the city wall was ·broken through [breached]. 3And all these officers of the king of Babylon came [Cinto Jerusalem] and sat down at the Middle Gate: Nergal-Sharezer ·of the district of Samgar [*or* Samgar-nebo]; Nebo-Sarsekim, a chief ·officer [*or* eunuch]; Nergal-Sharezer, ·an important leader [*or* the Rabmag]; and all the other important officers.

4When Zedekiah king of Judah and all his soldiers saw them, they ·ran away [fled]. They ·left [went out of] Jerusalem at night and went out ·from [Lby way of] the king's garden. They went through the gate that was between the two walls and then headed toward the ·Jordan Valley [LArabah]. 5But the ·Babylonian [LChaldean] army ·chased [pursued] them and ·caught up with [overtook] Zedekiah in the plains of Jericho. They captured him and took him to Nebuchadnezzar king of Babylon, who was at the town of Riblah in the land of Hamath [Cnorth of Israel, in Syria]. There Nebuchadnezzar passed ·his sentence [judgment] on Zedekiah. 6At Riblah the king of Babylon ·killed [slaughtered] Zedekiah's sons and all the ·important officers [nobles] of Judah ·as Zedekiah watched [Lbefore his eyes]. 7Then he ·put out [blinded] Zedekiah's eyes. He put bronze chains on Zedekiah and took him to Babylon.

8The ·Babylonians [LChaldeans] ·set fire to [Lburned with fire] the ·palace [Lhouse of the king] and to the houses of the people, and they ·broke [tore] down the walls around Jerusalem. 9Nebuzaradan, commander of the king's special guards, took the people left in Jerusalem, those captives who had ·surrendered [deserted; defected; Lfell] to him earlier, and the rest of the people of Jerusalem, and he ·took them all away [exiled them all] to Babylon. 10But Nebuzaradan, commander of the guard, left some of the poorest people of Judah behind. They owned nothing, but that day he gave them vineyards and fields.

11Nebuchadnezzar king of Babylon had ·given these orders [commanded] about Jeremiah through Nebuzaradan, commander of the guard: 12"Find Jeremiah and take care of him. Do not ·hurt [do evil to] him, but do for him whatever he asks you." 13So Nebuchadnezzar sent these men for Jeremiah: Nebuzaradan, commander of the guards; Nebushazban, a chief ·officer [*or* eunuch]; Nergal-Sharezer, ·an important leader [*or* the Rabmag]; and all the other officers of the king of Babylon. 14They had Jeremiah taken out of the courtyard of the guard. Then they turned him over to Gedaliah son of Ahikam son of Shaphan [Cthe new governor of the Babylonian province of Judah; 40:5], who had orders to take Jeremiah back home. So they took him home, and he stayed among the people left in Judah.

15While Jeremiah was guarded in the courtyard, the LORD spoke his word to him: 16"Jeremiah, go and tell Ebed-Melech the Cushite [CEthiopian; 38:7–13] this message: 'This is what the LORD ·All-Powerful [Almighty; of Heaven's Armies; Tof hosts], the God of Israel, says: Very soon I will make my words about this city [CJerusalem] come true ·through [for] ·disaster [evil; trouble], not ·through [for] ·good times [good]. You will see everything come true with your own eyes. 17But I will ·save [rescue; deliver] you on that day, Ebed-Melech, says the LORD. You will not be handed over to the people you fear. 18I will surely ·save [rescue] you [CEbed-Melech]. You will not ·die from [Lfall by] a sword, but ·you will escape and live [Lyour life will be plunder]. This will happen because you have ·trusted [confidence] in me, says the LORD.' "

Jeremiah Is Set Free

40 The LORD spoke his word to Jeremiah after Nebuzaradan, commander of the guards, had ·set Jeremiah free at the city of [released/Lsent him from] Ramah. He had found Jeremiah in Ramah bound in ·chains [fetters] with all the ·captives [exiles] from Jerusalem and Judah who were being ·taken away [exiled] to Babylon. 2When commander ·Nebuzaradan [Lof the guards] ·found [Ltook] Jeremiah, Nebuzaradan said to him, "The LORD your God announced this ·disaster [evil; trouble] would come to this place. 3And now the LORD has done everything he ·said [promised] he would do. This ·disaster [evil; trouble] happened because you [Cthe people of Judah] sinned against the LORD and did not ·obey him [Llisten to his voice]. 4But today I am ·freeing [releasing] you from the ·chains [fetters] on your ·wrists [Lhands]. If ·you want to [Lit is good in your eyes], come with me to Babylon, and I will ·take good care of you [Lset my eyes on you]. But if ·you don't want to come [Lit is wrong/evil/bad in your eyes to come with me to Babylon], then ·don't [fine]. Look, the whole country is open to you. Go wherever ·you wish [Lit is good and right in your eyes]." 5Before Jeremiah turned to leave, Nebuzaradan said, "Or go back to Gedaliah son of Ahikam, the son of Shaphan. The king of Babylon has ·chosen [appointed] him to be governor over the towns of Judah. Go and ·live [stay] with Gedaliah among the people, or go anywhere ·you want [Lit is right in your eyes]."

Then Nebuzaradan gave Jeremiah some ·food [provisions] and a ·present [gift] and let him go. 6So Jeremiah went to Gedaliah son of Ahikam at Mizpah [Cperhaps Tell en-Nasbeh eight miles north of Jerusalem; Judg. 20:1–3; 1 Sam. 7:5–14; 10:17–24] and stayed with him there. He lived among the people who ·were left behind in Judah [Lremained in the land].

The Short Rule of Gedaliah

7Some officers and their men from the army of Judah were still out in the open country. They heard that the king of Babylon had ·put [appointed] Gedaliah son of Ahikam ·in charge of the people [Lgovernor of those] who ·were left [remained] in the land: the men, women, and children who were the poorest. They were the ones who were not ·taken to Babylon as captives [exiled to Babylon]. 8So these soldiers came to Gedaliah at Mizpah: Ishmael son of Nethaniah, Johanan and Jonathan sons of Kareah, Seraiah son of Tanhumeth, the sons of Ephai the Netophathite, Jaazaniah son of the Maacathite, and their men.

9Gedaliah son of Ahikam, the son of Shaphan, ·made a promise [swore] to them, saying, "Do not be afraid to serve the ·Babylonians [LChaldeans]. Stay in the land and serve the king of Babylon. Then everything will go well for you. 10I myself will live in Mizpah and will ·speak for you [represent you; Lstand] before the ·Babylonians [LChaldeans] who come to us here. Harvest the wine, the summer fruit, and the oil, and put what you harvest in your storage jars. Live in the towns you control."

11The ·Jews [LJudeans] in Moab, ·Ammon [Lthe sons of Ammon], Edom, and other countries also heard that the king of Babylon had left a ·few Jews alive in the land [Lremnant in Judea]. And they heard the king of Babylon had ·chosen [appointed] Gedaliah as governor over them. (Gedaliah was the son of Ahikam, the son of Shaphan.) 12When the people of Judah heard this news, they came back to Judah from all the countries where they had been scattered. They came to Gedaliah at Mizpah and gathered a large harvest of wine and summer fruit.

13Johanan son of Kareah and all the army officers of Judah still in the open country came to Gedaliah at Mizpah. 14They said to him, "Don't you know that Baalis king of the ·Ammonite people [Lsons of Ammon] wants you dead? He has sent Ishmael son of Nethaniah to ·kill you [Lstrike your life]." But Gedaliah son of Ahikam ·did [*or* would] not believe them.

15Then Johanan son of Kareah spoke to Gedaliah in ·private [secret] at Mizpah. He said, "Let me go and ·kill [Lstrike] Ishmael son of Nethaniah. No one will know anything about it. ·We should not let Ishmael [LWhy should he…?] ·kill you [Lstrike your life]. Then all ·the Jews [LJudah] gathered around you would be scattered to different countries again, and the ·few people of Judah who are left alive [Lthe remnant of Judah] would ·be lost [perish]."

16But Gedaliah son of Ahikam said to Johanan son of Kareah, "Do not ·kill Ishmael [Ldo this thing]! The things you are saying about Ishmael are ·not true [false; lies]."

41 In the seventh month Ishmael son of Nethaniah and ten of his men came to Gedaliah son of Ahikam [Cthe Babylonian appointed governor] at Mizpah [40:6]. (Nethaniah was the son of Elishama.) Now Ishmael was a member of the ·king's [royal] family and had been one of the officers of the king of Judah. While they were eating ·a meal with Gedaliah [Lbread together] at Mizpah, 2Ishmael and his ten men got up and killed Gedaliah son of Ahikam, the son of Shaphan, with a sword. (Gedaliah was the man the king of Babylon had ·chosen [appointed] as governor over Judah.) 3Ishmael also killed all the ·Jews [LJudeans] and the ·Babylonian [LChaldean] soldiers who were there with Gedaliah at Mizpah.

4The day after Gedaliah was murdered, before anyone knew about it, 5eighty men came to Mizpah bringing ·grain [Lgift; tribute] offerings [Lev. 2:1] and incense to the ·Temple [Lhouse] of the LORD. Those men from Shechem, Shiloh, and Samaria [Cimportant centers in northern Israel] had shaved off their beards, torn their clothes, and ·cut [gashed] themselves [Cmourning rituals]. 6Ishmael son of Nethaniah went out from Mizpah to meet them, crying as he walked. When he ·met [encountered] them, he said, "Come with me to meet Gedaliah son of Ahikam." 7So they went into Mizpah. Then Ishmael son of Nethaniah and his men ·killed [slaughtered] seventy of them and threw the bodies into a deep ·well [cistern; pit]. 8But the ten men who were ·left alive [Lstill found] said to Ishmael, "Don't kill us! We have stores of wheat and barley and oil and honey that we have hidden in a field." So ·Ishmael let them live [Lhe stopped] and did not kill them with the others. 9Now the ·well [cistern; pit] where he had thrown all the bodies had been made by King Asa [Cruled 913–873 BC] as a part of his defenses against Baasha king of Israel [Cruled 900–877 BC; 1 Kin. 15:9–24; 15:33—16:7]. But Ishmael son of Nethaniah put dead bodies in it until it was full.

10Ishmael captured all the other people in Mizpah: the king's daughters and all the other people who ·were left [remained] there. They were the ones whom Nebuzaradan commander of the guard had ·chosen Gedaliah son of Ahikam to take care of [appointed Gedaliah son of Ahikam as governor over]. So Ishmael son of Nethaniah captured those people, and he started to cross over to the country of the ·Ammonites [Lsons of Ammon].

11Johanan son of Kareah [40:13–14] and all his army officers with him heard about all the ·evil things [crimes] Ishmael son of Nethaniah had

done. 12So they took their men and went to fight Ishmael son of Nethaniah
and ·caught [[L]found] him near the ·big pool of water [[L]many waters] at
Gibeon [[C]southwest of Mizpah; 2 Sam. 2:8–17]. 13When ·the captives
Ishmael had taken [[L]all the people who were with Ishmael] saw Johanan
and the army officers, they were glad. 14So all the people Ishmael had
taken captive from Mizpah turned around and ran to Johanan son of
Kareah. 15But Ishmael son of Nethaniah and eight of his men escaped
from Johanan and ran away to the ·Ammonites [[L]sons of Ammon].

16So Johanan son of Kareah and all his army officers ·saved [[L]took] the
captives that Ishmael son of Nethaniah had taken from Mizpah after he
·murdered [[L]struck] Gedaliah son of Ahikam. Among those left alive were
soldiers, women, children, and ·palace officers [*or* eunuchs]. And Johanan
brought them back from the town of Gibeon.

The Escape to Egypt

17-18Johanan and the other army officers were afraid of the ·Babylonians
[[L]Chaldeans]. Since the king of Babylon had chosen Gedaliah son of
Ahikam to be governor of Judah but Ishmael son of Nethaniah had ·mur-
dered [[L]struck] him, Johanan was afraid that the Babylonians would be
angry. So they decided to run away to Egypt. On the way they stayed at
Geruth Kimham, near the town of Bethlehem.

42 While there, Johanan son of Kareah and Jezaniah [*or*
Azariah; 43:2] son of Hoshaiah ·went to [approached]
Jeremiah the prophet. All the army officers and all the people, from the
least important to the greatest, went along, too. 2They said to him,
"Jeremiah, ·please listen to what we ask [[L]let our pleas for help/supplica-
tions fall before you]. Pray to the LORD your God for all ·the people left
alive from the family of Judah [[L]this remnant]. At one time there were
many of us, but ·you can see that [[L]as your eyes can see] there are few of
us now. 3So pray that the LORD your God will tell us ·where we should go
[[L]the path on which we should go] and what we should do."

4Then Jeremiah the prophet answered, "I ·understand what you want
me to do [[L]hear]. I will pray to the LORD your God ·as you have asked
[[L]according to your works]. I will tell you ·everything he says [all his
answers] and not ·hide [[L]keep back] anything from you."

5Then the people said to Jeremiah, "May the LORD be a true and ·loyal
[faithful] witness against us if we don't do everything the LORD your God
sends you to tell us. 6·It does not matter if we like the message or not
[[L]Whether good or bad...]. We will ·obey [listen to] the LORD our God, to
whom we are sending you. We will ·obey [listen to] what he says so good
things will happen to us."

7Ten days later the LORD spoke his word to Jeremiah. 8Then Jeremiah
called for Johanan son of Kareah, the army officers with him, and all the
other people, from the least important to the greatest. 9Jeremiah said to
them, "You sent me to ·ask the LORD for what you wanted [[L]make your
supplications/fall before him]. This is what the God of Israel says: 10'If
you will stay in this land [[C]Judah], I will build you up and not tear you
down. I will plant you and not ·pull [tear] you up [1:10], because I am
·sad [sorry] about the ·disaster [evil; trouble] I ·brought on [[L]did to] you.
11Now you fear the king of Babylon, but don't be afraid of him. Don't be
afraid of him,' says the LORD, 'because I am with you. I will save you and
·rescue [protect] you from his ·power [[L]hand]. 12I will be ·kind [compas-
sionate; merciful] to you, and he will also treat you with ·mercy [kindness;
compassion] and ·let you stay [restore you] in your land.'

13"But if you say, 'We will not stay in this land [CJudah],' you will ·dis-
obey [not listen to the voice of] the LORD your God. 14Or you might say,
'No, we will go and live in Egypt. There we will not see war, or hear the
trumpets of ·war [battle], or ·be hungry [famine].' 15If you say that, listen
to the message of the LORD, ·you who are left alive from [remnant of]
Judah. This is what the LORD ·All-Powerful [Almighty; of Heaven's Armies;
Tof hosts], the God of Israel, says: 'If you ·make up your mind [are deter-
mined] to go and live in Egypt, these things will happen: 16·You are afraid
of war, but it will find you [LThe sword you fear will overtake you there,]
in the land of Egypt. And ·you are worried about hunger, but it will follow
you into [Lthe famine you dread will cling after you there in] Egypt, and
you will die there. 17Everyone who ·goes to live in [Lsets their face to go to]
Egypt will die ·in war [Lby sword] or from ·hunger [famine] or ·terrible
disease [plague; pestilence]. ·No one who goes to Egypt will live; no one
will escape [LThere will be no remnant or survivor from] the ·terrible
things [harm; Levil] I will bring to them.'

18"This is what the LORD ·All-Powerful [Almighty; of Heaven's Armies;
Tof hosts], the God of Israel, says: 'I ·showed [poured out] my anger
against the people of Jerusalem. In the same way I will ·show [pour out]
my anger against you when you go to Egypt. Other nations will speak evil
of you. People will be ·shocked [horrified] by what will happen to you.
You will become a curse word, and people will ·insult [ridicule] you. And
you will never see this place [CJudah] again.'

19"·You who are left alive in [Remnant of] Judah, the LORD has told you,
'Don't go to Egypt.' Be sure you ·understand [know] this; I warn you
today 20that you ·are making a mistake that will cause your deaths [made
a fatal mistake; Lhave erred with your life]. You sent me to the LORD your
God, saying, 'Pray to the LORD our God for us. Tell us everything the LORD
our God says, and we will do it.' 21So today I have ·told [proclaimed to]
you, but you have not ·obeyed [listened to the voice of] the LORD your
God in all that he sent me to tell you. 22So now be sure you ·understand
[know] this: You want to go to live in Egypt, but you will die there by ·war
[Lsword], ·hunger [famine], or ·terrible diseases [plague; pestilence]."

43 So Jeremiah finished telling the people the message from the
LORD their God; he told them everything the LORD their God
had sent him to tell them.

2Azariah son of Hoshaiah [42:1], Johanan son of Kareah, and some
other men were ·too proud [arrogant]. They said to Jeremiah, "You are
lying! The LORD our God did not send you to say, 'You must not go to
Egypt to ·live [sojourn; wander] there.' 3Baruch son of Neriah [CJeremiah's
assistant; chs. 35; 45] is causing you to be against us. He wants you to
hand us over to the ·Babylonians [LChaldeans] so they can kill us or ·cap-
ture us and take [exile] us to Babylon."

4So Johanan, the army officers, and all the people ·disobeyed the LORD's
command [did not listen to the voice of the LORD] to stay in Judah. 5But
Johanan son of Kareah and the army officers ·led away [Ltook] ·those who
were left alive from [the remnant of] Judah. They were the people who
had ·run away from the Babylonians [been driven] to other countries but
then had ·come back to live in [returned to] Judah. 6They ·led away
[Ltook] the men, women, and children, and the king's daughters.
Nebuzaradan commander of the guard had ·put Gedaliah son of Ahikam
son of Shaphan in charge of those people [Lleft with Gedaliah son of

Ahikam son of Shaphan; [Cwho had been appointed governor]. **Johanan also took Jeremiah the prophet and Baruch son of Neriah. 7These people did not listen to the voice of the LORD. So they all went to Egypt to the city of Tahpanhes** [Cin the eastern region of the Nile Delta].

8In Tahpanhes the LORD spoke his word to Jeremiah: 9"Take some large stones. Bury them in the clay in the brick pavement in front of the ·king of Egypt's palace [Lhouse of Pharaoh] **in Tahpanhes. Do this ·while the Jews are watching you** [Lbefore the eyes of the Judeans]. **10Then say to them, 'This is what the LORD ·All-Powerful** [Almighty; of Heaven's Armies; Tof hosts], **the God of Israel, says: I will soon send for my servant, Nebuchadnezzar king of Babylon. I will set his throne over these stones I have buried, and he will spread his ·covering for shade** [canopy] **above them. 11He will come here and ·attack** [Lstrike] **Egypt. He will bring death to those who are supposed to die. He will make ·prisoners** [exiles] **of those who are to be ·taken captive** [exiled], **and he will bring ·war to** [Lto the sword] **those who are to be killed with a sword. 12Nebuchadnezzar will ·set** [kindle a] **fire to the ·temples** [Lhouses] **of the gods of Egypt and burn them. And he will take ·the idols** [Lthem] **away as captives. As a shepherd ·wraps himself in** [*or* picks lice from] **his clothes, so Nebuchadnezzar ·will wrap Egypt around him** [*or* picks the land of Egypt clean]. **Then he will safely leave Egypt. 13He will ·destroy** [break] **the stone pillars in the ·temple** [Lhouse] **of the sun god in Egypt, and he will burn ·down** [Lwith fire] **the ·temples** [Lhouses] **of the gods of Egypt.'"**

Disaster in Egypt

44 Jeremiah received a message from the LORD for all the ·Jews [LJudeans] **living in Egypt—in the cities of Migdol** [Ca city in the Nile Delta], **Tahpanhes** [43:7], **Memphis** [Ca capital city in central Egypt], **and in ·southern Egypt** [Lthe land of Pathros]. **This was the message: 2"The LORD ·All-Powerful** [Almighty; of Heaven's Armies; Tof hosts], **the God of Israel, says: You saw all the ·terrible things** [disasters; evil; troubles] **I brought on Jerusalem and the towns of Judah, which are ruins today with no one living in them. 3It is because the people who lived there did evil. They made me angry by burning incense and ·worshiping** [serving] **other gods that neither they nor you nor your ·ancestors** [fathers] **ever knew. 4I sent all my servants, the prophets, to you again and again. By them I said to you, 'Don't do this ·terrible** [abominable] **thing that I hate.' 5But they did not listen or ·pay attention** [Lincline their ear]. **They did not ·stop doing** [turn back from] **evil things and burning incense to other gods. 6So I showed my great anger against them. I poured out my anger in the towns of Judah and the streets of Jerusalem so they are only ruins and ·piles of stones** [a desolation] **today.**

7"Now the LORD ·All-Powerful [Almighty; of Heaven's Armies; Tof hosts], **the God of Israel, says: Why are you doing such great ·harm** [damage; evil] **to yourselves? You are cutting off the men and women, children and ·babies** [suckling infants] **from the ·family** [Lmidst] **of Judah, leaving yourselves without ·anyone from the family of Judah** [La remnant]. **8Why do you want to make me angry by ·making idols** [Lthe work of your hands]**? Why do you ·burn incense** [make offerings] **to the gods of Egypt, where you have come to ·live** [sojourn; wander]**? You will ·destroy** [Lcut off] **yourselves. Other nations will ·speak evil of** [curse] **you and ·make fun of** [reproach] **you. 9Have you forgotten about the evil things your ·ancestors** [fathers] **did? And have you forgotten the evil the kings and**

·queens [Ltheir wives] of Judah did? Have you forgotten about the evil you and your wives did? These things were done in the country of Judah and in the streets of Jerusalem. [10]Even to this day the people of Judah ·are still too proud [have shown no remorse]. They have not ·learned to respect [feared] me or ·to follow [Lwalked in] my ·teachings [laws; instructions]. They have not obeyed the ·laws [statutes; requirements; ordinances] I gave you and your ·ancestors [fathers].

[11]"So this is what the LORD ·All-Powerful [Almighty; of Heaven's Armies; Tof hosts], the God of Israel, says: I am ·determined [Lsetting my face against you] to bring ·disasters [evil; trouble] on you. I will ·destroy [Lcut off] ·the whole family of [Lall] Judah. [12]The ·few who were left alive [remnant] from Judah ·were determined [Lset their face] to go to Egypt and ·settle [sojourn; wander] there, but they will all die in Egypt. They will be killed ·in war [Lby the sword] or ·die from hunger [Lby famine]. From the least important to the greatest, they will be killed ·in war [Lby sword] or ·die from hunger [Lby famine]. Other nations will ·speak evil about [Lcurse] them. People will be shocked by what has happened to them. They will become a curse word, and people will ·insult [reproach] them. [13]I will punish those people who have gone to live in Egypt, just as I punished Jerusalem, using swords, ·hunger [famine], and ·terrible diseases [plague; pestilence]. [14]Of the ·people of Judah who were left alive [remnant of Judah] and have gone to ·live [wander; sojourn] in Egypt, none will escape ·my punishment [Lor survive]. They want to return to Judah and live there, but none of them will live to return to Judah, except a few people who will escape."

[15]A large group of the people [Cof Judah] who lived in ·southern Egypt [LPathros] were ·meeting [assembling] together. Among them were many women who were ·burning incense [*or* making offerings] to other gods, and their husbands knew it. All these people said to Jeremiah, [16]"We will not listen to the ·message from [Lthe word in the name of] the LORD that you spoke to us. [17]We promised to make sacrifices to the Queen Goddess [Ca female astral deity, probably Ashtart or Asherah], and we will certainly do everything ·we promised [Lthat came out of our mouths]. We will ·burn incense [*or* make offerings] and pour out drink offerings to worship her, just as we, our ·ancestors [fathers], kings, and officers did in the past. All of us did these things in the towns of Judah and in the streets of Jerusalem. At that time we had plenty of food and were ·successful [fine], and ·nothing bad happened to us [Lwe saw/experienced no evil]. [18]But since we stopped ·making sacrifices [*or* offering incense] to the Queen Goddess and stopped pouring out drink offerings to her, we have ·had great problems [Llacked everything]. Our people have also been killed ·in war [Lby sword] and by ·hunger [famine]."

[19]The women said, "Our husbands knew what we were doing. We had their permission to ·burn incense [*or* make offerings] to the Queen Goddess and to pour out drink offerings to her. Our husbands knew we were making cakes ·that looked like her [with her image] and were pouring out drink offerings to her."

[20]Then Jeremiah spoke to all the people—men and women—who answered him. [21]He said to them, "·The LORD remembered [LDid not the LORD remember…?] that you and your ·ancestors [fathers], kings and officers, and the people of the land ·burned incense [*or* made offerings] in the towns of Judah and in the streets of Jerusalem. He remembered and

·thought [set/Llifted up his mind/heart] about it. 22Then he could not be
patient with you any longer. He hated the ·terrible things [abominations]
you did. So he made your country an ·empty desert [desolation and a
ruin], where no one lives. Other people curse that country. And so it is
today. 23All this happened because you ·burned incense to other gods [*or*
made offerings]. You sinned against the LORD. You did not ·obey him
[Llisten to the voice of the LORD] or follow his ·teachings [laws; instructions; LTorah] or the ·laws [statutes; requirements; ordinances] he gave
you. You did not ·keep your part of the agreement with him [Lwalk in his
testimonies]. So this ·disaster [evil; trouble] has happened to you. ·It is
there for you to see [L...according to this day]."

24Then Jeremiah said to all those men and women, "People of Judah
who are now in Egypt, hear the word of the LORD: 25The LORD ·All-Powerful
[Almighty; of Heaven's Armies; Tof hosts], the God of Israel, says: You and
your wives did what you said you would do. You said, 'We will certainly
keep the ·promises [vows] we made. We ·promised [vowed] to ·make sacrifices [*or* offer incense] to the Queen Goddess and to pour out drink
offerings to her.' So, go ahead. Do the things you ·promised [vowed], and
keep your ·promises [vows]. 26But hear the word of the LORD. Listen, all
you ·Jews [LJudeans] living in Egypt. The LORD says, 'I have sworn by my
great name: The people of Judah now living in Egypt will never again ·use
[pronounce] my name to make promises. They will never again say in
Egypt, "As surely as the Lord GOD lives..." 27I am watching over them, not
·to take care of them, but to hurt them [Lfor good but for evil/harm]. The
·Jews [LJudeans] who live in Egypt will die from swords or ·hunger [fam-
ine] until they are all ·destroyed [annihilated]. 28A few will escape being
killed by the sword and will come back to Judah from Egypt. Then, of the
people of Judah who came to ·live [sojourn; wander] in Egypt, ·those who
are left alive [the remnant] will know ·if my word or their word came true
[Lwhose word will stand, theirs or mine]. 29I will give you a sign that I will
punish you here in this place [CEgypt],' says the LORD. 'When you see it
happen, you will know that my ·promises to hurt you will really happen
[Lwords for you will be carried out for harm/evil].' 30This is what the LORD
says: 'Hophra king of Egypt [Calso known as Apries, ruled 587–570 BC] has
enemies who ·want to kill him [Lseek his life]. Soon I will hand him over to
his enemies just as I handed Zedekiah king of Judah over to Nebuchadnezzar king of Babylon, who ·wanted to kill him [Lsought his life; 39:5–7].'"

A Message to Baruch

45 It was the fourth year that Jehoiakim son of Josiah was king
of Judah [C605 BC]. Jeremiah the prophet told these things to
Baruch son of Neriah [32:12–13; 36; 43:1–3], and Baruch wrote them on
a scroll: 2"This is what the LORD, the God of Israel, says to you, Baruch:
3You have said, '·How terrible it is for [Woe is] me! The LORD has given
me sorrow along with my pain. I am tired because of my ·suffering
[groaning] and cannot rest.'"

4The LORD said, "Say this to Baruch: 'This is what the LORD says: I will
soon ·tear [break] down what I have built, and I will ·pull [pluck] up what
I have planted everywhere in all this land [CJudah]. 5Baruch, you are
·looking [seeking] for great things for yourself. Don't ·look for [seek]
them, because I will bring ·disaster [evil; trouble] on all ·the people
[Lflesh], says the LORD. You will have to go many places, but I will ·let you
escape alive [Lgive you your life as plunder] wherever you go.'"

Messages to the Nations

46 The LORD spoke this word to Jeremiah the prophet about the nations [Cchapters 46–51 are oracles against the foreign nations; see also Is. 13–23; Ezek. 25–32; Amos 1–2; Nah.; Obad.]:

2This message is to Egypt. It is about the army of Neco king of Egypt [Cruled 610–595 BC], which ·was defeated at [Lstruck] the city of Carchemish on the Euphrates River by Nebuchadnezzar king of Babylon. This was in the fourth year that Jehoiakim son of Josiah was king of Judah [C605 BC]. This is the LORD's message to Egypt:

3"Prepare your shields, large and small,
and ·march out [advance] for battle!
4Harness the horses
and ·get on them [Lmount the steeds]!
·Go to your places for battle [Take your station]
and put on your helmets!
·Polish [Burnish] your spears.
Put on your ·armor [coats of mail]!
5What do I see?
That army is terrified,
and the soldiers ·are running away [have turned back].
Their warriors are defeated.
They ·run away [flee] quickly
without looking back.
There is terror on every side [6:5; 20:3, 10; 49:29]!" says the LORD.
6"The fast runners cannot ·run away [flee];
the strong soldiers cannot escape.
They stumble and fall
in the north, by the Euphrates River.
7Who is this, rising up like the Nile River,
like ·strong, fast rivers [rivers whose waters surge]?
8Egypt rises up like the Nile River,
like ·strong, fast rivers [rivers whose waters surge].
Egypt says, 'I will rise up and cover the earth.
I will destroy cities and the people in them!'
9·Horsemen [*or* Horses], ·charge into battle [advance]!
·Chariot drivers [*or* Chariots], drive hard!
·March on [LGo out], brave soldiers—
soldiers from the countries of Cush [CEthiopia] and Put [CLibya]
who carry shields,
soldiers from Lydia [Cfrom eastern Asia Minor] who ·use [Lgrasp and draw] bows.

10"But that day belongs to the Lord GOD ·All-Powerful [Almighty; of Heaven's Armies; Tof hosts].
At that time he will give ·those people [his foes] the punishment they deserve.
The sword will ·kill [Ldevour] until it is ·finished [satisfied; sated],
until it ·satisfies its thirst for [Lgets satiated/drunk with] their blood.
The Lord GOD ·All-Powerful [Almighty; of Heaven's Armies; Tof hosts]
will offer a sacrifice
in the land of the north, by the Euphrates River [CBabylon].

11"Go up to Gilead and get some balm [8:22],
·people [Lvirgin daughter] of Egypt!
You have prepared many medicines,
·but they will not work [in vain];
you will not be healed.
12The nations have heard of your ·shame [humiliation],
and your cries fill all the earth.
One warrior has ·run into [Lstumbled over] another;
both of them have fallen down together!"
13This is the message the LORD spoke to Jeremiah the prophet about
Nebuchadnezzar king of Babylon's coming to ·attack [Lstrike] Egypt:
14"·Announce this message [Declare] in Egypt, and ·preach it [Lmake it heard] in Migdol.
·Preach it [LMake it heard] also in the cities of Memphis and Tahpanhes [44:1]:
'·Get ready for war [Take your stations and be ready],
because the ·battle is [Lsword devours] all around you.'
15Egypt, why ·were your warriors killed [was it swept away; *or* has Apis fled; Cthe sacred bull of Egypt]?
They could not stand because the LORD pushed them down.
16They stumbled again and again
and fell over each other.
They said, 'Get up. Let's go back
to our own people and our homeland.
·We must get away from our enemy's sword [L...because of the destroyer's/oppressor's sword]!'
17·In their homelands those soldiers [LThere they] called out,
'The king of Egypt is only a lot of noise.
He missed his chance [Cfor glory]!' "

18The King's name is the LORD ·All-Powerful [Almighty; of Heaven's Armies; Tof hosts].
He says, "As surely as I live,
one [Ca powerful leader] will come.
He will be like Mount Tabor among the mountains,
like Mount Carmel by the sea [Cdistinctive and majestic mountains].
19·People [LDaughter] of Egypt, pack your things
to be taken away as ·captives [exiles],
because Memphis will be ·destroyed [a desolation].
It will be a ruin, and no one will live there.

20"Egypt is like a beautiful ·young cow [heifer],
but a ·horsefly [gadfly] is coming
from the north [CBabylon] to attack her [Cthough small, gadflies are annoying].
21·The hired soldiers in Egypt's army [LIts mercenaries]
are like fat calves,
because even they all turn and ·run away [flee] together;
they do not stand [Cstrong against the attack].
Their ·time of destruction [Lday of their devastation/calamity] is coming;
·they will soon be punished [Lthe time of their punishment].

[22]Egypt is like a hissing snake that is trying to escape.
The ·enemy [[L]army] comes closer and closer.
They come against it [[C]Egypt] with axes
like men who cut down trees.
[23]They will ·chop [cut] down her forest [[C]Egypt's army]
·as if it were a great forest [*or* for they cannot be numbered; [C]could refer either to the Babylonians or the Egyptians]," says the LORD.
"There are more [[C]enemy soldiers] than locusts;
there are too many to count.
[24]The people of Egypt will be ·ashamed [humiliated].
They will be handed over to the enemy from the north [[C]Babylon]."
[25]The LORD ·All-Powerful [Almighty; of Heaven's Armies; [T]of hosts],
the God of Israel, says: "Very soon I will punish Amon, the god of the city
of Thebes [[C]a sun god]. And I will punish Egypt, her ·kings [[L]Pharaohs],
her gods, and the people who ·depend on [have confidence in] the king.
[26]I will hand those people over to ·their enemies, who want to kill them
[[L]those who seek their life]. I will give them to Nebuchadnezzar king of
Babylon and his ·officers [[L]servants]. But in the future, Egypt will live as
it once did of old [[C]in peace]," says the LORD.

A Message to Israel

[27]"People of Jacob, my servants, don't be afraid;
don't be frightened, Israel.
I will surely ·save [rescue] you from those faraway places
and your ·children [[L]seed] from the lands where they are captives.
The people of Jacob will have peace and safety again,
and no one will make them afraid.
[28]People of Jacob, my servants, do not be afraid,
because I am with you," says the LORD.
"I will ·completely destroy the many different [[L]make an end of all the] nations
where I ·scattered [drove] you.
But I will not ·completely destroy [[L]make an end of] you.
I will ·punish [chastise; discipline] you ·fairly [with justice],
but I will not let you escape your punishment."

A Message to the Philistines

47 Before the king of Egypt ·attacked [[L]struck] the city of Gaza, the
LORD spoke his word to Jeremiah the prophet. This message is
to the Philistine people [[C]to the west of Israel; Gen. 10:14; 21:32, 34].
[2]This is what the LORD says:
"See, waters are rising from the north [[C]representing the overwhelming force of the Babylonians].
They will become like an overflowing ·stream [torrent]
and will cover the whole country ·like a flood [[L]and its fullness],
even the towns and the people living in them.
Everyone living in that country
will cry for help;
the people will ·cry painfully [wail].
[3]They will hear the sound of the ·running horses [[L]hoofs of the chargers]
and the noisy chariots
and the rumbling chariot wheels.
·Parents [Fathers] will not ·help their children to safety [turn back for their children],
because ·they will be too weak to help [[L]their hands will be weak].

4The ·time [Lday] has come
to destroy all the Philistines.
It is time to ·destroy [Lcut off] all who ·are left alive [survive]
who could help the cities of Tyre and Sidon [Cthe two most important Phoenician cities; the Philistines, Egypt's allies, could no longer help them].
The LORD will soon destroy the Philistines,
·those left alive from the island of Crete [Lthe remnant of the coastline of Caphtor].
5·The people from the city of Gaza will be sad and shave their heads [LBaldness will come to Gaza].
The people from the city of Ashkelon will be made silent.
·Those left alive [Remnant] from the valley,
how long will you ·cut [gash] yourselves [Ca mourning ritual]?

6"·You cry [LAh], 'Sword of the LORD,
how long ·will you keep fighting [Lbefore you rest]?
Return to your ·holder [sheath].
Stop and be still.'
7But how can his sword rest
when the LORD has given it a command?
He has ·ordered [assigned] it
to attack Ashkelon and the seacoast."

A Message to Moab

48 This message is to the country of Moab [Cto the east of Israel; Gen. 19; Num. 25; Deut. 23:3–6].
This is what the LORD ·All-Powerful [Almighty; of Heaven's Armies; Tof hosts], the God of Israel, says:
"·How terrible it will be for the city of [Woe to] Nebo,
because it will be ·ruined [desolate].
The town of Kiriathaim [Num. 32:37; Josh. 13:19; Ezek. 25:9] will be disgraced and captured;
the ·strong [fortified] city will be disgraced and shattered.
2Moab will not be praised again.
Men in the town of Heshbon plan ·Moab's defeat [Lits disaster].
They say, 'Come, let us ·put an end to [Lcut off] that nation!'
Town of Madmen you will also be silenced.
The sword will ·chase [Lcome after] you.
3Listen to the cries from the town of Horonaim,
·cries of much confusion and destruction [Ldesolation and great fracture].
4Moab will be broken up.
·Her little children will cry for help [*or* Their cries are heard as far as Zoar].
5Moab's people go up the path to the town of Luhith,
crying ·loudly [continually] as they go.
On the road down to Horonaim,
cries of pain and suffering can be heard.
6·Run [Flee]! ·Run for [LEscape with] your lives!
Go like a ·bush [*or* wild ass; *or* Aroer] in the ·desert [wilderness].
7You ·trust [have confidence] in the things you do and in your ·wealth [Lstorehouses; *or* arsenals],
so you also will be captured.

The god Chemosh [Cthe chief god of Moab] **will go into ·captivity** [exile]
and his priests and officers with him.
8**The destroyer will come against every town;**
not one town will escape.
The valley will ·be ruined [perish],
and the high plain will be destroyed,
as the Lord has said.
9**Give ·wings** [*or* salt; Ca symbol of complete destruction; Judg. 9:45] **to Moab,**
because she will surely leave her land.
Moab's towns will become ·empty [desolate],
with no one to live in them.
10**A curse will be on anyone who ·doesn't do what the Lord says** [Lis slack in doing the Lord's work],
and a curse will be on anyone who holds back his sword from ·killing [Lblood].

11**"The people of Moab have ·never known trouble** [Lbeen at ease since its youth].
They are like wine left to settle;
they have never been poured from one jar to another.
They have not ·been taken into captivity [Lgone into exile].
So ·they taste as they did before [Ltheir flavor stands],
and their ·smell [aroma] **has not changed.**
12**·A time is** [LDays are] **coming," says the Lord,**
"When I will send people to ·pour [decant] **you from your jars.**
They will empty Moab's jars
and smash their jugs [Ca fitting image since Moab produced much wine; 16:8–10].
13**The ·people** [Lhouse] **of Israel ·trusted** [had confidence in] **that god in the town of Bethel** [1 Kin. 13:26–33; Amos 7:13],
and they were ·ashamed [humiliated] **when there was no help.**
In the same way Moab will be ·ashamed of [humiliated by] **their god Chemosh.**

14**"·You cannot** [LHow can you…?] **say, 'We are warriors!**
We are brave men in battle!'
15**The destroyer of Moab and her towns has arrived.**
Her best young men will be ·killed [slaughtered]**!" says the King,**
whose name is the Lord ·All-Powerful [Almighty; of Heaven's Armies; Tof hosts].
16**"The ·end** [disaster; calamity] **of Moab is near,**
and ·she will soon be destroyed [Lher disaster comes quickly].
17**All you who live around Moab,**
all you who know ·her [Lher name], **·cry** [mourn] **for her.**
Say, 'The ·ruler's power [Lstrong scepter] **is broken;**
·Moab's power and glory are gone [L…the glorious/beautiful staff].'

18**"·You people living in the town of** [LEnthroned daughter] **Dibon, come down from ·your place of honor** [glory]
and sit on the dry ground,
because the destroyer of Moab has come against you.
And he has destroyed your ·strong, walled [fortified] **cities.**

19You people living in the town of Aroer,
stand next to the road and watch.
See the man ·running away [fleeing] and the woman escaping.
Ask them, 'What happened?'
20Moab is filled with ·shame [humiliation], because she is ruined.
·Cry [Wail], Moab, cry out!
Announce at the Arnon River
that Moab is destroyed.
21People on the high plain have been ·punished [judged].
Judgment has come to these towns:
Holon, Jahzah, and Mephaath;
22 Dibon, Nebo, and Beth Diblathaim;
23 Kiriathaim, Beth Gamul, and Beth Meon;
24 Kerioth and Bozrah [Call cities on the Moabite plateau].
Judgment has come to all the towns of Moab, far and near.
25Moab's ·strength [Lhorn; Ca symbol of strength] has been cut off,
and its arm broken!" says the LORD.

26"The people of Moab thought they were greater than the LORD,
so ·punish them until they act as if they are drunk [Lmake them drunk].
Moab will ·fall and roll around [wallow; *or* overflow] in its own vomit,
and people will even make fun of it [Cthey would drink from the cup of wrath; 25:15–38; Is. 19:14; 51:17; Nah. 1:10].
27Moab, you made fun of Israel.
Israel was ·caught [*or* not found] in the middle of a gang of thieves.
When you spoke about Israel,
you shook your head [Cacting as if Moab were better].
28People in Moab, ·leave your towns empty [Labandon; forsake]
and go live among the ·rocks [crags].
Be like a dove that makes its nest
at the entrance of a cave.

29"We have heard that the people of Moab are ·proud [arrogant],
very ·proud [arrogant].
They are proud, very ·proud [arrogant],
and in their hearts ·they think they are important [Lare exalted; Ps. 131]."
30The LORD says,
"I know ·Moab's great pride [Lhis insolence], but it is ·useless [false].
Moab's bragging accomplishes nothing.
31So I ·cry sadly [wail] for Moab,
for everyone in Moab.
I ·moan [mourn] for the people from the town of Kir Hareseth.
32I cry with the people of the town of Jazer
for you, the grapevines of the town of Sibmah.
In the past your vines spread all the way to the sea,
as far as the sea of Jazer.
But the destroyer has ·taken over [Lfallen on]
your ·fruit [summer fruits] and ·grapes [vintage].
33Joy and happiness are gone
from the ·large, rich fields [fruitful/garden lands] of Moab.

I have stopped the flow of wine from the winepresses.
No one walks on the grapes with shouts of joy.
There are shouts,
but not shouts of joy.

34"Their ·crying [cry for help] can be heard from Moabite towns,
from Heshbon to Elealeh and Jahaz.
It can be heard from Zoar as far away as Horonaim and Eglath Shelishiyah.
Even the waters of Nimrim are ·dried up [desolate].
35I will stop Moab
from making burnt offerings [Lev. 1:1–17] at the ·places of worship [[L]high places; [C]sites associated with pagan worship or inappropriate worship of God] and from ·burning incense [*or* making offerings] to their gods," says the LORD.

36"My heart ·cries sadly [wails] for Moab like a ·flute [reed-pipe; [C]an instrument that plays funeral songs].
It ·cries [wails] like a ·flute [reed-pipe] for the people from Kir Hareseth.
The money they made has all ·been taken away [perished].
37Every head has been shaved
and every beard cut off.
Everyone's hands are ·cut [gashed],
and everyone wears ·rough cloth around his waist [sackcloth; burlap; [C]mourning rituals].
38People are ·crying [mourning] on every roof [[C]flat roofs were living space] in Moab
and in every public square.
There is nothing but ·sadness [lament],
because I have broken Moab
like a jar no one wants [19:1–13; 22:28; Ps. 2:9]," says the LORD.
39"·Moab [[L]How it] is shattered! The people are ·crying [wailing]!
·Moab turns away [[L]How it turns its neck] in ·shame [humiliation]!
People all around her make fun of her.
The things that happened fill them with great fear [Is. 16:6–12]."

40This is what the LORD says:
"Look! Someone is coming, like an eagle ·diving down from the sky [swooping down]
and spreading its wings over Moab [49:22; Ezek. 17:3–4; Hos. 8:1].
41The towns of Moab will be captured,
and the ·strong, walled cities [fortresses] will be ·defeated [seized].
·At that time [[L]On that day] ·Moab's warriors will be frightened, [[L]the heart of Moab's warriors will be]
like ·a [[L]the heart of a] woman who is ·having a baby [in labor].
42The nation of Moab will be destroyed,
because they ·thought they were greater than [magnified themselves over] the LORD.
43Fear, deep pits, and traps wait for you,
people of Moab," says the LORD.
44"People will ·run [flee] from fear,
but they will fall into the pits.

Anyone who climbs out of the pits
will be caught in the traps.
I will bring the year of punishment to Moab," says the LORD.

45"People ·have run [flee] from the ·powerful enemy [Lstrong]
and ·have gone to Heshbon for safety [Lstand in the shadow of Heshbon].
But fire ·started in [Lhas come out from] Heshbon;
a ·blaze [Lflame] has spread from the ·hometown [Lhouse] of Sihon [Cearly king of Moab; Num. 21:28].
It ·burned up [Ldevoured] the ·leaders [*or* forehead] of Moab
and ·destroyed those proud people [Lthe pate of the sons of tumult].
46·How terrible it is for [Woe to] you, Moab!
The people of Chemosh [Cthe chief god of Moab] have been destroyed.
Your sons have been taken ·captive [into exile],
and your daughters ·have been taken away [into captivity].

47"But in ·days to come [the latter days],
I will ·make good things happen again to [restore the fortunes of] Moab," says the LORD.
This ends the judgment on Moab.

A Message to Ammon

49 This message is to the ·Ammonite people [Lsons of Ammon; Gen. 19:30–38; Deut. 2:19; 23:3–6].
This is what the LORD says:
"Do you think that Israel has no children?
Do you think there is no ·one to take the land when the parents die [Lheir]?
If that were true, why did Molech [Cthe chief god of Ammon] take Gad's [Ca tribe in the north of Israel] land
and why did Molech's people settle in Gad's towns [Ca bitter reference to the sacrifice of children to Molech]?"
2The LORD says,
"The ·time will come [Ldays are coming] when I will make Rabbah of the Ammonites [Cits capital], hear the battle cry.
It will become a ·hill covered with ruins [desolate ruin],
and the ·towns [villages; Ldaughters] around it will be burned with fire.
Those people ·forced [dispossessed] Israel out of that land,
but now Israel will ·force them out [dispossess them]!" says the LORD.
3"People in the town of Heshbon, ·cry sadly [wail] because the town of Ai is destroyed!
·Those who live in [LDaughters of] Rabbah, cry out!
Put on your ·rough cloth to show your sadness [sackcloth; burlap], and ·cry loudly [mourn; wail].
Run here and there for safety inside the walls,
because Molech will be taken ·captive [into exile]
and his priests and officers with him.
4·You [LWhy do you…?] brag about your valleys
and about the fruit in your valleys.

You are like an ·unfaithful [rebellious] ·child [Ldaughter]
who ·believes her treasures will save her [Ltrusts/has confidence in her treasures/arsenals].
You think, 'Who would attack me?'
5I will soon bring terror on you
from everyone around you,"
says the Lord God ·All-Powerful [Almighty; of Heaven's Armies; Tof hosts].
"You will all be ·forced to run [driven] away,
and no one will be able to gather you.

6"But the time will come
when I will ·make good things happen to [restore the fortunes of] the ·Ammonites [Lsons of Ammon] again,"
says the Lord.

A Message to Edom

7This message is to Edom [Gen. 36; Num. 20:14–21; Ps. 137:7; Lam. 4:22;
Obad. 10–14]. This is what the Lord ·All-Powerful [Almighty; of Heaven's
Armies; Tof hosts] says:
"Is there no more wisdom in the town of Teman [Job 2:11]?
Can the wise men [Cof Edom] no longer give good advice?
Have they lost their wisdom?
8You people living in the town of Dedan,
·run away [flee] and hide in deep caves,
because I will bring ·disaster [calamity] on the people of Esau.
It is time for me to punish them.
9If workers came and picked the grapes from your vines,
they would leave ·a few grapes [gleanings] behind.
If robbers came at night,
they would steal only enough for themselves.
10But I will strip Esau [CEdom] bare.
I will ·find [expose] all their hiding places,
so they will not be able to hide from me.
The ·children [Lseed], ·relatives [brothers], and neighbors will die,
And they [CEdom] will be no more.
11·Leave [Abandon; Forsake] the orphans, and I will ·take care of them [keep them alive].
Your widows also can ·trust [have confidence] in me."
12This is what the Lord says: "Some people did not deserve to be punished, but they had to drink from the cup [Cof suffering; 25:15–38;
48:26–28] anyway. You [Cpeople of Edom] deserve to be punished, so you
will not escape punishment. You must certainly drink from the cup."
13The Lord says, "I swear by ·my own name [Lmyself] that the city of
Bozrah will become a pile of ruins! People will be shocked by what happened there. They will ·insult [reproach] that city and ·speak evil of
[curse] it. And all the towns around it will become ruins forever."
14I have heard a message from the Lord.
A ·messenger [herald] has been sent among the nations, saying,
"Gather [Cyour armies] to attack it!
·Get ready [LRise up] for battle!"

15"Soon I will make you the smallest of nations,
and you will be greatly ·hated [despised] by everyone.
16Edom, you ·frightened [terrorized] other nations,
but your ·pride [arrogance] has ·fooled [deceived] you.
You live in the hollow places of the ·cliff [rock; crag]
and ·control [seize] the high places of the hills.
Even if you build your home as high as an eagle's nest,
I will bring you down from there," says the LORD.

17"Edom will be ·destroyed [desolate].
People who pass by will be shocked to see the destroyed cities,
and they will ·be amazed [hiss] at all her ·injuries [disasters].
18Edom will be ·destroyed [overturned] like the cities of Sodom and Gomorrah [Gen. 18—19]
and the towns around them," says the LORD.
"No one will live there!
No one will ·stay [sojourn; wander] in it [CEdom].

19"Like a lion coming up from the thick bushes near the Jordan River
to attack ·a strong pen for sheep [*or* perennial pastures; 50:44],
I will suddenly chase it [CEdom] from its land.
Who is the one I have ·chosen [appointed] to do this?
·There is no one [LWho is…?] like me,
·no one who [Lwho…?] can take me to court.
·None of their leaders [LWho is the shepherd who…?] can stand up against me."

20So listen to ·what the LORD has planned to do against Edom [Lthe counsel/advice of the LORD].
Listen to ·what he has decided to do to [Lhis plans against] the people in the town of Teman.
He will surely drag away the young of the flock [Cthe youth of Edom].
Their ·hometowns [Lpasture] will surely be shocked at what happens to them.
21At the sound of their [CEdom's] fall, the earth will shake.
Their cry will be heard all the way to the ·Red [Reed] Sea [50:20; Ex. 10:19].
22The LORD is like an eagle swooping down
and spreading its wings over the city of Bozrah.
At that time Edom's soldiers will become very frightened,
like a woman ·having a baby [in labor; 48:40; Ezek. 17:3–4; Hos. 8:1].

A Message to Damascus

23This message is to the city of Damascus:
"The towns of Hamath and Arpad are ·put to shame [humiliated],
because they have heard ·bad [disastrous] news.
They ·are discouraged [Lmelt; Cin fear].
They are troubled like the ·tossing sea [sea that cannot be quieted].
24The city of Damascus has become weak.
The people ·want to run away [turn to flee];
·they are ready to panic [panic seized them].
·The people feel pain and suffering [LAnguish and distress have grabbed them],
like a woman ·giving birth to a baby [in labor; 48:41; 49:22; 50:43].

[25]Damascus was a city of my joy.
Why have the people not ·left [abandoned; forsaken] that famous city yet?
[26]Surely the young men will die in the city squares,
and all her soldiers will be ·killed [[L]stilled; quieted] ·at that time [[L]on that day]," says the LORD ·All-Powerful [Almighty; of Heaven's Armies; [T]of hosts].
[27]"I will ·set [kindle a] fire to the walls of Damascus,
and it will completely ·burn [consume] the ·strong cities [strongholds; citadels] of King Ben-Hadad [[C]a name taken by many kings of Damascus]."

A Message to Kedar and Hazor

[28]This message is to the tribe of Kedar [Song 1:5; Ezek. 27:21] and the
kingdoms of Hazor, which Nebuchadnezzar king of Babylon ·defeated
[[L]struck]. This is what the LORD says:
"·Go [[L]Rise up] and attack the people of Kedar,
and destroy the ·people of the East [[L]sons of Kedar].
[29]Their tents and flocks will be taken away.
Their belongings will be carried off—
their tents, all their goods, and their camels.
Men will shout to them,
'Terror on every side [6:25; 20:3, 10; 46:5]!'

[30]"·Run away [Flee] quickly!
People in Hazor, ·find a ·good [[L]deep] place to hide [hide in deep places]!" says the LORD.
"Nebuchadnezzar king of Babylon has made plans against you
and ·wants to defeat [[L]makes plans against] you.

[31]"·Get [[L]Rise] up! Attack the nation that is ·comfortable [at ease],
that is ·sure [confident; [C]that no one will defeat it]," says the LORD.
"It does not have gates or ·fences [[L]bars; [C]to protect it].
Its people live alone.
[32]The enemy will ·steal [[L]plunder; despoil] their camels
and their large herds of cattle as ·war prizes [plunder; booty].
I will scatter the people who ·cut their hair short [shave their temples; Deut. 14:1] to ·every part of the earth [[L]the wind],
and I will bring disaster on them from everywhere," says the LORD.
[33]"The city of Hazor will become a ·home [den; haunt] for ·wild dogs [jackals; 9:11; 10:22];
it will be ·an empty desert [desolate] forever.
No one will live there,
and no one will ·stay [sojourn; wander] in it."

A Message to Elam

[34]·Soon after Zedekiah became [[L]At the beginning of the reign of
Zedekiah the] king of Judah [[C]beginning in 597 BC], the LORD spoke this
word to Jeremiah the prophet. This message is to the nation of Elam
[[C]located on the Iranian plateau].
[35]This is what the LORD ·All-Powerful [Almighty; of Heaven's Armies;
[T]of hosts] says:
"I will soon break Elam's bow [Is. 22:6],
its greatest strength.
[36]I will bring the four winds against Elam
from the four corners of the ·skies [heavens].

I will scatter its people ·everywhere the four winds blow [Lto all four winds];
its ·captives [exiles] will go to every nation.
37I will terrify Elam in front of their enemies,
who ·want to destroy them [Lseek their life].
I will bring ·disaster [evil; trouble] to Elam
and show them how angry I am!" says the LORD.
"I will send a sword ·to chase Elam [Lafter them]
until I have ·killed [ended; annihilated] them all.
38I will set up my throne in Elam,
and I will destroy its king and its officers!" says the LORD.

39"But I will ·make good things happen to [restore the fortunes of] Elam again
in the ·future [Llatter days]," says the LORD.

A Message to Babylon

50 This is the message the LORD spoke to Babylon and the
·Babylonian people [LChaldeans] through Jeremiah the
prophet.
2"·Announce [Proclaim] this to the nations [Land let them hear].
Lift up a banner [Ca battle standard] and ·tell them [make them hear].
·Speak the whole message [LDo not conceal anything] and say:
'Babylon will be captured.
The god Bel [Canother name for Marduk] will be ·put to shame [humiliated],
and the god Marduk [Cthe chief god of the Babylonians] will be ·afraid [terrified].
·Babylon's gods [LIts images] will be ·put to shame [humiliated],
and her idols will be ·afraid [terrified]!'
3A nation from the north will attack Babylon [CPersia]
and make it like an ·empty desert [desolation].
No one will live there;
both people and animals will ·run away [flee]."

4The LORD says, "At that time [Land in those days]
the ·people [Lsons] of Israel and Judah will come together.
They will cry and ·look for [Lseek] the LORD their God.
5Those people will ask ·how to go [Lthe way/path] to ·Jerusalem [LZion; Cthe location of the Temple]
and will start in that direction.
They will come and join themselves to the LORD.
They will make an ·agreement [covenant; treaty] with him that will last forever,
an ·agreement [covenant; treaty] that will never be forgotten [31:31–34].

6"My people have been like lost sheep.
Their ·leaders [Lshepherds] have led them ·in the wrong way [astray]
and made them wander around in the mountains and hills.
They forgot where their ·resting place [fold] was [Ps. 23].
7Whoever ·saw [Lfound] my people ·hurt [Ldevoured] them.
And those ·enemies [foes] said, 'We ·did nothing wrong [are not guilty].

Those people sinned against the LORD, their ·true [Lrighteous] ·resting place [fold],
the God their fathers ·trusted [hoped in].'

8"·Run away [Flee] from Babylon,
and leave the land of the ·Babylonians [LChaldeans].
Be like the goats that lead the flock.
9I will soon ·arouse [Lstir up] and bring against Babylon
·many great nations [a large assembly of nations] from the north [Cled by Persia].
They will take their places for war against it,
and it will be captured ·by people from the north [Lfrom there].
Their arrows are like trained soldiers
who do not return [Cfrom war] with empty hands.
10The ·enemy will take all the wealth from the Babylonians [LChaldeans will be plundered].
·Those enemy soldiers will get all they want [LThe plunderers will be satisfied/sated]," says the LORD.

11"Babylon, you are excited and happy,
because you took my ·land [Linheritance; CIsrael].
You ·dance around [run free] like a young cow ·in the grain [during the threshing; Deut. 25:4].
·Your laughter is like the neighing of male horses [LYou neigh like a stallion].
12Your mother will be ·very ashamed [humiliated];
the woman who gave birth to you will be disgraced.
·Soon Babylonia will be the least important of all [LIt brings up the backside of] the nations.
She will be an empty, dry ·desert [wilderness].
13Because of the LORD's anger,
no one will live there.
She will be completely ·empty [desolate].
Everyone who passes by Babylon will be shocked.
They will shake their heads when they see all her injuries.

14"Take your positions for war against Babylon,
all ·you soldiers with [Lwho draw] bows.
Shoot your arrows at Babylon! Do not ·save any of them [Lspare any arrows],
because Babylon has sinned against the LORD.
15·Soldiers around Babylon [LOn every side], shout the war cry!
Babylon has surrendered, her ·towers [defenses] have fallen,
and her walls have been ·torn down [demolished].
The LORD is giving her people the punishment they deserve.
·You nations should give her what she deserves;
do to her what she has done to others [LJust as it did, they did].
16·Don't let the people from Babylon plant their crops [LCut the sower off from Babylon]
·or gather [Lseize the sickle wielder at the time of] the harvest.
·The soldiers treated their captives cruelly [L...before the sword of the oppressor].
Now, let everyone ·go back home [Lturn face toward his people].

Let everyone ·run [flee] to his own country [Cafter the fall of
Babylon, the Persians allowed the exiled people to return to their
own lands; Ezra 1].

17"The people of Israel are like a flock of sheep that are scattered
from being ·chased [driven] by lions.
The first lion to eat them up
was the king of Assyria [CSennacherib defeated the northern
kingdom of Israel in 722 BC].
The last lion to ·crush [gnaw] their bones
was Nebuchadnezzar king of Babylon [Cdefeated the southern
kingdom of Judah in 586 BC]."
18So this is what the LORD ·All-Powerful [Almighty; of Heaven's Armies;
Tof hosts], the God of Israel, says:
"I will punish the king of Babylon and his country
as I punished the king of Assyria [Cdefeated by Babylon at the end of
the seventh century BC].
19But I will bring the people of Israel back to their own pasture.
They will ·eat [feed] on Mount Carmel and in Bashan [Cparticularly
lush areas].
They will ·eat and be full [be sated]
on the hills of Ephraim and Gilead."
20The LORD says,
"At that time and in those days people will try to find Israel's guilt,
but there will be no guilt.
People will try to find Judah's sins,
but no sins will be found,
because I will leave a ·few people alive from Israel and Judah [remnant],
and I will forgive their sins.

21"Attack the land of Merathaim.
Attack the people who live in Pekod [Calternate names for Babylon].
·Chase them, kill them [LPut them to the sword], and ·completely
destroy [annihilate] them.
Do everything I commanded you!" says the LORD.

22"The noise of battle can be heard all over the country;
it is the noise of ·much destruction [Lgreat fracture].
23·Babylon was the hammer of the whole earth,
but how broken and shattered that hammer is now [LHow cut down
and broken is the hammer of the whole earth].
·It is truly the most ruined
of [LHow Babylon has become a horror among] all the nations.
24I set a trap for you [CBabylon],
and you were caught before you knew it.
You ·fought against [challenged] the LORD,
so you were found and ·taken prisoner [captured].
25The LORD has opened up his storeroom
and brought out the weapons of his anger,
because the Lord GOD ·All-Powerful [Almighty; of Heaven's Armies;
Tof hosts] has work to do
in the land of the ·Babylonians [LChaldeans].

26Come against it [CBabylon] from far away.
Break open her storehouses of grain.
Pile them up [Cdead bodies] like heaps of grain.
·Completely destroy Babylon [LAnnihilate it]
and ·do not leave anyone alive [Llet there be no remnant].
27·Kill [LPut to the sword] all its bulls [Cthe young men in Babylon];
let them go down to the slaughter [Ckilled like animals].
·How terrible it will be for [Woe to] them, because ·the time has come
for their defeat [Ltheir day has come];
it is time for them to be punished.
28Listen to the people ·running [fleeing] to escape the country of Babylon!
They are telling ·Jerusalem [LZion; Cthe location of the Temple]
how the LORD our God is punishing Babylon as it deserves
for destroying his Temple.

29"Call for ·the archers [Lall those who draw the bow]
to come against Babylon.
·Tell them to surround the city [LCamp all around it],
and let no one escape.
Pay her back for what she has done;
do to her what she has done to other nations.
Babylon acted with ·pride [arrogance] against the LORD,
the Holy One of Israel.
30So her young men will be killed in her streets.
All her soldiers will ·die [Lbe silenced] on that day," says the LORD.
31"You [CBabylon] are too ·proud [arrogant], and I am against you,"
says the Lord GOD ·All-Powerful [Almighty; of Heaven's Armies; Tof
hosts].
"·The time has come [LYour day is coming]
·for you to be punished [Lthe time of your punishment].
32The ·proud [arrogant; CBabylon] will stumble and fall,
and no one will help her get up.
I will ·start [kindle] a fire in her towns,
and it will ·burn up [Ldevour] everything around her."
33This is what the LORD ·All-Powerful [Almighty; of Heaven's Armies;
Tof hosts] says:
"The people of Israel
and Judah are ·slaves [oppressed].
·The enemy took them as prisoners [LTheir captors have seized them]
and won't let them go.
34But ·God is strong and will buy them back [Ltheir redeemer is strong].
His name is the LORD ·All-Powerful [Almighty; of Heaven's Armies;
Tof hosts].
He will surely ·defend them with power [take up their cause/case]
so he can give rest to their land.
But ·he will not give rest [turmoil] to those living in Babylon."
35The LORD says,
"Let a sword ·kill the people living in Babylon [Lbe against the
Chaldeans]
and her officers and wise men!
36Let a sword ·kill [Lbe against] her ·false prophets [diviners],
and they will become fools.

Let a sword ·kill [Lbe against] her warriors,
and they will be full of terror.
37Let a sword ·kill [Lbe against] her horses and chariots
and all the soldiers hired from other countries!
Then they will be like women [Cfrightened].
Let a sword ·attack [Lbe against] her treasures,
so they will be ·taken away [Lplundered].
38Let a sword ·attack [Lbe against] her waters
so they will be dried up.
She is a land of idols,
and the people go ·crazy [mad] with fear over them.

39"Desert animals and hyenas will live there,
and ·owls [*or* ostriches] will live there [Critually unclean birds that live in desolate places],
but no people will ever live there again.
She will never be ·filled with people [resided in] again.
40God ·completely destroyed [Loverturned] the cities of Sodom and Gomorrah
and ·the towns around them [Ltheir neighbors; 20:6; 23:13–15; 49:18; Gen. 18–19]," says the LORD.
"In the same way no people will live there [CBabylon],
and no human being will stay there.

41"Look! An army is coming from the north [CPersia and its allies].
A powerful nation and many kings
are ·coming together [Lstirred up] from all around the world.
42·Their armies have [LThey have grabbed] bows and spears.
The soldiers are ·cruel [fierce; violent] and have no ·mercy [compassion].
As the soldiers come riding on their horses,
the sound is loud like the ·roaring [thundering] sea.
They stand in their places, ready for battle.
They are ready to attack you, city of Babylon.
43The king of Babylon heard ·about those armies [Lthe news/report],
and ·he became helpless with fear [Lhis hands grew slack/feeble].
Distress has gripped him.
His pain is like that of a woman ·giving birth to a baby [in labor; 6:22–24].

44"Like a lion coming up from the thick bushes near the Jordan River
to attack a ·strong pen for sheep [*or* perennial pastures],
I will suddenly chase them away [Cpeople of Babylon from their land].
Who is the one I have ·chosen [appointed] to do this?
·There is no one [LWho is…?] like me,
·no one who [LWho…?] can take me to court.
·None of their leaders [LWho is the shepherd who…?] can stand up against me [49:19]."

45So listen to ·what the LORD has planned to do against Babylon [Lcounsel/advice of the LORD].
Listen to ·what he has decided to do to [Lhis plans against] the people in the city of Babylon.

He will surely drag away the young of the flock [Cthe youth of Babylon].
Their ·hometowns [Lpasture] will surely be shocked at what happens to them.
46At the sound of Babylon's capture, the earth will shake.
People in all nations will hear Babylon's cry of distress.

51 This is what the LORD says:
"I will soon ·cause [arouse; stir up] a destroying ·wind [*or* spirit]
against Babylon and the ·Babylonian people [Linhabitants of Leb Qemai; Ca coded reference to Chaldea (Babylon)].
2I will send ·foreign people [strangers; *or* winnowers] to ·destroy [Lwinnow] Babylon.
They will ·destroy [Lempty] the land.
Armies will surround the city
when the day of ·disaster [evil; trouble] comes upon her.
3Don't let the archers [Cof Babylon] ·prepare [draw] their bows to shoot.
Don't even let them put on their ·armor [coat of mail].
Don't ·feel sorry for [pity] the young men of Babylon,
but ·completely destroy [annihilate] her army.
4·They will be killed [LCorpses will fall] in the land of the ·Babylonians [LChaldeans]
and ·will die [Lthe wounded] in her streets.
5The Lord GOD ·All-Powerful [Almighty; of Heaven's Armies; Tof hosts]
did not ·leave [Lwidow] Israel and Judah,
even though ·they were completely guilty [Ltheir land was full of guilt]
in the presence of the Holy One of Israel.
6"·Run away [Flee] from Babylon
and ·save your lives [rescue yourselves]!
Don't stay and be killed because of Babylon's sins.
It is time for the LORD to ·punish Babylon [Lavenge himself];
he will give Babylon the punishment she deserves.
7Babylon was like a gold cup in the LORD's hand
that made the whole earth drunk [CGod used Babylon to administer his cup of wrath].
The nations drank Babylon's wine,
so they went ·crazy [mad].
8Babylon has suddenly fallen and been broken.
·Cry [Wail] for her!
Get balm [8:22; 46:11] for her pain,
and maybe she can be healed.

9"Foreigners in Babylon say, 'We tried to heal Babylon,
but she cannot be healed.
So let us leave her and each go to his own country [Cafter the fall of Babylon, the Persians allowed the exiled people to return to their own lands; Ezra 1].
Babylon's ·punishment [judgment] ·is as high as [reaches; touches] the ·sky [heavens];
it ·reaches [Llifts up] to the ·clouds [*or* skies].'

10"The people of Judah say, 'The LORD has ·shown us to be right

[brought about/forth our vindication].
Come, let us ·tell [recount] **in ·Jerusalem** [LZion; Cthe location of the Temple]
what the LORD our God has done.'

11**"Sharpen the arrows!**
·Pick up your shields [*or* Fill the quivers]**!**
The LORD has stirred up the kings of the Medes,
because he ·wants [Lpurposes] **to destroy Babylon.**
The LORD will punish them as they deserve
for destroying his Temple.
12**Lift up a banner** [Ca battle standard] **against the walls of Babylon!**
·Bring more [LStrengthen the] **guards.**
Put the watchmen in their places,
and ·get ready for a secret attack [prepare an ambush]**!**
The LORD will certainly do what he has planned
and what he said he would do against the people of Babylon.
13**You** [CBabylon] **live near ·much** [mighty] **water** [Cthe Euphrates]
and are rich with many treasures,
but your end as a nation has come.
·It is time to stop you from robbing other nations [*or* Your destiny is fixed].
14**The LORD ·All-Powerful** [Almighty; of Heaven's Armies; Tof hosts] **has promised ·in his own name** [Lby himself]:
'I will surely fill you [CBabylon] **with so many men** [Cenemy soldiers] **they will be like locusts** [46:23; Judg. 6:5; 7:12; Nah. 3:15–17; Rev. 9:7].
They will ·stand [raise] **over you and shout their victory.'**

15**"The LORD made the earth by his power.**
He used his wisdom to ·build [Lestablish] **the world**
and his understanding to stretch out the ·skies [heavens; Prov. 3:19–20; 8:22–31].
16**When he ·thunders** [Lgives forth his voice]**, the waters in the skies roar.**
He makes ·clouds [mist] **rise ·all over** [Lfrom the ends of] **the earth.**
He sends lightning with the rain
and brings out the wind from his storehouses.

17**"People are so stupid and know so little.**
Goldsmiths are ·made ashamed [humiliated] **by their idols,**
because those statues are ·only false gods [Ldeceptive].
They have no breath in them.
18**They are worth nothing; ·people make fun of them** [*or* works of delusion].
·When they are judged [LAt the time of their punishment]**, they will be destroyed.**
19**But Jacob's Portion** [CGod] **is not like the idols.**
He ·made [formed; shaped] **everything,**
and ·he chose Israel to be his special people [Israel is the tribe of his inheritance].
The LORD ·All-Powerful [Almighty; of Heaven's Armies; Tof hosts] **is his name.**

20"You are my war club,
my battle weapon.
I use you to ·smash [shatter; [C]and so throughout this passage] nations.
I use you to destroy kingdoms.
21I use you to smash horses and riders.
I use you to smash chariots and drivers.
22I use you to smash men and women.
I use you to smash old people and young people.
I use you to smash young men and young women.
23I use you to smash shepherds and flocks.
I use you to smash farmers and oxen.
I use you to smash governors and ·officers [officials; leaders].
24"But I will pay back Babylon and all the ·Babylonians [[L]Chaldeans]
for all the ·evil things [disasters; troubles] they did to ·Jerusalem [[L]Zion;
[C]the location of the Temple] in your ·sight [[L]eyes]," says the LORD.
25The LORD says,
"Babylon, you are a destroying mountain,
and I am against you.
You have destroyed the whole land.
I will ·put [reach; stretch] my hand out against you.
I will roll you off the ·cliffs [rocks; crags],
and I will make you a burned-out mountain.
26People will not ·find any rocks in Babylon big enough for [[L]take from you] cornerstones.
People will not take any rocks from you for a foundation [[C]of a building],
because your city will be ·just a pile of ruins [a desolation] forever,"
says the LORD.

27"Lift up a banner [[C]a battle standard] in the land!
Blow the ·trumpet [ram's horn] among the nations!
·Get the nations ready for battle against Babylon [[L]Consecrate the nations against it].
Call these kingdoms of Ararat, Minni, and Ashkenaz [[C]near Lake Urmia and Lake Van to the northwest of Babylon, and part of the coalition against it] against her [[C]to fight].
Choose a commander ·to lead the army against Babylon [[L]against it].
·Send [[L]Bring up] so many horses that they are like a swarm of locusts.
28·Get the nations ready for battle against Babylon [[L]Consecrate the nations against it]—
the kings of the Medes,
their governors and all their officers,
and all the countries they rule.
29The land shakes and ·moves in pain [writhes],
because the LORD will do what he has planned to Babylon.
He will make Babylon an ·empty desert [desolation],
where no one will live.
30Babylon's warriors have stopped fighting.
They stay in their ·protected cities [strongholds].
Their strength is gone,
and they have become like women [[C]frightened].
Babylon's houses are burning.
The bars [[C]of its gates] are broken.

31One runner meets another runner;
messenger meets messenger.
They announce to the king of Babylon
that his whole city has been captured.
32The river crossings have been ·captured [seized],
and the swamplands are burning with fire.
All of the soldiers [Cof Babylon] are terribly afraid."
33This is what the LORD ·All-Powerful [Almighty; of Heaven's Armies;
Tof hosts], the God of Israel, says:
"The ·city [Ldaughter] of Babylon is like a threshing floor,
where people trod [Con grain at harvest time].
The time to harvest [CBabylon] is coming soon."

34"Nebuchadnezzar king of Babylon has ·defeated [Ldevoured;
consumed] and ·destroyed [crushed] us.
We became like an empty jar [Cprobably a reference to the exile].
He was like a ·giant snake [monster; dragon; Is. 27:1; 51:9; Ezek. 29:3;
32:2; Job 7:1; Ps. 74:13] that swallowed us.
He filled his stomach with our ·best things [delicacies].
Then he spit us out.
35·Babylon did terrible things to hurt us.
Now let those things happen to Babylon [LMay the violence done to
me and my flesh be on Babylon],"
say the people of ·Jerusalem [LZion; Cthe location of the Temple].
"·The people of Babylon killed our people.
Now let them be punished for what they did [LMay my blood be on
the Chaldeans]," says Jerusalem.
36So this is what the LORD says:
"I will ·soon defend you [Lpresent your case; Caddressed to Judah],
and make sure that Babylon is punished.
I will dry up Babylon's sea
and make her springs become dry [Is. 24:4; Nah. 1:4].
37Babylon will become a pile of ruins,
a ·home [den; haunt] for wild dogs [jackals; 9:11; 10:22; 49:33;
Lam. 5:18].
People will be shocked and hiss at what happened there.
No one will live there anymore.
38Babylon's people roar like young lions;
they growl like baby lions.
39While they are ·stirred [heated] up,
I will give ·a feast for [drinks to] them
and make them drunk.
They will shout and laugh.
And they will sleep forever and never wake up!" says the LORD.
40"I will take them [Cpeople of Babylon] to be ·killed [slaughtered].
They will be like lambs,
like sheep and goats [11:19; 12:3].

41"How ·Babylon [LSheshach; Can alternate name for Babylon; 25:26] has
been ·defeated [captured]!
The pride of the whole earth has been ·taken captive [seized].

·People from other nations are shocked at what happened to Babylon,
and the things they see make them afraid [LHow Babylon has become
a horror among the nations].
42The sea has risen over Babylon;
its ·roaring [tumultuous] waves cover her.
43·Babylon's [LIts] towns are ·ruined and empty [desolate].
It has become a dry, desert land,
a land where no one lives.
People do not even travel through it .
44I will punish the god Bel [Canother name for Marduk, the chief god of
Babylon] in Babylon.
I will make him spit out what he has swallowed.
Nations will no longer ·come [Lstream] to Babylon;
even the wall around the city will fall.

45"Come out of it [CBabylon], my people!
·Run for [Escape with] your lives!
·Run [Escape] from the LORD's great anger.
46Don't lose ·courage [heart];
rumors will spread through the land, but don't be afraid.
One rumor comes this year, and another comes the next year.
There will be rumors of ·terrible fighting [violence] in the country,
of rulers fighting against rulers.
47The ·time will surely come [Ldays are coming]
when I will punish the idols of Babylon,
and the whole land will be disgraced.
There will be many ·dead people [corpses] ·lying all around [Lfalling
in its midst].
48Then heaven and earth and all that is in them
will shout for joy about Babylon.
They will shout because the army comes from the north [CPersia and
its allies]
to destroy Babylon," says the LORD.

49"Babylon must fall, because ·she killed people from [Lof the corpses of]
Israel.
·She killed people from everywhere on [L...and the corpses of all the]
earth.
50You who have escaped being killed with swords,
·leave Babylon [go; flee; depart]! Don't wait!
Remember the LORD in the faraway land
and ·think about Jerusalem [Llet Jerusalem come up in your heart/
mind]."

51"We people of Judah are disgraced,
because we have been ·insulted [reproached].
·We have been shamed [LShame/Humiliation covers our face],
because strangers have gone into
the holy places of the LORD's Temple [Lhouse]!"

52So the LORD says, "The ·time is [Ldays are] coming soon
when I will punish the idols of Babylon.

Wounded people will ·cry with pain [groan]
all over that land.
53Even if Babylon grows until she touches the ·sky [heavens],
and even if she ·makes her highest cities strong [fortifies her lofty stronghold],
I will send people to destroy her," says the LORD.
54"Sounds of people crying are heard in Babylon.
Sounds of ·people destroying things [great destruction]
are heard in the land of the Babylonians.
55The LORD is destroying Babylon
and making the loud sounds of the city become silent.
Enemies come roaring in like ocean waves.
The roar of their voices is heard all around.
56·The army has come to destroy [LDestroyers have come to] Babylon.
Her soldiers have been captured,
and their bows are broken,
because the LORD is a God who punishes people for the evil they do.
He ·gives them the full punishment they deserve [repays them in full].
57I will make Babylon's rulers and wise men drunk [Cwith the cup of God's wrath; 25:15–38],
and her governors, officers, and soldiers, too.
Then they will sleep forever and never wake up [v. 39]," says the King,
whose name is the LORD ·All-Powerful [Almighty; of Heaven's Armies; Tof hosts].

58This is what the LORD ·All-Powerful [Almighty; of Heaven's Armies; Tof hosts] says:
"Babylon's ·thick [broad] wall will be completely ·pulled down [leveled]
and her high gates burned with fire.
The people will ·work hard [weary themselves], but it won't help;
their work will only become fuel for the flames!"

A Message to Babylon

59This is the message that Jeremiah the prophet gave to the officer
Seraiah son of Neriah, who was the son of Mahseiah [Cprobably Baruch's
brother; 32:12]. Seraiah went to Babylon with Zedekiah king of Judah in
the fourth year Zedekiah was king of Judah [C593 BC]. ·His duty was to
arrange the king's food and housing on the trip [LHe was the quartermas-
ter]. 60Jeremiah had written on a scroll all the ·terrible [disastrous; evil]
things that would happen to Babylon, all these words about Babylon.
61Jeremiah said to Seraiah, "As soon as you come to Babylon, be sure to
read this message so all the people can hear you. 62Then say, 'LORD, you
have said that you will ·destroy [Lcut off] this place so that no people or
animals will live in it. It will be an ·empty ruin [desolation] forever.'
63After you finish reading this scroll, tie a stone to it and throw it into the
Euphrates River. 64Then say, 'In the same way Babylon will sink and will
not rise again because of the ·terrible [disastrous; evil] things I will make
happen here. Her people will fall.' "

·The words of Jeremiah end here [Thus far are the words of Jeremiah].

The Fall of Jerusalem

52 Zedekiah was twenty-one years old when he became king, and
he was king in Jerusalem for eleven years [Cfrom 597–586 BC].
His mother's name was Hamutal daughter of Jeremiah [Cnot the prophet],
and she was from Libnah. 2Zedekiah did ·what the LORD said was wrong
[Levil in the eyes of the LORD], just as Jehoiakim [Chis brother who ruled

from 609–597 BC] had done. 3All this happened in Jerusalem and Judah because the LORD was angry with them. Finally, he threw them out of his presence.

Zedekiah ·turned [rebelled] against the king of Babylon. 4Then Nebuchadnezzar king of Babylon marched against Jerusalem with his whole army. They made a camp around the city and built ·devices [siege towers] all around the city walls to attack it. This happened on Zedekiah's ninth year, tenth month, and tenth day as king [CJanuary 15, 588]. 5And the city was under ·attack [siege] until Zedekiah's eleventh year as king [C586 BC].

6By the ninth day of the fourth month [CJuly 18], the ·hunger [famine] was ·terrible [severe] in the city; there was no food for the people to eat. 7Then the city wall was ·broken through [breeched], and the whole army [Cof Judah] ·ran away [fled] at night. They left the city through the gate between the two walls by the king's garden. Even though the ·Babylonians [LChaldeans] were surrounding the city, Zedekiah and his men headed toward the ·Jordan Valley [LArabah].

8But the ·Babylonian [LChaldean] army chased King Zedekiah and caught him in the ·plains [LArabah] of Jericho. All of his army was scattered from him. 9So the Babylonians ·captured [seized] Zedekiah and took him to the king of Babylon at the town of Riblah in the land of Hamath. There he ·passed sentence on [judged] Zedekiah. 10At Riblah the king of Babylon ·killed [slaughtered] Zedekiah's sons ·as he watched [Lbefore his eyes]. The king also ·killed [slaughtered] all the officers of Judah. 11Then he ·put out Zedekiah's eyes [blinded the eyes of Zedekiah], and put bronze chains on him, and took him to Babylon. And the king kept Zedekiah in prison there until the day he died.

12Nebuzaradan, commander of the king's special guards and servant of the king of Babylon, came to Jerusalem on the tenth day of the fifth month. This was in Nebuchadnezzar's nineteenth year as king of Babylon [CAugust 17, 586 BC]. 13Nebuzaradan set fire to the ·Temple [Lhouse] of the LORD, the ·palace [Lhouse of the king], and all the houses of Jerusalem; every ·important building [Lgreat/big house] was burned. 14The whole ·Babylonian [LChaldean] army, led by the commander of the king's special guards, ·broke down [demolished] all the walls around Jerusalem. 15Nebuzaradan, the commander of the king's special guards, took captive some of the poorest people, those who ·were left [remained] in Jerusalem, those who had ·surrendered [deserted; defected] to the king of Babylon, and the ·skilled craftsmen [artisans] who were left in Jerusalem. 16But Nebuzaradan left behind some of the poorest people of the land to take care of the vineyards and fields.

17The ·Babylonians [LChaldeans] broke into pieces the bronze pillars [1 Kin. 7:15–22], the bronze stands [1 Kin. 7:27], and the large bronze ·bowl [basin], called the Sea [1 Kin. 7:23–26], which were in the ·Temple [Lhouse] of the LORD. Then they carried all the bronze pieces to Babylon. 18They also took the pots, shovels, ·wick trimmers [snuffers], bowls, dishes, and all the bronze objects used to serve in the Temple. 19The commander of the king's special guards took away bowls, ·pans for carrying hot coals [firepans], large bowls, pots, lampstands, pans, and bowls used for drink offerings. He took everything that was made of pure gold or silver.

20There was so much bronze that it could not be weighed: two pillars, the large bronze bowl called the Sea with the twelve bronze bulls under it, and the movable stands, which King Solomon had made for the Temple of the LORD.

[21]Each of the pillars was about ·twenty-seven feet [Leighteen cubits] high, eighteen feet [Ltwelve cubits] around, and hollow inside. The wall of each pillar was ·three inches [Lfour fingers] thick. [22]The bronze capital on top of the one pillar was about ·seven and one-half feet [Lfive cubits] high. It was decorated with ·a net design [network; latticework] and bronze pomegranates all around it. The other pillar also had pomegranates and was like the first pillar. [23]There were ninety-six pomegranates on the sides of the pillars. There was a total of a hundred pomegranates above the ·net design [network; latticework].

[24]The commander of the king's special guards took as prisoners Seraiah the chief priest, Zephaniah the priest next in rank, and the three doorkeepers. [25]He also took from the city the officer in charge of the soldiers, seven people ·who advised the king [of the king's council], the ·royal secretary [scribe] who selected people for the army, and sixty other men from Judah who were in the city when it fell. [26]Nebuzaradan, the commander, took these people and brought them to the king of Babylon at the town of Riblah. [27]There at Riblah, in the land of Hamath, the king had them killed.

So the people of Judah were led away from their country as ·captives [exiles]. [28]This is the number of the people Nebuchadnezzar took away as ·captives [exiles]: in the seventh year [C597 BC], 3,023 ·Jews [LJudeans]; [29]in Nebuchadnezzar's eighteenth year [C586 BC], 832 people from Jerusalem; [30]in Nebuchadnezzar's twenty-third year [C582 BC], Nebuzaradan, commander of the king's special guards, took 745 ·Jews [LJudeans] as ·captives [exiles].

In all 4,600 people were ·taken captive [exiled].

Jehoiachin Is Set Free

[31]Jehoiachin king of Judah was in prison in Babylon for thirty-seven years. The year Evil-Merodach became king of Babylon [Ca son of Nebuchadnezzar, he ruled 562–560 BC] he let Jehoiachin king of Judah out of ·prison [Lhouse of confinement]. He set Jehoiachin free on the twenty-fifth day of the twelfth month [CMarch 31, 561 BC]. [32]Evil-Merodach spoke kindly to Jehoiachin and gave him a seat of honor above the seats of the other kings who were with him in Babylon [Che honored him above other defeated vassal kings]. [33]So Jehoiachin put away his prison clothes, and for the rest of his life, he ate at the king's table. [34]Every day the king of Babylon gave Jehoiachin an allowance. This lasted as long as he lived, until the day Jehoiachin died.

LAMENTATIONS

Jerusalem Cries over Her Loss

1 **How lonely sits the city** [CJerusalem],
once so full of people.
She is like a widow,
once great among the nations [Ps. 122:3].
She was like a queen ·of all the other cities [Lamong the provinces],
but now she is a ·slave [forced laborer; vassal].

2**She** [CJerusalem pictured as a widow] **cries loudly at night,**
and tears are on her cheeks.
There is no one to comfort her;
·all who loved her are gone [Lamong all her lovers; Creferring to other nations to whom she unfaithfully turned for help].
All her friends have ·turned against [betrayed] **her**
and are now her enemies.

3**Judah has gone into ·captivity** [exile; Cto Babylon; 2 Kin. 25:8–21; 2 Chr. 36:17–21; Jer. 39:1–10; 51:12–30]
where she ·suffers [is oppressed/afflicted] **·and works hard** [under slavery/harsh servitude].
She lives among other nations,
but she has found no rest.
Those who ·chased [pursued; persecuted] **her caught her**
·when she was in trouble [Lbetween her distresses].

4**The roads to ·Jerusalem** [LZion; Cthe location of the Temple] **·are sad** [mourn],
because no one comes for the feasts [CPassover, Pentecost, Tabernacles].
·No one passes through her gates [LAll her gates are desolate].
Her priests groan,
her young women are ·suffering [afflicted],
and ·Jerusalem suffers terribly [Lshe is bitter].

5**Her foes are now her masters.**
Her enemies ·enjoy the wealth they have taken [prosper].
The LORD is ·punishing [tormenting; afflicting] **her**
for her many ·sins [transgressions].
Her ·children [little ones] **have gone away**
as captives of the ·enemy [foe].

6**The ·beauty** [splendor; majesty] **of ·Jerusalem** [Lthe daughter of Zion; Cthe location of the Temple; Ps. 48:1–3]
has gone away.

Her rulers are like deer
that cannot find ·food [[L]pasture].
They ·are weak [[L]go without strength]
·and run from the hunters [[L]before those who pursue/chase/persecute them].

7**Jerusalem ·is suffering and homeless.**
She [[L]...in the days of her affliction and homelessness] **remembers all the ·good** [desirable; coveted] **things**
from the ·past [[L]former days].
But her people ·were defeated by the enemy [[L]fell to the power/hand of the foe],
and there was no one to help her.
When her ·enemies [foes] **saw her,**
they laughed ·to see her ruined [at her downfall].

8**Jerusalem sinned terribly,**
so she has become ·unclean [*or* an object of mockery].
Those who honored her now ·hate [despise] **her,**
because they have seen her nakedness.
She groans
and turns away.

9**She made herself ·dirty** [defiled] **·by her sins** [[L]in her skirts; [C]Jerusalem is pictured as a defiled woman; Lev. 15:19–30]
and did not think about what would happen to her.
Her ·defeat [downfall] **was surprising,**
and no one could comfort her.
She says, "Lord, see how I ·suffer [am afflicted],
because the enemy has won."

10**The ·enemy** [foe] **·reached out and took** [spread his hands on]
all her ·precious [desired; coveted] **things.**
She even saw ·foreigners [nations]
enter her ·Temple [[L]holy place; Ps. 74:4–8].
·The Lord had commanded foreigners [[L]...those you commanded]
never to enter the meeting place of ·his [[L]your] **people.**

11**All of ·Jerusalem's** [[L]its] **people groan,**
·looking for [seeking] **bread.**
They ·are trading [[L]give] **their ·precious** [desired; coveted] **things for food**
so they can stay alive.
The city says, "Look, Lord, and see.
I am ·hated [despised]."

12**Jerusalem says, "You who pass by on the road ·don't seem to care** [is it nothing to you...?; [L]No, to you].
Come, look at me and see:
Is there any ·pain [sorrow] **like ·mine** [[L]my pain/sorrow]?
·Is there any pain like that he has caused me [...which has come upon me]?

The LORD has ·punished [afflicted; tormented] me
on the day of his great anger.

13"He sent fire from above
that went ·down [deep] into my bones.
He ·stretched [spread] out a net for my feet
and turned me back.
He made me so ·sad and lonely [desolate]
that I am ·weak [faint; sick] all day.

14"He ·has noticed my sins [*or* bound my transgressions into a yoke];
they are ·tied together [intertwined] by his hands;
they hang around my neck.
·He has turned my strength into weakness [LMy strength falters].
The Lord has handed me over
to those who ·are stronger than I [LI cannot stand against].

15"The Lord has rejected
all my mighty men ·inside my walls [Lin my midst].
He ·brought an army [*or* proclaimed a time] against me
to ·destroy [break] my young men.
As if in a winepress, the Lord has ·crushed [trampled]
the ·capital city [Lvirgin daughter] of Judah [Is. 63:1–6].

16"I cry about these things;
my eyes overflow with tears.
·There is no one near to comfort me [LA comforter is far from me],
no one who can ·give me strength again [Lrestore my soul].
My children are ·left sad and lonely [desolate],
because the enemy has ·won [prevailed]."

17·Jerusalem [LZion; Cthe location of the Temple] ·reaches [spreads] out
her hands,
but there is no one to comfort her.
The LORD commanded the people of Jacob
to be surrounded by their ·enemies [foes].
Jerusalem is now unclean [1:8–9]
·like [Lamong] those around her.

18Jerusalem says, "The LORD is ·right [righteous],
but I ·refused to obey him [Lhave rebelled against his mouth].
Listen, all you people,
and look at my ·pain [sorrow].
My young women and men
have gone into captivity [1:3].

19"I called out to my ·friends [Llovers; 1:2],
but they ·turned against [deceived] me.
My priests and my elders
have died in the city
while ·looking for [seeking] food
to ·stay alive [revive their strength].

20"Look at me, Lord. I am ·upset [distressed]
and ·greatly troubled [Lmy innards/stomach/bowels are agitated].
My heart is ·troubled [Loverturned within me],
because I have been so ·stubborn [rebellious].
Out in the streets, the sword ·kills [bereaves];
inside the houses, ·death destroys [Lit is like death].

21"People have heard my groaning,
and there is no one to comfort me.
All my enemies have heard of my trouble,
and they are happy you have done this to me.
Now bring that day you have announced
so that ·my enemies [Lthey] will be like me.

22"·Look at all their evil [LLet all their evil come before you].
Do to them what you have done to me
because of all my ·sins [transgressions].
I groan over and over again,
and ·I am afraid [Lmy heart is sick/faint/weak]."

The Lord Destroyed Jerusalem

2 Look how the Lord in his anger
has ·brought Jerusalem to shame [Ltreated the daughter of Zion with contempt; *or* brought a cloud over the daughter of Zion].
He has thrown down the ·greatness [splendor; beauty] of Israel
from the ·sky [heavens] to the earth;
he did not remember his footstool [Cthe Temple; Ps. 99:5; 132:7],
on the day of his anger.

2The Lord swallowed up without ·mercy [pity]
all the ·houses [homes; dwellings] of the people of Jacob;
in his anger he ·pulled down [demolished]
the strong places of [Lthe daughter of] Judah.
He threw her kingdom and its rulers
down to the ground in dishonor.

3In his anger he has ·removed [cut to pieces]
all the ·strength [Lhorn; Ca symbol of pride and power] of Israel;
he took away his ·power [Lright hand] from Israel
when the enemy came.
He burned against the people of Jacob [Canother name for Israel] like a flaming fire
that burns up everything around it.

4Like an enemy, he ·prepared to shoot [bent; drew] his bow,
and his right hand was against us [Ps. 7:12–13].
Like an ·enemy [foe], he killed
all ·the good-looking people [Lwhich eye desired];
he poured out his anger like fire
on the tents of ·Jerusalem [Lthe daughter of Zion; Cthe location of the Temple].

5 **The Lord was like an enemy;**
he swallowed up Israel.
He swallowed up all her palaces
and destroyed all her strongholds.
He has ·caused more [multiplied] **moaning and groaning**
for ·Judah [Lthe daughter of Judah].

6 **He ·cut down** [laid waste to; violently treated] **his ·Temple** [Lbooth] **like a ·garden** [vineyard];
he destroyed the meeting place.
The Lord has made ·Jerusalem [LZion; Cthe location of the Temple] **forget**
the ·set feasts [*or* meeting place] **and Sabbath days.**
He has ·rejected [despised] **the king and the priest**
in his great anger.

7 **The Lord has rejected his altar**
and ·abandoned [disavowed] **his ·Temple** [LHoly Place; Ezek. 9–11].
He has ·handed over to [Ldelivered into the hand of] **the enemy**
the walls of its [Cprobably Jerusalem's] **palaces.**
·Their uproar [LThey gave forth voice] **in the Lord's ·Temple** [Lhouse]
was like that of a feast day.

8 **The Lord planned to destroy**
the wall around ·Jerusalem [Lthe daughter of Zion; Cthe location of the Temple].
He ·measured the wall [Lextended a measuring line; Cusually used in construction but here in demolition]
and did not stop himself from ·destroying [Lswallowing] **it.**
He made the walls and ·defenses [ramparts] **·sad** [mourn];
together they have ·fallen [languished].

9 **·Jerusalem's** [LIts] **gates have ·fallen** [sunk] **to the ground;**
he destroyed and smashed the bars [Cof the gates; Ps. 107:16; Is. 45:2; Jer. 51:30; Nah. 3:13].
Her king and her princes are among the nations.
The ·teaching [law; instruction; CGod's law] **has stopped,**
and the prophets do not have
visions from the Lord.

10 **The elders of ·Jerusalem** [Lthe daughter of Zion; Cthe location of the Temple]
sit on the ground in silence.
They throw dust on their heads
and put on ·rough cloth [sackcloth; burlap; signs of grief or repentance].
The young women of Jerusalem
bow their heads to the ground [Cin sorrow].

11 **My eyes ·have no more tears** [Lare exhausted from tears],
and ·I am sick to my stomach [Lmy innards/stomach/bowels are agitated].

·I feel empty inside [LMy bile/gall is poured out on the ground],
because ·my people [Lthe daughter of my people] have been
·destroyed [shattered; broken].
Children and ·babies [nurslings] are fainting
in the ·streets [public areas] of the city.

12They ask their mothers,
"Where is the grain and wine?"
They faint like wounded soldiers
in the ·streets [public areas] of the city
and ·die [Lpour out their lives] in their mothers' ·arms [Lbosom].

13What can I ·say [testify] about you, [Ldaughter] Jerusalem?
What can I compare you to?
What can I say you are like?
How can I comfort you, ·Jerusalem [Lvirgin daughter Zion; Clocation
of the Temple]?
Your ·ruin [wound] is as ·deep [great] as the sea.
·No one [LWho…?] can heal you.

14Your prophets saw visions,
but they were ·false [empty] and ·worth nothing [insipid; nonsense;
Ezek. 10:10–12].
They did not ·point out [expose] your ·sins [guilt]
to ·keep you from being captured [*or* restore your fortunes].
They ·preached what was [Lsaw oracles for you that were] ·false
[empty]
and ·led you wrongly [fraudulent].

15All who pass by on the road
clap their hands at you [Cin approval of Jerusalem's destruction;
Ezek. 25:6];
they ·make fun of [hiss at; Cin scorn; 1 Kin. 9:8; Jer. 19:8; Zeph. 2:15]
[Lthe daughter of] Jerusalem
and shake their heads.
They ask, "Is this the city that people called
the most beautiful city,
the ·happiest place on [joy of the whole] earth [Ps. 48:2]?"

16All your enemies ·open [Lcrack] their mouths
to speak against you.
They make fun and ·grind [gnash] their teeth [Cin anger].
They say, "We have swallowed you up.
This is the day we were ·waiting [hoping] for!
We have finally seen it happen."

17The LORD has done what he planned;
he has ·kept [fulfilled] his ·word [threat; Cthe covenant curses;
Deut. 28:45–50]
that he commanded ·long ago [Lin days of old].
He has ·destroyed [demolished] without ·mercy [pity],
and he has let your enemies laugh at you [Csuch as Edom; Obad. 1–21].

He has ·strengthened [Lexalted the horn of; Csymbol of pride and power] **your enemies.**

18·**The people** [LTheir hearts] **cry out to the Lord.**
Wall of ·Jerusalem [Lthe daughter of Zion; Cthe location of the Temple],
let your tears flow
like a ·river [torrent; wadi] **day and night.**
Do not ·stop [Lallow yourself relaxation]
or let your eyes rest.

19**Get up, cry out in the night,**
·even as the night begins [Lat the beginning of the night watches; Cthe night was divided into three four-hour watches].
Pour out your heart like water
·in prayer to [Lbefore the presence/face of] **the Lord.**
Lift up your hands in prayer to him
for the life of your children
who are ·fainting [growing weak] **with hunger**
·on every street corner [Lat the head of every street].

20**Jerusalem says: "Look, Lord, and see**
to whom you have done this.
·Women [LShould women…?] **eat their own ·babies** [Lfruit; Cshort for "fruit of their womb"],
the children ·they have cared for [they have nursed/borne; *or* which are well-formed; Deut. 28:53–55; Jer. 19:6–9].
·Priests and prophets are [LShould priests and prophets be…?] **killed in the ·Temple** [Lholy place] **of the Lord.**

21**"People young and old**
lie outside on the ground.
My young women and young men
have ·been killed [Lfallen] **by the sword.**
You killed them on the day of your anger;
you ·killed [slaughtered] **them without ·mercy** [pity].

22**"You invited ·terrors** [*or* enemies] **to come against me on every side,**
as if ·you were inviting them to a feast [Lon an appointed/feast day].
No one escaped or remained alive
on the day of the Lord's anger.
My enemy has ·killed [annihilated]
those I ·cared for [nursed; bore] **and brought up."**

The Meaning of Suffering

3 **I am a man** [Csymbolizing Jerusalem] **who has seen the ·suffering** [affliction]
that comes from the rod of ·the Lord's [Lhis] **anger.**
2**He ·led** [Lguided and brought] **me**
into darkness, not light.
3**He turned his hand against me**
again and again, all day long [Jer. 21:5].

4He ·wore out [wasted away] my flesh and skin
and broke my bones.
5He ·surrounded me with sadness
and attacked me with grief [Lhas built up and besieged me with bitterness/*or* poverty and hardship].
6He made me sit in the dark,
like those who have been dead a long time.

7He ·shut me [Lwalled me] in so I could not get out;
he put heavy chains on me.
8I cry out and beg for help,
but he ·ignores [obstructs] my prayer.
9He ·blocked [Lwalled in] my way with ·a stone wall [Lcut stones]
and ·led me in the wrong direction [Ltwisted my paths; Job 19:7–12].

10He is like a bear ready to ·attack [ambush] me,
like a lion in hiding [Hos. 13:8; Amos 5:19].
11He led me the wrong way and ·let me stray [*or* tore me to pieces]
and left me ·without help [desolate].
12He ·prepared to shoot [has drawn] his bow
and made me the target for his arrows.

13He shot me in the kidneys
with the arrows from his ·bag [quiver; Job 16:13].
14I was a joke to all my people,
who make fun of me with ·songs [mocking songs] all day long [Ps. 22:7; 69:12; 119:51].
15·The LORD [LHe] filled me with ·misery [bitterness];
he made me drunk with ·suffering [affliction; Lwormwood; gall; Ca bitter-tasting herb].

16He ·broke [made me gnash] my teeth with gravel
and trampled me into the ·dirt [dust; ashes].
17·I have no more peace [LMy life/soul is rejected from peace].
I have forgotten ·what happiness is [prosperity; Lgood].
18I said, "My ·strength [luster; *or* endurance] ·is gone [has perished],
and I have no hope in the LORD."

19LORD, remember my ·suffering [affliction] and my ·misery [*or* wanderings; homelessness; 1:7],
·my sorrow and trouble [Lit is wormwood and gall; 3:15].
20Please remember me
and think about ·me [Lmy life].
21But I have hope
when I ·think of this [Lreturn to my mind/heart]:

22The LORD's ·love [loyalty] never ends;
his ·mercies [compassion] never stop.
23They are new every morning;
LORD, your ·loyalty [faithfulness] is ·great [abundant; Ps. 33:4; 92:2; 143:1].
24I say to myself, "The LORD is ·mine [Lmy lot/portion],
so I hope in him."

25The LORD is good to those who ·hope in [wait for] him,
to those who seek him.
26It is good to wait ·quietly [silently]
for the LORD to ·save [be victorious].
27It is good for someone to ·work hard [Lcarry/bear the yoke]
while he is young.

28He should sit alone and be ·quiet [silent];
·the LORD has given him hard work to do [Lwhen it is imposed/heavy on him].
29He should ·bow down to the ground [Lput his mouth in the dust];
maybe there is still hope.
30He should ·let anyone slap [Lgive to the striker] his cheek;
he should be ·filled [sated] with ·shame [scorn].

31The Lord will not reject
his people forever.
32Although he brings ·sorrow [grief],
he also has ·mercy [compassion] and great ·love [loyalty].
33He does not ·like to punish people [Lafflict from his heart]
or make them ·sad [grieve].

34·He sees [LDoes he not see…?] if any prisoner of the earth
is crushed under ·his [*or* their; Cthe wicked oppressors'] feet;
35·he sees [Ldoes he not see…?] if ·someone is treated unfairly [human rights are distorted]
before the Most High God;
36·the Lord sees [Ldoes the Lord not see…?]
if someone is cheated in his case in court.

37·Nobody [LWho…?] can speak and have it happen
unless the Lord commands it.
38·Both [LDo not…?] bad and good things
come by the command of the Most High God [Job 2:10].
39No ·one [Lliving person] should complain
·when he is punished for [Lbefore] his sins.

40Let us ·examine [check] and ·see [investigate] ·what we have done [Lour ways]
and then return to the LORD [Crepent; Jer. 17:9–10; Ps. 139:23–24].
41Let us lift up our hands ·and pray from [as well as] our hearts
to God in heaven:
42"We have ·sinned [transgressed] and ·turned [rebelled] against you,
and you have not forgiven us.

43"You ·wrapped [covered] yourself in anger and ·chased [pursued] us;
you killed us without ·mercy [pity].
44You ·wrapped [covered] yourself in a cloud [Ex. 40:34–38],
and no prayer could ·get [pass] through.
45You made us like ·scum [sweepings] and trash
·among the other nations [Lin the midst of the peoples].

46"**All of our enemies**
·open [[L]crack] **their mouths and speak against us** [2:16].
47**We have been ·frightened** [terrified] **and fearful,**
ruined and ·destroyed [broken]."
48**·Streams of tears** [[L]Channels of water] **flow from my eyes,**
because ·my people are destroyed [[L]of the fracture of my people].

49**My tears flow ·continually** [without ceasing],
without ·stopping [respite; relaxation],
50**until the LORD looks down**
and sees from heaven.
51**·I am sad when I see** [[L]My eyes torment my life/soul]
·what has happened to all the women [because of all the daughters]
of my city.

52**Those who are my enemies ·for no reason** [without cause;
Ps. 7:4; 35:7]
hunted me like a bird [Ps. 91:3; Prov. 6:5; 7:23].
53**They ·tried to kill me** [destroyed my life/soul] **in a pit** [Ps. 7:15; 9:15];
they threw stones at me.
54**Water came up over my head** [Ps. 69:1–2],
and I said, "I am ·going to die [lost; [L]cut off]."
55**I called out ·to you** [[L]your name], **LORD,**
from the ·bottom [depth] **of the pit** [Ps. 130:1].
56**You heard ·me calling** [[L]my voice], **"Do not close your ears**
·and ignore my gasps and shouts [to my cries for relief]."
57**You came near ·when** [[L]in the day] **I called to you;**
you said, "Don't be afraid."

58**Lord, ·you have taken my case** [you defend/have defended me]
and ·given me back [[L]redeem; redeemed] **my life.**
59**LORD, you have seen how I have been wronged.**
Now judge my case for me.
60**You have seen ·how my enemies took revenge on me** [[L]all their
vengeance]
·and made evil plans against me [[L]all their plots against me].

61**LORD, you ·have heard** [hear] **their ·insults** [scorn]
and all their ·evil plans [plots] **against me.**
62**The ·words** [whispers; [L]lips] **and ·thoughts** [mumblings; murmurs] **of**
·my enemies [[L]those who rise up against me]
are against me all the time.
63**Look! In ·everything they do** [[L]their sitting and their rising up]
they ·make fun of me with songs [sing mocking songs; Ps. 69:7–12].

64**Pay them back, LORD,**
·for what they have done [[L]according to the acts of their hands].
65**Make them ·stubborn** [[L]insolent of heart],
and put your curse on them.
66**·Chase** [Pursue] **them in anger, LORD,**
and destroy them from under ·your [[L]the LORD's] **heavens.**

The Attack on Jerusalem

4 **See how the gold has ·lost its shine** [lost its luster; [L]become dim/dark],
how the pure gold has ·dulled [changed]!
The stones of the ·Temple [[L]Holy Place] **are scattered**
at ·every street corner [[L]the top of every street].

[2]**The precious ·people** [children; sons] **of ·Jerusalem** [[L]Zion; [C]the location of the Temple]
were ·more valuable than [worth their weight in] **gold,**
but now they are thought of as clay jars
·made by [[L]the work of] **the hands of a potter.**

[3]**Even ·wild dogs** [jackals] **·give their milk** [[L]prepare the breast]
to ·feed [suckle; nurse] **their young,**
but [[L]the daughter of] **my people are ·cruel** [violent]
like ostriches in the ·desert [wilderness; Job 39:14–16].

[4]**The ·babies** [[L]nurslings] **are so thirsty**
their tongues stick to ·the roofs of their mouths [[L]their palates].
Children ·beg [ask] **for bread,**
but no one ·gives [offers] **them any.**

[5]**Those who once ate ·fine foods** [delicacies; [C]the food of the rich; Prov. 23:3, 6]
are ·now starving [[L]desolate] **in the streets.**
People who ·grew up [were nurtured] **·wearing nice clothes** [[L]in purple/*or* crimson; [C]expensive clothes often associated with royalty]
now ·pick through [cling to] **·trash piles** [ash heaps; 1 Sam. 2:8; Job 2:8; Ps. 113:7].

[6]**·My people have been punished**
more than Sodom was [[L]The iniquity/*or* punishment of the daughter of my people is greater than the sin/*or* punishment of Sodom].
·Sodom [[L]...which] **was ·destroyed** [[L]overturned] **suddenly,**
and no hands ·reached out to help her [*or* were wrung; Gen. 19; Deut. 29:23; Is. 1:9–10; Jer. 23:14; Ezek. 16:46–56; Matt. 10:15; Jude 7; Rev. 11:8].

[7]**·Our** [*or* Her] **princes were purer than snow,**
and whiter than milk.
Their bodies were redder than ·rubies [*or* coral];
they looked like ·sapphires [lapis lazuli].

[8]**But now ·they** [[L]their faces] **are blacker than coal,**
and no one recognizes them in the streets.
Their skin ·hangs [*or* shrivels] **on their bones;**
it is as dry as wood.

[9]**Those who were ·killed** [[L]pierced] **·in the war** [[L]by the sword] **were better off**
than those ·killed [[L]pierced] **by ·hunger** [famine].
They ·starve in pain and die [drain/waste away],
·because there is no food from the field [[L]deprived of the produce of the field; Jer. 11:22; 14:12–18].

[10]With their own hands ·kind [compassionate] women
·cook [boil] their own children.
They became food
when ·my [Lthe daughter of my] people were ·destroyed [fractured; broken; Deut. 28:56–57].

[11]The LORD turned loose all of his anger;
he poured out his ·strong [Lhot] anger.
He set fire to ·Jerusalem [LZion; Cthe location of the Temple; Ps. 74:4–7],
·burning it down to the [Lconsuming its] foundations.

[12]Kings of the earth and ·people [Lthe inhabitants] of the world
could not believe
that enemies and foes
could enter the gates of Jerusalem [Csince God had made his presence known there; Ps. 48:1–2].

[13]It happened because her prophets sinned
and her priests did evil [Jer. 1:17–19; 2:7–8, 26; 4:9; 13:12–14].
They ·killed [Lpoured out blood] in ·the city [Lits midst]
·those who did what was right [the righteous].

[14]They wandered in the streets
as if they were blind.
They were ·dirty [defiled; Cin a ritual sense] with blood [Cas if covered with menstrual blood; Lev. 15],
so no one ·would [was able to] touch their clothes.

[15]"·Go away [Turn aside]! ·You are unclean [LUnclean!; Cin a ritual sense]," people shouted at them.
"·Get away [Turn aside]! ·Get away [Turn aside]! Don't touch us!"
So they ran away and wandered.
Even the other nations said, "Don't stay here."

[16]The LORD himself ·scattered [dispersed] them
and did not ·look after [regard] them anymore.
No one respects the priests
or ·honors [has favor for] the elders.

[17]Also, our eyes ·grew tired [failed],
looking for help ·that never came [in vain; without purpose; 2:11; Ps. 69:3; 119:82, 123].
We kept watch ·from our towers [*or* eagerly]
for a nation ·to save us [Lthat could not save us/give us victory; CJudah had hoped that Egypt would rescue them from Babylon; Jer. 2:18, 36].

[18]·Our enemies [LThey] ·hunted [dogged] ·us [Lour steps],
so we could not even walk in the ·streets [public areas].
Our end is near. Our ·time [Ldays] ·is [Lfill] up.
Our end has come.

[19]Those who ·chased [pursued] us
were faster than eagles in the ·sky [heavens].
They ·ran [chased] us into the mountains
and ambushed us in the ·desert [wilderness].

[20]The LORD's ·appointed king [anointed; [C]Judah's king], ·who was our very breath [[L]the breath of our life/nostrils],
was caught in their traps [2 Kin. 25:5–7].
We had said about him, "We will ·be protected by him [[L]live in his shadow/shade]
among the nations."

[21]Be happy and ·glad [rejoice], ·people [[L]daughter] of Edom,
you who live in the land of Uz [[C]city in Edom; Job 1:1; Jer. 25:20].
The cup [[C]of God's judgment] will ·come [pass] to you;
then you will get drunk and go naked [Jer. 25:15–38; 49:12–13].

[22]Your ·punishment [*or* iniquity] is complete, ·Jerusalem [[L]daughter of Zion; [C]the location of the Temple].
He will not send you into ·captivity again [exile].
But the LORD will punish the ·sins [iniquity] of Edom;
he will ·uncover [expose] your ·evil [sin].

A Prayer to the Lord

5 Remember, LORD, what happened to us [[C]a call to God for help and revenge].
Look and see our ·disgrace [scorn].
[2]Our ·land [[L]inheritance] has been turned over to strangers;
our houses have been given to foreigners.
[3]We are like orphans with no father;
our mothers are like widows [[C]defenseless and vulnerable].
[4]We have to buy the water we drink;
·we must pay for the firewood [[L]our wood comes with a price].
[5]·Those who chase after us want to catch us [[L]We are pursued] by the neck.
We are ·tired [exhausted] and find no rest.
[6]We ·made an agreement with [[L]gave a hand to] Egypt
and with Assyria to get enough food [Is. 28:1—33:34; Jer. 2:35].
[7]Our ·ancestors [fathers] sinned against you, but they are ·gone [[L]no more];
now we ·suffer because of their sins [[L]bear their iniquity].
[8]·Slaves [Servants] ·have become our rulers [[L]rule over us; Prov. 19:10; 30:21–22; Eccl. 10:5–7; Is. 24:2],
and no one can ·save us from them [[L]tear them off us].
[9]We risk our lives to get our ·food [bread];
·we face death in the desert [[L]because of the sword in the wilderness; [C]fields were outside the walls of the city where the enemy camped].
[10]Our skin is ·hot [*or* black] like an oven;
·we burn with [from the heat/fever of] ·starvation [famine].
[11]·The enemy [[L]They] ·abused [violated; raped] the women ·of Jerusalem [[L]in Zion; [C]the location of the Temple]
and the ·girls [[L]virgins] in the ·cities [towns] of Judah.
[12]Princes were hung by the hands;
they did not respect our ·elders [*or* old men].

[13]The young men ·ground grain at the mill [are forced to grind],
and boys stumbled under loads of wood.
[14]The ·elders [*or* old men] ·no longer sit at the city [[L]have left the] gates
[[C]the center of government and business];
the young men no longer sing.
[15]·We have no more joy in [[L]Joy has left] our hearts;
our dancing has turned to ·sadness [mourning].
[16]The crown has fallen from our head.
·How terrible it is [[L]Woe to us] because we sinned.
[17]Because of this ·we are afraid [[L]our hearts are sick],
and now our eyes ·are dim [grow dark; Ps. 69:23].
[18]Mount Zion [[C]Jerusalem] is ·empty [desolate],
and ·wild dogs [jackals] wander around it [Jer. 9:11; 10:22].

[19]But you ·rule [sit; [C]as king] forever, LORD.
·You will be King [[L]Your throne] ·from now on [[L]from generation to
generation].
[20]Why have you forgotten us for so long?
Have you ·left [abandoned; forsaken] us ·forever [[L]for length of days]?
[21]Bring us back to you, LORD, and we will ·return [be restored].
·Make [[L]Renew] our days as they were before,
[22]or have you completely rejected us?
Are you so angry with us?

EZEKIEL

Ezekiel's Vision of Living Creatures

1 **It was the thirtieth year, on the fifth day of the fourth month** [Cof Ezekiel's life, or of Nabopolassar's reign, or since King Josiah's reforms]. **I was by the Kebar ·River** [Canal; Ca branch of the Euphrates River south of Babylon] **among the ·people who had been carried away as captives** [exiles]. **The ·sky** [heavens] **opened, and I saw visions of God.**

2It was the fifth day of the month of the fifth year that King Jehoiachin had been ·a prisoner [in exile/captivity; C593 BC; 2 Kin. 24:12, 15]. **3The ·LORD spoke his word** [Lword of the LORD came] **to Ezekiel son of Buzi in the land of the Babylonians by the Kebar ·River** [Canal; 1:1]. **There ·he felt the power of the LORD** [Lthe hand of the LORD was on him].

4When I looked, I saw a ·stormy wind [windstorm] **coming from the north** [Cstorms often represent the presence of God; Jer. 23:19]. **There was a great cloud with ·a bright light** [*or* lightning flashing] **around it and ·fire flashing out of** [*or* brightness all around] **it. Something that looked like glowing ·metal** [*or* amber] **was in the center of the fire. 5Inside ·the cloud** [*or* the fire; Lits midst] **was what looked like four living creatures** [Rev. 4:6–8], **who ·were shaped like** [had the appearance of] **humans, 6but each of them had four faces and four wings. 7Their legs were straight. Their feet were like a calf's hoofs and ·sparkled** [gleamed] **like ·polished** [burnished] **bronze** [Rev. 1:15]. **8The living creatures had human hands under their wings on their four sides. All four of them had faces and wings, 9and their wings touched each other. The living creatures did not turn when they moved, but each went straight ahead.**

10Their faces looked like this: Each living creature had ·a human face [*or* the face of a man] **and the face of a lion on the right side and the face of an ox on the left side. And each one also had the face of an eagle. 11That was what their faces looked like. Their wings were spread out above. Each had two wings that touched one of the other living creatures and two wings that covered its body. 12Each went straight ahead. Wherever the ·spirit** [*or* wind] **would go, the living creatures would also go, without turning. 13The living creatures looked like burning coals of fire or like torches. Fire went back and forth among the living creatures. It was ·bright** [radiant], **and lightning flashed from it. 14The living creatures ·ran** [darted] **back and forth like ·bolts** [flashes] **of lightning.**

15Now as I looked at the living creatures, I saw a wheel on the ground by each of the living creatures with its four faces. 16The wheels and ·the way they were made [their construction/structure] **·were like this** [had this appearance]: **They looked like sparkling ·chrysolite** [*or* topaz; *or* beryl]. **All four of them looked the same, like one wheel ·crossways inside**

[Lin the middle of] another wheel. 17When they moved, they went in any
one of the four directions, without turning as they went. 18The rims of
the wheels were high and ·frightening [or awesome] and were full of eyes
all around.
19When the living creatures moved, the wheels moved beside them.
When the living creatures ·were lifted up [rose] from the ground, the
wheels also ·were lifted up [rose]. 20Wherever the ·spirit [or wind] would
go, the living creatures would go. And the wheels ·were lifted up [rose]
beside them, because the spirit of the living creatures was in the wheels.
21When the living creatures moved, the wheels moved. When the living
creatures stopped, the wheels stopped. And when the living creatures
·were lifted [rose] from the ground, the wheels ·were lifted [rose] beside
them, because the spirit of the living creatures was in the wheels.
22Now, ·over [stretched over] the heads of the living creatures was something like a ·dome [vault; expanse; or platform; Gen. 1:2] that sparkled like
·ice [crystal] and was ·frightening [or awesome]. 23And under the ·dome
[vault; expanse; or platform] the wings of the living creatures were stretched
out straight toward one another. Each living creature also had two wings
covering its body. 24I heard the sound of their wings, like the ·roaring sound
of the sea [Lsound of many waters], as they moved. It was like the voice of
·God Almighty [Lthe Almighty], a ·roaring sound [tumult] like a noisy
army. When the living creatures stopped, they lowered their wings.
25A voice came from above the ·dome [vault; expanse; or platform] over
the heads of the living creatures. When the living creatures stopped, they
lowered their wings. 26Now above the ·dome [vault; expanse; or platform]
there was something that looked like a throne. It looked like ·a sapphire
gem [or lapis lazuli]. And on the throne high above was a ·shape [form;
figure] like a ·human [man]. 27Then I noticed that from the waist up the
shape looked like glowing ·metal [or amber] with fire inside. From the waist
down it looked like fire, and a bright light was all around. 28The surrounding ·glow [radiance; brightness] looked like the rainbow in the clouds on a
rainy day. ·It seemed to look like [LThis was the appearance of the likeness
of] the glory of the Lord [Chis manifest presence]. So when I saw it, I ·bowed
[fell] facedown on the ground and heard a voice speaking.

The Lord Speaks to Ezekiel

2 He said to me, "·Human [TSon of man; Cused 93 times in the book
to address the prophet; it means "human being" and stresses the
frailty of humanity in contrast to the sovereignty of God], stand up on
your feet so I may speak with you." 2While he spoke to me, ·the Spirit [or
a spirit; or a wind] entered me and put me on my feet. Then I heard ·the
Lord [Lhim] speaking to me.
3He said, "·Human [TSon of man; 2:1], I am sending you to the ·people
[Lsons; Tchildren] of Israel, that nation of rebels who have ·turned [rebelled]
against me. They and their ·ancestors [fathers] have ·sinned [revolted;
transgressed] against me ·until [to] this very day. 4I am sending you to people who are ·stubborn [impudent] and ·who do not obey [stubborn;
obstinate]. You will say to them, 'This is what the Lord God says.' 5They may
listen, or they may not, since they are a ·people who have turned against me
[Lrebellious house]. But they will know that a prophet has been among
them. 6You, ·human [Tson of man; 2:1], don't be afraid of ·the people
[Lthem] or their words. Even though ·they may be like thorny branches and
stickers [Lbriars and thorns are] all around you, and though you ·may feel

like you live with stinging [Lsit among; or dwell among] scorpions, don't be
afraid. Don't be afraid of their words or terrified by their looks, because
they are a ·people who turn against me [Lrebellious house]. 7But speak my
words to them. They may listen, or they may not, because they ·turn against
me [are rebellious]. 8But you, ·human [Tson of man; 2:1], listen to what I say
to you. Don't ·turn against me [rebel] ·as those people do [Llike that rebellious house]. Open your mouth and eat what I am giving you."
9Then I looked and ·saw [Tbehold] a hand stretched out to me, and a
·scroll [scroll with writing on it; Lscroll of a document/book] was in it [Jer.
36:2; Rev. 10:2]. 10He ·opened [unrolled] the scroll in front of me. Written
on the front and back were ·funeral songs, sad writings, and warnings
about disaster [Lwords of lament, mourning, and woe].

3 Then the LORD said to me, "·Human [TSon of man; 2:1], eat what
·you find [you see; is before you]; eat this scroll. Then go and
speak to the ·people [Lhouse] of Israel." 2So I opened my mouth, and he
·gave [fed] me the scroll to eat.
3He said to me, "·Human [TSon of man; 2:1], eat this scroll which I am
giving you, and fill your stomach with it." Then I ate it, and it was as sweet
as honey in my mouth [Jer. 15:16; Rev. 10:9, 10].
4Then he said to me, "·Human [TSon of man; 2:1], go to the ·people
[Lhouse] of Israel, and speak my words to them. 5[LFor; Because] You are
not being sent to people ·whose speech you can't understand [of obscure/
foreign language; Ldeep of lip], ·whose language is difficult [Land heavy
tongue]. You are being sent to [Lthe house of] Israel. 6You are not being
sent to many nations ·whose speech you can't understand [of obscure/
foreign language; Ldeep of lip], ·whose language is difficult [Land heavy
tongue], whose words you cannot understand. If I had sent you to them,
they would have listened to you. 7But the ·people [Lhouse] of Israel will
not be willing to listen to you, because they are not willing to listen to me.
Yes, all the ·people [Lhouse] of Israel are ·stubborn [hardheaded] and ·will
not obey [hardhearted]. 8·See [TBehold], I now make ·you as stubborn
[Lyour face as strong as their face] and ·as hard as they are [Lyour forehead
as strong as their forehead]. 9I am making ·you [Lyour forehead] as hard as
·a diamond [or flint; or the hardest stone], harder than ·stone [or flint].
Don't be afraid of them or be ·frightened [terrified; dismayed] by them,
though they are a ·people who turn against me [Lrebellious house]."
10Also, he said to me, "·Human [TSon of man; 2:1], ·believe [Ltake in
your heart] all the words I will speak to you, and ·listen carefully to them
[Lhear with your ears]. 11Then go to the ·captives [exiles], ·your own [Lthe
sons of your] people, and say to them, 'The Lord GOD says this.' Tell them
this whether they listen or not."
12Then ·the Spirit [or the spirit; or a wind] lifted me up, and I heard a
loud rumbling ·sound [or voice] behind me, ·saying, "Praise the glory of
the LORD [Chis manifest presence] in heaven [or as the glory of the LORD
rose from its place]." 13·I heard [or It was the sound of] the wings of the
living creatures touching each other and the sound of the wheels by them.
It was a loud rumbling sound. 14So ·the Spirit [or the spirit; or a wind]
lifted me up and took me away. I ·was unhappy and angry [Lwent in bitterness in the heat/wrath of my spirit], and I felt the great ·power [Lhand]
of the LORD. 15I came to the ·captives [exiles] from Judah, who lived by the
Kebar ·River [Canal; 1:1] at Tel Abib. I sat there seven days where these
people lived, feeling ·shocked [stunned; overwhelmed; distressed].

Israel's Warning

16·After [LAt the end of] seven days the ·LORD spoke his word [Lword of the LORD came] to me again. He said, 17"·Human [TSon of man; 2:1], I ·now make [*or* have made] you a watchman for [Lthe house of] Israel. Any time you hear a word from my mouth, warn them for me. 18·When [*or* If] I say to the wicked, 'You will surely die,' but you don't speak out to warn them to stop their evil ways, they will die ·in their sin [for their iniquity]. But I will hold you ·responsible [accountable] for their death. 19But if you warn the wicked and they do not turn from their wickedness or their ·evil ways [wicked lifestyle], they will die because of their sin. But you will have saved your ·life [soul].

20"Again, ·those who do right [the righteous] may turn away from ·doing good [righteousness] and ·do evil [commit iniquity/injustice]. If I ·make something bad happen to [Llay a stumbling block before] them, they will die. Because you have not warned them, they will die because of their sin, and the ·good [righteous things] they did will not be remembered. But I will hold you ·responsible [accountable] for their deaths. 21But if you have warned ·those good people [the righteous] not to sin, and they do not sin, they will surely live, because they ·believed [took; received] the warning. And you will have saved your ·life [soul]."

22Then I felt the ·power [Lhand] of the LORD there. He said to me, "Get up and go out to the ·plain [*or* valley]. There I will speak to you." 23So I got up and went out to the ·plain [*or* valley]. ·I saw [TAnd behold] the glory of the LORD [Chis manifest presence] standing there, like the glory I saw by the Kebar ·River [Canal; 1:1], and I ·bowed [fell] facedown on the ground.

24Then the Spirit entered me and ·made me stand [set me] on my feet. He spoke to me and said, "Go, shut yourself up in your house. 25As for you, ·human [Tson of man; 2:1], the people will tie you up with ·ropes [cords] so that you will not be able to go out among them. 26Also, I will make your tongue stick to the roof of your mouth so you will be silent [CEzekiel would be mute for seven and a half years (see dates in 1:1–3 and 33:21–22), except when the Lord opened his mouth with prophetic revelations; v. 27]. You will not be able to ·argue with [rebuke; reprove] the people, ·even though they turn against me [Lfor they are a rebellious house]. 27But when I speak to you, I will open your mouth, and you will say to them, 'The Lord GOD says this.' Those who will listen, let them listen. Those who refuse, let them refuse, because they are a ·people who turn against me [rebellious house].

The Map of Jerusalem

4 "Now, ·human [Tson of man; 2:1], get yourself a brick, put it in front of you, and ·draw [inscribe; engrave] ·a map [Lthe city] of Jerusalem on it. 2Then ·surround it with an army [lay a siege against it]. Build ·battle [siege] works against the city and a ·dirt road to the top of the city walls [siege ramp/mound against it]. Set up camps around it, and put ·heavy logs in place to break down the walls [battering rams all around]. 3Then get yourself an iron ·plate [pan] and set it up like an iron wall between you and the city. Turn your face toward the city ·as if to attack it [*or* and it will be under siege] and then ·attack [besiege it]. This is a sign to [Lthe house of] Israel.

4"Then lie down on your left side, and take the ·guilt [punishment; iniquity] of [Lthe house of] Israel on yourself. Their ·guilt [punishment; iniquity] will be on you for the number of days you lie on your left side. 5I have ·given [assigned to] you the same number of days as the years of

the people's sin. So you will have the ·guilt of Israel's sin on you [punish-
ment/iniquity of the house of Israel] for three hundred ninety days.
[6]"After you have finished these days, lie down a second time, on your
right side. You will then have the ·guilt [punishment; iniquity] of [[L]the
house of] Judah on you. I will give it to you for forty days, a day for each
·year of their sin [[L]year]. [7]Then you will ·look [[L]turn your face] toward
Jerusalem, which is being ·attacked [besieged]. With your arm bare, you
will prophesy against Jerusalem. [8][[L]And look/[T]behold] I will put ·ropes
[cords] on you so you cannot turn from one side to the other until you
have finished the days of your ·attack on Jerusalem [siege].
[9]"Take wheat, barley, beans, ·small peas [lentils], millet and spelt [[C]a
kind of wheat; all foods common to Babylon, where Ezekiel was exiled],
and put them in one ·bowl [vessel; container], and make them into bread
for yourself. You will eat it the three hundred ninety days you lie on your
side. [10]You will eat ·eight ounces [[L]twenty shekels] of food ·every day at set
times [[L]from time to time]. [11]You will ·drink [[L]measure out and drink]
·about two-thirds of a quart [[L]a sixth of a hin] of water ·every day at set
times [[L]from time to time]. [12]Eat your food as you would eat a barley
cake, baking it over human dung where the people can see." [13]Then the
LORD said, "In the same way [[L]the sons/[T]children of] Israel will eat unclean
food [[C]ritually; Lev. 11] among the nations where I ·force them to go
[drive/banish them]."
[14]But I said, "·No [Ah], Lord GOD! I have never ·been made unclean
[defiled myself; [C]ritually]. From the time I was young until now I've never
eaten anything that died ·by itself [naturally; [C]a carcass] or was ·torn
[mauled] by ·animals [wild beasts]. ·Unclean [Impure; [C]ritually] meat has
never entered my mouth."
[15]"Very well," he said. "Then I will give you cow's dung instead of
human dung to use for your fire to bake your bread."
[16]He also said to me, "·Human [[T]Son of man; 2:1], I am going to cut off
the supply of bread to Jerusalem. They will eat the bread that is measured
out to them, and they will ·worry as they eat [eat anxiously]. They will
drink water that is measured out to them, and they will be in ·shock [ter-
ror; dismay] as they drink it. [17]This is because bread and water will be
hard to find [[C]because of the siege] The people will be ·shocked [terrified;
dismayed] at the sight of each other, and they will ·become weak [waste
away] because of their ·sin [punishment; iniquity].

Ezekiel Cuts His Hair

5 "Now, ·human [[T]son of man; 2:1], take a sharp sword, and use it
like a barber's razor to shave your head and beard. Then take
scales and weigh and divide the hair. [2]Burn one-third with fire ·in the
middle of [inside] the city when the days of the ·attack on Jerusalem
[[L]siege] are over. Then take one-third and cut it up with the ·knife [sword]
all around the city. And scatter one-third to the wind. This is how I will
chase them with ·a sword [unsheathed sword]. [3]Also take a few of these
hairs and ·tie [bind; tuck] them in the ·folds [edge] of your clothes. [4]Take
a few more and throw them into the fire and burn them up. From there a
fire will spread to all the ·people [[L]house] of Israel.
[5]"This is what the Lord GOD says: This is Jerusalem. I have put her at
the center of the nations with countries all around her. [6]But she has
·refused to obey [rebelled against] my ·laws [judgments] and has been
more ·evil [wicked] than the nations. She has refused to ·obey [[L]walk in]

my ·rules [statutes; ordinances; requirements], even more than ·nations [lands] around her. The people of Jerusalem have rejected my ·laws [judgments] and have not ·lived by [Lwalked in] my ·rules [statutes; ordinances; requirements].

7"So this is what the Lord God says: You have ·caused more trouble [been more insubordinate/arrogant] than the nations around you. You have not followed my ·rules [statutes; ordinances; requirements] or obeyed my ·laws [judgments]. You have not even obeyed the ·laws [judgments] of the nations around you.

8"So this is what the Lord God says: [LLook; TBehold] I myself am against you, and I will ·punish you [Lexecute judgments in your midst] ·as the nations watch [in the sight of the nations]. 9I will do things ·among [to] you that I have not done before and that I will never do anything like again, because ·you do the things I hate [of your detestable practices/*or* idols]. 10So ·parents [fathers] among you will eat their ·children [sons], and ·children [sons] will eat their ·parents [fathers; Cbecause of horrific starvation during the siege; Deut. 28:53–57; Jer. 19:9; Lam. 4:10]. I will ·punish you [execute judgments] and will scatter to the winds all ·who are left alive [the survivors]. 11So the Lord God says: You have ·made my Temple unclean [defiled my sanctuary] with all your ·evil idols [abominations] and ·the hateful things you do [your detestable practices/*or* idols]. Because of this, as surely as I live, I will ·cut you off [*or* shave you; Ca humiliation]. ·I will have [LMy eye will show] no pity, and I will show no mercy. 12A third of you will die by ·disease [plague; pestilence] or be ·destroyed [overcome; consumed] by ·hunger [famine] inside your walls. A third will fall dead by the sword ·outside your walls [all around]. And a third I will scatter in every direction as I chase them with a ·sword [Ldrawn/unsheathed sword]. 13Then my anger will ·come to an end [be finished]. ·I will use it up against them [...and my wrath will cease], and then I will be ·satisfied [calmed; appeased]. Then they will know that I, the Lord, have spoken. After I have carried out my ·anger [wrath] against them, they will know ·how strongly I felt [my zeal/jealousy].

14"I will make you a ruin and a ·shame [reproach; object of mockery] among the nations around you, ·to be seen by [Lin the eyes of] all who pass by. 15Then you will be ·shamed [a reproach/object of mockery] and ·made fun of [taunted] by the nations around. You will be a warning and a ·terror [horror] to them. This will happen when I ·punish [execute judgments against] you in my ·great anger [Langer, wrath, and furious rebukes]. I, the Lord, have spoken. 16I will ·send a time of hunger [Lshoot deadly and destructive arrows of famine] to destroy you, and then I will make your ·hunger [famine] get even worse, and I will cut off your supply of food. 17I will send a time of hunger and wild animals against you, and they will ·kill your children [Lbereave you]. ·Disease [Plague; Pestilence] and death will sweep through your people, and I will bring the sword against you to kill you. I, the Lord, have spoken."

Prophecies Against the Mountains

6 Again the ·Lord spoke his word [Lword of the Lord came] to me, saying: 2"·Human [TSon of man; 2:1], ·look [Lset your face] toward the mountains of Israel, and prophesy against them. 3Say, 'Mountains of Israel, listen to the word of the Lord God. The Lord God says this to the mountains, the hills, the ravines, and the valleys: [LLook; TBehold] I ·will [*or* am about to] bring a sword against you, and I will destroy your ·places

of idol worship [Lhigh places; Cpagan worship sites; Deut. 12; 2 Kin. 23:8].
4Your altars will be ·destroyed [desolated] and your incense altars ·broken
down [smashed]. ·Your people will be killed [LI will throw down your
slain] in front of your idols. 5I will lay the dead bodies of the Israelites in
front of their idols, and I will scatter your bones around your altars. 6In
all the places you live, cities will become ·empty [desolate; laid waste]. The
·places of idol worship [Lhigh places; 6:3] will be ruined; your altars will
become ·lonely [wasted] ruins. Your idols will be ·broken [smashed] and
·brought to an end [ruined]. Your incense altars will be cut down, and
·the things you made [your works; *or* the idols/religious objects you have
made] will be wiped out. 7·Your people will be killed and [LThe slain will]
fall among you. Then you will know that I am the LORD.
8" 'But I will leave some people alive; some will ·not be killed by the
nations [Lescape the sword] when you are scattered among the foreign
lands. 9Then those who have escaped will remember me, as they live
among the nations where they have been taken as captives. They will
remember how I was ·hurt [grieved; crushed] ·because they were unfaithful to me [Lby their adulterous heart] and turned away from me and
·desired to worship [by their eyes that have prostituted themselves with]
their idols. They will ·hate [loathe] themselves because of ·the evil things
they did that I hate [their abominations/detestable practices]. 10Then they
will know that I am the LORD. I did not ·bring this terrible thing on them
for no reason [*or* threaten in vain this catastrophe against them].
11" 'This is what the Lord GOD says: Clap your hands, stamp your feet,
and ·groan [Lsay, "Ah!"] because of all the ·hateful, evil things [evil and
detestable practices] the ·people [Lhouse] of Israel have done. They will
·die by war [Lfall by the sword], ·hunger [famine], and ·disease [plague;
pestilence; Lev. 26:25–26]. 12The person who is far away will die by ·dis-
ease [plague; pestilence]. The one who is nearby will ·die in war [fall by
the sword]. The person who ·is still alive [Lremains and is spared] and has
escaped these will die from ·hunger [famine]. So I will ·carry out [spend;
exhaust] my ·anger [wrath; fury] on them. 13Their people will lie dead
among their idols around the altars, on every high hill, on all the mountain tops, and under every green tree and leafy oak—all the places where
they offered ·sweet-smelling [fragrant; *or* pleasing] incense to their idols.
Then you will know that I am the LORD. 14I will ·use my power [Lstretch
out my hand] against them to make the land ·empty [desolate] and wasted
from the ·desert [wilderness] to ·Diblah,*n* wherever they live. Then they
will know that I am the LORD.' "

Ezekiel Tells of the End

7 Again the ·LORD spoke his word to me [Lword of the LORD came],
saying: 2"·Human [TSon of man; 2:1], the Lord GOD says this to the
land of Israel: An end! The end has come on the four corners of the land.
3Now the end has come for you, and I will send my anger against you. I will
judge you for the way you have lived, and I will ·make you pay [punish you;
or hold you accountable; Lplace upon you] for all your ·actions that I hate
[detestable/abominable practices]. 4·I will have no pity on [LMy eye will not
pity] you; I will not ·hold back punishment from [spare] you. Instead, I will
make you pay for the way you have lived and for your ·actions that I hate
[detestable/abominable practices]. Then you will know that I am the LORD.

6:14 Diblah Hebrew copies read "Diblah," an unknown place. The Latin Vulgate reads "Riblah," a city north of Damascus

5"This is what the Lord GOD says: Disaster ·on top of [*or* unheard of]
disaster ·is [[L]look/[T]behold, it is] coming. 6The end has come! The end has
come! It has ·stirred itself up [aroused; awakened] against you! Look! It
·has come [*or* is coming]! 7·Disaster [Doom] has come for you who live in
the land! The time has come; the day of is near. It will be a day of ·confu-
sion [panic], not ·celebration [shouts of joy], on the mountains. 8Soon I
will pour out my ·anger [wrath] against you; I will ·carry out [spend;
exhaust] my anger against you. I will judge you for the way you have lived
and will ·make you pay [punish you; *or* hold you accountable] for ·every-
thing you have done that I hate [your detestable/abominable practices].
9·I will show no pity [[L]My eye will not pity you], and I will not ·hold back
punishment [spare you]. I will ·pay you back [punish you; *or* hold you
accountable] for ·the way you have lived and the things you have done
that I hate [your detestable/abominable practices]. Then you will know
that I am the LORD who ·punishes [strikes you].

10"·Look [[T]Behold], the day is here. ·Look [[T]Behold] It has come.
·Disaster [Doom] has ·come [gone out], ·violence has grown [[L]the rod has
budded; Num. 17; [C]may refer to Nebuchadnezzar, the instrument of God's
judgment], ·and there is more pride than ever [[L]pride/arrogance has blos-
somed]. 11Violence has grown into a ·weapon [rod; staff] for punishing
wickedness. None of the people will be left—none of that crowd, none of
their wealth, and ·nothing of value [*or* none of their prominent ones].
12The time has come; the day has arrived. Don't let the buyer ·be happy
[rejoice] or the seller ·be sad [grieve; mourn], because my ·burning anger
[wrath] is against the whole crowd. 13Sellers will not ·return to the land
[*or* recover the property] they have sold as long as they live, because the
vision against all that crowd will not be ·changed [revoked; reversed].
Because of their ·sins [iniquity], they will not ·save [preserve] their lives.
14They have blown the trumpet, and everything is ready. But no one is
going to the battle, because my ·anger [wrath] is against all that crowd.

15"The sword is outside, and ·disease [pestilence; plague] and ·hunger
[famine] are inside [6:12]. Whoever is in the field will die by the sword.
·Hunger [Famine] and ·disease [pestilence; plague] will destroy those in
the city. 16·Those who are left alive and [The survivors] who escape will be
on the mountains, moaning like doves of the valleys about their own ·sin
[iniquity]. 17All hands ·will hang weakly with fear [are weak/limp], and all
knees will ·become weak as water [*or* be wet with urine; [L]run with water].
18They will put on ·rough cloth to show how sad they are [burlap; sack-
cloth]. ·They will tremble all over with fear [[L]Terror/Horror covers them].
Their faces will show their shame, and all their heads will be shaved. 19The
people will throw their silver into the streets, and their gold will be like
·trash [filth; an unclean thing]. Their silver and gold will not save them
from the LORD's ·anger [wrath]. It will not satisfy their hunger or fill their
stomachs, because it ·caused them to fall [was their stumbling block] into
sin. 20·They were proud of their beautiful jewelry [*or* They used God's
ornaments for their own prideful means; [C]the ornaments could refer to the
temple treasures] and used it to make their ·idols [abominable images] and
their ·evil statues, which I hate [detestable/abominable idols]. So I will
turn their wealth into ·trash [filth; an unclean thing]. 21I will give it to foreigners as loot from war and to the ·evil [*or* most wicked] people in the
world as ·treasure [plunder], and they will ·dishonor [desecrate; defile;
[C]ritually] it. 22I will also turn [[L]my face] away from the ·people [[L]house] of

Israel, and they will ·dishonor [desecrate; defile; Critually] my treasured
place. Then robbers will enter and ·dishonor [desecrate; defile; Critually] it.
23“·Make chains for captives [LPrepare/Forge the chains], because the
land is full of bloody crimes and the city is full of violence. 24So I will
bring the ·worst [most evil/wicked/ruthless] of the nations to take over
the people's houses. I will also end the pride of the strong, and their ·holy
places [sanctuaries] will be ·dishonored [desecrated; defiled; Critually].
25·When the people are suffering greatly [*or* Terror/Anguish is coming!],
they will look for peace, but there will be none. 26Disaster will come on
top of disaster, and rumor will be added to rumor. Then they will ·try to
get [seek] a vision from a prophet; the ·teachings of God [Llaws; instruc-
tions] from the priest and the ·advice [counsel] from the elders ·will be
lost [perishes]. 27The king will ·cry greatly [mourn], the prince will ·give
up hope [Lbe clothed/wrapped in despair], and the hands of the people of
land will shake with fear. I will ·punish [deal with] them for the way they
have lived. The way they have judged others is the way I will judge them.
Then they will know that I am the LORD.”

Ezekiel's Vision of Jerusalem

8 It was the sixth year [Csince king Jehoiachin's exile (1:2)], on the
fifth day of the sixth month [CSeptember 17, 592 BC; this vision is
the subject of chapters 8–11]. I was sitting in my house with the elders of
Judah in front of me. There ·I felt the power of the Lord GOD [Lthe hand
of the Lord GOD came upon me]. 2I looked and saw something that looked
like a ·human [man]. From the waist down it looked like fire, and from
the waist up it looked like bright glowing ·metal [*or* amber]. 3·It [*or* He]
stretched out the shape of a hand and caught me by the hair on my head.
·The Spirit [*or* A spirit; *or* The wind] lifted me up between the earth and
·the sky [heaven]. He took me in visions of God to Jerusalem, to the
entrance to the north gate of the inner courtyard of the Temple. In the
courtyard was the ·idol that caused God to be jealous [Limage of jealousy;
2 Kin. 21:7; 2 Chr. 33:7, 15]. 4I saw the glory of the God of Israel [Chis
manifest presence] there, as I had seen ·on the plain [in the valley].
5Then he said to me, “·Human [TSon of man; 2:1], now look toward the
north.” So I looked up toward the north, and in the entrance north of the
gate of the altar was the ·idol that caused God to be jealous [image of
jealousy].
6He said to me, “·Human [TSon of man; 2:1], do you see what they are
doing? Do you see how many ·hateful [detestable; abominable] things the
·people [Lhouse] of Israel are doing here that drive me far away from my
·Temple [sanctuary]? But you will see things more ·hateful [detestable;
abominable] than these.”
7Then he brought me to the entry of the courtyard. When I looked, I
saw a hole in the wall. 8He said to me, “·Human [TSon of man], dig through
the wall.” So I dug through the wall and saw an ·entrance [doorway].
9Then he said to me, “Go in and see the ·hateful [detestable; abomina-
ble], ·evil [wicked] things they are doing here.” 10So I entered and looked,
and ·I saw [Llook; Tbehold] every kind of crawling thing [Lev. 11:20] and
hateful beast [Cunclean animal, ritually] and all the idols of the ·people
[Lhouse] of Israel, ·carved [engraved] on the wall all around [Csuch images
were idolatrous; Deut. 4:16–18; Rom. 1:23). 11Standing in front of these
carvings and idols were seventy of the elders of [Lthe house of] Israel and
Jaazaniah son of Shaphan. Each man had his ·pan for burning incense

[censer] in his hand, and a ·sweet-smelling [fragrant] cloud of incense was
rising.
12Then he said to me, "·Human [TSon of man; 2:1], have you seen what
the elders of [Lthe house of] Israel are doing in the dark? Have you seen
each man in the ·room [chamber; shrine] of his own ·idol [carved image]?
They say, 'The LORD doesn't see us. The LORD has ·left [abandoned; for-
saken] the land.' " 13He also said to me, "You will see even more ·hateful
[detestable; abominable] things that they are doing."
14Then he brought me to the entrance of the north gate of the ·Temple
[Lhouse] of the LORD, where I saw women sitting and crying for Tammuz [Ca
Babylonian god of fertility and rain, whose annual death marked the change
of seasons]. 15He said to me, "Do you see, ·human [Tson of man; 2:1]? You
will see things even more ·hateful [detestable; abominable] than these."
16Then he brought me into the inner courtyard of the ·Temple [Lhouse
of the LORD]. There I saw about twenty-five men at the entrance to the
·Temple [Lhouse] of the LORD, between the ·porch [portico] and the altar.
With their backs turned to the Temple of the LORD, they faced east and
were worshiping the sun in the east.
17He said to me, "Do you see, ·human [Tson of man; 2:1]? Is it ·unim-
portant [a trivial thing] that the ·people [Lhouse] of Judah are doing the
·hateful [detestable; abominable] things they have done here? They have
filled the land with violence and ·made me continually angry [provoked
me to still greater anger]. ·Look [TBehold], they are ·insulting me every
way they can [Lputting the branch to their nose; Cperhaps part of the worship of the sun god]. 18So I will act ·in anger [with wrath]. I will have no
pity, nor will I ·show mercy [spare them]. Even if they shout in my ears, I
won't listen to them."

Vision of the Angels

9Then he shouted with a loud voice in my ears, "You who are ·cho-
sen [appointed] to ·punish [execute judgment on] this city, come
near with your ·weapon [weapon of destruction] in your hand." 2Then six
men came from the direction of the upper gate, which faces north, each
with his ·powerful weapon [war club] in his hand. Among them was a
man dressed in linen with a writing case at his side. The men went in and
stood by the bronze altar [Ex. 27:1–8].
3Then the glory of the God of Israel [Chis manifest presence] went up
from above the ·creatures with wings [Lcherubim], where it had been, to the
place in the ·Temple where the door opened [Lthreshold of the house]. He
called to the man dressed in linen who had the writing case at his side. 4The
LORD said to the man, "Go through Jerusalem and put a mark on the foreheads of the people who groan and cry about all the ·hateful [detestable;
abominable] things being done among them [Rev. 3:12; 7:3; 9:4; 14:1; 22:4]."
5As I listened, he said to the other men, "Go through the city behind
the man dressed in linen and ·kill [strike]. Don't [Llet your eye] pity anyone, and don't ·show mercy [spare them]. 6Kill and destroy old men,
young men and ·women [virgins], little children, and older women, but
don't touch any who have the mark on them. Start at my ·Temple [sanctu-
ary]." So they started with the ·elders [*or* old men] who were in front of
the ·Temple [Lhouse].
7Then he said to the men, "·Make the Temple unclean [Defile the temple; Critually], and fill the courtyards with ·those who have been killed
[the slain]. Go out!" So the men went out and killed the people in the city.

8While they were ·killing the people [striking them down], I was left alone. I bowed facedown on the ground and I cried out, "Oh, Lord GOD! Will you destroy ·everyone left alive in [the whole remnant of] Israel when you ·turn loose your anger [pour out your wrath] on Jerusalem?"

9Then he said to me, "The sin of the ·people [Lhouse] of Israel and Judah is very great. The land is filled with people who murder, and the city is full of ·people who are not fair [injustice; corruption]. The people say, 'The LORD has ·left [abandoned; forsaken] the land, and the LORD does not see.' 10But ·I [Lmy eye] will have no pity, nor will I ·show mercy [spare]. I will bring their ·evil [deeds; Lway] back on their heads."

11Then the man dressed in linen with the writing case at his side reported, "I have done just as you commanded me."

The Coals of Fire

10 Then I looked and ·saw [Tbehold] in the ·dome [vault; expanse; *or* platform; 1:22] above the heads of the ·living creatures [Lcherubim] something like a ·sapphire [*or* lapis lazuli] gem which looked like a throne. 2The LORD said to the man dressed in linen, "Go in between the wheels under the living creatures, fill your hands with ·coals of fire [burning coals] from between the ·living creatures [Lcherubim], and scatter the coals over the city."

As I watched, the man with linen clothes went in. 3Now the ·living creatures [Lcherubim] were standing on the south side of the ·Temple [Lhouse] when the man went in. And a cloud filled the inner courtyard. 4Then the glory of the LORD [Chis manifest presence] went up from the ·living creatures [Lcherubim] and stood over the ·door [threshold] of the ·Temple [Lhouse]. The ·Temple [Lhouse] was filled with the cloud [Ex. 40:34–38], and the courtyard was full of the brightness from the glory of the LORD. 5The sound of the wings of the ·living creatures [Lcherubim] was heard all the way to the outer courtyard. It was like the voice of God Almighty when he speaks.

6When the LORD commanded the man dressed in linen, "Take fire from between the wheels, from between the ·living creatures [Lcherubim]," the man went in and stood by a wheel. 7·One living creature [LThe cherub] put out his hand to the fire that was among them, took some of the fire, and put it in the hands of the man dressed in linen. Then the man took the fire and went out.

The Wheels and the Creatures

8Something that looked like a human hand could be seen under the wings of the ·living creatures [Lcherubim]. 9I ·saw [Llooked and saw/ Tbehold] the four wheels by the ·living creatures [Lcherubim], one wheel by each ·living creature [Lcherub]. The wheels looked like shining ·chrysolite [*or* topaz; *or* beryl]. 10All four wheels looked alike: Each looked like a wheel ·crossways inside [Lin the middle of] another wheel. 11When the wheels moved, they went in any of the directions that the four ·living creatures [Lcherubim] faced. The wheels did not turn about, and the ·living creatures [Lcherubim] did not turn their bodies as they went. 12All their bodies, their backs, their hands, their wings, and the wheels were full of eyes all over. Each of the four living creatures had a wheel. 13I heard the wheels being called "·whirling wheels [*or* the wheelwork]." 14Each ·living creature [Lone] had four faces. The first face was the face of a ·creature with wings [Lcherub]. The second face was a ·human [man's] face, the third was the face of a lion, and the fourth was the face of an eagle.

15Then the ·living creatures [cherubim] ·flew [mounted; rose] up. They

were the same living creatures I had seen by the Kebar ·River [Canal; 1:1].
16When the ·living creatures [Lcherubim] moved, the wheels moved
beside them. When the ·living creatures [Lcherubim] lifted their wings to
fly up from the ground, the wheels did not leave their place beside them.
17When the ·living creatures [Lcherubim] stopped, the wheels stopped.
When the creatures went up, the wheels went up also, because the spirit
of the living creatures was in the wheels.
18Then the glory of the LORD [Chis manifest presence] left the ·door [thresh-
old] of the ·Temple [Lhouse] and stood over the ·living creatures [Lcherubim].
19·As I watched [Before my eyes], the ·living creatures [Lcherubim] spread
their wings and flew up from the ·ground [earth], with the wheels beside
them. They stood where the east gate of the ·Temple [Lhouse] of the LORD
opened, and the glory of the God of Israel was over them.
20These were the living creatures I had seen under the God of Israel by
the Kebar ·River [Canal; 1:1]. I knew they were called cherubim. 21Each
one had four faces and four wings, and under their wings were things that
looked like human hands. 22Their faces looked the same as the ones I had
seen by the Kebar ·River [Canal; 1:1]. They each went straight ahead.

Prophecies Against Evil Leaders

11 ·The Spirit [*or* A spirit/*or* wind] lifted me up and brought me
to the ·front [Leastern] gate of the ·Temple [Lhouse] of the
LORD, which faces east. ·I saw [TAnd behold] twenty-five men at the
entrance of the gate, among them Jaazaniah son of Azzur and Pelatiah
son of Benaiah, who were ·leaders [princes; officials] of the people.
2Then the LORD said to me, "·Human [TSon of man; 2:1], these are the
men who plan evil and give wicked advice in this city [CJerusalem].
3They say, '·It is almost time [*or* Isn't it a good time…?; *or* The time is not
near] for us to build houses [Cmeaning either (1) let's keep building,
since no judgment is coming, or (2) we don't need to build our own
houses, since we can seize the houses of others (Mic. 2:1–2)]. This city is
·like a cooking pot [the cauldron], and we are ·like the best meat [Lthe
meat; Cthe city will protect them; see 24:3–11 for the same image used
differently].' 4So prophesy against them, prophesy, ·human [Tson of
man; 2:1]."
5Then the ·Spirit [*or* spirit] of the LORD ·entered [fell upon] me and
told me to say: "This is what the LORD says: You have said these things,
·people [Lhouse] of Israel, and I know ·what you are thinking [Lthe steps
of your spirits]. 6You have killed many people in this city, filling its streets
with ·their bodies [the slain].
7"So this is what the Lord GOD says: Those people you have killed and
left in the middle of the city are ·like the best meat [Lthe meat], and this city
is ·like the cooking pot [Lthe cauldron]. But I will ·force [drive; take] you out
of the city. 8You have feared the sword, ·but [so] I will bring a sword against
you, says the Lord GOD. 9I will ·force [drive; take] you out of the city and
hand you over to ·strangers [foreigners] and ·punish [execute judgments
upon] you. 10You will die by the sword. I will ·punish [judge] you at the
border of Israel so you will know that I am the LORD. 11This city will not be
·your cooking pot [the cauldron], and you will not be ·the best meat [Lmeat]
in the middle of it. I will ·punish [judge] you at the border of Israel. 12Then
you will know that I am the LORD. You did not live by my ·rules [statutes] or
obey my ·laws [rules; judgments]. Instead, you ·did the same things as
[obeyed the laws/rules/judgments of] the nations around you."

13 While I was prophesying, Pelatiah son of Benaiah died. Then I
·bowed [fell] facedown on the ground and ·shouted [cried out] with a
loud voice, "·Oh no [Ah], Lord God! Will you completely destroy the
·Israelites who are left alive [remnant of Israel]?"

Promise to Those Remaining

14 The ·Lord spoke his word [Lword of the Lord came] to me, saying,
15 "·Human [TSon of man; 2:1], the people still in Jerusalem have spoken
about your ·own relatives" [Lbrothers, your kinsmen redeemers; Lev.
25:25–55] and all the ·people [Lhouse] of Israel, saying, 'They are far from
the Lord. This land has been given to us as our ·property [possession].'
16 "So say, 'This is what the Lord God says: I sent the people far away
among the nations and scattered them among the countries. But ·for a
little while [*or* in a small measure] I have become a ·Temple [sanctuary] to
them in the countries where they have gone.'
17 "So say: 'This is what the Lord God says: I will gather you from the
nations and bring you together from the countries where you have been
scattered. Then I will give you back the land of Israel.'
18 "When they come to this land, they will remove all the ·evil idols
[detestable things] and all the ·hateful images [abominations]. 19 I will give
them ·a desire to respect me completely [a unified heart; Lone heart], and ·I
will put inside them a new way of thinking [La new spirit]. I will take away
their ·stubborn heart [Lheart of stone], and I will give them an ·obedient
heart [*or* tender heart; Lheart of flesh]. 20 Then they will ·live by my rules
[walk in my statutes/decrees] and obey my ·laws [rules; judgments] and
keep them. They will be my people, and I will be their God. 21 But those who
·want to serve [are devoted to; pursue] their ·evil statues [detestable things]
and ·hateful idols [abominations], I will ·pay back for their evil ways [Lbring
their way/path down upon their head], says the Lord God."

Ezekiel's Vision Ends

22 Then the ·living creatures [Lcherubim] lifted their wings with the
wheels beside them, and the glory of the God of Israel [Chis manifest
presence] was above them. 23 The glory of the Lord went up from inside
Jerusalem and stopped on the mountain on the east side of the city. 24 ·The
Spirit [*or* A wind/*or* spirit] lifted me up and brought me to the ·captives
[exiles] who had been taken from Judah to ·Babylonia [LChaldea]. This
happened in a vision given by the ·Spirit [spirit] of God, and then the
vision I had seen ·ended [Lwent up from me]. 25 And I told the ·captives
[exiles] from Judah all the things the Lord had shown me.

Ezekiel Moves Out

12 Again the ·Lord spoke his word [Lword of the Lord came] to
me, saying: 2 "·Human [TSon of man; 2:1], you are living
among a ·people who refuse to obey [Lrebellious house]. They have eyes
to see, but they do not see, and they have ears to hear, but they do not
hear [Is. 42:18; Matt. 13:13], because they are a ·people who refuse to
obey [Lrebellious house].
3 "So, ·human [Tson of man; 2:1], ·pack your things as if you will be
taken away captive [Lmake yourself bags of exile], and ·walk away like a
captive [go into exile] in the daytime with the people watching. Move
from your place to another with the people watching. Maybe they will
understand, even though they are a ·people who refuse to obey [Lrebellious
house]. 4 During the day when the people are watching, bring out ·the

11:15 relatives Hebrew copies read "kinsmen redeemers." Greek and Syriac copies read "brothers and fellow exiles"

things you would pack as captive [your bags of exile]. At evening, with the people watching, leave your place like those ·who are taken away as captives from their country [going out as exiles]. 5Dig a hole through the wall while they watch, and bring your things out through it. 6Lift them onto your shoulders with the people watching, and carry them out in the dark. Cover your face so you cannot see the ·ground [*or* land], because I have made you a sign to the ·people [Lhouse] of Israel."

7I did these things as I was commanded. In the daytime I brought what I had packed as ·if I were being taken away captive [bags of exile]. Then in the evening I dug through the wall with my hands. I brought my things out in the dark and carried them on my shoulders as the people watched.

8Then in the morning the ·LORD spoke his word [Lword of the LORD came] to me, saying: 9"·Human [TSon of man; 2:1], didn't [Lthe house of] Israel, ·who refuses to obey [Lthe rebellious house], ask you, 'What are you doing?'

10"Say to them, 'This is what the Lord GOD says: This ·message [oracle; burden] is about the ·king [prince; ruler; Creferring to King Zedekiah] in Jerusalem and all the ·people [Lhouse] of Israel who live there.' 11Say, 'I am a sign to you.'

"The same things I have done will be done to the people in Jerusalem. They will be taken ·away from their country [into exile] as captives. 12The ·king [prince; ruler] among them will put his things on his shoulder in the dark and will leave. ·The people[n] [LThey] will dig a hole through the wall to bring him out. He will cover his face so he cannot see the ·ground [land] with his eyes. 13But I will spread my net over him, and he will be caught in my ·trap [snare]. Then I will bring him to Babylon in the land of the ·Babylonians [LChaldeans]. He will not see that land, but he will die there. 14All who are around the king—his ·helpers [attendants] and all his ·army [troops]—I will scatter ·in every direction [Lto every wind], and I will ·chase them with a sword [Ldraw/unsheathe a sword after them].

15"They will know that I am the LORD when I ·scatter [disperse] them among the nations and ·spread [scatter] them among the countries. 16But I will save a few of them from the sword and from ·hunger [famine] and ·disease [plague; pestilence]. Then they can tell about their ·hateful [detestable; abominable] actions among the nations where they go. Then they will know that I am the LORD."

The Lesson of Ezekiel's Shaking

17The ·LORD spoke his word [Lword of the LORD came] to me, saying: 18"·Human [TSon of man; 2:1], tremble as you eat your ·food [bread], and shake with fear as you drink your water. 19Then say to the people of the land: 'This is what the Lord GOD says about the ·people who live in [inhabitants of] Jerusalem in the land of Israel: They will eat their food with ·fear [anxiety] and drink their water in ·shock [dread; despair], because their land will be stripped bare because of the violence of the people who live in it. 20The ·cities [towns] where people live will become ruins, and the land will become ·empty [desolate; devastated]. Then you will know that I am the LORD.' "

The Visions Will Come True

21The ·LORD spoke his word [Lword of the LORD came] to me, saying: 22"·Human [TSon of man; 2:1], what is this ·saying [proverb] you have in the land of Israel: 'The days ·go by [pass slowly; grow long] and every vision comes to nothing'? 23So say to them, 'This is what the Lord GOD

12:12 The people Hebrew copies read, "They." Greek and Syriac copies read "He."

says: I will ·make them stop saying this [Lput an end to this proverb], and
nobody in Israel will use this ·saying [proverb] anymore.' But tell them,
'The ·time is [days are] near when every vision will ·come true [be ful-
filled]. 24There will be no more false visions or ·pleasing prophecies
[flattering omens/divinations] inside the ·nation [Lhouse] of Israel, 25but
I, the LORD, will speak. What I say will be done, and it will not be delayed.
You ·refuse to obey [are a rebellious house], but in your ·time [days] I will
say the word and do it, says the Lord GOD.' "

26The ·LORD spoke his word [Lword of the LORD came] to me, saying:
27"·Human [TSon of man; 2:1], the ·people [Lhouse] of Israel are saying,
'The vision that Ezekiel sees is for a time many ·years [Ldays] from now.
He is prophesying about times far away.'

28"So say to them: 'The Lord GOD says this: None of my words will be
delayed anymore. ·What I have said [LThe word I speak] will be done, says
the Lord GOD.' "

Ezekiel Speaks Against False Prophets

13 The ·LORD spoke his word [Lword of the LORD came] to me,
saying: 2"·Human [TSon of man; 2:1], prophesy against the
prophets of Israel. Say to those who ·make up their own prophecies
[prophesy from their hearts/imagination]: 'Listen to the word of the
LORD. 3This is what the Lord GOD says: ·How terrible it will be for [LWoe
to] the foolish prophets who follow their own ·ideas [Lspirit] and have
·not seen a vision from me [Lseen nothing]! 4People of Israel, your prophets have been like ·wild dogs [jackals] among ruins. 5You have not gone
up into the ·broken places [breaches] or repaired the wall for the ·nation
[Lhouse of] Israel [CIsrael is portrayed as a house or fortress in ruins]. So
how can Israel ·hold back the enemy [stand firm] in the battle on the
·LORD's day of judging [LDay of the LORD]? 6·Your prophets [LThey] see
false visions and ·prophesy [their divinations are] lies. They say, "This is
the message of the LORD," when the LORD has not sent them. But they
still hope their words will ·come true [stand]. 7You said, "This is the
message of the LORD," but ·you have seen false visions and your prophecies are lies [Lhave you not seen a false vision and uttered a lying
divination…?], because I have not spoken.

8" 'So this is what the Lord GOD says: Because you prophets spoke
things that are false and saw ·visions that do not come true [lying visions],
[Llook; Tbehold] I am against you, says the Lord GOD. 9·I will punish [LMy
hand will be against] the prophets who see false visions and ·prophesy lies
[utter lying divinations]. They will ·have no place among [Lnot be in the
council of] my people. Their names will not be written on the ·list
[records; registry] of the ·people [Lhouse] of Israel, and they will not enter
the land of Israel. Then you will know that I am the Lord GOD.

10" 'It is because they lead my people ·the wrong way [astray] by saying,
"Peace!" when there is no peace. When the people build a ·weak [flimsy]
wall, the prophets cover it with whitewash [Cto make it look strong or to
cover its flaws]. 11So tell those who cover ·a weak wall [Lit] with whitewash
that it will fall down. ·Rain will pour down [There will be a deluge of
rain], hailstones will fall, and a windstorm will break the wall down.
12When the wall has fallen, people will ask you, "Where is the whitewash
you used on the wall?"

13" 'So this is what the Lord GOD says: I will break the wall with a windstorm. In my ·anger [wrath; rage] ·rain will pour down [there will be a

deluge of rain], and hailstones will ·destroy the wall [fall with destructive
fury]. 14I will tear down the wall on which you put whitewash. I will level
it to the ground so that ·people will see the wall's foundation [Lits foundations will be laid bare/exposed]. And when the wall falls, you will ·be
destroyed [perish] ·under [*or* within] it. Then you will know that I am the
LORD. 15So I will ·carry out my anger [spend my wrath/rage] on the wall
and against those who covered it with whitewash. Then I will tell you,
"The wall is gone, and those who covered it with whitewash are gone.
16The prophets of Israel who prophesy ·to [*or* about] Jerusalem and who
see visions of peace for the city, when there is no peace, will be gone, says
the Lord GOD."'

False Women Prophets

17"Now, ·human [Tson of man; 2:1], look toward the ·women among
[Ldaughters of] your people who ·make up their own prophecies [Lprophesy
from their own hearts/imaginations]. Prophesy against them. 18Say, 'This
is what the Lord GOD says: ·How terrible it will be for [LWoe to the] women
who sew ·magic charms [Lbands] on their wrists and make ·veils [*or* head-
bands] of every length to trap people! You ·ruin [entrap; ensnare] the ·lives
[souls] of my people but ·try to [will you…?] save your own ·lives [souls].
19For handfuls of barley and ·pieces [scraps] of bread, you have ·dishon-
ored [profaned; Critually] me among my people. By lying to my people,
who listen to lies, you have ·killed people [put to death souls] who should
not die, and you have kept alive those who should not live.

20" 'So this is what the Lord GOD says: I am against your magic ·charms
[bands], by which you ·trap [ensnare; hunt] ·people [souls] as if they were
birds. I will tear ·those charms [Lthem] off your arms, and I will free those
·people [souls] you have ·trapped [ensnare; hunt] like birds. 21I will also
tear off your ·veils [*or* headbands] and save my people from your hands.
They will no longer be ·trapped by your power [Lprey in your hand]. Then
you will know that I am the LORD. 22By your lies you have ·caused those
who did right to be sad [disheartened the righteous], when I did not
·make them sad [grieve them]. And you have encouraged the wicked not
to ·stop being wicked [turn from their wicked ways], which would have
saved their lives. 23So you will not see false visions or ·prophesy [practice
divination] anymore, and I will save my people from your ·power [Lhands]
so you will know that I am the LORD.' "

Stop Worshiping Idols

14 Some of the elders of Israel came to me and sat down in front
of me. 2Then the ·LORD spoke his word [Lword of the LORD
came] to me, saying: 3"·Human [TSon of man; 2:1], these people ·want to
worship idols [Lhave set up idols in their hearts]. They put up ·evil things
that cause people to sin [Lwicked stumbling blocks/obstacles before their
faces]. Should I allow them to ·ask me for help [consult me]? 4So speak
to them and tell them, 'This is what the Lord GOD says: When any of the
·people [Lhouse] of Israel ·want to worship idols [sets up idols in their
heart] and put up ·evil things that cause people to sin [Lwicked stumbling blocks/obstacles before their faces] and then ·come to the [consult
a] prophet, I, the LORD, will answer them myself ·for worshiping idols
[Lin accordance with the multitude of their idols]. 5Then I will ·win back
[take hold of/recapture the hearts of] my people Israel, who have left me
because of all their idols.'

6"So say to the ·people [Lhouse] of Israel, 'This is what the Lord GOD
says: ·Change your hearts and lives [Repent], and ·stop worshiping [Lturn

from your] idols. ·Stop doing [[L]Turn your faces from] all ·the things I hate
[your abominations/detestable practices]. 7 Any of the Israelites or foreigners in Israel can separate themselves from me by ·wanting to worship idols
[[L]setting up idols in their hearts] or by putting ·up things that cause people
to sin [[L]before their face a wicked stumbling block/obstacle]. Then if they
come to the prophet to ·ask me questions [consult me], I, the LORD, will
answer them myself. 8 I will ·reject [[L]set my face against] them. I will make
them a sign and an ·example [proverb; byword], and I will ·separate them
[[L]cut them off] from my people. Then you will know that I am the LORD.
9 " 'But if the prophet is ·tricked [deceived; *or* enticed] into giving a
prophecy, it is because I, the LORD, have ·tricked [deceived; *or* enticed]
that prophet to speak. Then I will ·use my power [[L]stretch out my hand]
against him and destroy him from among my people Israel. 10 The prophet
will be ·as guilty [*or* punished the same] as the one who asks him for help;
both will ·be responsible [*or* bear the punishment] for their guilt. 11 Then
the ·nation [[L]house] of Israel will ·not leave me anymore [no longer go
astray] or ·make themselves unclean [defile themselves; [C]ritually] anymore with all their sins. They will be my people, and I will be their God,
says the Lord GOD.' "

Jerusalem Will Not Be Spared

12 The ·LORD spoke his word [[L]word of the LORD came] to me, saying:
13 "·Human [[T]Son of man; 2:1], if ·the people of a country [[L]a country/land]
sin against me by not being ·loyal [faithful], I will ·use my power [[L]stretch
out my hand] against them. I will cut off their supply of ·food [bread] and
send ·a time of hunger [famine], destroying both people and animals.
14 Even if three great men like Noah, Daniel [[C]either the prophet Daniel
(who was still a young man at this time) or an ancient Canaanite hero
known for his wisdom and justice], and Job were in that country, their
·goodness [righteousness] could save only themselves, says the Lord GOD.
15 "Or I might send wild animals into that land, leaving the land ·empty
[desolate] and ·without children [bereaved]. Then no one would pass
through it because of the ·animals [beasts]. 16 As surely as I live, says the
Lord GOD, even if ·Noah, Daniel, and Job [[L]these three men; v. 14] were in
the land, they could not save their own sons or daughters. They could
save only themselves, but that country would become ·empty [desolate].
17 "Or I might bring a ·war [[L]sword] against that ·country [land]. I
might say, 'Let a ·war be fought in [[L]sword pass through] that land,' in this
way ·destroying [cutting off] its people and its animals. 18 As surely as I
live, says the Lord GOD, even if those three men were in the land, they
could not save their sons or daughters. They could save only themselves.
19 "Or I might cause a ·disease [plague; pestilence] to spread in that
country. I might pour out my ·anger [[L]rage/wrath with blood] against it,
destroying and killing people and animals. 20 As surely as I live, says the
Lord GOD, even if Noah, Daniel [v. 14], and Job were in the land, they
could not save their son or daughter. They could save only themselves
·because they did what was right [by their righteousness].
21 "This is what the Lord GOD says: ·My plans for Jerusalem are much
worse [[L]How much more for Jerusalem]! I will send my four terrible punishments against it—·war [[L]sword], ·hunger [famine], wild animals, and
·disease [pestilence; plague]—to destroy its people and animals. 22 But
[[L]look; [T]behold] some ·people will escape [survivors will be left]; some
sons and daughters will be led out. They will come out to you, and you

will see ·what happens to people who live as they did [Ltheir ways and
deeds]. Then you will be ·comforted [consoled] after the disasters I have
brought against Jerusalem, after all the things I have brought against it.
23·You will be comforted [They will console you] when you see ·what happens to them for living as they did [Ltheir ways and deeds], because you
will know ·there was a good reason for [it was not without cause that I
did] what I did to Jerusalem, says the Lord GOD."

Story of the Vine

15 The ·LORD spoke his word [Lword of the LORD came] to me,
saying: 2"·Human [TSon of man; 2:1], is the wood of the vine
better than the wood of any tree in the forest? 3Can wood be taken from
the vine to make anything? Can you use it to make a peg on which to
hang something? 4If the vine is thrown into the fire for fuel, and the fire
burns up both ends and ·starts to burn [chars] the middle, is it useful for
anything? 5 [LLook; TBehold] When the vine was whole, it couldn't be
made into anything. When the fire has burned it completely, ·it certainly cannot [how much less can it] be made into anything."
6So this is what the Lord GOD says: "Out of all the trees in the forest, I
have given the wood of the vine as fuel for fire. In the same way I have
given up the people who live in Jerusalem 7and will ·turn [Lset my face]
against them. Although they came through one fire, fire will still ·destroy
[consume] them. When I ·turn [Lset my face] against them, you will know
that I am the LORD. 8So I will make the land ·empty [desolate], because the
people have not been ·loyal [faithful], says the Lord GOD."

The Lord's Kindness to Jerusalem

16 The ·LORD spoke his word [Lword of the LORD came] to me,
saying: 2"·Human [TSon of man; 2:1], tell Jerusalem about her
·hateful [detestable; abominable] actions. 3Say, 'This is what the Lord
GOD says to Jerusalem: Your ·beginnings [origin] and your ·ancestors
[Lbirth] were in the land of the Canaanites. Your father was an Amorite,
and your mother was a Hittite. 4On the day you were born, your cord
[Cumbilical cord] was not cut. You were not washed with water to clean
you. You were not rubbed with salt or wrapped in ·cloths [Tswaddling
cloths; Luke 2:7, 12; Ctypical care for newborns in the ancient Near East].
5No ·one felt sorry enough for [Leye took pity on] you to do any of these
things for you. No, you were thrown out into the open field, because you
were ·hated [detested; despised] on the day you were born.
6" 'When I passed by and saw you kicking about in your blood, I said to
you ·as you lay in your blood [Lin your blood], "Live!"[n] 7I made you ·grow
[flourish] like a plant in the field. You grew up and ·became tall [*or*
matured; developed] and ·became like a beautiful jewel [*or* entered
puberty; reached womanhood]. Your breasts formed, and your hair grew,
but you were naked and ·without clothes [bare; exposed].
8" 'Later when I passed by you and looked at you, ·I saw that [Tbehold]
you were old enough for love. So I spread ·my robe [Lthe corner of my
garment; Deut. 22:30; Ruth 3:9] over you and covered your nakedness. I
also ·made a promise [swore; made a vow] to you and entered into an
·agreement [covenant; treaty; Ex. 19:5] with you so that you became mine,
says the Lord GOD.
9" 'Then I bathed you with water, washed all the blood off of you, and

16:6 Live Some Hebrew, Greek and Syriac copies repeat the phrase, "I said to you in your blood, 'Live!'"

·put oil on you [anointed you with oil/ointment]. 10I put ·beautiful clothes made with needlework [embroidered clothing] on you and put sandals of fine leather on your feet. I wrapped you in fine linen and covered you with silk. 11I put jewelry on you: bracelets on your arms, a ·necklace [chain] around your neck, 12a ring in your nose, earrings in your ears, and a beautiful ·crown [tiara] on your head. 13So you ·wore [were adorned with] gold and silver. Your clothes were made of fine linen, silk, and ·beautiful needlework [embroidery]. You ate fine flour, honey, and olive oil. You were very beautiful and became ·a queen [royalty]. 14Then ·you became famous [your fame spread] among the nations, because you were so beautiful. Your beauty was perfect, because of the ·glory [splendor] I gave you, says the Lord GOD.

Jerusalem Becomes a Prostitute

15" 'But you trusted in your beauty. You used your fame to become a prostitute. You ·had sexual relations with [lavished sexual favors on] anyone who passed by. 16You took some of your clothes and made your ·places of worship [high places; 6:3] ·colorful [decorated; gaudy]. There you carried on your prostitution. ·These things should not happen; they should never occur [*or* You went to him and became his; *or* How could such a thing ever have happened? Cthe Hebrew here is obscure]. 17You also took your beautiful jewelry, made from my gold and silver I had given you, and you made for yourselves male idols so you could be a prostitute with them [2 Kin. 23:7]. 18Then you took your ·clothes with beautiful needlework [embroidered clothing] and covered the idols. You gave my oil and incense as an offering to them. 19Also, you took the ·bread [food] I gave you, the fine flour, oil, and honey I gave you to eat, and you offered them before the gods as a ·pleasing smell [fragrant incense]. This is what happened, says the Lord GOD.

20" 'But your ·sexual sins [acts of prostitution] were not enough for you. You also took your sons and daughters who ·were my children [you bore to me], and you sacrificed them to the idols as food. 21You ·killed [slaughtered] my children and offered them up in fire to the idols [Lev. 18:21; 20:2; Deut. 12:31; 18:10; 2 Kin. 16:3; 21:6; 23:10; Jer. 32:35]. 22While you did all your ·hateful [detestable; abominable] acts and ·sexual sins [prostitution], you did not remember ·when you were young [Lthe days of your youth], when you were naked and had no clothes and were ·left [Lkicking about] in your blood.

23" '·How terrible [LWoe]! ·How terrible it will be for you [LWoe to you], says the Lord GOD. After you did all these evil things, 24you built yourself a ·place to worship gods [pagan shrine; *or* chamber; *or* mound]. You made for yourself a ·place of worship [lofty shrine; pavilion] in every city square. 25You built a place of worship at the ·beginning [head; corner] of every street. You made your beauty ·hateful [defiled; disgraced; detestable; an abomination], ·offering your body for sex [Lspreading your legs] to anyone who passed by, ·so your sexual sins became worse and worse [multiplying your promiscuity/prostitution]. 26You also ·had sexual relations [engaged in prostitution] with the ·Egyptians [Lsons of Egypt], who were your ·neighbors and partners in sexual sin [*or* well-endowed neighbors; *or* lusty neighbors]. Your ·sexual sins [prostitution; promiscuity] became even worse, and ·they caused me to be angry [provoked me to anger]. 27So then, [Llook; Tbehold] I ·used my power [Lstretched out my hand] against you and ·took away some of your land [reduced your

boundaries; *or* cut off your rations]. I **·let you be defeated by** [[L]delivered
you to the greed/desire of] **·those who hate you** [your enemies], **the
Philistine ·women** [[L]daughters], **who were ashamed of your ·evil ways**
[obscene/lewd behavior; [C]even the pagan Philistines were shocked at
Israel's outrageous sins]. **28Also, you ·had sexual relations** [engaged in
prostitution] **with the Assyrians, because you could not be satisfied. Even
though you ·had sexual relations** [prostituted yourself] **with them, you
still were not satisfied. 29You ·did many more sexual sins** [multiplied your
prostitution/promiscuity] **in ·Babylonia** [[L]Chaldea], **the land of ·traders**
[merchants], **but even this did not satisfy you.**

30" '·Truly your will is weak [*or* How sick/feverish is your heart; *or* I am
filled with anger against you], **says the Lord God. You do all the things a
·stubborn** [bold; brazen; shameless] **prostitute does. 31You built your
·place to worship gods** [pagan shrines; *or* chambers; *or* mounds] **at the
·beginning** [head; corner] **of every street, and you made ·places of worship**
[lofty shrines; pavilions; v. 24] **in every city square. But you were not like a
prostitute when you ·refused to accept** [scorned; scoffed at] **payment.**

32" 'You adulterous wife! You ·desire [prefer; receive] **strangers instead
of your husband. 33Men ·pay** [*or* give gifts to] **prostitutes, but you ·pay all**
[give gifts to] **your lovers, bribing them to come to you. And they come
from all around for ·sexual relations** [your prostitution]. **34So you are ·dif-
ferent from** [the opposite of] **other prostitutes. No man ·asks** [solicited]
**you to be a prostitute, and you pay money instead of having money paid
to you. Yes, you are ·different** [the opposite].

The Prostitute Is Judged

**35" 'So, prostitute, hear the word of the Lord. 36This is what the Lord
God says: You ·showed your nakedness** [[L]poured out your lust] **and
·uncovered your body** [[L]exposed your nakedness] **in your ·sexual sins**
[prostitution; promiscuity] **with your lovers and with all your ·hateful**
[detestable; abominable] **idols. You killed your children and offered their
blood to your idols. 37So** [[L]look; [T]behold] **I will gather all your lovers with
whom you found pleasure. Yes, I will gather all those you loved and those
you hated. I will gather them against you from all around, and I will strip
you naked in front of them so they can see your nakedness** [[C]an act of
humiliation and shame; Jer. 13:22, 26; Nah. 3:5]. **38I will punish you as
women guilty of adultery or as ·murderers** [[L]those who shed blood] **are
punished. I will ·put you to death** [[L]bring blood upon you; *or* avenge your
bloody deeds] **because I am angry and jealous. 39I will also ·hand you over
to your lovers** [[L]give you into their hands]. **They will tear down your
·places of worship** [pagan shrines; chambers; mounds] **and destroy ·other
places where you worship gods** [your lofty shrines; *or* pavilions; v. 24].
They will ·tear [strip] **off your clothes and take away your beautiful jewelry, leaving you naked and bare. 40They will bring a crowd against you to
throw stones at you and to cut you into pieces with their swords. 41They
will burn down your houses and will ·punish you** [execute judgments] **in
·front** [the sight of] **of many women. I will put an end to your ·sexual sins**
[prostitution], **and you will no longer ·pay** [give gifts to] **your lovers.
42Then I will ·rest from** [exhaust; satisfy] **my ·anger** [wrath] **against you,
and ·I will stop being jealous** [[L]my jealousy will turn away from you]. **I
will be ·quiet** [calm] **and not angry anymore.**

43" 'Because you didn't remember ·when you were young [[L]the days of
your youth], **but have ·made me angry** [enraged me] **in all these ways, I will**

·repay you for what you have done [Lbring these ways upon your head], says
the Lord GOD. Didn't you add ·sexual sins [lewd acts; obscenities] to all your
·other acts which I hate [detestable practices; abominations]?

44" 'Everyone who uses ·wise sayings [proverbs] will say this about you:
"·The daughter is like her mother [LLike mother, like daughter]." 45You are
·like your mother [Lthe daughter of your mother], who ·hated [detested;
loathed] her husband and ·children [sons]. You are ·also like your sisters
[Lthe sister of your sisters], who ·hated [detested; loathed] their husbands
and ·children [sons]. Your mother was a Hittite, and your father was an
Amorite [v. 3]. 46Your older sister is Samaria, who lived north of you with
her daughters; your younger sister is Sodom, who lived south of you with
her daughters [Gen. 19; CSodom is a symbol of evil in Scripture; Deut.
29:23; 32:32; Is. 1:9–10; 3:9; Jer. 23:14; Lam. 4:6; Matt. 10:15; 11:23–24;
Jude 7]. 47You not only ·followed [walked in] their ways and did the ·hate-
ful [detestable; abominable] things they did, but you were ·soon worse
[more corrupt/depraved] than they were in all your ways. 48As surely as I
live, says the Lord GOD, your sister Sodom and her daughters never did
what you and your daughters have done.

49" 'This was the ·sin [iniquity; guilt] of your sister Sodom: She and her
daughters were proud and had plenty of food and lived in ·great comfort
[secure ease], but she did not ·help [Lstrengthen the hand of] the poor and
needy. 50So Sodom and her daughters were ·proud [haughty] and did
·things I hate [detestable/abominable things] in front of me. So I ·got rid of
[removed] them when I saw what they did. 51Also, Samaria [Cthe northern
kingdom] did not do half the sins you do; you have done more ·hateful
[detestable; abominable] things than they did. So you make your sisters
·look good [appear righteous] because of all the ·hateful [detestable; abomi-
nable] things you have done. 52You will ·suffer [bear your] disgrace, because
you have ·provided an excuse [Linterceded with your sins] for your sisters.
They ·are better [appear more righteous] than you are. Your sins were even
more ·terrible [vile; abominable] than theirs. Feel ashamed and suffer disgrace, because you made your sisters ·look good [appear righteous].

53" 'But I will ·give back [restore] to Sodom and her daughters ·the good
things they once had [their fortunes]. I will give back to Samaria and her
daughters ·the good things they once had [their fortunes]. And with them
I will also give back ·the good things you once had [your fortunes] 54so you
may ·suffer [bear your] disgrace and feel ashamed for all the things you
have done. You even gave comfort to your sisters in their sins. 55Your sisters, Sodom with her daughters and Samaria with her daughters, will
return to ·what they were before [their former status]. You and your
daughters will also return to ·what you were before [their former status].
56You ·humiliated [spoke contemptuously about; Lmade a byword in your
mouth] your sister Sodom ·when you were proud [Lin the day of your
pride/majesty], 57before your ·evil [wickedness] was uncovered [exposed].
And now the Edomite ·women[n] [Ldaughters] and their neighbors ·humili-
ate [scorn] you. Even the Philistine women ·humiliate [scorn] you. Those
around you ·hate [despise] you. 58·This is your punishment [LYou bear the
penalty] for your ·terrible sins [lewdness] and for ·actions that I hate [your
detestable practices/abominations], says the LORD.

16:57 Edomite women Hebrew copies read "daughters of Edom." Some Hebrew copies read "daughters of Aram."

God Keeps His Promises

59“ ‘This is what the Lord God says: I will ·do to you what you have
done [give you what you deserve]. You ·hated [despised] and broke the
·agreement [covenant; treaty] you ·promised [swore; made an oath] to
keep. 60But I will remember my ·agreement [covenant; treaty] I made
with you ·when you were young [Lin the days of your youth], and I will
make an ·agreement [covenant; treaty] that will continue forever with
you [Jer. 31:31–34]. 61Then you will remember ·what you have done [your
ways] and feel ashamed when you receive your sisters—both your older
and your younger sisters. I will give them to you like daughters, but not
because they share in my ·agreement [covenant; treaty] with you. 62I will
·set up my agreement [establish my covenant/treaty] with you, and you
will know that I am the Lord. 63You will remember what you did and feel
ashamed. You will not open your mouth again because of your shame,
when I ·forgive [make atonement for] you for all the things you have
done, says the Lord God.’ ”

The Eagle and the Vine

17 The ·Lord spoke his word [Lword of the Lord came] to me,
saying: 2“·Human [TSon of man; 2:1], give a ·riddle [allegory]
and tell a ·story [parable] to the ·people [Lhouse] of Israel. 3Say, ‘This is
what the Lord God says: A ·giant [great; mighty] eagle with ·big [great]
wings and long ·feathers [Lfeathers and plumage] of many different colors [16:10] came to Lebanon and took hold of the top of a cedar tree. 4He
pulled off the top ·branch [shoot] and brought it to a land of ·traders
[merchants; CBabylon], where he planted it in a city of traders [Cthe eagle
symbolizes King Nebuchadnezzar; v. 12].
5“ ‘The eagle took ·some seed [*or* a seedling] from the land and planted
it in ·a good field [fertile soil] near plenty of water. He planted it to grow
like a willow tree. 6It sprouted and became a low vine that spread over the
ground. The branches turned toward the eagle, but the roots were under
·the eagle [*or* itself; Lit]. So the seed became a vine, and its ·branches
[shoots] grew, sending out ·leaves [*or* branches; boughs].
7“ ‘But there was another ·giant [great; mighty] eagle with ·big [great]
wings and ·many feathers [full plumage]. The vine then ·bent [sent] its
roots toward this eagle. It ·sent [stretched; shot] out its branches from the
·area [bed; plot] where it was planted toward the eagle ·so he could water
it [to get water]. 8It had been planted in ·a good field [good soil] by plenty
of water so it could grow branches and bear fruit. It could have become a
·fine [beautiful; splendid] vine.’
9“Say to them, ‘This is what the Lord God says: ·The vine will not continue to grow [LWill it thrive/prosper?]. ·The first eagle will [LWill he
not...?] pull up the vine’s roots and strip off its fruit. Then the vine and
all its new leaves will ·dry up and die [wither]. It will not take a strong
arm or many people to pull the vine up by its roots. 10[LLook; TBehold]
Even if it is planted again, ·it will not [Lwill it...?] ·continue to grow
[thrive]. ·It will [LWill it not...?] completely ·dry up and die [wither]
when the east wind hits it. ·It will [*or* Will it not...?] ·dry up and die
[wither] in the ·area [bed; plot] where it ·grew [sprouted].’ ”

Zedekiah Against Nebuchadnezzar

11Then the ·Lord spoke his word [Lword of the Lord came] to me, saying:
12“Say now to the ·people who refuse to obey [Lrebellious house]: ‘Don’t
you know what these things mean?’ Say: ‘[LLook; TBehold] The king of
Babylon came to Jerusalem and took the king [CJehoiachin; 2 Kin. 24:12]
and ·important men [nobles; officials] of Jerusalem and brought them to

Babylon. 13Then he took ·a member of the family of the king of Judah
[Lfrom the royal offspring/seed; CZedekiah, Jehoiachin's uncle; 2 Kin. 24:17]
and made an ·agreement [covenant; treaty] with him, ·forcing him to take
an [putting him under] oath. The king also took away the leaders of ·Judah
[Lthe land] 14to ·make the kingdom weak [humble/bring low the kingdom]
so it would not ·be strong [rise; exalt itself] again. Then the kingdom of
Judah ·could continue only [would stand] by keeping its ·agreement [cov-
enant; treaty] with the king of Babylon. 15But ·the king of Judah [Lhe;
Creferring to Zedekiah; 2 Kin. 24:20] ·turned [rebelled] against the king of
Babylon by sending his ·messengers [emissaries] to Egypt and asking them
for horses and many soldiers [2 Kin. 24:20]. Will ·the king of Judah succeed
[he prosper/succeed]? Will the one who does such things escape? ·He cannot [LCan he…?] break the ·agreement [covenant; treaty] and escape.
16" 'As surely as I live, says the Lord God, he will die in Babylon, in the land
of the king who made him king of Judah. The king of Judah ·hated [despised]
his ·promise [oath] to the king of Babylon and broke his ·agreement [cove-
nant; treaty] with him. 17·The king of Egypt [LPharaoh] with his mighty army
and ·many people [vast horde] will not help ·the king of Judah [Lhim] in the
war. The Babylonians will build ·devices [ramps and siege walls] to attack the
cities and to ·kill [destroy; cut off] many people. 18The king of Judah showed
that he ·hated [despised] the ·promise [oath] by breaking the ·agreement
[covenant; treaty]. He ·promised to support Babylon [Lgave his hand (in
pledge)], but he did all these things. So he will not escape.
19" 'So this is what the Lord God says: As surely as I live, I will ·pay back
the king of Judah [Lbring down on his head] for ·hating [despising] my
·promise [oath] and breaking my ·agreement [covenant; treaty]. 20I will
spread my net over him, and he will be caught in my ·trap [snare]. Then I
will bring him to Babylon, where I will ·punish [execute judgment on] him
for the ·unfaithful acts [treachery] he did against me. 21All the ·best" [choice
men] of his soldiers will die by the sword, and those who live will be scattered to every wind. Then you will know that I, the Lord, have spoken.
22" 'This is what the Lord God says: I myself will also take a ·young
branch [shoot; sprig] from the top of a tall cedar tree, and I will plant it. I
will cut off a ·small [tender] twig from the top of the tree's young branches,
and I will plant it on a ·very high [Lhigh and lofty] mountain. 23I will plant
it on the ·high mountain [mountain heights] of Israel. Then it will grow
branches and give fruit and become a ·great [beautiful; majestic] cedar
tree. Birds of every kind will build nests in it and live in the ·shelter
[shade] of the tree's branches. 24Then all the trees in the ·countryside
[field] will know that I am the Lord. I bring down the high tree and make
the low tree tall. I ·dry up [wither] the green tree and make the dry tree
·grow [thrive; flourish]. I am the Lord. I have spoken, and I will do it.' "

God Is Fair

18 The ·Lord spoke his word [Lword of the Lord came] to me,
saying: 2"What do you mean by ·using [quoting; repeating]
this ·saying [proverb] about the land of Israel:

'The ·parents [fathers] have eaten sour grapes,
and ·that caused the children to grind their teeth from the sour taste
[Tthe children's teeth are set on edge; Cthe children suffer for their
parents' sins; Jer. 31:29–30]'?

17:21 best Some Hebrew copies read "choice men." Other Hebrew copies read "fugitives."

3“As surely as I live, says the Lord GOD, you will not use this ·saying
[proverb] in Israel anymore. 4Every ·living thing [soul] belongs to me.
The ·life [soul] of the ·parent [father] is mine, and the ·life [soul] of the
child is mine. The ·person [soul] who sins is the one who will die.
5“Suppose a ·person [man] is good and does what is ·fair [just] and
right. 6He does not eat ·at the mountain places of worship [Lupon the
mountains; Cat pagan worship sites]. He does not ·look for help [Llift his
eyes] to the idols of [Lthe house of] Israel. He does not ·have sexual relations with [Ldefile] his neighbor’s wife or ·with [Lcome near; Ca euphemism
for sexual relations] a woman during her time of ·monthly bleeding
[impurity; Lev. 18:19]. 7He does not ·mistreat [oppress] anyone but returns
what was given ·as a promise for a loan [in pledge; as collateral]. He does
not rob other people. He gives bread to the hungry and ·clothes to those
who have none [Lcovers the naked with clothing]. 8He does not lend money
for interest or profit [Ex. 22:25; Ps. 15:5]. He keeps his hand from doing
wrong. He ·judges fairly [practices true justice] between one person and
another. 9He ·lives by [Lwalks in] my ·rules [statutes; ordinances; require-
ments] and obeys my ·laws [judgments] faithfully. Whoever does these
things is ·good [righteous] and will surely live, says the Lord GOD.
10“But suppose this person ·has [bears; begets] a ·wild [violent] son
who ·murders people [Lsheds blood] and who does any of these other
things. 11(But the father himself has not done any of these things.) This
son eats ·at the mountain places of worship [upon the mountains; v. 6].
He ·has sexual relations with [Ldefiles] his neighbor’s wife. 12He ·mistreats
[oppresses] the poor and needy. He steals and refuses to return what was
·promised for a loan [given in pledge/as collateral; v. 7]. He ·looks for help
[Llifts up his eyes] to idols. He does ·things which I hate [detestable/abom-
inable things]. 13He lends money for interest and profit [v. 8]. Will this
son live? No, he will not live! He has done all these ·hateful [detestable;
abominable] things, so he will surely be put to death. ·He will be responsible for his own death [LHis blood will be upon himself].
14“Now suppose this son has a son who has seen all his father’s sins,
but after seeing them does not do those things. 15He does not eat ·at the
mountain places of worship [Lupon the mountains; v. 6]. He does not
·look for help [Llift his eyes] to the idols of [Lthe house of] Israel. He does
not ·have sexual relations with [Ldefile] his neighbor’s wife [v. 6]. 16He
does not ·mistreat [oppress] anyone or keep something promised ·for a
loan [in pledge; as collateral] or steal. He gives bread to the hungry and
·clothes to those who have none [Lcovers the naked with clothing; v. 7].
17He keeps his hand from doing wrong. He does not take interest or
profit when he lends money [v. 8]. He obeys my ·laws [rules; judgments]
and ·lives by [walks in] my ·rules [statutes]. He will not die for his father’s
sin; he will surely live. 18But his father ·took other people’s money
unfairly [practiced extortion/fraud] and robbed his ·brother [*or* coun-
tryman] and did what was wrong among his people. So he will die for his
own sin.
19“But you ask, ‘Why is the son not punished for the father’s ·sin [iniq-
uity; guilt]?’ The son has done what is ·fair [just] and right. He obeys all
my ·rules [statutes; ordinances; requirements], so he will surely live. 20The
person who sins is the one who will die. A ·child [son] will not be punished for a ·parent’s [father’s] ·sin [iniquity; guilt], and a ·parent [father]
will not be punished for a ·child’s [son’s] ·sin [iniquity; guilt]. ·Those who

do right [The righteous] will enjoy the results of their ·own goodness [righteousness]; ·evil people [the wicked] will suffer the results of their ·own evil [wickedness].

21“But suppose the wicked ·stop doing all [turn away from] the sins they have done and obey all my ·rules [statutes; ordinances; requirements] and do what is ·fair [just] and right. Then they will surely live; they will not die. 22None of their ·sins [transgressions] will be ·held [Lremembered] against them. Because they have done what is ·right [righteous], they will live. 23·I do not really want the wicked to die [LDo I take pleasure in the death of the wicked…?], says the Lord GOD. ·I [Do I not…?] want them to ·stop [turn from] their ·bad ways [Lways] and live.

24“But suppose ·good people [the righteous] ·stop doing good [turn from righteousness] and do wrong and do the same ·hateful [detestable; abominable] things the wicked do. Will they live? All their ·good [righteous] acts will ·be forgotten [Lnot be remembered], because they became unfaithful. They have sinned, so they will die because of their sins.

25“But you say, ‘·What the Lord does [LThe way of the Lord] isn’t ·fair [just].’ Listen, ·people [Lhouse] of Israel. ·I am fair [LIs my way unjust?]. It is what you do that is not ·fair [just]! 26When ·good people [the righteous] ·stop [turn from] doing good and do wrong, they will die because of it. They will die, because they did wrong. 27When the wicked ·stop being wicked [turn from wickedness] and do what is ·fair [just] and right, they will save their ·lives [souls]. 28Because they thought about it and ·stopped [turned from] doing all the sins they had done, they will surely live; they will not die. 29But the ·people [Lhouse] of Israel still say, ‘·What the Lord does [LThe way of the LORD] isn’t ·fair [just].’ ·People [LHouse] of Israel. ·I am fair [LIs my way unjust?]. It is what you do that is not ·fair [just].

30“So I will judge you, ·people [Lhouse] of Israel; I will judge each of you ·by what you do [Laccording to your ways], says the Lord GOD. ·Change your hearts [Repent] and ·stop all [turn from] your ·sinning [transgressions] so sin will not ·bring your ruin [be your downfall/stumbling block]. 31·Get rid of [Throw away] all the ·sins [transgressions; offenses] you have done, and ·get [make] for yourselves a new heart and a new ·way of thinking [spirit]. Why ·do you want to [should you] die, ·people [Lhouse] of Israel? 32I ·do not want anyone to die [Ltake no pleasure/delight in anyone’s death], says the Lord GOD, so ·change your hearts and lives so you may [Lrepent and] live.

A Sad Song for Israel

19 “Sing a ·funeral song [lament; dirge] for the ·leaders [princes] of Israel. 2Say:

‘Your mother was a lioness [Creferring either to the Davidic dynasty or to Hamutal, the wife of Josiah and mother of Jehoahaz and Zedekiah; Gen. 49:9; 2 Kin. 23:31–34].
She lay down among the young lions [Cthe kings of Judah].
She ·had many [reared her] cubs.
3When she ·brought up [reared] one of her cubs,
he became a ·strong [Lyoung] lion [CKing Jehoahaz; 2 Kin. 23:31–34; Jer. 22:10–12].
He learned to tear ·the animals he hunted [prey],
and he ·ate [devoured] people.
4The nations heard about him.

He was trapped in their pit,
and they brought him with hooks
to the land of Egypt.
5“ ‘The mother lion waited and saw
that there was no hope for her cub.
So she took another one of her cubs
and made him a ·strong [Lyoung] lion [Ceither Jehoiachin (2 Kin. 24:8) or Zedekiah (2 Kin. 25:7)].
6This cub ·roamed [prowled] among the lions.
He was now a ·strong [Lyoung] lion.
He learned to tear ·the animals he hunted [prey],
and he ·ate [devoured] people.
7He tore down their ·strong places [strongholds; fortresses]
and ·destroyed [devastated] their cities.
The land and everything in it
were terrified by the sound of his roar.
8Then the nations came against him
from areas all around,
and they spread their net over him.
He was trapped in their pit.
9Then they put him into a ·cage with chains [collar]
and brought him to the king of Babylon.
They put him into prison
so his ·roar [voice] could not be heard again
on the mountains of Israel [2 Kin. 24:8–17; 2 Chr. 36:8–10].

10“ ‘Your mother was like a vine in your vineyard,
planted beside the water.
The vine had many branches and gave much fruit,
because there was plenty of water.
11The vine had strong ·branches [boughs],
good enough for a king's scepter.
The vine became tall
among the thick branches.
And it ·was seen [stood out], because it was tall
with many branches.
12But it was pulled up by its roots in anger
and thrown down to the ground.
The east wind dried it up.
Its fruit was ·torn [stripped] off.
Its strong branches were broken off
and burned up.
13Now the vine is planted in the ·desert [wilderness],
in a dry and thirsty land.
14Fire spread from the vine's main branch,
·destroying [consuming] its fruit.
There is not a strong branch left on it
·that could become a [Lno] scepter for a king.’
This is a ·funeral song [lament]; it ·is to be used as [*or* has become] a funeral song.”

Israel Has Refused God

20 It was the seventh year [Csince Jehoiachin's exile (1:2)], in the fifth month, on the tenth day of the month [CAugust 14, 591 BC]. Some of the elders of Israel came to ask about the LORD and sat down in front of me.

2The ·LORD spoke his word [Lword of the LORD came] to me, saying: 3"·Human [TSon of man; 2:1], speak to the elders of Israel and say to them: 'This is what the Lord GOD says: Did you come to ·ask me questions [inquire of/consult me]? As surely as I live, I will not let you ·ask me questions [inquire of/consult me].'

4"Will you judge them? Will you judge them, ·human [Tson of man; 2:1]? Let them know the ·hateful [detestable; abominable] things their ·ancestors [fathers] did. 5Say to them: 'This is what the Lord GOD says: ·When [LOn the day when] I chose Israel, I ·made a promise [Llifted my hand] to the ·descendants [offspring; seed] of Jacob. I made myself known to them in the land of Egypt, and I ·promised them [Llifted my hand to them, saying], "I am the LORD your God." 6·At that time [On that day] I ·promised them I would [Llifted my hand to them to] bring them out of Egypt into a land I had ·found [searched out] for them, a ·fertile land [land flowing with milk and honey; Ex. 3:8], the ·best [most beautiful] land in the world. 7I said to them, "Each one of you must throw away the ·hateful idols [detestable/abominable things] you have ·seen and liked [Lset your eyes on]. Don't ·make yourselves unclean [defile yourselves] with the idols of Egypt. I am the LORD your God."

8" 'But they ·turned [rebelled] against me and refused to listen to me. They did not throw away the ·hateful idols [detestable/abominable things] which they ·saw and liked [Lset your eyes on]; they did not give up the idols of Egypt. Then I decided to pour out my anger against them while they were still in Egypt. 9But I acted for the sake of my name so it would not be ·dishonored [profaned; Critually] in ·full view [Lthe eyes] of the nations where the Israelites lived. I made myself known to ·the Israelites [Lthem] by bringing them out of Egypt ·while the nations were watching [before their eyes]. 10So I took them out of Egypt and brought them into the ·desert [wilderness]. 11I gave them my ·rules [statutes; ordinances; requirements] and told them about my ·laws [judgments], by which people will live if they ·obey [do; practice] them. 12I also gave them my Sabbaths [Ex. 20:8–11; Deut. 5:12–15] to be a sign [Ex. 31:13] between us so they would know that I am the LORD who ·made them holy [sanctified them; set them apart].

13" 'But in the ·desert [wilderness] ·Israel [Lthe house of Israel] ·turned [rebelled] against me. They did not follow my ·rules [statutes], and they rejected my ·laws [rules; judgments], by which people will live if they obey them. They ·dishonored [desecrated; profaned; Critually] my Sabbaths. Then I decided to pour out my ·anger [wrath] against them and destroy them in the ·desert [wilderness]. 14But I acted for the sake of my name so it would not be ·dishonored [profaned; Critually] in ·full view [Lthe eyes] of the nations ·who watched as [before whose eyes] I had brought the Israelites out of Egypt. 15And in the ·desert [wilderness] I ·swore [Llifted my hand] to the Israelites that I would not bring them into the land I had given them. It is a ·fertile land [land flowing with milk and honey; Ex. 3:8], the ·best [most beautiful] land in the world. 16This was because they rejected my ·laws [judgments] and did not ·follow [Lwalk in] my ·rules [statutes; ordinances; requirements]. They ·dishonored [desecrated; profaned; Critually] my Sabbaths and ·wanted to worship [Ltheir hearts went after] their idols. 17But I ·had pity on [*or* spared] them. I did not destroy them or put an end to them in the ·desert [wilderness]. 18I said to their children in the ·desert [wilderness], "Don't ·live by [Lwalk in] the ·rules [statutes; ordinances; requirements] of your ·parents [fathers], or obey their ·laws [judgments]. Don't ·make yourselves unclean [defile yourselves] with their idols. 19I am the LORD your God. ·Live by [LWalk in] my ·rules [statutes; ordinances; requirements], obey my ·laws [judgments], and follow them. 20Keep my Sabbaths holy, and they will be a sign between me and you [Ex. 31:13]. Then you will know that I am the LORD your God."

21" 'But the children turned against me. They did not ·live by [walk in] my ·rules [statutes; ordinances; requirements], nor were they careful to obey my ·laws [judgments], by which people will live if they obey them. They ·dishonored [desecrated; profaned; Critually] my Sabbaths. So I decided to pour out my anger and ·rage [Lvent/exhaust my rage] against them in the ·desert [wilderness]. 22But I ·held back my anger [Lwithdrew my hand]. I acted for the sake of my name so it would not be ·dishonored [profaned; Critually] in ·full view [Lthe eyes] of the nations ·who watched as [Lbefore whose eyes] I brought the Israelites out. 23And in the ·desert [wilderness] I swore to the Israelites that I would scatter them among the nations and spread them among the ·countries [lands], 24because they had not obeyed my ·laws [judgments]. They had rejected my ·rules [statutes; ordinances; requirements] and ·dishonored [profaned; Critually] my Sabbaths and ·worshiped [Lset their eyes on] the idols of their ·parents [fathers]. 25I also allowed them to follow ·rules [statutes] that were not good and ·laws [judgments] by which they could not live. 26I ·let the Israelites make themselves unclean [Ldefiled them; Critually] by the gifts they brought to their gods when they sacrificed their first children in the fire [16:20–21]. I wanted to ·terrify [*or* devastate] them so they would know that I am the LORD.'

27"So, ·human [Tson of man; 2:1], speak to the ·people [Lhouse] of Israel. Say to them, 'This is what the Lord GOD says: Your ·ancestors [fathers] ·spoke against [blasphemed] me by being unfaithful to me in another way. 28When I had brought them into the land I ·promised [Llifted my hand] to give them, they saw every high hill and every leafy tree. There they offered their sacrifices to gods. They brought offerings that ·made me angry [provoked my anger] and burned their incense and poured out their drink offerings. 29Then I said to them: What is this high place where you go to worship?' " (It is still called ·High Place [LBamah] today.)

30"So say to the ·people [Lhouse] of Israel: 'This is what the Lord GOD says: Are you going to ·make yourselves unclean [defile yourselves; Critually] as your ·ancestors [fathers] did? Are you going to ·be unfaithful and desire [prostitute yourselves with] their ·hateful idols [detestable/abominable things]? 31When you offer your children as gifts and sacrifice them in the fire, you ·are making yourselves unclean [defile yourselves; Critually] with all your idols even today. So, ·people [Lhouse] of Israel, should I let you ·ask me questions [consult with me]? As surely as I live, says the Lord GOD, I will not ·accept questions from you [let you seek/inquire of me].

32" 'What you ·want [*or* plan] will not come true. You say, "We want to be like the other nations, like the ·people [clans; families] in other lands. We want to worship ·idols made of wood and stone [Lwood and stone]." 33As surely as I live, says the Lord GOD, ·I will use my great power and

strength and anger to [Lwith a mighty hand and an outstretched arm I
will; Deut. 4:34; 5:15] ·rule [be king] over you. 34I will bring you out from
the foreign nations. With ·my great power and strength [La mighty hand
and an outstretched arm] and anger I will gather you from the lands
where you are scattered. 35I will bring you into the ·desert [wilderness] of
the ·peoples [nations]. There I will judge you face to face. 36I will judge
you the same way I judged your ·ancestors [fathers] in the ·desert [wilder-
ness] of the land of Egypt, says the Lord God. 37I will ·count you like
sheep [Lmake you pass under the rod/shepherd's staff; Lev. 27:32] and will
bring you into ·line with [Lthe bond of] my ·agreement [covenant; treaty].
38I will ·get rid of [purge out] those who ·refuse to obey me [revolt] and
·who turn [rebel] against me. I will bring them out of the land where they
are now living, but they will never enter the land of Israel. Then you will
know that I am the Lord.

39" 'This is what the Lord God says: ·People [LHouse] of Israel, go serve
your idols for now. ·But later you will [*or*...if you will not] listen to me;
you will not continue to ·dishonor [profane; Critually] my holy name with
your gifts and ·gods [idols]. 40[LFor] On my holy mountain [CMount
Zion; Ps. 2:6; 3:4; 15:1], the high mountain of Israel, all [Lthe house of]
Israel will serve me in the land, says the Lord God. There I will accept you.
There I will ·expect [require] your ·offerings [contributions], ·the first
harvest of your offerings [*or* your choicest gifts], and all your holy gifts.
41I will accept you like ·the pleasing smell of sacrifices [a pleasing aroma;
a fragrant incense; Ps. 141:2] when I bring you out from the nations and
gather you from the lands where you are scattered. Then through you I
will ·show how holy I am [manifest/display my holiness] ·so the nations
will see [Lin the eyes/sight of the nations]. 42When I bring you into the
land of Israel, the land I ·promised [swore to] your ancestors, you will
know that I am the Lord. 43There you will remember ·everything you did
[Lyour ways and deeds] that ·made you unclean [defiled you; Critually],
and then you will ·hate [despise; loathe] yourselves for all the evil things
you have done. 44I will deal with you for the sake of my name, not because
of your evil ways or ·unclean [corrupt] actions. Then you will know I am
the Lord, ·people [Lhouse] of Israel, says the Lord God.' "

Babylon, the Lord's Sword

45Now the ·Lord spoke his word [Lword of the Lord came] to me, saying:
46"·Human [TSon of man; 2:1], ·look [Lset your face] toward the south.
Prophesy against the south and against the ·forest [*or* shrubland] of the
·southern area [LNegev]. 47Say to that ·forest [*or* shrubland]: 'Hear the word
of the Lord. This is what the Lord God says: I am ready to start a fire in you
that will destroy all your green trees and all your dry trees. The flames that
burn will not be put out. Every face from south to north will ·feel their heat
[*or* be scorched by it]. 48Then all ·the people [Lflesh] will see that I, the Lord,
have ·started the fire [kindled it]. It will not be ·put out [extinguished].' "

49Then I said, "Ah, Lord God! The people are saying about me, '·He is
only [LIsn't he just...?] telling ·stories [parables].' "

21 Then the ·Lord spoke his word [Lword of the Lord came] to
me, saying: 2"·Human [TSon of man; 2:1], ·look [Lset your
face] toward Jerusalem and speak against the ·holy place [sanctuary].
Prophesy against the land of Israel. 3Say to Israel: 'This is what the Lord
says: [LLook; TBehold] I am against you. I will pull my sword out of its
·holder [sheath], and I will cut off from you both the wicked and ·those

who do right [the righteous]. 4Because I am going to cut off the wicked
and ·those who do right [the righteous], my sword will ·come out from
its holder [be unsheathed] and attack all ·people [Lflesh] from south to
north. 5Then all people will know that I, the LORD, have pulled my sword
out from its ·holder [sheath]. My sword will not go back in again.'

6"So, ·human [Tson of man; 2:1], groan with breaking heart and ·great
sadness [bitter grief]. Groan ·in front of the people [Lbefore their eyes].
7When they ask you, 'Why are you groaning?' you will say, 'Because of
what I have heard is going to happen. When it happens, every heart will
melt with fear, and all hands will become ·weak [limp; feeble]. ·Everyone
[LEvery spirit] will ·be afraid [faint]; all knees will ·become weak as water
[*or* be wet with urine]. ·Look [TBehold], it is coming, and it will happen,
says the Lord GOD.'"

8The ·LORD spoke his word [Lword of the LORD came] to me, saying:
9"·Human [TSon of man; 2:1], prophesy and say, 'This is what the Lord says:

A sword, a sword,
  sharpened and polished.
10It is sharpened for the ·killing [slaughter].
  It is polished to flash like lightning.

"'·You are not happy [*or* Should you rejoice…?] ·about this horrible
punishment by the sword [Lin the scepter of my son]. ·But my son Judah,
you did not change when you were only beaten with a rod [LThe sword
despises every stick].

11The sword ·should [Lis appointed to] be polished.
  It is meant to be ·held [grasped] in the hand.
It is sharpened and polished,
  ready for the hand of a ·killer [slayer].
12Shout and ·yell [wail], ·human [Tson of man; 2:1],
  because the sword is meant for my people,
  for all the ·rulers [princes] of Israel.
They ·will be killed by [Lare thrown to] the sword,
  along with my people.
  So beat your chest [Ca sign of grief or sadness].

13"'The test will come. ·And [LWhat if…?] the scepter [Csymbolizing
Judah; Gen. 49:10], who is hated by the sword [Crepresenting the armies
of Babylon], will not last, says the Lord GOD.'

14"So, ·human [Tson of man; 2:1], prophesy
  and ·clap [strike together] your hands [Ca sign of scorn].
Let the sword strike
  two or three times.
It is a sword meant for ·killing [slaughter],
  a sword meant for ·much killing [great slaughter].
  This sword ·surrounds [*or* closes in on] ·the people to be killed [Lthem].
15Their hearts will ·melt with fear [Lmelt],
  and many people will ·die [stumble; fall].
I have placed the ·killing sword [sword for slaughter]
  at all their city gates.
Oh! The sword is made to flash like lightning.
  It is ·held [drawn], ready for killing.
16Sword, ·cut [slash; cut sharp] on the right side;
  then ·cut on [swing; Lput to] the left side.
  Cut anywhere your ·blade [*or* face] is turned.

17I will also clap my hands [v. 14; Ca sign of scorn]
  and ·use up [satisfy; exhaust] my ·anger [wrath].
I, the LORD, have spoken."

Jerusalem to Be Destroyed

18The ·LORD spoke his word [Lword of the LORD came] to me, saying: 19"·Human [TSon of man; 2:1], mark two roads that the king of Babylon and his sword can follow. Both of these roads will start from the same country. And make signs where the road divides and one way goes toward the city. 20Mark one sign to show the road ·he can take with his sword [Lfor the sword to come] to Rabbah in the land of the Ammonites. Mark the other sign to show the road to Judah and Jerusalem, which is protected with strong walls [Cmoving south from Syria, the roads branch east and west of the Jordan River]. 21The king of Babylon has come to where the road divides, and he is using ·magic [divination]. He ·throws lots with [Lshakes] arrows and ·asks questions of his family idols [Lconsults the teraphim]. He looks at the ·liver of a sacrificed animal [Lliver; Cmethods of divination, used here to determine which road to take]. 22The lot in his right hand tells him to go to Jerusalem. It tells him to use ·logs to break down the city gates [battering rams], to shout the battle cry and give the ·order to kill [command for slaughter], and to build ·a dirt road to the top of the walls [siege ramps] and ·devices to attack the walls [siege walls]. 23The people of Jerusalem will think this ·prediction is wrong [is a false omen/divination] because of their ·agreement with Babylon [*or* treaty with other nations; *or* covenant with God; Lsworn oaths/allegiance] But ·the king of Babylon will remind them of their rebellion [*or* the siege will remind them of their guilt] and they will be captured.

24"So this is what the Lord GOD says: 'You have ·shown how sinful you are [Lcaused your guilt to be remembered] by ·turning against the LORD [Luncovering your trangressions]. Your sins are ·seen [revealed] in all the things you do. Because of this proof against you, you will be taken captive by the enemy.

25" 'You ·unclean [profane; Critually] and evil ·leader [prince] of Israel, ·you will be killed [Lwhose day has come]! The time of your final punishment has come. 26This is what the Lord GOD says: Take off the royal turban, and remove the crown. Things will change. ·Those who are unimportant now will be made important [The lowly will be exalted], and ·those who are important now will be made unimportant [the exalted will be made lowly]. 27A ruin! A ruin! I will make it a ruin! ·This place will not be rebuilt [*or* The kingdom will not be restored] until the one comes ·who has a right to be king [to whom judgment belongs; Gen. 49:10]. Then I will give ·him that right [it to him].'

The Punishment of Ammon

28"And you, ·human [Tson of man; 2:1], prophesy and say: 'This is what the Lord GOD says about the people of Ammon and their ·insults [mockery; *or* humiliation]:

A sword, a sword
  is ·pulled out of its holder [drawn] ·to kill [for slaughter].
It is polished to ·destroy [consume],
  to flash like lightning!
29·Prophets [LThey] see false visions about you
  and ·prophesy lies [false divinations] about you.
The sword will be put on the necks
  of these ·unclean [profane; Critually] and ·evil [wicked] people.

Their ·day of judging [Lday] has come;
the time of final punishment has come.
30Put the sword back in its ·holder [sheath].
I will judge you
in the place where you were created,
in the land where you were born.
31I will pour out my anger against you
and ·blast you with [breathe/blow out] the fire of my anger.
I will hand you over to ·cruel [brutal] men,
experts in destruction.
32You will be fuel for the fire;
·you will die in [Lyour blood will be in the midst of] the land.
You will not be remembered,
because I, the LORD, have spoken.' "

The Sins of Jerusalem

22 The ·LORD spoke his word [Lword of the LORD came] to me,
saying: 2"And you, ·human [Tson of man; 2:1], will you judge?
Will you judge the city of ·murderers [bloodshed; CJerusalem]? Then tell
her about all her ·hateful [detestable; abominable] acts. 3You are to say:
'This is what the Lord GOD says: You are a city that ·kills those who come
to live there [Lsheds blood in her midst]. You ·make yourself unclean
[defile yourself; Critually] by making idols. 4You have become guilty of
·murder [bloodshed] and have become ·unclean [defiled] by your idols
which you have made. So you have brought your ·time of punishment
[Ldays] near; you have come to the end of your years. That is why I have
made you a ·shame [object of scorn] to the nations and ·why all lands
laugh at you [La mockery/laughingstock to all lands]. 5Those near and
those far away ·laugh at [mock] you with your ·bad [defiled] name, you
city full of ·confusion [turmoil].
6" 'See how each ·ruler [prince; leader] of Israel in you [CJerusalem; v.
2] has been trying to ·kill people [shed blood]. 7The people in you ·hate
[treat with contempt] their fathers and mothers. They ·mistreat [oppress]
the foreigners in you and wrong the ·orphans [fatherless] and widows in
you. 8You ·hate [despise] my holy things and ·dishonor [desecrate; profane; Critually] my Sabbaths. 9The ·lying [slanderous] men in you ·cause
the death of others [shed blood]. The people in you eat ·food offered to
idols at the mountain places of worship [Lon the mountains], and they
take part in ·sexual sins [Llewd/obscene acts among you]. 10The men in
you ·have sexual relations with their fathers' wives [Luncover their father's
nakedness] and ·with [Lviolate] women who are unclean [Critually], during their time of ·monthly bleeding [Limpurity]. 11One man in you does a
·hateful [detestable; abominable] act with his neighbor's wife, while
another has shamefully ·made his daughter-in-law unclean sexually
[Ldefiled his daughter-in-law; Critually]. And another ·forces his half sister
to have sexual relations [Lviolates his father's daughter] with him [Call
forbidden in the Law; Lev. 18:9, 15, 20]. 12The people in you take ·money
[bribes] to ·kill others [shed blood; Deut. 27:25]. You take ·interest [usury;
18:13, 17; Lev. 25:36] and profits and make profits by ·mistreating [extort-
ing] your neighbor. And you have forgotten me, says the Lord GOD.
13" '·So, Jerusalem, [LLook; TBehold] I will ·shake my fist [Lstrike my
hand] at you for ·stealing money [your dishonest gain] and for ·murder-
ing people [bloodshed]. 14Will ·you still be brave [Lyour heart stand] and

·strong [Lyour hands be strong] when I ·punish [deal with] you? I, the
Lord, have spoken, and I will act. 15I will scatter you among the nations
and spread you through the countries. ·That is how I will get rid of [LI will
remove] your uncleanness [Critually]. 16But you, yourself, will be ·dishon-
ored [defiled; profaned; Critually] in the ·sight [eyes] of the nations. Then
you will know that I am the Lord.' "

Israel Is Worthless

17The ·Lord spoke his word [Lword of the Lord came] to me, saying:
18"·Human [TSon of man; 2:1], the ·people [Lhouse] of Israel have become
·scum [dross; Cuseless] to me. They are like the ·copper [*or* bronze], tin,
iron, and lead left in the furnace when silver is purified. 19So this is what
the Lord God says: 'Because you have become ·scum [dross], I am going
to bring you together inside Jerusalem. 20Just as people put silver, ·copper
[*or* bronze], iron, lead, and tin together inside a furnace to melt them
down in a blazing fire, so I will gather you in my hot anger and put you
together in Jerusalem and melt you down. 21I will ·put [gather] you
together and ·make you feel [Lblow on you with] the ·heat [fire] of my
·anger [fury; wrath]. You will be melted down ·inside Jerusalem [Lin the
midst of it]. 22As silver is melted in a furnace, you will be melted inside
·the city [Lit]. Then you will know that I, the Lord, have poured out my
·anger [wrath] on you.' "

Sins of the People

23The ·Lord spoke his word [Lword of the Lord came] to me, saying:
24"·Human [TSon of man; 2:1], say to the land, 'You are a land that ·has
not had rain or [*or* is not cleansed with] showers ·when God is angry [Lin
the day of wrath/indignation].' 25Like a roaring lion that tears ·the animal
it has caught [its prey], Israel's ·rulers[n] [princes] ·make evil plans [con-
spire]. They have ·destroyed [devoured] lives and have taken treasure and
·valuable [precious] things. They have caused many women to become
widows. 26·Israel's [LHer; Its] priests do ·cruel things [violence] to my
·teachings [laws; instructions; LTorah] and ·do not honor [profane;
Critually] my holy things. They make no difference between holy and
·unholy [common; profane; Critually] things, and they teach there is no
difference between clean and unclean things [Critually]. They ·do not
remember [disregard; Lclose their eyes to] my Sabbaths, so I am ·dishon-
ored by [profaned among; Critually] them. 27Like wolves tearing ·a dead
animal [their prey], ·Jerusalem's leaders [Lher princes/officials] have
·killed people [Lshed blood and destroy lives] for profit. 28And the prophets ·try to cover this up by [whitewash their actions with; 13:10–15] false
visions and by lying ·messages [divinations]. They say, 'This is what the
Lord God says' when the Lord has not spoken. 29The people of the land
·cheat others [practice extortion] and ·steal [commit robbery]. They ·hurt
[oppress] the poor and needy. They ·cheat [mistreat; extort] foreigners
and ·do not treat them fairly [deny them justice].

30"I looked for someone to ·build up [repair; 13:5] the walls and to
stand before me ·where the walls are broken [in the gap/breach] ·to defend
these people [Lon behalf of the land] so I would not have to destroy them.
But I could not find anyone. 31So I ·let them see [poured out] my ·anger
[wrath]. I destroyed them with an anger that was like fire ·because of all
the things [Lbringing down on their heads all] they have done, says the
Lord God."

22:25 rulers Some Greek copies read "princes." Hebrew copies read "prophets."

Samaria and Jerusalem

23 The ·Lord spoke his word [[L]word of the Lord came] to me, saying: 2“·Human [[T]Son of man; 2:1], a woman had two daughters. 3While they were young, they went to Egypt and became prostitutes. They let men ·touch [fondle] and hold their virgin breasts. 4The older girl was named Oholah, and her sister was named Oholibah. They became my wives and had sons and daughters. Oholah is Samaria, and Oholibah is Jerusalem [[C]both names are related to the Hebrew word for “tent,” and refer to the two kingdoms of Israel and Judah].

5“While ·still my wife [[L]she was mine], ·Samaria [[L]Oholah] ·had sexual relations with other men [engaged in prostitution]. She ·had great sexual desire for [lusted after] her lovers, men from Assyria. The Assyrians were warriors ·and 6wore blue uniforms [clothed in blue]. They were all ·handsome [desirable] young men, ·captains [*or* governors] and ·lieutenants [commanders] riding on horseback. 7·Samaria [[L]She] became a prostitute for all the ·important [elite] men in Assyria and ·made herself unclean [defiled herself] with all the idols of everyone she desired. 8She ·continued [did not give up] the prostitution she began in Egypt. When she was young, she had slept with men, and they ·touched [fondled] her virgin breasts and ·had sexual relations with [[L]poured out their lust on] her.

9“So I handed her over to her lovers, the Assyrians, ·that she wanted so badly [for whom she lusted]. 10They ·stripped her naked [[L]uncovered her nakedness; 16:37] and took away her sons and daughters. Then they killed her with a sword [[C]referring to the fall of Samaria to the Assyrians in 722–721 BC]. ·Women everywhere began talking [It became notorious/a byword among women] about how she had been punished.

11“Her sister ·Jerusalem [[L]Oholibah; v. 4] saw what happened, but she became ·worse [more depraved/corrupt] than her sister in her sexual ·desire [lust] and prostitution. 12She also desired the Assyrians, who were all soldiers in ·beautiful uniforms [full dress; *or* full armor]—·handsome [desirable] young ·captains [*or* governors] and ·lieutenants [commanders] riding horses. 13I saw that both girls were alike; both were ·prostitutes [defiled; [C]ritually].

14“But ·Jerusalem went [[L]she increased her prostitution] even further. She saw carvings of ·Babylonian [[L]Chaldean] men on a wall. They wore red [Jer. 22:14] 15and had belts around their waists and turbans on their heads. They all looked like chariot officers ·born in Babylonia [[L]the image of sons of Babel, natives of Chaldea]. 16When she saw them, she ·wanted to have sexual relations with [lusted after] them and sent messengers to them in ·Babylonia [[L]Chaldea; [C]depicting Judah’s attempt at alliances with Babylon; 2 Kin. 20:12–15; 23:34—24:1]. 17So these Babylonian men came ·and had sexual relations with her [to her bed of love] and ·made her unclean [[L]defiled her with their lust; [C]ritually]. After that, she ·became sick of them [turned away in disgust]. 18But she ·continued her prostitution so openly that everyone knew about it [[L]uncovered her prostitution and uncovered her nakedness]. And I ·finally became sick of her [turned away from her in disgust], as I had her sister. 19But she remembered how she was a young prostitute in Egypt, so she took part in even more prostitution. 20She ·wanted men [lusted after lovers] ·who behaved like animals in their sexual desire [*or* whose genitals/[L]flesh were the size/[L]flesh of donkeys and seminal emission like that of horses]. 21In the same way you ·desired to do the sinful things you had done [longed for the lewdness of your youth] in Egypt. There men ·touched [fondled] and ·held [caressed] your young breasts.

God's Judgment on Jerusalem

22“So, ·Jerusalem [LOholibah; v. 4], this is what the Lord GOD says: You ·are tired of [turned in disgust from] your lovers. So [Llook; Tbehold] now I will ·make them angry with [Lstir them up against] you and ·have them attack [Lbring them against] you from all sides [Ca description of the siege of Jerusalem]. 23Men from Babylon and all ·Babylonia [Lthe Chaldeans] and men from Pekod, Shoa, and Koa attack you [Cpeople groups from the Mesopotamian region]. All the Assyrians will attack you: ·handsome [desirable] young ·captains [*or* governors] and ·lieutenants [commanders], all of them ·important men [officers and nobles] and all riding horses. 24Those men will attack with ·great armies [a host of people/nations] and with their weapons, chariots, and wagons. They will ·surround you [Ltake up positions against you on every side] with large and small shields and with helmets. And I will ·give them the right to punish you [Lassign judgment to them], and they will ·give you their own kind of punishment [*or* judge you by their own standards]. 25Then ·you will see how strong my anger can be [*or* I will direct my jealous anger against you] when they ·punish [deal with] you in their anger. They will cut off your noses and ears [Cacts of torture and humiliation]. They will ·take away [seize] your sons and daughters, and those who are left will be ·burned [consumed/devoured by fire]. 26They will ·take [strip] off your clothes and steal your beautiful jewelry. 27I will put a stop to the ·sinful life [lewd/obscene behavior] you began when you were in Egypt so that you will not ·desire it [*or* seek their help; Llift up your eyes to them] or remember Egypt anymore.

28“This is what the Lord GOD says: You became ·tired of [disgusted with] your lovers, but I am going to hand you over to those men you now hate. 29They will treat you with hate and take away everything you worked for, leaving you empty and naked. ·Everyone will know about the sinful things you did [LThe nakedness of your prostitution will be uncovered]. Your ·sexual sins [lewdness and promiscuity] 30have brought this on you. You have ·had sexual relations with [prostituted yourself with] the nations and ·made yourselves unclean [defiled yourself] by worshiping their idols. 31You ·did the same things your sister did [Lwent the way of your sister; vv. 9–10], so ·you will get the same punishment, like a bitter cup to drink [LI will put her cup in your hand].

32“This is what the Lord GOD says:

You will drink the same cup your sister did,
  and that cup is deep and wide [Cthe cup of judgment; Jer. 25:15–29].
·Everyone will make fun of you [You will be mocked and derided],
  because the cup ·is full [holds much].
33It will ·make you miserable and drunk [Lfill you with drunkenness and sorrow].
  It is the cup of ·fear [horror; *or* ruin] and ·ruin [devastation].
  It is the cup of your sister Samaria.
34You will drink ·everything in [Land drain] it,
  and then you will ·smash it [*or* chew on its pieces]
  and tear at your breasts.
I have spoken, says the Lord GOD.

35“So this is what the Lord GOD says: You have forgotten me and ·turned your back on me [Lcast me behind your back]. So you ·will be punished [must bear the consequences] for your ·sexual sins [Llewdness and prostitution].”

Judgment on Samaria and Jerusalem

36 The LORD said to me: "·Human [[T]Son of man; 2:1], will you judge
·Samaria [[L]Oholah] and ·Jerusalem [[L]Oholibah], ·showing [declaring to]
them their ·hateful [detestable; abominable] acts? 37 They are guilty of adultery and ·murder [[L]blood is on their hands]. They have taken part in adultery
with their idols. They even offered ·our children [[L]the children they bore to
me] as sacrifices in the fire to be food for these idols. 38 They have also done
this to me: They ·made my Temple unclean [defiled my sanctuary; [C]ritually]
at the same time they ·dishonored [defiled; profaned; [C]ritually] my Sabbaths.
39 They ·sacrificed [slaughtered] their children to their idols. Then they
entered my Temple at that very time to ·dishonor [desecrate; profane;
[C]ritually] it. That is what they did inside my ·Temple [[L]house]!
40 "They even sent for men from far away, who came after a messenger
was sent to them. You bathed yourselves for them, painted your eyes, and
put on jewelry [2 Kin. 9:30; Jer. 4:30]. 41 You sat on a ·fine bed [luxurious
couch] with a table set before it, on which you put my incense and my oil.
42 "There was the noise of a ·reckless [*or* carefree] crowd in the city.
Common people gathered, and ·drunkards [*or* Sabaeans; [C]inhabitants of
Sheba, in present-day Yemen] were brought from the ·desert [wilderness].
They put bracelets on the wrists of the two sisters and beautiful crowns
on their heads. 43 Then I said about the one who was worn out by her acts
of adultery, 'Let them continue their ·sexual sins [prostitution] with her.
·She is nothing but a prostitute [[L]…even her].' 44 They kept going to her as
they would go to a prostitute. So they continued to go to ·Samaria
[[L]Oholah] and ·Jerusalem [[L]Oholibah; v. 4], these ·shameful [lewd;
obscene] women. 45 But men who ·do right [are righteous] will ·punish
them as they punish [judge them with the judgment against] women who
take part in adultery and who ·murder people [shed blood], because they
are guilty of adultery and ·murder [[L]blood is on their hands].
46 "This is what the Lord GOD says: Bring together a mob against
·Samaria and Jerusalem [[L]them] and hand them over to ·be frightened
and robbed [terror and plunder]. 47 Let the ·mob [army; host] stone them,
and let them cut them down with their swords. Let them kill their sons
and daughters and burn their houses down.
48 "So I will put an end to ·sexual sins [lewdness; obscenity] in the land.
Then all women will be warned, and they will not ·do the sexual sins you
have done [practice the same wickedness]. 49 ·You will be punished [[L]They
will repay you] for your ·sexual sins [lewdness; obscenity] and the sin of
worshiping idols. Then you will know that I am the Lord GOD."

The Pot and the Meat

24 The ·LORD spoke his word [[L]word of the LORD came] to me in
the ninth year [[C]since King Jehoiachin's exile (1:2)], in the
tenth month, on the tenth day of the month [[C]January 15, 588 BC]. He
said: 2 "·Human [[T]Son of man; 2:1], write down ·today's date [[L]the name
of this day], this very ·date [[L]day]. The king of Babylon has ·surrounded
[laid siege to] Jerusalem this very day. 3 And tell a ·story [parable] to the
·people who refuse to obey me [[L]rebellious house]. Say to them: 'This is
what the Lord GOD says:

Put on the pot; put it on
  and pour water in it.
4 Put in the pieces of meat,
  the best pieces—the ·legs [thighs] and the shoulders.
  Fill it with the best bones.

5 Take the best of the flock,
and pile ·wood [*or* bones] under the pot.
Boil the pieces of meat
until even the bones are cooked.
6" 'This is what the Lord GOD says:
·How terrible it will be for [LWoe to] the city of ·murderers [Lblood]!
·How terrible it will be for [LWoe to] the ·rusty [corroded; rotted] pot
whose ·rust [corrosion; rot] will not come off!
Take the meat out of it, piece by piece.
·Don't choose any special piece [*or* Don't cast lots for any of it].

7" 'The blood ·from her killings [Lshe shed] is still in ·the city [her midst].
She poured the blood on the bare rock.
She did not pour it on the ground
where dust would cover it.
8To stir up my ·anger [wrath] and ·revenge [vengeance],
I put ·the blood she spilled [Lher blood] on the bare rock
so it will not be covered.
9" 'So this is what the Lord GOD says:
·How terrible it will be for [LWoe to] the city of ·murderers [Lblood]!
I myself will pile the wood high [Cfor burning].
10Pile up the wood
and ·light [kindle] the fire.
Cook the meat well.
·Mix in the spices [*or* Pour out all the broth],
and let the bones burn.
11Then set the empty pot on the coals
so it may become hot and its copper sides glow.
·The dirty scum stuck inside it [So that its impurities/uncleanness]
may then melt
and its ·rust [corrosion; rot] burn away.
12·But efforts to clean the pot have failed [LIt has wearied itself with toil].
Its heavy ·rust [corrosion; rot] cannot be removed,
·even in the fire [*or* Into the fire with its rust/corrosion!]).
13" 'By your ·sinful action [lewdness; obscenity] you have become
·unclean [defiled; Critually]]. I wanted to cleanse you, but you are still
unclean. You will never be cleansed from your sin until my ·anger [wrath]
against you is ·carried out [satisfied; exhausted].
14" 'I, the LORD, have spoken. The time has come for me to act. I will not
·hold back punishment [relent] or feel pity or ·change my mind [*or* be
sorry]. I will judge you by your ways and actions, says the Lord GOD.' "

The Death of Ezekiel's Wife

15Then the ·LORD spoke his word [Lword of the LORD came] to me, saying: 16"·Human [TSon of man; 2:1], I am going to take ·your wife from
you, the woman you look at with love [Lthe delight of your eyes]. ·She will
die suddenly [...with a stroke/blow/jolt], but you must not ·be sad
[lament] or ·cry loudly [weep] for her or shed any tears. 17Groan silently;
do not ·cry loudly [mourn] for the dead. ·Tie [Wrap; Bind] on your turban [Cnormally taken off for mourning], and put your sandals on your
feet. Do not cover your ·face [lower face; *or* mustache], and do not eat the
·food people eat when they are sad about a death [*or* food brought by others; Lbread of men]."

18 So I spoke to the people in the morning, and my wife died in the evening. The next morning I did as I had been commanded.

19 Then the people asked me, "·Tell [LWon't you tell…?] us, what do the things you are doing mean for us?"

20 Then I said to them, "The ·Lord spoke his word [Lword of the Lord came] to me. He said, 21 'Say to the ·people [Lhouse] of Israel, This is what the Lord God says: I am going to ·dishonor [desecrate; profane; Critually] my ·Temple [sanctuary]. ·You are proud of the strength it gives you [L…the pride of your power] and ·you look at it with love and tenderness [L…the delight of your eyes and the desire of your soul]. But your sons and daughters that you left behind in Jerusalem will fall dead by the sword. 22 When that happens, you will act as I have: you will not cover your ·face [lower face; *or* mustache], and you will not eat the ·food people eat when they are sad about a death [*or* food brought by others; Lbread of men]. 23 Your turbans will stay on your heads, and your sandals on your feet. You will not ·cry loudly [mourn or weep], but you will rot away ·in your sins [*or* because of your sins/iniquities] and groan to each other. 24 So Ezekiel is to be an ·example [sign; object lesson] for you. You will do all the same things he did. When all this happens, you will know that I am the Lord God.'

25 "And as for you, ·human [Tson of man; 2:1], this is how it will be. I will take away ·the Temple that gives them strength and joy, that makes them proud [Ltheir stronghold, their joy, and glory]. ·They look at it with love, and it makes them happy [L…the delight of their eyes and the desire of their soul; v. 21]. And I will take away their sons and daughters also. 26 ·At that time [LOn that day] a ·person who escapes [fugitive] will come to you with information for you to hear. 27 ·At that time [LOn that day] your mouth will be opened. You will speak and be silent no more. So you will be a sign for them, and they will know that I am the Lord."

Prophecy Against Ammon

25 The ·Lord spoke his word [Lword of the Lord came] to me, saying: 2 "·Human [TSon of man; 2:1], ·look [Lset your face] toward the people of Ammon and prophesy against them. 3 Say to them, 'Hear the word of the Lord God. This is what the Lord God says: You ·were glad [Lsaid, "Aha!"] when my ·Temple [sanctuary] was ·dishonored [defiled; profaned; Critually], when the land of Israel was ·ruined [made desolate], and when the ·people [Lhouse] of Judah ·were taken away as captives [went into exile]. 4 So [LLook; TBehold] I am going to give you to the people of the East ·to be theirs [Las a possession]. They will set up their camps among you and make their ·homes [dwelling places] among you. They will eat your fruit and drink your milk. 5 I will make the city of Rabbah a pasture for camels and the land of Ammon a resting place for sheep. Then you will know that I am the Lord. 6 For this is what the Lord God says: You have clapped your hands and stamped your feet; you have ·laughed about all the insults you made [Lrejoiced with the scorn/malice of your soul] against the land of Israel. 7 So I will ·use my power [Lstretch out my hand] against you. I will give you to the nations as ·if you were treasures taken in war [plunder]. I will cut you off from the ·nations [peoples] and wipe you out of the ·countries [lands], and I will destroy you. Then you will know that I am the Lord.'

Prophecy Against Moab and Edom

8 "This is what the Lord God says: 'Moab and ·Edom [LSeir] say, "[LLook; TBehold] The ·people [Lhouse] of Judah are like all the other nations." 9 So I am going to ·take away the cities that protect Moab's borders [open up

Moab's flank, starting with its frontier towns], the ·best cities in [Lglory of] that land: Beth Jeshimoth, Baal Meon, and Kiriathaim. 10 Then I will give Moab, along with the Ammonites, to the people of the East as their possession. Then, along with the Ammonites, Moab will not be a nation anymore. 11 So I will ·punish [execute judgments upon] the people of Moab, and they will know that I am the LORD.'

Prophecy Against Edom

12 "This is what the Lord GOD says: 'Edom took ·revenge [vengeance] on the ·people [Lhouse] of Judah, and the Edomites became guilty because of it. 13 So this is what the Lord GOD says: I will ·use my power [Lstretch out my hand] against Edom, killing every human and animal in it. And I will ·destroy [lay waste; make desolate] Edom all the way from Teman [Cdistrict in central Edom] to Dedan [Cterritory in southern Edom] as they ·die in battle [Lfall by the sword]. 14 I will use my people Israel to take revenge on Edom. ·So the Israelites will do to Edom what my hot anger demands [L… according to my anger and according to my wrath]. Then the Edomites will know what my ·revenge [vengeance] feels like, says the Lord GOD.'

Prophecy Against Philistia

15 "This is what the Lord GOD says: 'The Philistines have taken revenge with ·hateful hearts [malice in their souls]. Because of their ·strong [*or* ancient; *or* never-ending] hatred, they have tried to destroy Judah. 16 So this is what the Lord GOD says: [LLook; TBehold] I will ·use my power [Lstretch out my hand] against the Philistines. I will ·kill [cut off] the Kerethites, and I will destroy those people still alive on the ·coast of the Mediterranean Sea [seacoast]. 17 I will do great acts of ·revenge [vengeance] to them and punish them in my anger. They will know that I am the LORD when I take ·revenge [vengeance] on them.'"

Prophecy Against Tyre

26 It was the eleventh year [Csince King Jehoiachin's exile (1:2); 586 BC], on the first day of the month. The ·LORD spoke his word [Lword of the LORD came] to me, saying: 2 "·Human [TSon of man; 2:1], the city of Tyre has spoken against Jerusalem: 'The ·city that traded with [Lgate of] the nations is ·destroyed [broken]. ·Now we can be the trading center [LIts doors have swung open to me]. Since ·the city of Jerusalem [Lit] is ruined, ·we can make money [LI will be filled].' 3 So this is what the Lord GOD says: [LLook; TBehold] I am against you, Tyre. I will bring many nations against you, like the sea ·beating its waves on your island shores [Lbrings up its waves]. 4 They will destroy the walls of Tyre and pull down her towers. I will also scrape away her ·ruins [rubble; soil] and make her a bare rock. 5 Tyre will be ·an island [Lin the midst of the sea] where fishermen dry their nets. I have spoken, says the Lord GOD. ·The nations will steal treasures from Tyre [LShe will become plunder for the nations]. 6 Also, her ·villages [settlements; Ldaughters] on the ·shore [mainland] across from the island will be ·destroyed by war [Lslaughtered by the sword]. Then they will know that I am the LORD.

Nebuchadnezzar to Attack Tyre

7 "This is what the Lord GOD says: [LLook; TBehold] I will bring a king from the north against Tyre. He is Nebuchadnezzar king of Babylon, ·the greatest king [Lking of kings], with his horses, chariots, horsemen, and a great army. 8 He will destroy your ·villages [settlements; Ldaughters] on the ·shore across from the island [mainland]. He will set up ·devices to attack you [siege works]. He will build a ·road of earth to the top of the walls [siege ramp]. He will raise his shields against you. 9 He will ·bring logs to pound through [direct blows of bat-

tering rams against] your city walls, and he will break down your
towers with his ·iron bars [*or* hammers; Lswords]. 10His horses will be
so many that they will cover you with their dust. Your walls will shake
at the noise of horsemen, wagons, and chariots. The king of Babylon
will enter your city gates as men enter a city where the walls are broken
through. 11The hoofs of his horses will ·run over [trample] your streets.
He will kill your ·army [*or* people] with the sword, and your strong pillars will fall down to the ground. 12Also, his men will ·take away
[plunder] your riches and will ·steal [loot] ·the things you sell [your
merchandise]. They will break down your walls and destroy your ·nice
[pleasant; luxurious] houses. They will throw your stones, ·wood [tim-
ber; trees], and ·trash [rubble; *or* soil] into the sea. 13So I will stop your
songs; the music of your ·harps [lyres] will not be heard anymore. 14I
will make you a bare rock, and you will be a place for ·drying [spread-
ing] fishing nets. You will not be built again, because I, the LORD, have
spoken, says the Lord GOD.
15"This is what the Lord GOD says to Tyre: ·The people who live along
the seacoast will [LWon't the coastlands…?] ·shake with fear [tremble]
·when they hear about your defeat [*or* at the sound of your fall]. ·The
injured will [L…when the wounded] groan as the ·killing [slaughter]
takes place in you. 16Then all the ·leaders [princes] of the ·seacoast [Lsea]
will get down from their thrones, take off their ·beautiful needlework
[embroidered] clothes, and ·show how afraid they are [Lclothe themselves
with trembling]. They will sit on the ground and tremble ·all the time
[continuously], ·shocked [appalled; aghast] when they see you. 17They
will begin singing a ·funeral song [lament; dirge] about you and will say
to you:

'Famous city [CTyre was a great maritime power], you have been
destroyed!
You have lost your sea power!
You and your ·people [inhabitants]
had great power on the seas.
You made everyone around you
afraid of you.
18Now the ·people who live by the coast [coastlands will] tremble,
·now that [Lon the day] you have fallen.
The ·islands [*or* coastlands] of the sea
are ·afraid [terrified; dismayed] ·because you have been defeated [at
your demise/passing].'

19"This is what the Lord GOD says: I will make you ·an empty city [des-
olate; a ruin], like cities that ·have no people living in them [are
uninhabited/deserted]. I will bring the ·deep ocean waters [Ldeep] over
you, and the ·Mediterranean Sea [Lgreat waters] will cover you. 20At that
time I will send you down to the ·place of the dead [pit] to ·join those who
died long ago [the people of old/antiquity]. I will make you live with the
dead ·below the earth [in the underworld] ·in places that are like old ruins
[among ancient ruins]. You will not ·come back from there [*or* be inhab-
ited] or have any place in the ·world [land] of the living again. 21·Other
people will be afraid of what happened to you [*or* I will bring you to a
terrible end], and it will be the end of you. People will look for you, but
they will never find you again, says the Lord GOD."

A Funeral Song for Tyre

27 **The ·LORD spoke his word** [Lword of the LORD came] **to me, saying:** [2]**"·Human** [TSon of man; 2:1]**, sing a ·funeral song** [lament; dirge] **for the city of Tyre.** [3]**Speak to Tyre, which ·has ports for the Mediterranean Sea** [Lsits at the gateway to the Sea] **and is a ·place for trade** [merchant] **for the people of many coastlands. 'This is what the Lord GOD says:**

Tyre, you have said,
"I am ·like a beautiful ship [Lperfect in beauty]**."**
[4]**·You were at home on** [LYour borders were in the heart of] **the high seas.**
Your builders made your beauty perfect.
[5]**They made all your boards**
of fir trees from ·Mount Hermon [LSenir]**.**
They took a cedar tree from Lebanon
to make a ship's mast for you.
[6]**They made your oars**
from oak trees from Bashan.
They made your deck
from cypress trees from the coast of ·Cyprus [LKittim]
·and set ivory into it [inlaid with ivory]**.**
[7]**Your sail of ·linen with designs sewed on it** [embroidered linen] **came from Egypt**
and ·became like a flag for you [served as your banner]**.**
Your ·cloth shades over the deck [awnings] **were blue and purple**
and came from the ·island [coastlands] **of ·Cyprus** [LElisha; Ca city on the east side of Cyprus and an older name for the island]**.**
[8]**·Men** [Residents; *or* Leaders] **from Sidon** [Ca major city twenty-five miles north of Tyre] **and Arvad** [Ca city on the Phoenician coast, north of Sidon] **used oars to row you.**
Tyre, your skilled men were ·the sailors [*or* captains; pilots] **on your deck.**
[9]**·Workers** [*or* Veteran craftsmen; LElders] **of Byblos were with you,**
putting caulk in your ship's seams.
All the ships of the sea and their sailors
came alongside to trade with you.

[10]**" 'Men of Persia, ·Lydia** [LLud; Ca city in Asia Minor]**, and ·Put** [Cpresent-day Libya, in North Africa]
were warriors in your ·navy [army]
and hung their shields and helmets on your sides.
They ·made you look beautiful [gave you splendor]**.**
[11]**Men of Arvad** [v. 8] **and ·Cilicia** [LHelech; Csoutheast Asia Minor]
guarded your city walls all around.
Men of Gammad [Can unknown location, perhaps northern Asia Minor]
were in your watchtowers
and hung their shields around your walls.
They made your beauty perfect.

[12]**" 'People of Tarshish** [Cprobably in southern Spain; Jonah 1:3] **became traders for you because of your great wealth. They ·traded** [exchanged] **your goods for silver, iron, tin, and lead.**

[13]**" 'People of ·Greece** [LJavan]**, Tubal, and Meshech** [Cboth in Asia Minor; 32:26] **became merchants for you. They traded your goods for slaves and items of bronze.**

14“ ‘People of Beth Togarmah [Ceastern Asia Minor; present-day
Armenia] traded your goods for ·work [*or* chariot] horses, war horses
[Ceither chariot of cavalry horses], and mules.
15“ ‘·People of [LSons of] Rhodes[n] [Can island off southwest coast of
Asia Minor] became merchants for you, selling your goods on many
coastlands. They brought back ivory tusks and ·valuable black wood
[ebony] as your payment.
16“ ‘People of Aram[n] [CSyria] ·became traders for [did business with]
you, because you had so many good things to sell. They traded your
goods for turquoise, purple cloth, ·cloth with designs sewed on [embroi-
dered work], fine linen, coral, and rubies.
17“ ‘People of Judah and Israel became merchants for you. They traded
your goods for wheat from Minnith [Ca town in Ammon, east of the
Jordan River], and for ·meal [millet], honey, olive oil, and balm.
18-19“ ‘People of Damascus [Cthe capital of Aram (Syria)] became traders
for you because you have many good things and great wealth. They traded
your goods for wine from Helbon [Ca town north of Damascus], wool from
Zahar [Can area northwest of Damascus], and barrels of wine[n] from Izal
[Cpossibly present-day Yemen]. They received wrought iron, cassia [Ca tree
similar to the cinnamon tree; Ex. 30:24], and ·sugar cane [*or* calamus; Ca
fragrant reed] in payment for your ·good things [wares; merchandise].
20“ ‘People of Dedan [Ca territory in southern Edom] became merchants for you, trading saddle blankets for riding.
21“ ‘People of Arabia and all the ·rulers [princes] of Kedar became traders for you. They received lambs, ·male sheep [rams], and goats in
payment for you.
22“ ‘The merchants of Sheba [Cthe southwestern Arabian peninsula,
present-day Yemen] and Raamah [Ca city in southern Arabia] became
merchants for you. They traded your goods for all the best spices, ·valu-
able gems [precious stones], and gold.
23“ ‘People of Haran [Ca city in present-day eastern Turkey], Canneh
[Cunknown location], Eden [Cin Mesopotamia near Haran], and the traders of Sheba [v. 22], Asshur [Ca city south of Nineveh], and Kilmad [Can
unknown location] became merchants for you. 24They were paid with the
best clothes, blue cloth, ·cloth with designs sewed on [embroidered work],
carpets of many colors, ·and tightly wound ropes [*or* rolled up and tied
with cords; *or* made of tightly knotted cords].

25“ ‘·Trading ships [*or* The ships of Tarshish]
carried ·the things you sold [your merchandise].
You were like a ship full of heavy cargo
in the ·middle [Lheart] of the sea.
26The men who rowed you
brought you out into the high seas,
but the east wind broke you to pieces
in the ·middle [Lheart] of the sea.
27Your wealth, your ·trade [products], your goods,
your seamen, your ·sailors [*or* captains], your ·workers [*or* caulkers],
your traders, your ·warriors [soldiers],
and everyone else on board

27:15 Rhodes Greek copies read "Rhodes." Hebrew copies read "Dedan." **27:16 Aram** Some Hebrew copies read "Edom." **27:18–19 barrels of wine** Some Hebrew copies read "Vedan and Javan."

sank into the ·sea [Lheart of the sea]
on the day ·your ship was wrecked [Lof your fall].
28The ·people on the shore shake with fear [Lcountryside shakes; *or* waves surge]
when your ·sailors [*or* captains] cry out.
29All the men who row
·leave [disembark from; *or* abandon] their ships;
the seamen and the ·sailors [*or* captains] of other ships
stand on the shore.
30They cry loudly about you;
they cry ·very much [bitterly].
They throw dust on their heads
and roll in ashes.
31They shave their heads for you,
and they put on ·rough cloth [burlap; sackcloth; Csigns of sorrow and distress].
They ·cry and sob for you [weep over you with bitter souls];
they ·cry loudly [mourn bitterly].
32And in their ·loud crying [wailing]
they sing a ·funeral song [lament; dirge] for you:
"·No one was ever destroyed [LWho was…?] like Tyre,
·surrounded by [*or* like a tower in the middle of; *or* now silent in the midst of] the sea."
33When the goods you traded went out over the seas,
you ·met the needs of [satisfied] many nations.
With your great wealth and ·goods [merchandise],
you made kings of the earth rich.
34But now you are ·broken [shipwrecked; shattered] by the sea
·and have sunk to the bottom [Lin the depths of the waters].
Your ·goods [merchandise] and all the people on board
have gone down with you.
35All those who live along the ·shore [coastland]
are ·shocked [appalled; aghast] by what happened to you.
Their kings are ·terribly afraid [horrified],
and their faces ·show their fear [are troubled/contorted].
36The traders among the nations hiss at you.
You have ·come to a terrible end [*or* become a horror],
and you are gone forever.'"

Prophecy Against the King of Tyre

28 The ·LORD spoke his word [Lword of the LORD came] to me, saying: 2"·Human [TSon of man; 2:1], say to the ruler of Tyre:
'This is what the Lord GOD says:
Because ·you are [Lyour heart is] proud,
you say, "I am a god.
I sit on the ·throne [seat] of a god
in the ·middle [Lheart] of the seas."
You think you are as wise as a god,
but you are a ·human [mortal; man], not a god.
3[LLook; TBehold] You ·think you are [Lare] wiser than Daniel [14:14].
·You think you can find out all secrets [LNo secret is hidden from you].
4Through your wisdom and understanding
you have made yourself rich.

You have ·gained [gathered] gold and silver
·and have saved it in [Lin] your ·storerooms [treasuries].
5Through your great skill in trading,
you have made your riches grow.
·You are too [LYour heart is] proud
because of your riches.
6"'So this is what the Lord GOD says:
[LBecause] You think you are wise
like a god,
7·but [Ltherefore, look/behold] I will bring foreign people against you,
the ·cruelest [most ruthless] nations.
They will draw their swords
·and destroy all that your wisdom has built [Lagainst your beauty and wisdom],
and they will ·dishonor [defile] your ·greatness [splendor].
8They will ·kill you [Lbring you down to the pit];
you will die a ·terrible [violent] death
·like those who are killed at sea [*or* in the heart of the sea].
9·While they are killing you [LIn the presence of those killing you],
·you will not [Lwill you…?] be able to say anymore, "I am a god."
You will be only a human, not a god,
·when your murderers kill you [Lin the hands of those who kill you].
10You will die ·like an unclean person [Lthe death of the uncircumcised];
·foreigners will kill you [L…in the hands of strangers/foreigners].
I have spoken, says the Lord GOD.'"

11The ·LORD spoke his word [Lword of the LORD came] to me, saying:
12"·Human [TSon of man; 2:1], sing a ·funeral song [lament; dirge] for the
king of Tyre. Say to him: 'This is what the Lord GOD says:
You were ·an example [the seal/signet] of what was perfect,
full of wisdom and perfect in beauty.
13You ·had a wonderful life,
as if you were in Eden [Lwere in Eden], the garden of God [Clike Adam; Gen. 1—2].
Every valuable gem ·was on [covered] you:
·ruby [*or* carnelian], ·topaz [*or* chysolite], and ·emerald [*or* diamond],
·yellow quartz [*or* chrysolite], onyx, and jasper,
·sapphire [*or* lapis lazuli], turquoise, and ·chrysolite [*or* beryl; *or* emerald].
Your ·jewelry [settings and mounts] was made of gold.
It was prepared on the day you were created.
14I appointed a ·living creature [Lcherub] to guard you.
I put you on the holy mountain of God.
You walked among the ·gems that shined like fire [fiery stones].
15·Your life was right and good [LYou were blameless in your ways]
from the day you were created,
until ·evil [wickedness; unrighteousness] was found in you.
16Because you traded with countries ·far away [*or* in abundance],
you ·learned to be cruel [Lwere filled with violence], and you sinned.
So I ·threw you down [banished you] in ·disgrace [*or* defilement] from the mountain of God.
And the ·living creature [Lcherub] who guarded you
·forced you out [expelled you] from among the ·gems that shined like fire [fiery stones].

[17]·You became too [LYour heart was] **proud**
because of your beauty.
You ·**ruined** [corrupted] **your wisdom**
because of your ·**greatness** [splendor].
I threw you down to the ground.
·**Your example taught a lesson to** [*or* I made a spectacle of you before]
other kings.
[18]**You** ·**dishonored** [desecrated; profaned; Critually] **your** ·**places of worship** [sanctuaries]
through your many sins and dishonest trade.
So I ·**set on fire the place where you lived** [Lsent fire out from your midst],
and the fire ·**burned you up** [consumed you].
I turned you into ashes on the ground
·**for all those watching to see** [Lbefore the eyes of all who saw you].
[19]**All the nations who knew you**
are ·**shocked** [appalled; aghast] **about you.**
Your punishment was so terrible,
and you are gone forever.'"

Prophecy Against Sidon

[20]**The** ·**Lord spoke his word** [Lword of the Lord came] **to me, saying:**
[21]"·**Human** [TSon of man; 2:1], ·**look** [Lset your face] **toward the city of**
Sidon and prophesy against her. [22]**Say: 'This is what the Lord God says:**
I am against you, Sidon,
and I will show my glory ·**among** [*or* within] **you** [Chis manifest presence].
People will know that I am the Lord
when I ·**have punished Sidon** [Lexecute judgments against her];
I will show my holiness ·**by defeating** [Lin] **her.**
[23]**I will send** ·**diseases** [a plague/pestilence] **to Sidon,**
and blood will flow in her streets.
·**Those who are wounded** [*or* The slain] ·**in Sidon will fall dead** [Lwill fall in her midst],
·**attacked from** [Lby the sword against it on] **all sides.**
Then they will know that I am the Lord.

God Will Help Israel

[24]" '**No more will neighboring nations be like** ·**thorny branches** [prick-
ling briars] **or sharp** ·**stickers** [thorns] **to** ·**hurt** [Ltreat with contempt/
scorn the house of] **Israel. Then they will know that I am the Lord God.**
[25]" '**This is what the Lord God says: I will gather the** ·**people** [Lhouse] **of**
Israel from the nations where they are scattered. I will show my holiness
·**when the nations see what I do for my people** [Lin them in the sight of the
nations]. **Then they will live in their own land—the land I gave to my servant**
Jacob. [26]**They will live safely in the land and will build houses and plant vine-**
yards. They will live in safety after I have ·**punished** [executed judgments
against] **all the nations around who** ·**hate them** [treat them with contempt;
scorn them]. **Then they will know that I am the Lord their God.'"**

Prophecy Against Egypt

29 **It was the tenth year** [Csince King Jehoiachin's exile (1:2)], **in**
the tenth month, on the twelfth day of the month [CJanuary
7, 587 BC]. **The** ·**Lord spoke his word** [Lword of the Lord came] **to me,**
saying: [2]"·**Human** [TSon of man; 2:1], ·**look** [Lset your face] **toward the**
king of Egypt, and prophesy against him and all Egypt. [3]**Say: 'This is**
what the Lord God says:

[LLook; TBehold] I am against you, Pharaoh, king of Egypt.
You are like a great ·crocodile [*or* monster; *or* dragon] that lies in the Nile River.
You say, "The Nile is mine;
I made it for myself."
4But I will put hooks in your jaws,
and I will make the fish of the Nile stick to your ·sides [scales].
I will pull you up out of your ·rivers [streams],
with all the fish of your streams sticking to your ·sides [scales].
5I will leave you in the ·desert [wilderness],
you and all the fish from your ·rivers [streams].
You will fall onto the ·ground [open field];
you will not be picked up or ·buried [Lgathered].
I have given you to the ·wild animals [Lbeasts of the earth]
and to the birds of the sky for food.
6Then all the people who live in Egypt will know that I am the LORD.

" '·Israel tried to lean on you for help, but you were like a crutch made
out of a weak stalk of grass [LBecause you were a reed staff for the house of
Israel…; Is. 36:6]. 7When their hands grabbed you, you ·splintered [broke]
and tore open their shoulders. When they leaned on you, you ·broke [splin-
tered] and made all their ·backs twist [*or* legs go wobbly; *or* loins shake].

8" 'So this is what the Lord GOD says: I will ·cause an enemy to attack
[Lbring a sword against] you and kill your people and animals. 9Egypt will
become an ·empty desert [desolate wasteland]. Then they will know that
I am the LORD.

" 'Because you said, "The Nile River is mine, and I have made it," 10I am
against you and your ·rivers [streams]. I will destroy the land of Egypt and
make it an ·empty desert [desolate wasteland] from Migdol [Cin the north]
to Aswan [Cin the south], all the way to the border of Cush [CEthiopia].
11No ·person or animal will walk [Lfoot of man shall pass through it and no
foot of beast will pass] through it, and no one will live in Egypt for forty
years. 12I will make the land of Egypt ·the most deserted country of all [La
desolation among desolate lands]. Her cities will be ·the most deserted of
all [a desolation among] ruined cities for forty years. I will scatter the
Egyptians among the nations, spreading them among the countries.

13" 'This is what the Lord GOD says: After forty years I will gather Egypt
from the nations where they have been scattered. 14I will ·bring back the
Egyptian captives [restore the fortunes of Egypt] and make them return
to ·southern Egypt [Lthe land of Pathros], to the land ·they came from [of
their ancestry/origin]. They will become a ·weak [lowly; insignificant]
kingdom there. 15It will be the ·weakest [most lowly/insignificant] kingdom, and it will never again ·rule [Lexalt itself over] other nations. I will
make it so ·weak [small] it will never again rule over the nations. 16The
Israelites will never again ·depend on [rely on; have confidence in] Egypt.
Instead, ·Egypt's punishment [Lit] will remind the Israelites of their sin in
turning to Egypt for help. Then they will know that I am the Lord GOD.' "

Egypt Is Given to Babylon

17It was the twenty-seventh year [Csince King Jehoiachin's exile (1:2)],
in the first month, on the first day of the month [CApril 26, 571 BC]. The
·LORD spoke his word [Lword of the LORD came] to me, saying: 18"·Human
[TSon of man; 2:1], Nebuchadnezzar king of Babylon made his army
·fight [Llabor] hard against Tyre. Every soldier's head was rubbed bare,

and every shoulder was rubbed raw. But Nebuchadnezzar and his army gained ·nothing [*or* no wages] from ·fighting Tyre [Lthe labor he performed against her]. 19So this is what the Lord GOD says: I will give the land of Egypt to Nebuchadnezzar king of Babylon. He will ·take away Egypt's people and its wealth and its treasures [Lcarry off its wealth and loot and plunder it] as pay for his army. 20I am giving Nebuchadnezzar the land of Egypt as ·a reward [compensation] for working hard for me, says the Lord GOD.

21"·At that time [LOn that day] I will ·make Israel grow strong again [Lcause a horn to sprout for the house of Israel; Ps. 132:17], and I will ·let you, Ezekiel, speak to them [Lgive you an open mouth among them]. Then they will know that I am the LORD."

Egypt Will Be Punished

30 The ·LORD spoke his word [Lword of the LORD came] to me, saying: 2"·Human [TSon of man; 2:1], prophesy and say, 'This is what the Lord GOD says:

·Cry [Wail] ·and say [Alas; LHah],
"·The terrible day is coming [L...for the day]."
3 [LFor] The day is near;
the ·LORD's day of judging [LDay of the LORD] is near.
It is a ·cloudy day [day of clouds; Cperhaps storm clouds, or indicating the presence of God; Joel 2:2; Ex. 19:9]
and a time ·when the nations will be judged [Lfor the nations].
4An ·enemy will attack [Lsword will come against] Egypt,
and Cush [CEthiopia] will ·tremble with fear [be in anguish].
When the ·killing begins [Lslain fall] in Egypt,
her wealth will be ·taken away [carried off],
and her foundations will be torn down.

5Cush, Put, ·Lydia [LLud; 27:10], all ·Arabia [*or* all the foreigners; *or* all the mercenaries], ·Libya [LKub], and ·some of my people who had made an agreement with Egypt [*or* the people of allied lands; Lthe sons of the land of the covenant] will fall ·dead in war [Lby the sword with them].

6" 'This is what the LORD says:
·Those who fight on Egypt's side [Egypt's supporters] will fall.
The power she is proud of will ·be lost [collapse; come down].
From Migdol [Cin northern Egypt] to ·Aswan [LSyene; Cin southern Egypt],
the people will fall ·dead in war [Lby the sword]
says the Lord GOD.
7They will be ·the most deserted [Ldesolate in the midst of desolate] lands.
Egypt's cities will be ·the worst [Lin the midst] of cities that lie in ruins.
8Then they will know that I am the LORD
when I set fire to Egypt
and when all ·those nations on her side [her helpers/allies] are crushed.

9" '·At that time [LOn that day] I will send messengers in ships to frighten Cush [CEthiopia], which ·now feels safe [is over-confident; *or* is complacent]. ·The people of Cush will tremble with fear [LAnguish will come upon them] ·when Egypt is punished [Lin the day of Egypt]. And [Llook; Tbehold] that time is sure to come.

[10]" 'This is what the Lord GOD says:
I will destroy ·great numbers of people in [Lthe hordes of] Egypt
·through the power [Lby the hand] of Nebuchadnezzar king of Babylon.
[11]Nebuchadnezzar and his ·army [*or* people],
the ·cruelest army [most ruthless] of any nation,
will be brought in to destroy the land.
They will draw their swords against Egypt
and will fill the land with ·those they kill [the slain].
[12]I will make the streams of the Nile River become dry land,
and then I will sell the land to evil people.
I will ·destroy [desolate] the land and everything in it
through the ·power [Lhand] of foreigners.
I, the LORD, have spoken.

Egypt's Idols Are Destroyed

[13]" 'This is what the Lord GOD says:
I will destroy the idols
and ·take away [put an end to] the ·statues of gods from the city of [Limages in] Memphis.
There will no longer be a ·leader [prince] in the land of Egypt,
and I will spread fear through the land of Egypt.
[14]I will make ·southern Egypt [LPathros] ·empty [a desolation]
and ·start a fire in [*or* set fire to] Zoan
and ·punish [execute judgment on] Thebes.
[15]And I will pour out my anger against Pelusium [Ca fortess in the eastern delta of the Nile River],
the ·strong place [stronghold] of Egypt.
I will ·destroy [cut off] ·great numbers of people in [the hordes/ armies of] Thebes.
[16]I will set fire to Egypt.
Pelusium [v. 15] will ·be in great pain [writhe in agony].
·The walls of Thebes will be broken open [Thebes will be breached],
and Memphis will ·have troubles [*or* face enemies] every day.
[17]The young men of ·Heliopolis [LOn; Csix miles northeast of Cairo] and Bubastis [Cthe capital of northern Egypt; forty miles northeast of Cairo]
will fall dead ·in war [Lby the sword],
and ·the people [*or* the cities; Lthey] will be taken away as captives.
[18]In Tahpanhes [Cin northeast Egypt] the day will be dark
when I break ·Egypt's power [Lthe yoke of Egypt].
Then ·she will no longer be proud of her power [her proud strength will cease].
A cloud will cover Egypt,
and her ·villages [Ldaughters] will be captured and taken away.
[19]So I will ·punish [execute judgments on] Egypt,
and they will know I am the LORD.' "

Egypt Becomes Weak

[20]It was in the eleventh year [Csince King Jehoiachin's exile (1:2)], in the
first month, on the seventh day of the month [CApril 29, 587 BC]. The
·LORD spoke his word [Lword of the LORD came] to me, saying: [21]"·Human
[TSon of man; 2:1], I have broken the ·powerful arm [Larm] of Pharaoh,
the king of Egypt. It has not been ·tied [bound] up, so it will not get well.
It has not been wrapped with a bandage, so it will not be strong enough

to hold a sword in war. 22So this is what the Lord God says: [LLook;
TBehold] I am against Pharaoh, the king of Egypt. I will break his arms,
both the strong arm and the broken arm, and I will make the sword fall
from his hand. 23I will scatter the Egyptians among the nations, spreading them among the countries. 24I will make the arms of the king of
Babylon strong and put my sword in his hand. But I will break the arms
of Pharaoh. Then ·when he faces the king of Babylon [Lbefore him] he
will ·cry out in pain [groan] like a ·dying [mortally wounded] person.
25So I will make the arms of the king of Babylon strong, but the arms of
the king of Egypt will ·fall [become limp]. Then people will know that I
am the Lord when I put my sword into the hand of the king of Babylon
and he ·uses it in war [wields it; extends it] against the land of Egypt.
26Then I will scatter the Egyptians among the nations, spreading them
among the countries. Then they will know that I am the Lord."

A Cedar Tree

31 It was in the eleventh year [Csince King Jehoiachin's exile
(1:2)], in the third month, on the first day of the month [CJune
21, 587 BC]. The ·Lord spoke his word [Lword of the Lord came] to me,
saying: 2"·Human [TSon of man; 2:1], say to the king of Egypt and his
people:

'·No one [LWho…?] is like you in your greatness.
3 [LLook; TBehold] Assyria was once like a cedar tree in Lebanon
with beautiful branches that shaded the forest.
It was ·very tall [a towering height];
its top was among the clouds.
4Much water made the tree grow;
the deep springs made it tall.
Rivers flowed
around ·the bottom of the tree [its place of planting]
and sent their ·streams [channels]
to all other trees ·in the countryside [of the field].
5So the tree was taller
than all the other trees ·in the countryside [of the field].
Its ·limbs [boughs] became large and its branches long
because of ·so much [abundant] water.
6All the birds of the ·sky [heavens]
made their nests in the tree's ·limbs [boughs; Dan. 4:12, 21].
And all the ·wild animals [beasts of the field]
gave birth under its branches.
All great nations
lived in the tree's shade.
7So the tree was great and beautiful,
with its long branches,
because its roots reached down to ·much [abundant] water.
8The cedar trees in the garden of God [CEden]
were not as great as it was.
The ·pine [fir; juniper] trees
·did not have such great [could not equal its] ·limbs [boughs].
The plane trees
did not have such branches.
No tree in the garden of God
was as beautiful as this tree.

9I made it beautiful
with many branches,
and all the trees of Eden in the garden of God
·wanted to be like [envied] it.
10“ ‘So this is what the Lord God says: The tree grew tall. Its top reached
the clouds, and it became proud of its height. 11So I handed it ·over to
[Linto the hand of] a mighty ruler of the nations for him to ·punish [deal
with] it. Because it was ·evil [wicked], I ·got rid of it [threw it out; cast it
aside]. 12The ·cruelest [most ruthless] foreign nation cut it down and left
it. The tree's branches fell on the mountains and in all the valleys, and its
·broken limbs [boughs] were in all the ravines of the land. All the nations
of the earth left the shade of that tree. 13The birds of the ·sky [heavens] live
on the fallen tree. The wild animals live among the tree's fallen branches.
14So the trees that grow by the water will not ·be proud to be [*or* grow so]
tall; they will not put their tops among the clouds. None of the trees that
are watered well will grow that tall, because they all are ·meant [appointed;
consigned] to die and go ·under the ground [*or* to the underworld; to the
depths of the earth]. They will be with ·people who have died [mortals;
Lsons of men] and ·have gone down [those who descend] to the ·place of
the dead [Lpit].
15“ ‘This is what the Lord God says: On the day ·when the tree [Lit;
CAssyria] went down to ·the place of the dead [LSheol], I ·made the deep
springs cry loudly [*or* caused mourning]. I ·covered them [*or* closed the
deep over it] and held back their rivers, and the great waters ·stopped
flowing [were restrained]. I dressed Lebanon ·in black [*or* with gloom; Cin
mourning for the great tree], and all the trees in the countryside ·were sad
about it [wilted; fainted]. 16I made the nations ·shake with fear [tremble;
quake] at the sound of the tree falling when I brought it down to ·the
place of the dead [Sheol]. It went to join those who ·have gone down
[descend] to the ·grave [pit; Cthe trees represent other great nations that
have fallen]. Then all the trees of Eden and the best and ·most beautiful
[choicest] trees of Lebanon, all the well-watered trees, were comforted in
the ·place of the dead below the earth [underworld; world below]. 17These
trees had also gone down with the great tree to ·the place of the dead
[LSheol]. They joined those who were killed ·in war [Lby the sword] and
those among the nations who had lived under the great tree's shade.
18“ ‘·So no tree [LWhich of the trees…?] in Eden is equal to you [CEgypt],
in ·greatness [glory; splendor] and ·honor [greatness; majesty], but you
will go down to join the trees of Eden in the ·place below the earth [underworld]. You will lie among ·unclean people [Lthe uncircumcised], with
those who were killed ·in war [Lby the sword].

“ ‘This is about Pharaoh and all his ·people [hordes; armies], says the Lord God.’ ”

A Funeral Song

32 It was in the twelfth year [Csince King Jehoiachin's exile (1:2)],
in the twelfth month, on the first day of the month [CMarch
3, 585 BC]. The ·Lord spoke his word [Lword of the Lord came] to me,
saying: 2“·Human [TSon of man; 2:1], sing a ·funeral song [lament;
dirge] about Pharaoh, the king of Egypt. Say to him:

‘You are like a young lion [19:1–9] among the nations.
You are like a ·crocodile [*or* monster; *or* dragon; 29:4] in the seas.
You ·splash [thrash] around in your streams

and stir up the water with your feet,
making the rivers muddy.
[3]" 'This is what the Lord God says:
I will spread my net over you,
and I will use a ·large group of [assembly of many] people
to ·pull [haul] you up in my net.
[4]Then I will ·throw [cast; *or* abandon] you on the land
·dropping [hurling] you onto the ·ground [open field].
I will let the birds of the ·sky [heavens] ·rest [settle] on you
and all the animals of the earth ·eat you until they are full [gorge themselves on you; Rev. 19:21].
[5]I will scatter your flesh on the mountains
and fill the valleys with ·what is left of you [your remains; [L]your height].
[6]I will drench the land with your flowing blood
as far as the mountains,
and the ravines will be full of your flesh.
[7]When I ·make you disappear [snuff/blot you out],
I will cover the ·sky [heavens] and make the stars dark.
I will cover the sun with a cloud,
and the moon will not shine.
[8]I will make all the shining lights in the ·sky [heavens]
become dark over you;
I will bring darkness over your land,
says the Lord God.
[9]I will ·cause many people to be afraid [[L]trouble the hearts of many peoples]
when I bring ·you as a captive into other [*or* about your destruction among the] nations,
to lands you have not known.
[10]I will cause many people to be shocked about you.
Their kings will tremble with ·fear [horror] because of you
when I ·swing [brandish] my sword in front of them.
They will ·shake [tremble] every moment
on the day ·you fall [of your downfall];
each ·king [one] will ·be afraid [tremble] for his own life.
[11]" 'So this is what the Lord God says:
The sword of the king of Babylon
will attack you.
[12]I will cause your people to fall
by the swords of mighty soldiers,
the most ·terrible [ruthless] ·in the world [of nations].
They will ·destroy [shatter] the pride of Egypt
and all its ·people [[L]hordes/armies will be destroyed].
[13]I will also destroy all Egypt's cattle
that live alongside much water.
The foot of a human will not ·stir [disturb] the water,
and the hoofs of cattle will not muddy it anymore.
[14]So I will let ·the Egyptians' [[L]their] water ·become clear [*or* calm; [L]sink; settle].
I will cause their rivers to run ·as smoothly as [[L]like] olive oil,
says the Lord God.

15 When I make the land of Egypt ·empty [a desolation]
and ·take [strip out; empty] everything that is in the land,
when I ·destroy [strike down] all those who live in Egypt,
then they will know that I am the LORD.'

16 "This is the ·funeral song [lament; dirge] people will sing for Egypt. The ·women [Ldaughters] of the nations will ·sing [chant] it; they will ·sing [chant] it for Egypt and all ·its people [her hordes/armies], says the Lord GOD."

Egypt to Be Destroyed

17 It was in the twelfth year [Csince King Jehoiachin's exile (1:2)], on the fifteenth day of the month [CMarch 17, 585 BC]. The ·LORD spoke his word [Lword of the LORD came] to me, saying: 18 "·Human [TSon of man; 2:1], ·cry [wail] for the people of Egypt. Bring down Egypt, together with the ·women [Ldaughters] of the powerful nations; bring them down to the ·place of the dead below the earth [underworld; world below] to join those who go to the ·place of the dead [Lpit]. 19 Say to them: 'Are you more ·beautiful [*or* favored] than others? Go lie down [Cin death] with ·those who are unclean [Lthe uncircumcised].' 20 ·The Egyptians [LThey] will fall among those killed ·in war [Lby the sword]. The sword is ·ready [drawn; *or* appointed]; ·the enemy [Lthey] will drag Egypt and all her ·people [hordes; armies] away. 21 From the ·place of the dead [Lmidst of Sheol] the ·leaders of the mighty ones [*or* mighty leaders; warrior chiefs] will speak ·about [*or* to] ·the king of Egypt and the nations which help him [Lhim and his allies]: 'The ·unclean [Luncircumcised], those killed ·in war [Lby the sword], have come down here and ·lie dead [Llie].'

22 "Assyria and all its ·army [assembly; company] lie dead there. ·The graves of their soldiers [LIts graves] are all around. All were ·killed in war [Lstruck down by the sword], 23 and their graves were put in the deepest parts of the ·place of the dead [Lpit]. ·Assyria's army [LHer assembly/company] lies around its grave. When they ·lived on earth [Lwere in the land of the living], they ·frightened people [spread terror], but now all of them have been ·killed in war [Lstruck down by the sword].

24 "The nation of Elam [Ca country east of Assyria; present-day Iran] is there with all its ·army [hordes] around its grave. All of them were ·killed in war [Lstruck down by the sword]. They had ·frightened people [Lspread terror] ·on earth [Lin the land of the living] and so went down ·unclean [Luncircumcised] to the ·lowest parts of the place of the dead [underworld; world below]. They must carry their shame with those who have gone down to the ·place of the dead [Lpit]. 25 A ·bed [resting place] has been made for Elam [v. 24] ·with all those killed in war [among the slain]. The graves of her ·soldiers [hordes] are all around her. All Elam's people are ·unclean [Luncircumcised], killed ·in war [Lby the sword]. They ·frightened people [spread terror] ·when they lived on earth [Lin the land of the living], but now they must carry their shame with those who have gone down to the ·place of the dead [Lpit]. ·Their graves are [*or* They are assigned a place; LThey are set] with the rest who were killed.

26 "·Meshech and Tubal [*or* Meshech-tubal; Cpeople from Asia Minor, southeast of the Black Sea; 27:13] are there with the graves of all their ·soldiers [hordes] around them. All of them are ·unclean [uncircumcised] and have been killed ·in war [Lby the sword]. They also ·frightened people [spread terror] ·when they lived on earth [Lin the land of the living]. 27 But they ·are not buried [Ldo not lie] with the ·other soldiers who were killed

in battle [fallen warriors of] long ago," those who went with their weapons of war to ·the place of the dead [LSheol]. These soldiers had their swords laid under their heads and their ·shields [*or* iniquities; guilt] resting on their ·bodies [Lbones]. These mighty soldiers used to ·frighten [terrorize] people ·when they lived on earth [Lin the land of the living].

28“You [Caddressing Pharaoh, king of Egypt] will be broken and lie among ·those who are unclean [Lthe uncircumcised], who were killed ·in war [Lby the sword].

29“Edom is there also, with its kings and all its ·leaders [princes]. They were mighty, but now they lie [Cin death] with those killed ·in war [Lby the sword], with those who are ·unclean [Luncircumcised], with those who have gone down to the ·place of the dead [Lpit].

30“All the ·rulers [princes] of the north and all the Sidonians are there. Their strength frightened people, but they have gone down in shame with those who were killed. They are ·unclean [Luncircumcised], lying with those killed ·in war [Lby the sword]. They carry their shame with those who have gone down to the ·place of the dead [Lpit].

31“·The king of Egypt [LPharaoh] and his army will see ·these who have been killed in war [Lthem]. Then he will be comforted for all his ·soldiers [hordes] killed ·in war [Lby the sword], says the Lord GOD. 32I ·made people afraid of the king of Egypt [*or* terrified him] ·while he lived on earth [Lin the land of the living]. But he and all his ·people [hordes; armies] will lie among those who are ·unclean [Luncircumcised], who were killed ·in war [Lby the sword], says the Lord GOD.”

Ezekiel Is Watchman for Israel

33 The ·LORD spoke his word [Lword of the LORD came] to me, saying: 2“·Human [TSon of man; 2:1], speak to your people and say to them: ‘Suppose I bring a war against a land. The people of the land may choose one of their men and make him their watchman. 3When he sees the ·enemy [Lsword] coming ·to attack [against] the land, he will blow the trumpet and warn the people. 4If they hear the sound of the trumpet but do ·nothing [not heed], the ·enemy [Lsword] will come and ·kill them [Ltake them away]. ·They will be responsible for their own deaths [LTheir blood will be on their own head]. 5They heard the sound of the trumpet but didn’t ·do anything [heed the warning]. So ·they are to blame for their own deaths [Ltheir blood will be on their own head]. If they had ·done something [taken the warning], they would have saved their own lives. 6But if the watchman sees the ·enemy [Lsword] coming to attack and does not blow the trumpet, the people will not be warned. Then if the ·enemy [Lsword] comes and ·kills [Ltakes away] any of them, they have died because of their own sin. But I will ·punish [hold accountable] the watchman for their ·deaths [Lblood].’

7“You, ·human [Tson of man; 2:1], are the one I have made a watchman for [Lthe house of] Israel. If you hear a word from my mouth, you must warn them for me. 8Suppose I say to the wicked: ‘Wicked people, you will surely die,’ but you don’t speak to warn the wicked to ·stop doing evil [turn from their ways]. Then they will die ·because they were sinners [for their iniquity], but I will ·punish you [hold you accountable] for their deaths. 9But if you warn the wicked to ·stop doing evil [turn from their ways] and they do not stop, they will die ·because they were sinners [for their iniquity]. But you have saved your life.

32:27 long ago Greek copies read “long ago.” Hebrew copies read “of the uncircumcised.”

10"So you, ·human [Tson of man; 2:1], say to [Lthe house of] Israel: 'You
have said: Surely our ·lawbreaking [transgressions] and sins are ·hurting
[Lupon] us. ·They will kill us [We are wasting/rotting away because of them].
What can we do so we will live?' 11Say to them: 'The Lord God says: As
surely as I live, I ·do not want any who are wicked to die [Ltake no pleasure
in the death of the wicked]. I want them to ·stop doing evil [turn from their
ways] and live. ·Stop [Turn]! ·Stop [Turn from] your wicked ways! ·You
don't want to die, do you [LWhy will you die], ·people [Lhouse] of Israel?'
12"·Human [TSon of man; 2:1], say to your people: 'The ·goodness [righ-
teousness] of ·those who do right [the righteous] will not save them ·when
they sin [Lin the day of their rebellion]. The ·evil of wicked people [wicked-
ness of the wicked] will not cause them to ·be punished [stumble] if they
stop doing it. If ·good people [the righteous] sin, they will not be able to live
by the ·good [righteousness] they did earlier.' 13If I tell ·good people [the
righteous], 'You will surely live,' they might ·think they have done enough
good [Ltrust in their righteousness] and then do evil. Then none of the ·good
[righteous] things they did will be remembered. They will die because of the
·evil [iniquity] they have done. 14Or, if I say to the wicked people, 'You will
surely die,' they may stop sinning and do what is right and ·honest [just].
15For example, ·they [Lthe wicked one] may ·return what somebody gave
them as a promise to repay a loan [restore the pledge], or pay back what they
stole. If they live by the ·rules [statutes] that give life and do not ·sin [do evil;
practice iniquity], then they will surely live, and they will not die. 16None of
the sins they have committed will be ·held [Lremembered] against them.
They now do what is right and ·fair [just], so they will surely live.
17"Your people say: 'The way of the Lord is not fair.' But it is their own
ways that are not ·fair [just]. 18When the ·good people [righteous] ·stop
doing good [turn from righteousness] and do evil, they will die for their
evil. 19But when the wicked ·stop doing evil [turn from sin] and do what
is right and ·fair [just], they will live. 20You still say: 'The way of the Lord
is not fair.' Israel, I will judge all of you ·by [according to] your own ways."

The Fall of Jerusalem Explained

21It was in the twelfth year [Csince King Jehoiachin's exile (1:2)], on the
fifth day of the tenth month [CJanuary 19, 585 BC]. A ·person who had
escaped [survivor; refugee; fugitive] from Jerusalem came to me and said,
"Jerusalem has been ·captured [struck down]." 22Now ·I had felt the
power of the Lord [Lthe hand of the Lord was] on me the evening before.
He had ·made me able to talk again [Lopened my mouth] before this person came to me. ·I could speak [LHe opened my mouth]; I was not without
speech anymore [Csee 3:24–27].
23Then the ·Lord spoke his word [Lword of the Lord came] to me, saying:
24"·Human [TSon of man; 2:1], people who live in the ruins in the land of
Israel are saying: 'Abraham was only one person, yet he was given the land
as his own. Surely the land has been given to us, who are many, as our ·very
own [possession].' 25So say to them: 'This is what the Lord God says: You eat
meat with the blood still in it [Cforbidden in the law; Lev. 19:26], you ·ask
your idols for help [Lraise your eyes to your idols], and you ·murder people
[Lshed blood]. Should you then ·have the land as your very own [possess the
land]? 26You depend on your sword and do ·terrible things that I hate
[detestable/abominable things]. Each of you ·has sexual relations with
[defiles] his neighbor's wife. So should you ·have [possess] the land?'
27"Say to them: 'This is what the Lord God says: As surely as I live, those

who are among the city ruins in Israel will ·be killed in war [Lfall by the
sword]. I will cause those who live in the ·country [open field] to be eaten by
wild animals. People ·hiding in [Lin] the strongholds and caves will die of
·disease [plague; pestilence]. 28I will make the land an ·empty desert [deso-
late wasteland]. ·The people's pride in the land's power [L…and her confident
pride] will end. The mountains of Israel will become ·empty [desolate] so
that no one will pass through them. 29They will know that I am the LORD
when I make the land an ·empty desert [desolate wasteland] because of the
things they have done that ·I hate [are detestable/abominable].'

30"But as for you, ·human [Tson of man; 2:1], your people are talking
about you by the walls and in the doorways of houses. They say to each
other: 'Come now, and hear the message from the LORD.' 31So they come
to you in crowds as ·if they were really ready to listen [*or* they usually do;
or people do]. They sit in front of you as if they were my people and hear
your words, but they will not ·obey [do] them. With their mouths they
·tell me they love me [*or* talk lustfully], ·but [*or* and] their hearts ·desire
[pursue] their selfish profits. 32[LLook; TBehold] To your people you are
nothing more than a singer who sings ·love [*or* sensual; lustful] songs and
has a beautiful voice and plays a musical instrument well. They hear your
words, but they will not ·obey [do] them.

33"When this comes true, and it surely will happen, then the people
will know that a prophet has been among them."

The Leaders Are like Shepherds

34 The ·LORD spoke his word [Lword of the LORD came] to me, saying: 2"·Human [TSon of man; 2:1], prophesy against the
shepherds of Israel [Cthe leaders]. Prophesy and say to them: 'This is what
the Lord GOD says: ·How terrible it will be for [LWoe to] the shepherds of
Israel who feed only themselves! ·Why don't [Shouldn't] the shepherds feed
the flock? 3You eat the ·milk curds [*or* fat], and you clothe yourselves with
the wool. You kill the ·fat sheep [choice/fat ones], but you do not feed the
flock. 4You have not ·made the weak strong [strengthened the weak]. You
have not healed the sick or put bandages on those that were hurt. You have
not brought back those who strayed away or searched for the lost [Matt.
18:12; Luke 15:4]. But you have ruled the sheep with ·cruel force [violence
and harshness]. 5The sheep were scattered, because there was no shepherd,
and they became food for every wild animal. 6My flock wandered over all
the mountains and on every high hill. They were scattered all over the face
of the earth, and no one searched or looked for them.

7" 'So, you shepherds, hear the word of the LORD. This is what the Lord
GOD says: 8As surely as I live, my flock has ·been caught [become prey] and
eaten by all the wild animals, because the flock has no shepherd. The shepherds did not search for my flock. No, they fed themselves instead of my
flock. 9So, you shepherds, hear the word of the LORD. 10This is what the
Lord GOD says: [LLook; TBehold] I am against the shepherds. I will ·blame
them for what has happened to my sheep [hold them accountable;
Ldemand my sheep from their hand] and will not let them tend the flock
anymore. Then the shepherds will stop feeding themselves, and I will ·take
[rescue] my flock from their mouths so they will no longer be their food.

11" 'This is what the Lord GOD says: I, myself, will search for my sheep
and ·take care of [look after; *or* look for] them. 12As a shepherd ·take care
of [looks after; *or* looks for] his scattered flock when ·it is found [*or* they
are with him], I will ·take care of [look after; *or* look for] my sheep. I will

·save [rescue] them from all the places where they were scattered on a
cloudy and dark day. 13 I will bring them out from the nations and gather
them from the countries. I will bring them to their own land and ·pasture
[feed] them on the mountains of Israel, in the ravines, and in all the
places where people live in the land. 14 I will feed them in a good pasture,
and they will ·eat grass [graze] on the ·high mountains [mountain
heights] of Israel. They will lie down on good ·ground where they eat
grass [pasture], and they will eat in rich grassland on the mountains of
Israel. 15 I will feed my flock and ·lead them to rest [have them lie down],
says the Lord God [Ps. 23; Is. 40:11]. 16 I will search for the lost, bring back
those that strayed away [v. 4], put bandages on those that were hurt, and
make the weak strong. But I will destroy those sheep that are fat and
strong. I will ·tend [shepherd; feed] the sheep with ·fairness [justice].
17 " 'This is what the Lord God says: As for you, my flock, I will judge
between one sheep and another, between the ·male sheep [rams] and the
male goats [Matt. 25:32–33]. 18 Is it not enough for you to eat grass in the
good ·land [pasture]? Must you ·crush [trample] the rest of the grass with
your feet? Is it not enough for you to drink clear water? Must you make the
rest of the water muddy with your feet? 19 Must my flock eat what you ·crush
[trample], and must they drink what you make muddy with your feet?
20 " 'So this is what the Lord God says to them: [LLook; TBehold] I, myself,
will judge between the fat sheep and the thin sheep. 21 You push with your side
and with your shoulder, and you ·knock down [butt; thrust at] all the weak
sheep with your horns until you have ·forced them away [*or* scattered them
abroad]. 22 So I will save my flock; they will ·not be hurt anymore [Lno longer
be prey]. I will judge between one sheep and another. 23 Then I will put over
them one shepherd, my servant David [Is. 11:1; Jer. 30:9; Hos. 3:5; Mic. 5:2;
Cthe Messiah envisioned as a new David]. He will feed them and tend them
and be their shepherd. 24 Then I, the Lord, will be their God, and my servant
David will be a ·ruler [prince] among them. I, the Lord, have spoken.
25 " 'I will make an ·agreement [covenant; treaty] of peace with ·my sheep
[Lthem] and will remove ·harmful animals [wild beasts] from the land. Then
the sheep will live safely in the ·desert [wilderness] and sleep in the woods.
26 I will ·bless them and let them live around my hill [*or* make them and the
regions around my hill a blessing]. I will cause ·the rains [showers] to come
·when it is time [in their season]; there will be showers to bless them. 27 Also
the trees ·in the countryside [Lof the field] will ·give [yield] their fruit, and
the land will give its ·harvest [produce; increase]. And the sheep will ·be safe
[live securely] on their land. Then they will know that I am the Lord when I
break the bars of their ·captivity [Lyoke] and ·save [rescue] them from the
·power [Lhand] of those who made them slaves. 28 They will not be ·led captive by [prey for] the nations again. The wild animals will not ·eat [devour]
them, but they will live safely, and no one will make them afraid. 29 I will give
them a place famous for its good crops, so they will no longer ·suffer from
hunger [be victims of famine] in the land. They will not suffer the insults of
other nations anymore. 30 Then they will know that I, the Lord their God, am
with them. The nation [Lhouse] of Israel will know that they are my people,
says the Lord God. 31 You, my sheep, are the human sheep ·I care for [Lof my
pasture; Ps. 95:7; 100:3], and I am your God, says the Lord God.' "

Prophecy Against Edom

35 The ·Lord spoke his word [Lword of the Lord came] to me,
saying: 2 "·Human [TSon of man; 2:1], look toward ·Edom
[LMount Seir] and prophesy against it. 3 Say to it: 'This is what the Lord

GOD says: I am against you, ·Edom [LMount Seir]. I will stretch out my hand against you and make you an ·empty desert [desolate waste]. 4I will destroy your cities, and you will become ·empty [desolate]. Then you will know that I am the LORD.

5" 'You have ·always been an enemy of [shown perpetual/ancient hatred toward the sons of] Israel. You ·let them be defeated in war [Lgave them over to the hand of the sword] ·when they were in trouble [at the time of their disaster/calamity] at the time of their final punishment [Obad. 13]. 6So the Lord GOD says, as surely as I live, I will ·let you be murdered [bring you bloodshed]. ·Murder [Bloodshed] will chase you. Since you did not hate ·murdering people [bloodshed; Lblood], ·murder [bloodshed; Lblood] will chase you. 7I will make ·Edom [LMount Seir] an ·empty ruin [desolate waste] and ·destroy [cut off] everyone who goes in or comes out of it. 8I will fill its mountains with those who are killed. Those killed ·in war [Lby the sword] will fall on your hills, in your valleys, and in all your ravines. 9I will make you a ·ruin forever [perpetual/eternal desolation]; no one will live in your cities. Then you will know that I am the LORD.

10" 'You said, "These two nations, Israel and Judah, and these two lands will be ours. We will take them for our ·own [possession]." But the LORD was there. 11So this is what the Lord GOD says: As surely as I live, I will treat you just as you treated them. You were angry and ·jealous [envious] because you hated them. So I will ·show the Israelites who I am [make myself known to them] when I ·punish [judge] you. 12Then you will know that I, the LORD, have heard all your insults against the mountains of Israel. You said, "They ·have been ruined [are desolate/laid waste]. They have been given to us to ·eat [devour]." 13You have ·not stopped your proud talk [Lexalted yourself against me and multiplied words] against me. I have heard you. 14This is what the Lord GOD says: All the earth will ·be happy [rejoice] when I make you an ·empty ruin [desolation]. 15You ·were happy [rejoiced] when the ·land [Linheritance of the house] of Israel was ·ruined [desolated], but I will do the same thing to you. Mount Seir and all Edom, you will become an ·empty ruin [desolation]. Then you will know that I am the LORD.'

Israel to Come Home

36 "·Human [TSon of man; 2:1], prophesy to the mountains of Israel and say: 'Mountains of Israel, hear the word of the LORD. 2This is what the Lord GOD says: The enemy has said about you, "[LAha!] ·Now the old places to worship gods [The ancient heights] have become ·ours [Lour possession]." ' 3So prophesy and say: 'This is what the Lord GOD says: They have made you an ·empty ruin [desolation] and have crushed you from all around. So you became a possession of the ·other [rest of the] nations. People have ·talked [gossiped] and ·whispered [slandered] against you. 4So, mountains of Israel, hear the word of the Lord GOD. The Lord GOD speaks to the mountains, hills, ravines, and valleys, to the ·empty ruins [desolate wasteland] and abandoned cities that have ·been ·robbed [plundered] and ·laughed at [ridiculed; derided] by the other nations. 5This is what the Lord GOD says: I speak ·in hot anger [with burning zeal] against the other nations. I speak against the people of Edom, who took my land for themselves with joy and with ·hate [contempt] in their hearts. They ·forced out the people and took their pastureland [seized their pastureland as spoil].' 6So prophesy about the land of Israel and say to the mountains, hills, ravines, and valleys: 'This is what the Lord GOD says: I speak in my jealous anger, because you have suffered the ·insults [scorn; reproach] of

the nations. 7So this is what the Lord GOD says: I ·promise [vow] that the
nations around you will also have to suffer ·insults [scorn; reproach].
8" 'But you, mountains of Israel, will grow branches and fruit for my people, who will soon come home. 9[LLook; TBehold] I am ·concerned about
[for] you; I ·am on your side [Lwill turn to you]. You will be plowed, and seed
will be planted in you. 10I will increase the number of people who live on
you, all the ·people [Lhouse] of Israel. The cities will ·have people living in
them [be inhabited], and the ruins will be rebuilt. 11I will ·increase the number of people and animals living [multiply man and beast] on you. They will
grow and ·have many young [be fruitful]. You will have people living on you
as ·you did before [in former times], and I will make you better off than at
the beginning. Then you will know that I am the LORD. 12I will cause my
people Israel to ·walk [live] on you and ·own [possess] you, and you will
·belong to them [become their inheritance]. You will never again ·take their
children away from them [bereave them of their children].
13" 'This is what the Lord GOD says: People say about you, "You ·eat
[devour] people and ·take children [bereave children] from your nation."
14But you will not ·eat [devour] people anymore or ·take away the [bereave
your nation of] children, says the Lord GOD. 15 I will not make you listen
to ·insults [taunts] from the nations anymore; you will not ·suffer shame
[endure scorn/disgrace] from them anymore. You will not cause your
nation to ·fall [stumble] anymore, says the Lord GOD.' "

The Lord Acts for Himself

16The ·LORD spoke his word to me [Lword of the LORD came] again, saying: 17"·Human [TSon of man; 2:1], when the ·nation [Lhouse] of Israel
was living in their own land, they ·made it unclean [defiled it; Critually] by
their ways and the things they did. Their ways were like ·a woman's
uncleanness in her time of monthly bleeding [menstrual impurity;
Critually]. 18So I poured out my anger against them, because they ·mur-
dered in [shed blood on] the land and because they made the land
·unclean [defiled] with their idols. 19I scattered them among the nations,
and they were ·spread [dispersed] through the countries. I ·punished
[judged] them for how they lived and what they did. 20They ·dishonored
[defiled; profaned; Critually] my holy name in the nations where they
went. The nations said about them, 'These are the people of the LORD, but
they had to leave the land which he gave them.' 21But I had concern for my
holy name, which the ·nation [Lhouse] of Israel had ·dishonored [defiled;
profaned; Critually] among the nations where they went.
22"So say to the ·people [Lhouse] of Israel, 'This is what the Lord GOD
says: [Lhouse of] Israel, I am going to act, but not for your sake. I will do
something to help my holy name, which you have ·dishonored [defiled;
profaned; Critually] among the nations where you went. 23I will prove the
holiness of my great name, which has been ·dishonored [defiled; profaned; Critually] among the nations. You have ·dishonored [defiled;
profaned; Critually] it among these nations, but the nations will know
that I am the LORD when I ·prove myself holy [vindicate my holiness]
before their eyes, says the Lord GOD.
24" 'I will take you from the nations and gather you out of all the lands
and bring you back into your own land. 25Then I will sprinkle clean water
on you, and you will be clean. I will cleanse you from all your uncleanness
[Critual impurity] and your idols. 26Also, I will give you a new heart, and I
will put a new ·way of thinking [Lspirit] inside you. I will ·take out [remove

from you] ·the stubborn hearts of stone from your bodies [Lyour heart of
stone], and I will give you ·obedient hearts [La heart] of flesh. 27I will put
my ·Spirit [*or* spirit] ·inside you [*or* among you; Cthe pronoun is plural]
and ·help you [cause you to] ·live by [walk in] my ·rules [statutes] and
carefully obey my ·laws [rules; judgments]. 28You will live in the land I gave
to your ·ancestors [fathers], and you will be my people, and I will be your
God. 29So I will save you from all your ·uncleanness [defilement; Critual]. I
will ·command [summon; call for] the grain to ·come and grow [multiply];
I will not ·allow a time of hunger to hurt [bring famine upon] you. 30I will
increase the harvest of fruit trees and the crops in the field so you will
never again suffer ·shame [disgrace] among the nations because of ·hun-
ger [famine]. 31Then you will remember your evil ways and actions that
were not good, and you will ·hate [loathe] yourselves because of your sins
and your ·terrible acts that I hate [detestable/abominable acts]. 32I want
you to know that I am not going to do this for your sake, says the Lord
God. Be ashamed and embarrassed about your ways, [Lhouse of] Israel.
33" 'This is what the Lord God says: This is what will happen on the day
I cleanse you from all your sins: I will ·cause the cities to have people living
in them again [repopulate/resettle your towns/cities], and the ·destroyed
places [ruins] will be rebuilt. 34The ·empty [desolate] land will be plowed
so it will no longer be a ·ruin [desolation] for everyone who passes by to
see. 35They will say, "This land was ·ruined [desolate], but now it has
become like the garden of Eden. The cities were destroyed, empty, and
ruined, but now they are ·protected [fortified] and ·have people living in
them [inhabited]." 36Then those nations still around you will know that I,
the Lord, have rebuilt ·what was destroyed [the ruins] and have planted
what was ·empty [desolate]. I, the Lord, have spoken, and I will do it.'
37"This is what the Lord God says: I will let myself be asked by the
·people [Lhouse] of Israel to do this for them again: I will ·make their
people grow in number [multiply their people] like a flock. 38They will be
as many as the flocks ·brought to Jerusalem during her holy feasts [for
offerings]. Her ruined cities will be filled with flocks of people. Then they
will know that I am the Lord."

The Vision of Dry Bones

37 I felt the ·power [Lhand] of the Lord on me, and he brought
me out by the ·Spirit [*or* spirit] of the Lord and put me down
in the middle of a valley. It was full of bones. 2He led me around among
the bones, and I saw that there were many bones in the valley and [Llook;
Tbehold] that they were very dry. 3Then he asked me, "·Human [TSon of
man; 2:1], can these bones live?"
I answered, "Lord God, only you know."
4He said to me, "Prophesy ·to [over] these bones and say to them, 'Dry
bones, hear the word of the Lord. 5This is what the Lord God says to the
bones: I will cause breath to enter you so you will come to life. 6I will put
·muscles [tendons; sinews] on you and flesh on you and cover you with
skin. Then I will put breath in you so you will come to life. Then you will
know that I am the Lord.' "
7So I prophesied as I was commanded. While I prophesied, there was a
noise and a rattling. The bones came together, bone to bone. 8I looked
and saw ·muscles [sinews; tendons] come on the bones, and flesh grew,
and skin covered the bones. But there was no breath in them.
9Then he said to me, "Prophesy to the ·wind [breath; Spirit]. Prophesy,

·human [Tson of man; 2:1], and say to the ·wind [breath; Spirit], 'This is
what the Lord God says: ·Wind [Breath; Spirit], come from the four
winds, and breathe on these ·people who were killed [slain] so they can
come back to life.' " 10So I prophesied as the Lord commanded me. And
the ·breath [wind; Spirit] came into them, and they came to life and stood
on their feet, a very large army.
11Then he said to me, "·Human [TSon of man; 2:1], these bones are like
all the ·people [Lhouse] of Israel. They say, 'Our bones are dried up, and our
hope has ·gone [perished]. We are ·destroyed [cut off].' 12So, prophesy and
say to them, 'This is what the Lord God says: [LLook; TBehold] My people, I
will open your graves and cause you to come up out of your graves. Then I
will bring you into the land of Israel. 13My people, you will know that I am
the Lord when I open your graves and cause you to come up from them.
14And I will put my ·Spirit [breath; wind] inside you, and you will come to
life. Then I will ·put [settle] you in your own land. And you will know that
I, the Lord, have spoken and ·done it [*or* will do it], says the Lord.' "

Judah and Israel Back Together

15The ·Lord spoke his word [Lword of the Lord came] to me, saying,
16"·Human [TSon of man; 2:1], take ·a [one] ·stick [branch] and write on
it, 'For Judah and all the Israelites with him.' Then take another ·stick
[branch] and write on it, 'The ·stick [branch] of Ephraim, for Joseph and
all the ·Israelites [Lhouse of Israel; Cthe northern kingdom] with him.'
17Then join them together into one stick so they will be one in your hand.
18"When your people say to you, 'Explain to us what you mean by this,'
19say to them, 'This is what the Lord God says: I will take the ·stick [branch]
for Joseph and the tribes of Israel with him, which is in the hand of Ephraim,
and I will put it with the ·stick [branch] of Judah. I will make them into one
·stick [branch], and they will be one in my hand [Cthe northern and southern kingdoms will be united again; 33:29; Jer. 3:18; 23:5–6; Hos. 1:11; Amos
9:11].' 20Hold the sticks on which you wrote these names in your hand ·so
the people can see them [Lbefore their eyes]. 21Say to the people, 'This is
what the Lord God says: [LLook; TBehold] I am going to take the ·people
[Lhouse] of Israel from among the nations where they have gone. I will
gather them from all around and bring them into their own land. 22I will
make them one nation in the land, on the mountains of Israel. One king
will rule all of them. They will never again be two nations; they will not be
divided into two kingdoms anymore. 23They will not continue to ·make
themselves unclean [defile themselves] by their idols, their ·statues of gods
which I hate [detestable things], or by ·their sins [all their transgressions/
offenses]. I will save them from all ·the ways they sin and turn against me
[their backsliding/unfaithfulness/apostasies], and I will ·make them clean
[purify them]. Then they will be my people, and I will be their God.
24" 'My servant David will be their king [34:23], and they will all have one
shepherd. They will ·live by [Lwalk in] my ·laws [rules; judgments] and be
careful to keep my ·rules [statutes]. 25They will live on the land I gave to my
servant Jacob, the land in which your ·ancestors [fathers] lived. They will all
live on the land forever: they, their children, and their grandchildren. David
my servant will be their king forever. 26I will make an ·agreement [covenant;
treaty] of peace with them, an ·agreement that continues forever [everlasting
covenant/treaty; Jer. 31:31–34]. I will ·put them in their land [establish them]
and ·make them grow in number [multiply them; Gen. 12:1–3]. Then I will
put my ·Temple [sanctuary] among them forever. 27·The place where I live

[My dwelling place] will be with them. I will be their God, and they will be
my people. [28]When my ·Temple [sanctuary] is among them forever, the
nations will know that I, the LORD, ·make Israel holy [sanctify Israel].'"

Prophecy Against Gog

38 The ·LORD spoke his word [Lword of the LORD came] to me, saying, [2]"·Human [TSon of man; 2:1], ·look [Lturn your face]
toward Gog of the land of Magog [Rev. 20:8], the chief ·ruler [prince] of
the nations of Meshech and Tubal [Ctwo nations in northeast Asia Minor;
32:26]. Prophesy against him [3]and say, 'The Lord GOD says this: [LLook;
TBehold] I am against you, Gog, chief ·ruler [prince] of Meshech and
Tubal. [4]I will turn you around and put hooks in your jaws. And I will
bring you out with all your army, horses, and horsemen, all of whom will
be dressed in ·beautiful uniforms [*or* full armor]. They will be a ·large
army [great horde/host] with large and small shields and all ·having
[brandishing; wielding] swords. [5]Persia, Cush [CEthiopia], and Put
[CLydia] will be with them, all of them having shields and helmets. [6]There
will also be Gomer [Cpeople living north of the Black Sea; Gen. 10:3; 1 Chr.
1:6] with all its ·troops [hordes] and the nation of Beth-Togarmah [27:14;
Gen. 10:3] from the far north with all its troops—many nations with you.
[7]" 'Be prepared. Be prepared, you and all the ·armies [hosts; hordes]
that have come together to ·make you their commander [*or* be a guard for
them]. [8]After ·a long time [Lmany days] you will be ·called for service
[called to arms; mustered]. ·After those [In the latter] years you will come
into a land that has been ·rebuilt [recovered; restored] from war. The people in the land will have been gathered from many nations to the mountains
of Israel, which were ·empty [in ruins; a wasteland] for a long time. These
people were brought out from the nations, and they will all be living in
safety. [9]You will ·come [advance] like a storm. You, all your troops, and the
many nations with you will be like a cloud covering the land.
[10]" 'This is what the Lord GOD says: ·At that time [LOn that day] ideas will
come into your mind, and you will ·think up [devise] an evil plan. [11]You
will say, "I will ·march [Lgo up] against a land of towns without walls. I will
·attack [Lcome to] those who are at rest and live in safety. All of them live
without city walls or gate bars or gates. [12]I will ·capture treasures [plunder]
and take loot. I will turn my ·power [Lhand] against the ·rebuilt [resettled;
inhabited] ruins that now have people living in them. ·I will attack [...and]
these people who have been gathered from the nations, who have become
rich with ·farm animals [livestock] and ·property [goods], who live at the
center of the world." [13]Sheba [27:22], Dedan [27:20], and the traders of
Tarshish [27:12], with all its ·villages [*or* warriors; Lyoung lions], will say to
you, "Did you come to ·capture treasure [plunder]? Did you bring your
troops together to take loot? Did you bring them to carry away silver and
gold and to take away ·farm animals [livestock] and property?" '
[14]"So prophesy, ·human [Tson of man; 2:1], and say to Gog, 'This is what
the Lord GOD says: ·Now [LOn the day] that my people Israel are living in
safety, you will know about it. [15]You will come with many people from your
place in the ·far [*or* remote parts of the] north. You will have ·a large group
[many nations/peoples] with you, a ·mighty army [great horde/host], all riding on horses. [16]You will ·attack [come up against] my people Israel like a
cloud that covers the land. This will happen in the ·days to come [latter days]
when I bring you against my land. Gog, then the nations will ·know
[acknowledge] me when ·they see me prove how holy I am [I vindicate my
holiness] in what I do through you.

17"'This is what the Lord GOD says: ·You are [LAre you…?] the one about whom I spoke in ·past [former] days. I spoke through my servants, the prophets of Israel, who prophesied for many years that I would bring you against them. 18This is what will happen: On the day Gog ·attacks [comes against] the land of Israel, ·I will become very angry [my wrath/fury will mount up/be aroused], says the Lord GOD. 19With ·jealousy [zeal] and ·great anger [fiery wrath] I tell you that ·at that time [on that day] there will surely be a great earthquake in Israel. 20The fish of the sea, the birds of the ·sky [heavens], the wild ·animals [beasts], everything that crawls on the ground, and all the people on the earth will ·shake with fear [tremble; quake] before me. Also the mountains will be thrown down, the cliffs will fall, and every wall will fall to the ground. 21Then I will call for a ·war [Lsword] against Gog on all my mountains, says the Lord GOD. Everyone's sword will ·attack the soldier next to him [Lbe against his brother]. 22I will ·punish [execute judgment on] Gog with ·disease [plague; pestilence] and ·death [bloodshed]. I will send a heavy rain with hailstones and ·burning sulfur [brimstone] on Gog, his ·army [hordes], and the many nations with him. 23Then I will show how great I am. I will show my holiness, and I will make myself known ·to the many nations that watch [Lin the eyes of many nations]. Then they will know that I am the LORD.'

The Death of Gog and His Army

39 "·Human [TSon of man; 2:1], prophesy against Gog and say, 'This is what the Lord GOD says: I am against you, Gog, chief ·ruler [prince] of Meshech and Tubal [38:2]. 2I will turn you around and ·lead [drag; *or* drive] you. I will bring you from the ·far [remotest] north and send you to attack the mountains of Israel. 3I will knock your bow out of your left hand and ·throw down [make fall] your arrows from your right hand. 4You, all your troops, and the nations with you will fall dead on the mountains of Israel. I will let you be ·food for [devoured by] every bird ·that eats meat [of prey; Rev. 19:21] and for every ·wild animal [beast of the field]. 5You will ·lie fallen on the ground [fall in the open field], because I have spoken, says the Lord GOD. 6I will send fire on Magog and those who live in safety on the coastlands. Then they will know that I am the LORD.

7"'I will make my holy name known among my people Israel, and I will not let my holy name be ·dishonored [defiled; profaned; Critually] anymore. Then the nations will know that I am the LORD, the Holy One in Israel. 8[LLook; TBehold] It is coming! It will happen, says the Lord GOD. The ·time [Lday] I talked about is coming.

9"'Then those who live in the cities of Israel will come out and make fires with the enemy's weapons. They will burn them, both large and small shields, bows and arrows, war clubs, and spears. They will use the weapons to burn in their fires for seven years. 10They will not need to take wood from the field or chop firewood from the forests, because they will make fires with the weapons. In this way they will ·take the treasures of [plunder] those who ·took their treasures [plundered them]; they will take the loot of those who took their loot, says the Lord GOD.

11"'·At that time [LOn that day] I will give Gog a burial place in Israel, in the Valley of the Travelers, east of the Dead Sea. It will block the road for travelers. Gog and all his ·army [hordes; multitudes] will be buried there, so people will call it The Valley of ·Gog's Army [LHamon-gog].

12"'The ·people [Lhouse] of Israel will be burying them for seven months to ·make the land clean again [cleanse the land]. 13All the people

in the land will bury them, and ·they will be honored [or it will be a
memorial for them; or their fame will spread] on the day ·of my victory [I
display my glory; Chis manifest presence], says the Lord God.
14"'The ·people [Lhouse] of Israel will ·choose [appoint] men to work
through the land to ·make it clean [cleanse/purify it]. Along with others,
they will bury ·Gog's soldiers still [Lthose] lying dead on the ground. After
the seven months, they will ·still search [or begin their search]. 15As they go
through the land, anyone who sees a human bone is to put a ·marker [sign]
by it. The sign will stay there until the gravediggers bury the bone in The
Valley of ·Gog's Army [LHamon-gog]. 16A city will be there named
Hamonah [Cperhaps a feminine form of Hamon-gog, meaning Army of
Gog]. So they will ·make the land clean again [cleanse/purify the land].'
17"·Human [TSon of man; 2:1], this is what the Lord God says: Speak to
every kind of bird and ·wild animal [all the beasts of the field]: '·Come
[Assemble] together, come! ·Come together [Gather] from all around to my
·sacrifice [or slaughter], a great ·sacrifice [or slaughter] which I will prepare
for you on the mountains of Israel. Eat flesh and drink blood [Rev. 19:17–
21]! 18You are to eat the flesh of the mighty and drink the blood of the
·rulers [princes] of the earth ·as if they were [Lall of them] fat animals from
Bashan: ·male sheep [rams], lambs, goats, and bulls. 19You are to eat and
drink from my sacrifice which I have prepared for you, eating fat until you
are ·full [satisfied; glutted] and drinking blood until you are drunk. 20At my
table you are to eat until you are full of horses and ·riders [or charioteers],
·mighty men [warriors] and all kinds of soldiers,' says the Lord God.
21"I will ·show [display] my glory [Cmanifest presence] among the
nations. All the nations will see ·my power when I punish [Lthe judgment
I executed and the hand I laid on] them. 22From that time onward the
·people [Lhouse] of Israel will know that I am the Lord their God. 23The
nations will know [Lthe house of] Israel ·was taken away captive [went
into exile] because they sinned and were unfaithful to me. So I ·turned
away [Lhid my face] from them and handed them over to their enemies
until all of them died ·in war [Lby the sword]. 24Because of their uncleanness [Critual] and their ·sins [transgressions], I ·punished [dealt with]
them and ·turned away [hid my face] from them.
25"So this is what the Lord God says: Now I will ·bring the people of
Jacob back from captivity [Lrestore the fortunes of Jacob], and I will have
·mercy [compassion] on the whole ·nation [Lhouse] of Israel. I will ·not
let them dishonor me [Lbe zealous/jealous for my holy name]. 26The people will forget their shame and ·how they rejected [their unfaithfulness
to] me when they live again in safety on their own land with no one to
make them afraid. 27I will bring the people back from ·other lands [the
nations/peoples] and gather them from the lands of their enemies. So I
will use my people to ·show many nations that I am holy [Ldisplay my
holiness in the eyes of many nations.]. 28Then my people will know that I
am the Lord their God, because I sent them into ·captivity [exile] among
the nations, but then I ·brought them back [gathered them] to their own
land, leaving no one behind. 29I will not ·turn away [Lhide my face] from
them anymore, because I will put my ·Spirit [or spirit] into the ·people
[Lhouse] of Israel, says the Lord God [11:19; 36:26–27; 37:14]."

The New Temple

40 It was the twenty-fifth year [Csince King Jehoiachin's exile
(1:2)], at the beginning of the year, on the tenth day of the
month [CApril 19, 573 BC]. It was in the fourteenth year after ·Jerusalem

was captured [Lthe city was struck down]. On that same day ·I felt the
power of the LORD [Lthe hand of the LORD was upon me], and he brought
me to Jerusalem. 2In the visions of God he brought me to the land of
Israel and put me down on a very high mountain. On the south of the
mountain there were some buildings that looked like a city. 3He took me
closer to the buildings, and ·I saw [Llook; Tbehold] a man ·who looked as
if he were made of [whose appearance was like] bronze, standing in the
gateway. He had a cord made of linen and a stick in his hand, both for
measuring. 4The man said to me, "·Human [TSon of man; 2:1], look with
your eyes and hear with your ears. ·Pay attention to [LSet your heart
upon] all that I will show you, because that's why you have been brought
here. Tell the ·people [Lhouse] of Israel all that you see."

The East Gateway

5·I saw [LAnd look/Tbehold] a wall that surrounded the ·Temple area
[Lhouse]. The measuring ·stick [rod] in the man's hand was ·ten and one-
half feet long [Lsix long cubits, each being a cubit and a handbreadth; Ca
regular cubit was eighteen inches long; this long cubit was about twenty-one
inches long]. So the man measured the wall, which was ·ten and one-half
feet [Lsix long cubits] thick and ·ten and one-half feet [Lone rod/stick] high.
6Then the man went to the east gateway. He went up its steps and measured the opening of the gateway. It was ·ten and one-half feet [Lone rod/
stick; v. 5] deep. 7The ·rooms for the guards [alcoves] were ·ten and one-
half feet [Lone rod/stick] long and ·ten and one-half feet [Lone rod/stick]
wide. ·The walls that came out between the guards' rooms [LBetween the
alcoves] were ·about nine feet [Lfive cubits; v. 5] thick. The ·opening
[threshold] of the gateway next to the ·porch [portico] that faced the
Temple was ·ten and one-half feet [Lone rod/stick] deep.
8Then the man measured the porch of the gateway. 9It was ·about fourteen feet [Leight cubits] deep, and its ·side walls [*or* jambs] were ·three and
one-half feet [Ltwo cubits] thick. The ·porch [portico] of the gateway
faced the Temple.
10On each side of the east gateway were three ·rooms [alcoves], which
·measured the same on each side [had the same measurement]. The ·walls
between each room [dividing walls; *or* jambs] ·were the same thickness [*or*
had the same measurement]. 11The man measured the width of the entrance
to the gateway, which was ·seventeen and one-half feet [Lten cubits; v. 5]
wide. The ·width [*or* length] of the gate was ·about twenty-three feet
[Lthirteen cubits]. 12And there was a low ·wall [barrier] ·about twenty-one
inches [Lone cubit] high in front of each ·room [alcove]. The ·rooms [alcoves]
were ·ten and one-half feet [Lsix cubits] on each side. 13The man measured
the gateway from the roof of one ·room [alcove] to the roof of the opposite
one. It was ·about forty-four feet [Ltwenty-five cubits] from one door to the
opposite door. 14The man also measured the ·porch [*or* jambs], which was
·about thirty-five feet [Ltwenty cubits] wide. The courtyard was around the
·porch [*or* jamb; Cthe meaning of this verse is uncertain]. 15From the front of
the ·outer side of the [entrance] gateway to the front of the porch of the
·inner side of the [inner] gateway was ·eighty-seven and one-half feet [Lfifty
cubits]. 16The ·rooms [alcoves] and porch had small windows on both sides.
The windows were narrower on the side facing the gateway. Carvings of
palm trees were on each side wall of the rooms.

The Outer Courtyard

17Then the man brought me into the outer courtyard ·where I saw
[Land look/Tbehold] rooms and a pavement of stones all around the

court. Thirty rooms ·were along the edge of [faced] the paved walkway.
18The pavement ran alongside the gates and was as deep as the gates were
wide. This was the lower pavement. 19Then the man measured from the
·outer wall [front of the lower gate] to the ·inner wall [Lexterior face of the
inner court]. The outer court between these two walls was ·one hundred
seventy-five feet [Lone hundred cubits] on the east and on the north.

The North Gateway

20The man measured the length and width of the north gateway leading
to the outer courtyard. 21Its three ·rooms [alcoves] on each side, its ·inner
walls [*or* jambs], and its ·porch [portico] measured the same as the first gateway. It was ·eighty-seven and one-half feet [Lfifty cubits] long and ·forty-four
feet [Ltwenty-five cubits] wide. 22Its windows, ·porch [portico], and carvings
of palm trees measured the same as the east gateway. Seven steps went up to
the gateway, and the gateway's ·porch [portico] was at the inner end. 23The
inner courtyard had a gateway across from the northern gateway like the
one on the east. The man measured it and found it was ·one hundred seventy-five feet [Lone hundred cubits] from inner gateway to outer gateway.

The South Gateway

24Then the man led me south ·where I saw [Land look/Tbehold] a gateway facing south. He measured its ·inner walls [*or* jambs] and its ·porch
[portico], and they measured the same as the other gateways. 25The gateway and its porch had windows all around like the other gateways. It was
·eighty-seven and one-half feet [Lfifty cubits] long and ·forty-four feet
[Ltwenty-five cubits] wide. 26Seven steps went up to this gateway. Its porch
was at the inner end, and it had carvings of palm trees on its inner walls.
27The inner courtyard had a gateway on its south side. The man measured from gate to gate on the south side, which was ·one hundred
seventy-five feet [Lone hundred cubits].

The Inner Courtyard

28Then the man brought me through the south gateway into the inner
courtyard. The inner south gateway measured the same as the gateways
in the outer wall. 29The inner south gateway's ·rooms [alcoves], ·inner
walls [*or* jambs], and ·porch [portico] measured the same as the gateways
in the outer wall. There were windows all around the gateway and its
porch. The gateway was ·eighty-seven and one-half feet [Lfifty cubits]
long and ·forty-four feet [Ltwenty-five cubits] wide. 30Each porch of each
inner gateway was ·about forty-four feet [Ltwenty-five cubits] long and
·about nine feet [Lfive cubits] wide. 31The inner south gateway's ·porch
[portico] faced the outer courtyard. Carvings of palm trees were on its
·side walls [*or* jambs], and its stairway had eight steps.

32The man brought me into the inner courtyard on the east side. He
measured the inner east gateway, and it was the same as the other gateways. 33The inner east gateway's ·rooms [alcoves], ·inside walls [*or* jambs],
and ·porch [portico] measured the same as the other gateways. Windows
were all around the gateway and its ·porch [portico]. The inner east gateway was ·eighty-seven and one-half feet [Lfifty cubits] long and ·forty-four
feet [Ltwenty-five cubits] wide. 34Its porch faced the outer courtyard.
Carvings of palm trees were on its ·inner walls [*or* jambs] on each side,
and its stairway had eight steps.

35Then the man brought me to the inner north gateway. He measured it,
and it was the same as the other gateways. 36Its ·rooms [alcoves], ·inside walls
[*or* jambs], and ·porch [portico] measured the same as the other gateways.
There were windows all around the gateway, which was ·eighty-seven and

one-half feet [Lfifty cubits] long and ·forty-four feet [Ltwenty-five cubits]
wide. 37Its ·porch [portico] faced the outer courtyard. Carvings of palm
trees were on its inner walls on each side, and its stairway had eight steps.

Rooms for Preparing Sacrifices

38There was a room with a door that opened onto the ·porch [portico]
of the inner north gateway. ·In this room the priests washed animals for
the burnt offerings [L...where the burnt offering was washed; Lev. 1:1–17].
39There were two tables on each side of the ·porch [portico], on which
animals for burnt offerings, ·sin [*or* purification] offerings [Lev. 4:3], and
·penalty [guilt; reparation] offerings [Lev. 5:14—6:7] were killed. 40Outside,
by each side wall of the ·porch [portico], at the entrance to the north gateway, were two more tables. 41So there were four tables inside the gateway,
and four tables outside. In all there were eight tables on which ·the priests
killed animals for sacrifices [Lto slaughter]. 42There were four tables made
of cut stone for the burnt offering [Lev. 1:1–17]. These tables were ·about
three feet [La cubit and a half] long, ·three feet [La cubit and a half] wide,
and ·about two feet [La cubit] high. On these tables the priests put their
tools which they used to kill animals for burnt offerings and the other
sacrifices. 43Double shelves*n* ·three inches [Lone handbreadth] wide were
put up on all the walls. The flesh for the offering was put on the tables.

The Priests' Rooms

44There were two rooms in the inner courtyard. One was beside the
north gateway and faced south. The other room was beside the south
gateway and faced north. 45The man said to me, "The room which faces
south is for the priests who ·serve in [*or* guard; *or* have charge of] the
Temple area, 46while the room that faces north is for the priests who
·serve at [*or* guard; *or* have charge of] the altar. This second group of
priests are descendants of Zadok, the only descendants of Levi who can
come near the LORD to ·serve [minister to] him."
47The man measured the inner courtyard. It was a square—·one hundred
seventy-five feet [Lone hundred cubits] long and ·one hundred seventy-five
feet [Lone hundred cubits] wide. The altar was in front of the Temple.

The Temple Porch

48The man brought me to the ·porch [portico] of the Temple and measured each ·side wall [*or* jamb] of the ·porch [portico]. Each was ·about
nine feet [Lfive cubits] thick. The doorway was ·twenty-four and one-half
feet [Lfourteen cubits] wide. The side walls of the doorway were each
·about five feet [Lthree cubits] wide. 49The ·porch [portico] was ·thirty-
five feet [Ltwenty cubits] long and ·twenty-one feet [Ltwelve cubits] wide,
with ten steps leading up to it. Pillars were by the ·side walls [*or* jambs],
one on each side of the entrance.

The Holy Place of the Temple

41 The man brought me to the ·Holy Place [outer sanctuary;
main hall] and measured its ·side walls [*or* jambs], which
were each ·ten and one-half feet [Lsix cubits] thick. 2The entrance was
·seventeen and one-half feet [Lten cubits] wide. The walls alongside the
entrance were each ·about nine feet wide [Lfive cubits]. The man measured the ·Holy Place [outer sanctuary; main hall], which was ·seventy
feet [Lforty cubits] long and ·thirty-five feet [Ltwenty cubits] wide.
3Then the man went ·inside [into the inner sanctuary] and measured
the ·side walls [*or* jambs] of the next doorway. Each was ·three and one-
half feet [Ltwo cubits] thick. The doorway was ·ten and one-half feet [Lsix

40:43 shelves Aramaic, Greek and Syriac copies read "shelves." Hebrew copies read "hooks."

cubits] wide, and the walls next to it were each more than ·twelve [Lseven
cubits] feet thick. 4Then the man measured the room ·at the end of [*or*
adjacent to] the ·Holy Place [outer sanctuary; main hall]. It was ·thirty-
five feet [Ltwenty cubits] long and ·thirty-five feet [Ltwenty cubits] long
wide. The man said to me, "This is the Most Holy Place."
5Then the man measured the wall of the ·Temple [Lhouse], which was
·ten and one-half feet [Lsix cubits] thick. There were side rooms ·seven
feet [Lfour cubits] wide all around the Temple. 6The side rooms were on
three different stories, each above the other, with thirty rooms on each
story. All around the Temple walls there were ledges for the side rooms.
The upper rooms rested on the ledges but were not attached to the Temple
walls. 7The side rooms around the Temple were wider on each higher
story, so rooms were wider on the top story. ·A stairway went [*or* So one
went] up from the lowest story to the highest through the middle story.
8I also saw that the Temple had a raised ·base [platform] all around. Its
edge was the foundation for the side rooms, and it was ·ten and one-half
feet thick [La full rod/stick of six cubits]. 9The outer wall of the side rooms
was ·about nine feet [Lfive cubits] thick. There was an open area between
the side rooms of the Temple 10and some other rooms. It was ·thirty-five
feet [Ltwenty cubits] wide and went all around the Temple. 11The side
rooms had doors which led to the open area around the outside of the
Temple. One door faced north, and the other faced south. The open area
was ·about nine feet [Lfive cubits] wide all around.
12The building facing the ·private area [temple courtyard] at the west
side was ·one hundred twenty-two and one-half feet [Lseventy cubits]
wide. The wall around the building was ·about nine feet [Lfive cubits] thick
and ·one hundred fifty-seven and one-half feet [Lninety cubits] long.
13Then the man measured the Temple. It was ·one hundred seventy-
five feet [Lone hundred cubits] long. The ·private area [temple courtyard],
including the building and its walls, was in all ·one hundred seventy-five
feet [Lone hundred cubits] long. 14Also the front of the Temple and the
·private area [courtyard] on its east side were ·one hundred seventy-five
feet [Lone hundred cubits] wide.
15The man measured the length of the building facing the ·private area
[courtyard] ·on the west side [*or* at the rear], and it was ·one hundred
seventy-five feet [Lone hundred cubits] ·from one wall to the other [*or*
with its galleries on each side].
The ·Holy Place, the Most Holy Place [*or* interior of the outer sanctu-
ary/main hall], and the outer porch 16had wood panels on the walls. By
the ·doorway [thresholds], the Temple had wood panels on the walls. The
wood covered all the walls from the floor up to the windows, 17up to the
part of the wall above the entrance.
All the walls inside the ·Most Holy Place and the Holy Place [inner and
outer sanctuary], and on the outside, in the ·porch [portico], 18had carvings of ·creatures with wings [Lcherubim] and palm trees. A palm tree was
between each ·carved creature [Lcherub], and every ·creature [Lcherub]
had two faces. 19One was a human face looking toward the palm tree on
one side. The other was a lion's face looking toward the palm tree on the
other side. They were carved all around the Temple walls. 20From the floor
to above the entrance, palm trees and ·creatures with wings [Lcherubim]
were carved. The walls of the Holy Place 21had square doorposts. In front
of the ·Most Holy Place [sanctuary] was something that looked like 22an

altar of wood. It was more than ·five feet [Lthree cubits] high and ·three feet [Ltwo cubits] wide. Its corners, base, and sides were wood. The man said to me, "This is the table that is ·in the presence of [before] the LORD." 23Both the ·Holy Place [main hall; outer sanctuary] and the ·Most Holy Place [inner sanctuary] had double doors. 24Each of the doors had two ·pieces [leaves] that would swing open. Two for one and two for the other. 25Carved on the doors of the ·Holy Place [main hall; outer sanctuary] were palm trees and ·creatures with wings [Lcherubim], like those carved on the walls. And there was a wood ·roof [canopy] over the front Temple ·porch [portico]. 26There were narrow windows and palm trees on both side walls of the ·porch [portico]. The side rooms of the Temple were also covered by a ·roof [canopy] over the stairway.

The Priests' Rooms

42 Then the man led me north out into the outer courtyard and to the rooms across from the ·private area [temple courtyard] and the building. 2These rooms on the north side were ·one hundred seventy-five feet [Lone hundred cubits] long and ·eighty-seven and one-half feet [Lfifty cubits] wide. 3There was ·thirty-five feet [Ltwenty cubits] of the inner courtyard between them and the Temple. On the other side, they faced the stone pavement of the outer courtyard. The rooms were built in three stories like steps ·and had balconies [with gallery facing gallery]. 4There was a ·path [passageway; walkway] in front of the rooms on the inner side, which was ·seventeen and one-half feet [Lten cubits] wide and ·one hundred seventy-five feet [Lone hundred cubits] long. The entrances to the rooms were on the north. 5The ·top [upper] rooms were narrower, because the ·balconies [galleries] took more space from them. The rooms on the first and second stories of the building were wider. 6The rooms were on three stories. They did not have pillars like the pillars of the courtyards. So the ·top [upper] rooms were farther back than those on the first and second stories. 7There was a wall outside parallel to the rooms and to the outer courtyard. It ran in front of the rooms for ·eighty-seven and one-half feet [Lfifty cubits]. 8The row of rooms along the outer courtyard was ·eighty-seven and one-half feet [Lfifty cubits] long, and the rooms that faced the ·Temple [main hall; sanctuary] were ·about one hundred seventy-five feet [Lone hundred cubits] long. 9The lower rooms had an entrance on the east side so a person could enter them from the outer courtyard, 10at the start of the wall beside the courtyard [Csome interpret this phrase as beginning the next sentence].

There were rooms on the south side, which were across from the ·private area [Temple courtyard] and the building. 11These rooms had a path in front of them. They were like the rooms on the north with the same length and width and the same exits, measurements and doors. 12The doors of the south rooms were like the doors of the north rooms. There was an entrance at the ·open end [*or* beginning] of a path beside the wall, so a person could enter at the east end.

13The man said to me, "The north and south rooms across from the ·private area [courtyard] are holy rooms. There the priests who ·go near [approach] the LORD will eat the most holy offerings. There they will put the most holy offerings: the ·grain [Lgift; tribute] offerings [Lev. 2:1], ·sin [*or* purification] offerings [Lev. 4:3], and the ·penalty [guilt; reparation] offerings [Lev. 5:14–6:7], because the place is holy. 14The priests who enter the Holy Place must leave ·their serving clothes [garments in which they minister] there before they go into the outer courtyard, because these ·clothes [garments] are holy. After they put on other ·clothes [garments], they may go to the part of the Temple area which is for the people."

Outside the Temple Area

15When the man finished measuring inside the Temple area, he brought me out through the east gateway. He measured the area all around. 16The man measured the east side with the measuring stick; it was ·eight hundred seventy-five feet [Lfive hundred cubits] by the measuring ·stick [rod]. 17He measured the north side; it was ·eight hundred seventy-five feet [Lfive hundred cubits] by the measuring stick. 18He measured the south side; it was ·eight hundred seventy-five feet [Lfive hundred cubits] by the measuring stick. 19He went around to the west side; it measured ·eight hundred seventy-five feet [Lfive hundred cubits] by the measuring stick. 20So he measured the Temple area on all four sides. The Temple area had a wall all around it that was ·eight hundred seventy-five feet long [Lfive hundred cubits] and ·eight hundred seventy-five feet [Lfive hundred cubits] wide. It separated what was holy from ·that which was not holy [the common/profane; Critually].

The Lord Among His People

43 Then the man led me to the outer east gateway, 2and [Llook; Tbehold] I saw the glory of the God of Israel [Chis manifest presence] coming from the east. It sounded like the roar of rushing water, and ·its brightness made the earth shine [the earth radiated/shone with his glory]. 3The vision I saw was like the vision I had seen when the LORD came to destroy the city [ch. 9] and also like the vision I had seen by the Kebar ·River [Canal; 1:1]. I ·bowed [fell] facedown on the ground. 4The glory of the LORD came into the ·Temple area [Lhouse] through the east gateway.

5Then ·the Spirit [*or* the spirit; *or* a wind; 2:2; 3:12] picked me up and brought me into the inner courtyard. ·There I saw [LAnd look/Tbehold] the LORD's glory filling the ·Temple [Lhouse]. 6As the man stood at my side, I heard someone speaking to me from inside the ·Temple [Lhouse]. 7The voice said to me, "·Human [TSon of man; 2:1], this is my throne and the place ·where my feet rest [Lfor the soles of my feet]. I will live here among the ·Israelites [Lsons/Tchildren or Israel] forever. The ·people [Lhouse] of Israel will not make my holy name ·unclean [defiled; Critually] again. Neither the people nor their kings will ·make it unclean [defile my holy name; Critually] with their ·sexual sins [prostitution] or with the ·dead bodies [Lcorpses in their death; *or* funeral monuments/pillars] of their kings. 8The kings ·made my name unclean [defiled my holy name; Critually] by putting their ·doorway [threshold] next to my ·doorway [threshold], and their doorpost next to my doorpost so only a wall separated me from them [Ckings erected monuments to themselves around the temple]. When they did their ·acts that I hate [detestable/abominable acts], they ·made my holy name unclean [defiled my holy name; Critually], and so I ·destroyed [consumed] them in my anger. 9Now let them stop their ·sexual sins [prostitution] and take the ·dead bodies [*or* funeral pillars; v. 7] of their kings far away from me. Then I will live among them forever.

10"·Human [TSon of man; 2:1], tell the ·people [Lhouse] of Israel about the ·Temple [Lhouse] so they will be ashamed of their ·sins [iniquities]. Let them ·think about the plan of the Temple [study its plan; *or* consider its perfection]. 11If they are ashamed of all they have done, let them know the design of the ·Temple [Lhouse] and how it is built. Show them its exits and entrances, all its designs, and also all its ·rules [statutes; ordinances; requirements] and

·teachings [laws; instructions]. Write it down ·as they watch [in their sight] so they will obey all its ·teachings [laws; instructions] and its ·rules [statutes; ordinances; requirements]. 12This is the ·teaching about [law of] the ·Temple [[L]house]: All the area around the top of the mountain is most holy. This is the ·teaching about [law/instruction of] the ·Temple [[L]house].

The Altar

13"These are the measurements of the altar, ·using the measuring stick [[L]in long cubits, each being a cubit and a handbreadth; 40:5]. The altar's ·gutter [base] is ·twenty-one inches [[L]one cubit] high and ·twenty-one inches [[L]one cubit] wide, and its rim is ·about nine inches [[L]one span] around its edge. And the altar is this tall: 14From the base on the ground up to the lower ledge, it measures ·three and one-half feet [[L]two cubits]. It is ·twenty-one inches [[L]one cubit] wide. It measures ·seven feet [[L]four cubits] from the smaller ledge to the larger ledge and is ·twenty-one inches [[L]one cubit] wide. 15The ·place where the sacrifice is burned on the altar [altar hearth] is ·seven feet [[L]four cubits] high, with its four ·corners shaped like horns and reaching up above it [horns projecting upward; Ex. 27:2]. 16It is square, ·twenty-one feet [[L]twelve cubits] long and ·twenty-one feet [[L]twelve cubits] wide. 17The upper ledge is also square, ·twenty-four and one-half feet [[L]fourteen cubits] long and ·twenty-four and one-half feet [[L]fourteen cubits] wide. The rim around the altar is ·ten and one-half inches [[L]one-half cubit] wide, and its ·gutter [base] is ·twenty-one inches [[L]one cubit] wide all around. Its steps ·are on the east side [[L]face east]."

18Then the man said to me, "·Human [[T]Son of man; 2:1], this is what the Lord GOD says: These are the ·rules [statutes; ordinances; requirements] for the altar. ·When [[L]On the day] it is built, use these rules to offer burnt offerings [Lev. 1:1–17] and to sprinkle blood on it [Lev. 1:5]. 19You must give a young bull as a ·sin [*or* purification] offering [Lev. 4:3] to the priests, the Levites who are from the ·family [seed; offspring] of Zadok and who come near me to ·serve [minister to] me, says the Lord GOD. 20Take some of the bull's blood and put it on the four ·corners [[L]horns; Ex. 27:2] of the altar, on the four corners of the ledge, and all around the rim. This is how you will ·make the altar pure [cleanse/purify the altar] and ·ready for God's service [[L]make atonement for it]. 21Then take the bull for the ·sin [*or* purification] offering [Lev. 4:3] and burn it in the ·proper [appointed; designated] place ·in the Temple area [[L]of the house], outside the ·Temple building [sanctuary].

22"On the second day offer a male goat ·that has nothing wrong with it [without blemish/defect] for a sin offering. The priests will ·make the altar pure and ready for God's service [cleanse/purify the altar] as they did with the young bull. 23When you finish ·making the altar pure and ready [purifying it], offer a young bull and a male sheep from the flock, ·which have nothing wrong with them [without blemish/defect]. 24You must offer them ·in the presence of [before] the LORD, and the priests are to throw salt on them and offer them as a burnt offering [Lev. 1:1–17] to the LORD.

25"You must prepare a goat every day for seven days as a sin offering. Also, the priests must prepare a young bull and ·male sheep [ram] from the flock, ·which have nothing wrong with them [without blemish/defect]. 26For seven days the priests are to make ·the altar pure and ready for God's service [[L]atonement for the altar and cleanse it]. Then they will ·give the altar to God [consecrate/dedicate it; [L]fill its hands]. 27·After these seven days [[L]When these days are completed], on the eighth day, the

priests must offer your burnt offerings [Lev. 1:1–17] and your ·fellowship
[*or* peace; well-being] offerings [Lev. 3:1] on the altar. Then I will accept
you, says the Lord God."

The Outer East Gate

44 Then the man brought me back to the outer east gateway of
the ·Temple area [sanctuary], but the gate was shut. 2The
Lord said to me, "This gate will stay shut; it will not be opened. No one
may enter through it, because the Lord God of Israel has entered through
it. So it must stay shut. 3Only the ·ruler [prince] himself may sit in the
gateway to eat ·a meal [Lbread; Cprobably his portion of the fellowship
offering; Lev. 7:15; Deut. 12:7] ·in the presence of [before] the Lord. He
must enter through the porch of the gateway and go out the same way."
4Then the man brought me through the outer north gate to the front
of the ·Temple [Lhouse]. As I looked, ·I saw [Llook; Tbehold] the glory of
the Lord [Chis manifest presence] filling the Temple of the Lord, and I
·bowed [fell] facedown on the ground.
5The Lord said to me, "·Human [TSon of man; 2:1], pay attention. Use
your eyes to see, and your ears to hear. See and hear everything I tell you
about all the ·rules [statutes; ordinances; requirements] and ·teachings
[laws; instructions] of the ·Temple [Lhouse] of the Lord. Pay attention to
the entrance to the Temple and to all the exits from the ·Temple area
[sanctuary]. 6Then speak to ·those who refuse to obey [the rebellious]. Say
to the ·people [Lhouse] of Israel, 'This is what the Lord God says: ·Stop
doing all [Enough of] your ·acts that I hate [detestable/abominable acts],
[Lhouse of] Israel! 7You brought foreigners into my ·Holy Place [sanctu-
ary] who were not circumcised in the flesh and ·had not given themselves
to serving me [Luncircumcised in the heart; Jer. 9:26; Acts 7:51]. You ·dis-
honored [defiled; profaned; Critually] my ·Temple [Lhouse] when you
offered me food, fat, and blood. You broke my ·agreement [covenant;
treaty] by all ·the things you did that I hate [your detestable/abominable
acts]. 8You did not take ·care [charge] of my holy things yourselves but put
·foreigners [*or* others] ·in charge of [to take care of] my ·Temple [sanctu-
ary]. 9This is what the Lord God says: Foreigners who ·do not give
themselves to serving me [Lare uncircumcised in heart] and who are uncircumcised in flesh may not enter my ·Temple [sanctuary]. Not even a
foreigner living among the ·people [Lsons/Tchildren] of Israel may enter.
10" 'But the Levites who ·stopped obeying [Lwent far from] me when
Israel ·left me [went astray] and who followed their idols must ·be punished [be responsible; bear the penalty] for their sin. 11These Levites are
to be ·servants in [ministers of] my ·Holy Place [sanctuary]. They may
guard the gates of the ·Temple [Lhouse] and serve in the ·Temple area
[Lhouse]. They may ·kill the animals for [Lslaughter] the burnt offering
[Lev. 1:1–17] and the sacrifices for the people. They may stand before
the people to ·serve [minister to] them. 12But these Levites ·helped the
people worship [Lministered to them before] their idols and caused the
·people [Lhouse] of Israel to ·fall [stumble], so I ·make this promise
[Lswear with uplifted hand]: They will ·be punished [be responsible; bear
the penalty] for their sin, says the Lord God. 13They will not come near
me to serve as priests, nor will they come near any of my holy things or
the most holy offerings. But they will ·be made ashamed of [bear the
shame for] ·the things they did that I hate [their detestable/abominable
actions]. 14Yet I will ·put them in charge of taking care [appoint them to

guard/keep charge] of the ·Temple area [Lhouse], all the work that must be done in it.

[15]" 'But the priests who are Levites and descendants of Zadok took care of my ·Holy Place [sanctuary] when [Lthe sons/Tchildren of] Israel ·left me [went astray], so they may come near to serve me. They may stand in my presence to offer me the fat and blood [Cof sacrificial animals], says the Lord GOD. [16]They ·are the only ones who may [Lwill] enter my ·Holy Place [sanctuary]. ·Only they [LThey] may come near my table to ·serve [minister to] me and ·take care of the things I gave them to do [keep my charge; *or* serve me as guards].

[17]" 'When they enter the gates of the inner courtyard, they must wear linen robes. They must not wear wool to ·serve [minister] at the gates of the inner courtyard or in the ·Temple [Lhouse]. [18]They will wear linen turbans on their heads and linen underclothes [Lev. 6:10]. They will not ·wear [bind/gird themselves with] anything that makes them perspire. [19]When they go out into the outer courtyard to the people, they must take off their serving ·clothes [garments] before they go. They must leave these clothes in the ·holy rooms [sacred chambers] and put on other ·clothes [garments]. Then they will not ·let their holy clothes hurt [*or* transmit holiness with their garments to] the people.

[20]" 'They must not shave their heads or let their hair grow long but must keep the hair of their heads trimmed [Lev. 21:5]. [21]None of the priests may drink wine when they enter the inner courtyard [Lev. 10:9]. [22]The priests must not marry widows or divorced women. They may marry only virgins from the ·people [Loffspring/seed of the house] of Israel or widows of priests [Lev. 21:7–8]. [23]They must teach my people the difference between what is holy and what is ·not holy [common; profane; Critually]. They must help my people know what is unclean [Critually] and what is clean.

[24]" 'In ·court [a dispute/controversy] they will act as judges. When they judge, they will follow my ·teachings [judgments]. They must obey my ·laws [teachings; instructions] and my ·rules [statutes; ordinances; requirements] at all my ·special feasts [appointed festivals] and keep my Sabbaths holy.

[25]" 'They must not go near a dead person, ·making themselves unclean [defiling themselves; Critually]. But they are allowed to ·make themselves unclean [defile themselves; Critually] if the dead person is their father, mother, son, daughter, brother, or a sister who has not married. [26]After a priest has been ·made clean again [cleansed; Critually], he must wait seven days. [27]Then he may go into the inner courtyard to serve in the ·Temple [sanctuary], but he must offer a sin offering for himself, says the Lord GOD [Lev. 21:1–4].

[28]" '·These are the rules about the priests and their property [LThis will be their inheritance]: ·They will have me instead of property [LI am their inheritance]. You will not give them any ·land to own [possessions] in Israel; I am ·what they will own [their possession]. [29]They will eat the ·grain [Lgift; tribute] offerings [Lev. 2:1], ·sin [*or* purification] offerings [Lev. 4:3], and ·penalty [guilt; reparation] offerings [Lev. 5:14—6:7]. ·Everything Israel gives to me [LEvery devoted thing in Israel] will be theirs. [30]The ·best [first] fruits of all the first harvests and all the special gifts offered to me will belong to the priests. You will also give to the priests the first part of your ·grain that you grind [dough] ·and so bring a blessing [Lthat a blessing may rest] on your family. [31]The priests must not eat any bird or animal that died a natural death or one that has been torn by wild animals.

The Land Is Divided

45 " 'When you divide the land for the Israelite tribes by throwing lots, you must give a part of the land to belong to the LORD.
It will be ·about seven miles [Ltwenty-five thousand cubits] long and
·about six miles [Ltwenty thousand cubits] wide; all of this land will be
holy. 2From this land, an area ·eight hundred seventy-five feet [Lfive hundred cubits] square will be for the ·Temple [sanctuary]. There will be an
open space around the Temple that is ·eighty-seven and one-half feet
[Lfifty cubits] wide. 3In the holy area you will measure a part ·about seven
miles [Ltwenty-five thousand cubits] long and ·three miles wide [Lten
thousand cubits], and in it will be the sanctuary, the Most Holy Place.
4This ·holy part [sacred portion] of the land will be for the priests who
·serve [minister] in the ·Temple [sanctuary], who come near to the LORD to
·serve [minister to] him. It will be a place for the priests' houses and ·for
the Temple [La holy place for the sanctuary]. 5Another area ·about seven
miles [Ltwenty-five thousand cubits] long and ·three miles wide [Lten
thousand cubits] will be for the Levites, who ·serve [minister] in the
Temple area. It will belong to them so they will have cities in which to live.
6" 'You must give the city an area that is ·about one and one-half miles
[Lfive thousand cubits] wide and ·about seven miles [Ltwenty-five thousand cubits] long, along the side of the holy area. It will belong to all the
·people [Lhouse] of Israel.
7" 'The ·ruler [prince] will have land on both sides of the holy ·area
[allotment; contribution] and the city. On the west of the holy area, his
land will reach to the eastern border [Capparently the Mediterranean Sea].
On the east of the holy area, his land will reach to the eastern border [Cof
the country]. It will be as long as the land given to each tribe. 8Only this
land will be the ruler's ·property [possession] in Israel. So my rulers will
not ·be cruel to [oppress] my people anymore [Csuch a large portion
would keep the king from wanting to seize land, as Ahab had done (1 Kin.
21); see v. 9], but they will let each tribe in the ·nation [Lhouse] of Israel
have its share of the land.
9" 'This is what the Lord GOD says: ·You have gone far enough [Enough!],
you ·rulers [princes] of Israel! Stop ·being cruel and hurting people [your
violence and oppression], and do what is right and ·fair [just]. Stop ·forc-
ing my people out of their homes [evicting my people], says the Lord GOD.
10You must have ·honest [just] scales, an ·honest [just] ·dry measurement
[Lephah] and an ·honest [just] ·liquid measurement [Lbath]. 11The dry
measure [Lephah] and the liquid measure [Lbath] will be the same: The
·liquid measure [Lbath] will always be a tenth of a homer [C the Hebrew
means "donkey-load," and was about five bushels of dry measure and 55
gallons of liquid measure], and the dry measure [Lephah] will always be a
tenth of a homer. The ·measurement they follow [standard measure] will
be the homer. 12The shekel [Ccoin weighing about two-fifths of an ounce]
will be worth twenty gerahs, and a mina will be worth ·sixty shekels
[Ltwenty shekels and twenty-five shekels and fifteen shekels].

Offerings and Holy Days

13" 'This is the ·gift [offering] you should offer: a sixth of an ephah [v.
11] from every homer [v. 11] of wheat, and a sixth of an ephah from every
homer of barley. 14The amount of oil you are to offer is a tenth of a bath
[v. 11] from each cor. (Ten baths make a homer and also make a cor.)
15You should give one sheep from each flock of two hundred from the
watering places of Israel. All these are to be offered for the ·grain [Lgift;

tribute] offerings [Lev. 2:1], burnt offerings [Lev. 1:1–17], and ·fellowship
[*or* peace; well-being] offerings [Lev. 3:1] to ·remove the sins of [make
atonement for] the people, says the Lord God. 16All people in the land will
give this special offering to the ·ruler [prince] of Israel. 17It will be the
·ruler's [prince's] responsibility to supply the burnt offerings [Lev. 1:1–
17], ·grain [Lgift; tribute] offerings [Lev. 2:1], and drink offerings. These
offerings will be given at the ·feasts [appointed festivals], at the New
Moons, on the Sabbaths, and at all the other feasts of [Lthe house of]
Israel. He will supply the ·sin [*or* purification] offerings [Lev. 4:3], ·grain
[Lgift; tribute] offerings, and ·fellowship [*or* peace; well-being] offerings
[Lev. 3:1] to pay for the sins of [Lthe house of] Israel.
18" 'This is what the Lord God says: On the first day of the first month
take a young bull ·that has nothing wrong with it [without blemish/defect].
Use it to ·make the Temple pure and ready for God's service [Lpurify the
sanctuary]. 19The priest will take some of the blood from this ·sin [*or* puri-
fication] offering [Lev. 4:3] and put it on the doorposts of the ·Temple
[Lhouse], on the four corners of the ledge of the altar, and on the posts of
the gate to the inner courtyard. 20You will do the same thing on the seventh
day of the month for anyone who has sinned ·by accident [unintentionally]
or ·without knowing it [through ignorance]. This is how you make ·the
Temple pure and ready for God's service [Latonement for the house].

Passover Feast Offerings

21" 'On the fourteenth day of the first month you will celebrate the
Feast of Passover [Ex. 12:1–20; Lev. 23:4–8; Num. 28:16–25; Deut. 16:1–
5]. It will be a feast of seven days when you eat ·bread made without yeast
[unleavened bread]. 22On that day the ·ruler [prince] ·must offer [will
provide] a bull for himself and for all the people of the land as a ·sin [*or*
purification] offering [Lev. 4:3]. 23During the seven days of the feast he
·must offer [will provide] seven bulls and seven ·male sheep [rams] ·that
have nothing wrong with them [without blemish/defect]. They will be
burnt offerings [Lev. 1:1–17] to the Lord, which the ruler will offer every
day of the seven days of the feast. He must also offer a male goat every day
as a ·sin [*or* purification] offering [Lev. 4:3]. 24The ruler ·must give [will
provide] as a ·grain [Lgift; tribute] offering [Lev. 2:1] ·one-half bushel [Lan
ephah; v. 11] for each bull and ·one-half bushel [Lan ephah] for each
sheep. He must give a ·gallon [Lhin] of olive oil for each half bushel.
25" 'Beginning on the fifteenth day of the seventh month, when you
celebrate the ·Feast of Shelters [LFeast/Festival; Lev. 23:33–44; Num.
28:12–40], the ruler will supply the same ·things [provisions] for seven
days: the ·sin [*or* purification] offerings [Lev. 4:3], burnt offerings [Lev.
1:1–17], ·grain [Lgift; tribute] offerings [Lev. 2:1], and the olive oil.

Rules for Worship

46 " 'This is what the Lord God says: The east gate of the inner
courtyard will stay shut on the six working days, but it will be
opened on the Sabbath day and on the day of the New Moon. 2The ·ruler
[prince] will enter from outside through the ·porch [portico] of the gateway and stand by the gatepost, while the priests offer the ·ruler's [prince's]
burnt offering [Lev. 1:1–17] and ·fellowship [*or* peace; well-being] offering
[Lev. 3:1]. The ruler will ·worship [bow down] at the ·entrance [threshold]
of the gateway, and then he will go out. But the gate will not be shut until
evening. 3The people of the land will worship at the entrance of that gateway ·in the presence of [before] the Lord on the Sabbaths and New Moons.
4This is the burnt offering [Lev. 1:1–17] the ruler will offer to the Lord on

the Sabbath day: six male lambs ·that have nothing wrong with them [without blemish/defect] and a ·male sheep [ram] ·that has nothing wrong with it [without blemish/defect]. 5He must give a ·half-bushel [[L]ephah; 45:11] ·grain [[L]gift; tribute] offering with the male sheep, but he ·may [*or* will] give as much grain offering with the lambs as ·he pleases [*or* he is able; [L]a gift of his hand]. He must also give a ·gallon [[L]hin] of olive oil for each ·half bushel [[L]ephah] of grain. 6On the day of the New Moon he must offer a young bull ·that has nothing wrong with it [without blemish/defect]. He must also offer six lambs and a male sheep ·that have nothing wrong with them [all without blemish/defect]. 7The ruler must give a ·half-bushel [[L]ephah] ·grain [[L]gift; tribute] offering [Lev. 2:1] with the bull and ·one-half bushel [[L]an ephah] with the ·male sheep [ram]. With the lambs, he ·may [*or* will] give as much grain ·as he pleases [*or* as he is able; [L]a gift of his hand]. But he must give a ·gallon [[L]hin] of olive oil for each half bushel of grain. 8When the ·ruler [prince] enters, he must go in through the ·porch [portico] of the gateway, and he must go out the same way.

9" 'When the people of the land come ·into the LORD's presence [before the LORD] at the ·special feasts [appointed festivals], those who enter through the north gate to worship must go out through the south gate. Those who enter through the south gate must go out through the north gate. They must not return the same way they entered; everyone must go out ·the opposite way [straight ahead]. 10The ·ruler [prince] will go in with the people when they go in and go out with them when they go out.

11" 'At the feasts and ·regular times of worship [appointed festivals] ·one-half bushel [[L]an ephah] of grain must be offered with a young bull, and ·one-half bushel [[L]an ephah] of grain must be offered with a ·male sheep [ram]. But with an offering of lambs, the ruler may give as much grain as ·he pleases [*or* he is able; [L]a gift of his hand]. He should give a ·gallon [[L]hin] of olive oil for each ·half bushel [[L]ephah] of grain. 12The ·ruler [prince] may give an ·offering as a special gift to the LORD [freewill offering]; it may be a burnt offering [Lev. 1:1–17] or ·fellowship [*or* peace; well-being] offering [Lev. 3:1]. When he gives it to the LORD, the ·inner east gate [gate facing east] is to be opened for him. He must offer his burnt offering or his ·fellowship [*or* peace; well-being] offering [Lev. 3:1] as he does on the Sabbath day. Then he will go out, and the gate will be shut after he has left.

13" 'Every day you will give a year-old lamb ·that has nothing wrong with it [without blemish/defect] for a burnt offering [Lev. 1:1–17] to the LORD. Do it ·every morning [morning by morning]. 14Also, you must offer a ·grain [[L]gift; tribute] offering [Lev. 2:1] with the lamb ·every morning [morning by morning]. For this you will give ·three and one-third quarts [[L]a sixth of an ephah] of grain and ·one and one-third quarts [[L]a third of an ephah] of olive oil, to make the fine flour moist, as a ·grain [[L]gift; tribute] offering [Lev. 2:1] to the LORD. This is a ·rule that must be kept from now on [perpetual statute; lasting ordinance]. 15So you must always give the lamb, together with the ·grain [[L]gift; tribute] offering [Lev. 2:1] and the olive oil, ·every morning [morning by morning] as a ·regular [perpetual] burnt offering [Lev. 1:1–17].

Rules for the Ruler

16" 'This is what the Lord GOD says: If the ·ruler [prince] gives a gift from his ·land [inheritance] to any of his sons, that land will belong to the son and then to the son's children. It is their property ·passed down from their family [[L]by inheritance]. 17But if the ruler gives a gift from his ·land [inheritance] to any of his servants, that land will belong to the servant only until the year of freedom [[C]the year of Jubilee; Lev. 25:8–15]. Then the land will go back to the ·ruler [prince]. ·Only the ruler's sons may keep a gift of land from the ruler [[L]His inheritance shall be only for his sons]. 18The ·ruler [prince] must not take any of the people's ·land [inheritance], forcing them out of their land. He must give his sons ·some of his own land [inheritance from his own property] so my people will not be scattered out of their own land.' "

The Special Kitchens

19The man led me through the entrance at the side of the gateway to the priests' ·holy rooms [sacred chambers] that face north. ·There I saw [[L]And look/[T]behold] a place at the far west end. 20The man said to me, "This is where the priests will boil the ·meat of the penalty [[L]penalty; *or* guilt; reparation] offering [Lev. 5:14—6:7] and ·sin [*or* purification] offering [Lev. 4:3] and bake the ·grain [[L]gift; tribute] offering [Lev. 3:1]. Then they will not need to bring these holy offerings into the outer courtyard, ·because that would hurt [[L]which would transmit holiness to] the people [[C]the purity of God's holiness would destroy sinful human beings; Lev. 16:2]."

21Then the man brought me out into the outer courtyard and led me to its four corners. [[L]And look/[T]behold] In each corner of the courtyard was a smaller courtyard. 22Small courtyards were in the four corners of the courtyard. Each small courtyard was the same size, ·seventy feet [[L]forty cubits] long and ·fifty-two and one-half feet [[L]thirty cubits] wide. 23A ·stone wall [[L]row] was around each of the four small courtyards, and ·places for cooking [fireplaces; boiling places] were built in each of the ·stone walls [rows]. 24The man said to me, "These are the kitchens where those who ·work [minister] in the Temple will boil the sacrifices offered by the people."

The River from the Temple

47 The man led me back to the door of the ·Temple [[L]house], and ·I saw [[L]look; [T]behold] water coming out from under the ·doorway [threshold] and flowing east. (The Temple faced east.) The water flowed down from the south side wall of the Temple and then south of the altar. 2The man brought me out through the outer north gate and led me around outside to the outer east gate. ·I found [[L]And look/[T]behold] the water ·coming [trickling] out on the south side of the gate.

3The man went toward the east with a measuring line in his hand and measured ·about one-third of a mile [[L]a thousand cubits]. Then he led me through water that came up to my ankles. 4The man measured ·about one-third of a mile [[L]a thousand] again and led me through water that came up to my knees. Then he measured ·about one-third of a mile [[L]a thousand] again and led me through water up to my waist. 5The man measured ·about one-third of a mile [[L]a thousand] again, but it was now a river that I could not cross. The water had risen too high; it was deep enough for swimming; it was a river that no one could cross. 6The man asked me, "·Human [[T]Son of man; 2:1], do you see this?"

Then the man led me back to the bank of the river. 7As I went back, I saw many trees on both sides of the river. 8The man said to me, "This water will flow toward the eastern areas and go down into the ·Jordan Valley [[L]Arabah]. When it enters the ·Dead Sea [[L]Sea], it will ·become fresh [[L]be healed; [C]the Dead Sea has no fish or other living creatures due to its high mineral content]. 9Everywhere the river goes, there will be many fish. Wherever this water goes the ·Dead Sea [[L]Sea] will become fresh, and so where the river goes there will be ·many [swarms of] living things. 10 Fishermen will stand by ·the Dead Sea [Lit]. From En Gedi [Cmidway along the western side of the Dead Sea] all the way to En Eglaim [Can unknown location, perhaps on the east bank of the Dead Sea] there will be places to spread fishing nets. There will be many kinds of fish there, as many as in the ·Mediterranean [LGreat] Sea. 11 But its swamps and marshes will not become fresh; they will ·be left for salt [*or* remain salty]. 12 All kinds of fruit trees will grow on both banks of the river. Their leaves will not ·dry and die [wither] and ·there will always be fruit on them [Ltheir fruit will not fail]. The trees will bear fruit every month, because the water for them comes from the ·Temple [sanctuary]. The fruit from the trees will be used for food, and their leaves for ·medicine [Lhealing]."

Borders of the Land

13 This is what the Lord God says: "These are the borders of the land to be divided for an inheritance among the twelve tribes of Israel. Joseph will have two parts of land [Cthe tribes of Ephraim and Manasseh, Joseph's two sons adopted by Jacob (Gen. 48:17–20)]. 14 You will divide the land equally. I ·promised [vowed; Lswore with uplifted hand] to give it to your ·ancestors [fathers], so this land will ·belong to you as family property [become your inheritance].

15 "This will be the ·border line [boundary] of the land: "On the north side it will start at the ·Mediterranean [LGreat] Sea. It will go through Hethlon, toward ·Lebo Hamath [*or* Lebo of Hamath; Coften identified as the northern limit of Israel; Num. 13:21; Josh. 13:5; 1 Kin. 8:65] and on to the towns of Zedad, 16 Berothah, and Sibraim on the border between Damascus [Ccapital of Aram (Syria)] and Hamath [Ccity 120 miles north of Damascus]. Then it will go on to the town of Hazer Hatticon on the border of the country of Hauran. 17 So the border line will go from the ·Mediterranean Sea [LSea] east to the town of Hazar Enan, where the land belonging to Damascus and Hamath lies on the north side. This will be the north side of the land.

18 "On the east side the border runs south from a point between Hauran and Damascus. It will go along the Jordan between Gilead and the land of Israel and will continue to the town of Tamar [Cprobaby En-Gedi; 2 Chr. 20:2] on the ·Dead [Leastern] Sea. This will be the east side of the land.

19 "On the south side the border line will go west from Tamar all the way to the waters of Meribah Kadesh [Clikely Kadesh Barnea (Num. 34:4), fifty miles south of Beersheba]. Then it will run along the brook of Egypt to the ·Mediterranean [LGreat] Sea. This will be the south side of the land.

20 "On the west side the ·Mediterranean [LGreat] Sea will be the ·border line [boundary] up to a place across from Lebo Hamath [v. 15]. This will be the west side of your land.

21 "You will divide this land among the tribes of Israel. 22 You will divide it as ·family property [an inheritance] for yourselves and for the foreigners who live and have children among you. You are to treat these foreigners the same as people born in Israel; they are to ·share the land [be allotted an inheritance] with the tribes of Israel. 23 In whatever tribe the foreigner lives, you will give him ·some land [Lhis inheritance]," says the Lord God.

Dividing the Land

48 "These are the ·areas of the tribes named here [Lnames of the tribes]: Dan will have one share at the northern border. It will go from the sea through Hethlon to Lebo Hamath [47:15], all the way to Hazar Enan [47:17], ·where Damascus lies to the north. It will

stop there next to Hamath [*or* ...which is located on the northern border
of Damascus next to Hamath]. This will be Dan's northern border from
the east side to the ·Mediterranean Sea on the west side [Lwest].
2"·South of [LBeside] Dan's border, Asher will have one share. It will go
from the east side to the west side.
3"·South of [LBeside] Asher's border, Naphtali will have one share. It
will go from the east side to the west side.
4"·South of [LBeside] Naphtali's border, Manasseh will have one share.
It will go from the east side to the west side.
5"·South of [LBeside] Manasseh's border, Ephraim will have one share.
It will go from the east side to the west side.
6"·South of [LBeside] Ephraim's border, Reuben will have one share. It
will go from the east side to the west side.
7"·South of [LBeside] Reuben's border, Judah will have one share. It will
go from the east side to the west side.
8"·South of [LBeside] Judah's border will be the ·holy area which you
are to give [portion set apart]. It will be ·about seven miles [Ltwenty-five
thousand cubits] wide and as long and wide as one of the tribes' shares. It
will run from the east side to the west side. The ·Temple [Lsanctuary] will
be in the middle of this area.
9"The share which you will give the LORD will be ·about seven miles
[Ltwenty-five thousand cubits] long and ·three miles [Lten thousand cubits]
wide. 10The ·holy area [sacred allotment] will be divided among these people. The priests will have land ·about seven miles [Ltwenty-five thousand
cubits] long on the north and south sides, and ·three miles [Lten thousand
cubits] wide on the west and east sides. The ·Temple [sanctuary] of the
LORD will be in the middle of it. 11This land is for the ·priests who are given
the holy duty of serving the LORD [Lconsecrated priests]. ·They [L...who]
are the ·descendants [sons] of Zadok who ·did my work [were faithful to
me; kept my charge] and did not ·leave me [go astray] when Israel and the
Levites ·left me [went astray]. 12They will have as their share a very holy
part of the holy portion of the land. It will be next to the land of the Levites.
13"Alongside the land for the priests, the Levites will have a share ·about
seven miles [Ltwenty-five thousand cubits] long and ·three miles [Lten
thousand cubits] wide; its full length will be ·about seven miles [Ltwenty-
five thousand cubits] and its full width ·about three miles [Lten thousand
cubits]. 14The Levites are not to sell or ·trade [exchange] any of this land.
They are not to ·let anyone else own [transfer; alienate] any of this best
part of the land, because it ·belongs [is set apart/holy] to the LORD.

City Property

15"The rest of the area will be ·about one and one-half miles [Lfive
thousand cubits] wide and ·seven miles [Ltwenty-five thousand cubits]
long. It will ·not be holy but [be for common use and] will belong to the
city and be used for homes and pastures. The city will be in the middle of
it. 16These are the city's measurements: the north side will be ·about one
mile [Lfour thousand five hundred cubits], the south side ·about one mile
[Lfour thousand five hundred cubits], the east side ·about one mile [Lfour
thousand five hundred cubits], and the west side ·about one mile [Lfour
thousand five hundred cubits]. 17The city's land for pastures will be ·about
four hundred thirty-seven feet [Ltwo hundred fifty cubits] on the north,
·four hundred thirty-seven feet [Ltwo hundred fifty cubits] on the south,
·four hundred thirty-seven feet [Ltwo hundred fifty cubits] on the east,

and ·four hundred thirty-seven feet [Ltwo hundred fifty cubits] on the west. 18Along the long side of the holy area there will be left ·three miles [Lten thousand cubits] on the east and ·three miles [Lten thousand cubits] on the west. It will be used to grow food for the city workers. 19The city workers from all the tribes of Israel will farm this land. 20This whole area will be square, ·seven miles [Ltwenty-five thousand cubits] by ·seven miles [Ltwenty-five thousand cubits]. You shall give to the LORD the holy share along with the city property.

21"Land that is left over on both sides of the holy area and city property will belong to the ·ruler [prince]. That land will extend eastward from the ·seven miles [Ltwenty-five thousand cubits] of the holy area to the eastern border and westward from the ·seven miles [Ltwenty-five thousand cubits] to the ·Mediterranean Sea [Lwestern border]. Both of these areas run the length of the lands of the tribes, and they belong to the ·ruler [prince]. The holy area with the ·Holy Place [sanctuary] of the ·Temple [Lhouse] will be in the middle. 22The Levites' land and the city property will be in the middle of the lands belonging to the ·ruler [prince]. Those lands will be between Judah's border and Benjamin's border.

The Other Tribes' Land

23"Here is what the rest of the tribes will receive: Benjamin will have one share. It will go from the east side to the ·Mediterranean Sea on the west side [Lwest side].

24"·South of [LBeside] Benjamin's land, Simeon will have one share. It will go from the east side to the west side.

25"·South of [LBeside] Simeon's land, Issachar will have one share. It will go from the east side to the west side.

26"·South of [LBeside] Issachar's land, Zebulun will have one share. It will go from the east side to the west side.

27"·South of [LBeside] Zebulun's land, Gad will have one share. It will go from the east side to the west side.

28"The southern border of Gad's land will go ·east from Tamar on the Dead Sea [Lfrom Tamar; 47:18] to the waters of Meribah Kadesh [47:19]. Then it will run along the brook of Egypt to the ·Mediterranean [LGreat] Sea.

29"This is the land you will divide among the tribes of Israel to be their shares," says the Lord GOD.

The Gates of the City

30"These will be the ·outside borders [*or* exits] of the city: The north side will measure ·more than one mile [Lfour thousand five hundred cubits]. 31There will be three gates facing north: Reuben's Gate, Judah's Gate, and Levi's Gate, named for the tribes of Israel.

32"The east side will measure ·more than one mile [Lfour thousand five hundred cubits]. There will be three gates facing east: Joseph's Gate, Benjamin's Gate, and Dan's Gate.

33"The south side will measure ·more than one mile [Lfour thousand five hundred cubits]. There will be three gates facing south: Simeon's Gate, Issachar's Gate, and Zebulun's Gate.

34"The west side will measure ·more than one mile [Lfour thousand five hundred cubits]. There will be three gates facing west: Gad's Gate, Asher's Gate, and Naphtali's Gate.

35"The city will measure ·about six miles around [Leighteen thousand cubits]. From then on the name of the city will be The LORD Is There."

DANIEL

Daniel Taken to Babylon

1 During the third year that Jehoiakim was king of Judah [C605 BC], **Nebuchadnezzar king of Babylon** [Cruled 605–562 BC] **came to Jerusalem and ·surrounded it with his army** [besieged/Lpressed it]. 2**The Lord ·allowed Nebuchadnezzar to capture Jehoiakim king of Judah** [Lgave Jehoiakim king of Judah into his hand; CGod was in control, not Nebuchadnezzar]. **Nebuchadnezzar also took some of the ·things** [articles; utensils; Ccups, forks, and other items used in ritual; 5:2–4; Ex. 27:9; 30:27; 31:8–9; Ezra 1:9–11] **from the ·Temple** [Lhouse] **of God, which he carried to ·Babylonia** [Lthe land of Shinar] **and put in the ·temple** [Lhouse of the treasury] **of his ·gods** [*or* god; Cprobably Marduk, the chief god of Babylon].

3**Then King Nebuchadnezzar ordered Ashpenaz, ·his chief officer** [*or* the chief of his eunuchs], **to bring some of the ·men of Judah into his palace. He wanted them to be from important families, including the family of the king of Judah** [L…sons of Israel, from the royal family and from the nobility]. 4**King Nebuchadnezzar wanted only ·young Israelite men** [Lchildren] **who had ·nothing wrong with them** [Lno blemish; 2 Sam. 14:25; Song 4:4]. **They were to be ·handsome** [Lof good appearance] **and ·well educated** [Lskilled in all wisdom], **·capable of learning** [Lknowing knowledge] **and understanding, and able to ·serve** [Lstand] **in his palace** [Gen. 41:33]. **Ashpenaz was to teach them the language and ·writings** [literature] **of the ·Babylonians** [LChaldeans; Cprobably Akkadian and Aramaic; the literature would include myths and legends as well as divination texts]. 5**The king ·gave the young men** [Lallotted/assigned to them] **·a certain amount of food and wine every day, just like the food he ate** [La daily ration of the royal food and wine he drank]. **The young men were to be ·trained** [educated] **for three years, and then they would ·become servants of the king of Babylon** [Lstand before the king]. 6**Among those young men were Daniel** [C"God is my judge"], **Hananiah** [C"The Lord is gracious to me"], **Mishael** [C"Who is like God"], **and Azariah** [C"The Lord is my helper"] **from the ·people** [Lsons] **of Judah.**

7**Ashpenaz, the chief ·officer** [*or* of the eunuchs], **gave them names** [CBabylonian, that is Akkadian, names]. **Daniel's new name was Belteshazzar, Hananiah's was Shadrach, Mishael's was Meshach, and Azariah's was Abednego** [Cthe new names praised Babylonian gods].

8**Daniel ·decided** [Lset his heart] **not to eat the king's food or drink his wine because that would ·defile** [contaminate] **him** [Cperhaps would make him ritually unclean, but more likely because he depended on God to sustain him]. **So he ·asked** [sought] **·Ashpenaz** [Lthe chief officer/*or* of the eunuchs] **for permission not to ·defile** [contaminate] **himself in this way.**

9 God made Ashpenaz, the chief ·officer [or of the eunuchs], want to be
·kind [loving] and ·merciful [gracious] to Daniel, 10 but ·Ashpenaz [Lthe
chief officer/or of the eunuchs] said to Daniel, "I am afraid of my master,
the king. He ·ordered me to give you this [Lallotted/assigned your] food
and drink. If you begin to look ·worse [thinner] than other ·young men
[children; youth] your age, the king will see this. Then ·he will cut off my
head because of you [Lyou will forfeit my head to the king]."
11 Daniel spoke to the ·guard [or attendant; steward] whom the chief
·officer [or of the eunuchs] had ·appointed [allotted/assigned] over
Daniel, Hananiah, Mishael, and Azariah, 12 "Please give us this test for ten
days: Don't give us anything but vegetables to eat and water to drink.
13 Then compare how we look with how the other ·young men [children;
youth] look who eat the king's ·food [rations]. See for yourself and then
decide how you want to treat us, your servants."
14 So the ·guard [or attendant; steward] ·agreed to test [Llistened to them
on this matter and tested] them for ten days. 15 After ten days they looked
healthier and ·better fed [Ltheir flesh was fatter] than all the ·young men
[children; youths] who ate the king's ·food [rations]. 16 So the ·guard [or
attendant; steward] took away the king's special food and wine, feeding
them vegetables instead.
17 God gave these four ·young men [children; youths] ·wisdom [knowl-
edge] and ·the ability to learn many things that people had written and
studied [insight into wisdom and literature]. Daniel could also understand visions and dreams.
18 At the end of the ·time [Ldays] ·set for them by the king [Lwhich the
king said to bring them; v. 5], ·Ashpenaz [Lthe chief officer/or of the
eunuchs] brought all the young men to King Nebuchadnezzar. 19 The king
talked to them and found that none of the young men were ·as good as
[Llike] Daniel, Hananiah, Mishael, and Azariah. So ·those four young men
became the king's servants [Lthey stood before the king]. 20 Every time the
king ·asked them about [Lsought from them] something important, they
showed much wisdom and understanding. They were ten times better
than all the ·magicians [enchanters] and ·fortune-tellers [diviners] in his
kingdom! 21 So Daniel ·continued to be the king's servant [was there]
until the first year Cyrus was king.

Nebuchadnezzar's Dream

2 During Nebuchadnezzar's second year as king [603–602 BC], ·he
had dreams that bothered [Lhis spirit agitated] him and ·kept him
awake at night [Lhis sleep left him]. 2 So the king ·called for [summoned]
his ·magicians [enchanters], ·fortune-tellers [diviners], ·wizards [sorcer-
ers], and ·wise men [LChaldeans; Ca group of astrologers], because he
wanted them to tell him what he had dreamed. They came in and stood
in front of the king.
3 Then the king said to them, "I had a dream ·that bothers me [Land my
spirit is agitated], and I want to know ·what it means [Lthe dream]."
4 The ·wise men [astrologers; LChaldeans] answered the king in the
Aramaic language [Cthe language of the text shifts to Aramaic until the
end of chapter 7; Aramaic was the everyday language of Babylon at this
time], "O king, live forever! Please tell us, your servants, your dream.
Then we will ·tell you what it means [interpret it]."
5 King Nebuchadnezzar said to ·them [the astrologers/LChaldeans], "·I
meant what I said [LThe matter has been determined by me]. You must

tell me the dream and what it means. If you don't, I will have you torn
·apart [limb from limb], and I will turn your houses into piles of stones
[Ezra 6:11]. 6But if you tell me my dream and its ·meaning [interpreta-
tion], I will reward you with gifts, a reward, and great honor. So tell me
the dream and ·what it means [its interpretation]."

7Again the wise men said to the king, "Tell us, your servants, the dream,
and we will tell you ·what it means [its interpretation]."

8·King Nebuchadnezzar [LThe king] answered, "I know you are ·trying
to get more [stalling for] time, because you know that ·I meant what I said
[Lthe matter has been determined by me]. 9If you don't tell me my dream,
·you will be punished [Lthere is one ordinance/verdict for you]. You have
all agreed to tell me lies and wicked things, hoping things will change.
Now, tell me the dream so that I will know you can tell me ·what it really
means [its interpretation]!"

10The ·wise men [astrologers; LChaldeans] answered the king, saying,
"No one on earth can ·do [reveal] what the king asks! No great and powerful king has ever asked the ·magicians [enchanters], ·fortune tellers
[diviners], or ·wise men [astrologers; LChaldeans] to do this [Cnormally
the dreamer would tell the dream, and the interpreter would interpret it
using a dream commentary]; 11the king is asking something that is too
hard. Only the gods could tell the king this, but ·the gods do not live
among people [Ltheir home/dwelling is not with flesh]."

12When the king heard their answer, he became very angry. He ordered
that all the wise men of Babylon be killed. 13So King Nebuchadnezzar's
·order [decree; edict] to kill the wise men was announced, and men ·were
sent to look [searched] for Daniel and his friends to kill them [Csince they
were also wise men].

14Arioch, the ·commander of the king's guards [Lchief butcher], was
going to kill the wise men of Babylon. But Daniel spoke to him with ·wis-
dom [prudence] and ·skill [deference], 15saying to Arioch, the royal
official, "Why did the king order such a ·terrible [severe] punishment?"
Then Arioch explained everything to Daniel. 16So Daniel went to King
Nebuchadnezzar and asked for ·an appointment [*or* some time] so that
he could tell the king what his dream meant.

17Then Daniel went to his house and ·explained the whole story [Lmade
the matter known] to his friends Hananiah, Mishael, and Azariah.
18Daniel asked his friends to ·pray [ask] that the God of heaven would
show them ·mercy [compassion] and help them understand this ·secret
[mystery] so he and his friends would not ·be killed [perish] with the
other wise men of Babylon.

19During the night God ·explained [revealed] the ·secret [mystery] to
Daniel in a vision. Then Daniel ·praised [blessed] the God of heaven.
20Daniel said:

"·Praise [Blessed be] ·God [Lthe name of God] forever and ever,
because he has wisdom and ·power [might].
21He changes the times and seasons of the year.
He ·takes away the power of [removes; deposes] kings
and ·gives their power to new [sets up] kings.
He gives wisdom to those who are wise
and knowledge to those who understand.
22He ·makes known [reveals] ·secrets that are deep and hidden [Ldeep
and secret things];

he knows what is hidden in darkness,
and light ·is all around [dwells with] him.
23I thank you and praise you, God of my ·ancestors [fathers],
because you have given me wisdom and ·power [might].
You told me what we asked of you;
you told us about the king's ·dream [Lmatter]."

The Meaning of the Dream

24Then Daniel went to Arioch, the man King Nebuchadnezzar had
·chosen [assigned; delegated] to ·kill [put to death; destroy] the wise men
of Babylon. Daniel said to him, "Don't ·put the wise men of Babylon to
death [kill/destroy the wise men of Babylon]. Take me to the king, and I
will ·tell him what his dream means [Lgive him its interpretation]."
25Very quickly Arioch took Daniel to the king and said, "I have found a
man among the ·captives [Lsons of the exiles] from Judah who can tell the
king ·what his dream means [its interpretation]."
26The king asked Daniel, ·who was also called [Lwhose name was]
Belteshazzar [1:7], "Are you able to tell me what I dreamed and ·what it
means [its interpretation]?"
27Daniel answered, "No wise man, magician [enchanter], ·fortune-teller
[diviner], or exorcist can explain to the king the ·secret [mystery; v. 11] he
has asked about. 28But there is a God in heaven who ·explains [reveals]
·secret things [mysteries], and he has ·shown [made known to] King
Nebuchadnezzar what will happen ·at a later time [in the future; Lin the latter days]. This is your dream, the vision ·you saw [Lof your head] while lying
on your bed: 29O king, as you were lying ·there [Lon your bed], you thought
about things to come. God, who can ·tell people about [Lreveal] ·secret
things [mysteries], ·showed [made known to] you what is going to happen.
30God also ·told [revealed] this ·secret [mystery] to me, not because I have
greater wisdom than any other living person, but so that you may know
·what it means [its interpretation]. In that way you will understand ·what
went through your mind [Lthe thoughts of your heart/mind].
31"O king, in your ·dream [Lvision] you saw a ·huge [great], ·shiny
[extraordinarily bright], and frightening statue in front of you. 32The
head of the statue was made of ·pure [fine] gold. Its chest and arms were
made of silver. Its ·stomach [middle; torso] and ·the upper part of its legs
[its thighs] were made of bronze. 33·The lower part of the [LIts] legs were
made of iron, while its feet were made partly of iron and partly of ·baked
clay [pottery; terra cotta]. 34While you were looking at the statue, you saw
a rock cut free [Cfrom a mountain, perhaps "the mountain of the God's
temple"; Is. 2:2; Mic. 4:1], but ·no human being touched the rock [Lnot by
hands; Cimplying God did it]. It hit the statue on its feet of iron and ·clay
[pottery; terra cotta; Cits weak point] and ·smashed them [broke them in
pieces]. 35Then the iron, ·clay [pottery; terra cotta], bronze, silver, and
gold broke to pieces ·at the same time [*or* totally]. They became like chaff
on a threshing floor in the summertime; the wind blew them away, and
there was nothing left. Then the rock that hit the statue became a very
large mountain that filled the whole earth.
36"That was your dream. Now we will tell the king ·what it means [its
interpretation]. 37O king, you are the ·greatest king [Lking of kings]. God of
heaven has given you a kingdom, ·power [sovereignty], strength, and
·glory [honor]. 38Wherever people, wild animals, and birds live, God made
you ruler over them. King Nebuchadnezzar, you are the head of gold.

39**"Another kingdom will ·come** [rise up] **after you, but ·it will not be as great as** [inferior to] **yours** [Cperhaps the Medes or the Medo-Persians]. **Next a third kingdom, the bronze part, will rule over the earth** [Cperhaps the Persians or the Greeks]. 40**Then there will be a fourth kingdom, strong as iron** [Cperhaps the Greeks or the Romans]. **In the same way that iron crushes and smashes things to pieces, the fourth kingdom will smash and crush all the other kingdoms** [Cthese kingdoms might not be specific kingdoms but symbolic of a series of unnamed oppressive nations].

41**"You saw that the statue's feet and toes were partly ·baked** [pottery] **clay and partly iron. That means the fourth kingdom will be a divided kingdom. It will have some of the strength of iron in it, just as you saw iron was mixed with ·clay** [*or* pottery; *or* terra cotta]. 42**The toes of the statue were partly iron and partly ·clay** [*or* pottery; *or* terra cotta]. **So the fourth kingdom will be partly strong** [Clike iron] **and partly ·breakable** [brittle; Clike baked clay]. 43**You saw the iron mixed with ·clay** [pottery; terra cotta], **but iron and ·clay** [pottery; terra cotta] **do not hold together. In the same way the people of the fourth kingdom will be a mixture, but they will not be united as one people.**

44**"During the ·time** [Ldays] **of those kings, the God of heaven will set up another kingdom that will never be destroyed** [Cthe kingdom of God] **or given to another group of people. This kingdom will crush all the other kingdoms and bring them to an end** [v. 40], **but it will ·continue** [stand] **forever.**

45**"King Nebuchadnezzar, you saw a rock cut from a mountain, but ·no human being touched it** [Lnot by hand]. **The rock broke the iron, bronze, ·clay** [*or* pottery; *or* terra cotta], **silver, and gold to pieces. In this way the great God ·showed** [made known to] **you what will happen. The dream is ·true** [certain], **and you can trust this ·explanation** [interpretation]."

46**Then King Nebuchadnezzar fell ·facedown on the ground** [Lon his face] **in front of Daniel. The king ·honored** [*or* worshiped] **him and commanded that an ·offering** [*or* grain/gift/tribute offering] **and incense be ·presented** [offered] **to him.** 47**Then the king said to Daniel, "Truly I know your God is the ·greatest of all** [LGod of] **gods, the Lord of all the kings. He ·tells people about things they cannot know** [reveals mysteries]. **I know this is true, because you were able to ·tell** [reveal] **these ·secret things** [mysteries] **to me."**

48**Then the king gave Daniel many gifts plus an important position in his kingdom. Nebuchadnezzar made him ruler over the ·whole area** [Lprovince] **of Babylon and put him in charge of all the wise men of Babylon.** 49**Daniel asked the king to ·make** [appoint] **Shadrach, Meshach, and Abednego leaders over the ·area** [Lprovince] **of Babylon, so the king did as Daniel asked. Daniel ·himself became one of the people who stayed** [stayed] **at the royal court.**

The Gold Idol and Blazing Furnace

3 King Nebuchadnezzar made a gold statue ·ninety feet [Lsixty cubits] **high and ·nine feet** [Lsix cubits] **wide** [Cunclear whether the statue was of Nebuchadnezzar or a Babylonian god like Marduk] **and set it up on the plain of Dura** [Cfrom a Babylonian word meaning "wall" or "fortress"] **in the ·area** [Lprovince] **of Babylon.** 2**Then he ·called for the leaders:** [L... sent for] **the ·governors** [satraps], **·assistant governors** [prefects], **·captains of the soldiers** [governors], **·people who advised the king** [counselors], **·keepers of the treasury** [treasurers], **·judges** [justices], **·rulers** [magistrates], and all other officers ·in his kingdom [Lof the provinces]. He wanted them to ·come [assemble] ·to the special service for [for the dedication of] the statue he had set up. 3So ·they all [Lthe satraps, prefects, governors, counselors, treasurers, justices, magistrates, and all other officers of the provinces] came for the ·special service [dedication] and stood in front of the statue that King Nebuchadnezzar had set up. 4Then the herald [Csomeone who made royal announcements] said in a loud voice, "People, nations, and those of every language, this is what you are commanded to do: 5When you hear the sound of the horns, flutes, lyres, zithers [Ca string instrument], harps, pipes, and all the other musical instruments, you must ·bow [Lfall] down and worship the gold statue that King Nebuchadnezzar has set up. 6Anyone who doesn't ·bow [Lfall] down and worship will immediately be thrown into a blazing furnace."

7Now people, nations, and those who spoke every language were there. When they heard the sound of the horns, flutes, lyres, zithers [v. 5], pipes, and all the other musical instruments, they ·bowed [Lfell] down and worshiped the gold statue King Nebuchadnezzar had set up.

8Then some ·Babylonians [LChaldeans] came up to the king and ·began speaking against [denounced; Late pieces of] the men of Judah. 9They said to King Nebuchadnezzar, "O king, live forever! 10O king, you ·gave a command [Lset a decree] that everyone who heard the horns, lyres, zithers [v. 5], harps, pipes, and all the other musical instruments would have to ·bow [Lfall] down and worship the gold statue. 11Anyone who wouldn't ·do this [Lfall down and worship] was to be thrown into a blazing furnace. 12O king, there are some men of Judah whom you ·made officers in [Lappointed/delegated over] the ·area [province] of Babylon that did not pay attention to your order. Their names are Shadrach, Meshach, and Abednego. They do not serve your gods and do not worship the gold statue you have set up."

13Nebuchadnezzar ·became very angry [flew into a rage] and called for Shadrach, Meshach, and Abednego. When they were brought to the king, 14Nebuchadnezzar said, "Shadrach, Meshach, and Abednego, is it true that you do not serve my gods nor worship the gold statue I have set up? 15In a moment you will again hear the sound of the horns, flutes, lyres, zithers [v. 5], harps, pipes, and all the other musical instruments. If you ·bow [Lfall] down and worship the statue I made, that will be good. But if you do not worship it, you will immediately be thrown into the blazing furnace. What god will be able to ·save [rescue; deliver] you from my ·power [Lhands] then?"

16Shadrach, Meshach, and Abednego answered the king, saying, "Nebuchadnezzar, we do not need to defend ourselves to you. 17If you throw us into the blazing furnace, the God we ·serve [Lfear; Prov. 1:7] is able to save us from the furnace. He will save us from your ·power [Lhand], O king. 18But even if God does not save us, we want you, O king, to know this: We will not serve your gods or worship the gold statue you have set up [Ex. 20:3–6]."

19Then Nebuchadnezzar was furious with Shadrach, Meshach, and Abednego, and ·he changed his mind [*or* his appearance changed; Lhis image/visage of his face changed]. He ordered the furnace to be heated seven times hotter than usual. 20Then he commanded some of the ·strongest soldiers in his army [Lmen mighty in strength] to ·tie up [bind] Shadrach, Meshach, and Abednego and throw them into the blazing furnace.

21So ·Shadrach, Meshach, and Abednego [Lthe men] were ·tied up
[bound] and thrown into the blazing furnace while still wearing their
·robes [tunics], trousers, turbans, and other clothes. 22The king's command was ·very strict [urgent], and the furnace was made so hot that the
flames killed the strong soldiers who threw Shadrach, Meshach, and
Abednego into the furnace. 23Firmly tied, Shadrach, Meshach, and
Abednego fell into the blazing furnace.
24Then King Nebuchadnezzar was so surprised that he ·jumped to his
feet [rose up in haste]. He asked the men who advised him, "Didn't we tie
up only three men and throw them into the fire?"
They answered, "·Yes [True], O king."
25The king said, "Look! I see four men walking around in the fire. They
are not ·tied [bound] up, and they are not ·burned [hurt]. The fourth
man looks like a son of the gods [Ca divine figure]."
26Then Nebuchadnezzar ·went to [approached] the opening of the
blazing furnace and shouted, "Shadrach, Meshach, and Abednego, come
out! Servants of the Most High God, come here!"
So Shadrach, Meshach, and Abednego came out of the fire. 27When
they came out, the ·governors [satraps], ·assistant governors [prefects],
·captains of the soldiers [governors], and ·royal advisers [counselors]
crowded around them and saw that the fire had ·not harmed [Lno power
over] their bodies. Their hair was not ·burned [singed], their ·robes
[tunics] were not burned, and they didn't even smell like smoke!
28Then Nebuchadnezzar said, "·Praise [Blessed be] the God of
Shadrach, Meshach, and Abednego. Their God has sent his ·angel [*or*
messenger] and ·saved [rescued; delivered] his servants from the fire!
These three men trusted their God and ·refused to obey [defied] ·my [Lthe
king's] command. They were willing to ·die [Lforfeit/yield up their bodies]
rather than serve or worship any god other than their own God. 29So I
now give this ·command [decree]: Anyone from any nation or ·language
[Ltongue] who says anything against the God of Shadrach, Meshach, and
Abednego will be torn ·apart [limb from limb] and have his house turned
into a pile of stones [2:5; Ezra 6:11]. No other god can ·save [rescue;
deliver] his people like this." 30Then the king promoted Shadrach,
Meshach, and Abednego in the ·area [province] of Babylon.

Nebuchadnezzar's Dream of a Tree

4 King Nebuchadnezzar to the people, nations, and ·those who speak
every language [Ltongues that live] in all the world [Ca typical letter
opening]:

·I wish you peace and great wealth [LMay your peace/prosper-
ity increase]!

2The Most High God has done ·miracles [signs] and wonderful things for me that I am happy to tell you about.
3His wonderful acts are great,
and his ·miracles [signs] are mighty.
His kingdom ·goes on forever [Lis an eternal kingdom],
and his ·rule [sovereignty] continues from ·now on [Lgeneration
to generation].
4I, Nebuchadnezzar, was ·happy [at ease] in my house and ·suc-
cessful [living luxuriously] at my palace, 5but I ·had [Lsaw] a dream
that ·made me afraid [disturbed me]. As I was lying on my bed, I

saw ·pictures [fantasies] and visions in my ·mind [head] that
·alarmed [scared; terrified] me. 6So I ·ordered [Lset a decree for]
all the wise men of Babylon to ·come [be presented] to me and
tell me ·what my dream meant [its interpretation]. 7The ·fortune-
tellers [diviners], ·magicians [enchanters], ·wise men [LChaldeans;
2:2], and exorcists came, and I told them about the dream. But
they could not tell me ·what it meant [its interpretation].

8Finally, Daniel came to me. (I called him Belteshazzar ·to
honor [Lafter the name of] my god [1:7], because ·the spirit of
the holy gods [*or* a holy, divine spirit] is in him.) I told my dream
to him. 9I said, "Belteshazzar, you are the ·most important of all
[Lchief of] the ·fortune-tellers [diviners]. I know that ·the spirit
of the holy gods [*or* a holy, divine spirit] is in you, so there is no
·secret [mystery] that is too ·hard for you to understand [diffi-
cult for you]. ·This was what I dreamed [LThe dream I saw]; tell
me ·what it means [its interpretation]. 10These are the visions
[Lof my head] I saw while I was lying in my bed: I looked, and
there in front of me was a tree standing in the ·middle [center] of
the earth. And it was very tall. 11The tree grew large and strong.
The top ·touched [reached] the ·sky [heavens] and could be seen
·from anywhere on [Lto the ends of the] earth. 12The leaves of the
tree were beautiful. It had plenty of good fruit on it, enough
food for everyone. The ·wild animals [Lanimals of the field]
found shelter under the tree, and the birds of the ·sky [heavens]
lived in its branches. Every animal ate from it.

13"As I was looking ·at those things in the vision while lying
[Lat the visions of my head] on my bed, I saw an ·observer, a holy
angel [Lholy watcher] coming down from heaven. 14He spoke
very loudly and said, 'Cut down the tree and cut off its branches.
Strip off its leaves and scatter its fruit. Let the animals under the
tree ·run away [flee], and ·let the birds in its branches fly away
[Lthe birds from its branches]. 15But leave the stump and its roots
in the ground with a band of iron and bronze around it; let it
stay in the field with the grass around it.

" 'Let the man become wet with dew of ·the sky [heaven], and
let him live among the animals [Lof the field] and ·plants [grass]
of the earth. 16Let ·him not think like a human any longer [Lhis
heart/mind be changed from human; Che will be deranged], but
let him have the ·mind [heart] of an animal for seven ·years
[Lperiods; times].

17" 'The ·observers [watchers; v. 13] gave this ·command
[decree]; the holy ones declared the ·sentence [decision]. This is
so all people may know that the Most High God ·rules [is sover-
eign] over every kingdom ·on earth [Lof humans]. God gives
those kingdoms to anyone he wants, and he chooses people to
rule them who are ·not proud [Llow].'

18"That is what I, King Nebuchadnezzar, dreamed. Now
Belteshazzar [Canother name for Daniel; 1:7], tell me ·what the
dream means [its interpretation]. None of the wise men in my
kingdom can explain ·it to me [its interpretation], but you can,
because ·the spirit of the holy gods [*or* a holy, divine spirit] is in
you."

Daniel Explains the Dream

19Then Daniel, ·who was called [Lwhose name is] Belteshazzar
[1:7], was very quiet for a while, because his understanding of
the dream ·frightened [scared; terrified] him. So the king said,
"Belteshazzar, do not let the dream or its ·meaning [interpreta-
tion] ·make you afraid [terrify you]."

Then Belteshazzar answered, "My master, I wish the dream
were about your enemies, and I wish its ·meaning [interpreta-
tion] were for those who are against you! 20You saw a tree in your
dream that grew large and strong. Its top ·touched [reached] the
·sky [heavens], and it could be seen from all over the earth. 21Its
leaves were beautiful, and it had plenty of fruit for everyone to
eat. It was a home for the ·wild animals [Lanimals of the field],
and its branches were nesting places for the birds of the ·sky
[heavens]. 22O king, you are that tree! You have become great
and powerful, like the tall tree that ·touched [reached] the ·sky
[heavens]. Your ·power [sovereignty] reaches to the ·far parts
[ends] of the earth.

23"O king, you saw an ·observer, a holy angel [Lholy watcher],
coming down from heaven who said, 'Cut down the tree and
destroy it. But leave the stump and its roots in the ground with a
band of iron and bronze around it; leave it in the field with the
grass. Let him become wet with dew and live like a ·wild animal
[Lanimal of the field] for seven ·years [Lperiods; times].'

24"This is the ·meaning of the dream [interpretation], O king.
The Most High God has ·commanded [decreed] these things to
happen to my master the king: 25You will be ·forced [driven]
away from people to live among the ·wild animals [Lanimals of
the field]. People will feed you grass like an ox, and dew from the
·sky [heavens] will make you wet. Seven ·years [Lperiods; times]
will pass, and then you will learn this lesson: The Most High
God is ·ruler [sovereign] over every kingdom on earth, and he
gives those kingdoms to anyone he chooses.

26"Since the stump of the tree and its roots were left in the
ground, your kingdom will be given back to you when you learn
that ·one in heaven rules your kingdom [Lheaven is sovereign].
27So, O king, please accept my advice. ·Stop sinning [Atone for/
LBreak off your sins] and ·do what is right [be righteous]. Stop
doing wicked things and be kind to the ·poor [oppressed]. Then
you might continue to be ·successful [prosperous]."

The King's Dream Comes True

28All these things happened to King Nebuchadnezzar. 29Twelve
months later as he was walking on the roof [Cthe flat roofs of
ancient Near Eastern houses were used as living space] of his palace in Babylon, 30he said, "·I have built this great Babylon as [LIs
this not Babylon the great which I built as...?] my royal home. I
built it by my power to show my glory and my majesty."

31The words were still in his mouth when a voice from heaven
said, "King Nebuchadnezzar, ·these things will happen to you
[Lto you it is declared]: ·Your royal power [LThe kingdom] has
been taken away from you. 32You will be ·forced [driven] away
from people. You will live with the ·wild animals [Lanimals of the
field] and will be fed grass like an ox. Seven ·years [Lperiods;

times] will pass before you learn this lesson: The Most High God
·rules [is sovereign] over every kingdom on earth and gives those
kingdoms to anyone he chooses [v. 25]."
33 Immediately the ·words [sentence] came true. Nebuchadnezzar was ·forced to go [driven] away from people, and he
began eating grass like an ox. He became wet from dew. His hair
grew long like the feathers of an eagle, and his nails grew like the
claws of a bird.
34 "At the end of ·that time [Lthe days], I, Nebuchadnezzar,
·looked up [Llifted my eyes] toward heaven [Cacknowledging
God's supremacy], and ·I could think normally again [Lmy reason was restored to me]! Then I ·gave praise to [blessed] the
Most High God; I gave honor and glory to him who lives
forever.

"God's ·rule is forever [Lsovereignty is an eternal sovereignty],
and his kingdom continues for ·all time [Lall generations].
35 People on earth
are ·not truly important [counted as nothing].
God does what he ·wants [wills]
with the ·powers [hosts; armies] of heaven [Cangelic powers]
and the people on earth.
No one can stop his powerful hand
or ·question what he does [Lsay, 'What are you doing?'].

36 "At that time ·I could think normally again [Lmy reason
returned to me], and God gave back my great honor and power
and returned the glory to my kingdom. ·The people who advised
me [My counselors] and the royal family came to me for help again.
I became king again and was even greater and more powerful than
before. 37 Now I, Nebuchadnezzar, praise and ·honor [extol] and
glorify the King of heaven. ·Everything he does [All his works] is
·right [truth] and ·fair [Lhis ways are just], and he is able to ·make
proud people humble [Lbring low those who walk in pride]."

The Writing on the Wall

5 King Belshazzar [Calong with his father, Nabonidus, the last ruler
of Babylon] ·gave a big banquet [Lserved a large meal] for a thousand ·royal [noble; important] guests and drank wine with ·them [Lthe
thousand]. 2 As Belshazzar ·was drinking his wine [Ltasted the wine; Che
was under the influence of the wine], he gave orders to bring the gold and
silver cups that his ·ancestor Nebuchadnezzar [Lfather; predecessor; Cnot
his literal father; v. 1] had taken from the Temple in Jerusalem [1:2]. This
was so the king, his ·royal [noble; important] guests, his wives, and his
·slave women [Lconcubines; Csecondary wives] could drink from those
cups. 3 So they brought the gold cups that had been taken from the Temple
of God in Jerusalem. And the king and his ·royal [noble; important]
guests, his wives, and his ·slave women [Lconcubines; v. 2] drank from
them. 4 As they were drinking, they praised their gods, which were made
from gold, silver, bronze, iron, wood, and stone.
5 Suddenly the fingers of a person's hand appeared and began writing
on the plaster of the wall, near the lampstand in the royal palace. The king
watched the hand as it wrote.
6 ·King Belshazzar was very frightened [LThe king's thoughts terrified
him]. His face turned ·white [pale], his knees knocked together, and ·he

could not stand up because his legs were too weak [the strength left his
legs; [L]his hips went loose; [C]the idiom may mean he wet himself]. 7The king
called loudly for the ·magicians [enchanters], ·wise men [[L]Chaldeans; [C]a
group of astrologers], and ·wizards [exorcists] of Babylon and said to
·them [[L]the wise men of Babylon], "Anyone who can read this writing and
explain ·it [[L]its interpretation] will be clothed in purple [[C]befitting a king]
and have a gold chain around his neck. And I will make that person the
third highest ruler in the kingdom [[C]after Nabonidus and Belshazzar; v. 1;
Gen. 41:42; Esth. 8:15]."

8Then all the king's wise men came in, but they could not read the writing or tell the king ·what it meant [its interpretation]. 9King Belshazzar
became even more ·afraid [terrified], and his face became even ·whiter
[paler]. His ·royal [important; noble] guests were ·confused [agitated].

10Then the queen [[C]the queen mother, since the king's wives were
already present], who had heard the ·voices [discussion] of the king and
his ·royal [noble; important] guests, came into the banquet room. She
said, "O king, live forever! Don't ·be afraid [[L]let your thoughts terrify you]
or let your face ·be white with fear [turn pale]! 11There is a man in your
kingdom who has ·the spirit of the holy gods [*or* a holy, divine spirit in
him]. In the days of your father [v. 2], this man showed understanding,
knowledge, and wisdom like the gods. Your father, King Nebuchadnezzar,
put this man in charge of all the ·wise men [[L]Chaldeans; [C]a group of
astrologers], ·fortune-tellers [enchanters], ·magicians [diviners], and
·wizards [exorcists]. 12The man I am talking about is named Daniel,
whom the king named Belteshazzar [1:7]. He ·was very wise [[L]has an
excellent spirit] and had knowledge and understanding. He could ·explain
[interpret] dreams and ·secrets [riddles] and ·could answer very hard
[unravel] problems. Call for Daniel. He will tell you ·what the writing on
the wall means [its interpretation]."

13So they brought Daniel to the king, and the king asked, "Are you
Daniel one of the ·captives [exiles] my father the king brought from
Judah [[C]trying to put Daniel in his place]? 14I have heard that ·the spirit of
the gods [*or* a divine spirit] is in you, and that you are very wise and have
knowledge and ·extraordinary [excellent] understanding. 15The wise men
and ·magicians [enchanters] were brought to me to read this writing and
to explain ·what it means [its interpretation], but they could not ·explain
it [give me its interpretation]. 16I have heard that you are able to ·explain
what things mean [give interpretations] and can ·find the answers to hard
[unravel] problems. Read this writing on the wall and ·explain it to me
[give me its interpretation]. If you can, I will clothe you in purple
[[C]befitting a king] and give you a gold chain to wear around your neck.
And you will become the third highest ruler in the kingdom [v. 7]."

17Then Daniel answered the king, "You may keep your gifts for yourself, or you may give those rewards to someone else. But I will read the
writing [[C]on the wall] for you and will explain to you ·what it means [its
interpretation].

18"O king, the Most High God ·made your father Nebuchadnezzar a
great, important, and powerful king [[L]gave your father Nebuchadnezzar a
kingdom, greatness, splendor, and glory]. 19Because God made him
·important [great], all the people, nations, and ·those who spoke every
language [[L]tongues] ·were very frightened [[L]trembled with fear in front]
of Nebuchadnezzar. If he wanted someone to die, he killed that person. If

he wanted someone to live, he let that person live. Those he wanted to ·promote [honor], he ·promoted [honored]. Those he wanted to ·be less important [abase; degrade], he ·made less important [abased; degraded].

20“But ·Nebuchadnezzar became too proud [Lhis heart was exalted/lifted up] and ·stubborn [Lhis spirit became hard with insolence], so he was taken off his royal throne. His glory was ·taken [stripped] away. 21He was ·forced away [driven] from people, and his mind became like the mind of an animal. He lived with the wild donkeys and was fed grass like an ox and became wet with dew. These things happened to him until he learned: The Most High God ·rules [is sovereign] over every kingdom ·on earth [Lof humans], and he sets anyone he chooses over those kingdoms.

22“Belshazzar, you, his [CNebuchadnezzar’s] ·son [descendant; *or* successor; Cnot his literal son; v. 1], already knew these things. Still you have not ·been sorry for what you have done [Lhumbled your heart]. 23Instead, you have ·set yourself [exalted yourself] against the Lord of heaven. You ordered the drinking cups from the Temple of the Lord to be brought to you. Then you and your ·royal [important; noble] guests, your wives, and your ·slave women [concubines; Csecondary wives] drank wine from them. You praised the gods of silver, gold, bronze, iron, wood, and stone that cannot see or hear or understand anything [Cthey are not really gods]. You did not honor God, who has power over your ·life [very breath] and ·everything you do [all your ways]. 24So ·God sent [Lbefore his presence was sent] the hand that wrote.

25“These are the words that were written: ‘Mene, mene, tekel, and parsin.’

26“This is ·what the words mean [Lthe interpretation of the matter]: Mene [C“Numbered”]: God has ·counted [numbered] the days until your kingdom will end. 27Tekel [C“Weighed”]: You have been weighed on the scales and found ·not good enough [deficient; lacking; Twanting]. 28Parsin [C“Divided”]: Your kingdom is being divided and will be given to the Medes and the Persians [Cfrom the Iranian plateau].”

29Then Belshazzar gave an order for Daniel to be dressed in purple clothes [Cbefitting a king] and to have a gold chain put around his neck. And it was announced that Daniel was the third highest ruler in the kingdom [v. 7]. 30That very same night Belshazzar, king of the ·Babylonian people [LChaldeans], was killed. 31So Darius the Mede ·became the new king [Lreceived the kingdom] when he was sixty-two years old [Cwhen the Persians defeated the Babylonians; 539 BC].

Daniel and the Lions

6 ·Darius thought it would be a good idea [LIt pleased Darius; 5:30] to ·choose [Lset over the kingdom] one hundred twenty ·governors [Lsatraps] who would ·rule his [Lbe over the] kingdom. 2He chose three men as ·supervisors [presidents; heads] over those ·governors [Lsatraps], and Daniel was one of the ·supervisors [presidents; heads]. The ·supervisors [presidents; heads] were to ensure that the ·governors did not try to cheat the king [Lking would not be troubled/disturbed]. 3Daniel ·showed that he could do the work better than [distinguished himself above] the other ·supervisors [presidents; heads] and ·governors [Lsatraps] because an ·excellent [extraordinary] spirit was in him, so the king planned to put Daniel in charge of the whole kingdom. 4Because of this, the other ·supervisors [presidents; heads] and ·governors [Lsatraps] tried to find reasons to accuse Daniel ·about his work in the government

[Lin regard to the kingdom]. But they could not find anything ·wrong with him or any reason to accuse him [in regard to complaint or corruption], because he was trustworthy and not lazy or ·dishonest [corrupt]. 5Finally these men said, "We will never find any reason to accuse Daniel unless it is about the law of his God."

6So the ·supervisors [presidents; heads] and ·governors [Lsatraps] ·went as a group to [*or* conspired against] the king and said: "King Darius, live forever! 7The ·supervisors [presidents; heads], ·assistant governors [prefects], ·governors [Lsatraps], ·the people who advise you [counselors], and the ·captains of the soldiers [governors] have ·all agreed [taken counsel] that you should ·make a new law [issue a decree] ·for everyone to obey [and enforce an edict]: For the next thirty days no one should pray to any god or human except to you, O king. Anyone who doesn't obey will be thrown into the lions' den. 8Now, O king, ·make the law [enforce the edict] and sign ·your name to it [Lthe document] so that it cannot be changed, because then it will be a law of the Medes and Persians and cannot be canceled." 9So King Darius signed the ·law [Ldocument and edict].

10Even though Daniel knew that the ·new law [document] had been ·written [signed], he went to pray in an upstairs room in his house, which had windows that opened toward Jerusalem. Three times each day Daniel would kneel down to pray and ·thank [praise] God, just as he always had done [1 Kin. 8:35–36; Ps. 55:17].

11Then those men ·went as a group [conspired] and found Daniel praying and ·asking God for help [seeking mercy from God]. 12So they ·went to [approached] the king and talked to him about the ·law he had made [edict]. They said, "Didn't you sign a ·law [edict] that says no one may pray to any god or human except you, O king? Doesn't it say that anyone who disobeys during the next thirty days will be thrown into the lions' den?"

The king answered, "Yes, ·that is the law [Lthe thing is certain], and the laws of the Medes and Persians cannot be canceled."

13Then they said to the king, "Daniel, one of the ·captives [exiles] from Judah, ·is not paying attention to [disregards] you, O king, or to the ·law [edict] you signed. Daniel still prays three times every day." 14The king ·became very upset [was displeased] when he heard ·this [Lthe word]. He ·wanted [Lset his mind] to ·save [rescue] Daniel, and he worked hard until sunset trying to think of a way to ·save [rescue] him.

15Then those men ·went as a group to [*or* conspired against] the king. They said, "·Remember [Know], O king, the law of the Medes and Persians says that no ·law [edict] or command given by the king can be changed."

16So King Darius gave the order, and Daniel was brought in and thrown into the lions' den. The king said to Daniel, "May the God you ·serve [fear; Prov. 1:7] all the time ·save [rescue] you!" 17A stone was brought and placed over the ·opening [Lmouth] of the lions' den. Then the king used his signet ring and the rings of his ·royal [noble; important] officers to put special seals on the rock [Crings with personal identification symbols that could be pressed into soft clay]. This ensured that ·no one would move the rock and bring Daniel out [Lnothing would be changed with Daniel]. 18Then King Darius went back to his palace. He ·did not eat [fasted] that night, ·he did not have any entertainment [Lnothing was; Creferring to food and/or women] brought to him, and he could not sleep.

19The next morning King Darius got up at dawn and ·hurried [*or* in agitation went] to the lions' den. 20As he came near the den, he was worried.

He called out to Daniel, "Daniel, servant of the living God! Has your God
that you always ·worship [fear; serve; Prov. 1:7] been able to ·save [rescue]
you from the lions?"
21Daniel answered, "O king, live forever! 22My God sent his ·angel [*or*
messenger] to close the lions' mouths [Heb. 11:33]. They have not ·hurt
[injured] me, because my God knows I am ·innocent [blameless]. I never
did anything ·wrong to [to injure] you, O king."
23King Darius was very happy and told his servants to lift Daniel out of
the lions' den. So they lifted him out and did not find any injury on him,
because Daniel had trusted in his God.
24Then the king commanded that the men who had ·accused [con-
spired against; Leaten pieces of] Daniel be brought to the lions' den. They,
their wives, and their children were thrown into the den. The lions
·grabbed [overpowered] them before they ·hit [reached] the floor of the
den and ·crushed their bones [*or* tore their bodies into pieces; Prov. 28:10].
25Then King Darius wrote a letter to all people and all nations, ·to
those who spoke every language [Land tongues] in the world:

I wish you great ·peace and wealth [prosperity].

26I ·am making a new law [Lset a decree] for people in every
part of my ·kingdom [kingly dominion]. All of you must ·fear
[tremble] and ·respect [fear] the God of Daniel.
For he is the living God;
he ·lives [endures] forever.
His kingdom will never be destroyed,
and his ·rule [sovereignty] will never end.
27God rescues and ·saves [delivers] people
and does ·mighty miracles [signs and wonders]
in heaven and on earth.
He is the one who ·saved [rescued] Daniel
from the ·power [Lhand] of the lions.

28So Daniel was ·successful [prosperous] during the time Darius was
king ·and [*or* even] when Cyrus the Persian was king [Cmay be two different names for the same king].

Daniel's Dream About Four Animals

7 In Belshazzar's first year as king of Babylon [Cperhaps 550 BC],
Daniel had a dream. He saw visions [Lin his head] as he was lying
on his bed, and he wrote ·down what he had dreamed [Lthe beginning of
the words/matter].
2Daniel said: "I saw my vision at night. In the vision the ·wind was
blowing from all four directions, which made the sea very rough [Lfour
winds of heaven stirred up the great sea; Ca picture of chaos]. 3I saw four
huge ·animals [beasts] come up from the sea, and each ·animal [beast]
was different from the others.
4"The first ·animal [beast] looked like a lion, but had wings like an
eagle. I watched this ·animal [beast] until its wings were torn off. It was
lifted from the ground so that it stood up on two feet like a human, and it
was given the ·mind [heart] of a human [Cperhaps representing Babylon].
5"Then I saw a ·second [Lanother] ·animal [beast] before me that
looked like a bear. It was raised up on one of its sides and had three ·ribs

[*or* tusks] **in its mouth between its teeth. It was told, 'Get up and eat ·all**
the meat you want [much flesh; many bodies; Cperhaps representing the
Medes or the Medes and Persians]**!'**
6“**After that, I looked, and there before me was another ·animal** [beast].
This ·animal [beast] **looked like a leopard with four wings on its back that**
looked like a bird's wings. This ·animal [beast] **had four heads and was given**
·power to rule [authority; Cperhaps representing the Persians or the Greeks].
7“**After that, in my vision at night I saw in front of me a fourth ·animal**
[beast] **that was ·cruel** [fearsome], **·terrible** [terrifying], **and very strong**
[Cperhaps the Greeks or Romans]. **It had large iron teeth. It crushed and**
ate what it killed, and then it ·walked on [Lstamped with its feet] **whatever**
was left. This fourth ·animal [beast] **was different from any ·animal** [beast]
I had seen before, and it had ten horns [Crepresenting strength and power].
8“**While I was ·thinking about** [reflecting on] **the horns, another horn**
grew up among them. It was a little horn with eyes like a human's eyes. It
also had a mouth, and the mouth was bragging. The little horn ·pulled
out [uprooted] **three of the other horns.**

9“**As I looked,**
thrones were put in their places,
and ·God, the Eternal One, [Lthe Ancient of Days] **sat on his throne.**
His clothes were white like snow,
and the hair on his head was like wool [Cwhite].
His throne was made from fire,
and the wheels of his throne were blazing with fire.
10**A river of fire was flowing**
from in front of him.
·Many [LA thousand] **thousands of angels were serving him,**
and ·millions [Lten thousand times ten thousand; Cangels] **stood**
before him.
Court ·was ready to begin [sat in judgment],
and the books were opened.

11“**I kept on looking because the horn** [Cthe little one] **was bragging. I**
kept watching until finally the ·animal [beast; Cthe fourth] **was killed. Its**
body was destroyed, and it was ·thrown [given over] **into the burning fire.**
12**(The ·power and rule** [authority; dominion; sovereignty] **of the ·other**
animals [rest of the beasts] **had been taken from them, but they were per-**
mitted to live for a ·certain period of time [Lseason and a time].**)**
13“**In my vision at night I saw in front of me someone ·who looked like**
a human being [Llike a son of man] **coming on the clouds in the ·sky**
[heavens; CGod's heavenly chariot; Ps. 18:10–19; 68:4; 104:3; Is. 19:1; Luke
21:27; Rev. 1:7]. **He came near ·God, who has been alive forever** [Lthe
Ancient of Days], **and he was ·led to God** [presented to him]. 14**He was**
given ·authority [dominion; sovereignty], **glory, and ·the strength of a**
king [kingship]. **People of every tribe, nation, and ·language** [Ltongue]
will ·serve [fear; Prov. 1:7] **him. His ·rule will last forever** [dominion/
sovereignty is an everlasting dominion/sovereignty], **and his ·kingdom**
[kingship] **will never be destroyed.**

The Meaning of the Dream

15“**I, Daniel, was ·worried** [troubled/disturbed in spirit]. **The visions that**
went through my ·mind [Lhead] **·frightened** [terrified] **me.** 16**I came near**
one of those standing there [Can angel, perhaps Gabriel who interprets
visions; 8:16; 9:21] **and asked ·what all this meant** [the truth of all this].

"So he told me and explained to me ·what these things meant [Lthe interpretation of the matter]: 17"The four great ·animals [beasts] are four ·kingdoms [*or* kings] that will come from the earth [vv. 4–7]. 18But the holy ·people [Lones; Ceither the saints or angels or both] who belong to the Most High God will receive the ·power to rule [kingdom] and will have the ·power to rule [kingdom] forever, from now on.'

19"Then I wanted to know what the fourth ·animal [beast] meant, because it was different from all the others. It was very ·terrible [fearsome] and had iron teeth and bronze claws. It was the ·animal [beast] that crushed and ate what it killed and then ·walked on [stamped with its feet] whatever was left [v. 7]. 20I also wanted to know about the ten horns on its head and about the other horn [Cthe little one] that grew there. It had ·pulled out [uprooted] three of the other ten horns and looked greater than the others. It had eyes and a mouth that kept bragging. 21As I watched, the horn [Cthe little one] began making war against ·God's holy people [Lthe holy ones; v. 18] and was defeating them 22until ·God, who has been alive forever, [Lthe Ancient of Days; v. 9] came. He judged in favor of the holy ·people [ones; v. 18] who belong to the Most High God; then the time came for them to receive the ·power to rule [Lkingdom].

23"And he explained this to me: 'The fourth ·animal [beast] is a fourth kingdom that will come on the earth. It will be different from all the other kingdoms and will ·destroy [consume] ·people all over the world [Lthe whole earth]. It will ·walk on [trample] and crush the whole earth. 24The ten horns are ten kings who will ·come [arise] from this fourth kingdom. After ·those ten kings are gone [Lthem], another king will ·come [arise]. He will be different from the ·kings who ruled before him [Lformer ones], and he will ·defeat [cause to fall] three of the other kings. 25This king will speak against the Most High God, and he will ·hurt and kill [Lwear out] ·God's holy people [Lthe holy ones of Most High God; v. 18]. He will try to change ·times [holy times] and laws that have already been set. ·The holy people that belong to God will be in that king's [LThey will be given into his] power for ·three and one-half years [La time, times, and half a time; Che will seem to grow but then be cut back].

26" 'But the court will ·decide what should happen [Lsit in judgment]. ·The power of the king [LHis dominion/sovereignty] will be taken away, and his kingdom will be completely destroyed. 27Then the holy ·people [ones] who belong to the Most High God [v. 18] will have the power to rule. They will rule over all the kingdoms under heaven with power and greatness, and their power to rule will last forever. People from all the other kingdoms will ·respect [fear] and ·serve [obey] them.'

28"That was the end of the ·dream [Lmatter]. I, Daniel, was ·very afraid [terrified]. My face became ·white from fear [pale], but I kept everything ·to myself [Lin my own heart/mind]."

Daniel's Vision

8 ·During [In] the third year of King Belshazzar's rule [Cperhaps 547 BC], I, Daniel, saw another vision, ·which was like the first one [Lafter the one that appeared to me in the beginning/previously; 7:1]. 2In this vision I saw myself in the ·capital city [*or* fortress city] of Susa, in the ·area [province] of Elam. I was standing by the Ulai ·Canal [*or* Gate] 3when I ·looked up and [Llifted my eyes I] saw a ·male sheep [ram] standing beside the ·canal [*or* gate]. It had two long horns, but one horn was longer and ·newer than the other [Lcame up second]. 4I watched the

·sheep [ram] charge to the west, the north, and the south. No animal could stand before him, and none could ·save [protect] another animal from his ·power [Lhand]. He did whatever he ·wanted [pleased] and became very ·powerful [great; strong].

5While I was ·watching this [*or* reflecting; pondering], I saw a male goat come from the west. This goat had ·one large horn between his eyes that was easy to see [La horn of vision; *or* a conspicuous horn between its eyes]. He crossed over the whole earth without touching the ground [Cbecause of its speed].

6·In his anger [*or* With angry power] the goat ·charged [Lcame up to] the ·sheep [ram] with the two horns that I had seen standing by the ·canal [*or* gate]. 7I watched the angry goat ·attack [approach] the ·sheep [ram] and break the ·sheep's [ram's] two horns. The ·sheep [ram] ·was not strong enough to stop him [Ldid not have the power/strength to stand before him]. The goat ·knocked [threw] the ·sheep [ram] to the ground and then ·walked all over him [trampled him]. No one was able to ·save [protect] the ·sheep [ram] from ·the goat [its power/Lhand], 8so the male goat became very ·great [powerful; strong]. But when he was strong, his ·big [*or* conspicuous] horn broke off and four horns grew in place of the one big horn. Those four horns ·pointed in four different directions [Lwere toward the four winds of heaven] and were ·easy to see [conspicuous].

9Then ·a little horn grew from one of those four horns [Lfrom one of them came out another horn, a little one; 7:8], and it became very ·big [great]. It grew to the south, the east, and toward the beautiful land [CJudah; Ezek. 20:6, 15]. 10That ·little horn [Lit] grew ·until it reached to the sky [Lto the hosts of heaven; Cthe angels and the stars]. It even threw some of the ·army of heaven [Lhosts and the stars] to the ground and ·walked on [trampled] them! 11·That little horn [LIt] set itself up as equal to the prince of ·heaven's armies [Lthe hosts; CGod]. It ·stopped [abolished] the ·daily [regular] sacrifices [Ex. 29:38–41; Num. 28:3–8] that were offered to him, and the ·Temple, the place where people worshiped him, [Lplace of the sanctuary] was ·pulled down [overthrown]. 12Because there was a ·turning away from God [rebellion; transgression], the people stopped the ·daily [regular] sacrifices. Truth was thrown down to the ground, and ·the horn [Lit] was successful in everything it did.

13Then I heard ·a holy angel [Lone of the holy ones] speaking. Another ·holy angel [Lholy one] asked the first one, "How long will the things in this vision last—the ·daily [regular] sacrifices [8:12], the ·turning away from God [rebellion; transgression] that brings ·destruction [desolation], the ·Temple [sanctuary] being pulled down, and the ·army of heaven [host] being ·walked on [trampled]?"

14The angel said to me, "This will happen for twenty-three hundred evenings and mornings [Ceither 2,300 or 1,150 days]. Then the ·holy place [sanctuary] will be ·repaired [restored; made right again]."

15I, Daniel, saw this vision and ·tried to understand what it meant [Lsought understanding]. I saw someone who looked like a man standing near me. 16And I heard a man's voice calling from the Ulai ·Canal [*or* Gate]: "Gabriel [Can angel], explain the vision to this man."

17·Gabriel [LHe] came to where I was standing. When he came close to me, I was ·very afraid [terrified; *or* overwhelmed] and ·bowed facedown on the ground [Lfell on my face]. But ·Gabriel [Lhe] said to me, "·Human being [LSon of man], understand that this vision is about the time of the end."

18While ·Gabriel [Lhe] was speaking, I fell into a ·deep sleep [trance]
with my face on the ground. Then he touched me [Cstrengthening him]
and ·lifted me to my feet [Lmade me stand in my place]. 19He said, "Now,
I will ·explain [make known; reveal] to you what will happen in the time
of anger. Your vision was about the ·set [appointed] time of the end.
20"You saw a ·male sheep [ram] with two horns, which are the kings of
Media and Persia. 21The male goat is the king of ·Greece [LJavan], and the
big horn between its eyes is the first king [CAlexander the Great, who
defeated Persia around 330 BC]. 22The four horns that grew in the place of
the broken horn are four kingdoms [CAlexander died in 323 BC and his
four most powerful generals carved up his empire between them]. Those
four kingdoms will come from ·the nation of the first king [Lhis nation], but
·they will not be as strong as the first king [Lnot with his power/strength].
23"When the end comes near for those kingdoms, a ·bold and cruel
[fierce/stern-faced] king who ·tells lies will come [Lunderstands riddles/
enigmas; CAntiochus Epiphanes, who terrorized the Jews in the mid-second
century BC]. This will happen when ·many people have turned against God
[rebellions/transgressions will reach their height]. 24·This king will be very
powerful [LHis power will be strong], but ·his power will not come from
himself [Lnot his own power]. He will cause ·terrible [fearful] destruction
and will be successful in everything he does. He will destroy powerful people and even ·God's holy people [Lthe people of the holy ones]. 25This king
will succeed by using ·lies and force [Lthe deceit in his hand/power]. He will
·think that he is very important [Lbe great in his heart]. He will destroy
many people ·without warning [*or* with ease]; he will ·try to fight [Lstand
against] even the Prince of princes! But ·that cruel king [Lhe] will be
·destroyed [Lbroken], and not by human ·power [Lhand].
26"The vision that has been shown to you about these evenings and
mornings is true. But seal up the vision, because ·those things won't happen for a long time [Lit concerns many days from now]."
27I, Daniel, became very weak and was sick for ·several days after that
vision [Lsome days]. Then I got up and went back to work for the king,
but I was very ·upset [dismayed; perplexed] about the vision. I didn't
understand what it meant.

Daniel's Prayer

9 These things happened during the first year Darius son of
Ahasuerus was king over ·Babylon [Lthe Chaldeans; C539 BC]. He
was ·a descendant [Lfrom the seed] of the Medes [Ca people group within
the Persian empire]. 2During Darius' first year as king, I, Daniel, was
·reading in [pondering/reflecting on] the Scriptures. I saw ·that the LORD
told Jeremiah that Jerusalem would be empty ruins for seventy years
[Lthe number of years which were according to the word of the LORD to
Jeremiah the prophet to fulfill the ruin of Jerusalem was seventy years; 2
Chr. 36:20–22; Jer. 25:11–12; 29:10].
3Then I turned [Lmy face] to the Lord God and ·prayed [Lsought in
prayer] and ·asked him for help [supplication]. ·To show my sadness, I
fasted, put on rough cloth, and sat in [L...with fasting, and sackcloth, and]
ashes. 4I prayed to the LORD my God and ·told him about all of our sins
[made confession]. I said, "Lord, you are a great ·God who causes fear and
wonder [Land awesome God]. You ·keep [guard] ·your agreement of love
[covenant and loyalty] with all who love you and ·obey [keep; guard] your
commands.

5“But we have sinned and done wrong. We have been wicked and
·turned [rebelled] against you, your commands, and your ·laws [judg-
ments]. 6We did not listen to your servants, the prophets, who spoke ·for
you [Lin your name] to our kings, our ·leaders [princes], our ·ancestors
[fathers], and all the people of the land.
7“Lord, ·you are good and right [Lto you is righteousness], but ·we are
full of shame [Lto us is shame of face] today—the people of Judah and
Jerusalem, all the people of Israel, those near and far whom you ·scat-
tered [drove away] among many nations because they were ·not loyal
[treacherous] to you. 8Lord, ·we are all ashamed [Lto us is shame of face].
Our kings and ·leaders [princes] and our ·fathers [ancestors] are ·ashamed
[shame-faced], because we have ·sinned against [*or* failed] you.
9“But, Lord our God, you ·show us mercy [have compassion] and forgive
us even though we have ·turned [rebelled] against you. 10We have not
·obeyed [Llistened to the voice of] the Lord our God or the ·teachings
[instructions; laws] he gave us through his servants, the prophets. 11All the
people of Israel have ·disobeyed [transgressed] your ·teachings [instruc-
tions; laws] and have turned away, refusing to ·obey you [Llisten to your
voice]. So you ·brought [poured] on us the curses and ·promises of punishment [oaths] written in the ·Teachings [Instructions; Laws] of Moses [Deut.
28:64–68], the servant of God, because we ·sinned against [failed] you.
12“·You said these things would happen to us and our ·leaders [judges],
and you made them happen; you brought on us a great disaster. Nothing
has ever been done ·on earth [Lunder all the heavens] like what was done
to Jerusalem. 13All this disaster came to us just as it is written in the
·Teachings [Instructions; Laws] of Moses [Deut. 28:15–68]. But we have
not ·pleaded [entreated] with the Lord our God. We have not ·stopped
[turned from] ·sinning [iniquity]. We have not ·paid attention to [consid-
ered; pondered; reflected on] your ·truth [faithfulness]. 14The Lord ·was
ready to bring [Lkept watch on and brought] the disaster on us, and he did
it because the Lord our God is ·right [righteous] in everything he does.
But we still did not ·obey him [Llisten to his voice].
15“Lord our God, ·you used your power and [Lby your strong hand you]
brought us out of Egypt [Ex. 12–15]. Because of that, your name is known
even today. But we have sinned and ·have done wrong [acted wickedly].
16Lord, ·you do what is right, but [Laccording to all your righteousness,]
·please do not be angry with [Lturn aside your anger and your wrath from]
Jerusalem, your city on your holy hill [CZion, the location of the Temple].
Because of our sins and the ·evil things [iniquity] done by our ·ancestors
[fathers], people all around ·insult and make fun of [scorn; reproach]
Jerusalem and your people.
17“Now, our God, hear the prayers of your servant. Listen to my ·prayer
for help [supplication], and for ·your [Lthe Lord’s] sake ·do good things
for [Lmake your face shine on] your ·holy place [sanctuary] that is in
ruins. 18My God, ·pay attention [Lextend/incline your ear] and hear me.
Open your eyes and see all ·the terrible things that have happened to us
[Lour desolation/destruction] and the city that is called by your name. We
do not ·ask these things [present our supplication] because ·we are good
[of our righteousness]; instead, we ask because of your ·mercy [compas-
sion]. 19Lord, listen! Lord, forgive! Lord, ·hear us [pay attention] and do
something! For your sake, don’t ·wait [delay], because your city and your
people are called by your name.”

Gabriel's Explanation

20While I was ·saying these things in my prayer [Lspeaking and praying] to the LORD, my God, confessing my sins and the sins of the people of Israel and ·praying [Llaying down my supplication] for God's holy hill [CZion, the location of the Temple], 21Gabriel came to me. (I had seen him in my ·last vision [Lvision in the beginning; 8:1].) ·He came flying quickly to me [*or*...when I was tired and weary] about the time of the evening sacrifice, while I was still praying. 22He ·taught me [Lmade me understand] and said to me, "Daniel, I have come [Lout now] to give you wisdom and to help you understand. 23·When you first started praying [LAt the beginning of your supplication], an ·answer [Lword] ·was given [Lwent out], and I came to tell you, because ·God loves you very much [Lyou are favored/coveted/desired]. So ·think about [consider; reflect; ponder] the ·message [Lword] and ·understand [consider; reflect; ponder] the vision.

24"·God has ordered four hundred ninety years [LSeventy sevens/weeks are given] for your people and your holy city [Cfor the following reasons]: to ·stop [finish] ·people from turning against God [transgression]; to put an end to sin; to ·take away [atone for] ·evil [iniquity]; to bring in ·goodness that continues forever [everlasting righteousness]; to ·bring about [seal] the vision and prophecy; and to ·appoint [anoint] a most holy place.

25"Learn and understand these things. A command will come to ·rebuild [Lrestore and build] Jerusalem. The time from this command until the ·appointed leader [anointed prince] comes will be ·forty-nine years [Lseven sevens/weeks] and ·four hundred thirty-four years [Lsixty-two sevens/weeks]. Jerusalem will be ·rebuilt [Lrestored and built] with ·streets [*or* public squares] and a ·trench filled with water around it [moat; *or* conduits], but it will be built in times of ·trouble [oppression]. 26After the ·four hundred thirty-four years [Lsixty-two sevens/weeks] the ·appointed leader [Lanointed one] will be ·killed [Lcut off]; he will have nothing. The ·people [*or* troops] of the ·leader [prince] who is to come will destroy the city and the holy place. The end of ·the city [Lit/*or* him] will come like a flood, and war will continue until the end. ·God has ordered that place to be completely destroyed [LDesolation/Destruction is decreed]. 27·That leader [LHe] will make firm an ·agreement [covenant; treaty] with many people for ·seven years [Lone seven/week]. He will ·stop [make cease] the offerings and sacrifices after ·three and one-half years [La half a seven/week]. ·A destroyer will do blasphemous things until the ordered end comes to the destroyed city [L...and upon a wing will be the horrible abominations until the decreed end overwhelms the desolator]."

Daniel's Vision of a Man

10 During Cyrus' third year as king of Persia [C536 BC], a ·message [Lword] was revealed to Daniel, whose name was Belteshazzar [1:7]. The ·message [Lword] was true and concerned a great ·war [conflict]. He understood the ·message [Lword] and understood the vision.

2·At that time [LIn those days] I, Daniel, had been ·very sad [mourning] for three ·weeks [sevens of days]. 3I did not eat any ·fancy [rich] food or meat, or drink any wine, or ·use any perfumed oil [anoint myself] ·for three weeks [Luntil the completion of the three weeks/sevens of days].

4On the twenty-fourth day of the first month, I was standing beside the great Tigris River [Calong with the Euphrates, one of the major rivers in Babylon, present-day Iraq]. 5I ·looked up [Llifted up my eyes] and saw a man dressed in linen clothes with a belt of gold of Uphaz [Csignifying high quality] wrapped around his waist. 6His body was like ·shiny yellow quartz [beryl; *or* chrysolite]. His face was like lightning [Cbright], and his eyes were like ·fire [Lflaming torches]. His arms and legs were ·shiny [gleaming] like polished bronze, and his voice sounded like the roar of a crowd [Ezek. 1:7, 13, 23, 24, 27; 9:2; Rev. 1:15].

7I, Daniel, was the only person who saw the vision. The men with me did not see it, because ·they were so frightened [Lgreat trembling fell on them] that they ·ran away [fled] and hid. 8So I was left alone, watching this great vision. ·I lost my strength [LNo strength was left in me], my ·face turned white like a dead person [Lsplendor was spoiled], and I ·was helpless [Lretained no strength]. 9Then I heard the ·man in the vision speaking [Lsound of his words]. As I ·listened [Lheard the sound of his words], I fell into a ·deep sleep [trance] with my face on the ground.

10Then a hand touched me and set me on my hands and knees. I was so afraid that I was ·shaking [trembling]. 11·The man in the vision [LHe] said to me, “Daniel, ·God loves you very much [Lyou are favored/coveted/desired]. Think carefully about the words I will speak to you, and stand up, because I have been sent to you.” When he said this, I stood up, but I was still ·shaking [trembling].

12Then the man said to me, “Daniel, do not be afraid. ·Some time ago [LFrom the first day] you ·decided [Lgave your heart/mind] to get understanding and to humble yourself before your God. ·Since that time God has listened to you [L…your words have been heard], and I have come because of your ·prayers [Lwords]. 13But the prince of the kingdom of Persia [Ca spiritual being; nations have their presiding angels; Deut. 32:8–9] ·has been fighting [Lstood] against me for twenty-one days. Then Michael, one of the most important ·angels [Lprinces], came to help me, because I had been left there with the king of Persia. 14Now I have come to ·explain to you [help you understand] what will happen to your people, because the vision is about a time in the future.”

15While he was speaking to me, I ·bowed facedown [Lplaced my face on the ground] and could not speak. 16Then one ·who looked like a man [Laccording to the likeness of a son of man] touched my lips, so I opened my mouth and started to speak. I said to the one standing in front of me, “Master, ·I am upset and afraid [Lpangs/anguish/pain came over me] because of what I saw in the vision. I ·feel helpless [Lcould not retain strength]. 17Master, how can I, your servant, talk with ·you [Lmy master]? ·My strength is gone [LFrom now strength does not remain in me], and ·it is hard for me to breathe [Lbreath does not remain in me].”

18The one ·who looked like a [like the appearance of a] man touched me again and gave me strength. 19He said, “Daniel, don’t be afraid. ·God loves you very much [LYou are favored/coveted/desired]. Peace be with you. Be strong now; be courageous.”

When he spoke to me, I became stronger and said, “Master, speak, since you have given me strength.”

20Then he said, “Daniel, do you know why I have come to you? Soon I must go back to fight against the prince of Persia [v. 13]. When I go, the prince of ·Greece [LJavan] will come, 21but I must first tell you what is ·written [inscribed] in the ·Book of Truth [*or* dependable writings]. No one stands with me against these enemies except Michael, ·the angel ruling over your people [Lyour prince].

11 “In the first year that Darius the Mede was king [C539 BC; 5:31], I [Cthe unnamed angel speaking to Daniel; 10:5] stood

up to support and strengthen him [CMichael, in his fight against the
prince of Persia].

Kingdoms of the South and North

2"Now then, Daniel, I tell you the truth: Three more kings will ·rule
[Larise] in Persia, and then a fourth king will come. He will be much
richer than all ·the kings of Persia before him [Lof them] and will use his
riches to get power [Cperhaps Darius III, the last king of Persia]. He will
stir up everyone against the kingdom of ·Greece [LJavan]. 3Then a ·mighty
[*or* warrior] king will ·come [Larise], who will rule with great power and
will do anything he wants [CAlexander the Great, who defeats Persia].
4After that king ·has come [Larises], his kingdom will be broken up and
divided out toward the four ·parts of the world [Lwinds of heaven]. His
kingdom will not go to his ·descendants [posterity], and ·it will not have
the power that he had [Lnot according to the dominion of his dominion],
because his kingdom will be pulled up and given to other people
[CAlexander's kingdom was divided among his four most powerful generals, the Diadochoi].
5"The king of the South [CPtolemy I; the South is the Ptolemaic kingdom with its chief city in Alexandria, Egypt] will become strong, but one
of his commanders will become even stronger [CSeleucus, the founding
king of the Seleucid kingdom with its chief city in Antioch, Syria]. He will
begin to rule his own kingdom with great power. 6Then ·after a few [Lat the
end of] years, ·a new friendship will develop [they will enter an alliance].
The daughter of the king of the South will ·marry [Lcome to] the king of
the North ·in order to bring peace [Lto establish an agreement; Ca marriage
alliance between Berenice, daughter of the Ptolemaic king, and Antiochus
II Theos of the Seleucid kingdom]. But she will not ·keep [retain] her
power, and his ·family [Lseed; *or* power] will not last. She, her husband, her
child, and those who ·brought her to that country [supported her] will be
·killed [Lgiven up; Cthey were poisoned in a political intrigue].
7"But a ·person from her family [Lbranch of her roots] will ·become king
of the South [Larise in his place] and will ·attack [Lcome against] the armies
of the king of the North [CPtolemy III waged war against Seleucus II]. He
will go into that king's ·strong, walled city [fortress] and will ·fight [act] and
win. 8He will take their gods, their metal idols, and their ·valuable [Lfavored;
coveted; desired] things made of silver and gold back to Egypt as plunder.
Then he will not bother the king of the North for a few years. 9Next, ·the
king of the North [Lhe] will ·attack [Lcome against] the king of the South,
but he will ·be beaten back [return] to his own ·country [land; Cthe battles
between the Seleucids and the Ptolemies would continue].
10"His [Cthe king of the North] sons [CSeleucus III and Antiochus III
the Great] will prepare for war. They will get a large ·army [multitude;
horde] together that will move through the land, like a flood [Cpowerfully
and quickly]. Later, that army will come back and fight all the way to the
·strong, walled city [fortress; Cof the king of the South, Ptolemy IV; the
fortress may refer to Gaza]. 11Then the king of the South will become very
angry and will march out to fight against the king of the North [Cthe
battle of Raphia between Ptolemy IV and Antiochus III in 217 BC]. The
king of the North will ·have [raise] a large ·army [multitude; horde], but
he will ·lose the battle [Lbe delivered into his hand], 12and the ·soldiers
[multitude; horde] will be carried away. ·The king of the South will then
be very proud [LHis heart will be lifted up] and will ·kill [Lfell] ·thousands

of soldiers [Lmyriads; tens of thousands] from the northern army, but he
will not ·continue to be successful [prevail; be victorious]. 13The king of
the North will gather another ·army [multitude; horde], larger than the
first one. After ·several [a period of] years he will attack with a large ·army
[force] and many ·weapons [*or* supplies].

14"In those times many people will ·be [Lrise up] against the king of the
South. ·Some of your own people who love to fight [Wild/Violent men;
LSons who make breaches among your people; CJewish men] will ·turn
[Llift themselves up] against the king of the South, ·thinking it is time for
God's promises to come true [Lto fulfill the vision]. But they will ·fail
[stumble; falter]. 15Then the king of the North will come. He will ·build
[throw up] ·ramps to the tops of the city walls [siege engines] and will
capture a ·strong, walled [fortified] city. The southern ·army [forces] will
not ·have the power to fight back [endure; last]; even their best soldiers
will not be strong enough to ·stop the northern army [endure; last]. 16So
the ·king of the North [Lone who invades him] will do whatever he ·wants
[pleases]; no one will be able to ·stand [endure; last] against him. He will
gain power and control in the beautiful land [Cof Judah; 8:9] and ·will
have the power to destroy it [Lall of it will be in his hand/power]. 17The
king of the North will ·decide [Lset his face] to ·use [bring] all his power
to fight against the king of the South, but he will make a peace agreement
with the king of the South. The king of the North will give one of his
daughters as a wife to the king of the South so that he can ·defeat [destroy]
him [CCleopatra was given to Ptolemy V in marriage to serve as a spy]. But
those plans will not ·succeed [stand; endure; last] or help him [CCleopatra
changed loyalties]. 18Then the king of the North will turn his attention to
the coastlines [Ccities along the coast of the Mediterranean Sea; Antiochus
was able to take some cities in Asia Minor] and will capture ·them [Lmany].
But a commander [Cthe Roman consul Lucius Cornelius Scipio commanded him to cease warfare] will put an end to ·the pride of the king of
the North [Lhis scorn], turning his ·pride [scorn] back on him. 19After
that happens the king of the North will go back to the ·strong, walled
[fortified] cities of his own country, but he will ·lose his power [Lstumble
and fall]. ·That will be the end of him [L...and not be found; CAntiochus
III died in 187 BC].

20"·The next king of the North will send out a tax collector so he will
have plenty of money [LThen one will arise in his place who will send out
a tax collector/despot/oppressor for/*or* to enhance the splendor of the
kingdom]. In ·a few years [Llater/after days] that ruler will be ·killed
[Lbroken], ·although he will not die in [Lnot by] anger or in a battle
[CSeleucus IV died in mysterious circumstances, perhaps killed by his
brother Antiochus IV also known as Epiphanes].

21"·That ruler will be followed by [LThen one will arise in his place who
is] ·a very cruel and hated man [Ldespised], who had not yet been given
the honor of royalty [CAntiochus Epiphanes, who will be the focus of
much of the rest of the chapter]. He will attack ·the kingdom when the
people feel safe [without warning], and he will take power by ·lying to the
people [intrigue]. 22He will sweep away in defeat ·large and powerful
[Lfloodlike] ·armies [forces] and even a prince who made an ·agreement
[covenant; treaty]. 23Many nations will make ·agreements [alliances] with
·that cruel and hated ruler [Lhim], but he will lie to them. He will gain
much power, but only a few people will support him. 24The richest ·areas

[*or* people of a province] will feel safe, but ·that cruel and hated ruler [Lhe] will attack them. He will succeed where his ·ancestors [Lfathers and father's fathers] did not. He will ·rob the countries he defeats and will give those things to his followers [Lscatter spoil, plunder, and goods to them]. He will plan ·to defeat and destroy strong cities [Lagainst strongholds], ·but he will be successful for only a short time [Luntil a time].

25"·That very cruel and hated ruler [LHe] will have a large army that he will use to stir up his strength and ·courage [Lheart]. He will attack the king of the South [Cthe Seleucid king Ptolemy VI]. The king of the South will gather a large and very powerful army and prepare for war. But ·the people who are against him will make secret plans, and the king of the South will be defeated [Lhe will not stand/endure because of the plans they planned against him]. 26People who ·were supposed to be his good friends [Leat his royal rations; CPtolemy VI's advisors Eulaeus and Lenaeus] will try to ·destroy [Lbreak] him. His army will be swept away in defeat; many ·of his soldiers will be killed in battle [Lcorpses will fall]. 27Those two kings will ·want to hurt each other [Lhave their hearts/minds toward evil/harm]. They will sit at the same table and lie to each other, but it will not ·do either one any good [succeed], because ·God has set a time for their end to come [the appointed time of the end has been set]. 28·The king of the North [LHe; CAntiochus] will go back to his own country with much wealth. Then he will decide to go against the holy ·agreement [covenant; treaty; Cas Antiochus returned to Syria from Egypt, he took aggressive action against the Jews in Jerusalem]. He will take action and then return to his own country.

29"At the ·right [appointed] time ·the king of the North [Lhe] will attack the king of the South again, but this time ·he will not be successful as he was before [Lit will not be as before]. 30Ships from ·the west [LKittim; CRome, which made Antiochus stand down from his attack on the South] will come and fight against ·the king of the North [Lhim], so he will be ·afraid [startled; *or* dismayed]. Then he will return and show his anger against the holy ·agreement [covenant; treaty]. He will be good to those who have ·stopped obeying [Labandoned; forsaken] the holy ·agreement [covenant; treaty; Cthe pro-Antiochus party among the Jewish people].

31"·The king of the North will send his army [LForces from him will arise] to ·make the Temple in Jerusalem unclean [Lprofane the Holy Place and fortress]. They will ·stop the people from offering [Lturn aside] the ·daily [regular] sacrifice [8:12], and then they will set up a ·blasphemous object that brings destruction [Labomination of desolation; Ca pagan object, perhaps a meteorite dedicated to Zeus, would be placed in the holy place; Matt. 24:15; Mark 13:14; also 1 Maccabees 1:44-47, 54 in the Apocrypha]. 32·The king of the North [LHe] will tell lies and cause those who have ·not obeyed God [Ltransgressed the agreement/covenant/treaty] to ·be ruined [Lbecome godless]. But those who know God and obey him will be strong and fight back.

33"Those who are ·wise [Linsightful among the people] will help ·the others [Lmany] understand what is happening. But they will ·be killed [Lstumble] with swords, or ·burned [Lwith flame], or ·taken captive [Lby exile], or ·robbed of their homes and possessions [Lby spoil]. These things will continue for many days. 34When ·the wise ones are suffering [Lthey stumble], they will get a little help, but many who join ·the wise ones [Lthem] will ·not help them in their time of need [Lbe insincere]. 35Some

of the ·wise [Linsightful] ones will ·be killed [Lstumble]. ·But the hard
times must come so they can be made stronger and purer and without
faults [L…in order to refine, to purify, and to cleanse them] until the time
of the end comes. Then, at the right time, the end will come.

The King Who Praises Himself

36 “·The king of the North [LThe king] will do whatever he ·wants
[pleases; desires]. He will ·brag about [exalt] himself and praise himself
and think he is even better than a god. He will say ·things [fantastic/hor-
rendous things] against the God of gods that no one has ever heard. And
he will be successful until ·all the bad things have happened [Lrage is com-
pleted]. Then what ·God has planned to happen [Lis determined] will
happen. 37 ·The king of the North [LHe] will ·not care about [pay no attention to] the gods ·his ancestors worshiped [Lof his ancestors/fathers; Che
replaced the worship of Apollos with that of Zeus] or the god ·that women
worship [Ldesired/coveted/favored by women; Cperhaps Adonis or Dio
nysius]. He won’t ·care about [pay attention to] any god. Instead, he will
·make himself more important than any god [Lexalt himself above all].
38 ·The king of the North [LHe] will ·worship [glorify] ·power and strength
[La god of fortresses in his place], ·which his ancestors did not worship [La
god his ancestors/fathers did not know]. He will ·honor [glorify] the god
of power with gold and silver, ·expensive jewels [precious stones] and
·gifts [Ldesired/coveted/favored things]. 39 That king will attack ·strong,
walled cities [fortresses] with the help of a foreign god. He will give much
·honor [glory; *or* wealth] to the people who ·join [acknowledge; recog-
nize] him, making them rulers in charge of many other people. And he
will ·make them pay him for the land they rule [Ldistribute the land for a
price].

40 “At the time of the end, the king of the South will ·fight a battle
[Lbutt] against ·the king of the North [Lhim]. The king of the North will
·attack [Lrush in on him] with chariots, soldiers on horses, and many
large ships. He will invade many countries and sweep through their lands
like a flood. 41 The king of the North will attack the beautiful land [CJudah;
8:9]. He will ·defeat many countries [Lcause many to stumble], but Edom,
Moab, and the ·leaders [Lheads; *or* main part] of Ammon will be saved
from ·him [Lhis hand]. 42 ·The king of the North [LHe] will ·show his power
in [Lsend his hand against] many countries; Egypt will not escape. 43 ·The
king [LHe] will ·get [Lrule over the] treasures of gold and silver and all the
riches of Egypt. The Libyan and ·Nubian [*or* Ethiopian; LCushite] people
will ·obey him [Lfollow in his tracks]. 44 But the king of the North will hear
·news [reports] from the east and the north that will make him ·afraid
[terrified] and angry. He will go to [Ldevastate and] destroy completely
many. 45 He will ·set up [pitch] his royal tents between the sea and the
beautiful holy mountain [CZion, the location of the Temple]. But, finally,
his end will come, and no one will help him.

The Time of the End

12 “At that time Michael, the great prince [Cangel] who ·protects
[Lstands by] your people [10:13, 21], will ·stand up [arise].
There will be a time of ·much trouble [distress], the worst time since
nations have been on earth, but at that time your people will be ·saved
[rescued]. ·Everyone whose name is written in God’s book will be saved
[LAll who are found written in the book; Cof life; Ex. 32:32; Ps. 69:28;
Rev. 20:12]. 2 Many people who ·have already died [Lare sleeping in the
land of the dust] will ·live again [Lwake up]. Some will wake up to life

forever, but some will wake up to ·shame [reproach] and ·disgrace
[abhorrence] **forever** [Is. 26:19]. **3The ·wise** [insightful; 11:33, 35] **people**
will shine like the ·brightness of the sky [firmament; dome; expanse;
Gen. 1:6]. **Those who teach ·others** [Lthe many] **·to live right** [righteous-
ness] **will shine like stars forever and ever.**
4"But you, Daniel, ·close up the book and seal it [Lkeep the words secret
and seal the book]. **·These things will happen at the time of the end** [L...
until the time of the end]. **Many people will go here and there to ·find true**
[Lincrease] **knowledge** [Amos 8:12]."
5Then I, Daniel, looked, and saw two other men. One was standing on
·my side [one bank] **of the river, and the other was standing on the ·far**
side [other bank]. **6The man who was dressed in linen was standing ·over**
the water in the river [*or* upstream]. **One of the two men spoke to him**
and asked, "How long will it be before these ·amazing things [wonders]
come ·true [to an end]?"
7The man dressed in linen, who stood ·over the water [*or* upstream],
raised his ·hands [Lright hand and his left; Ca solemn vow] **toward heaven.**
And I heard him swear by the ·name of God who lives forever [Llife of the
Eternal One], **"It will be for ·three and one-half years** [La time; two times,
and half]. **The ·power** [Lhand] **of the holy people will finally be ·broken**
[shattered], **and then all these things will ·come true** [be completed]."
8I ·heard the answer [Llistened], **but I did not really understand, so I**
asked, "Master, what will ·happen after all these things come true [Lbe the
outcome of these things]?"
9He answered, "Go your way, Daniel. The ·message [Lword] **is ·closed**
up [secret] **and sealed until the time of the end. 10Many people will be**
made clean, pure, and ·spotless [refined], **but the wicked will continue to**
be wicked. Those wicked people will not understand these things, but the
·wise [insightful] **will understand them.**
11"The ·daily [regular] **sacrifice** [8:12] **will be ·stopped** [turned away].
Then, after 1,290 days from that time, ·a blasphemous object that brings
destruction [Lthe abomination of desolation; 11:31] **will be set up. 12Those**
who wait for the end of the 1,335 days will be ·happy [blessed].
13"As for you, Daniel, go your way until the end. You will get your rest,
and at the end you will rise to receive your reward."

HOSEA

1 The ·LORD spoke his word [Lword of the LORD that was] to Hosea son of Beeri ·during the time [Lin the days] that Uzziah, Jotham, Ahaz, and Hezekiah were kings of Judah and Jeroboam son of Jehoash was king of Israel [CHosea prophesied about 760–722 BC].

Hosea's Wife and Children

2When the LORD began speaking through Hosea, the LORD said to him, "Go, and ·marry [Ltake for yourself] an ·unfaithful woman [*or* prostitute; Lwoman/wife of prostitution/harlotries] and have ·unfaithful children [Lchildren of prostitution/harlotries], because ·the people in this country [Lthis land] have ·been completely unfaithful to [practiced prostitution/harlotry against] the LORD [Cthey have been spiritually unfaithful; CGomer may have been a prostitute or promiscuous woman before the marriage, or only afterward]." 3So Hosea ·married [Lwent and took] Gomer daughter of Diblaim, and she ·became pregnant [conceived] and gave birth to Hosea's son.

4The LORD said to Hosea, "Name him Jezreel [CHebrew: "God sows"], because soon I will punish the ·family [Lhouse] of Jehu for the ·people they killed at [Lblood of] Jezreel [CJehu slaughtered the family of king Ahab; 2 Kin. 9:7—10:28]. In ·the future [Lthat day] I will put an end to the kingdom of [Lthe house of] Israel 5and break the ·power of Israel's army [Lbow of Israel] in the Valley of Jezreel."

6Gomer ·became pregnant [conceived] again and gave birth to a daughter. The LORD said to Hosea, "Name her Lo-Ruhamah [CHebrew: "no pity/mercy" or "not loved"], because I will not ·pity [have mercy on; show love to] Israel anymore, nor will I forgive them. 7But I will show ·pity [mercy; love] to the people of Judah. I will save them, but not by using bows or swords, horses or horsemen, or ·weapons of war [*or* battle; war]. I, the LORD their God, will save them."

8After Gomer had stopped nursing Lo-Ruhamah, she ·became pregnant [conceived] again and gave birth to another son. 9The LORD said, "Name him Lo-Ammi [C"not my people"], because you are not my people, and I am not your God.

God's Promise to Israel

10"But the number of the Israelites will become like the grains of sand of the sea, which no one can measure or count [Gen. 22:17; 32:12]. ·They were called [*or* Although it was said to them; *or* In the place where it was said to them], 'You are not my people,' but later ·they will be called [it will be said to them] 'children of the living God.' 11The people of Judah and Israel will ·join [come; be gathered] together again and will ·choose [appoint] one leader for themselves. They will come up from the land, because the day of Jezreel [C"God plants/sows," alluding here to the rebirth of the once desolate nation; see vv. 4–5; 2:22–23] will be truly great.

2 "You are to call your brothers, 'my people [LAmmi; 1:9],' and your sisters, 'you have been shown pity [LRuhama; 1:6–8].'

God Speaks About Israel

2"·Plead with [*or* Rebuke; *or* Accuse; Bring charges against] your mother [Cthe nation Israel].
·Plead with [*or* Rebuke; *or* Accuse; Bring charges against] her, because she is ·no longer [Lnot] my wife,
and I am ·no longer [Lnot] her husband.
Tell her to ·stop acting like a prostitute [*or* take off her prostitute's make-up; Lset aside her harlotries from her presence/face],
·to stop behaving like an unfaithful wife [Land set aside unfaithfulness from between her breasts].
3If she refuses, I will strip her naked
and ·leave her bare [expose her] like the day she was born.
I will make her dry like a desert,
like a ·land without water [parched land],
and I will kill her with thirst.
4I will not ·take pity [have mercy/compassion] on her children,
because they are the children of ·a prostitute [*or* adultery; harlotry].
5Their mother has ·acted like a prostitute [been unfaithful; committed adultery];
the one who ·became pregnant with [conceived] them has acted ·disgracefully [shamefully].
She said, 'I will ·chase [seek; go] after my lovers [Cthe idol-worshiping nations around Israel],
who give me my ·food [bread] and water,
wool and flax, ·wine [Ldrinks] and olive oil.'
6So I will ·block her road [*or* fence/hedge her in] with thornbushes;
I will ·build a wall around her [wall her in]
so she cannot find her way.
7She will ·run after [pursue] her lovers,
but she won't catch them.
She will look for them,
but she won't find them.
Then she will say, 'I will go back to my first husband [CGod],
because life was better then for me than it is now.'
8But she does not ·know [acknowledge] that I was the one
who gave her grain, new wine, and oil.
I ·gave her much [lavished on her] silver and gold,
but ·she [Lthey; Cthe nation] used it for Baal.

9"So I will come back and take away my grain ·at harvest time [Lin its time]
and my new wine ·when it is ready [Lin its season/appointed time].
I will take back my wool and ·linen [flax]
that covered her nakedness.
10So I will ·show her nakedness [uncover her lewdness/shamelessness] to her lovers,
and no one will ·save [rescue] her from ·me [Lmy hand].
11I will put an end to all her ·celebrations [merrymaking]:
her yearly festivals, her New Moon festivals, and her Sabbaths.
I will stop all of her ·special [appointed] feasts.

12I will destroy her vines and fig trees,
which she said were her pay from her lovers.
I will turn them into a ·forest [overgrown thicket],
and ·wild animals [beasts of the field] **will eat them.**
13I will punish her for all the ·times [days; [C]pagan feast days]
she burned incense to the Baals [[C]the local gods of the Canaanites worshiped by the Israelites].
She ·put on her [adorned herself with] **·rings** [*or* earrings] **and jewelry**
and went ·chasing after [out to] **her lovers,**
but she forgot me!"
says the LORD.

14"So I am going to ·attract [allure; woo] **her;**
I will lead her into the ·desert [wilderness; [C]as in the Exodus, when God rescued Israel from slavery and cared for her; Ex. 12–17]
and speak tenderly to her.
15There I will give her back her vineyards,
and I will make the Valley of ·Trouble [[L]Achor; [C]see Josh. 7:1–26] **a door of hope.**
There she will ·respond [*or* sing] **as ·when she was young** [[L]in the days of her youth],
as when she came out of Egypt."

16The LORD says, "In the future she[n] **will call me 'my husband';**
no longer will she[n] **call me 'my baal** [[C]"baal" can mean "husband," "master," or "Baal" (the Canaanite god); in this wordplay, Israel has replaced one husband (the LORD) with another (Baal)].'
17I will ·never let her say [remove from her lips] **the names of Baal again;**
people won't ·use [utter; invoke; *or* remember] **their names anymore.**
18At that time I will make an ·agreement [covenant; treaty] **for them**
with the ·wild animals [[L]beasts of the field], **the ·birds** [[L]birds of the sky/heavens], **and the ·crawling things** [[T]creeping things of the ground].
I will ·smash [shatter; abolish] **from the land**
the bow and the sword and ·the weapons of war [*or* war; battle],
so my people will ·live [[L]lie down] **in safety.**
19And I will ·make you my promised bride [[L]betroth you to me] **forever.**
I will ·be good and fair [[L]betroth you in righteousness and justice];
I will show you my ·love [loyalty; unfailing love; lovingkindness] **and mercy.**
20I will ·be true to you as my promised bride [[L]betroth you in faithfulness],
and you will ·know [*or* acknowledge me as] **the LORD.**

21"At that time I will ·speak to you [answer; respond]," **says the LORD.**
"I will ·speak to [answer; respond to] **the ·skies** [*or* heavens],
and they will ·give rain to [[L]answer; respond to] **the earth.**
22The earth will ·produce [[L]answer/respond with] **grain, new wine, and oil;**
·much will grow because my people are called [[L]and they will answer/respond to] **Jezreel** [[C]"God plants"; 1:4, 11].

2:16 she Greek, Aramaic and Latin copies read "she." Hebrew copies read "you."

[23]I will plant ·my people [[L]her for myself] in the land,
and I will show pity to the one I had called '·not shown pity [[L]Lo-Ruhamah; 1:6–7].'
I will say, 'You are my people'
to those I had called '·not my people [[L]Lo-Ammi; 1:9].'
And they will say to me, 'You are our God.' "

Hosea Redeems His Wife

3 The LORD said to me again, "Go, show your love to a woman [[C]probably Gomer (1:3), who has since deserted him] ·loved by [*or* who loves] someone else, who ·has been unfaithful to you [is committing adultery]. In the same way the LORD loves the ·people [[L]sons; [T]children] of Israel, even though they ·worship [turn to] other gods and love to eat the raisin cakes [[C]food eaten at pagan temples]."

[2]So I bought her for six ·ounces of silver [shekels] and ·ten bushels [[L]a homer and a lethek; [C]a homer was 5-6 bushels; a lethek was about half that] of barley.
[3]Then I told her, "You must ·wait for [*or* live with] me for many days. You must not be a prostitute, and you must not have sexual relations with any other man. I will act the same way toward you."

[4]In the same way the ·people [[L]sons; [T]children] of Israel will live many days without a king or ·leader [prince], without sacrifices or holy stone pillars [[C]used in pagan worship; 2 Kin. 3:2; 10:26–28; 17:10], and without ·the holy vest [ephod; Ex. 28:6–14; Judg. 8:27] or ·an idol [household idols; [L]teraphim; Gen. 31:19].
[5]After this, the people of Israel will return and ·follow [seek] the LORD their God and ·the king from David's family [[L]David their king; [C]an heir from David's line]. In the last days they will ·turn in fear [come in reverence/awe] to the LORD, and he will bless them.

The Lord's Word Against Israel

4 ·People [[L]Sons; [T]Children] of Israel, ·listen to the LORD's message [hear the word of the LORD].
The LORD has a ·charge [case; lawsuit; *or* dispute] to bring
against you who live in the land:
"·The people are not true, not loyal to God [[L]There is no truth/faithfulness, there is no mercy/lovingkindness],
nor do those who live in the land even know him [there is no knowledge of God in the land].
[2][[L]There is only] Cursing, lying, ·killing [murder], stealing and adultery are everywhere.
·One murder follows another [[L]They break out and blood touches blood].
[3]Because of this the land ·dries up [*or* mourns],
and all its ·people [inhabitants] ·are dying [languish; waste away].
Even the ·wild animals [[L]beasts of the field] and the birds of the air
and the fish of the sea are ·dying [gathered; taken/swept away].

God's Case Against the Priests

[4]"·No one should [Let no one] ·accuse [bring a charge]
or ·blame [contend against] another person.
·Don't blame the people, you priests,
when they quarrel with you [*or* For my case is against you, the priests].
[5]You will ·be ruined [stumble] in the day,
and your prophets will ·be ruined [stumble] with you in the night.
I will also destroy your mother [[C]Israel].
[6]My people ·will be [*or* are being] destroyed,
because they ·have no [lack] knowledge.

You have ·refused to learn [rejected knowledge; *or* failed to acknowledge me],
so I will ·refuse to let you be [reject you as] priests to me.
You have forgotten the ·teachings [law; [C]Hebrew: *Torah*] of your God,
so I will forget your children.
7The more priests ·there are [increase],
the more they sin against me.
·I will take away their honor
and give them shame
[*or* They have exchanged the glory of God
for the shamefulness (of idols); Rom. 1:23].
8Since the priests ·live off [[L]eat; feed on] the ·sin offerings [*or* sin] of the people,
they ·want the people to sin more and more [relish/long for their iniquity].
9·The priests are as wrong as the people [[L]And it will be: like people, like priest],
and I will punish them both for ·what they have done [their ways].
I will repay them for the ·wrong [[L]acts; deeds] they have done.

10"They will eat
but not have enough;
they will ·have sexual relations with the prostitutes [*or* behave like prostitutes],
but they will not ·have children [*or* gain anything; [L]multiply; increase],
because they have ·left [deserted; abandoned] the LORD
to give themselves to 11·prostitution [immorality],
to old and new wine,
which take away ·their ability to understand [[L]the heart].

God's Case Against the People

12"My people ask wooden idols for ·advice [counsel];
they ask ·those sticks of wood [*or* divining rods/staffs] to advise them!
·Like prostitutes, they have chased after other gods [[L]A spirit/wind of prostitution leads/blows them astray]
·and have left [committing adultery against; being unfaithful to] their own God.
13They make sacrifices on the tops of the mountains [[C]places of pagan worship].
They burn offerings on the hills,
under oaks, poplars, and ·other trees [terebinths],
because their shade is ·nice [pleasant].
So your daughters become prostitutes [[C]cultic prostitutes in pagan temples],
and your daughters-in-law are guilty of adultery.

14"But I will not punish your daughters
for becoming prostitutes,
nor your daughters-in-law
for their sins of adultery.
I will not punish them,
because the men ·have sexual relations [go off] with prostitutes

and offer sacrifices with the ·temple [cult; shrine] prostitutes.
A ·foolish people [people without knowledge/discernment] will be ·ruined [destroyed].

15"Israel, you ·act like a prostitute [*or* commit adultery],
but do not let Judah be guilty toward the LORD.
Don't go to Gilgal [Ca city where false worship was taking place]
or go up to Beth Aven [C"house of wickedness," a derogatory name for Bethel, "house of God"].
Don't ·make promises [swear],
saying, 'As surely as the LORD lives...'
16The people of Israel are stubborn
like a stubborn ·young cow [heifer].
·Now the LORD will [*or* Should the LORD now...?] feed them
like lambs in ·the open country [a broad meadow].
17·The Israelites [LEphraim; Cthe leading tribe of the northern kingdom of Israel] ·have chosen to worship [Lis joined to] idols,
so leave ·them [Lhim] alone.
18When they finish their drinking,
they ·completely [*or* constantly] ·give themselves to being prostitutes [engage in prostitution; *or* go off with prostitutes];
·they [*or* their rulers; Ltheir shields] love these ·disgraceful [shameful] ways.
19They will be ·swept away as if by [wrapped up in] a whirlwind,
and their sacrifices will bring them only shame.

God's Word Against the Leaders

5 "·Listen [Hear this], you priests.
Pay attention, ·people [Lhouse] of Israel.
Listen, ·royal family [Lhouse of the king],
because you will all be judged.
You have been like a ·trap [snare] at Mizpah
and like a net spread out at Mount Tabor [Chunting places in Israel].
2·You have done many evil things [LThe rebels are deep into slaughter; *or* You have dug a deep pit at Shittim/Acacia],
so I will ·punish [discipline] you all.
3I know all about Ephraim [CIsrael; 4:17];
what Israel has done is not hidden from me.
Now Ephraim acts like a prostitute,
and Israel has ·made itself unclean [Ldefiled himself].

4"·They will not give up their deeds
and [*or* Their deeds won't let them] return to their God.
·They are determined to be unfaithful to me [LFor a spirit of prostitution is within them];
they do not know the LORD.
5Israel's ·pride [arrogance] testifies against them.
·The people of Israel [LIsrael and Ephraim; 4:17] will stumble because of their ·sin [iniquity],
and ·the people of Judah [LJudah] will stumble with them.
6They will come to ·worship [Lseek] the LORD,
bringing their flocks and herds,
but they will not be able to find him,
because he has ·left [withdrawn from] them.

[7]They have ·not been true to [been unfaithful to; dealt treacherously with] the LORD;
they ·are children who do not belong to him [*or* bear illegitimate/alien children].
So ·their false worship [[L]a new moon; [C]a festival]
will ·destroy [[L]devour] them and their ·land [wealth; portion].

[8]"Blow the ·horn [trumpet; ram's horn] in Gibeah
and the trumpet in Ramah [[C]used to sound a warning or call to battle].
·Give the warning [Sound the alarm; Raise the battle cry] at Beth Aven [4:15],
·and be first into battle [*or* lead on; *or* we are with you], ·people of Benjamin [[L]Benjamin].
[9]·Israel [[L]Ephraim; 4:17] will be ·ruined [laid waste; desolate]
on the day of ·punishment [rebuke; reckoning].
To the tribes of Israel
I ·tell the truth [[L]make known what is certain].
[10]The ·leaders [princes] of Judah are like those
who ·steal other people's land [[L]move boundary markers; [C]a serious crime in the ancient world; Deut. 19:14; 27:17; Prov. 15:25].
I will pour my ·punishment over [wrath on] them
like ·a flood of water [[L]water].
[11]·Israel [[L]Ephraim; 4:17] is ·beaten down [oppressed] and crushed by the ·punishment [judgment],
because it ·decided [was determined] to follow ·idols [*or* worthless things; *or* human precepts].
[12]I am like a moth to ·Israel [[L]Ephraim; 4:17],
like ·a rot [wood rot; decay] to the ·people [[L]house] of Judah.

[13]"When ·Israel [[L]Ephraim; 4:17] saw its illness
and Judah saw its ·wounds [*or* sores],
·Israel [[L]Ephraim] went to Assyria for help
and sent to the great ·king of Assyria [[L]king].
But he cannot heal you
or cure your wounds.
[14]I will be like a lion to ·Israel [[L]Ephraim; 4:17],
like a young lion to ·Judah [[L]the house of Judah].
·I will attack them
and tear them to pieces [[L]I, even I, will tear them and go away].
I will drag them off,
and no one will be able to ·save [rescue] them.
[15]Then I will go back to my ·place [lair; dwelling place]
until they ·suffer for [*or* admit] their guilt and ·turn back to me [[L]seek my face].
In their ·trouble [distress; affliction] they will look for me."

The People Are Not Faithful

6 "Come, let's ·go back [return] to the LORD.
He has ·hurt us [torn us to pieces], but he will heal us.
He has wounded us, but he will ·bandage [bind up] our wounds.
[2]·In [After] two days he will ·put new life in [revive; restore] us;
on the third day he will raise us up [[C]in a short time]
so that we may live in his presence [3]and know him.

Let's ·try [press on] to ·learn about [know] the LORD;
he will come to us as surely as the dawn comes.
He will come to us ·like rain [*or* as sure as the winter rains come],
like the ·spring [latter] rain that waters the ·ground [earth]."

4The LORD says, "·Israel [LEphraim; 4:17], what should I do with you?
Judah, what should I do with you?
Your faithfulness is like a morning mist,
like the dew that goes away early in the day.
5I have ·warned you [Lcut you into pieces; hewn you] by my prophets
that I will kill you with ·my words [Lthe words of my mouth].
My ·justice [judgment] comes out like ·bright light [*or* the morning dawn].
6I ·want [desire; delight in] ·faithful love [mercy; lovingkindness]
·more than I want animal sacrifices [Land not sacrifice].
I want ·people to know me [the knowledge of God]
more than I want burnt offerings [Lev. 1:1–17].
7But they ·have broken [transgressed] the ·agreement [covenant] as
·Adam did [*or* human beings did; *or* they did at Adamah; Josh. 3:16];
they have ·been unfaithful to [dealt treacherously with] me.
8Gilead is a city of ·people who do evil [sinners; evildoers];
·their footprints are bloody [tracked with bloody footprints].
9The ·priests [Lcompany of priests] are like robbers ·waiting [lying in ambush] to attack people;
they murder people on the road to Shechem [Ca city of refuge for someone who committed involuntary manslaughter; Josh. 20:7; 21:21; 1 Chr. 6:67]
and do wicked things.
10I have seen horrible things in ·Israel [*or* the temple of Israel; Lthe house of Israel].
Look at ·Israel's [LEphraim's; 4:17] prostitution;
Israel has become ·unclean [defiled].

11"Judah, I have ·set [appointed] a harvest time for you
when I will ·make the lives of my people good again [restore the fortunes of my people; *or* return my people from captivity].
7 When I heal Israel,
Israel's sin will ·go away [*or* be revealed/exposed],
and so will Samaria's evil.

"They ·cheat a lot [practice deceit; commit fraud]!
Thieves ·break into houses [Lcome in],
and ·robbers [gangs] ·are in the streets [raid/pillage outside].
2·It never enters their minds [LThey never say in their hearts]
that I remember all their evil deeds.
The bad things they do ·are all around [engulf; surround] them;
they are ·right in front of me [always before my face].

Israel's Evil Kings

3"They make the king happy with their wickedness;
their ·rulers [princes] are glad with their lies.
4But all of them are ·traitors [Ladulterers].
They are like an oven heated by a baker.

·While he mixes the dough [LFrom the kneading of the dough until it is leavened],
he does not need to stir up the fire.
5The kings get so drunk they get sick ·every day [*or* on the festival day; Lon the day].
The ·rulers [princes] become ·crazy [inflamed] with wine;
they ·make agreements [conspire; Lstretch out their hands] with ·those who do not know the true God [mockers; scoffers].
6Their hearts burn like an oven;
as they plot [Can assassination] against him.
All night long their anger ·is low [smolders],
but when morning comes, it becomes a roaring fire.
7All ·these people [Lof them] are as hot as an oven;
they ·burn up [consume; devour] their rulers.
All their kings fall,
and no one calls on me.

Israel and the Other Nations

8"·Israel [LEphraim; 4:17] mixes with other nations;
he is like a ·pancake [cake; flat loaf] ·cooked only on one side [*or* burned on one side; Lnot turned].
9·Foreign nations [Strangers; Foreigners] have ·eaten up [devoured; sapped] his strength,
but he doesn't know it.
·Israel is weak and feeble, like an old man [LGrey hair is scattered on him],
but he doesn't know it.
10Israel's ·pride [arrogance] ·will cause their defeat [*or* testifies against him; Lanswers in his face];
they will not ·turn back [return] to the LORD their God
or ·look to him for help [Lseek him] in all this.
11Israel has become like a ·pigeon [dove]—
·easy to fool [silly] and ·stupid [senseless].
First they call to Egypt for help.
Then they ·run [turn; go] to Assyria.
12When they go, I will ·catch them in a net [throw my net over them],
I will bring them down like birds from the sky;
I will ·punish [discipline] them ·countless times for their evil [*or* when I hear them flocking together; *or* according to the report given to the congregation].
13·How terrible for [LWoe to] them because they ·left [fled/strayed from] me!
They will be destroyed, because they ·turned [rebelled] against me.
I want to ·save [redeem] them,
but they have spoken lies against me.
14They do not ·call [cry out] to me from their hearts.
They just lie on their beds and ·cry [wail].
They ·come together [assemble themselves; *or* gash/slash themselves; Ca ritual practiced by pagan Canaanite priests (Deut. 14:1; 1 Kin. 18:28; Jer. 16:6)] to ask for grain and new wine,
but they really ·turn away from [rebel against] me.
15Though I trained them and ·gave them strength [Lstrengthened their arms],

they have ·made evil plans [plotted evil] against me.
16They ·did not turn to [*or* turn, but not to] the Most High God.
They are like a ·loose bow that can't shoot [faulty bow].
Because ·their leaders brag about their strength [of their indignant/insolent tongue],
they will ·be killed with swords [fall by the sword],
and the people in Egypt
will ·laugh at [ridicule; deride] them.

Israel Has Trusted Wrong Things

8 "Put the trumpet to your lips [Cto warn of danger or call to battle]!
The enemy ·swoops down on [*or* circles over] the LORD's ·people [*or* temple; Lhouse] like an eagle.
The Israelites have broken my ·agreement [covenant; treaty]
and have ·turned [rebelled] against my ·teachings [law; LTorah].
2Israel cries out to me,
'Our God, we in Israel ·know [acknowledge] you!'
3But Israel has rejected what is good,
so the enemy will ·chase [pursue] them.
4They ·chose their own [appointed; enthroned] kings
·without asking my permission [Lbut not from me].
They chose their own ·leaders [princes],
people I did not ·know [acknowledge; approve].
They made their silver and gold into idols,
and for all this they will be destroyed.
5I ·hate [have rejected] ·the calf-shaped idol of Israel [Lyour calf, Samaria; Ex. 32; 1 Kin. 12:26–30]!
·I am very angry with the people [LMy anger burns against them].
How long will they remain ·unclean [impure; guilty]?
6The idol is something a craftsman made;
it is not God.
·Israel's calf-shaped idol [LThe calf of Samaria; v. 5]
will surely be smashed to pieces.

7"·Israel's foolish plans are like planting the wind [LThey sow the wind],
·but they will harvest a storm [Land reap the whirlwind].
Like a stalk with no head of grain,
it produces ·nothing [Lno flour].
Even if it produced something,
·other nations [foreigners] would ·eat [devour] it.
8Israel is ·eaten [swallowed] up;
the people are ·mixed among [Lamong] the other nations
and have become ·useless to me [a useless pot/utensil/vessel].
9Israel is like a wild donkey ·all by itself [wandering alone].
They have ·run [Lgone up] to Assyria;
·They have hired other nations to protect them [LEphraim has hired lovers; *or* Ephraim has sold herself to lovers].
10Although Israel ·is mixed [*or* hired; *or* hired herself out] among the nations,
I will gather them together.
They will ·become weaker and weaker [begin to waste away]
·as they suffer under [from the burden/oppression of] the ·great king of Assyria [Lking of princes].

11"Although ·Israel [LEphraim; 4:17] built more altars to remove sin,
they have become altars for sinning.
12I have written many ·teachings [laws; instructions] for them,
but they think the teachings are ·strange and foreign [alien; irrelevant].
13The Israelites offer sacrifices to me as gifts
and eat the meat,
but the LORD ·is not pleased with [does not accept] them.
He remembers ·the evil they have done [their wickedness/iniquity],
and he will punish them for their sins.
They will ·be slaves again as they were in [Lreturn to] Egypt.
14Israel has forgotten its Maker and has built palaces;
Judah has built many ·strong, walled [fortified] cities.
But I will send fire on their cities
and ·destroy [Lit will devour/consume] their ·strong buildings
[strongholds; citadels]."

Israel's Punishment

9 Israel, do not rejoice;
don't shout for joy as the other nations do.
You have been ·like a prostitute against [unfaithful to] your God.
You love the pay of prostitutes on every threshing floor.
2But the threshing floor and the winepress will not feed the people,
and ·there won't be enough new wine [*or* the new wine will deceive
them].
3The people will not stay in the LORD's land.
·Israel [LEphraim] will return ·to being captives as they were in [Lto]
Egypt,
and in Assyria they will eat ·food that they are not allowed to eat
[Lunclean food; Cfood forbidden by the law; Lev. 11].
4The Israelites will not ·give [pour out] offerings of wine to the LORD;
and their sacrifices will not please him.
Their sacrifices will be like ·food that is eaten at a funeral [mourners
bread; Deut. 26:14];
it is unclean, and everyone who eats it becomes unclean [Cbecause
touched by someone who has touched a dead body; Num. 19:22].
Their food will only satisfy their hunger;
·they cannot sacrifice it in [Lit will not come into] the Temple.
5What will you do then on the day of ·feasts [your appointed festivals]
and on the day of the LORD's festival?
6 [LLook; TBehold] Even if the people ·are not destroyed [escape
destruction],
Egypt will ·capture [*or* receive; Lgather] them;
Memphis [Ca city in Egypt famous for its tombs] will bury them.
·Weeds [Briers; Nettles] will grow over their silver treasures,
and thorns will ·drive them out of [possess; inherit] their tents.
7The time of punishment has come,
the ·time to pay for sins [Ldays of recompense/vengeance].
Let Israel know this:
·You think the [LThe] prophet is a fool,
and ·you say the [Lthe] ·spiritual person [Spirit-inspired person] is
crazy.
·You [*or* This is because you] have sinned very much,
and your hatred is great.

8·Is Israel a watchman?
Are God's people prophets? [*or* The prophet is a watchman over Ephraim on God's behalf]
·Everywhere Israel goes, traps are set for him [*or* ...yet traps/snares await him on all his paths].
·He is an enemy [*or* ...and hatred even] in God's house.
9·The people of Israel [LThey] have gone deep into ·sin [depravity; corruption]
as ·the people of Gibeah did [Lin the days of Gibeah; Judg. 19–20].
The Lord will remember ·the evil things they have done [their wickedness/iniquity],
and he will punish their sins.

10"When I found Israel,
it was like finding grapes in the ·desert [wilderness].
Your ·ancestors [fathers; forefathers] were like
finding the first figs on the fig tree.
But when they came to Baal Peor,
they ·began worshiping an idol [Lconsecrated/dedicated themselves to a shameful thing; Num. 25:3–18],
and they became as ·hateful [detestable] as the thing they ·worshiped [Lloved].
11·Israel's [LEphraim's; 4:17] glory will fly away like a bird;
there will be no more pregnancy, no more births, no more conception.
12But even if ·the Israelites [Lthey] bring up children,
I will take them all away.
·How terrible it will be for [LWoe to] them
when I ·go away [turn away; depart] from them!
13I have seen Israel, like ·Tyre [*or* a young palm],
·given [Lplanted in] a pleasant place.
But ·the people of Israel [LEphraim; 4:17] will soon bring out
their children to ·be killed [slaughter; *or* the slayer]."
14Lord, ·give them what they should have [Lgive them].
What will you give them?
·Make their women unable to have children [LGive them wombs that miscarry];
give them ·dried-up breasts that cannot feed their babies [Ldry breasts].

15"The Israelites were very wicked in Gilgal [Ca center of false worship in Israel; 4:15],
so I have hated them there.
Because of the sinful things they have done,
I will ·force them to leave [drive them out of] my land.
I will no longer love them;
their ·leaders [princes] ·have turned against me [are rebels/rebellious].
16·Israel [LEphraim] is ·beaten down [struck down; *or* blighted];
its root is ·dying [withered; dried up], and it ·has [bears] no fruit.
If they have more children,
I will kill the ·children they love [Lcherished offspring of their womb]."

[17]My God will reject them,
because they have not obeyed him;
they will ·wander [be wanderers/fugitives] among the nations.

Israel Will Pay for Sin

10 Israel is like a ·large [spreading; lush; luxuriant] vine
that produced plenty of fruit.
As ·the people became richer [[L]his fruit increased],
they built more altars [[C]for idols].
As their land ·became better [prospered; improved],
they ·put up better [*or* adorned their] ·stone pillars to honor gods [sacred pillars].
[2]Their heart was ·false [*or* divided; fickle],
and now they must ·pay for [bear] their guilt.
The LORD will break down their altars;
he will destroy their holy stone pillars.

[3]Then they will say, "We have no king,
because we didn't ·honor [revere; fear] the LORD [Prov. 1:7].
As for the king,
·he couldn't do anything [[L]what could he do…?] for us."
[4]With words that mean nothing they make ·false [empty] ·promises [oaths]
and ·agreements [covenants; treaties] which they don't keep.
So ·people sue each other in court [[L]lawsuits/judgments spring up];
they are like poisonous weeds growing in [[L]the rows/furrows of] a plowed field.
[5]The people from ·Israel [[L]Samaria; [C]the capital of the northern kingdom of Israel] are worried about
the ·calf-shaped idol [calf; heifer; 1 Kin. 12:28] at Beth Aven [4:15].
The people will ·cry about [mourn over] it,
and the ·priests [idol-priests] will ·cry about [lament/wail over] it.
They used to ·shout for joy [rejoice] about its glory,
but ·it has been taken from them into exile [*or* its glory has departed].
[6]It will be carried off to Assyria
as a gift to ·the great king [*or* King Jareb; [C]this may be a title or a personal name].
·Israel [[L]Ephraim; 4:17] will be disgraced,
and ·the people [[L]Israel] will be ashamed for ·not obeying [*or* its counsel; *or* its wooden idol].
[7]·Israel [[L]Samaria; v. 5] will be destroyed;
its king will be like a ·chip of wood [twig] floating on the water.
[8]The ·places of false worship [[L]high places of wickedness; *or* high places of Aven; v. 5; 4:15] will be destroyed,
the places where Israel sins.
Thorns and ·weeds [thistles] will grow up
and cover their altars.
Then they will say to the mountains, "Cover us!"
and to the hills, "Fall on us! [Luke 23:30; Rev. 6:16]"

[9]"Israel, you have sinned since the ·time [[L]days] of Gibeah [9:9; Judg. 19–21],
and ·the people there have continued sinning [[L]there they have remained; *or* there they took their stand].

·But war will surely overwhelm [LDid not war overtake...?] **them in**
Gibeah,
because of the evil they have done there.
10**When I ·am ready** [desire; please],
I will come to ·punish [discipline] **them.**
Nations will come together against them,
and they will be ·punished [bound in chains] **for their ·double** [Ltwo]
sins [Ccould mean "twice the punishment" (Is. 40:2) or the two
sins of rejecting God and his anointed Davidic king].
11**·Israel** [LEphraim; 4:17] **is like a well-trained ·young cow** [heifer]
that likes to thresh grain.
I will put a ·yoke [*or* a fine yoke] **on her ·neck** [*or* fair neck]
and ·make her work hard in the field [drive Ephraim hard].
Israel will plow,
and Judah will break up the ground.
12**I said, '·Plant goodness** [Sow righteousness],
·harvest the fruit of loyalty [reap mercy/lovingkindness],
·plow the new ground of knowledge [Lbreak up the unplowed/fallow
ground].
·Look for [*or* For it is time to seek] **the LORD until he comes**
and ·pours goodness on you like water [Lrains/showers righteousness/
justice on you].'
13**But you have plowed ·evil** [wickedness; iniquity]
and ·harvested [reaped] **·trouble** [evil; injustice];
you have eaten the fruit of ·your lies [deception; treachery].
Because you have trusted in your own ·power [*or* chariots]
and your many ·soldiers [warriors],
14**·your people will hear** [Lagainst your people will rise] **the ·noise** [roar;
tumult] **of battle,**
and all your ·strong, walled cities [fortresses] **will be destroyed.**
It will be like the time King Shalman
destroyed Beth Arbel in battle [2 Kin. 17:3],
when mothers and their children were ·bashed to death [dashed to
pieces].
15**The same will happen to you, ·people of Bethel** [LBethel],
because ·you did so much evil [your wickedness is great].
·When the sun comes up [*or* When judgment day dawns; *or* As swiftly
as the dawn; LAt dawn],
the king of Israel will ·die [Lbe completely cut off].

God's Love for Israel

11 **"When Israel was a ·child** [youth], **I loved him,**
and I called my son out of Egypt [Cthe Exodus; Ex. 4:22; Matt. 2:15].
2**But when I called ·the people of Israel** [Lthem],
they went away from me.
They offered sacrifices to the Baals
and burned incense to ·the idols [images].
3**It was I who taught ·Israel** [LEphraim; 4:17] **to walk,**
and I took them by the arms,
but they did not ·understand [*or* acknowledge]
that I had healed them.
4**I led them with cords of ·human kindness** [humanity; *or* leather],
with ropes of love.

I lifted ·the yoke from their neck [*or* them like a little child to my cheek]
and bent down and fed them.

5"·The Israelites will become captives again, as they were in [*or* Will they not return to...? *or* They will not return to] Egypt,
and ·Assyria will [*or* will not Assyria...?] become their king,
because they refuse to turn back to God.
6·War will sweep through [LA sword will slash/flash in] their cities
and will destroy ·them [their gates; *or* their priests]
and ·kill [devour] them because of their ·wicked plans [counsels].
7My people ·have made up their minds [are determined]
to ·turn away [desert; backslide] from me.
·The prophets call them to turn to me [*or* They call me Most High; *or* They call to Baal],
but ·none of them honors me at all [*or* I will not exalt them; *or* he will never exalt them].
8"·Israel [LEphraim; 4:17], how can I give you up?
How can I ·give you away [hand you over], Israel?
·I don't want to [LHow can I...?] make you like Admah
or treat you like Zeboiim [Ctwo cities destroyed together with Sodom and Gomorrah; Gen. 19:24–25; Deut. 4:25–31].
My heart ·beats for you [*or* has changed within me; *or* is torn within me],
and my ·love for you stirs up my pity [compassion is aroused/stirred up/kindled].
9I won't ·punish you in my [unleash my burning] anger,
and I won't destroy ·Israel [LEphraim; 4:17] again.
I am God and not a human;
I am the Holy One, and I am among you.
I will not come against ·you in anger [you with terror; *or* your cities].
10They will ·go after [follow] the LORD,
and he will roar like a lion.
When he roars,
his children will ·hurry [Lcome trembling] to him from the west [CGod's people would return not only from Babylon and Assyria in the east but from every direction].
11They will come ·swiftly [*or* trembling]
like birds from Egypt
and like doves from Assyria.
I will settle them again in their homes,"
says the LORD.

The Lord Is Against Israel

12·Israel [LEphraim; 4:17] has surrounded me with lies;
the ·people have made [Lhouse of Israel with] evil plans.
·And [*or* But] Judah ·turns against [*or* roams away from; *or* still walks with] God,
·the faithful [*or* and is faithful to the] Holy One.

12 ·What Israel does is as useless as chasing [LEphraim feeds on] the wind;
he chases the east wind all day [Eccl. 1:14, 17; 2:11, 17, 26].
They ·tell more and more lies
and do more and more violence [multiply lies and violence].

They make ·agreements [a covenant/treaty] **with Assyria,**
and they send ·a gift of olive oil [Loil] **to Egypt** [Cas tribute or to gain support].
2**The** Lord **also has ·some things** [a case/lawsuit; *or* a dispute; 4:1] **against Judah.**
He will punish ·Israel [LJacob] **for what they have done;**
he will ·give [repay] **them ·what they deserve** [according to their deeds].
3**·Their ancestor Jacob** [LHe] **·held on to his brother's heel** [*or* struggled with/supplanted his brother]
·while the two of them were being born [Lin the womb; Gen. 25:19–26].
·When he grew to be a man [LIn his strength/manhood],
he ·wrestled [struggled] **with God.**
4**When Jacob ·wrestled** [struggled] **with the angel and ·won** [prevailed],
he ·cried [wept] **and ·asked for his blessing** [pleaded for/sought his favor; Gen. 32:22–32].
Later, ·God met with him [he found him] **at Bethel**
and spoke with him there [Gen. 35:1].
5**It was the** Lord **God ·All-Powerful** [Almighty; of Heaven's Armies; Tof hosts];
the Lord **is his ·great** [memorial; memorable] **name.**
6**You must return to your God;**
·love him, do what is just [*or* act with love and justice],
and always ·trust in him as [wait for] **your God.**

7**The merchants use dishonest scales;**
they like to ·cheat people [oppress].
8**·Israel** [LEphraim; 4:17] **said, "I am rich! I ·am someone with power** [have made my fortune]**!"**
·All their money will do them no good
because of the sins they have done [*or* "With all the wealth I've gained, no one can accuse me of sin"; Ceither self-vindication (continuing the quotation), or the prophet's pronouncement of guilt].

9**"But I am the** Lord **your God,**
·who brought you [*or* ever since you came] **out of Egypt.**
I will make you live in tents again
as you used to do on ·worship days [the appointed festivals; Cthe feast of tabernacles, which commemorated the wilderness wanderings].
10**I spoke to the prophets**
and gave them many visions;
through them, I ·taught my lessons [spoke in parables; *or* spoke oracles of doom] **to you."**

11**·The people of Gilead are evil** [*or* Is Gilead wicked? *or* In Gilead there was idolatry],
they ·are worth nothing [are worthless; *or* will come to nothing].
·People [*or* Do they…?] **sacrifice bulls at Gilgal** [4:15].
But their altars will become like piles of stone
in a plowed field.
12**·Your ancestor Jacob** [LJacob] **fled to ·northwest Mesopotamia** [LAram; Gen. 28:5]
where he ·worked [served; Chis uncle Laban] **to get a wife** [CRachel (and Leah); Gen. 29:20, 28];
he tended sheep to pay for her.

[13]Later the LORD used a prophet [[C]Moses; Deut. 18:15]
to bring ·Jacob's descendants [[L]Israel] out of Egypt;
he used a prophet
to ·take care of [tend; preserve; guard] the Israelites.
[14]But ·the Israelites [[L]Ephraim; 4:17] ·made the Lord angry [bitterly provoked the Lord];
So the Lord ·will make them pay for the blood they have shed [[L]leave on him the guilt of his bloodshed]
and for the ·disgraceful things they have done [*or* contempt they have shown].

The Final Word Against Israel

13 ·People used to fear the tribe of Ephraim [[L]When Ephraim spoke, there was trembling];
they were ·important people [[L]exalted] in Israel.
But they sinned by worshiping Baal,
·so they must die [[L]and died].
[2]But they still keep on sinning more and more.
They make ·idols of their silver [metal images],
idols that are ·cleverly [skillfully] made,
the work of a craftsman.
·Yet the people of Israel say to each other [*or* It is said of them],
"·Kiss those calf idols and sacrifice to them [*or* Those who sacrifice to the calf idol are calf kissers!; *or* They offer human sacrifices and kiss calf-idols]."
[3]So those people will be like the morning mist;
they will disappear like the morning dew.
They will be like chaff ·blown [that swirls away] from the threshing floor,
like smoke going out a window.

[4]"I, the LORD, have been your God
since you were in the land of Egypt.
You ·should have known no [must not acknowledge any] other God except me [Ex. 20:3].
·I am the only one who saves [[L]There is no savior but me].
[5]I ·cared for them [[L]knew you] in the ·desert [wilderness]
·where it was hot and dry [in the land of drought].
[6]I gave them ·food [pasture], and they became full and satisfied.
But then they became too proud and forgot me.
[7]That is why I will be like a lion to them,
like a leopard ·waiting [lurking] by the ·road [path].
[8]I will ·attack [meet them] like a bear robbed of her cubs,
ripping their ·bodies [chest] open.
I will devour them like a lion
and tear them apart like a wild animal.

[9]"Israel, I will destroy you.
·Who will be your helper then [*or* ...because you are against me, your helper]?
[10]·What good [[L]Where] is your king?
Can he save you in any of your towns?
·What good are [[L]Where are] your leaders
about whom you said, 'Give us a king and leaders'?

11So I gave you a king, but only in anger,
and I took him away in my ·great anger [wrath].
12The ·sins [guilt; iniquity] of Israel are ·on record [bound up in a scroll],
stored away, waiting for punishment.
13The pain of birth will come for him,
but he is like a ·foolish [senseless; unwise] baby
who won't come out of its mother's womb.
14Will I save them from ·the place of the dead [the power of the grave; [L]the hand of Sheol]?
Will I ·rescue [redeem] them from death?
·Where are [*or* Bring on…!] your plagues, death?
·Where is [*or* Bring on…!] your ·pain [destruction], ·place of death [O grave]?
·I will show them no mercy [[L]Pity/compassion is hidden from my eyes].
15·Israel is doing well among the nations [[L]He is fruitful among his brothers],
but the LORD will send a wind from the east,
coming from the ·desert [wilderness],
that will dry up his springs and wells of water.
He will ·destroy [plunder] from their treasure houses ·everything of value [every precious/desirable thing].
16·The nation of Israel [[L]Samaria; 10:5] will ·be ruined [*or* bear its guilt],
because it ·fought [rebelled] against God.
·The people of Israel will die in war [[L]They will fall by the sword];
their ·children [infants; little ones] will be ·torn to [dashed in] pieces,
and their pregnant women will be ripped open."

Israel Returns to God

14 Israel, return to the LORD your God,
because your sins have made you ·fall [stumble].
2·Come back [Return] to the LORD
and ·say these words to him [[L]take words with you]:
"Take away all our sin
and ·kindly receive us [accept our prayers],
·and we will keep the promises we made to you [[L]so that we may offer the sacrifices of our lips; *or* so that we may offer our lips as sacrificial bulls].
3Assyria cannot save us,
nor will we ·trust in our [mount and ride] horses.
We will not say again, 'Our gods,'
to the things our hands have made.
You show ·mercy [compassion] to ·orphans [the fatherless]."

4The LORD says,
"I will forgive ·them for leaving me [their apostasy/waywardness]
and will love them freely,
because ·I am not angry with them anymore [[L]my anger has turned away from them].
5I will be like the dew to Israel,
and they will blossom like a lily.

Like the cedar trees in Lebanon,
·their roots will be firm [they will take root].
6 **·They will be like spreading branches** [[L]His shoots will spread out],
like the beautiful olive trees
and the sweet-smelling cedars in Lebanon.
7 **·The people of Israel will again live under my protection** [*or* People will again live under Israel's protection/shade].
They will ·grow [flourish] **like the grain,**
they will bloom like a vine,
and they will be as famous as the wine of Lebanon.
8 **·Israel** [[L]Ephraim; 4:17], **have nothing to do with idols.**
I, the LORD, am the one who answers your prayers and ·watches over [cares for] **you.**
I am like a ·green [flourishing; evergreen] **·pine tree** [*or* juniper; *or* cypress];
your ·blessings [[L]fruit] **come from me."**

9 **·A wise person will know these things** [[L]Who is wise? Let him understand these things],
·and an understanding person will take them to heart [[L]Who is discerning? Let him understand them].
The LORD's ways are right.
·Good people [The righteous] **·live by following** [[L]walk in] **them,**
but ·those who turn against God [the rebellious/transgressors] **·die because of them** [[L]stumble in them].

JOEL

Locusts Destroy the Crops

1 ·The LORD spoke his word [[L]The word/message of the LORD that was (given)] to Joel son of Pethuel:

[2]Elders, listen to this message.
·Listen to [Hear] me, all you who live in the land.
·Nothing like this has [[L]Has anything like this…?] ever happened
·during your lifetime [[L]in your days]
or during your ·ancestors' [fathers'] ·lifetimes [[L]days].
[3]Tell your children about these things,
let your children tell their children,
and let ·your grandchildren [[L]their children] tell ·their children [the next generation].
[4]What the ·cutting [chewing; *or* swarming] locusts have left,
the ·swarming [*or* great] locusts have eaten;
what the ·swarming [*or* great] locusts have left,
the ·hopping [*or* crawling; *or* young] locusts have eaten,
and what the ·hopping [*or* crawling; *or* young] locusts have left,
the ·destroying [consuming] locusts have eaten [[C]these Hebrew terms could mean different species, different stages of development, or different destructive actions; they symbolize God's judgment against Israel through foreign invaders].

[5]Drunks, wake up and ·cry [weep]!
All you ·people who drink wine [wine-drinkers], ·cry [wail]!
Cry because your ·wine [sweet/new wine]
has been ·taken away [snatched; [L]cut off] from your mouths.
[6]A ·powerful [mighty] nation has ·come into [invaded; come up against] my land
·with too many soldiers to count [[L]without number].
It has teeth like a lion,
·jaws [fangs] like a ·female lion [lioness].
[7]It has made my grapevine a waste
and made my fig tree ·a stump [*or* splintered].
It has ·stripped all [[L]stripped and thrown away] the bark off my trees
and left the branches white.

[8]·Cry [Lament; Wail] as a young woman ·cries [[L]clothed in sackcloth]
·when the man she was going to marry has died [[L]for the husband/*or* betrothed of her youth].
[9]·There will be no more grain or drink offerings
to offer in [[L]The grain/gift/tribute (Lev. 2:1) and drink offerings are cut off from] the ·Temple [[L]house] of the LORD.

Because of this, the priests,
the servants of the LORD, are ·sad [in mourning].
10 The fields are ·ruined [destroyed];
the ground ·is dried up [*or* mourns].
·The [L...because the] grain is destroyed,
the new wine is dried up,
and the olive oil ·runs out [fails].
11 Be ·sad [in despair; *or* ashamed; embarrassed], farmers.
·Cry loudly [Wail], you who grow grapes.
Cry for the wheat and the barley.
Cry because the harvest of the field is ·lost [ruined; destroyed].
12 The vines have ·become dry [dried up],
and the fig trees ·are dried up [have withered/languish].
The pomegranate trees, the date palm trees, the apple trees—
all the trees in the field ·have died [are dried up].
And the ·happiness [joy; gladness] of the ·people [Lsons/children of man/humanity] has died, too.
13 Priests, put on your ·rough cloth [sackcloth] and ·cry to show your sadness [mourn; lament].
·Servants [Ministers] of the altar, ·cry out loud [wail].
Servants of my God,
·keep your rough cloth on all night to show your sadness [spend the night in sackcloth].
Cry because there will be no more grain [Lgift; tribute; Lev. 2:1] or drink offerings
to offer in the ·Temple [Lhouse] of your God.
14 ·Call for [Declare; Appoint; Consecrate] a ·day when everyone fasts [fast]!
·Tell everyone to stop work [LCall a sacred assembly]!
·Bring [Assemble] the elders
and everyone who lives in the land
to the ·Temple [Lhouse] of the LORD your God,
and cry out to the LORD.
15 ·What a terrible day it will be [LAh, for the day]!
The ·LORD's day of judging [Lday of the LORD] is near [2:1, 11, 31; Is. 13:6, 9; Jer. 46:10],
when ·punishment [destruction] will come
like a destroying attack from the Almighty [C"destroying" (*shod*) and "Almighty" (*shaddai*) are related words in Hebrew].

16 Our food is ·taken away [Lcut off]
·while we watch [Lin front of our eyes].
Joy and ·happiness [gladness] are gone
from the ·Temple [Lhouse] of our God.
17 ·Though we planted fig seeds,
they lie dry and dead in the dirt [LThe seed shrivels under the clods/ *or* shovels].
The ·barns [storehouses] are ·empty and falling down [desolate].
The ·storerooms for grain [granaries] have been broken down,
because the grain has dried up.
18 The animals are groaning!
The herds of cattle ·wander around confused [mill about; are restless/ distraught],

because they have no ·grass to eat [pasture];
even the flocks of sheep suffer.
19LORD, I am calling to you for help,
because fire has ·burned up [devoured] the ·open [*or* wilderness] pastures,
and flames have burned all the trees in the field.
20Wild animals ·also [even] ·need your help [cry out to you; long/pant for you].
The ·streams of water [water brooks; riverbeds] have dried up,
and fire has ·burned up [devoured] the ·open [*or* wilderness] pastures.

The Coming Day of Judgment

2 Blow the trumpet in ·Jerusalem [LZion; Cthe location of the Temple];
·shout a warning [sound the alarm; *or* raise the battle cry] on my holy mountain.
Let all the people who live in the land shake with fear,
because the ·LORD's day of judging [Lday of the LORD; 1:15] is coming;
it is near.
2It will be a ·dark, gloomy day [day/time of darkness and gloom],
cloudy and black.
Like ·the light at sunrise [spreading dawn; *or* spreading darkness],
a great and powerful army will spread over the mountains.
There has never been anything like it before,
and there will never be anything like it ·again [Lfor generations to come].

3In front of them a fire ·destroys [devours];
in back of them a flame burns.
The land in front of them is like the garden of Eden [Gen. 2:8–14];
the land behind them is like an ·empty desert [desolate wilderness].
Nothing will escape from them.
4·They look [Their appearance is] like horses,
and they ·run [charge] like ·war horses [*or* cavalry].
5It is like the noise of chariots
·rumbling [*or* leaping] over the tops of the mountains,
like the noise of a roaring fire
·burning dry stalks [devouring stubble].
They are like a ·powerful army [mighty nation] lined up for battle.
6·When they see them [Before them], ·nations [people] shake with fear,
and everyone's face becomes pale.

7They charge like soldiers;
they ·climb over [scale] the wall like warriors.
They all march ·straight ahead [in formation]
and do not ·move off their path [swerve from their course; break ranks].
8They do not ·run into [jostle; push] each other,
because each walks ·in line [straight ahead; in his column].
They ·break through all efforts to stop them [burst through defences; *or* fall upon the sword; Lfall upon weapons]
and ·keep coming [do not halt/break ranks].
9They ·run [rush; swarm] into the city.
They run at the wall
and climb into the houses,
entering through windows like thieves.

[10]Before them the earth shakes
and sky trembles.
The sun and the moon become dark,
and the stars ·stop shining [[L]withhold their brightness; 3:15].
[11]The LORD ·shouts out orders [cries out; thunders]
·to [*or* at the head of] his army.
His ·army [encampment] is very large!
Those who ·obey him [execute his word] are very strong!
The ·LORD's day of judging [[L]day of the LORD; 1:15]
is an ·overwhelming [awesome; great] and terrible day.
·No one can stand up against it! [[L]Who can endure it?]

Change Your Hearts

[12]The LORD says, "Even now, come back to me with all your heart.
Fast, ·cry [weep], and ·be sad [mourn]."

[13]·Tearing your clothes is not enough to show you are sad;
let your heart be broken [[L]Tear/Rend your hearts and not your garments; [C]true repentance, not just a show of grief].
Come back to the LORD your God,
because he is ·kind [gracious; merciful] and ·shows mercy [compassionate].
·He doesn't become angry quickly [...slow to anger],
and he has great ·love [loyalty; mercy; lovingkindness].
He ·can change his mind about [relents from] doing harm.
[14]Who knows? Maybe he will ·turn back to you [grant a reprieve; [L]turn and relent]
and leave behind a blessing for you.
·Grain [[L]Gift; Tribute; Lev. 2:1] and drink offerings ·belong to [*or* for] the LORD your God.

[15]Blow the trumpet in ·Jerusalem [[L]Zion; 2:1];
·call for [declare; appoint; consecrate] a ·day when everyone fasts [fast; 1:14].
·Tell everyone to stop work [[L]Call a sacred assembly]!
[16]·Bring the people together [Assemble/Gather the people]
and ·make the meeting holy for the LORD [consecrate/sanctify the congregation/assembly].
Bring together the elders,
as well as the children,
and even babies that still feed at their mothers' breasts.
·The bridegroom should [[L]Let the bridegroom] come from his room [[C]indicating urgency; newly married men were exempt from military service; Deut. 20:7; 24:5],
the bride from her ·bedroom [chamber].
[17]·The [[L]Let the] priests, ·the LORD's servants [who minister before the LORD], should ·cry [weep]
between the altar and the ·entrance to the Temple [portico; vestibule].
·They should [[L]Let them] say, "LORD, ·have mercy on [spare] your people.
Don't let ·them [[L]your inheritance/possession] be ·put to shame [mocked; a reproach];
don't let other nations make ·fun of them [them a byword].

·Don't let [LWhy should the] **people in other nations ask,**
'Where is their God?' "

The Lord Restores the Land

18Then the LORD became ·concerned about [jealous/zealous for] his land
and ·felt sorry [had compassion] for his people.
19He ·said to [answered] them:
"[LLook; TBehold] I will send you grain, new wine, and olive oil,
so that you will ·have plenty [be satisfied].
No more will I ·shame you [make you a reproach/object of scorn]
among the nations.
20I will ·force the army from the north to leave your land [Ldrive the
northern one far from you]
and go into a dry, ·empty [desolate] land.
·Their soldiers [LThose] in front will be forced into the ·Dead
[LEastern] Sea,
and those in the rear into the ·Mediterranean [LWestern] Sea.
·Their bodies will rot and stink [His stench and foul smell will rise].
The LORD has surely done ·a wonderful thing [great things]!"

21Land, don't be afraid;
be ·happy [glad] and ·full of joy [rejoice],
because the LORD has done ·a wonderful thing [great things].
22·Wild animals [LBeasts of the field], don't be afraid,
because the ·open [wilderness] pastures ·have grown grass [Lare
sprouting green].
The trees ·have given [bear] fruit;
the fig trees and the grapevines ·have grown much fruit [provide riches].
23So be happy, ·people of Jerusalem [Lsons/children of Zion; 2:1];
·be joyful [rejoice] in the LORD your God.
Because he ·does what is right,
he has brought you rain [*or* has vindicated you by giving you rain];
he has sent the ·fall [Learly] rain
and the ·spring [Llate] rain for you, as before.
24And the threshing floors will be full of grain;
the ·barrels [vats] will overflow with new wine and olive oil.

The Lord Speaks

25"Though I sent my great army against you—
those ·swarming [*or* great] locusts and ·hopping [*or* crawling; *or*
young] locusts,
the ·destroying [consuming] locusts and the ·cutting [chewing; *or*
swarming] locusts that ate your crops [see 1:4]—
I will ·pay you back
for [*or* restore to you] those ·years of trouble [Lyears].
26Then you will have plenty to eat
and be ·full [satisfied].
You will praise the name of the LORD your God,
who has ·done miracles [*or* acted wondrously/marvelously] for you.
My people will never again be shamed.
27Then you will know that I am ·among [in the midst of] the people of
Israel,
that I am the LORD your God,
and there is no ·other God [Lother].
My people will never be shamed again.

28"After this,
I will pour out my Spirit on all ·kinds of people [humanity; flesh; Acts 2:17–21; Is. 32:15; Ezek. 39:29; Zech. 12:10].
Your sons and daughters will prophesy,
your old men will dream dreams,
and your young men will see visions.
29·At that time [LIn those days] I will pour out my Spirit
·also [even] on male ·slaves [servants] and female ·slaves [servants].
30I will show ·miracles [wonders; portents]
in the ·sky [heavens] and on the earth:
blood, fire, and ·thick [columns/billows of] smoke.
31The sun will ·become dark [turn to darkness],
the moon ·red as blood [Lto blood; Rev. 6:12],
before the ·overwhelming [great] and ·terrible [awesome] day of the Lord comes.
32·Then [LAnd it will happen that] ·anyone [all] who calls on the [Lname of the] Lord
will be ·saved [rescued],
because on Mount Zion and in Jerusalem
there will be people who will ·be saved [escape; be delivered],
just as the Lord has said.
·Those left alive after the day of punishment [The remnant/survivors]
are the people whom the Lord called.

Punishment for Judah's Enemies

3 "[LFor look/Tbehold] In those days and at that time,
when I will ·make things better for [restore the fortunes of; *or* return the exiles/captives of] Judah and Jerusalem,
2I will gather all the nations together
and bring them down into the Valley ·Where the Lord Judges [Lof Jehoshaphat; CJehoshaphat means "the Lord judges"].
There I will ·judge [enter into judgment against] them,
because those nations scattered my ·own people [Lpeople, my heritage] Israel
·and forced them to live in other [Lamong the] nations.
They divided up my land
3and ·threw [Tcast] lots for my people.
They traded boys for prostitutes,
and they sold girls to buy wine to ·drink [get drunk].
4"Tyre and Sidon and all of you regions of Philistia! What did you have
against me? Were you ·punishing me [paying me back; taking vengeance]
for something I did, ·or were you doing something to hurt me? [*or* If you
were trying to pay me back,] I will very quickly ·do to you [Lreturn on
your heads] what you have done to me. 5You took my silver and gold, and
you put my ·precious [costly; rich; prized] treasures in your ·temples [*or*
palaces]. 6You sold the ·people [sons; descendants] of Judah and Jerusalem
to the [Lsons/descendants of the] Greeks so that you could ·send [remove]
them far from their ·land [Lborder].
7"[LLook; TBehold] You sent my people to that faraway place, but I will
·get them [rouse them; stir them up] and bring them back, and I will ·do
to you [Lreturn on your heads] what you have done to them. 8I will sell
your sons and daughters to the people of Judah, and they will sell them to
the Sabean people [CArab merchants from the southeast; Job 1:15] far
away." The Lord said this.

God Judges the Nations

9·Announce [Proclaim] this among the nations:
Prepare for war!
·Wake up [Rouse; Call out] the ·soldiers [warriors; mighty men]!
Let all the men of war come near and attack.
10·Make swords from your plows [TBeat your plowshares into swords],
and make spears from your ·hooks for trimming trees [pruning hooks; Cthe opposite of Is. 2:4].
Let even the weak person say,
"I am ·a soldier [a warrior; *or* strong]."
11All of you nations, hurry,
and ·come together [assemble] in that place.
LORD, ·send your soldiers
to gather the nations [Lbring down your warriors].

12"·Wake up, nations [*or* Let the nations be roused],
and come ·to attack in [up to] the Valley ·Where the LORD Judges [Lof Jehoshaphat; v. 2].
There I will sit to judge
all the nations on every side.
13Swing the ·cutting tool [sickle],
because the harvest is ripe.
Come, ·walk on them as you would walk on grapes to get their juice [Ltrample the grapes],
because the winepress is full
and the ·barrels [vats] are ·spilling over [overflowing],
because ·these people are so evil [their wickedness/evil is great]!"

14·There are huge numbers of people [LMultitudes, multitudes]
in the Valley of Decision [Cthe place of the Lord's verdict against the nations; vv. 2, 12],
because the ·LORD's day of judging [Lday of the LORD; 1:15] is near
in the Valley of Decision.
15The sun and the moon will become dark,
and the stars will ·stop shining [Lwithhold their brightness; 2:10].
16The LORD ·will roar like a lion from Jerusalem [Lroars from Zion];
his loud voice will thunder from ·that city [LJerusalem],
and the ·sky [heavens] and the earth will shake.
But the LORD will be a ·safe place [refuge] for his people,
a ·strong place of safety [stronghold] for the ·people [Lsons; Tchildren] of Israel.

17"Then you will know that I, the LORD your God,
live on my holy Mount Zion.
Jerusalem will be a holy place,
and ·strangers [foreigners] will never even go through it again [Cas invaders].

A New Life Promised for Judah

18"On that day ·wine [sweet/new wine] will drip from the mountains,
milk will flow from the hills [Csymbols of bounty and prosperity],
and water will run through all the ·ravines [streambeds] of Judah.
A fountain will flow from the ·Temple [Lhouse] of the LORD
and give water to the valley of ·acacia trees [LShittim; Cperhaps a proper name; Num. 25:1].

19But Egypt will ·become empty [be desolate],
and Edom an ·empty desert [deserted wilderness],
because ·they were cruel [of their violence] to the ·people [Lsons; descendants] of Judah.
They ·killed innocent people [Lshed innocent blood] in that land.
20But ·there will always be people living in Judah [Judah will be inhabited forever],
and ·people will live in Jerusalem from now on [LJerusalem from generation to generation].
21·Egypt and Edom killed my people,
so I will definitely punish them [LI will avenge/punish their blood, which I have not yet avenged/punished]."

The LORD ·lives [dwells] in Jerusalem!

AMOS

1 These are the words of Amos, one of the shepherds from the town
of Tekoa [[C]a small town in the highlands of Judah, ten miles south
of Jerusalem]. **·He saw this vision about** [[L]...which he saw concerning]
Israel two years before the earthquake [Zech. 14:5]. **·It was at the time** [...
[L]in the days when] **Uzziah was king of Judah** [[C]ruled 769–733 BC] **and**
Jeroboam son of Jehoash was king of Israel [[C]ruled 800–784 BC].
2 **Amos said,**
"The Lord will roar [Joel 3:16] **from ·Jerusalem** [[L]Zion; [C]the location
of the Temple];
he ·will send his voice [*or* thunders; bellows; [L]gives his voice] **from**
Jerusalem.
The pastures of the shepherds will ·become dry [*or* mourn],
and even the top of Mount Carmel [9:3] **will ·dry up** [wither]."

Israel's Neighbors Are Punished

The People of Aram

3 **This is what the Lord says:**
"For ·the many [[L]three, even four] **·crimes** [sins; transgressions] **of**
Damascus,
I will ·punish them [[L]not turn back/grant a reprieve].
They ·drove over [beat down; [L]threshed] **the people of Gilead**
with threshing boards ·that had iron teeth [[L]of iron].
4 **So I will send fire upon the house of Hazael** [[C]the royal dynasty of
Syria (Aram), founded by Hazael (842–796 BC); 2 Kin. 8:7–15]
that will destroy the strong towers of Ben-Hadad [[C]either Hazael's
predecessor (whom he assassinated), or Hazael's son, who took the
same name].
5 **I will break down the bar of the gate to Damascus** [[C]the huge beam
used to lock the gate]
and destroy the ·king who is in [*or* the inhabitants of; [L]the one who
sits/dwells in] **the Valley of ·Aven** [*or* Wickedness; Hos. 4:15],
as well as the ·leader [[L]one who holds the scepter] **of Beth Eden**
[[C]either Bit Adini, a city-state near the Euphrates, or a mocking
name for Damascus, meaning "city of delight"].
The people of ·Aram [Syria] **will be taken captive to the country of**
Kir [[C]where the Syrians originated (9:7); ironically, they would
return there as captives; 2 Kin. 16:9]," **says the Lord.**

The People of Philistia

6 **This is what the Lord says:**
"For ·the many [[L]three, even four; v. 3] **·crimes** [sins; transgressions] **of**
Gaza,
I will ·punish them [[L]not turn back/grant a reprieve].
They sold ·all the people of one area [whole communities]
·as slaves [into captivity] **to Edom.**

7So I will send a fire on the walls of Gaza
that will ·destroy [devour; consume] the city's ·strong buildings [fortresses; palaces].
8I will destroy the ·king [*or* inhabitants; [L]the one who sits; v. 5] of the city of Ashdod,
as well as the ·leader [[L]one who holds the scepter] of Ashkelon.
Then I will turn [[L]my hand] against ·the people of the city of Ekron [[L]Ekron],
and the ·last [rest; remnant] of the Philistines will ·die [perish]," says the Lord God.

The People of Phoenicia

9This is what the Lord says:
"For ·the many [[L]three, even four; vv. 3, 6] ·crimes [sins; transgressions] of Tyre,
I will ·punish them [[L]not turn back/grant a reprieve].
They sold ·all the people of one area [whole communities]
·as slaves to Edom [into captivity],
and they forgot the ·agreement among relatives they had made with Israel [[L]covenant/treaty of brotherhood].
10So I will send fire on the walls of Tyre
that will ·destroy [devour; consume] the city's ·strong buildings [fortresses; palaces]."

The People of Edom

11This is what the Lord says:
"For ·the many [[L]three, even four; vv. 3, 6, 9] ·crimes [sins; transgressions] of Edom,
I will ·punish them [[L]not turn back/grant a reprieve].
·They hunted down their relatives, the Israelites, [[L]He pursued his brother; [C]Esau (Edom) was the brother of Jacob/Israel and so the Israelites were related to the Edomites] with the sword,
·showing them no mercy [*or* wiping out their allies; *or* destroying their women].
·They were angry all the time [His anger raged unceasingly]
and ·kept on being very angry [[L]he preserved his wrath forever].
12So I will send fire on the city of Teman
that will even ·destroy [consume; devour] the ·strong buildings [fortresses; palaces] of Bozrah [[C]the whole country; Teman was in northern Edom and Bozrah in the south]."

The People of Ammon

13This is what the Lord says:
"For ·the many [[L]three, even four; vv. 3, 6, 9, 11] ·crimes [sins; transgressions] of Ammon,
I will ·punish them [[L]not turn back/grant a reprieve].
They ripped open the pregnant women in Gilead
·so they could take over that land
and make their own country larger [[L]to enlarge their borders].
14So I will send fire on the city wall of Rabbah
that will ·destroy [consume; devour] its ·strong buildings [fortresses; palaces].
·It will come during [[L]Amid shouting/war cries on] a day of battle,
during a stormy day with ·strong winds [a whirlwind].
15Then their king will be taken ·captive [into exile];
he and his ·leaders [officials; princes] will all be taken away together," says the Lord.

The People of Moab

2 This is what the LORD says:
"For ·the many [[L]three, even four; 1:3, 6, 9, 11, 13] ·crimes [sins;
transgressions] of Moab,
I will ·punish them [[L]not turn back/grant a reprieve].
They burned the bones of the king of Edom into lime [[C]desecrating a
tomb was a serious offense in the ancient Near East].
2So I will send fire on Moab
that will ·destroy [consume; devour] the ·strong buildings [fortresses;
palaces] of the city of Kerioth.
·The people of Moab [[L]Moab] will die in a great ·noise [uproar;
tumult],
in the middle of ·the sounds of war [shouting; war cries] and trumpets.
3So I will ·bring an end to [destroy; [L]cut off] the king of Moab,
and I will kill all its ·leaders [officials; princes] with him," says the LORD.

The People of Judah

4This is what the LORD says:
"For ·the many [[L]three, even four; 2:1] ·crimes [sins; transgressions] of
Judah,
I will ·punish them [[L]not turn back/grant a reprieve].
They rejected the ·teachings [law; [L]Torah] of the LORD
and did not ·keep [guard] his ·commands [statutes; ordinances;
requirements];
they ·followed the same gods [*or* have been led astray by the same lies]
as their ·ancestors [fathers] had followed.
5So I will send fire on Judah,
and it will ·destroy [consume; devour] the ·strong buildings
[fortresses; palaces] of Jerusalem."

Israel Is Punished

6This is what the LORD says:
"For ·the many [[L]three, even four; 2:1] ·crimes [sins; transgressions] of
Israel,
I will ·punish them [[L]not turn back/grant a reprieve].
For silver, they sell ·people who have done nothing wrong [the
innocent/righteous];
they sell the ·poor [needy] to buy a pair of sandals.
7They ·walk [trample] on ·poor people [[L]the heads of the poor] as if
they were ·dirt [[L]the dust of the ground/earth],
and they ·refuse to be fair to [deny justice to; *or* push away] those
who are ·suffering [afflicted].
Fathers and sons ·have sexual relations with [[L]go in to] the same woman,
and so they ·ruin [defile; profane] my holy name.
8·As they worship at their altars [[L]Beside every altar],
they lie down on clothes taken ·from the poor [[L]in pledge; [C]as
collateral for a debt; Deut. 24:12–13].
They fine people,
and with that money they buy wine to drink in the house of their god.
9"But it was I who destroyed the Amorites before them,
who were tall like cedar trees and as strong as oaks—
I destroyed ·them completely [[L]their fruit above and roots below].
10It was I who brought you from the land of Egypt
and led you for forty years through the ·desert [wilderness]
·so I could give you [[L]to possess] the land of the Amorites.

[11]I made some of your children to be prophets
and some of your young people to be Nazirites [Num. 6:2].
·People [[L]Sons/[T]Children] **of Israel, isn't this true?" says the LORD.**
[12]"But you made the Nazirites drink wine [[C]violating their vows; Num. 6:3]
and ·told [commanded] **the prophets not to prophesy.**
[13]Now I ·will make you get stuck [*or* will crush/press you down; *or* am burdened by you],
as a wagon loaded with grain ·gets stuck [*or* is weighed/pressed down].
[14]No one will ·escape [find refuge], **not even the fastest runner.**
Strong people will not be strong enough;
warriors will not be able to save themselves.
[15]Soldiers with bows and arrows will not ·stand and fight [hold their ground],
and even fast runners will not get away;
soldiers on horses will not escape alive.
[16]At that time even the bravest warriors
will run away ·without their armor [[L]naked]," **says the LORD.**

Warning to Israel

3 Listen to this word that the LORD has spoken against you, ·people [[L]sons; [T]children] **of Israel, against the whole family he brought out of Egypt.**
[2]"I have ·chosen [known; [C]selected for a special relationship] **only you**
out of all the families of the earth,
so I will punish you
for all your sins."

[3]·Two people will not [[L]Can two…?] **walk together**
unless they have agreed ·to do so [*or* to meet; *or* on the direction].
[4]·A lion in the forest does not [[L]Does a lion in the forest…?] **roar**
unless it has caught ·an animal [[L]its prey];
·it does not [[L]does a young lion…?] **growl in its den**
when it has caught nothing.
[5]·A bird will not [[L]Does a bird…?] **fall into a trap**
where there is no bait;
·the trap will not [[L]does the trap…?] **spring shut**
if there is nothing to catch.
[6]When a trumpet ·blows a warning [[L]sounds] **in a city,**
[[L]do not…?] **the people tremble.**
When ·trouble [disaster] **comes to a city,**
·the LORD has [[L]has not the LORD…?] **caused it.**
[7]Before the Lord GOD does anything,
he tells his plans to his servants the prophets.
[8]The lion has roared [[C]a symbol of coming judgment]**!**
Who wouldn't be afraid?
The Lord GOD has spoken.
Who will not prophesy?
[9]Announce this to the ·strong buildings [fortresses; palaces] **of Ashdod** [[C]a city in Philistia]
and to the ·strong buildings [fortresses; palaces] **of Egypt:**
"·Come to [Assemble yourselves on] **the mountains of Samaria,**
where you will see great ·confusion [chaos; tumult]
and ·people hurting others [oppression in her midst]."

[10]"The people don't know how to do what is right," says the LORD.
"Their ·strong buildings [fortresses; palaces] are filled with ·treasures
they took by force from others [the spoils of violence and robbery]."
[11]So this is what the Lord GOD says:
"An enemy will ·take over [overrun; *or* encircle] the land
and pull down your strongholds;
he will ·take the treasures out of [plunder] your ·strong buildings
[fortresses; palaces]."
[12]This is what the LORD says:
"A shepherd might save from a lion's mouth
only two leg bones or a scrap of an ear of his sheep.
In the same way only a few Israelites in Samaria will be saved—
·people who now sit on their beds
and on their couches [*or* only a corner of a bed or a part of a couch
will be saved]."
[13]"Listen and ·be witnesses [testify] against the family of Jacob
[CIsrael]," says the Lord GOD, the God ·All-Powerful [Almighty; of
Heaven's Armies; Tof hosts].
[14]"·When [LOn the day] I punish Israel for their sins,
I will also destroy the altars at Bethel [Can important worship center
in Israel; 1 Kin. 12:25–33].
The ·corners [Lhorns] of the altar will be cut off,
and they will fall to the ground.
[15]I will tear down the winter house,
together with the summer house.
The houses ·decorated with [*or* filled with; Lof] ivory will be destroyed,
and the great houses will ·come to an end [*or* be swept away]," says
the LORD.

Israel Will Not Return

4 [1]Listen to this message, you cows of Bashan on the Mountain of
Samaria [Cmocking the wealthy women of Samaria].
You ·take things from [oppress] the poor
and crush people who are in need.
Then you command your husbands,
"Bring us something to drink!"
[2]The Lord GOD has ·promised [sworn] this:
"Just as surely as I am a holy God,
the time will come
when you will be taken away ·by hooks [*or* in baskets],
and what is left of you with fishhooks.
[3]You will go straight out of the city
through ·holes [breaches] in the walls,
and you will be thrown ·on the garbage dump [on the dung heap; *or*
out toward Harmon]," says the LORD.

[4]"Come to the city of Bethel and ·sin [rebel; transgress];
come to Gilgal and ·sin [rebel; transgress] even more [CBethel and
Gilgal were important worship centers in Israel].
Offer your sacrifices every morning,
and bring ·one-tenth of your crops [your tithes] every three days.
[5]Offer bread made with yeast as a sacrifice to show your thanks,
and ·brag about [publicly announce] the ·special [voluntary; freewill]
offerings you bring,

because this is what you love to do, ·Israelites [Lsons/Tchildren of
Israel]," says the Lord God.

6"I ·did not give you any food [Lgave you cleanness of teeth; Can idiom
meaning "empty stomachs" and indicating starvation] in your cities,
and there was not enough to eat in any of your towns,
but you did not come back to me," says the Lord.
7"I held back the rain from you
three months before harvest time.
Then I let it rain on one city
but not on another.
Rain fell on one field,
but another field got none and dried up.
8·People weak from thirst went from town to town [LTwo or three cities
wandered to one] for water,
but they could not get enough to drink.
Still you did not come back to me," says the Lord.
9"I ·made your crops die from [Lstruck you with] ·disease [blight] and
mildew.
When your gardens and your vineyards got larger,
locusts ·ate [devoured] your fig and olive trees.
But still you did not come back to me," says the Lord.
10"I sent ·disasters [a plague/pestilence] against you,
as I did to Egypt.
I killed your young men with swords,
and your horses were taken from you.
I made ·you smell the stink from all the dead bodies [Lthe stench of
your camp rise into your nostrils],
but still you did not come back to me," says the Lord.
11"I ·destroyed [overthrew] some of you
as I destroyed Sodom and Gomorrah [Gen. 19].
You were like a burning stick pulled from a fire,
but still you did not come back to me," says the Lord.
12"So this is what I will do to you, Israel;
because I will do this to you,
get ready to meet your God, Israel."

13 [LFor look/Tbehold] He is the one who ·makes [forms] the mountains
and creates the wind
and makes his thoughts known to people.
He changes the dawn into darkness
and ·walks [treads; marches] ·over the mountains [on the heights] of
the earth.
His name is the Lord God ·All-Powerful [Almighty; of Heaven's
Armies; Tof hosts].

Israel Needs to Repent

5 Listen to this ·funeral song [dirge; word of lamentation] that I ·sing
about [*or* take up against] you, ·people [Lhouse] of Israel.
2"The ·young girl [virgin] Israel has fallen,
and she will not rise up again.
She was ·left alone [abandoned; forsaken] in her own land,
and there is no one to ·help [raise; lift] her up."
3This is what the Lord God says:

"If a thousand soldiers leave a city,
only a hundred will ·return [*or* remain];
if a hundred soldiers leave a city,
only ten will ·return [*or* remain]."
4 This is what the LORD says to the ·nation [Lhouse] of Israel:
"·Come to [Seek] me and live.
5 But do not ·look in [seek] Bethel [Cironic, since Bethel means "house of God"; 4:4]
or go to Gilgal,
and do not go down to Beersheba [Cimportant centers of worship in Israel; 4:4].
The people of Gilgal will ·be taken away as captives [surely go into exile],
and Bethel will become nothing."
6 ·Come to [Seek] the LORD and live,
or he will ·move [sweep through; Lrush] like fire against the ·descendants [Lhouse] of Joseph.
The fire will ·burn [consume; devour] Bethel [4:4],
and there will be no one to ·put it out [quench it].
7 You turn justice ·upside down [Linto bitterness/*or* wormwood; Ca bitter plant; 6:12],
and you throw on the ground ·what is right [rightousness; justice].

8 ·God is the one [LHe] who made the constellations Pleiades and Orion;
he changes darkness into the morning light,
and the day into dark night.
He calls for the waters of the sea
to pour out on the ·earth [Lsurface/face of the earth].
The LORD is his name.
9 He ·destroys [brings ruin upon; flashes destruction on] the protected city;
he ·ruins [destroys] the strong, walled city.

10 ·You [LThey] hate those who ·speak in court against evil [Lrebuke/reprove at the gate; Cwhere court was held],
and ·you [Lthey] ·can't stand [despise; detest] those who tell the truth.
11 You ·walk [trample; *or* levy a tax] on poor people,
·forcing them to give you [imposing a tax on their] grain.
You have built fancy houses of cut stone,
but you will not live in them.
You have planted ·beautiful [pleasant] vineyards,
but you will not drink the wine from them [Deut. 28:30].
12 I know your many ·crimes [trangressions],
your ·terrible [numerous; great] sins.
You ·hurt [oppress] ·people who do right [the righteous/innocent],
you take ·money to do wrong [bribes],
and you keep the poor from getting justice in ·court [Lthe gate; v. 10].
13 In such times the wise person will keep quiet,
because it is a ·bad [evil] time.

14 ·Try to do [Seek] good, not evil,
so that you will live,
and the LORD God ·All-Powerful [Almighty; of Heaven's Armies; Tof hosts] will be with you
just as you ·say [claim] he is.

[15]**Hate evil and love good;**
·be fair in the courts [[L]establish justice in the gate; v. 10].
Maybe the LORD God ·All-Powerful [Almighty; of Heaven's Armies; [T]of hosts] **will ·be kind to** [have mercy on; be gracious to] **the ·people of Joseph who are left alive** [remnant of Joseph; [C]a reference to the tribes of Ephraim and Manasseh (Joseph's sons), representing the northern kingdom].
[16]**This is what the Lord, the LORD God ·All-Powerful** [Almighty; of Heaven's Armies; [T]of hosts], **says:**
"People will be ·crying [wailing] **in all the streets;**
they will be saying, 'Oh, no!' in the public places.
They will call the farmers to ·come and weep [mourning]
and ·will pay people [[L]those who know lamentation; [C]professional mourners paid to weep] **to ·cry out loud** [wail] **for them.**
[17]**People will be ·crying** [wailing] **in all the vineyards,**
because I will pass ·among you to punish you [[L]through your midst; [C]as the angel of death passed through Egypt (Ex. 12:12)]," **says the LORD.**

The Lord's Day of Judging

[18]**·How terrible it will be for** [[L]Woe to] **you who want**
the ·LORD's day of judging [[L]day of the LORD] **to come.**
Why do you want that day to come?
It will bring darkness for you, not light.
[19]**It will be like someone who runs from a lion**
and meets a bear,
or like someone who goes into his house
and ·puts [leans] **his hand on the wall,**
and then is bitten by a snake.
[20]**So the ·LORD's day of judging** [[L]day of the LORD] **will bring darkness, not light;**
it will be ·very dark [deep gloom], **not ·light at all** [brightness].
[21]**The LORD says, "I ·hate and reject** [despise] **your ·feasts** [religious festivals];
I ·cannot stand [take no delight in] **your ·religious meetings** [sacred assemblies].
[22]**If you offer me burnt offerings** [Lev. 1:1–17] **and ·grain** [[L]gift; tribute] **offerings** [Lev. 2:1],
I won't accept them.
You bring your best ·fellowship [*or* peace; well-being] **offerings** [Lev. 3:1] **of fattened cattle,**
but I will ·ignore [have no regard for] **them** [Is. 1:11].
[23]**Take ·the noise of your songs** [*or* your noisy songs] **away from me!**
I won't listen to the music of your ·harps [stringed instruments].
[24]**But let justice ·flow** [roll] **like a river,**
and let ·goodness [righteousness; justice] **flow like a ·never-ending** [ever-flowing] **stream.**
[25]**"·People** [[L]House] **of Israel, you did not bring me sacrifices and offerings while you traveled in the desert for forty years.**
[26]**You have ·carried with you** [lifted up]
·your king, the god Sakkuth [*or* the shrine of your idol-king],
·and Kaiwan your idol [*or* the pedestal of your idols; [C]either names of Mesopotamian star gods, or general terms for idols],
the star gods you have made for yourselves.

[27]So I will send you ·away as captives [into exile] beyond Damascus,"
says the LORD, whose name is the God ·All-Powerful [Almighty; of
Heaven's Armies; [T]of hosts].

Israel Will Be Destroyed

6 ·How terrible it will be for [[L]Woe to] those who ·have an easy life [are
complacent/at ease] in Jerusalem,
for those who feel ·safe living [secure] on Mount Samaria.
You think you are ·the important people [notable/renowned men] of
the ·best nation in the world [first among the nations];
the ·Israelites [[L]house of Israel] come to you for help.
[2]Go look at the city of Calneh,
and from there go to the great city Hamath [[C]Aramean city-states
under the control of Israel];
then go down to Gath of the Philistines.
·You are no better than these kingdoms [[L]Are they better than your
kingdoms?].
·Your land is no larger than theirs [[L]Is their territory greater than yours?].
[3]You put off the ·day of punishment [day of disaster/doom; [L]evil day],
but you ·bring near [establish] ·the day when you can do evil to
others [a reign of terror; [L]the seat of violence].
[4]You lie on beds ·decorated with ivory [[L]of ivory]
and stretch out on your couches.
You eat ·tender lambs [[L]lambs from the flock]
and ·fattened calves [[L]calves from the midst of the stall].
[5]You ·make up songs [*or* strum away; *or* sing idly] on your ·harps
[stringed instruments],
and, like David, you ·compose [*or* improvise] songs on musical
instruments.
[6]You drink wine by the bowlful
and ·use [anoint yourselves with] the ·best perfumed lotions [finest oils].
But you ·are not sad [do not grieve; are unconcerned] over the ruin
of Israel,
[7]so you will be some of the first ones ·taken as slaves [to go into exile].
Your ·feasting and lying around [reclining at banquets] will come to
an end.

[8]The Lord GOD ·made this promise [[L]has sworn by himself]; the LORD
God ·All-Powerful [Almighty; of Heaven's Armies; [T]of hosts] says:
"I ·hate [abhor] the pride of ·the Israelites [[L]Jacob],
and I ·hate [detest] their ·strong buildings [fortresses; palaces],
so I will ·let the enemy take [deliver up] the city
and everything in it."

[9]·At that time there might be only [[L]If there are] ten people left alive in
just one house, but they will also die. [10]When the relatives come to take
the bodies out of the house to ·bury them [*or* burn them; *or* anoint them
for burial], one of them will call to ·the other [*or* any survivors] and ask,
"Are there any other dead bodies with you?"

That person will answer, "No."

Then the one who asked will say, "Hush! We must not say the name of
the LORD." [[C]This could mean do not say the Lord's name lest he return
with more judgment, or do not pronounce a eulogy using the Lord's name
on those already judged by God, or do not acknowledge the Lord because
of resentment of his judgment.]

[11]The LORD has given the command;
the large house will be ·broken [smashed] into pieces,
and the small house into bits.
[12]·Horses do not [LCan horses…?] run on rocks,
and ·people do not [Lcan people…?] plow ·rocks [*or* the sea] with oxen.
But you have changed ·fairness [justice] into poison;
you have changed ·what is right [Lthe fruit of righteousness] into ·a bitter taste [Lwormwood; 5:7].
[13]You ·are happy that the town of Lo Debar was captured [Lrejoiced over Lo Debar; Ca town across the Jordan whose name means "nothing," mocking Israel's conquest of it as insignificant],
and you say, "We have taken Karnaim [Canother insignificant town across the Jordan conquered by the Israelites] by our own strength."
[14]The LORD God ·All-Powerful [Almighty; of Heaven's Armies; Tof hosts] says,
"·Israel [LHouse of Israel], I will bring a nation against you
that will ·make your people suffer [oppress you] from Lebo Hamath [Cin the far north]
to the valley ·south of the Dead Sea [Lof the Arabah; Cin the far south; 2 Kin. 14:25; Israel had oppressed others, but would now be oppressed]."

The Vision of Locusts

7 This is what the Lord GOD showed me: He was forming a swarm
of locusts, after the ·king had taken his share of the first crop
[Lking's harvest/mowing] and the ·second [Llate] crop had just begun
growing [Cthe second of two agricultural seasons; vegetables planted to
coincide with the spring rains]. [2]When the locusts ate all the ·crops [veg-
etation; grass] in the country, I said, "Lord GOD, forgive us. How could
·Israel [LJacob] ·live through this [Lstand]? It is too small already!"
[3]So the LORD ·changed his mind about this [relented]. "It will not happen," said the LORD.

The Vision of Fire

[4]This is what the Lord GOD showed me: [LLook; TBehold] The Lord GOD
was calling for ·fire to come down like rain [*or* a judgment of fire]. It burned
up the ·deep water [great deep; deep abyss] and ·was going to burn up
[Lconsumed; devoured] the land. [5]Then I cried out, "Lord GOD, stop! How
could ·Israel [LJacob] ·live through this [Lstand]? It is too small already."
[6]So the LORD ·changed his mind about this [relented]. "It will not happen," said the Lord GOD.

The Vision of the Plumb Line

[7]This is what he showed me: The Lord stood by a ·straight wall [Lwall
built with a plumb line], with a plumb line in his hand. [8]The LORD said to
me, "Amos, what do you see?"
I said, "A plumb line."
Then the Lord said, "·See [TBehold], I will put a plumb line among my
people Israel [Cto show how crooked they are]. I will not ·look the other
way [spare them; Lpass by them] any longer.

[9]"·The places where Isaac's descendants worship [LThe high places of Isaac; Cplaces of pagan worship] will be destroyed,
Israel's ·holy places [sanctuaries] will be turned into ruins,
and I will ·attack [Lrise up against] King Jeroboam's ·family [house] with the sword."

Amaziah Speaks Against Amos

10Amaziah, a priest at Bethel [4:4], sent this message to Jeroboam king
of Israel: "Amos is ·making evil plans [conspiring] against you ·with the
people of Israel [*or* in the very heart of Israel; Lin the midst of the house of
Israel]. ·He has been speaking so much that this land can't hold all [LThis
land cannot bear/endure] his words. 11This is what Amos has said:
'Jeroboam will die by the sword,
and the people of Israel will be taken ·as captives [into exile]
out of their own country.' "
12Then Amaziah said to Amos, "Seer [Canother name for a prophet], go
back right now to the land of Judah. Do your prophesying and ·earn your
living [Leat bread] there, 13but don't prophesy anymore here at Bethel.
This is the king's ·holy place [sanctuary], and it is the ·nation's temple [*or*
royal palace; Lhouse of the kingdom]."
14Then Amos answered Amaziah, "·I do not make my living as a
prophet, nor am I a member of a group of prophets [LI was not a prophet
nor a prophet's son/disciple]. I ·make my living as [Lwas] a shepherd, and
·I take care [a tender] of ·sycamore [*or* sycamore-fig] trees. 15But the LORD
took me away from tending the flock and said to me, 'Go, prophesy to my
people Israel.' 16So listen to the LORD's word. You tell me,
'Don't prophesy against Israel,
and stop ·prophesying [preaching; spouting off; Ldripping] against
the ·descendants [house] of Isaac.'
17"Because you have said this, the LORD says:
'Your wife will become a prostitute in the city,
and your sons and daughters will ·be killed with swords [Lfall by the
sword].
Your land will be divided ·among themselves [Lwith a measuring line],
and you will die in a ·foreign [Lunclean; defiled] country.
The people of Israel will definitely be taken
from their own land ·as captives [into exile].' "

The Vision of Ripe Fruit

8 This is what the Lord GOD showed me: [Llook; Tbehold] a basket of
summer fruit. 2He said to me, "Amos, what do you see?"
I said, "A basket of summer fruit."
Then the LORD said to me, "An end [Cthe Hebrew word for "end" sounds
like the word for "summer fruit"] has come for my people Israel, because
I will not ·overlook their sins [Lpass by them] anymore.
3"On that day the ·palace [*or* temple] songs will become ·funeral songs
[Lwailing]," says the Lord GOD. "·There will be dead bodies [LMany bodies/
corpses] thrown everywhere! ·Silence! [*or* …and carried out in silence.]"
4Listen to me, you who ·walk on helpless people [trample the needy],
you who are trying to ·destroy [do away with] the poor people of this
country, saying,
5"When will the New Moon festival be over
so we can sell grain?
When will the Sabbath be over
so we can bring out wheat to sell?
We can ·give them less [Lmake the ephah small; Ca unit of dry measure]
and ·charge them more [Lthe shekel great; Ca unit of money],
and we can change the scales to cheat the people.
6We will buy poor people for silver,
and needy people for a pair of sandals [2:6].

We will even sell the ·wheat that was swept up from the floor [Lchaff
of the wheat]."
7The LORD has sworn by ·his name, the Pride of Jacob [*or* the arrogance
of Jacob], "I will never forget everything that these people did.
8The whole ·land [*or* earth] will shake because of it,
and everyone who lives in the land will ·cry for those who died [mourn].
The whole land will rise like the Nile;
it will be ·shaken [stirred/heaved up], and then it will ·fall [sink; subside]
like the Nile River in Egypt [Cthe Nile flooded its banks each year]."
9The Lord GOD says:
"·At that time [LIn that day] I will cause the sun to go down at noon
and make the earth dark ·on a bright day [in broad daylight].
10I will change your festivals into ·days of crying for the dead
[mourning],
and all your songs will become ·songs of sadness [dirges;
lamentation; weeping].
I will ·make all of you wear rough cloth to show your sadness [Lput
sackcloth on every waist];
·I will make you shave your heads as well [L…and baldness on every
head].
I will make it like ·a time of crying [mourning] for the death of an only son,
and its end like the end of an ·awful [bitter] day."
11The Lord GOD says: "[LLook; TBehold] The days are coming
when I will ·cause a time of hunger in [send a famine throughout]
the land.
·The people will not be hungry for bread or thirsty for water [L… not a
famine of food or a thirst for water],
but ·they will be hungry for words from [Lfor hearing the words of]
the LORD.
12They will ·wander [*or* stagger] from the ·Mediterranean Sea to the
Dead Sea [Lsea to sea; Cacross the whole land],
from the north to the east.
They will ·search for [run to and fro seeking] the word of the LORD,
but they won't find it.
13·At that time [LIn that day] the beautiful ·young women [virgins] and
the young men
will ·become weak [faint] from thirst.
14They ·make promises [swear oaths] by the ·idol in [Lsin of] Samaria
and say, 'As surely as the god of Dan lives … [1 Kin. 12:29]'
and, 'As surely as the ·god of [Lway to; Cperhaps the pilgrimage route
to the pagan worship there] Beersheba lives, we promise….' [CDan
was the city farthest north in Israel and Beersheba farthest south.]
So they will fall
and never get up again."

Israel Will Be Destroyed

9 I saw the Lord standing by the altar, and he said:
"·Smash [Strike] the top of the pillars
so that even the ·bottom of the doors [thresholds] will shake.
·Make the pillars fall [LStrike/Shatter them] on the people's heads;
anyone left alive I will kill with a sword.
Not one person will get away;
no one will escape.

[2]If they dig down ·as deep as the place of the dead [*or* into the depths of the earth; [L]into Sheol],
·I [[L]My hand] will pull them up from there.
If they climb up into heaven,
I will bring them down from there.
[3]If they hide at the top of Mount Carmel,
I will ·find them [hunt them down] and ·take them away [seize them].
If they try to hide from me at the bottom of the sea,
I will command ·a snake [*or* the serpent; [C]perhaps the mythological beast symbolic of chaos] to bite them.
[4]If they are ·captured and taken away [driven into exile] by their enemies,
I will command the sword to ·kill [slay] them.
I will ·keep watch over them [fix my eyes on them],
but ·I will keep watch to give them trouble, not to do them good [[L]for evil/harm, not for good/prosperity]."

[5]The Lord God ·All-Powerful [Almighty; of Heaven's Armies; [T]of hosts] touches the land,
and the land ·shakes [dissolves; melts].
Then everyone who lives in the land ·cries for the dead [mourns].
The whole ·land [*or* earth] rises like the Nile River
and ·falls [sinks; subsides] like the river of Egypt [8:8].
[6]The Lord builds his ·upper rooms [*or* steps] ·above the skies [in the heavens];
he sets their foundations on the earth.
He calls for the waters of the sea
and pours them out on the ·land [[L]face of the earth/land; [C]as rain].
The Lord is his name.
[7]The Lord says,
"Israel, you are no different to me than the people of Cush [[C]Ethiopia].
·I brought [[L]Did I not bring…?] Israel out of the land of Egypt,
and the Philistines from ·Crete [[L]Caphtor],
and the Arameans [[C]Syrians] from Kir.
[8][[L]Look; [T]Behold] I, the Lord God, am watching the sinful kingdom [[C]Israel].
I will destroy it
from ·off [[L]the face of] the earth,
but I will not completely destroy
·Jacob's descendants [[L]the house of Jacob]," says the Lord.
[9]"[[L]For look/[T]behold] I am giving the command
to ·scatter [[L]shake] the nation of Israel among all nations.
It will be like someone shaking grain through a ·strainer [sieve],
but not even a ·tiny stone [pebble; *or* kernel of grain] falls ·through [[L]to the ground].
[10]All the sinners among my people
will die by the sword—
those who say,
'·Nothing bad will happen to us [[L]Disaster will not approach and meet us].'

The Lord Promises to Restore Israel

[11]In that day I will ·restore [rebuild; raise up] the ·tent [hut; shack; [C]referring to the weakened state of the Davidic dynasty] of David that has fallen,
and ·mend [repair] its broken places.

I will ·rebuild [restore; raise up] its ruins
as it was ·before [in days long ago/of antiquity].
12Then Israel ·will take over [possess; conquer] ·what is left [the
remnant] of Edom
and the other nations that ·belong to me [Lare called by my name],"
says the LORD,
who will make it happen.

13The LORD says, "The time is coming when there will be all kinds of food.
·People will still be harvesting crops
when it's time to plow again [LThe plowman will overtake the reaper].
·People will still be taking the juice from grapes
when it's time to plant again [L...and the treader of grapes (will
overtake) the one who sows the seed].
Wine will drip from the mountains
and pour from the hills [Csymbols of great prosperity].
14I will bring my people Israel back from ·captivity [exile];
they will build the ruined cities again,
and they will live in them.
They will plant vineyards and drink the wine from them;
they will plant ·gardens [*or* orchards] and eat their fruit.
15I will plant my people on their land,
and they will not be ·pulled out again [uprooted]
from the land which I have given them,"
says the LORD your God.

OBADIAH

The Lord Will Punish the Edomites

1This is the vision of Obadiah.

This is what the Lord God says about Edom [Cthe Edomites were descendants of Esau, Jacob's twin brother (Gen. 25); they were often in conflict with Israel]:
We have heard a ·message [report] from the Lord.
A ·messenger [envoy] has been sent among the nations, saying,
"·Attack [LRise up]! Let's go ·attack [Lrise to battle against] Edom!"

The Lord Speaks to the Edomites

2"·Soon [LLook; TBehold] I will make you ·the smallest of [or weak among the] nations.
You will be greatly ·hated [despised] by everyone.
3Your pride has ·fooled [deceived] you,
you who live in the ·hollow places of the cliff [Tclefts of the rock].
Your home is ·up high [on the heights],
you who say to yourself,
'·No one can [LWho can…?] bring me down to the ground.'
4Even if you ·fly high [soar] like the eagle
and make your nest among the stars,
I will bring you down from there," says the Lord.
5"You will really be ·ruined [Lcut off]!
If thieves came to you,
if ·robbers [plunderers] came by night,
they would steal only enough for themselves.
If workers came and picked the grapes from your vines,
they would leave ·a few behind [some for the poor; the gleanings].
6But you, Edom, will ·really lose everything [be cleaned/Lsearched out]!
People will find all your hidden treasures!
7All ·the people who are your friends [your allies; Lthe people of your covenant/treaty]
will force you ·out of the land [Lto the border].
The people ·who are at peace with you [or who promised you peace; Lof your peace]
will ·trick [deceive] you and ·defeat [overpower] you.
Those who eat your bread [Cindicating fellowship and friendship] with you now
are planning a trap for you,
and you will ·not notice it [be taken by surprise; have no understanding]."

8The Lord says, "On that day

I will surely destroy the wise people from Edom,
and those with understanding from the mountains of Edom.
9Then, city of Teman, your ·best warriors [mighty men] will be ·afraid [dismayed],
and everyone from the mountains of Edom will be ·killed [Lcut down in the slaughter].
10You did violence to your ·relatives, the Israelites [Lbrother Jacob; verse 1; Gen. 25],
so you will be covered with shame
and destroyed forever.
11You stood ·aside without helping [aloof]
·while [Lon the day] strangers carried Israel's ·treasures [wealth; *or* army] away.
When foreigners entered Israel's city gate
and threw lots to decide ·what part of Jerusalem they would take [Lfor Jerusalem],
you were like one of them.

Commands That Edom Broke

12"Edom, ·do not laugh at [*or* you should not have gloated over] your ·brother Israel [Lbrother] in his time of ·trouble [misfortune]
or ·be happy [rejoice] about the ·people [sons; descendants] of Judah ·when they are destroyed [Lon the day of destruction].
Do not ·brag [boast; act with arrogance] ·when cruel things are done to them [Lon the day of distress].
13Do not enter the city gate of my people [Cto plunder their goods]
in their ·time [Lday] of ·trouble [disaster; Cthe Hebrew word for "trouble" sounds like Edom]
or ·laugh at their problems [gloat over them]
in their ·time [Lday] of ·trouble [disaster].
Do not ·take their treasures [loot their wealth]
in their ·time [Lday] of ·trouble [disaster].
14Do not stand at the crossroads
to ·destroy [Lcut off] ·those who are trying to escape [their fugitives].
Do not capture ·those who escape alive [their survivors] and turn them over to their enemy
in their ·time [Lday] of ·trouble [adversity].

The Nations Will Be Judged

15"The ·LORD's day of judging [Lday of the LORD] is ·coming soon [near] to all the nations.
·The same evil things you did to other people [LAs you have done]
·will happen [Lit will be done] to you;
·they [Lrecompense; reprisal] will come back upon your own head.
16Because you drank in my ·Temple [Lholy mountain],
all the nations will drink ·on and on [continually].
They will drink and ·drink [Lswallow]
·until they disappear [Land be as though they were not].
17But on Mount Zion ·some will escape the judgment [Lthere will be escape],
and it will be a holy place.
The ·people [Lhouse] of Jacob will ·take back their land
from those who ·took it from them [Lpossess their possessions].
18The ·people [Lhouse] of Jacob will be like a fire
and the ·people [Lhouse] of Joseph [Cthe Israelite tribes of Ephraim

and Manasseh (Joseph's sons, Jacob's grandsons), representing the northern kingdom] **like a flame.**
But the ·people [Lhouse] **of Esau** [Cthe Edomites] **will be like ·dry stalks** [stubble].
The ·people [Lhouse] **of Jacob will set them on fire and burn them up.**
There will be no ·one left [survivors] **of the ·people** [Lhouse] **of Esau."**
·This will happen because [LFor] **the Lord has said it.**

19 **·Then God's people will regain southern Judah from Edom;**
they will take back [LThe Negev shall possess] **the mountains of ·Edom** [LEsau].
·They will take back the western hills
from [LThe Shephelah/foothills shall possess] **the Philistines.**
They will ·regain [possess] **the ·lands** [Lfields] **of Ephraim and Samaria,**
and Benjamin will ·take over [possess] **Gilead** [Ceast of the Jordan River].
20 **·People from** [LThis host of the sons/Tchildren of] **Israel who once were ·forced to leave their homes** [exiled]
will take the land of the Canaanites,
all the way to Zarephath [Cin Phoenicia in the far northeast].
·People from Judah who once were forced to leave Jerusalem and [LThe exiles of Jerusalem who] **live in Sepharad** [Cunknown location, perhaps Sardis (in present-day Turkey)]
will take back the cities of ·southern Judah [Lthe Negev].
21 **·Powerful warriors** [Deliverers; Saviors; *or* Those who have been rescued/delivered] **will go up on Mount Zion,**
where they will rule ·the people living on Edom's mountains [LMount Esau].
And the kingdom will belong to the Lord.

JONAH

God Calls and Jonah Runs

1 **The ·LORD spoke his word** [Lword of the LORD came] **to Jonah son of Amittai: 2"Get up, go to the great city of Nineveh** [Cthe capital of Assyria; Gen. 10:11, 12; 2 Kin. 19:36], **and ·preach** [cry out] **against it, because ·I see the evil things they do** [its wickedness has come to my attention/Lup before me]**."**

3But Jonah got up to run away from the LORD by going to Tarshish [Cprobably Tartessos in southwest Spain, the opposite direction from Nineveh]**. He went to the city of Joppa, where he found a ship that was going to the city of Tarshish. Jonah paid for the trip and went aboard, planning to go to Tarshish to run away from the LORD.**

4But the LORD ·sent [hurled] **a great wind on the sea, which made the sea so stormy that the ship was in danger of breaking apart. 5The sailors were afraid, and each man cried to his own god. They began throwing the cargo from the ship into the sea to make the ship lighter.**

But Jonah had gone down far inside the ship to lie down, and he fell fast asleep. 6The captain of the ship came and said, "Why are you sleeping? Get up and pray to your god! Maybe your god will ·pay attention to [take notice of] **us, and we won't die!"**

7Then the men said to each other, "Let's throw lots to see who caused these troubles to happen to us."

When they threw lots, the lot ·showed that the trouble had happened because of [singled out; Lfell upon] **Jonah. 8Then they said to him, "Tell us, who caused our trouble? What is your job? Where do you come from? What is your country? Who are your people?"**

9Then Jonah said to them, "I am a Hebrew. I ·fear [worship] **the LORD, the God of heaven, who made the sea and the land** [Gen. 1]**."**

10The men were very afraid, and they asked Jonah, "What terrible thing did you do?" (They knew he was running away from the LORD because he had told them.)

11Since the wind and the waves of the sea were becoming much stronger, they said to him, "What should we do to you to make the sea calm down for us?"

12Jonah said to them, "Pick me up, and throw me into the sea, and then it will calm down. I know it is my fault that this great storm has come on you."

13Instead, the men ·tried [Ldug in] **to row the ship back to the land, but they could not, because the sea was becoming more stormy.**

Jonah's Punishment

14So the men cried to the LORD, "LORD, please don't let us die because of this man's life; please don't ·think we are [hold us] **guilty of ·killing an innocent person** [Linnocent blood]**. LORD, you have caused all this to happen; you wanted it this way." 15So they picked up Jonah and threw him**

into the sea, and the sea ·became calm [ceased raging]. 16Then they began
to fear the LORD very much; they offered a sacrifice to the LORD and made
·promises [vows] to him.

17The LORD ·caused [appointed; provided] a big fish to swallow Jonah,
and Jonah was ·inside [in the belly of] the fish three days and three nights.

2 While Jonah was ·inside [Lin the belly/innards of] the fish, he
prayed to the LORD his God and said,

2"When I was in ·danger [distress],
I called to the LORD,
and he answered me.
·I was about to die [LFrom the belly of Sheol; Cthe place of the dead],
so I cried to you,
and you heard my voice.
3You threw me into the ·sea [ocean depths; deep],
down, down into the ·deep [Lheart of the] sea.
The ·water [flood] ·was all around [engulfed] me,
and your ·powerful [surging; billowing] waves ·flowed [swept] over me.
4I said, 'I was ·driven out of your presence [banished from your sight],
·but I hope to see [yet I will look toward] your Holy Temple again.'
5The waters of the sea closed around my ·throat [*or* soul].
The deep sea ·was all around [surrounded; closed in on] me;
seaweed was wrapped around my head.
6When I ·went [sank] down to ·where the mountains of the sea start to
rise [Lthe roots of the mountains],
·I thought I was locked in this prison [the earth's bars held me] forever,
but you ·saved me [Lbrought up my life] from the pit of death,
LORD my God.

7"When my life ·had almost gone [was slipping/fainting away],
I remembered the LORD.
·I prayed [LMy prayer went up] to you,
·and you heard my prayers in [Lin] your Holy Temple.

8"People who ·worship [cling to] ·useless [worthless; false] idols
·give up their loyalty to you [*or* forfeit the mercy/lovingkindness that
is theirs].
9But ·I will praise and thank you
while I [Lwith a voice of thanksgiving I will] give sacrifices to you,
and I will ·keep my promises to you [Lpay what I have vowed].
Salvation comes from the LORD!"

10Then the LORD spoke to the fish, and the fish ·threw up [vomited]
Jonah onto the dry land.

God Calls and Jonah Obeys

3 The ·LORD spoke his word [Lword of the LORD came] to Jonah
·again [a second time] and said, 2"Get up, go to the great city
Nineveh [1:2], and ·preach [cry out] to it what I tell you to say."

3So Jonah obeyed the LORD and got up and went to Nineveh. It was a very
large city; just to walk ·across it [*or* through it all] took a person three days.
4After Jonah had entered the city and walked for one day, he preached to the
people, saying, "After forty days, Nineveh will be ·destroyed [overthrown]!"

5The people of Nineveh believed God. They ·announced that they
would fast [called for/decreed a fast], and they put on ·rough cloth [burlap;

9because Samaria's wound ·cannot be healed [is incurable].
It ·will spread [or has spread] to Judah;
it ·will reach [or has reached] the city gate of my people [Cwhere the city's affairs were conducted],
all the way to Jerusalem.
10Don't tell it in Gath [Csounds like Hebrew for "tell"; Gath and the cities in this list were in Assyria's path of destruction in 701 BC].
Don't cry ·in Acco [or at all; Cthe Hebrew for "cry" sounds like Acco].
Roll in the dust
at Beth Ophrah [C"house of dust"].
11Pass on your way, naked and ashamed,
you who live in Shaphir [C"beautiful" or "pleasant"].
Those who live in Zaanan [Csounds like Hebrew for "come out"]
won't come out.
The people in Beth Ezel [C"house of nearness"] ·will cry [are in mourning],
but they will not give you any support.
12Those who live in Maroth [Csounds like Hebrew for "sad" or "miserable"]
·will be anxious [hope] for good news to come,
because ·trouble [disaster] ·will [or has] come from the LORD,
all the way to the gate of Jerusalem.
13You people living in Lachish [Ca large town in Judah; Lachish sounds like the Hebrew for "horse" or "steed"],
harness the fastest ·horses [steeds] to the chariot.
·Jerusalem's [LDaughter of Zion's; Cthe location of the Temple] sins ·started in [began with] you;
yes, Israel's ·sins [transgressions; rebellion] were found in you.
14So you must give ·farewell gifts [a dowry]
to Moresheth in Gath.
The houses in Aczib [C"deception"] ·will be false help
to [or have deceived/betrayed] the kings of Israel.
15I will bring against you people who will ·take [possess; conquer] your land,
you who live in Mareshah [Csounds like Hebrew for "conqueror"].
The ·glory [or nobles; leaders] of Israel
will go in to Adullam [Cperhaps to hide in its caves].
16·Cut off your hair [Shave your head; Make yourself bald; Ca sign of mourning or sadness]
for the children ·you love [in whom you delight].
Make yourself bald like the eagle,
because your children will be taken away ·to a foreign land [in exile/captivity].

The Evil Plans of People

2 ·How terrible it will be for people [LWoe to those] who plan wickedness,
who lie on their beds and make evil plans.
When the morning light comes, they do what they planned,
because they have the power to do so.
2They ·want [covet] fields, so they take them;
they ·want [covet] houses, so they ·take them away [seize them].
They ·cheat [defraud; oppress] people to get their houses;
they rob them even of their ·property [inheritance].

3That is why the LORD says:
"Look, I am planning ·trouble [disaster] against such people,
·and you won't be able to save yourselves [Lfrom which you cannot
remove your necks; Clike a yoke].
You will no longer walk ·proudly [arrogantly],
because it will be a ·terrible time [time of calamity/catastrophe/evil].
4·At that time [LIn that day] people will ·make fun of [ridicule; sing a
taunt against] you
and ·sing this sad song [Llament with a lamentation] about you:
'We are completely ·ruined [destroyed];
the LORD has taken away my people's ·land [possession; inheritance].
Yes, he has taken it away from me
and divided our fields among ·our enemies [renegades; *or* the
traitors]!'"
5So you will have no one from the LORD's ·people [assembly]
to throw lots to divide the land.

Micah Is Asked Not to Prophesy

6The ·prophets [*or* preachers] say, "Don't ·prophesy [*or* preach] to us!
Don't ·prophesy [preach] about these things!
·Nothing to make us feel bad will happen [LDisgrace/Humiliation
will not overtake us]!"
7But I must say this, ·people [Lhouse] of Jacob:
·The LORD is becoming angry [*or* Does not the LORD grow
impatient…?] about what you have done.
·My words are welcome [*or* Are not my words good…?]
to the person who ·does what is right [Lwalks uprightly].
8But ·you are fighting against my people like an enemy [*or* my people
have risen up against me as an enemy].
You ·take the coats [strip off the rich robe] from people who pass by
peacefully;
·you plan war [*or* …like men returning from war].
9You have ·forced [cast out; evicted] the women of my people
from their ·nice [pleasant] houses;
you have taken my glory
from their children forever.
10·Get up [Arise] and leave.
This is not your place of rest anymore.
You have made this place ·unclean [defiled],
and it is doomed to destruction.
11·But you people want a false prophet
who will tell you nothing but lies
[LIf a man, coming as wind/spirit and lies,
should lie to you…].
You want one who ·promises to prophesy good things for you
if you give him wine and beer [*or* will prophesy wine and beer for you].
He's just the prophet for you.

The Lord Promises to Rescue His People

12"Yes, ·people of Jacob [LJacob], I will ·bring [assemble] all of you
together;
I will bring together ·all those left alive in [the remnant of] Israel.
I will put them together like sheep in a pen,
like a flock in its pasture;
the place will be filled with ·many people [*or* a noisy crowd].

13Someone will ·open the way [break out] and ·lead the people out [Lgo up before them].
The people will break through the gate and ·leave the city where they were held captive [Lgo out].
Their king will ·go out in front of [pass through before] them,
and the LORD will lead them."

The Leaders of Israel Are Guilty of Evil

3 Then I said,
"Listen, leaders of ·the people of Jacob [LJacob];
listen, you rulers of the ·nation [Lhouse] of Israel.
·You should [LShould you not…?] know ·how to decide cases fairly [justice],
2 but you hate good and love evil.
You skin my people alive
and tear the flesh off their bones.
3You ·eat [devour] my people's flesh
and skin them and break their bones;
you chop them up like meat for the pot,
like meat in a cooking pan.
4Then they will cry to the LORD,
but he won't answer them.
At that time he will hide his face from them,
because what they have done is evil."
5The LORD says this about the prophets who ·teach his people the
wrong way of living [mislead/lead astray my people]:
"If these prophets are given food to eat,
they shout, 'Peace!'
But if someone doesn't ·give them what they ask for [Lplace food in their mouths],
they ·call for a holy war [declare war] against that person.
6So it will become like night for them, without visions [Crevelation from God will cease].
It will become dark for them, without ·any way to tell the future [divination].
The sun is about to set for the prophets;
their day will become dark.
7The seers [Canother name for prophets] will be ashamed;
the ·people who see the future [diviners] will be ·embarrassed [disgraced; humiliated].
Yes, all of them will cover their ·mouths [*or* lips; *or* faces],
because there will be no answer from God."

Micah Is an Honest Prophet of God

8But I am filled with power,
with the Spirit of the LORD,
and with justice and ·strength [might],
to ·tell the people of Jacob [Ldeclare to Jacob] ·how they have turned against God [Lhis transgression],
and ·the people of Israel [LIsrael] how they have sinned.
9Leaders of [Lthe house of] Jacob and rulers of [Lthe house of] Israel,
listen to me,
you who hate ·fairness [justice]
and ·twist [pervert; distort] what is ·right [straight].
10You build ·Jerusalem [LZion; Cthe location of the Temple] ·by murdering people [Lwith bloodshed];

you build it with ·evil [wickedness; iniquity].
11Its ·judges take money
to decide who wins in court [Lrulers judge for a bribe].
Its priests only teach for ·pay [a price],
and its prophets ·only look into the future when they get paid [tell fortunes/practice divination for money].
But they lean on the LORD and say,
"The LORD is here with us,
so ·nothing bad [no harm] will ·happen to [overtake; come upon] us."
12 [LTherefore] Because of you,
Jerusalem will be plowed like a field.
·The city [LZion; v. 10] will become a ·pile of rocks [heap of rubble/ruins],
and the ·hill [mountain] ·on which the Temple stands [Lof the house] will be ·covered with bushes [an overgrown hill; wooded heights].

The Mountain of the Lord

4 In the last days
the mountain ·on which the LORD's Temple stands [Lof the house of the LORD]
will become the ·most important [Lhead] of all mountains.
It will be raised above the hills,
and people from other nations will come streaming to it.
2Many nations will come and say,
"Come, let us go up to the mountain of the LORD,
to the ·Temple [Lhouse] of the God of Jacob,
so that he can teach us his ways,
and we can ·obey his teachings [Lwalk in his paths]."
His ·teachings [instruction; law; LTorah] will go out from ·Jerusalem [LZion],
the word of the LORD from ·that city [LJerusalem].
3The Lord will ·judge [*or* arbitrate between] many nations;
he will ·make decisions about [settle disputes between] strong nations that are far away.
They will ·hammer [beat] their swords into ·plow blades [Tplowshares]
and their spears into ·hooks for trimming trees [pruning hooks; Is. 2:4; Joel 3:10].
Nations will no longer raise swords against other nations;
they will not train for war anymore.
4Everyone will sit under his own grapevine and fig tree [Csymbols of prosperity],
and no one will make him afraid,
because the LORD ·All-Powerful [Almighty; of Heaven's Armies; Tof hosts] has said it.
5All other nations ·may follow [Lwalk in the name of] their own gods,
but we will ·follow [Lwalk in the name of] the LORD our God forever and ever.
6The LORD says, "·At that time [LIn that day],
I will gather the ·crippled [lame];
I will ·bring together [assemble; gather] ·those who were sent away [the outcast/exile],
those whom I ·caused to have trouble [afflicted; filled with grief].
7I will ·keep alive those who were crippled [make the lame a remnant],

and I will make a strong nation of those who were ·sent away [outcasts; exiles].
The LORD will ·be their king [reign over them] in Mount Zion from now on and forever.
8And you, ·watchtower of the flocks [*or* Migdal-eder], ·hill [*or* stronghold] of ·Jerusalem [LDaughter Zion],
to you ·will come the kingdom [dominion will be restored] as in the past.
·Jerusalem [LDaughter Jerusalem], the ·right to rule [kingship; sovereignty] will come again to you."

Why the Israelites Must Go to Babylon

9Now, why do you cry so loudly?
·Is your king gone [Have you no king/King; Ceither a human king or God]?
Have you lost your ·helper [counselor; wise guide],
so that you are in pain, like a woman ·trying to give birth [in labor]?
10·People of Jerusalem [LDaughter Zion], ·strain and be in pain [writhe and groan].
Be like a woman ·trying to give birth [in labor],
because now you must leave the city
and live in the field.
You will go to Babylon,
but you will be ·saved [rescued] from that place.
The LORD will go there
and ·buy you back [redeem you] from [Lthe hand of] your enemies.

11But now many nations
have ·come to fight [gathered; assembled] against you,
saying, "·Let's destroy Jerusalem [LLet her be defiled/desecrated].
We will ·look at her and be glad we have defeated [gloat over; Llet our eye look upon] ·her [LZion]."
12But they don't know
·what the LORD is thinking [the thoughts of the LORD];
they don't understand his plan.
He has gathered them like ·bundles of grain [sheaves] to the threshing floor.

13"Get up and ·beat them [thresh], ·people of Jerusalem [Daughter Zion].
I will make you ·strong as if you had horns of iron [horns of iron]
and hoofs of bronze.
You will beat many nations into small pieces
and ·give [devote; consecrate] their ·wealth [gains; spoils] to the LORD,
their ·treasure [wealth] to the Lord of all the earth."

5 So, ·strong city [Ldaughter of troops], ·gather [marshal; muster] your ·soldiers [troops] together,
because we are ·surrounded and attacked [besieged].
They will ·hit [strike] the ·leader [ruler; judge] of Israel
·in the face [on the cheek] with a ·club [rod; *or* scepter].

The Ruler to Be Born in Bethlehem

2"But you, Bethlehem Ephrathah,
though you are ·too small to be [*or* small; insignificant] among the ·army groups from [clans of] Judah,

from you will come one who will rule Israel for me [Cthe Messiah; Is. 9:1–7; 11:1–16; Matt. 2:6].
·He comes [His origins are; LHis goings out are] from ·very old [ancient] times,
from days long ago."

3The LORD will ·give up [abandon] his people
until the one who is ·having a baby [in labor] gives birth;
then the rest of his ·relatives [brothers] will return
to the people of Israel.
4At that time ·the ruler of Israel [Lhe] will stand
and ·take care of his people [Lshepherd his flock]
with the LORD's strength
and with the ·power [majesty] of the name of the LORD his God.
·The Israelites [LThey] will live in safety,
because his greatness will reach ·all over [Lto the ends of] the earth.
5 He will ·bring [Lbe] peace.

Rescue and Punishment

·Assyria will surely [*or* When the Assyrians…; *or* If the Assyrians should…] come into our ·country [land]
and ·walk over [march through] our ·large buildings [fortresses].
We will ·set up [raise against them] seven shepherds [Csymbolic of completeness],
eight ·leaders [princes] of the people.
6They will ·destroy [*or* rule; shepherd] the Assyrians with their swords;
they will ·conquer [*or* rule; shepherd] the land of ·Assyria [LNimrod; Ca famous hunter, said to have founded Assyria; Gen. 10:8–9] ·with their swords drawn [*or* at its gates].
They will rescue us from the Assyrians when they come into our land,
when they ·walk [march] over our borders.

7Then the ·people of Jacob who are left alive [remnant of Jacob]
will be ·to other [Lin the midst of many] people
like dew from the LORD
or ·rain [showers] on the grass—
it does not wait for human beings;
it does not pause for ·any person [Lthe sons/children of man/Adam].
8·Those of Jacob's people who are left alive [The remnant of Jacob]
will be scattered among many nations and [Lin the midst of many] peoples.
They will be like a lion among the animals of the forest,
like a young lion in a flock of sheep:
As it goes, it jumps on them
and tears them to pieces,
and no one can ·save [rescue] them.
9So ·you will raise your fist in victory [Lyour hand will be lifted] over your ·enemies [adversaries],
and all your enemies will be ·destroyed [Lcut off].

10The LORD says, "·At that time [LIn that day],
I will ·take [Lcut off; destroy] your horses from you
and destroy your chariots.

[11]I will destroy the cities in your ·country [land]
and tear down all your ·defenses [strongholds; fortresses].
[12]I will ·take away [destroy] ·the magic charms you use [your sorcery/witchcraft]
so you will have no more fortune-tellers.
[13]I will destroy your ·statues of gods [carved images]
and the stone pillars you worship
so that you will no longer ·worship [bow down to]
what your hands have made.
[14]I will ·tear down [uproot your] ·Asherah idols [LAsherahs; Csacred trees or poles dedicated to the goddess Asherah] from you
and destroy your cities.
[15]In my anger and ·rage [wrath],
I will ·pay back [seek vengeance on] the nations that have not ·listened [obeyed]."

The Lord's Case

6 Now hear what the Lord says:
"Get up; plead ·your [*or* my] case in front of the mountains;
let the hills hear your ·story [Lvoice].
[2]Mountains, listen to the Lord's ·legal case [accusation; indictment].
·Strong [Enduring] foundations of the earth, listen.
The Lord has a ·legal case [accusation; indictment] against his people,
and he will ·accuse [contend with] Israel."

[3]He says, "My people, what did I do to you?
How ·did I make you tired of me [have I wearied you]?
·Tell [Answer] me.
[4]I brought you from the land of Egypt [Ex. 12:51]
and ·freed [redeemed] you from slavery;
I sent Moses, Aaron, and Miriam [Ex. 15:20] to you.
[5]My people, remember
the evil plans of Balak king of Moab [Num. 22:5]
and what Balaam son of Beor told Balak [Num. 22–24].
Remember what happened from Acacia to Gilgal [Josh. 3:1; 4:19–24]
so that you will know the ·Lord does what is right [righteousness/justice of the Lord]!"

[6]You say, "What can I bring with me
when I come before the Lord,
when I bow before ·God on high [the exalted God]?
Should I come before him with burnt offerings [Lev. 1:1–17],
with year-old calves?
[7]Will the Lord be pleased with a thousand ·male sheep [rams]?
Will he be pleased with ten thousand rivers of oil?
Should I give my ·first child [firstborn] for ·the evil I have done [my transgression]?
Should I give ·my very own child [Lthe fruit of my body] for ·my sin [Lthe sin of my soul]?"
[8]The Lord has told you, ·human [TO man], what is good;
he has told you what ·he wants [the Lord requires] from you:
to do what is ·right to other people [just],

love ·being kind to others [mercy; lovingkindness],
and ·live humbly, obeying [walk humbly with] your God.

9The voice of the LORD ·calls [cries out] to the city,
and ·the wise person [Lwisdom] ·honors him [Lsees/acknowledges his name].
So ·pay attention [listen] to the ·rod of punishment [Lrod];
pay attention to the One who ·threatens to punish [appointed it].
10Are there still in the wicked house
wicked treasures
and the cursed false measure?
11Can I forgive people who cheat others
with ·wrong [wicked] weights and [Ldeceptive] scales [Prov. 11:1]?
12The rich people of the city
·do cruel things [Lare full of violence].
Its people tell lies;
·they do not tell the truth [Ltheir tongues in their mouths are deceitful].
13As for me, I will make you sick.
I will ·attack [strike] you, ruining you because of your sins.
14You will eat, but you won't ·become full [be satisfied];
you will still be hungry and empty.
You will store up, but save nothing,
and what you store up, ·the sword will destroy [LI will give to the sword].
15You will plant,
but you won't harvest.
You will ·step on your [press; tread] olives,
but you won't ·get any oil from them [anoint yourself with oil].
You will ·crush [tread] the grapes,
but you will not drink the new wine.
16This is because you ·obey [keep; observe] the ·laws [statutes] of King Omri [Ca wicked king of Israel; 1 Kin. 16:25, 26]
and do all the things that Ahab's family does [Canother wicked king of Israel; 1 Kin. 16:30–33; 21:25, 26];
you follow their ·advice [*or* traditions; policies].
So I will ·let you be destroyed [make you a desolation].
The people in your city will be ·laughed at [taunted; La hissing],
and other nations will ·make fun of [mock] you.

The Evil That People Do

7 ·Poor [Woe to] me! I am like a hungry man,
and all the summer fruit has been picked—
there are no grapes left to eat,
none of the early figs I ·love [crave].
2All of the faithful people ·are gone [Lhave perished from the land/earth];
there is not one ·good [upright] person left in this country.
Everyone ·is waiting to kill someone [Llies in wait for blood];
everyone ·is trying to trap someone else [Lhunts his brother with a net].
3With both hands they are doing evil.
Rulers ask for ·money [gifts],
and judges' decisions are bought for a ·price [bribe].
·Rich [Influential; Great] people ·tell what they want [make demands],
and they get it.

[4]Even the best of them is like a ·thornbush [brier];
the most ·honest [upright] of them is worse than a ·prickly plant [thorn hedge].
The day ·that your watchmen warned you about [Lof your watchmen; Cthe coming exile predicted by the prophets] has come.
Now they will be confused [Cwithout the guidance of the prophets].
[5]Don't ·believe [trust] your neighbor
or ·trust [put confidence in] a friend.
·Don't say anything [LGuard the doors of your mouth],
even to ·your wife [Lthe one who lies on your bosom].
[6]A son will not honor his father,
a daughter will ·turn against [defy; rise up against] her mother,
and a daughter-in-law will be against her mother-in-law;
a person's enemies will be ·members of his own family [*or* the servants of his household; Lthe men/people of his house; Matt. 10:36].

The Lord's Kindness

[7]Israel says, "I will look to the LORD for help.
I will wait for God ·to save me [my savior];
my God will hear me.
[8]Enemy, don't ·laugh at [gloat over] me.
I have fallen, but I will get up again.
I sit in ·the shadow of trouble now [Ldarkness],
but the LORD will be a light for me.
[9]I sinned against the LORD,
so ·he was angry with me [LI will bear the wrath of the LORD],
but he will ·defend my case in court [plead my case].
He will ·bring about what is right [accomplish justice] for me.
Then he will bring me out into the light,
and I will see ·him set things right [his righteousness/justice/vindication].
[10]Then my enemies will see this,
and they will be ·ashamed [Lcovered wth shame],
those who said to me,
'Where is the LORD your God?'
I will ·look down on [gloat over] them.
They will ·get walked on [be trampled down], like mud in the street."

Israel Will Return

[11]The ·time [Lday] will come when your walls will be built again,
when your ·country will grow [borders will be extended].
[12]·At that time [LIn that day] your people will come back to you
from Assyria and the cities of Egypt,
and from Egypt to the ·Euphrates River [LRiver],
and from sea to sea and mountain to mountain.
[13]The earth will be ·ruined [desolate] ·for [*or* because of] the people who live in it
·because [Lfor the fruit] of their deeds.

A Prayer to God

[14]So shepherd your people with your ·stick [shepherd's staff];
tend the flock of ·people who belong to you [Lyour inheritance/possession].
That flock now lives alone in the forest
in the middle of ·a garden land [pasturelands; *or* Carmel].

Let them ·feed [graze] in Bashan and Gilead
as in days long ago.

15"As in the days when I brought you out of Egypt,
I will show them ·miracles [wonders]."

16When the nations see those miracles,
they will ·no longer brag [be ashamed/disappointed] about their power.
They will put their hands over their mouths,
·refusing to listen [and their ears will be deaf].
17They will ·crawl in the [Llick] dust like a snake,
like ·insects crawling [*or* serpents; Lcrawling things] on the ground.
They will come trembling from their ·holes [*or* strongholds] to the
LORD our God
and will turn in fear before you.
18There is no God like you.
You forgive those who are guilty of sin;
you ·don't look at the sins [pass over the transgressions] of ·your people
who are left alive [Lthe remnant of your inheritance].
You will not stay angry forever,
because you ·enjoy [delight in] ·being kind [mercy; lovingkindness].
19You will have ·mercy [compassion] on us again;
you will conquer our sins.
You will ·throw away [hurl; cast] all our sins
into the ·deepest part [depths] of the sea.
20You will be ·true [faithful] to ·the people of Jacob [LJacob],
and you will ·be kind [show mercy/lovingkindness] to ·the people of
Abraham [LAbraham]
as you promised to our ·ancestors [fathers] long ago.

NAHUM

1 **This is the ·message** [oracle; burden] **for the city of Nineveh** [Cthe capital of the Assyrian empire]**. This is the book of the vision of Nahum, ·who was from the town of Elkosh** [Lthe Elkoshite; Cof uncertain location]**.**

The Lord Is Angry with Nineveh

[2]**The LORD is a ·jealous** [zealous] **God** [Ex. 20:5; 34:14; Deut. 4:24; 5:9; Josh. 24:19] **who ·punishes** [avenges];
the LORD ·punishes [avenges] **and is filled with ·anger** [wrath].
The LORD ·punishes [takes vengeance on] **·those who are against him** [his adversaries/enemies],
and he ·stays angry with [*or* vents his wrath against] **his enemies.**
[3]**The LORD ·does not become angry quickly** [Lis slow to anger; Ex. 34:6; Num. 14:18; Neh. 9:17; Ps. 86:15; 145:8; Joel 2:13; Jon. 4:2],
and his power is great.
The LORD will not let the guilty go unpunished.
·Where the LORD goes, there are [LHis way/path is in] **whirlwinds and storms,**
and the clouds are the dust beneath his feet [CGod's awesome power is seen in nature; the clouds are his chariot; Ps. 68:4; 104:3; Dan. 7:13; Matt. 24:30; 26:64; Rev. 1:7].
[4]**He ·speaks to** [rebukes] **the sea and makes it dry** [Ps. 106:9; Matt. 8:26; Luke 8:24];
he dries up all the rivers.
The areas of Bashan and Carmel dry up,
and the ·flowers [blossoms] **of Lebanon dry up** [Careas known for their lush vegetation and fertile land].
[5]**The mountains ·shake** [tremble] **in front of him,**
and the hills melt.
The earth ·trembles [heaves] **·when he comes** [before him],
the world and all who live in it.
[6]**·No one** [LWho…?] **can ·stay alive** [withstand/stand before] **·when he is angry** [his indignation/anger];
no one can ·survive [endure] **his ·strong** [fierce; burning] **anger.**
His ·anger [wrath] **is poured out like fire;**
the rocks ·are smashed by [crumble before] **him.**

[7]**The LORD is good,**
·giving protection [a stronghold; refuge] **in ·times** [Lthe day] **of trouble.**
He ·knows [cares for] **those who trust in him.**

[8]But like a ·rushing [overwhelming] **flood,**
he will ·completely destroy [make an end of] **·Nineveh** [her place; [C]Nineveh was destroyed in 612 BC, after Nahum wrote];
he will ·chase [pursue] **his enemies ·until he kills them** [into darkness].

[9]**The LORD will completely destroy**
·anyone making plans [*or* whatever you plot/conspire] **against him.**
Trouble will not come a second time.
[10]**Those people will be ·like tangled** [*or* entangled among] **thorns**
or like people drunk from their wine;
they will be ·burned up quickly [consumed] **like ·dry weeds** [stubble].
[11]**Someone has come from ·Nineveh** [[L]you]
who ·makes evil plans [plots evil] **against the LORD**
and gives wicked ·advice [counsel; strategy].
[12]**This is what the LORD says:**
"Although Assyria ·is strong [*or* has allies] **and has many people,**
it will be ·defeated [destroyed] **and ·brought to an end** [pass away].
Although I have ·made you suffer, Judah [[L]afflicted you],
I will ·make you suffer [afflict you] **no more.**
[13]**Now I will ·free you from their control** [[L]break his yoke from you]
and tear away your ·chains [shackles]."

[14]**The LORD has given you this command, Nineveh:**
"You will not have ·descendants [[L]seed] **to carry on your name.**
I will ·destroy [[L]cut off] **the ·idols** [carved images] **and metal images**
that are in the ·temple [[L]house] **of your gods.**
I will ·make [prepare] **a grave for you,**
because you are ·wicked [vile; despicable]."

[15]**Look, there on the ·hills** [mountains],
·someone is [[L]the feet of one] **bringing good news** [Is. 52:7]!
He is announcing peace!
Celebrate your ·feasts [festivals], **people of Judah,**
and ·give your promised sacrifices to God [[L]fulfill your vows].
The wicked will not come to attack you again;
they have been completely ·destroyed [[L]cut off].

Nineveh Will Be Defeated

2 **The ·destroyer** [attacker; scatterer] **is coming ·to attack** [against] **·you,**
Nineveh [[L]you; [C]the Babylonians and Medes destroyed Nineveh].
Guard the ·defenses [fortress; ramparts].
Watch the road.
·Get ready [[T]Gird your loins].
Gather all your strength!
[2]**·Destroyers** [Plunderers] **have ·destroyed** [plundered] **God's people**
and ruined their vines,
but the LORD will ·bring back [restore] **Jacob's ·greatness** [splendor; majesty]
like Israel's ·greatness [splendor; majesty].

[3]**The shields of his soldiers are red** [[C]either dyed red or splattered with blood];
the army is dressed in ·red [scarlet].
The metal on the chariots ·flashes like fire [shines; glistens]

·when [Lon the day] they are ready to attack;
·their horses are excited [*or* their cypress spears are brandished].
4The chariots ·race [storm; charge insanely] through the streets
and rush back and forth through the city squares.
They look like torches;
they run like lightning.

5He [Cprobably the king of Assyria] ·calls [*or* remembers] his officers,
but they stumble on the way.
They hurry to the city wall,
and the ·shield [*or* siege tower] is put into place.
6The river gates are thrown open,
and the palace ·is destroyed [collapses; dissolves; melts].
7It has been ·announced [decreed] that ·the people of Nineveh [Lshe]
will be ·captured [exiled; *or* stripped; exposed] and carried away.
The slave girls moan like doves
and beat their breasts [Ca sign of grief].
8Nineveh is like a pool,
and now its water is draining away.
"Stop! Stop!" the people yell,
but no one turns back.
9·Take [Plunder] the silver!
·Take [Plunder] the gold!
There is no end to the treasure—
piles of wealth of every ·kind [precious/desirable thing].
10·Nineveh is robbed [LEmpty!], ·ruined [desolate!], and destroyed.
·The people lose their courage [LTheir hearts melt], and their knees knock.
·Stomachs ache [Bodies/Loins in anguish], and everyone's face grows pale.

11Where is the lions' den [Cthe lion was a symbol of Assyria]
and the place where they feed their young?
Where did the lion, lioness, and cubs go
without being afraid?
12The lion killed enough for his cubs,
·enough [Land strangled prey] for his ·mate [Llionesses].
He filled his cave with ·the animals he caught [prey];
he filled his den with ·meat he had killed [Ltorn (flesh)].

13"I am against ·you, Nineveh [Lyou],"
says the LORD ·All-Powerful [Almighty; of Heaven's Armies; Tof hosts].
"I will burn up your chariots in smoke,
and the sword will ·kill [devour] your young lions.
I will ·stop you from hunting down others on [Lcut off your prey from] the earth,
and your messengers' voices
will no longer be heard."

It Will Be Terrible for Nineveh

3 ·How terrible it will be for [LWoe to] the city ·that has killed so many [Lof blood].
It is full of lies
and ·goods stolen from other countries [plunder].

It is ·always killing somebody [Lnever empty of prey].
2Hear the sound of whips
and the ·noise [rumble; shaking] of the wheels.
Hear horses galloping
and chariots bouncing along!
3·Horses [Cavalry; Horsemen] are charging,
swords are ·shining [flashing],
spears are gleaming!
Many are ·dead [slain];
their bodies are piled up—
too many to count.
People stumble over the dead bodies.
4·The city was like a prostitute [For her many acts of prostitution];
she was ·charming [graceful] and a ·lover of magic [Lmistress of sorceries].
She made nations slaves with her prostitution
and her ·witchcraft [sorcery; charms].

5"I am against ·you, Nineveh [Lyou]," says the Lord ·All-Powerful [Almighty; of Heaven's Armies; Tof hosts].
"I will pull your dress up over your face
and show the nations your nakedness
and the kingdoms your shame [Cthe punishment of a prostitute in the ancient Near East].
6I will throw filthy garbage on you
and ·make a fool of you [treat you with contempt].
I will make ·people stare at you [you a spectacle].
7Everyone who sees you will ·run away [or turn away in disgust] and say,
'Nineveh is in ruins. Who will ·cry [grieve; lament] for her?'
Nineveh, where will I find anyone to comfort you?"

8You are no better than ·Thebes [LNo Amon; Cmeaning "city of (the god) Amon"; This capital of Upper Egypt, thought to be impregnable, was destroyed by the Assyrians in 663 BC),
who sits by the Nile River
with water all around her.
The river was her ·defense [rampart];
the waters were like a wall around her.
9Cush [Cancient Ethiopia or Nubia] and Egypt gave her endless strength;
Put and Libya supported her [Cneighboring countries allied with Egypt].
10But Thebes was captured
and went into ·captivity [exile].
Her ·small children [infants] were ·beaten to death [dashed to pieces]
at every street corner.
Lots were thrown for her ·important men [nobles; Cparceled out as slaves],
and all of her ·leaders [great ones] were put in chains.

11You [CNineveh] will be drunk, too.
You will hide;
you will ·look for a place safe [seek refuge] from the enemy.

12All your ·defenses [fortresses] are like fig trees with ripe fruit.
When the tree is shaken, the figs fall into the mouth of the eater.
13Look at your soldiers.
They are all women [Cmeaning helpless or physically weak]!
The gates of your land
are wide open for your enemies;
fire has ·burned [consumed; devoured] the bars of your gates.

14·Get enough water before the long war begins [Draw water for the siege].
Make your defenses strong!
Get mud,
mix clay,
·make bricks [strengthen the brickwork]!
15There the fire will ·burn you up [consume/devour you].
The sword will ·kill you [cut you down];
·like grasshoppers eating crops, the battle will completely destroy you [it will devour you like locusts].
Grow in number like ·hopping [*or* young] locusts;
grow in number like ·swarming [*or* flying] locusts!
16Your ·traders [merchants] are more than the stars in the sky,
but like locusts they ·strip the land [*or* shed their skin] and then fly away.
17Your guards are like locusts.
Your officers are like swarms of locusts
that ·hang [settle; encamp] on the walls on a cold day.
When the sun comes up, they fly away,
and no one knows where they have gone.
18King of Assyria, your ·rulers [Lshepherds] are asleep;
your ·important men [nobles; officers] lie down ·to rest [*or* dead].
Your people have been scattered on the mountains [Clike sheep],
and there is no one to ·bring them back [gather them].
19Nothing can heal your wound;
your ·injury [wound] ·will not heal [is fatal].
Everyone who hears ·about you applauds [will clap their hands over you],
because ·everyone has [Lwho has not…?] felt your endless cruelty.

HABAKKUK

1 This is the ·message [oracle; burden] Habakkuk the prophet received.

Habakkuk Complains

2LORD, how long must I ·ask [cry; call] for help
and you ·ignore [do not hear] me?
I cry out to you ·about violence [*or* "Violence!"],
but you do not ·save [rescue] us!
3Why do you make me see ·wrong things [evil; iniquity; injustice]
and make me look at ·trouble [wrongdoing]?
·People are destroying things and hurting others [LDestruction and violence are] in front of me;
·they are arguing and fighting [Lstrife and conflict arise].
4So the ·teachings [law; instruction; LTorah] are ·weak [paralyzed],
and justice never comes.
Evil people ·gain while good people lose [Lsurround/hem in the righteous];
·the judges no longer make fair decisions [Lso justice is perverted].

The Lord Answers

5"Look at the nations!
Watch them and be ·amazed and shocked [utterly astounded].
I will do something in your ·lifetime [Ldays]
that you won't believe even when you are told about it.
6I will ·use [raise up] the ·Babylonians [LChaldeans],
those ·cruel [ruthless; bitter] and ·wild [impetuous; hasty] people
who march across the earth
and ·take lands [Lseize dwellings] that don't belong to them.
7They scare and ·frighten [terrify] people.
·They do what they want to do
and are good only to themselves [LTheir justice/judgment and dignity proceed from themselves].
8Their horses are faster than leopards
and ·quicker [fiercer] than wolves ·at sunset [Lof the evening].
Their ·horse soldiers [cavalry] attack quickly;
they come from places far away.
They attack quickly, like an ·eagle [*or* vulture] ·swooping down for food [swift to devour].
9They all come ·to fight [Lfor violence].
·Nothing can stop them [*or* …a horde moving like an east wind; *or* … their faces set forward].
Their prisoners are ·as many as the grains of [Llike] sand.
10They ·laugh at [mock] kings
and make fun of rulers.

They laugh at all the ·strong, walled [fortified] cities
and build ·dirt piles to the top of the walls [earthen siege ramps] to capture them.
11Then they ·leave [sweep by] like the wind and move on.
They are guilty of ·worshiping their own strength [making their strength their god; *or* ascribing their strength to their gods]."

Habakkuk Complains Again

12LORD, ·you live forever [Lare you not from everlasting…?],
my God, my holy God.
We will not die.
LORD, you ·have chosen the Babylonians to punish people [appointed them for judgment];
our Rock [Ps. 61:2], you picked them to punish.
13Your eyes are too ·good [pure] to look at evil;
you cannot ·stand to see [tolerate; look on] those who do wrong.
So how can you put up with those ·evil [treacherous] people?
How can you be quiet when the wicked swallow up people who are ·better [more righteous] than they are?
14You ·treat [*or* made] people like fish in the sea,
like sea animals without a ·leader [ruler].
15·The enemy [LHe] brings them in with hooks.
He catches them in his net
and ·drags [gathers] them in his ·fishnet [dragnet].
So he rejoices and ·sings for joy [is glad].
16The enemy offers sacrifices to his net
and burns incense to ·worship it [Lhis dragnet],
because it lets him live ·like the rich [in luxury]
and enjoy ·the best [*or* plentiful] food.
17Will he keep on ·taking riches with [Lemptying] his net?
Will he go on destroying ·people [nations] without showing mercy?

2 I will stand like a guard to watch
and ·place [station] myself at the tower.
I will wait to see what he will say to me;
I will wait to learn how ·God will answer [*or* I will answer concerning] my complaint.

The Lord Answers

2The LORD answered me:
"Write down the vision;
write it ·clearly [plainly] on clay tablets
so whoever reads it can run to tell others.
3·It is not yet time for the message to come true [LFor the vision awaits an appointed time],
·but that time is coming soon [it hastens to the end; *or* it speaks about the end];
the message will ·come true [not lie].
·It may seem like a long time,
but [Though it tarries/lingers] be patient and wait for it,
because it will surely come;
it will not be delayed.
4[LLook; TBehold] ·The evil nation [LHe] is ·very proud of itself [puffed up];
·it [Lhis soul] is not ·living as it should [upright].
But ·those who are right with God [the righteous] will live ·by faith [*or* because of their faithfulness; Rom. 1:17; Gal. 3:11; Heb. 10:38].

5"Just as wine ·can trick [betrays] a person,
those who are too proud will not ·last, [have rest; settle down]
·because their desire is like a grave's desire for death [Lhe opens wide his throat like Sheol; Cthe grave or the underworld],
and like death they always want more.
They gather other nations for themselves
and collect for themselves all the ·countries [peoples].
6But all ·the nations the Babylonians have hurt [Lthese] will ·laugh at [taunt] them.
They will ·make fun of the Babylonians [ridicule with riddles]
and say, '·How terrible it will be for [LWoe to] the one that ·steals many things [Lpiles up what is not his].
How long will that nation get rich by ·forcing others to pay them [extortion; goods taken in pledge]?'

7"·One day the people from whom you have taken money will [LWill not your creditors…?] turn against you.
They will ·realize what is happening [Lwake up] and make you shake with fear.
Then ·they will take everything you have [Lyou will become their plunder].
8Because you have ·stolen from [plundered] many nations,
those who are left will ·take much from [plunder] you.
·This is because you have killed many people [For the human blood you have shed],
·destroying [violently attacking] countries and cities and everyone in them.

9"·How terrible it will be for the nation [LWoe to him] that ·becomes rich by doing wrong [builds his house with unjust gain; *or* acquires evil gain for his own house],
thinking they will ·live in a safe place [Lset his nest on high]
and escape ·harm [Lthe hand of evil].
10Because you have ·made plans [plotted; schemed] to ·destroy [Lcut off] many people,
you have brought shame to your house.
Because of it, you will ·lose your lives [forfeit your soul/life].
11The stones of the walls [Cof the "house" of Babylon] will cry out against you,
and the ·boards that support the roof [beams of the woodwork] will ·agree that you are wrong [echo the complaint; Lanswer back].

12"·How terrible it will be for the nation [LWoe to him] that ·kills people [uses bloodshed] to build a city,
that ·wrongs others [uses injustice] to start a town.
13[LLook; TBehold] The LORD ·All-Powerful [Almighty; of Heaven's Armies; Tof hosts] will send fire
to destroy what those people have built;
all the nations' ·work [weariness] will be for nothing.
14Then, just as water covers the sea,
·people everywhere will know [Lthe earth will be filled with the knowledge of] the LORD's glory.

15"·How terrible for the nation that [LWoe to him who] makes its
neighbors drink,
pouring ·from the jug of wine [*or* out your wrath] until they are drunk
so that it can look at their naked bodies.
16·You Babylonians [LYou] will be filled with ·disgrace [shame], not
·respect [glory].
It's your turn to drink and ·fall to the ground [*or* expose your
uncircumcision] like a drunk person.
The ·cup of anger [Lcup; Jer. 25:15–29] from the LORD's right hand is
coming around to you.
You will receive ·disgrace [shame], not ·respect [glory].
17You ·hurt many people [did violence] in Lebanon,
but now you will be ·hurt [overwhelmed by it].
You killed many animals there,
and now you must be afraid
because of ·what you did [the blood and violence you did]
to that land, those cities, and the people who lived in them.

The Message About Idols

18"·An idol does no good [LWhat value does an idol have…?], because a
human made it;
it is only a ·statue [metal image] that teaches lies.
The one who made it ·expects his own work to help him [trusts in his
own creation],
but he makes idols that can't even speak!
19·How terrible it will be for [LWoe to] the one who says to a wooden
statue, '·Come to life [Wake up]!'
·How terrible it will be for [LWoe to] the one who says to a silent
stone, '·Get up [Arise]!'
It cannot ·tell you what to do [teach/guide us].
It is only a statue covered with gold and silver;
there is no ·life [breath] in it.
20The LORD is in his Holy Temple;
all the earth should be silent ·in his presence [before him]."

Habakkuk's Prayer

3 This is the prayer of Habakkuk the prophet, on shigionoth
[Cprobably a literary or musical term].
2LORD, I have heard the ·news [report] about you;
I am ·amazed [in awe; afraid] at what you have done.
LORD, do great things once again in ·our time [Lthe midst of the years];
make ·those things happen again [Lthem known] in ·our own days
[Lthe midst of the years].
Even when you are angry,
remember to be ·kind [compassionate].

3God is coming from Teman [Cnear Edom, south of Israel];
the Holy One comes from Mount Paran [Con the Sinai peninsula south
of Israel; the language recalls God's revelation at Mount Sinai;
Deut. 33:2]. *Selah*
His glory covers the ·skies [heavens],
and his praise fills the earth.
4He is like ·a bright light [flashing lightning; *or* brightness at dawn].
Rays of light ·shine [flash] from his hand,
and there he hides his power.

5·Sickness [Plague] goes before him,
and ·disease [pestilence] follows ·behind him [Lat his feet].
6He stands and ·shakes [*or* measures] the earth.
He looks, and the nations ·shake [*or* jump] with fear.
The ·mountains, which stood for ages, [eternal mountains] ·break into pieces [crumble];
the ·old [age-old; everlasting] hills ·fall [sink] down.
·God has always done this [Ancient paths/ways are his].

7I saw that the tents of Cushan [Clocated in southern Transjordan] were in ·trouble [distress]
and that the ·tents [curtains] of the land of Midian trembled [Ex. 15:14–16; Josh. 2:9–10].
8Lord, were you angry at the rivers,
or ·were you angry at [was your wrath against] the streams?
Were you ·angry [enraged] with the sea
when you rode your horses and chariots of victory?
9You ·uncovered [pulled out; brandished] your bow
and commanded many arrows to be brought to you. *Selah*
You split the earth with rivers.
10The mountains saw you and ·shook with fear [writhed; trembled].
The ·rushing [raging; torrents of] water ·flowed [swept by].
The ·sea [deep] ·made a loud noise [shouted; roared],
and ·its waves rose high [Llifted its hands high].
11The sun and moon stood still in ·the sky [Llofty dwelling place];
they stopped when they saw the flash of your flying arrows
and the ·gleam [glint] of your ·shining [flashing] spear.
12In ·anger [indignation] you marched on the earth;
in anger you ·punished [trampled; threshed] the nations.
13You came out to ·save [rescue] your people,
to save your ·chosen one [anointed].
You crushed the ·leader [head] of the ·wicked ones [Lhouse of the wicked]
and ·took everything he had [lay him bare], from ·head to toe [Lfoundation to neck]. *Selah*
14With the enemy's own ·spear [*or* arrows] you ·stabbed the leader of his army [Lpierced his head; *or* pierced the heads of his soldiers/warriors].
His ·soldiers [warriors] rushed out like a storm to scatter us.
·They were happy [Rejoicing; Shouting with joy]
as they were ·robbing [plundering] the poor people in secret.
15But you ·marched through [trampled on] the sea with your horses,
stirring the great waters.

16I hear these things, and my body trembles;
my lips ·tremble [quiver] when I hear the sound.
My bones ·feel weak [Lrot away],
and my legs shake.

But I will wait patiently for the day of ·disaster [calamity]
that will come to the people who ·attack [invade] us.
17Fig trees may not ·grow figs [Lblossom; bud],
and there may be no grapes on the vines.

·There may be no olives growing [[L]The produce of the olive fails/
disappoints]
and no food growing in the fields.
There may be no sheep in the ·pens [fold]
and no cattle in the ·barns [stalls].
18But I will still ·be glad [rejoice] in the LORD;
I will ·rejoice [be joyful] in God my Savior.
19The Lord GOD is my strength.
He makes ·me like a deer that does not stumble [[L]my feet like a deer's]
so I can walk on the ·steep mountains [heights].
For the director of music. On my stringed instruments.

ZEPHANIAH

1 **This is the word of the LORD that came through Zephaniah while Josiah** [[C]ruled 640–609 BC] **son of Amon was king of Judah. Zephaniah was the son of Cushi, who was the son of Gedaliah. Gedaliah was the son of Amariah, who was the son of Hezekiah.**

The Lord's Judgment

2**“I will sweep away everything**
from the [[L]face of the] **earth,” says the LORD.**
3**“I will sweep away the people and animals;**
I will ·destroy [sweep away] **the birds in the air**
and the fish of the sea.
I will ·ruin the evil people [reduce the wicked to rubble; [L]destroy the stumbling blocks with the wicked],
and I will remove human beings from the [[L]face of the] **earth,” says the LORD.**

The Future of Judah

4**“I will ·punish** [[L]stretch out my hand against] **Judah**
and all the people living in Jerusalem.
I will remove from this place
·all signs [every trace; the remnant] **of Baal, ·the** [every memory of; [L]the names of] **·false** [idolatrous] **priests, and the other priests.**
5**I will destroy those who ·worship** [bow down to]
the ·stars [starry host; host of heaven] **from the roofs** [[C]roofs were flat and used for living space],
and those who ·worship [bow down] **and ·make promises** [swear oaths]
by both the LORD and the god ·Molech [*or* Malkam; *or* the king],
6**and those who turned away from the LORD,**
and those who quit following the LORD and ·praying to him for direction [[L]seeking or inquiring of him].
7**Be silent before the Lord GOD,**
because the ·LORD's day for judging people [[L]day of the LORD; Is. 13:6, 9; Jer. 46:10; Joel 2:1, 11, 31; Amos 5:18–20; Zech. 14:1] **is ·coming soon** [near].
The LORD has prepared a sacrifice;
he has ·made holy [consecrated] **his invited guests.**
8**On the day of the LORD's sacrifice,**
I, the LORD, will punish the ·princes [officials] **and the king's sons**
and all those who wear foreign clothes [[C]indicating adoption of pagan culture and religion].
9**On that day I will punish those who ·worship Dagon** [[L]leap over the threshold; [C]thought to be part of worship of the Philistine god Dagon; 1 Sam. 5:5],

those who fill the ·temple [[L]house] of their ·gods [*or* king; [L]master]
with violence and deceit.

10"On that day," says the LORD,
"a cry will be heard at the Fish Gate.
A wail will come from the ·new area of the city [[L]Second Quarter],
and a loud crash will echo from the hills.
11·Cry [Wail], you people living in ·the market area [*or* the lower town; *or* Mortar; [C]possibly a place name],
because all the merchants will ·be dead [be destroyed; *or* disappear];
all the silver traders will be ·gone [[L]cut off].
12At that time I, the LORD, will search Jerusalem with lamps.
I will punish those who are ·satisfied with themselves [complacent; *or* entrenched in sin; [L]thickened in their dregs/sediment],
who think, 'The LORD won't ·help us or punish us [[L]do good or evil].'
13Their wealth will be ·stolen [plundered]
and their houses ·destroyed [ruined; laid waste].
They may build houses,
but they will not live in them.
They may plant vineyards,
but they will not drink any wine from them.

The Lord's Day of Judging

14"The ·LORD's day of judging [great day of the LORD; 1:7] is ·coming soon [near];
it is near and coming fast.
The cry will be ·very sad [bitter] on the day of the LORD;
·even soldiers will cry [*or* soldiers will shout a battle cry].
15That day will be a day of ·anger [wrath],
a day of ·terror [distress] and ·trouble [anguish],
a day of ·destruction [devastation] and ruin,
a day of darkness and gloom,
a day of clouds and blackness,
16a day of ·alarms [trumpet blasts; [L]a ram's horn] and battle cries.
·'Attack [*or* …against] the ·strong, walled [fortified] cities!
·Attack [*or* …against] the corner towers!'
17I will ·make life hard [bring distress] on ·the people [*or* humanity];
they will ·walk [grope] around like the blind,
because they have sinned against the LORD.
Their blood will be poured out like dust,
and their ·insides [flesh] will be dumped like ·trash [refuse; dung].
18On the day ·that God will show his anger [[L]of the LORD's wrath],
neither their silver nor gold will save them.
·The LORD's anger will be like a fire [[L]In the fire of his jealousy; Nah. 1:2]
that will ·burn up [consume; devour] the whole world;
suddenly he will bring an end, yes, an end
to ·everyone on [all who live on] earth."

The Lord Asks People to Change

2 Gather together, gather,
you ·unwanted [shameful; undesirable] people.
2Do it before ·it's too late [[L]the decree takes effect],
before ·you are blown away like chaff [*or* the day passes like chaff],
before the LORD's ·terrible [fierce; burning] anger reaches you,

before the day of the LORD's anger comes to you.
3·Come to [Seek] the LORD, all you who are ·not proud [humble; meek],
who obey his ·laws [commands].
·Do what is right [Seek righteousness]. ·Learn [Seek] to be humble.
Maybe you will ·escape [be protected; [L]be hidden]
on the day the LORD shows his anger.

Philistia Will Be Punished

4·No one will be left in the city of Gaza [[L]Gaza will be abandoned; [C]Gaza
sounds like Hebrew for "abandoned"; all four of these were cities
in Philistia],
and the city of Ashkelon will be ·destroyed [desolated; a heap of ruins].
Ashdod will be empty by noon,
and the people of Ekron will be ·chased away [[L]uprooted; [C]Ekron
sounds like Hebrew for "uprooted"].
5·How terrible it will be for [[L]Woe to] you who live by the
·Mediterranean Sea [[L]sea],
you ·Philistines [[L]nation of Cerethites; [C]either another name for the
Philistines or a neighboring people group; the name suggests they
came from the island of Crete; 2 Sam. 8:18; Ezek. 25:16]!
The word of the LORD is against you,
Canaan, land of the Philistines.

"I will destroy you
so that no ·one [inhabitant] will be left."
6The land by the ·Mediterranean Sea, in which you live [[L]sea],
will become pastures, ·fields [*or* shelters; *or* having wells] for
shepherds, and pens for ·sheep [flocks].
7It will ·belong to [[L]be for] the ·descendants of Judah who are left alive
[[L]remnant of the house of Judah].
There they will ·let their sheep eat grass [graze; find pasture].
At night they will ·sleep [lay down]
in the houses of Ashkelon.
The LORD their God will ·pay attention to [care for] them
and will ·make their life good again [restore their fortunes; *or* return
their exiles].

Moab and Ammon Will Be Punished

8"I have heard the ·insults [taunts] of Moab[[C]the country]
and the ·threats [insults; reproach] of the ·people [[L]sons/descendants]
of Ammon.
They have ·insulted [taunted] my people
and ·have taken [*or* harrassed; threatened; *or* boasted about] their
·land [borders]."
9So the LORD ·All-Powerful [Almighty; of Heaven's Armies; [T]of hosts],
the God of Israel, says,
"As surely as I live,
Moab will ·be destroyed [[L]become] like Sodom,
and ·Ammon [[L]the sons/descendant of Ammon] will ·be destroyed
[become] like Gomorrah [[C]two cities destroyed for their great
wickedness; Gen. 19]—
a heap of weeds, a pit of salt,
and a ·ruin [wasteland] forever.
·Those of my people who are left alive [The remnant of my people]
will ·take whatever they want from [plunder] them;

·those who are left from my nation [the survivors] will ·take their
land [[L]inherit/possess them]."

10This is what Moab and Ammon get for being proud,
because they ·insulted [taunted] and ·made fun of [boasted against]
the people of the Lord ·All-Powerful [Almighty; of Heaven's
Armies; [T]of hosts].
11The Lord will ·frighten [terrify; be awesome against] them,
because he will ·destroy [*or* weaken; *or* starve] all the gods of the earth.
Then everyone in ·faraway places [*or* the coastlands of the nations]
will ·worship [bow down to] him wherever they are.

Cush and Assyria Will Be Destroyed

12"You ·Cushites [Ethiopians] also
will be ·killed [slain] by my sword."
13Then the Lord will ·turn [[L]stretch out his hand] against the north
and destroy Assyria.
He will make Nineveh
a ·ruin [desolation] as dry as a desert.
14Flocks and herds will lie down there,
and all ·wild animals [kinds of beasts].
The ·owls [horned owls; *or* pelicans] and ·crows [*or* screech owls; *or*
hedgehogs] will sit
on ·the stone pillars [her columns/capitals].
The owl will hoot through the windows,
·trash [rubble; devastation] will be in the ·doorways [thresholds],
and the ·wooden boards [cedar work] of the buildings will be ·gone
[*or* exposed].
15This is the ·happy [boisterous; exultant] and ·safe [secure] city
that ·thinks [[L]said in her heart] ·there is no one else as strong as it is
[[L]"I am it, and there is no one besides me"].
But what a ruin it will be,
a place where wild animals live.
All those who pass by will ·make fun [scoff; [L]hiss]
and shake their fists.

Jerusalem Will Be Punished

3 ·How terrible for [[L]Woe to] the ·wicked, stubborn [rebellious and
polluted/defiled] ·city of Jerusalem [[L]city],
which ·hurts its own people [oppresses].
2It obeys no voice;
it ·can't be taught to do right [receives/accepts no correction].
It doesn't trust the Lord;
it doesn't ·worship [[L]draw near to] its God.
3Its ·officers [princes] are like roaring lions.
Its ·rulers [*or* judges] are ·like hungry wolves that attack in the
evening [[L]evening wolves],
and in the morning ·nothing is left of those they attacked [[L]there is
no gnawing].
4Its prophets are proud;
they are ·people who cannot be trusted [treacherous people].
Its priests ·don't respect [profane] ·holy things [*or* the sanctuary];
they ·break [[L]do violence to] God's ·teachings [law; [L]Torah].
5But the Lord is ·good [righteous; just], and he is there in that city.
He does no ·wrong [iniquity; injustice].

Every morning he ·governs the people fairly [provides justice];
·every day [Lat the light/dawn] he ·can be trusted [never fails].
But evil people ·are not ashamed of what they do [know no shame].

6"I have ·destroyed [Lcut off] nations;
their ·towers [fortresses; strongholds] were ruined.
I made their streets ·empty [deserted]
so no one ·goes there [passes through] anymore.
Their cities are ·ruined [desolate];
no one lives there at all.
7I said, 'Surely now ·Jerusalem [Lyou] will ·respect [fear] me [Prov. 1:7]
and will accept my ·teaching [correction].'
Then the place where they lived would not be destroyed,
and I would not have to punish them.
But they were still eager
to ·do evil [act corruptly] in everything they did.
8Just ·wait [be patient]," says the LORD.
"Someday I will stand up ·as a witness [to testify; *or* to plunder].
I have decided that I will gather nations
and assemble kingdoms.
I will pour out my ·anger [wrath; indignation] on them,
all my ·strong [fierce; burning] anger.
My anger will be like fire
that will ·burn up [consume; devour] the whole world.

A New Day for God's People

9"Then I will ·give [restore to] the ·people of all nations [Lnations] pure
·speech [Llips; Cpure because they worship God instead of idols]
so that all of them will ·speak [call on] the name of the LORD
and worship me ·together [as one; side-by-side].
10People will come from ·where the Nile River begins [Lthe rivers of
Cush/Ethiopia];
my worshipers, ·my scattered people [Lthe daughter of my dispersed
ones] will come with ·gifts [offerings] for me.
11·Then [LOn that day] Jerusalem will not be ashamed
of the ·wrongs [rebellious deeds] done against me,
because I will remove from this city
those who ·like to brag [arrogantly boast];
there will never be any more ·proud people [haughty]
on my holy ·mountain in Jerusalem [Lmountain; hill; CZion, the
location of the Temple].
12But I will leave in ·the city [Lyour midst]
the humble and ·those who are not proud [meek; lowly],
and they will ·trust [*or* find refuge] in the [Lname of the] LORD.
13·Those who are left alive in [LThe remnant of] Israel won't do wrong or
tell lies;
·they won't trick people with their words [No deceitful tongue will be
found in their mouth].
They will ·eat [*or* graze; feed their flocks] and lie down
with no one to make them afraid."

A Happy Song

14·Sing [*or* Shout joyfully], Jerusalem.
Israel, shout ·for joy [out]!
·Jerusalem [LDaughter Jerusalem], be happy

and rejoice with all your heart.
15The LORD has ·stopped punishing you [taken away your judgments];
he has ·sent [swept; cleared; turned] your enemies away.
The King of Israel, the LORD, is with you;
you will never again be afraid of ·being harmed [disaster; evil].
16On that day Jerusalem will be told,
"Don't be afraid, ·city of Jerusalem [LZion; Cthe location of the Temple].
Don't ·give up [Llet your hands grow weak/hang limp].
17The LORD your God is ·with you [in your midst];
the mighty One will save you.
He will ·rejoice over you [take delight in you].
·You will rest [*or* He will quiet you; *or* He won't rebuke you] in his love;
he will sing and be joyful about you."

18"I will take away the sadness ·planned for you [*or* over the loss of your appointed festivals],
which would have made you very ashamed.
19At that time I will ·punish [Ldeal with]
all those who ·harmed [oppressed] you.
I will ·save my people who cannot walk [rescue the lame]
and gather ·my people who have been thrown out [the scattered; Cperhaps shepherd imagery].
I will give them praise and ·honor [fame; renown]
in every place where they were shamed.
20At that time I will gather you;
at that time I will ·bring you back home [gather you].
I will give you ·honor [fame; renown] and praise
·from people everywhere [Lamong all the peoples/nations of the earth]
when I ·make things go well again for you [restore your fortunes; *or* return your exiles],
·as you will see with your own [Lbefore your] eyes," says the LORD.

HAGGAI

It Is Time to Build the Temple

1 The prophet Haggai spoke the word of the LORD to Zerubbabel
son of Shealtiel, the governor of Judah [Ezra 2:2; 3:2; Zech.
6:9–14], and to Joshua son of Jehozadak, the high priest [Calso known
as Jeshua; Ezra 2:2; 3:2; 5:2; Zech. 3:1–10]. This message came in the
second year that Darius was king [520 BC], on the first day of the sixth
month [CAugust 29; Elul 1 on the Hebrew calendar]:
2“This is what the LORD ·All-Powerful [Almighty; of Heaven's Armies;
Tof hosts] says: ‘The people say the right time has not come to rebuild
the ·Temple [Lhouse] of the LORD.’ ”
3Then Haggai the prophet spoke the word of the LORD: 4“Is it right for
you to be living in ·fancy [Lpaneled] houses while ·the Temple [Lthis
house] is still in ruins?”
5This is what the LORD ·All-Powerful [Almighty; of Heaven's Armies;
Tof hosts] says: “·Think about what you have done [Consider your ways].
6You have planted much, but you harvest little. You eat, but you do not
become full. You drink, but you are still thirsty. You put on clothes, but
you are not warm enough. You earn ·money [wages], ·but then you lose it
all as if you had [Lto] put it into a purse full of holes.”
7This is what the LORD ·All-Powerful [Almighty; of Heaven's Armies; Tof
hosts] says: “·Think about what you have done [Consider your ways]. 8Go
up to the mountains, bring back wood, and build the ·Temple [Lhouse].
Then I will be pleased with it and be honored,” says the LORD. 9“You look
for much, but ·you find little [it came to little]. When you bring it home, I
·destroy it [Lblew it away]. Why?” asks the LORD ·All-Powerful [Almighty;
of Heaven's Armies; Tof hosts]. “Because you all ·work hard for [are busy
with; Lrun to] your own houses while my house is still in ruins! 10Because
of what you have done, the sky holds back its ·rain [dew] and the ground
holds back its crops. 11I have called for a ·time without rain [drought] on
the land, and on the ·mountains [hill country], and on the grain, the new
wine, the olive oil, the plants which the earth produces, the people, the
·farm animals [livestock], and all the work of your hands.”
12Zerubbabel son of Shealtiel and Joshua son of Jehozadak, the high
priest [1:1], and all the ·rest of the people who were left alive [remnant of
the people; Cthose who returned from exile in Babylon] obeyed the [Lvoice
of the] LORD their God and the message from Haggai the prophet, because
the LORD their God had sent him. And the people ·feared [were in awe of]
the LORD.
13Haggai, the LORD's messenger, gave the LORD's message to the people,
saying, “The LORD says, ‘I am with you.’ ” 14The LORD stirred up [Lthe spirit
of] Zerubbabel son of Shealtiel, the governor of Judah, and Joshua son of

Jehozadak, the high priest, and all the ·rest of the people who were left
alive [remnant of the people; v. 12]. So they came and worked on the
·Temple [Lhouse] of their God, the Lord ·All-Powerful [Almighty; of
Heaven's Armies; Tof hosts]. 15They began on the twenty-fourth day of the
sixth month in the second year Darius was king [v. 1].

The Beauty of the Temple

2 On the twenty-first day of the seventh month [COct. 17, 520 BC;
Tishri 21 on the Hebrew calendar; the same date Solomon finished the temple 440 years earlier (960 BC); 1 Kin. 6:38; 8:2], the Lord
spoke his word through Haggai the prophet, saying, 2"Speak to Zerubbabel
son of Shealtiel, governor of Judah, and to Joshua son of Jehozadak, the
high priest [1:1], and to the ·rest of the people who are left alive [remnant
of the people; 1:12]. Say, 3'Do any of you remember ·how great the Temple
was [the former glory of this house] before it was destroyed? What does it
look like now? Doesn't it seem like nothing to you?' 4But the Lord says,
'Zerubbabel, be ·brave [strong]. Also, Joshua son of Jehozadak, the high
priest, be ·brave [strong]. And all you people who live in the land, be
·brave [strong],' says the Lord. 'Work, because I am with you,' says the
Lord ·All-Powerful [Almighty; of Heaven's Armies; Tof hosts]. 5'I made a
promise to you when you came out of Egypt, and my Spirit ·is still with
[remains among] you. So don't be afraid.'

6"This is what the Lord ·All-Powerful [Almighty; of Heaven's Armies; Tof
hosts] says: 'In a short time I will once again shake the heavens and the earth,
the sea and the dry land. 7I will shake all the nations, and ·they will bring
their wealth [Lthe treasures of the nations shall come]. Then I will fill this
·Temple [Lhouse] with glory [CGod's manifest presence],' says the Lord ·All-
Powerful [Almighty; of Heaven's Armies; Tof hosts]. 8'The silver is mine, and
the gold is mine,' says the Lord ·All-Powerful [Almighty; of Heaven's Armies;
Tof hosts]. 9'The ·new Temple [Lglory of this second/latter house] will be
greater than the one before,' says the Lord ·All-Powerful [Almighty; of
Heaven's Armies; Tof hosts]. 'And in this place I will give peace,' says the Lord
·All-Powerful [Almighty; of Heaven's Armies; Tof hosts]."

10On the twenty-fourth day of the ninth month [CDecember 18, 520
BC; Kislev 24 on the Hebrew calendar] in the second year Darius was
king, the Lord spoke his word to Haggai the prophet, saying, 11"This is
what the Lord ·All-Powerful [Almighty; of Heaven's Armies; Tof hosts]
says: 'Ask the priests ·for a teaching [about the law; for guidance/instruc-
tion]. 12Suppose a person carries in the fold of his clothes some meat
made holy for the Lord. If that fold touches bread, ·cooked food [stew],
wine, olive oil, or some other food, will that be made holy?' "

The priests answered, "No."

13Then Haggai said, "If a person who is ·unclean [Cceremonially] from
touching a dead body touches any of these foods, will the food become
unclean, too?"

The priests answered, "Yes, it would become unclean."

14Then Haggai answered, "The Lord says, 'This is also true for the people of this nation. They are ·unclean [defiled], and everything they do
with their hands is unclean to me. Whatever they offer at the altar is also
·unclean [defiled].

15" '·Think about [Consider; LSet your heart on] this from now on! Think
about how it was before you started laying stones on top of stones to build
the ·Temple [Lhouse] of the Lord. 16A person used to come to a ·pile of grain

expecting to find twenty basketfuls [[L]heap of twenty measures/ephahs], but
there were only ten. And a person used to come to the wine vat to take out
fifty ·jarfuls [measures; [L]baths], but only twenty were there. 17I ·destroyed
your work [struck all the work of your hands] with ·diseases [blight], mildew, and hail, but you still did not come back to me,' says the LORD. 18"It is
the twenty-fourth day of the ninth month [December 18, 520 BC; Kislev 24
on the Hebrew calendar], the day in which the people finished working on
the foundation of the ·Temple [[L]house] of the LORD. From ·now [[L]this day]
on, think about these things: 19Do you have seeds for crops still in the barn?
Your vines, fig trees, pomegranates, and olive trees have not given fruit yet.
But from ·now [[L]this day] on I will bless you!' "

The Lord Makes a Promise to Zerubbabel

20Then the LORD spoke his word a second time to Haggai on the twenty-
fourth day of the month [December 18, 520 BC; Kislev 24 on the Hebrew
calendar]. He said, 21"Tell Zerubbabel, the governor of Judah, 'I am going
to shake the heavens and the earth. 22I will ·destroy [overthrow] the ·for-
eign [[L]thrones of] kingdoms and ·take away [shatter] the power of the
kingdoms of the nations. I will destroy the chariots and their riders. The
horses will fall with their riders, ·as people kill each other with swords
[[L]each one by the sword of his brother].' 23The LORD ·All-Powerful
[Almighty; of Heaven's Armies; [T]of hosts] says, 'On that day I will take you,
Zerubbabel son of Shealtiel, my servant,' says the LORD, 'and I will make
you ·important like [[L]like] my signet ring, because I have chosen you!' says
the LORD All-Powerful [Almighty; of Heaven's Armies; [T]of hosts]."

ZECHARIAH

The Lord Calls His People Back

1 In the eighth month [[C]October/November on our calendar; the
Hebrew month of Cheshvan] of the second year Darius was king
[[C]520 BC; Darius was king of Persia 522–486 BC], the ·LORD spoke his
word [[L]word of the LORD came] to the prophet Zechariah son of Berekiah,
who was the son of Iddo [[C]a priestly family; Neh. 12:4, 16]. The LORD
said, 2“The LORD was very angry with your ·ancestors [fathers]. 3So tell
the people: This is what the LORD ·All-Powerful [Almighty; of Heaven's
Armies; [T]of hosts] says: ‘Return to me, and I will return to you,’ says the
LORD ·All-Powerful [Almighty; of Heaven's Armies; [T]of hosts]. 4Don't be
like your ·ancestors [fathers]. ·In the past the [The former/earlier] prophets said to them: This is what the LORD ·All-Powerful [Almighty; of Heaven's
Armies; [T]of hosts] says: ‘·Stop [Turn from] your evil ways and evil actions.’
But they wouldn't listen or pay attention to me, says the LORD. 5Your
·ancestors [fathers] ·are dead [[L]where are they…?], and those prophets
·didn't [[L]do they…?] live forever. 6I commanded my words and ·laws [stat-
utes] to my servants the prophets, and ·they preached to [*or* they came
true to; [L]did they not overtake…?] your ·ancestors [fathers], who returned
to me. They said, ‘The LORD ·All-Powerful [Almighty; of Heaven's Armies;
[T]of hosts] did as he ·said he would [determined to do]. He punished us for
·the way we lived and for what we did [[L]our ways and deeds].’ ”

The Vision of the Horses

7It was on the twenty-fourth day of the eleventh month [[C]February 15,
519 BC], which is the month of Shebat, in Darius's second year as king [v.
1]. The ·LORD spoke his word [[L]word of the LORD came] to the prophet
Zechariah son of Berekiah, who was the son of Iddo.
8During the night I had a vision. I saw a man ·riding [*or* sitting on] a
red horse. He was standing among some myrtle trees in a ravine, with
red, brown, and white horses behind him [Rev. 6].
9I asked, “What are these, ·sir [*or* my lord]?”
The ·angel [messenger] who was talking with me answered, “I'll show
you what they are.”
10Then the man standing among the myrtle trees explained, “They are
the ones the LORD ·sent [[L]sent to walk/patrol] through all the earth.”
11Then they spoke to the ·LORD's angel [*or* angel of the LORD; [C]an OT
figure closely identified with the LORD himself; Gen. 16:11; 22:11–12], who
was standing among the myrtle trees. They said, “We have ·gone [walked;
patrolled] through all the earth, and [[L]look; [T]behold] everything is calm
and quiet.”
12Then the ·LORD's angel [angel of the LORD; v. 11] asked, “LORD ·All-
Powerful [Almighty; of Heaven's Armies; [T]of hosts], how long will ·it be
before you show [[L]you withhold] mercy to Jerusalem and the cities of

Judah? You have been angry with them for seventy years now." [13]So the LORD answered the ·angel [messenger] who was talking with me, and his words were comforting and good.

[14]Then the ·angel [messenger] who was talking to me said to me, "Announce this: This is what the LORD ·All-Powerful [Almighty; of Heaven's Armies; [T]of hosts] says: 'I ·have a strong love [am very jealous/zealous; Nah. 1:2] for Jerusalem. [15]And I am very angry with the nations that feel so ·safe [secure; at ease]. I was only a little angry at them, but they ·made things worse [added to/increased the calamity/disaster].'

[16]"So this is what the LORD says: 'I will return to Jerusalem with mercy. My ·Temple [[L]house] will be rebuilt,' says the LORD ·All-Powerful [Almighty; of Heaven's Armies; [T]of hosts], 'and the measuring line will be ·used to rebuild [[L]stretched out over] Jerusalem.'

[17]"Also announce: This is what the LORD ·All-Powerful [Almighty; of Heaven's Armies; [T]of hosts] says: 'My towns will ·be rich again [[L]overflow with prosperity]. The LORD will comfort Jerusalem again, and I will again choose Jerusalem.' "

The Vision of the Horns

[18]Then I looked up and saw four ·animal horns [[L]horns; [C]animal horns symbolized strength]. [19]I asked the ·angel [messenger] who was talking with me, "What are these?"

He said, "These are the horns that scattered the people of Judah, Israel, and Jerusalem."

[20]Then the LORD showed me four craftsmen. [21]I asked, "What are they coming to do?"

He answered, "They have come to ·scare [terrify] and throw down the horns. These horns scattered the people of Judah so that no one could even lift up his head. These horns stand for the nations that ·attacked [[L]lifted up their horns against] the people of Judah and scattered them."

The Vision of the Measuring Line

2 Then I looked up and saw a man holding a line for measuring things. [2]I asked him, "Where are you going?"

He said to me, "I am going to measure Jerusalem, to see how wide and how long it is."

[3]Then the ·angel [messenger] who was talking with me left, and another ·angel [messenger] came out to meet him. [4]The second ·angel [messenger] said to him, "Run and tell that young man, 'Jerusalem will become a city without walls, because there will be so many people and ·cattle [livestock] in it. [5]I will be a wall of fire around it,' says the LORD. 'And I will be the glory within it.'

[6]"·Oh no! Oh no [*or* Come! Come; *or* Up! Up]! Run away from ·Babylon [[L]the land of the north], because I have scattered you like the four winds of heaven," says the LORD.

[7]"·Oh no [*or* Come; *or* Up], ·Jerusalem [[L]Zion; [C]the location of the Temple]! Escape, you who live in ·Babylon [[L]Daughter Babylon]." [8]This is what the LORD ·All-Powerful [Almighty; of Heaven's Armies; [T]of hosts] says: "After ·he has honored me and [*or* the Glorious One; *or* for his own glory he] sent me against the nations who ·took your possessions [plundered you]—because whoever touches you ·hurts [[L]touches] ·what is precious to me [[T]the apple of his eye; [L]the pupil/little man of his eye]—[9]I will ·shake my hand [raise my fist] against them so that their slaves will ·rob [plunder] them."

Then you will know that the LORD ·All-Powerful [Almighty; of Heaven's Armies; [T]of hosts] sent me.

10"Shout and be glad, ·Jerusalem [LDaughter Zion]. [LFor look/TBehold] I am coming, and I will live among you," says the LORD. 11"At that time people from many nations will join with the LORD and will become my people. Then I will live among you, and you will know that the LORD ·All-Powerful [Almighty; of Heaven's Armies; Tof hosts] has sent me to you. 12The LORD will ·take [possess; inherit] Judah as his own part of the holy land, and ·Jerusalem will be his chosen city again [Lwill again choose Jerusalem]. 13Be silent, ·everyone [Lall flesh], in the presence of the LORD. He ·is coming [has roused himself] out of ·the holy place where he lives [his holy dwelling]."

The Vision of the High Priest

3 Then he showed me Joshua, the high priest, standing in front of the ·LORD's angel [angel of the LORD; 1:11]. And ·Satan [*or* the Accuser/Adversary; Job 1–2; 1 Chr. 21:1] was standing by Joshua's [Hag. 1:1] right ·side [hand] to accuse him. 2The LORD said to ·Satan [*or* the Accuser/Adversary], "The LORD ·says no to [rebuke] you, ·Satan [Adversary; Accuser]! The LORD who has chosen Jerusalem ·says no to [rebukes] you! ·This man was [LIsn't this man…?] like a burning stick ·pulled [snatched] from the fire."

3Joshua was wearing ·dirty [filthy] clothes and was standing in front of the ·angel [messenger]. 4The ·angel [messenger] said to those standing in front of him, "Take off those ·dirty [filthy] clothes."

Then ·the angel [Lhe] said to Joshua, "Look, I have taken away your ·sin [iniquity] from you, and I am giving you beautiful, ·fine clothes [festal robes; fine vestments]."

5Then I said, "Put a clean turban on his head." So they put a clean turban on his head and dressed him while the ·LORD's angel [angel of the LORD; 1:11] stood there.

6Then the ·LORD's angel [angel of the LORD; 1:11] ·said [spoke solemnly; gave this charge] to Joshua, 7"This is what the LORD ·All-Powerful [Almighty; of Heaven's Armies; Tof hosts] says: 'If you ·do as I tell you [walk in my ways] and ·serve me [carefully keep my requirements], you will be in charge of my ·Temple [Lhouse] and my courtyards. And I will let you be with ·these angels [Lthese] who are standing here.

8" 'Listen, Joshua, the high priest, and your ·friends [colleagues; associates] who are sitting in front of you. They are ·symbols [a sign] of what will happen. [LLook; TBehold] I am going to bring my servant, the Branch [Cthe Messiah; Ps. 132:17; Is. 11:1; 42:1; Jer. 23:5; 33:15]. 9Look, I put this stone in front of Joshua, a stone with seven ·sides [Leyes]. I will ·carve a message [engrave an inscription] on it,' says the LORD ·All-Powerful [Almighty; of Heaven's Armies; Tof hosts]. 'And in one day I will ·take away the sin [remove the iniquity] of this land.'

10"The LORD ·All-Powerful [Almighty; of Heaven's Armies; Tof hosts] says, 'In that day, each of you will invite your neighbor to sit under your own grapevine and under your own fig tree [Csymbols of security and prosperity; Is. 36:16; Mic. 4:4].' "

The Vision of the Lampstand

4 Then the ·angel [messenger] who was talking with me returned and woke me up as if I had been asleep. 2He asked me, "What do you see?"

I said, "I see a solid gold ·lampstand [menorah] with a bowl at the top. And there are seven lamps and also seven ·places [pipes; spouts] for wicks. 3There are two olive trees by it, one on the right of the bowl and the other on the left."

4I asked the ·angel [messenger] who talked with me, "·Sir [My lord],
what are these?"
5·The angel [LHe] said, "Don't you know what they are?"
"No, sir," I said.
6Then he told me, "This is the word of the LORD to Zerubbabel: '·You
will not succeed by your own strength or by your own power [TNot by
might, nor by power], but by my Spirit,' says the LORD ·All-Powerful
[Almighty; of Heaven's Armies; Tof hosts].
7"Who are you, ·big [mighty; great] mountain? ·In front of [Compared
with] Zerubbabel you will become ·flat land [a level plain], and he will bring
out the ·topmost stone [capstone], ·shouting [*or* amid shouting], '·It's beautiful! It's beautiful [*or* Blessings, Blessings upon it; LGrace, Grace to it]!' "
8Then the ·LORD spoke his word [Lword of the LORD came] to me again,
saying, 9"[LThe hands of] Zerubbabel has laid the foundation of this
·Temple [Lhouse; Ezra 3:7–13], and he will complete it [Ezra 6:13–18].
Then you will know that the LORD ·All-Powerful [Almighty; of Heaven's
Armies; Tof hosts] has sent me to you.
10"·The people should not think that small beginnings are unimportant [LFor who despises the day of small things?]. ·They [*or* These seven
eyes] will ·be happy [rejoice] when they see Zerubbabel with ·tools [*or* his
plumb line; *or* the chosen capstone], building the Temple.
"(These are the seven eyes of the LORD, which look back and forth
across the earth.)"
11Then I asked the ·angel [messenger], "What are the two olive ·trees
[*or* branches] on the right and left of the lampstand?"
12·I also [*or* Again I] asked him, "What are the two olive branches beside
the two gold pipes, from which the olive oil ·flows to the lamps [pours out]?"
13He answered, "Don't you know what they are?"
"No, ·sir [my lord]," I said.
14So he said, "They are symbols of the two ·who have been appointed
to serve [anointed ones who stand by] the Lord of all the earth."

The Vision of the Flying Scroll

5 I ·looked up again [Lturned and lifted my eyes] and saw a flying
scroll.
2·The angel [LHe] asked me, "What do you see?"
I answered, "I see a flying scroll, ·thirty feet [Ltwenty cubits] long and
·fifteen feet [Lten cubits] wide."
3And he said to me, "This is the curse that ·will go [*or* is going out] all
over the land. One side says every thief will be ·taken away [banished;
purged]. The other side says everyone who ·makes false promises [swears
falsely] will be ·taken away [banished; purged]. 4The LORD ·All-Powerful
[Almighty; of Heaven's Armies; Tof hosts] says, 'I will send it to the houses
of thieves and to those who ·use my name to make false promises [swear
falsely]. The scroll will stay in that person's house and destroy it with its
wood and stones.' "

The Vision of the Woman

5Then the ·angel [messenger] who was talking with me came forward
and said to me, "·Look up [LLift up your eyes] and see what is ·going out
[*or* coming; appearing]."
6"What is it?" I asked.
He answered, "It is a ·measuring basket [Lephah] going out." He also
said, "It is ·a symbol of the people's sins [Ltheir iniquity; *or* their appearance; Ltheir eye] in all the land."

[7]Then the lid made of lead was raised, and there was a woman sitting inside the basket. [8]The angel said, "The woman ·stands for [[L]is] wickedness." Then he pushed her back into the basket and put the lid back down.

[9]Then I ·looked up [[L]lifted my eyes] and saw two women going out with the wind in their wings. Their wings were like those of a stork, and they lifted up the basket between earth and the ·sky [heaven].

[10]I asked the ·angel [messenger] who was talking with me, "Where are they taking the basket?"

[11]"They are going to Babylonia to build a ·temple [[L]house] for it," he answered. "When ·the temple [[L]it] is ready, they will set the basket there ·in its place [*or* on its base/pedestal]."

The Vision of the Four Chariots

6 I looked up again and saw four chariots ·going [coming] out between two mountains, mountains of bronze. [2]Red horses pulled the first chariot. Black horses pulled the second chariot. [3]White horses pulled the third chariot, and strong, ·spotted [dappled] horses pulled the fourth chariot. [4]I asked the ·angel [messenger] who was talking with me, "What are these, sir?"

[5]He said, "These are the four spirits of heaven. They have just come from ·the presence of [*or* presenting themselves before] the Lord of the whole world. [6]The chariot pulled by the black horses will go to the land of the north. The white horses will go ·to the land of the west [*or* after them], and the spotted horses will go to the land of the south."

[7]When the powerful horses went out, they were ·eager [seeking] to go through all the earth. So he said, "Go ·through all [*or* and patrol] the earth," and they did.

[8]Then he ·called [cried out] to me, "Look, the horses that went north have caused my ·spirit to rest [anger to be appeased; *or* Spirit to rest] in the land of the north."

A Crown for Joshua

[9]The LORD spoke his word to me, saying, [10]"Take silver and gold from Heldai, Tobijah, and Jedaiah, who were captives in Babylon. Go that same day to the house of Josiah son of Zephaniah, who came from Babylon [[C]may refer to the three men rather than to Josiah]. [11]Make the silver and gold into a crown, and put it on the head of Joshua son of Jehozadak, the high priest. [12]Tell him this is what the LORD ·All-Powerful [Almighty; of Heaven's Armies; [T]of hosts] says: 'A man whose name is the Branch [3:8] will branch out from where he is, and he will build the Temple of the LORD. [13]It is he who will build the Temple of the LORD and will ·receive honor [*or* be clothed in splendor/majesty]. He will sit on his throne and rule [[C]referring to Zerubbabel and ultimately to the Messiah]. And there will be a priest on his throne [[C]referring to Joshua the high priest and ultimately to the Messiah]. And ·these two will work together in peace [[L]the counsel of peace will be between the two].' [14]The crown will be kept in the Temple of the LORD to remind ·Heldai [[L]Helem; [C]probably another name for Heldai], Tobijah, Jedaiah, and ·Josiah [[L]Hen; [C]perhaps a nickname for Josiah, meaning "gracious one"] son of Zephaniah. [15]People living far away will come and build the Temple of the LORD. Then you will know the LORD ·All-Powerful [Almighty; of Heaven's Armies; [T]of hosts] has sent me to you. This will happen if you completely obey the [[L]voice of the] LORD your God."

The People Should Show Mercy

7 In the fourth year Darius was king, on the fourth day of the ninth
month, which is called Kislev [December 7, 518 BC], the ·LORD
spoke his word [Lword of the LORD came] to Zechariah. 2The city of Bethel
sent Sharezer, Regem-Melech, and their men to ·ask the LORD a question
[*or* seek the LORD's favor]. 3They went to the prophets and priests who
were at the ·Temple [Lhouse] of the LORD ·All-Powerful [Almighty; of
Heaven's Armies; Tof hosts]. The men said, "For years in the fifth month
of each year we have ·shown our sadness [mourned; wept] and fasted.
Should we continue to do this?"
4The ·LORD All-Powerful spoke his word [Lword of the LORD All-Powerful/
of Heaven's Armies/Tof hosts came] to me, saying, 5"Tell the priests and the
people in the land: 'For seventy years you fasted and ·cried [mourned] in
the fifth and seventh months, but ·that was not [Lwas it…?] really for me.
6And when you ate and drank, ·it was really [Lwas it not…?] for yourselves.
7Wasn't this the same thing the LORD said through the ·earlier [former]
prophets, when Jerusalem and the surrounding towns were at peace and
wealthy, and people lived in the ·southern area [LNegev] and the ·western
hills [*or* lowland; LShephelah]?' "
8And the ·LORD spoke his word [Lword of the LORD came] to Zechariah
again, saying, 9"This is what the LORD ·All-Powerful [Almighty; of
Heaven's Armies; Tof hosts] says: '·Do what is right and true [Administer
true justice]. Be kind and ·merciful [compassionate] to each other. 10Don't
·hurt [oppress] widows and ·orphans [the fatherless], foreigners or the
poor [Ex. 22:21–24; 23:9; Lev. 19:33–34; Deut 24:17–18]; don't ·even think
of doing evil to [*or* secretly plot evil against] somebody else.'
11"But they refused to pay attention; they ·were stubborn [turned their
backs; Lgave a stubborn shoulder] and ·did not want to listen anymore
[covered their ears]. 12They made their hearts ·as hard as rock [like flint]
and would not listen to the ·teachings [law; LTorah] of the LORD ·All-
Powerful [Almighty; of Heaven's Armies; Tof hosts]. And they would not
hear the words he sent by his Spirit through the earlier prophets. So the
LORD ·All-Powerful [Almighty; of Heaven's Armies; Tof hosts] became
very angry.
13" 'When I called to them, they would not listen. So when they called
to me, I would not listen,' says the LORD ·All-Powerful [Almighty; of
Heaven's Armies; Tof hosts]. 14'I scattered them like a ·hurricane [whirl-
wind] ·to other countries [among all the nations] they did not know. This
good land was left so ·ruined behind them [desolate] that no one ·could
live there [*or* traveled through it]. They had made the ·desired [pleasant]
land ·a ruin [desolate; a wasteland].' "

The Lord Will Bless Jerusalem

8 ·A message from [LThe word of] the LORD ·All-Powerful [Almighty;
of Heaven's Armies; Tof hosts] came to me, saying, 2This is what
the LORD ·All-Powerful [Almighty; of Heaven's Armies; Tof hosts] says: "I
·have a very strong love [am jealous/zealous/passionate] for ·Jerusalem
[LZion; 2:7]. My strong love [jealousy; zeal; passion] for her ·is like a fire
burning in me [*or* will mean wrath for her enemies]."
3This is what the LORD says: "I will return to Jerusalem and ·live in
[dwell in the midst of] it. Then it will be called the City of ·Truth [*or*
Faithfulness], and the mountain of the LORD ·All-Powerful [Almighty; of
Heaven's Armies; Tof hosts] will be called the Holy Mountain [CZion, the
location of the Temple]."

4This is what the LORD ·All-Powerful [Almighty; of Heaven's Armies; Tof hosts] says: "Old men and old women will again sit along Jerusalem's streets, each carrying a cane because of age [Clong life due to peace and security]. 5And the streets will be filled with boys and girls playing."

6This is what the LORD ·All-Powerful [Almighty; of Heaven's Armies; Tof hosts] says: "·Those who are left alive then [The remnant] may think it is too ·difficult [marvelous] to happen, but ·it is not [Lis it…?] too ·difficult [marvelous] for me," says the LORD ·All-Powerful [Almighty; of Heaven's Armies; Tof hosts]. 7This is what the LORD ·All-Powerful [Almighty; of Heaven's Armies; Tof hosts] says: "[LLook; TBehold] I will save my people from countries in the east and west. 8I will bring them back, and they will live in Jerusalem. They will be my people, and I will be their ·loyal [faithful; true] and ·good [righteous] God."

9This is what the LORD ·All-Powerful [Almighty; of Heaven's Armies; Tof hosts] says: "·Work hard [LLet your hands be strong], you who are hearing these words today. The prophets spoke these words when the foundation was laid for the house of the LORD ·All-Powerful [Almighty; of Heaven's Armies; Tof hosts], for the building of the Temple. 10Before that time there was no money to hire people or animals. People could not ·safely [peacefully] come and go because of the enemies; I had turned everyone against his neighbor. 11But I will not do to ·these people who are left [this remnant of the people] what I did in the past," says the LORD ·All-Powerful [Almighty; of Heaven's Armies; Tof hosts].

12"They will plant their seeds in peace, their grapevines will have fruit, the ground will give good crops, and the sky will send ·rain [dew]. I will give ·all this [this as an inheritance/possession] to the ·people who are left alive [remnant of this people]. 13Judah and Israel, your names have been ·used as curses in [*or* viewed as accursed by] other nations. But I will save you, and you will become a blessing. So don't be afraid; ·work hard [Llet your hands be strong]."

14This is what the LORD ·All-Powerful [Almighty; of Heaven's Armies; Tof hosts] says: "When your ·ancestors [fathers] made me angry, I planned to ·punish [bring disaster on] you. I did not ·change my mind [relent]," says the LORD ·All-Powerful [Almighty; of Heaven's Armies; Tof hosts]. 15"But ·now [Lin these days] I am planning to do good to Jerusalem and Judah. So don't be afraid. 16These are the things you should do: Tell each other the truth. In ·the courts [Lyour gates; Ccourt was held at the city gate] judge with truth and ·complete fairness [sound justice; judgments of peace]. 17Do not ·make plans to hurt [Lplan/plot evil in your hearts against] your neighbors, and don't love false ·promises [oaths]. I hate all these things," says the LORD.

18·A message from [LThe word of the] LORD ·All-Powerful [Almighty; of Heaven's Armies; Tof hosts] came to me again. 19This is what the LORD ·All-Powerful [Almighty; of Heaven's Armies; Tof hosts] says: "The ·special days when you fast in [fasts of] the fourth, fifth, seventh, and tenth months will become good, joyful, happy feasts ·in [Lfor the house of] Judah. ·But you must [So; Therefore] love truth and peace."

20This is what the LORD ·All-Powerful [Almighty; of Heaven's Armies; Tof hosts] says: "·Many people from [LInhabitants of] many cities will still come to Jerusalem. 21·People [The inhabitants] from one city will go and say to those from another city, '·We are going [Let us go] to ·pray to [entreat] the LORD and to ·ask for help from [*or* worship; Lseek] the LORD ·All-Powerful

[Almighty; of Heaven's Armies; [T]of hosts]. ·Come and go with us [[L]I, even I
(am going)].' [22]Many people and powerful nations will come to worship the
LORD ·All-Powerful [Almighty; of Heaven's Armies; [T]of hosts] in Jerusalem
and to ·pray for help from [*or* worship; [L]seek] the LORD."

[23]This is what the LORD ·All-Powerful [Almighty; of Heaven's Armies;
[T]of hosts] says: "At that time, ten men from ·different countries [[L]all languages of the nations] will come and take hold of a ·Judean [Jew] by his
coat. They will say to him, 'Let us go with you, because we have heard that
God is with you.'"

Punishment on Israel's Enemies

9 ·This message is [An oracle/burden of] the word of the LORD.
The message is against the land of Hadrach [[C]region north of Israel]
and ·the city of Damascus [[L]Damascus its resting place].
·All [[L]For the eyes of all] people, including all the tribes of Israel
·belong to [*or* are on] the LORD.
[2]The message is also against the city of Hamath, on the border,
and against Tyre and Sidon [[C]cities on the coast northwest of Israel],
·with their skill [*or* though they are very wise/clever].
[3]Tyre has built a ·strong wall [fortress; stronghold] for herself.
She has piled up silver like dust
and gold like the mud in the streets.
[4]But [[L]look; [T]behold] the Lord will take away all she has
and ·destroy her power on [*or* throw her fortifications into] the sea.
That city will be ·destroyed [consumed; devoured] by fire.
[5]·The city of Ashkelon [[L]Ashkelon] will see it and be afraid.
·The people of Gaza [[L]Gaza] will ·shake with fear [writhe in anguish],
and ·the people of Ekron [[L]Ekron] ·will lose hope [*or* their hope will
wither].
No king will be left in Gaza,
and no one will live in Ashkelon anymore.
[6]·Foreigners [A mixed/mongrel people] will live in Ashdod,
and I will ·destroy [[L]cut off] the pride of the Philistines.
[7]I will ·stop them from drinking blood [[L]take the blood from their
mouths; Lev. 3:17; Deut. 12:16, 23]
and ·from eating forbidden food [[L]its abominations from between
its teeth].
Those left alive will belong to God.
They will be ·leaders [*or* like a clan] in Judah,
and Ekron will become like the Jebusites [[C]ancient inhabitants of
Jerusalem who were assimilated into Judah].
[8]I will ·protect [encamp around] my ·Temple [[L]house]
from armies who would come or go.
No ·one [oppressor] will ·hurt [overrun; pass over] my people again,
because now I ·am watching them [[L]see with my eyes].

The King Is Coming

[9]Rejoice greatly, ·people of Jerusalem [[L]Daughter Zion]!
Shout for joy, ·people of Jerusalem [[L]Daughter Jerusalem]!
[[L]Look; [T]Behold] Your king is coming to you.
He ·does what is right [is righteous/just], and he saves.
He is ·gentle [lowly; humble] and riding on a donkey,
on ·the colt [[L]a colt, the foal] of a donkey [Matt. 21:5; John 12:15].
[10]I will ·take away [[L]cut off] the chariots from Ephraim
and the ·horses [warhorses] from Jerusalem.

The bows used in war will be broken.
The king will ·talk about [announce; bring] **peace to the nations.**
His ·kingdom [dominion; rule] **will go from sea to sea,**
and from the ·Euphrates River [LRiver] **to the ends of the earth.**

11**As for you, because of the blood of ·the agreement** [my covenant/treaty] **with you**
I will set your prisoners free from the waterless pit.
12**You prisoners who have hope,**
return to ·your place of safety [the fortress/stronghold].
Today I ·am telling you [announce; declare]
that I will ·give you back twice as much as before [return double what you lost].
13**I will ·use** [Lbend] **Judah like a bow**
and Ephraim like the arrows.
·Jerusalem [LZion; Cthe location of the Temple], **I will ·use your men** [Lrouse your sons/children]
·to fight the men of [against your sons/children,] **Greece.**
I will use you like a warrior's sword.

14**Then the LORD will appear above them,**
and his arrows will shoot like lightning.
The Lord GOD will blow the trumpet,
and he will march in the ·storms [whirlwinds] **of the south.**
15**The LORD ·All-Powerful** [Almighty; of Heaven's Armies; Tof hosts] **will protect them;**
they will ·destroy [Leat and subdue] **the enemy with slingshots.**
They will drink and shout like drunks.
They will be filled like a bowl
used for sprinkling blood ·at [*or* and drenched with blood like] **the corners of the altar.**
16**On that day the LORD their God will save them**
as ·if his people were sheep [Lthe flock of his people].
They will shine in his land
like jewels in a crown.
17**They will be so ·pretty** [fine; good] **and beautiful.**
The young men will grow strong on the grain
and the young women on new wine.

The Lord's Promises

10 **Ask the LORD for rain during the ·springtime** [Llatter] **rains.**
The LORD is the one who makes the storm clouds.
He sends the showers
and gives everyone ·green [plants in the] **fields.**
2**·Idols** [Household gods; LTeraphim; Gen. 31:19] **·tell lies** [*or* give worthless counsel];
fortune-tellers see ·false [lying] **visions**
and tell about false dreams.
The comfort they give is ·worth nothing [in vain].
So the people ·are [wander] **like lost sheep.**
They are ·abused [oppressed; *or* in distress], **because there is no shepherd.**

3The LORD says, "·I am angry [My anger burns] at my shepherds,
and I will punish the ·leaders [Llead goats].
I, the LORD ·All-Powerful [Almighty; of Heaven's Armies; Tof hosts], care
for my flock, the ·people [Lhouse] of Judah.
I will make them like my ·proud [majestic] war horses.
4From ·Judah [Lhim] will come the cornerstone,
and the tent peg,
the battle bow,
and every ruler.
5Together they will be like ·soldiers [mighty men]
·marching to battle [*or* trampling their enemies] through muddy streets.
The LORD is with them,
so they will fight and ·defeat [Lput to shame] the horsemen.

6"I will strengthen the ·people [Lhouse] of Judah
and save the ·people [Lhouse] of Joseph.
I will bring them back,
because I ·care about [have compassion on] them.
It will be as though
I had never ·left [rejected] them,
because I am the LORD their God,
and I will ·answer [hear] them.
7The people of Ephraim will be strong like ·soldiers [mighty men];
·they will be glad [Ltheir hearts will rejoice] as when they have drunk wine.
Their children will see it and rejoice;
they will ·be happy [rejoice] in the LORD.
8I will ·call [signal/whistle for] my people
and gather them together.
I will ·save [redeem] them,
and they grow as numerous as they were before.
9I have scattered them among the nations,
but in those faraway places, they will remember me.
They and their children will ·live [survive; sprout forth] and return.
10I will bring them back from the land of Egypt
and gather them from Assyria.
I will bring them to Gilead and Lebanon
until there isn't enough room for them all.
11·They [*or* The LORD; LHe] will come through the sea of trouble [Cas at the Red/*or* Reed Sea; Ex. 14:22].
The waves of the sea will be calm,
and the ·Nile River [Ldepths of the Nile/River] will dry up.
I will ·defeat [bring down; humble] Assyria's pride
and destroy Egypt's ·power over other countries [Lscepter; Cruling authority].
12I will make my people strong [Lin the LORD],
and they will ·live as I say [Lwalk in my name]," says the LORD.

11 Lebanon, open your ·gates [doors]
so fire may ·burn [consume; devour] your cedar trees.
[2]·Cry [Wail], pine trees, because the cedar has fallen,
because the ·tall [majestic; glorious] trees are ruined.
·Cry [Wail], oaks in Bashan,
because the ·mighty [thick; dense] forest has been cut down [[C]trees
probably symbolize wicked rulers].
[3]Listen to the shepherds ·crying [wailing]
because their ·rich pastures [*or* glory; magnificence] are destroyed.
Listen to the lions roaring
because the ·lovely land [lush thicket] of the Jordan River is ruined.

The Two Shepherds

[4]This is what the LORD my God says: "·Feed [Shepherd] the flock that are
·about to be killed [set aside for slaughter]. [5]Their buyers ·kill [slaughter]
them and ·are not punished [are not held liable; *or* feel no remorse]. Those
who sell them say, '·Praise [Blessed be] the LORD, I am rich.' Even the shepherds don't ·feel sorry for [have compassion on; *or* spare] their sheep. [6]I
don't ·feel sorry [have compassion] anymore for the ·people [inhabitants]
of this country," says the LORD. "I will let everyone ·be under the power [[L]fall
into the hand] of his neighbor and king. They will ·bring trouble to [devas-
tate] the country, and I will not save anyone from ·them [[L]their hand]."
[7]So I ·fed [shepherded] the flock ·about to be killed [marked for slaugh-
ter], particularly the ·weakest [oppressed] ones. Then I took two ·sticks
[staffs]; I called one ·Pleasant [*or* Favor] and the other Union, and I ·fed
[shepherded] the flock. [8]In one month I got rid of three shepherds. The
flock ·did not pay attention to [*or* detested; loathed] me, and I ·got impatient [grew weary] with them. [9]I said, "I will no longer ·take care of you
like a shepherd [shepherd you]. Let those that are dying die, and let those
that are ·to be destroyed be destroyed [perishing perish]. Let those that
are left eat ·each other [[L]the flesh of his neighbor]."
[10]Then I broke the ·stick [staff] named ·Pleasant [*or* Favor] to ·break
[revoke] the ·agreement [covenant; treaty] God made with all the ·nations
[peoples]. [11]That day it was ·broken [revoked]. The ·weak [oppressed]
ones in the flock who were watching me knew this ·message was from
[[L]was the word of] the LORD.
[12]Then I said, "If ·you want [it seems right to you; [L]it is good in your
eyes] to pay me, pay me. If not, ·then don't [keep it]." So they ·paid
[weighed out to] me thirty pieces of silver [Ex. 21:32; Matt. 26:15].
[13]The LORD said to me, "Throw the money to the potter." ·That is how
little they thought I was worth [...this magnificent price at which they
valued me"; [C]sarcastic, since the sum was about the cost of a slave]. So I
took the thirty pieces of silver and threw them to the potter in the ·Temple
[[L]house] of the LORD [Matt. 27:9, 10].
[14]Then I broke the second ·stick [staff], named Union, to break the
brotherhood between Judah and Israel.
[15]Then the LORD said to me, "·Get the things used by a foolish shepherd
again, [16]because [[L]look; [T]behold] I am going to ·get [raise up] a new shepherd for the country. He will not care for the ·dying sheep [lost; perishing],
or look for the young ones, or heal the injured ones, or feed the healthy. But
he will ·eat [devour the flesh of] the ·best [fat] sheep and tear off their hoofs.
[17]"·How terrible it will be for [[L]Woe to] the ·useless [worthless] shepherd
who abandoned the flock.

A sword will strike his arm and his right eye.
His arm will ·lose all its strength [wither away],
and his right eye will go blind.”

Jerusalem Will Be Saved

12 ·This message is [The oracle/burden of] the word of the LORD ·to [*or* concerning] Israel. This is what the LORD says, who stretched out the ·skies [heavens], and laid the foundations of the earth [Gen. 1], and ·put [forms] the human spirit within: 2“I will make Jerusalem like a cup of ·poison [staggering; reeling; drunkenness] to the nations around her. They will come and ·attack [besiege] Jerusalem and Judah. 3·One [LAnd it shall be on that] day all the nations on earth will come together to attack Jerusalem, but I will make it like a ·heavy [immovable] rock; anyone who tries to ·move [carry] it will ·get hurt [be injured]. 4At that time I will ·confuse [strike with panic] every horse and cause its rider to go crazy,” says the LORD. “I will ·watch over [Lopen my eyes to] the ·people [Lhouse] of Judah, but I will blind all the horses of the ·enemies [nations; peoples]. 5Then the ·leaders [*or* clans] of Judah will say to themselves, ‘The ·people [inhabitants] of Jerusalem are strong, because the LORD ·All-Powerful [Almighty; of Heaven’s Armies; Tof hosts] is their God.’

6“At that time I will make the ·leaders [*or* clans] of Judah like a ·fire burning [firepot on] a stack of wood or like a ·fire burning straw [burning torch among sheaves]. They will ·destroy [consume; devour] all the people around them left and right. But the people of Jerusalem will remain ·safe [Lsettled in their place].

7“The LORD will save the ·homes [Ltents] of Judah first so that the ·honor given to [glory of] ·David’s family [Lthe house of David] and to the people of Jerusalem won’t be greater than the ·honor given to [glory of] Judah [Cthe defenseless countryside would be saved before the fortified city, showing the victory was due to the Lord]. 8·At that time [LOn that day] the LORD will ·protect [defend] the people in Jerusalem. Then even the weakest of them will be strong like David. And the ·family [house] of David will be like God, like ·an [*or* the] angel of the LORD in front of them [Gen. 48:16; Ex. 14:19; 23:20]. 9·At that time [LOn that day] I will ·go [set out; begin] to destroy all the nations that attack Jerusalem.

Crying for the One They Pierced

10“I will pour out on ·David’s family [Lthe house of David] and the ·people in [inhabitants of] Jerusalem a spirit of ·kindness [grace] and ·mercy [prayer; supplication]. They will look at me, the one they have ·stabbed [pierced], and they will ·cry [Lmourn/lament for him] like someone ·crying [mourning; lamenting] over the death of an only ·child [son]. They will ·be as sad [grieve bitterly] as someone who has lost a firstborn son. 11·At that time [LOn that day] there will be much crying in Jerusalem, like the crying for Hadad Rimmon in the plain of Megiddo [Ceither where Judah mourned the death of king Josiah (2 Chr. 35:25), or ritualistic mourning associated with the Canaanite storm god (Ezek. 8:14; 2 Kin. 5:18)]. 12The land will ·cry [mourn], each ·family [clan] by itself: the ·family [clan] of [Lthe house of] David by itself and their wives by themselves, the ·family [clan] of Nathan [2 Sam. 5:14] by itself and their wives by themselves, 13the ·family [clan] of Levi [Num. 3:17–18, 21] by itself and their wives by themselves, the ·family [clan] of Shimei [Ca clan of Levites; Ex. 6:16–17] by itself and their wives by themselves, 14and all the rest of the ·families [clans] by themselves and their wives by themselves.

13 "·At that time [[L]In that day] a fountain will be open for
·David's descendants [[L]the house of David] and for the ·people
[inhabitants] of Jerusalem to cleanse them of their sin and ·uncleanness
[impurity; defilement]."
2The LORD ·All-Powerful [Almighty; of Heaven's Armies; [T]of hosts]
says, "·At that time [[L]On that day] I will ·get rid of [remove; cut off] the
names of the idols from the land; no one will remember them anymore. I
will also remove the prophets and ·unclean spirits [*or* spirit of unclean-
ness/impurity] from the land [[C]unlike true prophecy from the Spirit of
God]. 3If a person continues to prophesy, his own father and mother, the
ones who gave birth to him, will tell him, 'You have told lies ·using [in]
the LORD's name, so you must die.' When he prophesies, his own father
and mother who gave birth to him will ·stab [pierce] him.
4"·At that time [[L]On that day] the prophets will be ashamed of their
visions and prophecies. They won't wear the prophet's clothes made of hair
[[C]like Elijah (1 Kin. 19:13) and Elisha (1 Kin. 19:19); cf. John the Baptist (Matt.
3:4)] to ·trick [deceive] people. 5Each of them will say, 'I am not a prophet. I
am a farmer ·and have been a farmer since I was young [[L]for a man sold me
in my youth; [C]as an indentured servant to work the land].' 6But someone will
ask, 'What are the ·deep cuts [wounds] ·on your body [*or* on your chest;
[L]between your hands; [C]pagan prophets often cut themselves to appeal to their
gods]?' And each will answer, 'I was ·hurt [wounded] at my friend's house.'

The Shepherd Is Killed

7"·Sword, hit the [[L]Awake, Sword, against my] shepherd.
·Attack [[L]...against] the man who is my ·friend [associate],"
says the LORD ·All-Powerful [Almighty; of Heaven's Armies; [T]of hosts].
"·Kill [Strike] the shepherd,
and the sheep will scatter [Matt. 26:31; Mark 14:27],
and I will ·punish [[L]turn my hand against] the little ones."
8The LORD says, "Two-thirds of the people
through all the land will die. They will be ·gone [struck down; [L]cut off],
and one-third will be left.
9The third that is left I will ·test with [[L]bring into the] fire,
·purifying [refining] them like silver,
testing them like gold.
Then they will call on ·me [my name],
and I will answer them.
I will say, 'These are my people,'
and they will say, 'The LORD is our God.' "

The Day of Punishment

14 The ·LORD's day of judging [[L]day of the LORD; Zeph. 1:7] is coming
when ·the wealth you have taken [your plunder] will be divided
·among you [in your midst; *or* right in front of you; while you watch].
2I will bring all the nations together to ·fight [wage war against]
Jerusalem. They will capture the city and ·rob [plunder; loot] the houses
and ·attack [rape] the women. Half the people will be taken away ·as captives [into exile], but the rest of the people won't be taken from the city.
3Then the LORD will go to war against those nations; he will fight as in a
day of battle. 4On that day ·he [[L]his feet] will stand on the Mount of Olives,
east of Jerusalem. The Mount of Olives will split in two, forming a deep
valley that runs east and west. Half the mountain will move toward the
north, and half will move toward the south. 5You will ·run [flee] through
this mountain valley, for it will extend to Azel [[C]unknown location east of

Jerusalem]. You will run just as you did from the earthquake when Uzziah
was king of Judah [Amos 1:1]. Then the LORD my God will come and all the
holy ones [Ceither angels or believers; Matt. 25:31; 1 Thess. 3:13; Jude 14;
Rev. 19:14] with him.
6On that day there will be no light, ·cold, or frost [*or* the sources of
lights will diminish]. 7There will be no other day like it, ·and the LORD
knows when it will come [La day known to the LORD]. There will be no day
or night; even at evening it will still be light.
8At that time ·fresh [bubbling; *or* living; life-giving] water will flow
from Jerusalem. Half of it will flow east to the ·Dead [Leastern] Sea, and
half will flow west to the ·Mediterranean [Lwestern] Sea. It will flow summer and winter.
9Then the LORD will be king over the whole world. ·At that time [LOn that
day] ·there will be only one LORD [Lthe LORD will be one; Deut. 6:4–5], and
his name ·will be the only name [Lone].
10All the land south of Jerusalem from Geba [Csix miles northeast of
Jerusalem, the northern boundary of Judah] to ·Rimmon [Cthirty-five miles
southwest of Jerusalem] will be ·turned into a plain [*or* like the Arabah; Cthe
Jordan Valley, from Mount Hermon to the Gulf of Aqaba]. Jerusalem will be
raised up, but it will stay in the same place. The city will reach from the
Benjamin Gate and to the First Gate to the Corner Gate, and from the
Tower of Hananel to the king's winepresses. 11People will live there, and it
will never be destroyed again. Jerusalem will ·be safe [dwell in security].
12But the LORD will bring a terrible ·disease [plague] on the nations that
fought against Jerusalem. Their flesh will rot away while they are still
standing up. Their eyes will rot in their sockets, and their tongues will rot
in their mouths. 13·At that time [LOn that day] the LORD will cause panic.
Everybody will grab ·his [Lthe hand of his] neighbor, and they will ·attack
each other [Lraise his hand against the hand of his neighbor]. 14·The people
of Judah [LJudah] will fight in Jerusalem. And the wealth of the nations
around them will be collected—much gold, silver, and clothes. 15A similar
·disease [plague] will strike the horses, mules, camels, donkeys, and all the
animals in the camps.
16All of those left alive of the ·people [nations] who came to fight
Jerusalem will come back to Jerusalem year after year to worship the King,
the LORD ·All-Powerful [Almighty; of Heaven's Armies; Tof hosts], and to
celebrate the Feast of ·Shelters [Booths; Tabernacles; Deut. 31:9–13].
17Anyone from the nations who does not go to Jerusalem to worship the
King, the LORD ·All-Powerful [Almighty; of Heaven's Armies; Tof hosts],
will not have rain fall on his land. 18If the Egyptians do not go to Jerusalem,
they will not have rain. Then the LORD will send them the same ·terrible
disease [plague] he sent the other nations that did not celebrate the Feast
of ·Shelters [Booths; Tabernacles]. 19This will be the punishment for Egypt
and any nation that does not go up to celebrate the Feast of Shelters.
20·At that time [LOn that day] the horses' bells will have written on them:
HOLY TO THE LORD. The cooking pots in the Temple of the Lord will be like the
holy altar bowls. 21Every pot in Jerusalem and Judah will be holy to the LORD
·All-Powerful [Almighty; of Heaven's Armies; Tof hosts], and everyone who
offers sacrifices will be able to take food from them and cook in them. ·At
that time [LOn that day] there will not be any ·buyers or sellers [*or* Canaanite]
in the Temple of the LORD [Matt. 21:12–13; John 2:13–16] ·All-Powerful
[Almighty; of Heaven's Armies; Tof hosts].

MALACHI

1 This ·message [oracle; burden] is the word of the LORD given to Israel through Malachi [C"my messenger"].

God Loves Israel

2 The LORD said, "I have loved you."

But you ask, "How have you loved us?"

The LORD said, "Esau and Jacob were brothers. I loved Jacob, 3 but I ·hated [rejected] Esau [Gen. 25:19–34]. I ·destroyed [laid waste] his mountain country and left his ·land [inheritance] to the ·wild dogs [jackals] of the ·desert [wilderness]."

4 The people of Edom [Ldescendants of Esau] might say, "We were ·destroyed [crushed; shattered], but we will go back and rebuild the ruins."

But the LORD ·All-Powerful [Almighty; of Heaven's Armies; Tof hosts] says, "If they rebuild them, I will ·destroy [demolish] them. ·People will say, 'Edom is a wicked country. The LORD is always angry with the Edomites.' [*or* They will be known as, 'The Wicked Land' and 'The people always under God's wrath.'] 5 You will see these things with your own eyes. And you will say, 'The LORD is great, even ·outside [beyond] the borders of Israel!' "

The Priests Don't Respect God

6 The LORD ·All-Powerful [Almighty; of Heaven's Armies; Tof hosts] says, "A son honors his father [Ex. 20:12; Deut. 5:16], and a ·servant [slave] honors his master." ·I am a [LIf I am your] father, so why don't you honor me? ·I am a [LIf I am your] master, so why don't you respect me? You priests ·do not respect me [Ldespise my name].

"But you ask, 'How have we ·shown you disrespect [Ldespised your name]?'

7 "You have shown it by bringing ·unclean [defiled] food to my altar.

"But you ask, 'What makes it ·unclean [defiled]?'

"It is ·unclean [defiled] because you ·don't respect [treat as contemptible] the altar of the LORD. 8 When you ·bring [offer] blind animals as sacrifices, ·that is [Lis that not…?] wrong. When you ·bring [offer] crippled and sick animals, ·that is [Lis that not…?] wrong [Lev. 1:3]. Try giving them to your governor. Would he be pleased with you? ·He wouldn't [LWould he…?] accept you," says the LORD ·All-Powerful [Almighty; of Heaven's Armies; Tof hosts].

9 "Now ·ask [plead with] God to ·be kind [show favor] to you, but he won't ·accept [show favor to] you with such offerings," says the LORD ·All-Powerful [Almighty; of Heaven's Armies; Tof hosts].

10 "I wish one of you would close the Temple doors so that you would not light ·useless [worthless; meaningless] fires on my altar! I am not pleased with you and will not accept ·your gifts [Lan offering from your hand]," says the LORD ·All-Powerful [Almighty; of Heaven's Armies; Tof

hosts]. 11“From the east to the west ·I [[L]my name] will be honored among
the nations. Everywhere they will bring incense and ·clean [pure; unde-
filed] offerings to me, because ·I will be honored [[L]my name will be great]
among the nations,” says the LORD ·All-Powerful [Almighty; of Heaven’s
Armies; [T]of hosts].
12“But you ·don’t honor [profane] me. You say about the Lord’s ·altar
[table], ‘It is ·unclean [defiled], and the food has no worth [is despicable/
contemptible].’ 13You say, ‘We are tired of doing this,’ and you ·sniff
[sneer] at it in disgust,” says the LORD ·All-Powerful [Almighty; of Heaven’s
Armies; [T]of hosts].
“And you bring ·hurt [*or* stolen], crippled, and sick animals as gifts.
You bring them as ·gifts [offerings], but I won’t accept them from ·you
[[L]your hands],” says the LORD. 14“The person who cheats will be cursed.
He has a male animal in his flock and promises to offer it, but then he
offers to the Lord an animal that ·has something wrong with it [is blem-
ished; Lev. 1:3]. I am a great king,” says the LORD ·All-Powerful [Almighty;
of Heaven’s Armies; [T]of hosts], “and ·I am [my name is] feared ·by all
[among] the nations.

Rules for Priests

2 “Priests, this ·command [warning] is for you. 2Listen to me. Pay
attention to what I say. Honor my name,” says the LORD ·All-Powerful
[Almighty; of Heaven’s Armies; [T]of hosts]. “If you don’t, I will send a curse
on you and on your blessings. I have already cursed them, because you don’t
·pay attention to what I say [take my warning to heart].
3“I will ·punish [discipline; rebuke] your descendants. I will smear
your faces with ·the animal insides [offal; entrails; *or* dung] left from your
feasts, and you will be thrown away with it. 4Then you will know that I am
giving you this ·command [warning] so my ·agreement [covenant; treaty]
with Levi will continue,” says the LORD ·All-Powerful [Almighty; of
Heaven’s Armies; [T]of hosts]. 5“My ·agreement [covenant; treaty] with ·the
Levites [[L]him; [C]Levi] was to bring life and peace so they would ·honor
[fear] me. And they did ·honor [fear] me and ·fear me [[L]stood in awe of
my name; Prov. 1:7]. 6·They taught the true teachings [True law/instruc-
tion/[L]Torah was in his mouth] and ·spoke no lies [no iniquity was found
on his lips]. With peace and ·honesty [integrity] they ·did what I said they
should do [walked with me], and they kept many people from sinning.
7“·A priest [[L]The lips of a priest] should ·teach what he knows [pre-
serve/guard knowledge; Deut. 33:10], and people should ·learn the
teachings [seek instruction] from ·him [[L]his mouth], because he is the
messenger of the LORD ·All-Powerful [Almighty; of Heaven’s Armies; [T]of
hosts]. 8But you priests have ·stopped obeying me [[L]turned from the way/
path]. With your teachings you have caused many people to ·do wrong
[stumble]. You have ·broken [corrupted] the ·agreement [covenant;
treaty] with ·the tribe of Levi [[L]Levi]!” says the LORD ·All-Powerful
[Almighty; of Heaven’s Armies; [T]of hosts]. 9“You have not been careful to
·do what I say [follow my ways/paths], but instead you ·take sides [show
favoritism/partiality] in ·court [legal] cases. So I have caused you to be
·hated [despised] and ·disgraced [humiliated] in front of everybody.”

Judah Was Not Loyal to God

10·We all have the same [[L]Do we not have one….?] father; the ·same
[one] God created us. So why do people ·break their promises to [betray]
each other and ·show no respect for [profane; defile] the ·agreement [cov-
enant; treaty] our ·ancestors [fathers] made with God [Ex. 19–24]? 11·The

people of Judah [LJudah] have ·broken their promises [been unfaithful]. They have done ·something God hates [an abomination/detestable thing] in Israel and Jerusalem: ·The people of Judah [LJudah] ·did not respect [desecrated] the ·Temple [sanctuary; *or* holy things] that the LORD loves, and the men of Judah married ·women who worship [Lthe daughter of] foreign gods. 12Whoever does this might bring offerings to the LORD ·All-Powerful [Almighty; of Heaven's Armies; Tof hosts], but the LORD will still cut that person off from the ·community of Israel [Ltents of Jacob].

13This is another thing you do. You cover the LORD's altar with your tears. You ·cry [weep] and moan, because he does not ·accept [look with favor on] your offerings and is not pleased with what you bring. 14You ask, "Why?" It is because the LORD ·sees how you treated [Lis the witness between you and] the wife ·you married when you were young [Lof your youth]. You ·broke your promise [have been unfaithful] to her, even though she was your partner and ·you had an agreement with her [your wife by solemn covenant]. 15·God made [LDid not God make…?] husbands and wives to become one body and one spirit for his purpose—so they would have ·children who are true to God [godly offspring].

So ·be careful [Lguard yourself in your spirit], and do not ·break your promise [be unfaithful] to the wife ·you married when you were young [Lof your youth].

16The LORD God of Israel says, "·I hate divorce. And I hate the person who [*or* The one who hates and divorces] ·does cruel things as easily as he puts on clothes [Lcovers his clothes in violence]," says the LORD ·All-Powerful [Almighty; of Heaven's Armies; Tof hosts].

So be ·careful [on your guard]. And do not ·break your trust [be unfaithful].

The Special Day of Judging

17You have ·tired [wearied] the LORD with your words.

You ask, "How have we ·tired [wearied] him?"

You did it by saying, "·The LORD thinks [LIn the LORD's eyes] anyone who does evil is good, and he is pleased with them." Or you asked, "Where is the God ·who is fair [of justice]?"

3 The LORD ·All-Powerful [Almighty; of Heaven's Armies; Tof hosts] says, "I will send my messenger, who will prepare the way for me [Is. 40:3; Matt. 11:10; Mark 1:2; Luke 7:27]. Suddenly, the Lord you are ·looking for [seeking] will come to his Temple; the messenger of the ·agreement [covenant; treaty], ·whom you want [in whom you delight], will come." 2·No one can live through [LWho can endure…?] ·that time [the day of his coming]; ·no one can survive [who can stand…?] when he ·comes [appears]. He will be like a ·purifying [refiner's] fire and like ·laundry [launderer's] soap. 3Like someone who ·heats [refines] and purifies silver, he will purify the ·Levites [Lsons/descendants of Levi] and ·make them pure [refine them] like gold and silver. Then they will bring offerings to the LORD in ·the right way [righteousness]. 4And the LORD will ·accept [be pleased with] the offerings from Judah and Jerusalem, as it was in ·the past [Ldays of antiquity and former years]. 5The LORD ·All-Powerful [Almighty; of Heaven's Armies; Tof hosts] says, "Then I will come to you and judge you. I will be quick to testify against those who take part in ·evil magic [sorcery], adultery, and ·lying under oath [perjury], those who cheat workers of their pay and who cheat widows and orphans, those who ·are unfair to [turn away; deprive of justice] ·foreigners [aliens; immigrants], and those who do not ·respect [fear] me [Prov. 1:7].

Stealing from God

6“I the LORD do not change. So you descendants of Jacob have not been
·destroyed [consumed]. 7·Since the time [LFrom the days] of your ·ancestors
[fathers], you have ·disobeyed [turned away from; spurned] my ·rules [decrees;
commands] and have not kept them. Return to me, and I will return to you,”
says the LORD ·All-Powerful [Almighty; of Heaven’s Armies; Tof hosts].
“But you ask, ‘How can we return?’
8“·Should [or Can] a person rob God? But you are robbing me.
“You ask, ‘How have we robbed you?’
“You have robbed me in your offerings and ·the tenth of your crops
[tithes]. 9So a curse is on you, because the whole nation has robbed me.
10Bring to the storehouse a full ·tenth of what you earn [tithe] so there will
be food in my house [Cthe temple; Deut. 14:22–28]. Test me in this,” says the
LORD ·All-Powerful [Almighty; of Heaven’s Armies; Tof hosts]. “I will open
the windows of heaven for you and pour out all the blessings you need. 11I
will stop the ·insects [pests; *or* plague; Lthe devourer] so they won’t ·eat
[destroy] your crops. The grapes won’t ·fall from your vines before they are
ready to pick [*or* fail to produce a crop],” says the LORD ·All-Powerful
[Almighty; of Heaven’s Armies; Tof hosts]. 12“All the nations will call you
blessed, because you will have a ·pleasant country [delightful land],” says
the LORD ·All-Powerful [Almighty; of Heaven’s Armies; Tof hosts].

The Lord’s Promise of Mercy

13The LORD says, “You have said ·terrible things about [Lhard things
against] me.
“But you ask, ‘What have we said about you?’
14“You have said, ‘It is ·useless [futile] to serve God. ·It did no good to
obey [LWhat profit is there to keep] his laws and to ·show that we were
sorry [Lwalk about in mourning] for what we did before the LORD ·All-
Powerful [Almighty; of Heaven’s Armies; Tof hosts]. 15So we say that
proud people are ·happy [blessed]. Evil people ·succeed [prosper]. They
·challenge [test] God and ·get away with it [escape harm].’ ”
16Then those who ·honored [feared] the LORD spoke with each other,
and the LORD listened and heard them. The names of those who ·respected
[feared] the LORD and honored ·him [Lhis name] were written in his presence in a ·book to be remembered [scroll of remembrance].
17The LORD ·All-Powerful [Almighty; of Heaven’s Armies; Tof hosts]
says, “They ·belong to me [shall be mine]; on that day they will be my
·very own [treasured possession; special treasure]. As a ·parent [father]
·shows mercy to [spares] his ·child [son] who serves him, I will ·show
mercy to [spare] my people. 18You will again see the difference between
·good [the righteous] and ·evil people [the wicked], between those who
serve God and those who don’t.

The Day of the Lord’s Judging

4 “[LFor look/Tbehold] There is a day coming that will burn like a
hot furnace, and all the ·proud [arrogant] and ·evil people [evil-
doers] will be like ·straw [chaff; stubble]. On that day they will be
completely burned up so that not a root or branch will be left,” says the
LORD ·All-Powerful [Almighty; of Heaven’s Armies; Tof hosts]. 2“But for
you who ·honor me [Lfear/revere my name], ·goodness will shine on you
like the sun [Lthe sun of righteousness will rise], with healing in its ·rays
[Lwings]. You will ·jump around [go out leaping], like ·well-fed calves
[Lcalves from the stall]. 3Then you will ·crush [trample] the wicked like
ashes under your feet on the day I will do this,” says the LORD ·All-Powerful
[Almighty; of Heaven’s Armies; Tof hosts].

4"Remember the ·teaching [law; [L]Torah] of Moses my servant, those ·laws [decrees] and rules I gave to him on ·Mount Sinai [[L]Horeb] for all the Israelites [Ex. 19–24].

5"But I will send you Elijah the prophet before that great and terrifying day of the ·LORD's judging [[L]LORD]. 6Elijah will ·help parents love [[L]turn the hearts of fathers/parents to] their children and ·children love [[L]turn children to] their parents. Otherwise, I will come and ·put a curse on the land [strike the land with a curse/destruction]."

New Testament

MATTHEW

The Family History of Jesus
(1:1–17; Luke 3:23–38)

1 **This is the ·family history** [record of the ancestors; genealogy; [L]book of the offspring/family; [C]perhaps a title for the entire book] **of Jesus ·Christ** [the Messiah]. **·He came from the family of David, and David came from the family of Abraham** [[L]...the son of David, the son of Abraham; [C]"son" can mean descendant].
2Abraham ·was the father of [fathered; [T]begot; [C]and so throughout the genealogy; the word can refer to more distant ancestry] **Isaac.**
Isaac was the father of Jacob.
Jacob was the father of Judah and his brothers.
3Judah was the father of Perez and Zerah.
(Their mother was Tamar [Gen. 38].**)**
Perez was the father of Hezron.
Hezron was the father of Ram.
4Ram was the father of Amminadab.
Amminadab was the father of Nahshon.
Nahshon was the father of Salmon.
5Salmon was the father of Boaz.
(Boaz's mother was Rahab [Josh. 2].**)**
Boaz was the father of Obed.
(Obed's mother was Ruth [Ruth 4:13–22].**)**
Obed was the father of Jesse.
6Jesse was the father of King David.
David was the father of Solomon.
(Solomon's mother had been Uriah's wife [[C]Bathsheba; 2 Sam. 11–12].**)**
7Solomon was the father of Rehoboam.
Rehoboam was the father of Abijah.
Abijah was the father of Asa.[n]
8Asa was the father of Jehoshaphat.
Jehoshaphat was the father of Joram [[C]a variant spelling of Jehoram; 1 Kin. 22:50].
Joram was the ·ancestor [*or* father; [C]see v. 2] **of Uzziah.**
9Uzziah was the father of Jotham.
Jotham was the father of Ahaz.
Ahaz was the father of Hezekiah.
10Hezekiah was the father of Manasseh.
Manasseh was the father of Amon.
Amon was the father of Josiah.
11Josiah was the ·grandfather [*or* father; [C]see v. 2] **of Jeconiah** [[C]another name for Jehoiachin; see 2 Kin. 24:6; 1 Chr. 3:16] **and his brothers.**

1:7 Asa Some Greek copies read "Asaph," another name for Asa (see 1 Chronicles 3:10).

(This was at the time ·that the people were taken [Lof the exile/deportation; 2 Kin. 24:8–17] to Babylon.)

12After ·they were taken [the exile/deportation] to Babylon:
Jeconiah was the father of Shealtiel.
Shealtiel was the ·grandfather [*or* father; Csee v. 2] of Zerubbabel [Ezra 2].
13Zerubbabel was the father of Abiud.
Abiud was the father of Eliakim.
Eliakim was the father of Azor.
14Azor was the father of Zadok.
Zadok was the father of ·Akim [Achim].
·Akim [Achim] was the father of Eliud.
15Eliud was the father of Eleazar.
Eleazar was the father of Matthan.
Matthan was the father of Jacob.
16Jacob was the father of Joseph.
Joseph was the husband of Mary,
and Mary ·was the mother of [gave birth to] Jesus, who is called the ·Christ [Messiah].

17So there were fourteen generations [Lin all] from Abraham to David. And there were fourteen generations from David until the ·people were taken [exile; deportation] to Babylon. And there were fourteen generations from the time ·when the people were taken [of the exile/deportation] to Babylon until ·Christ [the Messiah] was born.

The Birth of Jesus Christ

18This is how the birth of Jesus ·Christ [the Messiah] came about. His mother Mary was ·engaged [pledged; Tbetrothed; Ca formal agreement between families that required a "divorce" to annul] to marry Joseph, but before they ·married [came to live together], she ·learned she was [*or* was found/discovered to be] ·pregnant [Twith child] ·by the power of [through] the Holy Spirit. 19Because Mary's husband, Joseph, was a ·good [righteous] man, he did not want to disgrace her in public, so he planned to ·divorce her [end the engagement] ·secretly [privately; quietly].

20While Joseph ·thought about [considered; decided; resolved to do] these things, [Llook; Tbehold] an angel of the Lord ·came [appeared] to him in a dream. The angel said, "Joseph, ·descendant [son] of David, don't be afraid to take Mary as your wife, because ·the baby [Lwhat is conceived] in her is from the Holy Spirit. 21She will give birth to a son, and you will name him Jesus, because he will save his people from their sins [Cthe name Jesus means "the Lord saves"]."

22All this happened to ·bring about [fulfill] what the Lord had ·said [spoken] through the prophet: 23"[LLook; TBehold] The virgin will ·be pregnant [Lconceive in her womb; Is. 7:14]. She will ·have [give birth to] a son, and they will name him Immanuel," which [Cin Hebrew] means "God is with us."

24When Joseph woke up, he did what the Lord's angel had ·told [commanded] him to do. Joseph took Mary as his wife, 25but he did not have sexual relations with her until she gave birth to a son. And ·Joseph [Lhe] named him Jesus.

Wise Men Come to Visit Jesus

2 ·When [After] Jesus was born in the town of Bethlehem in Judea during the time when Herod was king, some ·wise men [astrologers; magi; Ca class of wise men and priests who practiced astrology] from the east came to Jerusalem. 2They asked, "Where is the ·baby who was born to be the king [*or* newborn king] of the Jews? We saw his star ·in

the east [*or* when it rose] and have come to ·worship him [pay him
homage]."
3When King Herod heard this, he was ·troubled [very disturbed; fright-
ened], as were all the people in Jerusalem. 4Herod ·called a meeting of
[assembled] all the ·leading [Tchief] priests and ·teachers of the law [scribes]
and ·asked [inquired of] them where the ·Christ [Messiah] would be born.
5They answered, "In the town of Bethlehem in Judea. ·The prophet wrote
about this in the Scriptures [LFor so it has been written by the prophet]:
6'·But [*or* And] you, Bethlehem, in the land of Judah,
are ·not just an insignificant village in [Lby no means least among the
rulers/ruling cities of] Judah [Mic. 5:2].
[LFor; Because] A ruler will come from you
who will ·be like a shepherd for [Lshepherd] my people Israel.'"
7Then Herod ·had a secret meeting with [privately summoned] the
·wise men [astrologers; magi; v. 1] and ·learned [inquired] from them the
exact time ·they first saw the star [the star appeared]. 8He sent the ·wise
men [astrologers; magi] to Bethlehem, saying, "·Look [Go and search]
carefully for the child. When you find him, ·come tell [report to] me so I
can [Lgo and] ·worship [pay homage to] him too."
9After the ·wise men [astrologers; magi] ·heard [listened to; had their
interview with] the king, they ·left [went on their way; set out]. [LAnd look]
The star that they had seen ·in the east [*or* when it rose] went ·before [ahead
of] them until it ·stopped [stood] above the place where the child was.
10When the ·wise men [astologers; magi] saw the star, they ·were filled with
joy [were overjoyed; Lrejoiced with exceedingly great joy]. 11They ·came to
[entered] the house where the child was and saw him with his mother,
Mary, and they ·bowed down [knelt; Lfell] and ·worshiped [paid homage to]
him. They opened their ·gifts [treasure chests; treasures] and gave him gifts
of gold, frankincense, and myrrh. 12·But God warned the wise men [LBeing
warned; Cthe passive verb implies God as subject] in a dream not to go back
to Herod, so they returned to their own country by a different way.

Jesus' Parents Take Him to Egypt

13After they left, an angel of the Lord ·came [appeared] to Joseph in a
dream and said, "Get up! Take the child and his mother and ·escape [flee]
to Egypt. Stay there until I tell you to return, because Herod is ·starting
[intending; going] to ·look [search] for the child so he can kill him."
14So Joseph got up and left for Egypt during the night with the child
and his mother. 15And Joseph stayed in Egypt until Herod died. This happened to ·bring about [fulfill] what the Lord had said through the
prophet: "I called my son out of Egypt [Hos. 11:1; CJesus fulfills the role of
Israel by leading a spiritual Exodus]."

Herod Kills the Baby Boys

16When Herod saw that the ·wise men [astologers; magi] had ·tricked
[outwitted; outsmarted] him, he was furious. So he ·gave an order [*or* sent
soldiers] to kill all the baby boys in Bethlehem and in the surrounding
area who were two years old or younger. This was ·in keeping with [based
on] the time he learned from the ·wise men [astologers; magi]. 17·So
[Then] what ·God had said [Lwas spoken; Cthe passive verb implies God as
subject] through the prophet Jeremiah ·came true [was fulfilled]:
18"A ·voice [cry; sound] was heard in Ramah [Cthe sending point from
which the Jews went into exile to Babylon; Jer. 40:1]
·of painful crying [weeping] and ·deep sadness [great mourning/
lamentation]:

Rachel ·crying [weeping] for her children.
She refused to be comforted,
because ·her children are dead [[L]they are no more; Jer. 31:15]."

Joseph and Mary Return

19After Herod died, an angel of the Lord ·spoke [appeared] to Joseph in a dream while he was in Egypt. 20The angel said, "Get up! Take the child and his mother and go to the land of Israel, because the people who were ·trying to kill [[L]seeking the life of] the child are now dead."

21So Joseph [[L]got up,] took the child and his mother and ·went [returned] to Israel. 22But he heard that Archelaus [[C]reigned from 4 BC to AD 6] was now ·king [reigning] in Judea ·since his father Herod had died [[L]in place of his father Herod]. So Joseph was afraid to go there. After being warned in a dream, he ·went [withdrew] to the ·area [region; district] of Galilee, 23to a town called Nazareth, and lived there. And so what ·God had said [was spoken; [C]the passive verb implies God as subject] through the prophets ·came true [was fulfilled]: "He will be called a Nazarene [[C]a person from the town of Nazareth; perhaps a reference to Is. 11:1, where the Hebrew word translated "branch" sounds like "Nazarene"]."

The Work of John the Baptist

(3:1–10; Mark 1:2–6; Luke 3:1–9; John 1:19–23)

3 ·About that time [In the course of time; [L]In those days] John the Baptist began preaching in the ·desert area [wilderness] of Judea. 2John said, "·Change your hearts and lives [Repent] because the kingdom of heaven ·is near [has drawn near; is at hand]." 3·John the Baptist [[L]For this] is the one Isaiah the prophet was talking about when he said:

"This is a voice of one
who ·calls out [shouts; cries out] in the ·desert [wilderness]:
'Prepare the way for the Lord.
Make ·the road straight [a clear path] for him [Is. 40:3].'"

4John's clothes were made from camel's hair, and he wore a leather belt around his waist [[C]reminiscent of the prophet Elijah; 2 Kin. 1:8]. For food, he ate locusts and wild honey [[C]signifies living off the land]. 5Many people came from Jerusalem and Judea and all the ·area [region] around the Jordan River to hear John. 6They confessed their sins, and he baptized them in the Jordan River.

7Many of the Pharisees and Sadducees came to the place where John was baptizing people. When John saw them, he said, "You ·are snakes [[T]brood/offspring of vipers]! Who warned you to ·run [slither; [L]flee] away from God's coming ·punishment [wrath; retribution]? 8·Do the things [[L]Produce the fruit] ·that show you really have changed your hearts and lives [that prove your repentance; [L]of repentance]. 9And don't ·think you can [presume to] say to yourselves, 'Abraham is our father [[C]a claim to be God's special people].' [[L]For] I tell you that God could ·make [create; [L]raise up] children for Abraham from these rocks. 10The ax ·is now ready to cut down [already lies at the root of] the trees, and every tree that does not produce good fruit will be cut down and thrown into the fire [[C]a metaphor for judgment].

John Preaches About the Christ

(3:11–12; Mark 1:7–8; Luke 3:15–18; John 1:24–28)

11"I baptize you with water ·to show that your hearts and lives have changed [for repentence]. But there is one coming after me who is ·greater [mightier; more powerful] than I am, whose sandals I am not ·good enough [fit; qualified] to carry. He will baptize you with the Holy Spirit and fire. 12·He will come ready [[L]The winnowing fork is in his hand] to clean the grain, ·separating the good grain from the chaff [[L]to clear his threshing floor]. He will put ·the good part of the grain [[L]the grain/wheat]

into his barn, but he will burn the chaff with ·a fire that cannot be put out
[never-ending/unquenchable fire; Ca metaphor for judgment, when Jesus
will separate the righteous from the wicked]."

Jesus Is Baptized by John
(3:13–17; Mark 1:9–11; Luke 3:21–22; John 1:29–34)

13**·At that time** [Then] **Jesus came from Galilee to the Jordan River ·and**
wanted John to baptize him [Lto be baptized by John]. 14**But John tried to**
·stop [deter; dissuade; prevent] **him, saying, "·Why do** [Do] **you come to**
me to be baptized? I need to be baptized by you!"
15**Jesus answered, "Let it ·be this way for** [happen] **now. ·We should do**
all things that are God's will [*or* In this way we will do what God requires;
LFor thus it is fitting for us to fulfill all righteousness]." **So John ·agreed to**
baptize Jesus [gave in; consented; allowed it].
16**As soon as Jesus was baptized, he came up out of the water. Then**
·heaven [the sky/heavens] **opened, and he saw God's Spirit ·coming down**
[descending and lighting/settling] **on him like a dove** [Ceither in the form
of a dove, or in bird-like descent]. 17**And a voice from heaven said, "This**
is my ·Son, whom I love [dearly beloved Son; Ps. 2:7; Gen. 22:2], **and I am**
·very [well] **pleased with him** [Is. 42:1]."

The Temptation of Jesus
(4:1–11; Mark 1:12–13; Luke 4:1–13)

4 Then the Spirit led Jesus [Lup; out] **into the ·desert** [wilderness] **to**
be tempted [*or* tested] **by the devil.** 2**Jesus fasted for forty days**
and nights [Canalogous to Israel's forty years in the desert]. **After this, he**
was ·very hungry [famished]. 3**The ·devil came to Jesus to tempt him**
[Ltempter/tester came to Jesus], **saying, "If you are the Son of God, ·tell**
[command] **these rocks to ·become bread** [turn into loaves]."
4**Jesus answered, "It is written in the Scriptures, 'A person lives not on**
bread alone, but by ·everything God says [Levery word that comes out of
God's mouth; Deut. 8:3].'"
5**Then the devil ·led** [took] **Jesus to the holy city** [CJerusalem] **and put**
him on ·a high place [the highest point; the pinnacle] **of the Temple.** 6**The**
devil said, "If you are the Son of God, ·jump [Lthrow yourself] **down,**
because it is written in the Scriptures:

'He ·has put his angels in charge of you [*or* will order his angels to
protect you; Lwill command his angel concerning you].
They will ·catch you in [lift you up with] **their hands**
so that you will not hit your foot on a rock [Ps. 91:11–12].'"

7**Jesus answered him, "It also says in the Scriptures, 'Do not test the**
Lord your God [Deut. 6:16].'"
8**·Then** [Again] **the devil took Jesus to a very high mountain and**
showed him all the kingdoms of the world and all their ·splendor [glory].
9**The devil said, "If you will ·bow** [fall] **down and worship me, I will give**
you all these things."
10**Jesus said to him, "·Go away from me** [Get out of here; Be gone],
Satan! [LFor] **It is written in the Scriptures, 'You must worship the Lord**
your God and serve only him [Deut. 6:13].'"
11**So the devil left Jesus, and angels came and ·took care of** [served;
ministered to] **him.**

Jesus Begins Work in Galilee
(4:12–16; Mark 1:14–15; Luke 4:14–15; John 4:43–46)

12**When Jesus heard that John had been ·put in prison** [arrested], **he**
·went back [withdrew] **to Galilee.** 13**He left Nazareth and went to live in**
Capernaum, ·a town near Lake Galilee [Lby the sea], **in the ·area near**
[region of] **Zebulun and Naphtali** [Ctwo northern tribes of Israel]. 14**Jesus**
did this to ·bring about [fulfill] **what the prophet Isaiah had said:**

15“Land of Zebulun and land of Naphtali
·along [on the road by; Lthe way of] the sea,
beyond the Jordan River.
·This is Galilee where the Gentiles live [LGalilee of the Gentiles/nations].
16These people who ·live [dwell; sit] in darkness
·will see [Lhave seen] a great light.
And on those ·living [dwelling; sitting] in ·a place covered with the
shadows of death [a land overshadowed by death; La/the region
and shadow of death],
a light ·will shine [Lhas dawned] on them [Is. 9:1–2].”

Jesus Chooses Some Followers
(4:17–22; Mark 1:16–20)

17From that time Jesus began to preach, saying, “·Change your hearts
and lives [Repent], because the kingdom of heaven is ·near [at hand].”
18As Jesus was walking by ·Lake Galilee [Tthe Sea of Galilee], he saw two
brothers, Simon (called Peter) and his brother Andrew. They were ·throw-
ing [casting] a net into the lake because they were fishermen. 19Jesus said,
“Come ·follow me [be my disciples], and I will ·make you [teach you how
to] ·fish for people [Tfishers of men].” 20So Simon and Andrew immediately left their nets and followed him.
21As Jesus ·continued walking by Lake Galilee [went on from there], he
saw two other brothers, ·James and John, the sons of Zebedee [LJames the
son of Zebedee, and his brother John]. They were in a boat with their
father Zebedee, ·mending [*or* preparing] their nets. Jesus ·told them to
come with him [called them]. 22Immediately they left the boat and their
father, and they followed Jesus.

Jesus Teaches and Heals People
(4:23–25; Mark 1:39; 3:7–13; Luke 4:44; 6:17–19)

23Jesus went everywhere in Galilee, teaching in the synagogues, preaching the ·Good News about [Gospel of] the kingdom, and healing ·all [*or*
every kind of] the people’s diseases and sicknesses. 24The ·news [fame]
about Jesus spread ·all over [*or* as far as] Syria, and people brought all the
sick to him. They were suffering from different kinds of diseases. Some
were in great pain, some ·had demons [were demon-possessed], some
were epileptics, and some were paralyzed. Jesus healed all of them.
25·Many people [Great crowds] from Galilee, the ·Ten Towns [LDecapolis;
Cthe area east of Lake Galilee that once had ten main towns], Jerusalem,
Judea, and ·the land across [beyond] the Jordan River followed him.

Jesus Teaches the People
(5:1–12; Luke 6:17–23)

5 When Jesus saw the crowds, he went up on ·a hill [the mountain]
and sat down. His ·followers [disciples] ·came to [gathered
around] him, 2and he began to teach them, saying:
3“·They are blessed [*or* Blessed are those…; Cand so through v. 10] who
·realize their spiritual poverty [Lare the poor in spirit],
for the kingdom of heaven ·belongs to them [is theirs].
4They are blessed who ·grieve [mourn],
for ·God will comfort them [Lthey will be comforted; Cthe passive
verb implies God as subject].
5They are blessed who are ·humble [meek; gentle],
for ·the whole earth will be theirs [Lthey shall inherit the earth; Ps. 37:11].
6They are blessed who hunger and thirst after ·justice [righteousness],
for they will be ·satisfied [filled].
7They are blessed who show mercy to others,
for ·God will show mercy to them [Lthey will be shown mercy; Cthe
passive verb implies God as subject].

8 They are blessed ·whose thoughts are pure [*or* whose hearts are pure;
TThe pure in heart],
for they will see God.
9 They are blessed who work for peace [TBlessed are the peacemakers],
for they will be called God's ·children [*or* sons].
10 They are blessed who are persecuted for ·doing good [doing what's
right; Lthe sake of righteousness],
for the kingdom of heaven ·belongs to them [is theirs].
11 "·You are blessed [TBlessed are you; *or* God will bless you] when people ·insult [mock; abuse; revile] you and ·hurt [persecute] you. They will
lie and say all kinds of evil things ·about [against] you because ·you follow [Lof] me. 12 Rejoice and be glad, because you have a great reward in
heaven. ·People did the same evil things to [LThey likewise persecuted]
the prophets who lived before you.

You Are Like Salt and Light
(5:13–16; Mark 9:49–50; 4:21; Luke 8:16; 14:34–35)

13 "You are the salt of the earth. But if the salt ·loses its salty taste
[becomes tasteless], ·it cannot [Lhow can it…?] be made salty again. It is
good for nothing, except to be thrown out and ·walked on [trampled].
14 "You are the light ·that gives light to [for; Lof] the world. A city that
·is built [stands; is set] on a hill cannot be hidden. 15 And people don't
light a lamp and then hide it under a ·bowl [*or* basket]. They put it on a
lampstand so the light shines for all the people in the house. 16 In the same
way let your light shine ·before others [for people to see], so that they will
see ·the good things you do [Lyour good deeds/works] and will ·praise
[glorify; give honor to] your Father in heaven.

The Importance of the Law and the Prophets
(5:17–20; Luke 16:16–17)

17 "Don't think that I have come to ·destroy [abolish; do away with] ·the
law of Moses or the teaching of the prophets [Lthe Law and the Prophets;
Creferring to the OT]. I have not come to destroy them but to ·bring about
what they said [fulfill/complete them]. 18 I tell you the truth, until heaven
and earth ·are gone [pass away; disappear], not even ·the smallest letter
[Tone jot; Lone *iota;* Cthe smallest Greek letter] or the smallest ·part [stroke;
Ttittle] of a letter will ·be lost [pass away; disappear] until everything ·has
happened [is accomplished/achieved]. 19 [LTherefore] Whoever ·refuses to
obey [ignores; breaks; annuls] ·any command [Lone of the least of these
commands] and teaches other people ·not to obey that command [Lto do
likewise] will be ·the least important [Lcalled/considered least] in the
kingdom of heaven. But whoever ·obeys [keeps; practices] the commands
and teaches other people to obey them will be [considered; Lcalled] great
in the kingdom of heaven. 20 [LFor] I tell you that ·if you are no more obedient than [Lunless your righteousness surpasses/exceeds that of] the
·teachers of the law [scribes] and the Pharisees, you will ·never [*or* certainly not] enter the kingdom of heaven.

Jesus Teaches About Anger
(5:21–26; Luke 12:57–59)

21 "You have heard that it was said to ·our people long ago [our ancestors; the ancients], 'You ·must [Lshall] not murder [Ex. 20:13; Deut. 5:17].
Anyone who murders another will be ·judged [subject to judgment].'
22 But I tell you, ·if you are [Leveryone who is] angry with a brother or
sister,ⁿ you will be ·judged [subject to judgment]. ·If you say [LWhoever
says] ·bad things ["Fool!"; L*Raca;* Can Aramaic term of derision] to a
brother or sister, you will be ·judged [subject/liable to judgment] by the
·council [Sanhedrin]. And if you call someone a ·fool [idiot; moron], you

5:22 sister Some Greek copies continue, "without a reason."

will be in danger of the fire of ·hell [[L]Gehenna; [C]a valley outside of Jerusalem where in the OT period children were sacrificed to a pagan god; later used as a burning trash heap; a metaphor for hell].

[23]**"So when you ·offer your gift to God** [present your offering/sacrifice] **at the altar, and you remember that your brother or sister has something against you,** [24]**leave your ·gift** [offering; sacrifice] **there at the altar. Go and ·make peace** [be reconciled] **with that person** [[L]first], **and then come and ·offer your gift** [present your offering/sacrifice].

[25]**"If your ·enemy** [opponent; adversary; accuser] **is taking you to court, ·become friends** [reach agreement; settle matters] **quickly, ·before you go** [on the way] **to court. Otherwise, your ·enemy** [opponent; adversary; accuser] **might turn you over to the judge, and the judge might give you to the ·guard** [officer; warden] **to ·put** [throw] **you in ·jail** [prison]. [26]**I tell you the truth, you will ·not** [never; certainly not] **leave there until you have paid ·everything you owe** [the last penny; [C]Greek: the last *quadrans*; a small copper coin of very low value].

Jesus Teaches About Sexual Sin
(5:27–30; Mark 9:43–48)

[27]**"You have heard that it was said, 'You ·must** [shall] **not ·be guilty of** [commit] **adultery** [Ex. 20:14; Deut. 5:18].**'** [28]**But I tell you that if anyone looks at a woman ·and wants to sin sexually with her** [lustfully; [L]with a desire for her], **in his ·mind** [heart] **he has already ·done that sin** [committed adultery] **with her.** [29]**If your right eye causes you to ·sin** [[L]stumble], **·take** [tear; gouge] **it out and throw it away.** [[L]For] **It is better to lose one part of your body than to have your whole body thrown into ·hell** [[L]Gehenna; v. 22]. [30]**If your right hand causes you to ·sin** [[L]stumble], **cut it off and throw it away. It is better to lose one part of your body than for your whole body to go into ·hell** [[L]Gehenna; v. 22].

Jesus Teaches About Divorce
(5:31–32; Luke 16:18)

[31]**"It was also said, 'Anyone who divorces his wife must give her a written divorce ·paper** [notice; certificate; Deut. 24:1].**'** [32]**But I tell you that anyone who divorces his wife ·forces** [causes; makes] **her ·to be guilty of** [commit] **adultery. ·The only reason for a man to divorce his wife is if she has sexual relations with another man** [[L]...except in the case of sexual immorality]. **And anyone who marries that divorced woman ·is guilty of** [commits] **adultery.**

Make Promises Carefully

[33]**"**[[L]Again] **You have heard that it was said to ·our people long ago** [our ancestors; the ancients], **'Don't break your ·promises** [vows; oaths], **but ·keep** [fulfill] **the ·promises** [vows; oaths] **you make to the Lord** [Lev. 19:12; Num. 30:2; Deut. 23:21].**'** [34]**But I tell you, do not swear an oath at all. ·Don't swear an oath using the name of heaven** [[L]...neither by heaven], **because heaven is God's throne.** [35]**·Don't swear an oath using the name of the earth** [[L]...nor by earth], **because the earth ·belongs to God** [[L]is his footstool; Is. 66:1]. **·Don't swear an oath using the name of Jerusalem** [...nor by Jerusalem], **because it is the city of the great King** [Ps. 48:2]. [36]**Don't even swear by your own head, because you cannot make one hair on your head become white or black.** [37]**·Say only yes if you mean yes, and no if you mean no** [[L]Let your word "yes" be "yes"; your "no" be "no"]. **·If you say more than yes or no, it** [[L]Anything more than this] **is from the Evil One.**

Don't Retaliate
(5:38–42; Luke 6:29–30)

[38]**"You have heard that it was said, 'An eye for an eye, and a tooth for a tooth** [Ex. 21:24; Lev. 24:20; Deut. 19:21].**'** [39]**But I tell you, don't ·stand up against** [resist; retaliate against] **an evil person. If someone ·slaps** [strikes] **you on the right cheek** [[C]either an insult or an act of violence], **turn to him**

the other cheek also. 40If someone wants to sue you in court and take your ·shirt [tunic], let him have your coat also. 41If someone forces you to go with him one mile, go with him two miles [Calluding to the practice of impressment, whereby a Roman soldier could command a civilian to carry his gear for a mile]. 42If a person asks you for something, give it to him. Don't ·refuse to give to [Lturn away from] someone who wants to borrow from you.

Love All People
(5:43–48; Luke 6:27–28, 32–36)

43"You have heard that it was said, 'Love your neighbor and hate your enemy [Lev. 19:18].' 44But I say to you, love your enemies. Pray for those who ·hurt [persecute] you." 45·If you do this, [...so that] you will be ·true children [Lchildren; *or* sons] of your Father in heaven. [LFor] He causes ·the [Lhis] sun to rise on evil people and on good people, and he sends rain ·to those who do right and to those who do wrong [Lon the just/righteous and the unjust/unrighteous]. 46[LFor] If you love only the people who love you, ·you will get no reward [what reward is there for that?]. ·Even [LDon't even...?] the tax collectors do that. 47And if you ·are nice only to your friends [Lgreet only your brothers; Cprobably meaning fellow Jews], ·you are no better than other people [Lwhat more are you doing (than others)?]. Even ·those who don't know God [the Gentiles; pagans] ·are nice to their friends [Ldo the same]. 48·So [Therefore] you must be perfect, just as your Father in heaven is perfect.

Jesus Teaches About Giving

6 "·Be careful! When you do good things, don't do them [*or* Be careful not to do/parade your righteous deeds] in front of people to be ·seen [noticed] by them. If you do that, you will ·have no [lose the] reward from your Father in heaven.

2"[LSo] When you give to the poor, don't be like the hypocrites. They blow trumpets [Ceither figuratively ("blow their own horn") or literally, since trumpets sometimes announced public events] in the synagogues and on the streets so that people will see them and ·honor [admire] them. I tell you the truth, those hypocrites already have their full reward [Cpraise from people, rather than reward from God]. 3So when you give to the poor, don't let ·anyone know what you are [Lyour left hand know what your right hand is] doing. 4Your giving should be done in ·secret [private]. Your Father can see what is done in ·secret [private], and he will reward you.

Jesus Teaches About Prayer
(6:5–15; Mark 11:25–26; Luke 11:1–4)

5"When you pray, don't be like the hypocrites. They love to stand in the synagogues and on the street corners and pray so people will ·see [notice] them. I tell you the truth, they already have their full reward. 6When you pray, you should go into your [private; inner] room and close the door and pray to your Father ·who cannot be seen [*or* who is in that secret place; *or* secretly; in private]. Your Father can see what is done in ·secret [private], and he will reward you.

7"And when you pray, don't be like ·those people who don't know God [the pagans/Gentiles/heathen]. They ·continue saying things that mean nothing [babble; repeat empty phrases], thinking ·that God will hear them [Lthey will be heard; Cthe passive verb implies God as subject] because of their many words. 8Don't be like them, because your Father knows the things you need before you ask him. 9So when you pray, you should pray like this:

'Our Father in heaven,
·may your name always be kept holy [THallowed be your name].

5:44 you Some Greek copies continue, "Bless those who curse you, do good to those who hate you." Compare Luke 6:28.

10May your kingdom come
·and what you want [Your will] be done,
here on earth as it is in heaven.
11Give us ·the food we need for each day [Ttoday our daily bread].
12Forgive us for our ·sins [Ldebts],
just as we have forgiven ·those who sinned against us [Lour debtors;
Csin is pictured as a debt owed].
13And ·do not cause us to be tempted [Tlead us not into temptation; *or*
do not put us to the test],
but ·save [rescue; deliver] us from ·the Evil One [*or* evil].'
|The kingdom, the power, and the glory are yours forever. Amen.|"
14·Yes, [For] if you forgive others for their ·sins [transgressions; failings;
trespasses], your Father in heaven will also forgive you. 15But if you don't
forgive others, your Father in heaven will not forgive your ·sins [trans-
gressions; failings; trespasses].

Jesus Teaches About Worship

16"When you fast [Cgiving up eating for spiritual purposes], don't put
on a ·sad [gloomy; somber] face like the hypocrites. They make their faces
·look sad [disheveled; disfigured; unattractive] to show people they are
fasting. I tell you the truth, those hypocrites already have their full reward
[v. 2]. 17So when you fast [v. 16], ·comb your hair [Lput oil on/anoint your
head; Ctypical first century grooming] and wash your face. 18Then people
will not know that you are fasting, but your Father, ·whom you cannot see
[who is hidden/in secret], will see you. Your Father sees what is done in
·secret [private], and he will reward you.

God Is More Important than Money

(6:19–24; Luke 11:34–36; 12:33–34; 16:13)

19"Don't store treasures for yourselves here on earth where moths and
rust will destroy them and thieves can break in and steal them. 20But store
·your [for yourselves] treasures in heaven where they cannot be destroyed
by moths or rust and where thieves cannot break in and steal them.
21Your heart will be where your treasure is.
22"The eye is ·a light [Lthe lamp] for the body. If your eyes are ·good
[healthy; clear], your whole body will be full of light. 23But if your eyes are
·evil [unhealthy; bad], your whole body will be full of darkness. And if the
·only light you have [*or* light you think you have; Llight in you] is really
darkness, then ·you have the worst darkness [how great that darkness is!].
24"No one can serve two ·masters [lords]. The person will hate one
master and love the other, or will ·follow [be devoted/loyal to] one master
and ·refuse to follow [despise] the other. You cannot serve both God and
·worldly riches [money; Lmammon].

Don't Worry

(6:25–34; Luke 12:22–32)

25"So I tell you, don't worry about the food or drink you need to live,
or about the clothes you need for your body. Life is more than food, and
the body is more than clothes. 26·Look at [Consider; Think of] the birds
in the air. They don't ·plant [sow] or ·harvest [reap] or ·store food in
[gather into] barns, but your heavenly Father feeds them. And ·you know
that you are [Laren't you…?] worth much more than the birds. 27·You cannot [LWho of you can…?] add ·any time [*or* one step; Lone cubit; Cabout
eighteen inches] to your ·life [*or* height; Cthe Greek probably refers to time
instead of stature] by worrying about it.
28"And why do you worry about clothes? ·Look at [Consider; Think] how
the lilies in the field grow. They don't ·work [toil] or ·make clothes for

6:13 The . . . Amen. Some Greek copies do not contain the bracketed text.

themselves [Lspin thread]. 29 But I tell you that even Solomon ·with his riches [Lin all his glory] was not dressed as beautifully as one of these flowers. 30 ·God clothes [LIf God clothes…?] the ·grass [wildflower] in the field, which is ·alive [here] today but tomorrow is thrown into the ·fire [Lfurnace; oven]. ·So you can be even more sure that God will [Will he not much more…?] clothe you. ·Don't have so little faith [*or* How little faith you have; TYou of little faith]! 31 Don't worry and say, 'What will we eat?' or 'What will we drink?' or 'What will we wear?' 32 The ·people who don't know God [Gentiles; pagans; unbelievers] ·keep trying to get [eagerly seek; run after] these things, and your Father in heaven knows you need them. 33 ·Seek first [Be concerned above all else with] God's kingdom and ·what God wants [Lhis righteousness]. Then all ·your other needs will be met as well [Lthese things will be given to you]. 34 So don't worry about tomorrow, because tomorrow will ·have its own worries [*or* worry about/take care of itself]. Each day has enough trouble of its own.

Be Careful About Judging Others
(7:1–6; Mark 4:24–25; Luke 6:37–42)

7 "Don't judge others, ·or you will [so that you will not] be judged. 2 You will be judged in the same way that you judge others, and ·the amount you give to others will be given to you [*or* the standard you use for others will be the standard used for you; Lwith the measure you measure, it will be measured to you].

3 "Why do you notice the ·little piece of dust [speck; tiny splinter] in your ·friend's [Lbrother's (or sister's)] eye, but you don't ·notice [consider] the ·big piece of wood [log; plank; beam] in your own eye? 4 How can you say to your ·friend [Lbrother], 'Let me take that ·little piece of dust [speck; splinter] out of your eye'? ·Look at yourself [TBehold]! You still have that ·big piece of wood [log; plank; beam] in your own eye. 5 You hypocrite! First, take the ·wood [log; plank; beam] out of your own eye. Then you will see clearly to take the ·dust [speck; splinter] out of your ·friend's [Lbrother's] eye.

6 "Don't give holy things to dogs, and don't throw your pearls ·before [to] ·pigs [Tswine]. ·Pigs will only trample on them, and dogs will turn to attack you [LThey will trample them and turn to attack you; Cpigs were ritually unclean and dogs were considered scavengers].

Ask God for What You Need
(7:7–11; Luke 11:9–13)

7 "·Ask [Keep asking], and ·God will give [Lit will be given; Cthe passive verb implies God as subject] to you. ·Search [Seek; Keep seeking], and you will find. ·Knock [Keep knocking], and the door will open for you. 8 ·Yes, [LFor; Because] everyone who asks will receive. Everyone who ·searches [seeks] will find. And everyone who knocks will have the door opened.

9 "If your children ask for bread, which of you would give them a stone? 10 Or [Lwhich of you] if your ·children ask [*or* son asks] for a fish, would you give them a snake? 11 ·Even though you are bad, you [If you, being evil,] know how to give good gifts to your children. How much more your heavenly Father will give good things to those who ask him!

The Most Important Rule
(7:12; Luke 6:31)

12 "[So always; So in everything] ·Do to others what [Treat others as] you want them to ·do to [treat] you. This ·is [sums up; is the essence of] the ·meaning of the law of Moses and the teaching of the prophets [LLaw and the Prophets; Creferring to the OT].

The Way to Heaven Is Hard
(7:13–14; Luke 13:23–24)

13 "Enter through the narrow gate. [LBecause] The gate is wide and the road is ·wide [broad; spacious; *or* easy] that leads to ·hell [Ldestruction; ruin], and many people enter through that gate. 14 But the gate is small and the road is ·narrow [*or* difficult; hard] that leads to true life. ·Only a few people [And there are few who] find that road.

People Know You by Your Actions
(7:15–23; Luke 6:43–46; 13:25–27)

15"·Be careful of [Beware of; Watch out for] false prophets. They come to you ·looking gentle like sheep [disguised like sheep; Lin sheep's clothing], but ·they are really dangerous like wolves [Lunderneath/inwardly they are ravenous/vicious/ferocious wolves]. 16You will know these people by ·what they do [Ltheir fruit]. ·Grapes don't come [LCan you pick grapes…?] from thornbushes, ·and figs don't come from [Land figs from…?] ·thorny weeds [thistles]. 17In the same way, every ·good [healthy; sound] tree produces good fruit, but a ·bad [rotten; diseased] tree produces bad fruit. 18A ·good [healthy; sound] tree cannot produce bad fruit, and a ·bad [rotten; diseased] tree cannot produce good fruit. 19Every tree that does not produce good fruit is cut down and thrown into the fire. 20In the same way, you will know ·these false prophets [Lthem] by ·what they do [Ltheir fruit].

21"Not all those who say [Lto me] ·'You are our Lord' [L'Lord! Lord!'] will enter the kingdom of heaven, but only those who do ·what my Father in heaven wants [the will of my Father in heaven]. 22On ·the last day [judgment day; Lthat day] many people will say to me, 'Lord, Lord, ·we spoke for you [LDid we not prophesy in your name…?], and ·through you we forced out demons [Lcast out demons in your name…?] and did many ·miracles [Lmighty works in your name…?].' 23Then I will ·tell them clearly [declare to them; publicly announce to them], 'I never knew you. ·Get away [Depart] from me, you who ·do evil [break God's law; practice lawlessness; Ps. 6:8].'

Two Kinds of People
(7:24–29; Mark 1:21–22; Luke 6:47–49)

24"Everyone who hears my words and ·obeys [acts on; practices] them is like a ·wise [sensible] man who built his house on rock. 25It rained hard, the ·floods came [rivers rose], and the winds blew and ·hit [beat; slammed against] that house. But it did not ·fall [collapse], because it was built on rock. 26Everyone who hears my words and does not ·obey [act on; practice] them is like a ·foolish [stupid] man who built his house on sand. 27It rained hard, the ·floods came [rivers rose], and the winds blew and ·hit [beat; slammed against] that house, and it ·fell [collapsed] with a big crash."

28When Jesus finished ·saying these things [Lthese words; Cthe end of the first of five major discourses in Matthew, all of which conclude with a similar phrase; see also 11:1; 13:53; 19:1; 26:1], the ·people [crowds] were amazed at his teaching, 29because he did not teach like their ·teachers of the law [scribes]. He taught like a person who had authority.

Jesus Heals a Sick Man
(8:1–4; Mark 1:40–45; Luke 5:12–16)

8 When Jesus came down from the ·hill [mountainside], ·great crowds [many people] followed him. 2Then a ·man with a skin disease [Tleper; Cthe term does not refer to modern leprosy (Hansen's disease), but to various skin disorders; see Lev. 14] came to Jesus. The man ·bowed down [knelt] before him and said, "Lord, you can ·heal me [Lmake me clean; Csuch skin disorders rendered the victim ceremonially unclean] if you ·will [choose; are willing]."

3Jesus reached out his hand and touched the man and said, "I ·will [do choose; am willing]. Be ·healed [Lcleansed]!" And immediately the man was ·healed [Lcleansed] from his disease. 4Then Jesus said to him, "Don't tell anyone about this. But go and show yourself to the priest and offer the ·gift [offering; sacrifice] Moses commanded for people who are made well [Lev. 14:1–32]. This will ·show the people [be a public testimony to; be evidence for] what I have done."

Jesus Heals a Soldier's Servant
(8:5–13; Luke 7:1–10; 13:28–29; John 4:46–54)

[5]When Jesus entered the city of Capernaum, an ·army officer
[Lcenturion] came to him, ·begging [pleading] for help. [6]The officer said,
"Lord, my servant is at home in bed. He ·can't move his body [is para-
lyzed] and ·is in much pain [suffering terribly]."
[7]Jesus said to the officer, "·I will go and heal him. [*or* Shall I go and heal
him?]"
[8]The officer answered, "Lord [*or* Sir], I ·am not worthy [do not deserve]
for you to come into my house. You only need to ·command it [Lsay the
word], and my servant will be healed. [9][LFor] I, too, am a man ·under the
authority of others [Lunder authority], and I have soldiers under my
command. I tell one soldier, 'Go,' and he goes. I tell another soldier,
'Come,' and he comes. I say to my ·servant [slave], 'Do this,' and my ·ser-
vant [slave] does it."
[10]When Jesus heard this, he was amazed. He said to those who were
following him, "I tell you the truth, ·this is the greatest faith I have
found [LI haven't found such faith], ·even in Israel [*or* in all Israel].
[11]Many people will come from the east and from the west and will ·sit
and eat [Lrecline; Cthe posture for a banquet or dinner party] with
Abraham, Isaac, and Jacob in the kingdom of heaven [Cthe messianic
banquet, a metaphor for God's restoration of creation; Is. 25:6–8]. [12]But
·those people who should be in [the heirs of; *or* the subjects of; Lthe sons
of] the kingdom will be thrown ·outside into the darkness [into the
outer darkness], where ·people will cry and grind their teeth with pain
[Lthere will be weeping and gnashing of teeth; Cmetaphors for agony and
torment]."
[13]Then Jesus said to the ·officer [Lcenturion], "Go home. ·Your servant
will be healed just as you believed he would [LLet it be done for you just
as you have believed]." And his servant was healed that ·same hour [exact
time].

Jesus Heals Many People
(8:14–17; Mark 1:29–34; Luke 4:38–41)

[14]When Jesus went to Peter's house, he saw that Peter's mother-in-
law was ·sick in bed [lying down] with a fever. [15]Jesus touched her hand,
and the fever left her. Then she stood up and began ·to serve [waiting
on] Jesus.
[16]That evening people brought to Jesus many who ·had demons
[were demon-possessed]. Jesus ·spoke and the demons left them
[Ldrove/cast out the demons with a word/command], and he healed all
the sick. [17]He did these things to ·bring about [fulfill] what Isaiah the
prophet had said:

"He took our ·suffering [sicknesses; weaknesses]
  and ·carried [bore; removed] our diseases [Is. 53:4]."

People Want to Follow Jesus
(8:18–22; Luke 9:57–62)

[18]When Jesus saw the crowd around him, he ·told [instructed; ordered]
his ·followers [disciples] to ·go [cross] to the other side of the lake. [19]Then
a ·teacher of the law [scribe] came to Jesus and said, "·Teacher [Master], I
will follow you any place you go."
[20]Jesus said to him, "The foxes have ·holes [dens] to live in, and the
birds [Lof the sky] have nests, but the Son of Man has no place to ·rest
[lay] his head."
[21]Another man, one of Jesus' ·followers [disciples], said to him, "Lord,
first let me go and bury my father."
[22]But Jesus told him, "Follow me, and let the people who are dead
[Cspiritually] bury their own dead."

Jesus Calms a Storm
(8:23–27; Mark 4:35–41; Luke 8:22–25)

23Jesus got into a boat, and his ·followers [disciples] ·went with [Lfollowed] him. 24[Suddenly; LAnd look/Tbehold] A ·great [fierce] storm arose on the ·lake [sea] so that waves ·covered [swept over] the boat, but Jesus was sleeping. 25His ·followers [disciples] went to him and woke him, saying, "Lord, save us! We ·will drown [Lare lost/perishing]!"

26Jesus answered, "Why are you ·afraid [cowardly]? ·You don't have enough faith [*or* How little faith you have!; TYou of little faith]." Then Jesus got up and ·gave a command to [reprimanded; rebuked] the wind and the waves, and it became completely calm [Cparalleling God's subduing of the waters representing chaos in the OT; Ps. 65:7; 89:9; 107:29].

27The men were amazed and said, "What kind of man is this? Even the wind and the ·waves [Lsea] obey him!"

Jesus Heals Two Men with Demons
(8:28–34; Mark 5:1–20; Luke 8:26–39)

28When Jesus arrived at the other side of the lake in the ·area [region; territory] of the Gadarene*n* people [Cfrom Gadara, an area southeast of Lake Galilee; the exact location is uncertain], two ·men who had demons in them [demon-possessed men; demoniacs] came out of the ·burial caves [tombs] and met him. These men were so ·dangerous [violent; fierce] that people could not ·use the road by those caves [Lpass that way]. 29They shouted, "·What do you want with us [*or* Leave us alone; What business do we have with each other?; LWhat to me and to you?], Son of God? Did you come here to ·torture [torment] us before the ·right time [*or* appointed time; Ltime; Cthe day of judgment]?"

30·Near that place there [In the distance] was a large herd of pigs feeding. 31The demons begged Jesus, "If you ·make us leave these men [Ldrive/cast us out], please send us into that herd of pigs [Critually unclean animals]."

32Jesus said to them, "Go!" So the demons ·left [came out of] the men and went into the pigs. Then [Llook; Tbehold] the whole herd rushed down the ·hill [steep bank; precipice] into the ·lake [sea] and ·were drowned [Ldied in the waters]. 33The herdsmen ·ran away [fled] and went into town, where they told about all of this and what had happened to the ·men who had demons [demon-possessed men; demoniacs]. 34Then [Llook; Tbehold] the whole town went out to ·see [meet] Jesus. When they saw him, they begged him to leave their ·area [region; territory].

Jesus Heals a Paralyzed Man
(9:1–8; Mark 2:1–12; Luke 5:17–26)

9 Jesus got into a boat and went back across the ·lake [sea] to his own town. 2[LAnd look/Tbehold] Some people brought to Jesus a man who was paralyzed and lying on a ·mat [cot; bed]. When Jesus saw ·the faith of these people [Ltheir faith], he said to the paralyzed man, "·Be encouraged [Have courage; Take heart], ·young man [son; child]. Your sins are forgiven."

3Some of the ·teachers of the law [scribes] said to themselves, "·This man speaks as if he were God. That is blasphemy [LThis man blasphemes]!"

4·Knowing [Perceiving] their thoughts, Jesus said, "Why are you thinking evil ·thoughts [Lin your hearts]? 5[LFor] Which is easier: to say, 'Your sins are forgiven,' or to tell him, 'Stand up and walk'? 6But ·I will prove to you [Lso that you may know] that the Son of Man [Ca title for the Messiah; Dan. 7:13–14] has authority on earth to forgive sins." Then Jesus said to the paralyzed man, "Stand up, ·take [pick up] your ·mat [cot; bed], and go home." 7And the man stood up and went home. 8When the ·people [crowds]

8:28 Gadarene Some Greek copies read "Gergesene"; others read "Gerasene."

saw this, they were ·amazed [filled with awe; afraid] and ·praised [glorified]
God for giving ·power like this [such authority] to ·human beings [man-
kind; Cthe language echoes the Son of Man title just used by Jesus (v. 6),
which the crowds misunderstand to mean simply "a human being"].

Jesus Chooses Matthew

(9:9–13; Mark 2:13–17; Luke 5:27–32)

9When Jesus was ·leaving [walking along], he saw a man named
Matthew sitting in the tax collector's booth [Cprobably a tariff booth for
taxing goods in transit]. Jesus said to him, "Follow me," and he stood up
and followed Jesus.
10As Jesus was ·having dinner [Lreclining; Caround a low table; the posture for a formal banquet or dinner party] at Matthew's house, many tax
collectors and sinners came and ·ate [Lreclined together] with Jesus and
his ·followers [disciples]. 11When the Pharisees saw this, they asked Jesus'
·followers [disciples], "Why does your teacher eat with tax collectors
[Cdespised because they worked for the Roman rulers and were notorious
for corruption and extortion] and sinners?"
12When Jesus heard them, he said, "It is not the healthy people who
need a doctor, but the sick. 13Go and learn what this means: 'I ·want
[desire; require; am pleased by] ·kindness [compassion; mercy] ·more
than I want [Lnot] animal sacrifices [Hos. 6:6].' [LFor] I did not come to
·invite [call] ·good people [the righteous; Cmeaning the "self-righteous"
who feel no need to repent] but to invite [call] sinners [Cthose who recognize their need to repent]."

Jesus' Followers Are Criticized

(9:14–17; Mark 2:18–22; Luke 5:33–39)

14Then the ·followers [disciples] of John [Cthe Baptist] came to Jesus
and said, "Why do we and the Pharisees often fast [Cgiving up eating for
spiritual purposes], but your ·followers [disciples] don't?"
15Jesus answered, "The ·friends of the bridegroom [*or* wedding guests;
Lchildren of the wedding hall] ·are not sad [Lcannot mourn] while he is
with them [CJesus is referring to himself; John 3:29; Rev. 19:7]. But the
·time [Ldays] will come when the bridegroom will be taken from them,
and then they will fast.
16"No one sews a patch of unshrunk [Cnew] cloth over a hole in an old
·coat [garment]. If he does, the patch will shrink and pull away from the
·coat [garment], making the ·hole [tear] worse. 17Also, people never pour
new wine into old ·leather bags [wineskins]. Otherwise, the ·bags [wine-
skins] will ·break [burst; Cbecause the fermenting wine expands], the wine
will spill, and the ·wine bags [wineskins] will be ruined. But people always
pour new wine into ·new [fresh] ·wine bags [wineskins]. Then both ·will
continue to be good [are preserved]."

Jesus Gives Life to a Dead Girl and Heals a Sick Woman

(9:18–26; Mark 5:21–43; Luke 8:40–56)

18While Jesus was saying these things, a ·leader of the synagogue [Lleader;
official; ruler; CMark 5:22 identifies him as a synagogue leader] came to him.
He ·bowed down [knelt] before Jesus and said, "My daughter has just died.
But if you come and lay your hand on her, she will live again." 19So Jesus
and his ·followers [disciples] stood up and ·went with [Lfollowed] him.
20·Then [LAnd look/Tbehold,] a woman who had been bleeding for
twelve years [Cprobably a chronic menstrual disorder] came behind Jesus
and touched the ·edge [*or* tassels; see Num. 15:38–39] of his ·coat [cloak;
garment]. 21[LFor] She was thinking, "If I can just touch his clothes, I will
·be healed [get well; be saved]."
22Jesus turned and saw the woman and said, "·Be encouraged [Have
courage; Take heart], ·dear woman [Ldaughter]. ·You are made well because

you believed [Your faith has saved/healed you]." And the woman was
·healed [made well; saved] from that moment on.
23Jesus continued along with the ·leader [ruler; official] and went into
his house. There he saw the ·funeral musicians [Lpipe/flute players] and
·many people crying [a noisy crowd]. 24Jesus said, "·Go away [Get out;
Leave]. [LFor] The girl is not dead, only asleep." But the people ·laughed
at [ridiculed] him. 25After the crowd had been ·thrown [sent; put] out of
the house, Jesus went into the girl's room and took hold of her hand, and
she ·stood up [arose]. 26The ·news [report] about this spread ·all around
the area [Lthroughout that whole land/region].

Jesus Heals Two Blind Men
(9:27–31; Mark 10:46–52; Luke 18:35–43)

27When Jesus was leaving there, two blind men followed him. They
cried out, "·Have mercy [Take pity] on us, Son of David [Ca title for the
Messiah, a descendant of King David; 2 Sam. 7:11–16]!"
28After Jesus went inside, the blind men went with him. He asked the
men, "Do you believe that I can ·make you see again [Ldo this]?"
They answered, "Yes, Lord."
29Then Jesus touched their eyes and said, "·Because you believe
[LAccording to your faith], ·it will happen [Llet it be done for you]." 30Then
·the men were able to see [Ltheir eyes were opened]. But Jesus warned
them strongly, saying, "·Don't tell anyone [LSee that no one knows] about
this." 31But the blind men left and spread the news about Jesus ·all around
that area [Lthroughout that whole land/region].

Jesus Heals a Demon Possessed Man
(9:32–34; Mark 3:22; Luke 11:14–15)

32When the two men were leaving, [Llook; behold] some people brought
to Jesus ·another man who could not talk because he had a demon in him
[a mute, demon-possessed man]. 33After Jesus ·forced the demon to leave
the man [drove/cast out the demon], he ·was able [began] to speak. The
crowd was amazed and said, "·We have never seen anything like this
[LNothing like this has ever been seen/happened] in Israel."
34But the Pharisees said, "He forces [drives; casts] demons out by the
power of the ·prince [ruler] of demons."

The Harvest Is Great
(9:35–38; Mark 6:6, 34; Luke 8:1; 10:2)

35Jesus traveled through all the towns and villages, teaching in their
synagogues, ·preaching [proclaiming] the ·Good News [Gospel] about
the kingdom, and healing all kinds of diseases and sicknesses. 36When he
saw the crowds, he ·felt sorry [had compassion] for them because they
were ·hurting [distressed; confused; harassed] and ·helpless [discouraged;
dejected], like sheep without a shepherd. 37Jesus said to his ·followers
[disciples], "·There are many people to harvest [LThe harvest is great/
large] but ·there are only a few workers [the workers/laborers are few].
38So pray to the Lord ·who owns [who is in charge of; Lof] the harvest, that
he will send more ·workers [laborers] ·to gather [Linto] his harvest."

Jesus Sends Out His Apostles
(10:1–15; Mark 3:13–19; 6:7–11; Luke 6:12–16; 9:1–5; 10:3)

10 Jesus called his twelve ·followers [disciples] together and gave
them authority to drive [force; cast] out ·evil [defiling;
Lunclean] spirits and to heal every kind of disease and sickness. 2These
are the names of the twelve apostles: first, Simon (also called Peter) and
his brother Andrew; James son of Zebedee, and his brother John; 3Philip
and Bartholomew; Thomas and Matthew, the tax collector; James son of
Alphaeus, and Thaddaeus; 4Simon the Zealot and Judas Iscariot, who
·turned against [betrayed] Jesus.
5Jesus sent out these twelve men with the following ·order [instructions]:
"Don't go ·to [Lon the way/road of] the ·Gentiles [non-Jewish people] or ·to

[Lenter] any town where the Samaritans live. 6But go to the ·people of Israel,
who are like lost sheep [Llost sheep of the house of Israel]. 7When you go,
·preach [announce; proclaim] this: 'The kingdom of heaven is ·near [at
hand].' 8Heal the sick, raise the dead to life again, ·heal [Lcleanse] ·those who
have skin diseases [Tthe lepers; see 8:2], and ·force demons out of people
[Lcast out demons]. ·I give you these powers freely, so help other people
freely [LFreely you have received, freely give]. 9Don't ·carry [*or* acquire] any
money ·with you [Lin your belts]—gold or silver or copper. 10Don't carry a
·bag [traveler's bag; *or* beggar's purse] or ·extra clothes [Ltwo tunics] or sandals or a ·walking stick [staff]. Workers ·should be given what they need
[deserve to be supported; Ldeserve their food/sustenance].

11"When you enter a city or town, ·find [seek out] some ·worthy [honor-
able; respected] person there and stay in that home until you leave. 12When
you enter that home, ·give it your blessing [Lgreet it; Ctypically, "Peace be
with you"; see Luke 10:5]. 13If the ·people there welcome you [Lhouse is
worthy], let your peace ·stay there [Lcome upon it]. But if ·they don't welcome you [Lit is not worthy], ·take back the peace you wished for them [Llet
your peace return to you]. 14And if ·a home or town [Lanyone] refuses to
welcome you or ·listen to you [heed your words/message], leave that ·place
[Lhome or town] and shake its dust off your feet [Cin protest and as a warning of judgment]. 15I tell you the truth, on the judgment day it will be ·better
[more bearable/tolerable] for the ·towns [Lland] of Sodom and Gomorrah
[Cevil cities destroyed by God; Gen. 19] than for the people of that town.

Jesus Warns His Apostles
(10:16–25; Mark 13:9–13; Luke 6:40; 12:11–12; 21:12–19)

16"·Listen [LLook; TBehold], I am sending you out like sheep among
wolves. So be as ·clever [wise; shrewd; cunning] as ·snakes [serpents] and
as ·innocent [harmless] as doves. 17·Be careful of [Beware of; Watch out
for] people, because they will ·arrest you and take you to court [hand you
over to the courts/councils; Clocal councils associated with Jewish syna-
gogues] and ·whip [flog; scourge] you in their synagogues. 18·Because of
me [On my account; For my sake] you will be taken to stand before governors and kings, ·and you will tell them and the Gentiles about me [Las a
witness/testimony to them and to the Gentiles]. 19When you are arrested,
don't worry about what to say or how to say it. [LFor] At that time you
will be given the things to say. 20It will not really be you speaking but the
Spirit of your Father speaking ·through [in] you.

21"Brothers will ·give [betray; hand over] their own brothers to ·be
killed [death], and fathers will give their own children to ·be killed
[death]. Children will ·fight [rebel; rise up] against their own parents and
have them put to death. 22All people will hate you because ·you follow me
[Lof my name], but those people who ·keep their faith [endure; stand
firm; persevere] until the end will be saved. 23When you are ·treated badly
[persecuted] in one city, ·run [flee] to ·another city [the next]. I tell you
the truth, you will not finish going through all the cities of Israel before
the Son of Man comes [Dan. 7:13–14].

24"A ·student [disciple; follower] is not ·better than [superior to; Labove]
his teacher, and a ·servant [slave] is not ·better than [superior to; Labove]
his ·master [lord]. 25·A student should be satisfied [LIt is enough for a
student/disciple/follower] to become like his teacher; ·a servant should be
satisfied to become [Land a servant/slave] like his master. If the head of
the family [Chere referring to Jesus] is called Beelzebul [Canother name for
Satan], ·then the other members of the family will be called worse names
[Lhow much more the members of his household]!

Fear God, Not People
(10:26–33; Luke 12:2–9)

26“So don’t be afraid of those people, because everything that is ·hidden
[concealed; covered up] will be ·shown [revealed; uncovered; disclosed].
Everything that is ·secret [hidden] will be made ·known [clear]. 27I tell you
these things in the dark, but I want you to tell them in the ·light [daylight].
What you hear whispered in your ear you should ·shout [proclaim] from the
housetops. 28Don’t be afraid of people, who can kill the body but cannot kill
the soul. The only one you should fear is the one who can destroy [Lboth]
the soul and the body in ·hell [LGehenna; 5:22]. 29Two sparrows are sold
[LAre not two sparrows sold…?] for only a penny [CGreek: *assarion*; a copper
coin of very low value], but not even one of them can ·die [Lfall to the ground]
·without your Father’s knowing it [*or* apart from your Father’s will]. 30God
even ·knows [numbers; counts] how many hairs are on your head. 31So don’t
be afraid. You are ·worth much more [more valuable] than many sparrows.
32“All those who ·stand before others and say they believe in me [Lconfess/
acknowledge me before people], I will ·say before my Father in heaven that
they belong to me [Lconfess/acknowledge them before my Father in heaven].
33But all who ·stand before others and say they do not believe in me [Ldeny/
disown me before people] I will ·say before my Father in heaven that they
do not belong to me [Lalso deny/disown them before my Father in heaven].

Divisions Within Households
(10:34–36; Luke 12:51–53)

34“Don’t ·think [suppose] that I came to bring peace to the earth. I did
not come to bring peace, but a sword. 35[LFor] I have come ·so that

‘a son will be [Lto turn a man] against his father,
a daughter ·will be against [against] her mother,
a daughter-in-law ·will be against [against] her mother-in-law.
36 A person’s enemies will be members of his own ·family [household;
Mic. 7:6].’

Conditions and Rewards of Discipleship
(10:37–42; Mark 9:41; Luke 10:16; 14:25–27; 17:33; John 12:25; 13:20)

37“·Those who love [LThe one who loves…] their father or mother
more than they love me are not worthy ·to be my followers [Lof me].
Those who love their son or daughter more than they love me are not
worthy ·to be my followers [Lof me]. 38Whoever ·is not willing to carry the
[Ldoes not take up his] cross and follow me is not worthy of me. 39Those
who ·try to hold on to [cling to; seek to preserve; Lfind] their lives will
·give up true life [lose them]. Those who ·give up [lose] their lives for ·me
[my sake] will ·hold on to true life [Lfind them]. 40Whoever ·accepts
[receives; welcomes] you also ·accepts [receives; welcomes] me, and whoever ·accepts [receives; welcomes] me also ·accepts [receives; welcomes]
the One who sent me. 41Whoever ·accepts [receives; welcomes] a prophet
·because he is a prophet [Lin the name of a prophet] will receive the
·reward of [same reward as] a prophet. And whoever ·accepts [receives;
welcomes] a ·good [righteous; upright] person because that person is
·good [righteous; upright] will receive the ·reward of [same reward as] a
·good [righteous; upright] person. 42Those who give one of these little
ones [even; so much as] a cup of cold water because they are my ·follow-
ers [disciples] will ·truly get [Lcertainly not lose] their reward.”

Jesus and John the Baptist
(11:1–19; Luke 7:18–35; 16:16)

11 After Jesus finished ·telling these things to [instructing; see
7:28] his twelve ·followers [disciples], he left there and went to
·the towns in Galilee [Ltheir towns] to teach and preach.
2John the Baptist was in prison, but he heard about ·what Christ was
doing [*or* the deeds/actions of the Messiah]. So John sent some of his ·fol-
lowers [disciples] to Jesus. 3They asked him, “Are you the ·One who is to

come [Expected One; [C]the Messiah], **or should we ·wait for** [look for;
expect] **someone else?"**

4 Jesus answered them, "Go ·tell [report to] **John what you hear and see:
5 The blind can see, the ·crippled** [lame] **can walk, and ·people with skin
diseases** [[T]lepers; see 8:2] **are ·healed** [[L]cleansed]. **The deaf can hear, the
dead are raised to life, and the ·Good News** [Gospel] **is preached to the
poor** [[C]signs of God's restoration of creation, predicted by the prophet
Isaiah; Is. 29:18–19; 35:5–6; 61:1–2]. **6 Those who ·do not stumble in their
faith** [are not offended] **because of me are blessed."**

7 As ·John's followers [[L]they] **were leaving, Jesus began talking to the
·people** [crowds] **about John. Jesus said, "What did you go out into the
·desert** [wilderness] **to see? A reed ·blown by** [shaken by; swaying in] **the
wind** [[C]a metaphor for something weak or wavering]? **8 What did you go
out to see? A man dressed in ·fine** [expensive] **clothes? No, those who
wear ·fine** [expensive; [L]soft] **clothes ·live** [are found] **in kings' ·palaces**
[houses]. **9 So why did you go out? To see a prophet? Yes, and I tell you,
John is more than a prophet. 10 This was written about him:**

'[[L]Look; [T]Behold] **I will send my messenger ahead of you,**
who will prepare ·the [your] **way ·for** [before; in front of] **you** [Mal. 3:1].**'**

**11 I tell you the truth, John the Baptist is greater than any other person
·ever born** [[L]born to women], **but even the least important person in the
kingdom of heaven is greater than John** [[C]because John prepares for, but
does not fully participate in the blessings of the kingdom]. **12 ·Since the
time** [[L]From the days] **John the Baptist came until now, the kingdom of
heaven has been ·going forward in strength** [advancing forcefully; *or* subject to violence; suffering violent attacks], **and ·forceful** [*or* violent] **people
have been trying to ·take it by force** [lay hold of it; *or* attack it]. **13 All the
prophets and the law of Moses ·told about what would happen**
[[L]prophesied] **until ·the time John came** [[L]John]. **14 And if you ·will believe
what they said, you will believe that John is Elijah** [[L]are willing to accept
it, he is Elijah], **whom they said would come. 15 ·Let those with ears use
them and listen**[[L]The one who has ears to hear, let him hear]!

16 "·What can I say about the people of this time? What are they like?
[[L]To what shall I compare this generation?] **They are like children sitting
in the marketplace, who call out to each other,**

17 'We played ·music [[L]the pipe/flute] **for you, but you did not dance;**
we sang a ·sad song [funeral song; dirge], **but you did not ·cry** [weep].**'**
[[C]The religious leaders wanted John to "dance" (lighten up his severe message) and wanted Jesus to "mourn" (follow their restrictive lifestyle).]

18 [[L]For] **John came and did not eat or drink like other people. So people say, 'He ·has** [is possessed by] **a demon.' 19 The Son of Man came, eating
and drinking, and people say, 'Look at him! ·He eats too much and drinks
too much wine** [[L]He's a glutton and a drunkard], **and he is a friend of tax
collectors and sinners.' But wisdom is ·proved to be right** [vindicated] **by
·what she does** [*or* its deeds/actions/results; [C]Wisdom is personified as a
woman (Prov. 8), her "children" being those who respond favorably to the
message of John and Jesus]."

Jesus Warns Unbelievers

(11:20–24; Luke 10:12–15)

20 Then Jesus began to ·criticize [denounce; reproach] **the cities where he
did ·most** [so many] **of his ·miracles** [powerful deeds], **because the people
did not ·change their lives and stop sinning** [repent]. **21 He said, "·How terrible for** [[L]Woe to] **you, Korazin! ·How terrible for** [[L]Woe to] **you, Bethsaida!**

If the same ·miracles [powerful deeds] **·I did** [Lthat occurred] **in you had happened in Tyre and Sidon** [Ccities in Phoenicia notorious for their wickedness], **those people would have ·changed their lives** [repented] **a long time ago. ·They would have worn rough cloth and put ashes on themselves to show they had changed** [L…in sackcloth/burlap and ashes; Csigns of sorrow and deep remorse]. 22**But I tell you, on the judgment day it will be ·better** [more bearable/tolerable] **for Tyre and Sidon than for you.** 23**And you, Capernaum** [Ca town in Galilee where Jesus lived and ministered], **will you be ·lifted up to** [honored/exalted in] **heaven? No! you will be thrown down to ·the depths** [the place of the dead; LHades; Is. 14:13, 15]. **If the ·miracles** [powerful deeds] **·I did** [Lthat occurred] **in you had happened in Sodom** [Ca city God destroyed because the people were so evil; Gen. 19], **it would ·still be a city** [Lhave remained until] **today** [Cbecause its people would have repented and judgment averted]. 24**But I tell you, on the judgment day it will be ·better** [more bearable/tolerable] **for** [Lthe region/land of] **Sodom than for you."**

Jesus Offers Rest to People
(11:25–27; Luke 10:21–22)

25**At that time Jesus said, "I ·praise** [bless; thank; acknowledge] **you, Father, Lord of heaven and earth, because you have hidden these things from the people who are wise and ·smart** [learned; intelligent]. **But you have ·shown** [revealed] **them to ·those who are like little children** [Llittle children; infants; Cthose with a childlike faith]. 26**Yes, Father,** [Lbecause] **this is what ·you really wanted** [pleased you].

27**"My Father has ·given** [entrusted/committed to] **me all things. No one knows the Son, except the Father. And no one knows the Father, except the Son and those whom the Son ·chooses** [desires; intends] **to ·tell** [reveal it].

28**"Come to me, all of you who are ·tired** [weary] **and ·have heavy loads** [overburdened; Theavy-laden] **and I will give you rest.** 29**·Accept my teachings** [LTake my yoke upon you] **and learn from me, because I am gentle and humble in ·spirit** [heart], **and you will find rest for your ·lives** [souls; Jer. 6:16]. 30**·The burden that I ask you to accept** [L…because my yoke] **is easy; ·the load I give you to carry** [Land my burden] **is light."**

Jesus Is Lord of the Sabbath
(12:1–8; Mark 2:23–28; Luke 6:1–5)

12 **At that time Jesus was walking through some fields of grain on a Sabbath day. His ·followers** [disciples] **were hungry, so they began to pick the grain and eat it** [Deut. 23:25]. 2**When the Pharisees saw this, they said to Jesus, "Look! Your ·followers** [disciples] **are doing what is ·unlawful to do** [forbidden] **on the Sabbath day."** [CGleaning was viewed as work, and therefore forbidden on the Sabbath; Ex. 34:21.]

3**Jesus answered, "Have you not read what David did when he and ·the people with him** [his companions] **were hungry?** 4**He went into God's house, and he and ·those with him** [his companions] **ate the ·holy bread** [consecrated bread; Lbread of presentation], **which was ·lawful** [allowed] **only for priests to eat** [Ex. 25:30; Lev. 24:5–9]. 5**And have you not read in the ·law of Moses** [LLaw] **that on every Sabbath day the priests in the Temple ·break this law about** [violate; desecrate; profane] **the Sabbath day** [Cby working when they offer sacrifices]**? But the priests are ·not wrong for doing that** [Linnocent; not guilty]. 6**I tell you that there is ·something** [*or* someone; Cmay refer to Jesus himself or to the arrival of the kingdom] **here that is greater than the Temple.** 7**The Scripture says, 'I want ·kindness more than I want animal sacrifices** [Lmercy and not sacrifice; Hos. 6:6].**' If you ·understood** [had known] **what these words mean, you would not have ·judged those who have done nothing wrong** [condemned the innocent/guiltless].

8**"·So** [For] **the Son of Man is ·Lord** [Master] **of the Sabbath day."**

Jesus Heals a Man's Hand
(12:9–14; Mark 3:1–6; Luke 6:6–11)

[9]Jesus left there and went into their synagogue, [10]·where [[L]and look/ [T]behold] there was a man with a ·crippled [paralyzed; deformed; shriveled] hand. They were looking for a reason to ·accuse [bring charges against] Jesus, so they asked him, "Is it ·right [lawful] to ·heal [cure] on the Sabbath day?"

[11]Jesus answered, "If any of you has a sheep, and it falls into a ·ditch [pit; hole] on the Sabbath day, ·you will [would you not…?] ·help [[L]grab it and lift] it out of the ditch. [12]·Surely a human being is more important [[L]How much better is a person] than a sheep. So it is ·lawful [permitted] to do ·good things [good] on the Sabbath day."

[13]Then Jesus said to the man, "·Hold [Stretch] out your hand." The man ·held [stretched] out his hand, and it ·became well again [was restored], ·like [[L]as healthy as] the other hand. [14]But the Pharisees left and ·made plans [plotted; conspired] to ·kill [destroy] Jesus.

Jesus Is God's Chosen Servant
(12:15–21; Mark 3:7–12; Luke 6:17–19)

[15]Jesus knew ·what the Pharisees were doing [[L]this], so he left that place. ·Many people [Large crowds] followed him, and he healed all who were sick. [16]But Jesus warned the people not to ·tell who he was [make him known]. [17]He did these things to ·bring about [fulfill] what Isaiah the prophet had said:

[18]"·Here is [[L]Behold; Look!] my servant whom I have chosen.
·I love him [The one I love; My beloved], ·and I am pleased with him [[L]in whom my soul delights/is well pleased].
I will put my Spirit upon him,
and he will ·tell of my [proclaim] justice to ·all people [the nations/ Gentiles].
[19]He will not ·argue [quarrel; fight] or ·cry out [shout];
no one will hear his voice in the streets.
[20]He will not break a ·crushed blade of grass [battered/bruised reed]
or ·put out [extinguish] ·even a weak flame [a flickering candle; [L]a smoldering wick]
until he ·makes justice win the [leads justice to] victory.
[21] In ·him [[L]his name] will the ·Gentiles [nations; non-Jewish people]
·find [put their] hope [Is. 42:1–4]."

Jesus' Power Is from God
(12:22–30; Mark 3:22–27; Luke 11:14–23)

[22]Then some people brought to Jesus a man who was blind and ·could not talk [mute], because he ·had a demon [was demon-possessed/demonized]. Jesus healed the man so that he could talk and see. [23]All the people were amazed and said, "Perhaps this man is the Son of David [[C]a title for the Messiah, a descendant of King David; 2 Sam. 7:11–16]!"

[24]When the Pharisees heard this, they said, "This man uses the power of Beelzebul [[C]another name for Satan], the ruler of demons, to ·force [drive; cast] demons out of people."

[25]Jesus knew what the Pharisees were thinking, so he said to them, "Every kingdom that is ·divided against [at war with] itself ·will be destroyed [is doomed/headed for ruin]. And any city or ·family [[L]house] that is ·divided against [at war with] itself will not ·continue [survive; stand]. [26]And if Satan ·forces out himself [[L]drives/casts out Satan], then Satan is ·divided against [at war with] himself, and ·his kingdom will not continue [[L]how will his kingdom stand?]. [27]You say that I use the power of Beelzebul [v. 24] to ·force [drive; cast] out demons. If that is true, then what power do your ·people [own exorcists; followers; [L]sons] use to ·force [drive; force] out demons? So they will be your judges. [28]But if I use the power of God's Spirit

to ·force [drive; cast] out demons, then the kingdom of God has ·come to
you [arrived among you; *or* overtaken you; caught you unaware].
29“·If anyone wants to [LOr how can anyone…?] enter a strong person’s
house and ·steal [seize; plunder] his things, he must first ·tie up [bind] the
strong person. Then he can ·steal [seize; plunder] the things from the
house. [CSatan is the strong man and his possessions are the people Jesus
is freeing from Satan’s power.]

The Sin Against the Holy Spirit

(12:31–32; Mark 3:28–30; Luke 6:43–45; 12:10)

30“Whoever is not with me is against me. Whoever does not ·work
[gather] with me ·is working against me [scatters; Cprobably a reference to
gathering or scattering a flock; John 10:12]. 31So I tell you, people can be
forgiven for every sin and ·everything they say against God [blasphemy].
But whoever ·speaks [blasphemes] against the ·Holy Spirit [LSpirit] will
not be forgiven. 32Anyone who speaks against the Son of Man can be forgiven, but anyone who speaks against the Holy Spirit will not be forgiven,
·now or in the future [Lneither in this age, nor the one to come].

People Know You by Your Words

33“If you want good fruit, you must ·make the tree good [grow a good/
healthy tree]. If ·your tree is not good [you grow a bad/unhealthy tree], it
will have bad fruit. A tree is ·known [identified; recognized] by the kind of
fruit it produces. 34You ·snakes [Tbrood/offspring of vipers]! You are evil
people, so how can you say anything good? [LFor] The mouth speaks the
things that ·are in [overflow from] the heart. 35Good people ·have good
things in their hearts, and so they say good things [Lbring forth good things
from the good treasure/storehouse]. But evil people ·have evil in their
hearts, so they say evil things [Lbring forth evil things from the evil treasure/
storehouse]. 36And I tell you that on the judgment day people will ·be
responsible [give an accounting; answer] for every ·careless [idle; thought-
less; unhelpful] ·thing [word] they have said. 37·The words you have said
will be used to judge you. Some of your words will prove you right, but
some of your words will prove you guilty [LFor by your words you will be
acquitted/justified, and by your words you will be condemned].”

The People Ask for a Miracle

(12:38–42; Mark 8:11–12; Luke 11:16, 24–32)

38Then some of the Pharisees and ·teachers of the law [scribes]
answered Jesus, saying, “Teacher, we want to see ·you work a miracle as a
sign [La sign from you].”
39Jesus answered, “Evil and sinful people [LAn evil and adulterous/
unfaithful generation] are the ones who ·want to see [seek after; ask for;
demand] ·a miracle for a sign [La sign]. But no sign will be given to them,
except the sign of the prophet Jonah. 40[LFor just as] Jonah was in the stomach of the ·big fish [sea monster; sea creature] for three days and three nights
[Jon. 1:17]. In the same way, the Son of Man will be in the ·grave [Lheart of
the earth] three days and three nights. 41On the judgment day the ·people [*or*
men] from Nineveh will stand up with ·you people who live now [this gen-
eration], and they will ·show that you are guilty [condemn you]. [LBecause]
When Jonah preached to them, they ·were sorry and changed their lives
[repented]. And ·I tell you that [Llook; Tbehold] ·someone [*or* something;
Ceither Jesus or the Kingdom of God] greater than Jonah is here. 42On the
judgment day, the Queen of the South will ·stand [rise] up with ·you people
who live today [this generation]. She will ·show that you are guilty [con-
demn you], because she came from ·far away [the ends of the earth] to listen
to Solomon’s wise teaching [1 Kin. 10:1–13]. And ·I tell you that [Llook;
Tbehold] ·someone [*or* something] greater than Solomon is here.

People Today Are Full of Evil
(12:43–45; Luke 11:24–26)

43“When an ·evil [defiling; Lunclean] spirit comes out of a person, it travels through ·dry [waterless; arid] places, looking for a place to rest, but it doesn't find it. 44So the spirit says, 'I will go back to the house [Cthe person] I left.' When the spirit comes back, it finds the house still empty, swept clean, and ·made neat [put in order; fixed up]. 45Then the evil spirit goes out and brings seven other spirits even more ·evil [wicked] than it is, and they go in and live there. So ·the person has even more trouble than before [Lthe last state of that person is worse than the first]. ·It is the same way [LSo it will be] with ·the evil people who live today [this evil generation].”

Jesus' True Family
(12:46–50; Mark 3:31–35; Luke 8:19–21; John 15:14)

46While Jesus was talking to the ·people [crowds], [Llook; Tbehold] his mother and ·brothers [*or* brothers and sisters; Cthe Greek word can mean “siblings”] stood outside, ·trying to find a way [seeking; asking] to talk to him. 47Someone told Jesus, “[LLook; TBehold] Your mother and brothers [and sisters] are standing outside, ·and they want [seeking; asking] to talk to you.”[n]

48He answered, “Who is my mother? Who are my brothers [and sisters]?” 49Then he ·pointed to [*or* stretched out his hand toward] his ·followers [disciples] and said, “·Here are [LLook; TBehold] my mother and my brothers. 50My true brother and sister and mother are those who do ·what my Father in heaven wants [the will of my Father in heaven].”

A Story About Planting Seed
(13:1–9; Mark 4:1–9; Luke 8:4–8)

13 That same day Jesus went out of the house and sat by the lake [Cthe Sea of Galilee]. 2Large crowds gathered around him, so he got into a boat and sat down, while the people stood on the shore. 3Then Jesus used ·stories [parables] to teach them many things. He said: “A ·farmer [sower] went out to ·plant [sow] his seed. 4While he was ·planting [sowing], some seed fell ·by the road [along the path], and the birds came and ate it all up. 5Some seed fell on rocky ground, where there wasn't much dirt. That seed ·grew [sprang up] very fast, because the ground was not deep. 6But when the sun rose, the plants ·dried up [were scorched and withered], because they did not have deep roots. 7Some other seed fell among thorny weeds, which grew and choked the good plants. 8Some other seed fell on good ground where it grew and produced ·a crop [grain]. Some plants made a hundred times more, some made sixty times more, and some made thirty times more. 9·Let those with ears use them and listen [LThe one who has ears to hear, let him hear].”

Why Jesus Used Stories to Teach
(13:10–17; Mark 4:10–12, 25; Luke 8:9–10, 18; 10:23–24)

10The ·followers [disciples] came to Jesus and asked, “Why do you ·use stories to teach the people [Lspeak to them in parables]?”

11Jesus answered, “·You have been chosen [LIt has been granted/given to you] to ·know [understand] the ·secrets [mysteries] about the kingdom of heaven, but ·others cannot know these secrets [Lit has not been given/granted to those others]. 12Those who ·have understanding [Lhave] will be given more, and they will have ·all they need [an abundance]. But those who do not ·have understanding [Lhave], even what they have will be taken away from them. 13This is why I ·use stories to teach the people [Lspeak in parables]: [LBecause] They ·see [look], but they don't ·really see [perceive]. They hear, but they don't really hear or understand. 14·So they show that the things Isaiah said about them are true [LIn them the prophecy of Isaiah is fulfilled that says]:

12:47 Someone . . . you.” Some Greek copies do not have verse 47.

'You will ·listen and listen [keep on hearing; *or* listen intently], but you
will not understand.
You will ·look and look [keep on seeing; *or* look intently], but you
will not ·learn [perceive; comprehend].
15For the ·minds [hearts] of these people have become ·stubborn [dull;
calloused; hardened].
They ·do not [hardly] hear with their ears,
and they have closed their eyes.
Otherwise they might see with their eyes
and hear with their ears.
They might really understand ·in their minds [with their hearts]
and ·come back [turn; return] to me and ·be healed [I would heal
them; Is. 6:9–10].'
16But ·you [Lyour eyes] are blessed, because you see with your eyes and
hear with your ears. 17I tell you the truth, many prophets and ·good [righ-
teous; just] people ·wanted [longed] to see the things that you now see,
but they did not see them. And they ·wanted [longed] to hear the things
that you now hear, but they did not hear them.

Jesus Explains the Seed Story
(13:18–23; Mark 4:13–20; Luke 8:11–15)

18"So listen to the ·meaning of that story about the farmer [parable of the
sower]. 19What is the seed that fell ·by the road [along the path]? That seed is
like ·the person [anyone] who hears the ·message [word; teaching] about the
kingdom but does not understand it. The Evil One comes and ·takes away
[snatches] what was ·planted [sown] in that person's heart. 20And what is the
seed ·that fell [sown] on rocky ground? That seed is like the person who
hears the ·teaching [word; message] and quickly ·accepts [receives] it with
joy. 21But ·he does not let the teaching go deep into his life, so [Lsince he has
no root in himself] ·he keeps it only a short time [he does not endure; it is
shortlived]. When trouble or persecution comes because of the ·teaching he
accepted [word, message], he ·quickly [immediately] ·gives up [falls away;
stumbles]. 22And what is the seed ·that fell [sown] among the thorny weeds?
That seed is like the person who hears the ·teaching [word; message] but lets
worries about this ·life [world; age] and the ·temptation [deceitfulness;
seduction] of wealth ·stop that teaching from growing [Lchoke the word/
message]. So the teaching does not produce fruit in that person's life. 23But
what is the seed ·that fell [sown] on the good ground? That seed is like the
person who hears the teaching and understands it. That person grows and
produces ·fruit [a crop], sometimes a hundred times more, sometimes sixty
times more, and sometimes thirty times more."

A Story About Wheat and Weeds

24Then Jesus ·told [presented to] them another ·story [parable]: "The
kingdom of heaven is like a man who ·planted [sowed] good seed in his field.
25That night, when everyone was asleep, his enemy came and ·planted
[sowed] ·weeds [Ttares; Ca noxious weed that looks like wheat] among the
wheat and then left. 26Later, the wheat sprouted and the heads of grain grew,
but the ·weeds [Ttares] also ·grew [appeared]. 27Then the man's ·servants
[slaves] came to him and said, '[Master; Sir] ·You planted [LDidn't you
sow…?] good seed in your field. Where did the ·weeds [Ttares] come from?'
28The man answered, 'An enemy ·planted weeds [Ldid this].' The ·servants
[slaves] asked, 'Do you want us to ·pull up the weeds [Lgo and gather them]?'
29The man answered, 'No, because when you ·pull up [gather] the ·weeds
[Ttares], you might also ·pull up [uproot] the wheat. 30Let ·the weeds and the
wheat [Lboth] grow together until the harvest time. At harvest time I will tell

the ·workers [reapers], "First gather the ·weeds [Ttares] and tie them ·together [in bundles] to be burned. Then gather the wheat and bring it to my barn." ' "

Stories of Mustard Seed and Yeast
(13:31–33; Mark 4:30–32; Luke 13:18–21)

31Then Jesus ·told [presented to them] another ·story [parable]: "The kingdom of heaven is like a mustard seed that a man ·planted [sowed] in his field. 32That seed is the smallest of all seeds [Cthe mustard seed was the smallest seed known to Jesus' hearers], but when it grows, it is one of the largest garden plants. It becomes ·big enough [La tree] for the ·wild birds [Lbirds of the sky] to come and build nests in its branches."

33Then Jesus told another ·story [parable]: "The kingdom of heaven is like ·yeast [leaven] that a woman took and ·hid [mixed] in a large tub [CGreek: three *sata*; about fifty pounds] of flour until ·it made all the dough rise [Lthe whole was leavened; Luke 13:20–21]."

34Jesus used ·stories [parables] to tell all these things to the people; he ·always used stories to teach them [Ldid not speak to them without parables; Mark 4:33–34]. 35This ·is as [fulfills what] the prophet said:

"I will ·speak using [Lopen my mouth in] ·stories [parables];
I will ·tell [announce; utter] things ·that have been secret [hidden] since
the ·world was made [creation/foundation of the world. Ps. 78:2]."

Jesus Explains About the Weeds

36Then Jesus left the crowd and went into the house. His ·followers [disciples] came to him and said, "Explain to us the meaning of the ·story [parable] about the ·weeds [Ttares] in the field."

37Jesus answered, "The man who ·planted [sowed] the good seed in the field is the Son of Man. 38The field is the world, and the good seed are ·all of God's children who belong to the kingdom [Lthe children/sons of the kingdom]. The ·weeds [Ttares] are ·those people who belong to the Evil One [Lthe children/sons of the Evil One]. 39And the enemy who ·planted [sowed] the bad seed is the devil. The harvest time is the end of the age, and the ·workers who gather [harvesters; reapers] are God's angels.

40"Just as the ·weeds [Ttares] are ·pulled up [gathered] and burned in the fire, so it will be at the end of the age. 41The Son of Man will send out his angels, and they will ·gather [remove; weed] out of his kingdom ·all who [*or* all things that] ·cause sin [Tare stumbling blocks] and all who ·do evil [break God's law]. 42The angels will throw them into the blazing furnace [Dan. 3:6], where ·the people will cry and grind their teeth with pain [Lthere will be weeping and gnashing of teeth; Cindicating agony and remorse]. 43Then the ·good people [righteous] will shine like the sun in the kingdom of their Father [Dan. 12:3]. ·Let those with ears use them and listen [LThe one who has ears to hear, let him hear.].

Stories of a Treasure and a Pearl

44"The kingdom of heaven is like a treasure hidden in a field. One day a man found the treasure, and then he hid it in the field again. He was so ·happy [joyful; excited] that he went and sold everything he owned to buy that field.

45"Also, the kingdom of heaven is like a merchant looking for fine pearls. 46When he found a very valuable pearl, he went and sold everything he had and bought it.

A Story of a Fishing Net

47"Also, the kingdom of heaven is like a ·net [dragnet; Ca net dragged between two boats, or between a boat and the shore] that was put into the ·lake [sea] and caught many different kinds of fish. 48When it was full, the fishermen pulled the net to the shore. They sat down and put all the good fish in baskets and threw away the ·bad [worthless] fish. 49It will be this way at the end of the age. The angels will come and separate the evil people from the ·good [righteous] people. 50The angels will throw the evil people into the blazing furnace [Dan. 3:11, 19–30], where ·people will cry and grind their teeth with pain [Lthere will be weeping and gnashing of teeth; v. 42]."

51Jesus asked his ·followers [disciples], "Do you understand all these things?"

They answered, "Yes."

52Then Jesus said to them, "So every ·teacher of the law [scribe] who has ·been taught about [become a disciple of] the kingdom of heaven is like the ·owner [head] of a house. He brings out both new things and old things ·he has saved [Lfrom his treasure/storeroom; Cknowledge of the Old Testament provides insight into Jesus' "new" message of the kingdom of God]."

Jesus Goes to His Hometown
(13:53–58; Mark 6:1–6; Luke 4:16–30)

53When Jesus finished teaching [see 7:28] with these ·stories [parables], he left there. 54He went to his hometown [CNazareth; 2:23; Luke 2:39] and taught the people in their synagogue, and they were ·amazed [astonished]. They said, "Where did this man get this wisdom and this power to do miracles? 55·He is just [Isn't this…?] the son of ·a [Lthe] carpenter. ·His mother is Mary [LIsn't his mother called Mary…?], and his brothers are James, Joseph, Simon, and Judas. 56And all his sisters are here with us. Where then does this man get all these things?" 57So the people were ·upset with [offended by] Jesus.

But Jesus said to them, "A prophet is ·honored everywhere [not dishonored] except in his hometown and in his own ·home [family; household]."

58So he did not do many miracles there because ·they had no faith [of their unbelief].

How John the Baptist Was Killed
(14:1–12; Mark 6:14–29; Luke 3:19–20; 9:7–9)

14 At that time Herod, the ·ruler of Galilee [Ltetrarch; see Luke 3:1], heard the reports about Jesus. 2So he said to his servants, "·Jesus [LThis] is John the Baptist, who has risen from the dead. That is why ·he can work these miracles [Lmiraculous powers are at work in him]."

3·Sometime before this, [LFor] Herod had arrested John, ·tied him up [chained/bound him], and put him into prison. Herod did this because of Herodias, who had been the wife of Philip, Herod's brother. 4[LFor] John had been telling Herod, "It is not lawful for you to ·be married to Herodias [have her]." 5Herod wanted to kill John, but he was afraid of the ·people [crowd], because they ·believed John was [regarded John as] a prophet.

6On Herod's birthday, the daughter of Herodias danced for Herod and his guests, and she [greatly] pleased him. 7So he ·promised [announced] with ·an oath [a vow] to give her anything she ·wanted [asked]. 8·Herodias told her daughter what to ask for, so [At her mother's urging/prompting] she said to Herod, "Give me the head of John the Baptist here on a platter." 9Although King Herod was very ·sad [sorry; grieved; distressed], he had made a ·promise [vow; oath], and his dinner guests had heard him. So Herod ·ordered [commanded] that what she asked for be done. 10He sent soldiers to the prison to cut off John's head. 11And they brought it on a platter and gave it to the girl, and she took it to her mother. 12John's ·followers [disciples] came and got his ·body [corpse] and buried it. Then they went and ·told [reported it to] Jesus.

More than Five Thousand Fed
(14:13–21; Mark 6:32–44; Luke 9:10–17; John 6:1–15)

13When Jesus heard what had happened to John, he left in a boat and
went to a ·lonely [isolated; deserted] place by himself. But the crowds
heard about it and followed him on foot from the towns. 14When he
·arrived [landed; came ashore], he saw a great crowd waiting. He ·felt
sorry [had compassion] for them and healed those who were sick.
15When it was evening, his ·followers [disciples] came to him and said,
"·No one lives in this [This is a remote/deserted] place, and it is already
late. Send the people away so they can go to the ·towns [villages] and buy
food for themselves."
16But Jesus answered, "They don't need to go away. You give them
something to eat."
17They said to him, "But we have only five loaves of bread and two fish."
18Jesus said, "Bring ·the bread and the fish [[L]them here] to me." 19Then
he ·told [commanded; ordered] the people to ·sit down [recline] on the
grass. He took the five loaves and the two fish and, looking to heaven, he
·thanked God for [blessed] the food. Jesus ·divided [broke] the bread and
gave it to his ·followers [disciples], who gave it to the people. 20All the
people ate and were satisfied. Then ·the followers [[L]they] filled twelve
baskets with the leftover pieces of food. 21There were about five thousand
men there who ate, not counting women and children.

Jesus Walks on the Water
(14:22–33; Mark 6:45–52; John 6:16–21)

22Immediately Jesus ·told [compelled; made] his ·followers [disciples]
to get into the boat and go ahead of him ·across the lake [to the other side].
He stayed there to ·send the people home [dismiss the crowds]. 23After he
had ·sent them away [dismissed them], he went by himself up into the
·hills [mountain] to pray. ·It was late, and [When evening/night came,]
Jesus was there alone. 24By this time, the boat was already ·far away [[L]many
stadia; [C]a stadion was about six hundred feet] from land. It was being ·hit
[buffeted; beaten] by waves, because the wind was blowing against it.
25·Between three and six o'clock in the morning [[L]And in the fourth
watch of the night], Jesus came to them, walking on the water. 26When his
·followers [disciples] saw him walking on the water, they were ·afraid [ter-
rified]. They said, "It's a ghost!" and cried out in fear.
27But Jesus ·quickly [immediately] spoke to them, "Have courage! It
is I. Do not be afraid."
28Peter said, "Lord, if it is really you, then ·command [tell] me to come
to you on the water."
29Jesus said, "Come."
And Peter left the boat and walked on the water ·to [[L]and came toward]
Jesus. 30But when Peter saw the wind,[n] he became ·afraid [terrified] and
began to sink. He shouted, "Lord, save me!"
31Immediately Jesus reached out his hand and ·caught [took hold of]
Peter. Jesus said, "·Your faith is small [What little faith you have; [T]You of
little faith]. Why did you doubt?"
32After they got into the boat, the wind ·became calm [stopped; died
down]. 33Then those who were in the boat worshiped Jesus and said,
"Truly you are the Son of God!"

Healings at Gennesaret
(14:34–36; Mark 6:53–56; John 6:22–25)

34When they had crossed the lake, they came to shore at Gennesaret.
35When the ·people there [*or* men of that place] recognized Jesus, they
·told people [sent word] all around there that Jesus had come, and they

---

14:30 wind Some Greek copies say "strong wind."

brought all their sick to him. 36They begged Jesus to let them touch just
the ·edge [*or* tassels; see Num. 15:38–39] of his ·coat [cloak], and all who
touched it were healed.

Obey God's Law
(15:1–20; Mark 7:1–23; Luke 6:39; 11:37–41)

15 Then some Pharisees and ·teachers of the law [scribes] came
to Jesus from Jerusalem. They asked him, 2"Why don't your
·followers [disciples] obey the ·unwritten laws which have been handed
down to us [Ltraditions of the elders]? [LFor] They don't wash their hands
before they eat [Ca Jewish ritual for ceremonial purity]."
3Jesus answered, "And why do you ·refuse to obey [break; violate]
God's command ·so that you can follow your own teachings [Lfor the sake
of your traditions]? 4God said, 'Honor your father and your mother [Ex.
20:12; Deut. 5:16],' and 'Anyone who ·says cruel things to [speaks evil of;
curses] his father or mother must be put to death [Ex. 21:17; Lev. 20:9].'
5But you say a person can tell his father or mother, 'I have something I
could use to help you, but I have ·given [dedicated; devoted] it to God
already [Ca practice known as Corban; see Mark 7:10–12].' 6You teach that
person ·not to [that he need not] honor his father or his mother. You
·rejected [invalidated; canceled; nullified] ·what God said [Lthe word of
God] for the sake of your own ·rules [tradition]. 7You are hypocrites!
Isaiah was right when he ·said [Lprophesied] about you:
8'These people show honor to me with ·words [Ltheir lips],
but their hearts are far from me.
9Their worship of me is ·worthless [futile; in vain].
The things [doctrines] they teach are nothing but human ·rules
[commandments; Is. 29:13].'"
10After Jesus called the crowd to him, he said, "Listen and ·understand
what I am saying [try to understand]. 11It is not what ·people put into
their mouths [Lgoes into the mouth] that ·makes them unclean [pollutes/
defiles the person]. It is what comes out of their mouths that ·makes them
unclean [pollutes/defiles the person]."
12Then his ·followers [disciples] came to him and asked, "Do you know
that the Pharisees are ·angry [offended; shocked] because of what you
said?"
13Jesus answered, "Every plant that my Father in heaven has not
planted himself will be pulled up by the roots. 14·Stay away from the
Pharisees [LLeave/Ignore them]; they are blind ·leaders [guides].*n* And if a
blind person ·leads [guides] a blind person, both will fall into a ·ditch [pit;
hole]."
15Peter said, "Explain the ·example [parable] to us."
16Jesus said, "·Do you still not understand [LAre you still so dull/fool-
ish]? 17·Surely you know [LDon't you know…?] that all the food that
enters the mouth goes into the stomach and then goes ·out of the body
[Linto the sewer/latrine]." 18But ·what people say with their mouths [Lthe
things that come out of the mouth] comes from the ·way they think [Lthe
heart]; these are the things that ·make people unclean [pollute/defiled a
person]. 19[LFor] Out of the ·mind [heart] come evil ·thoughts [inten-
tions; ideas], murder, adultery, sexual sins, stealing, ·lying [false witness/
testimony], and ·speaking evil of others [slander; blasphemy]. 20These
things make people ·unclean [polluted; defiled]; eating with unwashed
hands does not make them ·unclean [polluted; defiled]."

15:14 leaders Some Greek copies continue, "of blind people."

Jesus Helps a Gentile Woman
(15:21–28; Mark 7:24–30)

21 **Jesus left that place and went to the ·area** [district; region] **of Tyre and Sidon** [C cities on the coast north of Israel]. 22 **A ·Canaanite** [C a non-Jewish (Gentile) resident of Palestine (Canaan was the ancient name for Palestine)] **woman from that area came to Jesus and cried out, "Lord, Son of David** [C a title for the Messiah], **have mercy on me! My daughter ·has a demon, and she is suffering very much** [is tormented; L is severely demon-possessed]."

23 **But Jesus did not ·answer the woman** [L answer her a word]. **So his ·followers** [disciples] **came to Jesus and ·begged** [asked; urged] **him, "Tell the woman to go away.** [L Because] **She is following us and ·shouting** [crying out]."

24 **Jesus answered, "·God sent me** [L I was sent] **only to the lost sheep, the ·people** [L house] **of Israel."**

25 **Then the woman came to Jesus again and bowed before him and said, "Lord, help me!"**

26 **Jesus answered, "It is not right to take the children's bread and ·give** [throw] **it to the dogs."** [C "Children" refers to Israel; "dogs" to the Gentiles.]

27 **The woman said, "Yes, Lord, but even the dogs eat the crumbs that fall from their masters' table."**

28 **Then Jesus answered, "**[L O] **Woman, you have great faith! ·I will do what you asked** [L Let it be done for you as you wish]." **And ·at that moment** [L from that hour] **the woman's daughter was healed.**

Jesus Heals Many People
(15:29–31; Mark 7:31–37)

29 **After leaving there, Jesus went along ·the shore of Lake Galilee** [T the Sea of Galilee]. **He went up on ·a hill** [*or* the mountain] **and sat there.**

30 **Great crowds came to Jesus, bringing with them the lame, the blind, the crippled, ·those who could not speak** [the mute/deaf; C the word can refer to speech or hearing; v. 31 suggests it here means "mute"], **and many others. They ·put** [laid] **them at Jesus' feet, and he healed them.** 31 **The crowd was ·amazed** [astonished; marveled] **when they saw that ·people who could not speak before** [the mute/deaf] **were now able to speak. The crippled were ·made strong** [well; whole]. **The lame could walk, and the blind could see. And they ·praised** [glorified] **the God of Israel for this.**

More than Four Thousand Fed
(15:32–39; Mark 8:1–10)

32 **Jesus called his ·followers** [disciples] **to him and said, "I ·feel sorry** [have compassion] **for these people, because they have already been with me three days, and they have nothing to eat. I don't want to send them away hungry. They might ·faint** [collapse] **while going home."**

33 **His ·followers** [disciples] **asked him, "·How** [L From where] **can we get enough bread in this ·remote place** [desolate place; desert] **to feed ·all these people** [L so great a crowd]?"

34 **Jesus asked, "How many loaves of bread do you have?"**

They answered, "Seven, and a few small fish."

35 **Jesus told the people to ·sit** [recline] **on the ground.** 36 **He took the seven loaves of bread and the fish and gave thanks to God. Then he ·divided the food** [L broke them] **and gave it to his ·followers** [disciples], **and they gave it to the people.** 37 **All the people ate and were satisfied. Then his ·followers** [disciples] **filled seven ·baskets** [large baskets; C a different word than in the feeding of the five thousand; 14:20] **with the leftover pieces of food.** 38 **There were about four thousand men there who ate, besides women and children.** 39 **After ·sending the people home** [dismissing the crowds], **Jesus got into the boat and went to the ·area** [region] **of Magadan** [C an unknown place, probably on the western shore of Lake Galilee; perhaps Magdala, the hometown of Mary Magdalene].

The Leaders Ask for a Miracle
(16:1–4; Mark 8:11–13; Luke 11:16, 29; 12:54–56)

16 The Pharisees and Sadducees came to Jesus, wanting to ·trick
[test] him. So they asked him to show them a ·miracle [sign]
from ·God [[L]heaven; [C]possibly a sign in the sky, but more likely a Jewish
way of saying "from God"].
2Jesus answered,[n] "·At sunset [In the evening] you say we will have good
weather, because the sky is red. 3And in the morning you say that it will be ·a
rainy day [stormy; bad weather], because the sky is red and ·dark [threaten-
ing; overcast]. You see ·these signs in [the appearance of] the sky and know
·what they mean [how to interpret them]. ·In the same way [*or* However; On
the other hand], you ·see the things that I am doing now, but you don't know
their meaning [[L]cannot interpret the signs of the times]. 4·Evil and sinful
people [[L]An evil/wicked and adulterous generation] ·ask for [seek; demand]
a miracle as a sign, but they will not be given any sign, except the sign of
Jonah [see 12:40; Jon. 1:17]." Then Jesus left them and went away.

Guard Against Wrong Teachings
(16:5–12; Mark 8:14–21; Luke 12:1)

5Jesus' ·followers [disciples] went ·across the lake [[L]to the other side],
but they had forgotten to bring bread. 6Jesus said to them, "·Be careful
[Watch out]! Beware of the ·yeast [leaven] of the Pharisees and the
Sadducees [[C]yeast or leaven refers here to the dangerous permeating
power of their influence]."
7·His followers [[L]They] discussed the meaning of this, saying, "He said
this because we forgot to bring bread."
8Knowing what they were talking about, Jesus asked them, "Why are
you ·talking [discussing; arguing] about not having bread? ·Your faith is
small [What little faith you have!; [T]You of little faith]. 9Do you still not
understand? Remember the five loaves of bread that fed the five thousand?
And remember that you filled many baskets with the leftovers? 10Or the
seven loaves of bread that fed the four thousand and the many [large]
baskets you filled then also? 11Why don't you understand that I was not
talking to you about bread? I am telling you to beware of the ·yeast [leaven]
of the Pharisees and the Sadducees." 12Then ·the followers [[L]they] understood that Jesus was not telling them to beware of the ·yeast [leaven] used
in bread but to beware of the teaching of the Pharisees and the Sadducees.

Peter Says Jesus Is the Christ
(16:13–20; Mark 8:27–30; Luke 9:18–21)

13When Jesus came to the area of Caesarea Philippi [[C]25 miles north of
Lake Galilee near Mount Hermon], he asked his ·followers [disciples],
"Who do people say the Son of Man is?"
14They answered, "Some say you are John the Baptist. Others say you
are Elijah [[C]some Jews expected Elijah to return in the end times; Mal. 4:5],
and still others say you are Jeremiah or one of the prophets [Deut. 18:15]."
15Then Jesus asked them, "·And [But] who do you say I am?"
16Simon Peter answered, "You are the ·Christ [Messiah], the Son of the
living God."
17Jesus answered, "You are blessed, Simon son of Jonah, because ·no
person taught you that [[L]flesh and blood did not reveal this to you]. [[L]But;
Rather] My Father in heaven ·showed you who I am [revealed it]. 18So I
tell you, you are Peter [[C]the Greek *petros,* like the Aramaic *cephas,* means
"rock" or "stone"]. On this rock I will build my church, and the ·power of
death [[L]gates of Hades/the underworld] will not be able to ·defeat [over-
power; conquer; prevail against] it. 19I will give you the keys of the
kingdom of heaven; ·the things [and whatever] you ·don't allow [forbid;

16:2–3 answered Some Greek copies do not have the rest of verse 2 and verse 3.

[L]bind] **on earth will be ·the things that God does not allow** [forbidden/
[L]bound in heaven], **and ·the things** [whatever] **you ·allow** [permit; [L]loose]
on earth will be ·the things that God allows [permitted/[L]loosed in
heaven]." 20**Then Jesus** [sternly] **warned his ·followers** [disciples] **not to
tell anyone he was the ·Christ** [Messiah].

Jesus Says that He Must Die
(16:21–28; Mark 8:31–9:1; Luke 9:22–27; John 6:67–71; 12:25)

21**From that time on Jesus began ·telling** [showing; making it clear to]
his ·followers [disciples] **that he must go to Jerusalem, where the Jewish
elders, the leading priests, and the ·teachers of the law** [scribes] **would
make him suffer ·many things** [greatly]. **He told them he must be killed
and then be raised from the dead on the third day.**
22**Peter took Jesus aside and ·told him not to talk like that** [[L]began to
reprimand/rebuke him]. **He said, "·God save you from those things** [God
forbid; May it never be; [L](God) Be merciful], **Lord! Those things ·will
never** [must certainly not] **happen to you!"**
23**Then Jesus turned and said to Peter, "·Go away from** [Get behind]
me, Satan! You are ·not helping [an obstacle/stumbling block to] **me! You
·don't care about** [are not setting your mind on/thinking about] **the things
of God, but only ·about the things people think are important** [on/about
human concerns]."
24**Then Jesus said to his ·followers** [disciples], **"If ·people want** [[L]anyone
wants] **to follow me, they must ·give up the things they want** [deny themselves; turn from selfishness; set aside their own interests]. **They must ·be
willing even to give up their lives to** [[L]take up their cross and] **follow me.**
25**Those who want to save their lives will ·give up true life** [[L]lose their life/
soul; [C]Greek *psychē* can mean "life" or "soul," producing this play on
words], **and those who ·give up** [lose; sacrifice] **their lives for ·me** [my
sake] **will ·have true life** [find life]. 26**·It is worthless** [What good/profit/
benefit is it…?] **to ·have** [gain] **the whole world if they ·lose** [forfeit] **their
souls. ·They could never pay enough** [[L]Or what could they give…?] **·to
buy back** [in exchange for] **their souls.** 27[[L]For] **The Son of Man will come
again with his Father's glory and with his angels. At that time, he will
·reward** [repay; give back; judge] **them for what they have done** [Ps. 62:12;
Prov. 24:12]. 28**I tell you the truth, some people standing here will not ·die**
[[L]taste death] **before they see the Son of Man** [Dan. 7:13–14] **coming with
his kingdom."** [[C]This may refer to the Transfiguration which follows
(17:1–8), Jesus' resurrection, or the destruction of Jerusalem in AD 70.]

The Transfiguration on the Mountain
(17:1–13; Mark 9:2–13; Luke 9:28–36)

17

**Six days later, Jesus took Peter, James, and John, the brother
of James,** [[L]and led them] **up on a high mountain by themselves.** 2**·While they watched** [In their presence; In front of them], **Jesus'
appearance was ·changed** [transformed; [T]transfigured]; **his face ·became
bright** [shined] **like the sun, and his clothes became white as light.** 3**Then
Moses and Elijah appeared to them, talking with Jesus.** [[C]God had given
the Law through Moses, and Elijah was an important prophet (see Mark
6:15); together they signify that Jesus fulfills the OT.]
4**Peter said to Jesus, "Lord, it is good that we are here. If you want, I will
put up three ·tents** [shelters; shrines; tabernacles; Lev. 23:42] **here—one
for you, one for Moses, and one for Elijah."** [[C]Perhaps Peter wanted to
prolong their stay or to commemorate their visit.]
5**While Peter was talking,** [[L]look; [T]behold] **a bright cloud ·covered**
[overshadowed; Ex. 24:15] **them. A voice came from the cloud and said,
"This is my ·Son, whom I love** [dearly beloved Son; Ps. 2:7; Gen. 22:2],

·and I am very pleased with him [in whom I take great delight; Is. 42:1; Matt. 3:17]. Listen to him [Deut. 18:15; Acts 3:22]!"

6When his ·followers [disciples] heard the voice, they were so frightened they fell ·to the ground [Lon their faces]. 7But Jesus went to them and touched them and said, "Stand up. Don't be afraid." 8·When they looked up [Lifting up their eyes], they saw ·Jesus was now alone [Lno one except Jesus alone].

9As they were coming down the mountain, Jesus ·commanded [instructed] them not to tell anyone about ·what they had seen [the vision] until the Son of Man had ·risen [been raised] from the dead.

10Then his ·followers [disciples] asked him, "Why do the ·teachers of the law [scribes] say that Elijah must come first [Cthat is, before the Messiah comes; Mal. 3:1; 4:5]?"

11Jesus answered, "·They are right to say that Elijah is coming and that [LElijah is indeed coming, and] he will ·make everything the way it should be [restore/prepare everything]. 12But I tell you that Elijah has already come, and they did not recognize him. They did to him whatever they wanted to do. It will be the same with the Son of Man; those same people will make the Son of Man suffer." 13Then the ·followers [disciples] understood that Jesus was talking about John the Baptist.

Jesus Heals a Sick Boy
(17:14–21; Mark 9:14–29; Luke 9:37–43; 17:6)

14When Jesus and his ·followers [disciples] came back to the crowd, a man came to Jesus and ·bowed [knelt] before him. 15The man said, "Lord, have mercy on my son. He ·has epilepsy [has seizures; *or* is demented/a lunatic; Cthe word for epilepsy could also mean "moonstruck" or demented; Mark 9:17 says the boy was demon possessed] and is suffering ·very much [terribly], because he often falls into the fire or into the water. 16I brought him to your ·followers [disciples], but they could not ·cure [heal] him."

17Jesus answered, "·You people have no faith, and your lives are all wrong [LO faithless/unbelieving and perverse/corrupt generation]. How long must I ·put up [stay; Lbe] with you? How long must I ·continue to be patient [put up] with you? Bring the boy here to me." 18Jesus ·commanded [reprimanded; rebuked] the demon and it came out of him, and the boy was healed from that ·time on [moment; Lhour].

19The ·followers [disciples] came to Jesus when he was alone and asked, "Why couldn't we ·force [drive; cast] the demon out?"

20Jesus answered, "Because ·your faith is too small [you have so little faith]. I tell you the truth, if your faith is ·as big as [as small as; the size of; Las; like] a mustard seed, you can say to this mountain, 'Move from here to there,' and it will move. ·All things will be possible [LNothing would be impossible] for you. |21That kind of spirit comes out only if you use prayer and fasting.|"[n]

Jesus Talks About His Death
(17:22–23; Mark 9:30–32; Luke 9:43–45)

22While Jesus' ·followers [disciples] were gathering in Galilee, he said to them, "The Son of Man will be ·handed over [betrayed/delivered over] to ·people [Lhuman hands], 23and they will kill him [Cthe "handing over" may be Judas' betrayal or God's actions in "giving up" his Son to accomplish salvation; Rom. 4:25]. But on the third day he will be raised from the dead." And the ·followers [disciples] were ·filled with sadness [greatly distressed].

Jesus Talks About Paying Taxes

24When ·Jesus and his followers [Lthey] came to Capernaum, the men who collected the ·Temple tax [Ltwo-drachma; Cthe annual tax paid to

17:21 That . . . fasting. Some Greek copies do not contain the bracketed text.

support the Temple (Ex. 30:13–16)] came to Peter. They asked, "Does
your teacher pay the ·Temple tax [Ltwo-drachma]?"
25Peter answered, "Yes."
Peter went into the house, but before he could speak, Jesus said to him,
"What do you think? From whom do the kings of the earth collect ·different
kinds of taxes [tribute/tolls or taxes]—the king's ·children [*or* own people/
citizens] or ·others [*or* foreigners; Cperhaps tribute paid by defeated nations]?"
26Peter answered, "·Other people pay the taxes [LFrom others]."
Jesus said to Peter, "Then the ·children [*or* people; citizens] of the king
·don't have to pay taxes [are exempt/free]. 27But we don't want to ·upset
[offend] these tax collectors. So go to the lake and ·fish [throw out your
hook]. After you catch the first fish, open its mouth and you will find a
·coin [shekel; CGreek: *stater,* worth four drachma, or two payments of the
Temple tax]. Take that coin and give it to the tax collectors for you and me."

Who Is the Greatest?
(18:1–9; Mark 9:33–37, 42–50; Luke 9:46–48; 14:34–35; 17:1–2; John 13:20)

18 At that time the ·followers [disciples] came to Jesus and asked,
"Who is greatest in the kingdom of heaven?"
2Jesus called a little child to him and stood the child before his ·follow-
ers [disciples]. 3Then he said, "I tell you the truth, you must ·change [*or*
turn from your sins; convert; Lturn] and become like little children.
Otherwise, you will never enter the kingdom of heaven. 4The greatest
person in the kingdom of heaven [Ltherefore] is the one who makes himself humble [and becomes] like this [little] child.
5"[LAnd] Whoever ·accepts [welcomes; receives] a child ·in my name [Cas
a representative or follower of Jesus] ·accepts [welcomes; receives] me
[Cindicates concern for the lowly; children had low social status]. 6If someone
causes one of these little children who believes in me to ·sin [lose faith; stum-
ble], it would be better for that person to have a ·large stone [large millstone;
Lmillstone of a donkey] tied around the neck and be ·drowned [Lthrown] in
the [Ldepths of the] sea. 7·How terrible for [LWoe to] ·the people of the world
[Lthe world] because of ·the things that cause them to sin [temptations to
sin; Lstumbling blocks]. ·Such things will happen [LIt is necessary for stumbling blocks to come], but ·how terrible for [Lwoe to] the one ·who causes
them to happen [Lthrough whom the stumbling block comes]! 8If your hand
or your foot causes you to ·sin [lose faith; stumble], cut it off and throw it
away. It is better for you ·to lose part of your body and live forever [Lto enter
life maimed or crippled] than to have two hands and two feet and be thrown
into the ·fire that burns forever [eternal fire]. 9If your eye causes you to ·sin
[lose faith; stumble], ·take [tear; gouge] it out and throw it away. It is better
for you to ·have only one eye and live forever [Lenter life one-eyed] than to
have two eyes and be thrown into the ·fire of hell [LGehenna of fire; 5:22].

A Lost Sheep
(18:10–14; Luke 15:3–7)

10"Be careful [Watch out; *or* See that you…]. Don't ·think these little
children are worth nothing [Ldespise/look down on one of these little
ones]. [LFor] I tell you that they have angels in heaven who are always
·with [in the presence of; Lsee the face of] my Father in heaven. |11The Son
of Man came to save ·lost people [that which was lost].|*n*
12"[LWhat do you think?] If a man has a hundred sheep but one of the
sheep ·gets lost [goes astray; wanders off], ·he will [Lwon't he…?] leave the
other ninety-nine on the ·hill [Lhills; mountains] and go to look for the
lost sheep. 13I tell you the truth, if he finds it he ·is happier about [rejoices

---

18:11 The . . . people. Some Greek copies do not contain the bracketed text.

more over] that one sheep than ·about [over] the ninety-nine that ·were
never lost [never went astray/wandered off]. 14In the same way, your
Father in heaven ·does not want [is not willing that] any of these little
children to ·be lost [perish].

When a Person Sins Against You
(18:15–18; Luke 17:3; John 20:23)

15"If your ·fellow believer [Lbrother (or sister)] sins against you," go
and ·tell him what he did wrong [Lreprove/convict/correct him] ·in private [Lbetween you and him alone]. If he listens to you, you have ·helped
that person to be your brother or sister again [Lgained/won back your
brother (or sister)]. 16But if he refuses to listen, go to him again and take
one or two other people with you. 'Every ·case [matter; charge] may be
proved by [the testimony of; Lthe mouth of] two or three witnesses' [Deut.
19:15]. 17If he refuses to listen to them, tell the church. If he refuses to
listen to the church, then treat him like a ·person who does not believe in
God [pagan; Gentile] or like a tax collector.
18"I tell you the truth, ·the things [whatever] you ·don't allow [forbid;
Lbind] on earth will be ·the things God does not allow [forbidden/bound
in heaven]. And ·the things [whatever] you ·allow [permit; Lloose] on
earth will be ·the things that God allows [permitted/Lloosed in heaven]."
19"·Also [Again], I tell you that if two of you on earth agree about
something ·and pray for it [Lfor which you have asked], it will be done for
you by my Father in heaven. 20·This is true because if [LFor where] two or
three people ·come [are assembled/gathered] together in my name, I am
there ·with them [among them; in their midst]."

An Unforgiving Servant
(18:21–22; Luke 17:4)

21Then Peter came to Jesus and asked, "Lord, when my ·fellow believer
[Lbrother (or sister)] sins against me, how many times ·must [should] I
forgive him? Should I forgive him as many as seven times?"
22Jesus answered, "I tell you, you must forgive him not just seven times,
but ·seventy times seven times [*or* seventy-seven times; Cthe Greek can
mean either 490 or 77; the point is unlimited forgiveness]!
23"[LTherefore; For this reason] The kingdom of heaven is like a king
who decided to ·collect the money his servants owed him [Lsettle accounts
with his servants/slaves]. 24When the king began ·to collect his money [the
settlement/reckoning], a ·servant [slave] who owed him ·several million
dollars [*or* billions of dollars; Lten thousand talents; Ca talent was worth
about six thousand days' wages; this is an impossibly high debt] was brought
to him. 25But ·the servant [Lhe] did not have enough money to pay his master. So the master ordered that ·the servant [Lhe] be sold, together with his
wife and children and everything he owned, and the debt paid.
26"But the ·servant [slave] fell ·on his knees [face down; in obeisance]
and begged, 'Be patient with me, and I will pay you everything I owe.'
27The master felt ·sorry [compassion] for ·his servant [that slave], so he
let him go free and ·forgave [canceled] the debt.
28"·Later [LAfter departing], that same ·servant [slave] found ·another
servant [a fellow servant/slave] who owed him a ·few dollars [hundred
denarii]. ·The servant [LHe] grabbed him ·around the neck [Land began
choking him] and said, 'Pay me the money you owe me!'
29"The ·other servant [fellow servant/slave] fell on his knees and begged
him, 'Be patient with me, and I will pay you everything I owe.'
30"But ·the first servant [Lhe] refused. He threw ·the other servant

18:15 against you Some Greek copies do not have "against you."

[him] into prison until he could pay everything he owed. 31When ·the
other servants [his fellow servants/slaves] saw what had happened, they
were very ·sorry [upset; distressed]. So they went and ·told [reported to]
their master all that had happened.
32"Then the master called ·his servant [Lhim] in and said, 'You ·evil
[wicked] ·servant [slave]! Because you ·begged [pleaded with] me, I forgave [canceled] all that debt. 33·You should have [LShouldn't you have…?]
showed mercy to ·that other servant [your fellow servant/slave], just as I
showed mercy to you.' 34The master was very angry and ·put the servant
in prison to be punished [Ldelivered him to the tormenters/torturers]
until he could pay everything he owed.
35"·This king did what [LSo also] my heavenly Father will do to you if
you do not forgive your brother or sister from your heart."

Jesus Teaches About Divorce
(19:1–12; Mark 10:1–12; Luke 9:51; 16:18)

19 After Jesus ·said all these things [Lfinished these words; see
7:28], he left Galilee and went into the ·area [region] of Judea
·on the other side of [beyond] the Jordan River. 2Large crowds followed
him, and he healed them there.
3Some Pharisees came to Jesus ·and tried to trick [to trap/test] him.
They asked, "Is it ·right [lawful; Caccording to the law of Moses] for a man
to divorce his wife for any reason he chooses?"
4Jesus answered, "·Surely you have [LHaven't you…?] read in the
Scriptures: ·When God made the world, 'he [LFrom the beginning, the
Creator] made them male and female' [Gen. 1:27; 5:2]. 5And God said, 'So
a man will leave his father and mother and be ·united with [joined to] his
wife, and the two will become ·one body [as though they were one person;
Tone flesh; Gen. 2:24].' 6So they are no longer two, but one. God has joined
the two together, so no one should separate them."
7The Pharisees asked, "Why then did Moses give a command for a man
to divorce his wife by giving her ·divorce papers [a certificate of divorce/
dismissal; Deut. 24:1]?"
8Jesus answered, "Moses ·allowed [permitted] you to divorce your
wives because ·you refused to accept God's teaching [Lof your hard-heart-
edness], but ·divorce was not allowed in the beginning [*or* this was not
God's intention at creation; Lfrom the beginning it was not like this]. 9I tell
you that anyone who divorces his wife and marries another woman ·is
guilty of [commits] adultery.[n] ·The only reason for a man to divorce his
wife is if his wife has sexual relations with another man [L…except in the
case of sexual immorality]."
10The ·followers [disciples] said to him, "If that is the ·only reason a
man can divorce his wife [situation/case between a husband and wife], it
is better not to marry."
11Jesus answered, "Not everyone can accept this ·teaching [word], but
·God has made some able to accept it [*or* only those given this gift of celi-
bacy; Lonly to those whom it has been given]. 12·There are different reasons
why some men cannot marry [LFor…]. Some men were born ·without the
ability to become fathers [Las eunuchs]. Others were made ·that way later
in life [Leunuchs] by other people [Cmales would sometimes be castrated as
punishment, or to serve in harems]. And some men have ·given up marriage because [Lmade themselves eunuchs for the sake] of the kingdom of

19:9 adultery Some Greek copies continue, "And anyone who marries a divorced woman is guilty of adultery." Compare Matthew 5:32.

heaven [[C]through abstinence, not necessarily castration]. ·But the person who can marry should accept this teaching about marriage [*or* The person who can accept this teaching about not marrying should accept it]."

Jesus Welcomes Children
(19:13–15; Mark 10:13–16; Luke 18:15–17)

[13]Then the people brought their little children to Jesus so he could ·put [lay] his hands on them [[C]an act of blessing] and pray for them. [[L]But] His ·followers [disciples] ·told them to stop [scolded/rebuked them], [14]but Jesus said, "Let the little children come to me. Don't ·stop [hinder] them, because the kingdom of heaven belongs to people who are like these children [[C]meaning humble and dependent]." [15]After Jesus ·put [lay] his hands on the children [[C]a sign of blessing; Mark 10:16], he left there.

A Rich Young Man's Question
(19:16–30; Mark 10:17–31; Luke 18:18–30; 22:28–30)

[16][At that time; [L]And look/[T]behold] A man came to Jesus and asked, "Teacher, what ·good thing [good deed; [L]good] must I do to have ·life forever [eternal life]?"

[17]Jesus answered, "Why do you ask me about what is good? Only ·God [[L]one] is good. But if you want to ·have life forever [have eternal life; [L]enter life], ·obey [keep] the ·commands [commandments]."

[18]The man asked, "Which commands?"

Jesus answered, "'You must not murder anyone; you must not ·be guilty of [commit] adultery; you must not steal; you must not ·tell lies about your neighbor [testify falsely; [T]bear false witness]; [19]honor your father and mother [Ex. 20:12–16; Deut. 5:16–20]; and love your neighbor as you love yourself [Lev. 19:18].'"

[20]The young man said, "I have ·obeyed [kept carefully; guarded] all these things. What ·else do I need to do [[L]do I still lack]?"

[21]Jesus answered, "If you want to be ·perfect [complete], then go and sell your possessions and give the money to the poor, and you will have treasure in heaven. Then come and follow me."

[22]But when the young man heard this, he left ·sorrowfully [grieving], because he ·was rich [had many possessions].

[23]Then Jesus said to his ·followers [disciples], "I tell you the truth, it will be hard for a rich person to enter the kingdom of heaven. [24]·Yes [[L]Again], I tell you that it is easier for a camel to go through the eye of a needle than for a rich person to enter the kingdom of God [[C]meaning it is impossible, by human effort; see v. 26]."

[25]When Jesus' ·followers [disciples] heard this, they were ·very surprised [astonished] and asked, "Then who can be saved?"

[26]Jesus looked at them and said, "·For people [Humanly speaking,] this is impossible, but for God all things are possible."

[27]Peter said to Jesus, "Look, we have left everything and followed you. So what will we ·have [get]?"

[28]Jesus said to them, "I tell you the truth, ·when the age to come has arrived [at the renewal of the world; [L]in the regeneration], the Son of Man [Dan. 7:13–14] will sit on his ·great [glorious] throne. All of you who followed me will also sit on twelve thrones, judging the twelve tribes of Israel. [29]And all those who have left houses, brothers, sisters, father, mother,[n] children, or ·farms [fields] ·to follow me [[L]for my name's sake] will ·get much more than they left [[L]receive a hundred times as much], and they will ·have life forever [[L]inherit eternal life]. [30][[L]But] Many who are first now will be last in the future. And many who are last now will be first in the future.

19:29 mother Some Greek copies continue, "or wife."

A Story About Workers
(20:1–16; Mark 10:31; Luke 13:30)

20 "[LFor] The kingdom of heaven is like a ·person who owned
some land [landowner; householder]. One morning, he went
out very early to hire some people to work in his vineyard. 2The man
agreed to pay the workers ·one coin [La denarius; Ctypical pay for a day
laborer] for working that day. Then he sent them into the vineyard to
work. 3About ·nine o'clock [Lthe third hour] the man went to the marketplace and saw some other people standing there, doing nothing. 4So he
said to them, 'If you go and work in my vineyard, I will pay you ·what
your work is worth [Lwhatever is right].' 5So they went to work in the
vineyard. The man went out again about ·twelve o'clock and three
o'clock [Lthe sixth and ninth hour] and did the same thing. 6About ·five
o'clock [Lthe eleventh hour] the man went to the marketplace again and
saw others standing there. He asked them, 'Why did you stand here all
day doing nothing?' 7They answered, 'No one ·gave us a job [hired us].'
The man said to them, 'Then you can go and work in my vineyard.'

8"·At the end of the day [When evening came], the owner of the vineyard said to the ·boss of all the workers [foreman; supervisor; steward],
'Call the workers and pay them [Ltheir wage]. Start with the last people I
hired and end with those I hired first.'

9"When the workers who were hired at ·five o'clock [Lthe eleventh hour]
came to get their pay, each received ·one coin [La denarius; v. 2]. 10When
the workers who were hired first came to get their pay, they ·thought
[expected; assumed] they would be paid more than the others. But each
one of them also received ·one coin [La denarius]. 11When they got their
coin, they ·complained to [grumbled at; protested to] the ·man who owned
the land [landowner; householder]. 12They said, 'Those people were hired
last and worked only one hour. But you ·paid them the same as you paid
[Lmade them equal to] us who ·worked hard all day in the hot sun [Lbore
the burden and heat of the day].' 13But the man who owned the vineyard
said to one of those workers, 'Friend, I am ·being fair [Lnot being unfair] to
you. ·You agreed [Did you not agree…?] to work for ·one coin [La denarius;
v. 2]. 14So take ·your pay [Lwhat is yours] and go. I ·want [choose] to give
the man who was hired last the same pay that I gave you. 15·I can [LDon't I
have the right to…?] do what I want with ·my own money [Lwhat is mine].
Are you jealous because I am ·good to those people [generous; Lgood]?'

16"So those who are last now will someday be first, and those who are
first now will someday be last."

Jesus Talks About His Own Death
(20:17–19; Mark 10:32–34; Luke 18:31–34)

17While Jesus was going [Lup] to Jerusalem [Ctravelers go "up" to
Jerusalem because it is built on a hill and because it is God's holy city], he
took his twelve followers aside privately and [as they walked; Lon the way]
said to them, 18"Look, we are going [Lup] to Jerusalem. The Son of Man
will be ·turned over [betrayed; delivered over; see 17:22] to the ·leading
[Tchief] priests and the ·teachers of the law [scribes], and they will ·say
that he must die [condemn him to death]. 19They will turn the Son of
Man over to the Gentiles [Cthe Roman authorities] to ·laugh at [mock]
him and ·beat him with whips [scourge/flog him] and crucify him. But on
the third day, he will be raised to life again."

A Mother Asks Jesus a Favor
(20:20–28; Mark 10:35–45; Luke 22:24–27)

20Then the mother of the sons of Zebedee [CJames and John] came to
Jesus with her sons. She ·bowed [knelt] before him and asked ·him to do
something for her [a favor of him].

21Jesus asked, "What do you want?"

She said, "·Promise [Grant; Declare; LSay] that one of my sons will sit at your right ·side [hand] and the other will sit at your left side in your kingdom [Cthe positions of highest authority beside the king]."

22 But Jesus said, "You don't understand what you are asking. ·Can you [Are you able to] drink the cup [Csymbolizing suffering, and perhaps God's judgment experienced by Jesus on the cross; Jer. 25:15–29] that I am about to drink?"

The sons answered, "Yes, we ·can [are able]."

23 Jesus said to them, "You will drink from my cup. But ·I cannot choose [it is not for me to grant/say] who will sit at my right or my left; those places belong to those for whom my Father has prepared them."

24 When the other ten ·followers [disciples] heard this, they were ·angry [indignant] with the two brothers.

25 Jesus called them together and said, "You know that the rulers of the ·Gentiles [nations] love to ·show their power [lord it] over the people. And their ·important leaders [high officials; Lgreat ones] love to ·use [exert] their authority [Lover them]. 26 But it ·should not be [must not be; is not to be] that way among you. [Instead, LBut] Whoever wants to become great among you must ·serve the rest of you like a servant [Lbe your servant]. 27 Whoever wants to become first among you must ·serve all of you like a slave [Lbe slave of all]. 28 In the same way, the Son of Man did not come to be served. He came to serve others and to give his life as a ransom for many people [Is. 53:12; John 11:49–50]."

Jesus Heals Two Blind Men

(20:29–34; Mark 10:46–52; Luke 18:35–43)

29 When ·Jesus and his followers [Lthey] were leaving Jericho, a ·great many people [large crowd] followed him. 30 [LAnd look/Tbehold] Two blind men sitting by the road heard that Jesus was going by, so they shouted, "Lord, Son of David [Ca title for the Messiah, a descendant of King David; 2 Sam. 7:11–16], ·have mercy [take pity] on us!"

31 The people ·warned [rebuked; scolded] the blind men to be quiet, but they shouted even more, "Lord, Son of David, ·have mercy [take pity] on us!"

32 Jesus stopped and said to the blind men, "What do you want me to do for you?"

33 They answered, "Lord, ·we want to see [Llet our eyes be opened]."

34 Jesus felt ·sorry [compassion] for the blind men and touched their eyes, and at once they could see. Then they followed Jesus.

Jesus Enters Jerusalem as a King

(21:1–9; Mark 11:1–10; Luke 19:28–40; John 12:12–19)

21 As Jesus and his ·followers [disciples] ·were coming closer to [approached] Jerusalem, they ·stopped at [Lcame to] Bethphage ·at [*or* on] the Mount of Olives. From there Jesus sent two of his ·followers [disciples] 2 and said to them, "Go to the town ·you can see there [ahead of you; *or* opposite you]. When you enter it, you will ·quickly [immediately] find a donkey tied there with its colt. Untie them and bring them to me. 3 If anyone asks you ·why you are taking the donkeys [Lanything], say that ·the Master [the Lord; *or* its Owner] needs them, and ·he will send them at once [*or* the Lord will return it soon; see Mark 11:3]."

4 This was to ·bring about [fulfill] what ·the prophet had said [Lhad been spoken through the prophet]:

5 "Tell ·the people of Jerusalem [Lthe daughter of Zion; Ca metaphor for
Israel],
'[LLook; TBehold,] Your king is coming to you.
He is ·gentle [humble] and ·riding [mounted] on a donkey,
on the colt of a donkey [Is. 62:11; Zech. 9:9].'"

6[So] **The ·followers** [disciples] **went and did what Jesus ·told them to**
do [instructed; commanded]. 7**They brought the donkey and the colt to**
Jesus and laid their ·coats [cloaks] **on them, ·and Jesus sat on them.**
8**·Many people** [A very large crowd; *or* Most of the crowd] **spread their**
coats on the road. Others cut branches from the trees and spread them on
the road. 9**The ·people** [crowds] **were walking ahead of Jesus and ·behind**
[following] **him, shouting,**

"**·Praise** [LHosanna! Ca Hebrew word originally used in praying for
help, but by this time a joyful shout of praise to God] **to the Son of**
David [Ca title for the Messiah]!
·God bless [Blessed is] **the One who comes in the name of the Lord**
[Ps. 118:26]!
·Praise to God in heaven [LHosanna in the highest; Ceither "in highest
heaven" or "to the Most High God"]!"

10**When Jesus entered Jerusalem, all the city was ·filled with excitement**
[stirred up; in an uproar]. **The people asked, "Who is this man?"**
11**The crowd said, "This man is Jesus, the prophet from the town of**
Nazareth in Galilee."

Jesus Goes to the Temple
(21:12–17; Mark 11:11, 15–17; Luke 19:45–46)

12**Jesus went into the ·Temple** [temple complex; Cthe large temple area,
not the inner building where only the priests could go] **and ·threw** [drove]
out all the people who were buying and selling there. He turned over the
tables of ·those who were exchanging different kinds of money [Lthe mon-
eychangers], **and he upset the benches of those who were selling doves** [*or*
pigeons; Cmoneychangers provided particular coins needed for the temple
tax; doves or pigeons were sold for sacrifices; Lev. 5:7]. 13**Jesus said to ·all**
the people there [Lthem], **"It is written in the Scriptures, 'My ·Temple**
[LHouse] **will be called a house for prayer** [Is. 56:7].**' But you are ·changing**
[making] **it into a ·hideout for robbers** [Tden of thieves; Jer. 7:11]."
14**The blind and ·crippled people** [lame] **came to Jesus in the Temple**
[courts; v. 12], **and he healed them.** 15[LBut when] **The ·leading** [Tchief]
priests and the ·teachers of the law [scribes] **saw that Jesus was doing**
wonderful things and that the children were praising him in the Temple
[courts; v. 12], **saying, "·Praise** [LHosanna; v. 9] **to the Son of David** [Ca
title for the Messiah; v. 9]." **All these things made the priests and the**
·teachers of the law [scribes] **·very angry** [indignant].
16**They asked Jesus, "Do you hear the things these children are**
saying?"
Jesus answered, "Yes. Haven't you read in the Scriptures, ·'You have
taught children and babies to sing praises' [L'From the mouths of infants
and nursing babes you have prepared/created praise'; Ps. 8:2 LXX]?"
17**Then Jesus left and went out of the city to Bethany, where he spent**
the night.

The Power of Faith
(21:18–22; Mark 11:12–14, 20–26)

18**Early the next morning, as Jesus was going back to the city, he became**
hungry. 19**Seeing a fig tree beside the road, Jesus went to it, but ·there were**
no figs [Lhe found nothing] **on the tree, only leaves** [Is. 5:1–7]. **So Jesus**
said to the tree, "·You will [May you] **never again have fruit." The tree**
immediately ·dried up [withered].
20**When his ·followers** [disciples] **saw this, they were amazed. They**
asked, "How did the fig tree ·dry up [wither] **·so quickly** [immediately]?"
21**Jesus answered, "I tell you the truth, if you have faith and do not**
doubt, you will be able to do what I did to this tree and even more. You

will be able to say to this mountain, '·Go, fall [LBe lifted up and thrown] into the sea.' And if you have faith, it will ·happen [be done]. 22If you ·believe [have faith], you will get anything you ask for in prayer."

Leaders Doubt Jesus' Authority

(21:23–27; Mark 11:27–33; Luke 20:1–8)

23Jesus went to the Temple [courts], and while he was teaching there, the ·leading [Tchief] priests and the elders of the people came to him. They said, "What authority do you have to do these things? [LAnd] Who gave you this authority?"

24Jesus answered, "I also will ask you a question. If you answer me, then I will tell you what authority I have to do these things. 25Tell me: When John baptized people, did that come from ·God [Lheaven; Ca reverential Jewish way of referring to God] or just from ·other people [human beings]?"

They argued about Jesus' question, saying, "If we answer, 'John's baptism was from ·God [Lheaven],' Jesus will say, 'Then why didn't you believe him?' 26But if we say, 'It was from ·people [human beings],' we are afraid of what the crowd will do because they all ·believe [think; hold] that John was a prophet."

27So they answered Jesus, "We don't know."

Jesus said to them, "Then I won't tell you what authority I have to do these things.

A Story About Two Sons

28"Tell me what you think about this: A man had two sons. He went to the ·first [elder] son and said, 'Son, go and work today in ·my [the] vineyard.' 29The son answered, 'I will not go.' But later the son ·changed his mind [regretted/thought better of it] and went. 30Then the father went to the other son and said, ·'Son, go and work today in my vineyard' [Lthe same thing]. The son answered, 'Yes, sir, I will,' but he did not go. 31Which of the two sons ·obeyed [Ldid the will of] his father?"

·The priests and leaders [LThey] answered, "The first son."

Jesus said to them, "I tell you the truth, the tax collectors and the prostitutes ·will enter [are going into] the kingdom of God ·before you do [ahead of you]. 32[LFor] John came to show you the ·right way to live [the way/path of righteousness]. You did not believe him, but the tax collectors and prostitutes believed him. Even after seeing this, you still refused to ·change your ways [change your mind; repent] and believe him.

The Story of the Evil Farmers

(21:33–46; Mark 12:1–12; Luke 20:9–19)

33"Listen to ·this story [another parable]: There was a ·man who owned [landowner who planted] a vineyard. He put a wall around it and dug a ·hole [vat; pit] for a winepress and built a tower [Cto protect against thieves; see Is. 5:1–7 for the background to this parable]. Then he leased the land to some [Ctenant] farmers and left for a trip [Cthe owner represents God, the farmers are Israel's religious leaders]. 34When it was time for the grapes to be picked, he sent his ·servants [slaves] to the farmers to get his share of the grapes. 35But the farmers grabbed the ·servants [slaves], beat one, killed another, and then ·killed a third servant with stones [Lstoned a third]. 36So the man sent some other ·servants [slaves] to the farmers, even more than he sent the first time. But the farmers did the same thing to them that they had done before [Cthe servants represent the prophets God sent to Israel]. 37·So [LFinally; Last of all] the man sent his son to the farmers [Cthe son represents Jesus]. He said, 'They will respect my son.' 38But when the farmers saw the son, they said to each other, 'This son will inherit the vineyard. Let's kill him, and we will get his inheritance!' 39Then the farmers grabbed the son, threw him out of the

vineyard, and killed him. 40So what will the ·owner [lord] of the vineyard
do to these farmers when he comes?”
41·The priests and leaders [LThey] said, “He will ·surely kill those evil
men [bring those wretches/evil men to a wretched/evil end]. Then he will
lease the vineyard to some other farmers who will give him his share of
the crop at harvest time [Creferring to the sinners who were responding to
Jesus’ call for repentance, and eventually to the Gentiles who would be
saved].”
42Jesus said to them, “·Surely you have read [LHaven’t you ever read…?]
this in the Scriptures:

‘The stone that the builders rejected
became the cornerstone [capstone; keystone; Lhead of the corner;
Cthe meaning is uncertain, but clearly refers to the most important
stone in the building; Jesus is the rejected stone].
The Lord did this,
and it is ·wonderful [amazing; marvelous] ·to us [for us to see; Lin
our eyes; Ps. 118:22–23].’

43“·So [For this reason; Therefore] I tell you that the kingdom of God
will be taken away from you and given to ·people [a nation] who ·do the
things God wants in his kingdom [Lwill produce its fruit]. 44The person
who ·falls on [stumbles over] this stone will be ·broken [shattered], and
on whomever that stone falls, that person will be crushed.”[n]
45When the ·leading [Tchief] priests and the Pharisees heard these ·sto-
ries [parables], they knew Jesus was talking about them. 46They ·wanted
[were seeking/trying] to arrest him, but they were afraid of the ·people
[crowds], because the people believed that Jesus was a prophet.

A Story About a Wedding Feast
(22:1–14; Luke 14:15–24)

22 Jesus again used ·stories [parables] to teach them. He said,
2“The kingdom of heaven is like a king who prepared a wedding ·feast [banquet] for his son. 3When the ·feast [banquet] was ready,
the king sent his servants to ·tell [inform; call] the people who had been
invited, but they refused to come.
4“Then the king sent other servants, saying, ‘Tell those who have been
invited that my ·feast [banquet] is ready. I have killed my best ·bulls [*or*
oxen] and [Lfattened] calves for the dinner, and everything is ready. Come
to the wedding ·feast [banquet].’
5“But the people ·refused to listen [paid no attention] to the servants
and ·left to do other things [went their own way]. One went to ·work in
his field [his field/farm], and another went to his business. 6·Some of the
other people [*or* The rest] grabbed the servants, ·beat [mistreated;
insulted] them, and killed them. 7The king was furious and sent his army
to ·kill [destroy] the murderers and burn their city [Cprobably an allusion
to the destruction of Jerusalam in AD 70].
8“After that, the king said to his servants, ‘The wedding ·feast [ban-
quet] is ready. I invited those people, but they ·were not worthy [do not
deserve] to come. 9So go to the ·street corners [crossroads; *or* main roads]
and invite everyone you find to come to my ·feast [banquet].’ 10So the
servants went into the streets and gathered all the people they could find,
both good and ·bad [evil]. And the wedding hall was filled with guests.
11“[LBut] When the king came in to see the guests, he saw a man who

21:44 The . . . crushed. Some Greek copies do not have verse 44.

was not dressed ·for a wedding [in wedding clothes]. 12The king said, 'Friend, how were you allowed to come in here? You are not dressed for a wedding.' But the man ·said nothing [was speechless/silent]. 13So the king told some servants, 'Tie this man's hands and feet. Throw him out into the ·darkness [darkness outside; *or* outermost darkness], where ·people will cry and grind their teeth with pain [Lthere will be weeping and gnashing of teeth; Csymbols of agony and torment].'

14"·Yes [LFor], many are ·invited [called], but only a few are chosen."

Is It Right to Pay Taxes or Not?
(22:15–22; Mark 12:13–17; Luke 20:20–26)

15Then the Pharisees left that place and ·made plans [plotted] to ·trap [catch] Jesus in ·saying something wrong [his words]. 16They sent some of their own ·followers [disciples] and some people from the group called Herodians [Ca political group that supported king Herod and his family]. They said, "Teacher, we know that you are ·an honest man [true; sincere] and that you teach ·the truth [with sincerity/honesty] about God's way. You are not ·afraid of [Lconcerned about] what other people think about you, because you ·pay no attention to who they are [play no favorites; are impartial; aren't swayed by appearances]. 17So tell us what you think. Is it ·right [permissible; lawful] to pay taxes to Caesar or not?" [CSaying "yes" would anger Jews who hated Roman rule; saying "no" could result in being charged with insurrection.]

18But knowing ·that these leaders were trying to trick him [their evil/malicious motives], Jesus said, "You hypocrites! Why are you ·trying to trap [testing] me? 19Show me a coin used for paying the tax." So the men ·showed him a coin [Lbrought him a denarius; Ca Roman coin worth a day's wages]. 20Then Jesus asked, "Whose ·image [likeness; portrait] and ·name [inscription] are on the coin?"

21The men answered, "Caesar's." [CIronically, the religious leaders were carrying coins bearing the idolatrous image of Caesar.]

Then Jesus said to them, "·Give [TRender] to Caesar the things that are Caesar's, and give to God the things that are God's."

22When the men heard what Jesus said, they were amazed and left him and went away.

Some Sadducees Try to Trick Jesus
(22:23–33; Mark 12:18–27; Luke 20:27–40)

23That same day some Sadducees came to Jesus and asked him a question. (Sadducees believed that people would not rise from the dead.) 24They said, "Teacher, Moses said if a married man dies without having children, his brother must marry the widow and ·have children [Lraise up offspring/seed] for him [Deut. 25:5]. 25Once there were seven brothers among us. The first one married and died. Since he had no ·children [offspring], his brother married the widow. 26Then the second brother also died. The same thing happened to the third brother ·and all the other brothers [Ldown to the seventh]. 27Finally, the woman died. 28Since all seven men had married her, ·when people rise from the dead [Lat the resurrection], whose wife will she be?"

29Jesus answered, "You ·don't understand [are mistaken/deceived], because you don't know what the Scriptures say, and you don't know about the power of God. 30[LFor] ·When people rise from the dead [LAt the resurrection], they will not marry, nor will they be given to someone to marry. They will be like the angels in heaven. 31·Surely you have read [LHave you not read…?] what God said to you ·about rising [concerning the resurrection] from the dead. 32God said, 'I am the God of Abraham, the God of Isaac, and the God of Jacob [Ex. 3:6; CGod is still the God of the patriarchs, so they must have a continued existence after death].' God is the God of the living, not the dead."

33 When the people heard this, they were ·amazed [astounded] at Jesus' teaching.

The Most Important Command
(22:34–40; Mark 12:28–34; Luke 10:25–28)

34 When the Pharisees learned that ·the Sadducees could not argue with Jesus' answers to them [[L]Jesus had silenced the Sadducees], the Pharisees met together. 35 One Pharisee, who was an expert on the law of Moses, asked Jesus this question to ·test [trap] him: 36 "Teacher, which command in the law is the ·most important [greatest]?"

37 Jesus answered, " 'Love the Lord your God with all your heart, all your soul, and all your mind [Deut. 6:5].' 38 This is the first and ·most important [greatest] command. 39 And the second command is like the first: 'Love your neighbor as you love yourself [Lev. 19:18].' 40 All the law and the ·writings of the prophets [[L]prophets] ·depend [are based; [L]hang] on these two commands."

Jesus Questions the Pharisees
(22:41–46; Mark 12:35–37; Luke 20:41–44)

41 While the Pharisees were together, Jesus asked them, 42 "What do you think about the ·Christ [Messiah]? Whose ·son [descendant] is he?"

They answered, "The Son of David [see 2 Sam. 7:12]."

43 Then Jesus said to them, "Then why did David call him 'Lord'? David, speaking ·by the power of the Holy Spirit [[L]in/by the Spirit], said,

44 'The Lord said to my Lord,
"Sit by me at my right ·side [[L]hand; [C]the place of greatest honor beside the king],
until I put your enemies ·under your control [[L]beneath your feet; [C]meaning defeated or made subject to your authority; Ps. 110:1]." '

45 David calls ·the Christ [the Messiah; [L]him] 'Lord,' so how can ·the Christ [the Messiah; [L]he] be his son?"

46 ·None of the Pharisees [[L]No one] could answer ·Jesus' question [a word], and after that day no one ·was brave enough [dared] to ask him any more questions.

Jesus Accuses Some Leaders
(23:1–36; Mark 12:37–40; Luke 20:45–47)

23 Then Jesus said to the crowds and to his ·followers [disciples], 2 "The ·teachers of the law [scribes] and the Pharisees ·have the authority to interpret what the law of Moses says [[L]sit in Moses' seat/chair]. 3 So you should ·obey [do; practice] and ·follow [keep; observe] whatever they tell you, but ·their lives are not good examples for you to follow [[L]do not follow their actions]. ·They tell you to do things, but they themselves don't do them [[L]For they say but do not do]. 4 They ·make strict rules [[L]tie up heavy loads/burdens that are hard to carry] and ·try to force people to obey them [[L]put them on people's shoulders], but they are unwilling to ·help those who struggle under the weight of their rules [lift a finger to move them; [L]move them with their finger].

5 "They do good things so that other people will see them. They enlarge ·the little boxes holding Scriptures that they wear [[L]their phylacteries; [C]leather cases worn on the left arm and forehead to literally fulfill Deut. 6:8; 11:18], and they ·make their special prayer clothes very long [[L]lengthen their tassels; [C]Jewish males were to wear tassels on the four corners of their garment; Num. 15:38; Deut. 22:12]. 6 Those Pharisees and teachers of the law love to have the ·most important seats [places of greatest honor] at ·feasts [banquets] and [[L]the best seats] in the synagogues.

7They love people to greet them with respect in the marketplaces, and
they love to have people call them ·'Teacher [LRabbi].'
8"But you must not be called '·Teacher [Rabbi],' because you have only
one Teacher, and you are all brothers and sisters together. 9And don't call
any person on earth 'Father,' because you have one Father, who is in
heaven. 10And you should not be called '·Master [Leader; Teacher;
Instructor]' because you have only one ·Master [Leader; Teacher; Instructor],
the ·Christ [Messiah]. 11·Whoever is your servant is the greatest among
you [LThe greatest among you will be your servant]. 12Whoever ·makes
himself great [lifts up/exalts himself] will be made humble. Whoever
makes himself humble will be ·made great [exalted; lifted up].
13"·How terrible for [LWoe to] you, ·teachers of the law [scribes] and
Pharisees! You are hypocrites! [LBecause] You ·close [shut; lock] the door
for people to enter the kingdom of heaven. You yourselves don't enter,
and you ·stop [don't allow] others who are trying to enter. |14·How terri-
ble for [LWoe to] you, ·teachers of the law [scribes] and Pharisees. You are
hypocrites. You ·take away [Ldevour] widows' houses, and you say long
prayers ·so that people will notice you [as a pretense]. So you will have a
worse ·punishment [condemnation].|n
15"·How terrible for [LWoe to] you, ·teachers of the law [scribes] and
Pharisees! You are hypocrites! You travel across land and sea to ·find one
person who will change to your ways [Lmake one convert/proseltye].
When you ·find that person [make that convert], you make him ·more fit
for hell than [Ltwice the son of hell/Gehenna that; 5:22] you are.
16"·How terrible for [LWoe to] you! ·You guide the people, but you are
blind [LBlind guides!]. You say, 'If people ·swear [make an oath/vow] by the
Temple when they make a promise, that means nothing. But if they swear by
the gold that is in the Temple, they ·must keep that promise [are obligated/
bound].' 17You are blind fools! Which is greater: the gold or the Temple that
makes that gold ·holy [sacred; sanctified]? 18And you say, 'If people ·swear
[make an oath/vow] by the altar when they make a promise, that means
nothing. But if they ·swear [make an oath/vow] by the ·gift [offering] on the
altar, they ·must keep that promise [are obligated/bound].' 19You are blind!
Which is greater: the ·gift [offering] or the altar that makes the gift ·holy
[sacred; sanctified]? 20[LSo; Therefore] The person who swears by the altar is
really swearing by the altar and also everything on the altar. 21And the person who swears by the Temple is really swearing by the Temple and the One
who ·lives [dwells] in the Temple. 22The person who swears by heaven is also
swearing by God's throne and the One who sits on that throne.
23"·How terrible for [LWoe to] you, ·teachers of the law [scribes] and
Pharisees! You are hypocrites! You ·give to God one-tenth of [pay tithe
on] everything you have—even your mint, dill, and cumin. But you ·don't
obey [ignore; neglect] the ·really important teachings [Lweightier mat-
ters] of the law—justice, mercy, and ·being loyal [faith; faithfulness].
These are the things you should do, ·as well as [without neglecting] those
other things. 24·You guide the people, but you are blind! [LBlind guides!]
You ·are like a person who picks a fly out of a drink and then swallows a
camel [Lstrain out a gnat, but swallow a camel; Cworrying about the smallest mistakes while committing the biggest sins]!
25"·How terrible for [LWoe to] you, ·teachers of the law [scribes] and

23:14 How . . . punishment. Some Greek copies do not contain the bracketed text.

Pharisees! You are hypocrites! You ·wash [clean] the outside of your cups and dishes [Cfor ceremonial purity], but inside they are full of ·things you got by cheating others and by pleasing only yourselves [Lgreed/robbery and self-indulgence]. 26Pharisees, you are blind! First make the inside of the cup[n] clean, and then the outside ·can be truly [*or* will also be] clean.

27"·How terrible for [LWoe to] you, ·teachers of the law [scribes] and Pharisees! You are hypocrites! You are like ·tombs that are painted white [whitewashed tombs]. Outside, those tombs ·look fine [appear beautiful], but inside, they are full of the bones of dead people and all kinds of ·unclean things [filth; corruption; impurity]. 28It is the same with you. ·People look at you and think you are good [*or* On the outside you look like righteous people], but on the inside you are full of hypocrisy and ·evil [lawlessness].

29"·How terrible for [LWoe to] you, ·teachers of the law [scribes] and Pharisees! You are hypocrites! You build tombs for the prophets, and you ·show honor to [decorate; adorn] the graves of ·those who lived good lives [Lthe righteous]. 30You say, 'If we had lived during the time of our ancestors, we would not have ·helped them kill [Lbeen partners in the blood of] the prophets.' 31But you ·give proof [Ltestify against yourselves] that you are ·descendants [sons; children] of those who murdered the prophets. 32·And you will complete the sin that your ancestors started [*or* Go ahead and finish what your fathers started!; LFill up the measure of your fathers].

33"You ·are snakes [serpents]! A ·family of poisonous snakes [Tbrood/offspring of vipers]! How are you going to escape ·God's judgment [the sentence/judgment/damnation of hell/Gehenna; 5:22]? 34·So I tell you this [For this reason]: I am sending to you prophets and wise men and ·teachers [scribes; experts in the law]. Some of them you will kill and crucify. Some of them you will ·beat [scourge; flog] in your synagogues and ·chase [hunt; persecute] from town to town. 35So ·you will be guilty for [Lupon you will come] ·the death of all the good people who have been killed on earth [Lall the righteous blood shed on the earth]—from the ·murder [Lblood] of that ·good [righteous] man Abel to the murder of Zechariah son of Berakiah, whom you murdered between the ·Temple [sanctuary] and the altar [Cin the book order of the Hebrew Old Testament, Abel (Gen. 4:8) and Zechariah (2 Chr. 24:21) were the first and last men to be murdered]. 36I tell you the truth, all of these things will happen to ·you people who are living now [Lthis generation].

Jesus Grieves for Jerusalem
(23:37–39; Luke 13:34–35)

37"Jerusalem, Jerusalem! You kill the prophets and stone to death those who are sent to you. ·Many times [How often] I wanted to gather your ·people [Lchildren] as a hen gathers her chicks under her wings, but you ·did not let me [refused]. 38·Now [LLook; TBehold] your house ·will be [Lis] left ·completely empty [abandoned; deserted; desolate; Jer. 22:5]. 39[LFor] I tell you, you will not see me again until that time when you will say, '·God bless [LBlessed is] the One who comes in the name of the Lord [Ps. 118:26].'"

The Temple Will Be Destroyed
(24:1–35; Mark 13:1–31; Luke 21:5–33)

24 As Jesus left the Temple [courts] and was walking away, his ·followers [disciples] came up to ·show [point out to] him the Temple's buildings. 2Jesus asked, "Do you see all these buildings? I tell you the truth, not one stone will be left on another. Every stone will be ·thrown [pulled; torn] down."

3Later, as Jesus was sitting on the Mount of Olives, his ·followers [disciples]

23:26 cup Some Greek copies add "and dish."

came to be alone with him. They said, "Tell us, when will these things happen?
And what will be the sign ·that it is time for you to come again [of your com-
ing/return] and ·for this age to end [the end/consummation of the age]?"
4Jesus answered, "·Be careful [Watch out] that no one ·fools [misleads;
deceives] you. 5Many will come in my name, saying, 'I am the ·Christ
[Messiah],' and they will ·fool [mislead; deceive] many people. 6You will hear
about wars and ·stories of wars that are coming [rumors/reports of wars],
but don't be ·afraid [alarmed]. These things must happen ·before the end
comes [*or* but that is not yet the end]. 7Nations will ·fight [Lrise up] against
other nations, and kingdoms against other kingdoms. There will be ·times
when there is no food for people to eat [famines], and there will be earthquakes in ·different [various] places. 8All these things are ·like the first pains
when something new is about to be born [Lthe beginning of the birth pains].
9"Then people will arrest you, hand you over to be ·hurt [persecuted;
tortured], and kill you. ·They [The world; LAll nations] will hate you
because ·you believe in me [you follow me; Lof my name]. 10At that time,
many will ·lose their faith [turn/fall away], and they will ·turn against
[betray] each other and hate each other. 11Many false prophets will ·come
[appear; arise] and ·cause many people to believe lies [deceive many].
12There will be more and more ·evil [sin; lawlessness] in the world, so
·most people will stop showing their love for each other [Lthe love of
many/most will grow cold]. 13But those people who ·keep their faith
[endure; stand firm; persevere] until the end will be saved. 14·The Good
News [This Gospel] about God's kingdom will be preached in all the
world, [Las a testimony] to every nation. Then the end will come.
15"You will see '·a blasphemous object that brings destruction [Tthe
abomination of desolation; Ca phrase taken from Dan. 9:27; 11:31; 12:11, and
originally referring to the desecration of the Temple by Antiochus Epiphanes
in 168 BC],' which Daniel the prophet spoke about. ·It [*or* He] will be standing in the holy place." (You who read this should understand what it means
[Cprobably a reference to the soon-to-occur destruction of Jerusalem in AD
70].) 16"At that time, the people in Judea should ·run away [flee] to the
mountains. 17If people are on the roofs of their houses [Croofs in Palestine
were flat and used as spare rooms and for storage], they must not go down to
get anything out of their houses. 18If people are in the fields, they must not
go back to get their ·coats [cloaks]. 19At that time, ·how terrible it will be for
[Lwoe to] women who are pregnant or have nursing babies! 20Pray that it
will not be ·winter [bad weather] or a Sabbath day when these things happen
and you have to run away, 21because at that time there will be much ·trouble
[distress; Ttribulation]. There will be more ·trouble [distress; Ttribulation].
than there has ever been since the beginning of the world until now, and
nothing as bad will ever happen again [Dan. 12:1]. 22·God has decided to
make that terrible time short [LIf those days had not been shortened (by
God)...; Cthe passive verb implies God as subject]. Otherwise, no one would
·go on living [survive; Lbe saved]. But God will make that time short ·to help
the people he has chosen [for the sake of the elect]. 23At that time, someone
might say to you, 'Look, there is the ·Christ [Messiah]!' Or another person
might say, 'There he is!' But don't believe them. 24False ·Christs [messiahs]
and false prophets will ·come [appear; rise up] and perform great ·wonders
[signs; miracles] and ·miracles [wonders; marvels]. They will try to ·fool
[mislead; deceive] even the ·people God has chosen [elect], if that is possible.
25Now I have warned you about this before it happens.

26"If people tell you, '[LLook,] ·the Christ [Lhe] is in the ·desert [wilderness],' don't go there. If they say, '[LLook,] he is ·in the inner room [*or* hiding here; in this secret place],' don't believe it. 27When the Son of Man comes [Dan. 7:13–14], he will be like lightning flashing from the east to the west [Che will be seen by everyone]. 28Wherever the ·dead body [carcass] is, there the vultures will gather.

29"Soon after the ·trouble [tribulation; distress] of those days,
'the sun will grow dark,
and the moon will not give its light.
The stars will fall from ·the sky [heaven].
And the ·powers of the heavens [celestial bodies] will be shaken
[Is. 13:10; 34:4; cf. Ezek. 32:7–8; Joel 2:10, 31].'

30"At that time, the sign of the Son of Man will appear in ·the sky [*or* heaven]. Then all the ·peoples [tribes] of the world will ·cry [mourn]. They will see the Son of Man coming on ·clouds in the sky [*or* the clouds of heaven] with great power and glory. 31He will use a loud trumpet to send his angels, and they will gather his ·chosen people [elect] ·from every part of the world [Lfrom the four winds, from one end of the sky/heavens to another].

32"Learn a ·lesson [parable; analogy] from the fig tree: When its branches ·become green and soft [become tender; sprout] and new leaves appear, you know summer is near. 33In the same way, when you see all these things happening, you will know that ·the time [*or* he] is near, ·ready to come [right at the door]. 34I tell you the truth, all these things will happen ·while the people of this time are still living [before this generation passes away; Ceither the generation that sees the destruction of Jerusalem (AD 70), or a future generation of the end times]. 35 ·Earth and sky will be destroyed [THeaven and earth will pass away], but the words I have said will never ·be destroyed [pass away].

When Will Jesus Come Again?
(24:36–44; Mark 13:32, 35; Luke 12:39–40; 17:26–36)

36"No one knows when that day or ·time [hour] will be, not the angels in heaven, not even the Son.[n] Only the Father knows. 37When the Son of Man comes [Dan. 7:13–14], it will be like what happened during Noah's time. 38[LFor] In those days before the flood, people were eating and drinking, marrying and giving their children to be married, until the day Noah entered the boat. 39They ·knew [understood] nothing about what was happening until the flood came and ·destroyed them [Ltook/swept them all away]. It will be the same when the Son of Man comes. 40Two men will be in the field. One will be taken, and the other will be left. 41Two women will be grinding grain with a ·mill [handmill; Ctwo large, round, flat rocks used for grinding grain to make flour]. One will be taken, and the other will be left.

42"So ·always be ready [stay alert; keep watching], because you don't know the day your Lord will come. 43·Remember [Know] this: If the owner of the house knew what time of night a thief was coming, the owner would ·watch [have stayed alert; kept watching] and not let ·the thief break in [Lhis house be broken into]. 44So you also must be ready, because the Son of Man will come at a ·time [hour] you don't expect him.

The Story of the Two Servants
(24:45-51; Luke 12:41-46)

45"Who is the ·loyal [faithful; trusted] and ·wise [sensible] ·servant [slave] that the master ·trusts [Lputs in charge of his household] to give ·the other servants [Lthem] their food at the right time? 46That servant will be ·blessed [happy; *or* rewarded] when the master comes and finds

24:36 not even the Son Some Greek copies do not have this phrase.

him doing his work. 47I tell you the truth, the master will ·choose that servant to take care [put him in charge] of everything he owns. 48But suppose that evil servant thinks to himself, 'My master ·will not come back soon [will be away for a long time; is delayed],' 49and he begins to beat the other servants and eat and ·get drunk with others like him [drink with drunkards]? 50The master [Lof that servant/slave] will come [Lon a day] when that servant is not ready and [Lat an hour when he] is not expecting him. 51Then the master will cut him in pieces and ·send him away to be [Lassign/appoint him a place] with the hypocrites, where ·people will cry and grind their teeth with pain [Tthere will be weeping and gnashing of teeth; Cindicating agony and remorse].

A Story About Ten Bridesmaids

25 "At that time the kingdom of heaven will be like ten ·bridesmaids [Lvirgins] who took their lamps and went to ·wait for [meet] the bridegroom. 2Five of them were foolish and five were ·wise [sensible; prudent]. 3The five foolish ·bridesmaids [Lvirgins] took their lamps, but they did not take more oil for the lamps to burn. 4The ·wise [sensible; prudent] ·bridesmaids [Lvirgins] took their lamps and more oil in ·jars [flasks]. 5Because the bridegroom was ·late [delayed], they became ·sleepy [drowsy] and went to sleep.

6"At midnight someone cried out, '·The bridegroom is coming [LLook, the bridegroom]! Come and meet him!' 7Then all the ·bridesmaids [Lvirgins] woke up and ·got their lamps ready [trimmed their lamps]. 8But the foolish ones said to the ·wise [sensible; prudent], 'Give us some of your oil, because our lamps are going out.' 9The ·wise [sensible; prudent] bridesmaids answered, 'No, the oil we have might not be enough ·for all of us [Lfor us and for you]. Go to the people who sell oil and buy some for yourselves.'

10"So while ·the five foolish bridesmaids [Lthey] went to buy oil, the bridegroom came. The bridesmaids who were ready went in with the bridegroom to the wedding feast. Then the door was ·closed and locked [Lshut].

11"Later the others came back and said, '·Sir, sir, [Lord, lord] open the door to let us in.' 12But the bridegroom answered, 'I tell you the truth, I don't know you.'

13"So ·always be ready [stay awake; be alert; keep watch], because you don't know the day or the hour [Cthe Son of Man will come].

A Story About Three Servants

(25:14–30; Mark 13:34; Luke 19:11–27)

14"·The kingdom of heaven [LIt] is like a man who was going ·to another place for a visit [on a journey/trip]. Before he left, he called for his servants and ·told them to take care of his things while he was gone [Lentrusted his possessions/wealth to them]. 15He gave one servant five ·bags of gold [Ltalents; Ca talent was worth about 6,000 denarii, or twenty years' wages for a laborer], another servant two ·bags of gold [Ltalents], and a third servant one ·bag of gold [Ltalent], to each one ·as much as he could handle [Laccording to his ability]. Then he left. 16The servant who got five ·bags [Ltalents] went quickly ·to invest the money [and traded with them; and put the money to work] and ·earned [gained] five more. 17In the same way, the servant who had two ·invested [traded with] them and ·earned [gained] two more. 18But the servant who got one went out and dug a hole in the ground and hid the master's money.

19"After a long time the master came home and ·asked the servants what they did with his money [settled/went over the accounts with them]. 20The servant who was given five ·bags of gold [Ltalents] brought five more ·bags [Ltalents] to the master and said, 'Master, you trusted me to care for five

·bags of gold [Ltalents], ·so I used your five to earn [Lsee, I have earned] five
more.' 21The master answered, 'You did well. You are a good and ·loyal [faith-
ful] servant. Because you were ·loyal [faithful] with ·small [a few] things, I
will ·let you care for [put you in charge of] ·much greater [many] things.
·Come and share my joy with me [LEnter into the joy of your master].'
22"Then the servant who had been given two ·bags of gold [Ltalents]
came to the master and said, 'Master, you ·gave me [trusted me with] two
·bags of gold [Ltalents] to care for, ·so I used your two bags to earn [Lsee, I
have earned] two more.' 23The master answered, 'You did well. You are a
good and ·loyal [faithful] servant. Because you were ·loyal [faithful] with
·small [a few] things, I will ·let you care for [put you in charge of] ·much
greater [many] things. ·Come and share my joy with me [LEnter into the
joy of your master].'
24"Then the servant who had been given one ·bag of gold [Ltalent] came
to the master and said, 'Master, I knew that you were a ·hard [harsh; exact-
ing; demanding] man. You ·harvest things [reap where] you did not ·plant
[sow]. You gather crops where you did not sow any seed. 25So I was afraid
and went and hid your ·money [Ttalent] in the ground. [LSee] Here is ·your
bag of gold [Lwhat is yours].' 26[LBut] The master answered, 'You are a wicked
and lazy servant! You say you knew that I ·harvest things [reap where] I did
not ·plant [sow] and that I gather crops where I did not sow any seed. 27So
you should have put my ·gold [money] in the bank. Then, when I came
home, I would have received ·my gold [what was mine] back with interest.'
28"·So the master told his other servants, '[LTherefore,] Take the ·bag of
gold [Ltalent] from that servant and give it to the servant who has ten
·bags of gold [Ltalents]. 29[LFor] Those who have much will ·get [be given]
more, and they will have ·much more than they need [an abundance]. But
those who do not have much will have ·everything [even what they have]
taken away from them.' 30Then the master said, 'Throw that ·useless
[worthless] servant ·outside, into the darkness [*or* into the outer darkness,] where ·people will cry and grind their teeth with pain [Tthere will
be weeping and gnashing of teeth; Cindicating agony and remorse].

The King Will Judge All People

31"The Son of Man will come again in his great glory [Dan. 7:13–14],
with all his angels. He will ·be King and sit on his [Lsit on his] ·great [glo-
rious] throne. 32All the nations of the world will be gathered before him,
and he will separate them ·into two groups [Lone from another] as a shepherd separates the sheep from the goats. 33The Son of Man will put the
sheep on his right and the goats on his left.
34"Then the King will say to the people on his right, 'Come, ·my Father
has given you his blessing [Lthose blessed by my Father]. ·Receive [Inherit]
the kingdom God has prepared for you ·since the world was made [Lfrom
the creation/foundation of the world]. 35[LFor; Because] I was hungry, and
you gave me food. I was thirsty, and you gave me something to drink. I was
·alone and away from home [a stranger], and you ·invited me into your
house [welcomed/received me]. 36I was ·without clothes [naked], and you
·gave me something to wear [clothed me]. I was sick, and you ·cared for
[visited; looked after] me. I was in prison, and you ·visited [came to] me.'
37"Then the ·good [righteous] people will answer, 'Lord, when did we
see you hungry and give you food, or thirsty and give you something to
drink? 38When did we see you ·alone and away from home [a stranger] and
·invite you into our house [welcome/receive you]? When did we see you

·without clothes [naked] and ·give you something to wear [clothe you]?
39When did we see you sick or in prison and ·care for [come to] you?'
40"Then the King will answer, 'I tell you the truth, anything you did for
even the least of my ·people here [Lbrothers (and sisters)], you also did for
me.'
41"Then the King will say to those on his left, '·Go away [Depart] from
me. You ·will be punished [are cursed]. Go into the ·fire that burns forever [eternal fire] that was prepared for the devil and his angels [Cthe
demons]. 42[LFor; Because] I was hungry, and you gave me nothing to eat.
I was thirsty, and you gave me nothing to drink. 43I was ·alone and away
from home [a stranger], and you did not ·invite me into your house [wel-
come/receive me]. I was ·without clothes [naked], and you ·gave me
nothing to wear [did not clothe me]. I was sick and in prison, and you did
not ·care for [visit; look after] me.'
44"Then those people will answer, 'Lord, when did we see you hungry
or thirsty or ·alone and away from home [a stranger] or ·without clothes
[naked] or sick or in prison? When did we see these things and not ·help
[serve; care for] you?'
45"Then the King will answer, 'I tell you the truth, ·anything [to the
extent] you refused to do for even the least of ·my people here [Lthese],
you refused to do for me.'
46"These people will go off to ·be punished forever [eternal punish-
ment], but the ·good people [righteous] ·will go to live forever [to eternal
life]."

The Plan to Kill Jesus
(26:1–5; Mark 14:1–2; Luke 22:1–2)

26 After Jesus finished saying all these things [Cthis is the end of
Jesus' fifth and final discourse in Matthew; see 7:28], he told
his ·followers [disciples], 2"You know that ·the day after tomorrow [Ltwo
days from now] is the day of the Passover Feast [Cthe festival during
which an unblemished lamb was sacrificed]. On that day the Son of Man
will be ·given to his enemies [handed over] to be crucified."
3Then the ·leading [Tchief] priests and the elders ·had a meeting
[assembled] at the ·palace [court] of the high priest, named Caiaphas. 4At
the meeting, they ·planned [plotted] ·to set a trap [to act secretly/treach-
erously] to arrest Jesus and kill him. 5But they said, "We must not do it
during the ·feast [Passover festival], because the people might cause a
riot."

Perfume for Jesus' Burial
(26:6–13; Mark 14:3–9; Luke 7:36–50; John 12:1–8)

6Jesus was in Bethany at the house of Simon, ·who had a skin disease [Lthe
leper; Cfor leprosy, see 8:2; Simon may have been healed by Jesus.]. 7While
Jesus was there, a woman approached him with an alabaster ·jar [vial] filled
with expensive perfume. She poured this perfume on Jesus' head while he
was ·eating [Lreclining; Cthe posture for a banquet or dinner party].
8His ·followers [disciples] were ·upset [indignant] when they saw the
woman do this. They asked, "Why waste that perfume? 9It could have
been sold for a great deal of money and the money given to the poor."
10Knowing what had happened, Jesus said, "Why are you ·troubling
[bothering; criticizing] this woman? She did an ·excellent thing [beauti-
ful/good deed] for me. 11You will always have the poor with you [Deut.
15:11], but you will not always have me. 12This woman poured perfume
on my body to prepare me for burial. 13I tell you the truth, wherever the
·Good News [Gospel] is preached in all the world, what this woman has
done will be told, and people will remember her."

Judas Betrays Jesus
(26:14–16; Mark 14:10–11; Luke 22:3–6)

14Then one of ·the twelve apostles [Lthe Twelve], [Lwho was called]
Judas Iscariot, went to talk to the ·leading [Tchief] priests. 15He said,
"What will you ·pay [give] me for ·giving [betraying; delivering] Jesus to
you?" And they ·gave him [weighed/counted out] thirty silver coins [Zech.
11:12]. 16After that, Judas watched for ·the best time [an opportunity] to
·turn Jesus in [betray him].

Jesus Eats the Passover Meal
(26:17–25; Mark 14:12–21; Luke 22:7–14, 21–23; John 13:21–30)

17On the first day of the Feast of Unleavened Bread, the ·followers [dis-
ciples] came to Jesus. They said, "Where do you want us to prepare for
you to eat the Passover meal?"
18Jesus answered, "Go into the city to a certain man and tell him, 'The
Teacher says: "·The chosen time is near [LMy time has come/drawn near].
I will ·have [celebrate; observe] the Passover with my ·followers [disci-
ples] at your house."'" 19The ·followers [disciples] did what Jesus told
them to do, and they prepared the Passover meal.
20In the evening Jesus was ·sitting at the table [Lreclining; Cthe posture
for a banquet] with his twelve ·followers [disciples]. 21As they were eating,
Jesus said, "I tell you the truth, one of you will ·turn against [betray] me."
22This made the ·followers [disciples] very ·sad [distressed; pained].
Each one began to say to Jesus, "·Surely, Lord, I am not the one, am I
[Surely not I, Lord; *or* Is it I, Lord]?"
23Jesus answered, "The man who has dipped his hand with me into the
bowl [Cprobably not a signal, but means "one who shares close fellowship
with me"] is the one who will ·turn against [betray] me. 24The Son of Man
will ·die [go to his fate; Lgo], just as the Scriptures say. But ·how terrible it
will be for [Lwoe to] the person ·who hands the Son of Man over to be
killed [Lby whom the Son of Man is betrayed]. It would be better for him
if he had never been born."
25Then Judas, who would ·give Jesus to his enemies [betray him], said to
Jesus, "·Teacher [LRabbi], ·surely I am not the one, am I [surely not I; *or* is it I]?"
Jesus answered, "·Yes, it is you [LYou have said it]."

The Lord's Supper
(26:26–30; Mark 14:22–26; Luke 22:15–20)

26While they were eating, Jesus took some bread and ·thanked God for
[blessed] it and ·broke [divided] it. Then he gave it to his ·followers [dis-
ciples] and said, "·Take this bread and eat it [LTake, eat]; this is my body."
27Then Jesus took a cup and ·thanked God for it [gave thanks] and gave
it to the ·followers [disciples]. He said, "Every one of you drink [Lfrom]
this. 28This is my blood ·which is the new[n] agreement that God makes
with his people [*or* which confirms/establishes the new covenant; Lof the
new covenant; Ex. 24:8. Jer. 31:31–34]. This blood is poured out for many
·to forgive their [Tfor the remission of] sins [Is. 53:12]. 29I tell you this: I
will not drink of this ·fruit of the vine [wine] again until that day when I
drink it new with you in my Father's kingdom."
30After singing a hymn [Cprobably the *Hallel* psalms (Ps. 113–118),
sung during the Passover meal], they went out to the Mount of Olives.

Jesus' Followers Will Leave Him
(26:31–35; Mark 14:27–31; Luke 22:31–34; John 13:36–38)

31Jesus told ·his followers [Lthem], "Tonight you will all ·stumble in
your faith [fall away; desert] on account of me, because it is written in the
Scriptures:
'I will ·kill [strike] the shepherd,
and the sheep [Lof the flock] will ·scatter [be scattered]' [Zech. 13:7].

26:28 new Some Greek copies do not have this word. Compare Luke 22:20.

32 But after ·I rise from the dead [LI am raised], I will go ahead of you into Galilee."

33 Peter said, "Everyone else may ·stumble in their faith [fall away; desert] because of you, but I will not."

34 Jesus said, "I tell you the truth, tonight before the rooster crows you will ·say three times you don't know me [deny/disown me three times]."

35 But Peter said, "Even if I must die with you, I will never ·say that I don't know [deny/disown] you!" And all the other ·followers [disciples] said the same thing.

Jesus Prays Alone

(26:36–46; Mark 14:32–42; Luke 22:39–46; John 12:27; 18:1)

36 Then Jesus went with his ·followers [disciples] to a place called Gethsemane. He said to them, "Sit here while I go over there and pray." 37 He took Peter and the two sons of Zebedee with him, and he began to be very ·sad [sorrowful] and ·troubled [anguished; distressed]. 38 He said to them, "My ·heart [soul] is ·full of sorrow [overwhelmed with grief], to the point of death. Stay here and ·watch [stay awake; be alert] with me."

39 After walking a little farther away from them, Jesus fell [with his face] to the ground and prayed, "My Father, if it is possible, ·do not give me [Llet pass from me] this ·cup of suffering [Lcup; Csuffering is metaphorically portrayed as something bitter to drink]. But do ·what you want [your will], not ·what I want [my will]." 40 Then Jesus went back to his ·followers [disciples] and found them asleep. He said to Peter, "You men could not ·stay awake [watch] with me for one hour? 41 ·Stay awake [Keep watch] and pray for strength ·against temptation [*or* not to fail the test]. The spirit ·wants to do what is right [is willing], but ·the body [*or* human nature; Tthe flesh] is weak."

42 Then Jesus went away a second time and prayed, "My Father, if it is not possible for ·this painful thing [Lthis thing; Cthe cup of suffering; v. 39] to be taken from me, and if I must ·do [drink] it, ·I pray that what you want [Lmay your] will be done."

43 Then he went back to his ·followers [disciples], and again he found them asleep, because their eyes were heavy. 44 So Jesus left them and went away and prayed a third time, saying the same thing.

45 Then Jesus went back to his ·followers [disciples] and said, "·Are you still sleeping and resting? [*or* Go ahead, sleep and have your rest!] The time has come for the Son of Man to be ·handed over to [Lbetrayed/delivered into the hands of] sinful people. 46 Get up, we must go. Look, here comes ·the man who has turned against me [my betrayer]."

Jesus Is Arrested

(26:47–56; Mark 14:43–52; Luke 22:47–53; John 18:2–12)

47 While Jesus was still speaking, Judas, one of ·the twelve apostles [the Twelve], came up. With him were many people carrying swords and clubs who had been sent from the ·leading [Tchief] priests and the Jewish elders of the people. 48 Judas had planned to give them a ·signal [sign], saying, "The man I kiss is ·Jesus [the one]. ·Arrest [Seize] him." 49 At once Judas went to Jesus and said, "Greetings, ·Teacher [LRabbi]!" and kissed him.

50 Jesus answered, "Friend, do what you came to do."

Then the people came and grabbed Jesus and arrested him. 51 ·When that happened [LAnd look/Tbehold], one of ·Jesus' followers [Lthose with Jesus] reached for his sword and pulled it out. He struck the servant of the high priest and cut off his ear.

52 Jesus said to the man, "Put your sword back in its place. [LFor] All who ·use swords [Ltake the sword] will ·be killed with swords [Ldie/perish by the sword]. 53 ·Surely [LDon't…?] you know I could ask my Father, and he would give me more than twelve ·armies [legions] of angels. 54 But ·it

must happen this way to bring about what the Scriptures say [[L]how, then,
could the Scriptures be fulfilled that say it must happen this way?]."
55 Then Jesus said to the crowd, "You came to get me with swords and
clubs as if I were a ·criminal [revolutionary; rebel; [L]robber; [C]the term
"robber" was used by the Romans of insurrectionists]. Every day I sat in
the Temple teaching, and you did not arrest me there. 56 But all these
things have happened ·so that it will come about as the prophets wrote
[[L]to fulfill the writings/scriptures of the prophets]." Then all of Jesus' ·fol-
lowers [disciples] ·left [deserted] him and ·ran away [fled].

Jesus Before the Leaders
(26:57–68; Mark 14:53–65; Luke 22:54–71; John 18:13–24)

57 Those people who ·arrested [seized] Jesus led him to the house of
Caiaphas, the high priest, where the ·teachers of the law [scribes] and the
elders were gathered. 58 Peter followed far behind to the courtyard of the
high priest's house, and he sat down with the guards to see ·what would
happen to Jesus [[L]the end/outcome].
59 The ·leading [[T]chief] priests and the whole ·Jewish council [Sanhedrin;
[C]the highest Jewish court] tried to find ·something false [false evidence/
testimony] against Jesus so they could ·kill [execute] him. 60 Many people
came and ·told lies about him [testified falsely], but the council could find
no real reason to kill him. ·Then [Finally] two people came and said,
61 "This man said, 'I can destroy the Temple of God and build it again in
three days.' "
62 Then the high priest stood up and said to Jesus, "Aren't you going to
answer? ·Don't you have something to say about their [*or* What about
these] ·charges [testimony] against you?" 63 But Jesus ·said nothing [was
silent; Is. 53:7].
Again the high priest said to Jesus, "I ·command you by the power of
[demand in the name of; put you under oath by] the living God: Tell us if
you are the ·Christ [Messiah], the Son of God."
64 Jesus answered, "·Those are your words [[L]You have said it/so; [C]an
indirect affirmation]. But I tell you, ·in the future [[L]from now on] you will
see the Son of Man sitting at the right hand of God, the ·Powerful One [*or*
the place of power; [L]power], and coming on ·clouds in the sky [the clouds
of heaven; Ps. 110:1; Dan. 7:13–14]."
65 When the high priest heard this, he tore his clothes [[C]a sign of sorrow
or outrage] and said, "This man has ·said things that are against God
[blasphemed]! ·We don't [Why should we…?] need any more witnesses;
you all heard ·him say these things against God [the blasphemy]. 66 What
·do you think [is your verdict]?"
The people answered, "He ·should [deserves to; is guilty and should] die."
67 Then the people there spat in Jesus' face and beat him with their fists.
Others slapped him. 68 They said, "·Prove to us that you are a prophet
[[L]Prophesy to/for us], you ·Christ [Messiah]! Tell us who hit you!"

Peter Says He Doesn't Know Jesus
(26:69–75; Mark 14:66–72; Luke 22:56–62; John 18:25–27)

69 At that time, as Peter was sitting [[L]outside] in the courtyard, a servant
girl came to him and said, "You also were with Jesus of Galilee."
70 But Peter denied it in front of everyone. He said, "I don't know what
you are talking about."
71 When he left the courtyard and was at the gate, another girl saw him.
She said to the people there, "This man was with Jesus of Nazareth."
72 Again, ·Peter said he was never with him, saying, "I swear [[L]he denied
it with an oath, saying,] I don't know this man Jesus!"
73 A short time later, some people standing there went to Peter and said,

"Surely you are one of those who followed Jesus. The way you talk shows it [CPeter's Galilean accent gave him away]."

74Then Peter began to place a curse on himself and swear, "I don't know the man." At once, a rooster crowed. 75And Peter remembered what Jesus had told him: "Before the rooster crows, you will ·say three times that you don't know me [deny/disown me three times]." Then Peter went outside and ·cried painfully [Twept bitterly].

Jesus Is Taken to Pilate
(27:1–2; Mark 15:1; Luke 23:1; John 18:28)

27 Early the next morning, all the ·leading [Tchief] priests and elders of the people ·decided that Jesus should die [*or* met together to plan Jesus' death]. 2They ·tied [bound] him, led him away, and turned him over to Pilate, the governor.

Judas Kills Himself

3Judas, the one who had ·given [betrayed] Jesus to his enemies, saw that ·they had decided to kill Jesus [Jesus had been condemned]. Then he was ·very sorry [filled with remorse] for what he had done. So he took the thirty silver coins back to the leading [Tchief] priests and the elders, 4saying, "I sinned; I ·handed over to you [betrayed] ·an innocent man [Linnocent blood]."

The leaders answered, "What ·is that to us [do we care]? That's your ·problem, not ours [responsibility; concern]."

5So Judas threw the ·money [silver coins] into the ·Temple [sanctuary]. Then he went off and hanged himself.

6The ·leading [Tchief] priests picked up the silver coins in the Temple and said, "·Our law does not allow us [*or* It is not right] to ·keep [put] this money ·with the Temple money [in the Temple treasury], because it ·has paid for a man's death [is blood money; Lis the price of blood]." 7So they decided to use the coins to buy ·Potter's Field [*or* the potter's field] as a place to bury ·strangers [*or* foreigners]. 8That is why that field is still called the Field of Blood. 9So what Jeremiah the prophet had said ·came true [was fulfilled]: "They took thirty ·silver coins [Tpieces of silver]. That is ·how little the Israelites thought he was worth [*or* the price at which he was valued by the Israelites; *or* the value of a man with a price on his head among the Israelites; Jer. 18:2–3; 19:1–13; 32:5–15; Zech. 11:12–13]. 10They used those thirty silver coins to buy ·Potter's Field [*or* the potter's field], as the Lord commanded me."

Pilate Questions Jesus
(27:11–14; Mark 15:2–5; Luke 23:2–5; John 18:29–38)

11Jesus stood before Pilate the governor, and Pilate asked him, "Are you the king of the Jews?"

Jesus answered, "·Those are your words [It is as you say; LYou say so; Can indirect affirmation]."

12When the ·leading [Tchief] priests and the elders accused Jesus, he ·said nothing [did not answer].

13So Pilate said to Jesus, "Don't you hear them accusing you of ·all these [so many] things?"

14But Jesus ·said nothing in answer to Pilate [did not answer a single charge], and ·Pilate [Lthe governor] was very ·surprised [amazed] at this.

Pilate Tries to Free Jesus
(27:15–31; Mark 15:6–21; Luke 23:17–32; John 18:39–40; 19:1–17)

15Every year at the ·time of Passover [festival/feast] the governor would free [Lfor the crowd] one prisoner whom the people chose. 16At that time there was a man in prison, named Barabbas,*n* who was ·known to be very bad [well known; notorious]. 17When the people gathered, Pilate said, "Whom do you want me to set free: Barabbas*n* or Jesus who is called the

27:16–17 Barabbas Some Greek copies read "Jesus Barabbas."

·Christ [Messiah]?" 18[LFor] Pilate knew that they turned Jesus in to him because they were jealous.

19While Pilate was sitting there on the judge's seat [Ca special seat for speeches or judicial pronouncements], his wife sent this message to him: "·Don't do anything to [*or* Have nothing to do with] that man, because he is ·innocent [righteous]. Today I had a dream about him, and it ·troubled me very much [caused me great pain/anguish]."

20But the ·leading [Tchief] priests and elders convinced the crowd to ask for Barabbas to be freed and for Jesus to be ·killed [executed].

21Pilate said, "Which of these two do you want me to set free for you?"

The people answered, "Barabbas."

22Pilate asked, "So what should I do with Jesus, the one called the ·Christ [Messiah]?"

They all answered, "Crucify him!"

23Pilate asked, "Why? What ·wrong [crime; evil] has he done?"

But they shouted louder, "Crucify him!"

24When Pilate saw that he ·could do nothing about this [was getting nowhere; was gaining nothing] and that a riot was starting, he took some water and washed his hands in front of the crowd. Then he said, "I am ·not guilty [innocent] of this man's ·death [Lblood]. ·You are the ones who are causing it [It is your responsibility now; *or* Take care of it yourselves]!"

25All the people answered, "·We and our children will be responsible for his death [LHis blood be on us and on our children]."

26Then he set Barabbas free. But he had Jesus ·beaten with whips [scourged; flogged] and handed over to the soldiers to be crucified.

27The governor's soldiers took Jesus into the ·governor's palace [fortress; headquarters; LPraetorium], and ·they all gathered around him [*or* the whole regiment/company/cohort was assembled; Ca cohort was about five hundred soldiers; here it may mean those of the cohort on duty]. 28They ·took off his clothes [stripped him] and put a ·red [scarlet] robe on him [Cprobably a scarlet military coat, whose color resembled purple, the color of royalty]. 29Using thorny branches, they made a crown, put it on his head, and put a ·stick [reed; staff] in his right hand [Cas a scepter]. Then the soldiers ·bowed [kneeled] before Jesus and ·made fun of [mocked] him, saying, "Hail, King of the Jews!" 30They spat on Jesus. Then they took his ·stick [reed; staff] and began to beat him on the head. 31After they ·finished [had mocked him], the soldiers took off the robe and put his own clothes on him again. Then they led him away to be crucified.

Jesus Is Crucified
(27:32–44; Mark 15:22–32; Luke 23:33–43; John 19:17–27)

32·As the soldiers were going out of the city with Jesus [LAs they went out], they ·met [found; came across] a man from Cyrene [Ca city in northern Africa, in present-day Libya], named Simon, and forced him to carry the cross for Jesus. 33They all came to the place called Golgotha, which means [Cin Aramaic] the Place of the Skull. 34·The soldiers [LThey; Cthis could be the soldiers or the women of Jerusalem] gave Jesus wine mixed with gall to drink [Cthe gall was either a sedative or further mockery, making the wine bitter; Ps. 69:21; Prov. 31:6]. He tasted the wine but refused to drink it. 35When the soldiers had crucified him, they threw lots [Csimilar to dice] to ·decide who would get [Ldivide up] his clothes[n] [Ps. 22:18]. 36The soldiers sat there and ·continued watching [kept guard over] him. 37They put a sign above Jesus'

27:35 clothes Some Greek copies continue, "So what God said through the prophet came true, 'They divided my clothes among them, and they threw lots for my clothing.'" See Psalm 22:18.

head with the charge against him. It said: THIS IS JESUS, THE KING OF THE JEWS.
38Two ·robbers [rebels; revolutionaries; Cthe term "robber" was used by the
Romans of insurrectionists] **were crucified beside Jesus, one on the right and
the other on the left** [Is. 53:12]. **39People walked by and ·insulted** [defamed;
slandered; Cthe same Greek word used to "blaspheme"] **Jesus and shook their
heads** [Ca gesture of derision; Ps. 22:7], **40saying, "You said you could destroy
the Temple and build it again in three days. So save yourself! Come down
from that cross if you are really the Son of God!"**

41The ·leading [Tchief] **priests, the teachers of the law, and the Jewish
elders were also ·making fun of** [mocking] **Jesus. 42They said, "He saved
others, but he can't save himself! He says he is the king of Israel! If he is
the king, let him come down now from the cross. Then we will believe in
him. 43He trusts in God, so let God ·save** [rescue; deliver] **him now, if God
really wants him** [Ps. 22:8]. **He himself said, 'I am the Son of God.' " 44And
in the same way, the robbers** [rebels; revolutionaries; v. 38] **who were
being crucified beside Jesus also ·insulted** [ridiculed; taunted] **him.**

Jesus Dies
(27:45–56; Mark 15:33–41; Luke 23:44–49; John 19:25–30)

45At ·noon [Lthe sixth hour] **the whole country became dark, and the
darkness lasted ·for three hours** [Luntil the ninth hour]. **46About ·three
o'clock** [Lthe ninth hour] **Jesus cried out in a loud voice, "Eli, Eli, lama
sabachthani?" This means, "My God, my God, why have you ·abandoned**
[forsaken] **me** [Ps. 22:1; Cthese words are a mixture of Hebrew and Aramaic]**?"**
**47Some of the people standing there who heard this said, "He is calling
Elijah."** [CThe prophet Elijah, associated with the end times (Mal. 4:5), was
also viewed as a helper in time of need.]

48·Quickly [At once] **one of them ran and got a sponge and filled it with
·vinegar** [*or* sour wine; Can inexpensive drink used by soldiers and slaves]
and tied it to a ·stick [reed] **and gave it to Jesus to drink** [Ps. 69:21]. **49But
the others said, "·Don't bother him** [Wait; Leave him alone]. **We want to
see if Elijah will come to save him."**

50But Jesus cried out again in a loud voice and ·died [Lreleased his spirit].
51·Then [TAnd behold] **the curtain in the Temple** [Cdividing the Most
Holy Place from the rest of the Temple] **was torn into two pieces, from the
top to the bottom** [Crepresenting new access to the presence of God, and
perhaps God's judgment against the Temple leadership]. **Also, the earth
shook and rocks broke apart. 52The graves opened, and many** [Lof the
bodies] **of ·God's people** [the saints] **who had ·died** [Lfallen asleep] **were
raised from the dead. 53They came out of the graves after ·Jesus was raised
from the dead** [Lhis resurrection] **and went into the holy city** [CJerusalem],
where they appeared to many people.

54When the ·army officer [centurion] **and ·the soldiers** [Lthose with
him] **guarding Jesus saw this earthquake and everything else that happened, they were ·very frightened** [filled with awe] **and said, "He really
was the Son of God!"**

55Many women who had followed Jesus from Galilee to ·help [provide
support for; minister to] **him were standing at a distance from the cross,
watching. 56Mary Magdalene, and Mary the mother of James and Joseph,
and the mother of James and John were ·there** [among them].

Jesus Is Buried
(27:57–61; Mark 15:42–47; Luke 23:50–56; John 19:38–42)

57That evening a rich man named Joseph, a ·follower [disciple] **of Jesus
from the town of Arimathea, ·came to Jerusalem** [*or* came forward;
Lcame]. **58Joseph went to Pilate and asked to have Jesus' body. So Pilate
gave orders for ·the soldiers to give it** [Lit to be given] **to Joseph. 59Then
Joseph took the body and wrapped it in a clean linen cloth. 60He put Jesus'**

body in his own new tomb that he had cut out of a wall of rock, and he rolled a very large stone to block the entrance of the tomb. Then Joseph went away. 61Mary Magdalene and the other woman named Mary were sitting ·near [across from; opposite] the tomb.

The Tomb of Jesus Is Guarded

62The next day, the day after Preparation Day, the ·leading [Tchief] priests and the Pharisees ·went to [assembled/gathered before] Pilate. 63They said, "Sir, we remember that while that ·liar [deceiver; impostor] was still alive he said, 'After three days I will rise from the dead.' 64So give the order for the tomb to be ·guarded closely [secured; sealed] till the third day. Otherwise, his ·followers [disciples] might come and steal the body and tell people that he has risen from the dead. ·That lie [LThe last deception] would be even worse than the first one."

65Pilate said, "·Take some soldiers [*or* You have a guard; Cthe phrase could mean Pilate sends Roman soldiers or that the leaders should use their own temple police] and go ·guard [secure] the tomb the best way you know." 66So they all went to the tomb and ·made it safe from thieves [secured it] ·by sealing [*or* by placing a wax seal on] the stone in the entrance and putting soldiers there to guard it.

Jesus Rises from the Dead
(28:1–10; Mark 16:1–11; Luke 24:1–12; John 20:1–18)

28 After the Sabbath day, at dawn on the first day the week, Mary Magdalene and ·another woman named Mary [Lthe other Mary; 27:56] went to look at the tomb.

2·At that time [Suddenly; TAnd behold] there was a strong earthquake. [LFor] An angel of the Lord came down from heaven, went to the tomb, and rolled the stone away from the entrance. Then he sat on the stone. 3·He was shining as bright as [LHis appearance was like] lightning, and his clothes were white as snow. 4The soldiers guarding the tomb shook with fear because of the angel, and they ·became like dead men [Cperhaps they were paralyzed by fear, or they fainted].

5The angel said to the women, "Don't be afraid. I know that you are looking for Jesus, who has been crucified. 6He is not here. He has ·risen [been raised] from the dead as he said he would. Come and see the place where ·his body was [he lay]. 7And go quickly and tell his ·followers [disciples], 'Jesus has risen from the dead. He is going into Galilee ahead of you, and you will see him there.' " Then the angel said, "·Now [LLook; TBehold] I have told you."

8The women left the tomb quickly. They were afraid, but they were also ·very happy [filled with great joy]. They ran to tell Jesus' ·followers [disciples] what had happened. 9·Suddenly [LAnd look/Tbehold], Jesus met them and said, "Greetings." The women came up to him, ·took hold of [clasped] his feet, and worshiped him. 10Then Jesus said to them, "Don't be afraid. Go and tell my ·followers [disciples] to go on to Galilee, and they will see me there."

The Soldiers Report to the Leaders

11While the women ·went to tell Jesus' followers [were on their way], some of the soldiers who had been guarding the tomb went into the city to tell the ·leading [Tchief] priests everything that had happened. 12Then the priests met with the elders and made a plan. They paid the soldiers a ·large amount of money [substantial bribe] 13and said to them, "Tell the people that Jesus' ·followers [disciples] came during the night and stole ·the body [him away] while you were asleep. 14If the governor hears about this, we will satisfy him and save you from trouble." 15So the soldiers kept the money and did as they were ·told [instructed]. And that story is still spread among the ·people [LJews] even ·today [to this day].

Jesus Talks to His Followers

16The eleven ·followers [disciples] **went to Galilee to the mountain**
where Jesus had ·told [designated; arranged for] **them to go. 17When they**
saw Jesus, they worshiped him, but some of them ·did not believe it was
really Jesus [doubted]. **18Then Jesus came to them and said, "All ·power**
[authority] **in heaven and on earth ·is** [has been] **given to me. 19So go and**
make ·followers [disciples] **of all ·people in the world** [the nations]. **Baptize**
them in the name of the Father and the Son and the Holy Spirit. 20Teach
them to obey everything that I have ·taught [commanded] **you, and I will**
be with you always, even until the end of ·this age [the world; time].

MARK

John Prepares for Jesus

(1:1–8; Matt 3:1–12; Luke 3:1–18; John 1:19–28)

1 This is the beginning of the ·Good News [Gospel] ·about [of] Jesus Christ, the Son of God,n 2as the prophet Isaiah wrote:

"[Look; TBehold,] I ·will send [am sending] my messenger ahead of you,
who will prepare your way [Mal. 3:1]."

3"This is a voice of one
who ·calls out [shouts; cries out] in the ·desert [wilderness]:
'Prepare the way for the Lord.
Make ·the road straight [a clear path] for him [Is. 40:3].'"

4John [Cthe Baptist] was baptizing people in the ·desert [wilderness] and preaching a baptism of ·changed hearts and lives [turning from sin; repentance] for the ·forgiveness [remission] of sins. 5All the people from Judea and Jerusalem were going out to him. They confessed their sins and were baptized by him in the Jordan River. 6John wore clothes made from camel's hair, had a leather belt around his waist [Creminiscent of the prophet Elijah; 2 Kin. 1:8], and ate locusts and wild honey [Csignifies living off the land]. 7This is what John preached to the people: "There is one coming after me who is ·greater [mightier; more powerful] than I; I am not ·good enough [fit; qualified] even to kneel down and untie [Lthe thong/strap of] his sandals [Ca task of a servant or slave]. 8I baptize you with water, but he will baptize you with the Holy Spirit."

Jesus Is Baptized and Tested

(1:9–13; Matt 3:13–17; 4:1–11; Luke 3:21–22; 4:1–13)

9·At that time [In those days] Jesus came from the town of Nazareth in Galilee and was baptized by John in the Jordan River. 10Immediately, as Jesus was coming up out of the water, he saw ·heaven [the sky] ·open [split open]. The ·Holy Spirit [LSpirit] ·came down [descended] on him like a dove [Ceither in the form of a dove, or in bird-like descent], 11and a voice came from heaven: "You are my ·Son, whom I love [dearly beloved Son; Ps. 2:7; Gen. 22:2], ·and I am very pleased with you [in whom I take great delight; Is. 42:1]."

12·Then [Immediately] the Spirit ·sent [drove; compelled] Jesus into the ·desert [wilderness]. 13He was in the ·desert [wilderness] forty days [Canalogous to Israel's forty years] and was ·tempted [*or* tested] by Satan [Cas both Adam and Eve and the nation Israel in the wilderness were tempted, but failed]. He was with the wild animals [Cdangerous or perhaps Eden-like conditions], and the angels came and ·took care of [served; ministered to] him.

Jesus Announces the Good News

(1:14–15; Matt 4:17)

14After John was put in prison [Cby Herod Antipas; cf. 6:14–29], Jesus went into Galilee, preaching the ·Good News [Gospel] ·from [about] God. 15He said, "The ·right time has come [Ltime is fulfilled]. ·The kingdom of God [God's sovereign rule] is ·near [at hand]. ·Change your hearts

---

1:1 the Son of God Some Greek copies do not have this phrase.

and lives [Turn from your sins; Repent] and believe the ·Good News [Gospel]!"

Jesus Chooses His First Followers
(1:16–20; Matt. 4:18–22; Luke 5:2–11; John 1:35–42)

16When Jesus was walking by ·Lake Galilee [Tthe Sea of Galilee], he saw Simon [CPeter; cf. 3:16] and his brother Andrew ·throwing [casting] a net into the lake because they were fishermen. 17Jesus said to them, "Come ·follow me [be my disciples], and I will ·make you [teach you how to] fish for people." 18So Simon and Andrew immediately left their nets and followed him.

19Going a little farther, Jesus saw two more brothers, ·James and John, the sons of Zebedee [LJames the son of Zebedee, and his brother John]. They were in a boat, ·mending [preparing] their nets. 20Jesus immediately called them, and they left their father Zebedee in the boat with the hired workers and followed Jesus.

Jesus Forces Out an Evil Spirit
(1:21–28; Luke 4:31–37)

21Jesus and his ·followers [disciples] went to Capernaum [Ca town on the northwest shore of Lake Galilee; it became Jesus' home base]. On the Sabbath day he went to the synagogue and began to teach. 22The people were amazed at his teaching, because he taught ·like [as] a person who had authority, not ·like [as] ·their teachers of the law [the scribes; Cexperts in the law of Moses]. 23Just then, a man was there in the synagogue who had an ·evil [defiling; Lunclean] spirit in him. [CDemons were viewed as "unclean" or defiling spirit-beings.] He shouted, 24"Jesus ·of Nazareth [the Nazarene]! ·What do you want with us? [Let us alone!; What business do we have with each other? LWhat to us and to you?] Did you come to destroy us? I know who you are—God's Holy One!"

25Jesus ·commanded [reprimanded; rebuked] the evil spirit, "Be quiet! Come out of the man!" 26The ·evil [defiling; Lunclean] spirit ·shook the man violently [threw him into convulsions], gave a ·loud cry [shriek], and then came out of him.

27The people were [Lall] so amazed they asked each other, "What is happening here? This man is teaching something new, and with authority. He even gives ·commands [orders] to ·evil [defiling; Lunclean; v. 23] spirits, and they obey him." 28And the ·news [report; fame] about Jesus spread quickly everywhere in the area of Galilee.

Jesus Heals Many People
(1:29-39; Matt. 8:14-17 Luke 4:38-43)

29As soon as Jesus and his ·followers [disciples] left the synagogue, they went to the home of Simon [CPeter; 3:16] and Andrew, together with James and John. 30Simon's mother-in-law was sick in bed with a fever, and ·the people [Lthey; Ceither the people or the disciples] told Jesus about her. 31So Jesus went to her bed, took her hand, and ·helped [raised] her up. The fever left her, and she began ·serving them [waiting on them; Cpresumably meal preparation].

32That evening, after the sun went down, the people brought to Jesus all who were sick and ·had demons in them [were demon-possessed]. 33The whole town gathered at the door. 34Jesus healed many who had different kinds of sicknesses, and he ·forced many demons to leave people [Ldrove/cast out many demons]. But he would not allow the demons to speak, because they knew who he was. [CThey knew he was the Messiah; Jesus wanted to avoid premature publicity.]

35 [Very] Early the next morning, while it was still dark, Jesus ·woke [got up] and left the house. He went to a ·lonely [isolated; deserted] place, where he prayed. 36Simon and his ·friends [companions] went to look for

Jesus. 37When they found him, they said, "Everyone is looking for you!"

38Jesus answered, "·We should [Let us] go to other towns around here so I can preach there too. That is the reason I came." 39So he went everywhere in Galilee, preaching in the synagogues and ·forcing [driving; casting] out demons.

Jesus Heals a Sick Man
1:40-45; Matt. 8:1-4; Luke 5:12-16

40A man with ·a skin disease [Tleprosy; Cthe term does not refer to modern leprosy (Hansen's disease), but to various skin disorders; Lev. 14] came to Jesus. He fell to his knees and begged Jesus, "You can ·heal me [Lmake me clean; Cleprosy rendered a person ceremonially defiled ("unclean"), and so unable to participate in Israel's religious life] if you ·will [are willing; want to]."

41Jesus felt ·sorry[n] [compassion] for the man, so he reached out his hand and touched him and said, "I ·will [am willing; want to]. Be ·healed [Lcleansed]!" 42Immediately the ·disease [Tleprosy] left the man, and he was ·healed [Lcleansed].

43Jesus told the man to go away at once, but he warned him strongly, 44"Don't tell anyone about this. But go and show yourself to the priest. And offer the ·gift [offering; sacrifices] Moses commanded for ·people who are made well [Lyour cleansing; Lev. 14:1–32]. This will ·show the people [be a public testimony to; be evidence for] what I have done." 45The man left there, but he began to tell everyone that Jesus had healed him, and so he spread ·the news about Jesus [Lthe message/word]. As a result, Jesus could not enter a town ·if people saw him [publicly]. He stayed in ·places where nobody lived [secluded/deserted places], but people ·came [kept coming] to him from everywhere.

Jesus Heals a Paralyzed Man
(2:1–12; Matt. 9:1–8; Luke 5:17–26)

2 A few days later, when Jesus came back to Capernaum, the news spread that he was at home. 2Many people gathered together so that there was no room in the house, not even ·outside [near; in front of] the door. And Jesus was ·teaching them God's message [Lspeaking the word to them]. 3Four people came, carrying a paralyzed man. 4Since they could not get to Jesus because of the crowd, they dug a hole in the roof right above where he was speaking. [CPalestinian roofs were generally flat and made of thatch and dried mud.] When they got through, they lowered the ·mat [cot] with the paralyzed man on it. 5When Jesus saw the faith of these people, he said to the paralyzed man, "·Young man [Child; Son], your sins are forgiven."

6Some of the ·teachers of the law [scribes] were sitting there, thinking to themselves, 7"Why does this man ·say things like that [speak this way]? He is ·speaking as if he were God [Lblaspheming]. ·Only God can forgive sins." [L"Who can forgive sins but God alone?"; cf. Is. 43:25].

8Jesus knew immediately [in his spirit] what these teachers of the law were thinking. So he said to them, "Why are you thinking these things [Lin your hearts]? 9Which is easier: to tell this paralyzed man, 'Your sins are forgiven,' or to tell him, 'Stand up. Take your ·mat [cot] and walk'? 10But ·I will prove to you [Lso that you may know] that the Son of Man [Ca title for the Messiah; Dan. 7:13–14] has authority on earth to forgive sins." So Jesus said to the paralyzed man, 11"I tell you, stand up, take your ·mat [cot], and go home." 12Immediately the paralyzed man stood up, took his ·mat [cot], and walked out while everyone was watching him.

1:41 felt sorry Some Greek copies read "was indignant."

The people were [all] amazed and praised God. They said, "We have never seen anything like this!"

Jesus Calls Levi to Follow Him
(2:13–17; Matt. 9:9–13; Luke 5:27–32)

13Jesus went to the lake again. The whole crowd ·followed him [came to him] there, and he taught them. 14While he was walking along, he saw a man named Levi son of Alphaeus sitting in the tax collector's booth [Cprobably a tariff booth for taxing goods in transit]. Jesus said to him, "Follow me," and he stood up and followed Jesus.

15Later, as Jesus was ·having dinner [Lreclining; Caround a low table, the posture for a formal banquet or dinner party] at Levi's house, many tax collectors and sinners were eating there with Jesus and his followers. Many people like this followed Jesus. 16When the ·teachers of the law [scribes] who were Pharisees saw Jesus eating with the tax collectors and sinners, they asked his followers, "Why does he eat with tax collectors and sinners?" [CTax collectors were despised because they worked for the Roman rulers and were notorious for corruption and extortion.]

17Jesus heard this and said to them, "It is not the healthy people who need a doctor, but the sick. I did not come to ·invite [call] ·good people [the righteous; Cmeaning the "self-righteous" who feel no need to repent] but to ·invite [call] sinners [Cthose who recognize their need to repent]."

Jesus Is Questioned About Fasting
(2:18–22; Matt. 9:14–17; Luke 5:33–39; John 3:29–30)

18Now the ·followers [disciples] of John [Cthe Baptist; 1:4–8] and the Pharisees often fasted [Cgiving up eating for spiritual purposes]. ·Some people [LThey] came to Jesus and said, "Why do John's ·followers [disciples] and the ·followers [disciples] of the Pharisees often fast, but your ·followers [disciples] don't?"

19Jesus answered, "The ·friends of the bridegroom [*or* wedding guests; Lchildren of the wedding hall] do not fast while the bridegroom is still with them [CJesus is referring to himself; John 3:29; Rev. 19:7]. As long as the bridegroom is with them, they cannot fast. 20But the ·time [Ldays] will come when the bridegroom will be taken from them, and ·then [in that day] they will fast.

21"No one sews a patch of unshrunk cloth over a hole in an old ·coat [garment]. Otherwise, the patch will shrink and pull away—the new patch will pull away from the old ·coat [garment]. Then the ·hole [tear] will be worse. 22Also, no one ever pours new wine into old ·leather bags [wineskins]. Otherwise, the new wine will break the ·bags [skins; Cas the wine ferments and expands], and the wine will be ·ruined [lost] along with the ·bags [skins]. But new wine should be put into new ·leather bags [wineskins]."

Jesus Is Lord of the Sabbath
(2:23–28; Matt. 12:1–8; Luke 6:1–5)

23One Sabbath day, as Jesus was walking through some fields of grain, his ·followers [disciples] began to [make a path and] pick some grain to eat [Deut. 23:25]. 24The Pharisees said to Jesus, "Why are your followers doing what is not lawful on the Sabbath day?" [CGleaning was viewed as work, and therefore forbidden on the Sabbath; Ex. 34:21.]

25Jesus answered, "Have you never read what David did when he and ·those with him [his companions] were hungry and needed food [1 Sam. 21:1–6]? 26·During the time of Abiathar [*or,* In the account about Abiathar] the high priest, David went into God's house and ate the ·holy bread [consecrated bread; Lbread of presentation], which is lawful only for priests to eat [Ex. 25:30; Lev. 24:5–9]. And David also gave some of the bread to those who were with him."

27Then Jesus said to the Pharisees, "The Sabbath day was made ·to help people [Tfor man]; ·they were not made to be ruled by [Tnot man for] the Sabbath day. 28So then, the Son of Man is ·Lord [Master] even of the Sabbath day."

Jesus Heals a Man's Hand
(3:1–6; Matt. 12:9–14; Luke 6:6–11)

3 Another time when Jesus went into a synagogue, a man with a ·crippled [paralyzed; deformed; shriveled] hand was there. 2·Some people [LThey; Cprobably the Pharisees; see 2:24, 27] watched Jesus closely to see if he would heal the man on the Sabbath day so they could accuse him.

3Jesus said to the man with the crippled hand, "Stand up here in ·the middle [front] of everyone."

4Then Jesus asked ·the people [Lthem; Cprobably the Pharisees], "Which is lawful [Caccording to the law of Moses] on the Sabbath day: to do good or to do evil, to save a life or to kill?" But they ·said nothing to answer him [remained silent].

5Jesus was angry as he looked at them, and he felt very ·sad [distressed; grieved] because ·they were stubborn [of their hard hearts]. Then he said to the man, "·Hold out [stretch out] your hand." The man ·held out [stretched out] his hand and it was ·healed [restored]. 6Then the Pharisees left and [immediately] began ·making plans [plotting] with the Herodians [Ca political group that supported king Herod and his family] about a way to ·kill [destroy] Jesus.

Many People Follow Jesus
(3:7–12; Matt. 12:15–16; Luke 6:17–19)

7Jesus left with his ·followers [disciples] for the lake, and a large crowd from Galilee followed him. 8Also many people came from Judea, from Jerusalem, from Idumea [Clocated to the south], from the lands across the Jordan River, and from the area of Tyre and Sidon [Clocated to the north]. When they heard what Jesus was doing, many people came to him. 9When Jesus saw the crowds, he told his ·followers [disciples] to get a boat ready for him to keep people from ·crowding against [crushing] him. 10He had healed many people, so all the sick were pushing toward him to touch him. 11When ·evil [defiling; Lunclean; see 1:23] spirits [within people] saw Jesus, they fell down before him and shouted, "You are the Son of God!" 12But Jesus strongly ·warned [rebuked; ordered] them not to tell who he was.

Jesus Chooses His Twelve Apostles
(3:13–19; Matt. 10:1–4; Luke 6:12–16)

13Then Jesus went up ·on a mountain [to the hills] and called to him those he wanted, and they came to him. 14Jesus ·chose [appointed] twelve [Cparalleling the twelve tribes of Israel] and called them apostles*n* [C"apostle" means a messenger, or someone sent with a commission]. He wanted them to be with him, and he wanted to send them out to preach 15and to have the authority to ·force [drive; cast] demons out of people. 16These are the twelve he ·chose [appointed]: Simon (Jesus named him Peter), 17James and John, the sons of Zebedee (Jesus named them Boanerges, which [Cin Aramaic] means "Sons of Thunder"), 18Andrew, Philip, Bartholomew, Matthew, Thomas, James the son of Alphaeus, Thaddaeus, Simon the Zealot [Ceither religiously zealous, or a (former) member of the revolutionary movement known as Zealots], 19and Judas Iscariot [CIscariot probably means "man of Kerioth"], who later ·turned against [betrayed] Jesus.

Some People Say Jesus Is Possessed by an Evil Spirit
(3:20–30; Matt. 9:32–34; 12:24–37; Luke 11:14–15, 17–23; 12:10)

20Then Jesus went ·home [into a house], but again a crowd gathered. There were so many people that Jesus and his followers could not eat. 21When his ·family [own people] heard this, they went to ·get [seize; take charge of] him because they thought he was out of his mind. 22But the ·teachers of the law [scribes] from Jerusalem were saying, "·Beelzebul

---

3:14 and called them apostles Some Greek copies do not have this phrase.

[Canother name for Satan] is ·living inside [possessing] him! He uses
power from the ·ruler [prince] of demons to ·force [drive; cast] demons
out of people."
23So Jesus called the people together and ·taught them with stories
[Lspoke to them in parables; CGreek *parabolē*, which can mean stories and
analogies of various kinds]. He said, ·"Satan will not force himself out of
people. [L"How can Satan drive out Satan?] 24A kingdom that is ·divided [at
war with itself] cannot ·continue [stand], 25and a ·family [household;
Lhouse] that is divided cannot ·continue [stand]. 26And if Satan ·is [rises;
rebels] against himself and ·fights against his own people [is divided], he
cannot ·continue [stand]; that is the end of Satan. 27No one can enter a
strong man's house and ·steal [seize; plunder] his things unless he first ·ties
up [binds] the strong man [Is. 49:24–25]. Then he can ·steal [seize; plun-
der] things from the house. [CSatan is the strong man and his possessions
are the people Jesus is freeing from Satan's power.] 28I tell you the truth, all
sins that people do and all ·the things people say against God [blasphe-
mies] can be forgiven. 29But anyone who ·speaks against [blasphemes] the
Holy Spirit will never be forgiven; he is guilty of ·a sin that continues forever [a sin with eternal consequences; Lan eternal sin]."
30Jesus said this because the teachers of the law said that he had an ·evil
[defiling; Lunclean] spirit inside him.

Jesus' True Family
(3:31–35; Matt. 12:46–50; Luke 8:19–21)

31Then Jesus' mother and ·brothers [*or* brothers and sisters; Cthe Greek
word can mean "siblings"; cf. 6:3] arrived. Standing outside, they sent
someone in to tell him to come out. 32Many people were sitting around
Jesus, and they said to him, "Your mother and brothers[n] are ·waiting
[looking; asking] for you outside."
33Jesus asked, "Who are my mother and my brothers [and sisters]?"
34Then he looked at those sitting around him and said, "·Here are [Look;
TBehold,] my mother and my brothers [and sisters]! 35My true brother and
sister and mother are those who do ·what God wants [the will of God]."

A Story About Planting Seed
(4:1–9; Matt. 13:1–9; Luke 8:4–8)

4 Again Jesus began teaching by the lake [Cthe Sea of Galilee]. A great
crowd gathered around him, so he sat down in a boat near the shore.
All the people stayed on the shore close to the water. 2Jesus taught them
many things, using ·stories [parables; see 3:23]. He said, 3"Listen! A ·farmer
[sower] went out to ·plant [sow] his seed. 4While he was ·planting [sowing],
some seed fell ·by the road [along the path], and the birds came and ate it up.
5Some seed fell on rocky ground where there wasn't much dirt. That seed
·grew [sprang up] very fast, because the ground was not deep. 6But when the
sun rose, the plants ·dried up [were scorched and withered] because they did
not have deep roots. 7Some other seed fell among thorny weeds, which grew
and choked the good plants. So those plants did not produce ·a crop [grain].
8Some other seed fell on good ground and began to grow. It got taller and
produced ·a crop [grain]. Some plants made thirty times more, some made
sixty times more, and some made a hundred times more."
9Then Jesus said, ·"Let those with ears use them and listen!" [L"Whoever
has ears to hear, let him hear."]

Jesus Tells Why He Used Stories
(4:10–12; Matt. 13:10–17; Luke 8:9–10)

10Later, when Jesus was alone, the twelve apostles and others around
him asked him about the ·stories [parables; see 3:23].
11Jesus said, "·You can know [To you has been given] the secret about

3:32 brothers Some Greek copies continue, "and sisters."

the kingdom of God. But to ·other people [outsiders] I tell everything by using ·stories [parables] 12so that:

'They will look and look, but they will not ·learn [perceive].
They will listen and listen, but they will not understand.
·If they did learn and understand [LOtherwise],
they ·would [might] ·come back [return] to me and be forgiven
[Is. 6:9–10; cf. Is. 43:8; Jer. 5:21; Ezek. 12:2].' "

Jesus Explains the Seed Story
(4:13–20; Matt. 13:18–23; Luke 8:11–15)

13Then Jesus said to ·his followers [Lthem], "Don't you understand this ·story [parable]? If you don't, how will you understand any ·story [parable; see 3:23]? 14·The farmer plants God's message in people [LThe sower sows the word]. 15Sometimes the ·teaching [word; message] falls ·on the road [along the path]. This is like the people who hear the ·teaching of God [word; message], but Satan quickly comes and takes away the ·teaching [word; message] that was ·planted [sown] in them. 16Others are like the seed ·planted [sown] on rocky ground. They hear the ·teaching [word; message] and quickly accept it with joy. 17·But since they don't allow the teaching to go deep into their lives [LBut since they have no root in themselves], they keep it only a short time. When trouble or persecution comes because of the ·teaching they accepted [word; message], they quickly ·give up [fall away; stumble]. 18Others are like the seed planted among the thorny weeds. They hear the ·teaching [word; message], 19but the worries of this ·life [world; age], the ·temptation [deceitfulness; seduction] of wealth, and ·many other evil desires [desires for other things] ·keep the teaching from growing and producing fruit in their lives [Lcome in and choke the word, making it unfruitful]. 20Others are like the seed ·planted [sown] in the good ground. They hear the ·teaching [word; message] and accept it. Then they grow and produce ·fruit [a crop]—sometimes thirty times more, sometimes sixty times more, and sometimes a hundred times more."

Use What You Have
(4:21–25; Luke 8:16–18)

21Then Jesus said to them, "Do you hide a lamp under a ·bowl [basket] or under a bed? No! You put the lamp on a lampstand. 22[For] Everything that is hidden will be ·made clear [revealed; disclosed] and every ·secret [concealed] thing will be ·made known [brought to light/into the open]. 23·Let those with ears use them and listen! [L"If anyone has ears to hear, let him hear."]

24[And he said to them,] "·Think carefully about [Pay attention to] what you hear. ·The way you give to others is the way God will give to you [*or* The standard you use to judge others will be the standard used for you; LWith the measure you measure, it will be measured to you], ·but God will give you even more [and even more will be added to you]. 25Those who ·have understanding [Lhave] will be given more. But those who do not ·have understanding [Lhave], even what they have will be taken away from them. [CThe Greek does not say *what* they have; but the context suggests spiritual understanding to comprehend the mysteries of the kingdom (v. 11).]

Jesus Tells a Story About Seed

26Then Jesus said, "The kingdom of God is like someone who ·plants seed in [scatters seed on] the ground. 27Night and day, whether the person is asleep or awake, the seed still [sprouts and] grows, but the person does not know how it grows. 28By itself the earth produces grain. First the ·plant [blade; stalk] grows, then the head, and then ·all the [the ripe] grain in the head. 29When the grain is ready, the farmer cuts it [with a sickle], because this is the harvest time."

A Story About Mustard Seed
(4:30–34; Matt. 13:31–32, 34; Luke 13:18–21)

30Then Jesus said, "How can I show you what the kingdom of God is
like? What ·story [parable; see 3:23] can I use to explain it? **31**The kingdom
of God is like a mustard seed, the smallest seed you plant in the ground.
[CThe mustard seed was the smallest seed known to Jesus' hearers.] **32**But
when planted, this seed grows and becomes the largest of all garden plants.
It produces large branches, and the wild birds can make nests in its shade."
33Jesus used many ·stories [parables] like these to teach the crowd
God's ·message [word]—as much as they could ·understand [hear]. **34**He
always used ·stories [parables] to teach them. But when he and his ·fol-
lowers [disciples] were alone, Jesus explained everything to them.

Jesus Calms a Storm
(4:35–41; Matt. 8:18, 23–27; Luke 8:22–25)

35That evening, Jesus said to ·his followers [Lthem], "Let's go across the
lake." **36**Leaving the crowd behind, they took him in the boat just as he was
[Cmeaning he was already in the boat; 4:1]. There were also other boats
with them. **37**A very strong wind came up on the lake. The waves came
over the sides and into the boat so that it was ·already full of water [nearly
swamped]. **38**Jesus was at the ·back of the boat [stern], sleeping on a cush-
ion. ·His followers [LThey] woke him and said, "Teacher, don't you care
that we are ·drowning [perishing]?"
39Jesus stood up and ·commanded [reprimanded; rebuked] the wind
and said to the ·waves [sea], "·Quiet! [TPeace!] Be still!" Then the wind
stopped, and it became completely calm. [CThis parallels God's subduing
of the waters representing chaos in the OT; Ps. 65:7; 89:9; 107:29.]
40Jesus said to ·his followers [Lthem], "Why are you afraid? Do you still
have no faith?"
41They were ·very afraid [terrified; filled with awe] and asked each
other, "Who is this? Even the wind and the ·waves [sea] obey him!"

A Man with Demons Inside Him
(5:1–20; Matt. 8:28–34; Luke 8:26–39)

5 ·Jesus and his followers [LThey] went to the other side of the lake
to the ·area [land; region] of the ·Gerasene*n* people [CGerasa was
southeast of Lake Galilee; the exact location is uncertain]. **2**When Jesus got
out of the boat, immediately a man with an ·evil [defiling; Lunclean] spirit
came to him from the ·burial caves [tombs; cemetery]. **3**This man lived in
the ·caves [tombs], and no one could tie him up [any more], not even
with a chain. **4**[For] Many times people had used [shackles and] chains to
tie the man's hands and feet, but he always ·broke them off [tore apart the
chains and smashed the shackles]. No one was strong enough to ·control
[subdue] him. **5**Day and night he would wander around the ·burial caves
[tombs] and on the hills, screaming and ·cutting [bruising] himself with
stones. **6**While Jesus was still far away, the man saw him, ran to him, and
·fell [bowed] down before him.
7The man shouted in a loud voice, "·What do you want with me [Let
me alone; What business do we have with each other; LWhat to me and to
you; see 1:24], Jesus, Son of the Most High God? I ·command [beg;
implore; swear to] you in God's name not to ·torture [torment] me!" **8**He
said this because Jesus was saying to him, "You ·evil [defiling; Lunclean]
spirit, come out of the man."
9Then Jesus asked him, "What is your name?"
He answered, "My name is Legion [Ca legion was about 5,000 soldiers in
the Roman army], because we are many spirits." **10**He begged Jesus again
and again not to send them out of that ·area [land; region].

5:1 Gerasene Some Greek copies read "Gergesene"; others read "Gadarene."

[11]A large herd of pigs was feeding on a hill near there. [12]The demons
begged Jesus, "Send us into the pigs; let us go into them." [13]So Jesus
allowed them to do this. The ·evil [defiling; [L]unclean] spirits left the man
and went into the pigs. Then the herd of pigs—about two thousand of
them—rushed down the ·hill [steep bank; precipice] into the lake and
were drowned.

[14]The herdsmen ran away and went to the town and to the countryside,
telling everyone about this. So people went out to see what had happened.
[15]They came to Jesus and saw the man who used to have ·the many evil
spirits [[L]the "legion"], sitting, clothed, and in his right mind. And they were
frightened. [16]The people who saw this told the others what had happened
to the man who had ·the demons living in him [been demon-possessed],
and they told about the pigs. [17]Then the people began to beg Jesus to leave
their area.

[18]As Jesus was getting back into the boat, the man who ·was freed from
the demons [had been demon-possessed] begged to go with him.

[19]But Jesus would not let him. He said, "Go home to your family and
tell them how much the Lord has done for you and how he has had mercy
on you." [20]So the man left and began to ·tell [proclaim/preach to] the people in the ·Ten Towns [*or* Decapolis; [C]a league of ten cities east of Lake
Galilee] about what Jesus had done for him. And everyone was amazed.

Jesus Gives Life to a Dead Girl and Heals a Sick Woman
(5:21–43; Matt. 9:18–26; Luke 8:40–56)

[21]When Jesus went in the boat back to the other side of the lake, a large
crowd gathered around him there. [22]A leader of the synagogue, named
Jairus, came there, saw Jesus, and ·fell [bowed; knelt] at his feet. [23]He
begged Jesus, ·saying again and again [earnestly saying], "My daughter is
dying. Please come and ·put [lay] your hands on her so she will be healed
and will live." [24]So Jesus went with him.

A large crowd followed Jesus and pushed very close around him.
[25]Among them was a woman who had been bleeding for twelve years
[[C]probably a chronic menstrual disorder]. [26]She had suffered very much
from many doctors and had spent all the money she had, but instead of
improving, she was getting worse. [27]When the woman heard about Jesus,
she came up behind him in the crowd and touched his ·coat [cloak; gar-
ment]. [28][[L]For] She ·thought [said], "If I can just touch his clothes, I will ·be
healed [get well; be saved]." [29]Instantly her bleeding stopped, and she felt in
her body that she was healed from her disease.

[30]At once Jesus ·felt [perceived] power go out from him. So he turned
around in the crowd and asked, "Who touched my clothes?"

[31]His ·followers [disciples] said, "Look at how many people are pushing against you! And you ask, 'Who touched me?' "

[32]But Jesus continued looking around to see who had touched him.
[33]The woman, knowing that she was healed, came and fell at Jesus' feet.
Shaking with fear, she told him the whole truth. [34]Jesus said to her, "·Dear
woman [[L]Daughter], ·you are made well because you believed [your faith
has saved/healed you]. Go in peace; be healed of your disease."

[35]While Jesus was still speaking, some people came from the house of
the synagogue leader. They said, "Your daughter is dead. ·There is no need
to bother the teacher anymore." [[L]Why trouble the teacher anymore?"]

[36]But Jesus ·paid no attention to [*or* overheard] what they said. He told
the synagogue leader, "Don't be afraid; just believe."

[37]Jesus let only Peter, James, and John the brother of James go with

him. 38When they came to the house of the synagogue leader, Jesus found many people there making lots of noise and ·crying loudly [Lweeping and wailing loudly]. 39Jesus entered the house and said to them, "Why are you ·crying [weeping] and making so much noise? The child is not dead, only asleep." 40But they ·laughed at [ridiculed] him. So, after ·throwing [putting] them [Lall] out of the house, Jesus took the child's father and mother and his three followers into the room where the child was. 41Taking hold of the girl's hand, he said to her, "Talitha, koum!" (This means [Cin Aramaic, the language Jesus commonly spoke], "Little girl, I tell you to stand up!") 42At once the girl stood right up and began walking. (She was twelve years old.) Everyone was completely amazed. 43Jesus gave them strict orders not to tell people about this. Then he told them to give the girl something to eat.

Jesus Goes to His Hometown

(6:1–6a; Matt. 13:53–58; Luke 4:16–30)

6 Jesus left there and went to his hometown [CNazareth; Matt. 2:23; Luke 2:39], and his ·followers [disciples] went with him. 2On the Sabbath day he ·taught [Lbegan to teach] in the synagogue. Many people heard him and were ·amazed [astonished], saying, "Where did this man get these ·teachings [Lthings]? What is this wisdom that has been given to him? And where did he get the power to do ·miracles [Lsuch mighty works done by his hands]? 3·He is just [LIsn't this…?] the carpenter, the son of Mary and the brother of James, Joseph [CGreek: *Joses*], Judas, and Simon. ·And his sisters are [LAre not his sisters…?] here with us." So the people were ·upset with [offended by] Jesus.

4Jesus said to them, "A prophet is ·honored everywhere [not dishonored] except in his hometown and with his own ·people [relatives; kin] and in his own ·home [household]." 5So Jesus was not able to work any miracles there except to heal a few sick people by ·putting [laying] his hands on them. 6He ·was amazed [wondered; marveled] ·at how many people had no faith [because of their unbelief].

Jesus Commissions the Twelve Apostles

(6:6b–13; Matt. 9:35; 10:1, 7–14; Luke 9:1–6)

Then Jesus went [around] to other villages in that area and taught. 7He called ·his twelve followers [Lthe Twelve] together and ·got ready [began] to send them out two by two and gave them authority over ·evil [defiling; Lunclean] spirits. 8This is what Jesus ·commanded [ordered; instructed] them: "Take nothing for your ·trip [journey; way] except a ·walking stick [staff]. Take no bread, no ·bag [traveler's bag; *or* beggar's purse], and no money in your ·pockets [money belts]. 9Wear sandals, but ·take only the clothes you are wearing [do not wear/pack two tunics]. 10When you enter a house, stay there until you leave ·that town [that area]. 11If the people in a certain place refuse to welcome you or listen to you, leave that place. Shake its dust off your feet [Ca sign of rejection and coming judgment] as a ·warning to [testimony against] them."[n]

12So ·the followers [Lthey] went out and preached that people should ·change their hearts and lives [turn from sin; repent]. 13They ·forced [drove; cast] many demons out and ·put olive oil on [anointed with oil] many sick people and healed them.

How John the Baptist Was Killed

(6:14–29; Matt. 14:1–12; Luke 3:19–20; 9:7–9)

14King Herod [CAntipas; a son of Herod the Great; Luke 3:1] heard about Jesus, because he was now well known. Some people said,[n] "He is

6:11 them Some Greek copies continue, "I tell you the truth, on the Judgment Day it will be better for the towns of Sodom and Gomorrah than for the people of that town." See Matthew 10:15.
6:14 Some people said Some Greek copies read "He said."

John the Baptist, who has risen from the dead. That is why ·he can work these miracles [Lmiraculous powers are at work in him]."

15Others said, "He is Elijah [Ca great OT prophet (1 Kin. 17), who was expected to return in the end times (Mal. 4:5)]."

Other people said, "Jesus is a prophet, like the prophets who lived long ago."

16When Herod heard this, he said, "I killed John by cutting off his head. Now he has risen from the dead!"

17Herod himself had ·ordered [sent] his soldiers to arrest John and ·put [bound; chained] him in prison ·in order to please [Lbecause of] his wife, Herodias. She had been the wife of Philip, Herod's brother, but then Herod had married her. 18John had been telling Herod, "It is not lawful for you to ·be married to [have] your brother's wife." 19So Herodias ·hated [had a grudge against] John and wanted to kill him. But she couldn't, 20because Herod was afraid of John and protected him. He knew John was a ·good [righteous] and holy man. Also, though John's preaching always ·bothered [disturbed; puzzled; perplexed] him, he enjoyed listening to John.

21Then the ·perfect [opportune] time came for Herodias to cause John's death. On Herod's birthday, he gave a ·dinner party [banquet] for ·the most important government leaders [his nobles/high officials], the commanders of his army, and ·the most important people [leaders] in Galilee. 22When the daughter of Herodias[n] came in and danced, she pleased Herod and the people eating with him.

So King Herod said to the girl, "Ask me for anything you want, and I will give it to you." 23He ·promised [swore/vowed to] her, "Anything you ask for I will give to you—up to half of my kingdom."

24The girl went [out] to her mother and asked, "What should I ask for?"

Her mother answered, "Ask for the head of John the Baptist."

25At once the girl ·went back [hurried back in] to the king and said to him, "I want [you to give me] the head of John the Baptist right now on a platter."

26Although the king was very ·sad [sorry; grieved; distressed], he had made a promise, and his dinner guests had heard it. So he did not want to refuse what she asked. 27Immediately the king sent ·a soldier [an executioner] to bring John's head. The ·soldier [executioner] went and cut off John's head in the prison 28and brought it back on a platter. He gave it to the girl, and the girl gave it to her mother. 29When John's ·followers [disciples] heard this, they came and got John's ·body [corpse] and put it in a tomb.

More than Five Thousand Fed
(6:30–44; Matt. 14:13–21; Luke 9:10–17; John 6:1–15)

30The apostles gathered around Jesus and told him about all the things they had done and taught. 31Crowds of people were coming and going so that Jesus and his ·followers [disciples] did not even have time to eat. He said to them, "Come away by yourselves, and we will go to a ·lonely [isolated; deserted] place to get some rest."

32So they went in a boat by themselves to a ·lonely [isolated; deserted] place. 33But many people saw them leave and recognized them. So from all the towns they ran to the place where Jesus was going, and they got there before him. 34When he ·arrived [landed; came ashore], he saw a great crowd

6:22 When . . . Herodias Some Greek copies read "When his daughter Herodias."

waiting. He ·felt sorry [had compassion] for them, because they were like sheep without a shepherd. So he began to teach them many things.

35 When it was late in the day, his ·followers [disciples] came to him and said, "·No one lives in this place [This is a remote/deserted place], and it is already very late. 36 Send the people away so they can go to the countryside and towns around here to buy themselves something to eat."

37 But Jesus answered, "You give them something to eat."

They said to him, ·"We would all have to work a month to earn enough money to buy that much bread!" [L"Should we go and buy two hundred denarii worth of bread and give it to them to eat?"]

38 Jesus asked them, "How many loaves of bread do you have? Go and see."

When they found out, they said, "Five loaves and two fish."

39 Then Jesus ·told [commanded; ordered] ·his followers [Lthem] to have the people sit [recline; Cthe posture for a banquet or dinner party; 2:15] in groups on the green grass. 40 So they sat in groups of hundreds and fifties. 41 Jesus took the five loaves and two fish and, looking up to heaven, he ·thanked God for [blessed] the food. He ·divided [broke] the bread and gave it to his ·followers [disciples] for them to give to the people. Then he divided the two fish among them all. 42 All the people ate and were satisfied. 43 ·The followers [LThey] filled twelve baskets with the leftover pieces of bread and fish. 44 There were five thousand men who ate.

Jesus Walks on the Water
(6:45–56; Matt. 14:22–36; John 6:16–25)

45 Immediately Jesus ·told [compelled; made] his ·followers [disciples] to get into the boat and go ahead of him to Bethsaida [Ca town on the northern shore of Lake Galilee, east of the Jordan River] across the lake. He stayed there to ·send the people home [dismiss the crowd]. 46 After ·sending them away [saying goodbye], he went into the hills to pray.

47 That night, the boat was in the middle of the lake, and Jesus was alone on the land. 48 He saw his ·followers [disciples] struggling hard to row the boat, because the wind was blowing against them. ·Between three and six o'clock in the morning [LAt about the fourth watch of the night], Jesus came to them, walking on the water, and he ·wanted [intended; was about] to ·walk past [pass by] the boat. 49 But when they saw him walking on the ·water [lake; sea], they thought he was a ghost and cried out. 50 They all saw him and were afraid. But ·quickly [immediately] Jesus spoke to them and said, "Have courage! It is I. Do not be afraid." 51 Then he got into the boat with them, and the wind ·became calm [ceased; stopped]. They were greatly amazed. 52 [For] They did not understand ·about the miracle of the five loaves [the significance of the loaves; Labout the loaves], because their ·minds were closed [hearts were hardened/stubborn/dull].

53 When they had crossed the lake, they came to shore at Gennesaret [Ceither the plain on the northwestern shore of the lake, or a town in that region] and tied the boat there. 54 When they got out of the boat, people immediately recognized Jesus. 55 They ran everywhere in that ·area [region] and began to bring sick people on ·mats [cots] wherever they heard he was. 56 And everywhere he went—into towns, cities, or countryside—the people brought the sick to the marketplaces. They begged him to let them touch just the ·edge [fringe; tassels] of his coat, and all who touched it were healed.

The Things that Truly Please God
(7:1–23; Matt. 15:1–20; Luke 6:39; 11:37–41)

7 When some Pharisees and some ·teachers of the law [scribes] came from Jerusalem, they gathered around Jesus. 2 They saw that some of Jesus' ·followers [disciples] ate food with hands that were not clean, that is, they hadn't [ceremonially] washed them. 3 ([For] The Pharisees and all the

Jews never eat before washing their hands ·in the way required [Lwith a fist;
Cthe meaning of the idiom is uncertain; it could mean "with a handful of
water," "with cupped hand," "up to the wrist" or something else] by ·their
unwritten laws [Lthe traditions of the elders]. 4·And when they buy something in the market, they never eat it [*or,* And when they come from the
market (where they might have touched something "unclean"), they do not
eat] until they wash themselves in a special way. They also ·follow [hold fast
to; observe] many other ·unwritten laws [traditions], such as the washing of
cups, pitchers, and pots.[n])

5The Pharisees and the ·teachers of the law [scribes] asked Jesus, "Why
don't your ·followers [disciples] ·obey [walk according to] the ·unwritten
laws which have been handed down to us [traditions of the elders]? Why
do they eat their food with hands that are ·not clean [defiled]?"

6Jesus answered, "Isaiah was right when he ·spoke [prophesied] about
you hypocrites. ·He wrote [As it is written],

'These people show honor to me with ·words [Ltheir lips],
but their hearts are far from me.
7Their worship of me is ·worthless [futile; in vain].
The things they teach are nothing but human ·rules
[commandments; Is. 29:13].'

8 You ·have stopped following [neglected; abandoned] the commands of
God, and you ·follow [hold on to] only human ·teachings[n] [traditions]."

9Then Jesus said to them, "You ·cleverly ignore [are very good at ignor-
ing/despising] the commands of God so you can follow your own
·teachings [tradition]. 10[For] Moses said, 'Honor your father and your
mother' [Ex. 20:12; Deut. 5:16], and 'Anyone who ·says cruel things to
[speaks evil of; curses] his father or mother must be put to death' [Ex.
21:17; Lev. 20:9]. 11But you say a person can tell his father or mother, 'I
have something I could use to help you, but it is Corban—a gift to God.'
[C*Corban* is a Hebrew term meaning dedicated or set aside to God.] 12You
no longer let that person ·use that money [do anything] for his father or
his mother. 13By your own ·rules [tradition], which you ·teach people
[have handed down], you are ·rejecting [nullifying; canceling] what God
said. And you do many things like that."

14After Jesus called the crowd to him again, he said, "Listen to me,
everyone, and understand what I am saying. 15There is nothing people put
into their bodies that ·makes them unclean [pollutes/defiles them]. [But
rather] People are ·made unclean [polluted; defiled] by the things that
come out of them. |16·Let those with ears use them and listen [see 4:23].|"[n]

17When Jesus left the ·people [crowd] and went into the house, his ·fol-
lowers [disciples] asked him about this ·story [parable; see 3:23]. 18Jesus said,
"·Do you still not understand [Are you so dull]? ·Surely you know [LDon't
you know…?] that nothing that enters someone from the outside can make
that person ·unclean [polluted; defiled]. 19[Because] It does not go into the
·mind [heart], but into the stomach. Then it goes ·out of the body [Linto the
sewer/latrine]." ·(When Jesus said this, he meant that no longer was any food
unclean for people to eat.) [*or,* (In this way, Jesus cleansed all food.)]

20And Jesus said, "The things that come out of people are the things
that make them ·unclean [defiled]. 21·All these evil things begin inside

---

7:4 pots Some Greek copies continue, "and dining couches." **7:8 teachings** Some Greek copies continue, "You wash pitchers and jugs and do many other such things." **7:16 Let . . . listen.** Some Greek copies do not contain the bracketed text.

people, in the mind [LFor from within, out of human hearts, come]: evil ·thoughts [intentions; ideas], sexual sins, stealing, murder, adultery, 22greed, ·evil actions [wickedness], ·lying [deceit], ·doing sinful things [indecency; lust; lewdness], ·jealousy [envy; Levil eye], ·speaking evil of others [slander; blasphemy], pride, and foolish living. 23All these evil things come from inside and make people ·unclean [defiled]."

Jesus Helps a Gentile Woman
(7:24–30; Matt. 15:21–28)

24Jesus left that place and went to the area around Tyre[n] [Ca Gentile city on the coast north of Israel]. When he went into a house, he did not want anyone to know he was there, but he could not stay hidden. 25A woman whose daughter had an ·evil [defiling; Lunclean] spirit in her heard that he was there. So she ·quickly [immediately] came to Jesus and ·fell [bowed] at his feet. 26She was ·Greek [a Gentile; C"Greek" is sometimes used for any non-Jew; Rom. 1:16], born in Phoenicia, in Syria. She ·begged [kept asking] Jesus to ·force [drive; cast] the demon out of her daughter.

27Jesus told the woman, "It is not right to take the children's bread and ·give [throw] it to the dogs. First let the children eat all they want." [C"Children" refers to Israel; "dogs" to the Gentiles.]

28But she answered, "Yes, Lord, but even the dogs under the table can eat the children's crumbs."

29Then Jesus said, "Because of your answer, you may go. The demon has left your daughter."

30The woman went home and found her daughter lying in bed; the demon was gone.

Jesus Heals a Deaf Man
(7:31–37; Matt. 15:29–31)

31Then Jesus left the area around Tyre and went through Sidon to Lake Galilee [Tthe Sea of Galilee], to the area of ·the Ten Towns [*or* Decapolis; Can area east of Lake Galilee that once had ten main towns; 5:20]. 32While he was there, some people brought a man to him who was deaf and ·could not talk plainly [had a speech impediment]. The people begged Jesus to put his hand on the man to heal him.

33Jesus led the man away from the crowd, by himself. He put his fingers in the man's ears and then spit and touched the man's tongue. [CThe use of saliva is mentioned in other ancient accounts of healing, and elsewhere in the Gospels; see 8:23; John 9:6.] 34Looking up to heaven, he sighed and said to the man, "Ephphatha!" (This means [Cin Aramaic], "Be opened.") 35Instantly the man was able to hear and to use his tongue so that he spoke clearly.

36Jesus ·commanded [ordered; instructed] the people not to tell anyone about what happened. But the more he ·commanded [ordered; instructed] them, the more they ·told about [proclaimed] it. 37They were completely amazed and said, "Jesus does everything well. He makes the deaf hear! And ·those who can't talk [the mute] he makes able to speak."

More than Four Thousand People Fed
(8:1–10; Matt. 15:32–39)

8 ·Another time [About this time] there was ·a [another] great crowd with Jesus that had nothing to eat. So Jesus called his ·followers [disciples] and said, 2"I ·feel sorry [have compassion] for these people, because they have already been with me for three days, and they have nothing to eat. 3If I send them home hungry, they will ·faint [collapse] on the way. Some of them ·live a long way from here [have come from far away]."

4Jesus' ·followers [disciples] answered, "·How [LFrom where] can ·we [Lanyone] get enough bread in this ·remote place [desolate place; desert] to feed them?"

7:24 Tyre Some Greek copies continue, "and Sidon."

5Jesus asked, "How many loaves of bread do you have?"

They answered, "Seven."

6Jesus told the people to ·sit [recline] on the ground. Then he took the seven loaves, gave thanks to God, and ·divided [broke] the bread. He gave the pieces to his ·followers [disciples] to give to the people, and they did so. 7·The followers [LThey] also had a few small fish. After Jesus ·gave thanks for [blessed] the fish, he told his ·followers [disciples] to give them to the people also. 8All the people ate and were satisfied. Then ·his followers [Lthey] filled seven ·baskets [large baskets; Ca different word than in the feeding of the 5,000; 6:43] with the leftover pieces of food. 9There were about four thousand people who ate. After they had eaten, Jesus ·sent them home [dismissed them]. 10Then ·right away [immediately] he got into a boat with his ·followers [disciples] and went to the area of Dalmanutha. [CThis place is unknown; it was probably on the western shore of Lake Galilee.]

The Leaders Ask for a Miracle
(8:11–13; Matt. 12:38–39; 16:1–4; Luke 11:16, 29; 12:54–56)

11The Pharisees came to Jesus and began to ·ask him questions [argue/dispute with him]. ·Hoping to trap [Trying to test] him, they asked Jesus for a ·miracle [sign] from ·God [Lheaven; Cpossibly a sign in the sky, but more likely a Jewish way of saying "from God"]. 12Jesus ·sighed [groaned] deeply and said, "Why ·do you people [Ldoes this generation] ask for a miracle as a sign? I tell you the truth, no sign will be given to ·you [this generation]." 13Then Jesus left the Pharisees and went in the boat to the other side of the lake.

Guard Against Wrong Teachings
(8:14–21; Matt. 16:5–12; Luke 12:1)

14His ·followers [disciples] had only one loaf of bread with them in the boat; they had forgotten to bring more. 15Jesus warned them, "·Be careful [Watch out]! Beware of the ·yeast [leaven] of the Pharisees and the ·yeast [leaven] of Herod [Cyeast or leaven refers here to the dangerous permeating power of their influence]."

16They discussed the meaning of this, saying, "He said this because we have no bread."

17Knowing what they were talking about, Jesus asked them, "Why are you ·talking [discussing; arguing] about not having bread? Do you still not see or understand? Are your ·minds closed [hearts hardened]? 18·You have eyes, but you don't really see. You have ears, but you don't really listen [Jer. 5:21; Ezek. 12:2]. ·Remember [LDon't you remember] when 19I ·divided [broke] five loaves of bread for the five thousand? How many baskets did you fill with leftover pieces of food?"

They answered, "Twelve."

20"And when I ·divided [broke] seven loaves of bread for the four thousand, how many [large] baskets did you fill with leftover pieces of food?"

They answered, "Seven."

21Then Jesus said to them, "Don't you understand yet?"

Jesus Heals a Blind Man

22Jesus and his followers came to Bethsaida [6:45]. There some people brought a blind man to Jesus and begged him to touch the man. 23So Jesus took the blind man's hand and led him out of the village. Then he spit on the man's eyes [see 7:33] and ·put [laid] his hands on the man and asked, "Can you see [anything] now?"

24The man looked up and said, "Yes, I see people, but they look like trees walking around."

25Again Jesus ·put [laid] his hands on the man's eyes. Then the man

·opened his eyes wide [stared intently] and ·they were healed [his sight
was restored], and he was able to see everything clearly. 26Jesus told him
to go home, saying, "Don't go into the town."[n] [CJesus wanted to avoid the
publicity that the healing would produce.]

Peter Says Jesus Is the Christ
(8:27–9:1; Matt 16:13-28; Luke 9:18-27)

27Jesus and his ·followers [disciples] went to the towns around Caesarea
Philippi [Ca city about 25 miles north of Lake Galilee]. While they were
traveling, Jesus asked them, "Who do people say I am?"
28They answered, "Some say you are John the Baptist. Others say you are
Elijah [a great prophet (1 Kin. 17), who was expected to return in the end
times (Mal. 4:5); see 6:15], and others say you are one of the prophets."
29Then Jesus asked, "But who do you say I am?"
Peter answered, "You are the ·Christ [Messiah]."
30Jesus [strongly] warned them not to tell anyone who he was.
31Then Jesus began to teach them that the Son of Man [Dan. 7:13–14]
must suffer many things and that he would be rejected by the Jewish
elders, the ·leading [Tchief] priests, and the ·teachers of the law [scribes].
He told them that the Son of Man must be killed and then rise from the
dead after three days. 32Jesus told them ·plainly [boldly; openly] what
would happen. Then Peter took Jesus aside and began to ·reprimand
[rebuke] him. 33But Jesus turned and looked at his ·followers [disciples].
Then he ·reprimanded [rebuked] Peter. He said, "·Go away from me [LGet
behind me], Satan [CJesus accuses Peter of doing Satan's work by obstruct-
ing God's plan]! You ·don't care about [are not setting your mind on/
thinking about] the things of God, but only ·about things people think
are important [on/about human concerns]."
34Then Jesus called the crowd to him, along with his ·followers [disci-
ples]. He said, "If ·people [Lanyone wants] want to follow me, they must
·give up the things they want [deny themselves; set aside their own inter-
ests]. They must ·be willing even to give up their lives to [Ltake up their
cross and] follow me. 35Those who want to save their lives will ·give up true
life [Llose their life/soul; CGreek *psychē* can mean "life" or "soul," producing
this play on words]. But those who ·give up [lose; sacrifice] their lives for
·me [my sake] and for the ·Good News [Gospel] will ·have true life [save
their lives/souls]. 36·It is worthless [What good/profit/benefit is it…?] to
·have [gain] the whole world if they ·lose [forfeit] their souls. 37·They could
never pay enough [LOr what could they give…?] ·to buy back [in exchange
for] their souls. 38If people of this ·sinful and evil time [adulterous and
sinful generation] are ashamed of me and my ·teaching [words; message],
the Son of Man will be ashamed of them when he ·comes [returns] with
his Father's glory and with the holy angels [Dan. 7:13–14]."

9 Then Jesus said to the people, "I tell you the truth, some people
standing here will not ·die [Ltaste death] before they see the kingdom of God ·come [arrive] with power." [C"Seeing the kingdom of God"
may refer to the Transfiguration that follows (9:1–8), Jesus' resurrection,
or the destruction of Jerusalem in AD 70.]

The Transfiguration on the Mountain
(9:2-13; Matt 17:1-13; Luke 9:28-36)

2Six days later, Jesus took Peter, James, and John [Land led them] up on
a high mountain by themselves. ·While they watched [In their presence;
In front of them], Jesus' appearance was ·changed [transformed;
Ttransfigured]. 3His clothes became shining white, whiter than any ·person

8:26 town Some Greek copies continue, "Don't even go and tell anyone in the town."

[launderer on earth] **could ·make them** [bleach them]. **4 Then Elijah and**
Moses appeared to them, talking with Jesus. [CGod had given the Law
through Moses, and Elijah was an important prophet (see 6:1); together
they signify that Jesus fulfills the OT.]
5 Peter said to Jesus, "·Teacher [LRabbi], **it is good that we are here. Let**
us make three ·tents [shelters; shrines; tabernacles; Lev. 23:42]**—one for**
you, one for Moses, and one for Elijah." [CPerhaps Peter wanted to prolong their stay or to commemorate their visit.] **6 Peter did not know what**
to say, because he and the others were so frightened.
7 Then a cloud came and ·covered [overshadowed; Ex. 24:15] **them, and**
a voice came from the cloud, saying, "This is my ·Son, whom I love [dearly
loved Son; Ps. 2:7; Gen. 22:2; Mark 1:11]. **Listen to him** [Deut. 18:15;
Acts 3:22]**!"**
8 Suddenly Peter, James, and John looked around, but they saw only
Jesus there alone with them.
9 As they were coming down the mountain, Jesus ·commanded
[instructed] **them not to tell anyone about what they had seen until the**
Son of Man had risen from the dead.
10 So they ·obeyed Jesus [kept this statement/matter to themselves], **but**
they discussed what he meant about rising from the dead.
11 Then they asked Jesus, "Why do the ·teachers of the law [scribes] **say**
that Elijah must come first [Mal. 3:1; 4:5]**?"**
12 Jesus answered, "·They are right to say that Elijah must come first
and [LElijah is indeed coming, and he will] **·make everything the way it**
should be [restore/prepare everything]. **But why does the Scripture say**
that the Son of Man will suffer much and ·that people will treat him as if
he were nothing [be despised; be treated with contempt; be rejected; Is.
52:13—53:12]**?** 13 [LBut] **I tell you that Elijah has already come. And ·peo-**
ple [Lthey] **did to him whatever they wanted to do, just as ·the Scriptures**
said it would happen [it is written about him]**."**

Jesus Heals a Sick Boy
(9:14–29; Matt 17:14–21; Luke 9:37–43)

14 When Jesus, Peter, James, and John came back to the other ·followers
[disciples], **they saw a great crowd around them and the ·teachers of the**
law [scribes] **arguing with them. 15 But as soon as the crowd saw Jesus, the**
people were ·surprised [amazed] **and ran to welcome him.**
16 Jesus asked, "What are you arguing about?"
17 A man [in the crowd] **answered, "Teacher, I brought my son to you.**
He has an evil spirit in him that ·stops him from talking [makes him
mute]. **18 When the spirit attacks him, it throws him on the ground. Then**
my son foams at the mouth, grinds his teeth, and becomes ·very stiff
[rigid]. **I asked your ·followers** [disciples] **to ·force** [drive; cast] **the evil**
spirit out, but they couldn't."
19 Jesus answered, "You ·people have no faith [unbelieving/faithless
generation]. **How long must I stay with you? How long must I put up with**
you? Bring the boy to me."
20 So ·the followers [Lthey] **brought him to Jesus. As soon as the evil spirit**
saw Jesus, it ·made the boy lose control of himself [threw the boy into con-
vulsions], **and he fell down and rolled on the ground, foaming at the mouth.**
21 Jesus asked the boy's father, "How long has this been happening?"
The father answered, "Since ·he was very young [childhood]. **22 The spirit**
often throws him into a fire or into water to ·kill [destroy] **him. If you can**
do anything for him, please have ·pity [compassion] **on us and help us."**

23Jesus said to the father, "You said, 'If you can!' All things are possible for the one who believes."

24Immediately the father cried out, "I do believe! Help ·me to believe more [me not to doubt; me overcome my unbelief; Lmy unbelief]!"

25When Jesus saw that a crowd was quickly gathering, he ·ordered [rebuked] the ·evil [defiling; Lunclean] spirit, saying, "You deaf and mute spirit, I command you to come out of this boy and never enter him again!"

26The evil spirit screamed and ·caused the boy to fall on the ground again [convulsed him violently]. Then the spirit came out. The boy looked as if he were dead, and many people said, "He is dead!" 27But Jesus took hold of the boy's hand and helped him to stand up.

28When Jesus went into the house, his ·followers [disciples] began asking him privately, "Why couldn't we ·force [drive; cast] that evil spirit out?"

29Jesus answered, "That kind of spirit can only be forced out by prayer."[n]

Jesus Again Talks About His Death
(9:30–32; Matt. 17:22–23; Luke 9:43–45)

30Then Jesus and his ·followers [disciples] left that place and went through Galilee. He didn't want anyone to know where he was, 31because he was teaching his ·followers [disciples]. He said to them, "The Son of Man will be ·handed over [delivered over; betrayed] to ·people [Lhuman hands], and they will kill him [Cthe "handing over" may be Judas' betrayal or God's actions in "giving up" his Son to accomplish salvation; Rom. 4:25]. After three days, he will rise from the dead." 32But they did not understand what Jesus meant, and they were afraid to ask him.

Who Is the Greatest?
(9:33–37; Matt. 18:1–5; Luke 9:46–48)

33Jesus and his ·followers [disciples] went to Capernaum. When they went into a house there, he asked them, "What were you ·arguing about [discussing] on the road?" 34But they did not answer, because their ·argument [discussion] on the road was about which one of them was the greatest.

35Jesus sat down and called ·the twelve apostles [the Twelve] to him. He said, "Whoever wants to be ·the most important [first] must be last of all and servant of all."

36Then Jesus took a small child and had ·him [*or* her; Cthe Greek here does not specify gender] stand among them. Taking the child in his arms, he said, 37"Whoever ·accepts [welcomes; receives] a child like this in my name [Cas a representative or follower of Jesus] accepts me. And whoever ·accepts [welcomes; receives] me accepts [not only me, but] the One who sent me." [CChildren had low social status, so the saying indicates concern for the lowly.]

Anyone Not Against Us Is for Us
(9:38–50; Matt. 10:42; 18:6–9; Luke 9:49–50; 17:1–2)

38Then John said, "Teacher, we saw someone using your name [Cinvoking your authority] to ·force [drive; cast] demons out of a person. We told him to stop, because he does not belong to our group."

39But Jesus said, "Don't stop him, because anyone who uses my name to do powerful things will not ·easily [quickly] say evil things about me. 40Whoever is not against us is ·with [for] us. 41I tell you the truth, whoever gives you a drink of water because you belong to the ·Christ [Messiah] will ·truly get [Lcertainly not lose] his reward.

42"If someone causes one of these little children who believes in me to

9:29 prayer Some Greek copies continue, "and fasting."

·sin [lose faith; stumble], it would be better for that person to have a ·large
stone [large millstone; Lmillstone of a donkey] tied around his neck and
be ·drowned [Lthrown] in the sea. 43If your hand causes you ·to sin [lose
faith; stumble], cut it off. It is better for you ·to lose part of your body and
live forever [Lto enter life maimed] than to have two hands and go to ·hell
[LGehenna; Ca valley outside of Jerusalem where in the OT period children
were sacrificed to a pagan god; later used as a burning trash heap; a meta-
phor for hell], where the fire never goes out. |44In hell the worm does not
die; the fire is never put out.|n 45If your foot causes you to ·sin [lose faith;
stumble], cut it off. It is better for you ·to lose part of your body and to
live forever [Lto enter life crippled] than to have two feet and be thrown
into ·hell [Gehenna; v. 43]. |46In hell the worm does not die; the fire is
never put out.|n 47If your eye causes you to ·sin [lose faith; stumble], take
it out. It is better for you to enter the kingdom of God with only one eye
than to have two eyes and be thrown into ·hell [Gehenna; v. 43]. 48In hell
the worm does not die; the fire is never put out. 49Every person will be
salted with fire. [CThe meaning of this proverb is uncertain; it may mean
that the testing of believers purifies (fire) and preserves (salt); or it may
refer to believers as God's covenant people, since salt and fire were part of
the OT sacrificial system; see Lev. 2:3; Num. 18:9.]
50"Salt is good, but if the salt loses its salty taste, you cannot make it salty
again. So, ·be full of salt [Lhave salt in/among yourselves; Csalt here may
symbolize fellowship within the covenant], and have peace with each other."

Jesus Teaches About Divorce
(10:1–12; Matt. 19:1–12; Luke 9:51; 16:18)

10 Then Jesus left that place and went into the ·area [region] of
Judea and across the Jordan River. Again, crowds came to him,
and he taught them as he usually did.
2Some Pharisees came to Jesus and tried to ·trick [test; trap] him. They
asked, "Is it ·right [lawful; Caccording to the law of Moses] for a man to
divorce his wife?"
3Jesus answered, "What did Moses command you to do?"
4They said, "Moses ·allowed [permitted] a man to write out divorce
papers and send her away [Deut. 24:1]."
5Jesus said, "Moses wrote that command for you because you were
·stubborn [hard hearted]. 6But ·when God made the world [from the
beginning of creation], 'he made them male and female' [Gen. 1:27; 5:2].
7'So a man will leave his father and mother and be ·united with [joined
to] his wife,n 8and the two will become ·one body [as though they were
one person; Tone flesh; Gen. 2:24]'. So they are no longer two, but one.
9God has joined the two together, so no one should separate them."
10Later, in the house, his ·followers [disciples] asked Jesus again about
·the question of divorce [Lthis matter]. 11He answered, "Anyone who
divorces his wife and marries another woman ·is guilty of [commits]
adultery against her. 12And the woman who divorces her husband and
marries another man ·is also guilty of [commits] adultery."

Jesus Accepts Children
(10:13–16; Matt. 19:13–15; Luke 18:15–17)

13Some people brought their little children to Jesus so he could touch
them, but his ·followers [disciples] ·told them to stop [scolded/rebuked
them]. 14When Jesus saw this, he was ·upset [angry; indignant] and said to

9:44 In . . . out. Some Greek copies do not contain the bracketed text. **9:46 In . . . out.** Some Greek copies do not contain the bracketed text. **10:7 and . . . wife** Some Greek copies do not have this phrase.

them, "Let the little children come to me. Don't stop them, because the kingdom of God belongs to people who are like these children [Cmeaning humble
and dependent]. 15I tell you the truth, you must accept the kingdom of God
as if you were a little child, or you will never enter it." 16Then Jesus took the
children in his arms, ·put [laid] his hands on them, and blessed them.

A Rich Young Man's Question
(10:17–31; Matt. 19:16–30; Luke 18:18–30)

17As Jesus started ·to leave [on his way; on a journey], a man ran to him
and ·fell on his knees [knelt] before Jesus. The man asked, "Good teacher,
what must I do to ·have life forever [Linherit eternal life]?"
18Jesus answered, "Why do you call me good? ·Only God is good [No
one is good except One—God; CJesus is not denying his own divinity, but
is challenging the man's understanding of goodness]. 19You know the
commands: 'You must not murder. You must not ·be guilty of [commit]
adultery. You must not steal. You must not ·tell lies about your neighbor
[testify falsely; Tbear false witness]. You must not ·cheat [defraud]. Honor
your father and mother' [Ex. 20:12–16; Deut. 5:16–20]."
20The man said, "Teacher, I have ·obeyed [kept carefully; guarded] all
these things since I was a boy."
21Jesus, looking at the man, loved him and said, "There is one more
thing you need to do. Go and sell everything you have, and give the
money to the poor, and you will have treasure in heaven. Then come and
follow me."
22He was ·very sad [shocked; appalled] to hear Jesus say this, and he left
·sorrowfully [grieving], because he ·was rich [had many possessions].
23Then Jesus looked [around] at his ·followers [disciples] and said,
"How hard it will be for ·the rich [those with many possessions] to enter
the kingdom of God!"
24The ·followers [disciples] were ·amazed [astonished] at what Jesus
said. [CIn Judaism wealth was generally viewed as a reward from God.] But
he said again, "My children, it is very hard[n] to enter the kingdom of God!
25It is easier for a camel to go through the eye of a needle than for a rich
person to enter the kingdom of God [Cmeaning it is impossible, by human
effort; see v. 27]."
26They were even more ·surprised [amazed] and said to each other,
"Then who can be saved?"
27Jesus looked at them and said, "·For people [Humanly speaking,] this
is impossible, but for God all things are possible."
28Peter ·said [spoke up] to Jesus, "Look, we have left everything and
followed you."
29Jesus said, "I tell you the truth, all those who have left houses, brothers,
sisters, mother, father, children, or ·farms [fields] for me and for the ·Good
News [Gospel] 30will get more than they left. Here in ·this world [the present
age] they will have a hundred times more homes, brothers, sisters, mothers,
children, and ·fields [farms]. And with those things, ·they will also suffer for
their belief [persecutions]. But in the ·age [world] that is coming they will
have ·life forever [eternal life]. 31Many who are first now will be last in the
future. And many who are last now will be first in the future."

Jesus Talks a Third Time About His Death
(10:32–34; Matt. 20:17–19; Luke 18:31–34)

32As Jesus and the people with him were on the road to Jerusalem, he was
leading the way. His ·followers [disciples] were ·amazed [surprised; puzzled;
alarmed], but others in the crowd who followed were afraid. Again Jesus
took ·the twelve apostles [the Twelve] aside and began to tell them what was

10:24 hard Some Greek copies continue, "for those who trust in riches."

about to happen [to him] in Jerusalem. 33He said, "Look, we are going [Lup]
to Jerusalem. The Son of Man will be ·turned over [betrayed; delivered over;
see 9:31] to the ·leading [Tchief] priests and the ·teachers of the law [scribes].
They will ·say that he must die [condemn him to death], and they will turn
him over to the ·Gentiles [Cthe Roman authorities], 34who will laugh at him
and spit on him. They will beat him with whips and ·crucify [Lkill] him. But
after three days, he will rise to life again."

Two Followers Ask Jesus a Favor
(10:35–45; Matt. 20:20–28)

35Then James and John, sons of Zebedee, came to Jesus and said, "Teacher,
we want ·to ask you to do something for us [you to do whatever we ask]."
36Jesus asked, "What do you want me to do for you?"
37They answered, "Let one of us sit at your right side and one of us sit
at your left side in your glory [Cthe messianic kingdom]."
38Jesus said, "You don't understand what you are asking. Can you drink
the cup that I must drink? And can you be baptized with the same kind of
baptism that I must go through?" [CBoth "cup" and "baptism" symbolize
suffering, and perhaps God's judgment experienced by Jesus on the cross;
Jer. 25:15–29.]
39They answered, "Yes, we can."
Jesus said to them, "You will drink the same cup that I will drink, and
you will be baptized with the same baptism that I must go through. 40But
·I cannot choose [it is not for me to grant/say] who will sit at my right or
my left; those places belong to those for whom they have been prepared."
41When ·the other ten followers [Lthe ten] heard this, they began to be
·angry [indignant] with James and John.
42Jesus called them together and said, "You know that the rulers of
·other nations [the Gentiles] love to ·show their power [lord it] over the
people, and their ·important leaders [high officials; Lgreat ones] love to
·use [exert] their authority [Lover them]. 43But it ·should not be [must not
be; is not to be] that way among you. [Instead, LBut] Whoever wants to
become great among you must ·serve the rest of you like a servant [Lbe
your servant]. 44Whoever wants to become the first among you must
·serve all of you like a slave [Lbe your slave]. 45In the same way, the Son of
Man did not come to be served. He came to serve others and to give his
life as a ransom for many people [Is. 53:12; John 11:49–50]."

Jesus Heals a Blind Man
(10:46–52; Matt. 20:29–34; Luke 18:35–43)

46Then they came to the town of Jericho. As Jesus was leaving there
with his ·followers [disciples] and a great many people, a blind beggar
named Bartimaeus [which means] son of Timaeus was sitting by the
road. 47When he heard that Jesus from Nazareth was walking by, he began
to shout, "Jesus, Son of David [Ca title for the Messiah, a descendant of
King David; 2 Sam. 7:11–16], ·have mercy [take pity] on me!"
48Many people ·warned [rebuked; scolded] the blind man to be quiet,
but he shouted even more, "Son of David, ·have mercy [take pity] on me!"
49Jesus stopped and said, "Tell the man to come here."
So they called the blind man, saying, "·Cheer up [Take courage]! Get to
your feet. Jesus is calling you." 50The blind man jumped up, ·left his coat
there [threw off his cloak], and went to Jesus.
51Jesus asked him, "What do you want me to do for you?"
The blind man answered, "·Teacher [LRabbouni], I want to see."
52Jesus said, "Go, ·you are healed because you believed [your faith has
healed you]." At once the man could see, and he followed Jesus on the road.

Jesus Enters Jerusalem as a King
(11:1–14; Matt. 21:1–19; Luke 19:28–46)

11 As Jesus and his ·followers [disciples] were coming closer to Jerusalem, they came to the towns of Bethphage and Bethany near the Mount of Olives. From there Jesus sent two of his ·followers [disciples] 2and said to them, "Go to the town ·you can see there [ahead of you; *or* opposite you Ceither Bethphage, Bethany, or another village]. When you enter it, you will ·quickly [immediately] find a ·colt [young donkey] tied, which no one has ever ridden. Untie it and bring it here to me. 3If anyone asks you why you are doing this, tell him ·its Master [the Lord; *or* its Owner] needs the colt and ·he will send it at once [*or* he will return it soon; C"he" could be either Jesus or the colt's owner]."

4They went into the town, found a colt tied in the street near the door of a house, and untied it. 5Some people were standing there and asked, "What are you doing? Why are you untying that colt?" 6They answered the way Jesus told them to answer, and the people let them take the colt.

7They brought the colt to Jesus and put their coats on it, and Jesus sat on it [Zech. 9:9]. 8Many people spread their coats on the road. Others cut [leafy] branches in the fields and spread them on the road. 9The people were walking ahead of Jesus and behind him, shouting,

"·Praise God! [LHosanna! CA Hebrew word originally used in praying for help, but by this time a joyful shout of praise to God.]
·God bless [Blessed is] the One who comes in the name of the Lord [Ps. 118:26]!
10·God bless [Blessed is] the coming kingdom of our father David!
·Praise to God in heaven [LHosanna in the highest]!"

11Jesus entered Jerusalem and went into the Temple. After he had looked [around] at everything, since it was already late, he went out to Bethany with ·the twelve apostles [the Twelve].

12The next day as Jesus was leaving Bethany, he became hungry. 13Seeing a fig tree in leaf from far away, he went to see if it had any figs on it. But he found no figs, only leaves, because it was not the right season for figs. 14So Jesus said to the tree, "May no one ever eat fruit from you again." And Jesus' ·followers [disciples] heard him say this.

Jesus Goes to the Temple
(11:15–19; Matt. 21:12–13; Luke 19:45–48)

15When Jesus ·returned [came] to Jerusalem, he went into the ·Temple [temple complex; Cthe large temple area, not the inner building where only the priests could go] and began to ·throw [drive] out those who were buying and selling there. He turned over the tables of ·those who were exchanging different kinds of money [L the moneychangers], and he upset the benches of those who were selling doves [*or* pigeons; Cmoneychangers provided particular coins for the temple tax; doves or pigeons were sold for sacrifices; Lev. 5:7]. 16Jesus refused to allow anyone to carry goods through the Temple courts. 17Then he taught the people, saying, "It is written in the Scriptures, 'My ·Temple [LHouse] will be called a house for prayer for people from all nations' [Is. 56:7]. But you ·are changing God's house [Lhave made it] into a ·'hideout for robbers' [Tden of thieves'; Jer. 7:11]."

18The ·leading [Tchief] priests and the ·teachers of the law [scribes] heard all this and began trying to find a way to kill Jesus. They were afraid of him, because all the people were amazed at his teaching. 19That evening, Jesus and his ·followers*n* [disciples] left the city.

The Power of Faith
(11:20–26; Matt. 6:14–15; 21:20–22)

20The next morning as Jesus was passing by with his ·followers [disciples],

11:19 his followers Some Greek copies mention only Jesus here.

they saw the fig tree ·dry and dead [withered], even to the roots. [21]Peter ·remembered the tree and said to Jesus, "·Teacher [LRabbi], look! The fig tree you cursed is ·dry and dead [withered]!"

[22]Jesus answered, "Have faith in God. [23]I tell you the truth, you can say to this mountain, '·Go [Be lifted up], fall into the sea.' And if you have no doubts in your ·mind [heart] and believe that what you say will happen, ·God will do it for you [it will be done for you]. [24]So I tell you to believe that you have received ·the things [everything] you ask for in prayer, and ·God will give them to you [you will receive them]. [25]When you ·are praying [Lstand praying], if you ·are angry with [have anything against] someone, forgive him so that your Father in heaven will also forgive your ·sins [transgressions; trespasses]. |[26]But if you don't forgive other people, then your Father in heaven will not forgive your ·sins [transgressions; trespasses].|"[n]

Leaders Doubt Jesus' Authority
(11:27–33; Matt. 21:23–27; Luke 20:1–8)

[27]Jesus and his ·followers [disciples] went again to Jerusalem. As Jesus was walking in the Temple [complex; area; courts; see 11:15], the ·leading [Tchief] priests, the ·teachers of the law [scribes], and the elders came to him. [28]They said to him, "What authority do you have to do these things? Who gave you this authority?"

[29]Jesus answered, "I will ask you one question. If you answer me, I will tell you what authority I have to do these things. [30]Tell me: When John baptized people, was that authority from ·God [Lheaven; Ca reverential Jewish way of referring to God] or just from ·other people [human beings]?"

[31]They argued about Jesus' question, saying, "If we answer, 'John's baptism was from ·God [Lheaven],' Jesus will say, 'Then why didn't you believe him?' [32]But if we say, 'It was from ·other people [human beings],' the crowd will be against us." (These leaders were afraid of the people, because all the people believed that John was a prophet.)

[33]So they answered Jesus, "We don't know."

Jesus said to them, "Then I won't tell you what authority I have to do these things."

The Story of the Evil Farmers
(12:1–12; Matt. 21:33–46; Luke 20:9–19)

12 [Then] Jesus began ·to use stories to teach the people [Lto speak to them in parables; see 3:23]. He said, "A man planted a vineyard. He put a wall around it and dug a ·hole [vat; pit] for a winepress and built a tower [Cto protect against thieves; see Is. 5:1–7 for the background to this parable]. Then he leased the land to some [Ctenant] farmers and left for a trip [Cthe owner represents God, the farmers are Israel's religious leaders]. [2]When it was time for the grapes to be picked, he sent a ·servant [slave] to the farmers to get his share of the grapes. [3]But the farmers grabbed ·the servant [Lhim] and beat him and sent him away empty-handed. [4]Then the man sent another ·servant [slave]. They ·hit [beat] him on the head and ·showed no respect for [humiliated; dishonored] him. [5]So the man sent another, whom they killed. The man sent many others; the farmers beat some of them and killed others [Cthe servants represent the prophets God sent to Israel].

[6]"The man had one person left to send, his son whom he loved [Crepresenting Jesus; see 1:11; 9:7]. He sent him last of all, saying, 'They will respect my son.'

[7]"But the farmers said to each other, 'This son will inherit the vineyard.

11:26 But . . . sins. Some Greek copies do not contain the bracketed text.

Let's kill him, and the inheritance will be ours.' 8So they took the son, killed him, and threw him out of the vineyard.

9"So what will the ·owner [lord] of the vineyard do? He will come and ·kill [destroy] those farmers and will give the vineyard to ·other farmers [Lothers; Creferring to the sinners who were responding to Jesus' call for repentance, and eventually to the Gentiles who would be saved]. 10·Surely you have read [LHave you never read…?] this Scripture:

'The stone that the builders rejected
  became the ·cornerstone [capstone; keystone; Lhead of the corner;
    Cthe meaning is uncertain, but clearly refers to the most important
    stone in the building; Jesus is the rejected stone].
11The Lord did this,
  and it is ·wonderful [amazing; marvelous] ·to us [for us to see; Lin
    our eyes; Ps. 118:22–23].'"

12The Jewish leaders knew that the ·story [parable] was about them. So they ·wanted to find a way [were seeking/trying] to arrest Jesus, but they were afraid of the people. So the leaders left him and went away.

Is It Right to Pay Taxes or Not?

(12:13–17; Matt 22:15–22; Luke 20:20–26)

13Later, the Jewish leaders sent some Pharisees and Herodians [Ca political group that supported king Herod and his family; 3:6] to Jesus to ·trap [catch] him in saying something wrong. 14They came to him and said, "Teacher, we know that you are ·an honest man [true; honest; sincere]. You are not ·afraid of [concerned about] what other people think about you, because you ·pay no attention to who they are [play no favorites; are impartial; aren't swayed by appearances]. And you teach ·the truth [with sincerity/honesty] about God's way. Tell us: Is it ·right [permissible; lawful] to pay taxes to Caesar or not? 15Should we pay them, or not?" [CSaying "yes" would anger Jews who hated Roman rule; saying "no" could result in being charged with insurrection.]

But knowing ·what these men were really trying to do [Ltheir hypocrisy], Jesus said to them, "Why are you ·trying to trap [testing] me? Bring me a ·coin [Ldenarius; Ca Roman coin worth a day's wages] to look at." 16They gave Jesus a coin, and he asked, "Whose ·image [likeness; portrait] and ·name [inscription] are on the coin?"

They answered, "Caesar's." [CIronically, the religious leaders carry coins bearing the idolatrous image of Caesar.]

17Then Jesus said to them, "·Give [TRender] to Caesar the things that are Caesar's, and give to God the things that are God's." They were amazed at what Jesus said.

Some Sadducees Try to Trick Jesus

(12:18–27; Matt 22:23–33; Luke 20:27–40)

18Then some Sadducees came to Jesus and asked him a question. (Sadducees believed that people would not rise from the dead.) 19They said, "Teacher, Moses wrote that if a man's brother dies, leaving a wife but no children, then that man must marry the widow and ·have children [Lraise up offspring/seed] for his brother [Deut. 25:5]. 20Once there were seven brothers. The first brother ·married [Ltook a wife] and died, leaving no children. 21So the second brother married the widow, but he also died and had no children. The same thing happened with the third brother. 22All seven brothers married her and died, and none of the brothers had any children. Finally the woman died too. 23Since all seven brothers had married her, ·when people rise from the dead [Lat the resurrection], whose wife will she be?"

24Jesus answered, "·You are mistaken [LAre you not mistaken/in error…?] because you don't know what the Scriptures say, and don't you

know about the power of God. 25[LFor] When people rise from the dead,
they will not marry, nor will they be given to someone to marry. They will
be like the angels in heaven. 26·Surely you have read [LHave you not
read…?] what God said about people rising from the dead. In the book in
which Moses wrote about the burning bush [Ex. 3:1–12], it says that God
told Moses, 'I am the God of Abraham, the God of Isaac, and the God of
Jacob [Ex. 3:6; CGod is still the God of the patriarchs, so they must have a
continued existence after death].' 27God is the God of the living, not the
dead. You Sadducees are ·wrong [greatly deceived; badly mistaken]!"

The Most Important Command
(12:28–34; Matt. 22:34–40; Luke 10:25–28)

28One of the ·teachers of the law [scribes] came and heard Jesus arguing with the Sadducees. Seeing that Jesus gave good answers to their
questions, he asked Jesus, "Which of the commands is most important?"
29Jesus answered, "The most important command is this: '·Listen, people of Israel [THear, O Israel]! The Lord our God is ·the only Lord [one
Lord]. 30Love the Lord your God with all your heart, all your soul, all your
mind, and all your strength' [Deut. 6:4–5; Cthese are the opening words of
the *Shema*, the prayer said by pious Jews twice a day]. 31The second command is this: 'Love your neighbor as you love yourself' [Lev. 19:18]. There
are no commands ·more important [greater] than these."
32The man answered, "·That was a good answer [Well said!], Teacher.
You were right when you said God is ·the only Lord [one] and there is no
other God besides him. 33One must love God with all his heart, all his
mind, and all his strength. And one must love his neighbor as he loves
himself. These commands are more important than all the ·animals
[burnt offerings] and sacrifices we offer to God [1 Sam. 15:22; Hos. 6:6;
Mic. 6:6–8]."
34When Jesus saw that the man answered him ·wisely [thoughtfully;
with insight], Jesus said to him, "You are close to the kingdom of God."
And after that, no one ·was brave enough [dared] to ask Jesus any more
questions.

The Question About David's Son
(12:35–40; Matt. 22:41–23:36; Luke 20:41–47)

35As Jesus was teaching in the Temple [courts; complex], he asked,
"Why do the ·teachers of the law [scribes] say that the ·Christ [Messiah]
is the ·son [descendant] of David [Csee 2 Sam. 7:12]? 36David himself,
speaking by the Holy Spirit, said:
'The Lord said to my Lord,
"Sit by me at my right ·side [Lhand; Cthe place of greatest honor beside
the king],
until I put your enemies ·under your control [Lbeneath your feet;
Cmeaning defeated or made subject to your authority;
Ps. 110:1]."'
37David himself calls ·the Christ [the Messiah; Lhim] 'Lord,' so how can
·the Christ [the Messiah; Lhe] be his son?" The large crowd listened to
Jesus with pleasure.
38Jesus continued teaching and said, "Beware of the ·teachers of the law
[scribes]. They like to walk around ·wearing fancy clothes [in long robes],
and they love for people to greet them with respect in the marketplaces.
39They love to have the most important seats in the synagogues and at
·feasts [banquets]. 40But they ·cheat widows and steal their houses
[Ldevour widows' homes] and then try to make themselves look good by
saying long prayers [in public]. They will receive a greater ·punishment
[judgment; condemnation]."

True Giving
(12:41–44; Luke 21:1–4)

41Jesus sat near the Temple ·money box [offering chest; *or* treasury] and watched the people put in their money. Many rich people gave large sums of money. 42Then a poor widow came and put in ·two small copper coins [Ltwo *lepta*], ·which were only worth a few cents [Lwhich is a *quadrans;* Ca Roman coin worth 1/64 of a denarius, or about 10 minutes of work for a day laborer].

43Calling his ·followers [disciples] to him, Jesus said, "I tell you the truth, this poor widow gave more than all those rich people. 44They gave ·only what they did not need [out of their surplus/abundance]. This woman is very poor, but she gave all she had—everything she had to live on."

The Temple Will Be Destroyed
(13:1–37; Matt. 24:1–51; Luke 21:5–36)

13 As Jesus was leaving the Temple (courts; complex), one of his ·followers [disciples] said to him, "Look, Teacher! ·How big the stones are! [LWhat stones!] ·How beautiful the buildings are! [LWhat buildings!]"

2Jesus said, "Do you see all these great buildings? Not one stone will be left on another. Every stone will be ·thrown [torn; pulled] down."

3Later, as Jesus was sitting on the Mount of Olives, ·opposite [across from] the Temple [complex], he was alone with Peter, James, John, and Andrew. They asked Jesus, 4"Tell us, when will these things happen? And what will be the sign that they are going to ·happen [be accomplished/fulfilled]?"

5Jesus began to answer them, "·Be careful [Watch out] that no one ·fools [deceives; misleads] you. 6Many people will come in my name, saying, 'I am ·the One [*or* he; CMessiah or savior],' and they will ·fool [deceive; mislead] many people. 7When you hear about wars and ·stories of wars that are coming [rumors/reports of wars], don't be afraid. These things must happen ·before the end comes [but that is not yet the end]. 8Nations will ·fight [Lrise up] against other nations, and kingdoms against other kingdoms. There will be earthquakes in ·different [various] places, and there will be ·times when there is no food for people to eat [famines]. These things are ·like the first pains when something new is about to be born [Lthe beginning of birth pains].

9"You must ·be careful [watch out; be on guard]. People will arrest you and take you to ·court [local councils] and ·beat [flog] you in their synagogues. You will be forced to stand before governors and kings to ·tell them [testify; bear witness] about me, ·because you follow me [on account of me]. 10But before these things happen, the ·Good News [Gospel] must be ·told [preached; proclaimed] to all ·people [nations]. 11When you are arrested and ·judged [brought to trial], don't worry ahead of time about what you should say. Say whatever is given you to say at that time, because it will not really be you speaking; it will be the Holy Spirit.

12"Brothers will ·give [betray; hand over] their own brothers to ·be killed [death], and fathers will give their own children to ·be killed [death]. Children will ·fight [rebel; rise up] against their own parents and cause them to be put to death. 13All people will hate you because ·you follow me [Lof my name], but those people who ·keep their faith [endure; stand firm; persevere] until the end will be saved.

14"You will see '·a blasphemous object that brings destruction' [Tthe abomination of desolation; Ca phrase taken from Dan. 9:27; 11:31; 12:11, and originally referring to the desecration of the Temple by Antiochus Epiphanes in 168 BC] standing where ·it [*or* he] should not be." (You who read this should understand what it means [Cprobably a reference to the

(soon-to-occur) destruction of Jerusalem in AD 70].) "At that time, the
people in Judea should ·run away [flee] to the mountains. 15If people are
on the roofs of their houses [Croofs in Palestine were flat and used as spare
rooms and for storage], they must not go down or go inside to get anything out of their houses. 16If people are in the fields, they must not go
back to get their ·coats [cloaks]. 17At that time, ·how terrible it will be for
[Lwoe to] women who are pregnant or have nursing babies! 18Pray that
these things will not happen in ·winter [bad weather], 19because those
days will be full of ·trouble [distress; Ttribulation]. There will be more
·trouble [distress; Ttribulation] than there has ever been since the beginning, when God made the world, until now, and nothing as bad will ever
happen again [Dan. 12:1]. 20·God has decided to make that terrible time
short [LIf the Lord had not shortened those days…]. Otherwise, no one
would ·go on living [survive; Lbe saved]. But God will make that time
short ·to help [for the sake of] ·the people [the elect] he has chosen. 21At
that time, someone might say to you, 'Look, there is the ·Christ [Messiah]!'
Or another person might say, 'There he is!' But don't believe them. 22False
·Christs [Messiahs] and false prophets will ·come [appear; rise up] and
perform ·great wonders [signs; miracles] and ·miracles [wonders; mar-
vels]. They will try to ·fool [mislead; deceive] even the ·people God has
chosen [elect], if that is possible. 23So ·be careful [watch out; be on guard].
I have warned you about all this before it happens.

24"During the days after this ·trouble [tribulation; distress] comes,
'the sun will grow dark,
and the moon will not give its light.
25The stars will fall from ·the sky [heaven].
And the ·powers of the heavens [celestial bodies] will be shaken'
[Is. 13:10; 34:4; cf. Ezek. 32:7–8; Joel 2:10, 31].

26"Then people will see the Son of Man coming in clouds with great
power and glory [Dan. 7:13]. 27Then he will send his angels to gather his
·chosen people [elect] from ·all around the earth [the four winds], from
·every part [the farthest end] of the earth and from ·every part [the farthest end] of heaven [Deut. 30:4; Zech. 2:6].

28"Learn a ·lesson [parable; analogy] from the fig tree: When its branches
·become green and soft [become tender; sprout] and new leaves appear, you
know summer is near. 29In the same way, when you see these things happening, you will know that ·the time [*or* he] is near, ·ready to come [right at the
door]. 30I tell you the truth, all these things will happen ·while the people of
this time are still living [before this generation passes away; Ceither the generation that sees the destruction of Jerusalem (AD 70), or a future generation
of the end times]. 31·Earth and sky will be destroyed [THeaven and earth will
pass away], but the words I have said will never ·be destroyed [pass away].

32"No one knows when that day or ·time [hour] will be, not the angels
in heaven, not even the Son. Only the Father knows. 33·Be careful [Watch
out; Be on guard]! Always be ·ready" [alert; watching], because you don't
know when that [appointed] time will be. 34It is like a man who goes on a
·trip [journey]. He leaves his house and lets his servants take care of it,
giving each one ·a special job [his own work] to do. The man tells the
servant guarding the door always to be watchful. 35So ·always be ready
[stay alert; keep watching], because you don't know when the ·owner

13:33 ready Some Greek copies continue, "and pray."

[master; lord] of the house will come back. It might be in the evening, or at midnight, or ·in the morning while it is still dark [[L]when the rooster crows], or when the sun rises. 36Always be ready. Otherwise he might come back suddenly and find you sleeping. 37I tell you this, and I say this to everyone: 'Be ·ready [alert; watchful]!' "

The Plan to Kill Jesus
(14:1–2; Matt 26:1–5; Luke 22:1–2)

14 It was now only two days before the Passover and the Feast of Unleavened Bread [[C]the annual festival that celebrates God's rescue of Israel from Egypt; Ex. 12]. The ·leading [[T]chief] priests and ·teachers of the law [scribes] were trying to find a ·trick [secret way] to arrest Jesus and kill him. 2But they said, "We must not do it during the feast, because the people might cause a riot."

A Woman with Perfume for Jesus
(14:3–9; Matt 26:6–13; Luke 7:36–50; John 12:1–8)

3Jesus was in Bethany at the house of ·Simon, who had a skin disease [[L]Simon the leper; [C]for leprosy, see 1:40; Simon may have been healed by Jesus]. While Jesus was ·eating there [[L]reclining; [C]the posture for a banquet or dinner party; 2:15], a woman approached him with an alabaster ·jar [vial] filled with very expensive perfume, made of pure nard. She ·opened [broke open] the ·jar [vial] and poured the perfume on Jesus' head.

4Some who were there became ·upset [indignant] and said to each other, "Why waste that perfume? 5It was worth ·a full year's work [[L]over three hundred denarii]. It could have been sold and the money given to the poor." And they ·got very angry with [harshly scolded] the woman.

6Jesus said, "Leave her alone. Why are you ·troubling [bothering; criticizing] her? She did an ·excellent thing [beautiful/good deed] for me. 7You will always have the poor with you, and you can help them anytime you want [Deut. 15:11]. But you will not always have me. 8This woman did the only thing she could do for me; she ·poured perfume on [anointed] my body to prepare me for burial. 9I tell you the truth, wherever the ·Good News [Gospel] is preached in all the world, what this woman has done will be told, and people will remember her."

Judas Betrays Jesus
(14:10–11; Matt 26:14–16; Luke 22:3–6)

10One of ·the twelve apostles [the Twelve], Judas Iscariot, went to talk to the ·leading [[T]chief] priests to offer to ·hand Jesus over [betray him] to them. 11These priests were pleased about this and promised to pay Judas money. So he watched for ·the best time [an opportunity] to ·turn Jesus in [betray him].

Jesus Eats the Passover Meal
(14:12–21; Matt 26:17–25; Luke 22:7–14, 21–23; John 13:21–30)

12It was now the first day of the Feast of Unleavened Bread when the Passover lamb was sacrificed. Jesus' ·followers [disciples] said to him, "Where do you want us to go and prepare for you to eat the Passover meal?"

13Jesus sent two of his ·followers [disciples] and said to them, "Go into the city and a man carrying a jar of water will meet you. Follow him. 14When he goes into a house, tell the owner of the house, 'The Teacher says: "Where is my guest room in which I can eat the Passover meal with my ·followers [disciples]?" ' 15The owner will show you a large ·room upstairs [[T]upper room] that is furnished and ready. ·Prepare the food [Make preparations] for us there."

16So the ·followers [disciples] left and went into the city. Everything happened as Jesus had said, so they prepared the Passover meal.

17In the evening, Jesus went to that house with the twelve. 18While they were all ·eating [[L]reclining and eating; see v. 3], Jesus said, "I tell you the truth, one of you will ·turn against [betray] me—one of you eating with me now."

19The ·followers [disciples] were very ·sad [distressed; pained] to hear
this. Each one began to say to Jesus, "·I am not the one, am I [Surely not
I; *or* Is it I]?"
20Jesus answered, "It is one of the twelve—one who dips his bread into
the bowl with me [Cprobably not a signal, but means "one who shares
close fellowship with me"]. 21The Son of Man will ·die [go to his fate; Lgo],
just as the Scriptures say. But ·how terrible it will be for [Lwoe to] the
person ·who hands the Son of Man over to be killed [Lby whom the Son
of Man is betrayed]. It would be better for him if he had never been born."

The Lord's Supper
(14:22–26; Matt. 26:26–30; Luke 22:15–20; 1 Cor. 11:23–25)

22While they were eating, Jesus took some bread and ·thanked God for
[blessed] it and broke it. Then he gave it to his ·followers [disciples] and
said, "Take it; this is my body."
23Then Jesus took a cup and ·thanked God for it [gave thanks] and gave
it to ·the followers [the disciples; them], and they all drank from the cup.
24Then Jesus said, "This is my blood ·which is the new[n] agreement that
God makes with his people [*or* which confirms/establishes the new covenant;
Lof the new covenant; Ex. 24:8. Jer. 31:31–34]. This blood is poured out for
many [Is. 53:12]. 25I tell you the truth, I will not drink of this fruit of the vine
[Cwine] again until that day when I drink it new in the kingdom of God."
26After singing a hymn [Cprobably the *Hallel* psalms (Ps. 113–118),
sung during the Passover meal], they went out to the Mount of Olives.

Jesus' Followers Will Leave Him
(14:27–31; Matt. 26:31–35; Luke 22:31–34; John 13:36–38)

27Then Jesus told them, "You will all ·stumble in your faith [fall away;
desert me], because it is written in the Scriptures:
'I will ·kill [strike] the shepherd,
and the sheep will ·scatter [be scattered]' [Zech. 13:7].
28But after ·I rise from the dead [LI am raised], I will go ahead of you into
Galilee."
29Peter said, "Everyone else may ·stumble in their faith [fall away; desert you], but I will not."
30Jesus answered, "I tell you the truth, tonight before the rooster crows
twice you will ·say three times you don't know me [deny/disown me three
times]."
31But Peter insisted, "Even if I must die with you, I will never ·say that
I don't know [deny/disown] you!" And all the others said the same thing.

Jesus Prays Alone
(14:32–42; Matt. 26:36–46; Luke 22:39–46; John 18:1)

32Jesus and his ·followers [disciples] went to a place called Gethsemane.
He said to them, "Sit here while I pray." 33Jesus took Peter, James, and
John with him, and he began to be very ·sad [distressed] and ·troubled
[anguished]. 34He said to them, "My ·heart [soul] is ·full of sorrow [over-
whelmed with grief], to the point of death. Stay here and ·watch [stay
awake; be alert]."
35After walking a little farther away from them, Jesus fell [with his face]
to the ground and prayed that, if possible, ·he would not have this time of
suffering [Lthe hour might pass him by]. 36He prayed, "Abba [CAramaic
for "father"], Father! You can do all things. ·Take away this cup of suffering [LTake this cup from me; Csuffering is metaphorically portrayed as
something bitter to drink; see 10:38]. But do ·what you want [your will],
not ·what I want [my will]."
37Then Jesus went back to his ·followers [disciples] and found them
asleep. He said to Peter, "Simon, are you sleeping? Couldn't you ·stay awake

14:24 new Some Greek copies do not have this word. Compare Luke 22:20.

[watch] with me for one hour? 38·Stay awake [Keep watch] and pray for strength ·against temptation [*or* not to fail the test]. The spirit ·wants to do what is right [is willing], but ·the body [human nature; [T]the flesh] is weak."

39Again Jesus went away and prayed the same thing. 40Then he went back to his ·followers [disciples], and again he found them asleep, because their eyes were very heavy. And they did not know what to say to him.

41After Jesus prayed a third time, he went back to his ·followers [disciples] and said to them, "·Are you still sleeping and resting? [*or* Go ahead, sleep and have your rest!] ·That's enough [It's over; The account is settled; [C]the meaning of this phrase is uncertain]. The time has come for the Son of Man to be ·handed over to [[L]betrayed/delivered into the hands of] sinful people. 42Get up, we must go. Look, here comes ·the man who has turned against me [my betrayer]."

Jesus Is Arrested
(14:43–52; Matt. 26:47–56; Luke 22:47–53; John 18:2–12)

43At once, while Jesus was still speaking, Judas, one of ·the twelve apostles [the Twelve], came up. With him were many people carrying swords and clubs who had been sent from the ·leading [[T]chief] priests, the ·teachers of the law [scribes], and the Jewish elders.

44·Judas [[L]The betrayer] had planned a signal for them, saying, "The man I kiss is Jesus. ·Arrest [Seize] him and guard him while you lead him away." 45So Judas went straight to Jesus and said, "·Teacher [[L]Rabbi]!" and kissed him. 46Then the people grabbed Jesus and arrested him. 47One of ·his followers [[L]those] standing nearby pulled out his sword and struck the servant of the high priest and cut off his ear.

48Then Jesus said, "You came to get me with swords and clubs as if I were a ·criminal [revolutionary; rebel; [L]robber; [C]the term "robber" was used by the Romans of insurrectionists]. 49Every day I was with you teaching in the Temple, and you did not arrest me there. But all these things have happened to ·make the Scriptures come true [fulfill the Scriptures]." 50Then ·all of Jesus' followers [[L]everyone] ·left [deserted] him and ·ran away [fled].

51A young man [[C]perhaps the author Mark himself], wearing only a linen ·cloth [sheet; shirt], was following Jesus, and the people also grabbed him. 52But the cloth [sheet; shirt] he was wearing came off, and he ran away naked.

Jesus Before the Leaders
(14:53–65; Matt. 26:57–68; John 18:13–24)

53The people who arrested Jesus led him to the house of the high priest, where all the ·leading [[T]chief] priests, the elders, and the ·teachers of the law [scribes] were gathered. 54Peter followed far behind and entered the courtyard of the high priest's house. There he sat with the guards, warming himself by the fire.

55The ·leading [[T]chief] priests and the whole ·Jewish council [Sanhedrin; [C]the highest Jewish court] tried to find ·something that Jesus had done wrong [evidence/testimony against him] so they could ·kill [execute] him. But the council could find no proof of anything. 56Many people came and ·told false things [gave false testimony] about him, but all said different things—none of them agreed.

57Then some people stood up and ·lied [gave false testimony] about Jesus, saying, 58"We heard this man say, 'I will destroy this Temple that people made. And three days later, I will build another Temple not made by people.' " 59But even ·the things these people said [their testimony] did not agree.

60Then the high priest stood before them and asked Jesus, "Aren't you going to answer? ·Don't you have something to say about their [*or* What

are these] ·charges [testimony] against you?" 61But Jesus ·said nothing
[was silent; Is. 53:7]; he did not answer.
The high priest asked Jesus another question: "Are you the ·Christ
[Messiah], the Son of ·the blessed God [Lthe blessed (one)]?"
62Jesus answered, "I am. And ·in the future you will see [Lyou will see]
the Son of Man sitting at the right ·side [Lhand; see 12:36] of God, the
Powerful One, and coming on clouds ·in the sky [of heaven; Ps. 110:1;
Dan. 7:13–14]."
63When the high priest heard this, he tore his clothes [Ca sign of sorrow
or outrage] and said, "Why do we need more witnesses? 64You all heard
·him say these things against God [the blasphemy]. What ·do you think
[is your verdict]?"
They all said that Jesus was guilty and ·should [deserved to] die. 65Some
of the people there began to spit at Jesus. They blindfolded him and beat
him with their fists and said, "·Prophesy! [Prove you are a prophet!]"
Then the guards led Jesus away and beat him.

Peter Denies Jesus
(14:66–72; Matt. 26:69–75; Luke 22:56–62; John 18:16–18, 25–27)

66While Peter was in the courtyard, a servant girl of the high priest came
there. 67She saw Peter warming himself at the fire and looked closely at him.
Then she said, "You also were with Jesus, that man from Nazareth."
68But Peter denied it. He said, "I don't know or understand what you
are talking about." Then Peter left and went toward the entrance of the
courtyard. And the rooster crowed.ⁿ
69The servant girl saw Peter there, and again she said to the people who
were standing nearby, "This man is one of those who followed Jesus."
70Again Peter ·said that it was not true [denied it].
A short time later, some people were standing near Peter saying,
"Surely you are one of those who followed Jesus, because you are from
Galilee, too [CPeter's Galilean accent gave him away; Matt. 26:73]."
71Then Peter began to place a curse on himself and swear, "I don't
know this man you're talking about!"
72At once, the rooster crowed the second time. Then Peter remembered
what Jesus had told him: "Before the rooster crows twice, you will ·say
three times that you don't know me [deny/disown me three times]." Then
Peter broke down and began to cry.

Pilate Questions Jesus
(15:1–5; Matt. 27:1–2, 11–14; Luke 23:1–5; John 18:28–38)

15 Very early in the morning, the ·leading [Tchief] priests, the
elders, the ·teachers of the law [scribes], and all the ·Jewish
council [Sanhedrin; see 14:55] decided what to do with Jesus. They ·tied
[bound] him, led him away, and turned him over to Pilate, the governor.
2Pilate asked Jesus, "Are you the king of the Jews?"
Jesus answered, "·Those are your words [It is as you say; LYou say so;
Can indirect affirmation]."
3The ·leading [Tchief] priests accused Jesus of many things. 4So Pilate
asked Jesus another question, "You can see that they are accusing you of
many things. Aren't you going to answer?"
5But Jesus still said nothing, so Pilate was ·very surprised [amazed].

Pilate Tries to Free Jesus
(15:6–15; Matt. 27:15–26; Luke 23:2–5, 13–25; John 18:39—19:15)

6Every year at the ·time of the Passover [festival/feast] the governor
would free one prisoner whom the people ·chose [requested]. 7At that
time, there was a man named Barabbas in prison, one of a group of rebels

14:68 And the rooster crowed. Some Greek copies do not have this phrase.

who had committed murder during ·a riot [the uprising/insurrection].
8The crowd came to Pilate and began to ask him to free a prisoner as he
always did.

9So Pilate asked them, "Do you want me to free the king of the Jews?"
10Pilate knew that the ·leading [Tchief] priests had turned Jesus in to him
because they were jealous. 11But the ·leading [Tchief] priests had ·per-
suaded [stirred up] the people to ask Pilate to free Barabbas, not Jesus.

12Then Pilate asked the crowd again, "So what should I do with this
man you call the king of the Jews?"

13They shouted, "Crucify him!"

14Pilate asked, "Why? What ·wrong [crime; evil] has he done?"

But they shouted even louder, "Crucify him!"

15Pilate wanted to ·please [satisfy] the crowd, so he freed Barabbas for
them. After having Jesus ·beaten with whips [flogged; scourged], he
handed Jesus over to the soldiers to be crucified.

The Soldiers Mock Jesus
(15:16–20; Matt. 27:27–31)

16The soldiers took Jesus into the [courtyard of the] governor's palace
(called the Praetorium) and called ·all the other soldiers [the whole
cohort] together [Ca cohort was about 500 soldiers; here it may mean those
of the cohort on duty]. 17They put a purple robe [Cprobably a scarlet military coat (Matt. 27:28), whose color resembled purple—the color of
royalty] on Jesus and used thorny branches to make a crown for his head.
18They began to ·call out to [greet; salute] him, "Hail, King of the Jews!"
19The soldiers beat Jesus on the head many times with a stick. They spit on
him and made fun of him by bowing on their knees and worshiping him.
20After they finished, the soldiers took off the purple robe and put his own
clothes on him again. Then they led him out of the palace to be crucified.

Jesus Is Crucified
(15:21–32; Matt. 27:31–44; Luke 23:26–43; John 19:17–27)

21A man named Simon from Cyrene, the father of Alexander and Rufus
[Cprobably two Christians known to Mark's readers], was coming from
the ·fields [countryside] to the city. The soldiers forced Simon to carry
the cross for Jesus. 22They led Jesus to the place called Golgotha, which
means [Cin Aramaic] the Place of the Skull. 23·The soldiers [L They; Cthis
could be the soldiers or the women of Jerusalem] tried to give Jesus wine
mixed with myrrh to drink [Ca narcotic meant to dull the pain; Prov. 31:6;
Ps. 69:21], but he refused. 24The soldiers crucified Jesus and divided his
clothes among themselves, throwing lots [Csimilar to dice] to decide what
each soldier would get [Ps. 22:18].

25It was ·nine o'clock in the morning [Lthe third hour] when they crucified Jesus. 26There was a sign with this charge against Jesus written on it:
THE KING OF THE JEWS. 27They also put two ·robbers [rebels; revolutionaries;
Cthe term "robber" was used by the Romans of insurrectionists] on crosses
beside Jesus, one on the right, and the other on the left. |28And the Scripture
came true that says, "They put him with criminals [Is. 53:12]."|[n] 29People
walked by and ·insulted [defamed; slandered; Cthe same Greek word used
to "blaspheme"] Jesus and shook their heads [Ca gesture of derision; Ps.
22:7], saying, "You said you could destroy the Temple and build it again in
three days. 30So save yourself! Come down from that cross!"

31The ·leading [Tchief] priests and the ·teachers of the law [scribes]
were also making fun of Jesus. They said to each other, "He saved other

---

15:28 And . . . criminals." Some Greek copies do not contain the bracketed text, which quotes from Isaiah 53:12.

people, but he can't save himself. 32If he is really the ·Christ [Messiah], the
king of Israel, let him come down now from the cross. When we see this,
we will believe in him." The robbers who were being crucified beside
Jesus also ·insulted [ridiculed; taunted] him.

Jesus Dies
(15:33–41; Matt. 27:45–56; Luke 23:44–49; John 19:25–30)

33At ·noon [Lthe sixth hour] the whole country became dark, and the
darkness lasted ·for three hours [Luntil the ninth hour]. 34At ·three o'clock
[Lthe ninth hour] Jesus cried in a loud voice, "Eloi, Eloi, lama sabachthani." This means [Cin Aramaic], "My God, my God, why have you
·abandoned [forsaken] me?" [Ps. 22:1]
35When some of the people standing there heard this, they said, "Listen!
He is calling Elijah." [CThe prophet Elijah was associated with the end
times (Mal. 4:5) and was also viewed as a helper in time of need.]
36Someone there ran and got a sponge, filled it with ·vinegar [*or* sour
wine; Can inexpensive drink used by soldiers and slaves], tied it to a ·stick
[reed], and gave it to Jesus to drink [Ps. 69:21]. He said, "[Leave him be;
Wait!] We want to see if Elijah will come to take him down from the cross."
37Then Jesus cried in a loud voice and ·died [breathed his last; Lexpired].
38The curtain [Cdividing the Most Holy Place from the rest of the tem-
ple] in the Temple was torn into two pieces, from the top to the bottom
[Crepresenting new access to the presence of God, and perhaps God's
judgment against the Temple leadership]. 39When the ·army officer [cen-
turion] who was standing in front of the cross saw ·what happened when
[*or* how] Jesus died,[n] he said, "This man really was the Son of God!"
40Some women were standing at a distance from the cross, watching;
among them were Mary Magdalene, Salome, and Mary the mother of
James and Joseph. (James was her youngest son.) 41These women had followed Jesus in Galilee and ·helped [cared for; supported] him. Many
other women were also there who had come with Jesus to Jerusalem.

Jesus Is Buried
(15:42–47; Matt. 27:57–61; Luke 23:50–56; John 19:38–42)

42This was Preparation Day. (That means the day before the Sabbath
day.) That evening, 43Joseph from Arimathea was ·brave [bold] enough to
go to Pilate and ask for Jesus' body. Joseph, an ·important [respected]
member of the ·Jewish council [Sanhedrin; see 14:55], was one of the
people who was waiting for the kingdom of God to come. 44Pilate was
amazed that Jesus would have already died, so he called the ·army officer
[centurion] and asked him if Jesus ·had already died [*or* had been dead
very long]. 45The officer told Pilate that he was dead, so Pilate told Joseph
he could have the body. 46Joseph bought some linen cloth, took the body
down from the cross, and wrapped it in the linen. He put the body in a
tomb that was cut out of a wall of rock. Then he rolled a [Clarge] stone to
block the entrance of the tomb. 47And Mary Magdalene and Mary the
mother of Joseph ·saw [took note of] the place where Jesus was laid.

Jesus Rises from the Dead
(16:1–8; Matt. 28:1–8; Luke 24:1–12; John 20:1–13)

16 The day after the Sabbath day, Mary Magdalene, Mary the
mother of James, and Salome bought some sweet-smelling
spices to ·put on [anoint] Jesus' body. 2Very early on that day, the first
day of the week, soon after sunrise, the women were on their way to the
tomb. 3They said to each other, "Who will roll away for us the stone that
covers the entrance of the tomb?"
4Then the women looked and saw that the stone had already been

15:39 when Jesus died Some Greek copies read "when Jesus cried out and died."

rolled away, even though it was very large. 5The women entered the tomb and saw a young man wearing a white robe and sitting on the right side, and they were ·afraid [alarmed; amazed].

6But the man said, "Don't be ·afraid [alarmed; amazed]. You are looking for Jesus from Nazareth, who has been crucified. He has risen from the dead; he is not here. Look, here is the place they laid him. 7Now go and tell his ·followers [disciples] and Peter, 'Jesus is going into Galilee ahead of you, and you will see him there as he told you before.' "

8The women were shaking with fear and ·confused [overwhelmed; bewildered], so they left the tomb and ran away. They did not tell anyone about what happened, because they were afraid.

Verses 9–20 are not included in some of the earliest surviving Greek copies of Mark and have significant stylistic differences from the rest of Mark's Gospel.

Some Followers See Jesus
(16:9–13; Matt. 28:9–10; Luke 24:13–35; John 20:14–18)

|9After Jesus rose from the dead early on the first day of the week, he showed himself first to Mary Magdalene. One time in the past, he had ·forced [driven; cast] seven demons out of her. 10After Mary saw Jesus, she went and told his followers, who were ·very sad [mourning; grieving] and were crying. 11But Mary told them that Jesus was alive. She said that she had seen him, but they did not believe her.

12Later, Jesus showed himself to two of ·his followers [his disciples; [L]them] while they were walking in the country, but he did not look the same as before. 13They went back to the others and told them what had happened, but again, they did not believe them.

Jesus Talks to the Disciples
(16:14–20; Matt. 28:16–20; Luke 24:36–43; John 20:19–23)

14Later Jesus showed himself to the eleven while they were ·eating [reclining at table; see 2:15], and he ·criticized [reprimanded; rebuked] them because they had no faith. They were ·stubborn [hard hearted] and refused to believe those who had seen him after he had risen from the dead.

15Jesus said to them, "Go everywhere in the world, and ·tell [preach; proclaim] the ·Good News [Gospel] to ·everyone [all creation]. 16Anyone who believes and is baptized will be saved, but anyone who does not believe will be ·punished [condemned]. 17And those who believe will be able to do these things as ·proof [signs]: They will use my name to ·force [drive; cast] out demons. They will speak in new ·languages [tongues]. 18They will pick up snakes and drink poison without being hurt. They will ·touch [lay hands on] the sick, and the sick will ·be healed [recover]."

19After the Lord Jesus said these things to them, he was carried up into heaven, and he sat at the right ·side [hand] of God. 20The ·followers [disciples] went everywhere in the world and ·told [preached; proclaimed] the ·Good News [Gospel] to people, and the Lord helped them. The Lord ·proved [confirmed] that the ·Good News [Gospel] they ·told [preached; proclaimed] was true by giving them power to work ·miracles [signs].|

LUKE

Luke Writes About Jesus' Life

1 **Many have ·tried to report on** [set out to compile an account/narrative of] **the things that ·happened** [have been fulfilled/accomplished] **among us** [John 20:31; Acts 1:1–3; 2 Pet. 1:16–19]. 2**They have written the same things that ·we learned from** [Lwere handed down by] **others—the ·people who saw those things** [Leyewitnesses] **from the beginning and ·served God by telling people his message** [Lwere servants of the word; Acts 10:39–41; 1 John 1:1–3]. 3**Since I myself have ·studied** [investigated; followed closely] **everything carefully from the beginning, most excellent** [Ca designation for someone with high social or political status] **Theophilus, it seemed ·good** [fitting] **for me to write it out for you. I arranged it ·in order** [*or* in an orderly manner], 4**to help you know that what you have been taught is ·true** [certain; reliable; John 20:31].

Zechariah and Elizabeth

5**During the time ·Herod ruled Judea** [Lof Herod, king of Judea], **there was a priest named Zechariah who belonged to ·Abijah's group** [the priestly division/order of Abijah; Cpriests were divided into twenty-four divisions; 2 Chr. 31:2]. **Zechariah's wife, Elizabeth, came from the ·family** [Ldaughters; Cfemale descendants] **of Aaron** [Cbrother of Moses and first high priest of Israel; for a priest like Zechariah to marry a woman of priestly ancestry was a special blessing]. 6[LBoth] **Zechariah and Elizabeth ·truly did what God said was good** [Lwere righteous before God]. **They ·did** [followed; walked in] **everything the Lord commanded and were ·without fault** [blameless] **in keeping his ·law** [regulations; requirements]. 7**But they had no children, because Elizabeth ·could not have a baby** [could not conceive; Twas barren], **and both of them were very old** [Gen. 17:17; 18:11].

8**One day Zechariah was serving as a priest before God, because his ·group** [order; division] **was on duty.** 9**According to the custom of the ·priests** [Lpriesthood], **he was chosen by lot** [Csimilar to dice; used to determine God's will] **to go into the Temple of the Lord and burn incense** [1 Chr. 6:49; Heb. 9:6]. 10**·There were a great many people** [LThe whole multitude of the people were] **outside praying at the ·time** [Lhour] **the incense was offered.** 11**Then an angel ·of** [sent by] **the Lord appeared to Zechariah, standing on the right side of the incense ·table** [altar]. 12**When he saw the angel, Zechariah was ·startled** [shaken] **and frightened.** 13**But the angel said to him, "Zechariah, don't be afraid. God has heard your ·prayer** [petition]. **Your wife, Elizabeth, will ·give birth to** [bear for you] **a son, and you will name him John.** 14**He will bring you joy and ·gladness** [delight], **and many people will ·be happy** [rejoice] **because of his birth.** 15[LFor; Because] **John will be a great man ·for** [in the eyes of; Lbefore] **the Lord. He will never drink wine or beer** [Cindicating he will be set apart to God for special service; Num. 6:3], **and even ·from birth** [*or* in his mother's womb; 1:41, 44], **he will be filled with the Holy**

Spirit. 16**He will help many ·people** [Lof the children] **of Israel return to the Lord their God** [1 Kin. 18:37]. 17**He will go before ·the Lord** [Lhim] **in** [the] **spirit and power ·like** [of] **Elijah. He will ·make peace between parents and** [Lturn the hearts of parents/fathers back to] **their children and will bring those who are not obeying God back to the ·right way of thinking** [*or* wisdom of the righteous], **·to make a people ready** [Lto prepare a people who are fit/ready] **for the ·coming of the Lord** [LLord; Mal. 4:5–6]."

18**Zechariah said to the angel, "How can I know ·that what you say is true** [Lthis]**?** [LFor] **I am an old man, and my wife is old, too** [Gen. 17:17]."

19**The angel answered him, "I am Gabriel** [Cone of two named angels in Scripture (the other is Michael); Dan. 8:16; 9:21; 10:10–14]. **I stand before God, who sent me to talk to you and to tell you this good news.** 20**Now, ·listen** [Llook; Tbehold]! **You will** [Lbe silent and] **not be able to speak until the day these things happen, because you did not believe ·what I told you** [Lmy words]. **·But they will really happen** [L...which will be fulfilled at their appointed time]."

21**Outside, the people were still waiting for Zechariah and were ·surprised that** [wondering why] **he was ·staying so long** [delayed] **in the Temple.** 22**When Zechariah came outside, he could not speak to them, and they knew he had seen a vision in the Temple. He could only ·make signs** [motion; gesture] **to them and remained unable to speak.** 23**When his ·time** [period; Ldays] **of service at the Temple was finished, he went home.**

24**·Later** [LAfter these days], **Zechariah's wife, Elizabeth, became pregnant and ·did not go out of her house** [went into seclusion; Lhid herself; Cthe reason is unknown, perhaps for quiet worship or to avoid gawking neighbors] **for five months. Elizabeth said,** 25**"·Look what** [This is what; LThus] **the Lord has done for me! He has** [Lwatched over me and] **taken away my disgrace among the people** [Cthe Jewish people thought it was a disgrace for a woman not to have children; Gen. 30:23]."

An Angel Appears to Mary

26**During Elizabeth's sixth month of pregnancy, God sent the angel Gabriel** [1:19] **to Nazareth, a town in Galilee,** 27**to a virgin. She was ·engaged to marry** [pledged to; Cengagement was a binding contract between two families and could only be broken by divorce] **a man named Joseph ·from the family** [a descendent; Lfrom the house] **of David. ·Her** [LThe virgin's] **name was Mary.** 28**The angel came to her and said, "·Greetings** [Hello; LRejoice; Ca common greeting]! **·The Lord has blessed you and is with you** [*or* ...favored one, the Lord is with you]."

29**But Mary was ·very startled** [disturbed; perplexed; troubled] **by what the angel said and wondered what ·this greeting might mean** [sort of greeting this was].

30**The angel said to her, "Don't be afraid, Mary;** [Lfor; because] **·God has shown you his grace** [Lyou have found favor/grace with God]. 31**·Listen** [LLook; TBehold]! **You will ·become pregnant** [Lconceive in your womb] **and give birth to a son, and you will name him Jesus** [Is. 7:14]. 32**He will be great and will be called the Son of the Most High. The Lord God will give him the throne of ·King David, his ancestor** [Lhis father David]. 33**He will ·rule** [reign] **over the ·people** [Lhouse] **of Jacob forever, and his kingdom will never end** [2 Sam. 7:13, 16; Dan. 7:14, 27]."

34**Mary said to the angel, "How ·will** [can] **this happen since ·I am a virgin** [LI have not known a man (sexually)]?"

35**The angel said to Mary, "The Holy Spirit will come ·upon** [over] **you,**

and the power of the Most High will ·cover [overshadow] you. For this reason the ·baby will be holy and [holy one to be born] will be called the Son
of God. 36·Now [[L]And look/[T]behold] Elizabeth, your relative, ·is also pregnant with [has also conceived] a son ·though she is very old [in her old age].
·Everyone thought she could not have a baby, but she has been pregnant for
six months. [[L]And this is the sixth month for the woman they called barren!] 37·God can do anything [...because nothing is impossible with God; *or*
...because no word/message from God will ever fail; Gen. 18:14; Jer. 32:17]!"
38Mary said, "[[L]Look; [T]Behold] I am the ·servant [bondservant;
[T]handmaid] of the Lord. Let this happen to me ·as you say [according to
your word]!" Then the angel ·went away [left her].

Mary Visits Elizabeth

39[[L]In those days] Mary got up and went quickly to a town in the hills
of Judea [[C]from Galilee in the north to southern Israel, about three or four
days journey by foot]. 40She ·came to [entered] Zechariah's house and
greeted Elizabeth. 41When Elizabeth heard Mary's greeting, the unborn
baby ·inside her [in her womb] ·jumped [leaped; kicked], and Elizabeth
was filled with the Holy Spirit. 42She cried out in a loud voice, "·God has
blessed you [[L]You are blessed] ·more than any other woman [[L]among
women], and ·he has blessed the baby to which you will give birth
[[L]blessed is the fruit of your womb]. 43[[L]But] Why ·has this good thing
happened to me [am I so honored], that the mother of my Lord comes to
me? 44[[L]For look/[T]behold] When I heard ·your voice [[L]the sound of your
greeting], the baby inside ·me [my womb] ·jumped [leaped; kicked] with
joy. 45·You are blessed because you [[L]Blessed is she who has] believed that
what the Lord said would ·really happen [be fulfilled]."

Mary Praises God

46Then Mary said,

"My soul ·praises [exalts; glorifies; magnifies] the Lord [1 Sam. 2:1–10];
47 my ·heart [spirit] rejoices in God my Savior [Ps. 35:9],
48because he has ·shown his concern for [noticed; looked favorably on]
his ·humble [lowly] servant girl [1 Sam. 1:11].
[[L]For look/[T]behold] From now on, all ·people [[L]generations] will ·say
that I am [call me] blessed [Ps. 138:6],
49 because the ·Powerful [Mighty] One has done great things for me.
His name is holy.
50·God will show his mercy [[L]His mercy is/continues] ·forever and ever
[[L]to generations and generations]
to those who ·worship and serve [[L]fear; reverence] him [Ps. 103:17].
51He has done mighty deeds ·by his power [[L]with his arm; [C]a metaphor
for strength].
He has scattered the people who are proud
·and think great things about themselves [*or* in the schemes they
devise; [L]in the thoughts/intentions of their hearts].
52He has brought down ·rulers [the powerful] from their thrones
and ·raised up [exalted] the ·humble [lowly].
53He has filled the hungry with good things [Ps. 107:9]
and sent the rich away ·with nothing [empty-handed].
54He has helped his servant, the people of Israel,
·remembering to show them [mindful of his] mercy
55as he promised to our ancestors,
to Abraham and to his ·children [descendants; [L]seed] forever
[Gen. 17:7, 19]."

56 Mary stayed with Elizabeth for about three months and then
returned home.

The Birth of John

57 When it was time for Elizabeth to give birth, she had a ·boy [L son].
58 Her neighbors and relatives heard how ·good [greatly merciful] the
Lord was to her, and they rejoiced with her.
59 When the baby was eight days old, they came to circumcise him
[Gen. 17:12]. They ·wanted [were about] to name him Zechariah because
this was his father's name, 60 but his mother said, "No! He will be named
John."
61 The people said to Elizabeth, "But no one in your family has this
name." 62 Then they made ·signs [gestures; motions] to his father to find
out what he would like to name him [C indicating that Zechariah was not
only mute but also deaf].
63 Zechariah ·asked [motioned] for a writing tablet and wrote, "His
name is John," and everyone ·was surprised [marveled; was amazed].
64 Immediately ·Zechariah could talk again [L his mouth was opened and
his tongue freed], and he began ·praising [blessing] God. 65 All their neighbors ·became alarmed [were afraid/in awe], and in all the ·mountains [hill
country] of Judea people continued talking about all these things. 66 The
people who heard about them ·wondered [L kept/pondered them in their
hearts], saying, "What will this child [turn out to] be?" because the [L hand
of the; C a metaphor for empowering presence] Lord was with him.

Zechariah Praises God

67 Then Zechariah, John's father, was filled with the Holy Spirit and
prophesied:

68 "·Let us praise [L Blessed be] the Lord, the God of Israel,
because he has ·come to help his people and has given them freedom
[L visited and accomplished redemption for his people].
69 He has ·given us a powerful Savior [L raised up a horn of salvation for
us; C referring to the horn of a powerful animal—a metaphor for
strength; 1 Sam. 2:1, 10; Ps. 132:17; Ezek. 29:21]
·from the family [L in the house] of God's servant David.
70 [L ...just as] He said that he would do this
through [L the mouth of] his holy prophets who lived long ago:
71 He promised he would save us from our enemies
and from the ·power [L hand; C indicating controlling power or
oppression] of all those who hate us.
72 He said he would give mercy to our ·ancestors [forefathers]
and that he would remember his holy ·promise [covenant].
73 ·God promised [L The oath that he swore to] Abraham, our father
[Gen. 22:16–18],
74 that he would ·save [rescue] us from the ·power [hand; v. 71] of our
enemies
so we could serve him without fear,
75 being holy and ·good [righteous] before God as long as we live.
76 "Now you, child, will be called ·a [*or* the] prophet of the Most High
God.
[L For] You will go before the Lord to prepare his ·way [*or* paths;
Mal. 3:1].
77 You will ·make his people know that they will be saved [L give his
people the knowledge of salvation]
by having their sins forgiven [Jer. 31:34].

78·With [*or* Because of] the ·loving [tender] mercy of our God,
·a new day from heaven will dawn upon us [Lthe sunrise/dawn from
heaven will visit us; Ca metaphor for the Messiah; Mal. 4:2].
79It will shine on those who ·live [dwell; sit] in darkness,
in the shadow of death [Is. 9:2].
It will guide ·us [Lour feet] into the path of peace [Is. 59:8]."
80And so the child grew up and became strong ·in spirit [*or* in the
Spirit]. John lived in the ·desert [wilderness] until the time when he ·came
out to preach [appeared; was revealed] to Israel.

The Birth of Jesus

2 At that time, Augustus Caesar sent an ·order [decree] that all people in the ·countries under Roman rule [empire; Roman world]
must ·list their names in a register [register for taxation]. 2·This was the
first registration; it was taken while Quirinius was governor of Syria [*or*
This was the first census while Quirinius was governor of Syria; *or* This
census occurred before Quirinius was governor of Syria]. 3And all went to
their own towns to be registered.
4So Joseph left Nazareth, a town in Galilee, and went to the town of
Bethlehem in Judea, known as the town of David [CBethlehem was David's
hometown]. Joseph went there because he was from the ·family [Lhouse
and family line] of David. 5Joseph registered with Mary, to whom he was
·engaged [pledged to be married; see 1:27] and who was now pregnant.
6While they were in Bethlehem, the time came for Mary to have the baby,
7and she gave birth to her first son. She wrapped the baby ·with pieces of
cloth [in cloths; Tin swaddling clothes] and laid him in a ·feeding trough
[Tmanger], because there ·were no rooms [was no space/room] left in the
·inn [*or* guest room (of a private residence); *or* caravan shelter].

Shepherds Hear About Jesus

8·That night [LAt night], some shepherds were [living out] in the fields
·nearby [Lin that region/place] watching their ·sheep [Lflock]. 9Then an
angel of the Lord stood before them. The glory of the Lord ·was shining
around [surrounded] them, and they became very frightened. 10The
angel said to them, "Do not be afraid. [L...for/because] I am bringing you
good news that will ·be a [*or* bring] great joy to all the people. 11Today
your Savior was born in the town of David. He is ·Christ [the Messiah],
the Lord. 12This ·is how you will know him [will be the sign for you]: You
will find a baby wrapped in ·pieces of cloth [cloths; Tswaddling clothes]
and lying in a ·feeding trough [Tmanger]."
13·Then [LAnd suddenly] a ·very large group [*or* great army] of angels
from heaven ·joined [appeared with] the first angel, praising God and
saying:
14"Give glory to God in ·heaven [the highest place/heaven],
and on earth let there be peace among the people ·who please God
[*or* he favors; Lof his pleasure/approval]."*n*
15When the angels left them and went back to heaven, the shepherds
said to each other, "Let's go to Bethlehem. Let's see this thing that has
happened which the Lord has told us about."
16So the shepherds went quickly and found Mary and Joseph and the
baby, who was lying in a ·feeding trough [Tmanger]. 17When they had seen
him, they ·told [spread the word about; let people know] what the angels had

2:14 and...God Some Greek copies read "and on earth let there be peace and goodwill among people."

said about this child. 18Everyone [Lwho heard] ·was amazed [wondered; marveled] at what the shepherds said to them. 19But Mary ·treasured [kept; preserved] these things and ·continued to think about them [Lpondered/considered them in her heart]. 20Then the shepherds went back to their sheep, ·praising [glorifying] God and ·thanking [praising] him for everything they had seen and heard. It had been just as the angel had told them.

21When ·the baby was eight days old [Leight days were fulfilled; Gen. 17:12; Lev. 12:3], he was circumcised [1:59] and was named Jesus, the name given by the angel before ·the baby began to grow inside Mary [Lhe was conceived in the womb].

Jesus Is Presented in the Temple

22When the ·time came [Ldays were fulfilled] for ·Mary and Joseph to do what the law of Moses taught about being made pure [Ltheir purification according the law of Moses; Can animal sacrifice and ritual cleansing forty days after the birth of a son; see Lev. 12:2–8], they took Jesus [Lup] to Jerusalem to present him to the Lord. 23([LJust as] It is written in the law of the Lord: "Every ·firstborn male [Lmale who opens the womb; Can idiom for a firstborn] shall be ·given [set apart; consecrated; Lcalled holy] to the Lord" [Ex. 13:2].) 24Mary and Joseph also went to offer a sacrifice, as the law of the Lord says: "You must sacrifice two ·doves [*or* turtledoves] or two young pigeons [Lev. 5:11; 12:8]."

Simeon Sees Jesus

25[Now; LAnd behold] In Jerusalem ·lived [Lwas] a man named Simeon who was ·a good man [righteous; just] and ·godly [devout; reverent]. He was waiting for the ·time when God would take away Israel's sorrow [restoration/consolation of Israel; Is. 40:1] and the Holy Spirit was ·in [*or* upon] him. 26·Simeon had been told [LIt had been revealed to him] by the Holy Spirit that he would not die before he saw ·the Christ promised by the Lord [Lthe Lord's Messiah/Anointed One]. 27The Spirit led Simeon to the Temple. When ·Mary and Joseph [Lthe parents] brought the ·baby [child] Jesus to the Temple to do [Lfor him] what ·the law said they must do [the custom of the law required], 28Simeon took the baby in his arms and ·thanked [praised; blessed] God:

29"Now, Lord, you can let me, your servant,
·die [Ldepart; be dismissed] in peace ·as you said [Laccording to your word].
30With my own eyes I have seen your salvation [Is. 52:10],
31 which you prepared ·before [in the presence of] all ·people [nations; people groups].
32It is a light ·for the Gentiles to see [Lof revelation for the Gentiles/nations; Is. 42:6; 49:6]
and ·an honor [the glory] for your people, ·the Israelites [LIsrael]."

33Jesus' father and mother were amazed at what Simeon had said about him. 34Then Simeon blessed them and said to ·Mary [Lhis mother], "·God has chosen this child [LLook/TBehold, this one is destined/appointed] to cause the fall and rise of many in Israel. ·He will be a sign from God that many people will not accept [L...and to be a sign that is spoken against] 35so that the thoughts of many [Lhearts] will be made known. And ·the things that will happen will make your heart sad, too [La sword will pierce your own soul; CMary will experience deep sorrow over the death of Jesus]."

Anna Sees Jesus

36There was a prophetess, ·Anna, [LHannah] ·from the family [Lthe daughter] of Phanuel ·in [who was from] the tribe of Asher. She was very old and had once been married for seven years. 37 Then her husband died, and she was a widow ·for [*or* to the age of] eighty-four years. She never left the Temple but worshiped God, ·going without food [fasting] and praying day and night. 38 ·Standing there [*or* Coming up to them] at that time, she ·thanked [praised; blessed] God and spoke about ·Jesus [L him] to all who were waiting for ·God to free [L the redemption/deliverance of] Jerusalem.

Joseph and Mary Return Home

39 When Joseph and Mary had done everything the law of the Lord commanded, they went home to Nazareth, their own town in Galilee [Matt. 2:22–23]. 40 The little child grew and became strong. He was filled with wisdom, and God's ·goodness [favor; grace] was upon him.

Jesus as a Boy

41 Every year Jesus' parents went to Jerusalem for the Passover ·Feast [festival; C annual festival that celebrates God's rescue of Israel from Egypt; Ex. 12]. 42 When he was twelve years old, they went to the ·feast [festival] ·as they always did [*or* according to Jewish custom]. 43 After the feast days were over, they started home. The boy Jesus stayed behind in Jerusalem, but his parents did not know it. 44 Thinking that Jesus was with them in the group, they traveled for a whole day. Then they began to look for him among their family and friends. 45 When they did not find him, they went back to Jerusalem to look for him there. 46 After three days [C probably three days since they left Jerusalem—one out, one back, and one searching] they found Jesus sitting in the Temple ·with [among; in the middle of] the teachers, listening to them and asking them questions. 47 All who heard him were amazed at his understanding and answers. 48 When Jesus' parents saw him, they were astonished. His mother said to him, "·Son [Child], why ·did you do this to us [have you treated us this way]? [L Look; T Behold] Your father and I were ·very worried [distressed; in pain] about you and have been looking for you."

49 Jesus said to them, "Why were you looking for me? Didn't you know that I must be ·in my Father's house [*or* about my Father's business]?" 50 But they did not understand the meaning of what he said.

51 Jesus went with them to Nazareth and ·was obedient to them [lived under their authority]. But his mother ·kept in her mind all that had happened [L kept/treasured all these things/words in her heart]. 52 Jesus ·became wiser and grew physically [grew in wisdom and stature/height]. ·People liked him, and he pleased God [...and in favor with God and people; 1 Sam. 2:26].

The Preaching of John

(3:1–20; Matt. 3:1–12; Mark 1:2–8; John 1:19–28)

3 It was the fifteenth year of the rule of Tiberius Caesar [C the Roman emperor, AD 14–37]. ·These men were under Caesar: Pontius Pilate, [L ...when Pontius Pilate was] the ·ruler [*or* governor; C his official title was "prefect"; Pilate governed from AD 26–36] of Judea; Herod [C Herod Antipas, son of Herod the Great], the ·ruler [L tetrarch; C the title meant "ruler of a fourth," but came to be used of any minor ruler] of Galilee; Philip [C another son of Herod the Great], the ·ruler [L tetrarch] of Iturea and Traconitis; and Lysanias, the ·ruler [L tetrarch] of Abilene. 2 Annas and Caiaphas were the high priests [C Annas was the former high priest and father-in-law of Caiaphas, the official high priest]. At this time, ·the word of [a message from] God came to John son of Zechariah in the ·desert [wilderness]. 3 He went all over the ·area [country; region] around the Jordan River preaching a baptism of ·changed

hearts and lives [repentance] for the forgiveness of sins. 4As it is written
in the ·book of [Lbook of the words/oracles of] Isaiah the prophet:

"This is a voice of one
who ·calls out [shouts; cries out] in the ·desert [wilderness]:
'Prepare the way for the Lord.
Make ·the road straight [a clear path] for him.
5Every ·valley [ravine; wadi] should be filled in,
and every mountain and hill should be made ·flat [level; low].
·Roads with turns [LCurved/TCrooked places] should be made straight,
and rough ·roads [paths; ways] should be made smooth.
6And all ·people [humanity; Tflesh] will ·know about [Lsee] the salvation
of God [Is. 40:3–5]!' "

7[LSo; Therefore] To the crowds of people who came to be baptized by
John, he said, "You ·are all snakes [Tbrood/offspring of vipers]! Who
warned you to ·run [slither; Lflee] away from God's coming ·punishment
[wrath; retribution]? 8·Do the things [LProduce the fruit] ·that show you
really have changed your hearts and lives [that prove your repentance; Lof
repentance]. Don't begin to say to yourselves, 'Abraham is our father [Ca
claim to be God's special people, since their ancestor Abraham was chosen
and blessed by God; Gen. 12:1–3].' [LFor] I tell you that God could ·make
[Lraise up] children for Abraham from these rocks. 9The ax ·is now ready
to cut down [Lalready lies at the root of] the trees, and every tree that does
not produce good fruit will be cut down and thrown into the fire [Ca
metaphor for judgment against those who disobey God]."

10The ·people [crowd] asked John, "Then what should we do?"

11John answered, "If you have two ·shirts [tunics], share with the person who does not have one. If you have food, share that also [Is. 58:7]."

12Even tax collectors came to John to be baptized [Ctax collectors were
despised because they worked for the Roman rulers and were notorious for
corruption and extortion]. They said to him, "Teacher, what should we do?"

13John said to them, "Don't take more taxes from people than ·you
have been ordered to take [is prescribed/authorized]."

14The soldiers asked John, "What about us? What should we do?"

John said to them, "Don't ·force people to give you [extort] money, and
don't ·lie about them [make false accusations]. Be satisfied with the pay
you get."

15Since the people were ·hoping [waiting expectantly] for the ·Christ
[Messiah] to come, they [Lall] wondered if John might be the ·one [LChrist;
Messiah].

16John answered everyone, "I baptize you with water, but there is one
coming who is ·greater [more powerful; mightier] than I am. I am not
·good enough [fit; qualified] to untie [Lthe thong/strap of] his sandals [Ca
task of a servant or slave]. He will baptize you with the Holy Spirit and
fire. 17·He will come ready [LThe winnowing fork is in his hand] to ·clean
the grain, separating the good grain from the chaff [Lclear his threshing
floor]. He will put ·the good part of the grain [Lthe grain/wheat] into his
·barn [storehouse], but he will burn the chaff with ·a fire that cannot be
put out [never-ending/unquenchable fire; Ca metaphor for judgment,
when Jesus will separate the righteous from the wicked]." 18And John continued to preach the ·Good News [Gospel], saying many other things to
·encourage [exhort] the people.

19But John ·spoke against [criticized; rebuked] Herod [CAntipas], the

·governor [Ltetrarch; 3:1], ·because of his sin with [Lconcerning] Herodias, the wife of Herod's brother [CHerod had divorced his wife and illicitly married the wife of his brother Philip; Lev. 18:16], and because of the many other evil things Herod did.
20So Herod ·did something even worse [Ladded this to all his sins]: He ·put [locked; shut up] John in prison.

Jesus Is Baptized by John
(3:21–22; Matt. 3:13–17; Mark 1:9–11; John 1:29–34)

21When all the people were being baptized by John, Jesus also was baptized. [LAnd] While Jesus was praying, heaven opened
22and the Holy Spirit came down on him in ·the form of [Lbodily appearance like] a dove. Then a voice came from heaven, saying, "You are my ·Son, whom I love [dearly beloved Son; Gen. 22:2; Ps. 2:7], ·and I am very pleased with you [in whom I take great delight [Is. 42:1]."

The Family History of Jesus
(3:23–38; Matt. 1:1–17)

23When Jesus began his ministry, he was about thirty years old. People thought that Jesus was Joseph's son [Cthey were unaware of the virginal conception].

Joseph was the son of Heli [C"son" in Hebrew can mean "descendant," so there may be gaps in the genealogy].
24Heli was the son of Matthat.
Matthat was the son of Levi.
Levi was the son of Melki.
Melki was the son of Jannai.
Jannai was the son of Joseph.
25Joseph was the son of Mattathias.
Mattathias was the son of Amos.
Amos was the son of Nahum.
Nahum was the son of Esli.
Esli was the son of Naggai.
26Naggai was the son of Maath.
Maath was the son of Mattathias.
Mattathias was the son of Semein.
Semein was the son of Josech.
Josech was the son of Joda.
27Joda was the son of Joanan.
Joanan was the son of Rhesa.
Rhesa was the son of Zerubbabel.
Zerubbabel was the son of Shealtiel.
Shealtiel was the son of Neri.
28Neri was the son of Melki.
Melki was the son of Addi.
Addi was the son of Cosam.
Cosam was the son of Elmadam.
Elmadam was the son of Er.
29Er was the son of Joshua.
Joshua was the son of Eliezer.
Eliezer was the son of Jorim.
Jorim was the son of Matthat.
Matthat was the son of Levi.
30Levi was the son of Simeon.
Simeon was the son of Judah.
Judah was the son of Joseph.
Joseph was the son of Jonam.
Jonam was the son of Eliakim.

[31]Eliakim was the son of Melea.
Melea was the son of Menna.
Menna was the son of Mattatha.
Mattatha was the son of Nathan.
Nathan was the son of David.
[32]David was the son of Jesse.
Jesse was the son of Obed.
Obed was the son of Boaz.
Boaz was the son of Salmon.[n]
Salmon was the son of Nahshon.
[33]Nahshon was the son of Amminadab.
Amminadab was the son of Admin.
Admin was the son of Arni.[n]
Arni was the son of Hezron.
Hezron was the son of Perez.
Perez was the son of Judah.
[34]Judah was the son of Jacob.
Jacob was the son of Isaac.
Isaac was the son of Abraham.
Abraham was the son of Terah.
Terah was the son of Nahor.
[35]Nahor was the son of Serug.
Serug was the son of Reu.
Reu was the son of Peleg.
Peleg was the son of Eber.
Eber was the son of Shelah.
[36]Shelah was the son of Cainan.
Cainan was the son of Arphaxad.
Arphaxad was the son of Shem.
Shem was the son of Noah.
Noah was the son of Lamech.
[37]Lamech was the son of Methuselah.
Methuselah was the son of Enoch.
Enoch was the son of Jared.
Jared was the son of Mahalalel.
Mahalalel was the son of Kenan.
[38]Kenan was the son of Enosh.
Enosh was the son of Seth.
Seth was the son of Adam.
Adam was the son of God.

Jesus Is Tempted by the Devil
(4:1–13; Matt 4:1–11; Mark 1:12–13)

4 Jesus, filled with the Holy Spirit, returned from the Jordan River.
The Spirit led Jesus into the ·desert [wilderness] [2]where the devil
·tempted [*or* tested] Jesus for forty days [[C]like Israel's forty years of testing in the wilderness]. Jesus ate nothing during that time, and when those days were ended, he was very hungry [Ex. 34:28].

[3]The devil said to Jesus, "If you are the Son of God, ·tell [command] this rock to become bread."

[4]Jesus answered, "It is written in the Scriptures: 'A person does not live on bread alone [Deut. 8:3].' "

3:32 Salmon Some Greek copies read "Sala." **3:33 Admin...Arni** Some Greek copies omit Admin and Arni from the genealogy; others include the names Ram (or Aram) and/or Joram.

5Then the devil took Jesus [Lup] and showed him all the kingdoms of the
world in an instant. 6The devil said to Jesus, "I will give you all these kingdoms and all their ·power [authority] and ·glory [splendor]. [L...because] It
has all been ·given [handed over] to me, and I can give it to anyone I wish.
7If you worship me, then it will all be yours."
8Jesus answered, "It is written in the Scriptures: 'You must worship the
Lord your God and serve only him [Deut. 6:13; 10:20].'"
9Then the devil led Jesus to Jerusalem and put him on ·a high place [the
pinnacle] of the Temple. He said to Jesus, "If you are the Son of God, ·jump
[throw yourself] down [Lfrom here]. 10[LFor] It is written in the Scriptures:

'He ·has put his angels in charge of you [*or* will order his angels to
protect you; Lwill command his angel concerning you]
to ·watch over you [guard you carefully; Ps. 91:11].'

11It is also written:

'They will ·catch you in [lift you up with] their hands
so that you will not ·hit your foot on [trip/stumble over] a rock
[Ps. 91:12].'"

12Jesus answered, "But it also says in the Scriptures: 'Do not test the
Lord your God [Deut. 6:16].'"
13After the devil had ·tempted [tested] Jesus ·in every way [*or* with all
these temptations], he left him to wait until a ·better [opportune] time.

Jesus Teaches the People
(4:14–30; Matt. 4:12–17; Mark 1:14–15)

14Jesus returned to Galilee ·in the power of [empowered by] the Holy
Spirit, and ·stories [news; reports] about him spread all through the ·area
[region; countryside]. 15He began to teach in their synagogues, and everyone ·praised [acclaimed; glorified] him.
16Jesus traveled to Nazareth, where he had grown up. On the Sabbath
day he went to the synagogue, as he always did, and stood up to read. 17The
·book [*or* scroll] of Isaiah the prophet was given to him. He ·opened
[Lunrolled] the ·book [*or* scroll] and found the place where this is written:

18"·The Lord has put his Spirit in me [LThe Spirit of the Lord is on me],
because he ·appointed [Lanointed; Cat Jesus' baptism he was anointed
by the Spirit as the Messiah, meaning the Anointed One] me to
·tell [proclaim; preach] the ·Good News [Gospel] to the poor.
He has sent me to ·tell the captives they are free [proclaim liberty/
release for the captives/prisoners]
and to tell the blind that they can see again [Is. 61:1].
God sent me to free ·those who have been treated unfairly [the
oppressed; Is. 58:6]
19 and to ·announce [proclaim] the ·time [year] when the Lord will
show his ·kindness [favor; Is. 61:2; Can allusion to the release of
slaves during the Jubilee year; Lev. 25]."

20Jesus ·closed the book [*or* rolled up the scroll], gave it back to the
·assistant [synagogue attendant], and sat down. ·Everyone [LAll the eyes]
in the synagogue was watching Jesus closely. 21He began to say to them,
"·While you heard these words just now, they were coming true [LToday
this Scripture has been fulfilled in your ears]!"
22All the people spoke well of Jesus and were amazed at the ·words of
grace [*or* gracious words] he spoke. They asked, "Isn't this Joseph's son?"
23Jesus said to them, "·I know that [No doubt; Surely] you will ·tell [quote]
me ·the old saying [this proverb]: '·Doctor [TPhysician], heal yourself.' You
want to say, 'We heard about the things you did in Capernaum [Ca town in

Galilee where Jesus lived and ministered]. **Do those things here in your own town!' " 24 Then Jesus said, "·I tell you the truth** [LTruly/Amen I say to you], **a prophet is not ·accepted** [welcomed] **in his hometown. 25 But I tell you ·the truth** [truly], **there were many widows in Israel during the time of Elijah. ·It did not rain** [LThe sky/heavens were shut] **in Israel for three and one-half years, and there was ·no food anywhere** [La great famine] **in the whole country** [1 Kin. 17]. **26 But Elijah was sent to none of those widows, only to a widow in Zarephath, a town in Sidon** [Ca Gentile city on the coast north of Israel]. **27 And there were many ·with skin diseases** [Tlepers] **living in Israel during the time of the prophet Elisha. But none of them were ·healed** [cured; cleansed], **only Naaman, ·who was from the country of Syria** [Lthe Syrian; 2 Kin. 5]."

28 When all the people in the synagogue heard these things, they ·became very angry [were furious; Lwere filled with wrath]. **29 They got up, ·forced** [drove] **Jesus out of town, and took him to the ·edge** [brow] **of the ·cliff** [hill] **on which the town was built. They planned to throw him off the ·edge** [cliff], **30 but Jesus ·walked** [passed] **through the crowd and went on his way.**

Jesus Forces Out an Evil Spirit
(4:31–37; Mark 1:21–28)

31 Jesus went to Capernaum [4:23], **a city in Galilee, and on the Sabbath day, he taught the people. 32 They were amazed at his teaching, because ·he spoke with** [his words/message had] **authority. 33 In the synagogue a man who had within him an ·evil spirit** [Lunclean spirit; Cdemons were viewed as "unclean" or defiling spirit-beings] **shouted in a loud voice, 34 "Jesus of Nazareth! What do you ·want** [have to do] **with us? Did you come to destroy us? I know who you are—God's Holy One!"**

35 Jesus ·commanded [reprimanded; rebuked] **the evil spirit, "Be quiet! Come out of the man!" The ·evil spirit** [Ldemon] **threw the man down to the ground before all the people and then left the man without ·hurting** [injuring] **him.**

36 [LAll] **The people were amazed and said to each other, "·What does this mean?** [*or* What words these are!] **With authority and power he ·commands** [gives orders to] **·evil** [defiling; Lunclean; v. 33] **spirits, and they come out." 37 And so the news about Jesus spread to every place in the whole area.**

Jesus Heals Many People
(4:38–43; Mark 1:29–38)

38 Jesus left the synagogue and went to the home of Simon [CPeter]. **Simon's mother-in-law was sick with a high fever, and they asked Jesus ·to help her** [Lconcerning her]. **39 He ·came to her side** [*or* stood over her] **and ·commanded the fever to leave** [Lrebuked the fever]. **It left her, and immediately she got up and ·began serving them** [*or* waiting on them; Cpresumably meal preparation].

40 ·When [*or* As] **the sun went down, the people brought those who were sick to Jesus. ·Putting** [Laying] **his hands on each sick person, he healed every one of them. 41 Demons** [Lalso] **came out of many people, shouting, "You are the Son of God." But Jesus ·commanded** [reprimanded; rebuked] **the demons and would not allow them to speak, because they knew Jesus was the ·Christ** [Messiah].

42 At daybreak, Jesus went to a ·lonely [isolated; deserted] **place, but the ·people** [crowds] **·looked** [were looking] **for him. When they ·found** [came to] **him, they tried to keep him from leaving. 43 But Jesus said to them, "I must preach** [Lthe good news] **about God's kingdom to other towns, too.** [L...because] **This is why I was sent."**

44 Then he kept on preaching in the synagogues of Judea.ⁿ

4:44 Judea Some Greek copies read "Galilee."

Jesus' First Followers

5 One day while Jesus was standing beside ·Lake Galilee [[L]the Lake of
Gennesaret; [C]another name for the Sea of Galilee], many people were
·pressing [crowding] all around him to hear the word of God. 2Jesus saw two
boats at the shore of the lake. The fishermen had left them and were washing
their nets. 3Jesus got into one of the boats, the one that belonged to Simon
[[C]Peter], and asked him to push off a little from the ·land [shore]. Then Jesus
sat down and continued to teach the people from the boat.
4When Jesus had finished speaking, he said to Simon, "Take the boat into
deep water, and ·put [let down] your nets in the water to catch some fish."
5Simon answered, "Master, we ·worked [labored] hard all night trying
to catch fish, and we caught nothing. But ·you say [because you say; [L]upon
your word] to put the nets in the water, so I will." 6When the fishermen
did as Jesus told them, they caught so many fish that the nets began to
·break [tear]. 7They ·called [signaled; motioned] to their partners in the
other boat to come and help them. They came and filled both boats so
full that they were almost sinking.
8When Simon Peter saw what had happened, he bowed down ·before [[L]at
the knees of] Jesus and said, "Go away from me, Lord. I am a sinful man!"
9[[L]For] He and the other fishermen were amazed at the many fish they
caught, as were 10James and John, the sons of Zebedee, Simon's partners.
Jesus said to Simon, "Don't be afraid. From now on you will ·fish for
people [catch people; [T]be fishers of men]." 11When the men brought their
boats to the shore, they left everything and followed Jesus.

Jesus Heals a Sick Man
(5:12–16; Matt. 8:1–4; Mark 1:40–45)

12When Jesus was in one of the towns, there was a man covered with ·a
skin disease [[T]leprosy; [C]the term does not refer to modern leprosy
(Hansen's disease), but to various skin disorders; see Lev. 14]. When he
saw Jesus, he ·bowed [[L]fell on his face] before him and ·begged [implored]
him, "Lord, you can ·heal me [[L]make me clean; [C]such skin disorders rendered the victim ceremonially unclean] if you ·will [choose; are willing]."
13Jesus reached out his hand and touched the man and said, "I ·will [do
choose; am willing]. Be ·healed [[L]cleansed]!" Immediately the disease
·disappeared [left him]. 14Then Jesus ·said [ordered; commanded], "Don't
tell anyone about this, but go and ·show yourself to [be examined by] the
priest [[C]only a priest could declare a person clean] and ·offer a gift [make
an offering; offer the sacrifices] for your ·healing [cleansing], as Moses
commanded [Lev. 14:1–32]. This will ·show the people [be a public testimony to; be evidence for] what I have done."
15But the news about Jesus spread even more. ·Many people [Great
crowds] came to hear Jesus and to be healed of their sicknesses, 16but
Jesus often ·slipped away [withdrew] to ·be alone [desolate/lonely/wilder-
ness places] so he could pray.

Jesus Heals a Paralyzed Man
(5:17–26; Matt. 9:1–8; Mark 2:1–12)

17One day as Jesus was teaching the people, the Pharisees and teachers
of the law from every town in Galilee and Judea and from Jerusalem were
there. ·The Lord was giving Jesus the power [[L]The power of the Lord was
upon him] to heal people. 18·Just then [[L]And look/[T]behold], some men
were carrying on a ·mat [cot; bed] a man who was paralyzed. They tried
to bring him in and put him down before Jesus. 19But because there were
so many people there, they could not find a way in. So they went up on
the roof and lowered the man on his ·mat [cot; bed] through the ·ceiling
[[L]tiles] into the middle of the crowd right ·before [in front of] Jesus.
20Seeing their faith, Jesus said, "·Friend [[L]Man], your sins are forgiven."

21The ·Jewish teachers of the law [scribes] and the Pharisees ·thought to themselves [Lbegan thinking/reasoning], "Who is this man who is speaking ·as if he were God [blasphemies]? ·Only God can forgive sins [LWho can forgive sins except God alone?; Is. 43:25]."

22But Jesus knew what they were thinking and said, "Why are you thinking these things [Lin your hearts]? 23Which is easier: to say, 'Your sins are forgiven,' or to say, 'Stand up and walk'? 24But ·I will prove to you [Lso that you may know] that the Son of Man [Ca title for the Messiah; Dan. 7:13–14] has authority on earth to forgive sins." So Jesus said to the paralyzed man, "I tell you, stand up, take your ·mat [cot; bed], and go home."

25At once the man stood up before them, picked up ·his mat [Lwhat he had been lying on], and went home, ·praising [glorifying] God. 26All the people were ·fully amazed [astounded; astonished] and began to ·praise [glorify] God. They were filled with ·much respect [awe; fear] and said, "Today we have seen ·amazing [remarkable; incredible] things!"

Levi Follows Jesus

(5:27–32; Matt. 9:9–13; Mark 2:13–17)

27After this, Jesus went out and saw a tax collector named Levi sitting in the tax collector's booth [Cprobably a tariff booth for taxing goods in transit]. Jesus said to him, "Follow me!" 28So Levi got up, left everything, and followed him.

29Then Levi gave a ·big dinner [great banquet] for Jesus at his house. Many tax collectors and other people were ·eating there [Lreclining; Caround a low table, the posture for a formal banquet or dinner party], too. 30But the Pharisees and ·the men who taught the law for the Pharisees [Ltheir scribes] began to ·complain [grumble] to Jesus' ·followers [disciples], "Why do you eat and drink with tax collectors and sinners?" [CTax collectors were despised because they worked for the Roman rulers and were notorious for corruption and extortion.]

31Jesus answered them, "It is not the healthy people who need a doctor, but the sick. 32I have not come to ·invite [call] ·good people [the righteous; Cmeaning the "self-righteous" who feel no need to repent] but sinners to ·change their hearts and lives [repentance]."

Jesus Answers a Question

(5:33–39; Matt. 9:14–17; Mark 2:18–22)

33They said to Jesus, "John's ·followers [disciples] often fast [Cgiving up eating for spiritual purposes] and pray, just as the ·Pharisees [*or* disciples of the Pharisees] do. But your ·followers [disciples] eat and drink all the time."

34Jesus said to them, "You cannot make the ·friends of the bridegroom [*or* wedding guests; Lchildren of the wedding hall] fast while he is still with them. 35But the ·time [Ldays] will come when the bridegroom will be taken away from them, and ·then [Lin those days] they will fast."

36Jesus told them this ·story [parable]: "No one ·takes [tears] cloth off a new ·coat [garment] to cover a hole in an old ·coat [garment]. If he does, he ·ruins [tears] the new ·coat [garment], and the cloth from the new will not match the old. 37Also, no one pours new wine into old ·leather bags [wineskins]. Otherwise, the new wine will ·break [tear; burst; Cbecause the fermenting new wine expands] the ·bags [wineskins], the wine will spill out, and the ·leather bags [wineskins] will be ruined. 38[LBut; Rather] New wine must be put into ·new [fresh] ·leather bags [wineskins]. 39No one after drinking old wine wants new wine, because he says, 'The old wine is ·better [fine; good].' " [CThe religious leaders are content with the old ways of Judaism and not interested in the "new wine" (salvation blessings) of the Kingdom.]

Jesus Is Lord over the Sabbath
(6:1–5; Matt. 12:1–8; Mark 2:23–28)

6 One Sabbath day Jesus was walking through some fields of grain. His ·followers [disciples] picked the heads of grain, rubbed them in their hands, and ate them [Deut. 23:25]. 2 Some Pharisees said, "Why do you do what is ·not lawful [forbidden] on the Sabbath day?" [C Gleaning was viewed as work, and therefore forbidden on the Sabbath; Ex. 34:21.]

3 Jesus answered, "Have you not read what David did when he and ·those with him [his companions] were hungry [1 Sam. 21:1–6]? 4 He went into God's house and took and ate the ·holy bread [consecrated bread; L bread of presentation], which is ·lawful [allowed] only for priests to eat [Ex. 25:30; Lev. 24:5–9]. And he gave some to ·the people who were with him [his companions]." 5 Then Jesus said to the Pharisees, "The Son of Man [C a title for the Messiah; Dan. 7:13–14] is ·Lord [Master] of the Sabbath day."

Jesus Heals a Man's Hand
(6:6–11; Matt. 12:9–14; Mark 3:1–6)

6 On another Sabbath day Jesus went into the synagogue and was teaching, and a man with a ·crippled [paralyzed; shriveled; T withered] right hand was there. 7 The ·teachers of the law [scribes] and the Pharisees were watching closely to see if Jesus would heal on the Sabbath day so they could ·accuse [make a charge against] him. 8 But he knew what they were thinking, and he said to the man with the ·crippled [paralyzed; shriveled; T withered] hand, "Stand up here in ·the middle [front] of everyone." The man got up and stood there. 9 Then Jesus said to them, "I ask you, which is lawful on the Sabbath day: to do good or to do ·evil [harm], to save a life or to destroy it?" 10 Jesus looked around at all of them and said to the man, "·Hold [Stretch] out your hand." The man ·held [stretched] out his hand, and it was ·healed [restored].

11 But the Pharisees and the ·teachers of the law [scribes] were very angry and discussed with each other what they could do to Jesus.

Jesus Chooses His Apostles
(6:12–16; Matt. 10:1–4; Mark 3:13–19)

12 At that time Jesus went off to a mountain to pray, and he spent the night praying to God. 13 ·The next morning [L When the day dawned], Jesus called his ·followers [disciples] to him and chose twelve of them, whom he ·named [designated] apostles: 14 Simon (Jesus named him Peter), his brother Andrew, James, John, Philip, Bartholomew, 15 Matthew, Thomas, James son of Alphaeus, Simon (called the Zealot), 16 Judas son of James, and Judas Iscariot, who later ·turned Jesus over to his enemies [L became a traitor].

Jesus Teaches and Heals
(6:17–26; Matt. 4:24–5:12; Mark 3:7–13a)

17 Jesus and the apostles ·came down from the mountain [L came down; C perhaps to a level place on the side of the mountain], and he stood on level ground. A ·large group [great crowd] of his ·followers [disciples] was there, as well as many people from all around Judea, Jerusalem, and the seacoast cities of Tyre and Sidon. 18 They all came to hear Jesus teach and to be healed of their ·sicknesses [diseases], and he healed those who were troubled by ·evil [defiling; L unclean; 4:33] spirits. 19 All the people were trying to touch Jesus, because power was coming from him and healing them all.

20 Jesus looked at his ·followers [disciples] and said,

"·You people who are poor are blessed [*or* Blessed are you…; C and so through v. 22],
because the kingdom of God ·belongs to you [is yours].
21 You people who are now hungry are blessed,
because you will be ·satisfied [filled].
You people who are now ·crying [weeping] are blessed,
because you will ·laugh with joy [L laugh].

22“·You are blessed [TBlessed are you; *or* God will bless you] when people hate you, ·shut you out [exclude/ostracize you], ·insult [mock] you,
and ·say you are [Lscorn/curse/defame your name as] evil because ·you
follow [Lof] the Son of Man. 23·Be full of joy [LRejoice and leap] at that
time, because you have a great reward in heaven. [LFor] Their ancestors
did the same things to the prophets [2 Chr. 36:16].
24“But ·how terrible it will be for [Lwoe to] you who are rich,
because you have ·had your easy life [Lalready received your comfort/
consolation].
25·How terrible it will be for [LWoe to] you who are ·full [well-fed] now,
because you will be hungry.
·How terrible it will be for [LWoe to] you who are laughing now,
because you will ·be sad and cry [mourn and weep].
26“·How terrible [LWoe to you] when everyone ·says only good things
[speaks well] about you, because their ancestors ·said the same things
about [Ldid the same things to] the false prophets.

Love Your Enemies
(6:27–36; Matt 5:38–48)

27“But I say to you who are listening, love your enemies. Do good to those
who hate you, 28bless those who curse you, pray for those who ·are cruel to
[hurt; mistreat] you. 29If anyone ·slaps [strikes; hits] you on one cheek
[Cprobably an insult or act of rejection, although it could be a stronger
punch], ·offer him [Tturn] the other cheek, too. If someone takes your coat,
do not ·stop him from taking [withhold] your ·shirt [tunic]. 30Give to everyone who asks you, and when someone takes something that is yours, don't
·ask for [demand] it back. 31·Do to others what [Treat others as] you would
want them to ·do to [treat] you. 32If you love only the people who love you,
what ·praise [credit] should you get? Even sinners love the people who love
them. 33If you do good only to those who do good to you, what ·praise
[credit] should you get? Even sinners do that! 34If you lend things to people,
·always hoping to get something back [*or* …from whom you expect to be
repaid], what ·praise [credit] should you get? Even sinners lend to other sinners ·so that they can get back the same amount [expecting to be repaid in
full]! 35But love your enemies, do good to them, and lend to them without
·hoping [expecting] to get anything back. Then you will have a great reward,
and you will be children of the Most High God, because he is kind even to
people who are ungrateful and ·full of sin [wicked; evil]. 36·Show mercy [Be
compassionate], just as your Father ·shows mercy [is compassionate].

Look at Yourselves
(6:37–42; Matt 7:1–5; Mark 4:24–25)

37“Don't judge others, and you will not be judged. Don't ·accuse others
of being guilty [condemn others], and you will not be ·accused of being
guilty [condemned]. ·Forgive [Pardon; Release], and you will be ·forgiven
[pardoned; released]. 38Give, and ·you will receive [Lit will be given to
you]. ·You will be given much [L…a good measure…]. ·Pressed down
[Compacted], shaken together, and running over, it will spill into your
lap [Cthe image is of grain overflowing its container]. The ·way you give to
[standard/measure you use with] others is the ·way God will give to [stan-
dard/measure God will use with] you."
39Jesus told them this ·story [parable]: "Can a blind person ·lead [guide]
another blind person? No! Both of them will fall into a ·ditch [pit; hole].
40A ·student [disciple] is not ·better than [above] the teacher, but ·the student [Leveryone] who has been fully trained will be like the teacher.
41“Why do you notice the ·little piece of dust [speck; tiny splinter] in
your ·friend's [Lbrother's (or sister's)] eye, but you don't ·notice [consider]

the ·big piece of wood [log; plank; beam] in your own eye? 42How can you
say to your ·friend [Lbrother], '·Friend [LBrother], let me take that ·little
piece of dust [speck; tiny splinter] out of your eye' when you cannot see
that ·big piece of wood [log; plank; beam] in your own eye! You hypocrite! First, take the ·wood [log; plank; beam] out of your own eye. Then
you will see clearly to take the ·dust [speck; tiny splinter] out of your
friend's [Lbrother's] eye.

Two Kinds of Fruit
(6:43–45; Matt. 7:15–20; 12:33–35)

43"[LFor] A good tree does not produce ·bad [rotten] fruit, nor does a
·bad [rotten] tree produce good fruit. 44[LFor] Each tree is ·known [identi-
fied] by its own fruit. [LFor] People don't ·gather [pick] figs from
thornbushes, and they don't get grapes from ·bushes [brambles; briers].
45Good people bring good things out of the good ·they stored [treasured]
in their hearts. But evil people bring evil things out of the evil ·they stored
[treasured] in their hearts. ·People speak the things that are in their hearts
[LFor the mouth speaks what overflows from the heart].

Two Kinds of People
(6:46–49; Matt. 7:21–27)

46"Why do you call me, 'Lord, Lord,' but do not do what I say? 47I will
show you what everyone is like who comes to me and ·hears [listens to]
my words and ·obeys [acts on them]. 48That person is like a man building
a house who dug deep and laid the foundation on rock. When the floods
came, the ·water [Lriver] ·tried to wash the house away [Lswept/burst
against that house], but it could not shake it, because the house was built
well. 49But the one who ·hears [listens to] my words and does not ·obey
[act on them] is like a man who built his house on the ground without a
foundation. When the ·floods [Lriver] ·came [swept/burst against it], the
house quickly ·fell [collapsed] and was completely destroyed."

Jesus Heals a Soldier's Servant
(7:1–10; Matt. 8:5–13; cf. John 4:46b–54)

7 When Jesus finished saying all these things to the people, he went
to Capernaum [4:23]. 2There was ·an army officer [La centurion]
who had a servant who was ·very important [of great value; precious] to
him. The servant was so sick he was ·nearly dead [about to die]. 3When
the officer heard about Jesus, he sent some Jewish elders to him to ask
Jesus to come and heal his servant. 4The men went to Jesus and ·begged
[urged] him [Learnestly; strongly], saying, "This officer ·is worthy of
[deserves] your help. 5[L...for/because] He loves our ·people [nation], and
he built us a synagogue."

6So Jesus went with the men. He was getting near the officer's house
when the ·officer [centurion] sent friends to say, "Lord, don't trouble
yourself, because I ·am not worthy [do not deserve] to have you come
into my house. 7That is why I did not [Lconsider myself worthy/deserving
to] come to you myself. But you only need to ·command it [Lsay a word],
and my servant will be healed. 8[LFor; Because] I, too, am a man under the
authority of others, and I have soldiers under my command. I tell one
soldier, 'Go,' and he goes. I tell another soldier, 'Come,' and he comes. I say
to my ·servant [slave], 'Do this,' and he does it."

9When Jesus heard this, he was amazed. Turning to the crowd that was
following him, he said, "I tell you, ·this is the greatest faith I have found
anywhere [LI haven't found such faith], ·even in Israel [*or* in all Israel]."

10Those who had been sent to Jesus went back to the house where they
found the servant in good health.

Jesus Brings a Man Back to Life

11Soon afterwards Jesus went to a town called Nain [Ca small village a
few miles south of Nazareth], and his ·followers [disciples] and a large

crowd traveled with him. 12When he came near the town gate, ·he saw a funeral [Llook/Tbehold, a dead man was being carried out]. A mother, who was a widow, had lost her only son. A large crowd from the town was with the mother while her son was being carried out. 13When the Lord saw her, he felt ·very sorry [compassion] **for her and said, "Don't cry." 14He went up and touched the ·coffin** [*or* bier; Cthe body was probably wrapped in cloths and lying on a wooden plank], **and the people who were carrying it stopped. Jesus said, "Young man, I tell you, get up!" 15And the ·son** [Ldead man] **sat up and began to talk. Then Jesus gave him back to his mother.**

16All the people were ·amazed [seized with fear; filled with awe] **and began ·praising** [glorifying] **God, saying, "A great prophet has ·come to** [Lappeared/arisen among] **us! God has ·come to help** [looked favorably on; visited; 1:68] **his people."**

17This ·news [account; word] **about Jesus spread through all Judea and into all the ·places around there** [surrounding region].

John Asks a Question
(7:18–23; Matt. 11:2–6)

18John's ·followers [disciples] **told him about all these things. He called for two of his ·followers** [disciples] **19and sent them to the Lord to ask, "Are you the ·One who is to come** [the Expected One; Cthe Messiah], **or should we ·wait for** [look for; expect] **someone else?"**

20When the men came to Jesus, they said, "John the Baptist sent us to you with this question: 'Are you the ·One who is to come [Expected One], **or should we ·wait for** [look for; expect] **someone else?'" 21At that time, Jesus healed many people of their sicknesses, diseases, and ·evil** [defiling; Lunclean; 4:33] **spirits, and he gave sight to many blind people. 22Then Jesus answered John's ·followers** [disciples], **"Go tell John what you saw and heard here. The blind can see, the ·crippled** [lame] **can walk, and ·people with skin diseases** [Tlepers; see 5:12] **are ·healed** [Lcleansed]. **The deaf can hear, the dead are raised to life, and the ·Good News** [Gospel] **is ·preached** [announced; proclaimed] **to the poor** [Csigns of God's restoration of creation, predicted by the prophet Isaiah; Is. 29:18–19; 35:5–6; 61:1–2]. **23Those who ·do not stumble in their faith** [are not offended] **because of me are blessed."**

Jesus Comments on John
(7:24–35; Matt. 11:7–19)

24When John's ·followers [Lmessengers] **left, Jesus began talking to the ·people** [crowds] **about John: "What did you go out into the ·desert** [wilderness] **to see? A reed ·blown by** [shaken by; swaying in] **the wind** [Csomething fragile and easily swept away]? **25**[LBut] **What did you go out to see? A man dressed in ·fine** [expensive; Lsoft] **clothes? No, people who have ·fine** [glorious; splendid] **clothes and much ·wealth** [luxury] **·live** [are] **in ·kings' palaces** [royal courts]. **26But what did you go out to see? A prophet? Yes, and I tell you, ·John is** [Lone who is] **more than a prophet. 27This was written about him:**

'[LLook; TBehold] **I will send my messenger ahead of you,**
who will prepare ·the [your] **way ·for** [before; in front of] **you**
[Mal. 3:1].'

28I tell you, John is greater than any other person ·ever born [Lborn to women], **but even the least important person in the kingdom of God is greater than John** [Cbecause John was part of the old age of preparation, those in the new kingdom age have greater blessings and status]."

29(When the people, including the tax collectors, heard this, they all agreed that God's ·teaching was good [way was right/just], **because they had been baptized by John. 30But the Pharisees and experts on the law**

·refused to accept [rejected] **God's ·plan** [purpose] **for themselves; they**
did not let John baptize them.)

31Then Jesus said, "·What shall I say about [LTo what, therefore, shall I
compare] **the people of this ·time** [Lgeneration]**? What are they like?**
32They are like children sitting in the marketplace, calling to one another
and saying,

> **'We played ·music** [Lthe pipe/flute] **for you, but you did not dance;**
> **we sang a ·sad song** [funeral song; dirge]**, but you did not ·cry**
> [weep].' [CThe religious leaders wanted John to "dance" (lighten up
> his severe message) and wanted Jesus to "mourn" (follow their
> restrictive lifestyle).]

33[LFor] **John the Baptist came and did not eat bread or drink wine, and**
you say, 'He ·has [is possessed by] **a demon in him.' 34The Son of Man**
came eating and drinking, and you say, 'Look at him! ·He eats too much
and drinks too much wine [LA glutton and a drunkard]**, and he is a friend**
of tax collectors and sinners!' 35But wisdom is ·proved to be right [vindi-
cated] **by ·what it does** [*or* the behavior of her followers; Lall her/its
children; CWisdom is personified as a woman (Prov. 8), her "children"
being those who respond favorably to the message of John and Jesus]**."**

A Woman Washes Jesus' Feet
(7:36–50; Matt. 26:6–13; Mark 14:3–9)

36One of the Pharisees ·asked [invited] **Jesus to eat with him, so Jesus**
went into the Pharisee's house and ·sat at the table [Lreclined; Cat a formal
meal guests would recline at a low table with their feet stretched out
behind them]. 37[LAnd look/Tbehold] **A ·sinful** [immoral] **woman in the**
town learned that Jesus was eating at the Pharisee's house. So she brought
an alabaster ·jar [vial; flask] **of perfume 38and stood behind Jesus at his**
feet, ·crying [weeping]**. She began to ·wash** [wet; drench] **his feet with her**
tears, and she ·dried [wiped] **them with her hair, kissing them many times**
and ·rubbing [anointing] **them with the perfume. 39When the Pharisee**
who asked Jesus to come to his house saw this, he thought to himself, "If
·Jesus [Lthis person] **were a prophet, he would know ·that the woman**
touching him is a sinner [Lwho is touching him and what kind of woman
she is—that she is a sinner]**!"**

40Jesus said to ·the Pharisee [Lhim]**, "Simon, I have something to say to**
you."

Simon said, "Teacher, tell me."

41Jesus said, "Two people owed money to ·the same banker [La certain
moneylender/creditor]**. One owed five hundred ·coins** [Ldenarii; Ca denarius was equal to a day's wage for a laborer] **and the other owed fifty. 42They**
had no money to pay what they owed, but ·the banker [Lhe] **·told both of**
them they did not have to pay him [Lforgave both (debts)]**. Which person**
[Ltherefore] **will love ·the banker** [Lhim] **more?"**

43Simon answered, "I ·think [suppose] **it would be the one ·who owed**
him the most money [Lfor whom he forgave the larger]**."**

Jesus said to Simon, "You are right." 44Then Jesus turned toward the
woman and said to Simon, "Do you see this woman? When I came into
your house, you gave me no water for my feet, but she ·washed [wet;
drenched] **my feet with her tears and ·dried** [wiped] **them with her hair.**
45You gave me no kiss of greeting, but she has ·been [not stopped] **kissing**
my feet since I came in. 46You did not ·put oil on [anoint] **my head, but**
she ·poured perfume on my feet [has anointed my feet with perfume].
47[LTherefore] **I tell you that her many sins are forgiven, ·so** [that is why]

she showed great love. But the person who is forgiven only a little will love only a little."

48Then Jesus said to her, "Your sins are forgiven."

49The people ·sitting at the table [Lreclining together; 7:36] began to say among themselves, "Who is this who even forgives sins?"

50Jesus said to the woman, "·Because you believed, you are saved from your sins [LYour faith has saved you]. Go in peace."

The Group with Jesus

8 After this, while Jesus was traveling through some ·cities [or towns] and ·small towns [villages], he preached and ·told [proclaimed; announced] the ·Good News [Gospel] about God's kingdom. The twelve apostles were with him, 2and also some women who had been healed of sicknesses and ·evil [defiling; Lunclean; 4:33] spirits: Mary, called Magdalene [Cprobably because she was from the town of Magdala], from whom seven demons had gone out; 3Joanna, the wife of ·Cuza [or Chuza] (the ·manager [Tsteward] of Herod's [CHerod Antipas; see 3:1] house); Susanna; and many others. These women used their own ·money [resources] to ·help [support] ·Jesus and his apostles [Lthem].

A Story About Planting Seed

(8:4–15; Matt 13:1–23; Mark 4:1–20)

4When a great crowd was gathered, and people were coming to Jesus from every town, he told them this ·story [parable]:

5"A ·farmer [sower] went out to ·plant [sow] his seed. While he was ·planting [sowing, scattering seed], some seed fell ·by the road [along the footpath]. People ·walked [trampled] on the seed, and the ·birds [Lbirds of the sky] ate it up. 6Some seed fell on rock, and when it began to grow, it ·died [withered; dried up] because it had no ·water [moisture]. 7Some seed fell among thorny weeds, but the weeds grew up with it and choked ·the good plants [Lit]. 8And ·some [Lother] seed fell on good ·ground [soil] and grew and made a hundred times more."

As Jesus finished the story, he called out, "·Let those with ears use them and listen [LThe one who has ears to hear, let him hear]!"

9Jesus' ·followers [disciples] asked him what this ·story [parable] meant.

10Jesus said, "·You have been chosen [LIt has been granted/given to you] to ·know [understand] the ·secrets [mysteries] about the kingdom of God. But I use ·stories [parables] to speak to ·other people [the rest] so that:

'They will ·look [see], but they may not ·see [perceive].
They will ·listen [hear], but they may not understand [Is. 6:9].'

11"This is what the ·story [parable] means: The seed is God's ·message [word]. 12The seed that fell ·beside the road [along the footpath] is like the people who hear God's teaching, but [Lthen] the devil comes and takes it away from ·them [Ltheir hearts] so they cannot believe it and be saved. 13The seed that fell on rock is like those who hear God's teaching and ·accept [receive] it ·gladly [Lwith joy], but they ·don't allow the teaching to go deep into their lives [Lhave no root]. They believe for a while, but when ·trouble [La time of temptation/testing] comes, they ·give up [fall away; depart]. 14The seed that fell among the thorny weeds is like those who hear God's teaching, but they let the ·worries [cares; anxieties], riches, and pleasures of this life ·keep them from growing and producing [Lchoke/crowd them and they do not produce] ·good [mature; ripe] fruit. 15And the seed that fell on the good ground is like those who hear ·God's teaching [the word] with good, honest hearts and ·obey [cling/hold to] it and ·patiently [with perseverance] produce good fruit.

Use What You Have
(8:16–18; Matt. 10:26; 13:12; Mark 4:21–25)

16“No one after lighting a lamp covers it with a bowl or hides it under a
bed. Instead, the person puts it on a lampstand so those who come in will
see the light. 17[LFor] Everything that is ·hidden [secret] will ·become clear
[be revealed; disclosed; brought into the open] and every ·secret [hidden;
concealed] thing will be made known [Land come to light]. 18So ·be careful
[pay attention; Lsee] how you listen. [LFor] Those who ·have understanding [Lhave] will be given more. But those who do not ·have understanding
[Lhave], even what they think they have will be taken away from them.”

Jesus' True Family
(8:19–21; Matt. 12:46–50; Mark 3:31–35; John 15:14)

19Jesus' mother and brothers came to see him, but there was such a
crowd they could not get to him. 20Someone ·said [reported] to Jesus,
“Your mother and your ·brothers [*or* brothers and sisters; Cthe Greek
word can mean “siblings”] are standing outside, wanting to see you.”
21Jesus answered them, “My mother and my ·brothers [*or* brothers and
sisters] are those who listen to God's ·teaching [word] and ·obey [do;
practice] it!”

Jesus Calms a Storm
(8:22–25; Matt. 8:23–27; Mark 4:35–41)

22One day Jesus and his ·followers [disciples] got into a boat, and he said
to them, “Let's go across the lake.” And so they started across. 23While they
were sailing, Jesus fell asleep. A very strong wind blew up on the lake, causing the boat to ·fill with water [nearly swamp], and they were in danger.
24The ·followers [disciples] went to Jesus and woke him, saying,
“Master! Master! We ·will drown [are perishing/going to die]!”
Jesus got up and ·gave a command to [reprimanded; rebuked] the wind
and the waves. They stopped, and it became calm [Cparalleling God's subduing of the waters (representing chaos); Ps. 65:7; 89:9; 107:29]. 25Jesus
said to ·his followers [Lthem], “Where is your faith?”
·The followers [LThey] were afraid and amazed and said to each other,
“Who [Lthen] is this that commands even the wind and the water, and
they obey him?”

A Man with Demons Inside Him
(8:26–39; Matt. 8:28–34; Mark 5:1–20)

26·Jesus and his followers [LThey] sailed across the lake from Galilee to
the area of the Gerasene*n* people [CGerasa was southeast of Lake Galilee;
the exact location is uncertain]. 27When Jesus got out on the land, a man
from the town who ·had demons inside him [was possessed by demons]
came to Jesus. For a long time he had worn no clothes and had lived in the
·burial caves [tombs], not in a house. 28When he saw Jesus, he ·cried out
[shouted; shrieked] and fell down before him. He said with a loud voice,
“·What do you want with me [Leave me alone; What business do we have
with each other; LWhat to me and to you], Jesus, Son of the Most High
God? I beg you, don't ·torture [torment] me!” 29He said this because Jesus
was commanding [reprimanding; rebuking] the ·evil [defiling; Lunclean;
4:33] spirit to come out of the man. Many times it had ·taken hold of
[seized; taken control of] him. Though he had been kept under guard and
chained hand and foot, he had broken his chains and had been ·forced
[driven] by the demon out into ·a lonely place [the desert/wilderness].
30Jesus asked him, “What is your name?”
He answered, “Legion,” because many demons ·were in [had entered]
him [Ca legion was about five thousand Roman soldiers; the sense here is
“many”]. 31The demons begged Jesus not to ·send them [Lcommand them
to depart] into ·eternal darkness [the bottomless pit; Lthe Abyss]. 32A large

---

8:26 Gerasene Some Greek copies read “Gadarene”; others read “Gergesene.”

herd of pigs [Cconsidered ritually unclean by Jews] was feeding on a hill,
and the demons begged Jesus to allow them to go into the pigs. So Jesus
allowed them to do this. 33When the demons came out of the man, they
went into the pigs, and the herd ·ran [rushed] down the ·hill [steep bank;
precipice] into the lake and was drowned.
34When the herdsmen saw what had happened, they ·ran away [fled]
and ·told about [reported] this in the town and the countryside. 35And
people went to see what had happened. When they came to Jesus, they
found the man sitting at Jesus' feet, clothed and in his right mind, because
the demons were gone. But the people were frightened. 36The people who
saw this happen told the others how Jesus had made the [Ldemon-
possessed] man well. 37All the ·people [crowd; multitude] of the Gerasene
·country [region] asked Jesus to leave [Lthem], because they were all ·very
afraid [overwhelmed/seized with great fear]. So Jesus got into the boat
and ·went back across the lake [left; Lreturned].
38The man ·whom Jesus had healed [Lfrom whom the demons had gone
out] begged to go with him, but Jesus sent him away, saying, 39"Go back
home and ·tell [explain to] people ·how much [*or* what great things] God
has done for you." So the man went all over town ·telling [proclaiming]
·how much [*or* what great things] Jesus had done for him.

Jesus Gives Life to a Dead Girl and Heals a Sick Woman

(8:40–56; Matt. 9:18–26; Mark 5:21–43)

40When Jesus ·got back to the other side of the lake [Lreturned], a crowd
welcomed him, because everyone was ·waiting for [expecting] him.
41[LAnd look/Tbehold] A man named Jairus, a leader of the synagogue,
came to Jesus and ·fell [bowed; knelt] at his feet, ·begging [urging; pleading with] him to come to his house. 42[L...because] Jairus' only daughter,
about twelve years old, was dying.
While Jesus was on his way to Jairus' house, the people were ·crowding
[crushing; pressing] all around him. 43A woman was in the crowd who
had been bleeding for twelve years*n* [Cprobably a chronic menstrual disor-
der], but no one was able to heal her. 44She came up behind Jesus and
touched the ·edge [*or* tassel; see Num. 15:38–39] of his ·coat [cloak; gar-
ment], and instantly her bleeding stopped. 45Then Jesus said, "Who
touched me?"
When all the people ·said they had not touched him [denied it], Peter
said, "Master, the people are all around you and are pushing against you."
46But Jesus said, "Someone did touch me, because I felt power go out
from me." 47When the woman saw she could not hide, she came forward,
·shaking [trembling], and fell down before Jesus. While all the people listened, she ·told [explained] why she had touched him and how she had
been instantly healed. 48Jesus said to her, "·Dear woman [LDaughter],
·you are made well because you believed [your faith has saved/healed
you]. Go in peace."
49While Jesus was still speaking, someone came from the house of the
synagogue leader and said to him, "Your daughter is dead. Don't ·bother
[trouble] the teacher anymore."
50When Jesus heard this, he said to Jairus, "Don't be afraid. Just believe,
and your daughter will be ·well [healed]."
51When Jesus ·went [came] to the house, he let only Peter, John, James,
and the girl's father and mother go inside with him. 52All the people were

8:43 years Some Greek copies continue, "and she had spent all the money she had on doctors."

crying and ·feeling sad [wailing; lamenting; mourning] because the girl
was dead, but Jesus said, "Stop crying. She is not dead, only asleep."
53The people ·laughed at [ridiculed] Jesus because they knew the girl
was dead. 54But Jesus took hold of her hand and called to her, "My child,
·stand up [arise]!" 55Her ·spirit came back into her [*or* breath/life
returned], and she ·stood up [arose] at once. Then Jesus ·ordered
[directed] that she be given something to eat. 56The girl's parents were
·amazed [overwhelmed; astonished], but Jesus ·told [commanded;
ordered] them not to tell anyone what had happened.

Jesus Sends Out the Apostles
(9:1–6; Matt. 10:1–14; Mark 6:6b–13)

9 Jesus called ·the twelve apostles [Lthe Twelve] together and gave
them power and authority ·over all [to cast out] demons and the
ability to heal ·sicknesses [diseases]. 2He sent the ·apostles [Lthem] out to
·tell about [preach; proclaim] God's kingdom and to heal the sick. 3He
said to them, "Take nothing for your ·trip [journey], neither a ·walking
stick [staff], ·bag [*or* beggar's bag], ·bread [food], money, or ·extra clothes
[Ltwo shirts/tunics]. 4When you enter a house, stay there ·until it is time
to leave [Land depart from there; Cprobably to avoid temptation to move
to better accommodations]. 5If people do not welcome you, shake the
dust off of your feet [Ca sign of rejection and coming judgment] as you
leave the town, as a ·warning to [testimony/evidence against] them."
6So the apostles went out and traveled ·through all the towns [from
town to town], ·preaching [proclaiming] the ·Good News [Gospel] and
healing people everywhere.

Herod Is Confused About Jesus
(9:7–9; Matt. 14:1–2; Mark 6:14–16)

7[LNow; But] Herod, the ·governor [Ltetrarch; CHerod Antipas; 3:1],
heard about all the things that were happening and was ·confused [puz-
zled; perplexed], because some people said, "·John the Baptist [LJohn] has
risen from the dead." 8Others said, "Elijah has ·come to us [reappeared;
Lappeared; Csome Jews expected Elijah to return in the end times; Mal.
4:5]." And still others said, "One of the prophets who lived long ago has
·risen from the dead [*or* appeared once again; Larisen]." 9Herod said, "I
·cut off John's head [had John beheaded], so who is this man I hear such
things about?" And Herod kept trying to see Jesus.

More than Five Thousand Fed
(9:10–17; Matt. 14:13–21; Mark 6:30–44)

10When the apostles returned, they told Jesus everything they had
done. Then Jesus took them with him to a town called Bethsaida where
they could be alone together. 11But the ·people [crowds] learned where
Jesus went and followed him. He welcomed them and talked with them
about God's kingdom and healed those who needed to be healed.
12Late in the afternoon, ·the twelve apostles [Lthe Twelve] came to Jesus
and said, "Send the ·people [crowd] away. They need to go to the ·towns [vil-
lages] and countryside around here and find places to sleep and something
to eat, because ·no one lives in this [Lwe are in a remote/deserted] place."
13But Jesus said to them, "You give them something to eat."
They said, "We have only five loaves of bread and two fish, unless we go
buy food for all these people." 14(There were about five thousand men there.)
Jesus said to his ·followers [disciples], "Tell the people to sit in groups
of about fifty people."
15So ·the followers [Lthey] did this, and all the people sat down. 16Then
Jesus took the five loaves of bread and two fish, and looking up to heaven,
he ·thanked God for [Lblessed] the food. Then he ·divided the food [broke
it into pieces] and gave it to the ·followers [disciples] to ·give to [distribute

to; [L]set before] **the people.** 17 **They all ate and were ·satisfied** [filled], **and**
what was left over was gathered up, filling twelve baskets.

Jesus Is the Christ
(9:18–20; Matt. 16:13–20; Mark 8:27–30)

18 **One time when Jesus was praying alone, his ·followers** [disciples] **were**
with him, and he asked them, "Who do the ·people [crowds] **say I am?"**
19 **They answered, "Some say you are John the Baptist. Others say you**
are Elijah [see 9:8; 1 Kin. 17]. **And others say you are one of the prophets**
from long ago who has ·come back to life [risen/appeared again]."
20 **Then Jesus asked, "But who do you say I am?"**
Peter answered, "You are ·the Christ from God [God's Messiah; the
Messiah sent from God]."

Jesus Speaks of His Crucifixion
(9:21–27; Matt. 16:21–28; Mark 8:31–9:1)

21 **Jesus ·warned** [sternly commanded] **them not to tell anyone, saying,**
22 **"The Son of Man** [[C]a title for the Messiah; Dan. 7:13–14] **must suffer**
many things. He will be rejected by the Jewish elders, the ·leading [[T]chief]
priests, and the ·teachers of the law [scribes]. **He will be killed and ·after**
three days [[L]on the third day] **will be raised from the dead."**
23 **Jesus said to all of them, "If ·people want** [[L]anyone wants] **to follow**
me, they must ·give up the things they want [deny themselves; set aside
their own interests]. **They must ·be willing to give up their lives** [[L]take up
their cross] **daily and follow me.** 24 [[L]For] **Those who want to save their**
lives will ·give up true life [[L]lose their life/soul; [C]Greek *psychē* can mean
"life" or "soul"]. **But those who ·give up** [lose; sacrifice] **their lives for ·me**
[my sake] **will ·have true life** [save their lives/souls]. 25 **·It is worthless**
[[L]What good/profit/benefit is it…?] **to ·have** [gain] **the whole world if**
they themselves are destroyed or lost. 26 **·If people are** [[L]For whoever is]
ashamed of me and my ·teaching [message; words], **then the Son of Man**
will be ashamed of them when he comes in his glory and with the glory
of the Father and the holy angels. 27 **I tell you the truth, some people**
standing here will not ·die [[L]taste death] **before they see the kingdom of**
God." [[C]"Seeing the kingdom of God" may refer to the Transfiguration
which follows (9:28–36), Jesus' resurrection, or the destruction of
Jerusalem in AD 70.]

The Transfiguration on the Mountain
(9:28–36; Matt. 17:1–9; Mark 9:2–10)

28 **About eight days after Jesus said these things, he took Peter, John,**
and James and went up on a mountain to pray. 29 **While Jesus was praying,**
the appearance of his face ·changed [was altered], **and his clothes ·became**
shining white [*or* flashed white like lightning]. 30 **Then** [[L]look; [T]behold]
two men, Moses and Elijah, were talking with Jesus. [[C]God had given the
Law through Moses, and Elijah was an important prophet (see 9:8);
together they signify that Jesus fulfills the OT.] 31 **They appeared in ·heav-**
enly glory [[L]glory], **talking about his departure** [[C]Greek: *exodos*, perhaps
recalling the Exodus from Egypt, and referring to Jesus' death, resurrection, and ascension] **which he ·would soon bring about** [[L]was about to
fulfill/accomplish] **in Jerusalem.** 32 [[L]Now; But] **Peter and the others were**
·very sleepy [[L]weighed down with sleep], **but when they awoke fully, they**
saw the glory of Jesus and the two men standing with him. 33 **When Moses**
and Elijah were ·about to leave [[L]leaving him], **Peter said to Jesus, "Master,**
it is good that we are here. Let us make three ·tents [shelters; shrines; tabernacles; Lev. 23:42]—**one for you, one for Moses, and one for Elijah."**
[[C]Perhaps Peter wanted to prolong their stay or to commemorate their
visit.] **(Peter did not ·know what he was talking about** [[L]realize/know
what he was saying].)

34While he was saying these things, a cloud came and ·covered [overshadowed] them, and they became afraid as ·the cloud covered them [Lthey entered the cloud]. 35[LAnd; Then] A voice came from the cloud, saying, "This is my Son [Ps. 2:7], ·whom I have chosen [*or* my Chosen One; Is. 42:1]. Listen to him [Deut. 18:15; Acts 3:22]!"

36When the voice finished speaking, only Jesus was there. Peter, John, and James ·said nothing [kept silent] and told no one at that time what they had seen.

Jesus Heals a Sick Boy
(9:37–43a; Matt. 17:14–21; Mark 9:14–29)

37The next day, when they came down from the mountain, a large crowd met Jesus. 38A man in the crowd ·shouted [cried out] to him, "Teacher, ·please [LI beg you to] come and look at my son, because he is my only child. 39[LAnd look/Tbehold] ·An evil spirit [LA spirit] seizes my son, and suddenly ·he [*or* it] screams. It causes him to ·lose control of himself [have convulsions] and foam at the mouth. The evil spirit ·keeps on hurting [batters; mauls] him and almost never leaves him. 40I begged your ·followers [disciples] to ·force [drive; cast] the evil spirit out, but they could not do it."

41Jesus answered, "·You people have no faith, and your lives are all wrong [LO unbelieving and corrupt/perverse generation]. How long must I stay with you and ·put up with [endure; bear with] you? Bring your son here."

42While the boy was coming, the demon threw him on the ground ·and made him lose control of himself [in convulsions]. But Jesus ·gave a strong command to [rebuked] the ·evil [defiling; Lunclean; 4:33] spirit and healed the boy and gave him back to his father. 43All the people were ·amazed [astonished; awestruck] at the ·great power [majesty; greatness] of God.

Jesus Talks About His Death
(9:43b–45; Matt. 17:22–23; Mark 9:30–32)

While everyone was ·wondering [marveling] about all that Jesus did, he said to his ·followers [disciples], 44"·Don't forget what I tell you now [LPut these words into your ears]: [LFor] The Son of Man will be ·handed over [betrayed; delivered] to ·people [his enemies; Lhuman hands]." 45But ·the followers [Lthey] did not understand ·what this meant [Lthis word/statement]; the meaning was hidden from them so they could not ·understand [perceive it; grasp it]. But they were afraid to ask Jesus about it.

Who Is the Greatest?
(9:46–48; Matt. 18:1–5; Mark 9:33–37)

46Jesus' followers began to have an argument about which one of them ·was [would be] the greatest. 47Jesus knew what they were thinking, so he took a little child and stood the child beside him. 48Then Jesus said, "Whoever ·accepts [welcomes; receives] this little child in my name ·accepts [welcomes; receives] me [Cchildren had low social status, so the saying indicates concern for the lowly]. And whoever ·accepts [welcomes; receives] me ·accepts [welcomes; receives] the One who sent me, because whoever is least among you all is really the greatest."

Anyone Not Against Us Is for Us
(9:49–50; Matt. 10:42; Mark 9:38–41)

49John answered, "Master, we saw someone using your name to ·force [drive; cast] demons out of people. We told him to stop, because he ·does not belong to our group [Ldoes not follow with us]."

50But Jesus said to him, "Don't ·stop [hinder; forbid] him, because whoever is not against you is for you."

A Town Rejects Jesus

51When the time was coming near for Jesus to ·depart [ascend], he ·was determined to go to [resolutely set out for; Lset his face toward] Jerusalem [Matt. 19:1–2; Mark 10:1]. 52He sent some messengers ahead of him, who went into a town in Samaria to make everything ready for him. 53But the people there would not ·welcome [receive] him, because he was ·set on going to [heading towards; ^{L}traveling with his face toward] Jerusalem [^{C}Samaritans worshiped at Mount Gerizim, not in Jerusalem]. 54 When James and John, ·followers [disciples] of Jesus, saw this, they said, "Lord, do you want us to call fire down from heaven and ·destroy [burn up; consume] those people[n] [2 Kin. 1:10]?"

55 But Jesus turned and ·scolded [rebuked] them. |And Jesus said, "You don't know what kind of spirit you belong to. 56 The Son of Man [^{C}a title for the Messiah; Dan. 7:13–14] did not come to destroy the ·souls [lives] of people but to save them."|[n] Then they went to another town.

Following Jesus
(9:57–62; Matt 8:18–22)

57 As they were going along the road, someone said to Jesus, "I will follow you ·any place [wherever] you go."

58 Jesus said to them, "The foxes have ·holes [dens] to live in, and the ·birds [^{L}birds of the sky] have nests, but the Son of Man has no place to ·rest [lay] his head."

59 Jesus said to another man, "Follow me!"

But he said, "Lord, first let me go and bury my father."

60 But Jesus said to him, "Let the people who are [^{C}spiritually] dead bury their own dead. You must go and ·tell about [proclaim] the kingdom of God."

61 Another man said, "I will follow you, Lord, but first let me go and say good-bye to my family."

62 Jesus said, "Anyone who ·begins to plow a field [^{L}puts a hand to the plow] but keeps looking back is ·of no use in [*or* not fit for] the kingdom of God."

Jesus Sends Out the Seventy-Two
(10:1–12; Matt 9:37–38; 10:7–16)

10 After this, the Lord ·chose [appointed] ·seventy-two[n] [^{C}the number may reflect the 70 nations listed in the "table of nations" in Genesis 10 (the Greek text of which reads "72") and so foreshadows the mission to the Gentiles] others and sent them out in pairs ahead of him into every town and place where he ·planned [was about] to go. 2 He said to them, "·There are a great many people to harvest [^{L}The harvest is great/large], but ·there are only a few workers [^{L}the workers/laborers are few]. So pray to the Lord ·who owns [who is in charge of; ^{L}of] the harvest, that he will send more ·workers [laborers] ·to gather [^{L}into] his harvest. 3 Go now, but ·listen [^{L}look; ^{T}behold]! I am sending you out like ·sheep [lambs] among wolves. 4 Don't carry ·a purse [money bag], a ·bag [traveling bag], or sandals, and don't ·waste time talking with people [greet anyone] on the road [^{C}because of the urgency of the task]. 5 ·Before [When] you go into a house, [^{L}first] say, 'Peace be with this house.' 6 If ·peace-loving people [^{L}a son/child of peace] live there, your ·blessing of peace [^{L}peace] will ·stay with [rest on] them, but if not, then ·your blessing [^{L}it] will come back to you. 7 Stay in the same house, eating and drinking what the people there give you. [^{L}For] A worker ·should be given his pay [deserves his wages; ^{T}is worthy of his hire; 1 Tim. 5:18]. Don't move from house to house [^{C}to avoid the temptation of constantly seeking better accommodations]. 8 If you go into a town and the people welcome you, eat what they give you. 9 Heal the sick who live there, and tell them, 'The kingdom of God is near you.' 10 But if you go into a town, and the people don't welcome you, then go into the streets and say, 11 'Even the

9:54 people Some Greek copies continue "as Elijah did." **9:55–56 And . . . them."** Some Greek copies do not contain the bracketed text. **10:1 seventy-two** Some Greek copies read "seventy."

·dirt [dust] **from your town that sticks to our feet we wipe off against you**
[Cin protest and as a warning of judgment]. **But ·remember** [know; recog-
nize] **that the kingdom of God ·is near** [has come near; is at hand].' [12]**I tell
you, on ·the Judgment Day** [Lthat day] **it will be ·better** [more bearable/
tolerable] **for the people of Sodom** [Ca city God destroyed because the
people were so evil; Gen. 19] **than for the people of that town.**

Jesus Warns Unbelievers
(10:13–15; Matt. 11:20–24)

[13]**"·How terrible for** [LWoe to] **you, Korazin! ·How terrible for** [LWoe
to] **you, Bethsaida** [Ctowns in Galilee where Jesus ministered]**! If the ·mir-
acles** [powerful deeds] **·I did** [Lthat occurred] **in you had happened in
Tyre and Sidon** [Ccities in Phoenicia notorious for their wickedness],
those people would have ·changed their lives [repented] **long ago. ·They
would have worn rough cloth and put ashes on themselves to show they
had changed** [L...sitting in sackcloth/burlap and ashes; Csigns of sorrow
and deep remorse]. [14]**But ·on the judgment day** [Lat the judgment] **it will
be ·better** [more bearable/tolerable] **for Tyre and Sidon than for you.**
[15]**And you, Capernaum** [Ca town in Galilee where Jesus lived and minis-
tered], **will you be ·lifted up to** [honored/exalted in] **heaven? No! You will
be thrown down to ·the depths** [the place of the dead; hell; LHades;
Is. 14:13–15]**!**
[16]**"Whoever listens to you listens to me** [Matt. 10:40; John 13:20], **and
whoever ·refuses to accept** [rejects] **you ·refuses to accept** [rejects] **me.
And whoever ·refuses to accept** [rejects] **me ·refuses to accept** [rejects] **the
One who sent me."**

Satan Falls

[17]When the ·seventy-two[n] came back, they were very ·happy [joyful]
and said, "Lord, even the demons ·obeyed [submit to] us ·when we used
your name [Lin your name]!"
[18]Jesus said, **"I saw Satan fall like lightning from heaven** [Csymbolically
in the exorcisms; Is. 14:12; Rev. 12:13]. [19]**·Listen** [LLook; TBehold], **I have
given you ·power** [authority] **to ·walk on** [trample] **snakes and scorpions,
·power that is greater than the enemy has** [L...and authority over all the
power of the enemy]. **So nothing will hurt you.** [20]**But you should not ·be
happy** [rejoice] **because the spirits ·obey** [submit to] **you but because
your names are ·written** [recorded] **in heaven."**

Jesus Prays to the Father
(10:21–24; Matt. 11:25–27; 13:16–17)

[21]·Then [At that time; LIn the same hour] Jesus ·rejoiced [was full of
joy] in the Holy Spirit and said, **"I ·praise** [bless; thank; acknowledge] **you,
Father, Lord of heaven and earth, because you have hidden these things
from the people who are wise and ·smart** [learned; intelligent]. **But you
have ·shown** [revealed] **them to ·those who are like little children** [Llittle
children; infants; Cthose with a childlike faith]. **Yes, Father,** [Lbecause] **this
is what ·you really wanted** [pleased you].
[22]**"My Father has ·given** [entrusted/committed to] **me all things. No
one knows who the Son is, except the Father. And no one knows who the
Father is, except the Son and those whom the Son ·chooses** [desires;
intends] **to ·tell** [Lreveal it to]**."**
[23]Then Jesus turned to his ·followers [disciples] and said privately,
"·You are blessed to [LBlessed are the eyes that] **see what you now see.**
[24][LFor] **I tell you, many prophets and kings wanted to see what you now
see, but they did not, and they wanted to hear what you now hear, but
they did not."**

10:17 seventy-two Some Greek copies read "seventy."

The Good Samaritan
(10:25–37; Matt. 22:34–40; Mark 12:28–34)

25Then an expert on the law stood up to test Jesus, saying, "Teacher, what must I do to ·get life forever [Linherit eternal life]**?"**

26Jesus said, "What is written in the law? ·What do you read there [*or* How do you interpret it]**?"**

27The man answered, "Love the Lord your God with all your heart, all your soul, all your strength, and all your mind [Deut. 6:5]**." Also, "Love your neighbor as you love yourself** [Lev. 19:18]**."**

28Jesus said to him, "Your answer is right. Do this and you will live."

29But the man, wanting to ·show the importance of his question [*or* justify his question; *or* justify himself/his own actions]**, said to Jesus, "And who is my neighbor?"**

30Jesus answered, "As a man was going down from Jerusalem to Jericho [Ca dangerous 17-mile trek through desolate territory]**, some robbers attacked him. They tore off his clothes, beat him, and left him lying there, almost dead. 31·It happened that** [*or* By chance] **a priest was going down that road. When he saw the man, he ·walked** [passed] **by on the other side. 32·Next** [LLikewise; So too]**, a Levite** [CLevites were members of the tribe of Levi who helped the priests in the temple; 1 Chr. 23:24–32] **came there, and ·after he went over and looked at the man** [Lseeing him]**, he ·walked** [passed] **by on the other side of the road. 33Then a Samaritan** [Ca people disliked by the Jews because they were only part Jewish and worshiped differently] **traveling down the road came to where the hurt man was. When he saw the man, he felt ·very sorry** [compassion] **for him. 34The Samaritan went to him, poured olive oil and wine on his wounds** [Cto soothe and clean them]**, and bandaged them. Then he put the hurt man on his own ·donkey** [Lanimal] **and took him to an inn where he cared for him. 35The next day, the Samaritan brought out two ·coins** [Ldenarii; Ceach equivalent to a day's wage]**, gave them to the innkeeper, and said, 'Take care of this man. If you spend more money on him, I will pay it back to you when I come again.' "**

36Then Jesus said, "Which one of these three men do you think was a neighbor to the man who was attacked by the robbers?"

37The expert on the law answered, "The one who showed him mercy."

Jesus said to him, "Then go and do ·what he did [the same; likewise]**."**

Mary and Martha

38While ·Jesus and his followers [Lthey] **were traveling, Jesus went into a ·town** [village]**. A woman named Martha ·let Jesus stay at her house** [Lwelcomed/received him]**. 39Martha had a sister named Mary, who was sitting at the Lord's feet and listening to ·him teach** [what he said; Lhis word/message; Csitting at a teacher's feet indicates the position of a disciple; see Acts 22:3]**. 40But Martha was ·busy** [worried; distracted] **with ·all the work to be done** [the many preparations]**. She went in and said, "Lord, don't you care that my sister has left me alone to ·do all the work** [serve; prepare the meal]**?** [Please; LTherefore] **Tell her to help me."**

41But the Lord answered her, "Martha, Martha, you are ·worried [anxious] **and upset about many things. 42Only one thing is ·important** [necessary; needed]**. Mary has chosen the better thing, and it will never be taken away from her."**

Jesus Teaches About Prayer
(11:1–4; Matt. 6:9–13)

11 One time Jesus was praying in a certain place. When he finished, one of his ·followers [disciples] **said to him, "Lord, teach us to pray as John taught his ·followers** [disciples]**."**

2Jesus said to them, "When you pray, say:
'Father, ·may your name always be kept holy [Thallowed be your name].
May your kingdom come [Csoon *or* fully].
3Give us ·the food we need for each day [Tour daily bread].
4Forgive us for our sins,
·because [as] we forgive everyone who ·has done wrong to us [sins
against us; Lis indebted to us; Csin is pictured as a debt owed].
And ·do not cause us to be tempted [*or* do not subject us to testing;
Tlead us not into temptation].' "[n]

Continue to Ask
(11:5–13; Matt. 7:7–11)

5Then Jesus said to them, "Suppose one of you went to your friend's
house at midnight and said to him, 'Friend, loan me three loaves of bread.
6A friend of mine has come ·into town [Lfrom the road] to visit me, but I
have nothing ·for him to eat [to offer him; Lto set before him].' 7Your friend
inside the house answers, 'Don't bother me! The door is already ·locked
[shut], and my children ·and I are [Lare with me] in bed [Ca small Palestinian
home where everyone slept in one room]. I cannot get up and give you anything.' 8I tell you, [Leven] if friendship is not enough to make him get up to
give you the bread, ·your boldness will make him [your shameless persis-
tence will make him; *or* in order not to be shamed before the community he
will] get up and give you whatever you need. 9So I tell you, ·ask [keep on ask-
ing], and God will give to you. ·Search [Keep on searching/seeking], and you
will find. ·Knock [Keep on knocking], and the door will open for you. 10·Yes,
[LFor; Because] everyone who asks will receive. The one who ·searches
[seeks] will find. And everyone who knocks will have the door opened. 11If
your ·children ask [*or* son asks] for[n] a fish, which of you fathers would give
them a snake instead? 12Or, if ·your children ask [*or* he asks] for an egg,
would you give them a scorpion? 13Even though you are ·bad [sinful; evil],
you know how to give good ·things [Lgifts] to your children. How much
more your heavenly Father will give the Holy Spirit to those who ask him!"

Jesus' Power Is from God
(11:14–23; Matt. 12:22–30; Mark 3:22–27)

14One time Jesus was ·sending [driving; casting] out a demon ·who
could not talk [*or* who was making a man mute]. When the demon came
out, the man who had been unable to speak, then spoke. The ·people were
[crowd was] amazed. 15But some of them said, "Jesus uses the power of
Beelzebul [Canother name for Satan], the ruler of demons, to ·force [drive;
cast] demons out of people."
16Other people, wanting to test Jesus, asked him to give them a sign
from heaven. 17But knowing their thoughts, he said to them, "Every kingdom that is ·divided against [at war with] itself ·will be destroyed [is
doomed/heading for ruin]. And a ·family [Lhouse] that is ·divided against
[at war with] itself will ·not continue [Lfall]. 18So if Satan is divided
against himself, ·his kingdom will not continue [Lhow will his kingdom
stand?]. [LFor] You say that I use the power of Beelzebul [v. 15] to ·force
[drive; cast] out demons. 19But if I use the power of Beelzebul to ·force
[drive; cast] out demons, what power do your ·people [own exorcists; followers; Lsons] use to ·force [drive; cast] demons out? So they will ·be your
judges. 20But if I use the ·power [Lfinger] of God to ·force [drive; cast] out
demons, then the kingdom of God has ·come to [arrived among] you.

11:2–4 'Father . . . tempted.' Some Greek copies include phrases from Matthew's version of this prayer (Matthew 6:9–13). **11:11 for** Some Greek copies include the phrase "for bread, which of you would give them a stone, or if they ask for . . ."

21“**When a strong person ·with many weapons** [fully armed] **guards his own ·house** [villa; *or* palace; Ca large building with a courtyard], **his possessions are safe.** 22**But when someone stronger comes and ·defeats** [overpowers; conquers] **him, the stronger one will take away the ·weapons** [armor] **·the first man trusted** [on which he relied] **and will ·give away the possessions** [Ldivide his plunder].

23“**Anyone who is not with me is against me, and anyone who does not ·work** [Lgather] **with me ·is working against me** [scatters; Cthe metaphor is probably to gathering or scattering a flock; John 10:12].

The Empty Person
(11:24–26; Matt. 12:43–45)

24“**When an ·evil** [defiling; Lunclean; 4:33] **spirit comes out of a person, it ·travels** [wanders] **through ·dry** [waterless; arid] **places, looking for a place to rest. But when it finds no place, it says, ‘I will go back to the house** [Cmeaning the person] **I left.’** 25**And when it comes back, it finds that house swept clean and ·made neat** [in order; fixed up]. 26**Then ·the evil spirit** [Lit] **goes out and brings seven other spirits more evil than it is, and they go in and live there. So ·the person has even more trouble than before** [Lthe last state of that person is worse than the first].”

People Who Are Truly Blessed

27**As Jesus was saying these things, a woman in the crowd called out to Jesus, “Blessed is the ·mother who gave birth to you** [Lthe womb that bore you] and [Lthe breasts that] **nursed you.”**

28**But Jesus said, “·No** [LRather; On the contrary], **blessed are those who hear the ·teaching** [word] **of God and ·obey** [practice; keep] **it.”**

The People Want a Miracle
(11:29–32; Matt. 12:38–42; Mark 8:11–12)

29**As the crowd grew larger, Jesus ·said** [began to say], **“·The people who live today are evil** [LThis generation is an evil/wicked generation]. **They ·want to see** [seek] **a ·miracle for a sign** [Lsign], **but no sign will be given them, except the sign of Jonah** [Matt. 12:39–40]. 30**As Jonah was a sign for those people who lived in Nineveh, the Son of Man will be a sign for ·the people of this time** [this generation]. 31**·On the judgment day** [At the judgment] **the Queen of the South** [Cthe Queen of Sheba] **will stand up with the people ·who live now** [of this generation]. **She will ·show they are guilty** [condemn them], **because she came from ·far away** [Lthe ends of the earth] **to listen to Solomon’s wise teaching** [1 Kin. 10:1–13]. **And ·I tell you that** [Llook; Tbehold] **·someone** [*or* something; Ceither Jesus or his message of the Kingdom of God] **greater than Solomon is here.** 32**·On the judgment day** [At the judgment] **the ·people** [*or* men; Cthe Greek term usually refers to males] **of Nineveh will stand up with ·the people who live now** [this generation], **and they will ·show that you are guilty** [condemn it]. [LBecause] **When Jonah preached to them, they ·were sorry and changed their lives** [repented]. **And I tell you that ·someone** [*or* something; v. 31] **greater than Jonah is here.**

Be a Light for the World
(11:33–36; Matt. 5:15; 6:22–23)

33“**No one lights a lamp and puts it in a ·secret place** [cellar] **or under a ·bowl** [*or* basket], **but on a lampstand so the people who come in can see** [Lthe light; Matt. 5:15; Mark 4:21]. 34**Your eye is ·a light** [Lthe lamp] **for the body. When your eyes are ·good** [healthy; clear], **your whole body will be full of light. But when your eyes are ·evil** [unhealthy; bad], **your whole body will be full of darkness.** 35**So be careful ·not to let the light in you become** [*or* that the light in you is not actually] **darkness.** 36**If your whole body is full of light, and none of it is dark, then you will ·shine bright** [be radiant; be filled with light], **as when a lamp shines** [brightly; Lwith its rays] **on you.”**

Jesus Accuses the Pharisees
(11:37–54; Matt. 15:1–9; 23:4–7, 25–36; Mark 7:1–9)

37After Jesus had finished speaking, a Pharisee asked Jesus to ·eat [dine]
with him. So Jesus went in and ·sat at the table [reclined; C the posture for
a banquet or dinner party; see 7:36]. 38But the Pharisee was surprised
when he saw that Jesus did not wash his hands before the meal [Ca Jewish
ritual for ceremonial purity]. 39The Lord said to him, "You Pharisees clean
the outside of the cup and the dish, but inside you are full of ·greed
[extortion; robbery] and ·evil [wickedness]. 40You foolish people! The
same one who made what is outside also made what is inside. 41So ·give
what is in your dishes [*or* give from your hearts; Lgive the inside things] ·to
the poor [as alms], and then ·you [everything] will be fully clean. 42·How
terrible for [LWoe to] you Pharisees! You ·give God one-tenth of [pay tithe
on] even your mint, your rue, and every other ·plant [herb] in your garden. But you ·fail to be fair to others [neglect to show justice] and to love
God. These are the things you should do ·while continuing [without
neglecting] to do those other things. 43·How terrible for [LWoe to] you
Pharisees, because you love to have the most ·important [honorable]
seats in the synagogues, and you love to be greeted with respect in the
marketplaces. 44·How terrible for [LWoe to] you, because you are like ·hid-
den [unmarked] graves, which people walk on without knowing."

Jesus Talks to Experts on the Law
(see parallels at 11:37)

45One of the experts on the law said to Jesus, "Teacher, when you say
these things, you are insulting us, too."
46Jesus answered, "·How terrible for [LWoe to] you, you experts on the
law! You ·make strict rules that are very hard for people to obey [Lburden
people with burdens hard to carry], but you yourselves don't even ·try to
follow those rules [*or* lift a finger to ease the burden]. 47·How terrible for
[LWoe to] you, because you build ·tombs [monuments; memorials] for
the prophets whom your ancestors killed! 48And now you ·show [are witnesses; testify] that you approve of what your ancestors did. They killed
the prophets, and you build ·tombs [monuments; memorials] for them!
49This is why ·in his wisdom God said [LGod's Wisdom said; Ca personification of wisdom; Prov. 8], 'I will send prophets and apostles to them.
·They will kill some, and they will treat others cruelly [*or* Some they will
persecute and kill].' 50So ·you who live now [this generation] will be ·pun-
ished for [charged with; held responsible for] the ·deaths of all the
prophets who were killed [Lblood of all the prophets shed] since the
·beginning [foundation; creation] of the world— 51from the ·killing
[blood] of Abel to the ·killing [blood] of Zechariah, who died between the
altar and the ·Temple [sanctuary; Lhouse (of God); Cin the arrangement of
the Hebrew OT, Abel and Zechariah were the first and last people to be
murdered; Gen. 4:4–8; 2 Chr. 24:20–21]. Yes, I tell you that ·you who are
alive now [this generation] will be ·punished [charged; held responsible]
for them all.
52"·How terrible for [LWoe to] you, you experts on the law. You have
taken away the key to ·learning about God [Lknowledge]. You yourselves
·would not learn [Ldid not enter], and you ·stopped [hindered; prevented]
others from ·learning [Lentering], too."
53When Jesus left, the ·teachers of the law [scribes] and the Pharisees
began to ·give him trouble [fiercely oppose him; act with hostility], ·ask-
ing him [provoking/attacking/besieging him with] questions about many
things, 54·trying [lying in wait; plotting an ambush; Cmetaphorically] to
catch him saying something wrong.

Don't Be Like the Pharisees
(12:1–7; Matt. 10:26–31; 16:5–6; Mark 8:14–15)

12 [LMeanwhile] So many thousands of people had gathered
that they were ·stepping [trampling] on each other. Jesus
began to speak first to his ·followers [disciples], saying, "Beware of the
·yeast [leaven] of the Pharisees, ·because they are hypocrites [Lwhich is
hypocrisy; Cthe evil influence of the Pharisees was like yeast that would
grow and affect everything around it; Mark 8:14–21]. 2 Everything that is
·hidden [concealed; covered up] will be ·shown [revealed; uncovered;
disclosed], and everything that is ·secret [hidden] will be made known.
3 What you have said in the dark will be heard in the light, and what you
have whispered ·in an inner room [*or* behind closed doors] will be
·shouted [proclaimed] from the housetops.
4 "I tell you, my friends, don't be afraid of people who can kill the body
but after that can do nothing more to hurt you. 5 I will ·show you [warn
you about] the one to fear. Fear the one who has the ·power [authority]
·to kill you and also [Lafter the killing] to throw you into ·hell [LGehenna;
Ca valley outside of Jerusalem where in the OT period children were sacrificed to a pagan god; later used as a burning trash heap; a metaphor for
hell]. Yes, this is the one you should fear.
6 "[LAre not...?] Five sparrows are sold for only two pennies [CGreek: *assa-
ria*; copper coins of very low value], ·and [yet] God does not forget any of
them. 7 But ·God even knows how many hairs you have on your head
[Leven the hairs on your head have all been numbered]. Don't be afraid.
You are worth much more than many sparrows.

Don't Be Ashamed of Jesus

8 "I tell you, all those who ·stand before others and say they believe in
me [Lconfess/acknowledge me before people], ·I, the Son of Man, [Lthe Son
of Man; Ca title for the Messiah; Dan. 7:13–14] will ·say before the angels of
God that they belong to me [Lconfess/acknowledge them before God's
angels]. 9 But all who ·stand before others and say they do not believe in me
[Ldeny/disown me before people], I will ·say before the angels of God that
they do not belong to me [Ldeny/disown them before God's angels].
10 "Anyone who speaks [La word] against the Son of Man can be forgiven, but anyone who ·speaks [Lblasphemes] against the Holy Spirit will
not be forgiven [Matt. 12:31–32; Mark 3:28–30].
11 "When you are brought into the synagogues before the leaders and
·other powerful people [authorities], don't worry about how to defend
yourself or what to say. 12 [LFor] At that time the Holy Spirit will teach you
what you ·must [ought/need to] say [Matt. 10:19–20; Mark 13:11]."

Jesus Warns Against Selfishness

13 Someone in the crowd said to Jesus, "Teacher, tell my brother to
divide with me the ·property our father left us [family inheritance]."
14 But Jesus said to him, "[LMan,] Who ·said I should judge or decide
[appointed me judge or arbiter] between you?" 15 Then Jesus said to them,
"Be careful and guard against all kinds of greed. Life ·is not measured by
[does not consist of] how much one owns."
16 Then Jesus told this ·story [parable]: "There was a rich man who had
some land, which grew a good crop. 17 He thought to himself, 'What will I
do? I have no place to keep all my crops.' 18 Then he said, 'This is what I
will do: I will tear down my barns and build bigger ones, and there I will
store all my grain and other goods. 19 Then I can say to ·myself [Lmy soul],
"I [LSoul, you] have enough good things stored to last for many years.
·Rest [Take it easy], eat, drink, and ·enjoy life [celebrate; Tbe merry]!"'
20 "But God said to him, 'Foolish man! Tonight your ·life [Lsoul] will be

·taken [demanded back] from you. So who will get those things you have
prepared for yourself?'
21"This is how it will be for those who store up ·things [wealth; trea-
sure] for themselves and are not rich ·toward [*or* in what matters to; *or* in
their relationship with] God."

Don't Worry
(12:22–31; Matt 6:25–33)

22Jesus said to his ·followers [disciples], "So I tell you, don't worry about
the food you need to live, or about the clothes you need for your body.
23[LFor] Life is more than food, and the body is more than clothes. 24·Look at
[Consider; Think of] the ·birds [Lravens]. They don't ·plant [sow] or ·harvest
[reap], they don't have storerooms or barns, but God feeds them. And you
are worth much more than birds. 25·You cannot [LWho of you can...?] add
·any time [*or* a step; La cubit; Cabout eighteen inches] to your ·life [*or* height;
Cthe Greek is ambiguous, but probably refers to time instead of stature] by
worrying about it. 26If you cannot ·do [change] even the little things [by
worrying], then why worry about the ·big things [Lthe rest]? 27·Consider
[Look; Think] how the lilies grow; they don't ·work [toil] or ·make clothes
for themselves [Lspin thread]. But I tell you that even Solomon ·with his
riches [Lin all his glory] was not dressed as beautifully as one of these flowers. 28God clothes [LIf God clothes...?] the ·grass [wildflower] in the field,
which is alive today but tomorrow is thrown into the ·fire [Lfurnace; oven].
So how much more will God clothe you? ·Don't have so little faith [*or* You
people of little faith; *or* How little faith you have]! 29Don't always think about
what you will eat or what you will drink, and don't keep worrying. 30All the
·people [nations; Gentiles; pagans] in the world are trying to get these things,
and your Father knows you need them. 31But seek God's kingdom, and ·all
your other needs will be met as well [Lthese things will be given to you].

Don't Trust in Money

32"Don't fear, little flock, because your Father ·wants [is glad/pleased]
to give you the kingdom. 33Sell your possessions and give ·to the poor
[alms]. ·Get [Make] for yourselves ·purses [moneybags] that will not wear
out, the treasure in heaven that never ·runs out [fails you], where thieves
can't ·steal [Lcome near] and moths can't destroy. 34·Your heart will be
where your treasure is [LFor where your treasure is, there your heart will
be also; Matt. 6:19–21].

Always Be Ready
(12:35–48; Matt 24:43–51)

35"·Be dressed, ready for service [TLet your loins be girded; Ctucking
garments into the waist belt to allow swift movement; a metaphor for pre-
paredness], and have your lamps ·shining [burning; lit]. 36Be like ·servants
[Lpeople] who are waiting for their ·master [lord] to come home from a
wedding party. When he comes and knocks, the servants immediately
open the door for him. 37·They [LThose servants/slaves] will be ·blessed
[happy; *or* rewarded] when their ·master [lord] comes home, because he
sees that they were ·watching [alert; awake] for him. I tell you the truth,
the master will dress himself to serve and tell the servants to ·sit at the
table [recline; Cthe posture for a banquet or dinner party; see 7:36], and he
will ·serve [wait on] them [Ca radical reversal in a culture where a master
would never wait on a slave]. 38Those servants will be ·blessed [happy; *or*
rewarded] when he comes in and finds them ·still waiting [Lthus; Calert
and ready], even ·if it is midnight or later [Leven in the second or third
watches; Cbetween 9 PM and 3 AM (by Roman reckoning)].
39"·Remember [Know] this: If the owner of the house knew what time a
thief was coming, he would not allow the thief to ·enter [break into] his

house. 40So you also must be ready, because the Son of Man [Ca title for the Messiah; Dan. 7:13–14] **will come at a time when you don't expect him!"**

Who Is the Trusted Servant?

41Peter said, "Lord, did you tell this ·story to [parable for] **us or ·to** [for] **all people?"**

42The Lord said, "Who is the ·trusted [faithful] **and ·wise** [sensible] **·servant** [household manager] **that the ·master** [lord] **·trusts** [Lputs in charge of the household servants] **to give ·the other servants** [Lthem] **their ·food** [food allowance; daily provisions] **at the right time? 43That ·servant** [slave] **will be ·blessed** [happy; *or* rewarded] **when the master comes and finds him doing his work. 44I tell you the truth, the master will ·choose that servant to take care** [put him in charge] **of everything he owns. 45But suppose the ·servant** [slave] **thinks to himself, 'My master ·will not come back soon** [is delayed in coming]**,' and he begins to beat the other servants, men and women, and to eat and drink and get drunk. 46The master** [Lof that servant/slave] **will come** [Lon a day] **when that servant is not ready and** [Lat an hour when he] **is not expecting him. Then the master will cut him in pieces and ·send him away to be** [assign/appoint him a place] **with the ·others who don't obey** [unfaithful; unbelievers; Ca metaphorical reference to Jesus, the ultimate Lord and Master, returning to judge his servants].

47"The ·servant [slave] **who knows what his master wants but is not ·ready** [prepared]**, or who does not do what the master wants, will ·be beaten with many blows** [beaten severely]**! 48But the servant who does not know what his master wants and does things that should be punished will be beaten ·with few blows** [lightly; Ca metaphor for judgment]**. From everyone who has been given much, much will be ·demanded** [required]**. And from the one trusted with much, much more will be expected.**

Jesus Causes Division
(12:49–53; Matt. 10:34–36)

49"I came to ·set [bring; cast] **fire to the world, and I wish it were already ·burning** [kindled]**! 50I have a baptism** [Ca metaphor for suffering, portrayed as an overwhelming deluge] **·to suffer through** [Lto be baptized with]**, and I feel very ·troubled** [distressed] **until it is over. 51Do you think I came to give peace to the earth? No, I tell you, I came to ·divide it** [bring division]. 52[LFor] **From now on, a ·family** [Lhouse] **with five people will be divided, three against two, and two against three. 53They will be divided: father against son and son against father, mother against daughter and daughter against mother, mother-in-law against daughter-in-law and daughter-in-law against mother-in-law** [Mic. 7:6]**."**

Understanding the Times
(12:54–56; Matt. 16:2–3)

54Then Jesus said to the ·people [crowds]**, "When you see clouds coming up in the west,** [Limmediately] **you say, 'It's going to rain,' and** [Lso; thus] **it happens. 55When you feel the wind begin to blow from the south** [Cthe desert]**, you say, 'It will be a hot day,' and it happens. 56Hypocrites! You know how to ·understand** [interpret] **the appearance of the earth and sky. Why don't you ·understand** [know how to interpret] **·what is happening now** [this present time; Cthe time of the coming of the Kingdom]?

Settle Your Problems
(12:57–59; Matt. 5:25–26)

57"Why can't you ·decide [judge] **for yourselves what is right? 58If your ·enemy** [opponent; accuser] **is taking you ·to court** [before the magistrate/ruler]**, try hard to settle it on the way. If you don't, your enemy might ·take** [drag] **you to the judge, and the judge might turn you over to the officer, and the officer might throw you into ·jail** [prison]**. 59I tell you, you will not get out of there until you have paid everything you owe** [CGreek: the last *lepton*; a copper or bronze coin of very little value]**."**

Change Your Hearts

13 At that time some people were there who told Jesus that Pilate
[CPontius Pilate, governor of Judea from AD 26 to 36; see 3:1]
had killed some people from Galilee while they were worshiping. He
mixed their blood with the blood of the animals they were sacrificing to
God. 2Jesus answered, "Do you think ·this happened to them [Lthey suffered these things] because they were more sinful than all others from
Galilee? 3No, I tell you. But unless you ·change your hearts and lives
[repent], you will [Lall] be destroyed as they were! 4[LOr] What about
those eighteen people who died when the tower of Siloam fell on them?
Do you think they were ·more sinful [more guilty; greater offenders]
than all the others who live in Jerusalem? 5No, I tell you. But unless you
·change your hearts and lives [repent], you will all be destroyed too!"

The Useless Tree

6Jesus told this ·story [parable]: "A man had a fig tree planted in his
vineyard. He came looking for some fruit on the tree, but he found none.
7So the man said to his gardener, '[LLook,] I have been looking for fruit on
this tree for three years, but I never find any. Cut it down. Why should it
·waste the ground [take up space]?' 8But the servant answered, '·Master
[Sir], let the tree have one more year to produce fruit. Let me dig up the
dirt around it and put on some ·fertilizer [manure]. 9If the tree produces
fruit next year, good. But if not, you can cut it down.' "

Jesus Heals on the Sabbath

10Jesus was teaching in one of the synagogues on the Sabbath day. 11A
woman was there who, for eighteen years, had an evil spirit in her that
made her ·crippled [disabled]. Her back was always bent; she could not
stand up straight. 12When Jesus saw her, he called her over and said,
"Woman, you are ·free [released; set free] from your ·sickness [disabil-
ity]." 13Jesus ·put [laid] his hands on her, and immediately she was able to
stand up straight and began ·praising [giving glory to] God.
14The synagogue leader was ·angry [indignant] because Jesus healed on the
Sabbath day. He said to the people, "There are six days when one has to work.
So come to be healed on one of those days, and not on the Sabbath day."
15The Lord answered, "You hypocrites! Doesn't each of you untie your
·work animals [Lox or donkey from the stall] and lead them to drink water
on the Sabbath day? 16This woman that I healed, a daughter of Abraham,
has been held by Satan for eighteen years. ·Surely it is not wrong [LWas it
not necessary…?] for her to be freed from ·her sickness [Lthis bond/
imprisonment] on a Sabbath day!" 17When Jesus said this, all of those
who were ·criticizing [opposing] him were ashamed, but the entire crowd
rejoiced at all the ·wonderful [glorious] things Jesus was doing.

Stories of Mustard Seed and Yeast

(13:18–21; Matt 13:31–33; Mark 4:30–32)

18Then Jesus said, "What is God's kingdom like? What can I compare it
with? 19It is like a mustard seed that a man plants in his garden. The seed
grows and becomes a tree, and the ·wild birds [Lbirds of the sky] build
nests in its branches."
20Jesus said again, "What can I compare God's kingdom with? 21It is
like ·yeast [leaven] that a woman took and ·hid [mixed] in a large tub
[CGreek: three *sata*; about fifty pounds] of flour until ·it made all the
dough rise [Lthe whole was leavened; Matt. 13:33]."

The Narrow Door

(13:22–30; Matt 7:13–14, 22–23; 8:11–12; 19:30; Mark 10:31)

22Jesus was teaching in every town and village as he traveled toward
Jerusalem. 23Someone said to Jesus, "Lord, will only a few people be saved?"
Jesus said, 24"·Try hard [Strive; Exert yourself] to enter through the
narrow door, because many people [LI tell you] will try to enter there, but
they will not be able. 25When the owner of the house gets up and closes

the door, you ·can [Lbegin to] stand outside and knock on the door and say, '·Sir [Lord], open the door for us.' But he will answer, 'I don't know you or where you come from.' 26Then you will say, 'We ate and drank with you, and you taught in the streets of our town.' 27But he will say to you, 'I don't know you or where you come from. Go away from me, all you who ·do evil [practice unrighteousness; Ps. 6:8]!' 28[LThere; In that place] You will cry and ·grind [gnash] your teeth [Cindicating pain and remorse, or perhaps anger at the master; see Ps. 35:16] when you see Abraham, Isaac, Jacob, and all the prophets in God's kingdom, but you yourselves thrown outside. 29People will come from the east, west, north, and south and will ·sit down at the table [Lrecline; Cthe posture for a banquet or dinner party] in the kingdom of God [Cthe messianic banquet, a metaphor for God's final salvation; Is. 25:6–8]. 30[Indeed; LLook; TBehold] There are those who are last now who will be first in the future. And there are those who are first now who will be last in the future."

Jesus Will Die in Jerusalem
(13:31–35; Matt. 23:37–39)

31At that ·time [*or* very hour] some Pharisees came to Jesus and said, "Go away from here! Herod [CAntipas; see 3:1] wants to kill you!"

32Jesus said to them, "Go tell that fox Herod, '[LLook; TBehold] Today and tomorrow I am ·forcing [driving; casting] demons out and healing people. Then, on the third day, I will ·reach my goal [accomplish my purpose; finish my work; Lfinish].' 33Yet I must be on my way today and tomorrow and the next day. Surely it ·cannot be right [is impossible; is unthinkable] for a prophet to be killed anywhere except in Jerusalem.

34"Jerusalem, Jerusalem! You kill the prophets and stone to death those who are sent to you. ·Many times [How often] I wanted to gather your ·people [Lchildren] as a hen gathers her chicks under her wings, but you would not let me [Matt. 23:37–39]. 35·Now [LLook!; TBehold!] your house is ·left completely empty [left desolate; abandoned; Jer. 22:5]. I tell you, you will not see me until that time when you will say, '·God bless [LBlessed is] the One who comes in the name of the Lord [Ps. 118:26].'"

Healing on the Sabbath

14 On a Sabbath day, when Jesus went to eat at the home of a leading Pharisee, ·the people [Lthey; Cprobably religious leaders] were watching Jesus very closely. 2And [LLook; TBehold] in front of him was a man with ·dropsy [Cswelling caused by bodily fluids; also called edema]. 3Jesus said to the Pharisees and experts on the law, "Is it ·right or wrong [permitted; lawful] to heal on the Sabbath day?" 4But they ·would not answer his question [Lkept silent]. So Jesus ·took [touched; took hold of] the man, healed him, and sent him away. 5Jesus said to ·the Pharisees and teachers of the law [Lthem], "If your child*n* or ox falls into a ·well [*or* pit] on the Sabbath day, will you not pull him out ·quickly [immediately; right away; Ex. 21:33–34]?" 6And they could not answer him.

Don't Make Yourself Important

7When Jesus noticed that some of the guests were choosing the ·best places [places of honor] to sit [Cseats were assigned according to social status], he told this ·story [parable]: 8"When someone invites you to a wedding feast, don't take the ·most important seat [place of honor], because someone more ·important [distinguished; honorable] than you may have been invited. 9The host, who invited both of you, will come to you and say, 'Give this person your seat.' Then you will be ·embarrassed [humiliated; disgraced; shamed] and will have to move to the ·last [least;

14:5 child Some Greek copies read "donkey."

lowest] place. 10·So [LBut] when you are invited, go ·sit in a seat that is not important [Lrecline in the last/lowest place; 7:36]. When the host comes to you, he may say, 'Friend, move up here to a ·more important [better; higher] place.' Then ·all the other guests will respect you [Lyou will be honored in the presence of all the guests]. 11[LFor; Because] All who ·make themselves great [exalt themselves] will be made humble, but those who make themselves humble will be ·made great [exalted]."

You Will Be Rewarded

12Then Jesus said to the man who had invited him, "When you give a lunch or a dinner, don't invite only your friends, your ·family [near relatives; Lbrothers; siblings], your other relatives, and your rich neighbors. At another time they will invite you to eat with them, and ·you will be repaid [*or* that will be your only payment]. 13Instead, when you give a ·feast [banquet], invite the poor, the crippled, the lame, and the blind. 14Then you will be blessed, because they have nothing and cannot pay you back [Csomething given was typically repaid with goods, favors, or honor]. ·But [For] you will be repaid ·when the good people rise from the dead [Lat the resurrection of the righteous]."

A Story About a Big Banquet

(14:15–24; Matt. 22:1–10)

15One of those ·at the table [Lreclining; see 5:29] with Jesus heard these things and said to him, "·Blessed [Happy] are the people who will ·share in the meal [Leat bread] in God's kingdom [Can allusion to the messianic banquet at the end of time; see 13:29; Is. 25:6–8]."

16Jesus said to him, "A man gave a ·big [great] banquet and invited many people. 17When it was time to eat, the man sent his ·servant [slave] to tell the guests [Cwho had accepted the invitation], 'Come. Everything is ready.'

18"But all the guests [one after another; *or* in a similar manner] began to make excuses [Ca great offense in that culture]. The first one said, 'I have just bought a field, and I must go look at it. Please excuse me.' 19Another said, 'I have just bought five ·pairs [Lyoke] of oxen; I must go and try them. Please excuse me.' 20A third person said, 'I just got married; I can't come [Cwhile newly married men were exempt from certain duties (Deut. 24:5), that is not a valid excuse for offending the host].' 21So the ·servant [slave] returned and told his master what had happened. Then the master [Lof the household] became angry and said, 'Go at once into the ·streets [squares] and ·alleys [lanes] of the town, and bring in the poor, the crippled, the blind, and the lame.' 22·Later [LAnd] the ·servant [slave] said to him, 'Master, I did what you commanded, but we still have room.' 23The master said to the servant, 'Go out to the roads and ·country lanes [hedgerows], and ·urge [compel] the people there to come so my house will be full [Cthose outside the city may refer to the Gentiles, who will come into the kingdom (see Acts 10–11)]. 24[LFor] I tell you, none of ·those [Lthose men; Creferring to the three who refused] whom I invited first will ·eat with me [Ltaste my banquet/dinner].'"

The Cost of Being Jesus' Follower

(14:25–33; Matt. 10:37–38)

25Large crowds were traveling with Jesus, and he turned and said to them, 26"If anyone comes to me but ·does not hate [*or* loves more than me; CJesus is using hyperbole to emphasize his point] his father, mother, wife, children, brothers, or sisters—or even ·life [life itself; *or* his own life]—he cannot be my ·follower [disciple]. 27Whoever ·is not willing to [Ldoes not] carry his own cross and follow me cannot be my ·follower [disciple]. 28·If you want [LFor which of you who wants…?] to build a tower, you first sit down and ·decide [calculate; figure out] how much it will cost, to see if you have enough money to finish the job. 29If you don't, you might lay the foundation, but you would not be able to finish. Then all who would see it would ·make fun of [mock; ridicule] you, 30saying, 'This person began to build but was not able to finish.'

31"If a king is going to ·fight [meet in battle; wage war against] another king, first ·he will [Lwill he not…?] sit down and plan. He will decide if he and his ten thousand soldiers can ·defeat [Lengage/meet in battle] the other king who has twenty thousand soldiers. 32If he can't, then while the other king is still far away, he will send ·some people [an embassy; a messenger] to speak to him and ask for [terms of] peace. 33In the same way, you must give up everything you have to be my ·follower [disciple].

Don't Lose Your Influence

(14:34–35; Matt. 5:13; Mark 9:49–50)

34"Salt is good, but if it loses its salty taste, ·you cannot make it salty again [Lhow can it be seasoned?]. 35It is no good for the soil or for ·manure [the manure pile]; it is thrown away.

"·Let those with ears use them and listen [LThe one who has ears to hear, let him hear]."

A Lost Sheep, a Lost Coin

(15:1–7; Matt. 18:12–14)

15 The tax collectors [Cwho were despised because they worked for the Roman rulers and were notorious for corruption and extortion] and sinners all ·came [drew near] to listen to Jesus. 2But the Pharisees and the ·teachers of the law [scribes] began to ·complain [murmur; grumble]: "Look, this man ·welcomes [associates with; receives] sinners and even eats with them [Cindicating social acceptance]."

3·Then [So] Jesus told them this ·story [parable]: 4"Suppose one of you has a hundred sheep but loses one of them. ·Then he will [LWon't he…?] leave the other ninety-nine sheep in the ·open field [wilderness; desert] and go out and look for the lost sheep until he finds it. 5And when he finds it, he ·happily [joyfully] puts it on his shoulders 6and goes home. He calls ·to [together] his friends and neighbors and says, '·Be happy [Rejoice] with me because I found my lost sheep.' 7In the same way, I tell you there is more joy in heaven over one sinner who ·changes his heart and life [repents], than over ninety-nine ·good [righteous; Cself-righteous] people who don't need to ·change [repent].

8"[LOr] Suppose a woman has ten silver coins [CGreek: *drachmas;* each equal to about a day's wage], but loses one. ·She will [Won't she…?] light a lamp, sweep the house, and ·look [search] carefully for the coin until she finds it. 9And when she finds it, she will call her friends and neighbors and say, '·Be happy [Rejoice] with me because I have found the ·coin [Ldrachma] that I lost.' 10In the same way, [LI tell you] there is joy in the presence of the angels of God when one sinner ·changes his heart and life [repents]."

The Son Who Left Home

11Then Jesus said, "A man had two sons. 12The younger son said to his father, 'Father, give me my share of the ·property [estate; Chis inheritance].' So the father divided the ·property [wealth; assets; Llife] between his two sons. 13·Then [Some time later; LAfter not many days] the younger son gathered up all that was his and traveled ·far away to another [to a distant] country. There he ·wasted [squandered; scattered] his money in ·foolish [wild; reckless] living. 14After he had spent everything, a time came when there was ·no food anywhere [La severe famine] in the country, and the son ·was poor and hungry [Lbegan to be in need]. 15So he ·got a job with [hired himself out to] one of the citizens there who sent the son into the fields to feed pigs [Cdegrading work, since pigs were ritually unclean and detestable animals to Jews]. 16The son was so hungry that he

wanted to ·eat [*or* fill his stomach with] **the pods the pigs were eating, but no one gave him anything.** 17**When he ·realized what he was doing** [came to his senses; [L]came to himself], **he thought, 'All of my father's ·servants** [hired workers] **have ·plenty of** [more than enough; abundant] **·food** [bread]. **But I am here, ·almost dying** [perishing] **with hunger.** 18**I will ·leave and return** [get up and go] **to my father and say to him, "Father, I have sinned against ·God** [[L]heaven; [C]Jews often used "heaven" for "God" out of reverence for the divine Name] **and against you.** 19**I am no longer worthy to be called your son, but ·let me be** [make me] **like one of your ·servants** [hired workers]**."'** 20**So the son left and went to his father.**

"While the son was still a long way off, his father saw him and felt ·sorry [compassion] **for his son. So the father ran to him** [[C]an undignified act for a family patriarch; evidence of his unrestrained love] **and hugged and kissed him.** 21**The son said, 'Father, I have sinned against ·God** [[L]heaven; v. 18] **and against you. I am no longer worthy to be called your son.'**[n] 22**But the father said to his ·servants** [slaves], **'Hurry! Bring the ·best clothes** [[L]first/best robe; [C]either the father's own, or a ceremonial robe for an honored guest] **and put them on him. Also, put a ring on his finger** [[C]probably a signet ring indicating sonship and authority; Gen. 41:42] **and sandals on his feet** [[C]slaves went barefoot]. 23**And get our ·fat** [fattened; [C]prepared for slaughter] **calf and kill it** [[C]people only occasionally ate meat; such a large animal indicates a major celebration] **so we can have a feast and celebrate.** 24**My son was dead, but now he is alive again! He was lost, but now he is found!' So they began to celebrate.**

25**"The older son was in the field, and as he came closer to the house, he heard the sound of music and dancing.** 26**So he ·called to** [summoned] **one of the** [household] **servants and asked what all this meant.** 27**The servant said, 'Your brother has come back, and your father killed the ·fat** [fattened; v. 23] **calf, because your brother came home ·safely** [healthy; safe and sound]**.'** 28**The older son was angry and ·would not** [had no desire to] **go in to the feast. So his father went out and ·begged** [urged; encouraged] **him to come in.** 29**But the older son ·said to** [answered] **his father, '**[[L]Look; [T]Behold] **I have served you like a slave for many years and have ·always obeyed** [never disobeyed; [L]never neglected] **your commands. But you never gave me even a young goat to ·have at a feast** [celebrate] **with my friends.** 30**But ·your other son** [[L]this son of yours], **who ·wasted** [squandered; devoured] **·all your money** [your property; [L]your life] **on prostitutes, comes home, and you kill the fat** [fattened; v. 23] **calf for him!'** 31**The father said to him, '·Son** [Child], **you ·are always with** [*or* have always stood by] **me, and all that I have is yours.** 32[[L]But] **We had to celebrate and ·be happy** [rejoice] **because ·your brother** [[L]this brother of yours; v. 30] **was dead, but ·now he is alive** [has come back to life]. **He was lost, but now he is found.'"**

True Wealth

16 Jesus also said to his ·followers [disciples], **"Once there was a rich man who had a manager to take care of his business. This manager was accused of ·cheating him** [wasting/squandering his assests/possessions]. 2**So he called the manager in and said to him, 'What is this I hear about you? Give me a ·report** [accounting] **of ·what you have done with my money** [[L]your management], **because you ·can't be my manager any longer** [are going to be fired]**.'** 3**The manager thought to himself,**

15:21 son Some Greek copies continue, "but let me be like one of your servants" (see verse 19).

'What will I do since my master is ·taking my job away from [about to fire]
me? I am not strong enough to ·dig ditches [*or* work the soil; [L]dig], and I
am ashamed to beg. 4I know what I'll do so that when I ·lose my job [[L]am
removed from management] people will welcome me into their homes.'
5"So the manager called in everyone who owed the master any money.
He asked the first one, 'How much do you owe [[L]my master]?' 6He
answered, 'Eight hundred gallons [[C]Greek: one hundred *batoi;* a *batos* was
about eight gallons] of olive oil.' The manager said to him, 'Take your bill,
sit down quickly, and write ·four hundred gallons [Greek: fifty (*batoi*)].'
7Then the manager asked another one, 'How much do you owe?' He
answered, '·One thousand bushels [Greek: one hundred *koroi;* a *koros* was
about ten bushels] of wheat.' Then the manager said to him, 'Take your
bill and write eight hundred bushels [[C]Greek: eighty (*koroi*)].' 8So, the
master praised the ·dishonest [unrighteous; unjust] manager for being
·clever [shrewd; prudent]. Yes, ·worldly people [[L]the children of this age]
are more ·clever [shrewd; prudent] with their own ·kind [contemporaries;
generation] than ·spiritual people [[L]the children of light] are.
9"I tell you, make friends for yourselves using ·worldly riches [[L]the
mammon/wealth of unrighteousness] so that when those riches ·are gone
[fail; run out], you will be welcomed in ·those homes that continue forever [eternal dwellings/tents; [C]God's presence]. 10Whoever ·can be trusted
[is faithful] with a little ·can also be trusted [is also faithful] with a lot, and
whoever is ·dishonest [unjust] with a little is ·dishonest [unjust] with a
lot. 11If [[L]therefore] you ·cannot be trusted [have not been faithful] with
·worldly riches [[L]unrighteous mammon], then who will trust you with
true riches? 12And if you ·cannot be trusted [have not been faithful] with
things that belong to someone else, who will give you things of your own?
13"No servant can serve two ·masters [lords]. [[L]For] The servant will
hate one master and love the other, or will ·follow [be devoted/loyal to]
one master and ·refuse to follow [despise] the other. You cannot serve
both God and ·worldly riches [money; [L]mammon]."

God's Law Cannot Be Changed

14The Pharisees, who loved money, were listening to all these things and
·made fun of [derided; ridiculed] Jesus. 15He said to them, "You ·make
yourselves look good [justify yourselves] in front of people, but God knows
what is really in your hearts. What is ·important to [exalted/esteemed by]
people is ·hateful [detestable; an abomination] in God's sight.
16"The law of Moses and the writings of the prophets [[C]the Old
Testament] ·were preached [*or* were in force; [L]were] until John [[C]the
Baptist] came [3:1–20; [C]John is the transitional figure between the age of
promise and the age of salvation]. Since then the ·Good News [Gospel]
about the kingdom of God is being ·told [preached; proclaimed], and
everyone ·tries to enter it by force [*or* is eager to get into it; *or* is strongly
urged to enter it]. 17It would be easier for heaven and earth to ·pass away
[disappear] than for ·the smallest part [[L]one stroke] of a letter in the law
to ·be changed [drop out; Matt. 5:18; 11:12–13].

Divorce and Remarriage
(16:18; Matt. 19:9; Mark 10:11–12)

18"If a man divorces his wife and marries another woman, he ·is guilty
of [commits] adultery, and the man who marries a divorced woman ·is
also guilty of [commits] adultery."

The Rich Man and Lazarus

19Jesus said, "There was a rich man who always dressed in ·the finest
clothes [[L]purple and fine linen] and ·lived in luxury [*or* feasted sumptuously]

every day. 20And a very poor man named Lazarus, whose body was covered with sores, was laid at the rich man's gate. 21He ·wanted [longed] to eat ·only the small pieces of food that fell [Lwhat fell] from the rich man's table. ·And [Even] the dogs would come and lick his sores [Cdogs were viewed as despicable scavengers, not household pets]. 22·Later [LNow it happened that], Lazarus died, and the angels carried him to ·the arms of Abraham [LAbraham's side/Tbosom; Cthe imagery of a banquet, with Abraham as host and Lazarus as honored guest]. The rich man died, too, and was buried. 23In ·the place of the dead [LHades], he was in ·much pain [torment]. ·Looking up [LLifting up his eyes,], the rich man saw Abraham far away with Lazarus ·at his side [Tin his bosom]. 24He called, 'Father Abraham, have mercy on me! Send Lazarus to dip his finger in water and cool my tongue, because I am ·suffering [in agony] in this fire [Is. 66:24]!' 25But Abraham said, 'Child, remember when you were alive you had the good things in life, but bad things happened to Lazarus. Now he is comforted here, and you are ·suffering [in agony]. 26Besides [Lall this], there is a ·big pit [great gulf/chasm set in place] between you and us, so no one can cross over to you, and no one can leave there and come ·here [Lto us].' 27The rich man said, 'Father, then ·please [I ask/beg you to] send Lazarus to my father's house. 28[LFor] I have five brothers, and Lazarus could warn them so that they will not come to this place of ·pain [torment].' 29But Abraham said, 'They have ·the law of Moses and the writings of the prophets [LMoses and the prophets]; let them ·learn from [listen to] them.' 30The rich man said, 'No, father Abraham! [LBut] If someone goes to them from the dead, they would ·believe and change their hearts and lives [Lrepent].' 31But Abraham said to him, 'If they will not listen to Moses and the prophets, they will not ·listen to [Lbe persuaded/convinced by] someone who comes back from the dead.' "

Sin and Forgiveness
(17:1–4; Matt 18:6–7, 15; Mark 9:42)

17 Jesus said to his ·followers [disciples], "·Things that cause people to sin [Stumbling blocks; Causes of sin; Temptations] ·will happen [are inevitable; Lit is impossible for them not to come], but ·how terrible for [Lwoe to] the person who causes them to happen! 2It would be better for ·you [Lhim; that person] to be thrown into the sea with a ·large [Lmill] stone around ·your [Lhis] neck than to cause one of these little ones to ·sin [stumble]. 3So ·be careful [watch yourselves]!

"If ·another follower [fellow believer; Lyour brother (or sister)] sins, ·warn [rebuke] him, and if he ·is sorry and stops sinning [repents], forgive him. 4If he sins against you seven times ·in one day [*or* each day] and ·says that he is sorry each time [repents seven times], forgive him."

How Big Is Your Faith?
(17:5–6; Matt 17:19–21; Mark 9:28–29)

5The apostles said to the Lord, "Give us more faith!"

6The Lord said, "If your faith were the size of a mustard seed, you could say to this mulberry tree, '·Dig yourself up [Be uprooted] and plant yourself in the sea,' and it would obey you.

Be Good Servants

7"Suppose one of you has a ·servant [slave] who has been plowing the ground or caring for the sheep. When the servant comes in from working in the field, would you say, 'Come in and ·sit down to eat [Lrecline; Cthe posture for a banquet or formal meal]'? 8No, ·you [Lhe] would say to him, 'Prepare something for me to eat. Then ·get yourself ready [*or* put on your apron; Lgird yourself] and ·serve [wait on] me. After I finish eating and drinking, you can eat and drink.' 9·The servant does not get any special thanks [LDoes he thank the servant…?] for doing what his master commanded. 10It is the same with you. When you have done everything you are told to do, you should say, 'We are ·unworthy [undeserving; worthless] servants; we have only done ·the work we should do [our duty; our obligation].' "

Be Thankful

11[[L]Now it happened that] While Jesus was on his way to Jerusalem, he was going through the ·area between [middle of; borderlands of] Samaria and Galilee. 12As he came into a ·small town [village], ten men ·who had a skin disease [[T]with leprosy; [C]the term does not refer to modern leprosy (Hansen's disease), but to various skin disorders; see Lev. 14] met him there. They ·did not come close to Jesus [[L]stood at a distance] 13but ·called [shouted; raised their voices] to him, "Jesus! Master! Have ·mercy [pity] on us!"

14When Jesus saw the men, he said, "Go and show yourselves to the priests [[C]only a priest could declare a person cleansed of such skin disorders; Lev. 14]."

As the ten men were going, they were ·healed [[L]cleansed; [C]skin disorders like this rendered the person afflicted ceremonially unclean]. 15When one of them saw that he was healed, he went back to Jesus, praising God in a loud voice. 16Then he ·bowed down [[L]fell on his face] at Jesus' feet and thanked him. (And this man was a Samaritan [[C]a shocking revelation, since Samaritans were despised by Jews].) 17Jesus said, "Weren't ten men ·healed [[L]cleansed; v. 14]? Where are the other nine? 18Is this ·Samaritan [[L]foreigner] the only one who came back to ·thank [[L]give glory to] God?" 19Then Jesus said to him, "Stand up and go on your way. ·You were healed because you believed [[L]Your faith has saved/healed you]."

God's Kingdom Is Within You

20Some of the Pharisees asked Jesus, "When will the kingdom of God come?"

Jesus answered, "God's kingdom ·is coming, but not in a way that you will be able to see with your eyes [[L]is not coming with observable/visible signs; [C]perhaps the heavenly signs described in Jewish apocalyptic literature]. 21People will not say, 'Look, here it is!' or, 'There it is!' because God's kingdom is ·within you [*or* among you; in your midst]."

When Jesus, the Son of Man, Comes Again

(17:22–37; Matt. 10:39; 24:17–28, 37–41; Mark 13:14–23)

22Then Jesus said to ·his followers [the disciples], "The time will come when you will ·want very much [long] to see one of the days of the Son of Man [[C]the full revelation of the kingdom at Jesus' return]. But you will not see it. 23People will say to you, 'Look, ·there he is [*or* over there]!' or, 'Look, ·here he is [*or* over here]!' ·Stay where you are [[L]Don't leave/go out]; don't go away and ·search [pursue; chase after].

24"For as the lightning flashes and lights up the sky from one side to the other, so ·it will be when the Son of Man comes again [[L]will be the Son of Man in his day]." 25But first he must suffer many things and be rejected by ·the people of this time [[L]this generation]. 26Just as it was ·when Noah lived [[L]in the days of Noah; Gen. 6–9], so it will be ·when the Son of Man comes again [[L]in the days of the Son of Man]. 27People were eating, drinking, marrying, and ·giving their children to be married [*or* being given in marriage] until the day Noah entered the boat. Then the flood came and ·killed [destroyed] them all. 28It will be the same as ·during the time [[L]in the days] of Lot. People were eating, drinking, buying, selling, planting, and building. 29But the day Lot left Sodom, fire and ·sulfur [[T]brimstone] rained down from ·the sky [heaven] and ·killed [destroyed] them all

17:24 day Some Greek copies do not have "in his day."

[Gen. 19]. 30This is how it will be ·when [Lthe day] the Son of Man ·comes
again [Lis revealed].
31“On that day, a person who is on the roof [Croofs were typically flat
and used as extra rooms] and whose belongings are in the house should
not ·go inside [Lcome down] to get them. A person who is in the field
should not ·go back home [Lturn back]. 32Remember Lot’s wife [Cwho was
judged for longingly looking back at Sodom; Gen. 19:15–17, 26]. 33Those
who try to ·keep [preserve; keep secure] their lives will lose them. But
those who ·give up [lose; let go of] their lives will save them. 34I tell you,
on that night two people will be sleeping in one bed; one will be taken and
the other will be left. 35There will be two women grinding grain together;
one will be taken, and the other will be left. |36Two people will be in the
field. One will be taken, and the other will be left.|”[n]
37·The followers [LThey] asked Jesus, “·Where will this be [LWhere], Lord?”
Jesus answered, “Where there is a ·dead body [corpse], there the vultures
will gather [Cthe carnage will make the place of judgment obvious to all].”

God Will Answer His People

18 Then Jesus used this ·story [parable] to ·teach his followers
[show the necessity] that they should always pray and never
·lose hope [become discouraged]. 2“In a certain town there was a judge
who did not ·respect [fear] God or ·care about people [*or* care what people thought]. 3In that same town there was a widow [Camong the most
vulnerable members of society] who kept coming to this judge, saying,
‘Give me ·my rights [justice] against my ·enemy [opponent; adversary].’
4For a while the judge refused to help her. But afterwards, he thought to
himself, ‘Even though I don’t ·respect [fear] God or ·care about people
[*or* care what people think], 5yet because she ·keeps bothering me [is
causing me such trouble], I will see that she gets ·her rights [justice].
Otherwise she will ·keep coming until she wears me out [*or* eventually
come and punch me/blacken my eye].’”
6The Lord said, “Listen to what the ·unfair [unjust; unrighteous] judge
said. 7God will always [LWill not God…?] ·give what is right [provide justice]
to his ·people [Lchosen people; elect] who cry to him day and night, and ·he
will not [Lwill he…?] ·be slow to answer them [*or* keep putting them off]. 8I
tell you, God will ·help [provide justice to] his people ·quickly [*or* suddenly].
·But [However; Yet] when the Son of Man comes again, will he find ·those on
earth who believe in him [Lfaith on the earth; CGod’s faithfulness is certain;
the only question is whether people will remain faithful to him]?”

Being Right with God

9Jesus told this ·story [parable] to some people who ·thought they were
very good [were confident of their own righteousness] and ·looked down
on [scorned; despised] everyone else: 10“Two men went up to the Temple
[courts] to pray, one a Pharisee and the other a tax collector [Cdespised by
their fellow Jews because they worked for the hated Romans and were
notorious for extortion]. 11The Pharisee ·stood alone and prayed [*or*
stood and prayed about himself], ‘God, I thank you that I am not like
other people—thieves, ·cheaters [evildoers; unrighteous people], adulterers—or even like this tax collector. 12I fast twice a week [CPharisees
commonly fasted on Monday and Thursday], and I ·give one-tenth of
[pay tithes on] everything I get!’
13“[LBut] The tax collector, standing at a distance, would not even ·look

17:36 Two . . . left. Some Greek copies do not contain the bracketed text.

up [Lraise his eyes] to heaven. But he beat on his chest [Ca sign of sorrow and remorse] and said, 'God, have mercy on me, a sinner.' 14I tell you, when this man went home, he was ·right with God [justified], ·but the Pharisee was not [Lrather than that (other) man]. [LBecause] All who ·make themselves great [exalt themselves] will be made humble, but all who make themselves humble will be ·made great [exalted]."

Who Will Enter God's Kingdom?
(18:15–17; Matt. 19:13–15; Mark 10:13–16)

15Some people brought even their babies to Jesus so he could touch them. When the ·followers [disciples] saw this, they ·told them to stop [scolded/rebuked them]. 16But Jesus called for the children, saying, "Let the little children come to me. Don't ·stop [hinder; forbid] them, because the kingdom of God belongs to people who are like these children [Cmeaning humble and dependent]. 17I tell you the truth, you must ·accept [receive] the kingdom of God as if you were a child, or you will never enter it."

A Rich Man's Question
(18:18–30; Matt. 19:16–30; Mark 10:17–31)

18A certain ·leader [ruler] asked Jesus, "Good Teacher, what must I do to ·have life forever [Linherit eternal life]?"

19Jesus said to him, "Why do you call me good? ·Only God is good [LNo one is good except one—God; CJesus is not denying his own divinity, but is challenging the man's understanding of goodness]. 20You know the commands: 'You must not ·be guilty of [commit] adultery. You must not murder anyone. You must not steal. You must not ·tell lies [testify falsely] about your neighbor. Honor your father and mother [Ex. 20:12–16; Deut. 5:16–20].' "

21But the leader said, "I have ·obeyed [kept carefully; guarded] all these commands since ·I was a boy [my youth]."

22When Jesus heard this, he said to him, "There is still one more thing you ·need to do [lack]. Sell everything you have and give it to the poor, and you will have treasure in heaven. Then come and follow me." 23But when the man heard this, he became very sad, because he was ·very [extremely] rich.

24·Jesus looked at him and [or When Jesus saw this reaction, he] said, "·It is very hard [LHow hard it is…!] for ·rich people [Lthose who have wealth] to enter the kingdom of God. 25[LFor; Indeed] It is easier for a camel to go through the eye of a needle than for a rich person to enter the kingdom of God [Cmeaning it is impossible, by human effort; see v. 27]."

Who Can Be Saved?

26When the people heard this, they asked, "Then who can be saved?"

27Jesus answered, "The things impossible ·for people [humanly speaking] are possible for God."

28Peter said, "Look, we have left ·everything [*or* our possessions; *or* our home] and followed you."

29Jesus said, "I tell you the truth, all those who have left houses, wives, brothers [*or* siblings], parents, or children ·for [for the sake of] the kingdom of God 30will get much more in this ·life [age; Ltime]. And in the ·age [aeon; world] that is coming, they will have ·life forever [eternal life]."

Jesus Will Rise from the Dead
(18:31–34; Matt. 20:17–19; Mark 10:32–34)

31Then Jesus took ·the twelve apostles [Lthe Twelve] aside and said to them, "[LLook; TBehold] We are going [Lup] to Jerusalem. Everything the prophets wrote about the Son of Man will ·happen [be fulfilled/completed/accomplished]. 32He will be turned over to the Gentiles [Cthe Roman authorities]. They will ·laugh at [mock] him, insult him, spit on him, 33·beat him with whips [flog him; Tscourge him], and kill him. But on the third day, he will rise to life again." 34·The apostles [LThey] did not understand this; the meaning was hidden from them, and they did not ·realize [comprehend] what was said.

Jesus Heals a Blind Man
(18:35–43; Matt. 20:29–34; Mark 10:46–52)

35 As Jesus came near the city of Jericho, a blind man was sitting beside
the road, begging. 36 When he heard the people ·coming down the road
[passing by], he asked, "What is happening?"
37 They told him, "Jesus, ·from Nazareth [*or* the Nazarene], is going by."
38 The blind man cried out, "Jesus, Son of David [Ca title for the Messiah, a
descendant of King David; 2 Sam. 7:11–16], ·have mercy [take pity] on me!"
39 The people leading the group ·warned [rebuked; scolded] the blind
man to be quiet. But the blind man shouted even more, "Son of David,
·have mercy [take pity] on me!"
40 Jesus stopped and ordered the blind man to be brought to him. When
he came near, Jesus asked him, 41 "What do you want me to do for you?"
He said, "Lord, I want to see."
42 Jesus said to him, "Then see. ·You are healed because you believed
[Your faith has healed/saved you]."
43 At once the man was able to see, and he followed Jesus, thanking
God. All the people who saw this praised God.

Zacchaeus Meets Jesus

19 Jesus [Lentered and] was going through the city of Jericho. 2 A
man was there named Zacchaeus, who was a ·very important
[chief; leading] tax collector [Cwith oversight over other tax collectors,
and so even more hated; see 18:10], and he was wealthy. 3 He ·wanted [was
trying] to see who Jesus was, but he was not able because he was too short
to see above the crowd. 4 He ran ahead to a place where Jesus ·would come
[was about to pass], and he climbed a sycamore tree so he could see him.
5 When Jesus came to that place, he looked up and said to him, "Zacchaeus,
hurry and come down! [LFor; Because] I must stay at your house today."
6 Zacchaeus came down quickly and welcomed him ·gladly [joyfully].
7 All the people saw this and began to ·complain [murmur; grumble], "Jesus
·is staying with [has gone in to lodge with/be the guest of] a sinner!"
8 But Zacchaeus stood and said to the Lord [Cthe scene presumably
changes here to a meal at Zacchaeus' home], "[LLook; TBehold] I ·will give
[*or* I am now giving] half of my possessions to the poor. And ·if I have
cheated anyone [*or* to those I have cheated/extorted], I will pay back four
times more [Ca generous response, since the law required only restitution
plus one-fifth; Lev. 6:1–5]."
9 Jesus said to him, "Salvation has come to this house today, because this
man also ·belongs to the family [Lis a son] of Abraham. 10 [LFor; Because]
The Son of Man came to ·find [seek out] lost people and save them."

A Story About Three Servants
(19:11–27; Matt. 25:14–30; Mark 13:34)

11 As ·the people [Lthey; Ceither the disciples, the guests of Zacchaeus, or
the larger crowd] were listening to this, Jesus told them a ·story [parable]
because he was near Jerusalem and ·they thought [it seemed to them]
God's kingdom would appear immediately. 12 He said: "A ·very important
man [nobleman] went to a country far away to ·be made a king [Lreceive
a kingdom] and then to return home [CJudean kings, like Herod the Great
and his son Archelaus, received their authority to rule from the emperor
in Rome]. 13 So he called ten of his ·servants [slaves] and gave a coin
[CGreek: *mina;* worth 100 denarii, or about 3 months' wages] to each servant. He said, '·Do business with [Invest; Trade with] this money until I
get back.' 14 But ·the people in the kingdom [Lhis citizens/subjects] hated
the man. So they sent a ·group [delegation; embassy] to follow him and
say, 'We don't want this man to ·be our king [Lrule/reign over us].'
15 "But the man ·became king [Lreceived the kingdom]. When he

returned home, he said, 'Call those ·servants [slaves] who have my money so I can know how much they earned with it.'

16"The first servant came and said, 'Sir, ·I earned ten coins with the one you gave me [Lyour mina has earned ten minas].' 17The king said to the servant, 'Excellent! ·You are a good servant [Good servant/slave!]. Since ·I can trust you [you have been faithful] with small things, I will let you ·rule [govern; Lhave authority] over ten of my cities.'

18"The second servant said, 'Sir, ·I earned five coins with your one [Lyour mina earned five minas].' 19The king said to this servant, 'You can ·rule [be; take charge] over five cities.'

20"Then another servant came in and said to the king, 'Sir, here is your ·coin [mina] which I ·wrapped [stored away] in a ·piece of cloth [handkerchief] and hid. 21[LFor; Because] I was afraid of you, because you are a ·hard [harsh; demanding; severe] man. You even take ·money that [Lout what] you didn't ·earn [Lput in] and ·gather food that [harvest what] you didn't ·plant [sow].' 22Then the king said to the servant, 'I will ·condemn [judge] you ·by your own words [Lfrom your mouth], you ·evil [wicked; *or* worthless] servant. You knew that I am a ·hard [harsh; demanding; severe] man, taking ·money that [Lout what] I didn't ·earn [Lput in]and ·gathering food that [Lharvesting what] I didn't ·plant [sow]. 23Why then didn't you put my money ·in the bank [Lon the table; Creferring to the banker's table]? Then when I came back, my money would have earned some interest.'

24"·The king [He] said to the men who were standing by, 'Take the ·coin [Lmina] away from this servant and give it to the servant who earned ten ·coins [Lminas].' 25They said, 'But sir, that servant already has ten ·coins [Lminas].' 26·The king said [LI say to you], 'Those who have will be given more, but those who do not have anything ·will have everything [Leven what they have will be] taken away from them. 27Now ·where are my enemies [*or* concerning those enemies] who didn't want me to ·be king [rule/reign over them]? Bring them here and ·kill [slay; slaughter] them before me.' "

Jesus Enters Jerusalem as a King
(19:28–40; Matt. 21:1–9; Mark 11:1–10)

28After Jesus said this, he went on [Lahead, going up] toward Jerusalem. 29As Jesus came near Bethphage and Bethany, towns near the hill called the Mount of Olives, he sent out two of his ·followers [disciples]. 30He said, "Go to the town ·you can see there [ahead of you; *or* opposite you; Cunclear whether Bethphage or Bethany]. When you enter it, you will find a ·colt [young donkey] tied there, which no one has ever ridden. Untie it and bring it here to me. 31If anyone asks you why you are untying it, say that ·the Master [the Lord; *or* its Owner] needs it."

32The two ·followers [Lwho were sent] went into town and found ·the colt [*or* the situation] just as Jesus had told them. 33As they were untying it, its ·owners [masters] came out and asked the followers, "Why are you untying our ·colt [young donkey]?"

34The followers answered, "·The Master [The Lord; Its Owner] needs it." 35So they brought it to Jesus, threw their ·coats [garments] on the ·colt's [young donkey's] back, and put Jesus on it. 36As Jesus rode toward Jerusalem, others spread their coats on the ·road [path; way] before him.

37As he was coming close to Jerusalem, on the way down the Mount of Olives, the whole crowd of ·followers [disciples] began joyfully shouting praise to God for all the ·miracles [mighty works] they had seen. 38They said,

"·God bless [Blessed is] the king who comes in the name of the Lord
[Ps. 118:26]!

·There is peace [or May there be peace; LPeace] in heaven and glory ·to
God [Lin the highest; Ceither "in highest heaven" or "to the Most High God"]!"
39Some of the Pharisees in the crowd said to Jesus, "Teacher, ·tell your
followers not to say these things [Lrebuke your disciples]."
40But Jesus answered, "I tell you, if ·my followers didn't say these things
[Lthey remained silent], then the stones would ·cry out [start shouting]."

Jesus Cries for Jerusalem

41As Jesus came near Jerusalem, he saw the city and ·cried for [wept
over] it, 42saying, "·I wish you [LIf you, even you,] ·knew [recognized]
today what would bring you peace. But now it is hidden from ·you [Lyour
eyes]. 43·The time is coming [LFor the days will come upon you] when
your enemies will build ·a wall around you [ramparts against your walls]
and will ·hold you in [Lsurround and close you in] on all sides. 44They will
·destroy you [level you; smash you to the ground] and all your ·people
[Lchildren within your walls], and not one stone will be left on another.
All this will happen because you did not recognize the time ·when God
came to save you [Lof your visitation; Cthe failure to recognize God's "visit"
in Jesus (see 1:68, 78) will result in a divine "visit" in judgment]."

Jesus Goes to the Temple

(19:45–48; Matt. 21:12–13; Mark 11:15–19)

45Jesus went into the Temple and began to ·throw [drive] out the people
who were selling things there. 46He said, "It is written in the Scriptures,
'My ·Temple [LHouse] will be a house for prayer [Is. 56:7].' But you have
·changed [made] it into a '·hideout for robbers' [Tden of thieves; Jer. 7:11]!"
47Jesus ·taught [was teaching] in the Temple every day. The ·leading
[Tchief] priests, the ·experts on the law [scribes], and some of the leaders
of the people ·wanted [were looking for a way] to ·kill [destroy] Jesus. 48But
they ·did not know how they could [could not find a way to] do it, because
all the people were ·listening closely to him [hanging on his every word].

Jewish Leaders Question Jesus

(20:1–8; Matt. 21:23–32; Mark 11:27–33)

20 One day Jesus was in the Temple, teaching the people and
·telling them the Good News [preaching the Gospel]. The
·leading [Tchief] priests, ·teachers of the law [scribes], and elders came
up to talk with him, 2saying, "Tell us what authority you have to do
these things? [LOr] Who gave you this authority?"
3Jesus answered, "I will also ask you a question. Tell me: 4When John
baptized people, was that authority from ·God [Lheaven; Ca reverent Jewish
way of referring to God] or just from ·other people [human beings]?"
5They ·argued about this [Ldiscussed this among themselves], saying,
"If we answer, 'John's baptism was from ·God [Lheaven],' Jesus will say,
'Then why did you not believe him?' 6But if we say, 'It was from ·other
people [human beings],' all the people will stone us to death, because they
·believe [are convinced that] John was a prophet." 7So they answered that
they didn't know where it came from.
8Jesus said to them, "Then I won't tell you what authority I have to do
these things."

The Story of the Evil Farmers

(20:9–19; Matt. 21:33–46; Mark 12:1–12)

9Then Jesus ·told [Lbegan/proceeded to tell] the people this ·story [parable]:
"A man planted a vineyard and leased it to some [Ctenant] farmers [CJesus
builds on Is. 5:1–7; the owner represents God; the farmers are Israel's religious
leaders]. Then he ·went away [took a journey] for a long time. 10·When it was
time for the grapes to be picked [LAt the (harvest) time], he sent a ·servant
[slave] to the farmers to get some of the grapes [Cthe portion of the harvest to
pay the rent]. But they beat him and sent him away empty-handed. 11Then he
sent another ·servant [slave]. They beat him also, and ·showed no respect for

[humiliated; dishonored] him, and sent him away empty-handed. 12So the man sent a third. The farmers wounded him and threw him out [Cthe servants represent the prophets God sent to Israel]. 13The owner of the vineyard said, 'What will I do now? I will send my son whom I love [Crepresenting Jesus; see 3:22]. ·Maybe [*or* Probably; *or* Surely] they will respect him.' 14But when the farmers saw the son, they said to each other, 'This ·son will inherit the vineyard [Lis the heir]. Let's kill him so the inheritance will be ours.' 15So the farmers threw the son out of the vineyard and killed him.

"What will the ·owner [lord] of the vineyard do to them? 16He will come and ·kill [destroy] those farmers and will give the vineyard to ·other farmers [Lothers; Creferring to the sinners who were responding to Jesus' call for repentance, and eventually to the Gentiles who would be saved]."

When the people heard this ·story [parable], they said, "·Let this never happen [TGod forbid; LMay it not happen]!"

17But Jesus looked [directly; intently] at them and said, "Then what does this Scripture passage mean:

'The stone that the builders rejected
became the ·cornerstone [*or* capstone; *or* keystone; Lhead of the corner]'? [CThis is the most important stone in the building; Jesus is the rejected stone; Ps. 118:22.]

18Everyone who falls on that stone will be broken [Is. 8:14], and the person on whom it falls, that person will be crushed [cf. Dan. 2:34]!"

19The ·teachers of the law [scribes] and the ·leading [Tchief] priests ·wanted [tried/sought] to ·arrest [seize; Llay hands on] Jesus at once, because they knew the ·story [parable] was ·about [told against] them. But they were afraid of what the people would do.

Is It Right to Pay Taxes or Not?

(20:20–26; Matt. 22:15–22; Mark 12:13–17)

20So they watched Jesus and sent some spies who acted as if they were ·sincere [honest; righteous]. They wanted to trap Jesus in saying something wrong so they could hand him over to the ·authority [jurisdiction; rule] and ·power [authority] of the governor. 21So the spies asked Jesus, "Teacher, we know that what you say and teach is ·true [right; correct]. You ·pay no attention to who people are [play no favorites; are impartial; aren't swayed by appearances], and you always teach ·the truth [with sincerity/honesty] about God's way. 22Tell us, is it ·right [permissible; lawful] for us to pay taxes to Caesar or not?" [CSaying yes would anger Jews who hated Roman rule; saying no could result in being charged with insurrection.]

23But Jesus, knowing ·they were trying to trick him [Ltheir craftiness/duplicity], said, 24"Show me a ·coin [Ldenarius]. Whose ·image [likeness; portrait] and ·name [inscription; title] are on it?"

They said, "Caesar's." [CIronically, the religious leaders carry coins bearing the idolatrous image of Caesar.]

25Jesus said to them, "Then ·give [give back; Trender] to Caesar the things that are Caesar's, and ·give [give back; Trender] to God the things that are God's."

26So they were not able to ·trap [catch] Jesus in anything he said in the presence of the people. And being amazed at his answer, they ·became silent [kept quiet].

Some Sadducees Try to Trick Jesus

(20:27–40; Matt. 22:23–33; Mark 12:18–27)

27Some Sadducees, who believed people would not rise from the dead, came to Jesus. 28They asked, "Teacher, Moses wrote that if a man's brother dies and leaves a wife but no children, then that man must marry the widow and ·have children [Lraise up offspring/seed] for his brother [Deut. 25:5–6]. 29Once there were seven brothers. The first brother ·married

[L took a wife] **and died, but had no children.** 30 **Then the second brother married the widow, and he died.** 31 **And the third brother married the widow, and he died. The same thing happened with all seven brothers; they died and had no children.** 32 **Finally, the woman died also.** 33 **Since all seven brothers had married her, whose wife will she be ·when people rise from the dead** [L at the resurrection]**?"**

34 **Jesus said to them, "·On earth, people** [L The children of this age] **marry and are given to someone to marry.** 35 **But those who will be worthy ·to be raised from the dead and live again** [L of the age to come and the resurrection] **will not marry, nor will they be given to someone to marry.** 36 [L For] **In that life they are ·like** [*or* equal to] **angels and cannot die. They are children of God, because they ·have been raised from the dead** [are children of the resurrection]. 37 **Even Moses clearly showed that the dead are raised to life. When he wrote about the burning bush** [Ex. 3:1–12], **he said that the Lord is 'the God of Abraham, the God of Isaac, and the God of Jacob** [Ex. 3:6; C God is still the God of the patriarchs, so they must have a continued existence after death]**.'** 38 **God is the God of the living, not the dead, because all people are alive to him."**

39 **Some of the ·teachers of the law** [scribes] **said, "Teacher, ·your answer was good** [well said!]**."** 40 **No one ·was brave enough** [dared] **to ask him another question.**

Is the Christ the Son of David?
(20:41–44; Matt. 22:41–46; Mark 12:35–37a)

41 **Then Jesus said, "Why do people say that the ·Christ** [Messiah] **is the Son of David** [2 Sam. 7:12–16]? 42 [L For; Since] **In the book of Psalms, David himself says:**

'The Lord said to my Lord,
"Sit by me at my right ·side [L hand],
43 **until I put your enemies ·under your control** [L as a footstool for your feet; C meaning defeated or made subject to your authority; Ps. 110:1]**."'**

44 **David calls ·the Christ** [the Messiah; L him] **'Lord,' so how can ·the Christ** [the Messiah; L he] **be his son?"**

Jesus Accuses Some Leaders
(20:45–47; Matt. 23:1–36; Mark 12:37b–40)

45 **While all the people were listening, Jesus said to his ·followers** [disciples], 46 **"Beware of the ·teachers of the law** [scribes]. **They like to walk around wearing ·fancy clothes** [*or* flowing robes], **and they love for people to greet them with respect in the marketplaces. They love to have the most important seats in the synagogues** [11:43] **and** [the place of highest honor] **at ·feasts** [banquets]. 47 **But they ·cheat widows and steal their houses** [L devour widows' homes] **and ·then try to make themselves look good by saying** [L with false motives pray] **long prayers. They will receive a greater ·punishment** [condemnation]**."**

True Giving
(21:1–4; Mark 12:41–44)

21 **As Jesus looked up, he saw some rich people putting their gifts into the Temple ·money box** [*or* treasury; C one of thirteen trumpet-shaped receptacles used to collect offerings]. 2 **Then he saw a poor widow putting two small copper coins** [C Greek: *lepta;* worth only 1/128 of a denarius, the daily wage of a worker] **into the box.** 3 **He said, "I tell you the truth, this poor widow gave more than all those rich people.** 4 [L For] **They gave ·only what they did not need** [out of their surplus/abundance]. **·This woman is very poor, but she gave** [L But she, out of her poverty, gave] **all she had to live on."**

The Temple Will Be Destroyed
(21:5–19; Matt. 24:1–14; Mark 13:1–13)

5 **Some ·people** [*or* of the disciples] **were talking about the Temple and how it was ·decorated** [adorned] **with beautiful stones and gifts offered to God.**

But Jesus said, 6 **"As for these things you are looking at, the ·time** [days] **will come when not one stone will be left on another. Every stone will be ·thrown** [torn] **down."**

7They asked Jesus, “Teacher, when will these things happen? What will
be the sign that they are about to take place?”
8Jesus said, “·Be careful [Watch out] so you are not ·fooled [deceived;
led astray]. [LFor; Because] Many people will come in my name, saying, ‘I
am ·the One [or he; Cthe Messiah]’ and, ‘The time ·has come [or is near]!’
But don’t follow them. 9When you hear about wars and ·riots [uprisings;
insurrections], don’t be afraid [terrified], because these things must happen first, but the end will ·come later [not come immediately].”
10Then he said to them, “Nations will ·fight [Lrise up] against other
nations, and kingdoms against other kingdoms. 11In various places there
will be great earthquakes, ·sicknesses [plagues; pestilences], and ·a lack of
food [famines]. ·Fearful [Terrifying] events and great signs will come
from heaven.
12“But before all these things happen, people will ·arrest [seize; Llay their
hands on] you and ·treat you cruelly [persecute you]. They will ·judge you in
their [drag you into the; Lhand you over to] synagogues and put you in jail
and force you to stand before kings and governors, because ·you follow me
[of your allegiance to me; Lof my name]. 13But this will give you an opportunity to ·tell [testify; bear witness] about me. 14[LSo; Therefore] ·Make up your
minds [Resolve; LPut it in your hearts] not to ·worry [or rehearse] ahead of
time about what you will say [12:11]. 15[LFor] I will give you ·the wisdom to
say things [words and wisdom] that none of your enemies will be able to
·stand against [resist] or ·prove wrong [refute; contradict]. 16Even your parents, brothers [and sisters], relatives, and friends will ·turn against you
[betray you; Lhand you over], and they will kill some of you. 17All people will
hate you because ·you follow me [Lof my name]. 18But ·none of these things
can really harm you [Lnot a hair on your head will perish; Ca metaphor for
living forever with God]. 19By ·continuing to have faith [your endurance/
perseverance] you will ·save your lives [or gain/win your souls].

Jerusalem Will Be Destroyed
(21:20–24; Matt. 24:15–22; Mark 13:14–20)

20“When you see armies all around Jerusalem, you will know ·it will
soon be destroyed [Lits desolation draws near/is at hand]. 21At that time,
the people in Judea should run away to the mountains. The people in
Jerusalem must get out, and those who are ·near the city [in the country-
side] should not go in. 22These are the days of ·punishment [vengeance;
retribution] to ·bring about [fulfill] all that is written in the Scriptures.
23·How terrible it will be for [LWoe to] women who are pregnant or have
nursing babies [Lin those days]! [LFor; Because] Great ·trouble [distress;
calamity] will come upon this land, and ·God will be angry with these
people [Lwrath will come against this people]. 24They will ·be killed by
[Lfall by the mouth of] the sword and taken as ·prisoners [captives] to all
nations. Jerusalem will be ·crushed [trampled] by Gentiles until the time
of the Gentiles is ·over [fulfilled].

Don’t Fear
(21:25–28; Matt. 24:29–31; Mark 13:24–27)

25“There will be signs in the sun, moon, and stars. On earth, nations
will be ·afraid [distressed] and confused because of the roar and ·fury
[surging waves] of the sea. 26People will be so afraid they will ·faint [or
lose all hope], wondering what is ·happening to [coming upon] the world,
because the ·powers of the heavens [or heavenly bodies] will be shaken.
27Then people will see the Son of Man coming in a cloud with power and
great glory [Dan. 7:13]. 28When these things begin to happen, ·look up [or
stand up] and hold your heads high, because ·the time when God will free
you [your redemption/liberation] is ·near [at hand]!”

Jesus' Words Will Live Forever
(21:29–33; Matt. 24:32–36; Mark 13:28–32)

29Then Jesus told this ·story [parable]: "Look at the fig tree and all the
other trees. 30When their leaves appear, you [Lsee for yourselves and]
know that summer is near. 31In the same way, when you see these things
happening, you will know that God's kingdom is near.
32"I tell you the truth, all these things will happen ·while the people of this
time are still living [Lbefore this generation passes away; Ceither the generation that sees the destruction of Jerusalem (AD 70), or a future generation of
the end times]. 33·Earth and sky will be destroyed [THeaven and earth will
pass away], but the words I have spoken will never ·be destroyed [pass away].

Be Ready All the Time

34"·Be careful [Watch yourselves] not to ·spend your time [*or* become
dulled by; Llet your hearts be weighed down by] ·feasting [carousing;
debauchery], ·drinking [drunkenness], or worrying about worldly things. If
you do, that day might come on you suddenly, 35·like a trap. For it will come
upon all people who live on the earth. [*or* Like a trap, it will come upon all
people who live on the earth.] 36So be ·ready [alert; watching] all the time.
Pray that you will be strong enough to escape all these things that ·will [are
about to] happen and that you will be able to stand before the Son of Man."
37During the day, Jesus taught the people in the Temple, and at night
he went out of the city and stayed on the Mount of Olives. 38Every morning all the people got up early to go to the Temple to listen to him.

Judas Betrays Jesus
(22:1–6; Matt. 26:1–5, 14–16; Mark 14:1–2, 10–11)

22 It was almost time for the Feast of Unleavened Bread, called the
Passover Feast [Ccelebrating God's rescue of Israel from Egypt;
Ex. 12]. 2The ·leading [Tchief] priests and ·teachers of the law [scribes] were
trying to find a way to ·kill [destroy; eliminate] Jesus, ·because [*or* but] they
were afraid of the people [Cbecause of Jesus' popularity].
3[LThen] Satan entered Judas [Lwho was called] Iscariot, one of ·Jesus'
twelve apostles [Lthe Twelve]. 4Judas went to the ·leading [Tchief] priests
and the officers of the Temple guard and talked to them about a way to
·hand Jesus over [betray Jesus] to them. 5They were ·pleased [delighted]
and agreed to give Judas money. 6He ·agreed [consented] and watched for
·the best [an opportune] time to ·hand Jesus over [betray Jesus] to them
when he was away from the crowd.

Jesus Eats the Passover Meal
(22:7–13; Matt. 26:17–20; Mark 14:12–17)

7The Day of Unleavened Bread came when the Passover lambs had to
be sacrificed. 8Jesus said to Peter and John, "Go and prepare the Passover
meal for us to eat."
9They asked, "Where do you want us to prepare it?" 10Jesus said to
them, "[Pay attention; LLook; TBehold] After you go into the city, a man
carrying a jar of water will meet you. Follow him into the house that he
enters, 11and tell the owner of the house, 'The Teacher says: "Where is the
guest room in which I may eat the Passover meal with my ·followers [dis-
ciples]?"' 12Then he will show you a large, furnished room upstairs.
Prepare the Passover meal there."
13So Peter and John left and found everything as Jesus had said. And
they prepared the Passover meal.

The Lord's Supper
(22:14–20; Matt. 26:26–29; Mark 14:22–25)

14When the ·time [hour] came, Jesus and the apostles ·were sitting at
the table [Lreclined; Cthe posture at a formal meal; see 7:36]. 15He said to
them, "I wanted very much to eat this Passover meal with you before I
suffer. 16[LFor I tell you] I will not eat another Passover meal until it is
·given its true meaning [Lfulfilled] in the kingdom of God."
17Then Jesus took a cup, gave thanks, and said, "Take this cup and share

it among yourselves. 18[LFor I tell you] **I will not drink again from the**
fruit of the vine [Cwine] **until God's kingdom comes."**
19**Then Jesus took some bread, gave thanks, broke it, and gave it to the**
apostles, saying, "This is my body,ⁿ **which I am giving for you. Do this ·to**
remember [as a memorial to; Tin remembrance of] **me."** 20**In the same**
way, after ·supper [they had eaten], **Jesus took the cup and said, "·This cup**
[*or* This cup that is poured out...] **is the new ·agreement** [covenant; Ca
binding relationship between God and his people; Jer. 31:31–34] **·that**
begins with [that is established by; *or* that is sealed with; Lin] **my blood,**
which is poured out for you [Cinterpreters differ as to whether it is the
"cup" or the "blood" that Jesus says is "poured out"].

Who Will Turn Against Jesus?
(22:21–23; Matt. 26:21–25; Mark 14:18–21)

21**"But** [LLook; TBehold] **one of you will ·turn against** [betray] **me, and**
·his hand is with mine on [*or* he is sharing a place with me at] **the table.**
22**·What God has planned for the Son of Man will happen** [LFor the Son of
Man is going (to his death) as it has been determined/decreed (by God)],
but ·how terrible it will be for [Lwoe to] **that one who ·turns against**
[betrays] **the Son of Man** [Ca title for the Messiah; Dan. 7:13–14]."
23**Then the apostles ·asked** [began to ask] **each other which one of them**
would do that.

Be Like a Servant
(22:24–30; Matt. 19:28; 20:24–28; Mark 10:41–45)

24**·The apostles also began to argue** [LThen an argument/dispute
occurred among them] **about which one of them was the ·most impor-**
tant [greatest]. 25**But Jesus said to them, "The kings of the Gentiles ·rule**
[lord it] **over them, and those who have authority over others like to be**
called ·'friends of the people' ['Benefactors']. 26**But you must not be like**
that. Instead, the greatest among you should be like the youngest, and the
leader should be like the servant. 27[LFor] **Who is more important: the**
one ·sitting at the table [Lreclining] **or the one serving? Is it not the one**
·sitting at the table [Lreclining]**? But I am like a servant among you.**
28**"·You** [LBut you are the ones who] **have stayed with me through my**
·struggles [trials]. 29**Just as my Father has ·given** [granted; conferred on]
me a kingdom, I also ·give [grant; confer on] **you a kingdom** 30**so you may**
eat and drink at my table in my kingdom. And you will sit on thrones,
judging the twelve tribes of Israel.

Don't Lose Your Faith!
(22:31–34; Matt. 26:30–35; Mark 14:26–31; John 13:36–38)

31**"Simon** [CPeter], **Simon,** [Llook; Tbehold,] **Satan has ·asked** [de-
manded; sought permission] **to ·test all of you as a farmer sifts his** [Lsift all
of you as] **wheat.** 32[LBut] **I have prayed** [Lfor you] **that ·you will not lose**
your faith [your faith will not fail]! **And when you ·come back to me**
[return; turn back], **help your brothers be stronger."**
33**But Peter said to Jesus, "Lord, I am ready to go with you to prison and**
even to die with you!"
34**But Jesus said, "**[LI tell you,] **Peter, before the rooster crows this day, you**
will ·say three times that you don't [Ldeny three times that you] **know me."**

Be Ready for Trouble

35**Then Jesus said to the apostles, "When I sent you out without ·a**
purse [money bag], **a ·bag** [traveling bag], **or sandals, did you ·need** [lack]
anything?"
They said, "·No [LNothing]."
36**He said to them, "But now if you have a ·purse** [money bag] **or a ·bag**
[traveling bag], **carry that with you. If you don't have a sword, sell your**

22:19b–20 body Some Greek copies do not have the rest of verse 19 or verse 20.

·coat [cloak] and buy one. 37[LFor] I tell you this scripture must ·have its full meaning [be fulfilled] ·with reference to me [Lin me]: 'He was ·treated like a criminal [counted/numbered among the wicked/lawless ones; Is. 53:12],' [Yes; LFor] What was written about me ·is happening now [is being fulfilled]."

38His ·followers [disciples] said, "Look, Lord, here are two swords."

He said to them, "·That is enough [*or* That's enough talk like that!]."

Jesus Prays Alone
(22:39–46; Matt. 26:36–46; Mark 14:32–42; John 12:27; 18:1)

39Jesus left the city and went to the Mount of Olives, as he often did, and his ·followers [disciples] ·went with [followed] him. 40When he reached the place, he said to them, "Pray for strength ·against temptation [*or* not to fail the test]."

41Then Jesus went about a stone's throw away from them. He kneeled down and prayed, 42"Father, if you are willing, take away this ·cup of suffering [Lcup; Csuffering or punishment is metaphorically portrayed as something bitter to drink]. But do ·what you want [Lyour will], not ·what I want [Lmy will]." 43Then an angel from heaven appeared to him to strengthen him. 44Being ·full of pain [in agony/anguish], Jesus prayed even harder. His sweat was like drops of blood falling to the ground. 45When he ·finished praying [Lrose from prayer], he went to his ·followers [disciples] and found them asleep ·because of their sadness [exhausted from grief]. 46Jesus said to them, "Why are you sleeping? Get up and pray ·for strength against temptation [that you won't give in to temptation; *or* that you won't be tempted/tested]."

Jesus Is Arrested
(22:47–53; Matt. 26:47–56; Mark 14:43–52; John 18:2–12)

47While Jesus was speaking, [Llook; Tbehold] a crowd came up, and [Lthe man called] Judas, one of the twelve apostles, was leading them. He came close to Jesus so he could kiss him.

48But Jesus said to him, "Judas, are you betraying the Son of Man with a kiss?"

49When those who were standing around him saw what was ·happening [about to happen], they said, "Lord, should we strike them with our swords?" 50And one of them struck the servant of the high priest and cut off his right ear.

51Jesus said, "Stop! No more of this." Then he touched the servant's ear and healed him.

52Then Jesus said to those who had come to arrest him, the ·leading [Tchief] priests, the officers of the temple guard, and the elders, "You came out here with swords and clubs as though I were a ·criminal [revolutionary; rebel; Lrobber; Ca term used by the Romans of insurrectionists]. 53I was with you every day in the Temple, and you didn't ·arrest [Lextend your hands against] me there. But this is your ·time [hour]—the time when darkness ·rules [has power/authority]."

Peter Says He Doesn't Know Jesus
(22:54–71; Matt. 26:57–68; Mark 14:53–65; John 18:13–24)

54They ·arrested [seized] Jesus, and led him away, and brought him into the house of the high priest. Peter followed ·far behind them [at a distance]. 55After ·the soldiers [Lthey] started a fire in the middle of the courtyard and sat together, Peter sat with them. 56A servant girl saw Peter sitting there in the firelight, and looking closely at him, she said, "This man was also with him."

57But Peter ·said this was not true [denied it]; he said, "Woman, I don't know him."

58A short time later, another person saw Peter and said, "You are also one of them."

But Peter said, "Man, I am not!"
59 About an hour later, another man insisted, "Certainly this man was
with him, because he is ·from Galilee [a Galilean], too."
60 But Peter said, "Man, I don't know what you are talking about!"
At once, while Peter was still speaking, a rooster crowed. 61 Then the
Lord turned and looked straight at Peter. And Peter remembered what
the Lord had said: "Before the rooster crows this day, you will ·say three
times that you don't know me [deny me three times]." 62 Then Peter went
outside and ·cried painfully [wept bitterly].

The People Make Fun of Jesus

63 The men who were guarding Jesus began ·making fun of [mocking]
him and beating him.
64 They blindfolded him and said, "·Prove that you are a prophet
[LProphesy!], and tell us who hit you." 65 They said many ·cruel [insulting;
blasphemous] things to Jesus.

Jesus Before the Leaders

66 When day came, the council of the elders of the people, both the
·leading [Tchief] priests and the ·teachers of the law [scribes], came
together and led Jesus to ·their highest court [the high council/Sanhedrin].
67 They said, "If you are the ·Christ [Messiah], tell us."
Jesus said to them, "If I tell you, you will not believe me. 68 And if I ask
you, you will not answer. 69 But from now on, the Son of Man will sit at the
right hand of the powerful God [Ps. 110:1]."
70 They all said, "Then are you the Son of God?"
Jesus said to them, "You say that I am [Can indirect affirmation]."
71 They said, "Why do we need ·witnesses [testimony] now? [LFor] We
·ourselves heard him say this [Lheard it from his mouth]."

Pilate Questions Jesus
(23:1–5; Matt. 27:1–2, 11–14; Mark 15:1–5; John 18:28–38)

23 Then the whole group stood up and led Jesus to Pilate
[CPontius Pilate, governor of Judea from AD 26 to 36; see 3:1].
2 They began to accuse Jesus, saying, "We caught this man ·misleading
[subverting] our ·people [nation]. He ·says that we should not pay
[opposes/forbids paying] taxes to Caesar, and he ·calls himself [claims
to be] the ·Christ [Messiah], a king."
3 Pilate asked Jesus, "Are you the king of the Jews?"
Jesus answered, "·Those are your words [*or* It is as you say; LYou say so;
Can indirect affirmation; see 22:70]."
4 Pilate said to the ·leading [Tchief] priests and the ·people [crowd], "I
find ·nothing against [no basis for a charge against; no guilt in] this man."
5 [LBut] They were insisting, saying, "But Jesus ·makes trouble with [is
inciting/stirring up] the people, teaching all around Judea. He began in
Galilee, and now he is here."

Pilate Sends Jesus to Herod

6 Pilate heard this and asked if ·Jesus [Lthe man] was ·from Galilee [a
Galilean]. 7 ·Since [LLearning that] Jesus was under Herod's authority,
Pilate sent Jesus to Herod [CAntipas; see 3:1], who was in Jerusalem at
that time. 8 When Herod saw Jesus, he was very glad, because he had heard
about Jesus and had wanted to ·meet [Lsee] him for a long time. He was
hoping to see Jesus ·work a miracle [perform a sign]. 9 Herod asked Jesus
many questions, but Jesus said nothing. 10 The ·leading [Tchief] priests
and ·teachers of the law [scribes] were standing there, ·strongly [vehe-
mently; vigorously] accusing Jesus. 11 After Herod and his soldiers had
·made fun of [ridiculed and mocked] Jesus, they dressed him in a ·kingly
[elegant; splendid; Lbright] ·robe [clothing] and sent him back to Pilate.

[12]In the past, Pilate and Herod had always been enemies, but on that day they became friends.

Jesus Must Die
(23:17–25; Matt. 27:15–26; Mark 15:6–15; John 18:39–40; 19:16)

[13]Pilate called together the ·leading [Tchief] priests, the ·rulers [leaders] and the people. [14]He said to them, "You brought this man to me, saying he ·makes trouble among [misleads; subverts; incites] the people. But I have questioned him before you all, and I have not found ·him guilty of what you say [any basis for the charges]. [15]Also, Herod found nothing wrong with him; [Lbecause] he sent him back to us. Look, he has done nothing ·for which he should die [worthy/deserving of death]. [16]So, after I ·punish him [have him flogged], I will let him go free." |[17]Every year at the Passover Feast, Pilate had to release one prisoner to the people.|*n*

[18]But ·the people [Lthey] shouted together, "Take this man away [Cfor execution]! ·Let Barabbas go free [LRelease Barabbas to/for us]!" [19](Barabbas was a man who was in prison for his part in a ·riot [insurrection] in the city and for murder.)

[20]Pilate wanted to let Jesus go free and [Lagain] ·told this to [appealed to; addressed] the crowd. [21]But they shouted again, "Crucify him! Crucify him!"

[22]A third time Pilate said to them, "Why? What ·wrong [crime; evil] has he done? I can find no reason to kill him. So I will have him ·punished [flogged] and set him free."

[23]But they continued to shout, demanding that Jesus be crucified. Their ·yelling became so loud [Lvoices prevailed so] that [24]Pilate decided to give them what they ·wanted [requested; demanded]. [25]He set free the man who was in jail for ·rioting [insurrection] and murder, and he handed Jesus over ·to them to do with him as they wished [*or* as they requested; Lto their will].

Jesus Is Crucified
(23:26–49; Matt. 27:31b–56; Mark 15:20b–41; John 19:17–30)

[26]As they led Jesus away, Simon, a man from Cyrene [Ca port city in North Africa (modern Libya)], was coming in from the ·fields [countryside; country; CSimon may be a Jewish pilgrim visiting Jerusalem for Passover or an immigrant living there]. They forced him to carry Jesus' cross and to walk behind him.

[27]A large crowd of people was following Jesus, including some women who were ·sad [mourning] and ·crying [wailing; lamenting] for him. [28]But Jesus turned and said to them, "·Women [LDaughters] of Jerusalem, don't ·cry [weep] for me. ·Cry [Weep] for yourselves and for your children. [29][LFor look/Tbehold] The ·time is [days are] coming when people will say, 'Blessed are ·the women who cannot have children [Lthe barren women and the wombs that never gave birth] and ·who have no babies to nurse [Lthe breasts that have never nursed].' [30]Then people will say to the mountains, 'Fall on us!' And they will say to the hills, '·Cover [Bury] us [Hos.10:8]!' [31]If they act like this now when ·life is good [Lthe tree is green], what will happen when ·bad times come [Lit is dry; Cprobably an allusion to the siege and destruction of Jerusalem in AD 70]?"

[32]There were also two criminals led out with Jesus to be ·put to death [executed]. [33]When they came to a place called the Skull, the soldiers crucified Jesus and the criminals—one on his right and the other on his left. [34]Jesus said, "Father, forgive them, because they don't know what they are doing."*n*

23:17 Every . . . people. Some Greek copies do not contain the bracketed text. **23:34 Jesus . . . doing."** Some Greek copies do not have this first part of verse 34.

The soldiers threw lots [Csimilar to dice] to decide who would get his clothes [Ps. 22:18]. 35The people stood there watching. And the leaders ·made fun of [sneered at; mocked] Jesus, saying, "He saved others. Let him save himself if he is ·God's Chosen One, the Christ [*or* God's Messiah, the Chosen One]."

36The soldiers also ·made fun of [mocked] him, coming to Jesus and offering him some ·vinegar [sour wine]. 37They said, "If you are the king of the Jews, save yourself!" 38·At the top of the cross these words were written [LAbove him there was also an inscription]: THIS IS THE KING OF THE JEWS.

39One of the criminals ·on a cross [Lwho was hanging there] began to ·shout insults at [slander; blaspheme] Jesus: "Aren't you the ·Christ [Messiah]? Then save yourself and us."

40But the other criminal ·stopped [rebuked] him and said, "·You should [LDon't you…?] fear God! You are getting the same punishment he is. 41We are punished justly, getting what we deserve for what we did. But this man has done nothing wrong." 42Then he said, "Jesus, remember me when you come into your kingdom."

43Jesus said to him, "I tell you the truth, today you will be with me in paradise [Cheaven or the presence of God]."

Jesus Dies

44It was about ·noon [Lthe sixth hour; Chours were counted from dawn, about 6 AM], and the whole land became dark until ·three o'clock in the afternoon [Lthe ninth hour], 45because the sun did not shine. The curtain in the Temple [Cdividing the Most Holy Place from the rest of the Temple] was torn ·in two [down the middle]. 46Jesus cried out in a loud voice, "Father, ·I give you my life [Linto your hands I entrust/commit my spirit; Ps. 31:5]." After Jesus said this, he ·died [expired; Tbreathed his last].

47When the ·army officer [Lcenturion] there saw what happened, he ·praised [glorified] God, saying, "Surely this was a ·good [righteous; *or* innocent] man!"

48When all the people who had gathered there to watch saw what happened, they returned home, beating their chests [Ca sign of sorrow and remorse]. 49But those who ·were close friends of Jesus [Lknew him], including the women who had followed him from Galilee, stood at a distance and watched [Lthese things].

Joseph Takes Jesus' Body

(23:50–56; Matt 27:57–61; Mark 15:42–47; John 19:38–42)

50[LAnd look/Tbehold] There was a good and ·religious [righteous; just] man named Joseph who was a member of the council. 51But he had not agreed to the other leaders' plans and actions against Jesus. He was from the town of Arimathea [in Judea; *or* a town of the Jews] and was waiting for the kingdom of God to come. 52Joseph went to Pilate to ask for the body of Jesus. 53He took the body down from the cross, wrapped it in [linen] cloth, and put it in a tomb that was cut out of a wall of rock. ·This tomb had never been used before [L…where no one had been laid; Cfamily tombs held multiple bodies, but this new one was empty]. 54This was late on Preparation Day, ·and when the sun went down, the Sabbath day would begin [Land the Sabbath was beginning].

55The women who had come from Galilee with Jesus followed Joseph and saw the tomb and how Jesus' body was laid. 56Then the women left to prepare spices and perfumes [Cused to honor the dead and cover the stench of decay].

On the Sabbath day they rested, ·as the law of Moses commanded [Laccording to the commandment].

Jesus Rises from the Dead
(24:1–12; Matt. 28:1–8; Mark 16:1–8; 20:1–13)

24 Very early on the first day of the week, at dawn, the women
came to the tomb, bringing the spices they had prepared.
2They found the stone rolled away from the entrance of the tomb, 3but
when they went in, they did not find the body of the Lord Jesus. 4While
they were ·wondering [puzzling; perplexed] about this, two men in ·shin-
ing [dazzling; gleaming like lightning; 9:29] clothes suddenly stood beside
them. 5The women were ·very afraid [terrified] and bowed their ·heads
[faces] to the ground. The men said to them, "Why are you looking for ·a
living person in this place for the dead [Lthe living among the dead]? 6He
is not here; he has risen from the dead. Do you remember what he told you
[Lwhile he was still] in Galilee? 7He said the Son of Man must be ·handed
over [betrayed] to sinful people, be crucified, and rise from the dead on
the third day." 8Then the women remembered what Jesus had said.
9The women ·left [returned from] the tomb and told all these things to
·the eleven apostles [Lthe Eleven] and ·the other followers [Lall the rest].
10It was Mary Magdalene, Joanna, Mary the mother of James, and some
other women who told the apostles ·everything that had happened at the
tomb [Lthese things]. 11But they did not believe the women, because it
·sounded [seemed] like nonsense. 12But Peter got up and ran to the tomb.
Bending down and looking in, he saw only the [linen] cloth that Jesus'
body had been wrapped in. Peter went away to his home, ·wondering
[amazed; marveling] about what had happened.

Jesus on the Road to Emmaus
(24:13–35; Mark 16:12–13)

13That same day two of Jesus' followers were going to a town named
Emmaus, about seven miles [CGreek: sixty *stadia;* a stadion was about 600
ft.] from Jerusalem. 14They were talking about everything that had happened. 15While they were talking and discussing, Jesus himself came near
and began walking with them, 16but ·they [Ltheir eyes] were kept from
recognizing him. 17Then he said, "What are these things you are ·talking
about [discussing] while you walk?"
The two followers stopped, looking ·very sad [downcast]. 18The one
named Cleopas answered, "·Are you the only visitor in Jerusalem who
does not [*or* Are you only a visitor in Jerusalem and don't] know what just
happened there?"
19Jesus said to them, "What ·are you talking about [Lthings]?"
They said, "About Jesus of Nazareth. He was a prophet ·who said and did
many powerful things [Lpowerful in deed and word] before God and all the
people. 20Our ·leading [Tchief] priests and ·leaders [rulers] handed him
over to be sentenced to death, and they crucified him. 21But we were hoping
that he would ·free [rescue; redeem] Israel. Besides [Lall] this, it is now the
third day since this happened. 22·And [LBut also; Moreover] some women
among us ·amazed [astonished] us. Early this morning they went to the
tomb, 23but they did not find his body there. They came and told us that
they had seen a vision of angels who said that Jesus was alive! 24So some of
our group went to the tomb, too. They found it just as the women said, but
they did not see Jesus."
25Then Jesus said to them, "·You are foolish [LO foolish ones] and slow [Lin
heart] to believe everything the prophets said. 26 ·They said [LWas it not necessary…?] that the ·Christ [Messiah] must suffer these things before he enters
his glory." 27Then starting with what Moses and all the prophets [Ca way of
referring to the whole Old Testament] had said about him, Jesus began to
explain everything that had been written about himself in [Lall] the Scriptures.

28 They came near the town ·of Emmaus [Lto which they were going], and
Jesus acted as if he were going farther. 29 But they ·begged [urged] him, "Stay
with us, because it is late; it is almost night." So he went in to stay with them.
30 When Jesus ·was at the table [Lreclined; Cthe posture of a formal meal]
with them, he took some bread, ·gave thanks [blessed it], ·divided [broke]
it, and gave it to them [CJesus, the guest, functions like the host in a
Eucharist-like meal]. 31 And then, ·they were allowed to recognize Jesus
[Ltheir eyes were opened]. But when they saw who he was, he disappeared.
32 They said to each other, "·It felt like a fire burning in [LDidn't our hearts
burn within...?] us when Jesus talked to us on the road and ·explained
[opened] the Scriptures to us."
33 So ·the two followers [Lthey] got up ·at once [Lthe same hour] and
went back to Jerusalem. There they found ·the eleven apostles [Lthe
Eleven] and others gathered. 34 They were saying, "The Lord really has
risen from the dead! He showed himself to Simon."
35 Then ·the two followers [Lthey] told what had happened on the road
and how they recognized Jesus when he ·divided [broke] the bread.

Jesus Appears to His Followers

(24:36–43; John 20:19–23)

36 While ·the two followers [they] were telling this, Jesus himself stood
right in the middle of them and said, "Peace be with you."
37 They were ·fearful [startled] and terrified and thought they were seeing
a ·ghost [spirit]. 38 But Jesus said, "Why are you ·troubled [frightened]? Why
do ·you doubt what you see [Ldoubts rise in your heart]? 39 Look at my hands
and my feet. It is ·I myself [really me]! Touch me and see, because a ·ghost
[spirit] does not have ·a living body [Lflesh and bones] as you see I have."
40 After Jesus said this, he showed them his hands and feet. 41 While they
still could not believe it because they were happy [joyful] and amazed,
Jesus said to them, "Do you have any food here?" 42 They gave him a piece
of broiled fish. 43 ·While the followers watched [In their presence; LIn front
of them], Jesus took the fish and ate it.
44 He said to them, "·Remember [LThis is what I said....] when I was with
you before? I said that everything written about me must ·happen [be ful-
filled]—everything in the law of Moses, the books of the prophets, and the
Psalms [Ca way of referring to the whole Old Testament; see v. 27]."
45 Then Jesus opened their minds so they could understand the
Scriptures. 46 He said to them, "It is written that the ·Christ [Messiah]
would suffer and rise from the dead on the third day 47 and that ·a change
of hearts and lives and [Lrepentance for the] forgiveness of sins would be
preached in his name to all nations, starting at Jerusalem. 48 You are witnesses of these things. 49 [LAnd look/Tbehold] I will send you what my
Father has promised, but you must stay in ·Jerusalem [Lthe city] until you
·have received [Lare clothed with] that power from ·heaven [Lon high]."

Jesus Goes Back to Heaven

50 Jesus led his followers as far as Bethany, and he raised his hands and
blessed them. 51 While he was blessing them, he ·was separated [parted]
from them and ·carried [taken up] into heaven. 52 They worshiped him
and returned to Jerusalem ·very happy [with great joy]. 53 They ·stayed in
the Temple all the time [were continually in the Temple], praising God.

JOHN

Christ Comes to the World

1 In the beginning [Gen. 1:1] **·there was the Word** [the Word already existed; Cthe Word refers to Christ, God's revelation of himself]. **The Word was ·with** [in the presence of; in intimate relationship with] **God** [Cthe Father], **and the Word was** [fully] **God.** **2He was ·with** [in the presence of; in intimate relationship with] **God in the beginning.** **3All things ·were made** [were created; came to be] **·by** [through] **him, and nothing ·was made** [came to be] **without him** [Prov. 8:22–31]. **4·In him there was life** [*or* What was made through him was life], **and that life was the light of all people.** **5The Light shines in the darkness, and the darkness has not ·overpowered** [defeated; *or* understood; comprehended] **it.**

6There was a man named John [Cthe Baptist; Matt. 3; Luke 3] **who was sent by God.** **7He came to ·tell people the truth** [testify; bear witness] **about the Light so that ·through him all people could hear about the Light and believe** [Leveryone might believe through him]. **8John was not the Light, but he came to ·tell people the truth** [testify; bear witness] **about the Light.** **9The true Light that ·gives light to** [shines on; illuminates; enlightens] **all** [people] **was coming into the world!** [*or* 9The true Light gives light to all who have come into the world.]

10·The Word [LHe] **was in the world, and the world ·was made** [was created; came into being] **·by** [through] **him, but the world did not ·know** [recognize] **him.** **11He came to ·the world that was his own** [*or* his own country; Lthat which was his own], **but his own people did not ·accept** [receive] **him.** **12But to all who did ·accept** [receive] **him and believe ·in him** [Lin his name; Cthe name indicating the character of the person] **he gave the ·right** [power; authority] **to become children of God.** **13They did not become his children ·in any human way** [by natural descent; by physical birth; Lby blood]**—by ·any human parents** [human passion/decision; Ldesire/will of the flesh] **or ·human desire** [a husband's decision; Ldesire/will of a man/husband]. **They were born of God.**

14The Word became ·a human [Tflesh] **and ·lived** [made his home; pitched his tabernacle; CGod's glorious presence dwelt in Israel's tabernacle in the wilderness] **among us. We saw his ·glory** [majesty]**—the glory that belongs to the ·only Son** [one and only; Tonly begotten] **·of** [who came from] **the Father—and he was full of ·grace and truth** [God's gracious love and faithfulness; Ex. 34:5–7]. **15John ·tells the truth about** [testifies concerning; witnesses about] **him and cries out, saying, "This is the One I told you about: 'The One who comes after me** [Cin time] **is greater than I am, because he ·was living** [existed] **before me** [Ca reference to Christ's preexistence; 1:1–2].' "

16·**Because he was full of grace and truth** [LFrom his fullness; 1:14], **from him we all received ·one gift after another** [Lgrace for grace; Cthis could mean abundant grace or that the grace under Christ replaced grace under the law]. 17**The law was given through Moses** [Ex. 19–24], **but grace and truth came through Jesus Christ.** 18**No one has ever seen God** [CGod the Father, who is pure spirit; 4:24]. **But ·God the only Son**[n] [God the one and only; the only Son who is himself God; TGod the only begotten] **is ·very close to** [by the side of; close to the heart of; Tin the bosom of] **the Father, and he has ·shown us what God is like** [made him known].

John the Baptist Tells People About Jesus

(1:19–34; Matt 3:1–17; Mark 1:2–11; Luke 3:1–22)

19**Here is the ·truth John told** [testimony John gave; witness of John; 1:6] **when the ·leaders** [Jewish leadership; LJews; CJohn often uses the term "Jews" to refer to the religious leaders in opposition to Jesus, rather than to the Jewish people generally] **in Jerusalem sent ·priests and Levites** [Cthe religious authorities; priests oversaw temple worship; Levites were members of the tribe of Levi who assisted them; 1 Chr. 23:24–32] **to ask him, "Who are you?"**

20**John ·spoke freely** [confessed] **and did not ·refuse to answer** [deny it]. **He said, "I am not the ·Christ** [Messiah]."

21**So they asked him, "Then who are you? Are you Elijah?"** [CElijah, an OT prophet, was expected to come back before the Messiah; 1 Kin. 17—2 Kin. 2; Mal. 4:5–6.]

He answered, "No, I am not."

"Are you the Prophet?" [Cthe Prophet like Moses predicted in Deut. 18:15–19] **they asked.**

He answered, "No."

22**Then they said, "Who are you? Give us an answer to tell those who sent us. What do you say about yourself?"**

23**John told them in the words of the prophet Isaiah:**

"I am the voice of one
calling out in the ·desert [wilderness]:
'Make ·the road straight [a clear path] **for the Lord** [Is. 40:3].'"

24**Some Pharisees** [Ca religious party which strictly observed OT laws and later customs] **who had been sent asked John:** 25**"If you are not the ·Christ** [Messiah] **or Elijah or the Prophet** [1:21], **why do you baptize people?"**

26**John answered, "I baptize with water, but there is one here with you that you don't ·know about** [recognize]. 27**He is the One who comes after me. I am not ·good enough** [worthy; fit] **to untie the ·strings** [straps] **of his sandals."** [CRemoving sandals was the task of a slave.]

28**This all happened at Bethany on the other side of the Jordan River** [Ca site east of the Jordan River, not the Bethany near Jerusalem], **where John was baptizing people.**

29**The next day John saw Jesus coming toward him. John said, "Look, the Lamb of God** [Clambs were used for sacrifice; Gen. 22:8], **who takes away the sin of the world!** 30**This is the One I was talking about** [1:15] **when I said, 'A man will come after me, but he is greater than I am, because he ·was living** [existed] **before me.'** 31**Even I did not ·know** [recognize] **who he was, although I came baptizing with water so that ·the people of Israel would know who he is** [he might be revealed to Israel]."

32-33**Then John ·said** [testified; bore witness], **"I saw the Spirit come**

1:18 But . . . Father Some Greek copies read "But the only Son."

down from heaven in the form of a dove and ·rest [remain] on him. Until then I did not know ·who the Christ was [*or* he was the one; [L]him]. But the God who sent me to baptize with water told me, 'You will see the Spirit come down and ·rest [remain] on a man; he is the One who will baptize with the Holy Spirit.' 34I have seen this happen, and I ·tell you the truth [testify; bear witness]: This man is the Son of God."[n]

The First Followers of Jesus

35The next day John [[C]the Baptist; 1:6] was [standing] there again with two of his ·followers [disciples]. 36When he saw Jesus walking by, he said, "Look, the Lamb of God [see 1:29]!"

37The two ·followers [disciples] heard John say this, so they followed Jesus. 38When Jesus turned and saw them following him, he asked, "What are you looking for?"

They said, "Rabbi, where are you staying?" ("Rabbi" means "Teacher.")

39He answered, "Come and see." So the two men went with Jesus and saw where he was staying and stayed there with him that day. It was about ·four o'clock in the afternoon [[L]the tenth hour; [C]hours were counted from dawn, about 6 AM].

40One of the two men who followed Jesus after they heard John speak about him was Andrew, Simon Peter's brother. 41The first thing Andrew did was to find his brother Simon and say to him, "We have found the Messiah." ("Messiah" means "Christ.") [[C]Both Hebrew *Mashiach* (Messiah) and Greek *Christos* (Christ) mean "Anointed One."]

42Then Andrew took Simon to Jesus. Jesus looked at him and said, "You are Simon son of John. You will be called Cephas." ("Cephas" means "Peter.") [[C]Both Aramaic *Cephas* and Greek *Petros* mean "rock."]

43The next day Jesus decided to go to Galilee [[C]a region about 50 miles north of Jerusalem]. He found Philip and said to him, "Follow me [[C]as a disciple]."

44Philip was from the town of Bethsaida [[C]a town just to the north of the Sea of Galilee], where Andrew and Peter lived. 45Philip found Nathanael and told him, "We have found the man that Moses wrote about in the law, and the prophets also wrote about him. [[C]The law and the prophets refer to the OT Scriptures.] He is Jesus, the son of Joseph, from Nazareth [[C]a village a few miles southwest of the Sea of Galilee]."

46But Nathanael said to Philip, "Can anything good come from Nazareth?" [[C]This is because of its insignificance and lack of mention in the OT.]

Philip answered, "Come and see."

47As Jesus saw Nathanael coming toward him, he said, "Here is truly an Israelite. There is ·nothing false [no deceit; no guile] in him."

48Nathanael asked, "How do you know me?"

Jesus answered, "I saw you when you were under the fig tree, before Philip ·told you about me [[L]called you]."

49Then Nathanael said to Jesus, "Teacher [[L]Rabbi], you are the Son of God; you are the King of Israel."

50Jesus said to Nathanael, "Do you believe simply because I told you I saw you under the fig tree? You will see greater things than that." 51And Jesus said to them, "·I tell you the truth [[L]Truly, truly I say to you], you will all see heaven open and 'angels of God going up and coming down' [[C]a reference to Jacob's dream in Gen. 28:12] on the Son of Man [[C]a title for the Messiah; Dan. 7:13–14]."

1:34 the Son of God Some Greek copies read "God's Chosen One."

The Wedding at Cana

2 ·Two days later [LOn the third day] there was a wedding in the
town of Cana in Galilee [Cof uncertain location, probably near
Nazareth]. Jesus' mother was there, 2and Jesus and his ·followers [disci-
ples] were also invited to the wedding. 3When all the wine was gone, Jesus'
mother said to him, "They have no more wine."
4Jesus answered, "·Dear woman [LWoman; Ca respectful form of address
in that culture], ·why come to me [what concern is that to me and to you;
Lwhat to me and to you]? My ·time [Lhour; Chere and throughout John,
Jesus' "hour" refers to his messianic sacrifice on the cross] has not yet come."
5His mother said to the servants, "Do whatever he tells you to do."
6In that place there were six stone water jars that the Jews used in their
washing ceremony [Ca Jewish ritual before eating, before worshiping in
the Temple, and at other special times]. Each jar held about twenty or
thirty gallons [CGreek: two or three *metretai;* each about nine gallons or
forty liters].
7Jesus said to the servants, "Fill the jars with water." So they filled the
jars to the ·top [brim].
8Then he said to them, "Now take some out and give it to the ·master
of the feast [chief steward; headwaiter]."
So they took the water to the master. 9When he tasted it, the water had
become wine. He did not know where the wine came from, but the servants who had brought the water knew. The ·master of the wedding [chief
steward; headwaiter] called the bridegroom 10and said to him, "People
always serve the ·best [expensive] wine first. Later, after the guests have
been drinking awhile [Cand are less discriminating], they serve the ·cheaper
[inferior] wine. But you have saved the ·best [expensive] wine till now."
11So in Cana of Galilee [see 2:1] Jesus did his first ·miracle [Lsign;
CJesus' miracles are called *semeia,* "signs," in John's Gospel]. There he
·showed [revealed; manifested] his ·glory [majesty], and his ·followers
[disciples] believed in him.

Jesus in the Temple

(2:14–22; Matt. 21:12–13; Mark 11:15–17; Luke 19:45–46)

12After this, Jesus went to the town of Capernaum [Ca town on the
northwest shore of the Sea of Galilee] with his mother, brothers, and
·followers [disciples]. They stayed there for just a few days. 13When it
was almost time for the Jewish Passover Feast [Cannual festival that celebrates God's rescue of Israel from Egypt; Ex. 12], Jesus ·went [Lwent up]
to Jerusalem. 14In the Temple [area; Cnot in the Temple proper, but in
the outer courtyard, the Court of the Gentiles] he found people selling
cattle, sheep, and ·doves [*or* pigeons; Cfor sacrifices in the Temple]. ·He
saw others sitting at tables, exchanging different kinds of money [L…
and moneychangers sitting; Cthe annual temple tax (Ex. 30:11–16) had
to be paid in Tyrian shekels, because of their high quality silver]. 15Jesus
made a whip out of cords and forced all of them, ·both [with] the sheep
and cattle, to leave the Temple. He turned over the tables and scattered
the money of ·those who were exchanging it [Lthe moneychangers].
16Then he said to those who were selling ·doves [*or* pigeons], "Take these
things out of here! Don't make my Father's house [Cthe Temple was
God's home on earth; 1 Kin. 8] a ·place for buying and selling [La house
of market/trade]!"
17When this happened, the ·followers [disciples] remembered what
was written [Cin the Scriptures]: ·"My strong love for your Temple completely controls me [L"Zeal for your house will consume me"; Ps. 69:9]."

18**Some of ·his people** [Lthe Jews] **·said to** [responded to; demanded of] **Jesus, "Show us a ·miracle** [Lsign] **to ·prove you have the right to do these things** [justify your actions]**."**

19**Jesus ·answered** [replied to] **them, "Destroy this temple, and I will ·build** [Lraise] **it again in three days** [Can allusion to his resurrection; 2:22; Matt. 26:61; 27:40]**."**

20**·They** [The Jewish leaders; LThe Jews] **answered, "It took forty-six years** [CHerod the Great began a reconstruction and expansion of the Temple complex in 20 BC, thus dating this statement to about AD 27] **to ·build** [reconstruct] **this Temple! Do you really believe you can ·build** [raise] **it again in three days?"**

21**(But the temple Jesus meant was his own body** [CJesus was claiming divinity, his body corresponding with the Temple, the home/dwelling place of God; 1:14]. 22**After Jesus was raised from the dead, his ·followers** [disciples] **remembered that Jesus had said this. Then they believed the Scripture** [compare Ps. 16:10] **and the words Jesus had said.)**

23**When Jesus was in Jerusalem for the Passover Feast** [see 2:13], **many people ·believed** [put their faith; trusted] **in ·him** [Lhis name] **because they saw the ·miracles** [Lsigns; 2:11] **he did** [4:48; Mark 8:11–13]. 24**But Jesus did not ·believe in** [entrust/commit himself to] **them because he knew them all.** 25**He did not need anyone to ·tell** [testify/witness to] **him about ·people** [human nature], **because he knew what was in ·people's minds** [people's hearts; Lpeople].

Nicodemus Comes to Jesus

3 There was a man named Nicodemus who was one of the Pharisees [Ca religious party which strictly observed OT laws and later customs] **and ·an important Jewish leader** [La ruler of the Jews; Cprobably a member of the Sanhedrin, the highest Jewish court of the time]. 2**·One night** [*or* By night; Cperhaps with connotations that he could not "see" spiritually] **Nicodemus came to Jesus and said, "·Teacher** [LRabbi], **we know you are a teacher sent from God, because no one can do the ·miracles** [Lsigns; 2:11] **you do unless God is with him."**

3**Jesus answered, "·I tell you the truth** [LTruly, truly I say to you], **unless you are born ·again** [*or* from above; Cthis may be a play on words, meaning both "again" and "from above"], **you cannot ·be in** [experience; Lsee] **God's kingdom."**

4**Nicodemus said to him, "But if a person is already old, how can he be born ·again** [*or* from above; 3:3]? **·He cannot enter his mother's womb again. So how can a person be born a second time** [LCan he enter his mother's womb a second time and be born]**?"**

5**But Jesus answered, "·I tell you the truth** [LTruly, truly I say to you], **unless you are born from water and the Spirit** [Cequivalent to being born again (3:3); water could symbolize physical birth, but more likely symbolizes spiritual cleansing which brings renewal; Ezek. 36:25–27], **you cannot enter God's kingdom.** 6**·Human life comes from human parents** [LThat which is born of the flesh is flesh; Cflesh here means human nature], **but ·spiritual life comes from the Spirit** [Lthat which is born of the Spirit is spirit]. 7**Don't be ·surprised** [amazed; astonished] **when I tell you, 'You** [Cplural, referring to the Jews or the Jewish leaders] **must be born ·again** [*or* from above; 3:3].' 8**The wind** [Cone word means both "wind" and "spirit" in Greek] **blows where it wants to and you hear the sound of it, but you don't know where the wind comes from or where it is going. It is**

the same with every person who is born from the Spirit." [CWe cannot
comprehend or control the Spirit, but we experience his effect.]
9 **Nicodemus ·asked** [replied], **"How can this ·happen** [be]**?"**
10 **Jesus ·said** [replied; answered], **"You are ·an important teacher in
Israel** [Lthe teacher of Israel], **and you don't ·understand** [know] **these
things?** 11 **·I tell you the truth** [LTruly, truly I say to you], **we talk about
what we know, and we ·tell** [testify; bear witness] **about what we have
seen, but you don't ·accept what we tell you** [Lreceive our testimony/wit-
ness]. 12 **I have told you about things here on earth** [Cthe teaching about
being born again], **and you do not believe me. ·So you will not** [LSo how
will you…?] **believe me if I tell you about things of heaven.** 13 **·The only
one who has ever gone up to heaven is** [LNo one has gone up into heaven
except] **the One who came down from heaven—the Son of Man**ⁿ [Ca title
for the Messiah; Dan. 7:13–14].
14 **"Just as Moses lifted up the ·snake** [Tserpent] **in the ·desert** [wilderness;
CMoses put a bronze snake statue on a pole, and those who looked at it were
healed of snake bites; Num. 21:4–9], **the Son of Man must also be lifted up**
[Can allusion to the cross and resurrection]. 15 **So that everyone who ·believes
can have eternal life in him** [*or* believes in him can have eternal life].
16 **"**[LFor] **God loved the world so much that he gave his ·one and only**
[only; unique; Tonly begotten; 1:14, 18] **Son so that whoever believes in
him may not ·be lost** [Tperish], **but have eternal life.** 17 [LFor; Indeed] **God
did not send his Son into the world to ·judge the world guilty** [condemn
the world], **but to save the world through him.** 18 **People who believe in
God's Son are not ·judged guilty** [condemned]. **Those who do not believe
have already been ·judged guilty** [condemned], **because they have not
believed in** [Lthe name of] **God's ·one and only** [only; unique; Tonly begotten; 3:16] **Son.** 19 **·They are judged by this fact** [LAnd this is the judgment/
condemnation/verdict]: **The Light** [CJesus, God's Son] **has come into the
world, ·but they did not want light. They wanted darkness** [Lbut people
loved the darkness more than the light], **because they were doing evil
things.** 20 **All who do evil hate the light and will not come to the light,
because it will show ·all the evil things they do** [Ltheir deeds/actions].
21 **But those who ·follow the true way** [do what is true; live by the truth]
come to the light, and it ·shows [may be seen] **that the things they do were
done ·through** [*or* in the sight of; *or* in obedience to; Lin] **God."**

Jesus and John the Baptist

22 **After this, Jesus and his ·followers** [disciples] **went into the ·area** [coun-
tryside] **of Judea, where he ·stayed** [spent time] **with his ·followers** [disciples]
and baptized people. 23 **John was also baptizing in Aenon** [Ca town (meaning "springs") of uncertain location on the Jordan River (but see note on
Salim)], **near Salim** [Ca town (meaning "peace") probably located either
near Shechem or just south of Bethshan, both of which are in a Samaritan
area], **because there was plenty of water there. People were going there to be
baptized.** 24 **(This was before John was put into prison** [Matt. 4:12]**.)**
25 **Some of John's ·followers** [disciples] **had an ·argument** [discussion;
debate] **with a Jew about ·religious washing** [ceremonial cleansing;
Lpurification; Cthe Jewish people washed themselves for ritual purposes
before eating, before worshiping in the Temple, and at other special times].
26 **So they came to John and said, "Teacher** [LRabbi], **remember the man**

3:13 the Son of Man Some Greek copies continue, "who is in heaven."

who was with you on the other side of the Jordan River, the one ·you
spoke about so much [Labout whom you have testified/witnessed]**? He is**
baptizing, and everyone is going to him."
27**John answered, "A ·man** [person] **can get only what ·God gives him**
[Lis given to him from heaven]. 28**You yourselves heard me ·say** [testify], **'I**
am not the ·Christ [Messiah], **but I am the one sent ·to prepare the way**
for him [Lbefore him; 1:20–28; compare Is. 40:3].**'** 29**The bride belongs**
only to the bridegroom. But the ·friend who helps the bridegroom [*or* the
best man] **stands by and listens to him. He ·is thrilled** [rejoices greatly]
that he gets to hear the bridegroom's voice. In the same way, ·I am really
happy [Lmy joy is fulfilled; Cin this analogy, John is the best man and Jesus
is the bridegroom]. 30**He must ·become greater** [increase], **and I must**
·become less important [decrease].

The One Who Comes from Heaven

31**"The One** [CJesus] **who comes from above is ·greater than** [Labove]
all. The one who is from the earth belongs to the earth and talks about
·things on the earth [earthly matters]. **But the One who comes from**
heaven is ·greater than [Labove] **all.** 32**He ·tells** [testifies to; bears witness
to] **what he has seen and heard, but no one ·accepts** [receives] **·what he**
says [his testimony; 3:11]. 33**Whoever ·accepts what he says** [receives his
testimony] **has ·proven** [certified; affirmed; Lset his seal] **that God is true.**
34[LFor] **The One whom God sent speaks the words of God, because God**
gives him the Spirit ·fully [Lwithout measure/limit]. 35**The Father loves**
the Son and has given ·him power over everything [him authority over
all; Lall things into his hand]. 36**Those who believe in the Son have eternal**
life, but those who ·do not obey [reject] **the Son will ·never have** [Lnot see]
life. God's ·anger [wrath] **·stays** [remains] **on them."**

Jesus and a Samaritan Woman

4 **The Pharisees** [Ca religious party which strictly observed OT laws
and later customs] **heard that Jesus was making and baptizing**
more ·followers [disciples] **than John,** 2**although Jesus himself did not**
baptize people, but his ·followers [disciples] **did.** 3**Jesus knew that the**
Pharisees had heard about him, so he left Judea [Cthe southern region of
Israel] **and went back to Galilee** [Cthe northern region of Israel; Mark 1:14].
4**But on the way he had to go through the country of Samaria** [Cthe central
region occupied by a people disliked because they were only partly Jewish].
5**In Samaria Jesus came to the town called Sychar** [Cperhaps Shechem or a
village near it; compare Gen. 33:18–19; 48:22], **which is near the ·field** [plot of
ground] **Jacob gave to his son Joseph.** 6**Jacob's well was there. Jesus was tired**
from ·his long trip [Lthe journey], **so he sat down beside the well. It was about**
·twelve o'clock noon [Lthe sixth hour; Chours were counted from dawn, about
6 AM]. 7**When a Samaritan woman came to the well to ·get some** [draw]
water, Jesus said to her, "·Please give [LGive] **me a drink."** 8**(This happened**
while Jesus' ·followers [disciples] **were in town buying some food.)**
9**The Samaritan woman said, "·I am surprised** [LHow is it…?] **that you**
ask me for a drink, since you are a ·Jewish man [La Jew] **and I am a**
Samaritan woman." (Jewish people ·are not friends [do not share things;
have no dealings] **with Samaritans.)**
10**Jesus ·said** [answered; replied], **"If you only knew the ·free gift** [Lgift]
of God and who it is that is asking you ·for water [L"Give me a drink"], **you**
would have asked him, and he would have given you living water." [C"Living
water" in Greek can mean fresh running water, but Jesus means "water
which gives eternal life"; the woman misunderstands this play on words.]

11The woman said, "Sir, where will you get this living water? The well is very deep, and you have ·nothing to get water with [Lno bucket]. 12Are you greater than Jacob, our father [Ca patriarch recognized by both Jews and Samaritans], who gave us this well and drank from it himself along with his sons and ·flocks [*or* livestock]?"

13Jesus answered, "Everyone who drinks this water will be thirsty again [Cbecause physical water only temporarily satisfies thirst], 14but whoever drinks the water I give will never be thirsty [Cbecause spiritual renewal/eternal life is forever]. [LBut; Indeed] The water I give will become a spring of water gushing up inside that person, giving eternal life [Is. 12:3; 49:10; 55:1–3; Rev. 7:16]."

15The woman said to him, "Sir, give me this water so I will never be thirsty again and will not have to come back here to ·get [draw] more water." [CHer response indicates she does not understand.]

16Jesus told her, "Go ·get [call] your husband and come back here."

17The woman answered, "I have no husband."

Jesus said to her, "You are right to say you have no husband. 18·Really [For] you have had five husbands, and the man you ·live with [Lhave] now is not your husband. You told the truth."

19The woman said to him, "Sir, I can see that you are a prophet. 20Our ·ancestors [forefathers; Lfathers] worshiped on this mountain [Cthe Samaritans worshiped on Mount Gerizim near Shechem], but you [Cplural, referring to the Jews] say that Jerusalem [CMount Zion, the location of the temple] is the place where people must worship."

21Jesus said to her, "Believe me, woman [Ca respectful form of address in that culture; 2:4]. The ·time [Lhour; Cthe time of salvation established by the death and resurrection of Christ; see 2:4] is coming when neither in Jerusalem nor on this mountain will you ·actually worship [Lworship] the Father. 22You Samaritans worship something you don't understand. We [CJews] understand what we worship, because salvation comes from the Jews [Cbecause the Messiah who brings salvation comes through the Jews]. 23[LBut] The ·time [Lhour; see 4:21] is coming when the true worshipers will worship the Father in ·spirit [*or* the Spirit] and truth, and that time ·is here already [has now come; is now here]. You see, the Father too is actively seeking such people to worship him. 24God is ·spirit [Spirit], and those who worship him must worship in ·spirit [Spirit] and truth."

25The woman said to him, "I know that the Messiah is coming." (Messiah is the One called Christ [Cboth Hebrew *Mashiach* and Greek *Christos* mean "Anointed One"; see 1:41].) "When ·the Messiah [Lthat one] comes, he will ·explain [report; announce] everything to us."

26Then Jesus said to her, "I am he—I, the one talking to you."

27Just then his ·followers [disciples] came back from town and were surprised to see him talking with a woman [Csome Jews thought it a waste of time for rabbis to teach women]. But none of them asked, "What do you want?" or "Why are you talking with her?"

28Then the woman left her water jar and went back to town. She said to the people, 29"Come and see a man who told me everything I ever did. Do you think he might be the ·Christ [Messiah]?" 30So the people left the town and ·went to see Jesus [Lwere coming toward him].

31Meanwhile, his ·followers [disciples] were ·begging [urging] him, "·Teacher [LRabbi], eat something."

32But Jesus answered, "I have food to eat that you know nothing about [Deut. 8:3]."

33So the ·followers [disciples] asked ·themselves [each other], "·Did
somebody already bring him food [LNo one brought him anything to eat,
did they]?"
34Jesus said to them, "My food is to do ·what the One who sent me wants
me to do [Lthe will of the One who sent me] and to ·finish [complete] his
work. 35·You have a saying [LDo you not say…?], 'Four more months till
harvest.' ·But [Look; TBehold] I tell you, ·open your eyes and look at [Llift up
your eyes and see] the fields ·ready [ripe; Lwhite] for harvest now. 36Already,
the one who ·harvests [reaps] is ·being paid [Lreceiving wages] and is gathering ·crops [fruit] for eternal life. So the one who ·plants [sows] and the one
who ·harvests [reaps] ·celebrate [rejoice] ·at the same time [together].
37[LFor] ·Here [in this case] the saying is true, 'One person ·plants [sows],
and another ·harvests [reaps].' 38I sent you to ·harvest a crop that [reap what]
you did not ·work [labor; toil] on. Others did the ·work [labor; toil], and you
·get to finish up [reap the benefits of; Lhave entered into] their work."
39Many of the Samaritans in that town believed in Jesus because of
·what the woman said [Lthe word of the woman who testified]: "He told me
everything I ever did." 40When the Samaritans came to Jesus, they ·begged
[urged; asked] him to stay with them, so he stayed there two more days.
41And many more believed because of ·the things he said [Lhis word].
42They said to the woman, "·First we believed in Jesus [LIt is no longer]
because of what you said, but now we believe because we heard him ourselves. We know that this man really is the Savior of the world."

Jesus Heals an Officer's Son
(4:43–54; Matt. 8:5–13; Luke 7:1–10)

43Two days later, Jesus left [Lfrom there] and went to Galilee [Cthe
northern region of Israel]. 44(Jesus had ·said [testified; witnessed] before
that a prophet ·is not respected [Lhas no honor] in his own ·country [*or*
hometown; Cprobably a reference to Galilee, but some think Judea].)
45When [Ltherefore] Jesus arrived in Galilee, the ·people there [LGalileans]
·welcomed [received] him. They had seen all the things he did at the
Passover Feast in Jerusalem, because they had been there, too.
46Jesus went again to visit Cana in Galilee where he had changed the
water into wine [2:1–11]. One of the king's important officers lived in the
city of Capernaum, and his son was sick. 47When he heard that Jesus had
come from Judea to Galilee, he went to Jesus and ·begged [urged; asked]
him to come to Capernaum and heal his son, because his son was almost
dead. 48Jesus said to him, "·You people must see signs and miracles before
you will believe in me [LUnless you see signs and wonders you will not
believe; 2:23–25; 6:26]."
49The [royal] officer said, "Sir, ·come [Lcome down] before my child dies."
50Jesus ·answered [said to him], "Go. Your son will live."
The man believed what Jesus told him [Che did not need "signs" and
miracles] and went home. 51On the way the man's ·servants [slaves; bond-
servants] came and met him and told him, "Your son is alive."
52[LSo/Then] The man asked, "What ·time [hour] did my son begin to
get well?"
They answered, "Yesterday at ·one o'clock [Lthe seventh hour; Chours
were counted from dawn, about 6 AM] the fever left him."
53[LSo/Then] The father knew that ·one o'clock was the exact time that
[Lin that hour] Jesus had said, "Your son will live." So the man and all ·the
people who lived in his house [his household] believed in Jesus.
54That was the second ·miracle [Lsign; Cthe first sign was turning water
into wine; 2:1–11] Jesus did after coming from Judea to Galilee.

Jesus Heals a Man at a Pool

5 ·Later [LAfter these things] Jesus went [Lup] to Jerusalem for a ·special feast [Lfeast/festival of the Jews]. 2 In Jerusalem there is a pool with five covered porches, which is called Bethesda[n] [Ca pool of water north of the temple thought to have curative powers] in the Hebrew language [Creferring to Aramaic, the native language of the Jews at the time]. This pool is near the Sheep Gate. 3 Many sick people were lying on the porches beside the pool. Some were blind, some were crippled, and some were paralyzed |, and they waited for the water to move. 4 ·Sometimes [At a certain time; From time to time] an angel of the Lord came down to the pool and stirred up the water. After the angel did this, the first person to go into the pool was healed from any sickness he had|[n]. 5 A man was lying there who had been ·sick [an invalid; disabled] for thirty-eight years. 6 When Jesus saw the man and knew that he had been ·sick [an invalid; disabled] for such a long time, Jesus asked him, "Do you want to be well?"

7 The ·sick man [invalid] answered [him], "Sir, there is no one to help me get into the pool when the water ·starts moving [is stirred up]. While I am coming to the water, someone else always ·gets in [goes down] before me."

8 Then Jesus said to him, "·Stand up [TRise]. Pick up your ·mat [bed; cot] and walk." 9 And immediately the man ·was well [was healed; became whole]; he picked up his ·mat [bed; cot] and began to walk.

The day this happened was a Sabbath day. 10 So the ·Jews [*or* Jewish leaders] said to the man who had been healed, "Today is the Sabbath. It is ·against our law [Lnot lawful/permitted] for you to carry your ·mat [bed; cot] on the Sabbath day [Cthe fourth commandment prohibited work on the Sabbath, but not specifically this action (Ex. 20:8–11)]."

11 But he answered them, "The man who made me well told me, 'Pick up your ·mat [bed; cot] and walk.' "

12 Then they asked him, "Who is the man who told you to pick up your ·mat [bed; cot] and walk?"

13 But the man who had been healed did not know who it was, because there were many people in that place, and Jesus had ·left [withdrawn; slipped away unnoticed].

14 Later, Jesus found the man at the Temple [area] and said to him, "See, you are well now. ·Stop sinning [TSin no more] so that something worse does not happen to you." [CSometimes, not always, suffering can be explained by sin.]

15 Then the man left and told ·his people [the Jewish leaders; Lthe Jews] that Jesus was the one who had made him well.

16 Because Jesus was doing ·this [Lthese things] on the Sabbath day, ·some evil people [the Jewish leaders; Lthe Jews] began to ·persecute [harass] him. 17 But Jesus ·said to [Lanswered] them, "My Father ·never stops [is always; is still] working [Ceven on the Sabbath], and so I keep working, too."

18 This made ·them [the Jewish leaders; Lthe Jews] try still harder to kill him. They said, "First Jesus was breaking the law about the Sabbath day. Now he says that God is his own Father, making himself equal with God!" [CBoth breaking the Sabbath and blasphemy against God were punishable by death; Ex. 35:2; Lev. 24:16.]

Jesus Has God's Authority

19 But Jesus ·said [answered them], "·I tell you the truth [LTruly, truly I say to you], the Son can do nothing ·alone [on his own initiative; by himself].

5:2 Bethesda Some Greek copies read "Bethzatha" or "Bethsaida," different names for the pool of Bethesda. **5:3–4 and . . . had** Some Greek copies do not contain all or most of the bracketed text.

The Son does only what he sees the Father doing, ·because the Son does whatever the Father does [Lfor whatever the Father does, the Son does likewise]. 20[LFor] The Father loves the Son and shows the Son all the things he himself does. But the Father will show the Son even greater things than this so that you can all ·be amazed [marvel; be astonished]. 21[LFor] Just as the Father raises the dead and gives them life, so also the Son gives life to those he ·wants to [wishes; wills]. 22·In fact, [*or* For] the Father judges no one, but he has ·given [entrusted to] the Son ·power to do all the judging [Lall judgment; Rev. 20:11–15] 23so that all people will honor the Son as much as they honor the Father. Anyone who does not honor the Son does not honor the Father who sent him.

24"·I tell you the truth [LTruly, truly I say to you], whoever ·hears [obeys] ·what I say [Lmy word/message] and believes in the One who sent me has eternal life. That person will not ·be judged guilty [Lcome into judgment/condemnation] but has ·already left death and entered life [Lpassed from death into life]. 25·I tell you the truth [LTruly, truly I say to you], the ·time [Lhour] is coming and is already here when the dead will ·hear [obey] the voice of the Son of God, and those who ·hear [obey] will ·have life [live]. 26[LFor] ·Life comes from the Father himself [just as the Father has life], ·and [so] he has ·allowed the Son to have [given the Son] life in himself as well. 27And the Father has given the Son the ·approval [authority; power; right] to ·judge [execute judgment], because he is the Son of Man [Ca title for the Messiah; Dan. 7:13–14]. 28Don't ·be surprised [marvel; be amazed] at this: A ·time [Lhour] is coming when all who are dead and in their graves will hear his voice. 29Then they will come out of their graves. Those who did good ·will rise and have life forever [Lto the resurrection resulting in life], but those who did evil ·will rise to be judged guilty [Lto the resurrection resulting in condemnation/judgment].

Jesus Is God's Son

30"I can do nothing ·alone [by myself; on my own initiative]. I judge ·only the way I am told [Las I hear], so my judgment is ·fair [just; right; righteous]. I don't ·try to please myself [Lseek my own will/desire], but ·I try to please [Lthe will of] the One who sent me.

31"If only I ·tell people [testify; witness] about myself, ·what I say [my testimony; witness] is not ·true [valid]. 32But there is another who ·tells [testifies; witnesses] about me, and I know that ·the things he says [Lthe witness/testimony he witnesses/testifies] about me are ·true [valid].

33"You have sent people to John, and he has ·told you [testified/witnessed to] the truth. 34It is not that I ·need [accept; depend on] ·what humans say [human testimony/witness]; I tell you this so you can be saved. 35John was like a burning and shining lamp, and you were ·happy to enjoy [Lwilling to rejoice in] his light for a while.

36"But I have a ·proof [testimony; witness] about myself that is ·greater [weightier] than that of John. [LFor] The ·things [Lworks] I do, which are the ·things [Lworks] my Father gave me to ·do [complete; finish; Cthe signs and miracles which point to his saving work on the cross], ·prove [testify; witness] that the Father sent me. 37And the Father himself who sent me has given ·proof [testimony; witness] ·about me [concerning me; on my behalf]. You have never heard his voice or seen ·what he looks like [his form; his outward appearance]. 38His ·teaching [word; message] does not ·live [remain; abide] in you, because you don't believe in the One the Father sent. 39You ·carefully study [search; examine] the Scriptures because

you think they give you eternal life. They do in fact ·tell [testify; witness]
·about me [concerning me; on my behalf], 40but you ·refuse [do not want]
to come to me to have that life.
41"I don't ·need [*or* accept; receive] ·praise [glory; honor] from people.
42But I know you—I know that you don't have God's love in you. 43I have
come ·from my Father and speak for him [Lin my Father's name], ·but [*or*
and] you don't ·accept [receive] me. But when another person comes,
·speaking only for himself [Lin his own name], you will ·accept [receive]
him. 44You try to ·get praise [receive glory/honor] from each other, but you
do not try to ·get the praise [receive glory/honor] that comes from the only
God. So how can you believe? 45Don't think that I will ·stand before the
Father and say you are wrong [Laccuse you before the Father]. The one
who ·says you are wrong [Laccuses you] is Moses, the one ·you hoped
would save you [Lin whom you hoped]. 46[LFor] If you really believed
Moses, you would believe me, because Moses wrote about me [Cin the
Torah, the first five books of the OT; for example, Deut. 18:15 quoted in
Acts 3:22]. 47But if you don't believe what Moses wrote, how can you
believe what I say?"

More than Five Thousand Fed
(6:1–15; Matt 14:13–21; Mark 6:32–44; Luke 9:10–17)

6 After this, Jesus went ·across [to the other side of] ·Lake [Tthe Sea
of] Galilee (or, Lake Tiberias). 2Many people followed him
because they saw the ·miracles [Lsigns; 2:11] he did ·to heal [Lfor; on
behalf of] the sick. 3Jesus went up on a ·hill [*or* mountain] and sat down
there with his ·followers [disciples]. 4It was almost the time for the Jewish
Passover Feast [Cthe annual festival that celebrates God's rescue of Israel
from Egypt; Ex. 12; John 2:13].
5When Jesus ·looked up [Lraised his eyes] and saw a large crowd coming toward him, he said to Philip [Cone of the twelve disciples; 1:43],
"Where can we buy enough bread for all these people to eat?" 6(Jesus
asked Philip this question to test him, because Jesus already knew what
he ·planned [was going] to do.)
7Philip answered [Lhim], "·Someone would have to work almost a year
to buy enough bread [LTwo hundred denarii worth of bread is not enough;
Ca denarius was a unit of money worth about a day's wages] for each person to have only a little piece."
8Another one of his ·followers [disciples], Andrew, Simon Peter's brother,
said to him, 9"Here is a boy with five loaves of barley bread and two little
fish, but ·that is not enough [Lwhat are these…?] for so many people."
10Jesus said, "·Tell [LMake] the people to sit down." There was plenty of
grass there, and about five thousand men sat down there. 11Then Jesus
took the loaves of bread, ·thanked God [Lgave thanks] for them, and ·gave
[distributed] them to the people who were sitting there. He did the same
with the fish, giving as much as the people wanted.
12When they ·had all had enough to eat [Lwere filled/satisfied], Jesus
said to his ·followers [disciples], "Gather the leftover ·pieces of fish and
bread [Lpieces] so that nothing is wasted." 13So they gathered up the
pieces and filled twelve baskets with the pieces left from the five barley
loaves [2 Kin. 4:42–44; CJesus' miracle surpasses that of Elisha].
14When the people saw this ·miracle [Lsign] that Jesus did, they said,
"He must truly be the Prophet [1:21; Cprobably the "prophet like Moses"
of Deut. 18:15–18] who is coming into the world."
15Jesus knew that the people ·planned [intended; were about] to come

and take him by force and make him their king, so he ·left [withdrew] and went into the ·hills [*or* mountains] alone.

Jesus Walks on the Water
(6:16–21; Matt. 14:22–33; Mark 6:45–52)

16That evening Jesus' ·followers [disciples] went down to ·Lake Galilee [Lthe lake/sea]. 17It was dark now, and Jesus had not yet ·come to [joined] them. The ·followers [disciples] got into a boat and started across the lake to Capernaum. 18By now a strong wind was blowing, and ·the waves on the lake were getting bigger [Lthe sea/lake rose up]. 19When they had rowed the boat about ·three or four miles [Ltwenty-five or thirty stadia; Ca stadion was about 600 feet], they saw Jesus walking on the ·water [sea; lake], coming toward the boat. The ·followers [disciples] were afraid, 20but Jesus said to them, "It is I [*or* "I am"; Cthere could be an echo here of Ex. 3:14]. Do not be afraid." 21Then they ·were glad [*or* were willing] to take him into the boat. ·At once [Immediately] the boat came to land at the place where they wanted to go. [CThe sea often stands for chaos, and God controls it.]

The People Seek Jesus

22The next day the ·people [Lcrowd] who had stayed on the ·other [opposite] side of the ·lake [sea] knew that Jesus had not gone in the boat with his ·followers [disciples] but that they had left ·without him [Lalone]. And they ·knew [Lsaw] that only one boat had been there. 23But then some boats came from Tiberias [Ca major city on the western shore of Lake Galilee] and landed near the place where the people had eaten the bread after the Lord had given thanks. 24When the ·people [Lcrowd] saw that Jesus and his ·followers [disciples] were not there now, they got into boats and went to Capernaum to find Jesus.

Jesus, the Bread of Life

25When ·the people [Lthey] found Jesus on the ·other [opposite] side of the ·lake [sea], they asked him, "·Teacher [LRabbi], when did you come here?"

26Jesus answered, "·I tell you the truth [LTruly, truly I say to you], you aren't looking for me because you saw ·me do miracles [Lsigns]. You are looking for me because you ate the bread and were ·satisfied [filled]. 27Don't work for the food that ·spoils [perishes]. Work for the food that ·stays good always and gives eternal life [Lendures/remains/abides for eternal life]. The Son of Man [Ca title for the Messiah; Dan. 7:13–14] will give you this food, because on him God the Father has ·put his power [Lset his seal; Ca seal impression signifies ownership and authority; 3:33]."

28The people asked Jesus, "What ·are the things God wants us to do [Lshould we do to work the works of God]?"

29Jesus answered, "·The work God wants you to do is this [LThis is the work of God]: Believe the One he sent."

30So ·the people [Lthey] asked, "What ·miracle will you do? If we see a miracle, we will believe you [Lsign will you do that we might see and believe you?]. What ·will you do [work will you perform]? 31Our ·ancestors [forefathers; Lfathers] ate the manna [Ca flaky breadlike food that God provided the Israelites in the wilderness; Ex. 16:13–36] in the ·desert [wilderness]. ·This is written in the Scriptures [LAs it is written]: 'He gave them bread from heaven to eat [compare Ex. 16:4; Neh. 9:15; Ps. 78:24].'"

32[LTherefore; So; Then] Jesus said to them, "·I tell you the truth [LTruly, truly I say to you], it was not Moses who gave you bread from heaven; it is my Father who is giving you the true bread from heaven. 33[LFor] God's bread is the One who comes down from heaven and gives life to the world."

34[LTherefore] ·the people [Lthey] said to him, "Sir, give us this bread always."

35Then Jesus said to them, "I am the ·bread that gives life [Tbread of life].
Whoever comes to me will never be hungry, and whoever believes in me will
never be thirsty. 36But as I told you before, you have seen me and still don't
believe. 37·The Father gives me the people who are mine. Every one of them
will come to me [LAll/Everything the Father gives me will come to me], and I
will ·always accept them [not reject them; Lnot cast them out]. 38[LFor] I
came down from heaven to do ·what God wants me to do [Lthe will of him
who sent me], not ·what I want to do [Lmy own will]. 39Here is ·what the One
who sent me wants me to do [Lthe will of him who sent me]: I must not lose
even one whom God gave me, but I must raise them all on the last day.
40Those who see the Son and believe in him have eternal life, and I will raise
them on the last day. This is ·what my Father wants [Lthe will of my Father]."
41·Some people [The Jewish leaders; LThe Jews] began to ·complain
[grumble; murmur] about Jesus because he said, "I am the bread that
comes down from heaven." 42They said, "·This is [LIs this not…?] Jesus,
the son of Joseph. We know his father and mother. How can he [Lnow]
say, 'I came down from heaven'?"
43But Jesus ·answered [responded], "Stop ·complaining to each other
[grumbling/murmuring among yourselves]. 44The Father is the One who
sent me. No one can come to me unless the Father draws him to me, and
I will raise that person up on the last day. 45It is written in the prophets,
'They will all be taught by God [Is. 54:13].' Everyone who listens to the
Father and learns from him comes to me. 46·No one has [*or* Not that anyone has] seen the Father except the One who is from God; only he has
seen the Father. [CSome interpreters put the previous sentence in paren-
theses as a side comment made by the author.] 47·I tell you the truth
[LTruly, truly I say to you], whoever believes has eternal life. 48I am the
·bread that gives life [Tbread of life]. 49Your ·ancestors [forefathers;
Lfathers] ate the manna [see 6:31] in the ·desert [wilderness], but still they
died. 50Here is the bread that comes down from heaven. Anyone who eats
this bread will never die. 51I am the living bread that came down from
heaven. Anyone who eats this bread will live forever. This bread is my
flesh, which I will give up so that the world may have life."
52Then the ·Jewish leaders [LJews] began to ·argue [dispute; quarrel]
among themselves, saying, "How can this man give us his flesh to eat?"
53[LSo] Jesus said to them, "·I tell you the truth [LTruly, truly I say to you],
you must eat the flesh of the Son of Man and drink his blood. Otherwise, you
won't have ·real life [Llife] in you. 54Those who ·eat [feed on; CJesus uses a different Greek word for "eat" in vv. 54–57 than in the previous verses; but the
difference is probably stylistic] my flesh and drink my blood have eternal life,
and I will raise them up on the last day. 55[LFor] My flesh is true food, and my
blood is true drink. 56Those who ·eat [feed on] my flesh and drink my blood
·live [remain; abide] in me, and I ·live [remain; abide] in them. 57The living
Father sent me, and I live because of the Father. So whoever ·eats [feeds on]
me will live because of me. 58I am not like the bread your ·ancestors [forefa-
thers; Lfathers] ate [Cthe manna; 6:31]. They ate that bread and still died. I am
the bread that came down from heaven, and whoever ·eats [feeds on] this
bread will live forever." 59Jesus said all these things while he was teaching in
the synagogue [Ca local congregation of Jews] in Capernaum [2:12].

The Words of Eternal Life

60When the ·followers [disciples; Ca broader circle of followers, not the
twelve disciples] of Jesus heard this, many of them said, "This teaching

[Cthat Jesus is the bread of life; 6:25–59] is ·hard [difficult; offensive]. Who can ·accept [obey; Lhear] it?"

61 Knowing that his ·followers [disciples] were ·complaining [grumbling] about this, Jesus said to them, "Does this teaching ·bother [offend] you? 62 Then ·will it also bother you to [Lwhat if you] see the Son of Man ·going back [Lgoing up; ascending] to the place ·where he came from [Lwhere he was before; Cheaven]? 63 It is the Spirit that gives life. The flesh ·doesn't give life [Lis useless; counts for nothing]. The words I told you ·are spirit, and they give life [*or* are from the Spirit who gives life]. 64 But some of you don't believe." ([LFor] Jesus knew from the beginning who did not believe and who would ·turn against [betray] him.) 65 Jesus said, "That is the reason I said, ·'If the Father does not bring a person to me, that one cannot come.' [L'No one can come to me unless the Father enables/grants him.']"

66 After Jesus said this, many of his ·followers [disciples] ·left him [Lturned back to previous things] and ·stopped following [Lno longer walked with] him.

67 Jesus asked ·the twelve followers [the Twelve], "Do you want to leave, too?"

68 Simon Peter answered him, "Lord [*or* Master], who would we go to? You have the words that give eternal life. 69 We believe and know that you are the Holy One from God."

70 Then Jesus answered them, "·I chose [LDid I not choose…?] all twelve of you, but one of you is ·a devil [*or* the Devil; CJesus equates the work of Judas with the work of Satan; compare Mark 8:33]."

71 Jesus was talking about Judas, the son of Simon Iscariot. Judas was one of the twelve, but later he was going to ·turn against [betray] Jesus.

Jesus' Brothers Don't Believe

7 After this, Jesus ·traveled [walked] around Galilee. He did not want to ·travel [walk] in Judea, because the ·Jewish leaders [LJews] there ·wanted [sought] to kill him [see 5:18]. 2 [LBut] It was [Lnear the] time for the Feast of ·Shelters [Tabernacles; Booths; Can important annual festival celebrating harvest, sometimes known as Ingathering, and commemorating the exodus from Egypt; Ex. 23:16; Lev. 23:33–44; Deut. 16:13–17]. 3 So Jesus' brothers [Cchildren of Joseph and Mary born after Jesus, or children of Joseph from a previous marriage; Mark 3:21, 31–35] said to him, "You should leave here and go to Judea so your ·followers [disciples] there can see the ·miracles [Lworks] you do. 4 [LFor] Anyone who wants to be ·well [publicly] known does not ·hide what he does [Lact in secret]. If you are doing these things, show yourself to the world." 5 ([LFor] Even Jesus' brothers did not believe in him.)

6 [LTherefore] Jesus said to his brothers, "·The right time for me [LMy time; 2:4] has not yet come, but any time is right for you [Cthey could go to Jerusalem anytime; but Jesus had a special destiny to fulfill there]. 7 The world cannot hate you [Cbecause they are part of it], but it hates me, because I ·tell it [testify concerning; witness to] ·the evil things it does [Lthat its works are evil]. 8 So you go [Lup] to the feast. I will not go [Lup] yet[n] to this feast, because ·the right time for me [my time] has not yet ·come [fully come; Lbeen fulfilled]." 9 After saying this, Jesus ·stayed [remained behind] in Galilee.

10 But after Jesus' brothers had gone [Lup] to the feast, Jesus went [Lup] also. But he did not ·let people see him [Lgo publicly, but in secret]. 11 At

7:8 yet Some Greek copies do not have this word.

the feast ·some people [the Jewish leaders; [L]the Jews] **were ·looking for** [watching for] **him and saying, "Where is that man?"**

[12]**Within the large crowd there, many people were ·whispering** [arguing; murmuring; grumbling] **to each other about Jesus. Some said, "He is a good man."**

Others said, "No, he ·fools [deceives; misleads] **the people."** [13]**But no one was brave enough to talk about Jesus openly, because they were afraid of the ·elders** [the Jewish leaders; [L]the Jews].

Jesus Teaches at the Feast

[14]**When the feast was about half over, Jesus went to the Temple** [courts; 2:14] **and began to teach.** [15]**The people ·were amazed** [marveled] **and said, "This man has never studied in school. How did he learn so much?"**

[16]**Jesus answered them, "The things I teach are not my own, but they come from him who sent me** [[C]God]. [17]**If people ·choose** [desire; want] **to do ·what God wants** [[L]God's will], **they will know that my teaching comes from God and not from me.** [18]**Those who ·teach their own ideas** [speak with their own authority] **are trying to get ·honor** [glory] **for themselves. But those who try to bring ·honor** [glory] **to the one who sent them speak the truth, and there is nothing ·false** [*or* unrighteous] **in them.** [[C]The Greek here is singular ("But the one who…"), so Jesus is speaking especially about himself.] [19]**Moses gave you the law** [[L]Has not Moses given you the law?; Ex. 34:29–32], **but none of you obeys that law. Why are you trying to kill me?"**

[20]**The people answered, "A demon has come into you** [[L]You have a demon]. **We are not trying to kill you** [[L]Who is trying to kill you?]**."**

[21]**Jesus ·said to** [answered] **them, "I did one ·miracle** [[L]work; deed; 5:1–15], **and you are all ·amazed** [astonished]. [22]**Moses gave you the law about circumcision** [Ex. 12:44–49]. **(But really Moses did not give you circumcision; it came from ·our ancestors** [[L]the fathers/patriarchs; Gen. 17:9–14].) **And yet you circumcise a ·baby boy** [[L]person] **on a Sabbath day.** [23]**If a ·baby boy** [[L]person] **can be circumcised on a Sabbath day ·to obey the law of Moses** [[L]so the law of Moses may not be broken], **why are you angry at me for healing a person's whole body on the Sabbath day?** [24]**Stop judging by ·the way things look** [outward appearances], **but judge by ·what is really right** [[L]right/just/righteous judgment]**."**

Is Jesus the Christ?

[25]**Then some of the people who lived in Jerusalem said, "·This is the man** [[L]Isn't this the man…?] **they are trying to kill.** [26]**But he is ·teaching where everyone can see and hear him** [[L]speaking publicly], **and no one is ·trying to stop** [[L]saying anything to] **him. Maybe the ·leaders** [rulers; authorities] **have ·decided** [come to recognize] **he really is the ·Christ** [Messiah]. [27]**But we know where this man is from. Yet when the real ·Christ** [Messiah] **comes, no one will know where he comes from."** [[C]Some Jewish traditions claimed the Messiah would be unknown until he came to deliver Israel.]

[28]**Jesus, teaching in the Temple** [courts; 2:14], **cried out, "Yes, you know me, and you know where I am from. But I have not come ·by my own authority** [on my own initiative; [L]from myself]. **I was sent by the One who is true, whom you don't know.** [29]**But I know him, because I am from him, and he sent me."**

[30]**When Jesus said this, they tried to ·seize** [arrest] **him. But no one was able to ·touch him** [[L]lay a hand on him], **because ·it was not yet the right time** [[L]his hour had not yet come; see 2:4]. [31]**But many ·of the people** [[L]in the crowd] **believed in Jesus. They said, "When the ·Christ** [Messiah] **comes, will he do more ·miracles** [[L]signs] **than this man has done?"**

The Leaders Try to Arrest Jesus

32 The Pharisees [see 1:24] heard the crowd ·whispering [arguing; murmuring; grumbling] these things about Jesus. So the leading priests and
the Pharisees sent some Temple ·guards [police; officers] to ·arrest [seize]
him. 33 [LTherefore] Jesus said, "I will be with you a little while longer.
Then I will go back to the One who sent me. 34 You will ·look for [seek] me,
but you will not find me. And you cannot come where I am [Cin heaven]."
35 [LTherefore] ·Some people [The Jewish leaders; LThe Jews] said to each
other, "Where will this man go so we cannot find him? Will he go to the
·Greek cities where our people live [Ldispersion/scattering among the Greeks;
Cever since the Babylonian exile many Jewish people had lived outside the
land of Israel] and teach the Greek people there? [CThe Jews often used
"Greeks" for Gentiles generally.] 36 What did he mean when he said, 'You will
look for me, but you will not find me,' and 'You cannot come where I am'?"

Jesus Talks About the Spirit

37 On the last and ·most important [Lgreatest] day of the feast Jesus
stood up and said in a loud voice, "Let anyone who is thirsty come to me
and drink. [CThe feast of Shelters/Tabernacles featured a water pouring
ritual that may stand in the background of Jesus' speech.] 38 If anyone
believes in me, rivers of living water will flow out from that person's
·heart [Lbelly; gut], as the Scripture says [Is. 55:1; 58:11; Ezek. 47:1–12;
Zech. 14:8, compare John 4:10–11; Rev. 7:17; 22:1]." 39 Jesus was talking
about the Holy Spirit. The Spirit had not yet been given, because Jesus
had not yet been ·raised to glory [glorified]. But later, those who believed
in Jesus would receive the Spirit.

The People Argue About Jesus

40 When the people heard Jesus' words, some of them said, "This man
really is the Prophet [1:21; Cthe "prophet like Moses" of Deut.
18:15–18]."
41 Others said, "He is the ·Christ [Messiah]."
Still others said, "The ·Christ [Messiah] will not come from Galilee.
42 The Scripture says that the ·Christ [Messiah] will come from David's
·family [offspring; Lseed; 2 Sam. 7:12–16; Ps. 89:3–4; Is. 9:7; 55:3] and
from Bethlehem, the ·town [village] where David lived [Mic. 5:2]." 43 So
·the people did not agree with each other [Lthere was a division in the
crowd] about Jesus. 44 Some of them wanted to ·arrest [seize] him, but no
one was able to ·touch [Llay a hand on] him.

Some Leaders Won't Believe

45 [LTherefore] The Temple ·guards [police; officers] went back to the
·leading [Tchief] priests and the Pharisees, who asked, "Why didn't you
bring Jesus?"
46 The ·guards [police; officers] answered, "·The words he says are
greater than the words of any other person who has ever spoken [LNo one
has ever spoken like this]!"
47 [LTherefore] The Pharisees answered them, "So Jesus has ·fooled
[deceived; led astray] you also! 48 Have any of the ·leaders [rulers; authori-
ties] or the Pharisees believed in him? No! 49 But ·these people [Lthis
crowd], who know nothing about the law, are ·under God's curse
[accursed]."
50 Nicodemus, who had gone to see Jesus before [see 3:1–21], was in
that group. He said, 51 "·Our law does not [LDoes our law…?] judge a person without hearing him and knowing what he has done."
52 They answered, "Are you from Galilee, too? ·Study the Scriptures,
and you will learn [LSearch and see] that no prophet comes from Galilee."

Some of the earliest surviving Greek copies do not contain 7:53—8:11.

|[53]And everyone left and went home.

The Woman Caught in Adultery

8 Jesus went to the Mount of Olives [[C]east of Jerusalem across the
Kidron Valley]. [2]But ·early in the morning [at dawn] he went back
to the Temple [courts; 2:14], and all the people came to him, and he sat
and taught them. [3]The ·teachers of the law [scribes; [C]experts in the law of
Moses] and the Pharisees brought a woman who had been caught in
adultery. They forced her to stand ·before [*or* in the midst of] the people.
[4]They said to Jesus, "Teacher, this woman was caught ·having sexual relations with a man who is not her husband [in the very act of committing
adultery]. [5]The law of Moses commands that we stone to death every
woman who does this [compare Lev. 20:10; Deut. 22:22–24]. What do you
say we should do?" [6]They were asking this to ·trick [trap; test] Jesus so
that they could have some ·charge [accusation] against him.
But Jesus ·bent over [stooped down] and started writing on the ground
with his finger [[C]we do not know what he is writing though there has been
much speculation]. [7]When they continued to ask Jesus their question, he
·raised up [straightened] and said, "Anyone here who ·has never sinned
[is guiltless; [T]is without sin] can throw the first stone at her [Deut. 13:9;
17:7; comp. Lev. 24:14]." [8]Then Jesus ·bent over [stooped down] again and
wrote on the ground.
[9]Those who heard Jesus began to leave one by one, first the ·older men
[elders] and then the others. Jesus was left there alone with the woman
standing before him. [10]Jesus ·raised up [straightened] again and asked
her, "Woman [[C]a respectful term of address in Greek; see 2:4], where are
they? Has no one ·judged you guilty [condemned you]?"
[11]She answered, "No one, sir."
Then Jesus said, "I also don't ·judge you guilty [condemn you]. ·You
may go now, but don't sin anymore [[T]Go, and sin no more]."|

Jesus Is the Light of the World

[12]Later, Jesus talked to the people again, saying, "I am the light of the
world [[C]the Feast of Shelters included a lamp lighting ritual that Jesus may
be alluding to; 7:37–39]. The person who follows me will never ·live
[[L]walk] in darkness but will have the light ·that gives life [[L]of life]."
[13]The Pharisees [see 1:24] said to Jesus, "When you ·talk [testify; witness]
about yourself, ·you are the only one to say these things are true. We cannot
accept what you say [[L]your testimony/witness is not true/valid; 5:31]."
[14]Jesus answered, "Yes, I am ·saying these things [witnessing; testifying]
about myself, but they are true [valid]. I know where I came from [[C]from
the Father or "from above"] and where I am going. But you don't know
where I came from or where I am going. [15]You judge ·by human standards
[[T]according to the flesh; [C]rather than guided by the Spirit]. I am not judging anyone. [16]But ·when [if] I do judge, ·I judge truthfully [[L]my judgment
is true], because I am not alone. The Father who sent me is with me.
[17]Your own law says that ·when two witnesses say the same thing, you
must accept what they say [[L]the testimony of two witnesses is true/valid;
Deut. 17:6; 19:15]. [18]I am one of the witnesses who speaks about myself,
and the Father who sent me is the other witness."

19[LTherefore] They asked him, "Where is your father?"
Jesus answered, "You don't know me or my Father. If you knew me, you
would know my Father, too." 20Jesus said these things while he was teaching in the Temple [courts], near ·where the money is kept [the treasury;
offering box]. But no one ·arrested [seized] him, because ·the right time
for him [Lhis hour; see 2:4] had not yet come.

The People Misunderstand Jesus

21Again, Jesus said to the people, "I will leave you [Cwhen he dies, is
raised, and ascends to the Father], and you will ·look for [seek; search for]
me, but you will die in your ·sins [Lsin; Cof unbelief]. You cannot come
where I am going."
22So the Jews asked, "Will he kill himself? Is that why he said, 'You cannot come where I am going'?"
23Jesus said, "You people are from here below [Cfrom the earth], but I
am from above [Cfrom heaven or from God]. You belong to this world,
but I ·don't belong to this world [Lam not of this world]. 24So I told you
that you would die in your sins. Yes, you will die in your sins if you don't
believe that ·I am he [LI am; Cthis may be an allusion to God's (Yahweh's)
self identification either from Ex. 3:14 (the great "I AM") or Is. 40–55,
where God repeatedly says, "I am he")]."
25[LTherefore] They asked, "Then who are you?"
Jesus answered them, "·I am what I have told you from the beginning
[*or* Why do I speak to you at all?]. 26I have many things to say and ·decide
about you [*or* condemn/judge you for]. But I tell ·people [the world] only
the things I have heard from the One who sent me, and he speaks the
truth."
27The people did not understand that he was talking to them about the
Father. 28So Jesus said to them, "When you lift up [Con the cross] the Son
of Man [Ca title for the Messiah; Dan. 7:13–14], you will know that ·I am
he [LI am; Csee 8:24]. You will know that these things I do are not ·by my
own authority [on my own] but that I say only what the Father has taught
me. 29The One who sent me is with me. I always do what is pleasing to
him, so he has not left me alone." 30While Jesus was saying these things,
many people believed in him.

Freedom from Sin

31So Jesus said to the Jews who believed in him, "If you ·continue to
obey my teaching [Lremain/abide in my word], you are truly my ·follow-
ers [disciples]. 32Then you will know the truth, and the truth will ·make
[set] you free."
33They answered, "We are Abraham's ·children [descendants; Lseed;
Gen. 12:1–3], and we have never been anyone's slaves. So why do you say
we will be free?"
34Jesus answered them, "·I tell you the truth [LTruly, truly I say to you],
everyone who ·lives in sin [commits/practices sin] is a slave to sin. 35A
slave does not ·stay with a family [live in the household] forever, but a son
·belongs to the family [lives in the household] forever. 36So if the Son
makes you free, you will be ·truly free [Tfree indeed]. 37I know you are
Abraham's ·children [descendants; Lseed], but you ·want [are trying; seek]
to kill me because ·you don't accept my teaching [Lmy word has no place
in you; Cthus showing they were Abraham's children only physically, not
spiritually; Jer. 9:25–26; Rom. 9:7; Gal. 4:21–31]. 38I am telling you ·what
my Father has shown me [Lwhat I have seen in the Father's presence], but
you do what ·your father [*or* the Father] has told you."

39They answered, "Our father is Abraham."
Jesus said to them, "If you were really Abraham's children, you would
do" the things Abraham did. 40I am a man who has told you the truth
which I heard from God, but you are trying to kill me. Abraham did
nothing like that. 41So you are doing the things your own father did."
But [*or* Therefore] they said to him, "We are not ·like children who
never knew who their father was [illegitimate children; Lborn from/of for-
nication]. God is our Father; he is the only Father we have."
42Jesus said to them, "If God were really your Father, you would love me,
because I came from God and now I am here. [LFor] I did not come ·by my
own authority [on my own]; God sent me. 43You don't understand [LWhy
don't you understand…?] what I say, because you cannot ·accept my teaching [Lhear my word/message]. 44You ·belong to [are from] your father the
devil, and you want to do what he wants. He was a murderer from the
beginning [Gen. 3; Rom. 5:12] and ·was against the truth [does not uphold
the truth], because there is no truth in him. When he tells a lie, ·he shows
what he is really like [he reveals his own nature; *or* he speaks his own language; Lhe speaks from his own], because he is a liar and the father of lies.
45But because I speak the truth, you don't believe me. 46·Can any of you
[LWho among you can…?] ·prove that I am guilty [convict me] of sin? If I
am telling the truth, why don't you believe me? 47The person who belongs
to God ·accepts what God says [Lhears/obeys the words of God]. But you
don't ·accept what God says [hear; obey], because you don't belong to God."

Jesus Is Greater than Abraham

48·They [The Jewish leaders; LThe Jews] answered, "We say you are a
Samaritan [Ca people disliked by the Jews; 4:4, 9] and ·have a demon in
you [are demon-possessed]. Are we not right?"
49Jesus answered, "I ·have no demon in me [am not demon-possessed].
I give honor to my Father, but you dishonor me. 50I am not trying to get
·honor [glory] for myself. There is One who wants this ·honor [glory] for
me, and he is the judge. 51·I tell you the truth [LTruly, truly I say to you],
whoever ·obeys my teaching will never die [Lkeeps my word will never see
death]."
52[LTherefore] ·They [The Jewish leaders; LThe Jews] said to Jesus, "Now
we know that you ·have a demon in you [are demon-possessed]! Even
Abraham and the prophets died. But you say, 'Whoever ·obeys my teaching
will never die [Lkeeps my word will never taste death].' 53Do you think you
are greater than our father Abraham, who died? And the prophets died, too.
·Who do you think you are [*or* Who are you claiming/pretending to be]?"
54Jesus answered, "If I give ·honor [glory] to myself, that ·honor [glory]
is worth nothing. The One who gives me ·honor [glory] is my Father, and
you say he is your God. 55You don't really know him, but I know him. If I
said I did not know him, I would be a liar like you. But I do know him,
and I ·obey what he says [Lkeep his word]. 56Your father Abraham ·was
very happy [rejoiced] that he would see my day [Cthe day of the Messiah's
arrival]. He saw that day and was glad."
57[LTherefore] ·They [The Jewish leaders; LThe Jews] said to him, "You
have never seen Abraham! You are not even fifty years old [CAbraham had
been dead for almost 2,000 years]."
58Jesus answered, "·I tell you the truth [LTruly, truly I say to you], before

8:39 If . . . do Some Greek copies read "If you are really Abraham's children, you will do."

Abraham was even born, ·I am!" [CA claim to deity; see comments at 8:24;
10:28.] 59When Jesus said this, the people picked up stones to throw at
him [Cbelieving he had committed blasphemy worthy of death]. But Jesus
hid himself, and then he left the Temple.

Jesus Heals a Man Born Blind

9 As Jesus ·was walking along [passed by; went along], he saw a man
who had been born blind. 2His ·followers [disciples] asked him,
"·Teacher [LRabbi], whose sin caused this man to be born blind—his own
sin or his parents' sin?" [CThe disciples, like the friends of Job, viewed suffering as the result of a person's own sins.]
3Jesus answered, "It is not this man's sin or his parents' sin that made
him blind. This man was born blind so that God's ·power [Lworks] could
be ·shown [displayed; revealed; manifest] in him. 4While it is daytime, we
must continue doing the work of the One who sent me. Night is coming
[CJesus' death], when no one can work. 5While I am in the world, I am the
light of the world [see 8:12]."
6After Jesus said this, he spit on the ground and made some mud with
·it [Lthe saliva] and ·put [spread; anointed] the mud on the man's eyes
[Cthe significance of the mud made with spit is unclear]. 7Then he told the
man, "Go and wash in the Pool of Siloam." (Siloam [Cfrom a Hebrew
word] means Sent.) So the man went, washed, and came back seeing.
8The neighbors and some people who had earlier seen this man begging said, "Isn't this the same man who used to sit and beg?"
9Some said, "He is the one," but others said, "No, he only looks like him."
The man himself said, "I am the man."
10[LTherefore] They asked him, "How [Lthen] ·did you get your sight
[Lwere your eyes opened]?"
11He answered, "The man named Jesus made some mud and ·put
[spread; anointed] it on my eyes. Then he told me to go to Siloam and
wash. So I went and washed, and then I could see."
12They asked him, "Where is this man?"
"I don't know," he answered.

Pharisees Question the Healing

13Then the people took to the Pharisees [Ca religious party which
strictly observed OT laws and later customs] the man who had been blind.
14The day Jesus had made mud and healed his eyes was a Sabbath day
[Con which no work was allowed]. 15So now the Pharisees asked the man,
"How did you get your sight?"
He answered, "He put mud on my eyes, I washed, and now I see."
16So some of the Pharisees were saying, "This man does not keep the
Sabbath day [Caccording to rabbinic tradition neither kneading nor healing were permitted on the Sabbath], so he is not from God."
But others said, "·A man who is a sinner can't [LHow can a man who is
a sinner…?] do ·miracles [Lsigns] like these." So ·they could not agree
with each other [Lthere was a division among them].
17[LTherefore; So; Then] They asked the man again, "What do you say
about him, since it was your eyes he opened?"
The man answered, "He is a prophet."
18·These leaders [LThe Jews; Cthe Pharisees] did not believe that he had
been blind and could now see again. So they sent for the ·man's parents
[Lparents of the man who could now see] 19and asked them, "Is this your
son who you say was born blind? Then how does he now see?"
20[LTherefore; So] His parents answered, "We know that this is our son

and that he was born blind. 21But we don't know how he can now see. We don't know who opened his eyes. Ask him. He is old enough to speak for himself [Cof legal age to give testimony]." 22His parents said this because they were afraid of the ·elders [Jewish leaders; LJews], who had already decided that anyone who ·said [confessed; acknowledged] Jesus was the ·Christ [Messiah] would be ·avoided [Lput out of the synagogue; Can act of expulsion or excommunication]. 23That is why his parents said, "He is old enough. Ask him."

24So for the second time, they called the man who had been blind. They said, "·You should give God the glory by telling the truth [LGive God the glory; Csee Josh. 7:19 where this phrase is a command to tell the truth]. We know that this man is a sinner."

25[LSo; Then] He answered, "I don't know if he is a sinner. One thing I do know: I was blind, and now I see."

26[LSo; Then] They asked, "What did he do to you? How did he ·make you see again [Lopen your eyes]?"

27He answered them, "I already told you, and you didn't listen. Why do you want to hear it again? Do you want to become his ·followers [disciples] too?"

28Then they ·insulted [ridiculed; reviled] him and said, "You are his ·follower [disciple], but we are ·followers [disciples] of Moses. 29We know that God spoke to Moses [Ex. 33:11; Num. 12:8; Deut. 34:10], but we don't even know where this man comes from."

30The man answered, "This is a very ·strange [astonishing; marvelous] thing. You don't know where he comes from, and yet he opened my eyes. 31We all know that God does not listen to sinners, but he listens to anyone who ·worships [is devout; is godfearing] and ·obeys him [Ldoes his will]. 32Nobody has ·ever [or since the beginning of the world; Lfrom the age/eternity] heard of anyone giving sight to a man born blind. 33If this man were not from God, he could do nothing."

34They answered, "You were born ·full of sin [or in utter sinfulness]! Are you trying to teach us?" And they threw him out [Cof the synagogue; an act of excommunication].

Spiritual Blindness

35When Jesus heard that they had ·thrown [cast; driven] him out [Cof the synagogue], Jesus found him and said, "Do you ·believe [trust] in the Son of Man [Ca title for the Messiah; Dan. 7:13–14]?"

36He asked, "Who is ·the Son of Man [Lhe], sir, so that I can ·believe [trust] in him?"

37Jesus said to him, "You have seen him. ·The Son of Man [LHe] is the one talking with you."

38He said, "·Lord [Cthe same word is rendered "sir" in v. 36, but here may have a more solemn sense], I ·believe [trust]!" Then the man ·worshiped [prostrated himself before] Jesus.

39Jesus said, "I came into this world ·so that the world could be judged [Lfor judgment]. I came so that the blind would see and so that those who see will become blind." [CThose who acknowledge they are spiritually blind will see the truth; and those who think they see spiritually (the Jewish religious leaders) are actually blind; Is. 6:10; 42:19.]

40Some of the Pharisees who were nearby heard Jesus say this and asked, "Are you saying we are blind, too?"

41Jesus said to them, "If you were blind, you would not be guilty of sin. But since you keep saying you see, your ·guilt [or sin] remains."

The Shepherd and His Sheep

10 Jesus said, "·I tell you the truth [LTruly, truly I say to you], the person who does not enter the ·sheepfold [sheep pen] by the ·door [gate], but climbs in some other way, is a thief and a robber. [CThe sheep represent the people of God; the thief/robber stands for those who would lead them astray; Ps. 23; Ezek. 34.] 2The one who enters by the ·door [gate] is the shepherd of the sheep. 3The ·one who guards the door [gatekeeper; watchman] opens it for him. And the sheep listen to the voice of the shepherd. He calls his own sheep by name and leads them out [compare Num. 27:15–17]. 4When he brings all his sheep out, he goes ahead of them, and they follow him because they know his voice. 5But they will never follow a stranger. They will run away from him because they don't know his voice." 6Jesus told the people this ·story [figure of speech; illustration; parable], but they did not understand what ·it meant [he was telling them].

Jesus Is the Good Shepherd

7So Jesus said again, "·I tell you the truth [LTruly, truly I say to you], I am the ·door [gate] for the sheep. [CJesus now refers to himself as the door rather than the shepherd.] 8All the people who came before me were thieves and robbers [Cothers who claimed to be the Messiah]. The sheep did not listen to them. 9I am the ·door [gate], and the person who enters through me will be saved and will be able to come in and go out and find pasture [compare Ps. 118:20]. 10A thief comes [Lonly] to steal and kill and destroy, but I came ·to give life [Lthat they might have life]—life in all its ·fullness [abundance].

11"I am the good shepherd [contrast Zech. 11:17]. The good shepherd ·gives [lays down] his life for the sheep. 12The ·worker who is paid to keep the sheep [Lhired hand] is different from the shepherd who owns them. When the worker sees a wolf coming, he runs away and leaves the sheep alone. Then the wolf ·attacks [*or* snatches; seizes] the sheep and scatters them. 13The man runs away because he is only a ·paid worker [hired hand] and does not really care about the sheep.

14"I am the good shepherd. I know my ·sheep [Lown], and my ·sheep [Lown] know me, 15just as the Father knows me, and I know the Father. I ·give [lay down] my life for the sheep. 16I have other sheep that are not in this ·flock [fold; pen; Ca reference to future Gentile followers of Christ], and I must bring them also. They will listen to my voice, and there will be one flock and one shepherd. 17The Father loves me because I ·give [lay down] my life so that I can ·take [receive] it back again. 18No one takes it away from me; I ·give [lay down] my own life ·freely [voluntarily; of my own free will]. I have the ·right [power; authority] to ·give [lay down] my life, and I have the ·right [power; authority] to ·take [receive] it back. This is what my Father commanded me to do."

19Again ·the leaders did not agree with each other [Lthere was a division among the Jews] because of these words of Jesus. 20Many of them said, "·A demon has come into him and made him crazy [LHe has a demon and is crazy]. Why listen to him?"

21But others said, "A man who is ·crazy with a demon [Ldemon-possessed] does not say things like this. Can a demon open the eyes of the blind?"

Jesus Is Rejected

22The time came for the ·Feast of Dedication [Calso called Hanukkah or the Feast of Lights, recalling the rededication of the Temple in 164 BC] at Jerusalem. It was winter, 23and Jesus was walking in the Temple in Solomon's ·Porch [Portico; Colonnade; Con the eastern side of the Temple area; at a later time Christians gathered there to worship; Acts 3:11; 5:12].

24·Some people [The Jewish leaders; LThe Jews] gathered around him and
said, "How long will you ·make us wonder [keep us in suspense] about
you? If you are the ·Christ [Messiah], tell us plainly."
25Jesus answered them, "I told you already, but you did not believe.
The ·miracles [Lworks] I do in my Father's name ·show who I am [testify/
bear witness about me]. 26But you don't believe, because you are not my
sheep. 27My sheep listen to my voice; I know them, and they follow me. 28I
give them eternal life, and they will never ·die [perish], and no one can
·steal [snatch] them out of my hand. 29My Father gave my sheep to me. He
is greater than all, and no person can ·steal [snatch] my sheep out of my
Father's hand. 30The Father and I are one."
31Again some of the ·people [Jewish leaders; LJews] picked up stones to
·kill [Lstone] Jesus. 32But he ·said to [answered] them, "I have ·done
[Lshown you] many good works from the Father. Which of these good
works are you ·killing [Lstoning] me for?"
33·They [The Jewish leaders; LThe Jews] answered him, "We are not
·killing [Lstoning] you because of any good work you did, but ·because
you speak against God [Lfor blasphemy]. You are only a human, but you
·say you are the same as God [claim to be God; Lmake yourself God]!"
34Jesus answered them, "·It is written [LIs it not written…?] in your law
that God said, 'I said, you are gods' [Ps. 82:6; Cthe "gods" here may be
Israel's judges, or the Israelites generally, or angelic powers]. 35This
Scripture called those people gods who received God's ·message [word],
and Scripture ·is always true [Lcannot be broken/annulled/set aside]. 36So
why do you say that I ·speak against God [Lblaspheme] because I said, 'I
am God's Son'? [CJesus is not denying he is God, but is making a lesser-to-
greater argument; if Scripture calls lesser beings "gods," why should they
object that he—the One God sent—calls himself the Son of God?] I am
the one ·God [Lthe Father] ·chose [consecrated; set apart] and sent into
the world. 37If I don't do ·what my Father does [Lthe works of my Father],
then don't believe me. 38But if I do ·what my Father does [the works of my
Father; Lthem], even though you don't believe in me, believe ·what I do
[Lthe works]. Then you will ·know [recognize; learn] and understand that
the Father is in me and I am in the Father."
39[LSo] They tried to ·take [seize; arrest] Jesus again [see 7:30], but he
escaped from ·them [Ltheir hands].
40Then he went back across the Jordan River to the place where John
had ·first [*or* earlier] baptized. Jesus stayed there, 41and many people came
to him and said, "John never did a ·miracle [Lsign], but everything John
said about this man is true." 42And in that place many believed in Jesus.

The Death of Lazarus

11 A man named Lazarus was sick. He lived in the town of
Bethany, where Mary and her sister Martha lived [Cnear
Jerusalem to the east, not the same Bethany as in 1:28]. 2Mary was the
woman who ·later put perfume on the Lord [Lanointed the Lord with
perfume/ointment/fragrant oil] and wiped his feet with her hair [12:1–
8]. Mary's brother was Lazarus, the man who was now sick. 3So ·Mary
and Martha [Lthe sisters] sent someone to tell Jesus, "Lord, the one you
love is sick."
4When Jesus heard this, he said, "This sickness will not end in death. It
is for the glory of God, to bring glory to the Son of God." 5Jesus loved
Martha and her sister and Lazarus. 6·But [*or* So] when he heard that

Lazarus was sick, he stayed where he was for two more days. 7Then Jesus
said to his ·followers [disciples], "Let's go back to Judea."
8The ·followers [disciples] said to him, "But Teacher [LRabbi], ·some
people [the Jewish leaders; Lthe Jews] there tried to stone you to death
only a short time ago. Now you want to go back there?"
9Jesus answered, "Are there not twelve hours ·in the day [of daylight]?
If anyone walks in the daylight, he will not stumble, because he can see by
·this world's light [Cthe sun]. 10But if anyone walks at night, he stumbles
because ·there is no light to help him see [Lthe light is not in him]."
11After Jesus said this, he added, "Our friend Lazarus has fallen asleep,
but I am going there to wake him."
12The ·followers [disciples] said, "But Lord, if he is only asleep, he will
·be all right [recover; get better; Lbe saved/healed]."
13[LBut] Jesus meant that Lazarus was dead, but his followers thought
he meant Lazarus was really sleeping. 14So then Jesus said to them plainly,
"Lazarus is dead. 15And I ·am glad [rejoice] for your sakes I was not there
so that you may believe. But let's go to him now."
16Then Thomas (the one called Didymus [Cmeaning, "the Twin"]) said
to ·the other followers [his fellow disciples], "Let us also go so that we can
die with him."

Jesus in Bethany

17When Jesus arrived, he learned that Lazarus had already been dead and
in the tomb for four days. [CSome Jews believed that a soul would stay near a
body for up to three days after death.] 18Bethany was about two miles [Lfifteen
stadia; Ca stadion was about 600 ft.] from Jerusalem. 19Many of the Jews had
come there to ·comfort [console] Martha and Mary about their brother.
20When Martha heard that Jesus was coming, she went out to meet
him, but Mary ·stayed [Lwas sitting at] home. 21Martha [Lthen] said to
Jesus, "Lord, if you had been here, my brother would not have died. 22But
I know that even now God will give you anything you ask."
23Jesus said, "Your brother will rise and live again."
24Martha answered, "I know that he will rise and live again in the resurrection on the last day." [CMany Jews, particularly Pharisees, believed in
a future bodily resurrection.]
25Jesus said to her, "I am the resurrection and the life. ·Those who believe
[LThe one who believes…] in me will have life even if they die. 26And everyone who lives and believes in me will never die. Do you believe this?"
27Martha answered, "Yes, Lord. I believe that you are the ·Christ [Messiah],
the Son of God, the One ·coming to [who was to come into] the world."

Jesus Weeps

28After Martha said this, she went back and ·talked to [summoned] her
sister Mary ·alone [privately]. Martha said, "The Teacher is here and he is
·asking for [summoning; calling for] you." 29When Mary heard this, she got
up quickly and went to Jesus. 30Jesus had not yet come into the town but was
still at the place where Martha had met him. 31The Jews were with Mary in
the house, ·comforting [consoling] her. When they saw her stand and leave
quickly, they followed her, thinking she was going to the tomb to weep there.
32But Mary went to the place where Jesus was. When she saw him, she
fell at his feet and said, "Lord, if you had been here, my brother would not
have died."
33When Jesus saw Mary weeping and the Jews who came with her also
weeping, he was ·upset [Ldisturbed in spirit] and was deeply troubled.
34He asked, "Where ·did you bury [Lhave you put] him?"

"Come and see, Lord," they said.

35 Jesus wept.

36 So the Jews said, "See how much he loved him."

37 But some of them said, "·If Jesus [LCould not the one who…] opened the eyes of the blind man, why couldn't he keep ·Lazarus [Lthis man] from dying?"

Jesus Raises Lazarus

38 Again feeling ·very upset [deeply disturbed/moved], Jesus came to the tomb. It was a cave with a large stone ·covering the entrance [Llying on/against it; CJews typically buried their dead in caves with stones covering the entrance]. 39 Jesus said, "Move the stone away."

Martha, the sister of the dead man, said, "But, Lord, it has been ·four days since he died [see 11:17]. There will be a ·bad smell [stench]."

40 Then Jesus said to her, "Didn't I tell you that if you believed you would see the glory of God?"

41 So they moved the stone away from the entrance. Then Jesus ·looked up [Lraised his eyes] and said, "Father, I thank you that you heard me. 42 I know that you always hear me, but I said these things ·because [for the benefit] of the people here around me. ·I want them to [Lso that they might] believe that you sent me." 43 After Jesus said this, he cried out in a loud voice, "Lazarus, come ·out [Tforth]!" 44 The dead man came out, his hands and feet wrapped with ·pieces of cloth [strips of linen; graveclothes; Cthe dead were wrapped in strips of cloth], and a cloth around his face.

Jesus said to them, "Take the cloth off of him and let him go."

The Plan to Kill Jesus

45 [LSo] Many of the ·people [LJews], who had come to visit Mary and saw what Jesus did, believed in him. 46 But some of them went to the Pharisees and told them what Jesus had done. 47 Then the ·leading [Tchief] priests and Pharisees called a meeting of the ·council [LSanhedrin; Cthe highest Jewish court of the time]. They asked, "·What should we do? [*or* What are we accomplishing?] This man is doing many ·miracles [Lsigns]. 48 If we let him continue doing these things, everyone will believe in him. Then the Romans will come and take away our ·Temple [Lplace; Cprobably a reference to *the* "holy place"—the Jerusalem Temple] and our nation."

49 One of the men there was Caiaphas, the high priest that year. [CHe was high priest between AD 18 and 36.] He said, "·You people know nothing [You don't know what you are talking about]! 50 You don't realize that it is better [Lfor you] for one man to die for the people than for the whole nation to be destroyed."

51 Caiaphas did not ·think of this himself [Lsay this from himself]. As high priest that year, he was really prophesying that Jesus would die for their nation 52 and for God's scattered children to bring them all together and make them one. [CAlthough Caiaphas was thinking politically, his words predicted spiritual salvation.]

53 [LSo from] That day they started ·planning [plotting] to kill Jesus. 54 So Jesus no longer ·traveled [Lwalked] openly among the ·people [Jews]. He ·left there [withdrew; departed] and went to a ·place [region] near the ·desert [wilderness], to a town called Ephraim and stayed there with his ·followers [disciples].

55 It was almost time for the ·Passover Feast [LPassover of the Jews; Cthe annual festival that celebrates God's rescue of Israel from Egypt; Ex. 12; John 2:13]. Many from the country went up to Jerusalem before the Passover to ·do the special things to make themselves pure [Lpurify/consecrate

themselves; Num. 9:6–13]. 56The people ·looked for [sought] Jesus and stood in the Temple [courts] asking each other, "·Is he [LSurely he is not] coming to the Feast? What do you think?" 57But the ·leading [Tchief] priests and the Pharisees had given orders that if anyone knew where Jesus was, he must tell them. Then they could ·arrest [seize] him.

Jesus with Friends in Bethany

12 [LTherefore] Six days before the Passover Feast, Jesus went to Bethany, where Lazarus lived. (Lazarus is the man Jesus raised from the dead.) 2There they had a dinner for Jesus. Martha served the food, and Lazarus was one of the people ·eating [Lreclining; Cit was customary to eat formal meals while reclining around a low table] with Jesus. 3[LThen] Mary brought in a pint [CGreek *litra;* about eleven ounces, weighing just under a pound] of very expensive ·perfume [ointment/fragrant oil] made from pure nard. She ·poured the perfume on [anointed; Cnot the word for royal or priestly anointing, but for hospitality or care] Jesus' feet, and then she wiped his feet with her hair. And the ·sweet smell [fragrance] from the perfume filled the whole house.

4Judas Iscariot, one of Jesus' ·followers [disciples] who would later ·turn against [betray] him, was there. Judas said, 5"This ·perfume [ointment/fragrant oil] was worth an ·entire year's wages [Lthree hundred denarii]. Why wasn't it sold and the money given to the poor?" 6But Judas did not really care about the poor; he said this because he was a thief. He was the one who kept the money ·box [*or* bag], and he often stole from it.

7[LTherefore] Jesus answered, "Leave her alone. It was right for her to save this perfume for today, the day for me to be prepared for burial. 8[LFor] You will always have the poor with you, but you will not always have me."

The Plot Against Lazarus

9A large crowd of ·people [LJews] ·heard [learned; came to know] that Jesus was ·in Bethany [Lthere]. So they went there to see not only Jesus but Lazarus, whom Jesus raised from the dead. 10So the leading [Tchief] priests ·made plans [plotted; counseled together] to kill Lazarus too. 11Because of Lazarus many of the Jews were ·leaving [going away from; deserting] them and believing in Jesus.

Jesus Enters Jerusalem
(12:12–19; Matt. 21:1–9; Mark 11:1–10; Luke 19:28–40)

12The next day a great crowd who had come to Jerusalem for the Passover Feast [Cthe annual festival celebrating God's rescue of Israel from Egypt; Ex. 12; John 2:13] heard that Jesus was coming there. 13So they took branches of palm trees [Ca symbol of the nation of Israel] and went out to meet Jesus, shouting,

"·Praise God [LHosanna; Can Aramaic cry to God for salvation, which became a shout of praise]!
·God bless [LBlessed is] the One who comes in the name of the Lord [Ps. 118:25–26]!
·God bless [LBlessed is] the King of Israel!"

14Jesus found a ·colt [young donkey] and sat on it. ·This was as the Scripture says [LAs it is written],

15"Don't be afraid, ·people of Jerusalem [LDaughter of Zion; Ca term of endearment for the people of Jerusalem]!
Your king is coming,
sitting on the colt of a donkey [Zech. 9:9; Criding a donkey rather than a warhorse, perhaps signaling that he was a different sort of king than their nationalist expectations anticipated]."

16The ·followers [disciples] of Jesus did not understand this at first. But

after Jesus was ·raised to glory [Lglorified], they remembered that this
had been written about him and that they had done these things to him.

People Tell About Jesus

17There had been ·many people [a crowd] with Jesus when he raised
Lazarus from the dead and told him to come out of the tomb. Now they were
·telling others [testifying; witnessing] about what Jesus did. 18·Many people
[A crowd] went out to meet Jesus, because they had heard ·about this miracle
[Lthat he had done this sign]. 19So the Pharisees said to each other, "You can
see that ·nothing is going right for us [we are getting nowhere; Lyou are gaining nothing]. Look! The whole world ·is following [has gone after] him."

Jesus Talks About His Death

20There were some Greek people [CGentiles—here meant to represent
people from all over the world; 12:19], too, who came to Jerusalem to worship at the Passover Feast. 21[LSo] They went to Philip, who was from
Bethsaida in Galilee, and ·said [requested], "Sir, we would like to ·see [meet]
Jesus." 22Philip told Andrew, and then Andrew and Philip told Jesus.
23Jesus ·said to [answered; replied to] them, "The ·time [Lhour] has
come for the Son of Man [Ca title for the Messiah; Dan. 7:13–14] to ·receive
his glory [be glorified; Cthrough his death, resurrection, and ascension].
24·I tell you the truth [LTruly, truly I say to you], a grain of wheat must fall
to the ground and die to make ·many seeds [Lmuch fruit]. But if it never
dies, it remains only a single ·seed [grain]. 25·Those who [LThe one who…]
love their lives will lose them, but those who hate their lives in this world
will ·keep [guard; preserve] ·true life forever [Lit for eternal life]. 26Whoever
serves me must follow me. Then my servant will be with me everywhere
I am. My Father will honor anyone who serves me.
27"Now ·I am very [Lmy soul is] troubled. Should I say, 'Father, save me
from this ·time [Lhour]'? No, ·I came to this time so I could suffer [Lfor
this reason I have come to this hour]. 28Father, ·bring glory to [glorify;
honor] your name!"
Then a voice came from heaven, "I have ·brought glory to [glorified] it,
and I will ·do [Lglorify; honor] it again."
29The crowd standing there, who heard the voice, said it was thunder.
But others said, "An angel has spoken to him."
30Jesus ·said [responded], "That voice was for your sake, not mine.
31Now is the time for the world to be judged; now the ·ruler [prince] of
this world [CSatan] will be ·thrown down [Lcast/driven out]. 32·If [*or*
When] I am lifted up from the earth, I will draw all people ·toward me [to
myself]." 33Jesus said this to show ·how [what kind of death] he would die.
34The crowd ·said [responded to him], "We have heard from the ·law
[Cthe Old Testament] that the ·Christ [Messiah] will ·live [remain] forever
[Ps. 89:35–37; Is. 9:7; Ezek. 37:25]. So why do you say, 'The Son of Man
must be lifted up'? Who is this 'Son of Man'?"
35Then Jesus said, "The light will be ·with [among] you for a little longer, so walk while you have the light. Then the darkness will not ·catch
[overtake] you. ·If you walk [LThe one who walks] in the darkness, you
will not know where you are going. 36·Believe [Put your trust] in the light
while you still have it so that you will become children of light." When
Jesus had said this, he left and hid himself from them.

Some People Won't Believe in Jesus

37Though Jesus had done many ·miracles [Lsigns; 2:11] in front of the
people, they still did not believe in him. 38This was to ·bring about
[Lfulfill] ·what [Lthe message/word that] Isaiah the prophet had said:

"Lord, who believed ·what we told them [Lour message/report]?
Who saw the Lord's ·power [Larm; Ca symbol of his power] in this
[Is. 53:1]?"
39This is why the people could not believe: Isaiah also had said,
40"He has blinded their eyes,
and he has ·closed their minds [Lhardened their heart].
Otherwise they would see with their eyes
and understand in their ·minds [Lheart]
and ·come back to me and be healed [Lturn/repent, and I would heal
them; Is. 6:10]."
41Isaiah said this because he saw Jesus' glory and spoke about him.
42But many believed in Jesus, even many of the ·leaders [authorities]. But
because of the Pharisees, they did not ·say they believed in him [Lconfess/
proclaim him/it] for fear they would be put out of the synagogue. 43They
loved ·praise [glory] from people more than ·praise [glory] from God.
44Then Jesus cried out, "Whoever believes in me is really believing in
the One who sent me. 45Whoever sees me sees the One who sent me. 46I
have come as light into the world so that whoever believes in me would
not ·stay [remain] in darkness.
47"Anyone who hears my words and does not ·obey [keep] them, I do
not judge, because I did not come to judge the world, but to save the world.
48There is a judge for those who ·refuse to believe in [reject] me and do not
accept my words. The word I have ·taught [spoken] will ·be their judge
[judge them] on the last day. 49The things I ·taught [spoke] were not from
myself. The Father who sent me ·told [commanded] me what to say and
what to ·teach [speak]. 50And I know that eternal life comes from what the
Father commands. So whatever I say is what the Father told me to say."

Jesus Washes His Followers' Feet

13 ·It was almost time for [LNow before…,] the Passover Feast
[12:12]. Jesus knew that it was ·time [Lthe hour] for him to
·leave [depart from] this world and go back to the Father. He had always
loved those who were his own in the world, and he loved them ·all the
way to the end [*or* completely; totally].
2·Jesus and his followers were at the evening meal [LIt was dinnertime].
The devil had already ·persuaded [Lput it into the heart of] Judas Iscariot,
the son of Simon, to ·turn against [betray] Jesus. 3Jesus knew that the Father
had ·given him power over everything [Lplaced everything into his hands]
and that he had come from God and was going back to God. 4So ·during the
meal [Lfrom supper] Jesus stood up and took off his outer clothing. Taking
a towel, he wrapped it around his waist. 5Then he poured water into a bowl
and began to wash the ·followers' [disciples'] feet, ·drying [wiping] them
with the towel that was wrapped around him. [CThis act was considered so
demeaning by some people that they only allowed Gentile slaves to do it.]
6Jesus came to Simon Peter, who said to him, "Lord, are you going to
wash my feet?"
7Jesus answered, "You don't understand now what I am doing, but you
will understand later."
8Peter said, "No, you will never wash my feet."
Jesus answered, "If I don't wash your feet, you ·are not one of my people [Lhave no share/part with me]."
9Simon Peter answered, "Lord, then wash not only my feet, but wash
my hands and my head, too!"

[10]Jesus said to him, "After a person has ·had a bath [washed; bathed], his whole body is clean. He needs only to wash his feet. And you men are clean, but not all of you." [11][LFor] Jesus knew who would ·turn against [betray] him, and that is why he said, "Not all of you are clean."

[12]When he had finished washing their feet, he put on his clothes and ·sat down [Lreclined; Cthe posture for a banquet or dinner party] again. He asked, "Do you understand what I have just done ·for [to] you? [13]You call me 'Teacher' and 'Lord' [Ctitles appropriately ascribed to an esteemed Rabbi, but which took on deeper meaning after his death and resurrection], and you are right, because that is what I am. [14]If I, your Lord and Teacher, have washed your feet, you also should wash each other's feet. [15]I did this as ·an example [a pattern] so that you should do as I have done for you. [16]·I tell you the truth [LTruly, truly, I say to you], a ·servant [slave; bond-servant] is not greater than his ·master [lord]. [LAnd] A messenger is not greater than the one who sent him. [17]If you know these things, you will be blessed if you do them.

[18]"I am not talking about all of you. I know those I have chosen. But this is to ·bring about what the Scripture said [Lfulfill the Scripture]: ·'The man who ate at my table has turned against me.' [L'The one who ate bread with me lifted his heel against me'; Ps. 41:9; Ceating with someone showed an intimate relationship, and lifting one's heel was an act of betrayal.] [19]I am telling you this now before it happens so that when it happens, you will believe that ·I am he [LI am; Cthis may be an allusion to God's (Yahweh's) self identification as "I AM" in Ex. 3:14, or to God's repeated claim that "I am he" throughout Is. 40–55; see John 8:24, 28, 58]. [20]·I tell you the truth [LTruly, truly, I say to you], whoever ·accepts [receives] anyone I send also ·accepts [receives] me. And whoever ·accepts [receives] me also ·accepts [receives] the One who sent me [Matt. 10:40]."

Jesus Talks About His Death
(13:21–30; Matt. 26:21–25; Mark 14:18–21; Luke 22:21–23)

[21]After Jesus said this, he was very troubled [Lin spirit]. He ·said openly [bore witness and said], "·I tell you the truth [LTruly, truly, I say to you], one of you will ·turn against [betray] me."

[22]The ·followers [disciples] all looked at each other, because they did not know whom Jesus was talking about. [23]One of the ·followers [disciples] ·sitting next to Jesus [Lreclining at his side/chest; Can honored position] was the ·follower [disciple] Jesus loved [Ca reference to John]. [24]Simon Peter motioned to him to ask Jesus whom he was talking about. [25]That ·follower [disciple] ·leaned [reclined] closer to Jesus and asked, "Lord, who is it?"

[26]Jesus answered, "I will dip this [piece/morsel of] bread into the dish. The man I give it to is the man who will ·turn against [betray] me." So Jesus took a piece of bread, dipped it, and gave it to Judas Iscariot, the son of Simon. [27]·As soon as [After] Judas took the [piece/morsel of] bread, Satan entered him. [LThen] Jesus said to him, "·The thing that you will do—do it quickly [TWhat you do, do quickly]." [28]No one ·at the table [Lof those reclining] understood why Jesus said this to Judas. [29]Since he was the one who kept the money ·box [*or* bag], some of the ·followers [disciples] thought Jesus was telling him to buy what was needed for the ·feast [festival] or to give something to the poor.

[30][LSo] Judas took the [piece/morsel of] bread Jesus gave him and immediately went out. It was night. [CThe night is both a time reference and a symbol of Judas' evil actions.]

[31]When Judas was gone, Jesus said, "Now the ·Son of Man [Ca title for

the Messiah; Dan. 7:13–14] ·receives his glory [is glorified], **and God ·receives glory** [is glorified] **through him. 32If God ·receives glory** [is glorified] **through him,**[n] **then God will ·give glory to** [glorify; honor] **the Son through himself. And God will ·give him glory** [glorify/honor him] **·quickly** [immediately; at once]**.”**

33Jesus said, “·My children [*or* Little children; [C]a term of endearment], **I will be with you only a little longer. You will ·look for** [seek] **me, and what I told the Jews** [7:33–34; 8:21], **I tell you now: Where I am going you cannot come.**

34“I give you a new ·command [commandment]: **Love ·each other** [[T]one another]. **You must love ·each other** [[T]one another] **as I have loved you. 35All people will know that you are my ·followers** [disciples] **if you love ·each other** [[T]one another]**.”**

Peter Will Say He Doesn't Know Jesus
(13:36–38; Matt. 26:30–35; Mark 14:26–31; Luke 22:31–34)

36Simon Peter asked Jesus, “Lord, where are you going?”

Jesus answered, “Where I am going you cannot follow now, but you will follow later.”

37Peter asked, “Lord, why can't I follow you now? I ·am ready to die for you [[L]will lay down my life for you]**!”**

38Jesus answered, “·Are you ready to die for me [[L]Will you lay down your life for me]**? ·I tell you the truth** [[L]Truly, truly, I say to you], **before the ·rooster** [cock] **crows, you will ·say three times that you don't know me** [deny/disown me three times]**.”**

Jesus Comforts His Followers

14 Jesus said, “Don't let your hearts be troubled. ·Trust [Believe] **in God, and ·trust** [believe] **in me** [*or* You trust/believe in God, trust/believe also in me]. **2There are many ·rooms** [places to live] **in my Father's house** [[C]heaven, metaphorically portrayed as a great palace]; **I would not tell you this if it were not true. I am going there to prepare a place for you. 3·After** [[L]And if] **I go and prepare a place for you, I will come back and take you to be with me so that you may be where I am. 4You know the way to the place where I am going**[n] [[C]because they know Jesus; 14:6]**.”**

5Thomas said to Jesus, “Lord, we don't know where you are going. So how can we know the way?”

6Jesus answered, “I am ·the way, and the truth, and the life [*or* the one true way to have life]. **·The only way to the Father is through me** [[L]No one comes to the Father except through me]. **7If you really knew me, you would know my Father, too. ·But now** [*or* From now on] **you do know him, and you have seen him.”**

8Philip said to him, “Lord, show us the Father. That is all we need.”

9Jesus answered, “I have been with you ·a long time now [all this time; for so long]. **Do you still not know me, Philip? Whoever has seen me has seen the Father. So why do you say, ‘Show us the Father’? 10Don't you believe that I am in the Father and the Father is in me? The words I say to you don't come ·from me** [on my own authority], **but the Father ·lives** [remains; abides] **in me and does his own work. 11Believe me when I say that I am in the Father and the Father is in me. Or believe because of ·the miracles I have done** [[L]the works themselves]. **12·I tell you the truth** [[L]Truly, truly, I say to you], **whoever believes in me will do the same things that I do. Those who believe will do even greater things than these, because I am**

13:32 If . . . him Some Greek copies do not have this phrase. **14:4 You . . . going.** Some Greek copies read "You know where I am going and the way to the place I am going."

going to the Father. [CThey will do greater things because all believers—not
just Jesus—will have the Holy Spirit living in them and empowering them.]
13And if you ask for anything in my name [Casking "in my name" means
acknowledging that Jesus is the mediator between God and human beings;
the name represents the person], I will do it for you so that ·the Father's
glory will be shown [Lthe Father might be glorified] ·through [*or* in] the
Son. 14If you ask me for anything in my name, I will do it.

The Promise of the Holy Spirit

15"·If you love me, you will obey my commands [*or* If you love me,
obey my commands; Cthis may be either a declaration or a command]. 16I
will ask the Father, and he will give you another ·Helper [Counselor;
Advocate; Cthe Holy Spirit] to be with you forever— 17the Spirit of truth.
The world cannot ·accept [receive] him, because it does not see him or
know him. But you know him, because he ·lives [remains; abides] with
you and he will be ·in [*or* among] you.
18"I will not leave you all alone like orphans [Corphans had little or no
support in ancient society]; I will ·come back [Lcome] to you. 19In a little
while the world will not see me anymore, but you will see me. Because I
live, you will live, too. 20On that day you will know that I am in my Father,
and that you are in me and I am in you. 21Those who ·know [Lhave] my
commands and ·obey [keep] them are the ones who love me, and my
Father will love those who love me. I will love them and will ·show [reveal]
myself to them."
22Then Judas (not Judas Iscariot [Cprobably Judas son of James; Luke 6:16;
Acts 1:13]) said, "But, Lord, ·why do [how is it that; what has happened that]
you plan to ·show [reveal] yourself to us and not to the rest of the world?"
23Jesus answered, "If people love me, they will ·obey my teaching [Lkeep
my word]. My Father will love them, and we will come to them and make
our home with them. 24Those who do not love me do not ·obey my teaching [Lkeep my words]. This ·teaching [word] that you hear is not really
mine; it is from my Father, who sent me.
25"I have told you all these things while I ·am [remain; abide] with you.
26But the ·Helper [Counselor; Advocate; see 14:15] will teach you ·every-
thing [all things] and will ·cause you to remember [remind you of] all
that I told you. This Helper is the Holy Spirit whom the Father will send
in my name.
27"I leave you peace [Cthe Greek word for "peace" reflects the Hebrew
shalom, a typical Hebrew farewell; but Jesus' peace, in the sense of wholeness, is also a characteristic of the messianic kingdom]; my peace I give you.
I do not give it to you as the world does. So don't let your hearts be troubled
or afraid. 28You heard me say to you, 'I am going, but I am coming back to
you.' If you loved me, you should ·be happy [rejoice] that I am going back
to the Father, because he is greater than I am. 29I have told you this now,
before it happens, so that when it happens, you will believe [13:19]. 30I will
not talk with you much longer, because the ·ruler [prince] of this world
[CSatan] is coming. He has ·no power [no claim/hold; Lnothing] over me,
31but the world must know that I love the Father, so I do ·exactly what [just
as] the Father ·told [commanded] me to do [Cgo to the cross].
"·Come now [LGet up; Rise up], let us go.

Jesus Is Like a Vine

15 "I am the ·true vine [Ccontrast Israel, the unreliable vine; Ps.
80:8–18; Is. 5:1–7]; my Father is the ·gardener [farmer; vine-
dresser]. 2He ·cuts off [*or* takes away] every branch ·of mine [Lin me]

that does not produce fruit [[C]whose lives bear no indication of a relationship with Christ]. And he ·trims and cleans [prunes; [C]the verb implies
both trimming and cleaning] every branch that produces fruit so that it
will produce even more fruit [Heb. 12:4–11]. 3You are already ·clean [*or*
pruned] because of the words I have spoken to you. 4·Remain [Abide] in
me, and I will ·remain [abide] in you. A branch cannot produce fruit
·alone [by itself] but must ·remain [abide] in the vine. In the same way,
you cannot produce fruit alone but must ·remain [abide] in me.

5"I am the vine, and you are the branches. If any ·remain [abide] in me
and I ·remain [abide] in them, they produce much fruit. But ·without [apart
from] me they can do nothing. 6If any do not ·remain [abide] in me, they are
like a branch that is thrown away and then ·dies [withers; dries up]. People
·pick up [gather together] dead branches, throw them into the fire, and burn
them. 7If you ·remain [abide] in me and ·follow my teachings [[L]my words
abide/remain in you], you can ask anything you want, and it will ·be given to
[be done for; come to] you. 8You should produce much fruit and ·show that
you are [*or* become] my ·followers [disciples], which ·brings glory to [glori-
fies] my Father. 9I loved you as the Father loved me. Now ·remain [abide] in
my love. 10I have ·obeyed [kept] my Father's commands, and I ·remain
[abide] in his love. In the same way, if you ·obey [keep] my commands, you
will ·remain [abide] in my love. 11I have told you these things so that ·you
can have the same joy I have [[L]my joy may be in you] and so that your joy
·will be the fullest possible joy [[L]might be complete].

12"This is my command: Love each other as I have loved you. 13·The
greatest love a person can show is to die for his friends [[L]No one has greater
love than this: to lay down one's life for one's friends; [C]Jesus' death is the
ultimate expression of this principle]. 14You are my friends if you do what
I command you. 15I no longer call you ·servants [slaves; bond-servants],
because a ·servant [slave; bond-servant] does not know what his ·master
[lord] is doing. But I call you friends, because I have made known to you
everything I heard from my Father. 16You did not choose me; I chose you.
And I ·gave you this work: [appointed you] to go and produce fruit, fruit
that will ·last [remain; abide]. Then the Father will give you anything you
ask for in my name [see 14:13]. 17This is my command: Love each other.

Jesus Warns His Followers

18"If the world hates you, remember that it hated me ·first [before you].
19If you ·belonged to [[L]were of] the world, it would love you as it loves its
own. But I have chosen you out of the world, ·so [because] you don't
belong to it. That is why the world hates you. 20Remember ·what [the
word] I told you: A ·servant [slave; bond-servant] is not greater than his
·master [lord; see 13:16]. If people ·did wrong to [persecuted] me, they will
·do wrong to [persecute] you, too. And if they ·obeyed my teaching [[L]kept
my word], they will ·obey [keep] yours, too. 21[[L]But] They will do all this
to you on account of ·me [[L]my name; 14:13], because they do not know the
One who sent me. 22If I had not come and spoken to them, they would not
be guilty of sin, but now they have no excuse for their sin. 23Whoever hates
me also hates my Father. 24I did works among them that no one else has
ever done. If I had not done these works, they would not be guilty of sin.
[[C]Jesus' words and actions resulted in their guilt because they rejected him
despite the evidence (the "signs") that God was working through him; see
Matt. 11:20–24; Luke 11:31–32.] But now they have seen what I have done,
and yet they have hated both me and my Father. 25But this happened so

that what is written in their law ·would be true [Lmight be fulfilled]**: 'They hated me for no reason** [Cthe quote could be from Ps. 35:19 or Ps. 69:4]**.'**

26**"I will send you the ·Helper** [Counselor; Advocate; Cthe Holy Spirit] **from the Father; he is the Spirit of truth who comes from the Father. When he comes, he will ·tell** [testify; witness] **about me,** 27**and you also must ·tell people** [testify; witness] **about me, because you have been with me from the beginning.**

16 **"I have told you these things to keep you from ·giving up** [stumbling; falling away; going astray]. 2**People will ·put you out of** [ban you from] **their synagogues. Yes, ·the time** [Lan hour; Can indefinite reference to a future time but likely connected to the period after the death and resurrection of Christ] **is coming when those who kill you will think they are offering ·service** [worship] **to God.** 3**They will do this because they have not known the Father and they have not known me.** 4**I have told you these things now so that when ·the time** [Ltheir hour; Cthe time of persecution] **comes you will remember that I ·warned** [told] **you** [about them].

The Work of the Holy Spirit

"I did not tell you ·these things [Cthat they would experience persecution] **·at** [from] **the beginning, because I was with you then.** 5**Now I am going back to the One who sent me. But none of you asks me, 'Where are you going?'** 6**Your hearts are filled with ·sadness** [grief; sorrow] **because I have told you these things.** 7**But I tell you the truth, it is ·better for you** [for your advantage] **that I go away.** [LFor] **When I go away, I will send the ·Helper** [Counselor; Advocate; Cthe Holy Spirit] **to you. If I do not go away, the Helper will not come** [to you]. 8**When the Helper comes, he will ·prove to the people of the world the truth about sin** [Lconvict/expose/convince the world about sin], **about ·being right with God** [Lrighteousness], **and about judgment** [Cthe meaning of this sentence is uncertain, as are the explanatory phrases in vv. 9–11]. 9**·He will prove to them that sin is not believing in me** [Lconcerning sin, because they do not believe in me]. 10**·He will prove to them that being right with God comes from my going to the Father and not being seen anymore** [Lconcerning righteousness, because I go to the Father and you will no longer see me; Cprobably means the Spirit will convict the world of its empty righteousness because Jesus is no longer present to model true righteousness]. 11**·And the Helper will prove to them that judgment happened when the ruler of this world was judged** [Lconcerning judgment, because the ruler of this world has been judged; Cprobably means the Spirit will convict the world that its judgments are false because Satan—the one they follow—has been condemned by Christ's victory on the cross].

12**"I** [Lstill] **have many more things to say to you, but ·they are too much for you** [Lyou cannot bear them] **now.** 13**But when the Spirit of truth** [Cthe Helper; see 16:7] **comes, he will ·lead** [guide] **you into all truth. He will not speak ·his own words** [from his own authority; Lfrom himself], **but he will speak only what he hears** [Cfrom the Father], **and he will ·tell** [announce/declare to] **you what is to come.** 14**The Spirit of truth will ·bring glory to** [glorify; honor] **me, because he will take what ·I have to say** [Lis mine] **and ·tell** [announce; declare] **it to you.** 15**All that the Father has is mine. That is why I said that the Spirit will take what ·I have to say** [Lwhat is mine] **and ·tell** [announce; declare] **it to you.**

Sadness Will Become Happiness

16**"After a little while you will not see me** [Cafter his crucifixion], **and then after a little while you will see me again** [Cafter his resurrection]**."**

17[LTherefore] Some of the ·followers [disciples] ·said to each other
[discussed among themselves], "What does Jesus mean when he says,
'After a little while you will not see me, and then after a little while you
will see me again'? And what does he mean when he says, 'Because I am
going to the Father'?" 18They also asked, "What does he mean by 'a little
while'? We don't understand what he is saying."
19Jesus ·saw [knew; was aware] that the ·followers [disciples] wanted to
ask him about this, so he said to them, "Are you ·asking each other [dis-
cussing among yourselves] what I meant when I said, 'After a little while
you will not see me, and then after a little while you will see me again'? 20·I
tell you the truth [LTruly, truly I say to you], you will ·cry and be sad [weep
and mourn/lament], but the world will be happy. You will ·be sad [grieve;
have pain], but your ·sadness [grief; pain] will become joy. 21When a
woman ·gives birth to a baby [goes into labor], she has pain, because her
·time [Lhour] has come. But when her baby is born, she ·forgets the pain
[does not remember the suffering/affliction], because ·she is so happy [Lof
the joy] that a ·child [Lhuman being] has been born into the world. 22It is
the same with you. Now you are ·sad [sorrowful; in pain; grieving], but I
will see you again and ·you [Lyour heart] will ·be happy [rejoice], and no
one will take away your joy. 23In that day [Cafter his resurrection] you will
not ask me for anything. ·I tell you the truth [LTruly, truly I say to you], my
Father will give you anything you ask for in my name [see 14:13]. 24Until
now you have not asked for anything in my name. Ask and you will receive,
so that your joy will be ·the fullest possible joy [complete; fulfilled].

Victory over the World

25"I have told you these things ·indirectly in stories [in parables/figura-
tive speech]. But ·the time [Lthe hour] will come when I will ·not [no longer]
use ·stories like that [parables; figurative speech; 10:6] to tell you things; I
will speak to you in plain words about the Father. 26In that day you will ask
the Father for things in my name. I mean, I will not need to ask the Father
for you. 27[LFor] The Father himself loves you. He loves you because you
loved me and believed that I came from God. 28I came from the Father into
the world. Now I am leaving the world and going back to the Father."
29Then the ·followers [disciples] of Jesus said, "You are speaking ·clearly
[plainly] to us now and are not using ·stories that are hard to understand
[parables; figurative speech]. 30We can see now that you know all things.
·You can answer a person's question even before it is asked. [LYou do not
need anyone to question you.] This makes us believe you came from God."
31Jesus answered, "So now you believe? 32Listen to me; ·a time [Lan
hour] is coming when you will be scattered, each to your own home
[compare Zech. 13:7]. That time is now here. You will leave me alone, but
I am ·never really [Lnot] alone, because the Father is with me.
33"I told you these things so that you can have peace in me. In this world
you will have ·trouble [persecution; suffering], but ·be brave [take courage/
heart]! I have ·defeated [victory over; conquered; overcome] the world."

Jesus Prays for His Followers

17 After Jesus said these things, he ·looked [Lraised his eyes]
toward heaven and ·prayed [Lsaid], "Father, the ·time [Lhour;
Cthe time of his death and resurrection] has come. ·Give glory to [Glorify;
Honor] your Son so that the Son can ·give glory to [glorify; honor] you.
2You gave the Son ·power [authority] over all ·people [Tflesh] so that the
Son could give eternal life to all those you gave him. 3And this is eternal
life: that people know you, the only true God, and that they know Jesus

Christ, the One you sent. 4Having ·finished [completed] the work you
gave me to do, I ·brought you glory [glorified/honored you] on earth
[Cby leading people to praise God]. 5And now, Father, ·give me glory
[glorify/honor me] ·with you [*or* in your presence]; give me the ·glory
[honor] I had with you before the world ·was made [existed; began].

6"I ·showed what you are like [Lrevealed your name; CGod's reputation/
character] to ·those [Lthe people] you gave me from the world. They belonged
to you, and you gave them to me, and they have ·obeyed your teaching [Lkept
your word]. 7Now they know that everything you gave me comes from you.
8[LBecause] I gave them the ·teachings [words; utterances] you gave me, and
they ·accepted [received] them. They knew that I truly came from you, and
they believed that you sent me. 9I am ·praying for them [asking on their
behalf]. I am not ·praying for [asking on behalf of] people in the world but
for those you gave me, because they are yours. 10·All I have is yours, and all
you have is mine [LAll mine are yours and all yours are mine]. And ·my glory
is shown [I am glorified] through them. 11I am coming to you; I will not stay
in the world any longer. But they are still in the world. Holy Father, ·keep
them safe by the power of [*or* keep them loyal to] your name, the name you
gave me, so that they will be one, just as you and I are one. 12While I was with
them, I kept them safe by the power of [*or* kept them loyal to] your name, the
name you gave me. I ·protected [guarded] them, and only one of them, the
·one worthy of destruction [Lson of destruction/perdition; CJudas], was lost
so that the Scripture would ·come true [Lbe fulfilled; Ps. 41:9].

13"I am coming to you now. But I ·pray [Lsay] these things while I am still
in the world so that ·these followers [these disciples; Lthey] can have all of
my joy [Lmade complete; fulfilled] in them. 14I have given them your ·teach-
ing [word]. And the world has hated them, because they don't belong to the
world, just as I don't belong to the world. 15I am not asking you to take
them out of the world but to ·keep them safe [protect them] from the ·Evil
One [*or* evil; Cthe Evil One is the Devil]. 16They don't belong to the world,
just as I don't belong to the world. 17·Make them ready for your service
[Sanctify them; Consecrate them; Csetting them apart for service] through
your truth; your ·teaching [word] is truth. 18I have sent them into the world,
just as you sent me into the world. 19For their sake, I am ·making myself
ready to serve [sanctifying/consecrating myself] so that they can be ·ready
for their service of [sanctified/consecrated by] the truth.

20"I ·pray for these followers [Lask not only for these], but I am also
·praying [Lasking] for all those who will believe in me because of their
·teaching [message; proclamation; Lword]. 21Father, I ·pray [Lask] that
they can be one. As you are in me and I am in you, I ·pray [Lask] that they
can also be ·one in us [Lin us]. Then the world will believe that you sent
me. 22I have given these people the ·glory [honor] that you gave me so
that they can be one, just as you and I are one. 23·I will be in them and you
will be in me [LI in them and you in me] so that they will be ·completely
one [in perfect unity]. ·Then [...so that] the world will know that you
sent me and that you loved them just as much as you loved me.

24"Father, I want these people that you gave me to be with me where I
am. ·I want them to [...so that they may] see my ·glory [honor], which
you gave me because you loved me before the ·world was made [founda-
tion/creation of the world]. 25·Father, you are the One who is good
[LRighteous Father,...]. The world does not know you, but I know you,
and these people know you sent me. 26I ·showed [made known to] them

·what you are like [Lyour name; 14:13], and I will ·show them again [con-
tinue to make it known]. ·Then [...so that] they will have the same love
that you have for me, and I will ·live [be] in them."

Jesus Is Arrested
(18:1–11; Matt. 26:36–56; Mark 14:32–52; Luke 22:39–46)

18 When Jesus finished ·praying [Lsaying these things], he went
with his ·followers [disciples] across the Kidron Valley [Ca deep
wadi or ravine separating Jerusalem on the east from the Mount of Olives].
On the other side there was a garden [*or* grove; CGethsemane; Matt. 26:36;
Mark 14:32], and Jesus and his ·followers [disciples] went into it.
2 Judas knew where this place was, because Jesus met there often with
his ·followers [disciples]. Judas was the one who ·turned against [betrayed]
Jesus. 3 So Judas came there with a group of soldiers [CRoman] and some
guards [CJewish temple police] from the ·leading [Tchief] priests and the
Pharisees. They were carrying torches, lanterns, and weapons.
4 Knowing everything that would happen to him, Jesus went out and
asked, "Who is it you are looking for?"
5 They answered him, "Jesus ·from Nazareth [Lthe Nazarene]."
"·I am he [LI am; Cthis may be an allusion to God's (Yahweh's) self identification as "I AM" in Ex. 3:14 or to God's repeated claim that "I am he"
throughout Is. 40–55; see John 8:24, 28, 58]," Jesus said. (Judas, the one
who ·turned against [betrayed] Jesus, was standing there with them.)
6 When Jesus said, "·I am he [LI am; see 18:5]," they moved back and fell to
the ground.
7 Jesus asked them again, "Who is it you are looking for?"
They said, "Jesus ·of Nazareth [Lthe Nazarene]."
8 "I told you that I am he [see 18:5]," Jesus ·said [answered]. "So if you
are looking for me, let the others go." 9 This happened so that the words
Jesus said before would ·come true [Lbe fulfilled]: "I have not lost any of
the ones you gave me [6:39; 17:12]."
10 [LThen] Simon Peter, who had a sword, pulled it out and struck the
·servant [slave; bond-servant] of the high priest, cutting off his right ear.
(The ·servant's [slave's; bond-servant's] name was Malchus.) 11 Jesus said
to Peter, "Put your sword back [Linto its sheath]. Shouldn't I drink the cup
the Father gave me?" [CThe prophets spoke of a cup of judgment; by dying
on the cross Jesus drinks it on our behalf; Jer. 25:15–29.]

Jesus Is Brought Before Annas

12 Then the soldiers [CRoman] with their commander and the guards
[CJewish temple police] arrested Jesus. They tied him 13 and led him first
to Annas, the father-in-law of Caiaphas, the high priest that year.
14 Caiaphas was the one who ·told [advised; counseled] the Jews that it
would be better if one man died ·for [on behalf of] all the people.

Peter Says He Doesn't Know Jesus
(18:15–27; Matt. 26:57, 69; Mark 14:54, 67; Luke 22:54, 56)

15 Simon Peter and another one of Jesus' ·followers [disciples] ·went along
after [followed] Jesus. This ·follower [disciple] knew the high priest, so he
went with Jesus into the high priest's courtyard. 16 But Peter waited outside
near the ·door [gate]. The ·follower [disciple] who knew the high priest came
back outside, spoke to the ·girl at the door [gatekeeper; doorkeeper], and
brought Peter inside. 17 The ·girl at the door [gatekeeper; doorkeeper] said to
Peter, "Aren't you also one of that man's ·followers [disciples]?"
Peter answered, "No, I am not!"
18 It was cold, so the ·servants [slaves; bond-servants] and guards [tem-
ple police] had built a [charcoal] fire and were standing around it, warming
themselves. Peter also was standing with them, warming himself.

The High Priest Questions Jesus

19The high priest asked Jesus questions about his ·followers [disciples]
and his teaching. 20Jesus answered him, "I have spoken ·openly [publicly]
to ·everyone [Lthe world]. I have always taught in synagogues and in the
Temple, where all the Jews come together. I never said anything in secret.
21So why do you question me? Ask the people who heard ·my teaching
[Lwhat I said to them]. They know what I said."
22When Jesus said this, one of the ·guards [officials; temple police]
standing there ·hit [slapped] him. The ·guard [official; temple policeman]
said, "Is that the way you answer the high priest?"
23Jesus answered him, "If I said something wrong, then ·show [testify to;
witness to] what it was. But if what I said is ·true [right], why do you hit me?"
24Then Annas sent Jesus, who was still tied, to Caiaphas the high priest.

Peter Says Again He Doesn't Know Jesus

(18:25–27; Matt 26:69-75; Mark 14:66-72; Luke 22:56-62)

25As Simon Peter was standing and warming himself, they said to him,
"Aren't you one of that man's ·followers [disciples]?"
Peter ·said it was not true [denied it]; he said, "No, I am not."
26One of the ·servants [slaves; bond-servants] of the high priest was there.
This servant was a relative of the man whose ear Peter had cut off [see 18:10].
The servant said, "Didn't I see you with him in the ·garden [grove]?"
27Again Peter ·said it wasn't true [denied it]. At once ·a rooster [Tthe
cock] crowed.

Jesus Is Brought Before Pilate

(18:28–19:16; Matt 27:1–2, 11–26; Mark 15:1–15; Luke 23:1–5, 13–25)

28Early in the morning they [Cthe Jewish leaders] led Jesus from Caiaphas's
house to the ·Roman governor's palace [*or* governor's headquarters;
LPraetorium]. They would not go inside the ·palace [LPraetorium], because
they did not want to make themselves ·unclean [Caccording to early Jewish
sources a Jew who entered the house of a Gentile would become ritually
unclean]; they wanted to eat the Passover meal. 29So Pilate [CPontius Pilate,
the Roman governor of Judea from AD 26 to 37] went outside to them and
asked, "What ·charges [accusation] do you bring against this man?"
30They answered, "If he were not a ·criminal [Levildoer], we wouldn't
have brought him to you."
31Pilate said to them, "Take him yourselves and judge him by your own
law."
"But ·we are not allowed [it is not legal for us] to put anyone to death,"
the Jews answered. [CThe Jewish people had to concede the authority for
capital punishment to their Roman occupiers.] 32(This happened so that
what Jesus said about how he would die [Cby crucifixion rather than ston-
ing] would ·come true [Lbe fulfilled; see 12:32–33].)
33Then Pilate went back inside the ·palace [headquarters; LPraetorium]
and called Jesus to him and asked, "Are you the king of the Jews?"
34Jesus ·said [answered], "Is that your own question, or did others tell
you about me?"
35Pilate answered, "·I am not one of you [LAm I a Jew?]. It was your
own ·people [nation] and their ·leading [Tchief] priests who ·handed you
over [*or* betrayed you] to me. What have you done wrong?"
36Jesus answered, "My kingdom ·does not belong to [Tis not of] this
world. If it belonged to this world, my servants would have fought to keep
me from being ·given over [betrayed; handed over] to the ·Jewish leaders
[LJews]. But my kingdom is from another place."
37Pilate said, "So you are a king!"
Jesus answered, "You are the one saying I am a king. This is why I was
born and came into the world: to ·tell people [testify/witness to] the truth.

And everyone ·who belongs to the [on the side of] truth ·listens to me
[[L]hears my voice]."
38 Pilate said, "What is truth?" After he said this, he went out to the
·crowd [[L]Jews] again and said to them, "I find ·nothing [no case; no basis
for a charge] against this man. 39 But it is your custom that I ·free [release]
one prisoner to you at Passover time. Do you want me to ·free [release]
the 'king of the Jews'?"
40 They shouted back, "No, not him! Let Barabbas ·go free [be released]!"
(Barabbas was a ·robber [bandit; revolutionary; terrorist; [C]the Romans
referred to insurrectionists as "robbers" or "criminals"].)

19 Then Pilate ordered that Jesus be taken away and ·whipped
[flogged]. 2 The soldiers ·made [wove; twisted together] a
crown ·from some thorny branches [[T]of thorns] and put it on Jesus' head
and put a purple robe [[C]purple was the color of royalty] around him.
3 Then they came to him many times and said, "Hail, King of the Jews!"
and ·hit him in the face [slapped/struck him].
4 Again Pilate came out and said to them, "Look, I am bringing Jesus out
to you. I want you to know that I find ·nothing [no case; no basis for a
charge] against him." 5 So Jesus came out, wearing the crown of thorns and
the purple robe. Pilate said to them, "·Here is the man [[T]Behold the man]!"
6 When the ·leading [[T]chief] priests and the ·guards [officials; temple
police] saw Jesus, they shouted, "Crucify him! Crucify him!"
But Pilate answered them, "Crucify him yourselves, because I find
·nothing [no case; no basis for a charge] against him."
7 The ·leaders [Jewish leaders; [L]Jews] answered [[L]him], "We have a law
[Lev. 24:16] that says he should die, because he ·said he is [made himself;
claimed to be] the Son of God."
8 When Pilate heard this [[L]statement; word], he was even more afraid. 9 He
went back inside the ·palace [headquarters; [L]Praetorium] and asked Jesus,
"Where do you come from?" But Jesus did not answer him. 10 Pilate said [[L]to
him], "You refuse to speak to me? Don't you know I have ·power [authority]
to ·set you free [release you] and ·power [authority] to have you crucified?"
11 Jesus answered [him], "The only ·power [authority] you have over
me is the ·power [authority] given to you ·by God [[L]from above]. The
man who ·turned me in to you [betrayed me; [C]Caiaphas or perhaps Judas]
is guilty of a greater sin."
12 ·After this [*or* For this reason], Pilate tried to let Jesus go. But ·some
in the crowd [[L]the Jews] ·cried out [shouted], "Anyone who makes himself
king ·is against [opposes] Caesar [[C]the Roman emperor]. If you let this
man go, you are no friend of Caesar."
13 When Pilate heard ·what they were saying [[L]these words], he brought
Jesus out and ·sat down [*or* seated him] on the judge's seat at the place
called The Stone Pavement. (In the ·Hebrew language [[C]more specifically,
Aramaic, the native language of the Jews at the time] the name is Gabbatha.)
14 It was about ·noon [[L]the sixth hour; [C]hours were counted from dawn,
about 6 AM] on Preparation Day of Passover week. Pilate said to ·the crowd
[[L]the Jews], "·Here is your king! [[L]Look, your king! *or* Look at your king!]"
15 They shouted, "Take him away! Take him away! Crucify him!"
Pilate asked them, "Do you want me to crucify your king?"
The ·leading [[T]chief] priests answered, "The only king we have is Caesar."
16 So Pilate handed Jesus over to them to be crucified.

Jesus Is Crucified

(19:16b–27; Matt. 27:31–37, 55–56; Mark 15:20–26, 40–41; Luke 23:26–34, 49)

The soldiers took charge of Jesus. 17Carrying his own cross, Jesus went out to a place called The Place of the Skull, which in the Hebrew [CAramaic; see v. 13] language is called Golgotha. 18There they crucified Jesus. They also crucified two other men, one on each side, with Jesus in the middle. 19Pilate wrote a ·sign [title; notice; inscription] and ·put [fastened] it on the cross. It read: JESUS ·OF NAZARETH [Lthe Nazarene], THE KING OF THE JEWS. 20The ·sign [title; notice; inscription] was written in Hebrew [CAramaic; 19:13], in Latin, and in Greek [Cthe languages spoken in Jerusalem at the time]. Many of the people read the sign, because the place where Jesus was crucified was near the city. 21The ·leading [Tchief] priests [Lof the Jews] said to Pilate, "Don't write, 'The King of the Jews.' But write, 'This man ·said [claimed], "I am the King of the Jews." ' "

22Pilate answered, "What I have written, I have written."

23After the soldiers crucified Jesus, they took his clothes and divided them into four parts, with each soldier getting one part [Cit was a custom that the executioners would get the victim's clothes]. They also took his ·long shirt [tunic; undergarment], which was ·all one piece of cloth [seamless], woven from top to bottom. 24So the soldiers said to each other, "We should not tear this into parts. Let's throw lots [Csimilar to dice] to see who will get it." This happened so that this Scripture would come true:

"They divided my clothes among them,
and they threw lots for my clothing [Ps. 22:18]."

So the soldiers did this.

25[LNow] Standing near his cross were Jesus' mother, his mother's sister, Mary the wife of Clopas, and Mary Magdalene. [CIt is unclear whether Mary the wife of Clopas is the same as Jesus' mother's sister or someone else.] 26When Jesus [Ltherefore] saw his mother and the ·follower [disciple] he loved [Cprobably John himself] standing nearby, he said to his mother, "·Dear woman [LWoman; see 2:4], ·here is [Tbehold] your son." 27Then he said to the ·follower [disciple], "·Here is [TBehold] your mother." From that time on, the ·follower [disciple] took her to live in his home.

Jesus Dies

(19:28–37; Matt. 27:45–54; Mark 15:33–39; Luke 23:44–48)

28After this, Jesus knew that everything had been ·done [finished; completed]. So that the Scripture would ·come true [be fulfilled], he said, "I ·am thirsty [Tthirst; Ps. 22:15; 69:21]." 29There was a jar full of ·vinegar [sour wine] there, so the soldiers soaked a sponge in it, put the sponge on a ·branch [stalk] of a hyssop plant, and lifted it to Jesus' mouth. 30When Jesus ·tasted [Lreceived] the ·vinegar [sour wine], he said, "It is ·finished [completed; accomplished]." Then he bowed his head and ·died [Lgave up/yielded his spirit].

31This day was Preparation Day [Cfor the celebration of Passover; 12:12], and the next day was a ·special [high; Lgreat] Sabbath day [Cspecial because it occurred during Passover]. Since the ·religious leaders [LJews] did not want the bodies to stay on the cross on the Sabbath day, they asked Pilate to order that the legs of the men be broken [Cso they would die quicker] and the bodies be taken away [Deut. 21:22–23]. 32So the soldiers came and broke the legs of the first man on the cross beside Jesus. Then they broke the legs of the man on the other cross beside Jesus. 33But when the soldiers came to Jesus and saw that he was already dead, they did not break his legs. 34But one of the soldiers ·stuck [pierced] his ·spear [lance; javelin] into Jesus' side, and at once blood and water came out [Cindicating his death as a human being]. 35(The one who saw this happen is the one who ·told us this [witnesses; testifies; Cagain probably an allusion to the disciple John], and ·whatever he says [his witness/testimony] is true. And he knows that he tells the truth, and he tells it so that you might believe [see 21:24].) 36[LFor] These things happened to ·make the Scripture come true [fulfill the Scripture]: "Not one of his bones will be broken [Ps. 34:20; see Ex. 12:46; Num. 9:12]." 37And [Lagain] another Scripture says, "They will look at the one they ·stabbed [pierced; Zech. 12:10]."

Jesus Is Buried
(19:38–42; Matt. 27:57–61; Mark 15:42–47; Luke 23:50–56)

38·Later [LAfter these things], Joseph from Arimathea asked Pilate if he could take the body of Jesus. (Joseph was a secret ·follower [disciple] of Jesus, because he was afraid of ·some of the leaders [the Jewish leaders; Lthe Jews].) Pilate gave his permission, so Joseph came and took Jesus' body away. 39Nicodemus, who earlier had come to Jesus at night [3:1–15; 7:50–52], went with Joseph. He brought about seventy-five pounds [CGreek: a hundred *litrai;* a *litra* was about 12 ounces] of [a mixture of] myrrh and aloes [Cused to cover a decomposing body to prevent the stench]. 40These two men took Jesus' body and wrapped it with the spices in pieces of linen cloth, ·which is how they bury the dead [Laccording to the burial custom of the Jews]. 41In the place where Jesus was crucified, there was a garden. In the garden was a new tomb that had never been used before. 42The men laid Jesus in that tomb because it was nearby, and ·they were preparing to start their Sabbath day [Lbecause it was the Jewish Day of Preparation].

Jesus' Tomb Is Empty
(20:1–9; Matt. 28:1–10; Mark 16:1–8; Luke 24:1–12)

20

Early on the first day of the week, Mary Magdalene went to the tomb while it was still dark. When she saw that the large stone had been moved away from the tomb, 2she ran to Simon Peter and the ·follower [disciple] whom Jesus loved [Cprobably John]. Mary said, "They have taken the Lord out of the tomb, and we don't know where they have put him."

3So Peter and the other ·follower [disciple] started for the tomb. 4They were both running, but the other ·follower [disciple] ran faster than Peter and reached the tomb first. 5He bent down and looked in and saw the strips of linen cloth lying there, but he did not go in. 6Then following him, Simon Peter arrived and went into the tomb and saw the strips of linen lying there. 7He also saw the [burial] cloth that had been around Jesus' head, which was ·folded [*or* rolled] up and laid [by itself] in a different place from the strips of linen. 8Then the other ·follower [disciple], who had reached the tomb first, also went in. He saw and believed. 9([LFor] They did not yet understand from the Scriptures that ·Jesus must rise [it was necessary for him to rise] from the dead.)

Jesus Appears to Mary Magdalene

10Then the ·followers [disciples] went back home. 11But Mary stood outside the tomb, ·crying [weeping]. As she was ·crying [weeping], she bent down and looked inside the tomb. 12She saw two angels dressed in white, sitting where Jesus' body had been, one at the head and one at the feet.

13They asked her, "Woman, why are you ·crying [weeping]?"

She answered, "They have taken away my Lord, and I don't know where they have put him." 14When Mary said this, she turned around and saw Jesus standing there, but she did not ·know [realize] it was Jesus.

15Jesus asked her, "Woman, why are you ·crying [weeping]? Whom are you looking for?"

Thinking he was the gardener, she said to him, "·Did you take him away, sir? [LIf you took him away, sir…] Tell me where you put him, and I will get him."

16Jesus said to her, "Mary."
Mary turned toward Jesus and said in the Hebrew [CAramaic] language,
"Rabboni [Ca variant of the more common Rabbi]." (This means "Teacher.")
17Jesus said to her, "Don't ·hold on to [cling to; *or* touch] me, because I
have not yet ·gone up [ascended] to the Father. But go to my brothers
[Chis disciples] and tell them, 'I am ·going back [ascending] to my Father
and your Father, to my God and your God.' "
18Mary Magdalene went and said to the ·followers [disciples], "I saw
the Lord!" And she told them what Jesus had said to her.

Jesus Appears to His Followers *(20:19–23; Luke 24:36–43)*

19When it was evening on the first day of the week, Jesus' ·followers
[disciples] were together. The doors were ·locked [shut], because they
were afraid of ·the elders [the Jewish leaders; Lthe Jews]. Then Jesus came
and stood right in the middle of them and said, "Peace be with you."
20After he said this, he showed them his hands and his side. His ·followers
[disciples] ·were thrilled [rejoiced] when they saw the Lord.
21Then Jesus said to them again, "Peace be with you. As the Father sent
me, I now send you." 22After he said this, he breathed on them [Gen. 2:7]
and said, "Receive the Holy Spirit. 23If you forgive anyone his sins, they
are forgiven. If you ·don't forgive them [withhold forgiveness; Lretain the
sins of any; Matt. 16:19; 18:18], they are not forgiven."

Jesus Appears to Thomas

24Thomas (called Didymus [Cmeaning "the Twin"]), who was one of
the twelve, was not with them when Jesus came. 25The other ·followers
[disciples] kept telling Thomas, "We saw the Lord."
But Thomas said, "I will not believe it until I see the nail marks in his
hands and put my finger where the nails were and put my hand into his side."
26·A week later [LAfter eight days] the ·followers [disciples] were in the house
again, and Thomas was with them. The doors were ·locked [shut], but Jesus
came in and stood right in the middle of them. He said, "Peace be with you."
27Then he said to Thomas, "Put your finger here, and look at my hands. Put
your hand here in my side. Stop ·being an unbeliever [doubting] and believe."
28Thomas ·said to [answered] him, "My Lord and my God!"
29Then Jesus told him, "You believe because you see me. ·Those who
believe without seeing me will be truly blessed [LBlessed are those who
have not seen and yet have believed]."

Why John Wrote This Book

30Jesus [Ltherefore] did many other ·miracles [Lsigns; 2:11] in the presence of his ·followers [disciples] that are not written in this book. 31But
these are written so that you may ·believe [*or* keep on believing] that Jesus
is the Christ [CGreek: *Christos,* for Hebrew *Mashiach,* the "anointed one"],
the Son of God. Then, by believing, you may have life through his name.

Jesus Appears to Seven Followers

21 ·Later [LAfter these things], Jesus ·showed [revealed] himself
to his ·followers [disciples] again—this time at ·Lake Galilee
[Lthe Sea of Tiberias; Can alternate name of Lake/the Sea of Galilee]. This
is how he ·showed [revealed] himself: 2Some of the ·followers [disciples]
were together: Simon Peter, Thomas (called Didymus [Cmeaning "the
Twin"]), Nathanael from Cana in Galilee, the two sons of Zebedee
[CJames and John], and two other ·followers [disciples]. 3Simon Peter
said to them, "I am going out to fish."
The others said [Lto him], "We will go with you." So they went out and
got into the boat. They fished that night but caught nothing.
4·Early the next morning [Just at daybreak] Jesus stood on the shore, but

the ·followers [disciples] did not ·know [realize] it was Jesus. 5Then he said to them, "·Friends [LChildren; Ca term of endearment], did you catch any fish?"

They answered, "No."

6He said to them, "Throw your net on the right side of the boat, and you will find some." So they did, and they caught so many fish they could not pull the net back into the boat.

7The ·follower [disciple] whom Jesus loved [CJohn] said to Peter, "It is the Lord!" [LSo] When Peter heard him say this, he wrapped his ·coat [outer garment] around himself. (·Peter had taken his clothes off [Lfor he was naked].) Then he jumped into the ·water [Lsea; lake]. 8The other ·followers [disciples] went to shore in the boat, ·dragging [towing] the net full of fish. They were not very far from shore, only about a hundred yards [Ltwo hundred cubits]. 9When the ·followers [disciples] ·stepped out of the boat and onto the shore [landed; disembarked], they saw a fire of hot coals. There were fish on the fire, and there was bread.

10Then Jesus said [Lto them], "Bring some of the fish you just caught."

11Simon Peter went into the boat and ·pulled [hauled] the net to the shore. It was full of big fish, one hundred fifty-three in all, but even though there were so many, the net did not tear. 12Jesus said to them, "Come and ·eat [*or* have breakfast]." None of the followers dared ask him, "Who are you?" because they knew it was the Lord. 13Jesus came and took the bread and gave it to them, along with the fish.

14This was now the third time [Csee 20:19–23; 20:26–29] Jesus ·showed [revealed; manifested] himself to his ·followers [disciples] after he was raised from the dead.

Jesus Talks to Peter

15When they finished eating, Jesus said to Simon Peter, "Simon son of John, do you love me more than these?" [C"These" probably refers to the other disciples (rather than the fishing gear), and could mean "Do you love me more than you love your friends?" or "Do you love me more than they love me?" The latter is more likely. This whole scene is the restoration of Peter after he had boasted of his loyalty to Jesus and then denied him.]

He answered, "Yes, Lord, you know that I love you."

Jesus said, "Feed my lambs."

16Again Jesus said, "Simon son of John, do you love me?"

He answered, "Yes, Lord, you know that I love you."

Jesus said, "·Take care of [Tend; Shepherd] my sheep."

17A third time he said, "Simon son of John, do you love me?"

Peter ·was hurt [grieved] because Jesus asked him the third time, "Do you love me?" Peter said, "Lord, you know everything; you know that I love you!"

He said to him, "Feed my sheep. [CIn verses 15 and 16 Jesus uses a different word for "love" (*agapaō*) than Peter uses (*phileō*); but then in v. 17 Jesus uses Peter's word (*phileō*). The two terms can be synonymous, and the difference is probably stylistic. The passage is not contrasting two kinds of love; rather, Peter's three affirmations counterbalance his three denials; see 18:15–18, 25–27] 18·I tell you the truth [LTruly, truly I say to you], when you were younger, you ·tied your own belt [dressed yourself] and went where you wanted. But when you are old, you will put out your hands and someone else will ·tie [dress] you and take you where you don't want to go." 19(Jesus said this to ·show [indicate; signify] how Peter would die to ·give glory to [glorify] God.) Then Jesus said to Peter, "Follow me!"

20Peter turned and saw that the ·follower [disciple] Jesus loved [CJohn]

was ·walking behind them [following]. (This was the ·follower [disciple]
who had leaned against Jesus at the supper and had said, "Lord, who will
·turn against [betray] you?" [see 13:24–25]) 21When Peter saw him behind
them, he asked Jesus, "Lord, what about him?"

22Jesus answered [Lhim], "If I want him to live until I come back, ·that
is not your business [Lwhat is that to you?]. You follow me."

23So a ·story [rumor; report; saying; Lword] spread among the ·follow-
ers [disciples; Lbrothers] that this one would not die. But Jesus did not say
he would not die. He only said, "If I want him to live until I come back,
·that is not your business [what is that to you?]."

24That ·follower [disciple] is the one who ·is telling [witnesses/testifies
to] these things and who has now written them down. We know that
·what he says [his testimony/witness] is true.

25There are many other things Jesus did. If every one of them were
written down, I suppose the whole world would not be big enough for all
the books that would be written.

ACTS

Luke's Second Volume

1 ·To [LO] Theophilus [Ca name meaning "Lover of God"; probably a specific individual, though possibly addressing all who love God].

The ·first [*or* former; previous] ·book [account; Ca reference to the Gospel of Luke] I wrote was about everything Jesus began to do and teach 2until the day he was taken up into heaven. Before this, ·with the help of [through] the Holy Spirit, Jesus ·told [instructed; commanded] the apostles he had chosen [Luke 6:13] what they should do. 3After his ·death [Lsuffering], he showed himself to them and ·proved [provided undeniable evidence] in many ways that he was alive [Luke 24:13–49]. The apostles saw Jesus during the forty days after he was raised from the dead, and he spoke to them about the kingdom of God. 4Once when he was ·eating [*or* staying; meeting] with them, he ·told [commanded] them not to leave Jerusalem. He said, "Wait here to receive the promise from the Father [Cthe gift of the Holy Spirit] which I told you about [Luke 24:49]. 5John baptized people ·with [*or* in] water [Luke 3:1–20], but in a few days you will be baptized ·with [by; *or* in] the Holy Spirit."

Jesus Is Taken Up into Heaven

6When the apostles were all together, they ·asked [kept asking] Jesus, "Lord, are you ·now [at this time] going to ·give the kingdom back [restore the kingdom] to Israel [CIsrael had lived for centuries under the oppression of foreign nations; Jer. 16:15; 23:8; Hos. 11:8–11; the disciples were expecting the messianic kingdom; Is. 9:1–7; 11:1–16]?"

7Jesus said to them, "The Father is the only One who has the ·authority [*or* power] to ·decide [set] dates and times [Mark 13:32]. These things are not for you to know. 8But when the Holy Spirit comes to you, you will receive power. You will be my witnesses—in Jerusalem [2:1—8:3], in all of Judea, in Samaria [8:4—11:18], and ·in every part of the world [to the ends of the earth; 11:19—28:31; Luke 24:45–48]."

9After he said this, as they were watching, he was lifted up, and a cloud ·hid him from [*or* took him out of; Ca reference to the cloud chariot; Dan. 7:13–14] their sight [Ca description of Christ's ascension into heaven]. 10As he was going, they were ·looking [staring; gazing] into the ·sky [heavens]. Suddenly, two men wearing white clothes [Cangels] stood beside them. 11They said, "Men of Galilee, why are you standing here ·looking into [staring at] ·the sky [heaven]? Jesus, whom you saw taken up from you into heaven, will come back in the same way you saw him go [Con a cloud; Luke 21:27]."

A New Apostle Is Chosen

12Then they went back to Jerusalem from the Mount ·of Olives [*or* called Olivet]. (This mountain is about ·half a mile [La Sabbath day's journey]

from Jerusalem.) 13 When they entered the city, they went to the upstairs
room where they were staying. Peter, John, James, Andrew, Philip, Thomas,
Bartholomew, Matthew, James son of Alphaeus, Simon (known as the
Zealot [Ceither a political revolutionary or one zealous for the Law of Moses;
Luke 6:15]), and Judas son of James were there. 14 They all ·continued [*or*
were constantly] praying together with some women [Cfollowers of Jesus
(Luke 8:3; 24:22) and perhaps wives of the apostles], including Mary the
mother of Jesus, and Jesus' brothers.

15 ·During this time [LIn those days] there was a meeting of the ·believers
[Lbrothers (and sisters)] (about one hundred twenty of them). Peter stood
up and said, 16-17 "·Brothers and sisters [LMen, brothers; CPeter is probably
specifically addressing the apostles], in the Scriptures the Holy Spirit ·said
[foretold] through [Lthe mouth of] David ·something that must happen
involving [Lconcerning] Judas. He was one of our own group and ·served
together with us [shared part of this ministry]. He ·led [guided] those who
arrested Jesus." 18 (Judas bought a field with the ·money [wages; reward] he
got for his ·evil [unjust] act. But he fell to his death, his body burst open,
and all his ·intestines [bowels; guts] poured out [Matt. 27:3–10]. 19 Everyone
in Jerusalem learned about this so they named this place Akeldama. In
their language [CAramaic] Akeldama means "Field of Blood.") 20 "[LFor] In
the Book of Psalms," Peter said, "this is written:

'May his ·place [dwelling; home] be ·empty [deserted];
leave no one to live in it [Ps. 69:25].'

And it is also written:

'Let another man ·replace him as leader [take his office/position of
leadership; Ps. 109:8].'

21-22 "So now a man must become a witness with us of Jesus' ·being
raised from the dead [resurrection]. He must be one of the men who were
part of our group during all the time the Lord Jesus ·was [Lwent in and
out] among us—·from the time John was baptizing people [*or* from
John's baptism of Jesus; Lfrom the baptism of John] until the day Jesus was
taken up from us to heaven."

23 They put the names of two men before the group. One was Joseph
Barsabbas, who was also called Justus. The other was Matthias. 24-25 The
apostles prayed, "Lord, you know the ·thoughts [hearts] of everyone. Show
us which one of these two you have chosen to ·do this work and to be an
apostle [Ltake this position of ministry and apostleship] in place of Judas,
who turned away and went where he belongs [Cto death, destruction, or
hell]." 26 Then they ·used [cast] lots to choose between them [Coften used as
a means to discern God's will in the OT; Lev. 16:8; Num. 26:55; 33:54; Josh.
19:1–4; 1 Sam. 23:6], and the lots showed that Matthias was the one. So he
·became [was counted as] an apostle with the other eleven.

The Coming of the Holy Spirit

2 When the day of Pentecost [Ca harvest festival fifty days after
Passover, celebrating the firstfruits of the crops (while on this day
the firstfruits of the Spirit); Ex. 34:22; Deut. 16:10, 16] ·came [arrived], they
were all together in one place. 2 Suddenly a ·noise [roar] like a ·strong [vio-
lent], ·blowing [rushing] wind came from heaven and filled the whole
house where they were sitting. 3 They saw something like ·flames [Ltongues]
of fire ·that were separated [that were divided; *or* that spread out] and ·stood
[came to rest] over each person there. 4 They were all filled with the Holy
Spirit, and they began to speak ·different [other; *or* foreign] ·languages

[Ltongues] by the power the Holy Spirit was giving them [Creversing the
confusion of languages at the Tower of Babel; Gen. 11:1–9].
5There were some ·religious [devout; God-fearing] Jews ·staying [liv-
ing] in Jerusalem who were from every ·country [nation] ·in the world
[Lunder heaven]. 6When they heard this noise, a crowd came together.
They were all ·surprised [*or* confused; bewildered], because each one
heard them speaking in his own language. 7They were ·completely
[Lastounded and] amazed at this. They said, "Look! Aren't all these people
that we hear speaking ·from Galilee [LGalileans]? 8Then how is it possible
that we each hear them in our own [native] languages? We are: 9Parthians,
Medes, Elamites, residents of Mesopotamia, Judea, Cappadocia, Pontus,
Asia [Ca Roman province, in present-day Turkey], 10Phrygia, Pamphylia,
Egypt, the areas of Libya near Cyrene, [visitors from] Rome 11(both Jews
and ·those who had become Jews [proselytes]), Crete, and Arabia. But we
hear them telling in our own ·languages [tongues] about the ·great things
[mighty acts] God has done!" 12They were all amazed and confused, asking each other, "What does this mean?"
13But others ·were making fun of them [sneered], saying, "They have
had too much [sweet; new] wine [Cthey accuse them of being intoxicated
and speaking nonsense]."

Peter Speaks to the People

14But Peter stood up with the eleven apostles, and in a loud voice he
·spoke to [addressed] the crowd: "·My fellow Jews [*or* Judeans], and all of you
who ·are [are living/staying] in Jerusalem, ·listen to me [Llet this be known to
you]. Pay attention to what I have to say. 15These people are not drunk, as
you think; it is only ·nine o'clock in the morning [Lthe third hour of the day]!
16But Joel the prophet wrote about what is happening here today:
17'God says: In the last days
I will pour out my Spirit on all ·kinds of people [people; humanity;
Tflesh].
Your sons and daughters will prophesy.
Your young men will see visions,
and your old men will dream dreams.
18At that time I will pour out my Spirit
also on my male ·slaves [servants] and female ·slaves [servants],
and they will prophesy.
19I will show ·miracles [wonders; marvels]
in the ·sky [*or* heaven] above
and ·signs [miracles] on the earth below:
blood, fire, and ·thick [La cloud/billow of] smoke.
20The sun will ·become dark [Lbe turned to darkness],
the moon ·red as blood [Lto blood],
before the ·overwhelming [great] and glorious day of the Lord will
come.
21Then anyone who calls on [Lthe name of] the Lord will be saved
[Joel 2:28–32].'
22"·People of Israel [LMen, Israelites], ·listen to [hear] these words:
Jesus ·from Nazareth [*or* the Nazarene] was a very special man. God
clearly ·showed [attested; pointed out] this to you by the ·miracles [mighty
deeds], wonders, and signs he did through Jesus. You all know this,
because it happened ·right here among you [Lin your midst]. 23Jesus was
·given [handed over] to you, and ·with the help [Lby the hands] of ·those

who don't know the law [*or* lawless ones; wicked people; Ca reference to
the Gentiles/Romans who crucified Jesus], **you put him to death by nailing him to a cross. But this was ·God's plan which he had made long ago**
[Laccording to God's predetermined plan]; **·he knew all this would happen**
[L...and his foreknowledge]. 24**God raised Jesus from the dead and set him
free from the ·pain** [agony; birthpains] **of death, because death could not
hold him.** 25**For David said this about him:**
'I ·keep [Lsaw] **the Lord before me always.**
Because he is ·close by my side [Lat my right hand; Ca soldier's
shieldbearer would stand at his right side to protect him],
[Lso that] **I will not be ·hurt** [Lshaken].
26**So ·I am** [Lmy heart was] **glad, and ·I rejoice** [Lmy tongue rejoiced].
Even my body ·has [Lwill live in; *or* will rest in] **hope,**
27**because you will not ·leave** [abandon] **·me** [Lmy soul/life] **in ·the grave**
[LHades; Cthe underworld].
You will not let your Holy One [experience; Lsee] **decay.**
28**You ·will teach me** [Lhave made known to me] **·how to live a holy life**
[Lthe way/path of life].
·Being with you [Your presence; LYour face] **will fill me with joy**
[Ps. 16:8–11]."
29"**·Brothers and sisters** [LMen, brothers], **I can tell you ·truly** [*or* with
confidence] **that David, ·our ancestor** [Lthe patriarch], **died and was buried.
His ·grave** [tomb] **is still here with us today.** 30[But because] **He was a prophet
and knew God had ·promised him** [sworn with an oath] **that he would
·make a person from David's family a king just as he was** [Lput one of his
descendants on his throne; Ca reference to the Davidic covenant; 2 Sam. 7:13;
Ps. 132:11]. 31**·Knowing this before it happened** [LForeseeing this], **David
talked about the ·Christ** [Messiah] **rising from the dead. He said:**
'He was not ·left [abandoned] **in ·the grave** [Hades].
His ·body [flesh] **did not ·rot** [Lsee/experience decay; 2:27].'
32**So Jesus is the One whom God raised from the dead. And we are all witnesses to this.** 33**Jesus was ·lifted up to heaven and is now at** [Lexalted to]
God's right ·side [Lhand; Ca position of highest honor beside the king].
**The Father has given the Holy Spirit to Jesus as he promised. So Jesus has
poured out that Spirit, and this is what you now see and hear.** 34**David was
not the one who ·was lifted up** [went up; ascended] **to heaven, but he said:**
'The Lord said to my Lord,
"Sit by me at my right ·side [Lhand; v. 33],
35 **until I ·put your enemies under your control** [Lmake your enemies a
footstool for your feet; Ps. 110:1]."'
36"**·So** [Therefore], **all the ·people** [Lhouse] **of Israel should know this
·truly** [with certainty]: **God has made Jesus—the man you ·nailed to the
cross** [crucified]**—both Lord and ·Christ** [Messiah]."
37**When the people heard this, they ·felt guilty** [were deeply distressed;
Lwere cut/pierced to the heart] **and asked Peter and the other apostles,
"What shall we do, ·brothers** [Lmen, brothers]?"
38**Peter said to them, "·Change your hearts and lives** [Repent] **and be
baptized, each one of you, in the name of Jesus Christ for the forgiveness of
your sins. And you will receive the gift of the Holy Spirit.** 39[LFor] **This
promise is for you, for your children, and for all who are far away** [Cboth in
space and time; may refer to Gentiles and/or Jews scattered outside the land
of Israel]. **It is for everyone the Lord our God calls to himself** [Joel 2:32]."

40Peter ·warned [testified to] them with many other ·words [arguments]. He ·begged [pleaded with; exhorted; urged] them, "Save yourselves from ·the evil of today's people [Lthis corrupt/crooked/perverse generation]!" 41Then those people who accepted what Peter said were baptized. About three thousand ·people [souls] were added to the number of believers that day. 42They ·spent [devoted] their time learning the apostles' teaching, ·sharing [fellowship], breaking bread [Cthis may refer to a meal as in v. 46, or to the Lord's Supper; Luke 22:14–20], and praying together.

The Believers Share

43The apostles were doing many miracles and signs, and ·everyone [every soul] felt great ·respect [fear; awe; Prov. 1:7] for God. 44All the believers were ·together [in one place; *or* in close fellowship] and ·shared everything [Lhad/held all things in common]. 45They would sell their land and the things they owned and then divide ·the money [the proceeds; Lthem] and give it to anyone who needed it. 46The believers met together in the Temple [Cnot the Temple building where only priests went, but the outer courts] every day. They ate together ·in their homes [*or* from home to home], sharing their food with joyful and ·sincere [*or* generous; *or* humble; *or* simple] hearts. 47They praised God and were ·liked by [looked upon favorably by] all the people. Every day the Lord added those who were being saved to the group of believers.

Peter Heals a Crippled Man

3 One day Peter and John went to the Temple at ·three o'clock [Lthe ninth hour; time was reckoned from dawn, traditionally set at 6 AM], ·the time set each day for the afternoon prayer service [Lthe hour of prayer]. 2There, at the Temple gate called Beautiful Gate [Cunknown location, perhaps one of several gates between various courtyards], was a man who had been ·crippled [lame] ·all his life [Lfrom his mother's womb]. Every day ·he was carried to [people would lay him at] this gate to beg for ·money [alms] from the people going into the Temple [Cthe Temple complex; 2:46]. 3The man saw Peter and John going into the Temple [Ccourts; 2:46] and asked them for ·money [alms; help]. 4Peter and John looked ·straight [intently] at him and said, "Look at us!" 5The man ·looked at [paid attention to] them, thinking they were going to give him ·some money [Lsomething]. 6But Peter said, "·I don't have any silver or gold, but ·I do have something else I can give you [Lwhat I do have, I give to you]. ·By the power [LIn the name] of Jesus Christ ·from Nazareth [*or* the Nazarene], stand up and walk [Luke 5:23]!" 7Then Peter took the man's right hand and ·lifted [raised] him up. Immediately the man's feet and ankles became strong. 8He ·jumped up [leaped], stood on his feet, and began to walk. He went into the Temple [Ccourts; 2:46] with them, walking and ·jumping [leaping] and praising God [Is. 35:4–6]. 9-10All the people recognized him as the ·crippled [lame] man who always sat by the Beautiful Gate [3:2] begging for ·money [alms; help]. Now they saw this same man walking and praising God, and they were amazed. ·They wondered how this could happen [*or* …and stunned/astonished at what had happened].

Peter Speaks to the People

11While the man was ·holding on [clinging] to Peter and John, all the people were ·amazed [astonished] and ran to them at Solomon's ·Porch [Portico; Colonnade; Ccolumns marked the outside perimeter of the large outer court of the Temple]. 12When Peter saw this, he ·said to [addressed] them, "·People of Israel [LMen, Israelites], why are you ·surprised [amazed]? ·You are [LOr why are you…?] ·looking [staring] at us as if it

were our own power or ·goodness [piety; godliness] that made this man
walk. 13The God of Abraham, Isaac, and Jacob, the God of our ·ancestors
[forefathers; fathers], ·gave glory to [has glorified/honored] Jesus, his ·ser-
vant [*or* child]. But you handed him over to be killed. Pilate decided to let
him go free, but you ·told Pilate you did not want [Ldisowned; rejected]
Jesus. 14You ·did not want [Ldisowned; rejected] the One who is holy and
·good [righteous] but asked Pilate to give you a murderer [CBarabbas;
Luke 23:18] instead. 15And so you killed the ·One who gives [Author/
Source/Ruler of] life, but God raised him from the dead. We are witnesses
to this. 16It was faith in [Lthe name of] Jesus that made this ·crippled
[lame] man ·well [strong]. You can see this man, and you know him. He
was made completely well because of ·trust [faith] in ·Jesus [Lthe name of
Jesus], ·and you all saw it happen [in front of you all]!
17"·Brothers and sisters [*or* Brothers; Cfellow Jews], I know you did those
things to Jesus because neither you nor your leaders [rulers] understood
what you were doing. 18God ·said [foretold; predicted] through [Lthe
mouth of all] the prophets that his ·Christ [Messiah] would suffer. And
now God has ·made these things come true [Lfulfilled these things] in this
way. 19So you must ·change your hearts and lives [repent]! ·Come back
[Return; Turn back] to God, and he will ·forgive [wipe out; erase] your
sins. Then the ·time [Ltimes; seasons] of ·rest [refreshment; comfort; Cthe
messianic age] will come from [Lthe presence of] the Lord. 20And he will
send Jesus, the One he ·chose [appointed] to be the ·Christ [Messiah].
21But ·Jesus must stay in heaven [Lheaven must receive/welcome him] until
the time comes when all things will be ·made right again [restored; made
new]. God ·told about [announced] this time long ago when he spoke
through his holy prophets. 22Moses said, 'The Lord your God will ·give you
[Lraise up for you] a prophet like me, ·who is one of your own people
[Lfrom among your brothers]. You must ·listen to [hear; obey] everything
he tells you. 23Anyone who does not listen to that prophet will ·die, cut off
[be utterly destroyed] from God's people [Lev. 23:29; Deut. 18:15–20].'
24Samuel, and all the other prophets who spoke for God after Samuel, ·told
[announced; foretold; predicted] about ·this time now [Lthese days; Cthere
are no specific messianic prophecies from Samuel, but he did anoint David
whose kingship anticipated the Messiah; 2 Sam. 7:12–16; Acts 13:22–23;
Heb. 5:1]. 25You are ·descendants [children; sons] of the prophets. You
have received the ·agreement [covenant; treaty] God made with your
·ancestors [Lfathers; patriarchs]. He said to your father Abraham, 'Through
your ·descendants [heirs; Lseed] all the ·nations [*or* families] on the earth
will be blessed [Gen. 22:18; 26:4].' 26God has raised up his ·servant [*or*
child] Jesus and sent him to you first [Cthe Jews were to receive the blessing
first, and through them God would bless all nations] to bless you by turning each of you away from ·doing evil [your wicked ways]."

Peter and John at the Council

4 While Peter and John were speaking to the people, they were
approached by priests, the captain of the soldiers that guarded
the Temple, and Sadducees [CJewish religious party with most influence in
the Jewish high court (Sanhedrin) and among the Temple leadership].
2They were ·upset [annoyed; disturbed] because the two apostles were
teaching the people and were ·preaching [proclaiming] ·that people will
rise from the dead through the power of Jesus [Lthe resurrection of the
dead in Jesus; CSadducees did not believe in the afterlife]. 3They ·grabbed

[seized; arrested] **Peter and John and put them in ·jail** [custody]**. Since it was already ·night** [evening]**, they kept them in jail until the next day. 4But many of those who had heard Peter and John preach believed the ·things they said** [message; Lword]**. ·There were now about five thousand in the group of believers** [*or* The number of men grew to about five thousand; Cprobably referring to adult males and so household units].

5The next day the rulers, the elders, and the ·teachers of the law [scribes] **·met** [assembled] **in Jerusalem. 6Annas the high priest, Caiaphas** [CAnnas was the former high priest and father-in-law of Caiaphas, the official high priest; Luke 3:2]**, John, and Alexander** [Cperhaps sons of Annas] **were there, as well as ·everyone** [*or* others] **from the high priest's family. 7They made Peter and John stand before them and then ·asked** [questioned; interrogated] **them, "By what power or ·authority** [Lin/by what name] **did you do this?"**

8Then Peter, filled with the Holy Spirit, said to them, "Rulers of the people and you elders, 9are you ·questioning [examining] **us** [Ltoday] **about a ·good thing** [good deed; act of kindness] **that was done to a ·crippled** [lame; sick] **man? Are you asking us ·who made him well** [*or* how he was made well/healed]**? 10We want all of you and all the people** [of Israel] **to know that this man was made well ·by the power** [Lin/by the name] **of Jesus Christ ·from Nazareth** [*or* the Nazarene]**. You crucified him, but God raised him from the dead. This man was ·crippled** [lame; sick]**, but he is now ·well** [healthy] **and able to stand here before you because of the ·power** [Lname] **of Jesus. 11Jesus is**

'the stone that you builders ·rejected [despised],
which has become the cornerstone [Ps. 118:22; CJesus is the central stone that holds up the building].'

12·Jesus is the only One who can save people [LSalvation is found/present in no one else]**. ·No one else** [LNo other name given to people] **·in the world** [Lunder heaven] **is able to save us."**

13The leaders saw that Peter and John were ·not afraid to speak [bold; confident]**, and they ·understood** [discovered; found out] **that these men ·had no special training or education** [*or* were common/ordinary and uneducated; Cno formal training from a rabbi in teaching Scripture]**. So they were amazed. Then they realized that Peter and John had been with Jesus. 14Because they saw the healed man standing there beside the two apostles, they could say nothing against them. 15After the leaders ordered them to leave the ·meeting** [*or* Sanhedrin; Ca council of the chief leaders of the Jewish people]**, they began to ·talk to** [confer with] **each other. 16They said, "What shall we do with these men? Everyone** [Lwho lives] **in Jerusalem knows they have done a great ·miracle** [Lsign]**, and we cannot say it is not true. 17But to keep it from spreading among the people, we must warn them not to talk to people anymore ·using that name** [*or* about that name/person]**."**

18So they called Peter and John in again and ·told [commanded; ordered] **them not to ·speak** [preach] **or to teach at all in the name of Jesus. 19But Peter and John answered them, "You ·decide** [judge] **what ·God would want** [Lis right before God]**. Should we ·obey** [listen to] **you or God? 20**[LFor] **We cannot ·keep quiet** [stop speaking] **about what we have seen and heard." 21The leaders ·warned** [threatened] **the apostles again and let them go free. They could not find a way to punish them, because all the people were praising God for what had ·been done** [happened]**. 22The man who received the ·miracle** [Lsign] **of healing was more than forty years old.**

The Believers Pray

23After Peter and John ·left the meeting of leaders [Lwere released], they went to their own group and ·told them [reported] everything the ·leading [Tchief] priests and the elders had said to them. 24When the believers heard this, they ·prayed [Lraised their voices] to God together, "·Lord [*or* Sovereign; Master], you are the One who made the sky, the earth, the sea, and everything in them [Gen. 1; Ps. 8; 19; 104]. 25By the Holy Spirit, through our father David your ·servant [*or* child], you said:

'Why are the ·nations [Gentiles] ·so angry [furious; raging]?
Why are the people ·making useless plans [plotting in vain]?
26The kings of the earth ·prepare to fight [take their stand],
and their ·leaders [rulers] ·make plans [*or* gather; assemble] together against the Lord
and his ·Christ [Messiah; Anointed One; Ps. 2:1–2; Cthe psalm describes the unrest of subject nations at the coronation of Israel's anointed king].'

27·These things really happened when [For truly; Indeed] Herod, Pontius Pilate, and ·some Jews [the people of Israel] and Gentiles all came together here in ·Jerusalem [Lthis city] against your holy ·servant [child] Jesus, the One you ·made to be the Christ [Lanointed; Luke 4:18; CChrist in Greek and Messiah in Hebrew mean "anointed one"]. 28These people made your plan happen because of your ·power [Lhand] and your ·will [purpose]. [*or* LThey did whatever your hand and your purpose predestined/determined beforehand to be done.] 29And now, Lord, ·listen to [consider] their threats. Lord, help us, your ·servants [slaves], to speak your ·word [message] ·without fear [Lwith all boldness/confidence]. 30·Show us your power [LStretch out your hand] to heal. Give ·proofs [signs] and ·make miracles happen [wonders] by the ·power [Lname] of Jesus, your holy ·servant [*or* child]."

31After they had prayed, the place where they were meeting was shaken. They were all filled with the Holy Spirit, and they spoke God's ·word [message] ·without fear [Lwith boldness/confidence/courage].

The Believers Share

32The group of believers were ·united in their hearts and spirit [Lone heart and mind/soul; Jer. 32:39]. ·All those in the group acted as though their private property belonged to everyone in the group [LNo one said any of their possessions was their own]. In fact, ·they shared everything [*or* everything was held in common]. 33With great power the apostles ·were telling people [gave testimony; witnessed] that the Lord Jesus was truly raised from the dead. And ·God blessed all the believers very much [Lgreat grace was on all of them]. 34[LFor] There were no needy people among them [Deut. 15:4]. [LBecause] From time to time those who owned fields or houses sold them, brought the money from the sale, 35and ·gave it to [Llaid it at the feet of] the apostles. Then the money was ·given [distributed] to anyone who needed it.

36One of the believers was named Joseph, a Levite [Cthe Israelite tribe set apart for priestly service] born in Cyprus [Can island to the west of the coast of Syria]. The apostles called him Barnabas (which means ·"one who encourages" [L"son of encouragement"]). 37Joseph owned a field, sold it, brought the money, and ·gave it to [Llaid it at the feet of] the apostles.

Ananias and Sapphira Die

5But a man named Ananias and his wife Sapphira sold ·some land [a piece of property]. 2He ·kept back [pilfered; skimmed off] part of the ·money [proceeds; price] for himself; his wife knew about this and agreed to it. But he brought the rest of the money and ·gave it to [Llaid it at the feet of] the apostles. 3Peter said, "Ananias, why did you let Satan ·rule your thoughts [Lfill your heart] to lie to the Holy Spirit and to ·keep [pilfer; skim off] for yourself part of the ·money [proceeds] you received for the land? 4Before you sold the land, it belonged to you. And even after you sold it, you could have used the ·money [proceeds] any way you wanted. Why did you think of doing this? You lied to God, not to us!" 5-6When Ananias heard this, he fell down and died. Some young men came in, wrapped up his body, carried it out, and buried it. And everyone who heard about this was filled with fear.

7About three hours later his wife came in, but she did not know what had happened. 8Peter said to her, "Tell me, was the ·money [payment] you got for your field this much?"

Sapphira answered, "Yes, that was the price."

9Peter said to her, "Why did you and your husband ·agree [conspire] to test the Spirit of the Lord [Gal. 6:7–8]? Look! The ·men [Lfeet of those] who buried your husband are at the door, and they will carry you out." 10·At that moment [Instantly] Sapphira fell down by his feet and died. When the young men came in and ·saw [discovered; found] that she was dead, they carried her out and buried her beside her husband. 11The whole church and all the others who heard about these things were filled with ·fear [terror; awe].

The Apostles Heal Many

12The apostles did many ·signs [miracles] and ·miracles [wonders] among the people. And they would all meet together on Solomon's Porch [see 3:11]. 13None of the others dared to join them, ·but [*or* even though] all the people ·respected [praised; highly regarded] them. 14More and more men and women believed in the Lord and were added to the ·group [crowd; multitude] of believers. 15[As a result] The people placed their sick on ·beds [cots] and mats in the streets, hoping that when Peter passed by at least his shadow might fall on [Lsome of] them. 16Crowds came from all the towns around Jerusalem, bringing their sick and those who were ·bothered [tormented] by ·evil [Lunclean; Cdemons were viewed as "unclean" or defiling spirit-beings] spirits, and all of them were healed.

Leaders Try to Stop the Apostles

17The high priest and all his friends (a ·group [sect; religious party] called the Sadducees [4:1]) became very ·jealous [indignant; *or* zealous; Cperhaps referring to their religious zeal]. 18They ·took [seized; arrested; Lput hands on] the apostles and put them in [public] ·jail [custody]. 19But during the night, an angel of the Lord opened the doors of the ·jail [prison] and led the apostles outside. The angel said, 20"Go stand in the Temple [Ccourts; 2:46] and tell the people ·everything [*or* the full message; Lall the words] about this new life." 21When the apostles heard this, they obeyed and went into the Temple [Ccourts; 2:46] early in the morning and ·continued [*or* began] teaching.

When the high priest and his friends arrived, they called a meeting of the ·leaders [LSanhedrin; 4:15] ·and [*or* that is,] ·all the important elders [Lthe whole senate/council of the sons of Israel]. They sent some men to the ·jail [prison] to bring the apostles to them. 22But, upon arriving, the ·officers [temple police] could not find the apostles. So they went back and reported to the leaders. 23They said, "·The jail was [LWe found the jail] closed and locked, and the guards were standing at the doors. But when we opened the doors, ·the jail was empty [Lwe found no one inside]!" 24Hearing this, the captain of the Temple guards and the ·leading [Tchief] priests were ·confused [puzzled; confounded] and wondered what ·was happening [*or* this might lead to].

25 Then someone came and told them, "Listen [L Look]! The men you put in ·jail [prison] are standing in the Temple [courts] teaching the people." 26 Then the captain and ·his men [the officers/attendants; C the temple police] went out and brought the apostles back. But they did not use force, because they were afraid the people would stone them to death.

27 They brought the apostles to the ·meeting [L Sanhedrin; 4:15] and made them stand before the leaders. The high priest questioned them, 28 saying, "We gave you strict orders not to continue teaching in that name [C of Jesus]. But look, you have filled Jerusalem with your teaching and are ·trying [wishing; intending] to make us responsible for this man's ·death [L blood]."

29 Peter and the other apostles answered, "We must obey God, not ·human authority [L people]! 30 You ·killed [murdered] Jesus by hanging him on a ·cross [L tree]. But God, the God of our ancestors, raised Jesus up from the dead! 31 Jesus is the One whom God ·raised [exalted] to be on his right ·side [L hand], as ·Leader [Prince; Ruler] and Savior. Through him, ·the people of Israel [L Israel] could ·change their hearts and lives [repent] and have their sins forgiven. 32 We ·saw all these things happen [L testify to/are witnesses of these things]. The Holy Spirit, whom God has given to all who obey him, also ·proves [*or* testifies that] these things are true."

33 When the leaders heard this, they became ·angry [furious] and wanted to kill them. 34 But a Pharisee [C a member of a religious party that strictly observed OT laws, added traditions, and represented a minority on the Sanhedrin] named Gamaliel [C Paul's teacher; 22:3] stood up in the ·meeting [L Sanhedrin; 4:15]. He was a teacher of the law, and all the people respected him. He ordered the ·apostles [L men] to leave the meeting for a little while. 35 Then he said, "·People of Israel [L Men, Israelites], be careful what you are planning to do to these men. 36 ·Remember when [*or* Some time ago] Theudas ·appeared [L rose up]? He ·said [claimed] he was ·a great man [L somebody], and about four hundred men joined him. But he was killed, and all his followers were scattered; they ·were able to do nothing [failed; came to nothing]. 37 Later, a man named ·Judas came from Galilee [*or* Judas the Galilean appeared/arose] at the time of the ·registration [census; C of people and possessions, for tax purposes; Judas led a tax revolt]. He also led a group of followers and ·was killed [perished], and all his followers were scattered. 38 And so now I tell you: Stay away from these men, and leave them alone. If their ·plan [*or* activity; endeavor] comes from human ·authority [*or* origin], it will fail. 39 But if it is from God, you will not be able to stop them. You might even ·be [find yourselves] fighting against God himself!"

The leaders ·agreed with [were convinced by] what Gamaliel said. 40 They called the apostles in, ·beat [flogged; whipped] them, and ·told [commanded] them not to speak in the name of Jesus again. Then they let them go free. 41 The apostles left the ·meeting [L presence of the Sanhedrin/council; 4:15] ·full of joy [rejoicing] because they were ·given the honor [*or* considered worthy by God] of suffering disgrace for ·Jesus [L the name]. 42 Every day in the Temple [courts] and in people's homes they continued teaching the people and ·telling [proclaiming] the ·Good News [Gospel]—that Jesus is the ·Christ [Messiah].

Seven Leaders Are Chosen

6 The number of ·followers [disciples] was ·growing [multiplying]. But during ·this same time [those days], the ·Greek-speaking followers [L Hellenists; C Jewish Christians who spoke primarily Greek and had returned to Israel after living abroad] ·had an argument with [began

grumbling/complaining against] the ·other followers [LHebrews; CAramaic
speaking Jewish Christians born in Israel]. The Greek-speaking widows
were ·not getting their share [being neglected/overlooked in the distribu-
tion] of the food that was given out every day. 2The ·twelve apostles
[Twelve] called the whole group of ·followers [Ldisciples] together and
said, "It is not right for us to ·stop our work of teaching God's word
[Lleave/abandon the word of God] in order to serve tables. 3So, ·brothers
and sisters [*or* brothers; Cuncertain whether women would have been
included in that culture], choose seven of your own men who ·are good
[have a good reputation], full of the Spirit and full of wisdom. We will
·put [appoint] them in charge of this ·work [responsibility; Lneed]. 4Then
we [apostles] can ·continue [devote ourselves] to pray and to ·teach [Lthe
ministry/service of] the word of God."

5The whole group ·liked [was pleased with] the idea, so they chose
these seven men: Stephen (a man ·with great [Lfull of] faith and full of the
Holy Spirit), Philip [Cnot the apostle of the same name], Procorus,
Nicanor, Timon, Parmenas, and Nicolas (a man from Antioch [Ca major
city in Syria] who ·had become a follower of the Jewish religion [Lwas a
prosylete; Ca Gentile convert to Judaism]. 6Then they ·put [presented]
these men before the apostles, who prayed and laid their hands [Ca ritual
of blessing and/or conferring of authority] on them.

7The word of God was continuing to spread. The ·group [number] of
·followers [disciples] in Jerusalem [quickly; *or* greatly] ·increased [multi-
plied], and a great number of the Jewish priests ·believed and obeyed
[Lbecome obedient to the faith].

Stephen Is Accused

8Stephen was ·richly blessed by God who gave him the power [Lfull of
grace and power] to do great ·miracles [wonders] and signs among the
people. 9But some people ·were [rose up] against him. They belonged to the
synagogue of Free Men [CJews who were freed slaves] (as it was called),
which included people from Cyrene, Alexandria [Cboth in North Africa],
Cilicia, and Asia [Cboth in Asia Minor, present-day Turkey]. They all ·came
[rose up; came forward] and ·argued [debated; disputed] with Stephen.

10But ·the Spirit was helping him to speak with wisdom, and his words
were so strong that they could not argue with him [Lthey could not resist
the wisdom and Spirit/spirit by which he spoke]. 11So they ·secretly urged
[*or* bribed] some men to say, "We heard Stephen ·speak [Lspeaking blasphemous words] against Moses and against God."

12They ·stirred up [roused; incited] the people, the elders, and the
teachers of the law. They ·came [*or* confronted] and grabbed Stephen and
brought him to ·a meeting of the leaders [Lthe Sanhedrin; 4:15]. 13They
brought in some ·people to tell lies about Stephen [Lfalse witnesses], saying, "This man is always speaking against this holy place [Cthe Temple]
and the law of Moses. 14We heard him say that Jesus ·from Nazareth [*or*
the Nazarene] will destroy this place and that Jesus will change the customs Moses gave us [Cfor a similar charge leveled against Jesus see Matt.
26:61; Mark 14:58]." 15All the people [who sat] in the ·meeting [LSanhedrin;
4:15] ·were watching Stephen closely [*or* stared intently at Stephen] ·and
[*or* because they] saw that his face looked like the face of an angel.

Stephen's Speech

7 The high priest said to Stephen, "Are these ·things [charges] true?"
2Stephen answered, "Brothers [LMen, brothers] and fathers, listen
to me. ·Our glorious God [The God of glory] appeared to Abraham, our

·ancestor [patriarch; Lfather], in Mesopotamia before he lived in Haran [Ca city in Syria where Abraham resided before reaching the Promised Land; Gen. 11:31]. 3God said to Abraham, 'Leave your country and your relatives, and go to the land I will show you [Gen. 12:1].' 4So Abraham left the ·country [land] of Chaldea [Canother name for southern Mesopotamia, the location of Ur] and went to live in Haran. After Abraham's father [CTerah] died, God sent him to this place where you now live. 5God did not give Abraham ·any of this land [Lan inheritance in it], not even a ·foot of it [La foot's length]. But God promised that he would give this land to him [Las a possession] and his ·descendants [Lseed; Gen. 12:2], even before Abraham had a child. 6This is what God said to him: 'Your ·descendants [Lseed] will be ·strangers [foreigners; resident aliens] in a ·land they don't own [foreign land; land belonging to others; CEgypt]. The people there will make them slaves and will ·mistreat [oppress] them for four hundred years. 7But I will ·punish [judge] the nation where they are slaves. Then ·your descendants [Lthey] will leave that land and will worship me in this place [Gen. 15:13–14; Ex. 3:12].' 8God made an ·agreement [covenant; Ca treaty-like relationship] with Abraham, the sign of which was circumcision [Gen. 17:9–14]. And so when Abraham ·had his son [became the father of; Tbegat] Isaac, Abraham circumcised him when he was eight days old. Isaac ·also circumcised his son Jacob [*or* became the father of Jacob], and Jacob ·did the same for his sons, [*or* became the father of] the twelve ·ancestors of our people [patriarchs; Cthe twelve sons of Jacob who were the "fathers" of the twelve tribes of Israel].

9"·Jacob's sons [LThe patriarchs] became jealous of Joseph and sold him to be a slave in Egypt. But God was with him 10and ·saved [rescued; delivered] him from all his ·troubles [afflictions]. God gave Joseph ·wisdom to gain the favor of [Lfavor and wisdom before] Pharaoh, king of Egypt. The king made him governor of Egypt and put him in charge of ·all the people in his palace [Lhis whole household].

11"Then all the land of Egypt and Canaan experienced a famine, and the people suffered very much. ·Jacob's sons, our ancestors, [LOur fathers] could not find anything to eat. 12But when Jacob heard there was grain in Egypt, he sent ·his sons [Lour fathers] there. This was their first trip to Egypt [Gen. 42]. 13When they went there a second time [Gen. 43–45], Joseph ·told his brothers who he was [made himself known to his brothers], and ·the king [LPharaoh] learned about Joseph's family. 14Then Joseph sent messengers to ·invite [summon; call] Jacob, his father, to come to Egypt along with all his relatives (seventy-five persons altogether). 15So Jacob went down to Egypt, where he and ·his sons [Lour fathers] died. 16Later their bodies were moved to Shechem and put in a grave there. (It was the same grave Abraham had bought for a sum of ·money [Lsilver] from the sons of Hamor in Shechem.) [CStephen combines two accounts, Abraham's purchase of a field in Hebron (Gen. 23:3–20) and Jacob's purchase of a field in Shechem (Josh. 24:32).]

17"The promise God made to Abraham [Gen. 15:12–16] was soon to come true, and the number of people in Egypt ·grew large [Lincreased/flourished and multiplied]. 18Then ·a new [Lanother] king, who ·did not know who Joseph was [*or* did not think Joseph was important], ·began to rule Egypt [Larose; Ex. 1:8]. 19This king ·tricked [exploited; dealt treacherously with] our ·people [Lrace] and was cruel to our ·ancestors [Lfathers], forcing them to ·leave [Lexpose; abandon] their babies outside to die [Csuch abandonment was a common ancient method of population control]. 20At this time Moses was born, and he was ·very beautiful [beautiful before/to God; *or* of high status in God's eyes]. **For three months Moses was cared for in his father's house.** 21**When ·they put Moses outside** [Lhe was abandoned/exposed; Cwhen Moses' mother "exposed" Moses to the elements, she was actually hiding him; Ex. 2:3–4], **·the king's** [LPharaoh's] **daughter adopted him and raised him as if he were her own son.** 22**·The Egyptians taught Moses everything they knew** [LSo Moses was instructed in all the wisdom of the Egyptians], **and he was a powerful man in ·what he said and did** [Lhis words and actions].

23**"When Moses was about forty years old, ·he thought it would be good** [Lit rose up in his heart] **to visit his own ·people** [relatives; Lbrothers (and sisters)], **the ·people** [Lsons; children] **of Israel.** 24**Moses saw an Egyptian ·mistreating** [wronging] **one of his people, so he defended the ·Israelite** [Loppressed man] **and ·punished the Egyptian by killing him** [Lavenged him by striking down the Egyptian; Ex. 2:11–12]. 25**Moses ·thought** [assumed] **his own ·people** [relatives; Lbrothers (and sisters)] **would understand that God was using him to save them, but they did not.** 26**The next day when Moses saw two men of Israel fighting, he tried to ·make peace between** [reconcile] **them. He said, 'Men, you are brothers. Why are you ·hurting** [wronging] **each other?'** 27**The man who was ·hurting** [wronging] **·the other** [Lhis neighbor] **pushed Moses away and said, 'Who made you our ruler and judge?** 28**·Are you going** [*or* Do you want] **to kill me as you killed the Egyptian yesterday** [Ex. 2:14]**?'** 29**When Moses heard him say this, he ·left Egypt** [Lfled] **and went to live in the land of Midian** [Ca land without distinct borders centered in northwestern Arabia] **where he was a ·stranger** [foreigner; resident alien; Ex. 2:15–25]. **While Moses lived in Midian, he had two sons.**

30**"Forty years later an angel appeared to Moses in the flames of a burning bush as he was in the ·desert** [wilderness] **near Mount Sinai** [Ex. 3]. 31**When Moses saw this, he was amazed** [Lat the sight/vision] **and went near to look closer. Moses heard the Lord's voice say,** 32**'I am the God of your ·ancestors** [forefathers; fathers], **the God of Abraham, Isaac, and Jacob** [Ex. 3:6]**.' Moses began to ·shake** [tremble] **with fear and ·was afraid** [did not dare] **to look.** 33**The Lord said to him, 'Take off your sandals, because you are standing on holy ground.** 34**I have** [surely; indeed] **seen the ·troubles** [wrongs; mistreatment; oppression] **my people have suffered in Egypt. I have heard their ·cries** [groans] **and have come down to ·save** [rescue; deliver] **them. And now, Moses, I am sending you back to Egypt** [Ex. 3:5, 7–8, 10]**.'**

35**"This Moses was the same man the two men of Israel rejected, saying, 'Who made you a ruler and judge** [Ex. 2:14; Ccompare the rejection of Jesus in v. 52]**?' This same man God sent to be a ruler and ·savior** [rescuer; liberator; redeemer], **with the ·help** [Lhand] **of the angel that ·Moses saw** [Lappeared to him] **in the burning bush.** 36**·So Moses** [LThis man] **led the people out of Egypt. He worked ·miracles** [wonders] **and signs in Egypt, at the Red Sea** [Cthe Hebrew OT calls it the Sea of Reeds; the Septuagint (the Greek OT) calls it the Red Sea; Ex. 13:18; 15:4], **and then in the ·desert** [wilderness] **for forty years.** 37**This is the same Moses that said to the ·people** [Lsons; children] **of Israel, 'God will ·give** [Lraise up for] **you a prophet like me, ·who is one of your own ·people** [Lfrom among your brothers; Deut. 18:15]**.'** 38**This is the Moses who was with the ·gathering of the Israelites** [assembly; congregation] **in the ·desert** [wilderness]. **He was with the angel that spoke to him at Mount Sinai, and he was with our ·ancestors** [forefathers; fathers]. **He received ·commands from God that give life** [life-giving messages; *or* living oracles], **and he gave those commands to us** [Ex. 19–24].

39"But our ·ancestors [forefathers; fathers] did not want to obey Moses.
They ·rejected him [pushed him away] and ·wanted to go [Lin their hearts
turned] back to Egypt. 40They said to Aaron, 'Make us gods who will ·lead
[Lgo before] us. Moses led us out of Egypt, but we don't know what has
happened to him [Ex. 32:1].' 41So [Lin those days] the people made an idol
that looked like a calf. Then they ·brought [*or* offered up] sacrifices to it
and ·were proud of [celebrated; Lrejoiced about] what they had made with
their own hands. 42But God turned ·against [*or* away from] them and did
not try to stop them from worshiping the ·sun, moon, and stars [Lhost of
heaven]. This is what is written in the book of the prophets: God says,

'·People [LHouse] of Israel, you did not ·bring [offer up to] me
sacrifices and offerings
while you traveled in the ·desert [wilderness] for forty years.
43You have carried with you
the tent to worship Molech [Ca pagan deity; Lev. 18:21; 20:2–5]
and the idols of ·the star god [*or* the star of your god] Rephan [Ca
pagan deity, perhaps associated with the planet Saturn] that you
made to worship.
So I will send you away [Cinto exile] beyond Babylon [Amos 5:25–27].'

44"The ·Holy Tent [LTent/TTabernacle of Testimony/Witness] where God
spoke to our ·ancestors [forefathers; fathers] was with them in the ·desert
[wilderness]. God told Moses how to make this ·Tent [TTabernacle], and he
made it like the ·plan [pattern] God showed him [Ex. 25–31]. 45Later, Joshua
led our ·ancestors [forefathers; fathers] to ·capture [take possession of] the
lands of the other nations. Our people went in, and God forced the other
people out [Josh. 1–12]. When our people went into this new land, they
took with them this same ·Tent [TTabernacle] they had received from their
·ancestors [forefathers; fathers]. They kept it until the time of David, 46who
·pleased [Lfound favor with] God and asked God to ·let him build a house
[Lfind a dwelling place] for him, the God of Jacob*n* [2 Sam. 7]. 47But Solomon
was the one who built ·the Temple [La house for him; 1 Kin. 7–8].

48"But the Most High does not live in houses that people build with
their hands. As the prophet says:

49'Heaven is my throne,
and the earth is my footstool.
·So do you think you can build a house [LWhat kind of house will you
build] for me? says the Lord.
·Do I need a place to rest [LOr what is my resting place]?
50·Remember, my hand made [LDid not my hand make…?] all these
things [Is. 66:1–2]!'"

51Stephen continued speaking: "You ·stubborn [Lstiff-necked] people!
You have ·not given your hearts to God, nor will you listen to him
[Luncircumcised hearts and ears]! You are always ·against [resisting] what
the Holy Spirit is trying to tell you, just as your ·ancestors [forefathers;
fathers] were. 52Was there ever a prophet your ·ancestors [forefathers;
fathers] did not ·try to hurt [persecute]? They even killed ·the prophets
[Lthose] who ·predicted [foretold; announced beforehand] the coming of
the ·One who is good [Righteous One; CJesus the Messiah]. And now you
have ·turned against [betrayed] and ·killed [murdered] the ·One who is

7:46 God of Jacob Some Greek copies read "for (or, with) the house of Jacob." This means the people of Israel.

good [Righteous One]. 53You received the law of Moses, which God gave you through his angels [Gal. 3:19; Heb. 2:2], but you haven't obeyed it."

Stephen Is Killed

54When the leaders heard this, they became furious [Lin their hearts]. They were so mad they were ·grinding [gnashing] their teeth at Stephen. 55But Stephen was full of the Holy Spirit. He looked up to heaven and saw the glory of God and Jesus standing at God's right ·side [*or* hand; Cthe place of highest honor beside a king]. 56He said, "Look! I see heaven open and the Son of Man [Ca title for the Messiah; Dan. 7:13–14] standing at God's right ·side [*or* hand]." [CNormally portrayed as "sitting" at God's right side (Ps. 110:1), Jesus is standing either to give testimony to Stephen's faithfulness, or to welcome him into God's presence.]

57Then they shouted loudly and covered their ears and all ·ran [rushed together; *or* rushed with one intent] at Stephen. 58They ·took [dragged] him out of the city and began to ·throw stones at him to kill [stone] him [Cthe customary way to execute a criminal]. And ·those who told lies against Stephen [*or* his accusers; those who provided testimony; Lthe witnesses] left their coats ·with [Lat the feet of] a young man named Saul [Clater known as Paul]. 59While they were ·throwing stones [stoning him], Stephen ·prayed [Lcalled out], "Lord Jesus, receive my spirit." 60He fell on his knees and cried in a loud voice, "Lord, do not hold this sin against them." After Stephen said this, he ·died [Lfell asleep; Cfor believers death is temporary, like sleep].

8 Saul ·agreed that the killing of Stephen was good [Lapproved of his execution/death].

Troubles for the Believers

On that day the church of Jerusalem began to be persecuted, and all the believers, except the apostles, were scattered throughout [Lthe countryside/regions of] Judea and Samaria [Cthe southern and central regions of Israel]. 2And some ·religious [devout; pious; godly] ·people [*or* men] buried Stephen and ·cried loudly [*or* mourned deeply] for him. 3[LBut] Saul ·was also trying to destroy [*or* began harassing/mistreating/doing harm to] the church, going from house to house, dragging ·out [*or* off] men and women and putting them in ·jail [prison]. 4But wherever the believers were scattered, they told people the ·Good News [Gospel].

Philip Preaches in Samaria

5Philip [Cone of the seven leaders chosen to serve; 6:5; 21:8] went to ·the city[n] [*or* a city; *or* the main city] of Samaria [Cperhaps the city of Sebaste, known in ancient times as Samaria] and ·preached about [proclaimed] the ·Christ [Messiah]. 6When the ·people [Lcrowds] there heard Philip and saw the ·miracles [signs] he was doing, they all [Lwith one accord/mind] listened carefully to what he said. 7Many of these people had ·evil [Lunclean; 5:16] spirits in them, but Philip made the evil spirits ·leave [come out]. The spirits made a loud ·noise [cry] when they came out. Philip also healed many ·weak [paralyzed] and ·crippled [lame] people there. 8So the people in that city were ·very happy [joyful; greatly rejoicing].

9But there was a man named Simon in that city. ·Before Philip came there, [LPreviously] Simon had practiced ·magic [sorcery] and amazed all the people of Samaria. He ·bragged and called himself [Lsaid he was] a great man. 10All the people—·the least important and the most important [Lfrom the smallest to the greatest]—paid attention to Simon, saying, "This man has the power of God, called '·the Great Power [LGreat]'!"

8:5 a city Some Greek copies read "a city."

11Simon had amazed them with his ·magic [sorcery] so long that the people ·became his followers [Lpaid attention to him]. 12But when Philip told them the ·Good News [Gospel] about the kingdom of God and the ·power [Lname] of Jesus Christ, men and women believed Philip and were baptized. 13Simon himself believed, and after he was baptized, he stayed very close to Philip. When he saw the ·miracles [signs] and the powerful things Philip did, Simon was amazed.

14When the apostles who were still in Jerusalem heard that the people of Samaria [8:1] had ·accepted [received] the word of God, they sent Peter and John to them. 15When Peter and John arrived, they prayed that the Samaritan believers might receive the Holy Spirit. 16These people had [Lonly] been baptized in the name of the Lord Jesus, but the Holy Spirit had not yet ·come [Lfallen] upon any of them. 17Then, when ·the two apostles [Lthey] began ·laying [placing] their hands on the people [Ca ritual of blessing and/or conferring of authority], they received the Holy Spirit.

18Simon saw that the Spirit was given to people when the apostles ·laid [placed] their hands on them. So he offered the apostles money, 19saying, "Give me also this power so that anyone on whom I ·lay [place] my hands will receive the Holy Spirit."

20Peter said to him, "·You and your money should both be destroyed [LMay your silver perish with you], because you thought you could ·buy [get; obtain] God's gift with money. 21You ·cannot [Lhave no part or] share with us in this ·work [ministry; Lthing; word] since your heart is not right before God. 22·Change your heart! Turn away from [LRepent of] this evil thing you have done, and pray to the Lord. Maybe he will forgive you for ·thinking this [Lthe intent of your heart]. 23[LFor] I see that you are full of ·bitter jealousy [Lthe gall/bile of bitterness; Ca metaphor; gall is a bitter fluid; Deut. 29:18] and ·ruled by sin [Lin bondage to wickedness/unrighteousness]."

24Simon answered, "Both of you pray for me to the Lord so the things you have said will not happen to me."

25After ·Peter and John [Lthey] ·told the people what they had seen Jesus do [Ltestified; bore witness] and after they had spoken the ·message [word] of the Lord, they went back to Jerusalem. On the way, they went through many Samaritan ·towns [villages] and preached the ·Good News [Gospel] to the people.

Philip Teaches an Ethiopian

26An angel of the Lord said to Philip, "Get ·ready [up] and go ·south [*or* at about noon] to the road that leads down to Gaza from Jerusalem [Ca distance of about fifty miles]—the ·desert [wilderness] road." 27So Philip got ·ready [up] and went. On the road he saw a man from Ethiopia [Cnot present-day Ethiopia (Abyssinia), but Nubia in northern Sudan], a eunuch [*or* court official; Croyal servants were sometimes made eunuchs (castrated males), especially if they served in the presence of females]. He was an important officer in the service of ·Candace [*or* the Kandáke; Ca title, not a name, meaning "queen"], the queen of the Ethiopians; he was responsible for ·taking care of all her money [her entire treasury]. He had gone to Jerusalem to worship. 28Now, as he was on his way home, he was sitting in his chariot reading from the ·Book of Isaiah, the prophet [Lthe prophet Isaiah]. 29The Spirit said to Philip, "Go to that chariot and ·stay near [join] it."

30So when Philip ran toward the chariot, he heard the man reading from Isaiah the prophet [Cancient peoples generally read aloud]. Philip asked, "Do you understand what you are reading?"

31He answered, "How can I understand unless someone ·explains it to [guides; directs] me?" Then he ·invited [urged] Philip to climb in and sit with him. 32The portion of Scripture he was reading was this:

"He was like a sheep being led to ·be killed [Lthe slaughter].
He was quiet, as a lamb is quiet ·while its wool is being cut [Lbefore its shearer];
he never opened his mouth.
33 He was shamed and was treated ·unfairly [unjustly].
·He died without children to continue his family [LWho can describe his generation?; Chaving no descendants was a mark of shame and failure].
[LFor] His life on earth ·has ended [was taken away; Is. 53:7–8]."

34The ·officer [Leunuch] said to Philip, "Please tell me, who is the prophet talking about—himself or someone else [Cthe idea of a suffering messiah was not commonly understood in Judaism]?" 35Philip ·began to speak [Lopened his mouth], and starting with this same Scripture, he told the man the ·Good News [Gospel] about Jesus.

36While they were traveling down the road, they came to some water. The ·officer [Leunuch] said, "Look, here is water. What is ·stopping [preventing] me from being baptized?" |37Philip answered, "If you believe with all your heart, you can." The officer said, "I believe that Jesus Christ is the Son of God."|n 38Then the officer commanded the chariot to stop. Both Philip and the ·officer [Leunuch] went down into the water, and Philip baptized him. 39When they came up out of the water, the Spirit of the Lord ·took [snatched; carried] Philip away; the officer ·never [*or* no longer] saw him again. And the ·officer [Leunuch] continued on his way home, ·full of joy [rejoicing]. 40But Philip ·appeared [*or* found himself; Lwas found] in a city called Azotus [Canother name for Ashdod, just to the north of Gaza] and ·preached [proclaimed] the ·Good News [Gospel] in all the towns on the way from Azotus to Caesarea [Ca city further north up the coast].

Saul Is Converted

9 ·In Jerusalem [LBut; Meanwhile] Saul was still ·threatening [Lbreathing threats against] the ·followers [disciples] of the Lord by saying he would kill them. So he went to the high priest [Cprobably Caiaphas; 4:6] 2and asked him to write letters to the synagogues in the city of Damascus [Cin Syria, 135 miles north of Jerusalem]. Then if Saul found any ·followers of Christ's Way [*or* who belonged to the Way; Ca name for the Christian movement], men or women, he would ·arrest [take them prisoner; Lbind] them and bring them back to Jerusalem.

3So Saul headed toward Damascus. As he came near the city, a bright light from heaven suddenly flashed around him [Cin the OT lightning sometimes signaled the appearance of God; Ex. 19:16]. 4Saul fell to the ground and heard a voice saying to him, "Saul, Saul! Why are you persecuting me?"

5Saul said, "Who are you, ·Lord [*or* sir]?"

The voice answered, "I am Jesus, whom you are persecuting. 6Get up now and go into the city. ·Someone there will tell you [LYou will be told] what you must do."

7The ·people [men] traveling with Saul stood there ·but said nothing [speechless; *or* unable to speak]. They heard the voice, but they saw no one. 8Saul got up from the ground and opened his eyes, but he could not

---

8:37 Philip . . . God." Some Greek copies do not contain the bracketed text.

see. So those with Saul took his hand and led him into Damascus. 9For three days Saul could not see and did not eat or drink.

10There was a ·follower of Jesus [Ldisciple] in Damascus named Ananias [22:12]. The Lord spoke to Ananias in a vision, "Ananias!"

Ananias answered, "Here I am, Lord."

11The Lord said to him, "Get up and go to Straight Street [Cthe main east-west street of the city]. Find the house of Judas [Cnot either of Jesus' disciples by that name; Judas was a common name], and ask for a man named Saul from the city of Tarsus [Ca town in Cilicia, a Roman province in southeastern Asia Minor (present-day Turkey)]. He is there now, praying. 12Saul has seen a vision in which a man named Ananias comes to him and ·lays [places] his hands on him. Then he is able to see again."

13But Ananias answered, "Lord, many people have told me about this man and the ·terrible [evil; harmful] things he did to your ·holy people [saints] in Jerusalem. 14Now he has come here to Damascus, and the ·leading [Tchief] priests have given him the ·power [authority] to ·arrest [bind] everyone who ·worships you [Lcalls on your name]."

15But the Lord said to Ananias, "Go! ·I have chosen Saul for an important work [LFor he is my chosen instrument/vessel]. ·He must tell about me [L…to take/carry my name] to the ·Gentiles [nations], to kings, and to the people of Israel. 16[LFor] I will show him how much he must suffer for my name."

17So Ananias went to the house of Judas. He ·laid [placed] his hands on Saul and said, "Brother Saul, the Lord Jesus sent me. He is the one ·you saw [Lwho appeared to you] on the road on your way here. He sent me so that you can see again and be filled with the Holy Spirit." 18Immediately, something that looked like ·fish scales [*or* flakes] fell from Saul's eyes, and he was able to see again! Then Saul got up and was baptized. 19After he ate some food, his strength returned.

Saul Preaches in Damascus

Saul stayed with the ·followers of Jesus [disciples] in Damascus for ·a few [several; some] days. 20·Soon [Immediately; At once] he began to ·preach about [proclaim] Jesus in the synagogues, saying, "·Jesus [LThis one; He] is the Son of God."

21All the people who heard him were amazed. They said, "·This is [LIsn't this…?] the man who was in Jerusalem ·trying to destroy [raising havoc for; attacking] those who ·trust in [*or* worship; Lcall on] this name [Cthe name of Jesus; the name represents the person]! He came here to ·arrest [bind] them and take them back to the ·leading [Tchief] priests."

22But Saul grew more ·powerful [capable; effective]. His proofs that Jesus is the Christ were so strong that ·his own people [Lthe Jews who lived] in Damascus ·could not argue with [were baffled/confounded by] him.

23·After many days [*or* Some time later], ·they [Lthe Jews] ·made plans [plotted] to kill Saul. 24They were watching the city gates day and night [Lin order to kill him], but Saul learned about their ·plan [plot]. 25One night some ·followers [disciples] of Saul helped him leave the city by lowering him in a basket through an opening in the city wall [2 Cor. 11:32–33].

Saul Preaches in Jerusalem

26When Saul went to Jerusalem [Gal. 1:18], he tried to ·join [associate with] the ·group of followers [disciples], but they were all afraid of him. They did not believe he was really a ·follower [disciple]. 27But Barnabas ·accepted [*or* took hold of] Saul and took him to the apostles. Barnabas explained to them that Saul had seen the Lord on the road and the Lord had spoken to Saul. Then he told them how ·boldly [fearlessly] Saul had preached in the name of Jesus in Damascus.

28 And so Saul stayed with the ·followers [disciples], ·going everywhere [*or* going around openly with them; Lgoing in and going out] in Jerusalem, preaching ·boldly [fearlessly] in the name of the Lord. 29 He would often talk and ·argue [debate] with the ·Jewish people who spoke Greek [LHellenists; CJews who spoke Greek and had returned to Israel after living abroad], but they were trying to kill him. 30 When the ·followers [Lbrothers] learned about this, they took Saul to Caesarea [Ccity on the Mediterranean coast] and from there sent him to Tarsus [9:11].

31 [Then; *or* Therefore] The church everywhere in Judea, Galilee, and Samaria [Careas that comprise ancient Israel] had a time of peace and ·became stronger [Lwas built up/edified]. ·Respecting the Lord by the way they lived [LWalking in the fear of the Lord], and being ·encouraged [comforted; exhorted] by the Holy Spirit, ·the group of believers [Lit] continued to grow.

Peter Heals Aeneas

32 As Peter was traveling through all the area, he ·visited [Lcame down also to] ·God's people [the saints] who lived in Lydda [COT Lod, 25 miles northwest of Jerusalem; 1 Chr. 8:12–13]. 33 There he ·met [Lfound] a man named Aeneas, who was paralyzed and had not been able to leave his ·bed [cot; mat] for the past eight years. 34 Peter said to him, "Aeneas, Jesus ·Christ [*or* the Messiah] heals you. Stand up and ·make your bed [roll up your mat; *or* prepare yourself a meal; Cthe idiom "spread for yourself" probably refers to his bed, but could refer to food]." Aeneas stood up immediately. 35 All the people living in Lydda and on ·the Plain of Sharon [LSharon; Cthe coastal plain] saw him and turned to the Lord.

Peter Heals Tabitha

36 In the city of Joppa [Con the Mediterranean coast, 35 miles northwest of Jerusalem; present-day Jaffa] there was a ·follower [disciple] named Tabitha (whose Greek name was Dorcas [Cboth mean "gazelle"]). She was always doing good deeds and ·kind acts [acts of charity; Lgiving alms]. 37 ·While Peter was in Lydda [LIn those days], Tabitha became sick and died. Her body was washed [Ca custom of preparation for burial] and put in a room upstairs. 38 Since Lydda is near Joppa and the ·followers [disciples] in Joppa heard that Peter was in Lydda, they sent two ·messengers [Lmen] to Peter. They begged him, "Hurry, please come to us!" 39 So Peter got ·ready [Lup] and went with them. When he arrived, they took him to the upstairs room where all the widows stood around Peter, crying. They showed him the ·shirts [tunics] and coats [clothing; garments; robes] ·Tabitha [LDorcas] had made when she was ·still alive [Lwith them]. 40 Peter sent everyone out of the room and kneeled and prayed. Then he turned to the body and said, "Tabitha, stand up." She opened her eyes, and when she saw Peter, she sat up. 41 He gave her his hand and helped her up. Then he called the believers and the widows into the room and showed them that Tabitha was alive. 42 People everywhere in Joppa learned about this, and many believed in the Lord. 43 Peter stayed in Joppa for many days with a man named Simon who was a tanner [*or* Simon Byrseus; C*Byrseus* means "tanner" (someone who works with animal skins), but could be a name or an occupation; the occupation was considered unclean by Jews since it involved the bodies of dead animals].

Peter Teaches Cornelius

10 **At Caesarea** [Ca coastal city, 25 miles south of Mount Carmel;
a center of Roman government for Palestine] **there was a man
named Cornelius, ·an officer** [La centurion; Can officer in charge of
about a hundred soldiers] **in the Italian ·group of the Roman army**
[Lcohort; regiment; Ca cohort was about six hundred soldiers]. **2Cornelius
was a ·religious** [pious; godly] **man. He and all ·the other people who
lived in his house** [his household] **·worshiped the true God** [Lfeared God;
C"God-fearers" were Gentiles who worshiped the one true God of Israel].
He gave much of his money to ·the poor [*or* the Jewish people; Lthe peo-
ple] **and prayed to God often. 3·One afternoon about three o'clock**
[LAbout the ninth hour of the day], **Cornelius clearly saw a vision. An
angel of God came to him and said, "Cornelius!"**
4Cornelius stared at the angel. He ·became afraid [was terrified] **and
said, "What do you want, ·Lord** [*or* sir]**?"**
**The angel said, "·God has heard your prayers. He has seen that you give
to the poor, and he remembers you** [LYour prayers and your alms have
gone up to God as a memorial/memorial offering]. **5Send some men now
to Joppa** [9:36] **to bring back a man named Simon who is also called
Peter. 6He is staying** [as a guest] **with a man, ·also named Simon, who is a
tanner** [*or* named Simon Byrseus; 9:43] **and has a house beside the sea."
7When the angel who spoke to Cornelius left, Cornelius called two of his
·servants** [household slaves/servants] **and a soldier, a ·religious** [devout;
pious; godly] **man who ·worked for him** [*or* was on his staff; *or* was loyal
to him]. **8Cornelius explained everything to them and sent them to Joppa.**
9About ·noon [Lthe sixth hour] **the next day as they ·came near Joppa**
[Ljourneyed and drew near the city], **Peter was going up to the roof** [Cin
ancient Israel flat roofs were used as living spaces and for storage] **to pray.
10He was hungry and wanted to eat, but while the food was being prepared, he ·had a vision** [*or* fell into a trance]. **11He saw heaven opened and
·something** [an object] **coming down that looked like a big sheet being
lowered to earth by its four corners. 12In it were all kinds of ·animals**
[Lfour-footed creatures], **reptiles, and birds** [Lof the air/sky]. **13Then a
voice said to Peter, "Get up, Peter; kill and eat."**
14But Peter said, "·No [Absolutely not], **Lord! I have never eaten food
that is ·unholy** [profane; common] **or ·unclean** [ritually defiled; Cthe OT
food laws differentiated Israelites from Gentiles; Lev. 11; Ezek. 4:13–15]**."**
**15But the voice said to him again, "God has made these things clean, so
don't call them ·'unholy'** ['profane'; 'common']**!" 16This happened three
times, and at once the ·sheet** [Lobject; thing] **was taken back to heaven.**
17While Peter was ·wondering [perplexed about] **what this vision
meant,** [Llook; Tbehold] **the men Cornelius sent had found Simon's house
and were standing at the gate. 18They asked, "Is ·Simon Peter** [LSimon
who is called Peter] **staying** [as a guest] **here?"**
**19While Peter was still thinking about the vision, the Spirit said to him,
"·Listen** [LLook; TBehold], **three men are looking for you. 20**[So; LBut] **Get
up and go downstairs. Go with them without ·doubting** [*or* hesitation],
because I have sent them to you."
**21So Peter went down to the men and said, "I am the one you are ·look-
ing** [searching] **for. Why did you come here?"**
22They said, "A holy angel spoke to Cornelius, ·an army officer [La cen-
turion] **and a ·good** [righteous] **man; he ·worships** [Lfears] **God. ·All the
people** [LThe whole Jewish nation] **·respect** [speak well of; Ltestify to] **him.**

The angel told Cornelius to ask you to come to his house so that he can
hear what you have to say." 23So Peter ·asked [invited] the men to come in
and ·spend the night [Lentertained them as guests; Can unusual gesture,
since Jews would not normally invite Gentiles into their homes].

The next day Peter got ·ready [up] and went with them, and some of
the ·followers [Jewish believers; Lbrothers] from Joppa joined him. 24On
the following day they came to Caesarea [10:1]. Cornelius was ·waiting
for [expecting] them and had called together his relatives and close
friends. 25When Peter entered, Cornelius met him, fell at his feet, and
worshiped him. 26But Peter helped him up, saying, "Stand up. I too am
only a ·human [mortal]." 27As he talked with Cornelius, Peter went inside
where he ·saw [Lfound] many people gathered. 28He said, "You people
understand that it is against our law for Jewish people to associate with or
visit anyone who is a ·foreigner [Gentile]. But God has shown me that I
should not call any person unholy [profane; common] or unclean
[defiled]. 29That is why I did not ·argue [object] when I was asked to come
here. Now, please tell me why you sent for me."

30Cornelius said, "Four days ago [10:3], I was praying in my house at
this same time—·three o'clock in the afternoon [Lat the ninth hour].
Suddenly, there was a man standing before me wearing ·shining [dazzling]
clothes. 31He said, 'Cornelius, God has heard your prayer and ·has seen
that you give to the poor and remembers you [Lyour alms have been
remembered by/before God]. 32So send some men to Joppa and ask Simon
[Lwho is called] Peter to come. Peter is staying [as a guest] in the house of
a man, ·also named Simon, who is a tanner [*or* named Simon Byrseus;
9:43] and has a house beside the sea [see 10:5–6].' 33So I sent for you immediately, and it was ·very good [kind] of you to come. Now we are all here
·before [in the presence of; *or* available to] God to hear everything the Lord
has commanded you to tell us."

34Peter ·began to speak [Lopened his mouth]: "I ·really [truly] understand now that ·to God every person is the same [God does not show
favoritism/partiality]. 35[LBut] In every ·country [nation] God accepts anyone who ·worships [Lfears] him and ·does what is right [practices
righteousness]. 36You know the ·message [word] that God has sent to the
people of Israel ·is the Good News that peace [announcing/proclaiming the
Gospel of peace that] has come through Jesus Christ. Jesus is the Lord of all
people [Cboth Jews and Gentiles]! 37You know what has happened all over
Judea, beginning in Galilee after John [Cthe Baptist] preached to the people
about baptism [Luke 3]. 38You know about Jesus from Nazareth, that God
·gave him [Lanointed him with] the Holy Spirit and power. You know how
Jesus went everywhere doing good and healing those who were ·ruled
[oppressed] by the devil, because God was with him. 39We ·saw [witnessed]
what Jesus did in [Lthe region/country of] Judea and in Jerusalem, but ·the
Jews in Jerusalem [Lthey] killed him by hanging him on a ·cross [Ltree].
40Yet, on the third day, God raised Jesus ·to life [*or* from the dead] and
caused him to be seen, 41not by all the people, but only by the witnesses
God had already chosen. And we are those witnesses who ate and drank
with him after he was raised from the dead. 42He ·told [commanded] us to
preach to the people and to ·tell them [testify; bear witness] that he is the
one whom God ·chose [appointed; determined] to be the judge of the living
and the dead. 43All the prophets ·say it is true [witnessed; testified] that all
who believe in Jesus will be forgiven of their sins through Jesus' name."

44While Peter was still saying ·this [[L]these words], the Holy Spirit ·came
down [[L]fell] on all those who ·were listening [[L]heard the word/message].
45The ·Jewish [[L]circumcised] believers who came with Peter were ·amazed
[astonished] that the gift of the Holy Spirit had been ·given [[L]poured out]
even to the ·nations [Gentiles]. 46[[L]For] ·These believers [[L]They] heard them
speaking in different languages [[L]tongues; [C]either other languages or ecstatic
utterance] and ·praising [magnifying] God. Then Peter said, 47"Can anyone
keep these people from being baptized with water? They have received the
Holy Spirit just as we did!" 48So Peter ordered that they be baptized in the
name of Jesus Christ. Then they asked Peter to stay with them for a few days.

Peter Returns to Jerusalem

11 The apostles and the ·believers [[L]brothers] in Judea heard
that some Gentiles had accepted ·God's teaching [[L]the word
of God] too. 2But when Peter ·came [went up] to Jerusalem, ·some people [[L]the circumcised; [C]Jewish Christians who believed that they should
continue to obey certain Jewish regulations] ·argued with [criticized]
him. 3They said, "You went into the homes of people who are not circumcised and ate with them!"

4So Peter ·started from the beginning [*or* began speaking] and explained
·the whole story [it in order/step by step] to them. 5He said, "I was in the city
of Joppa [9:36], and as I was praying, I had a vision while in a trance [10:10].
I saw ·something [[L]an object] that looked like a big sheet being lowered from
heaven by its four corners. It came very close to me. 6I looked [intently]
inside it and saw ·animals [[L]four-footed creatures], wild beasts, reptiles, and
birds [[L]of the sky/air]. 7I heard a voice say to me, 'Get up, Peter. Kill and eat.'
8But I said, '·No [Absolutely not], Lord! I have never eaten anything that is
unholy [profane; common] or ·unclean [ritually defiled; 10:14].' 9But the
voice from heaven spoke again, 'God has made these things clean, so don't
call them ·unholy [profane; common].' 10This happened three times. Then
the whole thing was ·taken back [*or* pulled up] to heaven. 11Right then
[[L]look; [T]behold] three men who were sent to me from Caesarea came to the
house where I was staying [10:17–19]. 12The Spirit told me to go with them
without ·doubting [*or* hesitation]. These six ·believers [[L]brothers] here also
·went with [accompanied] me, and we entered the house of ·Cornelius [[L]the
man]. 13He told us about the angel he saw standing in his house. The angel
said to him, 'Send some men to Joppa and ·invite [summon; send for] Simon
[[L]who is also called] Peter to come. 14By the ·words [message] he will say to
you, you and all your ·family [*or* household] will be saved.' 15When I began
·my speech [[L]to speak], the Holy Spirit ·came [[L]fell] on them just as he came
on us at the beginning. 16Then I remembered the words of the Lord. He said,
'John baptized ·with [*or* in] water, but you will be baptized ·with [*or* in; *or*
by] the Holy Spirit [1:5; Matt. 3:11; Mark 1:8; Luke 3:16].' 17[[L]Therefore]
Since God gave them the same gift he gave us who believed in the Lord Jesus
Christ, how could I ·stop [prevent; hinder] the work of God?"

18When ·the believers [[L]they] heard this, they ·stopped arguing [ceased
their objections; remained silent]. They ·praised [glorified] God and said,
"So God ·is allowing [has given] even ·other nations [the Gentiles] ·to
turn to him and live [[L]repentance (leading) to life]."

The Good News Comes to Antioch

19Many of the believers were scattered when they were persecuted after
Stephen was killed. Some of them went as far as Phoenicia [[C]northwest of
Israel on the coast], Cyprus [[C]an island to the west of the coast of Syria],
and Antioch [[C]an important city in Syria] telling the message to others,

but only to Jews. 20 Some of these believers were people from Cyprus and
Cyrene [C a city in North Africa]. When they came to Antioch, they spoke
also to ·Greeks[n] [*or* Hellenists (see textual note); C in 6:1 and 9:29 the word
refers to Greek-speaking Jews; here it refers to Greek-speaking Gentiles],
telling them the ·Good News [Gospel] about the Lord Jesus. 21 ·The Lord
was helping the believers [L The hand of the Lord was with them], and a
large group of people believed and turned to the Lord.

22 The church in Jerusalem heard about all of this, so they sent Barnabas
[4:36; 9:26–27] to Antioch. 23–24 Barnabas was a good man, full of the Holy
Spirit and full of faith. When he reached Antioch and saw ·how God had
blessed the people [L the grace of God], he ·was glad [rejoiced]. He ·encour-
aged [exhorted; urged] all the believers in Antioch always to ·obey [*or*
remain true to] the Lord with ·all their hearts [resolved/resolute hearts],
and many people ·became followers of [L were added to] the Lord.

25 Then Barnabas went to the city of Tarsus [C Paul's hometown in Cilicia;
9:11] to look for Saul, 26 and when he found Saul, he brought him to Antioch.
For a whole year Saul and Barnabas met with the church and taught many
people there. In Antioch the ·followers [disciples] were called Christians for
the first time [C highlighting that they were followers of Christ, and perhaps
that they were no longer viewed as merely a sect within Judaism].

27 ·About that time [L In those days] some prophets came [L down] from
Jerusalem to Antioch. 28 One of them, named Agabus [21:10], stood up
and spoke ·with the help of [by the power of; through] the Holy Spirit. He
said, "A severe famine is coming to the whole ·world [*or* inhabited world;
C probably meaning the Roman empire]." (This happened when Claudius
[C Roman emperor from AD 41–54] ruled.) 29 The ·followers [disciples] all
decided to ·help [send relief to; L send (something) as a ministry for] the
·believers [brothers] who lived in Judea, as much as each one could.
30 They ·gathered the money [L did this] and ·gave it to Barnabas and Saul,
who brought it to the elders in Judea [L sent it to the elders through the
hand of Barnabas and Saul].

Herod Agrippa Hurts the Church

12 During that same time King Herod [C Agrippa I, who lived 10
BC–AD 44; he was the grandson of Herod the Great (Luke
1:5)] ·began to mistreat [L laid hands on to harm/do evil to] some who
belonged to the church. 2 He ordered James, the brother of John, to be
killed by the sword [C execution by beheading]. 3 Herod saw that ·some of
the people liked this [L this pleased the Jews/Jewish leaders], so he decided
to arrest Peter, too. (This happened during the time of the Feast of
Unleavened Bread.)

4 After Herod ·arrested [seized] Peter, he put him in ·jail [prison] and
handed him over to be guarded by ·sixteen [L four squads of four] soldiers.
Herod planned to bring Peter ·before the people for trial [L to the people;
C an idiom for a public trial] after the Passover Feast. 5 So Peter was kept in
·jail [prison], but the church prayed earnestly to God for him.

Peter Released by an Angel

6 The night before Herod was to bring him ·to trial [L out; C either for
trial or for execution], Peter was sleeping between two soldiers, bound
with two chains. Other soldiers were guarding the door of the jail.
7 Suddenly, an angel of the Lord stood there, and a light shined in the cell.
The angel ·struck [tapped; poked] Peter on the side and woke him up.

11:20 Greeks Some Greek copies read "Hellenists," non-Greeks who spoke Greek.

"Hurry! Get up!" the angel said. And the chains fell off Peter's ·hands [wrists]. 8Then the angel told him, "·Get dressed [*or* Put on your belt] and put on your sandals." And Peter did. Then the angel said, "·Put on your coat [LWrap your coat/cloak around you] and follow me." 9So Peter followed him out, but he did not know if what the angel was doing was real; he thought he might be seeing a vision. 10They went past the first and second guards and came to the iron gate that ·separated them from [Lled to] the city. The gate opened by itself for them, and they went through it. When they had walked down one street, the angel suddenly left him.

11Then Peter ·realized what had happened [came to himself]. He thought, "Now I know that the Lord really sent his angel to me. He rescued me ·from [Lfrom the hands of] Herod and from all the things the [LJewish] people thought would happen."

12When he ·considered [realized] this, he went to the home of Mary, the mother of John [Lwho was also called] Mark [12:25; 13:5; 15:37; Col. 4:10; 2 Tim. 4:11; Philem. 24; 1 Pet. 5:13]. Many people were gathered there, praying. 13Peter knocked on the ·outside door [*or* courtyard gate], and a servant girl named Rhoda came to answer it. 14When she recognized Peter's voice, she was so happy she forgot to open the ·door [gate]. Instead, she ran inside and told the group, "Peter is at the ·door [gate]!"

15They said to her, "You are ·crazy [insane; mad]!" But she kept on ·saying [insisting] it was true, so they said, "It must be Peter's angel."

16[LBut; Meanwhile] Peter continued to knock, and when they opened the door, they saw him and were ·amazed [astonished]. 17Peter ·made a sign [motioned] with his hand to tell them to be quiet. He ·explained [recounted] how the Lord led him out of the ·jail [prison], and he said, "Tell James [Cnot the son of Zebedee (who had been executed, 12:2), but the half-brother of Jesus, who would become the senior leader in the Jerusalem church; 15:13–21; 21:18] and the other ·believers [Lbrothers] what happened." Then he left to go to another place.

18The next ·day [*or* morning] ·the soldiers were very upset [Lthere was no small commotion among the soldiers; Csoldiers who allowed a prisoner to escape would suffer the prisoner's punishment] and wondered what had happened to Peter. 19Herod ·looked [searched] everywhere for him but could not find him. So he questioned the guards and ordered that they be ·killed [Lled away; Cpresumably to be executed].

The Death of Herod Agrippa

Later Herod ·moved [*or* took a trip] from Judea and went to the city of Caesarea, where he stayed. 20Herod was very angry with the people of Tyre and Sidon [Cmajor cities on the Phoenician coast north of Israel], but the people of those cities all ·came in a group [*or* agreed together to come] to him. After convincing Blastus, the ·king's personal servant [chamberlain; Lone in charge of his bedroom], to ·be on their side [*or* support their position], they asked Herod for peace, because their country got its food from his country.

21On ·a chosen [an appointed] day Herod put on his royal robes, sat on his ·throne [judgment seat; rostrum; platform], and made a speech to the people. 22They shouted, "This is the voice of a god, not a human!" 23Because Herod did not give the glory to God, an angel of the Lord immediately ·caused him to become sick [Lstruck him down], and he was ·eaten [*or* infected] by worms [Cperhaps intestinal roundworms] and died.

24God's ·message [word] continued to spread and reach people.

25 After Barnabas and Saul finished their ·task in Jerusalem [mission],
they returned to Antioch,[n] taking John [L also called] Mark with them.

Barnabas and Saul Are Chosen

13 1 In the church at Antioch there were these prophets and teachers: Barnabas [4:36], Simeon (also called Niger [C meaning
"Black"; Luke 23:26]), Lucius (from the city of Cyrene [C a city in North
Africa]), Manaen (who ·had grown up with Herod [*or* was a close friend of
Herod; *or* was a member of Herod's court], the ·ruler [L tetrarch; C a Roman
political title; see Luke 3:1]), and Saul. 2 They were all ·worshiping [*or* serv-
ing] the Lord and fasting [C giving up eating for spiritual purposes]. During
this time the Holy Spirit said to them, "Set apart for me Barnabas and
Saul to do ·a special [L the] work for which I have ·chosen [called] them."
3 So after they fasted and prayed, they laid their hands on [C a ritual of
blessing and/or conferring of authority] Barnabas and Saul and sent
them out.

Barnabas and Saul in Cyprus

4 Barnabas and Saul, sent out by the Holy Spirit, went to the city of
Seleucia [C a Syrian city 15 miles from Antioch]. From there they sailed to
the island of Cyprus [C an island off the coast of Syria, and Barnabas'
homeland; 4:36]. 5 When they came to Salamis [C the main city of Cyprus],
they preached the ·Good News [Gospel; L word] of God in the synagogues
[L of the Jews]. John Mark was ·with them to help [their assistant].
6 They went across the whole island to Paphos [C the capital city of
Cyprus, on the southwest coast] where they met a ·magician [sorcerer]
named Bar-Jesus [C meaning "son of Jesus/Joshua"]. He was a Jewish false
prophet 7 who ·always stayed close to [L was with; C perhaps an assistant or
advisor] Sergius Paulus, the ·governor [proconsul] and a ·smart [intelli-
gent; discerning] man. He asked Barnabas and Saul to come to him,
because he wanted to hear the ·message [L word] of God. 8 But Elymas, the
magician (that is what his name means), was against them [C Elymas probably comes either from an Arabic word meaning "wise man" or an Aramaic
word meaning "interpreter of dreams"—hence a "magician"]. He tried to
·stop [turn away] the ·governor [proconsul] from ·believing in Jesus [L the
faith]. 9 But Saul, who was also called Paul [C Saul was his Jewish name; Paul
his Roman name (both probably given at birth)], was filled with the Holy
Spirit. He looked ·straight [intently] at Elymas 10 and said, "You son of the
devil! You are an enemy of ·everything that is right [all righteousness]! You
are full of ·lies [deceit] and ·evil tricks [fraud; evil schemes], ·always trying
to change the Lord's truths into lies [L will you never stop making crooked/
perverting the straight paths of the Lord?]. 11 Now [L look; T behold] the
[L hand of the] Lord will touch you, and you will be blind. For a time you
will not be able to see anything—not even the light from the sun."
Then ·everything became dark for [L mist and darkness fell upon] Elymas,
and he walked around, trying to find someone to lead him by the hand.
12 When the ·governor [proconsul] saw this, he believed because he was
amazed at the teaching about the Lord.

Paul and Barnabas Leave Cyprus

13 Paul and ·those with him [his companions] sailed from Paphos [v. 6]
and came to Perga, in Pamphylia [C a Roman province in southern Turkey;
Perga was a major city]. There John Mark left them to return to Jerusalem
[15:38]. 14 They continued their trip from Perga and went to Antioch, a

12:25 to Antioch Some early Greek copies read "from Jerusalem." Others read "to Jerusalem."

city in Pisidia [Ca Roman province in southcentral Turkey; this Antioch
should not be confused with Antioch in Syria (11:19–20)]. On the Sabbath
day they went into the synagogue and sat down. 15 After the law of Moses
and the writings of the prophets were read [Cpart of the traditional synagogue service], the leaders of the synagogue sent a message to Paul and
Barnabas: "Brothers, if you have any ·message that will encourage the
people [Lword of encouragement/exhortation; Cthey are invited to give the
homily, or sermon], please speak."

16 Paul stood up, ·raised [*or* motioned with] his hand, and said, "·You
Israelites [Men, Israelites] and you who ·worship [Lfear] God [CGentiles
who worshiped the God of Israel; 10:2], please listen! 17 The God of the
Israelites chose our ·ancestors [Lfathers; CAbraham, Isaac, and Jacob; Gen.
12–36]. He made the people great during the time they lived [as foreign-
ers/aliens] in Egypt, and he brought them out of that country with ·great
power [La raised/uplifted arm]. 18 And he ·was patient with [put up with]
them[n] for forty years in the ·desert [wilderness; Ex. 16–Deut. 34]. 19 God
destroyed seven nations in the land of Canaan and gave the land to his
people [Las an inheritance]. 20 All this happened in about four hundred
fifty years [Ca round number of the time Israel was in Egypt, wandering in
the wilderness, and conquering the land].

"After this, God gave them judges [Judg. 1–21] until the time of Samuel
the prophet [1 Sam. 1:1—25:1; 28]. 21 Then the people asked for a king, so
God gave them Saul son of Kish. Saul was from the tribe of Benjamin and
was king for forty years [1 Sam. 8–2 Sam. 1]. 22 After God ·took him away
[removed/deposed him], God ·made David [Lraised up David as] their
king [2 Sam. 2–7]. God ·said [witnessed; testified] about him: 'I have
found in David son of Jesse ·the kind of man I want [a man whose heart
is like mine; Ta man after my own heart; 1 Sam. 13:14; Ps. 89:20]. He will
·do [*or* accomplish] all ·I want him to do [Lmy will].' 23 So God has brought
Jesus, one of David's ·descendants [Lseed], to Israel to be its Savior, as he
promised [2 Sam. 7:12–16; Is. 11:1–16]. 24 Before Jesus came, John [Cthe
Baptist] preached to all the people of Israel about a baptism of ·changed
hearts and lives [Lrepentance; Matt. 3; Mark 1:2–8; Luke 3]. 25 When he
was finishing his ·work [race; course; mission], he said, 'Who do you think
I am? I am not ·the Christ [the Messiah; Lhe; Cthe anointed king from
David's line]. He is coming later, and I am not worthy to untie his sandals
[Ca gesture of subservience fit for a slave].'

26 "·Brothers, [LMen, brothers] ·sons [*or* descendants] of the family of
Abraham, and others who ·worship [fear; 13:16] God, listen! The ·news
[word; message] about this salvation has been sent to us. 27 Those who live
in Jerusalem and their leaders ·did not realize that Jesus was the Savior
[Lwere ignorant of this; *or* did not recognize him]. They did not understand the ·words that the prophets wrote [Lvoices of the prophets], which
are read every Sabbath day. But they ·made them come true [Lfulfilled
them] when they ·said Jesus was guilty [Lcondemned him]. 28 They could
not find any real ·reason [cause; basis] for Jesus to be put to death, but
they asked Pilate to have him ·killed [executed]. 29 When they had done to
him all that ·the Scriptures had said [Lwas written about him], they took
him down from the ·cross [Ltree; 5:30; 10:39; Deut. 21:23; Gal. 3:13] and
laid him in a tomb. 30 But God raised him up from the dead! 31 After this,

13:18 And . . . them Some Greek copies read "And he cared for them."

for many days, ·those who had gone with Jesus from Galilee to Jerusalem
saw him [*or* he appeared to those…Jerusalem]. They are now his witnesses to the people. 32We tell you the ·Good News [Gospel] about the
promise God made to our ·ancestors [forefathers; fathers; Gen. 12:1–3; 2
Sam. 7:12–16]. 33·God has made this promise come true [He has fulfilled
this promise] for us, their ·children [descendants], by raising Jesus from
the dead. We read about this also in the second psalm:

'You are my Son.
Today I have ·become your Father [fathered you; Tbegotten you;
Ps. 2:7].'

34God raised Jesus from the dead, and he will never go back to ·the grave
and become dust [Lcorruption; decay]. So God said:

'I will give you the holy and ·sure blessings [Lfaithful things]
that I promised to David [Is. 55:3].'

35But in another place God says:

'You will not let your Holy One ·experience [Lsee] ·decay [corruption;
Ps. 16:10].'

36[LFor; Now] David ·did God's will [served God's purpose] during his
·lifetime [Lgeneration]. Then he ·died [Lslept; Ca euphemism for death]
and was ·buried [Lplaced] beside his ·ancestors [Lfathers], and his body
·experienced [Lsaw] ·decay [corruption] in the grave. 37But the One God
raised from the dead did not ·experience [Lsee] ·decay [corruption].
38[LTherefore] ·Brothers [LMen, brothers], ·understand what we are telling you [know this]: ·You can have forgiveness of your sins [LForgiveness
of sins is announced to you] through ·Jesus [Lthis man]. 39The law of
Moses could not ·free you from your sins [justify you; make you righ-
teous]. But through Jesus everyone who believes is ·free from all sins
[justified; made/declared righteous]. 40[LSo; Therefore] ·Be careful [Watch
out]! Don't let what the prophets said happen to you:

41'·Listen [LLook; TBehold], you ·people who doubt [scoffers; mockers]!
·You can wonder [Be amazed], and then ·die [Lperish; vanish].
I ·will do something [Lam working a work] in your ·lifetime [Ldays]
that you won't believe even when you are told about it [Hab. 1:5]!'"

42While ·Paul and Barnabas [Lthey] were leaving the synagogue, the
people ·asked [urged; encouraged] them to tell them more about these
things on the next Sabbath. 43When the meeting was over, many of the
Jews and devout ·converts to Judaism [Lproselytes] followed Paul and
Barnabas from that place. Paul and Barnabas were persuading them to
continue trusting in God's grace.

44On the next Sabbath day, almost everyone in the city ·came [gathered]
to hear the word of the Lord. 45Seeing the crowd, the Jewish people became
very jealous and said ·insulting [blasphemous] things and ·argued against
[contradicted] what Paul said. 46But Paul and Barnabas spoke very ·boldly
[fearlessly; courageously], saying, "·We must [It was necessary for us to]
speak the ·message [word] of God to you first. But [Lsince] you ·refuse to
listen [*or* reject it]. You are judging yourselves not worthy of having eternal life! So we will now ·go [Lturn] to the ·people of other nations [Gentiles].
47[LFor] This is what the Lord ·told us to do [commanded us], saying:

'I have ·made [appointed] you a light for the ·nations [Gentiles];
·you will show people all over the world the way to be saved [Lto
bring salvation to the ends of the earth; Is. 42:6; 49:6; Acts 1:8].'"

48When the Gentiles heard Paul say this, they ·were happy [rejoiced]

and ·gave honor to [praised] **the ·message** [word] **of the Lord. And the**
people who were ·chosen [destined; appointed] **to have life forever**
·believed the message [Lbelieved].
49So the ·message [word] **of the Lord was spreading through the whole**
·country [area; region]. **50But the Jewish people ·stirred up** [incited] **some**
of the ·important religious women [devout/God-fearing women of high
social status] **and the ·leaders** [*or* prominent men] **of the city. They**
·started trouble [stirred up persecution] **against Paul and Barnabas and**
forced them out of their ·area [region]. **51So Paul and Barnabas shook the**
dust off their feet [Ca sign of rejection and protest] **and went to Iconium**
[Ca city in the interior of south central Asia Minor, present-day Turkey].
52But the ·followers [disciples] **were filled with joy and the Holy Spirit.**

Paul and Barnabas in Iconium

14 In Iconium [13:51], **·Paul and Barnabas** [Lthey] **went as usual to**
the Jewish synagogue [Cthey typically appealed to their fellow
Jews first]. **They spoke ·so well** [Lin such a way] **that a great many Jews and**
Greeks believed. 2But the Jews who did not believe ·excited [stirred up] **the**
Gentiles and ·turned them [poisoned their minds; Lharmed/did evil to
their souls] **against the ·believers** [Lbrothers (and sisters)]. 3 [LSo; Therefore]
·Paul and Barnabas [LThey] **stayed in Iconium a long time and spoke**
·bravely [*or* boldly] **for the Lord. He ·showed** [testified; confirmed] **that**
their ·message [word] **about his grace was true by giving them the power**
to work [miraculous] **signs and ·miracles** [wonders]. **4But** [Lthe people/
population of] **the city was divided. Some of the people agreed with the**
Jews, and others ·believed [Lwere with] **the apostles.**
5Some Gentiles, some Jews, and some of their rulers ·wanted [intended;
plotted] **to mistreat Paul and Barnabas and to stone them to death.**
6When ·Paul and Barnabas [Lthey] **learned about this, they ·ran away**
[fled; escaped] **to Lystra** [Ceighteen miles south of Iconium] **and Derbe**
[Csixty miles southeast from Lystra], **cities in Lycaonia** [Cthe administrative district], **and to the areas around those cities. 7They ·announced the**
Good News [preached the Gospel] **there, too.**

Paul in Lystra and Derbe

8In Lystra [v. 6] **there sat a man who had been ·born crippled** [Llame from
the womb of his mother]; **he had never walked. 9As this man was listening to**
Paul speak, Paul looked straight at him and saw that he ·believed [had faith
that] **God could heal him. 10So he ·cried out** [Lsaid with a loud voice], **"Stand**
up on your feet!" The man jumped up and began walking around. 11When
the crowds saw what Paul did, they shouted in the Lycaonian language, "The
gods have ·become like humans [*or* taken on human form] **and have come**
down to us!" 12Then the people began to call Barnabas "Zeus" [Cmain god of
the Greek pantheon] **and Paul "Hermes,"** [Cthe Greek god who delivered
messages] **because he was the main speaker. 13The priest in the temple of**
Zeus, which was ·near [*or* beside; at the entrance of] **the city, brought some**
·bulls [*or* oxen] **and ·flowers** [garlands; wreaths] **to the ·gates** [temple gates;
or city gates; Cbut it is doubtful that Lystra had city walls at this time]. **He and**
the people wanted to offer a sacrifice to Paul and Barnabas. 14But when the
apostles, Barnabas and Paul, heard about it, they tore their clothes
[Cindicating outrage or sorrow]. **They ran in among the people, shouting,**
15"·Friends [LMen], **why are you doing these things? We are only human**
beings ·like [of the same nature as] **you. We are bringing you the ·Good**
News [Gospel] **and are telling you to turn away from these worthless things**
and turn to the living God. He is the One who made the sky, the earth, the

sea, and everything in them [Ex. 20:11; Ps. 146:6]. 16In the past [Lgenerations],
God let all the nations ·do what they wanted [Lgo their own way]. 17Yet he
·proved he is real [Lhas not left himself without a witness] by ·showing kindness [doing good], by giving you rain from heaven and crops at the right
·times [seasons], by ·giving you [satisfying/filling you with] food and filling
your hearts with joy [Ps. 104:13–15]." 18Even with these words, they were
barely able to keep the crowd from offering sacrifices to them.

19Then some Jews [Cthose who had opposed them earlier; 13:50–51;
14:2, 5] came from Antioch and Iconium and persuaded the people to
turn against Paul. So they threw stones at him [2 Cor. 11:25; Cstoning was
the main Jewish method of execution] and dragged him out of town,
thinking they had killed him. 20But the ·followers [disciples] ·gathered
around him [*or* surrounded him; Ceither to protect from further attack or
to check on his condition], and he got up and went back into the town
[Cperhaps a miracle; certainly evidence of Paul's perseverance]. The next
day he and Barnabas left and went to the city of Derbe [v. 6].

The Return to Antioch in Syria

21·Paul and Barnabas [LThey] ·told the Good News [preached the
Gospel] in Derbe, and many became ·followers [disciples]. ·Paul and
Barnabas [LThey] returned to Lystra [14:6], Iconium, and Antioch,
22·making the followers of Jesus stronger [Lstrengthening the souls/lives of
the disciples] and ·helping them stay [Lencouraging/exhorting them to
remain/persevere] in the faith. They said, "We must ·suffer many things
[endure/pass through many trials/persecutions] to enter God's kingdom."
23They ·chose [appointed; *or* elected] elders [1 Tim. 5:17–20; Titus 1:5–9]
for each church, ·by [after; Lwith] praying and fasting [Cgiving up eating
for spiritual purposes]. These elders had ·trusted [believed in] the Lord,
so Paul and Barnabas ·put them in [committed them to] the Lord's care.

24Then they went through Pisidia [13:14] and came to Pamphylia
[13:13]. 25When they had ·preached the message [Lspoken the word] in
Perga [13:13], they went down to Attalia [Ceight miles southwest of Perga].
26And from there they sailed away to Antioch [Cin Syria about 400 miles
away] where ·the believers had put them into God's care [Lthey had been
delivered over to God's grace] to do the work that they had now ·finished
[completed; fulfilled].

27When they arrived in Antioch, ·Paul and Barnabas [Lthey] gathered
the church together. They ·told [reported/recounted to] the church all
about what God had done with them and how God had ·made it possible
for the Gentiles to believe [Lopened a door of faith to the Gentiles]. 28And
they stayed there ·a long [a considerable; Lno little] time with the ·follow-
ers [disciples].

The Meeting in Jerusalem

15 Then some people came to Antioch from Judea and began
teaching the Gentile believers [Lbrothers (and sisters)]: "You
cannot be saved if you are not circumcised ·as Moses taught us [Laccording
to the custom of Moses; compare Gen. 17:9–14]." 2Paul and Barnabas
·were against this teaching and argued [Lhad no small argument and
debate] with them about it. So the church ·decided to send [commis-
sioned; appointed] Paul, Barnabas, and some others to Jerusalem where
they could talk more about this disagreement with the apostles and elders.

3The church ·helped them leave [sent them] on the trip, and they went
through the countries of Phoenicia and Samaria, telling all about ·how
the other nations had turned to God [Lthe conversion of the Gentiles].

This made all the ·believers [Lbrothers (and sisters)] very ·happy [joyful].
4When they arrived in Jerusalem, they were welcomed by the apostles, the
elders, and the church. They told about everything God had done with
them. 5But some of the believers who belonged to the Pharisee ·group
[sect; party; faction] ·came forward [Lstood up] and said, "·The Gentile
believers [LThey] must be circumcised. They must be ·told to obey
[ordered to keep] the law of Moses."

6The apostles and the elders gathered to consider this ·problem [matter].
7After a long debate, Peter stood up and said to them, "[LMen,] Brothers, you
know that in the early days God chose me from among you to preach the
·Good News [Gospel] to the ·nations [Gentiles]. They heard the ·Good News
[Gospel] from ·me [Lmy mouth], and they believed. 8God, who knows the
·thoughts of everyone [Lheart], ·accepted [showed his approval of; Ltestified
for] them. He showed this to us by giving them the Holy Spirit, just as he did
to us. 9To God, those people are not different from us. When they believed,
he made their hearts ·pure [clean]. 10So now why are you testing God by
putting a ·heavy load around [Lyoke on] the necks of the ·Gentile believers
[Ldisciples]? It is a ·load [yoke] that neither we nor our ·ancestors [forefa-
thers; fathers] were ·able [strong enough] to ·carry [bear]. 11But we believe
that we are saved by the grace of the Lord Jesus, just as they are."

12Then the whole ·group [assembly] became quiet. They listened to Paul
and Barnabas tell about all the [miraculous] signs and ·miracles [wonders]
that God did through them among the Gentiles. 13After they finished
speaking, James said, "[LMen,] Brothers, listen to me. 14·Simon [CPeter; v. 7]
has told us how God ·showed his love for [cared for; intervened with; vis-
ited] the Gentiles [Acts 10–11]. For the first time he is ·accepting [taking;
selecting] from among them a people ·to be his own [Lfor his name]. 15The
words of the prophets agree with this too [Las it is written]:

16'After these things I will return.
And I will rebuild the tent of David, which has fallen [Ceither the
Davidic dynasty of kings (the "house of David"), or the nation
Israel generally].
But I will rebuild its ruins,
and I will ·set it up [restore it].
17Then ·those people who are left alive [the remnant; Lthe rest of the
people] may ·ask the Lord for help [Lseek the Lord],
and the ·other nations [Gentiles] ·that belong to me [Lwho are called
by my name],
says the Lord,
who will make it happen.
18And these things have been known ·for a long time [from long ago;
Amos 9:11–12; Ca reference to God's promise that he would restore
the "remnant" of Israel and save the Gentiles].'

19"So I ·think [conclude; judge] we should not ·bother [trouble; cause
trouble for] the Gentiles who are turning to God. 20Instead, we should write
a letter to them telling them these things: Stay away from food ·that has been
offered to idols (which makes it unclean) [Lpolluted by idols], ·any kind of
sexual sin [*or* prohibited marriages; Cthe Greek word could mean any sexual
sin, or marriages viewed as incestuous by OT law], eating animals that have
been strangled [Cleaving the blood inside, which the OT law prohibited; Gen.
9:4], and blood [Cconsuming blood was forbidden in the OT law; Lev. 17:10–
12]. 21They should do these things, because for a long time in every city ·the

law of Moses has been taught [LMoses has been preached/proclaimed; Creferring to the Torah (the Law)]. **And it is still read in the synagogue every Sabbath day."** [CThese guidelines were to keep from offending pious Jews in the community and so promote unity in the Church.]

Letter to Gentile Believers

22**The apostles, the elders, and the whole church decided to send some of their men with Paul and Barnabas to Antioch. They chose Judas** [Lcalled] **Barsabbas** [1:23] **and Silas** [15:40; 1 Thess. 1:1], **who were ·respected by** [*or* leaders among] **the ·believers** [Lbrothers (and sisters)]. 23**·They sent the following letter with them** [LWriting by their hand; Can idiom for composing and sending a letter]:

From the apostles and elders, your brothers.

To all the Gentile ·believers [Lbrothers (and sisters)] **in Antioch, Syria, and Cilicia:**

Greetings!

24**We have heard that some of our group have come to you and said things that trouble and ·upset you** [unsettle your minds/souls]. **But we did not ·tell** [instruct; authorize; order] **them to do this.** 25**We have ·all** [unanimously; with one accord] **agreed to choose some ·messengers** [Lmen] **and send them to you with our ·dear friends** [beloved] **Barnabas and Paul—** 26**people who have ·given** [dedicated; *or* risked] **their lives ·to serve** [Lfor the name of] **our Lord Jesus Christ.** 27**So we are sending Judas and Silas, who will tell you the same things** [in person; Lthrough word]. 28**It has pleased the Holy Spirit that you should not have a heavy ·load** [burden] **to carry, and we agree. You need to do only these things:** 29**Stay away from any food that has been ·offered** [sacrificed] **to idols, eating any animals that have been strangled, and blood, and any kind of sexual sin** [see v. 20]. **If you stay away from these things, you will do well.**

·Good-bye [Best wishes; May you fare well].

30**So they ·left Jerusalem** [were sent off/dismissed] **and went to Antioch where they gathered the ·church** [congregation; assembly] **and ·gave them** [delivered] **the letter.** 31**When they read it, they ·were very happy** [rejoiced] **because of the encouraging message.** 32**Judas and Silas, who were ·also** [themselves] **prophets, said many things to encourage the ·believers** [Lbrothers (and sisters)] **and make them stronger.** 33**After some time ·Judas and Silas** [Lthey] **were sent off in peace by the ·believers** [Lbrothers (and sisters)], **and they went back to those who had sent them|,** 34**but Silas decided to remain there|.**[n]

35**But Paul and Barnabas stayed in Antioch and, along with many others, preached the ·Good News** [Gospel] **and taught the people the ·message** [Lword] **of the Lord.**

Paul and Barnabas Separate

36**After some ·time** [days], **Paul said to Barnabas, "·We should** [Let's] **go back to visit the ·believers** [Lbrothers (and sisters)] **in all those ·towns** [*or* cities] **where we preached the ·message** [Lword] **of the Lord** [chs. 13–14] **and see how they are doing."**

37**Barnabas wanted to take John** [Lwho is called] **Mark with them** [CJohn Mark was a cousin of Barnabas; Col. 4:10]. 38**But Paul ·did not think it was a good idea to** [*or* insisted that they should not] **take him,**

15:34 but... there Some Greek copies do not contain the bracketed text.

since Mark had ·left [deserted] them at Pamphylia and had not continued
with them in the work [13:13]. 39 Paul and Barnabas had such a ·serious
argument [sharp disagreement] about this that they ·separated and went
different ways [parted company; [L]separated from one another]. Barnabas
took Mark and sailed to Cyprus [[C]an island off the coast of Syria, and the
homeland of Barnabas; 4:36; 13:4], 40 but Paul chose Silas [v. 32; 16:37; 2
Cor. 1:19; 1 Thess. 1:1; 2 Thess. 1:1] and left. The ·believers [[L]brothers
(and sisters)] in Antioch ·put [commended; entrusted] Paul ·into the
Lord's care [[L]to the grace of the Lord], 41 and he went through Syria and
Cilicia, ·giving strength to [building up; encouraging] the churches.

Timothy Goes with Paul

16 Paul came to Derbe and Lystra [14:6], where a ·follower [dis-
ciple] named Timothy lived. Timothy's mother was Jewish
[[C]her name was Eunice (2 Tim. 1:5; 3:15)] and a believer, but his father
was a Greek.

2 The ·believers [[L]brothers (and sisters)] in Lystra and Iconium [13:51]
·respected Timothy and ·said good things about [spoke well of; [L]testified
about] him. 3 Paul wanted Timothy to travel with him, but all the people
living in that area knew that Timothy's father was Greek. So Paul circumcised Timothy ·to please his mother's people [[L]because of the Jews in
those places]. 4 ·Paul and those with him [[L]They] traveled from town to
town and ·gave [delivered; passed on] the ·decisions [decrees] made by
the apostles and elders in Jerusalem for the people to obey. 5 So the
churches became stronger in the faith and grew larger every day.

Paul Is Called to Macedonia

6 ·Paul and those with him [[L]They] went through the areas of Phrygia
[[C]a region in north central Asia Minor; 18:23] and Galatia [[C]either the
Roman province of Galatia or the old kingdom of Galatia in its north]
since the Holy Spirit ·did not let them [prohibited them to; [C]either
through circumstances or divine revelation] ·preach the Good News
[[L]speak the word] in Asia [[C]a Roman province, in present-day Turkey].
7 When they came ·near [*or* opposite] the country of Mysia [[C]the northwest section of Asia Minor, present-day Turkey], they tried to go into
Bithynia [[C]northern Asia Minor further east than Mysia], but the Spirit of
Jesus did not let them. 8 So they passed by Mysia and went to Troas [[C]a city
in northwest Asia Minor]. 9 That night Paul saw in a vision a man from
Macedonia [[C]an area across the Aegean Sea in mainland Greece]. The man
stood and ·begged [urged; encouraged], "Come over to Macedonia and help
us." 10 After Paul had seen the vision, we [[C]the switch to first person plural
("we") indicates that the author, Luke, joined them (see also 20:5—21:18;
27:1—28:16)] immediately ·prepared [made plans; attempted] to leave for
Macedonia, ·understanding [*or* convinced] that God had called us to ·tell
the Good News [preach the Gospel] to those people.

Lydia Becomes a Christian

11 We ·left [embarked/put out to sea from] Troas and sailed straight to
the island of Samothrace [[C]a mountainous island in the north Aegean].
The next day we sailed to Neapolis [[C]city in Macedonia, the first city Paul
visited on the continent of Europe]. 12 Then we went by land to Philippi, a
Roman colony [[C]a town begun by Romans with Roman laws, customs,
and privileges] and ·the leading city in that part [*or* one of the leading cities in that district; *or* a city in the first district] of Macedonia. We stayed
there for several days.

13 On the Sabbath day we went outside the city gate to the river where

we ·thought [expected] we would find a special place for prayer [CPhilippi evidently had no synagogue because of its small Jewish population]. Some women had gathered there, so we sat down and talked with them. 14One of the listeners was a woman named Lydia from the city of Thyatira [Cin western Asia Minor] ·whose job was selling [who was a dealer/merchant in] purple cloth [Cthe most expensive type of material]. She was a worshiper of God [Ca God-fearing Gentile; 10:2], and the Lord opened her ·mind [Lheart] to pay attention to what Paul was saying. 15She and ·all the people in her house [her household] were baptized. Then she ·invited us to her home [Lurged us], saying, "If you ·think I am truly [Lhave judged me to be] ·a believer in [*or* faithful to] the Lord, then come stay in my house." And she ·persuaded us [urged us strongly] to stay with her.

Paul and Silas in Jail

16Once, while we were going to the place for prayer, a ·servant [slave] girl met us. She had a ·special spirit [spirit/demon of divination/prediction; LPython spirit; CPython was the serpent god that guarded the Delphic oracle; the term came to be used of the ability to predict the future] in her, and she earned a lot of money for her owners by telling fortunes. 17This girl followed Paul and us, shouting, "These men are ·servants [slaves] of the Most High God. They are telling you ·how you can be saved [Lthe way/path of salvation]."

18She kept this up for many days. This ·bothered [annoyed; exasperated] Paul, so he turned and said to the spirit, "By the ·power [Lname] of Jesus Christ, I command you to come out of her!" ·Immediately, [LThat very hour] the spirit came out.

19When the owners of the ·servant [slave] girl saw that their ·source for making money [hope of profit] was gone, they grabbed Paul and Silas and dragged them before the ·city rulers [leaders; authorities] in the marketplace. 20They brought Paul and Silas to the ·Roman rulers [magistrates] and said, "These men are Jews and are ·making trouble in [disturbing] our city. 21They are ·teaching things [advocating customs] that are not ·right [permitted; lawful] for us as Romans to [Ladopt/accept or to] do."

22The crowd joined the attack against them. The ·Roman officers [magistrates] ·tore [stripped off] the clothes of Paul and Silas and ·had [ordered] them beaten with rods [2 Cor. 11:25]. 23After ·being severely beaten [Lmany blows were laid on them], ·Paul and Silas [Lthey] were thrown into ·jail [prison], and the jailer was ordered to guard them ·carefully [securely]. 24When he heard this order, he put them far inside the ·jail [prison] and ·pinned [secured; fastened] their feet ·down between large blocks of wood [in stocks; Lin wood].

25About midnight Paul and Silas were praying and singing ·songs [hymns; praise songs] to God as the other prisoners listened. 26Suddenly, there was a ·strong [great; violent] earthquake that shook the foundation of the ·jail [prison]. Then all the doors of the ·jail [prison] broke open, and all the prisoners were freed from their chains. 27The jailer woke up and saw that the ·jail [prison] doors were open. Thinking that the prisoners had already escaped, he got his sword and was about to kill himself [Cbeing responsible, he would suffer punishment and shame for their escape]. 28But [Lwith a great/loud voice] Paul shouted, "Don't hurt yourself! We are all here."

29The jailer ·told someone to bring a light [Lasked for lights]. Then he ·ran [rushed] inside and, shaking with fear, fell down before Paul and

Silas. 30He brought them outside and said, "·Men [LLords; Sirs], what
must I do to be saved?"
31They said to him, "Believe in the Lord Jesus and you will be saved—
you and ·all the people in your house [your household]." 32So ·Paul and
Silas [Lthey] told the ·message [word] of the Lord to the jailer and all the
people in his ·house [household]. 33At that hour of the night the jailer
took Paul and Silas and washed their wounds. Then he and all his ·people
[*or* family; household] were baptized immediately. 34After this the jailer
took Paul and Silas home and gave them food. He and his ·family
[Lhousehold] ·were very happy [rejoiced; celebrated] because they now
believed in God.
35The next morning, the ·Roman officers [magistrates] sent the police
to tell the jailer, "Let these men go free."
36The jailer ·said [Lreported these words] to Paul, "The ·officers [magis-
trates] have sent an order to let you go free. You can leave now. Go in peace."
37But Paul said to ·the police [Lthem], "They beat us in public ·without a
trial [Luncondemned], even though we are Roman citizens [CRoman law
stated that citizens could not be beaten without a trial]. And they threw us
in ·jail [prison]. Now they want to ·make us go away [get rid of us; throw us
out] ·quietly [in secret]. No! Let them come themselves and bring us out."
38The police ·told [reported to] the ·Roman officers [magistrates] what
Paul said. When ·the officers [Lthey] heard that ·Paul and Silas [Lthey] were
Roman citizens, they were afraid. 39So they came and ·told Paul and Silas
they were sorry [apologized to them; appeased them] and took them out
of ·jail [prison] and asked them to leave the city. 40So when they came out
of the ·jail [prison], they went to Lydia's house where they saw some of the
·believers [Lbrothers (and sisters)] and encouraged them. Then they left.

Paul and Silas in Thessalonica

17 ·Paul and Silas [LThey] traveled through Amphipolis and
Apollonia and came to Thessalonica [Ca city on the Via Egnatia,
the major road on the northern Aegean coast] where there was a synagogue. 2Paul went into the synagogue as he ·always [customarily] did
[Cspeaking to the Jews first], and on each Sabbath day for three weeks, he
·talked [discussed; *or* argued; reasoned] with ·his fellow Jews [Lthem]
about the Scriptures. 3He explained and proved that the ·Christ [Messiah;
CChrist in Greek and Messiah in Hebrew mean "anointed one"] must ·die
[Lsuffer] and then rise from the dead [3:18]. He said, "This Jesus I am ·tell-
ing you about [proclaiming to you] is the ·Christ [Messiah]." 4Some of
them were ·convinced [persuaded] and joined Paul and Silas, along with
many of the Greeks who ·worshiped God [were devout; Csometimes called
"God-fearers," these were Gentiles who worshiped the one true God of
Israel; 10:2; 13:43] and ·many [Lnot a few] of the important women [13:50].
5But ·some others [Lthe Jews] became jealous. So they got some evil
men ·from the marketplace [*or* loitering in the streets; from the marketplace rabble], formed a mob, and ·started a riot [put the city in an uproar].
They ran to Jason's house, looking for ·Paul and Silas [Lthem], wanting to
bring them out to the ·people [assembly; crowd]. 6But when they did not
find them, they dragged Jason and some other ·believers [Lbrothers] to
the ·leaders of the city [city authorities; Lpolitarchs]. The people were yelling, "These people have ·made trouble [agitated; stirred up rebellion]
everywhere in the world, and now they have come here too! 7Jason ·is
keeping [has welcomed/received/harbored] them in his house. All of

them ·do things against [defy; oppose] the ·laws [decrees] of Caesar, saying there is another king, called Jesus."

8When the ·people [crowd] and the ·leaders of the city [city authorities; Lpolitarchs] heard these things, they ·became very upset [were disturbed]. 9They made Jason and the others ·put up a sum of money [pay bail; post a bond]. Then they let ·the believers [Lthem] go free.

Paul and Silas Go to Berea

10That same night the ·believers [Lbrothers] sent Paul and Silas to ·Berea [Ca Macedonian city to the south] where [Lupon arriving] they went to the synagogue [Lof the Jews]. 11These people were more ·willing to listen [open-minded; fair-minded; noble in character] than the people in Thessalonica. The Bereans ·were eager to hear what Paul and Silas said [Leagerly received the word/message] and ·studied [examined] the Scriptures every day to find out if these things were true [Cto confirm Paul's teaching was in line with Scripture]. 12So, many of them believed, as well as ·many [Lnot a few] ·important [prominent; socially high-standing] Greek women and men [17:4]. 13But the Jews [Cwho had opposed Paul earlier] in Thessalonica learned that Paul was preaching the word of God in Berea, too. So they came there, ·upsetting [stirring up] the ·people [crowd] and ·making trouble [causing a disturbance]. 14The ·believers [Lbrothers (and sisters)] ·quickly [immediately] sent Paul away to the ·coast [Lsea], but Silas and Timothy stayed ·in Berea [behind; Lthere]. 15The people ·leading [escorting; accompanying] Paul went with him to Athens [Cthe leading city in Greece]. Then they carried ·a message [instructions; an order] from Paul back to Silas and Timothy for them to ·come to [rejoin] him as soon as they could.

Paul Preaches in Athens

16While Paul was waiting for ·Silas and Timothy [Lthem] in Athens, ·he [Lhis spirit] was ·troubled [very distressed] because he saw that the city was full of idols. 17In the synagogue, he ·talked [*or* argued; reasoned] with the Jews and the ·Greeks who worshiped God [God-fearing Gentiles; Lpious/devout ones; see 17:4]. He also ·talked [*or* argued; reasoned] every day with ·people [Lthose who happened to be present] in the ·marketplace [*or* public square].

18Some of the Epicurean [Cwho believed the goal of life was pleasure and did not believe the soul survived death] and Stoic philosophers [Cwho believed life should be lived with indifference to pleasure and pain, and did not believe the soul was immortal] ·argued [conversed; debated] with him, saying, "What is this ·babbler [*or* charlatan; *or* ignorant show-off; Lword-scatterer] trying to say?" Others said, "He seems to be telling us about ·some other gods [foreign gods; strange deities]," because Paul was ·telling them [preaching the Good News/Gospel] about Jesus and ·his rising from the dead [the resurrection]. 19They got Paul and took him to ·a meeting of the Areopagus [*or* the Hill of Ares; *or* Mars Hill; CAres (Greek name) or Mars (Roman name) was the god of thunder and war; the council of Areopagus was the oldest and most prestigious court for intellectual and moral matters], where they said, "Please explain to us this new idea you have been teaching. 20[LFor; Because] The things you are saying ·are new [*or* sound strange] to us, and we want to know what ·this teaching means [Lthese things mean]." 21(All the people of Athens and ·those from other countries [foreigners] who lived there spent all their time talking about and listening to the newest ideas.)

22Then Paul stood ·before the meeting [Lin the midst] of the Areopagus and said, "·People of Athens [LMen, Athenians], I can see you are very religious in ·all things [every way]. 23[LFor; Because] As I was going through

your city, I ·saw [observed closely] the objects you worship. I found an altar
that had these words written on it: TO·A GOD WHO IS NOT KNOWN [TAN UNKNOWN
GOD]. ·You worship a god that you don't know, and this is the God I am telling you about [LWhat therefore you worship as unknown, this I proclaim to
you]! 24The God who made the whole world and everything in it [Deut. 4:39;
Ps. 146:6] is the Lord of the ·sky and the land [*or* heaven and earth]. He does
not live in ·temples [shrines] built by human hands. 25This God is the One
who gives life, breath, and everything else to ·people [Lall; everyone; Gen.
1:29; 2:7]. He ·does not need any help from them [Lis not served by human
hands]; he has everything he needs. 26·God began by making one person,
and from him came all the different people [LFrom one, God made every
nation of people] ·who live everywhere in the world [*or* in order to inhabit
the whole earth]. God ·decided exactly [determined; *or* allotted] ·when [*or*
their appointed time in history; *or* the seasons of their year] and ·where they
must live [*or* the boundaries of their lands]. 27God wanted them to ·look for
[seek] him and perhaps ·search all around for [grope for; reach out to; feel
their way towards] him and find him, though he is not far from any of us:
28'[LFor] ·By his power [*or* In him] we live and move and ·exist [have our
being; Ca quotation from the Cretan philosopher Epimenides, from about
600 BC].' [LAs] Some of your own poets have said: 'For we are his ·children
[offspring; Ca quotation from Aratus, a Stoic philosopher from Cilicia, who
lived about 315–240 BC].' 29Since we are God's ·children [offspring], you
must not think that ·God [the deity; *or* the divine nature] is like ·something
[an image/likeness] ·that people imagine or make [Lmade by human skill and
imagination] from gold, silver, or rock. 30·In the past, people did not understand God, and he ignored this [*or* God overlooked such times of ignorance].
But now, God ·tells [commands] all people in the world to ·change their
hearts and lives [repent]. 31[LBecause] God has ·set [fixed; established] a day
that he will judge all the world with ·fairness [righteousness], by the man he
·chose [appointed] long ago. And God has ·proved [*or* given assurance of]
this to everyone by raising that man from the dead!"

32When the people heard about ·Jesus being raised [Lthe resurrection]
from the dead, some of them ·laughed [mocked; scoffed]. But others said,
"We will hear more about this from you ·later [Lagain]." 33So Paul went
away from them. 34But some of the ·people [Lmen] ·believed Paul [became
believers] and joined him. Among those who believed was Dionysius, a
member of the Areopagus, a woman named Damaris, and some others.

Paul in Corinth

18 ·Later [LAfter this] Paul left Athens and went to Corinth [Ca city
about thirty miles southwest of Athens]. 2Here he ·met [Lfound]
a Jew named Aquila ·who had been born in [*or* whose family was from; a
native of] the country of Pontus [Ca province just south of the Black Sea in
northeast Asia Minor]. But Aquila and his wife, Priscilla, had recently
moved to Corinth from Italy, because Claudius [CRoman emperor from
AD 41–54] commanded that all Jews must leave Rome [Can edict issued in
AD 49 because of rioting, perhaps between Jews and Jewish Christians].
Paul ·went to visit [*or* came in contact with; *or* approached] Aquila and
Priscilla. 3[LAnd] Because they were ·tentmakers [*or* leatherworkers], just
as he was, he stayed with them and worked with them. 4Every Sabbath day
he ·talked [reasoned; argued] with the Jews and Greeks in the synagogue,
trying ·to persuade them to believe in Jesus [Lto persuade them].

5Silas and Timothy came from Macedonia [Cthe northern region of

Greece] and joined Paul in Corinth. After this, Paul ·spent all his time
telling people the Good News [Ldevoted himself to (preaching) the word],
·showing [testifying to] the Jews that Jesus is the Christ [Messiah; 17:3].
6But they ·would not accept Paul's teaching [Lopposed/resisted him] and
·said some evil things [*or* reviled him; *or* blasphemed; 13:45]. So he shook
off the dust from his clothes [Ca sign of protest and that he was done with
them, leaving them to God's judgment; 13:51] and said to them, "·If you
are not saved, it will be your own fault [LYour blood is on your heads]! ·I
have done all I can do [*or* My conscience is clear; LI am innocent/pure]!
·After this [From now on], I will go to ·other nations [the Gentiles]." 7Paul
left ·the synagogue [Lthere] and moved into the home of a man named
Titius Justus, next to the synagogue. This man worshiped God [Ca Gentile
"God-fearer," who worshiped the true God of Israel; 10:2; 13:43; 17:4].
8Crispus was the ·leader [official] of that synagogue, and he and all the
people ·living in his house [of his household] believed in the Lord. Many
others in Corinth also listened to Paul and believed and were baptized.

9During the night, the Lord told Paul in a vision [10:9–16; 16:9–10]:
"Don't be afraid. ·Continue talking to people [Speak out] and don't be
·quiet [silent]. 10[LFor] I am with you, and no one will [Llay a hand on you
to] ·hurt [*or* do evil to] you because many of my people are in this city
[Deut. 31:6; Josh. 1:5; Is. 41:10; 43:5; Jer. 1:7–9]." 11Paul stayed there [Cin
Corinth] for a year and a half, teaching God's word to the people.

Paul Is Brought Before Gallio

12When Gallio was the ·governor [Lproconsul; Cfrom AD 51 to 52] of
Achaia [Ca Roman province in present-day southern Greece], ·some people
[Lthe Jews] ·came together [made a united attack] against Paul and took him
to the ·court [tribunal; judgment seat]. 13They said, "This man is ·teaching
[Lpersuading] people to worship God in a way that is against our law."

14Paul was about to ·say something [Lopen his mouth], but Gallio spoke
[Lto the Jews], saying, "I would [Lreasonably; justifiably] listen to you [LO
Jews,] if you were complaining about a crime or some ·wrong [evil wrongdoing; moral evil]. 15But the things you are saying are only questions about
words and names [Cthe debate over whether Jesus is the Messiah]—arguments about your own law. ·So you must solve this problem [LSee to it]
yourselves. I don't want to be a judge of these things." 16And ·Gallio [Lhe]
·made them leave [threw them out of] the ·court [tribunal; judgment seat].

17Then they[n] [Cprobably Greeks, using the opportunity to vent their
dislike for the Jewish population; less likely, the Jews, angry at Sosthenes
for losing the case] all grabbed Sosthenes [Cperhaps the person mentioned
in 1 Cor. 1:1], the ·leader [official] of the synagogue, and beat him there
before the ·court [tribunal; judgment seat]. But this ·did not bother [was
of no concern to; was ignored by] Gallio.

Paul Returns to Antioch

18Paul stayed with the ·believers [Lbrothers (and sisters)] for many
more days. Then he ·left [said farewell] and sailed for Syria, with Priscilla
and Aquila. At Cenchrea [Ca port city east of Corinth] Paul cut off his hair
[Ca ritual sometimes performed when a promise was accomplished; perhaps this was a Nazirite vow; Num. 6:1–21], because he had made a
·promise to God [Lvow]. 19Then they went to Ephesus [Ca major city
across the Aegean Sea in western Asia Minor], where Paul left ·Priscilla
and Aquila [Lthem]. While Paul was there, he went into the synagogue

18:17 they Some Greek copies say "the Greeks." A few say "the Jews."

and talked [*or* argued; reasoned] **with the ·people** [LJews]. 20**When they**
asked him to stay with them longer, he ·refused [declined]. 21**But as he**
·left [said farewell], **he said, "I will come back to you again if God ·wants**
me to [wills]." **And so he sailed away from Ephesus.**
22**When Paul landed at Caesarea** [Ca port city to the west of Jerusalem on
the Mediterranean], **he went** [Lup] **and gave greetings to the ·church in**
Jerusalem [Lthe church; Cthe Greek does not mention Jerusalem, but going
"up" implies the church in Jerusalem; less likely, it could be the church in
Caesarea]. **After that, Paul went** [Ldown] **to Antioch** [Cin Syria; the church
that sent Paul out]. 23**He stayed there for a while and then left and went**
through the regions of Galatia and Phrygia [Cregions in north central Asia
Minor; 16:6]. **·He traveled from town to town in these regions** [...traveling
from place to place; L...passing through sequentially], **·giving strength to**
[building up; encouraging; 15:41] **all the ·followers** [disciples].

Apollos in Ephesus and Corinth

24[LNow; Meanwhile] **A Jew named Apollos came to Ephesus. He was**
·born in the city [a native] **of Alexandria and was ·a good speaker** [*or* a
learned man] **who ·knew the Scriptures well** [Lwas powerful/competent in
the Scriptures]. 25**He had been taught about the ·way** [*or* Way; 9:2] **of the**
Lord and was always ·very excited [enthusiastic; Lfervent in spirit] **when he**
spoke and taught ·the truth [Laccurately the things] **about Jesus. But the**
only baptism Apollos knew about was the baptism that John [Cthe Baptist]
taught [Cbaptism of repentance before the ministry of Jesus began; Luke 3].
26**Apollos began to speak ·very boldly** [confidently; fearlessly] **in the syna-**
gogue, and when Priscilla and Aquila heard him, they ·took him to their
home [*or* took him aside; Lreceived/took him] **and ·helped him better**
understand [explained more accurately/precisely] **the ·way** [*or* Way; 9:2] **of**
God. 27**Now Apollos wanted to ·go** [cross over] **to Achaia** [v. 12]. **So the**
·believers [Lbrothers (and sisters)] **·helped** [encouraged] **him and wrote a**
letter to the ·followers [disciples] **there, asking them to ·accept** [welcome]
him. ·When Apollos arrived, he was a great help to those who, by God's
grace, had believed in Jesus [*or* When Apollos arrived, by God's grace he was
a great help...]. 28[LFor] **He ·argued very strongly with** [vigorously refuted]
the Jews ·before all the people [Lin public (debate)], **clearly ·proving** [*or*
showing] **with the Scriptures that Jesus is the ·Christ** [Messiah; 17:3; 18:5].

Paul in Ephesus

19 **While Apollos was in Corinth, Paul traveled through the**
interior regions [Cthe mountainous northern route through
the interior of Phrygia; 18:23] **to Ephesus** [Ca major city in western Asia
Minor; 18:23]. **There he found some ·followers** [disciples] 2**and asked**
them, "Did you receive the Holy Spirit ·when [*or* after] **you believed?"**
They said, "We have never even heard ·of [*or* that there is] **a Holy Spirit."**
3**So he asked, "·What kind of baptism did you have** [LInto what were
you baptized]?"
They said, "·It was the baptism that John taught [LInto John's bap-
tism]." [CThese followers of John the Baptist either (1) knew only of John's
ministry but had not heard that Jesus was the Messiah, or less likely, (2)
believed in Jesus as Messiah, but had not been baptized in his name to
receive the Holy Spirit.]
4**Paul said, "John's baptism was a baptism of ·changed hearts and lives**
[repentance; Cin preparation for the Messiah]. **He told people to believe in**
the one who would come after him, and that one is Jesus."
5**When they heard this, they were baptized ·in** [*or* into] **the name of the**

Lord Jesus. 6Then Paul ·laid [placed] his hands on them [Ca ritual of blessing and/or conferring of authority], and the Holy Spirit came upon them. They began speaking ·different languages [*or* in tongues; ecstatic utterance] and prophesying. 7There were about twelve people in this group.

8Paul went into the synagogue and spoke out ·boldly [confidently; fearlessly] for three months. He ·talked [reasoned; argued] with the people and persuaded them ·to accept the things he said about [Lconcerning] the kingdom of God. 9But some of them became ·stubborn [hardened]. They refused to believe and ·said evil things about [slandered; cursed] ·the Way of Jesus [Lthe Way; Canother name for the Christian movement; 9:2; 18:25; 22:4] before ·all the people [the crowd]. So Paul left them, and taking the ·followers [disciples] with him, he went to the ·school [lecture hall] of a man named Tyrannus. There Paul ·talked [discussed; reasoned; debated] with people every day 10for two years. Because of his work, ·everyone who lived in [the whole population of] the province of Asia, both Jews and Greeks, heard the word of the Lord.

The Sons of Sceva

11God ·used Paul to do [Lthrough the hands of Paul did] some ·very special [extraordinary] miracles. 12Some people took ·handkerchiefs [face cloths] and ·clothes [work aprons; *or* hand towels] ·that Paul had used [that had touched Paul; Lfrom his skin] and put them on the sick. When they did this, ·the sick were healed [Lthe diseases left them] and evil spirits ·left [Lcame out of] them.

13But some ·people also were traveling around and making evil spirits go out of people [Ltraveling/itinerant Jewish exorcists…]. They tried to ·use [invoke; Lname] the name of the Lord Jesus to force the evil spirits out. They would say, "By the same Jesus that Paul ·talks about [Lpreaches; proclaims], I ·order [command; adjure] you to come out!" 14Seven sons of Sceva, a ·leading [LJewish chief] priest, were doing this.

15But one time ·an [Lthe] evil spirit said to them, "I know Jesus, and I ·know about [recognize] Paul, but who are you?"

16Then the man who had the evil spirit ·jumped on [leaped on; attacked] them. Because he ·was so much stronger than all of them [violently overpowered them], they ran away from the house naked and ·hurt [wounded]. 17All the people [Lwho lived] in Ephesus—Jews and Greeks—learned about this and were filled with fear and ·gave great honor to [praised/magnified the name of] the Lord Jesus. 18Many of ·the believers [those who now believed] began to confess openly and ·tell all the evil things they had done [Ldisclose their (evil/magical) practices]. 19·Some [*or* A significant number] of them who had ·used magic [practiced sorcery/witchcraft] brought their magic ·books [*or* scrolls] and burned them before everyone. Those books were worth about fifty thousand silver coins [Cprobably drachmas, each worth a day's wages].

20·So in a powerful way [LIn this way; Thus] the word of the Lord kept spreading and ·growing [*or* grew strong; prevailed].

21After these things [Lhad been fulfilled/accomplished], Paul decided [Lin his spirit; *or* in the Spirit] to go to Jerusalem, planning to go through Macedonia [Cnorthern Greece] and Achaia [Csouthern Greece] and then on to Jerusalem. He said, "After I have been ·to Jerusalem [Lthere], I must also ·visit [Lsee] Rome." 22Paul sent Timothy and Erastus, two of his ·helpers [assistants], ahead to Macedonia, but he himself stayed in [Cthe province of] Asia for a while.

Trouble in Ephesus

[23]And during [*or* about; at] that time, there was ·some serious trouble
[[L]no small disturbance] in Ephesus about ·the Way of Jesus [[L]the Way;
[C]another name for the Christian movement; 9:2; 18:25; 22:4]. [24]A man
named Demetrius, who worked with silver, made little silver ·models that
looked like the temple [[L]shrines; [C]probably reliefs depicting the goddess in
her temple] of the goddess Artemis [[C]Greek goddess of fertility, worshiped
particularly in Ephesus]. ·Those who did this work [The artisans/crafts-
men] made much money [[L]had no little business]. [25]·Demetrius [[L]He]
had a meeting with them and ·some others [[L]workers] who did ·the same
kind of work [*or* similar trades]. He told them, "Men, you know that ·we
make a lot of money [our wealth/livelihood comes] from this business.
[26]But ·look at [[L]you have seen and heard] what this man Paul is doing. He
has ·convinced [persuaded] and ·turned away [*or* led astray] many people,
not only in Ephesus, but in almost all of [[C]the province of] Asia! He says
the gods made by human hands are not ·real [[L]gods (at all); Is. 44:9–20;
46:1–7; 1 Cor. 8:4–6]. [27]There is a danger that our business will ·lose its
good name [be discredited], but there is also another danger: People will
begin to think that the temple of the great goddess Artemis is not important, and the goddess herself, whom everyone in [[C]the province of] Asia
and the whole world worships, will ·lose [be deposed of/stripped of] her
majesty [magnificence; greatness].

[28]When the others heard this, they became ·very angry [enraged; furious]
and shouted, "Great is Artemis of the Ephesians!" [29]The whole city ·became
confused [was filled with confusion; was in an uproar]. The people grabbed
Gaius and Aristarchus [20:4; 27:2; Col. 4:10; Philem. 24], who were from
Macedonia and were traveling with Paul, and ·ran [rushed together] to the
theater. [30]Paul wanted to ·go in and talk to the crowd [appear before the
assembly], but the ·followers [disciples] did not let him. [31]Also, some ·leaders
of Asia [provincial authorities; [L]of the Asiarchs; [C]a group of wealthy political
leaders who had religious functions] who were friends of Paul sent him a
message, ·begging [urging; encouraging] him not to ·go [venture; take the
risk of going] into the theater. [32]Some people were shouting one thing, and
some were shouting another. The ·meeting [assembly] was completely confused; most of them did not know why they had come together. [33]The Jews
·pushed forward [put in front] a man named Alexander, and some of them
[[C]either the crowd or the Jews] ·told him to explain [*or* gave him advice on
what to say; *or* assumed he was responsible for the trouble]. Alexander
·waved [gestured with] his hand [[C]for silence] so he could ·explain things to
[*or* make a defense before] the ·people [crowd]. [34]But when they ·saw [recog-
nized] that Alexander was a Jew [[C]Jews opposed idol worship, so the crowd
was suspicious of him], they all shouted ·the same thing [in unison; [L]with
one voice] for two hours: "Great is Artemis of the Ephesians!"

[35]Then the city clerk [[C]the head of the assembly and the senior local offi-
cial] quieted [calmed down] the crowd. He said, "·People of Ephesus [[L]Men,
Ephesians], ·everyone knows [[L]who does not know…?] that Ephesus is the
city that ·keeps [guards] the temple of the great goddess Artemis and her
·holy stone [*or* image; *or* statue] that fell from heaven [[C]probably a meteorite that resembled the many-breasted image of Artemis]. [36]Since no one can
say this is not true, you should ·be quiet [keep calm]. ·Stop and think before
you do anything [Do nothing reckless/rash]. [37]You brought these men here,
but they have not ·said anything evil against [[L]blasphemed] our goddess or
·stolen anything from [*or* committed sacrilege against] her temple. [38]If

Demetrius and ·those who work [Lthe artisans/craftmen] **with him have a ·charge** [complaint; grievance; Lword] **against anyone, ·they should go to the courts and judges** [Lthe courts are open/in session and there are proconsuls] **where they can ·argue with** [*or* bring charges against] **each other.** 39**If there is something else you want to talk about, it ·can** [*or* must] **be decided at the ·regular town meeting of the people** [legal assembly; Cwhich met three times a month]. 40**I say this because** [Lwe are in danger that] **some people might see this trouble today and ·say that we are** [accuse us of; charge us with] **rioting. We could not explain this, because there is no real reason for this ·meeting** [*or* uproar; commotion]**."** 41**After the city clerk said these things, he ·told the people to go home** [Ldismissed the assembly].

Paul in Macedonia and Greece

20 **When the ·trouble stopped** [uproar ended]**, Paul sent for the ·followers** [disciples] **to come to him. After he encouraged them and then told them good-bye, he left and went to Macedonia** [Cnorthern Greece; 16:9]. 2**He ·said many things to strengthen the followers** [Lencouraged them with many words] **in the different places on his way through Macedonia. Then he ·went to** [arrived in] **Greece** [probably Achaia (southern Greece)], 3**where he stayed for three months** [Cprobably in Corinth; at this time he wrote his letter to the Romans]. **He was ready to sail for Syria, but some of the Jews were ·planning** [plotting] **something against him. So Paul decided to go back through Macedonia to Syria.** 4**The men who went with him were Sopater** [Rom. 16:21] **son of Pyrrhus, from the city of Berea** [17:10–15]; **Aristarchus** [19:29; Col. 4:10; Philem. 24] **and Secundus, from the city of Thessalonica** [17:1–9]; **Gaius** [19:29], **from Derbe** [14:20–21]; **Timothy** [Rom. 16:21]; **and Tychicus** [Eph. 6:21; Col. 4:7; 2 Tim. 4:12] **and Trophimus** [21:29; 2 Tim. 4:20], **two men from Asia** [Call representatives of the Gentile churches delivering a financial gift to the church in Jerusalem]. 5**These men went on ahead and waited for us at Troas** [Chere begins the second "we" section in Acts, indicating that the author, Luke, has rejoined Paul (16:10–17; 20:5—21:18; 27:1—28:16)]. 6**We sailed from Philippi after the Feast of Unleavened Bread** [Canother name for Passover; Ex. 12:14–20]. **Five days later we met them in Troas** [16:8], **where we stayed for seven days.**

Eutychus Raised from the Dead at Troas

7**On the first day of the week** [CSunday; or perhaps Saturday night since the Jewish day began in the evening (Greeks reckoned from the morning)], **we all met together to break bread** [Cprobably a reference to the Lord's Supper; Luke 22:14–20], **and Paul ·spoke to** [*or* was having a discussion with] **the group. Because he was planning to leave the next day, he kept on talking until midnight.** 8**We were all together in a room upstairs, and there were many lamps in the room** [Cusing up oxygen and causing drowsiness]. 9**A young man named Eutychus was sitting in the window. As Paul continued talking, Eutychus was falling into a deep sleep. Finally, he went sound asleep and fell to the ground from the third floor. When they picked him up, he was dead.** 10**Paul went down to Eutychus, ·knelt down** [*or* threw himself on him; Clike Elisha; 2 Kin. 4:32–35], **and ·put his arms around** [embraced] **him. He said, "Don't ·worry** [fear]. **·He is alive now** [LFor his life/soul is in him]**."** 11**Then Paul went upstairs again, broke bread, and ate. He spoke to them a long time, until ·it was early morning** [dawn], **and then he left.** 12**They took the young man home alive and were ·greatly** [Lnot in a small measure] **comforted.**

The Trip from Troas to Miletus

13We went on ahead of Paul and sailed for the city of Assos [Con the
east coast of the Aegean in the Gulf of Adramyttium], where we ·intended
[planned] to take Paul on board. Paul ·planned [arranged] it this way
because he wanted to go to Assos by land. 14When he met us there, we
took him aboard and went to Mitylene [Cthe main city on the island of
Lesbos in the Aegean]. 15We sailed from ·Mitylene [Lthere] and the next
day came to a place ·near [opposite; across from] Kios [Can island five
miles off the coast in the Aegean]. The following day we sailed to Samos
[Canother island off the coast in the Aegean], and the next day we reached
Miletus [Ca city on the western coast of Asia Minor]. 16[LFor] Paul had
already decided ·not to stop at [Lto sail past] Ephesus [18:19], because he
did not want to stay too long in [Cthe province of] Asia [Cwith so many
friends in Ephesus (ch. 19), a short stop would be impossible]. He was
hurrying to be in Jerusalem on the day of Pentecost [Cone of three great
Jewish festivals, celebrated 50 days after Passover], if that were possible.

The Elders from Ephesus

17Now from Miletus [20:15] Paul sent to Ephesus [18:19; 19:1–41] and
called for the elders [14:23; 1 Tim. 5:17] of the church. 18When they came
to him, he said, "You know about my life from the first day I came to Asia
[18:19]. You know the way I lived all the time I was with you [19:1–41].
19·Some Jewish opponents [LThe Jews] ·made plans [plotted] against me,
which ·troubled me very much [severely tested/tried me]. But you know I
always served the Lord ·unselfishly [Lwith humility], and ·I often cried [in
sorrowful times; Lwith tears]. 20You know I preached to you and did not
hold back anything that would help you. You know that I taught you in
public and ·in your homes [from house to house]. 21I ·warned [witnessed/
testified to] both Jews and Greeks to ·change their lives and turn to God
[repent] and believe in our Lord Jesus. 22But now [Lindeed; Tbehold] ·I
must obey the Holy Spirit and [Lbound/compelled by the Spirit, I must] go
to Jerusalem. I don't know what will happen to me there. 23I know only
that in every city the Holy Spirit ·tells [warns; testifies to] me that ·troubles
and even jail [Lchains and persecutions/afflictions] wait for me. 24[LBut] I
don't ·care about my own life [consider my life worth anything]. ·The most
important thing [*or* My only goal] is that I ·complete [finish] my ·mission
[task; course; Lrace; 2 Tim. 4:7; Heb. 12:1], the ·work [ministry; service]
that ·the Lord Jesus gave me [LI received from the Lord Jesus]—to ·tell
people [testify/witness to] the ·Good News [Gospel] about God's grace.
25"And now [Llook; Tbehold], I know that none of you among whom I
was ·preaching [proclaiming] the ·kingdom of God [Lkingdom] will ever
see ·me [Lmy face] again. 26So today I ·tell [testify/witness to] you that ·if
any of you should be lost, I am not responsible [LI am innocent/clean of
the blood of everyone; Ezek. 33:9], 27because I ·have told [Lhave not held
back from telling] you ·everything God wants you to know [*or* the whole
purpose/plan/will of God]. 28·Be careful for [Keep watch over] yourselves
and for all the ·people [Lflock] the Holy Spirit has ·given to you to oversee
[Lmade you overseers/guardians; John 21:16]. You must be like shepherds
to the church of God,ⁿ which he ·bought [*or* obtained] with the ·death of
his own Son [Lwith the blood of his own (Son); *or* with his own blood]. 29I
know that after ·I leave [my departure; I am gone], ·some people will come
like wild wolves [Lwild/savage wolves will come in among you] and ·try to

---

20:28 of God Some Greek copies read "of the Lord."

destroy [will not spare] the flock. 30·Also, [*or* Even] some from your own
group will rise up and ·twist the truth [Lspeak perversions/distortions] and
will ·lead away [lure; entice] ·followers [disciples] after them. 31So ·be careful [keep watch]! Always remember that for three years, day and night, I
never stopped warning [admonishing; instructing] each of you, ·and I
often cried over you [Lwith tears].
32"Now I ·am putting you in the care of [commend/commit/entrust you
to] God and the ·message [word] about his grace. It is able to ·give you
strength [edify you; build you up], and it will give you the ·blessings God
has [Linheritance] ·for [*or* among] all ·his holy people [those who are sanctified; those set apart for himself]. 33When I was with you, I never ·wanted
[coveted] anyone's ·money [Lsilver or gold] or fine clothes [Ex. 20:17; Deut.
5:21; 1 Sam. 12:3]. 34You [Lyourselves] know I always worked [Lwith my
own hands] to take care of my own needs and the needs of those who were
with me. 35I ·showed [provided an example to] you ·in all things [in everything I did] that you should work as I did and help the weak. I taught you
to remember the words Jesus said: 'It is more blessed to give than to receive
[Ca saying of Jesus not recorded elsewhere in Scripture].'"
36·When [After] Paul had said this, he knelt down with all of them and
prayed. 37-38And they all ·cried [wept loudly/a great deal] because Paul
had said they would never see ·him [Lhis face] again. They ·put their arms
around him [embraced/hugged him] and kissed him. Then they ·went
with [escorted; accompanied] him to the ship.

Paul Goes to Jerusalem

21 After we ·all said good-bye to [tore ourselves away from] them,
we sailed ·straight [a straight course] to the island of Cos
[Cbetween Ephesus and Rhodes]. The next day we reached Rhodes [Can
island off the southwest Coast of Asia Minor], and from there we went to
Patara [Ca seaport on the southwest coast of Asia Minor]. 2There we found
a ship ·going [crossing over] to Phoenicia [Ca coastal region north of Israel;
present-day Lebanon], so we went aboard and sailed away. 3We sailed near
the island of Cyprus [11:19], ·seeing [Lleaving] it to the ·north [Lleft], but
we sailed on to Syria. We ·stopped [landed] at Tyre [12:20] because the
ship needed to unload its cargo there. 4We ·found [sought out] some ·fol-
lowers [disciples] in Tyre and stayed with them for seven days. Through
the ·Holy Spirit [LSpirit] they ·warned [*or* kept warning] Paul not to go to
Jerusalem. 5When ·we finished our visit [Lour days there were finished],
we left and continued our trip. All ·the followers [Lof them], even the
women and children, came outside the city with us. After we all knelt on
the beach and prayed, 6we said good-bye and got on the ship, and ·the followers [Lthey] went back home.
7We ·continued [*or* finished] our trip from Tyre and arrived at
Ptolemais [Ca town on the Mediterranean coast about half way between
Tyre and Caesarea, also known as Acco], where we greeted the ·believers
[Lbrothers (and sisters)] and stayed with them for a day. 8The next day we
left Ptolemais and went to the city of Caesarea [10:1]. There we went into
the home of Philip the ·preacher [*or* evangelist], one of the ·seven helpers
[LSeven; 6:1–6; 8:4–40], and stayed with him. 9He had four ·unmarried
[Lvirgin] daughters who ·had the gift of prophesying [Lprophesied].
10After we had been there for ·some time [Lmany days], a prophet named
Agabus [11:27–28] ·arrived [Lcame down] from Judea. 11He came to us
and ·borrowed [took] Paul's belt and used it to tie his own hands and feet.

He said, "The Holy Spirit says, 'This is how the Jews in Jerusalem will ·tie up [*or* bind (in chains)] the man ·who wears this belt [Lwhose belt this is]. Then they will ·give [deliver; hand over; betray] him to the Gentiles.' "

12When we all heard this, we and the people there ·begged [encouraged; urged; pleaded with] Paul not to go to Jerusalem. 13But he ·said [Lresponded], "Why are you crying and ·making me so sad [Lbreaking my heart]? I am not only ready to be ·tied up [*or* bound; imprisoned] in Jerusalem, I am ready to die for the [Lname of the] Lord Jesus!"

14We could not ·persuade him to stay away from Jerusalem [Lpersuade/convince him]. So we ·stopped begging him [Lremained silent] and said, "·We pray that what the Lord wants will [LLet the Lord's will] be done."

15After ·this [Lthese days], we ·got ready [made preparations; packed our bags] and ·started on our way [Lwent up] to Jerusalem. 16Some of the ·followers [disciples] from Caesarea went with us and took us to the home of Mnason, where we would stay. He was from Cyprus and was one of the ·first [*or* early; *or* original] ·followers [disciples].

Paul Visits James

17[LArriving] In Jerusalem the ·believers [Lbrothers (and sisters)] ·were glad to see us [welcomed us warmly]. 18The next day Paul went with us to visit James, and all the elders [14:23] were there. 19Paul greeted them and ·told [recounted for] them ·everything [*or* in detail what; *or* one by one the things] God had done among the ·other nations [Gentiles] through ·him [Lhis ministry/service]. 20When they heard this, they ·praised [gave glory to] God. Then they said to ·Paul [Lhim], "Brother, you can see that many thousands of ·our people [Lthe Jews] have become believers [2:41, 47; 4:4]. And they ·think it is very important to obey [Lare passionate about; are zealots for] ·the law of Moses [Lthe Law]. 21They have ·heard [been informed] about your teaching, that you tell ·our people [Lthe Jews] who live among the ·nations [Gentiles] to ·leave the law of Moses [Lforsake/abandon Moses]. They have heard that you tell them not to circumcise their children and not to ·obey [observe; Lwalk in] our ·customs [*or* traditional way of life]. 22What [Lthen; therefore] should we do? They will [Lsurely] ·learn [hear] that you have come. 23So ·we will tell you what to do [Ldo what we say]: Four of our men have made a ·promise to God [Lvow]. 24Take these men with you and share in their ·cleansing ceremony [ritual purification]. Pay their expenses so they can shave their heads [Ca ritual that indicates the end of a Nazirite's vows; Num. 6:13–20]. Then ·it will prove to everyone [Leveryone will know] that what they have heard about you is not true and that you ·follow [Lindeed keep/observe] the law of Moses in your own life. 25We have already sent a letter [Lwith our judgment/decision] to the Gentile believers [Cthe decision of the council of Jerusalem; 15:6–21]. The letter said: 'Do not eat food that has been offered to idols, or blood, or animals that have been strangled. Do not take part in sexual sin [15:20].' "

26The next day Paul took the four men and shared in the ·cleansing ceremony [ritual purification] with them. Then he went to the Temple and announced the time when the days of the ·cleansing ceremony [ritual purification] would be finished and an ·offering [sacrifice] would be ·given [offered] for each of the men.

27When the seven days were almost over [Cthe period of time for purification; Num. 19:12], some of ·his people [Lthe Jews] from [Cthe province of] Asia saw Paul at the Temple. They ·caused all the people to be upset [stirred up/incited the whole crowd] and grabbed Paul. 28They shouted,

"·People of Israel [[L]Men, Israelites], help us! This is the man who goes
everywhere teaching against our people [[C]Israel], against ·the law of
Moses [[L]the Law], and against this ·Temple [[L]place]. Now he has brought
some Greeks into the Temple and has ·made this holy place unclean
[defiled this holy place]!" 29(They said this because they had seen
Trophimus [20:4; 2 Tim. 4:20], ·a man from Ephesus [[L]the Ephesian], with
Paul in ·Jerusalem [[L]the city]. They ·thought [supposed; assumed] that
Paul had brought him into the Temple [[C]God-fearing Gentiles were only
allowed in the outer courtyard, known as the "court of the Gentiles"].)
30·All the people in Jerusalem [[L]The whole city] became ·upset [aroused].
Together they ·ran [*or* rushed together; came running], took Paul, and
dragged him out of the Temple. The Temple doors were closed immediately. 31While they were trying to kill ·Paul [[L]him], the ·commander of the
Roman army in Jerusalem [[L]tribune/commander of the regiment; [C]a tribune (Greek: *chiliarch*) oversaw about a thousand soldiers] ·learned
[received the report] that ·there was trouble in the whole city [[L]all Jerusalem
was in confusion/an uproar]. 32Immediately he took some ·officers and
soldiers [[L]soldiers and centurions; [C]centurions oversaw about a hundred
soldiers] and ran to the place where the crowd was gathered. When the
people saw ·them [[L]the tribune and the soldiers], they stopped beating
Paul. 33The ·commander [tribune] went to Paul and arrested him. He told
his soldiers to ·bind [shackle] Paul with two chains. Then he ·asked
[inquired about] who he was and what he had done wrong. 34Some in the
crowd were yelling one thing, and some were yelling another. Because of
all this ·confusion and shouting [uproar; noise; tumult], the commander
could not learn ·what had happened [the truth/facts]. So he ordered the
soldiers to take Paul to the ·army building [barracks; [C]probably the Roman
garrison known as the Antonia fortress, overlooking the temple from the
north]. 35When ·Paul [[L]he] came to the steps [[C]leading up to the Antonia
fortress], the soldiers had to carry him because ·the people were ready to
hurt him [[L]of the violence of the mob/crowd]. 36[[L]For] The whole mob was
following them, shouting, "·Kill [*or* Away with] him!"
37As ·the soldiers [[L]they] were about to take Paul into the ·army building [barracks], he spoke to the ·commander [tribune], "May I say
something to you?"
·The commander [[L]He] said, "Do you speak Greek? 38·I thought you
were [[L]Are you not…?] the Egyptian who started ·some trouble against
the government [a revolt; an insurrection] ·not long ago [*or* some time
ago; [C]according to the Jewish historian Josephus, the event occurred about
three years prior to this] and led four thousand ·killers [terrorists; cut-
throats; [L]of the sicarii; [C]Josephus identifies sicarii ("dagger-men") as
assassins who mingled with crowds and used daggers to murder Romans
and their collaborators] out to the desert."
39Paul said, "No, I am a Jew from Tarsus [9:11] in the ·country [prov-
ince] of Cilicia [6:9]. I am a citizen of that ·important [[L]not insignificant]
city. ·Please [[L]I beg/urge you], let me speak to the people."
40·The commander [[L]He] gave permission, so Paul stood on the steps
and ·waved [signaled/gestured with] ·his hand to quiet the people [[L]his
hand]. When there was silence, he spoke to them in the Hebrew language
[[C]probably Aramaic; the biblical writers do not distinguish between these
related languages, calling both "Hebrew"].

Paul Speaks to the People

22 Paul said, "[LMen,] Brothers and fathers, listen to my defense to you." 2When they heard him ·speaking [addressing them in] the Hebrew [*or* Aramaic; 21:40] language, they became ·very [even more] quiet. Paul said, 3"I am a Jew, born in Tarsus [9:11] in the ·country [province] of Cilicia [6:9], but I ·grew up [was brought up; *or* was educated] in this city [CJerusalem]. I was ·a student of [Linstructed at the feet of; Cidiom indicating the role of a disciple] Gamaliel [Ca famous teacher of the Pharisees; 5:34], who ·carefully [*or* strictly] taught me everything about the law of our ·ancestors [forefathers; fathers]. I was ·very serious about serving [Lzealous/passionate for] God, just as are all of you here today. 4I persecuted the people who followed ·the Way of Jesus [Lthis Way; Canother name for the Christian movement; 9:2; 18:25; 19:23], ·and some of them were even killed [Lup to the point of death; 7:60]. I ·arrested [Lbound] men and women and put them in jail. 5The high priest and the whole council of elders can ·tell you this is true [testify about me]. They gave me letters to the brothers [Ctheir fellow Jewish leaders] in Damascus. So I was going there to ·arrest [Lbind] these people and bring them back to Jerusalem to be punished.

6"About noon when I came near Damascus, a bright light from heaven suddenly ·flashed [shone] all around me. 7I fell to the ground and heard a voice saying, 'Saul, Saul, why are you persecuting me?' 8I asked, 'Who are you, Lord?' ·The voice [LHe] said, 'I am Jesus ·of Nazareth [*or* the Nazarene] whom you are persecuting.' 9Those who were with me did not ·understand [*or* hear; Cthe word can mean either "hear" or "understand," but 9:7 suggests the latter] the voice [Lthat was speaking to me], but they saw the light. 10I said, 'What shall I do, Lord?' The Lord answered, 'Get up and go to Damascus. There you will be told about all the things ·I have planned [*or* assigned; appointed] for you to do.' 11I could not see, because ·the bright light had made me blind [Lof the glory/brilliance of that light]. So ·my companions [Lthose with me] led me [Lby the hand] into Damascus.

12"There a man named Ananias came to me. He was a ·religious [devout; God-fearing] man; ·he obeyed the law of Moses [L…according to the law], and all the Jews who lived there ·respected [spoke well of] him. 13He [Lcame to me and] stood by me and said, 'Brother Saul, ·see again [Llook up; Can idiom for regaining sight]!' ·Immediately [LAt that hour] I ·was able to see [Llooked up at] him. 14He said, 'The God of our ·ancestors [forefathers; fathers] ·chose [appointed] you long ago to know his ·plan [will; purpose], to see the Righteous One [CJesus], and to hear ·words [a divine message; La voice] from ·him [Lhis mouth]. 15You will be his witness to all people, telling them about what you have seen and heard. 16Now, ·why wait any longer [what are you waiting for]? Get up, be baptized, and wash your sins away, ·trusting in him to save you [Lcalling on his name].'

17"Later, when I returned to Jerusalem, I was praying in the Temple, and I ·saw a vision [*or* fell into a trance]. 18I saw ·the Lord [Lhim] saying to me, 'Hurry! Leave Jerusalem ·now [*or* quickly]! The people here will not accept ·the truth [Lyour testimony/witness] about me.' 19But I said, 'Lord, they [Lthemselves; very well] know that in every synagogue I put ·the believers [Lthose who believe in you] in jail and beat them. 20They also know I was there when Stephen, your ·witness [*or* martyr], ·was killed [Lhad his blood shed]. I [myself; indeed] stood there agreeing and ·holding [guarding; keeping] the coats of those who were killing him!' 21But the Lord said to me, '·Leave now [Go!]. I will send you far away to the ·other nations [Gentiles].'"

22·The crowd [LThey] listened to ·Paul [him] until he said ·this [Lthis word]. Then they ·began shouting [Lraised their voice saying], "·Get rid of him [Kill him; LRemove this one from the earth]! He doesn't deserve to live!" 23They ·shouted [yelled; screamed], threw off their coats, and threw dust into the air [Cdemonstrations of anger and disgust].

24Then the ·commander [tribune] ordered the soldiers to take ·Paul [Lhim] into the ·army building [barracks] and ·beat him [Lquestion him by whipping/flogging]. ·He wanted [L…in order] to make Paul tell why the people were shouting against him like this [Cflogging was commonly used to gain information]. 25But as the soldiers were ·tying him up [*or* stretching him out (on the posts)], preparing to ·beat [whip; flog] him, Paul said to an officer nearby, "Do you have the right to ·beat [whip; flog] a Roman citizen who ·has not been proven guilty [Lis uncondemned; Cthis was against Roman law]?"

26When the ·officer [Lcenturion; 21:32] heard this, he went to the ·commander [tribune] and reported it. The officer said, "·Do you know what you are doing [*or* What are you about to do]? This man is a Roman citizen."

27The ·commander [tribune] came to ·Paul [Lhim] and said, "Tell me, are you really a Roman citizen?"

He answered, "Yes."

28The ·commander [tribune] ·said [Lresponded], "I paid a lot of money to become a Roman citizen."

But Paul said, "I was born a citizen."

29[LTherefore] The men who were preparing to question Paul ·moved away from him [withdrew] immediately. The ·commander [tribune] was frightened because he had already ·tied [bound] ·Paul [Lhim], and Paul was a Roman citizen.

Paul Speaks to the Jewish Council

30The next day ·the commander [Lhe] ·decided [desired] to learn [with certainty; the true reason] why the Jews were accusing ·Paul [Lhim]. So he ordered the ·leading [Tchief] priests and the ·council [Sanhedrin; CJewish high court comprised of 70 Jewish leaders; 4:15] to meet. ·The commander [LHe] ·took Paul's chains off [Lreleased him]. Then he brought Paul out and stood him before their meeting.

23 Paul looked [Lintently] at the ·council [Sanhedrin; 22:30] and said, "[LMen,] Brothers, I have ·lived my life [conducted myself; Llived as a citizen] ·without guilt feelings [Lwith a good/clear conscience] before God up to this day." 2Ananias, the high priest [Chigh priest from AD 47 to 58; not the man named in 22:12], heard this and told the men who were standing near Paul to ·hit [strike] him on the mouth. 3Paul said to ·Ananias [Lhim], "God ·will [*or* is about to] ·hit [strike] you, too! You ·are like a wall that has been painted white [whitewashed wall!; Ca wall with many flaws covered only by a coat of paint]. ·You sit [LDo you sit…?] there and judge me, using the ·law of Moses [Llaw], but you are telling them to hit me, and that is against the law."

4The men standing near Paul said to him, "·You cannot insult [*or* How dare you insult; LAre you insulting…?] God's high priest like that!"

5Paul said, "Brothers, I did not know this man was the high priest [Cperhaps because of poor eyesight (Gal. 4:15; 6:11), or because the high priest was not in his formal vestments, or Paul is speaking ironically]. It is written in the Scriptures, 'You must not ·curse [Lspeak evil of] a leader of your people [Ex. 22:28].'" 6Some of the men in the meeting were Sadducees

[CJewish religious party with most influence in the Jewish high court
(Sanhedrin) and among the Temple leadership; 4:1], **and others were**
Pharisees [Creligious party that strictly observed OT laws and added traditions; 5:34]. **·Knowing** [*or* Realizing] **this, Paul ·shouted** [called out] **·to**
them [Lin the council/Sanhedrin], **"My brothers, I am a Pharisee, ·and my**
father was a Pharisee [*or* descended from Pharisees; La son of Pharisees]. **I**
am on trial here because ·I believe that people will rise from the dead [Lof
the hope and the resurrection]**."**

7**When Paul said this, there was an argument between the Pharisees**
and the Sadducees, and the ·group [assembly] **was divided.** 8([LFor] **The**
Sadducees ·do not believe that people will rise from the dead [Lsay there
is no resurrection] **nor do they believe in angels or spirits. But the**
Pharisees believe in them all.) 9**So there was a great ·uproar** [commotion;
outcry]. **Some of the ·teachers of the law** [scribes], **who were Pharisees,**
stood up and ·argued [protested violently/vehemently], **"We find ·noth-**
ing wrong [no fault; nothing evil] **with this man. ·Maybe** [LWhat if...?] **an**
angel or a spirit did speak to him."

10**The argument was ·beginning to turn into such a fight** [becoming so
great] **that the ·commander** [tribune] **was afraid they would tear Paul to**
pieces. So he told the soldiers to go down and take Paul away and ·put
him in [bring him to] **the ·army building** [barracks].

11**The next night the Lord came and stood by Paul. He said, "Be brave** [*or*
Don't be afraid; Rest assured]! [LFor just as] **You have ·told** [testified to] **peo-**
ple in Jerusalem about me. You must ·do the same [Ltestify to me] **in Rome."**

12**In the morning ·some of Paul's Jewish opponents** [Lthe Jews] **·made a**
plan [entered a conspiracy] **to kill Paul, and they took an oath not to eat**
or drink anything until they had killed him. 13**There were more than forty**
men who ·made this plan [formed this conspiracy]. 14**They went to the**
·leading [Tchief] **priests and the elders and said, "We have ·taken** [sworn]
an oath not to ·eat or drink [Ltaste anything] **until we have killed Paul.**
15**So** [Lnow] **this is what we want you** [Ltogether with the Sanhedrin] **to do:**
Send a message to the ·commander [tribune] **to bring Paul out to you as**
though you want to ·ask him more questions [Ldetermine more accurately
the facts of his case]. **We will be waiting to kill him ·while he is on the way**
[before he arrives] **here."**

16**But ·Paul's nephew** [Lthe son of Paul's sister] **heard about this ·plan**
[plot; Lambush plan] **and went to the ·army building** [barracks] **and told**
Paul. 17**Then Paul called one of the ·officers** [centurions] **and said, "Take**
this young man to the ·commander [tribune]. [LFor] **He has ·a message**
for him [Lsomething to report to him]**."**

18**So ·the officer** [Lhe] **brought ·Paul's nephew** [Lhim] **to the ·commander**
[tribune] **and said, "The prisoner, Paul,** [Lcalled me over and] **asked me to**
bring this young man to you. He wants to tell you something."

19**The ·commander** [tribune] **took the young man's hand and led him**
to a place where they could be alone. He asked, "What do you ·want to tell
[have to report to] **me?"**

20**·The young man** [LHe] **said, "The Jews have ·decided** [conspired;
agreed] **to ask you to bring Paul down to ·their council meeting** [the
Sanhedrin] **tomorrow. They want you to think they are going to ·ask him**
more questions [Linquire more accurately concerning him]. 21**But don't**
·believe [be persuaded by] **them!** [LBecause] **More than forty men are**
·hiding and waiting to kill Paul [Lwaiting in ambush for him]. **They have**

all taken an oath not to eat or drink until they have killed him. Now they are [Lready,] waiting for you to agree."

22[LTherefore] The ·commander [tribune] sent the young man away, ordering him, "Don't tell anyone that you have ·told [revealed to] me ·about their plan [Lthese things]."

Paul Is Sent to Caesarea

23Then ·the commander [Lhe] called two ·officers [centurions] and said, "Prepare two hundred soldiers, seventy horsemen, and two hundred men with spears to leave for Caesarea at ·nine o'clock tonight [Lat the third hour of the night; Cnight begins about 6 PM]. 24Get ·some horses [mounts; Lanimals] for Paul to ride so he can be taken to Governor Felix [Cheld office from AD 52–59] safely." 25And he wrote a letter ·that said [of this kind; to this effect; Lpossessing this type/pattern]:

26From Claudius Lysias.
To the Most Excellent Governor Felix:
Greetings.

27Some of the Jews had ·taken [seized] this man and ·planned [were about] to kill him. But I learned that he is a Roman citizen, so I went with my soldiers and ·saved [rescued] him. 28I wanted to know ·why [Lthe charge/reason] they were accusing him, so I brought him before their ·council meeting [Sanhedrin]. 29I ·learned [Lfound; discovered] that the accusation had to do with ·questions [debates; disputed matters] about their own law [Cthe law of Moses], but no charge was worthy of death or ·jail [chains]. 30When I was ·told [informed] that ·some of them were planning to kill Paul [Lthere was a plot against the man], I sent him to you at once. I also ·told [ordered] ·them [Lhis accusers] to tell you what they have against him.

31So the soldiers ·did what they were told [followed orders] and took Paul and brought him to the city of Antipatris [Ccity 40 miles from Jerusalem and 25 miles from Caesarea] that night. 32The next day the horsemen ·went [were sent] with ·Paul to Caesarea [Lhim], but the other soldiers went back to the ·army building in Jerusalem [Lbarracks]. 33When ·the horsemen [Lthey] came to Caesarea and ·gave [delivered] the letter to the governor, they turned Paul over to him. 34The governor read the letter and asked Paul, "What ·area [province] are you from?" When he learned that Paul was from Cilicia [9:11], 35he said, "I will hear your case when ·those who are against you [your accusers] come here, too." Then the governor gave orders for Paul to be kept under guard in Herod's ·palace [headquarters; Praetorium].

Paul Is Accused

24 Five days later Ananias, the high priest [23:1], ·went to the city of Caesarea [Lcame down] with some of the elders and a ·lawyer [orator; Cone who speaks in court] named Tertullus. They had come to make charges against Paul before the governor. 2Paul was called into the meeting, and Tertullus began to accuse him, saying, "Most Excellent Felix! Our people enjoy ·much [*or* a long period of] peace because of you, and many ·wrong things in our country are being made right [*or* improvements/reforms have been made] through your ·wise help [*or* foresight]. 3We ·accept [acknowledge] these things always and in every place, ·and we are thankful for them [*or* …with much gratitude/thanksgiving]. 4But not wanting to ·take any more of your time [detain you; *or* bore you], I ·beg [encourage; urge] you ·to be kind and [*or* because you are kind/patient to] listen to our few words. 5We have found this man to be a ·troublemaker

[pest; plague], ·stirring up [*or* instigating riots among] ·his people [LJews]
everywhere in the world. He is a ·leader [ringleader] of the Nazarene
·group [party; faction; sect]. 6Also, he was trying to ·make the Temple
unclean [defile/profane/desecrate the Temple], but we ·stopped [*or*
grabbed; arrested] him. |And we wanted to judge him by our own law. 7But
the ·officer [tribune] Lysias came and used much force to take him from
us. 8And Lysias commanded ·those who wanted to accuse Paul [his accus-
ers] to come to you.|n By ·asking him questions [cross-examining him]
yourself, you can ·decide [learn; come to know] ·if all these things are true
[*or* the nature of our accusations]." 9The ·others [LJews] ·agreed [*or* joined
in the attack] and said that all of this was true.

10When the governor ·made a sign [motioned; gestured] for ·Paul [Lhim]
to speak, Paul ·said [responded], "I know you have been a judge over this
nation for ·a long time [Lmany years]. So I ·am happy to [gladly; confi-
dently] defend myself before you. 11You can ·learn [find out; verify] for
yourself that I went to worship in Jerusalem ·only [Lno more than] twelve
days ago. 12·Those who are accusing me [LThey] did not find me arguing
with anyone in the Temple or stirring up the ·people [crowd] in the synagogues or in the city. 13They cannot prove the ·things they are saying
[charges; accusations] against me now. 14But I will ·tell you this [admit/
confess this to you]: I worship the God of our ·ancestors [forefathers;
fathers] as a follower of ·the Way of Jesus [Lthe Way; 22:4], which they call a
·sect [faction; cult]. But I believe everything that is ·taught in [*or* in agreement with; Laccording to] the law of Moses and that is written in the books
of the Prophets. 15I have the same hope in God that they ·have [accept]—
the hope that all people, ·good and bad [righteous and unrighteous], will
surely be ·raised from the dead [resurrected; Cthe righteous to salvation, the
wicked for judgment; Is. 26:19; Dan. 12:2]. 16This is why I always try to ·do
what I believe is right [Lhave a clear conscience] before God and people.

17"After being away from Jerusalem for ·several [Lmany] years, I went
back to bring ·money [alms; gifts for the poor] to my ·people [nation;
Rom. 15:26; 1 Cor. 16:1; 2 Cor. 8:4; 9:1, 13] and to ·offer sacrifices [present
offerings]. 18I was doing this when they found me in the Temple. I ·had
finished the cleansing ceremony [*or* I was ritually pure; 21:20–29] ·and
had not made any trouble; no people were gathering around me [Lwith
neither crowd nor trouble]. 19But there were some ·people [LJews] from
Asia who should be here, standing before you. If ·I have really done anything wrong [Lthey have anything against me], they are the ones who
should accuse me. 20Or ·ask these people here [Llet these people themselves state] if they found any ·wrong [crime; unrighteousness] in me
when I stood before the ·council in Jerusalem [Sanhedrin]. 21But I did
shout one thing when I stood before them: '·You are judging me [*or* I am
on trial before you] today ·because I believe that people will rise from [*or*
with respect to the issue of the resurrection of] the dead!' "

22Felix already ·understood much about [Lknew accurately the facts about]
the ·Way of Jesus [LWay; 22:4]. He ·stopped the trial [adjourned the hearing]
and said, "When ·commander [tribune] Lysias comes ·here [Ldown], I will
decide your case." 23Felix ·told [Lordered] the ·officer [centurion] to keep
·Paul [Lhim] guarded but to give him some freedom and to let his ·friends
[Lown people] ·bring what he needed [meet his needs; Lserve him].

24:6–8 And . . . you. Some Greek copies do not contain the bracketed text.

Paul Speaks to Felix and His Wife

24After some days Felix came with his wife, Drusilla, who was Jewish,
and asked for Paul to be brought to him. He listened to Paul talk about
·believing [faith] in Christ Jesus. 25But Felix became afraid when Paul spoke
about ·living right [righteousness; justice], self-control, and the ·time when
God will judge the world [Lcoming judgment]. He said, "·Go away [*or* That's
enough for] now. When I have ·more time [another opportunity], I will call
for you." 26At the same time Felix hoped that ·Paul [Lhe] would give him
·some money [*or* a bribe], so he often sent for Paul and talked with him.
27But after two years, Felix was ·replaced [succeeded] by Porcius Festus
as governor [Cfrom AD 59–62]. But Felix had left Paul in prison to please
the Jews.

Paul Asks to See Caesar

25 Three days after Festus ·became governor [Larrived in the
province], he went [Lup] from Caesarea to Jerusalem. 2There
the ·leading [Tchief] priests and the important leaders [Lof the Jews]
made charges against Paul before Festus. 3They ·asked [urged] Festus to
do them a favor. They wanted him to send Paul back to Jerusalem,
because they ·had a plan [Lplanned an ambush] to kill him on the way.
4But Festus answered that Paul would be kept in Caesarea and that he
himself was returning there soon. 5He said, "[LTherefore,] Some of your
·leaders [authorities] should go with me. They can accuse the man there
in Caesarea, if he has really done something wrong."
6·Festus [LHe] stayed ·in Jerusalem [Lamong them] another eight or ten
days and then went ·back [Ldown] to Caesarea. The next day he ·told the
soldiers to bring Paul [Lordered Paul to be brought] before him. Festus
was seated on the ·judge's seat [tribunal] 7when Paul came into the room.
The ·people [LJews] who had come [Ldown] from Jerusalem stood around
him, making serious charges against him, which they could not prove.
8This is what Paul said to defend himself: "I have done ·nothing wrong
[committed no offense/sin/crime] against the law [Lof the Jews], against
the Temple, or against Caesar."
9But Festus wanted to ·please [curry favor with; *or* do a favor for] the
·people [LJews]. So he asked Paul, "·Do you want [*or* Are you willing] to go
[Lup] to Jerusalem for me to ·judge [try] you there on these charges?"
10Paul said, "I am standing at Caesar's ·judgment seat [*or* court; tribu-
nal] now, where I should be ·judged [tried]. I have done nothing wrong to
·them [Lthe Jews]; you ·know this is true [clearly recognize this]. 11If I have
done something wrong and ·the law says I must die [Lworthy of death], I
do not ask to be saved from death. But if these charges are ·not true [base-
less], then no one can ·give me [hand me over; *or* make me a gift; CPaul
detects Festus' desire to gain favor with the Jews] to them. I ·want Caesar
to hear my case [appeal to Caesar/the emperor; Cthe right of a Roman citizen for a capital offense]!"
12Festus talked about this with his ·advisers [council]. Then he said,
"You have ·asked to see [appealed to] Caesar, so you will go to Caesar!"

Paul Before King Agrippa

13A few days later King Agrippa [CAgrippa II, the Jewish king who ruled
parts of Palestine from AD 52 to 92] and Bernice [CAgrippa's sister and
probably his lover] came to Caesarea to ·visit [*or* welcome; pay their respects
to] Festus. 14They stayed there for ·some time [Lmany days], and Festus told
the king about Paul's case. Festus said, "There is a man that Felix left in
prison. 15When I went to Jerusalem, the ·leading [Tchief] priests and the
elders there made charges against him, asking me to ·sentence him to death

[Lsentence/condemn him]. **16But I answered, 'When a man is accused of a crime, ·Romans do not** [Lit is not a custom for Romans to] **hand him over until he has been allowed to face his accusers and defend himself against their charges.' 17So when these people came here ·to Caesarea for the trial** [Lwith me], **I did not ·waste time** [postpone/delay the case]. **The next day I sat on the ·judge's seat** [tribunal] **and commanded that the man be brought in. 18·They stood up and accused him** [LThe accusers stood up (to speak)], **but not of any ·serious crime** [evil deeds] **as I ·thought they would** [expected]. **19The things they ·said** [disputed] **were about their own ·religion** [*or* superstition] **and about a man named Jesus who died. But Paul ·said** [claimed] **that he is still alive. 20·Not knowing** [At a loss] **how to ·find out about** [investigate] **these questions, I asked Paul, '·Do you want** [*or* Are you willing] **to go to Jerusalem and be ·judged** [tried] **there** [Lconcerning these things]**?' 21But he asked to be ·kept in Caesarea** [Lheld in custody]. **He wants a decision from ·the emperor** [*or* His Majesty; the Revered/August One; CA title for Caesar, the ruler of the Roman world, first given to Caesar "Augustus"; here it refers to Nero]. **So I ordered that he be held** [in custody] **until I could send him to Caesar."**

22Agrippa said to Festus, "I would also like to hear this man myself."

Festus said, "Tomorrow you will hear him."

23 [LTherefore] **The next day Agrippa and Bernice ·appeared** [entered] **with great ·show** [pomp; fanfare]. **They went into the ·judgment room** [audience hall] **with the ·army leaders** [tribunes] **and the important men of ·Caesarea** [Lthe city]. **Then Festus ·ordered the soldiers** [Lgave the order] **to bring Paul in. 24Festus said, "King Agrippa and all who ·gathered** [*or* present] **here with us, you see this man. ·All the people** [The Jewish community; LAll the multitude of the Jews], **here and in Jerusalem, have ·complained to** [*or* petitioned] **me about him, shouting that he should not live any longer. 25But I found ·no reason to order his** [Lhe had done nothing deserving] **death. But since he ·asked to be judged by Caesar** [appealed to the emperor], **I decided to send him. 26But I have nothing definite to write the ·emperor** [Llord; sovereign] **about him. So I have brought him before all of you—especially you, King Agrippa. ·I hope you can question him and give me** [L...so that from this examination, I might have] **something to write. 27**[LFor] **I think it is ·foolish** [unreasonable] **to send a prisoner to Caesar without telling what charges are against him."**

Paul Defends Himself

26 Agrippa said to Paul, "You may now speak for yourself."

Then Paul ·raised [stretched out] **his hand and began to defend himself. 2He said, "King Agrippa, I am very ·blessed** [*or* fortunate] **to stand before you and will ·answer** [Ldefend myself against] **all the charges the Jews make against me. 3·You know so much** [You especially know; *or* I am especially blessed because you know] **about all the customs and the ·things they argue about** [controversies of the Jews], **so ·please** [I urge/beg you to] **listen to me patiently.**

4"All ·my people [Lthe Jews] **know about my ·whole life** [Lmanner of life from youth], **how I lived from the beginning ·in my own country and later** [*or* among my own people and] **in Jerusalem. 5They have known me for a long time. If they ·want** [are willing] **to, they can ·tell** [testify to] **you that I ·was a good** [Llived as a] **Pharisee. ·And the Pharisees obey the laws of my tradition more carefully than any other group** [L...the strictest sect/party of our religion]. **6Now I ·am** [stand here] **on trial because I**

hope for the promise that God made to our ·ancestors [forefathers;
fathers; [C]either the hope of the Messiah or the resurrection from the dead].
7This is the promise that the twelve tribes of our people hope to receive as
they ·serve [*or* worship] God day and night. My king, ·they [[L]the Jews]
have accused me because ·I hope for this same promise [[L]of this hope]!
8Why do any of you people think it is ·impossible [unbelievable] for God
to raise people from the dead?

9"I, too, thought ·I ought [it was necessary] to do many things against
[[L]the name of] Jesus ·from Nazareth [*or* the Nazarene]. 10And that is what
I did in Jerusalem. The ·leading [[T]chief] priests gave me the ·power
[authority] to put many of ·God's people [God's holy people; the saints]
in ·jail [prison], and when they were ·being killed [*or* condemned to die],
I ·agreed it was a good thing [[L]cast my vote against them]. 11In every synagogue, I often punished them and tried to make them ·speak against
[blaspheme; curse] Jesus. I was so ·angry [enraged] against them I even
went to ·other [*or* foreign] cities to ·find them and punish [pursue; *or*
persecute] them.

12"One time the ·leading [[T]chief] priests gave me ·permission [com-
mission] and the ·power [authority] to go to Damascus. 13On the ·way
[road] there, at noon, [[L]O king,] I saw a light from heaven. It was brighter
than the sun and ·flashed [shone] all around me and those who were traveling with me. 14We all fell to the ground. Then I heard a voice speaking
to me in the Hebrew language [[C]probably Aramaic, the common language
of the people in that area; 21:40], saying, 'Saul, Saul, why are you persecuting me? ·You are only hurting yourself by fighting me [[L]It is hard for
you to kick against the goads; Eccl. 12:11; [C]a goad was a sharp instrument
to herd cattle].' 15I said, 'Who are you, Lord?' The Lord said, 'I am Jesus,
the one you are persecuting. 16·Stand up [[L]Get up and stand on your feet]!
This is why I have come [appeared] to you today: I have ·chosen
[appointed] you to be my servant and my witness—you will tell people
the things that you have seen and the things that I will show you. 17I will
·keep you safe [rescue you] from your own people and also from the
·Gentiles [nations]. I am sending you to them 18to open their eyes so that
they may turn away from darkness to the light, away from the ·power [*or*
authority] of Satan and to God. ·Then [*or* …so that] their sins can be
forgiven, and they can have a place with those people who have been
·made holy [sanctified] by ·believing [faith] in me.'

19"[[L]So; Therefore] King Agrippa, after I had this vision from heaven, I
·obeyed [[L]was not disobedient to] it. 20[Indeed; *or* On the contrary] I began
telling people that they should ·change their hearts and lives and turn to
God [repent] and do ·things [works] ·to show they really had changed
[[L]worthy of repentance]. I told this first to those in Damascus, then in
Jerusalem, and ·in every part [all throughout the countryside] of Judea, and
also to ·people everywhere [[L]the Gentiles; the nations]. 21This is why the Jews
·took [seized] me and were trying to kill me in the Temple [[C]courts; 2:46].
22But God has helped me [from that day until now; [L]until this day], and so I
stand here today, ·telling [testifying/witnessing to] all people, small and
great, what I have seen. But I am saying only what the prophets and Moses
[[C]meaning the whole OT] said would happen— 23that the ·Christ [Messiah;
[C]the promised king and Savior] would ·die [[L]suffer; 3:17; 17:3], and as the
first to rise from the dead, he would ·bring [[L]proclaim] light to his own people [[C]the Jews] and to ·the Gentiles [the nations; people everywhere]."

Paul Tries to Persuade Agrippa

24While Paul was saying these things to defend himself, Festus said
loudly, "Paul, you are ·out of your mind [insane]! Too much ·study [learn-
ing] has driven you ·crazy [insane; mad]!"
25Paul said, "Most excellent Festus, I am not crazy. My words are true
and ·sensible [sober; rational]. 26[LFor] ·King Agrippa [LThe king] knows
about these things, and I can speak ·freely [boldly] to him. [LFor] I ·know
[Lam convinced/persuaded] ·he has heard about all of these things [Lnone
of these things were hidden from him], because they did not happen off
in a corner. 27King Agrippa, do you believe ·what the prophets wrote [Lthe
prophets]? I know you believe."
28King Agrippa said to Paul, "Do you think you can persuade me to
become a Christian in such a short time? [*or* In a short time you will persuade me to become a Christian!]"
29Paul said, "Whether it is a short or a long time, I pray to God that not
only you but every person listening to me today ·would be saved and be
[Lmight become] like me—except for these chains I have."
30Then ·King Agrippa [Lthe king], ·Governor Festus [Lthe governor],
Bernice, and all the people sitting with them stood up 31and left the room.
Talking to each other, they said, "This man has done nothing ·that
deserves [worthy of] death or ·imprisonment [chains]." 32And Agrippa
said to Festus, "We could let this man go free, ·but he has [Lif he had not]
·asked Caesar to hear his case [Lappealed to Caesar]."

Paul Sails for Rome

27 It was decided that we would sail for Italy. An ·officer [centu-
rion] named Julius, who served in the ·emperor's army
[Imperial/Augustan regiment; Ca military unit directly under Caesar],
·guarded [took charge of] Paul and some other prisoners. 2We got on a
ship that was from the city of Adramyttium [Ca seaport on the northwest
coast of Asia Minor] and was about to sail to different ports in Asia [Ca
Roman province, in present-day Turkey]. Aristarchus [19:29; 20:4; Col.
4:10; Philem. 24], a man from the city of Thessalonica [17:1] in
Macedonia [16:9], went with us. 3The next day we ·came to [landed at]
Sidon [12:20]. Julius was very ·good [kind; considerate] to Paul and gave
him freedom to go visit his friends, who took care of his needs. 4We left
Sidon and sailed ·close to [to the north of; Lunder the lee/shelter of] the
island of Cyprus [11:19], because the wind was blowing against us. 5We
·went [Lsailed] across the sea by Cilicia [6:9; 9:11] and Pamphylia [13:13]
and landed at the city of Myra [Ca significant city on the Andracus River]
in Lycia [Ca province in southeastern Asia Minor]. 6There the ·officer
[centurion] found a ship from Alexandria [Ca major city in Egypt] that
was going to Italy, so he put us on it.
7We sailed slowly for many days. We had a hard time reaching Cnidus
[Ca port on the southwest side of Asia Minor] because the wind was blowing against us, and we could not go any farther. So we sailed ·by the south
side [Lunder the shelter/lee] of the island of Crete [Ca large island off the
southern coast of Asia Minor] near Salmone [Ca promontory on the eastern coast of Crete, present-day Cape Sidero]. 8Sailing past it was hard.
Then we came to a place called Fair Havens [Ca bay on the southern coast
of Crete], near the ·city [town] of Lasea [Ca nearby Cretan city].
9We had lost much time, and it was now dangerous to sail, because it
was already after ·the Day of Cleansing [Lthe Fast; Cthe Day of Atonement;
Yom Kippur in Hebrew; Lev. 16; either late September or early October].

So Paul ·warned [advised] them, 10“Men, I can see there will be ·a lot of
trouble [Ldisaster and heavy loss] on this trip. The ship, the cargo, and
even our lives may be lost.” 11But the centurion was more persuaded by
the ·captain [pilot] and the owner of the ship than by what Paul said.
12Since that harbor was not a ·good [suitable; safe] place for the ship to
stay for the winter, ·most of the men [the majority] decided that the ship
·should leave [put to sea]. They hoped we could go to Phoenix and stay
there for the winter. Phoenix, a ·city [*or* port; *or* harbor] on the island of
Crete, had a harbor which faced southwest and northwest.

The Storm

13When a ·good [moderate; gentle] wind began to blow from the south,
the men on the ship thought they ·could reach their goal [*or* had achieved
their objective; *or* had the opportunity they were waiting for]. So they
pulled up the anchor, and we sailed very close to the island of Crete. 14But
·then [Lnot long after this] a ·very strong [violent; hurricane-like] wind
named the “northeaster” came from ·the island [Lit]. 15The ship was
caught in it and could not sail against it. So we stopped trying and ·let the
wind carry us [Lwere driven along]. 16When we went ·below [under the
lee/shelter of] a small island named Cauda [C23 miles off the south coast
of Crete], we were barely able to bring in the lifeboat. 17After the men
took the lifeboat in, they tied ·ropes [*or* cables] ·around [*or* under] the
ship to hold it together. The men were afraid that the ship would ·hit [run
aground on] the sandbanks of Syrtis [Coff the coast of North Africa], so
they lowered the ·sail [*or* sea anchor; Lgear] and let the wind carry the
ship. 18The next day the storm was blowing us so hard that the men threw
out some of the cargo. 19·A day later [LOn the third day] with their own
hands they threw out the ship’s ·equipment [rigging; tackle; gear]. 20When
we could not see the sun or the stars for many days, and ·the storm was
very bad [Lno small storm raged], we lost all hope of being saved.
21After ·the men [many] had ·gone without food [*or* lost their appetite]
for a long time, Paul stood up before them and said, “Men, you should
have ·listened to me [obeyed me; taken my advice]. You should not have
sailed from Crete. Then you would not have all this trouble and loss.
22But now I ·tell [urge; advise] you to ·cheer up [keep up your courage]
because none of you will ·die [be lost]. Only the ship will be lost. 23·Last
[LThis] night an angel ·came to [Lstood by] me from the God I belong to
and worship. 24The angel said, ‘Paul, do not be afraid. You must stand
before Caesar. And God has ·promised you that he will save the lives of
[graciously granted safety to] everyone sailing with you.’ 25So men, have
courage. [LFor] I trust in God that everything will happen as ·his angel
told me [LI have been told]. 26But we will ·crash [run aground] on ·an
[Lsome/a certain] island.”
27On the fourteenth night we were still ·being carried [drifting; *or*
being driven] around in the Adriatic Sea [Cthe sea between Greece and
Italy including the central Mediterranean]. About ·midnight [Lthe middle
of the night] the sailors thought we were close to land, 28so they ·lowered
a rope with a weight on the end of it into the water [took a sounding].
They found that the water was one hundred twenty feet deep [Ltwenty
fathoms]. They went a little farther and ·lowered the rope again [took a
sounding]. It was ninety feet [Lfifteen fathoms] deep. 29·The sailors
[LThey] were afraid that we would ·hit the rocks [run aground], so they
threw four anchors ·into the water [Lfrom the stern] and prayed for day-

light to come. 30Some of the sailors wanted to leave the ship, and they lowered the lifeboat, pretending they were throwing more anchors from the ·front of the ship [bow]. 31But Paul told the ·officer [centurion] and the other soldiers, "If these men do not stay in the ship, your lives cannot be saved." 32So the soldiers cut the ropes and let the lifeboat fall into the water.

33Just before dawn Paul ·began persuading [begged; encouraged; urged] all the people to ·eat something [Ltake food]. He said, "·For the past fourteen days [LToday is the fourteenth day] you have been ·waiting and watching [in suspense] and ·not eating [Lgoing without food, taking nothing]. 34Now I ·beg [urge; encourage] you to ·eat something [Ltake food]. You need it to ·stay alive [survive]. None of you will lose even one hair off your heads." 35After he said this, Paul took some bread and thanked God for it before all of them. He broke off a piece and began eating [Creflecting language associated with the Lord's Supper]. 36They all felt ·better [encouraged] and ·started eating [Ltook bread], too. 37·There were [LWe were in all] two hundred seventy-six people on the ship. 38When they had eaten all they wanted, they began making the ship lighter by throwing the ·grain [wheat] into the sea.

The Ship Is Destroyed

39When daylight came, they did not recognize the land, but they saw a bay with a beach and wanted to sail the ship ·to [up on] the beach if they could. 40So they ·cut the ropes to [Lcast off] the anchors and left ·the anchors [Lthem] in the sea. At the same time, they untied the ropes that were holding the rudders. Then they raised the front sail into the wind and sailed toward the beach. 41But the ship hit a ·sandbank [reef; shoal; *or* cross-current; Lplace of two seas]. The front of the ship stuck there and could not move, but the ·back of the ship [stern] began to break up from the big waves.

42The soldiers ·decided [made a decision] to kill the prisoners so none of them could swim away and escape. 43But ·Julius, the officer, [Lthe centurion] wanted to ·let Paul live [Lsave Paul] and ·did not allow the soldiers to kill the prisoners [Lstopped them from their plan]. Instead he ordered everyone who could swim to jump into the water first and swim to land. 44The rest were to follow using wooden boards or pieces of the ship. And this is how all the people made it safely to land.

Paul on the Island of Malta

28 When we ·were safe on land [reached safety], we learned that the island was called Malta [C58 miles southwest of Sicily]. 2The ·people who lived there [native people; Lbarbarians; Ca term referring to non-Greek speakers] were very ·good [kind] to us. Because it was raining and very cold, they made a fire and welcomed all of us. 3Paul gathered a pile of ·sticks [brushwood] and was putting them on the fire when a ·poisonous snake [viper] came out because of the heat and ·bit [Lfastened itself to] him on the hand. 4The ·people living on the island [native people; 28:2] saw the ·snake [Lcreature; animal] hanging from Paul's hand and said to each other, "This man must be a murderer! He ·did not die in [Lescaped from] the sea, but Justice [LDikē; Cpronounced di-káy); the goddess of justice] ·does not want [has not allowed] him to live." 5But Paul shook the ·snake [Lcreature; animal] off into the fire and ·was not hurt [suffered no harm]. 6·The people [LThey] thought that Paul would swell up or fall down dead. They waited and watched him for a long time, but nothing ·bad [Lunusual] happened to him. So they changed their minds and said, "He is a god!"

7There ·were some fields [*or* was an estate] around there owned by Publius, ·an important man [*or* the chief official; governor] on the island.

He ·welcomed [received] **us into his home and ·was very good to us** [provided generous hospitality; treated us as honored guests] **for three days.** **[8]Publius' father was sick in bed with a fever and dysentery** [Ca serious illness that includes cramping and severe diarrhea]. **Paul went to him, prayed, and ·put** [*or* laid] **his hands on the man and healed him.** **[9]After this, ·all the other** [Lthe rest of the] **sick people on the island came to Paul, and he healed them, too.** **[10-11]The people on the island gave us many honors. When we were ready to leave, they gave us the ·things** [provisions] **we needed.**

Paul Goes to Rome

After three months we got on a ship from Alexandria [27:6] **that had stayed on the island during the winter. On the front of the ship was the sign of the ·twin gods** [CCastor and Pollux, the twin sons of Zeus; protectors of sailors]. **[12]We ·stopped** [put in] **at Syracuse** [Ca major city on the island of Sicily] **for three days.** **[13]From there we ·sailed to** [Lset sail and arrived at] **Rhegium** [Ca port city on the Italian mainland across from Sicily]. **The next day a wind began to blow from the south, and ·a day later** [Lon the second day] **we came to Puteoli** [Ca bit further north on the southwestern coast of Italy]. **[14]We found some ·believers** [Lbrothers (and sisters)] **there who ·asked** [invited] **us to stay with them for ·a week** [Lseven days]. **·Finally** [LAnd so in this way], **we came to Rome.** **[15]The ·believers** [Lbrothers (and sisters)] **in Rome heard that we were there and came out as far as the ·Market** [LForum] **of Appius** [Cabout 40 miles from Rome] **and the Three Inns** [Ceight miles toward Rome from the Market of Appius] **to meet us. When Paul saw them, he thanked God and ·was encouraged** [took courage].

Paul in Rome

[16]When we arrived at Rome, Paul was allowed to live alone, with the soldier who guarded him.

[17]Three days later ·Paul [Lhe] **sent for the leaders of the ·Jewish community** [LJews] **there. When they came together, he said, "**[LMen,] **Brothers, I have done nothing against our people or the customs of our ·ancestors** [forefathers; fathers]. **But I was ·arrested** [made a prisoner] **in Jerusalem and given ·to** [Linto the hands of] **the Romans.** **[18]After they ·asked me many questions** [examined me; tried my case], **they wanted to let me go free because they could find no reason why I should be ·killed** [given the death penalty]. **[19]But the Jews there ·argued against that** [objected], **so I had to ·ask to come to Rome to have my trial before** [Lappeal to] **Caesar. But I have no ·charge** [accusation] **to bring against my own ·people** [nation]. **[20]That is why I wanted to see you and talk with you. I am bound with this chain because ·I believe in** [Lof] **the hope of Israel."**

[21]They ·answered [said to] **Paul, "We have received no letters from Judea about you. None of our Jewish brothers who have come from there brought news or told us anything bad about you.** **[22]But we ·want to hear** [consider it worth hearing] **your ideas, because we know that people everywhere are speaking against this ·religious group** [sect]."

[23]Paul and the people ·chose [arranged; appointed] **a day for a meeting and on that day ·many more of the Jews** [La great number] **met with Paul at the place he was staying. He spoke to them ·all day long** [Lfrom morning until evening]. **Using the law of Moses and the prophets' writings** [Cthe whole Old Testament], **he explained** [Lby testifying/bearing witness about] **the kingdom of God, and he tried to persuade them to believe these things about Jesus.** **[24]Some ·believed** [Lwere persuaded by] **what Paul said, but others ·did** [were] **not.** **[25]So they ·argued** [disagreed with each other] **and began leaving after Paul said one more thing to them:**

"The Holy Spirit spoke the truth to your ·ancestors [fathers] **through**
Isaiah the prophet, saying,

26'Go to this people and say:
You will ·listen and listen [*or* certainly listen], **but you will not**
understand.
You will ·look and look [*or* certainly look], **but you will not ·learn**
[perceive],
27because [Lthe heart of] **these people have become ·stubborn** [dull].
They ·don't hear with their ears [*or* hardly hear with their ears; are
hard of hearing],
and they have closed their eyes.
Otherwise, they might see with their eyes
and hear with their ears.
They might really understand in their ·minds [hearts]
and come back to me and ·be healed [LI would heal them; Is. 6:9–10].'

28"[LTherefore,] **I want you to know that God has also sent his salvation**
to ·all nations [the Gentiles], **and they will listen!"** |**29·After** [*or* When] **·Paul**
[Lhe] **said this, the Jews left. They were arguing very much with each other.**|*n*
30Paul stayed two full years ·in his own rented house [*or* at his own
expense] **and welcomed all people who came to visit him. 31He ·boldly**
[confidently] **·preached about** [proclaimed] **the kingdom of God and**
taught about the Lord Jesus Christ, ·and no one stopped him [freely;
without hindrance].

28:29 After . . . other. Some Greek copies do not contain the bracketed text.

ROMANS

1 **From Paul, a ·servant** [slave; bondservant] **of Christ Jesus. ·God called me** [L...called] **to be an ·apostle** [messenger] **and ·chose me** [set me apart; appointed me] **to tell the ·Good News** [Gospel].

2**God promised this ·Good News** [Gospel] **·long ago** [beforehand; previously] **through his prophets, as it is written in the Holy Scriptures.** 3**The Good News is about God's Son. ·As a man** [*or* With reference to his earthly life; LAccording to the flesh], **he was born ·from the family** [a descendant; Lof the seed] **of David** [2 Sam. 7:11–14]. 4**But through the Spirit of holiness** [Ca Jewish way of referring to the Holy Spirit] **he was ·declared** [*or* designated; appointed] **to be God's Son with great power by rising from the dead** [Cthough eternally the Son of God, Jesus was appointed such "with power" at his resurrection; see Ps. 2:7; 110:1–2]. **He is Jesus Christ our Lord.** 5**Through ·Christ** [Lwhom], **·God gave me the special work of an apostle** [Lwe have received apostleship; C"we" could be a formal way of saying "I," or could refer to Paul and the other apostles], **which was to lead ·people of all nations** [the Gentiles] **to ·believe and obey** [*or* the obedience that comes from faith; *or* the obedience that is faith]. **I do this work for ·him** [Lhis name]. 6**And you who are in Rome are also among those** [CGentiles] **called to belong to Jesus Christ.**

7**To all of you in Rome whom God loves and has called to be ·his holy people** [Tsaints]:

Grace and peace to you from God our Father and the Lord Jesus Christ.

A Prayer of Thanks

8**First I want to say that I thank my God through Jesus Christ for all of you, because people everywhere in the world are talking about your faith.** 9**God, whom I serve ·with my whole heart** [in/with my spirit] **·by telling** [*or* for the sake of; Lin] **the ·Good News** [Gospel] **about his Son, ·knows** [Lis my witness] **that I ·always** [continually; never cease to] **mention you** 10**every time I pray. I pray that now at last ·if God wants it** [by God's will] **I will ·be allowed to come** [succeed in coming] **to you.** 11**I ·want very much** [long] **to see you, to ·give** [impart to; *or* share with] **you some spiritual gift to make you strong.** 12**I mean that I want us to ·help each other** [be mutually encouraged/comforted] **·with the faith we have** [by each other's faith]. **·Your faith will help me, and my faith will help you** [L...both yours and mine]. 13**Brothers and sisters, I want you to know that I ·planned** [intended] **many times to come to you, but ·this has not been possible** [Lhave been hindered/ unsuccessful until now]. **I wanted to come so that I could ·help you grow spiritually** [Lharvest some fruit among you] **as I have ·helped the other** [Lamong the rest of the] **Gentiles.**

14**I have a ·duty** [obligation; debt] **to all people—Greeks and ·those who are not Greeks** [*or* barbarians; Cthis pairing could mean (1) ethnic Greeks

and other Gentiles; (2) Greek speakers (people in the Roman empire) and
non-Greek speakers (those outside the Roman empire); or (3) cultured
people and uncultured people], **the wise and the foolish** [Cperhaps contrasting educated with uneducated, or philosophically sophisticated (1 Cor.
1:18–31) with simple-minded]. 15 **That is why I ·want so much** [am so
eager] **to preach the ·Good News** [Gospel] **to you in Rome.**

16 [LFor] **I am not ashamed of the ·Good News** [Gospel], **because it is**
the power God uses to save everyone who believes—to save the Jews first,
and then to save ·Gentiles [Lthe Greeks; Chere meaning anyone who is not
Jewish; contrast v. 14]. 17 **The ·Good News** [Gospel] **shows ·how God**
makes people right with himself [*or* God's righteous character; Lthe righteousness of/from God]—**·that it begins and ends with faith** [*or* that
advances from one believing person to the next; *or* that begins with God's
faithfulness and results in people's faith; Lfrom faith to faith]. **As the**
Scripture says, "But ·those who are right with God will live by faith [*or*
those made righteous through faith will live (eternally); Hab. 2:4]."

All People Have Sinned

18 [LFor] **God's ·anger** [wrath; retribution] **is ·shown** [being revealed]
from heaven against all the ·evil [ungodly] **and ·wrong** [wicked; unrigh-
teous] **things people do. By their ·own evil lives** [wickedness; unrigh
teousness] **they ·hide** [suppress] **the truth.** 19 **God ·shows** [reveals] **his**
·anger [wrath; retribution] **because ·some knowledge of** [what can be
known about] **him has been made ·clear** [plain; evident] **to them. Yes, God**
has ·shown himself [revealed/disclosed it] **to them.** 20 **For since the creation**
of the world, God's invisible qualities—his eternal power and ·all the
things that make him God [his divine nature]—**have been clearly ·seen**
[perceived], **understood through what God has made. So people have no**
excuse. 21 **They knew God, but they did not give glory to God or thank him.**
Their thinking became ·useless [futile; pointless]. **Their ·foolish** [ignorant;
uncomprehending] **·minds** [Lhearts] **were ·filled with darkness** [darkened].
22 **They claimed to be wise, but they became fools.** 23 **They ·traded**
[exchanged] **the glory of ·God who lives forever** [the immortal/imperish-
able God] **for the worship of ·idols** [images] **made to look like ·earthly**
[mortal; perishable] **people, birds, animals, and reptiles.**

24 **Because they did these things, God ·abandoned them to** [allowed
them to pursue; gave them over to] **·their sinful desires** [Lthe desires of
their hearts], **resulting in ·sexual impurity** [Luncleanness; impurity] **and**
the dishonoring of their bodies with one another. 25 **They ·traded**
[exchanged] **the truth of God for ·a lie** [*or* the lie; see Gen. 3:4–5] **and wor-**
shiped and served ·the creation [*or* the creature; *or* created things] **instead**
of the Creator, who ·should be praised [*or* is blessed] **forever. Amen.**

26 **Because people did those things, God ·abandoned them to** [allowed
them to pursue; gave them over to] **·shameful** [dishonorable; degrading]
·lusts [passions]. [LTheir] **Women ·stopped having natural sex and started**
having sex with other women [Lexchanged natural (heterosexual) relations for unnatural ones]. 27 **In the same way, men ·stopped having**
[abandoned] **natural ·sex** [Lrelations with women] **and ·began wanting**
[Lwere inflamed in their lust for] **each other. Men did shameful things**
with other men, and in ·their bodies [Lthemselves] **they received the ·pun-**
ishment [recompense; due penalty] **for ·those wrongs** [their error].

28 [LAnd since/just as] **People did not ·think it was important** [consider it
worthwhile; see fit] **to ·have a true knowledge of** [*or* acknowledge] **God. So**

God ·abandoned them to [allowed them to pursue; gave them over to]
·their own worthless thinking [a depraved/corrupted mind] to do things
they should not do. 29They are filled with every kind of ·sin [unrighteous-
ness; injustice], ·evil [wickedness], ·selfishness [greed], and ·hatred [evil;
malice; depravity]. They are full of ·jealousy [envy], murder, ·fighting
[strife; quarreling], ·lying [deceit; treachery], and ·thinking the worst about
each other [spite; maliciousness]. They are gossips 30and ·say evil things
about each other [slanderers; backstabbers]. They hate God. They are
·rude [insolent; haughty] and ·conceited [proud; arrogant] and ·brag
about themselves [boastful]. They invent ways of doing evil. They do not
·obey [respect] their parents. 31They are ·foolish [senseless; undiscerning],
they ·do not keep their promises [*or* are covenant-breakers], and they show
no ·kindness [love; affection] or ·mercy [pity] to others. 32They know
God's ·law says [righteous decree; just requirement] that those who live
like this should die. But they themselves not only continue to do these evil
things, they ·applaud [approve of; encourage] others who do them.

You People Also Are Sinful

2 [LTherefore] If you think you can judge others, [LO man,] you are
·wrong [Lwithout excuse]. [LFor] When you judge them, you are
really judging yourself guilty, because you [Lwho are judging] do the same
things they do. 2God judges those who do ·wrong [Lsuch] things, and we
know that his judging is ·right [just; justified; Lbased on truth]. 3You judge
those who do ·wrong [Lsuch things], but you do ·wrong [Lthe same things]
yourselves. Do you think [LO man,] you will be able to escape the judgment
of God? 4You [LDo you…?] ·think nothing of [despise; have contempt for;
disregard] his kindness, ·tolerance [forbearance] and patience. Perhaps you
do not understand that God is kind to you so you will ·change your hearts
and lives [repent]. 5But because you are stubborn and ·refuse to change
[Lhave an unrepentant heart], you are ·making your own punishment even
greater [Lstoring up wrath for yourself] on the day ·he shows his anger [of
(God's) wrath]. ·On that day everyone will see [L…and the day of the revelation of] God's ·right [righteous; just] judgments. 6God will ·reward or
punish [give back to; repay] every person for what that person has done.
7Some people, by ·always continuing [persevering] to do good, ·live for
[seek after; aim for] ·God's glory [Lglory], for honor, and for ·life that has no
end [immortality]. God will give them ·life forever [eternal life]. 8But other
people are ·selfish [self-seeking], ·refusing to follow [disobeying; *or* disbe-
lieving] truth and instead ·following [obeying; *or* believing] evil. God will
give them his ·punishment [wrath] and anger. 9·He will give [*or* There will
be] ·trouble [affliction; tribulation] and ·suffering [distress] to everyone
who does evil—to the Jews first and also to ·those who are not Jews [Lthe
Greek; Chere meaning all Gentiles; see 1:13, 14, 16]. 10But ·he will give [*or*
there will be] glory, honor, and peace to everyone who does good—to the
Jews first and also to ·those who are not Jews [Lthe Greek; v. 9]. 11For ·God
judges all people in the same way [Lthere is no partiality with God].
12·People [*or* For all those] who do not have the law [CGentiles without
the written law of Moses] and who are sinners will ·be lost [perish],
although they do not have the law. And, in the same way, those who have
the law [CJews who have the law of Moses] and are sinners will be judged
by the law. 13Hearing the law does not make people ·right with [righteous/
justified before] God. It is those who obey the law who will be ·right with
[justified/declared righteous before] him. 14(·Those who are not Jews

[Gentiles] **do not have the law, but when they ·freely** [by nature; instinctively] **do what the law commands, they ·are the law for themselves** [*or* reveal their awareness of God's law]. **This is true even though they do not have the law** [Cthe written law of Moses]. **15They show that ·in their hearts they know what is right and wrong, just as the law commands** [Lthe requirements of the law are written on their hearts]. **And they show this by their consciences** [Lbearing witness]. **Sometimes their thoughts ·tell them they did wrong** [Laccuse them], **and sometimes their thoughts ·tell them they did right** [defend them].) **16·All these things** [*or* This] **will happen on the day when, according to ·my Gospel** [the Good News I preach], **God, through Christ Jesus, will judge people's secret thoughts.**

The Jews and the Law

17What about you? You call yourself a Jew. You ·trust in [rely on] **the ·law of Moses** [Llaw] **and ·brag that you are close to God** [Lboast in God]. **18You know ·what he wants you to do** [his will] **and ·what is important** [can discern/test what is best/superior], **because you have ·learned** [been instructed in] **the law. 19You ·think** [are convinced/confident that] **you are a guide for the blind and a light for those who are in darkness. 20You think you ·can show foolish people what is right** [Lare an instructor to the foolish] **and ·teach** [La teacher for] **·those who know nothing** [the immature/ignorant; *or* children/infants]. **You have the law; so you think you ·know everything and have all truth** [Lhave the embodiment/formulation of knowledge and truth]. **21You teach others, so why don't you teach yourself? You ·tell** [preach to] **others not to steal, but do you steal? 22You say that others must not commit adultery, but do you commit adultery? You ·hate** [abhor; detest] **idols, but do you steal from temples** [Cperhaps (1) profiting by selling stolen idols to Gentiles; or (2) withholding what is due to God and so "robbing" his temple]? **23You ·brag** [boast] **about ·having God's law** [Lthe law], **but do you ·bring shame to** [dishonor] **God by breaking his law? 24It is just as the Scriptures say: "God's name is blasphemed among the Gentiles because of you** [Is. 52:5; Ezek. 36:20]."

25If you follow the law, your circumcision [Ca key distinctive of Jewish identity; Gen. 17] **has ·meaning** [value; benefit]. **But if you ·break** [transgress; disobey] **the law, it is as if you were never circumcised. 26If those who are not circumcised ·do** [keep; obey] **·what the law says** [*or* the law's righteous requirements], **it is as if they were circumcised. 27Those who are not circumcised in their bodies, but still ·obey** [fulfill; carry out] **the law, will ·pass judgment on** [condemn] **you who, though having the written law and circumcision, ·break** [transgress; disobey] **the law. 28They can do this because a person is not a true Jew if he is only a Jew ·in his physical body** [Lby (physical) appearance]; **true circumcision is not ·only on the outside of the body** [Lthe appearance of the flesh]. **29A person is a Jew only if he is a Jew ·inside** [inwardly]; **true circumcision is done in the heart by the Spirit, not by the written law. Such a person gets praise from God rather than from people.**

3 So what advantage does a Jew have? [LOr] **Is there ·anything special** [any benefit/advantage] **about being circumcised? 2Yes, there are great benefits in ·every way** [*or* all different ways]. **·The most important thing is this** [LFirst]: **God ·trusted** [entrusted] **the Jews with his ·teachings** [revelation; oracles]. **3·If** [LWhat if] **some Jews were not faithful to him, will their unfaithfulness ·stop God from doing what he promised** [Lnullify God's faithfulness]? **4·No** [Absolutely not; May it never be]! **·God**

will continue to be true even when every person is false [[L]Let God be true
and every person a liar]. As the Scriptures say:
"So you will be ·shown to be right [justified] ·when you speak [[L]in your
words],
and you will ·win your case in court [[L]prevail when you are judged; *or*
prevail when you judge (sin); Ps. 51:4]."
5 But if ·what we do wrong [our unrighteousness] ·shows more clearly
[highlights] ·that God is right [God's righteousness], ·how can we say
[[L]what shall we say?] that God is ·wrong [unrighteous; unjust] to ·punish
[[L]inflict wrath on] us? (I am talking ·as people might talk [*or* in limited
human terms].) 6 ·No [Absolutely not; May it never be; v. 4]! If God could
not punish us, ·he could not [[L]how could he…?] judge the world.
7 A person might say, "When I lie, it really ·gives him [[L]increases his]
glory, because my lie shows God's truth. So why am I ·judged [condemned
as] a sinner?" 8 It would be the same to say, "We should do evil so that
good will come." Some people ·find fault with [slander] us and say we
teach this, but ·they are wrong and deserve the punishment they will
receive [[L]their condemnation is just].

All People Are Guilty

9 ·So [[L]What then?] ·are we Jews [*or* are we Christians; [L]are we] ·better
than others [*or* making excuses for ourselves]? ·No [[L]Not at all]! We have
already ·said [charged; made the accusation] that Jews and Gentiles alike
are all ·guilty of [*or* under the power of; [L]under] sin. 10 As the Scriptures say:
"There is no one who ·always does what is right [[L]is righteous],
not even one.
11 There is no one who understands.
There is no one who ·looks to God for help [[L]seeks God].
12 All have turned away.
Together, everyone has become ·useless [worthless].
There is no one who ·does anything good [*or* shows kindness];
there is not even one [Ps. 14:1–3]."
13 "Their throats are like open graves [[C]either their words are like rotting
corpses, or their speech is murderous];
they use their tongues ·for telling lies [to deceive; Ps. 5:9]."
"·Their words are like snake poison [[L]Asp/Viper venom is on their lips;
Ps. 140:3]."
14 "Their mouths are full of cursing and ·hate [bitterness; Ps. 10:7]."
15 "·They [[L]Their feet] are ·always ready [eager; quick] to ·kill people
[[L]shed blood].
16 ·Everywhere they go [[L]Along their paths/ways] they cause ·ruin
[destruction; havoc] and misery.
17 They don't know ·how to live in [[L]the way of] peace [Is. 59:7–8]."
18 "They have no fear of God [Ps. 36:1]."
19 We know that ·the law's commands [[L]what the law says] are for those
who ·have [are under/subject to; [L]are in] the law. This ·stops all excuses
[[L]silences every mouth] and brings the whole world under God's judgment, 20 because no one can be ·made right [justfied; declared righteous]
with God [Ps. 143:2] ·by following [[L]through the works of] the law. [[L]For]
The law only ·shows us our [brings awareness of] sin.

How God Makes People Right

21 But now ·God's way to make people right with him [[L]the righteousness
of God] ·without [apart from] the law has been ·shown to us [revealed;
made known], a way ·told to us [testified to; attested] by the law and the

prophets. 22**·God makes people right with himself** [LThis righteousness comes] **through ·their faith in** [*or* the faithfulness of] **Jesus Christ. This is true for all who believe in Christ, because ·all people are the same** [there is no distinction/difference; Cbetween Jews and Gentiles]: 23[LFor; Because] **Everyone has sinned and ·fallen short** [*or* is not worthy] **of God's ·glorious standard** [*or* glorious presence; Lglory], 24**and all need to be ·made right with God** [justfied; declared righteous] **as a free gift by his grace, ·by being set free from sin** [Lthrough the redemption that is] **·through** [*or* in] **Jesus Christ.** 25**God ·sent** [*or* appointed; *or* presented] **him ·to die in our place to take away our sins** [as a sacrifice of atonement; *or* as the mercy seat; Tas a propitiation; Cthe Greek term could mean the place where sacrificial blood was dripped (the mercy seat) or the sacrifice itself; it implies an atoning sacrifice that turns away divine wrath]. **We receive forgiveness through faith in ·the blood of Jesus' death** [Lhis blood]. **This showed ·that God always does what is right and fair** [Lhis righteousness], **as in the past when he was patient and ·did not punish people for their sins** [Lpassed over/delayed punishment for previously committed sins]. 26**And God gave Jesus to show ·today** [*or* at this present time (of salvation)] **·that he does what is right** [Lhis righteousness/justice]. **God did this so he could ·judge rightly** [*or* be shown to be just/righteous] **and so he could ·make right** [declare righteous; justify] **any person ·who has faith in Jesus** [*or* on the basis of Jesus' faithfulness; see v. 22]. [CChrist's sacrificial death shows that God is both just (sin is justly punished) and merciful (God saves undeserving sinners).]

27**·So do we have a reason to brag about ourselves? No!** [LWhere, then, is boasting? It is excluded.] **·And why not** [LBy what law/principle]**? It is the ·way** [law; principle] **of faith that stops all ·bragging** [boasting], **not the ·way** [law; principle] **of ·trying to obey the law** [Lworks]. 28**For we ·conclude** [maintain; assert] **a person is ·made right with God** [justified; declared righteous] **through faith, not through ·obeying** [Lthe works of] **the law.** 29[LOr] **Is God only the God of the Jews? Is he not also the God of the Gentiles?** 30**Of course he is, because ·there is only one God** [*or* God is one; Deut. 6:4]. **He will ·make Jews right with him** [Ljustify/make righteous the circumcised] **by their faith, and he will also ·make Gentiles right with him** [Ljustify/declare righteous the uncircumcised] **through their faith.** 31**So do we ·destroy** [nullify; annul] **the law by ·following the way of faith** [Lfaith]**? ·No** [Absolutely not; May it never be; v. 6]**! ·Faith causes us to be what the law truly wants** [LWe uphold/establish/support the law; Cliving by faith captures the true spirit and purpose of the law; the law pointed out sin and the need for grace, thereby pointing to Christ].

The Example of Abraham

4 **So what can we say that Abraham, ·the father of our people** [Lour forefather according to the flesh; Gen. 12–25], **·learned about faith** [discovered in this regard; Lhas found]? 2**If Abraham was ·made right** [justified; declared righteous] **by ·the things he did** [Lthe works of the law], **he had a reason to ·brag** [boast]. **·But this is not God's view** [*or* …but he could not boast before God], 3**because the Scripture says, "Abraham believed God, and ·God accepted Abraham's faith, and that faith made him right with God** [Lit was credited/counted to him for righteousness; Gen. 15:6]."

4**When people work, their ·pay** [wage] **is not ·given** [credited; counted] **as ·a gift** [grace], **but as something ·earned** [due to them]. 5**·But people cannot do any work that will make them right with God. So they must trust in him** [LBut for the one who does not work, but trusts in God], **who**

·makes even evil people right in his sight [justifies/makes righteous the
ungodly]. **Then God ·accepts their faith, and that makes them right with
him** [Lcredits/counts their faith for righteousness]. 6**David said the same
thing. He said that people are ·truly blessed** [happy; spiritually fulfilled]
when God, ·without paying attention to their deeds [apart from works],
·makes people right with himself [Lcredits/counts righteousness to them].
7"**·Blessed** [Happy; Spiritually fulfilled] **are they**
  whose ·sins [lawless deeds] **are forgiven,**
  whose ·wrongs [sins] **are ·pardoned** [covered; blotted out].
8**·Blessed** [Happy; Spiritually fulfilled] **is the person**
  whom the Lord does not ·consider guilty [Lcount sin against;
    Ps. 32:1–2]."
9**Is this ·blessing** [happiness; spiritual fulfillment] **only for those who are
circumcised or also for those who are not circumcised? We have already
said that ·God accepted Abraham's faith and that faith made him right
with God** [Lfaith was credited/counted to Abraham for righteousness; v. 3].
10**So how did this happen? Did God accept Abraham before or after he was
circumcised? It was not after, but before his circumcision.** 11**Abraham ·was
circumcised** [Lreceived the sign of circumcision; Gen. 17:9–14] **·to show
that he was right with God** [Las a seal/guarantee of the righteousness he
had] **through faith before he was circumcised. So Abraham is the father of
all those who believe but are not circumcised, so that ·they too may be
accepted as being right with God** [righteousness may be credited/counted
to them also]. 12**And Abraham is also the father of those who have been
circumcised and who ·live following** [Lwalk in the footsteps of] **the faith
that our father Abraham had before he was circumcised.**

God Keeps His Promise

13[LFor] **The promise Abraham and his ·descendants** [seed] **received that
they would inherit the ·whole world** [Lworld] **·did not come through** [was
not based on his obedience to] **the law, but through ·being right with God
by his faith** [the righteousness that comes by faith]. 14[LFor] **If people ·could
receive what God promised** [Lare heirs] **by following the law, then faith is
worthless. And ·God's promise to Abraham** [Lthe promise] **is ·worthless**
[nullified; canceled], 15**because the law can only bring God's ·anger** [wrath].
But if there is no law, there is ·nothing to disobey [no transgression/viola-
tion; Cthe law points out sin (5:13), but it cannot save from sin].
16**So people receive God's promise by having faith. This happens so the
promise can be ·a free gift** [by grace]. **Then all of Abraham's ·children**
[descendants; offspring; Lseed] **can ·have** [be guaranteed; be certain to
have] **that promise. It is not only for those who live under the law of
Moses but for anyone who lives with faith like that of Abraham, who is
the father of us all.** 17**As it is written in the Scriptures: "I ·am making**
[Lhave made] **you a father of many nations** [Gen. 17:5]." **This is true
·before** [in the presence of] **God, the God Abraham believed, the God
who gives life to the dead and who ·creates something out of nothing**
[Lcalls things that did not exist into existence].
18**·Though there was no hope that Abraham would have children** [*or*
When all seemed hopeless; LAgainst hope…], **Abraham believed God and
continued hoping, and so he became the father of many nations** [Gen.
17:5]. **As God told him, "·Your descendants also will be too many to count**
[LSo shall your seed/offspring be; Gen. 15:5]." 19**Abraham was almost a
hundred years old, ·much past the age for having children** [Lhis own body

(as good as) dead], **and ·Sarah could not have children** [LSarah's womb was dead]. **Abraham ·thought about all** [considered; *or* acknowledged] **this, but his faith in God did not become weak.** [20]**He never ·doubted or stopped believing** [*or* wavered through unbelief] **that God would keep his promise. He grew stronger in his faith and gave ·praise** [glory] **to God.** [21]**Abraham ·felt sure** [was fully convinced] **that God was able to do what he had promised.** [22]**So, "·God accepted Abraham's faith, and that faith made him right with God** [Lit was credited/counted to him for righteousness; Gen. 15:6]." [23]**Those words ("·God accepted Abraham's faith** [Lit was credited/counted to him]") **were written not only for Abraham** [24]**but also for us. ·God will accept us also** [L...to whom it will be credited/counted] **because we believe in the One who raised Jesus our Lord from the dead.** [25]**Jesus was ·given to die** [handed/delivered over; 8:32] **·for** [because of] **our ·sins** [violations; transgressions], **and he was raised from the dead ·to make us right with God** [for our justification; *or* to confirm our justification].

Right with God

5 [LTherefore,] **Since we have been ·made right with God** [declared righteous; justified] **by our faith, we have[n] peace with God. This happened through our Lord Jesus Christ,** [2]**·who through our faith[n] has brought us into that blessing of** [Lthrough whom we have access by faith to] **God's grace ·that we now enjoy** [Lin which we stand/live]. **And we ·are happy** [rejoice; boast] **because of the hope we have ·of sharing** [*or* of experiencing; Lof] **God's glory.** [3][LNot only this, but] **We also ·have joy** [rejoice; boast] **·with our troubles** [through suffering/trials/persecution], **because we know that ·these troubles** [suffering; trials; persecution] **produce ·patience** [endurance]. [4]**And ·patience** [endurance] **produces** [tested and proven] **character, and** [tested and proven] **character produces hope.** [5]**And this hope will never ·disappoint us** [let us down; *or* put us to shame; dishonor us; Chonor and shame were among the most important values in first century culture], **because God has ·poured out his love to fill our hearts** [*or* flooded our hearts with his love]. **He gave us his love through the Holy Spirit, whom God has given to us.**

[6][LFor] **When we were ·unable to help ourselves** [Lstill helpless/weak], **at the ·right** [*or* appointed] **time, Christ died for ·us sinners** [Lthe ungodly/wicked]. [7]**·Very few people will** [*or* Rarely/Scarcely will anyone] **die for a ·righteous** [just; pious] **person. Although perhaps for a ·good** [truly good; noble] **person someone might possibly die** [Cthe "righteous" person may be someone who is outwardly religious, while the "good" person is genuinely generous and loving]. [8]**But God ·shows** [demonstrates; proves] **his ·great** [Lown] **love for us in this way: Christ died for us while we were still sinners.**

[9]**And since we have now been ·made right with God** [declared righteous; justified] **by ·the blood of Christ's death** [Lhis blood], **·we will surely also** [Lhow much more shall we...!] **be saved through Christ from ·God's anger** [final punishment; Lthe wrath]. [10][LFor if] **While we were God's enemies, ·he made us his friends** [Lwe were reconciled to God] **through the death of his Son. ·Surely** [LHow much more...?], **·now that we are his friends** [Lhaving been reconciled], **he will save us through his Son's life.** [11]**And not only that, but now we ·are also very happy** [also rejoice/boast] **in God through our Lord Jesus Christ. Through him we ·are now God's friends again** [have now received reconciliation].

5:1 we have Some Greek copies read "let us have." **5:2 through our faith** Some Greek copies do not have this phrase.

Adam and Christ Compared

12[LTherefore, just as] Sin came into the world ·because of what one man
did [Lthrough one man], and with sin came death. ·This is why [L…and so;
or and in this way] ·everyone must die [death spread/passed to all people]—
because everyone sinned. 13Sin was in the world before ·the law of Moses
[Lthe law], but sin is not ·counted against us as breaking a command [charged
to one's account; recorded as sin] when there is no law [4:15]. 14But from the
time of Adam to the time of Moses, ·everyone had to die [Ldeath reigned/
ruled], even those who had not sinned ·by breaking a command, as Adam
had [Lin the likeness of Adam's disobedience/transgression].

Adam was ·like [a type/pattern/prefigurement of] the One who was
coming in the future. 15But ·God's free gift [Lthe gift] is not like Adam's
·sin [violation; transgression]. [LFor if] Many people died because of the
·sin [violation; transgression] of that one man. ·But the grace from God
was much greater, since many people received God's gift of life [L…how
much more did God's grace and gift abound/multiply to the many] by the
grace of the one man, Jesus Christ [Cthe death of the "one" saved the
"many"; see v. 19; Is. 53:11]. 16But the gift of God is different from ·Adam's
[Lthe one man's] sin. After Adam sinned once, ·he was judged guilty [Lhis
judgment brought condemnation]. [LBut] God's free gift came after many
·sins [violations; transgressions], and it ·makes people right with God
[Lbrought justification]. 17[LFor if] One man's ·sin [violation; transgres-
sion] caused death to ·rule over all people [Lreign; rule] because of that
one man. How much more, then, will those people who ·accept [receive]
·God's full grace [Lthe abundance of grace] and the great gift of ·being
made right with him [righteousness] ·have true life and rule [*or* rule in
the future life; Lreign/rule in life] through the one man, Jesus Christ. [CJust
as death "ruled" in Adam, so believers "rule" over death through Christ.]

18So as one ·sin of Adam [Lviolation; trangression] brought ·the punishment of death [condemnation] to all people, so too one ·good act that Christ
did [Lrighteous act/deed] ·makes all people right with God, bringing them
true life [Lbrings justification of life to all people]. 19[LFor just as…] One man
disobeyed God, and many became sinners. ·In the same way, [L…so also]
one man obeyed God, and many will be made ·right [righteous]. 20The law
came ·to make sin worse [*or* to reveal the true extent of sin; Lto increase the
violation/transgression]. But when sin ·grew worse [increased; multiplied],
God's grace ·increased [multiplied/abounded all the more]. 21·Sin once used
death to rule us [LJust as sin reigned in death…], ·but God gave people more
of his grace so that grace could rule [L…so grace will reign] ·by making people right with him [through justification/righteousness]. And this brings ·life
forever [eternal life] through Jesus Christ our Lord.

Dead to Sin but Alive in Christ

6 ·So [LWhat then shall we say?] ·do you think we should [Lshall we]
continue sinning so that ·God will give us even more grace [Lgrace
may increase/Tabound]? 2·No [Absolutely not; May it never be; 3:31]! We
died to ·our old sinful lives [Lsin], so how can we continue living ·with [*or*
in] sin? 3·Did you forget [*or* Don't you know] that all of us who ·became
part of Christ Jesus when we were baptized [Lwere baptized into Christ
Jesus] ·shared his death in that baptism [*or* participated in his death through
that baptism; Lwere baptized into his death]. 4[LTherefore] When we were
baptized, we were buried with Christ ·and shared his [and participated in
his; Linto] death. So, just as Christ was raised from the dead by the ·wonder-
ful power [glorious power; Lglory] of the Father, we also can live a new life.

5**Christ died, and we have been ·joined with** [united with; grafted into] **him ·by dying too** [*or* by participating in his death; Lin the likeness of his death]. **So we will also be ·joined with** [united with; grafted into] **him by rising from the dead as he did.** 6**We know that our old ·life** [self; Lperson] **died with Christ on the cross so that our ·sinful selves** [*or* body controlled by sin; Lbody of sin] **would have no power over us and we would not be slaves to sin.** 7**Anyone who has died is ·made free** [justified; declared righteous] **from ·sin's control** [Lsin].

8[LNow; But] **If we died with Christ, we ·know** [have confidence; believe] **we will also live with him.** 9**Christ was raised from the dead, and we know that he cannot die again. Death has no ·power** [mastery; dominion] **over him now.** 10**·Yes** [LFor; Because], **when Christ died, he died ·to defeat the power of sin** [to take away sin; *or* with reference to sin] **·one time—enough for all time** [once for all; Heb. 7:27]. [LBut] **He now has a new life, and his new life is ·with** [*or* for the glory of; *or* with reference to] **God.** 11**In the same way, you should ·see** [count; consider] **yourselves as being dead to ·the power of sin** [Lsin] **and alive ·with** [to; with reference to] **God ·through** [*or* in; in union with] **Christ Jesus.**

12**So, do not let sin ·control your life** [Lreign; rule over you] **·here on earth** [Lin your mortal body] **so that you ·do what your sinful self wants to do** [Lobey/submit to its (evil/sinful) desires]. 13**Do not offer ·the parts of your body** [*or* any part of yourself; Lyour parts/members] **to serve sin, as ·things to be used in doing** [Linstruments/weapons of] **·evil** [unrighteousness; injustice]. **Instead, offer yourselves to God as people who have died and now live. Offer ·the parts of your body** [*or* every part of yourself; Lyour parts/members] **to God ·to be used in doing good** [Las instruments/weapons of righteousness/justice]. 14[LFor] **Sin will not ·be your master** [exercise dominion/power over you], **because you are not under law but under God's grace.**

Be Slaves of Righteousness

15**·So what should we do** [LWhat then; 3:9]? **Should we sin because we are under grace and not under law? ·No** [Absolutely not; May it never be; v. 2]! 16**·Surely you know** [LDon't you know…?] **that when you submit yourselves to someone as obedient slaves, ·the person you obey is your master** [Lyou are slaves to the one you obey]. [LEither] **You can ·follow** [be slaves to] **sin, which brings ·spiritual death** [Ldeath], **or you can ·obey God** [L(be slaves) to obedience], **which ·makes you right with him** [leads to righteousness]. 17**In the past ·sin controlled you** [Lyou were slaves to sin]. **But thank God, you ·fully obeyed** [Lobeyed from the heart] **the ·things** [accepted/orthodox teaching; Lexample/pattern of teaching] **·that you were taught** [*or* that have claimed your allegiance; Lto which you were delivered/entrusted]. 18**You were set free from sin, and now you are slaves to ·goodness** [righteousness]. 19**I use ·this example** [*or* an analogy from everyday life; *or* an inadequate human illustration (like slavery)] **because ·this is hard for you to understand** [Lof the limitations/weakness of your human nature/flesh]. **In the past you offered ·the parts of your body** [*or* yourselves; Lyour parts/members] **to be slaves to ·sin** [impurity; defilement] **and ·evil** [lawlessness; wickedness]; **·you lived only for evil** [*or* …leading to even more lawlessness/wickedness]. **In the same way now you must offer ·yourselves** [Lyour parts/members] **to be slaves of ·goodness** [righteousness]. **·Then you will live only for God** [L…leading to holiness/sanctification].

20[LFor] **When you were slaves to sin, ·goodness did not control you** [Lyou were free (from obligation) to righteousness]. 21**And what ·was the result of**

[benefit/fruit did you reap from] **doing those things that now make you**
ashamed? [LFor] **·Those things only bring** [LThe end/result of those things is]
death. 22**But now you are free from sin and have become slaves of God. This**
·brings you [reaps the benefit/fruit of] **·a life that is only for God** [holiness;
sanctification], **and ·this gives you life forever** [Lthe end/result is eternal life].
23[LFor; Because] **The ·payment** [wages] **for sin is death. But God gives us the**
free gift of ·life forever [eternal life] **in Christ Jesus our Lord.**

An Example from Marriage

7 **Brothers and sisters, all of you understand the ·law of Moses** [Llaw].
So surely you know that the law ·rules [has authority] **over people**
only while they are alive. 2**For example, a ·woman must stay married**
[Lmarried woman is bound by law] **to her husband as long as he is alive. But**
if her husband dies, she is free from the law of marriage. 3**But if she ·marries**
[*or* lives with] **another man while her husband is still alive, ·the law says she**
is guilty of adultery [Lshe will be called/labeled an adulteress]. **But if her**
husband dies, she is free from the ·law of marriage [Llaw]. **Then if she mar-**
ries another man, she is not ·guilty of adultery [Lan adulteress].
4**In the same way, my brothers and sisters, ·your old selves died, and you**
became free from the law [Lyou died to the law] **through the body of Christ.**
This happened so that you might belong to someone else—the One who
was raised from the dead—and so that we might ·be used in service to [Lbear
fruit for] **God.** 5[LFor] **When we were ·ruled by** [controlled by; living in; Lin]
·our sinful selves [our sinful nature; Tthe flesh], **sinful ·desires** [passions]
stirred up by the law were at work ·in our bodies [*or* within us; Lin our mem-
bers/parts], **so the things we did ·were bringing us** [Lproduced fruit leading
to] **death.** 6**But now we have been freed from the law, since we have died to**
that which ·held us like prisoners [controlled us; Lheld us]. **So now we serve**
God in a new way ·with [by means of; in the power of] **the Spirit, and not in**
the old way ·with written rules [*or* of the written law; Lof the letter].

Our Fight Against Sin

7**·You might think I am saying that sin and the law are the same thing**
[LWhat, then, shall we say? Is the law sin?]. **·That is not true** [Absolutely not!;
May it never be!; 6:15]. **But the law was the only way I could learn what sin**
meant. I would never have known what it means to ·want to take something
belonging to someone else [selfishly desire; covet] **if the law had not said,**
"You must not ·want to take your neighbor's things [selfishly desire; covet;
Ex. 20:17; Deut. 5:21]**."** 8**And sin ·found a way** [seized the occasion/opportu-
nity] **to use that command and ·cause me to want all kinds of things I**
should not want [Lproduce in me all kinds of desires/coveting]. **But without**
the law, sin ·has no power [Lis dead]. 9**I was alive ·before I knew** [*or* before I
recognized the demands of; Lapart from] **the law** [CPaul thought he was
righteous; see Phil. 3:6]. **But when the law's command ·came to me** [*or* came
to my attention; Lcame], **then sin ·began to live** [sprang to life], **and I died**
[Cthe law revealed Paul's sinfulness and confirmed he was spiritually dead].
10**The command was meant to bring life, but for me it brought death.** 11**Sin**
·found a way [seized the occasion/opportunity; v. 8] **to ·fool** [deceive] **me by**
using the command to make me die.
12**So the law is holy, and the command is holy and ·right** [righteous]
and good. 13**Does this mean that something that is good ·brought** [*or*
became] **death to me? No** [Absolutely not; May it never be; v. 7]**! Sin used**
something that is good to bring death to me. This happened so that ·I
could see what sin is really like [Lsin might be shown as sin]; **the com-**
mand was used to show that sin is ·very evil [exceedingly/terribly sinful].

The War Within Us

14[LFor] We know that the law is spiritual, but I am ·not spiritual [fleshly; carnal] ·since sin rules me as if I were its slave [Lsold to sin; Cas a slave]. 15[LFor] I do not understand the things I do. [LFor] I do not do what I want to do, and I do the things I hate. 16And if I do what I do not want to do, that means I agree that the law is good [CPaul's acknowledgement that his behavior is wrong confirms the law's righteous standards]. 17But [Lnow] I am not really the one who is doing these hated things; it is sin living in me that does them. 18·Yes [LFor…], I know that nothing good lives in me—I mean nothing good lives in ·the part of me that is earthly and sinful [my sinful self; my sinful nature; Tmy flesh]. [LFor] I want to do the things that are good, but I ·do not [*or* cannot] do them. 19[LFor] I do not do the good things I want to do, but I do the ·bad [evil] things I do not want to do. 20So if I do things I do not want to do, then I am not the one doing them. It is sin living in me that does those things.

21So I ·have learned this rule [*or* find this principle/law at work]: When I want to do good, evil is ·there with me [present within me; close at hand]. 22[LFor] In ·my mind [my inmost self; Lthe person within], I ·am happy with [delight in] God's law. 23But I see ·another law [a different standard; *or* another power] working in my ·body [*or* outward actions; Lmembers; parts], which makes war against the ·law [standards] that my mind accepts. That other ·law [standard; *or* power] working in my ·body [*or* outward actions; Lmembers; parts] is the law of sin, and it makes me its prisoner. 24What a ·miserable [wretched] man I am! Who will ·save [free; rescue; deliver] me from this ·body that brings me death [body doomed to die; *or* burden of death]? 25·I thank God for saving me [LThanks be to God!] through Jesus Christ our Lord!

So [Lthen] in my mind I am a slave to God's law, but in my ·sinful self [sinful nature; Tflesh] I am a slave to the ·law [principle; *or* power] of sin.

Be Ruled by the Spirit

8 So now, those who are in Christ Jesus are not ·judged guilty[n] [condemned; punished for their sins]. 2[LFor] ·Through [*or* In] Christ Jesus the ·law [principle; *or* power] of the Spirit that brings life set you[n] free from the ·law [principle; *or* power] that brings sin and death. 3The law [Cof Moses] was without power, because the law was made weak by our ·sinful selves [sinful nature; Tflesh]. But God did what the law could not do. He sent his own Son to earth ·with the same human life that others use for sin [*or* in a body like ours, prone to sin; Lin the likeness of sinful flesh]. By sending his Son ·to be an offering for sin [Lconcerning sin], God ·used a human life to destroy sin [Lcondemned sin in the flesh]. 4He did this so that ·we could be the kind of people that the law demands that we be [Lthe law's righteous/just requirements would be fulfilled in us]. Now we do not ·live [walk; Clife's journey] following our ·sinful selves [sinful nature; Tflesh], but following the Spirit.

5Those who live following their ·sinful selves [sinful nature; Tflesh] ·think only about [have their minds set on; *or* have their outlook shaped by] things that their ·sinful selves [sinful nature; Tflesh] want. But those who live following the Spirit ·are thinking about [have their minds set on; *or* have their outlook shaped by] the things ·the Spirit wants them to do [Lof the Spirit]. 6If people's ·thinking is controlled by [*or* outlook/mind is set on] the ·sinful self [sinful nature; Tflesh], ·there is [the result is] death.

8:1 guilty Some Greek copies continue, "those who do not live in the power of their sinful selves, but in the power of the Spirit." **8:2 you** Some Greek copies read "me."

But if their ·thinking is controlled by [or outlook/mind is set on] the
Spirit, ·there is [the result is] life and peace. 7When people's ·thinking is
controlled by [or outlook/mind is set on] the ·sinful self [sinful nature;
Tflesh], they are ·against [hostile to] God, because they refuse to ·obey
[submit to] God's law and really are not even able to ·obey [submit to]
God's law. 8Those people who are ·ruled by [or under the control of; Lin]
·their sinful selves [their sinful nature; Tthe flesh] cannot please God.
9But you are not ·ruled by [controlled by; or in] ·your sinful selves
[your sinful nature; Tthe flesh], but ·by [or in] the Spirit, if that Spirit of
God really lives in you. But the person who does not have the Spirit of
Christ does not belong to Christ. 10Your body ·will always be [Lis] dead
because of sin. But if Christ is in you, then the Spirit ·gives you [Lis] life,
because ·Christ made you right with God [Lof righteousness]. 11God
raised Jesus from the dead, and if God's Spirit is living in you, the One
who raised Christ from the dead will also give life to your mortal bodies
that die, through[n] his Spirit who lives in you.
12So, my brothers and sisters, we ·must not be ruled by [Lare not obligated to] ·our sinful selves [our sinful nature; Tthe flesh] or live ·the way
our sinful selves want [according to the sinful nature/Tflesh]. 13[LFor] If
you ·use your lives to do the wrong things your sinful selves want [Llive
according to the flesh], you will ·die spiritually [Ldie]. But if you ·use the
Spirit's help to [Lby the Spirit] ·stop doing the wrong things you do with
[Lput to death the deeds of] your body, you will ·have true life [Llive].
14For all those who are led by the Spirit of God are the ·children [or sons]
of God. 15·The Spirit you received does not make you slaves again to fear [or
You did not receive the spirit of slavery, leading to fear]; instead, you received
the Spirit ·who adopts you as God's children [Lof adoption]. ·With [Through]
that Spirit we cry out, "Abba [CAramaic for "Father"; Mark 14:36], Father."
16And the Spirit himself ·joins with [or testifies to] our spirits to say we are
God's children. 17If we are God's children, we ·will receive blessings from
God together with Christ [Lare heirs—heirs of God and co-heirs with Christ].
·But we must [L...if indeed we] ·suffer as Christ suffered [share in his suffer-
ings] so that we ·will have glory as Christ has glory [may share in his glory].

Our Future Glory

18[LFor I consider that] The sufferings we have now are nothing compared to the great glory that will be ·shown [revealed] to us. 19·Everything
God made [LThe creation] is waiting with ·excitement [eager expectation]
for ·God to show his children's glory completely [the revelation of the
children/sons of God]. 20·Everything God made [LFor the creation] was
·changed to become useless [subjected to futility/meaninglessness; Gen. 3;
Eccl. 1:2], not by its own wish but because God ·wanted [Lsubjected] it
·and because all along there was this hope [yet with the hope...]: 21that
·everything God made [the creation itself] would be set free from ·ruin
[inevitable decay; Lthe slavery of decay] to have the ·freedom and glory [or
glorious freedom] that belong to God's children.
22We know that ·everything God made [all creation] has been ·waiting
until now in pain, like a woman ready to give birth [Lgroaning with labor
pains until now]. 23Not only the world, but we also ·have been waiting
with pain inside us [Lgroan within ourselves]. We have the Spirit as the
·first part of God's promise [Lfirstfruits; Cas the first crops confirmed the
future harvest, so the Spirit's presence confirms believers' final salvation].

8:11 through Some Greek copies read "because of."

So we are [eagerly] **waiting for ·God to finish making us his own children** [Lour adoption], **which means ·our bodies will be made free** [Lthe redemption of our bodies]. 24**We were saved, ·and we have this hope** [*or* ...by this hope; Lin hope]. **If we see what we are waiting for, that is not really hope. ·People do not hope** [LFor who hopes...?] **for something they already have.** 25**But we are hoping for something we do not have yet, and we are waiting for it ·patiently** [with perseverance].

26**·Also** [*or* In the same way], **the Spirit helps us ·with** [*or* in] **our weakness. We do not know ·how to pray as we should** [*or* what we ought to pray for]. **But the Spirit himself ·speaks to God for us** [intercedes] **with ·deep feelings** [Lgroanings] **·that words cannot explain** [*or* that are inexpressible; *or* that are unspoken; *or* too deep for words]. 27**·God can see what is in people's hearts and** [LThe one who searches hearts] **knows what is in the mind of the Spirit, because the Spirit ·speaks to God** [intercedes; appeals] **for ·his people** [*or* his holy people; Tthe saints] **·in the way God wants** [*or* in harmony with God; Laccording to God].

28**We know that ·in everything God works** [*or* God works everything together; *or* everything works together (*see text note*)] **for the good of those who love him.**n **They are the people he called, ·because that was his plan** [L... according to his purpose]. 29**·God knew them before he made the world** [LFor those whom he foreknew...], **·and he chose them** [...he also predestined/chose beforehand] **to be ·like** [molded to the pattern of; conformed to the image of] **his Son so that Jesus would be the firstborn** [Cthe preeminent one, but also indicating others will follow] **of many brothers and sisters** [CJesus' resurrection confirms that his followers will also share in God's glory]. 30**And those God ·chose to be like his Son** [predestined; chose beforehand], **he also called; and those he called, he also ·made right with him** [declared righteous; justified]; **and those he ·made right** [declared righteous; justified], **he also glorified** [Cboth a past act in Christ, and a future transformation].

God's Love in Christ Jesus

31**So what should we say ·about this** [in response to these things]? **If God is for us, ·no one can defeat us** [Lwho is against us?]. 32**He did not spare his own Son but ·gave him** [*or* delivered him over; Cto death] **for us all. So with Jesus, ·God will surely** [how could he not...?] **give us all things.** 33**Who can ·accuse** [bring an accusation/charge against] **the people God has chosen? No one, because God is the One who ·makes them right** [declares them righteous; justifies them]. 34**Who can ·say God's people are guilty** [condemn; pronounce punishment]? **No one, because Christ Jesus died, but he was also raised from the dead, and now he is on God's right ·side** [hand; Ps. 110:1], **·appealing to God** [interceding; pleading] **for us.** 35**·Can anything** [*or* Who can] **separate us from the love Christ has for us? Can ·troubles** [trials; tribulations] **or ·problems** [distress; hardship] **or ·sufferings** [persecution] **or ·hunger** [famine] **or ·nakedness** [destitution] **or danger or ·violent death** [Lsword]? 36**As it is written in the Scriptures:**

"**For ·you** [your sake] **we are ·in danger of death** [Lbeing put to death]
all the time.
·People think we are worth no more than [LWe were considered like]
sheep ·to be killed [about to be slaughtered; Ps. 44:22]."

37**But in all these things we are completely victorious through ·God** [*or* Christ; Lthe One] **who showed his love for us.** 38**Yes, I am ·sure** [convinced]

8:28 We . . . him. Some Greek copies read "We know that everything works together for good for those who love God."

that neither death, nor life, nor angels, nor ·ruling spirits [*or* heavenly rulers; *or* demons; Lrulers; Tprincipalities]**, nothing ·now** [in the present]**, nothing in the future, no ·powers** [*or* spiritual powers/authorities], 39**·nothing above us** [*or* no powers in the sky], **·nothing below us** [*or* nor powers in the depths], **nor ·anything else in the whole world** [any created thing] **will ever be able to separate us from the love of God that is in Christ Jesus our Lord.**

God and the Jewish People

9 I am telling you the truth ·as a follower of Christ [*or* with Christ as my witness; Lin Christ]**; I do not lie. My conscience is ·ruled by** [*or* guided by] **the Holy Spirit, and it ·tells** [testifies to] **me I am not lying.** 2**I have great sorrow and ·always feel much sadness** [unceasing/constant anguish]. 3[LFor] **I would even wish that I were cursed and cut off from ·Christ** [*or* the Messiah] **·if that would help** [for the sake of] **my Jewish brothers and sisters, my ·people** [countrymen; Lrelatives according to the flesh]. 4**They are the people of Israel, God's ·chosen** [Ladopted] **children. They ·have seen** [*or* have] **the glory of God, and they have the ·agreements that God made between himself and his people** [Lcovenants]. **God gave them the law of Moses and the ·right way of worship** [*or* temple worship] **and his promises.** 5**·They are the descendants of our great ancestors** [LThey have the fathers/patriarchs], **and ·they are the earthly family into which Christ was born** [*or* from their descendants the Messiah came], **·who is God over all. Praise him forever** [*or* May God, who is over all, be praised forever]**! Amen.**

6**It is not that ·God failed to keep his promise to them** [LGod's word failed]. **·But only some of the people of Israel are truly God's people** [LBecause not all those (descended) from Israel are Israel], 7**·and only some of Abraham's descendants are true children of Abraham** [Lnor are all of Abraham's seed/descendants (true) children]. **But God said to Abraham: "·The descendants I promised you will be from Isaac** [*or* Through Isaac your descendants will carry on your name; Gen. 21:12]**."** 8**This means that ·not all of Abraham's descendants** [Lit is not the children of the flesh who] **are God's true children.** [LBut; Rather] **·Abraham's true children** [LThose counted as Abraham's descendants/seed] **are ·those who become God's children because of the promise God made to Abraham** [Lthe children of the promise]. 9**God's promise to Abraham was this: "·At the right time** [At the appointed time; *or* About this time next year] **I will return, and Sarah will have a son** [Gen. 18:10, 14]**."** 10**And that is not all. Rebekah's sons ·had the same father,** [*or* were conceived at the same time by] **our ·father** [ancestor; forefather] **Isaac.** 11-12**But before the two boys were born, God told Rebekah, "The older will serve the younger** [Gen. 25:23]**." This was before the boys had done anything good or bad. God said this so that ·the one chosen would be chosen because of God's own plan** [*or* the plan/purpose God had chosen would continue/prevail]. **·Jacob was chosen** [*or* God's plan continued] **not because of ·anything Jacob did** [Lworks], **but because ·he was the one God wanted to call** [*or* of the One who called him]. 13**As the Scripture says, "I loved Jacob, but I hated Esau** [Mal. 1:2–3]**."**

14**So what should we say about this? Is God ·unfair** [unjust]**? ·In no way** [Absolutely not!; May it never be!; 7:13]. 15[LFor] **God said to Moses, "I will show ·kindness** [mercy] **to anyone to whom I want to show ·kindness** [mercy], **and I will show ·compassion** [pity] **to anyone to whom I want to show ·compassion** [pity; Ex. 33:19]**."** 16**So God's choice does not depend on ·what people want** [human desire; *or* human will] **or ·try to do** [effort; exertion], **but on God's ·mercy** [kindness]. 17**The Scripture says to ·the**

king of Egypt [[L]Pharaoh]: "I ·made you king [[L]raised you up] for this reason: to show my power in you so that my name will be ·talked about
[proclaimed] in all the earth [Ex. 9:16]." 18So God shows mercy where he
wants to show mercy, and he ·makes stubborn [hardens] the people he
wants to ·make stubborn [harden].
19So one of you will ask me: "Then why does God ·blame us for our sins
[[L]blame; find fault]? Who can ·fight [resist; oppose] his will?" 20·You are
only human, and human beings have no right to question God [[L]Who are
you, a mere human being, to talk back to God?]. ·An object [*or* A thing
molded] should not ask the ·person who made it [molder], "Why did you
make me like this? [Is. 29:16; 45:9]" 21·The potter can make anything he
wants to make [[L]Doesn't the potter have authority over the clay?]. He can
use the same ·clay [[L]lump] to make one ·thing [vessel; pot] for ·special
[honorable] use and another thing for ·daily [common; dishonorable] use.
22·It is the same way with God. He [[L]What if he…?] wanted to show his
·anger [wrath] and to let people see his power. But he ·patiently stayed
with [endured with great patience] those ·people he was angry with
[[L]vessels/objects of wrath]—people who were ·made ready [prepared] to
be destroyed. 23He waited with patience so that he could make known ·his
rich glory [the riches of his glory] to the ·people who receive his [[L]vessels/
objects of] mercy. He has prepared these people ·to have his glory [to
experience his glory; [L]for glory], 24and we are those people whom God
called. He called us not from the Jews only but also from the Gentiles.
25As ·the Scripture [*or* God] says in Hosea:

"I will ·say, 'You are my people' [call them 'my people']
to those who were not my people.
And I will ·show my love [call her 'beloved']
to ·those people [her] I did not love [Hos. 2:1, 23; [C]in Hosea, a
reference to apostate Israel; here applied to the Gentiles]."
26"And in the same place where they were called,
'You are not my people,'
there they will be called
'children of the living God [Hos. 1:10].'"

27And Isaiah cries out about Israel:

"[[L]Though] The ·people [[L]children; sons] of Israel are numbered
like the grains of sand ·by [*or* of] the sea.
But only ·a few of them [the remnant] will be saved,
28 because the Lord will quickly and completely ·punish the people
[carry out/execute his sentence; settle his account] on the earth
[Is. 10:22–23]."

29It is as Isaiah said:

"If the Lord ·All-Powerful [of Hosts; of Heaven's Armies]
had not ·allowed a few of our descendants to live [left us offspring/
seed],
We would have become like Sodom
and would resemble Gomorrah [Is. 1:9; [C]OT cities destroyed by God
because of their wickedness; Gen. 19]."

30·So what does all this mean [[L]What, then, shall we say]? Those who
are Gentiles ·were not trying to make themselves right with God [[L]did not
pursue righteousness], but they ·were made right with God [obtained
righteousness] ·because of their faith [[L]—that is, a righteousness that is by
faith]. 31The people of Israel tried to ·follow [pursue] a law ·to make

themselves right with God [Lof righteousness]. **But they did not ·succeed**
[reach/attain it], 32[LWhy?] **because they tried to make themselves right**
by ·the things they did [works] **instead of ·trusting in God to make them**
right [Lby faith]. **They stumbled over the stone that causes people to**
stumble. 33**As it is written in the Scripture:**

"[LLook; TBehold] **I will put in ·Jerusalem** [LZion; Ca poetic term for
Jerusalem and symbolizing the nation Israel] **a stone that causes**
people to stumble,
a rock that makes them fall [Is. 8:14].
Anyone who ·trusts [believes; has faith] **in him will never be**
·disappointed [put to shame; disgraced; Is. 28:16]."

10 **Brothers and sisters, the ·thing I want most** [pleasure/desire of
my heart] **and my prayer to God is for ·all the Jews to be saved**
[Ltheir salvation]. 2**·I can say this about them** [LFor I testify about them
that...]: **They ·really try to follow God** [Lhave a zeal for God], **but ·they do**
not know the right way [their zeal is misguided/uninformed/undiscern-
ing; Lnot according to knowledge]. 3**Because they ·did not know** [*or*
ignored] **the ·way that God makes people right with him** [righteousness
of God], **they ·tried to make themselves right in their own way** [Lsought
to establish their own righteousness]. **So they did not ·accept God's way**
of making people right [Lsubmit to God's righteousness]. 4[LFor] **Christ**
·ended [is the end/culmination/fulfillment of] **the law so that everyone**
who believes in him may ·be right with God [have righteousness].

5[LFor] **Moses writes about ·being made right** [the righteousness
attained] **by following the law. He says, "A person who ·obeys** [Ldoes] **these**
things will live ·because of [*or* by means of] **them** [Lev. 18:5]." 6**But ·this is**
what the Scripture says about being made right through faith [Lthe righteousness by faith says; Crighteousness is personified as speaking]: **"Don't**
say ·to yourself [Lin your heart; Deut. 9:4], **'Who will ·go up** [ascend] **into**
heaven [Deut. 30:12]?'" **(That means, "Who will go up to heaven and**
bring Christ down to earth [Ca reference to the Incarnation, Christ coming
to earth as a human being]?") 7**"And do not say, 'Who will go down into the**
·world below [*or* depths; *or* place of the dead; Labyss; Deut. 30:13; Ps.
107:26]?'" **(That means, "Who will go down and bring Christ up from the**
dead?") [CSuch impossible tasks are not needed for our salvation, since
Christ already did them for us.] 8**·This is what the Scripture says** [LBut what
does it say?]: **"The word is near you; it is in your mouth and in your heart**
[Deut. 30:14; CGod's salvation has been brought near through Christ and is
received by faith]." **That is the ·teaching** [message; word] **of faith that we**
·are telling [preach; proclaim]. 9**If you ·declare** [confess] **with your mouth,**
"Jesus is Lord," and if you believe in your heart that God raised Jesus from
the dead, you will be saved. 10[LFor] **We believe with our hearts, and so we**
·are made right with God [are justified; receive righteousness]. **And we**
·declare [confess] **with our mouths, ·and so we are saved** [leading to salva-
tion]. 11**As the Scripture says, "Anyone who ·trusts** [believes] **in him will**
never be ·disappointed [*or* put to shame; Is. 28:16]." 12**·That Scripture says**
"anyone" because [LFor] **there is no difference between Jews and Gentiles.**
[LFor; Because] **The same Lord is the Lord of all and gives ·many blessings**
[generously; (spiritual) riches] **to all who trust in him,** 13**as the Scripture**
says, "Anyone who calls on the Lord will be saved [Joel 2:32]."

14**·But before people can ask the Lord for help, they must believe in him**

[LHow, then, can they call on one in whom they have not believed?]; and
·before they can believe in him, they must hear about him [Lhow can they
believe in one of whom they have not heard?]; and ·for them to hear about
the Lord, someone must tell them [Lhow can they hear without someone
preaching to them?]; 15and ·before someone can go and tell them, that
person must be sent [Lhow can they preach unless they are sent?]. [LAs] It
is written, "How ·beautiful [*or* welcome; *or* timely] ·is the person [Lare the
feet of those] who comes ·to bring [proclaiming; preaching] good news
[Is. 52:7]." 16But not ·all the Jews [Leveryone] ·accepted [heeded; obeyed]
the good news. [LFor] Isaiah said, "Lord, who believed ·what we told them
[our message/report; Is. 53:1]?" 17·So [Thus; Consequently] faith comes
from ·hearing the Good News [Lhearing], and ·people hear the Good
News [hearing comes; *or* the message/report arrives] ·when someone tells
them [through the word/message] ·about [*or* proclaimed by; Lof] Christ.
18But I ask: Didn't ·people [Lthey; CIsrael] ·hear the Good News [Lhear]?
Yes, they heard—as the Scripture says:

"Their ·message [voice] went out to all the earth;
their words ·go everywhere on [Lto the ends of] the world [Ps. 19:4]."

19Again I ask: Didn't ·the people of Israel [LIsrael] understand? Yes, they
did understand [Cthis sentence is implied, but not stated, in the Greek].
First, Moses says:

"I will use those who are not a nation [Cthe Gentiles] to make you
jealous.
I will use a nation that ·does not understand [is foolish/senseless] to
make you angry [Deut. 32:21]."

20Then Isaiah is bold enough to say:

"I was found by those who were not ·asking me for help [seeking/
looking for me].
I ·made myself known [revealed myself] to people who were not
·looking for [asking about/for] me [Is. 65:1]."

21But about Israel ·God [*or* Isaiah; Lhe] says,

"All day long I ·stood ready to accept [Lheld out my hands to]
people who ·disobey [disbelieve] and are ·stubborn [defiant;
rebellious; Is. 65:2]."

God Shows Mercy to All People

11 So I ask: Did God ·throw out [cast away; reject] his people? ·No
[Absolutely not; May it never be; 9:14]! I myself am an Israelite
from the ·family [descendants; Lseed] of Abraham, from the tribe of
Benjamin. 2God has not ·thrown out [cast away; rejected] his people, whom
he ·chose [*or* knew] ·long ago [from the beginning; Lbeforehand]. ·Surely
you know [LDo you not know...?] what the Scripture says about Elijah, how
he ·prayed [appealed; complained] to God against the people of Israel.
3"Lord," he said, "they have killed your prophets, and they have ·destroyed
[torn/burned down] your altars. I am the only one left, and now they are
·trying to kill me, too [seeking my life; 1 Kin. 19:10, 14]." 4But what ·answer
did God give Elijah [Lwas the divine response]? He said, "But I have ·left
[kept for myself] seven thousand ·people [*or* men] in Israel who have not
bowed ·down [Lthe knee] before Baal [1 Kin. 19:18]." 5It is the same now.
There ·are a few people [is a remnant] that God has chosen by his grace.
6And if he chose them by grace, it is not ·for the things they have done [by
works]. If they could be made God's people by ·what they did [works],
God's gift of grace would ·not really [*or* no longer] be a gift.

7·So this is what has happened [What follows from this? LWhat then?]: ·The people of Israel [LIsrael] did not ·succeed in [attain; obtain; find] what they were ·striving [looking; seeking] for, but the ·ones God chose [elect] did ·succeed [attain/obtain/find it]. The ·others [rest] were ·made stubborn and refused to listen to God [Lhardened]. 8As it is written in the Scriptures:

"God gave the people a ·dull mind [Lspirit of stupor/insensitivity] so
they could not understand [Is. 29:10]."
"He ·closed their eyes so they [*or* gave them eyes that] could not see
and ·their ears so they [*or* gave them ears that] could not hear.
This continues until today [Deut. 29:4]."

9And David says:

"Let their ·own feasts [Ltable] ·trap them and cause their ruin
[Lbecome a snare and a trap],
becoming a ·stumbling block [pitfall] and ·paying them back [their
retribution].
10Let their eyes be ·closed [Ldarkened] so they cannot see
and their backs be ·forever [*or* continually] ·weak from troubles
[Lbent over; Ps. 69:22–23]."

11So I ask: When ·the Jews [Lthey] fell, did ·that fall destroy them [*or* they fall beyond recovery]? ·No [Absolutely not; May it never be; 11:1]! But their ·failure [transgression; violation] brought salvation to the Gentiles, in order to make ·the Jews [Lthem] jealous. 12[LBut if…] Their ·failure [transgression/violation] brought ·rich blessings [Lriches] for the world, and their ·loss [defeat; failure] brought ·rich blessings [Lriches] for the Gentiles. ·So surely the world will receive much richer blessings [LHow much more…!] ·when enough Jews become the kind of people God wants [*or* when the appointed number of Jews is saved; *or* when the nation as a whole is restored; Lat their fullness].

13Now I am speaking to you Gentiles. ·Since [*or* As long as] I am an apostle to the Gentiles [Acts 9:15; 22:21; Gal. 2:8], I ·will make the most of [glory in; take pride in; magnify] my ministry. 14·I hope […if somehow] I can make my own ·people [flesh] jealous and, in that way, help some of them to be saved. 15[LFor] If ·God's rejection of Israel [Ltheir loss/rejection] meant he ·became friends with [was reconciled to] the world, what will Israel's acceptance mean? It will be like ·bringing the dead back to life [life from the dead].

16If the ·first piece of bread is offered to God [Lfirstfruits are holy; Cthe dough made from the first crops harvested], then the whole ·loaf [batch; Llump of dough] is made holy. If the roots of a tree are holy, then the tree's branches are holy too [Csince Abraham and the patriarchs were God's chosen people, so were their Jewish descendants].

17It is as if some of the branches from an olive tree [Csymbolizing Israel] have been broken off. You Gentiles are like the branch of a wild olive tree that has been ·joined [grafted] to that first tree. You now share the ·strength and life [nourishment; Lrich/fat root] of the first tree [Cthe Gentiles now share in the rich blessings promised to Israel through their "root," Abraham and the patriarchs]. 18So do not ·brag about [boast over; consider yourselves superior to] those branches that were broken off. If you ·brag [boast], remember that you do not support the root, but the root supports you. 19[LThen] You will say, "Branches were broken off so that I could be ·joined to their tree [grafted in]." 20That is true. But those branches were broken off because they ·did not believe [were unfaithful], and you ·continue to be part of the tree only because you believe [Lstand

by faith]. Do not be ·proud [arrogant], but be ·afraid [in awe]. 21[LFor] If
God did not spare the natural branches, then he will not spare you either.
22·So you see [Notice; Consider] that God is kind and also ·very strict
[stern; severe; harsh]. He ·punishes [is strict/severe/harsh toward] those
who ·stop following him [have fallen]. But God is kind to you, if you continue ·following in [trusting in; Lin] his kindness. If you do not, you will also
be cut off from the tree. 23And if ·the Jews [Lthey] ·will believe in God again
[Ldo not continue in unbelief], ·he will accept them back [Lthey will be
grafted in]. [LFor] God is able to ·put them back where they were [graft
them in again]. 24[LFor] If ·you Gentiles [you] were cut off from a wild olive
tree and, contrary to nature, ·joined to [grafted into] a ·good [cultivated]
olive tree, how much more will these natural branches [CJews presently
rejecting the gospel] be ·joined to [grafted into] their own olive tree again.
25I ·want you to understand [Ldo not want you to be ignorant of] this
·secret [mystery; Csomething God had not previously disclosed; Eph. 1:9],
brothers and sisters, so you will ·understand that you do not know everything [not become conceited/arrogant/superior-minded]: ·Part of Israel
has been made stubborn [*or* A partial hardening has happened to Israel],
·but that will change when [Luntil] the ·complete number [*or* appointed
number; Lfullness] of the Gentiles have come ·to God [*or* into the kingdom; Lin]. 26And ·that is how [in this way; *or* so it will be that; *or* so in the
end] all Israel will be saved. [LAs; Just as] It is written in the Scriptures:
"The ·Savior [Rescuer; Deliverer] will come from ·Jerusalem [LZion; Ca
poetic term for Jerusalem symbolizing the nation Israel];
he will take away ·all evil [wickedness; godlessness] from ·the family
of Jacob [LJacob; CAbraham's grandson (renamed "Israel"), whose
sons became the twelve tribes of Israel; Is. 59:20–21].
27And I will make this ·agreement [covenant] with those people
when I take away their sins [Is. 27:9]."
28·The Jews refuse to accept the Good News, so [LWith regard to the
Gospel,] they are God's enemies. ·This has happened to help you who are
not Jews [L…for your sake; CIsrael's rejection resulted in the proclamation
of the Good News to the Gentiles; vv. 11, 12]. But ·the Jews are still God's
chosen people, and he loves them very much [Lwith regard to election, they
are beloved] because of ·the promises he made to their ancestors [Lthe
ancestors/fathers/patriarchs]. 29·God never changes his mind about the
people he calls and the things he gives them [LFor God's gifts and calling
are irrevocable]. 30[LFor] At one time you refused to obey God. But now
you have received mercy, because those people refused to obey. 31And now
the Jews refuse to obey, ·because God showed mercy to you. But this happened so that they also can[n] receive mercy from him [*or* but this happened
so that they also can[n] receive mercy from him, because of the mercy God
showed to you]. 32God has ·given [imprisoned] all people ·over to their
stubborn ways [Lto/in disobedience] so that he can show mercy to all.

Praise to God

33·Yes [LO], ·how great are [Lthe depth of] ·God's riches and wisdom
and knowledge [*or* the riches of God's wisdom and knowledge]! ·No one
can explain [LHow unsearchable are…] ·the things God decides [God's
judgments] ·or understand [L…and untraceable…!] his ·ways [paths].
34As the Scripture says,

11:31 can Some Greek copies read "can now."

“[LFor] Who has known the mind of the Lord,
or who has been ·able to give him advice [his counselor; Is. 40:13]?”
35“·No one [LOr who…?] has ever given God anything
that he must pay back [Job 41:11].”
36·Yes, God made all things, and everything continues through him
and for him [LBecause all things come from him, through him and for
him]. To him be the glory forever! Amen.

Give Your Lives to God

12 ·So [Therefore] brothers and sisters, since God has shown us
great mercy, I ·beg [urge; appeal to] you to offer your ·lives
[selves; Lbodies] as a living sacrifice to him. Your offering must be ·only for
God [holy] and pleasing to him, which is the ·spiritual [*or* authentic; true;
or appropriate; fitting; *or* rational; reasonable] way for you to worship. 2Do
not be ·shaped by [conformed to; pressed into a mold by] this ·world [age];
instead be ·changed within [transformed] by ·a new way of thinking [*or*
changing the way you think; Lthe renewing of your mind]. Then you will be
able to ·decide [discern; test and approve] what ·God wants for you [is
God’s will]; you will know what is good and pleasing to him and what is
perfect. 3Because God has given me ·a special gift [his grace], I have something to say to everyone among you. Do not think you are better than you
are. [Instead] You must ·decide what you really are [think sensibly; think
with sober discernment] ·by [based on; in accordance with] the amount of
faith God has given you. 4[LFor just as] Each one of us has ·a [Lone] body
with many parts, and these parts all have different ·uses [functions]. 5In
the same way, we are many, but in Christ we are all one body, and each part
belongs to all the other ·parts [Lmembers]. 6We all have different gifts, each
of which came because of the grace God gave us. The person who has the
gift of prophecy should use that gift ·in agreement with the faith [*or* in
proportion to their faith]. 7Anyone who has the gift of serving should serve.
Anyone who has the gift of teaching should teach. 8Whoever has the gift of
·encouraging [exhorting] others should ·encourage [exhort]. Whoever has
the gift of giving to others should give ·freely [generously]. Anyone who
has the gift of being a leader should ·try hard when he leads [lead diligently/
enthusiastically]. Whoever has the gift of showing mercy to others should
do so with ·joy [cheerfulness].

9Your love must be ·real [sincere; unhypocritical]. ·Hate [Abhor;
Despise] what is evil, and ·hold on [cling] to what is good. 10·Love [Be
devoted to] each other ·like brothers and sisters [with family/brotherly
affection]. ·Give each other more honor than you want for yourselves [*or*
Outdo one another in showing honor; *or* Be eager to show honor to one
another]. 11Do not be ·lazy but work hard [Llacking in zeal], serving the
Lord with ·all your heart [La fervent/eager/enthusiastic spirit]. 12·Be joyful
because you have hope [LRejoice in hope]. ·Be patient [Endure] ·when
trouble comes [Lin suffering/tribulation], and pray ·at all times [faith-
fully; with persistence/perseverance]. 13Share with ·God’s people [Tthe
saints] who need help. ·Bring strangers in need into your homes [Pursue/
Be eager to show hospitality].

14·Wish good for [Bless] those who ·harm [persecute] you; ·wish them
well [bless] and do not curse them. 15·Be happy [Rejoice] with those who
·are happy [rejoice], and ·be sad [weep] with those who ·are sad [weep].
16Live in ·peace [harmony] with each other. Do not be ·proud [arrogant;
haughty], but ·make friends with those who seem unimportant [associate

with the humble/those of low social status; *or* be willing to do lowly tasks].
Do not think how ·smart [wise; superior] you are.
17·If someone does wrong to you, do not pay him back by doing wrong
to him [LRepay no one evil for evil]. ·Try to do [*or* Consider carefully]
what ·everyone thinks is right [others view as good/honorable; Lis good/
noble before all people]. 18·Do your best to [LIf possible, from your part,]
live in peace with everyone. 19My friends, do not ·try to punish others
when they wrong you [take revenge; avenge yourselves], but ·wait for God
to punish them with his anger [Lleave room for (God's) wrath]. [LFor] It
is written: "·I will punish those who do wrong [LVengeance is mine]; I will
repay them [Deut. 32:35]," says the Lord. 20But you should do this:

"If your enemy is hungry, feed him;
if he is thirsty, give him a drink.
Doing this will be like ·pouring [heaping] burning coals on his head
[Prov. 25:21–22]."

21Do not let evil ·defeat [conquer; overcome] you, but ·defeat [conquer;
overcome] evil by doing good.

Christians Should Obey the Law

13 All of you must ·yield [obey; submit; be subject] to the government ·rulers [authorities]. [LBecause; For] ·No one rules
[LThere is no authority] ·unless God has given him the power to rule
[Lexcept by/through God], and ·no one rules now without that power
from God [Lthose that exist are appointed/established by God]. 2So those
who ·are against the government [rebel/resist the authority] are really
·against [resisting; opposing] what God has ·commanded [ordained; insti-
tuted]. And they will bring ·punishment [judgment] on themselves.
3[LFor] Those who do ·right [good] do not have to fear the rulers; only
those who do ·wrong [evil] fear them. Do you want to be unafraid of the
·rulers [Lauthority]? Then do what is ·right [good], and they will ·praise
[commend] you. 4The ruler is God's servant ·to help you [for your good].
But if you do wrong, then be afraid. ·He has the power to punish [LFor he
does not bear the sword in vain]; he is God's servant ·to punish [an avenger
for (God's) wrath to] those who do wrong. 5So you must ·yield [submit; be
subject] to the government, not only because ·you might be punished [Lof
wrath], but because ·you know it is right [of (your) conscience].
6This is also why you pay taxes. [LBecause] Rulers are ·working for God
[God's servants/ministers] ·and give their time to [devoting themselves to]
their work. 7Pay everyone what you owe them: taxes to those you owe taxes,
·fees [tolls] to those you owe ·fees [tolls], ·respect [reverence; fear] to those
you owe ·respect [reverence; fear], and honor to those you owe honor.

Loving Others

8Do not owe ·people [Lanyone] anything, except always owe love to
each other, because the person who loves others has ·obeyed all [fulfilled]
the law. 9[LFor] The law says, "You must not be guilty of adultery. You
must not murder anyone. You must not steal. You must not ·want to take
your neighbor's things [covet; Ex. 20:13–15, 17; Deut. 5:17–21]." All these
commands and all others are really summed up in this one ·rule [com-
mand; word]: "Love your neighbor as you love yourself [Lev. 19:18]."
10Love never ·hurts [does wrong/evil to] a neighbor, so loving is ·obeying
all [fulfilling] the law.
11Do this ·because you know the times in which we live [Lknowing the
time/season]. It is ·now [*or* already the] ·time [hour] for you to wake up
from your sleep, because our salvation is nearer now than when we first

believed. 12 The night [C a metaphor for the present evil age] is ·almost finished [advancing], and the day [C the time of final judgment and reward] is ·almost here [near; *or* at hand]. So we should ·stop doing [put aside; cast off] ·things that belong to [L the deeds/works of] darkness and ·take up the weapons [*or* put on the armor] ·used for fighting in [*or* that belong to; L of] the light. 13 Let us ·live [walk] ·in a right way [properly; decently], like people who belong to the day. We should not have wild parties or get drunk. There should be no ·sexual sins of any kind [L sexual immorality or debauchery/sensuality], no ·fighting [strife; quarrels] or jealousy. 14 But clothe yourselves with the Lord Jesus Christ and ·forget about satisfying [*or* give no opportunity to the desires of; *or* don't think about ways to gratify] ·your sinful self [the sinful nature; T the flesh].

Do Not Criticize Other People

14 ·Accept into your group [L Welcome; Receive] someone who is weak in ·faith [*or* convictions; C on debatable issues], and do not argue about ·opinions [doubtful/debatable issues]. 2 One person believes it is right to eat all kinds of food. But another, who is weak, believes it is right to eat only vegetables [C possibly the issue of whether to keep the OT dietary laws, and/or whether to avoid food sacrificed to idols (see 1 Cor. 8–10)]. 3 The one who ·knows that it is right to eat any kind of food [L eats; v. 14; see Mark 7:18–19] must not ·reject [despise; look down on] the one who ·eats only vegetables [L does not eat]. And the person who ·eats only vegetables [L does not eat] must not ·think that the one who eats all foods is wrong [L judge the one who eats], because God has accepted that person. 4 ·You cannot [L Who are you to…?] judge another person's servant. ·The master decides if the servant is doing well or not [L Before his own lord/master he stands or falls]. And the Lord's servant will ·do well [stand] because the Lord ·helps him do well [L can make him stand].

5 Some ·think [decide; judge] that one day is more ·important [sacred; holy] than another, and others think that every day is the same [C the issue is whether to observe the Jewish Sabbath]. Let all be ·sure [fully convinced] ·in their own mind [according to their convictions/conscience]. 6 Those who ·think one day is more important than other days [L observe the day] are doing that for the Lord. And those who ·eat all kinds of food [L eat] are doing that for the Lord, ·and [since; for] they give thanks to God. Others who ·refuse to eat some foods [L do not eat] do that for the Lord, and they give thanks to God. 7 [L For] We do not live for ourselves, and we do not die for ourselves. 8 If we live, we are living for the Lord, and if we die, we are dying for the Lord. So living or dying, we belong to the Lord.

9 The reason Christ died and ·rose from the dead to live again [L lived] was so he would be Lord over both the dead and the living. 10 So why do you judge your brothers or sisters in Christ? And why do you ·think you are better than they are [L despise/look down on your brother or sister]? [L For] We will all stand before ·God to be judged [the judgment seat of God], 11 because it is written in the Scriptures:

"'As surely as I live,' says the Lord,
'·Everyone [L Every knee] will bow before me;
·everyone [L every tongue] will ·say that I am [confess; acknowledge;
or praise] God [Is. 45:23].'"

12 So each of us will ·have to answer [give an account of ourselves] to God.

Do Not Cause Others to Sin

13 For that reason ·we should [*or* let us] stop judging each other. We must make up our minds not to ·do anything that will make another Christian

sin [Lplace a stumbling block or obstacle before a brother or sister]. **14·I am in the Lord Jesus, and I know** [LI know and am persuaded in the Lord Jesus] **that there is ·no food that is wrong to eat** [Lnothing impure/unclean/defiling in itself]. **But if a person ·believes** [considers; regards] **something is ·wrong** [impure; unclean; defiling], **that thing is ·wrong** [impure; unclean; defiling] **for him. 15If ·you hurt your brother's or sister's faith** [your brother or sister is distressed/grieved] **because of something you eat, you are ·not really following the way of** [Lno longer walking/living in] **love. ·Do not destroy someone's faith by eating food he thinks is wrong, because Christ died for him** [LBy your eating do not destroy that one for whom Christ died!; Cso trivial a matter as food must not negate the tremendous sacrifice Christ made]. **16Do not allow what you think is good to ·become what others say is evil** [be criticized/regarded as evil; Lbe slandered/blasphemed]. **17·In the kingdom of God, eating and drinking are not important** [LFor the kingdom of God is not (about) eating and drinking]. **The important things are ·living right with God** [righteousness], **peace, and joy in the Holy Spirit. 18Anyone who serves Christ by living this way is pleasing God and will be ·accepted** [approved; respected] **by other people.**

19So let us try to do what makes peace and ·helps [builds up; edifies] **one another. 20Do not let the eating of food ·destroy** [tear down] **the work of God. All foods are ·all right to eat** [clean; ritually undefiled], **but it is wrong to eat food that causes someone else to ·sin** [stumble; fall]. **21It is ·better** [good] **not to eat meat or drink wine or do anything that will cause your brother or sister to ·sin** [stumble; fall].

22Your beliefs about these things should be kept secret between you and God. ·People are happy [Blessed are those] **·if they can do what they think is right without feeling guilty** [Lwho do not condemn themselves concerning issues they have examined and approved]. **23But those who eat something ·without being sure it is right** [while doubting; with misgivings] **are ·wrong** [condemned] **because they did not believe it was right. Anything that ·is done without believing it is right** [*or* does not come from faith] **is sin.**

15 We who are ·strong in faith [Lstrong] **should ·help** [bear with; be patient with] **the weak with their ·weaknesses** [failings; struggles], **and not please only ourselves. 2Let each of us please our neighbors for their good, to ·help them be stronger in faith** [edify them; build them up]. 3[LFor] **Even Christ did not live to please himself. It was as the Scriptures said: "·When people insult you, it hurts me** [LThe insults of those who insulted you have fallen on me; Ps. 69:9]." 4[LFor] **Everything that was written in the past was written to teach us. The Scriptures give us ·patience** [endurance] **and encouragement so that we can have hope. 5May ·the patience and encouragement that come from God** [Lthe God of patience and encouragement] **·allow you to live in harmony with each other the way Christ Jesus wants** [*or* grant you the same attitude with each other that Christ Jesus had]. **6·Then** [L...so that] **·you will all be joined together and** [Ltogether with one voice/mouth] **you will give glory to God the Father of our Lord Jesus Christ. 7Accept each another, just as Christ accepted you. ·This will bring glory to God** [*or* In this way Christ brought glory to God; L...to the glory of God]. 8[LFor] **I tell you that Christ became a servant of the ·Jews** [Lcircumcised] **to ·show** [confirm] **that God's promises to the ·Jewish ancestors** [patriarchs; fathers] **are true. 9And he also did this so that the Gentiles could**

give glory to God for the mercy he gives to them. [LJust as] It is written
in the Scriptures:
"So I will ·praise [confess] you among the ·Gentiles [nations].
I will sing ·praises [psalms] to your name [Ps. 18:49]."
10·The Scripture also [LAnd again it] says,
"·Be happy [Rejoice; Celebrate], you ·Gentiles [nations], together with
his people [Deut. 32:43]."
11·Again the Scripture says [LAnd again],
"All you ·Gentiles [nations], praise the Lord.
All you people, sing praises to him [Ps. 117:1]."
12And [Lagain] Isaiah says,
"·A new king will come from the family of Jesse [The root of Jesse will
come/sprout; CJesse was the father of King David].
He will ·come [rise up] to rule over the ·Gentiles [nations],
and they will ·have hope because of [put their hope in] him [Is. 11:10]."
13I pray that the God who gives hope will fill you with ·much [Lall] joy
and peace ·while you trust [because you trust; through your faith] in him.
Then your hope will overflow by the power of the Holy Spirit.

Paul Talks About His Work

14My brothers and sisters, I am ·sure [fully convinced] that you are
[indeed] full of goodness. I know that you ·have all the knowledge you
need [Lare filled with all knowledge] and that you are able to ·teach
[instruct; admonish; warn] each other. 15But I have written to you very
·openly [boldly] about some ·things [points; Lparts] I wanted you to
remember. I did this because ·God gave me this special gift [*or* of the
grace God gave me]: 16to be a ·minister [servant] of Christ Jesus to the
Gentiles. I ·served God [*or* perform priestly service] ·by teaching his Good
News [for the Good News/Gospel of/about God], so that the Gentiles
could be an offering that God would accept—an offering ·made holy
[sanctified; purified] by the Holy Spirit.
17So I ·am proud [have a reason to boast] of what I have done for God in
Christ Jesus. 18I will not [dare] talk about anything except what Christ has
done through me in leading the Gentiles to obey God. They have obeyed
God because of what I have said and done, 19because of the power of ·mira-
cles [signs] and ·the great things they saw [wonders; marvels], ·and because
of [*or* acccomplished through] the power of the Spirit of God. I have ·fin-
ished my work of preaching [fulfilled my commission to preach; *or* fully
preached] the ·Good News [Gospel] from Jerusalem all the way around to
Illyricum [Ca Roman province northwest of Macedonia; modern Albania,
Serbia and Montenegro]. 20[So; In this way] I always ·want [*or* try; make it
my ambition] to preach the ·Good News [Gospel] in places where ·people
have never heard of Christ [LChrist has not been named], ·because I do not
want [*or* in order not] to build on the ·work someone else has already started
[Lfoundation of others]. 21But [Las; just as] it is written in the Scriptures:
"Those who were not told about him will see,
and those who have not heard about him will understand [Is. 52:15]."

Paul's Plan to Visit Rome

22This is the reason I was ·stopped [hindered; *or* delayed] many times
from coming to you. 23[LBut] Now I have ·finished my work here [Lno
more place (to work) in these regions]. Since for many years I have wanted
to come to you, 24I hope to visit you [while passing through] on my way
to Spain. After I enjoy being with you for a while, I hope you can ·help
[assist; support] me on my trip. 25Now I am going to Jerusalem to ·help

[minister to; provide a service for] ·God's people [^T the saints]. 26The
believers in Macedonia [^C northern Greece] and Achaia [^C southern
Greece] were ·happy [pleased; *or* resolved] to ·give their money to help
[make a contribution to; 1 Cor. 16:1–4; 2 Cor. 8–9] the poor among ·God's
people [^T the saints] at Jerusalem. 27They were ·happy [pleased; *or* resolved]
to do this, and really they ·owe it [^L are debtors] to them. These Gentiles
have shared in the Jews' spiritual blessings, so they should use their material ·possessions [*or* blessings] to ·help the Jews [^L render service to them].
28[^L Therefore] After I have completed this collection and ·delivered the
money safely to them [^L sealed this fruit for them; ^C uncertain idiom, likely
indicating secure packaging or safe arrival of cargo], I will leave for Spain
and stop and visit you. 29I know that when I come to you ·I will bring
Christ's full blessing [*or* Christ will richly bless our time together; ^L I will
come in the fullness of Christ's blessing].

30Brothers and sisters, I ·beg [urge; encourage] you to ·help [join; strive
together with] me in my work by praying to God for me. Do this because
of our Lord Jesus and the love ·that the Holy Spirit gives us [^L of the Spirit].
31Pray that I will be ·saved [rescued; delivered] from the nonbelievers in
Judea and that ·this help I bring [my ministry/service] to Jerusalem will
·please [be acceptable to; be well received by] ·God's people [^T the saints]
there. 32Then, ·if God wants me to [by God's will], I will come to you with
joy, and together you and I will ·have a time of rest [be refreshed]. 33[Now
may] The God who gives peace be with you all. Amen.

Greetings to the Christians

16 1I ·recommend [commend] to you our sister Phoebe, who is a
·helper [*or* servant; *or* minister; *or* deacon; 1 Tim. 3:11] in the
church in Cenchrea [^C Phoebe may have been the messenger carrying this
letter]. 2I ask you to ·accept [welcome] her in the Lord in the way ·God's
people should [worthy of the saints]. Help her with anything she needs,
because she has ·helped [been a benefactor/patron to] many people,
·including [*or* especially] me.

3Give my greetings to Priscilla and Aquila [Acts 18:2, 18, 26], ·who
work together with me [^L my coworkers] in Christ Jesus 4and who risked
their own ·lives [neck] ·to save [^L for] my life. I am thankful to them, and
[^L not only I, but] all the Gentile churches are thankful as well. 5Also, greet
for me the church that meets at their house.

Greetings to my dear friend Epenetus, who was the ·first person in Asia to
follow Christ [^L firstfruit of Asia for Christ]. 6Greetings to Mary, who worked
very hard for you. 7Greetings to Andronicus and Junia [^C Junia is probably a
woman's name, though not certainly], my ·relatives [*or* fellow Jews], ·who
were in prison with me [and fellow prisoners]. They are ·very important
[prominent; *or* well known to/among the] apostles. They were believers in
Christ before I was. 8Greetings to Ampliatus, my ·dear [beloved] friend in
the Lord. 9Greetings to Urbanus, a worker together with me for Christ. And
greetings to my ·dear [beloved] friend Stachys. 10Greetings to Apelles, ·who
was tested and proved that he truly loves Christ [*or* a proven servant of
Christ; ^L approved in Christ]. Greetings to all those who are in the family of
Aristobulus. 11Greetings to Herodion, my ·fellow citizen [*or* fellow Jew; *or*
relative]. Greetings to all those in the family of Narcissus who ·belong to
[^L are in] the Lord. 12Greetings to Tryphena and Tryphosa, ·women who
work very hard for [^L laborers in] the Lord. Greetings to ·my dear friend [the
beloved] Persis, who also has worked very hard ·for [^L in] the Lord. 13Greetings

to Rufus, who is ·a special person [Lchosen] in the Lord, and to his mother,
who has been like a mother to me also. 14Greetings to Asyncritus, Phlegon,
Hermes, Patrobas, Hermas, and all the brothers and sisters who are with
them. 15Greetings to Philologus and Julia, Nereus and his sister, and
Olympas, and to all ·God's people [Tthe saints] with them. 16Greet each other
with a holy kiss. All of Christ's churches send greetings to you.

17Brothers and sisters, I ·ask [urge; encourage] you to look out for those
who cause ·divisions [dissension] and who ·upset other people's faith [create
obstacles/stumbling blocks]. ·They [*or* Such things] are against the true
teaching you learned, so stay away from them. 18Such people are not serving
our Lord Christ but are ·only doing what pleases themselves [serving their
own appetites/Lbellies]. They use ·fancy [smooth] talk and ·fine words [flat-
tery] to ·fool [deceive] the ·minds of those who do not know about evil
[Lhearts of the innocent/naive]. 19All the believers have heard ·that you obey
[about your obedience/faithfulness], so I ·am very happy [rejoice] because of
you. But I want you to be wise in what is good and innocent in what is evil.

20The God ·who brings [Lof] peace will soon ·defeat Satan and give you
power over him [crush Satan under your feet; Gen. 3:15].

The grace of our Lord Jesus be with you.

21Timothy [Acts 16:1–2; 1 Tim. 1:2; 2 Tim. 1:2], ·a worker together with
me [my coworker], sends greetings, as well as Lucius, Jason, and Sosipater,
my ·relatives [*or* fellow Jews].

22I am Tertius, and I am writing this letter from Paul [CTertius was the
scribe, or amanuensis, to whom Paul was dictating the letter]. I send greetings to you in the Lord.

23Gaius [1 Cor. 1:14; Acts 19:29] is ·letting me and the whole church
here use his home [Lhost to me and to the whole church; Cchurches met in
homes at this time]. He also sends greetings to you, as do Erastus, the city
treasurer, and our brother Quartus. [24The grace of our Lord Jesus Christ
be with all of you. Amen.][n]

25·Glory to God [LNow to the one] who can make you strong in faith ·by
[*or* in accord with] ·the Good News that I tell people [Lmy Gospel] and ·by
[*or* in accord with] the ·message [preaching; proclamation] about Jesus
Christ. The message about Christ is the ·secret [mystery; 11:25] that was
hidden for long ages past but is now ·made known [revealed; disclosed].
26It has been ·made clear [revealed; disclosed] through the writings of the
prophets. And by the command of the eternal God it is ·made known
[revealed; disclosed] to all ·nations [Gentiles] ·that they might believe and
obey [*or* for the obedience that follows faith; Lfor the obedience of faith].

27To the only wise God be glory forever through Jesus Christ! Amen.

16:24 The . . . Amen. Some Greek copies do not contain the bracketed text.

1 CORINTHIANS

1 From Paul. ·God called me [L…called] **to be an ·apostle** [messenger] **of Christ Jesus ·because that is what God wanted** [Lby the will of God]. **Also from Sosthenes** [Ca coworker; Paul may be dictating the letter to him; see 16:21; perhaps the synagogue leader mentioned in Acts 18:15–17], **our ·brother in Christ** [Lbrother].

2To the church of God in Corinth [Can important city in southern Greece; Paul started the church on his second missionary journey, around AD 52; Acts 18], **to you who have been ·made holy** [sanctified; dedicated/set apart to God] **in Christ Jesus. You were called to be ·God's holy people** [Tsaints] **with all people everywhere who pray in the name of the Lord Jesus Christ—·their Lord and ours** [Ltheirs and ours]:

3Grace and peace to you from God our Father and the Lord Jesus Christ.

Paul Gives Thanks to God

4I always thank my God for you because of the ·grace [gift; favor] **God has given you in Christ Jesus. 5I thank God because in Christ you have been ·made rich** [enriched] **in every way, in all your ·speaking** [*or* spiritual gifts of speaking] **and in all your ·knowledge** [*or* gifts of spiritual knowledge]. **6Just as our ·witness** [testimony; message] **about Christ has been ·guaranteed to** [*or* confirmed among] **you, 7so you ·have every** [Ldo not lack any] **·gift from God** [spiritual gift; Lgift] **while you wait for the ·return** [Lrevelation] **of our Lord Jesus Christ. 8·Jesus** [L…who] **will keep you strong until the end so that ·there will be no wrong in you** [you will be blameless/faultless] **on the day ·our Lord Jesus Christ comes again** [Lof our Lord Jesus Christ; Cthe final day of judgment, known in the OT as "the Day of the Lord"]. **9God, who has called you into ·fellowship** [partnership; relationship] **with his Son, Jesus Christ our Lord, is faithful.**

Problems in the Church

10I ·beg [urge; appeal to] **you, brothers and sisters, ·by the name** [*or* by the authority; *or* as followers] **of our Lord Jesus Christ that all of you agree with each other and not be ·split into groups** [divided into factions]. **I beg that you be ·completely joined together** [fully united; *or* made complete] **by having the same ·kind of thinking** [Lmind] **and the same ·purpose** [intention; conviction]. **11My brothers and sisters, some people from Chloe's ·family** [household; Cthese could be family members, servants, or business agents] **have ·told me quite plainly** [reported to me] **that there are ·quarrels** [conflicts; rivalries] **among you. 12This is what I mean: One of you says, "I follow Paul"; another says, "I follow Apollos"; another says, "I follow ·Peter** [LCephas; CPeter's name in Aramaic; 3:22; 9:5; 15:5; Mark 1:30; John 1:42]"; **and another says, "I follow Christ." 13·Christ has been divided up into different groups!** [*or* Is Christ divided?] **Did Paul die on the cross for you? No!**

Were you baptized in the name of Paul? No! [C"No!" is implied but not stated
in the Greek.] 14**I thank God I did not baptize any of you except Crispus and
Gaius** 15**so that now no one can say you were baptized in my name.** 16**(I also
baptized the ·family** [household] **of Stephanas, but I do not remember if I
baptized anyone else.)** 17[LFor] **Christ did not send me to baptize people but
to preach the ·Good News** [Gospel], **and not using ·words of human wisdom**
[*or* eloquent language; clever speech] **so that the cross of Christ** [Cthe message of Christ's sacrificial death on the cross] **would not ·lose its power** [*or*
become meaningless; Lbe emptied].

Christ Is God's Power and Wisdom

18[LFor] **The ·teaching** [message; word] **about the cross is ·foolishness**
[folly] **to those who are ·being lost** [headed for destruction; perishing],
but to us who are being saved it is the power of God. 19[LFor] **It is written
in the Scriptures:**
"I will destroy the wisdom of the wise;
And I will ·reject [thwart; bring to nothing] **the ·intelligence** [discern-
ment; cleverness] **of the ·intelligent** [discerning; clever; Is. 29:14]**."**
20**Where is the wise person? Where is the ·educated person** [scholar; *or*
scribe; teacher of the law]? **Where is the ·skilled talker** [orator; debater;
philosopher] **of this ·world** [age]? **·God has** [LHas not God…?] **made the
wisdom of the world foolish.** 21**·In the wisdom of God the world did** [*or*
God wisely determined that the world would] **not know God through its
own wisdom. So God ·chose** [was pleased] **to use the ·message that sounds
foolish** [Lfolly/foolishness of what was preached] **to save those who
believe.** 22[LFor; Since] **The Jews ·ask for** [demand] **·miracles** [Lsigns], **and
the Greeks ·want** [seek; look for] **wisdom.** 23**But we preach ·that Christ
was crucified** [Christ crucified; *or* a crucified Messiah]. **This ·causes the
Jews to stumble** [is a stumbling block/offense/obstacle to Jews] **and is
·foolishness** [folly] **to Gentiles.** 24**But to those people God has called—
both Jews and Greeks—Christ is the power of God and the wisdom of
God.** 25[LFor] **Even the foolishness of God is wiser than human wisdom,
and the weakness of God is stronger than human strength.**
26**Brothers and sisters, look at what you were when God called you. Not
many of you were wise ·in the way the world judges wisdom** [by human
standards; Laccording to the flesh]. **Not many of you ·had great influence**
[were powerful/strong]. **Not many of you ·came from important families**
[were well-born; were of high social status]. 27**But God chose the foolish
things of the world to shame the wise, and he chose the weak things of the
world to shame the strong.** 28**He chose what the world thinks is ·unim-
portant** [insignificant; lowly] **and what the world ·looks down on**
[despises] **and thinks is nothing in order to destroy what the world thinks
is ·important** [something special]. 29**God did this so that no one can ·brag**
[boast] **in his presence.** 30**Because of God you are ·in** [united with; in relationship with] **Christ Jesus, who has become for us wisdom from God. ·In
Christ we are put right with God, and have been made holy, and have
been set free from sin** [L…and became for us righteousness, holiness, and
redemption]. 31**So, as the Scripture says, "If people want to ·brag** [boast],
they should ·brag [boast] **only about the Lord** [Jer. 9:24]**."**

The Message of Christ's Death

**2 Dear brothers and sisters, when I came to you, I did not come
preaching God's ·secret**[n] [mystery; Csomething God had not

2:1 God's secret Some Greek copies read "God's message."

previously disclosed; Eph. 1:9] with ·fancy [superior; eloquent] words or a show of human wisdom. 2[LFor] I ·decided [resolved] that while I was with you I would ·forget about everything [Lnot know anything] except Jesus Christ and his death on the cross. 3So when I came to you, I was weak and fearful and trembling. 4My ·teaching [message; speech] and preaching were not with words of human wisdom that ·persuade [*or* entice] people but with ·proof of the power that the Spirit gives [*or* proof powerfully revealed by the Spirit; *or* demonstrations of the Spirit and of power]. 5This was so that your faith would be in God's power and not in human wisdom.

God's Wisdom

6However, we speak wisdom to those who are mature. But this wisdom is not from this ·world [age] or from the rulers of this ·world [age], who ·are losing their power [will soon disappear; are passing away]. 7We speak God's ·secret wisdom [*or* wisdom in a mystery; 2:1], which he has kept hidden. Before the ·world began [ages], God ·planned [decreed; destined] this wisdom for our glory. 8None of the rulers of this ·world [age] understood it. If they had, they would not have crucified the ·Lord of glory [glorious Lord]. 9But as it is written in the Scriptures:

"No ·one [Leye] has ever seen this,
and no ·one [Lear] has ever heard about it.
No ·one [Lhuman heart] has ever imagined
what God has prepared for those who love him [Is. 64:4]."

10But God has ·shown [revealed to] us these things through the Spirit. [LFor] The Spirit ·searches out [examines; scrutinizes] all things, even the ·deep secrets [deep things; depths] of God. 11Who knows the thoughts that another person has? Only a person's spirit that lives within him knows his thoughts. It is the same with God. No one knows the thoughts of God except the Spirit of God. 12Now we did not receive the spirit of the world, but we received the Spirit that is from God so that we can know all that God has [freely] given us. 13And we speak about these things, not with words taught us by human wisdom but with words taught us by the Spirit. And so we explain spiritual truths ·to spiritual people [*or* to those who have the Spirit; *or* with the Spirit's words]. 14A ·person who does not have the Spirit [*or* natural person] does not accept the ·truths [Lthings] that come from the Spirit of God. That person thinks they are foolish and cannot understand them, because they can only be ·judged to be true [discerned; assessed] by the Spirit. 15The ·spiritual person [*or* person with the Spirit] is able to ·judge [discern; assess] all things, but no one can ·judge [discern; assess] him. ·The Scripture says [LFor]:

16"Who has known the mind of the Lord?
Who has been able to ·teach [advise; counsel] him [Is. 40:13]?"

But we have the mind of Christ [Cthe Holy Spirit reveals God and his ways to us; Rom. 11:34].

Following People Is Wrong

3 Brothers and sisters, in the past I could not talk to you as I talk to ·spiritual people [*or* people who have the Spirit]. I had to talk to you as I would to ·people without the Spirit [unspiritual/carnal/fleshly people]—·babies [infants] in Christ. 2·The teaching I gave you was like milk [LI gave you milk to drink], not solid food, because you were not yet able to take solid food [Cthe comparison is between basic and advanced teaching]. And even now you are not ready. 3You are still ·not spiritual [carnal; fleshly; living by your sinful nature], because there is ·jealousy [envy] and ·quarreling [conflict; rivalry] among you, and this shows that

you are ·not spiritual [carnal; fleshly; living by your sinful nature]. **You are ·acting** [living; Lwalking] **·like people of the world** [*or* like ordinary/unsaved people; *or* on a merely human level; Laccording to man]. **4One of you says, "I belong to Paul," and another says, "I belong to Apollos." When you say things like this, ·you are** [Lare you not…?] **·acting like people of the world** [*or* living on a merely human level; Lpeople; human beings].

5·Is Apollos important? No! [LWhat, then, is Apollos?] **·Is Paul important? No!** [LAnd what is Paul?] **We are only servants of God who helped you believe. Each one of us did the work the Lord gave us to do. 6I planted the seed, and Apollos watered it. But God is the One who made it grow. 7So the one who plants is not ·important** [Lanything], **and the one who waters is not ·important** [Lanything], **but only God, who makes things grow. 8The one who plants and the one who waters ·have the same purpose** [*or* are equal; Lare one], **and each will ·be rewarded** [receive wages] **for his own work. 9We are ·God's workers, working together** [coworkers belonging to God; coworkers in God's service]; **you are God's ·farm** [field], **God's building.**

10·Using [*or* Because of] **the ·gift** [grace] **God gave me, I laid the foundation of that building like an ·expert** [skilled; wise] **builder. Others are building on that foundation, but ·all people** [Leach one] **should be careful how they build on it. 11The foundation that has already been laid is Jesus Christ, and no one can lay down any other foundation. 12But if ·people** [anyone; someone] **build on that foundation, using gold, silver, ·jewels** [precious stones], **wood, ·grass** [*or* hay], **or straw, 13their work will be ·clearly seen** [*or* shown for what it is], **because the ·day of judgment** [Lday] **will make it ·visible** [clear; obvious]. **That day will ·appear** [*or* reveal it; expose it] **with fire, and the fire will test everyone's work to show what sort of work it was. 14If the ·building that has been put on the foundation** [Lwork] **still stands, the builder will get ·a reward** [*or* wages]. **15But if the ·building** [Lwork] **is burned up, the builder will ·suffer loss** [*or* be fined; *or* be punished]. **The builder will be saved, but it will be as one who escaped ·from a fire** [Lthrough fire].

16Don't ·you [you all; Cthe verb is plural] **know that you are God's temple and that God's Spirit lives in you** [Cjust as God's presence filled the tabernacle; Ex. 40:34–38]? **17If anyone destroys God's temple, God will destroy that person, because God's temple is holy ·and you are that temple** [*or* and you are holy; Lwhich is what you are].

18Do not ·fool [deceive] **yourselves. If you think you are wise in this ·world** [age], **you should become a fool so that you can become truly wise, 19because the wisdom of this world is ·foolishness** [folly] **with God.** [LFor] **It is written in the Scriptures, "He catches those who are wise in their own ·clever traps** [craftiness; cunning; Job 5:13]." **20·It is also written in the Scriptures** [LAnd again], **"The Lord knows ·what wise people think** [Lthe thoughts/reasoning/machinations of the wise]. **He knows their thoughts are ·worthless** [pointless; useless; futile; Ps. 94:11]." **21So you should not ·brag** [boast] **about ·human leaders** [Lpeople]. **All things belong to you: 22Paul, Apollos, and ·Peter** [LCephas; CPeter's name in Aramaic; see 1:12]; **the world, life, death, the present, and the future—all these belong to you. 23And you belong to Christ, and Christ belongs to God.**

Apostles Are Servants of Christ

4 People should think of us as servants of Christ, ·the ones God has trusted with his [and stewards/household managers of God's] **·secrets** [mysteries]. **2Now in this way ·those who are trusted with something**

valuable [stewards; household managers] **must ·show they are worthy of**
that trust [[L]be found faithful]. 3**As for myself, ·I do not care** [*or* it is of no
consequence; [L]it is a minor thing] **if I am judged by you or by any human**
court. I do not even judge myself. 4**I know of no wrong I have done, but this**
does not make me ·right before the Lord [innocent; acquitted; justified]. **The**
Lord is the One who judges me. 5**So do not judge before the ·right** [appointed]
time; wait until the Lord comes. He will bring to light things that are now
hidden in darkness, and will make known the secret ·purposes [motives] **of**
people's hearts. Then God will ·praise [give appropriate commendation to]
each one of them.

6**Brothers and sisters, I have used Apollos and myself as examples so**
you could learn through us the meaning of the saying, "·Follow only [[L]Do
not go beyond] **·what is written in the Scriptures** [*or* what I have already
written to you; [L]what is written]." **Then you will not ·be more proud of**
one person than another [*or* arrogantly support one person over another].
7[[L]For] **Who ·says you are better than others** [made you so important; *or*
sees anything different in you]? **What do you have that was not given to**
you? And if it was given to you, why do you ·brag [boast] **as if you did not**
·receive it as a gift [[L]receive it]?

8**·You think you already have everything you need** [[L]Already you have
been satisfied/filled up!; [C]the Corinthians believed they had reached a
higher spiritual status because of their wisdom]. **·You think you are rich**
[[L]Already you are rich!]. **You ·think you have become kings** [have begun to
reign…!] **without us. I wish you really were ·kings** [reigning] **so we could**
·be kings [reign] **together with you.** 9**But it seems to me that God has put**
us apostles ·in last place [*or* on display at the end of the procession], **like**
those sentenced to die [[C]the image is of prisoners of war being led through
the city in disgrace, condemned to die in the arena]. **We are like a ·show**
[spectacle; display] **for the whole world to see—angels and people.** 10**We**
are fools for Christ's sake, but you are very wise in Christ. We are weak,
but you are strong. You receive honor, but we are ·shamed [disgraced;
dishonored]. 11**Even ·to this very hour** [*or* now] **we do not have enough to**
eat or drink or to wear. We are often beaten, and we have no homes in
which to live. 12**We work hard with our own hands** [[C]Paul earned his own
living so as not to burden the church and to avoid accusations of profiting
from the Gospel; 1 Thess. 2:9]. **When people ·curse** [insult; revile] **us, we**
bless them. When they ·hurt [persecute] **us, we ·put up with it** [endure;
persevere]. 13**When they ·tell evil lies about** [slander] **us, we ·speak nice**
words about them [answer gently; *or* humbly appeal; entreat]. **Even today,**
we are treated as though we were the garbage of the world—·the filth of
the earth [[L]everyone's scum/filth; *or* scum/filth in everyone's eyes].

14**I am not writing this to make you feel ashamed, but to ·warn** [admon-
ish; correct] **you as my own ·dear** [beloved] **children.** 15**For though you**
may have ten thousand ·teachers [guardians; tutors] **in Christ, you do not**
have many fathers. [[L]For; Because] **Through the ·Good News** [Gospel] **I**
became your father in Christ Jesus, 16**so I ·beg** [urge; encourage; exhort]
you, ·please follow my example [[L]be imitators of me]. 17**That is why I am**
sending to you Timothy, my ·dear [beloved] **and faithful son in the Lord.**
He will ·help you remember [remind you about] **my way of life in Christ**
Jesus, just as I teach it in all the churches everywhere.

18**Some of you have become ·proud** [arrogant; puffed up], **thinking**
that I will not come to you again. 19**But I will come to you very soon if the**

Lord ·wishes [wills; allows]. Then I will ·know [find out; learn] ·what the
proud ones do, not what they say [Lnot just the talk/word of these arrogant people, but also their power], 20because the kingdom of God ·is
present [*or* consists] not in talk but in power. 21Which do you want: that I
come to you with ·punishment [La rod] or with love and ·gentleness [*or* a
gentle spirit]?

Wickedness in the Church

5 It is actually being ·said [reported] that there is sexual sin among
you. And it is a kind that ·does not happen [*or* is not tolerated]
even among ·people who do not know God [pagans; Gentiles]. A man
there ·has [is living in sin with; is sleeping with] his father's wife [Cprobably
his stepmother; Lev. 18:7–8; 20:11]. 2And you are ·proud [arrogant; puffed
up]! ·You should [LShould you not…?] have been filled with ·sadness
[grief; mourning] so that the man who did this should be put out of your
group. 3I am not there with you in person, but I am with you in spirit. And
I have already ·judged [condemned] the man who did that sin as if I were
really there. 4When you meet together in the name of our Lord Jesus, and
I meet with you in spirit with the power of our Lord Jesus, 5then hand this
man over to Satan. So his ·sinful self will be destroyed [sinful nature will
be purged; *or* body/flesh will be destroyed; *or* body will be beaten down by
sin], and his spirit will be saved on the day of the Lord.
6Your ·bragging [boasting] is not good. You know the saying, "Just a
little ·yeast [*or* leaven; Cleaven is a small lump of fermented dough used to
make a loaf rise, as yeast is today] makes the whole batch of dough rise
[Cyeast/leaven symbolizes the permeating influence of this man's sin
within the community; Gal. 5:9]." 7·Take out all [Cleanse; Purge] the old
·yeast [leaven] so that you will be a new batch of dough without ·yeast
[leaven], which you really are. For Christ, our Passover lamb, has been sacrificed [CChrist's sacrificial death rescued us from spiritual death, just as the
blood of the first Passover lambs rescued the children of Israel; Ex. 11–12].
8So let us celebrate this feast [Ca new kind of Passover feast], but not with
the bread that has the old ·yeast [leaven]—the ·yeast [leaven] of ·sin [evil;
malice] and wickedness [Cunleavened bread was used in the Passover celebration; Ex. 12:15; Deut. 16:3]. Let us celebrate this feast with the bread that
has no ·yeast [leaven]—the bread of ·goodness [sincerity] and truth.
9I wrote you in my earlier letter not to associate with those who sin
sexually. 10But I did not [Lat all] mean you should not associate with those
of this world who sin sexually, or with the greedy, or ·robbers [*or* swin-
dlers], or those who worship idols. To get away from them you would
have to leave this world. 11I am writing to tell you that you must not associate with those who call themselves ·believers in Christ [a brother or
sister] but who sin sexually, or are greedy, or worship idols, or ·abuse others with words [slander], or get drunk, or ·cheat [swindle] people. Do not
even eat with people like that.
12-13It is not my business to judge those who are ·not part of the
church [Loutside]. God will judge them. But you must judge the people
who are ·part of the church [Linside]. The Scripture says, "You must ·get
rid of [expel; remove] the evil person among you [Deut. 17:7; 19:19;
22:21, 24; 24:7]."

Judging Problems Among Christians

6 When you have ·something against [a legal dispute with; a grievance against] another Christian, how can you ·bring yourself
[dare] to go before ·judges who are not right with God [*or* the pagan

courts; [Lthe unrighteous] **instead of before ·God's people** [Tthe saints]?
2**·Surely** [LDon't…?] **you know that ·God's people** [Tthe saints] **will judge**
the world. So if you are to judge the world, are you not able to judge
·small [trivial; the smallest of] **cases as well?** 3**·You** [LDon't you…?] **know**
that we will judge angels, so surely we can judge the ·ordinary things of
[*or* matters pertaining to] **this life.** 4**If you have ·ordinary cases** [cases/legal
disputes of this life] **that must be judged, ·are you going to appoint people**
as judges who mean nothing to the church? [will you appoint judges with
no standing in/whose lifestyle is rejected by the church?; *or* go ahead and
appoint the least members of the church to judge them! Cin the latter
interpretation, Paul speaks sarcastically.] 5**I say this to shame you. ·Surely**
there is someone [LIs there no one…?] **among you wise enough to judge**
a ·complaint [dispute; conflict] **between ·believers** [La brother]. 6**But now**
one ·believer [brother] **goes to court against another ·believer** [Lbrother]—
and you do this in front of unbelievers!

7**The fact that you have lawsuits against each other shows that you are**
already defeated. Why not ·let yourselves be wronged [suffer the injus-
tice]? **Why not let yourselves be cheated?** 8**But you yourselves ·do wrong**
[act unjustly] **and cheat, and you do this to ·other believers** [Lbrothers]!

9-10**·Surely** [LDon't…?] **you know that the ·people who do wrong**
[unrighteous; wicked; unjust] **will not inherit God's kingdom. Do not be**
·fooled [deceived]. **Those who sin sexually, worship idols, take part in**
adultery, those who are ·male prostitutes [*or* passive homosexual part-
ners], **or ·men who have sexual relations with other men** [*or* active
homosexual partners], **those who steal, are greedy, get drunk, ·lie about**
others [slander others; use abusive language], **or ·rob** [swindle]**—these**
people will not inherit God's kingdom. 11**In the past, some of you were like**
that, but you were washed clean. You were ·made holy [sanctified], **and**
you were ·made right with God [justified; declared righteous] **in the name**
of the Lord Jesus Christ and ·in [*or* by; through] **the Spirit of our God.**

Use Your Bodies for God's Glory

12**"·I am allowed to do all things** [LAll things are lawful/permissible for
me; Cprobably a slogan the Corinthians were using; see also 7:1; 8:1, 4;
10:23]**," but not all things are ·good for me to do** [profitable; beneficial].
"·I am allowed to do all things [LAll things are lawful/permissible for me]**,"**
but I will not let anything make me its slave. 13**"Food is for the stomach,**
and the stomach for food, but God will ·destroy [do away with] **them**
both [Cprobably another Corinthian slogan (v. 12), meaning only the
spirit matters, not what we do with our physical bodies; Paul disagrees]**."**
The body is not for sexual sin but for the Lord, and the Lord is for the
body. 14**By his power God has raised the Lord from the dead and will also**
raise us from the dead. 15**·Surely** [Don't…?] **you know that your bodies**
are ·parts [members] **of Christ himself. Should I take the ·parts** [mem-
bers] **of Christ and join them to a prostitute? ·Never** [Absolutely not; May
it never be]! 16**Don't you know that anyone who joins with a prostitute**
[Cin a sexual relationship] **becomes one body with the prostitute? For it is**
written in the Scriptures, "The two will become one ·body [flesh; Gen.
2:24]**."** 17**But the one who joins with the Lord** [Cin spiritual union] **is one**
spirit with the Lord.

18**So ·run away from** [flee; stay away from] **sexual sin. Every other sin**
people do is outside their bodies, but those who sin sexually sin against
their own bodies. 19**·You should** [LDon't you…?] **know that your body is a**

temple for the Holy Spirit who is in you and was given to you by God. So
you do not belong to yourselves, 20because you were ·bought by God
[Lbought] for a price. So honor God with your bodies.

About Marriage

7 Now ·I will discuss [Lconcerning] the things you wrote me about
[Cin a letter from the Corinthians; see 8:1; 12:1; 16:1]. It is good for
a man not to ·have sexual relations with [Ltouch; Ca euphemism for sex] a
woman [Cprobably another slogan (6:12; 8:1, 4; 10:23) asserting that a
celibate lifestyle was spiritually superior]. 2But because ·sexual sin is a
danger [of sexual temptations; Lof sexual sins], each man should ·have [*or*
have sexual relations with] his own wife, and each woman should ·have
[*or* have sexual relations with] her own husband. 3The husband should
give his wife all that he owes her as his wife [Cmeet her sexual needs]. And
the wife should give her husband all that she owes him as her husband
[Cmeet his sexual needs]. 4The wife does not have ·full rights [Lauthority]
over her own body; her husband shares them. And the husband does not
have ·full rights [authority] over his own body; his wife shares them
[Crevolutionary teaching in the first century, when wives were generally
viewed as the possession of their husbands]. 5Do not ·refuse to give your
bodies to [refuse sex to; Ldeprive] each other, unless you both agree to stay
away from sexual relations for a time so you can ·give your time [devote
yourselves] to prayer. Then ·come together again [resume your sexual
relationship] so Satan cannot tempt you because of a lack of self-control.
6I say this ·to give you permission to stay away from sexual relations for a
time [Las a concession/allowance]. It is not a command to do so. 7I wish
that everyone were like me [Cunmarried], but each person has his own
gift from God. One has one gift, another has another gift.

8Now for those who are not married and for the widows I say this: It is
good for them to stay unmarried as I am. 9But if they cannot ·control
themselves [exercise self-control], they should marry. It is better to marry
than ·to burn with sexual desire [Lto burn].

10Now I give this command for the married people. (The command is
not from me; it is from the Lord [CJesus taught on divorce; Mark 10:5–
12].) A wife should not ·leave [separate from; *or* divorce] her husband.
11But if she does ·leave [*or* divorce], she must not marry again, or she
should ·make up [reconcile] with her husband. Also the husband should
not ·divorce [*or* leave] his wife.

12For ·all the others [the rest] I say this (I am saying this, not the Lord
[CJesus gave no instruction on this, but Paul still speaks with authority as an
apostle]): If a ·Christian man [Lbrother] has a wife who is not a believer, and
she is ·happy [content; willing] to live with him, he must not ·divorce [*or*
leave] her. 13And if a Christian woman has a husband who is not a believer,
and he is ·happy [content; willing] to live with her, she must not ·divorce [*or*
leave] him. 14The husband who is not a believer is ·made holy [sanctified;
touched by holiness] through his believing wife. And the wife who is not a
believer is ·made holy [sanctified; touched by holiness] through her believing husband. If this were not true, your children would ·not be clean [be
spiritually impure; *or* be without spiritual influence], but now your children
are holy [Csome Corinthians said an unbeliever defiled a Christian marriage; Paul reverses this and says believers "sanctify" the marriage].

15But if those who are not believers decide to ·leave [*or* divorce], let
them ·leave [*or* divorce]. When this happens, the ·Christian man [Lbrother]

or ·woman [Lsister] is ·free [Lnot bound; Cto the marriage covenant]. But God called us[n] to ·live in peace [Lpeace]. 16Wife, you don't know; maybe you will save your husband. And husband, you don't know; maybe you will save your wife.

Live as God Called You

17But in any case each one of you should continue to live ·the way [*or* in the situation] God has given you to live—the way you were when God called you. This is a ·rule [instruction] I make in all the churches. 18If a man was already circumcised when he was called, he should not undo his circumcision. If a man was without circumcision when he was called, he should not be circumcised. 19·It is not important if a man is circumcised or not [LCircumcision is nothing and uncircumcision is nothing]. The important thing is ·obeying [keeping] God's commands. 20Each one of you should stay ·the way you were [in the situation you were in] when God called you. 21If you were a slave when God called you, do not let that bother you. But if you can ·be free [gain your freedom], ·then make good use of your freedom [*or* then take that opportunity; *or* instead remain and make use of your opportunities as a slave]. 22[LFor] Those who were slaves when the Lord called them are free persons who belong to the Lord. In the same way, those who were free when they were called are now Christ's slaves. 23You all were bought at a great price, so do not become slaves of people. 24Brothers and sisters, each of you should stay as you were when you were called, ·and stay there with God [*or* with God at your side; Lwith God].

Questions About Getting Married

25Now I write about ·people who are not married [*or* those never married; *or* betrothed women; Lvirgins]. I have no command from the Lord about this; I give my ·opinion [perspective; judgment]. But I can be trusted, because the Lord has shown me mercy. 26Because ·the present time is a time of trouble [of the present crisis/distress/trouble], I think it is ·good [best] for you to stay the way you are. 27If you ·have a wife [Lare bound to a wife; *or* are pledged to a woman], do not try to ·become free from [*or* divorce] her. If you are not married, do not try to find a wife. 28But if you decide to marry, you have not sinned. And if a ·girl who has never married [*or* betrothed woman; Lvirgin] decides to marry, she has not sinned. But those who marry will have ·trouble [trials; tribulation] in ·this life [this world; Lthe flesh], and I want ·you to be free [to spare you] from trouble [Cduring times of persecution, those with family obligations suffer the most].

29Brothers and sisters, this is what I mean: ·We do not have much time left [The time is short/limited/coming to an end]. So starting now, those who have wives should live as if they had no wives. 30Those who are ·crying [weeping; mourning] should live as if they were not ·crying [weeping; mourning]. Those who ·are happy [rejoice] should live as if they were not ·happy [rejoicing]. Those who buy things should live as if they ·own [*or* could keep/hold on to] nothing. 31Those who use ·the things of the world [Lthe world] should live as if they were not ·using [engrossed in; dependent upon] them, because this world in its present form ·will soon be gone [is passing away].

32I want you to be free from ·worry [concern]. A man who is not married is ·busy [concerned] with the Lord's work, trying to please the Lord. 33But a man who is married is ·busy [concerned] with things of the world,

7:15 us Some Greek copies read "you."

trying to please his wife. [34]He ·must think about two things—pleasing his
wife and pleasing the Lord [[L]is divided]. A woman who is not married or
a ·girl who has never married [*or* betrothed woman; [L]virgin] is ·busy
[concerned] with the ·Lord's work [[L]things of the Lord]. She wants to be
holy in body and spirit. But a married woman is ·busy [concerned] with
things of the world, as to how she can please her husband. [35]I am saying
this to help you, not to ·limit [restrain] you. But I want you to live ·in the
right way [*or* in a proper/orderly manner; *or* above criticism], to ·give
yourselves fully [be devoted] to the Lord without ·concern for other
things [distraction].

[36]If a man thinks he is ·not doing the right thing with [*or* acting
improperly toward] ·the girl he is engaged to [[L]his virgin; [C]it is possible,
but less likely, that the passage concerns a father's decision to allow his
virgin daughter to marry; a third option is that it is about a couple in a
"spiritual" (celibate) marriage deciding whether to consummate it], if ·she
is almost past the best age to marry [*or* his passions are too strong; [L]he/she
is at the highest point] and ·he feels he should marry her [[L]it ought to be
so], he should do what he wants. They should get married. It is no sin.
[37]But if a man is ·sure [resolved; firm] in his ·mind [conviction; heart]
that there is no ·need for marriage [obligation; necessity], and has his
own ·desires [*or* will] under control, and has decided ·not to marry the
one to whom he is engaged [to keep her a virgin], he is doing the right
thing. [38]So the man who marries his ·fiancée [[L]virgin] does right, but the
man who does not marry will do better.

[39]A woman ·must stay with [is bound to] her husband as long as he
lives. But if her husband dies, she is free to marry any man she wants, but
she must marry ·another believer [[L]in the Lord]. [40]The woman is ·happier
[better off; more blessed] if she ·does not marry again [[L]remains as she is].
This is my ·opinion [perspective; judgment], but I believe I also have
God's Spirit [[C]Paul affirms he is speaking for God].

About Food Offered to Idols

8 Now ·I will write about [*or* concerning your question about;
[L]concerning; see 7:1; 12:1; 16:1] meat that is sacrificed to idols. We
know that "we all have knowledge [[C]probably a slogan used by the
Corinthians; see 6:12, 13; 7:1; 8:4; 10:23]." Knowledge puffs you up with
pride, but love builds up. [2]If you think you know something, you do not
yet know as ·well as you should [[L]you ought to know]. [3]But if any person
loves God, that person is known by God.

[4]So ·this is what I say about [[L]concerning] eating meat sacrificed to
idols: We know that an idol is really nothing in the world, and we know
there is ·only one God [no God but one; Deut. 4:35, 39; [C]these may be
other slogans the church was using to justify their behavior; see v. 1]. [5]Even
though there are things called gods, in heaven or on earth (and there are
many "gods" and "lords"), [6]for us there is only one God—the Father. All
things came from him, and we live for him. And there is only one Lord—
Jesus Christ. All things were made through him, and we also ·were made
[exist; live] through him.

[7]But not all people know this. Some people are still so used to idols
that when they eat meat, they still think of it as being sacrificed to an idol.
Because their conscience is weak, when they eat it, ·they feel guilty [[L]their
conscience is defiled]. [8]But food will not ·bring us closer [make us accept-
able] to God. Refusing to eat does not make us ·less pleasing to God [any

worse; Llacking], and eating does not make us ·better in God's sight [any better; Labounding].

9But be careful that ·your freedom [this right/authority of yours] does not ·cause those who are weak in faith to fall into sin [Lbecome a stumbling block to the weak]. 10Suppose one of you who has knowledge eats in an idol's temple. Someone who ·is weak in faith [*or* has a weak conscience] might see you eating there and be ·encouraged [emboldened] to eat meat sacrificed to idols ·while thinking it is wrong to do so [*or* as a result of his weak conscience]. 11This weak ·believer [Lbrother] for whom Christ died is ·ruined [destroyed] because of your "knowledge." 12When you sin against your brothers and sisters in Christ like this and ·cause them to do what they feel is wrong [Lwound their weak conscience], you are also sinning against Christ. 13So if the food I eat causes them to fall into sin, I will never eat meat again so that I will not cause any of them to ·sin [stumble; fall into sin].

Paul Is like the Other Apostles

9 ·I am a free man [LAm I not free?]. ·I am [LAm I not…?] an apostle. ·I have [Haven't I…?] seen Jesus our Lord. ·You people are all an example of [LAre you not…?] my work in the Lord. 2If others do not accept me as an apostle, surely you do, because you are ·proof that I am an apostle [Lthe seal/verification of my apostleship] in the Lord.

3This is the answer I give people who want to ·judge me [examine me; question my credentials]: 4Do we not have the right to eat and drink [Creceive hospitality and support for their missionary work]? 5Do we not have the right to ·bring a believing wife with us when we travel [*or* be married to a believer; Ltake along a wife who is a sister] as do the other apostles and the Lord's brothers [Matt. 13:55; Acts 1:14] and ·Peter [LCephas; CPeter's name in Aramaic; see 1:12]? 6Are Barnabas [Acts 13–14] and I the only ones who ·must work to earn our living [Ldon't have the authority/right not to work]? 7·No soldier [LWho…?] ever serves in the army and pays his own salary. ·No one [LWho…?] ever plants a vineyard without eating some of the grapes. ·No person [LWho…?] takes care of a flock without drinking some of the milk.

8I do not say this ·by human authority [from human experience; Laccording to man]; God's law also says the same thing. 9[LFor] It is written in the law of Moses: "Do not muzzle an ox when it is ·working in [treading; threshing] the grain [Deut. 25:4]." When God said this, was he ·thinking only [concerned] about oxen? No. 10He was ·really [surely] talking ·about us [for our benefit]. Yes, that Scripture was written for us, because it goes on to say: "The one who plows and the one who ·works in the grain [threshes] should hope to get some of the grain for their work." 11·Since [If] we ·planted [sowed] spiritual seed among you, is it too much if we should harvest material things from you [Creceive support for ministry]? 12If others have the right to get something from you, surely we have this right, ·too [*or* even more so]. But we ·do not use it [have not exercised this right]. No, we put up with everything ourselves so that we will not ·keep anyone from believing [Lput up a hindrance to] the ·Good News [Gospel] of Christ. 13·Surely [LDon't…?] you know that those who ·work at the Temple [perform priestly temple service] get their food from the Temple, and those who serve at the altar get part of what is offered at the altar. 14In the same way, the Lord has commanded that those who ·tell the Good News [proclaim/preach the Gospel] should get their living from ·this work [Lthe Gospel].

15But I have not used any of these rights. And I am not writing this now

to get anything from you. I would rather die than to have my reason for
·bragging [boasting] taken away. 16·Telling the Good News [Preaching the
Gospel] does not give me any reason for ·bragging [boasting]. Telling the
Good News is my duty—something I must do. And ·how terrible it will
be for [Lwoe to] me if I do not ·tell the Good News [preach the Gospel].
17If I preach ·because it is my own choice [voluntarily], I have a reward.
But if I preach ·and it is not my choice to do so [without volunteering], I
am ·only doing the duty that was given to me [Lentrusted with a steward-
ship/responsibility]. 18So what ·reward [payment; wages] do I get? Only
this: that when I tell the ·Good News [Gospel] I can offer it ·freely [free of
charge]. I do not ·use [take advantage of; *or* misuse] my full rights in ·my
work of preaching the Good News [Lthe Gospel].

19I am free and belong to no one. But I make myself a slave to all people
to win as many as I can. 20To the Jews I became like a Jew to win the Jews.
I myself am not ·ruled by [subject to; Lunder] the law. But to those who
are ·ruled by [subject to; Lunder] the law I became like a person who is
·ruled by [subject to; Lunder] the law. I did this to win those who are
·ruled by [subject to; Lunder] the law. 21To those who are without the law
[CGentiles] I became like a person who is without the law. I did this to win
those people who are without the law. (But really, I am not without God's
law—I am ·ruled by [Lunder] Christ's law.) 22To those who are weak [Cin
faith; 8:7–13], I became weak so I could win the weak. I have become all
things to all people so I could save some of them in any way possible. 23I
do all this because of the ·Good News [Gospel] and so I can ·share in its
blessings [*or* be a participant in it].

24·You [LDon't you…?] know that in a ·race [Lstadium] all the runners run,
but only one gets the prize. So run to win! 25All those who compete in the
games ·use self-control [train with strict discipline] so they can win a ·crown
[victor's wreath]. That ·crown [victor's wreath] is ·an earthly thing that lasts
only a short time [Lperishable], but our crown ·will never be destroyed [Lis
imperishable]. 26So I do not run ·without a goal [aimlessly]. I fight like a
boxer who is hitting something—not just the air. 27I ·treat my body hard
[discipline/subdue/pummel my body] and ·make it my slave [subdue it] so
that I myself will not be disqualified after I have preached to others.

Warnings from Israel's Past

10 Brothers and sisters, I ·want you to know [Ldon't want you to
be ignorant of] what happened to our ancestors. They were
all under the cloud [Cthe Israelites were guided in the wilderness by a
cloud, a symbol of God's presence; Ex. 13:21; Num. 9:15–23] and all went
through the sea [Cthe miraculous passage through the Red Sea; Ex.
14:22]. 2They were all baptized ·as followers of [Linto] Moses in the cloud
and in the sea [Cjust as believers are baptized "into Christ" (Rom. 6:3), so
the Israelites were "baptized" into Moses, their leader-redeemer]. 3They
all ate the same spiritual food [Cthe manna God provided from heaven;
Ex. 16:15, 35], 4and all drank the same spiritual drink [Cthe water mirac-
ulously provided from a rock; Ex. 17:6; Num. 20:7–13]. They drank from
that spiritual rock that followed them [Cin Jewish tradition, the rock
travelled with the Israelites, providing continual refreshment], and that
rock was Christ [Ca type of Christ, who provides spiritual sustenance].
5But God was not pleased with most of them, so they ·died [*or* were
struck down; *or* (their bodies) were scattered] in the desert [Cas judgment for unbelief and refusing to enter the Promised Land; Num. 13–14].

6And these things happened as examples for us, to stop us from ·want-
ing [desiring; craving] evil things as those people did. 7Do not worship
idols, as some of them did. Just as it is written in the Scriptures: "The
people sat down to eat and drink, and then they got up and ·sinned sexually [Lplayed; Ca euphemism for immoral revelry; Ex. 32:6]." 8We must not
take part in sexual sins, as some of them did. In one day twenty-three
thousand of them ·died because of their sins [Lfell; Num 25:1–9]. 9We
must not test Christ as some of them did; they were ·killed [destroyed] by
snakes. 10Do not ·complain [grumble] as some of them did; they were
killed by the ·angel that destroys [Ldestroyer; Num. 16:41–50; Ex. 12:23].
11The things that happened to those people are examples. They were
written down to ·teach [instruct; warn] us ·who live in the final days of
this age [Lfor whom the end/climax/culmination of the ages has come].
12[LSo; Therefore] If you think you are ·strong [Lstanding (firm)], you
should be careful not to fall. 13The only ·temptation [*or* trials] that has
come to you is ·that which everyone has [L(common to) human life]. But
·you can trust God [God is faithful], who will not permit you to be
tempted more than you can stand. But when you are tempted, he will also
give you a way to escape so that you will be able to ·stand [endure] it.
14So, my ·dear friends [beloved], ·run away from [flee; stay away from]
the worship of idols. 15I am speaking to you as to ·reasonable [sensible;
discerning] people; ·judge [consider] for yourselves what I say. 16We give
thanks for the cup of blessing [Cused in the Lord's Supper], ·which is [Lis
this not…?] a ·sharing [participation; fellowship] in the blood of Christ.
And the bread that we break ·is [Lis it not…?] a ·sharing [participation;
fellowship] in the body of Christ. 17Because there is one loaf of bread, we
who are many are one body, because we all share that one loaf.
18Think about ·the Israelites [LIsrael according to the flesh]: Do not those
who eat the sacrifices ·share [participate] in the altar [Cby eating the sacrificial food, priests in the Jerusalem temple participate in the worship of God]?
19·I do not mean [LWhat, then, am I saying…?] that the food sacrificed to an
idol is important or that an idol is anything at all. 20But I say that what is
sacrificed to idols is offered to demons, not to God. And I do not want you
to ·share anything [be participants; share fellowship] with demons. 21You
cannot drink the cup of the Lord and the cup of demons also. You cannot
·share in [partake of] the Lord's table and the table of demons. 22Are we
trying to make the Lord jealous? We are not stronger than he is, are we?

How to Use Christian Freedom

23"·We are allowed to do all things [LAll things are lawful/permissible],"
but not all things are ·good for us to do [profitable; beneficial]. "·We are
allowed to do all things [LAll things are lawful/permissible]," but not all
things ·help others grow stronger [Lbuild up; Cthe quotations were probably slogans the Corinthians used; 6:12, 13; 7:1; 8:1, 4]. 24Do not look out
only for yourselves. Look out for the good of others.
25Eat any meat that is sold in the meat market. Do not ask questions
·about it [Lfor conscience's sake]. 26You may eat it, "because the earth
belongs to the Lord, and ·everything in it [its fullness/abundance/bounty;
Ps. 24:1; 50:12; 89:11]."
27Those who are not believers may invite you to eat with them. If you
want to go, eat anything that is put before you. Do not ask questions
·about it [Lfor conscience's sake]. 28But if anyone says to you, "That food
was offered to idols," do not eat it. Do not eat it because of that person

who told you and ·because eating it might be thought to be wrong [Lfor conscience's sake]. 29I don't mean ·you think it is wrong [your conscience], but the ·other person might [the concience of the other person]. ·But why, you ask, [*or* For why] should my freedom be judged by someone else's conscience? 30If I eat the meal with thankfulness, why am I criticized because of something for which I thank God?

31·The answer is [*or* Therefore; In summary], if you eat or drink, or if you do anything, do it all for the glory of God. 32Never do anything that might hurt others—Jews, Greeks, or God's church— 33just as I, also, try to please everybody in every way. I am not trying to do what is ·good [advantageous] for me but what is ·good [advantageous] for most people so they can be saved.

11 ·Follow my example [Imitate me], as I ·follow the example of [imitate] Christ.

Being Under Authority

2I praise you because you ·remember me in everything [are always thinking of me], and you follow closely the ·teachings [traditions] just as I ·gave them [passed them on] to you. 3But I want you to understand this: The head of every man is Christ, the head of a woman is ·the man [*or* her husband], and the head of Christ is God. 4Every man who prays or prophesies ·with his head covered [*or* with long hair; Lhaving down the head; Cmost scholars think the passage concerns head coverings; others long or short hair (see v. 14)] brings shame to his head [Cmeaning shame to Christ, who is the head of the man; v. 3]. 5But every woman who prays or prophesies with ·her head uncovered [*or* no covering (of hair); v. 4] brings shame to her head. She is the same as a woman who has her head shaved. 6If a woman does not cover her head, she should have her hair cut off. But since it is shameful for a woman to cut off her hair or to shave her head, she should cover her head. 7But a man should not cover his head, because he is the likeness and glory of God. But woman is man's glory [CGod's glory should be unveiled (revealed), while human glory should be veiled]. 8[LFor] Man did not come from woman, but woman came from man. 9And man was not made for woman, but woman was made for man [Gen. 2:18]. 10So that is why a woman should have a ·symbol of authority on [*or* authority over] her head, because of the angels [Cthe significance of the angels is unclear; perhaps their presence at worship calls for reverence and propriety].

11But in the Lord women are not independent of men, and men are not independent of women. 12This is true because woman came from man, but also man is born from woman. But everything comes from God. 13·Decide [Judge] this for yourselves: Is it ·right [fitting; proper] for a woman to pray to God with her head uncovered? 14·Even [LDoes not...?] ·nature [*or* custom; culture] itself teaches you that wearing long hair is shameful for a man [CGreco-Roman men normally wore their hair short]. 15But long hair is a woman's glory. Long hair is given to her as a covering. 16·Some people [LIf anyone] may still want to argue about this, but I would add that neither we nor the churches of God have any other ·practice [custom].

The Lord's Supper

17In the ·things [instructions; commands] I tell you now I do not praise you, because ·when you come together you [your meetings as a congregation] do more harm than good. 18First, I hear that when you meet together as a church ·you are divided [there are divisions among you], and I believe some of this. 19(It is necessary to have ·differences [factions] among you so

that it may be clear which of you really have God's approval [C controversy
is necesssary because error must be opposed].) 20 When you ·come together
[meet as a congregation], you are not really eating the Lord's Supper [C the
worship meal Jesus told his followers to celebrate to remember his death;
Luke 22:14–20]. 21 This is because when you eat, each person eats without
waiting for the others [C the wealthy church members were arriving early to
avoid sharing with the poorer members; such social distinctions were common throughout the Greco-Roman world]. Some people do not get
enough to eat, while others ·have too much to drink [get drunk]. 22 Don't
you have homes in which to eat and drink? Or do you ·despise [have contempt for; have no regard for] God's church and so ·embarrass [humiliate]
those who ·are poor [have nothing]? What should I tell you? Should I
praise you? I will not praise you for doing this [C the Corinthians were
turning a time meant for unity into one of discrimination].

23 [L For] The teaching I ·gave [passed on to] you is the same teaching I
received from the Lord: On the night when the Lord Jesus was ·handed over
to be killed [betrayed], he took bread 24 and gave thanks for it. Then he broke
the bread and said, "This is my body; it is[n] for you. Do this to remember me."
25 In the same way, after ·they ate [the meal; supper], Jesus took the cup. He
said, "This cup is the new ·agreement [covenant; Ex. 24:8; Jer. 31:31–34] ·that
is sealed with the blood of my death [L in my blood]. When you drink this, do
it to remember me [Matt. 26:26–28; Mark 14:22–24; Luke 22:19, 20]." 26 [L For]
Every time you eat this bread and drink this cup you ·are telling others
about [proclaim; announce] the Lord's death until he comes.

27 So a person who eats the bread or drinks the cup of the Lord in ·a way
that is not worthy of it [*or* an inappropriate manner] will be ·guilty of
sinning against [*or* held responsible for; liable for; L guilty of] the body
and the blood of the Lord. 28 ·Look into your own hearts [L Let a person
examine himself] before you eat the bread and drink the cup, 29 because
all who eat the bread and drink the cup without ·recognizing [discerning;
careful regard for] the body eat and drink judgment against themselves.
30 That is why many in your group are sick and weak, and ·some [a num-
ber] of you have ·died [L fallen asleep; C a euphemism for death]. 31 But if we
·judged ourselves in the right way [evaluated/examined ourselves], ·God
would not judge us [L we would not be judged/punished]. 32 But when the
Lord judges us, he disciplines us so that we will not be ·destroyed [con-
demned] along with the world.

33 So my brothers and sisters, when you ·come together [gather as a
congregation] to eat, wait for each other. 34 Anyone who is too hungry
should eat at home so that in meeting together you will not bring God's
judgment on yourselves. I will tell you what to do about ·the other things
[additional matters] when I come.

Gifts from the Holy Spirit

12 Now, brothers and sisters, I don't want you to ·misunder-
stand [be uninformed] ·about [concerning; *or* in regard to
your question about; see 7:1; 8:1; 16:1] spiritual gifts. 2 You know the way
you lived ·before you were believers [L when you were pagans/Gentiles].
You let yourselves be influenced and led away to worship idols—things
that could not speak. 3 So I want you to understand that no one who is
speaking ·with the help of [by means of; in the power of] God's Spirit

11:24 it is Some Greek copies read "it is broken."

says, "Jesus be cursed." And no one can say, "Jesus is Lord," ·without the help of [Lexcept by means of/in the power of] **the Holy Spirit.**

4There are different kinds of gifts, but they are all from the same Spirit. 5There are different ·ways to serve [ministries] **but the same Lord to serve. 6And there are different ·ways that God works through people** [kinds of action; activities] **but the same God works ·in all of us in everything we do** [Lall things in all people]. **7·Something from the Spirit can be seen in** [LThe manifestation/disclosure of the Spirit is given to] **each person, for the common good. 8The Spirit gives one person the ·ability to speak with wisdom** [message/word of wisdom], **and the same Spirit gives another the ·ability to speak with knowledge** [message/word of knowledge]. **9The same Spirit gives faith to one person. And, to another, that one Spirit gives gifts of healing. 10The Spirit gives to another person ·the power to do miracles** [works of power], **to another ·the ability to prophesy** [Lprophecy]. **And he gives to another the ·ability to know the difference between good and evil** [Ldiscernment/distinguishing of] **spirits. The Spirit gives one person the ability to speak in different kinds of ·languages** [*or* ecstatic utterance; Ltongues] **and to another the ·ability to interpret those languages** [Linterpretation of tongues]. **11One Spirit, the same Spirit, does all these things, and the Spirit ·decides what to give** [Ldistributes just as he wishes to] **each person.**

The Body of Christ Works Together

12A person's body is ·one thing [a unity; Lone], **but it has many parts. Though there are many parts to a body, all those parts make only one body. Christ is like that also. 13Some of us are Jews, and some are Greeks. Some of us are slaves, and some are free. But we were all baptized into one body ·through** [by; in] **one Spirit. And we were all made to ·share in** [Ldrink of] **the one Spirit.**

14[LFor] **The ·human body** [Lbody] **is not made up of one part, but of many. 15The foot might say, "Because I am not a hand, I am not part of the body." But saying this would not stop the foot from being a part of the body. 16The ear might say, "Because I am not an eye, I am not part of the body." But saying this would not stop the ear from being a part of the body. 17If the whole body were an eye, ·it would not be able to** [Lhow would it…?] **hear. If the whole body were an ear, ·it would not be able to** [Lhow would it…?] **smell. 18-19If each part of the body were the same part, ·there would be no body** [Lwhere would the body be?]. **But truly God put all the parts, each one of them, in the body as he wanted them. 20So then there are many parts, but only one body.**

21The eye cannot say to the hand, "I don't need you!" And the head cannot say to the foot, "I don't need you!" 22·No! [LOn the contrary,] **Those parts of the body that seem to be the weaker are ·really necessary** [essential; indispensable]. **23And the parts of the body we think are less ·deserving** [honorable] **are the parts to which we give ·the most** [special; greater] **honor. We ·give special respect to** [*or* treat with special modesty] **the parts ·we want to hide** [that are shameful/unpresentable]. **24The more ·respectable** [presentable] **parts of our body need no special care. But God put the body together and gave ·more** [special] **honor to the parts that need it 25so ·our body would not be divided** [*or* there would be no division in the body]. **God wanted the different parts to care the same for each other. 26If one part of the body suffers, all the other parts suffer with it. Or if one part of our body is ·honored** [glorified], **all the other parts ·share its honor** [Lrejoice with it].

27·Together you [[L]You; [C]the Greek is plural] are the body of Christ, and each one of you is a part of that body. 28In the church God has ·given a place first to [appointed/placed first] apostles, second to prophets, and third to teachers, then those who do ·miracles [acts of powers], those who have gifts of healing, those who can help others, those who are able to ·govern [lead], and those who can speak ·in different languages [*or* with ecstatic utterance; [L]different kinds of tongues; v. 10]. 29·Not all are apostles [[L]Not all are apostles, are they? [C]vv. 29–30 are all rhetorical questions assuming a negative answer]. Not all are prophets. Not all are teachers. Not all do miracles. 30Not all have gifts of healing. Not all speak ·in different languages [*or* with ecstatic utterance; [L]in tongues]. Not all interpret those ·languages [[L]tongues]. 31But ·you should truly want to have [eagerly desire; be zealous for] the greater gifts.

Love Is the Greatest Gift

And now I will show you ·the best way of all [a better/superior way].

13 I may speak in ·different languages [[L]tongues; 12:10, 29, 30] of people or even angels. But if I do not have love, I am only a ·noisy [resounding] ·bell [gong] or a ·crashing [clanging] cymbal. 2I may have the gift of prophecy. I may understand all ·the secret things of God [[L]mysteries] and have all knowledge, and I may have faith so great I can move mountains. But even with all these things, if I do not have love, then I am nothing. 3I may give away everything I have, and I may even give my body ·as an offering to be burned [[L]to be burned]." But I gain nothing if I do not have love.

4Love is patient and kind. Love is not ·jealous [envious], it does not brag, and it is not ·proud [arrogant; conceited; puffed up]. 5Love is not ·rude [disrespectful], is not ·selfish [self-serving], and ·does not get upset with others [is not easily provoked/angered]. Love does not ·count up [keep a record of] wrongs that have been done. 6Love ·takes no pleasure [does not rejoice] in ·evil [wrongdoing; injustice] but rejoices over the truth. 7Love ·patiently accepts all things [[T]bears all things; *or* always protects], ·always trusts [[T]believes all things], ·always hopes [[T]hopes all things], and ·always endures [[T]endures all things].

8Love never ·ends [fails; falls short]. There are gifts of prophecy, but they will ·be ended [cease; pass away]. There are gifts of ·speaking in different languages [*or* ecstatic utterance; [L]tongues], but those gifts will ·stop [cease; fall silent]. There is the gift of knowledge, but it will ·come to an end [pass away; be set aside]. 9·The reason is that [For] ·our knowledge and our ability to prophesy are not perfect [[L]we know in part/imperfectly and we prophesy in part/incompletely]. 10But when ·perfection [the perfect; completeness; wholeness] comes, the ·things that are not perfect [partial] will ·end [pass away; be set aside]. 11When I was a child, I talked like a child, I thought like a child, I reasoned like a child. When I became a man, I ·stopped [set aside] those childish ways. 12·It is the same with us [[L]For…]. Now we see ·a dim reflection [obscurely; *or* indirectly], ·as if we were looking into a mirror [[T]through a glass darkly], but then we shall see ·clearly [[L]face to face]. Now I know only a part, but then I will know fully, as ·God has known me [[L]I am fully known]. 13So these three things ·continue forever [endure; remain]: faith, hope, and love. And the greatest of these is love.

13:3 give… burned Other Greek copies read "hand over my body in order that I may brag."

Desire Spiritual Gifts

14 ·You should seek after [Pursue; Make your aim] love, and ·you should truly want to have [eagerly desire; be zealous for] the spiritual gifts, especially the gift of prophecy. 2·I will explain why. [LFor] Those who ·have the gift of speaking in different languages [*or* speak with ecstatic utterance; Lspeak in a tongue; 12:10, 29, 30; 13:1] are not speaking to people; they are speaking to God. No one understands them; they are speaking ·secret things [mysteries] ·through [by; in; with] the Spirit. 3But those who prophesy are speaking to people ·to give them strength [for edification/upbuilding], encouragement, and ·comfort [consolation]. 4The ones who speak in different languages are ·helping [edifying; building up] only themselves, but those who prophesy are ·helping [edifying; building up] the whole church. 5I wish all of you ·had the gift of speaking in different kinds of languages [Lspoke in tongues; v. 2], but more, I wish you would prophesy. Those who prophesy are greater than those who ·can only speak in different languages [Lspeak in tongues; v. 2]—unless someone ·is there who can explain what is said [Linterprets (the tongues)] so that the whole church can be ·helped [edified; built up].

6Brothers and sisters, how will it help you if I come to you speaking in ·different languages [Ltongues; v. 2], unless I bring you a ·new truth [revelation] or ·some new knowledge [Lknowledge], or prophecy, or teaching? 7It is the same as with lifeless things that make sounds—like a flute or a harp. If they do not make ·clear [distinct] musical notes, ·you will not [Lhow will you…?] know what is being played. 8And in a war, if the trumpet does not give a clear sound, who will prepare for battle? 9It is the same with you. Unless you speak ·clearly [intelligible words] with your tongue, ·no one can [Lhow will anyone…?] understand what you are saying. You will be talking into the air! 10It may be true that there are all kinds of sounds in the world, and none is without meaning. 11But unless I understand the meaning of what someone says to me, we will be like ·foreigners [barbarians] to each other. 12It is the same with you. Since you ·eagerly desire [are zealous for] ·spiritual gifts [*or* manifestations of the Spirit], seek ·most of all to have [to excel in] the gifts that ·help the church grow stronger [build up/edify the church].

13[LTherefore] The one who has the gift of ·speaking in a different language [*or* ecstatic utterance; Ltongues] should pray for the gift to interpret what is spoken. 14If I pray ·in a different language [*or* with ecstatic utterance; Lin a tongue], my spirit is praying, but my mind ·does nothing [Lis unfruitful]. 15So what should I do? I will pray with my spirit, but I will also pray with my mind. I will ·sing [sing praises/psalms] with my spirit, but I will also ·sing [sing praises/psalms] with my mind. 16[LOtherwise] If you ·praise God [*or* pronounce a blessing] with your spirit, those persons there ·without understanding [*or* without the gift; *or* who are inquirers/seekers; vv. 23, 24] cannot say "Amen" [Cfrom a Hebrew term meaning "it is true"; 1 Chr. 16:36] to your prayer of thanks, because they do not know what you are saying. 17You may be thanking God ·in a good way [well enough], but the other person is not ·helped [edified; built up].

18I thank God that I speak ·in different kinds of languages [*or* with ecstatic utterance; Lin tongues] more than all of you. 19But in the church meetings I would rather speak five words ·I understand [Lwith my mind] in order to teach others than thousands of words ·in a different language [*or* with ecstatic utterance; Lin a tongue].

20Brothers and sisters, do not think like children. In evil things be like ·babies [infants], but in your thinking you should be ·like adults [mature; grown-up]. 21It is written in the ·Scriptures [LLaw; Creferring here to all of Scripture]:

"With people who use ·strange words [Ldifferent tongues/languages]
and ·foreign languages [Ldifferent lips]
I will speak to these people.
But even then they will not ·listen to [*or* obey] me [Is. 28:11–12; see also Deut. 28:49],"

says the Lord. [CIsrael didn't listen when God used foreign-speaking Assyrians to punish them; similarly people won't benefit from hearing tongues they don't understand.]

22So ·the gift of speaking in different kinds of languages [*or* ecstatic utterance; Ltongues] is a sign for believers, not for unbelievers [Ctongues served as a warning of judgment and a call to repentance; see Acts 2:4, 21, 38–40]. And prophecy is for believers, not for unbelievers. 23Suppose the whole church meets together and everyone speaks in ·different languages [Ltongues]. If some people come in who ·do not understand [*or* are inquirers/seekers; v. 16] or are unbelievers, they will say you are ·crazy [insane; Cunintelligible tongues sound like babbling]. 24But suppose everyone is prophesying and unbelievers or ·those who does not understand [*or* inquirers/seekers] come in. If everyone is prophesying, ·their sin will be shown to them [Lthey will be convicted by all], and they will be judged by ·all that they hear [Lall]. 25The secret things in their hearts will be made known. So they will ·bow down [Lfall face down] and worship God saying, "Truly, God is ·with you [among you; in your midst]." [CThough prophecy is for believers (v. 22), it also convicts unbelievers better than uninterpreted (and so incoherent) tongues (see vv. 27–28), since it is a coherent message from God.]

Meetings Should Help the Church

26So, brothers and sisters, what should you do? When you meet together, one person has a ·song [psalm; hymn], and another has a teaching. Another has a ·new truth from God [Lrevelation]. Another speaks ·in a different language [*or* with ecstatic utterance; Ltongue], and another person ·interprets that language [Lan interpretation]. The purpose of all these things should be ·to help the church grow strong [Lfor edification/building up]. 27When you meet together, if anyone speaks ·in a different language [*or* with ecstatic utterance; Lin a tongue], it should be only two, or not more than three, who speak. They should speak one after the other, and someone should interpret. 28But if there is no interpreter, then they should ·be quiet [remain silent] in the church meeting. They should speak only to themselves and to God.

29Only two or three prophets should speak, and the others should ·judge [evaluate; consider; weigh] what they say. 30If a ·message from God [Lrevelation] comes to another person who is sitting, the first speaker should stop. 31[LFor] You can all prophesy one after the other. In this way all the people can be taught and encouraged. 32The spirits of prophets are ·under the control of [subject to] the prophets themselves [Cunlike in pagan religions, where a spirit would seize control of a speaker, causing frenzy, mania or ecstasy]. 33[LFor] God is not a God of ·confusion [disorder] but a God of peace.

As is true in all the ·churches [assemblies] of ·God's people [Tthe saints; Csome commentators take this clause as part of the previous sentence],

34·women [*or* wives] **should keep quiet in the ·church meetings** [churches; assemblies; Cthe context here may be the evaluation of prophecy (v. 29), rather than general worship (where women presumably could speak; see 11:2–16)]. [LFor] **They are not allowed to speak, but they must ·yield to this rule** [*or* be in submission; *or* keep their ordered place] **as the law says** [Cperhaps Gen. 3:16, or a nonbiblical Jewish tradition]. 35**If they want to ·learn something** [*or* ask questions], **they should ask their own husbands at home. It is ·shameful** [disgraceful; improper] **for a woman to speak in ·the church meeting** [the assembly; church]. 36**Did ·God's teaching** [the word of God] **·come from** [originate with] **you? Or are you the only ones to whom it has come?** [CApparently, some women were being disruptive during meetings.]

37**Those who think they are prophets or spiritual persons should ·understand** [*or* acknowledge] **that what I am writing to you is the Lord's command.** 38**Those who ignore this will ·be ignored by God** [*or* themselves be ignored].[n]

39**So my brothers and sisters, you should ·truly want** [be eager] **to prophesy. And do not ·stop people from using the gift of speaking in different kinds of languages** [Lforbid/hinder speaking in tongues]. 40**But let everything be done in a ·right** [proper; fitting] **and orderly way.**

The Good News About Christ

15 Now, brothers and sisters, I want you to ·remember [*or* be clear about] **the ·Good News** [Gospel] **I brought to you. You received this ·Good News** [Gospel] **·and continue strong in it** [*or* and have based your faith on it; Lin which you stand]. 2**And you are being saved by it if you ·continue believing** [Lhold firm to] **·what I told you** [Lthe Gospel message I proclaimed to you], **unless you believed ·for nothing** [in vain; *or* superficially; *or* in something of no value].

3[LFor] **I passed on to you what I received, which is ·of greatest importance** [*or* the first thing I told you]: **that Christ died for our sins, ·as the Scriptures say** [Laccording to the Scripture; Is. 53:5–6]; 4**that he was buried and was raised to life on the third day ·as the Scriptures say** [Laccording to the Scripture; Ps. 16:8–11]; 5**and that he was seen by ·Peter** [LCephas; CPeter's name in Aramaic; see 1:12] **and then by ·the twelve apostles** [Lthe Twelve; Luke 24:33–36]. 6**After that, Jesus was seen by more than five hundred of the ·believers** [Lbrothers (and sisters)] **at the same time. Most of them ·are still living today** [Lremain until now], **but some have ·died** [Lfallen asleep; Ca euphemism for death]. 7**Then he was seen by ·James** [Jesus' brother; Mark 6:3; Acts 15:13; Gal. 1:19] **and later by all the apostles** [Acts 1:6–11]. 8**Last of all he was seen by me** [Acts 9]**—as by a person ·not born at the normal time** [prematurely/abnormally born; CChrist's appearance to Paul was unique, occurring after Jesus' ascension]. 9**For I am the least of the apostles. I am not even ·good enough** [worthy] **to be called an apostle, because I persecuted the church of God.** 10**But God's grace has made me what I am, and his grace to me was not ·wasted** [in vain; without effect]. [LOn the contrary; Indeed] **I worked harder than all ·the other apostles** [of them]. **(But it was not I really; it was God's grace that was with me.)** 11**So whether I preached to you or ·the other apostles** [Lthey] **preached to you, ·we all preach the same thing** [this is what we preach; Cthe message of Christ's death and resurrection; vv. 3–8], **and this is what you believed.**

14:38 Those… God. Some Greek copies read "Those who are ignorant of this will stay ignorant."

We Will Be Raised from the Dead

12 Now ·since we preached that Christ was [L if Christ is preached as] raised from the dead, why do some of you say that people will not be raised from the dead [C some Corinthians denied the resurrection of the body]? 13 If ·no one is ever raised [L there is no resurrection] from the dead, then Christ has not been raised. 14 And if Christ has not been raised, then our preaching is ·worth nothing [futile; useless; empty], and your faith is ·worth nothing [futile; useless; empty]. 15 And also, we are ·guilty of lying [L found to be false witnesses] about God, because we testified ·of him [L against God] that he raised Christ from the dead. But if people are not raised from the dead, then God never raised Christ. 16 If the dead are not raised, Christ has not been raised either. 17 And if Christ has not been raised, then your faith ·has nothing to it [is futile/useless/empty]; you are still ·guilty of [*or* a slave to; L in] your sins. 18 ·And [Consequently; Therefore] those in Christ who have ·already died [L fallen asleep; v. 6] ·are lost [have perished]. 19 If our hope in Christ is for this life only, we should be pitied more than ·anyone else in the world [L all people].

20 But Christ has truly been raised from the dead—the ·first one and proof that those who sleep in death will also be raised [L firstfruits of those who have fallen asleep; C unlike others who had been raised to mortal life, Christ was the first to be raised to everlasting life]. 21 Death has come ·because of what one man did [through a man/human being], but the rising from death also comes ·because of one man [through a man/human being]. 22 In Adam all of us die. In the same way, in Christ all of us will be made alive again [Rom. 5:12–21]. 23 But ·everyone [each] will be raised to life in the right order. Christ was ·first to be raised [L the firstfruits]. When Christ comes again, those who belong to him will be raised to life, 24 and then the end will come. At that time Christ will ·destroy [abolish] all rulers, authorities, and powers, and he will hand over the kingdom to God the Father. 25 [L For] Christ must ·rule [reign] until he puts all enemies under his ·control [L feet; Ps. 110:1]. 26 The last enemy to be destroyed will be death. 27 ·The Scripture says that God put [L For he has subjected] all things under his ·control [L feet; Ps. 8:6]. When it says "all things" are ·under [subjected to] him, it is clear this does not include the One [C God the father] who put everything under his control. 28 After everything has been ·put under [subjected to] the Son, then he will ·put himself under [be subjected to] ·God [L the One…], who had put all things under him. ·Then [*or* …so that] God will be ·the complete ruler over everything [*or* supreme in every place and in every way; L all in all].

29 If the dead are never raised, what will people do who are being baptized for the dead [C it is unclear what this practice was or whether Paul approves or disapproves]? If the dead are not raised at all, why are people being baptized for them?

30 And what about us? Why do we put ourselves in danger every hour? 31 I ·die [face death] every day. ·That is true, brothers and sisters, just as it is true that I brag about you [L (I swear) by my boasting in you, brothers (and sisters), which I have] in Christ Jesus our Lord. 32 If I fought wild animals in Ephesus [C probably a metaphor for human opponents, though possibly beasts in the arena (Acts 19; 2 Cor. 1:8–11; 2 Tim. 4:16–18)] ·only with human hopes [*or* from a human point of view; L according to man], I have gained nothing. If the dead are not raised, "Let us eat and drink, because tomorrow we will die [Is. 22:13; 56:12]."

33 Do not be ·fooled [deceived; misled]: "Bad ·friends [company] will ruin good ·habits [*or* character; morals; C a quote from the Greek poet

Menander (c. 342–291 BC)]." 34·Come back to your right way of thinking
[Come to your senses; *or* Sober up as you should] and stop sinning. Some
of you ·do not know [*or* are ignorant about] God—I say this to shame you.

What Kind of Body Will We Have?

35But someone may ask, "How are the dead raised? What kind of body
will they have?" 36Foolish person! When you sow a seed, it must die in the
ground before it can ·live and grow [come to life]. 37And when you sow it,
it does not have the same "body" it will have later. [LBut; On the contrary]
What you sow is only a bare seed, maybe wheat or something else. 38But
God gives it a body that he ·has planned [wants; has chosen] for it, and
God gives each kind of seed its own body. 39All things made of flesh are
not the same: People have one kind of flesh, animals have another, birds
have another, and fish have another. 40Also there are heavenly bodies and
earthly bodies. But the ·beauty [splendor; glory] of the heavenly bodies is
one kind, and the ·beauty [splendor; glory] of the earthly bodies is
another. 41The sun has one kind of ·beauty [splendor; glory], the moon
has another ·beauty [splendor; glory], and the stars have another. And
each star is different in its ·beauty [splendor; glory].

42It is the same with the dead who are raised to life. ·The body that is
"planted" will ruin and decay [LIt is sown/buried in corruption], but it is
raised ·to a life that cannot be destroyed [imperishable; Lin incorruption].
43·When the body is "planted," it is without honor [LIt is sown/buried in
dishonor], but it is raised in glory. ·When the body is "planted," it is weak
[LIt is sown/buried in weakness], but ·when it is raised, it is powerful [Lit
is raised in power]. 44·The body that is "planted" is a physical body [LIt is
sown/buried a natural/physical/soulish body]. ·When it is raised, it is [LIt
is raised] a spiritual body.

There is a ·physical [natural; soulish] body, and there is also a spiritual
body. 45[LSo also] It is written in the Scriptures: "The first man, Adam,
became a living ·person [soul; Gen. 2:7]." But the last Adam [CChrist]
became a spirit that gives life. 46[LBut] The spiritual did not come first, but
the ·physical [natural; soulish] and then the spiritual. 47The first man came
from the dust of the earth. The second man came from heaven. 48People
who ·belong to the earth [*or* are of dust] are like the first man of ·earth
[dust]. But those people who belong to heaven are like the man of heaven.
49Just as we ·were made like [Lhave borne the image of] the man of earth,
so we will[n] also ·be made like [bear the image of] the man of heaven.

50I tell you this, brothers and sisters: Flesh and blood cannot ·have a part
in [inherit] the kingdom of God. ·Something that will ruin cannot [...nor
can the perishable/corruptible] ·have a part in something that never ruins
[inherit the imperishable/incorruptible]. 51But look! I tell you ·this secret [a
mystery; 2:1]: We will not all ·sleep in death [Lsleep; Ca euphemism for
death], but we will all be changed. 52It will ·take only a second [happen in a
flash]—as quickly as an eye ·blinks [*or* twinkles]—when the last trumpet
sounds. The trumpet will sound, and those who have died will be raised ·to
live forever [imperishable; incorruptible], and we will be changed [1 Thess.
4:13–17]. 53[LFor] This body that ·can be destroyed [is perishable/corrupt-
ible] must clothe itself with ·something that can never be destroyed [the
imperishable/incorruptible]. And this ·body that dies [Lmortal] must clothe
itself with ·something that can never die [immortality]. 54So when this

15:49 so we will Some Greek copies read "so let us."

body that ·can be destroyed [is perishable/corruptible] will clothe itself with
that which ·can never be destroyed [is imperishable/incorruptible], and this
·body that dies [Lmortal] will clothe itself with ·that which can never die
[immortality], then this Scripture will ·be made true [come to pass]:
"Death is ·destroyed forever [Lswallowed up] in victory [Is. 25:8]."
55"[LO] Death, where is your victory?
Death, where is your ·pain [Lsting; Hos. 13:14]?"
56Death's ·power to hurt [Lsting] is sin, and the power of sin is the law.
57But we thank God! He gives us the victory through our Lord Jesus Christ.
58So my ·dear [beloved] brothers and sisters, stand strong. Do not let
anything move you. Always ·give yourselves fully to [excel in] the work of
the Lord, because you know that your work in the Lord is ·never wasted
[not useless/in vain].

The Gift for Other Believers

16 Now ·I will write about [*or* concerning your question about;
Lconcerning; 7:1; 8:1; 12:1] the collection of money for ·God's
people [Tthe saints; 2 Cor. 8–9; Rom. 15:25–28]. Do the same thing I told
the Galatian churches to do [CGalatia was a Roman province in present-
day central Turkey where Paul started churches on his first missionary
journey (Acts 13–14)]: 2On the first day of every week [CSunday], each one
of you should put aside money ·as you have been blessed [*or* what you can
afford; Lwhatever one prospers]. Save it up so you will not have to collect
money after I come. 3When I arrive, I will send ·with letters of introduction whomever you approve [*or* whomever you authorize with your letters]
to take your gift to Jerusalem. 4And if it seems ·good [appropriate; advis-
able; *or* worthwhile] for me to go also, they will go along with me.

Paul's Plans

5I will come to you after I go through Macedonia—for I am planning to
go through Macedonia [Cthe northern part of present-day Greece; Acts
19:21; 20:1, 2; 2 Cor. 1:15–16]. 6Perhaps I will stay with you for a time or even
all winter. Then you can help me on my trip, wherever I go. 7[LFor] I do not
want to see you now just in passing. I hope to stay a longer time with you if
the Lord allows it. 8But I will stay at Ephesus [Ca prominent city in the
Roman province of Asia, present-day western Turkey; Acts 19] until Pentecost
[Cthe Jewish festival held on the fiftieth day after Passover (late spring)],
9because a ·good opportunity for a great and growing work has been given
[Lgreat and effective door (of opportunity) has opened up] to me now. And
there are many ·people working against me [opponents; adversaries].
10If Timothy comes to you, see to it that ·he has nothing to fear with
you [*or* you put him at ease; you don't intimidate him], because he is
working for the Lord just as I am. 11So none of you should treat Timothy
·as unimportant [*or* with contempt], but ·help [send] him on his trip in
peace so that he can come back to me. I am expecting him to come with
the ·brothers [other believers].
12Now about our brother Apollos: I strongly encouraged him to visit
you with the other brothers. He did not at all want to come now; he will
come when he has the opportunity.

Paul Ends His Letter

13Be ·alert [watchful; on your guard]. ·Continue strong [Stand firm] in
the faith. ·Have courage [*or* Act like men (ready for battle)], and be strong.
14Do everything in love.
15You know that the ·family [household] of Stephanas were the ·first
believers in [Lfirstfruits of] Achaia [Csouthern Greece] and that they have

given themselves to the service of ·God's people [Tthe saints]**. I ask you,**
brothers and sisters, 16**to ·follow the leading of** [*or* submit to the authority
of] **people like these and anyone else who ·works and serves with them**
[*or* works hard in our common task]**.**
17**I ·am happy** [rejoice] **that Stephanas, Fortunatus, and Achaicus have**
come. ·You are not here, but they have filled your place [*or* They have supplied the help you could not]. 18[LFor] **They have refreshed my spirit and**
yours. You should ·recognize the value of [*or* give recognition to] **people**
like these.
19**The churches in Asia** [Cthe Roman province, in present-day Turkey]
send greetings to you. Aquila and Priscilla [Acts 18:2–3, 18, 26] **greet you**
in the Lord, as does the church that meets in their house. 20**All the broth-**
ers and sisters here send greetings. Greet each other with a holy kiss.
21**I, Paul, am writing this greeting with my own hand** [Cthe rest of the letter was evidently dictated to a scribe, called an amanuensis; see Rom. 16:22].
22**If anyone does not love the Lord, let him be ·separated from God—**
lost forever [Lanathema]**!**
·Come, O Lord [LMaranatha; CAramaic phrase meaning either "Our
Lord, Come!" or "Our Lord has come"]**!**
23**The grace of the Lord Jesus be with you.**
24**My love be with all of you in Christ Jesus.**n

16:24 My... Jesus. Some Greek copies add "Amen."

2 CORINTHIANS

1 From Paul, an ·apostle [messenger] of Christ Jesus. ·I am an
apostle because that is what God wanted [L…by the will of
God]. Also from Timothy [Acts 16:1–5; 1 Cor. 16:10–11; Phil. 2:19–24;
1–2 Timothy] our ·brother in Christ [Lbrother].
To the church of God in Corinth, and to all ·of God's people [Tthe
saints] everywhere in Achaia [Cthe Roman province where the city of
Corinth was located, present day southern Greece]:
2Grace and peace to you from God our Father and the Lord Jesus
Christ.

Paul Gives Thanks to God

3·Praise be to [Blessed is/be] the God and Father of our Lord Jesus
Christ, the Father who is full of ·mercy [compassion] and all ·comfort
[encouragement]. 4He ·comforts [encourages] us ·every time we have [Lin
all our] ·troubles [trials; tribulation], so when others have ·trouble [any
trials/tribulation], we can ·comfort [encourage] them with the same
·comfort [encouragement] God gives us. 5[LFor just as] ·We share in the
many sufferings of Christ [LChrist's sufferings abound in us]. In the same
way, ·much comfort comes to us [Lour comfort abounds] through Christ.
6If we have ·troubles [trials; tribulation], it is for your ·comfort [encour-
agement] and salvation, and if we ·have comfort [are encouraged], ·you
also have comfort [*or* it is for your comfort/encouragement]. This helps
you to accept patiently the same sufferings we have. 7Our hope for you is
·strong [unshaken; firm], knowing that as you share in our sufferings,
you will also share in the ·comfort [encouragement] we receive.
8Brothers and sisters, we want you to know about the ·trouble [trial; tribu-
lation] we suffered in Asia [Ca Roman province in present-day western Turkey].
We had great burdens there that were beyond our own strength, so that we
even ·gave up hope of living [Ldespaired of life]. 9Truly, in our own hearts we
believed we ·would die [Lhad been sentenced to death]. But this happened so
we would not trust in ourselves but in God, who raises people from the dead.
10God ·saved [rescued; delivered] us from these great dangers of death, and he
will continue to ·save [rescue; deliver] us. We have put our hope in him, and
he will ·save [rescue; deliver] us again. 11·And you can [*or* …as you] help us
with your prayers. Then many people will give thanks for us—·that God
blessed [for the gift/favor given to] us because of their many prayers.

The Change in Paul's Plans

12This is ·what we are proud of [Lour boast], ·and I can say it with a clear
conscience [Lthe testimony/witness of our conscience]: In everything we
have done in the world, and especially with you, we have had an ·honest*n* [*or*
generous] and sincere heart from God. We did this by God's grace, not by

1:12 honest Some Greek copies read "holy."

·the kind of wisdom the world has [worldly/fleshly wisdom]. 13-14We write to
you ·only what you can read and understand [*or* in a clear and straightfor-
ward manner]. And I hope that as you have understood ·some things [part
of the situation; Lin part] about us, you may come to ·know everything
[understand fully] about us [Csome of Paul's previous contacts and corre-
spondence had produced misunderstanding or conflict; 2:1]. Then you can
·be proud [boast] of us, as we will ·be proud [boast] of you on the day ·our
Lord Jesus Christ comes again [Lof our Lord Jesus Christ; Cjudgment day].
15I was so sure of all this that I made plans to visit you first so you
could ·be blessed twice [Lhave a second grace]. 16I planned to visit you on
my way to Macedonia [Cthe northern part of present-day Greece; Acts
19:21; 20:1, 2] and again on my way back [Cthe visit anticipated in 1 Cor.
16:5]. I wanted to ·get help from you for my trip [Lbe sent by you] to
Judea. 17[LSo; Therefore] Do you think that I made these plans ·without
really meaning it [lightly; with vacillation]? Or maybe you think I make
plans ·as the world does [*or* using only human standards/reason; Laccording to the flesh], so that I say yes, yes and at the same time no, no.
18But ·since you can believe God [LGod is trustworthy/faithful], you can
believe that what we tell you is never both yes and no. 19[LFor] The Son of
God, Jesus Christ, that Silas and Timothy and I preached to you, was not
yes and no. [LBut; Rather] In ·Christ [Lhim] it has always been yes. 20The yes
to all of God's promises is in ·Christ [Lhim], and through Christ we say ·yes
[Lamen; Cfrom a Hebrew term meaning "yes," or "it is true"] to the glory of
God. 21Remember, God is the One who makes you and us ·strong [stand
firm; established] in Christ. God ·made us his chosen people [*or* commissioned us; Lanointed us]. 22He put his ·mark on us to show that we are his
[Lseal on us; Cof ownership], and he put his Spirit in our hearts ·to be a
guarantee for all he has promised [Las a pledge/deposit/downpayment].
23Now I ·ask [call on; appeal to] God to be my witness ·that this is true
[*or* staking my life on it; Lagainst my soul/life; Ca very serious vow or oath]:
The reason I did not come back to Corinth was to ·keep you from being
punished or hurt [Lspare you]. 24We are not trying to ·control [rule; lord
it over] your faith. You ·are strong [stand firm; are well established] in
faith. But we are workers with you for your own joy.

2 So I decided that my next visit to you would not be another ·one to
make you sad [painful/sorrowful one; CPaul's first visit (1:16; 1 Cor.
16:5) had resulted in conflict, rejection, and hurt feelings]. 2If I ·make you
sad [cause you pain/sorrow], who will make me glad? Only you can make
me glad—·particularly the person [*or* those] whom I made sad [Ceither the
church generally, or a particular opponent (vv. 5–10)]. 3I wrote you a letter
for this reason: that when I came to you I would not be made ·sad [sorrow-
ful] by the people who should ·make me happy [bring me joy; CPaul wrote
a severe letter (now lost) after his painful visit (v. 1) to call the church to
repentance]. I felt sure of all of you, that you would share my joy. 4When I
wrote to you before [v. 3], I was very ·troubled [distressed] and ·unhappy
[anguished] in my heart, and I wrote with many tears. I did not write to
make you ·sad [sorrowful], but to let you know how much I love you.

Forgive the Sinner

5·Someone [LIf someone…; Cevidently the ringleader who opposed Paul
on his previous visit (v. 1)] there among you has caused sadness, ·not [L…it
is not] to me, but to all of you. I mean he caused sadness to all ·in some way
[*or* to some extent]. (I do not want to ·make it sound worse than it really

is [exaggerate; put it too severely].) **6The punishment that ·most of you** [the majority] **gave him is enough for him** [Cthe church as a whole has now sided with Paul and disciplined this individual]. **7But now you should forgive him and ·comfort** [encourage] **him to keep him from ·having too much sadness and giving up completely** [being overwhelmed/swallowed up by excessive sorrow/grief]. **8So I ·beg** [urge; encourage] **you to ·show** [reaffirm] **that you love him. 9I wrote you to test you and to see if you obey in everything** [CPaul's "severe" letter (vv. 1, 3) evidently called the church to submit again to his authority]. **10If you forgive someone, I also forgive him. And what I have forgiven—if I had anything to forgive—I forgave it for you, ·as if Christ were with me** [*or* in the presence of Christ]. **11I did this so that Satan would not ·win anything from** [outwit; take advantage of] **us, because we ·know very well** [Lare not ignorant of] **what Satan's ·plans** [schemes; intentions] **are.**

Paul's Concern in Troas

12When I came to Troas [Ca city in northwest Asia Minor; Acts 16:8, 11; 20:5–6; 2 Tim. 4:13] **to preach the Good News of Christ, ·the Lord gave me a good opportunity there** [La door opened for me by/in the Lord]. **13But I had no ·peace** [Lrest in my spirit], **because I did not find my brother Titus** [Gal. 2:1–3; Titus 1:4–5]. **So I said good-bye to them at Troas and went to Macedonia** [1:16; Acts 20:1–3]. [CPaul evidently sent his severe letter (vv. 1, 3, 9) with Titus, and now awaited the church's response. Starting in v. 14 he digresses into a long expression of joy because of their favorable reaction (2:14—7:1). He picks up the story again in 7:5.]

Victory Through Christ

14But thanks be to God, who always leads us as captives in Christ's victory ·parade [procession; Cthe image is of a victorious Roman general leading his army and his captives through the streets]. **God uses us to spread ·his knowledge everywhere like a sweet-smelling perfume** [Lthe aroma/fragrance of the knowledge of him; Cincense or spices were burned during such victory parades]. **15·Our offering to God is this:** [*or* For God's sake; *or* To God] **We are the ·sweet smell** [aroma; fragrance] **of Christ among those who are being saved and among those who are ·being lost** [perishing; headed for destruction]. **16To those who are ·lost** [perishing; headed for destruction], **we are the ·smell** [aroma] **of death that brings death, but to those who are being saved, we are the ·smell** [aroma] **of life that brings life. So who is ·able** [qualified; adequate] **to do this work? 17We do not ·sell** [peddle] **the word of God for a profit as many other people do. But in Christ we speak the truth ·before** [in the presence of] **God, as ·messengers of** [envoys of; Lfrom] **God.**

Servants of the New Agreement

3 Are we starting to ·brag about [praise; commend] **ourselves again? Do we need letters of ·introduction** [recommendation] **to you or from you, like some other people** [CPaul's opponents evidently carried letters of reference (perhaps from Jerusalem)]? **2You yourselves are our letter, written on our hearts, known and read by everyone** [Cthe changed lives of the Corinthians prove Paul's credibility as an apostle of Jesus Christ]. **3You show that you are a letter from Christ ·sent through us** [delivered by us; *or* produced by us; the result of our ministry]. **This letter is not written with ink but ·with** [by] **the Spirit of the living God. It is not written on stone tablets** [Cthe law of Moses was written on stone tablets; Ex. 24:12; 32:16] **but on human hearts** [Lhearts of flesh; Jer. 31:33; Ezek. 11:19; 36:26].

4We can say this, because through Christ we ·feel certain before God [have confidence in God's presence; *or* can trust in God]. **5We are not saying**

that we ·can do this work ourselves [Lare able/competent/adequate to consider anything as from ourselves]. ·It is God who makes us able to do all that
we do [LBut our ability/competence/adequacy is from God]. 6He made us
·able [adequate; competent] to be servants of a new ·agreement from himself to his people [covenant; Jer. 31:31–34; Luke 22:20]. This new ·agreement
[covenant] is not ·a written law [Lof the letter], but it is of the Spirit. The
·written law [Lletter] brings death, but the Spirit gives life.

7The ·law [*or* old system; Lministry] that brought death was ·written in
words [Lengraved with letters] on stone. It came with ·God's glory [Lglory],
which made Moses' face so ·bright [glorious] that the ·Israelites [Lchildren
of Israel] could not ·continue to look [gaze] at it. But that glory ·later disappeared [was fading; *or* was made ineffective (by the veil on his face)]. 8So
·surely [Lwill not…?] the ·new way that brings [Lministry of] the Spirit has
even more glory. 9[LFor] If the ·law that judged people guilty of sin
[Lministry of condemnation] had glory, surely the ·new way that makes
people right with God [Lministry of righteousness] has much greater glory.
10For that which had glory [Cthe law] ·really loses its glory [Lhas no glory]
when it is compared to the much greater glory [Cthe new way through the
Spirit]. 11[LFor] If that which ·disappeared [faded; was made ineffective;
Cthe law; v. 7] came with glory, then that which ·continues forever [remains;
abides; Cthe new way through the Spirit] has much greater glory.

12We have this hope, so we ·are very bold [*or* speak with boldness/confi-
dence]. 13We are not like Moses, who put a ·covering [veil] over his face so
the ·Israelites [Lchildren of Israel] would not see it [Ex. 34:29–35]. The glory
was ·disappearing [fading; *or* made ineffective], and Moses did not want
them to see it end. 14But their minds were ·closed [stubborn; hardened],
and even today that same ·covering [veil] ·hides the meaning [Lremains]
when they read the old ·agreement [covenant]. That covering is ·taken away
[Lnot lifted, because it is removed] only through Christ. 15Even today, when
they read ·the law of Moses [LMoses], there is a ·covering over [Lveil laying
upon] their ·minds [hearts]. 16But when a person ·changes and follows
[Lturns to] the Lord, that ·covering [veil] is taken away [Ex. 34:34]. 17The
Lord is the Spirit, and where the Spirit of the Lord is, there is freedom.
18·Our faces, then, are not covered [LWith an unveiled face…]. We all ·show
[reflect; *or* behold; *or* contemplate] the Lord's glory, and we are being
·changed [transformed] ·to be like him [Linto the same image]. This change
in us ·brings ever greater glory [*or* is from one degree of glory to another; Lis
from glory to glory], which comes from the Lord, who is the Spirit.

Preaching the Good News

4 [LTherefore,] Since God in his mercy gave us this ·work to do
[ministry], we don't ·give up [lose heart; become discouraged].
2But we have ·turned away from [rejected; renounced] ·secret [under-
handed] and shameful ways. We ·use no trickery [Ldo not walk in
deception], and we do not ·change [distort] the ·teaching [word] of God.
We ·teach the truth plainly [fully/openly disclose the truth], ·showing
everyone who we are so that they can know in their hearts what kind of
people we are [Lcommending ourselves to every person's conscience] in
God's sight. 3If the ·Good News [Gospel] that we preach is ·hidden [veiled],
it is ·hidden [veiled] only to those who are ·lost [perishing]. 4The ·devil
who rules this world [Lgod of this age] has blinded the minds of ·those who
do not believe [unbelievers]. [L…so that] They cannot see the light of the
Good News—the Good News ·about [that reveals] the glory of Christ,

who is ·exactly like [Lthe image of] God. 5[LFor] We do not preach about
ourselves, but we preach that Jesus Christ is Lord and that we are your
·servants [slaves; bondservants] for Jesus. 6[LFor; Because] God who said,
"Let the light shine out of the darkness [Gen. 1:3; Is. 9:2]," is the same God
who made his light shine in our hearts ·by letting us know [*or* to give us the
knowledge of] the glory of God that is in the face of Christ.

Spiritual Treasure in Clay Jars

7[LBut] We have this treasure ·from God, but we are like clay jars that hold
the treasure [Lin clay jars]. This shows that the ·great [extraordinary; tran-
scendent] power is from God, not from us. 8We have ·troubles all around us
[*or* all kinds of troubles/trials], but we are not ·defeated [crushed]. We ·do
not know what to do [are perplexed/bewildered], but we do not ·give up the
hope of living [despair]. 9We are ·persecuted [pursued], but ·God does not
leave us [not abandoned/left behind]. We are ·hurt [Lstruck down; knocked
over] sometimes, but we are not destroyed. 10We always carry the death of
Jesus in our own bodies [CPaul was in constant danger of the kind of violent
death Jesus experienced] so that the life of Jesus [Cresurrection life] can also
be ·seen [revealed; manifested] in our bodies. 11[LFor] We are alive, but for
Jesus we are always ·in danger of [Lbeing handed over to] death so that the
life of Jesus can be ·seen [revealed; manifested] in our ·bodies that die [mor-
tal flesh]. 12So death is working in us, but life is working in you.
13It is written in the Scriptures, "I believed, so I spoke [Ps. 116:10]."
·Our faith is like this, too [LHaving the same spirit of faith,…]. We also
believe, and so we speak. 14We know that ·God [Lthe one] who raised the
Lord Jesus from the dead will also raise us with Jesus and will ·bring us
together with you into his presence [Lpresent (us) with you]. 15All these
things are for ·you [your benefit], so that the grace of God that is ·being
given [expanding; increasing] to more and more people will bring increasing thanks to God for his glory.

Living by Faith

16So we do not ·give up [despair; lose heart]. Though our ·physical
body [Louter person] is ·becoming older and weaker [decaying; being
destroyed], our ·spirit inside us [Linner (person)] is ·made new [being
renewed] every day. 17·We have small troubles for a while now, but they
[LFor our brief and insignificant trials/tribulations] are ·helping us gain
[*or* producing in us] an eternal ·glory [Lburden/weight of glory] that ·is
much greater than [overwhelmingly exceeds] the troubles. 18We set our
eyes not on what we see but on what we cannot see. [LFor; Because] What
we see ·will last only a short time [Lis temporary/transitory], but what we
cannot see ·will last forever [Lis eternal].

5 [LFor] We know that ·when [if] our ·body [Learthly house]—the
tent we live in here on earth—is destroyed, ·God will have a house
for us [Lwe have a building from God]. It will not be made by human
hands, but will be an eternal home ·in heaven [*or* in the heavens]. 2But
now we ·groan [sigh] in this ·tent [*or* body; Lone], longing to be clothed in
our heavenly ·home [dwelling place], 3because it will clothe us so we will
not be naked. 4While we live in this ·body [Ltent], we ·have burdens [are
weighed down], and we ·groan [sigh]. We do not want to be ·naked
[stripped; unclothed], but we want to be clothed with our heavenly home.
Then ·this body that dies [Lthe mortal] will be ·fully covered with
[Lswallowed up by] life [Is. 25:8; 1 Cor. 15:54]. 5This is what God ·made
[designed; prepared] us for, and he has given us the Spirit to be a ·guaran-
tee for this new life [deposit; down payment; 1:22].

6So we always have courage. We know that while we ·live [Lare at home]
in this body, we are ·away [absent; *or* exiles] from the Lord. 7We ·live [walk]
by ·what we believe [faith], not by ·what we can see [sight]. 8So I say that
we ·have courage [*or* are confident]. We really ·want [would prefer] to be
·away [absent; *or* exiled] from this body and be at home with the Lord.
9Our only ·goal [aim; ambition] is to please ·God [Lhim] whether we ·live
here [are at home] or ·there [are absent/exiled], 10because we must all
stand before ·Christ to be judged [Lthe Bema/judgment seat of Christ; Cthe
Bema was a raised platform from which civic leaders made pronounce-
ments and rendered judgment]. [L...so that] Each of us will receive what
we should get—good or bad—for the things we did in the earthly body.

Becoming Friends with God

11[LTherefore] Since we know what it means to fear the Lord, we try to
persuade people [Ceither about the truth of the Gospel or about Paul's
good motives]. God knows what we really are, and I hope that in your
·hearts [consciences] you know, too. 12We are not trying to ·prove [com-
mend] ourselves to you again, but we are giving you a ·reason
[opportunity] to ·be proud of [boast about] us. Then you will have an
answer for those who ·are proud [boast] about ·things that can be seen
[outward appearance] rather than what is in the heart. 13If we are out of
our minds, it is for God. If we have our right minds, it is for you. 14[LFor]
The love of Christ ·controls [compels; drives] us, because we ·know [are
convinced; have concluded] that One died for all, so all have died [Cwe
died spiritually with Christ, the penalty for our sins]. 15Christ died for all
so that those who live would ·not continue to [no longer] live for themselves, but for him who died for them and was raised from the dead.
16[LSo; As a result] From ·this time [now] on we do not think of anyone
·as the world does [*or* from a merely human perspective; Laccording to the
flesh]. [LAlthough] In the past we thought of Christ ·as the world thinks
[*or* as nothing more than a man; Laccording to the flesh], but we no longer
think of him in that way. 17If anyone belongs to Christ, ·there is a new
creation [the new creation has arrived; *or* that person has become a new
creation]. The old things have gone; [Llook; Tbehold] ·everything is made
new [the new has come]! 18All this is from God, who through Christ ·made
peace between us and [reconciled us to] himself, and gave us the ·work of
telling everyone about the peace we can have with him [Lministry/service
of reconciliation]. 19[LFor] God was in Christ, ·making peace between the
world and [reconciling the world to] himself. In Christ, God did not ·hold
the world guilty of its sins [Lcount their trespasses against them]. And he
·gave [committed/entrusted to] us this message of ·peace [reconciliation].
20So we ·have been sent to speak [Lare ambassadors] for Christ. It is as if
God is ·calling to [urging; exhorting; encouraging] you through us. We
speak for Christ when we ·beg [implore; urge] you to be ·at peace with
[reconciled to] God. 21God made ·Christ [Lthe one] who ·had no sin [*or*
never sinned; Ldid not know sin] to become sin for us, so that in ·Christ
[Lhim] we could become ·right with [Lthe righteousness of] God.

6 We are working together [Cwith fellow believers, or with God, or
with Christ], so we ·beg [urge; appeal to; encourage] you: Do not
·let the grace that you received from God be for nothing [Lreceive God's
grace in vain]. 2[LFor] God says,

"At the ·right [favorable; acceptable] time I heard your prayers.
On the day of salvation I helped you [Is. 49:8]."

·I tell you that [TBehold; LLook] **the "·right** [favorable; acceptable] **time" is now, ·and** [Tbehold; Llook] **the "day of salvation" is now.**

3**We try not to ·be a problem** [cause offense; place an obstacle/stumbling block] **for anyone in any way, so that no one will find fault with our ·work** [ministry]. 4**But in every way ·we show we are servants of God** [*or* as God's servants/ministers, we commend ourselves]: **·in accepting many hard things** [in/with great endurance], **in ·troubles** [trials; tribulation], **in ·difficulties** [hardships; times of need], **·and in great problems** [in distress/calamities/Ltight spots]. 5**·We are beaten** [L...in beatings/floggings] **·and thrown into prison** [Lin imprisonments]. **·We meet those who become upset with us and start riots** [L...in riots/rebellions]. **·We work hard** [L...in hard labors], **·and sometimes we get no sleep** [L...in sleepless nights] **·or food** [L...in hunger]. 6**·We show we are servants of God by our pure lives** [L...in/by purity; CPaul continues the same list, but moves to positive character traits], **·our understanding** [L...in/by knowledge], **patience, and kindness, by the Holy Spirit, by ·true** [sincere; unhypocritical] **love,** 7**by ·speaking the truth** [*or* the message/word of truth; Cthe Gospel], **and by God's power. ·We use our right living** [L...with weapons of righteousness] **·to defend ourselves against everything** [*or* both to attack (with a sword) and defend (with a shield); Lin our right hands and in our left]. 8**·Some people honor us, but others blame us** [L...through honor/glory and dishonor/disgrace...]. **·Some people say evil things about us, but others say good things** [L...through slander and praise...]. **·Some people say we are liars, but we speak the truth** [L...(treated) as deceivers, yet true...]. 9**·We are not known, but we are well known** [L...as unknown, yet known...]. **·We seem to be dying, but we continue to live** [L...as dying, yet look/behold we live!]. **·We are punished** [L...as punished/scourged], **but we are not killed.** 10**·We have much sadness** [L...as sorrowful/grieving], **but we are always rejoicing. ·We are poor** [L...as poor], **but we are making many people ·rich in faith** [Lrich]. **·We have** [L...as having] **nothing, but really we have everything.**

11**We have spoken ·freely** [openly; frankly] **to you, ·Corinthian friends** [LCorinthians], **and have opened our hearts to you.** 12**·Our feelings of love for you have not stopped** [We have not withheld our affection from you; LYou are not constrained/held back by us], **but you have ·stopped your feelings of love** [Lconstrained/held back your affection] **for us.** 13**I speak to you ·as if you were** [Las] **my children. ·Do to us as we have done** [As a fair exchange]**—open your hearts to us** [v. 11].

Warning About Non-Christians

14**Do not ·join yourselves to** [become partners with; Lbe mismatched/unevenly yoked with] **unbelievers. ·Good and bad do not belong together** [LFor what partnership has righteousness and wickedness/lawlessness?]. **·Light and darkness cannot share together** [Or what fellowship/partnership can light have with darkness?]. 15**How can Christ and Belial** [Cthe devil; Satan] **have any ·agreement** [harmony; accord]**? What can a believer ·have together** [share in common] **with a nonbeliever?** 16**What ·agreement** [union] **can the temple of God have with idols? For we are the temple of the living God** [1 Cor. 3:16]. **As God said: "I will live with them and walk with them. And I will be their God, and they will be my people** [Lev. 26:11–12; Jer. 32:38; Ezek. 37:27]."

17"[LTherefore] **·Leave those people** [LCome out from their midst],
and be separate, says the Lord.

Touch nothing that is ·unclean [polluted, defiled],
and I will ·accept [receive; welcome] you [Is. 52:11; Ezek. 20:41]."
18"I will be your father,
and you will be my sons and daughters,
says the Lord Almighty [2 Sam. 7:14]."

7 [LTherefore] ·Dear friends [Beloved], we have these promises
from God, so we should make ourselves pure—free from ·any-
thing that makes body or soul unclean [Levery defilement of flesh and
spirit]. ·We should try to become holy in the way we live [*or* ...and in this
way bring our holiness to completion/perfection], ·because we respect
[out of reverence for; in the fear of] God.

Paul's Joy

2·Open your hearts to [LMake room for] us. We have not done wrong to
anyone, we have not ·ruined the faith of [Lruined; corrupted] anyone, and
we have not ·cheated [exploited] anyone. 3I do not say this to ·blame [con-
demn] you. [LFor] I told you before that ·we love you so much [Lyou are in
our hearts so that] we would live or die with you. 4I ·feel very sure of you
[am very confident in you; *or* have spoken very boldy/frankly to you] and
am very proud of you. You give me much ·comfort [encouragement], and
in all of our ·troubles [trials; tribulation] I ·have great [overflow with] joy.
5[LFor] When we came into Macedonia [1:16], ·we [our body/flesh] had
no rest [CHere Paul picks up his account where he left off at 2:13]. We
found ·trouble [trial; tribulation] all around us. We had ·fighting [battles;
conflicts] on the outside and fear on the inside. 6But God, who ·comforts
[encourages] those who are ·troubled [downcast; discouraged], ·com-
forted [encouraged] us when Titus [2:13] came. 7We were ·comforted
[encouraged], not only by his ·coming [arrival; presence] but also by the
comfort you gave him. Titus told us about your ·wish to see me [Llonging]
and ·that you are very sorry for what you did [Lyour sorrow/mourning;
Cregret for their treatment of Paul during his previous visit; 1:23; 2:1]. He
also told me about your great ·care [*or* loyalty; Lzeal] for me, and when I
heard this, I ·was much happier [rejoiced even more].
8[LFor] Even if my letter [CPaul's "severe" letter that he wrote after his
painful visit; see 2:3–4, 9] made you ·sad [grieve], I am not sorry I wrote
it. At first I was sorry, because it made you ·sad [grieve], but you ·were sad
[grieved] only for a short time. 9Now I ·am happy [rejoice], not because
you were ·made sad [grieved], but because your sorrow ·made you change
your lives [led to repentance]. You ·became sad [grieved] in the way God
wanted you to, so you were not ·hurt by [*or* punished because of] us in
any way [Cthe Corinthians' repentance prevented further sorrow as well as
discipline from God]. 10[LFor] The kind of sorrow God wants makes people ·change their hearts and lives [repent], leading to salvation, and ·you
cannot be sorry for that [*or* there can be no regret for that kind of sorrow;
Lwithout regret]. But the kind of sorrow the world has ·brings [leads to;
results in] death. 11[LFor] See what this sorrow—the sorrow God wanted
you to have—has ·done to [led to/produced in] you: It has made you very
·serious [eager; earnest; zealous]. It made you want to ·restore [vindicate;
defend] yourselves. It made you ·angry [indignant] and afraid. It made
you ·want to see me [long for reconciliation]. It made you ·care [zealous].
It made you want to ·do the right thing [see justice done]. In every way
you have ·regained your innocence [*or* proved yourselves innocent]. 12I
wrote that letter, not because of the one who did the wrong or because of

the person who was ·hurt [wronged]. I wrote the letter so you could see, before God, the great ·care [eagerness; zeal] you have for us. 13That is why we were ·comforted [encouraged].

Not only were we very ·comforted [encouraged], we ·were even happier [rejoiced even more] to see that Titus [2:13] was so ·happy [joyful], because all of you ·made him feel much better [Lrefreshed his spirit]. 14[LFor] I ·bragged [boasted] to Titus about you, and ·you showed that I was right [LI was not put to shame]. Everything we said to you was true, and you have proved that what we ·bragged [boasted] about to Titus is true. 15And his ·love [affection; feeling] for you is ·stronger [greater still] when he remembers that you were all ready to obey. You ·welcomed [received] him with ·respect and fear [Lfear and trembling]. 16I ·am very happy [rejoice] that I can ·trust you fully [have complete confidence in you].

Christian Giving

8 And now, brothers and sisters, we want you to know about the grace God gave the churches in Macedonia [1:16]. 2Although they have been tested by great ·troubles [trials; tribulation] ·and are very poor, they gave much because of their great joy [Ltheir deep poverty and abundant joy overflowed into rich generosity]. 3I can ·tell you [testify] that they gave as much as they were able and even more than they could afford. No one told them to do it. 4But they begged and pleaded with us ·to let them [Lfor the privilege/grace to] share in this service for ·God's people [Tthe saints]. 5And they gave in a way we did not expect: They first gave themselves to the Lord and to us. ·This is what God wants [...by the will of God]. 6So we ·asked [urged; encouraged] Titus [2:13] to help you finish this special work of grace since he is the one who started it. 7You ·are rich [excel] in everything—in faith, in speaking, in knowledge, in ·truly wanting to help [eagerness; zeal], and in the love ·you learned [Lthat is in you] from us.ⁿ In the same way, ·be strong [excel] also in the grace of giving.

8I am not commanding you to give. But I want to ·see [test; prove] if your love is true by comparing you with ·others that really want to help [Lthe zeal/eagerness of others]. 9[LFor] You know the ·grace [gift] of our Lord Jesus Christ. Though he was rich, for your sake he became poor so that by his becoming poor you might become rich.

10This is ·what I think you should do [Lmy opinion on this matter for your benefit]: Last year you were the first to want to give, and you were the first who gave. 11So now finish the work you started. Then your ·"doing" [Lcompletion] will be equal to your ·"wanting to do" [eager desire]. Give from what you have. 12If you ·want [are eager/willing] to give, your gift will be accepted. It will be judged by what you have, not by what you do not have. 13[LFor] We do not want you to have ·troubles [hardships; trials] while other people ·are at ease [have relief], but we want everything to be equal [Cgiving is not intended to impoverish the giver, but to distribute God's resources]. 14At this time ·you have plenty and what you have [Lyour abundance] can help others who are in need. ·Then later, when they have plenty, they [*or* In the same way, their abundance] can help you when you are in need, and all will be equal [CPaul may be saying, (1) that the Jerusalem church may one day reciprocate by helping the Corinthians financially; or, (2) that the Corinthians' *financial* gift will be reciprocated through Jerusalem's *spiritual* gifts]. 15As it is written in the Scriptures, "The person

8:7 in... us Some Greek copies read "in your love for us."

who gathered more did not have too much, nor did the person who gathered less have too little [Ex. 16:18]."

Titus and His Companions Help

16·I thank [[L]Thanks be to] God because he ·gave [[L]put into the heart of] Titus [2:13] the same ·love [[L]eagerness; zeal] for you that I have. 17[[L]For] Titus accepted what we asked him to do. He ·wanted very much [was eager] to go to you, and this was ·his own idea [of his own accord]. 18We are sending with him the brother who is praised by all the churches because of his service ·in preaching the Good News [[L]in the Gospel; [C]unknown person, possibly Luke]. 19Also, this brother was ·chosen [appointed] by the churches to go with us ·when we deliver this gift of money [*or* in this ministry/administration of grace]. We are doing this ·service [ministry] to bring glory to the Lord and to show ·that we really want [our eagerness/willingness] to help.

20We are being careful so that no one will ·criticize [blame] us for the way we are handling this ·large [abundant; generous] gift. 21[[L]For] We are trying hard to do what is right, not only before the Lord but also before people [Prov. 3:4].

22Also, we are sending with them our brother, who has proved to us in many ways that he is always ·ready [eager; zealous] to help. He wants to help even more now, because he has much ·faith [confidence] in you.

23·Now [*or* If there is any question] about Titus [2:13]—he is my partner ·who is working with me [and coworker] to help you. ·And [*or* If there is any question] about the other brothers—they are ·sent [messengers] from the churches, and ·they bring glory to [*or* they are the glory of] Christ. 24So show these men the proof of your love and the reason we ·are proud [boast] of you. ·Then [*or* ...so that] all the churches can see it.

Help for Fellow Christians

9 I really do not need to write you about this ·help [service; ministry] for ·God's people [[T]the saints]. 2[[L]For; Because] I know ·you want [your eagerness/willingness] to help. I have been ·bragging [boasting] about this to the ·believers in Macedonia [[L]Macedonians; 8:1], telling them that you in Achaia [[C]southern Greece; 1:1] have been ready to give since last year. And your ·desire to give [[L]zeal; enthusiasm] has ·made most of them ready to give also [[L]aroused/provoked the majority]. 3But I am sending the brothers to you so that our ·bragging [boasting] about you in this matter will not be empty words. I want you to be ready, as I said you would be. 4If any of the ·believers from Macedonia [[L]Macedonians] come with me and find that you are not ready, we will be ·ashamed [embarrassed; dishonored] that we were so sure of you. (And you will be ·ashamed [embarrassed; dishonored], too!) 5So I thought I should ·ask [urge; encourage] these brothers to go to you before we do. They will finish getting in order the ·generous gift [blessing] you promised so it will be ready when we come. And it will be a ·generous gift [blessing]—not one ·that you did not want to give [required from you; grudgingly given].

6Remember this: The person who ·plants a little [sows sparingly] will ·have a small harvest [also reap sparingly], but the person who ·plants a lot [sows generously/bountifully] will ·have a big harvest [also reap generously/bountifully]. 7Each of you should give as you have decided in your heart to give. You should not ·be sad when you give [*or* give reluctantly], and you should not give ·because you feel forced to give [out of compulsion]. [[L]For] God loves the person who gives ·happily [cheerfully]. 8And God can ·give you more blessings than you need [[L]overflow/abound all grace to you].

Then ·you will always have plenty of everything [Lin all things at all times you will have all you need]— **·enough to give to** [abounding/overflowing in] **every good work.** 9[LJust as] **It is written in the Scriptures:**

"**He ·gives** [Lscatters (seed) and gives] **freely to the poor.**
·The things he does are right and will continue forever [*or* His righteousness endures forever; Ps. 112:9]."

10[LFor] **God is the One who gives seed to the farmer and bread for food. He will ·give you all the seed you need and make it grow** [Lsupply and multiply your seed] **so there will be a great harvest ·from your goodness** [of your righteousness]. 11**He will make you rich in every way so that you can always give ·freely** [generously]. **And your giving through us will ·cause many to give thanks** [Lproduce thanksgiving] **to God.** 12**This ·service you do** [Lministry of service] **not only helps the needs of ·God's people** [Tthe saints], **it also brings many more thanks to God.** 13**It is a proof of your faith. Many people will ·praise** [glorify] **God because you ·obey** [submit to] **the ·Good News** [Gospel] **of Christ—the gospel you ·say you believe** [confess]**—and because you ·freely** [generously] **share with them and with all others.** 14**And when they pray for you, they will ·wish they could be with** [Llong for] **you because of the great grace that God has given you.** 15**Thanks be to God for his ·gift that is too wonderful for words** [indescribable/inexpressible gift].

Paul Defends His Ministry

10 **I, Paul, ·am begging** [urge; appeal to] **you with the gentleness and the kindness of Christ. ·Some people say that I am** [L…—I who am; CPaul is answering an accusation; see v. 10] **·easy on you** [lenient; *or* timid] **when I am with you and bold when I am away** [CPaul here confronts those still resisting his authority]. 2**I ·beg** [ask] **you that when I ·come** [am present] **I will not need to use that same boldness with you that I expect to use with those who ·think** [*or* claim] **we ·live** [walk] **·in a worldly way** [by the world's standards; Laccording to the flesh]. 3[LFor] **Although we ·live in the world** [Lwalk in the flesh], **we do not ·fight** [wage war] **·in the same way the world fights** [Laccording to the flesh]. 4**We fight with weapons that are ·different from those the world uses** [not merely human weapons; Lnot of the flesh]. **Our weapons have power from God that can destroy ·the enemy's strong places** [Lstrongholds; fortresses]. **We destroy ·people's arguments** [human reasoning; sophistries] 5**and every ·proud thing** [pretension; exalted opinion; Lhigh thing] **that raises itself against the knowledge of God. We capture every thought and make it obey Christ.** 6**We are ready to ·punish** [avenge] **·anyone there who does not obey** [Levery disobedience], **·but first we want you to obey fully** [Lonce/after your obedience is fulfilled; Conce the church as a whole repents, Paul will discipline those who refuse].

7**You ·must look at the facts before you** [*or* are looking only at outward appearances]. **If you ·feel sure** [are confident] **that you belong to Christ, you must ·remember** [consider again] **that we belong to Christ just as you do.** 8**·It is true that we brag freely** [LIf I boast too much…] **about the authority the Lord gave us. But this authority is to build you up, not to tear you down. So I will not be ashamed.** 9**I do not want you to think I am trying to scare you with my letters.** 10**Some people say** [v. 1], **"Paul's letters are ·powerful** [forceful] **and ·sound important** [weighty; *or* demanding], **but ·when he is with us, he** [his physical presence] **is weak. And his ·speaking is nothing** [speaking skills are deplorable; *or* speeches

are worthless; CGreek culture highly valued rhetorical skill]." 11They
should ·know [consider] this: ·The authority we show by letter [LWhat we
are in word] while we are ·away [absent], we will ·demonstrate in our
actions [Lbe in deed] when we ·come to you [Lare present].
12[LFor] We do not dare to classify or compare ourselves with those who
·think they are very important [commend/promote themselves; 3:1]. They
use themselves to measure themselves, and they judge themselves by what
they themselves are. ·This shows that they know nothing [*or* What ignorance!; *or* What fools!]. 13But we will not ·brag [boast] ·about things outside
the work that was given us to do [Lbeyond the limits]. We will limit our
·bragging [boasting] to the ·work [sphere of ministry] that God gave us,
·and this includes our work with you [Lwhich reaches even to you]. 14[LFor]
We are not ·bragging too much [*or* going beyond our commission;
Loverreaching/overextending ourselves], as we would be if we had not
already come to you. But we have come to you with the Good News of
Christ [CPaul's opponents claimed the Corinthians were their sphere of
ministry; Paul counters that he first brought the Gospel to Corinth (Acts
18)]. 15We limit our ·bragging [boasting] to the work that is ours, not what
others have done. We hope that as your faith continues to grow, ·the scope
of our work among you will greatly increase [*or* our work among you will
greatly increase within the sphere/limits God has given us]. 16·We want to
[L…so that we may] ·tell the Good News [preach the Gospel] in the areas
beyond ·your city [Lyou]. We do not want to ·brag [boast] about work that
has already been done in another person's area. 17But, "·If people want to
brag, they should brag only [LLet the one who boasts, boast] about the
Lord [Jer. 9:24; 1 Cor. 1:31]." 18[LFor] It is not those who ·say they are good
[Lcommend/promote themselves; v. 12] who are ·accepted [approved] but
those the Lord ·thinks are good [commends].

Paul and the False Apostles

11 I wish you would be patient with me even ·when I am a little
foolish [in a little foolishness], but you are already doing that.
2[LFor] I am jealous over you with a ·jealousy that comes from God [*or*
godly jealousy]. I promised to give you to Christ, as your only husband. I
want to give you as his pure ·bride [Lvirgin]. 3But I am afraid that your
minds will be ·led away [*or* corrupted] from your ·true [sincere] and pure
following of Christ just as Eve was ·tricked [deceived] by the ·snake [ser-
pent] with his ·evil ways [cunning; craftiness; Gen. 3:1–6]. 4You ·are very
patient with [willingly put up with; gladly tolerate] anyone who comes to
you and preaches a different Jesus from the one we preached. You are very
willing to accept a spirit that is different from the Spirit you received, or a
gospel that is different from the one you ·accepted [*or* received from us].
5I do not think that those "·great [super-] apostles" are any better than
I am. 6I may not be a trained speaker, but I do have knowledge. We have
shown this to you clearly in every way.
7Was it ·wrong [a sin] for me to ·humble [lower] myself and ·honor
[exalt; lift up] you by preaching God's ·Good News [Gospel] to you without pay? 8I accepted pay from other churches, ·taking their money
[L"robbing" them] so I could serve you. 9If I needed something when I
was with you, I did not ·trouble [burden] any of you. The brothers who
came from Macedonia gave me all that I needed. I did not allow myself to
·depend on [become a burden to] you in any way, and I will ·never depend
on you [Lkeep doing this]. 10No one in Achaia [Csouthern Greece; 1:1] will

stop me from ·bragging [boasting] about that. ·I say this with the truth of Christ in me [or By Christ's truth in me! Ca strong vow or oath]. 11·And why do I not depend on you [LWhy]? Do you think it is because I do not love you? ·God knows that I love you [LGod knows!].

12And I will continue doing what I am doing now, because I want to stop those people from having a reason to ·brag [boast]. They ·would like [are looking for an opportunity] to say that the work they ·brag [boast] about is ·the same as [equal to] ours. 13Such men are ·not true apostles [false apostles; pseudo-apostles] but are ·workers who lie [deceitful workers]. ·They change themselves to look like [...disguising themselves as; ...masquerading as] apostles of Christ. 14·This does not surprise us [And no wonder, since...]. Even Satan ·changes himself to look like [disguises himself as; masquerades as] an ·angel [messenger] of light [Ctrying to fool people into thinking he is from God, who is pure light]. 15So it does not surprise us if Satan's servants also ·make themselves look like [masquerade as] servants ·who work for what is right [of righteousness]. But ·in the end they will be punished for what they do [Ltheir end will match their deeds].

Paul Tells About His Sufferings

16I tell you again: No one should think I am a fool. But if you think so, accept me as you would accept a fool. Then I can ·brag [boast] a little, too. 17·When I brag because I feel sure of myself [By boasting so confidently], I am not talking ·as the Lord would talk [or with the Lord's authority; Laccording to the Lord] but as a fool. 18Many people are ·bragging [boasting] ·about their lives in the world [or as the world does; or by human standards; Laccording to the flesh]. So I will ·brag [boast] too. 19You are wise, so you will gladly be patient with fools! [CPaul sarcastically suggests that the "wise" Corinthians, who listened to the false apostles, would surely listen to his "foolishness."] 20You ·are even patient [bear; put up] with those who ·order you around [Lenslave you], or ·use you [exploit you; Ldevour (your possessions)], or ·trick [take advantage of] you, or ·think they are better than you [act arrogantly; put on airs], or ·hit [slap] you in the face. 21It is shameful to me to say this, but we were too "weak" to do those things to you!

But if anyone else ·is brave enough [dares] to ·brag [boast], then I also will ·be brave and brag [dare to boast]. (I am talking as a fool.) 22Are they Hebrews? So am I. Are they Israelites? So am I. Are they from Abraham's ·family [descendants; Lseed]? So am I. 23Are they servants of Christ? I am serving him more. (I am crazy to talk like this.) I have worked much harder than they. I have been in prison more often [Acts 16:23–40]. I have been ·hurt more in beatings [flogged more severely; Acts 16:22]. I have been near death many times. 24Five times the Jews have given me ·their punishment of thirty-nine lashes with a whip [Lforty minus one; Ca shorthand phrase for the standard Jewish punishment; Deut. 25:1–3 allowed a maximum of forty lashes; the Jews gave thirty-nine to avoid breaking the law]. 25Three different times I was beaten with rods [Ca Roman punishment]. One time I was almost stoned to death [Acts 14:19]. Three times I was in ships that wrecked, and one of those times I spent a night and a day in the sea [CPaul's shipwreck in Acts 27 occurred after writing this (c. AD 60), so he experienced at least four shipwrecks]. 26I have gone on many travels and have been in danger from rivers, from ·thieves [bandits], from my own people [Cthe Jews], and from the Gentiles. I have been in danger in cities, in ·places where no one lives [the desert/wilderness], and on the sea. And I have been in danger with false ·Christians [Lbrothers]. 27I have

done hard and tiring work, and many times I did not sleep. I have been
hungry and thirsty, and many times I have been without food. I have been
cold and ·without clothes [*or* destitute; Lnaked]. 28Besides all this, there is
on me every day the ·load [pressure] of my ·concern [anxiety] for all the
churches. 29I feel weak every time someone is weak [LWho is weak, and I
am not weak?], and ·I feel upset every time someone is led into sin [LWho
is led into sin, and I am not indignant/Lburning (with anger)?].

30If I must ·brag [boast], I will ·brag [boast] about the things that show
I am weak. 31The God and Father of the Lord Jesus Christ, who is to be
praised forever, knows I am not lying. 32When I was in Damascus, the
·governor [Lethnarch; Ca title for a minor ruler] under King Aretas wanted
to arrest me, so he put guards around the city. 33But ·my friends lowered
me [LI was lowered] in a basket through ·a hole [*or* window] in the city
wall. So I escaped from ·the governor [Lhis hands].

A Special Blessing in Paul's Life

12 I must continue to ·brag [boast]. It will do no good, but I will
talk now about visions and revelations from the Lord. 2I
know a man in Christ [Ca believer] who was ·taken up [caught up;
snatched away] to the third heaven [Cthe presence of God] fourteen years
ago [CPaul is indirectly referring to himself]. I do not know whether the
man was in his body or out of his body, but God knows. 3-4And I know
that this man was ·taken up [caught up; snatched away] to paradise
[Canother name for heaven; Luke 23:43; Rev. 2:7]. I don't know if he was
in his body or away from his body, but God knows. He heard things ·he
is not able to explain [inexpressible; ineffable], things that no human is
allowed to tell. 5I will ·brag [boast] about a man like that, but I will not
·brag [boast] about myself, except about my weaknesses. 6But if I wanted
to ·brag [boast] about myself, I would not be a fool, because I would be
telling the truth. But I will ·not brag about myself [spare you; refrain
from this] because I do not want people to think more of me than what
they see me do or hear me ·say [*or* say, or because of these extraordinary
revelations; Cthis phrase may go here or with the next sentence].

7So that I would not become too proud ·of the wonderful things that
were shown to me [*or* because of these extraordinary revelations; Cthis
phrase may be part of the previous sentence], a ·painful physical problem
[Lthorn in the flesh] was given to me. This problem was a messenger from
Satan, sent to ·beat [torment; harrass; trouble] me and keep me from being
too proud. 8I ·begged [pleaded with] the Lord three times ·to take this
problem away from [Lthat it might leave] me. 9But he said to me, "My grace
is ·enough for you [sufficient for you; all you need]. ·When you are weak,
my power is made perfect in you [LFor (my) power is perfected in weak-
ness]." So I am very happy to ·brag [boast] about my weaknesses. Then
Christ's power can ·live [reside; *or* rest] in me. 10For this reason I am ·happy
[pleased; content] when I have weaknesses, insults, ·hard times [times of
need], ·sufferings [persecutions], and ·all kinds of troubles [distress] ·for
[for the sake of] Christ. Because when I am weak, then I am truly strong.

Paul's Love for the Christians

11I have ·been talking like [Lbecome] a fool, but you ·made me [com-
pelled me to] do it. You are the ones who should ·say good things about
[have commended] me. Even if I am ·worth nothing [Lnothing], I am not
at all inferior to those "·great [super-] apostles."

12·When I was with you, I patiently did the things that prove I am an
apostle [LThe signs of an apostle were performed among you, with all

patience/perseverance]—signs, wonders, and ·miracles [powerful deeds].
13In what way were you treated worse than the rest of the churches, except
that I was not a burden to you? Forgive me for this ·wrong [injustice]!
14[TBehold; LLook] I am now ready to visit you the third time [2:1, 3],
and I will not be a burden to you. I want nothing from you, except you.
[LFor] Children should not have to save up to give to their parents.
[LRather,] Parents should save to give to their children. 15So I ·am happy
to [most gladly] ·give everything I have for you, even myself [Lspend and
be spent for your lives/souls]. If I love you more, will you love me less?
16·It is clear [Granting that; *or* Be that as it may] I was not a burden to
you, but ·you think I was tricky and lied to catch you [Lbeing so crafty, I
took you by deceit!; CPaul is being sarcastic]. 17Did I ·cheat [take advantage
of] you by using any of the messengers I sent to you? [CThe Greek question assumes a negative answer.] 18I ·asked [urged; encouraged] Titus
[2:13] to go to you, and I sent our brother with him [8:18, 22]. Titus did
not cheat you, did he? ·No, you know that Titus and I did the same thing
[LDid we not walk in the same footsteps…?] and with the same spirit.
19·Do you think we have been defending ourselves to you all this time
[*or* All this time have you been thinking that we are defending ourselves to
you]? We have been speaking in Christ and ·before [in the presence of]
God, ·dear friends [beloved], and everything we do is to ·make you stronger [build you up]. 20[LFor] I am afraid that when I come, you will not be
what I want you to be, and I will not be what you want me to be. I am
afraid that among you there may be ·arguing [quarreling], jealousy, anger,
selfish ·fighting [*or* ambition], ·evil talk [slander], gossip, ·pride [arro-
gance], and ·confusion [disorder]. 21I am afraid that when I come to you
again, my God will ·make me ashamed [*or* humble/humiliate me] before
you. I may ·be saddened by [*or* mourn/grieve over] many of those who
have sinned because they have not ·changed their hearts or turned
[repented] from their ·impurity [uncleanness], sexual sins and the
·shameful things [debauchery; licentiousness] they have done.

Final Warnings and Greetings

13 I will come to you for the third time [2:1, 3; 12:14]. "Every
·case [accusation; matter] must be ·proved [established] by
two or three witnesses [Deut. 19:15]." 2When I was with you the second
time [2:1–2], I gave a warning to those who had sinned. Now I am away
from you, and I give a warning to all the others. When I come to you
again, I will not ·be easy with [spare] them. 3·You want [*or* …since you
are demanding] proof that Christ is speaking through me. My proof is
that he is not weak among you, but he is powerful. 4It is true that he was
weak when he was ·killed on the cross [crucified], but he lives now by
God's power. It is true that we are weak in Christ, but ·for you [*or* when
dealing with you; *or* in your presence] we will be alive with Christ by
God's power [CChrist's resurrection turns weakness into strength].
5·Test [Examine] yourselves to see if you are ·living in [Lin] the faith.
·Look closely at [Test; Examine] yourselves. ·You [LOr don't you…?] know
that Jesus Christ is in you—·unless [*or* if not,] you fail the test. 6But I
hope you will see that we ourselves have not failed the test. 7We pray to
God that you will not do anything ·wrong [evil]. It is not important ·to
see [that people see; *or* for it to appear] that we have passed the test, but it
is important that you do what is ·right [good], even if it seems we have
failed. 8[LFor] We cannot do anything against the truth, but only for the

truth. 9We ·**are happy to be** [rejoice whenever we are] **weak, if you are**
strong, and we pray that you will become ·**complete** [mature; *or* fully
equipped/restored]. **10I am writing this while I am away from you so that**
when I come I will not have to be ·**harsh** [severe] **in my use of authority.**
The Lord gave me this authority to build you up, not to tear you down.

11·**Now** [Finally], **brothers and sisters,** ·**I say good-bye** [*or* be joyful;
Lrejoice; Ca common greeting and farewell]. ·**Live in harmony** [Seek restoration; *or* Mend your ways]. ·**Do what I have asked you to do** [Follow my
exhortation; *or* Encourage/Exhort one another]. ·**Agree with each other** [Live
in unity], **and live in peace. Then the God of love and peace will be with you.**

12Greet each other with a holy kiss. 13All ·**of God's holy people** [Tthe
saints] **send greetings to you.**

14The grace of the Lord Jesus Christ, the love of God, and the fellow-
ship of the Holy Spirit be with you all.

GALATIANS

1 From Paul, an ·apostle [messenger]. ·I was not chosen to be an apostle by human beings, nor was I sent from human beings [L...not from men/humans or by a man/human authority]. ·I was made an apostle [L...but] through Jesus Christ and God the Father who raised Jesus from the dead. [2]This letter is also from all ·those of God's family [Lthe brothers (and sisters)] who are with me.

To the churches in Galatia [Ca Roman province in present-day central Turkey; Paul started churches in Galatia on his first missionary journey (Acts 13–14)]:

[3]Grace and peace to you from God our Father and the Lord Jesus Christ, [4]who gave himself for our sins to ·free [rescue; deliver] us from this ·evil world we live in [present evil age], as God the Father ·planned [willed; desired]. [5]·The glory belongs to God [L...to whom be glory] forever and ever. Amen.

The Only Good News

[6]I am amazed that you are so quickly ·turning away from [deserting; forsaking] ·God [Lthe one] who called you by ·his grace given through Christ [Lthe grace of Christ], and are believing ·something different than the Good News [La different Gospel]. [7]·Really, there is no other Good News [L...which is not another]. But some people are ·confusing [troubling; disturbing] you; they want to ·change [distort] the ·Good News [Gospel] of Christ. [8]But even if we ourselves or an angel from heaven were to preach to you a different message than the Good News we preached, ·we should be [Llet him be] ·judged guilty [condemned; accursed; Lanathema]! [9]I said this before, and now I say it again: If anyone is preaching a different message than the one you received, ·that person should be [Llet him be] ·judged guilty [condemned; accursed; Lanathema]!

[10]Do you think I am now trying to ·make people accept me [seek human favor/acceptance]? ·No, God is the One I am trying to please [L...or (the favor of) God?]. Am I trying to please people? If I still wanted to please people, I would not be a ·servant [slave; bondservant] of Christ.

Paul's Authority Is from God

[11]Brothers and sisters, I want you to know that the ·Good News [Gospel] I preached to you was not ·made up by human beings [devised by man; of human origin]. [12]I did not get it from ·humans [a human source; man], nor did anyone teach it to me, but ·Jesus Christ showed it to me [Lby a revelation of/from/about Jesus Christ; Acts 9].

[13][LFor] You have heard about my past life in the Jewish religion. I ·attacked [intensely/severely persecuted] the church of God and tried to destroy it. [14]I was ·becoming a leader in the Jewish religion [Ladvancing/progressing in Judaism], doing better than most other Jews of my age. I

·tried harder than anyone else [was exceedingly zealous] to follow the ·teachings handed down by our [traditions of my] ·ancestors [forefathers].

15 But God ·set me apart [*or* chose/appointed me] for his work ·even before I was born [Lfrom my mother's womb]. He called me through his grace 16 and ·showed [revealed] his son to me so that I might ·tell the Good News [preach the Gospel] about him to the Gentiles [Acts 9:15; 22:21]. When God called me, I did not ·get advice or help from [confer/consult with] ·any person [Lflesh and blood]. 17 I did not go up to Jerusalem to see those who were apostles before I was. ·But [Instead; Rather] I went away to Arabia [Cprobably the Nabatean kingdom south of Damascus] and later went back to Damascus.

18 Then after three years I went up to Jerusalem to ·meet [get to know; *or* confer with; gain information from] ·Peter [LCephas, Peter's name in Aramaic; John 1:42] and stayed with him for fifteen days. 19 I ·met [*or* saw] no other apostles, except James [Acts 12:17; 15:13–21; 21:18; James 1:1], the brother of the Lord. 20 ·God knows that [*or* I swear before God that; LBefore God,] these things I write are not lies. 21 Later, I went to the areas of Syria [Ca Roman province north of Israel] and Cilicia [Ca Roman province in present-day southeastern Turkey; Paul's hometown Tarsus was in Cilicia].

22 In Judea the churches in Christ had never met me. 23 They had only heard it said, "This man who was ·attacking [persecuting] us is now preaching the same faith that he once tried to destroy." 24 And these believers ·praised [glorified] God because of me.

Other Apostles Accepted Paul

2 [LThen] After fourteen years I went to Jerusalem again, this time with Barnabas [Acts 4:36; 9:26–27; 11:22, 25, 30; 13:2–4; 15:36–39]. I also took Titus [2 Cor. 2:13; Titus 1:4–5] with me. 2 I went because ·God showed me I should go [Lof a revelation]. There I met in private with ·the leaders of the church [*or* those who seemed to be leaders; *or* the prominent/influential ones] and I ·told [presented to; set before] them the ·Good News [Gospel] that I preach to the Gentiles. ·I did not want my past work and the work I am now doing to be wasted [L…to make sure I was not running or had run in vain]. 3 Titus was with me, but he was not ·forced [compelled] to be circumcised [Gen. 17], even though he was a Greek. 4 ·We talked about this problem [This issue arose] because some false ·believers [Lbrothers] had come into our group secretly. They came in ·like spies to overturn [to sabotage; Lto spy on] the freedom we have in Christ Jesus. They wanted to make us slaves. 5 But we did not give in to ·those false believers [Lthem] for a minute, so that the truth of the ·Good News [Gospel] would ·continue [be preserved; not be compromised] for you.

6 Those leaders who ·seemed to be important [*or* were prominent/influential] did not ·change the Good News that I preach [*or* add anything to my message]. (It doesn't matter to me if they were ·"important" [prominent; influential] or not. To God everyone is the same.) 7 But these leaders saw that I had been ·given the work of telling the Good News [Lentrusted with the Gospel] to the ·Gentiles [non-Jewish people; Luncircumcised], just as Peter ·had the work of telling the Jews [Lto the circumcised]. 8 [LFor] ·God [LThe one] who gave Peter the power to work as an apostle for the ·Jewish people [Lcircumcised] also gave me the power to work as an apostle for the Gentiles. 9 James, Peter, and John, who seemed to be ·the leaders [Lpillars], ·understood [recognized; acknowledged] that God had given me this special grace, so they ·accepted [shook hands in partnership with;

[Lgave the right hand of fellowship/partnership to] **Barnabas and me. They**
agreed that we should go to the Gentiles and they would go to the ·Jewish
people [Lcircumcised]. **10 The only thing they asked us was to remember to**
help the poor [Cmeaning especially the poor believers in Jerusalem; Acts
11:27–30]**—something I ·really wanted** [myself was eager/zealous] **to do.**

Paul Shows that Peter Was Wrong

11 [LBut] **When ·Peter** [LCephas; CPeter's name in Aramaic; 1:18] **came to**
Antioch, I challenged him to his face, because he ·was wrong [Lstood con-
demned]. 12 [LFor; Because] **·Peter** [LHe] **ate with the Gentiles until ·some**
Jewish people [Lcertain people] **sent from James** [1:19] **came to Antioch**
[Ca major city in Syria]. **When they arrived, Peter ·stopped eating with**
those who weren't Jewish [Lbacked off; withdrew], **and he separated him-**
self from them. [...because] **He was afraid of the ·Jews** [circumcised; *or*
the pro-circumcision group]. **13 Then the rest of the ·Jewish believers**
[LJews] **joined him in this hypocrisy. Even Barnabas was ·influenced**
[swept along; carried away] **by their hypocrisy.** 14 [LBut] **When I saw they**
were not ·following [acting in line with] **the truth of the ·Good News**
[Gospel], **I spoke to ·Peter** [LCephas; v. 11] **in front of them all. I said, "You**
are a Jew, but you are living like a Gentile and not a Jew. So how can you
now try to force Gentiles to live like Jews?"
15 We were not born as Gentile "sinners," but as Jews. 16 Yet we know that
a person is ·made right with God [justified; declared righteous] **not by**
·following [Lthe works of] **the law, but by ·trusting in** [faith in; *or* the
faithfulness of] **Jesus Christ. So we, too, have put our faith in Christ Jesus,**
that we might be ·made right with God [justified; declared righteous]
·because we trusted in [through faith in; *or* because of the faithfulness of]
Christ. It is not ·because we followed [Lby the works of] **the law, because**
no ·one [human being; Lflesh] **can be ·made right with God** [justified;
declared righteous] **by ·following** [Lthe works of] **the law.**
17 ·We Jews came to Christ, trying to be made right with God, and it
became clear that we are sinners, too [*or* But if we ourselves, also, by seeking to be justified in Christ, were found to be sinners...]. **Does this mean**
that Christ ·encourages [Lis a servant/minister of] **sin? ·No** [Absolutely
not; May it never be]**! 18 But I would ·really be wrong** [*or* prove myself to
be a lawbreaker/sinner] **·to begin teaching again those things that I gave**
up [Lif I rebuild those things I tore down; Cdependance on the law for sal-
vation]. **19 ·It was the law that put me to death** [*or* Trying to keep the law
condemned me to death; LFor through the law I died to the law], **and I**
died to the law so that I can now live for God [Cno longer depending on
the law for salvation, Paul now depends on God's grace]. **20 I ·was put to**
death on the cross [Lhave been crucified] **with Christ, and I do not live**
anymore—it is Christ who lives in me. I still live in my ·body [flesh], **but**
I live ·by faith in [*or* because of the faithfulness of] **the Son of God who**
loved me and gave himself ·to save me [Lfor me; on my behalf]. **21 By say-**
ing these things I ·am not going against [Ldo not set aside/nullify] **God's**
grace. ·Just the opposite [LFor...], **if the law could make us right with**
God, then Christ's death would be ·useless [in vain; for nothing].

Blessing Comes Through Faith

3 ·You [LO] **·foolish** [stupid] **Galatians! Who has ·tricked** [*or* cast a
spell on; bewitched] **you? ·You were told very clearly about the**
death of Jesus Christ on the cross [LBefore your eyes Jesus Christ was publicly portrayed/announced as crucified]. **2 Tell me this one thing: How did**
you receive the Holy Spirit? Did you receive the Spirit by ·following [Lthe

works of] the law? ·No, you received the Spirit [L...or] ·because you heard
the Good News and believed it [by believing what you heard]. 3·Are you so
foolish [How can you be so stupid]? You began ·your life in Christ by [Lby;
or through] the Spirit. Now are you trying to ·make it complete [finish; *or*
be perfected] by ·your own power [human effort; Lthe flesh]? 4·Were all your
experiences wasted [*or* Have you suffered so much for nothing]? ·I hope not
[*or* Surely it was not for nothing; L—if indeed for nothing]! 5Does God give
you the Spirit and work miracles among you ·because you follow [Lby the
works of] the law? ·No, he does these things [L...or] ·because you heard the
Good News and believed it [by your believing what you heard; v. 2].

6·The Scriptures say the same thing about Abraham [LJust as (it says)]:
"Abraham believed God, and ·God accepted Abraham's faith, and that faith
made him right with God [Lit (Abraham's faith) was credited to him as righteousness; Gen. 15:6; Rom. 4]." 7So you should know that the true children
of Abraham are those who have faith. 8·The Scriptures, telling what would
happen in the future, said [LScripture foresaw; CScripture is personified as
foreseeing and speaking] that God would ·make the Gentiles right [justify
the Gentiles] through their faith. This ·Good News was told [Gospel was
proclaimed] to Abraham beforehand, as the Scripture says: "All nations will
be blessed through you [Gen. 12:3; 18:18]." 9So all who ·believe as Abraham
believed [rely on faith; have faith; Lare of faith] are blessed ·just as Abraham
was [Lwith faithful Abraham; *or* with Abraham, the man of faith]. 10·But
[LFor] those who depend on ·following [Lthe works of] the law to make
them right are under a curse, because the Scriptures say, "·Anyone [All;
Everyone] will be cursed who does not ·always obey what [keep doing
everything that] is written in the Book of the Law [Deut. 27:26]." 11Now it is
clear that no one can be ·made right with [justified/declared righteous
before] God by the law, because the Scriptures say, "·Those who are right
with God will live by faith [The righteous will live by faith; *or* Those made
righteous by faith will live; Gen. 15:6; Hab. 2:4]." 12The law is not based on
faith. ·It says [LRather; On the contrary], "A person who ·obeys [does; prac-
tices] these things will ·live because of [gain life by/in] them [Lev. 18:5]."
13Christ ·took away [redeemed us from; bought our freedom from] the
curse ·the law put on us [Lof the law]. ·He changed places with us and put
himself under that curse [L...by becoming a curse for us]. [LFor; Because] It
is written in the Scriptures, "Anyone ·whose body is displayed [Lwho is
hung] on a tree is cursed [Deut. 21:23; Can executed man's body was hung
on a stake or tree for humiliation and warning; Paul here applies it to Christ's
crucifixion as the curse/judgment for our sin]." 14Christ did this so that
God's blessing promised to Abraham [Gen. 12:2–3] might come through
Jesus Christ to the Gentiles. ·Jesus died so that by our believing [...so that
by faith] we could receive the Spirit that God promised.

The Law and the Promise

15Brothers and sisters, let us think ·in human terms [*or* of an example
from everyday life; Laccording to man]: Even in the case of a human
·agreement [covenant; *or* will and testament], after it has been ·accepted
[ratified; put into affect] no one can ·set it aside [annul it] or add anything
to it. 16God made promises both to Abraham and to his ·descendant
[seed]. God did not say, "and to your ·descendants [seeds]." That would
mean many people. But God said, "and to your ·descendant [seed; Gen.
12:7; 13:15; 17:7; 24:7]." That means only one person; that person is
Christ. 17This is what I mean: The law, which came four hundred thirty

years later, cannot ·change [cancel; nullify] that ·agreement [covenant] previously made by God and so ·destroy [nullify; render invalid] God's promise to Abraham. 18If the law could give us ·Abraham's blessing [Lthe inheritance], then ·the promise would not be necessary [*or* it is not based on a promise]. But that is not possible, because God freely gave ·his blessings [Lit] to Abraham through the promise he had made.

19So what was the law for? It was ·given to show that the wrong things people do are against God's will [Ladded because of transgressions]. And it continued until the ·special descendant [seed], who had been promised, came. The law was given through angels [Acts 7:53; Heb. 2:2] ·who used Moses for a mediator to give the law to people [Lby the hand of a mediator/intermediary]. 20But a mediator is not needed when there is only one side, and God is only one.

The Purpose of the Law of Moses

21Does this mean that the law is against God's promises? ·Never [Absoluely not; May it never be]! That would be true only if the law could make us ·right with God [righteous]. But God did not give a law that can bring life. 22Instead, the Scriptures ·showed that the whole world is bound by sin [Limprisoned all things under (the power of) sin; CScripture is personified as the jailer]. This was so the promise would be given ·through faith to people who believe in Jesus Christ [*or* because of Christ's faithfulness, to all who believe].

23Before this faith came, we were all held prisoners by the law. We ·had no freedom [were locked up] until ·God showed us the way of faith that was coming [Lthe coming faith would be revealed]. 24In other words, the law was our ·guardian [child-minder; tutor; Can attendant slave who watched over a child in a wealthy Greco-Roman household] ·leading us to [*or* until] Christ so that we could be ·made right with God [declared righteous; justified] through faith. 25Now ·the way of faith [Lfaith] has come, and we no longer live under a ·guardian [child-minder; tutor; v. 24].

26[LFor] ·You are all children of God through faith in Christ Jesus [*or* In Christ Jesus you are all children/sons of God through faith]. 27[LFor] All of you who were baptized into Christ have clothed yourselves with Christ. 28In Christ, there is ·no difference between Jew and Greek [Lneither Jew nor Greek], slave and free person, male and female. You are all ·the same [*or* united; Lone] in Christ Jesus. 29·You [LIf you…] belong to Christ, so you are Abraham's ·descendants [seed]. ·You will inherit all of God's blessings because of the promise God made to Abraham [L…heirs according to the promise].

4 ·I want to tell you this [*or* This is what I mean; LI am saying]: While those who will inherit their fathers' property are still children, they are no different from slaves. It does not matter that the children ·own everything [*or* are masters/lords over the whole estate]. 2They must obey ·those chosen to care for them [Ltheir guardians and administrators/trustees] until the time set by their father. 3It is the same for us. We were once like children, slaves to the ·useless rules [*or* spiritual forces; *or* elementary principles/powers] of this world. 4But when the ·right [appropriate; *or* appointed; Lfullness of] time came, God sent his Son who was born of a woman and ·lived [Lborn] under the law. 5God did this so he could ·buy freedom for [redeem] those who were under the law and so we could ·become his children [*or* receive adoption as heirs; Ca Roman legal term for adopting an heir to carry on one's name].

6Since you are God's ·children [*or* sons], God sent the Spirit of his Son into your hearts, and the Spirit cries out, "Abba [CAramaic for "Father," a term of intimacy], Father." 7So you are no longer a slave; you are God's ·child [or son], and ·because you are his child, God will give you the blessing he promised [Lif a son/child, then also an heir through God].

Paul's Love for the Christians

8In the past you did not know God. You were slaves to gods that were not real. 9But now you know the true God. Really, it is God who knows you. So ·why do [Lhow can] you turn back to those weak and ·useless [bankrupt; Lpoor] ·rules [or spiritual forces; or elementary principles/powers; v. 3] you followed before? Do you want to be slaves to those things again? 10You still ·follow teachings about [are observing/keeping] special days, months, seasons, and years [Cprobably Jewish Sabbaths and festivals, which Paul's opponents claimed must be observed to be saved]. 11I am afraid for you, that my work for you has been wasted.

12Brothers and sisters, I became like you [Cliving like a Gentile to win them to Christ; 1 Cor. 9:21], so I beg you to become like me [Cdepending on God's grace, not the Jewish law, for salvation]. You ·were very good to me before [Ldid me no wrong]. 13You remember that it was because of an illness that I came to you the first time, preaching the ·Good News [Gospel]. 14Though my sickness was a ·trouble for you [trial for you; or test of your concern], you did not ·hate [despise] me or ·make me leave [reject me]. Instead, you welcomed me as an angel from God, as if I were Christ Jesus himself! 15But where is that ·joy [happiness; blessedness] you had then? I am ready to testify that you would have taken out your eyes and given them to me if that were possible. 16Now am I your enemy because I tell you the truth?

17Those people [Cthe false teachers; 1:7] ·are working hard to persuade you [or show great interest in you; or are eager to win your favor; Lare zealous for you], but ·this is not good for you [for no good purpose; or their intentions are not good]. They want to persuade you to ·turn against [reject; exclude] us and ·follow only [care only for; Lbe zealous for] them. 18It is good ·for people to show interest in you [or to be passionate/enthusiastic; Lto be zealous/the object of zeal], but only if their ·purpose [intention] is good. This is always true, not just when I am with you. 19My little children, again I feel the pain of childbirth for you until ·you truly become like Christ [LChrist is formed in you]. 20I wish I could be with you now and could change ·the way I am talking to you [or my tone of voice; Lmy voice], because I ·do not know what to think about [or don't know how to help; or am perplexed/at wit's end about] you.

The Example of Hagar and Sarah

21Some of you still want to be under the law. Tell me, do you know what the law says? 22[LFor] The Scriptures say that Abraham had two sons. The mother of one son was a slave woman, and the mother of the other son was a free woman. 23Abraham's son from the slave woman was born ·in the normal human way [or through human effort/plan; Laccording to the flesh; CIshmael; Gen. 16]. But the son from the free woman was born ·because of the promise God made to Abraham [Lthrough the promise; CIsaac; Gen. 17; 21].

24This story ·teaches something else [or may be read allegorically/figuratively/as an illustration]: The two women are ·like the two agreements between God and his people [Ltwo covenants]. One is ·the law that God made on Mount Sinai [Lfrom Mount Sinai; Cthe mountain in Arabia where God delivered his law to Israel through Moses; Ex. 19–31], ·and the people who are under this agreement are like slaves [L…bearing children for slavery].

·The mother named Hagar is like that agreement [LThis is Hagar]. 25She is
like Mount Sinai in Arabia and ·is a picture of [corresponds to; represents]
the ·earthly city of [Lpresent] Jerusalem. This city and ·its people [Lher chil-
dren] are ·slaves to the law [Lslaves]. 26But the ·heavenly Jerusalem, which is
above [LJerusalem above], is like the free woman. She is our mother. 27[LFor]
It is written in the Scriptures:

"·Be happy [Rejoice], barren one [CJerusalem].
You are like a woman who never gave birth to children.
·Start singing [Burst out] and ·shout for joy [cry out].
You never ·felt the pain of giving birth [*or* went into labor],
but you who are ·childless [Ldesolate; *or* deserted] will have more children
than the woman who has a husband [Is. 54:1]."

28My brothers and sisters, you are ·God's children because of his promise [Lchildren of the promise], as Isaac was then. 29[LFor just as] The son
who was born ·in the normal way [*or* through human effort/plan;
Laccording to the flesh] treated the other son badly. It is the same today
[Ca reference to Jewish persecution of Christians]. 30But what does the
Scripture say? "Throw out the slave woman and her son. The son of the
slave woman will not share in the inheritance with the son of the free
woman [Gen. 21:10]." 31So, my brothers and sisters, we are not children of
the slave woman, but of the free woman.

Keep Your Freedom

5 Christ set us free ·so that we could live in freedom [to a place of
freedom; *or* by means of freedom; 4:31]. So stand strong. Do not
·change and go back into the slavery of the law [Lsubmit/be fastened to a
yoke of slavery]. 2Listen, I Paul tell you that if you ·go back to the law by
being [Llet yourself be] circumcised, Christ does you no good. 3Again, I
warn every man: If you allow yourselves to be circumcised, you ·must follow [are obligated to obey] all the law. 4If you try to be ·made right with
God [justified] through the law, ·your life with Christ is over [Lyou are
alienated/separated/severed from Christ]—you have ·left [fallen away from]
God's grace. 5For by the Spirit and through faith we wait eagerly for ·a right
relationship with God [Lrighteousness]—the object of our hope. 6·When
we are [LFor] in Christ Jesus, ·it is not important if we are circumcised or
not [Lneither circumcision nor uncircumcision accomplishes anything].
The important thing is faith—the kind of faith that works through love.

7You were running a good race. Who ·stopped [hindered] you from
·following [*or* obeying; *or* your conviction about] the ·true way [truth]?
8This ·change [persuasion; enticement] did not come from the One who
·chose [called] you. 9Be careful! "Just a little ·yeast [leaven; 1 Cor. 5:6–7]
makes the whole batch of dough rise [Ca little error will spread through
the whole community]." 10But I ·trust [Lhave confidence/am persuaded
about you] in the Lord that you will ·not believe those different ideas
[take no different view]. Whoever is ·confusing [troubling] you with such
ideas will ·be punished [pay the penalty; Lbear the condemnation], ·no
matter who he is [Lwhoever he may be].

11My brothers and sisters, if I am still preaching ·that a man must be
circumcised [Lcircumcision; Csome were evidently accusing Paul of this],
why am I still being ·attacked [persecuted]? If I still taught circumcision,
·my preaching about the cross would not be a problem [the scandal/
offense of the cross has been removed/abolished]. 12I wish the people who
are bothering you would ·castrate themselves [make themselves eunuchs;

Lcut it off]! [CPaul sarcastically says that if circumcision is so helpful, why
not go even further?]
13My brothers and sisters, God called you to ·be free [Lfreedom], but do
not use your freedom as an ·excuse to do what pleases [opportunity/occa-
sion for] your ·sinful self [sinful nature; flesh]. [LBut; Rather] Serve each
other with love. 14[LFor] The whole law is ·made complete [summed up;
fulfilled] in this one command: "Love your neighbor as you love yourself
[Lev. 19:18]." 15[LBut] If you go on ·hurting each other and tearing each
other apart [Lbiting and devouring one another], be careful, or you will
completely ·destroy [*or* consume] each other.

The Spirit and Human Nature

16So I tell you: ·Live [Walk] ·by following [guided by; in the power of; Lby]
the Spirit. Then you will not do what your ·sinful self [sinful nature; Tflesh]
·wants [desires; craves]. 17Our ·sinful self [sinful nature; Tflesh] ·wants
[desires] what is against the Spirit, and the Spirit ·wants [desires] what is
against our ·sinful self [sinful nature; Tflesh]. [LFor] The two are ·against
[opposed to; *or* hostile toward] each other, so you cannot do just what you
·please [want]. 18But if the Spirit is leading you, you are not under the law.
19The ·wrong things the sinful self does [works of the flesh/sinful
nature] are ·clear [evident; obvious]: ·being sexually unfaithful [sexual
immorality], ·not being pure [impurity], ·taking part in sexual sins
[depravity; promiscuity], 20·worshiping gods [idolatry], ·doing witchcraft
[sorcery], ·hating [hostility; antagonism], ·making trouble [discord;
strife], being jealous, ·being angry [rage], ·being selfish [rivalries], ·mak-
ing people angry with each other [dissensions], ·causing divisions among
people [factions], 21feeling envy, being drunk, ·having wild and wasteful
parties [carousings; orgies], and doing other things like these. I warn you
now as I warned you before: Those who do these things will not inherit
God's kingdom. 22But the ·Spirit produces the fruit of [Lfruit of the Spirit
is] love, joy, peace, patience, kindness, goodness, ·faithfulness [*or* faith],
23gentleness, self-control. ·There is no law that says these things are wrong
[*or* No law can oppose such things]. 24Those who belong to Christ Jesus
have crucified ·their own sinful selves [the sinful nature; the flesh]. They
have given up ·their old selfish feelings and the evil things they wanted to
do [Lits passions and desires]. 25·We [LIf/Since we…] ·get our new life from
the Spirit [live by the Spirit], so we should ·follow [be guided by; walk in
step with] the Spirit. 26We must not be ·proud [conceited] or ·make trouble with [provoke] each other or be ·jealous [envious] of each other.

Help Each Other

6 Brothers and sisters, if ·someone in your group [La person] ·does
something wrong [*or* is overcome by some trangression/sin; *or* is dis-
covered/caught in some trangression/sin], you who are spiritual should go
to that person and ·gently help make him right again [restore him gently/
with a gentle spirit]. But be careful, ·because you might [*or* so that you won't]
be tempted to sin, too. 2By ·helping each other with your troubles [Lbearing
each other's burdens], you truly ·obey [accomplish; fulfill] the law of Christ.
3If anyone thinks he is ·important [Lsomething] when he really is not, he is
only ·fooling [deceiving; deluding] himself. 4Each person should ·judge
[examine; test] his own ·actions [*or* achievements; Lwork] and not compare
himself with others. Then he can be proud for what he himself has done.
5Each person ·must be responsible for himself [Lwill carry their own load].
6Anyone who is ·learning the teaching of God [being instructed in the
word] should share all the good things he has with his teacher.

Life Is like Planting a Field

7Do not be ·fooled [deceived; mistaken]**: You cannot ·cheat** [mock; make a fool of] **God. People ·harvest only what they plant** [reap what they sow]. **8If they plant ·to satisfy** [*or* in the field of; Linto; to] **their ·sinful selves** [sinful nature; flesh]**, ·their sinful selves will bring them ruin** [Lthey will reap destruction from the flesh]. **But if they plant ·to please** [*or* in the field of; Linto; to] **the Spirit, they will ·receive** [reap; harvest] **eternal life from the Spirit. 9We must not become ·tired** [*or* discouraged] **of doing good. We will receive our harvest of eternal life ·at the right** [*or* in due] **time if we do not give up.** 10[LTherefore; So then] **When we have the opportunity to ·help** [do good to] **anyone, we should do it. But ·we should give special attention** [Lespecially] **to those who are in the ·family** [household] **of ·believers** [Lfaith].

Paul Ends His Letter

11See what large letters I use to write this ·myself [Lwith my own hand; Cadded to authenticate the letter; the rest had likely been dictated]. **12Some people are trying to force you to be circumcised ·so the Jews will accept them** [*or* to impress others by external standards; Lto make a good showing in the flesh]. **They do this only to avoid persecution for the cross of Christ** [Cthe Gospel message of Christ's sacrificial death on the cross]. 13[LFor] **Those who are circumcised do not obey the law themselves, but they want you to be circumcised so they can ·brag** [boast] **·about what they forced you to do** [Lin your flesh]. **14·I hope I will never** [LMay it never be that I] **·brag** [boast] **about anything except the cross of our Lord Jesus Christ. ·Through that cross** [*or* Through Jesus Christ; L...through which/whom] **the world has been crucified to me and I have been crucified to the world. 15It ·is not important** [makes no difference; is nothing] **if a man is circumcised or uncircumcised. The important thing is ·being the new people God has made** [La new creation; 2 Cor. 5:17]. **16Peace and mercy to those who ·follow** [walk/live by] **this rule—and to ·all of God's people** [Lthe Israel of God; Ceither: (1) Jewish Christians or (2) the church as the "new Israel"].

17·So [*or* In conclusion; *or* From now on] **do not give me any more trouble.** [LFor] **I ·have scars on my body that show I belong to Jesus** [Lbear the marks of Jesus on my body; Cfrom his many beatings for the Gospel; perhaps also indicating his "branding" as a slave of Jesus Christ].

18My brothers and sisters, the grace of our Lord Jesus Christ be with your spirit. Amen.

EPHESIANS

1 From Paul, an ·apostle [messenger] of Christ Jesus. ·I am an
apostle because that is what God wanted [[L]…by the will of God].
To ·God's holy people [[T]the saints] living in Ephesus[n] [[C]a prominent
city in the Roman province of Asia, present-day western Turkey; Acts
19], ·believers in [*or* who are faithful to] Christ Jesus:
[2]Grace and peace to you from God our Father and the Lord Jesus
Christ.

Spiritual Blessings in Christ

[3]·Praise be to [*or* Blessed is] the God and Father of our Lord Jesus
Christ. In Christ, God has given us every spiritual blessing in the heavenly ·world [realms; places]. [4]·That is [*or* Just as; *or* For; Because], in
Christ, he chose us before the ·world was made [[L]foundation of the world]
so that we would be his holy people—people ·without blame [*or* unblemished; [C]as are sacrificial animals] before him. [5]Because of his love [[C]this
phrase may go with the previous sentence], God ·had already decided to
make us his own children [[L]predestined us for adoption] through Jesus
Christ. That was what he wanted and what pleased him, [6]and it brings
praise to God because of his ·wonderful [glorious] grace. God gave that
grace to us freely, in ·Christ, the One he loves [[L]the Beloved]. [7]In ·Christ
[[L]him] we ·are set free [have been redeemed/purchased] by ·the blood of
his death [[L]his blood; [C]blood signifies his sacrificial death], and so we have
forgiveness of sins. ·How rich is [*or* This redemption reveals the wealth of;
[L]…according to the riches of] God's grace, [8]which he has ·given to us so
fully and freely [lavished on us]. With ·full [all] wisdom and understanding [[C]this phrase may go with the previous sentence], [9]God let us know
·his secret purpose [*or* the mystery of his will; [C]a "mystery" in Scripture is
something God had not previously disclosed]. This was what ·God wanted
[pleased him], and he ·planned to do it [*or* set it forth; publicly revealed it]
through Christ. [10]His goal was to carry out his plan, ·when the right time
came [*or* at the time of fulfillment; [L]in the fullness of the times], that all
things in heaven and on earth would be ·joined together [unified; *or*
summed up; *or* renewed] in Christ as the head.
[11]In Christ we ·were chosen to be God's people [have received/were
given our part of an inheritance], ·because from the very beginning God
had decided this [[L]having been predestined] in keeping with his plan. And
he is the One who ·makes everything agree [*or* accomplishes everything in
accord] with what he decides and wants. [12]We are the first people who
hoped in ·Christ [the Messiah], and we were chosen so that we would
bring praise to God's glory. [13]So it is with you. When you heard the ·true

---

1:1 in Ephesus Some Greek copies do not have this phrase.

teaching [message/word of truth]—the ·Good News about [Gospel of]
your salvation—you believed in Christ. ·And in Christ, God put his special mark of ownership on you by giving you [L...having been sealed
with] the Holy Spirit that he had promised. 14That Holy Spirit is the
·guarantee [down payment; deposit] ·that we will receive what God promised for his people [Lof our inheritance] until ·God gives full freedom to
those who are his [*or* we acquire possession of it; Lthe redemption of the
possession; v. 7]—to bring praise to God's glory.

Paul's Prayer

15That is why ·since [*or* because] I heard about your faith in the Lord Jesus
and your love for all ·God's people [Tthe saints], 16I ·have not stopped [never
cease] giving thanks to God for you. I always remember you in my prayers,
17asking the God of our Lord Jesus Christ, the glorious Father, to give you ·a
spirit of wisdom [*or* spiritual wisdom; *or* the Spirit of wisdom] and revelation so that you will know him better. 18I pray also that ·you will have greater
understanding in your heart [Lthe eyes of your heart may be enlightened] so
you will ·know [comprehend] the hope to which he has called us and that
you will know ·how rich and glorious are the blessings God has promised
[the riches of his glorious inheritance for; *or* the glorious wealth of an inheritance that God possesses in] ·his holy people [Tthe saints]. 19And you will
know that God's power is ·very [exceedingly; overwhelmingly] great for us
who believe. That power ·is the same as [*or* was demonstrated in] the great
strength 20God ·used [exerted] to raise Christ from the dead and ·put [Lseat]
him at his right ·side [Lhand; Ps. 110:1; Acts 2:34] in the heavenly ·world
[realm; places]. 21God has put Christ ·over [far above] all rulers, authorities,
powers, and ·kings [lords; dominion], and every other ·title given [Lname
that is named] not only in this ·world [age] but also in the ·next [coming
one]. 22God ·put [subjected] everything under his ·power [Lfeet; Ps. 8:6] and
·made him the head over everything for the church [*or* gave him to the
church as head over all things], which is his body. 23·The church is filled with
Christ [*or* The church completes Christ; L...the fullness of the one], who fills
·everything in every way [*or* all things everywhere; Lall in all].

We Now Have Life

2 In the past you were ·spiritually dead [Ldead] ·because of [*or* in]
your sins and ·the things you did against God [transgressions].
2Yes, in the past you ·lived [walked] ·the way the world lives [Laccording to
the course/ways/age of this world], following the ruler [CSatan] of the ·evil
powers that are above the earth [Ldominion/authority of the air; Cprobably
demonic forces]. That same spirit is now working in ·those who refuse to
obey God [Lthe children/sons of disobedience]. 3In the past all of us lived
·like [*or* among] them, ·trying to please [*or* giving in to the cravings of]
our ·sinful selves [sinful nature; flesh] and doing all the things our ·bodies
[flesh] and minds wanted. We ·should have suffered God's anger because
we were sinful by nature [Lwere by nature children/sons of wrath]. ·We
were the same as all other people [L...just like the rest; Cof mankind].

4But ·God's mercy is great [LGod is rich in mercy], and he loved us very
much. 5Though we were spiritually dead because of ·the things we did
against God [our transgressions], he ·gave us new life [brought us to life]
with Christ. You have been saved by God's grace. 6And he raised us up with
Christ and gave us a seat with him in the ·heavens [heavenly places/realms].
He did this for those in Christ Jesus 7so that ·for all future time [Lin the ages
to come] he could show the ·very great [exceeding; overwhelming] riches of
his grace by being kind to us in Christ Jesus. 8·I mean that [*or* For; Because]

you have been saved by grace through ·believing [faith]. You did not save
yourselves; it was a gift from God. 9It was not the result of ·your own efforts
[works], so ·you cannot [no one can] ·brag about it [boast]. 10·God has
made us what we are [LFor we are his handiwork/workmanship/work of
art]. In Christ Jesus, God ·made [created] us to do good works, which God
planned in advance for us to live our lives doing.

One in Christ

11[LTherefore] Remember that you ·were born as Gentiles [are Gentiles
in the flesh], the ones called "uncircumcised" by those who call themselves
"circumcised." (·Their circumcision is only something they themselves do
on their bodies [...Lperformed in the flesh by hands].) 12Remember that ·in
the past [at that time/season] you were without ·Christ [the Messiah]. You
were ·not citizens [Lexcluded from the citizenship] of Israel, and you ·had
no part in [Lwere aliens/strangers to] the ·agreements with the promise that
God made to his people [Lcovenants of promise; Cthe Abrahamic (Gen.
12:1–3), Mosaic (Ex. 19–24), and Davidic (2 Sam. 7) covenants.] You had no
hope, and you did not know God. 13But now in Christ Jesus, you who were
far away from God are brought near through the blood of ·Christ's death
[LChrist; Cblood symbolizing his sacrificial death]. 14Christ himself is our
peace. He made ·both Jews and Gentiles one people [Lboth one], and broke
down the wall of ·hate [hostility; enmity] that divided them [Cthe wall
beyond which Gentiles could not pass in the Jerusalem temple, or the law of
Moses that distinguished Jew from Gentile (see v. 15)] ·by giving his own
body [Lin his flesh; Cthis phrase may go with the following sentence]. 15He
did this by ·ending [setting aside; nullifying] the law of commands and
rules ·by giving his own body [Lin his flesh; Cthis phrase may go with the
previous sentence]. His purpose was to make the two groups of people
become one new ·people [humanity; person; man] in him and in this way
make peace. 16It was also Christ's purpose to ·end [Lput to death; kill] the
·hatred [hostility; enmity] between the two groups, to make them into one
body, and to ·bring them back [reconcile them] to God. ·Christ did all this
with his death on the cross [L...through the cross]. 17Christ came and
·preached [proclaimed the Good News of] peace [Is. 52:7] to you who were
·far away from God [Lfar away/off], and to those who were ·near to God
[Lnear; Is. 57:19]. 18·Yes, it is [For; *or* So that] through Christ we all have ·the
right to come [free access] to the Father ·in [by] one Spirit.

19Now you Gentiles are not foreigners or strangers any longer, but are
citizens together with ·God's holy people [Tthe saints]. You belong to God's
·family [household]. 20·You are like a building that was built [...having
been built] on the foundation of the apostles and prophets. Christ Jesus
himself is the ·most important stone [cornerstone; *or* capstone; Is. 28:16; 1
Cor. 3:11] in that building, 21and that whole building is joined together in
Christ. He makes it grow and become a holy temple in the Lord. 22And in
Christ you, too, are being ·built together with the Jews [Lbuilt together]
into a place where God lives through the Spirit.

Paul's Work in Telling the Good News

3 ·So [For this reason] I, Paul, a prisoner [CPaul is probably writing
from house arrest in Rome, about AD 60; see Acts 28:30–31] of
Christ Jesus ·for [for the sake of] you Gentiles—[CPaul is about to pray for
the Ephesians, but instead digresses into a description of his ministry until v.
14]. 2Surely you have heard that God gave me this ·work [task; stewardship;
commission] ·to tell you about his grace [Lof God's grace for you]. 3He let me
know his ·secret [mystery; 1:9] by ·showing it to me [revelation]. I have

already written ·a little [briefly] about this [Ceither earlier in this letter or previously]. [4]·If you read what I wrote then [*or* By reading this], you can see that I truly understand the ·secret [mystery] ·about [*or* revealed by; *or* that consists of; Lof] ·Christ [*or* the Messiah]. [5]·People [LThe sons of men; Ca Hebrew way of referring to people] who lived in other ·times [generations] were not told that secret. But now, through the Spirit, God has ·shown [revealed] that secret to his holy apostles and prophets. [6]This is that ·secret [mystery]: that through the ·Good News [Gospel] the Gentiles ·will share with the Jews in God's blessing [Lare co-heirs]. They belong to the same body, and they share together in the promise that God made in Christ Jesus.

[7]By God's special gift of grace given to me through ·his power [Lthe working out/exercise of his power], I became a servant ·to tell that Good News [of this Gospel]. [8]I am the least important of all ·God's people [Tthe saints], but God gave me this ·gift [*or* grace]—to tell the Gentiles the ·Good News [Gospel] about the riches of Christ, which are ·too great to understand fully [unfathomable; *or* boundless]. [9]And God gave me the work of ·telling [making plain; enlightening] all people about the ·plan for [administration of; Cthe same word translated "work" in v. 2] his ·secret [mystery], which has been hidden ·in [*or* by] him ·since the beginning of time [Lfrom the ages]. He is the One who created everything. [10]His purpose was that through the church all the rulers and powers in the heavenly ·world [realm; places; 1:3, 20; 2:6] will now know God's ·wisdom, which has so many forms [multi-faceted/multi-dimensional wisdom]. [11]·This agrees with [L...according to] ·the plan God had since the beginning of time [his eternal purpose/plan], which he accomplished ·through [*or* in] Christ Jesus our Lord. [12]In Christ we ·can come before [have access to] God with ·freedom [boldness; freedom to speak] and ·without fear [with confidence]. We can do this ·through faith in Christ [*or* because of Christ's faithfulness]. [13]So I ·ask you not to become [*or* pray that you would not be] discouraged because of the ·sufferings [trials] I am having for you. My ·sufferings [trials; affliction] are ·for your glory [to bring you honor/eternal glory].

The Love of Christ

[14]So [CPaul begins again the prayer he started in v. 1] I ·bow in prayer [kneel] before the Father [15]from whom ·every [*or* the whole] ·family [Ca play on words, since the words "father" and "family" are related] in heaven and on earth gets its true name. [16]I ask the Father ·in his great glory [*or* from the treasures of his glory; *or* out of his glorious riches] to give you the power to be strong ·inwardly [Lin the inner person] through his Spirit. [17]I pray that Christ will ·live [make his home] in your hearts by faith and that your life will be ·strong in love and be built on love [Lrooted and grounded in love]. [18]And I pray that you and all ·God's holy people [Tthe saints] will have the power to ·understand [comprehend; grasp] the greatness of Christ's love—how wide and how long and how high and how deep that love is. [19]Christ's love is ·greater than anyone can ever know [beyond comprehension/knowledge], but I pray that you will be able to know that love. ·Then [L...so that] you can be filled with the fullness of God.

[20]·Glory be to God, who can [LNow to the One who is able to] do much, much more than anything we can ask or imagine through his power working in us. [21]To him be glory in the church and in Christ Jesus for all ·time [generations], forever and ever. Amen.

The Unity of the Body

4 [LTherefore,] As a prisoner [3:1] ·for [because I belong to; *or* in]
the Lord, I urge you to ·live [walk] in a manner worthy of the
calling ·you have received [Lto which you were called]. 2·Always be [*or* Be
completely] humble, gentle, and patient, ·accepting [putting up/bearing
with] each other in love. 3Make every effort to preserve the unity ·of
[provided by; available through] the Spirit ·in [through] the ·peace that
joins us together [Lbond of peace]. 4There is one body and one Spirit,
and God called you to ·have one hope [Lone hope of your calling]. 5There
is one Lord, one faith, and one baptism. 6There is one God and Father of
everything. ·He rules everything and is everywhere and is in everything
[L...who is over all and through all and in all].
7Each one of us has been given the ·special gift of grace [Lgrace; *or* gift],
·showing how generous Christ is [*or* in proportion to Christ's gift; Laccording
to the measure of Christ's gift]. 8That is why it says in the Scriptures,
"When he ·went up [ascended] to the heights,
he ·led a parade of captives [*or* took captives into captivity],
and he gave gifts to people [Ps. 68:18]."
9When it says, "He ·went up [ascended]," what does it mean? ·It means
[L...except] that he first ·came down [descended] to the ·earth [*or* lower
regions, namely the earth; *or* the depths of the earth; Cprobably refers to (1)
the Incarnation, though possibly (2) Christ's descent to Hades after his
death (1 Pet. 3:19–20), or (3) Christ's descent through the Spirit at Pentecost
(Acts 2)]. 10So the one who ·came down [descended] is the same one who
·went up [ascended] above all the heavens. ·Christ did that [L...in order] to
fill ·everything with his presence [Lall things]. 11And ·Christ gave gifts to
people—he made some to be apostles, some to be prophets, some to go and
tell the Good News, and some to have the work of caring for and teaching
God's people [Lhe himself gave apostles, prophets, evangelists, pastors/shep-
herds, and teachers]. 12·Christ gave those gifts to prepare [L...to equip]
God's holy people for the work of serving, to make the body of Christ
stronger. 13This work must continue until we ·are all joined together in the
same faith [*or* all reach unity in the faith] and in the same knowledge of the
Son of God. We must become like ·a mature person [*or* the perfect Man;
CChrist], ·growing until we become like Christ and have his perfection [Lto
the measure of the stature of Christ's fullness].
14Then we will no longer be ·babies [children]. We will not be tossed
about like a ship that the waves carry one way and then another. We will
not be ·influenced by every new teaching [Lcarried along by every wind of
(false) teaching] we hear from people who are trying to ·fool [trick] us.
They ·make plans [scheme] and try any kind of trick to fool people into
following ·the wrong path [error; false teaching]. 15·No! [Instead; Rather]
·Speaking [*or* Living out; Practicing] the truth with love, we will grow up
in every way into Christ, who is the head. 16·The whole body depends on
Christ, and [L...through/by whom] all the parts of the body are joined
and held together. Each ·part [supporting joint/ligament] ·does its own
work [performs its function] to make the whole body grow and ·be strong
with [to build itself up in] love.

The Way You Should Live

17·In the Lord's name [*or* By the Lord's authority; LIn the Lord], I ·tell
you [Lspeak and testify to] this. Do not continue ·living [walking] like
·those who do not believe [the pagans; Lthe Gentiles], whose thoughts are
·worth nothing [futile]. 18They ·do not understand [Lare darkened in their

minds/understanding] and they are ·separated [excluded; alienated] from the life ·God gives [or God has; Lof God] because of their ignorance ·and because of [or caused by] ·their stubbornness [or their closed minds; Lthe stubbornness of their heart/mind]. 19They have lost ·all feeling of shame [or any sense of right and wrong; Lall feeling/sensitivity], and they ·use their lives for doing evil [abandon themselves to indecency/depravity]. They ·continually want to do [or greedily pursue] all kinds of ·evil [impurity]. 20But ·what you learned in Christ was not like this [or that is not how you learned about Christ; Lyou did not learn Christ that way]. 21·I know that [L...if indeed] you heard ·about him [or him], and you ·are in him, so you were taught the truth that is in Jesus [or were taught by him, because the truth is in Jesus]. 22You were taught to ·leave [put off; lay aside] your old ·self [Lperson]—to stop living the evil way you lived before. That old self ·becomes worse [is decaying/being corrupted], because ·people are fooled by the evil things they want to do [Lof the deceitfulness of their desires]. 23But you were taught to be made new in ·your hearts [the spirit/attitude of your minds], 24to ·become [put on; clothe yourself with] the new ·self [Lperson; or Man; Cbecome like Christ]. That new person is created ·to be like God [or in God's image; Laccording to God]—truly good and holy [or in the righteousness and holiness that comes from truth].

25So you must stop telling lies. ·Tell each other the truth [LLet each one of you speak truthfully to his neighbor; Zech. 8:16], because we ·all belong to each other in the same body [Lare members of one another]. 26·When you are angry, [or Be angry, and] do not sin [Ps. 4:4; Cthere is a time for righteous anger, but it must not result in sin], and ·be sure to stop being angry before the end of the day [Ldon't let the sun set on your anger]. 27Do not give the devil a ·way to defeat you [foothold; opportunity]. 28Those who are stealing must stop stealing and start working. They should ·earn an honest living for themselves [do something good/useful with their hands]. Then they will have something to share with those who ·are poor [Lhave need].

29Don't ·say anything that will hurt others [Llet any rotten/unhealthy word come from your mouth], but only say what is ·helpful [good] to ·make others stronger [build others up] ·and meet [Laccording to] their needs. Then what you say will ·do good [give grace; be a gift] to those who listen to you. 30And do not ·make the Holy Spirit sad [grieve/bring sorrow to the Holy Spirit]. ·The Spirit is God's proof that you belong to him and he will make you free when the final day comes [...by whom you were sealed for the day of redemption]. 31Do not be bitter or angry or ·mad [raging]. Never shout angrily or ·say things to hurt [slander; insult] others. ·Never do anything [Get rid of all kinds of] evil. 32Be kind and ·loving [compassionate; tenderhearted] to each other, and forgive each other just as God forgave you in Christ.

Living in the Light

5 You are God's children whom he loves, so ·try to be like [imitate] him. 2·Live a life of love [Walk in love] just as Christ loved us and gave himself for us as a ·sweet-smelling [fragrant] offering and sacrifice to God.

3But there must be ·no [no hint/mention/rumor of] sexual sin among you, or any kind of ·evil [impurity] or greed. Those things are not ·right [proper; fitting] for God's holy people. 4Also, there must be no ·evil talk [obscenity; filthiness] among you, and you must not speak foolishly or tell ·evil [crude; coarse; vulgar] jokes. These things are ·not right for you

[out of place/character]. Instead, you should be giving thanks to God.
5[LFor] You can be sure of this: No one will have a ·place [inheritance] in
the kingdom of Christ and of God who sins sexually, or does ·evil
[impure] things, or is greedy. Anyone who is greedy is ·serving a false god
[Lan idolater].
6Do not let anyone ·fool [deceive] you ·by telling you things that are not
true [*or* with shallow philosophies; Lwith empty words], because these
things will bring God's ·anger [wrath] on ·those who do not obey him
[Lthe children/sons of disobedience]. 7So ·have nothing to do with them [*or*
do not partner/associate with them]. 8In the past you were ·full of darkness
[Ldarkness], but now you are ·full of light [Llight] in the Lord. So ·live
[walk] like children ·who belong to [living in; Lof] the light. 9·Light brings
[LFor the fruit of the light is] every kind of goodness, ·right living [righ-
teousness], and truth. 10·Try to learn [Discern; Test and prove] what pleases
the Lord. 11·Have nothing to do with [Take no part in] the things done in
darkness, which are ·not worth anything [Lunfruitful]. But ·show that they
are wrong [expose them]. 12[LFor] It is shameful even to talk about what
those people do in secret. 13But the light makes all things ·easy to see [vis-
ible; exposed], 14and everything that is ·made easy to see [visible; exposed]
·can become [*or* becomes a; Lis] light. This is why it is said:

"Wake up, sleeper!
Rise from death,
and Christ will ·shine on [give light to] you [Clikely an early Christian
hymn based on Is. 26:19 and 60:1–2]."

15So be very careful how you ·live [walk]. Do not ·live [walk] like those
who are ·not wise [foolish], but ·live wisely [like those who are wise].
16·Take advantage of every opportunity [*or* Make the most of your time;
L…redeeming the time/season], because ·these are evil times [Lthe days
are evil]. 17So do not be ·foolish [ignorant] but ·learn what the Lord wants
you to do [*or* understand the Lord's will]. 18Do not be drunk with wine,
which ·will ruin you [is debauchery/reckless living], but be filled with the
Spirit. 19·Speak [L…speaking] to each other with psalms, hymns, and spiritual songs, singing and making music in your hearts to the Lord.
20·Always give [L…always giving] thanks to God the Father for everything,
in the name of our Lord Jesus Christ.

Wives and Husbands

21·Yield [Submit; Be subject; L…yielding/submitting; Cgrammatically
linked to the previous sentence, and so part of being filled with the Spirit]
to each other out of ·reverence [respect; fear; awe] for Christ.
22Wives, ·yield to [submit to; be subject to; Lto] your husbands, as you
do to the Lord, 23because the husband is the head of the wife, as Christ is
the head of the church. And he is the Savior of the body, which is the
church. 24As the church ·yields [submits; is subject] to Christ, so you
wives should ·yield [submit; be subject] to your husbands in everything
[Col. 3:18; 1 Pet. 3:1–6].
25Husbands, love your wives as Christ loved the church [Col. 3:19;
1 Pet. 3:7] and gave himself for her 26to ·make her holy [sanctify her],
cleansing her in the washing of water by the word [Cthe "washing" may be
(1) baptism, (2) spiritual cleansing (Titus 3:5), or (3) an analogy drawn
from the Jewish prenuptial bath (Ezek. 16:8–14); the "word" may be (1)
the Gospel, (2) a baptismal formula, or (3) the confession of the one bap-
tized]. 27He did this so that he could present the church to himself ·like a

bride in all her beauty [in splendor; glorious], with no ·evil or sin [Lstain or wrinkle] or any other ·wrong thing in it [Lsuch thing], but ·pure [holy] and ·without fault [blameless]. 28In the same way, husbands should love their wives as they love their own bodies. The man who loves his wife loves himself. 29[LFor] No one ever hates his own ·body [Tflesh], but feeds and takes care of it. And that is what Christ does for the church, 30because we are ·parts [members] of his body. 31The Scripture says, "·So [For this reason] a man will leave his father and mother and be ·united [joined] with his wife, and the two will become one ·body [flesh; Gen. 2:24]." 32This ·secret [mystery] is ·very important [*or* great; profound]—I am talking about Christ and the church. 33·But [However; In any case; *or* To sum up] each one of you must love his wife as he loves himself, and a wife must ·respect [reverence; v. 21] her husband.

Children and Parents

6 Children, obey your parents ·as the Lord wants [Lin the Lord], because this is ·the right thing to do [right; just]. 2The command says, "Honor your father and mother [Ex. 20:12; Deut. 5:16]." This is the first command that has a promise with it—3"Then everything will be well with you, and you will have a long life on the earth [Ex. 20:12; Deut. 5:16]."

4·Fathers [*or* Parents; Heb. 11:23], do not make your children angry, but raise them with the ·training [discipline] and ·teaching [instruction] of the Lord [Col. 3:21].

Slaves and Masters

5·Slaves [Bondservants], obey your ·masters here on earth [human masters; Lmasters according to the flesh; Col. 3:22; 1 Pet. 2:18–25] with ·respect [fear] and ·fear [trembling] and from a sincere heart, ·just as you [*or* as you would] obey Christ. 6You must do this not only ·while they are watching you [Lwith eye-service], ·to please them [Las people-pleasers]. But as ·slaves [bondservants] of Christ, do ·what God wants [God's will] ·with all your [*or* from the] heart. 7Do your work ·with enthusiasm [willingly; cheerfully]. Work as if you were serving the Lord, not people. 8·Remember [L…knowing] that the Lord will give ·a reward [*or* back] to everyone, slave or free, for doing good.

9Masters, treat your slaves the same way. Do not threaten them. Remember that the One who is your Master and their Master is in heaven, and he ·treats everyone alike [has no favorites; shows no favoritism].

Wear the Full Armor of God

10Finally, be strong in the Lord and in his ·great [strong; mighty] power. 11Put on the full armor of God so that you can fight against the devil's ·evil tricks [schemes]. 12[For] Our ·fight [conflict; struggle] is not against ·people on earth [Lflesh and blood] but against the rulers and authorities and the ·powers [*or* cosmic powers/rulers] of this ·world's darkness [Ldarkness], against the spiritual powers of evil in the heavenly ·world [realm; places]. 13·That is why you need to [LFor this reason,] put on God's full armor. Then on the day of evil [Cpersecution generally or end-time tribulation] you will be able to ·stand strong [keep your ground; resist the enemy]. And ·when you have finished the whole fight [Lafter you have done/accomplished everything], you will still be standing. 14So stand ·strong [*or* ready], with the belt of truth tied around your waist and the ·body armor [breastplate] of ·right living [a righteous life; *or* God's own righteousness/justice; Lrighteousness]. 15On your feet wear the ·Good News [Gospel] of peace ·to help you stand strong [for firm footing; *or* to be fully prepared]. 16And ·also [in addition to all this; *or* in all circumstances] use the shield of faith

with which you can ·stop [extinguish] **all the ·burning arrows** [Tfiery darts]
of the Evil One. 17**·Accept** [Receive; *or* Take] **the helmet of salvation, and**
take the sword of the Spirit, which is the ·word [message] **of God.** 18**Pray**
·in [*or* in dependence on] **the Spirit at all times with all ·kinds of prayers**
[Lprayers and requests], **asking for everything you need. To do this you**
must always be ·ready [alert] **·and never give up** [Lwith all perseverance].
Always pray for all ·God's people [Tthe saints].

19**Also pray for me that when I ·speak** [Lopen my mouth], **God will give**
me words so that I can tell the ·secret [mystery] **of the ·Good News**
[Gospel] **·without fear** [confidently; boldly]. 20**·For this Good News** [...for
which] **I am an ambassador in ·prison** [Lchains; 3:1]. **Pray that I will speak**
·it [*or* for him; *or* in him] **·without fear** [boldly; confidently], **as I should.**

Final Greetings

21**Tychicus** [Acts 20:4; Col. 4:7; 2 Tim. 4:12; Titus 3:12], **our ·brother**
whom we love [dear/beloved brother] **and a faithful servant ·of the Lord's**
work [*or* in the Lord] **will tell you everything that is happening with me.**
Then you will know how I am and what I am doing. 22**I am sending him**
to you for this reason—so that you will know how we are, and he can
encourage ·you [Lyour hearts].

23**Peace and love with faith to you brothers and sisters from God the**
Father and the Lord Jesus Christ. 24**Grace to all of you who love our Lord**
Jesus Christ with ·love that never ends [an imperishable/undying love].

PHILIPPIANS

1 From Paul and Timothy [2:19–24; Acts 16:1–5; 1 Cor. 16:10–11;
1 and 2 Timothy], ·servants [slaves; bondservants] of Christ Jesus.
To all of ·God's holy people [Tthe saints] in Christ Jesus who live in
Philippi [Ca city located in Macedonia, present-day northern Greece;
Acts 16], including your ·overseers [Tbishops; Cperhaps the same as
elders] and ·deacons [servants; ministers]:
2Grace and peace to you from God our Father and the Lord Jesus
Christ.

Paul's Prayer

3I thank my God every time I remember you, 4always praying with joy
for all of you. 5I thank God for ·the help you gave me [Lyour partnership/
participation] in ·spreading the Good News [Lthe Good News/Gospel]
from the first day you believed until now. 6God began doing a good work
in you, and I am ·sure [confident; persuaded] he will continue it until it is
·finished [completed; perfected] ·when Jesus Christ comes again [Lon the
day of Christ Jesus; Cthe final day of judgment and reward].
7And I know that I am right to think like this about all of you, because
·I have you in my [*or* you have me in your] heart. All of you ·share [are
partners/co-sharers] in God's grace with me while I am in ·prison [chains;
CPaul is probably writing from house arrest in Rome, about AD 60; see
Acts 28:30–31] and while I am defending and ·proving the truth of [con-
firming] the ·Good News [Gospel]. 8[LFor] God ·knows [Lis my witness]
that I ·want [long] to see you very much, because I love all of you with the
·love [affection] of Christ Jesus.
9This is my prayer for you: that your love will ·grow [increase; abound]
more and more; that you will have knowledge and ·understanding
[insight; discernment] with your love; 10that you will ·see the difference
between good and bad and will choose the good [Ldiscern/test and prove
what is best]; that you will be pure and ·without wrong [blameless] ·for
the coming [in the day; v. 6] of Christ; 11that you will be filled with the
·good things produced in your life by Christ [Lfruit of righteousness that
comes through Christ] to bring glory and praise to God.

Paul's Troubles Help the Work

12I want you brothers and sisters to know that what has happened to me
has helped to ·spread [advance] the ·Good News [Gospel]. 13All the ·palace
guards [imperial guard; Lpraetorium; CCaesar's elite troops] and everyone
else knows that I am in ·prison [chains] ·because I am a believer in [*or* for
the cause of] Christ. 14Because I am in prison, most of the ·believers
[Lbrothers (and sisters)] have become more ·bold [confident] in the Lord
and ·are not afraid [Ldare without fear] to speak the word of God.
15It is true that some preach about Christ because of ·jealousy [envy]

and ·ambition [rivalry], but others preach about Christ because ·they
want to help [of good will/intentions]. 16 They preach because they have
love, and they know that ·God gave me the work of [I have been appointed
for; *or* I have been put here (in prison) for] defending the ·Good News
[Gospel]. 17 But the others preach about Christ for ·selfish [selfish ambi-
tion; *or* rivalry] and ·wrong reasons [not sincerely], wanting to make
trouble for me in ·prison [my chains].

18 ·But it doesn't matter [What difference does it make? *or* What is the
result? LFor what?]. The important thing is that in every way, whether ·for
right or wrong reasons [from false motives or true], they are preaching
about Christ. So ·I am happy [Lin this I rejoice], ·and [indeed] I will continue to ·be happy [rejoice]. 19 Because I know ·this trouble [Lthis] will
·bring my [result in] ·freedom [deliverance; *or* salvation], through your
prayers and the ·help of [support from] the Spirit of Jesus Christ. 20 I
expect and hope that I will not ·fail Christ in [Lbe ashamed about] anything but that I will have the ·courage [boldness] now, as always, ·to show
the greatness of Christ [*or* so that Christ will be exalted] in my ·life here
on earth [Lbody], whether I live or die. 21 [LFor] To me ·the only important
thing about living [Lto live] is Christ, and ·dying would be profit for me
[Lto die is gain/profit]. 22 If I continue living in my ·body [flesh], ·I will be
able to work for the Lord [Lthis is productive/fruitful work for me]. I do
not know what to choose—living or dying. 23 ·It is hard to choose [I am
torn/hard pressed] between the two. I ·want [desire; long] to leave this life
and be with Christ, which is much better, 24 but ·you need me here [*or* it is
better for you that I remain] in ·my body [the flesh]. 25 Since I am sure of
this, I know I will stay with you ·to help you grow and have [Lfor your
progress/success and] joy in your faith. 26 [L...so that] ·You will be very
happy [*or* Because of me, your confidence/pride will increase; LYour boasting in me will abound] in Christ Jesus when I am with you again.

27 ·Only one thing concerns me [*or* Whatever happens; LOnly]: Be sure
that you ·live [conduct yourselves; live as citizens] in a way that ·brings
honor to [is worthy of] the ·Good News [Gospel] of Christ. ·Then [L...so
that] whether I come and ·visit [see] you or am away from you, I will hear
that you are standing strong ·with one purpose [with one spirit; *or* in the
one Spirit], that you work together ·as one [with one mind/soul] for the
faith ·of [*or* that is; *or* in] the ·Good News [Gospel], 28 and that you are not
·frightened [intimidated] in any way by ·those who are against you [your
opponents]. All of this is ·proof [evidence; a sign] that ·your enemies
[they] will be destroyed but that you will be saved. And ·this salvation [*or*
this proof/evidence/sign; Lthis] is from God. 29 ·God gave you the honor
[LFor it has been granted/given to you] not only of believing in Christ but
also of suffering for him. 30 You yourselves are having the same kind of
struggles that you saw ·I had when I was with you [Lin me], and ·you hear
that I am still having now [Lnow hear in me].

2 [LTherefore,] ·Does your life in Christ give you strength? [LIf there is
any encouragement in Christ...] ·Does his love comfort you? [L...if
any comfort from (his) love...] ·Do we share together in the Spirit? [L...if
any fellowship/sharing of the Spirit...] ·Do you have mercy and kindness?
[L...if any mercy/affection and kindness/compassion...] 2 ·If so [...then],
·make me very happy [Lfulfill/complete my joy] by ·having the same thoughts
[being like-minded/of one mind], sharing the same love, and having one

·mind [heart; soul] and ·purpose [goal; mind]. 3When you do things, do not
let ·selfishness [rivalry; selfish ambition] or pride be your guide. Instead, be
humble and give more ·honor [regard; value] to others than to yourselves.
4Do not ·be interested only in your own life [look out for your own inter-
ests], but ·be interested in the lives of others [look out for others' interests].

Be Unselfish like Christ

5In your lives you must ·think and act like [have the same attitude as]
Christ Jesus. [CWhat follows may be from an early Christian hymn.]
6·Christ himself was like God in everything [LWho, being in the form of
God].
But he did not think that being equal with God was something to be
·used for his own benefit [or grasped; seized; held on to].
7But he ·gave up his place with God and made himself nothing
[Lemptied himself].
He ·became like [Ltook the form of] a ·servant [slave; bondservant]
and was born ·as a man [Lin the likeness of humanity/men].
8And ·when he was living [Lbeing found in appearance/likeness] as a
·man [human being],
he humbled himself and was fully obedient to God,
even ·when that caused his [to the point of] death—death on a cross.
9So God ·raised [exalted] him to the highest place.
God ·made his name [or gave him the name] ·greater than [far above]
every other name
10so that every knee will bow to the name of Jesus—
everyone in heaven, on earth, and under the earth.
11And ·everyone [Levery tongue] will confess that Jesus Christ is Lord
and bring glory to God the Father.

Be the People God Wants You to Be

12My ·dear friends [beloved], you have always obeyed God when I was
with you. It is even more important that you obey now while I am away
from you. ·Keep on working to complete [Continue working out] your
salvation with ·fear [awe; reverence] and trembling, 13because God is
working in you ·to help you want to do and be able to do [Lboth to will/
desire and to work] what pleases him.
14Do everything without ·complaining [grumbling] or arguing. 15Then
you will be ·innocent [blameless] and ·without any wrong [innocent; pure;
harmless], God's children without ·fault [blemish; Cas are sacrificial animals].
·But you are living with people that are crooked and evil [L…in the midst of
a crooked and perverse generation; Deut. 32:5], among whom you shine like
stars in the ·dark world [or sky; Lworld]. 16You ·offer [or hold firmly/fast to]
the ·teaching that gives life [message/word of life]. So ·when Christ comes
again [Lon the day of Christ; Cjudgment day], I can ·be happy [Lbe proud;
boast] because I ·ran the race and won [Ldid not run for nothing/in vain].
·My work was not wasted [L…nor did I labor for nothing/in vain].
17Your faith makes you offer your lives as a sacrifice in serving God.
[LEven] If I ·have to offer my own blood [Lam poured out as a drink offer-
ing] with your sacrifice, I will be ·happy [rejoicing] and full of joy with all
of you. 18You also should be ·happy [rejoicing] and full of joy with me.

Timothy and Epaphroditus

19I hope in the Lord Jesus to send Timothy to you soon. [L…so that] I
will be ·happy [encouraged] to learn how you are. 20I have no one else like
Timothy [1:1], who ·truly [genuinely] cares for you. 21Other people ·are
interested only in their own lives [pursue their own interests/concerns],

not ·in the work [the interests/concerns; [L]the things] **of Jesus Christ. [22]You**
know ·the kind of person Timothy is [his tested and proven character].
You know he has served with me in ·telling the Good News [[L]the Gospel],
as a son serves his father. [2][[L]Therefore] **I ·plan** [hope] **to send him to you**
quickly when I know what will happen to me [[C]probably referring to the
outcome of Paul's trial in Rome]. **[24]I am ·sure** [confident] **·that the Lord**
will help me to [[L]in the Lord that I will] **come to you soon.**

[25][[L]But; *or* Meanwhile,] **I thought ·I should** [it necessary to] **send back**
to you Epaphroditus [4:18], **my ·brother in Christ** [[L]brother] **and**
coworker, ·who serves with me in Christ's army [[L]and fellow soldier]. **He**
was your messenger, sent as a ·servant [minister] **to meet my needs. [26]I**
am sending him because he ·wants very much to see [greatly misses;
[L]longs for] **all of you. He is ·worried** [distressed] **because you heard that**
he was sick. [27]Yes, he was sick, and nearly died, but God had mercy on him
and me too so that I would not have ·more sadness [[L]sorrow upon sor-
row]. **[28]I ·want very much** [am very eager] **to send him to you so that**
when you see him you can ·be happy [rejoice], **and I can stop worrying**
about you. [29]Welcome him in the Lord with much joy. Give honor to peo-
ple like him, [30]because he almost died for the work of Christ. He risked
his life to give me the help you could not give in your service to me.

The Importance of Christ

3 [Furthermore, *or* Finally,] **My brothers and sisters, ·be full of joy**
[rejoice] **in the Lord. It is no trouble for me to write the same**
things to you again, and it ·will help you to be more ready [[L]is a safeguard/
protection for you]. **[2]·Watch out for** [Beware] **those who do evil, ·who are**
like dogs [[L]beware the dogs; [C]a derogatory reference to Paul's opponents],
·who demand to cut the body [[L]beware the mutilation; [C]a mocking reference to those who demand circumcision of Gentile believers]. [3][[L]For] **We**
are the ·ones who are truly circumcised [[L](true) circumcision]. **We ·wor-**
ship [serve] **God ·through** [*or* in] **his Spirit, and ·our pride is** [we boast/
glory] **in Christ Jesus. We do not put ·trust** [reliance; confidence] **in ·our-**
selves or anything we can do [human ability/effort; [T]the flesh], **[4]although**
I might be able to put ·trust [reliance; confidence] **in ·myself** [human abil-
ity/effort; [T]the flesh]. **If anyone thinks he has a reason to ·trust** [rely; have
confidence] **in ·himself** [human ability/effort; [T]the flesh], **he should know**
that I have greater reason. [5]I was circumcised eight days after my birth
[Gen. 17:12; Lev. 12:3]. **I am from the people of Israel and the tribe of**
Benjamin. I am a ·Hebrew, and my parents were Hebrews [*or* true Hebrew;
Hebrew through and through; [L]Hebrew of Hebrews]. **With regard to the**
·law of Moses [[L]law], **I was a Pharisee** [[C]Pharisees strictly followed the OT
law and expanded on it with many traditions]. **[6]·I was so enthusiastic**
[[L]With regard to (religious) zeal,] **I persecuted the church. With regard to**
·obedience to the law of Moses [[L]righteousness based on the law] **I was**
·faultless [blameless]. **[7]Those things were ·important** [valuable; *or* assets]
to me, but now I think they are ·worth nothing [*or* liabilities; [L]a loss]
because of Christ. [8]Not only those things, but I think that all things are
·worth nothing [*or* liabilities; [L]a loss] **·compared with** [*or* because of] **the**
·greatness [superior/supreme value] **of knowing Christ Jesus my Lord.**
Because of him, I have lost all those things, and now I ·know they are
[consider them] **·worthless trash** [garbage; refuse; excrement]. **·This**
allows me to have [[L]...so that I may gain] **Christ [9]and to ·belong to** [be
united with; [L]be found in] **him. ·Now I am right with God, not because I**

followed the law [L...not having my own righteousness from the law], but
because ·I believed in Christ [of faith in Christ; *or* of the faithfulness of
Christ]. This is the ·right relationship with [*or* righteousness of/from]
God that comes through ·faith [*or* the faithfulness (of Christ)]. [10]I want to
know Christ and the power ·that raised him from the dead [Lof his resur-
rection]. I want to share in his sufferings and become like him in his
death. [11]·Then I have hope that [L...if somehow] I myself will ·be raised
[reach/attain to the resurrection] from the dead.

Continuing Toward Our Goal

[12]·I do not mean [LNot] that I have already ·achieved [obtained; taken
hold of] it or have already ·been perfected [become mature; *or* reached
the goal]. But I keep ·trying [pressing forward; striving; pursuing] to ·take
hold of that for which [*or* make it my own because] Christ ·took hold of
me [*or* made me his own]. [13]Brothers and sisters, I know that I have not
·yet reached that goal [taken hold of it], but there is one thing I always do.
Forgetting the ·past [Lthings that are behind] and ·straining toward
[stretching/reaching forward to] what is ahead, [14]I keep ·trying to reach
[pursuing; chasing] the goal and get the prize for which God called me ·to
the life above [heavenward; Lupward] ·through [*or* in] Christ Jesus.
[15]All of us who are ·spiritually mature [perfect; complete] should think
this way, too. And if there are things you ·do not agree with [Lthink differently about], God will ·make them clear [*or* reveal this] to you. [16]But we
should ·continue following the truth [*or* live up to the standard] we
already have.
[17]Brothers and sisters, ·all of you should try to follow my example
[Lbecome imitators of me] and ·to copy [Lwatch closely; pay attention to]
those who ·live [walk] the way we ·showed [modeled it for] you. [18][LFor]
Many people ·live [walk] like enemies of the cross of Christ. I have often
told you about them, and ·it makes me cry to [Lwith tears I] tell you about
them now. [19]·In the end, they will be destroyed [Their end/destiny is
destruction]. ·They do whatever their bodies want [LTheir god is their
stomach/belly], ·they are proud of their shameful acts [Ltheir glory is in
their shame], and they think only about earthly things. [20]But our ·home-
land [*or* citizenship] is in heaven, and we are waiting for our Savior, the
Lord Jesus Christ, to come from heaven. [21]By his power to ·rule [Lsubject
to himself] all things, he will ·change [transform; transfigure] our humble
bodies and make them like his own glorious body.

What the Christians Are to Do

4 [LTherefore; So then] My brothers and sisters, ·I love you and
want to see you [Lmy beloved and longed-for ones]. ·You bring me
joy and make me proud of you [L...my joy and crown; 1 Thess. 2:19; Ca
wreath bestowed for victory or honor], so stand ·strong [firm] in the Lord
as I have told you, ·dear friends [beloved].
[2]I ·ask [urge; encourage; exhort] Euodia and Syntyche [Ctwo women in
the Philippian congregation] to agree in the Lord. [3]And I ask you, my
·faithful [true; genuine] ·friend [companion; Lyoke-partner; Cpossibly a
proper name: Syzygos], to help these women. They ·served [struggled;
labored] with me in telling the ·Good News [Gospel], together with
Clement and ·others who worked with me [Lthe rest of my coworkers],
whose names are written in the book of life [Rev. 3:5; 21:27].
[4]·Be full of joy [Rejoice] in the Lord always. I will say again, ·be full of
joy [rejoice].
[5]Let everyone see that you are ·gentle [kind; considerate; patient]. The

Lord is ·coming soon [or close at hand; [L]near]. 6Do not ·worry [be anxious]
about anything, but pray and ·ask God for everything you need [or make
your requests known to God], always giving thanks. 7And God's peace,
which ·is so great we cannot understand it [transcends/surpasses all com-
prehension], will ·keep [guard] your hearts and minds in Christ Jesus.

8[[L]Finally; In conclusion; or Now then] Brothers and sisters, ·think
about [focus your thoughts on; fill your minds with] things that are true
and honorable and ·right [just] and pure and ·beautiful [lovely] and
·respected [commendable]. If there is anything that is ·good [morally
excellent] and worthy of praise, ·think about [focus your thoughts on; fill
your minds with] these things. 9Do what you learned and received and
heard ·from [[L]in] me, and what you saw ·me do [[L]in me]. And the God
·who gives [[L]of] peace will be with you.

Paul Thanks the Christians

10I ·am very happy [[L]rejoiced greatly] in the Lord that you have ·shown
[renewed; revived] your ·care [concern] for me again. You continued to
·care [be concerned] about me, but ·there was no way for you [you had no
opportunity] to show it. 11I am not telling you this because I need anything. [[L]For] I have learned to be ·satisfied [content] ·whatever the
circumstances [or with whatever I have]. 12I know how to live when I am
·poor [in humble circumstances], and I know how to live when I have
plenty. I have learned the ·secret of being happy [[L]secret] ·at any time in
everything that happens [or in any and all circumstances], when I have
enough to eat and when I go hungry, when I have ·more than I need
[plenty; an abundance] and when I do not have enough. 13I can do all
things through ·Christ, because he [[L]the one who] gives me strength.

14·But [However; Nevertheless] it was good that you ·helped [shared/part-
nered with] me ·when I needed it [[L]in my trouble/trial]. 15You Philippians
remember ·when I first preached the Good News there [or when you first
believed the Good News/Gospel; [L]in the beginning of the Good News/Gospel;
Acts 16:11–40]. When I left Macedonia [[C]the northern part of present-day
Greece; Acts 17:14–15], ·you were the only church that [[L]no church except
you alone] ·gave me help [[L]shared/partnered with me in matters of giving and
receiving; [C]business terminology; the Philippians "invested" in Paul's ministry
and received back spiritual blessings]. 16[[L]For] Even when I was in Thessalonica
[[C]shortly after leaving Philippi; Thessalonica is southwest of Philippi; Acts
17:1–9] ·several times [[L]both once and twice] you sent me things I needed.
17Really, it is not that I ·want to receive gifts from you [[L]seek the gift], but I
·want you to have the good that comes from giving [[L]seek the profit/fruit that
increases to your account; [C]more business terminology; v. 15]. 18And now I
have ·everything [or received full payment], and more. I ·have all I need [or
am fully supplied/filled up], because Epaphroditus [2:25] brought your gifts
to me. They are ·like a sweet-smelling offering to God [[L]a fragrant aroma], a
sacrifice that is acceptable and pleasing to him. 19[[L]And] My God will ·meet
[supply; fulfill] all of your needs ·from [[L]according to] his ·wonderful riches
[glorious riches; or riches in heaven/glory] in Christ Jesus. 20Glory to our God
and Father forever and ever! Amen.

21Greet each ·of God's people [[T]saint] in Christ Jesus. ·Those [[L]The brothers
(and sisters)] who are with me send greetings to you. 22All of ·God's people
[[T]the saints] greet you, particularly those from ·the palace of Caesar [[L]Caesar's
household; [C]the soldiers, slaves, and freedmen engaged in imperial service].

23The grace of the Lord Jesus Christ be with ·you all [your spirit].

COLOSSIANS

1 From Paul, an ·apostle [messenger] of Christ Jesus. ·I am an apostle because that is what God wanted [L...by the will of God]. Also from Timothy [Acts 16:1–5; 1 Cor. 16:10–11; Phil. 2:19–24; 1 and 2 Timothy], our brother.

[2]To the ·holy [Tsaints] and faithful brothers and sisters in Christ that live in Colossae [a city located in the Lycus Valley in the Roman province of Phrygia, present-day central Turkey]:

Grace and peace to you from God our Father.[n]

[3]In our prayers for you we always thank God, the Father of our Lord Jesus Christ, [4]·because we have [*or* ever since we; Lhaving] heard about the faith you have in Christ Jesus and the love you have for all ·of God's people [Tthe saints]. [5]You have this faith and love because of your hope, and what you hope for is ·kept safe [stored up; reserved] for you in heaven. You learned about this hope when you heard the ·message about the truth [*or* true message; Lword of truth], the ·Good News [Gospel] [6]that ·was told [Lhas come] to you. [L...just as] Everywhere in the world that ·Good News [Gospel] is ·bringing blessings [Lbearing fruit] and is growing. This has happened with you, too, ·since [Lfrom the day] you heard and ·understood the truth about [*or* truly understood] the grace of God. [7]You learned about ·God's grace [Lit] from Epaphras, our ·dear [beloved; much loved] fellow ·servant [slave; bondservant], who is a faithful ·servant [minister] of Christ ·for us[n] [on our behalf]. [CEpaphras apparently established the church at Colossae during Paul's three-year ministry in Ephesus; Acts 19:10.] [8]He also told us about the love you have ·from [*or* in] the Holy Spirit.

[9]Because of this, since the day we heard about you, we have ·continued [not ceased] praying for you, asking God ·that you will know fully what he wants [Lto fill you with the knowledge of his will], ·and that you will have great [Lin all] ·spiritual wisdom and understanding [*or* wisdom and understanding from the Spirit] [10]so that you will live the kind of life that ·honors [is worthy of] and pleases the Lord in every way. You will produce fruit in every good work and grow in the knowledge of God. [11]·God will strengthen you [L...being strengthened] with ·his own great power [Lall power according to his glorious might] so that you will not give up when troubles come, but you will ·be patient. [12]And you will joyfully give thanks [*or* ...have patience with joy, [12]giving thanks] to the Father who has made you[n] able to have a share in ·all that he has prepared for his

---

1:2 Father Some Greek copies continue, "and the Lord Jesus Christ." **1:7 for us** Some Greek copies read "for you." **1:12 you** Some Greek copies read "us."

people in the kingdom of light [Lthe inheritance of the saints/holy ones in
the light]. 13**·God** [L...who] **has ·freed** [rescued; delivered] **us from the
·power** [authority; dominion] **of darkness, and he brought us into the
kingdom of his ·dear** [dearly loved; beloved] **Son,** 14**·who purchased our
freedom**[n] [Lin whom we have redemption] **·and forgave our sins** [*or* which
is the forgiveness of sins].

The Importance of Christ

15**The Son** [L...who] **is ·the image of** [exactly like; the visible representa-
tion of] **the invisible God** [John 1:18; Heb. 1:3]. **He ·ranks higher than** [Lis
the firstborn of/over] **·everything that has been made** [all creation; Prov.
8:22–30]. 16**·Through his power** [LIn him; *or* By him] **all things were created** [John 1:3; Heb. 1:2]**—things in heaven and on earth, things seen and
unseen, all ·powers** [*or* heavenly authorities; Lthrones], **·authorities**
[dominions; kingdoms], **·lords** [rulers], **and ·rulers** [authorities; Cthese
four may refer to angelic hierarchies, or to earthly and heavenly rulers]. **All
things were created through Christ and for Christ.** 17**He ·was there before
anything was made** [Lis before all things], **and all things ·continue** [endure;
or hold together; unite] **·because of** [*or* in] **him.** 18**He is the head of the
body, which is the church. He is the beginning** [Cmeaning (1) the source
of the church; (2) the creator of all things; or (3) the beginning/initiator of
the end-time resurrection]. **He is the ·first one who was raised** [Lfirstborn]
from the dead. So in all things Jesus has ·first place [supremacy]. 19**God
was pleased for all ·of himself** [that he is; Lof his fullness] **to live in ·Christ**
[*or* the Son; Lhim]. 20**And through ·Christ** [Lhim], **God has ·brought all
things back to himself again** [Lreconciled all things to himself]**—things
on earth and things in heaven. ·God made** [L...by making] **peace through
the blood of ·Christ's death on the cross** [Lhis cross].
21**At one time you were ·separated** [alienated; estranged] **from God. You
were his enemies in your minds, ·and the evil things you did were against
God** [*or* because of your evil deeds]. 22**But now God has ·made you his
friends again** [reconciled you] **through Christ's death in ·the body** [his
physical body; Lthe body of his flesh], **so that he might bring you into God's
presence as people who are holy, ·with no wrong** [without blemish; Cas were
sacrificial animals], **and ·with nothing of which God can judge you guilty**
[blameless; innocent; free of accusation]. 23**This will happen if you continue
·strong** [grounded; established] **and ·sure** [firm; steadfast] **in your faith. You
must not ·be moved** [shift; drift] **away from the hope ·brought to you by** [*or*
found in; Lof] **the ·Good News** [the Gospel] **that you heard. That same
·Good News** [Gospel] **has been ·told** [preached; proclaimed] **to ·everyone**
[Levery creature; *or* in all creation] **·in the world** [Lunder heaven], **and I,
Paul, ·help in preaching** [Lam a servant/minister of] **it.**

Paul's Work for the Church

24[LNow] **I ·am happy** [rejoice] **in my sufferings for you. And I ·accept**
[fill up; complete] **in my ·body** [flesh] **what ·Christ must still suffer** [*or* is
lacking in the suffering of Christ] **·through** [*or* on behalf of] **his body, the
church.** [CBy suffering while spreading the Gospel, Paul both participates in
Christ's death and helps complete God's plan.] 25**I became a ·servant** [min-
ister] **of the church because God gave me a ·special work to do** [stewardship;
commission] **·that helps you** [Lfor you], **and that work is to ·tell fully** [*or*
complete; *or* preach everywhere; Lfulfill] **the ·message** [word] **of God.**
26**This message is the ·secret** [mystery; Csomething God had not previously

1:14 freedom Some Greek copies continue, "with his blood."

disclosed; Eph. 1:9] **that was hidden from ·everyone since the beginning of**
time [Lages and generations], **but now it is made known to ·God's holy**
people [Tthe saints]. 27**God ·decided** [chose; willed] **to let his people know**
this rich and glorious ·secret [mystery; 1:26] **which he has for ·all people**
[the nations/Gentiles]. **This ·secret** [mystery] **is ·that Christ lives in you.**
He is our only hope for glory [LChrist in you, the hope of glory]. 28**So we**
continue to ·preach [proclaim; announce] **Christ to each person, using all**
wisdom to ·warn [instruct; admonish] **and to teach everyone, in order to**
bring each one into God's presence as a mature person in Christ. 29**To do**
this, I ·work [toil; labor] **and struggle, using ·Christ's** [Lhis] **great strength**
that works so powerfully in me.

2 [LFor] **I want you to know how hard I ·work** [contend; struggle] **for**
you, those in Laodicea [Ca city northwest of Colossae; 4:16; Rev.
3:14–22], **and others who have never ·seen me** [met me personally; Lseen my
face in the flesh]. 2**I want ·them** [Ltheir hearts] **to be ·strengthened** [encour-
aged; comforted] **and joined together with love so that they may be rich in**
their ·understanding [Lassurance of understanding]. **This leads to their**
knowing fully God's ·secret [mystery; 1:26], **that is, Christ himself.** 3**In him**
all the treasures of wisdom and knowledge are ·safely kept [hidden].

4**I say this so that no one can ·fool** [deceive] **you by ·arguments that**
seem good, but are false [persuasive/enticing/specious arguments]. 5[LFor]
Though I am absent from you in my body, ·my heart is [in spirit I am] **with**
you, and I ·am happy [rejoice] **to see your ·good lives** [discipline; orderly
lives; *or* unbroken ranks] **and your ·strong** [firm; steadfast] **faith in Christ.**

Continue to Live in Christ

6[LTherefore] **As you received Christ Jesus the Lord, so continue to ·live**
[walk] **in him.** 7**Keep your roots deep in him and have your lives built on**
him. Be ·strong [established] **in the faith, just as you were taught, ·and**
always be thankful [abounding/overflowing with gratitude].

8**·Be sure** [Be careful; Watch; See] **that no one ·leads you away** [takes you
captive; captivates you] **with ·false** [deceptive] **and ·empty** [worthless] **teach-**
ing that is ·only human [Laccording to human traditions], **which comes from**
the ·ruling spirits [elemental spiritual forces (demons); *or* elementary teach-
ings] **of this world, and not from Christ.** 9**·All of God lives fully in Christ**
[LFor in him all the fullness of deity dwells] **·in a human body** [bodily;
embodied], 10**and you have ·a full and true life in Christ** [Lbeen filled in him],
who is ·ruler [Lhead] **over every ruler and ·power** [authority].

11**In Christ you were also circumcised, but not with a circumcision**
done by hands [Rom. 2:28; Phil. 3:3]. **It was ·a circumcision done by**
Christ [Lthe circumcision of Christ], **which ·freed you from** [put off; cut
away] **·the power of your sinful self** [your sinful nature; Lthe body of flesh;
Cjust as OT circumcision cut off the physical flesh, so Christ's circumcision
"cuts off" the "flesh"—the power of our sinful self]. 12**When you were**
baptized, you were buried with Christ, and you were raised up with him
through your faith in the ·power [working; active agency] **of God, who**
raised Christ from the dead. 13**When you were ·spiritually dead** [Ldead]
·because of [*or* in] **your sins and ·because you were not free from the**
power [Lin the uncircumcision] **of your ·sinful self** [sinful nature; flesh],
God made you alive with Christ, and he forgave all our ·sins [transgres-
sions]. 14**He ·canceled** [wiped out; erased] **the ·record** [certificate] **of debt,**
·which listed all the rules we failed to follow [Lwith its decrees that were
against us; Cthe record of sins revealed through the OT law; Eph. 2:15]. **He**

·took it away [set it aside; destroyed it] **and nailed it to the cross.** 15**·God** [*or* Christ; LHe] **·stripped the spiritual rulers and powers of their authority** [Ldisarmed/despoiled the rulers and authorities]. **With the cross, he won the victory and ·showed the world that they were powerless** [publicly shamed them; made a public spectacle of them; Clike a triumphant general displaying his captives in a victory parade].

Don't Follow People's Rules

16**So do not let anyone ·make rules for** [*or* criticize; judge; *or* condemn] **you about eating and drinking or about a religious ·feast** [festival], **a New Moon Festival** [2 Kin. 4:23; Neh. 10:33], **or a Sabbath day** [Creligious observances that false teachers pressured the Colossians to keep]. 17**These things ·were like** [Lare] **a shadow of what was to come. But ·what is true and real has come and is found in Christ** [*or* the reality/substance belongs to Christ; Lthe body (is) of Christ]. 18**Do not let anyone disqualify you by ·insisting on** [*or* delighting in] **self-denial** [asceticism; *or* false humility] **and worship of angels. Such people ·enter into** [*or* talk endlessly about; *or* pin their hopes on] **visions, which ·fill them** [puff them up] **with ·foolish pride** [*or* empty notions] **because of their ·human way of thinking** [unspiritual/worldly/carnal minds; Lmind of the flesh]. 19**They ·do not hold tightly** [*or* have no connection] **to the head** [CChrist]. **It is from him that all the parts of the body are ·cared for** [supported] **and held together through its joints and ligaments. So it grows in the way God ·wants** [*or* causes] **it to grow.**

20**Since you died with Christ and were made free from the ·ruling spirits** [elemental spiritual forces (demons); *or* elementary teachings; v. 8] **of the world, why do you act as if you still ·belong to** [Lare living in] **this world by following rules like these:** 21**"Don't handle this," "Don't taste that," "Don't even touch that thing"?** 22**These rules refer to ·earthly things that are gone as soon as they are used** [Lthings that all perish with use]. **They are only human commands and teachings.** 23**They ·seem to be wise** [have an appearance of wisdom], **with their ·religious devotion** [*or* forced piety; *or* asceticism], **false humility, and ·harsh treatment** [severe discipline] **of their bodies. But they ·do not really control** [have no value against] **the ·evil desires** [indulgence] **of the ·sinful self** [sinful nature; flesh].

Your New Life in Christ

3 [LTherefore] **Since you were ·raised from the dead** [Lraised] **with Christ, ·aim at** [aspire to; seek after; focus on] **·what is in heaven** [Lthe things above], **where Christ is sitting at the right hand of God.** 2**·Think only about** [Set your minds on; Fix your thoughts on] **the things ·in heaven** [Labove], **not the things on earth.** 3[LFor] **·Your old sinful self has** [LYou] **died, and your new life is ·kept** [hidden] **with Christ in God.** 4**When Christ, who is your**[n] **life, ·comes again** [appears; Lis revealed], **you will ·share in his** [Lbe revealed with him in] **glory.**

5**So put all ·evil** [earthly; worldly] **things ·out of your life** [Lto death]: **sexual sinning, ·doing evil** [impurity; defilement], **·letting evil thoughts control you** [lust; passion], **·wanting things that are evil** [selfish desires], **and greed, which is ·serving a false god** [idolatry]. 6**Because of these things, God's ·judgment** [anger; wrath] **is coming.**[n] 7**You also used to ·do these things** [live/walk this way] **when you were ·part of the world** [Lliving among/in them].

8**But now also put these things out of your life: anger, ·bad temper** [rage], **·hatred** [malice; evil], **·saying things to hurt others** [slander; blasphemy],

3:4 your Some Greek copies read "our." **3:6 Because... coming** Some Greek copies continue, "against the people who do not obey God."

and ·using evil words [abusive/filthy/obscene language] ·when you talk
[Lfrom your mouth]. 9Do not lie to each other. You have ·left [taken/stripped
off; *or* disarmed; 2:15] your old ·sinful life [self; person; man] and ·the
things you did before [Lits deeds/practices]. 10You have ·begun to live the
new life [Lput on the new person/man], in which you are being ·made new
[renewed] in ·the true knowledge of God [Lknowledge] ·and are becoming
like [Laccording to the image of] the One who created you [Gen. 1:26–27].
11In the new life there is no difference between Greeks and Jews, those who
are circumcised and those who are not circumcised, or ·people who are
foreigners [barbarians], or Scythians [Cfrom the northern coast of the Black
Sea, considered uncivilized and violent]. There is no difference between
slaves and free people. But Christ is ·all that is important and is in all believers [Lall and in all].
12·God loves you and has chosen you and made you his holy people. So
[LAs God's chosen, holy and beloved ones; Ex. 19:6; 1 Pet. 2:9] you should
always clothe yourselves with ·mercy [La heart of compassion], kindness,
humility, gentleness, and patience. 13·Bear with [Make allowances for; Be
patient with] each other, and forgive each other. If someone ·does wrong
to you [Lhas a grievance/complaint against someone], forgive that person
because the Lord forgave you. 14·Even more than all this [Above all],
clothe yourself in love, which ·holds you all together in perfect unity [*or*
binds everything together; Lis the bond of perfection/completeness]. 15Let
the peace ·that Christ gives [of Christ] ·control [rule; arbitrate] your
·thinking [hearts], because you were all called together in one body [Cthe
church as the body of Christ] to have peace. Always be thankful. 16Let the
·teaching [message; word] of Christ ·live in [*or* dwell among] you richly.
Use all wisdom to teach and ·instruct [warn; admonish] each other by
singing psalms, hymns, and spiritual songs with ·thankfulness [gratitude;
grace] in your hearts to God. 17Everything you do or say should be done
·to obey [*or* as a representative of; Lin the name of] the Lord Jesus. And in
all you do, give thanks to God the Father through Jesus.

Your New Life with Other People

18Wives, ·yield to the authority of [submit to] your husbands, because
this is ·the right thing to do [appropriate; fitting] in the Lord [Eph. 5:22–
24; 1 Pet. 3:1–6].
19Husbands, love your wives and ·be gentle with [Ldon't be harsh
toward/embittered against] them [Eph. 5:25–33; 1 Pet. 3:7].
20Children, obey your parents in all things, because this pleases the
Lord [Eph. 6:1–3].
21Fathers [*or* Parents; Heb. 11:23], do not ·nag [aggravate; exasperate;
provoke] your children [Eph. 6:4]. If you are too hard to please, they may
·want to stop trying [become discouraged; lose heart].
22·Slaves [Bondservants], obey your ·human [earthly] masters in all
things [Eph. 6:5–9; 1 Pet. 2:18–25]. Do not obey just ·when they are
watching you [Lwith eye-service], ·to gain their favor [Las people-pleas-
ers], but serve them ·honestly [with a sincere heart], because you ·respect
[reverence; fear] the Lord [Prov. 1:7]. 23In all the work you are doing,
·work the best you can [do it heart and soul; Lfrom the soul]. Work as if
you were doing it for the Lord, not for people. 24·Remember [L…know-
ing] that you will receive from the Lord the reward ·which he promised to
his people [Lof an inheritance]. You are serving the Lord Christ. 25But
remember that anyone who does wrong will be ·punished [repaid] for

that wrong, and ·the Lord treats everyone the same [Lthere is no favorit-
ism/partiality].

4 Masters, give what is good and fair to your slaves. Remember that
you have a Master in heaven.

What the Christians Are to Do

2·Continue praying [Be devoted to prayer], keeping alert, and always
thanking God. 3Also pray for us that God will ·give us an opportunity
[Lopen a door for us] to tell people his ·message [word]. Pray that we can
preach the ·secret that God has made known about Christ [Lmystery of
Christ; 1:26]. This is why I am in ·prison [chains; CPaul is probably writing
from house arrest in Rome, about AD 60; see Acts 28:30–31]. 4Pray that I
can speak in a way that will make it clear, as I should.
5Be wise in the way you ·act with [behave towards] people who are not
believers, making the most of every opportunity. 6When you talk, you
should always be ·kind [gracious] and ·pleasant [winsome; engaging; *or*
wholesome; Lseasoned with salt] so you will be able to answer everyone in
the way you should.

News About the People with Paul

7Tychicus [Acts 20:4; Eph. 6:21; 2 Tim. 4:12; Titus 3:12] is my ·dear
[beloved] brother in Christ and a faithful ·minister [servant] and ·servant
with me [fellow slave/bondservant] in the Lord. He will tell you all the
things that are happening to me. 8This is why I am sending him: so you
may know how we are[n] and he may encourage ·you [Lyour hearts]. 9I send
him with Onesimus [Philem. 10], a faithful and ·dear [beloved] ·brother
in Christ [Lbrother], and one of your ·group [*or* own people; *or* fellow-
citizens]. They will tell you all that has happened here.
10Aristarchus [Acts 19:29; 20:4; Philem. 24], a prisoner with me, and
Mark [Acts 12:25; 13:13; 15:37–39], the cousin of Barnabas [Acts 4:36;
9:26–27; 11:22, 25, 30; 13:2–4; 15:36–39], greet you. (·I have already told
you what to do [LYou have received instructions] about Mark. If he comes,
welcome him.) 11Jesus, who is called Justus, also greets you. These are the
only ·Jewish believers [Lones of the circumcision] who work with me for
the kingdom of God, and they have been a comfort to me.
12Epaphras [1:7], a ·servant [slave; bondservant] of Jesus Christ, from
your ·group [*or* people; *or* city], also greets you. He always ·prays [prays
earnestly; Lwrestles/struggles in prayer] for you that you will ·grow to be
spiritually mature [*or* stand complete/perfect] and ·confident that you are
in God's will [Lfully assured in all the will of God]. 13I ·know [can testify/bear
witness that] he has worked hard for you and ·the people [*or* the churches;
Lthose] in Laodicea [2:1] and in Hierapolis [Ca city north of Colossae, in
present-day southwest Turkey]. 14Demas [2 Tim. 4:10; Philem. 24] and our
·dear [beloved] friend Luke [2 Tim. 4:11; Philem. 24], the doctor, greet you.
15Greet the brothers and sisters in Laodicea [2:1]. And greet Nympha
and the church that meets in her house. 16After this letter is read to you,
be sure it is also read to the church in Laodicea. And you read the letter
·that I wrote to [Lfrom] Laodicea. 17Tell Archippus [Philem. 2], "Be sure to
·finish [fulfill] the ·work [ministry; service] ·the Lord gave you [Lyou
received in the Lord]."
18I, Paul, write this greeting with my own hand. Remember ·me in
prison [Lmy chains]. Grace be with you.

4:8 so... are Some Greek copies read "so he may know how you are."

1 THESSALONIANS

1 From Paul, Silas [Acts 15:22, 40], and Timothy [Acts 16:1–5;
1 Cor. 16:10–11; Phil. 2:19–24; 1 and 2 Timothy].
To the church in Thessalonica [Lof the Thessalonians; Ca city in
Macedonia, present-day northern Greece], the church in God the
Father and the Lord Jesus Christ:
Grace and peace to you.

The Faith of the Thessalonians

2 We always thank God for all of you and mention you when we pray.
3 We continually recall before God our Father ·the things you have done
because of your faith [Lyour work of/from faith], ·the work you have
done because of your love [Lyour labor of/from love] and your ·continu-
ing strength because of your hope [Lendurance of/from hope] in our Lord
Jesus Christ.
4 Brothers and sisters, God loves you, and we know he has chosen you,
5 because the ·Good News [Gospel] we brought to you came not only with
words, but with power, with the Holy Spirit, and with ·sure knowledge that
it is true [great conviction]. You know how we lived when we were with
you ·in order to help you [for your sake]. 6 And you became ·like us and like
[imitators of us and of] the Lord. You ·suffered much [experienced many
trials/much persecution], but still you accepted the teaching with the joy
that comes from the Holy Spirit. 7 So you became an ·example to [model
for] all the believers in Macedonia [Cthe Roman province in which
Thessalonica was located, present-day northern Greece] and Achaia
[Cpresent-day southern Greece]. 8 And the Lord's ·teaching [message; word]
·spread [rang out; sounded forth] from you not only into Macedonia and
Achaia, but now your faith in God has ·become known [gone forth] everywhere. So we do not need to say anything about it. 9 ·People everywhere
[LFor they themselves] are ·telling [reporting; announcing] about the way
you ·accepted [welcomed] us when we were there with you. They tell how
you ·stopped worshiping idols [Lturned to God from idols] to serve the
living and true God, 10 and to wait for his Son from heaven, whom God
raised from the dead. He is Jesus, who ·saves [rescues; delivers] us from
·God's angry judgment that is sure to come [Lthe coming wrath].

Paul's Work in Thessalonica

2 Brothers and sisters, you ·know [yourselves know; are well aware
that] our ·visit [coming] to you was not ·a failure [without results;
in vain; Acts 17:1–9]. 2 Before we came to you, we suffered and were ·insulted
[mistreated] in Philippi [Ca city in Macedonia (1:7); Acts 16:6–40], as you
know. But ·our God helped us to be brave and [Lwe were emboldened in our
God] to tell you ·his Good News [the Gospel of God] in spite of great opposition. 3 [LFor] Our ·appeal [encouragement; exhortation] does not come
from ·lies [error] or ·wrong reasons [false motives; Limpurity], nor ·were we

trying to trick you [with guile/deceit]. **4But we speak the ·Good News** [Gospel] **because God ·tested** [approved] **us and ·trusted us to do** [*or* entrusted us with] **it. When we speak, we are not trying to please people, but God, who ·tests** [examines; approves] **our hearts. 5You know that we never ·tried to influence you by saying nice things about you** [Lcame with words of flattery]. **·We were not trying to get your money; we had no selfishness to hide from you** [L...nor with hidden motives of greed]. **God ·knows that this is true** [Lis (our) witness]. **6We were not looking for human ·praise** [glory], **from you or anyone else, 7even though as apostles of Christ we could have ·used our authority over you** [thrown our weight around; exercised our prerogatives].

But we were very gentle with you,n **like a ·mother** [nurse; nursing mother] **caring for her** [Lown] **little children. 8Because we ·loved** [had such affection for/devotion to] **you, we were ·happy** [pleased; delighted] **to share not only God's ·Good News** [Gospel] **with you, but ·even** [also] **our own lives. You had become so ·dear** [beloved] **to us! 9Brothers and sisters, ·I know** [surely] **you remember our hard work and ·difficulties** [hardship; labor]. **We worked night and day so we would not burden any of you while we preached God's ·Good News** [Gospel] **to you.**

10When we were with you, we lived in a holy and ·honest [righteous; just] **way, ·without fault** [blameless; innocent]. **You ·know this is true, and so does** [Lare witnesses, and so is] **God. 11You know that we treated each of you as a father treats his own children. 12We ·encouraged** [exhorted; urged] **you, we ·urged** [encouraged; comforted] **you, and we ·insisted** [appealed/bore witness to you] **that you ·live good lives for** [Lwalk worthy of] **God, who calls you to his ·glorious kingdom** [Lkingdom and glory].

13·Also [LFor this reason], **we always thank God because when you ·heard his message** [received the message you heard] **from us, you accepted it not as ·merely human words** [a human message], **but for what it truly is—·the word of** [a message from] **God, which ·works in** [transforms] **you who believe. 14**[LFor] **Brothers and sisters, ·your experiences have been like those** [*or* you became imitators] **of God's churches in Christ Jesus that are in Judea** [Cthe original church in Jerusalem and others nearby]. **You suffered the same things from the people of your own country, as they suffered from the Jews 15who killed both the Lord Jesus and the prophets and ·forced us to leave that country** [drove us out; *or* persecuted us]. **They do not please God and are ·against** [hostile/opposed to] **all people. 16·They try** [*or* ...because they try; *or* ...by trying] **to stop us from ·teaching** [speaking/preaching to] **the Gentiles so they may be saved. By doing this, they are ·increasing** [filling/heaping up] **their sins to the limit. The ·anger** [wrath] **of God ·has come to** [*or* has drawn near to; *or* will overtake] **them ·at last** [*or* completely; *or* until the end (of the age)].

Paul Wants to Visit Them Again

17Brothers and sisters, though we were ·separated [torn away; orphaned] **from you for a short time, ·our thoughts were still with you** [physically, not spiritually...; Lin face, not in heart...]. **We wanted very much to see you and tried hard to do so. 18We wanted to come to you. I, Paul, tried to come ·more than once** [again and again; Lboth once and twice], **but Satan ·stopped** [hindered; prevented] **us. 19·You are** [LFor who is...?] **our hope, our joy, and the crown we will ·take pride in** [boast about] **when our Lord Jesus Christ comes. 20Truly you are our glory and our joy.**

2:7 But... you Some Greek copies read "But we were like infants among you."

3 When we could ·not wait any [endure it no] longer, we decided it was best to stay in Athens alone 2and send Timothy to you. Timothy, our brother, ·works with us [is our coworker] for God ·and helps us tell people the Good News about [Lin the Gospel of] Christ. We sent him to strengthen and ·encourage [comfort; *or* exhort] you in your faith 3so none of you would be ·upset [disturbed; shaken] by these ·troubles [trials]. [LFor] You yourselves know that we ·must face these troubles [Lare destined/appointed for this]. 4[LFor] Even when we were with you, we told you [Lin advance] we all would have to ·suffer [be persecuted; suffer hardship/affliction], and you know it has happened. 5Because of this, when I could ·wait [endure it] no longer, I sent Timothy to you so I could learn about your faith. I was afraid ·the devil [Lthe tempter] had tempted you, and perhaps our hard work would have been ·wasted [in vain; for nothing].

6But Timothy now has come back to us from you and has brought us good news about your faith and love. He told us that you always remember us in a good way and that you ·want [long] to see us just as much as we ·want [long] to see you. 7So, brothers and sisters, ·while we have much [Lin all of our] ·trouble [distress] and ·suffering [trials; persecution], we are ·encouraged [comforted; reassured] about you because of your faith. 8·Our life is really full [LFor now we live/are alive (again)] ·if you stand [since you are standing] ·strong [firm; fast] in the Lord. 9·We cannot thank God enough [LFor what thanks can we give to God…?] for all the joy we feel ·in God's presence [before our God] because of you. 10Night and day we continue praying ·with all our heart [most earnestly] that we can see you again and ·give you all the things you need [Lstrengthen/supply what is lacking] to make your faith strong.

11Now may our God and Father himself and our Lord Jesus ·prepare [clear; direct] the way for us to come to you. 12May the Lord make your love grow more and ·multiply [abound; overflow] for each other and for all people ·so that you will love others as we love you [*or* just as our love abounds for you]. 13·May your hearts [L…so that your hearts may] be made strong so that you will be holy and ·without fault [blameless] before our God and Father when our Lord Jesus comes with all his ·holy ones [Tsaints; *or* holy angels].

A Life that Pleases God

4 [LFinally; *or* Now then; Furthermore] Brothers and sisters, we taught you how to ·live [walk] in a way that will please God, and you are living that way. Now we ask and ·encourage [urge; appeal to] you in the Lord Jesus to ·live that way [excel; abound] even more. 2[LFor] You know what ·we told [instructions/commands we gave] you to do ·by the authority of [Lthrough] the Lord Jesus. 3·God wants you to be holy and [*or* For this is God's will, your sanctification:] to stay away from sexual sins. 4He wants each of you to ·learn to control your own body [*or* take a wife for yourself; *or* live with your own wife; Lgain/possess his own vessel] in a way that is holy and honorable. 5·Don't use your body for sexual sin [L…not in lustful passion] like the ·people [LGentiles] who do not know God. 6Also, do not ·wrong [exploit; transgress] or ·cheat [take advantage of] another ·Christian [Lbrother (or sister)] in this way. The Lord ·will punish people who do those [Lis the avenger concerning these] things as we have already told you and ·warned [solemnly testified to] you. 7[LFor] God did not call us to ·a life of sin [Limpurity], but to holiness. 8·So [Therefore] the person who ·refuses to obey [disregards; rejects; despises] this teaching is not simply

·disobeying [disregarding; rejecting; despising] ·a human being [human
authority], but God, who gives you his Holy Spirit.
9We do not need to write you about ·having love for your Christian
family [Lbrotherly love], because God has already taught you to love each
other. 10And truly you do love the ·Christians [Lbrothers (and sisters)] in
all of Macedonia [1:7]. Now we encourage you, brothers and sisters, to
·love them [excel; abound; v. 1] even more. 11·Do all you can [...and to
aspire] to live a peaceful life. ·Take care of [Attend to; Mind] your own
business, and ·do your own work [Lwork with your hands] as we have
already ·told [instructed; commanded] you. 12If you do, then you will ·win
the respect of [*or* live a respectable/proper life before] ·unbelievers
[Loutsiders], and you will not have to depend on others for what you need.

The Lord's Coming

13Brothers and sisters, we ·want you to know [do not want you to be
uninformed] about those ·Christians who have died [Lwho sleep; Ca euphemism for death] so you will not ·be sad [grieve], as ·others [Lthe rest] who
have no hope. 14[LFor] We believe that Jesus died and that he rose again.
·So, through him, God will raise with Jesus those who have died [*or* So
God will bring with Jesus those who have died/Lfallen asleep in him].
15What we tell you now is ·the Lord's own message [Lby the word of the
Lord]. We who are ·living [still alive] when the Lord comes again will
[Lcertainly; surely] not go before those who have ·already died [Lfallen
asleep]. 16The Lord himself will come down from heaven with a loud ·com-
mand [*or* shout], ·with [*or* accompanied by; *or* preceded by] the voice of
the archangel [Ca leading or ruling angel; Dan. 10:13; Jude 9], and with the
trumpet call of God. And ·those who have died believing [Lthe dead] in
Christ will rise first [1 Cor. 15:51–57]. 17After that, we who are ·still alive
[*or* alive and are left] will be ·gathered [caught; taken] up with them in the
clouds to meet the Lord in the air. And [Lso; in this way] we will be with the
Lord forever. 18So ·encourage [comfort] each other with these words.

Be Ready for the Lord's Coming

5 Now, brothers and sisters, we do not need to write you about
times and ·dates [seasons; Crelated to end-time events]. 2You know
·very well [accurately] that the ·day the Lord comes again [Lday of the
Lord; Cthe time of Christ's return and the judgments associated with it]
will ·be a surprise, like a thief that comes in the night [Lcome like a thief
in the night]. 3While people are saying, "·We have peace and we are safe
[LPeace and safety/security]," they will be destroyed ·quickly [suddenly].
It is like pains that come quickly to a woman having a baby. Those people
will not escape. 4But you, brothers and sisters, are not ·living in darkness
[Lin darkness], and so that day will not ·surprise you [*or* overtake you] like
a thief. 5[LFor] You are all ·people who belong to the light [Lchildren/sons
of the light] and ·who belong to [Lchildren/sons of] the day. We do not
belong to the night or to darkness. 6So we should not be like other people
who are sleeping [Cspiritually], but we should be ·alert [awake] and ·have
self-control [sober]. 7[LFor] Those who sleep sleep at night. Those who
get drunk get drunk at night. 8But we belong to the day, so we should
·control ourselves [be sober]. We should ·wear faith and love to protect us
[Lput on the breastplate/body armor of faith and love], and the hope of
salvation should be our helmet [Is. 59:17]. 9God did not ·choose [appoint;
destine] us ·to suffer his anger [Lfor wrath] but to ·have [receive; gain;
possess] salvation through our Lord Jesus Christ. 10·Jesus [L...who] died
for us so that we can live together with him, whether we are ·alive [Lawake]

or ·dead [Lasleep] when he comes. 11So encourage each other and ·give each other strength [build each other up], just as you are doing now.

Final Instructions and Greetings

12Now, brothers and sisters, we ask you to ·appreciate [acknowledge; respect] those who work hard among you, who ·lead [*or* care for] you in the Lord and ·teach [instruct; admonish] you. 13·Respect [Regard; Esteem] them ·with a very special [*or* very highly with your] love because of the work they do.

Live in peace with each other. 14We ·ask [urge; exhort; encourage] you, brothers and sisters, to ·warn [admonish; rebuke] those who ·do not work [are idle; *or* are undisciplined]. ·Encourage [Comfort] the people who are ·afraid [apprehensive; fainthearted; discouraged]. Help those who are weak. Be patient with everyone. 15·Be sure [See to it] that no one pays back ·wrong [evil] for ·wrong [evil], but always ·try to do [strive for; Lpursue] what is good for each other and for all people.

16Always ·be joyful [rejoice]. 17Pray ·continually [without ceasing], 18and give thanks ·whatever happens [in all circumstances; in everything]. That is ·what God wants [God's will] for you in Christ Jesus.

19Do not ·hold back the work of [stifle; quench; extinguish] the Holy Spirit. 20Do not treat ·prophecy [Lprophecies; Coccurring in the church] ·as if it were unimportant [with contempt]. 21But test everything. ·Keep [Hold on to] what is good, 22and stay away from ·everything that is [every form/kind of] evil.

23Now may God himself, the God of peace, ·make you holy in every way [sanctify you completely/through and through]. May your whole self—spirit, soul, and body—be kept ·faultless [blameless] when our Lord Jesus Christ comes. 24The One who calls you is ·trustworthy [faithful], and he will ·do this [make this happen].

25Brothers and sisters, pray for us.

26Greet all ·believers [Lthe brothers (and sisters)] with a holy kiss. 27I ·tell [solemnly charge; adjure] you ·by the authority of [*or* before; *or* in] the Lord to read this letter to all the believers.

28The grace of our Lord Jesus Christ be with you.

2 THESSALONIANS

1 **From Paul** [Acts 15:22, 40], **Silas, and Timothy** [Acts 16:1–5; 1 Cor. 16:10–11; Phil. 2:19–24; 1 and 2 Timothy].

To the church ·in Thessalonica [L of the Thessalonians; C a city in Macedonia, present-day northern Greece] **in God our Father and the Lord Jesus Christ:**

2 **Grace and peace to you from God the Father and the Lord Jesus Christ.**

Paul Talks About God's Judgment

3 **We ·must** [ought to] **always thank God for you, brothers and sisters. This is only right, because your faith is growing more and more, and the love that every one of you has for each other is increasing.** 4 **So we ·brag** [boast] **about you to the other churches of God. We tell them about the way you ·continue to be strong** [persevere; endure] **and have faith even though you are being ·treated badly** [persecuted] **and are suffering many ·troubles** [trials; hardships].

5 **This is ·proof** [evidence] **that God is ·right** [just; righteous] **in his judgment. ·He wants you to be counted** […so that you will be considered; *or* … to make you] **worthy of his kingdom for which you are suffering.** 6 [L For] **God ·will do what is right** [is just/righteous]. **He will ·give trouble to** [pay back with trials/hardship] **those who ·trouble** [inflict trials/hardships on] **you.** 7 **And he will give rest to you who are ·troubled** [suffering trials/hardships] **and to us also when the Lord Jesus ·appears** [is revealed] **·with blazing fire from heaven** [*or* from heaven; C "with blazing fire" may go with the next sentence] **with his powerful angels.** 8 **Then he will ·punish** [*or* punish with blazing fire] **those who do not know God** [Jer. 10:25] **and who do not obey the ·Good News about** [Gospel of] **our Lord Jesus.** 9 **Those people will be punished with a ·destruction that continues forever** [eternal destruction], **·separated from** [L …from] **the presence of the Lord and from ·his great power** [*or* the glory of his strength; *or* his glorious strength]. 10 **This will happen on the day when ·the Lord Jesus** [L he] **comes to ·receive glory** [be glorified] **·because of** [*or* among; *or* in; *or* from] **his holy people. And all the people who have believed will ·be amazed at** [marvel at] **Jesus. You will be in that group, because you believed ·what we told** [our testimony to] **you.**

11 **·That is why** [To that end; In this regard] **we always pray for you, asking our God to ·help you live the kind of life he called you to live** [make/consider you worthy of his calling]. **We pray that with his power God will ·help you do the good things you want** [L fulfill every desire for goodness] **and ·perform the works that come from your** [L every work of] **faith.** 12 **We pray all this so that the name of our Lord Jesus Christ will ·have glory** [be glorified] **in you, and you ·will have glory in him** [L in him]. **That glory comes from the grace of our God and the Lord Jesus Christ.**

Evil Things Will Happen

2 Brothers and sisters, ·we have something to say about [Lconcerning] **the coming of our Lord Jesus Christ and ·the time when we will meet** [our assembly/being gathered] **together with him.** 2**·Do not** [We ask/request that you don't] **become ·easily** [quickly] **·upset** [unsettled; shaken] **in your thinking or ·afraid** [disturbed; alarmed] **if you hear that the day of the Lord has already come** [Cthe time of Christ's return and the judgments associated with it]**. Someone may have said this ·in a prophecy** [Lby a spirit; *or* by the Spirit] **or ·in a message** [*or* by word of mouth] **or in a letter as if it came from us** [Ca forged letter]. 3**Do not let anyone ·fool** [deceive] **you in any way. That day of the Lord** [v. 2] **will not come until the ·turning away from God** [great rebellion; apostasy; Matt. 24:11–12; 1 Tim. 4:1; 2 Tim. 3:1–5; 2 Pet. 2:3; Jude 18] **happens and the Man of ·Evil**[n] [Wickedness; LLawlessness; Cprobably the Antichrist; 1 John 2:18; Rev. 13], **·who is on his way to hell** [Lthe son of destruction; John 17:12], **appears.** 4**He will ·be against** [defy; oppose] **and ·put himself above** [exalt himself against] **any so-called god or ·anything that** [any object that; *or* any place where] **people worship** [Is. 14:13–14; Ezek. 28:2–9; Dan. 11:36] **·and** [*or* so that] **he will even go into the Temple of God and sit there and ·say that he is** [present himself as] **God.**

5**Don't you remember that when I was with you I told you that all this would happen?** 6**And ·now** [so] **you know what is ·stopping that Man of Evil** [Lrestraining him; holding him back; 2:3] **so he will ·appear** [be revealed] **at ·the right** [the proper; Lhis own] **time.** 7**The ·secret power** [*or* mystery] **of ·evil** [lawlessness; wickedness] **is already ·working in the world** [*or* at work], **but there is one who is ·stopping that power** [restraining it]**. And ·he** [*or* it] **will continue to ·stop** [restrain] **it until ·he** [*or* it] **is taken out of the way** [Cthis restrainer may be the Holy Spirit or human government, among other possibilities]. 8**Then that ·Man of Evil** [Levil/lawless one; 2:3] **will ·appear** [be revealed], **and the Lord Jesus**[n] **will ·kill** [destroy] **him with the breath that comes from his mouth** [Is. 11:4] **and will ·destroy** [annihilate; put an end to] **him with the ·glory** [brightness; splendor; *or* appearance; manifestation] **of his ·coming** [arrival; presence]. 9**·The Man of Evil** [L...who; 2:3] **will ·come** [arrive] **·by the power** [*or* at the instigation; Lin accordance with the work/activity] **of Satan ·and will have** [*or* with; accompanied by] **·all kinds** [*or* every kind] **of ·false** [counterfeit] **·miracles** [powers], **signs, and wonders.** 10**He will use every ·kind of evil to trick** [*or* wicked deception against/toward] **those who are ·lost** [perishing; heading toward destruction], **because they refused to love the truth that would save them.** 11**For this reason God sends them ·something powerful that leads them away from the truth** [La powerful/compelling/effective deception/error] **so they will believe ·a lie** [what is false]. 12**So all those will be ·judged guilty** [condemned] **who did not believe the truth, but ·enjoyed doing** [delighted in; approved of] **·evil** [wickedness; unrighteousness; injustice].

You Are Chosen for Salvation

13**Brothers and sisters, whom the Lord loves, God chose you from the beginning**[n] **to be saved. So we ·must** [ought to] **always thank God for you. You are saved by the ·Spirit that makes you holy** [sanctifying work of the Spirit] **and by your faith in the truth.** 14**God used the ·Good News** [Gospel] **that we preached to call you to be saved so you can ·share in** [obtain; possess] **the glory of our Lord Jesus Christ.** 15**So, brothers and sisters, stand**

2:3 Man of Evil Some Greek copies read "Man of Sin." **2:8 Jesus** Some Greek copies do not have "Jesus."
2:13 God . . . beginning Some Greek copies read "God chose you as the firstfruits of the harvest."

·strong [firm] and ·continue to believe [hold fast to; grasp firmly] the
·teachings we gave you [Ltraditions you were taught] ·in our speaking and
in our [Lwhether through our word or our] letter.
16May our Lord Jesus Christ himself and God our Father, who loved us
and through his grace gave us eternal ·comfort [encouragement] and a
good hope, 17·encourage [comfort] you and strengthen you in every good
thing you do and say.

Pray for Us

3 ·And now [*or* Finally], brothers and sisters, pray for us that the
Lord's ·teaching [message; word] ·will continue to spread quickly
[Lmight run (forward)] and ·that people will give honor to that teaching
[Lbe honored/glorified], just as happened with you. 2And pray that we will
be ·protected [*or* rescued; delivered] from ·stubborn [*or* perverse; worthless; wicked] and evil people, because not all people ·believe [have faith].
3But the Lord is faithful and will give you strength and will protect you
from the Evil One [CSatan]. 4·The Lord makes us feel sure [LWe have confidence about you in the Lord] that you are doing and will continue to do
the things we ·told [instructed; commanded] you. 5May the Lord ·lead
[guide; direct] your hearts into God's love and Christ's ·patience [endur-
ance; perseverance].

The Duty to Work

6Brothers and sisters, ·by the authority [Lin the name] of our Lord Jesus
Christ we command you to stay away from any ·believer [Lbrother (or sister)] who ·refuses to work [*or* behaves irresponsibly; Llives/walks in
idleness/disorder] and does not follow the ·teaching we gave you [Ltradition
you received from us]. 7[LFor] You yourselves know that you should ·live as
we live [follow our example; imitate us]. [LBecause] We were not ·lazy [idle;
undisciplined] when we were with you. 8And when we ate another person's
·food [bread], we always paid for it. We worked ·very hard [Lwith labor and
toil] night and day so we would not be an ·expense [financial burden] to
any of you. 9·We had [LIt was not because we do not have] the right to ask
you to help us, but we worked ·to take care of ourselves so we would [Lin
order to] be an example for you to ·follow [imitate]. 10[LFor even] When we
were with you, we gave you this ·rule [instruction; command]: "Anyone
who ·refuses [is not willing] to work should not eat."
11[LFor; *or* Yet] We hear that some people in your group ·refuse to work
[*or* are behaving irresponsibly; Lare living/walking in idleness/disorder].
They do nothing but ·busy themselves [meddle; interfere] in other people's lives. 12We command ·those [such] people and ·beg [urge; encourage;
exhort] them in the Lord Jesus Christ to ·work quietly [*or* settle down]
and ·earn [Leat] their own ·food [bread]. 13But you, brothers and sisters,
never become tired of doing good.
14If some people do not obey what we tell you in this letter, then take
note of them. ·Have nothing to do [Do not associate] with them so they will
·feel ashamed [*or* be shamed]. 15But do not ·treat [regard] them as enemies.
·Warn [Admonish] them as ·fellow believers [La brother (or sister)].

Final Words

16Now may the Lord of peace [Lhimself] give you peace at all times and
in every way. The Lord be with all of you.
17I, Paul, ·end this letter now [write this greeting] in my own ·hand-
writing [Lhand]. All my letters have this ·to show they are from me [sign].
This is the way I write.
18The grace of our Lord Jesus Christ be with you all.

1 TIMOTHY

1 From Paul, an ·apostle [messenger] of Christ Jesus, by the command of God our Savior and Christ Jesus our hope.

[2]To Timothy [Acts 16:1–5; 1 Cor. 16:10–11; Phil. 2:19–24], a ·true [genuine] child to me ·because you believe [*or* in the faith]:

Grace, mercy, and peace from God the Father and Christ Jesus our Lord.

Warning Against False Teaching

[3]I ·asked [urged; encouraged] you to stay longer in Ephesus [[C]a major port city in the Roman province of Asia, present-day western Turkey; Acts 19] when I went into Macedonia [[C]a Roman province in present-day northern Greece] so you could ·command [charge; instruct] some people there ·to stop teaching [*or* not to teach] ·false things [[L]different doctrine/teachings; [C]different from Paul's Gospel, and so false]. [4]Tell them not to ·spend their time on [occupy themselves with; devote themselves to] ·stories that are not true [myths] and ·on long lists of names in family histories [endless/useless genealogies; Titus 3:9]. These things only bring ·arguments [controversy; *or* useless speculation]; they do not help God's ·work [plan; redemptive purpose], which ·is done in [*or* operates by; *or* is received by; *or* is known by] faith. [5]The ·purpose [goal; aim] of this ·command [charge; instruction] is for people to have love, a love that comes from a pure heart and a ·good [clear] conscience and a ·true [genuine; sincere] faith. [6]Some people have ·missed [departed/deviated from] these things and turned to ·useless talk [empty/meaningless/foolish discussion]. [7]They want to be teachers of the law, but they do not understand either what they are talking about or what they ·are sure about [so confidently assert].

[8]But we know that the law [[C]the OT law of Moses] is good if someone uses it ·lawfully [legitimately; as God intended]. [9]·We also know [*or* … recognizing this:] that the law is not ·made [intended; laid down] for ·good people [[L]the just/righteous person] but for those who are ·against the law [lawbreakers; lawless] and for ·those who refuse to follow it [rebels; criminals]. It is for people who are ·against God [godless; ungodly] and are sinful, who are unholy and ·ungodly [irreverent; profane], who ·kill [*or* strike] their fathers and mothers, who murder, [10]who take part in sexual sins, who ·have sexual relations with people of the same sex [are practicing homosexuals], who ·sell slaves [are kidnappers/slave traders], who tell lies, who speak falsely, and ·who do anything against [*or* all who live contrary to] the true teaching of God. [11]That teaching ·is part of [accords with; conforms to] the ·Good News [Gospel] of the blessed God that he ·gave me to tell [entrusted to me].

Thanks for God's Mercy

12I thank Christ Jesus our Lord, who gave me strength, because he ·trusted
me [considered me trustworthy/faithful] and ·gave me this work of serving
him [placed me in his service; appointed me to ministry]. 13[Even though] In
the past I ·spoke against Christ [Lwas a blasphemer] and persecuted him and
·did all kinds of things to hurt him [was an arrogant/insolent/violent man;
Acts 8:3]. But God showed me mercy, because I acted in ignorance and
unbelief. 14But the grace of our Lord ·was fully given [overflowed; abounded]
to me, and with that grace came the faith and love that are in Christ Jesus.
15·What I say is true [*or* This saying/word is trustworthy; 3:1; 4:9; 2 Tim.
2:11; Titus 3:8], and ·you should fully accept it [Lworthy of full acceptance; Cwhat follows may be an early Christian hymn]: Christ Jesus came
into the world to save sinners, of whom I am the ·worst [Lfirst; foremost].
16But [Lfor that reason] I was given mercy so that in me, the worst of all
sinners, Christ Jesus could show that he has ·unlimited [immense; perfect; Lall] patience. His patience with me made me an example for those
who would believe in him and have ·life forever [eternal life]. 17To the
·King who rules forever [eternal King; LKing of the ages], ·who will never
die [immortal; incorruptible], ·who cannot be seen [invisible], the only
God, be honor and glory forever and ever. Amen.
18Timothy, my child, I am giving you ·a command [this charge/instruc-
tion] that agrees with the prophecies that were given about you in the past
[4:14; 6:12]. I tell you this so that ·by following [*or* by recalling; Lby] them
you can fight the good fight. 19Continue to have faith and ·do what you
know is right [La good conscience]. Some people have rejected this, and
their faith has been shipwrecked. 20Hymenaeus [2 Tim. 2:17] and Alexander
[2 Tim. 4:14] have done that, and I have ·given them [handed them over] to
Satan so they will learn not to ·speak against God [Lblaspheme].

Some Rules for Men and Women

2 First of all, then, I ·tell [urge; exhort] you to ·pray for all people,
asking God for what they need and being thankful to him [Lmake
petitions, prayers, intercessions, and thanksgivings for all people]. 2Pray
for ·rulers [kings] and for all who have authority so that we can have
quiet and peaceful lives ·full of worship and respect for God [Lin all godliness and dignity/reverence]. 3This is good, and it ·pleases [is acceptable
to] God our Savior, 4who wants all people to be saved and to know the
truth. 5[LFor] There is one God and one ·mediator [intermediary] ·so that
human beings can reach God [Lbetween God and human beings], Christ
Jesus, who is himself human. 6He gave himself as a ·payment to free [ran-
som for] all people, ·proof that came [*or* revealing God's purpose; Lthe
testimony/witness] at ·the right [the appointed; God's own] time. 7That is
why I was ·chosen [appointed] to ·tell the Good News [be a herald/
preacher] and to be an apostle. (I am telling the truth; I am not lying.) I
was ·chosen [appointed] ·to teach the Gentiles to believe and to know the
truth [*or* as a true and faithful teacher of the Gentiles].
8So, I want the men everywhere to pray, lifting up ·their hands in a holy
manner [their hands in reverence; Lholy hands], without anger and ·argu-
ments [quarreling; disputing].
9·Also [Similarly; Likewise], women should wear ·proper [modest;
respectable] clothes that show ·respect [modesty] and ·self-control [good
sense], not using ·braided hair [elaborate hairstyles] or gold or pearls or
expensive clothes. 10Instead, they should do good deeds, which is ·right
[proper] for women who ·say they worship God [profess reverence for God].

11Let a woman learn ·by listening quietly [in silence] and ·being ready to cooperate in everything [Lin full/all submission]. 12But I do not allow a woman to teach or to ·have [assume; exercise] authority over ·a man [*or* her husband], but to ·listen quietly [be quiet], 13because Adam was formed first and then Eve [Gen. 2:8, 18, 22]. 14And Adam was not ·tricked [deceived; led astray], but the woman was ·tricked [deceived; led astray] and became a ·sinner [transgressor; Gen. 3:1–6]. 15But she will be saved through ·having children [*or* motherhood; Cless likely, a reference to the birth of Christ] if she continues in faith, love, and holiness, with ·self-control [propriety; good sense].

Elders in the Church

3 ·What I say is true [*or* This saying/word is trustworthy; 1:15; 4:9; 2 Tim. 2:11; Titus 3:8]: Anyone ·wanting [aspiring] to become an ·overseer [Tbishop; Cperhaps the same as elder; 3:6, 7; 5:17; Titus 1:5–6] desires a ·good [honorable; noble] ·work [role; position]. 2An overseer must ·not give people a reason to criticize him [have a good reputation; be above reproach], and he must ·have only one wife [*or* be faithful to his wife]. He must be ·self-controlled [sober], ·wise [have good judgment], respected by others, ·ready to welcome guests [hospitable], and able to teach. 3He must not drink too much wine or ·like to fight [be violent/a troublemaker], but rather be gentle and ·peaceable [not quarrelsome/contentious], not ·loving money [avaricious; greedy]. 4He must ·be a good family leader [Lmanage/lead his own household well], having children ·who cooperate with full respect [who obey and respect him; *or* whom he controls with dignity]. 5(If someone does not know how to ·lead [manage] his own ·family [household], how can that person take care of God's church?) 6But an elder must not be a ·new believer [recent convert], or he might ·be too proud of himself [become arrogant] and ·be judged guilty just as the devil was [*or* incur the same punishment as the devil; 1:20]. 7An elder must also have ·the respect of [a good reputation among] ·people who are not in the church [Loutsiders] so he will not ·be criticized by others [fall into disgrace; be caught in a scandal] ·and [*or* and in this way] ·caught [ensnared] in the devil's trap.

Deacons in the Church

8In the same way, deacons must be ·respected by others [dignified], not ·saying things they do not mean [insincere; two-faced; deceitful]. They must not drink too much wine or ·try to get rich by cheating others [be greedy for money/profit]. 9With a clear conscience they must ·follow [hold on to] ·the secret of the faith that God made known to us [*or* God's revealed truths; Lthe mystery of the faith; Ca mystery being something previously unknown but now revealed by God; Eph. 1:9]. 10Test them first. Then let them serve as deacons if you find ·nothing wrong in them [them blameless]. 11In the same way, ·women [*or* women who are deacons; *or* deacon's wives] must be ·respected by others [dignified]. They must not ·speak evil of others [be slanderers/gossips]. They must be ·self-controlled [sober] and ·trustworthy [honest; faithful] in everything. 12Deacons must ·have only one wife [*or* be faithful to their wife] and be good ·leaders [managers] of their children and their own ·families [households]. 13Those who serve well as deacons ·are making an honorable place [gain good standing] for themselves, and they will ·be very bold [*or* have greater confidence/assurance] in their faith in Christ Jesus.

The Secret of Our Life

14Although I hope I can come to you ·soon [quickly], I am writing these things to you now. 15Then, even if I am delayed, you will know ·how [Lhow it is necessary] to live in the ·family [household] of God, which is the ·church [assembly] of the living God, the ·support [pillar] and foundation of the truth. 16·Without doubt [*or* And we all agree], ·the secret of our life of worship [*or* the truth revealed in our faith/worship; [L]the mystery of godliness; v. 9] is great [[C]what follows may be from an early Christian hymn]:

He[n] ·was shown to us [appeared; was revealed] in ·a human body [[T]the flesh],
·proved right [vindicated] ·in spirit [*or* by the Spirit],
and seen by angels.
He was proclaimed ·to [among] the ·nations [Gentiles],
believed in ·by [*or* in; throughout] the world,
and taken up in glory.

A Warning About False Teachers

4 Now the ·Holy Spirit [[L]Spirit] clearly says that in the later times some people will ·stop believing [abandon; desert] the faith [2 Thess. 2:3–9; 2 Tim. 3:1]. They will ·follow [occupy themselves with; devote themselves to] ·spirits that lie [deceiving spirits] and teachings of demons. 2Such teachings come ·from the false words [*or* through the hypocrisy] of liars whose consciences are ·destroyed [seared; *or* branded] as if by a hot iron. 3They forbid people to marry and tell them not to eat certain foods which God created to be ·eaten [received] with thanks by people who believe and know the truth. 4[[L]For] Everything God created is good, and nothing should be ·refused [rejected] if it is accepted with thanks, 5because it is ·made holy [sanctified] by ·what God has said [the word/pronouncement of God] and by prayer.

Be a Good Servant of Christ

6By ·telling [pointing out] these things to the brothers and sisters, you will be a good servant of Christ Jesus. You will be ·made strong [nourished; nurtured] by the words of the faith and the good teaching which you have been following. 7But ·do not follow [reject] ·foolish stories that disagree with God's truth [[T]godless myths and old wives tales], but train yourself ·to serve God [for godliness/piety]. 8[[L]For] ·Training your body [Physical exercise] helps you in ·some [*or* small] ways, but ·serving God [godliness] helps you in every way ·by bringing you blessings [[L]since it holds promise] in this life and in the future life, too. 9What I say is true [*or* This saying/word is trustworthy; 1:15; 3:1; 2 Tim. 2:11; Titus 3:8], and ·you should fully accept it [[L]worthy of full acceptance]. 10This is why we work and struggle,[n] because we have put our hope in the living God who is the Savior of all people, especially of those who believe.

11Command and teach these things. 12Do not let anyone ·treat you as if you are unimportant [despise/disregard/look down on you] because you are young. Instead, be an example to the believers with your words, your ·actions [conduct; behavior], your love, your ·faith [faithfulness], and your ·pure life [purity]. 13Until I come, ·continue to read the Scriptures to the people [attend/devote yourself to the public reading (of Scripture)], ·strengthen [encourage; exhort] them, and teach them. 14·Use [[L]Do not neglect] the ·gift from the Spirit [spiritual gift; [L]gift] ·you have [that is in you], which was given to you through prophecy when the group of elders laid their hands on you [[C]a way of dedicating someone to Christian service; 1:18; 5:22]. 15·Continue [Take care; Be diligent] to do those things; give your life to doing them so your progress may be seen by everyone. 16Be ·careful

3:16 He Some Greek copies read "God." **4:10 struggle** Some Greek copies read "suffer."

[conscientious] ·in your life [Labout yourself] and in your teaching. If you
·continue to live and teach rightly [Lpersevere in these things], you will save
both yourself and those who listen to you.

Rules for Living with Others

5 Do not ·speak angrily to [rebuke; speak harshly to] an older man,
but ·plead with [exhort; encourage] him as if he were your father.
Treat younger men like brothers, 2older women like mothers, and younger
women like sisters. ·Always treat them in a pure way [L…with complete
purity].

3·Take care of [Provide support for; *or* Honor; Show respect to; Cboth honor
and financial help are likely in mind] widows who are truly widows. 4But if a
widow has children or grandchildren, let them first learn to ·do their duty to
[*or* practice their piety/godliness toward] their own ·family [household] and
to repay their parents or grandparents. [LFor] That pleases God. 5The true
widow, who is all alone, puts her hope in God and continues ·to pray night
and day for God's help [Lin petitions and prayers night and day]. 6But the
widow who ·uses her life to please herself [lives in luxury; is self-indulgent] is
really dead while she is alive. 7·Tell [Command; Instruct] the believers to do
these things so that ·no one can criticize them [they may be blameless/above
reproach]. 8Whoever does not care for his ·own relatives [Lown], especially his
own family members, has ·turned against [denied; rejected] the faith and is
worse than ·someone who does not believe in God [Lan unbeliever].

9To be on the list of widows [Cprobably a list of those widows who received
regular support from the church], a woman must be at least sixty years old.
She must have been ·faithful to her husband [*or* married only once; *or* the
wife of one husband]. 10She must be known for her good works—works
such as raising her children, ·welcoming strangers [practicing hospitality],
washing the feet of ·God's people [Tthe saints], helping those in ·trouble [dis-
tress; hardship], and ·giving [devoting] her life to do all kinds of good deeds.

11But do not put younger widows on that list. After they give themselves to Christ, they are pulled away from him by their physical desires,
and then they want to marry again. 12They will be judged for ·not doing
what they first promised to do [breaking/despising their first pledge].
13Besides that, they learn to ·waste their time [be idle], going from house
to house. And they not only ·waste their time [are idlers] but also begin to
gossip and ·busy themselves with other people's lives [become busybod-
ies/meddlers], saying things they should not say. 14So I want the younger
widows to marry, have children, and manage their homes. Then ·no
enemy will [*or* the adversary will not; CSatan] have any ·reason [*or* oppor-
tunity] ·to criticize them [*or* for maligning/slandering (us/them)]. 15But
some have already ·turned [wandered; strayed] away to follow Satan.

16If any woman who is a believer has widows in her family, she should
·care for [provide support for] them herself. The church should not ·have
to care for them [Lcarry this burden]. Then it will be able to ·take care of
[support] those who are truly widows.

17The elders who lead the church well should receive ·double honor [*or*
both honor and remuneration; Cprobably includes both respect and financial support; see v. 3], especially those who work hard by ·speaking
[preaching] and teaching, 18because the Scripture says: "When an ox is
·working in the grain [threshing], do not ·cover its mouth to keep it from
eating [muzzle it; Deut. 25:4]," and "A worker ·should be given his pay
[deserves his wages; Tis worthy of his hire; Luke 10:7]."

19Do not listen to someone who accuses an elder, without two or three witnesses [Deut. 19:15]. 20·Reprimand [Rebuke] those who continue sinning. Do this in front of the whole church so that the others will ·have a warning [Lfear; *or* show reverence].

21Before God and Christ Jesus and the ·chosen [elect] angels, I ·command [solemnly charge] you to ·do [keep; guard] these things without ·taking sides [prejudice] or showing favoritism of any kind.

22·Think carefully before you [LDo not quickly/hastily] ·appoint someone to leadership [Llay your hands on anyone; 4:14; Ca way of dedicating someone to Christian service], and don't share in the sins of others. Keep yourself pure.

23Stop drinking only water, but drink a little wine to help your stomach and your frequent sicknesses.

24The sins of some people are ·easy to see [obvious; evident] ·even before they are judged [*or* arriving at the judgment before they do; *or* preceding them into court; Lgoing before them to judgment], but the sins of others ·are seen only later [arrive later; Lfollow after]. 25So also good deeds are ·easy to see [obvious; evident], but even those that are not easily seen cannot stay hidden [Csince they will be revealed on judgment day].

6 All who are ·slaves [Lslaves under a yoke] should show full ·respect [honor] to their masters so no one will ·speak against [revile; blaspheme] God's name and ·our teaching [*or* Christian doctrine; Lthe teaching]. 2The slaves whose masters are believers should not ·show their masters any less respect [disrespect them; *or* take advantage of them] because they are believers. They should serve their masters even better, because they are helping believers ·they love [*or* loved by God; Lwho are beloved].

You must teach and ·preach [encourage/exhort them about] these things.

False Teaching and True Riches

3Anyone who has a different teaching and does not agree with the ·true teaching [sound/healthy words] of our Lord Jesus Christ and the teaching that ·shows the true way to serve God [promotes piety/godliness]—4that person is ·full of pride [arrogant; conceited] and understands nothing, but ·is sick with a love for [has an unhealthy interest in] ·arguing [controversies; debate] and ·fighting about [quarrels over] words. This brings ·jealousy [envy], ·fighting [strife; division], ·speaking against others [slander; blasphemy], evil ·mistrust [suspicions], 5and constant ·quarrels [bickering; disputes] from those who have ·evil [depraved; corrupted] minds and have ·lost [been deprived of] the truth. They think that ·serving God [godliness; piety] is a way to ·get rich [make a profit].

6[LBut] ·Serving God [Godliness; Piety] does ·make us very rich [bring great profit], ·if we are satisfied with what we have [when accompanied by contentment]. 7[LFor] We brought nothing into the world, so we can take nothing out. 8But, if we have food and clothes, we will be satisfied with that. 9Those who want to become rich ·bring temptation to themselves [Lfall into temptation] and are caught in a trap. They ·want [desire] many foolish and harmful things that ·ruin and destroy people [Lplunge people into ruin and destruction]. 10[LFor] The love of money ·causes [Lis the root of] all kinds of evil. Some people have ·left [strayed/wandered from] the faith, because they wanted ·to get more money [Lit], ·but they have caused themselves much sorrow [Land have pierced themselves with many pains].

Some Things to Remember

11But you, man of God, ·run away from [flee] all those things. Instead, chase after [pursue] ·a right relationship with God [righteousness], a godly life [godliness; piety], faith, love, ·patience [perseverance; endurance], and gentleness. 12·Fight the good fight [*or* Run the good race] of faith, grabbing hold of ·the life that continues forever [eternal life]. You were called to have that life when you confessed the good confession before many witnesses [1:18]. 13·In the sight of [In the presence of; LBefore] God, who gives life to everything, and of Christ Jesus, I ·give you a command [exhort/encourage/charge you]. Christ Jesus made the good confession when he stood before Pontius Pilate [Matt. 27:11–26; Mark 15:1–15; Luke 23:1–24; John 18:28—19:16]. 14·Do what you were commanded to do [Keep/Obey the command] without ·wrong [spot; stain] or blame until our Lord Jesus Christ ·comes again [returns; appears]. 15God will ·make that happen [Lreveal it] at ·the right [the appointed; his own] time. He is the blessed and only ·Ruler [Sovereign], the King of all kings and the Lord of all lords. 16He is the only One who ·never dies [has immortality]. He lives in light ·so bright no one can go near it [unapproachable]. No one has ever seen God, or can see him. May honor and power belong to God forever. Amen.

17Command those who are rich ·with things of this world [Lin the present age] not to be ·proud [arrogant; haughty]. Tell them to hope in God, not in their uncertain riches. God richly gives us everything to enjoy. 18Tell ·the rich people [Lthem] to do good, to be rich in doing good deeds, to be generous and ready to share. 19By doing that, they will be ·saving [storing up] a treasure for themselves as a strong foundation for the future. Then they will be able to ·have [take hold of] the life that is true life.

20Timothy, guard what God has ·trusted to [entrusted/deposited with] you. Stay away from foolish, ·useless [irreverent; godless] talk and from the ·arguments [absurdities; contradictions] of what is falsely called "knowledge." 21By ·saying they have that "knowledge" [Lclaiming/professing it], some have ·missed [strayed/lost their way from] the true faith.

Grace be with you.

2 TIMOTHY

1 From Paul, an ·apostle [messenger] of Christ Jesus by the will
of God. ·God sent me to tell about [L...according to] the promise of life that is in Christ Jesus.
2To Timothy [Acts 16:1–5; 1 Cor. 16:10–11; Phil. 2:19–24], a ·dear
[beloved] child to me [1 Tim. 1:2]:

Grace, mercy, and peace to you from God the Father and Christ Jesus our Lord.

Encouragement for Timothy

3I thank God as I always ·mention [remember] you in my prayers,
day and night. I serve him, ·doing what I know is right [with a clear con-
science] as my ancestors did. 4Remembering your tears [Cprobably at
Paul's departure], I ·want very much [long] to see you so I can be filled
with joy. 5I remember your ·true [sincere] faith. That faith first lived in
your grandmother Lois and in your mother Eunice, and I ·know [am
sure/persuaded] you now have that same faith. 6This is why I remind you
to ·keep using [rekindle; fan into flames] the gift God gave you when I laid
my hands on you [Ca way of dedicating someone to Christian service;
1 Tim. 4:14]. 7[LFor] God did not give us ·a spirit [*or* the Spirit] that makes
us ·afraid [timid] but ·a spirit [*or* the Spirit] of power and love and ·self-
control [self-discipline; *or* good judgment].
8So do not be ashamed to ·tell people [testify; bear witness] about our
Lord, and do not be ashamed of me, ·in prison for the Lord [Lhis prisoner;
CPaul was in prison in Rome for a second time and would soon be exe-
cuted]. But suffer with me for the ·Good News [Gospel]. God, who gives
us the strength to do that, 9saved us and ·made us his holy people [Lcalled
us to a holy calling]. That was not because of anything we did ourselves
but because of ·God's [Lhis own] purpose and grace. That grace was given
to us through Christ Jesus before ·time began [Leternal times], 10but it is
now ·shown [revealed; manifested] to us by the ·coming [appearing; man-
ifestation] of our Savior Christ Jesus. He ·destroyed [broke the power of;
abolished] death, and through the ·Good News [Gospel] he ·showed us
the way to have [Lilluminated; brought to light] ·life that cannot be
destroyed [immortal life; Llife and immortality]. 11I was ·chosen
[appointed] ·to tell that Good News [La preacher/herald] and to be an
apostle and a teacher. 12I am suffering now ·because I tell the Good News
[Lfor this reason], but I am not ashamed, because I know the One in
whom I have ·believed [put my trust/faith]. And I am ·sure [convinced;
confident] he is able to ·protect [guard; keep safe] what ·he has trusted me
with [*or* I have entrusted with him; Lmy deposit/entrustment] until that
day [Cthe final day of judgment and reward]. 13·Follow the pattern [*or*
Hold to the standard/norm] of true teachings that you heard from me ·in

[*or* accompanied by the] **faith and love, which are ·available in** [Lin] **Christ**
Jesus. 14**·Protect** [Guard] **the ·truth that you were given** [Lthe good deposit
entrusted to you]; **·protect** [guard] **it ·with the help of** [by the power of;
Lthrough; by] **the Holy Spirit who lives in us.**
15**You know that everyone in Asia** [Ca Roman province in present-day
western Turkey] **has left me, even Phygelus and Hermogenes.** 16**May the**
Lord show ·mercy [kindness] **to the family of Onesiphorus** [4:20; Cthe reference to the "family" rather than the man may indicate that Onesiphorus
has since died], **who has often ·helped** [encouraged; refreshed] **me and was**
not ashamed ·that I was in prison [Lof my chains]. 17**When he came to**
Rome, he ·looked eagerly [searched diligently] **for me until he found me.**
18**May the Lord ·allow him to find** [grant/give him] **mercy from the Lord**
on that day [Cthe final day of judgment and reward]. **You know very well**
how many ways he ·helped [served] **me in Ephesus** [Ca major port city in
the Roman province of Asia, present-day western Turkey; Acts 19].

A Loyal Soldier of Christ Jesus

2 **You then, Timothy, my child, be strong in the grace we have in**
Christ Jesus. 2**You should ·teach** [entrust to; *or* pass on to] **people**
·whom you can trust [who are faithful/reliable] **the things you have heard**
me say ·in the presence of [*or* confirmed by] **many witnesses. Then they**
will be able to teach others. 3**·Share in the troubles we have** [*or* Join me in
suffering] **like a good soldier of Christ Jesus.** 4**A soldier wants to please**
the ·enlisting [*or* commanding] **officer, so no one serving in the army**
·wastes time with [gets involved/entangled with] **·everyday matters** [civil-
ian affairs]. 5**Also an athlete who takes part in a contest must ·obey all**
[play by] **the rules in order to ·win** [Lbe crowned; Cwith the victor's
wreath]. 6**The farmer who works hard should be the first person to get**
some of the food that was grown. 7**Think about what I am saying, because**
the Lord will give you the ability to understand everything.
8**Remember Jesus Christ, who was raised from the dead, who is from**
the ·family [Lseed] **of David** [2 Sam. 7:12–16]. **·This is the Good News I**
preach [L...according to my Gospel], 9**and I am suffering because of it to**
the point of being bound with chains like a criminal. But God's ·teaching
[message; word] **is not in chains.** 10**So I ·patiently accept** [endure] **all these**
troubles so that those whom God has chosen can ·have [receive; obtain]
the salvation that is in Christ Jesus. With that salvation comes ·glory that
never ends [eternal glory].
11**This ·teaching is true** [saying/word is trustworthy; 1 Tim. 1:15; 3:1;
4:9; Titus 3:8; Cwhat follows may be an early Christian hymn]:
If we died with him, we will also live with him.
12**If we ·accept suffering** [endure; persevere], **we will also ·rule** [reign]
with him.
If we ·say we don't know [deny; disown; renounce] **him, he will ·say he**
doesn't know [deny; disown; renounce] **us.**
13**If we are not faithful, he will still be faithful,**
because he ·must be true to who he is [Lcannot deny/disown himself].

A Worker Pleasing to God

14**·Continue teaching** [LRemind them of] **these things, ·warning people**
[Lsolemnly testifying/declaring] **in God's presence not to ·argue** [quarrel]
about words. It ·does not help anyone [is good for nothing], **and it ruins**
those who listen. 15**·Make every effort** [Do your best; Be diligent] **to ·give**
[present] **yourself to God as the kind of person he will approve. Be a worker**
who ·is not ashamed [*or* will not be shamed] **and who ·uses the true teaching**

in the right way [correctly handles the true message/word of truth; *or* holds
carefully to the true message/word of truth]. 16**Stay away from ·foolish, useless talk** [godless/irreverent chatter; 1 Tim. 1:3–4; 4:7; 6:20]**, because that will
lead people ·further away from God** [into even more ungodliness]. 17**Their
evil teaching will spread like ·a sickness inside the body** [Lgangrene].
Hymenaeus [1 Tim. 1:20] **and Philetus are like that** [Cprobably false teachers
and opponents of Paul from Ephesus]. 18**They have ·left** [strayed away from]
the ·true teaching [truth]**, saying that the ·rising from the dead** [resurrec-
tion] **has already taken place, and so they are ·destroying** [undermining;
overturning] **the faith of some people.** 19**But God's strong foundation continues to stand, ·sealed** [inscribed; engraved] **with these words: "The Lord
knows those who belong to him** [Num. 16:5]**," and "Everyone who ·wants to
belong to** [Lnames the name of] **the Lord must ·stop doing wrong** [Lturn
away from wickedess/injustice]**."**

20**In a ·large house** [wealthy household] **there are not only ·things** [ves-
sels; dishes] **made of gold and silver, but also ·things** [vessels; dishes]
made of wood and clay. Some things are used for ·special [honorable;
noble] **purposes, and others are made for ·ordinary** [dishonorable; igno-
ble] **jobs** [Csuch as garbage or excrement]. 21**All who make themselves
clean from ·evil** [Lthese things; Cthe false teaching described in vv. 16–18]
will be used for ·special [honorable; noble] **purposes. They will be made
holy, useful to the Master, ready to do any good work.**

22**But ·run away from** [flee] **the ·evil desires** [passions; desires] **of youth.
·Try hard to live right and to have** [LPursue righteousness,] **faith, love, and
peace, together with those who ·trust in** [Lcall upon] **the Lord from pure
hearts.** 23**·Stay away from** [Avoid; Having nothing to do with] **foolish and
·stupid** [ignorant] **·arguments** [controversies; speculation]**, because you
know they ·grow into** [breed; beget] **quarrels.** 24**And a ·servant** [slave; bond-
servant] **of the Lord must not quarrel but must be kind to everyone, a ·good**
[qualified; able] **teacher, and patient.** 25**·The Lord's servant must gently
teach** [L...gently instructing/correcting] **those who ·disagree** [are oppo-
nents]. **Then ·maybe** [perhaps] **God will ·let them change their minds**
[Lgrant them repentance] **·so they can accept** [Lleading to knowledge of] **the
truth.** 26**And they may ·wake up** [come to their senses] **and escape from the
·trap** [snare] **of the devil, who catches them to do ·what he wants** [his will].

The Last Days

3 **·Remember** [Know] **this! In the last days there will be ·many troubles** [Ldifficult/terrible times]**,** 2**because people will love themselves,
love money, ·brag** [boast]**, and be ·proud** [arrogant]. **They will ·say evil
things against others** [speak abusively; *or* blaspheme] **and will not obey
their parents or be ·thankful** [grateful] **or be ·the kind of people God wants**
[holy; pious]. 3**They will not love others, will refuse to ·forgive** [reconcile],
will ·gossip [slander], **and will not control themselves. They will be ·cruel**
[brutal], **will ·hate** [Lnot love] **what is good,** 4**will ·turn against their friends**
[be treacherous/traitors], **and will ·do foolish things without thinking** [be
reckless]. **They will be conceited, will love pleasure instead of God,** 5**·and
will act as if they serve God** [Lhaving a form/appearance of godliness/piety]
but will ·not have his [*or* deny his/its] **power. ·Stay away from** [Avoid]
those people. 6[LFor] **Some of them ·go** [sneak; worm their way; talk their
way] **into homes and ·get control of** [captivate; gain influence over] **·silly**
[vulnerable; *or* idle] **women who are ·full of** [*or* burdened with (the guilt
of)] **sin and are ·led** [swayed; controlled] **by ·many** [all kinds of] **evil**

desires. 7These women are always ·learning [*or* seeking out] new teachings,
but they are never able to ·understand [arrive at] the truth fully. 8Just as
Jannes and Jambres were against Moses [Cthe traditional names (not found
in the OT) of the Egyptian magicians who opposed Moses; Ex. 7:11], these
people are against the truth. Their ·thinking has been ruined [minds/
thoughts are corrupted/depraved], and they ·have failed in trying to follow
the faith [*or* are teaching a counterfeit faith]. 9But they will not ·be successful in what they do [*or* get much further], because as with Jannes and
Jambres, everyone will see ·that they are foolish [their folly/ignorance].

Obey the Teachings

10But you have followed what I teach, the way I live, my ·goal [pur-
pose/aim (in life)], faith, patience, and love. ·You know I never give up
[L...my endurance]. 11·You know how I have been hurt and have suffered
[...my persecution and suffering], as in Antioch [Acts 13:14–52],
Iconium [Acts 14:1–5], and Lystra [Acts 14:6–20]. I have ·suffered
[Lendured such persecutions], but the Lord ·saved [rescued; delivered]
me from all those troubles. 12[LIndeed; In fact] Everyone who wants to
live ·as God desires [in a godly manner], in Christ Jesus, will be persecuted. 13But people who are evil and ·cheat others [impostors; charlatans]
will go from bad to worse. ·They will fool others, but they will also be
fooling themselves [L...deceiving and being deceived].

14But you should continue following the teachings you learned. You
·know [are confident] they are true, ·because you trust those who taught you
[Lknowing from whom you learned them]. 15Since you were a ·child [infant]
you have known the ·Holy Scriptures [*or* sacred writings] which are able to
make you wise. And that wisdom leads to salvation through faith in Christ
Jesus. 16All Scripture is ·inspired by God [breathed out by God; LGod-
breathed] and is useful for teaching, for ·showing people what is wrong in
their lives [refuting error; rebuking], for correcting faults, and for ·teaching
how to live right [training in righteousness]. 17·Using the Scriptures, [L...so
that] ·the person who serves God [LGod's person] will be ·capable [compe-
tent], ·having all that is needed [fully equipped] to do every good work.

4 I ·give you a command [solemnly charge you] in the presence of
God and Christ Jesus, the One who will judge the living and the
dead, and by his ·coming [appearing] and his kingdom: 2Preach the ·Good
News [Gospel]. Be ready ·at all times [whether it is convenient or incon-
venient; in season or out of season], and ·tell people what they need to do
[correct; reprove]. ·Tell them when they are wrong [Rebuke]. ·Encourage
[Comfort; Exhort] them with ·great patience and careful teaching [Lall
patience and teaching], 3because the time will come when people will not
·listen to [put up with; endure] the ·true [sound; healthy] teaching but
will ·find many more [gather around themselves; accumulate] teachers
who ·please them [meet their needs/desires] by saying the things ·they
want to hear [their ears itch for]. 4They will ·stop listening to [Lturn their
ears/hearing away from] the truth and will ·begin to follow [wander/turn
aside to] ·false stories [myths]. 5But you should ·control yourself [be
sober-minded] at all times, ·accept troubles [endure hardships], do the
work of ·telling the Good News [Lan evangelist], and ·complete all the
duties of a servant of God [Lfulfill your service/ministry].

6[LFor] My life is being ·given as an offering to God [Lpoured out as a
drink offering; Num. 28:24; Phil. 2:17], and the time has come for ·me to
leave this life [Lmy departure]. 7I have ·fought the good fight [*or* competed

well], I have finished the race, I have kept the faith. 8Now, a ·crown [vic-
tor's wreath] is ·being held [reserved] for me—a ·crown [victor's wreath]
·for being right with God [Lof righteousness]. The Lord, the ·judge who
judges rightly [Lrighteous/just judge], will give the ·crown [victor's
wreath] to me on that day [Cthe final day of judgment and reward]—not
only to me but to all those who have ·waited with love for him to come
again [Lloved his appearing].

Personal Words

9·Do your best [Make every effort; Be diligent] to come to me as soon as
you can, 10because Demas [Col. 4:14; Philem. 24], who loved this ·world
[Lpresent age], ·left [deserted] me and went to Thessalonica [Ca city in
Macedonia, present-day northern Greece; 1 Thess. 1:1; 2 Thess. 2:1]. Crescens
went to Galatia [Ca Roman province in present-day central Turkey; Gal. 1:2],
and Titus [2 Cor. 2:13; Gal. 2:1–3; Titus 1:1] went to Dalmatia [Ca Roman
province, mostly in present-day Croatia]. 11Luke [Col. 4:14; Philem. 24] is the
only one still with me. Get Mark [Acts 12:25; 13:13; 15:37–39; Col. 4:10] and
bring him with you when you come, because he can help me in my work
here. 12I sent Tychicus [Acts 20:4; Eph. 6:21; Col. 4:7; Titus 3:12] to Ephesus
[1:18; 1 Tim. 1:3]. 13When I was in Troas [Ca city in northwest Asia Minor;
Acts 16:8, 11; 20:5–6], I left my ·coat [cloak] there with Carpus. So when you
come, bring it to me, along with my ·books [*or* scrolls], particularly the ones
written on parchment [Cwriting material made from animal skins].
14Alexander the ·metalworker [*or* coppersmith; 1 Tim. 1:20] did many
·harmful [evil] things against me. The Lord will ·punish [repay] him for
what he did [Ps. 28:4]. 15You also should be ·careful that he does not hurt
you [Lon your guard], because he ·fought strongly against [strongly
opposed] our ·teaching [message; words].
16·The first time I defended myself [*or* At my first defense/court hear-
ing], no one ·helped me [appeared on my behalf]; everyone ·left [deserted]
me. May ·they be forgiven [Lit not be counted/reckoned against them].
17But the Lord ·stayed [stood] with me and gave me strength so I could
fully tell the ·Good News [Gospel; Lproclamation] for all the ·Gentiles
[nations] to hear. So I was ·saved [rescued; delivered] from the lion's
mouth [Ca reference to literal or, more likely, figurative death; the lion may
represent the Roman emperor Nero]. 18The Lord will ·save [rescue;
deliver] me ·when anyone tries to hurt me [Lfrom every evil deed], and he
will ·bring me safely [Lsave me] to his heavenly kingdom. Glory forever
and ever be ·the Lord's [Lto him]. Amen.

Final Greetings

19Greet ·Priscilla [LPrisca] and Aquila [Acts 18:2, 18, 26; Rom. 16:3–4;
1 Cor. 16:19] and the family of Onesiphorus [1:17]. 20Erastus [Acts 19:22;
Rom. 16:23] stayed in Corinth [Ca major city in Achaia, present-day southern
Greece; Acts 18; 1 Cor. 1:1; 2 Cor. 1:1], and I left Trophimus [Acts 20:4; 21:29]
sick in Miletus [Ca coastal city near Ephesus; Acts 20:15, 17]. 21·Try as hard as
you can [Make every effort; Do your best] to come to me before winter.
Eubulus sends greetings to you. Also Pudens, Linus, Claudia, and all
the brothers and sisters in Christ greet you.
22The Lord be with your spirit. Grace be with you.

TITUS

1 **From Paul, a ·servant** [slave; bondservant] **of God and an ·apostle** [messenger] **of Jesus Christ. I was sent ·to help** [*or* in the service of; *or* to bring about] **the faith of God's ·chosen people** [elect] **and to help them know the truth that ·shows people how to serve God** [*or* leads to godliness/piety]. **2That faith and that knowledge ·come from** [*or* lead to] **the ·hope for** [confidence/certainty of] **·life forever** [eternal life], **which God, who never lies, promised to us before ·time began** [Leternal times]. **3At ·the right** [the appointed; his own] **time God ·let the world know about that life** [Lrevealed/manifested his word/message] **through preaching. He ·trusted** [entrusted] **me with that work by the command of God our Savior.**

4To Titus [2 Cor. 2:13; 7:6; 8:16; Gal. 2:1–3], **my ·true** [genuine] **child in the faith we share:**

Grace and peace from God the Father and Christ Jesus our Savior.

Titus' Work in Crete

5I left you in Crete [Can island in the Mediterranean southeast of Greece] **so you could ·finish doing** [organize; straighten out] **the things that still needed to be done and so you could appoint elders in every ·town** [city], **as I directed you. 6An elder** [1 Tim. 3:1–7] **must ·not be guilty of doing wrong** [be blameless], **must ·have only one wife** [*or* be faithful to his wife], **and must have ·believing** [*or* faithful] **children. They must not be ·known as children who are** [accused of being] **·wild** [reckless] **and ·do not cooperate** [unruly; undisciplined; rebellious]. **7As God's ·managers** [stewards], **overseers** [Cprobably the same church office as elder; 1 Tim. 3:1, 6, 7; 5:17] **must be ·innocent of wrongdoing** [blameless], **·unselfish** [not arrogant/self-willed], **not ·quick-tempered** [easily angered]. **They must not ·drink too much wine** [be a drunkard], **·like to fight** [be violent/a brawler], **or ·try to get rich by cheating others** [be greedy for gain/dishonest in business]. **8Overseers must be ·ready to welcome guests** [hospitable], **love what is good, be ·wise** [self-controlled; sensible], **·live right** [upright; just], **and be ·holy** [devout] **and ·self-controlled** [disciplined]. **9By holding ·on** [firmly] **to the ·trustworthy** [faithful] **·word** [message] **just as it was taught to them, overseers can ·encourage** [exhort] **people with ·true** [sound; healthy] **teaching, and they can ·correct** [reprove; refute] **those who are against it.**

10There are many ·people who refuse to cooperate [unruly/rebellious people], **who talk about ·worthless** [empty; useless] **things and ·lead others into the wrong way** [deceive others]**—·mainly** [especially] **those ·who insist on circumcision to be saved** [*or* among the Jewish Christians; Lof the circumcision]. **11These people must be ·stopped** [Lsilenced], **because they are ·upsetting** [misleading; ruining; overthrowing] **whole families by teaching things they should not teach, which they do ·to get rich by cheating people**

[for dishonest gain]. 12Even one of their own prophets said, "Cretans are always liars, evil ·animals [beasts], and lazy ·people who do nothing but eat [gluttons; Ca quote from Epimenides, a poet from Crete (sixth century BC)]." 13·The words that prophet said are [LThis testimony is] true. So ·firmly [severely; sharply] ·tell those people they are wrong [rebuke/admonish them] so they may become ·strong [sound; healthy] in the faith, 14not ·accepting [paying attention to; wasting time with] Jewish ·false stories [myths; 1 Tim. 1:4; 4:7; 2 Tim. 4:4] and the commands of people who ·reject [turn their backs on] the truth. 15To those who are pure, all things are pure, but to those who are ·full of sin [defiled; polluted (with sin)] and ·do not believe [unfaithful], nothing is pure. Both their minds and their consciences have been ·ruined [defiled; polluted]. 16They ·say [claim; confess] they know God, but their actions show they ·do not accept [deny] him. They are ·hateful people [detestable; abominable], they refuse to obey, and they are ·useless [unfit; disqualified] for doing anything good.

Follow the True Teaching

2 But you must tell everyone what ·to do to follow [*or* is consistent with] ·the true [sound; healthy] teaching. 2Teach older men to be ·self-controlled [sober], ·serious [dignified; worthy of respect], ·wise [self-controlled], ·strong [sound; healthy] in faith, in love, and in ·patience [endurance].

3In the same way, teach older women to be ·holy [reverent] in their behavior, not ·speaking against [slandering; gossiping about] others or enslaved to ·too much wine [excessive drinking], but teaching what is good. 4Then they can ·teach [train] the young women to love their husbands, to love their children, 5to be ·wise [sensible; self-controlled] and pure, to be ·good workers at home [devoted to home life], to be kind, and to ·yield [submit] to their husbands. Then no one will be able to ·criticize [discredit; malign; blaspheme] the ·teaching God gave us [word of God].

6In the same way, encourage young men to be ·wise [self-controlled]. 7In every way be an example of doing good deeds. When you teach, do it with ·honesty [integrity] and ·seriousness [dignity]. 8Speak ·the truth [a sound message] so that you cannot be ·criticized [condemned]. Then those who are against you will be ashamed because there is nothing bad to say about us.

9·Slaves [Bondservants] should ·yield [submit] to their own masters at all times, trying to please them and not ·arguing with [talking back to] them. 10They should not ·steal [pilfer] from them but should show their masters ·they can be fully trusted [*or* that their faith is good/productive; Lall good faith] so that in everything they do they will ·make attractive [adorn; show the beauty of] the teaching of God our Savior.

11·That is the way we should live, because [LFor] God's grace that can save everyone has ·come [appeared; been revealed]. 12It ·teaches [trains; disciplines] us to ·turn away from [reject; deny] ungodly living and ·the evil things the world wants to do [*or* worldly desires; sinful pleasures]. Instead, that grace teaches us to live in the present age in a ·wise [self-controlled] and ·right [upright; just] way and in a ·way that shows we serve God [godly manner]. 13We should live like that while we wait for our ·great [happy; blessed] hope and the ·coming of the glory [glorious appearing/manifestation] of our great God and Savior Jesus Christ. 14He gave himself for us so he might ·pay the price to free [redeem; ransom] us from all ·evil [wickedness; lawlessness] and to make us pure people who

belong only to him—people who are always ·wanting [eager; zealous] to
do good deeds.
15Say these things and ·encourage [exhort] the people and ·tell them
what is wrong in their lives [rebuke/admonish them], with all authority.
Do not let anyone ·treat you as if you were unimportant [look down on/
despise/disregard you].

The Right Way to Live

3 Remind the believers to ·yield to the authority of [submit/be subject to] rulers and ·government leaders [authorities], to obey them,
to be ready to do ·good [whatever is good; Levery good work], 2to ·speak no
evil about anyone [slander no one], to ·live in peace [avoid fighting], and
to be gentle and ·polite [considerate; courteous] to all people.
3In the past we also were foolish. We did not obey, we were ·wrong
[mislead; deceived], and we were slaves to ·many things our bodies wanted
and enjoyed [Lvarious passions and pleasures]. We spent our lives doing
evil and being ·jealous [envious]. People hated us, and we hated each
other. 4But when the kindness and ·love [love of humanity] of God our
Savior ·was shown [appeared; was revealed], 5he saved us because of his
mercy. It was not because of ·good deeds we did to be right with him [*or*
righteous deeds we did]. He saved us through the washing ·that made us
new people [Lof new-birth/regeneration and renewal] ·through [by] the
Holy Spirit. 6God poured out ·richly [generously; abundantly] upon us
that Holy Spirit through Jesus Christ our Savior. 7Being [L…so that having been] ·made right with God [justified; declared righteous] by his
grace, we could ·have the hope of receiving [Lbecome heirs with the hope/
expectation of] ·the life that never ends [eternal life].
8This ·teaching is true [saying/word is trustworthy; 1 Tim. 1:15; 3:1; 4:9;
2 Tim. 2:11], and I want you to ·be sure the people understand [*or* insist
on] these things. Then those who ·believe [trust; have faith] in God will
·be careful to use their lives for [devote themselves to; *or* take the lead in]
doing good. These things are good and will ·help [be beneficial for]
everyone.
9But ·stay away from [avoid] foolish ·arguments [controversies;
debates] and ·talk about useless family histories [Lgenealogies; 1 Tim. 1:4]
and ·arguments [quarrels; disputes] and ·quarrels [fights] about the law
[1:10, 14; 1 Tim. 1:3–7]. Those things are ·worth nothing [unprofitable]
and ·will not help anyone [empty]. 10After a first and second warning,
·avoid [reject; have nothing to do with] someone who ·causes arguments
[is divisive; causes factions]. 11You can know that such people are ·evil
[warped; perverted; corrupt] and sinful; ·their own sins prove them
wrong [L…being self-condemned].

Some Things to Remember

12When I send Artemas or Tychicus [Acts 20:4; Eph. 6:21; Col. 4:7; 2
Tim. 4:12] to you, make every effort to come to me at Nicopolis [Ca city
located on the west coast of Greece], because I have decided to stay there
this winter. 13·Do all you can [Make every effort] to help Zenas the lawyer
and Apollos [Acts 18:24, 27; 1 Cor. 1:12; 3:4–6] on their journey so that
they have everything they need. 14Our people must learn to ·use their
lives for [devote themselves to; *or* take the lead in] doing good deeds to
·provide what is necessary [meet urgent needs] so that their lives will not
be ·useless [unfruitful].
15All who are with me greet you. Greet those who love us in the faith.
Grace be with you all.

PHILEMON

1 From Paul, a prisoner of Christ Jesus, and from Timothy [Acts 16:1–5; 1 Cor. 16:10–11; Phil. 2:19–24]**, our brother.**

To Philemon, our ·dear friend [brother] **and ·worker with us** [coworker]**; 2 to Apphia** [Cperhaps Philemon's wife]**, our sister; to Archippus** [Cpossibly Philemon's son]**, ·a worker with us** [Lour fellow soldier]**; and to the church that meets in your home:**

3 Grace and peace to you from God our Father and the Lord Jesus Christ.

Philemon's Love and Faith

4 I always thank my God when I ·mention [remember] **you in my prayers, 5 because I hear about the love you have for all ·God's holy people** [Tthe saints] **and the faith you have in the Lord Jesus. 6 I pray that the ·faith you share** [the sharing/fellowship of your faith] **may ·make you** [enable/empower you to] **understand every blessing we have in Christ. 7 I have great joy and comfort, my brother, because the love you have shown to ·God's people** [Tthe saints] **has refreshed ·them** [their hearts; Ltheir inward parts; Cthe seat of emotions].

Accept Onesimus as a Brother

8 So, in Christ, I could be bold and order you to do what is ·right [required; proper; your duty]. **9 But because I love you, I am ·pleading with** [appealing to; urging; encouraging] **you instead. I, Paul, an old man now and also a prisoner** [Cin Rome, about AD 60; Acts 28:16–31; Phil. 1:7] **for Christ Jesus, 10 am ·pleading with** [appealing to; urging; encouraging] **you for my child Onesimus, ·who became my child** [Lwhom I begat/fathered; CPaul evidently led Onesimus to Christ in Rome] **while I was in prison. 11 In the past he was ·useless** [unprofitable; worthless] **to you, but now he has become ·useful** [helpful; valuable] **for both you and me** [Ca play on words, since Onesimus means "useful" or "helpful"].

12 I am sending him back to you, and ·with him I am sending my own heart [*or* he is my very heart]. **13 I wanted to keep him with me so that ·in your place** [*or* on your behalf] **he might ·help** [serve] **me while I am in prison for the ·Good News** [Gospel]. **14 But I did not want to do anything without ·asking you first** [your consent] **so that any good you do for me will be because you want to do it, not ·because I forced you** [out of compulsion]. 15 [LFor] **Maybe Onesimus was separated from you for a short time so you could have him back forever— 16 no longer as a slave, but better than a slave, as a loved brother. ·I love him very much, but you will love him even more** [L…especially to me, but more so to you]**, both ·as a person** [*or* in the natural realm; Lin the flesh] **and ·as a believer in the Lord** [*or* in the spiritual realm; Lin the Lord].

17 So if you consider me your partner, ·welcome [receive; accept]

Onesimus as you would ·welcome [receive; accept] **me.** [18]**If he has ·done**
anything wrong to [defrauded; harmed] **you or if he owes you anything,**
charge that to me. [19]**I, Paul, am writing this with my own hand** [Ccontrary
to his usual practice of using a scribe, or amanuensis; Rom. 16:22]. **I will**
pay it back, and I will ·say nothing about what [make no mention that]
you owe me for your ·own life [very self; CPaul had evidently led Philemon
to Christ]. [20]**·So** [LYes], **my brother, I ask ·that you do this for me** [for this
benefit/favor from you] **in the Lord: Refresh my heart in Christ.** [21]**I write**
this letter, ·knowing [Lconfident of your obedience/compliance, knowing]
that you will do what I ask you and even more.

[22]**One more thing—prepare a ·room** [guest room] **for me in which to**
stay, because I hope God will answer your prayers and I will be ·able to
come [restored; Lgranted] **to you.**

Final Greetings

[23]**Epaphras** [Col. 1:7; 4:12], **a prisoner with me for Christ Jesus, sends**
greetings to you. [24]**And also Mark** [Acts 12:25; 13:13; 15:37–39; Col. 4:10],
Aristarchus [Acts 19:29; Col. 4:10], **Demas** [Col. 4:14; 2 Tim. 4:10], **and**
Luke [Col. 4:14; 2 Tim. 4:11], **·workers together with me** [my coworkers],
send greetings.

[25]**The grace of our Lord Jesus Christ be with your spirit.**

HEBREWS

God Spoke Through His Son

1 **·In the past** [Long ago] **God spoke to our ·ancestors** [forefathers; fathers] **through the prophets ·many times** [*or* in a fragmentary/partial way; Lin many parts] **and in many different ways.** **2But now in these last days God has spoken to us through ·his Son** [*or* a son; 1:3]. **God has ·chosen** [appointed] **his Son to ·own** [be heir/inheritor of] **all things, and through him he made the ·world** [universe; ages; Ccomprising both space and time; John 1:3]. **3The Son ·reflects** [*or* radiates; shines forth] **the glory of God** [John 1:14] **and ·shows exactly what God is like** [Lis the exact representation/imprint/stamp of his being/essence/nature]. **He ·holds everything together** [sustains/upholds all things] **with his powerful word. When the Son ·made people clean from their** [Lprovided purification/cleansing for] **sins** [9:14], **he sat down at the right ·side** [Lhand; Cthe most honored position beside a king; Ps. 110:1] **of ·God, the Great One in heaven** [Lthe Majesty/Preeminence in the highest places; Ca Jewish way to avoid saying the divine name of God]. **4The Son became much ·greater** [superior; better] **than the angels, ·and** [*or* just as; in the same way that] **·God gave him** [Lhe inherited] **a name** [Ceither "Son" (v. 5), or referring to his nature or reputation] **that is ·much greater than** [far superior to] **theirs.**

5This is because God never said to any of the angels,

"You are my Son.
Today I have ·become your Father [Tbegotten you; Ps. 2:7; see Heb. 5:5; Acts 13:33]."

·Nor did God say of any angel [LAnd again],

"I will be his Father,
and he will be my Son [2 Sam. 7:14]."

6And [Lagain] **when God brings ·his firstborn Son** [Lthe firstborn; Rom. 8:29] **into the world, he says,**

"Let all God's angels worship him [Ps. 97:7 (in the Greek version of the OT); Csimilar words are found in the Greek version of Deut. 32:43 and in a Hebrew copy among the Dead Sea Scrolls]."

7This is what God said about the angels:

"·God makes his angels become like winds [*or* God makes winds into his messengers].
He makes ·his servants become like flames of fire [*or* flames of fire to be his servants; Ps. 104:4]."

8But God said this about his Son:

"·God, your throne [LYour throne, O God;] **will last forever and ever.**
You will rule your kingdom with ·fairness [La just/righteous scepter; Ca scepter symbolizes royal authority].
9You love ·right [righteousness] **and hate ·evil** [wickedness; lawlessness],

so ·God [LGod, your God,] has ·chosen [Lanointed] you ·from among your friends [*or* above your peers; above anyone else];
he has ·set you apart with much joy [Lanointed you with the oil of joy/rejoicing; Ps. 45:6–7]."
10God also says,
"Lord, in the beginning you ·made [Llaid the foundations of] the earth,
and your hands made the ·skies [heavens].
11They will be destroyed, but you ·will remain [continue; Cforever].
They will all wear out like ·clothes [a garment].
12You will ·fold them [roll them up] like a ·coat [robe].
And, like ·clothes [a garment], you will change them.
But you ·never change [are the same; 13:8],
and your ·life [Lyears] will never ·end [fail; run out; Ps. 102:25–27]."
13And God never said this to an angel:
"Sit by me at my right ·side [hand; v. 3]
until I put your enemies ·under your control [Las a footstool under your feet; Ps. 110:1]."
14·All the angels are [LAre they not...?] ·spirits who serve God [*or* min-
istering spirits] and are sent to ·help [serve] those who will ·receive
[Linherit] salvation.

Our Salvation Is Great

2 ·So [For this reason] we must ·be more careful to follow [pay even
closer attention to] what we ·were taught [have heard]. Then we
will not ·stray [drift] away from the truth. 2·The teaching [LIf/Since the
message/word...] God spoke through angels [Acts 7:53] was shown to be
·true [firm; reliable], and ·anyone who did not follow it or obey it [every
violation/transgression and disobedience] received the punishment that
·was earned [it deserved; was just]. 3·So surely we also will be punished
[LHow will we escape...?] if we ignore ·this [such a] great salvation. The
Lord himself first ·told about [announced] this salvation, and those who
heard him ·testified [confirmed to us] it was true. 4God also ·testified to
the truth of the message [joined in/confirmed their testimony] by using
great signs, wonders, many kinds of ·miracles [acts of power], and by ·giv-
ing people [Lthe distribution/apportioning of] gifts through the Holy
Spirit, ·just as he wanted [*or* however he desired].

Christ Became like Us

5[LFor] God did not ·choose angels to be the rulers of the new world
that was coming [Lsubject the world to come to angels], which is what we
have been talking about. 6·It is written in the Scriptures [LSomeone has
testified somewhere],
"·Why are people even important to you [LWhat is man/humanity that you remember/think about him/them]?
·Why do you take care of human beings [LOr the son of man/children of Adam that you care for/about them]?
7You made ·them [*or* him] ·a little [*or* for a little while] lower than the angels
and crowned ·them [*or* him] with glory and honor.[n]
8You ·put all things under their control [Lsubjected everything under his feet; Ps. 8:4–6]."
[LFor] When God ·put everything under their control [Lsubjected everything

2:7 You ... honor. Some Greek copies continue, "You put them in charge of everything you made." See Psalm 8:6.

to him], **there was nothing left ·that they did not rule** [uncontrolled; not
subjected]. **Still,** [Lnow; at the present time] **we do not yet see ·them** [*or*
him; Creferring to humanity] **ruling over everything.** **9But we see Jesus,
who for a short time was made lower than the angels. This was so that, by
God's grace, he could ·die** [Ltaste death] **for everyone. And now, because
he suffered and died, he is ·wearing a crown of** [Lcrowned with] **glory and
honor.** [CJesus fulfills humanity's destiny: to be crowned with glory and
honor; Ps. 8 (cited above).]

10God is the One ·who made all things, and all things are for his glory
[Lthrough whom and for whom all things exist]. **He wanted to ·have many
children share his** [lead/bring many children/sons to] **glory, so** [Lit was
fitting/appropriate that] **he made the ·One who leads people to** [Leader/
Pioneer/Source of their] **salvation perfect through suffering.**

11[LFor indeed] **·Jesus,** [Lthe one] **who makes people holy, and those
who are made holy ·are from the same family** [*or* have the same Father; *or*
have one origin; Lare all from one]. **·So** [For this reason] **he is not ashamed
to call them his brothers and sisters.** **12He says,**

"Then, I will ·tell my brothers and sisters about you [Lproclaim your
name to my brothers (and sisters)];
I will ·praise [sing hymns/praise songs to] **you in the ·public meeting**
[midst of the assembly; Ps. 22:22]."

13He also says,

"I will ·trust [put my confidence] **in ·God** [Lhim; Is. 8:17]."

And he also says,

"I am here, and with me are the children God has given me [Is. 8:18]."

14[LTherefore] **Since these children ·are people with physical bodies**
[have in common their flesh and blood], **Jesus himself ·became like them**
[shared their humanity; Llikewise shared the same things]. **He did this so
that, by dying, he could destroy the one who has the power of death—the
devil—** **15and free those who were ·like slaves** [held in slavery] **all their
lives because of their fear of death.** 16[LFor] **Clearly, it is not angels that
Jesus helps, but the ·people who are from** [seed/descendants of] **Abraham**
[Cthe father of the Jewish nation; Gen. 12–25]. **17For this reason Jesus had
to be made like his brothers and sisters in every way so he could ·be their**
[Lbecome a] **merciful and faithful high priest in ·service** [Lthe things per-
taining] **to God. Then Jesus could ·die in their place to take away** [make
atonement for; be the sacrifice that pays for; be the sacrifice that appeases
God's wrath against] **·their sins** [Lthe sins of the people]. **18And now he
can help those who are ·tempted** [*or* tested], **because he himself suffered
and ·was tempted** [*or* was tested; *or* passed the test].

Jesus Is Greater than Moses

3 **·So all of you** [LTherefore] **holy brothers and sisters, who ·were
called by God** [are partners/partakers in a heavenly calling], **·think
about** [consider; focus on] **Jesus, who ·was sent to us** [*or* is our apostle; Ca
commissioned messenger] **and is the high priest ·of our faith** [*or* whom
we acknowledge/confess; Lof our confession]. **2Jesus was faithful to God
who appointed him just as Moses was faithful in God's ·family** [house-
hold; house]. **3Jesus ·has** [deserves; is worthy of] **more honor than Moses,
just as the builder of a house has more honor than the house itself.** 4[LFor]
**Every house is built by someone, but the builder of everything is God
himself.** **5Moses was faithful in ·God's family** [Lall of God's house; Num.
12:7] **as a servant, and he ·told** [testified to] **what God would say in the**

future. 6But Christ is faithful as a Son over God's house. And we are God's
house if we ·confidently maintain our hope [*or* maintain our courage and
confident hope].

We Must Continue to Follow God

7So it is as the Holy Spirit says:
"Today ·listen to what he says [[L]if you hear his voice...].
8Do not ·be stubborn [[L]harden your hearts] as in the past
·when you turned against God [[L]as in the rebellion; Ex. 17:1–7],
when you tested God in the desert.
9There your ancestors tried me and tested me
and saw the things I did for forty years.
10I was angry with ·them [[L]that generation].
I said, '·They are not loyal to me [[L]Their hearts are always wandering]
and have not ·understood my ways [*or* discerned/obeyed my will].'
11I was angry and ·made a promise [[L]swore an oath],
'They will never enter my rest [Ps. 95:7–11; [C]referring to the
generation of Israel that disobeyed God and so were not allowed to
enter the Promised Land (Num. 14:23)].'"

12So brothers and sisters, ·be careful [see to it] that none of you has an evil,
unbelieving heart that will ·turn you away from [desert; forsake] the living
God. 13But encourage each other every day while it is "today" [[C]meaning the
time of opportunity to be saved; v. 7]. ·Help [Encourage] each other so none
of you will become hardened ·because sin has tricked you [by sin's decep-
tion]. 14[[L]For] We all ·share in [*or* have become partners with] Christ if
[indeed; in fact] we ·keep [hold firm] till the end the sure ·faith [conviction;
confidence] we had in the beginning. 15This is what the Scripture says:
"Today ·listen to what he says [[L]if you hear his voice...].
Do not ·be stubborn [[L]harden your hearts] as in the past
·when you turned against God [[L]as in the rebellion; Ps. 95:7–8;
[C]referring to Ex. 17:1–7]."
16Who heard God's voice and ·was against [rebelled against; provoked]
him? ·It was [[L]Was it not...?] all those people Moses led out of Egypt.
17And with whom was God angry for forty years? ·He was angry [[L]Was it
not...?] with those who sinned, ·who died [[L]whose corpses/bodies fell] in
the desert [Num. 14:29, 32]. 18And to whom ·was God talking when he
promised [[L]did he swear] that they would never enter his rest [v. 11]? He
was talking to those who did not ·obey [*or* believe] him. 19So we see they
were not allowed to enter [[C]the Promised Land and God's promised rest]
because ·they did not believe [of unbelief/faithlessness].

4 ·Now [Therefore], since ·God has left us the promise [the promise
remains/still stands] that we may enter his rest, let us ·be very
careful [beware; be wary/afraid] so none of you will ·fail to enter [appear/
be found to fall short]. 2[[L]For] The ·Good News [Gospel] was preached to
us just as it was to them. But the ·teaching [message; word] they heard did
not help them, because they heard it but did not ·accept [combine; join]
it with faith.[n] 3[[L]For; Now] We who have believed are able to enter ·and
have God's rest [[L]the rest]. As God has said,
"I was angry and ·made a promise [declared/swore an oath],
'They will never enter my rest [Ps. 95:11].'"
But God's work was finished from the ·time he made [foundation/creation

---

4:2 because... faith Some Greek copies read "because they did not share the faith of those who heard it."

of] the world. 4·In the Scriptures [[L]For somewhere] he talked about the
seventh day of the week: "And on the seventh day God rested from all his
works [Gen. 2:2]." 5And again in ·the Scripture [*or* this passage; [C]Psalm 95,
the passage the author has been discussing] God said, "They will never
enter my rest [Ps. 95:11]."

6·It is still true that some people will [*or* This passage shows that some
can still] enter God's rest, but those who ·first [*or* formerly] ·heard the
way to be saved [[L]had the Good News/Gospel proclaimed to them] did
not enter, because they did not ·obey [believe; remain faithful]. 7So God
·planned [set; established; ordained] another day, called "today" [3:13].
He spoke about that day through David a long time later in the ·same
Scripture used before [words quoted before]:

"Today ·listen to what he says [[L]if you hear his voice…].
Do not ·be stubborn [[L]harden your hearts; Ps. 95:7–8]."

8[[L]For; Now] If Joshua [[C]Moses' successor, who led God's people into the
Promised Land; Josh. 3–4] had ·led the people into that [[L]given them] rest,
God would not have spoken later about another day. 9This shows that the
·rest [[L]Sabbath rest; [C]sharing in the rest God enjoyed after Creation] for
God's people ·is still coming [*or* is still available; [L]remains]. 10[[L]For] Anyone
who enters God's rest ·will rest [*or* has also rested] from his work as God
did. 11Let us ·try as hard as we can [strive; make every effort] to enter ·God's
[[L]that] rest so that no one will ·fail [be lost; [L]fall] by following the example
of those who ·refused to obey [*or* did not believe; were unfaithful].

12[[L]For] God's word is alive and ·working [active; powerful; effective]
and is sharper than a double-edged sword. It ·cuts all the way into us,
where the soul and the spirit are joined, to the center of our joints and
bones [[L]penetrates until it divides even soul and spirit, joints and marrow]. And it ·judges [discerns] the ·thoughts [ideas] and ·feelings
[attitudes; intentions] in our hearts. 13·Nothing in all the world [Nothing
in all creation; *or* No creature] can be hidden from God. Everything is
·clear [naked] and ·lies open before him [[L]exposed to his eyes], and to him
we must ·explain the way we have lived [give an account; answer].

Jesus Is Our High Priest

14[[L]Therefore] Since we have a great high priest [2:17–18], Jesus the
Son of God, who has ·gone into [ascended to; *or* passed through] ·heaven
[*or* the heavens], let us hold ·on [firmly] to ·the faith we have [[L]the confession/profession; [C]of our faith]. 15·For our high priest is able [[L]For we do
not have a high priest who is unable] to ·understand [sympathize with]
our weaknesses. He was tempted in every way that we are, but he did not
sin. 16Let us, then, ·feel very sure that we can come before [[L]confidently
approach] God's throne ·where there is grace [[L]of grace; [C]as opposed to a
throne of judgment and condemnation]. There we can receive mercy and
·grace [[L]find grace] to help us ·when we need it [[L]at the right time].

5 [[L]For] Every high priest is chosen from among ·the people
[human beings; [C]to represent humans, the priest must himself be
human] and is ·given the work of going before God for them [[L]appointed
to represent people in things related to God] to offer gifts and sacrifices
for sins. 2Since he himself is weak [[C]subject to human frailty, both physical
and moral], he is able to be gentle with those who ·do not understand [are
ignorant] and who are ·doing wrong things [easily deceived; wayward;
going astray]. 3Because he is weak, the high priest must offer sacrifices for
his own sins and also for the sins of the people [Lev. 16].

**4To be a high priest is an honor, but no one ·chooses himself for this
work** [takes this office by his own authority; Ltakes this honor for himself].
He must be ·called [chosen] **by God as Aaron was** [CMoses' brother and
Israel's first high priest; Ex. 28:1]. **5So also ·Christ** [*or* the Messiah; Ceither
a proper name or a title] **did not ·choose himself to have the honor of
being** [Lglorify/exalt himself by becoming] **a high priest, but God ·chose**
[glorified; exalted] **him. God said to him,**

"You are my Son.
Today I have ·become your Father [Tbegotten you; Ps. 2:7]."

6And in another Scripture God says,

"You are a priest forever,
·a priest like [Lin the priestly order/line of] **Melchizedek** [Ps. 110:4]."
[CSee 7:1–10; Melchizedek was a priest and king in the time of
Abraham; Gen. 14:17–24.]

7·While Jesus lived on earth [LIn the days of his flesh/earthly life], **he
·prayed to God and asked God for help** [Loffered prayers and petitions].
**He prayed with loud cries and tears to the One who could save him from
death, and his prayer was heard because ·he trusted God** [Lof his rever-
ence/devotion; Creferring especially to Jesus' prayer in Gethsemane; Matt.
26:39; Mark 14:36; Luke 22:41, 44]. **8Even though Jesus was ·the Son of
God** [*or* a son; Cwith all the rights and privileges of an heir], **he learned
obedience by what he suffered** [Cthrough total obedience to God, Jesus
achieved the glorified or perfected state God originally intended for
human beings; 2:3–9]. **9And ·because his obedience was perfect** [*or* having
achieved perfection], **he ·was able to give** [Lbecame the source/means of]
eternal salvation to all who obey him. 10In this way God ·made [desig-
nated; appointed] **Jesus a high priest, ·a priest like** [Lin the priestly order/
line of] **Melchizedek** [v. 6; Ps. 110:4].

Warning Against Falling Away

**11We have much to say about this, but it is hard to explain because you
are so ·slow to understand** [hard of hearing; Cspiritually]. **12By now you
should be teachers, but you need someone to teach you again the ·first
lessons** [elementary truths; basic principles] **of God's ·message** [revela-
tion; oracles]. **You still need ·the teaching that is like milk** [Lmilk]. **You are
not ready for solid food. 13**[LFor] **Anyone who lives on milk is still a baby
and ·knows nothing about** [*or* is unskilled/inexperienced with] **·right
teaching** [*or* the message about righteousness]. **14But solid food is for
those who are ·grown up** [mature]. **·They are mature enough** […who
through practice/exercise have trained their faculties/senses] **to know the
difference between good and evil.**

6 ·So [Therefore] **let us ·go on to grown-up teaching** [Lmove forward to maturity/completeness]. **Let us ·not go back over** [Lleave
behind] **the ·beginning** [rudimentary; elementary] **·lessons** [teaching;
Lword] **we learned about ·Christ** [*or* the Messiah; 5:5]. **We should not
again ·start teaching** [Llay a foundation] **about ·turning away** [repen-
tance] **from ·those acts that lead to death** [*or* useless works; Ldead works]
**and about faith in God. 2We should not return to the teaching about bap-
tisms** [Ceither Christian baptism or Jewish ceremonial washings], **about
laying on of hands** [Ca ritual of blessing and/or conferring of authority],
about the raising of the dead and eternal judgment [Cthese may be Jewish
practices or foundational Christian teaching]. **3And we will ·go on to
grown-up teaching** [Ldo this] **if God allows.**

4For it is impossible to ·bring back again to a changed life [[L]renew
again to repentance] those who were once ·in God's light [enlightened],
and ·enjoyed [experienced; [L]tasted] ·heaven's gift [*or* the heavenly gift;
[C]perhaps the gift of salvation], and ·shared in [partook of] the Holy Spirit.
5They ·found out [[L]tasted] how good God's word is, and ·they received
[[L]tasted] the ·powers [miracles] of ·his new world [the coming age/world].
6If they have ·fallen away [committed apostasy], it is impossible to ·bring
them back to a changed life again [[L]renew them again to repentance],
because they are nailing the Son of God to a cross again and are ·shaming
him in front of others [making a public disgrace/exhibition of him].
7·Some people are like land that gets plenty of rain and [[L]Land that
drinks in the abundance of rain] produces a ·good [useful] crop for those
who ·work [farm] it. That land receives God's blessings. 8·Other people
are like land that [[L]But if it…] grows thorns and ·weeds [thistles] and is
worthless. It is about to be cursed by God and ·will be destroyed by fire
[[L]its end/fate is burning].
9·Dear friends [Loved ones; [T]Beloved], we are saying this to you, but
we ·really expect [are convinced/confident of] better things from you
that ·will lead to [*or* accompany; come with] your salvation. 10[For] God
is ·fair [[L]not unjust]; he will not forget the work you did and the love you
showed ·for him [[L]in his name] by ·helping [serving] his ·people [holy
people; [T]saints]. And he will remember that you are still ·helping [serv-
ing] them. 11We ·want [desire for] each of you to ·go on with the same
hard work [demonstrate the same zeal/diligence] ·all your lives [[L]until
the end] ·so you will surely get what you hope for [*or* until your hope is
fulfilled/attained]. 12We do not want you to become ·lazy [sluggish; [C]in
contrast to diligent; v. 11]. Be ·like [[L]imitators of] those who through
faith and ·patience [endurance] will ·receive [inherit] what God has
promised.
13[[L]For] God made a promise to Abraham. And as there is no one
greater than God, he ·used himself [vowed by his own name; [L]swore by
himself] when he swore to Abraham, 14saying, "I will ·surely [*or* greatly]
bless you and ·give you many [greatly multiply your] descendants [Gen.
22:17]." 15Abraham ·waited patiently for this to happen [persevered], and
he received what God promised.
16[[L]For] People always ·use the name of [[L]swear by] someone greater
than themselves when they swear. The oath ·proves [is confirmation] that
what they say is true, and this ·ends all arguing [*or* settles the dispute; [C]an
oath by a higher authority is taken as a legal guarantee]. 17God wanted to
·make very clear [demonstrate convincingly] to ·those who would get
what he promised [[L]the heirs of the promise] that his ·purposes [*or* plans]
never change, so he ·made [[L]confirmed/guaranteed it with] an oath.
18These two things cannot change: God cannot lie when he makes a
promise, and he cannot lie when he makes an oath. These things greatly
encourage us, who ·came [[L]have fled] to God for safety, to hold on to the
hope ·we have been given [[L]set before us]. 19We have this hope as an
anchor for ·the soul [our lives], ·sure [stable; secure] and ·strong [reliable;
unshifting]. It enters behind the curtain in the ·Most Holy Place in heaven
[[L]inner place/sanctuary], 20where Jesus has gone ·ahead of us [[L]as a fore-
runner] ·and for us [on our behalf]. He has become the high priest
forever, a priest like Melchizedek [Ps. 110:4; Heb. 5:6, 10; 7:1–17].

The Priest Melchizedek

7 **Melchizedek** [C a priest and king in the time of Abraham; Gen. 14:17–24; Heb. 5:6, 10; 6:20] **was the king of Salem** [C another name for Jerusalem, meaning "peace"; v. 2] **and a priest for God Most High. He met Abraham when Abraham was coming back after ·defeating** [L the slaughter of] **the kings** [Gen. 14:17–19]. **When they met, Melchizedek blessed Abraham,** 2**and Abraham ·gave** [L apportioned/divided to] **him a ·tenth** [tithe] **·of everything he had brought back from the battle** [L of everything]. **First, Melchizedek's name means "king of ·goodness** [righteousness; justice]**," and he is king of Salem** [C another name for Jerusalem], **which means "king of peace."** 3**·No one knows who Melchizedek's father or mother was** [L ...without father, without mother], **·where he came from** [L without genealogy], **·when he was born, or when he died** [L having neither beginning of days, nor end of life; C something unstated was assumed not to exist]. **Melchizedek is like the Son of God; he continues being a priest forever** [C Melchizedek's unmentioned genealogy in Genesis is, by analogy, like Jesus' eternal Sonship and priesthood].

4**You can see how great Melchizedek was. Abraham, the ·great father** [patriarch], **gave him a tenth of ·everything that he won in battle** [the spoils/booty/plunder]. 5**Now the law ·says** [authorizes; commands] **that those ·in the tribe** [L of the sons/descendants] **of Levi who become priests must collect a ·tenth** [tithe] **from the people—their ·own people** [L brothers (and sisters)]**—even though ·the priests and the people** [L they] **·are from the family** [are also descendants; L have come from the loins/body] **of Abraham.** 6[L But] **Melchizedek was not ·from the tribe of Levi** [L descended from them; v. 3; C he was not from the Levitical line of priests], **but he collected a ·tenth** [tithe] **from Abraham. And he blessed Abraham, the man who had God's promises** [Gen. 12:1–3]. 7**Now ·everyone knows** [it is indisputable] **that the ·more important person blesses the less important person** [L lesser/inferior is blessed by the greater/superior]. 8**·Priests receive a tenth, even though they are only men who live and then die** [L In the one case, mortal men receive a tithe,...]. **·But Melchizedek, who received a tenth from Abraham, continues living, as the Scripture says** [L ...but in the other case, the one (receives the tithe) who is declared (by Scripture) to be alive]. 9**We might even say that Levi, who receives a ·tenth** [tithe], **also paid it when Abraham paid Melchizedek a tenth.** 10**Levi was not yet born, but he was in the ·body** [loins] **of his ancestor when Melchizedek met Abraham** [C the Levitical priesthood is considered inferior to Melchizedek's (and Christ's) priesthood, since Levi paid tithes to Melchizedek through his ancestor Abraham].

11**·The people were given the law concerning the system of priests from the tribe of Levi, but they could not be made perfect through that system** [L If perfection could be attained through the Levitical priesthood, established for the people in the law...]. **·So there was** [L ...why was there...?] **a need for another priest to come, a priest ·like** [L in the priestly order/line of] **Melchizedek, not** [L in the priestly order/line of] **Aaron** [C Moses' brother and Israel's first high priest (5:4; Ex. 28:1); the existence of Melchizedek's priestly line implies that the priesthood through Levi and Aaron was inadequate]. 12**And when a different ·kind of priest** [priesthood; priestly line] **comes, the law must be changed, too.** 13**·We are saying these things about Christ, who** [L For the one about whom these things are said] **belonged to a different tribe** [C Jesus belonged to the tribe of Judah, not Levi]. **No one from that tribe** [C Judah] **ever served as a priest at the altar.** 14**It is clear that our Lord came from the tribe of Judah, and Moses said nothing about priests belong-**

ing to that tribe [[C]the kings from David's line (including Jesus) came from the tribe of Judah, but the OT priesthood came through Levi and Aaron].

Jesus Is like Melchizedek

15 And this becomes even more clear ·when we see that [[L]if] another priest ·comes [arises; appears on the scene] who is like Melchizedek [vv. 1–14]. 16 He was not made a priest by ·human rules and laws [*or* regulations about physical descent/ancestry] but through the power of his life, which ·continues forever [*or* is indestructable]. 17 [[L]For] It is said about him,

"You are a priest forever,
·a priest like [[L]in the priestly order/line of] Melchizedek [Ps. 110:4; Heb. 5:6, 10]."

18 The ·old [former] ·rule [commandment; regulation] is now ·set aside [nullified; abolished], because it was weak and ·useless [ineffective]. 19 The law [[C]of Moses] could not make anything perfect. But now a better hope has been given to us, and ·with [by means of; through] this hope we can ·come near to [approach] God. 20 ·It is important that God did this with an oath [[L]And it was not without an oath]. Others became priests without an oath, 21 but ·Christ [[L]he] became a priest with an oath, ·when God said [[L]by the one who said] to him:

"The Lord has ·made a promise [[L]sworn; [C]an oath]
and will not change his mind.
'You are a priest forever [v. 17; Ps. 110:4].' "

22 ·This means that [Because of this oath,] Jesus is the guarantee of a better ·agreement from God to his people [covenant; contract; 8:7–13; Jer. 31:31–34; [C]the new covenant is greater than the old (the law of Moses) because it provides true forgiveness of sins].

23 When one of the other priests died, he could not continue being a priest. So there were many priests. 24 But because Jesus ·lives [remains; abides] forever, he ·will never stop serving as priest [[L]has a permanent/eternal priesthood]. 25 So he is able ·always to save [*or* to save completely/forever] those who come to God through him because he always lives, ·asking God to help [interceding for] them.

26 ·Jesus is the kind of high priest we need [[L]For such a high priest is indeed suited/fitting for us]. He is holy, ·sinless [innocent; blameless], ·pure [undefiled], ·not influenced by [set apart from] sinners, and he is ·raised above the heavens [*or* having the highest place in heaven]. 27 He is not like the other priests who had to offer sacrifices every day, first for their own sins, and then for the sins of the people. Christ offered his sacrifice only once and for all time [9:12; 10:10] when he offered himself. 28 The law ·chooses [designates; appoints] high priests who are people with weaknesses [5:2], but the word of God's oath came later than the law. It made God's Son to be the high priest, and that Son has been made perfect forever [2:10; 5:9].

Jesus Is Our High Priest

8 Here is the [main; most important] point of what we are saying: We have a high priest who sits on the right side of ·God's [[L]the Majesty's] throne in heaven. 2 Our high priest ·serves [ministers; performs priestly service] in the ·Most Holy Place [sanctuary; [L]holy things], the true ·place of worship [Tabernacle; Holy Tent; Ex. 33:7] that was made by the Lord, not by humans.

3 [[L]For] Every high priest ·has the work of offering [is appointed to offer] gifts and sacrifices to God. So our high priest must also ·offer something to God [[L]have something to offer]. 4 If our high priest were now living on earth, he would not be a priest, because there are already priests here who follow

the law by offering gifts to God. 5·The work they do as priests [*or* The sanctuary in which they serve] is only a ·copy [model; prototype] and a shadow of what is in heaven. This is why God warned Moses when he was ready to build the ·Holy Tent [TTabernacle]: "Be very careful to make everything by the ·plan [pattern; design] I showed you on the mountain [Ex. 25:40]." 6But the priestly ·work [service; ministry] that has been given to Jesus is ·much greater than [far superior to] the work that was given to the other priests. In the same way, the new ·agreement [covenant; contract] that Jesus ·brought from God to his people [Lmediates] is much ·greater [better] than the old one. And the new ·agreement [covenant; contract] is ·based [founded; legally enacted] on ·promises of better things [Lbetter promises; Call God's promises are reliable, but these promises bring greater blessings].

7If there had been ·nothing wrong [no fault] with the first ·agreement [covenant; contract; Cgiven to Israel through Moses at Mount Sinai], there would have been no ·need for [*or* reason to look for; *or* occasion for God to establish] a second ·agreement [Lone; Cthe Mosaic covenant was insufficient because it did not provide true forgiveness of sins; 10:1]. 8But God
·found something wrong with his people and said [*or* found fault with the covenant, and said to his people]:*n*

"·Look [TBehold], the ·time is [days are] coming, says the Lord,
when I will ·make [complete; establish] a new ·agreement [covenant; contract]
with the ·people [Lhouse] of Israel
and the ·people [Lhouse] of Judah.
9It will not be like the ·agreement [covenant]
I made with their ·ancestors [forefathers; fathers]
when I took them by the hand
to bring them out of [Lthe land of] Egypt.
But they ·broke [Ldid not abide by] that ·agreement [covenant; contract],
and I ·turned away from [abandoned; stopped caring for] them, says the Lord.
10[For; But] This is the ·agreement [covenant; contract] I will make
with the ·people [Lhouse] of Israel ·at that time [Lafter those days], says the Lord.
I will put my ·teachings [Llaws] in their minds
and write them on their hearts.
I will be their God,
and they will be my people.
11People will no longer have to teach their ·neighbors [fellow citizens]
and ·relatives [Lbrothers (and sisters)]
·to know the Lord [Lsaying, "Know the Lord"],
because all people will know me,
from the least to the ·most important [greatest].
12I will ·forgive them for [be merciful with regard to] ·the wicked things they did [their unrighteousness/wickedness],
and I will not remember their sins anymore [Jer. 31:31–34; Luke 22:20]."

13God called this a new ·agreement [covenant; contract], so he has made

8:8 But . . . said Some Greek copies read "But God found something wrong and said to his people."

·the first agreement [Lthe first one] ·old [obsolete; outdated]. And anything
that is ·old [obsolete; outdated] and worn out is ready to disappear.

The Old Agreement

9 The first ·agreement [covenant; contract; Cgiven to Israel through
Moses; 8:7, 13] had ·rules [regulations; requirements] for worship
and a ·place on earth for worship [Learthly sanctuary/holy place]. 2The
·Holy Tent [TTabernacle; Ex. 25:8–9; 26:1] was ·set up [constructed; pre-
pared] for this. The first area in the Tent was called the Holy Place. In it
were the lampstand [Ex. 25:31–39] and the table [Ex. 25:23–30] with the
·bread that was made holy for God [consecrated bread; bread of presenta-
tion/offering; Ex. 25:30; Lev. 24:5–8]. 3Behind the second curtain was a
·room [section; Ltent] called the ·Most Holy Place [THoly of Holies; Ex.
26:31–34]. 4In it was a golden altar for burning incense [Lev. 16:12–13]
and the ·Ark [box; chest] ·that held the old agreement [Lof the covenant/
contract; Ex. 25:10; 26:33], covered [Lcompletely; on all sides] with gold.
Inside this Ark was a golden jar of manna [Ex. 16:33–34], Aaron's rod that
once grew leaves [Num. 17:1–11], and the stone tablets of the ·old agreement [covenant; contract; Ex. 25:16; 40:20; Deut. 10:2]. 5Above the Ark
were the ·creatures that showed God's glory [*or* glorious cherubim; Ex.
25:18–22; Cangelic beings representing God's presence and glory; Gen.
3:24; Ezek. 9:3; 10:1–22], ·whose wings reached over [Lovershadowing] the
·lid [mercy seat; atonement cover; Lev. 16:2]. But we cannot ·tell everything about [discuss in detail] these things now.

6When everything was made ready in this way, the priests went into the
·first room [outer room; Lfirst tent] ·every day [regularly] to ·worship
[serve; minister; perform their priestly duties; Num. 28:3]. 7But only the
high priest could go into the ·second room [inner room; Lsecond one], and
he did that only once a year [Ex. 30:10; Lev. 16:15, 34]. He could never
enter the inner room without taking blood [Cfrom the sacrificial animal]
with him, which he offered to God for himself and for sins the people did
·without knowing they did them [unintentionally; in ignorance]. 8The
Holy Spirit uses this to show that the way into the ·Most Holy Place [sanc-
tuary; Lholy things; THoly of Holies] ·was not open [*or* had not yet been
revealed] while the ·system of the old Holy Tent [*or* outer room of the
Tabernacle; Lfirst tent/Tabernacle] was still ·being used [in place; standing].
9This is an ·example [illustration; symbol] for the present time. It shows
that the gifts and sacrifices offered cannot make the conscience of the worshiper ·perfect [clear; pure]. 10These gifts and sacrifices were only about
food and drink and special [ceremonial; ritual] washings. They were ·rules
for the body [*or* external regulations], ·to be followed [in force; applying]
until the time of God's ·new way [reformation; new order].

The New Agreement

11But when Christ came as the high priest of the good things ·we now
have*n* [Lthat have come], he entered the greater and more perfect ·tent
[Ttabernacle]. It is not made ·by humans [Lwith hands] and does not
belong to this ·world [creation; created order]. 12Christ entered the ·Most
Holy Place [sanctuary; Lholy things; THoly of Holies] ·only once—and for
all time [Lonce for all; 7:27; 10:10]. ·He did not take with him [L...not by
means of] the blood of goats and calves. ·His sacrifice was [L...but by
means of] his own blood, and by it he ·set us free from sin forever
[Lobtained/secured eternal redemption/liberation]. 13The blood of goats

9:11 good . . . have Some Greek copies read "good things that are to come."

and bulls [Lev. 16:14–16] **and the ashes of a ·cow** [young cow; heifer; Num. 19:2, 17–18] **are sprinkled on the people who are** [[C]ritually] **unclean, and this ·makes their bodies clean again** [restores their body to ritual purity]. 14 **How much more is done by the blood of Christ. He offered himself through the eternal ·Spirit** [*or* spirit; [C]most likely the Holy Spirit, though possibly Christ's own eternal spirit, or as a "spiritual" and eternal sacrifice] **as a ·perfect** [unblemished] **sacrifice to God. His blood** [[C]signifying his sacrificial death] **will make our consciences ·pure** [cleansed] **from ·useless acts** [*or* acts that lead to death; [L]dead works; 6:1] **so we may ·serve** [worship; offer priestly service for] **the living God.**

15 **For this reason Christ ·brings a new agreement from God to his people** [[L]is the mediator of a new covenant/contract]. **Those who are called by God can now receive the eternal ·blessings** [inheritance] **he has promised. They can have those things because Christ died to ·set them free** [redeem them] **from the ·sins** [transgressions; violations] **committed under the first agreement** [covenant; contract].

16 **When there is a ·will** [last will and testament; [C]the same Greek word translated "agreement" in v. 15; the author develops his illustration from the various meanings of the word], **it must be proven that the one who wrote that ·will** [last will and testament] **is dead.** 17 [[L]For; Because] **A ·will** [last will and testament] **·means nothing** [carries no force] **while the person is alive; it can ·be used** [take effect] **only after the person dies.** 18 **This is why even the first ·agreement** [covenant; contract; [C]the same Greek word as "will" in vv. 16–17] **could not ·begin** [be inaugurated/put into effect] **without blood** [[C]the death of a sacrificial animal]. 19 **First, Moses told all the people every command in the law. Next he took the blood of calves**[n] **and mixed it with water. Then he used ·red** [scarlet] **wool and a branch of the hyssop plant to sprinkle it on the book of the law and on all the people.** 20 **He said, "This is the blood ·that begins** [that seals/confirms; [L]of] **the ·Agreement** [Covenant; Contract] **that God commanded you to ·obey** [keep; Ex. 24:8]." 21 **In the same way, Moses sprinkled the blood on the ·Holy Tent** [[T]Tabernacle] **and over all the ·things** [vessels; utensils] **used in worship.** 22 **The law says that almost everything must be ·made clean** [purified; cleansed] **by blood, and sins cannot be forgiven without ·blood to show death** [the shedding of blood; [C]signifying death to pay the penalty of sin].

Christ's Death Takes Away Sins

23 **So the ·copies** [symbols; models; prototypes] **of the real things in heaven had to be ·made clean** [purified; cleansed] **by animal sacrifices. But the real things in heaven need much better sacrifices.** 24 [[L]For] **Christ did not go into ·the Most Holy Place** [a sanctuary; [L]holy things] **made by ·humans** [[L]hands], **which is only a ·copy** [model; *or* prefiguration] **of the real one. He went into heaven itself and ·is there** [appears] **now ·before** [in the presence of] **God ·to help us** [for us; on our behalf]. 25 **The high priest enters the ·Most Holy Place** [sanctuary; [L]holy things; [T]Holy of Holies] **once every year with blood that is not his own. But Christ did not offer himself many times.** 26 **·Then** [Otherwise; In such a case,] **he would have had to suffer many times ·since the world was made** [from the foundation/creation of the world]. **But Christ ·came** [appeared] **·only once and for all time** [once for all; 7:27; 9:12, 26; 10:10] **at the ·end** [culmination; climax] **of ·the present age** [time; [L]the ages] **to ·take away all** [nullify; abolish] **sin by sacrificing**

9:19 calves Some Greek copies read "calves and goats."

himself. [27]Just as ·everyone [[L]people] ·must [is/are destined/appointed to] die once and ·then be judged [[T]after this the judgment], [28]so Christ was offered as a sacrifice one time to ·take away [bear] the sins of many people [Is. 53:12]. And he will ·come [appear] a second time, not to offer himself for sin, but to bring salvation to those who are waiting for him.

10 The law is only an ·unclear picture [[L]shadow] of the good things coming in the future; it is not the ·real thing [reality itself; true image of them]. The people under the law offer the same sacrifices every year, but these sacrifices can never make perfect those who come near to worship God. [2]If the law could make them perfect, the sacrifices would have already ·stopped [ceased; been abolished]. The worshipers would ·be made clean [[L]have been cleansed/purified once for all; [C]forever], and they would no longer have a ·sense of [consciousness of; feeling of guilt about] sin. [3]But these sacrifices remind them of their sins every year, [4]because it is impossible for the blood of bulls and goats to take away sins.

[5]So when ·Christ [[L]he] came into the world, he said:

"You did not ·want [desire] sacrifices and offerings,
but you have ·prepared a body for me [*or* given me a body].
[6]You ·did not ask for [were not pleased with; took no delight in] burnt offerings
and offerings to take away sins.
[7]Then I said, '·Look [*or* Here I am; [T]Behold], I have come.
It is written about me in the ·book [scroll].
·God [[L]O God], I have come to do ·what you want [your will; Ps. 40:6–8].' "

[8]In this Scripture ·he first said [*or* cited above he said], "You did not ·want [desire] sacrifices and offerings. You ·did not ask for [were not pleased with; took no delight in] burnt offerings and offerings to take away sins [v. 6]." (These are all sacrifices that the law ·commands [requires; prescribes].) [9]Then he said, "·Look [*or* Here I am; [T]Behold], I have come to do ·what you want [your will; v. 7]." God ·ends [abolishes; takes away] the ·first system of sacrifices [[L]first] so he can ·set up [establish] the ·new system [[L]second]. [10]And ·because of this [[L]by God's will/desire/intention], we are ·made holy [sanctified; set apart to God] through the sacrifice Christ made in his body ·once and for all time [[L]once for all; 7:27; 9:12, 26].

[11]·Every day [Day after day] ·the priests [[L]every priest] stand and do their ·religious [priestly] service, ·often [again and again] offering the same sacrifices. Those sacrifices can never take away sins. [12]But after ·Christ [[L]this one; [C]this priest] offered one sacrifice for sins, forever, he sat down at the right ·side [[L]hand] of God [1:3, 13; Ps. 110:1a]. [13]And now ·Christ [[L]he] waits there for his enemies to be ·put under his power [[L]made a footstool for his feet; 1:13; Ps. 110:1b]. [14]With one ·sacrifice [offering] he made perfect forever those who are being ·made holy [sanctified; set apart to God].

[15]The Holy Spirit also ·tells [testifies/bears witness to] us about this. First he says:

[16]"This is the ·agreement [covenant; contract] I will make
with them ·at that time [[L]after those days], says the Lord.
I will put my ·teachings [laws] in their hearts
and write them on their minds [8:10; Jer. 31:33]."

[17]Then he says:

"Their sins and ·the evil things they do [their lawless/wicked actions]—
I will not remember anymore [8:12; Jer. 31:34]."

18Now when these have been forgiven, there is no more need for a ·sacrifice
[offering] **for sins.**

Continue to Trust God

19So, brothers and sisters, ·we are completely free [Lsince we have confidence…; Cthis "since" clause continues through v. 22] **to enter the ·Most
Holy Place** [sanctuary; Lholy things; THoly of Holies] **without fear ·because
of** [*or* by means of] **the blood of Jesus' death. 20We can enter through a new
and living way that Jesus ·opened** [*or* restored; renewed; *or* inaugurated] **for
us. It leads through the curtain—Christ's ·body** [Tflesh; Clike the curtain of
the Most Holy Place, Christ's body, sacrificed for us, provides access to the
presence of God]. **21And since we have a great priest over God's house, 22let
us come near to God with a ·sincere** [true] **heart and a ·sure** [confident]
faith, because we have ·been made free [Lhad our hearts sprinkled; Csacrificial
blood was sprinkled on people and things to purify them] **from a ·guilty**
[evil] **conscience, and our bodies have been washed with pure water** [Cwater
was used in Judaism for ritual purification]. **23Let us hold ·firmly** [without
wavering] **to the hope that we have confessed, because ·we can trust God to
do what he promised** [Lthe one who promised is faithful].

24Let us think about ·each other and help each other [*or* how to pro-
voke/rouse/encourage each another] **to show love and do good deeds.
25You should not ·stay away from** [neglect; forsake] **·the church meetings**
[meeting together], **as some are doing** [Csome were abandoning
Christianity and returning to Judaism], **but you should encourage each
other** [Cto stay faithful to Christ and to other believers], **and even more so
as you see the day coming** [Cthe day of the Lord, when Christ will return].

26If we ·decide to [deliberately] **go on sinning after we have learned the
·truth** [Lknowledge of the truth], **there is no longer any sacrifice for sins.
27There is nothing but ·fear in waiting for the** [a fearful/terrifying expecta-
tion/prospect of] **judgment and the ·terrible** [raging; furious] **fire that
will ·destroy** [consume; devour] **·all those who live against God** [the enemies of God; Lthose who oppose; the adversaries]. **28Anyone who ·refused
to obey** [rejected; disregarded] **the law of Moses was put to death without
mercy on the basis of the ·evidence** [testimony] **provided by two or three
witnesses** [Deut. 17:6]. **29So how much worse punishment do you think is
deserved by those who ·do not respect** [trample on; show contempt for]
**the Son of God, who ·look at the blood of the agreement that made them
holy as no different from others' blood** [Lprofane/treat as unholy/com-
mon the blood of the covenant], **who insult the Spirit of God's grace?
30We know that God said, "·I will punish those who do wrong** [TVengeance
is mine]; **I will repay them** [Deut. 32:35]**." And he also said, "The Lord will
judge his people** [Deut. 32:36; Ps. 135:14]**." 31It is a ·terrible** [dreadful; ter-
rifying] **thing to fall into the hands of the living God.**

32Remember those ·days in the past [*or* early days of your faith] **when
you first ·learned the truth** [Lwere enlightened]. **You ·remained strong**
[endured; persevered] **through a hard struggle with many sufferings.
33Sometimes you were ·hurt and attacked before crowds of people** [Lexposed
to public shame/ridicule and persecution/oppression], **and sometimes you
shared with those who were being treated that way. 34You ·helped** [had
sympathy for; *or* suffered with] **the prisoners** [Cprobably Christians imprisoned for their faith]. **You even had joy when ·all that you owned** [your
property] **was ·taken from you** [seized; confiscated], **because you knew you
had ·something** [La possession; property] **better and more lasting.**

11**·He was too old to have children, and Sarah** [*or* Sarah was too old and] **·could not have children** [was barren/sterile]. **It was by faith that ·Abraham was made able to become a father, because he** [*or* Sarah was made able to bear children, because she] **·trusted God** [Lconsidered God faithful/trustworthy] **to do what he had promised**n [Gen. 21:2]. 12**This man was so old he was ·almost** [as good as] **dead, but from ·him** [Lone man] **·came** [Lwere fathered/ Tbegotten] **as many descendants as there are stars in the sky. Like the sand on the seashore, they could not be counted** [Gen. 15:5; 22:17; 32:12].

13**All these great people died in faith. They did not ·get** [receive] **the things that God promised his people, but they saw them ·coming far in the future** [Lfrom afar] **and ·were glad** [welcomed/greeted them]. **They ·said** [acknowledged/recognized that] **they were like ·strangers** [foreigners] **and ·visitors** [sojourners; refugees; resident aliens] **on earth.** 14**When people say such things, they show they are looking for a ·country that will be their own** [homeland]. 15**If they had been thinking about the country they had left, they ·could have gone back** [Lwould have had an opportunity to return]. 16**But** [as it is; Lnow] **they were ·waiting** [desiring; longing] **for a better country—a heavenly one. So God is not ashamed to be called their God, because he has prepared a city for them.**

17**It was by faith that Abraham, when God tested him, offered his son Isaac as a sacrifice** [Gen. 22:1–10]. **·God made the promises to Abraham, but Abraham** [LThe one who received the promises] **was ready to offer his ·own** [unique; one of a kind; John 3:16] **son as a sacrifice.** 18**God had said, "·The descendants I promised you will be from Isaac** [Through Isaac your offspring/seed will carry on your name; Gen. 21:12]." 19**Abraham ·believed** [considered; reasoned] **that God ·could** [had the power to] **raise the dead, and ·really** [in one sense; in a manner of speaking; figuratively speaking], **it was as if Abraham ·got** [received] **Isaac back from death.**

20**It was by faith that Isaac blessed Jacob and Esau ·in regard to their future** [Lconcerning things to come; Gen. 27]. 21**It was by faith that Jacob, as he was dying, blessed each one of Joseph's sons** [Gen. 49]. **Then he ·worshiped** [*or* bowed in reverent worship] **as he leaned on the top of his ·walking stick** [staff; Gen. 47:31].

22**It was by faith that Joseph, while he was dying, spoke about ·the Israelites leaving Egypt** [Lthe exodus of the children/sons of Israel] **and ·gave instructions** [commanded] **about ·what to do with his body** [Lhis bones; Gen. 50:24–25; Ex. 13:19].

23**It was by faith that Moses' parents hid him for three months after he was born** [Ex. 2:2–3]. [L...because] **They saw that Moses was a ·beautiful baby** [*or* special child], **and they were not ·afraid to disobey** [intimidated by; Lafraid of] **the king's order.**

24**It was by faith that Moses, when he grew up, refused to be called the son of ·the king of Egypt's** [LPharaoh's] **daughter** [Ex. 2:10]. 25**He chose to ·suffer** [be mistreated/oppressed] **with God's people instead of enjoying ·sin for a short time** [Lthe temporary/fleeting pleasures of sin]. 26**He thought it was better to suffer ·for** [the disgrace/stigma/ humilation of] **·Christ** [*or* the Messiah/Anointed One] **than to have all the treasures of Egypt, because ·he was looking for** [*or* his eyes were fixed on] **God's reward.** 27**It was by faith that Moses left Egypt and was not afraid of the king's anger** [Ex. 10:28–29]. **Moses ·continued strong** [persevered; was

---

11:11 It . . . promised. Some Greek copies refer to Sarah's faith, rather than Abraham's.

resolute] as if he could see the ·God that no one can see [Lone who is invisible; v. 13]. 28It was by faith that Moses ·prepared [celebrated; kept] the
Passover [Ex. 12] and ·spread the blood on the doors [Lthe sprinkling of
blood; 10:22] so the ·one who brings death [destroyer] would not ·kill
[Ltouch] the firstborn sons of Israel [Ex. 12:7, 13, 29–30].
29It was by faith that the people crossed the Red Sea as if it were dry
land [Ex. 14:21–30]. But when the Egyptians tried it, they were ·drowned
[destroyed; Lswallowed].
30It was by faith that the walls of Jericho fell after the people had
·marched around [encircled] them for seven days [Josh. 6].
31It was by faith that Rahab, the prostitute, ·welcomed [Lwelcomed
with peace] the spies and ·was not killed [did not perish] with ·those who
refused to obey God [the disobedient; *or* the unbelievers; Josh. 2].
32·Do I need to give more examples [LWhat more shall I say]? I do not
have time to tell you about Gideon [Judg. 6–8], Barak [Judg. 4], Samson
[Judg. 13–16], Jephthah [Judg. 10:6—12:15], David [1 Sam. 16–1 Kin. 2],
Samuel [1 Sam. 1–16], and the prophets. 33Through their faith they defeated
kingdoms. They ·did what was right [practiced righteousness; *or* adminis-
tered justice], received ·God's promises [*or* what God promised], and shut
the mouths of lions [Dan. 6]. 34They ·stopped [quenched; extinguished]
great fires and ·were saved [escaped; fled] from being killed with swords.
·They were weak, and yet were made strong [Their strength was turned to
weakness; *or* They recovered from illnesses]. They were powerful in battle
and ·defeated [routed; drove back] ·other [foreign] armies. 35Women
received their dead relatives raised back to life [1 Kin. 17:22; 2 Kin. 4:35].
[But] Others were tortured and refused to accept ·their freedom [release;
redemption] so they could ·be raised from the dead [gain/obtain a resurrec-
tion] to a better life. 36Some were ·laughed at [mocked] and ·beaten [flogged;
scourged]. Others were put in chains and thrown into prison [Gen. 39:20;
Jer. 20:2; 37:15]. 37They were stoned to death [1 Kin. 21:13], they were ·cut
[sawn] in half [CJewish tradition reported that Isaiah was martyred this
way],n and they were killed with swords [1 Kin. 19:10; Jer. 26:23]. Some
·wore [Ltraveled about in] the skins of sheep and goats. They were ·poor
[destitute], ·abused [persecuted; oppressed], and treated badly. 38The world
was not ·good enough for [worthy of] them! They wandered in deserts and
mountains, living in caves and holes in the earth.
39All these people ·are known for [were commended for; *or* won approval
through] their faith, but none of them received what God had promised.
40God ·planned to give us [had provided] something better so that they
would be made perfect, but ·only together with us [Lnot without us].

Follow Jesus' Example

12 Therefore, since we are surrounded by a great cloud of ·people
whose lives tell us what faith means [Lwitnesses], let us run the
race that is before us ·and never give up [with endurance/perseverance].
·We should [Let us] ·remove from our lives [get rid of; cast aside] anything that ·would get in the way [impedes/hinders us] and the sin that so
easily ·holds us back [entangles/clings to us]. 2Let us ·look only to [keep
our eyes on] Jesus, the ·One who began [Pioneer/Founder of; *or* Leader/
Prince of] our faith and who ·makes it perfect [completes it]. He ·suffered
death on [Lendured] the cross, ·accepting the shame as if it were nothing

11:37 they were cut in half Some Greek copies also include, "they were tested."

[[L]disregarding/despising the shame] **because of the joy that ·God put**
before [lay ahead for] **him. And now he is sitting at the right ·side** [[L]hand]
of God's throne [1:3; 13; Ps. 110:1]. 3 **Think about Jesus, who endured such**
·hostility [opposition] **from sinful people, so that you will not ·get tired**
[grow weary; get discouraged] **and ·stop trying** [give up].

God Is like a Father

4 **You are struggling against sin, but your ·struggles** [resistance; opposi-
tion] **have not yet ·caused you to be killed** [resulted in bloodshed/[L]blood].
5 **·You have forgotten** [*or* Have you forgotten…?] **the ·encouraging words**
[exhortation] **that ·call you his** [*or* address you as] **·children** [*or* sons]:

> **"My ·child** [*or* son], **don't ·think the Lord's discipline is worth nothing**
> [scorn/treat lightly/make light of the Lord's discipline],
> **and don't ·stop trying** [get discouraged] **when he ·corrects** [rebukes] **you.**
> 6 [[L]For; Because] **The Lord disciplines those he loves,**
> **and he ·punishes** [chastises; severely disciplines] **everyone he accepts**
> **as his child** [Prov. 3:11–12]."

7 **·So hold on through your sufferings, because they are like a father's**
discipline [[L]Persevere in discipline]. **God is treating you as ·children** [*or*
sons]. **·All children are** [[L]For what child/son is not…?] **disciplined by their**
fathers. 8 **If you are never disciplined (and every ·child** [*or* son] **must be**
disciplined), you are ·not true children [[L]illegitimate and not (true) chil-
dren/sons]. 9 [Furthermore; Moreover] **We have all had ·fathers** [*or*
parents] **here on earth who disciplined us, and we respected them. So it is**
even more important that we accept discipline from ·the Father of our
spirits [*or* our spiritual Father; *or* the Father of all spirit beings; 12:23;
Num. 16:22] **so we will have** [[C]eternal or true spiritual] **life.** 10 **·Our fathers**
on earth [[L]They] **disciplined us for a short time in the way they thought**
was best. But God disciplines us ·to help us [for our good/benefit], **so we**
can ·become holy as he is [[L]share in his holiness]. 11 **We do not enjoy being**
disciplined. It is painful at the time, but later, after we have ·learned from
[been trained by] **it, ·we have peace** [[L]it produces/bears the fruit of peace],
·because we start living in the right way [*or* …and righteousness].

Be Careful How You Live

12 **·You have become weak, so make yourselves strong again** [[L]Therefore,
strengthen your drooping arms/hands and your weak/disabled knees; Is.
35:3]. 13 **·Keep on the right path** [[L]Make straight/clear paths for your feet;
Prov. 4:27], **so the ·weak** [lame] **will not ·stumble** [be disabled; put out of
joint] **but rather be ·strengthened** [healed].

14 **·Try to live in** [[L]Pursue] **peace with all people, and ·try to live free**
from sin [[L]pursue holiness/sanctification]. [[L]For] **Anyone whose life is not**
·holy [sanctified] **will never see the Lord.** 15 **·Be careful** [See to it; Take
heed] **that no one ·fails to receive** [falls short of] **God's grace and ·begins**
to cause trouble among you [[L]that no bitter root/plant grows up to cause
trouble]. **·A person like that** [Such a root/plant] **can ·ruin** [defile; pollute;
corrupt] **many of you.** 16 **·Be careful** [See to it; Take heed] **that no one takes**
part in sexual sin or is like Esau and ·never thinks about God [is godless/
profane/worldly-minded]. **·As the oldest son, Esau would have received**
everything from his father, but he sold all that for a single meal [[L]…who
sold his own birthright for one meal; Gen. 25:29–34]. 17 **You remember**
that after Esau did this, he wanted to ·get [[L]inherit] **his father's blessing,**
but ·his father refused [[L]he was rejected]. **Esau could find no way to**
·change [*or* repent of] **what he had done, even though he ·wanted** [pleaded
for; sought] **the blessing so much that he cried** [Gen. 27:34–41].

18 **You have not come to ·a mountain** [Lsomething] **that can be touched**
and that is burning with fire [Ca description of Mount Sinai when Israel
received the Law; Ex. 19:18; Deut. 4:11]. **You have not come to darkness,**
gloom, and ·storms [a whirlwind]. 19 **You have not come to the noise of a**
trumpet [Ex. 19:16, 19] **or to the sound of ·a voice** [Lwords] **like the one**
the people of Israel heard and begged not to hear another word [Cfearing
God's wrath, Israel asked Moses to mediate God's message; Ex. 20:19;
Deut. 5:5; 18:16]. 20 [L For] **They ·did not want to hear** [could not bear/
endure] **the command: "If anything, even an animal, touches the moun-**
tain, it must be put to death with stones [Ex. 19:12–13]**."** 21 [Indeed,] **What**
they saw was so ·terrible [terrifying] **that Moses said, "I am ·shaking**
[trembling] **with fear** [Deut. 9:19]**."**
22 **But you have come to Mount Zion** [Canother name for Jerusalem, here
meaning the spiritual city of God's people; Gal. 4:26; Rev. 21:2], **to the city**
of the living God, the heavenly Jerusalem [11:10]. **You have come to ·thou-**
sands of [tens of thousands/myriads of; countless] **angels ·gathered**
together with joy [in joyful assembly; Deut. 33:2]. 23 **You have come to the**
·meeting [assembly; congregation; *or* church] **of God's firstborn** [Cthe first
son in a Jewish family received special privileges and a greater share of the
inheritance; all God's people are "firstborn"] **children ·whose names are**
written [who are registered as citizens; Luke 10:20; Rev. 21:27] **in heaven.**
You have come to God, the judge of ·all people [everything; all], **and to the**
spirits of ·good [righteous] **people who have been made perfect.** 24 **You**
have come to Jesus, the ·One who brought [mediator of] **the new ·agree-**
ment from God to his people [covenant; contract; 8:1–13; Jer. 31:31–34],
and you have come to the sprinkled blood [CJesus' blood shed on the cross;
Heb. 9:19–22] **that ·has a better message** [speaks of something better; *or*
pleads more insistently] **than the blood of Abel** [Cmurdered by his brother
Cain; Abel's "blood cried out" to God for vengeance (Gen. 4:10), but Jesus'
blood cries out with a message of forgiveness and reconciliation].
25 **So ·be careful and** [see that you] **do not refuse to listen when God**
speaks. If those who refused to listen to him when he warned them on
earth did not escape, how much worse will it be for us if we refuse to lis-
ten to God who warns us from heaven? 26 **When he spoke ·before** [then],
his voice shook the earth, but now he has promised, "Once again I will
shake not only the earth but also the heavens [Hag. 2:6, 21]**."** 27 **The words**
"once again" clearly show us that everything that was made—things that
can be shaken—will be ·destroyed [removed]. [So that] **Only the things**
that cannot be shaken will remain.
28 **So let us be thankful, because we ·have** [are receiving] **a kingdom that**
cannot be shaken. [As a result; *or* In this way] **We should worship God in**
a way that pleases him with ·respect [reverence; devotion] **and ·fear** [awe],
29 **because our God is ·like a fire that burns things up** [La consuming/
devouring fire; Deut. 4:24; 9:3].

13 **Keep on loving each other as brothers and sisters.** 2 **·Remember**
[Do not forget/neglect] **to ·welcome** [show hospitality to]
strangers, because some who have done this have welcomed angels with-
out knowing it [Gen. 18:1–16; 19:1–22]. 3 **Remember those who are in**
prison as if you were in prison with them. Remember those who are ·suf-
fering [mistreated] **·as if you were suffering with them** [*or* since you are
vulnerable to the same treatment; Lbeing in a/the body yourselves].
4 **Marriage should be honored by everyone, and ·husband and wife**

should keep their marriage [Lthe marriage bed should be kept] **·pure**
[undefiled]. **God will ·judge as guilty** [Ljudge] **·those who take part in**
sexual sins [Lthe sexually immoral and adulterers]. **5Keep your lives free**
from the love of money, and be ·satisfied [content] **with what you have.**
[LFor] **God has said,**

"I will never leave you;
I will never ·abandon [Tforsake] **you** [Deut. 31:6]."

6So we can be ·sure [confident; bold] **when we say,**

"I will not be afraid, because the Lord is my helper.
·People can't do anything [LWhat can people do...?] **to me** [Ps. 118:6]."

7Remember your leaders who ·taught [proclaimed; spoke] **God's ·mes-**
sage [word] **to you. ·Remember** [Consider; Reflect on] **·how they lived**
and died [*or* the outcome/result of their way of life], **and ·copy** [imitate]
their faith. 8Jesus Christ is the same yesterday, today, and forever.

9Do not let all kinds of strange teachings ·lead you into the wrong way
[take you off course; lead you astray]. **·Your hearts should be strength-**
ened by [*or* Inner strength comes from] **God's grace, not by obeying rules**
about foods [Creferring to Jewish dietary laws; Lev. 11; Mark 7:19; Acts 10;
Col. 2:16], **which ·do not help** [*or* have never benefited] **those who ·obey**
[observe; live by] **them.**

10We have a ·sacrifice [Laltar], **but the priests who serve in the ·Holy**
Tent [TTabernacle] **·cannot** [Lhave no authority/right to] **eat from it. 11The**
high priest carries the blood of animals into the ·Most Holy Place [sanc-
tuary; Lholy things; THoly of Holies] **where he offers this blood for sins.**
But the bodies of the animals are burned outside the camp [Lev. 6:11].
12So Jesus also suffered outside the ·city [Lgate] **to ·make his people holy**
[sanctify the people] **·with** [through] **his own blood. 13So let us go to Jesus**
outside the camp, ·holding on as he did when we are abused [Lbearing the
abuse/humiliation he bore].

14[LFor] **Here on earth we do not have a city that ·lasts forever**
[endures], **but we are ·looking for** [seeking] **the city that ·we will have in**
the future [is to come]. **15So through Jesus let us ·always** [continu-
ously] **offer to God our sacrifice of praise, ·coming from** [Lwhich is the
fruit of] **lips that ·speak** [profess; acknowledge] **his name. 16Do not ·for-**
get [neglect] **to do good to others, and share with them, because such**
sacrifices please God.

17·Obey [*or* Have confidence in] **your leaders and ·act under** [*or* submit
to] **their authority.** [LFor; Because] **They are watching over you, because**
they ·are responsible [will give an account (to God)] **for ·your souls** [*or*
you]. **·Obey them** [Do this; Act this way] **so that they will do this work**
with joy, not ·sadness [*or* complaint; groaning], **for that would be of no**
·benefit [advantage; help] **to you.**

18Pray for us. We are ·sure [convinced] **that we have a clear conscience,**
·because [*or* and] **we always want to ·do the right thing** [act honorably].
19I especially ·beg [urge; exhort] **you to pray so that ·God will send me**
back [LI may be restored] **to you soon.**

20-21·I pray that the God of peace will [*or* May the God of peace] **·give you**
[equip/prepare you with] **every good thing you need so you can do ·what he**
wants [his will]. **This God of peace raised from the dead our Lord Jesus, the**
Great Shepherd of the sheep [Ps. 23; John 10:11–18], **·because of** [*or* through;
by] **the ·blood of his death** [Lblood] **·that began the eternal agreement that**
God made with his people [Lof the eternal covenant/contract; 8:1–13]. **I pray**

that God will do in us what ·pleases [is acceptable to] **him, through Jesus**
Christ, and to him be glory forever and ever. Amen.
22**My brothers and sisters, I ·beg** [urge; exhort] **you to ·listen patiently to**
[bear with] **this message I have written to ·encourage** [exhort] **you, because**
·it is not very long [LI have written to you briefly]. 23**I want you to know**
that our brother Timothy [Acts 16:1–5; 1 Cor. 16:10–11; Phil. 2:19–24;
1 and 2 Timothy] **has been ·let out of prison** [Lreleased]. **If he arrives soon,**
·we will both come [he will come with me] **to see you.**
24**Greet all your leaders and all ·of God's people** [Tthe saints]. **Those**
from Italy send greetings to you.
25**Grace be with you all.**

JAMES

1 **From James** [Cone of Jesus' brothers and a leader in the early
church; Gal. 1:19; Acts 12:17; 15:13–21; 21:17], **a ·servant** [slave;
bond-servant] **of God and of the Lord Jesus Christ.**
To ·all of God's people [Lthe twelve tribes; Can allusion to the twelve
tribes of Israel; referring either to Jewish Christians or all believers as the
new covenant people of God] **·who are scattered everywhere in the world**
[Lin the Diaspora/Dispersion; Ca reference to the scattering of the Jews
during the Babylonian captivity, now applied to the church]**: Greetings.**

Faith and Wisdom

2**My brothers and sisters** [Cfellow believers], **when you have many
kinds of ·troubles** [trials; testing], **·you should be full of joy** [Lconsider it
all/pure joy], 3**because you know that these troubles test your faith, and
this will give you ·patience** [perserverance; endurance]. 4[LAnd] **Let your
·patience** [perserverance; endurance] **·show itself perfectly in what you do**
[have its full effect; finish its work]. **Then you will be ·perfect and complete** [mature and whole; *or* completely mature] **and will ·have everything
you need** [Llack nothing]. 5**But if any of you ·needs** [lacks] **wisdom, you
should ask God for it** [Prov. 2:6]. **He is generous to everyone and will give
you wisdom ·without criticizing you** [without finding fault; ungrudg-
ingly; Matt. 7:7]. 6**But when you ask God, you must ·believe** [ask with
faith] **and not doubt. Anyone who doubts is like a wave in the sea, ·blown
up and down** [driven and tossed] **by the wind.** 7-8[LFor] **Such doubters are
·thinking two different things at the same time** [Ldouble-minded], **and
they ·cannot decide about anything they do** [Lare unstable in all they do].
They should not ·think [expect] **they will receive anything from the Lord.**

True Riches

9**·Believers** [Brothers or sisters] **who are ·poor** [in lowly/humble circum-
stances] **should ·take pride** [boast] **·that God has made them spiritually rich**
[in being raised up; in their exaltation; in their high position]. 10[LBut] **Those
who are ·rich** [wealthy] **should ·take pride** [boast] **·that God has shown them
that they are spiritually poor** [in their humiliation; in their lowly state; Jer.
9:23–24]. [LBecause] **The rich will ·die** [pass away; wither] **like a ·wild flower
in the grass** [*or* flower in the field]. 11[LFor] **The sun rises with ·burning**
[scorching] **heat and ·dries up** [withers] **the ·plants** [*or* grass]. **The flower
falls off, and its beauty is ·gone** [destroyed]. **In the same way the rich will ·die**
[Lwither away] **·while they are still taking care of business** [in the midst of
their pursuits; Lin his journeys; Ps. 49:16–17; 103:15–16; Is. 40:6–8].

Temptation Is Not from God

12**·When people are tempted and still continue strong, they should be
happy** [LBlessed is the one who perserveres/endures trials/temptations].
After they have ·proved their faith [stood/endured/passed the test], **·God will
reward them with life forever** [Lthey will receive the crown of life; Calludes to

the devil [1 Pet. 5:9], **and the devil will ·run** [flee] **from you.** 8**Come near to
God, and God will come near to you. You sinners, ·clean sin out of your
lives** [Lcleanse/purify your hands; Ca metaphor for cleaning up your behav-
ior]. **·You who are trying to follow God and the world at the same time**
[LYou double-minded ones], **·make your thinking pure** [Lpurify your
hearts; Ca metaphor for cleaning up your interior life]. 9**·Be sad** [Lament],
·cry [mourn], **and weep! Change your laughter into ·crying** [mourning]
and your joy into ·sadness [gloom; sorrow]. 10**Humble yourself in the
Lord's presence, and he will ·honor you** [Lexalt you; lift you up; 1 Pet. 5:6].

You Are Not the Judge

11**Brothers and sisters** [Cfellow believers], **do not ·tell evil lies about**
[slander] **each other** [Lev. 19:16]. **If you ·speak against** [slander] **your ·fel-
low believers** [La brother or sister] **or judge them, you are judging and
·speaking against** [slandering] **the law** [Cbecause the law commanded
love]. **And when you are judging the law, you are no longer a ·follower**
[Ldoer] **of the law. You have become a judge** [Csitting in judgment over the
law]. 12**·God is the only** [LThere is one] **·Lawmaker** [Lawgiver] **and Judge.
He is the only One who can save and destroy** [Matt. 10:28]. **·So it is not
right for you** [LSo who are you…?] **to judge your neighbor** [Lev. 19:18].

Let God Plan Your Life

13**·Some of you say** [LCome now, you who say], **"Today or tomorrow we
will go to some city. We will stay there a year, do business, and make
money."** 14**But you do not know what will happen tomorrow! Your life is
like a ·mist** [vapor; puff of smoke]. **·You can see it** [It appears] **for a short
time, but then it ·goes away** [vanishes; Prov. 27:1]. 15**·So** [*or* Instead] **you
should say, "If the Lord ·wants** [wills; wishes], **we will live and do this or
that** [Matt. 6:10]." 16**But now you are ·proud** [arrogant; Cprobably referring
to their plans for the future] **and you brag** [boast]. **All of this bragging**
[boasting] **is wrong** [Levil; wicked; 3:14]. 17[LTherefore] **Anyone who knows
the right thing to do, but does not do it, ·is sinning** [Lfor him it is sin].

A Warning to the Rich

5 **You rich people, ·listen** [LCome now; 4:13]! **Cry** [Weep] **and be very
sad because of the ·troubles** [miseries] **that are coming to you.**
2**Your riches have rotted, and your clothes have been eaten by moths.** 3**Your
gold and silver have ·rusted** [corroded], **and that ·rust** [corrosion] **will be a
·proof that you were wrong** [Lwitness/testimony/evidence against you]. **It
will eat your ·bodies** [flesh] **like fire. You ·saved** [hoarded; stored up] **your
treasure ·for** [*or* in] **the last days** [Cjust before judgment day, when such
treasures will be useless]. 4[LListen; TBehold] **The ·pay** [wages] **you ·did not
give** [defrauded from] **the workers who mowed your fields cries out against
you** [Lev. 19:13; Deut. 24:14–15], **and the cries of the ·workers** [Lharvesters]
have ·been heard by [Lreached the ears of] **the Lord ·All-Powerful** [of Hosts/
Armies; LSabaoth; CGod's warrior name referring to the angelic army]. 5**Your
life on earth was full of ·rich living** [luxury] **and ·pleasing yourselves with
everything you wanted** [pleasure; self-indulgence]. **You made ·yourselves**
[Lyour hearts] **fat, ·like an animal ready to be killed** [in/for a day of slaughter; Ca farm animal gorging itself, unaware it is being fattened for slaughter].
6**You have ·judged guilty** [condemned] **and then murdered innocent people, who ·were not against** [did not resist/oppose] **you.**

Be Patient

7[LTherefore] **Brothers and sisters** [Cfellow believers], **be patient until
the Lord comes again.** [LSee; TBehold,] **A farmer patiently waits for his
·valuable** [precious] **·crop** [fruit] **to grow from the earth and for it to
receive the ·autumn and spring** [Learly and late] **rains** [Deut. 11:14]. 8**You,**

too, must be patient. ·Do not give up hope [LStrengthen your hearts],
because ·the Lord is coming soon [Lthe Lord's coming draws near/is at
hand]. [9]Brothers and sisters [Cfellow believers], do not ·complain [grum-
ble] against each other or you will be judged guilty [Matt. 7:1]. ·And
[LLook; TBehold] the Judge is ·ready to come [Lstanding at the door]!
[10]Brothers and sisters [Cfellow believers], follow the example of the prophets who spoke ·for [Lin the name of] the Lord. They suffered many hard
things, but they ·were patient [endured]. [11][LLook; *or* Indeed] ·We say they
are happy [*or* We consider them blessed] because they ·did not give up
[endured; persevered]. You have heard about Job's ·patience [*or* endur-
ance; perseverance], and you know the Lord's purpose for him in the end.
You know the Lord is full of mercy and is ·kind [compassionate].

Be Careful What You Say

[12]My brothers and sisters [Cfellow believers], above all, do not ·use an
oath when you make a promise [swear; take a vow]. Don't use the name
of heaven, earth, or anything else to prove what you say. ·When you mean
yes, say only yes, and when you mean no, say only no [TLet your "Yes" be
yes and your "No" be no; Matt. 5:33–37] so you will not be ·judged guilty
[condemned].

The Power of Prayer

[13]Anyone who is ·having troubles [suffering] should pray. Anyone who is
·happy [joyful] should ·sing praises [sing psalms]. [14]Anyone who is sick
should call the church's elders. They should pray for and ·pour oil on the
person [Lanoint that person with olive oil; Canointing probably indicates
dedicating or setting aside the person to God's care; Mark 6:13] in the name
of the Lord. [15]And the prayer that is said with faith will ·make the sick person well [save the sick; Cthe same Greek word is commonly used for both
physical healing and spiritual salvation]; the Lord will ·heal [Lraise up] that
person [1 Cor. 12:9, 28]. And if the person has sinned, the sins will be forgiven. [16][LTherefore,] Confess your sins to each other and pray for each
other so God can heal you. ·When a believing person prays, great things
happen [LThe prayer of a righteous person is powerful and effective].
[17]Elijah was a human being just like us. He prayed [earnestly; Lwith prayer]
that it would not rain, and it did not rain on the land for three and a half
years! [18]Then Elijah prayed again, and ·the rain came down from the sky [*or*
heaven gave rain], and the land produced crops again [1 Kin. 17–18].

Saving a Soul

[19]My brothers and sisters [Cfellow believers], if one of you ·wanders
away [strays] from the truth, and someone helps that person come back,
[20]·remember [Lknow] this: Anyone who brings a sinner back from the
·wrong way [Lerror/wandering of his ways] will save that sinner's soul from
death and will ·cause many sins to be forgiven [Lcover a multitude of sins].

1 PETER

1 From Peter, an apostle of Jesus Christ. To God's ·chosen [elect]
people who are ·away from their homes [exiles; temporary residents; refugees; foreigners] ·and are scattered [Lof the Diaspora/
Dispersion; Can analogy to the Jewish people scattered around the
known world since the Babylonian exile] all around Pontus, Galatia,
Cappadocia, Asia, and Bithynia [Call located in Asia Minor, present-day
Turkey]. 2God the Father ·planned long ago to choose you [Lchose you
according to his foreknowledge] ·by making you his holy people, which
is the Spirit's work [*or* by the sanctifying/purifying work of the Spirit; *or*
by setting you apart by means of the Spirit]. God wanted you to obey him
and to be ·made clean [Lsprinkled] by the blood of the death of Jesus
Christ. [CIn the OT blood from animal sacrifices was sprinkled on persons
and objects to indicate purification or forgiveness of sins; Ex. 24:3–8.]
Grace and peace be ·yours more and more [Lmultiplied to you].

We Have a Living Hope

3·Praise be to [LBlessed be] the God and Father of our Lord Jesus Christ.
In God's ·great [abundant] mercy he has caused us to be born ·again
[anew; John 3:5–8] into a living hope, ·because Jesus Christ rose [*or* by
means of the resurrection of Jesus Christ] from the dead. 4·Now we hope
for [*or* This new birth provides us with] ·the blessings God has for his children [Lan inheritance]. ·These blessings [*or* This inheritance], which
cannot be destroyed or be ·spoiled [corrupted; defiled] or lose their beauty,
·are [is] kept in heaven for you [Matt. 6:19–21; Luke 12:33]. 5God's power
protects you through your faith until ·salvation is shown to you [*or* the
coming of the salvation that is ready to be revealed] ·at the end of [in the
last] time. 6·This makes you very happy [*or* Rejoice in this], even though
now for a short time ·different kinds of troubles may make you sad [you
have had to suffer various kinds of trials/testings]. 7These ·troubles [trials;
testings] come ·to prove that your faith is pure [to test and prove the
authenticity of your faith; Ca test that proves the genuineness of a valuable
metal]. This ·purity of faith [*or* tested and proven authenticity] is ·worth
more [more precious; more valuable] than gold, which can be ·proved to
be pure [tested and proven authentic] by fire [Ps. 66:10; Prov. 17:3; 27:21;
Zech. 13:9; Mal. 3:3] but ·can [*or* will] be destroyed. But the ·purity [tested
and proven authenticity] of your faith will bring you praise and glory and
honor ·when Jesus Christ is shown to you [Lat the revelation of Jesus
Christ]. 8You have not seen ·Christ [Lhim], but still you love him. You cannot see him now, but you believe in him. So you ·are filled [rejoice] with ·a
joy that cannot be explained, a joy full of glory [an inexpressible and glorious joy]. 9·And you are receiving [*or* ...because you are receiving] the ·goal
[outcome; purpose] of your faith—the salvation of your souls.

10The prophets [C of the Old Testament] searched carefully and ·tried to
learn [diligently inquired/investigated] about this salvation. They prophesied about the grace that was coming to you. 11The Spirit of Christ was
in the prophets, ·telling [witnessing; testifying] in advance about the sufferings of Christ and about the glory that would follow those sufferings
[Luke 24:25–27, 45–49]. The prophets ·tried to learn [inquired; investi-
gated] about what the Spirit was showing them, ·when those things would
happen, and what the world would be like at that time [about the circumstances and time; *or* about the person and time]. 12It was ·shown [revealed
to] them that their service was not for themselves but for you, when they
·told about [announced] the truths [L things] you have now heard. Those
who preached the ·Good News [Gospel] to you ·told you [announced]
those things with the help of the Holy Spirit who was sent from heaven—
things into which angels desire to look.

A Call to Holy Living

13·So [Therefore; For this reason] ·prepare your minds for service [pre-
pare your minds for action; *or*, be alert; L gird the loins of your mind] and
·have self-control [be disciplined]. ·All your hope should be for [Focus all
your hope on] the gift of grace that will be ·yours [brought/given to you]
·when Jesus Christ is shown to you [L at the revelation of Jesus Christ]. 14·Now
that you are [As; *or* Like] obedient ·children of God [L children] ·do not live
as you did in the past. You did not understand, so you did the evil things you
wanted [L do not be shaped by the desires/lusts of your former ignorance].
15But be holy in all ·you do [your behavior/conduct], just as ·God, the One
[L the One] who called you, is holy. 16[L For; Because] It is written in the
Scriptures: "You must be holy, because I am holy [Lev. 11:45; 19:2; 20:7]."
17·You pray to God and call him Father, and he [L Since you address as
Father the one who] judges each person's ·work [deeds] ·equally [impartially;
without prejudice]. So while you are ·here on earth [living as exiles/strangers/
sojourners], you should live with ·respect [fear] for God [Prov. 1:7]. 18[L For]
You know that in the past you were living in a ·worthless [meaningless; futile;
vain; Eccl. 1:2] way, a way passed down from ·the people who lived before you
[your ancestors]. But you were saved [ransomed; redeemed] from that useless life. You were ·bought [ransomed; redeemed; C like a slave whose freedom
was purchased by a payment], not with something that ·ruins [perishes;
spoils] like silver or gold, 19but with the precious blood of Christ [Is. 52:3],
who was like ·a pure and perfect lamb [a lamb without defect or blemish; Lev.
1:3]. 20Christ was ·chosen [destined; L foreknown] before ·the world was made
[L the foundation/creation of the world], but he was ·shown to the world
[revealed] in these last times for your sake. 21Through Christ you ·believe
[have faith/trust] in God, who raised Christ from the dead and gave him
glory. So your faith and your hope are in God.
22Now that your obedience to the truth has purified your ·souls [*or* lives],
you can have ·true [genuine; sincere] love for your Christian brothers and
sisters. So love each other ·deeply [earnestly] ·with all your [L from the]
heart.n 23You have been born ·again [*or* anew], and this new life did not
come from ·something that dies [L a perishable seed], but from ·something
that cannot die [L an imperishable seed]. You were born ·again [*or* anew]
through ·God's living message that continues forever [L the living and abid-
ing/enduring word of God]. 24·The Scripture says [L For; Therefore],

1:22 with all your heart Some Greek copies read "with a pure heart."

"All ·people are [Tflesh is] like the grass,
and all their glory is like the flowers of the ·field [Lgrass].
The grass ·dies [withers] and the flowers ·fall [drop off],
25 but the word of the Lord ·will live [remains; abides; endures] forever [Is. 40:6–8]."
And this is the word that was ·preached [*or* proclaimed as Good News/Gospel] to you.

Jesus Is the Living Stone

2 So then, rid yourselves of all evil, all ·lying [deceit], hypocrisy, ·jealousy [envy], and ·evil speech [slander; Call traits that destroy relationships; Rom. 13:13; Eph. 4:25–32; Col. 3:8]. 2As newborn babies want milk, you should want the ·pure [sincere; unadulterated] and ·simple [*or* spiritual] ·teaching [Lmilk; Cprobably referring to the word of God; see 1:23–25]. By it you can ·mature [grow; reach maturity] in your salvation, 3because you have already ·examined and seen [Ltasted] how good the Lord is [Ps. 34:8].

4Come to the Lord Jesus, the ·"stone" that lives [La living stone; CJesus is the most important stone in the spiritual temple described in v. 5]. ·The people of the world did not want this stone, but he was the stone God chose, and he was precious [L…rejected by people, but chosen and precious/valuable to God]. 5You also are like living stones, so let yourselves be used to build a spiritual ·temple [house]—to be holy priests who offer spiritual sacrifices that are ·acceptable [pleasing] to God ·through [*or* because they are mediated by] Jesus Christ. 6The Scripture ·says [Lcontains]:

"[LSee; Look,] I will ·put a stone in the ground in Jerusalem [Llay a stone in Zion; CZion is a poetic term for Jerusalem].
·Everything will be built on this important and precious rock [La chosen and precious cornerstone; Cthe stone that supports the others].
Anyone who ·trusts [believes; has faith] in him
will never be ·disappointed [Lput to shame; Is. 28:16]."

7·This stone is worth much to you who believe [*or* You who believe see the honor/value/preciousness of the stone; LThe honor is to you who believe]. But to the people who do not believe,

"the stone that the builders rejected
has become ·the cornerstone [Lhead of the corner; Cthe precise meaning is uncertain, but clearly refers to the most important stone in a building; Ps. 118:22; compare Mark 12:10–11; Acts 4:11; Eph. 2:20–22]."

8·Also, he is [LAnd]

"a stone that causes people to stumble,
a rock that ·makes them fall [trips them; snares them; causes them to sin; offends them; Is. 8:14; Rom. 9:32–33]."

They stumble because they do not obey ·what God says [the message/word], which is what God ·planned to happen to [destined/appointed for] them.

9But you are a chosen ·people [*or* generation; Is. 43:21], royal ·priests [Lpriesthood], a holy nation, a people ·for God's own possession [who belong to God; Ex. 19:5–6]. You were chosen to ·tell about the wonderful acts of God, who [proclaim the praises/virtues of him who] called you out of darkness into his ·wonderful [marvelous] light. 10At one time you were not a people, but now you are God's people. In the past you had ·never [Lnot] received mercy, but now you have received God's mercy [Hos. 2:23].

Live for God

11·Dear friends [LBeloved], I ·beg [urge; exhort] you as ·foreigners
[strangers; sojourners; resident aliens; 1:17] and ·strangers in this world
[exiles; temporary residents; refugees; foreigners; 1:1; Gen. 23:4] to ·avoid
[abstain from] the ·evil things your bodies want to do [Lfleshly/worldly
desires] that fight against your soul. 12Live such good lives among unbelievers [Lthe Gentiles/pagans] that, even though they might ·say that you
are doing wrong [slander you; accuse you of doing evil], they will see the
good things you do and will give glory to God ·on the day when Christ
comes again [when Christ comes to judge; Lon the day of visitation].

Yield to Every Human Authority

13For the Lord's sake, ·yield [submit; be subject] to ·the people who have
authority in this world [*or* every human institution/creation; Rom. 13:1–7;
Titus 3:1]: the ·king [*or* emperor], who is the ·highest [supreme] authority,
14and the ·leaders [governors] who are ·sent [commissioned] by him to
punish those who do wrong and to praise those who do right. 15[LFor;
Because] It is ·God's desire [Lthe will of God] that by doing good you should
·stop foolish people from saying stupid things about you [Lsilence the ignorant talk of foolish people]. 16Live as free people, but do not use your
freedom as an ·excuse [cover-up; pretext] to do evil. Live as ·servants [slaves]
of God. 17·Show respect for [Honor] all people: Love the ·brothers and sisters of God's family [community of believers; brotherhood], ·respect [fear]
God [Prov. 1:7], honor the king [*or* emperor; Rom. 13:1].

Follow Christ's Example

18·Slaves [Servants; Cthe term refers to household slaves], ·yield [submit;
be subject; Cput the other person's interests first] to the authority of your
masters with all ·respect [fear; deference; Eph. 6:5–9; Col. 3:22—4:1], not
only those who are good and ·kind [gentle; considerate], but also those
who are ·dishonest [*or* cruel; Lcrooked]. 19A person might have to suffer
even when it is ·unfair [unjust], but if ·through awareness of God (*or*
because of his God-given conscience) he endures the ·pain [grief], ·God is
pleased [*or* this is commendable; Lthis is favor/credit/grace]. 20If you are
beaten for ·doing wrong [sin], ·there is no reason to praise you [what
credit/honor is that for you…?] for ·being patient in your punishment
[enduring it]. But if you suffer for doing good, and you ·are patient [endure
it], ·then God is pleased [this is commendable to God; Lthis is favor/credit/
grace from God]. 21[LFor] This is what you were called to do, because
Christ suffered for you ·and gave you [leaving you] an example to follow.
So you should ·do as he did [Lfollow in his footsteps].
22"He ·had never sinned [committed no sin],
  and ·he had never lied [Lno deceit was found in his mouth; Is. 53:9]."
23People ·insulted [abused; reviled] Christ, but he did not ·insult [abuse;
revile] them in return. Christ suffered, but he did not threaten. ·He let
God, the One who judges rightly, take care of him [LHe delivered/
entrusted himself to the One who judges justly/rightly]. 24Christ [Lhimself]
·carried [bore] our sins in his body on the ·cross [Ltree; Deut. 21:23; Gal.
3:13] so we would ·stop living for [die to] sin and start living for ·what is
right [righteousness]. And you are healed ·because of [by] his wounds.
25[LFor] You were like sheep that wandered away [Is. 53:6], but now you
have come back to the Shepherd and ·Overseer [Guardian] of your souls.

Wives and Husbands

3 In the same way [2:18], you wives should ·yield [submit; be subject; Eph. 5:21–24; Col. 3:18; Cputting the other person's interests
first] to your husbands. Then, if some husbands do not ·obey [*or* believe]

·God's teaching [Lthe word/message], they will be ·persuaded to believe [won over; Lgained] without anyone's saying a word to them. They will be ·persuaded [won over; Lgained] by ·the way their wives live [their wives' conduct/behavior]. 2Your husbands will see the pure lives you live ·with your respect for God [Lin reverence/fear; Cfear in the positive sense of reverence for God; Prov. 1:7]. 3It is not [Lexternal things like] ·fancy [braided; elaborate] hair, gold jewelry, or fine clothes that should ·make you beautiful [Lbe your adornment]. 4No, your beauty should come from ·within you [your inner self; Lthe hidden/secret person of the heart]—the beauty of a gentle and quiet spirit that will never ·be destroyed [fade; perish] and is ·very precious [very valuable; of great worth] to God [Prov. 31:30]. 5In this same way the holy women who lived long ago and ·followed [Lput their hope in] God ·made themselves beautiful [Ladorned themselves], ·yielding [submitting; subjecting themselves] to their own husbands. 6Sarah obeyed Abraham, her husband, and called him her ·master [lord; Gen. 18:12]. And you women are true children of Sarah if you always do what is ·right [good] and ·are not afraid [Lfear no fear/intimidation].

7In the same way [2:18; 3:1], you husbands should live with your wives in an ·understanding [considerate] way [Eph. 5:25–33; Col. 3:19], since they are ·weaker than you [the weaker sex; *or* the less empowered one; Lthe weaker vessel; Cwomen are typically physically weaker, but in Greco-Roman and Jewish society, they also had less power and authority]. But ·show them respect [pay/give them honor], because ·God gives them the same blessing he gives you—[Lthey are co-heirs of] ·the grace that gives true life [*or* God's gift of life; Lthe grace of life]. Do this so that nothing will ·stop [hinder] your prayers.

Suffering for Doing Right

8Finally, all of you should ·be in agreement [be like-minded; live in harmony], ·understanding each other [sympathetic], ·loving each other as family [Lshowing brotherly love], being ·kind [tender; compassionate] and humble. 9Do not ·do wrong to repay a wrong, and do not insult to repay an insult [Lrepay evil for evil or insult for insult]. But repay with a blessing, because you yourselves were called [Cby God] to do this so that you might ·receive [Linherit] a blessing [Luke 6:27–28]. 10·The Scripture says [LFor],

"·A person must do these things [LThe one who wants]
to ·enjoy [Llove] life and have many happy days.
He must ·not say evil things [Lkeep his tongue from evil],
and he must ·not tell lies [Lkeep his lips from speaking lies].
11He must ·stop doing [turn away from] evil and do good.
He must ·look for [seek] peace and ·work for [Lpursue] it.
12·The Lord sees the good people [LThe eyes of the Lord are on the righteous]
and ·listens to [Lhis ears on] their prayers.
But the [Lface of the] Lord is against
those who do evil [Ps. 34:12–16; compare Rom. 12:9–17]."

13If you are ·trying hard [eager; zealous; passionate] to do good, ·no one [Lwho…?] can really ·hurt [harm; do evil to; mistreat] you. 14But even if you suffer for ·doing right [righteousness], you are blessed [Matt. 5:10].

"Don't be afraid of ·what they fear [*or* their threats/intimidation];
do not ·dread those things [be disturbed/intimidated; Is. 8:12–13]."

15But ·respect Christ as the holy Lord [Lsanctify Christ as Lord; Is. 8:13] in your hearts [Cthat is, acknowledge his holiness and sovereignty in your life]. **Always be ready to ·answer** [*or* give a defense to] **everyone who asks you to explain about the hope ·you have** [Lthat is in you], 16**but answer in a ·gentle** [humble] **way and ·with respect** [*or* with fear/reverence for God]. **Keep a ·clear** [good] **conscience so that ·those who speak evil of** [Lwhen you are accused, those slanderers of] **your good ·life** [behavior; conduct] **in Christ will be made ashamed.** 17**It is better to suffer for doing good than for doing wrong** [evil] **if that is ·what God wants** [the will of God]. 18**Christ himself suffered for sins ·once** [*or* once for all; Conly his suffering has the power to redeem others]. **·He was not guilty, but he suffered for those who are guilty** [L...the righteous for the unrighteous] **to bring you to God. ·His body was killed** [LHe was put to death in the flesh/body], **but he was made alive in the ·spirit** [*or* Spirit; Cat his resurrection in a glorified body]. 19**And in the ·spirit** [*or* Spirit] **he went and preached to the spirits in prison** [Cprobably either fallen angels, imprisoned by God (see Gen. 6:1–4; 2 Peter 2:4; Jude 6) or the spirits of the people who rejected Noah's preaching; see v. 20] 20**who refused to obey God long ago in the time of Noah** [Gen. 6:1—8:22], **when ·God was waiting patiently** [Lthe patience of God waited] **while Noah was building the ·boat** [ark]. [In this ark; LIn it] **Only a few people—eight in all—were saved ·by** [*or* through] **water.** 21**And that water ·is like** [anticipates; foreshadows; symbolizes; prefigures] **baptism that now saves you—not the ·washing** [removal] **of dirt from the body, but the ·promise** [pledge; appeal; *or* response] **made to God from a ·good** [clear] **conscience. And this is ·because Jesus Christ was raised from the dead** [*or* through the resurrection of Jesus Christ]. 22**Now Jesus has gone into heaven and is at God's right side** [Cthe place of honor] **·ruling over angels, authorities, and powers** [Lwith angels, authorities, and powers made subject to him].

Change Your Lives

4 [LTherefore] **Since Christ suffered while he was in his ·body** [Tflesh], **·strengthen** [arm] **yourselves with the same ·way of thinking Christ had** [intention; attitude; resolve]. [LBecause] **The person who has suffered in the ·body** [Tflesh] **·is finished with sin** [*or* has broken from the power of sin]. 2**·Strengthen** [Arm] **yourselves so that you will live ·here on earth** [Lthe rest of the time in the flesh] **doing ·what God wants** [the will of God], **·not the evil things people want** [*or* not pursuing your own human desires]. 3**·In the past you wasted too much time** [*or* For you have spent enough time in the past] **doing what ·nonbelievers** [Gentiles; pagans] **enjoy. You were guilty of sexual sins, evil desires, drunkenness, wild and drunken parties, and ·hateful** [lawless; detestable] **idol worship.** 4**·Nonbelievers** [The Gentiles/pagans] **think it is ·strange** [surprising] **that you do not ·do the many wild and wasteful things they do** [Lrun with them into the same flood/excess of debauchery], **so they ·insult you** [abuse/slander you; *or* blaspheme]. 5**But they will have to ·explain** [Tgive account of] **this to God, who is ready to judge the living and the dead.** 6**For this reason the ·Good News** [Gospel] **was preached to those who are now dead. Even though they were judged ·like all people** [Laccording to human beings in the flesh], **the Good News was preached to them so they could live ·in the spirit as God lives** [*or* in the Spirit as God lives; Laccording to God in the spirit/Spirit; Cthough Christians will die physically, because of the Good News they will live forever with God].

Use God's Gifts Wisely

7**The ·time is near when all things will end** [Tend of all things is near]. **So ·think clearly** [be serious/alert] **and ·control** [discipline] **yourselves so you will be able to pray.** 8**Most importantly, love each other ·deeply** [earnestly], because love ·will cause people to forgive each other for many sins [Lcovers a multitude of sins; Prov. 10:12; Luke 7:46–47]. 9·Open your homes [Be hospitable] to each other, without ·complaining [grumbling]. 10Each of you has received a gift to use to serve others. Be good ·servants [stewards; managers] of God's various gifts of grace [Rom. 5:15–16; 6:23]. 11Anyone who speaks should speak ·words from God [*or* oracles from God; *or* as one bringing God's message]. Anyone who serves should serve with the strength God gives so that in everything God will be ·praised [glorified] through Jesus Christ. Glory and power belong to him forever and ever [Col. 3:17]. Amen.

Suffering as a Christian

12·My friends [Beloved], do not be surprised at the ·terrible trouble [fiery ordeal; Zech. 13:9; Mal. 3:1–3] which now comes to test you. Do not think that something strange is happening to you. 13But ·be happy [rejoice] that you are sharing in Christ's sufferings so that you will ·be happy and full of joy [Lrejoice exulting/joyously] ·when Christ comes again in glory [Lat the revelation of his glory]. 14When people ·insult [ridicule] you ·because you follow Christ [Lfor the name of Christ], you are blessed, because the glorious Spirit, the Spirit of God, ·is with [rests on] you [Is. 11:1–2]. 15Do not suffer for murder, theft, or any other crime, nor ·because you trouble other people [as a meddler/troublemaker]. 16But if you suffer because you are a Christian, do not be ashamed. ·Praise [Glorify] God ·because you wear that name [*or* because you are called by his name; Lin that name]. 17[LFor] It is time for judgment to begin with ·God's family [Tthe household of God; 2:4–5]. And if that judging begins with us, what will ·happen to [Lbe the end for] those people who do not obey the ·Good News [Gospel] of God?

18"If it is very hard for a ·good [righteous] person to be saved,
·the wicked person and the sinner will surely be lost! [*or* What will happen to the wicked person and the sinner?; Prov. 11:31]"

19So those who suffer ·as God wants [*or* because God has allowed it; Laccording to the will of God] should trust their souls to the faithful Creator as they continue to do what is ·right [good].

The Flock of God

5 ·Now [LTherefore] I ·have something to say to [exhort; appeal to] the elders in your group. I also am an elder. I ·have seen [was a witness to] ·Christ's [*or* the Messiah's] sufferings [Matt. 16:13–23; Mark 8:27–33; Luke 9:18–22], and I will share in the glory that will be ·shown [revealed] to us. I ·beg [exhort; urge] you to 2·shepherd [tend] God's flock [John 21:15–19], ·for whom you are responsible [which is under your care]. ·Watch over [Oversee] them because you want to, not because you are forced. That is how God wants it. Do it because you are ·happy [eager] to serve, not because ·you want money [of greed]. 3Do not ·be like a ruler over people [Tlord it over those; dominate those; Matt. 20:25–27; Mark 10:42–45; Luke 22:25–27] ·you are responsible for [under your care; Lthose allotted (to you)], but be good examples to ·them [Lthe flock]. 4Then when the Chief Shepherd [CChrist] ·comes [Lappears], you will get a glorious crown that will never ·lose its beauty [fade away; Ccrowns for athletic success made from flowers wilted quickly; 1 Cor. 9:25].

5In the same way, younger people should be willing to ·be under [submit/be subject to] ·older people [*or* the elders]. And all of you should ·be very humble with each other [Lclothe yourselves with humility toward one another]. [LBecause:]

"God ·is against [resists; opposes] the proud,
but he gives grace to the humble [Prov. 3:34]."

6Be humble [Ltherefore] under God's powerful hand so he will ·lift you
up [exalt you] ·when the right time comes [in due time]. 7·Give all your
worries to him [Cast all your anxiety on him], because he cares about you.
8·Control [Discipline] yourselves and be ·careful [alert]! The devil,
your enemy, ·goes around [prowls] like a roaring lion looking for someone
to ·eat [devour]. 9·Refuse to give in to [Resist] him, by standing strong in
your faith. You know that your ·Christian family [community of believers;
Lbrotherhood] all over the world is having the same kinds of suffering.
10And after you suffer ·for a short time [*or* a little], God, who gives all
grace, will ·make everything right [Lrestore you]. He will make you strong
and support you and keep you from falling. He called you ·to share in his
glory in Christ, a glory that will continue forever [Linto his eternal glory in
Christ]. 11·All power is his [*or* To him be the power] forever and ever. Amen.

Final Greetings

12I wrote this short letter ·with the help of Silas [Lthrough Silvanus; Ca
variant of Silas; he either helped write the letter or carried it], who I know
is a faithful brother in Christ. I wrote to ·encourage [exhort] you and to
·tell [testify/witness to] you that this is the true grace of God. Stand strong
in that grace.
13·The church in Babylon [LShe who is in Babylon; C"Babylon" is probably a veiled (and negative) name for Rome], who was chosen like you,
sends you greetings. Mark, ·my son in Christ [Lmy son; Cbut probably a
spiritual rather than a physical relationship], also greets you. 14·Give each
other a kiss of Christian love when you meet [LGreet one another with a
kiss of love].
Peace to all of you who are in Christ.

2 PETER

1 **From ·Simon** [LSimeon; Ca version of Simon closer to the Hebrew
name] **Peter, a ·servant** [slave] **and apostle of Jesus Christ.**
To ·you [Lthose] **who have received a faith as ·valuable** [precious;
privileged] **as ours, ·because our God and Savior Jesus Christ does what
is right** [*or* through the righteousness/justice of our God and Savior
Jesus Christ].
2[May] **Grace and peace be ·given to you more and more** [lavished
upon you; multiplied to you], **·because you truly know** [*or* as you grow in
your knowledge; Lthrough/in the knowledge of] **God and Jesus our Lord.**

God Has Given Us Blessings

3**·Jesus has the power of God, by which he has given us** [LHis divine power
has given us] **everything we need ·to live and to serve God** [*or* to live a godly
life; Lfor life and godliness]. **We have these things ·because we know** [*or* as we
better come to know; Lthrough the knowledge of] **·Jesus, who called us** [Lthe
one who called us; Cmay refer to Jesus or God the Father] **by his glory and
·goodness** [virtue; moral excellence]. 4**Through these he gave us the very
great and precious promises.** [L…so that] **With these gifts you can ·share in**
[partake of; participate in] **·God's nature** [Lthe divine nature; Cwhich enables
us to live forever], **·and the world will not ruin you with its evil desires** [*or*
having escaped the world's decay that was caused by its evil desires].
5**·Because you have these blessings** [LFor this very reason; Cthe reasons
stated in vv. 3–4], **·do your best** [make every effort; strive] **to ·add these
things to** [*or* increase these things in] **your lives: to your faith, add ·good-
ness** [virtue; moral excellence]; **and to your ·goodness** [virtue; moral
excellence], **add knowledge;** 6**and to your knowledge, add self-control; and
to your self-control, add ·patience** [*or* perseverance]; **and to your ·patience**
[*or* perseverance], **add ·service for God** [devotion; piety; godliness]; 7**and to
your ·service for God** [devotion; piety; godliness], **add ·kindness for your
brothers and sisters in Christ** [affection for fellow believers; Lbrotherly
love/affection; CGreek: *philadelphia*]; **and to ·this kindness** [affection;
Lbrotherly love/affection], **add love** [CGreek: *agapē*]. 8**If all these things are
in you and are ·growing** [increasing], **they will ·help you to be useful and
productive** [Lkeep you from being ineffective/idle and unfruitful/unpro-
ductive] **in your knowledge of our Lord Jesus Christ.** 9**·But** [*or* For] **anyone
who does not have these things ·cannot see clearly** [is nearsighted]. **He is
blind** [1 John 2:11; Rev. 3:17] **·and** [*or* because he] **has forgotten that he
was made clean from his past sins.**
10[LTherefore] **My brothers and sisters, ·try hard** [make every effort;
strive] **to ·be certain that you really are called and chosen by God**
[Lconfirm your calling and election]. [LFor] **If you do all these things, you
will never ·fall** [stumble]. 11**·And** [For in this way] **you will be given a very**

·**great** [rich; lavish] ·**welcome** [entrance; arrival] **into the eternal kingdom of our Lord and Savior Jesus Christ.**

12 **You know these things, and you are ·very strong** [established] **in the truth** [that has come to you; that you now have], **but I will always ·help you remember** [remind you of] **them.** 13 **I think it is right for me to ·help you remember** [[L]arouse you with a reminder] **as long as I am in this ·body** [[L]tent; [C]a metaphor for the transitory earthly body]. 14 **I know I must soon ·leave this body** [[L]put off my tent; [C]die; 1:13; 2 Cor. 5:1, 4], **as our Lord Jesus Christ ·has shown** [made clear to] **me** [John 21:18]. 15 **I will ·try my best** [make every effort; strive] **so that you may be able** [[L]always] **to remember these things even after ·I am gone** [[L]my departure; [C]Peter's death].

We Saw Christ's Glory

16 [[L]For] **When we ·told** [made known to] **you about the ·powerful coming** [*or* power and coming] **of our Lord Jesus Christ, we were not ·telling** [following; repeating] ·**just clever stories that someone invented** [*or* cleverly-concocted myths]. **But we ·saw the greatness of Jesus with our own eyes** [[L]were eyewitness of his majesty]. 17 [[L]For] ·**Jesus heard the voice of God, the Greatest Glory** [[L]When that voice came to him from the Majestic Glory], **when he received honor and glory from God the Father. The voice said, "This is my Son, whom I love, and I am very pleased with him** [[C]a reference to the Transfiguration; Matt. 17:5; Mark 9:7; Luke 9:35]**."** 18 **We heard that voice from heaven while we were with Jesus on the ·holy** [sacred] **mountain.**

19 ·**This makes us more sure about the message the prophets gave** [*or* And we also have a reliable message from the prophets; [L]And we have the prophetic word confirmed; [C]probably referring to the Old Testament]. ·**It is good for you** [You do well] **to follow closely what they said as you would follow a ·light** [[L]lamp] **shining in a dark place, until the day ·begins** [[L]dawns] **and the morning star rises in your hearts** [Num. 24:17; Rev. 22:16; [C]the planet Venus as seen before sunrise, here symbolizing Christ]. 20 ·**Most** [First] **of all, you must understand this: No prophecy in the Scriptures ·ever comes from the prophet's own interpretation** [*or* is a matter of one's own interpretation]. 21 **No prophecy ever came from ·what a person wanted to say** [[L]human will/intention], **but people ·led** [carried; moved] **by the Holy Spirit spoke words from God.** [[C]True prophecy originates with God, not with the prophet.]

False Teachers

2 **There used to be false prophets among God's people** [Deut. 13:1–5; 18:14–22; Jer. 28] **just as you will have some false teachers ·in your group** [[L]among you; Jude 4]. **They will secretly ·teach** [bring in; introduce] ·**things that are wrong—teachings that will cause people to be lost** [[L]destructive heresies/opinions/factions]. **They will even ·refuse to accept** [[L]deny] **the Master** [[C]Jesus] **who bought ·their freedom** [[L]them; [C]as a master purchases a slave; 1 Cor. 6:20; 1 Pet. 1:18]. **So they will bring quick ·ruin** [destruction] **on themselves.** 2 **Many will follow their ·evil** [depraved; debauched; licentious] **ways and ·say evil things about** [malign; slander] **the way of truth.** 3 ·**Those false teachers only want your money, so** [[L]In their greed] **they will ·use** [exploit] **you ·by telling you lies** [with deceptive/false words]. **Their judgment spoken against them long ago is ·still coming** [not idle], **and their ruin ·is certain** [does not sleep].

4 [[L]For if] **When angels sinned, God did not ·let them go free without punishment** [spare them]. [[L]But] **He sent them to ·hell** [[L]Tartarus; [C]a Greek term for the underworld] **and put them in caves**[n] **of darkness where they**

2:4 caves Some Greek copies read "chains."

are being held for judgment [Gen. 6:1–4; Jude 6]. 5**And God ·punished the world long ago** [Ldid not spare the ancient world] **when he brought a flood to the world that was full of ·people who were against him** [the ungodly]. **But God ·saved** [protected; kept] **Noah, ·who preached about being right with God** [a preacher of righteousness; CJewish tradition described Noah preaching repentance], **and seven other people with him** [Chis wife plus his three sons and their wives; Gen. 6–9]. 6**And God also ·destroyed** [condemned] **the evil cities of Sodom and Gomorrah by burning them until they were ashes** [Gen. 19; Jude 7]. **He made those cities an example ·of what will happen to** [*or* for future generations of] **·those who are against God** [Lthe ungodly; Jude 7]. 7**But he saved Lot from those cities. Lot, a ·good** [righteous] **man, was ·troubled** [distressed; *or* oppressed] **because of the ·filthy lives** [depraved behavior] **of ·evil** [lawless] **people.** 8**(Lot was a ·good** [righteous] **man, but because he lived with evil people ·every day** [day after day], **his ·good heart** [righteous soul] **was ·hurt** [tormented] **by the ·evil things** [lawless deeds] **he saw and heard.)** 9**So the Lord knows how to save ·those who serve him** [the godly] **·when troubles come** [from trial/testing/temptation]. **He will hold ·evil people** [the wicked/unrighteous] **·and punish them, while waiting for the judgment day** [*or* while they wait for their punishment on judgment day]. 10**That punishment is especially for those who ·live by doing the evil things their sinful selves want** [Lgo after the flesh with defiling passion/lust] **and who ·hate** [despise] **authority** [Jude 8].

These false teachers are bold and ·do anything they want [arrogant; self-willed]. **They ·are not afraid** [Ldo not tremble] **to ·speak against** [slander; blaspheme] **·the angels** [Lthe glorious ones; Cprobably angelic beings; unclear whether referring to good or evil angels; Jude 8]. 11**But even the angels, who are much stronger and more powerful ·than false teachers** [*or* than the evil angels; Cunclear whether referring to false teachers or to "the glorious ones" (seen as evil angels) of v. 10], **do not ·accuse them with insults** [Lbring a slanderous charge against them] **before**[n] **the Lord** [see Jude 9]. 12**But these people ·speak against** [slander; blaspheme] **things they do not understand. They are like ·animals that act without thinking** [irrational animals], **animals** [of simple instinct] **born to be caught and killed. And, ·like animals, these false teachers will be destroyed** [*or* like the evil angels, these false teachers will be destroyed; Lin their destruction they will be destroyed; Jude 10]. 13**·They have caused many people to suffer, so they themselves will suffer. That is their pay for what they have done** [L…suffering harm as the wage of unrighteousness; Ca wordplay based on the similarity of the Greek words translated "suffering harm" and "unrighteousness"]. **They take pleasure in ·openly doing evil** [doing evil/carousing in the daylight], **so they are like dirty spots and ·stains** [blemishes] **among you. They delight in deceiving you while ·eating meals** [*or* feasting] **with you** [Cperhaps an allusion to the fellowship meal, or "love feast," celebrated with the Lord's Supper; Jude 12]. 14**·Every time they look at a woman they want her** [LThey have eyes full of adultery], **and ·their desire for sin is never satisfied** [*or* they never stop sinning]. **They ·lead weak people into the trap of sin** [ensnare/entice/lure unstable people/souls], **and they have ·taught** [exercised; trained] **their hearts to be greedy. ·God will punish them** [LAccursed children; Cunder God's curse]! 15**These false teachers ·left** [abandoned] **the ·right** [*or* straight] **road and ·lost their way** [wandered away; went astray], **following the way**

2:11 before Some Greek copies read "from."

Balaam went. Balaam, the son of ·Beor [*or* Bosor], **loved ·being paid for**
doing wrong [Lthe wages of unrighteousness; Num. 25; 31:16; Rev. 2:14].
16 **But a donkey, which cannot talk, ·told Balaam he was sinning** [Lrebuked
his wrongdoing]. **It spoke with a ·man's** [human] **voice and stopped the**
prophet's ·crazy thinking [madness; Num. 22:21–35; Jude 11].

17 **Those false teachers are like ·springs** [*or* wells] **without water and**
·clouds [*or* mists] **blown by a ·storm** [whirlwind; squall; Jude 12]. **A place**
in the ·blackest [deepest; Lgloomy] **darkness has been kept for them** [Jude
12–13]. 18 **They ·brag with** [speak with bombastic, boastful] **words that**
·mean nothing [are empty]. **By their ·evil** [fleshly] **desires they ·lead people**
into the trap of sin—[entice] **people who ·are just beginning to escape** [*or*
have barely escaped] **from others who live in error.** 19 **They promise them**
freedom [Cperhaps from the law or from fear of judgment], **but they them-**
selves are not free. They are slaves of ·things that will be destroyed
[corruption; depravity]. **For people are slaves of anything that ·controls**
[masters; overpowers; defeats] **them** [Cthis last sentence may be a common
proverb]. 20 **They ·were made free** [escaped] **from the ·evil** [depravity;
defilement] **in the world by knowing our Lord and Savior Jesus Christ. But**
if they ·return to [Lget entangled again with] **evil things and those things**
·control [master; overpower; defeat] **them, then ·it is worse for them than**
it was before [their last/final state is worse than the first; Matt. 12:45; Luke
11:26]. 21 **·Yes,** [LFor] **it would be better for them to have never known the**
·right way [*or* the way of righteousness] **than to know it and to turn away**
from the holy ·teaching [Lcommandment; law] **that was ·given** [passed on;
handed down] **to them.** 22 **What they did is like this true ·saying** [proverb;
parable]: **"A dog ·goes back to what it has thrown up** [Treturns to its vomit;
Prov. 26:11]**," and, "After a pig is washed, it goes back and rolls in the mud."**

Jesus Will Come Again

3 **·My friends** [LBeloved], **this is** [Lnow] **the second letter I have writ-**
ten you [Cthe first is probably 1 Peter] **to ·help your honest minds**
remember [Lawaken/arouse your sincere understanding/intentions with a
reminder]. 2 **I want you to ·think about** [remember; recall] **the words the**
holy prophets spoke in the past, and remember the command our Lord
and Savior gave us through your apostles [Jude 17]. 3 **It is most important**
for you to understand what will happen in the last days. ·People [LScoffers]
will ·laugh at [scoff at; ridicule] **you. They will ·live doing the evil things**
they want to do [indulge their own desires/lusts; Jude 18]. 4 [LAnd] **They**
will say, "·Jesus promised to come again. Where is he [LWhere is his promised coming]? [LFor] **Our ·fathers** [ancestors] **have ·died** [Lfallen asleep],
but ·the world [Lall things] **continues the way it has been since ·it was made**
[it began with creation]**."** 5 **But they ·do not want to remember** [willfully
forget/ignore] **what happened long ago. By the word of God heaven ·was**
made [came to be; Gen. 1:3–20; Ps. 33:6; 148:5; Heb. 11:3], **and the earth**
was made from water [Gen. 1:2; Ps. 24:2] **and with water** [Gen. 1:6–7, 9; Ps.
33:7; 136:6; Prov. 8:27–29]. 6 **·Then** [LThrough these; Ceither the water and
the word of God, or the heavens and earth which poured forth their water;
Gen. 7:11] **the world was flooded and destroyed ·with water** [Lbeing del-
uged with water; Gen. 6–9]. 7 **And that same word of God is ·keeping**
[reserving; holding in store] **heaven and earth that we now have in order to**
be destroyed by fire [Deut. 32:22; Is. 66:15–16; Zeph. 1:18; Mal. 4:1]. **They**
are being kept for the judgment day and the destruction of ·all who are
against God [Lthe ungodly/impious people].

8 But do not forget [ignore; miss] this one thing, ·dear friends [Lbeloved]:
To the Lord one day is like a thousand years, and a thousand years is like
one day [Cour perception of time is not the same as God's; Ps. 90:4]. 9 The
Lord is not ·slow [*or* late] in doing what he promised—the way some people understand ·slowness [lateness; Hab. 2:3]. But God is being patient
with you [Ex. 34:6]. He does not want anyone to ·be lost [perish], but he
wants all people to ·change their hearts and lives [Lcome to repentance].
10 But the day of the Lord will come like a thief [Cwith surprise and dan-
ger]. The ·skies [heavens] will ·disappear [pass away; Matt. 5:18; 24:35;
Mark 13:31; Luke 16:17; 21:33] with a loud noise. ·Everything in them
[LThe elements; Ceither everything in the cosmos or specifically the heavenly bodies] will be ·destroyed [*or* dissolved] by ·fire [heat; burning], and
the earth and ·everything in it [*or* all the deeds done on it] will be exposed.[n]
11 In that way everything will be ·destroyed [*or* dissolved]. So what kind of
people should you be? You should live holy lives and ·serve God [be godly/
pious], 12 as you wait for and ·look forward to [strive for; *or* hurry; hasten]
the coming of the day of God. When that day comes, the ·skies [*or* heav-
ens] will be ·destroyed [*or* dissolved] with fire, and ·everything in them
[the elements; 3:10] will melt with ·heat [fire; burning]. 13 But God made a
promise to us [Is. 65:17; 66:22], and we are waiting for a new heaven and a
new earth where ·goodness [righteousness] ·lives [makes its home].
14 [LTherefore] ·Dear friends [LBeloved], ·since [*or* while] you are waiting for this to happen, ·do your best [make every effort; strive] to be
[Lfound] without ·sin [Lspot] and without ·fault [Lblemish; Cthe character-
istics of the false teachers in 2:13]. ·Try [Make every effort; Strive] to be at
peace with God. 15 ·Remember [Consider; Bear in mind] that ·we are saved
because our Lord is patient [Lour Lord's patience is our salvation; Chis
delay in coming allows more to be saved]. Our ·dear [Lbeloved] brother
Paul told you the same thing when he wrote to you with the wisdom that
God gave him. 16 He writes about ·this [Lthese things] in all his letters.
Some things in Paul's letters are hard to understand, and people who are
·ignorant [untaught] and ·weak in faith [unstable] ·explain these things
falsely [Ltwist/distort them]. They also ·falsely explain [Ltwist; distort] the
other Scriptures, ·but they are destroying themselves by doing this [*or*
which will lead to their destruction].
17 [LTherefore] ·Dear friends [LBeloved], since you already ·know [are
forewarned] about this, be ·careful [on guard]. Do not let those ·evil [law-
less; unprincipled] people lead you away ·by the wrong they do [*or* by
their deception; *or* into error]. Be ·careful [on guard] so you will not fall
from your own ·strong faith [stability; firm position]. 18 But grow in the
grace and knowledge of our Lord and Savior Jesus Christ. Glory be to
him now and ·forever [Lto the day of eternity]! ·Amen [So be it].

3:10 and . . . exposed Some Greek copies read "and everything in it will be burned up."

1 JOHN

1 We ·write [announce/proclaim to] you now about what ·has
always existed [was from the beginning; Gen. 1:1; John 1:1],
which we have heard, [[L]which] we have seen with our own eyes, [[L]which]
we have looked at, and we have touched with our hands. We ·write
[announce/proclaim] to you about the ·Word that gives life [Word of life;
[C]associating the *logos* or "word" with Jesus suggests he is God's communi-
cation with humanity; John 1:4; 11:25; 14:6]. 2·He who gives life [[L]The
life] ·was shown [appeared; was revealed] to us. We saw him and can ·give
proof about [testify/witness to] it. And now we ·announce [proclaim;
declare] to you ·that he has life that continues forever [[L]the eternal life]. He
was with ·God the Father [[L]the Father] and ·was shown [appeared; was
revealed] to us. 3We ·announce [proclaim; declare] to you what we have
seen and heard, ·because we want you also to have [so that you also may
have] fellowship with us. Our fellowship is with ·God the Father [[L]the
Father] and with his Son, Jesus Christ. 4We write this to you so ·we[n] may be
full of joy [our joy may be complete/perfect/come to full expression].

God Forgives Our Sins

5Here is the message we have heard from ·Christ [[L]him] and now
·announce [proclaim; declare] to you: God is light [[C]referring to God's truth
and goodness], and in him there is no darkness [[C]referring to falsehood and
evil] at all. 6So if we say we have fellowship with God, but we ·continue living
[[L]are walking] in darkness, we are liars and do not ·follow [perform; practice;
act according to] the truth [John 8:12; 12:35]. 7But if we ·live [[L]walk] in the
light, as ·God [[L]he] is in the light, we ·can share [have] fellowship with each
other. Then the blood of Jesus, God's Son, cleanses us from every sin.
8If we say we ·have no sin [*or* have no sin nature; *or* are not guilty of
sinning], we are ·fooling [deceiving] ourselves, and the truth is not in us.
9But if we confess our sins, he will forgive our sins, because ·we can trust
God to do what is right [[L]he is faithful and righteous/just; Deut. 32:4]. He
will ·cleanse [purify] us from all ·the wrongs we have done [unrighteous-
ness]. 10If we ·say [claim] we have not sinned, we make God a liar, and ·we
do not accept God's teaching [[L]his word is not in us].

Jesus Is Our Helper

2 My ·dear children [[L]little children; [C]a term of endearment], I write
·this letter [[L]these things] to you so you will not sin. But if anyone
does sin, we have a ·helper [counselor; advocate; Rom. 8:34] in the presence of the Father—Jesus Christ, ·the One who does what is right [*or* the
Righteous One]. 2He ·died in our place to take away [is the atoning sacri-
fice/[T]propitiation for] our sins [[C]his death pays the penalty and removes

---

1:4 we Some Greek copies read "you."

God's anger from us; 4:10; Rom. 3:25; Heb. 2:17], **and not only our sins**
but the sins of ·all people [Lthe whole world].
[3]**We ·can be sure** [know] **that we know ·God** [Lhim] **if we ·obey** [keep]
his commands. [4]**Anyone who says, "I know ·God** [Lhim]**," but does not**
·obey [keep] **·God's** [Lhis] **commands is a liar, and the truth is not in that**
person. [5]**But if someone ·obeys** [keeps] **·God's teaching** [Lhis word], **then**
in that person ·God's love [*or* love for God] **has ·truly reached its goal**
[been fulfilled/perfected/completed]. **This is how we can be sure we are**
·living in God [Lin him]: [6]**Whoever says that he ·lives** [abides; remains] **in**
God must ·live [Lwalk] **as ·Jesus lived** [Lhe walked].

The Command to Love Others

[7]**·My dear friends** [LBeloved], **I am not writing a new command to you**
but an old command you have had from the beginning [3:23; John 13:34].
It is the ·teaching [Lword] **you have already heard.** [8]**But also I am writing**
a new command to you, ·and you can see its truth in Jesus [Lwhich is true
in him] **and in you, ·because** [*or* that] **the darkness is passing away, and**
the true light is already shining.
[9]**Anyone who ·says** [claims; Cas do the false teachers; see 2:18–19], **"I am**
in the light," [Cfollowing God's goodness and truthfulness] **but hates a**
brother or sister [Cfellow Christian], **is still in the darkness.** [10]**Whoever loves**
a brother or sister ·lives [abides; remains] **in the light and ·will not cause**
anyone to stumble in his faith [*or* he will not stumble in his faith; Lthere is
no cause of stumbling in him; Cthe "stumbling" may be either by apostasy or
sin; John 6:61; 16:1; Rom. 14:13; Rev. 2:14]. [11]**But whoever hates a brother**
or sister is in darkness, ·lives [Lwalks] **in darkness, and does not know where**
to go, because the darkness has ·made that person blind [Lblinded his eyes].
[12]**I write to you, dear children** [2:1],
because your sins are forgiven ·through Christ [Lon account of his
name; Cthe name represents the person].
[13]**I write to you, fathers** [Cprobably senior members of the congregation],
·because [*or* that] **you know the One who existed from the beginning**
[CChrist; John 1:1].
I write to you, young people,
·because [*or* that] **you have ·defeated** [conquered; overcome] **the Evil**
One.
[14]**I ·write** [*or* have written] **to you, children,**
·because [*or* that] **you ·know** [have come to know] **the Father.**
I ·write [*or* have written] **to you, fathers,**
·because [*or* that] **you ·know** [have come to know] **the One who**
existed from the beginning [2:13].
I ·write [*or* have written] **to you, young people,**
·because [*or* that] **you are strong;**
the ·teaching [Lword] **of God ·lives** [abides; remains] **in you,**
and you have ·defeated [conquered; overcome] **the Evil One.**
[15]**Do not love the world or the things ·in** [associated with] **the world. If**
you love the world, the love ·of [*or* for] **the Father is not in you** [James
4:4]. [16][LFor] **·These are the ways of** [All that is in/associated with] **the**
world: ·wanting to please our sinful selves [Lthe desire/lust of the flesh],
·wanting the sinful things we see [Lthe desire/lust of the eyes], **and ·being**
too proud of what we have [Lthe pride of life/possessions]. **None of these**
come from the Father, but all of them come from the world. [17]**The world**
and ·everything that people want in it [Lits desire/lust] **are passing away**

[1 Cor. 7:31], **but the person who does ·what God wants** [the will of God]
·lives [abides; remains] **forever.**

Reject the Enemies of Christ

18 **My dear children** [2:1], **·these are the last days** [L it is the last hour;
C suggesting urgency, though not claiming the end was near]. [L Just as] **You
have heard that the ·enemy of Christ** [L antichrist] **is coming, and now
many ·enemies of Christ** [L antichrists; C false teachers; 2:22; 2 John 7] **are
already here. This is how we know that ·these are the last days** [L it is the
last hour]. 19 **·These enemies of Christ were in our fellowship, but they left
us** [L They went out from us; C probably to form a rival fellowship]. **They
never really belonged to us** [L But they were not of us]; [L For] **if they had
been a part of us, they would have ·stayed** [remained; abided] **with us. But
they left, ·and this shows** [*or* so that it would be shown] **that none of them
really belonged to us.**

20 **You have the ·gift** [L anointing; C probably the Holy Spirit and/or the
spiritual gift of the Word of God applied to their hearts; v. 24; 1 Sam.
16:13; Is. 61:1; John 16:13; 2 Cor. 1:21–22] **that the Holy One gave you**
[L from the Holy One; C a reference to God the Father (Ps. 71:22) or more
likely Jesus Christ (Mark 1:24; John 6:69)], **so you all ·know the truth**" [*or*
have knowledge; L know]. 21 **I do not write to you because you do not know
the truth but because you do know the truth. And you know that no lie
comes from the truth.**

22 **Who is the liar? It is the person who ·does not accept** [denies; repudi-
ates] **Jesus as the ·Christ** [Messiah; Anointed One]. **This is the ·enemy of
Christ** [L antichrist]: **the person who ·does not accept** [denies; repudiates]
the Father and ·his [the] **Son.** 23 **Whoever ·does not accept** [denies; repudi-
ates] **the Son does not have the Father. But whoever ·confesses**
[acknowledges; accepts] **the Son has the Father, too.**

24 [L As for you] **Be sure you ·continue to follow** [abide/remain in] **·the
teaching** [L what] **you heard from the beginning** [C when they first became
Christians; 1 Tim. 6:3; 2 Tim. 1:13; Titus 1:9; 2 Pet. 3:2; Jude 17, 20]. **If you
·continue to follow** [abide/remain in] **what you heard from the beginning, you will** [L also; indeed] **·stay** [abide; remain] **in the Son and in the
Father.** 25 **And this is ·what the Son** [L the promise which he himself] **promised to us—·life forever** [eternal life; 1 Tim. 4:8; 2 Tim. 1:1].

26 **I ·am writing** [*or* have written] **·this letter** [L these things] **about those
people who are ·trying to lead you the wrong way** [deceiving you; leading
you astray]. 27 [L As for you] **·Christ gave you a special gift that is still in
you** [L The anointing that you received from him abides/remains in you;
2:20], **so you do not need ·any other teacher** [L anyone to teach you; Jer.
31:34]. [L But just as] **His ·gift** [L anointing] **teaches you about everything,
and it is true, not false. So ·continue to live in Christ, as his gift taught you**
[L just as he taught you, abide/remain in him].

28 **·Yes** [Now], **my dear children** [2:1], **·live** [abide; remain] **in him so
that when ·Christ comes back** [L he appears/is revealed], **we can be ·with-
out fear** [confident] **and not be ashamed** [L of him] **·in his presence** [at his
coming]. 29 **·Since** [If] **you know that ·Christ** [L he] **is righteous, you know
that all who ·do right** [practice righteousness] **·are God's children** [L have
been born of/begotten by him].

2:20 you . . . truth Some Greek copies read "so you know all things."

We Are God's Children

3 ·The Father has loved us so much [LSee what sort of love the
Father has given us…!] that we are called children of God. ·And
we really are his children [LAnd we are!]. The reason ·the people in the
world do [Lthe world does] not know us is that they have not known him.
2·Dear friends [LBeloved], now we are children of God, and ·we have not
yet been shown [it has not yet been revealed] what we will be in the future.
But we know that when ·Christ comes again [Lhe/it is revealed], we will be
like him, because we will see him as he really is. 3And all who have this
hope in ·Christ [Lhim] keep themselves pure, just as ·Christ [Lhe] is pure.
4·The person [LEveryone] who ·sins [commits sin] ·breaks God's law
[commits lawlessness/iniquity; Creferring to the false teachers; 2:19–20]. Yes,
sin is ·living against God's law [lawlessness; iniquity]. 5You know that ·Christ
came [Lhe has appeared/was revealed] to take away sins and that there is no
sin in ·Christ [Lhim]. 6So anyone who ·lives [abides; remains] in ·Christ
[Lhim] does not ·go on sinning [*or* sin; Cthe Christian ideal, an implicit call to
avoid sin]. Anyone who ·goes on sinning [*or* sins] has ·never really understood Christ and has never known him [Lneither seen him nor known him].
7Dear children [2:1], do not let anyone ·lead you the wrong way [deceive
you]. The one who does what is right is righteous, just as ·Christ [Lhe] is
righteous. 8Anyone who ·continues to sin [*or* sins] belongs to the devil [John
8:44], because the devil has been sinning since the beginning. The Son of
God ·came [was revealed; appeared] for this purpose: to destroy the devil's
work [Matt. 4:1–11; 12:25–29; Luke 10:18; John 12:31; Rev. 12:7–12; 20:1–3].
9·Those [LAll] who are ·God's children [Lborn of/begotten by God; 2:29]
do not ·continue sinning [*or* sin], because ·the new life from God [*or* God's
message; *or* God's Spirit; Lhis seed/sperm] ·remains [abides] in them. They
are not able to ·go on sinning [*or* sin], because they ·have become children
of God [Lare born of/begotten by God]. 10·So we can see [LIn this way it is
apparent/revealed/evident] who God's children are and who the devil's
children are: Those who do not ·do what is right [practice righteousness]
are not ·God's children [Lfrom/of God], and those who do not love their
brothers and sisters are not ·God's children [Lfrom/of God].

We Must Love Each Other

11This is the ·teaching [message] you have heard from the beginning:
We must love each other [Cas Jesus himself taught: John 13:34–35; 15:12].
12Do not be like Cain who belonged to the Evil One and ·killed [mur-
dered] his brother [Gen. 4; John 8:44]. And why did he ·kill [murder]
him? Because the things Cain did were evil, and the things his brother did
were ·good [righteous; just].
13Brothers and sisters [Cfellow believers], do not ·be surprised [be
amazed; wonder] ·when [*or* that; *or* if] ·the people of the world hate [Lthe
world hates] you. 14We know we have ·left death and have come into life
[passed/crossed from death to life; John 5:24] because we love ·each other
[Lthe brothers and sisters]. Whoever does not love ·is still dead [abides/
remains/continues in death]. 15Everyone who hates a brother or sister
[Cfellow believer] is a murderer [Cbecause they have killed that person in
their heart; Matt. 5:21–26], and you know that no murderers have eternal
life [Labiding; remaining] in them. 16This is how we know what real love
is: ·Jesus [Lhe] ·gave [laid down] his life for us [John 15:13]. So we should
·give [lay down] our lives for our brothers and sisters [Cfellow believers;
John 15:12]. 17Suppose someone has ·enough to live [Lthe world's posses-
sions/goods] and sees a brother or sister [Cfellow believer] in need, but

·does not help [Lcloses off his heart/compassion from him]. ·Then God's love is not living in that person [LHow does God's love abide/remain in him?]. 18My children [2:1], we should love people not only ·with words and talk [Lin word and tongue], but ·by our actions and true caring [*or* by showing true love through our actions; Lin deed and truth].

19–20·This is the way [LBy this] we ·know [Lwill know; Cperhaps in a future moment of crisis] that we belong to the ·way of truth [Ltruth]. ·When [*or* If] our hearts [Cour conscience] make us feel guilty [condemn/ convict us], ·we can still have peace before God [our hearts can be reassured before him]. God is greater than our hearts, and he knows everything [1 Cor. 4:3–5]. 21·My dear friends [LBeloved], if our hearts do not ·make us feel guilty [condemn/convict us], we ·can come without fear into God's presence [Lhave boldness/confidence before God]. 22And ·God gives us [Lwe receive from him] what we ask for because we obey ·God's [Lhis] commands and do what pleases him [John 14:14; 16:23]. 23This is ·what God commands [Lhis command]: that we believe in [Lthe name of] his Son, Jesus Christ, and that we love each other, just as he commanded. 24The people who ·obey [keep] God's commands ·live [abide; remain] in God, and God ·lives [abides; remains] in them. We know that God ·lives [abides; remains] in us ·because of [by; from] the Spirit God gave us.

Warning Against False Teachers

4 ·My dear friends [LBeloved], many false prophets [Deut. 13:1–5; 18:14–22; Mark 13:22] have gone out into the world. So do not ·believe [trust] every spirit, but test the spirits to see if they are from God [Cthe false teachers evidently claimed that their teaching was from the Spirit; 1 Cor. 12:1–3; 14:29; 1 Thess. 5:19–21]. 2This is how you can ·know [recognize] God's Spirit: Every spirit [Ca teacher/prophet claiming inspiration from the Spirit] who ·confesses [acknowledges] that Jesus Christ came ·to earth as a human [Lin the flesh] is from God. 3And every spirit who ·refuses to say this about Jesus [Ldoes not confess/acknowledge Jesus] is not from God [2 John 7]. It is the spirit of the ·enemy of Christ [Lantichrist; 2:18, 22], which you have heard is coming, and now he is already in the world.

4·My dear children [2:1], you ·belong to [Lare from] God and have ·defeated [conquered; overcome] them [Cthe antichrists/false teachers]; because ·God's Spirit, who is in you, is greater than the devil, who is in the world [Lthat which is in you is greater than that which is in the world]. 5And they ·belong to [Lare from] the world, so what they say is from the world, and the world ·listens to [hears; obeys] them. 6But we ·belong to [are from] God, and those who know God ·listen to [hear; obey] us. But those who are not from God do not ·listen to [hear; obey] us. That is how we ·know [recognize] the Spirit that is true and the spirit that ·is false [deceives; errs].

Love Comes from God

7·Dear friends [LBeloved], ·we should [let us] love each other, because love comes from God. Everyone who loves has ·become God's child [Lbeen begotten/fathered by God] and knows God. 8Whoever does not love does not know God, because God is love. 9This is how God ·showed [revealed] his love to us: He sent his one and only Son into the world so that we could have life through him. 10This is what real love is: It is not our love for God; it is God's love for us. He sent his Son ·to die in our place to take away our sins [as the atoning sacrifice/Tpropitiation for our sins; see 2:2].

11·Dear friends [Beloved], if God loved us ·that much [*or* in this way; John 3:16] we also should love each other. 12No one has ever seen God [CGod the Father; John 1:18], but if we love each other, God ·lives [remains;

abides] ·in [*or* among] us, and his love ·is made perfect [is made complete; comes to full expression] in us.

13 [LBy this] We know that we ·live [abide; remain] in God and he ·lives [abides; remains] in us, because he gave us [Lof; from; 3:24] his Spirit [Cwe share in his Spirit]. 14 We have seen and can ·testify [witness; proclaim] that the Father sent his Son ·to be [*or* as] the Savior of the world. 15 Whoever ·confesses [acknowledges] that Jesus is the Son of God has God ·living [abiding; remaining] inside, and that person ·lives [abides; remains] in God. 16 And so we ·know [have come to know] the love that God has for us, and we ·trust [believe; rely on] that love.

God is love. Those who ·live [abide; remain] in love ·live [abide; remain] in God, and God ·lives [abides; remains] in them. 17 This is how love ·is made perfect [is made complete; comes to full expression] ·in [*or* among] us: that we can ·be without fear [have boldness; have confidence; 2:28; 3:21; 5:14] on the day of judgment, because in this world we are like him [Cprobably referring to Christ, our example of love]. 18 ·Where God's love is, there is no fear [LThere is no fear in love], because ·God's perfect love drives out fear [Tperfect love casts out fear]. It is punishment that makes a person fear, so love is not made ·perfect [complete] in the person who fears [Cfear of punishment, not an appropriate fear of God; compare Prov. 1:7; 2 Cor. 7:15; Phil. 2:12].

19 We love because ·God [Lhe] first loved us. 20 If people say, "I love God," but hate their brothers or sisters [Cfellow believers], they are liars. [LFor] Those who do not love their brothers and sisters [Cfellow believers], whom they have seen, cannot love God, whom they have never seen. 21 And ·God gave us this command [Lwe have this command from him]: Those who love God must also love their brothers and sisters [Cfellow believers; John 13:34].

Faith in the Son of God

5 Everyone who believes that Jesus is the ·Christ [Messiah] is ·God's child [Lborn of/begotten by God], and whoever loves the Father also loves the ·Father's children [Lone born of/begotten by him]. 2 ·This is how [By/In this] we know we love God's children: when we love God and ·obey [perform; carry out] his commands. 3 ·Loving God means [LFor this is the love of God:] ·obeying [keeping] his commands. And God's commands are not ·too hard [burdensome] for us [Matt. 11:30], 4 because everyone who is ·a child of [Lborn of; begotten of] God ·conquers [defeats; overcomes] the world. And this is the ·victory [conquest] that ·conquers [defeats; overcomes] the world—our faith. 5 ·So the one who conquers the world is [*or* Who is it that conquers/defeats/overcomes the world but…?] the person who believes that Jesus is the Son of God.

6 Jesus Christ is the One who came by water [Clikely a reference to Jesus' baptism] and blood [Ca reference to his death]. He did not come by water only, but by water and blood. And the Spirit ·says that this is true [is the one who testifies/bears witness; Mark 1:11; John 1:32–34], because the Spirit is the truth. 7 ·So [*or* For] there are three ·witnesses[n] [who testify/bear witness]: 8 the Spirit, the water, and the blood; and these three witnesses ·agree [Lare one]. 9 ·We believe people when they say something is true. But what God says is more important [LIf we accept the witness/testimony of people, the witness/testimony of God is better], ·and he has

---

5:7–8 So . . . witnesses A few very late Greek copies and the Latin Vulgate continue, "in heaven: the Father, the Word, and the Holy Spirit, and these three witnesses agree. 8 And there are three witnesses on earth:"

told us the truth about his own Son [Lbecause this is the witness/testimony God has given about his Son]. 10**Anyone who believes in the Son of God ·has the truth that God told us** [*or* has the internal testimony of the Holy Spirit; *or* has the testimony of the eyewitnesses (see 1:1–4); Lhas the witness/testimony in himself]. **Anyone who does not believe makes God a liar** [1:10], **because that person does not believe ·what God told us** [Lthe witness/testimony that God witnessed/testified to] **about his Son.** 11**This is ·what God told us** [Lthe witness/testimony]. **God has given us eternal life, and this life is in his Son.** 12**Whoever has the Son has life, but whoever does not have the Son of God does not have life.**

We Have Eternal Life Now

13**·I write this letter** [LI have written these things] **to you who believe in the** [Lname of the] **Son of God so you will know you have eternal life.** 14**And this is the ·boldness** [confidence] **we have ·in God's presence** [Lbefore God; 3:21]: **that if we ask God for anything ·that agrees with what he wants** [Laccording to his will], **he hears us.** 15[LAnd] **If we know he hears us ·every time we ask him** [in whatever we ask], **we know we have what we ask from him** [3:21–22; Mark 11:24].

16**If anyone sees a brother or sister** [Cfellow believer] **sinning (sin that does not lead to ·eternal death** [Ldeath]), **that person should ·pray** [ask; intercede], **and God will give the sinner life. I am talking about people whose sin does not lead to ·eternal death** [Ldeath]. **There is ·sin** [*or* a sin] **that leads to** [eternal] **death** [Cprobably referring to the false teachers, their rejection of the Spirit's work having put them beyond repentance; compare Mark 3:29]. **I do not mean that a person should ·pray** [ask; intercede] **about that sin.** 17**·Doing wrong is always sin** [LAll unrighteousness is sin], **but there is sin that does not lead to ·eternal death** [Ldeath].

18**We know that those who ·are God's children** [Lare born of/begotten by God] **do not ·continue to sin** [Lsin; 3:6, 9]. **The ·Son of God** [Lthe one born of/begotten by God; CJesus] **·keeps them safe** [protects them], **and the Evil One** [Cthe Devil] **cannot ·touch** [harm] **them.** 19**We know that we ·belong to God** [*or* are children of God; Lare of God], **but the Evil One controls the whole world.** 20**We also know that the Son of God has come and has given us understanding so that we can know the True One. And ·our lives** [Lwe] **are in the True One and in his Son, Jesus Christ. He is the true God and the eternal life.**

21**So, dear children** [2:1], **·keep yourselves away** [guard yourselves] **from ·false gods** [Lidols; Ceither literal idols or false ideas about God].

2 JOHN

Do Not Help False Teachers

1From the ·Elder [*or* old man; CGreek: *presbyteros,* referring to advanced
age, a church office, or both; 1 Tim. 5:17; Titus 1:5; 1 Pet. 5:1; see 3 John 1].
To the ·chosen [elect] lady [Cmost likely a metaphor for a church]
and her children [Cthe members of that church]:
I love all of you in the truth [Cthe truth about the Gospel of Jesus
Christ], and all those who know the truth love you. 2We love you
because of the truth that ·lives [abides; remains] in us and will be with
us forever.
3Grace, mercy, and peace from God the Father and his Son, Jesus
Christ, will be with us in truth and love.
4I ·was very happy [rejoiced greatly] to learn that some of your children
are ·following the way of [living by; Lwalking in] truth [Cliving as the Gospel
requires], as the Father commanded us. 5And now, dear lady, this is not a
new command [LI am writing] but is the same command we have had from
the beginning. I ask you that we all love each other. 6And ·love means [Lthis
is love:] ·living the way God commanded us to live [Lwalking according to his
commands]. As you have heard from the beginning, his command is this:
·Live a life of love [LYou must walk in it; Cthat is, in love; Rom. 13:1–10].
7[LFor] Many ·false teachers [deceivers] ·are in [Lhave gone out into] the
world now [Mark 13:5–6, 22] who do not confess that Jesus Christ came to
earth ·as a human [Tin the flesh]. Anyone who does not confess this is ·a
false teacher [Lthe deceiver] and ·an enemy of Christ [Lthe antichrist; Cone
who radically opposes Christ; 1 John 2:18, 22; 4:3]. 8·Be careful [Watch]
yourselves that you do not lose everything you[n] have worked for, but that
you receive your full reward.
9Anyone who ·goes beyond [runs ahead of] Christ's teaching and does
not ·continue to follow only his teaching [Labide/remain in it] does not
have God. But whoever ·continues to follow [Labides/remains in] ·the
teaching of Christ [Lthe teaching] has both the Father and the Son. 10If
someone comes to you and does not bring this teaching, do not ·greet
[welcome] that person or ·accept [receive] them into your house. 11If you
welcome such a person, you ·share [participate] in the evil work.
12I have many things to write to you, but I do not want to use paper and
ink. Instead, I hope to ·come to [visit] you and talk face to face so ·we can be
full of joy [our joy can be complete]. 13The children of your ·chosen [elect]
sister [see 1:1; Cprobably refers to another church] greet you [3 John 13–14].

8 you Some Greek copies read "we."

3 JOHN

Help Christians Who Teach Truth

1From the Elder [*or* old man; CGreek: *presbyteros*, referring to advanced age, a church office, or both; 1 Tim. 5:17; 1 Pet. 5:1; see 2 John 1].

To ·my dear friend [Lthe beloved] **Gaius** [Can otherwise unknown Christian leader], **whom I love in the truth** [Cthe truth about the Gospel of Jesus Christ]:

2**·My dear friend** [LBeloved], **I pray that you are ·doing well** [prospering] **in ·every way** [all respects] **and that your health is good, just as ·your soul is doing fine** [it is well with your soul; your soul is prospering]. 3[LFor] **I was very happy when some brothers and sisters came and ·told me** [testified] **about the truth in your life and how you are ·following** [Lwalking in] **the way of truth** [2 John 4]. 4**Nothing gives me greater joy than to hear that my children** [Cmembers of the church under his spiritual care] **are ·following the way of truth** [walking in the truth].

5**·My dear friend** [LBeloved], **·it is good that** [you are living out your faith when] **you help the brothers and sisters, even those ·you do not know** [Lwho are strangers]. 6**They ·told** [testified before] **the church about your love. ·Please help them** [You will do well] **to continue their trip** [Cas missionaries] **in a way worthy of God.** 7[LFor] **They ·started out in service to Christ** [Ldeparted for the sake of the name], **and they have been accepting ·nothing** [no support] **from nonbelievers** [LGentiles; pagans]. 8**So we should ·help** [show hospitality to; support] **such people; when we do, we ·share in their work** [become coworkers] **for the truth.**

9**I wrote something to the church, but Diotrephes, who loves to be ·their leader** [first], **will not ·listen to us** [receive us; *or* accept our authority]. 10**So if I come, I will ·talk about** [call to mind; bring attention to] **what Diotrephes** [Cnothing further is known about this man] **is doing, about how he ·lies and says evil things about us** [slanders us with evil/malicious words]. **But ·more than** [not satisfied with] **that, he refuses to ·accept** [welcome; receive] **the other brothers and sisters; he even ·stops** [prevents] **those who do want to ·accept** [welcome; receive] **them and ·puts them out of** [expels them from] **the church.**

11**·My dear friend** [Beloved], **do not ·follow** [imitate] **what is ·bad** [evil]; **·follow** [imitate] **what is good** [1 Cor. 4:16; 11:1; 1 Thess. 1:6; 2:14; 2 Thess. 3:7; Heb. 6:12; 13:7]. **The one who does good ·belongs to** [is from] **God. But the one who does evil has never ·known** [Lseen] **God.**

12**Everyone ·says** [witnesses/testifies to] **good things about Demetrius** [Clikely the bearer of the letter to Gaius; otherwise unknown], **and the truth agrees with what they say. We also ·speak** [witness; testify] **well of him, and you know ·what we say** [our witness/testimony] **is true.**

13**I have many things I want to write you, but I do not want to use pen and ink.** 14**I hope to see you soon and talk face to face.** 15**Peace to you. The friends here greet you. Please greet each friend there by name** [2 John 12–13].

JUDE

[1]From Jude [Mark 6:3; Acts 1:14], a ·servant [slave; bondservant] of
Jesus ·Christ [the Messiah] and a brother of James [Cthe half-brother of
Jesus; James 1:1].

To all who have been ·called [chosen] by God. God the Father loves
you, and you have been kept safe ·in [*or* for; *or* by] Jesus Christ:
[2]Mercy, peace, and love be yours ·richly [in abundance; more and
more].

God Will Punish Sinners

[3]·Dear friends [Loved ones; Beloved], I ·wanted very much [*or* was
making every effort; *or* was just about] to write you about ·the salvation we
all share [our common salvation]. But I felt the need to write you about
something else: I want to ·encourage [exhort; urge; appeal to] you to ·fight
hard for [earnestly contend for; defend] the faith [Cthe authentic gospel
message] that was ·given [handed down to; entrusted to] the ·holy people
of God [Tsaints] once and for all time. [4][LFor] Some people have ·secretly
entered [sneaked in; infiltrated; wormed their way into] your group [2 Pet.
2:1]. Long ago ·the prophets wrote about these people who will be judged
guilty [their condemnation was written about/predetermined]. They are
·against God [ungodly] and have ·changed [perverted; distorted] the grace
of our God [Cwith its freedom from legalistic rules] into ·a reason for sexual sin [Ldebauchery; licentiousness; immorality]. They also ·refuse to
accept [deny; have turned against] our only Master and Lord, Jesus Christ.
[5]I want to remind you of some things you already know ·well [fully]:
Remember that the Lord[n] ·saved [rescued; delivered] his people by bringing them out of the land of Egypt. But later he destroyed all those who
·did not believe [were unfaithful]. [6]And remember the angels who did not
keep their ·place of power [position of authority; Lown domain/rule] but
left their proper ·home [dwelling place]. The Lord has kept these angels in
·darkness [gloom; Cthe nether world or underworld; the place of the
dead], bound with everlasting chains, to be judged on the great day [Cthe
final day of judgment; 2 Pet. 2:4]. [7]Also remember the cities of Sodom and
Gomorrah [Cdestroyed by God for their evil; Gen. 19; 2 Pet. 2:6] and the
other towns around them. In the same way they were full of sexual sin
and people who ·desired sexual relations that God does not allow [pur-
sued sexual perversion; Ldeparted after different flesh]. They suffer the
punishment of eternal fire, as an ·example [warning] for all to see.
[8]It is the same with these people [Cthe false teachers; v. 4]. They are
guided by dreams ·and make themselves filthy with sin [and live immoral
lives/pollute their bodies; *or* to defile the flesh]. They ·reject [despise] ·God's

---

5 the Lord Some Greek copies read "Jesus."

authority [Lauthority] **and ·speak against** [insult; slander; blaspheme] **·the**
angels [celestial beings; Lglorious ones; 2 Pet. 2:10–11]. 9**Not even the arch-**
angel Michael [Ca leader among God's angels; Dan. 10:13, 21; 12:1; Rev. 12:7],
when he ·argued [contended] **with the devil ·about who would have**
[Labout] **the body of Moses, dared to ·judge the devil guilty** [Lbring a slan-
derous/blasphemous judgment]. **Instead, he said, "The Lord ·punish**
[rebuke] **you** [Cprobably a story told in the *Testament of Moses,* a Jewish
writing of the early first century AD]." 10**But these people ·speak against**
[slander; blaspheme] **things they do not understand** [2 Pet. 2:12]. **And what**
they do know, ·by feeling [instinctively], **like ·dumb** [unreasoning; irratio-
nal] **animals, are the very things that destroy them.** 11**·It will be terrible for**
them [LWoe to them!]. **They have followed the way of Cain** [Cwho murdered his brother Abel; Gen. 4], **and ·for money** [because of greed; Lfor
wages] **they have ·given themselves** [poured themselves out] **to doing the**
·wrong [error] **that Balaam did** [Num. 22–24; 2 Pet. 2:15–16]. **·They have**
rebelled against God as Korah did, and like Korah, they surely will be
destroyed [LIn the rebellion of Korah, they were destroyed; Num. 16]. 12**They**
are like ·dirty spots [blemishes; *or* dangerous hidden reefs/rocks] **in your**
·special Christian meals you share [fellowship meals; love feasts]. **They eat**
with you and have no ·fear [qualms; *or* shame], **·caring only for themselves**
[*or* shepherds feeding themselves]. **They are clouds without ·rain** [Lwater],
which the wind blows around [2 Pet. 2:17]. **They are autumn trees without**
fruit that are ·pulled out of the ground [uprooted]. **So they are twice dead**
[Cbecause they are both barren and uprooted; or perhaps a reference to both
the physical *and* spiritual death of the false teachers]. 13**They are like wild**
waves of the sea, ·tossing up their own shameful actions like foam [Lfoaming
up their own shame]. **They are like ·stars that wander in the sky** [Cperhaps
a reference to planets, whose variable positions, unlike those of the stars,
provide mariners no guidance]. **A place in the ·blackest darkness** [Lgloom of
darkness; v. 7] **has been kept for them forever** [2 Pet. 2:17].

14**Enoch, the seventh descendant from Adam** [Ccounting Adam first;
Gen. 5:18–24], **·said** [Lprophesied] **about these people: "·Look** [TBehold],
the Lord is coming with many thousands of his ·holy angels [Lholy ones]
to 15**judge every person. He is coming to ·punish** [convict] **·all** [every per-
son/soul] **who are against God for all ·the evil they have done against him**
[Ltheir ungodly deeds committed in an ungodly manner]. **And he will**
punish the ·sinners who are against God [ungodly sinners] **for all the ·evil**
[harsh/defiant words; insults] **they have said against him."** [CJude appears
to be quoting here from the nonbiblical Jewish book of 1 Enoch (1:9),
although he may be drawing generally from Jewish tradition.]

16**These people ·complain and blame others** [are grumblers and fault-
finders], **·doing the evil things they want to do** [Lpursuing their own
desires/lusts]. **·They brag about themselves** [LTheir mouths speak boastful
words], **and they ·flatter** [impress; astound] **others ·to get what they want**
[to gain an advantage; Lfor the sake of gain].

A Warning and Things to Do

17[LBut you] **·Dear friends** [Beloved], **remember what the apostles of our**
Lord Jesus Christ ·said before [predicted; prophesied; foretold; 2 Pet. 3:2].
18[LFor] **They said to you, "In the ·last times** [end time] **there will be ·people**
who laugh about God [scoffers; mockers], **·following** [pursuing] **their own**
·evil [ungodly] **·desires** [passions; lusts; 2 Pet. 3:3]." 19**These are the people**
who ·divide you [cause divisions], **people ·whose thoughts are only of this**

world [who are worldly; *or* who live by natural instincts/desires], **who do not have the Spirit** [Cliving within them and guiding them].

[20]**But** [Lyou] **·dear friends** [beloved], **·use your most holy faith to build yourselves up** [*or* build yourselves up on the foundation of your most holy faith; Cthe whole body of true Christian doctrine and practice], **praying ·in** [in dependence on; *or* as directed by; *or* according to the will of] **the Holy Spirit.** [21]**Keep yourselves in God's love as you wait for the mercy of the Lord Jesus Christ ·to give you** [that leads to] **·life forever** [eternal life].

[22]**Show mercy to ·some people who have doubts** [those who waver; Cin their faith]. [23]**·Take others out of the fire, and save them** [LSave/Rescue others by snatching them from the fire; Cfire represents judgment]. **Show mercy mixed with fear to others** [Cfear inspired by God's righteous judgment against sin], **hating even their clothes which are ·dirty from sin** [Lstained by the sinful nature/flesh].

Praise God

[24]**·God is strong and can** [LNow to the one who is able to] **·help you not to fall** [keep/guard you from falling/stumbling]. **·He can bring you** [L…and to present you] **before his ·glory** [glorious presence] **·without any wrong in you** [faultless; blameless; spotless] **and ·can give you great joy** [with gladness/jubilation/rejoicing]. [25]**To the only God, ·the One who saves us** [Lour Savior], **be glory, ·greatness** [majesty], **·power** [might], **and authority through Jesus Christ our Lord for all ·time past** [the ages], **now, and forever. Amen.**

REVELATION

John Tells About This Book

1 **This is the revelation ·of Jesus Christ** [about Jesus Christ; *or* given by Jesus Christ; Cthe author could be intentionally ambiguous], **which God gave to him, to show his servants what must ·soon** [quickly] **happen. And Jesus sent his angel to ·show it** [make it known] **to his servant John, 2who has ·told** [witnessed; testified to] **everything he has seen. It is the word of God; it is the ·message** [witness; testimony] **from Jesus Christ. 3·Blessed** [Happy] **is the one who reads the words of ·God's message** [Lthe prophecy], **and ·blessed** [happy] **are the people who hear this message and ·do** [keep; obey] **what is written in it** [Cthe context envisioned is a leader reading to a congregation]. ·The time is near when all of this will happen [LFor the time is near].

Jesus' Message to the Churches

4From John.

To the seven churches in Asia [Cthe Roman province of Asia, today part of western Turkey]:

Grace and peace to you from the One who is and [the One who] was and [the One who] is coming [Cthese three descriptions function like titles for God; Ex. 3:14–15], and from ·the seven spirits [Creferring either to angels or to the "sevenfold Spirit"—the Holy Spirit portrayed in his perfection (the number seven indicating completeness)] before his throne, 5and from Jesus Christ. Jesus is ·the faithful witness [*or* the faithful one, the witness], the ·first among those raised from [Lfirstborn of/from among] the dead. He is the ruler of the kings of the earth.

·He is the One [LTo him] who loves us, who made us free[n] from our sins ·with the blood of his death [Lby his blood]. 6He made us to be a ·kingdom of priests [*or* kingdom and priests; *or* kingdom, that is, priests; Ex. 19:6] who serve ·God his Father [Lhis God and Father]. To ·Jesus Christ [Lhim] be glory and ·power [dominion] forever and ever! Amen.

7Look [TBehold], Jesus is coming with the clouds [Dan. 7:13–14], and ·everyone [Levery eye] will see him, even those who ·stabbed [pierced] him [Ca reference to the crucifixion; Zech. 12:10]. And all ·peoples [people groups; tribes] of the earth will ·cry loudly [wail; mourn] because of him. ·Yes, this will happen [So it shall be; LYes]! Amen.

8The Lord God says, "I am the Alpha and the Omega [Cthe first and last letters of the Greek alphabet; 21:6; 22:13]. I am the One who is and [the One who] was and [the One who] is coming [see 1:4]. I am the ·Almighty [All-powerful]."

9I, John, ·am your brother. All of us share [Lyour brother and partner] ·with Jesus [*or* in Jesus; Creferring to salvation as joining oneself to Christ]

1:5 who made us free Some Greek copies read "who washed us."

in ·suffering [persecution], in the kingdom, and in ·patience to continue
[perseverance]. I was on the island of Patmos [C a small island in the
Aegean Sea near Asia Minor, present-day Turkey], because ·I had preached
[L of] the word of God and the ·message [witness; testimony] about Jesus.
10 On the Lord's day [C probably a reference to the first day of the week,
Sunday, when Christians met for worship] I was in the ·Spirit [*or* spirit; C a
state of deep spiritual communion with God], and I heard a loud voice
behind me that sounded like a trumpet [C trumpet blasts often precede a
divine appearance or speech; Ex. 19:16, 19]. 11 The voice said, "Write what
you see in a ·book [scroll] and send it to the seven churches: to Ephesus,
Smyrna, Pergamum, Thyatira, Sardis, Philadelphia, and Laodicea
[C locations in western Asia Minor, present-day Turkey]."
12 I turned to see who was talking to me. When I turned, I saw seven
golden lampstands 13 and someone among the lampstands who was "like
a Son of Man [C referring to Jesus; the title he most often used to refer to
himself; Dan. 7:13–14]." He was dressed in a long robe and had a gold
·band [sash] around his chest [C the clothes of a dignitary; Dan. 10:5].
14 His head and hair were white like wool, as white as snow [Dan. 7:9], and
his eyes were like ·flames of [blazing] fire [Dan. 10:6]. 15 His feet were like
bronze ·that glows hot [refined; fired] in a furnace [Dan. 10:6], and his
voice was like the noise of ·flooding water [rushing water; L many waters;
Ezek. 43:2]. 16 He held seven stars in his right hand, and a sharp double-
edged sword came out of his mouth. ·He [L His face] looked like the sun
shining ·at its brightest time [*or* with full power/force; L in its strength].
17 When I saw him, I fell down at his feet like a dead man. He put his right
hand on me and said, "Do not be afraid. I am the First and the Last. 18 I am
the One who lives; I was dead, but ·look [T behold], I am alive forever and
ever! And I hold the keys to death and ·to the place of the dead [L Hades].
19 So write the things you ·see [*or* have seen], ·what is now [L what is] and
what will happen ·later [L after these things]. 20 Here is the ·secret [mystery]
of the seven stars that you saw in my right hand and the seven golden lampstands: The seven stars are the ·angels [*or* messengers; C these may be
guardian angels, human leaders, or the personified "spirit" of each church]
of the seven churches, and the seven lampstands are the seven churches.

To the Church in Ephesus

2 "Write this to the ·angel [*or* messenger; see 1:20] of the church in
Ephesus [C an important city in western Asia Minor]:
"The One who holds the seven stars in his right hand and walks among
the seven golden lampstands [C the resurrected Jesus; 1:16, 20] says ·this
[L these things]: 2 I know ·what you do [L your works], ·how you work hard
[L your toil] and ·never give up [L your perseverence/endurance]. I know
you do not put up with ·the false teachings of evil people [L evildoers; *or*
evil]. You have tested those who say they are apostles but really are not,
and you found they are ·liars [*or* false]. 3 You have ·patience [perseverance;
endurance] and have ·suffered troubles [endured much] for my name
and have not ·given up [L grown weary].
4 "But I have this against you: You have ·left [abandoned] ·the love you
had in the beginning [*or* your first love]. 5 So ·remember [consider] ·where
you were before you fell [L how far you have fallen]. ·Change your hearts
[Repent] and do ·what [L the works] you did at first. If you do not ·change
[repent], I will come to you and will take away your lampstand from its
place. 6 But ·there is something you do that is right [L this you have]: You

hate what the Nicolaitans do [[C]we know little about this heresy, which possibly entailed false worship and immorality], **as much as I.**

7**“Every person who has ears should ·listen to** [hear; obey] **what the Spirit says to the churches. To those who ·win the victory** [overcome; conquer] **I will give the right to eat the fruit from the ·tree of life, which is in the ·garden** [*or* paradise] **of God** [22:2; Gen. 2:9].

To the Church in Smyrna

8**“Write this to the ·angel** [*or* messenger; see 1:20] **of the church in Smyrna** [[C]a major city in western Asia Minor, identified with present-day Izmir, Turkey]:

“The One who is the First and the Last, who died and came to life again [[C]the resurrected Jesus; 1:17–18], **says ·this** [[L]these things]: 9**I know your ·troubles** [persecution; affliction] **and that you are poor, but really you are rich! I know the ·bad things** [slander; blasphemy] **some people say about you. They say they are Jews, but they are not true Jews. They are a synagogue ·that belongs to** [[L]of] **Satan.** 10**Do not be afraid of what you are about to suffer. I tell you, the devil will put some of you in prison to test you, and you will ·suffer** [be persecuted/afflicted] **for ten days** [[C]perhaps a symbolic number meaning a significant and definite time]. **But be faithful, even if you have to die, and I will give you the ·crown** [[C]a wreath worn to indicate high status or as a reward] **of life.**

11**“Everyone who has ears should ·listen to** [hear; obey] **what the Spirit says to the churches. Those who ·win the victory** [overcome; conquer] **will not be hurt by the second death** [[C]the spiritual death after physical death; 20:6, 14; 21:8].

To the Church in Pergamum

12**“Write this to the ·angel** [messenger; see 1:20] **of the church in Pergamum** [[C]a rich city in western Asia Minor]:

“The One who has the sharp, double-edged sword [[C]the resurrected Jesus; 1:16] **says this** [[L]these things]: 13**I know where you live. It is where Satan has his throne** [[C]a reference to false worship; Pergamum was a center of emperor worship]. **But you ·are true to me** [[L]hold fast to my name]. **You did not ·refuse to tell about** [deny] **your faith in me even during the time of Antipas, my faithful witness who was killed ·in your city** [[L]among you; [C]we know nothing further about Antipas], **where Satan lives.**

14**“But I have a few things against you: You have some there who follow the teaching of Balaam. He taught Balak how to ·cause the people of Israel to sin** [[L]put a stumbling block before the children of Israel] **by eating food offered to idols and by taking part in sexual sins** [Num. 22–24; 31:8; Deut. 23:4–5; 2 Pet. 2:15; Jude 11]. 15**You also have some who follow the teaching of the Nicolaitans** [see 2:6]. 16**So ·change your hearts and lives** [repent]. **If you do not, I will come to you quickly and ·fight** [make war] **against them with the sword that comes out of my mouth** [[C]the judgment he enacts by merely speaking; 1:16].

17**“Everyone who has ears should ·listen to** [hear; obey] **what the Spirit says to the churches.**

“I will give some of the hidden manna [[C]perhaps alluding to a Jewish tradition that the manna placed in the ark is hidden until the messianic age; ultimately referring to the spiritual life Christ provides; John 6:32–35] **to everyone who ·wins the victory** [overcomes; conquers]. **I will also give to each one who ·wins the victory** [overcomes; conquers] **a white stone with a new name written on it** [[C]an unknown cultural image, which, along with the manna, points to salvation in Christ]. **No one knows this new**

name except the one who receives it [Cthe name could be God's or Christ's,
but more likely refers to a new name given to the people of God].

To the Church in Thyatira

18"Write this to the ·angel [messenger; see 1:20] of the church in
·Thyatira [Ca small city in western Asia Minor]:
"The Son of God, who has eyes that blaze like fire [1:14] and feet like
shining bronze [1:15; Cthe resurrected Jesus], says ·this [Lthese things]: 19I
know ·what you do [your works]. I know about your love, your faith, your
service, and your ·patience [endurance; perseverance]. I know that ·you
are doing more now than you did at first [Lyour last works are greater than
the first].
20"But I have this against you: You ·let that woman Jezebel spread false
teachings [Ltolerate the woman Jezebel; Cprobably the leader of the
Nicolaitans, here given the name of the notorious Baal-worshiping queen;
1 Kin. 16:31–34; 21:25–26; 2 Kin. 9:22]. She ·says she is [calls herself] a
prophetess, but ·by her teaching she leads [teaches and misleads/deceives]
my ·people [Lservants] to take part in sexual sins and to eat food that is
offered to idols. 21I have given her time to ·change her heart and turn
away from her sin [repent of her sexual immorality], but she does not
want to ·change [repent]. 22·So [LLook!] I will throw her on ·a bed of suffering [*or* a sickbed; Cthe bed used for sexual sin is now a bed of suffering].
And all those who take part in adultery with her will suffer greatly if they
do not ·turn away from the wrongs she does [repent of her works/deeds].
23I will also kill her ·followers [Lchildren]. Then all the churches will know
I am the One who searches hearts and minds, and I will repay each of you
for ·what you have done [your works/deeds].
24"But ·others [the rest] of you in Thyatira have not followed her teaching and have not learned what some call Satan's deep secrets. I say to you
that I will not put any other ·load [burden] on you. 25Only ·continue in
your loyalty [Lhold fast to what you have] until I come.
26"I will give ·power [authority] over the nations to everyone who
·wins the victory [overcomes; conquers] and ·continues to be obedient to
me [*or* keeps working for me; Lkeeps/obeys my works] until the end.
27'·You [Lhe; Cthe one who overcomes] will ·rule over [Lshepherd] them
with an iron ·rod [*or* scepter],
·as when pottery is broken into pieces [*or* and will break them into
pieces like pottery; Ps. 2:9].'
28This is the same ·power [authority] I received from my Father. I will also
give him the morning star [Cusually the planet Venus as seen before sunrise, but here symbolically Christ at his return; 22:16; Num. 24:17; 2 Pet.
1:19]. 29Everyone who has ears should ·listen to [hear; obey] what the
Spirit says to the churches.

To the Church in Sardis

3 "Write this to the ·angel [messenger; see 1:20] of the church in
·Sardis [Cthe capital of the Roman province of Lydia in western
Asia Minor]:
"The One [Cthe resurrected Jesus] who has the ·seven spirits [Creferring
either to angels or to the "sevenfold Spirit"—the Holy Spirit portrayed in
his perfection; 1:4] and the seven stars [1:16] says ·this [Lthese things]: I
know ·what you do [your works]. ·People say [LYou have a name/reputa-
tion] that you are alive, but really you are dead. 2Wake up! Strengthen
what you have left ·before it dies completely [*or* which is about to die]. I
have found that ·what you are doing is less than what my God wants

[Lyour works are incompleted/unfulfilled before my God]. 3**So ·do not forget** [Lremember] **what you have received and heard. Obey it, and ·change your hearts and lives** [repent]. **·So you must wake up, or** [LBut if you do not wake up,] **I will come like a thief, and you will not know ·when** [Lat what hour] **I will come ·to** [upon; against] **you.** 4**But you have a ·few** [few people; Lfew names] **there in Sardis who have kept their clothes ·unstained** [unsoiled; undefiled], **so they will walk with me ·and will wear white clothes** [Lin white], **because they are worthy.** 5**Those who ·win the victory** [overcome; conquer] **will be dressed in white clothes like them. And I will ·not** [never; Can emphatic negation] **erase** [wipe out; blot out] **their names from the ·book** [scroll] **of life** [Ex. 32:32–33; Ps. 69:28; Dan. 12:1], **but I will ·say they belong to me** [Lconfess their names] **before my Father and before his angels.** 6**Everyone who has ears should ·listen to** [hear; obey] **what the Spirit says to the churches.**

To the Church in Philadelphia

7**"Write this to the ·angel** [messenger; see 1:20] **of the church in ·Philadelphia** [a city in the Roman province of Lydia in western Asia Minor]:

"This is what the One who is holy and true, who holds the key of David [Cthe resurrected Jesus; holding the key of David signifies access to the king; Is. 22:22], **says. When he opens a door, no one can close it. And when he closes it, no one can open it** [CJesus controls access to God]. 8**I know ·what you do** [your works]. **I have put an open door before you, which no one can close. I know you have little ·strength** [power], **but you have ·obeyed my teaching** [Lkept my word] **and ·were not afraid to speak** [Lhave not denied] **my name.** 9**Those in the synagogue ·that belongs to Satan** [Lof Satan] **say they are Jews, but they are not true Jews; they are liars. I will make them come before you and bow at your feet, and they will ·know** [acknowledge; learn] **that I have loved you.** 10**You have ·obeyed my teaching** [Lkept my word] **about ·not giving up your faith** [endurance; perseverance]. **So I will keep you from the ·time** [hour] **of ·trouble** [trial; testing] **that ·will come** [*or* is about to come] **to the whole world to test those who live on earth.**

11**"I am coming ·soon** [quickly]. **·Continue strong in your faith** [LHold on to what you have] **so no one will take away your crown** [Cwreath indicating honor or victory; 2:10]. 12**I will make those who ·win the victory** [overcome; conquer] **pillars in the temple of my God** [Can image of stability and security close to the glory of God], **and they will never have to leave it** [Cfrequent earthquakes often forced Philadelphians to live outdoors]. **I will write on them the name of my God and the name of the city of my God, the new Jerusalem, that comes down out of heaven from my God** [Cthe believers' eternal dwelling place; see chs. 21–22]. **I will also write on them my new name.** 13**Everyone who has ears should ·listen to** [hear; obey] **what the Spirit says to the churches.**

To the Church in Laodicea

14**"Write this to the ·angel** [*or* messenger; see 1:20] **of the church in Laodicea** [Ca city in Phrygia, a mountainous province of western Asia]:

"The Amen [CHebrew for "so be it"; here referring to Jesus], **the faithful and true witness, ·the ruler of all God has made** [1:5; Prov. 8:30–31; Cthe resurrected Jesus], **says this** [Lthese things]: 15**I know ·what you do** [your works], **that you are not hot or cold. I wish that you were hot or cold** [Cboth positive images, alluding to cold refreshing mountain streams and healing hot springs near Laodicea]! 16**But because you are lukewarm—neither hot,**

nor cold—I am ready to ·spit [vomit] you out of my mouth. 17[LFor] You
say, 'I am rich, and I have become wealthy and do not need anything.' But
you do not know that you are really ·miserable [wretched], pitiful, poor,
blind, and naked. 18I advise you to buy from me gold ·made pure in [refined
by] fire so you can be truly rich. Buy from me white clothes [Cindicating
purity] so you can be clothed and so you can cover your shameful nakedness. Buy from me ·medicine [salve; ointment] to put on your eyes so you
can truly see.

19"I ·correct [rebuke] and ·punish [discipline] those whom I love. So be
·eager to do right [zealous; earnest], and ·change your hearts and lives
[repent]. 20·Here I am [LLook; TBehold]! I stand at the door and knock. If
·you [Lanyone] hear my voice and open the door, I will come in and eat
with you, and you will eat with me.

21"Those who ·win the victory [overcome; conquer] will sit with me on
my throne in the same way that I ·won the victory [overcame; conquered;
Cover death, by his resurrection] and sat down with my Father on his
throne. 22Everyone who has ears should ·listen to [hear; obey] what the
Spirit says to the churches."

John Sees Heaven

4 After the vision of these things I looked, and [Llook; Tbehold] there
before me was an open door in heaven. And the ·same [Lfirst] voice
that spoke to me before, that sounded like a trumpet [1:8], said, "Come up
here, and I will show you what must happen after this." 2Immediately I was
in the ·Spirit [or spirit; Ca state of deep spiritual communion with God;
1:10], and [Llook; Tbehold] before me was a throne in heaven, and someone was sitting on it. 3The One who sat on the throne looked like precious
stones, like jasper and carnelian [Ca symbol of great beauty, purity and
value]. All around the throne was a ·rainbow [*or* halo] ·the color of [*or* that
looked like] an emerald. 4Around the throne there were twenty-four other
thrones with twenty-four elders sitting on them [Cprobably angelic lead-
ers]. They were dressed in white and had golden crowns [Cwreaths
symbolizing honor or victory; see 2:10] on their heads. 5Lightning flashes
and ·noises and thunder [*or* the rumbling of thunder; Cphenomena associated with God's appearance at Mount Sinai; Ex. 19:16–18] came from the
throne. Before the throne seven lamps were burning, which are the seven
spirits [Ceither angels or the "sevenfold Spirit"—the Holy Spirit portrayed
in his perfection; 3:1] of God. 6Also before the throne there was something
that looked like a sea of glass, clear like crystal.

In the center and around the throne were four living creatures ·with eyes
all over them [full of eyes], in front and in back. 7The first living creature
was like a lion. The second was like an ·ox [*or* calf]. The third had a face like
a man. The fourth was like a flying eagle [Ezek. 1:10; Cangelic beings identified with the most powerful example of various species]. 8Each of these four
living creatures had six wings and was ·covered all over with eyes [full of
eyes], inside and out. Day and night they never ·stop [rest from] saying:

"Holy, holy, holy is the Lord God ·Almighty [All-powerful].
He was, he is, and he is coming [1:4, 8]."

9[LWhenever] These living creatures give glory, honor, and thanks to
the One who sits on the throne, who lives forever and ever. 10Then the
twenty-four elders bow down before the One who sits on the throne, and
they worship him who lives forever and ever. They ·put their crowns
down [cast/lay their crowns; 4:4] before the throne and say:

11"You are worthy, our Lord and God,
to receive glory and honor and ·power [strength],
because you made all things.
Everything existed and was made,
·because you wanted it [by your will]."

5 Then I saw a scroll in the right hand of the One sitting on the throne.
The scroll had writing on both sides and was ·kept closed [Lsealed]
with seven seals [Ca wax stamp that sealed a document shut]. 2And I saw a
·powerful [mighty] angel ·calling [proclaiming] in a loud voice, "Who is
worthy to break the seals and open the scroll?" 3But there was no one in
heaven or on earth or under the earth who could open the scroll or look
inside it. 4I cried ·bitterly [Lmuch] because there was no one who was worthy
to open the scroll or look inside. 5But one of the elders said to me, "Do not
cry! [LLook; TBehold] The Lion from the tribe of Judah [Ca messianic title;
Gen. 49:9–10], ·David's descendant [Lthe root of David; Ca messianic title
applied to Christ; Is. 11:10], has ·won the victory [overcome; conquered] so
that he is able to open the scroll and its seven seals."
6Then I saw a Lamb [CJesus] standing ·in the center of the throne and in
the middle of the four living creatures and the elders [*or* between the throne
and the living creatures and among the elders]. The Lamb looked as if he had
been ·killed [slaughtered; slain]. He had seven horns and seven eyes, which
are the seven spirits of God [Ceither angels or the "sevenfold Spirit"; see 1:4]
that were sent into all the world. 7The Lamb came and ·took [received] the
scroll from the right hand of the One sitting on the throne. 8When he took
the scroll, the four living creatures and the twenty-four elders [4:4] ·bowed
down [fell] before the Lamb. Each one of them had a harp and golden bowls
full of incense, which are the prayers of God's holy people [Ps. 141:2]. 9And
they all sang a new song [Ps. 33:3; 40:3; 98:1] to the Lamb:
"You are worthy to take the scroll
and to open its seals,
because you were ·killed [slaughtered; slain],
and with ·the blood of your death [Lyour blood] you ·bought
[ransomed; purchased; redeemed] people for God
from every tribe, language, people, and nation.
10You made them to be a kingdom ·of priests [*or* and priests; Ex. 19:6]
for our God,
and they will ·rule [reign; Cother manuscripts have "they reign"
(present tense)] on the earth."
11Then I looked, and I heard the voices of many angels around the
throne, and the four living creatures, and the elders. There were ·thou-
sands and thousands [Lmyriads of myriads and thousands of thousands;
Ca myriad can mean either ten thousand or many thousands; here means
"countless"] of angels, 12saying in a loud voice:
"The Lamb who was ·killed [slaughtered; slain] is worthy
to receive power, wealth, wisdom, and strength,
honor, glory, and ·praise [*or* blessing]!"
13Then I heard all creatures in heaven and on earth and under the
earth and in the sea saying:
"To the One who sits on the throne
and to the Lamb
be ·praise [*or* blessing] and honor and glory and power
forever and ever."

14The four living creatures said, "Amen [CHebrew for "so be it"]," and
the elders ·bowed down [fell] and worshiped.

6 Then I watched while the Lamb opened the first of the seven seals
[5:1]. I heard one of the four living creatures say with a voice like
thunder, "·Come [*or* Go; CChrist, the Lamb, calls forth the four riders who
bring bloody judgment on the world]!" 2I looked, and ·there before me was
[Llook; Tbehold] a white horse. The rider on the horse held a bow [Csignifying
war], and he was given a crown [Cindicating victory; see 2:10], and he rode
out, ·determined to win the victory [Lconquering and in order to conquer].
3When the Lamb opened the second seal, I heard the second living
creature say, "·Come [*or* Go; 6:1]!" 4Then another horse came out, a ·red
[Lfiery/bright red; Cpossibly signifying blood] one. Its rider was given
·power [permission] to take away peace from the earth and to make people ·kill [slaughter] each other, and he was given a ·big [great] sword
[Csignifying civil war].
5When the Lamb opened the third seal, I heard the third living creature
say, "·Come [*or* Go]!" I looked, and ·there before me was [Llook; Tbehold] a
black horse [Cindicating mourning brought on by the rider], and its rider
held a pair of scales in his hand [Cfor use in commerce; Prov. 11:1; 16:11].
6Then I heard something that sounded like a voice coming from the middle
of the four living creatures. The voice said, "A quart of wheat for a ·day's
pay [Ldenarius; Ca Roman coin equal to a day's wage], and three quarts of
barley for a ·day's pay [Ldenarius; Cinflated prices caused by famine], and do
not damage the olive oil and wine [Cindicates only partial destruction; vines
and olive trees endured drought better than wheat and barley]!"
7When the Lamb opened the fourth seal, I heard the voice of the fourth
living creature say, "·Come [*or* Go; 6:1]!" 8I looked, and ·there before me
was [Llook; Tbehold] a ·pale [*or* pale green] horse. Its rider was named
death, and Hades [Cthe realm of the dead, also known as Sheol] was following close behind him. They were given ·power [authority] over a fourth of
the earth to kill people by ·war [Lthe sword], by ·starvation [famine], by
·disease [pestilence; plague], and by the wild animals of the earth.
9When the Lamb opened the fifth seal, I saw under the altar [Cprobably
the bronze altar where sacrifices were offered] the souls of those who had
been ·killed [slaughtered; slain] because ·they were faithful to [Lof] the
word of God and to the ·message [witness; testimony] they had ·received
[*or* given; *or* maintained]. 10These souls ·shouted [cried out] in a loud
voice, "Holy and true ·Lord [Master], how long until you judge the people
of the earth and ·punish them for killing us [Lavenge our blood]?" 11Then
each one of them was given a white robe [Csignifying high status and
purity] and was told to ·wait [*or* rest] a short time longer. There were still
some of their fellow servants and ·brothers and sisters in the service of
Christ [Ltheir brothers; Cthe Greek term may include men and women]
who ·must be [were soon to be] killed as they were. They had to wait until
all of this was ·finished [fulfilled; completed].
12Then I watched while the Lamb opened the sixth seal, and there was
a great earthquake. The sun became black like ·rough black cloth
[Lsackcloth made of goat hair; Cclothing used in mourning], and the whole
moon became red like blood [Csignifying destruction; apocalyptic literature often describes nature falling apart at the end time; Joel 2:31]. 13And
the stars in the sky fell to the earth like ·figs [*or* unripe figs] falling from a
fig tree when ·the wind blows [Lshaken by a strong wind/gale]. 14The sky

·disappeared [vanished] as a scroll when it is rolled up [Is. 34:4], and
every mountain and island was moved from its place.
15Then the kings of the earth, the ·rulers [princes; nobles; magnates], the
generals, the rich people, the powerful people, ·the slaves, and the free people [Land everyone, both slave and free; Cpeople of every status and economic
level] hid themselves in caves and in the rocks on the mountains. 16They
called to the mountains and the rocks, "Fall on us. Hide us from the face of
the One who sits on the throne and from the ·anger [wrath] of the Lamb!
17[LBecause] The great day for their ·anger [wrath] has come [Cthe final
judgment], and who can stand against it [Ca rhetorical question]?"

The 144,000 People of Israel

7 After ·the vision of these things [Lthis] I saw four angels standing
at the four corners [Cfrom every direction] of the earth. The
angels were ·holding [restraining] the four winds [Dan. 7:2; 8:8; 11:4] of
the earth to keep them from blowing on the land or on the sea or on any
tree. 2Then I saw another angel coming up from the ·east [Lrising of the
sun] who had the seal [5:1] of the living God. And he ·called out [cried
out; shouted] in a loud voice to the four angels to whom God had given
power to ·harm [damage] the earth and the sea. 3He said to them, "Do not
·harm [damage] the land or the sea or the trees until we ·mark with a sign
[place a seal upon] the foreheads [Cto spare them from harm; Ezek. 9:4–6]
of the ·people who serve [Lthe slaves/servants of] our God." 4Then I heard
how many people were ·marked with the sign [sealed]. There were one
hundred forty-four thousand [Cthe square of 12 multiplied by 1000; a
symbolic number indicating completeness] from every tribe of the ·peo-
ple [children; sons] of Israel.

5From the tribe of Judah twelve thousand were ·marked with the sign
[sealed],
from the tribe of Reuben twelve thousand,
from the tribe of Gad twelve thousand,
6from the tribe of Asher twelve thousand,
from the tribe of Naphtali twelve thousand,
from the tribe of Manasseh [Cone of the two sons of Joseph; he replaces
Dan in the list, perhaps because the tribe of Dan fell into idolatry;
Judg. 18] twelve thousand,
7from the tribe of Simeon twelve thousand,
from the tribe of Levi twelve thousand,
from the tribe of Issachar twelve thousand,
8from the tribe of Zebulun twelve thousand,
from the tribe of Joseph twelve thousand [Cin OT lists Manasseh and
Ephraim are named instead of their father Joseph; here Joseph
replaces Ephraim, perhaps because of Ephraim's bad reputation],
and from the tribe of Benjamin twelve thousand were ·marked with
the sign [sealed].

The Great Crowd Worships God

9After ·the vision of these things [Lthese things] I looked, and ·there was
a great number of people [Lbehold a great crowd/multitude], so many that
no one could count them. They were from every nation, tribe, people, and
language of the earth. They were all standing before the throne and before
the Lamb, wearing white robes [Csignifying high status and purity] and
holding palm branches [Cused to celebrate a festive occasion, specifically a
victory] in their hands. 10They were ·shouting [crying out] in a loud voice,
"Salvation belongs to our God, who sits on the throne, and to the Lamb."

11[LAnd] All the angels were standing around the throne and the elders [4:4] and the four living creatures. They all ·bowed [fell] down on their faces before the throne and worshiped God, 12saying, "Amen [CHebrew for "so be it"]! ·Praise [Blessing], glory, wisdom, thanks, honor, power, and ·strength [might] belong to our God forever and ever. Amen!"

13Then one of the elders asked me, "Who are these people dressed in white robes? Where did they come from?"

14I answered, "You know, ·sir [*or* my lord]."

And the elder said to me, "These are the people who have come out of the great ·distress [persecution; tribulation]. They have washed their robes and made them white in the blood of the Lamb [Chaving believed in Jesus, their sins are forgiven through Christ's death and resurrection]. 15Because of this, they are before the throne of God. They worship him day and night in his temple. And the One who sits on the throne will ·be present with [dwell with; *or* shelter; spread his tent over] them. 16Those people will never be hungry again, and they will never be thirsty again. The sun will not ·hurt [strike; beat on; Is. 49:10] them, and no [scorching] heat will burn them, 17because the Lamb at the center of the throne will be their shepherd [Ps. 23; John 10]. He will ·lead [guide] them to springs of ·water that give life [living water; the water of life; John 4:14]. And God will wipe away every tear from their eyes [21:4; Is. 25:8]."

The Seventh Seal

8 When the Lamb opened the seventh seal [Cthe final and climactic seal; 5:1], there was silence in heaven for about half an hour [Ca dramatic pause induced by awe]. 2And I saw the seven angels who stand before God and to whom were given seven trumpets [Ctrumpets often announce God's appearance, accompanied by judgment and victory; Josh. 6].

3Another angel came and stood at the altar, holding a golden ·pan for incense [censer; incense burner]. He was given much incense to offer with the prayers of all ·God's holy people [Tthe saints; Ps. 141:2]. The angel put this offering on the golden altar before the throne. 4The smoke from the incense went up from the angel's hand ·to [in the presence of] God with the prayers of ·God's people [Tthe saints]. 5Then the angel filled the ·incense pan [censer; incense burner] with fire from the altar and threw it on the earth, and there ·were thunder and loud noises [was rumbling thunder], flashes of lightning, and an earthquake [4:5].

The Seven Angels and Trumpets

6Then the seven angels who had the seven trumpets prepared to blow them [8:2].

7The first angel blew his trumpet, and hail and fire mixed with blood were ·poured [thrown; hurled] down on the earth [Csimilar to the seventh plague against Egypt; Ex. 9:13–35; Joel 2:30–31]. And a third of the earth [Lwas burned up], and a third of the trees [Lwas burned up], and all the green grass were burned up.

8Then the second angel blew his trumpet, and something that looked like a ·big [great] mountain, burning with fire, was thrown into the sea [Cperhaps referring to a volcano or a flaming meteorite; Jer. 51:25]. And a third of the sea became blood [Cechoes the first plague against Egypt; Ex. 7:14–21], 9a third of the living ·things [creatures] in the sea died, and a third of the ships were destroyed.

10Then the third angel blew his trumpet, and a ·large [great] star, burning like a torch, fell from ·the sky [*or* heaven; Cperhaps a meteorite]. It fell on a third of the rivers and on the springs of water. 11[LAnd] The name of the star is Wormwood [Ca plant with a greenish, bitter oil; a symbol of bitter sorrow; Prov. 5:4; Jer. 9:15; 23:15]. And a third of all the water became ·bitter [Lwormwood; Cagain an allusion to the first Egyptian plague], and many people died from ·drinking the water [Lthe water] that ·was [became; was made] bitter.

12Then the fourth angel blew his trumpet, and a third of the sun, and a third of the moon, and a third of the stars were struck. So a third of them became dark, and a third of the day was ·without light [kept from shining], and also the night [Cechoing the ninth Egyptian plague; Ex. 10:21–23].

13While I watched, I heard an ·eagle [*or* vulture] that was flying ·high in the air [Lin mid-heaven] cry out in a loud voice, "·Trouble! Trouble! Trouble [LWoe! Woe! Woe; Creminiscent of OT funeral laments, signifying their doom; Nah. 3:1] for those who live on the earth because of the remaining ·sounds [blasts] of the trumpets that the other three angels are about to blow!"

9 Then the fifth angel blew his trumpet, and I saw a star fall from ·the sky [*or* heaven] to the earth. The star was given the key to the ·deep hole [shaft] ·that leads to the bottomless pit [Lof the Abyss; Cthe place of the dead and/or a prison for fallen angels; Luke 8:31; Rom. 10:7]. 2Then ·it [*or* he] opened up the ·hole that leads to the bottomless pit [shaft of the Abyss], and smoke came up from the ·hole [shaft] like smoke from a ·big [great; giant] furnace. Then the sun and ·sky [air] became dark because of the smoke from the ·hole [shaft]. 3Then locusts came down to the earth out of the smoke [Csimilar to the eighth Egyptian plague; Ex. 10:1–20; see also Joel 1:2—2:10], and they were given the power ·to sting like [Llike the power of] scorpions [Lof the earth]. 4They were told not to ·harm [damage] the grass on the earth or any ·plant [greenery] or tree. They could ·harm [damage] only the people who did not have the ·sign [seal] of God on their foreheads [7:3]. 5These locusts were not ·given the power [permitted] to kill anyone, but to ·cause pain to [torture; torment] the people for five months [Cperhaps referring to the limited life span of a locust]. And ·the pain they felt was like the pain a scorpion gives [Ltheir torture/torment was like the torture/torment of a scorpion] when it stings someone. 6During those days people will ·look for a way to die [Lseek death], but they will not find it. They will ·want [long; desire] to die, but death will ·run away [flee] from them.

7The locusts looked like horses ·prepared [equipped; trained] for battle [Joel 2:4]. On their heads they wore what looked like crowns of gold [Cindicating their victory; 2:10], and their faces looked like human faces. 8Their hair was like women's hair, and their teeth were like lions' teeth [Joel 1:6]. 9Their chests looked like iron breastplates, and the sound of their wings was like the noise of many horses and chariots ·hurrying [charging; running] into battle [Joel 2:5]. 10The locusts had tails with stingers like scorpions, and in their tails was their ·power [authority] to ·hurt [damage; harm] people for five months. 11The locusts had a king who was the ·angel [*or* messenger] of the ·bottomless pit [LAbyss; 9:1]. His name in the Hebrew language is Abaddon and in the Greek language is Apollyon [Cboth mean "Destroyer"; perhaps a reference to Satan].

12The first ·trouble [Lwoe] is past; there are still two other ·troubles [Lwoes] that will come [8:13].

13Then the sixth angel blew his trumpet, and I heard a voice coming from the horns [Csome ancient manuscripts specify that there are four horns; protrusions on the four corners of the altar symbolizing God's

strength] on the golden altar [Cthe incense altar; Ex. 30:1–10] that is before
God. 14The voice said to the sixth angel who had the trumpet, "·Free
[Release] the four angels who are ·tied [bound] at the great river Euphrates
[7:1]." 15And they ·let loose [released] the four angels who had been ·kept
ready [prepared] for this hour and day and month and year so they could
kill a third of ·all people on the earth [Lhumanity; mankind]. 16I heard how
many troops on horses were in their army—two hundred million.

17The horses and their riders I saw in the vision looked like this: They
had breastplates that were fiery red, dark blue [Lhyacinth-colored], and
yellow like sulfur [brimstone]. The heads of the horses looked like heads
of lions, with fire, smoke, and sulfur coming out of their mouths. 18A third
of ·all the people on earth [humanity; mankind] were killed by these three
·terrible disasters [plagues] coming out of the horses' mouths: the fire, the
smoke, and the sulfur. 19The horses' ·power [authority] was in their mouths
and in their tails; their tails were like snakes with heads [12:9; Gen. 3:1–7],
and with them they ·hurt [damaged; injured; wounded] people.

20The ·other [rest of the] people who were not killed by these ·terrible
disasters [plagues] still did not ·change their hearts and turn away from
what they had made with their own hands [Lrepent from the works of
their hands]. They did not stop worshiping demons and idols made of
gold, silver, bronze, stone, and wood—things that cannot see or hear or
walk [Ps. 115:4–7; 135:17; Jer. 10:1–16]. 21These people did not ·change
their hearts and turn away from [repent of] murder or ·evil magic [sor-
cery], from their ·sexual sins [fornication] or stealing.

The Angel and the Small Scroll

10 Then I saw another ·powerful [mighty; strong] ·angel [mes-
senger; 5:2] coming down from heaven ·dressed [wrapped;
robed] in a cloud with a ·rainbow [*or* halo] over his head. His face was
like the sun, and his ·legs [*or* feet] were like pillars of fire. 2The angel was
holding a small scroll open in his hand. He put his right foot on the sea
and his left foot on the land. 3Then he ·shouted [cried out] loudly like the
roaring of a lion [Hos. 11:10; Amos 3:8]. And when he ·shouted [cried
out], the voices of seven thunders [Ps. 29] spoke. 4When the seven thunders spoke, I ·started [was about] to write. But I heard a voice from
heaven say, "·Keep hidden [LSeal up; Dan. 12:4] what the seven thunders
said, and do not write them down."

5Then the angel I saw standing on the sea and on the land raised his
right hand to heaven [Cas when taking an oath; Ex. 6:8; Deut. 32:40], 6and
he ·made a promise [swore an oath] ·by the power of the One [Lby the
One] who lives forever and ever [Dan. 12:7]. He is the One who ·made
[created] the ·skies [*or* heavens] and all that is in them, the earth and all
that is in it, and the sea and all that is in it [Gen. 1]. The angel ·promised
[swore an oath], "There will be no ·more waiting [delay; Ltime]! 7[LBut] In
the days when the seventh angel is ready to blow his trumpet, God's
·secret [mystery; hidden plan] will be ·finished [completed]. This ·secret
[mystery; hidden plan] is ·the Good News God told [*or* just as he
announced] to his servants, the prophets [Amos 3:7; 1 Pet. 1:10–12]."

8Then I heard the same voice from heaven again, saying to me: "Go
and take the open scroll that is in the hand of the angel that is standing
on the sea and on the land."

9So I went to the angel and told him to give me the small scroll. And he
said to me, "Take the scroll and eat it [Ca symbol of internalizing the

word]. **It will be ·sour** [bitter] **in your stomach** [Cbecause it is a message of
judgment], **but in your mouth it will be sweet as honey** [Cbecause it is
God's word and because it brings salvation and vindication to his people;
Ps. 119:103; Jer. 15:16; Ezek. 2:8—3:3]." 10**So I took the small scroll from
the angel's hand and ate it. In my mouth it tasted sweet as honey, but after
I ate it, it was ·sour** [bitter] **in my stomach.** 11**Then I was told, "You must
prophesy again about many peoples, nations, languages, and kings** [Che
must share the word he just received]."

The Two Witnesses

11 **I was given a ·measuring stick** [Ca reed or cane used for measur-
ing] **like a ·rod** [staff; walking stick], **and I was told, ·Go** [Get up]
and measure the temple of God and the altar, ·and count [*or* including] **the
people worshiping there** [Cprobably to show God's control and protection
of his people; Ezek. 40:3, 5]. 2**But do not measure the ·yard** [courtyard]
outside the temple. Leave it ·alone [out], **because it has been given to ·those
who are not God's people** [the Gentiles; the nations]. **And they will trample
on the holy city** [CJerusalem] **for forty-two months** [Ca period of oppression—either literal or symbolic—equal to three and a half years; see Dan.
7:25; 12:7, 11–12]. 3**And I will ·give power to** [*or* appoint; Lgive to] **my two
witnesses to prophesy for one thousand two hundred sixty days** [C42
months reckoned as 30 days each], **·and they will be dressed in rough cloth
to show their sadness** [Ldressed in sackcloth; Cmourning clothes]."

4**These two witnesses are the two olive trees and the two lampstands
that stand before the Lord of the earth** [Creminiscent of Zerubbabel and
Joshua whom God used to build the second temple in spite of opposition;
Zech. 4:2–6]. 5**And if anyone ·tries** [wants] **to ·hurt** [harm; damage] **them,
fire comes from their mouths and ·kills** [consumes; devours] **their enemies** [Jer. 5:14]. **And if anyone ·tries** [wants] **to ·hurt** [harm; damage]
them in whatever way, in that same way that person ·will [*or* must] **die.**
6**These witnesses have the ·power** [authority] **to ·stop the sky** [close the
heavens] **from raining during the time they are prophesying** [1 Kin. 17:1].
And they have ·power [authority] **to make the waters become blood** [8:8;
16:3–4; Ex. 7:17–21], **and they have ·power** [authority] **to send every kind
of ·trouble** [plague] **to the earth as many times as they want.**

7**When the two witnesses have finished ·telling their message** [giving
their witness/testimony], **the beast** [Cprobably the Antichrist; 13:1; 17:8;
Dan. 7] **that comes up from the ·bottomless pit** [Abyss; 9:1] **will fight a war
against them. He will ·defeat** [conquer] **them and kill them.** 8**The ·bodies**
[corpses] **of the two witnesses will lie in the ·street** [public square; Cto be left
unburied as a sign of disdain] **of the great city where the Lord was ·killed**
[Lcrucified; CJerusalem, perhaps here symbolic of the world's opposition to
God]. **·This city is named Sodom and Egypt, which has a spiritual meaning**
[L...which is figuratively/symbolically/spiritually called Sodom and Egypt;
CJerusalem is symbolically named after places judged by God for wickedness
(Sodom) and for oppressing God's people (Egypt); Gen. 19; Ex. 7–12].
9**Those from every race of people, tribe, language, and nation will look at
the bodies of the two witnesses for three and one-half days, and they will
·refuse to bury them** [Lnot let them be placed in a tomb]. 10**People who live
on the earth will rejoice and ·be happy** [celebrate] **because these two are
dead. They will send each other gifts, because these two prophets brought
much ·suffering** [torment] **to those who live on the earth.**

11**But after** [Lthe] **three and one-half days, ·God put the breath of life**

into the two prophets again [[L]a breath/spirit of life from God entered
them; Gen. 2:7]. **They stood on their feet, and everyone who saw them**
became very afraid. 12**Then the two prophets heard a loud voice from**
heaven saying, "Come up here!" And they went up into heaven in a cloud
as their enemies watched.
13**In the same hour there was a ·great** [violent] **earthquake, and a tenth**
of the city ·was destroyed [collapsed; [L]fell]. **Seven thousand people were**
killed in the earthquake, and those who did not die were very afraid and
gave glory to the God of heaven [Ezek. 38:19–20; Zech. 14:4].
14**The second ·trouble** [[L]woe] **is finished. ·Pay attention** [Look; [T]Behold]:
The third ·trouble [[L]woe] **is coming ·soon** [quickly; 8:13].

The Seventh Trumpet

15**Then the seventh angel blew his trumpet. And there were loud voices**
in heaven, saying:
"**·The power to rule the world now belongs to** [*or* The kingdom of the
world has become the kingdom of] **our Lord and his Christ**
[[C]Greek for Messiah or Anointed One],
and he will ·rule [reign] **forever and ever** [2 Sam. 7:16; Dan. 7:14, 18;
Luke 1:32–33]."
16**Then the twenty-four elders** [4:4], **who sit on their thrones before**
God, ·bowed down [fell] **on their faces and worshiped God.** 17**They said:**
"**We give thanks to you, Lord God ·Almighty** [All-powerful],
[the One] **who is and** [the One] **who was** [[C]in contrast with 1:4, 8;
4:8, this lacks the future reference, "who is coming," because here
God has commenced his future reign],
because you have ·used [*or* taken; *or* received] **your great power**
and have begun to rule!
18**The ·people of the world** [nations; Gentiles] **were angry** [Ps. 2:1],
but your ·anger [wrath] **has come.**
The time has come to judge the dead [Dan. 12:2],
and to reward your servants the prophets
and your ·holy people [[T]saints],
·all who respect you [[L]those who fear your name], **small and great.**
The time has come to destroy those who destroy the earth!"
19**Then God's temple in heaven was opened. The ·Ark that holds the**
agreement God gave to his people [[L]Ark of his Covenant] **could be seen in**
his temple. Then there were flashes of lightning, ·noises, thunder [rumbling
thunder], **an earthquake, and a great hailstorm** [[C]typical accompaniments
to the arrival of God; 4:5].

The Woman and the Dragon

12 **And then a great ·wonder** [sign; portent; [C]symbolic descriptions of heavenly/spiritual realities] **appeared in heaven: A**
woman was clothed with the sun, and the moon was under her feet
[[C]indicating authority or victory; Gen. 37:9], **and a crown** [[C]a reward of
victory] **of twelve stars was on her head** [[C]representing the twelve tribes of
Israel; the woman is a symbol of the persecuted people of God]. 2**She was**
·pregnant [[L]in the womb] **and cried out with** [[L]labor] **pain, because she**
was about to give birth [[C]to the Messiah]. 3**Then another ·wonder** [sign;
portent; 12:1] **appeared in heaven: There was a giant red dragon with**
seven heads [[C]reminiscent of the many-headed Leviathan representing
evil and chaos, here representing Satan; Ps. 74:14; Is. 27:1; Dan. 7:1–9] **and**
seven ·crowns [diadems; royal crowns] **on each head. He** [*or* It; [C]the Greek
masculine pronoun can refer to a person or thing] **also had ten horns**

[Csymbols of strength and power; Dan. 7:7–8, 20, 24]. **4His tail swept a
third of the stars out of ·the sky** [*or* heaven] **and ·threw** [cast; hurled; Dan.
8:10] **them down to the earth** [Crepresenting an early victory against
God's people; 12:1]. **He stood in front of the woman who was ready to
give birth so he could ·eat** [devour] **her ·baby** [child; CJesus the Messiah]
as soon as it was born. 5Then the woman gave birth to ·a son [La son, a
male child,] **who will ·rule** [*or* shepherd] **all the nations with an iron ·rod**
[sceptre; 19:15; Ps. 2:9]. **And her child was ·taken up** [*or* snatched away;
Cprobably a symbolic reference to the resurrection, where Satan's victory
was thwarted] **to God and to his throne. 6The woman ·ran away** [fled]
into the ·desert [wilderness] **to a place God prepared for her where she
would ·be taken care of** [nourished; fed] **for one thousand two hundred
sixty days** [Cequal to three and one-half years; see 11:3].

7Then there was a war in heaven. Michael [Can archangel and protector
of God's people; Dan. 10:13, 21; 12:1; Jude 9] **and his angels fought against
the dragon, and the dragon and his angels fought back. 8But the dragon was
not strong enough, and he and his angels lost their place in heaven. 9The
·giant** [great] **dragon was ·thrown down** [cast; hurled] **out of heaven. (He is
that ·old snake** [ancient serpent] **called the devil or Satan** [Gen. 3:1, 15],
who ·tricks [deceives; leads astray] **the whole world.) The dragon with his
angels was ·thrown down** [cast; hurled] **to the earth.**

10Then I heard a loud voice in heaven saying:

"The salvation and the power and the kingdom of our God
and the ·authority [power] **of his ·Christ** [Messiah; Anointed One]
have now come [Dan. 7:14].
[LFor] **The accuser** [Cthe name Satan means "Accuser" in Hebrew; Job
1:6–12; 2:1–6; Zech. 3:1–2] **of our brothers and sisters,**
who accused them day and night before our God,
has been ·thrown [cast; hurled] **down.**
11And our brothers and sisters ·defeated [conquered] **him**
by the blood of the ·Lamb's death [LLamb; Cby means of Christ's
sacrificial death]
and by the ·message they preached [Lword of their witness/testimony].
[LAnd] **They did not love their lives so much**
that they ·were afraid of [avoided] **death.**
12So rejoice, you heavens
and all who live there!
But ·it will be terrible for [Lwoe to] **the earth and the sea,**
because the devil has come down to you!
He is filled with ·anger [wrath],
because he knows he ·does not have much time [Lhas little time]."

13When the dragon saw he had been ·thrown [cast; hurled] **down to the
earth, he ·hunted for** [pursued; *or* persecuted] **the woman who had given
birth to the ·son** [boy; Lmale]. **14But the woman was given the two wings of a
great ·eagle** [*or* vulture; Ex. 19:4; Deut. 32:10–11; Is. 40:31] **so she could fly to
the place prepared for her in the ·desert** [wilderness]. **There she would be
·taken care of** [nourished; fed] **for ·three and one-half years** [La time, times,
and half a time; 11:2, 3; 13:5; Dan. 7:25; 12:7], **away from the ·snake** [serpent;
CGod will spiritually nourish his people though they are persecuted]. **15Then
the ·snake** [serpent] **·poured** [spewed; Lthrew] **water out of its mouth like a
river ·toward** [after] **the woman so the flood would ·carry** [sweep] **her away**
[Coverwhelming water signifies overwhelming trouble; Ps. 18:4; 69:2]. **16But**

the earth ·helped [rescued] the woman by opening its mouth and swallow-
ing the river that ·came [spewed; Lwas thrown] from the mouth of the
dragon. 17Then the dragon was ·very angry [furious; full of wrath] at the
woman, and he went off to make war against ·all her other children [Lthe rest
of her seed/offspring]—those who obey God's commands and who ·have
the message Jesus taught [*or* hold fast to their testimony about Jesus].
18And the dragon[n] stood on the ·seashore [Lsand of the sea; Csome commentators and translations take this verse as the introduction to the episode
in chapter 13].

The Two Beasts

13 Then I saw a beast coming up out of the sea [Cthe sea was a
symbol of chaos in the ancient world; Dan. 7:1–8]. It [*or* He]
had ten horns [Csymbols of power and strength] and seven heads [12:3],
and there was a ·crown [diadem; royal crown; Cindicating a king of evil] on
each horn. A ·name against God [Lblasphemous name; some manuscripts
read the plural "names"] was written on each head. 2This beast looked like
a leopard, with feet like a bear's feet and a mouth like a lion's mouth. And
the dragon gave the beast all of his ·power [authority] and his throne and
great authority. 3One of the heads of the beast looked as if it ·had been
killed by a wound [had a fatal/mortal wound; Lwas slain to death; Can evil
imitation of the Lamb that was slain; 5:6], but this ·death wound [fatal/
mortal wound; Lwound of its death] was healed [Ca false imitation of the
resurrection]. Then the whole world was amazed and followed the beast.
4People worshiped the dragon because he had given his ·power [authority]
to the beast. And they also worshiped the beast, asking, "Who is like the
beast [Ex. 15:11]? Who can make war against ·it [*or* him]?"
5The beast was ·allowed [Lgiven a mouth] to say ·proud words [Lgreat
things; Dan. 7:8, 11, 20] and ·words against God [Lblasphemies; Dan. 11:36],
and it was allowed to ·use [exercise] its ·power [authority] for forty-two
months [11:2]. 6It ·used [opened] its mouth ·to speak [blaspheme] against
God, against God's name, against ·the place where God lives [his dwelling/
tabernacle], and against all those who ·live [dwell] in heaven. 7It was given
·power [authority] to make war against ·God's holy people [Tthe saints] and
to ·defeat [conquer] them. It was given ·power [authority] over every tribe,
people, language, and nation [Dan. 7:21]. 8And all who live on earth will
worship ·the beast [Lit; *or* him]—all the people since the ·beginning [foun-
dation] of the world whose names are not written in the Lamb's book [scroll]
of life [3:5; 17:8; Ex. 32:32–33]. ·The Lamb is the One who was killed [*or* The
Lamb who was killed/slaughtered before the creation/foundation of the
earth]. [CSome commentators link the phrase "since the beginning/founda-
tion of the world" with "all who live on the earth"; others link it with "written
in the Lamb's book of life"; and still others with "the Lamb who was slain."]
9Anyone who has ears should ·listen [hear; obey]:
10If you are to be ·a prisoner [Ltaken into captivity],
then you will ·be a prisoner [Lgo into captivity].
If you are to be killed with the sword,
then you will be killed with the sword [Jer. 15:2; 43:11].
This means that ·God's holy people [Tthe saints] must have ·patience
[perseverance; endurance] and faith.
11Then I saw another beast ·coming up [rising] out of the earth [Dan. 7:17].

12:18 the dragon Some Greek copies read "I."

It [*or* He] **had two horns like a ·lamb** [*or* ram; Dan. 8:3], **but it spoke like a dragon** [Cacting like a prophetic spokesperson for the dragon (see 16:13); along with the dragon and the first beast, this second beast forms an evil trinity]. 12**This beast ·stands before the first beast and uses the same power the first beast has** [*or* uses all the authority of the first beast on its behalf]. **By this ·power** [authority] **it makes ·everyone living on earth** [Lthe earth and its inhabitants] **worship the first beast, who had the ·death wound** [fatal/mortal wound; Lwound of its death] **that was healed.** 13**And the second beast ·does great miracles** [performs great signs] **so that it even makes fire come down from heaven to earth** [1 Kin. 18:38; 2 Kin. 1:10, 12] **·while people are watching** [Lbefore people]. 14**It ·fools** [deceives; tricks] **those who live on earth by the ·miracles** [signs; Cthese are counterfeit miracles] **it has been given the power to do. It does these ·miracles** [signs] **·to serve the first beast** [Lbefore/in the presence of the first beast]. **The second beast orders** [tells] **people to make an ·idol** [image] **to honor the first beast, the one that ·was wounded by the deadly** [Lhas the wound of the] **sword but ·sprang to life again** [lives]. 15**The second beast was ·given power** [*or* allowed] **to give ·life** [breath; a spirit] **to the idol of the first one so that the idol could speak. And the second beast was ·given power** [allowed] **to ·command** [cause; make] **all who will not worship the ·image** [idol] **of the beast to be killed.** 16**The second beast also ·forced** [caused; made] **all people, small and great, rich and poor, free and slave, to have a ·mark** [brand; stamp; Cto show allegiance to the first beast] **on their right hand or on their forehead** [compare 7:2–4; 14:1]. 17[LSo that] **No one could buy or sell without this mark, which is the name of the beast or the number of its name** [CGreek and Hebrew letters had a numerical equivalent, and so could represent names—a practice known as *gematria*]. 18**This ·takes** [calls for; Lis] **wisdom** [Dan. 12:10]. **Let the one who has understanding ·find the meaning of** [calculate; figure out] **the number** [Lof the beast], **which is the number of a ·person** [*or* man]. **Its number is 666**[n] [Ca symbolic number signifying imperfection and sin; some speculate it represents the name of a Roman emperor, perhaps Nero or Domitian].

The Song of the Saved

14 Then I looked, and there before me was the Lamb standing on Mount Zion [Ca mountain near Jerusalem where the temple was located, representing the presence of God]. **With him were one hundred forty-four thousand people** [7:4] **who had his name and his Father's name written on their foreheads** [13:16]. 2**And I heard a sound from heaven like the noise of ·flooding water** [rushing water; Lmany waters; 1:15] **and like the ·sound** [peal] **of loud thunder** [19:6]. **The sound I heard was like ·people** [Lharpists] **playing harps.** 3**And they sang a new song** [Ca song celebrating divine deliverance; 5:9; Ps. 33:3; 40:3; 96:1; 98:1; 144:9; 149:1] **before the throne and before the four living creatures and the elders** [4:4]. **No one could learn the new song except the one hundred forty-four thousand** [7:4] **who had been ·bought** [redeemed] **from the earth.** 4**These are the ones who did not ·do sinful things** [defile themselves] **with women, because they ·kept themselves pure** [Lare virgins]. **They follow the Lamb every place he goes. ·These one hundred forty-four thousand** [LThey] **were ·bought** [redeemed] **from ·among the people of the earth** [Lhumanity; mankind] **as ·people to be offered** [Lfirstfruits; Cthe earliest part of the harvest was offered to God] **to God and the Lamb.** 5**·They were not guilty of telling lies** [LNo lie was found in their mouth]; **they are ·without fault** [blameless].

13:18 666 Some Greek copies read "616."

The Three Angels

6Then I saw another angel flying ·high in the air [L in mid-heaven; 8:13].
He had the eternal ·Good News [Gospel] to preach to those who ·live
[dwell] on earth—to every nation, tribe, language, and people. 7He
·preached [L spoke] in a loud voice, "Fear God and give him ·praise [glory],
because the ·time has come for God to judge all people [L hour of his judgment has come]. So worship God who made the heavens, and the earth,
and the sea, and the springs of water."
8Then the second angel followed the first angel and said, "·Ruined,
ruined [L Fallen, fallen] is ·the great city of Babylon [L Babylon the Great;
C the capital of the empire that destroyed Jerusalem in 586 BC, a symbol for
the evil world system opposing God; 2 Kin. 24–25; Is. 21:9; Dan. 4:30]! She
made all the nations drink the wine of the ·anger [*or* passion; C the Greek
word *thymos* can mean either anger or passion; see v. 10 for a possible play
on words] of her ·adultery [*or* sexual immorality]."
9Then a third angel followed the first two angels, saying in a loud voice:
"If anyone worships the beast and his ·idol [image] and ·gets [receives;
takes] the beast's ·mark [brand; stamp] on the forehead or on the hand,
10that one also will drink the wine of God's anger [C perhaps a play on words
with v. 8; Babylon's "passion" will bring on God's "wrath"], which is prepared ·with all its strength [undiluted; L unmixed; C wine was often mixed
with water] in the cup of his anger [C God's judgment is often portrayed in
the OT as a "cup" of wine poured out; Jer. 25:15–29]. And that person will
be ·put in pain [tortured; tormented] with ·burning sulfur [L fire and sulfur]
before the holy angels and the Lamb. 11And the smoke from their ·burning
pain [torture; torment] will rise forever and ever. There will be no rest, day
or night, for those who worship the beast and his ·idol [image] or who get
the ·mark [brand; stamp] of his name." 12This means ·God's holy people
[T the saints] must ·be patient [persevere; endure]. They must ·obey [keep]
God's commands and ·keep their faith in [remain faithful to] Jesus.
13Then I heard a voice from heaven saying, "Write this: ·Blessed [*or*
Happy] are the dead who die from now on in the Lord."
The Spirit says, "Yes, they will rest from their hard work, ·and the reward
of all they have done stays with them [L for their deeds will follow them]."

The Earth Is Harvested

14Then I looked, and there before me was a white cloud, and sitting on
the white cloud was One who looked like a ·Son of Man [*or* human being;
C a designation Jesus applied to himself; Dan. 7:13–14]. He had a gold
crown on his head and a sharp sickle [C a curved blade used to harvest
grain] in his hand. 15Then another angel came out of the temple and
called out in a loud voice to the One who was sitting on the cloud, "Take
your sickle and ·harvest [reap] from the earth, because the time to ·har-
vest [reap] has come, ·and [L because] the ·fruit [L harvest] of the earth is
ripe." 16So the One who was sitting on the cloud swung his sickle over the
earth, and the earth was ·harvested [reaped].
17Then another angel came out of the temple in heaven, and he also
had a sharp sickle. 18And then another angel, who has ·power [authority;
charge] over the fire, came from the altar. This angel called to the angel
with the sharp sickle, saying, "Take your sharp sickle and gather the
bunches [clusters] of grapes from the earth's vine, because its grapes are
ripe." 19Then the angel swung his sickle over the earth. He gathered the
earth's grapes and threw them into the great winepress of God's ·anger
[wrath; Is. 63:2–3, 6; Lam. 1:15]. 20They were trampled in the winepress

outside the city, and blood flowed out of the winepress as high as horses'
bridles for a distance of about ·one hundred eighty miles [[L]one thousand
six hundred stadia].

The Last Troubles

15 Then I saw another ·wonder [sign; miracle; portent] in heaven
that was great and amazing. There were seven angels bringing
seven ·disasters [plagues]. These are the last ·disasters [plagues], because
·after [*or* in] them, God's ·anger [wrath] is ·finished [completed; ended].
2 I saw what looked like a sea of glass [1 Kin. 7:23–26; Ezek. 1:22] mixed
with fire [19:20; 20:10]. All of those who had ·won the victory over [con-
quered] the beast and his ·idol [image] and over the number of his name
[13:17] were standing by the sea of glass. They had harps ·that God had
given them [[L]of/from God]. 3 They sang the song of Moses [Ex. 15:1; Deut.
31:30], the servant of God, and the song of the Lamb:

"·You do great and wonderful things [[L]Great and marvelous/amazing
are your works; Ps. 111:2],
Lord God ·Almighty [All-powerful].
·Everything the Lord does is [[L]Your ways are] ·right [just] and true
[Ps. 145:17],
King of the nations."
4 ·Everyone will respect you [[L]Who will not fear you…?], Lord [Jer. 10:7],
and ·will honor you [[L]honor/glorify your name].
[[L]Because; For] Only you are holy.
All the nations will come
and worship [[L]before] you [Ps. 86:9–10],
because the right things you have done
are now made known [Deut. 32:4]."

5 After ·this [[L]these things] I saw that the temple (the ·Tent [Tabernacle] of
the ·Agreement [Testimony; Covenant Law]) in heaven was opened. 6 And
the seven angels bringing the seven ·disasters [plagues] came out of the temple. They were dressed in ·clean [pure], ·shining [bright] linen and wore
golden ·bands [sashes] tied around their chests [[C]garments worn by priests].
7 Then one of the four living creatures gave to the seven angels seven golden
bowls filled with the ·anger [wrath] of God, who lives forever and ever. 8 The
temple was filled with smoke [[C]smoke often symbolizes the presence of God;
Ex. 40:34–38] from the glory and the power of God, and no one could enter
the temple until the seven ·disasters [plagues] of the seven angels were ·fin-
ished [completed; ended; [C]accomplished their purpose].

The Bowls of God's Anger

16 Then I heard a loud voice from the temple saying to the seven
angels, "Go and pour out the seven bowls of God's ·anger
[wrath] on the earth."
2 The first angel left and poured out his bowl on the land. Then ·ugly
[foul] and painful sores [[C]reminiscent of the sixth Egyptian plague; Ex.
9:9–11; Job 2] came upon all those who had the ·mark [brand] of the
beast and who worshiped his ·idol [image].
3 The second angel poured out his bowl on the sea, and it became blood
like that of a ·dead man [corpse; [C]reminiscent of the first Egyptian plague;
Ex. 7:14–21; see also 8:8–9], and every living thing in the sea died.
4 The third angel poured out his bowl on the rivers and the springs of
water, and they became blood [[C]also similar to the first Egyptian plague].

15:3 King . . . nations Some Greek copies read "King of the ages."

5Then I heard the angel of the waters saying:
"[LO] Holy One, you are the One who is and who was.
You are ·right [just] ·to decide to punish [*or* because you judged]
these ·evil people [Lthings].
6[LBecause] They have poured out the blood of your ·holy people
[Tsaints] and your prophets.
So now you have given them blood to drink as they deserve [Is.
49:26]."
7And I heard ·a voice coming from the altar [Lthe altar] saying:
"Yes, Lord God ·Almighty [All-powerful],
·the way you punish evil people is [Lyour judgments are] ·right [true]
and ·fair [just; righteous]."
8The fourth angel poured out his bowl on the sun, and ·he [*or* it; Ceither
the sun or the angel] was given ·power [authority] to ·burn [scorch] the
people with fire. 9They were ·burned [scorched] by the great heat, and
they ·cursed [blasphemed] the name of God, who had ·control [authority;
power] over these ·disasters [plagues]. But the people ·refused to change
their hearts and lives [Ldid not repent] and give ·glory [honor] to God.
10The fifth angel poured out his bowl on the throne of the beast, and
darkness covered its kingdom [8:12; Creminiscent of the ninth Egyptian
plague; Ex. 10:21–29]. People ·gnawed [bit] their tongues because of the
·pain [agony]. 11They also cursed the God of heaven because of their pain
and the sores they had, but they refused to ·change their hearts and turn
away [repent] from ·the evil things they did [Ltheir deeds].
12The sixth angel poured out his bowl on the great river Euphrates so
that the water in the river was dried up to prepare the way for the kings
from the east to come [Creminiscent of the splitting of the Red Sea and the
Jordan; Ex. 14:21–22; Josh. 3:13–17]. 13Then I saw three ·evil [Lunclean]
spirits that looked like frogs [Creminiscent of the second Egyptian plague;
Ex. 8:1–15] coming out of the mouth of the dragon, out of the mouth of
the beast, and out of the mouth of the false prophet. 14[LFor] These evil
spirits are the spirits of demons, ·which have power to do miracles [Lthat
perform signs]. They go out to the kings of the whole world to gather them
together for the battle on the great day of God ·Almighty [All-powerful].
15"Listen [LLook; TBehold]! I will come as a thief comes [Cthat is, without warning]! ·Blessed [Happy] are those who stay ·awake [alert] and
keep their clothes on [Ca metaphor for staying faithful and pure] so that
they will not walk around naked and have people see their shame."
16Then ·the evil spirits [Lthey] gathered the kings together to the place
that is called Armageddon in the Hebrew language [Cmeaning "Mountain
of Megiddo," a strategic pass in northern Israel].
17The seventh angel poured out his bowl into the air. Then a loud voice
came out of the temple from the throne, saying, "It ·is finished [is done; has
come to pass]!" 18Then there were flashes of lightning, ·noises, thunder
[rumbling thunder], and a ·big [great] earthquake [4:5; 11:19]—the ·worst
[greatest; most violent] earthquake that has ever happened since people
have been on earth. 19The great city split into three parts, and the cities of
the nations ·were destroyed [fell; collapsed]. And God remembered ·the
sins of Babylon [LBabylon] the Great, so he gave that city the cup filled with
the wine of ·his terrible anger [Lthe anger/fury of his wrath; 14:8]. 20Then
every island ·ran away [fled], and mountains ·disappeared [Lwere not to be
found]. 21Giant hailstones, each weighing about ·a hundred pounds [La talent],

fell from the sky upon people [Creminiscent of the seventh Egyptian plague;
11:19; Ex. 9:13–35]. People ·cursed [blasphemed] God for the ·disaster
[plague] of the hail, because this ·disaster [plague] was so terrible.

The Woman on the Animal

17 Then one of the seven angels who had the seven bowls came
and spoke to me. He said, "Come, and I will show you the ·pun-
ishment [judgment] that will be given to the great ·prostitute [whore], the
one sitting [*or* ruling] over many waters [Creferring to the Euphrates River
and its many waterways (Jer. 51:13), or symbolically to the cosmic forces of
evil]. 2The kings of the earth ·sinned sexually [prostituted themselves;
committed fornication] with her, and the people of the earth became
drunk from the wine of her ·sexual sin [prostitution; fornication; 14:8]."

3Then the angel carried me away ·by the Spirit [*or* in the spirit] to the
·desert [wilderness]. There I saw a woman sitting on a ·red [scarlet] beast. It
was covered with ·names against God written on it [blasphemous names],
and it had seven heads and ten horns. 4The woman was dressed in purple
and ·red [scarlet] and was ·shining [glittering; adorned] with the gold, precious jewels, and pearls she was wearing. She had a golden cup in her hand,
a cup filled with ·evil [abominable; detestable] things and the uncleanness
of her ·sexual sin [prostitution; fornication]. 5On her forehead a ·title
[name] was written that was ·secret [a mystery]. This is what was written:

THE GREAT BABYLON
MOTHER OF ·PROSTITUTES [whores]
AND OF THE ·EVIL [abominable; detestable] THINGS
OF THE EARTH

6Then I saw that the woman was drunk with the blood of ·God's holy
people [Tthe saints] and with the blood of ·those who were killed because
of their faith in [witnesses to; *or* martyrs for] Jesus.

When I saw the woman, I was ·very amazed [greatly astonished; Lamazed
with great amazement]. 7Then the angel said to me, "Why are you amazed
[astonished]? I will tell you the ·secret [mystery] of this woman and the
beast ·she rides [that carries her]—the one with seven heads and ten horns.
8The beast you saw ·was once alive but is not alive now [Lwas, and is not;
13:3, 12, 14]. But soon it will come up out of the ·bottomless pit [Abyss;
9:1] and go away to ·be destroyed [its destruction]. There are people who
live on earth whose names have not been written in the ·book [scroll] of
life [3:5] since the ·beginning [foundation; creation] of the world. They
will be amazed when they see the beast, because he was ·once alive, is not
alive now, but will come again [Lwas, is not, but is to come; Cimitating the
divine title of the Lamb (1:18; 2:8) and God (1:4, 8; 4:8)].

9"You need a wise mind to understand this. The seven heads on the
beast are seven ·mountains [*or* hills; CRome was built on seven hills] where
the woman sits. 10·And they are seven kings. Five of the kings have ·already
been destroyed [Lfallen], one of the kings ·lives now [Lis], and another has
not yet come. When he comes, he must stay a short time. 11The beast that
·was once alive [Lwas], but ·is not alive now [Lis not], is also an eighth king.
He belongs to the first seven kings, and he ·will go away to be destroyed
[is heading to destruction].

12"The ten horns [Dan. 7:7–8, 20–25] you saw are ten kings who have
not yet ·begun to rule [received a kingdom], but they will receive ·power
[authority] to rule with the beast for one hour [Ca short time]. 13All ten of
these kings have ·the same [Lone] ·purpose [intention], and they will give

their power and authority to the beast. [14]They will make war against the
Lamb [CJesus], but the Lamb will ·defeat [conquer; be victorious over]
them, because he is Lord of lords and King of kings. ·He will defeat them
with his called, chosen, and faithful followers [*or* Those with him are
called, chosen and faithful]."

[15]Then the angel said to me, "The waters that you saw, where the ·prosti-
tute [whore] sits, are peoples, ·races [multitudes; crowds], nations, and
languages. [16]The ten horns and the beast you saw will hate the ·prostitute
[whore]. They will ·take everything she has [make her desolate] and leave
her naked. They will eat her body and burn her with fire [Ezek. 23:25–29].
[17][LFor] God ·made the ten horns want [Lput it into their hearts] to carry out
his ·purpose [intention] by agreeing to give the beast their ·power to rule
[kingdom], until ·what God has said comes about [Lthe word of God has
been fulfilled/completed]. [18]The woman you saw is the great city that rules
over the kings of the earth." [CWhether symbolized by Rome, Babylon,
Sodom or apostate Jerusalem, this city is ultimately the human world system
ruled by Satan standing in opposition to the city of God, the new Jerusalem.]

Babylon Is Destroyed

18 After ·the vision of these things [Lthese things], I saw another
angel coming down from heaven. This angel had great ·power
[authority], and his ·glory [splendor] ·made the earth bright [illumined
the earth]. [2]He ·shouted [cried out] in a ·powerful [mighty; strong] voice:

"·Ruined, ruined [LFallen, fallen] is ·the great city of Babylon
[LBabylon the great]!
She has become a ·home [haunt; dwelling place] for demons
and a ·prison [*or* haunt] for every ·evil [Lunclean] spirit,
and a ·prison [*or* haunt] for every unclean bird and unclean beast.
[3]She has ·been ruined [fallen], because all the ·peoples [nations] of the earth
have ·drunk [some manuscripts read "have fallen from"] the wine of the ·desire [passion] of her ·sexual sin [promiscuity; fornication; 14:8; 17:2].
She has been ruined also because the kings of the earth
have ·sinned sexually [fornicated] with her,
and the merchants of the earth
have grown rich from the ·great wealth [power] of her ·luxury [sensuality]."

[4]Then I heard another voice from heaven saying:

"Come out of that city, my people,
so that you will not share in her sins,
so that you will not receive ·the disasters that will come to her [Lher plagues; Gen. 19:15, 17].
[5][LBecause] Her sins have ·piled up [heaped; reached] as high as ·the sky [heaven],
and God has ·not forgotten [remembered] ·the wrongs she has done [her crimes; her sins].
[6]·Give [Pay back] that city the same as she ·gave to [paid] others.
Pay her back ·twice as much as [double what] she did.
·Prepare wine for her that is twice as strong
as the wine she prepared for others [LIn the cup she mixed, mix double for her; 14:8].
[7]She gave herself much glory and ·rich living [sensual luxury].

Give her that much ·suffering [torment; torture] and ·sadness [grief; mourning].
She says ·to herself [[L]in her heart], 'I am a queen sitting on my throne.
I am not a widow; I will never ·be sad [know grief; mourn].'
8So these ·disasters [plagues] will come to her in one day:
death, and ·crying [sadness; grief; mourning], and ·great hunger [famine],
and she will be ·destroyed [consumed; burned up] by fire,
because the Lord God who judges her is ·powerful [strong]."

9The kings of the earth who ·sinned sexually [fornicated] with her and
·shared her wealth [lived in luxury/sensuality with her] will see the smoke
from her burning. Then they will ·cry [weep] and ·be sad [mourn]
because of her death. 10They will be afraid of her ·suffering [torment;
torture] and stand far away and say:

"·Terrible! How terrible for you [[L]Woe, woe; 8:13], great city,
·powerful [strong; mighty] city of Babylon,
because your ·punishment [judgment; doom] has come ·in one hour [suddenly]!"

11And the merchants of the earth will ·cry [weep] and be sad about her,
because now there is no one to buy their cargoes— 12cargoes of gold, silver, ·jewels [precious stones], pearls, fine linen, purple cloth, silk, ·red
[scarlet] cloth; all kinds of citron wood and all kinds of things made from
ivory, expensive wood, bronze, iron, and marble; 13[and cargoes of] cinnamon, spice, incense, myrrh, frankincense, wine, olive oil, fine flour,
wheat, cattle, sheep, horses, carriages [wagons], ·slaves, and human lives
[[L]bodies and human souls].

14The merchants will say [[C]implied by the context],
"Babylon, the ·good things [[L]fruit] you ·wanted [desired; longed for] are gone from you.
All your ·rich [expensive; luxurious] and ·fancy [glamorous; [L]shining] things have disappeared.
You will never ·have [find] them again."

15The merchants [[L]of these things] who became rich ·from selling to her
[[L]from her] will be afraid of her ·suffering [torment; torture] and will
stand far away. They will ·cry [weep] and ·be sad [mourn] 16and say:

"·Terrible! How terrible [[L]Woe, woe; 8:13] for the great city!
She was dressed in fine linen, purple and ·red [scarlet] cloth,
and she was ·shining [glittering; adorned] with gold, precious jewels, and pearls [17:4]!
17All these riches have been ·destroyed [made desolate] in one hour [[C]suddenly or in a short time]!"

Every sea captain, every passenger, the sailors, and all those who ·earn
their living from [trade; work on] the sea stood far away from Babylon.
18As they saw the smoke from her burning, they cried out loudly, "·There
was never a city [What city was…?] like this great city!" 19And they threw
dust on their heads [[C]a ritual of mourning] and cried out, weeping and
·being sad [mourning]. They said:

"·Terrible! How terrible [[L]Woe, woe] for the great city!
[[L]In which] All the people who had ships on the sea
became rich because of her wealth!
But she has been ·destroyed [made desolate] in one hour [[C]suddenly or in a short time]!

20·Be happy [rejoice] ·because of this [Lover her], heaven!
·Be happy [Rejoice], ·God's holy people [Tsaints] and apostles and prophets!
[LFor] God has ·punished [judged] her ·because of what she did to you [*or* on your behalf; *or* for the judgment/punishment she imposed on you]."

21Then a ·powerful [strong; mighty] angel picked up a large stone, like
·one used for grinding grain [a millstone], and threw it into the sea [Jer.
51:63–64]. He said:

"In the same way, the great city of Babylon will be thrown down [with violence],
and it will never be found again.
22The ·music [Lsound] of ·people playing harps [harpists] and ·other instruments [musicians; singers], ·flutes [flutists], and ·trumpets [trumpeters],
will never be heard in you again.
No ·workman [craftsman] doing any ·job [trade]
will ever be found in you again.
The sound of ·grinding grain [the millstone]
will never be heard in you again.
23The light of a lamp
will never shine in you again,
and the voices of a bridegroom and bride
will never be heard in you again.
[LFor; Because] Your merchants were the world's great people,
and all the nations were ·tricked [deceived; led astray] by your ·magic [sorcery].
24·You are guilty of the death of the prophets and God's holy people [LIn you was found the blood of the prophets and the saints]
and all who have been ·killed [slaughtered; slain] on earth."

People in Heaven Praise God

19 After ·this vision and announcement [Lthese things] I heard
·what sounded like a great many people [Lthe loud voice/
sound of a great crowd] in heaven saying:

"·Hallelujah! [CFrom the Hebrew meaning "Praise the LORD/Yahweh!]
Salvation, ·glory [honor], and power belong to our God,
2 because his judgments are true and ·right [just].
He has ·punished [judged] the [Lgreat] ·prostitute [whore]
who ·made the earth evil [corrupted the earth] with her ·sexual sin [fornication].
He has ·paid her back for [avenged] the ·death [Lblood] of his servants [which she shed; Lby her hand]."

3Again they said:

"Hallelujah [see 19:1]!
She is burning [Cimplied by the context], and her smoke will rise forever and ever."

4Then the twenty-four elders [4:4] and the four living creatures ·bowed
[fell] down and worshiped God, who sits on the throne. They said:

"Amen [Cmeaning, "So be it!"], Hallelujah [see 19:1]!"

5Then a voice came from the throne, saying:

"Praise our God, all ·you who serve him [his servants/slaves]
and all you who ·honor [Lfear; Prov. 1:7] him, both small and great!"

6Then I heard ·what sounded like a great many people [Lthe voice/
sound of a great crowd], like the noise of ·flooding water [many waters],
and like the noise of loud thunder. The people were saying:

"Hallelujah [19:1]!
[LFor] Our Lord God, the ·Almighty [All-powerful], ·rules [reigns].
7Let us rejoice and ·be happy [exult]
and give ·God [Lhim] ·glory [honor],
because the ·wedding [marriage] of the Lamb has come,
and the Lamb's bride has made herself ready.
8Fine linen, bright and ·clean [pure], was given to her to wear."

(The fine linen ·means [is; stands for] the ·good things done by God's
holy people [Lrighteousness/righteous deeds of the saints/holy ones].)

9And the angel said to me, "Write this: ·Blessed [Happy] are those who
have been invited to the wedding ·meal [supper; banquet] of the Lamb!"
And the angel said [Lto me], "These are the true words of God."

10Then I ·bowed down [fell] at the angel's feet to worship him, but he
said to me, "·Do not worship me [Don't do that!; LSee, not]! I am a ·ser-
vant like you [fellow servant with you] and your brothers and sisters who
have the ·message [witness; testimony] of Jesus. Worship God, because
the ·message [witness; testimony] ·about [*or* from] Jesus ·is the spirit that
gives all prophecy [*or* is the essence of true prophecy; *or* is Spirit-inspired
prophecy; Lis the spirit/Spirit of prophecy]."

The Rider on the White Horse

11Then I saw heaven opened, and there before me was a white horse.
The rider [CJesus] on the horse is called Faithful and True, and ·he is right
when [with justice/righteousness] he judges and makes war [Ps. 96:13;
98:9]. 12His eyes are like ·burning [blazing; flames of] fire [Dan. 10:6], and
on his head are many ·crowns [diadems; royal crowns; Ccontrast 12:3;
13:1]. He has a name written on him, which no one but himself knows.
13He is dressed in a ·robe [garment] dipped in blood [Cindicating judgment; Is. 63:1–3], and his name is the Word of God [John 1:1]. 14The
armies of heaven, dressed in fine linen, white and ·clean [pure], were following him on white horses. 15Out of the rider's mouth comes a sharp
sword [1:16] that he will use to ·defeat [strike down] the nations [Is. 11:4],
and he will ·rule [*or* shepherd] them with a ·rod [staff; scepter] of iron [Ps.
2:9]. He will ·crush out [tread; stomp] the wine in the winepress of the
·terrible anger [furious wrath] of God the ·Almighty [All-powerful; 19:13;
Is. 63:1–6]. 16On his robe and on his upper leg was written this name: KING
OF KINGS AND LORD OF LORDS [17:14; Deut. 10:17; Dan. 2:47].

17Then I saw an angel standing in the sun, and he called with a loud
voice to all the birds flying in ·the sky [Lmid-heaven]: "Come and gather
together for the great ·feast [supper; banquet] of God 18so that you can
eat the ·bodies [flesh] of kings, ·generals [captains; officers], mighty people, horses and their riders, and the bodies of all people—free, slave,
small, and great [13:16; Ezek. 39:17–20]."

19Then I saw the beast and the kings of the earth. Their armies were gathered together to make war against the rider on the horse [CJesus] and his
army. 20But the beast was captured and with him the false prophet who ·did
the miracles [performed signs] ·for the beast [on his behalf; in his presence].
The false prophet had used these ·miracles [signs] to ·trick [deceive; lead
astray] those who had the ·mark [brand; stamp] of the beast and worshiped
his ·idol [image]. ·The false prophet and the beast [LThe two] were thrown

alive into the lake of fire that burns with sulfur. 21And ·their armies [Lthe rest] were killed with the sword that came out of the mouth of the rider on the horse, and all the birds ·ate the bodies until they were full [Lwere gorged/filled up with their flesh].

The Thousand Years

20 I saw an angel coming down from heaven. He had the key to the ·bottomless pit [Abyss; 9:1] and a ·large [great] chain in his hand. 2The angel ·grabbed [seized] the dragon, that ·old snake [ancient serpent] who is the devil and Satan [12:9; Gen. 3:15], and ·tied him up [bound him; Mark 3:27] for a thousand years. 3Then he threw him into the ·bottomless pit [Abyss], ·closed [*or* locked] it, and ·locked it [Lsealed it; *or* placed a seal on it] over him. The angel did this so he could not ·trick [deceive; lead astray] the ·people of the earth [nations] anymore until the thousand years were ·ended [finished; completed]. After ·a thousand years [Lthese things] he must be set free for a short time.

4Then I saw some thrones and people sitting on them who had been given the power to judge. And I saw the souls of those who had been ·killed [Lbeheaded] because ·they were faithful to the message [of their testimony/witness] of Jesus and [Lbecause of] the ·message from [word of] God. They had not worshiped the beast or his ·idol [image], and they had not received the ·mark [brand; stamp] of the beast on their foreheads or on their hands. They came back to life and ·ruled [reigned] with Christ for a thousand years. 5(The others that were dead did not live again until the thousand years were ended.) This is the first ·raising of the dead [resurrection]. 6·Blessed [Happy] and holy are those who ·share [have a part] in this first ·raising of the dead [resurrection]. The second death [Cbeing cast in the lake of fire] has no ·power [authority] over them. They will be priests for God and for Christ and will ·rule [reign] with him for a thousand years.

7When the thousand years are over, Satan will be set free from his prison. 8Then he will go out to ·trick [deceive; lead astray] the nations in ·all [Lthe four corners of] the earth—Gog and Magog—to gather them for battle [Ezek. 38–39]. ·There are so many people [LIn number] they will be like ·sand on the seashore [*or* the sand of the sea]. 9And ·Satan's army [Lthey] marched across [Lthe breadth of; *or* the broad plain of] the earth and ·gathered around [surrounded] the camp of ·God's people [Tthe saints] and the city God loves. But fire came down from heaven and ·burned them up [consumed/devoured them; 13:13; 1 Kin. 18:38; 2 Kin. 1:10, 12]. 10And ·Satan [Lthe Devil], who ·tricked them [deceived them; led them astray], was thrown into the lake of ·burning sulfur [Lfire and sulfur] with the beast and the false prophet. There they will be ·punished [tormented; tortured] day and night forever and ever.

People of the World Are Judged

11Then I saw a great white throne and the One who was sitting on it. Earth and ·sky [heaven] ·ran away [fled] from ·him [Lhis presence/face] and ·disappeared [Lno place was found for them]. 12And I saw the dead, great and small, standing before the throne. Then ·books [scrolls] were opened, and [Lanother book/scroll, which is] the ·book [scroll] of life was opened [3:5; Dan. 12:1–2]. The dead were judged by what they had done, which was ·written [recorded] in the ·books [scrolls]. 13The sea gave up the dead who were in it, and Death and Hades [Cthe realm of the dead, also known as Sheol; 6:8] gave up the dead who were in them. Each person was judged by what he had done. 14And Death and Hades were thrown into the lake of fire. The lake of fire is the second death. 15And

anyone whose name was not found written in the book [scroll] of life was
thrown into the lake of fire.

The New Jerusalem

21 Then I saw a new heaven and a new earth [Is. 65:17; 66:22;
2 Pet. 3:13]. [LFor] The first heaven and the first earth had
·disappeared [passed away], and there was no sea anymore [Cthe sea represents chaos and evil, so its absence indicates peace and security]. 2And I
saw the holy city, the new Jerusalem [Cthe believers' eternal dwelling
place; 3:12], coming down out of heaven from God. It was prepared like
a bride ·dressed [adorned] for her husband [19:7, 9]. 3And I heard a loud
voice from the throne, saying, "[LLook; TBehold] Now God's ·presence
[dwelling; tabernacle] is with people, and he will ·live [dwell; tabernacle;
John 1:14] with them, and they will be his people [Ex. 29:45; Jer. 31:33;
Ezek. 37:27]. God himself will be with them and will be their God." 4He
will wipe away every tear from their eyes [7:17; Is. 25:8], and there will be
no more death [Is. 25:8; 1 Cor. 15:54], ·sadness [mourning], crying, or
pain, because ·all the old ways [the old order; Lthe first things] are gone."
5The One who was sitting on the throne [CJesus] said, "Look! I am
making everything new!" Then he said, "Write this, because these words
are ·true and can be trusted [Lfaithful/reliable and true]."
6The One on the throne said to me, "It is ·finished [done; accom-
plished]. I am the Alpha and the Omega [Cthe first and last letters of the
Greek alphabet; 1:8], the Beginning and the End. I will give ·free water
[Lfreely] from the spring of the water of life to anyone who is thirsty [Is.
55:1; John 7:37]. 7Those who ·win the victory [conquer] will ·receive
[inherit] ·this [Lthese things; CGod's promise], and I will be their God, and
they will be my children [21:3; 2 Sam. 7:14]. 8But cowards, those ·who
refuse to believe [without faith], who do ·evil [vile; detestable] things,
who kill, who sin sexually, who do ·evil magic [sorcery], who worship
idols, and who tell lies—all these will have ·a place [Ltheir part] in the lake
of burning sulfur. This is the second death [20:6]."
9Then one of the seven angels who had the seven bowls full of the seven
last ·troubles [plagues] came to me, saying, "·Come with me [LCome], and I
will show you the bride, the wife of the Lamb [Cthe church; Eph. 5:27–29]."
10And the angel carried me away ·by the Spirit [*or* in the spirit] to a very large
and high mountain. He showed me the holy city, Jerusalem, coming down
out of heaven from God. 11It ·was shining with [possessed; Lhad] the glory of
God and was ·bright [radiant; brilliant] like a ·very expensive jewel [precious
stone], like a jasper, clear as crystal. 12The city had a great high wall with
twelve gates with twelve angels at the gates, and on each gate was written the
name of one of the twelve tribes of Israel. 13There were three gates on the
east, three on the north, three on the south, and three on the west [Ezek.
48:30–35]. 14The walls of the city were built on twelve foundation stones,
and on the stones were written the names of the twelve apostles of the Lamb.
15The angel who talked with me had a measuring rod made of gold to
measure the city, its gates, and its wall. 16The city ·was built in a square [Llies
foursquare], and its length was equal to its width. The angel measured the
city with the rod. The city was ·1,500 miles long, 1,500 miles wide, and 1,500
miles high [L1,200 stadia—its length and width and height are equal; Cthe
unit of measure called a stadium was approximately 600 feet]. 17The angel
also measured the wall. It was ·216 feet [L144 cubits] ·high [*or* thick; Cthe

21:3 and . . . God Some Greek copies do not have this phrase.

Greek is ambiguous], by human measurements, which the angel was using. 18The wall was made of jasper, and the city was made of pure gold, as pure as glass. 19The foundation stones of the city walls were ·decorated [ornamented] with every kind of ·jewel [precious stone; Ex. 28:15–21; Is. 54:11–12]. The first foundation was jasper, the second was sapphire, the third was ·chalcedony [agate], the fourth was emerald, 20the fifth was ·onyx [sardonyx], the sixth was carnelian, the seventh was ·chrysolite [yellow quartz], the eighth was beryl, the ninth was topaz, the tenth was ·chrysoprase [turquoise], the eleventh was jacinth, and the twelfth was amethyst [Cthe specific identity of some of these jewels is uncertain]. 21The twelve gates were twelve pearls, each gate having been made from a single pearl. And the ·street [main street; square] of the city was made of pure gold as clear as glass.

22I did not see a temple in the city, because the Lord God ·Almighty [All-powerful] and the Lamb are the city's temple [Ca temple representing the presence of God is not needed because God's presence is throughout the city]. 23The city does not need the sun or the moon to shine on it, because the glory of God ·is its [gives it] light, and the Lamb is the city's lamp [Is. 60:19]. 24By its light the ·people of the world [nations] will walk, and the kings of the earth will bring their glory into it [Is. 60:1–3]. 25The city's gates will never be shut on any day [Is. 60:11], because there is no night there. 26The glory and the honor of the nations will be brought into it [Cas gifts to God]. 27Nothing ·unclean [impure; profane; common] and no one who does ·shameful [detestable; abominable] things or tells lies will ever go into it. Only those whose names are written in the Lamb's ·book [scroll] of life [3:5] will enter the city.

22 Then the angel showed me the river of the ·water of life [*or* living water]. It was ·shining [bright; clear] like crystal and was flowing from the throne of God and of the Lamb 2down the middle of the ·street [main street; square] of the city [Gen. 2:10; Ezek. 47:1–12]. The tree of life was on each side of the river [Gen. 2:9; Cheaven is like Eden, only better]. It produces ·fruit twelve times a year, once each month [*or* twelve kinds of fruit, producing fruit each month]. The leaves of the tree are for the healing of all the nations. 3·Nothing that God judges guilty will be in that city [Nothing accursed will be there; *or* There will no longer be any curse; Gen. 3:16–19; Zech. 14:11]. The throne of God and of the Lamb will be there, and God's servants will ·worship [serve] him. 4They will see his face, and his name will be written on their foreheads [Cdenoting ownership; 3:12; 7:3; contrast 13:16; Ex. 28:36–38]. 5There will never be night again. They will not need the light of a lamp or the light of the sun, because the Lord God will give them light. And they will ·rule as kings [reign] forever and ever.

6The angel said to me, "These words ·can be trusted and are [are faithful and] true." The Lord, the God of the spirits of the prophets [Cthe spirit that inspires the prophets; 1 Cor. 14:32], sent his angel to show his servants the things that must happen ·soon [quickly].

7"·Listen [LLook; TBehold]! I am coming ·soon [quickly]! ·Blessed [Happy] is the one who obeys the words of prophecy in this ·book [scroll]."

8I, John, am the one who heard and saw these things. When I heard and saw them, I ·bowed [fell] down to worship at the feet of the angel who showed these things to me. 9But the angel said to me, "·Do not worship me [Don't do that!; LSee, not]! I am a ·servant like you [fellow servant with you], your brothers the prophets, and all those who ·obey [keep] the words in this ·book [scroll]. Worship God!"

[10]Then the angel told me, "Do not ·keep secret [[L]seal; contrast 10:4] the
words of prophecy in this ·book [scroll], because the time is near for all
this to happen. [11]Let whoever is doing ·evil [wrong; harm] continue to do
evil [wrong; harm; Dan. 12:10]. Let whoever is ·unclean [vile; impure;
filthy] continue to be ·unclean [vile; impure; filthy]. Let whoever is ·doing
right [righteous; just] continue to do ·right [righteousness; justice]. Let
whoever is holy continue to be holy."

[12]"·Listen [[L]Look; Behold]! I am coming ·soon [quickly]! ·I will bring my
reward with me [[L]and my reward is with me; Is. 40:10], and I will repay ·each
one of you [[L]each person] for what you have done. [13]I am the Alpha and the
Omega, the First and the Last, the Beginning and the End [1:8; 21:6].

[14]"·Blessed [Happy] are those who wash their robes [[C]an image of spiritual cleansing] so that they will receive the ·right [power; authority] to
eat the fruit from the tree of life and may ·go through [enter] the gates
into the city. [15]Outside the city are the ·evil people [[L]dogs], those who do
·evil magic [sorcery], who ·sin sexually [fornicate], who murder, who
worship idols, and who love lies and tell lies.

[16]"I, Jesus, have sent my angel to ·tell you [testify/witness to] these
things for the churches. I am the ·descendant from the family of David
[root and descendant/offspring of David; [C]a messianic title applied to
Jesus; 5:4; Is. 11:10], and I am the bright morning star [2:28; Num. 24:17;
[C]a messianic title]."

[17]The Spirit and the bride say, "Come!" Let the one who hears this say,
"Come!" Let whoever is thirsty come; whoever wishes may ·have [take;
receive] the water of life ·as a free gift [freely].

[18]I ·warn [testify to] everyone who hears the words of the prophecy of
this ·book [scroll]: If anyone adds anything to these words, God will add
to that person the ·disasters [plagues] written about in this ·book [scroll].
[19]And if anyone takes away from the words of this ·book [scroll] of prophecy, God will take away that one's ·share [part] of the tree of life and of the
holy city, which are written about in this ·book [scroll; Deut. 4:2; 12:32].

[20]·Jesus, the One who says these things are true, [[L]The One who witnesses
to these things] says, "Yes, I am coming ·soon [quickly]."

·Amen [[C]Hebrew for "so be it"]. Come, Lord Jesus!

[21]The grace of the Lord Jesus be with all. Amen.

SUBJECT INDEX

Major events and topics of the Bible,
and the chapters in which they can be studied.